ISBN 978-0-428-94778-1
PIBN 11297820

This book is a reproduction of an important historical work. Forgotten Books uses
state-of-the-art technology to digitally reconstruct the work, preserving the original format
whilst repairing imperfections present in the aged copy. In rare cases, an imperfection in
the original, such as a blemish or missing page, may be replicated in our edition. We do,
however, repair the vast majority of imperfections successfully; any imperfections that
remain are intentionally left to preserve the state of such historical works.

tional Institute
Mental Health

**The National Clearinghouse
for Mental Health Information**

OL. 19 CUMULATIVE INDEX June 1982

sy....pharmacology Abstracts

onal Institute
ental Health

The National Clearinghouse
for Mental Health Information

L. 19 CUMULATIVE INDEX June 1982

ychopharmacology Abstracts

PSYCHOPHARMACOLOGY ABSTRACTS is a publication of the National Clearinghouse for Mental Health Information of the National Institute of Mental Health. It is a specialized information medium designed to assist the Institute in meeting its obligation to foster and support laboratory and clinical research into the nature and causes of mental disorders and methods of treatment and prevention. Specifically, this information service is designed to meet the needs of investigators in the field of psychopharmacology for rapid and comprehensive information about new developments and research results. For information or correspondence with the National Institute of Mental Health concerning *Psychopharmacology Abstracts*, changes of address, or removal of names from the mailing list see the inside back cover page.

The Secretary of Health and Human Services has determined that the publication of this periodical is necessary in the transaction of the public business required by law of this Department. Use of funds for printing this periodical has been approved by the Director of the Office of Management and Budget through November 15, 1982.

NATIONAL CLEARINGHOUSE FOR MENTAL HEALTH INFORMATION
PSYCHOPHARMACOLOGY ABSTRACTS

Volume 19

Cumulative Index

June 1982

Carrie Lee Rothgeb, *Editor*
Bette L. Shannon, *Managing Editor*

U.S. DEPARTMENT OF HEALTH AND HUMAN SERVICES
Public Health Service

Alcohol, Drug Abuse, and Mental Health Administration
National Institute of Mental Health
National Clearinghouse for Mental Health Information
5600 Fishers Lane
Rockville, Maryland 20857

DHHS Publication No. (ADM) 83-150
Printed 1983

For sale by the Superintendent of Documents, U.S. Government Printing Office, Washington, D.C. 20402.

CROSS-REFERENCE LIST

The use of a Key-Word-out-of-Context (KWOC) index, while saving time and money, poses a problem to users seeking to locate relevant references on a given topic, as all references are not found under one entry. To alleviate this problem, we have prepared the following cross-reference list.

A

Ability   see also
  Learning ability
Abuse   see also
  Drug abuse
Access   see
  Continuous access
Accidents   see
  Cerebrovascular accidents
Acetylcholine   see also
  ACH
Acetylsalicylic acid   see also
  Aspirin
ACH   see also
  Acetylcholine
Acid   see also
  Names of individual acid:
Act   see
  Controlled substances ac
ACTH   see also
  Adrenocorticotropin
Acting   see
  Centrally acting
  CNS acting
  Long-acting
  Short-acting
Action(s)   see
  Anorectic actions
  Behavioural actions
  Biochemical action
  Central action(s)
  Dual action(s)
  Hypotensive action
  Inhibitory actions
  Mechanism-of-action
  Neurotoxic action(s)
  Neurotropic action
  Psychotropic action
  Site-of-action
Activated   see
  Dopamine-activated
  Na-K-activated
Active   see
  Centrally active
  Highly active
Activity   see
  Alpha-adrenergic activity

Anorectic activity
Antiarrhythmic activity
Anticandidal activity
Anticholinergic activity
Anxiolytic activity
Behavioral activity
Binding activity
Bioelectric activity
Bioelectrical activity
Biological activity
Central activity
Dopaminergic activity
Electrical activity
Exploratory activity
Fast Activity
General activity
Hypersynchronous activity
Locomotor activity
Motor activity
Parasympathetic activity
Social activity
Structure-activity
Thyroid activity
AD-810   see
  Sulfamoylmethylbenzisoxazole
AD-1308   see
  Ethyl-2-piperazinyl-4-phenyl-
  quinoline-HCl
Adenosine monophosphate   see
  AMP
  C-AMP
  Cyclic AMP
Adenosine triphosphatase   see also
  ATPASE
Adenosine triphosphate   see
  ATP
Administered   see
  Centrally administered
  Self-administered
Administration   see also
  Route-of-administration
  Self-administration
Adrenaline   see also
  Epinephrine
Adrenocorticotropin   see also
  ACH

1

ADTN   see also
  Aminodihydroxytetrahydro-
  naphthalene
AEP   see also
  Evoked potential
Affective disorders   see also
  Bipolar
  Depression
  Manic-depressive
  Unipolar
Affinity   see also
  High affinity
Agent(s)   see
  Addictive agents
  Anorectic agents
  Antianxiety agents
  Anticonvulsant agents
  Antiepileptic agents
  Blocking agents
  Catecholamine depleting agent
  Convulsant agents
  Depolarizing agent
  Disinhibiting agent
  Dopaminergic agent(s)
  Hallucinogenic agent
  Narcotic agents
  Neuroactive agents
  Neuroleptic agents
  Neuropharmacological agents
  Neuropsychiatric agents
  Oxotremorine-like agent
  Pharmaceutic agents
  Pharmacologic agents
  Pharmacological agents
  Psychopharmacologic agents
  Psychopharmacological agents
  Psychotropic agent
  Releasing agents
  Serotonergic agents
  Vasoactive agents
AHR-1118   see
  Pridefine
Aids   see
  Sleeping aids
Alcohol   see also
  Ethanol
  Ethylalcohol
Alteration   see also
  Attentional alteration
  Rate altering
Amine(s)   see also
  Biogenic amine
  Brain amine
  Monoamine(s)

Names of specific amines
Sympathomimetic amines
Aminobutyric acid   see also
  GABA
Aminodihydroxytetrahydronaphthalene
  see also
  ADTN
Amphetamine   see also
  D-Amphetamine
  Dextroamphetamine
  L-Amphetamine
  Methamphetamine
  Methylamphetamine
Analysis   see also
  Behavioral analysis
  Behavioural analysis
  Mass spectral analysis
  Mass spectrometric analysis
  Microanalysis
  Psychometric analysis
  Signal detection analysis
  Symptom profile analysis
  Video analysis
Analyzed   see
  Computer analyzed
AMPT   see
  Methyl-p-tyrosine
Antidepressant   see also
  Names of specific compounds
  Nontricyclic antidepressant
  Polycyclic antidepressants
  Tetracyclic antidepressant(s)
  Tricyclic antidepressant(s)
Antihypertensive effects   see also
  Hypotensive effect
Anxiety   see also
  Panic anxiety
  Phobic anxiety
AOAA   see
  Aminooxyacetic acid
Apnea   see
  Sleep apnea
Application(s)   see
  Microiontophoretic applications
Approach(es)   see
  Psychodynamic approach
  Psychotherapeutic approaches
Area   see
  Preoptic area
Artery(ies)   see also
  Cerebral artery(ies)
  Mensenteric arteries
  Pial arteries
  Pulmonary arteries
  Vertebral artery

2

Aspect(s)   see
    Associative aspects
    Behavioral aspect
    Biochemical aspects
    Clinical aspects
    Metabolic aspects
    Nonassociative aspects
    Pathophysiological aspects
    Pharmacological aspects
    Psychiatric aspects
    Technical aspect
Aspirin   see also
    Acetylsalicylic-acid
Assay   see also
    Microassay
Assessment   see also
    Electromyographic assessment
Associations   see also
    Verbal associations
ATPASE   see also
    Adenosine-triphosphatase
Autoreceptor(s)   see also
    Alpha2-adrenergic autoreceptor
    Dopamine autoreceptor(s)
    GABA autoreceptors
    Presynaptic autoreceptors
    Serotoninergic autoreceptor
Availability   see also
    Commercially available
Aversion(s)   see also
    Taste aversion(s)
Avoidance   see also
    High avoidance
    Low avoidance
    Passive avoidance
    Shock avoidance
    Sidman avoidance

                    B

Barnetil   see
    Sultopride
Barrier   see
    Blood brain barrier
Based   see
    Community based
Basis; Bases   see
    Biochemical basis
    Neurochemical bases
    Neurophysiological basis
    Pathophysiologic basis
    Pharmacokinetic bases
    Pharmacological bases

Battery   see
    Neuropsychological battery
Behavior(s)   see also
    Abnormal behavior
    Abstinence behavior
    Acquisition behavior
    Addictive behavior
    Aggressive behavior
    Ataxic behaviors
    Avoidance behavior
    Bar-pressing behavior
    Conflict behavior
    Defensive behavior
    Drinking behavior
    Eating behavior
    Escape behavior
    Exploratory behavior
    Fighting behavior
    Head-shaking behavior
    Homing behavior
    Hyperactive behavior
    Learned behavior
    Maternal behavior
    Mating behavior
    Maze behavior
    Mothering behavior
    Motor behavior
    Mouse-killing behavior
    Nest-building behavior
    Nonverbal behavior
    Nursing behavior
    Operant behavior
    Pathological behavior
    Pecking behavior
    Punished behavior
    Reaching behavior
    Rotational behavior
    Scent-marking behavior
    Sexual behavior
    Shaking behavior
    Social behavior
    Stereotyped behavior
    Sterotypic behavior
    Violent behavior
    Yawning behavior
Behaviour   see also
    Abstinence behaviour
    Aggressive behaviour
    Agonistic behaviour
    Avoidance behaviour
    Circling behaviour
    Climbing behaviour
    Disturbed behaviour
    Exploratory behaviour

Rotational behaviour
Scratching behaviour
Sexual behaviour
Social behaviour
Sociosexual behaviour
Stereotyped behaviour
Timid behaviour
Biochemistry   see also
  Brain biochemistry
Bipolar   see also
  Affective disorders
  Depression
  Manic-depressive
  Unipolar
Biting   see
  Self-biting
Blind   see
  Double blind
  Single blind
  Time blind
Blues   see
  Maternity blues
Bodies   see also
  Dense bodies
  Lafora bodies
Bound   see also
  Membrane bound
Boy(s)   see also
  Hyperactive boys
  Hyperkinetic boys
  Schizophrenic boy
Brain   see also
  Anterior forebrain
  Blood brain barrier
  Forebrain
  Midbrain
  Mouse brain
  Rat brain
  Rat forebrain
  Rat midbrain
  Rat whole brain
Bulb(s)   see
  Olfactory bulb

C

C-AMP   see also
  Cyclic-adenosine monophosphate
  Cyclic-AMP
C-GMP   see
  Cyclic-GMP
  Cyclic-guanosine monophosphate
Ca   see also
  Calcium
  45Ca

Calcium   see also
  Ca
  45Ca
Capacity   see also
  Mental capacity
Care   see also
  Sheltered care
Cardiac   see also
  Heart
CAT-scan   see
  Computerized axial tomography
Catecholamine-O-methyltransferase
  see
  COMT-A
  COMT-B
Cation(s)   see also
  Divalent cation(s)
Caused   see
  Psychotropic caused
CCK-8   see
  Cholecystokinin octapeptide
CEEG   see also
  Comp-EEG
  CSEEG
Cell(s)   see also
  Purkinje cell(s)
  Red blood cell(s)
  Schwann cell
Center   see also
  Day treatment center
  Residential center
Central nervous system   see also
  CNS
Cerebellum   see also
  Rat cerebellum
Cerebral cortex   see also
  Frontal cerebral cortex
  Rat cerebral cortex
Cerebrospinal fluid   see also
  CSF
CG-3033   see
  Supidimide
Chain   see
  Branched chain
Chamber   see
  Anterior chamber
Change(s)   see also
  Behavior change
  Behavioral changes
  Behavioural changes
  Biochemical changes
  Developmental change
  Electrocardiographic changes
  Electrocortical changes
  Electrophysiological changes

Electroretinographic changes
Mechanical changes
Channel(s) see
Calcium channel
Ion channel(s)
Characterization see also
Biochemical characterization
Check see
Methodical check
Child; Children see also
Borderline children
Cerebral palsied child
Depressed child
Epileptic children
Hyperactive child(ren)
Hyperkinetic children
Special child
Chlorpromazine see also
CPZ
Cholinoceptor see also
Muscurinic cholinoceptor
Chorea see also
Huntingtons chorea
Chromatography see also
Gas Chromatography
Gas liquid chromatography
Liquid chromatography
Thin layer chromatography
TLC
Circadian see also
Ultradian
Circuit see also
Short circuit
Classification see also
Pharmacoclinical classification
Clinic see also
Mental hygiene clinic
CNS see also
Central nervous system
Coated see
Enteric coated
Colony see
Social colony
Comfort see
Social comfort
Communication see also
Preliminary communication
Comp-EEG see also
CEEG
CSEEG
Comparison see also
Controlled comparison
Complaint(s) see
Psychosomatic complaints

Complication see also
Neurological complications
Ocular complication
Component see
Two component
Compound(s) see
Hypnotic compounds
Names of specific compounds
Computer see also
Microcomputer
Concentration(s) see also
High concentrations
Conditioning see also
Appetitive conditioning
CS
Pavlovian conditioning
Conditions see also
Depressive conditions
Psychopathological conditions
Conductance see also
Ion conductance
Consequences see
Behavioral consequences
Biochemical consequences
Neurochemical consequences
Considerations see also
Behavioral considerations
Biochemical considerations
Methodological considerations
Pharmacological considerations
Control(led) see also
Autonomic control
Placebo controlled
Schedule controlled
Weight control
Cord see
Spinal cord
Correlates see
Behavioral correlates
Biochemical correlates
Biomedical correlates
Cortical correlates
Electrophysiological correlates
Metabolic correlates
Neurochemical correlates
Neuropsychological correlates
Peripheral correlates
Pharmacological correlates
Physiological correlates
Correlation see also
Biochemical correlation
Clinical correlation
Neuropsychiatric correlations

5

Cortex see also
  Cerebellar cortex
  Cerebral cortex
  Frontal cerebral cortex
  Frontal cortex
  Motor cortex
  Occipital cortex
  Olfactory cortex
  Prefrontal cortex
  Rat brain cortex
  Rat cerebral cortex
  Rat cerebral cortical
  Rat cortex
  Rat frontal cortex
Cortisol see also
  Hydrocortisone
Course see
  Time course
Court see
  Federal court
CP-36584 see
  Flutroline
CPZ see also
  Chlorpromazine
CS-386 see
  Mexazolam
CSD see
  Cysteine sulphinic acid-
    decarboxylase
CSF see also
  Cerebrospinal fluid
Culture see also
  Cell culture
Current see
  Outward current
Curve see also
  Response curve
Cycle(s); Cycling see also
  Circadian cycles (cycling)
  Estrous cycle
Cyclic-adenosine monophosphate
  see also
  C-AMP
  Cyclic-AMP
Cyclic AMP see also
  C-AMP
  Cyclic-adenosine monophosphate
Cyclic-GMP see also
  Cyclic-guanosine monophosphate
Cyclic-guanosine monophosphate
  see also
  Cyclic-GMP
Cylert see
  Pemoline

D

D-12524 see
  Lopirazepam
D-Amphetamine see also
  Amphetamine
  Dextroamphetamine
  L-Amphetamine
  Methamphetamine
  Methylamphetamine
DA see
  Dopamine
DAergic see
  Dopaminergic
Damage(d) see also
  Brain damage(d)
Dapotum-D see
  Fluphenazine decanoate
Data see also
  Biochemical data
  Pathophysiological data
DBH see
  Dopamine-beta-hydroxylase
Deaza-siba see
  Deoxyisobutylthio-3-deazaadenosine
Deficiencies see also
  Behavioral deficiencies
Deficits see also
  Avoidance deficits
  Behavioral deficits
Delirium see also
  Alcoholic delirium
Delta sleep see
  DSIP
Dementia see also
  Senile dementia
Deoxycorticosterone see also
  DOCA
Depakene see
  Valproic acid
Depakine see also
  Dipropylacetate
  Dipropylacetic acid
  Sodium dipropylacetate
  Sodium valproate
  Valproic acid
Dependent(ence) see also
  Age dependent
  Barbiturate dependence
  Behavior dependent
  Ca++-dependent
  DNA dependent
  Dopamine dependent

6

Dose dependent
Meal dependent
Morphine dependence(ent)
Na+-dependent
Opiate dependent
Physical dependence
Prostacyclin dependent
Rate depencency
Sodium dependent
State dependent
Time dependent
Depression   see also
  Affective disorders
  Behavioral depression
  Bipolar
  Childhood depression
  Manic-depressive
  Motor depression
  Unipolar
Deprived   see also
  Maternally deprived
  Sleep deprivation (ed)
  Water deprived
Desensitization   see also
  Behavioral desensitization
Desipramine   see also
  Desmethylimipramine
  DMI
Desmethylimipramine   see also
  Desipramine
  DMI
Despair   see
  Behavioural despair
Detection   see also
  Electrochemical detection
Determination   see also
  Liquid chromatographic determination
Deviants; Deviations   see
  Sexual deviants; deviations
Dextroamphetamine   see also
  Amphetamine
  D-Amphetamine
  L-Amphetamine
  Methamphetamine
  Methylamphetamine
DHT   see also
  Dihydroxytryptamine
Diagnosis   see also
  Psychiatric diagnosis
Difference(s)   see
  Sex difference(s)
  Species difference(s)
Difficulties   see
  Sexual difficulties

Diflunisal   see
  Difluorophenylsalicylic acid
Dihydroxyergotoxine   see also
  Hydergine
Dihydroxyphenylacetic acid   see also
  DOPAC
Dihydroxyphenethylamine   see
  Dopamine
Dihydroxyphenylalanine   see also
  DOPA
  L-DOPA
  Levodopa
Dihydroxytryptamine   see also
  DHT
Diisopropylfluorophosphate   see
  DFP
Dimethoxy-4-methylamphetamine
  see also
  DOM
Dimethylaminoethanol   see
  DEANOL
Diphenylhydantoin   see also
  Phenytoin
Dipropylacetate; Dipropylacetic acid
  see also
  Depakine
  Sodium dipropylacetate
  Sodium valproate
  Valproic acid
DIPT   see
  Diisopropyltryptamine
Disability(ies)   see
  Learning disabilities
  Reading disabled
Discharge   see also
  Epileptic discharge
Disease(s)   see
  Alzheimers disease
  Cerebrovascular diseases
  Chagas disease
  Gilles de la Tourettes disease
  Heart disease
  Hepatic disease
  Huntington(s) disease
  Mental diseases
  Names of specific diseases
  Parkinson(s) disease
  Psychosomatic diseases
  Renal disease
  Respiratory disease
Disorder(s)(ed)   see also
  Affective disorder(s)
  Anxiety disorders
  Astheno-depressive disorders

Attention disordered
Behavior disorders
Behavioural disorders
Deficit disorders
Depressive disorder(s)
Dystonic disorders
Extrapyramidal disorders
Gilles de la Tourettes disorder
Learning disorders
Leukopenia disorders
Manic melancholic disorders
Mental disorders
Mood disorders
Movement disorders
Obsessive compulsive disorder(s)
Panic disorder
Personality disorder
Psychiatric disorders
Psychotic disorders
Schizoaffective disorder
Sexual disorders
Sleep disorders
Sleep wake disorders
Distalgesic   see
  Dextropropoxyphene
Disturbances   see also
  Behavioral disturbances
  Memory disturbances
  Mental disturbances
  Organic brain disturbance
  Psychiatric disturbance
  Sensory disturbances
  Sleep disturbances
DMI   see also
  Desipramine
  Desmethylimipramine
DN-1417   see
  Butyrolactone-gamma-carbonyl-
  histidyl-prolinamide
DOCA   see also
  Deoxycorticosterone
Dogs   see also
  Beagle dogs
DOM   see also
  Dimethoxy-4-methylamphetamine
DOPA   see also
  Dihydroxyphenylalanine
  L-DOPA
  Levodopa
DOPAC   see also
  Dihydroxyphenylacetic acid
DOPEG-SO$_4$ see
  Dihydroxyphenylethylene-glycol-
  sulfate

Dose(es) (ages)   see also
  High dosage(es)
  Hyperthermic dose
  Large doses
  Large single doses
  Log dose
  Low dose(s) (age)
  Minimum doses
  Multiple dose
  Overdose(age)
  Single bedtime dose
  Single daily dose(s)
  Single dosage(e) (es)
  Single nightly dose
  Single oral dosages (e)
  Single therapeutic dose
  Small dose
Doubt   see
  Reasonable doubt
DPEA   see
  Dichloro-6-phenylphenoxyethylamine-
  HBr
Drugs   see also
  Analgesic drugs
  Anorectic drugs
  Antialcoholism drug
  Antianxiety drug(s)
  Anticholinergic drugs
  Anticonvulsant drug(s)
  Antidepressant drug(s)
  Antidepressive drug(s)
  Antiepileptic drugs
  Antihypoxidotic drugs
  Antiinflammatory drugs
  Antiparkinson drugs
  Antiparkinsonian drugs
  Antipsychotic drug(s)
  Antischizophrenic drugs
  Anxiolytic drugs
  Blocking drugs
  Cholinergic drugs
  Hallucinogenic drugs
  Hypnotic drug(s)
  Names of specific drugs
  Narcotic drugs
  Neuroleptic drug(s)
  Neuropharmacological drugs
  Neurotropic drugs
  Nicotinic drugs
  Nootropic drugs
  Opiate-like drugs
  Psychedelic drugs
  Psychiatric drug(s)
  Psychoactive drug(s)

8

Psycholeptic drugs
Psychotherapeutic drug(s)
Psychotropic drug(s)
Stimulant drugs
Tranquilizing drugs
Two-drug
Duration   see also
  Long duration
Dysfunction(s)   see also
  Attention dysfunction
  Brain dysfunction
  Minimal brain dysfunction
  Sensorimotor dysfunctions
  Sexual dysfunction(s)
Dyskinesia(s)   see also
  Paroxystic dyskinesias
  Tardive dyskinesia (s)

E

ECG   see
  EKG
  Electrocardiogram
ECS   see
  ECT
  Electroconvulsive shock
  Electroconvulsive therapy
  Electroconvulsive treatment
  Electroshock
ECT   see also
  Electroconvulsive shock
  Electroconvulsive therapy
  Electroconvulsive treatment
  Electroshock
EEG   see also
  CEEG
  Comp-EEG
  Electroencephalography
  PharmacoEEG
Effect(s)   see
  Adverse effects
  Anorectic effect
  Antagonistic effects
  Antianxiety effects
  Anticholinergic effects
  Antidopaminergic effects
  Antiepileptic effect
  Antihypertensive effects
  Antimanic effect
  Antinociceptive effect
  Antinuretic effect
  Antipsychotic effect
  Associative effects
  Autonomic effects

Aversive effect(s)
Behavioral effects
Behavioural effects
Biochemical effects
Biological effects
Biphasic effects
Cardiovascular effects
Cataleptic effect(s)
Choleretic effect
Clinical effect(s)
Comparative effect(s)
Contrasting effects
Convulsant effect(s)
Differential effect(s)
Dipsogenic effect
Dissociative effects
Dopaminergic effects
Dose effects
Drug effect(s)
Electrocortical effects
Electroencephalographic effects
Electrophysiological effects
Endocrine effects
Epileptogenic effect
Experimental effects
Extrapyramidal effects
Hormonal effects
Hyperthermic effects
Hypnotic effects
Hypotensive effect
Hypothermic effects
Inhibitory effect(s)
Interactive effects
Joint effects
Laryngeal effects
Locomotor effects
Lytic effects
Metabolic effects
Motor effects
Neurochemical effects
Neuroleptic effect(s)
Neurophysiological effects
Neuropsychologic effects
Opiate effects
Opposite effects
Paradoxical effect(s)
Perceptual effects
Pharmacologic effects
Pharmacological effects
Placebo effect(s)
Prohypnotic effects
Psychiatric effects
Psychic effects
Psychoactive drug effect

9

Psycholeptic effects
Psychopharmacological effects
Psychophysiological effects
Residual effects
Retinotoxic effects
Side effect(s)
Stimulant effect(s)
Subjective effects
Thermoregulatory effects
Transient effect
Efficacy   see also
   Antipsychotic efficacy
   Clinical efficacy
   Therapeutic efficacy
EKG   see also
   Electrocardiogram
Electrocardiogram   see also
   EKG
Electroconvulsive shock   see also
   ECT
   Electroconvulsive therapy
   Electroconvulsive treatment
   Electroshock
Electroconvulsive therapy   see also
   ECT
   Electroconvulsive shock
   Electroconvulsive treatment
   Electroshock
Electroconvulsive treatment   see also
   ECT
   Electroconvulsive shock
   Electroconvulsive therapy
   Electroshock
Electroencephalography   see also
   CEEG
   Comp-EEG
   CSEEG
   EEG
Electromyographic   see also
   EMG
Elements   see
   Mineral elements
   Names of specific elements
Elicited   see
   Amphetamine-elicited
   Apomorphine-elicited
   Shock-elicited
Emergency(ies)   see also
   Medical emergencies
   Psychiatric emergencies
EMG   see also
   Electromyographic
Eminence   see
   Median eminence

Ending   see
   Nerve ending(s)
Enhanced   see
   GABA-enhanced
Enriched   see
   K+-enriched
Entheogenic   see
   Hallucinogenic
Enuresis   see also
   Childhood enuresis
Epilepsy   see also
   Childhood epilepsy
   Focal epilepsy
   Petit mal
Epinephrine   see also
   Adrenaline
Episode   see
   Affective episode
   Schizophrenic episodes
ERG   see
   Electroretinography
Escape   see also
   Water escape
Estimation   see
   Microestimation
ET-495   see
   Piribedil
Ethanol   see also
   Alcohol
   Ethyl alcohol
Ethyl alcohol   see also
   Alcohol
   Ethanol
Euhypnos-forte   see
   Temazepam
Evaluation   see also
   Clinical evaluation
   Preclinical evaluation
   Self-evaluation
Events   see
   Behavioral events
   Biochemical event
   Endocrine events
Evidence   see also
   Behavioral evidence
   Biochemical evidence
Evoked   see also
   Barbiturate-evoked
   Dopamine-evoked
   Flash-evoked
   GABA-evoked
   K+-evoked
   Stimulation-evoked
   Stimulus-evoked
   Striatally-evoked

Evoked Potential   see also
  AEP
Exchange   see
  Gas exchange
Execretion   see also
  Circadian excretion
Experiences   see also
  Aversive experiences
  Clinical experiences
  Psychedelic experiences
Exposed   see also
  Stress exposed
Extracts   see also
  Coca extracts

F

Facilitation   see
  Behavioral facilitation
Factor(s)   see also
  Antihemophilic factor
  Bass scale factors
  Growth factor
  Psychopharmacologic factors
  Psychosocial factors
  Risk factors
  Thyrotrophin-releasing factor
FDA   see also
  Food and Drug Administration
Fear   see also
  Learned fear
Feeding   see also
  Freely feeding
Fiber   see also
  Thin fiber
Field   see
  Open field
  Terminal fields
Fighting   see also
  Shock-induced fighting
Findings   see
  Preliminary findings
Firing   see also
  Burst firing
Fluid   see also
  Amniotic fluid
  Crebrospinal fluid
  CSF
  Jejunal fluid
  Spinal fluid
Flux   see also
  Ca++-flux
  Ca-flux
  Calcium flux

Focus; Foci   see
  Epileptic focus (foci)
  Epileptogenic focus
Food and Drug Administration
  see also
  FDA
Forebrain   see also
  Anterior forebrain
  Rat forebrain
Fragmentography   see
  Mass fragmentography
Frequency   see also
  High frequency
FSH   see
  Follicle-stimulating hormone
Function(ing)   see also
  Affective functions
  Autonomic functioning
  Mixed functions
  Sexual function(s)
  Thyroid function

G

GABA   see also
  Aminobutyric acid
GAD   see also
  Glutamic acid decarboxylase
Gain   see
  Weight gain
Gas liquid chromatography
  see also
  GLC
GBL   see
  Butyrolactone
GC   see
  Gas chromatography
Generation   see also
  F1 generation
  Second generation
Gerbil(s)   see also
  Mongolian gerbil
GH   see also
  Growth hormone
Gilles de la Tourette syndrome
  see also
  Tourette syndrome
Gland   see
  Adrenal gland
  Pineal gland
  Pituitary glands
  Salivary gland
  Submarxillary gland
  Thymus gland
  Thyroid gland

11

GLC   see also
  Gas liquid chromatography
Glutamic acid decarboxylase   see also
  GAD
Growth Hormone   see also
  GH
GS-385   see
  Chloro-4-phenylsuccinimidobenzene-
  sulfonamide
Guanosine triphosphate   see
  GTP
Gum   see also
  Chewing gum

H

H-77-77   see
  Dimethyl-m-tyramine
Haldol   see
  Haloperidol
Handicapped   see also
  Intellectually handicapped
  Mentally handicapped
Headaches   see also
  Cluster headaches
Health   see
  Mental health
Heart   see also
  Cardiac
Helplessness   see
  Learned helplessness
Hepatic   see also
  Liver
HIAA   see also
  Hydroxyindoleacetic acid
Histamine receptors   see also
  H1-receptors
  H2-receptors
Holidays   see
  Drug holidays
Homes   see
  Nursing homes
  Sheltered care homes
Hormones   see also
  Adrenal hormones
  Follicle-stimulating hormone
  GH
  Glucocortical hormones
  Gonadotropin-releasing hormone
  Growth hormone
  LH
  Luteinizing hormone
  Melanocorticotropic hormone
  Melanocyte-stimulating hormone

  Names of specific hormones
  Parathyroid hormones
  Peptide hormones
  Pituitary hormones
  Sex hormone
  Steroid hormones
  STH
  Thyroid hormones
  Thyrotrophin-releasing hormone
  TRH
  TSH
Hospital   see also
  Day hospital
  General hospital
  Lima State Hospital
  Psychiatric hospital
  State hospital
HT   see also
  Hydroxytryptamine
  Serotonin
HTP   see also
  Hydroxytryptophan
Hydergine   see also
  Dihydroxyergotoxine
Hydrocortisone   see also
  Cortisol
Hydroxyindoleautic acid   see also
  HIAA
Hydroxydopamine   see also
  OHDA
Hydroxytryptamine   see also
  HT
  Serotonin
Hydroxytryptaminergic   see also
  Serotonergic
  Serotoninergic
Hydroxytryptophan   see also
  HTP
Hydroxyvanillic acid   see
  HVA
Hyperactivity   see also
  Hyperkinesis
Hyperkinesis (ia)   see also
  Hyperactivity
  Tardive hyperkinesia
Hypoactivity   see also
  Hypokinesia
Hypokinesia   see also
  Hypoactivity
Hypotensive effect   see also
  Antihypertensive effect
H1-receptors   see also
  Histamine receptors
H2-receptors   see also
  Histamine receptors

12

I

ICS   see
  Intracranial stimulation
Illness; Ill   see also
  Affective illness
  Chronically ill
  Depressive illness
  Lupus like illness
  Manic-depressive illness
  Medically ill
  Mental illness
  Psychosomatic illness
IMAP   see
  Fluspirilene
IMI   see
  Imipramine
Impact   see
  Pathophysiologic impact
Implication   see
  Clinical implications
Independent   see also
  Ca++-independent
  Na+-independent
  Voltage independent
Induced   see also
  ACTH-induced
  Adrenaline-induced
  Agonist-induced
  Ala2-met5-enkephalinamide-induced
  Aminophylline-induced
  Amphetamine-induced
  Analgesic-induced
  Angiotensin-II-induced
  Anticonvulsant-induced
  Apomorphine-induced
  Barbiturate-induced
  Bicuculline-induced
  Caffeine-induced
  Cannabinoid-induced
  Carbachol-induced
  Carbamazepine-induced
  Chemically-induced
  Chloralose-induced
  Chlorophenylalanine-induced
  Chlorpromazine-induced
  Chlorea-toxin-induced
  Cimetidine-induced
  Clonidine-induced
  Cocaine-induced
  Cyclophosphamide-induced
  D-amphetamine-induced
  Denervation-induced
  Depolarization-induced

Desipramine-induced
Di-n-propylacetate-induced
Diazepam-induced
Dihydroxytryptamine-induced
Diphenylhydantoin-induced
Disease-induced
Dopamine-induced
Drug-induced
Electrically-induced
Electroshock-induced
Endogenously-induced
Endorphin-induced
Endotoxin-induced
Enkephalin-induced
Enzyme-inducing
Ethanol-induced
Exogenously-induced
Experimentally-induced
Flurazepam-induced
Haloperidol-induced
Handling-induced
Harmaline-induced
Hexobarbital-induced
Homocysteine-induced
HTP-induced
Hydroxytryptamine-induced
Insulin-induced
Iron-induced
Isolation-induced
Isoprenaline-induced
Isoproterenol-induced
Kainic-acid-induced
L-dopa-induced
Lesion-induced
Lithium-induced
LSD-induced
MAOI-induced
Methadone-induced
Methamphetamine-induced
Methylmercury-induced
Methylphenidate-induced
Metrazol-induced
Morphine-induced
Naloxone-induced
Narcotic-induced
Neuroleptic-induced
Neurotensin-induced
Opiate-induced
Organophosphate-induced
Pemoline-induced
Penicillin-induced
Pentobarbital-induced
Pentylenetetrazol-induced
Peripherally-induced

13

Pethidine-induced
Phencyclidine-induced
Potassium-induced
Psychotropic-drug-induced
Reflex-induced
Reserpine-induced
Schedule-induced
Scopolamine-induced
Self-induced
Shock-induced
Sound-induced
Stimulation-induced
Stimulus-induced
Stress-induced
Stretch-induced
Strychnine-induced
Sulpiride-induced
Tetrabenazine-induced
THC-induced
Thiazide-induced
Thyroid-induced
Tricyclic-antidepressant-induced
Triethyltin-induced
Tryptophan-induced
Tryptophol-induced
Infarction   see
  Myocardial infarction
Influence(d)   see
  Parasympathomimetic influence
  Serotonergially influenced
Infusion   see also
  Microinfusion
Inhibition(or)   see also
  MAOI
  MAO inhibition(or)
  Monoamine-oxidase inhibition(or)
Injection   see also
  Microinjection
  Self-injection
Injury   see also
  Self-injury
Inpatient(s)   see also
  Depressed inpatients
  Insomniac inpatients
  Psychiatric inpatients
  Psychogeriatric inpatients
Interaction   see also
  Behavioral interactions
  Biologic interaction
  Biological interaction
  Drug interactions
  Hypnotic interactions
  Monoaminergic interaction
  Paradoxical interaction

Pharmacokinetic interaction
  Social interaction(s)
Interval   see also
  Fixed interval
Intervention   see
  Behavioral intervention
  Psychiatric intervention
Interperitoneal   see also
  IP
Investigation(s)   see also
  Psychopharmacological investigation
Ion(s)   see
  Calcium ions
  Lithium ion
  Sodium ion
Ionization   see also
  Chemical ionization
  Flame ionization
Iontophoresis   see also
  Microiontophoresis
IP   see also
  Intraperitoneal
Isolation   see also
  Social isolation
Isomers   see also
  Cis-isomers
  D-isomers
  L-isomers
  Optical isomers
  Trans-isomers
Issue(s)   see
  Methodological issues

K

K   see also
  Potassium
Kidney   see also
  Renal
Killing   see
  Mouse-killing
  Pup-killing

L

L-Amphetamine   see also
  Amphetamine
  D-Amphetamine
  Dextroamphetamine
  Methamphetamine
  Methylamphetamine
L-DOPA   see also
  Dihydroxyphenylalanine
  DOPA
  Levodopa

14

LAAM   see
  Acetylmethadol
Labeled   see also
  Isotope labeled
  Spiroperidol labeled
Lasting   see
  Long-lasting
Learning   see also
  Maze learning
  Motor learning
Level(s)   see
  High levels
Levodopa   see also
  Dihydroxyphenylalanine
  DOPA
  L-DOPA
LH   see also
  Luteinizing hormone
LHM   see
  Lisuride hydrogen maleate
Li   see also
  Lithium
LiCl   see also
  Lithium chloride
Life   see also
  Sex life
Lilly-110140   see
  Fluoxetine
Lithium   see also
  Li
Lithium carbonate   see also
  Li_2CO_3
Lithium chloride   see also
  LiCl
Liver   see also
  Hepatic
Li_2CO_3 see also
  Lithium carbonate
Localization   see also
  Biochemical localization
Loss   see also
  Hair loss
LSD   see also
  Lysergic acid diethylamide
LU-10-171 · see
  Citalopram
Luteinizing hormone   see also
  LH
Lyorodin   see
  Fluphenazine-HCl
Lysergic acid diethylamide   see also
  LSD

M

Maladjustments   see

  Social maladjustments
Manic-depressive   see also
  Affective-disorders
  Bipolar
  Depression
  Unipolar
Manifestations   see also
  Psychic manifestations
Manipulation   see also
  Behavioural manipulation
MAO   see also
  Monoamine oxidase
MAOI   see also
  MAO inhibition
  Monamine oxidase inhibition
Maze   see also
  T-Maze
  Y-Maze
MBD   see
  Minimal brain dysfunction
Measurements   see also
  Biochemical measurements
Mechanism(s)   see also
  Autonomic mechanisms
  Biochemical mechanism
  Dual mechanism
Mediated   see
  Adrenoceptor-mediated
  Agonist-mediated
  Alpha-adrenoceptor-mediated
  Aminobutyric-acid-mediated
  Dopamine-mediated
  GABA-mediated
  H1-receptor-mediated
  Receptor-mediated
Medication; Medicine   see also
  Antipsychotic medications
  Neuroleptic medication; medicine
  Psychoactive medication
  Psychosomatic medicine
  Psychotropic medication
  Self-medication
Medulla   see
  Adrenal medulla
  Pons medulla
Meeting   see
  Psychopharmacological meeting
Memory   see also
  Verbal memory
MEO-DIPT   see
  Methoxydiisopropyltryptamine
Merital   see
  Nomifensine
Met-enkephalin   see also
  Methionine enkephalin

15

Methamphetamine   see also
  Amphetamine
  D-Amphetamine
  Dextroamphetamine
  L-Amphetamine
  Methylamphetamine
Methionine enkephalin   see also
  Met-enkephalin
Method(s)   see also
  Electrochemical method
  Electromyographic method
Methoxy-4-hydroxyphenylglycol
  see also
  MHPG
Methylamphetamine   see also
  Amphetamine
  D-Amphetamine
  Dextroamphetamine
  L-Amphetamine
  Methamphetamine
Methylphenidate   see also
  Ritalin
MHPG   see also
  Methoxy-4-hydroxyphenylglycol
Mianserin   see also
  ORG-GB-94
MIF   see also
  Pro-leu-gly-NH$_2$
MIlk   see also
  Mothers milk
Minnesota Multiphasic Inventory   see
  MMPI
MK-647   see
  Difluorophenylsalicylic acid
MMH   see
  Monomethylhydrazine
Model   see also
  Animal model(s)
  Medical model
Modification; Modifying; Modified
  see also
  Behavior modification
  Behaviour modifying
  Synthetically modified
Modulated   see
  Stress modulated
Monitored (ing) .see also
  Holtor monitored
  Ion-monitoring
Monkey(s)   see also
  Macaca mulatta
  Pigtail macaque
  Rhesus macaque
  Rhesus monkey(s)

  Squirrel monkey(s)
  Talapoin monkeys
  Vervet monkeys
Monoamine(s)   see also
  Brain monoamine
Monoamine oxidase   see also
  MAO
Monoamine oxidase inhibitor
  see also
  MAO inhibitor
  MAOI
MOPEG   see
  Methoxy-4-hydroxyphenylethylene-
  glycol
Motivation   see
  Sexual motivation
Movement(s)   see also
  Abnormal movements
  Choreic movements
  Dyskinetic movements
  Eye movements
  Involuntary movements
  Psychiatric movements
  Rapid eye movement
  REM
MS   see
  Mass spectrometry
MSH   see
  Melanocyte-stimulating hormone
MT   see
  Methyl-p-tyrosine
Muscle   see also
  Anococcygeus muscle
  Cardiac muscle
  Intestinal muscle
  Skeletal muscle
  Smooch muscle
  Ventricular muscle
Mutilation   see
  Self-mutilation

                      N

Na   see also
  Sodium
NaCl   see also
  Sodium chloride
Nerve   see also
  Hepatic nerve
  Phrenic nerve
  Sciatic nerve
  Sympathetic nerve
Neuralgia   see
  Trigeminal neuralgia

16

Neurochemistry see also
  Behavioral neurochemistry
Neurones   see also
  Rat cortical neurones
Neurosis   see also
  Depressive neurosis
  Obsessive-compulsive neurosis
  War neurosis
Neurotransmission   see also
  Transmission
Neurotransmitter   see also
  Transmitter
NH_4-tyr-pro-phe-pro-$CONH_2$ see
  Morphiceptin
Nigrostriatal   see also
  Striatonigral
Node   see
  Lymph node
Noradrenaline   see also
  Norepinephrine
Norepinephrine   see also
  Noradrenaline
Noveril; Noveril-240   see
  Dibenzepine
Nuclear magnetic resonance   see
  NMR
Nucleotide(s)   see also
  Cyclic nucleotides
  Guanine nucleotides
  Guanyl nucleotides
Nucleus (Nuclei)   see also
  Caudate nucleus
  Preopticus medialis nucleus
  Trigeminal nucleus

O

Observations   see also
  Biochemical observations
Ocytocin   see also
  Oxytocin
Offenders   see also
  Criminally insane offenders
  Sex offenders
  Sexual offenders
OHDA   see also
  Hydroxydopamine
Opening   see
  Ring opening
ORAP   see
  Pimozide
Order   see
  Higher order
  Randomized order

Second order
ORG-GB-94   see also
  Mianserin
Organ   see also
  Pineal organ
Outpatient(s)   see also
  Depressed outpatients
  Psychiatric outpatients
  Psychotic outpatients
  Schizophrenic outpatients
Oxidase(s)   see also
  Amine oxidase
  Cu amine oxidase(s)
  MAO
  Monoamine-oxidase(s)
Oxytocin   see also
  Ocytocin

P

Papers   see
  Clinical papers
Parameters   see also
  Biochemical parameters
Parlodel   see
  Bromo-alpha-ergocriptine
Parnate   see
  Tranylcypromine
Patient(s)   see also
  Aggressive patients
  Alcoholic patients
  Autistic patients
  Bipolar-I patients
  Bipolar patients
  Borderline patients
  Cancer patients
  Depressed patient(s)
  Depressive patients
  Dysthymic patients
  Elderly patients
  Epileptic patients
  Fibrositis patients
  Geriatric patients
  Gerontopsychiatric patient(s)
  Hospitalized patients
  Hyperprolactinaemic patients
  Hypertensive patients
  Hypothyroid patients
  Involuntary patients
  Manic patients
  Manic-depressive patient(s)
  Melancholic depressed patients
  Mental patients
  Mentally handicapped patients
  Mentally subnormal patients

17

Neurotic patients
Parkinson patients
Parkinsonian patients
Physically handicapped patients
Psychiatric patients
Psychogeriatric patient(s)
Psychotic patients
Schizoaffective patients
Schizophrenic patients
Subnormal patients
Patterns   see also
  Drinking patterns
  Mood-swing patterns
PCP   see also
  Phencyclidine
PCPA   see
  Chlorophenylalanine
PEA   see
  Phenethylamine
  Phenylethylamine
Pemoline   see also
  Cylert
Peptides   see also
  Bombesin-like peptides
  Cholecystokinin peptides
  Hexapeptide
  Names of specific peptides
  Neuroleptic peptides
  Neuropeptide(s)
  Opiate pentapeptide
  Opiod peptide(s)
  Pyrimidine peptide
  Tetrapeptide
Performance(s)   see also
  High performance
  Maze performance
Periodicity   see also
  Circadian periodicity
Perspective   see also
  Biopsychosocial perspective
  Historical perspective
  Neurobiological perspective
  Psychiatric perspective
  Therapeutic perspectives
Pharmacology   see also
  Behavioral pharmacology
  Biochemical pharmacology
  Cardiovascular pharmacology
  Clinical pharmacology
  Neurochemical pharmacology
  Neurovascular pharmacology
Pharmacotherapy   see also
  Behavioral pharmacotherapy
Phencyclidine   see also
  PCP

Phenethylamine   see also
  Phenylethylamine
Phenylethylamine   see also
  Phenethylamine
Phenytoin   see also
  Diphenylhydantoin
Picture   see
  Clinical picture
Pills   see also
  Sleeping pill(s)
Placebo   see also
  Double placebo
Platelets   see also
  Blood platelets
Postassium   see also
  K
Potential(s)   see also
  Evoked potential(s)
  VEP
  Visually-evoked-potentials
Practice   see
  Clinical practice
  General medical practice
  General practice
  Pediatric practice
  Psychiatric practice
Practitioner(s)   see
  General practitioner(s)
Predictors   see also
  Behavioral predictors
Preparations   see
  Anxiolytic preparations
Pressure   see also
  Blood pressure
  Micropressure
Primed   see
  Estrogen-primed
Probe(s)   see also
  Pharmacologic probes
  Pharmacological probes
Problem(s)   see
  Methodological problem
  Personality problems
Procedures   see also
  Psychopharmacological procedures
Process   see
  Creative process
Processing   see also
  Information processing
Prone   see
  Epilepsy prone
Properties   see
  Anorectic properties
  Antidyskinetic properties
  Antipsychotic properties

18

Arrythmogenic properties
Biochemical properties
Microproperties
Pharmacological properties
Prothieden   see
  Dothiepin
Psychiatry   see also
  Biological psychiatry
  Child psychiatry
  Social psychiatry
Psychopharmacology   see also
  Pediatric psychopharmacology
Psychosis   see also
  Affective psychosis
  Epileptic psychosis
  Manic-depressive psychosis
  Manic psychosis
  Schizoaffective psychoses
  Schizophrenic psychoses
Pulp   see
  Tooth pulp
Pump   see
  Lithium-pump
  Na-pump
  Sodium-pump
Pursuit   see
  Smooth pursuit
Putamen   see
  Caudate-putamen

Q

Questionnaire   see also
  Leeds-Sleep-Evaluation-Questionnaire

R

R 33812   see
  Domperidone
Radiation; Ray   see
  Gamma radiation (ray)
Radioreceptor(s)   see also
  Dopamine radioreceptor
Rapid eye movement   see also
  REM
Rate   see also
  Firing rate
  Turnover rate(s)
Rating   see also
  Self-rating
Ratio   see
  Fixed ratio
  Progressive ratio
RBC   see
  Red blood cell

Reaction(s)   see also
  Adverse reactions
  Behavioral reactions
  Hypomanic reaction
Receptivity   see
  Sexual receptivity
Receptor(s)   see also
  Acetylcholine receptor(s)
  ACH receptor
  Adenosine receptors
  Adrenergic receptor(s)
  Alpha-adrenergic receptor(s)
  Alpha-receptors
  Alpha1-adrenergic receptors
  Alpha1-receptors
  Alpha2-receptors
  Aminobutyric acid receptor(s)
  Apomorphine receptors
  Benzodiazepine receptor(s)
  Beta-adrenergic receptor(s)
  Beta-receptor
  Bradykinesia receptor(s)
  Catecholamine receptors
  Cholinergic receptor(s)
  Delta-receptor(s)
  Diazepam receptor
  Dopamine receptor(s)
  Dopaminergic receptor(s)
  Drug receptors
  Enkepalin receptors
  GABA receptor(s)
  Glucocorticord receptor
  Glutamate receptors
  Histamine receptors
  HT receptor
  HTP receptors
  Hydroxytryptamine receptors
  H1-receptor(s)
  H2-receptor(s)
  Ionophore receptor
  Kappa-receptor(s)
  Monamine receptor(s)
  Monoaminergic receptor
  Mu-receptors
  Muscarinic receptor(s)
  Neuroleptic receptor(s)
  Neuropeptide receptor
  Neurotensin receptor
  Neurotransmitter receptor(s)
  Nicotine receptors
  Noradrenaline receptors
  Noradrenergic-alpha2 receptors
  Norepinephrine receptor
  Opiate receptor(s)
  Opiod receptor(s)

19

Postsynaptic receptors
Presynaptic receptors
Progestin receptors
Quisqualate receptors
Serotonergic receptors
Serotonin receptor(s)
Recorded   see
  EMG recorded
Redergine   see
  Dihydroergotoxine
  Hydergine
Reflex(es)   see also
  Biting reflex
  Motor reflexes
  Sexual reflexes
Refusal   see
  Drug refusal
Refuse   see also
  Right-to-refuse
Region   see
  Hippocampal CA1-region
Regulation   see also
  Central regulation
Reinforced   see
  Cocaine reinforced
  Drug reinforced
  Emotionally reinforced
  Narcotic reinforced
Related   see
  Age related
  Dose related
  Drug related
  Event related
  Sleep related
Relaxant(s)   see
  Muscle relaxant(s)
Release   see also
  Controlled release
  Sustained release
REM   see also
  Rapid eye movement
Renal   see also
  Kidney
Report(s)   see
  Case report
  Preliminary report
  Task force report
Research   see also
  Psychiatric research
  Psychobiological research
  Psychopharmacological research
  Psychoneuropharmacologic research
Resistance   see
  Drug resistance

Galvanic skin resistance
Skin resistance
Stress resistance
Resistant   see also
  Atropine resistant
  Drug resistant
  Therapeutically resistant
  Therapy resistant
Responding   see
  FI responding
  Operant responding
  Punished responding
Response(s)   see
  Behavioral responses
  Behavioural responses
  Biochemical response
  CR
  Clinical response
  Dose response
  Early response
  Evoked response(s)
  Glycemic response
  Hyperthermic response
  Motor response
  Operant response
  Pharmacologic responses
Results   see
  Preliminary results
Resuscitation   see
  Neurosurgical resuscitation
Retardate(s); Retarded   see also
  Mental retardates
  Mentally retarded
Reversal   see also
  Behavioral reversal
Review   see also
  Minireview
Rhythm(s)   see
  Biological rhythm
  Circadian rhythm(s)
Rhythmicity   see
  Biological rhythmicity
Ribonucleic acid   see
  RNA
Rich   see
  Terminal rich
Risk   see also
  High risk
Ritalin   see also
  Methylphenidate
Roipnol   see
  Flunitrazepam
Rodent   see also
  Guinea pig

20

S

Sample   see also
  Matching-to-sample
  Psychiatric sample
Satisfaction   see
  Job satisfaction
Scale(s)   see also
  Behavioral rating scales
  Clinical scale
  Hamilton Depression Rating Scale
Schedule   see also
  Automaintenance schedule
  Multiple schedule
Schizophrenics (ia)   see also
  Childhood schizophrenia
  Chronic schizophrenics
Scores   see
  T-scores
Seizure(s)   see also
  Audiogenic seizure(s)
  Cephalgic seizures
  Convulsive seizure.
  Epileptic seizures
  Organic brain seizures
Selection   see also
  Self-selection
Selective   see also
  Behaviorally selective
  Biochemically selective
Sensitive   see also
  Calcium sensitive
  Dopamine sensitive
  HT sensitive
  Opiate sensitive
  Serotonin sensitive
Sensitivity   see also
  Behavioral sensitivity
  High sensitivity
Sensitization   see also
  Behavioral sensitization
Sequelae   see also
  Behavioral sequelae
Serotonergic   see also
  Hydroxytryptaminergic
  Serotoninergic
Serotonin   see also
  HT
  Hydroxytryptamine
Serotoninergic   see also
  Hydroxytryptaminergic
  Serotonergic
Serum   see also
  Umbilical cord serum

Service(s)   see
  Health care services
  Inpatient service
Sheet   see
  Fact sheet
Shake(s)   see
  Wet dog shake(s)
Shock(s)   see also
  Convulsive shock
  ECS
  Electric shock
  Electroconvulsive shock
  Electroshock
  Footshock
  Stimulus shock
  Tail shock
  Two shock
SIF   see
  Shock-induced fighting
Site(s)   see
  Binding sites
  XQ fragile site
Situations   see
  Aversive situations
  Conflict situation
  Stressful situation
SKF-525-A   see
  Diethylaminoethyldiphenylpropyl-
  acetate
SKF-69634   see
  Clopipazan
Sleep   see also
  DSIP
  Paradoxical sleep
  REM
Sleep-walking   see also
  Somnambulism
Sodium   see also
  Na
Sodium chloride   see also
  NaCl
Sodium dipropylacetate   see also
  Depakine
  Dipropylacetate
  Dipropylacetic acid
  Sodium valproate
  Valproic acid
Sodium valproate   see also
  Depakine
  Dipropylacetate
  Dipropylacetic acid
  Sodium diproprylacetate
  Valproic acid
Solvent   see also
  Industrial solvent

21

Somnambulism   see also
  Sleep-walking
Specific   see
  Age-specific
  Brain specific
  Opiod specific
Spectrometry   see
  Audio-spectrometry
  Mass spectrometry
Spider   see
  Black widow spider
Stability   see also
  Biological stability
  Photochemical stability
State(s)   see
  Behavioral state
  Confusional state
  Depressive states
  Manic state
  Mental state
  Phobic state
  Steady state
Stay   see
  Long-stay
Stimulation(ed)   see also
  Behavioral stimulation
  Brain stimulation
  Electric stimulation
  Electrical stimulation
  GABA stimulated
  Intracranial stimulation
  Locomotor stimulation
  Pentagastrin stimulated
  Self-stimulation
Stimulus   see also
  Discriminative stimulus
  UCS
  Unconditioned stimulus
Strategies   see also
  Video strategies
Stress(ed)   see also
  Emotional stress
  Ether stressed
  Psychological stress
  Psychosomatic stress
Striatonigral   see also
  Nigrostriatal
Study   see
  Behavioral studies
  Biochemical study(ies)
  Biological studies
  Case study(ies)
  Clinical study(ies)
  Collaborative study

Comparative study(ies)
Controlled comparative study
Controlled study
Cross-study
Drug studies
Early activity studies
Electrocytochemical study
Electrophysiological study(ies)
Empirical study
Endocrine study
Experimental study(ies)
Histochemical study
Interaction studies
Metabolic study(ies)
Microiontophoretic study
Morphological study
Multicenter study
Multiclinical study
Multiinstitutional study
Neuroanatomical study
Neurochemical study(ies)
Neuroendocrine study(ies)
Neurological study
Neuropharmacological study(ies)
Neurophysiological study
Neuropsychopharmacological studies
Neuropsychopharmacology study
Ontogenetic studies
Open study
Pathophysiological studies
Pharmacokinetic study
Pharmacologic studies
Pharmacological study(ies)
Pharmacomanometric studies
Physiological studies
Pilot study
Placebo controlled study
Polygraphic study
Polygraphical studies
Preliminary study(ies)
Psychopharmacological studies
Psychophysiologic studies
Relapse studies
Scientific study
Subject(s)   see
  Epileptic subjects
  Phobic subjects
Substance(s)   see also
  Psychoactive substances
  Psychotropic substances
Supersensitivity   see also
  Behavioral supersensitivity
  Cholinergic supersensitivity
  Dopaminergic supersensitivity

Suppression   see also
  Behavioral suppression
Sustained   see
  Self-sustained
Symposium   see
  Mini-symposium
Symptom(s)   see also
  Depressive symptoms
  Manic symptoms
  Mental symptoms
  Obsessive symptoms
  Psychotic symptoms
  Schizophrenic symptoms
Symptomatology   see also
  Depressive symptomatology
  Schizophrenic symptomatology
Syndrome(s)   see also
  Abstinence syndrome
  Anticholinergic syndrome
  Anxious depressive syndromes
  Asthenic depressive syndromes
  Astheno-depressive syndromes
  Behavioral syndrome
  Behavioural syndromes
  Borderline syndromes
  Brain damage syndrome
  Catatonia syndrome
  Chronic brain syndromes
  DeLange syndrome
  Depressive syndrome(s)
  Dissociative syndromes
  Down syndrome
  Downs syndrome
  Episodic dyscontrol syndrome
  Extrapyramidal syndromes
  Forum-fruste-du-syndrome-malin
  Gilles de la Tourette(s) syndrome
  Hyperactive child syndrome
  Hyperactivity syndrome
  Hyperkinetic syndrome
  Hypertension syndrome
  Hyperventilation syndrome
  Kleine Levin syndrome
  Lennox Gastaut syndrome
  Lesch Nyhaus syndrome
  Malignant hyperthermic syndromes
  Malignant syndrome
  Nelsons syndrome
  Neurological syndrome
  Organic brain syndrome
  Organic mental syndrome
  Organic psychosyndromes
  Parkinsonian syndrome

  Phobic anxiety syndrome
  Premenstrual syndrome
  Psychiatric syndromes
  Sleep apnea syndrome
  Stereotypic behavior syndrome
  Stretch yawning syndrome
  Tourette syndrome
  Transient syndromes
  Withdrawal syndrome(s)
Synthesis   see also
  Gas chromatographic synthesis
System(s)   see   .
  Cardiovascular system
  Central nervous system
  Dopaminergic system(s)
  HLA system
  Limbic system
  Sympathetic nervous system

                    T

Table   see
  Life table
Techniques   see also
  Behavioural techniques
Temperature   see also
  Body temperature
Term   see
  Long-term
  Short-term
Terrors   see
  Night terrors
Test(s)   see also
  Behavioral tests
  Clinical tests
  Dexamethasone Suppression Test(s)
  Electroshock test
  Neuroendocrine tests
  Psychometric test
  Psychophysiological tests
  Screening test
  Shock escape test
Testing   see also
  Behavioral testing
  Clinical testing
Tetrahydrocannabinol   see also
  THC
Tetrahydroisoxazolopyridin-3-ol
  see
  THIP
THC   see also
  Tetrahydrocannabinol

23

Therapy see also
  Behavioral therapy
  Behaviour therapy
  Cognitive therapy
  Drug therapy
  Electroconvulsive therapy
  Maintenance therapy
  Monotherapy
  Psychopharmaceutical therapy
Thin layer chromatography see also
  TLC .
Thyrotropin-releasing hormone
  see also
  TRH
Thyrotophin-stimulating hormone
  see
  TSH
Time see also
  Reaction time
  Sleeping time
TLC see also
  Thin layer chromatography
Tolerance(ant) see also
  Behavioral tolerance
  Cross-tolerance
  Morphine tolerance (ant)
  Opiate tolerant
  Opiod tolerance
Tomography see
  Computed tomography
  Computerized axial tomography
  Positron tomography
Tourette syndrome see also
  Gilles de la Tourette syndrome
Tranquilizer(s) see also
  Major tranquilizers
  Minor tranquilizer(s)
  Names of specific tranquilizers
Transfer see also
  Ion transfer
Transmission see also
  Neurotransmission
Transmitter see also
  Neurotransmitter
Transport see also
  Cellular transport
Treatment(s) see also
  Behavioral treatments
  Chronic treatment
  Drug treatment
  Convulsive shock treatment
  Electroconvulsive treatment
  Electroshock treatment

Long-term treatment
Maintenance treatment
Pharmacological treatment
Psychiatric treatment
Psychologic treatment
Psychological treatment
Psychopharmacological treatment
Subchronic treatment
TRF see
  Thyrotrophin-releasing factor
TRH see also
  Thyrotropin-releasing hormone
Trial(s) see also
  Clinical trial(s)
  Comparative trial
  Controlled trial
  Multicenter trail
  Placebo controlled trial
  Preliminary trial
  Prospective trial
  Randomised trial
Tumescence see
  Penile tumescence
Turning see also
  Head turning
Twitch(es) see
  Head twitches

U

U-14-624 see
  Phenyl-2-thiazolyl-2-thiourea
UCS see also
  Unconditioned stimulus
Ulcers see
  Gastric ulcers
  Peptic ulcers
  Stress ulcers
Ultradian see also
  Circadian
Unconditioned stimulus see also
  UCS
Unipolar see also
  Affective disorders
  Bipolar
  Depression
  Manic-depressive

V

Valproic acid see also
  Depakine
  Dipropylacetate

24

SUBJECT INDEX

[The Subject Index is machine generated. Keywords in the titles of abstracts appear alphabetically in the the left hand margin; under each keyword is a list of titles in which the keyword appears. The spelling of words in the titles of abstracts has not been changed; hence, two spellings of the same word may appear in this index — for example, BEHAVIOR and BEHAVIOUR.]

ABANDONMENT
SELF-MEDICATION, ABANDONMENT, MANIPULATION, AND DEPENDENCE IN DRUG-THERAPY IN PSYCHOSOMATIC-ILLNESS: COMPARATIVE POLYCENTRIC RESEARCH ON VARIOUS PSYCHOTROPIC-DRUGS.
002189 02-11

ABILITIES
MOTOR-LEARNING ABILITIES IN SUBJECTS TREATED WITH LITHIUM-SALTS AND TRICYCLIC-ANTIDEPRESSANTS.
002058 02-09

ABILITY
A COMPARISON OF HUMAN TACTILE STIMULUS VELOCITY DISCRIMINATION WITH THE ABILITY OF S-I CORTICAL NEURONS IN AWAKE RHESUS-MONKEYS TO SIGNAL THE SAME VELOCITY DIFFERENCES BEFORE AND AFTER NONANESTHETIC DOSES OF PENTOBARBITAL.
000055 01-03
ABILITY OF AGED RATS TO ALTER BETA-ADRENERGIC-RECEPTORS OF BRAIN IN RESPONSE TO REPEATED ADMINISTRATION OF RESERPINE AND DESMETHYLIMIPRAMINE.
000113 01-03
THE HYPOTHERMIC-EFFECTS OF CLONIDINE AND OTHER IMIDAZOLIDINES IN RELATION TO THEIR ABILITY TO ENTER THE CENTRAL-NERVOUS-SYSTEM IN MICE.
003933 04-03

ABNORMAL
THE ALBINO LOCUS PRODUCES ABNORMAL RESPONSES TO OPIATES IN THE MOUSE.
001675 02-04
ABNORMAL REGULATION OF PROLACTIN RELEASE IN IDIOPATHIC PARKINSONS-DISEASE.
002255 02-13
CORRECTION BY PROPRANOLOL OF THE ABNORMAL ADRENALINE DISCHARGE INDUCED BY EMOTIONAL-STRESS IN CEREBRAL HEMORRHAGE PATIENTS.
002295 02-13
ABNORMAL MATURATION OF CEREBRAL-CORTEX AND BEHAVIORAL-DEFICIT IN ADULT RATS AFTER NEONATAL ADMINISTRATION OF ANTIBODIES TO GANGLIOSIDE.
003025 03-04
ABNORMAL TRANSMETHYLATION REACTION DURING THE METABOLISM OF DOPAMINE, TRYPTAMINE, AND SEROTONIN, AND SCHIZOPHRENIC-SYMPTOMS; A CRITICAL REVIEW.
003404 03-13
PREVALENCE OF PERSISTENT ABNORMAL INVOLUNTARY-MOVEMENTS AMONG PATIENTS IN A NIGERIAN LONG-STAY PSYCHIATRIC UNIT.
004334 04-08
ABNORMAL MOVEMENTS INDUCED BY PSYCHOTROPIC-DRUGS.
004652 04-15

ABNORMAL-BEHAVIOR
PSYCHONEUROENDOCRINOLOGY AND ABNORMAL-BEHAVIOR.
002347 02-14

ABNORMALITIES
PROTEIN ABNORMALITIES IN MACROPHAGES BEARING ASBESTOS. (UNPUBLISHED PAPER).
001037 02-01
VITAMIN RESPONSIVE GENETIC ABNORMALITIES. (UNPUBLISHED PAPER).
001388 02-03
HORMONAL ABNORMALITIES IN ANOREXIA-NERVOSA (AN).
002099 02-11
ABNORMALITIES OF LITHIUM TRANSPORT IN PATIENTS WITH AFFECTIVE-DISORDERS.
002269 02-13
DOPAMINERGIC ABNORMALITIES IN POSTMORTEM SCHIZOPHRENIC BRAIN.
002575 02-17
METABOLIC AND SYMPATHOADRENAL ABNORMALITIES IN THE OBESE ZUCKER RAT: EFFECT OF CHRONIC PHENOXYBENZAMINE TREATMENT.
003905 04-03

ABNORMALITY
DEVELOPMENT AND USE OF PHARMACOLOGICAL-PROBES OF THE CNS IN MAN; EVIDENCE OF CHOLINERGIC ABNORMALITY IN PRIMARY AFFECTIVE-ILLNESS.
002506 02-16

ABRUPT
PANIC-ANXIETY AFTER ABRUPT DISCONTINUATION OF AMITRIPTYLINE.
003223 03-09
CLINICAL AND BIOCHEMICAL-CORRELATIONS IN ABRUPT DISCONTINUATION OF PSYCHOPHARMACOTHERAPY.
004330 04-08

ABSCESSES
ABSCESSES FOLLOWING PROLONGED INTRAMUSCULAR ADMINISTRATION OF PERPHENAZINE-ENANTATE.
000888 01-15

ABSORPTION
ABSORPTION OF 14C LABELED METHADONE BY PORTAL AND EXTRAPORTAL VENOUS CIRCULATIONS FOLLOWING INTRAPERITONEAL AND INTRODUODENAL ADMINISTRATION.
000094 01-03
EFFECT OF DOSE ON PHENYTOIN ABSORPTION.
000773 01-13
MEAL-DEPENDENT ABSORPTION OF ENTERIC-COATED SODIUM-VALPROATE.
000777 01-13
MICROSCOPIC EVIDENCE OF LYMPHOGENIC ABSORPTION OF OIL IN HUMANS RECEIVING NEUROLEPTIC OILY DEPOT PREPARATIONS INTRAMUSCULARLY.
000890 01-15
PREDICTION OF THE VOLUME OF DISTRIBUTION FROM IN VITRO DATA AND USE FOR ESTIMATING THE ABSOLUTE EXTENT OF ABSORPTION.
000907 01-16
ABSORPTION OF LEVODOPA AFTER RECTAL ADMINISTRATION.
003406 03-13
ORAL AND RECTAL ABSORPTION OF CHLORAL-HYDRATE AND ITS BETAINE COMPLEX.
004554 04-13
CLINICAL-PHARMACOLOGY: DRUG ABSORPTION.
004740 04-17

ABSTINENCE
ENKEPHALIN LEVELS DECREASE IN RAT STRIATUM DURING MORPHINE ABSTINENCE.
000027 01-03
AN ELECTROMYOGRAPHIC-METHOD FOR THE ASSESSMENT OF NALOXONE-INDUCED ABSTINENCE IN MORPHINE-DEPENDENT RATS.
000433 01-04
NARCOTIC ANTAGONIST PRECIPITATED ABSTINENCE; RELATIONSHIP TO WITHDRAWAL INDUCING BENZAZOCINES. (PH.D. DISSERTATION).
001518 02-03
CYCLIC-AMP-INDUCED CHANGES IN THE ELECTROENCEPHALOGRAM AND IN BEHAVIOR DURING MORPHINE-DEPENDENCE AND ABSTINENCE IN THE RAT.
003078 03-04
EFFECTS OF NARCOTIC ABSTINENCE ON SCHEDULE-CONTROLLED BEHAVIOR IN DEPENDENT RATS.
004230 04-04
SUPPRESSION OF MORPHINE ABSTINENCE IN HEROIN ADDICTS BY BETA ENDORPHIN.
004489 04-11
DOPAMINE AND 5 HT SUPERSENSITIVITY IN NONORGANIC CENTRAL PAIN AND IN MORPHINE ABSTINENCE; FORTUITOUS OR REAL ANALOGY?
004553 04-13

ABSTINENCE-BEHAVIOR
EFFECTS OF BRANCHED-CHAIN FATTY-ACIDS ON GABA DEGRADATION AND BEHAVIOR; FURTHER EVIDENCE FOR A ROLE OF GABA IN QUASI-MORPHINE ABSTINENCE-BEHAVIOR.
001809 02-04

ABSTINENCE-BEHAVIOUR
DIPROPYLACETATE-INDUCED ABSTINENCE-BEHAVIOUR AS A POSSIBLE CORRELATE OF INCREASED GABAERGIC ACTIVITY IN THE RAT.
001606 02-04

ABSTINENCE-SYNDROME
AN ABSTINENCE-SYNDROME FOLLOWING CHRONIC ADMINISTRATION OF DELTA9 TETRAHYDROCANNABINOL IN RHESUS-MONKEYS.
001621 02-04
THE SHORT-TERM AND LONG-TERM EFFECTS OF BETA ENDORPHIN ON THE OPIATE ABSTINENCE-SYNDROME IN RATS.
001643 02-04
DOSE-RESPONSE STUDY OF THE PRECIPITATED ABSTINENCE-SYNDROME FOR MORPHINE; SYSTEMIC VS PERIAQUEDUCTAL GRAY NALOXONE. (PH.D. DISSERTATION).
002979 03-04
POSSIBLE INFLUENCE OF OPIOID NORMETABOLITES ON THE ONSET, MAGNITUDE AND QUALITY OF THE OPIOID ABSTINENCE-SYNDROME.
004610 04-15
CASE-REPORT OF UNUSUAL DIAZEPAM ABSTINENCE-SYNDROME.
004643 04-15

ABSTINENT
SEXUAL-BEHAVIOUR OF MORPHINE-DEPENDENT AND ABSTINENT MALE RATS.
000438 01-04

ABSTRACTS
ABSTRACTS OF THE ANNUAL GENERAL CONFERENCE OF THE EUROPEAN-BRAIN-AND-BEHAVIOUR-SOCIETY, HELD AT LOUVAIN-LA-NEUVE, BELGIUM, ON NOVEMBER 13-15TH, 1980.
003617 03-17

Subject Index

ABUNDANCE
ABUNDANCE AND LOCATION OF 125I SALMON CALCITONIN BINDING-SITE IN RAT-BRAIN.
001320 02-03

ABUNDANT
THE HIGH-AFFINITY CHOLINE UPTAKE SYSTEM WITH RESPECT TO THE MUSCARINIC-RECEPTORS USING A SYNAPTOSOMAL FRACTION ABUNDANT IN PRESYNAPTIC MEMBRANES.
004028 04-03

ABUSE
ISSUES FOR INPATIENT TREATMENT OF CHRONIC PCP ABUSE.
000736 01-12
EPIDEMIOLOGY OF PCP ABUSE: THE MIDWEST PERSPECTIVE.
000740 01-12
PCP ABUSE: DIAGNOSTIC AND PSYCHOPHARMACOLOGICAL-TREATMENT APPROACHES.
000746 01-12
USE AND ABUSE OF BENZODIAZEPINES.
000877 01-15
CHRONIC PHENCYCLIDINE (PCP) ABUSE: A PSYCHIATRIC-PERSPECTIVE.
000935 01-17
MEDICAL AND PSYCHIATRIC-COMPLICATIONS OF PENTAZOCINE AND TRIPELENNAMINE ABUSE.
000955 01-17
THE BENZODIAZEPINES – USE AND ABUSE.
000960 01-17
ABUSE OF THE ANTIPARKINSON-DRUGS: A REVIEW OF THE LITERATURE.
000989 01-17
ABUSE POTENTIAL OF LOPERAMIDE.
002413 02-15
RELAPSE TO NARCOTIC SELF-ADMINISTRATION IN MORPHINE POSTADDICT RATS: A POSSIBLE MODEL FOR PREDICTING ABUSE LIABILITY OF NARCOTIC-DRUGS. (PH.D. DISSERTATION).
003097 03-04
PSYCHOACTIVE-MEDICATION USE AND ABUSE AMONG AN ADULT RURAL POPULATION. (PH.D. DISSERTATION).
003627 03-17
LONG-TERM USE AND ABUSE OF BENZODIAZEPINES.
004598 04-15
A MULTIVARIATE ANALYSIS OF THE INFRARED SPECTRA OF DRUGS OF ABUSE.
004688 04-16

ABUSER
PHARMACODYNAMICS AND PHARMACOKINETICS OF DIAZEPAM IN AN ABUSER.
000867 01-15

ABUSERS
OUTPATIENT TREATMENT ISSUES AND STRATEGIES FOR ACUTE AND CHRONIC PCP ABUSERS.
000919 01-17

ACCELERATION
ACCELERATION OF DESIPRAMINE-INDUCED DECREASE OF RAT CORTICOCEREBRAL BETA-ADRENERGIC-RECEPTORS BY YOHIMBINE.
000326 01-03
CORTICAL RECOVERY FROM EFFECTS OF MONOCULAR DEPRIVATION: ACCELERATION WITH NOREPINEPHRINE AND SUPPRESSION WITH 6 HYDROXYDOPAMINE.
003024 03-04
CONDITIONED DRUG-EFFECTS OF D-AMPHETAMINE-INDUCED AND MORPHINE-INDUCED MOTOR ACCELERATION IN MICE: EXPERIMENTAL APPROACH FOR PLACEBO-EFFECT.
004128 04-04

ACCIDENTAL
ACCIDENTAL INTRAARTERIAL INJECTION OF DIAZEPAM.
002598 02-17

ACCLIMATIZATION
CORE TEMPERATURE CHANGES FOLLOWING ADMINISTRATION OF NALOXONE AND NALTREXONE TO RATS EXPOSED TO HOT AND COLD AMBIENT TEMPERATURES. EVIDENCE FOR THE PHYSIOLOGICAL ROLE OF ENDORPHINS IN HOT AND COLD ACCLIMATIZATION.
004034 04-03

ACCUMBENS
BEHAVIOURAL-RESPONSES TO STEREOTACTICALLY CONTROLLED INJECTIONS OF MONOAMINE NEUROTRANSMITTERS INTO THE ACCUMBENS AND CAUDATE-PUTAMEN NUCLEI.
001708 02-04

ACCUMULATION
INHIBITORY-EFFECTS OF ANTICONVULSANT-DRUGS ON CYCLIC-NUCLEOTIDE ACCUMULATION IN BRAIN.
000090 01-03
ADENOSINE REGULATES VIA TWO DIFFERENT TYPES OF RECEPTORS, THE ACCUMULATION OF CYCLIC-AMP IN CULTURED BRAIN CELLS.
000308 01-03
EFFECT OF DESMETHYLIMIPRAMINE ON THE KINETICS OF CHLORPHENTERMINE ACCUMULATION IN ISOLATED PERFUSED RAT LUNG.
000524 01-05
CHANGE IN PYRUVATE-DEHYDROGENASE ACTIVITY INFLUENCE PYRUVATE SUPPORTED CALCIUM ACCUMULATION BY BRAIN MITOCHONDRIA. (UNPUBLISHED PAPER).
001147 02-03

REGULATION OF STRIATAL ACETYLCHOLINE CONCENTRATION BY D2 DOPAMINE-RECEPTORS.
000269 01-03

IN VITRO ACETYLCHOLINE RELEASE FROM RAT CAUDATE-NUCLEUS AS A NEW MODEL FOR TESTING DRUGS WITH DOPAMINE-RECEPTOR ACTIVITY.
000289 01-03

THE EFFECTS OF MUSCARINIC-RECEPTOR BLOCKERS ON THE TURNOVER-RATE OF ACETYLCHOLINE IN VARIOUS REGIONS OF THE RAT-BRAIN.
000328 01-03

TOLERANCE TO INCREASES IN STRIATAL ACETYLCHOLINE CONCENTRATIONS AFTER REPEATED ADMINISTRATION OF APOMORPHINE-DIPIVALOYL-ESTER.
000464 01-04

REGULATION OF ACETYLCHOLINE RELEASE DURING INCREASED NEURONAL ACTIVITY. (UNPUBLISHED PAPER).
001061 02-01

EFFECT OF THE NEW GAMMA AMINOBUTYRIC-ACID AGONIST SL-76-002 ON STRIATAL ACETYLCHOLINE: RELATION TO NEUROLEPTIC-INDUCED EXTRAPYRAMIDAL ALTERATIONS.
001119 02-03

FACTORS INFLUENCING THE RELEASE OF LABELLED GAMMA AMINOBUTYRIC-ACID AND ACETYLCHOLINE EVOKED BY ELECTRICAL-STIMULATION WITH ALTERNATING POLARITY FROM RAT CORTICAL SLICES.
001130 02-03

EFFECT OF MOXESTROL ON HALOPERIDOL-INDUCED CHANGES IN STRIATAL ACETYLCHOLINE LEVELS AND DOPAMINE TURNOVER.
001218 02-03

LONG-TERM ADMINISTRATION OF ATROPINE, IMIPRAMINE, AND VILOXAZINE ALTERS RESPONSIVENESS OF RAT-CORTICAL-NEURONES TO ACETYLCHOLINE.
001306 02-03

ASCORBIC-ACID, AN ENDOGENOUS FACTOR REQUIRED FOR ACETYLCHOLINE RELEASE FROM THE SYNAPTIC VESICLES.
001322 02-03

DIRECT EVIDENCE AGAINST ACETYLCHOLINE AS THE DILATOR TRANSMITTER IN THE CAT CEREBRAL-ARTERY.
001336 02-03

ACETYLCHOLINE AND AMINO-ACID NEUROTRANSMITTERS IN EPIDURAL CUPS OF FREELY-MOVING-RATS: EFFECT OF ACUTE AND CHRONIC-TREATMENT WITH ANTISCHIZOPHRENIC-DRUGS.
001386 02-03

EFFECTS OF DIAZEPAM ON ADENOSINE AND ACETYLCHOLINE RELEASE FROM RAT-CEREBRAL-CORTEX: FURTHER EVIDENCE FOR A PURINERGIC MECHANISM IN ACTION OF DIAZEPAM.
001414 02-03

EFFECT OF ANTINOCICEPTIVE DOSES OF OXOTREMORINE ON MOUSE-BRAIN ACETYLCHOLINE TURNOVER-RATE.
001513 02-03

ACTIONS OF ENKEPHALIN, MU AND PARTIAL AGONIST ANALGESICS ON ACETYLCHOLINE TURNOVER IN RAT-BRAIN.
001541 02-03

GLYCINE, ACETYLCHOLINE, AND SEROTONIN: NEUROTRANSMITTERS OR NEUROMODULATORS?
002271 02-13

THE EXCITATORY ACTION OF ACETYLCHOLINE ON HIPPOCAMPAL NEURONES OF THE GUINEA-PIG AND RAT MAINTAINED IN VITRO.
002704 03-03

THE PRESYNAPTIC STIMULATING EFFECT OF ACETYLCHOLINE ON DOPAMINE RELEASE IS SUPPRESSED DURING ACTIVATION OF NIGROSTRIATAL DOPAMINERGIC NEURONS IN THE CAT.
002733 03-03

MODULATION BY ENDOGENOUS DOPAMINE OF THE RELEASE OF ACETYLCHOLINE IN THE CAUDATE-NUCLEUS OF THE RABBIT.
002751 03-03

PIRACETAM DIMINISHES HIPPOCAMPAL ACETYLCHOLINE LEVELS IN RATS.
002934 03-03

THE EFFECTS OF ACETYLCHOLINE AND GLUTAMATE ON SEPTAL NEURONS IN VITRO.
002941 03-03

RELEASE OF ACETYLCHOLINE FROM RAT-BRAIN SYNAPTOSOMES STIMULATED WITH LEPTINOTARSIN, A NEW NEUROTOXIN.
003148 03-06

MODULATORY EFFECT OF BRAIN ACETYLCHOLINE ON REFLEX-INDUCED BRADYCARDIA AND TACHYCARDIA IN CONSCIOUS RATS.
003744 04-03

COMPARISON OF THE EFFECTS OF THE STEREOISOMERS OF FENFLURAMINE ON THE ACETYLCHOLINE CONTENT OF RAT STRIATUM, HIPPOCAMPUS AND NUCLEUS-ACCUMBENS.
003758 04-03

OXOTREMORINE DOES NOT ENHANCE ACETYLCHOLINE RELEASE FROM RAT DIAPHRAGM PREPARATIONS.
003819 04-03

ALTERATIONS OF ACETYLCHOLINE AND CHOLINE METABOLISM IN MAMMALIAN PREPARATIONS TREATED WITH BETA BUNGAROTOXIN.
003820 04-03

PRESYNAPTIC REGULATION OF THE RELEASE OF ACETYLCHOLINE BY 5 HYDROXYTRYPTAMINE.
003843 04-03

INVESTIGATION OF ACTION OF ENKEPHALIN ON THE SPONTANEOUS AND EVOKED RELEASE OF ACETYLCHOLINE FROM RAT CORTICAL AND STRIATAL SLICES.
003862 04-03

ACTION OF ENKEPHALIN ANALOGUES AND MORPHINE ON BRAIN ACETYLCHOLINE RELEASE: DIFFERENTIAL REVERSAL BY NALOXONE AND AN OPIATE-PENTAPEPTIDE.
003863 04-03

THE EFFECT OF CHRONIC NICOTINE AND WITHDRAWAL ON INTRAAXONAL TRANSPORT OF ACETYLCHOLINE AND RELATED ENZYMES IN SCIATIC-NERVE OF THE RAT.
003897 04-03

THE EFFECT OF ACETYLCHOLINE RELEASE ON CHOLINE FLUXES IN ISOLATED SYNAPTIC TERMINALS.
003924 04-03

ACETYLCHOLINE AND CHOLINE-ACETYLTRANSFERASE.
003930 04-03

CORRELATIONS BETWEEN NA-K-ATPASE ACTIVITY AND ACETYLCHOLINE RELEASE IN RAT CORTICAL SYNAPTOSOMES.
003937 04-03

EFFECTS OF ETHANOL ON ACETYLCHOLINE AND ADENOSINE EFFLUX FROM THE IN VIVO RAT-CEREBRAL-CORTEX.
003969 04-03

INHIBITION OF THE SYNTHESIS OF ACETYLCHOLINE IN RAT-BRAIN SLICES BY (-) HYDROXYCITRATE AND CITRATE.
004044 04-03

5' TRIPHOSPHATE RECYCLES INDEPENDENTLY OF ACETYLCHOLINE IN CHOLINERGIC SYNAPTIC VESICLES.
004063 04-03

CHOLINE REVERSES NALOXONE-INDUCED DECREASES IN HIPPOCAMPAL ACETYLCHOLINE CONTENT AND SUPPRESSES ESCAPE-BEHAVIOR IN OPIATE-DEPENDENT RATS.
004076 04-04

ANTITREMOR ACTION OF C10DICHOL, A PERIPHERAL ACETYLCHOLINE SYNTHESIS INHIBITOR.
004096 04-04

ACETYLCHOLINE TURNOVER AND AGGRESSION IN RELATED THREE STRAINS OF MICE.
004151 04-04

ACETYLCHOLINE-INDUCED
ACETYLCHOLINE-INDUCED MODULATION OF HIPPOCAMPAL PYRAMIDAL NEURONS.
003728 04-03

ACETYLCHOLINE-RECEPTOR
PHOSPHORYLATION OF THE MEMBRANE-BOUND ACETYLCHOLINE-RECEPTOR: INHIBITION BY DIPHENYLHYDANTOIN.
001257 02-03

ENZYMATIC CARBOXYMETHYLATION OF THE NICOTINIC ACETYLCHOLINE-RECEPTOR. (UNPUBLISHED PAPER).
001318 02-03

MUSCARINIC ACETYLCHOLINE-RECEPTOR. (UNPUBLISHED PAPER).
002667 03-03

ACETYLCHOLINE-RECEPTORS
LITHIUM REDUCES THE NUMBER OF ACETYLCHOLINE-RECEPTORS IN SKELETAL-MUSCLE.
000232 01-03

THE BINDING OF SOME ANTIDEPRESSANT-DRUGS TO BRAIN MUSCARINIC ACETYLCHOLINE-RECEPTORS.
001253 02-03

PSYCHOTHERAPEUTIC-DRUGS, HISTAMINE H1-RECEPTORS AND MUSCARINIC ACETYLCHOLINE-RECEPTORS.
004737 04-17

ACETYLCHOLINESTERASE
ACTION OF BARBITURATES ON ACTIVITY OF ACETYLCHOLINESTERASE FROM SYNAPTOSOMAL MEMBRANES.
000224 01-03

ACETYLCHOLINESTERASE AND CHOLINESTERASE ACTIVITIES IN THE MOUSE CEREBELLUM FOLLOWING MISONIDAZOLE TREATMENT.
003123 03-05

INHIBITION OF AMINOPEPTIDASE AND ACETYLCHOLINESTERASE BY PUROMYCIN AND PUROMYCIN ANALOGS.
003835 04-03

INSEPARABILITY OF ACETYLCHOLINESTERASE AND NERVE EXCITATION.
003875 04-03

ACETYLENIC-GABA
EFFECTS OF GAMMA ACETYLENIC-GABA AND GAMMA VINYL-GABA ON ELECTRICALLY-INDUCED SPINAL-CORD CONVULSIONS AND ON SPINAL-CORD GABA CONCENTRATION.
000145 01-03

MAPPING OF DYSKINETIC-MOVEMENTS INDUCED BY LOCAL APPLICATION OF PICROTOXIN OR () GAMMA ACETYLENIC-GABA ON THE RAT MOTOR-CORTEX.
000458 01-04

GAMMA ACETYLENIC-GABA IN TARDIVE-DYSKINESIA.
002101 02-11

MULTIPLE EFFECTS OF REPEATED ADMINISTRATION OF GAMMA ACETYLENIC-GABA ON RAT-BRAIN METABOLISM.
002878 03-03

TREATMENT OF HUNTINGTON-DISEASE WITH GAMMA ACETYLENIC-GABA, AN IRREVERSIBLE INHIBITOR OF GABA-TRANSAMINASE: INCREASED CSF GABA AND HOMOCARNOSINE WITHOUT CLINICAL AMELIORATION.
003458 03-14

ACETYLENIC-GAMMA-AMINOBUTYRIC-ACID
CHANGES IN PRIMARY AFFERENT DEPOLARIZATION AFTER ADMINISTRATION OF GAMMA ACETYLENIC-GAMMA-AMINOBUTYRIC-ACID (GAG), A GAMMA AMINOBUTYRIC-ACID-TRANSAMINASE (GABA-TRANSAMINASE) INHIBITOR.
000174 01-03

ACETYLESTERS
GAS-CHROMATOGRAPHY/MASS-SPECTROMETRY STABLE ISOTOPIC ANALYSES FOR DEANOL, CHOLINE, AND THEIR ACETYLESTERS.
004683 04-16

ACETYLMANNOSAMINE
INCORPORATION OF N ACETYLMANNOSAMINE INTO RAT-BRAIN SUBCELLULAR GANGLIOSIDES: EFFECT OF PENTYLENETETRAZOL-INDUCED CONVULSIONS IN BRAIN GANGLIOSIDES.
002937 03-03

ACETYLMETHADOL
PHARMACODYNAMIC PROFILES OF L ALPHA ACETYLMETHADOL (LAAM) AND ITS N DEMETHYLATED METABOLITES, NORLAAM AND DINORLAAM, DURING SELF-ADMINISTRATION IN THE DEPENDENT RAT.
000505 01-04
OCCURRENCE OF CORNEAL OPACITIES IN RATS AFTER ACUTE ADMINISTRATION OF L ALPHA ACETYLMETHADOL.
001853 02-05
A CHARACTERIZATION OF THE BEHAVIORAL-EFFECTS OF LEVO ALPHA ACETYLMETHADOL IN THE RAT AND IN THE PIGEON. (PH.D. DISSERTATION).
003047 03-04
A CLINICAL, CONTROLLED-STUDY OF L ALPHA ACETYLMETHADOL IN THE TREATMENT OF NARCOTIC ADDICTION.
003335 03-11
EFFECTS OF LEVO ALPHA ACETYLMETHADOL (LAAM) ON MORPHINE SELF-ADMINISTRATION IN THE RAT.
004170 04-04
MORPHINE CHALLENGES IN LEVO ALPHA ACETYLMETHADOL (LAAM) POSTADDICT RATS.
004259 04-04

ACETYLSALICYLIC-ACID
BEHAVIOURAL-EFFECTS OF ACETYLSALICYLIC-ACID, PARACETAMOL, CAFFEINE, GUAIPHENESIN AND THEIR COMBINATIONS.
001805 02-04

ACH
INHIBITION OF ACH RELEASE BY PROSTAGLANDIN-E1 IN THE RABBIT SUPERIOR-CERVICAL-GANGLION.
001205 02-03

ACH-RECEPTOR
IMMUNODETECTION OF ACH-RECEPTOR IN THE CNS. (UNPUBLISHED PAPER).
003670 04-01
5 HYDROXYTRYPTAMINE CONTROLS ACH-RECEPTOR SENSITIVITY OF BULLFROG SYMPATHETIC GANGLION CELLS.
003710 04-03

ACID
THE CONTRIBUTION OF ALPHA1 ACID GLYCOPROTEIN, LIPOPROTEINS, AND ALBUMIN TO THE PLASMA BINDING OF PERAZINE, AMITRIPTYLINE, AND NORTRIPTYLINE IN HEALTHY MAN.
002214 02-13
BINDING OF PERAZINE TO ALPHA1 ACID GLYCOPROTEIN.
002290 02-13
PARTIAL PURIFICATION OF ACID SPHINGOMYELINASE FROM NORMAL AND PATHOLOGICAL (λ.. NIEMANN-PICK TYPE C) HUMAN BRAIN.
003671 04-01
THE EFFECTS OF NEFOPAM ON BLOOD ACID BASE STATUS IN THE RABBIT: INTERACTIONS WITH MORPHINE IN THE MOUSE AND RABBIT.
004279 04-05

ACIDIC
REVERSIBLE RING-OPENING REACTIONS OF NIMETAZEPAM AND NITRAZEPAM IN ACIDIC MEDIA AT BODY-TEMPERATURE.
004517 04-13

ACOUSTIC
5 METHOXYDIMETHYLTRYPTAMINE: SPINAL-CORD AND BRAINSTEM MEDIATION OF EXCITATORY EFFECTS ON ACOUSTIC STARTLE.
001605 02-04
SPINAL MODULATION OF THE ACOUSTIC STARTLE RESPONSE: THE ROLE OF NOREPINEPHRINE, SEROTONIN AND DOPAMINE.
002950 03-04

ACQUISITION
EFFECT OF BETA ENDORPHIN AND NALOXONE ON ACQUISITION, MEMORY, AND RETRIEVAL OF SHUTTLE AVOIDANCE AND HABITUATION LEARNING IN RATS.
000410 01-04
THE EFFECTS OF PIPRADROL ON THE ACQUISITION OF RESPONDING WITH CONDITIONED REINFORCEMENT: A ROLE FOR SENSORY PRECONDITIONING.
001572 02-04

EFFECTS OF A LOW-DOSE AND A HIGH-DOSE OF BETA ENDORPHIN ON ACQUISITION AND RETENTION IN THE RAT.
001663 02-04
L-DOPA ENHANCES ACQUISITION OF AN INHIBITORY AVOIDANCE RESPONSE.
001711 02-04
EFFECTS OF PHENCYCLIDINE, PENTOBARBITAL, AND D-AMPHETAMINE ON THE ACQUISITION AND PERFORMANCE OF CONDITIONAL DISCRIMINATIONS IN MONKEYS.
001723 02-04
CUMULATIVE AFTERDISCHARGE AS THE PRINCIPAL FACTOR IN THE ACQUISITION OF KINDLED SEIZURES.
002862 03-03
EFFECT OF P CHLOROPHENYLALANINE ON THE ACQUISITION OF TOLERANCE TO THE HYPNOTIC-EFFECTS OF PENTOBARBITAL, BARBITAL, AND ETHANOL.
003883 04-03
RAPID ACQUISITION OF A TWO-DRUG DISCRIMINATION: TIME OF DAY EFFECT UPON SALINE STATE.
004214 04-04

ACQUISITION-BEHAVIOR
EFFECTS OF METHYLPHENIDATE-HYDROCHLORIDE ON REPEATED ACQUISITION-BEHAVIOR IN HYPERKINETIC-CHILDREN. (PH.D. DISSERTATION).
003386 03-11
EFFECTS OF DEXTROAMPHETAMINE-SULFATE ON REPEATED ACQUISITION-BEHAVIOR AND MOOD IN HUMANS: A PRELIMINARY REPORT.
003459 03-14

ACRYLAMIDE
THE ETIOLOGY OF TOXIC PERIPHERAL NEUROPATHIES: IN VITRO EFFECTS OF ACRYLAMIDE AND 2,5 HEXANEDIONE ON BRAIN ENOLASE AND OTHER GLYCOLYTIC ENZYMES.
000131 01-03
NEUROTRANSMITTER-RECEPTORS IN BRAIN REGIONS OF ACRYLAMIDE TREATED RATS. I: EFFECTS OF A SINGLE EXPOSURE TO ACRYLAMIDE.
004264 04-05
NEUROTRANSMITTER-RECEPTORS IN BRAIN REGIONS OF ACRYLAMIDE TREATED RATS. II: EFFECTS OF EXTENDED EXPOSURE TO ACRYLAMIDE.
004265 04-05

ACTH
CHANGES OF ACTH, STH, TSH AND PROLACTIN LEVELS IN ENDOTOXIN SHOCK IN RATS.
000119 01-03
OPIATE-RECEPTORS MAY MEDIATE THE SUPPRESSIVE BUT NOT THE EXCITATORY ACTION OF ACTH ON MOTOR-ACTIVITY IN RATS.
000337 01-04
ACTH MODULATION OF MEMORY STORAGE PROCESSING. (UNPUBLISHED PAPER).
001250 02-03
ACTH MEDIATION OF LEARNED-FEAR: BLOCKADE BY NALOXONE AND NALTREXONE.
001597 02-04
ACTH POTENTIATES MORPHINE-INDUCED CONDITIONED TASTE-AVERSION.
001781 02-04
TRIAL OF A PEPTIDE FRACTION OF ACTH (ACTH4-10) IN THE ALCOHOLIC BRAIN-DAMAGE-SYNDROME.
002318 02-14
EXPLORATION AND MOTOR-ACTIVITY AFTER INTRAVENTRICULAR ACTH, MORPHINE AND NALOXONE.
002991 03-04

ACTH-INDUCED
ACTH-INDUCED GROOMING INVOLVES HIGH-AFFINITY OPIATE-RECEPTORS.
002985 03-04

ACTH-LIKE
ACTH-LIKE PEPTIDES, PITUITARY ADRENOCORTICAL FUNCTION AND AVOIDANCE-BEHAVIOR.
004109 04-04

ACTH1-24
EFFECTS OF ACUTE CENTRAL AND PERIPHERAL ACTH1-24 ADMINISTRATION ON LORDOSIS BEHAVIOR.
002975 03-04
TESTOSTERONE POTENTIATION OF THE EFFECTIVENESS OF ACTH1-24 ON THE INDUCTION OF THE STRETCH-YAWNING-SYNDROME (SYS) IN MALE GUINEA-PIGS.
003074 03-04
HORMONAL STIMULATION AFTER INJECTION OF THYROTROPHIN-RELEASING-FACTOR (TRF) AND ACTH1-24 IN PATIENTS FOLLOWING CHRONIC-TREATMENT WITH NEUROLEPTICS: PRELIMINARY-STUDY.
004505 04-13

ACTH4-10
ACTH4-10 AND MEMORY IN ECT TREATED AND UNTREATED PATIENTS. I. EFFECT ON CONSOLIDATION.
001982 02-09
ACTH4-10 AND MEMORY IN ECT TREATED PATIENTS AND UNTREATED CONTROLS. II. EFFECT ON RETRIEVAL.
001983 02-09
TRIAL OF A PEPTIDE FRACTION OF ACTH (ACTH4-10) IN THE ALCOHOLIC BRAIN-DAMAGE-SYNDROME.
002318 02-14

POSSIBLE MECHANISMS OF EFFECT OF ACTH4-10 AND ITS ANALOG, CONTAINING D ISOMER OF PHENYLALANINE, ON BEHAVIOR.
002949 03-04
IMITATION, SOCIAL FACILITATION, AND THE EFFECTS OF ACTH4-10 ON RATS BAR-PRESSING-BEHAVIOR.
003009 03-04

ACTH4-9
Y-MAZE BEHAVIOR AFTER AN ANALOG OF ACTH4-9. EVIDENCE FOR AN ATTENTIONAL-ALTERATION.
001676 02-04
EFFECTS OF AN ACTH4-9 RELATED PEPTIDE UPON INTRACRANIAL SELF-STIMULATION AND GENERAL-ACTIVITY IN THE RAT.
001679 02-04
INDUCTION OF ANALGESIA BY CENTRAL ADMINISTRATION OF ORG-2766, AN ANALOG OF ACTH4-9.
003112 03-04
A SYNTHETIC ACTH4-9 ANALOGUE (ORGANON-2766) AND SLEEP IN HEALTHY MAN.
004574 04-14

ACTINOMYCIN-D
INHIBITION OF BEHAVIORAL-EFFECTS OF COCAINE BY ACTINOMYCIN-D IN RATS.
000346 01-04

ACTIVATION
ACTIVATION OF CORTICAL CIRCUITS DURING INTERICTAL SPIKES.
000056 01-03
THE ROLE OF INTRANEURONAL 5 HT AND OF TRYPTOPHAN-HYDROXYLASE ACTIVATION IN THE CONTROL OF 5 HT SYNTHESIS IN RAT-BRAIN SLICES INCUBATED IN K-ENRICHED MEDIUM.
000123 01-03
ANALYSIS OF THE ACTIVATION OF DOPAMINE METABOLISM BY A SEROTONIN UPTAKE INHIBITOR.
000315 01-03
METERGOLINE ANTAGONISM OF 5 HYDROXYTRYPTAMINE-INDUCED ACTIVATION OF RAT-CEREBRAL-CORTICAL NA-K-ATPASE.
000329 01-03
BRADYKININ-RECEPTOR STIMULATION OF C-AMP INVOLVES PHOSPHOLIPID METHYLATION, CA-FLUX, PHOSPHOLIPASE-A2 ACTIVATION AND PROSTAGLANDIN FORMATION. (UNPUBLISHED PAPER).
001002 02-01
CENTRAL LEVELS OF NORADRENALINE, 3 METHOXY-4-HYDROXYPHENYLETHYLENEGLYCOL AND CYCLIC-AMP IN THE RAT AFTER ACTIVATION OF LOCUS-COERULEUS NEURONS: INFLUENCE OF SINGLE AND REPEATED NEUROLEPTIC TREATMENT.
001095 02-03
PROSTACYCLIN-DEPENDENT ACTIVATION OF ADENYLATE-CYCLASE IN A NEURONAL SOMATIC CELL HYBRID: PROSTANOID STRUCTURE-ACTIVITY RELATIONSHIPS.
001132 02-03
MIANSERIN: DIRECT ACTIVATION OF BRAIN NOREPINEPHRINE NEURONS BY BLOCKING ALPHA2-RECEPTORS.
001214 02-03
ACTIVATION OF PRESYNAPTIC ALPHA NORADRENALINE-RECEPTORS IN RAT-BRAIN BY THE POTENT DOPAMINE-MIMETIC N,N DIPROPYL-ADTN.
001390 02-03
BRAIN STRIATAL TYROSINE-HYDROXYLASE: ACTIVATION OF THE ENZYME BY CYCLIC-AMP INDEPENDENT PHOSPHORYLATION.
001423 02-03
THE EFFECT OF NALOXONE ON THE ACTIVATION OF EMOTIONALLY POSITIVE REACTION PRODUCED BY DRUGS WITH A DEPENDENCE LIABILITY.
001556 02-03
ACTIVATION AND LATERALIZATION OF SENSORIMOTOR FIELD FOR PERIORAL BITING-REFLEX BY INTRANIGRAL GABA AGONIST AND BY SYSTEMIC APOMORPHINE IN THE RAT.
001657 02-04
VARIATIONS IN PSYCHOPHYSIOLOGICAL ACTIVATION RESPONSES IN DEPRESSIVE-STATES.
001965 02-09
STRETCH-INDUCED MYOTUBE GROWTH CORRELATES WITH NA-PUMP ACTIVATION. (UNPUBLISHED PAPER).
002087 02-10
THE PRESYNAPTIC STIMULATING EFFECT OF ACETYLCHOLINE ON DOPAMINE RELEASE IS SUPPRESSED DURING ACTIVATION OF NIGROSTRIATAL DOPAMINERGIC NEURONS IN THE CAT.
002733 03-03
LEVONANTRADOL, A POTENT CANNABINOID RELATED ANALGESIC, ANTAGONIZES HALOPERIDOL-INDUCED ACTIVATION OF STRIATAL DOPAMINE SYNTHESIS.
002786 03-03
IDENTICAL RESPONSES OF THE TWO HIPPOCAMPAL THETA GENERATORS TO PHYSIOLOGICAL AND PHARMACOLOGICAL ACTIVATION.
002792 03-03
ACTIVATION OF SOLUBLE STRIATAL TYROSINE-HYDROXYLASE IN THE RAT BRAIN AFTER CDP-CHOLINE ADMINISTRATION.
002816 03-03
EFFECT OF DOPAMINE ON ACTIVATION OF RAT STRIATAL ADENYLATE-CYCLASE BY FREE MG2 AND GUANYL-NUCLEOTIDES.
002825 03-03

BARBITURATE ENHANCEMENT OF GABA-MEDIATED INHIBITION AND ACTIVATION OF CHLORIDE ION-CONDUCTANCE: CORRELATION WITH ANTICONVULSANT AND ANESTHETIC ACTIONS.
002885 03-03
EFFECT OF SODIUM-VALPROATE ON MOTOR FUNCTION REGULATED BY THE ACTIVATION OF GABA-RECEPTORS.
003033 03-04
NEUROLEPTICS: ACTIVATION OR INHIBITION OF THE DOPAMINERGIC-SYSTEM?
003424 03-13
DOES P CHLOROPHENYLALANINE PRODUCE DISTURBED WAKING, DISTURBED SLEEP OR ACTIVATION BY PONTO-GENICULO-OCCIPITAL WAVES IN CATS?
003704 04-02
AN EVALUATION OF THE MECHANISM BY WHICH SEROTONERGIC ACTIVATION DEPRESSES RESPIRATION.
003917 04-03
BETA PHENYLETHYLAMINE REVERSAL OF CHLORPROMAZINE-INDUCED ACTIVATION OF STRIATAL TYROSINE-HYDROXYLASE AND CATALEPSY.
004018 04-03
INHIBITORY-ACTION OF THE COMBINATION OF AMINOPYRINE AND SECOBARBITAL ON EEG ACTIVATION, NEOCORTICAL RECRUITING AND AUGMENTING RESPONSES IN RABBITS.
004022 04-03
EFFECTS OF PROPRANOLOL ON THE LOCOMOTOR-STIMULATION INDUCED BY ACTIVATION OF POSTSYNAPTIC CATECHOLAMINE-RECEPTORS.
004126 04-04
REDUCTION IN OPIATE ACTIVATION AFTER CHRONIC ELECTROCONVULSIVE-SHOCK -- POSSIBLE ROLE FOR ENDORPHINS IN THE BEHAVIORAL-EFFECTS OF CONVULSIVE-SHOCK-TREATMENT. (UNPUBLISHED PAPER).
004154 04-04
CONTRIBUTION OF SOCIAL FACTORS TO OPIATE-INDUCED ACTIVATION IN THE MOUSE.
004156 04-04
A COMPARATIVE EVALUATION OF THE USEFULNESS OF PSYCHOPHYSIOLOGICAL-TESTS DURING VARIOUS LEVELS OF ACTIVATION OF THE CENTRAL-NERVOUS-SYSTEM.
004543 04-13

ACTIVATORS
PSYCHOMOTOR STIMULANTS AS ACTIVATORS OF NORMAL AND PATHOLOGICAL-BEHAVIOR: IMPLICATIONS FOR THE EXCESSES IN MANIA. (UNPUBLISHED PAPER).
002353 02-14

ACTOMETRIC
THE ANOREXIC AND ACTOMETRIC EFFECTS OF COCAINE AND TWO COCA-EXTRACTS.
000344 01-04

ACYLASE
AN EVALUATION OF THE USEFULNESS OF THE ACYLASE TEST IN NEUROLEPTIC TREATMENT.
004426 04-10

ACYLCYANAMIDES
ACYLCYANAMIDES, ACYLUREA, AND VARIOUS SUBSTITUTED ARYLALLOPHANATES; EFFECT ON THE CNS.
003689 04-02

ACYLUREA
ACYLCYANAMIDES, ACYLUREA, AND VARIOUS SUBSTITUTED ARYLALLOPHANATES; EFFECT ON THE CNS.
003689 04-02

ADAPTATION
NEUROTRANSMITTER RELATED ADAPTATION IN THE CENTRAL-NERVOUS-SYSTEM FOLLOWING CHRONIC MONOAMINE-OXIDASE-INHIBITION.
000038 01-03
CENTRAL NORADRENERGIC ADAPTATION TO LONG-TERM-TREATMENT WITH IMIPRAMINE IN RHESUS-MONKEYS.
000182 01-03
LONG-TERM-TREATMENT WITH NEUROLEPTIC-AGENTS: ADAPTATION PHENOMENA AND THEIR SIGNIFICANCE WITH REGARD TO SCHIZOPHRENIC-SYMPTOMATOLOGY AND SIDE-EFFECTS.
002370 02-15
IN VITRO CELLULAR ADAPTATION OF SEROTONERGIC PROCESSES AFTER CHRONIC CENTRAL PHENOBARBITAL ADMINISTRATION.
002813 03-03
THERAPY AND SOCIAL ADAPTATION OF OLIGOPHRENICS (REVIEW OF THE LITERATURE).
004444 04-11

ADAPTATIONS
RECEPTOR ADAPTATIONS TO CENTRALLY ACTING DRUGS.
003585 03-17

ADAPTIVE
ADAPTIVE CHANGES OF THE STRIATAL DOPAMINE SYSTEM INDUCED BY REPEATED ADMINISTRATION OF NEUROLEPTICS AND ERGOT DERIVATIVES.
001156 02-03

ADDICTION
IATROGENIC OPIATE ADDICTION: SUCCESSFUL DETOXIFICATION WITH CLONIDINE.
000666 01-11

Subject Index

THE TREATMENT OF OPIATE ADDICTION USING METHADONE-CHLORHYDRATE.
002600 02-17

A CLINICAL, CONTROLLED-STUDY OF L ALPHA ACETYLMETHADOL IN THE TREATMENT OF NARCOTIC ADDICTION.
003335 03-11

ACTION ON THE EMOTIONALLY-REINFORCED BRAIN SYSTEM AS A MEANS OF TREATING ALCOHOLISM AND DRUG ADDICTION PATHOGENETICALLY.
003641 03-17

ADDICTIVE-AGENTS
ADDICTIVE-AGENTS AND INTRACRANIAL-STIMULATION (ICS): MORPHINE, NALOXONE, AND PRESSING FOR AMYGDALOID ICS.
000371 01-04

ADDICTIVE-BEHAVIOR
ADDICTIVE-BEHAVIOR.
002114 02-11

ADDICTS
A PRELIMINARY OPEN-STUDY OF THE USE OF AMINEPTINE OF THE DEFICIENT SYNDROME OF HEBEPHRENICS AND OF ADDICTS DURING WITHDRAWAL.
004445 04-11

METHADONE TREATMENT OF HEROIN ADDICTS IN SWITZERLAND.
004452 04-11

SUPPRESSION OF MORPHINE ABSTINENCE IN HEROIN ADDICTS BY BETA ENDORPHIN.
004489 04-11

ADENINE-NUCLEOTIDES
ADENINE-NUCLEOTIDES AND SYNAPTIC TRANSMISSION IN THE IN VITRO RAT HIPPOCAMPUS.
000080 01-03

REACTIVITY OF ISOLATED CANINE CEREBRAL-ARTERIES TO ADENINE-NUCLEOTIDES AND ADENOSINE.
000210 01-03

ADENOSINE
REACTIVITY OF ISOLATED CANINE CEREBRAL-ARTERIES TO ADENINE-NUCLEOTIDES AND ADENOSINE.
000210 01-03

BLOCKADE OF STRIATAL NEURONE RESPONSES TO MORPHINE BY AMINOPHYLLINE: EVIDENCE FOR ADENOSINE MEDIATION OF OPIATE ACTION.
000229 01-03

ADENOSINE REGULATES VIA TWO DIFFERENT TYPES OF RECEPTORS, THE ACCUMULATION OF CYCLIC-AMP IN CULTURED BRAIN CELLS.
000308 01-03

INHIBITION OF (3H)DIAZEPAM BINDING TO RAT-BRAIN CORTICAL SYNAPTOSOMAL MEMBRANES BY ADENOSINE UPTAKE BLOCKERS.
000330 01-03

MORPHINE ENHANCES ADENOSINE RELEASE FROM THE IN VIVO RAT-CEREBRAL-CORTEX.
000451 01-04

ADENOSINE ANALOGS AS SUBSTRATES AND INHIBITORS OF 5 ADENOSYLHOMOCYSTEINE-HYDROLASE. (UNPUBLISHED PAPER).
001021 02-01

REGIONAL RELEASE OF (3H)ADENOSINE DERIVATIVES FROM RAT-BRAIN IN VIVO: EFFECT OF EXCITATORY AMINO-ACIDS, OPIATE AGONISTS, AND BENZODIAZEPINES.
001303 02-03

INHIBITORY ACTION OF ADENOSINE ON SYNAPTIC TRANSMISSION IN THE HIPPOCAMPUS OF THE GUINEA-PIG IN VITRO.
001401 02-03

AMINOPHYLLINE AND THEOPHYLLINE DERIVATIVES AS ANTAGONISTS OF NEURONAL DEPRESSION BY ADENOSINE: A MICROIONTOPHORETIC-STUDY.
001410 02-03

EFFECTS OF DIAZEPAM ON ADENOSINE AND ACETYLCHOLINE RELEASE FROM RAT-CEREBRAL-CORTEX: FURTHER EVIDENCE FOR A PURINERGIC MECHANISM IN ACTION OF DIAZEPAM.
001414 02-03

ALPHA2-ADRENERGIC AMINES, ADENOSINE AND PROSTAGLANDINS INHIBIT LIPOLYSIS AND CYCLIC-AMP ACCUMULATION IN HAMSTER ADIPOCYTES IN THE ABSENCE OF EXTRACELLULAR SODIUM.
002728 03-03

METHYLXANTHINES MODULATE ADENOSINE RELEASE FROM SLICES OF CEREBRAL-CORTEX.
002907 03-03

DO BENZODIAZEPINES BIND AT ADENOSINE UPTAKE SITES IN CNS?
002933 03-03

EFFECTS OF MORPHINE AND CAFFEINE ON ADENOSINE RELEASE FROM RAT-CEREBRAL-CORTEX: IS CAFFEINE A MORPHINE ANTAGONIST.
003864 04-03

THE EFFECT OF ADENOSINE AND GUANOSINE ON THE CONTENT OF SEROTONIN AND CATECHOLAMINES IN THE BRAIN IN THE RESTORATION PERIOD FOLLOWING EXPERIMENTAL CLINICAL DEATH.
003882 04-03

ADENOSINE AND CYCLIC-AMP IN RAT-CEREBRAL-CORTICAL-SLICES: EFFECTS OF ADENOSINE UPTAKE INHIBITORS AND ADENOSINE-DEAMINASE INHIBITORS.
003950 04-03

S-

ON THE QUESTION OF PARENCHYMAL DAMAGE CAUSED BY LONG-TERM
THERAPY WITH PSYCHOTROPICS IN ADOLESCENCE.
004626 04-15

ADOLESCENT
PREDICTORS OF ADOLESCENT HEIGHT AND WEIGHT IN HYPERKINETIC-
BOYS TREATED WITH METHYLPHENIDATE.
003509 03-15
PHENYTOIN TOXICITY IN A BRAIN-DAMAGE ADOLESCENT: A CASE-
REPORT.
003512 03-15
MAOI-INDUCED RAPID CYCLING BIPOLAR AFFECTIVE-DISORDER IN AN
ADOLESCENT.
004637 04-15

ADOLESCENTS
MARIJUANA: A REVIEW OF MEDICAL RESEARCH WITH IMPLICATIONS
FOR ADOLESCENTS.
000871 01-15
INITIAL PRESCRIPTION OF PSYCHOTROPIC-MEDICATIONS FOR
ADOLESCENTS IN A MEDICAL/PROFESSIONAL INSTITUTE, AND THE
ROLE OF THE PSYCHIATRIST IN A MEDICAL/PROFESSIONAL INSTITUTE.
002621 02-17
LATE RESULTS OF LITHIUM TREATMENT OF ADOLESCENTS WITH ATTACK
LIKE SCHIZOPHRENIA.
003177 03-08
ON THE EFFECTS OF SULTOPRIDE ADMINISTERED IN LOW-DOSAGES TO
OLDER CHILDREN AND ADOLESCENTS.
003230 03-09
TREATMENT OF ANXIETY IN CHILDREN AND ADOLESCENTS.
003349 03-11
PHARMACOLOGICAL INFLUENCE OF SEXUAL-FUNCTIONS IN ADOLESCENTS.
004436 04-11
DRUG-INDUCED PSYCHOSIS AND SCHIZOPHRENIA IN ADOLESCENTS.
004596 04-15
EMOTIONAL-DISORDERS IN CHILDREN AND ADOLESCENTS: MEDICAL AND
PSYCHOLOGICAL APPROACHES TO TREATMENT.
004743 04-17

ADRENAL
RELEASE OF ARACHIDONIC-ACID FROM ADRENAL CHROMAFFIN CELL-
CULTURES DURING SECRETION OF EPINEPHRINE. (UNPUBLISHED
PAPER).
001027 02-01
INFLUENCE OF DRUGS AFFECTING THE PITUITARY ADRENAL AXIS ON
CHROMAFFIN CELLS.
001183 02-03

ADRENAL-GLAND
EFFECT OF OXOTREMORINE ON ORNITHINE-DECARBOXYLASE ACTIVITY OF
THE ADRENAL-GLAND IN RAT.
000246 01-03
IDENTIFICATION AND QUANTIFICATION OF 1,2,3,4 TETRAHYDRO-BETA-
CARBOLINE, 2 METHYL-TETRAHYDRO-BETA-CARBOLINE, AND 6
METHOXY-TETRAHYDRO-BETA-CARBOLINE AS IN VIVO CONSTITUENTS
OF RAT-BRAIN AND ADRENAL-GLAND.
002636 03-01

ADRENAL-HORMONES
ADRENAL-HORMONES AND ETHANOL INGESTION IN C57BL/CRGL AND
C3H/CRGL/2 MICE.
002739 03-03

ADRENAL-MEDULLA
REGULATION OF CHOLINERGIC TRANSMISSION IN ADRENAL-MEDULLA.
(UNPUBLISHED PAPER).
001182 02-03
BETA ENDORPHIN-INDUCED HYPERGLYCEMIA IS MEDIATED BY INCREASED
CENTRAL SYMPATHETIC OUTFLOW TO ADRENAL-MEDULLA.
002924 03-03
EFFECTS OF TAIPOXIN ON THE ULTRASTRUCTURE OF CHOLINERGIC AXON
TERMINALS IN THE MOUSE ADRENAL-MEDULLA.
003916 04-03

ADRENALECTOMIZED
CORTICOSTERONE INCREASES THE SYNTHESIS OF A SOLUBLE PROTEIN IN
PITUITARY-GLANDS FROM ADRENALECTOMIZED MALE RATS WHICH
PRECIPITATES WITH ANTI-RAT GROWTH-HORMONE ANTISERUM.
(UNPUBLISHED PAPER).
001122 02-03

ADRENALINE
INCREASED ADRENALINE, BETA-ADRENERGIC-RECEPTOR STIMULATION
AND PHOSPHOLIPID METHYLATION IN PINEAL-GLAND OF
SPONTANEOUSLY HYPERTENSIVE-RATS. (UNPUBLISHED PAPER).
001458 02-03
CORRECTION BY PROPRANOLOL OF THE ABNORMAL ADRENALINE
DISCHARGE INDUCED BY EMOTIONAL-STRESS IN CEREBRAL
HEMORRHAGE PATIENTS.
002295 02-13
ADRENALINE: A SECRET AGENT IN MEMORY.
002345 02-14

ADRENALINE-INDUCED
THE BLOOD-BRAIN-BARRIER IN ADRENALINE-INDUCED HYPERTENSION.
000147 01-03

Subject Index

ADRENERGIC

SEIZURES AND RELATED EPILEPTIFORM ACTIVITY IN HIPPOCAMPUS TRANSPLANTED TO THE ANTERIOR-CHAMBER OF THE EYE: MODULATION BY CHOLINERGIC AND ADRENERGIC INPUT.
000095 01-03

THE RELEASE OF CATECHOLAMINES FROM ADRENERGIC NEURONS.
000974 01-17

AN EXAMINATION OF FACTORS INFLUENCING ADRENERGIC TRANSMISSION IN THE PITHED RAT, WITH SPECIAL REFERENCE TO NORADRENALINE UPTAKE MECHANISMS AND POSTJUNCTIONAL ALPHA-ADRENOCEPTORS.
001196 02-03

ADRENERGIC NONSPECIFIC POTENTIATION OF YOHIMBINE TOXICITY IN MICE BY ANTIDEPRESSANTS AND RELATED DRUGS AND ANTIYOHIMBINE ACTION OF ANTIADRENERGIC AND SEROTONERGIC DRUGS.
001330 02-03

INDIRECT ADRENERGIC EFFECT OF HISTAMINE IN CAT CEREBRAL-ARTERIES.
001355 02-03

RETROGRADE AMNESIA PRODUCED BY ELECTRICAL-STIMULATION OF THE AMYGDALA: ATTENUATION WITH ADRENERGIC ANTAGONISTS. (UNPUBLISHED PAPER).
001488 02-03

AMPHETAMINE STEREOTYPIES AND POLYRIBOSOMAL DISAGGREGATION IN RATS: EFFECTS OF ADRENERGIC AND SEROTONERGIC BLOCKING-AGENTS.
001531 02-03

DORSAL TEGMENTAL BUNDLE DESTRUCTION: EFFECTS ON OPERANT-BEHAVIOR, BRAIN CATECHOLAMINE LEVELS, AND BEHAVIORAL-SUPPRESSION PRODUCED BY ADRENERGIC AGONISTS.
001726 02-04

ADRENERGIC MODULATION OF THE HYPOTHALAMIC CHOLINERGIC MECHANISM IN THE CONTROL OF EMOTIONAL DEFENSIVE-BEHAVIOR IN THE CAT.
001761 02-04

THE CORRELATION OF CATECHOLAMINE AND ADRENERGIC PARAMETERS WITH DRUG-THERAPY OF NEUROTIC AND ENDOGENOUS DEPRESSIONS.
002047 02-09

CHANGES IN BODY-TEMPERATURE AFTER ADMINISTRATION OF ADRENERGIC AND SEROTONERGIC-AGENTS AND RELATED DRUGS INCLUDING ANTIDEPRESSANTS.
002532 02-17

ADRENERGIC REGULATION OF THE REDUCTION IN ACETYL-COENZYME-A:ARYLAMINE-N-ACETYLTRANSFERASE IN THE RAT PINEAL.
002654 03-03

DIFFERENTIAL-EFFECT OF CHRONIC DESIPRAMINE AND AMITRIPTYLINE TREATMENT ON RAT-BRAIN ADRENERGIC AND SEROTONERGIC-RECEPTORS.
002914 03-03

ROLE OF ADRENERGIC BLOCKING-AGENTS AND GLUCOCORTICOIDS ON THE REGULATION OF PITUITARY OPIOID-PEPTIDES LEVELS.
003801 04-03

NYSTAGMIC RESPONSES OF HIPPOCAMPAL ORIGIN WITH REFERENCE TO EXCITABILITY OF CHOLINERGIC AND ADRENERGIC COMPONENTS INVOLVED IN THE HIPPOCAMPUS OF RABBITS.
003842 04-03

SUBSTANCE-P INCREASES HYPOTHALAMIC BLOOD FLOW VIA AN INDIRECT ADRENERGIC CHOLINERGIC INTERACTION.
003887 04-03

THE IMPORTANCE OF CATECHOLAMINE UPTAKE INHIBITION IN THE REVERSAL OF GUANETHIDINE BLOCKADE OF ADRENERGIC NEURONS.
003900 04-03

SPINAL-CORD PHARMACOLOGY OF ADRENERGIC AGONIST-MEDIATED ANTINOCICEPTION.
004206 04-04

RETROGRADE AMNESIA PRODUCED BY ELECTRICAL-STIMULATION OF THE AMYGDALA: ATTENUATION WITH ADRENERGIC ANTAGONISTS.
004231 04-04

PERIPHERAL SEROTONERGIC AND ADRENERGIC RESPONSES IN DEPRESSION.
004364 04-09

THE STATE OF THE ADRENERGIC AND CHOLINERGIC SYSTEMS IN SCHIZOPHRENIC-PATIENTS DURING PSYCHPHARMACOTHERAPY.
004526 04-13

ADRENERGIC-RECEPTOR

MORPHINE WITHDRAWAL CAUSES SUBSENSITIVITY OF ADRENERGIC-RECEPTOR RESPONSE.
002838 03-03

ADRENERGIC-RECEPTORS

ASSESSMENT OF ADRENERGIC-RECEPTORS IN VIVO IN EXPERIMENTAL ANIMALS AND MAN. (UNPUBLISHED PAPER).
001034 02-01

ACUTE AND CHRONIC EFFECTS OF PSYCHOACTIVE-DRUGS ON ADRENERGIC-RECEPTORS AND CALMODULIN.
004750 04-17

ADRENOCEPTOR

A NEUROENDOCRINE-STUDY OF ADRENOCEPTOR FUNCTION IN ENDOGENOUS DEPRESSION.
004362 04-09

A TEST OF A NEUROTRANSMITTER MODEL OF THE AFFECTIVE-DISORDERS.
(PH.D. DISSERTATION).
003063 03-04

THE EFFECT OF SODIUM-VALPROATE ON MANIA: THE GABA HYPOTHESIS
OF AFFECTIVE-DISORDERS.
003218 03-09

PSYCHOTROPIC-DRUGS AND THEIR RELATIONSHIP WITH
PSYCHOPATHOLOGY OF AFFECTIVE-DISORDERS.
004361 04-09

LITHIUM IN THE PROPHYLAXIS OF RECURRENT AFFECTIVE-DISORDERS
(EFFECTIVENESS OF LOW PLASMA LEVELS AND PREDICTORS TO
CLINICAL-RESPONSE).
004365 04-09

LITHIUM USE IN AFFECTIVE-DISORDERS.
004367 04-09

EFFECT OF LITHIUM ON GLYCINE LEVELS IN PATIENTS WITH AFFECTIVE-
DISORDERS.
004606 04-15

KIDNEY FUNCTION IN PATIENTS WITH AFFECTIVE-DISORDERS WITH AND
WITHOUT LITHIUM THERAPY.
004664 04-15

AFFECTIVE-EPISODE
AFFECTIVE-EPISODE FREQUENCY AND LITHIUM THERAPY.
000587 01-09

AFFECTIVE-FUNCTIONS
COGNITIVE AND AFFECTIVE-FUNCTIONS IN PATIENTS WITH AFFECTIVE-
DISORDERS TREATED WITH LITHIUM: AN ASSESSMENT BY
QUESTIONNAIRE.
000604 01-09

AFFECTIVE-ILLNESS
ANTIDEPRESSANT POTENTIATION OF 5 HYDROXYTRYPTOPHAN BY L
DEPRENIL IN AFFECTIVE-ILLNESS.
000608 01-09

AMPHETAMINE AND PIRIBEDIL IN AFFECTIVE-ILLNESS.
000618 01-09

SENSITIZATION AND OSCILLATION FOLLOWING REPEATED STIMULATION:
RELATIONSHIP TO AFFECTIVE-ILLNESS AND ITS TREATMENT WITH
LITHIUM AND CARBAMAZEPINE.
002031 02-09

DEVELOPMENT AND USE OF PHARMACOLOGICAL-PROBES OF THE CNS IN
MAN: EVIDENCE OF CHOLINERGIC ABNORMALITY IN PRIMARY
AFFECTIVE-ILLNESS.
002506 02-16

BIOLOGICAL-RHYTHM DISTURBANCES IN AFFECTIVE-ILLNESS.
002628 02-17

THYROTROPHIN RESPONSE TO THYROTROPHIN-RELEASING-HORMONE IN
UNIPOLAR AND BIPOLAR AFFECTIVE-ILLNESS.
003237 03-09

UNWANTED EFFECTS OF LITHIUM-CARBONATE USED IN THE PREVENTION
OF RELAPSES OF AFFECTIVE-ILLNESS.
004625 04-15

AFFECTIVE-PSYCHOSES
COMPARATIVE CHARACTERISTICS OF THE PROPHYLACTIC PROPERTIES OF
SHORT-TERM AND LONG-ACTING LITHIUM-CARBONATE PREPARATIONS
IN ENDOGENOUS AFFECTIVE-PSYCHOSES.
004390 04-09

AFFECTIVE-PSYCHOSIS
BIPOLAR AFFECTIVE-PSYCHOSIS WITH ONSET BEFORE AGE 16 YEARS:
REPORT OF 10 CASES.
002001 02-09

AN ATTEMPT TO ASSESS THE EFFECT OF LITHIUM ON THE NEUTROPHIL
LEUKOCYTE SYSTEM IN AFFECTIVE-PSYCHOSIS.
004416 04-09

AFFERENT
CHANGES IN PRIMARY AFFERENT DEPOLARIZATION AFTER
ADMINISTRATION OF GAMMA ACETYLENIC-GAMMA-AMINOBUTYRIC-
ACID (GAG), A GAMMA AMINOBUTYRIC-ACID-TRANSAMINASE
(GABA-TRANSAMINASE) INHIBITOR.
000174 01-03

DEMONSTRATION OF SUBSTANCE-P IN AORTIC NERVE AFFERENT FIBERS
BY COMBINED USE OF FLOURESCENT RETROGRADE NEURONAL
LABELING AND IMMUNOCYTOCHEMISTRY. (UNPUBLISHED PAPER).
001024 02-01

AFFERENTS
SELECTIVE SYNAPTIC ANTAGONISM BY ATROPINE AND ALPHA
AMINOADIPATE OF PULVINAR AND CORTICAL AFFERENTS TO THE
SUPRASYLVIAN VISUAL AREA (CLARE-BISHOP AREA).
002752 03-03

EVIDENCE THAT THE OPIATE-RECEPTORS OF THE SUBSTANTIA-
GELATINOSA CONTRIBUTE TO THE DEPRESSION, BY INTRAVENOUS
MORPHINE, OF THE SPINAL TRANSMISSION OF IMPULSES IN
UNMYELINATED PRIMARY AFFERENTS.
002767 03-03

NALOXONE EFFECTS ON THE BLOOD-PRESSURE RESPONSE INDUCED BY
THIN-FIBER MUSCULAR AFFERENTS.
002794 03-03

SUPRASPINAL INHIBITION OF THE EXCITATION OF DORSAL-HORN NEURONES BY IMPULSES IN UNMYELINATED PRIMARY AFFERENTS: LACK OF EFFECT BY STRYCHNINE AND BICUCULLINE.
003778 04-03

AFFINITIES
THE AFFINITIES OF ERGOT COMPOUNDS FOR DOPAMINE AGONIST AND DOPAMINE ANTAGONIST RECEPTOR SITES.
001254 02-03
GABA-RECEPTORS REGULATE THE AFFINITIES OF ANIONS REQUIRED FOR BRAIN SPECIFIC BENZODIAZEPINE BINDING.
002903 03-03

AFFINITY
ON THE CAPACITY OF PRESYNAPTIC ALPHA-RECEPTORS TO MODULATE NOREPINEPHRINE RELEASE FROM SLICES OF RAT NEOCORTEX AND THE AFFINITY OF SOME AGONISTS AND ANTAGONISTS FOR THESE RECEPTORS.
000323 01-03
AFFINITY CHROMATOGRAPHY OF THE BETA-ADRENERGIC-RECEPTOR AND CHARACTERIZATION OF ANTIBODIES RAISED AGAINST PURIFIED RECEPTOR PREPARATIONS.
001009 02-01
NEGLIGIBLE AFFINITY OF HISTAMINE H2-RECEPTOR ANTAGONISTS FOR CENTRAL ALPHA1-ADRENOCEPTORS.
001508 02-03
MULTIPLE CNS RECEPTOR INTERACTIONS OF ERGOT ALKALOIDS: AFFINITY AND INTRINSIC ACTIVITY ANALYSIS IN IN VITRO BINDING SYSTEMS.
001516 02-03
MU-RECEPTORS AND DELTA OPIATE-RECEPTORS: CORRELATION WITH HIGH-AFFINITY AND LOW AFFINITY OPIATE BINDING-SITES.
001554 02-03
RELATIONSHIPS BETWEEN STRUCTURE AND ALPHA-ADRENERGIC-RECEPTOR AFFINITY OF CLONIDINE AND AND SOME RELATED CYCLIC-AMIDINES.
002698 03-03
PENTOBARBITAL: DUAL-ACTIONS TO INCREASE BRAIN BENZODIAZEPINE-RECEPTOR AFFINITY.
002896 03-03
EFFECT OF THE POSITION OF THE PHENOLIC GROUP IN MORPHINANS ON THEIR AFFINITY FOR OPIATE-RECEPTOR BINDING.
003702 04-02

AFTERCARE
DOUBLE-BLIND COMPARISON OF HALOPERIDOL AND THIOTHIXENE WITH AFTERCARE TREATMENT EVALUATION IN PSYCHIATRIC-OUTPATIENTS WITH SCHIZOPHRENIA.
000574 01-17
FOLLOWUP TREATMENT AND AFTERCARE OF DISCHARGED SCHIZOPHRENIC-PATIENTS.
000944 01-17

AFTERDISCHARGE
FLASH-EVOKED AFTERDISCHARGE IN RAT AS A MODEL OF THE ABSENCE SEIZURE: DOSE-RESPONSE STUDIES WITH THERAPEUTIC DRUGS.
000160 01-03
THE ROLE OF BIOGENIC-AMINES IN AMYGDALAR KINDLING. I. LOCAL AMYGDALAR AFTERDISCHARGE.
000327 01-03
RELATION OF MONOMETHYLHYDRAZINE (MMH) SEIZURE THRESHOLDS TO AFTERDISCHARGE THRESHOLDS WITH AMYGDALOID STIMULATION IN CATS.
000474 01-04
A STUDY ON EFFECTS OF ANTIEPILEPTIC-DRUGS UPON THE HIPPOCAMPAL AFTERDISCHARGE.
002844 03-03
CUMULATIVE AFTERDISCHARGE AS THE PRINCIPAL FACTOR IN THE ACQUISITION OF KINDLED SEIZURES.
002862 03-03
POWER SPECTRAL ANALYSIS OF THE FLASH-EVOKED AFTERDISCHARGE.
003133 03-06

AFTERDISCHARGES
INFLUENCE OF CARBAMAZEPINE ON THALAMOCORTICAL AND HIPPOCAMPOCORTICAL SELF-SUSTAINED AFTERDISCHARGES IN RATS.
001356 02-03
THE EFFECT OF ELECTRICAL-STIMULATION OF THE LOCUS-COERULEUS AND INTRAPERITONEAL INJECTION OF CERTAIN PHARMACOLOGICAL SUBSTANCES ON THE THRESHOLD OF HIPPOCAMPAL AFTERDISCHARGES.
003885 04-03

AFTEREFFECTS
PERSONALITY AND DRUGS IN VISUAL FIGURAL AFTEREFFECTS.
004581 04-14

AG-3-5
PHARMACOLOGICAL-ASPECTS OF SHAKING-BEHAVIOR PRODUCED BY TRH, AG-3-5, AND MORPHINE WITHDRAWAL.
004248 04-04

AGE
AGE, DEMENTIA, DYSKINESIAS, AND LITHIUM RESPONSE.
000594 01-09
EFFECTS OF AGE AND OTHER DRUGS ON BENZODIAZEPINE KINETICS.
000681 01-11
EFFECT OF AGE AND ROUTE-OF-ADMINISTRATION ON LD50 OF LITHIUM-CHLORIDE IN THE RAT.
001413 02-03

BIPOLAR AFFECTIVE-PSYCHOSIS WITH ONSET BEFORE AGE 16 YEARS: REPORT OF 10 CASES.
002001 02-09
OPEN-STUDY OF L 5 HTP IN MELANCHOLIC-DEPRESSED-PATIENTS OVER 50 YEARS OF AGE.
002016 02-09
SPECIFIC 3H IMIPRAMINE BINDING IN HUMAN PLATELETS: INFLUENCE OF AGE AND SEX.
002254 02-13
CHANGES IN PREVALENCE, SEVERITY, AND RECOVERY IN TARDIVE-DYSKINESIA WITH AGE.
002455 02-15
AGE DEPENDENT CHANGES IN THE BETA ENDORPHIN CONTENT OF DISCRETE RAT-BRAIN NUCLEI.
002635 03-01
MIND/BRAIN IN THE AGE OF PSYCHOPHARMACOLOGY: A CROSSROADS FOR MEDICINE AND MINISTRY.
003624 03-17
PIRACETAM ACTIVITY MAY DIFFER ACCORDING TO THE AGE OF THE RECIPIENT MOUSE.
003705 04-02
EFFECTS OF AGE ON DOPAMINERGIC-SUPERSENSITIVITY INDUCED BY CHRONIC FLUPHENAZINE.
003940 04-03
EFFECTS OF ANIMAL AGE AND PHENOBARBITAL ON RAT LIVER GLUCOSE-6-PHOSPHATASE ACTIVITY.
003997 04-03
EFFECTS OF ANISOMYCIN ON RETENTION OF THE PASSIVE-AVOIDANCE HABIT AS A FUNCTION OF AGE.
004097 04-04

AGE-DEPENDENT
AGE-DEPENDENT MODIFICATION OF DRUG INTERFERENCE ON THE ENZYMATIC ACTIVITIES OF THE RAT-BRAIN.
003730 04-03

AGE-RELATED
AGE-RELATED ELECTROPHYSIOLOGICAL CHANGES IN RAT-CEREBELLUM.
000197 01-03
AGE-RELATED CHANGES IN BODY-TEMPERATURE RESPONSES TO MORPHINE IN RATS.
001366 02-03
AGE-RELATED FACTORS AFFECTING ANTIDEPRESSANT-DRUG METABOLISM AND CLINICAL-RESPONSE.
002035 02-09
CLINICAL PHARMACOKINETICS IN NEWBORNS AND INFANTS: AGE-RELATED DIFFERENCES AND THERAPEUTIC IMPLICATIONS.
003343 03-11
PHARMACOTHERAPY FOR AGE-RELATED BEHAVIORAL-DEFICIENCIES.
003391 03-11

AGE-SPECIFIC
AGE-SPECIFIC DOSES OF LORMETAZEPAM AS A NIGHT SEDATIVE IN CASES OF CHRONIC SLEEP-DISTURBANCE.
004309 04-07

AGED
ABILITY OF AGED RATS TO ALTER BETA-ADRENERGIC-RECEPTORS OF BRAIN IN RESPONSE TO REPEATED ADMINISTRATION OF RESERPINE AND DESMETHYLIMIPRAMINE.
000113 01-03
DRUGS AND THE AGED.
002593 02-17
ALTERATIONS IN DIHYDROMORPHINE BINDING IN CEREBRAL HEMISPHERES OF AGED MALE RATS.
003936 04-03
PSYCHOPHARMACOTHERAPY OF SEXUAL-DISORDERS IN THE AGED.
004466 04-11
AN OVERVIEW OF PHARMACOLOGIC-TREATMENT OF COGNITIVE DECLINE IN THE AGED.
004482 04-11
PSYCHOPHARMACOLOGY FOR THE AGED.
004701 04-17

AGENT
ADRENALINE: A SECRET AGENT IN MEMORY.
002345 02-14

AGES
MORPHINE TREATMENT AT DIFFERENT INFANT AGES: INFLUENCE ON LATER MORPHINE EFFECTS IN RATS. (PH.D. DISSERTATION).
000511 01-05

AGGRAVATED
A CASE OF PETIT-MAL EPILEPSY AGGRAVATED BY LITHIUM.
004641 04-15

AGGREGATED
POSSIBLE MECHANISM FOR THE ENHANCED LETHALITY OF MORPHINE IN AGGREGATED MICE.
000437 01-04

AGGREGATES
EFFECTS OF ISOPROTERENOL ON THE DEVELOPMENT OF BETA-ADRENERGIC-RECEPTORS IN BRAIN CELL AGGREGATES.
002932 03-03

AGGREGATION
PLATELET AGGREGATION, 5 HYDROXYTRYPTAMINE UPTAKE AND RELEASE IN HUNTINGTONS-CHOREA.
002112 02-11
CANALIZATION OF AROUSAL IN THE PREWEANLING RAT: EFFECTS OF AMPHETAMINE ON AGGREGATION WITH SURROGATE STIMULI.
002965 03-04
SELECTIVE INHIBITORY-EFFECTS OF CHLORPROMAZINE AND IMIPRAMINE ON PLATELET AGGREGATION.
004518 04-13

AGGRESSION
ALCOHOL AND CHLORDIAZEPOXIDE INCREASE SUPPRESSED AGGRESSION IN MICE.
000434 01-04
PSYCHOPHARMACOLOGY OF AGGRESSION.
000721 01-11
PSYCHOPHARMACOLOGY OF AGGRESSION.
000995 01-17
COMPARATIVE-STUDY OF AGGRESSIVE-BEHAVIOUR AFTER INJECTION OF CHOLINOMIMETICS, ANTICHOLINESTERASES, NICOTINIC, AND MUSCARINIC GANGLIONIC STIMULANTS INTO THE CEREBRAL VENTRICLES OF CONSCIOUS CATS: FAILURE OF NICOTINIC-DRUGS TO EVOKE AGGRESSION.
001568 02-04
NALOXONE PRETREATMENT ENHANCES SHOCK-ELICITED AGGRESSION.
001615 02-04
AN IMPROVED MODEL OF INTRASPECIFIC AGGRESSION: DOSE-RESPONSE ANALYSIS OF APOMORPHINE-INDUCED-FIGHTING AND STEREOTYPY IN THE RAT.
002983 03-04
DRUG REGIMENS FACILITATING AGGRESSION: BEHAVIOR, AMINE, AND RECEPTOR ALTERATIONS.
002987 03-04
AGGRESSION ALTERING EFFECTS OF CYCLIC-AMP.
003021 03-04
LITHIUM AND PORCINE AGGRESSION.
003048 03-04
PHARMACOLOGICAL EVIDENCE FOR CATECHOLAMINE INVOLVEMENT IN ANIMAL AGGRESSION.
003052 03-04
FACILITATED SHOCK-INDUCED AGGRESSION AFTER CHRONIC-TREATMENT WITH ANTIDEPRESSANT-DRUGS IN THE RAT.
003058 03-04
FAILURE TO FIND SEX-DIFFERENCES IN TESTOSTERONE ACTIVATED AGGRESSION IN TWO STRAINS OF RATS.
003107 03-04
PHARMACOLOGICAL EVIDENCE FOR CATECHOLAMINE INVOLVEMENT IN ANIMAL AGGRESSION.
003140 03-06
ERGOT DRUGS SUPPRESS PLASMA PROLACTIN AND LACTATION BUT NOT AGGRESSION IN PARTURIENT MICE.
003159 03-07
PRENATAL EXPOSURE TO SYNTHETIC PROGESTINS INCREASES POTENTIAL FOR AGGRESSION IN HUMANS.
003527 03-15
ACETYLCHOLINE TURNOVER AND AGGRESSION IN RELATED THREE STRAINS OF MICE.
004151 04-04

AGGRESSIVE
BICUCULLINE ANTAGONIZES EFFECTS OF DIAZEPAM ON AGGRESSIVE AND TIMID-BEHAVIOUR IN MICE.
000485 01-04
COMPARISON OF SCH-12679 AND THIORIDAZINE IN AGGRESSIVE MENTAL-RETARDATES.
002119 02-11
LITHIUM THERAPY IN AGGRESSIVE MENTALLY-SUBNORMAL-PATIENTS.
002316 02-14
MOLINDONE-HYDROCHLORIDE IN THE TREATMENT OF AGGRESSIVE, HOSPITALIZED CHILDREN.
003321 03-11
EFFECTS OF LITHIUM-CARBONATE AND HALOPERIDOL ON COGNITION IN AGGRESSIVE, HOSPITALIZED SCHOOL-AGE CHILDREN.
003360 03-11
EFFECTS OF LITHIUM-CARBONATE AND HALOPERIDOL ON COGNITION IN AGGRESSIVE HOSPITALIZED SCHOOL-AGE CHILDREN.
003361 03-11
POSSIBLE MUSCARINIC CHOLINERGIC MEDIATION OF PATTERNED AGGRESSIVE REFLEXES IN THE CAT.
004153 04-04

AGGRESSIVE-BEHAVIOR
ROLE OF BRAIN DOPAMINERGIC MECHANISMS IN RODENT AGGRESSIVE-BEHAVIOR: INFLUENCE OF (OR -)N N PROPYLNORAPOMORPHINE ON THREE EXPERIMENTAL MODELS.
000340 01-04
EFFECTS OF SODIUM-DIPROPYLACETATE, MUSCIMOL-HYDROBROMIDE AND (R,S) NIPECOTIC-ACID-AMIDE ON ISOLATION-INDUCED AGGRESSIVE-BEHAVIOR IN MICE.
001756 02-04
INHIBITION OF AGGRESSIVE-BEHAVIOR IN RHESUS-MONKEYS BY BUSPIRONE.
003103 03-04

AGGRESSIVE-BEHAVIOR INDUCED BY APOMORPHINE IN RATS SUBMITTED TO FOUR STRESSFUL-SITUATIONS.
003163 03-07
LITHIUM AND AGGRESSIVE-BEHAVIOR.
004409 04-09

AGGRESSIVE-BEHAVIOUR
COMPARATIVE-STUDY OF AGGRESSIVE-BEHAVIOUR AFTER INJECTION OF CHOLINOMIMETICS, ANTICHOLINESTERASES, NICOTINIC, AND MUSCARINIC GANGLIONIC STIMULANTS INTO THE CEREBRAL VENTRICLES OF CONSCIOUS CATS: FAILURE OF NICOTINIC-DRUGS TO EVOKE AGGRESSION.
001568 02-04

AGGRESSIVE-BEHAVIOURAL-PHENOMENA
THE PHARMACOLOGY OF AGGRESSIVE-BEHAVIOURAL-PHENOMENA ELICITED BY MUSCARINE INJECTED INTO THE CEREBRAL VENTRICLES OF CONSCIOUS CATS.
001569 02-04

AGGRESSIVE-PATIENT
ACUTE MANAGEMENT OF THE VIOLENT AGGRESSIVE-PATIENT.
000586 01-09

AGING
SERUM PROLACTIN DURING AGING AND THE EFFECTS OF ERGOTS.
001171 02-03
BRAIN CATECHOLAMINES, MENTAL-ILLNESSES, AGING AND SENILE-DEMENTIA: BIOCHEMICAL-CONSIDERATIONS AND PHARMACOLOGICAL-CONSIDERATIONS.
001550 02-03
PSYCHOPHARMACOLOGY OF THE AGING.
002142 02-11
NEUROPSYCHIATRIC SIDE-EFFECTS OF DRUGS IN THE ELDERLY. VOL. 9, AGING.
002573 02-17
THE PSYCHOBIOLOGY OF AGING.
003861 04-03
MEMORY, OPIATE-RECEPTORS, AND AGING.
004143 04-04
PSYCHOPHARMACOLOGY OF AGING.
004710 04-17

AGITATED
TREATMENT OF TARDIVE-DYSKINESIA IN AN AGITATED, DEPRESSED-PATIENT.
002038 02-09

AGITATION
AGITATION, DISORIENTATION, AND HALLUCINATIONS IN PATIENTS ON CIMETIDINE: A REPORT OF THREE CASES AND LITERATURE REVIEW.
000896 01-15

AGONIST
CLENBUTEROL, A CENTRAL BETA-ADRENOCEPTOR AGONIST.
000120 01-03
DIFFERENTIAL REGULATION OF MUSCARINIC AGONIST BINDING-SITES FOLLOWING CHRONIC CHOLINESTERASE INHIBITION.
000279 01-03
INTRAVENOUS GABA AGONIST ADMINISTRATION STIMULATES FIRING OF A10 DOPAMINERGIC NEURONS.
000320 01-03
TRANSIENT ABOLITION OF GENERALIZED PHOTOSENSITIVE EPILEPTIC-DISCHARGE IN HUMANS BY APOMORPHINE, A DOPAMINE-RECEPTOR AGONIST.
000774 01-11
EFFECT OF THE NEW GAMMA AMINOBUTYRIC-ACID AGONIST SL-76-002 ON STRIATAL ACETYLCHOLINE: RELATION TO NEUROLEPTIC-INDUCED EXTRAPYRAMIDAL ALTERATIONS.
001119 02-03
EFFECT OF GABA AGONIST AND ANTAGONISTS ON CARDIOVASCULAR AND SYMPATHETIC RESPONSES IN SHR AND WKY RATS. (UNPUBLISHED PAPER).
001224 02-03
THE AFFINITIES OF ERGOT COMPOUNDS FOR DOPAMINE AGONIST AND DOPAMINE ANTAGONIST RECEPTOR SITES.
001254 02-03
UNITARY DOPAMINERGIC-RECEPTOR COMPOSED OF COOPERATIVELY LINKED AGONIST AND ANTAGONIST SUBUNIT BINDING-SITES.
001342 02-03
BENZODIAZEPINES MODIFY THE AGONIST RESPONSES AT A PRESYNAPTIC GABA-RECEPTOR.
001377 02-03
SOME CENTRAL-EFFECTS OF IMPROMIDINE, A POTENT AGONIST OF HISTAMINE H2-RECEPTORS.
001417 02-03
ACTIONS OF ENKEPHALIN, MU AND PARTIAL AGONIST ANALGESICS ON ACETYLCHOLINE TURNOVER IN RAT-BRAIN.
001541 02-03
ACTIVATION AND LATERALIZATION OF SENSORIMOTOR FIELD FOR PERIORAL BITING-REFLEX BY INTRANIGRAL GABA AGONIST AND BY SYSTEMIC APOMORPHINE IN THE RAT.
001657 02-04

MORPHINE ANALGESIA AFTER INTRATHECAL ADMINISTRATION OF A
NARCOTIC AGONIST, CHLOROXYMORPHAMINE AND ANTAGONIST,
CHLORNALTREXAMINE.
001695 02-04

PHENCYCLIDINE AS AN INDIRECT DOPAMINE AGONIST.
001719 02-04

NEUROCHEMICAL EVIDENCE AND BEHAVIORAL-EVIDENCE FOR A
SELECTIVE PRESYNAPTIC DOPAMINE-RECEPTOR AGONIST.
002236 02-13

PERGOLIDE, A POTENT LONG-ACTING DOPAMINE-RECEPTOR AGONIST.
002257 02-13

DOPAMINE ANTAGONIST AND AGONIST TREATMENT OF TARDIVE-
DYSKINESIA.
002377 02-15

PIPERIDINE-4-SULPHONIC-ACID, A NEW SPECIFIC GABA AGONIST.
002647 03-02

EFFECT OF KAINIC-ACID LESIONS ON MUSCARINIC AGONIST RECEPTOR
SUBTYPES IN RAT STRIATUM.
002679 03-03

DIFFERENTIAL REGULATION BY GUANINE-NUCLEOTIDES OF OPIATE
AGONIST AND ANTAGONIST RECEPTOR INTERACTIONS.
002688 03-03

CHRONOLOGY OF NEUROCHEMICAL ALTERATIONS INDUCED BY GABA
AGONIST ADMINISTRATION.
002713 03-03

PROPERTIES OF DOPAMINE AGONIST AND ANTAGONIST BINDING-SITES IN
MAMMALIAN RETINA.
002814 03-03

THE NEUROLATHYROGEN, BETA N OXALYL-L-ALPHA-BETA-
DIAMINOPROPIONIC-ACID, IS A POTENT AGONIST AT GLUTAMATE
PREFERRING RECEPTORS IN THE FROG SPINAL-CORD.
002858 03-03

DOPAMINERGIC AGONIST AND ANTAGONIST EFFECTS ON STRIATAL
TYROSINE-HYDROXYLASE DISTRIBUTION.
002898 03-03

EFFECTS OF ACUTE OR CHRONIC ADMINISTRATION OF LOW-DOSES OF A
DOPAMINE AGONIST ON DRINKING AND LOCOMOTOR-ACTIVITY IN THE
RAT.
002982 03-04

CLINICAL-PHARMACOLOGY OF MIXED AGONIST ANTAGONIST DRUGS.
003329 03-11

MORPHICEPTIN (NH4-TYR-PRO-PHE-PRO-CONH2): A POTENT AND
SPECIFIC AGONIST FOR MORPHINE MU-RECEPTORS.
003746 04-03

RESPONSE OF STRIATONIGRAL SUBSTANCE-P SYSTEMS TO A DOPAMINE-
RECEPTOR AGONIST AND ANTAGONIST.
003826 04-03

ON THE IMPORTANCE OF AGONIST CONCENTRATION GRADIENTS WITHIN
ISOLATED TISSUES. INCREASED MAXIMAL RESPONSES OF RAT VASA-
DEFERENTIA TO (-) NORADRENALINE AFTER BLOCKADE OF NEURONAL
UPTAKE.
003879 04-03

BINDING OF (3H) MUSCIMOL, A POTENT GAMMA AMINOBUTYRIC-ACID-
RECEPTOR AGONIST, TO MEMBRANES OF THE BOVINE RETINA.
003954 04-03

ACTIONS OF MU, KAPPA, SIGMA, DELTA AND AGONIST/ANTAGONIST
OPIATES ON STRIATAL DOPAMINERGIC FUNCTION.
004053 04-03

HYPERACTIVITY FOLLOWING INJECTION OF A GLUTAMATE AGONIST AND
6,7 ADTN INTO RAT NUCLEUS-ACCUMBENS AND ITS INHIBITION BY
THIP.
004066 04-04

PHARMACOLOGICAL-STUDIES WITH AN ALKYLATING NARCOTIC
AGONIST, CHLOROXYMORPHAMINE, AND ANTAGONIST,
CHLORNALTREXAMINE.
004082 04-04

AGONIST-INDUCED
AGONIST-INDUCED CHANGES IN BETA-ADRENERGIC-RECEPTOR DENSITY
AND RECEPTOR-MEDIATED RESPONSIVENESS IN SLICES OF RAT-
CEREBRAL-CORTEX.
000072 01-03

AGONIST-MEDIATED
SPINAL-CORD PHARMACOLOGY OF ADRENERGIC AGONIST-MEDIATED
ANTINOCICEPTION.
004206 04-04

AGONISTIC-BEHAVIOUR
EFFECTS OF SCOPOLAMINE ON AGONISTIC-BEHAVIOUR IN MICE.
001690 02-04

EFFECT OF PIRACETAM ON AGONISTIC-BEHAVIOUR IN MICE.
001796 02-04

AGONISTS
EFFECTS OF DOPAMINERGIC AGONISTS AND ANTAGONISTS ON
(3H)APOMORPHINE BINDING TO STRIATAL MEMBRANES: SULPIRIDE
LACK OF INTERACTIONS WITH POSITIVE COOPERATIVE
(3H)APOMORPHINE BINDING.
000099 01-03

COMPARTMENTATION OF CATECHOLAMINES IN RAT-BRAIN: EFFECTS OF
AGONISTS AND ANTAGONISTS.
000125 01-03

COMPARISON OF OPIATE AGONISTS AND THEIR N ALLYL DERIVATIVES IN THE PRODUCTION OF PHYSICAL-DEPENDENCE IN THE RAT.
001841 02-05

THE ROLE OF DIFFERENTIAL BLOCKADE OF ALPHA-ADRENERGIC AGONISTS IN CHLORPROMAZINE-INDUCED HYPOTENSION.
001851 02-05

ANTIPSYCHOTIC-PROPERTIES AND ANTIDYSKINETIC-PROPERTIES OF ERGOT DOPAMINE AGONISTS.
002178 02-11

DOPA AND DOPAMINE AGONISTS IN DEPRESSION.
002310 02-13

TARDIVE-HYPERKINESIA. EFFECTS OF SULPIRIDE AND GABA SYSTEM AGONISTS.
002405 02-15

AN OBSERVATIONAL METHOD FOR QUANTIFYING THE BEHAVIOURAL-EFFECTS OF DOPAMINE AGONISTS: CONTRASTING-EFFECTS OF D-AMPHETAMINE AND APOMORPHINE.
002484 02-16

HETEROGENEOUS DEPRESSION OF GLUCOSE UTILIZATION IN THE CAUDATE-NUCLEUS BY GABA AGONISTS.
002640 03-01

EFFECTS OF ELECTROCONVULSIVE-TREATMENT ON GROWTH-HORMONE SECRETION INDUCED BY MONOAMINE-RECEPTOR AGONISTS IN RESERPINE PRETREATED RATS.
002664 03-03

A COMPARISON OF THE CONTRACTILE RESPONSES OF THE RABBIT BASILAR AND PULMONARY-ARTERIES TO SYMPATHOMIMETIC AGONISTS: CHARACTERISTICS.
002670 03-03

GABA-AUTORECEPTORS: STRUCTURE-ACTIVITY RELATIONSHIPS FOR AGONISTS.
002678 03-03

GABA AGONISTS AS ANTIEPILEPTIC-AGENTS.
002826 03-03

ESTROGEN POTENTIATES THE STEREOTYPY INDUCED BY DOPAMINE AGONISTS IN THE RAT.
002968 03-04

INFLUENCE OF THE DOPAMINERGIC AGONISTS BROMOCRIPTINE, PIRIBEDIL AND NOMIFENSINE ON THE SYMPATHETIC NEURAL TRANSMISSION IN THE NICTITATING MEMBRANE OF THE CAT.
003822 04-03

DOPAMINERGIC MECHANISMS IN THE TELEOST RETINA. I. DOPAMINE-SENSITIVE ADENYLATE-CYCLASE IN HOMOGENATES OF CARP RETINA; EFFECTS OF AGONISTS, ANTAGONISTS AND ERGOTS.
004051 04-03

A COMPARISON OF THE RESPONSES TO SOME DOPAMINE-RECEPTOR AGONISTS AND ANTAGONISTS IN THE ISOLATED PERFUSED RAT KIDNEY.
004054 04-03

GENETIC VARIATIONS IN MIDBRAIN DOPAMINE CELL NUMBER: PARALLEL WITH DIFFERENCES IN RESPONSES TO DOPAMINERGIC AGONISTS AND IN NATURALISTIC BEHAVIORS MEDIATED BY CENTRAL DOPAMINERGIC-SYSTEMS. (UNPUBLISHED PAPER).
004112 04-04

INTERACTIONS BETWEEN NARCOTIC AGONISTS, PARTIAL AGONISTS AND ANTAGONISTS EVALUATED BY SCHEDULE-CONTROLLED BEHAVIOR.
004127 04-04

DOPAMINERGIC AGONISTS DIFFERENTIALLY AFFECT OPEN-FIELD ACTIVITY OF RATS WITH A10 LESIONS.
004135 04-04

MINI-SYMPOSIUM: III. SIMPLE IN VIVO TESTS THAT DIFFERENTIATE PROTOTYPE AGONISTS AT OPIATE-RECEPTORS.
004289 04-06

SPECIFIC GABA-RECEPTOR AGONISTS AND UPTAKE INHIBITORS: DESIGN, DEVELOPMENT AND STRUCTURE-ACTIVITY STUDIES.
004725 04-17

AGRANULOCYTOSIS
MIANSERIN: A POSSIBLE CAUSE OF NEUTROPENIA AND AGRANULOCYTOSIS.
003517 03-15

A CASE OF ACUTE AGRANULOCYTOSIS DURING TREATMENT WITH CLOZAPINE.
004642 04-15

AIMS
LONG-TERM CHANGES IN AIMS RATINGS AND THEIR RELATION TO MEDICATION HISTORY.
003537 03-15

AIRCRAFT
AIRCRAFT NOISE AND MENTAL-HEALTH: II. USE OF MEDICINES AND HEALTH-CARE-SERVICES.
003647 03-17

AKINESIA
IMPORTANCE OF AKINESIA: PLASMA CHLORPROMAZINE AND PROLACTIN LEVELS.
000891 01-15

PARADOXICAL AKINESIA INDUCED BY ANTIDEPRESSANT-DRUGS.
002378 02-15

AKINETON
A COMPARISON OF BIPERIDEN-HYDROCHLORIDE (AKINETON) AND BENZHEXOL (ARTANE) IN THE TREATMENT OF DRUG-INDUCED PARKINSONISM.
002146 02-11

ALANINE
LOCALIZATION OF SENSITIVE SITES TO TAURINE, GAMMA AMINOBUTYRIC-ACID, GLYCINE AND BETA ALANINE IN THE MOLECULAR LAYER OF GUINEA-PIG CEREBELLAR SLICES.
001402 02-03

MODULATORY INTERACTIONS BETWEEN NOREPINEPHRINE AND TAURINE, BETA ALANINE, GAMMA AMINOBUTYRIC-ACID AND MUSCIMOL APPLIED IONTOPHORETICALLY TO CEREBELLAR PURKINJE-CELLS.
004058 04-03

ALA2-MET-ENKEPHALINAMIDE
SELF-ADMINISTRATION OF D ALA2-MET-ENKEPHALINAMIDE AT HYPOTHALAMIC SELF-STIMULATION SITES.
001738 02-04

ALA2-METHIONINE-ENKEPHALIN
DIFFERENCE IN THE DEVELOPMENT OF TOLERANCE TO MORPHINE AND D ALA2-METHIONINE-ENKEPHALIN IN C57 BL/6J AND DBA/2J MICE.
003126 03-05

ALA2-METHIONINE-ENKEPHALINAMIDE
ELECTROENCEPHALOGRAPHIC AND BEHAVIORAL-TOLERANCE TO AND CROSS-TOLERANCE BETWEEN D ALA2-METHIONINE-ENKEPHALINAMIDE AND MORPHINE IN THE RAT.
004038 04-03

ALA2-MET5-ENKEPHALINAMIDE-INDUCED
NALOXONE REVERSIBLE EFFECTS OF D ALA2-MET5-ENKEPHALINAMIDE-INDUCED BEHAVIORAL-ACTIVITY IN RATS.
000402 01-04

ALBINO
THE ALBINO LOCUS PRODUCES ABNORMAL RESPONSES TO OPIATES IN THE MOUSE.
001675 02-04

ALBINO-RATS
INFERENCES DERIVED FROM ELECTROENCEPHALOGRAPHIC RESPONSES TO ACUTE ADMINISTRATION OF CLOMIPHENE-CITRATE IN MALE ALBINO-RATS.
000155 01-03

ALBUMIN
EFFECTS OF LEAD ON MOVEMENT OF ALBUMIN INTO BRAIN.
000076 01-03

ALBUMIN BINDING INTERACTIONS OF SODIUM-VALPROATE.
000762 01-13

THE CONTRIBUTION OF ALPHA1 ACID GLYCOPROTEIN, LIPOPROTEINS, AND ALBUMIN TO THE PLASMA BINDING OF PERAZINE, AMITRIPTYLINE, AND NORTRIPTYLINE IN HEALTHY MAN.
002214 02-13

EFFECTS OF ALBUMIN, AMINO-ACIDS, AND CLOFIBRATE ON THE UPTAKE OF TRYPTOPHAN BY THE RAT-BRAIN.
002673 03-03

ALCOHOL
ALCOHOL AND CHLORDIAZEPOXIDE INCREASE SUPPRESSED AGGRESSION IN MICE.
000434 01-04

IN UTERO ALCOHOL HEIGHTENS JUVENILE REACTIVITY.
000510 01-05

PHARMACOPSYCHOLOGICAL INVESTIGATION OF CHANGES IN MOOD INDUCED BY DIPOTASSIUM-CHLORAZEPATE WITH AND WITHOUT SIMULTANEOUS ALCOHOL ADMINISTRATION.
000825 01-14

INFLUENCE OF CHRONIC ALCOHOL INTOXICATION ON CIRCADIAN-RHYTHM OF NEUROSECRETORY CENTERS OF RAT HYPOTHALAMUS.
001549 02-03

POSTNATAL ALCOHOL EXPOSURE IN THE RAT: ITS EFFECTS ON AVOIDANCE CONDITIONING, HEBB-WILLIAMS MAZE-PERFORMANCE, MATERNAL-BEHAVIOR, AND PUP DEVELOPMENT.
001580 02-04

ACTION OF TOFISOPAM ON THE ERGONOMIC VIGILANCE LEVEL. ITS INTERACTION WITH THE EFFECTS OF ALCOHOL. CLINICAL PHARMACOLOGICAL-STUDY.
001891 02-07

SODIUM-VALPROATE IN THE TREATMENT OF ALCOHOL WITHDRAWAL-SYNDROME.
002139 02-11

USE OF INJECTABLE LORAZEPAM IN ALCOHOL WITHDRAWAL.
002176 02-11

THE EFFECTS OF ALCOHOL AND CAFFEINE ON CONCENTRATION TEST PERFORMANCE.
002337 02-14

ALCOHOL WITHDRAWAL-SYNDROME: TREATMENT WITH TRAZODONE.
002356 02-14

EFFECTS OF LITHIUM, AND LITHIUM AND ALCOHOL ADMINISTRATION ON NA-K-ATPASE.
002744 03-03

COMBINED EFFECTS OF ALCOHOL AND LITHIUM ON BODY COMPOSITION IN THE RAT MODEL.
002928 03-03

PINEAL-GLAND AND MELATONIN INFLUENCE ON CHRONIC ALCOHOL CONSUMPTION BY HAMSTERS.
003076 03-04

ALCOHOL WITHDRAWAL USING TIAPRIDE: QUANTITATIVE PSYCHOPATHOLOGY.
003293 03-11

DOUBLE-BLIND COMPARISON OF ALPRAZOLAM AND DIAZEPAM FOR SUBCHRONIC WITHDRAWAL FROM ALCOHOL.
003332 03-11

SMOOTH-PURSUIT EYE-MOVEMENTS: EFFECTS OF ALCOHOL AND CHLORAL-HYDRATE.
003448 03-14

INTERACTIONS BETWEEN ALCOHOL AND MEDICATIONS.
003629 03-17

SUPPRESSION OF ALCOHOL DRINKING WITH BRAIN ALDEHYDE-DEHYDROGENASE INHIBITION.
004220 04-04

MEMORY: THE EFFECTS OF ALCOHOL AND OF MARIHUANA.
004570 04-14

DRUGS, ALCOHOL AND SEX.
004706 04-17

ALCOHOL-DEHYDROGENASE
INHIBITION OF ALCOHOL-DEHYDROGENASE BY DISULFIRAM; POSSIBLE RELATION TO THE DISULFIRAM ETHANOL REACTION.
000270 01-03

ALCOHOLIC
ADVANTAGE OF MONOTHERAPY WITH CLOBAZAM IN THE TREATMENT AND POSTTREATMENT OF ALCOHOLIC WITHDRAWAL.
002140 02-11

TRIAL OF A PEPTIDE FRACTION OF ACTH (ACTH4-10) IN THE ALCOHOLIC BRAIN-DAMAGE-SYNDROME.
002318 02-14

CLINICAL PHARMACOKINETICS OF CHLORDIAZEPOXIDE IN PATIENTS WITH ALCOHOLIC HEPATITIS.
004473 04-11

DISULFIRAM AND NOCTURNAL PENILE-TUMESCENCE IN THE CHRONIC ALCOHOLIC.
004556 04-13

TRICYCLIC-ANTIDEPRESSANTS AND ALCOHOLIC BLACKOUTS.
004617 04-15

BEHAVIOR AND LEARNING DIFFICULTIES IN CHILDREN OF NORMAL INTELLIGENCE BORN TO ALCOHOLIC MOTHERS.
004658 04-15

ALCOHOLIC-DELIRIUM
CHOICE OF TACTICS IN TREATING ALCOHOLIC-DELIRIUM.
000688 01-11

ALCOHOLIC-PATIENTS
SALIVA BENZODIAZEPINE LEVELS AND CLINICAL OUTCOME IN DETOXIFYING ALCOHOLIC-PATIENTS.
004671 04-16

ALCOHOLICS
CONCENTRATION OF SEROTONIN METABOLITES IN THE CEREBROSPINAL-FLUID FROM ALCOHOLICS BEFORE AND DURING SULFIRAM THERAPY.
002095 02-11

SEXUAL-DIFFICULTIES AMONG CONVALESCING ALCOHOLICS: INTEREST IN PRAZEPAM TREATMENT IN 30 CASES.
003296 03-11

ALCOHOLISM
TOFIZOPAM IN THE TREATMENT OF CHRONIC ALCOHOLISM.
000706 01-11

POSSIBILITIES OF INFLUENCE ON THE ORGANIC-PSYCHOSYNDROME WITH NOOTROPIC-DRUGS IN CHRONIC ALCOHOLISM.
000707 01-11

A POSSIBLE ECOPHARMACOGENETIC MODEL IN NEUROPSYCHOPHARMACOLOGY ASPECTS IN ALCOHOLISM AND PHARMACODEPENDENCE.
002596 02-17

ACTION ON THE EMOTIONALLY-REINFORCED BRAIN SYSTEM AS A MEANS OF TREATING ALCOHOLISM AND DRUG ADDICTION PATHOGENETICALLY.
003641 03-17

ALDEHYDE-DEHYDROGENASE
SUPPRESSION OF ALCOHOL DRINKING WITH BRAIN ALDEHYDE-DEHYDROGENASE INHIBITION.
004220 04-04

ALDOSTERONE
RENIN AND ALDOSTERONE SECRETIONS DURING HYPOVOLEMIA IN RATS: RELATION TO NACL INTAKE.
000484 01-04

ALERTING
CHANGES IN THE HORIZONTAL VESTIBULO-OCULAR REFLEX OF THE RHESUS-MONKEY WITH BEHAVIORAL AND PHARMACOLOGICAL ALERTING.
002997 03-04

ALEXIA
REVERSIBLE ALEXIA, MITOCHONDRIAL MYOPATHY, AND LACTIC-ACIDEMIA.
000723 01-11

ALGORITHMS
PHENCYCLIDINE (PCP) INTOXICATION: DIAGNOSIS IN STAGES AND ALGORITHMS OF TREATMENT.
003525 03-15

ALIMENTARY
INTRAHYPOTHALAMIC MICROINJECTIONS OF NORADRENALINE WITH AND WITHOUT INDUCTION OF THE ALIMENTARY DRIVE AS A REWARD IN A T-MAZE LEARNING IN RATS.
001604 02-04

THE EFFECTS OF IMIPRAMINE TREATMENT ON THE UNCONDITIONED ALIMENTARY BEHAVIOR AND CLASSICAL CONDITIONED SALIVARY REACTIONS IN DOGS.
003030 03-04

INHIBITION OF MONOAMINE-OXIDASE BY FURAZOLIDONE IN THE CHICKEN AND THE INFLUENCE OF THE ALIMENTARY FLORA THEREON.
003711 04-03

ALIVAL
COOPERATIVE PSYCHIATRIC-STUDY OF ALIVAL: PRELIMINARY RESULTS.
002045 02-09

ALIVAL: NEW CLINICAL APPLICATIONS, STUDIES IN PROGRESS, AND NEW POSSIBILITIES.
002530 02-17

ALIVALS
ROUNDTABLE DISCUSSION: ALIVALS PLACE IN PSYCHIATRIC-PRACTICE.
002585 02-17

ALKALOID
HYPERTHERMIC-RESPONSE TO (-) CATHINONE, AN ALKALOID OF CATHA-EDULIS (KHAT).
003694 04-02

SINGLE-CASE STUDY OF CLINICAL-RESPONSE TO HIGH-DOSE ERGOT ALKALOID TREATMENT FOR DEMENTIA. PRELIMINARY REPORT.
004493 04-11

ALKALOIDS
SELECTIVE INFLUENCE OF ERGOT ALKALOIDS ON CORTICAL AND STRIATAL DOPAMINERGIC-RECEPTORS AND SEROTONERGIC-RECEPTORS.
001447 02-03

MULTIPLE CNS RECEPTOR INTERACTIONS OF ERGOT ALKALOIDS: AFFINITY AND INTRINSIC ACTIVITY ANALYSIS IN IN VITRO BINDING SYSTEMS.
001516 02-03

DESIGN ASPECTS OF CLINICAL-TRIALS WITH ERGOT ALKALOIDS: A COMPARISON OF TWO GERIATRIC BEHAVIORAL-RATING-SCALES.
002512 02-16

ALKOXYALKYL
N TETRAHYDROFURYLALKYL AND N ALKOXYALKYL DERIVATIVES OF (-) NORMETAZOCINE, COMPOUNDS WITH DIFFERENTIATED OPIOID ACTION PROFILES.
000013 01-02

ALKYLATED
N ALKYLATED 2 AMINOTETRALINS: CENTRAL DOPAMINE-RECEPTOR STIMULATING ACTIVITY.
000399 01-04

STRUCTURE-ACTIVITY RELATIONSHIPS AMONG SOME D N ALKYLATED AMPHETAMINES.
001542 02-03

ALKYLATING
PHARMACOLOGICAL-STUDIES WITH AN ALKYLATING NARCOTIC AGONIST, CHLOROXYMORPHAMINE, AND ANTAGONIST, CHLORNALTREXAMINE.
004082 04-04

IN VIVO EFFECTS OF TWO NOVEL ALKYLATING BENZODIAZEPINE, IRAZEPINE AND KENAZEPINE,
004251 04-04

ALL-NIGHT
THE EFFECT OF BUTOCTAMIDE-HYDROGEN-SUCCINATE ON NOCTURNAL SLEEP: ALL-NIGHT POLYGRAPHICAL-STUDIES.
002350 02-14

ALL-OR-NONE
A STUDY OF THE QUANTAL (ALL-OR-NONE) CHANGE IN REFLEX LATENCY PRODUCED BY OPIATE ANALGESICS.
000425 01-04

ALLERGIC-ENCEPHALOMYELITIS
ENHANCED TRANSFER OF EXPERIMENTAL ALLERGIC-ENCEPHALOMYELITIS WITH STRAIN-13 GUINEA-PIG LYMPH-NODE CELLS: REQUIREMENT FOR CULTURE WITH SPECIFIC ANTIGEN AND ALLOGENIC PERITONEAL EXUDATE CELLS. (UNPUBLISHED PAPER).
001201 02-03

ENHANCED TRANSFER OF EXPERIMENTAL ALLERGIC-ENCEPHALOMYELITIS WITH LEWIS-RAT LYMPH-NODE CELLS. (UNPUBLISHED PAPER).
001434 02-03

CENTRAL SEROTONIN-RECEPTOR SENSITIVITY IN RATS WITH EXPERIMENTAL ALLERGIC-ENCEPHALOMYELITIS.
001821 02-04

ALLOGENIC
ENHANCED TRANSFER OF EXPERIMENTAL ALLERGIC-ENCEPHALOMYELITIS WITH STRAIN-13 GUINEA-PIG LYMPH-NODE CELLS: REQUIREMENT FOR CULTURE WITH SPECIFIC ANTIGEN AND ALLOGENIC PERITONEAL EXUDATE CELLS. (UNPUBLISHED PAPER).
001201 02-03

ALLOXAN
GLUCOSE OXIDATION IN THE VENTROMEDIAL HYPOTHALAMUS IS NOT
AFFECTED BY INSULIN OR OUABAIN BUT DEPRESSED BY ALLOXAN
TREATMENT.
001145 02-03

ALLYL
COMPARISON OF OPIATE AGONISTS AND THEIR N ALLYL DERIVATIVES IN
THE PRODUCTION OF PHYSICAL-DEPENDENCE IN THE RAT.
001841 02-05

ALLYLNORCOCAINE
DISCRIMINATIVE-STIMULUS PROPERTIES OF COCAINE, NORCOCAINE, AND
N ALLYLNORCOCAINE.
002954 03-04

ALPHA-ADRENERGIC
MORPHINE ACTS THROUGH ALPHA-ADRENERGIC AND SEROTONINERGIC
NEURONS TO STIMULATE GROWTH-HORMONE SECRETION IN THE DOG.
000088 01-03
CHANGES IN ALPHA-ADRENERGIC-RECEPTORS IN RAT-BRAIN IN VITRO BY
PREINCUBATION WITH ALPHA-ADRENERGIC LIGANDS.
001272 02-03
CENTRAL PHARMACOLOGICAL CONTROL OF CORTICOSTERONE SECRETION
IN THE INTACT RAT. DEMONSTRATION OF CHOLINERGIC AND
SEROTONINERGIC FACILITATORY AND ALPHA-ADRENERGIC INHIBITORY
MECHANISMS.
001487 02-03
THE ROLE OF DIFFERENTIAL BLOCKADE OF ALPHA-ADRENERGIC AGONISTS
IN CHLORPROMAZINE-INDUCED HYPOTENSION.
001851 02-05
AMITRIPTYLINE: LONG-TERM-TREATMENT ELEVATES ALPHA-ADRENERGIC
AND MUSCARINIC-RECEPTOR BINDING IN MOUSE-BRAIN.
002875 03-03
FLUORESCENT PROBES OF ALPHA-ADRENERGIC AND BETA-ADRENERGIC
AND OPIATE-RECEPTORS: BIOCHEMICAL AND HISTOCHEMICAL
EVALUATION.
003685 04-02
EFFECTS OF ALPHA-ADRENERGIC AND BETA-ADRENERGIC BLOCKERS ON
CHLORPROMAZINE-INDUCED ELEVATION OF PLASMA GLUCOSE AND
CYCLIC-AMP IN FED MICE.
003946 04-03

ALPHA-ADRENERGIC-ACTIVITY
CYCLOHEXYLPHENOXYAMIDOXIMES AND IMIDAZOLINES WITH
ANTIDEPRESSIVE AND ALPHA-ADRENERGIC-ACTIVITY.
001051 02-01

ALPHA-ADRENERGIC-RECEPTOR
PERIPHERAL ALPHA-ADRENERGIC-RECEPTOR SUBTYPES.
000901 01-16
RELATIONSHIPS BETWEEN STRUCTURE AND ALPHA-ADRENERGIC-
RECEPTOR AFFINITY OF CLONIDINE AND AND SOME RELATED CYCLIC-
AMIDINES.
002698 03-03
CHARACTERIZATION AND QUANTITATION OF ALPHA-ADRENERGIC-
RECEPTOR SUBTYPES IN RAT HYPOTHALAMUS.
002839 03-03

ALPHA-ADRENERGIC-RECEPTORS
AMITRIPTYLINE BINDING TO SPECIFIC ALPHA-ADRENERGIC-RECEPTORS IN
VITRO.
000181 01-03
(3H)QUINUCLIDINYL-BENZILATE BINDING TO MUSCARINIC-RECEPTORS
AND (3H)WB-4101 BINDING TO ALPHA-ADRENERGIC-RECEPTORS IN
RABBIT IRIS: COMPARISON OF RESULTS IN SLICES AND MICROSOMAL
FRACTIONS.
000299 01-03
TRICYCLIC-ANTIDEPRESSANT DRUG-INTERACTIONS WITH HISTAMINE AND
ALPHA-ADRENERGIC-RECEPTORS.
000791 01-13
CHANGES IN ALPHA-ADRENERGIC-RECEPTORS IN RAT-BRAIN IN VITRO BY
PREINCUBATION WITH ALPHA-ADRENERGIC LIGANDS.
001272 02-03
CHARACTERIZATION BY (3H)DIHYDROERGOCRYPTINE BINDING OF ALPHA-
ADRENERGIC-RECEPTORS IN NEUROBLASTOMA X GLIOMA HYBRID
CELLS.
003823 04-03

ALPHA-ADRENOCEPTOR
SUPPRESSION OF SEROTONERGIC NEURONAL FIRING BY ALPHA-
ADRENOCEPTOR ANTAGONISTS: EVIDENCE AGAINST GABA
MEDIATION.
000024 01-03
EFFECTS OF ALPHA-ADRENOCEPTOR AGONISTS AND ANTAGONISTS AND
OF ANTIDEPRESSANT-DRUGS ON PRESYNAPTIC AND POSTSYNAPTIC
ALPHA-ADRENOCEPTORS.
001146 02-03
EFFECTS OF ALPHA-ADRENOCEPTOR STIMULATING DRUGS ON
BARORECEPTOR REFLEXES IN CONSCIOUS CATS.
001514 02-03
POSSIBLE ROLE OF AN ENDOGENOUS OPIATE IN THE CARDIOVASCULAR-
EFFECTS OF CENTRAL ALPHA-ADRENOCEPTOR STIMULATION IN
SPONTANEOUSLY HYPERTENSIVE-RATS.
003791 04-03
PRESYNAPTIC AND POSTSYNAPTIC ALPHA-ADRENOCEPTOR ANTAGONISM
BY NEUROLEPTICS IN VIVO.
003966 04-03

ALPHA-ADRENOCEPTOR-MEDIATED
ALPHA-ADRENOCEPTOR-MEDIATED MODULATION OF 5
HYDROXYTRYPTAMINE RELEASE FROM RAT-BRAIN-CORTEX SLICES.
000111 01-03

ALPHA-ADRENOCEPTORS
COMPARISON OF MIANSERIN WITH DESIPRAMINE, MAPROTILINE AND
PHENTOLAMINE ON CARDIAC PRESYNAPTIC AND VASCULAR
POSTSYNAPTIC ALPHA-ADRENOCEPTORS AND NORADRENALINE
REUPTAKE IN PITHED NORMOTENSIVE-RATS.
000044 01-03
THE EFFECTS OF BROMOCRIPTINE ON PRESYNAPTIC AND POSTSYNAPTIC
ALPHA-ADRENOCEPTORS IN THE MOUSE VAS-DEFERENS.
000108 01-03
EFFECTS OF ALPHA-ADRENOCEPTOR AGONISTS AND ANTAGONISTS AND
OF ANTIDEPRESSANT-DRUGS ON PRESYNAPTIC AND POSTSYNAPTIC
ALPHA-ADRENOCEPTORS.
001146 02-03
AN EXAMINATION OF FACTORS INFLUENCING ADRENERGIC
TRANSMISSION IN THE PITHED RAT, WITH SPECIAL REFERENCE TO
NORADRENALINE UPTAKE MECHANISMS AND POSTJUNCTIONAL
ALPHA-ADRENOCEPTORS.
001196 02-03
PRESYNAPTIC ALPHA-ADRENOCEPTORS AND THE ACTION OF TRICYCLIC-
ANTIDEPRESSANT DRUGS IN BEHAVIOURAL-DESPAIR IN RATS.
001829 02-04
FUNCTIONAL CHARACTERIZATION OF CENTRAL ALPHA-ADRENOCEPTORS
BY YOHIMBINE DIASTEREOMERS.
002748 03-03
THE TETRACYCLIC-ANTIDEPRESSANT MIANSERIN: EVALUATION OF ITS
BLOCKADE OF PRESYNAPTIC ALPHA-ADRENOCEPTORS IN A SELF-
STIMULATION MODEL USING CLONIDINE.
003016 03-04
PHARMACOLOGICAL DIFFERENTIATION OF PRESYNAPTIC INHIBITORY
ALPHA-ADRENOCEPTORS AND OPIATE-RECEPTORS IN THE CAT
NICTITATING MEMBRANE.
003777 04-03
EFFECTS ON THE PINNA-REFLEX OF DRUGS ACTING AT ALPHA-
ADRENOCEPTORS.
004078 04-04

ALPHA-ADRENORECEPTOR
ALPHA-ADRENORECEPTOR MEDIATED ALTERATION OF ETHANOL EFFECTS
ON NA-K-ATPASE OF RAT NEURONAL MEMBRANES.
001425 02-03

ALPHA-PATTERN
THE TWO SURVIVAL CASES OF ALPHA-PATTERN COMA CAUSED BY
LARGE AMOUNTS OF HYPNOTICA AND NEUROLEPTICA.
004608 04-15

ALPHA-RECEPTORS
ON THE CAPACITY OF PRESYNAPTIC ALPHA-RECEPTORS TO MODULATE
NOREPINEPHRINE RELEASE FROM SLICES OF RAT NEOCORTEX AND THE
AFFINITY OF SOME AGONISTS AND ANTAGONISTS FOR THESE
RECEPTORS.
000323 01-03
ALPHA METHYLEPINEPHRINE, A METHYLDOPA METABOLITE THAT BINDS
TO ALPHA-RECEPTORS IN RAT-BRAIN.
002734 03-03

ALPHA1
THE CONTRIBUTION OF ALPHA1 ACID GLYCOPROTEIN, LIPOPROTEINS,
AND ALBUMIN TO THE PLASMA BINDING OF PERAZINE,
AMITRIPTYLINE, AND NORTRIPTYLINE IN HEALTHY MAN.
002214 02-13
BINDING OF PERAZINE TO ALPHA1 ACID GLYCOPROTEIN.
002290 02-13

ALPHA1-ADRENERGIC-RECEPTORS
ONTOGENY OF MAMMALIAN CARDIAC ALPHA1-ADRENERGIC-
RECEPTORS.
001545 02-03

ALPHA1-ADRENOCEPTOR
DIFFERENTIAL INHIBITION OF ALPHA1-ADRENOCEPTOR AND ALPHA2-
ADRENOCEPTOR MEDIATED PRESSOR RESPONSES IN PITHED RATS.
004057 04-03

ALPHA1-ADRENOCEPTORS
3H PRAZOSIN BINDS SPECIFICALLY TO ALPHA1-ADRENOCEPTORS IN RAT-
BRAIN.
000205 01-03
NEGLIGIBLE AFFINITY OF HISTAMINE H2-RECEPTOR ANTAGONISTS FOR
CENTRAL ALPHA1-ADRENOCEPTORS.
001508 02-03
THE DOPAMINE-RECEPTOR ANTAGONIST DOMPERIDONE IS ALSO A
COMPETITIVE ANTAGONIST AT ALPHA1-ADRENOCEPTORS.
003785 04-03
REGULATION OF ALPHA1-ADRENOCEPTORS IN THE CEREBRAL-CORTEX OF
THE RAT BY THYROID-HORMONES.
003816 04-03
ALPHA1-ADRENOCEPTORS AND ALPHA2-ADRENOCEPTORS IN RAT-
CEREBRAL-CORTEX: EFFECT OF FRONTAL LOBOTOMY.
003944 04-03

ALPHA1-RECEPTORS
AN IN VIVO MODEL FOR INVESTIGATING ALPHA1-RECEPTORS AND ALPHA2-RECEPTORS IN THE CNS: STUDIES WITH MIANSERIN.
000053 01-03

ALPHA2-ADRENERGIC
ALPHA2-ADRENERGIC AMINES, ADENOSINE AND PROSTAGLANDINS INHIBIT LIPOLYSIS AND CYCLIC-AMP ACCUMULATION IN HAMSTER ADIPOCYTES IN THE ABSENCE OF EXTRACELLULAR SODIUM.
002728 03-03

ALPHA2-ADRENERGIC-AUTORECEPTOR
ANTIDEPRESSANTS AND ALPHA2-ADRENERGIC-AUTORECEPTOR DESENSITIZATION.
004659 04-15

ALPHA2-ADRENERGIC-RECEPTORS
HUMAN PLATELET ALPHA2-ADRENERGIC-RECEPTORS: LABELING WITH 3H YOHIMBINE, A SELECTIVE ANTAGONIST LIGAND.
004676 04-16

ALPHA2-ADRENOCEPTOR
EFFECTS OF DESIPRAMINE AND YOHIMBINE ON ALPHA2-ADRENOCEPTOR AND BETA-ADRENOCEPTOR SENSITIVITY.
001305 02-03
DIFFERENTIAL INHIBITION OF ALPHA1-ADRENOCEPTOR AND ALPHA2-ADRENOCEPTOR MEDIATED PRESSOR RESPONSES IN PITHED RATS.
004057 04-03

ALPHA2-ADRENOCEPTORS
ALPHA2-ADRENOCEPTORS IN RAT-BRAIN: THE DIVALENT-CATION SITE.
001246 02-03
THE BLOCKADE OF ALPHA2-ADRENOCEPTORS BY THE PNMT INHIBITOR SKF-64139.
001255 02-03
THE INABILITY OF CHRONIC MIANSERIN TO BLOCK CENTRAL ALPHA2-ADRENOCEPTORS.
001492 02-03
ALPHA1-ADRENOCEPTORS AND ALPHA2-ADRENOCEPTORS IN RAT-CEREBRAL-CORTEX: EFFECT OF FRONTAL LOBOTOMY.
003944 04-03

ALPHA2-ADRENORECEPTORS
TRICYCLIC-ANTIDEPRESSANT DRUG-TREATMENT DECREASES ALPHA2-ADRENORECEPTORS ON HUMAN PLATELET MEMBRANES.
003408 03-13
ALPHA2-ADRENORECEPTORS IN RAT-BRAIN ARE DECREASED AFTER LONG-TERM TRICYCLIC-ANTIDEPRESSANT DRUG-TREATMENT.
004008 04-03

ALPHA2-NORADRENERGIC-RECEPTOR
MULTIPLE ALPHA2-NORADRENERGIC-RECEPTOR SITES IN RAT-BRAIN: SELECTIVE REGULATION OF HIGH-AFFINITY (3H)CLONIDINE BINDING BY GUANINE-NUCLEOTIDES AND DIVALENT-CATIONS.
003992 04-03
CLONIDINE-INDUCED HYPERPHAGIA IN MONKEYS: EVIDENCE FOR ALPHA2-NORADRENERGIC-RECEPTOR MEDIATION.
004215 04-04

ALPHA2-RECEPTORS
AN IN VIVO MODEL FOR INVESTIGATING ALPHA1-RECEPTORS AND ALPHA2-RECEPTORS IN THE CNS: STUDIES WITH MIANSERIN.
000053 01-03
MIANSERIN: DIRECT ACTIVATION OF BRAIN NOREPINEPHRINE NEURONS BY BLOCKING ALPHA2-RECEPTORS.
001214 02-03

ALPRAZOLAM
ANXIOLYTIC EFFICACY OF ALPRAZOLAM COMPARED TO DIAZEPAM AND PLACEBO.
000648 01-10
DOUBLE-BLIND CLINICAL ASSESSMENT OF ALPRAZOLAM, A NEW BENZODIAZEPINE DERIVATIVE, IN THE TREATMENT OF MODERATE TO SEVERE ANXIETY.
002070 02-10
DOUBLE-BLIND COMPARISON OF ALPRAZOLAM AND DIAZEPAM FOR SUBCHRONIC WITHDRAWAL FROM ALCOHOL.
003332 03-11
ALPRAZOLAM, A NEW TYPE ANXIOLYTIC IN NEUROTIC-PATIENTS: A PILOT-STUDY.
004422 04-10

ALTERATION
ALTERATION OF PHARMACOKINETIC PARAMETERS FOR PENTOBARBITAL BY ISCHEMIC STROKE AND REVERSION TO NORMAL BY DEXAMETHASONE TREATMENT.
000321 01-03
ELECTIVE ALTERATION OF THE STATE OF CONSCIOUSNESS SUBJECTED TO THE EFFECTS OF PSYCHOACTIVE-SUBSTANCES.
000994 01-17
ALTERATION OF PROLACTIN SECRETION BY CENTRALLY-ACTING DRUGS.
001127 02-03
ALPHA-ADRENORECEPTOR MEDIATED ALTERATION OF ETHANOL EFFECTS ON NA-K-ATPASE OF RAT NEURONAL MEMBRANES.
001425 02-03
BENZODIAZEPINE-RECEPTORS: THE EFFECT OF GABA ON THEIR CHARACTERISTICS IN HUMAN BRAIN AND THEIR ALTERATION IN HUNTINGTONS-DISEASE.
002163 02-11

CEEG STUDY ON PATIENTS UNDER THE PSYCHIATRIC-DRUG TREATMENT; THE CORRELATION BETWEEN EEG ALTERATION AND CLINICAL EVOLUTION.
002165 02-11
ENDOCRINE CHANGES AND BEHAVIORAL-CHANGES IN DEPRESSION AFTER THYROTROPIN-RELEASING-HORMONE (TRH): ALTERATION BY PRETREATMENT WITH THYROID-HORMONES.
002259 02-13
HIGH-AFFINITY RENAL (3H)FLUNITRAZEPAM BINDING: CHARACTERIZATION, LOCALIZATION, AND ALTERATION IN HYPERTENSION.
002874 03-03
QUANTITATION AND COMPARISON OF PHENOBARBITAL LEVELS IN THE PLASMA, SALIVA, AND CEREBROSPINAL-FLUID OF THE RAT, AND THE DEMONSTRATION OF AN ALTERATION OF DRUG PASSAGE BY ETHANOL.
003725 04-03
STRESS-MODULATED ALTERATION OF BRAIN BIOGENIC-AMINES IN THE RAT: EFFECTS OF L TRYPTOPHAN.
003978 04-03

ALTERATIONS
LONG-TERM ANTIDEPRESSANT TREATMENT: ALTERATIONS IN CEREBRAL CAPILLARY PERMEABILITY.
000239 01-03
GABA LEVELS IN HUMAN CEREBROSPINAL-FLUID: ALTERATIONS IN PSYCHIATRIC-DISORDERS. (UNPUBLISHED PAPER).
000764 01-13
EFFECT OF THE NEW GAMMA AMINOBUTYRIC-ACID AGONIST SL-76-002 ON STRIATAL ACETYLCHOLINE. RELATION TO NEUROLEPTIC-INDUCED EXTRAPYRAMIDAL ALTERATIONS.
001119 02-03
ALTERATIONS IN BASAL FIRING-RATE AND AUTORECEPTOR SENSITIVITY OF DOPAMINE NEURONS IN THE SUBSTANTIA-NIGRA FOLLOWING ACUTE AND EXTENDED EXPOSURE TO ESTROGEN.
001167 02-03
DRUG-INDUCED ALTERATIONS IN NEUROTRANSMITTER-RECEPTOR BINDING AND FUNCTION.
001215 02-03
CHRONOLOGY OF NEUROCHEMICAL ALTERATIONS INDUCED BY GABA AGONIST ADMINISTRATION.
002713 03-03
DRUG REGIMENS FACILITATING AGGRESSION: BEHAVIOR, AMINE, AND RECEPTOR ALTERATIONS.
002987 03-04
BEHAVIORAL AND METABOLIC ALTERATIONS IN PROGENY OF METHADONE-TREATED RATS. (PH.D. DISSERTATION).
003113 03-04
ALTERATIONS IN CEREBROSPINAL-FLUID DOPAMINE METABOLITES FOLLOWING PHYSOSTIGMINE INFUSION.
003477 03-15
ALTERATIONS OF ACETYLCHOLINE AND CHOLINE METABOLISM IN MAMMALIAN PREPARATIONS TREATED WITH BETA BUNGAROTOXIN.
003820 04-03
ALTERATIONS IN DIHYDROMORPHINE BINDING IN CEREBRAL HEMISPHERES OF AGED MALE RATS.
003936 04-03
ALTERATIONS IN GAMMA AMINOBUTYRIC-ACID-RECEPTOR SENSITIVITY FOLLOWING ACUTE AND CHRONIC ETHANOL TREATMENTS.
004037 04-03
ALTERATIONS OF EVOKED-POTENTIALS LINK RESEARCH IN ATTENTION-DYSFUNCTION TO PEPTIDE RESPONSE SYMPTOMS OF SCHIZOPHRENIA.
004316 04-08
ALTERATIONS IN NORADRENERGIC FUNCTION DURING CLORGYLINE TREATMENT.
004393 04-09
DRUG-INDUCED ALTERATIONS OF THE HYPOTHALAMUS HYPOPHYSIS AXIS.
004535 04-13

ALTERING
BEHAVIOURAL-RESPONSES TO DRUGS RELEASING 5 HYDROXYTRYPTAMINE AND CATECHOLAMINES: EFFECTS OF TREATMENTS ALTERING PRECURSOR CONCENTRATIONS IN BRAIN.
002990 03-04
AGGRESSION ALTERING EFFECTS OF CYCLIC-AMP.
003021 03-04
LITHIUM DRUG INTERACTIONS ALTERING THE INTRACELLULAR LITHIUM LEVEL: AN IN VITRO STUDY.
003142 03-06
CHLORPROMAZINE EFFECTS ON COCAINE-REINFORCED RESPONDING IN RHESUS-MONKEYS: RECIPROCAL MODIFICATION OF RATE ALTERING EFFECTS OF THE DRUGS.
004133 04-04
MECHANISMS AND PHARMACOLOGICAL IMPLICATIONS OF ALTERING CALMODULIN ACTIVITY.
004751 04-17

ALTERNATION
AROUSAL AND SHORT-TERM MEMORY: EFFECTS OF CAFFEINE AND TRIAL SPACING ON DELAYED ALTERNATION PERFORMANCE.
000487 01-04

ALTERNATIVE
ELECTROLYTIC MICROINFUSION TRANSDUCER SYSTEM: AN ALTERNATIVE METHOD OF INTRACRANIAL DRUG APPLICATION.
001861 02-06

ALTHESIN
EFFECTS OF ALTHESIN IN PSYCHOTHERAPY OF SCHIZOPHRENICS: PRELIMINARY REPORT.
004331 04-08

ALUMINUM
ORAL ALUMINUM AND NEUROPSYCHOLOGICAL FUNCTIONING: A STUDY OF DIALYSIS PATIENTS RECEIVING ALUMINUM-HYDROXIDE GELS.
002283 02-13

ALUMINUM-HYDROXIDE
ORAL ALUMINUM AND NEUROPSYCHOLOGICAL FUNCTIONING: A STUDY OF DIALYSIS PATIENTS RECEIVING ALUMINUM-HYDROXIDE GELS.
002283 02-13

ALZHEIMER-LIKE
USE OF THA IN TREATMENT OF ALZHEIMER-LIKE DEMENTIA: PILOT-STUDY IN TWELVE PATIENTS.
003377 03-11

ALZHEIMER-TYPE
CHOLINE-BITARTRATE TREATMENT OF ALZHEIMER-TYPE DEMENTIAS.
000675 01-11

ALZHEIMERS-DISEASE
LECITHIN AND MEMORY TRAINING IN ALZHEIMERS-DISEASE. (PH.D. DISSERTATION).
003299 03-11
EFFECTS OF CHOLINERGIC-DRUGS ON MEMORY IN ALZHEIMERS-DISEASE.
003454 03-14

ALZHEIMERS-TYPE
THE EFFECTS OF LECITHIN ON MEMORY IN PATIENTS WITH SENILE-DEMENTIA OF THE ALZHEIMERS-TYPE.
003385 03-11

AMANITIN
RNA-POLYMERASE-II IN C6-GLIOMA CELLS: ALPHA AMANITIN BLOCKADE OF CYCLIC-AMP-PHOSPHODIESTERASE INDUCTION BY BETA-ADRENERGIC STIMULATION. (UNPUBLISHED PAPER).
003998 04-03

AMANTADINE
REVIEW OF 38 CASES OF SUBACUTE SCLEROSING PANENCEPHALITIS: EFFECT OF AMANTADINE ON THE NATURAL COURSE OF THE DISEASE.
000718 01-11
LITHIUM-INDUCED COGWHEEL RIGIDITY: TREATMENT WITH AMANTADINE.
000748 01-13
CLINICAL-TRIAL WITH AMANTADINE AND HYDERGINE IN ELDERLY-PATIENTS.
002093 02-11
EDEMAS AND MYOCLONIES IN A PATIENT WITH PARKINSONS-DISEASE TREATED BY AMANTADINE: PROBLEM WITH ASSOCIATED MEDICATIONS.
002389 02-15
THE EFFECT OF AMANTADINE ON PROLACTIN LEVELS AND GALACTORRHEA ON NEUROLEPTIC TREATED PATIENTS.
003373 03-11
COMPARATIVE-EFFECTS OF AMANTADINE AND AMFONELIC-ACID ON DOPAMINE METABOLISM IN RAT-BRAIN.
003796 04-03
ACCUMULATION OF AMANTADINE BY ISOLATED CHROMAFFIN GRANULES.
003866 04-03

AMBIENT
THE EFFECTS OF THEOPHYLLINE AND CAFFEINE ON THERMOREGULATORY FUNCTIONS OF RATS AT DIFFERENT AMBIENT TEMPERATURES.
003907 04-03
CORE TEMPERATURE CHANGES FOLLOWING ADMINISTRATION OF NALOXONE AND NALTREXONE TO RATS EXPOSED TO HOT AND COLD AMBIENT TEMPERATURES. EVIDENCE FOR THE PHYSIOLOGICAL ROLE OF ENDORPHINS IN HOT AND COLD ACCLIMATIZATION.
004034 04-03

AMBLYOPIA
ROLE OF INTRACORTICAL INHIBITION IN DEPRIVATION AMBLYOPIA: REVERSAL BY MICROIONTOPHORETIC BICUCULLINE.
002684 03-03

AMBULATORY
COVERT DYSKINESIA IN AMBULATORY SCHIZOPHRENIA.
000836 01-15
EVALUATIONS OF LOXAPINE-SUCCINATE IN THE AMBULATORY TREATMENT OF ACUTE SCHIZOPHRENIC-EPISODES.
004345 04-08
PHARMACOTHERAPY AND PSYCHOTHERAPY FOR AMBULATORY DEPRESSION: EFFICACY AND CHOICES.
004413 04-09

AMELIORATES
CLONIDINE AMELIORATES GILLES-DE-LA-TOURETTE-SYNDROME.
002106 02-11

AMELIORATION
TREATMENT OF HUNTINGTON-DISEASE WITH GAMMA ACETYLENIC-GABA, AN IRREVERSIBLE INHIBITOR OF GABA-TRANSAMINASE:

INCREASED CSF GABA AND HOMOCARNOSINE WITHOUT CLINICAL AMELIORATION.
003458 03-14
LITHIUM AMELIORATION OF RESERPINE-INDUCED HYPOACTIVITY IN RATS.
004167 04-04

AMERICA
THE TRANQUILIZING OF AMERICA.
003602 03-17

AMERICAN-PSYCHIATRIC-ASSOCIATION
TARDIVE-DYSKINESIA: SUMMARY OF A TASK-FORCE-REPORT OF THE AMERICAN-PSYCHIATRIC-ASSOCIATION.
000875 01-15

AMFONELIC-ACID
DIFFERENT DOPAMINERGIC MECHANISMS FOR AMFONELIC-ACID, AMPHETAMINE AND APOMORPHINE.
000465 01-04
DIVERGENT RESERPINE EFFECTS ON AMFONELIC-ACID AND AMPHETAMINE STIMULATION OF SYNAPTOSOMAL DOPAMINE FORMATION FROM PHENYLALANINE.
001113 02-03
COMPARATIVE-EFFECTS OF AMANTADINE AND AMFONELIC-ACID ON DOPAMINE METABOLISM IN RAT-BRAIN.
003796 04-03

AMILORIDE
ATTENUATION OF THE LITHIUM-INDUCED DIABETES-INSIPIDUS-LIKE SYNDROME BY AMILORIDE IN RATS.
002717 03-03

AMINE
TRICYCLIC-ANTIDEPRESSANT DRUGS AND INDIVIDUAL DIFFERENCES IN THE EXPLORATORY-ACTIVITY OF RATS: CONTRASTING-EFFECTS OF TERTIARY AND SECONDARY AMINE COMPOUNDS.
000401 01-04
DOPAMINE BIOSYNTHESIS IS REGULATED BY THE AMINE NEWLY RECAPTURED BY DOPAMINERGIC NERVE-ENDINGS.
001163 02-03
QUINACRINE AND SEROTONIN BINDING BY SYNTHETIC MODELS FOR HUMAN PLATELET DENSE-BODIES: EVALUATION OF THE ROLE OF BINDING IN AMINE STORAGE. (UNPUBLISHED PAPER).
002219 02-13
DRUG REGIMENS FACILITATING AGGRESSION: BEHAVIOR, AMINE, AND RECEPTOR ALTERATIONS.
002987 03-04
CROSS-OVER STUDY OF ZIMELIDINE AND DESIPRAMINE IN DEPRESSION: EVIDENCE FOR AMINE SPECIFICITY.
003250 03-09
NONCOMPETITIVE AMINE UPTAKE INHIBITION BY THE NEW ANTIDEPRESSANT PRIDEFINE.
003771 04-03
AMINE UPTAKE INHIBITORS: CRITERIA OF SELECTIVITY.
003921 04-03
THE INTERACTION OF AMINE LOCAL ANESTHETICS WITH MUSCARINIC-RECEPTORS.
004031 04-03
A SIMPLE HISTOCHEMICAL SCREENING METHOD FOR AMINE UPTAKE.
004295 04-06
A RAPID AND SENSITIVE RADIORECEPTOR ASSAY FOR TERTIARY AMINE TRICYCLIC-ANTIDEPRESSANTS.
004689 04-16

AMINE-OXIDASE
ESR STUDIES OF BOVINE PLASMA AMINE-OXIDASE: PROBING OF THE ENVIRONMENT ABOUT THE SUBSTRATE LIBERATED SULFHYDRYL GROUPS IN THE ACTIVE SITE. (UNPUBLISHED PAPER).
001066 02-01
CU-AMINE-OXIDASES: STUDIES RELATED TO THE MECHANISM-OF-ACTION OF BOVINE PLASMA AMINE-OXIDASE (UNPUBLISHED PAPER).
003680 04-01

AMINEPTINE
AMINEPTINE: CLINICAL REVIEW.
001896 02-07
AMINEPTINE, A NEW ANTIDEPRESSANT: PHARMACOLOGICAL REVIEW.
001898 02-07
THE IMPORTANCE OF AMINEPTINE IN THE TREATMENT OF NONPSYCHOTIC DEPRESSIVE-STATES IN THE ELDERLY.
001999 02-09
COMPARATIVE EXPERIMENT OF THE ANTIDEPRESSANT EFFECTS OF AMINEPTINE AND CHLORIMIPRAMINE.
002029 02-09
ANTIDEPRESSANT ACTION OF AMINEPTINE: CONTROLLED DOUBLE-BLIND STUDY.
002030 02-09
DOUBLE-BLIND CONTROLLED EXPERIMENT: AMINEPTINE VERSUS AMITRIPTYLINE USING THE HAMILTON-DEPRESSION-RATING-SCALE.
002050 02-09
DOUBLE-BLIND CONTROLLED-STUDY: AMINEPTINE VERSUS TRIMIPRAMINE.
002051 02-09

COMPARATIVE CROSS-STUDY ON THE EFFECTS OF AMINEPTINE AND MAPROTILINE.
002065 02-10

DOUBLE-BLIND CONTROLLED-STUDY ON THE PSYCHOLEPTIC-EFFECTS OF AMINEPTINE IN MENTALLY-HANDICAPPED CHILDREN WITHOUT PERSONALITY-PROBLEMS.
002116 02-11

A PRELIMINARY OPEN-STUDY OF THE USE OF AMINEPTINE OF THE DEFICIENT SYNDROME OF HEBEPHRENICS AND OF ADDICTS DURING WITHDRAWAL.
004445 04-11

AMINERGIC
CENTRAL AMINERGIC AND PEPTIDERGIC MECHANISMS IN SPONTANEOUSLY (GENETIC) HYPERTENSIVE-RATS. (UNPUBLISHED PAPER).
001459 02-03

SELF-ADMINISTRATION OF D-AMPHETAMINE AND AMINERGIC SYSTEMS IN THE RAT.
001696 02-04

AMINES
PHARMACOLOGY OF PHENETHYLAMINE TRACE AMINES IN THE DOG – DISCUSSION.
000469 01-04

ALPHA2-ADRENERGIC AMINES, ADENOSINE AND PROSTAGLANDINS INHIBIT LIPOLYSIS AND CYCLIC-AMP ACCUMULATION IN HAMSTER ADIPOCYTES IN THE ABSENCE OF EXTRACELLULAR SODIUM.
002728 03-03

EVIDENCE FOR THE PRESENCE OF TWO TYPES OF MONOAMINE-OXIDASE IN RABBIT CHOROID PLEXUS AND THEIR ROLE IN BREAKDOWN OF AMINES INFLUENCING CEREBROSPINAL-FLUID FORMATION.
002807 03-03

REGULATION OF BIOGENESIS OF PSYCHOTOMIMETIC AMINES. (UNPUBLISHED PAPER).
003818 04-03

EFFECTS OF MOLINDONE AND FLUPHENAZINE ON THE BRAIN CONCENTRATION OF SOME PHENOLIC AND CATECHOLIC AMINES IN THE MOUSE AND THE RAT.
003870 04-03

AMINO-ACID
INTERACTIONS OF NOREPINEPHRINE WITH PURKINJE-CELL RESPONSES TO PUTATIVE AMINO-ACID NEUROTRANSMITTERS APPLIED BY MICROIONTOPHORESIS.
000209 01-03

ACETYLCHOLINE AND AMINO-ACID NEUROTRANSMITTERS IN EPIDURAL CUPS OF FREELY-MOVING-RATS: EFFECT OF ACUTE AND CHRONIC-TREATMENT WITH ANTISCHIZOPHRENIC-DRUGS.
001386 02-03

THE INTERACTION BETWEEN BARBITURATE ANESTHETICS AND EXCITATORY AMINO-ACID RESPONSES ON CAT SPINAL NEURONES.
002799 03-03

ACTIONS OF BETA BUNGAROTOXIN ON AMINO-ACID TRANSMITTER RELEASE.
002897 03-03

PHARMACOLOGICAL ANTAGONISTS OF EXCITANT AMINO-ACID ACTION.
003587 03-17

EXCITATORY AMINO-ACID TRANSMITTERS.
003648 03-17

BACLOFEN: STEREOSELECTIVE INHIBITION OF EXCITANT AMINO-ACID RELEASE.
003867 04-03

CHANGES IN REGIONAL BRAIN LEVELS OF AMINO-ACID PUTATIVE NEUROTRANSMITTERS AFTER PROLONGED TREATMENT WITH THE ANTICONVULSANT-DRUGS DIPHENYLHYDANTOIN, PHENOBARBITONE, SODIUM-VALPROATE, ETHOSUXIMIDE, AND SULTHIAME IN THE RAT.
003961 04-03

DRUG-INDUCED CHANGES IN THE COMPOSITION OF THE CEREBRAL FREE AMINO-ACID POOL.
004039 04-03

AMINO-ACIDS
INFLUENCE OF CELLULAR-TRANSPORT ON THE INTERACTION OF AMINO-ACIDS WITH GAMMA AMINOBUTYRIC-ACID-RECEPTORS (GABA) IN THE ISOLATED OLFACTORY-CORTEX OF THE GUINEA-PIG.
000034 01-03

EFFECTS OF L AND D AMINO-ACIDS ON ANALGESIA AND LOCOMOTOR-ACTIVITY OF MICE: THEIR INTERACTION WITH MORPHINE.
000336 01-04

LITHIUM-INDUCED CHANGES IN THE BRAIN LEVELS OF FREE AMINO-ACIDS IN STRESS-EXPOSED RATS.
001217 02-03

REGIONAL RELEASE OF (3H)ADENOSINE DERIVATIVES FROM RAT-BRAIN IN VIVO: EFFECT OF EXCITATORY AMINO-ACIDS, OPIATE AGONISTS, AND BENZODIAZEPINES.
001303 02-03

EFFECTS OF ALBUMIN, AMINO-ACIDS, AND CLOFIBRATE ON THE UPTAKE OF TRYPTOPHAN BY THE RAT-BRAIN.
002673 03-03

SENSITIVITY OF IDENTIFIED MEDIAL HYPOTHALAMIC NEURONS TO GABA, GLYCINE AND RELATED AMINO-ACIDS; INFLUENCE OF BICUCULLINE, PICROTOXIN AND STRYCHNINE ON SYNAPTIC INHIBITION.
002674 03-03

TRANSPORT OF NEUTRAL AMINO-ACIDS AT THE BLOOD-BRAIN-BARRIER.
002764 03-03

L HISTIDINE: EFFECTS ON SENSITIVITY OF CAT SPINAL NEURONES TO AMINO-ACIDS.
002808 03-03

LAMINAR DISTRIBUTION OF PUTATIVE NEUROTRANSMITTER AMINO-ACIDS AND LIGAND BINDING-SITES IN THE DOG OLFACTORY-BULB.
002836 03-03

EFFECTS OF D AMINOLAEVULINIC-ACID, PORPHOBILINOGEN, AMINO-ACIDS AND BARBITURATES ON CALCIUM ACCUMULATION BY CULTURED NEURONS.
002859 03-03

AMINO-3-ETHOXYCARBONYL-4-PHENYLTHIOPHENE
SYNTHESIS AND PHARMACOLOGY OF 2 AMINO-3-ETHOXYCARBONYL-4-PHENYLTHIOPHENE DERIVATIVES.
001083 02-02

AMINO-4-METHYLPYRIDINE
ON THE MECHANISM-OF-ACTION OF 2 AMINO-4-METHYLPYRIDINE, A MORPHINE-LIKE ANALGESIC.
001574 02-04

AMINO-4-PHOSPHONOBUTYRIC-ACID
2 AMINO-4-PHOSPHONOBUTYRIC-ACID: A NEW PHARMACOLOGICAL TOOL FOR RETINA RESEARCH.
003145 03-06

AMINO-4H-5-TRIAZOLOBENZODIAZEPINES
6 SUBSTITUTED AMINO-4H-5-TRIAZOLOBENZODIAZEPINES AND 4 SUBSTITUTED AMINO-6H-5-TRIAZOLOBENZODIAZEPINES WITH POTENTIAL ANTIANXIETY ACTIVITY.
001076 02-02

AMINO-6H-5-TRIAZOLOBENZODIAZEPINES
6 SUBSTITUTED AMINO-4H-5-TRIAZOLOBENZODIAZEPINES AND 4 SUBSTITUTED AMINO-6H-5-TRIAZOLOBENZODIAZEPINES WITH POTENTIAL ANTIANXIETY ACTIVITY.
001076 02-02

AMINOADIPATE
TOXIC EFFECTS OF ALPHA AMINOADIPATE ON CULTURED CEREBELLAR CELLS.
002729 03-03

SELECTIVE SYNAPTIC ANTAGONISM BY ATROPINE AND ALPHA AMINOADIPATE OF PULVINAR AND CORTICAL AFFERENTS TO THE SUPRASYLVIAN VISUAL AREA (CLARE-BISHOP AREA).
002752 03-03

DEPRESSION OF VENTRAL ROOT DORSAL ROOT POTENTIAL BY DL ALPHA AMINOADIPATE IN FROG SPINAL-CORD.
002755 03-03

AMINOADIPIC-ACID
LOCALIZATION OF GABA-RECEPTOR AND DOPAMINE-RECEPTOR SITES IN RETINAL GLIAL CELLS USING DL ALPHA AMINOADIPIC-ACID.
002828 03-03

AMINOALKYL-6-ARYL-4H-5-TRIAZOLOBENZODIAZEPINES
1 AMINOALKYL-6-ARYL-4H-5-TRIAZOLOBENZODIAZEPINES WITH ANTIANXIETY AND ANTIDEPRESSANT ACTIVITY.
001074 02-02

AMINOBUTYRIC-ACID
DIFFERENTIAL-EFFECTS OF N DIPROPYLACETATE AND AMINOOXYACETIC-ACID ON GAMMA AMINOBUTYRIC-ACID LEVELS IN DISCRETE AREAS OF RAT-BRAIN.
000140 01-03

GAMMA AMINOBUTYRIC-ACID AGONISTS: AN IN VITRO COMPARISON BETWEEN DEPRESSION OF SPINAL SYNAPTIC ACTIVITY AND DEPOLARIZATION OF SPINAL ROOT FIBRES IN THE RAT.
001104 02-03

EFFECT OF THE NEW GAMMA AMINOBUTYRIC-ACID AGONIST SL-76-002 ON STRIATAL ACETYLCHOLINE: RELATION TO NEUROLEPTIC-INDUCED EXTRAPYRAMIDAL ALTERATIONS.
001119 02-03

FACTORS INFLUENCING THE RELEASE OF LABELLED GAMMA AMINOBUTYRIC-ACID AND ACETYLCHOLINE EVOKED BY ELECTRICAL-STIMULATION WITH ALTERNATING POLARITY FROM RAT CORTICAL SLICES.
001130 02-03

ROLES OF SEROTONIN AND GAMMA AMINOBUTYRIC-ACID IN OPIOID EFFECTS.
001140 02-03

PRESYNAPTIC ACTIONS OF 4 AMINOPYRIDINE AND GAMMA AMINOBUTYRIC-ACID ON RAT SYMPATHETIC GANGLIA IN VITRO.
001244 02-03

BENZODIAZEPINE BINDING IN CHICKEN RETINA AND ITS INTERACTION WITH GAMMA AMINOBUTYRIC-ACID.
001287 02-03

LOCALIZATION OF SENSITIVE SITES TO TAURINE, GAMMA AMINOBUTYRIC-ACID, GLYCINE AND BETA ALANINE IN THE MOLECULAR LAYER OF GUINEA-PIG CEREBELLAR SLICES.
001402 02-03

THE ROLE OF GAMMA AMINOBUTYRIC-ACID IN ACUTE AND CHRONIC NEUROLEPTIC ACTION.
001465 02-03

A STUDY OF A GLIAL GAMMA AMINOBUTYRIC-ACID SYSTEM: ITS
REGULATION, FUNCTION AND THE EFFECTS OF DIAZEPAM. (PH.D.
DISSERTATION).
001524 02-03
PRELIMINARY-STUDIES ON CSF GAMMA AMINOBUTYRIC-ACID LEVELS IN
PSYCHIATRIC-PATIENTS BEFORE AND DURING TREATMENT WITH
DIFFERENT PSYCHOTROPIC-DRUGS.
001959 02-08
INCREASED CSF GAMMA AMINOBUTYRIC-ACID AFTER TREATMENT WITH
GAMMA VINYL-GABA.
002237 02-13
INHIBITION OF VASOPRESSIN RELEASE TO CAROTID OCCLUSION BY
GAMMA AMINOBUTYRIC-ACID AND GLYCINE.
002715 03-03
DOPAMINE-RECEPTOR SUPERSENSITIVITY IN THE CORPUS-STRIATUM
FOLLOWING CHRONIC ELEVATION OF BRAIN GAMMA AMINOBUTYRIC-
ACID.
002716 03-03
CENTRAL HYPOTENSIVE-EFFECT OF GAMMA AMINOBUTYRIC-ACID IN
ANESTHETIZED DOGS.
003772 04-03
A STUDY OF GAMMA AMINOBUTYRIC-ACID UPTAKE IN NORMAL AND
DOWNS-SYNDROME PLATELETS.
003787 04-03
THE EFFECT OF SODIUM-DIPROPYLACETATE ON GAMMA AMINOBUTYRIC-
ACID DEPENDENT INHIBITION IN THE RAT-CORTEX AND SUBSTANTIA-
NIGRA IN RELATION TO ITS ANTICONVULSANT ACTIVITY.
003880 04-03
CHANGES IN GAMMA AMINOBUTYRIC-ACID SHUNT ENZYMES IN
REGIONS OF RAT-BRAIN WITH KETAMINE ANESTHESIA.
003891 04-03
STUDIES ON THE MECHANISM-OF-ACTION OF AVERMECTIN-B1A:
STIMULATION OF RELEASE OF GAMMA AMINOBUTYRIC-ACID FROM
BRAIN SYNAPTOSOMES.
003973 04-03
STUDIES ON GAMMA AMINOBUTYRIC-ACID TRANSPORT IN COBALT
EXPERIMENTAL EPILEPSY IN THE RAT.
003990 04-03
MODULATORY INTERACTIONS BETWEEN NOREPINEPHRINE AND TAURINE,
BETA ALANINE, GAMMA AMINOBUTYRIC-ACID AND MUSCIMOL
APPLIED IONTOPHORETICALLY TO CEREBELLAR PURKINJE-CELLS.
004058 04-03
ANTAGONISM OF SOME CENTRAL-EFFECTS OF D TUBOCURARINE BY
GAMMA AMINOBUTYRIC-ACID.
004102 04-04

AMINOBUTYRIC-ACID-MEDIATED
REDUCTION OF GAMMA AMINOBUTYRIC-ACID-MEDIATED (GABA)
TRANSMISSION BY A CONVULSANT BENZODIAZEPINE.
000015 01-02

AMINOBUTYRIC-ACID-RECEPTOR
DIFFERENCES IN GAMMA AMINOBUTYRIC-ACID-RECEPTOR SENSITIVITY IN
INBRED STRAINS OF MICE.
000303 01-03
SUSTAINED GAMMA AMINOBUTYRIC-ACID-RECEPTOR STIMULATION AND
CHRONIC NEUROLEPTIC-EFFECTS.
001345 02-03
BINDING OF (3H) MUSCIMOL, A POTENT GAMMA AMINOBUTYRIC-ACID-
RECEPTOR AGONIST, TO MEMBRANES OF THE BOVINE RETINA.
003954 04-03
THE EFFECTS OF ACUTE AND CHRONIC ETHANOL ADMINISTRATION AND
ITS WITHDRAWAL ON GAMMA AMINOBUTYRIC-ACID-RECEPTOR
BINDING IN RAT-BRAIN.
004035 04-03
ALTERATIONS IN GAMMA AMINOBUTYRIC-ACID-RECEPTOR SENSITIVITY
FOLLOWING ACUTE AND CHRONIC ETHANOL TREATMENTS.
004037 04-03

AMINOBUTYRIC-ACID-RECEPTORS
INFLUENCE OF CELLULAR-TRANSPORT ON THE INTERACTION OF AMINO-
ACIDS WITH GAMMA AMINOBUTYRIC-ACID-RECEPTORS (GABA) IN THE
ISOLATED OLFACTORY-CORTEX OF THE GUINEA-PIG.
000034 01-03

AMINOBUTYRIC-ACID-TRANSAMINASE
CHANGES IN PRIMARY AFFERENT DEPOLARIZATION AFTER
ADMINISTRATION OF GAMMA ACETYLENIC-GAMMA-AMINOBUTYRIC-
ACID (GAG), A GAMMA AMINOBUTYRIC-ACID-TRANSAMINASE
(GABA-TRANSAMINASE) INHIBITOR.
000174 01-03
INHIBITION OF GAMMA AMINOBUTYRIC-ACID-TRANSAMINASE WITH 6
AMINONICOTINAMIDE IN REGIONS OF THE RAT-BRAIN.
002868 03-03
THE INACTIVATION OF GAMMA AMINOBUTYRIC-ACID-TRANSAMINASE IN
DISSOCIATED NEURONAL CULTURES FROM SPINAL-CORD.
003980 04-03

AMINODIHYDROXYTETRAHYDRONAPHTHALENE
(3H) 2 AMINODIHYDROXYTETRAHYDRONAPHTHALENE (ADTN):
REGIONAL DISTRIBUTION AND IN VIVO BINDING AFTER ACUTE AND
CHRONIC DRUG-TREATMENT.
000052 01-03

AMINOHIPPURIC-ACID
STUDIES ON THE EFFECT OF ALPHA MELANOCYTE-STIMULATING-
HORMONE AND RELATED PEPTIDES ON THE ACCUMULATION OF P

AMINOHIPPURIC-ACID IN RENAL CORTICAL SLICES. (UNPUBLISHED
PAPER).
001372 02-03

AMINOLAEVULINIC-ACID
EFFECTS OF D AMINOLAEVULINIC-ACID, PORPHOBILINOGEN, AMINO-
ACIDS AND BARBITURATES ON CALCIUM ACCUMULATION BY
CULTURED NEURONS.
002859 03-03

AMINOMETHYLCYCLOPROPANECARBOXYLIC-ACID
THE SYNTHESIS AND ACTIVITY OF CIS AND TRANS 2
AMINOMETHYLCYCLOPROPANECARBOXYLIC-ACID AS
CONFORMATIONALLY RESTRICTED ANALOGUES OF GABA.
002633 03-01

AMINONICOTINAMIDE
INHIBITION OF GAMMA AMINOBUTYRIC-ACID-TRANSAMINASE WITH 6
AMINONICOTINAMIDE IN REGIONS OF THE RAT-BRAIN.
002868 03-03

AMINOOXYACETIC-ACID
EFFECT OF AMINOOXYACETIC-ACID (AOAA) ON GABA LEVELS IN SOME
PARTS OF THE RAT-BRAIN.
000040 01-03
DIFFERENTIAL-EFFECTS OF N DIPROPYLACETATE AND AMINOOXYACETIC-
ACID ON GAMMA AMINOBUTYRIC-ACID LEVELS IN DISCRETE AREAS
OF RAT-BRAIN.
000140 01-03
EFFECT OF AMINOOXYACETIC-ACID AND BICUCULLINE ON PROLACTIN
RELEASE IN CASTRATED MALE RATS.
001194 02-03
CONVULSANT-EFFECTS OF AMINOOXYACETIC-ACID DURING ONTOGENESIS
IN RATS.
001439 02-03

AMINOPEPTIDASE
INHIBITION OF AMINOPEPTIDASE AND ACETYLCHOLINESTERASE BY
PUROMYCIN AND PUROMYCIN ANALOGS.
003835 04-03

AMINOPHYLLINE
EFFECTS OF RESERPINE, PROPRANOLOL, AND AMINOPHYLLINE ON
SEIZURE ACTIVITY AND CNS CYCLIC-NUCLEOTIDES.
000115 01-03
BLOCKADE OF STRIATAL NEURONE RESPONSES TO MORPHINE BY
AMINOPHYLLINE: EVIDENCE FOR ADENOSINE MEDIATION OF OPIATE
ACTION.
000229 01-03
AMINOPHYLLINE AND THEOPHYLLINE DERIVATIVES AS ANTAGONISTS OF
NEURONAL DEPRESSION BY ADENOSINE: A MICROIONTOPHORETIC-
STUDY.
001410 02-03
AMINOPHYLLINE AND IMIDAZOLE AS CONVULSANTS.
004232 04-04

AMINOPHYLLINE-INDUCED
CAFFEINE-INDUCED AND AMINOPHYLLINE-INDUCED SEIZURES.
002689 03-03

AMINOPYRIDINE
PRESYNAPTIC ACTIONS OF 4 AMINOPYRIDINE AND GAMMA
AMINOBUTYRIC-ACID ON RAT SYMPATHETIC GANGLIA IN VITRO.
001244 02-03
EFFECTS OF 4 AMINOPYRIDINE ON THE TURNOVER OF MONOAMINES IN
THE CENTRAL-NERVOUS-SYSTEM OF THE RAT.
002658 03-03
ACTION OF 4 AMINOPYRIDINE ON THE CEREBRAL CIRCULATION.
003781 04-03
4 AMINOPYRIDINE BLOCKADE OF NEURONAL DEPRESSANT RESPONSES TO
ADENOSINE-TRIPHOSPHATE.
003963 04-03

AMINOPYRINE
INHIBITORY-ACTION OF THE COMBINATION OF AMINOPYRINE AND
SECOBARBITAL ON EEG ACTIVATION, NEOCORTICAL RECRUITING AND
AUGMENTING RESPONSES IN RABBITS.
004022 04-03

AMINOSULFONIC-ACIDS
EFFECT OF INTRAVENTRICULAR INJECTIONS OF ALPHA AMINOSULFONIC-
ACIDS ON THE CENTRAL-NERVOUS-SYSTEM OF CONSCIOUS MICE.
000009 01-02

AMINOTETRALINS
PRODRUGS OF SOME DOPAMINERGIC 2 AMINOTETRALINS: A REVIEW OF
THEIR SYNTHESES AND NEUROCHEMICAL PROFILES.
000004 01-01
N ALKYLATED 2 AMINOTETRALINS: CENTRAL DOPAMINE-RECEPTOR
STIMULATING ACTIVITY.
000399 01-04

AMITRIPTYLINE
AMITRIPTYLINE BINDING TO SPECIFIC ALPHA-ADRENERGIC-RECEPTORS IN
VITRO.
000181 01-03
A REEXAMINATION OF THE CLINICAL-EFFECTS OF IMIPRAMINE AND
AMITRIPTYLINE IN DEPRESSIVE-ILLNESS.
000579 01-09
STUDY OF INTRAVENOUS AMITRIPTYLINE IN ACUTE DEPRESSIONS.
000581 01-09

PREDICTION OF STEADY-STATE PLASMA LEVELS OF AMITRIPTYLINE AND NORTRIPTYLINE FROM A SINGLE-DOSE 24-HR. LEVEL IN DEPRESSED-PATIENTS.
000582 01-09

COMPARATIVE-STUDY OF THE CARDIOTOXICITY OF AMITRIPTYLINE AND MAPROTILINE IN DEPRESSIVE-PATIENTS.
000595 01-09

ON THE RELATIONSHIP OF NORTRIPTYLINE: AMITRIPTYLINE RATIO TO CLINICAL IMPROVEMENT OF AMITRIPTYLINE TREATED DEPRESSIVE-PATIENTS.
000599 01-09

D-AMPHETAMINE AS A PREDICTOR FOR RESPONSE TO IMIPRAMINE AND AMITRIPTYLINE.
000621 01-09

URINARY MHPG AND CLINICAL-RESPONSE TO AMITRIPTYLINE IN DEPRESSED-PATIENTS.
000631 01-09

INTERACTION BETWEEN AMITRIPTYLINE AND PHENOTHIAZINE IN MAN: METABOLITE NORTRIPTYLINE AND THE CORRELATION WITH CLINICAL-RESPONSE.
000640 01-09

AMITRIPTYLINE THERAPY OF OBSESSIVE-COMPULSIVE-NEUROSIS.
000656 01-10

AMITRIPTYLINE, NORTRIPTYLINE PLASMA LEVELS AND CLINICAL-RESPONSE IN WOMEN WITH AFFECTIVE-DISORDERS.
000757 01-13

STIMULUS INTENSITY CONTROL IN DEPRESSION: A STUDY OF THE COMPARATIVE-EFFECT OF DOXEPIN AND AMITRIPTYLINE ON CORTICAL EVOKED-POTENTIALS.
000763 01-13

HYPNAGOGIC AND HYPNOPOMPIC HALLUCINATIONS DURING AMITRIPTYLINE TREATMENT.
000850 01-15

POSSIBLE INVOLVEMENT OF CYCLIC-AMP AND FRONTAL-CORTEX IN AMITRIPTYLINE MEDIATED SUPPRESSION OF THE HYPOTENSIVE-EFFECT OF CLONIDINE.
001259 02-03

ANTIARRHYTHMIC-ACTIVITY OF AMITRIPTYLINE ANALOGUES IN CONSCIOUS DOGS AFTER MYOCARDIAL-INFARCTION: CYPROHEPTADINIUM-METHIODIDE.
001534 02-03

EFFECTS OF AMITRIPTYLINE AND CLOMIPRAMINE IN THE ISOLATED, PERFUSED RABBIT HEART.
001852 02-05

EFFECT OF AMITRIPTYLINE ANTIDOTES ON REPETITIVE EXTRASYSTOLE THESHOLD.
001856 02-05

AMITRIPTYLINE PLASMA CONCENTRATION AND CLINICAL-EFFECT: A WORLD-HEALTH-ORGANIZATION COLLABORATIVE-STUDY.
001976 02-09

DOUBLE-BLIND CONTROLLED EXPERIMENT: AMINEPTINE VERSUS AMITRIPTYLINE USING THE HAMILTON-DEPRESSION-RATING-SCALE.
002050 02-09

BLOOD LEVEL OF AMITRIPTYLINE, NORTRIPTYLINE, NORADRENALINE, SEROTONIN AND THERAPEUTIC RESPONSE.
002057 02-09

TRICHOTILLOMANIA TREATED WITH AMITRIPTYLINE.
002083 02-10

THE CONTRIBUTION OF ALPHA1 ACID GLYCOPROTEIN, LIPOPROTEINS, AND ALBUMIN TO THE PLASMA BINDING OF PERAZINE, AMITRIPTYLINE, AND NORTRIPTYLINE IN HEALTHY MAN.
002214 02-13

CARDIOVASCULAR-EFFECTS OF AMITRIPTYLINE, MIANSERIN AND ZIMELIDINE IN DEPRESSED-PATIENTS.
002215 02-13

HIGH-LEVELS OF AMITRIPTYLINE AND CLINICAL-RESPONSE.
002266 02-13

INTERINDIVIDUAL DIFFERENCES IN AMITRIPTYLINE DEMETHYLATION.
002282 02-13

THE PERIPHERAL ANTICHOLINERGIC-ACTIVITY OF TRICYCLIC-ANTIDEPRESSANTS: COMPARISON OF AMITRIPTYLINE AND DESIPRAMINE IN HUMAN VOLUNTEERS.
002298 02-13

THYMOANALEPTIC TREATMENT CONTROL THROUGH MEASUREMENT OF PLASMA CONCENTRATIONS OF AMITRIPTYLINE AND ITS METABOLITE NORTRIPTYLINE.
002304 02-13

TERATOGENICITY OF IMIPRAMINE AND AMITRIPTYLINE IN FETAL HAMSTERS.
002410 02-15

HYPOMANIC-REACTION TO AMITRIPTYLINE IN A DEPRESSED-CHILD.
002418 02-15

CARDIOVASCULAR-EFFECTS OF MIANSERIN AND AMITRIPTYLINE IN HEALTHY VOLUNTEERS.
002469 02-15

A METHOD FOR THE DETERMINATION OF AMITRIPTYLINE AND ITS METABOLITES NORTRIPTYLINE, 10 HYDROXYAMITRIPTYLINE, AND 10 HYDROXYNORTRIPTYLINE IN HUMAN PLASMA USING STABLE ISOTOPE DILUTION AND GAS-CHROMATOGRAPHY CHEMICAL-IONIZATION MASS-SPECTROMETRY.
002486 02-16

AMITRIPTYLINE: LONG-TERM-TREATMENT ELEVATES ALPHA-ADRENERGIC AND MUSCARINIC-RECEPTOR BINDING IN MOUSE-BRAIN.
002875 03-03

DIFFERENTIAL-EFFECT OF CHRONIC DESIPRAMINE AND AMITRIPTYLINE TREATMENT ON RAT-BRAIN ADRENERGIC AND SEROTONERGIC-RECEPTORS.
002914 03-03

AMITRIPTYLINE PROVIDES LONG-LASTING IMMUNIZATION AGAINST SUDDEN CARDIAC DEATH FROM COCAINE.
003122 03-05

AMOXAPINE AND AMITRIPTYLINE IN THE OUTPATIENT TREATMENT OF ENDOGENOUS DEPRESSION.
003217 03-09

PANIC-ANXIETY AFTER ABRUPT DISCONTINUATION OF AMITRIPTYLINE.
003223 03-09

DOUBLE-BLIND STUDY OF MIANSERIN AND AMITRIPTYLINE.
003231 03-09

A DOUBLE-BLIND COMPARISON BETWEEN AMOXAPINE AND AMITRIPTYLINE IN DEPRESSED-INPATIENTS.
003234 03-09

DEPRESSION SUBTYPES AFFECT THE STEADY-STATE PLASMA LEVELS AND THERAPEUTIC-EFFICACY OF AMITRIPTYLINE AND NORTRIPTYLINE.
003244 03-09

PHENELZINE AND AMITRIPTYLINE IN NEUROTIC DEPRESSION. (UNPUBLISHED PAPER).
003248 03-09

EFFECTS OF PHENELZINE AND AMITRIPTYLINE ON DEPRESSION.
003249 03-09

BEHAVIORAL-PREDICTORS OF AMITRIPTYLINE RESPONSE IN DEPRESSION.
003253 03-09

PHARMACOKINETICS OF AMITRIPTYLINE, IMIPRAMINE, AND MAPROTILINE IN THE ELDERLY.
003324 03-11

CARDIOVASCULAR-EFFECTS OF MIANSERIN — A COMPARATIVE-STUDY WITH AMITRIPTYLINE AND A PLACEBO IN HEALTHY SUBJECTS.
003503 03-15

A TARDIVE-DYSKINESIA-LIKE SYNDROME AFTER AMITRIPTYLINE TREATMENT.
003552 03-15

FIRST RESULTS OF AN ORIGINAL METHOD FOR MEASURING BLOOD LEVELS OF ANTIDEPRESSANTS (AMITRIPTYLINE AND NORTRIPTYLINE).
003559 03-16

INTERACTION OF THE TRICYCLIC-ANTIDEPRESSANT AMITRIPTYLINE WITH PREJUNCTIONAL ALPHA AND MUSCARINIC-RECEPTORS IN THE DOG SAPHENOUS VEIN.
003756 04-03

DRUG-INTERACTIONS OF AMITRIPTYLINE AND NORTRIPTYLINE WITH WARFARIN IN THE RAT.
003912 04-03

REGULATION OF SEROTONIN2-RECEPTORS (5 HT2) LABELED WITH (3H)SPIROPERIDOL BY CHRONIC-TREATMENT WITH THE ANTIDEPRESSANT AMITRIPTYLINE.
003964 04-03

COMPARATIVE-EFFECTS OF PHENELZINE AND AMITRIPTYLINE: A PLACEBO-CONTROLLED-TRIAL.
004402 04-09

THE RELATIONSHIPS BETWEEN CLINICAL-RESPONSE, PSYCHOPHYSIOLOGICAL-VARIABLES AND PLASMA LEVELS OF AMITRIPTYLINE AND NORTRIPTYLINE IN NEUROTIC-OUTPATIENTS.
004423 04-10

AMITRIPTYLINE AND NORTRIPTYLINE PLASMA LEVELS MONITORING. PERSPECTIVE IN CLINICAL-PRACTICE.
004675 04-16

AMITRIPTYLINE-HYDROCHLORIDE

NMR SPECTRAL STUDY OF PROTON TRANSFER IN AMITRIPTYLINE-HYDROCHLORIDE CHLORDIAZEPOXIDE-HYDROCHLORIDE COMBINATIONS IN DIPOLAR APROTIC SOLVENTS.
003654 04-01

SIMULTANEOUS HIGH-PERFORMANCE LIQUID-CHROMATOGRAPHIC-DETERMINATION OF AMITRIPTYLINE-HYDROCHLORIDE IN TWO-COMPONENT TABLET FORMULATIONS.
004673 04-16

AMMONIA

EFFECT OF PYRITINOL AND PIRACETAM ON CHANGES IN FREE AMMONIA LEVEL IN CNS TISSUE AFTER PARADOXICAL SLEEP-DEPRIVATION IN RATS.
001199 02-03

AMMONIA AND DISINHIBITION IN CAT MOTOR-CORTEX BY AMMONIUM-ACETATE, MONOFLUOROACETATE AND INSULIN-INDUCED HYPOGLYCEMIA.
004276 04-05

AMMONIUM-ACETATE

AMMONIA AND DISINHIBITION IN CAT MOTOR-CORTEX BY AMMONIUM-ACETATE, MONOFLUOROACETATE AND INSULIN-INDUCED HYPOGLYCEMIA.
004276 04-05

AMNESIA
RETROGRADE AMNESIA PRODUCED BY ELECTRICAL-STIMULATION OF THE AMYGDALA: ATTENUATION WITH ADRENERGIC ANTAGONISTS. (UNPUBLISHED PAPER).
001488 02-03
BETA ENDORPHIN CAUSES RETROGRADE AMNESIA AND IS RELEASED FROM THE RAT-BRAIN BY VARIOUS FORMS OF TRAINING AND STIMULATION.
001664 02-04
TIME-DEPENDENT CHANGES IN ANTEROGRADE SCOPOLAMINE-INDUCED AMNESIA IN RATS.
004182 04-04
RETROGRADE AMNESIA PRODUCED BY ELECTRICAL-STIMULATION OF THE AMYGDALA: ATTENUATION WITH ADRENERGIC ANTAGONISTS.
004231 04-04
USE OF LYSINE-VASOPRESSIN IN THE TREATMENT OF POSTTRAUMATIC AMNESIA.
004583 04-14

AMNIOTIC-FLUID
CONCENTRATIONS OF CIS(Z) FLUPENTHIXOL IN MATERNAL SERUM, AMNIOTIC-FLUID, UMBILICAL-CORD-SERUM, AND MILK.
002423 02-15

AMOXAPINE
AMOXAPINE IN EXPERIMENTAL PSYCHOPHARMACOLOGY: A NEUROLEPTIC OR AN ANTIDEPRESSANT?
001070 02-02
AMOXAPINE AND AMITRIPTYLINE IN THE OUTPATIENT TREATMENT OF ENDOGENOUS DEPRESSION.
003217 03-09
A DOUBLE-BLIND COMPARISON BETWEEN AMOXAPINE AND AMITRIPTYLINE IN DEPRESSED-INPATIENTS.
003234 03-09
AMOXAPINE AND IMIPRAMINE IN THE TREATMENT OF DEPRESSED-OUTPATIENTS: A CONTROLLED-STUDY.
003254 03-09
CLINICAL-RESPONSE AND BLOOD LEVELS IN THE TREATMENT OF DEPRESSION WITH A NEW ANTIDEPRESSANT-DRUG, AMOXAPINE.
004356 04-09
AMOXAPINE: A REVIEW OF LITERATURE.
004702 04-17

AMP
STUDY ON THE STABILITY OF THE FACTORIAL STRUCTURE OF THE AMP SYSTEM DURING TREATMENT.
004696 04-16

AMPHETAMINE
COMPARISON OF THE EFFECTS OF THE ISOMERS OF AMPHETAMINE, METHYLPHENIDATE AND DEOXYPIPRADROL ON THE UPTAKE OF L (3H)NOREPINEPHRINE AND (3H)DOPAMINE BY SYNAPTIC VESICLES FROM RAT-WHOLE-BRAIN, STRIATUM AND HYPOTHALAMUS.
000091 01-03
ACUTE AND CHRONIC EFFECTS OF NEUROLEPTICS AND ACUTE EFFECTS OF APOMORPHINE AND AMPHETAMINE ON DOPAMINE TURNOVER IN CORPUS-STRIATUM AND SUBSTANTIA-NIGRA OF THE RAT-BRAIN.
000215 01-03
DECREASED SPIROPERIDOL AND LSD BINDING IN RAT-BRAIN AFTER CONTINUOUS AMPHETAMINE.
000216 01-03
LONG-TERM EFFECTS OF CONTINUOUS EXPOSURE TO AMPHETAMINE ON BRAIN DOPAMINE CONCENTRATION AND SYNAPTOSOMAL UPTAKE IN MICE.
000287 01-03
INFLUENCE OF AMPHETAMINE AND PHENYLPROPANOLAMINE ON FOOD INTAKE, ACTIVITY, AND BODY-TEMPERATURE IN RATS WITH VENTROMEDIAL HYPOTHALAMIC OR DORSOLATERAL TEGMENTAL DAMAGE.
000322 01-03
REWARD SYSTEM DEPRESSION FOLLOWING CHRONIC AMPHETAMINE: ANTAGONISM BY HALOPERIDOL.
000342 01-04
CONSEQUENT EVENTS AS DETERMINANTS OF DRUG-EFFECTS ON SCHEDULE-CONTROLLED BEHAVIOR: MODIFICATION OF EFFECTS OF COCAINE AND D-AMPHETAMINE FOLLOWING CHRONIC AMPHETAMINE ADMINISTRATION.
000350 01-04
DISRUPTION OF SELECTIVE ATTENTION BY APOMORPHINE, BUT NOT AMPHETAMINE, IN THE MONGOLIAN-GERBIL.
000358 01-04
RELATIONSHIPS BETWEEN SELECTIVE DENERVATION OF DOPAMINE TERMINAL-FIELDS IN THE ANTERIOR-FOREBRAIN AND BEHAVIORAL-RESPONSES TO AMPHETAMINE AND APOMORPHINE.
000384 01-04
EFFECTS OF 6 HYDROXYDOPAMINE AND AMPHETAMINE ON RAT MOTHERING-BEHAVIOR AND OFFSPRING DEVELOPMENT.
000452 01-04
FACILITATION OF SELF-STIMULATION OF THE PREFRONTAL-CORTEX IN RATS FOLLOWING CHRONIC ADMINISTRATION OF SPIROPERIDOL OR AMPHETAMINE.
000457 01-04
DIFFERENT DOPAMINERGIC MECHANISMS FOR AMFONELIC-ACID, AMPHETAMINE AND APOMORPHINE.
000465 01-04

TEMPORAL PROPERTIES OF THE REWARDING AND AVERSIVE-EFFECTS OF AMPHETAMINE IN RATS.
000471 01-04
THE INFLUENCE OF GABAERGIC SUBSTANCES ON THE EFFECTS OF STIMULATION OF THE CAUDATE-NUCLEUS AND AMPHETAMINE STEREOTYPY IN CATS.
000489 01-04
CHRONIC AMPHETAMINE ADMINISTRATION TO CATS: BEHAVIORAL-EVIDENCE AND NEUROCHEMICAL EVIDENCE FOR DECREASED CENTRAL SEROTONERGIC FUNCTION.
000491 01-04
ATTENUATION OF AMPHETAMINE ANOREXIA IN RATS FOLLOWING SUBCHRONIC-TREATMENT WITH A TRICYCLIC-ANTIDEPRESSANT.
000501 01-04
AMPHETAMINE AND PIRIBEDIL IN AFFECTIVE-ILLNESS.
000618 01-09
REINFORCING, DISCRIMINATIVE AND ACTIVATING PROPERTIES OF AMPHETAMINE.
000804 01-14
DIVERGENT RESERPINE EFFECTS ON AMFONELIC-ACID AND AMPHETAMINE STIMULATION OF SYNAPTOSOMAL DOPAMINE FORMATION FROM PHENYLALANINE.
001113 02-03
EPINEPHRINE IS RELEASED FROM HYPOTHALAMUS BY DEPOLARIZING-AGENTS AND AMPHETAMINE.
001155 02-03
A COMPARISON OF THE EFFECTS OF METHYLPHENIDATE AND AMPHETAMINE ON THE SIMULTANEOUS RELEASE OF RADIOLABELLED DOPAMINE AND P OR M TYRAMINE FROM RAT STRIATAL SLICES.
001207 02-03
LONG-TERM DECREASES IN SPONTANEOUS FIRING OF CAUDATE NEURONS INDUCED BY AMPHETAMINE IN CATS.
001340 02-03
DEVELOPMENT OF AND RECOVERY FROM SUBSENSITIVITY OF THE NORADRENERGIC CYCLIC-AMP GENERATING SYSTEM IN BRAIN: EFFECT OF AMPHETAMINE FOLLOWING INHIBITION OF ITS AROMATIC HYDROXYLATION BY IPRINDOLE.
001353 02-03
MODIFICATION OF DOPAMINE-RECEPTORS IN BRAIN BY CONTINUOUS AMPHETAMINE ADMINISTRATIONS TO RATS.
001395 02-03
SUPERSENSITIVITY AND THE EFFECTS OF LONG-TERM AMPHETAMINE IN THE RAT NIGROSTRIATAL SYSTEM. (PH.D. DISSERTATION).
001485 02-03
AMPHETAMINE STEREOTYPIES AND POLYRIBOSOMAL DISAGGREGATION IN RATS: EFFECTS OF ADRENERGIC AND SEROTONERGIC BLOCKING-AGENTS.
001531 02-03
REDUCTION OF DOPAMINERGIC-SUPERSENSITIVITY BY A SINGLE-DOSE OF AMPHETAMINE.
001642 02-04
BRAIN LOCATIONS CONTROLLING THE BEHAVIORAL-EFFECTS OF CHRONIC AMPHETAMINE INTOXICATION.
001653 02-04
EFFECTS OF RESERPINE AND AMPHETAMINE ON THE DEVELOPMENT OF HYPERACTIVITY IN MATERNALLY-DEPRIVED RAT PUPS.
001654 02-04
ENHANCED LATERAL HYPOTHALAMIC SELF-STIMULATION RESPONDING AFTER CHRONIC EXPOSURE TO AMPHETAMINE.
001688 02-04
EFFECTS OF CHRONIC AMPHETAMINE OR RESERPINE ON SELF-STIMULATION RESPONDING: ANIMAL-MODEL OF DEPRESSION?
001699 02-04
GENETIC AND EXPERIMENTAL FACTORS AFFECTING THE PARADOXICAL-EFFECTS OF AMPHETAMINE IN DOGS.
001704 02-04
INTERACTION OF PROSTAGLANDINS AND THE EFFECTS OF MORPHINE AND AMPHETAMINE IN RATS. (PH.D. DISSERTATION).
001732 02-04
AMPHETAMINE AND MATERNAL-BEHAVIOR: DOSE-RESPONSE RELATIONSHIPS.
001752 02-04
APPARENT TOLERANCE TO SOME ASPECTS OF AMPHETAMINE STEREOTYPY WITH LONG-TERM-TREATMENT.
001758 02-04
GO-HERE-GO-THERE PERFORMANCE AFTER AMPHETAMINE: THE IMPORTANCE OF THE RESPONSE REQUIREMENT IN SUCCESSIVE DISCRIMINATION.
001759 02-04
EFFECTS OF AMPHETAMINE AND PHENYLPROPANOLAMINE ON FOOD INTAKE IN RATS WITH VENTROMEDIAL HYPOTHALAMIC OR DORSOLATERAL TEGMENTAL DAMAGE.
001818 02-04
A SILICONE PELLET FOR LONG-TERM CONTINUOUS ADMINISTRATION OF AMPHETAMINE.
001875 02-06
DIFFERENTIAL-EFFECTS OF AMPHETAMINE AND NEUROLEPTICS ON NEGATIVE VS. POSITIVE SYMPTOMS IN SCHIZOPHRENIA.
001906 02-08

PARADOXICAL IMPROVEMENT FOLLOWING IV AMPHETAMINE IN
SCHIZOPHRENIA. (UNPUBLISHED PAPER).
001951 02-08
REGIONAL CEREBRAL BLOOD FLOW IN A CASE OF AMPHETAMINE
INTOXICATION.
002210 02-13
EFFECTS OF AMPHETAMINE ON VIGILANCE PERFORMANCE IN NORMAL
AND HYPERACTIVE-CHILDREN.
002359 02-14
SUBJECTIVE DRUG-EFFECTS AND DRUG PREFERENCE IN HEALTHY
VOLUNTEERS AS A MODEL OF A DRUGS REINFORCING EFFECTS;
STUDIES ON NOMIFENSINE, AMPHETAMINE AND PLACEBO.
002362 02-14
SEX-DIFFERENCES IN THE AMPHETAMINE STIMULATED RELEASE OF
CATECHOLAMINES FROM RAT STRIATAL TISSUE IN VITRO.
002668 03-03
MIDBRAIN DOPAMINE NEURONS; DIFFERENTIAL RESPONSES TO
AMPHETAMINE ISOMERS.
002680 03-03
COCAINE AND AMPHETAMINE ANTAGONIZE THE DECREASE OF
NORADRENERGIC NEUROTRANSMISSION ELICITED BY OXYMETAZOLINE
BUT POTENTIATE THE INHIBITION BY ALPHA METHYLNOREPINEPHRINE
IN THE PERFUSED CAT SPLEEN.
002801 03-03
INCREASED AMPHETAMINE STEREOTYPY AND LONGER HALOPERIDOL
CATALEPSY IN SPONTANEOUSLY HYPERTENSIVE-RATS.
002891 03-03
CANALIZATION OF AROUSAL IN THE PREWEANLING RAT; EFFECTS OF
AMPHETAMINE ON AGGREGATION WITH SURROGATE STIMULI.
002965 03-04
HYPERACTIVITY IN DEVELOPING RATS; SEX-DIFFERENCES IN 6
HYDROXYDOPAMINE AND AMPHETAMINE EFFECTS.
002970 03-04
ANIMAL-MODEL OF PSYCHOSIS; HALLUCINATORY BEHAVIORS IN
MONKEYS DURING THE LATE STAGE OF CONTINUOUS AMPHETAMINE
INTOXICATION.
002988 03-04
THE ROLE OF CALCIUM AND DOPAMINE MEMBRANE CARRIER IN
MEDIATING THE BEHAVIORAL-EFFECTS AND BIOCHEMICAL-EFFECTS OF
AMPHETAMINE. (PH.D. DISSERTATION).
002996 03-04
GONADECTOMY AND SEX-DIFFERENCES IN THE BEHAVIORAL-RESPONSES
TO AMPHETAMINE AND APOMORPHINE OF RATS.
003084 03-04
RELATIVE POTENCY OF AMPHETAMINE ISOMERS IN CAUSING THE
SEROTONIN BEHAVIORAL-SYNDROME IN RATS.
003094 03-04
COMPUTER-ANALYZED EEG IN AMPHETAMINE RESPONSIVE
HYPERACTIVE-CHILDREN.
003338 03-11
THE STIMULATING EFFECT OF AMPHETAMINE ON THE VISUAL SYSTEM.
003398 03-13
EFFECT OF AMPHETAMINE ON THE METABOLISM AND INCORPORATION
OF (3H) THYMIDINE INTO DNA OF DEVELOPING RAT-BRAIN.
003729 04-03
UNIT ACTIVITY IN MEDIAL THALAMUS; COMPARATIVE-EFFECTS OF
CAFFEINE AND AMPHETAMINE.
003752 04-03
EFFECTS OF ACUTE AND CHRONIC AMPHETAMINE TREATMENT ON
PURKINJE NEURON DISCHARGE IN RAT CEREBELLUM.
003793 04-03
EFFECT OF AMPHETAMINE ON PLASMA CORTICOSTERONE IN THE
CONSCIOUS RAT.
003888 04-03
EFFECTS OF IN VIVO AMPHETAMINE ADMINISTRATION ON DOPAMINE
SYNTHESIS REGULATION IN RAT-BRAIN STRIATAL SYNAPTOSOMES.
(UNPUBLISHED PAPER).
003960 04-03
SUSTAINED DECREASE IN FAT CONSUMPTION PRODUCED BY
AMPHETAMINE IN RATS MAINTAINED ON A DIETARY SELF-SELECTION
REGIME.
004150 04-04
HABITUATION OF THE THE HEAD-POKE RESPONSE; EFFECTS OF AN
AMPHETAMINE BARBITURATE MIXTURE, PLG AND FENFLURAMINE.
004159 04-04
AN ANALYSIS OF VISUAL OBJECT REVERSAL LEARNING IN THE
MARMOSET AFTER AMPHETAMINE AND HALOPERIDOL.
004208 04-04
SELECTIVE EFFECTS OF BARBITURATE AND AMPHETAMINE ON
INFORMATION-PROCESSING AND RESPONSE EXECUTION.
004563 04-14
INTERACTION OF P CHLOROPHENYLALANINE, MIANSERINE AND
DANITRACEN WITH AMPHETAMINE.
004599 04-15

AMPHETAMINE-ELICITED
SEX-DIFFERENCES IN AMPHETAMINE-ELICITED ROTATIONAL-BEHAVIOR
AND THE LATERALIZATION OF STRIATAL DOPAMINE IN RATS.
004459 01-04

AMPHETAMINE-INDUCED
AMPHETAMINE-INDUCED HYPERSENSITIVITY IN GUINEA-PIGS.
000498 01-04

DOSE-DEPENDENT, AMPHETAMINE-INDUCED CHANGES IN PERMEABILITY
OF THE BLOOD-BRAIN-BARRIER OF NORMOTENSIVE-RATS AND
SPONTANEOUSLY HYPERTENSIVE-RATS.
001197 02-03
5,7 DIHYDROXYTRYPTAMINE LESIONS OF THE AMYGDALA REDUCE
AMPHETAMINE-INDUCED AND APOMORPHINE-INDUCED STEREOTYPED-
BEHAVIOUR IN THE RAT.
001589 02-04
INFLUENCE OF BENZODIAZEPINE TRANQUILIZERS ON AMPHETAMINE-
INDUCED LOCOMOTOR-STIMULATION IN MICE.
001767 02-04
SUPPRESSION OF AMPHETAMINE-INDUCED EEG AROUSAL IN THE
HIPPOCAMPUS OF HALOPERIDOL TREATED RABBITS.
002683 03-03
AMPHETAMINE-INDUCED ROTATION IN NORMAL CATS.
003002 03-04
AMPHETAMINE-INDUCED MOTILITY AND NIGROSTRIATAL IMPULSE FLOW.
003005 03-04
A PRIMATE ANALOGUE OF AMPHETAMINE-INDUCED BEHAVIORS IN
HUMANS.
003006 03-04
AMPHETAMINE-INDUCED OVEREATING AND OVERWEIGHT IN RATS.
003015 03-04
EFFECTS OF DORSOLATERAL TEGMENTAL LESIONS ON AMPHETAMINE-
INDUCED AND LITHIUM-INDUCED TASTE-AVERSIONS.
003114 03-04
NEUROTENSIN BLOCKS CERTAIN AMPHETAMINE-INDUCED BEHAVIOURS.
004111 04-04
THE EFFECT OF DOPAMINE UPTAKE BLOCKING-AGENTS ON THE
AMPHETAMINE-INDUCED CIRCLING-BEHAVIOR IN MICE WITH
UNILATERAL NIGROSTRIATAL LESIONS.
004117 04-04
NALOXONE FAILS TO BLOCK AMPHETAMINE-INDUCED ANOREXIA AND
CONDITIONED TASTE-AVERSION.
004121 04-04
CENTRAL AND PERIPHERAL EFFECTS OF LITHIUM ON AMPHETAMINE-
INDUCED HYPERACTIVITY IN RATS.
004223 04-04

AMPHETAMINE-LIKE
A CONSTITUENT OF KHAT-LEAVES WITH AMPHETAMINE-LIKE RELEASING
PROPERTIES.
001307 02-03
AMPHETAMINE-LIKE REACTIONS TO PHENYLPROPANOLAMINE.
003480 03-15

AMPHETAMINES
STRUCTURE-ACTIVITY RELATIONSHIPS AMONG SOME D N ALKYLATED
AMPHETAMINES.
001542 02-03

AMPHETAMINIL
AMPHETAMINIL IN THE TREATMENT OF DISTURBED ERECTION POTENCY.
002129 02-11

AMYGDALA
EFFECT OF NALOXONE, HALOPERIDOL AND PROPRANOLOL ON CYCLIC-
ADENOSINE-MONOPHOSPHATE CONTENT OF RAT AMYGDALA.
000071 01-03
LOCOMOTOR AND CONVULSIVE RESPONSES TO PICROTOXIN IN
AMYGDALA KINDLED RATS.
000416 01-04
EFFECTS OF MORPHINE ON EVOKED-POTENTIALS RECORDED FROM THE
AMYGDALA BY TOOTH-PULP STIMULATION IN CATS.
001379 02-03
A PHARMACOLOGICAL ANALYSIS OF THE ROLE OF THE AMYGDALA IN
THE CONTROL OF GONADOTROPIN AND PROLACTIN SECRETION.
001418 02-03
RETROGRADE AMNESIA PRODUCED BY ELECTRICAL-STIMULATION OF THE
AMYGDALA; ATTENUATION WITH ADRENERGIC ANTAGONISTS.
(UNPUBLISHED PAPER).
001488 02-03
5,7 DIHYDROXYTRYPTAMINE LESIONS OF THE AMYGDALA REDUCE
AMPHETAMINE-INDUCED AND APOMORPHINE-INDUCED STEREOTYPED-
BEHAVIOUR IN THE RAT.
001589 02-04
AMYGDALA OPIATE-SENSITIVE MECHANISMS INFLUENCE FEAR
MOTIVATED RESPONSES AND MEMORY PROCESSES FOR AVERSIVE-
EXPERIENCES. (UNPUBLISHED PAPER).
001628 02-04
MODULATION OF OPIATE-RECEPTOR BINDING IN STRIATUM AND
AMYGDALA BY SELECTIVE MESENCEPHALIC LESIONS.
001629 02-04
INVOLVEMENT OF CAUDATE-NUCLEUS, AMYGDALA OR RETICULAR
FORMATION IN NEUROLEPTIC AND NARCOTIC CATALEPSY.
002986 03-04
EFFECT OF PHENTOLAMINE ADMINISTRATION INTO THE AMYGDALA
COMPLEX OF RATS ON TIME-DEPENDENT MEMORY PROCESSES.
002998 03-04
THE EFFECT OF AMYGDALA KINDLING ON SPONTANEOUS AND COCAINE-
INDUCED MOTOR-ACTIVITY AND LIDOCAINE SEIZURES.
003067 03-04

OPIATE-EFFECTS IN THE AMYGDALA CENTRAL NUCLEUS ON HEART RATE
CONDITIONING IN RABBITS.
003798 04-03
EFFECTS OF 3 SULFAMOYLMETHYL-BENZISOXAZOLE (AD-810) AND SOME
ANTIEPILEPTICS ON THE KINDLED SEIZURES IN THE NEOCORTEX,
HIPPOCAMPUS AND AMYGDALA IN RATS.
004149 04-04
SEROTONERGIC MECHANISM IN SEIZURES KINDLED FROM THE RABBIT
AMYGDALA.
004227 04-04
RETROGRADE AMNESIA PRODUCED BY ELECTRICAL-STIMULATION OF THE
AMYGDALA: ATTENUATION WITH ADRENERGIC ANTAGONISTS.
004231 04-04
LESIONS OF AMYGDALA, PYRIFORM CORTEX AND OTHER BRAIN
STRUCTURES DUE TO DIPIPERIDINOETHANE INTOXICATION.
004273 04-05

AMYGDALAR
THE ROLE OF BIOGENIC-AMINES IN AMYGDALAR KINDLING. I. LOCAL
AMYGDALAR AFTERDISCHARGE.
000327 01-03

AMYGDALOID
MODIFICATION OF DOPAMINERGIC-RECEPTOR SENSITIVITY IN RAT-BRAIN
AFTER AMYGDALOID KINDLING.
000106 01-03
ADDICTIVE-AGENTS AND INTRACRANIAL-STIMULATION (ICS): MORPHINE,
NALOXONE, AND PRESSING FOR AMYGDALOID ICS.
000371 01-04
RELATION OF MONOMETHYLHYDRAZINE (MMH) SEIZURE THRESHOLDS
TO AFTERDISCHARGE THRESHOLDS WITH AMYGDALOID STIMULATION
IN CATS.
000474 01-04
BEHAVIORAL-ANALYSIS OF AMYGDALOID KINDLING IN BEAGLE-DOGS
AND THE EFFECTS OF CLONAZEPAM, DIAZEPAM, PHENOBARBITAL,
DIPHENYLHYDANTOIN, AND FLUNARIZINE ON SEIZURE
MANIFESTATION.
000496 01-04
ENHANCED SENSITIVITY OF AMYGDALOID NEURONS TO SEROTONIN AND
NOREPINEPHRINE AFTER CHRONIC ANTIDEPRESSANT TREATMENT.
001523 02-03
BARBITURATE SERUM LEVELS AND PROTECTION AGAINST KINDLED
AMYGDALOID SEIZURES IN THE RAT.
001559 02-04
PHARMACOLOGICAL MODIFICATION OF AMYGDALOID KINDLED
SEIZURES.
001588 02-04
NALOXONE FACILITATES AMYGDALOID KINDLING IN RATS.
001644 02-04
VALPROIC-ACID SERUM LEVELS AND PROTECTION AGAINST KINDLED
AMYGDALOID SEIZURES IN THE RAT.
002946 03-04
THE EFFECTS OF VARIOUS ANESTHETICS ON AMYGDALOID KINDLED
SEIZURES.
002959 03-04
DIFFERENTIAL ACTIONS OF CLASSICAL AND ATYPICAL ANTIPSYCHOTIC-
DRUGS ON SPONTANEOUS NEURONAL ACTIVITY IN THE AMYGDALOID
COMPLEX.
003131 03-05

AMYLOBARBITONE
AMYLOBARBITONE AND FORGETTING.
001763 02-04

AMYOTROPHY
THE USE OF LITHIUM-CARBONATE FOR TREATING KUGELBERG-WELANDER
SPINAL AMYOTROPHY PATIENTS.
003326 03-11

ANAFRANIL
THE BIOAVAILABILITY OF ORAL AND PARENTERAL CHLORIMIPRAMINE
(ANAFRANIL).
002232 02-13

ANALGESIA
COMPARATIVE-STUDY OF ANALGESIA INDUCED BY N VAL5-ENKEPHALIN
AND PRO5-ENKEPHALIN ANALOGS.
000021 01-03
REVERSIBLE INACTIVATION OF RAPHE-MAGNUS NEURONS: EFFECTS ON
NOCICEPTIVE THRESHOLD AND MORPHINE-INDUCED ANALGESIA.
000240 01-03
THE POSSIBILITY THAT A COMPONENT OF MORPHINE-INDUCED
ANALGESIA IS CONTRIBUTED INDIRECTLY VIA THE RELEASE OF
ENDOGENOUS OPIOIDS.
000263 01-03
A FURTHER CHARACTERIZATION OF THE DIFFERENTIAL-EFFECTS OF
LEUCINE-ENKEPHALIN, METHIONINE-ENKEPHALIN AND THEIR ANALOGS
ON MORPHINE-INDUCED ANALGESIA.
000311 01-03
EFFECTS OF L AND D AMINO-ACIDS ON ANALGESIA AND LOCOMOTOR-
ACTIVITY OF MICE: THEIR INTERACTION WITH MORPHINE.
000336 01-04
METHIONINE-ENKEPHALIN ANTAGONISM AND ENDORPHIN POTENTIATION
OF NARCOTIC-INDUCED ANALGESIA.
000357 01-04

PSYCHOPHARMACOLOGY OF ANALGESIA AND PAIN. (UNPUBLISHED
PAPER).
001411 02-03
EFFECTS OF RAPHE-MAGNUS AND RAPHE-PALLIDUS LESIONS ON
MORPHINE-INDUCED ANALGESIA AND SPINAL-CORD MONOAMINES.
001420 02-03
MORPHINE ANALGESIA FOLLOWING ITS INFUSION INTO DIFFERENT
LIQUOR SPACES IN RAT-BRAIN.
001429 02-03
DIFFERENTIAL-EFFECTS OF SYSTEMIC VERSUS INTRACRANIAL INJECTION
OF OPIATES ON CENTRAL, OROFACIAL AND LOWER BODY
NOCICEPTION: SOMATOTYPY IN BULBAR ANALGESIA SYSTEMS.
001446 02-03
INFLUENCE OF THYROTROPIN-RELEASING-HORMONE AND HISTIDYL-
PROLINE-DIKETOPIPERAZINE ON SPONTANEOUS LOCOMOTOR-ACTIVITY
AND ANALGESIA INDUCED BY DELTA9 TETRAHYDROCANNABINOL IN
THE MOUSE.
001575 02-04
ANTAGONISTIC-EFFECTS OF PSYCHOLEPTIC-DRUGS ON STRESS-INDUCED
ANALGESIA.
001609 02-04
ETHANOL-INDUCED ANALGESIA IN RATS SELECTIVELY BRED FOR ETHANOL
SENSITIVITY.
001625 02-04
MORPHINE ANALGESIA AFTER INTRATHECAL ADMINISTRATION OF A
NARCOTIC AGONIST, CHLOROXYMORPHAMINE AND ANTAGONIST,
CHLORNALTREXAMINE.
001695 02-04
OPIATE AND PEPTIDE INTERACTION: EFFECT OF ENKEPHALINS ON
MORPHINE ANALGESIA.
001698 02-04
BRIEF SOCIAL-ISOLATION, PAIN RESPONSIVITY, AND MORPHINE
ANALGESIA IN YOUNG RATS.
001744 02-04
AN INHIBITOR OF OPIOID-PEPTIDE DEGRADATION PRODUCES ANALGESIA
IN MICE.
001780 02-04
ASPIRIN ANALGESIA EVALUATED BY EVENT-RELATED POTENTIALS IN
MAN: POSSIBLE CENTRAL-ACTION IN BRAIN.
002195 02-12
MECHANISMS OF OPIATE ANALGESIA AND THE ROLE OF ENDORPHINS IN
PAIN SUPPRESSION. (UNPUBLISHED PAPER).
002275 02-13
ENKEPHALIN-LIKE CHARACTER AND ANALGESIA.
002650 03-02
PHARMACOLOGICAL-STUDIES ON STIMULATION PRODUCED ANALGESIA
IN MICE.
002964 03-04
DYNORPHIN: A POSSIBLE MODULATORY PEPTIDE ON MORPHINE OR BETA
ENDORPHIN ANALGESIA IN MOUSE.
002994 03-04
NALOXONE REVERSIBLE DUPLICATION BY LANTHANUM OF OPIATE
ANALGESIA EFFECTS ON OROFACIAL, LOWER BODY AND CENTRAL
NOCICEPTION.
003028 03-04
CLONIDINE ANALGESIA AND SUPPRESSION OF OPERANT RESPONDING:
DISSOCIATION OF MECHANISM.
003046 03-04
SUBSTANCE-P, HEXAPEPTIDE-PGLU6(SP6-11), ANALGESIA AND
SEROTONIN DEPLETION.
003050 03-04
FOOTSHOCK ANALGESIA: PREVENTION BY BEHAVIOURAL-MANIPULATION
BUT NOT BY NALOXONE.
003073 03-04
EVIDENCE FOR INVOLVEMENT OF SEPARATE MECHANISMS IN THE
PRODUCTION OF ANALGESIA BY ELECTRICAL-STIMULATION OF THE
NUCLEUS-RETICULARIS-PARAGIGANTOCELLULARIS AND NUCLEUS-
RAPHE-MAGNUS IN THE RAT.
003083 03-04
EFFECTS OF METHYSERGIDE AND NALOXONE ON ANALGESIA INDUCED BY
THE PERIPHERAL ELECTRIC-STIMULATION IN MICE.
003093 03-04
A NEUROANATOMICAL-STUDY OF ANALGESIA AND CATATONIA INDUCED
BY ETORPHINE IN THE RAT. (PH.D. DISSERTATION).
003102 03-04
INDUCTION OF ANALGESIA BY CENTRAL ADMINISTRATION OF ORG-2766,
AN ANALOG OF ACTH4-9.
003112 03-04
A COMPARISON OF THE EFFECTS OF MORPHINE-SULPHATE AND NITROUS-
OXIDE ANALGESIA ON CHRONIC PAIN STATES IN MAN.
003442 03-14
ANALGESIA FOLLOWING INTRAVENTRICULAR ADMINISTRATION OF 2
DEOXY-D-GLUCOSE.
004074 04-04
NALOXAZONE, A LONG-ACTING OPIATE ANTAGONIST: EFFECTS ON
ANALGESIA IN INTACT ANIMALS AND ON OPIATE-RECEPTOR BINDING
IN VITRO.
004198 04-04

BETA ENDORPHIN: CENTRAL SITES OF ANALGESIA, CATALEPSY AND BODY-TEMPERATURE CHANGES IN RATS.
004238 04-04

ANALGESIC
INHIBITION OF (3H)NALOXONE BINDING IN HOMOGENATES OF RAT-BRAIN BY ESEROLINE, A DRUG, WITH ANALGESIC ACTIVITY, RELATED TO PHYSOSTIGMINE.
000104 01-03
CHANGES IN BRAIN N DEMETHYLATION AND OPIATE-RECEPTOR CONTENT CORRELATE WITH ANALGESIC EFFECTIVENESS OF MORPHINE.
000400 01-04
ANALGESIC ACTIVITY OF DIFLUNISAL (MK-647; 5 2,4 DIFLUOROPHENYLSALICYLIC-ACID) IN RATS WITH HYPERALGESIA INDUCED BY FREUNDS-ADJUVANT.
000502 01-04
THE ANALGESIC AND RESPIRATORY EFFECTS OF MEPTAZINOL, MORPHINE AND PENTAZOCINE IN THE RAT.
000516 01-05
MECHANISMS OF PAIN AND ANALGESIC COMPOUNDS.
000916 01-17
BETA ENDORPHIN: DISSOCIATION OF RECEPTOR BINDING-ACTIVITY FROM ANALGESIC POTENCY.
001081 02-02
ON THE MECHANISM-OF-ACTION OF 2 AMINO-4-METHYLPYRIDINE, A MORPHINE-LIKE ANALGESIC.
001574 02-04
ANALGESIC ACTION OF INTRATHECAL AND INTRACEREBRAL BETA ENDORPHIN IN RATS: COMPARISON WITH MORPHINE.
001691 02-04
OPIATE ANTAGONISTS AND LONG-TERM ANALGESIC REACTION INDUCED BY INESCAPABLE SHOCK IN RATS.
001707 02-04
NEUROCHEMICAL-STUDIES OF AN ANALGESIC, 1,3 DIPHENYL-5-2-DIMETHYLAMINOPROPIONAMIDE-PYRAZOLE (DIFENAMIZOLE).
002771 03-03
LEVONANTRADOL, A POTENT CANNABINOID RELATED ANALGESIC, ANTAGONIZES HALOPERIDOL-INDUCED ACTIVATION OF STRIATAL DOPAMINE SYNTHESIS.
002786 03-03
ANALGESIC TOLERANCE PRODUCED BY MORPHINE PELLETS IS FACILITATED BY ANALGESIC TESTING.
002943 03-04
ENVIRONMENTAL MODULATION OF ANALGESIC TOLERANCE INDUCED BY MORPHINE PELLETS.
002944 03-04
ANALGESIC PROPERTIES OF THE GABAMIMETIC THIP.
003013 03-04
COMPARATIVE ANALGESIC, BEHAVIORAL, AND DEPENDENCE PROPERTIES OF MORPHINE AND O METHOXYLPHENYLCARBAMOYLDIETHYLAMINOPROPIOPHENONEOXIME HCL.
003707 04-02
ANALGESIC AND OTHER PHARMACOLOGICAL ACTIVITIES OF A NEW NARCOTIC ANTAGONIST ANALGESIC (-) 1 3 METHYLBUTENYLHYDROXYPHENYLPHENYLETHYLPIPERAZINE AND ITS ENANTIOMORPH IN EXPERIMENTAL ANIMALS.
004185 04-04

ANALGESIC-DRUGS
EFFECTS OF CHANGES IN THE STRUCTURE OF ENKEPHALINS AND OF NARCOTIC ANALGESIC-DRUGS ON THEIR INTERACTIONS WITH MU-RECEPTORS AND DELTA-RECEPTORS.
000168 01-03
THE EFFECT OF PSYCHOTROPIC-SUBSTANCES AND NARCOTIC ANALGESIC-DRUGS ON 14C NORADRENALINE UPTAKE BY SYNAPTOSOMES OF THE CEREBRAL-CORTEX OF RATS.
001363 02-03
GUIDELINES FOR THE CLINICAL-EVALUATION OF ANALGESIC-DRUGS.
002584 02-17

ANALGESIC-INDUCED
EFFECT OF QUIPAZINE AND FLUOXETINE ON ANALGESIC-INDUCED CATALEPSY AND ANTINOCICEPTION IN THE RAT.
001709 02-04

ANALGESICS
INFLUENCE OF GLUCOSE (IN VIVO OR IN VITRO) ON DURATION OF NARCOTIC ANALGESICS AND ON THE KINETICS OF DRUG METABOLISM.
000292 01-03
ANTINOCICEPTIVE-EFFECT OF MORPHINE, OPIOID ANALGESICS AND HALOPERIDOL INJECTED INTO THE CAUDATE-NUCLEUS OF THE RAT.
000414 01-04
A STUDY OF THE QUANTAL (ALL-OR-NONE) CHANGE IN REFLEX LATENCY PRODUCED BY OPIATE ANALGESICS.
000425 01-04
THE INFLUENCE OF 5 HT-RECEPTOR BLOCKING-AGENTS ON THE BEHAVIORAL-EFFECTS OF ANALGESICS IN RATS.
000429 01-04
INTERACTION-STUDIES BETWEEN NARCOTIC ANALGESICS, NARCOTIC ANTAGONISTS AND ETHANOL. STUDIES DURING ACUTE AND CHRONIC-TREATMENT AND WITHDRAWAL STATES IN RATS AND MICE. (PH.D. DISSERTATION).
001165 02-03

ACTIONS OF ENKEPHALIN, MU AND PARTIAL AGONIST ANALGESICS ON ACETYLCHOLINE TURNOVER IN RAT-BRAIN.
001541 02-03
NARCOTIC ANALGESICS AND STEREOTYPED-BEHAVIOUR IN MICE.
001694 02-04
CLASSIFICATION OF ANALGESICS.
002570 02-17
STRUCTURE-ACTIVITY AND RECEPTOR BINDING OF ANTAGONIST ANALGESICS.
003611 03-17
BLOCKADE BY L LYSINE OF NONNARCOTIC ANALGESICS.
003857 04-03
EFFECTS OF ANALGESICS AND CNS-ACTING DRUGS ON STRUGGLING FOLLOWING REPETITIVE STIMULATION OF THE TAIL, AND FLEXOR REFLEX TO A SINGLE STIMULATION OF THE SCIATIC-NERVE IN RATS.
004148 04-04

ANALOG
UNUSUAL DOSE-RELATED EFFECT OF AN ENDORPHIN ANALOG IN A COMPLEX MAZE.
001674 02-04
Y-MAZE BEHAVIOR AFTER AN ANALOG OF ACTH4-9, EVIDENCE FOR AN ATTENTIONAL-ALTERATION.
001676 02-04
METKEPHAMID, A SYSTEMICALLY ACTIVE ANALOG OF METHIONINE-ENKEPHALIN WITH POTENT OPIOID DELTA-RECEPTOR ACTIVITY.
002720 03-03
POSSIBLE MECHANISMS OF EFFECT OF ACTH4-10 AND ITS ANALOG, CONTAINING D ISOMER OF PHENYLALANINE, ON BEHAVIOR.
002949 03-04
GAMMA BUTYROLACTONE-GAMMA-CARBONYL-HISTIDYL-PROLINAMIDE CITRATE (DN-1417): A NOVEL TRH ANALOG WITH POTENT EFFECTS ON THE CENTRAL-NERVOUS-SYSTEM.
003057 03-04
INDUCTION OF ANALGESIA BY CENTRAL ADMINISTRATION OF ORG-2766, AN ANALOG OF ACTH4-9.
003112 03-04
HIGH-AFFINITY BINDING-SITES FOR A SOMATOSTATIN-28 ANALOG IN RAT-BRAIN.
003985 04-03
GLC MASS-SPECTROMETRIC-DETERMINATION OF MAPROTILINE AND ITS MAJOR METABOLITE USING STABLE ISOTOPE-LABELED ANALOG AS INTERNAL STANDARD.
004291 04-06

ANALOGS
COMPARATIVE-STUDY OF ANALGESIA INDUCED BY N VAL5-ENKEPHALIN AND PRO5-ENKEPHALIN ANALOGS.
000021 01-03
THE EFFECTS OF TWO ANALOGS OF DOPAMINE ON GANGLIONIC TRANSMISSION IN THE SYMPATHETIC-NERVOUS-SYSTEM.
000162 01-03
STRUCTURE-ACTIVITY RELATIONSHIPS IN THE EFFECTS OF PHENACEMIDE ANALOGS ON SERUM CREATININE AND ANTICONVULSANT ACTIVITY.
000249 01-03
A FURTHER CHARACTERIZATION OF THE DIFFERENTIAL-EFFECTS OF LEUCINE-ENKEPHALIN, METHIONINE-ENKEPHALIN AND THEIR ANALOGS ON MORPHINE-INDUCED ANALGESIA.
000311 01-03
ROTATIONAL-BEHAVIOR INDUCED BY COCAINE ANALOGS IN RATS WITH UNILATERAL 6 HYDROXYDOPAMINE LESIONS OF THE SUBSTANTIA-NIGRA: DEPENDENCE UPON DOPAMINE UPTAKE INHIBITION.
000404 01-04
HISTORY AND PHARMACOLOGY OF PCP AND PCP RELATED ANALOGS.
000737 01-12
IRREVERSIBLE INHIBITION OF S ADENOSYLHOMOCYSTEINE-HYDROLASE BY NUCLEOSIDE ANALOGS. (UNPUBLISHED PAPER).
001010 02-01
ADENOSINE ANALOGS AS SUBSTRATES AND INHIBITORS OF S ADENOSYLHOMOCYSTEINE-HYDROLASE. (UNPUBLISHED PAPER).
001021 02-01
BETA ENDORPHIN AND ANALOGS: 360 MHZ PROTON NMR SPECTROSCOPY.
001028 02-01
SYNTHESIS OF 180 ANALOGS OF BIOGENIC-AMINES. (UNPUBLISHED PAPER).
001044 02-01
DIHYDROXY AND TRIHYDROXY ANALOGS OF CHLORPROMAZINE INFLUENCE THE CENTRAL-ACTIVITY OF ADENYLATE-CYCLASE AND CYCLIC-AMP-PHOSPHODIESTERASE.
001405 02-03
MOTOR-ACTIVITY AND ROTATIONAL-BEHAVIOR AFTER ANALOGS OF COCAINE: CORRELATION WITH DOPAMINE UPTAKE BLOCKADE.
001650 02-04
ENKEPHALIN ANALOGS AND PHYSICAL-DEPENDENCE.
003572 03-16
SYNTHESIS AND BIOLOGICAL-ACTIVITY OF HUMAN BETA ENDORPHIN ANALOGS WITH DISULFIDE BRIDGES.
003655 04-01

SYNTHESIS AND PHARMACOLOGICAL-STUDY OF SOME ENKEPHALIN ANALOGS IN RELATION TO THE PLURALITY OF OPIATE-RECEPTORS.
003682 04-02
CENTRALLY ACTIVE N SUBSTITUTED ANALOGS OF 3,4 METHYLENEDIOXYPHENYLISOPROPYLAMINE (3,4 METHYLENEDIOXYAMPHETAMINE).
003683 04-02
INHIBITION OF AMINOPEPTIDASE AND ACETYLCHOLINESTERASE BY PUROMYCIN AND PUROMYCIN ANALOGS.
003835 04-03
OPIOIDS, NORADRENALINE AND GTP ANALOGS INHIBIT CHOLERA-TOXIN ACTIVATED ADENYLATE-CYCLASE IN NEUROBLASTOMA-X GLIOMA HYBRID CELLS.
003975 04-03
N,N DIISOPROPYLTRYPTAMINE (DIPT) AND 5 METHOXYDIISOPROPYLTRYPTAMINE (5 MEO-DIPT). TWO ORALLY ACTIVE TRYPTAMINE ANALOGS WITH CNS ACTIVITY.
004310 04-07

ANALOGUE
AN ANALOGUE OF THYROTROPIN-RELEASING-HORMONE WITH IMPROVED BIOLOGICAL-STABILITY BOTH IN VITRO AND IN VIVO.
000032 01-03
EFFECTS OF ENKEPHALIN ANALOGUE AND NALOXONE ON CAT SPINAL-CORD DORSAL ROOT POTENTIALS.
000236 01-03
APPLICATION OF A SYNTHETIC ENKEPHALIN ANALOGUE DURING HEROIN WITHDRAWAL.
000685 01-11
CONTRALATERAL CIRCLING-BEHAVIOUR INDUCED BY INTRANIGRAL INJECTION OF MORPHINE AND ENKEPHALIN ANALOGUE FK-33-824 IN RATS.
001669 02-04
BIPHASIC-EFFECTS OF A POTENT ENKEPHALIN ANALOGUE D MET2-PRO5-ENKEPHALINAMIDE AND MORPHINE ON LOCOMOTOR-ACTIVITY IN MICE.
001799 02-04
A PRIMATE ANALOGUE OF AMPHETAMINE-INDUCED BEHAVIORS IN HUMANS.
003006 03-04
BIOLOGICAL EVALUATION OF A TRH ANALOGUE WITH A MODIFIED PROLINE RESIDUE.
003662 04-01
INTERACTIONS BETWEEN A MONOFLUORINATED ANALOGUE OF P CHLOROAMPHETAMINE AND 5 HYDROXYTRYPTAMINE IN BRAIN.
003719 04-03
A SYNTHETIC ACTH4-9 ANALOGUE (ORGANON-2766) AND SLEEP IN HEALTHY MAN.
004574 04-14

ANALOGUES
FLUORINATED ANALOGUES OF THE TRICYCLIC NEUROLEPTICS: 2,3 DIFLUORO DERIVATIVE OF CLOROTEPIN.
000001 01-01
EFFECT OF GABA ANALOGUES ON BLOOD-PRESSURE AND CENTRAL GABA METABOLISM IN THE RAT.
000231 01-03
DISPLACEMENT OF (3H)CLONIDINE BINDING BY CLONIDINE ANALOGUES IN MEMBRANES FROM RAT-CEREBRAL-CORTEX.
000536 01-06
THE EFFECTS OF LSD AND SOME ANALOGUES ON THE RESPONSES OF SINGLE CORTICAL NEURONS OF THE CAT TO OPTICAL-STIMULATION.
000738 01-12
ANTIARRHYTHMIC-ACTIVITY OF AMITRIPTYLINE ANALOGUES IN CONSCIOUS DOGS AFTER MYOCARDIAL-INFARCTION: CYPROHEPTADINIUM-METHIODIDE.
001534 02-03
CONFORMATIONALLY RESTRICTED TRICYCLIC-ANTIDEPRESSANTS. 1. OCTAHYDRODIBENZAZEPINONAPHTHYRIDINES AS RIGID IMIPRAMINE ANALOGUES.
001710 02-04
THE EFFECT OF SOME STRUCTURAL GABA ANALOGUES ON THE SEROTONIN AND DOPAMINERGIC MECHANISMS.
001736 02-04
THE SYNTHESIS AND ACTIVITY OF CIS AND TRANS 2 AMINOMETHYLCYCLOPROPANECARBOXYLIC-ACID AS CONFORMATIONALLY RESTRICTED ANALOGUES OF GABA.
002633 03-01
GABA ANALOGUES ACTIVATE CHANNELS OF DIFFERENT DURATION ON CULTURED MOUSE SPINAL NEURONS.
002665 03-03
KINETIC DATA ON THE INHIBITION OF HIGH-AFFINITY CHOLINE TRANSPORT INTO RAT-FOREBRAIN SYNAPTOSOMES BY CHOLINE-LIKE COMPOUNDS AND NITROGEN-MUSTARD ANALOGUES.
002879 03-03
DISCRIMINATIVE-STIMULUS PROPERTIES OF PHENCYCLIDINE AND FIVE ANALOGUES IN THE SQUIRREL-MONKEY.
002961 03-04
SYNTHESIS AND BIOCHEMICAL AND PHARMACOLOGIC PROPERTIES OF ANALOGUES AND DERIVATIVES OF P CHLOROPHENYLALANINE.
003691 04-02

EFFECTS OF CONFORMATIONALLY RESTRAINED ANALOGUES OF SEROTONIN ON ITS UPTAKE AND BINDING IN RAT-BRAIN.
003794 04-03
IBOTENIC-ACID ANALOGUES AS INHIBITORS OF (3H)GLUTAMIC-ACID BINDING TO CEREBELLAR MEMBRANES.
003848 04-03
ACTION OF ENKEPHALIN ANALOGUES AND MORPHINE ON BRAIN ACETYLCHOLINE RELEASE: DIFFERENTIAL REVERSAL BY NALOXONE AND AN OPIATE-PENTAPEPTIDE.
003863 04-03

ANALYSE
THE USE OF PSYCHOPHARMACOLOGICAL-PROCEDURES TO ANALYSE THE ONTOGENY OF LEARNING AND RETENTION: ISSUES AND CONCERNS.
000482 01-04

ANALYSES
MULTIDIMENSIONAL ANALYSES OF BEHAVIOR IN MICE TREATED WITH ALPHA ENDORPHIN.
003020 03-04
STATISTICAL ANALYSES OF PHYSIOLOGIC DATA FROM FEMALE PATIENTS WITH AN ENDOMORPHOUS DEPRESSIVE COURSE: A TRIAL, INTERACTIONS BETWEEN PHYSIOLOGIC PARAMETERS, TEST JUNCTURES IN THIS PHASE.
003251 03-09
CONSISTENCY IN CATECHOLAMINE EXCRETION IN LABORATORY AND NATURAL SETTINGS: CORRELATIONAL AND VARIANCE COMPONENTS ANALYSES.
004508 04-13
GAS-CHROMATOGRAPHY/MASS-SPECTROMETRY STABLE ISOTOPIC ANALYSES FOR DEANOL, CHOLINE, AND THEIR ACETYLESTERS.
004683 04-16

ANALYSIS
ANALYSIS FOR DIAZEPAM AND NORDIAZEPAM BY ELECTRON-CAPTURE GAS-CHROMATOGRAPHY AND BY LIQUID-CHROMATOGRAPHY
000006 01-01
NONLINEAR REGRESSION ANALYSIS OF NOREPINEPHRINE RESPONSE KINETICS IN CEREBRAL VASCULATURE.
000256 01-03
ANALYSIS OF THE ACTIVATION OF DOPAMINE METABOLISM BY A SEROTONIN UPTAKE INHIBITOR.
000315 01-03
DRUG-VARIABLES IN THE ETIOLOGY OF TARDIVE-DYSKINESIA: APPLICATION OF DISCRIMINANT FUNCTION ANALYSIS.
000844 01-15
AN HPLC AND RIA ANALYSIS OF THE CHOLECYSTOKININ-PEPTIDES IN RAT-BRAIN. (UNPUBLISHED PAPER).
001004 02-01
DECOMPOSITION OF PHARMACOLOGICAL ACTIVITY INDICES INTO MUTUALLY INDEPENDENT COMPONENTS USING PRINCIPAL COMPONENT ANALYSIS.
001039 02-01
QUANTITATIVE ANALYSIS OF 6 HYDROXYMELATONIN IN HUMAN URINE BY GAS-CHROMATOGRAPHY NEGATIVE CHEMICAL-IONIZATION MASS-SPECTROMETRY. (UNPUBLISHED PAPER).
001058 02-01
REGIONAL 5 HT ANALYSIS IN ROMAN HIGH-AVOIDANCE AND LOW-AVOIDANCE RATS FOLLOWING MAO-INHIBITION.
001202 02-03
AUTOCORRELATION ANALYSIS OF SINGLE NEURON ACTIVITY AFTER ADMINISTRATION OF PENTOBARBITAL.
001268 02-03
ACUTE AND CHRONIC OPIATE-EFFECTS ON SINGLE UNITS AND EEG OF MEDIAL THALAMUS AND HIPPOCAMPUS: A LATENCY ANALYSIS.
001344 02-03
A PHARMACOLOGICAL ANALYSIS OF THE ROLE OF THE AMYGDALA IN THE CONTROL OF GONADOTROPIN AND PROLACTIN SECRETION.
001418 02-03
MULTIPLE CNS RECEPTOR INTERACTIONS OF ERGOT ALKALOIDS: AFFINITY AND INTRINSIC ACTIVITY ANALYSIS IN IN VITRO BINDING SYSTEMS.
001516 02-03
AN ANALYSIS OF SOME PERCEPTUAL-EFFECTS OF MORPHINE, CHLORPROMAZINE, AND LSD.
001652 02-04
NEUROPHARMACOLOGICAL ANALYSIS OF HANDLING-INDUCED SEIZURES IN GERBILS.
001876 02-06
PSYCHOACTIVE-DRUG-EFFECTS IN A HYPERACTIVE-CHILD: A CASE-STUDY ANALYSIS OF BEHAVIOR-CHANGE AND TEACHER ATTENTION.
002313 02-14
VIGILANCE IMPAIRING DRUGS: ANALYSIS OF SUBJECTIVE RESPONSES.
002332 02-14
USE OF SURVIVAL CURVES IN ANALYSIS OF ANTIPSYCHOTIC RELAPSE-STUDIES.
002481 02-16
RESPONDERS AND NONRESPONDERS TO CHLORDIAZEPOXIDE AND PLACEBO: A DISCRIMINANT FUNCTION ANALYSIS.
002482 02-16
COORDINATING CLINICAL-TRIALS IN PSYCHOPHARMACOLOGY: PLANNING, DOCUMENTATION, AND ANALYSIS.
002574 02-17

A QUANTITATIVE REGIONAL ANALYSIS OF PROTEIN SYNTHESIS INHIBITION IN THE RAT-BRAIN FOLLOWING LOCALIZED INJECTION OF CYCLOHEXIMIDE.
002780 03-03

AN IMPROVED MODEL OF INTRASPECIFIC AGGRESSION: DOSE-RESPONSE ANALYSIS OF APOMORPHINE-INDUCED-FIGHTING AND STEREOTYPY IN THE RAT.
002983 03-04

AN ANALYSIS OF SPECIFICITY OF DRUG-INDUCED CHANGES IN DRUG-REINFORCED RESPONDING. (PH.D. DISSERTATION).
003010 03-04

THE PHARMACOLOGICAL ANALYSIS OF MONOAMINERGIC MECHANISMS OF THE MEDIAL HYPOTHALAMUS IN FOOD PROCURING CONDITIONED REFLEXES IN RATS.
003100 03-04

POWER SPECTRAL ANALYSIS OF THE FLASH-EVOKED AFTERDISCHARGE.
003133 03-06

ANALYSIS OF SINGLE-BLIND, DOUBLE-BLIND PROCEDURES, MAINTENANCE OF PLACEBO-EFFECTS, AND DRUG-INDUCED DYSKINESIA WITH MENTALLY-RETARDED PERSONS -- BRIEF REPORT.
003298 03-11

PSYCHOTROPIC-DRUG-INDUCED CHANGES IN AUDITORY AVERAGED EVOKED-POTENTIALS: RESULTS OF A DOUBLE-BLIND TRIAL USING AN OBJECTIVE FULLY AUTOMATED AEP ANALYSIS METHOD.
003412 03-13

OPERANT ANALYSIS OF HUMAN HEROIN SELF-ADMINISTRATION AND THE EFFECTS OF NALTREXONE.
003449 03-14

TIME-BLIND ANALYSIS AND OTHER VIDEO-STRATEGIES IN PHASE II TRIALS OF PSYCHOTROPIC-DRUGS.
003568 03-16

DRUG DEPENDENCE: REFLECTIONS ON AND ANALYSIS OF AN EXPERIENCE IN THE PROVINCE OF RIGGIO-EMILIA.
003591 03-17

AN ANALYSIS OF DRUG DECISIONS IN A STATE PSYCHIATRIC-HOSPITAL.
003593 03-17

FURTHER ANALYSIS OF THE MECHANISMS OF ACTION OF BATRACHOTOXIN ON THE MEMBRANE OF MYELINATED NERVE.
003884 04-03

RX-336-M, A NEW CHEMICAL TOOL IN THE ANALYSIS OF THE QUASI-MORPHINE WITHDRAWAL-SYNDROME.
004093 04-04

AN ANALYSIS OF VISUAL OBJECT REVERSAL LEARNING IN THE MARMOSET AFTER AMPHETAMINE AND HALOPERIDOL.
004208 04-04

PRESENCE OF CONJUGATED CATECHOLAMINES IN RAT-BRAIN: A NEW METHOD OF ANALYSIS OF CATECHOLAMINE-SULFATES.
004286 04-06

PROPHYLACTIC-EFFECT OF LITHIUM AGAINST DEPRESSION IN CYCLOTHYMIC-PATIENTS: A LIFE-TABLE ANALYSIS.
004391 04-09

RESPONDERS AND NONRESPONDERS TO CHLORDIAZEPOXIDE AND PLACEBO. A DISCRIMINANT FUNCTION ANALYSIS. (UNPUBLISHED PAPER).
004420 04-10

ANALYSIS OF SINGLE-BLIND AND DOUBLE-BLIND PROCEDURES, MAINTENANCE OF PLACEBO-EFFECTS AND DRUG-INDUCED DYSKINESIA WITH MENTALLY-RETARDED PERSON.
004437 04-11

MECHANISM OF LITHIUM INCLUDED ELEVATION IN RED-BLOOD-CELL CHOLINE CONTENT: AN IN VITRO ANALYSIS.
004511 04-13

COMPUTERIZED ANALYSIS OF SLEEP RECORDINGS APPLIED TO DRUG EVALUATION: MIDAZOLAM IN NORMAL SUBJECTS.
004564 04-14

CHLORPROMAZINE ANALYSIS IN HUMAN PLASMA. (UNPUBLISHED PAPER).
004591 04-15

MILD, MODERATE, SEVERE -- THE STATISTICAL ANALYSIS OF SHORT ORDINAL SCALES.
004677 04-16

GLC/TLC ANALYSIS OF CODEINE AND MORPHINE IN URINE VIA DERIVATIZATION TECHNIQUES.
004687 04-16

A MULTIVARIATE ANALYSIS OF THE INFRARED SPECTRA OF DRUGS OF ABUSE.
004688 04-16

ANALYTICAL
THE MYTHOLOGEM OF REVERSIBLE DEATH. THE ANALYTICAL CONFRONTATION OF ENDOGENOUS DELIRIUM WITH DELUSIONS IN PSYCHEDELIC-EXPERIENCES.
002200 02-12

ANALYZING
STUDIES ON THE TREATMENT AND DIAGNOSIS OF NEUROTIC VERTIGO FROM THE VIEWPOINT OF NEUROOTOLOGY: OBSERVATION OF THE BALANCE TEST FOR ANALYZING NEUROTIC VERTIGO.
004387 04-09

ANASTOMOSIS
ORAL BIOAVAILABILITY OF APOMORPHINE IN THE RAT WITH A PORTACAVAL VENOUS ANASTOMOSIS.
001158 02-03

ANATOMICOPHYSIOLOGICAL
ANATOMICOPHYSIOLOGICAL AND NEUROCHEMICAL-STUDY OF THE LIMBIC-SYSTEM: EFFECT OF NOMIFENSINE.
001160 02-03

ANATOMOBIOCHEMICAL
ANATOMOBIOCHEMICAL MAPPING OF THE BRAIN: NEUROPSYCHIATRIC-CORRELATIONS.
002630 02-17

ANATOMY
STEREOCHEMICAL ANATOMY OF MORPHINOMIMETICS.
002197 02-12

ANESTHESIA
THE INFLUENCE OF CHLORALOSE ANESTHESIA ON THE ACTIVITY OF RED NUCLEUS NEURONS IN CATS.
000245 01-03

INTRACELLULAR REDOX STATES UNDER HALOTHANE AND BARBITURATE ANESTHESIA IN NORMAL, ISCHEMIC, AND ANOXIC MONKEY BRAIN.
000295 01-03

ON THE MECHANISM OF A DIFFERENT DRUG DISTRIBUTION DURING CONVULSIVE-SEIZURE IN COMPARISON TO ANESTHESIA.
001151 02-03

INFLUENCE OF IMIPRAMINE AND PARGYLINE ON THE ARRHYTHMOGENICITY OF EPINEPHRINE DURING HALOTHANE, ENFLURANE OR METHOXYFLURANE ANESTHESIA IN DOGS.
001539 02-03

REDUCTION OF BARBITURATE ANESTHESIA BY NEW GLUTARIMIDE COMPOUNDS IN MICE.
001748 02-04

ACCELERATED EXTINCTION AFTER POSTTRIAL HALOTHANE ANESTHESIA IN RATS: AN AVERSIVE-EFFECT.
003001 03-04

EFFECTS OF ANESTHESIA ON PATIENTS TAKING PSYCHOTROPIC-DRUGS.
003603 03-17

CHANGES IN GAMMA AMINOBUTYRIC-ACID SHUNT ENZYMES IN REGIONS OF RAT-BRAIN WITH KETAMINE ANESTHESIA.
003891 04-03

RESPIRATORY DEPRESSION PRODUCED BY DIAZEPAM IN CATS: EFFECT OF ANESTHESIA.
004272 04-05

ANESTHETIC
ANTICONVULSANT AND ANESTHETIC BARBITURATES: DIFFERENT POSTSYNAPTIC ACTIONS IN CULTURED MAMMALIAN NEURONS.
000194 01-03

REGULATION OF THE STATE OF PHOSPHORYLATION OF SPECIFIC NEURONAL PROTEINS IN MOUSE-BRAIN BY IN VIVO ADMINISTRATION OF ANESTHETIC AND CONVULSANT-AGENTS.
000291 01-03

BARBITURATE ENHANCEMENT OF GABA-MEDIATED INHIBITION AND ACTIVATION OF CHLORIDE ION-CONDUCTANCE: CORRELATION WITH ANTICONVULSANT AND ANESTHETIC ACTIONS.
002885 03-03

ANESTHETICS
FACTORS INFLUENCING SEIZURE DURATION AND NUMBER OF SEIZURES APPLIED IN UNILATERAL ELECTROCONVULSIVE-THERAPY: ANESTHETICS AND BENZODIAZEPINES.
000792 01-13

INHIBITION BY LOCAL ANESTHETICS, PHENTOLAMINE AND PROPRANOLOL OF (3H)QUINUCLYDINYL-BENZYLATE BINDING TO CENTRAL MUSCARINIC-RECEPTORS.
001097 02-03

THE INTERACTION BETWEEN BARBITURATE ANESTHETICS AND EXCITATORY AMINO-ACID RESPONSES ON CAT SPINAL NEURONES.
002799 03-03

THE EFFECTS OF VARIOUS ANESTHETICS ON AMYGDALOID KINDLED SEIZURES.
002959 03-04

ANESTHETICS AND THE HABENULO-INTERPEDUNCULAR SYSTEM: SELECTIVE SPARING OF METABOLIC ACTIVITY.
003833 04-03

THE INTERACTION OF AMINE LOCAL ANESTHETICS WITH MUSCARINIC-RECEPTORS.
004031 04-03

ANESTHETIZED
MORPHINE AND SUPRASPINAL INHIBITION OF SPINAL NEURONES: EVIDENCE THAT MORPHINE DECREASES TONIC DESCENDING INHIBITION IN THE ANESTHETIZED CAT.
001203 02-03

DIFFERENCES IN CUTANEOUS SENSORY RESPONSE PROPERTIES OF SINGLE SOMATOSENSORY CORTICAL NEURONS IN AWAKE AND HALOTHANE ANESTHETIZED RATS.
002687 03-03

METHYSERGIDE AND SUPRASPINAL INHIBITION OF THE SPINAL TRANSMISSION OF NOCICEPTIVE INFORMATION IN THE ANESTHETIZED CAT.
002740 03-03

SENSITIVE DEPRESSANT EFFECT OF BENZODIAZEPINES ON THE CROSSED EXTENSOR REFLEX IN CHLORALOSE ANESTHETIZED RATS.
003027 03-04

CENTRAL HYPOTENSIVE-EFFECT OF GAMMA AMINOBUTYRIC-ACID IN ANESTHETIZED DOGS.
003772 04-03

PRESSOR EFFECTS OF ELECTRICAL-STIMULATION OF THE DORSAL AND MEDIAN RAPHE NUCLEI IN ANESTHETIZED RATS.
003892 04-03

ANGINA
TREATMENT OF UNSTABLE ANGINA BY DILTIAZEM.
004307 04-07

ANGIOTENSIN
REGULATION OF RECEPTOR BINDING INTERACTIONS OF 125I ANGIOTENSIN-II AND 125I SARCOSINE1-LEUCINE8-ANGIOTENSIN-II, AN ANGIOTENSIN ANTAGONIST, BY SODIUM-ION.
001124 02-03

CAPTOPRIL GIVEN INTRACEREBROVENTRICULARLY, SUBCUTANEOUSLY OR BY GAVAGE INHIBITS ANGIOTENSIN CONVERTING ENZYME ACTIVITY IN THE RAT-BRAIN.
001614 02-04

ANGIOTENSIN-II
EVIDENCE OF A DIRECT ACTION OF ANGIOTENSIN-II ON NEURONES IN THE SEPTUM AND IN THE MEDIAL PREOPTIC-AREA.
000272 01-03

REGULATION OF RECEPTOR BINDING INTERACTIONS OF 125I ANGIOTENSIN-II AND 125I SARCOSINE1-LEUCINE8-ANGIOTENSIN-II, AN ANGIOTENSIN ANTAGONIST, BY SODIUM-ION.
001124 02-03

RECEPTOR BINDING INTERACTIONS OF THE ANGIOTENSIN-II ANTAGONIST, 125I SARCOSINE1-LEUCINE8-ANGIOTENSIN-II, WITH MAMMALIAN BRAIN AND PERIPHERAL TISSUES.
001125 02-03

NEURONAL SENSITIVITY OF SOME BRAIN REGIONS TO ANGIOTENSIN-II IN RABBITS.
003716 04-03

CENTRAL-EFFECTS OF ANGIOTENSIN-II IN WATER AND SALINE LOADED RATS.
003845 04-03

ANGIOTENSIN-II-INDUCED
INTRACRANIAL INJECTION PARAMETERS WHICH AFFECT ANGIOTENSIN-II-INDUCED DRINKING.
000534 01-06

ANIMAL
CHOLINERGIC ASPECTS OF TARDIVE-DYSKINESIA: HUMAN AND ANIMAL STUDIES.
000928 01-17

ANIMAL ACTIVITY MONITOR FOR CHRONIC DRUG-STUDIES. (UNPUBLISHED PAPER).
001794 02-04

QUANTITATIVE STUDY OF THE DISTRIBUTION OF LITHIUM IN THE MOUSE-BRAIN FOR VARIOUS DOSES OF LITHIUM GIVEN TO THE ANIMAL.
002299 02-13

PHARMACOLOGICAL EVIDENCE FOR CATECHOLAMINE INVOLVEMENT IN ANIMAL AGGRESSION.
003052 03-04

PHARMACOLOGICAL EVIDENCE FOR CATECHOLAMINE INVOLVEMENT IN ANIMAL AGGRESSION.
003140 03-06

POSITRON-TOMOGRAPHY. A NEW METHOD FOR IN VIVO BRAIN STUDIES OF BENZODIAZEPINE, IN ANIMAL AND IN MAN.
003564 03-16

EFFECTS OF ANIMAL AGE AND PHENOBARBITAL ON RAT LIVER GLUCOSE-6-PHOSPHATASE ACTIVITY.
003997 04-03

THE EFFECT OF PROPYLNORANTIFEIN ON BEHAVIORAL-REACTIONS, ADRENOCORTICAL ACTIVITY, AND ENERGY METABOLISM IN THE ANIMAL BRAIN.
004075 04-04

EFFECTS OF PAIN, MORPHINE AND NALOXONE ON THE DURATION OF ANIMAL HYPNOSIS.
004081 04-04

LACK OF SPECIFICITY OF AN ANIMAL BEHAVIOR MODEL FOR HALLUCINOGENIC DRUG ACTION.
004250 04-04

ANIMAL-MODEL
BIOCHEMICAL-STUDY OF THE ANIMAL-MODEL DEPRESSION INDUCED BY TETRABENAZINE.
001506 02-03

DOPAMINERGIC INVOLVEMENT IN ATTENTION A NOVEL ANIMAL-MODEL.
001678 02-04

EFFECTS OF CHRONIC AMPHETAMINE OR RESERPINE ON SELF-STIMULATION RESPONDING: ANIMAL-MODEL OF DEPRESSION?
001699 02-04

PRESYNAPTIC AND POSTSYNAPTIC SEROTONERGIC MANIPULATIONS IN AN ANIMAL-MODEL OF DEPRESSION.
001730 02-04

A PHARMACOLOGICAL INVESTIGATION OF AN ANIMAL-MODEL OF THE PETIT-MAL SEIZURE. (PH.D. DISSERTATION).
001870 02-06

EFFECTS OF D-AMPHETAMINE AND APOMORPHINE IN A NEW ANIMAL-MODEL OF PETIT-MAL EPILEPSY.
002493 02-16

ANIMAL-MODEL OF PSYCHOSIS: HALLUCINATORY BEHAVIORS IN MONKEYS DURING THE LATE STAGE OF CONTINUOUS AMPHETAMINE INTOXICATION.
002988 03-04

DOPAMINE AND DEMENTIA. AN ANIMAL-MODEL WITH DESTRUCTION OF THE MESOCORTICAL DOPAMINERGIC PATHWAY: A PRELIMINARY STUDY.
003085 03-04

ANTAGONISM OF DOPAMINE SUPERSENSITIVITY BY ESTROGEN: NEUROCHEMICAL-STUDIES IN AN ANIMAL-MODEL OF TARDIVE-DYSKINESIA.
004268 04-05

THE SIMULTANEOUS INFUSION OF DRUGS VIA THE LEFT AND RIGHT VERTEBRAL-ARTERY OF THE CAT; A MODIFIED ANIMAL-MODEL FOR THE STUDY OF POSSIBLE CENTRAL-ACTIONS OF DRUGS UPON THE LOWER BRAINSTEM.
004297 04-06

ANIMAL-MODELS
ANIMAL-MODELS OF ANXIETY AND BENZODIAZEPINE ACTIONS.
000531 01-06

INTERACTION OF PSYCHOPHARMALOGIC-FACTORS AND PSYCHOSOCIAL-FACTORS IN THE TREATMENT OF ANIMAL-MODELS OF HYPOINHIBITORY (HYPERKINETIC) BEHAVIOR.
001602 02-04

ANIMAL-MODELS OF PSYCHIATRIC-DISORDERS.
001871 02-06

ANIMAL-MODELS OF RELEVANCE TO BIOLOGICAL-PSYCHIATRY.
002490 02-16

ANIMAL-MODELS OF TARDIVE-DYSKINESIA.
003476 03-15

ANIMALS
IMIPRAMINE AND REM SLEEP: CHOLINERGIC MEDIATION IN ANIMALS.
000406 01-04

ASSESSMENT OF ADRENERGIC-RECEPTORS IN VIVO IN EXPERIMENTAL ANIMALS AND MAN. (UNPUBLISHED PAPER).
001034 02-01

A CLASSIFICATION OF OPIATE-RECEPTORS THAT MEDIATE ANTINOCICEPTION IN ANIMALS.
001807 02-04

BEHAVIOURAL-ANALYSIS OF FEEDING: IMPLICATIONS FOR THE PHARMACOLOGICAL MANIPULATION OF FOOD INTAKE IN ANIMALS AND MAN.
002527 02-17

MORPHOLOGICAL CHANGES IN RAT-BRAIN INDUCED BY L CYSTEINE INJECTION IN NEWBORN ANIMALS.
002774 03-03

PLASMA IMIPRAMINE LEVELS AND DEMETHYLASE ACTIVITY IN THE LIVER OF STRESSED ANIMALS.
002793 03-03

POTENTIATION OF BARBITURATE HYPNOSIS BY PROBENECID: DIFFERENTIAL-EFFECT IN TOLERANT ANIMALS.
003038 03-04

SPECIFIC AND NONSPECIFIC MULTIPLE UNIT ACTIVITIES DURING PENTYLENETETRAZOL SEIZURES. I. ANIMALS WITH ENCEPHALE ISOLE.
004046 04-03

ANALGESIC AND OTHER PHARMACOLOGICAL ACTIVITIES OF A NEW NARCOTIC ANTAGONIST ANALGESIC (-) 1 3 METHYLBUTENYLHYDROXYPHENYLPHENYLETHYLPIPERAZINE AND ITS ENANTIOMORPH IN EXPERIMENTAL ANIMALS.
004185 04-04

NALOXAZONE, A LONG-ACTING OPIATE ANTAGONIST: EFFECTS ON ANALGESIA IN INTACT ANIMALS AND ON OPIATE-RECEPTOR BINDING IN VITRO.
004198 04-04

LITHIUM AND MOTOR-ACTIVITY OF ANIMALS: EFFECTS AND POSSIBLE MECHANISM-OF-ACTION.
004222 04-04

THE EFFECT OF MEBICAR ON THE CONDITION OF ANIMALS UNDER CERTAIN EXTREME CIRCUMSTANCES.
004262 04-04

ANIONS
GABA-RECEPTORS REGULATE THE AFFINITIES OF ANIONS REQUIRED FOR BRAIN SPECIFIC BENZODIAZEPINE BINDING.
002903 03-03

ANISAMIDE
NEUROPHYSIOLOGICAL-STUDY OF TWO O ANISAMIDE DERIVATIVES: SULPIRIDE AND SULTOPRIDE.
001170 02-03

ANISAMIDES
PHARMACOLOGICAL REFLECTIONS ON O ANISAMIDES.
002292 02-13

ANISOMYCIN
EFFECTS OF ANISOMYCIN ON RETENTION OF THE PASSIVE-AVOIDANCE HABIT AS A FUNCTION OF AGE.
004097 04-04

ANOCOCCYGEUS-MUSCLE
EFFECT OF MIANSERIN ON NORADRENERGIC TRANSMISSION IN THE RAT ANOCOCCYGEUS-MUSCLE.
000075 01-03

ANORECTIC-ACTIONS
DOUBLE-BLIND EVALUATION OF REINFORCING AND ANORECTIC-ACTIONS OF WEIGHT-CONTROL MEDICATIONS: INTERACTION OF PHARMACOLOGICAL-TREATMENT AND BEHAVIORAL-TREATMENTS.
002314 02-14
THE EFFECT OF THE DOPAMINE-RECEPTOR BLOCKING-DRUG PIMOZIDE ON THE STIMULANT AND ANORECTIC-ACTIONS OF DEXTROAMPHETAMINE IN MAN.
004580 04-14

ANORECTIC-ACTIVITY
EFFECT OF DESMETHYLIMIPRAMINE ON TISSUE DISTRIBUTION AND ANORECTIC-ACTIVITY OF CHLORPHENTERMINE IN RATS.
004179 04-04

ANORECTIC-AGENTS
EFFECTS OF SPIPERONE ALONE AND IN COMBINATION WITH ANORECTIC-AGENTS ON FEEDING PARAMETERS IN THE RAT.
001598 02-04
INTERACTIONS OF CHLORDIAZEPOXIDE AND ANORECTIC-AGENTS ON RATE AND DURATION PARAMETERS OF FEEDING IN THE RAT.
001600 02-04

ANORECTIC-DRUGS
PSYCHOPHARMACOLOGY OF ANORECTIC-DRUGS IN MAN.
002607 02-17

ANORECTIC-EFFECT
ANORECTIC-EFFECT OF LISURIDE AND OTHER ERGOT DERIVATIVES IN THE RAT.
000042 01-03

ANORECTIC-PROPERTIES
ANORECTIC-PROPERTIES OF A NEW LONG ACTING SEROTONIN UPTAKE INHIBITOR.
004105 04-04

ANOREXIA
ATTENUATION OF AMPHETAMINE ANOREXIA IN RATS FOLLOWING SUBCHRONIC-TREATMENT WITH A TRICYCLIC-ANTIDEPRESSANT.
000501 01-04
THE EFFECTS OF PARA CHLOROAMPHETAMINE ON FENFLURAMINE ANOREXIA IN AD LIBITUM AND STIMULATION-INDUCED FEEDING IN THE RAT.
001823 02-04
DIFFERENTIAL-EFFECTS OF PHARMACOLOGICAL-AGENTS ACTING ON MONOAMINERGIC SYSTEMS ON DRUG-INDUCED ANOREXIA.
002533 02-17
SUBSTITUTED PHENETHYLAMINES AND ANOREXIA.
002541 02-17
EVIDENCE THAT IT IS POSSIBLE TO CAUSE ANOREXIA BY INCREASING RELEASE AND/OR DIRECTLY STIMULATING POSTSYNAPTIC SEROTONIN-RECEPTORS IN THE BRAIN.
002602 02-17
EFFECTS OF A HIGH-DOSE TREATMENT OF METHAMPHETAMINE ON CAUDATE DOPAMINE AND ANOREXIA IN RATS.
004073 04-04
NALOXONE FAILS TO BLOCK AMPHETAMINE-INDUCED ANOREXIA AND CONDITIONED TASTE-AVERSION.
004121 04-04

ANOREXIA-NERVOSA
BODY-WEIGHT AND RESPONSES TO LHRH INFUSION IN ANOREXIA-NERVOSA.
002062 02-10
HORMONAL ABNORMALITIES IN ANOREXIA-NERVOSA (AN).
002099 02-11
NALOXONE IN THE TREATMENT OF ANOREXIA-NERVOSA: EFFECT ON WEIGHT-GAIN AND LIPOLYSIS.
003342 03-11
TREATMENT OF UNDERNUTRITION AND ELECTROLYTE-DISTURBANCES IN ANOREXIA-NERVOSA.
004531 04-13
ANOREXIA-NERVOSA. SYMPTOMS, COURSE AND POSSIBILITIES FOR TREATMENT.
004711 04-17

ANOREXIC
THE ANOREXIC AND ACTOMETRIC EFFECTS OF COCAINE AND TWO COCA-EXTRACTS.
000344 01-04

ANOSMIA
EFFECTS OF OLFACTORY-BULBECTOMY AND PERIPHERALLY-INDUCED ANOSMIA ON THERMOREGULATION IN THE RAT: SUSCEPTIBILITY TO ANTIDEPRESSANT-DRUGS.
004113 04-04

ANOXIC
INTRACELLULAR REDOX STATES UNDER HALOTHANE AND BARBITURATE ANESTHESIA IN NORMAL, ISCHEMIC, AND ANOXIC MONKEY BRAIN.
000295 01-03

ANTAGONISM
CONVULSANTS ANTAGONISE INHIBITION IN THE OLFACTORY-CORTEX SLICE.
001466 02-03

ANTAGONISES
ETHYL-BETA-CARBOLINE-3-CARBOXYLATE ANTAGONISES THE EFFECT OF DIAZEPAM ON A FUNCTIONAL GABA-RECEPTOR.
001378 02-03

ANTAGONISM
NALOXONE ANTAGONISM OF GABA-EVOKED MEMBRANE POLARIZATIONS IN CULTURED MOUSE SPINAL-CORD NEURONS.
000116 01-03
ANTAGONISM OF INTRASTRIATAL AND INTRAVENOUS KAINIC-ACID BY 1 NUCIFERINE: COMPARISON WITH VARIOUS ANTICONVULSANTS AND GABAMIMETICS.
000188 01-03
METERGOLINE ANTAGONISM OF 5 HYDROXYTRYPTAMINE-INDUCED ACTIVATION OF RAT-CEREBRAL-CORTICAL NA-K-ATPASE.
000329 01-03
MORPHINE EFFECTS UPON DISCRIMINATED APPROACH AND DISCRIMINATED AVOIDANCE IN RATS: ANTAGONISM BY NALOXONE.
000338 01-04
REWARD SYSTEM DEPRESSION FOLLOWING CHRONIC AMPHETAMINE: ANTAGONISM BY HALOPERIDOL.
000342 01-04
METHIONINE-ENKEPHALIN ANTAGONISM AND ENDORPHIN POTENTIATION OF NARCOTIC-INDUCED ANALGESIA.
000357 01-04
STEREOSPECIFIC, DOSE-DEPENDENT ANTAGONISM BY NALOXONE OF NONOPIATE BEHAVIOR IN MICE.
000411 01-04
ANTAGONISM BY CLASSICAL ANTIEPILEPTICS AND SODIUM-VALPROATE OF CEFAZOLIN-INDUCED EXPERIMENTAL EPILEPSY IN RATS.
000442 01-04
THE NEW ANTIDEPRESSANT PIRLINDOLE: ANTAGONISM OF ACUTE OVERDOSAGE IN THE MOUSE.
001082 02-02
ANTAGONISM OF THE RENAL VASODILATOR ACTIVITY OF DOPAMINE BY METOCLOPRAMIDE.
001265 02-03
ANTAGONISM OF 5 HYDROXYTRYPTAMINE-RECEPTORS BY QUIPAZINE.
001329 02-03
ANTAGONISM OF 2 DEOXY-D-GLUCOSE-INDUCED HYPERPHAGIA BY NALOXONE: POSSIBLE INVOLVEMENT OF ENDORPHINS.
001773 02-04
LITHIUM ANTAGONISM OF ETHANOL-INDUCED DEPLETION OF CEREBELLAR GUANOSINE-CYCLIC-MONOPHOSPHATE AND STIMULATION OF STRIATAL DOPAMINE RELEASE.
002242 02-13
APOMORPHINE HALOPERIDOL INTERACTIONS: DIFFERENT TYPES OF ANTAGONISM IN CORTICAL AND SUBCORTICAL BRAIN REGIONS.
002662 03-03
SELECTIVE SYNAPTIC ANTAGONISM BY ATROPINE AND ALPHA AMINOADIPATE OF PULVINAR AND CORTICAL AFFERENTS TO THE SUPRASYLVIAN VISUAL AREA (CLARE-BISHOP AREA).
002752 03-03
CALCIUM ANTAGONISM OF THE INHIBITORY-EFFECTS OF FENTANYL ON THE CONTRACTION OF THE NICTITATING MEMBRANE IN CATS.
002876 03-03
ANTAGONISM BY CHLORNALTREXAMINE OF SOME EFFECTS OF DELTA9 TETRAHYDROCANNABINOL IN RATS.
003104 03-04
ANTAGONISM OF INTRAVENOUS COCAINE LETHALITY IN NONHUMAN PRIMATES.
003127 03-05
CHLORPROMAZINE, HALOPERIDOL, METOCLOPRAMIDE AND DOMPERIDONE RELEASE PROLACTIN THROUGH DOPAMINE ANTAGONISM AT LOW CONCENTRATIONS BUT PARADOXICALLY INHIBIT PROLACTIN RELEASE AT HIGH-CONCENTRATIONS.
003731 04-03
ANTAGONISM OF ETHANOL-INDUCED DECREASE IN LH BY P CHLOROPHENYLALANINE: LACK OF CORRELATION WITH ALTERED SEROTONERGIC MECHANISMS.
003748 04-03
PRESYNAPTIC AND POSTSYNAPTIC ALPHA-ADRENOCEPTOR ANTAGONISM BY NEUROLEPTICS IN VIVO.
003966 04-03
USE OF THE INTRACEREBRAL INJECTION TECHNIQUE TO ELUCIDATE MECHANISMS OF APOMORPHINE CLIMBING AND ITS ANTAGONISM IN THE MOUSE.
004092 04-04
ANTAGONISM OF SOME CENTRAL-EFFECTS OF D TUBOCURARINE BY GAMMA AMINOBUTYRIC-ACID.
004102 04-04
IS DOPAMINE ANTAGONISM A REQUISITE OF NEUROLEPTIC ACTIVITY?
004122 04-04
BENZODIAZEPINE ANTAGONISM BY HARMANE AND OTHER BETA CARBOLINES IN VITRO AND IN VIVO.
004211 04-04
ANTAGONISM BY PHENOXYBENZAMINE AND PENTAZOCINE OF THE ANTINOCICEPTIVE-EFFECTS OF MORPHINE IN THE SPINAL-CORD.
004213 04-04
ANTAGONISM OF DOPAMINE SUPERSENSITIVITY BY ESTROGEN: NEUROCHEMICAL-STUDIES IN AN ANIMAL-MODEL OF TARDIVE-DYSKINESIA.
004268 04-05

ANTAGONISMS
DIFFERENTIATION OF KAINATE AND QUISQUALATE-RECEPTORS IN THE CAT SPINAL-CORD BY SELECTIVE ANTAGONISMS WITH GAMMA D(AND L) GLUTAMYLGLYCINE.
002696 03-03

ANTAGONIST
THE CRYSTAL AND MOLECULAR STRUCTURE OF THE ACETYLCHOLINE ANTAGONIST DIMETHYLAMINOBUTYNYLCYCLOHEXYLHYDROXY 2 PHENYLACETATE HCL.
000003 01-01
ALPHA FLUPENTHIXOL: AN ANTAGONIST OF DOPAMINE-EVOKED FLUID SECRETION BY AN INSECT SALIVARY-GLAND PREPARATION.
000031 01-03
HYPOALGESIA INDUCED BY MICROINJECTION OF A NOREPINEPHRINE ANTAGONIST IN THE RAPHE-MAGNUS: REVERSAL BY INTRATHECAL ADMINISTRATION OF A SEROTONIN ANTAGONIST.
000121 01-03
CHLOROETHYLNORAPOMORPHINE, A PROPOSED LONG-ACTING DOPAMINE ANTAGONIST: INTERACTIONS WITH DOPAMINE-RECEPTORS OF MAMMALIAN FOREBRAIN IN VITRO.
001114 02-03
REGULATION OF RECEPTOR BINDING INTERACTIONS OF 125I ANGIOTENSIN-II AND 125I SARCOSINE1-LEUCINEB-ANGIOTENSIN-II, AN ANGIOTENSIN ANTAGONIST, BY SODIUM-ION.
001124 02-03
RECEPTOR BINDING INTERACTIONS OF THE ANGIOTENSIN-II ANTAGONIST, 125I SARCOSINE1-LEUCINEB-ANGIOTENSIN-II, WITH MAMMALIAN BRAIN AND PERIPHERAL TISSUES.
001125 02-03
THE AFFINITIES OF ERGOT COMPOUNDS FOR DOPAMINE AGONIST AND DOPAMINE ANTAGONIST RECEPTOR SITES.
001254 02-03
UNITARY DOPAMINERGIC-RECEPTOR COMPOSED OF COOPERATIVELY LINKED AGONIST AND ANTAGONIST SUBUNIT BINDING-SITES.
001342 02-03
EFFECTS OF HALOPERIDOL, A DOPAMINE-RECEPTOR ANTAGONIST, ON A DELAYED TYPE HYPERSENSITIVITY REACTION TO 1 CHLORODINITROBENZENE IN MICE.
001473 02-03
NARCOTIC ANTAGONIST PRECIPITATED ABSTINENCE: RELATIONSHIP TO WITHDRAWAL INDUCING BENZAZOCINES. (PH.D. DISSERTATION).
001518 02-03
MORPHINE ANALGESIA AFTER INTRATHECAL ADMINISTRATION OF A NARCOTIC AGONIST, CHLOROXYMORPHAMINE AND ANTAGONIST, CHLORNALTREXAMINE.
001695 02-04
DOPAMINE ANTAGONIST AND AGONIST TREATMENT OF TARDIVE-DYSKINESIA.
002377 02-15
RECEPTOR BINDING PROFILE OF R-41-468, A NOVEL ANTAGONIST AT 5 HT2-RECEPTORS.
002648 03-02
DIFFERENTIAL REGULATION BY GUANINE-NUCLEOTIDES OF OPIATE AGONIST AND ANTAGONIST RECEPTOR INTERACTIONS.
002688 03-03
OPIATE ANTAGONIST IMPROVES NEUROLOGIC RECOVERY AFTER SPINAL INJURY.
002714 03-03
PROPERTIES OF DOPAMINE AGONIST AND ANTAGONIST BINDING-SITES IN MAMMALIAN RETINA.
002814 03-03
DOPAMINERGIC AGONIST AND ANTAGONIST EFFECTS ON STRIATAL TYROSINE-HYDROXYLASE DISTRIBUTION.
002898 03-03
A COMPARISON OF HUMAN MUSCARINIC CHOLINERGIC-RECEPTOR RESPONSE TO A NUMBER OF PSYCHOTROPICS UTILIZING THE RADIOLABELED ANTAGONIST, (3H) QUINUCLIDINYL-BENZILATE. (PH.D. DISSERTATION).
002918 03-03
ENHANCEMENT OF APOMORPHINE-INDUCED CLIMBING IN MICE BY REVERSIBLE AND IRREVERSIBLE NARCOTIC ANTAGONIST DRUGS.
003068 03-04
MORPHINE-LIKE STIMULUS EFFECTS IN THE MONKEY: OPIOIDS WITH ANTAGONIST PROPERTIES.
003086 03-04
GABA AND SCHIZOPHRENIA: STUDY OF THE ACTION OF A GABAERGIC ANTAGONIST. PROGABIDE OR SL-76-002.
003175 03-08
THE USE OF A MORPHINE ANTAGONIST (NALOXONE) IN THE TREATMENT OF DISSOCIATIVE-SYNDROMES.
003194 03-08
CLINICAL-PHARMACOLOGY OF MIXED AGONIST ANTAGONIST DRUGS.
003329 03-11
STRUCTURE-ACTIVITY AND RECEPTOR BINDING OF ANTAGONIST ANALGESICS.
003611 03-17
THE DOPAMINE-RECEPTOR ANTAGONIST DOMPERIDONE IS ALSO A COMPETITIVE ANTAGONIST AT ALPHA1-ADRENOCEPTORS.
003785 04-03

RESPONSE OF STRIATONIGRAL SUBSTANCE-P SYSTEMS TO A DOPAMINE-RECEPTOR AGONIST AND ANTAGONIST.
003826 04-03
ISOMERIZATION OF THE MUSCARINIC-RECEPTOR ANTAGONIST COMPLEX.
003860 04-03
EFFECTS OF MORPHINE AND CAFFEINE ON ADENOSINE RELEASE FROM RAT-CEREBRAL-CORTEX: IS CAFFEINE A MORPHINE ANTAGONIST.
003864 04-03
ACTIONS OF MU, KAPPA, SIGMA, DELTA AND AGONIST/ANTAGONIST OPIATES ON STRIATAL DOPAMINERGIC FUNCTION.
004053 04-03
PHARMACOLOGICAL-STUDIES WITH AN ALKYLATING NARCOTIC AGONIST, CHLOROXYMORPHAMINE, AND ANTAGONIST, CHLORNALTREXAMINE.
004082 04-04
ANALGESIC AND OTHER PHARMACOLOGICAL ACTIVITIES OF A NEW NARCOTIC ANTAGONIST ANALGESIC (-) 1 3 METHYLBUTENYLHYDROXYPHENYLPHENYLETHYLPIPERAZINE AND ITS ENANTIOMORPH IN EXPERIMENTAL ANIMALS.
004185 04-04
NALOXAZONE, A LONG-ACTING OPIATE ANTAGONIST: EFFECTS ON ANALGESIA IN INTACT ANIMALS AND ON OPIATE-RECEPTOR BINDING IN VITRO.
004198 04-04
HUMAN PLATELET ALPHA2-ADRENERGIC-RECEPTORS: LABELING WITH 3H YOHIMBINE, A SELECTIVE ANTAGONIST LIGAND.
004676 04-16

ANTAGONISTIC-EFFECTS
ANTAGONISTIC-EFFECTS OF PROPRANOLOL UPON ETHANOL-INDUCED NARCOSIS IN MICE.
000439 01-04
ANTAGONISTIC-EFFECTS OF PSYCHOLEPTIC-DRUGS ON STRESS-INDUCED ANALGESIA.
001609 02-04

ANTAGONISTS
SUPPRESSION OF SEROTONERGIC NEURONAL FIRING BY ALPHA-ADRENOCEPTOR ANTAGONISTS: EVIDENCE AGAINST GABA MEDIATION.
000024 01-03
EFFECTS OF DOPAMINERGIC AGONISTS AND ANTAGONISTS ON (3H)APOMORPHINE BINDING TO STRIATAL MEMBRANES; SULPIRIDE LACK OF INTERACTIONS WITH POSITIVE COOPERATIVE (3H)APOMORPHINE BINDING.
000099 01-03
HYPOALGESIA FOLLOWING MICROINJECTION OF NORADRENERGIC ANTAGONISTS IN THE NUCLEUS-RAPHE-MAGNUS.
000122 01-03
COMPARTMENTATION OF CATECHOLAMINES IN RAT-BRAIN: EFFECTS OF AGONISTS AND ANTAGONISTS.
000125 01-03
EFFECTS OF NORADRENERGIC AGONISTS AND ANTAGONISTS ON GROWTH-HORMONE SECRETION UNDER GAMMA HYDROXYBUTYRATE NARCOANALGESIA IN THE RAT.
000262 01-03
EFFECTS OF ANTICONVULSANTS AND GLUTAMATE ANTAGONISTS ON THE CONVULSIVE ACTION OF KAINIC-ACID.
000288 01-03
ON THE CAPACITY OF PRESYNAPTIC ALPHA-RECEPTORS TO MODULATE NOREPINEPHRINE RELEASE FROM SLICES OF RAT NEOCORTEX AND THE AFFINITY OF SOME AGONISTS AND ANTAGONISTS FOR THESE RECEPTORS.
000323 01-03
POSTSWIM GROOMING IN MICE INHIBITED BY DOPAMINE-RECEPTOR ANTAGONISTS AND BY CANNABINOIDS.
000359 01-04
NORADRENERGIC AGONISTS AND ANTAGONISTS: EFFECTS ON CONDITIONED FEAR AS MEASURED BY THE POTENTIATED STARTLE PARADIGM.
000372 01-04
ROTATION INDUCED BY INTRANIGRAL INJECTIONS OF GABA AGONISTS AND ANTAGONISTS: ZONE-SPECIFIC EFFECTS.
000422 01-04
BETA-ADRENOCEPTOR ANTAGONISTS: STUDIES ON BEHAVIOUR (DELAYED DIFFERENTIATION) IN THE MONKEY (MACACA-MULATTA).
000440 01-04
NOREPINEPHRINE UPTAKE INHIBITORS AS BIOCHEMICALLY-SELECTIVE AND BEHAVIORALLY-SELECTIVE ANTAGONISTS OF THE LOCOMOTOR-STIMULATION INDUCED BY INDIRECTLY ACTING SYMPATHOMIMETIC-AMINES IN MICE.
000492 01-04
GUANINE-NUCLEOTIDES INHIBIT BINDING OF AGONISTS AND ANTAGONISTS TO SOLUBLE OPIATE-RECEPTORS. (UNPUBLISHED PAPER).
001035 02-01
EFFECTS OF ALPHA-ADRENOCEPTOR AGONISTS AND ANTAGONISTS AND OF ANTIDEPRESSANT-DRUGS ON PRESYNAPTIC AND POSTSYNAPTIC ALPHA-ADRENOCEPTORS.
001146 02-03

Subject Index

INTERACTION-STUDIES BETWEEN NARCOTIC ANALGESICS, NARCOTIC ANTAGONISTS AND ETHANOL: STUDIES DURING ACUTE AND CHRONIC-TREATMENT AND WITHDRAWAL STATES IN RATS AND MICE. (PH.D. DISSERTATION).
001165 02-03

A PROPOSED MODE OF ACTION FOR NARCOTIC AGONISTS AND ANTAGONISTS.
001168 02-03

EFFECT OF GABA AGONIST AND ANTAGONISTS ON CARDIOVASCULAR AND SYMPATHETIC RESPONSES IN SHR AND WKY RATS. (UNPUBLISHED PAPER).
001224 02-03

ATTEMPTS TO DEVELOP SUPERSENSITIVITY OR SUBSENSITIVITY RETINAL DOPAMINE-RECEPTORS AFTER VARIOUS TREATMENTS WITH ANTAGONISTS OR AGONISTS.
001350 02-03

AMINOPHYLLINE AND THEOPHYLLINE DERIVATIVES AS ANTAGONISTS OF NEURONAL DEPRESSION BY ADENOSINE: A MICROIONTOPHORETIC-STUDY.
001410 02-03

RETROGRADE AMNESIA PRODUCED BY ELECTRICAL-STIMULATION OF THE AMYGDALA: ATTENUATION WITH ADRENERGIC ANTAGONISTS. (UNPUBLISHED PAPER).
001488 02-03

NEGLIGIBLE AFFINITY OF HISTAMINE H2-RECEPTOR ANTAGONISTS FOR CENTRAL ALPHA1-ADRENOCEPTORS.
001508 02-03

OPIATE ANTAGONISTS AND LONG-TERM ANALGESIC REACTION INDUCED BY INESCAPABLE SHOCK IN RATS.
001707 02-04

OPIATE ANTAGONISTS AND FEMALE FUNCTIONING. (UNPUBLISHED PAPER).
001735 02-04

LACK OF EFFECT OF CHOLINE AND NARCOTIC ANTAGONISTS UPON APOMORPHINE DISCRIMINATION.
001770 02-04

BIPHASIC-EFFECTS OF DIRECT, BUT NOT INDIRECT, GABAMIMETICS AND ANTAGONISTS ON HALOPERIDOL-INDUCED CATALEPSY.
001826 02-04

DISPOSITION AND ACTIVITY OF BETA-ADRENOCEPTOR ANTAGONISTS IN THE RAT USING AN EX VIVO RECEPTOR BINDING ASSAY.
001878 02-06

CHARACTERIZATION OF ERGOT AND NONERGOT SEROTONIN ANTAGONISTS BY PROLACTIN AND GROWTH-HORMONE PROFILES DURING WAKEFULNESS AND SLEEP.
002217 02-13

EFFECT OF OPIATES AND OPIATE ANTAGONISTS ON SOMATOSENSORY EVOKED-POTENTIALS IN PATIENTS WITH SCHIZOPHRENIA AND NORMAL ADULTS.
002222 02-13

SELECTIVE ANTAGONISTS OF BENZODIAZEPINES.
002646 03-02

GABA ANTAGONISTS ENHANCE DOPAMINE TURNOVER IN THE RAT RETINA IN VIVO.
002772 03-03

THE EFFECTS OF OPIATE ANTAGONISTS ON THE DISCRIMINATIVE STIMULUS PROPERTIES OF ETHANOL.
002947 03-04

THE EFFECTS OF OPIATE ANTAGONISTS ON FOOD INTAKE ARE STEREOSPECIFIC.
003080 03-04

SUPERSENSITIVITY TO THE BEHAVIORAL-EFFECTS OF OPIATE ANTAGONISTS.
003096 03-04

THE RELATIONSHIP BETWEEN THE ACUTE BEHAVIORAL-EFFECTS OF NARCOTIC ANTAGONISTS AND THE NARCOTIC DEPENDENT STATE.
003106 03-04

INFUSIONS INTO THE OCULOMOTOR NUCLEUS OR NERVE: A METHOD OF ESTIMATING THE DOSAGE AT WHICH TRANSMITTER ANTAGONISTS INFUSED INTRACRANIALLY PRODUCE NONSPECIFIC BLOCKING OF NEURAL ACTIVITY.
003134 03-06

PHARMACOLOGICAL ANTAGONISTS OF EXCITANT AMINO-ACID ACTION.
003587 03-17

PRESYNAPTIC MODULATION OF SYNAPTIC TRANSMISSION IN HELIX-POMATIA: THE EFFECTS OF SEROTONIN AND DOPAMINE ANTAGONISTS.
003869 04-03

DOPAMINERGIC MECHANISMS IN THE TELEOST RETINA. I. DOPAMINE-SENSITIVE ADENYLATE-CYCLASE IN HOMOGENATES OF CARP RETINA; EFFECTS OF AGONISTS, ANTAGONISTS AND ERGOTS.
004051 04-03

A COMPARISON OF THE RESPONSES TO SOME DOPAMINE-RECEPTOR AGONISTS AND ANTAGONISTS IN THE ISOLATED PERFUSED RAT KIDNEY.
004054 04-03

HISTAMINE AS A PUNISHER IN SQUIRREL-MONKEYS: EFFECTS OF PENTOBARBITAL, CHLORDIAZEPOXIDE AND H1-RECEPTOR AND H2-RECEPTOR ANTAGONISTS ON BEHAVIOR AND CARDIOVASCULAR RESPONSE.
004119 04-04

CHOLINERGIC, DOPAMINERGIC, NORADRENERGIC, OR GLUTAMINERGIC STIMULATION VENTRAL TO THE ANTERIOR SEPTUM DOES NOT SPECIFICALLY SUPPRESS DEFENSIVE-BEHAVIOR.
002945 03-04

ROLE OF THE ANTERIOR PITUITARY GABA-RECEPTOR IN THE CONTROL OF PROLACTIN RELEASE.
003809 04-03

EFFECTS OF CAFFEINE ON ANTERIOR PITUITARY AND THYROID-FUNCTION IN THE RAT.
004014 04-03

ANTERIOR-CHAMBER
SEIZURES AND RELATED EPILEPTIFORM ACTIVITY IN HIPPOCAMPUS TRANSPLANTED TO THE ANTERIOR-CHAMBER OF THE EYE: MODULATION BY CHOLINERGIC AND ADRENERGIC INPUT.
000095 01-03

ANTERIOR-FOREBRAIN
RELATIONSHIPS BETWEEN SELECTIVE DENERVATION OF DOPAMINE TERMINAL-FIELDS IN THE ANTERIOR-FOREBRAIN AND BEHAVIORAL-RESPONSES TO AMPHETAMINE AND APOMORPHINE.
000384 01-04

ANTEROGRADE
TIME-DEPENDENT CHANGES IN ANTEROGRADE SCOPOLAMINE-INDUCED AMNESIA IN RATS.
004182 04-04

ANTI-BETA-ENDORPHIN
SUPPRESSION OF SERUM PROLACTIN BY NALOXONE BUT NOT BY ANTI-BETA-ENDORPHIN ANTISERUM IN STRESSED AND UNSTRESSED RATS.
002871 03-03

ANTI-DELTA9-TETRAHYDROCANNABINOL
IN VIVO AND IN VITRO PROPERTIES OF ANTI-DELTA9-TETRAHYDROCANNABINOL ANTIBODY.
003751 04-03

ANTI-RAT
CORTICOSTERONE INCREASES THE SYNTHESIS OF A SOLUBLE PROTEIN IN PITUITARY-GLANDS FROM ADRENALECTOMIZED MALE RATS WHICH PRECIPITATES WITH ANTI-RAT GROWTH-HORMONE ANTISERUM. (UNPUBLISHED PAPER).
001122 02-03

ANTI-THY-1-2
ANTI-THY-1-2 MONOCLONAL ANTIBODY LINKED TO RICIN IS A POTENT CELL TYPE SPECIFIC TOXIN. (UNPUBLISHED PAPER).
001064 02-01

ANTIADRENERGIC
ADRENERGIC NONSPECIFIC POTENTIATION OF YOHIMBINE TOXICITY IN MICE BY ANTIDEPRESSANTS AND RELATED DRUGS AND ANTIYOHIMBINE ACTION OF ANTIADRENERGIC AND SEROTONERGIC DRUGS.
001330 02-03

ANTIALCOHOLISM-DRUG
ARCALION-200 PRESCRIBED AS A PSYCHIATRIC-DRUG AND ANTIALCOHOLISM-DRUG ON AN OUTPATIENT AND INPATIENT BASIS.
002103 02-11

ANTIANDROGENS
PHARMACOTHERAPY FOR SEXUAL-OFFENDERS: REVIEW OF THE ACTION OF ANTIANDROGENS WITH SPECIAL REFERENCE TO THEIR PSYCHIC-EFFECTS.
004455 04-11

CLINICAL APPLICATION OF ANTIANDROGENS IN PSYCHIATRY.
004457 04-11

ANTIANXIETY
1 AMINOALKYL-6-ARYL-4H-S-TRIAZOLOBENZODIAZEPINES WITH ANTIANXIETY AND ANTIDEPRESSANT ACTIVITY.
001074 02-02

2,4 DIHYDRO-6-PHENYL-1H-S-TRIAZOLOBENZODIAZEPIN-1-ONES WITH ANTIANXIETY AND ANTIDEPRESSANT ACTIVITY.
001075 02-02

6 SUBSTITUTED AMINO-4H-S-TRIAZOLOBENZODIAZEPINES AND 4 SUBSTITUTED AMINO-6H-S-TRIAZOLOBENZODIAZEPINES WITH POTENTIAL ANTIANXIETY ACTIVITY.
001076 02-02

PHARMACOLOGY OF 1 DICHLOROBENZYL-TETRAHYDROPYRIMIDONE, A NOVEL ANTIDEPRESSANT COMPOUND WITH ANTIANXIETY ACTIVITY.
003688 04-02

THE EFFECTS OF ANTIANXIETY AND ANTIPSYCHOTIC-DRUGS ON SEXUAL-BEHAVIOR.
004657 04-15

AN EVALUATION OF THE ANTIANXIETY ACTION AND SIDE-EFFECTS OF PROPRANOLOL.
004660 04-15

ANTIANXIETY-AGENT
HOSTILITY PRODUCTION AS A COMMON FEATURE OF ANTIANXIETY-AGENT ACTION.
004654 04-15

ANTIANXIETY-AGENTS
ANTIANXIETY-AGENTS AND SYNAPTIC TRANSMISSION IN THE BRAIN: ELECTROPHYSIOLOGICAL-STUDIES. (PH.D. DISSERTATION).
002840 03-03

ANTIANXIETY-DRUG
PERSONALITY TRAIT AND ANTIANXIETY-DRUG EFFECTS ON PSYCHOMOTOR PERFORMANCE.
002336 02-14

ANTIANXIETY-DRUGS
EFFECT OF ANTIANXIETY-DRUGS ON FEAR AND STRESS.
000801 01-14

POSSIBLE LIMBIC SITES OF ACTION OF ANTIANXIETY-DRUGS.
002069 02-10

DISINHIBITION OF BEHAVIOR BY ANTIANXIETY-DRUGS.
002403 02-15

ANTIANXIETY-EFFECTS
METHODS AND METHODOLOGICAL-CONSIDERATIONS IN MEASURING ANTIANXIETY-EFFECTS OF TRANQUILIZING-DRUGS.
002537 02-17

ANTIARRHYTHMIC-ACTIVITY
ANTIARRHYTHMIC-ACTIVITY OF AMITRIPTYLINE ANALOGUES IN CONSCIOUS DOGS AFTER MYOCARDIAL-INFARCTION: CYPROHEPTADINIUM-METHIODIDE.
001534 02-03

ANTIAVOIDANCE
CORRELATION BETWEEN ANTIAVOIDANCE ACTIVITIES OF ANTIPSYCHOTIC-DRUGS IN RATS AND DAILY CLINICAL DOSES.
003032 03-04

ANTIBIOTICS
EFFECTS OF THREE ANTIBIOTICS ON THEOPHYLLINE KINETICS.
000784 01-13

ANTIBODIES
AFFINITY CHROMATOGRAPHY OF THE BETA-ADRENERGIC-RECEPTOR AND CHARACTERIZATION OF ANTIBODIES RAISED AGAINST PURIFIED RECEPTOR PREPARATIONS.
001009 02-01

ABNORMAL MATURATION OF CEREBRAL-CORTEX AND BEHAVIORAL-DEFICIT IN ADULT RATS AFTER NEONATAL ADMINISTRATION OF ANTIBODIES TO GANGLIOSIDE.
003025 03-04

BEHAVIOURAL-CHANGES IN ADULT RATS FOLLOWING ADMINISTRATION OF ANTIBODIES AGAINST BRAIN GANGLIOSIDES.
003071 03-04

ANTIBODY
PRODUCTION OF A SPECIFIC ANTISERUM TO RAT-BRAIN GLUTAMIC-ACID-DECARBOXYLASE (GAD) BY INJECTION OF AN ANTIGEN ANTIBODY COMPLEX. (UNPUBLISHED PAPER).
001047 02-01

ANTI-THY-1-2 MONOCLONAL ANTIBODY LINKED TO RICIN IS A POTENT CELL TYPE SPECIFIC TOXIN. (UNPUBLISHED PAPER).
001064 02-01

IN VIVO AND IN VITRO PROPERTIES OF ANTI-DELTA9-TETRAHYDROCANNABINOL ANTIBODY.
003751 04-03

ANTICANDIDAL-ACTIVITY
ANTICANDIDAL-ACTIVITY OF PYRIMIDINE-PEPTIDE CONJUGATES.
001059 02-01

ANTICHOLINERGIC
DIAZEPAM IN COMBINATION WITH TACRINE DERIVATIVES ANTAGONIZES BEHAVIOURAL-EFFECTS OF ANTICHOLINERGIC PSYCHOTOMIMETICS IN RATS.
000420 01-04

LONG-TERM APPLICATION OF HALOPERIDOL; EFFECT OF ANTICHOLINERGIC TREATMENT ON THE RATE OF DOPAMINE SYNTHESIS.
001490 02-03

ANTICHOLINERGIC-ACTIVITY
THE PERIPHERAL ANTICHOLINERGIC-ACTIVITY OF TRICYCLIC-ANTIDEPRESSANTS: COMPARISON OF AMITRIPTYLINE AND DESIPRAMINE IN HUMAN VOLUNTEERS.
002298 02-13

SELF-STIMULATION AND LOCOMOTOR CHANGES INDICATING LATENT ANTICHOLINERGIC-ACTIVITY BY AN ATYPICAL NEUROLEPTIC (THIORIDAZINE).
0035^0 03-16

ANTICHOLINERGIC-DRUGS
INDIVIDUAL DIFFERENCES IN EFFECTS OF TRICYCLIC-ANTIDEPRESSANTS AND ANTICHOLINERGIC-DRUGS ON OPERANT-BEHAVIOR IN THE SQUIRREL-MONKEY.
004176 04-04

ANTICHOLINERGIC-EFFECTS
STUDIES ON THE PUTATIVE ANTICHOLINERGIC-EFFECTS OF DESMETHYLIMIPRAMINE.
000228 01-03

ANTICHOLINERGIC-EFFECTS AND PLASMA DESIPRAMINE LEVELS.
004550 04-13

ANTICHOLINERGIC-SYNDROME
THE INTERACTION OF ANTICHOLINESTERASES AND DIAZEPAM IN THE TREATMENT OF ANTICHOLINERGIC-SYNDROME IN DOGS.
000389 01-04

ANTICHOLINERGICS
ANTICHOLINERGICS PROMOTE NEUROLEPTIC-INDUCED TARDIVE-DYSKINESIA.
001834 02-05

ANTICHOLINESTERASES
THE INTERACTION OF ANTICHOLINESTERASES AND DIAZEPAM IN THE TREATMENT OF ANTICHOLINERGIC-SYNDROME IN DOGS.
000389 01-04

COMPARATIVE-STUDY OF AGGRESSIVE-BEHAVIOUR AFTER INJECTION OF
CHOLINOMIMETICS, ANTICHOLINESTERASES, NICOTINIC, AND
MUSCARINIC GANGLIONIC STIMULANTS INTO THE CEREBRAL
VENTRICLES OF CONSCIOUS CATS: FAILURE OF NICOTINIC-DRUGS TO
EVOKE AGGRESSION.
001568 02-04

ANTICONFLICT
RELATIONSHIP OF ANTICONFLICT ACTIVITY OF BENZODIAZEPINES TO
BRAIN RECEPTOR BINDING, SEROTONIN, AND GABA.
000057 01-03

MULTIPLE BENZODIAZEPINE-RECEPTORS: EVIDENCE OF A DISSOCIATION
BETWEEN ANTICONFLICT AND ANTICONVULSANT PROPERTIES BY PK-
8165 AND PK-9084 (TWO QUINOLINE DERIVATIVES).
003898 04-03

ANTICONVULSANT
EFFECT OF DOPAMINERGIC AND GABAERGIC DRUGS GIVEN ALONE OR IN
COMBINATION ON THE ANTICONVULSANT ACTION OF PHENOBARBITAL
AND DIPHENYLHYDANTOIN IN THE ELECTROSHOCK-TEST IN MICE.
000163 01-03

SINGLE-DOSE PHARMACOKINETICS AND ANTICONVULSANT EFFICACY OF
PRIMIDONE IN MICE.
000177 01-03

ANTICONVULSANT AND ANESTHETIC BARBITURATES: DIFFERENT
POSTSYNAPTIC ACTIONS IN CULTURED MAMMALIAN NEURONS.
000194 01-03

STRUCTURE-ACTIVITY RELATIONSHIPS IN THE EFFECTS OF PHENACEMIDE
ANALOGS ON SERUM CREATININE AND ANTICONVULSANT ACTIVITY.
000249 01-03

CORRELATION BETWEEN BENZODIAZEPINE-RECEPTOR OCCUPATION AND
ANTICONVULSANT EFFECTS OF DIAZEPAM.
000450 01-04

PROCONVULSANT AND ANTICONVULSANT ACTION OF MORPHINE IN
RATS.
000494 01-04

3 CHLORO-4-PHENYLSUCCINIMIDOBENZENESULFONAMIDE (GS-385), A
NEW ANTICONVULSANT: ITS QUANTITATIVE DETERMINATION,
PHARMACOKINETICS AND METABOLISM USING HIGH-PERFORMANCE
LIQUID-CHROMATOGRAPHY.
000705 01-11

EVALUATION OF CLORAZEPATE (TRANXENE) AS AN ANTICONVULSANT --
A PILOT-STUDY.
000728 01-11

ON THE GENETIC SIDE-EFFECTS OF PSYCHOTROPIC-SUBSTANCES: I.
PSYCHOPHARMACEUTICALS, NARCOTICS, AND ANTICONVULSANT.
000845 01-15

CONVULSANT AND ANTICONVULSANT BARBITURATES. 1. MOLECULAR
CONFORMATIONS FROM CLASSICAL POTENTIAL ENERGY
CALCULATIONS.
001029 02-01

EEG AND ANTICONVULSANT EFFECTS OF DIPROPYLACETIC-ACID AND
DIPROPYLACETAMIDE IN THE BABOON PAPIO-PAPIO.
001210 02-03

ANTICONVULSANT PROPERTIES OF S ADENOSYL-L-HOMOCYSTEINE.
001227 02-03

DRUG-INDUCED ELEVATION OF GABA AFTER INTRACEREBRAL
MICROINJECTION: SITE OF ANTICONVULSANT ACTION.
001627 02-04

SUBACUTE CANNABINOID TREATMENT: ANTICONVULSANT ACTIVITY AND
WITHDRAWAL EXCITABILITY IN MICE.
001671 02-04

THE ANTICONVULSANT PROPERTIES OF MELATONIN ON KINDLED
SEIZURES IN RATS.
002653 03-03

BARBITURATE ENHANCEMENT OF GABA-MEDIATED INHIBITION AND
ACTIVATION OF CHLORIDE ION-CONDUCTANCE: CORRELATION WITH
ANTICONVULSANT AND ANESTHETIC ACTIONS.
002885 03-03

CORRELATION OF (14C)MUSCIMOL CONCENTRATION IN RAT-BRAIN WITH
ANTICONVULSANT ACTIVITY.
003045 03-04

KETAMINE: CONVULSANT OR ANTICONVULSANT?
003060 03-04

A POSSIBLE ROLE FOR CATECHOLAMINE NEUROTRANSMITTERS IN THE
ANTICONVULSANT ACTIVITY OF CHLORDIAZEPOXIDE.
003119 03-04

ON THE ANTICONVULSANT BLOOD LEVEL IN THERAPY-RESISTANT
EPILEPTIC-PATIENTS.
003300 03-11

A PROSPECTIVE RANDOMISED-TRIAL ON THE EFFECT OF MONITORING
PLASMA ANTICONVULSANT LEVELS IN EPILEPSY.
003314 03-11

ANTICONVULSANT PROPERTIES OF SELECTED PYRROLOPYRIMIDINEDIONES
AND INTERMEDIATES.
003700 04-02

THE EFFECT OF SODIUM-DIPROPYLACETATE ON GAMMA AMINOBUTYRIC-
ACID DEPENDENT INHIBITION IN THE RAT-CORTEX AND SUBSTANTIA-
NIGRA IN RELATION TO ITS ANTICONVULSANT ACTIVITY.
003880 04-03

MULTIPLE BENZODIAZEPINE-RECEPTORS: EVIDENCE OF A DISSOCIATION
BETWEEN ANTICONFLICT AND ANTICONVULSANT PROPERTIES BY PK-
8165 AND PK-9084 (TWO QUINOLINE DERIVATIVES).
003898 04-03

ANTICONVULSANT ACTIVITY OF METABOLITES OF VALPROIC-ACID.
004168 04-04

BIOCHEMICAL-STUDIES OF HUMAN EPILEPTICS DURING ANTICONVULSANT
THERAPY.
004490 04-11

ANTICONVULSANT-AGENTS
SYNTHESIS OF PHENYLURETHANS OF 1,2 DIALKYL-4-PYRAZOLIDINOLS AS
ANTICONVULSANT-AGENTS.
003695 04-02

ANTICONVULSANT-DRUG
3 SULFAMOYLMETHYL-1-2-BENZISOXAZOLE, A NEW TYPE OF
ANTICONVULSANT-DRUG: PHARMACOLOGICAL PROFILE.
000012 01-02

3 SULFAMOYLMETHYL-1-2-BENZISOXAZOLE, A NEW TYPE OF
ANTICONVULSANT-DRUG: ELECTROENCEPHALOGRAPHIC PROFILE.
000142 01-03

PERINATAL EFFECTS OF PSYCHOTROPIC-DRUGS: THE ANTICONVULSANT-
DRUG DIPHENYLHYDANTOIN. (UNPUBLISHED PAPER).
001842 02-05

CONVULSANT AND ANTICONVULSANT-DRUG BINDING-SITES RELATED TO
GABA REGULATED CHLORIDE ION-CHANNELS.
002848 03-03

ANTICONVULSANT-DRUGS
INHIBITORY-EFFECTS OF ANTICONVULSANT-DRUGS ON CYCLIC-
NUCLEOTIDE ACCUMULATION IN BRAIN.
000090 01-03

COMPARATIVE-STUDY OF THE INHIBITION OF GABA-AMINOTRANSFERASE
BY DIFFERENT ANTICONVULSANT-DRUGS.
000192 01-03

PREGNANCY AND EPILEPSY: SHOULD ANTICONVULSANT-DRUGS BE
CONTINUED?
000679 01-11

ANTICONVULSANT-DRUGS AND CANCER.
000855 01-15

PSYCHIATRIC IMPLICATIONS OF ANTICONVULSANT-DRUGS.
002463 02-15

EFFECT OF ANTICONVULSANT-DRUGS ON INHIBITORY AND EXCITATORY
PATHWAYS.
002724 03-03

ACCELERATED METABOLISM OF PROBENECID DURING LONG-TERM-
TREATMENT OF RATS WITH ANTICONVULSANT-DRUGS: EFFECT ON
CENTRAL SEROTONIN TURNOVER STUDIES.
002890 03-03

CHANGES IN REGIONAL BRAIN LEVELS OF AMINO-ACID PUTATIVE
NEUROTRANSMITTERS AFTER PROLONGED TREATMENT WITH THE
ANTICONVULSANT-DRUGS DIPHENYLHYDANTOIN, PHENOBARBITONE,
SODIUM-VALPROATE, ETHOSUXIMIDE, AND SULTHIAME IN THE RAT.
003961 04-03

VARIOUS ASPECTS OF THE EFFECT OF ANTICONVULSANT-DRUGS ON
MEMORY.
004602 04-15

PHARMACOKINETICS OF ANTICONVULSANT-DRUGS.
004738 04-17

ANTICONVULSANT-INDUCED
ANTICONVULSANT-INDUCED STATUS-EPILEPTICUS IN LENNOX-GASTAUT-
SYNDROME.
003467 03-15

ANTICONVULSANTS
CORRELATION BETWEEN MONOAMINE-OXIDASE-INHIBITORS AND
ANTICONVULSANTS.
000081 01-03

ANTAGONISM OF INTRASTRIATAL AND INTRAVENOUS KAINIC-ACID BY 1
NUCIFERINE: COMPARISON WITH VARIOUS ANTICONVULSANTS AND
GABAMIMETICS.
000188 01-03

EFFECTS OF ANTICONVULSANTS AND GLUTAMATE ANTAGONISTS ON THE
CONVULSIVE ACTION OF KAINIC-ACID.
000288 01-03

ANTICONVULSANTS SPECIFIC FOR PETIT-MAL ANTAGONIZE
EPILEPTOGENIC-EFFECT OF LEUCINE-ENKEPHALIN.
000477 01-04

ANTICONVULSANTS AND TREATMENT OF EPILEPSY.
000661 01-11

EFFECTS OF ANTICONVULSANTS AND METHOTREXATE ON CALCIUM
DISPOSITION.
001840 02-05

PLASMA HDL CHOLESTEROL AND GROWTH-HORMONE IN EPILEPTICS
TREATED WITH ANTICONVULSANTS.
002260 02-13

THE QUESTION OF MINIMUM-DOSES OF ANTICONVULSANTS IN THE
TREATMENT OF EPILEPSY.
002306 02-13

CLINICAL-TRIALS OF DEPAKENE (VALPROIC-ACID) COADMINISTERED WITH
OTHER ANTICONVULSANTS IN EPILEPTIC-PATIENTS.
002367 02-14

THE ROLE OF FOLATE DEFICIENCY IN THE DEVELOPMENT OF PERIPHERAL NEUROPATHY CAUSED BY ANTICONVULSANTS.
002402 02-15

HEPATOTOXICITY OF SODIUM-VALPROATE AND OTHER ANTICONVULSANTS IN RAT HEPATOCYTE CULTURES.
002422 02-15

A RAPID GAS-LIQUID-CHROMATOGRAPHY METHOD FOR SIMULTANEOUS DETERMINATION OF VARIOUS ANTICONVULSANTS.
002501 02-16

SAFETY OF ANTICONVULSANTS IN HEPATIC PORPHYRIAS.
003132 03-05

ADULT-ONSET STUTTERING TREATED WITH ANTICONVULSANTS.
003290 03-11

SYNTHESIS OF POTENTIAL ANTICONVULSANTS: CONDENSATION OF ISATINS WITH ACETONE AND RELATED KETONES.
003699 04-02

GUANYLATE-CYCLASE ~ CYCLIC-GMP IN MOUSE CEREBRAL-CORTEX AND CEREBELLUM: MODIFICATION BY ANTICONVULSANTS.
003956 04-03

THERAPEUTIC PLASMA LEVELS OF SOME ANTICONVULSANTS IN FOCAL EPILEPSY IN RELATION TO COMPUTERIZED-AXIAL-TOMOGRAPHY.
004439 04-11

SERUM CONCENTRATION OF ANTICONVULSANTS. PHARMACOKINETIC FINDINGS AND THEIR PRACTICAL APPLICATION.
004443 04-11

ANTICONVULSANTS AND MENTAL-SYMPTOMS.
004649 04-15

ANTICONVULSIVE
VALPROIC-ACID IN CHILDHOOD-EPILEPSY: ANTICONVULSIVE EFFICACY IN RELATION TO ITS PLASMA LEVELS.
004525 04-13

ANTIDEPRESSANT
A PHARMACOLOGICAL-STUDY OF THE NEW SOVIET ANTIDEPRESSANT INKASAN.
000008 01-02

HISTAMINE H1-RECEPTORS LABELED IN VIVO: ANTIDEPRESSANT AND ANTIHISTAMINE INTERACTIONS.
000074 01-03

ANTIDEPRESSANT PROPERTIES OF 2 4 ETHYL-2-PIPERAZINYL-4-PHENYLQUINOLINE-HCL (AD-1308) AND ITS MECHANISM-OF-ACTION AS COMPARED WITH TRICYCLIC-ANTIDEPRESSANTS.
000152 01-03

LONG-TERM ANTIDEPRESSANT TREATMENT DECREASES SPIROPERIDOL-LABELED SEROTONIN-RECEPTOR BINDING.
000230 01-03

LONG-TERM ANTIDEPRESSANT TREATMENT: ALTERATIONS IN CEREBRAL CAPILLARY PERMEABILITY.
000239 01-03

ACTION OF THE ANTIDEPRESSANT PRIDEFINE (AHR-1118) ON BIOGENIC-AMINES IN THE RAT-BRAIN.
000312 01-03

ANTIDEPRESSANT TREATMENT BY INTRAVENOUS ADMINISTRATION COMPARED TO PERORAL ADMINISTRATION: A DOUBLE-BLIND STUDY OF QUINUPRAMINE.
000552 01-08

ANTIDEPRESSANT POTENTIATION OF 5 HYDROXYTRYPTOPHAN BY L DEPRENIL IN AFFECTIVE-ILLNESS.
000608 01-09

THE INFLUENCE OF LITHIUM-SALTS AND ANTIDEPRESSANT MEDICATION ON SERUM PROLACTIN LEVEL.
000780 01-13

MHPG AS A PREDICTOR OF ANTIDEPRESSANT RESPONSE TO IMIPRAMINE AND MAPROTILINE.
000787 01-13

EXPERIMENTAL EVALUATION OF ANTIDEPRESSANT ACTIVITY OF CLOMIPRAMINE, A NEW TRICYCLIC-ANTIDEPRESSANT DRUG.
001068 02-02

AMOXAPINE IN EXPERIMENTAL PSYCHOPHARMACOLOGY: A NEUROLEPTIC OR AN ANTIDEPRESSANT?
001070 02-02

1 AMINOALKYL-6-ARYL-4H-S-TRIAZOLOBENZODIAZEPINES WITH ANTIANXIETY AND ANTIDEPRESSANT ACTIVITY.
001074 02-02

2,4 DIHYDRO-6-PHENYL-1H-S-TRIAZOLOBENZODIAZEPIN-1-ONES WITH ANTIANXIETY AND ANTIDEPRESSANT ACTIVITY.
001075 02-02

THE NEW ANTIDEPRESSANT PIRLINDOLE: ANTAGONISM OF ACUTE OVERDOSAGE IN THE MOUSE.
001082 02-02

THE NEUROVASCULAR-PHARMACOLOGY AND CARDIOVASCULAR-PHARMACOLOGY OF RS-51324, A POTENTIAL ANTIDEPRESSANT.
001091 02-02

THE NEW ANTIDEPRESSANT PIRLINDOLE: A COMPARISON WITH IMIPRAMINE AND TRANYLCYPROMINE.
001360 02-03

ENHANCED SENSITIVITY OF AMYGDALOID NEURONS TO SEROTONIN AND NOREPINEPHRINE AFTER CHRONIC ANTIDEPRESSANT TREATMENT.
001523 02-03

PHARMACOLOGICAL-STUDIES ON A NEW THYMOLEPTIC ANTIDEPRESSANT. DIMETHYLAMINOPROPYL-5-METHYL-3-PHENYL-1H-INDAZOLE (FS-32).
001659 02-04

AMINEPTINE, A NEW ANTIDEPRESSANT: PHARMACOLOGICAL REVIEW.
001898 02-07

ANTIDEPRESSANT ACTION OF INJECTABLE 1694.
001960 02-09

PROFILE OF THE ANTIDEPRESSANT ACTION OF NOMIFENSINE.
002025 02-09

COMPARATIVE EXPERIMENT OF THE ANTIDEPRESSANT EFFECTS OF AMINEPTINE AND CHLORIMIPRAMINE.
002029 02-09

ANTIDEPRESSANT ACTION OF AMINEPTINE: CONTROLLED DOUBLE-BLIND STUDY.
002030 02-09

EFFECT OF PIRIBEDIL (ET-495) ON PLASMA NOREPINEPHRINE: RELATIONSHIP TO ANTIDEPRESSANT RESPONSE.
002034 02-09

RATING OF ANTIDEPRESSANT ACTIVITY.
002487 02-16

NEW DEVELOPMENT IN ANTIDEPRESSANT MEDICATION -- A REVIEW.
002558 02-17

REPEATED ANTIDEPRESSANT TREATMENTS INDUCE A LONG-LASTING DOPAMINE-AUTORECEPTOR SUBSENSITIVITY: IS DAILY TREATMENT NECESSARY FOR CLINICAL EFFICACY?
002659 03-03

INFLUENCE OF A CHRONIC NEW POTENTIAL ANTIDEPRESSANT, DIMETHYLAMINOPROPYL-5-METHYL-3-PHENYL-1H-INDAZOLE (FS-32) AND ITS N DESMETHYLATED-COMPOUND (FS-97): TREATMENT ON MONOAMINERGIC-RECEPTOR SENSITIVITY IN THE RAT-BRAIN.
002787 03-03

AN ENHANCED SENSITIVITY OF MUSCARINIC CHOLINERGIC-RECEPTOR ASSOCIATED WITH DOPAMINERGIC-RECEPTOR SUBSENSITIVITY AFTER CHRONIC ANTIDEPRESSANT TREATMENT.
002788 03-03

THE ANTIDEPRESSANT ACTION OF SULPHO-ADENOSYL-L-METHIONINE (SAME) COMPARED WITH THAT OF CHLORIMIPRAMINE: HYPOTHETICAL INTERPRETATIONS OF THE MECHANISM-OF-ACTION.
003150 03-07

RAPIDITY OF CLINICAL ANTIDEPRESSANT RESPONSE TO IMIPRAMINE. (UNPUBLISHED PAPER).
003164 03-07

THERAPEUTIC TRIAL OF A NEW ANTIDEPRESSANT: MIANSERIN.
003208 03-09

CLINICAL-EFFICACY OF THE NEW ANTIDEPRESSANT BUPROPION (WELLBUTRIN).
003227 03-09

RELATIONSHIP BETWEEN BLOOD CONCENTRATIONS AND CLINICAL-EFFECTS OF A NEW ANTIDEPRESSANT MAPROTILINE.
003271 03-09

HEPATIC SIDE-EFFECTS OF ANTIDEPRESSANT MEDICATIONS.
003523 03-15

SYNTHESIS AND STRUCTURE-ACTIVITY RELATIONSHIP OF A PYRIMIDOPYRIMIDINE DERIVATIVE WITH ANTIDEPRESSANT ACTIVITY.
003653 04-01

PHARMACOLOGY OF 1 DICHLOROBENZYL-TETRAHYDROPYRIMIDONE, A NOVEL ANTIDEPRES" 4NT COMPOUND WITH ANTIANXIETY ACTIVITY.
003688 04-02

SUPERSENSITIVITY OF CENTRAL NORADRENERGIC PRESYNAPTIC-AUTORECEPTORS FOLLOWING CHRONIC-TREATMENT WITH THE ANTIDEPRESSANT MIANSERIN.
003745 04-03

NONCOMPETITIVE AMINE UPTAKE INHIBITION BY THE NEW ANTIDEPRESSANT PRIDEFINE.
003771 04-03

REGULATION OF SEROTONIN2-RECEPTORS (5 ᴴT2) LABELED WITH (3H)SPIROPERIDOL BY CHRONIC-TREATMENT WITH THE ANTIDEPRESSANT AMITRIPTYLINE.
003964 04-03

PHARMACOLOGICAL-PROPERTIES OF 2,3,3A,4,5,6 HEXAHYDROMETHYL-1H-PYRAZINOCARBAZOL-HCL (PIRLINDOLE), A NEW ANTIDEPRESSANT.
004174 04-04

THE EFFECT OF THE NEW ANTIDEPRESSANT INKAꞱAN ON THE BIOELECTRICAL-ACTIVITY OF THE BRAIN AND ON CONDITIONED REFLEXES.
004212 04-04

ELECTROCARDIOGRAPHIC-CHANGES IN RATS DURING CHRONIC-TREATMENT WITH ANTIDEPRESSANT AND NEUROLEPTIC-DRUGS.
004284 04-05

THE ANTIDEPRESSANT EFFECTS OF TRAZODONE AND INHIBITION OF PLATELET SEROTONIN REUPTAKE.
004383 04-09

TOWARD A BIOCHEMICAL CLASSIFICATION OF DEPRESSIVE-DISORDERS IV: PRETREATMENT URINARY MHPG LEVELS AS PREDICTORS OF ANTIDEPRESSANT RESPONSE TO IMIPRAMINE.
004406 04-09

MAPROTILINE, NOMIFENSINE, MIANSERIN, ZIMELIDINE; A REVIEW OF ANTIDEPRESSANT EFFICACY IN INPATIENTS.
004731 04-17

ANTIDEPRESSANT-DRUG
3H MIANSERIN BINDING IN CALF CAUDATE; POSSIBLE INVOLVEMENT OF SEROTONIN-RECEPTORS IN ANTIDEPRESSANT-DRUG ACTION.
000325 01-03
AGE-RELATED FACTORS AFFECTING ANTIDEPRESSANT-DRUG METABOLISM AND CLINICAL-RESPONSE.
002035 02-09
FACTORS WHICH AFFECT ANTIDEPRESSANT-DRUG RESPONSE IN A MULTICENTER-TRIAL.
003239 03-09
FLUVOXAMINE AS AN ANTIDEPRESSANT-DRUG.
003775 04-03
THE PHARMACOLOGICAL PROFILE OF LOFEPRAMINE, A NEW ANTIDEPRESSANT-DRUG.
004006 04-03
PHARMACOLOGICAL AND BIOCHEMICAL-PROPERTIES OF BRL-14342, A NOVEL POTENTIAL ANTIDEPRESSANT-DRUG.
004086 04-04
CLINICAL-RESPONSE AND BLOOD LEVELS IN THE TREATMENT OF DEPRESSION WITH A NEW ANTIDEPRESSANT-DRUG, AMOXAPINE.
004356 04-09

ANTIDEPRESSANT-DRUGS
RELATION BETWEEN THE EFFECTS OF ANTIDEPRESSANT-DRUGS ON THE UPTAKE OF MONOAMINES AND ON THE SPONTANEOUS ACTIVITY OF CENTRAL NEURONS.
000267 01-03
PROGNOSTIC FACTORS DETERMINING RESPONSE TO ANTIDEPRESSANT-DRUGS IN PSYCHIATRIC-OUTPATIENTS AND GENERAL-PRACTICE.
000638 01-09
EFFECTS OF ALPHA-ADRENOCEPTOR AGONISTS AND ANTAGONISTS AND OF ANTIDEPRESSANT-DRUGS ON PRESYNAPTIC AND POSTSYNAPTIC ALPHA-ADRENOCEPTORS.
001146 02-03
NEW DATA ON THE USE OF ANTIDEPRESSANT-DRUGS.
001195 02-03
THE BINDING OF SOME ANTIDEPRESSANT-DRUGS TO BRAIN MUSCARINIC ACETYLCHOLINE-RECEPTORS.
001253 02-03
ANTIDEPRESSANT-DRUGS SLOW CIRCADIAN-RHYTHMS IN BEHAVIOR AND BRAIN NEUROTRANSMITTER-RECEPTORS.
001536 02-03
SEROTONINMIMETIC AND ANTIDEPRESSANT-DRUGS ON PASSIVE-AVOIDANCE LEARNING BY OLFACTORY BULBECTOMISED RATS.
001585 02-04
ENHANCEMENT OF 5 HYDROXYTRYPTAMINE-INDUCED BEHAVIORAL-EFFECTS FOLLOWING CHRONIC ADMINISTRATION OF ANTIDEPRESSANT-DRUGS.
001667 02-04
CLASSIFICATION OF THE ANTIDEPRESSANT-DRUGS.
002015 02-09
TREATMENT OF CHRONIC PAIN WITH ANTIDEPRESSANT-DRUGS.
002048 02-09
OBSESSIVE-SYMPTOM RESPONSE TO BEHAVIOUR-THERAPY AND TO ANTIDEPRESSANT-DRUGS.
002084 02-10
PARADOXICAL AKINESIA INDUCED BY ANTIDEPRESSANT-DRUGS.
002378 02-15
REFLECTIONS ON THE CLASSIFICATION OF ANTIDEPRESSANT-DRUGS.
002610 02-17
NEW PERSPECTIVES ON THE MODE OF ACTION OF ANTIDEPRESSANT-DRUGS.
002617 02-17
HOW ANTIDEPRESSANT-DRUGS ACT.
002694 03-03
3H SEROTONIN BINDING-SITES IN RAT-BRAIN; EFFECTS OF REPEATED ADMINISTRATION OF ANTIDEPRESSANT-DRUGS. (PH.D. DISSERTATION).
002881 03-03
FACILITATED SHOCK-INDUCED AGGRESSION AFTER CHRONIC-TREATMENT WITH ANTIDEPRESSANT-DRUGS IN THE RAT.
003058 03-04
SYNAPTIC AND BEHAVIOURAL-ACTIONS OF ANTIDEPRESSANT-DRUGS; FURTHER THOUGHTS ON THE IMPLICATIONS FOR THEORIES OF DEPRESSION.
003229 03-09
EFFECTS OF ANTIDEPRESSANT-DRUGS ON DIFFERENT RECEPTORS IN THE BRAIN.
003824 04-03
DIFFERENTIAL-EFFECTS OF ELECTROCONVULSIVE-SHOCK AND ANTIDEPRESSANT-DRUGS ON SEROTONIN2-RECEPTORS IN RAT-BRAIN.
003878 04-03
EFFECTS OF OLFACTORY-BULBECTOMY AND PERIPHERALLY-INDUCED ANOSMIA ON THERMOREGULATION IN THE RAT; SUSCEPTIBILITY TO ANTIDEPRESSANT-DRUGS.
004113 04-04
POTENTIATION OF THE EFFECT OF ANTIDEPRESSANT-DRUGS BY TRYPTOPHAN.
004412 04-09

CARDIOTOXICITY OF ANTIDEPRESSANT-DRUGS.
004597 04-15
NEW ANTIDEPRESSANT-DRUGS AND THE SEIZURE THRESHOLD.
004662 04-15
THE USE OF CLINICAL KINETIC DATA IN TREATMENT WITH ANTIDEPRESSANT-DRUGS.
004686 04-16
RECEPTOR TECHNIQUES IN THE STUDY OF PLASMA LEVELS OF NEUROLEPTICS AND ANTIDEPRESSANT-DRUGS.
004694 04-16
PHARMACOLOGICAL-PROPERTIES OF SOME SECOND-GENERATION ANTIDEPRESSANT-DRUGS.
004726 04-17
DOWN REGULATION OF NORADRENERGIC-RECEPTOR FUNCTION BY ANTIDEPRESSANT-DRUGS; FUNCTIONAL SIGNIFICANCE AND DISTINCTION FROM ANTIPSYCHOTIC-DRUGS. (UNPUBLISHED PAPER).
004746 04-17

ANTIDEPRESSANTS
EFFECT OF CHRONIC-TREATMENT WITH ANTIDEPRESSANTS ON BETA-ADRENERGIC-RECEPTOR BINDING IN GUINEA-PIG BRAIN.
000135 01-03
THE EFFECT OF ANTIDEPRESSANTS ON L 5 HTP-INDUCED CHANGES IN RAT PLASMA CORTICOSTEROIDS.
000170 01-03
INTERACTION OF ANTIDEPRESSANTS WITH CLONIDINE ON RAT-BRAIN TOTAL 3 METHOXY-4-HYDROXYPHENYLGLYCOL.
000300 01-03
PHARMACOLOGY: CURRENT ANTIDEPRESSANTS.
000793 01-13
PHARMACOLOGY: NEW ANTIDEPRESSANTS.
000936 01-17
ADRENERGIC NONSPECIFIC POTENTIATION OF YOHIMBINE TOXICITY IN MICE BY ANTIDEPRESSANTS AND RELATED DRUGS AND ANTIYOHIMBINE ACTION OF ANTIADRENERGIC AND SEROTONERGIC DRUGS.
001330 02-03
ELECTROMYOGRAPHIC-ASSESSMENT OF SPINAL REFLEXES IN EXPERIMENTALLY DEPRESSED DOGS TREATED WITH ANTIDEPRESSANTS.
001620 02-04
NEUROCHEMICAL BASIS OF THE ACTION OF ANTIDEPRESSANTS ON LEARNED-HELPLESSNESS.
001775 02-04
CARDIOTOXICITY OF ANTIDEPRESSANTS.
001843 02-05
DEXAMETHASONE-SUPPRESSION-TEST IDENTIFIES SUBTYPES OF DEPRESSION WHICH RESPOND TO DIFFERENT ANTIDEPRESSANTS.
001971 02-09
CLINICAL-EXPERIENCE WITH SECOND-GENERATION ANTIDEPRESSANTS IN ENDOGENOUS DEPRESSIONS.
001975 02-09
USE OF ANTIDEPRESSANTS; PHARMACOKINETIC-BASES.
001981 02-09
EVALUATION OF THE CLINICAL-EFFICACY OF SINGLE-DAILY-DOSES OF ANTIDEPRESSANTS.
001985 02-09
EFFECTS OF ANTIDEPRESSANTS ON PITUITARY HORMONAL SECRETIONS IN HEALTHY TEST SUBJECTS, NEUROTIC-PATIENTS, AND ENDOGENOUS DEPRESSIVE-PATIENTS.
002009 02-09
INNOVATIONS IN TREATMENT WITH ANTIDEPRESSANTS.
002019 02-09
TARDIVE-DYSKINESIA IN DEPRESSED-PATIENTS; SUCCESSFUL THERAPY WITH ANTIDEPRESSANTS AND LITHIUM.
002037 02-09
SECOND-GENERATION ANTIDEPRESSANTS.
002042 02-09
MECHANISMS OF ACTION OF THE ANTIDEPRESSANTS.
002218 02-13
ON THE PROPOSED MECHANISM-OF-ACTION OF ANTIDEPRESSANTS.
002256 02-13
PSYCHIATRIC-ASPECTS OF ACUTE POISONING WITH TRICYCLIC AND RELATED ANTIDEPRESSANTS – 1980.
002458 02-15
CHANGES IN BODY-TEMPERATURE AFTER ADMINISTRATION OF ADRENERGIC AND SEROTONERGIC-AGENTS AND RELATED DRUGS INCLUDING ANTIDEPRESSANTS.
002532 02-17
ANTIPSYCHOTICS AND ANTIDEPRESSANTS: NEW TRENDS AND EXPECTED FUTURE.
002539 02-17
THE RESEARCH FOR NEW ANTIDEPRESSANTS: PRESENT ORIENTATIONS.
002543 02-17
RESPECTIVE POSITION OF ANTIDEPRESSANTS IN THERAPEUTICS.
002581 02-17
STUDY OF METABOLISM AND BLOOD LEVELS OF ANTIDEPRESSANTS; TOWARDS A RATIONALIZATION OF THEIR THERAPEUTIC USE.
002625 02-17

EFFECTS OF ACUTELY AND CHRONICALLY ADMINISTERED ANTIDEPRESSANTS ON THE CLONIDINE-INDUCED DECREASE IN RAT-BRAIN 3 METHOXY-4-HYDROXYPHENYLETHYLENEGLYCOL-SULPHATE CONTENT.
002908 03-03

THE DEXAMETHASONE-SUPPRESSION-TEST IN THE IDENTIFICATION OF SUBTYPES OF DEPRESSION DIFFERENTIALLY RESPONSIVE TO ANTIDEPRESSANTS.
003211 03-09

LIFE EVENTS AND RESPONSE TO ANTIDEPRESSANTS.
003238 03-09

NOVEL ANTIDEPRESSANTS: A CLINICAL-TRIAL OF MIANSERIN.
003240 03-09

COMPARISON OF STANDARD AND HOLTOR-MONITORED EKGS IN A PATIENT TREATED WITH SEVERAL ANTIDEPRESSANTS.
003304 03-11

FIRST RESULTS OF AN ORIGINAL METHOD FOR MEASURING BLOOD LEVELS OF ANTIDEPRESSANTS (AMITRIPTYLINE AND NORTRIPTYLINE).
003559 03-16

THERAPEUTIC INTEREST OF BLOOD LEVELS DETERMINATION FOR ANTIDEPRESSANTS: METHODOLOGICAL APPROACH.
003571 03-17

THE USE OF ANTIDEPRESSANTS IN PSYCHIATRY.
003597 03-17

SECOND-GENERATION ANTIDEPRESSANTS: A CLINICAL PHARMACOTHERAPEUTIC RESEARCH STRATEGY.
003632 03-17

THE EFFECTS OF ANTIDEPRESSANTS ON THE RETENTION AND METABOLISM OF (3H) NOREPINEPHRINE IN RAT-BRAIN SLICES.
003763 04-03

STUDIES ON THE KINETIC PROPERTIES OF TRYPTOPHAN-HYDROXYLASE OF RABBIT MESENCEPHALON AND PONS-MEDULLA: EFFECT OF LONG-TERM-TREATMENT WITH NEUROLEPTICS AND ANTIDEPRESSANTS.
003852 04-03

THE EFFECT OF ANTIDEPRESSANTS ON THE HYPOTENSIVE-EFFECT OF CLOFELIN IN RATS.
003934 04-03

ON THE KINETICS OF IMIPRAMINE AND RELATED ANTIDEPRESSANTS.
003945 04-03

INTERACTIONS BETWEEN ANTIDEPRESSANTS AND OTHER DRUGS.
004371 04-09

CLINICAL NEUROPHYSIOLOGICAL PROPERTIES OF ANTIDEPRESSANTS.
004373 04-09

CHANGES IN PSYCHOPATHOLOGIC SYMPTOMS DURING 20 DAYS OF TREATMENT WITH ANTIDEPRESSANTS AND NEUROLEPTIC-DRUGS.
004415 04-09

SEXUAL-EFFECTS OF ANTIDEPRESSANTS AND PSYCHOMOTOR STIMULANT-DRUGS.
004646 04-15

ANTIDEPRESSANTS AND ALPHA2-ADRENERGIC-AUTORECEPTOR DESENSITIZATION.
004659 04-15

DO WE NEED ANY MORE ANTIDEPRESSANTS?
004707 04-17

ANTIDEPRESSANTS AND THE SEROTONIN UPTAKE IN PLATELETS.
004727 04-17

ANTIDEPRESSIVE
ANTIDEPRESSIVE TREATMENT AND MOOD-SWING-PATTERNS IN ENDOGENOUS DEPRESSION.
000633 01-09

ANTIDEPRESSIVE TREATMENT IN PARKINSONS-DISEASE: A CONTROLLED-TRIAL OF THE EFFECT OF NORTRIPTYLINE IN PATIENTS WITH PARKINSONS-DISEASE TREATED WITH L-DOPA.
000659 01-11

CYCLOHEXYLPHENOXYAMIDOXIMES AND IMIDAZOLINES WITH ANTIDEPRESSIVE AND ALPHA-ADRENERGIC-ACTIVITY.
001051 02-01

CAN THE ANTIDEPRESSIVE PROPERTIES OF LITHIUM BE DETERMINED EXPERIMENTALLY?
003089 03-04

ANTIDEPRESSIVE-DRUGS
EFFECTS OF ANTIDEPRESSIVE-DRUGS UPON THE HEART AND CIRCULATION.
000863 01-15

ANTIDEPRESSIVES
ANTIDEPRESSIVES IN RENAL FAILURE.
002284 02-13

ANTIDOPAMINERGIC
DISCRIMINATION OF FUNCTIONALLY HETEROGENEOUS RECEPTOR SUBPOPULATIONS: ANTIPSYCHOTIC AND ANTIDOPAMINERGIC PROPERTIES OF METOCLOPRAMIDE.
002877 03-03

ANTIDOPAMINERGIC EFFECT OF ESTROGENS AT THE STRIATAL LEVEL.
003789 04-03

ANTIDOPAMINERGIC PROPERTIES OF YOHIMBINE.
003995 04-03

ANTIDOPAMINERGIC-EFFECTS
BEHAVIORAL-EFFECTS, ANTIDOPAMINERGIC-EFFECTS, AND PROHYPNOTIC-EFFECTS OF NEUROLEPTICS DURING AND AFTER PROLONGED TREATMENT.
001577 02-04

ANTIDOTES
EFFECT OF AMITRIPTYLINE ANTIDOTES ON REPETITIVE EXTRASYSTOLE THESHOLD.
001856 02-05

ANTIDYSKINETIC-PROPERTIES
ANTIPSYCHOTIC-PROPERTIES AND ANTIDYSKINETIC-PROPERTIES OF ERGOT DOPAMINE AGONISTS.
002178 02-11

ANTIENURETIC-EFFECT
CHILDHOOD-ENURESIS: II. PSYCHOPATHOLOGY, TRICYCLIC CONCENTRATION IN PLASMA, AND ANTIENURETIC-EFFECT.
002354 02-14

ANTIEPILEPTIC
TRANSFER FROM MULTIPLE TO SINGLE ANTIEPILEPTIC DRUG-THERAPY.
003316 03-11

ANTIEPILEPTIC THERAPY WITH PHENYTOIN: WHICH IS THE OPTIMUM SERUM LEVEL?
004586 04-14

THE PROGNOSIS OF EPILEPSY AND THE STRATEGY FOR TERMINATING ANTIEPILEPTIC THERAPY
004724 04-17

ANTIEPILEPTIC-AGENTS
GABA AGONISTS AS ANTIEPILEPTIC-AGENTS.
002826 03-03

ANTIEPILEPTIC-DRUGS
SOCIAL AND CLINICAL SIGNIFICANCE OF DETERMINING THE BARBITURATE LEVEL IN THE BLOOD SERUM OF PATIENTS TREATED WITH ANTIEPILEPTIC-DRUGS.
000695 01-11

INFLUENCE OF DEXTROPROPOXYPHENE ON STEADY-STATE SERUM LEVELS AND PROTEIN BINDING OF THREE ANTIEPILEPTIC-DRUGS IN MAN.
000767 01-13

INTERRELATION AT PLASMATIC LEVEL BETWEEN ANTIEPILEPTIC-DRUGS AND LIPIDS. ITS IMPLICATIONS IN THE EFFICIENCY OF TREATMENT IN EPILEPSY. I. CHANGES INDUCED BY PHENOBARBITAL OR/AND DIPHENYLHYDANTOIN IN SERUM LIPIDS.
002281 02-13

CORRELATIONS BETWEEN PLASMA LEVELS OF ANTIEPILEPTIC-DRUGS AND EEG INTENSIVE MONITORING.
002288 02-13

MULTIINSTITUTIONAL-STUDY ON THE TERATOGENICITY AND FETAL TOXICITY OF ANTIEPILEPTIC-DRUGS: A REPORT OF A COLLABORATIVE-STUDY GROUP IN JAPAN.
002442 02-15

A STUDY ON EFFECTS OF ANTIEPILEPTIC-DRUGS UPON THE HIPPOCAMPAL AFTERDISCHARGE.
002844 03-03

SIMULTANEOUS ADMINISTRATION OF FIVE ANTIEPILEPTIC-DRUGS IN PLASMA THROUGH GAS-LIQUID-CHROMATOGRAPHY.
003563 03-16

BEHAVIORAL-INTERACTIONS BETWEEN OPIATE AND ANTIEPILEPTIC-DRUGS IN THE MOUSE.
004155 04-04

ASPECTS OF PHARMACOLOGICAL-EFFECTS OF ANTIEPILEPTIC-DRUGS.
004462 04-11

ANTIEPILEPTIC-EFFECT
ANTIEPILEPTIC-EFFECT OF CLOBAZAM IN LENNOX-GASTAUT-SYNDROME.
004479 04-11

ANTIEPILEPTICS
ANTAGONISM BY CLASSICAL ANTIEPILEPTICS AND SODIUM-VALPROATE OF CEFAZOLIN-INDUCED EXPERIMENTAL EPILEPSY IN RATS.
000442 01-04

SERUM CONCENTRATION AND CLINICAL-EFFECT OF ANTIEPILEPTICS.
003315 03-11

EFFECTS OF 3 SULFAMOYLMETHYL-BENZISOXAZOLE (AD-810) AND SOME ANTIEPILEPTICS ON THE KINDLED SEIZURES IN THE NEOCORTEX, HIPPOCAMPUS AND AMYGDALA IN RATS.
004149 04-04

ANTIGEN
PRODUCTION OF A SPECIFIC ANTISERUM TO RAT-BRAIN GLUTAMIC-ACID-DECARBOXYLASE (GAD) BY INJECTION OF AN ANTIGEN ANTIBODY COMPLEX. (UNPUBLISHED PAPER).
001047 02-01

ENHANCED TRANSFER OF EXPERIMENTAL ALLERGIC-ENCEPHALOMYELITIS WITH STRAIN-13 GUINEA-PIG LYMPH-NODE CELLS: REQUIREMENT FOR CULTURE WITH SPECIFIC ANTIGEN AND ALLOGENIC PERITONEAL EXUDATE CELLS. (UNPUBLISHED PAPER).
001201 02-03

ANTIHEMOPHILIC-FACTOR
EFFECT OF PSYCHIATRIC-INTERVENTION ON USE OF ANTIHEMOPHILIC-FACTOR CONCENTRATE.
000945 01-17

ANTIHISTAMINE
ANTIHISTAMINE EFFECT ON SYNAPTOSOMAL UPTAKE OF SEROTONIN, NOREPINEPHRINE AND DOPAMINE.
000035 01-03

HISTAMINE H1-RECEPTORS LABELED IN VIVO: ANTIDEPRESSANT AND ANTIHISTAMINE INTERACTIONS.
000074 01-03

Subject Index

ANTIHYPERTENSIVE
DIETARY PROTEIN INTAKE INFLUENCES THE ANTIHYPERTENSIVE POTENCY
OF METHYLDOPA IN SPONTANEOUSLY HYPERTENSIVE-RATS.
004025 04-03

ANTIHYPERTENSIVE-EFFECTS
FENFLURAMINE POTENTIATION OF ANTIHYPERTENSIVE-EFFECTS OF
THIAZIDES.
002138 02-11

ANTIHYPOXIDOTIC-DRUGS
ANTIHYPOXIDOTIC-DRUGS AND NOOTROPIC-DRUGS: PROOF OF THEIR
ENCEPHALOTROPIC AND PHARMACODYNAMIC PROPERTIES BY
ENCEPHALOTROPIC AND PHARMACODYNAMIC PROPERTIES BY
QUANTITATIVE EEG INVESTIGATIONS.
002166 02-11

ANTIINFLAMMATORY-DRUGS
LOWERING OF THE CONVULSIVE THRESHOLD BY NONSTEROIDAL
ANTIINFLAMMATORY-DRUGS.
002904 03-03

ANTILEPTAZOL
SPECIES-DIFFERENCES IN CLOBAZAM METABOLISM AND ANTILEPTAZOL
EFFECT.
001157 02-03

ANTILYMPHOCYTIC
PROSPECTS FOR THE TREATMENT OF POSTENCEPHALITIC PARKINSONISM
WITH ANTILYMPHOCYTIC IMMUNOGLOBULIN.
004572 04-14

ANTIMANIC-EFFECT
ANTIMANIC-EFFECT OF CLONIDINE.
000598 01-09

ANTINEOPHOBIC
FOOD PREFERENCE FOLLOWING ACUTE OR CHRONIC CHLORDIAZEPOXIDE
ADMINISTRATION: TOLERANCE TO AN ANTINEOPHOBIC ACTION.
004090 04-04

ANTINEOPLASTIC
THE IMMUNOSTIMULANT ANTINEOPLASTIC ACTION OF SOME
PSYCHOTROPIC-DRUGS OF THE SYDNONIMINE SERIES.
001520 02-03

ANTINOCICEPTION
CHLORDIAZEPOXIDE ANTINOCICEPTION: CROSS-TOLERANCE WITH
OPIATES AND WITH STRESS.
000348 01-04
STRAIN DEPENDENT EFFECTS OF KETAMINE ON LOCOMOTOR-ACTIVITY
AND ANTINOCICEPTION IN MICE.
000382 01-04
EFFECT OF QUIPAZINE AND FLUOXETINE ON ANALGESIC-INDUCED
CATALEPSY AND ANTINOCICEPTION IN THE RAT.
001709 02-04
EFFECT OF SELECTIVE DESTRUCTION OF SEROTONERGIC NEURONS IN
NUCLEUS-RAPHE-MAGNUS ON MORPHINE-INDUCED ANTINOCICEPTION.
001724 02-04
FURTHER STUDIES ON OPIATE-RECEPTORS THAT MEDIATE
ANTINOCICEPTION: TOOTH-PULP STIMULATION IN THE DOG.
001782 02-04
A CLASSIFICATION OF OPIATE-RECEPTORS THAT MEDIATE
ANTINOCICEPTION IN ANIMALS.
001807 02-04
ATTENUATION OF PETHIDINE-INDUCED ANTINOCICEPTION BY ZIMELIDINE,
AN INHIBITOR OF 5 HYDROXYTRYPTAMINE REUPTAKE.
004118 04-04
SPINAL-CORD PHARMACOLOGY OF ADRENERGIC AGONIST-MEDIATED
ANTINOCICEPTION.
004206 04-04

ANTINOCICEPTIVE
ANTINOCICEPTIVE COMPARISON OF QUIPAZINE AND MORPHINE.
000435 01-04
EFFECT OF ANTINOCICEPTIVE DOSES OF OXOTREMORINE ON MOUSE-
BRAIN ACETYLCHOLINE TURNOVER-RATE.
001513 02-03
ANTINOCICEPTIVE ACTION OF MORPHINE AND PENTAZOCINE ON UNIT
ACTIVITY IN THE NUCLEUS-CENTRALIS-LATERALIS, NUCLEUS-
VENTRALIS-LATERALIS AND NEARBY STRUCTURES OF THE CAT.
002837 03-03

ANTINOCICEPTIVE-EFFECT
ANTINOCICEPTIVE-EFFECT OF MORPHINE, OPIOID ANALGESICS AND
HALOPERIDOL INJECTED INTO THE CAUDATE-NUCLEUS OF THE RAT.
000414 01-04
THE ANTINOCICEPTIVE-EFFECT OF INTRACEREBROVENTRICULARLY
ADMINISTERED PROSTAGLANDIN-E1 IN THE RAT.
001769 02-04

ANTINOCICEPTIVE-EFFECTS
A REEVALUATION OF THE NEUROCHEMICAL-EFFECTS AND
ANTINOCICEPTIVE-EFFECTS OF INTRATHECAL CAPSAICIN IN THE RAT.
004184 04-04
ANTAGONISM BY PHENOXYBENZAMINE AND PENTAZOCINE OF THE
ANTINOCICEPTIVE-EFFECTS OF MORPHINE IN THE SPINAL-CORD.
004213 04-04

ANTIPARKINSON-DRUG
ADVERSE-EFFECTS OF ANTIPARKINSON-DRUG WITHDRAWAL.
(UNPUBLISHED PAPER).
004623 04-15

Subject Index

ANTISECRETORY
INHIBITION OF PENTAGASTRIN-STIMULATED AND OVERNIGHT GASTRIC
SECRETION BY LM24056, A NEW PHENOTHIAZINE DERIVED
ANTISECRETORY DRUG.
004306 04-07

ANTISERUM
PRODUCTION OF A SPECIFIC ANTISERUM TO RAT-BRAIN GLUTAMIC-ACID-
DECARBOXYLASE (GAD) BY INJECTION OF AN ANTIGEN ANTIBODY
COMPLEX. (UNPUBLISHED PAPER).
001047 02-01
CORTICOSTERONE INCREASES THE SYNTHESIS OF A SOLUBLE PROTEIN IN
PITUITARY-GLANDS FROM ADRENALECTOMIZED MALE RATS WHICH
PRECIPITATES WITH ANTI-RAT GROWTH-HORMONE ANTISERUM.
(UNPUBLISHED PAPER).
001122 02-03
SUPPRESSION OF SERUM PROLACTIN BY NALOXONE BUT NOT BY ANTI-
BETA-ENDORPHIN ANTISERUM IN STRESSED AND UNSTRESSED RATS.
002871 03-03

ANTISOMATOSTATIN
ADMINISTRATION OF ANTISOMATOSTATIN SERUM TO RATS REVERSES
THE INHIBITION OF PULSATILE GROWTH-HORMONE SECRETION
PRODUCED BY INJECTION OF METERGOLINE BUT NOT YOHIMBINE.
(UNPUBLISHED PAPER).
000019 01-03

ANTISTEREOTYPIC
DIFFERENTIAL REVERSAL BY SCOPOLAMINE AND THIP OF THE
ANTISTEREOTYPIC AND CATALEPTIC-EFFECTS OF NEUROLEPTICS.
002948 03-04

ANTITREMOR
ANTITREMOR ACTION OF C10DICHOL, A PERIPHERAL ACETYLCHOLINE
SYNTHESIS INHIBITOR.
004096 04-04

ANTITUSSIVE
HIGH-AFFINITY BINDING OF THE ANTITUSSIVE DEXTROMETHORPHAN TO
GUINEA-PIG BRAIN.
000061 01-03

ANTITUSSIVES
INVESTIGATION OF NARCOTICS AND ANTITUSSIVES USING DRUG
DISCRIMINATION TECHNIQUES.
000447 01-04

ANTIVIRAL
ANTIVIRAL ACTIVITY OF 3 DEAZAADENOSINE AND 5'
DEOXYISOBUTYLTHIO-3-DEAZAADENOSINE (3 DEAZA-SIBA).
(UNPUBLISHED PAPER).
001006 02-01

ANTIWITHDRAWAL
CLONIDINE AND THE PRIMATE LOCUS-COERULEUS: EVIDENCE SUGGESTING
ANXIOLYTIC AND ANTIWITHDRAWAL EFFECTS. (UNPUBLISHED PAPER).
003982 04-03

ANTIYOHIMBINE
ADRENERGIC NONSPECIFIC POTENTIATION OF YOHIMBINE TOXICITY IN
MICE BY ANTIDEPRESSANTS AND RELATED DRUGS AND
ANTIYOHIMBINE ACTION OF ANTIADRENERGIC AND SEROTONERGIC
DRUGS.
001330 02-03

ANXIETY
BENZODIAZEPINES: A TOOL TO EXPLORE THE BIOCHEMICAL-BASIS AND
NEUROPHYSIOLOGICAL-BASIS OF ANXIETY.
000397 01-04
ANIMAL-MODELS OF ANXIETY AND BENZODIAZEPINE ACTIONS.
000531 01-06
THE EFFECT OF BETADRENOL ON EXAMINATION ANXIETY.
000650 01-10
KETAZOLAM AND DIAZEPAM IN ANXIETY: A CONTROLLED-STUDY.
000655 01-10
ANXIETY AND THYROID-ACTIVITY IN PSYCHIATRIC-PATIENTS.
000786 01-13
ANXIETY RECONCEPTUALIZED.
000951 01-17
RATIONAL USE OF BENZODIAZEPINES FOR ANXIETY AND INSOMNIA.
002063 02-10
DOUBLE-BLIND CLINICAL ASSESSMENT OF ALPRAZOLAM, A NEW
BENZODIAZEPINE DERIVATIVE, IN THE TREATMENT OF MODERATE TO
SEVERE ANXIETY.
002070 02-10
KETAZOLAM COMPARED TO DIAZEPAM AND PLACEBO IN THE
TREATMENT OF ANXIETY.
002074 02-10
CORONARY-HEART-DISEASE: TREATING THE ANXIETY COMPONENT.
002088 02-10
CLINICAL-ASPECTS OF ANXIETY AND ITS THERAPY.
002089 02-10
ANXIETY AND SEDATION DURING A STRESSFUL-SITUATION AFTER SINGLE-
DOSE OF DIAZEPAM VERSUS N DESMETHYLDIAZEPAM -- A
CONTROLLED-TRIAL.
002329 02-14
EFFECTS OF ANXIETY REDUCTION BY BEHAVIOURAL-TECHNIQUES AND
MEPROBAMATE ON CERTAIN PARAMETERS OF INFORMATION THEORY.
003108 03-04

37

Subject Index

CURRENT BIOLOGIC STRATEGIES FOR ANXIETY.
003276 03-10

COMPARISON OF ANXIETY REDUCING SUBSTANCES. (PH.D. DISSERTATION).
003278 03-10

BENZODIAZEPINE TREATMENT OF SPECIFIC ANXIETY STATES.
003284 03-10

TREATMENT OF ANXIETY IN CHILDREN AND ADOLESCENTS.
003349 03-11

A DOUBLE-BLIND TRIAL: THE USE OF OXPRENOLOL AND DIAZEPAM IN ANXIETY.
004428 04-10

CLINICAL-REVIEW OF BETA-BLOCKERS IN ANXIETY.
004464 04-11

NEW BIOLOGICAL RESEARCH RELEVANT TO ANXIETY.
004705 04-17

PSYCHOPHARMACOLOGY AND PSYCHOTHERAPY IN THE TREATMENT OF ANXIETY.
004712 04-17

ANXIETY-DISORDERS
PROPRANOLOL IN CHRONIC ANXIETY-DISORDERS: A CONTROLLED-STUDY.
002073 02-10

RECENT ADVANCES IN THE DIAGNOSIS AND TREATMENT OF ANXIETY-DISORDERS.
003275 03-10

ANXIOGENIC
DISCRIMINATIVE-STIMULUS PROPERTIES OF COCAINE RELATED TO AN ANXIOGENIC ACTION.
004219 04-04

ANXIOLYTIC
ANXIOLYTIC EFFICACY OF ALPRAZOLAM COMPARED TO DIAZEPAM AND PLACEBO.
000648 01-10

COMPARATIVE ANXIOLYTIC AND HYPNOTIC-EFFECTS OF 3 BENZODIAZEPINES ON BABOONS.
001581 02-04

CLONIDINE AND THE PRIMATE LOCUS-COERULEUS: EVIDENCE SUGGESTING ANXIOLYTIC AND ANTIWITHDRAWAL EFFECTS. (UNPUBLISHED PAPER).
003982 04-03

ALPRAZOLAM, A NEW TYPE ANXIOLYTIC IN NEUROTIC-PATIENTS: A PILOT-STUDY.
004422 04-10

DOXEPIN PLASMA LEVELS AND ANXIOLYTIC RESPONSE.
004477 04-11

ANXIOLYTIC-ACTIVITY
SYNTHESIS AND ANXIOLYTIC-ACTIVITY OF A SERIES OF PYRAZINOBENZODIAZEPINE DERIVATIVES.
001089 02-02

THE USE OF SOCIAL-INTERACTION AS A METHOD FOR DETECTING ANXIOLYTIC-ACTIVITY OF CHLORDIAZEPOXIDE-LIKE DRUGS.
001866 02-06

DIAZEPAM ANXIOLYTIC-ACTIVITY IN HIPPOCAMPUS.
003743 04-03

ANXIOLYTIC-DRUGS
TWO BASS-SCALE-FACTORS AND RESPONSE TO PLACEBO AND ANXIOLYTIC-DRUGS.
000649 01-10

ANXIOLYTIC-PREPARATIONS
THE EFFECTS OF COMBINED SEDATIVE AND ANXIOLYTIC-PREPARATIONS ON SUBJECTIVE ASPECTS OF SLEEP AND OBJECTIVE MEASURE OF AROUSAL AND PERFORMANCE THE MORNING FOLLOWING NOCTURNAL MEDICATION: II. REPEATED DOSES.
002331 02-14

ANXIOLYTICS
TO THE CLINICAL-EVALUATION OF ANXIOLYTICS (TOFISOPAM).
002494 02-16

THERAPEUTICS VI – ANXIOLYTICS (BENZODIAZEPINES).
003546 03-15

AVOIDANCE ENHANCEMENT AND DISCRIMINATIVE RESPONSE CONTROL BY ANXIOLYTICS WITH DRUGS ACTING ON THE GABA SYSTEM.
004193 04-04

ANXIOMIMETIC
THE ANXIOMIMETIC PROPERTIES OF PENTYLENETETRAZOL IN THE RAT. (PH.D. DISSERTATION).
003092 03-04

ANXIOUS-DEPRESSED
TREATMENT OF ANXIOUS-DEPRESSED OUTPATIENTS WITH A FIXED COMBINATION (NOMIFENSINE/CLOBAZAM) IN COMPARISON TO A MONOSUBSTANCE (DOXEPINE).
002028 02-09

ANXIOUS-DEPRESSIVE
PRAZEPAM: A NEW BENZODIAZEPINE FOR THE TREATMENT OF ANXIOUS-DEPRESSIVE STATES.
004419 04-10

ANXIOUS-DEPRESSIVE-SYNDROME
ANXIOUS-DEPRESSIVE-SYNDROME. CLINICAL-STUDY OF A NEW BENZODIAZEPINE, PRAZEPAM.
004354 04-09

ANXIOUS-DEPRESSIVE-SYNDROMES
THE TREATMENT OF ANXIOUS-DEPRESSIVE-SYNDROMES WITH TOFIZOPAM.
000615 01-09

EFFECT OF APOMORPHINE ON MORPHINE-INDUCED DECREASE IN
LOCOMOTOR-ACTIVITY AND INCREASE IN DOPAMINE TURNOVER IN
RATS.
001728 02-04
STEREOTYPED-BEHAVIOUR AND ELECTROCORTICAL-CHANGES AFTER
INTRACEREBRAL MICROINFUSION OF DOPAMINE AND APOMORPHINE
IN FOWLS.
001734 02-04
LACK OF EFFECT OF CHOLINE AND NARCOTIC ANTAGONISTS UPON
APOMORPHINE DISCRIMINATION.
001770 02-04
PSYCHOPHARMACOLOGICAL-EFFECTS OF LOW-DOSES AND HIGH-DOSES
OF APOMORPHINE DURING ONTOGENY.
001774 02-04
SUPERSENSITIVITY TO APOMORPHINE IN EXPERIMENTALLY-INDUCED
HYPOKINESIA AND DRUG-INDUCED MODIFICATIONS OF THE
APOMORPHINE RESPONSE.
001814 02-04
TOLERANCE TO FLUPHENAZINE AND SUPERSENSITIVITY TO APOMORPHINE
IN CENTRAL DOPAMINERGIC-SYSTEMS AFTER CHRONIC FLUPHENAZINE-
DECANOATE TREATMENT.
001820 02-04
APOMORPHINE HYPOTHERMIA: AN INDEX OF CENTRAL DOPAMINE-
RECEPTOR FUNCTION IN MAN.
002221 02-13
APOMORPHINE: SELECTIVE INHIBITION OF THE AVERSIVE COMPONENT OF
LATERAL HYPOTHALAMIC SELF-STIMULATION.
002476 02-16
AN OBSERVATIONAL METHOD FOR QUANTIFYING THE BEHAVIOURAL-
EFFECTS OF DOPAMINE AGONISTS: CONTRASTING-EFFECTS OF D-
AMPHETAMINE AND APOMORPHINE.
002484 02-16
EFFECTS OF D-AMPHETAMINE AND APOMORPHINE IN A NEW ANIMAL-
MODEL OF PETIT-MAL EPILEPSY.
002493 02-16
SPONTANEOUS ACTIVITY AND APOMORPHINE STEREOTYPY DURING AND
AFTER WITHDRAWAL FROM 3 1/2 MONTHS CONTINUOUS
ADMINISTRATION OF HALOPERIDOL: SOME METHODOLOGICAL-ISSUES.
002509 02-16
APOMORPHINE HALOPERIDOL INTERACTIONS: DIFFERENT TYPES OF
ANTAGONISM IN CORTICAL AND SUBCORTICAL BRAIN REGIONS.
002662 03-03
THREE CLASSES OF DOPAMINE-RECEPTOR (D-2, D-3, D-4) IDENTIFIED BY
BINDING STUDIES WITH 3H APOMORPHINE AND 3H DOMPERIDONE.
002900 03-03
BIPHASIC-EFFECTS AND OPPOSITE-EFFECTS OF DOPAMINE AND
APOMORPHINE ON ENDOGENOUS GABA RELEASE IN THE RAT
SUBSTANTIA-NIGRA.
002923 03-03
POTENTIATION OF APOMORPHINE AND D-AMPHETAMINE EFFECTS BY
NALOXONE.
002942 03-04
SINGLE OR REPEATED ADMINISTRATION OF SMALL DOSES OF
APOMORPHINE ON WATER INTAKE AND ACTIVITY IN WATER-
DEPRIVED RATS.
002981 03-04
GONADECTOMY AND SEX-DIFFERENCES IN THE BEHAVIORAL-RESPONSES
TO AMPHETAMINE AND APOMORPHINE OF RATS.
003084 03-04
AGGRESSIVE-BEHAVIOR INDUCED BY APOMORPHINE IN RATS SUBMITTED
TO FOUR STRESSFUL-SITUATIONS.
003163 03-07
PRESYNAPTIC AND POSTSYNAPTIC STRIATAL DOPAMINE-RECEPTORS:
DIFFERENTIAL SENSITIVITY TO APOMORPHINE INHIBITION OF
(3H)DOPAMINE AND (14C)GABA RELEASE IN VITRO.
003741 04-03
PREJUNCTIONAL ACTIONS OF PIRIBEDIL ON THE ISOLATED KIDNEY OF THE
RABBIT: COMPARISON WITH APOMORPHINE.
003749 04-03
PHARMACOLOGICAL DIFFERENCE OF L-DOPA, APOMORPHINE, AND
BROMOCRIPTINE AGAINST METOCLOPRAMIDE.
003790 04-03
EFFECTS OF DOPAMINE, APOMORPHINE, GAMMA HYDROXYBUTYRIC-
ACID, HALOPERIDOL AND PIMOZIDE ON REFLEX BRADYCARDIA IN
RATS.
004085 04-03
USE OF THE INTRACEREBRAL INJECTION TECHNIQUE TO ELUCIDATE
MECHANISMS OF APOMORPHINE CLIMBING AND ITS ANTAGONISM IN
THE MOUSE.
004092 04-04
INDUCTION OF BEHAVIORAL-SUPERSENSITIVITY TO APOMORPHINE BY
DFP TREATMENT.
004099 04-04
APOMORPHINE IN SCHIZOPHRENIA.
004327 04-08
APOMORPHINE, HALOPERIDOL AND THE AVERAGE EVOKED-POTENTIALS
IN NORMAL HUMAN VOLUNTEERS.
004549 04-13

APOMORPHINE-DIPIVALOYL-ESTER
TOLERANCE TO INCREASES IN STRIATAL ACETYLCHOLINE
CONCENTRATIONS AFTER REPEATED ADMINISTRATION OF
APOMORPHINE-DIPIVALOYL-ESTER.
000464 01-04
APOMORPHINE-ELICITED
EFFECTS OF THIORIDAZINE ON APOMORPHINE-ELICITED STEREOTYPIC-
BEHAVIOR AND MOTOR-ACTIVITY.
000424 01-04
APOMORPHINE-INDUCED
EFFECTS OF THE POTENTIAL NEUROLEPTIC-PEPTIDE DES-TYR1-GAMMA-
ENDORPHIN AND HALOPERIDOL ON APOMORPHINE-INDUCED
BEHAVIOURAL-SYNDROMES IN RATS AND MICE.
000441 01-04
5,7 DIHYDROXYTRYPTAMINE LESIONS OF THE AMYGDALA REDUCE
AMPHETAMINE-INDUCED AND APOMORPHINE-INDUCED STEREOTYPED-
BEHAVIOUR IN THE RAT.
001589 02-04
MODULATION OF APOMORPHINE-INDUCED STEREOTYPY BY ESTROGEN:
TIME-COURSE AND DOSE-RESPONSE.
001636 02-04
EMERGENCE OF APOMORPHINE-INDUCED VACUOUS CHEWING DURING 6
MONTHS CONTINUOUS TREATMENT WITH FLUPHENAZINE-DECANOATE.
001817 02-04
EFFECT OF L TRYPTOPHAN ON APOMORPHINE-INDUCED GROWTH-
HORMONE SECRETION IN NORMAL SUBJECTS.
002253 02-13
EFFECTS OF CHOLECYSTOKININ-OCTAPEPTIDE ON STRIATAL DOPAMINE
METABOLISM AND ON APOMORPHINE-INDUCED STEREOTYPED CAGE
CLIMBING IN MICE.
003031 03-04
ENHANCEMENT OF APOMORPHINE-INDUCED CLIMBING IN MICE BY
REVERSIBLE AND IRREVERSIBLE NARCOTIC ANTAGONIST DRUGS.
003068 03-04
EFFECT OF L HISTIDINE AND CHLORCYCLIZINE ON APOMORPHINE-INDUCED
CLIM   -BEHAVIOUR AND METHAMPHETAMINE STEREOTYPY IN
MICEBING
004147 04-04
PHARMACOKINETIC-STUDY OF APOMORPHINE-INDUCED STEREOTYPY IN
FOOD DEPRIVED RATS.
004247 04-04
APOMORPHINE-INDUCED STEREOTYPY IN MATURE AND SENESCENT RATS
FOLLOWING CESSATION OF CHRONIC HALOPERIDOL TREATMENT.
004651 04-15
APOMORPHINE-INDUCED-FIGHTING
AN IMPROVED MODEL OF INTRASPECIFIC AGGRESSION: DOSE-RESPONSE
ANALYSIS OF APOMORPHINE-INDUCED-FIGHTING AND STEREOTYPY IN
THE RAT.
002983 03-04
APOMORPHINE-RECEPTORS
3H APOMORPHINE-RECEPTORS IN VARIOUS RAT-BRAIN REGIONS: A
STUDY OF SPECIFIC AND NONSPECIFIC BINDING AND THE INFLUENCE OF
CHRONIC NEUROLEPTIC TREATMENT.
001846 02-05
APPETITIVE
INTRAVENTRICULAR CORTICOSTERONE INJECTION FACILITATES MEMORY
OF AN APPETITIVE DISCRIMINATIVE TASK IN MICE.
003051 03-04
APPETITIVE-CONDITIONING
SENSORY AND ASSOCIATIVE-EFFECTS OF LSD ON CLASSICAL APPETITIVE-
CONDITIONING OF THE RABBIT JAW MOVEMENT RESPONSE.
001637 02-04
APROTIC
NMR SPECTRAL STUDY OF PROTON TRANSFER IN AMITRIPTYLINE-
HYDROCHLORIDE CHLORDIAZEPOXIDE-HYDROCHLORIDE COMBINATIONS
IN DIPOLAR APROTIC SOLVENTS.
003654 04-01
ARACHIDONIC-ACID
RELEASE OF ARACHIDONIC-ACID FROM ADRENAL CHROMAFFIN CELL-
CULTURES DURING SECRETION OF EPINEPHRINE. (UNPUBLISHED
PAPER).
001027 02-01
IGE MEDIATED HISTAMINE RELEASE IN RAT BASOPHILIC LEUKEMIA
CELLS: RECEPTOR ACTIVATED PHOSPHOLIPID METHYLATION, CA-FLUX
AND RELEASE OF ARACHIDONIC-ACID. (UNPUBLISHED PAPER).
001188 02-03
ARCALION-200
ARCALION-200 PRESCRIBED AS A PSYCHIATRIC-DRUG AND
ANTIALCOHOLISM-DRUG ON AN OUTPATIENT AND INPATIENT BASIS.
002103 02-11
ARCHITECTURE
THE MOLECULAR ARCHITECTURE OF ERGOPEPTIDES: A BASIS FOR
BIOLOGICAL-INTERACTION.
001527 02-03
AREA-POSTREMA
ABSENCE OF LITHIUM-INDUCED TASTE-AVERSION AFTER AREA-POSTREMA
LESION.
000456 01-04

Subject Index

ARECOLINE
CHRONIC ADMINISTRATION OF HALOPERIDOL DURING DEVELOPMENT: LATER PSYCHOPHARMACOLOGICAL RESPONSES TO APOMORPHINE AND ARECOLINE.
001470 02-03

ARM
HEXAMETHONIUM MODIFICATION OF CARDIOVASCULAR ADJUSTMENTS DURING COMBINED STATIC DYNAMIC ARM EXERCISE IN MONKEYS.
001242 02-03

AROMATIC
DEVELOPMENT OF AND RECOVERY FROM SUBSENSITIVITY OF THE NORADRENERGIC CYCLIC-AMP GENERATING SYSTEM IN BRAIN: EFFECT OF AMPHETAMINE FOLLOWING INHIBITION OF ITS AROMATIC HYDROXYLATION BY IPRINDOLE.
001353 02-03

AROMATIC-L-AMINO-ACID-DECARBOXYLASE
IRREVERSIBLE INHIBITION OF AROMATIC-L-AMINO-ACID-DECARBOXYLASE BY ALPHA DIFLUOROMETHYL-DOPA AND METABOLISM OF THE INHIBITOR.
000248 01-03

AROUSAL
AROUSAL AND SHORT-TERM MEMORY: EFFECTS OF CAFFEINE AND TRIAL SPACING ON DELAYED ALTERNATION PERFORMANCE.
000487 01-04
THE EFFECT OF SMALL AND MODERATE DOSES OF D-AMPHETAMINE ON HUNGER, MOOD, AND AROUSAL IN MAN.
000807 01-14
THE EFFECTS OF COMBINED SEDATIVE AND ANXIOLYTIC-PREPARATIONS ON SUBJECTIVE ASPECTS OF SLEEP AND OBJECTIVE MEASURE OF AROUSAL AND PERFORMANCE THE MORNING FOLLOWING NOCTURNAL MEDICATION: II. REPEATED DOSES.
002331 02-14
SUPPRESSION OF AMPHETAMINE-INDUCED EEG AROUSAL IN THE HIPPOCAMPUS OF HALOPERIDOL TREATED RABBITS.
002683 03-03
CATECHOLAMINERGIC INVOLVEMENT IN PHASIC VERSUS TONIC ELECTROCORTICAL AROUSAL.
002723 03-03
CANALIZATION OF AROUSAL IN THE PREWEANLING RAT: EFFECTS OF AMPHETAMINE ON AGGREGATION WITH SURROGATE STIMULI.
002965 03-04
EFFECT OF FLURAZEPAM, PENTOBARBITAL, AND CAFFEINE ON AROUSAL THRESHOLD.
003439 03-14
AUDITORY AROUSAL THRESHOLDS OF GOOD SLEEPERS AND POOR SLEEPERS WITH AND WITHOUT FLURAZEPAM.
003446 03-14

ARRHYTHMIA
ARRHYTHMIA INDUCED BY A TRICYCLIC-ANTIDEPRESSANT IN A PATIENT WITH UNDIAGNOSED MITRAL-VALVE PROLAPSE.
003521 03-15

ARRHYTHMOGENIC-PROPERTIES
CORTICAL CONTROL OF NEURALLY MEDIATED ARRHYTHMOGENIC-PROPERTIES OF DESACETYLLANATOSIDE-C.
003124 03-05

ARRHYTHMOGENICITY
INFLUENCE OF IMIPRAMINE AND PARGYLINE ON THE ARRHYTHMOGENICITY OF EPINEPHRINE DURING HALOTHANE, ENFLURANE OR METHOXYFLURANE ANESTHESIA IN DOGS.
001539 02-03

ARSENIC
PRUSSIAN-BLUE: SPECIFIC TREATMENT OF THALLIUM, ARSENIC, INDUSTRIAL-SOLVENT INTOXICATION, AND OTHER POLYNEUROPATHOLOGIES. A POSSIBLE ANTIPSYCHOTIC-AGENT.
003348 03-11

ARTANE
A COMPARISON OF BIPERIDEN-HYDROCHLORIDE (AKINETON) AND BENZHEXOL (ARTANE) IN THE TREATMENT OF DRUG-INDUCED PARKINSONISM.
002146 02-11

ARTIFACT
HIGH-AFFINITY BINDING OF TRICYCLIC-ANTIDEPRESSANTS TO HISTAMINE H1-RECEPTORS: FACT AND ARTIFACT.
001880 02-06

ARYLALLOPHANATES
ACYLCYANAMIDES, ACYLUREA, AND VARIOUS SUBSTITUTED ARYLALLOPHANATES; EFFECT ON THE CNS.
003689 04-02

ARYLAMINE-N-ACETYLTRANSFERASE
ADRENERGIC REGULATION OF THE REDUCTION IN ACETYL-COENZYME-A:ARYLAMINE-N-ACETYLTRANSFERASE IN THE RAT PINEAL.
002654 03-03

ARYLDIALKENYLPIPERAZINES
ARYLDIALKENYLPIPERAZINES AS SELECTIVE AND VERY POTENT INHIBITORS OF DOPAMINE UPTAKE.
000005 01-01

ARYLSULPHATASE
INHIBITION BY ARYLSULPHATASE A OF NA-INDEPENDENT (3H) GABA AND (3H) MUSCIMOL BINDING TO BOVINE CEREBELLAR SYNAPTIC MEMBRANES.
001208 02-03

ASSAYS
PSYCHOTROPIC-DRUGS DO NOT INTERFERE WITH RADIOLIGAND ASSAYS FOR PROLACTIN, CORTISOL, AND GROWTH-HORMONE.
002511 02-16

ASSERTIVENESS
THE EFFECT OF ASSERTIVENESS TRAINING, PROVERA AND SEX OF THERAPIST IN THE TREATMENT OF GENITAL EXHIBITIONISM.
000697 01-11

ASSESSMENT
ASSESSMENT OF TOLERANCE TO AND PHYSICAL-DEPENDENCE ON PENTOBARBITAL, INDUCED BY MULTIPLE PELLET IMPLANTATION.
000385 01-04

AN ELECTROMYOGRAPHIC-METHOD FOR THE ASSESSMENT OF NALOXONE-INDUCED ABSTINENCE IN MORPHINE-DEPENDENT RATS.
000433 01-04

CLINICAL ASSESSMENT OF ONCE A DAY PHENOTHIAZINE ADMINISTRATION.
000573 01-08

COGNITIVE AND AFFECTIVE-FUNCTIONS IN PATIENTS WITH AFFECTIVE-DISORDERS TREATED WITH LITHIUM: AN ASSESSMENT BY QUESTIONNAIRE.
000604 01-09

CLASSIFICATION AND ASSESSMENT OF CEREBRAL BIOAVAILABILITY OF LOPIRAZEPAM (D-12524) BY QUANTITATIVE EEG AND PSYCHOMETRIC-ANALYSIS.
000720 01-11

ASSESSMENT OF MULTIVARIATE RELATIONSHIPS IN REACTIVITY OF PATIENTS RECEIVING LITHIUM THERAPY.
000819 01-14

A NEW APPROACH TO THE ASSESSMENT OF THE POTENCY OF REVERSIBLE MONOAMINE-OXIDASE-INHIBITORS IN VIVO, AND ITS APPLICATION TO D-AMPHETAMINE, P METHOXYAMPHETAMINE AND HARMALINE.
000900 01-16

AN ASSESSMENT PROGRAM TO REDUCE DRUG USE WITH THE MENTALLY-RETARDED.
000937 01-17

ASSESSMENT OF ADRENERGIC-RECEPTORS IN VIVO IN EXPERIMENTAL ANIMALS AND MAN. (UNPUBLISHED PAPER).
001034 02-01

DOUBLE-BLIND CLINICAL ASSESSMENT OF ALPRAZOLAM, A NEW BENZODIAZEPINE DERIVATIVE, IN THE TREATMENT OF MODERATE TO SEVERE ANXIETY.
002070 02-10

TOLERANCE TO DEXTROAMPHETAMINE-SULFATE IN HYPERACTIVE-CHILDREN: ASSESSMENT USING AN EMPIRICAL NEUROPSYCHOLOGICAL PARADIGM -- A PILOT-STUDY.
002126 02-11

QUANTITATIVE ASSESSMENT OF SMOOTH-PURSUIT EYE-MOVEMENTS IN HEALTHY AND EPILEPTIC-SUBJECTS.
002376 02-15

CASE 3: ASSESSMENT AND TREATMENT OF DRUG-INDUCED TREMOR.
002407 02-15

SUBJECTIVE ASSESSMENT OF SEXUAL-DYSFUNCTION OF PATIENTS ON LONG-TERM ADMINISTRATION OF DIGOXIN.
002443 02-15

ELECTROPHYSIOLOGIC ASSESSMENT OF RECEPTOR CHANGES FOLLOWING CHRONIC DRUG-TREATMENT.
003136 03-06

DRUG PREFERENCE AND MOOD IN HUMANS: REPEATED ASSESSMENT OF D-AMPHETAMINE.
003445 03-14

EVALUATION OF DRUG EFFICACY IN DEMENTIA: A COMPUTERIZED COGNITIVE ASSESSMENT SYSTEM.
003557 03-16

PHARMACOLOGICAL-BASES OF PSYCHONEUROENDOCRINOLOGY: PRECLINICAL ASSESSMENT OF CLINICAL FACTS.
003735 04-03

OPIATE-DEPENDENCE FOLLOWING ACUTE INJECTIONS OF MORPHINE AND NALOXONE: THE ASSESSMENT OF VARIOUS WITHDRAWAL SIGNS.
004209 04-04

ASSESSMENTS
EEG ASSESSMENTS OF DOSAGE AND SLEEP PROFILES FOR A HYPNOTIC-DRUG OF THE TRIAZOLOTHIENODIAZEPINE SERIES.
002338 02-14

ASSIMILATION
LITHIUM, ASSIMILATION OF NUTRIENTS AND REPRODUCTION. (UNPUBLISHED PAPER).
002777 03-03

ASSOCIATION
HUMAN PLATELET 5 HT-RECEPTORS: CHARACTERISATION AND FUNCTIONAL ASSOCIATION.
001412 02-03

THE ASSOCIATION OF RETARD NEUROLEPTICS TO OTHER NEUROLEPTICS IN THE REHABILITATION OF PSYCHOTIC-PATIENTS.
002108 02-11

HYPERPARATHYROIDISM IN ASSOCIATION WITH LITHIUM THERAPY.
003489 03-15

ASSOCIATIVE-ASPECTS
INTERFERENCE WITH INGESTIONAL AVERSION LEARNING PRODUCED BY PREEXPOSURE TO THE UNCONDITIONED-STIMULUS: ASSOCIATIVE-ASPECTS AND NONASSOCIATIVE-ASPECTS.
001610 02-04

ASSOCIATIVE-EFFECTS
SENSORY AND ASSOCIATIVE-EFFECTS OF LSD ON CLASSICAL APPETITIVE-CONDITIONING-OF THE RABBIT JAW MOVEMENT RESPONSE.
001637 02-04

ASTERIXIS
ASTERIXIS ASSOCIATED WITH SODIUM-VALPROATE.
003468 03-15

ASTHENIA
ATTEMPT AT PSYCHOLOGICAL UNDERSTANDING AND TREATMENT OF PSYCHOLOGICAL ASTHENIA AND ASTHENO-DEPRESSIVE-SYNDROMES USING ERGADYL.
001974 02-09

DOSE-EFFECT OF DEAE ON SUBJECTIVE PROBLEMS, VERTIGO, DEPRESSION, ASTHENIA, CEPHALALGIA, AND TONIC POSTURAL ACTIVITY PROBLEMS RECORDED WITH STATOKINESIMETER IN POSTCONCUSSIONAL-SYNDROME.
004472 04-11

ASTHENIC-DEPRESSIVE-SYNDROMES
CLINICAL-TESTING OF MINAPRINE ON ELDERLY SUBJECTS WITH THE ASTHENIC-DEPRESSIVE-SYNDROMES.
002123 02-11

ASTHENO-DEPRESSIVE-DISORDERS
TREATMENT OF ASTHENO-DEPRESSIVE-DISORDERS WITH MINAPRINE (CANTOR). MULTICENTER-STUDY OF 248 CASES EVALUATED WITH THE FATIGUE STUDY GROUPS NO. 4 CLINICAL-SCALE.
001980 02-09

ASTHENO-DEPRESSIVE-SYNDROMES
ATTEMPT AT PSYCHOLOGICAL UNDERSTANDING AND TREATMENT OF PSYCHOLOGICAL ASTHENIA AND ASTHENO-DEPRESSIVE-SYNDROMES USING ERGADYL.
001974 02-09

ASTHMA
NEUROPSYCHOLOGICAL-CORRELATES OF ASTHMA: EFFECT OF HYPOXIA OR DRUGS?
003482 03-15

NEUROPSYCHOLOGICAL-CORRELATES OF ASTHMA: BRAIN-DAMAGE OR DRUG-EFFECTS?
003538 03-15

ASTHMA THERAPY MAY UNDERCUT KIDS AT SCHOOL.
004475 04-11

ASTROCYTES
BENZODIAZEPINE-RECEPTORS ON PRIMARY CULTURES OF MOUSE ASTROCYTES.
004029 04-03

ASTROGLIAL
DOXEPIN, A TRICYCLIC-ANTIDEPRESSANT, BINDS TO NORMAL, INTACT ASTROGLIAL CELLS IN CULTURES AND INHIBITS THE ISOPROTERENOL-INDUCED INCREASE IN CYCLIC-AMP PRODUCTION.
003836 04-03

ASYMMETRY
POSTURAL ASYMMETRY AND DIRECTIONALITY OF ROTATION IN RATS.
001729 02-04

DOES POSTURAL ASYMMETRY INDICATE DIRECTIONALITY OF ROTATION IN RATS: ROLE OF SEX AND HANDLING.
003061 03-04

ATARACTIC-DRUG
PHARMACOLOGICAL PECULIARITIES OF A BENZODIAZEPINE/ATARACTIC-DRUG AND ITS THERAPEUTIC RELEVANCE: THE SPECIAL STATUS OF CLORAZEPATE-DIPOTASSIUM (TRANXILIUM).
004527 04-13

ATAXIA
ORAL CHOLINE IN CEREBELLAR ATAXIA.
000722 01-11

DIAZEPAM-INDUCED ATAXIA IN TROTTING SQUIRREL-MONKEYS.
004138 04-04

ATAXIC-BEHAVIORS
EFFECTS OF CHRONIC ADMINISTRATION OF PHENCYCLIDINE ON STEREOTYPED-BEHAVIORS AND ATAXIC-BEHAVIORS IN THE RAT.
003095 03-04

ATENOLOL
EFFECTS OF ATENOLOL AND PROPRANOLOL ON HUMAN PERFORMANCE AND SUBJECTIVE FEELINGS.
002340 02-14

ATMOSPHERE
CORRELATED STUDY OF THE EFFECTS OF SE-5023 IN AN HYPOXIC ATMOSPHERE ON QUANTIFIED EEG, VIGILANCE, MEMORY, AND MOOD.
003440 03-14

ATP
ATP COMPLEXES WITH THE ATPASE INHIBITOR QUERCETIN.
000045 01-03

ATPASE
ATP COMPLEXES WITH THE ATPASE INHIBITOR QUERCETIN.
000045 01-03

Subject Index

THE INFLUENCE OF PENTIFYLLINE AND THEOPHYLLINE ON REACTION KINETICS OF CATECHOLAMINE STIMULATED ATPASE FROM RAT-BRAIN.
001052 02-01

EFFECTS OF MALNUTRITION AND QUIPAZINE ON RAT-CEREBRAL-CORTEX ATPASE ACTIVITY DURING DEVELOPMENT.
001276 02-03

ATPASES
CERTAIN MECHANISMS OF THE ACTION OF PSYCHOTROPIC-DRUGS ON TRANSPORT ATPASES.
001331 02-03

ATRIAL
IMIPRAMINE AFFECTS AUTONOMIC-CONTROL OF SINOATRIAL RATE IN ISOLATED RIGHT ATRIAL PREPARATIONS.
000195 01-03

ATROPHY
IN VIVO EFFECT OF PROTEASE INHIBITORS IN DENERVATION ATROPHY.
000290 01-03

ATROPINE
THE EFFECT OF DIAZEPAM ON EEG CHANGES FOLLOWING INTRASEPTAL ADMINISTRATION OF ATROPINE.
000127 01-03

BEHAVIOR-DEPENDENT EVOKED-POTENTIALS IN THE HIPPOCAMPAL-CA1 REGION OF THE RAT. II. EFFECTS OF ESERINE, ATROPINE, ETHER AND PENTOBARBITAL.
000184 01-03

THE EFFECT OF CLONAZEPAM ON ATROPINE SPIKES IN THE LIMBIC-SYSTEM.
001274 02-03

LONG-TERM ADMINISTRATION OF ATROPINE, IMIPRAMINE, AND VILOXAZINE ALTERS RESPONSIVENESS OF RAT-CORTICAL-NEURONES TO ACETYLCHOLINE.
001306 02-03

ATROPINE AND NATURAL SLEEP: ACTIVITY DATA OF THE STRIATUM IN RATS.
001551 02-03

SELECTIVE SYNAPTIC ANTAGONISM BY ATROPINE AND ALPHA AMINOADIPATE OF PULVINAR AND CORTICAL AFFERENTS TO THE SUPRASYLVIAN VISUAL AREA (CLARE-BISHOP AREA).
002752 03-03

SLEEP ELICITED BY OLFACTORY TUBERCLE STIMULATION AND THE EFFECT OF ATROPINE.
002955 03-04

THE EXCITATORY EFFECT OF ATROPINE ON THE NEURONS OF THE FROG SYMPATHETIC GANGLIA.
004041 04-03

DEVELOPMENTAL-CHANGE IN REARING RESPONSE TO ATROPINE IN RATS TREATED WITH 6 HYDROXYDOPA.
004191 04-04

ATROPINE-RESISTANT
MONOAMINE REPLACEMENT AFTER RESERPINE: CATECHOLAMINERGIC AGONISTS RESTORE MOTOR-ACTIVITY BUT PHENYLETHYLAMINE RESTORES ATROPINE-RESISTANT NEOCORTICAL LOW VOLTAGE FAST-ACTIVITY.
000309 01-03

RESERPINE ABOLISHES MOVEMENT CORRELATED ATROPINE-RESISTANT NEOCORTICAL LOW VOLTAGE FAST-ACTIVITY.
000310 01-03

ATTACK
LATE RESULTS OF LITHIUM TREATMENT OF ADOLESCENTS WITH ATTACK LIKE SCHIZOPHRENIA.
003177 03-08

ATTACKS
DIFFERENTIAL DIAGNOSIS AND TREATMENT OF PANIC ATTACKS AND PHOBIC-STATES.
004424 04-10

A MODIFIED VERSION OF THE SIMULTANEOUS DISCONTINUATION OF PSYCHOTROPIC-DRUGS (COMBINED WITH THE ADMINISTRATION OF DIURETICS) AS A METHOD OF HALTING PROLONGED ATTACKS OF SCHIZOPHRENIA.
004584 04-14

ATTEMPTS
ATTEMPTS TO REINSTATE LORDOSIS REFLEX IN ESTROGEN-PRIMED SPINAL FEMALE RATS WITH MONOAMINE AGONISTS.
000421 01-04

ATTEMPTS TO DEVELOP SUPERSENSITIVITY OR SUBSENSITIVITY RETINAL DOPAMINE-RECEPTORS AFTER VARIOUS TREATMENTS WITH ANTAGONISTS OR AGONISTS.
001350 02-03

PRESENT ATTEMPTS AT TREATING TARDIVE-DYSKINESIA.
004629 04-15

ATTENDING
BEHAVIORAL-INTERVENTION FOR SELF-STIMULATORY, ATTENDING AND SEIZURE BEHAVIOR IN A CEREBRAL-PALSIED-CHILD.
002104 02-11

ATTENTION
DISRUPTION OF SELECTIVE ATTENTION BY APOMORPHINE, BUT NOT AMPHETAMINE, IN THE MONGOLIAN-GERBIL.
000358 01-04

THE EFFECTS OF NOREPINEPHRINE PERFUSION OF THE MESENCEPHALIC RETICULAR FORMATION ON BEHAVIOR IN THE RAT: INTERACTION

AUDIOGENIC-SEIZURE
DIFFERENCES IN ACTIVITY IN CEREBRAL METHYLTRANSFERASES AND
MONOAMINE-OXIDASES BETWEEN AUDIOGENIC-SEIZURE SUSCEPTIBLE
AND RESISTANT MICE AND DEERMICE.
000377 01-04
EFFECT OF RO-4-1284 ON AUDIOGENIC-SEIZURE SUSCEPTIBILITY AND
INTENSITY IN EPILEPSY-PRONE RATS.
003865 04-03

AUDIOGENIC-SEIZURES
AUDIOGENIC-SEIZURES: INCREASED BENZODIAZEPINE-RECEPTOR BINDING
IN A SUSCEPTIBLE STRAIN OF MICE. .
000252 01-03
THE EFFECTS OF NOOTROPIC-DRUGS ON THE SUSCEPTIBILITY TO
AUDIOGENIC-SEIZURES IN RATS.
001571 02-04
EFFECTS OF WITHDRAWAL FROM LONG-TERM DIPHENYLHYDANTOIN
TREATMENT ON AUDIOGENIC-SEIZURES AND MAXIMAL
ELECTROSHOCK-INDUCED SEIZURES IN RATS.
004101 04-04

AUDITORY
BRAINSTEM AUDITORY EVOKED-POTENTIALS AND MYELIN CHANGES IN
TRIETHYLTIN-INDUCED EDEMA IN YOUNG ADULT RATS.
000509 01-05
EFFECTS OF HIPPOCAMPAL BRAIN-DAMAGE ON AUDITORY AND VISUAL
RECENT MEMORY: COMPARISON WITH MARIJUANA INTOXICATED
SUBJECTS.
002320 02-14
PHASIC ACTIVITY INDUCED BY P CHLOROPHENYLALANINE IN THE
AUDITORY PATHWAY.
002661 03-03
PSYCHOTROPIC-DRUG-INDUCED CHANGES IN AUDITORY AVERAGED
EVOKED-POTENTIALS: RESULTS OF A DOUBLE-BLIND TRIAL USING AN
OBJECTIVE FULLY AUTOMATED AEP ANALYSIS METHOD.
003412 03-13
AUDITORY BRAINSTEM EVOKED-RESPONSES IN HOSPITALIZED-PATIENTS
UNDERGOING DRUG-TREATMENT OR ECT.
003430 03-13
AUDITORY AROUSAL THRESHOLDS OF GOOD SLEEPERS AND POOR
SLEEPERS WITH AND WITHOUT FLURAZEPAM.
003446 03-14
THE BRAINSTEM AUDITORY EVOKED-RESPONSE AS A TOOL IN
NEUROBEHAVIORAL TOXICOLOGY AND MEDICINE.
004277 04-05

AUGMENTER
CHANGES IN THE AUGMENTER REDUCER TENDENCY AND IN PAIN
MEASURES AS A RESULT OF TREATMENT WITH A SEROTONIN
REUPTAKE INHIBITOR ZIMELIDINE.
002305 02-13

AUGMENTING
INHIBITORY-ACTION OF THE COMBINATION OF AMINOPYRINE AND
SECOBARBITAL ON EEG ACTIVATION, NEOCORTICAL RECRUITING AND
AUGMENTING RESPONSES IN RABBITS.
004022 04-03

AUTHORITIES
QUALITY OF REPORTS OF CLINICAL-TRIALS SUBMITTED BY THE DRUG
INDUSTRY TO THE FINNISH AND SWEDISH CONTROL AUTHORITIES.
003599 03-17

AUTISM
THE BIOLOGICAL-EFFECTS AND CLINICAL-EFFECTS OF ORAL MAGNESIUM
AND ASSOCIATED MAGNESIUM VITAMIN-B6 ADMINISTRATION ON
CERTAIN DISORDERS OBSERVED IN INFANTILE AUTISM.
003291 03-11

AUTISTIC-PATIENT
TARDIVE TOURETTE-SYNDROME IN AN AUTISTIC-PATIENT AFTER LONG-
TERM NEUROLEPTIC ADMINISTRATION.
000887 01-15

AUTOCORRELATION
AUTOCORRELATION ANALYSIS OF SINGLE NEURON ACTIVITY AFTER
ADMINISTRATION OF PENTOBARBITAL.
001268 02-03

AUTOINDUCTION
THE AUTOINDUCTION OF CARBAMAZEPINE DURING LONG-TERM
THERAPY.
000785 01-13

AUTOMAINTENANCE-SCHEDULE
DRUG-EFFECTS ON THE PERFORMANCE OF PIGEONS UNDER A NEGATIVE
AUTOMAINTENANCE-SCHEDULE.
001754 02-04

AUTOMATED
AN AUTOMATED ELECTROCHEMICAL-METHOD FOR IN VIVO MONITORING
OF CATECHOLAMINE RELEASE.
001873 02-06
AN AUTOMATED METHOD FOR STUDYING STEREOTYPED GNAWING.
002500 02-16
PSYCHOTROPIC-DRUG-INDUCED CHANGES IN AUDITORY AVERAGED
EVOKED-POTENTIALS: RESULTS OF A DOUBLE-BLIND TRIAL USING AN
OBJECTIVE FULLY AUTOMATED AEP ANALYSIS METHOD.
003412 03-13

AUTONOMIC
THE EFFECTS OF ALPHA AND BETA NEUROTOXINS FROM THE VENOMS OF
VARIOUS SNAKES ON TRANSMISSION IN AUTONOMIC GANGLIA.
003750 04-03

AUTONOMIC-ACTIVITY
THE INFLUENCE OF METHYLPHENIDATE ON SPONTANEOUS AUTONOMIC-
ACTIVITY AND BEHAVIOR IN CHILDREN DIAGNOSED AS HYPERACTIVE.
003363 03-11

AUTONOMIC-CONTROL
IMIPRAMINE AFFECTS AUTONOMIC-CONTROL OF SINOATRIAL RATE IN
ISOLATED RIGHT ATRIAL PREPARATIONS.
000195 01-03

AUTONOMIC-EFFECTS
AUTONOMIC-EFFECTS OF DEXTROAMPHETAMINE IN NORMAL MEN:
IMPLICATIONS FOR HYPERACTIVITY AND SCHIZOPHRENIA.
003437 03-13

AUTONOMIC-FUNCTIONING
PREDICTING OUTCOME FROM MEASURES OF ATTENTION AND
AUTONOMIC-FUNCTIONING.
003205 03-08

AUTONOMIC-MECHANISMS
PERIPHERAL AUTONOMIC-MECHANISMS AND PAVLOVIAN-CONDITIONING
IN THE RABBIT (ORYCTOLAGUS-CUNICULUS).
001560 02-04

AUTORADIOGRAPHIC
AUTORADIOGRAPHIC STUDIES ON DISTRIBUTION OF L-3,4
DIHYDROXYPHENYLALANINE (L-DOPA) 14C AND L 5
HYDROXYTRYPTOPHAN (L 5 HTP) 14C IN THE CAT BRAIN.
003941 04-03
AUTORADIOGRAPHIC LOCALIZATION OF DRUG AND NEUROTRANSMITTER-
RECEPTORS IN THE BRAIN.
004292 04-06

AUTORADIOGRAPHICAL
BENZODIAZEPINE-RECEPTORS: AUTORADIOGRAPHICAL AND
IMMUNOCYTOCHEMICAL EVIDENCE FOR THEIR LOCALIZATION IN
REGIONS OF GABAERGIC SYNAPTIC CONTACTS.
002643 03-01

AUTORADIOGRAPHY
IN VITRO AUTORADIOGRAPHY OF OPIATE-RECEPTORS IN RAT-BRAIN
SUGGESTS LOCI OF OPIATE-ERGIC PATHWAYS. (UNPUBLISHED PAPER).
001025 02-01
NEUROTENSIN-RECEPTOR LOCALIZATION BY LIGHT MICROSCOPIC
AUTORADIOGRAPHY IN RAT-BRAIN.
002938 03-03

AUTORECEPTOR
REPEATED TRICYCLIC-ANTIDEPRESSANTS INDUCE A PROGRESSIVE SWITCH
IN THE ELECTROPHYSIOLOGICAL RESPONSE OF DOPAMINE NEURONS TO
AUTORECEPTOR STIMULATION.
000046 01-03
ALTERATIONS IN BASAL FIRING-RATE AND AUTORECEPTOR SENSITIVITY
OF DOPAMINE NEURONS IN THE SUBSTANTIA-NIGRA FOLLOWING
ACUTE AND EXTENDED EXPOSURE TO ESTROGEN.
001167 02-03

AUTOSHAPED
DISRUPTION OF AUTOSHAPED RESPONDING TO A SIGNAL OF BRAIN-
STIMULATION REWARD BY NEUROLEPTIC-DRUGS.
004199 04-04

AVAILABILITY
SWIMMING CAPACITY OF MICE AFTER PROLONGED TREATMENT WITH
PSYCHOSTIMULANTS: II. EFFECT OF METHAMPHETAMINE ON
SWIMMING PERFORMANCE AND AVAILABILITY OF METABOLIC
SUBSTRATES.
001613 02-04
AVAILABILITY OF ISOSORBIDE-DINITRATE, DIAZEPAM AND
CHLORMETHIAZOLE, FROM I.V. DELIVERY SYSTEMS.
003558 03-16

AVERAGE
APOMORPHINE, HALOPERIDOL AND THE AVERAGE EVOKED-POTENTIALS
IN NORMAL HUMAN VOLUNTEERS.
004549 04-13

AVERAGED
PSYCHOTROPIC-DRUG-INDUCED CHANGES IN AUDITORY AVERAGED
EVOKED-POTENTIALS: RESULTS OF A DOUBLE-BLIND TRIAL USING AN
OBJECTIVE FULLY AUTOMATED AEP ANALYSIS METHOD.
003412 03-13

AVERMECTIN-B1A
STUDIES ON THE MECHANISM-OF-ACTION OF AVERMECTIN-B1A:
STIMULATION OF RELEASE OF GAMMA AMINOBUTYRIC-ACID FROM
BRAIN SYNAPTOSOMES.
003973 04-03
IN VITRO MODULATION BY AVERMECTIN-B1A OF THE GABA/
BENZODIAZEPINE-RECEPTOR COMPLEX OF RAT-CEREBELLUM.
004023 04-03

AVERSION
INTERFERENCE WITH INGESTIONAL AVERSION LEARNING PRODUCED BY
PREEXPOSURE TO THE UNCONDITIONED-STIMULUS: ASSOCIATIVE-
ASPECTS AND NONASSOCIATIVE-ASPECTS.
001610 02-04

ETHANOL AVERSION INDUCED BY PARENTERALLY ADMINISTERED ETHANOL ACTING BOTH AS CS AND UCS.
001721 02-04

AVERSIONS
LITHIUM-CHLORIDE AND DELTA9 THC LEAD TO CONDITIONED AVERSIONS IN THE PIGEON.
003003 03-04

AVERSIVE
APOMORPHINE: SELECTIVE INHIBITION OF THE AVERSIVE COMPONENT OF LATERAL HYPOTHALAMIC SELF-STIMULATION.
002476 02-16

PHARMACOLOGICAL EVIDENCE ON THE SPECIALIZATION OF CNS MECHANISMS RESPONSIBLE FOR MOTOR ACT INHIBITION BY AVERSIVE EVENTS.
002671 03-03

AVERSIVE-EFFECT
ACCELERATED EXTINCTION AFTER POSTTRIAL HALOTHANE ANESTHESIA IN RATS: AN AVERSIVE-EFFECT.
003001 03-04

AVERSIVE-EFFECTS
REWARDING AND AVERSIVE-EFFECTS OF MORPHINE: TEMPORAL AND PHARMACOLOGICAL-PROPERTIES.
000470 01-04

TEMPORAL PROPERTIES OF THE REWARDING AND AVERSIVE-EFFECTS OF AMPHETAMINE IN RATS.
000471 01-04

CALCITONIN: AVERSIVE-EFFECTS IN RATS?
002977 03-04

CALCITONIN: AVERSIVE-EFFECTS IN RATS?
002992 03-04

AVERSIVE-EXPERIENCES
AMYGDALA OPIATE-SENSITIVE MECHANISMS INFLUENCE FEAR MOTIVATED RESPONSES AND MEMORY PROCESSES FOR AVERSIVE-EXPERIENCES. (UNPUBLISHED PAPER)
001628 02-04

AVERSIVE-PROPERTIES
A COMPARISON BETWEEN THE EFFECTS OF MORPHINE ON THE REWARDING AND AVERSIVE-PROPERTIES OF LATERAL HYPOTHALAMIC AND CENTRAL GRAY STIMULATION.
001771 02-04

AVERSIVE-SITUATIONS
DIFFERENTIAL-EFFECTS OF NALOXONE AGAINST THE DIAZEPAM-INDUCED RELEASE OF BEHAVIOR IN RATS IN THREE AVERSIVE-SITUATIONS.
000480 01-04

AVERSIVENESS
SOCIAL CROWDING ENHANCES AVERSIVENESS OF NALOXONE IN RATS.
004201 04-04

AVFAIL
DEPENDENCE OF THE AVFAIL EFFECT ON THE SEQUENCE OF TRAINING OPERATIONS.
001086 02-02

AVOIDANCE
ENHANCED SUPPRESSION OF CONDITIONED AVOIDANCE RESPONSE BY HALOPERIDOL BUT NOT PHENOXYBENZAMINE IN RATS WITH BILATERAL PARAFASCICULAR LESIONS.
000334 01-04

MORPHINE EFFECTS UPON DISCRIMINATED APPROACH AND DISCRIMINATED AVOIDANCE IN RATS: ANTAGONISM BY NALOXONE.
000338 01-04

EFFECT OF BETA ENDORPHIN AND NALOXONE ON ACQUISITION, MEMORY, AND RETRIEVAL OF SHUTTLE AVOIDANCE AND HABITUATION LEARNING IN RATS.
000410 01-04

POSTNATAL ALCOHOL EXPOSURE IN THE RAT: ITS EFFECTS ON AVOIDANCE CONDITIONING, HEBB-WILLIAMS MAZE-PERFORMANCE, MATERNAL-BEHAVIOR, AND PUP DEVELOPMENT.
001580 02-04

TWO-WAY AVOIDANCE LEARNING UNDER THE INFLUENCE OF NOOTROPIC-DRUGS.
001647 02-04

L-DOPA ENHANCES ACQUISITION OF AN INHIBITORY AVOIDANCE RESPONSE.
001711 02-04

AVOIDANCE ENHANCEMENT AND DISCRIMINATIVE RESPONSE CONTROL BY ANXIOLYTICS WITH DRUGS ACTING ON THE GABA SYSTEM.
004193 04-04

EFFECTS OF CHLORPROMAZINE ON ESCAPE AND AVOIDANCE RESPONSES: A CLOSER LOOK.
004226 04-04

AVOIDANCE RESPONSE IN RATS AFTER INJECTION OF DOPAMINE INTO THE NEOSTRIATUM.
004255 04-04

AVOIDANCE-BEHAVIOR
IMPAIRMENT OF AVOIDANCE-BEHAVIOR FOLLOWING SHORT-TERM INGESTION OF ETHANOL, TERTIARY BUTANOL, OR PENTOBARBITAL IN MICE.
000479 01-04

INTERACTION AMONG D-AMPHETAMINE, SCOPOLAMINE AND GENOTYPE IN AVOIDANCE-BEHAVIOR OF RATS.
003082 03-04

ACTH-LIKE PEPTIDES, PITUITARY ADRENOCORTICAL FUNCTION AND AVOIDANCE-BEHAVIOR.
004109 04-04

AVOIDANCE-BEHAVIOUR
EFFECTS OF MORPHINE AND CHLORDIAZEPOXIDE ON AVOIDANCE-BEHAVIOUR IN TWO INBRED STRAINS OF MICE.
002973 03-04

AVOIDANCE-DEFICITS
THE USE OF EXTINCTION TO INVESTIGATE THE NATURE OF NEUROLEPTIC-INDUCED AVOIDANCE-DEFICITS.
000345 01-04

THE USE OF CONDITIONED SUPPRESSION TO EVALUATE THE NATURE OF NEUROLEPTIC-INDUCED AVOIDANCE-DEFICITS.
004070 04-04

AVOIDING
APPROACHES TO THE PROBLEM OF PREVENTING HAZARDS OF LONG-TERM NEUROLEPTIC TREATMENT AND OF AVOIDING UNNECESSARY DRUGS.
002426 02-15

AVP
DIFFERENTIAL-EFFECTS OF VARIOUS STIMULI ON AVP LEVELS IN BLOOD AND CEREBROSPINAL-FLUID.
001370 02-03

AWAKE
A COMPARISON OF HUMAN TACTILE STIMULUS VELOCITY DISCRIMINATION WITH THE ABILITY OF S-I CORTICAL NEURONS IN AWAKE RHESUS-MONKEYS TO SIGNAL THE SAME VELOCITY DIFFERENCES BEFORE AND AFTER NONANESTHETIC DOSES OF PENTOBARBITAL.
000055 01-03

DIFFERENCES IN CUTANEOUS SENSORY RESPONSE PROPERTIES OF SINGLE SOMATOSENSORY CORTICAL NEURONS IN AWAKE AND HALOTHANE ANESTHETIZED RATS.
002687 03-03

TEMPORAL PATTERNING OF NEURONAL ACTIVITY DURING THERMAL AND NEUROCHEMICAL STIMULATION OF THE PREOPTIC/ANTERIOR HYPOTHALAMUS OF THE AWAKE RABBIT.
002737 03-03

AWAKENING
COMPARATIVE-STUDY OF SLEEP AND STATE ON AWAKENING WITH TWO HYPNOTIC DIAZEPINES.
000817 01-14

AXIS
INFLUENCE OF DRUGS AFFECTING THE PITUITARY ADRENAL AXIS ON CHROMAFFIN CELLS.
001183 02-03

DEVELOPMENT OF ACUTE TOLERANCE TO THE EFFECTS OF NALOXONE ON THE HYPOTHALAMIC PITUITARY LUTEINIZING-HORMONE AXIS IN THE MALE RAT.
002853 03-03

DRUG-INDUCED ALTERATIONS OF THE HYPOTHALAMUS HYPOPHYSIS AXIS.
004535 04-13

AXON
EFFECTS OF TAIPOXIN ON THE ULTRASTRUCTURE OF CHOLINERGIC AXON TERMINALS IN THE MOUSE ADRENAL-MEDULLA.
003916 04-03

AXONAL
BIOSYNTHESIS, AXONAL TRANSPORT AND RELEASE OF POSTERIOR PITUITARY-HORMONES. (UNPUBLISHED PAPER).
001148 02-03

PAPAIN-DERIVED FRAGMENT IIC TETANUS-TOXIN: ITS BINDING TO ISOLATED SYNAPTIC MEMBRANES AND RETROGRADE AXONAL TRANSPORT.
003734 04-03

STUDIES ON AXONAL TRANSPORT IN DOPAMINERGIC NEURONS: EFFECT OF NEUROPHARMACOLOGIC LESIONS.
003858 04-03

RESERPINE EFFECT ON THE AXONAL TRANSPORT OF DOPAMINE-BETA-HYDROXYLASE AND TYROSINE-HYDROXYLASE IN RAT-BRAIN.
003904 04-03

AXONS
ABSENCE OF POTASSIUM CONDUCTANCE IN CENTRAL MYELINATED AXONS.
000166 01-03

AZETIDINYLBUTYNYL
SYNTHESIS AND PHARMACOLOGICAL PROPERTIES OF N-4 1 AZETIDINYLBUTYNYL 2 PYRROLIDONE, A HIGHLY POTENT OXOTREMORINE-LIKE-AGENT.
003701 04-02

A10
INTRAVENOUS GABA AGONIST ADMINISTRATION STIMULATES FIRING OF A10 DOPAMINERGIC NEURONS.
000320 01-03

DOPAMINERGIC AGONISTS DIFFERENTIALLY AFFECT OPEN-FIELD ACTIVITY OF RATS WITH A10 LESIONS.
004135 04-04

BABOON
EEG AND ANTICONVULSANT EFFECTS OF DIPROPYLACETIC-ACID AND
DIPROPYLACETAMIDE IN THE BABOON PAPIO-PAPIO.
001210 02-03

BABOONS
PROGRESSIVE-RATIO AND FIXED-RATIO SCHEDULES OF COCAINE
MAINTAINED RESPONDING IN BABOONS.
000395 01-04

COMPARATIVE ANXIOLYTIC AND HYPNOTIC-EFFECTS OF 3
BENZODIAZEPINES ON BABOONS.
001581 02-04

BACKGROUND
THE BIOCHEMICAL BACKGROUND TO TARDIVE-DYSKINESIA.
004588 04-15

BACKWARD
THE ROLE OF CENTRAL SEROTONERGIC MECHANISMS ON HEAD-TWITCH
AND BACKWARD LOCOMOTION INDUCED BY HALLUCINOGENIC-DRUGS.
003397 03-12

BACLOFEN
CIRCLING-BEHAVIOUR INDUCED BY INTRANIGRAL INJECTION OF
BACLOFEN IN RATS.
000415 01-04

MANIC-PSYCHOSIS FOLLOWING RAPID WITHDRAWAL FROM BACLOFEN.
000832 01-15

THE EFFECTS OF ETHANOL, PHENOBARBITAL, AND BACLOFEN ON
ETHANOL WITHDRAWAL IN THE RHESUS-MONKEY.
001802 02-04

BACLOFEN IN TRIGEMINAL-NEURALGIA: ITS EFFECT ON THE SPINAL
TRIGEMINAL-NUCLEUS: A PILOT-STUDY.
002122 02-11

EFFECT OF SODIUM-VALPROATE AND BACLOFEN IN TARDIVE-DYSKINESIA:
CLINICAL-STUDIES AND NEUROENDOCRINE-STUDIES.
002441 02-15

CROSS-TOLERANCE OF DOPAMINE METABOLISM TO BACLOFEN, GAMMA
BUTYROLACTONE AND HA-966 IN THE STRIATUM AND OLFACTORY
TUBERCLE OF THE RAT.
002681 03-03

GABA AND BACLOFEN POTENTIATE THE K-EVOKED RELEASE OF
METHIONINE-ENKEPHALIN FROM RAT STRIATAL SLICES.
002882 03-03

BACLOFEN: BROADER ASPECTS OF ACTIVITY.
003429 03-13

3H BACLOFEN AND 3H GABA BIND TO BICUCULLINE INSENSITIVE GABAB
SITES IN RAT-BRAIN.
003839 04-03

BACLOFEN: STEREOSELECTIVE INHIBITION OF EXCITANT AMINO-ACID
RELEASE.
003867 04-03

CENTRAL CARDIOVASCULAR-EFFECTS AND BIOCHEMICAL-EFFECTS OF
BACLOFEN IN THE CONSCIOUS RAT.
003965 04-03

BACLOFEN IN THE TREATMENT OF TARDIVE-DYSKINESIA: OPEN LABEL
STUDY.
004619 04-15

BACTERIAL
SYNTHETIC IMMUNOSTIMULANTS DERIVED FROM THE BACTERIAL CELL
WALL.
001080 02-02

BAR-PRESSING-BEHAVIOR
FIRST DOSE BEHAVIORAL-TOLERANCE TO PHENCYCLIDINE ON FOOD
REWARDED BAR-PRESSING-BEHAVIOR IN THE RAT.
000462 01-04

IMITATION, SOCIAL FACILITATION, AND THE EFFECTS OF ACTH4-10 ON
RATS BAR-PRESSING-BEHAVIOR.
003009 03-04

BARBITAL
EFFECT OF P CHLOROPHENYLALANINE ON THE ACQUISITION OF
TOLERANCE TO THE HYPNOTIC-EFFECTS OF PENTOBARBITAL, BARBITAL,
AND ETHANOL.
003883 04-03

BARBITURATE
INTRACELLULAR REDOX STATES UNDER HALOTHANE AND BARBITURATE
ANESTHESIA IN NORMAL, ISCHEMIC, AND ANOXIC MONKEY BRAIN.
000295 01-03

SOCIAL AND CLINICAL SIGNIFICANCE OF DETERMINING THE BARBITURATE
LEVEL IN THE BLOOD SERUM OF PATIENTS TREATED WITH
ANTIEPILEPTIC-DRUGS.
000695 01-11

INTRAVENOUS PHENOBARBITAL THERAPY IN BARBITURATE AND OTHER
HYPNOSEDATIVE WITHDRAWAL REACTIONS: A KINETIC APPROACH.
000703 01-11

BARBITURATE SERUM LEVELS AND PROTECTION AGAINST KINDLED
AMYGDALOID SEIZURES IN THE RAT.
001559 02-04

REDUCTION OF BARBITURATE ANESTHESIA BY NEW GLUTARIMIDE
COMPOUNDS IN MICE.
001748 02-04

THE INTERACTION BETWEEN BARBITURATE ANESTHETICS AND
EXCITATORY AMINO-ACID RESPONSES ON CAT SPINAL NEURONES.
002799 03-03

BARBITURATE ENHANCEMENT OF GABA-MEDIATED INHIBITION AND
ACTIVATION OF CHLORIDE ION-CONDUCTANCE: CORRELATION WITH
ANTICONVULSANT AND ANESTHETIC ACTIONS.
002885 03-03

POTENTIATION OF BARBITURATE HYPNOSIS BY PROBENECID:
DIFFERENTIAL-EFFECT IN TOLERANT ANIMALS.
003038 03-04

NEUTRALIZATION OF THE EFFECT OF DELTA9 TETRAHYDROCANNABINOL
ON BARBITURATE SLEEPING-TIME BY SPECIFIC ACTIVE IMMUNIZATION.
003803 04-03

HABITUATION OF THE THE HEAD-POKE RESPONSE: EFFECTS OF AN
AMPHETAMINE BARBITURATE MIXTURE, PLG AND FENFLURAMINE.
004159 04-04

SELECTIVE EFFECTS OF BARBITURATE AND AMPHETAMINE ON
INFORMATION-PROCESSING AND RESPONSE EXECUTION.
004563 04-14

BARBITURATE-DEPENDENCE
BARBITURATE-DEPENDENCE IN MICE: EFFECTS OF PROPRANOLOL ON THE
WITHDRAWAL-SYNDROME (40798).
000313 01-03

BARBITURATE-DEPENDENCE AND DRUG PREFERENCE.
004235 04-04

BARBITURATE-EVOKED
A BARBITURATE-EVOKED INTENSIFICATION OF POSTSYNAPTIC INHIBITION
IN THE PREOPTIC OVULATORY TRIGGER REGION OF THE
HYPOTHALAMUS.
002818 03-03

BARBITURATE-INDUCED
TOLERANCE TO BARBITURATE-INDUCED CENTRAL-NERVOUS-SYSTEM
DEPRESSION: INVOLVEMENT OF STIMULUS SECRETION COUPLING IN
DISCRETE BRAIN AREAS. (PH.D. DISSERTATION).
001213 02-03

BARBITURATES
ANTICONVULSANT AND ANESTHETIC BARBITURATES: DIFFERENT
POSTSYNAPTIC ACTIONS IN CULTURED MAMMALIAN NEURONS.
000194 01-03

ACTION OF BARBITURATES ON ACTIVITY OF ACETYLCHOLINESTERASE
FROM SYNAPTOSOMAL MEMBRANES.
000224 01-03

CONVULSANT AND ANTICONVULSANT BARBITURATES. 1. MOLECULAR
CONFORMATIONS FROM CLASSICAL POTENTIAL ENERGY
CALCULATIONS.
001029 02-01

LACK OF INFLUENCE OF BRAIN CATECHOLAMINES ON ACUTE EFFECTS OF
BARBITURATES.
001138 02-03

EXPERIMENTAL DEPENDENCE ON BARBITURATES: II. RELATIONSHIP
BETWEEN DRUG LEVELS IN SERUM AND BRAIN AND THE
DEVELOPMENT OF DEPENDENCE IN RATS.
001800 02-04

THE EFFECT OF BARBITURATES ON THE DEGRADATION OF ENKEPHALIN BY
BRAIN ENZYMES.
002656 03-03

BARBITURATES AND GABA-RECEPTORS.
002769 03-03

EFFECTS OF D AMINOLAEVULINIC-ACID, PORPHOBILINOGEN, AMINO-
ACIDS AND BARBITURATES ON CALCIUM ACCUMULATION BY
CULTURED NEURONS.
002859 03-03

MECHANISM-OF-ACTION OF BARBITURATES.
003600 03-17

EFFECTS OF BARBITURATES ON INHIBITORY AND EXCITATORY RESPONSES
TO APPLIED NEUROTRANSMITTERS IN APLYSIA.
003762 04-03

SOME BARBITURATES ENHANCE THE EFFECT OF MUSCIMOL ON
DOPAMINE TURNOVER IN THE RAT RETINA.
003873 04-03

INTERACTION OF STEREOISOMERS OF BARBITURATES WITH (3H)ALPHA
DIHYDROPICROTOXININ BINDING-SITES.
004036 04-03

SEPARATION OF BARBITURATES USING REVERSE PHASE THIN-LAYER-
CHROMATOGRAPHY.
004670 04-16

BARORECEPTOR
EVIDENCE SUGGESTING A TRANSMITTER OR NEUROMODULATORY ROLE
FOR SUBSTANCE-P AT THE FIRST SYNAPSE OF THE BARORECEPTOR
REFLEX.
001264 02-03

EFFECTS OF ALPHA-ADRENOCEPTOR STIMULATING DRUGS ON
BARORECEPTOR REFLEXES IN CONSCIOUS CATS.
001514 02-03

BASAL
PROSTAGLANDIN-E RELEASE BY RAT MEDIAL BASAL HYPOTHALAMUS IN
VITRO. INHIBITION BY MELATONIN AT SUBMICROMOLAR
CONCENTRATIONS.
001159 02-03

ALTERATIONS IN BASAL FIRING-RATE AND AUTORECEPTOR SENSITIVITY
OF DOPAMINE NEURONS IN THE SUBSTANTIA-NIGRA FOLLOWING
ACUTE AND EXTENDED EXPOSURE TO ESTROGEN.
001167 02-03
DENERVATION IN THE DOPAMINERGIC MESOLIMBIC SYSTEM:
FUNCTIONAL CHANGES FOLLOWED USING (-)N N
PROPYLNORAPOMORPHINE DEPEND ON THE BASAL ACTIVITY LEVELS
OF RATS.
001603 02-04
BASAL AND STIMULATED LEVELS OF PROLACTIN, TSH AND LH IN SERUM
OF CHRONIC SCHIZOPHRENIC-PATIENTS, LONG-TERM TREATED WITH
NEUROLEPTICS.
001935 02-08
BASAL AND STIMULATED LEVELS OF PROLACTIN, TSH, AND LH IN SERUM
OF CHRONIC SCHIZOPHRENIC-PATIENTS LONG-TERM TREATED WITH
NEUROLEPTICS: RELATIONS TO PSYCHOPATHOLOGY.
001936 02-08
ANTIPSYCHOTIC-DRUGS: DIFFERENTIAL-EFFECTS ON DOPAMINE NEURONS
IN BASAL GANGLIA AND MESOCORTEX FOLLOWING CHRONIC
ADMINISTRATION IN HUMAN AND NONHUMAN PRIMATES.
002285 02-13
BASAL GANGLIA DOPAMINERGIC CONTROL OF SENSORIMOTOR
FUNCTIONS RELATED TO MOTIVATED BEHAVIOR.
002815 03-03
KAINIC-ACID AND NEUROTRANSMITTER INTERACTIONS IN THE BASAL
GANGLIA.
002824 03-03
GLUCOSE SUPPRESSES BASAL FIRING AND HALOPERIDOL-INDUCED
INCREASES IN THE FIRING-RATE OF CENTRAL DOPAMINERGIC
NEURONS.
002880 03-03
SELECTIVE MODIFICATION BY OPIATES OF NEURONAL ACTIVITY OF THE
MEDIAL BASAL HYPOTHALAMUS.
003773 04-03
BASAL PROLACTINAEMIA AND RESPONSES TO TRH AND SULPIRIDE IN
DIFFERENT CATEGORIES OF MALE SEXUAL-DYSFUNCTIONS.
004503 04-13

BASELINE
EFFECTS OF SINGLE-ORAL-DOSAGES OF STEROIDS ON HUMAN EEG
BASELINE CROSSING T-SCORES SHOWN BY MULTIVARIATE STATISTICS
AND STANDARD PROFILES.
002239 02-13

BASILAR
A COMPARISON OF THE CONTRACTILE RESPONSES OF THE RABBIT
BASILAR AND PULMONARY-ARTERIES TO SYMPATHOMIMETIC
AGONISTS: CHARACTERISTICS.
002670 03-03

BASOPHILIC
IGE MEDIATED HISTAMINE RELEASE IN RAT BASOPHILIC LEUKEMIA
CELLS: RECEPTOR ACTIVATED PHOSPHOLIPID METHYLATION, CA-FLUX
AND RELEASE OF ARACHIDONIC-ACID. (UNPUBLISHED PAPER).
001188 02-03

BASS-SCALE-FACTORS
TWO BASS-SCALE-FACTORS AND RESPONSE TO PLACEBO AND
ANXIOLYTIC-DRUGS.
000649 01-10

BATRACHOTOXIN
FURTHER ANALYSIS OF THE MECHANISMS OF ACTION OF
BATRACHOTOXIN ON THE MEMBRANE OF MYELINATED NERVE.
003884 04-03

BEAGLE-DOGS
BEHAVIORAL-ANALYSIS OF AMYGDALOID KINDLING IN BEAGLE-DOGS
AND THE EFFECTS OF CLONAZEPAM, DIAZEPAM, PHENOBARBITAL,
DIPHENYLHYDANTOIN, AND FLUNARIZINE ON SEIZURE
MANIFESTATION.
000496 01-04

BEARING
PROTEIN ABNORMALITIES IN MACROPHAGES BEARING ASBESTOS.
(UNPUBLISHED PAPER).
001037 02-01

BED
CONSISTENT UNMASKING OF DOPAMINE-INDUCED DILATION OF THE
CANINE FEMORAL VASCULAR BED.
003911 04-03

BEHAVIOR
TRANYLCYPROMINE STEREOISOMERS, MONOAMINERGIC
NEUROTRANSMISSION AND BEHAVIOR. A MINIREVIEW.
000016 01-02
SCHEDULE-CONTROLLED BEHAVIOR IN THE MORPHINE-DEPENDENT AND
POSTDEPENDENT RAT.
000349 01-04
CONSEQUENT EVENTS AS DETERMINANTS OF DRUG-EFFECTS ON
SCHEDULE-CONTROLLED BEHAVIOR: MODIFICATION OF EFFECTS OF
COCAINE AND D-AMPHETAMINE FOLLOWING CHRONIC AMPHETAMINE
ADMINISTRATION.
000350 01-04
BEHAVIORAL-PHARMACOLOGY AND THE STIMULUS CONTROL OF
BEHAVIOR.
000381 01-04

STEREOSPECIFIC, DOSE-DEPENDENT ANTAGONISM BY NALOXONE OF
NONOPIATE BEHAVIOR IN MICE.
000411 01-04
DIFFERENTIAL-EFFECTS OF NALOXONE AGAINST THE DIAZEPAM-INDUCED
RELEASE OF BEHAVIOR IN RATS IN THREE AVERSIVE-SITUATIONS.
000480 01-04
CONFIRMATION BEHAVIOR OF PHENCYCLIDINES AND BIOLOGICAL-
ACTIVITY.
001031 02-01
ANTIDEPRESSANT-DRUGS SLOW CIRCADIAN-RHYTHMS IN BEHAVIOR AND
BRAIN NEUROTRANSMITTER-RECEPTORS.
001536 02-03
THE EFFECTS OF NOREPINEPHRINE PERFUSION OF THE MESENCEPHALIC
RETICULAR FORMATION ON BEHAVIOR IN THE RAT: INTERACTION
WITH SEVERAL NEUROLEPTIC-DRUGS ON A MEASURE OF SUSTAINED
ATTENTION. (PH.D. DISSERTATION).
001563 02-04
ACUTE AND CHRONIC EFFECTS OF DELTA9 TETRAHYDROCANNABINOL ON
COMPLEX BEHAVIOR OF SQUIRREL-MONKEYS.
001583 02-04
EFFECTS OF LILLY-110140 (FLUOXETINE) ON SELF-STIMULATION
BEHAVIOR IN THE DORSAL AND VENTRAL REGIONS OF THE LATERAL
HYPOTHALAMUS IN THE MOUSE.
001590 02-04
INTERACTION OF PSYCHOPHARMALOGIC-FACTORS AND PSYCHOSOCIAL-
FACTORS IN THE TREATMENT OF ANIMAL-MODELS OF
HYPOINHIBITORY (HYPERKINETIC) BEHAVIOR.
001602 02-04
THE BEHAVIOR OF RATS IN THE OPEN-FIELD WITHOUT STRESS, UNDER
ACUTE AND PERSISTING INFLUENCE OF IMIPRAMINE AND
TRANYLCYPROMINE AS WELL AS ON THE INDIVIDUAL REACTION TYPE
(EMOTIVE AND NONEMOTIVE).
001624 02-04
INTERACTIONS BETWEEN NALTREXONE AND NONOPIATE DRUGS
EVALUATED BY SCHEDULE-CONTROLLED BEHAVIOR.
001645 02-04
Y-MAZE BEHAVIOR AFTER AN ANALOG OF ACTH4-9, EVIDENCE FOR AN
ATTENTIONAL-ALTERATION.
001676 02-04
THE EFFECTS OF D-AMPHETAMINE, CHLORDIAZEPOXIDE, AND
PENTOBARBITAL ON BEHAVIOR MAINTAINED BY ESCAPE FROM
PUNISHMENT IN PIGEONS. (PH.D. DISSERTATION).
001713 02-04
INTERRELATIONS AMONG PRIOR EXPERIENCE AND CURRENT CONDITIONS
IN THE DETERMINATION OF BEHAVIOR AND THE EFFECTS OF DRUGS.
001715 02-04
EFFECTS OF NEONATAL 6 HYDROXYDOPA ON BEHAVIOR IN FEMALE
RATS.
001717 02-04
EFFECTS OF ACUTE VS. CHRONIC PHENCYCLIDINE ON BRAIN-
BIOCHEMISTRY AND BEHAVIOR.
001789 02-04
EFFECTS OF BRANCHED-CHAIN FATTY-ACIDS ON GABA DEGRADATION
AND BEHAVIOR: FURTHER EVIDENCE FOR A ROLE OF GABA IN QUASI-
MORPHINE ABSTINENCE-BEHAVIOR.
001809 02-04
BEHAVIOR MAINTAINED BY INTRAVENOUS INJECTION OF CODEINE,
COCAINE, AND ETORPHINE IN THE RHESUS-MACAQUE AND THE
PIGTAIL-MACAQUE.
001828 02-04
BEHAVIORAL-INTERVENTION FOR SELF-STIMULATORY, ATTENDING AND
SEIZURE BEHAVIOR IN A CEREBRAL-PALSIED-CHILD.
002104 02-11
DISINHIBITION OF BEHAVIOR BY ANTIANXIETY-DRUGS.
002403 02-15
THE EFFECT OF ALTERED DOPAMINERGIC-ACTIVITY ON FOOD INTAKE IN
THE RAT: EVIDENCE FOR AN OPTIMAL LEVEL OF DOPAMINERGIC-
ACTIVITY FOR BEHAVIOR.
002632 02-17
FUNDAMENTAL MECHANISMS UNDERLYING ALTERED BEHAVIOR
FOLLOWING CHRONIC ADMINISTRATION OF PSYCHOMOTOR
STIMULANTS.
002711 03-03
BASAL GANGLIA DOPAMINERGIC CONTROL OF SENSORIMOTOR
FUNCTIONS RELATED TO MOTIVATED BEHAVIOR.
002815 03-03
POSSIBLE MECHANISMS OF EFFECT OF ACTH4-10 AND ITS ANALOG,
CONTAINING D ISOMER OF PHENYLALANINE, ON BEHAVIOR.
002949 03-04
FACILITATION OF LORDOSIS BEHAVIOR IN THE OVARIECTOMIZED
ESTROGEN-PRIMED RAT BY DIBUTYRYL-C-AMP.
002957 03-04
EFFECTS OF ACUTE CENTRAL AND PERIPHERAL ACTH1-24
ADMINISTRATION ON LORDOSIS BEHAVIOR.
002975 03-04
VASOTOCIN, PROSTAGLANDIN, AND FEMALE REPRODUCTIVE BEHAVIOR
IN THE FROG, RANA-PIPIENS.
002978 03-04

DRUG REGIMENS FACILITATING AGGRESSION: BEHAVIOR, AMINE, AND RECEPTOR ALTERATIONS.
002987 03-04
CONFLICT-SITUATION BASED ON INTRACRANIAL SELF-STIMULATION BEHAVIOR AND THE EFFECT OF BENZODIAZEPINES.
003004 03-04
MULTIDIMENSIONAL ANALYSES OF BEHAVIOR IN MICE TREATED WITH ALPHA ENDORPHIN.
003020 03-04
THE EFFECTS OF IMIPRAMINE TREATMENT ON THE UNCONDITIONED ALIMENTARY BEHAVIOR AND CLASSICAL CONDITIONED SALIVARY REACTIONS IN DOGS.
003030 03-04
SUPPRESSION OF ACTIVE SLEEP BY CHRONIC-TREATMENT WITH CHLORIMIPRAMINE DURING EARLY POSTNATAL DEVELOPMENT: EFFECTS UPON ADULT SLEEP AND BEHAVIOR IN THE RAT.
003056 03-04
CYCLIC-AMP-INDUCED CHANGES IN THE ELECTROENCEPHALOGRAM AND IN BEHAVIOR DURING MORPHINE-DEPENDENCE AND ABSTINENCE IN THE RAT.
003078 03-04
RESEARCH STRATEGIES FOR ASSESSING THE EFFECTS OF METHYLMERCURY ON BEHAVIOR.
003128 03-05
THE INFLUENCE OF METHYLPHENIDATE ON SPONTANEOUS AUTONOMIC-ACTIVITY AND BEHAVIOR IN CHILDREN DIAGNOSED AS HYPERACTIVE.
003363 03-11
SENSORY PROCESSING, CARDIOVASCULAR REACTIVITY, AND THE TYPE A CORONARY-PRONE BEHAVIOR PATTERN.
003405 03-13
COMPARISON OF THE EFFECTS OF FOUR BENZODIAZEPINES ON FRAME OF MIND AND BEHAVIOR IN HEALTHY SUBJECTS.
003441 03-14
EFFECTS OF NORCOCAINE AND SOME NORCOCAINE DERIVATIVES ON SCHEDULE-CONTROLLED BEHAVIOR OF PIGEONS AND SQUIRREL-MONKEYS.
004012 04-03
EFFECTS OF DOPAMINERGIC DRUGS ON PHENCYCLIDINE-INDUCED BEHAVIOR IN THE RAT.
004083 04-04
HISTAMINE AS A PUNISHER IN SQUIRREL-MONKEYS: EFFECTS OF PENTOBARBITAL, CHLORDIAZEPOXIDE AND H1-RECEPTOR AND H2-RECEPTOR ANTAGONISTS ON BEHAVIOR AND CARDIOVASCULAR RESPONSE.
004119 04-04
INTERACTIONS BETWEEN NARCOTIC AGONISTS, PARTIAL AGONISTS AND ANTAGONISTS EVALUATED BY SCHEDULE-CONTROLLED BEHAVIOR.
004127 04-04
EFFECTS OF NARCOTIC ABSTINENCE ON SCHEDULE-CONTROLLED BEHAVIOR IN DEPENDENT RATS.
004230 04-04
STUDIES OF CARBACHOL-INDUCED WET-DOG-SHAKE BEHAVIOR IN RATS.
004241 04-04
LACK OF SPECIFICITY OF AN ANIMAL BEHAVIOR MODEL FOR HALLUCINOGENIC DRUG ACTION.
004250 04-04
BEHAVIOR OF RATS AND MICE ADMINISTERED ACTIVE METABOLITES OF FLUPHENAZINE, 7 HYDROXYFLUPHENAZINE AND FLUPHENAZINE-SULFOXIDE.
004256 04-04
DOSAGE FORM DESIGN FOR IMPROVEMENT OF BIOAVAILABILITY OF LEVODOPA III: INFLUENCE OF DOSE ON PHARMACOKINETIC BEHAVIOR OF LEVODOPA IN DOGS AND PARKINSONIAN-PATIENTS.
004551 04-13
SEROTONERGIC APPROACHES TO THE MODIFICATION OF BEHAVIOR IN THE LESCH-NYHANS-SYNDROME.
004576 04-14
BEHAVIOR AND LEARNING DIFFICULTIES IN CHILDREN OF NORMAL INTELLIGENCE BORN TO ALCOHOLIC MOTHERS.
004658 04-15

BEHAVIOR-CHANGE
PSYCHOACTIVE-DRUG-EFFECTS IN A HYPERACTIVE-CHILD: A CASE-STUDY ANALYSIS OF BEHAVIOR-CHANGE AND TEACHER ATTENTION.
002313 02-14

BEHAVIOR-DEPENDENT
BEHAVIOR-DEPENDENT EVOKED-POTENTIALS IN THE HIPPOCAMPAL-CA1 REGION OF THE RAT. II. EFFECTS OF ESERINE, ATROPINE, ETHER AND PENTOBARBITAL.
000184 01-03

BEHAVIOR-DISORDERS
UNDERSTANDING AND USE OF CHEMOTHERAPY BY LEARNING-DISABILITIES AND BEHAVIOR-DISORDERS TEACHERS.
000965 01-17
THE MANAGEMENT OF CHRONIC BEHAVIOR-DISORDERS IN MENTALLY-RETARDED ADULTS WITH LITHIUM-CARBONATE.
003376 03-11
PREVALENCE OF DRUG-TREATMENT FOR HYPERACTIVITY AND OTHER CHILDHOOD BEHAVIOR-DISORDERS.
004713 04-17

BEHAVIOR-MODIFICATION
A CONTROLLED-TRIAL OF BEHAVIOR-MODIFICATION AND METHYLPHENIDATE IN HYPERACTIVE-CHILDREN.
000678 01-11
EVALUATION OF THE RELATIVE EFFECTIVENESS OF METHYLPHENIDATE AND COGNITIVE BEHAVIOR-MODIFICATION IN THE TREATMENT OF KINDERGARTEN-AGED HYPERACTIVE-CHILDREN.
003306 03-11

BEHAVIORAL
BEHAVIORAL CONFIRMATION OF DIFFUSE NOXIOUS INHIBITORY CONTROLS (DNIC) AND EVIDENCE FOR A ROLE OF ENDOGENOUS OPIATES.
002791 03-03
THE EFFECTS OF INJECTIONS OF BOMBESIN INTO THE CEREBRAL VENTRICLES ON BEHAVIORAL THERMOREGULATION.
002952 03-04
BRIEF COMMUNICATION: BEHAVIORAL RECOVERY AFTER TOLUENE EXPOSURE IN RATS.
002969 03-04
CHANGES IN THE HORIZONTAL VESTIBULO-OCULAR REFLEX OF THE RHESUS-MONKEY WITH BEHAVIORAL AND PHARMACOLOGICAL ALERTING.
002997 03-04
BOMBESIN ALTERS BEHAVIORAL THERMOREGULATION IN FISH.
003026 03-04
BEHAVIORAL AND METABOLIC ALTERATIONS IN PROGENY OF METHADONE-TREATED RATS. (PH.D. DISSERTATION).
003113 03-04
A RADIOIMMUNOASSAY FOR EPENDYMINS BETA AND GAMMA: TWO GOLDFISH BRAIN PROTEINS INVOLVED IN BEHAVIORAL PLASTICITY.
003677 04-01
DOM AND RELATED 2,5 DIMETHOXY-4-ALKYLPHENYLISOPROPYLAMINES: BEHAVIORAL AND SEROTONIN-RECEPTOR PROPERTIES.
003690 04-02
COMPARATIVE ANALGESIC, BEHAVIORAL, AND DEPENDENCE PROPERTIES OF MORPHINE AND O METHOXYLPHENYLCARBAMOYLDIETHYLAMINOPROPIOPHENONEOXIME HCL.
003707 04-02
BEHAVIORAL AND REGIONAL NEUROCHEMICAL SEQUELAE OF HIPPOCAMPAL DESTRUCTION IN THE RAT.
003721 04-03
THE EFFECT OF SMALL DOSES OF HALOPERIDOL AND CLOZAPINE ON BEHAVIORAL SHIFTS IN CATS, ARISING AFTER CESSATION OF ELECTRICAL-STIMULATION OF THE CAUDATE-NUCLEUS.
004067 04-04
BEHAVIORAL AND BIOCHEMICAL-STUDIES OF THE SCOPOLAMINE-INDUCED REVERSAL OF NEUROLEPTIC ACTIVITY.
004195 04-04
PHYSIOLOGICAL AND BEHAVIORAL APPROACHES TO THE STUDY OF THE QUASI-MORPHINE WITHDRAWAL-SYNDROME.
004242 04-04
A MICROCOMPUTER SYSTEM FOR THE CONTROL OF BEHAVIORAL EXPERIMENTS.
004287 04-06

BEHAVIORAL-ACTIVITY
NALOXONE REVERSIBLE EFFECTS OF D ALA2-MET5-ENKEPHALINAMIDE-INDUCED BEHAVIORAL-ACTIVITY IN RATS.
000402 01-04
COMPARISON OF BIOLOGICAL-ACTIVITY AND BEHAVIORAL-ACTIVITY OF ALPHA AND GAMMA MELANOCYTE-STIMULATING-HORMONES. (UNPUBLISHED RESULTS).
001398 02-03
THE EFFECT OF NEUROPEPTIDE FRAGMENTS OF ADRENOCORTICOTROPIN AND VASOPRESSIN ON BEHAVIORAL-ACTIVITY IN RATS.
001812 02-04

BEHAVIORAL-ANALYSIS
MORPHINE VERSUS HALOPERIDOL CATALEPSY IN THE RAT: A BEHAVIORAL-ANALYSIS OF POSTURAL SUPPORT MECHANISMS.
000376 01-04
BEHAVIORAL-ANALYSIS OF AMYGDALOID KINDLING IN BEAGLE-DOGS AND THE EFFECTS OF CLONAZEPAM, DIAZEPAM, PHENOBARBITAL, DIPHENYLHYDANTOIN, AND FLUNARIZINE ON SEIZURE MANIFESTATION.
000496 01-04

BEHAVIORAL-ASPECT
MECHANISM-OF-ACTION OF THE BENZODIAZEPINES: BEHAVIORAL-ASPECT.
000468 01-04

BEHAVIORAL-ASPECTS
THE ROLE OF NICOTINE IN THE BEHAVIORAL-ASPECTS OF CIGARETTE SMOKING.
004575 04-14

BEHAVIORAL-CHANGES
ENDOCRINE CHANGES AND BEHAVIORAL-CHANGES IN DEPRESSION AFTER THYROTROPIN-RELEASING-HORMONE (TRH): ALTERATION BY PRETREATMENT WITH THYROID-HORMONES.
002259 02-13

BEHAVIORAL-CHANGES AND BIOCHEMICAL-CHANGES AFTER HIPPOCAMPAL DAMAGE. (PH.D. DISSERTATION).
003069 03-04

BEHAVIORAL-CONSEQUENCES
LARGE-DOSES OF VITAMINS AND BEHAVIORAL-CONSEQUENCES. (PH.D. DISSERTATION).
001633 02-04
BEHAVIORAL-CONSEQUENCES OF LONG-TERM-TREATMENT WITH NEUROLEPTIC-DRUGS.
001661 02-04

BEHAVIORAL-CONSIDERATIONS
RAPID TREATMENT OF ACUTE PSYCHOTIC-SYMPTOMS WITH HIGH-DOSE AND LOW-DOSE HALOPERIDOL: BEHAVIORAL-CONSIDERATIONS.
003346 03-11

BEHAVIORAL-CORRELATES
BEHAVIORAL-CORRELATES AND BIOCHEMICAL-CORRELATES AFTER HALOPERIDOL AND CLOZAPINE LONG-TERM-TREATMENT.
001422 02-03

BEHAVIORAL-DEFICIENCIES
PHARMACOTHERAPY FOR AGE-RELATED BEHAVIORAL-DEFICIENCIES.
003391 03-11

BEHAVIORAL-DEFICIT
PHENYLACETATE AND THE ENDURING BEHAVIORAL-DEFICIT IN EXPERIMENTAL PHENYLKETONURIA.
000388 01-04
ABNORMAL MATURATION OF CEREBRAL-CORTEX AND BEHAVIORAL-DEFICIT IN ADULT RATS AFTER NEONATAL ADMINISTRATION OF ANTIBODIES TO GANGLIOSIDE.
003025 03-04

BEHAVIORAL-DEPRESSION
BEHAVIORAL-DEPRESSION AND ITS NEUROCHEMICAL-CORRELATES AT HIGH-DOSES OF D-AMPHETAMINE IN RATS.
001601 02-04

BEHAVIORAL-DESENSITIZATION
BEHAVIORAL-DESENSITIZATION OF PHOBIC-ANXIETY USING THIOPENTAL-SODIUM.
002352 02-14

BEHAVIORAL-DISORDERS
PLASMA CHLORPROMAZINE CONCENTRATIONS IN CHILDREN WITH BEHAVIORAL-DISORDERS AND MENTAL-ILLNESS.
000717 01-11
INVESTIGATION INTO THE EFFECT OF FLUPHENAZINE-HCL (LYORODIN) IN CHILDREN WITH BEHAVIORAL-DISORDERS BY MEANS OF PSYCHOPHYSIOLOGICAL PARAMETERS.
003344 03-11
POLYPHARMACY REGIMEN AS AN EXACERBATING RISK IN THERAPY-RESISTANT EPILEPTIC-SEIZURES AND BEHAVIORAL-DISORDERS.
004720 04-17

BEHAVIORAL-DISTURBANCES
BEHAVIORAL-DISTURBANCES IN PSYCHIATRY: A THERAPEUTIC APPROACH.
002321 02-14

BEHAVIORAL-EFFECTS
INHIBITION OF BEHAVIORAL-EFFECTS OF COCAINE BY ACTINOMYCIN-D IN RATS.
000346 01-04
ENHANCEMENT OF THE BEHAVIORAL-EFFECTS OF 2,5 DIMETHOXY-4-METHYLAMPHETAMINE (DOM) BY PRETREATMENT WITH P CHLOROPHENYLALANINE.
000364 01-04
THE INFLUENCE OF 5 HT-RECEPTOR BLOCKING-AGENTS ON THE BEHAVIORAL-EFFECTS OF ANALGESICS IN RATS.
000429 01-04
BEHAVIORAL-EFFECTS AND ELECTROCORTICAL-EFFECTS AFTER INTRASTRIATAL CEFAZOLIN IN RATS ARE ANTAGONIZED BY DRUGS ENHANCING GABAERGIC TRANSMISSION.
000443 01-04
NALOXONE OVERCOMES THE DOPAMINERGIC, EEG, AND BEHAVIORAL-EFFECTS OF GAMMA HYDROXYBUTYRATE.
000478 01-04
CHRONIC ADMINISTRATION OF HALOPERIDOL DURING DEVELOPMENT: BEHAVIORAL-EFFECTS AND PSYCHOPHARMACOLOGICAL-EFFECTS.
000481 01-04
BEHAVIORAL-EFFECTS OF ETHYNYL ESTROGENS IN THE FEMALE RAT.
000483 01-04
DEXTROAMPHETAMINE: COGNITIVE AND BEHAVIORAL-EFFECTS IN NORMAL AND HYPERACTIVE-BOYS AND NORMAL ADULT MALES.
000716 01-11
BEHAVIORAL-EFFECTS OF DRUGS: THE ROLE OF THE STIMULUS REINFORCER CONTINGENCY. (PH.D. DISSERTATION).
001537 02-03
BEHAVIORAL-EFFECTS, ANTIDOPAMINERGIC-EFFECTS, AND PROHYPNOTIC-EFFECTS OF NEUROLEPTICS DURING AND AFTER PROLONGED TREATMENT.
001577 02-04
BEHAVIORAL-EFFECTS AND ELECTROPHYSIOLOGICAL-EFFECTS OF OPIOID-PEPTIDES IN CATS.
001612 02-04
BEHAVIORAL-EFFECTS OF HASHISH IN MICE: II. NURSING-BEHAVIOR AND DEVELOPMENT OF THE SUCKLINGS.
001626 02-04

BRAIN LOCATIONS CONTROLLING THE BEHAVIORAL-EFFECTS OF CHRONIC AMPHETAMINE INTOXICATION.
001653 02-04
DIFFERENT BEHAVIORAL-EFFECTS FOLLOWING INTRACEREBRAL, INTRACEREBROVENTRICULAR OR INTRAPERITONEAL INJECTION OF NALOXONE IN THE RAT.
001665 02-04
ENHANCEMENT OF 5 HYDROXYTRYPTAMINE-INDUCED BEHAVIORAL-EFFECTS FOLLOWING CHRONIC ADMINISTRATION OF ANTIDEPRESSANT-DRUGS.
001667 02-04
NEUROCHEMICAL-EFFECTS AND BEHAVIORAL-EFFECTS OF CHRONIC D-AMPHETAMINE TREATMENT IN GENETICALLY OBESE (OBOB) MICE. (PH.D. DISSERTATION).
001739 02-04
BEHAVIORAL-EFFECTS OF HASHISH IN MICE: III. SOCIAL-INTERACTIONS BETWEEN TWO RESIDENTS AND AN INTRUDER MALE.
001776 02-04
BEHAVIORAL-EFFECTS OF HASHISH IN MICE: I. SOCIAL-INTERACTIONS AND NEST-BUILDING-BEHAVIOR OF MALES.
001777 02-04
BEHAVIORAL-EFFECTS OF DOPAMINE AGONISTS ACROSS THE ESTROUS-CYCLE IN RATS.
001792 02-04
BEHAVIORAL-EFFECTS AND SUBJECTIVE-EFFECTS OF BETA-ADRENERGIC BLOCKADE IN PHOBIC-SUBJECTS.
002060 02-10
MOOD AND BEHAVIORAL-EFFECTS OF PHYSOSTIGMINE ON HUMANS ARE ACCOMPANIED BY ELEVATIONS IN PLASMA BETA ENDORPHIN AND CORTISOL.
002280 02-13
BIOCHEMICAL-EFFECTS AND BEHAVIORAL-EFFECTS OF ACUTE ETHANOL IN RATS AT DIFFERENT ENVIRONMENTAL TEMPERATURES.
002864 03-03
THE ROLE OF CALCIUM AND DOPAMINE MEMBRANE CARRIER IN MEDIATING THE BEHAVIORAL-EFFECTS AND BIOCHEMICAL-EFFECTS OF AMPHETAMINE. (PH.D. DISSERTATION).
002996 03-04
A CHARACTERIZATION OF THE BEHAVIORAL-EFFECTS OF LEVO ALPHA ACETYLMETHADOL IN THE RAT AND IN THE PIGEON. (PH.D. DISSERTATION).
003047 03-04
2,4,5 TRICHLOROPHENOXYACETIC-ACID CAUSES BEHAVIORAL-EFFECTS IN CHICKENS AT ENVIRONMENTALLY RELEVANT DOSES.
003079 03-04
SUPERSENSITIVITY TO THE BEHAVIORAL-EFFECTS OF OPIATE ANTAGONISTS.
003096 03-04
THE RELATIONSHIP BETWEEN THE ACUTE BEHAVIORAL-EFFECTS OF NARCOTIC ANTAGONISTS AND THE NARCOTIC DEPENDENT STATE.
003106 03-04
BEHAVIORAL-EFFECTS OF METHADONE IN SCHIZOPHRENIC-PATIENTS.
003178 03-08
BEHAVIORAL-EFFECTS AND BIOLOGICAL-EFFECTS OF ACUTE BETA ENDORPHIN INJECTION IN SCHIZOPHRENIC-PATIENTS AND DEPRESSED-PATIENTS.
003357 03-11
THE BEHAVIORAL-EFFECTS OF D-AMPHETAMINE ALONE AND IN COMBINATION WITH ACUTE AND CHRONIC MORPHINE TREATMENTS IN RATS.
003915 04-03
A COMMON MECHANISM FOR LYSERGIC-ACID, INDOLEALKYLAMINE AND PHENETHYLAMINE HALLUCINOGENS: SEROTONERGIC MEDIATION OF BEHAVIORAL-EFFECTS IN RATS.
004007 04-03
REDUCTION IN OPIATE ACTIVATION AFTER CHRONIC ELECTROCONVULSIVE-SHOCK — POSSIBLE ROLE FOR ENDORPHINS IN THE BEHAVIORAL-EFFECTS OF CONVULSIVE-SHOCK-TREATMENT. (UNPUBLISHED PAPER).
004154 04-04
SAME OR DIFFERENT? AN EXPLORATION OF THE BEHAVIORAL-EFFECTS OF BENZAMIDES.
004207 04-04
INTRACEREBRAL SUBSTANCE-P IN MICE: BEHAVIORAL-EFFECTS AND NARCOTIC-AGENTS.
004218 04-04
BEHAVIORAL-EFFECTS OF SELF-ADMINISTERED COCAINE: RESPONDING MAINTAINED ALTERNATELY BY COCAINE AND ELECTRIC-SHOCK IN SQUIRREL-MONKEYS.
004225 04-04
CANNABINOIDS. I. BEHAVIORAL-EFFECTS.
004228 04-04

BEHAVIORAL-EVENTS
BRAIN GLUCOCORTICOID-RECEPTOR: CORRELATION OF IN VIVO.UPTAKE OF CORTICOSTERONE WITH BEHAVIORAL-EVENTS, ENDOCRINE-EVENTS, AND NEUROPHARMACOLOGICAL EVENTS.
002515 02-17

BEHAVIORAL-EVIDENCE
CHRONIC AMPHETAMINE ADMINISTRATION TO CATS: BEHAVIORAL-EVIDENCE AND NEUROCHEMICAL EVIDENCE FOR DECREASED CENTRAL SEROTONERGIC FUNCTION.
000491 01-04
NEUROCHEMICAL EVIDENCE AND BEHAVIORAL-EVIDENCE FOR A SELECTIVE PRESYNAPTIC DOPAMINE-RECEPTOR AGONIST.
002236 02-13
BEHAVIORAL-EVIDENCE THAT SUBSTANCE-P MAY BE A SPINAL-CORD SENSORY NEUROTRANSMITTER.
004200 04-04

BEHAVIORAL-FACILITATION
BEHAVIORAL-FACILITATION FOLLOWING CHRONIC ADMINISTRATION OF N N PROPYLNORAPOMORPHINE.
001822 02-04

BEHAVIORAL-INTERACTIONS
BEHAVIORAL-INTERACTIONS BETWEEN OPIATE AND ANTIEPILEPTIC-DRUGS IN THE MOUSE.
004155 04-04

BEHAVIORAL-INTERVENTION
BEHAVIORAL-INTERVENTION FOR SELF-STIMULATORY, ATTENDING AND SEIZURE BEHAVIOR IN A CEREBRAL-PALSIED-CHILD.
002104 02-11

BEHAVIORAL-NEUROCHEMISTRY
BEHAVIORAL-NEUROCHEMISTRY OF BENZODIAZEPINES.
000991 01-17

BEHAVIORAL-PHARMACOLOGY
BEHAVIORAL-PHARMACOLOGY AND THE STIMULUS CONTROL OF BEHAVIOR.
000381 01-04
CUMULATIVE DOSE RESPONSE-CURVES IN BEHAVIORAL-PHARMACOLOGY.
001883 02-06
ADVANCES IN BEHAVIORAL-PHARMACOLOGY. VOL. 2.
002364 02-14
BEHAVIORAL-PHARMACOLOGY OF TETRAHYDROCANNABINOL CONVULSIONS IN RABBITS.
004288 04-06

BEHAVIORAL-PHARMACOTHERAPY
A COMBINED BEHAVIORAL-PHARMACOTHERAPY APPROACH TO OBSESSIVE-COMPULSIVE-DISORDERS.
002082 02-10

BEHAVIORAL-PREDICTORS
BEHAVIORAL-PREDICTORS OF AMITRIPTYLINE RESPONSE IN DEPRESSION.
003253 03-09

BEHAVIORAL-PROFILE
EEG AND BEHAVIORAL-PROFILE OF FLUTROLINE (CP-36-584), A NOVEL ANTIPSYCHOTIC-DRUG.
001071 02-02

BEHAVIORAL-RATING-SCALES
DESIGN ASPECTS OF CLINICAL-TRIALS WITH ERGOT ALKALOIDS: A COMPARISON OF TWO GERIATRIC BEHAVIORAL-RATING-SCALES.
002512 02-16

BEHAVIORAL-REACTIONS
ON CORRELATION OF BEHAVIORAL-REACTIONS AND NEURONAL ACTIVITY IN THE HYPOTHALAMUS UNDER SUBCUTANEOUS GASTRIN INJECTION.
002892 03-03
THE EFFECT OF PROPYLNORANTIFEIN ON BEHAVIORAL-REACTIONS, ADRENOCORTICAL ACTIVITY, AND ENERGY METABOLISM IN THE ANIMAL BRAIN.
004075 04-04

BEHAVIORAL-RESPONSES
RELATIONSHIPS BETWEEN SELECTIVE DENERVATION OF DOPAMINE TERMINAL-FIELDS IN THE ANTERIOR-FOREBRAIN AND BEHAVIORAL-RESPONSES TO AMPHETAMINE AND APOMORPHINE.
000384 01-04
EFFECTS OF CHRONIC ADMINISTRATION OF DELTA9 TETRAHYDROCANNABINOL ON THE CARDIOVASCULAR SYSTEM, AND PRESSOR AND BEHAVIORAL-RESPONSES TO BRAIN-STIMULATION IN FREELY-MOVING-RATS.
000417 01-04
EFFECTS OF DELTA9 TETRAHYDROCANNABINOL ON THE CARDIOVASCULAR-SYSTEM, AND PRESSOR AND BEHAVIORAL-RESPONSES TO BRAIN-STIMULATION IN RATS.
001681 02-04
GONADECTOMY AND SEX-DIFFERENCES IN THE BEHAVIORAL-RESPONSES TO AMPHETAMINE AND APOMORPHINE OF RATS.
003084 03-04

BEHAVIORAL-REVERSAL
5,7 DIHYDROXYTRYPTAMINE-INDUCED MOUSE-KILLING AND BEHAVIORAL-REVERSAL WITH VENTRICULAR ADMINISTRATION OF SEROTONIN IN RATS.
001562 02-04

BEHAVIORAL-SENSITIVITY
THE INFLUENCE OF GENOTYPE AND SEX ON BEHAVIORAL-SENSITIVITY TO NICOTINE IN MICE.
001648 02-04

BEHAVIORAL-SENSITIZATION
DRUG ENVIRONMENT INTERACTION: CONTEXT DEPENDENCY OF COCAINE-INDUCED BEHAVIORAL-SENSITIZATION.
002866 03-03

BEHAVIORAL-STIMULATION
NEUROPHARMACOLOGICAL-STUDIES OF PHENCYCLIDINE-INDUCED BEHAVIORAL-STIMULATION IN MICE.
001622 02-04

BEHAVIORAL-STUDIES
BEHAVIORAL-STUDIES AND NEUROCHEMICAL-STUDIES OF LESCH-NYHANS-SYNDROME.
001743 02-04
PHYSIOLOGICAL-STUDIES AND BEHAVIORAL-STUDIES WITH MUSCIMOL.
002538 02-17

BEHAVIORAL-SUPERSENSITIVITY
SELECTIVE INHIBITION OF MESOLIMBIC BEHAVIORAL-SUPERSENSITIVITY BY NALOXONE.
000467 01-04
INDUCTION OF BEHAVIORAL-SUPERSENSITIVITY TO APOMORPHINE BY DFP TREATMENT.
004099 04-04
THE EFFECT OF CHRONIC LEVODOPA ON HALOPERIDOL-INDUCED BEHAVIORAL-SUPERSENSITIVITY IN THE GUINEA-PIG.
004249 04-04

BEHAVIORAL-SUPPRESSION
DORSAL TEGMENTAL BUNDLE DESTRUCTION: EFFECTS ON OPERANT-BEHAVIOR, BRAIN CATECHOLAMINE LEVELS, AND BEHAVIORAL-SUPPRESSION PRODUCED BY ADRENERGIC AGONISTS.
001726 02-04

BEHAVIORAL-SYNDROME
RELATIVE POTENCY OF AMPHETAMINE ISOMERS IN CAUSING THE SEROTONIN BEHAVIORAL-SYNDROME IN RATS.
003094 03-04

BEHAVIORAL-TEST
BEHAVIORAL-TEST FOR DETECTION OF SUBCLINICAL BRAIN-DAMAGE: AN EXPERIMENTAL MODEL.
003120 03-04

BEHAVIORAL-TESTING
CYCLOPHOSPHAMIDE-INDUCED SPERMATOGENIC EFFECTS DETECTED IN THE F1-GENERATION BY BEHAVIORAL-TESTING.
003121 03-05

BEHAVIORAL-TESTS
EFFECT OF DRUGS ON LEARNING AND MEMORY PROCESSES IN SIMPLE BEHAVIORAL-TESTS.
000809 01-14

BEHAVIORAL-THERAPY
PSYCHOPHARMACOLOGY AND BEHAVIORAL-THERAPY.
003584 03-17

BEHAVIORAL-TOLERANCE
FIRST DOSE BEHAVIORAL-TOLERANCE TO PHENCYCLIDINE ON FOOD REWARDED BAR-PRESSING-BEHAVIOR IN THE RAT.
000462 01-04
ELECTROENCEPHALOGRAPHIC AND BEHAVIORAL-TOLERANCE TO AND CROSS-TOLERANCE BETWEEN D ALA2-METHIONINE-ENKEPHALINAMIDE AND MORPHINE IN THE RAT.
004038 04-03

BEHAVIORAL-TREATMENT
BEHAVIORAL-TREATMENT AND PHARMACOLOGICAL-TREATMENT OF OBSESSIVE-COMPULSIVE-DISORDERS.
000657 01-10

BEHAVIORAL-TREATMENTS
DOUBLE-BLIND EVALUATION OF REINFORCING AND ANORECTIC-ACTIONS OF WEIGHT-CONTROL MEDICATIONS: INTERACTION OF PHARMACOLOGICAL-TREATMENT AND BEHAVIORAL-TREATMENTS.
002314 02-14

BEHAVIORALLY-SELECTIVE
NOREPINEPHRINE UPTAKE INHIBITORS AS BIOCHEMICALLY-SELECTIVE AND BEHAVIORALLY-SELECTIVE ANTAGONISTS OF THE LOCOMOTOR-STIMULATION INDUCED BY INDIRECTLY ACTING SYMPATHOMIMETIC-AMINES IN MICE.
000492 01-04

BEHAVIORS
EFFECTS OF PHENCYCLIDINE AND METHYLPHENIDATE ON D-AMPHETAMINE-INDUCED BEHAVIORS IN RESERPINE PRETREATED RATS.
001616 02-04
DIFFERENTIAL DOPAMINERGIC FUNCTION IN YOUNG AND OLD FEMALE RATS AS MEASURED BY THREE BEHAVIORS.
001683 02-04
DRUG-EFFECTS ON SCHEDULE-INDUCED BEHAVIORS. (PH.D. DISSERTATION).
001786 02-04
ANIMAL-MODEL OF PSYCHOSIS: HALLUCINATORY BEHAVIORS IN MONKEYS DURING THE LATE STAGE OF CONTINUOUS AMPHETAMINE INTOXICATION.
002988 03-04
A PRIMATE ANALOGUE OF AMPHETAMINE-INDUCED BEHAVIORS IN HUMANS.
003006 03-04
GENETIC VARIATIONS IN MIDBRAIN DOPAMINE CELL NUMBER: PARALLEL WITH DIFFERENCES IN RESPONSES TO DOPAMINERGIC AGONISTS AND IN NATURALISTIC BEHAVIORS MEDIATED BY CENTRAL DOPAMINERGIC-SYSTEMS. (UNPUBLISHED PAPER).
004112 04-04

HIPPOCAMPAL INVOLVEMENT IN THE PHARMACOLOGIC INDUCTION OF WITHDRAWAL-LIKE BEHAVIORS.
004140 04-04

PERIPHERAL-CORRELATES OF SEROTONERGICALLY-INFLUENCED BEHAVIORS IN VERVET-MONKEYS (CERCOPITHECUS-AETHIOPS-SABAEUS).
004204 04-04

BEHAVIOUR
BETA-ADRENOCEPTOR ANTAGONISTS: STUDIES ON BEHAVIOUR (DELAYED DIFFERENTIATION) IN THE MONKEY (MACACA-MULATTA).
000440 01-04

EPILEPSY: NEUROTRANSMITTER, BEHAVIOUR AND PREGNANCY.
002466 02-15

EFFECTS OF NEONATAL TESTOSTERONE AND ESTROGEN ON OPEN-FIELD BEHAVIOUR IN RATS.
003098 03-04

EFFECTS OF LITHIUM ON BEHAVIOUR AND CENTRAL MONOAMINES.
004110 04-04

ATTENUATION OF DELTA9 TETRAHYDROCANNABINOL-INDUCED WITHDRAWAL-LIKE BEHAVIOUR BY DELTA9 TETRAHYDROCANNABINOL.
004243 04-04

ON MONOAMINERGIC-INTERACTION WITH BEHAVIOUR MODIFYING PEPTIDE-HORMONES.
004700 04-17

BEHAVIOUR-THERAPY
CONTROLLED-TRIAL OF BEHAVIOUR-THERAPY, PHARMACOTHERAPY, AND THEIR COMBINATION IN THE TREATMENT OF OBESITY.
000725 01-11

OBSESSIVE-SYMPTOM RESPONSE TO BEHAVIOUR-THERAPY AND TO ANTIDEPRESSANT-DRUGS.
002084 02-10

BEHAVIOURAL
BEHAVIOURAL AND NEUROCHEMICAL PROPERTIES OF 1 1 INDOL-3-YLMETHYLPIPERID-4-YL-3-BENZOYLUREA (WY-25093) IN RODENTS.
003686 04-02

BEHAVIOURAL-ACTIONS
SYNAPTIC AND BEHAVIOURAL-ACTIONS OF ANTIDEPRESSANT-DRUGS: FURTHER THOUGHTS ON THE IMPLICATIONS FOR THEORIES OF DEPRESSION.
003229 03-09

BEHAVIOURAL-ANALYSIS
BEHAVIOURAL-ANALYSIS OF FEEDING: IMPLICATIONS FOR THE PHARMACOLOGICAL MANIPULATION OF FOOD INTAKE IN ANIMALS AND MAN.
002527 02-17

BEHAVIOURAL-CHANGES
GABA DEPLETION AND BEHAVIOURAL-CHANGES PRODUCED BY INTRAVENTRICULAR PUTRESCINE IN CHICKS.
000218 01-03

BEHAVIOURAL-CHANGES INDUCED BY N,N DIMETHYLTRYPTAMINE IN RODENTS.
000413 01-04

BEHAVIOURAL-CHANGES IN ADULT RATS FOLLOWING ADMINISTRATION OF ANTIBODIES AGAINST BRAIN GANGLIOSIDES.
003071 03-04

BEHAVIOURAL-DESPAIR
PRESYNAPTIC ALPHA-ADRENOCEPTORS AND THE ACTION OF TRICYCLIC-ANTIDEPRESSANT DRUGS IN BEHAVIOURAL-DESPAIR IN RATS.
001829 02-04

BEHAVIOURAL-EFFECTS
DIAZEPAM IN COMBINATION WITH TACRINE DERIVATIVES ANTAGONIZES BEHAVIOURAL-EFFECTS OF ANTICHOLINERGIC PSYCHOTOMIMETICS IN RATS.
000420 01-04

OXOTREMORINE BEHAVIOURAL-EFFECTS AS A SCREENING-TEST IN MICE.
001072 02-02

STUDIES ON THE BIOCHEMICAL-EFFECTS AND BEHAVIOURAL-EFFECTS OF ORAL NICOTINE.
001115 02-03

THE INFLUENCE OF ANTERIOR NEOSTRIATAL LESIONS ON THE BEHAVIOURAL-EFFECTS OF SPIROPERIDOL IN RATS.
001702 02-04

BEHAVIOURAL-EFFECTS AND ENDOCRINE-EFFECTS OF NALTREXONE IN MALE TALAPOIN-MONKEYS.
001718 02-04

ENHANCED BEHAVIOURAL-EFFECTS, ELECTROCORTICAL-EFFECTS AND HYPERTHERMIC-EFFECTS OF SEROTONIN-LIKE AGENTS AFTER IMPAIRMENT OF SEROTONIN TRANSMISSION IN FOWL BRAIN.
001733 02-04

BEHAVIOURAL-EFFECTS OF ACETYLSALICYLIC-ACID, PARACETAMOL, CAFFEINE, GUAIPHENESIN AND THEIR COMBINATIONS.
001805 02-04

ELECTROENCEPHALOGRAPHIC-EFFECTS AND BEHAVIOURAL-EFFECTS OF SODIUM-VALPROATE IN PATIENTS WITH PHOTOSENSITIVE EPILEPSY. A SINGLE-DOSE TRIAL.
002154 02-11

AN OBSERVATIONAL METHOD FOR QUANTIFYING THE BEHAVIOURAL-EFFECTS OF DOPAMINE AGONISTS: CONTRASTING-EFFECTS OF D-AMPHETAMINE AND APOMORPHINE.
002484 02-16

A COMPARISON BETWEEN SOME BIOCHEMICAL-EFFECTS AND BEHAVIOURAL-EFFECTS PRODUCED BY NEUROLEPTICS.
004116 04-04

BEHAVIOURAL-MANIPULATION
FOOTSHOCK ANALGESIA: PREVENTION BY BEHAVIOURAL-MANIPULATION BUT NOT BY NALOXONE.
003073 03-04

BEHAVIOURAL-RESPONSES
BEHAVIOURAL-RESPONSES TO STEREOTACTICALLY CONTROLLED INJECTIONS OF MONOAMINE NEUROTRANSMITTERS INTO THE ACCUMBENS AND CAUDATE-PUTAMEN NUCLEI.
001708 02-04

EFFECT OF ACUTE AND CHRONIC TRIIODOTHYRONINE (T3) ADMINISTRATION TO RATS ON CENTRAL 5 HT AND DOPAMINE-MEDIATED BEHAVIOURAL-RESPONSES AND RELATED BRAIN-BIOCHEMISTRY.
002951 03-04

BEHAVIOURAL-RESPONSES TO DRUGS RELEASING 5 HYDROXYTRYPTAMINE AND CATECHOLAMINES: EFFECTS OF TREATMENTS ALTERING PRECURSOR CONCENTRATIONS IN BRAIN.
002990 03-04

BEHAVIOURAL-SEQUELAE
NEUROLEPTIC TREATMENT FOR A SUBSTANTIAL PROPORTION OF ADULT LIFE: BEHAVIOURAL-SEQUELAE OF 9 MONTHS HALOPERIDOL ADMINISTRATION.
001858 02-05

BEHAVIOURAL-STATE
THE BEHAVIOURAL-STATE DURING CLIMAX (HATCHING) IN THE DOMESTIC-FOWL (GALLUS-DOMESTICUS).
001564 02-04

BEHAVIOURAL-STRATEGIES
ROLE OF THE NEOSTRIATAL DOPAMINERGIC-ACTIVITY IN SEQUENCING AND SELECTING BEHAVIOURAL-STRATEGIES: FACILITATION OF PROCESSES INVOLVED IN SELECTING THE BEST STRATEGY IN A STRESSFUL-SITUATION.
000366 01-04

BEHAVIOURAL-STUDIES
EVIDENCE FOR A GABAERGIC NIGROTHALAMIC PATHWAY IN THE RAT: I. BEHAVIOURAL-STUDIES AND BIOCHEMICAL-STUDIES.
000158 01-03

EFFECT OF SINGLE AND REPEATED ELECTROCONVULSIVE-SHOCK ON SEROTONERGIC SYSTEM IN RAT-BRAIN — II. BEHAVIOURAL-STUDIES.
001697 02-04

BEHAVIOURAL-SYNDROMES
EFFECTS OF THE POTENTIAL NEUROLEPTIC-PEPTIDE DES-TYR1-GAMMA-ENDORPHIN AND HALOPERIDOL ON APOMORPHINE-INDUCED BEHAVIOURAL-SYNDROMES IN RATS AND MICE.
000441 01-04

BEHAVIOURAL-TECHNIQUES
EFFECTS OF ANXIETY REDUCTION BY BEHAVIOURAL-TECHNIQUES AND MEPROBAMATE ON CERTAIN PARAMETERS OF INFORMATION THEORY.
003108 03-04

BEHAVIOURS
THE DIFFERENTIAL NEUROCHEMICAL-BASES OF THE BEHAVIOURS ELICITED BY SEROTONERGIC-AGENTS AND BY THE COMBINATION OF A MONOAMINE-OXIDASE-INHIBITOR AND L-DOPA.
002976 03-04

NEUROTENSIN BLOCKS CERTAIN AMPHETAMINE-INDUCED BEHAVIOURS.
004111 04-04

BELGIUM
ABSTRACTS OF THE ANNUAL GENERAL CONFERENCE OF THE EUROPEAN-BRAIN-AND-BEHAVIOUR-SOCIETY, HELD AT LOUVAIN-LA-NEUVE, BELGIUM, ON NOVEMBER 13-15TH, 1980.
003617 03-17

BELIEFS
THE INFLUENCE OF PATIENT BELIEFS ON COMPLIANCE TO THERAPY FOR DIABETES-MELLITUS. (PH.D. DISSERTATION).
003631 03-17

BENSERASIDE
THE TREATMENT OF PARKINSONS-DISEASE USING A COMBINATION OF L-DOPA AND DECARBOXYLASE INHIBITORS (CARBIDOPA, BENSERASIDE). A CLINICAL AND BIOCHEMICAL COMPARATIVE INVESTIGATION.
000712 01-11

BENSERAZIDE
EFFECTS OF BENSERAZIDE AND CARBIDOPA ON THE METABOLISM OF L TRYPTOPHAN BY ISOLATED RAT LIVER CELLS.
002899 03-03

BENSERAZIDE-HCL
COMPARATIVE-STUDIES OF L-DOPA ALONE AND COMBINATION WITH A PERIPHERAL DOPA-DECARBOXYLASE INHIBITOR, BENSERAZIDE-HCL, ON PARKINSONS-DISEASE — PART II: PHARMACOKINETIC-STUDY.
002309 02-13

BENZAMIDE
STEREOSELECTIVE ACTIONS OF SUBSTITUTED BENZAMIDE DRUGS ON CEREBRAL DOPAMINE MECHANISMS.
001301 02-03

NEUROPSYCHOPHARMACOLOGICAL-STUDIES ON SOME BENZAMIDE DERIVATIVES.
002220 02-13

COMPARISON OF THE POTENCIES OF CLEBOPRIDE AND OTHER SUBSTITUTED BENZAMIDE DRUGS ON ISOLATED GASTROINTESTINAL TRACT OF THE GUINEA-PIG AND RAT.
003928 04-03

BENZAMIDES
SODIUM-DEPENDENT INTERACTION OF BENZAMIDES WITH DOPAMINE-RECEPTORS.
000285 01-03
THE EFFECTS OF SUBSTITUTED BENZAMIDES ON FROG RECTUS-ABDOMINIS.
001228 02-03
CLINICAL-EXPERIENCE WITH SUBSTITUTED BENZAMIDES IN FRENCH-SPEAKING COUNTRIES.
002036 02-09
SAME OR DIFFERENT? AN EXPLORATION OF THE BEHAVIORAL-EFFECTS OF BENZAMIDES.
004207 04-04

BENZAZOCINES
NARCOTIC ANTAGONIST PRECIPITATED ABSTINENCE: RELATIONSHIP TO WITHDRAWAL INDUCING BENZAZOCINES. (PH.D. DISSERTATION).
001518 02-03

BENZHEXOL
A COMPARISON OF BIPERIDEN-HYDROCHLORIDE (AKINETON) AND BENZHEXOL (ARTANE) IN THE TREATMENT OF DRUG-INDUCED PARKINSONISM.
002146 02-11

BENZILATE
QUINUCLIDINYL BENZILATE BINDING IN HOUSEFLY HEADS AND RAT-BRAIN.
003868 04-03

BENZOCTAMINE
THE INFLUENCE OF BENZOCTAMINE ON DOPAMINE AND NOREPINEPHRINE CONTENTS OF THE SUBSTANTIA-NIGRA AND ON THE MUSCLE STRETCH REFLEX OF THE CAT.
000054 01-03
ACUTE EFFECT OF BENZOCTAMINE (10 MG), SODIUM-HYDROXYBUTYRATE (2 G) AND FENCAMFAMINE (10 MG) ON VERBAL-ASSOCIATIONS.
000806 01-14

BENZODIAZEPINE
REDUCTION OF GAMMA AMINOBUTYRIC-ACID-MEDIATED (GABA) TRANSMISSION BY A CONVULSANT BENZODIAZEPINE.
000015 01-02
GABA BENZODIAZEPINE INTERACTIONS: PHYSIOLOGICAL, PHARMACOLOGICAL AND DEVELOPMENTAL ASPECTS.
000103 01-03
ANIMAL-MODELS OF ANXIETY AND BENZODIAZEPINE ACTIONS.
000531 01-06
EFFECTS OF AGE AND OTHER DRUGS ON BENZODIAZEPINE KINETICS.
000681 01-11
DIFFERENTIAL-EFFECTS ON BENZODIAZEPINE DISPOSITION BY DISULFIRAM AND ETHANOL.
000789 01-13
INTROVERSION AND SEVERITY OF THE BENZODIAZEPINE WITHDRAWAL.
000923 01-17
THE REGULATION OF GABA-RECEPTORS AS A POSSIBLE MECHANISM FOR GABA 1,4 BENZODIAZEPINE INTERACTIONS. (UNPUBLISHED PAPER).
001012 02-01
ETHANOL ENHANCES (3H)DIAZEPAM BINDING AT THE BENZODIAZEPINE GABA-RECEPTOR IONOPHORE COMPLEX.
001154 02-03
PHARMACOLOGICAL EVIDENCE AND BIOCHEMICAL-EVIDENCE FOR AN INTERACTION BETWEEN THE BENZODIAZEPINE AND GABA-RECEPTORS.
001261 02-03
GABA-MODULIN REGULATES SOLUBILIZED BENZODIAZEPINE AND GABA RECOGNITION SITES. (UNPUBLISHED PAPER).
001263 02-03
BENZODIAZEPINE BINDING IN CHICKEN RETINA AND ITS INTERACTION WITH GAMMA AMINOBUTYRIC-ACID.
001287 02-03
RENAL BENZODIAZEPINE BINDING INCREASES DURING DEOXYCORTICOSTERONE/SALT HYPERTENSION IN RATS.
001430 02-03
MULTIPLE BENZODIAZEPINE-RECEPTOR COMPLEXES; SOME BENZODIAZEPINE RECOGNITION SITES ARE COUPLED TO GABA-RECEPTORS AND IONOPHORES.
001484 02-03
CHARACTERIZATION OF BENZODIAZEPINE BINDING-SITES. (UNPUBLISHED PAPER).
001503 02-03
BENZODIAZEPINE BINDING-SITES: PROPERTIES AND MODULATION. (UNPUBLISHED PAPER).
001504 02-03
INFLUENCE OF BENZODIAZEPINE TRANQUILIZERS ON AMPHETAMINE-INDUCED LOCOMOTOR-STIMULATION IN MICE.
001767 02-04
INFLUENCE OF BENZODIAZEPINE TRANQUILIZERS ON SCOPOLAMINE-INDUCED LOCOMOTOR-STIMULATION IN MICE.
001768 02-04
CLINICAL ACTIVITY OF A NEW BENZODIAZEPINE: CLOXAZOLAM.
001904 02-07

DOUBLE-BLIND CLINICAL ASSESSMENT OF ALPRAZOLAM, A NEW BENZODIAZEPINE DERIVATIVE, IN THE TREATMENT OF MODERATE TO SEVERE ANXIETY.
002070 02-10
THE REGULATION OF BENZODIAZEPINE RECOGNITION SITES BY ENDOGENOUS MODULATORS.
002642 03-01
RADIOHISTOCHEMICAL STUDIES OF BENZODIAZEPINE AND GABA-RECEPTORS AND THEIR INTERACTIONS.
002644 03-01
BENZODIAZEPINE RECOGNITION SITES ON GABA-RECEPTORS.
002730 03-03
THE EFFECTS OF A BENZODIAZEPINE ON THE HYPERPOLARIZING AND THE DEPOLARIZING RESPONSES OF HIPPOCAMPAL CELLS TO GABA.
002763 03-03
IDENTIFICATION OF TWO BENZODIAZEPINE BINDING-SITES ON CELLS CULTURED FROM RAT-CEREBRAL-CORTEX.
002820 03-03
THE BENZODIAZEPINE GABA-CHLORIDE IONOPHORE-RECEPTOR COMPLEX: COMMON SITE OF MINOR-TRANQUILIZER ACTION.
002857 03-03
GABA-RECEPTORS REGULATE THE AFFINITIES OF ANIONS REQUIRED FOR BRAIN SPECIFIC BENZODIAZEPINE BINDING.
002903 03-03
BENZODIAZEPINE BINDING-SITES: PROPERTIES AND MODULATION.
002912 03-03
INTERACTION BETWEEN PURINE AND BENZODIAZEPINE: INOSINE REVERSES DIAZEPAM-INDUCED STIMULATION OF MOUSE EXPLORATORY-BEHAVIOR.
002972 03-04
BENZODIAZEPINE TREATMENT OF SPECIFIC ANXIETY STATES.
003284 03-10
SEVERE WITHDRAWAL-SYNDROME AFTER CESSATION OF BENZODIAZEPINE TREATMENT: SIX CLINICAL CASES.
003505 03-15
BENZODIAZEPINE WITHDRAWAL SYMPTOMS AND PROPRANOLOL.
003543 03-15
POSITRON-TOMOGRAPHY. A NEW METHOD FOR IN VIVO BRAIN STUDIES OF BENZODIAZEPINE, IN ANIMAL AND IN MAN.
003564 03-16
BENZODIAZEPINE ANTAGONISM BY HARMANE AND OTHER BETA CARBOLINES IN VITRO AND IN VIVO.
004211 04-04
IN VIVO EFFECTS OF TWO NOVEL ALKYLATING BENZODIAZEPINE, IRAZEPINE AND KENAZEPINE.
004251 04-04
ANXIOUS-DEPRESSIVE-SYNDROME. CLINICAL-STUDY OF A NEW BENZODIAZEPINE, PRAZEPAM.
004354 04-09
PRAZEPAM: A NEW BENZODIAZEPINE FOR THE TREATMENT OF ANXIOUS-DEPRESSIVE STATES.
004419 04-10
CLINICAL USE OF A NEW BENZODIAZEPINE, PRAZEPAM.
004421 04-10
PHARMACOLOGICAL PECULIARITIES OF A BENZODIAZEPINE/ATARACTIC-DRUG AND ITS THERAPEUTIC RELEVANCE: THE SPECIAL STATUS OF CLORAZEPATE-DIPOTASSIUM (TRANXILIUM).
004527 04-13
EFFECTS OF A SHORT-ACTING BENZODIAZEPINE ON BRAIN ELECTRICAL-ACTIVITY DURING SLEEP.
004568 04-14
PROLONGED BENZODIAZEPINE COMA.
004653 04-15
SALIVA BENZODIAZEPINE LEVELS AND CLINICAL OUTCOME IN DETOXIFYING ALCOHOLIC-PATIENTS.
004671 04-16
A SENSITIVE BENZODIAZEPINE RADIOIMMUNOASSAY OF BROAD SPECIFICITY.
004693 04-16

BENZODIAZEPINE-LIKE
BRAIN-SPECIFIC BENZODIAZEPINE-RECEPTORS AND PUTATIVE ENDOGENOUS BENZODIAZEPINE-LIKE COMPOUNDS.
000225 01-03
PHARMACOLOGY OF 2 O CHLOROBENZOYL-CHLORO-METHYL-NA-GLYCYLGLYCINANILIDE HYDRATE (45-0088-S), A COMPOUND WITH BENZODIAZEPINE-LIKE PROPERTIES.
003692 04-02

BENZODIAZEPINE-RECEPTOR
AUDIOGENIC-SEIZURES: INCREASED BENZODIAZEPINE-RECEPTOR BINDING IN A SUSCEPTIBLE STRAIN OF MICE.
000252 01-03
PURINES AS ENDOGENOUS LIGANDS OF THE BENZODIAZEPINE-RECEPTOR.
000276 01-03
CORRELATION BETWEEN BENZODIAZEPINE-RECEPTOR OCCUPATION AND ANTICONVULSANT EFFECTS OF DIAZEPAM.
000450 01-04
CHARACTERIZATION OF GABA-STIMULATED BENZODIAZEPINE-RECEPTOR BINDING.
001309 02-03

DECREASED BENZODIAZEPINE-RECEPTOR DENSITY IN RAT-CEREBELLUM FOLLOWING NEUROTOXIC DOSES OF PHENYTOIN.
001373 02-03

BENZODIAZEPINE-RECEPTOR: LOCALIZATION BY PHOTOAFFINITY LABELING AND ISOLATION OF A POSSIBLE ENDOGENOUS LIGAND.
001381 02-03

HARMALINE-INDUCED TREMOR: THE BENZODIAZEPINE-RECEPTOR AS A SITE-OF-ACTION.
001436 02-03

1 METHYL-BETA-CARBOLINE (HARMANE), A POTENT ENDOGENOUS INHIBITOR OF BENZODIAZEPINE-RECEPTOR BINDING.
001440 02-03

INCREASED BENZODIAZEPINE-RECEPTOR NUMBER ELICITED IN VITRO BY A NOVEL PURINE, EMD-28422.
001475 02-03

MULTIPLE BENZODIAZEPINE-RECEPTOR COMPLEXES: SOME BENZODIAZEPINE RECOGNITION SITES ARE COUPLED TO GABA-RECEPTORS AND IONOPHORES.
001484 02-03

MODULATION BY PICROTOXIN AND IPTBO OF 3H FLUNITRAZEPAM BINDING TO THE GABA/BENZODIAZEPINE-RECEPTOR COMPLEX OF RAT-CEREBELLUM.
002775 03-03

THE BENZODIAZEPINE-RECEPTOR: AN UPDATE.
002833 03-03

PENTOBARBITAL: DUAL-ACTIONS TO INCREASE BRAIN BENZODIAZEPINE-RECEPTOR AFFINITY.
002896 03-03

ACTION OF PYRAZOLOPYRIDINES AS MODULATORS OF (3H)FLUNITRAZEPAM BINDING TO THE GABA/BENZODIAZEPINE-RECEPTOR COMPLEX OF THE CEREBELLUM.
002909 03-03

A STEROID DERIVATIVE, R-5135, ANTAGONIZES THE GABA/BENZODIAZEPINE-RECEPTOR INTERACTION.
003851 04-03

IN VITRO MODULATION BY AVERMECTIN-B1A OF THE GABA/BENZODIAZEPINE-RECEPTOR COMPLEX OF RAT-CEREBELLUM.
004023 04-03

BENZODIAZEPINE-RECEPTOR: HETEROGENEITY IN RABBIT BRAIN.
004060 04-03

BENZODIAZEPINE-RECEPTORS

DISSIMILAR EFFECTS OF NICOTINAMIDE AND INOSINE, PUTATIVE ENDOGENOUS LIGANDS OF THE BENZODIAZEPINE-RECEPTORS, ON PENTYLENETETRAZOL SEIZURES IN FOUR STRAINS OF MICE.
000173 01-03

BRAIN-SPECIFIC BENZODIAZEPINE-RECEPTORS AND PUTATIVE ENDOGENOUS BENZODIAZEPINE-LIKE COMPOUNDS.
000225 01-03

PENTOBARBITAL POTENTIATES GABA-ENHANCED (3H) DIAZEPAM BINDING TO BENZODIAZEPINE-RECEPTORS.
000275 01-03

BRAIN-SPECIFIC BENZODIAZEPINE-RECEPTORS ARE LOCALIZED IN THE INNER PLEXIFORM LAYER OF RAT RETINA.
000277 01-03

BENZODIAZEPINE-RECEPTORS.
000918 01-17

TWO OR MORE CONFORMATIONS OF BENZODIAZEPINE-RECEPTORS DEPENDING ON GABA-RECEPTORS AND OTHER VARIABLES.
001139 02-03

STUDIES ON BENZODIAZEPINE-RECEPTORS.
001502 02-03

GABA-RECEPTORS AND BENZODIAZEPINE-RECEPTORS IN THE OFFSPRING OF DAMS RECEIVING DIAZEPAM: ONTOGENETIC-STUDIES.
001849 02-05

BENZODIAZEPINE-RECEPTORS: THE EFFECT OF GABA ON THEIR CHARACTERISTICS IN HUMAN BRAIN AND THEIR ALTERATION IN HUNTINGTONS-DISEASE.
002163 02-11

DIFFERENTIAL-EFFECTS OF KAINIC-ACID ON BENZODIAZEPINE-RECEPTORS, GABA-RECEPTORS, AND GABA-MODULIN IN THE CEREBELLAR-CORTEX.
002477 02-16

BENZODIAZEPINE-RECEPTORS: AUTORADIOGRAPHICAL AND IMMUNOCYTOCHEMICAL EVIDENCE FOR THEIR LOCALIZATION IN REGIONS OF GABAERGIC SYNAPTIC CONTACTS.
002643 03-01

BENZODIAZEPINE-RECEPTORS IN CHICK RETINA: DEVELOPMENT AND CELLULAR LOCALIZATION.
002655 03-03

BETA CARBOLINE-3-CARBOXYLATES AND BENZODIAZEPINE-RECEPTORS.
002676 03-03

EFFECT OF PICROTOXIN ON BENZODIAZEPINE-RECEPTORS AND GABA-RECEPTORS WITH REFERENCE TO THE EFFECT OF CHLORIDE ION.
002725 03-03

GABA-RECEPTORS AND BENZODIAZEPINE-RECEPTORS. STUDIES ON THEIR LOCALIZATION IN THE HIPPOCAMPUS AND THEIR INTERACTION WITH CENTRAL DOPAMINE NEURONS IN THE RAT-BRAIN.
002727 03-03

KAINIC-ACID INDUCED LESION OF RAT RETINA: DIFFERENTIAL-EFFECT ON CYCLIC-GMP AND BENZODIAZEPINE-RECEPTORS AND GABA-RECEPTORS.
002743 03-03

NEURONAL LOCALIZATION OF BENZODIAZEPINE-RECEPTORS IN THE MURINE CEREBELLUM.
002902 03-03

MULTIPLE BENZODIAZEPINE-RECEPTORS.
003579 03-17

ENDOGENOUS LIGANDS FOR BENZODIAZEPINE-RECEPTORS.
003615 03-17

BRAIN BENZODIAZEPINE-RECEPTORS AND THEIR RAPID CHANGES AFTER SEIZURES IN THE MONGOLIAN-GERBIL.
003717 04-03

NEURONAL LOCALISATION OF BENZODIAZEPINE-RECEPTORS IN CEREBELLUM.
003739 04-03

MULTIPLE BENZODIAZEPINE-RECEPTORS: EVIDENCE OF A DISSOCIATION BETWEEN ANTICONFLICT AND ANTICONVULSANT PROPERTIES BY PK-8165 AND PK-9084 (TWO QUINOLINE DERIVATIVES).
003898 04-03

THE INSENSITIVITY OF DEVELOPING BENZODIAZEPINE-RECEPTORS TO CHRONIC-TREATMENT WITH DIAZEPAM, GABA AND MUSCIMOL IN BRAIN CELL-CULTURES.
004002 04-03

BENZODIAZEPINE-RECEPTORS: EFFECT OF TISSUE PREINCUBATION AT 37 DEGREES C.
004013 04-03

BENZODIAZEPINE-RECEPTORS ON PRIMARY CULTURES OF MOUSE ASTROCYTES.
004029 04-03

BENZODIAZEPINES

RELATIONSHIP OF ANTICONFLICT ACTIVITY OF BENZODIAZEPINES TO BRAIN RECEPTOR BINDING, SEROTONIN, AND GABA.
000057 01-03

ELECTROPHYSIOLOGICAL ACTIONS OF BENZODIAZEPINES.
000107 01-03

RELATIONSHIPS BETWEEN PLASMA CORTICOSTEROIDS AND BENZODIAZEPINES IN STRESS.
000176 01-03

CARDIOVASCULAR RESPONSE TO THE INTERACTION OF ETHANOL AND SOME BENZODIAZEPINES IN RATS.
000332 01-03

BENZODIAZEPINES: A TOOL TO EXPLORE THE BIOCHEMICAL-BASIS AND NEUROPHYSIOLOGICAL-BASIS OF ANXIETY.
000397 01-04

MECHANISM-OF-ACTION OF THE BENZODIAZEPINES: BEHAVIORAL-ASPECT.
000468 01-04

FACTORS INFLUENCING SEIZURE DURATION AND NUMBER OF SEIZURES APPLIED IN UNILATERAL ELECTROCONVULSIVE-THERAPY: ANESTHETICS AND BENZODIAZEPINES.
000792 01-13

THE DIFFERENTIAL-EFFECTS OF SHORT-ACTING AND LONG-ACTING BENZODIAZEPINES UPON NOCTURNAL SLEEP AND DAYTIME PERFORMANCE.
000822 01-14

USE AND ABUSE OF BENZODIAZEPINES.
000877 01-15

USE OF BENZODIAZEPINES IN PSYCHIATRIC-INPATIENTS.
000910 01-17

PHARMACOKINETICS OF BENZODIAZEPINES: SHORT-ACTING VERSUS LONG-ACTING.
000920 01-17

BENZODIAZEPINES AND NEUROTRANSMITTERS.
000925 01-17

THE PRESENT STATUS OF BENZODIAZEPINES IN PSYCHOPHARMACOLOGY.
000948 01-17

THE PRESENT STATUS OF THE BENZODIAZEPINES IN PSYCHIATRY AND MEDICINE.
000954 01-17

THE BENZODIAZEPINES -- USE AND ABUSE.
000960 01-17

THE SHORT-TERM USE OF BENZODIAZEPINES.
000962 01-17

BEHAVIORAL-NEUROCHEMISTRY OF BENZODIAZEPINES.
000991 01-17

REGIONAL RELEASE OF (3H)ADENOSINE DERIVATIVES FROM RAT-BRAIN IN VIVO: EFFECT OF EXCITATORY AMINO-ACIDS, OPIATE AGONISTS, AND BENZODIAZEPINES.
001303 02-03

BENZODIAZEPINES MODIFY THE AGONIST RESPONSES AT A PRESYNAPTIC GABA-RECEPTOR.
001377 02-03

COMPARATIVE ANXIOLYTIC AND HYPNOTIC-EFFECTS OF 3 BENZODIAZEPINES ON BABOONS.
001581 02-04

RATIONAL USE OF BENZODIAZEPINES FOR ANXIETY AND INSOMNIA.
002063 02-10

THE LONG-TERM TREATMENT WITH BENZODIAZEPINES: SUGGESTIONS FOR FURTHER RESEARCH.
002085 02-10

MECHANISM-OF-ACTION OF BENZODIAZEPINES.
002302 02-13
BENZODIAZEPINES CAUSE SMALL LOSS OF BODY-WEIGHT.
002446 02-15
DEPENDENCE ON BENZODIAZEPINES.
002464 02-15
BENZODIAZEPINES: CLINICAL-PHARMACOLOGY AND THERAPEUTIC USE.
002521 02-17
SELECTIVE ANTAGONISTS OF BENZODIAZEPINES.
002646 03-02
THE ACTION OF BENZODIAZEPINES ON THE LIMBIC-SYSTEM COMPARED TO OTHER TRANQUILIZERS.
002731 03-03
DO BENZODIAZEPINES BIND AT ADENOSINE UPTAKE SITES IN CNS?
002933 03-03
CONFLICT-SITUATION BASED ON INTRACRANIAL SELF-STIMULATION BEHAVIOR AND THE EFFECT OF BENZODIAZEPINES.
003004 03-04
SENSITIVE DEPRESSANT EFFECT OF BENZODIAZEPINES ON THE CROSSED EXTENSOR REFLEX IN CHLORALOSE ANESTHETIZED RATS.
003027 03-04
BENZODIAZEPINES, STRESS AND RAT PLASMA CORTICOSTEROIDS: THE ROLE OF INDOLEAMINES.
003034 03-04
COMPARISON OF THE EFFECTS OF FOUR BENZODIAZEPINES ON FRAME OF MIND AND BEHAVIOR IN HEALTHY SUBJECTS.
003441 03-14
THERAPEUTICS VI -- ANXIOLYTICS (BENZODIAZEPINES).
003546 03-15
PATIENT CHARACTERISTICS AND CLINICIAN ATTITUDES INFLUENCING THE PRESCRIBING OF BENZODIAZEPINES.
003598 03-17
NEW TRENDS CONCERNING THE BIOCHEMICAL-MECHANISM OF ACTION OF BENZODIAZEPINES.
003642 03-17
THE BENZODIAZEPINES AND INOSINE ANTAGONIZE CAFFEINE-INDUCED SEIZURES.
004172 04-04
CLINICAL PHARMACOKINETICS OF BENZODIAZEPINES.
004524 04-13
LONG-TERM USE AND ABUSE OF BENZODIAZEPINES.
004598 04-15
BENZODIAZEPINES IN SCHIZOPHRENIA: A NEED FOR REASSESSMENT.
004733 04-17
BENZTROPINE-MESYLATE
THE EFFECT OF BENZTROPINE-MESYLATE ON THE PROLACTIN RESPONSE TO HALOPERIDOL.
002238 02-13
BENZYL
ON-COLUMN GAS-CHROMATOGRAPHIC-SYNTHESIS OF 1,3 DIALYKYL (C=1-10), BENZYL, AND CYCLOHEXYLBARBITURATE DERIVATIVES.
003656 04-01
BENZYLTETRAHYDROPYRIMIDONES
1 SUBSTITUTED BENZYLTETRAHYDROPYRIMIDONES: A SERIES WITH STIMULANT AND DEPRESSANT ACTIVITIES.
003687 04-02
BETA-ADRENERGIC
ISOLATION INCREASES THE RESPONSES TO BETA-ADRENERGIC STIMULATION IN MICE.
001232 02-03
BEHAVIORAL-EFFECTS AND SUBJECTIVE-EFFECTS OF BETA-ADRENERGIC BLOCKADE IN PHOBIC-SUBJECTS.
002060 02-10
SIDE-EFFECTS OF BETA-ADRENERGIC BLOCKING-DRUGS: A METHODOLOGICAL-PROBLEM.
002395 02-15
PROPRANOLOL (INDERAL) FOR TARDIVE-DYSKINESIA AND EXTRAPYRAMIDAL SIDE-EFFECTS FROM NEUROLEPTICS: POSSIBLE INVOLVEMENT OF BETA-ADRENERGIC MECHANISMS.
002470 02-15
FLUORESCENT PROBES OF ALPHA-ADRENERGIC AND BETA-ADRENERGIC AND OPIATE-RECEPTORS: BIOCHEMICAL AND HISTOCHEMICAL EVALUATION.
003685 04-02
BETA-ADRENERGIC INFLUENCE ON CARDIAC DYNAMICS DURING SHOCK-AVOIDANCE IN DOGS.
003813 04-03
EFFECTS OF ALPHA-ADRENERGIC AND BETA-ADRENERGIC BLOCKERS ON CHLORPROMAZINE-INDUCED ELEVATION OF PLASMA GLUCOSE AND CYCLIC-AMP IN FED MICE.
003946 04-03
RNA-POLYMERASE-II IN C6-GLIOMA CELLS: ALPHA AMANITIN BLOCKADE OF CYCLIC-AMP-PHOSPHODIESTERASE INDUCTION BY BETA-ADRENERGIC STIMULATION. (UNPUBLISHED PAPER).
003998 04-03
BETA-ADRENERGIC-RECEPTOR
AGONIST-INDUCED CHANGES IN BETA-ADRENERGIC-RECEPTOR DENSITY AND RECEPTOR-MEDIATED RESPONSIVENESS IN SLICES OF RAT-CEREBRAL-CORTEX.
000072 01-03

EFFECT OF CHRONIC-TREATMENT WITH ANTIDEPRESSANTS ON BETA-ADRENERGIC-RECEPTOR BINDING IN GUINEA-PIG BRAIN.
000135 01-03
COMPARISON OF BETA-ADRENERGIC-RECEPTOR SUBTYPES IN MAMMALIAN TISSUES.
000207 01-03
DOPAMINE-BETA-HYDROXYLASE: A MODULATOR OF BETA-ADRENERGIC-RECEPTOR ACTIVITY.
000302 01-03
AFFINITY CHROMATOGRAPHY OF THE BETA-ADRENERGIC-RECEPTOR AND CHARACTERIZATION OF ANTIBODIES RAISED AGAINST PURIFIED RECEPTOR PREPARATIONS.
001009 02-01
LONG-TERM HALOPERIDOL TREATMENT OF MICE: A CHANGE IN BETA-ADRENERGIC-RECEPTOR RESPONSIVENESS.
001206 02-03
REGULATION BY A BETA-ADRENERGIC-RECEPTOR OF A CA-INDEPENDENT ADENOSINE-CYCLIC-MONOPHOSPHATE-PHOSPHODIESTERASE IN C6-GLIOMA CELLS. (UNPUBLISHED PAPER).
001403 02-03
INCREASED ADRENALINE, BETA-ADRENERGIC-RECEPTOR STIMULATION AND PHOSPHOLIPID METHYLATION IN PINEAL-GLAND OF SPONTANEOUSLY HYPERTENSIVE-RATS. (UNPUBLISHED PAPER).
001458 02-03
THE EFFECT OF BETA-ADRENERGIC-RECEPTOR BLOCKING-DRUGS ON CEREBRAL BLOOD FLOW IN HYPERTENSIVE-PATIENTS.
002071 02-10
BETA-ADRENERGIC-RECEPTOR SUBTYPES: PROPERTIES, DISTRIBUTION, AND REGULATION.
002829 03-03
BETA-ADRENERGIC-RECEPTORS
ABILITY OF AGED RATS TO ALTER BETA-ADRENERGIC-RECEPTORS OF BRAIN IN RESPONSE TO REPEATED ADMINISTRATION OF RESERPINE AND DESMETHYLIMIPRAMINE.
000113 01-03
ACCELERATION OF DESIPRAMINE-INDUCED DECREASE OF RAT CORTICOCEREBRAL BETA-ADRENERGIC-RECEPTORS BY YOHIMBINE.
000326 01-03
MODULATION OF BETA-ADRENERGIC-RECEPTORS AND CALMODULIN FOLLOWING ACUTE AND CHRONIC-TREATMENT WITH NEUROLEPTICS.
001529 02-03
MEPACRINE TREATMENT PREVENTS IMMOBILIZATION-INDUCED DESENSITIZATION OF BETA-ADRENERGIC-RECEPTORS IN RAT HYPOTHALAMUS AND BRAINSTEM.
002919 03-03
EFFECTS OF ISOPROTERENOL ON THE DEVELOPMENT OF BETA-ADRENERGIC-RECEPTORS IN BRAIN CELL AGGREGATES.
002932 03-03
DEVELOPMENTAL-CHANGE OF BETA-ADRENERGIC-RECEPTORS IN RAT-BRAIN.
004050 04-03
BETA-ADRENOCEPTOR
CLENBUTEROL, A CENTRAL BETA-ADRENOCEPTOR AGONIST.
000120 01-03
BETA-ADRENOCEPTOR ANTAGONISTS: STUDIES ON BEHAVIOUR (DELAYED DIFFERENTIATION) IN THE MONKEY (MACACA-MULATTA).
000440 01-04
EFFECTS OF DESIPRAMINE AND YOHIMBINE ON ALPHA2-ADRENOCEPTOR AND BETA-ADRENOCEPTOR SENSITIVITY.
001305 02-03
EFFECTS OF THE BETA-ADRENOCEPTOR BLOCKING-AGENT SOTALOL ON CNS: SLEEP, EEG, AND PSYCHOPHYSIOLOGICAL PARAMETERS.
001570 02-04
DISPOSITION AND ACTIVITY OF BETA-ADRENOCEPTOR ANTAGONISTS IN THE RAT USING AN EX VIVO RECEPTOR BINDING ASSAY.
001878 02-06
BETA-ADRENORECEPTOR
REVERSAL OF NORADRENALINE DENERVATION-INDUCED INCREASE OF BETA-ADRENORECEPTOR BINDING IN RAT NEOCORTEX BY NORADRENALINE INFUSION.
002672 03-03
BETA-BLOCKERS
BETA-BLOCKERS IN PSYCHIATRY.
002109 02-11
CLINICAL-REVIEW OF BETA-BLOCKERS IN ANXIETY.
004464 04-11
PSYCHIATRIC USES OF BETA-BLOCKERS.
004709 04-17
BETA-RECEPTOR
FAILURE OF ISOPRENALINE AND BETA-RECEPTOR BLOCKING-DRUGS TO MODIFY DEPRESSOR RESPONSE AND BRADYCARDIA INDUCED BY ELECTRICAL-STIMULATION OF THE ANTERIOR HYPOTHALAMUS OF CATS.
000520 01-05
EFFECTS OF PROLONGED TREATMENT WITH LITHIUM AND TRICYCLIC-ANTIDEPRESSANTS ON DISCHARGE FREQUENCY, NOREPINEPHRINE RESPONSES AND BETA-RECEPTOR BINDING IN RAT-CEREBELLUM: ELECTROPHYSIOLOGICAL AND BIOCHEMICAL COMPARISON.
002884 03-03

HYPERVENTILATION-SYNDROME AND BETA-RECEPTOR FUNCTION --
CLINICAL-EFFECT OF BETA BLOCKER UPON THE SYNDROME.
004459 04-11
BETA-SYMPATHOMIMETICS
SPONTANEOUS MOTOR-ACTIVITY IN RATS GIVEN REPEATEDLY BETA-
SYMPATHOMIMETICS -- ISOPRENALIN AND SALBUTAMOL.
001804 02-04
BETADRENOL
THE EFFECT OF BETADRENOL ON EXAMINATION ANXIETY.
000650 01-10
BETAINE
ORAL AND RECTAL ABSORPTION OF CHLORAL-HYDRATE AND ITS BETAINE
COMPLEX.
004554 04-13
BETTA-SPLENDENS
BETTA-SPLENDENS MAZE-BEHAVIOR UNDER THE INFLUENCE OF THE BETA
FENIL-ISOPROPIL-AMINA-SULFATE.
001558 02-04
BIBLIOGRAPHY
BIBLIOGRAPHY ON THE BIOLOGY AND PHARMACOLOGY OF LITHIUM.
003630 03-17
BICUCULLINE
BICUCULLINE ANTAGONIZES EFFECTS OF DIAZEPAM ON AGGRESSIVE AND
TIMID-BEHAVIOUR IN MICE.
000485 01-04
EFFECT OF AMINOOXYACETIC-ACID AND BICUCULLINE ON PROLACTIN
RELEASE IN CASTRATED MALE RATS.
001194 02-03
SENSITIVITY OF IDENTIFIED MEDIAL HYPOTHALAMIC NEURONS TO GABA,
GLYCINE AND RELATED AMINO-ACIDS; INFLUENCE OF BICUCULLINE,
PICROTOXIN AND STRYCHNINE ON SYNAPTIC INHIBITION.
002674 03-03
ROLE OF INTRACORTICAL INHIBITION IN DEPRIVATION AMBLYOPIA;
REVERSAL BY MICROIONTOPHORETIC BICUCULLINE.
002684 03-03
SUPRASPINAL INHIBITION OF THE EXCITATION OF DORSAL-HORN
NEURONES BY IMPULSES IN UNMYELINATED PRIMARY AFFERENTS:
LACK OF EFFECT BY STRYCHNINE AND BICUCULLINE.
003778 04-03
3H BACLOFEN AND 3H GABA BIND TO BICUCULLINE INSENSITIVE GABAB
SITES IN RAT-BRAIN.
003839 04-03
EFFECTS OF 5 HYDROXYTRYPTAMINE ON CENTRAL NEURONES
ANTAGONIZED BY BICUCULLINE AND PICROTOXIN.
003931 04-03
BICUCULLINE-INDUCED
EFFECTS OF BICUCULLINE-INDUCED SEIZURES ON CEREBRAL METABOLISM
AND CIRCULATION OF RATS RENDERED HYPOGLYCEMIC BY
STARVATION.
001134 02-03
BRAIN AND SERUM CALCIUM CONCENTRATIONS FOLLOWING
ELECTROCONVULSIVE-SHOCK OR BICUCULLINE-INDUCED CONVULSIONS
IN RATS.
003736 04-03
EFFECT OF GAMMA VINYL-GABA ON BICUCULLINE-INDUCED SEIZURES.
004157 04-04
BICYCLIC
CLINICAL-TRIALS WITH NEW BICYCLIC AND TETRACYCLIC COMPOUNDS:
ZIMELIDINE AND MAPROTILINE.
003213 03-09
BILE
COMPARISON OF BLOOD AND BILE LEVELS OF OXYPROTHEPIN AND
DOCLOXYTHEPIN IN RATS.
000242 01-03
BIND
DO BENZODIAZEPINES BIND AT ADENOSINE UPTAKE SITES IN CNS?
002933 03-03
3H BACLOFEN AND 3H GABA BIND TO BICUCULLINE INSENSITIVE GABAB
SITES IN RAT-BRAIN.
003839 04-03
BINDING
OXAZEPAM-ESTERS. 2. CORRELATION OF HYDROPHOBICITY WITH SERUM
BINDING, BRAIN PENETRATION, AND EXCRETION.
000011 01-02
3H IMIPRAMINE BINDING IN NEURONAL AND GLIAL FRACTIONS OF
HORSE STRIATUM.
000033 01-03
(3H) 2 AMINODIHYDROXYTETRAHYDRO.!APHTHALENE (ADTN):
REGIONAL DISTRIBUTION AND IN VITRO BINDING AFTER ACUTE AND
CHRONIC DRUG-TREATMENT.
000052 01-03
RELATIONSHIP OF ANTICONFLICT ACTIVITY OF BENZODIAZEPINES TO
BRAIN RECEPTOR BINDING, SEROTONIN, AND GABA.
000057 01-03
HIGH-AFFINITY BINDING OF THE ANTITUSSIVE DEXTROMETHORPHAN TO
GUINEA-PIG BRAIN.
000061 01-03
CHARACTERISTICS OF 3H CIS FLUPENTHIXOL BINDING TO CALF BRAIN
MEMBRANES.
000062 01-03

REDUCTION OF OPIATE BINDING TO BRAINSTEM SLICES ASSOCIATED
WITH THE DEVELOPMENT OF TOLERANCE TO MORPHINE IN RATS.
000066 01-03
STEREOSPECIFIC BINDING OF 3H HALOPERIDOL IN RAT DORSAL SPINAL-
CORD.
000070 01-03
INCREASED MESOLIMBIC 3H SPIROPERIDOL BINDING IN 4 WEEK OLD
OFFSPRING OF NURSING RAT MOTHERS TREATED WITH PENFLURIDOL.
000087 01-03
EFFECTS OF DOPAMINERGIC AGONISTS AND ANTAGONISTS ON
(3H)APOMORPHINE BINDING TO STRIATAL MEMBRANES: SULPIRIDE
LACK OF INTERACTIONS WITH POSITIVE COOPERATIVE
(3H)APOMORPHINE BINDING.
000099 01-03
INHIBITION OF (3H)NALOXONE BINDING IN HOMOGENATES OF RAT-
BRAIN BY ESEROLINE, A DRUG, WITH ANALGESIC ACTIVITY, RELATED
TO PHYSOSTIGMINE.
000104 01-03
HIGH-AFFINITY BINDING OF 3H ETHYLKETOCYCLAZOCINE IN RAT-BRAIN
HOMOGENATE.
000124 01-03
3H ETHYLKETOCYCLAZOCINE BINDING: LACK OF EVIDENCE FOR A
SEPARATE KAPPA-RECEPTOR IN RAT CNS.
000128 01-03
EFFECT OF CHRONIC-TREATMENT WITH ANTIDEPRESSANTS ON BETA-
ADRENERGIC-RECEPTOR BINDING IN GUINEA-PIG BRAIN.
000135 01-03
CHARACTERIZATION OF 3H GABA-RECEPTOR BINDING TO RAT-BRAIN
SYNAPTOSOMAL MEMBRANES: EFFECT OF NONGABAERGIC
COMPOUNDS.
000139 01-03
AMITRIPTYLINE BINDING TO SPECIFIC ALPHA-ADRENERGIC-RECEPTORS IN
VITRO.
000181 01-03
DECREASED SPIROPERIDOL AND LSD BINDING IN RAT-BRAIN AFTER
CONTINUOUS AMPHETAMINE.
000216 01-03
INHIBITION OF IN VIVO 3H SPIPERONE BINDING BY THE PROPOSED
ANTIPSYCHOTIC DES-TYR1-GAMMA-ENDORPHIN.
000226 01-03
LONG-TERM ANTIDEPRESSANT TREATMENT DECREASES SPIROPERIDOL-
LABELED SEROTONIN-RECEPTOR BINDING.
000230 01-03
CHRONIC SYMPATHETIC DENERVATION INCREASES MUSCARINIC-
CHOLINOCEPTOR BINDING IN THE RAT SUBMAXILLARY-GLAND.
000235 01-03
AUDIOGENIC-SEIZURES: INCREASED BENZODIAZEPINE-RECEPTOR BINDING
IN A SUSCEPTIBLE STRAIN OF MICE.
000252 01-03
EFFECTS OF CHRONIC HALOPERIDOL ON CAUDATE 3H SPIROPERIDOL
BINDING IN LESIONED RATS.
000255 01-03
PENTOBARBITAL POTENTIATES GABA-ENHANCED (3H) DIAZEPAM
BINDING TO BENZODIAZEPINE-RECEPTORS.
000275 01-03
CHANGES IN MOUSE-BRAIN DIAZEPAM-RECEPTOR BINDING AFTER
PHENOBARBITAL ADMINISTRATION.
000281 01-03
BIOCHEMICAL-PROPERTIES OF SPIPERONE BINDING TO RAT-BRAIN
MEMBRANES.
000294 01-03
(3H)QUINUCLIDINYL-BENZILATE BINDING TO MUSCARINIC-RECEPTORS
AND (3H)WB-4101 BINDING TO ALPHA-ADRENERGIC-RECEPTORS IN
RABBIT IRIS; COMPARISON OF RESULTS IN SLICES AND MICROSOMAL
FRACTIONS.
000299 01-03
3H MIANSERIN BINDING IN CALF CAUDATE: POSSIBLE INVOLVEMENT OF
SEROTONIN-RECEPTORS IN ANTIDEPRESSANT-DRUG ACTION.
000325 01-03
INHIBITION OF (3H)DIAZEPAM BINDING TO RAT-BRAIN CORTICAL
SYNAPTOSOMAL MEMBRANES BY ADENOSINE UPTAKE BLOCKERS.
000330 01-03
INCREASED DOPAMINE-RECEPTOR BINDING IN THE STRIATUM OF RATS
AFTER LONG-TERM ISOLATION.
000398 01-04
DISPLACEMENT OF (3H)CLONIDINE BINDING BY CLONIDINE ANALOGUES
IN MEMBRANES FROM RAT-CEREBRAL-CORTEX.
000536 01-06
VALPROIC-ACID DOSAGE AND PLASMA PROTEIN BINDING AND
CLEARANCE.
000755 01-13
ALBUMIN BINDING INTERACTIONS OF SODIUM-VALPROATE.
000762 01-13
INFLUENCE OF DEXTROPROPOXYPHENE ON STEADY-STATE SERUM LEVELS
AND PROTEIN BINDING OF THREE ANTIEPILEPTIC-DRUGS IN MAN.
000767 01-13
SPECIFIC BINDING FOR OPIATE-LIKE-DRUGS IN THE PLACENTA.
000797 01-13

TECHNIQUES FOR PLASMA PROTEIN BINDING OF DEMETHYLCHLORIMIPRAMINE.
000897 01-16

DISEASE-INDUCED CHANGES IN THE PLASMA BINDING OF BASIC DRUGS.
000975 01-17

GUANINE-NUCLEOTIDES INHIBIT BINDING OF AGONISTS AND ANTAGONISTS TO SOLUBLE OPIATE-RECEPTORS. (UNPUBLISHED PAPER).
001035 02-01

HISTAMINE-RECEPTORS IN THE BRAIN: CHARACTERIZATION BY BINDING STUDIES AND BIOCHEMICAL-EFFECTS.
001054 02-01

INHIBITION BY LOCAL ANESTHETICS, PHENTOLAMINE AND PROPRANOLOL OF (3H)QUINUCLYDINYL-BENZYLATE BINDING TO CENTRAL MUSCARINIC-RECEPTORS.
001097 02-03

REGULATION OF RECEPTOR BINDING INTERACTIONS OF 125I ANGIOTENSIN-II AND 125I SARCOSINE1-LEUCINE8-ANGIOTENSIN-II, AN ANGIOTENSIN ANTAGONIST, BY SODIUM-ION.
001124 02-03

RECEPTOR BINDING INTERACTIONS OF THE ANGIOTENSIN-II ANTAGONIST, 125I SARCOSINE1-LEUCINE8-ANGIOTENSIN-II, WITH MAMMALIAN BRAIN AND PERIPHERAL TISSUES.
001125 02-03

IN VIVO (3H)SPIPERONE BINDING TO THE RAT HIPPOCAMPAL FORMATION: INVOLVEMENT OF DOPAMINE-RECEPTORS.
001131 02-03

ETHANOL ENHANCES (3H)DIAZEPAM BINDING AT THE BENZODIAZEPINE GABA-RECEPTOR IONOPHORE COMPLEX.
001154 02-03

RADIOLIGAND BINDING STUDIES: EVIDENCE FOR MULTIPLE DOPAMINE-RECEPTORS.
001186 02-03

HIGH-AFFINITY BINDING OF (3H)MIANSERIN TO RAT-CEREBRAL-CORTEX.
001204 02-03

INHIBITION BY ARYLSULPHATASE A OF NA-INDEPENDENT (3H) GABA AND (3H) MUSCIMOL BINDING TO BOVINE CEREBELLAR SYNAPTIC MEMBRANES.
001208 02-03

DRUG-INDUCED ALTERATIONS IN NEUROTRANSMITTER-RECEPTOR BINDING AND FUNCTION.
001215 02-03

THE EFFECT OF GABAMIMETICS ON NEUROTRANSMITTER-RECEPTOR BINDING AND FUNCTION IN RAT-BRAIN. (PH.D. DISSERTATION).
001221 02-03

THE BINDING OF SOME ANTIDEPRESSANT-DRUGS TO BRAIN MUSCARINIC ACETYLCHOLINE-RECEPTORS.
001253 02-03

OPIATES AND SPECIFIC RECEPTOR BINDING OF (3H)CLONIDINE.
001256 02-03

PERSISTENT EFFECTS OF HIGH-CONCENTRATIONS OF CHLORPROMAZINE ON 3H PROPYLBENZILYLCHOLINE-MUSTARD BINDING TO MUSCARINIC-RECEPTORS IN GUINEA-PIG INTESTINAL-MUSCLE STRIPS.
001266 02-03

BENZODIAZEPINE BINDING IN CHICKEN RETINA AND ITS INTERACTION WITH GAMMA AMINOBUTYRIC-ACID.
001287 02-03

NO EVIDENCE FOR INCREASED DOPAMINE-RECEPTOR BINDING IN SUPERRESPONSIVE MICE AFTER A SINGLE-DOSE OF NEUROLEPTICS.
001292 02-03

EVIDENCE FOR AN ENDOGENOUS COMPOUND INTERFERING WITH 3H DIAZEPAM BINDING TO RAT-BRAIN MEMBRANES.
001308 02-03

CHARACTERIZATION OF GABA-STIMULATED BENZODIAZEPINE-RECEPTOR BINDING.
001309 02-03

INCREASED MUSCARINIC-RECEPTOR BINDING IN RAT-FOREBRAIN AFTER SCOPOLAMINE.
001351 02-03

DOPAMINE-SENSITIVE ADENYLATE-CYCLASE AND DOPAMINE/NEUROLEPTIC-RECEPTOR BINDING: EFFECT OF NEUROLEPTIC-DRUGS.
001358 02-03

CHARACTERIZATION AND RADIOAUTOGRAPHY OF (3H)LSD BINDING BY RAT-BRAIN SLICES IN VITRO: THE EFFECT OF 5 HYDROXYTRYPTAMINE.
001369 02-03

FURTHER CHARACTERIZATION OF THE BINDING OF SUBSTANCE-P TO A FRACTION FROM RABBIT BRAIN ENRICHED IN SYNAPTIC MEMBRANES.
001394 02-03

RENAL BENZODIAZEPINE BINDING INCREASES DURING DEOXYCORTICOSTERONE/SALT HYPERTENSION IN RATS.
001430 02-03

1 METHYL-BETA-CARBOLINE (HARMANE), A POTENT ENDOGENOUS INHIBITOR OF BENZODIAZEPINE-RECEPTOR BINDING.
001440 02-03

CHRONIC LITHIUM REDUCES (3H)SPIROPERIDOL BINDING IN RAT STRIATUM.
001443 02-03

INCREASED RENAL NEUROLEPTIC BINDING IN SPONTANEOUSLY HYPERTENSIVE-RATS.
001444 02-03

EFFECTS OF HALOPERIDOL AND D-AMPHETAMINE ON IN VIVO 3H SPIROPERIDOL BINDING IN THE RAT-FOREBRAIN.
001461 02-03

DECREASE IN (3H) SEROTONIN BINDING IN RAT-BRAIN PRODUCED BY THE REPEATED ADMINISTRATION OF EITHER MONOAMINE-OXIDASE-INHIBITORS ON CENTRALLY-ACTING SEROTONIN AGONISTS.
001463 02-03

MULTIPLE CNS RECEPTOR INTERACTIONS OF ERGOT ALKALOIDS: AFFINITY AND INTRINSIC ACTIVITY ANALYSIS IN IN VITRO BINDING SYSTEMS.
001516 02-03

BINDING OF (3H)PERGOLIDE-MESYLATE TO DOPAMINE-RECEPTORS OF MAMMALIAN BRAINS.
001538 02-03

(3H) PHENCYCLIDINE BINDING TO SPECIFIC BRAIN RECEPTOR SITES.
001555 02-03

MODULATION OF OPIATE-RECEPTOR BINDING IN STRIATUM AND AMYGDALA BY SELECTIVE MESENCEPHALIC LESIONS.
001629 02-04

3H APOMORPHINE-RECEPTORS IN VARIOUS RAT-BRAIN REGIONS: A STUDY OF SPECIFIC AND NONSPECIFIC BINDING AND THE INFLUENCE OF CHRONIC NEUROLEPTIC TREATMENT.
001846 02-05

STUDIES ON THIORIDAZINE AND MESORIDAZINE METABOLISM. I. PROTEIN BINDING.
001867 02-06

DISPOSITION AND ACTIVITY OF BETA-ADRENOCEPTOR ANTAGONISTS IN THE RAT USING AN EX VIVO RECEPTOR BINDING ASSAY
001878 02-06

HIGH-AFFINITY BINDING OF TRICYCLIC-ANTIDEPRESSANTS TO HISTAMINE H1-RECEPTORS: FACT AND ARTIFACT.
001880 02-06

BINDING OF PHENCYCLIDINE TO RAT-BRAIN MEMBRANES: TECHNICAL-ASPECT.
001882 02-06

COMPARATIVE PROTEIN BINDING OF DIAZEPAM AND DESMETHYLDIAZEPAM.
002206 02-13

THE COMPETITION OF ALPHA1 ACID GLYCOPROTEIN, LIPOPROTEINS, AND ALBUMIN TO THE PLASMA BINDING OF PERAZINE, AMITRIPTYLINE, AND NORTRIPTYLINE IN HEALTHY MAN.
002214 02-13

QUINACRINE AND SEROTONIN BINDING BY SYNTHETIC MODELS FOR HUMAN PLATELET DENSE-BODIES: EVALUATION OF THE ROLE OF BINDING IN AMINE STORAGE. (UNPUBLISHED PAPER).
002219 02-13

SPECIFIC 3H IMIPRAMINE BINDING IN HUMAN PLATELETS: INFLUENCE OF AGE AND SEX.
002254 02-13

EFFECTS OF CAFFEINE ON PLASMA FREE FATTY-ACIDS, URINARY CATECHOLAMINES, AND DRUG BINDING.
002272 02-13

INTERACTION BETWEEN PHENYTOIN AND VALPROIC-ACID; PLASMA PROTEIN BINDING AND METABOLIC-EFFECTS.
002276 02-13

BINDING OF PERAZINE TO ALPHA1 ACID GLYCOPROTEIN.
002290 02-13

THE EFFECTS OF ACUTE AND CHRONIC MORPHINE ADMINISTRATION ON GABA-RECEPTOR BINDING.
002301 02-13

DEMONSTRATION AND CHARACTERIZATION OF AN ENDOGENOUS INHIBITOR OF GABA-ENHANCED (3H) DIAZEPAM BINDING FROM BOVINE CEREBRAL-CORTEX.
002645 03-01

RECEPTOR BINDING PROFILE OF R-41-468, A NOVEL ANTAGONIST AT 5 HT2-RECEPTORS.
002648 03-02

REVERSAL OF NORADRENALINE DENERVATION-INDUCED INCREASE OF BETA-ADRENORECEPTOR BINDING IN RAT NEOCORTEX BY NORADRENALINE INFUSION.
002672 03-03

NA-INDEPENDENT BINDING OF (3H)GABA AND (3H)MUSCIMOL TO SUBCELLULAR PARTICLES OF NEURAL PRIMARY CULTURES AND WHOLE BRAIN.
002699 03-03

THE EFFECT OF GUANOSINE-NUCLEOTIDES ON (3H)SULPIRIDE BINDING TO RAT STRIATAL MEMBRANES.
002722 03-03

SIMILARITIES BETWEEN THE BINDING OF 3H PIFLUTIXOL AND 3H FLUPENTIXOL TO RAT STRIATAL DOPAMINE-RECEPTORS IN VITRO.
002760 03-03

MODULATION BY PICROTOXIN AND IPTBO OF 3H FLUNITRAZEPAM BINDING TO THE GABA/BENZODIAZEPINE-RECEPTOR COMPLEX OF RAT-CEREBELLUM.
002775 03-03

IMIPRAMINE: EFFECT OF OVARIAN STEROIDS ON MODIFICATIONS IN SEROTONIN-RECEPTOR BINDING.
002778 03-03

THE EFFECT OF SPECIFIC BRAIN LESIONS ON THE HIGH-AFFINITY BINDING OF GABA IN THE SUBSTANTIA-NIGRA.
002795 03-03

ASCORBATE DECREASES LIGAND BINDING TO NEUROTRANSMITTER-RECEPTORS.
002804 03-03

BRAIN MUSCARINIC CHOLINERGIC-RECEPTOR BINDING IN ROMAN HIGH-AVOIDANCE AND LOW-AVOIDANCE RATS.
002852 03-03

TWO DISTINCT SEROTONIN-RECEPTORS: REGIONAL VARIATIONS IN RECEPTOR BINDING IN MAMMALIAN BRAIN.
002861 03-03

HIGH-AFFINITY RENAL (3H)FLUNITRAZEPAM BINDING: CHARACTERIZATION, LOCALIZATION, AND ALTERATION IN HYPERTENSION.
002874 03-03

AMITRIPTYLINE: LONG-TERM-TREATMENT ELEVATES ALPHA-ADRENERGIC AND MUSCARINIC-RECEPTOR BINDING IN MOUSE-BRAIN.
002875 03-03

EFFECTS OF PROLONGED TREATMENT WITH LITHIUM AND TRICYCLIC-ANTIDEPRESSANTS ON DISCHARGE FREQUENCY, NOREPINEPHRINE RESPONSES AND BETA-RECEPTOR BINDING IN RAT-CEREBELLUM: ELECTROPHYSIOLOGICAL AND BIOCHEMICAL COMPARISON.
002884 03-03

EFFECTS OF PROTEIN AND MEMBRANE MODIFYING AGENTS ON THE BINDING OF L (3H)GLUTAMATE TO CEREBELLAR SYNAPTIC MEMBRANES.
002888 03-03

THREE CLASSES OF DOPAMINE-RECEPTOR (D-2, D-3, D-4) IDENTIFIED BY BINDING STUDIES WITH 3H APOMORPHINE AND 3H DOMPERIDONE.
002900 03-03

GABA-RECEPTORS REGULATE THE AFFINITIES OF ANIONS REQUIRED FOR BRAIN SPECIFIC BENZODIAZEPINE BINDING.
002903 03-03

ACTION OF PYRAZOLOPYRIDINES AS MODULATORS OF (3H)FLUNITRAZEPAM BINDING TO THE GABA/BENZODIAZEPINE-RECEPTOR COMPLEX OF THE CEREBELLUM.
002909 03-03

REGULATION BY CATIONS OF (3H)SPIROPERIDOL BINDING ASSOCIATED WITH DOPAMINE-RECEPTORS OF RAT-BRAIN.
002922 03-03

3H IMIPRAMINE BINDING IN HUMAN PLATELETS: DIMINUTION OF BINDING-SITES IN DEPRESSED-PATIENTS.
003427 03-13

DIFFERENTIAL BINDING OF CHLORPROMAZINE TO HUMAN BLOOD CELLS: APPLICATION OF THE HYGROSCOPIC DESORPTION METHOD.
003556 03-16

HIGH-AFFINITY 3H IMIPRAMINE BINDING: A NEW BIOLOGICAL TOOL FOR STUDIES IN DEPRESSION.
003610 03-17

STRUCTURE-ACTIVITY AND RECEPTOR BINDING OF ANTAGONIST ANALGESICS.
003611 03-17

EFFECT OF THE POSITION OF THE PHENOLIC GROUP IN MORPHINANS ON THEIR AFFINITY FOR OPIATE-RECEPTOR BINDING.
003702 04-02

EFFECT OF CHRONIC SULPIRIDE ON STRIATAL SPIPERONE BINDING.
003720 04-03

PAPAIN-DERIVED FRAGMENT IIC TETANUS-TOXIN: ITS BINDING TO ISOLATED SYNAPTIC MEMBRANES AND RETROGRADE AXONAL TRANSPORT.
003734 04-03

INHIBITION OF (3H)DIAZEPAM BINDING BY AN ENDOGENOUS FRACTION FROM RAT-BRAIN SYNAPTOSOMES.
003768 04-03

EFFECTS OF CONFORMATIONALLY RESTRAINED ANALOGUES OF SEROTONIN ON ITS UPTAKE AND BINDING IN RAT-BRAIN.
003794 04-03

COMPARISON OF THE BINDING CHARACTERISTICS OF TRITIATED OPIATES AND OPIOID-PEPTIDES.
003802 04-03

CHARACTERIZATION BY (3H)DIHYDROERGOCRYPTINE BINDING OF ALPHA-ADRENERGIC-RECEPTORS IN NEUROBLASTOMA X GLIOMA HYBRID CELLS.
003823 04-03

SPECIFIC, HIGH-AFFINITY (3H)ETHYLKETOCYCLAZOCINE BINDING IN RAT CENTRAL-NERVOUS-SYSTEM: LACK OF EVIDENCE FOR KAPPA-RECEPTORS.
003840 04-03

REGIONAL CHANGES IN (3H)DIAZEPAM BINDING IN THE BRAINS OF MICE AFTER REMOVAL OF THE OLFACTORY-BULBS.
003848 04-03

IBOTENIC-ACID ANALOGUES AS INHIBITORS OF (3H)GLUTAMIC-ACID BINDING TO CEREBELLAR MEMBRANES.
003868 04-03

QUINUCLIDINYL BENZILATE BINDING IN HOUSEFLY HEADS AND RAT-BRAIN.
003872 04-03

INCREASED MESOLIMBIC DOPAMINE BINDING FOLLOWING CHRONIC HALOPERIDOL TREATMENT.
003872 04-03

OPIOID BINDING PROPERTIES OF BRAIN AND PERIPHERAL TISSUES: EVIDENCE FOR HETEROGENEITY IN OPIOID LIGAND BINDING SITES.
003902 04-03

THE EFFECT OF TYPICAL AND ATYPICAL NEUROLEPTICS ON BINDING OF (3H)SPIROPERIDOL IN CALF CAUDATE.
003906 04-03

EFFECTS OF HALOPEMIDE ON GABA-RECEPTOR BINDING, UPTAKE AND RELEASE.
003913 04-03

ALTERATIONS IN DIHYDROMORPHINE BINDING IN CEREBRAL HEMISPHERES OF AGED MALE RATS.
003936 04-03

DOPAMINE-RECEPTORS IN SUBCELLULAR FRACTIONS FROM BOVINE CAUDATE: ENRICHMENT OF (3H)SPIPERONE BINDING IN A POSTSYNAPTIC MEMBRANE FRACTION.
003948 04-03

BINDING OF (3H) MUSCIMOL, A POTENT GAMMA AMINOBUTYRIC-ACID-RECEPTOR AGONIST, TO MEMBRANES OF THE BOVINE RETINA.
003954 04-03

REGIONAL DISTRIBUTION OF (3H)IMIPRAMINE BINDING IN RAT-BRAIN.
003955 04-03

DOES HIGH-AFFINITY (3H) IMIPRAMINE BINDING LABEL SEROTONIN REUPTAKE SITES IN BRAIN AND PLATELET?
003962 04-03

MULTIPLE ALPHA2-NORADRENERGIC-RECEPTOR SITES IN RAT-BRAIN: SELECTIVE REGULATION OF HIGH-AFFINITY (3H)CLONIDINE BINDING BY GUANINE-NUCLEOTIDES AND DIVALENT-CATIONS.
003992 04-03

L ASPARTATE BINDING-SITES IN RAT-CEREBELLUM: A COMPARISON OF THE BINDING OF L (3H)ASPARTATE AND L (3H)GLUTAMATE TO SYNAPTIC MEMBRANES.
004000 04-03

DOPAMINE-RECEPTOR BINDING IN BOVINE INTERMEDIATE LOBE PITUITARY MEMBRANES.
004003 04-03

CATION REGULATION DIFFERENTIATES SPECIFIC BINDING OF (3H)SULPIRIDE AND (3H)SPIPERONE TO RAT STRIATAL PREPARATIONS.
004032 04-03

THE EFFECTS OF ACUTE AND CHRONIC ETHANOL ADMINISTRATION AND ITS WITHDRAWAL ON GAMMA AMINOBUTYRIC-ACID-RECEPTOR BINDING IN RAT-BRAIN.
004035 04-03

RELEVANCE OF DOPAMINE-RECEPTOR BINDING STUDIES FOR EVALUATION OF ANTIPARKINSONIAN-DRUGS.
004120 04-04

THE RELATIONSHIP BETWEEN LOSS OF DOPAMINE NERVE TERMINALS, STRIATAL (3H)SPIROPERIDOL BINDING AND ROTATIONAL-BEHAVIOR IN UNILATERALLY 6 HYDROXYDOPAMINE LESIONED RATS.
004129 04-04

NALOXAZONE, A LONG-ACTING OPIATE ANTAGONIST: EFFECTS ON ANALGESIA IN INTACT ANIMALS AND ON OPIATE-RECEPTOR BINDING IN VITRO.
004198 04-04

SPECIFIC IN VIVO BINDING OF 77BR P BROMOSPIROPERIDOL IN RAT-BRAIN: A POTENTIAL TOOL FOR GAMMA-RAY IMAGING.
004293 04-06

PROTEIN BINDING OF CHLORPROMAZINE IN CEREBROSPINAL-FLUID AND SERUM.
004311 04-08

DECREASED 3H IMIPRAMINE BINDING IN DEPRESSED MALES AND FEMALES.
004349 04-09

(3H) IMIPRAMINE BINDING IN HUMAN PLATELETS: A NEW BIOCHEMICAL-PARAMETER IN DEPRESSION.
004358 04-09

BINDING-ACTIVITIES
DOPAMINE-SENSITIVE ADENYLATE-CYCLASE AND RECEPTOR BINDING-ACTIVITIES FOLLOWING ACUTE AND CHRONIC NEUROLEPTIC-DRUG TREATMENT. (UNPUBLISHED PAPER).
001172 02-03

BINDING-ACTIVITY
IDENTIFICATION AND PARTIAL PURIFICATION OF A HYDROPHOBIC PROTEIN COMPONENT ASSOCIATED WITH (3H)SPIROPERIDOL BINDING-ACTIVITY. (UNPUBLISHED PAPER).
001007 02-01

BETA ENDORPHIN: DISSOCIATION OF RECEPTOR BINDING-ACTIVITY FROM ANALGESIC POTENCY.
001081 02-02

SYNTHESIS AND GABA-RECEPTOR BINDING-ACTIVITY OF TWO FLUOROAMINOMETHYLPHENOLS.
003693 04-02

BINDING-SITE
ABUNDANCE AND LOCATION OF 125I SALMON CALCITONIN BINDING-SITE IN RAT-BRAIN.
001320 02-03

A HIGH-AFFINITY GTP BINDING-SITE IN RAT-BRAIN. (UNPUBLISHED PAPER).
001442 02-03

THE PHARMACOLOGICAL RELEVANCE OF THE COCAINE BINDING-SITE IN MOUSE-BRAIN.
001772 02-04

BINDING-SITES
LOCALIZATION OF ALPHA BUNGAROTOXIN BINDING-SITES IN SYNAPSES OF THE DEVELOPING CHICK RETINA.
000065 01-03

(3H)5 HT BINDING-SITES AND 5 HT-SENSITIVE ADENYLATE-CYCLASE IN GLIAL CELL MEMBRANE FRACTION.
000093 01-03

EVIDENCE FOR, AND LOCALIZATION OF, A UNITARY DOPAMINE-RECEPTOR COMPOSED OF COOPERATIVELY LINKED SUBUNIT BINDING-SITES IN RAT STRIATUM.
000186 01-03

SEROTONIN-SENSITIVE ADENYLATE-CYCLASE AND (3H)SEROTONIN BINDING-SITES IN THE CNS OF THE RAT -- I. KINETIC PARAMETERS AND PHARMACOLOGICAL-PROPERTIES.
000213 01-03

SEROTONIN-SENSITIVE ADENYLATE-CYCLASE AND (3H)SEROTONIN BINDING-SITES IN THE CNS OF THE RAT -- II. RESPECTIVE REGIONAL AND SUBCELLULAR DISTRIBUTIONS AND ONTOGENETIC DEVELOPMENTS.
000214 01-03

REGIONAL DISTRIBUTION AND BIOCHEMICAL-PROPERTIES OF 125I TYR8-SUBSTANCE-P BINDING-SITES IN SYNAPTIC VESICLES.
000259 01-03

DIFFERENTIAL REGULATION OF MUSCARINIC AGONIST BINDING-SITES FOLLOWING CHRONIC CHOLINESTERASE INHIBITION.
000279 01-03

PROPERTIES OF (3H)DIAZEPAM BINDING-SITES ON RAT BLOOD-PLATELETS.
000317 01-03

SOLUBILIZATION OF THE DIHYDROPICROTOXININ BINDING-SITES.
001192 02-03

DOWN REGULATION OF DIHYDROALPRENOLOL AND IMIPRAMINE BINDING-SITES IN BRAIN OF RATS REPEATEDLY TREATED WITH IMIPRAMINE.
001317 02-03

UNITARY DOPAMINERGIC-RECEPTOR COMPOSED OF COOPERATIVELY LINKED AGONIST AND ANTAGONIST SUBUNIT BINDING-SITES.
001342 02-03

LOCALIZATION OF NALOXONE SENSITIVE (3H)DIHYDROMORPHINE BINDING-SITES WITHIN THE HIPPOCAMPUS OF THE RAT.
001368 02-03

CHARACTERIZATION OF BENZODIAZEPINE BINDING-SITES. (UNPUBLISHED PAPER).
001503 02-03

BENZODIAZEPINE BINDING-SITES: PROPERTIES AND MODULATION. (UNPUBLISHED PAPER).
001504 02-03

COMPARED PROPERTIES OF CENTRAL AND PERIPHERAL BINDING-SITES FOR PHENCYCLIDINE.
001521 02-03

MU-RECEPTORS AND DELTA OPIATE-RECEPTORS; CORRELATION WITH HIGH-AFFINITY AND LOW AFFINITY OPIATE BINDING-SITES.
001554 02-03

KAINATE LESION DISSOCIATES STRIATAL DOPAMINE-RECEPTOR RADIOLIGAND BINDING-SITES.
002803 03-03

PROPERTIES OF DOPAMINE AGONIST AND ANTAGONIST BINDING-SITES IN MAMMALIAN RETINA.
002814 03-03

IDENTIFICATION OF TWO BENZODIAZEPINE BINDING-SITES ON CELLS CULTURED FROM RAT-CEREBRAL-CORTEX.
002820 03-03

LAMINAR DISTRIBUTION OF PUTATIVE NEUROTRANSMITTER AMINO-ACIDS AND LIGAND BINDING-SITES IN THE DOG OLFACTORY-BULB.
002836 03-03

CONVULSANT AND ANTICONVULSANT-DRUG BINDING-SITES RELATED TO GABA REGULATED CHLORIDE ION-CHANNELS.
002848 03-03

3H SEROTONIN BINDING-SITES IN RAT-BRAIN: EFFECTS OF REPEATED ADMINISTRATION OF ANTIDEPRESSANT-DRUGS. (PH.D. DISSERTATION).
002881 03-03

BENZODIAZEPINE BINDING-SITES: PROPERTIES AND MODULATION.
002912 03-03

3H IMIPRAMINE BINDING IN HUMAN PLATELETS: DIMINUTION OF BINDING-SITES IN DEPRESSED-PATIENTS.
003427 03-13

CHARACTERIZATION OF TWO (3H)GLUTAMATE BINDING-SITES IN RAT HIPPOCAMPAL MEMBRANES.
003726 04-03

INHIBITION OF DOPAMINE D-1 AND D-2 BINDING-SITES IN NEURONAL TISSUE BY ASCORBATE.
003876 04-03

HIGH-AFFINITY BINDING-SITES FOR A SOMATOSTATIN-28 ANALOG IN RAT-BRAIN.
003985 04-03

L ASPARTATE BINDING-SITES IN RAT-CEREBELLUM: A COMPARISON OF THE BINDING OF L (3H)ASPARTATE AND L (3H)GLUTAMATE TO SYNAPTIC MEMBRANES.
004000 04-03

INTERACTION OF STEREOISOMERS OF BARBITURATES WITH (3H)ALPHA DIHYDROPICROTOXININ BINDING-SITES.
004036 04-03

BIOAVAILABILITY
BIOAVAILABILITY OF 14C SULPIRIDE IN DOGS.
000017 01-03

CLASSIFICATION AND ASSESSMENT OF CEREBRAL BIOAVAILABILITY OF LOPIRAZEPAM (D-12524) BY QUANTITATIVE EEG AND PSYCHOMETRIC-ANALYSIS.
000720 01-11

BIOAVAILABILITY OF SULPIRIDE TABLET AND CAPSULE IN DOGS.
001101 02-03

ORAL BIOAVAILABILITY OF APOMORPHINE IN THE RAT WITH A PORTACAVAL VENOUS ANASTOMOSIS.
001158 02-03

LOW ORAL CPZ BIOAVAILABILITY IN CHRONIC SCHIZOPHRENIA. (UNPUBLISHED PAPER).
001938 02-08

BIOAVAILABILITY AND KINETICS OF MAPROTILINE.
002204 02-13

THE BIOAVAILABILITY OF ORAL AND PARENTERAL CHLORIMIPRAMINE (ANAFRANIL).
002232 02-13

BIOAVAILABILITY AND RELATED PHARMACOKINETICS IN MAN OF ORALLY ADMINISTERED L 5 HYDROXYTRYPTOPHAN IN STEADY-STATE.
002261 02-13

PHARMACOKINETICS AND BIOAVAILABILITY OF CHLORDIAZEPOXIDE IN HUMANS.
002564 02-17

EFFECT OF DOSE ON BIOAVAILABILITY OF ORAL DIGOXIN.
003161 03-07

DOSAGE FORM DESIGN FOR IMPROVEMENT OF BIOAVAILABILITY OF LEVODOPA III: INFLUENCE OF DOSE ON PHARMACOKINETIC BEHAVIOR OF LEVODOPA IN DOGS AND PARKINSONIAN-PATIENTS.
004551 04-13

BIOCHEMICAL
THE TREATMENT OF PARKINSONS-DISEASE USING A COMBINATION OF L-DOPA AND DECARBOXYLASE INHIBITORS (CARBIDOPA, BENSERASIDE). A CLINICAL AND BIOCHEMICAL COMPARATIVE INVESTIGATION.
000712 01-11

EFFECTS OF PROLONGED TREATMENT WITH LITHIUM AND TRICYCLIC-ANTIDEPRESSANTS ON DISCHARGE FREQUENCY, NOREPINEPHRINE RESPONSES AND BETA-RECEPTOR BINDING IN RAT-CEREBELLUM: ELECTROPHYSIOLOGICAL AND BIOCHEMICAL COMPARISON.
002884 03-03

RECENT REVIEWS OF BIOCHEMICAL, NEUROCHEMICAL, AND PHARMACOLOGICAL TOPICS.
003649 03-17

BIOCHEMICAL AND IMMUNOLOGICAL PROPERTIES OF THE MOUSE BRAIN ENOLASES PURIFIED BY A SIMPLE METHOD.
003668 04-01

FLUORESCENT PROBES OF ALPHA-ADRENERGIC AND BETA-ADRENERGIC AND OPIATE-RECEPTORS: BIOCHEMICAL AND HISTOCHEMICAL EVALUATION.
003685 04-02

SYNTHESIS AND BIOCHEMICAL AND PHARMACOLOGIC PROPERTIES OF ANALOGUES AND DERIVATIVES OF P CHLOROPHENYLALANINE.
003691 04-02

BIOCHEMICAL INVESTIGATIONS INTO THE MODE OF ACTION OF TRAZODONE.
003753 04-03

TOWARD A BIOCHEMICAL CLASSIFICATION OF DEPRESSIVE-DISORDERS IV: PRETREATMENT URINARY MHPG LEVELS AS PREDICTORS OF ANTIDEPRESSANT RESPONSE TO IMIPRAMINE.
004406 04-09

PROLACTIN AND NEUROLEPTIC-DRUGS: A BIOCHEMICAL INDEX OF CLINICAL-RESPONSE?
004539 04-13

THE BIOCHEMICAL BACKGROUND TO TARDIVE-DYSKINESIA.
004588 04-15

BIOCHEMICAL AND NEUROENDOCRINE APPROACHES TO A MALIGNANT-SYNDROME OF NEUROLEPTIC.
004589 04-15

BIOCHEMICAL-ACTION
CLINICAL AND BIOCHEMICAL-ACTION OF PIRACETAM (NOOTROPIL) IN DRUG-RESISTANT DEPRESSION.
000600 01-09

BIOCHEMICAL-ASPECTS
SOME PHARMACOLOGICAL-ASPECTS AND BIOCHEMICAL-ASPECTS OF TRH: EXPERIMENTAL AND CLINICAL DATA.
001189 02-03

CLOMIPRAMINE TREATMENT OF OBSESSIVE-COMPULSIVE-DISORDER: II. BIOCHEMICAL-ASPECTS.
002300 02-13

BIOCHEMICAL-BASIS
BENZODIAZEPINES: A TOOL TO EXPLORE THE BIOCHEMICAL-BASIS AND NEUROPHYSIOLOGICAL-BASIS OF ANXIETY.
000397 01-04

BIOCHEMICAL-CHANGES
BEHAVIORAL-CHANGES AND BIOCHEMICAL-CHANGES AFTER HIPPOCAMPAL DAMAGE. (PH.D. DISSERTATION).
003069 03-04

BIOCHEMICAL-CHARACTERIZATION
BIOCHEMICAL-CHARACTERIZATION OF THE RAT SYMPATHETIC GANGLION: PHARMACOLOGICAL-EFFECTS OF RESERPINE ON GANGLIONIC CATECHOLAMINES.
000153 01-03

BIOCHEMICAL-CHARACTERIZATION AND PHARMACOLOGICAL CHARACTERIZATION OF A PEPTIDE FROM THE HEMODIALYSATE OF PSYCHOTIC-PATIENTS.
001049 02-01

BIOCHEMICAL-CONSEQUENCES
THE DOPAMINE-RECEPTOR COMPLEX: BIOCHEMICAL-CONSEQUENCES OF SUPERSENSITIVITY INDUCED BY TREATMENT WITH 6 HYDROXYDOPAMINE OR MORPHINE.
003958 04-03

BIOCHEMICAL-CONSIDERATIONS
BRAIN CATECHOLAMINES, MENTAL-ILLNESSES, AGING AND SENILE-DEMENTIA: BIOCHEMICAL-CONSIDERATIONS AND PHARMACOLOGICAL-CONSIDERATIONS.
001550 02-03

BIOCHEMICAL-CORRELATES
SODIUM-VALPROATE IN SCHIZOPHRENIA: SOME BIOCHEMICAL-CORRELATES.
000561 01-08

RECEPTOR PLASTICITY: BIOCHEMICAL-CORRELATES AND PHARMACOLOGICAL SIGNIFICANCE.
001181 02-03

BEHAVIORAL-CORRELATES AND BIOCHEMICAL-CORRELATES AFTER HALOPERIDOL AND CLOZAPINE LONG-TERM-TREATMENT.
001422 02-03

BIOCHEMICAL-CORRELATION
CLINICAL-CORRELATION, BIOCHEMICAL-CORRELATION, AND PSYCHOPHARMACOLOGICAL-CORRELATION IN PATIENTS WITH DEPRESSIVE-SYMPTOMATOLOGY.
002018 02-09

BIOCHEMICAL-CORRELATIONS
CLINICAL AND BIOCHEMICAL-CORRELATIONS IN ABRUPT DISCONTINUATION OF PSYCHOPHARMACOTHERAPY.
004330 04-08

BIOCHEMICAL-DATA
CLINICAL AND BIOCHEMICAL-DATA ON THE ACTION OF MAPROTILINE AND CLOMIPRAMINE IN DEPRESSIVE-STATES (PRELIMINARY OBSERVATION).
002032 02-09

BIOCHEMICAL-EFFECTS
HISTAMINE-RECEPTORS IN THE BRAIN: CHARACTERIZATION BY BINDING STUDIES AND BIOCHEMICAL-EFFECTS.
001054 02-01

STUDIES ON THE BIOCHEMICAL-EFFECTS AND BEHAVIOURAL-EFFECTS OF ORAL NICOTINE.
001115 02-03

BIOCHEMICAL-EFFECTS OF ZIMELIDINE IN MAN.
001967 02-09

BIOCHEMICAL-EFFECTS AND BEHAVIORAL-EFFECTS OF ACUTE ETHANOL IN RATS AT DIFFERENT ENVIRONMENTAL TEMPERATURES.
002864 03-03

THE ROLE OF CALCIUM AND DOPAMINE MEMBRANE CARRIER IN MEDIATING THE BEHAVIORAL-EFFECTS AND BIOCHEMICAL-EFFECTS OF AMPHETAMINE. (PH.D. DISSERTATION).
002996 03-04

CENTRAL CARDIOVASCULAR-EFFECTS AND BIOCHEMICAL-EFFECTS OF BACLOFEN IN THE CONSCIOUS RAT.
003965 04-03

A COMPARISON BETWEEN SOME BIOCHEMICAL-EFFECTS AND BEHAVIOURAL-EFFECTS PRODUCED BY NEUROLEPTICS.
004116 04-04

LONG-TERM NEUROLEPTIC TREATMENT OF CHRONIC SCHIZOPHRENIC-PATIENTS: CLINICAL AND BIOCHEMICAL-EFFECTS OF WITHDRAWAL.
004344 04-08

BIOCHEMICAL-EVENT
PHOSPHOLIPID METHYLATION: A BIOCHEMICAL-EVENT OF SIGNAL TRANSDUCTION. (UNPUBLISHED PAPER).
001279 02-03

BIOCHEMICAL-EVIDENCE
BIOCHEMICAL-EVIDENCE FOR TYPE-1 AND TYPE-2 OPIATE-RECEPTORS. (UNPUBLISHED PAPER).
001050 02-01

PHARMACOLOGICAL EVIDENCE AND BIOCHEMICAL-EVIDENCE FOR AN INTERACTION BETWEEN THE BENZODIAZEPINE AND GABA-RECEPTORS.
001261 02-03

BIOCHEMICAL-EVIDENCE FOR OSTEOMALACIA WITH CARBAMAZEPINE THERAPY.
002445 02-15

BIOCHEMICAL-LOCALIZATION
BIOCHEMICAL-LOCALIZATION AND CHARACTERIZATION OF BOMBESIN-LIKE-PEPTIDES IN DISCRETE REGIONS OF RAT-BRAIN. (UNPUBLISHED PAPER).
001046 02-01

BIOCHEMICAL-MEASUREMENTS
BIOCHEMICAL-MEASUREMENTS DURING (-)DEPRENYL TREATMENT OF PARKINSONISM.
000673 01-11

BIOCHEMICAL-MECHANISM
BIOCHEMICAL-MECHANISM OF SIGNAL TRANSDUCTION ACROSS BIOMEMBRANES. (UNPUBLISHED PAPER).
001026 02-01

NEW TRENDS CONCERNING THE BIOCHEMICAL-MECHANISM OF ACTION OF BENZODIAZEPINES.
003642 03-17

BIOCHEMICAL-OBSERVATIONS
TREATMENT OF MYOCLONUS WITH L 5 HYDROXYTRYPTOPHAN AND CARBIDOPA: CLINICAL, ELECTROPHYSIOLOGICAL, AND BIOCHEMICAL-OBSERVATIONS.
002180 02-11

BIOCHEMICAL-PARAMETER
(3H) IMIPRAMINE BINDING IN HUMAN PLATELETS: A NEW BIOCHEMICAL-PARAMETER IN DEPRESSION.
004358 04-09

BIOCHEMICAL-PARAMETERS
DRUG INTERFERENCE ON SOME BIOCHEMICAL-PARAMETERS OF RAT-CEREBRAL-CORTEX DURING POSTISCHEMIC RECOVERY.
001126 02-03

BIOCHEMICAL-PHARMACOLOGY
NEUROCHEMICAL-PHARMACOLOGY AND BIOCHEMICAL-PHARMACOLOGY.
003639 03-17

BIOCHEMICAL-PROPERTIES
REGIONAL DISTRIBUTION AND BIOCHEMICAL-PROPERTIES OF 125I TYR8-SUBSTANCE-P BINDING-SITES IN SYNAPTIC VESICLES.
000259 01-03

BIOCHEMICAL-PROPERTIES OF SPIPERONE BINDING TO RAT-BRAIN MEMBRANES.
000294 01-03

PHARMACOLOGICAL AND BIOCHEMICAL-PROPERTIES OF BRL-14342, A NOVEL POTENTIAL ANTIDEPRESSANT-DRUG.
004086 04-04

BIOCHEMICAL-RESPONSE
RELATIONSHIPS BETWEEN CHLORPROMAZINE CONCENTRATIONS IN PLASMA AND CEREBROSPINAL-FLUID AND CLINICAL-RESPONSE AND BIOCHEMICAL-RESPONSE IN PSYCHOTIC-PATIENTS.
001905 02-08

BIOCHEMICAL-STUDIES
EVIDENCE FOR A GABAERGIC NIGROTHALAMIC PATHWAY IN THE RAT: I. BEHAVIOURAL-STUDIES AND BIOCHEMICAL-STUDIES.
000158 01-03

BIOCHEMICAL-STUDIES AFTER CHRONIC ADMINISTRATION OF NEUROLEPTICS TO MONKEYS.
000523 01-05

TARDIVE-DYSKINESIA: BIOCHEMICAL-STUDIES. (UNPUBLISHED PAPER).
002245 02-13

BEHAVIORAL AND BIOCHEMICAL-STUDIES OF THE SCOPOLAMINE-INDUCED REVERSAL OF NEUROLEPTIC ACTIVITY.
004195 04-04

BIOCHEMICAL-STUDIES OF HUMAN EPILEPTICS DURING ANTICONVULSANT THERAPY.
004490 04-11

BIOCHEMICAL-STUDY
EFFECT OF CHLORPROMAZINE ON CELL PROLIFERATION IN THE DEVELOPING RAT-BRAIN. A COMBINED BIOCHEMICAL-STUDY AND MORPHOLOGICAL-STUDY.
001407 02-03

BIOCHEMICAL-STUDY OF THE ANIMAL-MODEL DEPRESSION INDUCED BY TETRABENAZINE.
001506 02-03

A BIOCHEMICAL-STUDY OF LUMBAR CEREBROSPINAL-FLUID IN EXTRAPYRAMIDAL-DISORDERS.
002186 02-11

BIOCHEMICAL-VARIABLES
RELATIONSHIPS AMONG BIOCHEMICAL-VARIABLES, CLINICAL-VARIABLES, AND PHARMACOKINETIC-VARIABLES IN NEUROLEPTIC TREATED SCHIZOPHRENIC-PATIENTS.
001946 02-08

BIOCHEMICALLY-SELECTIVE
NOREPINEPHRINE UPTAKE INHIBITORS AS BIOCHEMICALLY-SELECTIVE AND BEHAVIORALLY-SELECTIVE ANTAGONISTS OF THE LOCOMOTOR-STIMULATION INDUCED BY INDIRECTLY ACTING SYMPATHOMIMETIC-AMINES IN MICE.
000492 01-04

BIOCHEMISTRY
INFLUENCE OF CANNABIS AND DELTA9 TETRAHYDROCANNABINOL ON THE BIOCHEMISTRY OF THE MALE REPRODUCTIVE ORGANS.
002686 03-03

BIOELECTRIC-ACTIVITY
THE EFFECT OF CLOFELIN ON THE BIOELECTRIC-ACTIVITY OF THE BRAIN.
001449 02-03
BIOELECTRICAL-ACTIVITY
BIOELECTRICAL-ACTIVITY OF THE RAT BRAIN AFTER PREMATURE
WEANING AND AFTER RNA ADMINISTRATION.
002865 03-03
THE EFFECT OF LITHIUM-HYDROXYBUTYRATE ON THE BIOELECTRICAL-
ACTIVITY OF THE CORTEX AND SOME SUBCORTICAL STRUCTURES OF
THE RABBIT BRAIN.
003994 04-03
THE EFFECT OF THE NEW ANTIDEPRESSANT INKASAN ON THE
BIOELECTRICAL-ACTIVITY OF THE BRAIN AND ON CONDITIONED
REFLEXES.
004212 04-04
BIOGENESIS
REGULATION OF BIOGENESIS OF PSYCHOTOMIMETIC AMINES.
(UNPUBLISHED PAPER).
003818 04-03
BIOGENIC-AMINE
INTERACTION OF BIOGENIC-AMINE SYSTEMS IN BRAIN. (UNPUBLISHED
PAPER).
001141 02-03
SHORT-TERM AND LONG-TERM EFFECTS OF METHAMPHETAMINE ON
BIOGENIC-AMINE METABOLISM IN EXTRASTRIATAL DOPAMINERGIC
NUCLEI.
001384 02-03
A SELECTED ION-MONITORING ASSAY FOR BIOGENIC-AMINE
METABOLITES AND PROBENECID, IN HUMAN LUMBAR
CEREBROSPINAL-FLUID.
003663 04-01
BIOGENIC-AMINES
REUPTAKE OF BIOGENIC-AMINES BY BRAIN SLICES: EFFECT OF
HYDROCORTISONE.
000187 01-03
ACTION OF THE ANTIDEPRESSANT PRIDEFINE (AHR-1118) ON BIOGENIC-
AMINES IN THE RAT-BRAIN.
000312 01-03
THE ROLE OF BIOGENIC-AMINES IN AMYGDALAR KINDLING. I. LOCAL
AMYGDALAR AFTERDISCHARGE.
000327 01-03
HIGH-SENSITIVITY NEGATIVE CHEMICAL-IONIZATION MASS-SPECTRAL-
ANALYSIS OF BIOGENIC-AMINES AND METABOLITES. (UNPUBLISHED
PAPER).
001042 02-01
SYNTHESIS OF 180 ANALOGS OF BIOGENIC-AMINES. (UNPUBLISHED
PAPER).
001044 02-01
BIOGENIC-AMINES AND NEUROPEPTIDES PLAY A ROLE IN THE CENTRAL-
REGULATION OF GENETIC HYPERTENSION. (UNPUBLISHED PAPER).
001455 02-03
CENTRAL BIOGENIC-AMINES AND NEUROPEPTIDES IN GENETIC
HYPERTENSION. (UNPUBLISHED PAPER).
001456 02-03
EFFECT OF LOW-DOSE LITHIUM ADMINISTRATION AND SUBSEQUENT
WITHDRAWAL ON BIOGENIC-AMINES IN RAT-BRAIN.
003708 04-03
STRESS-MODULATED ALTERATION OF BRAIN BIOGENIC-AMINES IN THE
RAT: EFFECTS OF L TRYPTOPHAN.
003978 04-03
THE EFFECT OF P CHLOROPHENYLALANINE ON THE DISTRIBUTION OF
BIOGENIC-AMINES IN THE BRAIN, AND ON MEMORY IN RATS.
004068 04-04
BIOLOGIC
CURRENT BIOLOGIC STRATEGIES FOR ANXIETY.
003276 03-10
BIOLOGIC-INTERACTION
BIOLOGIC-INTERACTION OF GAMMA-RADIATION WITH
PHENYLBUTAZONE, PHENYTOIN, OR HYDRALAZINE.
000518 01-05
BIOLOGICAL
INFLUENCE OF NICERGOLINE ON MOLECULAR BIOLOGICAL PROCESSES IN
THE BRAIN AND LEARNING-ABILITY OF THE RAT.
000449 01-04
LITHIUM LEVEL IN SOME BIOLOGICAL FLUIDS AT ITS PROPHYLACTIC
THERAPEUTIC APPLICATION.
000605 01-09
DETERMINATION OF TRICYCLIC-ANTIDEPRESSANTS AND TETRACYCLIC-
ANTIDEPRESSANTS AND OF THEIR METABOLIC PRODUCTS IN
BIOLOGICAL FLUIDS.
002498 02-16
HIGH-AFFINITY 3H IMIPRAMINE BINDING: A NEW BIOLOGICAL TOOL FOR
STUDIES IN DEPRESSION.
003610 03-17
BIOLOGICAL EVALUATION OF A TRH ANALOGUE WITH A MODIFIED
PROLINE RESIDUE.
003662 04-01
PREPARATION AND BIOLOGICAL ACTIONS OF N 2,2,2 TRIFLUOROETHYL-
DIHYDROXYPHENYLETHYLAMINE.
003697 04-02

NEW BIOLOGICAL RESEARCH RELEVANT TO ANXIETY.
004705 04-17
BIOLOGICAL AND PHYSIOLOGICAL PREDICTORS OF DRUG RESPONSE.
(UNPUBLISHED PAPER).
004708 04-17
BIOLOGICAL-ACTIVITY
MODIFICATION OF THE PROLINE RESIDUE OF TRH ENHANCES BIOLOGICAL-
ACTIVITY AND INHIBITS DEGRADATION.
000351 01-04
CONFIRMATION BEHAVIOR OF PHENCYCLIDINES AND BIOLOGICAL-
ACTIVITY.
001031 02-01
COMPARISON OF BIOLOGICAL-ACTIVITY AND BEHAVIORAL-ACTIVITY OF
ALPHA AND GAMMA MELANOCYTE-STIMULATING-HORMONES.
(UNPUBLISHED PAPER).
001398 02-03
BIOLOGICAL-ACTIVITY OF THE TETRAHYDROCANNABINOLS.
002556 02-17
DIFFERENTIAL LOSS OF BIOLOGICAL-ACTIVITY OF THE ENKEPHALINS
INDUCED BY CURRENT.
002783 03-03
SYNTHESIS AND BIOLOGICAL-ACTIVITY OF HUMAN BETA ENDORPHIN
ANALOGS WITH DISULFIDE BRIDGES.
003655 04-01
BIOLOGICAL-EFFECTS
BIOLOGICAL-EFFECTS OF CHLORPROMAZINE IN CHRONIC
SCHIZOPHRENICS. III. THE MUTUAL RELATION OF EACH INDEX.
003179 03-08
THE BIOLOGICAL-EFFECTS AND CLINICAL-EFFECTS OF ORAL MAGNESIUM
AND ASSOCIATED MAGNESIUM VITAMIN-B6 ADMINISTRATION ON
CERTAIN DISORDERS OBSERVED IN INFANTILE AUTISM.
003291 03-11
BEHAVIORAL-EFFECTS AND BIOLOGICAL-EFFECTS OF ACUTE BETA
ENDORPHIN INJECTION IN SCHIZOPHRENIC-PATIENTS AND DEPRESSED-
PATIENTS.
003357 03-11
BIOLOGICAL-EFFECTS OF CHLORPROMAZINE IN CHRONIC
SCHIZOPHRENICS. I. WITH REFERENCE TO PITUITARY-HORMONES.
003415 03-13
BIOLOGICAL-EFFECTS OF CHLORPROMAZINE IN CHRONIC
SCHIZOPHRENICS. II. WITH REFERENCE TO SYMPATHETIC NEURONAL
FUNCTION.
003416 03-13
BIOLOGICAL-INTERACTION
THE MOLECULAR ARCHITECTURE OF ERGOPEPTINES: A BASIS FOR
BIOLOGICAL-INTERACTION.
001527 02-03
BIOLOGICAL-MATERIAL
A SPECIFIC AND SENSITIVE MICROASSAY FOR HYDROXYINDOLES IN
BIOLOGICAL-MATERIAL -- APPLICATION FOR CEREBRAL MICROVESSELS,
BRAIN, AND PINEAL-ORGAN OF THE RAT.
002503 02-16
BIOLOGICAL-PSYCHIATRY
ANIMAL-MODELS OF RELEVANCE TO BIOLOGICAL-PSYCHIATRY.
002490 02-16
DISCUSSION OF WHO ACTIVITY IN BIOLOGICAL-PSYCHIATRY WITH
SPECIAL REFERENCE TO TRAINING.
002520 02-17
CONVERGENCES AND DIVERGENCES BETWEEN BIOLOGICAL-PSYCHIATRY
AND PSYCHOTHERAPY.
002536 02-17
BIOLOGICAL-PSYCHIATRY TODAY -- VOL. B.
002588 02-17
BIOLOGICAL-PSYCHIATRY TODAY -- VOL. A.
002589 02-17
A QUANTITATIVE PROBE FOR BIOLOGICAL-PSYCHIATRY: SELECTED ION-
MONITORING.
004685 04-16
THE PROMISE OF BIOLOGICAL-PSYCHIATRY.
004752 04-17
BIOLOGICAL-RHYTHM
BIOLOGICAL-RHYTHM DISTURBANCES IN AFFECTIVE-ILLNESS.
002628 02-17
BIOLOGICAL-RHYTHMICITY
THE INFLUENCE OF DAILY BIOLOGICAL-RHYTHMICITY ON THE HOMING-
BEHAVIOR, PSYCHOPHARMACOLOGICAL RESPONSIVENESS, LEARNING
AND RETENTION OF SUCKLING RATS. (PH.D. DISSERTATION).
001660 02-04
BIOLOGICAL-STABILITY
AN ANALOGUE OF THYROTROPIN-RELEASING-HORMONE WITH IMPROVED
BIOLOGICAL-STABILITY BOTH IN VITRO AND IN VIVO.
000032 01-03
BIOLOGICAL-STUDIES
CLINICAL-STUDIES AND BIOLOGICAL-STUDIES OF L TRYPTOPHAN IN
DEPRESSION.
001977 02-09
BIOLOGY
BIOLOGY OF MANIC-MELANCHOLIC-DISORDERS.
000978 01-17

BIOLOGY AND THERAPY OF VIOLENT-BEHAVIOUR IN CHILDREN.
002608 02-17
BIBLIOGRAPHY ON THE BIOLOGY AND PHARMACOLOGY OF LITHIUM.
003630 03-17
BIOMEDICAL-CORRELATES
LECITHIN ADMINISTRATION IN TARDIVE-DYSKINESIA: CLINICAL AND
BIOMEDICAL-CORRELATES.
003496 03-15
BIOMEMBRANES
BIOCHEMICAL-MECHANISM OF SIGNAL TRANSDUCTION ACROSS
BIOMEMBRANES. (UNPUBLISHED PAPER).
001026 02-01
BIOPSY
RENAL FUNCTION AND BIOPSY IN PATIENTS ON LITHIUM THERAPY.
000830 01-15
BIOPSYCHOSOCIAL-PERSPECTIVE
LITHIUM: A BIOPSYCHOSOCIAL-PERSPECTIVE.
003247 03-09
BIOPTERIN
THE INFLUENCE OF D-AMPHETAMINE ON RAT-BRAIN STRIATAL REDUCED
BIOPTERIN CONCENTRATION.
003922 04-03
BIOSYNTHESIS
HYPOTHALAMIC CATECHOLAMINE BIOSYNTHESIS IN VITRO AS
MEASURED BY LIQUID-CHROMATOGRAPHY AND ELECTROCHEMICAL-
DETECTION.
000537 01-06
BIOSYNTHESIS OF POSTERIOR PITUITARY-HORMONES. (UNPUBLISHED
PAPER).
001053 02-01
INHIBITORS OF PHENYLETHANOLAMINE-N-METHYLTRANSFERASE AND
EPINEPHRINE BIOSYNTHESIS. 2. 1,2,3,4 TETRAHYDROISOQUINOLINE-7-
SULFONANILIDES.
001069 02-02
BIOSYNTHESIS, AXONAL TRANSPORT AND RELEASE OF POSTERIOR
PITUITARY-HORMONES. (UNPUBLISHED PAPER).
001148 02-03
DOPAMINE BIOSYNTHESIS IS REGULATED BY THE AMINE NEWLY
RECAPTURED BY DOPAMINERGIC NERVE-ENDINGS.
001163 02-03
EFFECT OF OPIATES ON MACROMOLECULE BIOSYNTHESIS.
001335 02-03
EFFECT OF MELANOSTATIN AND THYROLIBERIN ON THE BIOSYNTHESIS
AND RELEASE OF DOPAMINE BY RAT-BRAIN STRIATAL P2-FRACTIONS.
001472 02-03
EFFECT OF PROSTAGLANDIN-E1 AND ITS BIOSYNTHESIS INHIBITOR
INDOMETHACIN ON DRINKING IN THE RAT.
001749 02-04
INFLUENCE OF PSYCHOACTIVE AND NONPSYCHOACTIVE CANNABINOIDS
ON CELL PROLIFERATION AND MACROMOLECULAR BIOSYNTHESIS IN
HUMAN CELLS.
002830 03-03
LONG-TERM-TREATMENT OF RATS WITH MORPHINE DECREASES IN VITRO
BIOSYNTHESIS IN AND RELEASE OF BETA ENDORPHIN FROM
INTERMEDIATE/POSTERIOR LOBES OF PITUITARY.
003846 04-03
BIOTRANSFORMATION
EFFECTS OF LISURIDE ON BODY-TEMPERATURE OF RATS AND RABBITS:
RELATION TO MICROSOMAL BIOTRANSFORMATION AND
DOPAMINERGIC-RECEPTOR STIMULATION.
001161 02-03
KINETICS AND BIOTRANSFORMATION OF LORMETAZEPAM: II.
RADIOIMMUNOLOGIC DETERMINATIONS IN PLASMA AND URINE OF
YOUNG AND ELDERLY SUBJECTS: FIRST-PASS EFFECT.
004516 04-13
BIPERIDEN-HYDROCHLORIDE
A COMPARISON OF BIPERIDEN-HYDROCHLORIDE (AKINETON) AND
BENZHEXOL (ARTANE) IN THE TREATMENT OF DRUG-INDUCED
PARKINSONISM.
002146 02-11
BIPHASIC
BIPHASIC RESPONSIVENESS OF RAT PIAL-ARTERIOLES TO DOPAMINE:
DIRECT OBSERVATIONS ON THE MICROCIRCULATION.
001105 02-03
BIPHASIC ACTIVITY OF MEMBRANE-BOUND ENZYMES IN BRAIN
MITOCHONDRIA AND SYNAPTOSOMES DURING THE DEVELOPMENT OF
TOLERANCE TO AND PHYSICAL-DEPENDENCE ON CHRONIC MORPHINE
ADMINISTRATION TO RATS.
001285 C2-03
APPARENT SEROTONERGIC MODULATION OF THE DOSE-DEPENDENT
BIPHASIC RESPONSE OF NEOSTRIATAL NEURONS PRODUCED BY D-
AMPHETAMINE.
003981 04-03
BIPHASIC-EFFECTS
BIPHASIC-EFFECTS OF PIMOZIDE ON SLEEP-WAKEFULNESS IN DOGS.
000495 01-04
BIPHASIC-EFFECTS OF A POTENT ENKEPHALIN ANALOGUE D MET2-PRO5-
ENKEPHALINAMIDE AND MORPHINE ON LOCOMOTOR-ACTIVITY IN
MICE.
001799 02-04

BIPHASIC-EFFECTS OF THYROTROPIN-RELEASING-HORMONE ON
EXPLORATORY-BEHAVIOR IN MICE.
001808 02-04
BIPHASIC-EFFECTS OF DIRECT, BUT NOT INDIRECT, GABAMIMETICS AND
ANTAGONISTS ON HALOPERIDOL-INDUCED CATALEPSY.
001826 02-04
BIPHASIC-EFFECTS AND OPPOSITE-EFFECTS OF DOPAMINE AND
APOMORPHINE ON ENDOGENOUS GABA RELEASE IN THE RAT
SUBSTANTIA-NIGRA.
002923 03-03
BIPOLAR
BIPOLAR AFFECTIVE-PSYCHOSIS WITH ONSET BEFORE AGE 16 YEARS:
REPORT OF 10 CASES.
002001 02-09
THYROTROPHIN RESPONSE TO THYROTROPHIN-RELEASING-HORMONE IN
UNIPOLAR AND BIPOLAR AFFECTIVE-ILLNESS.
003237 03-09
MAOI-INDUCED RAPID CYCLING BIPOLAR AFFECTIVE-DISORDER IN AN
ADOLESCENT.
004637 04-15
BIPOLAR-I-PATIENTS
PROPHYLACTIC LITHIUM WITH AND WITHOUT IMIPRAMINE FOR BIPOLAR-
I-PATIENTS: A DOUBLE-BLIND STUDY.
003233 03-09
BIPOLAR-II
LITHIUM AND IMIPRAMINE IN THE PROPHYLAXIS OF UNIPOLAR AND
BIPOLAR-II DEPRESSION: A PROSPECTIVE, PLACEBO-CONTROLLED
COMPARISON.
003252 03-09
BIPOLAR-PATIENTS
THE RELATIVE PROPHYLACTIC EFFICACY OF LITHIUM AGAINST MANIC
AND DEPRESSIVE RECURRENCES IN BIPOLAR-PATIENTS.
002040 02-09
BIS-TETRAHYDRO-2-FURANYL-5-FLUOROPYRIMIDINEDIONE
EFFECTS OF 1,3 BIS-TETRAHYDRO-2-FURANYL-5-
FLUOROPYRIMIDINEDIONE (FD-1) ON THE CENTRAL-NERVOUS-SYSTEM:
1. EFFECTS OF MONOAMINES IN THE BRAIN.
001857 02-05
BISFLUOROPHENYL-BUTYLPIPERIDYLBENZIMIDAZOLINONE-HCL
THE CRYSTAL AND MOLECULAR STRUCTURE OF THE NEUROLEPTIC
PIMOZIDE-HYDROCHLORIDE, BISFLUOROPHENYL-
BUTYLPIPERIDYLBENZIMIDAZOLINONE-HCL.
001015 02-01
BITING-REFLEX
ACTIVATION AND LATERALIZATION OF SENSORIMOTOR FIELD FOR
PERIORAL BITING-REFLEX BY INTRANIGRAL GABA AGONIST AND BY
SYSTEMIC APOMORPHINE IN THE RAT.
001657 02-04
BLACK-WIDOW-SPIDER
METABOLISM OF 3H NORADRENALINE RELEASED FROM ISOLATED RAT
HYPOTHALAMUS BY EXTRACTS OF BLACK-WIDOW-SPIDER GLANDS.
000223 01-03
BLACKOUTS
TRICYCLIC-ANTIDEPRESSANTS AND ALCOHOLIC BLACKOUTS.
004617 04-15
BLEPHAROPTOSIS
EFFECTS OF NARCOTIC ANTAGONISTS ON L-DOPA REVERSAL OF
RESERPINE-INDUCED CATALEPSY AND BLEPHAROPTOSIS IN MICE.
004186 04-04
BLINK
BLINK RATES AND RECEPTOR SUPERSENSITIVITY.
003022 03-04
DRUG-EFFECT ON BLINK RATES IN RHESUS-MONKEYS: PRELIMINARY
STUDIES.
003023 03-04
EARLY DETECTION OF HUNTINGTONS-DISEASE. BLINK REFLEX AND
LEVODOPA LOAD IN PRESYMPTOMATIC AND INCIPIENT SUBJECTS.
003311 03-11
BLINKS
EYE BLINKS. (UNPUBLISHED PAPER).
001672 02-04
BLOCK
THE INABILITY OF CHRONIC MIANSERIN TO BLOCK CENTRAL ALPHA2-
ADRENOCEPTORS.
001492 02-03
DIPHENYLHYDANTOIN-INDUCED BLOCK OF THE RAT PHRENIC-NERVE
DIAPHRAGM PREPARATION PRETREATED WITH P
HYDROXYMERCURIBENZOATE.
002749 03-03
A CRITICAL EVALUATION OF THE USE OF TOXINS FROM DENDROASPIS
VIRIDIS TO BLOCK NICOTINIC RESPONSES AT CENTRAL AND
GANGLIONIC SYNAPSES.
002870 03-03
WHY DOES SULPIRIDE NOT BLOCK THE EFFECT OF DOPAMINE ON THE
DOPAMINE-SENSITIVE ADENYLATE-CYCLASE?
004055 04-03
NALOXONE FAILS TO BLOCK AMPHETAMINE-INDUCED ANOREXIA AND
CONDITIONED TASTE-AVERSION.
004121 04-04

BLOCKADE

BLOCKADE OF METHAMPHETAMINE-INDUCED DEPRESSION OF TYROSINE-HYDROXYLASE BY GABA-TRANSAMINASE INHIBITORS.
000130 01-03

BLOCKADE OF STRIATAL NEURONE RESPONSES TO MORPHINE BY AMINOPHYLLINE: EVIDENCE FOR ADENOSINE MEDIATION OF OPIATE ACTION.
000229 01-03

REDUCTION IN THE NUMBER OF SEROTONIN-RECEPTORS IN THE BRAINSTEM OF MORPHINE-DEPENDENT RATS: RELATION TO BLOCKADE OF NALOXONE PRECIPITATED JUMPING BY SEROTONIN AGONISTS.
000258 01-03

5 HT BLOCKADE AND THE STIMULANT-EFFECTS OF D-AMPHETAMINE AND L-AMPHETAMINE: NO INTERACTION IN SELF-STIMULATION OF PREFRONTAL-CORTEX, HYPOTHALAMUS, OR DORSAL TEGMENTUM. UNEXPECTED LETHALITY IN HIPPOCAMPAL SITES.
000387 01-04

EXTINCTION AND DOPAMINE-RECEPTOR BLOCKADE AFTER INTERMITTENT REINFORCEMENT TRAINING: FAILURE TO OBSERVE FUNCTIONAL EQUIVALENCE.
000490 01-04

THE BLOCKADE OF ALPHA2-ADRENOCEPTORS BY THE PNMT INHIBITOR SKF-64139.
001255 02-03

DOPAMINE-RECEPTOR BLOCKADE IN RAT-BRAIN AFTER ACUTE AND SUBCHRONIC-TREATMENT WITH TRICYCLIC-ANTIDEPRESSANTS.
001314 02-03

PSYCHOTROPIC-DRUG BLOCKADE OF HISTAMINE H1-RECEPTORS.
001432 02-03

ACTH MEDIATION OF LEARNED-FEAR: BLOCKADE BY NALOXONE AND NALTREXONE.
001597 02-04

MOTOR-ACTIVITY AND ROTATIONAL-BEHAVIOR AFTER ANALOGS OF COCAINE: CORRELATION WITH DOPAMINE UPTAKE BLOCKADE.
001650 02-04

DOPAMINE-RECEPTOR BLOCKADE BY IMIDOLINE AND ITS PROPOSED ACTIVE CONFORMATION.
001687 02-04

OPIOID BLOCKADE AND SOCIAL-COMFORT IN CHICKS.
001745 02-04

HANDEDNESS IN RATS; BLOCKADE OF REACHING-BEHAVIOR BY UNILATERAL 6 DHDA INJECTIONS INTO SUBSTANTIA-NIGRA AND CAUDATE-NUCLEUS.
001778 02-04

THE ROLE OF DIFFERENTIAL BLOCKADE OF ALPHA-ADRENERGIC AGONISTS IN CHLORPROMAZINE-INDUCED HYPOTENSION.
001851 02-05

BEHAVIORAL-EFFECTS AND SUBJECTIVE-EFFECTS OF BETA-ADRENERGIC BLOCKADE IN PHOBIC-SUBJECTS.
002060 02-10

DURING ONE YEARS NEUROLEPTIC TREATMENT IN RATS STRIATAL DOPAMINE-RECEPTOR BLOCKADE DECREASES BUT SERUM PROLACTIN LEVELS REMAIN ELEVATED.
002707 03-03

NALOXONE REVERSAL OF THE PENTOBARBITAL-INDUCED BLOCKADE OF OVULATION IN THE RAT.
002817 03-03

PLASMA CATECHOLAMINES IN RATS EXPOSED TO COLD: EFFECTS OF GANGLIONIC AND ADRENORECEPTOR BLOCKADE.
002863 03-03

THE TETRACYCLIC-ANTIDEPRESSANT MIANSERIN: EVALUATION OF ITS BLOCKADE OF PRESYNAPTIC ALPHA-ADRENOCEPTORS IN A SELF-STIMULATION MODEL USING CLONIDINE.
003016 03-04

BLOCKADE OF ENDOGENOUS OPIATES REDUCES ACTIVITY IN THE RAT.
003111 03-04

NEUROLEPTIC MALIGNANT-SYNDROME: A PATHOGENETIC ROLE FOR DOPAMINE-RECEPTOR BLOCKADE?
003492 03-15

BLOCKADE BY L LYSINE OF NONNARCOTIC ANALGESICS.
003857 04-03

ON THE IMPORTANCE OF AGONIST CONCENTRATION GRADIENTS WITHIN ISOLATED TISSUES. INCREASED MAXIMAL RESPONSES OF RAT VASA-DEFERENTIA TO (-) NORADRENALINE AFTER BLOCKADE OF NEURONAL UPTAKE.
003879 04-03

THE IMPORTANCE OF CATECHOLAMINE UPTAKE INHIBITION IN THE REVERSAL OF GUANETHIDINE BLOCKADE OF ADRENERGIC NEURONS.
003900 04-03

4 AMINOPYRIDINE BLOCKADE OF NEURONAL DEPRESSANT RESPONSES TO ADENOSINE-TRIPHOSPHATE.
003963 04-03

RNA-POLYMERASE-II IN C6-GLIOMA CELLS: ALPHA AMANITIN BLOCKADE OF CYCLIC-AMP-PHOSPHODIESTERASE INDUCTION BY BETA-ADRENERGIC STIMULATION. (UNPUBLISHED PAPER).
003998 04-03

PHENYTOIN INHIBITION OF CYCLIC-GUANOSINE-MONOPHOSPHATE (C-GMP) ACCUMULATION IN NEUROBLASTOMA CELLS BY CALCIUM-CHANNEL BLOCKADE.
004020 04-03

PHYSIOLOGICAL SIGNIFICANCE OF DOPAMINE-AUTORECEPTORS AS STUDIED FOLLOWING THEIR SELECTIVE BLOCKADE BY MOLINDONE.
004065 04-04

BLOCKADE BY IMIPRAMINE OR DESIPRAMINE OF PANIC-INDUCED BY SODIUM-LACTATE.
004427 04-10

IN NORMAL YOUNG MEN ACUTE DOPAMINERGIC BLOCKADE DOES NOT IMPAIR FREE WATER EXCRETION FOLLOWING A STANDARD WATER LOAD.
004600 04-15

BLOCKER

HYPERVENTILATION-SYNDROME AND BETA-RECEPTOR FUNCTION -- CLINICAL-EFFECT OF BETA BLOCKER UPON THE SYNDROME.
004459 04-11

BLOCKERS

ACUTE VERSUS CHRONIC EFFECTS OF SEROTONIN UPTAKE BLOCKERS ON POTENTIATION OF THE SEROTONIN SYNDROME.
000050 01-03

CGP-6085-A, A NEW, SPECIFIC, INHIBITOR OF SEROTONIN UPTAKE: NEUROCHEMICAL CHARACTERIZATION AND COMPARISON WITH OTHER SEROTONIN UPTAKE BLOCKERS.
000316 01-03

THE EFFECTS OF MUSCARINIC-RECEPTOR BLOCKERS ON THE TURNOVER-RATE OF ACETYLCHOLINE IN VARIOUS REGIONS OF THE RAT-BRAIN.
000328 01-03

INHIBITION OF (3H)DIAZEPAM BINDING TO RAT-BRAIN CORTICAL SYNAPTOSOMAL MEMBRANES BY ADENOSINE UPTAKE BLOCKERS.
000330 01-03

EFFECTS OF ALPHA-ADRENERGIC AND BETA-ADRENERGIC BLOCKERS ON CHLORPROMAZINE-INDUCED ELEVATION OF PLASMA GLUCOSE AND CYCLIC-AMP IN FED MICE.
003946 04-03

EFFECT OF NOREPINEPHRINE UPTAKE BLOCKERS ON NOREPINEPHRINE KINETICS.
004506 04-13

BLOCKING

MIANSERIN: DIRECT ACTIVATION OF BRAIN NOREPINEPHRINE NEURONS BY BLOCKING ALPHA2-RECEPTORS.
001214 02-03

INFUSIONS INTO THE OCULOMOTOR NUCLEUS OR NERVE: A METHOD OF ESTIMATING THE DOSAGE AT WHICH TRANSMITTER ANTAGONISTS INFUSED INTRACRANIALLY PRODUCE NONSPECIFIC BLOCKING OF NEURAL ACTIVITY.
003134 03-06

A COMPARISON OF DOPAMINE-RECEPTOR BLOCKING ASSAY WITH PLASMA DRUG LEVELS OF HALOPERIDOL IN SCHIZOPHRENIC-PATIENTS.
003182 03-08

BLOCKING-AGENT

EFFECTS OF THE BETA-ADRENOCEPTOR BLOCKING-AGENT SOTALOL ON CNS: SLEEP, EEG, AND PSYCHOPHYSIOLOGICAL PARAMETERS.
001570 02-04

BLOCKING-AGENTS

THE INFLUENCE OF 5 HT-RECEPTOR BLOCKING-AGENTS ON THE BEHAVIORAL-EFFECTS OF ANALGESICS IN RATS.
000429 01-04

METOCLOPRAMIDE AND SULPIRIDE AS SELECTIVE BLOCKING-AGENTS PRESYNAPTIC AND POSTSYNAPTIC DOPAMINE-RECEPTORS.
001102 02-03

AMPHETAMINE STEREOTYPIES AND POLYRIBOSOMAL DISAGGREGATION IN RATS: EFFECTS OF ADRENERGIC AND SEROTONERGIC BLOCKING-AGENTS.
001531 02-03

ROLE OF ADRENERGIC BLOCKING-AGENTS AND GLUCOCORTICOIDS ON THE REGULATION OF PITUITARY OPIOID-PEPTIDES LEVELS.
003801 04-03

THE EFFECT OF DOPAMINE UPTAKE BLOCKING-AGENTS ON THE AMPHETAMINE-INDUCED CIRCLING-BEHAVIOR IN MICE WITH UNILATERAL NIGROSTRIATAL LESIONS.
004117 04-04

BLOCKING-DRUG

THE EFFECT OF THE DOPAMINE-RECEPTOR BLOCKING-DRUG PIMOZIDE ON THE STIMULANT AND ANORECTIC-ACTIONS OF DEXTROAMPHETAMINE IN MAN.
004580 04-14

BLOCKING-DRUGS

FAILURE OF ISOPRENALINE AND BETA-RECEPTOR BLOCKING-DRUGS TO MODIFY DEPRESSOR RESPONSE AND BRADYCARDIA INDUCED BY ELECTRICAL-STIMULATION OF THE ANTERIOR HYPOTHALAMUS OF CATS.
000520 01-05

INTERACTION OF HISTAMINE H2-RECEPTOR BLOCKING-DRUGS WITH THE NORADRENERGIC SYSTEM IN RAT-BRAIN AND HEART.
001397 02-03

THE EFFECT OF BETA-ADRENERGIC-RECEPTOR BLOCKING-DRUGS ON CEREBRAL BLOOD FLOW IN HYPERTENSIVE-PATIENTS.
002071 02-10

SIDE-EFFECTS OF BETA-ADRENERGIC BLOCKING-DRUGS: A METHODOLOGICAL-PROBLEM.
002395 02-15

BLOCKS

PREEXPOSURE TO DELTA9 THC BLOCKS THC-INDUCED CONDITIONED
TASTE-AVERSION IN RATS.
001618 02-04

DISRUPTION OF 5 HYDROXYTRYPTAMINERGIC NEURONAL FUNCTION
BLOCKS THE ACTION OF MORPHINE ON TUBEROINFUNDIBULAR
DOPAMINERGIC NEURONS.
002700 03-03

CAFFEINE BLOCKS THE DELAYED K OUTWARD-CURRENT OF MOLLUSCAN
NEURONS.
003834 04-03

NEUROTENSIN BLOCKS CERTAIN AMPHETAMINE-INDUCED BEHAVIOURS.
004111 04-04

BLOOD

COMPARISON OF BLOOD AND BILE LEVELS OF OXYPROTHEPIN AND
DOCLOXYTHEPIN IN RATS.
000242 01-03

SOCIAL AND CLINICAL SIGNIFICANCE OF DETERMINING THE BARBITURATE
LEVEL IN THE BLOOD SERUM OF PATIENTS TREATED WITH
ANTIEPILEPTIC-DRUGS.
000695 01-11

PARASYMPATHOMIMETIC-INFLUENCE OF CARBACHOL ON LOCAL
CEREBRAL BLOOD FLOW IN THE RABBIT BY A DIRECT VASODILATOR
ACTION AND AN INHIBITION OF THE SYMPATHETIC MEDIATED
VASOCONSTRICTION.
001109 02-03

EFFECT OF PAPAVERINE ON REGIONAL CEREBRAL BLOOD FLOW AND
SMALL VESSEL BLOOD CONTENT.
001177 02-03

EFFECTS OF RATE OF BLOOD FLOW ON FRACTIONAL EXTRACTION AND ON
UPTAKE OF INFUSED NORADRENALINE BY BROWN ADIPOSE TISSUE IN
VIVO.
001231 02-03

DIFFERENTIAL-EFFECTS OF VARIOUS STIMULI ON AVP LEVELS IN BLOOD
AND CEREBROSPINAL-FLUID.
001370 02-03

THE EFFECT OF SODIUM-SALICYLATE ON CEREBRAL BLOOD FLOW AND
METABOLISM.
001416 02-03

SUBCUTANEOUS SILASTIC IMPLANTS: MAINTENANCE OF HIGH BLOOD
ETHANOL LEVELS IN RATS DRINKING A LIQUID DIET.
001865 02-06

ENDOGENOUS DEPRESSION AND IMIPRAMINE LEVELS IN THE BLOOD.
001979 02-09

BLOOD LEVEL OF AMITRIPTYLINE, NORTRIPTYLINE, NORADRENALINE,
SEROTONIN AND THERAPEUTIC RESPONSE.
002057 02-09

THE EFFECT OF BETA-ADRENERGIC-RECEPTOR BLOCKING-DRUGS ON
CEREBRAL BLOOD FLOW IN HYPERTENSIVE-PATIENTS.
002071 02-10

REGIONAL CEREBRAL BLOOD FLOW IN A CASE OF AMPHETAMINE
INTOXICATION.
002210 02-13

CARDIOVASCULAR-EFFECTS OF THERAPEUTIC DOSES OF TRICYCLIC-
ANTIDEPRESSANTS: IMPORTANCE OF BLOOD LEVEL MONITORING.
002456 02-15

NEUROLEPTIC BLOOD LEVELS AND THERAPEUTIC EFFECT.
002480 02-16

HALOPERIDOL STIMULATION OF PROLACTIN SECRETION: HOW MANY
BLOOD SAMPLES ARE NEEDED TO DEFINE THE HORMONE RESPONSE?
002505 02-16

THE CHANGE OF BLOOD PROLACTIN LEVEL DUE TO THE WITHDRAWAL OF
MAINTENANCE NEUROLEPTICS.
002559 02-17

STUDY OF METABOLISM AND BLOOD LEVELS OF ANTIDEPRESSANTS:
TOWARDS A RATIONALIZATION OF THEIR THERAPEUTIC USE.
002625 02-17

STEADY-STATE LITHIUM BLOOD LEVEL FLUCTUATIONS IN MAN
FOLLOWING ADMINISTRATION OF A LITHIUM-CARBONATE
CONVENTIONAL AND CONTROLLED-RELEASE DOSAGE FORM.
003151 03-07

PROGNOSIS IN SCHIZOPHRENIA: INDIVIDUAL DIFFERENCES IN
PSYCHOLOGICAL RESPONSE TO A TEST DOSE OF ANTIPSYCHOTIC-DRUG
AND THEIR RELATIONSHIP TO BLOOD AND SALIVA LEVELS AND
TREATMENT OUTCOME.
003189 03-08

CORRELATIONS BETWEEN LITHIUM LEVELS IN CEREBROSPINAL-FLUID AND
LITHIUM LEVELS IN BLOOD PLASMA AND ERYTHROCYTES.
003210 03-09

RELATIONSHIP BETWEEN BLOOD CONCENTRATIONS AND CLINICAL-
EFFECTS OF A NEW ANTIDEPRESSANT MAPROTILINE.
003271 03-09

ON THE ANTICONVULSANT BLOOD LEVEL IN THERAPY-RESISTANT
EPILEPTIC-PATIENTS.
003300 03-11

PLASMA FREE AND TOTAL TRYPTOPHAN, BLOOD SEROTONIN, AND THE
HYPERACTIVITY-SYNDROME: NO EVIDENCE FOR THE SEROTONIN
DEFICIENCY HYPOTHESIS.
003312 03-11

PHENYTOIN CONCENTRATIONS IN VENOUS VERSUS CAPILLARY BLOOD OF
GERIATRIC-PATIENTS.
003381 03-11

LEVELS OF 5 HYDROXYINDOLEACETIC-ACID AND TRYPTOPHAN IN
LUMBAR CEREBROSPINAL-FLUID AND BLOOD OF PATIENTS WITH
DEMENTIA AND NORMAL PRESSURE HYDROCEPHALUS AFTER
TRYPTOPHAN ADMINISTRATION.
003419 03-13

DIFFERENTIAL BINDING OF CHLORPROMAZINE TO HUMAN BLOOD CELLS:
APPLICATION OF THE HYGROSCOPIC DESORPTION METHOD.
003556 03-16

FIRST RESULTS OF AN ORIGINAL METHOD FOR MEASURING BLOOD
LEVELS OF ANTIDEPRESSANTS (AMITRIPTYLINE AND NORTRIPTYLINE).
003559 03-16

THERAPEUTIC INTEREST OF BLOOD LEVELS DETERMINATION FOR
ANTIDEPRESSANTS: METHODOLOGICAL APPROACH.
003571 03-16

SUBSTANCE-P INCREASES HYPOTHALAMIC BLOOD FLOW VIA AN
INDIRECT ADRENERGIC CHOLINERGIC INTERACTION.
003887 04-03

EFFECTS OF METHAMPHETAMINE ON BLOOD FLOW IN THE CAUDATE-
PUTAMEN AFTER LESIONS OF THE NIGROSTRIATAL DOPAMINERGIC
BUNDLE IN THE RAT.
003910 04-03

THE EFFECTS OF NEFOPAM ON BLOOD ACID BASE STATUS IN THE RABBIT:
INTERACTIONS WITH MORPHINE IN THE MOUSE AND RABBIT.
004279 04-05

CHANGES IN BLOOD PLASMA OSMOLALITY AND STATES OF MANIA.
004352 04-09

CLINICAL-RESPONSE AND BLOOD LEVELS IN THE TREATMENT OF
DEPRESSION WITH A NEW ANTIDEPRESSANT-DRUG, AMOXAPINE.
004356 04-09

BLOOD LEVEL MEASUREMENTS OF TRICYCLIC DRUGS AS A DIAGNOSTIC
TOOL.
004368 04-09

CORRECTION OF THE EXTRAPYRAMIDAL NEUROLEPTIC-SYNDROME BY
TRYPTOPHAN AND THE TIME-COURSE OF ITS CONTENT IN THE BLOOD
OF PATIENTS.
004434 04-11

THE EFFECT OF CHLORPROMAZINE AND MAGEPTIL ON THE
PROLIFERATION OF PERIPHERAL BLOOD LYMPHOCYTES IN CULTIVATION
WITH PHYTOHEMAGGLUTININ.
004541 04-13

SIMULTANEOUS DETERMINATION OF MORPHINE AND CODEINE IN BLOOD
BY USE OF SELECT ION-MONITORING AND DEUTERATED INTERNAL
STANDARDS.
004690 04-16

COMPARISON OF SPECTROFLUOROMETRIC AND GAS-
CHROMATOGRAPHY/MASS-SPECTROMETRY PROCEDURES FOR THE
QUANTITATION OF MORPHINE IN BLOOD AND BRAIN.
004692 04-16

BLOOD-BRAIN-BARRIER

THE BLOOD-BRAIN-BARRIER IN ADRENALINE-INDUCED HYPERTENSION.
000147 01-03

DOSE-DEPENDENT, AMPHETAMINE-INDUCED CHANGES IN PERMEABILITY
OF THE BLOOD-BRAIN-BARRIER OF NORMOTENSIVE-RATS AND
SPONTANEOUSLY HYPERTENSIVE-RATS.
001197 02-03

INFLUENCE OF RESPIRATORY STRESS AND HYPERTENSION UPON THE
BLOOD-BRAIN-BARRIER.
001437 02-03

TRANSPORT OF NEUTRAL AMINO-ACIDS AT THE BLOOD-BRAIN-BARRIER.
002764 03-03

INDICATIONS FOR A BRAIN UPTAKE OF LABELLED VASOPRESSIN AND
OCYTOCIN AND THE PROBLEM OF THE BLOOD-BRAIN-BARRIER.
003669 04-01

H2-RECEPTORS MEDIATE INCREASES IN PERMEABILITY OF THE BLOOD-
BRAIN-BARRIER DURING ARTERIAL HISTAMINE INFUSION.
003817 04-03

PASSAGE THROUGH THE BLOOD-BRAIN-BARRIER OF THYROTROPIN-
RELEASING-HORMONE ENCAPSULATED IN LIPOSOMES.
004298 04-06

BLOOD-PLATELET

THE ACTIVITY OF BLOOD-PLATELET MONOAMINE-OXIDASE IN
ENDOGENOUS DEPRESSION.
004547 04-13

BLOOD-PLATELETS

LITHIUM LEVELS IN BLOOD-PLATELETS, SERUM, RED-BLOOD-CELLS AND
BRAIN REGIONS IN RATS GIVEN ACUTE OR CHRONIC LITHIUM-SALT
TREATMENTS.
000082 01-03

PROPERTIES OF (3H)DIAZEPAM BINDING-SITES ON RAT BLOOD-
PLATELETS.
000317 01-03

DECREASED UPTAKE OF 5 HYDROXYTRYPTAMINE IN BLOOD-PLATELETS
FROM PATIENTS WITH ENDOGENOUS DEPRESSION.
000637 01-09

TETRAHYDRO-BETA-CARBOLINES AND CORRESPONDING TRYPTAMINES: IN VITRO INHIBITION OF SEROTONIN AND DOPAMINE UPTAKE BY HUMAN BLOOD-PLATELETS.
001067 02-02
EFFECT OF DOXEPIN ON SEROTONIN METABOLISM IN RAT-BRAIN AND SEROTONIN UPTAKE BY HUMAN BLOOD-PLATELETS.
002243 02-13
LIBERATION OF CATECHOLAMINES AND 5 HYDROXYTRYPTAMINE FROM HUMAN BLOOD-PLATELETS.
003967 04-03

BLOOD-PRESSURE
EFFECT OF GABA ANALOGUES ON BLOOD-PRESSURE AND CENTRAL GABA METABOLISM IN THE RAT.
000231 01-03
CENTRAL BLOOD-PRESSURE EFFECTS OF GUANYLYLIMIDODIPHOSPHATE AND CYCLIC-GUANOSINE-MONOPHOSPHATE.
000266 01-03
TYROSINE ADMINISTRATION REDUCES BLOOD-PRESSURE AND ENHANCES BRAIN NOREPINEPHRINE RELEASE IN SPONTANEOUSLY HYPERTENSIVE-RATS.
000296 01-03
HALLUCINATORY AND DELUSIONAL-STATES IN CONNECTION WITH BLOOD-PRESSURE AND EEG.
000814 01-14
EFFECT OF PROSTAGLANDINS ON PLASMA CATECHOLAMINES, HEART AND BLOOD-PRESSURE RESPONSES TO HEMORRHAGE. (UNPUBLISHED PAPER).
001223 02-03
NALOXONE EFFECTS ON THE BLOOD-PRESSURE RESPONSE INDUCED BY THIN-FIBER MUSCULAR AFFERENTS.
002794 03-03
COVARIANCE OF PLASMA FREE 3 METHOXY-4-HYDROXYPHENETHYLENEGLYCOL AND DIASTOLIC BLOOD-PRESSURE.
003418 03-13
BLOOD-PRESSURE AND COGNITIVE FUNCTIONING.
004492 04-11

BLOOD-PRESSURES
NICOTINE INGESTION REDUCES ELEVATED BLOOD-PRESSURES IN RATS AND SQUIRREL-MONKEYS.
002759 03-03

BODIES
EFFECT OF REPEATED TREATMENT WITH NEUROLEPTICS ON DOPAMINE METABOLISM IN CELL BODIES AND TERMINALS OF DOPAMINERGIC-SYSTEMS IN THE RAT-BRAIN.
001464 02-03

BODY
EFFECTS OF CHRONIC-TREATMENT WITH L SULPIRIDE AND HALOPERIDOL ON CENTRAL DOPAMINE TURNOVER EVALUATED IN DOPAMINE CELL BODY AND NERVE TERMINAL-RICH AREAS.
001096 02-03
DIFFERENTIAL-EFFECTS OF SYSTEMIC VERSUS INTRACRANIAL INJECTION OF OPIATES ON CENTRAL, OROFACIAL AND LOWER BODY NOCICEPTION: SOMATOTYPY IN BULBAR ANALGESIA SYSTEMS.
001446 02-03
COMBINED EFFECTS OF ALCOHOL AND LITHIUM ON BODY COMPOSITION IN THE RAT MODEL.
002928 03-03
NALOXONE REVERSIBLE DUPLICATION BY LANTHANUM OF OPIATE ANALGESIA EFFECTS ON OROFACIAL, LOWER BODY AND CENTRAL NOCICEPTION.
003028 03-04

BODY-TEMPERATURE
EFFECTS OF GAMMA HYDROXYBUTYRIC-ACID ON METABOLIC, RESPIRATORY AND VASOMOTOR ACTIVITIES AND BODY-TEMPERATURE IN RATS.
000189 01-03
INFLUENCE OF AMPHETAMINE AND PHENYLPROPANOLAMINE ON FOOD INTAKE, ACTIVITY, AND BODY-TEMPERATURE IN RATS WITH VENTROMEDIAL HYPOTHALAMIC OR DORSOLATERAL TEGMENTAL DAMAGE.
000322 01-03
EFFECTS OF LISURIDE ON BODY-TEMPERATURE OF RATS AND RABBITS: RELATION TO MICROSOMAL BIOTRANSFORMATION AND DOPAMINERGIC-RECEPTOR STIMULATION.
001161 02-03
THE MECHANISM-OF-ACTION OF DELTA9 TETRAHYDROCANNABINOL ON BODY-TEMPERATURE IN MICE.
001190 02-03
COMPARISON OF THE EFFECTS OF CENTRAL ADMINISTRATION OF SERINE AND GLYCINE ON BODY-TEMPERATURE OF THE RABBIT.
001248 02-03
AGE-RELATED CHANGES IN BODY-TEMPERATURE RESPONSES TO MORPHINE IN RATS.
001366 02-03
PHENOBARBITAL EFFECTS ON WEIGHT-GAIN AND CIRCADIAN-CYCLING OF FOOD INTAKE AND BODY-TEMPERATURE.
001409 02-03
EFFECTS OF KAINIC-ACID ON BODY-TEMPERATURE OF RATS: ROLE OF CATECHOLAMINERGIC AND SEROTONERGIC SYSTEMS.
001515 02-03

THE EFFECTS OF BOMBESIN INJECTED INTO THE ANTERIOR AND POSTERIOR HYPOTHALAMUS ON BODY-TEMPERATURE AND OXYGEN CONSUMPTION.
001544 02-03
CHRONIC DELTA9 TETRAHYDROCANNABINOL IN RATS: EFFECT ON SOCIAL-INTERACTIONS, MOUSE-KILLING, MOTOR-ACTIVITY, CONSUMMATORY-BEHAVIOR, AND BODY-TEMPERATURE.
001722 02-04
CHANGES IN BODY-TEMPERATURE AFTER ADMINISTRATION OF ADRENERGIC AND SEROTONERGIC-AGENTS AND RELATED DRUGS INCLUDING ANTIDEPRESSANTS.
002532 02-17
INTERACTION BETWEEN THE EFFECTS OF STRESS AND MORPHINE ON BODY-TEMPERATURE IN RATS.
002906 03-03
THE EFFECT OF PHARMACOLOGICAL DESTRUCTION OF HYPOTHALAMIC MONOAMINERGIC STRUCTURES ON BODY-TEMPERATURE AND GAS-EXCHANGE DURING EXTREME COOLING.
004016 04-03
BETA ENDORPHIN: CENTRAL SITES OF ANALGESIA, CATALEPSY AND BODY-TEMPERATURE CHANGES IN RATS.
004238 04-04
REVERSIBLE RING-OPENING REACTIONS OF NIMETAZEPAM AND NITRAZEPAM IN ACIDIC MEDIA AT BODY-TEMPERATURE.
004517 04-13

BODY-WEIGHT
BODY-WEIGHT, FEEDING, AND DRINKING-BEHAVIORS IN RATS WITH KAINIC-ACID-INDUCED LESIONS OF STRIATAL NEURONS -- WITH A NOTE ON BODY-WEIGHT SYMPTOMATOLOGY IN HUNTINGTONS-DISEASE.
000463 01-04
EFFECTS OF BODY-WEIGHT LEVELS ON CANNABIS SELF-INJECTION.
001801 02-04
BODY-WEIGHT AND RESPONSES TO LHRH INFUSION IN ANOREXIA-NERVOSA.
002062 02-10
BENZODIAZEPINES CAUSE SMALL LOSS OF BODY-WEIGHT.
002446 02-15
SUSTAINED INTRACEREBROVENTRICULAR INFUSION OF BRAIN FUELS REDUCES BODY-WEIGHT AND FOOD INTAKE IN RATS.
004098 04-04

BOLUS
PHARMACOKINETIC PROFILE OF VALPROIC-ACID IN RHESUS-MONKEYS FOLLOWING SINGLE BOLUS AND CONSTANT RATE INTRAVENOUS ADMINISTRATIONS.
002797 03-03

BOMBESIN
THE EFFECTS OF BOMBESIN INJECTED INTO THE ANTERIOR AND POSTERIOR HYPOTHALAMUS ON BODY-TEMPERATURE AND OXYGEN CONSUMPTION.
001544 02-03
BOMBESIN PRODUCES TASTE-AVERSION IN RATS.
002702 03-03
THE EFFECTS OF INJECTIONS OF BOMBESIN INTO THE CEREBRAL VENTRICLES ON BEHAVIORAL THERMOREGULATION.
002952 03-03
BOMBESIN ALTERS BEHAVIORAL THERMOREGULATION IN FISH.
003026 03-04
ENHANCEMENT OF ETHANOL-INDUCED SEDATION AND HYPOTHERMIA BY CENTRALLY ADMINISTERED NEUROTENSIN, BETA ENDORPHIN AND BOMBESIN.
003037 03-04
BOMBESIN INHIBITS STRESS-INDUCED EATING.
003059 03-04

BOMBESIN-LIKE-PEPTIDES
BIOCHEMICAL-LOCALIZATION AND CHARACTERIZATION OF BOMBESIN-LIKE-PEPTIDES IN DISCRETE REGIONS OF RAT-BRAIN. (UNPUBLISHED PAPER).
001046 02-01

BONDS
COMT-A AND COMT-B: CATALYTIC DIFFERENCES AND ROLE OF DISULFIDE BONDS.
003927 04-03

BORDERLINE-CHILDREN
IMIPRAMINE TREATMENT OF BORDERLINE-CHILDREN: CASE-REPORTS WITH A CONTROLLED-STUDY.
003356 03-11

BORDERLINE-PATIENT
THE INTERACTION OF PSYCHOPHARMACOLOGY AND PSYCHOANALYSIS IN THE BORDERLINE-PATIENT.
004430 04-10

BORDERLINE-SYNDROMES
EXTRAPYRAMIDAL-DISORDERS AND BORDERLINE-SYNDROMES: EREDOATAXIAS AND DEMENTIA.
003518 03-15

BORN
BEHAVIOR AND LEARNING DIFFICULTIES IN CHILDREN OF NORMAL INTELLIGENCE BORN TO ALCOHOLIC MOTHERS.
004658 04-15

BOUND
ISOLATION OF SELECTIVE 3H CHLORNALTREXAMINE BOUND COMPLEXES, POSSIBLE OPIOID-RECEPTOR COMPONENTS IN BRAINS OF MICE.
001162 02-03
DISSOCIATION BETWEEN FREE AND BOUND PHENYTOIN LEVELS IN PRESENCE OF SODIUM-VALPROATE.
003367 03-11

BOVINE
ESR STUDIES OF SPIN LABELLED BOVINE LIVER MONOAMINE-OXIDASE-B. (UNPUBLISHED PAPER).
001065 02-01
ESR STUDIES OF BOVINE PLASMA AMINE-OXIDASE: PROBING OF THE ENVIRONMENT ABOUT THE SUBSTRATE LIBERATED SULFHYDRYL GROUPS IN THE ACTIVE SITE. (UNPUBLISHED PAPER).
001066 02-01
INHIBITION BY ARYLSULPHATASE A OF NA-INDEPENDENT (3H) GABA AND (3H) MUSCIMOL BINDING TO BOVINE CEREBELLAR SYNAPTIC MEMBRANES.
001208 02-03
DEMONSTRATION AND CHARACTERIZATION OF AN ENDOGENOUS INHIBITOR OF GABA-ENHANCED (3H) DIAZEPAM BINDING FROM BOVINE CEREBRAL-CORTEX.
002645 03-01
PHYSICAL AND KINETIC PROPERTIES OF CHOLINE-ACETYL-TRANSFERASE FROM RAT AND BOVINE BRAIN.
003676 04-01
CU-AMINE-OXIDASES: STUDIES RELATED TO THE MECHANISM-OF-ACTION OF BOVINE PLASMA AMINE-OXIDASE (UNPUBLISHED PAPER).
003680 04-01
DOPAMINE-RECEPTORS IN SUBCELLULAR FRACTIONS FROM BOVINE CAUDATE: ENRICHMENT OF (3H)SPIPERONE BINDING IN A POSTSYNAPTIC MEMBRANE FRACTION.
003948 04-03
BINDING OF (3H) MUSCIMOL, A POTENT GAMMA AMINOBUTYRIC-ACID-RECEPTOR AGONIST, TO MEMBRANES OF THE BOVINE RETINA.
003954 04-03
ELECTROPHYSIOLOGICAL-EFFECTS OF IMIPRAMINE ON BOVINE VENTRICULAR-MUSCLE AND PURKINJE-FIBRES.
003988 04-03
DOPAMINE-RECEPTOR BINDING IN BOVINE INTERMEDIATE LOBE PITUITARY MEMBRANES.
004003 04-03

BOYS
EFFECTS OF METHYLPHENIDATE ON SELECTIVE AND SUSTAINED ATTENTION IN HYPERACTIVE, READING-DISABLED, AND PRESUMABLY ATTENTION-DISORDERED BOYS.
002118 02-11
ACUTE EFFECTS OF CAFFEINE IN NORMAL PREPUBERTAL BOYS.
003310 03-11
EFFECT OF PIRACETAM ON EEG SPECTRA OF BOYS WITH LEARNING-DISORDERS.
003383 03-11

BRADYCARDIA
FAILURE OF ISOPRENALINE AND BETA-RECEPTOR BLOCKING-DRUGS TO MODIFY DEPRESSOR RESPONSE AND BRADYCARDIA INDUCED BY ELECTRICAL-STIMULATION OF THE ANTERIOR HYPOTHALAMUS OF CATS.
000520 01-05
BRADYCARDIA, PERSISTENT DIABETES-INSIPIDUS, AND TARDIVE-DYSKINESIA WITH LITHIUM INTOXICATION.
002427 02-15
MODULATORY EFFECT OF BRAIN ACETYLCHOLINE ON REFLEX-INDUCED BRADYCARDIA AND TACHYCARDIA IN CONSCIOUS RATS.
003744 04-03
EFFECTS OF DOPAMINE, APOMORPHINE, GAMMA HYDROXYBUTYRIC-ACID, HALOPERIDOL AND PIMOZIDE ON REFLEX BRADYCARDIA IN RATS.
004085 04-04

BRADYKININ
CENTRALLY INDUCED CARDIOVASCULAR AND SYMPATHETIC-NERVE RESPONSES TO BRADYKININ IN RATS.
003099 03-04

BRADYKININ-LIKE
INHIBITORY ACTION OF MORPHINE ON THE RELEASE OF A BRADYKININ-LIKE SUBSTANCE AFTER SCIATIC-NERVE STIMULATION.
001293 02-03

BRADYKININ-RECEPTOR
BRADYKININ-RECEPTOR STIMULATION OF C-AMP INVOLVES PHOSPHOLIPID METHYLATION, CA-FLUX, PHOSPHOLIPASE-A2 ACTIVATION AND PROSTAGLANDIN FORMATION. (UNPUBLISHED PAPER).
001002 02-01

BRAIN
OXAZEPAM-ESTERS. 1. CORRELATION BETWEEN HYDROLYSIS RATES AND BRAIN APPEARANCE OF OXAZEPAM.
000010 01-02
OXAZEPAM-ESTERS. 2. CORRELATION OF HYDROPHOBICITY WITH SERUM BINDING, BRAIN PENETRATION, AND EXCRETION.
000011 01-02

PHARMACOLOGICAL ACTIVITIES OF CLOBAZAM AND DIAZEPAM IN THE RAT: RELATION TO DRUG BRAIN LEVELS.
000036 01-03
RELATIONSHIP OF ANTICONFLICT ACTIVITY OF BENZODIAZEPINES TO BRAIN RECEPTOR BINDING, SEROTONIN, AND GABA.
000057 01-03
ACUTE CHANGES IN BRAIN TRYPTOPHAN AND SEROTONIN FOLLOWING CARBOHYDRATE OR PROTEIN INGESTION BY DIABETIC RATS. (UNPUBLISHED PAPER).
000060 01-03
HIGH-AFFINITY BINDING OF THE ANTITUSSIVE DEXTROMETHORPHAN TO GUINEA-PIG BRAIN.
000061 01-03
CHARACTERISTICS OF 3H CIS FLUPENTHIXOL BINDING TO CALF BRAIN MEMBRANES.
000062 01-03
EFFECTS OF LEAD ON MOVEMENT OF ALBUMIN INTO BRAIN.
000076 01-03
LITHIUM LEVELS IN BLOOD-PLATELETS, SERUM, RED-BLOOD-CELLS AND BRAIN REGIONS IN RATS GIVEN ACUTE OR CHRONIC LITHIUM-SALT TREATMENTS.
000082 01-03
INHIBITION OF BRAIN SYNAPTOSOMAL UPTAKE OF CHOLINE BY SOME 2 CARBOXAMIDOSTRYCHNINE DERIVATIVES WITH MUSCLE-RELAXANT PROPERTIES.
000084 01-03
RELATIONSHIPS BETWEEN SEIZURE ACTIVITY AND CYCLIC-NUCLEOTIDE LEVELS IN BRAIN.
000089 01-03
INHIBITORY-EFFECTS OF ANTICONVULSANT-DRUGS ON CYCLIC-NUCLEOTIDE ACCUMULATION IN BRAIN.
000090 01-03
ABILITY OF AGED RATS TO ALTER BETA-ADRENERGIC-RECEPTORS OF BRAIN IN RESPONSE TO REPEATED ADMINISTRATION OF RESERPINE AND DESMETHYLIMIPRAMINE.
000113 01-03
ACTIONS OF CHLORPROMAZINE, HALOPERIDOL AND PIMOZIDE ON LIPID METABOLISM IN GUINEA-PIG BRAIN SLICES.
000129 01-03
THE ETIOLOGY OF TOXIC PERIPHERAL NEUROPATHIES: IN VITRO EFFECTS OF ACRYLAMIDE AND 2,5 HEXANEDIONE ON BRAIN ENOLASE AND OTHER GLYCOLYTIC ENZYMES.
000131 01-03
EFFECT OF CHRONIC-TREATMENT WITH ANTIDEPRESSANTS ON BETA-ADRENERGIC-RECEPTOR BINDING IN GUINEA-PIG BRAIN.
000135 01-03
REUPTAKE OF BIOGENIC-AMINES BY BRAIN SLICES: EFFECT OF HYDROCORTISONE.
000187 01-03
SUBSENSITIVITY OF THE NOREPINEPHRINE-RECEPTOR COUPLED ADENYLATE-CYCLASE SYSTEM IN BRAIN: EFFECTS OF NISOXETINE VERSUS FLUOXETINE.
000208 01-03
THE MECHANISM OF EFFECT OF NEUROPHARMACOLOGICAL-DRUGS. VI: EFFECT OF NORADRENALINE AND 5 HYDROXYTRYPTAMINE ON BRAIN FREE FATTY-ACIDS.
000274 01-03
LONG-TERM EFFECTS OF CONTINUOUS EXPOSURE TO AMPHETAMINE ON BRAIN DOPAMINE CONCENTRATION AND SYNAPTOSOMAL UPTAKE IN MICE.
000287 01-03
INTRACELLULAR REDOX STATES UNDER HALOTHANE AND BARBITURATE ANESTHESIA IN NORMAL, ISCHEMIC, AND ANOXIC MONKEY BRAIN.
000295 01-03
TYROSINE ADMINISTRATION REDUCES BLOOD-PRESSURE AND ENHANCES BRAIN NOREPINEPHRINE RELEASE IN SPONTANEOUSLY HYPERTENSIVE-RATS.
000296 01-03
ADENOSINE REGULATES VIA TWO DIFFERENT TYPES OF RECEPTORS, THE ACCUMULATION OF CYCLIC-AMP IN CULTURED BRAIN CELLS.
000308 01-03
ROLE OF BRAIN DOPAMINERGIC MECHANISMS IN RODENT AGGRESSIVE-BEHAVIOR: INFLUENCE OF (OR -)N N PROPYLNORAPOMORPHINE ON THREE EXPERIMENTAL MODELS.
000340 01-04
POSTINGESTION INTERFERENCE WITH BRAIN FUNCTION PREVENTS ATTENTUATION OF NEOPHOBIA IN RATS.
000352 01-04
HANDLING IN INFANCY, TASTE-AVERSION, AND BRAIN LATERALITY IN RATS.
000375 01-04
CHANGES IN BRAIN N DEMETHYLATION AND OPIATE-RECEPTOR CONTENT CORRELATE WITH ANALGESIC EFFECTIVENESS OF MORPHINE.
000400 01-04
INFLUENCE OF NICERGOLINE ON MOLECULAR BIOLOGICAL PROCESSES IN THE BRAIN AND LEARNING-ABILITY OF THE RAT.
000449 01-04

RELATIONSHIP BETWEEN DELTA9 TETRAHYDROCANNABINOL-INDUCED
MOUSE-KILLING-BEHAVIOR ON THE RAT AND THE METABOLISM OF
MONOAMINES IN THE BRAIN, PARTICULARLY THE OLFACTORY-BULB.
000472 01-04

BRAIN FUNCTION IN OLD-AGE: EVALUATION OF CHANGES AND
DISORDERS.
000684 01-11

INFLUENCING BRAIN CONCUSSION BY NOOTROPIL.
000724 01-11

ELECTRON MICROSCOPIC STUDIES OF BRAIN SLICES: THE EFFECTS OF
HIGH-FREQUENCY STIMULATION ON DENDRITIC ULTRASTRUCTURE.
(UNPUBLISHED PAPER).
001036 02-01

ASSAYING GABA-MODULIN ACTIVITY IN BRAIN EXTRACTS: RESOLUTION
OF INHERENT DIFFICULTIES. (UNPUBLISHED PAPER).
001045 02-01

COMPARISON OF CYSTEINE-SULPHINIC-ACID-DECARBOXYLASE (CSD)
ISOENZYMES AND GLUTAMIC-ACID-DECARBOXYLASE (GAD) IN RAT: IS
BRAIN CSD-I IDENTICAL WITH LIVER CSD AND BRAIN CSD-II WITH
GAD? (UNPUBLISHED PAPER).
001048 02-01

HISTAMINE-RECEPTORS IN THE BRAIN: CHARACTERIZATION BY BINDING
STUDIES AND BIOCHEMICAL-EFFECTS.
001054 02-01

THE EFFECT OF PHENELZINE AND SOME OF ITS PARA HALOGENATED
DERIVATIVES ON THE LEVELS OF BRAIN TYRAMINE AND OCTOPAMINE
IN THE MOUSE.
001077 02-02

DYNAMICS OF ENDOGENOUS CATECHOLAMINE RELEASE FROM BRAIN
FRAGMENTS OF MALE AND FEMALE RATS.
001121 02-03

RECEPTOR BINDING INTERACTIONS OF THE ANGIOTENSIN-II ANTAGONIST,
125I SARCOSINE1-LEUCINE8-ANGIOTENSIN-II, WITH MAMMALIAN
BRAIN AND PERIPHERAL TISSUES.
001125 02-03

LACK OF INFLUENCE OF BRAIN CATECHOLAMINES ON ACUTE EFFECTS OF
BARBITURATES.
001138 02-03

INTERACTION OF BIOGENIC-AMINE SYSTEMS IN BRAIN. (UNPUBLISHED
PAPER).
001141 02-03

CHANGE IN PYRUVATE-DEHYDROGENASE ACTIVITY INFLUENCE PYRUVATE
SUPPORTED CALCIUM ACCUMULATION BY BRAIN MITOCHONDRIA.
(UNPUBLISHED PAPER).
001147 02-03

BRAIN SEROTONIN AND 5 HYDROXYINDOLEACETIC-ACID
CONCENTRATIONS AND SEROTONIN SYNTHESIS FOLLOWING
TETRAHYDRO-BETA-CARBOLINE ADMINISTRATION IN MICE.
001152 02-03

ROLE OF PROTEIN-KINASES IN OPIATE ACTIONS IN BRAIN.
001173 02-03

EFFECT OF TABERNANTHINE ON THE TURNOVER TIME OF BRAIN
CATECHOLAMINES IN NORMAL AND HYPOBARIC HYPOXIC RATS.
001187 02-03

TOLERANCE TO BARBITURATE-INDUCED CENTRAL-NERVOUS-SYSTEM
DEPRESSION: INVOLVEMENT OF STIMULUS SECRETION COUPLING IN
DISCRETE BRAIN AREAS. (PH.D. DISSERTATION).
001213 02-03

MIANSERIN: DIRECT ACTIVATION OF BRAIN NOREPINEPHRINE NEURONS
BY BLOCKING ALPHA2-RECEPTORS.
001214 02-03

EFFECT OF LITHIUM ON STRESS-INDUCED CHANGES IN THE BRAIN LEVELS
OF MONOAMINES IN RATS.
001216 02-03

LITHIUM-INDUCED CHANGES IN THE BRAIN LEVELS OF FREE AMINO-ACIDS
IN STRESS-EXPOSED RATS.
001217 02-03

TRYPTOPHOL-INDUCED CHANGE IN BRAIN 5 HYDROXYTRYPTAMINE
METABOLISM.
001236 02-03

EFFECTS OF CHRONIC NEUROLEPTIC TREATMENT ON TYROSINE-
HYDROXYLASE IN DOPAMINERGIC TERMINALS: COMPARISONS
BETWEEN DRUGS AND BRAIN REGIONS REVEALS DIFFERENT
MECHANISMS OF TOLERANCE.
001243 02-03

THE BINDING OF SOME ANTIDEPRESSANT-DRUGS TO BRAIN MUSCARINIC
ACETYLCHOLINE-RECEPTORS.
001253 02-03

SEX-DIFFERENCE IN BRAIN IRON. (UNPUBLISHED PAPER).
001278 02-03

BIPHASIC ACTIVITY OF MEMBRANE-BOUND ENZYMES IN BRAIN
MITOCHONDRIA AND SYNAPTOSOMES DURING THE DEVELOPMENT OF
TOLERANCE TO AND PHYSICAL-DEPENDENCE ON CHRONIC MORPHINE
ADMINISTRATION TO RATS.
001285 02-03

THE INFLUENCE OF EXTERNAL SODIUM AND POTASSIUM ON LITHIUM
UPTAKE BY PRIMARY BRAIN CELL CULTURES AT THERAPEUTIC LITHIUM
CONCENTRATION.
001300 02-03

DOWN REGULATION OF DIHYDROALPRENOLOL AND IMIPRAMINE
BINDING-SITES IN BRAIN OF RATS REPEATEDLY TREATED WITH
IMIPRAMINE.
001317 02-03

INTERACTION OF TRIAZOLAM WITH DESIPRAMINE: EFFECTS OF SINGLE
AND REPEATED TREATMENT ON CERTAIN PHARMACOLOGIC-
RESPONSES AND BRAIN CATECHOLAMINE LEVELS.
001323 02-03

DEVELOPMENT OF AND RECOVERY FROM SUBSENSITIVITY OF THE
NORADRENERGIC CYCLIC-AMP GENERATING SYSTEM IN BRAIN: EFFECT
OF AMPHETAMINE FOLLOWING INHIBITION OF ITS AROMATIC
HYDROXYLATION BY IPRINDOLE.
001353 02-03

SUBCELLULAR REACTION OF THE BRAIN TO HYPOXIA.
001354 02-03

FURTHER CHARACTERIZATION OF THE BINDING OF SUBSTANCE-P TO A
FRACTION FROM RABBIT BRAIN ENRICHED IN SYNAPTIC MEMBRANES.
001394 02-03

MODIFICATION OF DOPAMINE-RECEPTORS IN BRAIN BY CONTINUOUS
AMPHETAMINE ADMINISTRATIONS TO RATS.
001395 02-03

BRAIN STRIATAL TYROSINE-HYDROXYLASE: ACTIVATION OF THE ENZYME
BY CYCLIC-AMP INDEPENDENT PHOSPHORYLATION.
001423 02-03

THYROTROPIN-RELEASING-HORMONE: NEUROCHEMICAL EVIDENCE FOR
THE POTENTIATION OF IMIPRAMINE EFFECTS ON THE METABOLISM
AND UPTAKE OF BRAIN CATECHOLAMINES.
001427 02-03

EVIDENCE FOR INVOLVEMENT OF DOPAMINE IN THE ACTION OF
DIAZEPAM: POTENTIATION OF HALOPERIDOL AND CHLORPROMAZINE
ACTION IN THE BRAIN.
001428 02-03

THE EFFECT OF CLOFELIN ON THE BIOELECTRIC-ACTIVITY OF THE BRAIN.
001449 02-03

PROSTAGLANDINS IN THE BRAIN OF RATS GIVEN, ACUTELY, AND
CHRONICALLY, A HYPERTHERMIC-DOSE OF MET-ENKEPHALIN.
001468 02-03

THE EFFECTS OF PIRACETAM ON FREE FATTY-ACIDS IN THE BRAIN.
001474 02-03

ROLE OF BRAIN CATECHOLAMINES AND 5 HYDROXYTRYPTAMINE IN
MORPHINE-INDUCED TEMPERATURE CHANGES IN NORMAL AND
TOLERANT RATS AND MICE.
001476 02-03

GLUCOCORTICOIDS AS A REGULATORY FACTOR FOR BRAIN TRYPTOPHAN-
HYDROXYLASE DURING DEVELOPMENT.
001500 02-03

ANTIDEPRESSANT-DRUGS SLOW CIRCADIAN-RHYTHMS IN BEHAVIOR AND
BRAIN NEUROTRANSMITTER-RECEPTORS.
001536 02-03

BRAIN CATECHOLAMINES, MENTAL-ILLNESSES, AGING AND SENILE-
DEMENTIA: BIOCHEMICAL-CONSIDERATIONS AND PHARMACOLOGICAL-
CONSIDERATIONS.
001550 02-03

(3H) PHENCYCLIDINE BINDING TO SPECIFIC BRAIN RECEPTOR SITES.
001555 02-03

BRAIN LOCATIONS CONTROLLING THE BEHAVIORAL-EFFECTS OF CHRONIC
AMPHETAMINE INTOXICATION.
001653 02-04

BRAIN CATECHOLAMINES MODIFICATIONS. THE EFFECTS ON MEMORY
FACILITATION INDUCED BY OXOTREMORINE IN MICE.
001658 02-04

DORSAL TEGMENTAL BUNDLE DESTRUCTION: EFFECTS ON OPERANT-
BEHAVIOR, BRAIN CATECHOLAMINE LEVELS, AND BEHAVIORAL-
SUPPRESSION PRODUCED BY ADRENERGIC AGONISTS.
001726 02-04

ENHANCED BEHAVIOURAL-EFFECTS, ELECTROCORTICAL-EFFECTS AND
HYPERTHERMIC-EFFECTS OF SEROTONIN-LIKE AGENTS AFTER
IMPAIRMENT OF SEROTONIN TRANSMISSION IN FOWL BRAIN.
001733 02-04

PLASMA AND BRAIN LEVELS OF DELTA6 THC AND SEVEN
MONOOXYGENATED METABOLITES CORRELATED TO THE CATALEPTIC-
EFFECT IN THE MOUSE.
001737 02-04

CHANGES OF PHYSICAL MORPHINE-DEPENDENCE IN RATS CHRONICALLY
TREATED WITH DRUGS ACTING ON BRAIN 5 HYDROXYTRYPTAMINE.
001764 02-04

P CHLOROAMPHETAMINE: EVALUATION OF A BRAIN METABOLITE.
001779 02-04

EXPERIMENTAL DEPENDENCE ON BARBITURATES: II. RELATIONSHIP
BETWEEN DRUG LEVELS IN SERUM AND BRAIN AND THE
DEVELOPMENT OF DEPENDENCE IN RATS.
001800 02-04

EFFECT OF L FUCOSE ON BRAIN PROTEIN METABOLISM AND RETENTION
OF A LEARNED-BEHAVIOR IN RATS:
001819 02-04

REGIONAL CHANGES IN BRAIN GLUCOSE UTILIZATION IN RATS GIVEN A
PYRETHROID INSECTICIDE.
001838 02-05

EFFECTS OF 1,3 BIS-TETRAHYDRO-2-FURANYL-5-
FLUOROPYRIMIDINEDIONE (FD-1) ON THE CENTRAL-NERVOUS-SYSTEM:
1. EFFECTS OF MONOAMINES IN THE BRAIN.
001857 02-05
THE IN VITRO BRAIN SLICE AS A USEFUL NEUROPHYSIOLOGICAL
PREPARATION FOR INTRACELLULAR RECORDING.
001864 02-06
ESTIMATING IN VIVO THE TURNOVER-RATE OF BRAIN ENKEPHALINS.
001884 02-06
TIME-COURSE OF THE ANTIPSYCHOTIC-EFFECT IN SCHIZOPHRENIA AND
SOME CHANGES IN POSTMORTEM BRAIN AND THEIR RELATION TO
NEUROLEPTIC-MEDICATION.
001911 02-08
BENZODIAZEPINE-RECEPTORS: THE EFFECT OF GABA ON THEIR
CHARACTERISTICS IN HUMAN BRAIN AND THEIR ALTERATION IN
HUNTINGTONS-DISEASE.
002163 02-11
ASPIRIN ANALGESIA EVALUATED BY EVENT-RELATED POTENTIALS IN
MAN: POSSIBLE CENTRAL-ACTION IN BRAIN.
002195 02-12
SPECIES-DIFFERENCES IN THE DEAMINATION OF DOPAMINE AND OTHER
SUBSTRATES FOR MONOAMINE-OXIDASE IN BRAIN.
002233 02-13
CLASSIFICATION OF ENDORPHINS/ENKEPHALINS IN BRAIN PHYSIOLOGY
AND PATHOLOGY (BASED ON EEG AND CLINICAL-STUDY OF
SYNTHETICALLY-MODIFIED METHIONINE-ENKEPHALIN).
002286 02-13
POSSIBLE INVOLVEMENT OF BRAIN DOPAMINERGIC-SYSTEMS IN THE
EXPRESSION OF EMOTIONS IN DREAMS.
002325 02-14
NOOTROPIC-DRUGS AND RELATED DRUGS INTERACTING WITH THE
INTEGRATIVE ACTIVITY OF THE BRAIN.
002327 02-14
A SPECIFIC AND SENSITIVE MICROASSAY FOR HYDROXYINDOLES IN
BIOLOGICAL-MATERIAL — APPLICATION FOR CEREBRAL MICROVESSELS,
BRAIN, AND PINEAL-ORGAN OF THE RAT.
002503 02-16
BRAIN GLUCOCORTICOID-RECEPTOR: CORRELATION OF IN VIVO UPTAKE
OF CORTICOSTERONE WITH BEHAVIORAL-EVENTS, ENDOCRINE-EVENTS,
AND NEUROPHARMACOLOGICAL EVENTS.
002515 02-17
DOPAMINERGIC ABNORMALITIES IN POSTMORTEM SCHIZOPHRENIC
BRAIN.
002575 02-17
EVIDENCE THAT IT IS POSSIBLE TO CAUSE ANOREXIA BY INCREASING
RELEASE AND/OR DIRECTLY STIMULATING POSTSYNAPTIC SEROTONIN-
RECEPTORS IN THE BRAIN.
002602 02-17
ANATOMOBIOCHEMICAL MAPPING OF THE BRAIN: NEUROPSYCHIATRIC-
CORRELATIONS.
002630 02-17
THE EFFECT OF BARBITURATES ON THE DEGRADATION OF ENKEPHALIN BY
BRAIN ENZYMES.
002656 03-03
APOMORPHINE HALOPERIDOL INTERACTIONS: DIFFERENT TYPES OF
ANTAGONISM IN CORTICAL AND SUBCORTICAL BRAIN REGIONS.
002662 03-03
NA-INDEPENDENT BINDING OF (3H)GABA AND (3H)MUSCIMOL TO
SUBCELLULAR PARTICLES OF NEURAL PRIMARY CULTURES AND WHOLE
BRAIN.
002699 03-03
DOPAMINE-RECEPTOR SUPERSENSITIVITY IN THE CORPUS-STRIATUM
FOLLOWING CHRONIC ELEVATION OF BRAIN GAMMA AMINOBUTYRIC-
ACID.
002716 03-03
EFFECT OF MAZINDOL ON BRAIN DOPAMINE TURNOVER IN SPIPERONE
TREATED RATS.
002726 03-03
EFFECT OF NEUROLEPTICS ON INDOLEAMINE-N-METHYLTRANSFERASE
ACTIVITY AND BRAIN METABOLISM OF BUFOTENIN.
002735 03-03
CANNABIS-SATIVA: EFFECTS ON BRAIN FUNCTION AND ULTRASTRUCTURE
IN RHESUS-MONKEYS.
002747 03-03
EFFECTS OF LITHIUM ON MORPHOLOGICAL CHARACTERISTICS OF
DISSOCIATED BRAIN CELLS IN CULTURE.
002765 03-03
THE FUNCTIONAL IMPORTANCE OF INCREASED BRAIN TRYPTOPHAN IN
THE SEROTONERGIC RESPONSE TO RESTRAINT STRESS.
002779 03-03
THE EFFECT OF SPECIFIC BRAIN LESIONS ON THE HIGH-AFFINITY BINDING
OF GABA IN THE SUBSTANTIA-NIGRA.
002795 03-03
ENHANCEMENT OF ETORPHINE BRAIN CONCENTRATIONS AND CHANGES
IN ETORPHINE NALOXONE PA2 VALUES IN MORPHINE PRETREATED
MICE.
002800 03-03
ACTIVATION OF SOLUBLE STRIATAL TYROSINE-HYDROXYLASE IN THE RAT
BRAIN AFTER CDP-CHOLINE ADMINISTRATION.
002816 03-03

ANTIANXIETY-AGENTS AND SYNAPTIC TRANSMISSION IN THE BRAIN:
ELECTROPHYSIOLOGICAL-STUDIES. (PH.D. DISSERTATION).
002840 03-03
BRAIN MUSCARINIC CHOLINERGIC-RECEPTOR BINDING IN ROMAN HIGH-
AVOIDANCE AND LOW-AVOIDANCE RATS.
002852 03-03
EFFECT OF TAURINE ON 45CA2 ACCUMULATION IN RAT BRAIN
SYNAPTOSOMES.
002855 03-03
TWO DISTINCT SEROTONIN-RECEPTORS: REGIONAL VARIATIONS IN
RECEPTOR BINDING IN MAMMALIAN BRAIN.
002861 03-03
BIOELECTRICAL-ACTIVITY OF THE RAT BRAIN AFTER PREMATURE
WEANING AND AFTER RNA ADMINISTRATION.
002865 03-03
PENTOBARBITAL: DUAL-ACTIONS TO INCREASE BRAIN BENZODIAZEPINE-
RECEPTOR AFFINITY.
002896 03-03
GABA-RECEPTORS REGULATE THE AFFINITIES OF ANIONS REQUIRED FOR
BRAIN SPECIFIC BENZODIAZEPINE BINDING.
002903 03-03
DIFFERENTIAL-EFFECTS OF SHORT-TERM AND LONG-TERM LITHIUM ON
TRYPTOPHAN UPTAKE AND SEROTONERGIC FUNCTION IN CAT BRAIN.
002911 03-03
BRAIN MECHANISMS OF LEARNING.
002916 03-03
EFFECTS OF ISOPROTERENOL ON THE DEVELOPMENT OF BETA-
ADRENERGIC-RECEPTORS IN BRAIN CELL AGGREGATES.
002932 03-03
INCORPORATION OF N ACETYLMANNOSAMINE INTO RAT-BRAIN
SUBCELLULAR GANGLIOSIDES: EFFECT OF PENTYLENETETRAZOL-
INDUCED CONVULSIONS IN BRAIN GANGLIOSIDES.
002937 03-03
BEHAVIOURAL-RESPONSES TO DRUGS RELEASING 5
HYDROXYTRYPTAMINE AND CATECHOLAMINES: EFFECTS OF
TREATMENTS ALTERING PRECURSOR CONCENTRATIONS IN BRAIN.
002990 03-04
INDUCTION OF HYPERSENSITIVITY OF BRAIN BY HYDRALAZINE
TREATMENT IN RATS.
003008 03-04
BEHAVIOURAL-CHANGES IN ADULT RATS FOLLOWING ADMINISTRATION
OF ANTIBODIES AGAINST BRAIN GANGLIOSIDES.
003071 03-04
DIFFERENTIATION OF OPIATE-RECEPTORS IN THE BRAIN BY THE SELECTIVE
DEVELOPMENT OF TOLERANCE.
003088 03-04
SIMULTANEOUS DETERMINATION OF FEMTOMOLE QUANTITIES OF 5
HYDROXYTRYPTOPHAN, SEROTONIN AND 5 HYDROXYINDOLEACETIC-
ACID IN BRAIN USING HPLC WITH ELECTROCHEMICAL-DETECTION.
003139 03-06
A NEW METHOD FOR APPLICATION OF HORSERADISH-PEROXIDASE INTO
A RESTRICTED AREA OF THE BRAIN.
003141 03-06
MODIFIED CUP TECHNIQUE FOR MICROESTIMATION OF THE RELEASE AND
UPTAKE OF NEUROTRANSMITTERS IN BRAIN SLICES.
003147 03-06
HUMAN BRAIN, PLASMA, AND CEREBROSPINAL-FLUID CONCENTRATION
OF SODIUM-VALPROATE AFTER 72 HOURS OF THERAPY.
003433 03-13
POSITRON-TOMOGRAPHY. A NEW METHOD FOR IN VIVO BRAIN STUDIES
OF BENZODIAZEPINE, IN ANIMAL AND IN MAN.
003564 03-16
MIND/BRAIN IN THE AGE OF PSYCHOPHARMACOLOGY: A CROSSROADS
FOR MEDICINE AND MINISTRY.
003624 03-17
ACTION ON THE EMOTIONALLY-REINFORCED BRAIN SYSTEM AS A MEANS
OF TREATING ALCOHOLISM AND DRUG ADDICTION
PATHOGENETICALLY.
003641 03-17
BIOCHEMICAL AND IMMUNOLOGICAL PROPERTIES OF THE MOUSE BRAIN
ENOLASES PURIFIED BY A SIMPLE METHOD.
003668 04-01
INDICATIONS FOR A BRAIN UPTAKE OF LABELLED VASOPRESSIN AND
OCYTOCIN AND THE PROBLEM OF THE BLOOD-BRAIN-BARRIER.
003669 04-01
PARTIAL PURIFICATION OF ACID SPHINGOMYELINASE FROM NORMAL
AND PATHOLOGICAL (M. NIEMANN-PICK TYPE C) HUMAN BRAIN.
003671 04-01
A RAPID AND SIMPLE METHOD FOR THE DETERMINATION OF PICOGRAM
LEVELS OF 3 METHOXYTYRAMINE IN BRAIN TISSUE USING LIQUID-
CHROMATOGRAPHY WITH ELECTROCHEMICAL DETECTION.
003674 04-01
PHYSICAL AND KINETIC PROPERTIES OF CHOLINE-ACETYL-TRANSFERASE
FROM RAT AND BOVINE BRAIN.
003676 04-01
A RADIOIMMUNOASSAY FOR EPENDYMINS BETA AND GAMMA: TWO
GOLDFISH BRAIN PROTEINS INVOLVED IN BEHAVIORAL PLASTICITY.
003677 04-01

NEURONAL SENSITIVITY OF SOME BRAIN REGIONS TO ANGIOTENSIN-II IN RABBITS.
003716 04-03
BRAIN BENZODIAZEPINE-RECEPTORS AND THEIR RAPID CHANGES AFTER SEIZURES IN THE MONGOLIAN-GERBIL.
003717 04-03
INTERACTIONS BETWEEN A MONOFLUORINATED ANALOGUE OF P CHLOROAMPHETAMINE AND 5 HYDROXYTRYPTAMINE IN BRAIN.
003719 04-03
EFFECT OF ALPHA METHYLPHENYLALANINE AND PHENYLALANINE ON BRAIN POLYRIBOSOMES AND PROTEIN SYNTHESIS.
003733 04-03
BRAIN AND SERUM CALCIUM CONCENTRATIONS FOLLOWING ELECTROCONVULSIVE-SHOCK OR BICUCULLINE-INDUCED CONVULSIONS IN RATS.
003736 04-03
MODULATORY EFFECT OF BRAIN ACETYLCHOLINE ON REFLEX-INDUCED BRADYCARDIA AND TACHYCARDIA IN CONSCIOUS RATS.
003744 04-03
EFFECT OF INTRAVENOUS ADMINISTRATION OF D LYSERGIC-ACID-DIETHYLAMIDE ON SUBSEQUENT PROTEIN SYNTHESIS IN A CELL-FREE SYSTEM DERIVED FROM BRAIN.
003761 04-03
SOLUBILIZATION OF NEUROLEPTIC/DOPAMINE-RECEPTORS OF HUMAN BRAIN STRIATUM.
003767 04-03
DOPAMINE, NORADRENALINE AND 3,4 DIHYDROXYPHENYLACETIC-ACID (DOPAC) LEVELS OF INDIVIDUAL BRAIN NUCLEI, EFFECTS OF HALOPERIDOL AND PARGYLINE.
003792 04-03
OPPOSITE EFFECTS OF NALOXONE ON SUBSTANCE-P-INDUCED IN BRAIN DOPA SYNTHESIS AND IN LOCOMOTOR-ACTIVITY IN RATS.
003799 04-03
EFFECTS OF ANTIDEPRESSANT-DRUGS ON DIFFERENT RECEPTORS IN THE BRAIN.
003824 04-03
COMPARISON OF THE EFFECT OF INTRAVENOUS ADMINISTRATION OF D LYSERGIC-ACID-DIETHYLAMIDE ON FREE AND MEMBRANE-BOUND POLYSOMES IN THE RABBIT BRAIN.
003831 04-03
CELL-FREE TRANSLATION OF FREE AND MEMBRANE-BOUND POLYSOMES AND POLYADENYLATED MRNA FROM RABBIT BRAIN FOLLOWING ADMINISTRATION OF D LYSERGIC-ACID-DIETHYLAMIDE IN VIVO.
003832 04-03
PHARMACOLOGIC MANIPULATION OF BRAIN AND PITUITARY ENDORPHIN CONTENT AND RELEASE.
003837 04-03
COMPARATIVE-EFFECTS OF SUBSTITUTED PHENYLETHYLAMINES ON BRAIN SEROTONERGIC MECHANISMS.
003854 04-03
ACTION OF ENKEPHALIN ANALOGUES AND MORPHINE ON BRAIN ACETYLCHOLINE RELEASE: DIFFERENTIAL REVERSAL BY NALOXONE AND AN OPIATE-PENTAPEPTIDE.
003863 04-03
EFFECTS OF MOLINDONE AND FLUPHENAZINE ON THE BRAIN CONCENTRATION OF SOME PHENOLIC AND CATECHOLIC AMINES IN THE MOUSE AND THE RAT.
003870 04-03
THE EFFECT OF ADENOSINE AND GUANOSINE ON THE CONTENT OF SEROTONIN AND CATECHOLAMINES IN THE BRAIN IN THE RESTORATION PERIOD FOLLOWING EXPERIMENTAL CLINICAL DEATH.
003882 04-03
OPIOID BINDING PROPERTIES OF BRAIN AND PERIPHERAL TISSUES: EVIDENCE FOR HETEROGENEITY IN OPIOID LIGAND BINDING SITES.
003902 04-03
EFFECT OF INHIBITORS OF GABA-AMINOTRANSFERASE ON THE METABOLISM OF GABA IN BRAIN TISSUE AND SYNAPTOSOMAL FRACTIONS.
003914 04-03
EFFECT OF DIAZEPAM ON STRESS-INDUCED CHANGES IN BRAIN HISTAMINE.
003932 04-03
THE EFFECT OF PRENATAL EXPOSURE TO ETHANOL OR OPIATES ON BRAIN CATECHOLAMINE ACTIVITY.
003939 04-03
AUTORADIOGRAPHIC STUDIES ON DISTRIBUTION OF L-3,4 DIHYDROXYPHENYLALANINE (L-DOPA) 14C AND L 5 HYDROXYTRYPTOPHAN (L 5 HTP) 14C IN THE CAT BRAIN.
003941 04-03
EVIDENCE TO SUGGEST THAT DOPAMINE-INDUCED INCREASE IN GABA CONCENTRATIONS IN CHICK BRAIN IS MEDIATED THROUGH CYCLIC-AMP.
003952 04-03
CHANGES IN REGIONAL BRAIN LEVELS OF AMINO-ACID PUTATIVE NEUROTRANSMITTERS AFTER PROLONGED TREATMENT WITH THE ANTICONVULSANT-DRUGS DIPHENYLHYDANTOIN, PHENOBARBITONE, SODIUM-VALPROATE, ETHOSUXIMIDE, AND SULTHIAME IN THE RAT.
003961 04-03
DOES HIGH-AFFINITY (3H) IMIPRAMINE BINDING LABEL SEROTONIN REUPTAKE SITES IN BRAIN AND PLATELET?
003962 04-03

STUDIES ON THE MECHANISM-OF-ACTION OF AVERMECTIN-B1A: STIMULATION OF RELEASE OF GAMMA AMINOBUTYRIC-ACID FROM BRAIN SYNAPTOSOMES.
003973 04-03
STRESS-MODULATED ALTERATION OF BRAIN BIOGENIC-AMINES IN THE RAT: EFFECTS OF L TRYPTOPHAN.
003978 04-03
EFFECT OF PROSTAGLANDIN-D2, PROSTAGLANDIN-E2 AND PROSTAGLANDIN-F2ALPHA ON CATECHOLAMINE RELEASE FROM SLICES OF RAT AND RABBIT BRAIN.
003983 04-03
PROPERTIES OF A CDP-DIGLYCERIDE-HYDROLASE FROM GUINEA-PIG BRAIN.
003987 04-03
EFFECT OF PRENATAL NEUROLEPTIC TREATMENT ON MEMBRANE RECEPTOR DEVELOPMENT IN THE BRAIN.
003989 04-03
THE EFFECT OF LITHIUM-HYDROXYBUTYRATE ON THE BIOELECTRICAL-ACTIVITY OF THE CORTEX AND SOME SUBCORTICAL STRUCTURES OF THE RABBIT BRAIN.
003994 04-03
THE INSENSITIVITY OF DEVELOPING BENZODIAZEPINE-RECEPTORS TO CHRONIC-TREATMENT WITH DIAZEPAM, GABA AND MUSCIMOL IN BRAIN CELL-CULTURES.
004002 04-03
THE ROLE OF OPIATE-RECEPTORS OF DIFFERENT BRAIN REGIONS IN DETERMINING THE EMOTIONAL REACTIONS OF RATS.
004017 04-03
OXIDATION OF BETA PHENYLETHYLAMINE BY BOTH TYPES OF MONOAMINE-OXIDASE: EXAMINATION OF ENZYMES IN BRAIN AND LIVER MITOCHONDRIA OF EIGHT SPECIES.
004024 04-03
EFFECT OF CHRONIC-TREATMENT WITH TRICYCLIC-ANTIDEPRESSANT DRUGS ON IDENTIFIED BRAIN NORADRENERGIC AND SEROTONERGIC NEURONS.
004026 04-03
INHIBITION BY CAFFEINE OF CALCIUM UPTAKE BY BRAIN MICROSOMAL VESICLES.
004042 04-03
POSTMORTEM STABILITY OF BRAIN 3 METHOXY-4-HYDROXYPHENYLETHYLENEGLYCOL AND 3,4 DIHYDROXYPHENYLETHYLENEGLYCOL IN THE RAT AND MOUSE.
004048 04-03
BENZODIAZEPINE-RECEPTOR: HETEROGENEITY IN RABBIT BRAIN.
004060 04-03
RELATIONSHIP BETWEEN PENTYLENETETRAZOL-INDUCED SEIZURES AND BRAIN PENTYLENETETRAZOL LEVELS IN MICE.
004061 04-03
EFFECTS OF TRICYCLIC-ANTIDEPRESSANTS ON TETRABENAZINE-INDUCED DEPLETION OF BRAIN MONOAMINES IN RATS. 1. NOREPINEPHRINE.
004062 04-03
THE EFFECT OF P CHLOROPHENYLALANINE ON THE DISTRIBUTION OF BIOGENIC-AMINES IN THE BRAIN, AND ON MEMORY IN RATS.
004068 04-04
THE EFFECT OF PROPYLNORANTIFEIN ON BEHAVIORAL-REACTIONS, ADRENOCORTICAL ACTIVITY, AND ENERGY METABOLISM IN THE ANIMAL BRAIN.
004075 04-04
DOES RAPID-EYE-MOVEMENT SLEEP PLAY A ROLE IN BRAIN DEVELOPMENT?
004091 04-04
SUSTAINED INTRACEREBROVENTRICULAR INFUSION OF BRAIN FUELS REDUCES BODY-WEIGHT AND FOOD INTAKE IN RATS.
004098 04-04
COCAINE AND SEIZURE PROTECTION IN MICE OF VARYING BRAIN WEIGHTS.
004103 04-04
EFFECT OF PRENATAL PHENYTOIN ADMINISTRATION ON BRAIN TRYPTOPHAN METABOLISM OF RAT OFFSPRING DURING THE PREWEANING PERIOD.
004108 04-04
RELATION BETWEEN BRAIN CATECHOLAMINE-RECEPTORS AND DOPAMINERGIC STEREOTYPY IN RAT STRAINS.
004131 04-04
MORPHINE DIFFERENTIALLY AFFECTS VENTRAL TEGMENTAL AND SUBSTANTIA-NIGRA BRAIN REWARD THRESHOLDS.
004187 04-04
THE EFFECT OF THE NEW ANTIDEPRESSANT INKASAN ON THE BIOELECTRICAL-ACTIVITY OF THE BRAIN AND ON CONDITIONED REFLEXES.
004212 04-04
SUPPRESSION OF ALCOHOL DRINKING WITH BRAIN ALDEHYDE-DEHYDROGENASE INHIBITION.
004220 04-04
NEUROTRANSMITTER-RECEPTORS IN BRAIN REGIONS OF ACRYLAMIDE TREATED RATS. I: EFFECTS OF A SINGLE EXPOSURE TO ACRYLAMIDE.
004264 04-05

Subject Index

NEUROTRANSMITTER-RECEPTORS IN BRAIN REGIONS OF ACRYLAMIDE
TREATED RATS. II: EFFECTS OF EXTENDED EXPOSURE TO ACRYLAMIDE.
004265 04-05

LESIONS OF AMYGDALA, PYRIFORM CORTEX AND OTHER BRAIN
STRUCTURES DUE TO DIPIPERIDINOETHANE INTOXICATION.
004273 04-05

EFFECTS OF A SINGLE-THERAPEUTIC-DOSE OF GLYCEROL ON CEREBRAL
METABOLISM IN THE BRAINS OF YOUNG MICE: POSSIBLE INCREASE IN
BRAIN GLUCOSE TRANSPORT AND GLUCOSE UTILIZATION.
004281 04-05

AUTORADIOGRAPHIC LOCALIZATION OF DRUG AND NEUROTRANSMITTER-
RECEPTORS IN THE BRAIN.
004292 04-06

LSD, PSYCHOTOGENIC PROCEDURES AND BRAIN NEUROHUMORS.
(UNPUBLISHED PAPER).
004448 04-11

EFFECTS OF A SHORT-ACTING BENZODIAZEPINE ON BRAIN ELECTRICAL-
ACTIVITY DURING SLEEP.
004568 04-14

THE USE OF EVENT-RELATED SLOW POTENTIALS OF THE BRAIN AS AN
OBJECTIVE METHOD TO STUDY THE EFFECTS OF CENTRALLY ACTING
DRUGS.
004669 04-16

COMPARISON OF SPECTROFLUOROMETRIC AND GAS-
CHROMATOGRAPHY/MASS-SPECTROMETRY PROCEDURES FOR THE
QUANTITATION OF MORPHINE IN BLOOD AND BRAIN.
004692 04-16

BRAIN DOPAMINE-RECEPTORS.
004741 04-17

BRAIN-AMINE
MONOAMINE-OXIDASE-INHIBITION AND BRAIN-AMINE METABOLISM
AFTER ORAL TREATMENT WITH TOLOXATONE IN THE RAT.
000156 01-03

BRAIN-BIOCHEMISTRY
EFFECTS OF ACUTE VS. CHRONIC PHENCYCLIDINE ON BRAIN-
BIOCHEMISTRY AND BEHAVIOR.
001789 02-04

CHANGES IN CEREBRAL DOPAMINE METABOLISM AND RECEPTORS
DURING ONE-YEAR NEUROLEPTIC ADMINISTRATION AND SUBSEQUENT
WITHDRAWAL: RELEVANCE TO BRAIN-BIOCHEMISTRY IN
SCHIZOPHRENIA.
002390 02-15

EFFECT OF ACUTE AND CHRONIC TRIIODOTHYRONINE (T3)
ADMINISTRATION TO RATS ON CENTRAL 5 HT AND DOPAMINE-
MEDIATED BEHAVIOURAL-RESPONSES AND RELATED BRAIN-
BIOCHEMISTRY.
002951 03-04

BRAIN-DAMAGE
EFFECTS OF HIPPOCAMPAL BRAIN-DAMAGE ON AUDITORY AND VISUAL
RECENT MEMORY: COMPARISON WITH MARIJUANA INTOXICATED
SUBJECTS.
002320 02-14

BEHAVIORAL-TEST FOR DETECTION OF SUBCLINICAL BRAIN-DAMAGE: AN
EXPERIMENTAL MODEL.
003120 03-04

PHENYTOIN TOXICITY IN A BRAIN-DAMAGE ADOLESCENT: A CASE-
REPORT.
003512 03-15

NEUROPSYCHOLOGICAL-CORRELATES OF ASTHMA: BRAIN-DAMAGE OR
DRUG-EFFECTS?
003538 03-15

BRAIN-DAMAGE-SYNDROME
TRIAL OF A PEPTIDE FRACTION OF ACTH (ACTH4-10) IN THE ALCOHOLIC
BRAIN-DAMAGE-SYNDROME.
002318 02-14

BRAIN-DAMAGED
ORAL DYSKINESIA IN BRAIN-DAMAGED RATS WITHDRAWN FROM A
NEUROLEPTIC: IMPLICATION FOR MODELS OF TARDIVE-DYSKINESIA.
000393 01-04

BRAIN-DYSFUNCTION
PHENYLACETATE AND BRAIN-DYSFUNCTION IN EXPERIMENTAL
PHENYLKETONURIA: SYNAPTIC DEVELOPMENT.
000191 01-03

BRAIN-MONOAMINE
EFFECTS OF BRAIN-MONOAMINE DEPLETION ON THERMOREGULATORY
RESPONSES OF RABBITS TO DIFFERENT HYPOTHALAMIC
TEMPERATURES.
000190 01-03

BRAIN-MONOAMINES
BRAIN-MONOAMINES IN THE RHESUS-MONKEY DURING LONG-TERM
NEUROLEPTIC ADMINISTRATION.
001471 02-03

EFFECT OF BROMOCRIPTINE ON EXPLORATORY-ACTIVITY, BRAIN-
MONOAMINES AND PLASMA CORTICOSTERONE IN THE
NORMOTENSIVE-RATS, GENETICALLY HYPERTENSIVE-RATS AND/OR
HYPERTENSIVE OBESE RATS.
001635 02-04

BRAIN-MONOAMINES AND THE HIGH PRESSURE NEUROLOGICAL-
SYNDROME.
001686 02-04

THE STUDY OF POSSIBLE CENTRAL-ACTIONS OF DRUGS UPON THE LOWER BRAINSTEM.
004297 04-06

BRANCHED-CHAIN
EFFECTS OF BRANCHED-CHAIN FATTY-ACIDS ON GABA DEGRADATION AND BEHAVIOR: FURTHER EVIDENCE FOR A ROLE OF GABA IN QUASI-MORPHINE ABSTINENCE-BEHAVIOR.
001809 02-04

BREAKDOWN
EVIDENCE FOR THE PRESENCE OF TWO TYPES OF MONOAMINE-OXIDASE IN RABBIT CHOROID PLEXUS AND THEIR ROLE IN BREAKDOWN OF AMINES INFLUENCING CEREBROSPINAL-FLUID FORMATION.
002807 03-03

BREAKING-POINT
DRUG-INDUCED STIMULUS CONTROL AND THE CONCEPT OF BREAKING-POINT: LSD AND QUIPAZINE.
003116 03-04

BRED
TOLERANCE TO ETHANOL-INDUCED IMPAIRMENT OF WATER-ESCAPE IN RATS BRED FOR ETHANOL SENSITIVITY.
001567 02-04

ETHANOL-INDUCED ANALGESIA IN RATS SELECTIVELY BRED FOR ETHANOL SENSITIVITY.
001625 02-04

BRIDGES
SYNTHESIS AND BIOLOGICAL-ACTIVITY OF HUMAN BETA ENDORPHIN ANALOGS WITH DISULFIDE BRIDGES.
003655 04-01

BRITISH-PHARMACOLOGICAL-SOCIETY
PROCEEDINGS OF THE BRITISH-PHARMACOLOGICAL-SOCIETY, 12TH-14TH SEPTEMBER, 1979, UNIVERSITY-OF-LEEDS.
000966 01-17

BRL-14342
PHARMACOLOGICAL AND BIOCHEMICAL-PROPERTIES OF BRL-14342, A NOVEL POTENTIAL ANTIDEPRESSANT-DRUG.
004086 04-04

BROMAZEPAM
CONTROLLED-STUDY WITH BROMAZEPAM AND CLOROTEPIN IN CHILD INSTABILITY.
002190 02-11

ACTIVITY OF BROMAZEPAM AND LORAZEPAM IN NEUROTIC DEPRESSIONS.
004384 04-09

BROMISM
BROMISM, HYSTERIA AND NARCOLEPSY.
002472 02-15

BROMO-ALPHA-ERGOCRIPTINE
PLASMA DOPAMINE-BETA-HYDROXYLASE ACTIVITY IN CHRONIC SCHIZOPHRENIC-PATIENTS TESTED WITH SINGLE-DOSE OF 2 BROMO-ALPHA-ERGOCRIPTINE (PARLODEL).
004343 04-08

BROMOCRIPTINE
THE EFFECTS OF BROMOCRIPTINE ON PRESYNAPTIC AND POSTSYNAPTIC ALPHA-ADRENOCEPTORS IN THE MOUSE VAS-DEFERENS.
000108 01-03

DISTRIBUTION AND EXCRETION IN THE RAT AND MONKEY OF (82BR) BROMOCRIPTINE.
000196 01-03

LONG-TERM EFFICACY OF BROMOCRIPTINE IN PARKINSONS-DISEASE.
000698 01-11

BROMOCRIPTINE AND DOPAMINERGIC FUNCTION IN HUNTINGTON-DISEASE.
000700 01-11

IMPROVEMENT OF L-DOPA-INDUCED DYSKINESIA AND OF ON-OFF-PHENOMENON BY BROMOCRIPTINE.
000813 01-14

NEUROPHARMACOLOGY OF BROMOCRIPTINE AND DIHYDROERGOTOXINE (HYDERGINE).
001346 02-03

EFFECT OF BROMOCRIPTINE ON EXPLORATORY-ACTIVITY, BRAIN-MONOAMINES AND PLASMA CORTICOSTERONE IN THE NORMOTENSIVE-RATS, GENETICALLY HYPERTENSIVE-RATS AND/OR HYPERTENSIVE OBESE RATS.
001635 02-04

USE OF LARGE-SINGLE-DOSES OF BROMOCRIPTINE IN SCHIZOPHRENIC-PATIENTS WITH ELEVATED SERUM PROLACTIN LEVELS AND EXTRAPYRAMIDAL SIDE-EFFECTS ASSOCIATED WITH NEUROLEPTIC TREATMENT.
001944 02-08

AN ATTEMPT TO TREAT THE SIDE-EFFECTS OF PSYCHOTROPIC THERAPY WITH BROMOCRIPTINE.
002094 02-11

A COMPARATIVE-STUDY OF BROMOCRIPTINE AND LEVODOPA IN PARKINSONS-DISEASE.
002117 02-11

BROMOCRIPTINE AND PARKINSONS-DISEASE: A 16-HOUR CLINICAL-EVALUATION.
002127 02-11

THE ROLE OF BROMOCRIPTINE IN THE TREATMENT OF PARKINSONS-DISEASE.
002177 02-11

THE USE OF BROMOCRIPTINE FOR TESTING CENTRAL DOPAMINERGIC REACTIVITY.
002205 02-13

THE PHARMACOKINETICS OF BROMOCRIPTINE IN MAN.
002291 02-13

BROMOCRIPTINE IN PARKINSONS-DISEASE: REPORT ON 106 PATIENTS TREATED FOR UP TO 5 YEARS.
002342 02-14

FURTHER EXPERIENCES WITH LOW-DOSES OF BROMOCRIPTINE IN PARKINSONS-DISEASE.
002401 02-15

LEVODOPA COMPARED WITH BROMOCRIPTINE IN THE TREATMENT OF PARKINSONS-DISEASE.
002406 02-15

PSYCHIATRIC-EFFECTS OF BROMOCRIPTINE AND LERGOTRILE IN PARKINSONIAN-PATIENTS.
002453 02-15

PHARMACOLOGICAL DIFFERENCE OF L-DOPA, APOMORPHINE, AND BROMOCRIPTINE AGAINST METOCLOPRAMIDE.
003790 04-03

INFLUENCE OF THE DOPAMINERGIC AGONISTS BROMOCRIPTINE, PIRIBEDIL AND NOMIFENSINE ON THE SYMPATHETIC NEURAL TRANSMISSION IN THE NICTITATING MEMBRANE OF THE CAT.
003822 04-03

PHENOXYBENZAMINE AND BROMOCRIPTINE ATTENUATE NEED FOR REM SLEEP IN RATS.
004203 04-04

BROMOCRYPTINE
EVIDENCE FOR AN IRREVERSIBLE INTERACTION OF BROMOCRYPTINE WITH CENTRAL DOPAMINE-RECEPTORS.
000023 01-03

BROMOSPIROPERIDOL
SPECIFIC IN VIVO BINDING OF 77BR P BROMOSPIROPERIDOL IN RAT-BRAIN: A POTENTIAL TOOL FOR GAMMA-RAY IMAGING.
004293 04-06

BROMPERIDOL
CLINICAL-EVALUATION OF BROMPERIDOL VERSUS HALOPERIDOL IN PSYCHOTIC-PATIENTS.
004562 04-14

BUCCOLINGUOFACIAL
THE TREATMENT OF BUCCOLINGUOFACIAL DYSKINESIA IN THE ELDERLY: THE CHOICE OF A NEUROLEPTIC-AGENT.
002223 02-13

BUFFERS
EFFECT OF STRUCTURE ON PHENOTHIAZINE CATION RADICAL REACTIONS IN AQUEOUS BUFFERS.
000014 01-02

BUFOTENIN
EFFECT OF NEUROLEPTICS ON INDOLEAMINE-N-METHYLTRANSFERASE ACTIVITY AND BRAIN METABOLISM OF BUFOTENIN.
002735 03-03

BULBECTOMISED
SEROTONINMIMETIC AND ANTIDEPRESSANT-DRUGS ON PASSIVE-AVOIDANCE LEARNING BY OLFACTORY BULBECTOMISED RATS.
001585 02-04

BULLFROG
CALCIUM LOCALIZATION IN THE SYMPATHETIC GANGLION OF THE BULLFROG AND EFFECTS OF CAFFEINE.
000098 01-03

5 HYDROXYTRYPTAMINE CONTROLS ACH-RECEPTOR SENSITIVITY OF BULLFROG SYMPATHETIC GANGLION CELLS.
003710 04-03

BUMETANIDE
THE EFFECT OF FRUSEMIDE PIRETANIDE AND BUMETANIDE ON COCHLEAR SUCCINIC-DEHYDROGENASE.
003757 04-03

BUNDLE
MALE RAT SEXUAL-BEHAVIOR COMPARED AFTER 6 OHDA AND ELECTROLYTIC LESIONS IN THE DORSAL NA BUNDLE REGION OF THE MIDBRAIN.
001593 02-04

DORSAL TEGMENTAL BUNDLE DESTRUCTION: EFFECTS ON OPERANT-BEHAVIOR, BRAIN CATECHOLAMINE LEVELS, AND BEHAVIORAL-SUPPRESSION PRODUCED BY ADRENERGIC AGONISTS.
001726 02-04

EFFECTS OF METHAMPHETAMINE ON BLOOD FLOW IN THE CAUDATE-PUTAMEN AFTER LESIONS OF THE NIGROSTRIATAL DOPAMINERGIC BUNDLE IN THE RAT.
003910 04-03

BUNGAROTOXIN
LOCALIZATION OF ALPHA BUNGAROTOXIN BINDING-SITES IN SYNAPSES OF THE DEVELOPING CHICK RETINA.
000065 01-03

ACTIONS OF BETA BUNGAROTOXIN ON AMINO-ACID TRANSMITTER RELEASE.
002897 03-03

ALTERATIONS OF ACETYLCHOLINE AND CHOLINE METABOLISM IN MAMMALIAN PREPARATIONS TREATED WITH BETA BUNGAROTOXIN.
003820 04-03

BUPRENORPHINE
A COMPARISON OF THE NEUROCHEMICAL-EFFECTS OF BUPRENORPHINE
WITH THOSE OF MORPHINE AND HALOPERIDOL IN RATS.
002701 03-03
BUPRENORPHINE: DEMONSTRATION OF PHYSICAL-DEPENDENCE LIABILITY.
004104 04-04

BUPROPION
CLINICAL-EFFICACY OF THE NEW ANTIDEPRESSANT BUPROPION
(WELLBUTRIN).
003227 03-09

BURST-FIRING
DOPAMINE INHIBITS BURST-FIRING OF NEUROSECRETORY CELL R-15 IN
APLYSIA-CALIFORNICA: ESTABLISHMENT OF A DOSE-RESPONSE
RELATIONSHIP.
003806 04-03

BURYING
CONDITIONING AND RETENTION OF DEFENSIVE BURYING AS A FUNCTION
OF ELAVIL AND THORAZINE INJECTION.
002974 03-04

BUSPIRONE
INHIBITION OF AGGRESSIVE-BEHAVIOR IN RHESUS-MONKEYS BY
BUSPIRONE.
003103 03-04

BUTACLAMOL
CALMODULIN RELEASE FROM STRIATAL MEMBRANES AFTER ACUTE AND
CHRONIC TREATMENT WITH BUTACLAMOL.
001249 02-03

BUTANOL
IMPAIRMENT OF AVOIDANCE-BEHAVIOR FOLLOWING SHORT-TERM
INGESTION OF ETHANOL, TERTIARY BUTANOL, OR PENTOBARBITAL IN
MICE.
000479 01-04

BUTOCTAMIDE-HYDROGEN-SUCCINATE
THE EFFECT OF BUTOCTAMIDE-HYDROGEN-SUCCINATE ON NOCTURNAL
SLEEP: ALL-NIGHT POLYGRAPHICAL-STUDIES.
002350 02-14

BUTORPHANOL
SERUM LEVELS OF BUTORPHANOL BY RADIOIMMUNOASSAY.
004691 04-16

BUTRIPTYLINE-HYDROCHLORIDE
ACTION OF BUTRIPTYLINE-HYDROCHLORIDE IN THE
GERONTOPSYCHIATRIC-PATIENT.
003358 03-11

BUTYROLACTONE
CROSS-TOLERANCE OF DOPAMINE METABOLISM TO BACLOFEN, GAMMA
BUTYROLACTONE AND HA-966 IN THE STRIATUM AND OLFACTORY
TUBERCLE OF THE RAT.
002681 03-03

BUTYROLACTONE-GAMMA-CARBONYL-HISTIDYL-PROLINAMIDE
GAMMA BUTYROLACTONE-GAMMA-CARBONYL-HISTIDYL-PROLINAMIDE
CITRATE (DN-1417): A NOVEL TRH ANALOG WITH POTENT EFFECTS ON
THE CENTRAL-NERVOUS-SYSTEM.
003057 03-04

BUTYROPHENONE
SLEEP PROFILE AND ULTRADIAN SLEEP PERIODICITY IN HUMANS UNDER
THE INFLUENCE OF A BUTYROPHENONE DERIVATIVE: I. SLEEP
CORRECTION IN SUBJECTS WITH OLIGOSYMPTOMATIC SLEEP-
DISORDERS.
001869 02-06
INCREASED SERUM PROLACTIN LEVELS DURING PHENOTHIAZINE AND
BUTYROPHENONE TREATMENT OF SIX POSTPARTUM WOMEN.
003318 03-11

C-AMP
HALOTHANE EFFECT ON C-AMP GENERATION AND HYDROLYSIS IN RAT-
BRAIN.
000305 01-03
BRADYKININ-RECEPTOR STIMULATION OF C-AMP INVOLVES
PHOSPHOLIPID METHYLATION, CA-FLUX, PHOSPHOLIPASE-A2
ACTIVATION AND PROSTAGLANDIN FORMATION. (UNPUBLISHED
PAPER).
001002 02-01

C-GMP
INCREASE OF C-GMP AND ACCUMULATION OF 45CA2 EVOKED BY DRUGS
ACTING ON SODIUM OR POTASSIUM CHANNELS.
003709 04-03
PHENYTOIN INHIBITION OF CYCLIC-GUANOSINE-MONOPHOSPHATE (C-
GMP) ACCUMULATION IN NEUROBLASTOMA CELLS BY CALCIUM-
CHANNEL BLOCKADE.
004020 04-03

C-TYPE
SELECTIVE NEUROTOXIC-ACTION OF CAPSAICIN ON GLOMERULAR C-TYPE
TERMINALS IN RAT SUBSTANTIA-GELATINOSA.
003143 03-06

CA
CA DIAZEPAM LINK? NO SCIENTIFIC TAKERS SO FAR.
003519 03-15

CA-DEPENDENT
SEROTONIN-RECEPTOR MEDIATED MODULATION OF CA-DEPENDENT 5
HYDROXYTRYPTAMINE RELEASE FROM NEURONES OF THE RAT-BRAIN-
CORTEX.
001258 02-03

CA-FLUX
IGE MEDIATED HISTAMINE RELEASE IN RAT BASOPHILIC LEUKEMIA
CELLS: RECEPTOR ACTIVATED PHOSPHOLIPID METHYLATION, CA-FLUX
AND RELEASE OF ARACHIDONIC-ACID. (UNPUBLISHED PAPER).
001188 02-03

CA-INDEPENDENT
REGULATION BY A BETA-ADRENERGIC-RECEPTOR OF A CA-INDEPENDENT
ADENOSINE-CYCLIC-MONOPHOSPHATE-PHOSPHODIESTERASE IN C6-
GLIOMA CELLS. (UNPUBLISHED PAPER).
001403 02-03

CA-FLUX
BRADYKININ-RECEPTOR STIMULATION OF C-AMP INVOLVES
PHOSPHOLIPID METHYLATION, CA-FLUX, PHOSPHOLIPASE-A2
ACTIVATION AND PROSTAGLANDIN FORMATION. (UNPUBLISHED
PAPER).
001002 02-01

CACTUS
CATECHOLAMINE METABOLISM IN A PSYCHOACTIVE CACTUS.
004722 04-17

CAERULEIN
CENTRAL DEPRESSANT EFFECTS OF CAERULEIN AND CHOLECYSTOKININ-
OCTAPEPTIDE (CCK-8) DIFFER FROM THOSE OF DIAZEPAM AND
HALOPERIDOL.
002652 03-02

CAFFEINE
CALCIUM LOCALIZATION IN THE SYMPATHETIC GANGLION OF THE
BULLFROG AND EFFECTS OF CAFFEINE.
000098 01-03
CAFFEINE PRODUCES REM SLEEP REBOUND IN RATS.
000244 01-03
AROUSAL AND SHORT-TERM MEMORY: EFFECTS OF CAFFEINE AND TRIAL
SPACING ON DELAYED ALTERNATION PERFORMANCE.
000487 01-04
BEHAVIOURAL-EFFECTS OF ACETYLSALICYLIC-ACID, PARACETAMOL,
CAFFEINE, GUAIPHENESIN AND THEIR COMBINATIONS.
001805 02-04
EFFECTS OF CAFFEINE ON PLASMA FREE FATTY-ACIDS, URINARY
CATECHOLAMINES, AND DRUG BINDING.
002272 02-13
THE EFFECTS OF ALCOHOL AND CAFFEINE ON CONCENTRATION TEST
PERFORMANCE.
002337 02-14
EFFECTS OF CAFFEINE ADMINISTRATION ON FOOD AND WATER
CONSUMPTION UNDER VARIOUS EXPERIMENTAL CONDITIONS.
003049 03-04
ACUTE EFFECTS OF CAFFEINE IN NORMAL PREPUBERTAL BOYS.
003310 03-11
EFFECT OF FLURAZEPAM, PENTOBARBITAL, AND CAFFEINE ON AROUSAL
THRESHOLD.
003439 03-14
UNIT ACTIVITY IN MEDIAL THALAMUS: COMPARATIVE-EFFECTS OF
CAFFEINE AND AMPHETAMINE.
003752 04-03
CAFFEINE BLOCKS THE DELAYED K OUTWARD-CURRENT OF MOLLUSCAN
NEURONS.
003834 04-03
EFFECTS OF MORPHINE AND CAFFEINE ON ADENOSINE RELEASE FROM
RAT-CEREBRAL-CORTEX: IS CAFFEINE A MORPHINE ANTAGONIST.
003864 04-03
THE EFFECTS OF THEOPHYLLINE AND CAFFEINE ON THERMOREGULATORY
FUNCTIONS OF RATS AT DIFFERENT AMBIENT TEMPERATURES.
003907 04-03
EFFECTS OF CAFFEINE ON ANTERIOR PITUITARY AND THYROID-FUNCTION
IN THE RAT.
004014 04-03
INHIBITION BY CAFFEINE OF CALCIUM UPTAKE BY BRAIN MICROSOMAL
VESICLES.
004042 04-03

CAFFEINE-INDUCED
CAFFEINE-INDUCED AND AMINOPHYLLINE-INDUCED SEIZURES.
002689 03-03
THE BENZODIAZEPINES AND INOSINE ANTAGONIZE CAFFEINE-INDUCED
SEIZURES.
004172 04-04

CAGE
REPEATED ELECTROCONVULSIVE-SHOCK DOES NOT INCREASE THE
SUSCEPTIBILITY OF RATS TO A CAGE CONVULSANT
(ISOPROPYLBICYCLOPHOSPHATE).
001184 02-03
EFFECTS OF CHOLECYSTOKININ-OCTAPEPTIDE ON STRIATAL DOPAMINE
METABOLISM AND ON APOMORPHINE-INDUCED STEREOTYPED CAGE
CLIMBING IN MICE.
003031 03-04

CAIMAN-SCLEROPS
INFLUENCE OF MONOAMINE DEPLETING PHARMACOLOGIC-AGENTS ON
LEVELS OF ACTIVITY IN CAIMAN-SCLEROPS.
001810 02-04

CALCITONIN
ABUNDANCE AND LOCATION OF 125I SALMON CALCITONIN BINDING-SITE IN RAT-BRAIN.
001320 02-03
IMMUNOREACTIVE CALCITONIN IN CEREBROSPINAL-FLUID OF MAN.
002637 03-01
EVOKED-POTENTIAL STUDIES OF PORCINE CALCITONIN IN RABBITS.
002936 03-03
CALCITONIN: AVERSIVE-EFFECTS IN RATS?
002977 03-04
CALCITONIN: AVERSIVE-EFFECTS IN RATS?
002992 03-04

CALCIUM
CALCIUM LOCALIZATION IN THE SYMPATHETIC GANGLION OF THE BULLFROG AND EFFECTS OF CAFFEINE.
000098 01-03
EFFECT OF MORPHINE ON CALCIUM UPTAKE BY LYSED SYNAPTOSOMES.
000117 01-03
EFFECTS OF CHLORDIAZEPOXIDE ON DEPOLARIZATION-INDUCED CALCIUM INFLUX INTO SYNAPTOSOMES.
000183 01-03
(3H)ACETYLCHOLINE AND (3H)5 HYDROXYTRYPTAMINE RELEASE FROM RAT-MIDBRAIN SLICES AND THE EFFECTS OF CALCIUM AND PHENOBARBITAL.
000251 01-03
TWENTY YEARS CLINICAL THERAPEUTIC EXPERIENCE WITH CALCIUM GLUTAMATES EFFICACY.
000963 01-17
ELECTRON PROBE MICROANALYSIS OF CALCIUM AND PHOSPHORUS IN DENSE-BODIES ISOLATED FROM HUMAN PLATELETS. (UNPUBLISHED PAPER).
001014 02-01
CHANGE IN PYRUVATE-DEHYDROGENASE ACTIVITY INFLUENCE PYRUVATE SUPPORTED CALCIUM ACCUMULATION BY BRAIN MITOCHONDRIA. (UNPUBLISHED PAPER).
001147 02-03
NERVE CELL CALCIUM AS A MESSENGER FOR OPIATE AND ENDORPHIN ACTIONS.
001450 02-03
EFFECTS OF ANTICONVULSANTS AND METHOTREXATE ON CALCIUM DISPOSITION.
001840 02-05
EFFECT OF LITHIUM ON POTASSIUM AND CALCIUM IN SERUM, ERYTHOCYTES AND IN URINE.
002054 02-09
INTERACTIONS OF NARCOTICS WITH SYNAPTOSOMAL CALCIUM TRANSPORT.
002712 03-03
EFFECTS OF NEOMYCIN ON CALCIUM AND POLYPHOSPHOINOSITIDE METABOLISM OF GUINEA-PIG SYNAPTOSOMES.
002741 03-03
EFFECTS OF D AMINOLAEVULINIC-ACID, PORPHOBILINOGEN, AMINO-ACIDS AND BARBITURATES ON CALCIUM ACCUMULATION BY CULTURED NEURONS.
002859 03-03
CALCIUM ANTAGONISM OF THE INHIBITORY-EFFECTS OF FENTANYL ON THE CONTRACTION OF THE NICTITATING MEMBRANE IN CATS.
002876 03-03
THE ROLE OF CALCIUM AND DOPAMINE MEMBRANE CARRIER IN MEDIATING THE BEHAVIORAL-EFFECTS AND BIOCHEMICAL-EFFECTS OF AMPHETAMINE. (PH.D. DISSERTATION).
002996 03-04
GLOMERULAR FILTRATION RATE AND CALCIUM METABOLISM IN LONG-TERM LITHIUM TREATMENT.
003542 03-15
BRAIN AND SERUM CALCIUM CONCENTRATIONS FOLLOWING ELECTROCONVULSIVE-SHOCK OR BICUCULLINE-INDUCED CONVULSIONS IN RATS.
003736 04-03
INVOLVEMENT OF CALCIUM CHANNELS IN SHORT-TERM DESENSITIZATION OF MUSCARINIC-RECEPTOR MEDIATED CYCLIC-GMP FORMATION IN MOUSE NEUROBLASTOMA CELLS.
003783 04-03
INHIBITION OF SYNAPTOSOMAL CALCIUM UPTAKE BY ETHANOL.
003827 04-03
INFLUENCE OF CALCIUM ON NORADRENALINE RELEASE EVOKED BY 5 HYDROXYTRYPTAMINE, TYRAMINE AND POTASSIUM FROM GOAT PIAL-ARTERIES.
003925 04-03
INHIBITION BY CAFFEINE OF CALCIUM UPTAKE BY BRAIN MICROSOMAL VESICLES.
004042 04-03

CALCIUM-ACTIVATED
REGULATION OF HIPPOCAMPAL GLUTAMATE-RECEPTORS: EVIDENCE FOR THE INVOLVEMENT OF A CALCIUM-ACTIVATED PROTEASE.
001120 02-03

CALCIUM-CARBIMIDE
A COMPARATIVE REVIEW OF THE PHARMACOLOGICAL AND TOXICOLOGICAL PROPERTIES OF DISULFIRAM AND CALCIUM-CARBIMIDE.
003522 03-15

CALCIUM-CHANNEL
PHENYTOIN INHIBITION OF CYCLIC-GUANOSINE-MONOPHOSPHATE (C-GMP) ACCUMULATION IN NEUROBLASTOMA CELLS BY CALCIUM-CHANNEL BLOCKADE.
004020 04-03

CALCIUM-FLUX
PHOSPHOLIPID METABOLISM, CALCIUM-FLUX AND THE RECEPTOR-MEDIATED INDUCTION OF CHEMOTAXIS IN RABBIT NEUTROPHILS. (UNPUBLISHED PAPER).
001118 02-03

CALCIUM-IONS
RELATIONSHIP BETWEEN THE ACTIONS OF CALCIUM-IONS, OPIOIDS, AND PROSTAGLANDIN-E1 ON THE LEVEL OF CYCLIC-AMP IN NEUROBLASTOMA-X GLIOMA HYBRID CELLS.
002677 03-03

CALCIUM-SENSITIVE
CALCIUM-SENSITIVE ACCUMULATION OF NOREPINEPHRINE IN RAT-CEREBRAL-CORTEX.
002685 03-03

CALCULATIONS
CONVULSANT AND ANTICONVULSANT BARBITURATES. 1. MOLECULAR CONFORMATIONS FROM CLASSICAL POTENTIAL ENERGY CALCULATIONS.
001029 02-01

CALF
CHARACTERISTICS OF 3H FLUPENTHIXOL BINDING TO CALF BRAIN MEMBRANES.
000062 01-03
3H MIANSERIN BINDING IN CALF CAUDATE: POSSIBLE INVOLVEMENT OF SEROTONIN-RECEPTORS IN ANTIDEPRESSANT-DRUG ACTION.
000325 01-03
THE EFFECT OF TYPICAL AND ATYPICAL NEUROLEPTICS ON BINDING OF (3H)SPIROPERIDOL IN CALF CAUDATE.
003906 04-03

CALM
PSYCHOPHARMACEUTICAL-THERAPY TO CALM DRIVE, ACTIVITY, AND RESTLESSNESS IN CHILDHOOD.
002604 02-17

CALMODULIN
CALMODULIN RELEASE FROM STRIATAL MEMBRANES AFTER ACUTE AND CHRONIC TREATMENT WITH BUTACLAMOL.
001249 02-03
ROLE OF CALMODULIN IN DOPAMINERGIC TRANSMISSION. (UNPUBLISHED PAPER).
001270 02-03
MODULATION OF BETA-ADRENERGIC-RECEPTORS AND CALMODULIN FOLLOWING ACUTE AND CHRONIC-TREATMENT WITH NEUROLEPTICS.
001529 02-03
CALMODULIN: ITS ROLE IN SYNAPTIC TRANSMISSION.
003162 03-07
PHARMACOLOGICAL REGULATION OF CALMODULIN.
004052 04-03
ACUTE AND CHRONIC EFFECTS OF PSYCHOACTIVE-DRUGS ON ADRENERGIC-RECEPTORS AND CALMODULIN.
004750 04-17
MECHANISMS AND PHARMACOLOGICAL IMPLICATIONS OF ALTERING CALMODULIN ACTIVITY.
004751 04-17

CANALIZATION
CANALIZATION OF AROUSAL IN THE PREWEANLING RAT: EFFECTS OF AMPHETAMINE ON AGGREGATION WITH SURROGATE STIMULI.
002965 03-04

CANCER
ANTICONVULSANT-DRUGS AND CANCER.
000855 01-15
INTRAVENOUS LORAZEPAM TO PREVENT NAUSEA AND VOMITING ASSOCIATED WITH CANCER CHEMOTHERAPY.
003614 03-17
TREATMENT OF CANCER PAIN.
003619 03-17

CANCER-PATIENTS
SERIAL COGNITIVE TESTING IN CANCER-PATIENTS RECEIVING CHEMOTHERAPY.
000876 01-15

CANINE
REACTIVITY OF ISOLATED CANINE CEREBRAL-ARTERIES TO ADENINE-NUCLEOTIDES AND ADENOSINE.
000210 01-03
PROTECTIVE EFFECT OF PRENYLAMINE AGAINST VULNERABILITY TO VENTRICULAR FIBRILLATION IN THE NORMAL AND ISCHEMIC CANINE MYOCARDIUM.
000265 01-03
CONSISTENT UNMASKING OF DOPAMINE-INDUCED DILATION OF THE CANINE FEMORAL VASCULAR BED.
003911 04-03

CANNABIDIOL
CHRONIC ADMINISTRATION OF CANNABIDIOL TO HEALTHY VOLUNTEERS AND EPILEPTIC-PATIENTS.
000669 01-11

THE EFFECTS OF DELTA9 TETRAHYDROCANNABINOL ALONE AND IN COMBINATION WITH CANNABIDIOL ON FIXED-INTERVAL PERFORMANCE IN RHESUS-MONKEYS.
001582 02-04

METABOLIC-STUDIES AND PSYCHOPHYSIOLOGIC-STUDIES OF CANNABIDIOL HEXOBARBITAL INTERACTION.
002209 02-13

EFFECT OF CANNABIDIOL ON CYTOCHROME-P-450 AND HEXOBARBITAL SLEEP-TIME.
002675 03-03

EFFECTS OF DELTA9 TETRAHYDROCANNABINOL AND CANNABIDIOL ON SODIUM-DEPENDENT HIGH-AFFINITY CHOLINE UPTAKE IN THE RAT HIPPOCAMPUS.
003908 04-03

CHARACTERISTICS OF THE STIMULUS PRODUCED BY THE MIXTURE OF CANNABIDIOL WITH DELTA9 TETRAHYDROCANNABINOL.
004263 04-04

CANNABINOID
ISOLATION OF PSYCHOACTIVE CANNABINOID PRECURSORS FROM CANNABIS OF SOVIET PROVENIENCE GROWN IN MISSISSIPPI.
001023 02-01

SUBACUTE CANNABINOID TREATMENT: ANTICONVULSANT ACTIVITY AND WITHDRAWAL EXCITABILITY IN MICE.
001671 02-04

INTERCANNABINOID AND CANNABINOID ETHANOL INTERACTIONS AND THEIR EFFECTS ON HUMAN PERFORMANCE.
002193 02-12

A SINGLE-DOSE STUDY OF NABILONE, A SYNTHETIC CANNABINOID.
002328 02-14

DIFFERENTIAL-EFFECTS OF CANNABINOID EXPOSURE AND STRESS ON PLASMA PROLACTIN, GROWTH-HORMONE AND CORTICOSTERONE LEVELS IN MALE MICE.
002695 03-03

LEVONANTRADOL, A POTENT CANNABINOID RELATED ANALGESIC, ANTAGONIZES HALOPERIDOL-INDUCED ACTIVATION OF STRIATAL DOPAMINE SYNTHESIS.
002786 03-03

CANNABINOID-INDUCED
CANNABINOID-INDUCED ENHANCEMENT AND DEPRESSION OF CAT MONOSYNAPTIC REFLEXES.
004040 04-03

CANNABINOIDS
EFFECTS OF SYSTEMIC AND INTRAVENTRICULAR ADMINISTRATION OF CANNABINOIDS ON SCHEDULE-CONTROLLED RESPONDING IN THE SQUIRREL-MONKEY.
000354 01-04

POSTSWIM GROOMING IN MICE INHIBITED BY DOPAMINE-RECEPTOR ANTAGONISTS AND BY CANNABINOIDS.
000359 01-04

INFLUENCE OF PSYCHOACTIVE AND NONPSYCHOACTIVE CANNABINOIDS ON CELL PROLIFERATION AND MACROMOLECULAR BIOSYNTHESIS IN HUMAN CELLS.
002830 03-03

INFLUENCE OF PSYCHOACTIVE AND NONPSYCHOACTIVE CANNABINOIDS ON CHROMATIN STRUCTURE AND FUNCTION IN HUMAN CELLS.
002831 03-03

EFFECTS OF CANNABINOIDS ON CATECHOLAMINE UPTAKE AND RELEASE IN HYPOTHALAMIC AND STRIATAL SYNAPTOSOMES.
003970 04-03

CANNABINOIDS. I. BEHAVIORAL-EFFECTS.
004228 04-04

CANNABINOIDS. II. CARDIOVASCULAR-EFFECTS.
004280 04-05

CANNABIS
INTERACTIVE-EFFECTS OF NUTRITION AND CANNABIS UPON RAT PERINATAL DEVELOPMENT.
000513 01-05

ISOLATION OF PSYCHOACTIVE CANNABINOID PRECURSORS FROM CANNABIS OF SOVIET PROVENIENCE GROWN IN MISSISSIPPI.
001023 02-01

EFFECTS OF BODY-WEIGHT LEVELS ON CANNABIS SELF-INJECTION.
001801 02-04

SIMILARITIES BETWEEN CANNABIS AND OPIUM.
002554 02-17

INFLUENCE OF CANNABIS AND DELTA9 TETRAHYDROCANNABINOL ON THE BIOCHEMISTRY OF THE MALE REPRODUCTIVE ORGANS.
002686 03-03

CANNABIS-SATIVA
CANNABIS-SATIVA: EFFECTS ON BRAIN FUNCTION AND ULTRASTRUCTURE IN RHESUS-MONKEYS.
002747 03-03

CANNED
TYRAMINE CONTENT OF CANNED AND PACKET SOUPS.
002394 02-15

CANNULA
QUICKLY-MADE CANNULA FOR REPEATED CEREBROSPINAL-FLUID SAMPLING IN RATS.
001879 02-06

CANTOR
TREATMENT OF ASTHENO-DEPRESSIVE-DISORDERS WITH MINAPRINE (CANTOR). MULTICENTER-STUDY OF 248 CASES EVALUATED WITH THE FATIGUE STUDY GROUPS NO. 4 CLINICAL-SCALE.
001980 02-09

CAPACITIES
CAPACITIES OF ATTENTION, STRESS-RESISTANCE, AND SLOW CEREBRAL POTENTIALS: EFFECTS OF CARPIPRAMINE ON CONTINGENT NEGATIVE VARIATION WAVES AND P-300.
003451 03-14

CAPACITY
ON THE CAPACITY OF PRESYNAPTIC ALPHA-RECEPTORS TO MODULATE NOREPINEPHRINE RELEASE FROM SLICES OF RAT NEOCORTEX AND THE AFFINITY OF SOME AGONISTS AND ANTAGONISTS FOR THESE RECEPTORS.
000323 01-03

SWIMMING CAPACITY OF MICE AFTER PROLONGED TREATMENT WITH PSYCHOSTIMULANTS: II. EFFECT OF METHAMPHETAMINE ON SWIMMING PERFORMANCE AND AVAILABILITY OF METABOLIC SUBSTRATES.
001613 02-04

EFFECTS OF PSYCHOPHARMACEUTICALS ON DRIVING CAPACITY.
003453 03-14

CAPILLARIES
DECARBOXYLATION OF EXOGENOUS L-DOPA IN RAT STRIATUM AFTER LESIONS OF THE DOPAMINERGIC NIGROSTRIATAL NEURONS: THE ROLE OF STRIATAL CAPILLARIES.
000202 01-03

CAPILLARY
LONG-TERM ANTIDEPRESSANT TREATMENT: ALTERATIONS IN CEREBRAL CAPILLARY PERMEABILITY.
000239 01-03

PHENYTOIN CONCENTRATIONS IN VENOUS VERSUS CAPILLARY BLOOD OF GERIATRIC-PATIENTS.
003381 03-11

THE EFFECT OF DIBENZAPINES (TRICYCLIC-ANTIDEPRESSANTS) ON CEREBRAL CAPILLARY PERMEABILITY IN THE RAT IN VIVO.
003974 04-03

CAPSAICIN
NEUROPHYSIOLOGICAL-EFFECTS AND THERMOREGULATORY-EFFECTS OF CAPSAICIN.
001421 02-03

SELECTIVE NEUROTOXIC-ACTION OF CAPSAICIN ON GLOMERULAR C-TYPE TERMINALS IN RAT SUBSTANTIA-GELATINOSA.
003143 03-06

INTRANIGRAL INJECTION OF CAPSAICIN ENHANCES MOTOR-ACTIVITY AND DEPLETES NIGRAL 5 HYDROXYTRYPTAMINE BUT NOT SUBSTANCE-P.
004100 04-04

A REEVALUATION OF THE NEUROCHEMICAL-EFFECTS AND ANTINOCICEPTIVE-EFFECTS OF INTRATHECAL CAPSAICIN IN THE RAT.
004184 04-04

CAPSULE
BIOAVAILABILITY OF SULPIRIDE TABLET AND CAPSULE IN DOGS.
001101 02-03

CAPTOPRIL
CAPTOPRIL GIVEN INTRACEREBROVENTRICULARLY, SUBCUTANEOUSLY OR BY GAVAGE INHIBITS ANGIOTENSIN CONVERTING ENZYME ACTIVITY IN THE RAT-BRAIN.
001614 02-04

POTENTIATION OF THE MORPHINE-INDUCED RESPIRATORY RATE DEPRESSION BY CAPTOPRIL.
004275 04-05

CAPTURE
A METHOD FOR MEASUREMENT OF TRANYLCYPROMINE IN RAT-BRAIN REGIONS USING GAS-CHROMATOGRAPHY WITH ELECTRON CAPTURE DETECTION.
003137 03-06

CARBACHOL
PARASYMPATHOMIMETIC-INFLUENCE OF CARBACHOL ON LOCAL CEREBRAL BLOOD FLOW IN THE RABBIT BY A DIRECT VASODILATOR ACTION AND AN INHIBITION OF THE SYMPATHETIC MEDIATED VASOCONSTRICTION.
001109 02-03

FUNCTIONAL ORGANIZATION OF THE CAUDATE-NUCLEUS AFTER ADMINISTRATION OF CARBACHOL.
001495 02-03

EFFECT OF MEDIAN RAPHE STIMULATION ON HIPPOCAMPAL SEIZURE DISCHARGE INDUCED BY CARBACHOL IN THE RABBIT.
003951 04-03

CARBACHOL-INDUCED
STUDIES OF CARBACHOL-INDUCED WET-DOG-SHAKE BEHAVIOR IN RATS.
004241 04-04

CARBAMAZEPINE
PHARMACOKINETICS OF CARBAMAZEPINE IN THE DOG.
000096 01-03

CARBAMAZEPINE-EPOXIDE DETERMINED BY EMIT CARBAMAZEPINE REAGENT.
000533 01-06

THE AUTOINDUCTION OF CARBAMAZEPINE DURING LONG-TERM THERAPY.
000785 01-13

CORRELATION BETWEEN DAILY FLUCTUATIONS OF CARBAMAZEPINE SERUM LEVELS AND INTERMITTENT SIDE-EFFECTS.
000851 01-15

CARBAMAZEPINE INTOXICATION DUE TO TRIACETYLOLEANDOMYCIN ADMINISTRATION IN EPILEPTIC-PATIENTS.
000873 01-15

VALUE OF SALIVA SAMPLES IN MONITORING CARBAMAZEPINE CONCENTRATIONS IN EPILEPTIC-PATIENTS.
000903 01-16

INFLUENCE OF CARBAMAZEPINE ON THALAMOCORTICAL AND HIPPOCAMPOCORTICAL SELF-SUSTAINED AFTERDISCHARGES IN RATS.
001356 02-03

SENSITIZATION AND OSCILLATION FOLLOWING REPEATED STIMULATION: RELATIONSHIP TO AFFECTIVE-ILLNESS AND ITS TREATMENT WITH LITHIUM AND CARBAMAZEPINE.
002031 02-09

CARBAMAZEPINE THERAPY IN TRIGEMINAL-NEURALGIA: CLINICAL-EFFECTS IN RELATION TO PLASMA CONCENTRATION.
002181 02-11

SALIVARY IMMUNOGLOBULIN CONCENTRATIONS IN PATIENTS WITH EPILEPSY TREATED WITH CARBAMAZEPINE.
002234 02-13

BIOCHEMICAL-EVIDENCE FOR OSTEOMALACIA WITH CARBAMAZEPINE THERAPY.
002445 02-15

A DOUBLE-BLIND, PLACEBO-CONTROLLED, CROSS-OVER TRIAL OF CARBAMAZEPINE IN OVERACTIVE, SEVERELY MENTALLY-HANDICAPPED PATIENTS.
003365 03-11

A PRELIMINARY DOUBLE-BLIND STUDY ON THE EFFICACY OF CARBAMAZEPINE IN PROPHYLAXIS OF MANIC-DEPRESSIVE-ILLNESS.
004388 04-09

MEASUREMENTS OF NERVE CONDUCTION VELOCITY DURING DECREASING TOXIC DIPHENYLHYDANTOIN LEVELS AND THE BEGINNING OF CARBAMAZEPINE MEDICATION: A CLINICAL NEUROPHYSIOLOGICAL REPORT.
004441 04-11

INFLUENCE OF CARBAMAZEPINE ON SERUM THYROXINE AND TRIIODOTHYRONINE IN PATIENTS WITH EPILEPSY.
004488 04-11

CONCENTRATIONS AND KINETICS OF CARBAMAZEPINE IN WHOLE SALIVA, PAROTID SALIVA, SERUM ULTRAFILTRATE, AND SERUM.
004545 04-13

CARBAMAZEPINE-EPOXIDE
CARBAMAZEPINE-EPOXIDE DETERMINED BY EMIT CARBAMAZEPINE REAGENT.
000533 01-06

CARBAMAZEPINE-ETHOSUXIMIDE
KINETICS OF A CARBAMAZEPINE-ETHOSUXIMIDE INTERACTION.
004558 04-13

CARBAMAZEPINE-INDUCED
REVERSAL BY PHENYTOIN OF CARBAMAZEPINE-INDUCED WATER INTOXICATION: A PHARMACOKINETIC-INTERACTION.
000783 01-13

CARBAMAZEPINE-INDUCED OROFACIAL DYSKINESIA.
002415 02-15

CARBIDINE
THE EFFECT OF CARBIDINE ON DOPAMINE TURNOVER IN THE CORPUS-STRIATUM OF THE BRAINS OF RATS.
001352 02-03

CARBIDOPA
THE TREATMENT OF PARKINSONS-DISEASE USING A COMBINATION OF L-DOPA AND DECARBOXYLASE INHIBITORS (CARBIDOPA, BENSERASIDE). A CLINICAL AND BIOCHEMICAL COMPARATIVE INVESTIGATION.
000712 01-11

TREATMENT OF MYOCLONUS WITH L 5 HYDROXYTRYPTOPHAN AND CARBIDOPA: CLINICAL, ELECTROPHYSIOLOGICAL, AND BIOCHEMICAL-OBSERVATIONS.
002180 02-11

INCREASED RATIO OF CARBIDOPA TO LEVODOPA IN TREATMENT OF PARKINSONS-DISEASE.
002182 02-11

EFFECTS OF BENSERAZIDE AND CARBIDOPA ON THE METABOLISM OF L TRYPTOPHAN BY ISOLATED RAT LIVER CELLS.
002899 03-03

ELECTRORETINOGRAPHY (ERG) AS A TOOL OF INVESTIGATION IN HUMAN PSYCHOPHARMACOLOGY. ELECTRORETINOGRAPHIC-CHANGES INDUCED BY A COMBINATION OF CARBIDOPA AND LEVODOPA.
004507 04-13

ELECTROENCEPHALOGRAPHIC CHANGE IN PARKINSONIAN-PATIENTS TREATED WITH LEVODOPA CARBIDOPA.
004557 04-13

CARBOHYDRATE
ACUTE CHANGES IN BRAIN TRYPTOPHAN AND SEROTONIN FOLLOWING CARBOHYDRATE OR PROTEIN INGESTION BY DIABETIC RATS. (UNPUBLISHED PAPER).
000060 01-03

CARBOLINE-3-CARBOXYLATES
BETA CARBOLINE-3-CARBOXYLATES AND BENZODIAZEPINE-RECEPTORS.
002676 03-03

CARBOLINES
BENZODIAZEPINE ANTAGONISM BY HARMANE AND OTHER BETA CARBOLINES IN VITRO AND IN VIVO.
004211 04-04

CARBOXAMIDOSTRYCHNINE
INHIBITION OF BRAIN SYNAPTOSOMAL UPTAKE OF CHOLINE BY SOME 2 CARBOXAMIDOSTRYCHNINE DERIVATIVES WITH MUSCLE-RELAXANT PROPERTIES.
000084 01-03

CARBOXYMETHYLATION
ENZYMATIC CARBOXYMETHYLATION OF THE NICOTINIC ACETYLCHOLINE-RECEPTOR. (UNPUBLISHED PAPER).
001318 02-03

CARDIAC
COMPARISON OF MIANSERIN WITH DESIPRAMINE, MAPROTILINE AND PHENTOLAMINE ON CARDIAC PRESYNAPTIC AND VASCULAR POSTSYNAPTIC ALPHA-ADRENOCEPTORS AND NORADRENALINE REUPTAKE IN PITHED NORMOTENSIVE-RATS.
000044 01-03

THE REGULATION OF CARDIAC MUSCARINIC CHOLINERGIC-RECEPTORS BY ISOPROTERENOL.
001441 02-03

ONTOGENY OF MAMMALIAN CARDIAC ALPHA1-ADRENERGIC-RECEPTORS.
001545 02-03

AMITRIPTYLINE PROVIDES LONG-LASTING IMMUNIZATION AGAINST SUDDEN CARDIAC DEATH FROM COCAINE.
003122 03-05

BETA-ADRENERGIC INFLUENCE ON CARDIAC DYNAMICS DURING SHOCK-AVOIDANCE IN DOGS.
003813 04-03

CARDIAC-MUSCLE
POTENTIATION OF THE EFFECTS OF ADENOSINE ON ISOLATED CARDIAC-MUSCLE AND SMOOTH-MUSCLE BY DIAZEPAM.
004266 04-05

CARDIOLOGICAL
PLASMA NOMIFENSINE CONCENTRATION: CARDIOLOGICAL EFFECTS AND CLINICAL-RESPONSE.
004639 04-15

CARDIOLOGY
INTERFACES OF PSYCHOPHARMACOLOGY AND CARDIOLOGY -- PART TWO.
003529 03-15

INTERFACES OF PSYCHOPHARMACOLOGY AND CARDIOLOGY -- PART ONE.
003530 03-15

CARDIOMYOPATHY
INTRAVENOUS QUINIDINE IN CONGESTIVE CARDIOMYOPATHY.
003352 03-11

CARDIOTOXICITY
COMPARATIVE-STUDY OF THE CARDIOTOXICITY OF AMITRIPTYLINE AND MAPROTILINE IN DEPRESSIVE-PATIENTS.
000595 01-09

CARDIOTOXICITY OF ANTIDEPRESSANTS.
001843 02-05

CARDIOTOXICITY OF ANTIDEPRESSANT-DRUGS.
004597 04-15

CARDIOVASCULAR
CARDIOVASCULAR RESPONSE TO THE INTERACTION OF ETHANOL AND SOME BENZODIAZEPINES IN RATS.
000332 01-03

EFFECTS OF CHRONIC ADMINISTRATION OF DELTA9 TETRAHYDROCANNABINOL ON THE CARDIOVASCULAR SYSTEM, AND PRESSOR AND BEHAVIORAL-RESPONSES TO BRAIN-STIMULATION IN FREELY-MOVING-RATS.
000417 01-04

A COMPARISON OF THE CARDIOVASCULAR EFFECTS OF HALOPERIDOL, THIORIDAZINE AND CHLORPROMAZINE-HCL.
000512 01-05

A CASE OF CARDIOVASCULAR COLLAPSE DURING LITHIUM-CARBONATE THERAPY.
000860 01-15

CARDIOVASCULAR EFFECTS OF NORTRIPTYLINE IN GERIATRIC-PATIENTS.
000882 01-15

DESIPRAMINE: CARDIOVASCULAR EFFECTS AND PLASMA LEVELS.
000884 01-15

EFFECT OF GABA AGONIST AND ANTAGONISTS ON CARDIOVASCULAR AND SYMPATHETIC RESPONSES IN SHR AND WKY RATS. (UNPUBLISHED PAPER).
001224 02-03

HEXAMETHONIUM MODIFICATION OF CARDIOVASCULAR ADJUSTMENTS DURING COMBINED STATIC DYNAMIC ARM EXERCISE IN MONKEYS.
001242 02-03

CENTRALLY INDUCED CARDIOVASCULAR AND SYMPATHETIC-NERVE RESPONSES TO BRADYKININ IN RATS.
003099 03-04

Subject Index

SENSORY PROCESSING, CARDIOVASCULAR REACTIVITY, AND THE TYPE A CORONARY-PRONE BEHAVIOR PATTERN.
003405 03-13

HISTAMINE AS A PUNISHER IN SQUIRREL-MONKEYS: EFFECTS OF PENTOBARBITAL, CHLORDIAZEPOXIDE AND H1-RECEPTOR AND H2-RECEPTOR ANTAGONISTS ON BEHAVIOR AND CARDIOVASCULAR RESPONSE.
004119 04-04

CARDIOVASCULAR-EFFECTS
CARDIOVASCULAR-EFFECTS OF AMITRIPTYLINE, MIANSERIN AND ZIMELIDINE IN DEPRESSED-PATIENTS.
002215 02-13

CARDIOVASCULAR-EFFECTS OF THERAPEUTIC DOSES OF TRICYCLIC-ANTIDEPRESSANTS: IMPORTANCE OF BLOOD LEVEL MONITORING.
002456 02-15

CARDIOVASCULAR-EFFECTS OF MIANSERIN AND AMITRIPTYLINE IN HEALTHY VOLUNTEERS.
002469 02-15

TYRAMINE PRESSOR TEST AND CARDIOVASCULAR-EFFECTS OF CHLORIMIPRAMINE AND NORTRIPTYLINE IN HEALTHY VOLUNTEERS.
003428 03-13

CARDIOVASCULAR-EFFECTS OF MIANSERIN — A COMPARATIVE-STUDY WITH AMITRIPTYLINE AND A PLACEBO IN HEALTHY SUBJECTS.
003503 03-15

POSSIBLE ROLE OF AN ENDOGENOUS OPIATE IN THE CARDIOVASCULAR-EFFECTS OF CENTRAL ALPHA-ADRENOCEPTOR STIMULATION IN SPONTANEOUSLY HYPERTENSIVE-RATS.
003791 04-03

CENTRAL CARDIOVASCULAR-EFFECTS AND BIOCHEMICAL-EFFECTS OF BACLOFEN IN THE CONSCIOUS RAT.
003965 04-03

CANNABINOIDS. II. CARDIOVASCULAR-EFFECTS.
004280 04-05

CARDIOVASCULAR-PHARMACOLOGY
THE NEUROVASCULAR-PHARMACOLOGY AND CARDIOVASCULAR-PHARMACOLOGY OF RS-51324, A POTENTIAL ANTIDEPRESSANT.
001091 02-02

CARDIOVASCULAR-SYSTEM
EFFECTS OF DELTA9 TETRAHYDROCANNABINOL ON THE CARDIOVASCULAR-SYSTEM, AND PRESSOR AND BEHAVIORAL-RESPONSES TO BRAIN-STIMULATION IN RATS.
001681 02-04

CARE
HOSPITAL AND OUTPATIENT CARE FOR PSYCHOTIC-PATIENTS DURING THE LAST THREE DECADES: SUBSEQUENT HOSPITAL AND OUTPATIENT TREATMENT OF PSYCHOTIC-PATIENTS HOSPITALIZED FOR THE FIRST TIME IN 1949-50, 1959-60 OR 1969-70.
000571 01-08

OUTPATIENT CARE OF DEPRESSIVE-PATIENTS WITH MIANSERIN.
002041 02-09

PSYCHOPHARMACOLOGY — AN AREA OF RESEARCH TO IMPROVE MENTAL-HEALTH CARE.
002586 02-17

THE MEDICATION SEMINAR AND PRIMARY CARE EDUCATION.
003592 03-17

CARNITINE
THE UPTAKE OF CARNITINE BY SLICES OF RAT-CEREBRAL-CORTEX.
003853 04-03

CAROTID
INHIBITION OF VASOPRESSIN RELEASE TO CAROTID OCCLUSION BY GAMMA AMINOBUTYRIC-ACID AND GLYCINE.
002715 03-03

CARP
STEREOSPECIFIC INHIBITION OF DOPAMINE-SENSITIVE ADENYLATE-CYCLASE IN CARP RETINA BY THE ENANTIOMERS OF (/-) 1 CYCLOPROPYLMETHYL TRIFLUOROMETHYLTHIODIBENZOCYCLOHEPTENYLIDENEPIPERIDINE.
003706 04-02

DOPAMINERGIC MECHANISMS IN THE TELEOST RETINA. II. FACTORS AFFECTING THE ACCUMULATION OF CYCLIC-AMP IN PIECES OF INTACT CARP RETINA.
003776 04-03

DOPAMINERGIC MECHANISMS IN THE TELEOST RETINA. I. DOPAMINE-SENSITIVE ADENYLATE-CYCLASE IN HOMOGENATES OF CARP RETINA; EFFECTS OF AGONISTS, ANTAGONISTS AND ERGOTS.
004051 04-03

CARPIPRAMINE
THE INTEREST OF THE STIMULATING EFFECT OF CARPIPRAMINE IN PSYCHOSOMATIC-MEDICINE.
002061 02-10

PERSPECTIVES ON PRAZINIL (CARPIPRAMINE): A DISINHIBITING-AGENT WITH NO NEUROLEPTIC ACTIVITY. A REVIEW OF 38 CASES.
003149 03-07

CARPIPRAMINE: A DISINHIBITORY DRUG COMPOUND IN CHRONIC SCHIZOPHRENIA.
003192 03-08

CAPACITIES OF ATTENTION, STRESS-RESISTANCE, AND SLOW CEREBRAL POTENTIALS: EFFECTS OF CARPIPRAMINE ON CONTINGENT NEGATIVE VARIATION WAVES AND P-300.
003451 03-14

5

THREE CASES OF UNIPOLAR DELUSIONAL DEPRESSION RESPONSIVE TO L-DOPA.
000628 01-09

REVIEW OF 38 CASES OF SUBACUTE SCLEROSING PANENCEPHALITIS: EFFECT OF AMANTADINE ON THE NATURAL COURSE OF THE DISEASE.
000718 01-11

TARDIVE-DYSKINESIAS (OBSERVATIONS CONCERNING THREE CASES).
000861 01-15

AGITATION, DISORIENTATION, AND HALLUCINATIONS IN PATIENTS ON CIMETIDINE: A REPORT OF THREE CASES AND LITERATURE REVIEW.
000896 01-15

THE DEVELOPMENT OF PROGENY IN CASES OF ANTENATAL EXPOSURE TO PHENAZEPAM.
001854 02-05

TREATMENT OF ASTHENO-DEPRESSIVE-DISORDERS WITH MINAPRINE (CANTOR). MULTICENTER-STUDY OF 248 CASES EVALUATED WITH THE FATIGUE STUDY GROUPS NO. 4 CLINICAL-SCALE.
001980 02-09

BIPOLAR AFFECTIVE-PSYCHOSIS WITH ONSET BEFORE AGE 16 YEARS: REPORT OF 10 CASES.
002001 02-09

MINAPRINE IN SEVERE PSYCHOPATHOLOGY: STUDY OF 20 CASES.
002135 02-11

MEDICAL PSYCHOLOGICAL AND COMBINED THERAPY IN THE CASES OF ENURESIS: A COMPARATIVE-STUDY.
002175 02-11

PERSPECTIVES ON PRAZINIL (CARPIPRAMINE): A DISINHIBITING-AGENT WITH NO NEUROLEPTIC ACTIVITY. A REVIEW OF 38 CASES.
003149 03-07

THE TREATMENT OF DEPRESSION USING CLOMIPRAMINE IN GENERAL-MEDICAL-PRACTICE: 48 CASES TREATED ON AN OUTPATIENT BASIS.
003268 03-09

SEXUAL-DIFFICULTIES AMONG CONVALESCING ALCOHOLICS: INTEREST IN PRAZEPAM TREATMENT IN 30 CASES.
003296 03-11

EXCESSIVE PLASMA CONCENTRATIONS OF TRICYCLIC-ANTIDEPRESSANTS RESULTING FROM USUAL DOSES: A REPORT OF SIX CASES.
003479 03-15

EXCEPTIONAL CASES OF DEATH CAUSED BY TRICYCLIC-ANTIDEPRESSANT AGENTS.
003490 03-15

SEVERE WITHDRAWAL-SYNDROME AFTER CESSATION OF BENZODIAZEPINE TREATMENT: SIX CLINICAL CASES.
003505 03-15

AGE-SPECIFIC DOSES OF LORMETAZEPAM AS A NIGHT SEDATIVE IN CASES OF CHRONIC SLEEP-DISTURBANCE.
004309 04-07

NEUROLOGICAL TOLERANCE OF LITHIUM AND PSYCHOTROPIC-DRUGS IN COMBINATION: 265 CASES.
004594 04-15

THE TWO SURVIVAL CASES OF ALPHA-PATTERN COMA CAUSED BY LARGE AMOUNTS OF HYPNOTICA AND NEUROLEPTICA.
004608 04-15

TWO CASES OF FORM-FRUSTE-DU-SYNDROME-MALIN WITH HIGH-LEVELS OF SERUM CPK.
004636 04-15

CASOMORPHINS
OPIOID ACTIVITIES OF BETA CASOMORPHINS.
003740 04-03

CASTRATED
MORPHINE EXERTS TESTOSTERONE-LIKE EFFECTS IN THE HYPOTHALAMUS OF THE CASTRATED MALE RAT.
000051 01-03

EFFECT OF AMINOOXYACETIC-ACID AND BICUCULLINE ON PROLACTIN RELEASE IN CASTRATED MALE RATS.
001194 02-03

SUPPRESSIVE EFFECT OF MORPHINE ON SERUM GONADOTROPIN LEVELS IN CASTRATED RATS.
001393 02-03

CAT
THE INFLUENCE OF BENZOCTAMINE ON DOPAMINE AND NOREPINEPHRINE CONTENTS OF THE SUBSTANTIA-NIGRA AND ON THE MUSCLE STRETCH REFLEX OF THE CAT.
000054 01-03

EFFECTS OF ALPHA CHLORALOSE ON THE ACTIVITY OF THE NIGROSTRIATAL DOPAMINERGIC SYSTEM IN THE CAT.
000217 01-03

EFFECTS OF ENKEPHALIN ANALOGUE AND NALOXONE ON CAT SPINAL-CORD DORSAL ROOT POTENTIALS.
000236 01-03

EFFECTS OF CENTRALLY-ADMINISTERED PENTAZOCINE AND ETHYLKETOCYCLAZOCINE ON THERMOREGULATION IN THE CAT.
000361 01-04

THE EFFECTS OF LSD AND SOME ANALOGUES ON THE RESPONSES OF SINGLE CORTICAL NEURONS OF THE CAT TO OPTICAL-STIMULATION.
000738 01-12

EVOKED-POTENTIAL CHANGES IN THE SUPERIOR-COLLICULUS PARALLEL THE LESION-INDUCED DEVELOPMENT OF GROOMING REFLEXES IN THE CAT. (PH.D. DISSERTATION).
001179 02-03

DEPRESSION AND FACILITATION OF SYNAPTIC RESPONSES IN CAT DORSAL-HORN BY SUBSTANCE-P ADMINISTERED INTO SUBSTANTIA-GELATINOSA.
001191 02-03

MORPHINE AND SUPRASPINAL INHIBITION OF SPINAL NEURONES: EVIDENCE THAT MORPHINE DECREASES TONIC DESCENDING INHIBITION IN THE ANESTHETIZED CAT.
001203 02-03

THE QUANTITATIVE MEASUREMENT OF CHANGES IN EEG FREQUENCY SPECTRA PRODUCED IN THE CAT BY SEDATIVE HYPNOTICS AND NEUROLEPTICS.
001220 02-03

METHYLDOPA PRODUCES CENTRAL INHIBITION OF PARASYMPATHETIC-ACTIVITY IN THE CAT.
001321 02-03

DIRECT EVIDENCE AGAINST ACETYLCHOLINE AS THE DILATOR TRANSMITTER IN THE CAT CEREBRAL-ARTERY.
001336 02-03

INDIRECT ADRENERGIC EFFECT OF HISTAMINE IN CAT CEREBRAL-ARTERIES.
001355 02-03

DOPAMINE-BETA-HYDROXYLASE ACTIVITY AND NORADRENALINE CONTENT IN PIAL-ARTERIES OF CAT AND GOAT.
001357 02-03

ADRENERGIC MODULATION OF THE HYPOTHALAMIC CHOLINERGIC MECHANISM IN THE CONTROL OF EMOTIONAL DEFENSIVE-BEHAVIOR IN THE CAT.
001761 02-04

IMMUNOHISTOCHEMICAL LOCALIZATION OF LEUCINE-ENKEPHALIN IN THE SPINAL-CORD OF THE CAT; ENKEPHALIN-CONTAINING MARGINAL NEURONS AND PAIN MODULATION.
002638 03-01

DIFFERENTIATION OF KAINATE AND QUISQUALATE-RECEPTORS IN THE CAT SPINAL-CORD BY SELECTIVE ANTAGONISMS WITH GAMMA D(AND L) GLUTAMYLGLYCINE.
002696 03-03

PRESYNAPTIC REGULATION OF THE RELEASE OF CATECHOLAMINES IN THE CAT HYPOTHALAMUS.
002703 03-03

THE PRESYNAPTIC STIMULATING EFFECT OF ACETYLCHOLINE ON DOPAMINE RELEASE IS SUPPRESSED DURING ACTIVATION OF NIGROSTRIATAL DOPAMINERGIC NEURONS IN THE CAT.
002733 03-03

METHYSERGIDE AND SUPRASPINAL INHIBITION OF THE SPINAL TRANSMISSION OF NOCICEPTIVE INFORMATION IN THE ANESTHETIZED CAT.
002740 03-03

POTENTIATION OF L GLUTAMATE AND L ASPARTATE EXCITATION OF CAT SPINAL NEURONES BY THE STEREOISOMERS OF THREO-3-HYDROXYASPARTATE.
002768 03-03

THE INTERACTION BETWEEN BARBITURATE ANESTHETICS AND EXCITATORY AMINO-ACID RESPONSES ON CAT SPINAL NEURONES.
002799 03-03

COCAINE AND AMPHETAMINE ANTAGONIZE THE DECREASE OF NORADRENERGIC NEUROTRANSMISSION ELICITED BY OXYMETAZOLINE BUT POTENTIATE THE INHIBITION BY ALPHA METHYLNOREPINEPHRINE IN THE PERFUSED CAT SPLEEN.
002801 03-03

L HISTIDINE: EFFECTS ON SENSITIVITY OF CAT SPINAL NEURONES TO AMINO-ACIDS.
002808 03-03

ANTINOCICEPTIVE ACTION OF MORPHINE AND PENTAZOCINE ON UNIT ACTIVITY IN THE NUCLEUS-CENTRALIS-LATERALIS, NUCLEUS-VENTRALIS-LATERALIS AND NEARBY STRUCTURES OF THE CAT.
002837 03-03

VOLTAGE CLAMP STUDY OF CAT SPINAL MOTONEURONS DURING STRYCHNINE-INDUCED SEIZURES.
002886 03-03

DIFFERENTIAL-EFFECTS OF SHORT-TERM AND LONG-TERM LITHIUM ON TRYPTOPHAN UPTAKE AND SEROTONERGIC FUNCTION IN CAT BRAIN.
002911 03-03

EFFECTS OF REPEATED ADMINISTRATIONS OF DIHYDROERGOTOXINE (REDERGINE) ON THE SLEEP-WAKEFULNESS CYCLE IN THE CAT.
003703 04-02

PHARMACOLOGICAL DIFFERENTIATION OF PRESYNAPTIC INHIBITORY ALPHA-ADRENOCEPTORS AND OPIATE-RECEPTORS IN THE CAT NICTITATING MEMBRANE.
003777 04-03

THE EFFECT OF NOOTROPIL ON THE TRANSCALLOSAL AND PRIMARY EVOKED-RESPONSES OF THE CAT CEREBRAL-CORTEX.
003780 04-03

INFLUENCE OF THE DOPAMINERGIC AGONISTS BROMOCRIPTINE, PIRIBEDIL AND NOMIFENSINE ON THE SYMPATHETIC NEURAL TRANSMISSION IN THE NICTITATING MEMBRANE OF THE CAT.
003822 04-03

AUTORADIOGRAPHIC STUDIES ON DISTRIBUTION OF L-3,4 DIHYDROXYPHENYLALANINE (L-DOPA) 14C AND L 5 HYDROXYTRYPTOPHAN (L 5 HTP) 14C IN THE CAT BRAIN.
003941 04-03

IN VIVO EVIDENCE FOR GABAERGIC CONTROL OF SEROTONIN RELEASE IN THE CAT SUBSTANTIA-NIGRA.
004011 04-03

CANNABINOID-INDUCED ENHANCEMENT AND DEPRESSION OF CAT MONOSYNAPTIC REFLEXES.
004040 04-03

NALOXONE SUPPRESSES FOOD/WATER CONSUMPTION IN THE DEPRIVED CAT.
004114 04-04

SELECTIVE EFFECT OF ETHANOL ON THE VESTIBULAR NUCLEUS NEURONS IN THE CAT.
004139 04-04

POSSIBLE MUSCARINIC CHOLINERGIC MEDIATION OF PATTERNED AGGRESSIVE REFLEXES IN THE CAT.
004153 04-04

AMMONIA AND DISINHIBITION IN CAT MOTOR-CORTEX BY AMMONIUM-ACETATE, MONOFLUOROACETATE AND INSULIN-INDUCED HYPOGLYCEMIA.
004276 04-05

THE SIMULTANEOUS INFUSION OF DRUGS VIA THE LEFT AND RIGHT VERTEBRAL-ARTERY OF THE CAT; A MODIFIED ANIMAL-MODEL FOR THE STUDY OF POSSIBLE CENTRAL-ACTIONS OF DRUGS UPON THE LOWER BRAINSTEM.
004297 04-06

CATABOLISM
DECREASED CEREBRAL CATABOLISM OF (3H)HISTAMINE IN VIVO AFTER S ADENOSYLMETHIONINE ADMINISTRATION
002883 03-03

PROPERTIES OF THE OPTICAL-ISOMERS AND METABOLITES OF KETAMINE ON THE HIGH-AFFINITY TRANSPORT AND CATABOLISM OF MONOAMINES.
004009 04-03

CATALEPSY
EFFECTS OF DOPAMINERGIC AND CHOLINERGIC-DRUGS, NALOXONE AND L PROLYL-LEUCYL-GLYCINAMIDE ON LSD-INDUCED CATALEPSY.
000360 01-04

MORPHINE VERSUS HALOPERIDOL CATALEPSY IN THE RAT: A BEHAVIORAL-ANALYSIS OF POSTURAL SUPPORT MECHANISMS.
000376 01-04

FAILURE OF NALOXONE TO REVERSE CATALEPSY ASSOCIATED WITH SCHIZOPHRENIA: A CASE-REPORT.
000560 01-08

STRESS-INDUCED FACILITATION OF OPIATE CATALEPSY IN THE RAT.
001680 02-04

EFFECT OF QUIPAZINE AND FLUOXETINE ON ANALGESIC-INDUCED CATALEPSY AND ANTINOCICEPTION IN THE RAT.
001709 02-04

BIPHASIC-EFFECTS OF DIRECT, BUT NOT INDIRECT, GABAMIMETICS AND ANTAGONISTS ON HALOPERIDOL-INDUCED CATALEPSY.
001826 02-04

INCREASED AMPHETAMINE STEREOTYPY AND LONGER HALOPERIDOL CATALEPSY IN SPONTANEOUSLY HYPERTENSIVE-RATS.
002891 03-03

INVOLVEMENT OF CAUDATE-NUCLEUS, AMYGDALA OR RETICULAR FORMATION IN NEUROLEPTIC AND NARCOTIC CATALEPSY.
002986 03-04

BETA PHENYLETHYLAMINE REVERSAL OF CHLORPROMAZINE-INDUCED ACTIVATION OF STRIATAL TYROSINE-HYDROXYLASE AND CATALEPSY.
004018 04-03

EFFECTS OF NARCOTIC ANTAGONISTS ON L-DOPA REVERSAL OF RESERPINE-INDUCED CATALEPSY AND BLEPHAROPTOSIS IN MICE.
004186 04-04

BETA ENDORPHIN: CENTRAL SITES OF ANALGESIA, CATALEPSY AND BODY-TEMPERATURE CHANGES IN RATS.
004238 04-04

CATALEPTIC-EFFECT
PLASMA AND BRAIN LEVELS OF DELTA6 THC AND SEVEN MONOOXYGENATED METABOLITES CORRELATED TO THE CATALEPTIC-EFFECT IN THE MOUSE.
001737 02-04

CATALEPTIC-EFFECTS
DIFFERENTIAL REVERSAL BY SCOPOLAMINE AND THIP OF THE ANTISTEREOTYPIC AND CATALEPTIC-EFFECTS OF NEUROLEPTICS.
002948 03-04

THE EFFECTS OF PEPTIDES ON TOLERANCE TO THE CATALEPTIC-EFFECTS AND HYPOTHERMIC-EFFECTS OF MORPHINE IN THE RAT.
004072 04-04

CATALYTIC
COMT-A AND COMT-B: CATALYTIC DIFFERENCES AND ROLE OF DISULFIDE BONDS.
003927 04-03

CATAPLEXY
CHOLINERGIC MECHANISMS AND CATAPLEXY IN DOGS.
000374 01-04

CATATONIA
EPIDURAL MORPHINE-INDUCED CATATONIA.
002400 02-15

A NEUROANATOMICAL-STUDY OF ANALGESIA AND CATATONIA INDUCED BY ETORPHINE IN THE RAT. (PH.D. DISSERTATION).
003102 03-04

MODIFICATION OF DRUG-INDUCED CATATONIA AND TREMORS BY QUIPAZINE IN RATS AND MICE.
004164 04-04

CATATONIA-SYNDROME
DISULFIRAM ENCEPHALOPATHY AS A CAUSE OF THE CATATONIA-SYNDROME.
000894 01-15

CATCH-UP
ACTIVITY AND CATCH-UP GROWTH IN HYPOTHYROID RATS.
004190 04-04

CATECHOL-O-METHYLTRANSFERASE
THE ACTIVITY OF ERYTHROCYTE CATECHOL-O-METHYLTRANSFERASE IN ENDOGENOUS DEPRESSIVE-SYNDROMES.
004546 04-13

CATECHOLAMINE
EFFECTS OF MORPHINE, BETA ENDORPHIN AND NALOXONE ON CATECHOLAMINE LEVELS AND SEXUAL-BEHAVIOR IN THE MALE RAT.
000430 01-04

EFFECTS OF L-DOPA AND L 5 HYDROXYTRYPTOPHAN ON LOCOMOTOR-ACTIVITY OF THE RAT AFTER SELECTIVE OR COMBINED DESTRUCTION OF CENTRAL CATECHOLAMINE AND SEROTONIN NEURONS.
000466 01-04

HYPOTHALAMIC CATECHOLAMINE BIOSYNTHESIS IN VITRO AS MEASURED BY LIQUID-CHROMATOGRAPHY AND ELECTROCHEMICAL-DETECTION.
000537 01-06

CATECHOLAMINE TRANSMITTER SYSTEMS.
000580 01-09

THE INFLUENCE OF PENTIFYLLINE AND THEOPHYLLINE ON REACTION KINETICS OF CATECHOLAMINE STIMULATED ATPASE FROM RAT-BRAIN.
001052 02-01

DYNAMICS OF ENDOGENOUS CATECHOLAMINE RELEASE FROM BRAIN FRAGMENTS OF MALE AND FEMALE RATS.
001121 02-03

INTERACTION OF TRIAZOLAM WITH DESIPRAMINE: EFFECTS OF SINGLE AND REPEATED TREATMENT ON CERTAIN PHARMACOLOGIC-RESPONSES AND BRAIN CATECHOLAMINE LEVELS.
001323 02-03

ERGOT AND CATECHOLAMINE POTENCIES AT CATECHOLAMINE-RECEPTORS.
001510 02-03

THE PHARMACOLOGY OF CATECHOLAMINE INVOLVEMENT IN THE NEURAL MECHANISMS OF REWARD.
001526 02-03

DOSE-DEPENDENT PHARMACOKINETICS OF ALPHA METHYL-P-TYROSINE (ALPHA MT) AND COMPARISON OF CATECHOLAMINE TURNOVER-RATES AFTER TWO DOSES OF ALPHA MT.
001532 02-03

DORSAL TEGMENTAL BUNDLE DESTRUCTION: EFFECTS ON OPERANT-BEHAVIOR, BRAIN CATECHOLAMINE LEVELS, AND BEHAVIORAL-SUPPRESSION PRODUCED BY ADRENERGIC AGONISTS.
001726 02-04

AN AUTOMATED ELECTROCHEMICAL-METHOD FOR IN VIVO MONITORING OF CATECHOLAMINE RELEASE.
001873 02-06

THE CORRELATION OF CATECHOLAMINE AND ADRENERGIC PARAMETERS WITH DRUG-THERAPY OF NEUROTIC AND ENDOGENOUS DEPRESSIONS.
002047 02-09

IMMUNOCYTOCHEMICAL LOCALIZATION OF CATECHOLAMINE SYNTHESIZING ENZYMES AND NEUROPEPTIDES IN AREA POSTREMA AND MEDIAL NUCLEUS-TRACTUS-SOLITARIUS OF RAT-BRAIN.
002634 03-01

CENTRAL AND PERIPHERAL CATECHOLAMINE FUNCTION IN LEARNING AND MEMORY PROCESSES.
002823 03-03

PHARMACOLOGICAL EVIDENCE FOR CATECHOLAMINE INVOLVEMENT IN ANIMAL AGGRESSION.
003052 03-04

A POSSIBLE ROLE FOR CATECHOLAMINE NEUROTRANSMITTERS IN THE ANTICONVULSANT ACTIVITY OF CHLORDIAZEPOXIDE.
003119 03-04

PHARMACOLOGICAL EVIDENCE FOR CATECHOLAMINE INVOLVEMENT IN ANIMAL AGGRESSION.
003140 03-06

CATECHOLAMINE TURNOVER IN RAT-CEREBRAL-CORTEX AND CAUDATE FOLLOWING REPEATED TREATMENT WITH DIHYDROERGOTOXINE.
003765 04-03

CATECHOLAMINE AND 5 HYDROXYTRYPTAMINE SYNTHESIS AND METABOLISM FOLLOWING INTRACEREBROVENTRICULAR INJECTION OF DIBUTYRYL-CYCLIC-AMP.
003769 04-03

CATECHOLAMINE SYNTHESIS REGULATION IN HYPOTHALAMIC SYNAPTOSOMES. (UNPUBLISHED PAPER).
003829 04-03

CHANGE IN CATECHOLAMINE SENSITIVE NA-K-ATPASE ACTIVITY IN THE RAT STRIATUM MICROSOMES FOLLOWING ELECTROLYTIC OR 6 HYDROXYDOPAMINE-INDUCED LESIONS OF DOPAMINERGIC NEURONS.
003871 04-03
THE IMPORTANCE OF CATECHOLAMINE UPTAKE INHIBITION IN THE REVERSAL OF GUANETHIDINE BLOCKADE OF ADRENERGIC NEURONS.
003900 04-03
THE EFFECT OF PRENATAL EXPOSURE TO ETHANOL OR OPIATES ON BRAIN CATECHOLAMINE ACTIVITY.
003939 04-03
CATECHOLAMINE MODULATION OF ENKEPHALIN-INDUCED ELECTROPHYSIOLOGICAL RESPONSES IN CEREBRAL-CORTEX.
003957 04-03
EFFECTS OF CANNABINOIDS ON CATECHOLAMINE UPTAKE AND RELEASE IN HYPOTHALAMIC AND STRIATAL SYNAPTOSOMES.
003970 04-03
EFFECT OF PROSTAGLANDIN-D2, PROSTAGLANDIN-E2 AND PROSTAGLANDIN-F2ALPHA ON CATECHOLAMINE RELEASE FROM SLICES OF RAT AND RABBIT BRAIN.
003983 04-03
CATECHOLAMINE SEROTONIN INTERACTION EFFECTS ON ACTIVITY IN RATS NEONATALLY TREATED WITH 6 HYDROXYDOPAMINE.
004194 04-04
CONSISTENCY IN CATECHOLAMINE EXCRETION IN LABORATORY AND NATURAL SETTINGS: CORRELATIONAL AND VARIANCE COMPONENTS ANALYSES.
004508 04-13
CATECHOLAMINE METABOLISM IN A PSYCHOACTIVE CACTUS.
004722 04-17

CATECHOLAMINE-DEPLETING-AGENT
EFFECT OF THE CATECHOLAMINE-DEPLETING-AGENT 1 PHENYL-2-THIAZOLYL-2-THIOUREA (U-14-624) ON DRUG METABOLISM IN THE RAT.
000280 01-03

CATECHOLAMINE-RECEPTORS
ERGOT AND CATECHOLAMINE POTENCIES AT CATECHOLAMINE-RECEPTORS.
001510 02-03
EFFECTS OF PROPRANOLOL ON THE LOCOMOTOR-STIMULATION INDUCED BY ACTIVATION OF POSTSYNAPTIC CATECHOLAMINE-RECEPTORS.
004126 04-04
RELATION BETWEEN BRAIN CATECHOLAMINE-RECEPTORS AND DOPAMINERGIC STEREOTYPY IN RAT STRAINS.
004131 04-04

CATECHOLAMINE-SULFATES
PRESENCE OF CONJUGATED CATECHOLAMINES IN RAT-BRAIN: A NEW METHOD OF ANALYSIS OF CATECHOLAMINE-SULFATES.
004286 04-06

CATECHOLAMINERGIC
MONOAMINE REPLACEMENT AFTER RESERPINE: CATECHOLAMINERGIC AGONISTS RESTORE MOTOR-ACTIVITY BUT PHENYLETHYLAMINE. RESTORES ATROPINE-RESISTANT NEOCORTICAL LOW VOLTAGE FAST-ACTIVITY.
000309 01-03
SEROTONERGIC AND CATECHOLAMINERGIC INFLUENCE ON THYROID-FUNCTION IN THE VERVET-MONKEY.
001385 02-03
EFFECTS OF KAINIC-ACID ON BODY-TEMPERATURE OF RATS: ROLE OF CATECHOLAMINERGIC AND SEROTONERGIC SYSTEMS.
001515 02-03
PATHOPHYSIOLOGIC-IMPACT OF CENTRAL CATECHOLAMINERGIC FUNCTION IN SCHIZOPHRENIA AND SCHIZOPHRENIA-LIKE PSYCHOSES.
002174 02-11
CATECHOLAMINERGIC INVOLVEMENT IN PHASIC VERSUS TONIC ELECTROCORTICAL AROUSAL.
002723 03-03

CATECHOLAMINES
COMPARTMENTATION OF CATECHOLAMINES IN RAT-BRAIN: EFFECTS OF AGONISTS AND ANTAGONISTS.
000125 01-03
BIOCHEMICAL-CHARACTERIZATION OF THE RAT SYMPATHETIC GANGLION: PHARMACOLOGICAL-EFFECTS OF RESERPINE ON GANGLIONIC CATECHOLAMINES.
000153 01-03
INCREASED URINARY EXCRETION OF CATECHOLAMINES AND THEIR METABOLITES IN STREPTOZOTOCIN DIABETIC RAT.
000154 01-03
FALSE LABELLING OF COMMERCIALLY-AVAILABLE 3H CATECHOLAMINES?
000535 01-06
THE RELEASE OF CATECHOLAMINES FROM ADRENERGIC NEURONS.
000974 01-17
LACK OF INFLUENCE OF BRAIN CATECHOLAMINES ON ACUTE EFFECTS OF BARBITURATES.
001138 02-03
EFFECT OF TABERNANTHINE ON THE TURNOVER TIME OF BRAIN CATECHOLAMINES IN NORMAL AND HYPOBARIC HYPOXIC RATS.
001187 02-03
EFFECT OF PROSTAGLANDINS ON PLASMA CATECHOLAMINES, HEART AND BLOOD-PRESSURE RESPONSES TO HEMORRHAGE. (UNPUBLISHED PAPER).
001223 02-03

PERIPHERAL CATECHOLAMINES AND MEMORY MODULATION. (UNPUBLISHED PAPER).
001251 02-03
EFFECTS OF PRENATAL METHADONE ON RAT-BRAIN CATECHOLAMINES.
001367 02-03
THYROTROPIN-RELEASING-HORMONE: NEUROCHEMICAL EVIDENCE FOR THE POTENTIATION OF IMIPRAMINE EFFECTS ON THE METABOLISM AND UPTAKE OF BRAIN CATECHOLAMINES.
001427 02-03
ROLE OF BRAIN CATECHOLAMINES AND 5 HYDROXYTRYPTAMINE IN MORPHINE-INDUCED TEMPERATURE CHANGES IN NORMAL AND TOLERANT RATS AND MICE.
001476 02-03
BRAIN CATECHOLAMINES, MENTAL-ILLNESSES, AGING AND SENILE-DEMENTIA: BIOCHEMICAL-CONSIDERATIONS AND PHARMACOLOGICAL-CONSIDERATIONS.
001550 02-03
BRAIN CATECHOLAMINES MODIFICATIONS. THE EFFECTS ON MEMORY FACILITATION INDUCED BY OXOTREMORINE IN MICE.
001658 02-04
OPIATE ACTIONS AND CATECHOLAMINES.
001662 02-04
EFFECTS OF CAFFEINE ON PLASMA FREE FATTY-ACIDS, URINARY CATECHOLAMINES, AND DRUG BINDING.
002272 02-13
SEX-DIFFERENCES IN THE AMPHETAMINE STIMULATED RELEASE OF CATECHOLAMINES FROM RAT STRIATAL TISSUE IN VITRO.
002668 03-03
PRESYNAPTIC REGULATION OF THE RELEASE OF CATECHOLAMINES IN THE CAT HYPOTHALAMUS.
002703 03-03
PLASMA CATECHOLAMINES IN RATS EXPOSED TO COLD: EFFECTS OF GANGLIONIC AND ADRENORECEPTOR BLOCKADE.
002863 03-03
BEHAVIOURAL-RESPONSES TO DRUGS RELEASING 5 HYDROXYTRYPTAMINE AND CATECHOLAMINES: EFFECTS OF TREATMENTS ALTERING PRECURSOR CONCENTRATIONS IN BRAIN.
002990 03-04
THE EFFECT OF ADENOSINE AND GUANOSINE ON THE CONTENT OF SEROTONIN AND CATECHOLAMINES IN THE BRAIN IN THE RESTORATION PERIOD FOLLOWING EXPERIMENTAL CLINICAL DEATH.
003882 04-03
LIBERATION OF CATECHOLAMINES AND 5 HYDROXYTRYPTAMINE FROM HUMAN BLOOD-PLATELETS.
003967 04-03
HYPOTENSION ALTERS THE RELEASE OF CATECHOLAMINES IN THE HYPOTHALAMUS OF THE CONSCIOUS RABBIT.
003968 04-03
PRESENCE OF CONJUGATED CATECHOLAMINES IN RAT-BRAIN: A NEW METHOD OF ANALYSIS OF CATECHOLAMINE-SULFATES.
004286 04-06

CATECHOLESTROGEN
DEVELOPMENTAL ASPECTS OF CATECHOLESTROGEN SYNTHESIS. (UNPUBLISHED PAPER).
001282 02-03

CATECHOLIC
EFFECTS OF MOLINDONE AND FLUPHENAZINE ON THE BRAIN CONCENTRATION OF SOME PHENOLIC AND CATECHOLIC AMINES IN THE MOUSE AND THE RAT.
003870 04-03

CATEGORIES
ON THE USE OF CERTAIN PHARMACOLOGICAL CATEGORIES IN HYSTERIA.
004347 04-09
BASAL PROLACTINAEMIA AND RESPONSES TO TRH AND SULPIRIDE IN DIFFERENT CATEGORIES OF MALE SEXUAL-DYSFUNCTIONS.
004503 04-13

CATHA-EDULIS
RELATIVE POTENCIES OF TWO PHENYLALKYLAMINES FOUND IN THE ABUSED PLANT CATHA-EDULIS, KHAT
001084 02-02
HYPERTHERMIC-RESPONSE TO (-) CATHINONE, AN ALKALOID OF CATHA-EDULIS (KHAT).
003694 04-02

CATHINONE
HYPERTHERMIC-RESPONSE TO (-) CATHINONE, AN ALKALOID OF CATHA-EDULIS (KHAT).
003694 04-02

CATION
EFFECT OF STRUCTURE ON PHENOTHIAZINE CATION RADICAL REACTIONS IN AQUEOUS BUFFERS.
000014 01-02
MEASUREMENT OF THE MEMBRANE POTENTIAL OF ISOLATED NERVE TERMINALS BY THE LIPOPHILIC CATION (3H)TRIPHENYLMETHYLPHOSPHONIUM-BROMIDE.
002746 03-03
CATION REGULATION DIFFERENTIATES SPECIFIC BINDING OF (3H)SULPIRIDE AND (3H)SPIPERONE TO RAT STRIATAL PREPARATIONS.
004032 04-03

Subject Index

CATIONS

REGULATION BY CATIONS OF (3H)SPIROPERIDOL BINDING ASSOCIATED WITH DOPAMINE-RECEPTORS OF RAT-BRAIN.
002922 03-03

SPECTRA OF RADICAL CATIONS OF PHENOTHIAZINE DERIVATIVES IN SOLUTION AND SOLID STATE.
003673 04-01

CATS

NEURONAL ACTIVITY IN CHRONIC FERRIC-CHLORIDE EPILEPTIC-FOCI IN CATS AND MONKEY.
000172 01-03

THE INFLUENCE OF CHLORALOSE ANESTHESIA ON THE ACTIVITY OF RED NUCLEUS NEURONS IN CATS.
000245 01-03

RELATION OF MONOMETHYLHYDRAZINE (MMH) SEIZURE THRESHOLDS TO AFTERDISCHARGE THRESHOLDS WITH AMYGDALOID STIMULATION IN CATS.
000474 01-04

THE INFLUENCE OF GABAERGIC SUBSTANCES ON THE EFFECTS OF STIMULATION OF THE CAUDATE-NUCLEUS AND AMPHETAMINE STEREOTYPY IN CATS.
000489 01-04

CHRONIC AMPHETAMINE ADMINISTRATION TO CATS: BEHAVIORAL-EVIDENCE AND NEUROCHEMICAL EVIDENCE FOR DECREASED CENTRAL SEROTONERGIC FUNCTION.
000491 01-04

FAILURE OF ISOPRENALINE AND BETA-RECEPTOR BLOCKING-DRUGS TO MODIFY DEPRESSOR RESPONSE AND BRADYCARDIA INDUCED BY ELECTRICAL-STIMULATION OF THE ANTERIOR HYPOTHALAMUS OF CATS.
000520 01-05

THE EFFECT OF EMOTIONAL-STRESS AND DIAZEPAM ON MONOAMINE METABOLITES IN THE CEREBROSPINAL-FLUID OF CATS. (PH.D. DISSERTATION).
001260 02-03

LONG-TERM DECREASES IN SPONTANEOUS FIRING OF CAUDATE NEURONS INDUCED BY AMPHETAMINE IN CATS.
001340 02-03

EFFECTS OF MORPHINE ON EVOKED-POTENTIALS RECORDED FROM THE AMYGDALA BY TOOTH-PULP STIMULATION IN CATS.
001379 02-03

INHIBITION OF NEUROSYMPATHETIC CEREBROARTERIAL CONSTRICTION BY CLONIDINE IN CATS.
001431 02-03

EFFECTS OF ALPHA-ADRENOCEPTOR STIMULATING DRUGS ON BARORECEPTOR REFLEXES IN CONSCIOUS CATS.
001514 02-03

COMPARATIVE-STUDY OF AGGRESSIVE-BEHAVIOUR AFTER INJECTION OF CHOLINOMIMETICS, ANTICHOLINESTERASES, NICOTINIC, AND MUSCARINIC GANGLIONIC STIMULANTS INTO THE CEREBRAL VENTRICLES OF CONSCIOUS CATS: FAILURE OF NICOTINIC-DRUGS TO EVOKE AGGRESSION.
001568 02-04

THE PHARMACOLOGY OF AGGRESSIVE-BEHAVIOURAL-PHENOMENA ELICITED BY MUSCARINE INJECTED INTO THE CEREBRAL VENTRICLES OF CONSCIOUS CATS.
001569 02-04

BEHAVIORAL-EFFECTS AND ELECTROPHYSIOLOGICAL-EFFECTS OF OPIOID-PEPTIDES IN CATS.
001612 02-04

EFFECT OF CHOLINE ON CONDITIONED FOOD MOTOR-REFLEXES IN CATS.
001731 02-04

CALCIUM ANTAGONISM OF THE INHIBITORY-EFFECTS OF FENTANYL ON THE CONTRACTION OF THE NICTITATING MEMBRANE IN CATS.
002876 03-03

AMPHETAMINE-INDUCED ROTATION IN NORMAL CATS.
003002 03-04

CATS DEVELOP TOLERANCE TO D-AMPHETAMINES EFFECTS UPON LOCOMOTION AND STEREOTYPED-BEHAVIORS.
003018 03-04

MODIFICATION OF MOTOR-ACTIVITY, PASSIVE-AVOIDANCE CONDITIONING AND EVOKED-POTENTIALS BY MICROINJECTIONS OF STRYCHNINE IN BOTH CAUDATE-NUCLEI IN CATS.
003101 03-04

DOES P CHLOROPHENYLALANINE PRODUCE DISTURBED WAKING, DISTURBED SLEEP OR ACTIVATION BY PONTO-GENICULO-OCCIPITAL WAVES IN CATS?
003704 04-02

THE EFFECT OF SMALL DOSES OF HALOPERIDOL AND CLOZAPINE ON BEHAVIORAL SHIFTS IN CATS, ARISING AFTER CESSATION OF ELECTRICAL-STIMULATION OF THE CAUDATE-NUCLEUS.
004067 04-04

RESPIRATORY DEPRESSION PRODUCED BY DIAZEPAM IN CATS: EFFECT OF ANESTHESIA.
004272 04-05

CAUDATE

EFFECTS OF CHRONIC HALOPERIDOL ON CAUDATE 3H SPIROPERIDOL BINDING IN LESIONED RATS.
000255 01-03

CELL-CULTURES

RELEASE OF ARACHIDONIC-ACID FROM ADRENAL CHROMAFFIN CELL-CULTURES DURING SECRETION OF EPINEPHRINE. (UNPUBLISHED PAPER).

001027 02-01

THE INSENSITIVITY OF DEVELOPING BENZODIAZEPINE-RECEPTORS TO CHRONIC-TREATMENT WITH DIAZEPAM, GABA AND MUSCIMOL IN BRAIN CELL-CULTURES.

004002 04-03

CELL-FREE

OPIOID DEPENDENT DUAL-REGULATION OF ADENYLATE-CYCLASE IN A CELL-FREE SYSTEM. (UNPUBLISHED PAPER).

001033 02-01

EFFECT OF INTRAVENOUS ADMINISTRATION OF D LYSERGIC-ACID-DIETHYLAMIDE ON SUBSEQUENT PROTEIN SYNTHESIS IN A CELL-FREE SYSTEM DERIVED FROM BRAIN.

003761 04-03

CELL-FREE TRANSLATION OF FREE AND MEMBRANE-BOUND POLYSOMES AND POLYADENYLATED MRNA FROM RABBIT BRAIN FOLLOWING ADMINISTRATION OF D LYSERGIC-ACID-DIETHYLAMIDE IN VIVO.

003832 04-03

CELLS

PSYCHOTROPIC-DRUGS AND HISTAMINE H1-RECEPTORS OF CULTURED MOUSE NEUROBLASTOMA CELLS.

000250 01-03

ADENOSINE REGULATES VIA TWO DIFFERENT TYPES OF RECEPTORS, THE ACCUMULATION OF CYCLIC-AMP IN CULTURED BRAIN CELLS.

000308 01-03

HYBRID PROTEINS USED TO STUDY THE MECHANISM OF TOXIN ENTRANCE INTO CELLS. (UNPUBLISHED PAPER).

001063 02-01

INFLUENCE OF DRUGS AFFECTING THE PITUITARY ADRENAL AXIS ON CHROMAFFIN CELLS.

001183 02-03

IGE MEDIATED HISTAMINE RELEASE IN RAT BASOPHILIC LEUKEMIA CELLS: RECEPTOR ACTIVATED PHOSPHOLIPID METHYLATION, CA-FLUX AND RELEASE OF ARACHIDONIC-ACID. (UNPUBLISHED PAPER).

001188 02-03

ENHANCED TRANSFER OF EXPERIMENTAL ALLERGIC-ENCEPHALOMYELITIS WITH STRAIN-13 GUINEA-PIG LYMPH-NODE CELLS: REQUIREMENT FOR CULTURE WITH SPECIFIC ANTIGEN AND ALLOGENIC PERITONEAL EXUDATE CELLS. (UNPUBLISHED PAPER).

001201 02-03

EXCITATORY ACTION OF OPIOID-PEPTIDES AND OPIATES ON CULTURED HIPPOCAMPAL PYRAMIDAL CELLS.

001241 02-03

REGULATION BY A BETA-ADRENERGIC-RECEPTOR OF A CA-INDEPENDENT ADENOSINE-CYCLIC-MONOPHOSPHATE-PHOSPHODIESTERASE IN C6-GLIOMA CELLS. (UNPUBLISHED PAPER).

001403 02-03

LITHIUM-ION ENTRY INTO CULTURED CELLS OF NEURAL ORIGIN.

001433 02-03

ENHANCED TRANSFER OF EXPERIMENTAL ALLERGIC-ENCEPHALOMYELITIS WITH LEWIS-RAT LYMPH-NODE CELLS. (UNPUBLISHED PAPER).

001434 02-03

STIMULATION OF THE PLASMA MEMBRANE ENZYME, 5' NUCLEOTIDASE, BY ETHANOL EXPOSURE TO NEURAL CELLS IN CULTURE.

001499 02-03

RELATIONSHIP BETWEEN THE ACTIONS OF CALCIUM-IONS, OPIOIDS, AND PROSTAGLANDIN-E1 ON THE LEVEL OF CYCLIC-AMP IN NEUROBLASTOMA-X GLIOMA HYBRID CELLS.

002677 03-03

A COMPARISON OF THE EFFECTS OF PENTOBARBITAL AND DIPHENYLHYDANTOIN ON THE GABA SENSITIVITY AND EXCITABILITY OF ADULT SENSORY GANGLION CELLS.

002692 03-03

TOXIC EFFECTS OF ALPHA AMINOADIPATE ON CULTURED CEREBELLAR CELLS.

002729 03-03

THE EFFECTS OF A BENZODIAZEPINE ON THE HYPERPOLARIZING AND THE DEPOLARIZING RESPONSES OF HIPPOCAMPAL CELLS TO GABA.

002763 03-03

EFFECTS OF LITHIUM ON MORPHOLOGICAL CHARACTERISTICS OF DISSOCIATED BRAIN CELLS IN CULTURE.

002765 03-03

IDENTIFICATION OF TWO BENZODIAZEPINE BINDING-SITES ON CELLS CULTURED FROM RAT-CEREBRAL-CORTEX.

002820 03-03

LOCALIZATION OF GABA-RECEPTOR AND DOPAMINE-RECEPTOR SITES IN RETINAL GLIAL CELLS USING DL ALPHA AMINOADIPIC-ACID.

002828 03-03

INFLUENCE OF PSYCHOACTIVE AND NONPSYCHOACTIVE CANNABINOIDS ON CELL PROLIFERATION AND MACROMOLECULAR BIOSYNTHESIS IN HUMAN CELLS.

002830 03-03

INFLUENCE OF PSYCHOACTIVE AND NONPSYCHOACTIVE CANNABINOIDS ON CHROMATIN STRUCTURE AND FUNCTION IN HUMAN CELLS.

002831 03-03

EFFECTS OF BENSERAZIDE AND CARBIDOPA ON THE METABOLISM OF L
TRYPTOPHAN BY ISOLATED RAT LIVER CELLS.
002899 03-03
LITHIUM UPTAKE IN RED CELLS OF CYCLOID AND UNIPOLAR DYSTHYMIC-
PATIENTS.
003258 03-09
DIFFERENTIAL BINDING OF CHLORPROMAZINE TO HUMAN BLOOD CELLS:
APPLICATION OF THE HYGROSCOPIC DESORPTION METHOD.
003556 03-16
5 HYDROXYTRYPTAMINE CONTROLS ACH-RECEPTOR SENSITIVITY OF
BULLFROG SYMPATHETIC GANGLION CELLS.
003710 04-03
INVOLVEMENT OF CALCIUM CHANNELS IN SHORT-TERM
DESENSITIZATION OF MUSCARINIC-RECEPTOR MEDIATED CYCLIC-GMP
FORMATION IN MOUSE NEUROBLASTOMA CELLS.
003783 04-03
CHARACTERIZATION BY (3H)DIHYDROERGOCRYPTINE BINDING OF
ALPHA-ADRENERGIC-RECEPTORS IN NEUROBLASTOMA X GLIOMA
HYBRID CELLS.
003823 04-03
DOXEPIN, A TRICYCLIC-ANTIDEPRESSANT, BINDS TO NORMAL, INTACT
ASTROGLIAL CELLS IN CULTURES AND INHIBITS THE ISOPROTERENOL-
INDUCED INCREASE IN CYCLIC-AMP PRODUCTION.
003836 04-03
OPIOIDS, NORADRENALINE AND GTP ANALOGS INHIBIT CHOLERA-TOXIN
ACTIVATED ADENYLATE-CYCLASE IN NEUROBLASTOMA-X GLIOMA
HYBRID CELLS.
003975 04-03
RNA-POLYMERASE-II IN C6-GLIOMA CELLS; ALPHA AMANITIN BLOCKADE
OF CYCLIC-AMP-PHOSPHODIESTERASE INDUCTION BY BETA-
ADRENERGIC STIMULATION. (UNPUBLISHED PAPER).
003998 04-03
PHENYTOIN INHIBITION OF CYCLIC-GUANOSINE-MONOPHOSPHATE (C-
GMP) ACCUMULATION IN NEUROBLASTOMA CELLS BY CALCIUM-
CHANNEL BLOCKADE.
004020 04-03
DESENSITIZATION OF HISTAMINE H1-RECEPTOR-MEDIATED CYCLIC-GMP
FORMATION IN MOUSE NEUROBLASTOMA CELLS.
004030 04-03
RELATIVE ACTIVITIES OF SUBSTANCES RELATED TO 5
HYDROXYTRYPTAMINE AS DEPOLARIZING-AGENTS OF SUPERIOR
CERVICAL GANGLION CELLS.
004047 04-03
DEMONSTRATION OF A MUSCARINIC-RECEPTOR-MEDIATED CYCLIC-GMP-
DEPENDENT HYPERPOLARIZATION OF THE MEMBRANE POTENTIAL OF
MOUSE NEUROBLASTOMA CELLS USING
(3H)TETRAPHENYLPHOSPHONIUM.
004049 04-03

CELLULAR
BENZODIAZEPINE-RECEPTORS IN CHICK RETINA: DEVELOPMENT AND
CELLULAR LOCALIZATION.
002655 03-03
IN VITRO CELLULAR ADAPTATION OF SEROTONERGIC PROCESSES AFTER
CHRONIC CENTRAL PHENOBARBITAL ADMINISTRATION.
002813 03-03

CELLULAR-TRANSPORT
INFLUENCE OF CELLULAR-TRANSPORT ON THE INTERACTION OF AMINO-
ACIDS WITH GAMMA AMINOBUTYRIC-ACID-RECEPTORS (GABA) IN THE
ISOLATED OLFACTORY-CORTEX OF THE GUINEA-PIG.
000034 01-03

CENTER
SATIETY CENTER NEUROANATOMY. (UNPUBLISHED PAPER).
003678 04-01

CENTERS
INFLUENCE OF CHRONIC ALCOHOL INTOXICATION ON CIRCADIAN-RHYTHM
OF NEUROSECRETORY CENTERS OF RAT HYPOTHALAMUS.
001549 02-03

CENTRAL
EVIDENCE FOR AN IRREVERSIBLE INTERACTION OF BROMOCRIPTINE
WITH CENTRAL DOPAMINE-RECEPTORS.
000023 01-03
EVIDENCE FOR A RECEPTOR SUPERSENSITIVITY FOLLOWING IMPAIRMENT
OF CENTRAL SEROTONERGIC ACTIVITY IN THE RABBIT.
000041 01-03
NUCIFERINE AND CENTRAL GLUTAMATE-RECEPTORS.
000063 01-03
CLENBUTEROL, A CENTRAL BETA-ADRENOCEPTOR AGONIST.
000120 01-03
ABSENCE OF POTASSIUM CONDUCTANCE IN CENTRAL MYELINATED
AXONS.
000166 01-03
CENTRAL NORADRENERGIC ADAPTATION TO LONG-TERM-TREATMENT
WITH IMIPRAMINE IN RHESUS-MONKEYS.
000182 01-03
EFFECT OF GABA ANALOGUES ON BLOOD-PRESSURE AND CENTRAL GABA
METABOLISM IN THE RAT.
000231 01-03
DIAZEPAM POTENTIATION OF PURINERGIC DEPRESSION OF CENTRAL
NEURONS.
000233 01-03

INVOLVEMENT OF CENTRAL CHOLINOCEPTORS IN METRAZOL-INDUCED
CONVULSIONS.
000247 01-03
CENTRAL BLOOD-PRESSURE EFFECTS OF GUANYLYLIMIDODIPHOSPHATE
AND CYCLIC-GUANOSINE-MONOPHOSPHATE.
000266 01-03
RELATION BETWEEN THE EFFECTS OF ANTIDEPRESSANT-DRUGS ON THE
UPTAKE OF MONOAMINES AND ON THE SPONTANEOUS ACTIVITY OF
CENTRAL NEURONS.
000267 01-03
A COMPARISON OF RATES OF DEPLETION AND RECOVERY OF
NORADRENALINE STORES OF PERIPHERAL AND CENTRAL
NORADRENERGIC NEURONES AFTER RESERPINE ADMINISTRATION:
IMPORTANCE OF NEURONAL ACTIVITY.
000314 01-03
N ALKYLATED 2 AMINOTETRALINS; CENTRAL DOPAMINE-RECEPTOR
STIMULATING ACTIVITY.
000399 01-04
EFFECTS OF L-DOPA AND L 5 HYDROXYTRYPTOPHAN ON LOCOMOTOR-
ACTIVITY OF THE RAT AFTER SELECTIVE OR COMBINED DESTRUCTION
OF CENTRAL CATECHOLAMINE AND SEROTONIN NEURONS.
000466 01-04
CHRONIC AMPHETAMINE ADMINISTRATION TO CATS: BEHAVIORAL-
EVIDENCE AND NEUROCHEMICAL EVIDENCE FOR DECREASED CENTRAL
SEROTONERGIC FUNCTION.
000491 01-04
CENTRAL EXCITATORY ACTIONS OF FLURAZEPAM.
000526 01-05
CENTRAL LEVELS OF NORADRENALINE, 3 METHOXY-4-
HYDROXYPHENYLETHYLENEGLYCOL AND CYCLIC-AMP IN THE RAT
AFTER ACTIVATION OF LOCUS-COERULEUS NEURONS: INFLUENCE OF
SINGLE AND REPEATED NEUROLEPTIC TREATMENT.
001095 02-03
EFFECTS OF CHRONIC-TREATMENT WITH L SULPIRIDE AND HALOPERIDOL
ON CENTRAL DOPAMINE TURNOVER EVALUATED IN DOPAMINE CELL
BODY AND NERVE TERMINAL-RICH AREAS.
001096 02-03
INHIBITION BY LOCAL ANESTHETICS, PHENTOLAMINE AND PROPRANOLOL
OF (3H)QUINUCLYDINYL-BENZYLATE BINDING TO CENTRAL
MUSCARINIC-RECEPTORS.
001097 02-03
CENTRAL SYMPATHETIC REACTIVITY INHIBITED BY INDORAMIN.
001193 02-03
CENTRAL MONOAMINE SYNAPSES AS SITES OF ACTION FOR ERGOT
DRUGS.
001238 02-03
EFFECTS OF CHRONIC-TREATMENT WITH L SULPIRIDE AND HALOPERIDOL
ON CENTRAL MONOAMINERGIC MECHANISMS.
001240 02-03
CENTRAL ADMINISTRATION OF SERINE CAUSES HYPOTHERMIA AND
INHIBITS FEVER IN RABBITS.
001247 02-03
COMPARISON OF THE EFFECTS OF CENTRAL ADMINISTRATION OF SERINE
AND GLYCINE ON BODY-TEMPERATURE OF THE RABBIT.
001248 02-03
METHYLDOPA PRODUCES CENTRAL INHIBITION OF PARASYMPATHETIC-
ACTIVITY IN THE CAT.
001321 02-03
TWO CONDUCTANCE MECHANISMS ACTIVATED BY APPLICATIONS OF L
GLUTAMIC-ACID, L ASPARTIC-ACID, DL HOMOCYSTEIC-ACID, N
METHYL-D-ASPARTIC-ACID, AND DL KAINIC-ACID TO CULTURED
MAMMALIAN CENTRAL NEURONES.
001349 02-03
EFFECTS OF DIFFERENT MONOAMINE-OXIDASE-INHIBITORS ON
RESPIRATORY ACTIVITY IN RATS WITH CHRONICALLY IMPAIRED
CENTRAL SEROTONERGIC FUNCTION.
001389 02-03
DIFFERENTIAL-EFFECTS OF SYSTEMIC VERSUS INTRACRANIAL INJECTION
OF OPIATES ON CENTRAL, OROFACIAL AND LOWER BODY
NOCICEPTION: SOMATOTYPY IN BULBAR ANALGESIA SYSTEMS.
001446 02-03
CENTRAL BIOGENIC-AMINES AND NEUROPEPTIDES IN GENETIC
HYPERTENSION. (UNPUBLISHED PAPER).
001456 02-03
CENTRAL AMINERGIC AND PEPTIDERGIC MECHANISMS IN
SPONTANEOUSLY (GENETIC) HYPERTENSIVE-RATS. (UNPUBLISHED
PAPER).
001459 02-03
CENTRAL PHARMACOLOGICAL CONTROL OF CORTICOSTERONE SECRETION
IN THE INTACT RAT. DEMONSTRATION OF CHOLINERGIC AND
SEROTONINERGIC FACILITATORY AND ALPHA-ADRENERGIC INHIBITORY
MECHANISMS.
001487 02-03
THE INABILITY OF CHRONIC MIANSERIN TO BLOCK CENTRAL ALPHA2-
ADRENOCEPTORS.
001492 02-03
NEGLIGIBLE AFFINITY OF HISTAMINE H2-RECEPTOR ANTAGONISTS FOR
CENTRAL ALPHA1-ADRENOCEPTORS.
001508 02-03

COMPARED PROPERTIES OF CENTRAL AND PERIPHERAL BINDING-SITES
FOR PHENCYCLIDINE.
001521 02-03
KAINIC-ACID-INDUCED WET-DOG-SHAKES IN RATS: THE RELATION TO
CENTRAL NEUROTRANSMITTERS.
001685 02-04
INVESTIGATIONS ON THE INTERACTION OF THYROTROPIN-RELEASING-
HORMONE (TRH) AND MK-771 WITH CENTRAL NORADRENERGIC
MECHANISMS.
001701 02-04
A COMPARISON BETWEEN THE EFFECTS OF MORPHINE ON THE
REWARDING AND AVERSIVE-PROPERTIES OF LATERAL HYPOTHALAMIC
AND CENTRAL GRAY STIMULATION.
001771 02-04
TOLERANCE TO FLUPHENAZINE AND SUPERSENSITIVITY TO APOMORPHINE
IN CENTRAL DOPAMINERGIC-SYSTEMS AFTER CHRONIC FLUPHENAZINE-
DECANOATE TREATMENT.
001820 02-04
CENTRAL SEROTONIN-RECEPTOR SENSITIVITY IN RATS WITH
EXPERIMENTAL ALLERGIC-ENCEPHALOMYELITIS.
001821 02-04
ELECTROPHYSIOLOGICAL-CHANGES AT A CENTRAL NORADRENERGIC
SYNAPSE DURING THALLIUM TOXICOSIS.
001848 02-05
CLINICAL PROCESSES AND CENTRAL DOPAMINERGIC-ACTIVITY IN
PSYCHOTIC-DISORDERS.
002098 02-11
PATHOPHYSIOLOGIC-IMPACT OF CENTRAL CATECHOLAMINERGIC
FUNCTION IN SCHIZOPHRENIA AND SCHIZOPHRENIA-LIKE PSYCHOSES.
002174 02-11
THE USE OF BROMOCRIPTINE FOR TESTING CENTRAL DOPAMINERGIC
REACTIVITY.
002205 02-13
APOMORPHINE HYPOTHERMIA: AN INDEX OF CENTRAL DOPAMINE-
RECEPTOR FUNCTION IN MAN.
002221 02-13
CENTRAL DOPAMINERGIC-EFFECTS OF ERGOLINE DERIVATIVES.
002540 02-17
CENTRAL NEUROPHARMACOLOGY OF ENDORPHINS.
002599 02-17
CENTRAL DEPRESSANT EFFECTS OF CAERULEIN AND CHOLECYSTOKININ-
OCTAPEPTIDE (CCK-8) DIFFER FROM THOSE OF DIAZEPAM AND
HALOPERIDOL.
002652 03-02
GABA-RECEPTORS AND BENZODIAZEPINE-RECEPTORS. STUDIES ON THEIR
LOCALIZATION IN THE HIPPOCAMPUS AND THEIR INTERACTION WITH
CENTRAL DOPAMINE NEURONS IN THE RAT-BRAIN.
002727 03-03
FUNCTIONAL CHARACTERIZATION OF CENTRAL ALPHA-ADRENOCEPTORS
BY YOHIMBINE DIASTEREOMERS.
002748 03-03
IN VITRO CELLULAR ADAPTATION OF SEROTONERGIC PROCESSES AFTER
CHRONIC CENTRAL PHENOBARBITAL ADMINISTRATION.
002813 03-03
CENTRAL AND PERIPHERAL CATECHOLAMINE FUNCTION IN LEARNING
AND MEMORY PROCESSES.
002823 03-03
IN VIVO VOLTAMMETRIC INVESTIGATIONS INTO THE ACTION OF HA-966
ON CENTRAL DOPAMINERGIC NEURONS.
002832 03-03
A CRITICAL EVALUATION OF THE USE OF TOXINS FROM DENDROASPIS
VIRIDIS TO BLOCK NICOTINIC RESPONSES AT CENTRAL AND
GANGLIONIC SYNAPSES.
002870 03-03
GLUCOSE SUPPRESSES BASAL FIRING AND HALOPERIDOL-INDUCED
INCREASES IN THE FIRING-RATE OF CENTRAL DOPAMINERGIC
NEURONS.
002880 03-03
ACCELERATED METABOLISM OF PROBENECID DURING LONG-TERM-
TREATMENT OF RATS WITH ANTICONVULSANT-DRUGS: EFFECT ON
CENTRAL SEROTONIN TURNOVER STUDIES.
002890 03-03
BETA ENDORPHIN-INDUCED HYPERGLYCEMIA IS MEDIATED BY INCREASED
CENTRAL SYMPATHETIC OUTFLOW TO ADRENAL-MEDULLA.
002924 03-03
ACTION OF CYCLIC-ADENOSINE-MONOPHOSPHATE ON CENTRAL
NEURONS.
002940 03-03
EFFECT OF ACUTE AND CHRONIC TRIIODOTHYRONINE (T3)
ADMINISTRATION TO RATS ON CENTRAL 5 HT AND DOPAMINE-
MEDIATED BEHAVIOURAL-RESPONSES AND RELATED BRAIN-
BIOCHEMISTRY.
002951 03-04
EFFECTS OF ACUTE CENTRAL AND PERIPHERAL ACTH1-24
ADMINISTRATION ON LORDOSIS BEHAVIOR.
002975 03-04
NALOXONE REVERSIBLE DUPLICATION BY LANTHANUM OF OPIATE
ANALGESIA EFFECTS ON OROFACIAL, LOWER BODY AND CENTRAL
NOCICEPTION.
003028 03-04

INDUCTION OF ANALGESIA BY CENTRAL ADMINISTRATION OF ORG-2766,
AN ANALOG OF ACTH4-9.
003112 03-04
THE ROLE OF CENTRAL SEROTONERGIC MECHANISMS ON HEAD-TWITCH
AND BACKWARD LOCOMOTION INDUCED BY HALLUCINOGENIC-DRUGS.
003397 03-12
SUPERSENSITIVITY OF CENTRAL NORADRENERGIC PRESYNAPTIC-
AUTORECEPTORS FOLLOWING CHRONIC-TREATMENT WITH THE
ANTIDEPRESSANT MIANSERIN.
003745 04-03
CENTRAL HYPOTENSIVE-EFFECT OF GAMMA AMINOBUTYRIC-ACID IN
ANESTHETIZED DOGS.
003772 04-03
POSSIBLE ROLE OF AN ENDOGENOUS OPIATE IN THE CARDIOVASCULAR-
EFFECTS OF CENTRAL ALPHA-ADRENOCEPTOR STIMULATION IN
SPONTANEOUSLY HYPERTENSIVE-RATS.
003791 04-03
OPIATE-EFFECTS IN THE AMYGDALA CENTRAL NUCLEUS ON HEART RATE
CONDITIONING IN RABBITS.
003798 04-03
CENTRAL DOPAMINERGIC NEURONS DURING DEVELOPMENT OF GENETIC
AND DOCA-SALT HYPERTENSION IN THE RAT.
003899 04-03
EFFECTS OF 5 HYDROXYTRYPTAMINE ON CENTRAL NEURONES
ANTAGONIZED BY BICUCULLINE AND PICROTOXIN.
003931 04-03
CENTRAL CARDIOVASCULAR-EFFECTS AND BIOCHEMICAL-EFFECTS OF
BACLOFEN IN THE CONSCIOUS RAT.
003965 04-03
OPIATE SYSTEM INFLUENCES CENTRAL RESPIRATORY CHEMOSENSORS.
003971 04-03
EFFECT OF IMIPRAMINE ON CENTRAL 5 HYDROXYTRYPTAMINE
TURNOVER AND METABOLISM IN RATS.
003999 04-03
EFFECTS OF LITHIUM ON BEHAVIOUR AND CENTRAL MONOAMINES.
004110 04-04
GENETIC VARIATIONS IN MIDBRAIN DOPAMINE CELL NUMBER: PARALLEL
WITH DIFFERENCES IN RESPONSES TO DOPAMINERGIC AGONISTS AND
IN NATURALISTIC BEHAVIORS MEDIATED BY CENTRAL DOPAMINERGIC-
SYSTEMS. (UNPUBLISHED PAPER).
004112 04-04
CENTRAL AND PERIPHERAL EFFECTS OF LITHIUM ON AMPHETAMINE-
INDUCED HYPERACTIVITY IN RATS.
004223 04-04
BETA ENDORPHIN: CENTRAL SITES OF ANALGESIA, CATALEPSY AND
BODY-TEMPERATURE CHANGES IN RATS.
004238 04-04
A POSSIBLE NEUROCHEMICAL BASIS OF THE CENTRAL STIMULATORY
EFFECTS OF PP'DDT.
004274 04-05
THE EFFICACY OF PIRACETAM IN VERTIGO: A DOUBLE-BLIND STUDY IN
PATIENTS WITH VERTIGO OF CENTRAL ORIGIN.
004478 04-11
DOPAMINE AND 5 HT SUPERSENSITIVITY IN NONORGANIC CENTRAL PAIN
AND IN MORPHINE ABSTINENCE: FORTUITOUS OR REAL ANALOGY?
004553 04-13

CENTRAL-ACTION
CENTRAL-ACTION OF INTRAVENTRICULARLY INJECTED MIDODRINE IN
RATS.
001684 02-04
ASPIRIN ANALGESIA EVALUATED BY EVENT-RELATED POTENTIALS IN
MAN: POSSIBLE CENTRAL-ACTION IN BRAIN.
002195 02-12

CENTRAL-ACTIONS
CENTRAL-ACTIONS OF NOREPINEPHRINE, PHENTOLAMINE AND 6
HYDROXYDOPAMINE IN SPONTANEOUSLY HYPERTENSIVE-RATS.
001553 02-03
KINETICS OF CENTRAL-ACTIONS OF ISOFLOXYTHEPIN, AN ORAL
NEUROLEPTIC-DRUG WITH PROLONGED ACTION IN RODENTS.
001720 02-04
ADENOSINE-RECEPTORS IN THE CENTRAL-NERVOUS-SYSTEM:
RELATIONSHIP TO THE CENTRAL-ACTIONS OF METHYLXANTHINES.
003766 04-03
THE SIMULTANEOUS INFUSION OF DRUGS VIA THE LEFT AND RIGHT
VERTEBRAL-ARTERY OF THE CAT; A MODIFIED ANIMAL-MODEL FOR
THE STUDY OF POSSIBLE CENTRAL-ACTIONS OF DRUGS UPON THE
LOWER BRAINSTEM.
004297 04-06

CENTRAL-ACTIVITY
DIHYDROXY AND TRIHYDROXY ANALOGS OF CHLORPROMAZINE
INFLUENCE THE CENTRAL-ACTIVITY OF ADENYLATE-CYCLASE AND
CYCLIC-AMP-PHOSPHODIESTERASE.
001405 02-03

CENTRAL-EFFECTS
MECHANISMS INVOLVED IN CENTRAL-EFFECTS OF PROSTAGLANDIN-
F2ALPHA. (UNPUBLISHED PAPER).
001222 02-03

SOME CENTRAL-EFFECTS OF IMPROMIDINE, A POTENT AGONIST OF HISTAMINE H2-RECEPTORS.
001417 02-03

CYCLIC-NUCLEOTIDES AND THE CENTRAL-EFFECTS OF OPIATES: AN OVERVIEW OF CURRENT RESEARCH.
001445 02-03

CENTRAL-EFFECTS OF SUBSTANCE-P IN FOWLS.
003075 03-04

CENTRAL-EFFECTS OF ANGIOTENSIN-II IN WATER AND SALINE LOADED RATS.
003845 04-03

ANTAGONISM OF SOME CENTRAL-EFFECTS OF D TUBOCURARINE BY GAMMA AMINOBUTYRIC-ACID.
004102 04-04

CENTRAL-NERVOUS-SYSTEM
EFFECT OF INTRAVENTRICULAR INJECTIONS OF ALPHA AMINOSULFONIC-ACIDS ON THE CENTRAL-NERVOUS-SYSTEM OF CONSCIOUS MICE.
000009 01-02

NEUROTRANSMITTER RELATED ADAPTATION IN THE CENTRAL-NERVOUS-SYSTEM FOLLOWING CHRONIC MONOAMINE-OXIDASE-INHIBITION.
000038 01-03

THE EFFECTS OF OPIATES ON THE LEVELS OF CYCLIC-GUANOSINE-MONOPHOSPHATE IN DISCRETE AREAS OF THE RAT CENTRAL-NERVOUS-SYSTEM.
000220 01-03

THE INVOLVEMENT OF SEROTONERGIC NEURONS IN THE CENTRAL-NERVOUS-SYSTEM AS THE POSSIBLE MECHANISM FOR SLOW HEAD-SHAKING-BEHAVIOR INDUCED BY METHAMPHETAMINE IN RATS.
000408 01-04

MOTOR-EFFECTS OF SEROTONIN IN THE CENTRAL-NERVOUS-SYSTEM.
000941 01-17

DERIVATIVES OF 11 1 PIPERAZINYL-5H-PYRROLOBENZODIAZEPINE AS CENTRAL-NERVOUS-SYSTEM AGENTS.
001093 02-02

CENTRAL-NERVOUS-SYSTEM DOPAMINE-RECEPTORS.
001185 02-03

TOLERANCE TO BARBITURATE-INDUCED CENTRAL-NERVOUS-SYSTEM DEPRESSION: INVOLVEMENT OF STIMULUS SECRETION COUPLING IN DISCRETE BRAIN AREAS. (PH.D. DISSERTATION).
001213 02-03

PERIPHERAL PRESYNAPTIC AND POSTSYNAPTIC DOPAMINE-RECEPTORS: ARE THEY DIFFERENT FROM DOPAMINE-RECEPTORS IN THE CENTRAL-NERVOUS-SYSTEM.
001252 02-03

FURTHER EVIDENCE FOR THE EXISTENCE OF MULTIPLE RECEPTORS FOR DOPAMINE IN THE CENTRAL-NERVOUS-SYSTEM.
001296 02-03

PINEAL INTERACTIONS WITH THE CENTRAL-NERVOUS-SYSTEM: NEUROENDOCRINE IMPLICATIONS. (PH.D. DISSERTATION).
001341 02-03

THE ELECTROPHYSIOLOGICAL-EFFECTS OF ENKEPHALIN AND PHENCYCLIDINE IN THE RAT CENTRAL-NERVOUS-SYSTEM. (PH.D. DISSERTATION).
001406 02-03

FUNCTIONAL ASPECTS OF THE NOREPINEPHRINE-RECEPTOR COUPLED ADENYLATE-CYCLASE SYSTEM IN THE CENTRAL-NERVOUS-SYSTEM.
001493 02-03

ON THE USE OF OPERANT-BEHAVIOR TO STUDY THE NEUROPSYCHOPHARMACOLOGY OF OPIATES WITH SPECIAL REFERENCE TO MORPHINE AND ITS RELATIONSHIP TO DOPAMINE IN THE CENTRAL-NERVOUS-SYSTEM.
001790 02-04

EFFECTS OF 1,3 BIS-TETRAHYDRO-2-FURANYL-5-FLUOROPYRIMIDINEDIONE (FD-1) ON THE CENTRAL-NERVOUS-SYSTEM: 1. EFFECTS OF MONOAMINES IN THE BRAIN.
001857 02-05

THEORY, PROCEDURE, AND APPLICATIONS OF THE RADIOACTIVE DEOXYGLUCOSE METHOD FOR THE MEASUREMENT OF LOCAL GLUCOSE UTILIZATION IN THE CENTRAL-NERVOUS-SYSTEM. (UNPUBLISHED PAPER).
001877 02-06

NEUROLEPTIC-INDUCED REINNERVATION SPROUTING IN THE CENTRAL-NERVOUS-SYSTEM (A MODEL FOR THE DEVELOPMENT OF TARDIVE-DYSKINESIA AND SUPERSENSITIVITY PSYCHOSIS).
002459 02-15

EFFECTS OF 4 AMINOPYRIDINE ON THE TURNOVER OF MONOAMINES IN THE CENTRAL-NERVOUS-SYSTEM OF THE RAT.
002658 03-03

GAMMA BUTYROLACTONE-GAMMA-CARBONYL-HISTIDYL-PROLINAMIDE CITRATE (DN-1417): A NOVEL TRH ANALOG WITH POTENT EFFECTS ON THE CENTRAL-NERVOUS-SYSTEM.
003057 03-04

ADENOSINE-RECEPTORS IN THE CENTRAL-NERVOUS-SYSTEM: RELATIONSHIP TO THE CENTRAL-ACTIONS OF METHYLXANTHINES.
003766 04-03

SPECIFIC, HIGH-AFFINITY (3H)ETHYLKETOCYCLAZOCINE BINDING IN RAT CENTRAL-NERVOUS-SYSTEM: LACK OF EVIDENCE FOR KAPPA-RECEPTORS.
003840 04-03

THE HYPOTHERMIC-EFFECTS OF CLONIDINE AND OTHER IMIDAZOLIDINES IN RELATION TO THEIR ABILITY TO ENTER THE CENTRAL-NERVOUS-SYSTEM IN MICE.
003933 04-03

KINETIC STUDIES ON THE ENTRY OF D-AMPHETAMINE INTO THE CENTRAL-NERVOUS-SYSTEM: I. CEREBROSPINAL-FLUID.
004005 04-03

A COMPARATIVE EVALUATION OF THE USEFULNESS OF PSYCHOPHYSIOLOGICAL-TESTS DURING VARIOUS LEVELS OF ACTIVATION OF THE CENTRAL-NERVOUS-SYSTEM.
004543 04-13

CENTRAL-REGULATION
BIOGENIC-AMINES AND NEUROPEPTIDES PLAY A ROLE IN THE CENTRAL-REGULATION OF GENETIC HYPERTENSION. (UNPUBLISHED PAPER).
001455 02-03

CENTRALLY-ACTING
EFFECTS OF MORPHINE AND OTHER CENTRALLY-ACTING DRUGS ON 3,4 DIHYDROXYPHENYLETHYLENE-GLYCOL-SULFATE (DOPEG-SO4) IN RAT-BRAIN.
000136 01-03

ALTERATION OF PROLACTIN SECRETION BY CENTRALLY-ACTING DRUGS.
001127 02-03

DECREASE IN (3H) SEROTONIN BINDING IN RAT-BRAIN PRODUCED BY THE REPEATED ADMINISTRATION OF EITHER MONOAMINE-OXIDASE-INHIBITORS ON CENTRALLY-ACTING SEROTONIN AGONISTS.
001463 02-03

THE EFFECT OF REPEATED ELECTROCONVULSIVE-SHOCK ON CORTICOSTERONE RESPONSES TO CENTRALLY-ACTING PHARMACOLOGICAL STIMULI IN THE MALE RAT.
001486 02-03

CENTRALLY-ACTIVE
A SIGNAL-DETECTION-ANALYSIS OF CENTRALLY-ACTIVE DRUGS IN MICE.
001631 02-04

CENTRALLY-ADMINISTERED
EFFECTS OF CENTRALLY-ADMINISTERED PENTAZOCINE AND ETHYLKETOCYCLAZOCINE ON THERMOREGULATION IN THE CAT.
000361 01-04

EFFECTS OF CENTRALLY-ADMINISTERED AND SYSTEMICALLY ADMINISTERED L TYROSINE AND L LEUCINE ON OVARIAN FUNCTION IN THE OLD RAT.
001180 02-03

THE HYPOTENSIVE-EFFECT OF CENTRALLY-ADMINISTERED TYROSINE.
001548 02-03

CENTURIES
THE OPIATES: TWO CENTURIES OF SCIENTIFIC-STUDY.
000952 01-17

CEPHALALGIA
DOSE-EFFECT OF DEAE ON SUBJECTIVE PROBLEMS, VERTIGO, DEPRESSION, ASTHENIA, CEPHALALGIA, AND TONIC POSTURAL ACTIVITY PROBLEMS RECORDED WITH STATOKINESIMETER IN POSTCONCUSSIONAL-SYNDROME.
004472 04-11

CEPHALGIC-SEIZURES
CEPHALGIC-SEIZURES.
002172 02-11

CERCOPITHECUS-AETHIOPS-SABAEUS
PERIPHERAL-CORRELATES OF SEROTONERGICALLY-INFLUENCED BEHAVIORS IN VERVET-MONKEYS (CERCOPITHECUS-AETHIOPS-SABAFUS).
004204 04-04

CEREBELLAR
CEREBELLAR GRANULE CELL GENESIS IN THE HYDROCORTISONE TREATED RAT.
000030 01-03

A PROBABLE SITE-OF-ACTION OF DIAZEPAM IN RAT CEREBELLAR GABA SYSTEM.
000151 01-03

DISTRIBUTION OF 14C PHENYTOIN IN RAT PURKINJE-CELLS, CEREBELLAR AND CEREBRAL NEURONAL TISSUE AFTER A SINGLE INTRAPERITONEAL INJECTION.
000261 01-03

ORAL CHOLINE IN CEREBELLAR ATAXIA.
000722 01-11

INHIBITION BY ARYLSULPHATASE A OF NA-INDEPENDENT (3H) GABA AND (3H) MUSCIMOL BINDING TO BOVINE CEREBELLAR SYNAPTIC MEMBRANES.
001208 02-03

LOCALIZATION OF SENSITIVE SITES TO TAURINE, GAMMA AMINOBUTYRIC-ACID, GLYCINE AND BETA ALANINE IN THE MOLECULAR LAYER OF GUINEA-PIG CEREBELLAR SLICES.
001402 02-03

LITHIUM ANTAGONISM OF ETHANOL-INDUCED DEPLETION OF CEREBELLAR GUANOSINE-CYCLIC-MONOPHOSPHATE AND STIMULATION OF STRIATAL DOPAMINE RELEASE.
002242 02-13

TOXIC EFFECTS OF ALPHA AMINOADIPATE ON CULTURED CEREBELLAR CELLS.
002729 03-03

INHIBITORY ACTIONS OF TAUROCYAMINE, HYPOTAURINE, HOMOTAURINE, TAURINE AND GABA ON SPIKE DISCHARGES OF PURKINJE-CELLS, AND LOCALIZATION OF SENSITIVE SITES, IN GUINEA-PIG CEREBELLAR SLICES.
002846 03-03

EFFECTS OF PROTEIN AND MEMBRANE MODIFYING AGENTS ON THE BINDING OF L (3H)GLUTAMATE TO CEREBELLAR SYNAPTIC MEMBRANES.
002888 03-03

EFFECTS OF PHENYTOIN ON MOUSE CEREBELLAR 5 HYDROXYTRYPTAMINE AND NOREPINEPHRINE.
003795 04-03

ACTION OF DRUGS ON THE CEREBELLAR ELECTRICAL-ACTIVITIES.
003804 04-03

IBOTENIC-ACID ANALOGUES AS INHIBITORS OF (3H)GLUTAMIC-ACID BINDING TO CEREBELLAR MEMBRANES.
003848 04-03

MODULATORY INTERACTIONS BETWEEN NOREPINEPHRINE AND TAURINE, BETA ALANINE, GAMMA AMINOBUTYRIC-ACID AND MUSCIMOL APPLIED IONTOPHORETICALLY TO CEREBELLAR PURKINJE-CELLS.
004058 04-03

CEREBELLAR-CORTEX
DIFFERENTIAL-EFFECTS OF KAINIC-ACID ON BENZODIAZEPINE-RECEPTORS, GABA-RECEPTORS, AND GABA-MODULIN IN THE CEREBELLAR-CORTEX.
002477 02-16

CEREBELLUM
GABA FACILITATION BY NORADRENALINE SHOWED SUPERSENSITIVITY IN CEREBELLUM AFTER 6 HYDROXYDOPAMINE.
001382 02-03

NEURONAL LOCALIZATION OF BENZODIAZEPINE-RECEPTORS IN THE MURINE CEREBELLUM.
002902 03-03

ACTION OF PYRAZOLOPYRIDINES AS MODULATORS OF (3H)FLUNITRAZEPAM BINDING TO THE GABA/BENZODIAZEPINE-RECEPTOR COMPLEX OF THE CEREBELLUM.
002909 03-03

ACETYLCHOLINESTERASE AND CHOLINESTERASE ACTIVITIES IN THE MOUSE CEREBELLUM FOLLOWING MISONIDAZOLE TREATMENT.
003123 03-05

THE EFFECTS OF LITHIUM ON MYOINOSITOL LEVELS IN LAYERS OF FRONTAL-CEREBRAL-CORTEX, IN CEREBELLUM, AND IN CORPUS-CALLOSUM OF THE RAT.
003712 04-03

NEURONAL LOCALISATION OF BENZODIAZEPINE-RECEPTORS IN CEREBELLUM.
003739 04-03

EFFECTS OF ACUTE AND CHRONIC AMPHETAMINE TREATMENT ON PURKINJE NEURON DISCHARGE IN RAT CEREBELLUM.
003793 04-03

ELECTROPHYSIOLOGICAL EVIDENCE FOR PRESYNAPTIC ACTIONS OF PHENCYCLIDINE ON NORADRENERGIC TRANSMISSION IN RAT CEREBELLUM.
003926 04-03

GUANYLATE-CYCLASE -- CYCLIC-GMP IN MOUSE CEREBRAL-CORTEX AND CEREBELLUM: MODIFICATION BY ANTICONVULSANTS.
003956 04-03

THE EFFECT OF PROPRANOLOL AND ITS ISOMERS ON PURKINJE NEURONES IN RAT CEREBELLUM.
004059 04-03

CEREBRAL
EFFECT OF ISOPROTERENOL ON CEREBRAL CIRCULATION IN DOGS.
000199 01-03

CEREBRAL CIRCULATORY AND METABOLIC-EFFECTS OF PIRIBEDIL.
000200 01-03

LONG-TERM ANTIDEPRESSANT TREATMENT: ALTERATIONS IN CEREBRAL CAPILLARY PERMEABILITY.
000239 01-03

IN VIVO OCCUPATION OF CEREBRAL HISTAMINE H1-RECEPTORS EVALUATED WITH 3H MEPYRAMINE MAY PREDICT SEDATIVE PROPERTIES OF PSYCHOTROPIC-DRUGS.
000241 01-03

NONLINEAR REGRESSION ANALYSIS OF NOREPINEPHRINE RESPONSE KINETICS IN CEREBRAL VASCULATURE.
000256 01-03

DISTRIBUTION OF 14C PHENYTOIN IN RAT PURKINJE-CELLS, CEREBELLAR AND CEREBRAL NEURONAL TISSUE AFTER A SINGLE INTRAPERITONEAL INJECTION.
000261 01-03

DIFFERENCES IN ACTIVITY IN CEREBRAL METHYLTRANSFERASES AND MONOAMINE-OXIDASES BETWEEN AUDIOGENIC-SEIZURE SUSCEPTIBLE AND RESISTANT MICE AND DEERMICE.
000377 01-04

IMPROVEMENT OF RESTITUTION FROM CEREBRAL ISCHEMIA IN HYPERGLYCEMIC RATS BY PENTOBARBITAL OR DIAZEPAM.
000475 01-04

CONTRIBUTION TO THE CLINICAL-STUDY OF CEREBRAL DOPAMINERGIC MECHANISMS: THE ACTION OF PIRIBEDIL IN PSYCHIATRY. FIRST RESULTS.
000616 01-09

CLASSIFICATION AND ASSESSMENT OF CEREBRAL BIOAVAILABILITY OF LOPIRAZEPAM (D-12524) BY QUANTITATIVE EEG AND PSYCHOMETRIC-ANALYSIS.
000720 01-11

CONTRIBUTION TO STUDY OF CEREBRAL DOPAMINERGIC MECHANISMS: REALITY OF THE PROBLEM.
000782 01-13

OPIOID MECHANISMS IN REGULATION OF CEREBRAL MONOAMINES IN VIVO.
001098 02-03

PARASYMPATHOMIMETIC-INFLUENCE OF CARBACHOL ON LOCAL CEREBRAL BLOOD FLOW IN THE RABBIT BY A DIRECT VASODILATOR ACTION AND AN INHIBITION OF THE SYMPATHETIC MEDIATED VASOCONSTRICTION.
001109 02-03

EFFECTS OF BICUCULLINE-INDUCED SEIZURES ON CEREBRAL METABOLISM AND CIRCULATION OF RATS RENDERED HYPOGLYCEMIC BY STARVATION.
001134 02-03

CHANGES IN CEREBRAL DOPAMINE FUNCTION INDUCED BY A YEARS ADMINISTRATION OF TRIFLUOPERAZINE OR THIORIDAZINE AND THEIR SUBSEQUENT WITHDRAWAL.
001175 02-03

EFFECT OF PAPAVERINE ON REGIONAL CEREBRAL BLOOD FLOW AND SMALL VESSEL BLOOD CONTENT.
001177 02-03

STEREOSELECTIVE ACTIONS OF SUBSTITUTED BENZAMIDE DRUGS ON CEREBRAL DOPAMINE MECHANISMS.
001301 02-03

LOCAL CEREBRAL GLUCOSE UTILIZATION (LCGU) IN RAT-BRAIN DURING HYPOXEMIA. (UNPUBLISHED PAPER).
001380 02-03

THE EFFECT OF SODIUM-SALICYLATE ON CEREBRAL BLOOD FLOW AND METABOLISM.
001416 02-03

COMPARATIVE-STUDY OF AGGRESSIVE-BEHAVIOUR AFTER INJECTION OF CHOLINOMIMETICS, ANTICHOLINESTERASES, NICOTINIC, AND MUSCARINIC GANGLIONIC STIMULANTS INTO THE CEREBRAL VENTRICLES OF CONSCIOUS CATS: FAILURE OF NICOTINIC-DRUGS TO EVOKE AGGRESSION.
001568 02-04

THE PHARMACOLOGY OF AGGRESSIVE-BEHAVIOURAL-PHENOMENA ELICITED BY MUSCARINE INJECTED INTO THE CEREBRAL VENTRICLES OF CONSCIOUS CATS.
001569 02-04

CEREBRAL VENTRICLES AND DOPAMINE IN SCHIZOPHRENIA. (UNPUBLISHED PAPER).
001928 02-08

THE EFFECT OF BETA-ADRENERGIC-RECEPTOR BLOCKING-DRUGS ON CEREBRAL BLOOD FLOW IN HYPERTENSIVE-PATIENTS.
002071 02-10

CEREBRAL SENESCENCE AND ITS PSYCHIC-MANIFESTATIONS. THE EFFECTIVENESS OF DEBRUMYL.
002105 02-11

LSD-INDUCED ULTRASTRUCTURAL MODIFICATIONS OF LIMBIC-SYSTEM NUCLEI AND OTHER CEREBRAL ZONES.
002198 02-12

REGIONAL CEREBRAL BLOOD FLOW IN A CASE OF AMPHETAMINE INTOXICATION.
002210 02-13

HEMODYNAMIC AND CEREBRAL METABOLIC-STUDY OF DIAZEPAM IN NEUROSURGICAL-RESUSCITATION.
002231 02-13

CORRECTION BY PROPRANOLOL OF THE ABNORMAL ADRENALINE DISCHARGE INDUCED BY EMOTIONAL-STRESS IN CEREBRAL HEMORRHAGE PATIENTS.
002295 02-13

CHANGES IN CEREBRAL DOPAMINE METABOLISM AND RECEPTORS DURING ONE-YEAR NEUROLEPTIC ADMINISTRATION AND SUBSEQUENT WITHDRAWAL: RELEVANCE TO BRAIN-BIOCHEMISTRY IN SCHIZOPHRENIA.
002390 02-15

A SPECIFIC AND SENSITIVE MICROASSAY FOR HYDROXYINDOLES IN BIOLOGICAL-MATERIAL -- APPLICATION FOR CEREBRAL MICROVESSELS, BRAIN, AND PINEAL-ORGAN OF THE RAT.
002503 02-16

PURSUING THE ACTIONS OF PSYCHOTROPIC-DRUGS: RECEPTOR SITES AND ENDOGENOUS CEREBRAL PROGRAMMES.
002578 02-17

NOREPINEPHRINE DEPLETION ALTERS CEREBRAL OXIDATIVE METABOLISM IN THE ACTIVE STATE.
002798 03-03

PHENOTHIAZINE ACTION ON CEREBRAL 5 HYDROXYTRYPTAMINE.
002850 03-03

LONG-ACTING ANTIPSYCHOTIC-DRUGS AND CEREBRAL 5 HYDROXYTRYPTAMINE.
002851 03-03

Subject Index

NOREPINEPHRINE AND DOPAMINE CEREBRAL LEVELS AFTER CHRONIC-TREATMENT WITH NOMIFENSINE.
002872 03-03

DECREASED CEREBRAL CATABOLISM OF (3H)HISTAMINE IN VIVO AFTER S ADENOSYLMETHIONINE ADMINISTRATION.
002883 03-03

THE EFFECTS OF INJECTIONS OF BOMBESIN INTO THE CEREBRAL VENTRICLES ON BEHAVIORAL THERMOREGULATION.
002952 03-04

DOSAGE OF INTRATUMORAL LITHIUM (CEREBRAL GLIOBLASTOMA): ON A FAILURE OF TREATMENT OF MANIC-DEPRESSIVE-PSYCHOSIS.
003226 03-09

CEREBRAL EVOKED-POTENTIAL CHANGES PRODUCED BY TREATMENT WITH LITHIUM-CARBONATE.
003263 03-09

CAPACITIES OF ATTENTION, STRESS-RESISTANCE, AND SLOW CEREBRAL POTENTIALS: EFFECTS OF CARPIPRAMINE ON CONTINGENT NEGATIVE VARIATION WAVES AND P-300.
003451 03-14

ACUTE PHARMACOTOXIC PSYCHOSES IN CHRONIC CEREBRAL CONDITIONS.
003475 03-15

ACTION OF 4 AMINOPYRIDINE ON THE CEREBRAL CIRCULATION.
003781 04-03

NA-GAMMA-HYDROXYBUTYRATE IN CEREBRAL PROTECTION DURING SEVERE HYPOXEMIA IN THE RAT.
003895 04-03

ALTERATIONS IN DIHYDROMORPHINE BINDING IN CEREBRAL HEMISPHERES OF AGED MALE RATS.
003936 04-03

THE EFFECT OF DIBENZAZEPINES (TRICYCLIC-ANTIDEPRESSANTS) ON CEREBRAL CAPILLARY PERMEABILITY IN THE RAT IN VIVO.
003974 04-03

DRUG-INDUCED CHANGES IN THE COMPOSITION OF THE CEREBRAL FREE AMINO-ACID POOL.
004039 04-03

CLASSICAL NEUROLEPTICS AND DECONDITIONING ACTIVITY AFTER SINGLE OR REPEATED TREATMENTS: ROLE OF DIFFERENT CEREBRAL NEUROTRANSMITTERS.
004115 04-04

EFFECTS OF A SINGLE-THERAPEUTIC-DOSE OF GLYCEROL ON CEREBRAL METABOLISM IN THE BRAINS OF YOUNG MICE: POSSIBLE INCREASE IN BRAIN GLUCOSE TRANSPORT AND GLUCOSE UTILIZATION.
004281 04-05

PECULIARITIES OF THE CEREBRAL PATHOMORPHOLOGY OF PATIENTS WITH SCHIZOPHRENIA TREATED WITH PSYCHOTROPIC-DRUGS (PHARMACOLOGICAL PATHOMORPHOSIS).
004528 04-13

CEREBRAL FLUORIDE IN MANIA AND THE EFFECT OF LITHIUM: A HYPOTHESIS.
004715 04-17

CEREBRAL-ARTERIES
REACTIVITY OF ISOLATED CANINE CEREBRAL-ARTERIES TO ADENINE-NUCLEOTIDES AND ADENOSINE.
000210 01-03

RESPONSIVENESS TO VASOACTIVE-AGENTS OF CEREBRAL-ARTERIES AND MESENTERIC-ARTERIES ISOLATED FROM CONTROL AND RESERPINE TREATED DOGS.
001273 02-03

INDIRECT ADRENERGIC EFFECT OF HISTAMINE IN CAT CEREBRAL-ARTERIES.
001355 02-03

CEREBRAL-ARTERY
RELEASE OF ENDOGENOUS NOREPINEPHRINE FROM A RABBIT CEREBRAL-ARTERY.
000079 01-03

DIRECT EVIDENCE AGAINST ACETYLCHOLINE AS THE DILATOR TRANSMITTER IN THE CAT CEREBRAL-ARTERY.
001336 02-03

CEREBRAL-CORTEX
FUNCTIONAL HYPERINNERVATION OF CEREBRAL-CORTEX BY NORADRENERGIC NEURONS RESULTS FROM FETAL LESIONS: PARALLELS WITH SCHIZOPHRENIA.
000059 01-03

THE EFFECT OF PSYCHOTROPIC-SUBSTANCES AND NARCOTIC ANALGESIC-DRUGS ON 14C NORADRENALINE UPTAKE BY SYNAPTOSOMES OF THE CEREBRAL-CORTEX OF RATS.
001363 02-03

OPIATE-RECEPTOR GRADIENTS IN MONKEY CEREBRAL-CORTEX: CORRESPONDENCE WITH SENSORY PROCESSING HIERARCHIES.
002641 03-01

DEMONSTRATION AND CHARACTERIZATION OF AN ENDOGENOUS INHIBITOR OF GABA-ENHANCED (3H) DIAZEPAM BINDING FROM BOVINE CEREBRAL-CORTEX.
002645 03-01

METHYLXANTHINES MODULATE ADENOSINE RELEASE FROM SLICES OF CEREBRAL-CORTEX.
002907 03-03

CORRELATIONS BETWEEN LITHIUM LEVELS IN CEREBROSPINAL-FLUID AND
LITHIUM LEVELS IN BLOOD PLASMA AND ERYTHROCYTES.
003210 03-09

LEVELS OF 5 HYDROXYINDOLEACETIC-ACID AND TRYPTOPHAN IN
LUMBAR CEREBROSPINAL-FLUID AND BLOOD OF PATIENTS WITH
DEMENTIA AND NORMAL PRESSURE HYDROCEPHALUS AFTER
TRYPTOPHAN ADMINISTRATION.
003419 03-13

DOPAMINE CONJUGATE IN CEREBROSPINAL-FLUID.
003432 03-13

HUMAN BRAIN, PLASMA, AND CEREBROSPINAL-FLUID CONCENTRATION
OF SODIUM-VALPROATE AFTER 72 HOURS OF THERAPY.
003433 03-13

ALTERATIONS IN CEREBROSPINAL-FLUID DOPAMINE METABOLITES
FOLLOWING PHYSOSTIGMINE INFUSION.
003477 03-15

CEREBROSPINAL-FLUID CONCENTRATIONS OF THIORIDAZINE AND ITS
MAIN METABOLITES IN PSYCHIATRIC-PATIENTS.
003569 03-16

A SELECTED ION-MONITORING ASSAY FOR BIOGENIC-AMINE
METABOLITES AND PROBENECID, IN HUMAN LUMBAR
CEREBROSPINAL-FLUID.
003663 04-01

QUANTITATION AND COMPARISON OF PHENOBARBITAL LEVELS IN THE
PLASMA, SALIVA, AND CEREBROSPINAL-FLUID OF THE RAT, AND THE
DEMONSTRATION OF AN ALTERATION OF DRUG PASSAGE BY
ETHANOL.
003725 04-03

KINETIC STUDIES ON THE ENTRY OF D-AMPHETAMINE INTO THE
CENTRAL-NERVOUS-SYSTEM: I. CEREBROSPINAL-FLUID.
004005 04-03

THE DYNAMICS OF SYSTEMIC VENOUS, ARTERIAL, AND CEREBROSPINAL-
FLUID PRESSURE UNDER I.V. ADMINISTRATION OF POLYETHYLENE-
GLYCOL.
004045 04-03

PROTEIN BINDING OF CHLORPROMAZINE IN CEREBROSPINAL-FLUID AND
SERUM.
004311 04-08

CEREBROSPINAL-FLUID VALUES OF HVA AND 5 HIAA IN PATIENTS WITH
ENDOGENOUS DEPRESSION DURING THE COURSE OF TREATMENT.
004382 04-09

CEREBROSPINAL-FLUID HOMOVANILLIC-ACID PATTERNS DURING
NEUROLEPTIC TREATMENT. (UNPUBLISHED PAPER).
004502 04-13

CONCENTRATIONS OF CHLORPROMAZINE AND TWO OF ITS ACTIVE
METABOLITES IN PLASMA AND CEREBROSPINAL-FLUID OF PSYCHOTIC-
PATIENTS TREATED WITH FIXED DRUG DOSES.
004559 04-13

CEREBROVASCULAR-ACCIDENTS
EFFECTS OF CYCLOSPASMOL UPON SENSORY PARAMETERS IN PATIENTS
RECOVERING FROM CEREBROVASCULAR-ACCIDENTS.
002360 02-14

CEREBROVASCULAR-DISEASES
THERAPEUTIC TREATMENT OF INSUFFICIENT PERFORMANCE IN
CEREBROVASCULAR-DISEASES.
004718 04-17

CESIUM
CESIUM.
001090 02-02

DISTRIBUTION OF CESIUM IN THE ORGANISM AND ITS EFFECT ON THE
NUCLEOTIDE METABOLISM ENZYMES.
003696 04-02

CESSATION
SEVERE WITHDRAWAL-SYNDROME AFTER CESSATION OF
BENZODIAZEPINE TREATMENT: SIX CLINICAL CASES.
003505 03-15

THE EFFECT OF SMALL DOSES OF HALOPERIDOL AND CLOZAPINE ON
BEHAVIORAL SHIFTS IN CATS, ARISING AFTER CESSATION OF
ELECTRICAL-STIMULATION OF THE CAUDATE-NUCLEUS.
004067 04-04

THE EFFECT OF AN INTENSIVE COURSE OF NEUROLEPTIC-DRUGS ON
SCHIZOPHRENIC-PATIENTS AND THEIR SUBSEQUENT COURSE
FOLLOWING THE CESSATION OF ALL NEUROLEPTIC-MEDICATION.
004341 04-08

WITHDRAWAL SYMPTOMS AFTER GRADUATED CESSATION OF
IMIPRAMINE IN CHILDREN.
004630 04-15

APOMORPHINE-INDUCED STEREOTYPY IN MATURE AND SENESCENT RATS
FOLLOWING CESSATION OF CHRONIC HALOPERIDOL TREATMENT.
004651 04-15

CF-25-397
TREATMENT OF DYSKINETIC AND DYSTONIC-DISORDERS WITH CF-25-
397: CLINICAL-ASPECTS AND PHARMACOLOGICAL ASPECTS.
002121 02-11

CFF
SMOKING AND VIGILANCE: THE EFFECTS OF TOBACCO SMOKING ON CFF
AS RELATED TO PERSONALITY AND SMOKING HABITS.
002368 02-14

CGP-6085-A
CGP-6085-A, A NEW, SPECIFIC, INHIBITOR OF SEROTONIN UPTAKE:
NEUROCHEMICAL CHARACTERIZATION AND COMPARISON WITH OTHER
SEROTONIN UPTAKE BLOCKERS.
000316 01-03

CH-757
PHARMACOKINETIC-STUDY IN MAN OF THE CH-757 PREPARATION.
004440 04-11

CHAGAS-DISEASE
EPILEPSY AND CHRONIC CHAGAS-DISEASE.
003328 03-11

CHALLENGE
PHENCYCLIDINE-HCL: A CHALLENGE TO MEDICINE.
003395 03-12

NEUROENDOCRINE-TESTS DURING TREATMENT WITH NEUROLEPTIC-
DRUGS: I. PLASMA PROLACTIN RESPONSE TO CHLORPROMAZINE
CHALLENGE.
004329 04-08

CHALLENGE-DOSE
THE EFFECT OF THIORIDAZINE ON PROLACTIN LEVELS IN ACUTELY
SCHIZOPHRENIC-PATIENTS: CHALLENGE-DOSE AND STEADY-STATE
LEVELS.
000558 01-08

CHALLENGES
MORPHINE CHALLENGES IN LEVO ALPHA ACETYLMETHADOL (LAAM)
POSTADDICT RATS.
004259 04-04

CLINICAL DEPRESSIONS: DIAGNOSTIC AND THERAPEUTIC CHALLENGES.
004350 04-09

CHANCES
SOME WAYS TO INCREASE CHANCES TO DISCOVER THE CNS DRUGS OF
THE FUTURE.
002528 02-17

CHANGE
A STUDY OF THE QUANTAL (ALL-OR-NONE) CHANGE IN REFLEX LATENCY
PRODUCED BY OPIATE ANALGESICS.
000425 01-04

HOW TO SUCCESSFULLY CHANGE A PATIENT FROM ONE DRUG TO
ANOTHER.
000913 01-17

CHANGE IN PYRUVATE-DEHYDROGENASE ACTIVITY INFLUENCE PYRUVATE
SUPPORTED CALCIUM ACCUMULATION BY BRAIN MITOCHONDRIA.
(UNPUBLISHED PAPER).
001147 02-03

LONG-TERM HALOPERIDOL TREATMENT OF MICE: A CHANGE IN BETA-
ADRENERGIC-RECEPTOR RESPONSIVENESS.
001206 02-03

TRYPTOPHOL-INDUCED CHANGE IN BRAIN 5 HYDROXYTRYPTAMINE
METABOLISM.
001236 02-03

EEG CHANGE IN THE CONSCIOUS RAT DURING IMMOBILITY INDUCED BY
PSYCHOLOGICAL-STRESS.
001297 02-03

CHANGE IN OVERINCLUSIVE THINKING OF SCHIZOPHRENIC-PATIENTS IS
RELATED TO PLASMA PHENOTHIAZINE CONCENTRATION.
001941 02-08

THERAPEUTIC RESULTS IN A PSYCHOGERIATRIC-WARD AFTER CHANGE OF
MEDICATION.
002136 02-11

THE CHANGE OF BLOOD PROLACTIN LEVEL DUE TO THE WITHDRAWAL OF
MAINTENANCE NEUROLEPTICS.
002559 02-17

CHANGE IN CATECHOLAMINE SENSITIVE NA-K-ATPASE ACTIVITY IN THE
RAT STRIATUM MICROSOMES FOLLOWING ELECTROLYTIC OR 6
HYDROXYDOPAMINE-INDUCED LESIONS OF DOPAMINERGIC NEURONS.
003871 04-03

SCHEDULE DEPENDENT CHANGE OF PUNISHED-RESPONDING AFTER
DIAZEPAM IN RATS.
004165 04-04

ELECTROENCEPHALOGRAPHIC CHANGE IN PARKINSONIAN-PATIENTS
TREATED WITH LEVODOPA CARBIDOPA.
004557 04-13

CHANGES
ACUTE CHANGES IN BRAIN TRYPTOPHAN AND SEROTONIN FOLLOWING
CARBOHYDRATE OR PROTEIN INGESTION BY DIABETIC RATS.
(UNPUBLISHED PAPER).
000060 01-03

AGONIST-INDUCED CHANGES IN BETA-ADRENERGIC-RECEPTOR DENSITY
AND RECEPTOR-MEDIATED RESPONSIVENESS IN SLICES OF RAT-
CEREBRAL-CORTEX.
000072 01-03

CHANGES IN PLASMA CORTICOSTERONE LEVELS AS A MEASURE OF
ACUTE DEPENDENCE UPON LEVORPHANOL IN RATS.
000085 01-03

CHANGES OF ACTH, STH, TSH AND PROLACTIN LEVELS IN ENDOTOXIN
SHOCK IN RATS.
000119 01-03

THE EFFECT OF DIAZEPAM ON EEG CHANGES FOLLOWING INTRASEPTAL ADMINISTRATION OF ATROPINE.
000127 01-03

CORTICAL NEUROCHEMICAL CHANGES AFTER INTRASTRIATAL INJECTION OF KAINIC-ACID.
000133 01-03

EFFECTS OF CHANGES IN THE STRUCTURE OF ENKEPHALINS AND OF NARCOTIC ANALGESIC-DRUGS ON THEIR INTERACTIONS WITH MU-RECEPTORS AND DELTA-RECEPTORS.
000168 01-03

THE EFFECT OF ANTIDEPRESSANTS ON L 5 HTP-INDUCED CHANGES IN RAT PLASMA CORTICOSTEROIDS.
000170 01-03

CHANGES IN PRIMARY AFFERENT DEPOLARIZATION AFTER ADMINISTRATION OF GAMMA ACETYLENIC-GAMMA-AMINOBUTYRIC-ACID (GAG), A GAMMA AMINOBUTYRIC-ACID-TRANSAMINASE (GABA-TRANSAMINASE) INHIBITOR.
000174 01-03

AGE-RELATED ELECTROPHYSIOLOGICAL CHANGES IN RAT-CEREBELLUM.
000197 01-03

CHANGES IN MOUSE-BRAIN DIAZEPAM-RECEPTOR BINDING AFTER PHENOBARBITAL ADMINISTRATION.
000281 01-03

CHANGES IN OPIATE ACTIVITY OF RAT PITUITARY FOLLOWING ACUTE ADMINISTRATION OF NEUROLEPTICS.
000282 01-03

CHANGES IN BRAIN N DEMETHYLATION AND OPIATE-RECEPTOR CONTENT CORRELATE WITH ANALGESIC EFFECTIVENESS OF MORPHINE.
000400 01-04

BRAINSTEM AUDITORY EVOKED-POTENTIALS AND MYELIN CHANGES IN TRIETHYLTIN-INDUCED EDEMA IN YOUNG ADULT RATS.
000509 01-05

BRAIN FUNCTION IN OLD-AGE: EVALUATION OF CHANGES AND DISORDERS.
000684 01-11

PROLACTIN CHANGES IN MAJOR DEPRESSIVE-DISORDERS.
000752 01-13

THE ULTRASTRUCTURAL CHANGES OF SYNAPSES IN RAT FOLLOWING LONG-TERM ADMINISTRATION OF THE NEUROLEPTICS RESERPINE AND HALOPERIDOL.
000795 01-13

PHARMACOPSYCHOLOGICAL INVESTIGATION OF CHANGES IN MOOD INDUCED BY DIPOTASSIUM-CHLORAZEPATE WITH AND WITHOUT SIMULTANEOUS ALCOHOL ADMINISTRATION.
000825 01-14

NEUROLOGICAL SIDE-EFFECTS OF LITHIUM: ORGANIC-BRAIN-SYNDROME, SEIZURES, EXTRAPYRAMIDAL SIDE-EFFECTS, AND EEG CHANGES.
000847 01-15

ENDOCRINOLOGICAL CHANGES IN PATIENTS WITH SEXUAL-DYSFUNCTION UNDER LONG-TERM NEUROLEPTIC TREATMENT.
000912 01-17

DISEASE-INDUCED CHANGES IN THE PLASMA BINDING OF BASIC DRUGS.
000975 01-17

INFERENTIAL CHANGES AFTER CHRONIC-TREATMENTS WITH LI, DMI, OR ETHANOL DETECTED BY ELECTROPHYSIOLOGICAL-CORRELATES.
001136 02-03

ADAPTIVE CHANGES OF THE STRIATAL DOPAMINE SYSTEM INDUCED BY REPEATED ADMINISTRATION OF NEUROLEPTICS AND ERGOT DERIVATIVES.
001156 02-03

CHANGES IN CEREBRAL DOPAMINE FUNCTION INDUCED BY A YEARS ADMINISTRATION OF TRIFLUOPERAZINE OR THIORIDAZINE AND THEIR SUBSEQUENT WITHDRAWAL.
001175 02-03

EVOKED-POTENTIAL CHANGES IN THE SUPERIOR-COLLICULUS PARALLEL THE LESION-INDUCED DEVELOPMENT OF GROOMING REFLEXES IN THE CAT. (PH.D. DISSERTATION).
001179 02-03

DOSE-DEPENDENT, AMPHETAMINE-INDUCED CHANGES IN PERMEABILITY OF THE BLOOD-BRAIN-BARRIER OF NORMOTENSIVE-RATS AND SPONTANEOUSLY HYPERTENSIVE-RATS.
001197 02-03

EFFECT OF PYRITINOL AND PIRACETAM ON CHANGES IN FREE AMMONIA LEVEL IN CNS TISSUE AFTER PARADOXICAL SLEEP-DEPRIVATION IN RATS.
001199 02-03

EFFECT OF LITHIUM ON STRESS-INDUCED CHANGES IN THE BRAIN LEVELS OF MONOAMINES IN RATS.
001216 02-03

LITHIUM-INDUCED CHANGES IN THE BRAIN LEVELS OF FREE AMINO-ACIDS IN STRESS-EXPOSED RATS.
001217 02-03

EFFECT OF MOXESTROL ON HALOPERIDOL-INDUCED CHANGES IN STRIATAL ACETYLCHOLINE LEVELS AND DOPAMINE TURNOVER.
001218 02-03

THE QUANTITATIVE MEASUREMENT OF CHANGES IN EEG FREQUENCY SPECTRA PRODUCED IN THE CAT BY SEDATIVE HYPNOTICS AND NEUROLEPTICS.
001220 02-03

CHANGES IN ALPHA-ADRENERGIC-RECEPTORS IN RAT-BRAIN IN VITRO BY PREINCUBATION WITH ALPHA-ADRENERGIC LIGANDS.
001272 02-03

AGE-RELATED CHANGES IN BODY-TEMPERATURE RESPONSES TO MORPHINE IN RATS.
001366 02-03

ROLE OF BRAIN CATECHOLAMINES AND 5 HYDROXYTRYPTAMINE IN MORPHINE-INDUCED TEMPERATURE CHANGES IN NORMAL AND TOLERANT RATS AND MICE.
001476 02-03

IN VIVO CHANGES IN THE GABA CONTENT OF NERVE-ENDINGS (SYNAPTOSOMES) INDUCED BY INHIBITORS OF GABA UPTAKE.
001540 02-03

NEUROPHARMACOLOGICAL-AGENTS MODIFYING ENDOTOXIN-INDUCED CHANGES IN MICE.
001543 02-03

DENERVATION IN THE DOPAMINERGIC MESOLIMBIC SYSTEM: FUNCTIONAL CHANGES FOLLOWED USING (-)N N PROPYLNORAPOMORPHINE DEPEND ON THE BASAL ACTIVITY LEVELS OF RATS.
001603 02-04

CHANGES OF PHYSICAL MORPHINE-DEPENDENCE IN RATS CHRONICALLY TREATED WITH DRUGS ACTING ON BRAIN 5 HYDROXYTRYPTAMINE.
001764 02-04

REGIONAL CHANGES IN BRAIN GLUCOSE UTILIZATION IN RATS GIVEN A PYRETHROID INSECTICIDE.
001838 02-05

LONG-TERM CHLORPROMAZINE IN RHESUS-MONKEYS: PRODUCTION OF DYSKINESIAS AND CHANGES IN SOCIAL-BEHAVIOR.
001850 02-05

TIME-COURSE OF THE ANTIPSYCHOTIC-EFFECT IN SCHIZOPHRENIA AND SOME CHANGES IN POSTMORTEM BRAIN AND THEIR RELATION TO NEUROLEPTIC-MEDICATION.
001911 02-08

CLINICAL AND EEG CHANGES IN DEPRESSIVE-PATIENTS AFTER A SINGLE INJECTION OF BETA ENDORPHIN.
001962 02-09

EEG CHANGES IN CHILDREN WITH TREATED PHENYLKETONURIA AFTER PHENYLALANINE LOAD.
002115 02-11

ENDOCRINE CHANGES AND BEHAVIORAL-CHANGES IN DEPRESSION AFTER THYROTROPIN-RELEASING-HORMONE (TRH): ALTERATION BY PRETREATMENT WITH THYROID-HORMONES.
002259 02-13

INTERRELATION AT PLASMATIC LEVEL BETWEEN ANTIEPILEPTIC-DRUGS AND LIPIDS. ITS IMPLICATIONS IN THE EFFICIENCY OF TREATMENT IN EPILEPSY. I. CHANGES INDUCED BY PHENOBARBITAL OR/AND DIPHENYLHYDANTOIN IN SERUM LIPIDS.
002281 02-13

CHANGES IN THE AUGMENTER REDUCER TENDENCY AND IN PAIN MEASURES AS A RESULT OF TREATMENT WITH A SEROTONIN REUPTAKE INHIBITOR ZIMELIDINE.
002305 02-13

CHANGES IN CEREBRAL DOPAMINE METABOLISM AND RECEPTORS DURING ONE-YEAR NEUROLEPTIC ADMINISTRATION AND SUBSEQUENT WITHDRAWAL: RELEVANCE TO BRAIN-BIOCHEMISTRY IN SCHIZOPHRENIA.
002390 02-15

ON THE MEASUREMENT IN RATS OF THE CONVULSANT-EFFECT OF DRUGS AND THE CHANGES WHICH FOLLOW ELECTROCONVULSIVE-SHOCK.
002444 02-15

CHANGES IN PREVALENCE, SEVERITY, AND RECOVERY IN TARDIVE-DYSKINESIA WITH AGE.
002455 02-15

CHANGES IN BODY-TEMPERATURE AFTER ADMINISTRATION OF ADRENERGIC AND SEROTONERGIC-AGENTS AND RELATED DRUGS INCLUDING ANTIDEPRESSANTS.
002532 02-17

AGE DEPENDENT CHANGES IN THE BETA ENDORPHIN CONTENT OF DISCRETE RAT-BRAIN NUCLEI.
002635 03-01

MORPHOLOGICAL CHANGES IN RAT-BRAIN INDUCED BY L CYSTEINE INJECTION IN NEWBORN ANIMALS.
002774 03-03

CHANGES IN THE CORTICAL ACTIVITY OF SUCCINATE-DEHYDROGENASE UNDER THE INFLUENCE OF CHLORPROMAZINE (A HISTOCHEMICAL-STUDY AND ELECTROCYTOCHEMICAL-STUDY).
002784 03-03

ENHANCEMENT OF ETORPHINE BRAIN CONCENTRATIONS AND CHANGES IN ETORPHINE NALOXONE PA2 VALUES IN MORPHINE PRETREATED MICE.
002800 03-03

LACK OF CORRELATION BETWEEN NALOXONE-INDUCED CHANGES IN SEXUAL-BEHAVIOR AND SERUM LH IN MALE RATS.
002821 03-03

CHANGES IN NORADRENERGIC TRANSMISSION ALTER THE CONCENTRATION OF CYTOPLASMIC PROGESTIN-RECEPTORS IN HYPOTHALAMUS.
002842 03-03

CHANGES IN THE HORIZONTAL VESTIBULO-OCULAR REFLEX OF THE RHESUS-MONKEY WITH BEHAVIORAL AND PHARMACOLOGICAL ALERTING.
002997 03-04
AN ANALYSIS OF SPECIFICITY OF DRUG-INDUCED CHANGES IN DRUG-REINFORCED RESPONDING. (PH.D. DISSERTATION).
003010 03-04
CYCLIC-AMP-INDUCED CHANGES IN THE ELECTROENCEPHALOGRAM AND IN BEHAVIOR DURING MORPHINE-DEPENDENCE AND ABSTINENCE IN THE RAT.
003078 03-04
ELECTROPHYSIOLOGIC ASSESSMENT OF RECEPTOR CHANGES FOLLOWING CHRONIC DRUG-TREATMENT.
003136 03-06
CEREBRAL EVOKED-POTENTIAL CHANGES PRODUCED BY TREATMENT WITH LITHIUM-CARBONATE.
003263 03-09
CHANGES IN THE PSYCHOPATHOLOGY OF PSYCHOSIS DUE TO NEUROLEPTIC TREATMENT.
003281 03-10
PSYCHOTROPIC-DRUG-INDUCED CHANGES IN AUDITORY AVERAGED EVOKED-POTENTIALS: RESULTS OF A DOUBLE-BLIND TRIAL USING AN OBJECTIVE FULLY AUTOMATED AEP ANALYSIS METHOD.
003412 03-13
INTRAOCULAR PRESSURE CHANGES FOLLOWING MODIFIED ECT.
003536 03-15
LONG-TERM CHANGES IN AIMS RATINGS AND THEIR RELATION TO MEDICATION HISTORY.
003537 03-15
CHANGES IN AND CURRENT PROGRESS OF NEUROLOGY AND PSYCHIATRY.
003550 03-15
SELF-STIMULATION AND LOCOMOTOR CHANGES INDICATING LATENT ANTICHOLINERGIC-ACTIVITY BY AN ATYPICAL NEUROLEPTIC (THIORIDAZINE).
003560 03-16
BRAIN BENZODIAZEPINE-RECEPTORS AND THEIR RAPID CHANGES AFTER SEIZURES IN THE MONGOLIAN-GERBIL.
003717 04-03
ETHANOL-INDUCED CHANGES IN CYCLIC-GUANOSINE-PHOSPHATE METABOLISM IN MOUSE VESTIBULAR REGION.
003784 04-03
CHANGES OF ELECTRORETINOGRAM AND NEUROCHEMICAL ASPECTS OF GABAERGIC NEURONS OF RETINA AFTER INTRAOCULAR INJECTION OF KAINIC-ACID IN RATS.
003807 04-03
REGIONAL CHANGES IN (3H)DIAZEPAM BINDING IN THE BRAINS OF MICE AFTER REMOVAL OF THE OLFACTORY-BULBS.
003844 04-03
CHANGES IN GAMMA AMINOBUTYRIC-ACID SHUNT ENZYMES IN REGIONS OF RAT-BRAIN WITH KETAMINE ANESTHESIA.
003891 04-03
THE EFFECT OF PSYCHOSTIMULANTS ON CHANGES IN THE EXCITABILITY OF THE VISUAL CEREBRAL-CORTEX.
003919 04-03
EFFECT OF DIAZEPAM ON STRESS-INDUCED CHANGES IN BRAIN HISTAMINE.
003932 04-03
CHANGES IN REGIONAL BRAIN LEVELS OF AMINO-ACID PUTATIVE NEUROTRANSMITTERS AFTER PROLONGED TREATMENT WITH THE ANTICONVULSANT-DRUGS DIPHENYLHYDANTOIN, PHENOBARBITONE, SODIUM-VALPROATE, ETHOSUXIMIDE, AND SULTHIAME IN THE RAT.
003961 04-03
THE EFFECT OF DIAZEPAM ON CYCLIC EXCITABILITY CHANGES IN AN EPILEPTIC-FOCUS IN THE CORTEX OF THE MAJOR HEMISPHERES.
003984 04-03
CORE TEMPERATURE CHANGES FOLLOWING ADMINISTRATION OF NALOXONE AND NALTREXONE TO RATS EXPOSED TO HOT AND COLD AMBIENT TEMPERATURES. EVIDENCE FOR THE PHYSIOLOGICAL ROLE OF ENDORPHINS IN HOT AND COLD ACCLIMATIZATION.
004034 04-03
DRUG-INDUCED CHANGES IN THE COMPOSITION OF THE CEREBRAL FREE AMINO-ACID POOL.
004039 04-03
TIME-DEPENDENT CHANGES IN ANTEROGRADE SCOPOLAMINE-INDUCED AMNESIA IN RATS.
004182 04-04
DOPAMINE-RECEPTOR CHANGES FOLLOWING DESTRUCTION OF THE NIGROSTRIATAL PATHWAY: LACK OF A RELATIONSHIP TO ROTATIONAL-BEHAVIOR.
004229 04-04
BETA ENDORPHIN: CENTRAL SITES OF ANALGESIA, CATALEPSY AND BODY-TEMPERATURE CHANGES IN RATS.
004238 04-04
CHANGES OF RESPONSE TO DOPAMINERGIC DRUGS IN RATS SUBMITTED TO REM SLEEP DEPRIVATION.
004239 04-04
METHYLMERCURY-INDUCED CHANGES IN OPERANT DISCRIMINATION BY THE PIGEON.
004271 04-05

CHANGES IN BLOOD PLASMA OSMOLALITY AND STATES OF MANIA.
004352 04-09
CHANGES IN PSYCHOPATHOLOGIC SYMPTOMS DURING 20 DAYS OF TREATMENT WITH ANTIDEPRESSANTS AND NEUROLEPTIC-DRUGS.
004415 04-09
ELECTROPHYSIOLOGICAL AND PSYCHOLOGICAL CHANGES INDUCED BY STEROID-HORMONES IN MEN AND WOMEN.
004500 04-13
EVENT-RELATED POTENTIAL CHANGES WITH MORPHINE IN NONADDICTED HUMANS.
004512 04-13
PATHOPHYSIOLOGICAL AND MORPHOLOGICAL CHANGES IN THE CNS DURING LONG-TERM ADMINISTRATION OF HALOPERIDOL.
004633 04-15
DEPOT FLUPHENAZINE MAINTENANCE-TREATMENT AND ASSOCIATED WEIGHT CHANGES.
004635 04-15
CHANGES IN THE CLINICAL-PICTURE AND THE COURSE OF PSYCHOSES DURING MASSIVE PSYCHOPHARMACOTHERAPY AND THE SIGNIFICANCE OF THESE CHANGES FOR IMPROVEMENTS IN PSYCHIATRIC-TREATMENT.
004699 04-17
FLURAZEPAM-INDUCED SLEEP-APNEA-SYNDROME IN A PATIENT WITH INSOMNIA AND MILD SLEEP-RELATED RESPIRATORY CHANGES.
004729 04-17

CHARACTER
ENKEPHALIN-LIKE CHARACTER AND ANALGESIA.
002650 03-02
EFFECTS OF PENTAZOCINE AND NALORPHINE ON MOTILITY IN CHRONICALLY MORPHINE TREATED RATS: A POTENTIAL SUBSTITUTION TEST TO DETECT THE NARCOTIC CHARACTER OF A DRUG.
003555 03-16
CHARACTER AND MEANING OF QUASI-MORPHINE WITHDRAWAL PHENOMENA ELICITED BY METHYLXANTHINES.
004087 04-04

CHARACTERISATION
HUMAN PLATELET 5 HT-RECEPTORS: CHARACTERISATION AND FUNCTIONAL ASSOCIATION.
001412 02-03

CHARACTERISTIC
CHARACTERISTIC HYPERPYREXIA INDUCED BY LICL AND TRANYLCYPROMINE IN RATS.
004278 04-05

CHARACTERISTICS
CHARACTERISTICS OF 3H CIS FLUPENTHIXOL BINDING TO CALF BRAIN MEMBRANES.
000062 01-03
CHARACTERISTICS OF OSCILLATORY CONTRACTIONS ELICITED BY NALOXONE IN ILEUM PREPARATION FROM MORPHINE-DEPENDENT GUINEA-PIGS.
001491 02-03
THE STRIATONIGRAL GABA PATHWAY: FUNCTIONAL AND NEUROCHEMICAL CHARACTERISTICS IN RATS WITH UNILATERAL STRIATAL KAINIC-ACID LESIONS.
001816 02-04
BENZODIAZEPINE-RECEPTORS: THE EFFECT OF GABA ON THEIR CHARACTERISTICS IN HUMAN BRAIN AND THEIR ALTERATION IN HUNTINGTONS-DISEASE.
002163 02-11
PHYSICAL AND PHYSIOLOGICAL CHARACTERISTICS OF MICROPRESSURE EJECTION OF DRUGS FROM MULTIBARRELED PIPETTES.
002502 02-16
A COMPARISON OF THE CONTRACTILE RESPONSES OF THE RABBIT BASILAR AND PULMONARY-ARTERIES TO SYMPATHOMIMETIC AGONISTS: CHARACTERISTICS.
002670 03-03
EFFECTS OF LITHIUM ON MORPHOLOGICAL CHARACTERISTICS OF DISSOCIATED BRAIN CELLS IN CULTURE.
002765 03-03
PATIENT CHARACTERISTICS AND CLINICIAN ATTITUDES INFLUENCING THE PRESCRIBING OF BENZODIAZEPINES.
003598 03-17
THERAPEUTIC (III): GENERAL CHARACTERISTICS OF ANTIPSYCHOTIC-DRUGS.
003644 03-17
COMPARISON OF THE BINDING CHARACTERISTICS OF TRITIATED OPIATES AND OPIOID-PEPTIDES.
003802 04-03
CHARACTERISTICS OF THE INHIBITION OF RAT-BRAIN MONOAMINE-OXIDASE IN VITRO BY MD780515.
003874 04-03
THE PHARMACOLOGICAL CHARACTERISTICS OF THE TRANQUILIZING EFFECT OF HYDIPHEN.
004261 04-04
CHARACTERISTICS OF THE STIMULUS PRODUCED BY THE MIXTURE OF CANNABIDIOL WITH DELTA9 TETRAHYDROCANNABINOL.
004263 04-04

COMPARATIVE CHARACTERISTICS OF THE PROPHYLACTIC PROPERTIES OF SHORT-TERM AND LONG-ACTING LITHIUM-CARBONATE PREPARATIONS IN ENDOGENOUS AFFECTIVE-PSYCHOSES.
004390 04-09

CHARACTERIZATION
ENDORPHIN-INDUCED HYPERTHERMIA: CHARACTERIZATION OF THE EXOGENOUSLY-INDUCED AND ENDOGENOUSLY-INDUCED EFFECTS.
000029 01-03
CHARACTERIZATION OF 3H GABA-RECEPTOR BINDING TO RAT-BRAIN SYNAPTOSOMAL MEMBRANES: EFFECT OF NONGABAERGIC COMPOUNDS.
000139 01-03
A FURTHER CHARACTERIZATION OF THE DIFFERENTIAL-EFFECTS OF LEUCINE-ENKEPHALIN, METHIONINE-ENKEPHALIN AND THEIR ANALOGS ON MORPHINE-INDUCED ANALGESIA.
000311 01-03
CGP-6085-A, A NEW, SPECIFIC, INHIBITOR OF SEROTONIN UPTAKE: NEUROCHEMICAL CHARACTERIZATION AND COMPARISON WITH OTHER SEROTONIN UPTAKE BLOCKERS.
000316 01-03
AFFINITY CHROMATOGRAPHY OF THE BETA-ADRENERGIC-RECEPTOR AND CHARACTERIZATION OF ANTIBODIES RAISED AGAINST PURIFIED RECEPTOR PREPARATIONS.
001009 02-01
PREPARATION AND CHARACTERIZATION OF SYNTHETIC MODELS FOR THE DENSE-BODIES OF HUMAN PLATELETS. (UNPUBLISHED PAPER).
001013 02-01
CHARACTERIZATION OF LRF-LIKE IMMUNOREACTIVITY IN THE FROG SYMPATHETIC GANGLIA: NONIDENTITY WITH LRF-DECAPEPTIDE. (UNPUBLISHED PAPER).
001018 02-01
BIOCHEMICAL-LOCALIZATION AND CHARACTERIZATION OF BOMBESIN-LIKE-PEPTIDES IN DISCRETE REGIONS OF RAT-BRAIN. (UNPUBLISHED PAPER).
001046 02-01
BIOCHEMICAL-CHARACTERIZATION AND PHARMACOLOGICAL CHARACTERIZATION OF A PEPTIDE FROM THE HEMODIALYSATE OF PSYCHOTIC-PATIENTS.
001049 02-01
HISTAMINE-RECEPTORS IN THE BRAIN: CHARACTERIZATION BY BINDING STUDIES AND BIOCHEMICAL-EFFECTS.
001054 02-01
CHARACTERIZATION OF GABA-STIMULATED BENZODIAZEPINE-RECEPTOR BINDING.
001309 02-03
CHARACTERIZATION AND RADIOAUTOGRAPHY OF (3H)LSD BINDING BY RAT-BRAIN SLICES IN VITRO: THE EFFECT OF 5 HYDROXYTRYPTAMINE.
001369 02-03
FURTHER CHARACTERIZATION OF THE BINDING OF SUBSTANCE-P TO A FRACTION FROM RABBIT BRAIN ENRICHED IN SYNAPTIC MEMBRANES.
001394 02-03
CHARACTERIZATION OF BENZODIAZEPINE BINDING-SITES. (UNPUBLISHED PAPER).
001503 02-03
CHARACTERIZATION OF ERGOT AND NONERGOT SEROTONIN ANTAGONISTS BY PROLACTIN AND GROWTH-HORMONE PROFILES DURING WAKEFULNESS AND SLEEP.
002217 02-13
OPIATE-RECEPTORS: PROBLEMS OF DEFINITION AND CHARACTERIZATION.
002620 02-17
DEMONSTRATION AND CHARACTERIZATION OF AN ENDOGENOUS INHIBITOR OF GABA-ENHANCED (3H) DIAZEPAM BINDING FROM BOVINE CEREBRAL-CORTEX.
002645 03-01
DISTRIBUTION OF MEMBRANE GLYCOPROTEINS AMONG THE ORGANELLES OF A SINGLE IDENTIFIED NEURON OF APLYSIA. II. ISOLATION AND CHARACTERIZATION OF A GLYCOPROTEIN ASSOCIATED WITH VESICLES.
002657 03-03
FUNCTIONAL CHARACTERIZATION OF CENTRAL ALPHA-ADRENOCEPTORS BY YOHIMBINE DIASTEREOMERS.
002748 03-03
CHARACTERIZATION AND QUANTITATION OF ALPHA-ADRENERGIC-RECEPTOR SUBTYPES IN RAT HYPOTHALAMUS.
002839 03-03
CHARACTERIZATION OF HALOPERIDOL MEDIATED EFFECTS ON RAT STRIATAL TYROSINE-HYDROXYLASE.
002867 03-03
HIGH-AFFINITY RENAL (3H)FLUNITRAZEPAM BINDING: CHARACTERIZATION, LOCALIZATION, AND ALTERATION IN HYPERTENSION.
002874 03-03
SUPPRESSION OF DRINKING BY NALOXONE IN THE RAT: A FURTHER CHARACTERIZATION.
002963 03-04
PHARMACOLOGICAL CHARACTERIZATION OF SCRATCHING-BEHAVIOUR INDUCED BY INTRACRANIAL INJECTION OF SUBSTANCE-P AND SOMATOSTATIN.
002980 03-04

A CHARACTERIZATION OF THE BEHAVIORAL-EFFECTS OF LEVO ALPHA ACETYLMETHADOL IN THE RAT AND IN THE PIGEON. (PH.D. DISSERTATION).
003047 03-04
CHARACTERIZATION OF THE ISOLATED PERFUSED MOUSE-BRAIN AS A SYSTEM FOR NEUROCHEMICAL-STUDIES.
003146 03-06
PHARMACOLOGIC CHARACTERIZATION AND LECITHIN TREATMENT OF A PATIENT WITH SPONTANEOUS ORAL FACIAL DYSKINESIA AND DEMENTIA.
003347 03-11
DOPAMINE-RECEPTOR PURIFICATION AND CHARACTERIZATION. (UNPUBLISHED PAPER).
003661 04-01
PURIFICATION AND CHARACTERIZATION OF RAT PHEOCHROMOCYTOMA DOPAMINE-BETA-HYDROXYLASE.
003664 04-01
CHARACTERIZATION OF THE BASIC PROTEINS FROM RODENT PERIPHERAL-NERVOUS-SYSTEM MYELIN.
003665 04-01
CHARACTERIZATION OF TWO (3H)GLUTAMATE BINDING-SITES IN RAT HIPPOCAMPAL MEMBRANES.
003726 04-03
CHARACTERIZATION BY (3H)DIHYDROERGOCRYPTINE BINDING OF ALPHA-ADRENERGIC-RECEPTORS IN NEUROBLASTOMA X GLIOMA HYBRID CELLS.
003823 04-03
CHARACTERIZATION OF ENKEPHALIN RELEASE FROM RAT STRIATUM.
003909 04-03

CHARGED
VOLUNTARY INTOXICATION FROM PHENCYCLIDINE. WILL IT RAISE A REASONABLE-DOUBT OF THE MENTAL-CAPACITY OF A PERSON CHARGED WITH A CRIME REQUIRING SPECIFIC INTENT OR MENTAL-STATE?.
000914 01-17

CHECKLIST
A REVISED CHECKLIST TO OBTAIN CONSENT TO TREATMENT WITH MEDICATION.
000984 01-17

CHEESE
IS THE FAILURE OF (-)DEPRENYL, A SELECTIVE MONOAMINE-OXIDASE-B-INHIBITOR, TO ALLEVIATE DEPRESSION RELATED TO FREEDOM FROM THE CHEESE EFFECT?
004640 04-15

CHEMICAL
GASTRIC AND PYLORIC MOTOR-RESPONSE TO SYMPATHETIC-NERVE STIMULATION AFTER CHEMICAL SYMPATHECTOMY. (UNPUBLISHED PAPER).
001337 02-03
THE EFFECT OF CYCLO-LEU-GLY ON CHEMICAL DENERVATION SUPERSENSITIVITY OF DOPAMINE-RECEPTORS INDUCED BY INTRACEREBROVENTRICULAR INJECTION OF 6 HYDROXYDOPAMINE IN MICE.
001435 02-03
A MODEL FOR PSYCHONEUROENDOCRINE INVESTIGATION: SPECIFIC CHEMICAL LESIONING OF THE MEDIAN-EMINENCE.
001478 02-03
CHEMICAL STRUCTURE OF SURVECTOR. STRUCTURE-ACTIVITY RELATIONSHIP.
002262 02-13
TIME-COURSE OF CLINICAL CHEMICAL PARAMETERS UNDER LONG-TERM LITHIUM TREATMENT.
003515 03-15
NEUROLEPTICS: INTERACTIONS WITH FOOD — CHEMICAL AND PHARMACODYNAMIC STUDIES ON THE INTERACTIONS OF COFFEE AND TEA.
003612 03-17
TISSUE CHOLINE STUDIED USING A SIMPLE CHEMICAL ASSAY.
003828 04-03
CONVERGENT PROPERTIES AND CHEMICAL SENSITIVITY OF MIDBRAIN RETICULAR FORMATION NEURONS OF UNANESTHETIZED RABBITS.
003972 04-03
RX-336-M, A NEW CHEMICAL TOOL IN THE ANALYSIS OF THE QUASI-MORPHINE WITHDRAWAL-SYNDROME.
004093 04-04

CHEMICAL-IONIZATION
HIGH-SENSITIVITY NEGATIVE CHEMICAL-IONIZATION MASS-SPECTRAL-ANALYSIS OF BIOGENIC-AMINES AND METABOLITES. (UNPUBLISHED PAPER).
001042 02-01
QUANTITATIVE ANALYSIS OF 6 HYDROXYMELATONIN IN HUMAN URINE BY GAS-CHROMATOGRAPHY NEGATIVE CHEMICAL-IONIZATION MASS-SPECTROMETRY. (UNPUBLISHED PAPER).
001058 02-01
A METHOD FOR THE DETERMINATION OF AMITRIPTYLINE AND ITS METABOLITES NORTRIPTYLINE, 10 HYDROXYAMITRIPTYLINE, AND 10 HYDROXYNORTRIPTYLINE IN HUMAN PLASMA USING STABLE ISOTOPE

DILUTION AND GAS-CHROMATOGRAPHY CHEMICAL-IONIZATION
MASS-SPECTROMETRY.
002486 02-16

CHEMICALLY-INDUCED
SENSORY NEUROTOXINS: CHEMICALLY-INDUCED SELECTIVE DESTRUCTION
OF PRIMARY SENSORY NEURONS.
003859 04-03

CHEMISTRY
CHEMISTRY OF BETA ENDORPHIN.
001038 02-01

CHEMOSENSORS
OPIATE SYSTEM INFLUENCES CENTRAL RESPIRATORY CHEMOSENSORS.
003971 04-03

CHEMOTAXIS
CHEMOTAXIS BY MOUSE MACROPHAGE CELL LINES. (UNPUBLISHED
PAPER).
001099 02-03
INHIBITION OF CHEMOTAXIS BY S 3 DEAZAADENOSYLHOMOCYSTEINE IN
A MOUSE MACROPHAGE CELL LINE. (UNPUBLISHED PAPER).
001100 02-03
PHOSPHOLIPID METABOLISM, CALCIUM-FLUX AND THE RECEPTOR-
MEDIATED INDUCTION OF CHEMOTAXIS IN RABBIT NEUTROPHILS.
(UNPUBLISHED PAPER).
001118 02-03
PHAGOCYTIC FUNCTION IN DOWN-SYNDROME -- I. CHEMOTAXIS.
003401 03-13

CHEMOTHERAPY
SERIAL COGNITIVE TESTING IN CANCER-PATIENTS RECEIVING
CHEMOTHERAPY.
000876 01-15
UNDERSTANDING AND USE OF CHEMOTHERAPY BY LEARNING-
DISABILITIES AND BEHAVIOR-DISORDERS TEACHERS.
000965 01-17
PHARMACOMANOMETRIC-STUDIES OF COLONIC MOTILITY AS A GUIDE
TO THE CHEMOTHERAPY OF SCHIZOPHRENIA.
001930 02-08
THE RELATIVE EFFICACY OF COGNITIVE-THERAPY AND CHEMOTHERAPY
FOR THE TREATMENT OF DEPRESSION AMONG THE RETIRED ELDERLY.
(PH.D. DISSERTATION).
002148 02-11
PSYCHIATRIC MORBIDITY AND PHYSICAL TOXICITY ASSOCIATED WITH
ADJUVANT CHEMOTHERAPY AFTER MASTECTOMY.
002433 02-15
ADVANCES IN PHARMACOLOGY AND CHEMOTHERAPY.
002546 02-17
CONSIDERATIONS ON LONG-ACTING CHEMOTHERAPY: AN EXPERIENCE
WITH FLUPHENAZINE-DECANOATE.
003173 03-08
REFLECTIONS ON ANTIPSYCHOTIC CHEMOTHERAPY: THE BEGINNING OF
PHARMACOLOGICAL-TREATMENT.
003292 03-11
INTRAVENOUS LORAZEPAM TO PREVENT NAUSEA AND VOMITING
ASSOCIATED WITH CANCER CHEMOTHERAPY.
003614 03-17

CHEWING
EMERGENCE OF APOMORPHINE-INDUCED VACUOUS CHEWING DURING 6
MONTHS CONTINUOUS TREATMENT WITH FLUPHENAZINE-DECANOATE.
001817 02-04

CHEWING-GUM
THE USE OF NICOTINE CHEWING-GUM AS AN AID TO STOPPING
SMOKING.
002343 02-14

CHICK
LOCALIZATION OF ALPHA BUNGAROTOXIN BINDING-SITES IN SYNAPSES
OF THE DEVELOPING CHICK RETINA.
000065 01-03
THE EFFECT OF FLA-63 ON PENTOBARBITONE-INDUCED SLEEP IN THE
CHICK.
001741 02-04
BENZODIAZEPINE-RECEPTORS IN CHICK RETINA: DEVELOPMENT AND
CELLULAR LOCALIZATION.
002655 03-03
GABA DEPLETION IN CHICK BRAINSTEM AFTER INTRAVENTRICULAR
INJECTION OF CEFAZOLIN.
002762 03-03
THE EFFECT OF COLCHICINE AND CYTOCHALASIN B ON THE RELEASE OF
TAURINE FROM THE CHICK RETINA.
002856 03-03
DEVELOPMENTALLY REGULATED LECTINS IN SLIME MOULDS AND CHICK
TISSUES -- ARE THEY CELL ADHESION MOLECULES?
003724 04-03
EVIDENCE TO SUGGEST THAT DOPAMINE-INDUCED INCREASE IN GABA
CONCENTRATIONS IN CHICK BRAIN IS MEDIATED THROUGH CYCLIC-
AMP.
003952 04-03

CHICKEN
BENZODIAZEPINE BINDING IN CHICKEN RETINA AND ITS INTERACTION
WITH GAMMA AMINOBUTYRIC-ACID.
001287 02-03

INHIBITION OF MONOAMINE-OXIDASE BY FURAZOLIDONE IN THE
CHICKEN AND THE INFLUENCE OF THE ALIMENTARY FLORA THEREON.
003711 04-03

CHICKENS
2,4,5 TRICHLOROPHENOXYACETIC-ACID CAUSES BEHAVIORAL-EFFECTS IN
CHICKENS AT ENVIRONMENTALLY RELEVANT DOSES.
003079 03-04
THE EFFECTS OF TRYPTOPHAN AND MANIPULATIONS OF SEROTONERGIC-
RECEPTORS ON TONIC IMMOBILITY IN CHICKENS.
004245 04-04

CHICKS
GABA DEPLETION AND BEHAVIOURAL-CHANGES PRODUCED BY
INTRAVENTRICULAR PUTRESCINE IN CHICKS.
000218 01-03
APOMORPHINE: EFFECTS ON THE TIMING AND SEQUENCING OF PECKING-
BEHAVIOR IN CHICKS.
000428 01-04
OPIOID BLOCKADE AND SOCIAL-COMFORT IN CHICKS.
001745 02-04
THE EFFECTS OF COLCHICINE AND VINBLASTINE ON MEMORY IN CHICKS.
004069 04-04

CHILD
THE PARENT CHILD INTERACTIONS OF HYPERACTIVE-CHILDREN AND THEIR
MODIFICATION BY STIMULANT-DRUGS.
002092 02-11
CONTROLLED-STUDY WITH BROMAZEPAM AND CLOROTEPIN IN CHILD
INSTABILITY.
002190 02-11
HALOPERIDOL-INDUCED TARDIVE-DYSKINESIA IN A CHILD WITH GILLES-
DE-LA-TOURETTES-DISEASE.
002437 02-15
CHILD PSYCHOPHARMACOLOGY.
004470 04-11
LSD: MY PROBLEM CHILD.
004497 04-12

CHILD-PSYCHIATRY
USE OF PIMOZIDE (ORAP) IN CHILD-PSYCHIATRY.
002100 02-11
THE USE OF MINAPRINE IN CHILD-PSYCHIATRY IN HOSPITALS AND
OUTPATIENT CLINICS.
002169 02-11
EXPERIMENTATION WITH MINAPRINE IN CHILD-PSYCHIATRY.
002344 02-14
CHILD-PSYCHIATRY AND PSYCHOPHARMACOTHERAPY IN GENERAL
PRACTICE, IN PEDIATRICS, AND IN NEUROLOGY.
003288 03-11

CHILDHOOD
PSYCHOPHARMACOLOGY IN CHILDHOOD: CURRENT STATUS AND FUTURE
PROSPECTIVES.
002192 02-11
PSYCHOPHARMACEUTICAL-THERAPY TO CALM DRIVE, ACTIVITY, AND
RESTLESSNESS IN CHILDHOOD.
002604 02-17
ON THE EVALUATION OF A PROVOCATIVE EEG METHOD USING
MEDICATION IN THE DIAGNOSIS OF ORGANIC-BRAIN-SEIZURES IN
CHILDHOOD, WITH SPECIAL EMPHASIS ON SLEEP INDUCTION THROUGH
MEDICATION.
003387 03-11
PREVALENCE OF DRUG-TREATMENT FOR HYPERACTIVITY AND OTHER
CHILDHOOD BEHAVIOR-DISORDERS.
004713 04-17

CHILDHOOD-DEPRESSION
CHILDHOOD-DEPRESSION.
000680 01-11

CHILDHOOD-ENURESIS
CHILDHOOD-ENURESIS: II. PSYCHOPATHOLOGY, TRICYCLIC
CONCENTRATION IN PLASMA, AND ANTIENURETIC-EFFECT.
002354 02-14

CHILDHOOD-EPILEPSY
VALPROIC-ACID IN CHILDHOOD-EPILEPSY: ANTICONVULSIVE EFFICACY IN
RELATION TO ITS PLASMA LEVELS.
004525 04-13

CHILDHOOD-SCHIZOPHRENIA
CLINICAL-RESPONSE AND SERUM NEUROLEPTIC LEVELS IN CHILDHOOD-
SCHIZOPHRENIA. (UNPUBLISHED PAPER).
000566 01-08

CHILDREN
OUR EXPERIENCE WITH PIRACETAM (NOOTROPIL-UCB) TREATMENT IN
CHILDREN FROM HIGH-RISK PREGNANCIES WITH SUBSEQUENT
MINIMAL-BRAIN-DYSFUNCTION.
000544 01-07
PYRITINOL ADMINISTRATION AS PART OF EPILEPSY TREATMENT IN
CHILDREN.
000671 01-11
CHILDREN ON MEDICATION: A PRIMER FOR SCHOOL PERSONNEL.
000676 01-11
PLASMA CHLORPROMAZINE CONCENTRATIONS IN CHILDREN WITH
BEHAVIORAL-DISORDERS AND MENTAL-ILLNESS.
000717 01-11

TARDIVE-DYSKINESIA AND OTHER MOVEMENT-DISORDERS IN CHILDREN TREATED WITH PSYCHOTROPIC-DRUGS.
000849 01-15
DYSKINETIC AND NEUROLOGICAL-COMPLICATIONS IN CHILDREN TREATED WITH PSYCHOTROPIC-MEDICATIONS.
000880 01-15
PHENYTOIN KINETICS IN CHILDREN.
002113 02-11
EEG CHANGES IN CHILDREN WITH TREATED PHENYLKETONURIA AFTER PHENYLALANINE LOAD.
002115 02-11
DOUBLE-BLIND CONTROLLED-STUDY ON THE PSYCHOLEPTIC-EFFECTS OF AMINEPTINE IN MENTALLY-HANDICAPPED CHILDREN WITHOUT PERSONALITY-PROBLEMS.
002116 02-11
5 HYDROXYTRYPTOPHAN AND PYRIDOXINE: THEIR EFFECTS IN YOUNG CHILDREN WITH DOWNS-SYNDROME.
002161 02-11
IMIPRAMINE AND EEG SLEEP IN CHILDREN WITH DEPRESSIVE-SYMPTOMS.
002339 02-14
EFFECTS OF IMIPRAMINE ON LEFT VENTRICULAR PERFORMANCE IN CHILDREN.
002385 02-15
THE INFLUENCE OF NEUROLEPTIC-DRUGS ON PROLACTIN SECRETION IN CHILDREN.
002409 02-15
BIOLOGY AND THERAPY OF VIOLENT-BEHAVIOUR IN CHILDREN.
002608 02-17
ON THE EFFECTS OF SULTOPRIDE ADMINISTERED IN LOW-DOSAGES TO OLDER CHILDREN AND ADOLESCENTS.
003230 03-09
LITHIUM IN CHILDREN OF LITHIUM RESPONDING PARENTS.
003242 03-09
MOLINDONE-HYDROCHLORIDE IN THE TREATMENT OF AGGRESSIVE, HOSPITALIZED CHILDREN.
003321 03-11
A COMPARATIVE-STUDY ON THE CLINICAL-EFFECTS OF RECTAL DIAZEPAM AND PENTOBARBITAL ON SMALL CHILDREN. RELATIONSHIP BETWEEN PLASMA LEVEL AND EFFECT.
003330 03-11
INVESTIGATION INTO THE EFFECT OF FLUPHENAZINE-HCL (LYORODIN) IN CHILDREN WITH BEHAVIORAL-DISORDERS BY MEANS OF PSYCHOPHYSIOLOGICAL PARAMETERS.
003344 03-11
TREATMENT OF ANXIETY IN CHILDREN AND ADOLESCENTS.
003349 03-11
EFFECTS OF LITHIUM-CARBONATE AND HALOPERIDOL ON COGNITION IN AGGRESSIVE, HOSPITALIZED SCHOOL-AGE CHILDREN.
003360 03-11
EFFECTS OF LITHIUM-CARBONATE AND HALOPERIDOL ON COGNITION IN AGGRESSIVE HOSPITALIZED SCHOOL-AGE CHILDREN.
003361 03-11
THE INFLUENCE OF METHYLPHENIDATE ON SPONTANEOUS AUTONOMIC-ACTIVITY AND BEHAVIOR IN CHILDREN DIAGNOSED AS HYPERACTIVE.
003363 03-11
HALOPERIDOL -- ITS USE IN CHILDREN.
003370 03-11
STOPPING MEDICATION IN CHILDREN WITH EPILEPSY.
004447 04-11
PREVALENCE OF HYPERACTIVITY AND RELATED TREATMENTS AMONG ELEMENTARY SCHOOL CHILDREN.
004469 04-11
TARDIVE-DYSKINESIA AND OTHER DRUG-INDUCED MOVEMENT-DISORDERS AMONG HANDICAPPED CHILDREN AND YOUTH.
004614 04-15
WITHDRAWAL SYMPTOMS AFTER GRADUATED CESSATION OF IMIPRAMINE IN CHILDREN.
004630 04-15
BEHAVIOR AND LEARNING DIFFICULTIES IN CHILDREN OF NORMAL INTELLIGENCE BORN TO ALCOHOLIC MOTHERS.
004658 04-15
EMOTIONAL-DISORDERS IN CHILDREN AND ADOLESCENTS; MEDICAL AND PSYCHOLOGICAL APPROACHES TO TREATMENT.
004743 04-17

CHILEAN
PLASMA LEVELS OF DIPHENYLHYDANTOIN AND THE CONTROL OF ADULT EPILEPTIC-SEIZURES; A CHILEAN EXPERIENCE.
000102 01-03

CHLORAL-HYDRATE
EFFICACY AND SIDE-EFFECTS OF CHLORAL-HYDRATE AND TRYPTOPHAN AS SLEEPING-AIDS IN PSYCHOGERIATRIC-PATIENTS.
002077 02-10
THE EFFICACY OF TRIAZOLAM AND CHLORAL-HYDRATE IN GERIATRIC INSOMNIACS.
002160 02-11
SMOOTH-PURSUIT EYE-MOVEMENTS: EFFECTS OF ALCOHOL AND CHLORAL-HYDRATE.
003448 03-14

ORAL AND RECTAL ABSORPTION OF CHLORAL-HYDRATE AND ITS BETAINE COMPLEX.
004554 04-13

CHLORALOSE
EFFECTS OF ALPHA CHLORALOSE ON THE ACTIVITY OF THE NIGROSTRIATAL DOPAMINERGIC SYSTEM IN THE CAT.
000217 01-03
THE INFLUENCE OF CHLORALOSE ANESTHESIA ON THE ACTIVITY OF RED NUCLEUS NEURONS IN CATS.
000245 01-03
SENSITIVE DEPRESSANT EFFECT OF BENZODIAZEPINES ON THE CROSSED EXTENSOR REFLEX IN CHLORALOSE ANESTHETIZED RATS.
003027 03-04

CHLORALOSE-INDUCED
OBSERVATIONS ON CHLORALOSE-INDUCED MYOCLONUS IN GUINEA-PIGS.
001164 02-03

CHLORCYCLIZINE
EFFECT OF L HISTIDINE AND CHLORCYLIZINE ON APOMORPHINE-INDUCED CLIMBING-BEHAVIOUR AND METHAMPHETAMINE STEREOTYPY IN MICE.
004147 04-04

CHLORDIAZEPOXIDE
THE SENSITIVITY OF THE RAT CORTICOSTERONE RESPONSE TO ENVIRONMENTAL MANIPULATIONS AND TO CHRONIC CHLORDIAZEPOXIDE TREATMENT.
000092 01-03
EFFECTS OF CHLORDIAZEPOXIDE ON DEPOLARIZATION-INDUCED CALCIUM INFLUX INTO SYNAPTOSOMES.
000183 01-03
CHLORDIAZEPOXIDE ANTINOCICEPTION: CROSS-TOLERANCE WITH OPIATES AND WITH STRESS.
000348 01-04
RATS REACTIONS TO A PREDATOR: MODIFICATION BY CHLORDIAZEPOXIDE.
000353 01-04
TOLERANCE TO SUPPRESSIVE EFFECTS OF CHLORDIAZEPOXIDE ON OPERANT-BEHAVIOR: LACK OF CROSS-TOLERANCE TO PENTOBARBITAL.
000356 01-04
EFFECTS OF CHLORDIAZEPOXIDE AND DIAZEPAM ON FEEDING PERFORMANCE IN A FOOD PREFERENCE TEST.
000367 01-04
EFFECTS OF ACUTE OR CHRONIC ADMINISTRATION OF CHLORDIAZEPOXIDE ON FEEDING PARAMETERS USING TWO FOOD TEXTURES IN THE RAT.
000368 01-04
WATER INTAKE AND TIME-COURSE OF DRINKING AFTER SINGLE OR REPEATED CHLORDIAZEPOXIDE INJECTIONS.
000369 01-04
ALCOHOL AND CHLORDIAZEPOXIDE INCREASE SUPPRESSED AGGRESSION IN MICE.
000434 01-04
CHLORDIAZEPOXIDE AND OXAZEPAM DISPOSITION IN CIRRHOSIS.
000790 01-13
INTERACTIONS OF CHLORDIAZEPOXIDE AND ANORECTIC-AGENTS ON RATE AND DURATION PARAMETERS OF FEEDING IN THE RAT.
001600 02-04
THE EFFECTS OF D-AMPHETAMINE, CHLORDIAZEPOXIDE, AND PENTOBARBITAL ON BEHAVIOR MAINTAINED BY ESCAPE FROM PUNISHMENT. IN PIGEONS. (PH.D. DISSERTATION).
001713 02-04
EFFECTS OF CHLORDIAZEPOXIDE MORPHINE COMBINATIONS ON SPONTANEOUS LOCOMOTOR-ACTIVITY IN THREE INBRED STRAINS OF MICE.
001766 02-04
ATTENUATION OF THE EFFECTS OF PUNISHMENT BY ETHANOL: COMPARISONS WITH CHLORDIAZEPOXIDE.
001813 02-04
SHORT-TERM ETHANOL ADMINISTRATION IMPAIRS THE ELIMINATION OF CHLORDIAZEPOXIDE (LIBR"'M) IN MAN.
002224 02-13
RESPONDERS AND NONRESPONDERS TO CHLORDIAZEPOXIDE AND PLACEBO: A DISCRIMINANT FUNCTION ANALYSIS.
002482 02-16
PHARMACOKINETICS AND BIOAVAILABILITY OF CHLORDIAZEPOXIDE IN HUMANS.
002564 02-17
INTERACTION OF CHLORDIAZEPOXIDE AND SODIUM-VALPROATE IN THE NUCLEUS-ACCUMBENS OF THE RAT.
002796 03-03
EFFECTS OF MORPHINE AND CHLORDIAZEPOXIDE ON AVOIDANCE-BEHAVIOUR IN TWO INBRED STRAINS OF MICE.
002973 03-04
EFFECTS OF CHLORDIAZEPOXIDE AND D-AMPHETAMINE ON RESPONDING SUPPRESSED BY CONDITIONED PUNISHMENT.
003105 03-04
A POSSIBLE ROLE FOR CATECHOLAMINE NEUROTRANSMITTERS IN THE ANTICONVULSANT ACTIVITY OF CHLORDIAZEPOXIDE.
003119 03-04

FOOD PREFERENCE FOLLOWING ACUTE OR CHRONIC CHLORDIAZEPOXIDE ADMINISTRATION: TOLERANCE TO AN ANTINEOPHOBIC ACTION.
004090 04-04

HISTAMINE AS A PUNISHER IN SQUIRREL-MONKEYS: EFFECTS OF PENTOBARBITAL, CHLORDIAZEPOXIDE AND H1-RECEPTOR AND H2-RECEPTOR ANTAGONISTS ON BEHAVIOR AND CARDIOVASCULAR RESPONSE.
004119 04-04

RESPONDERS AND NONRESPONDERS TO CHLORDIAZEPOXIDE AND PLACEBO. A DISCRIMINANT FUNCTION ANALYSIS. (UNPUBLISHED PAPER).
004420 04-10

CLINICAL PHARMACOKINETICS OF CHLORDIAZEPOXIDE IN PATIENTS WITH ALCOHOLIC HEPATITIS.
004473 04-11

CHLORDIAZEPOXIDE-HCL
THE EFFECTS OF CHLORDIAZEPOXIDE-HCL ADMINISTRATION UPON PUNISHMENT AND CONDITIONED SUPPRESSION IN THE RAT.
001757 02-04

CHLORDIAZEPOXIDE-HYDROCHLORIDE
NMR SPECTRAL STUDY OF PROTON TRANSFER IN AMITRIPTYLINE-HYDROCHLORIDE CHLORDIAZEPOXIDE-HYDROCHLORIDE COMBINATIONS IN DIPOLAR APROTIC SOLVENTS.
003654 04-01

CHLORDIAZEPOXIDE-LIKE
THE USE OF SOCIAL-INTERACTION AS A METHOD FOR DETECTING ANXIOLYTIC-ACTIVITY OF CHLORDIAZEPOXIDE-LIKE DRUGS.
001866 02-06

CHLORIDE
EFFECT OF PICROTOXIN ON BENZODIAZEPINE-RECEPTORS AND GABA-RECEPTORS WITH REFERENCE TO THE EFFECT OF CHLORIDE ION.
002725 03-03

CONVULSANT AND ANTICONVULSANT-DRUG BINDING-SITES RELATED TO GABA REGULATED CHLORIDE ION-CHANNELS.
002848 03-03

BARBITURATE ENHANCEMENT OF GABA-MEDIATED INHIBITION AND ACTIVATION OF CHLORIDE ION-CONDUCTANCE: CORRELATION WITH ANTICONVULSANT AND ANESTHETIC ACTIONS.
002885 03-03

CHLORIMIPRAMINE
PROLONGATION OF THE EJACULATION LATENCY IN THE MALE RAT BY THIORIDAZINE AND CHLORIMIPRAMINE.
000335 01-04

COMPARATIVE EXPERIMENT OF THE ANTIDEPRESSANT EFFECTS OF AMINEPTINE AND CHLORIMIPRAMINE.
002029 02-09

THE BIOAVAILABILITY OF ORAL AND PARENTERAL CHLORIMIPRAMINE (ANAFRANIL).
002232 02-13

INTRAVENOUS CHLORIMIPRAMINE AFFECTS REM CYCLE IN PATIENTS WITH EXCESSIVE DAYTIME SLEEPINESS AND CONTROL SUBJECTS.
002341 02-14

SUPPRESSION OF ACTIVE SLEEP BY CHRONIC-TREATMENT WITH CHLORIMIPRAMINE DURING EARLY POSTNATAL DEVELOPMENT: EFFECTS UPON ADULT SLEEP AND BEHAVIOR IN THE RAT.
003056 03-04

THE ANTIDEPRESSANT ACTION OF SULPHO-ADENOSYL-L-METHIONINE (SAME) COMPARED WITH THAT OF CHLORIMIPRAMINE: HYPOTHETICAL INTERPRETATIONS OF THE MECHANISM-OF-ACTION.
003150 03-07

TYRAMINE PRESSOR TEST AND CARDIOVASCULAR-EFFECTS OF CHLORIMIPRAMINE AND NORTRIPTYLINE IN HEALTHY VOLUNTEERS.
003428 03-13

A DOUBLE-BLIND MULTICENTRE-TRIAL COMPARING THE EFFICACY AND SIDE-EFFECTS OF MIANSERIN AND CHLORIMIPRAMINE IN DEPRESSED-INPATIENTS AND DEPRESSED-OUTPATIENTS.
004395 04-09

CHLORMETHIAZOLE
SORPTION OF CHLORMETHIAZOLE BY INTRAVENOUS INFUSION GIVING SETS.
002508 02-16

AVAILABILITY OF ISOSORBIDE-DINITRATE, DIAZEPAM AND CHLORMETHIAZOLE, FROM I.V. DELIVERY SYSTEMS.
003558 03-16

CHLORNALTREXAMINE
ISOLATION OF SELECTIVE 3H CHLORNALTREXAMINE BOUND COMPLEXES, POSSIBLE OPIOID-RECEPTOR COMPONENTS IN BRAINS OF MICE.
001162 02-03

MORPHINE ANALGESIA AFTER INTRATHECAL ADMINISTRATION OF A NARCOTIC AGONIST, CHLOROXYMORPHAMINE AND ANTAGONIST, CHLORNALTREXAMINE.
001695 02-C

ANTAGONISM BY CHLORNALTREXAMINE OF SOME EFFECTS OF DELTA9 TETRAHYDROCANNABINOL IN RATS.
003104 03-04

PHARMACOLOGICAL-STUDIES WITH AN ALKYLATING NARCOTIC AGONIST, CHLOROXYMORPHAMINE, AND ANTAGONIST, CHLORNALTREXAMINE.
004082 04-04

CHLORO-4-PHENYLSUCCINIMIDOBENZENESULFONAMIDE
3 CHLORO-4-PHENYLSUCCINIMIDOBENZENESULFONAMIDE (GS-385), A NEW ANTICONVULSANT: ITS QUANTITATIVE DETERMINATION, PHARMACOKINETICS AND METABOLISM USING HIGH-PERFORMANCE LIQUID-CHROMATOGRAPHY.
000705 01-11

CHLOROAMPHETAMINE
COMPARATIVE-EFFECTS OF P CHLOROAMPHETAMINE AND L P CHLOROPHENYLPIPERAZINE ON 5 HYDROXYINDOLE CONCENTRATION IN RAT-BRAIN.
000101 01-03

P CHLOROAMPHETAMINE: EVALUATION OF A BRAIN METABOLITE.
000101 01-03

P CHLOROAMPHETAMINE: EVALUATION OF A BRAIN METABOLITE.
001779 02-04

THE EFFECTS OF PARA CHLOROAMPHETAMINE ON FENFLURAMINE ANOREXIA IN AD LIBITUM AND STIMULATION-INDUCED FEEDING IN THE RAT.
001823 02-04

INTERACTIONS BETWEEN A MONOFLUORINATED ANALOGUE OF P CHLOROAMPHETAMINE AND 5 HYDROXYTRYPTAMINE IN BRAIN.
003719 04-03

THE EFFECTS OF P CHLOROAMPHETAMINE ADMINISTRATION ON LOCOMOTOR-ACTIVITY AND SEROTONIN IN NEONATAL AND ADULT RATS. (UNPUBLISHED PAPER).
004169 04-04

CHLOROBENZOYL-CHLORO-METHYL-NA-GLYCYLGLYCINANILIDE
PHARMACOLOGY OF 2 0 CHLOROBENZOYL-CHLORO-METHYL-NA-GLYCYLGLYCINANILIDE HYDRATE (45-0088-S), A COMPOUND WITH BENZODIAZEPINE-LIKE PROPERTIES.
003692 04-02

CHLORODIMETHYLAMINOETHOXYDIBENZOTHIEPINE
PHARMACOKINETICS AND METABOLISM OF CHLORODIMETHYLAMINOETHOXYDIBENZOTHIEPINE (ZOTEPINE) IN RAT, MOUSE, DOG AND MAN.
000219 01-03

PHARMACOLOGICAL-STUDY OF CHLORODIMETHYLAMINOETHOXYDIBENZOTHIEPINE (ZOTEPINE), A NEW NEUROLEPTIC-DRUG.
000493 01-04

TOXICOLOGICAL AND TERATOLOGICAL STUDIES OF CHLORODIMETHYLAMINOETHOXYDIBENZOTHIEPINE (ZOTEPINE), A NEW NEUROLEPTIC-DRUG.
000515 01-05

CHLORODINITROBENZENE
EFFECTS OF HALOPERIDOL, A DOPAMINE-RECEPTOR ANTAGONIST, ON A DELAYED TYPE HYPERSENSITIVITY REACTION TO 1 CHLORODINITROBENZENE IN MICE.
001473 02-03

CHLOROETHYLNORAPOMORPHINE
CHLOROETHYLNORAPOMORPHINE, A PROPOSED LONG-ACTING DOPAMINE ANTAGONIST: INTERACTIONS WITH DOPAMINE-RECEPTORS OF MAMMALIAN FOREBRAIN IN VITRO.
001114 02-03

CHLOROPHENYL-CYCLOPROPYLAMINE
EFFECT OF 2 P CHLOROPHENYL-CYCLOPROPYLAMINE ON 5 HYDROXYINDOLE CONCENTRATION AND MONOAMINE-OXIDASE ACTIVITY IN RAT-BRAIN.
001237 02-03

CHLOROPHENYL-4-HYDROXYPIPERIDINE-4-FLUOROBUTYROPHENONE
THE STRUCTURE OF HALOPERIDOL-HYDROBROMIDE (CHLOROPHENYL-4-HYDROXYPIPERIDINE-4-FLUOROBUTYROPHENONE HBR).
000002 01-01

CHLOROPHENYLALANINE
ENHANCEMENT OF THE BEHAVIORAL-EFFECTS OF 2,5 DIMETHOXY-4-METHYLAMPHETAMINE (DOM) BY PRETREATMENT WITH P CHLOROPHENYLALANINE.
000364 01-04

EFFECT OF P CHLOROPHENYLALANINE ON DIAZEPAM WITHDRAWAL SIGNS IN RATS.
001797 02-04

PHASIC ACTIVITY INDUCED BY P CHLOROPHENYLALANINE IN THE AUDITORY PATHWAY.
002661 03-03

EFFECT OF P CHLOROPHENYLALANINE AND TRYPTOPHAN ON SLEEP, EEG AND MOTOR-ACTIVITY IN THE RAT.
002958 03-04

SYNTHESIS AND BIOCHEMICAL AND PHARMACOLOGIC PROPERTIES OF ANALOGUES AND DERIVATIVES OF P CHLOROPHENYLALANINE.
003691 04-02

DOES P CHLOROPHENYLALANINE PRODUCE DISTURBED WAKING, DISTURBED SLEEP OR ACTIVATION BY PONTO-GENICULO-OCCIPITAL WAVES IN CATS?
003704 04-02

ANTAGONISM OF ETHANOL-INDUCED DECREASE IN LH BY P CHLOROPHENYLALANINE: LACK OF CORRELATION WITH ALTERED SEROTONERGIC MECHANISMS.
003748 04-03

EFFECT OF P CHLOROPHENYLALANINE ON THE ACQUISITION OF TOLERANCE TO THE HYPNOTIC-EFFECTS OF PENTOBARBITAL, BARBITAL, AND ETHANOL.
003883 04-03

THE EFFECT OF P CHLOROPHENYLALANINE ON THE DISTRIBUTION OF BIOGENIC-AMINES IN THE BRAIN, AND ON MEMORY IN RATS.
004068 04-04

INTERACTION OF P CHLOROPHENYLALANINE, MIANSERINE AND DANITRACEN WITH AMPHETAMINE.
004599 04-15

CHLOROPHENYLALANINE-INDUCED
REVERSAL OF PARA CHLOROPHENYLALANINE-INDUCED INSOMNIA BY 5 HYDROXYTRYPTOPHAN IN THE RAT.
000423 01-04

CHLOROPHENYLPIPERAZINE
COMPARATIVE-EFFECTS OF P CHLOROAMPHETAMINE AND L P CHLOROPHENYLPIPERAZINE ON 5 HYDROXYINDOLE CONCENTRATION IN RAT-BRAIN.
000101 01-03

1-M CHLOROPHENYLPIPERAZINE: A METABOLITE OF TRAZODONE ISOLATED FROM RAT URINE.
000204 01-03

DISPOSITION AND PHARMACOLOGICAL-EFFECTS OF M CHLOROPHENYLPIPERAZINE IN RATS.
002995 03-04

5 HYDROXYTRYPTAMINE-LIKE PROPERTIES OF M CHLOROPHENYLPIPERAZINE: COMPARISON WITH QUIPAZINE.
004210 04-04

CHLOROXYMORPHAMINE
MORPHINE ANALGESIA AFTER INTRATHECAL ADMINISTRATION OF A NARCOTIC AGONIST, CHLOROXYMORPHAMINE AND ANTAGONIST, CHLORNALTREXAMINE.
001695 02-04

PHARMACOLOGICAL-STUDIES WITH AN ALKYLATING NARCOTIC AGONIST, CHLOROXYMORPHAMINE, AND ANTAGONIST, CHLORNALTREXAMINE.
004082 04-04

CHLORPHENTERMINE
EFFECT OF DESMETHYLIMIPRAMINE ON THE KINETICS OF CHLORPHENTERMINE ACCUMULATION IN ISOLATED PERFUSED RAT LUNG.
000524 01-05

EFFECT OF DESMETHYLIMIPRAMINE ON TISSUE DISTRIBUTION AND ANORECTIC-ACTIVITY OF CHLORPHENTERMINE IN RATS.
004179 04-04

CHLORPROMAZINE
ACTIONS OF CHLORPROMAZINE, HALOPERIDOL AND PIMOZIDE ON LIPID METABOLISM IN GUINEA-PIG BRAIN SLICES.
000129 01-03

MECHANISM OF CHLORPROMAZINE ACTION ON PLASMA GLUCOSE AND CYCLIC-AMP LEVELS.
000211 01-03

PRIOR AND ONGOING EXPERIENCE AS DETERMINANTS OF THE EFFECTS OF D-AMPHETAMINE AND CHLORPROMAZINE ON PUNISHED-BEHAVIOR.
000339 01-04

EXPERIMENTAL DYSTONIA INDUCED BY QUATERNARY CHLORPROMAZINE.
000461 01-04

EFFECT OF MORPHINE IN COMBINATION WITH CHLORPROMAZINE AND HALOPERIDOL ON OPERANT-BEHAVIOR.
000486 01-04

EFFECTS OF TRIFLUOPERAZINE, CHLORPROMAZINE, AND HALOPERIDOL UPON TEMPORAL INFORMATION-PROCESSING BY SCHIZOPHRENIC-PATIENTS.
000554 01-08

COMPARATIVE ENZYME-INDUCING EFFECTS OF CHLORPROMAZINE AND FLUPHENAZINE THERAPIES IN PSYCHOTIC-PATIENTS.
000682 01-11

PLASMA CHLORPROMAZINE CONCENTRATIONS IN CHILDREN WITH BEHAVIORAL-DISORDERS AND MENTAL-ILLNESS.
000717 01-11

PLASMA CHLORPROMAZINE SERUM PROLACTIN RELATIONSHIP IN A SINGLE-DOSE EXPERIMENT.
000761 01-13

PHARMACOKINETICS OF CHLORPROMAZINE IN NORMAL VOLUNTEERS.
000778 01-13

PLASMA AND SALIVA LEVELS OF CHLORPROMAZINE AND SUBJECTIVE RESPONSE.
000826 01-14

IMPORTANCE OF AKINESIA: PLASMA CHLORPROMAZINE AND PROLACTIN LEVELS.
000891 01-15

PERSISTENT EFFECTS OF HIGH-CONCENTRATIONS OF CHLORPROMAZINE ON 3H PROPYLBENZILYLCHOLINE-MUSTARD BINDING TO MUSCARINIC-RECEPTORS IN GUINEA-PIG INTESTINAL-MUSCLE STRIPS.
001266 02-03

DIHYDROXY AND TRIHYDROXY ANALOGS OF CHLORPROMAZINE INFLUENCE THE CENTRAL-ACTIVITY OF ADENYLATE-CYCLASE AND CYCLIC-AMP-PHOSPHODIESTERASE.
001405 02-03

EFFECT OF CHLORPROMAZINE ON CELL PROLIFERATION IN THE DEVELOPING RAT-BRAIN. A COMBINED BIOCHEMICAL-STUDY AND MORPHOLOGICAL-STUDY.
001407 02-03

EVIDENCE FOR INVOLVEMENT OF DOPAMINE IN THE ACTION OF DIAZEPAM: POTENTIATION OF HALOPERIDOL AND CHLORPROMAZINE ACTION IN THE BRAIN.
001428 02-03

MECHANISMS OF CHLORPROMAZINE AND CHLORPROMAZINE ISOSTERES ON THE GLYCEMIC-RESPONSE IN MICE. (PH.D. DISSERTATION).
001525 02-03

AN ANALYSIS OF SOME PERCEPTUAL-EFFECTS OF MORPHINE, CHLORPROMAZINE, AND LSD.
001652 02-04

CORRELATION BETWEEN DAILY DOSAGE OF CHLORPROMAZINE AND SUBSEQUENT SUPERSENSITIVITY.
001845 02-05

LONG-TERM CHLORPROMAZINE IN RHESUS-MONKEYS: PRODUCTION OF DYSKINESIAS AND CHANGES IN SOCIAL-BEHAVIOR.
001850 02-05

RELATIONSHIPS BETWEEN CHLORPROMAZINE CONCENTRATIONS IN PLASMA AND CEREBROSPINAL-FLUID AND CLINICAL-RESPONSE AND BIOCHEMICAL-RESPONSE IN PSYCHOTIC-PATIENTS.
001905 02-08

PHARMACOKINETIC INTERACTION BETWEEN PROPRANOLOL AND CHLORPROMAZINE IN SCHIZOPHRENIC-PATIENTS.
001940 02-08

THE RELATIONSHIP OF ALPHA AND DELTA EEG FREQUENCIES TO PAIN AND MOOD IN FIBROSITIS-PATIENTS TREATED WITH CHLORPROMAZINE AND L TRYPTOPHAN.
002152 02-11

LUPUS-LIKE-ILLNESS ASSOCIATED WITH CHLORPROMAZINE.
002408 02-15

THE DISTRIBUTION OF CHLORPROMAZINE BETWEEN PLASMA AND ERYTHROCYTES.
002496 02-16

EFFECTS OF CHLORPROMAZINE ON DOPAMINERGIC-RECEPTOR FUNCTIONS IN RAT-BRAIN – DIFFERENCE OF THE RESPONSE OF SEVERAL DOPAMINERGIC-SYSTEMS AFTER CHRONIC ADMINISTRATION.
002773 03-03

CHANGES IN THE CORTICAL ACTIVITY OF SUCCINATE-DEHYDROGENASE UNDER THE INFLUENCE OF CHLORPROMAZINE (A HISTOCHEMICAL-STUDY AND ELECTROCYTOCHEMICAL-STUDY).
002784 03-03

BIOLOGICAL-EFFECTS OF CHLORPROMAZINE IN CHRONIC SCHIZOPHRENICS. III. THE MUTUAL RELATION OF EACH INDEX.
003179 03-08

CHLORPROMAZINE LEVELS AND THE OUTCOME OF TREATMENT IN SCHIZOPHRENIC-PATIENTS.
003188 03-08

PLASMA LEVELS OF CHLORPROMAZINE AND CLINICAL-RESPONSE.
003201 03-08

BIOLOGICAL-EFFECTS OF CHLORPROMAZINE IN CHRONIC SCHIZOPHRENICS. I. WITH REFERENCE TO PITUITARY-HORMONES.
003415 03-13

BIOLOGICAL-EFFECTS OF CHLORPROMAZINE IN CHRONIC SCHIZOPHRENICS. II. WITH REFERENCE TO SYMPATHETIC NEURONAL FUNCTION.
003416 03-13

DIFFERENTIAL BINDING OF CHLORPROMAZINE TO HUMAN BLOOD CELLS: APPLICATION OF THE HYGROSCOPIC DESORPTION METHOD.
003556 03-16

CHLORPROMAZINE, HALOPERIDOL, METOCLOPRAMIDE AND DOMPERIDONE RELEASE PROLACTIN THROUGH DOPAMINE ANTAGONISM AT LOW CONCENTRATIONS BUT PARADOXICALLY INHIBIT PROLACTIN RELEASE AT HIGH-CONCENTRATIONS.
003731 04-03

THE EFFECT OF LONG-TERM CONCURRENT ADMINISTRATION OF CHLORPROMAZINE AND LITHIUM ON THE STRIATAL AND FRONTAL CORTICAL DOPAMINE METABOLISM IN RATS.
003788 04-03

INHIBITION OF LYSOSOMAL LIPASES BY CHLORPROMAZINE: A POSSIBLE MECHANISMS OF STABILIZATION.
003993 04-03

INTERACTIONS BETWEEN CHLORPROMAZINE AND SOME OF ITS METABOLITES.
004001 04-03

CHLORPROMAZINE EFFECTS ON COCAINE-REINFORCED RESPONDING IN RHESUS-MONKEYS: RECIPROCAL MODIFICATION OF RATE ALTERING EFFECTS OF THE DRUGS.
004133 04-04

EFFECTS OF CHLORPROMAZINE ON ESCAPE AND AVOIDANCE RESPONSES: A CLOSER LOOK.
004226 04-04

PROTEIN BINDING OF CHLORPROMAZINE IN CEREBROSPINAL-FLUID AND SERUM.
004311 04-08

CHOLECYSTOKININ-LIKE
EFFECTS OF CHOLECYSTOKININ-LIKE PEPTIDES ON REARING ACTIVITY AND
HEXOBARBITAL-INDUCED SLEEP.
000507 01-04

CHOLECYSTOKININ-OCTAPEPTIDE
INHIBITION OF THE ACTION OF CHOLECYSTOKININ-OCTAPEPTIDE ON THE
GUINEA-PIG ILEUM MYENTERIC PLEXUS BY DIBUTYRYL-CYCLIC-
GUANOSINE-MONOPHOSPHATE.
001291 02-03

CENTRAL DEPRESSANT EFFECTS OF CAERULEIN AND CHOLECYSTOKININ-
OCTAPEPTIDE (CCK-8) DIFFER FROM THOSE OF DIAZEPAM AND
HALOPERIDOL.
002652 03-02

EFFECTS OF CHOLECYSTOKININ-OCTAPEPTIDE ON STRIATAL DOPAMINE
METABOLISM AND ON APOMORPHINE-INDUCED STEREOTYPED CAGE
CLIMBING IN MICE.
003031 03-04

OPERANT FEEDING AND DRINKING IN PIGS FOLLOWING
INTRACEREBROVENTRICULAR INJECTION OF SYNTHETIC
CHOLECYSTOKININ-OCTAPEPTIDE.
003064 03-04

INTRAVENTRICULAR CHOLECYSTOKININ-OCTAPEPTIDE PRODUCES
HYPERGLYCEMIA IN RATS.
003943 04-03

CHOLECYSTOKININ-PEPTIDES
AN HPLC AND RIA ANALYSIS OF THE CHOLECYSTOKININ-PEPTIDES IN
RAT-BRAIN. (UNPUBLISHED PAPER).
001004 02-01

HPLC SEPARATION OF CHOLECYSTOKININ-PEPTIDES -- TWO SYSTEMS.
(UNPUBLISHED PAPER).
001005 02-01

CHOLECYSTOKININ-PEPTIDES PRODUCE MARKED REDUCTION OF
DOPAMINE TURNOVER IN DISCRETE AREAS IN THE RAT-BRAIN
FOLLOWING INTERAVENTRICULAR INJECTION.
001239 02-03

CHOLERA-TOXIN
OPIOIDS, NORADRENALINE AND GTP ANALOGS INHIBIT CHOLERA-TOXIN
ACTIVATED ADENYLATE-CYCLASE IN NEUROBLASTOMA-X GLIOMA
HYBRID CELLS.
003975 04-03

CHOLERA-TOXIN-INDUCED
CHOLERA-TOXIN-INDUCED EPILEPTOGENIC-FOCUS -- SPECIAL REFERENCE
TO CYCLIC-AMP METABOLISM AND EPILEPTOGENIC-FOCUS.
000522 01-05

CHOLERETIC-EFFECT
DISPOSITION OF VALPROIC-ACID IN THE RAT: DOSE-DEPENDENT
METABOLISM, DISTRIBUTION, ENTEROHEPATIC RECIRCULATION AND
CHOLERETIC-EFFECT.
000073 01-03

CHOLESTEROL
PLASMA HDL CHOLESTEROL AND GROWTH-HORMONE IN EPILEPTICS
TREATED WITH ANTICONVULSANTS.
002260 02-13

CHOLINE
INHIBITION OF HIGH-AFFINITY CHOLINE UPTAKE: STRUCTURE-ACTIVITY
STUDIES.
000026 01-03

INHIBITION OF BRAIN SYNAPTOSOMAL UPTAKE OF CHOLINE BY SOME 2
CARBOXAMIDOSTRYCHNINE DERIVATIVES WITH MUSCLE-RELAXANT
PROPERTIES.
000084 01-03

ORAL CHOLINE IN CEREBELLAR ATAXIA.
000722 01-11

EFFECTS OF CHOLINE CONTAINING COMPOUNDS ON TARDIVE-DYSKINESIA
AND OTHER MOVEMENT-DISORDERS.
000942 01-17

EFFECTS OF HEMICHOLINIUM-3 AND CHOLINE ON HIPPOCAMPAL
ELECTRICAL-ACTIVITY DURING IMMOBILITY VS. MOVEMENT.
001438 02-03

EFFECT OF CHOLINE ON CONDITIONED FOOD MOTOR-REFLEXES IN CATS.
001731 02-04

LACK OF EFFECT OF CHOLINE AND NARCOTIC ANTAGONISTS UPON
APOMORPHINE DISCRIMINATION.
001770 02-04

EFFECTS OF ORAL CHOLINE ON HUMAN COMPLEX PARTIAL SEIZURES.
002149 02-11

USE OF CHOLINE AND LECITHIN IN THE TREATMENT OF TARDIVE-
DYSKINESIA.
002473 02-15

KINETIC DATA ON THE INHIBITION OF HIGH-AFFINITY CHOLINE
TRANSPORT INTO RAT-FOREBRAIN SYNAPTOSOMES BY CHOLINE-LIKE
COMPOUNDS AND NITROGEN-MUSTARD ANALOGUES.
002879 03-03

ALTERATIONS OF ACETYLCHOLINE AND CHOLINE METABOLISM IN
MAMMALIAN PREPARATIONS TREATED WITH BETA BUNGAROTOXIN.
003820 04-03

TISSUE CHOLINE STUDIED USING A SIMPLE CHEMICAL ASSAY.
003828 04-03

EFFECTS OF DELTA9 TETRAHYDROCANNABINOL AND CANNABIDIOL ON SODIUM-DEPENDENT HIGH-AFFINITY CHOLINE UPTAKE IN THE RAT HIPPOCAMPUS.
003908 04-03
THE EFFECT OF ACETYLCHOLINE RELEASE ON CHOLINE FLUXES IN ISOLATED SYNAPTIC TERMINALS.
003924 04-03
CNS EFFECTS OF CHOLINE ADMINISTRATION: EVIDENCE FOR TEMPORAL DEPENDENCE.
003996 04-03
THE HIGH-AFFINITY CHOLINE UPTAKE SYSTEM WITH RESPECT TO THE MUSCARINIC-RECEPTORS USING A SYNAPTOSOMAL FRACTION ABUNDANT IN PRESYNAPTIC MEMBRANES.
004028 04-03
CHOLINE REVERSES NALOXONE-INDUCED DECREASES IN HIPPOCAMPAL ACETYLCHOLINE CONTENT AND SUPPRESSES ESCAPE-BEHAVIOR IN OPIATE-DEPENDENT RATS.
004076 04-04
MECHANISM OF LITHIUM INCLUDED ELEVATION IN RED-BLOOD-CELL CHOLINE CONTENT: AN IN VITRO ANALYSIS.
004511 04-13
A MECHANISM FOR THE ACCUMULATION OF CHOLINE IN ERYTHROCYTES DURING TREATMENT WITH LITHIUM.
004520 04-13
ERYTHROCYTE CHOLINE CONCENTRATIONS ARE ELEVATED IN MANIC-PATIENTS.
004521 04-13
GAS-CHROMATOGRAPHY/MASS-SPECTROMETRY STABLE ISOTOPIC ANALYSES FOR DEANOL, CHOLINE, AND THEIR ACETYLESTERS.
004683 04-16

CHOLINE-ACETYL-TRANSFERASE
PHYSICAL AND KINETIC PROPERTIES OF CHOLINE-ACETYL-TRANSFERASE FROM RAT AND BOVINE BRAIN.
003676 04-01

CHOLINE-ACETYLTRANSFERASE
ACETYLCHOLINE AND CHOLINE-ACETYLTRANSFERASE.
003930 04-03

CHOLINE-BITARTRATE
CHOLINE-BITARTRATE TREATMENT OF ALZHEIMER-TYPE DEMENTIAS.
000675 01-11

CHOLINE-CHLORIDE
HUMAN MEMORY AND THE EFFECTS OF PHYSOSTIGMINE AND CHOLINE-CHLORIDE.
002317 02-14
PHARMACOKINETIC-STUDIES WITH CHOLINE-CHLORIDE: A PRELIMINARY REPORT.
004514 04-13
CLINICAL AND PRECLINICAL EXPERIENCE WITH CHOLINE-CHLORIDE IN HUNTINGTONS-DISEASE AND TARDIVE-DYSKINESIA: UNANSWERED QUESTIONS.
004604 04-15

CHOLINE-LIKE
KINETIC DATA ON THE INHIBITION OF HIGH-AFFINITY CHOLINE TRANSPORT INTO RAT-FOREBRAIN SYNAPTOSOMES BY CHOLINE-LIKE COMPOUNDS AND NITROGEN-MUSTARD ANALOGUES.
002879 03-03

CHOLINERGIC
SEIZURES AND RELATED EPILEPTIFORM ACTIVITY IN HIPPOCAMPUS TRANSPLANTED TO THE ANTERIOR-CHAMBER OF THE EYE: MODULATION BY CHOLINERGIC AND ADRENERGIC INPUT.
000095 01-03
ENKEPHALINS PRESYNAPTICALLY INHIBIT CHOLINERGIC TRANSMISSION IN SYMPATHETIC GANGLIA.
000167 01-03
CHOLINERGIC MECHANISMS AND CATAPLEXY IN DOGS.
000374 01-04
IMIPRAMINE AND REM SLEEP: CHOLINERGIC MEDIATION IN ANIMALS.
000406 01-04
CHOLINERGIC MECHANISMS IN SCENT-MARKING-BEHAVIOR BY MONGOLIAN-GERBILS (MERIONES-UNGUICULATUS).
000504 01-04
CHOLINERGIC ASPECTS OF TARDIVE-DYSKINESIA: HUMAN AND ANIMAL STUDIES.
000928 01-17
INTERACTIONS OF NEUROPEPTIDES WITH CHOLINERGIC SEPTOHIPPOCAMPAL PATHWAY: INDICATION FOR A POSSIBLE TRANSSYNAPTIC REGULATION. (UNPUBLISHED PAPER).
001062 02-01
MARIJUANA AND CHOLINERGIC DYNAMICS. (UNPUBLISHED PAPER).
001166 02-03
REGULATION OF CHOLINERGIC TRANSMISSION IN ADRENAL-MEDULLA. (UNPUBLISHED PAPER).
001182 02-03
OPIATE INTERACTIONS WITH CHOLINERGIC NEURONS.
001198 02-03
LONG-TERM EFFECTS OF HALOPERIDOL, CLOZAPINE, AND METHADONE ON RAT STRIATAL CHOLINERGIC AND DOPAMINERGIC DYNAMICS.
001325 02-03
INTRINSIC CHOLINERGIC EXCITATION IN THE RAT NEOSTRIATUM: NICOTINIC AND MUSCARINIC-RECEPTORS.
001374 02-03

CENTRAL PHARMACOLOGICAL CONTROL OF CORTICOSTERONE SECRETION IN THE INTACT RAT. DEMONSTRATION OF CHOLINERGIC AND SEROTONINERGIC FACILITATORY AND ALPHA-ADRENERGIC INHIBITORY MECHANISMS.
001487 02-03
INTERACTION OF CHOLINERGIC AND DOPAMINERGIC INFLUENCES ON YAWNING-BEHAVIOR.
001656 02-04
ADRENERGIC MODULATION OF THE HYPOTHALAMIC CHOLINERGIC MECHANISM IN THE CONTROL OF EMOTIONAL DEFENSIVE-BEHAVIOR IN THE CAT.
001761 02-04
INVOLVEMENT OF CHOLINERGIC AND GABAERGIC SYSTEMS IN SCHIZOPHRENIA.
001907 02-08
INCREASED VULNERABILITY TO CHOLINERGIC STIMULATION IN AFFECTIVE-DISORDER PATIENTS.
002003 02-09
CHOLINERGIC ASPECTS OF TARDIVE-DYSKINESIA.
002102 02-11
DEVELOPMENT AND USE OF PHARMACOLOGICAL-PROBES OF THE CNS IN MAN: EVIDENCE OF CHOLINERGIC ABNORMALITY IN PRIMARY AFFECTIVE-ILLNESS.
002506 02-16
DYSFUNCTIONS OF CHOLINERGIC PROCESSES IN SCHIZOPHRENIA.
002611 02-17
TRIMETHADIONE EFFECTS ON CHOLINERGIC RESPONSES IN APLYSIA NEURONS.
002782 03-03
CHOLINERGIC, DOPAMINERGIC, NORADRENERGIC, OR GLUTAMINERGIC STIMULATION VENTRAL TO THE ANTERIOR SEPTUM DOES NOT SPECIFICALLY SUPPRESS DEFENSIVE-BEHAVIOR.
002945 03-04
INJECTIONS OF DOPAMINERGIC, CHOLINERGIC, SEROTONINERGIC AND GABAERGIC DRUGS INTO THE NUCLEUS-ACCUMBENS: EFFECTS ON LOCOMOTOR-ACTIVITY IN THE RAT.
003019 03-04
PHYSOSTIGMINE IN TOURETTE-SYNDROME: EVIDENCE FOR CHOLINERGIC UNDERACTIVITY.
003286 03-10
CHOLINERGIC REBOUND IN NEUROLEPTIC WITHDRAWAL-SYNDROMES.
003506 03-15
THE EFFECT OF CHOLINERGIC SUBSTANCES ON NOCICEPTIVE EVOKED-RESPONSES IN SPECIFIC NUCLEI OF THE THALAMUS.
003770 04-03
NYSTAGMIC RESPONSES OF HIPPOCAMPAL ORIGIN WITH REFERENCE TO EXCITABILITY OF CHOLINERGIC AND ADRENERGIC COMPONENTS INVOLVED IN THE HIPPOCAMPUS OF RABBITS.
003842 04-03
SUBSTANCE-P INCREASES HYPOTHALAMIC BLOOD FLOW VIA AN INDIRECT ADRENERGIC CHOLINERGIC INTERACTION.
003887 04-03
EFFECTS OF TAIPOXIN ON THE ULTRASTRUCTURE OF CHOLINERGIC AXON TERMINALS IN THE MOUSE ADRENAL-MEDULLA.
003916 04-03
5' TRIPHOSPHATE RECYCLES INDEPENDENTLY OF ACETYLCHOLINE IN CHOLINERGIC SYNAPTIC VESICLES.
004063 04-03
POSSIBLE MUSCARINIC CHOLINERGIC MEDIATION OF PATTERNED AGGRESSIVE REFLEXES IN THE CAT.
004153 04-04
CHOLINERGIC MECHANISMS IN MANIA AND DEPRESSION: QUESTIONS OF SPECIFICITY.
004374 04-09
THE STATE OF THE ADRENERGIC AND CHOLINERGIC SYSTEMS IN SCHIZOPHRENIC-PATIENTS DURING PSYCHPHARMACOTHERAPY.
004526 04-13

CHOLINERGIC-DRUGS
EFFECTS OF DOPAMINERGIC AND CHOLINERGIC-DRUGS, NALOXONE AND L PROLYL-LEUCYL-GLYCINAMIDE ON LSD-INDUCED CATALEPSY.
000360 01-04
THE EFFECTS OF CHOLINERGIC-DRUGS ON THE INVOLUNTARY-MOVEMENTS OF TARDIVE-DYSKINESIA.
000726 01-11
EFFECTS OF CHOLINERGIC-DRUGS ON MEMORY IN ALZHEIMERS-DISEASE.
003454 03-14

CHOLINERGIC-RECEPTOR
AN ENHANCED SENSITIVITY OF MUSCARINIC CHOLINERGIC-RECEPTOR ASSOCIATED WITH DOPAMINERGIC-RECEPTOR SUBSENSITIVITY AFTER CHRONIC ANTIDEPRESSANT TREATMENT.
002788 03-03
BRAIN MUSCARINIC CHOLINERGIC-RECEPTOR BINDING IN ROMAN HIGH-AVOIDANCE AND LOW-AVOIDANCE RATS.
002852 03-03
A COMPARISON OF HUMAN MUSCARINIC CHOLINERGIC-RECEPTOR RESPONSE TO A NUMBER OF PSYCHOTROPICS UTILIZING THE RADIOLABELED ANTAGONIST, (3H) QUINUCLIDINYL-BENZILATE. (PH.D. DISSERTATION).
002918 03-03

CHOLINERGIC-RECEPTORS
THE REGULATION OF CARDIAC MUSCARINIC CHOLINERGIC-RECEPTORS BY
ISOPROTERENOL.
001441 02-03
CHOLINERGIC-SUPERSENSITIVITY
THE ROLE OF CHOLINERGIC-SUPERSENSITIVITY IN THE MEDICAL
SYMPTOMS ASSOCIATED WITH WITHDRAWAL OF ANTIPSYCHOTIC-
DRUGS.
000869 01-15
CHOLINESTERASE
DIFFERENTIAL REGULATION OF MUSCARINIC AGONIST BINDING-SITES
FOLLOWING CHRONIC CHOLINESTERASE INHIBITION.
000279 01-03
ACETYLCHOLINESTERASE AND CHOLINESTERASE ACTIVITIES IN THE
MOUSE CEREBELLUM FOLLOWING MISONIDAZOLE TREATMENT.
003123 03-05
CHOLINOCEPTORS
INVOLVEMENT OF CENTRAL CHOLINOCEPTORS IN METRAZOL-INDUCED
CONVULSIONS.
000247 01-03
CHOLINOLYTIC
SCOPOLAMINE IN CHOLINOLYTIC TREATMENT.
004468 04-11
CHOLINOMIMETICS
COMPARATIVE-STUDY OF AGGRESSIVE-BEHAVIOUR AFTER INJECTION OF
CHOLINOMIMETICS, ANTICHOLINESTERASES, NICOTINIC, AND
MUSCARINIC GANGLIONIC STIMULANTS INTO THE CEREBRAL
VENTRICLES OF CONSCIOUS CATS: FAILURE OF NICOTINIC-DRUGS TO
EVOKE AGGRESSION.
001568 02-04
CHOLINOMIMETICS IN HUNTINGTONS-DISEASE.
004442 04-11
CHOLINOMIMETICS IN MANIA, SCHIZOPHRENIA, AND MEMORY-
DISORDERS.
004703 04-17
CHOREA
PEMOLINE-INDUCED CHOREA.
003516 03-15
CHOREIC-MOVEMENTS
CHOREIC-MOVEMENTS INDUCED BY THE USE OF METHADONE.
002467 02-15
CHORIONIC
INCREASES IN TESTOSTERONE LEVELS AND IN COPULATORY-BEHAVIOR OF
MALE RHESUS-MONKEYS FOLLOWING TREATMENT WITH HUMAN
CHORIONIC GONADOTROPHIN.
003012 03-04
CHOROID
EVIDENCE FOR THE PRESENCE OF TWO TYPES OF MONOAMINE-OXIDASE
IN RABBIT CHOROID PLEXUS AND THEIR ROLE IN BREAKDOWN OF
AMINES INFLUENCING CEREBROSPINAL-FLUID FORMATION.
002807 03-03
CHROMAFFIN
RELEASE OF ARACHIDONIC-ACID FROM ADRENAL CHROMAFFIN CELL-
CULTURES DURING SECRETION OF EPINEPHRINE. (UNPUBLISHED
PAPER).
001027 02-01
INFLUENCE OF DRUGS AFFECTING THE PITUITARY ADRENAL AXIS ON
CHROMAFFIN CELLS.
001183 02-03
ACCUMULATION OF AMANTADINE BY ISOLATED CHROMAFFIN
GRANULES.
003866 04-03
CHROMATIN
INFLUENCE OF PSYCHOACTIVE AND NONPSYCHOACTIVE CANNABINOIDS
ON CHROMATIN STRUCTURE AND FUNCTION IN HUMAN CELLS.
002831 03-03
CHROMATOGRAPHY
AFFINITY CHROMATOGRAPHY OF THE BETA-ADRENERGIC-RECEPTOR AND
CHARACTERIZATION OF ANTIBODIES RAISED AGAINST PURIFIED
RECEPTOR PREPARATIONS.
001009 02-01
GAS-CHROMATOGRAPHY, MASS-SPECTROMETRY, AND COMBINED
CHROMATOGRAPHY MASS-SPECTROMETRY.
004290 04-06
CHROMOSOMES
FRAGILE SITES IN HUMAN CHROMOSOMES I. THE EFFECT OF METHIONINE
ON THE XQ-FRAGILE-SITE.
004515 04-13
CHRONIC-BRAIN-SYNDROMES
PROPRANOLOL IN THE TREATMENT OF RAGE AND VIOLENT-BEHAVIOR IN
PATIENTS WITH CHRONIC-BRAIN-SYNDROMES.
003394 03-11
CHRONIC-OUTPATIENTS
USING DRUG-HOLIDAYS FOR CHRONIC-OUTPATIENTS.
004742 04-17
CHRONIC-SCHIZOPHRENICS
THE EFFECTS OF A DRUG-HOLIDAY ON RELAPSE AND TARDIVE-
DYSKINESIA IN CHRONIC-SCHIZOPHRENICS.
003487 03-15

CHRONIC-TREATMENT
EFFECT OF CHRONIC-TREATMENT WITH ANTIDEPRESSANTS ON BETA-
ADRENERGIC-RECEPTOR BINDING IN GUINEA-PIG BRAIN.
000135 01-03
EFFECTS OF CHRONIC-TREATMENT WITH L SULPIRIDE AND HALOPERIDOL
ON CENTRAL DOPAMINE TURNOVER EVALUATED IN DOPAMINE CELL
BODY AND NERVE TERMINAL-RICH AREAS.
001096 02-03
INTERACTION-STUDIES BETWEEN NARCOTIC ANALGESICS, NARCOTIC
ANTAGONISTS AND ETHANOL: STUDIES DURING ACUTE AND CHRONIC-
TREATMENT AND WITHDRAWAL STATES IN RATS AND MICE. (PH.D.
DISSERTATION).
001165 02-03
EFFECTS OF CHRONIC-TREATMENT WITH L SULPIRIDE AND HALOPERIDOL
ON CENTRAL MONOAMINERGIC MECHANISMS.
001240 02-03
REGULATION OF TYROSINE-HYDROXYLASE AFTER CHRONIC-TREATMENT
WITH CLASSIC AND ATYPICAL ANTISCHIZOPHRENIC-DRUGS.
001262 02-03
ACETYLCHOLINE AND AMINO-ACID NEUROTRANSMITTERS IN EPIDURAL
CUPS OF FREELY-MOVING-RATS: EFFECT OF ACUTE AND CHRONIC-
TREATMENT WITH ANTISCHIZOPHRENIC-DRUGS.
001386 02-03
MODULATION OF BETA-ADRENERGIC-RECEPTORS AND CALMODULIN
FOLLOWING ACUTE AND CHRONIC-TREATMENT WITH NEUROLEPTICS.
001529 02-03
CHRONIC-TREATMENT WITH VALIUM (DIAZEPAM) FAILS TO AFFECT THE
REPRODUCTIVE SYSTEM OF THE MALE RAT.
001535 02-03
DIFFERENTIAL-EFFECTS OF CLOMIPRAMINE AND CLORGYLINE ON THE
SENSITIVITY OF CORTICAL NEURONS TO SEROTONIN: EFFECT OF
CHRONIC-TREATMENT.
002847 03-03
NOREPINEPHRINE AND DOPAMINE CEREBRAL LEVELS AFTER CHRONIC-
TREATMENT WITH NOMIFENSINE.
002872 03-03
SUPPRESSION OF ACTIVE SLEEP BY CHRONIC-TREATMENT WITH
CHLORIMIPRAMINE DURING EARLY POSTNATAL DEVELOPMENT:
EFFECTS UPON ADULT SLEEP AND BEHAVIOR IN THE RAT.
003056 03-04
FACILITATED SHOCK-INDUCED AGGRESSION AFTER CHRONIC-TREATMENT
WITH ANTIDEPRESSANT-DRUGS IN THE RAT.
003058 03-04
SUPERSENSITIVITY OF CENTRAL NORADRENERGIC PRESYNAPTIC-
AUTORECEPTORS FOLLOWING CHRONIC-TREATMENT WITH THE
ANTIDEPRESSANT MIANSERIN.
003745 04-03
REGULATION OF SEROTONIN2-RECEPTORS (5 HT2) LABELED WITH
(3H)SPIROPERIDOL BY CHRONIC-TREATMENT WITH THE
ANTIDEPRESSANT AMITRIPTYLINE.
003964 04-03
THE INSENSITIVITY OF DEVELOPING BENZODIAZEPINE-RECEPTORS TO
CHRONIC-TREATMENT WITH DIAZEPAM, GABA AND MUSCIMOL IN
BRAIN CELL-CULTURES.
004002 04-03
EFFECT OF CHRONIC-TREATMENT WITH TRICYCLIC-ANTIDEPRESSANT
DRUGS ON IDENTIFIED BRAIN NORADRENERGIC AND SEROTONERGIC
NEURONS.
004026 04-03
ELECTROCARDIOGRAPHIC-CHANGES IN RATS DURING CHRONIC-
TREATMENT WITH ANTIDEPRESSANT AND NEUROLEPTIC-DRUGS.
004284 04-05
HORMONAL STIMULATION AFTER INJECTION OF THYROTROPHIN-
RELEASING-FACTOR (TRF) AND ACTH1-24 IN PATIENTS FOLLOWING
CHRONIC-TREATMENT WITH NEUROLEPTICS: PRELIMINARY-STUDY.
004505 04-13
CHRONIC-TREATMENTS
INFERENTIAL CHANGES AFTER CHRONIC-TREATMENTS WITH LI, DMI, OR
ETHANOL DETECTED BY ELECTROPHYSIOLOGICAL-CORRELATES.
001136 02-03
CHRONICALLY-ILL
CHRONIC DRUG-TREATMENT OF THE CHRONICALLY-ILL: BENEFITS AND
RISKS.
003625 03-17
CHRONOLOGICAL
CHRONOLOGICAL ELECTROENCEPHALOGRAPHIC AND
NEUROPHARMACOLOGICAL-STUDY IN CORTICAL KINDLING RABBITS.
002761 03-03
CHRONOLOGY
CHRONOLOGY OF EXTRAPYRAMIDAL-EFFECTS OF NEUROLEPTIC-DRUGS
AND THE NIGROSTRIATAL DOPAMINERGIC-SYSTEM.
002449 02-15
CHRONOLOGY OF NEUROCHEMICAL ALTERATIONS INDUCED BY GABA
AGONIST ADMINISTRATION.
002713 03-03
CICLAZINDOL
INFLUENCE OF CICLAZINDOL ON MONOAMINE UPTAKE AND CNS
FUNCTION IN NORMAL SUBJECTS.
002268 02-13

CIGARETTE
NALOXONE REDUCES CIGARETTE SMOKING.
000808 01-14
THE ROLE OF NICOTINE IN THE BEHAVIORAL-ASPECTS OF CIGARETTE SMOKING.
004575 04-14

CIMETIDINE
SYNERGISTIC ACTIONS OF PROPANTHELINE-BROMIDE WITH CIMETIDINE AND THIOPROPAZATE-HYDROCHLORIDE IN THE PREVENTION OF STRESS-ULCER FORMATION IN RATS.
000064 01-03
DELAYED CLEARANCE OF DIAZEPAM DUE TO CIMETIDINE.
000164 01-03
CIMETIDINE TOXICITY MANIFESTED AS PARANOIA AND HALLUCINATIONS.
000829 01-15
AGITATION, DISORIENTATION, AND HALLUCINATIONS IN PATIENTS ON CIMETIDINE: A REPORT OF THREE CASES AND LITERATURE REVIEW.
000896 01-15
INFLUENCE OF CIMETIDINE ON THE PHARMACOKINETICS OF DESMETHYLDIAZEPAM AND OXAZEPAM.
002249 02-13

CIMETIDINE-INDUCED
A CASE-REPORT OF CIMETIDINE-INDUCED DEPRESSIVE-SYNDROME.
000839 01-15
DIFFERENTIAL DIAGNOSIS OF CIMETIDINE-INDUCED DELIRIUM.
003488 03-15

CIRCADIAN-CYCLES
THE EFFECTS OF PROGESTERONE ON THE CIRCADIAN-CYCLES AND ESTROUS-CYCLES IN THE RAT. (PH.D. DISSERTATION).
001111 02-03

CIRCADIAN-CYCLING
PHENOBARBITAL EFFECTS ON WEIGHT-GAIN AND CIRCADIAN-CYCLING OF FOOD INTAKE AND BODY-TEMPERATURE.
001409 02-03

CIRCADIAN-EXCRETION
EFFECT OF FLUPHENAZINE ON THE CIRCADIAN-EXCRETION OF CYCLIC-NUCLEOTIDES AND ELECTROLYTES IN THE URINE OF CHRONIC SCHIZOPHRENICS.
001927 02-08

CIRCADIAN-PERIODICITY
EFFECT OF LITHIUM-CARBONATE ON CIRCADIAN-PERIODICITY IN HUMANS.
000772 01-13

CIRCADIAN-RHYTHM
CIRCADIAN-RHYTHM OF CYCLIC-NUCLEOTIDE AND GABA LEVELS IN THE RAT-BRAIN.
000049 01-03
INFLUENCE OF CHRONIC ALCOHOL INTOXICATION ON CIRCADIAN-RHYTHM OF NEUROSECRETORY CENTERS OF RAT HYPOTHALAMUS.
001549 02-03

CIRCADIAN-RHYTHMS
ANTIDEPRESSANT-DRUGS SLOW CIRCADIAN-RHYTHMS IN BEHAVIOR AND BRAIN NEUROTRANSMITTER-RECEPTORS.
001536 02-03

CIRCADIAN-VARIATION
CIRCADIAN-VARIATION OF CYCLIC-AMP IN THE RAT PINEAL-GLAND.
003938 04-03

CIRCLING
MORPHINE-DEPENDENCE AND DOPAMINERGIC-ACTIVITY: TESTS OF CIRCLING RESPONSES IN RATS WITH UNILATERAL NIGRAL LESIONS.
001641 02-04
CIRCLING PRODUCED BY SEROTONIN AND DOPAMINE AGONISTS IN RAPHE LESIONED RATS: A SEROTONIN MODEL.
001783 02-04
INVOLVEMENT OF DOPAMINE IN CIRCLING RESPONSES TO MUSCIMOL DEPENDS ON INTRANIGRAL SITE OF INJECTION.
004158 04-04

CIRCLING-BEHAVIOR
THE EFFECT OF DOPAMINE UPTAKE BLOCKING-AGENTS ON THE AMPHETAMINE-INDUCED CIRCLING-BEHAVIOR IN MICE WITH UNILATERAL NIGROSTRIATAL LESIONS.
004117 04-04

CIRCLING-BEHAVIOUR
CIRCLING-BEHAVIOUR INDUCED BY INTRANIGRAL INJECTION OF BACLOFEN IN RATS.
000415 01-04
CONTRALATERAL CIRCLING-BEHAVIOUR INDUCED BY INTRANIGRAL INJECTION OF MORPHINE AND ENKEPHALIN ANALOGUE FK-33-824 IN RATS.
001669 02-04
CONTRALATERAL CIRCLING-BEHAVIOUR INDUCED BY INTRANIGRAL INJECTION OF TAURINE IN RATS.
001670 01-04
THE ROLE OF NIGRAL PROJECTIONS TO THE THALAMUS IN DRUG-INDUCED CIRCLING-BEHAVIOUR IN THE RAT.
004205 04-04

CIRCUITS
ACTIVATION OF CORTICAL CIRCUITS DURING INTERICTAL SPIKES.
000056 01-03

CIRCULATION
EFFECT OF ISOPROTERENOL ON CEREBRAL CIRCULATION IN DOGS.
000199 01-03
EFFECTS OF ANTIDEPRESSIVE-DRUGS UPON THE HEART AND CIRCULATION.
000863 01-15
EFFECTS OF BICUCULLINE-INDUCED SEIZURES ON CEREBRAL METABOLISM AND CIRCULATION OF RATS RENDERED HYPOGLYCEMIC BY STARVATION.
001134 02-03
ACTION OF 4 AMINOPYRIDINE ON THE CEREBRAL CIRCULATION.
003781 04-03

CIRCULATIONS
ABSORPTION OF 14C LABELED METHADONE BY PORTAL AND EXTRAPORTAL VENOUS CIRCULATIONS FOLLOWING INTRAPERITONEAL AND INTRODUODENAL ADMINISTRATION.
000094 01-03

CIRCULATORY
CEREBRAL CIRCULATORY AND METABOLIC-EFFECTS OF PIRIBEDIL.
000200 01-03

CIRCUMSTANCES
THE EFFECT OF MEBICAR ON THE CONDITION OF ANIMALS UNDER CERTAIN EXTREME CIRCUMSTANCES.
004262 04-04

CIRCUMVENTRICULAR
INHIBITION OF MONOAMINE-OXIDASE BY CLORGYLINE AND DEPRENYL IN CIRCUMVENTRICULAR STRUCTURES OF RAT-BRAIN.
000159 01-03
MONOAMINE-OXIDASE-B ACTIVITIES TOWARD BETA PHENYLETHYLAMINE IN DISCRETE HYPOTHALAMIC AND CIRCUMVENTRICULAR NUCLEI OF THE RAT.
002781 03-03

CIRRHOSIS
CHLORDIAZEPOXIDE AND OXAZEPAM DISPOSITION IN CIRRHOSIS.
000790 01-13

CIS-ISOMERS
THE PHOTOCHEMICAL-STABILITY OF CIS-ISOMERS AND TRANS-ISOMERS OF TRICYCLIC NEUROLEPTIC-DRUGS.
001872 02-06
PLASMA LEVELS OF THE CIS-ISOMERS AND TRANS-ISOMERS OF DOXEPIN AND DESMETHYLDOXEPIN AFTER ADMINISTRATION OF DOXEPIN TO PATIENTS.
004355 04-09

CISMETHRIN
THE EFFECT OF CISMETHRIN ON THE RAT DORSAL ROOT POTENTIALS.
000528 01-05

CITALOPRAM
INITIAL, CLINICAL-TRIAL OF A NEW, SPECIFIC 5 HT REUPTAKE INHIBITOR, CITALOPRAM (LU-10-171).
000591 01-09
EFFECT OF CITALOPRAM (LU-10-171) ON TRANYLCYPROMINE AND TRYPTOPHAN-INDUCED WET-DOG-SHAKES IN RATS.
001682 02-04

CITICOLINE
OBSERVATIONS ON THE USE OF CITICOLINE IN DYSTHYMIC-PATIENTS.
003207 03-09

CITRATE
GAMMA BUTYROLACTONE-GAMMA-CARBONYL-HISTIDYL-PROLINAMIDE CITRATE (DN-1417): A NOVEL TRH ANALOG WITH POTENT EFFECTS ON THE CENTRAL-NERVOUS-SYSTEM.
003057 03-04
INHIBITION OF THE SYNTHESIS OF ACETYLCHOLINE IN RAT-BRAIN SLICES BY (-) HYDROXYCITRATE AND CITRATE.
004044 04-03
LITHIUM EFFECTS ON CITRATE METABOLISM IN HUMANS AND RATS.
004537 04-13

CLAMP
VOLTAGE CLAMP STUDY OF CAT SPINAL MOTONEURONS DURING STRYCHNINE-INDUCED SEIZURES.
002886 03-03

CLARE-BISHOP
SELECTIVE SYNAPTIC ANTAGONISM BY ATROPINE AND ALPHA AMINOADIPATE OF PULVINAR AND CORTICAL AFFERENTS TO THE SUPRASYLVIAN VISUAL AREA (CLARE-BISHOP AREA).
002752 03-03

CLASSIC
REGULATION OF TYROSINE-HYDROXYLASE AFTER CHRONIC-TREATMENT WITH CLASSIC AND ATYPICAL ANTISCHIZOPHRENIC-DRUGS.
001262 02-03

CLASSICALLY
EFFECTS OF SUBCHRONIC DESMETHYLIMIPRAMINE (DMI) TREATMENT OF THE CLASSICALLY CONDITIONED EYEBLINK RESPONSE IN RABBITS.
004180 04-04

CLASSIFICATION
CLASSIFICATION AND ASSESSMENT OF CEREBRAL BIOAVAILABILITY OF LOPIRAZEPAM (D-12524) BY QUANTITATIVE EEG AND PSYCHOMETRIC-ANALYSIS.
000720 01-11

CRITERIA FOR CLINICAL DEVELOPMENT AND CLASSIFICATION OF
NOOTROPIC-DRUGS. AN EXAMPLE: PIRACETAM.
000988 01-17
A CLASSIFICATION OF OPIATE-RECEPTORS THAT MEDIATE
ANTINOCICEPTION IN ANIMALS.
001807 02-04
AN OBJECTIVE CLASSIFICATION OF PSYCHOACTIVE-DRUGS.
001894 02-07
CLASSIFICATION OF PSYCHOTROPIC-DRUGS IN PEDIATRIC-
PSYCHOPHARMACOLOGY.
001903 02-07
DIAGNOSTIC CLASSIFICATION AND THE ENDORPHIN HYPOTHESIS OF
SCHIZOPHRENIA: INDIVIDUAL DIFFERENCES AND
PSYCHOPHARMACOLOGICAL STRATEGIES. (UNPUBLISHED PAPER).
001910 02-08
CLASSIFICATION OF THE ANTIDEPRESSANT-DRUGS.
002015 02-09
CLASSIFICATION OF ENDORPHINS/ENKEPHALINS IN BRAIN PHYSIOLOGY
AND PATHOLOGY (BASED ON EEG AND CLINICAL-STUDY OF
SYNTHETICALLY-MODIFIED METHIONINE-ENKEPHALIN).
002286 02-13
CLASSIFICATION OF DRUGS AND PATIENTS TO ACHIEVE MAXIMUM
THERAPEUTIC RESPONSE.
002560 02-17
CLASSIFICATION OF ANALGESICS.
002570 02-17
CLASSIFICATION AND PSYCHOTROPIC-DRUGS.
002605 02-17
REFLECTIONS ON THE CLASSIFICATION OF ANTIDEPRESSANT-DRUGS.
002610 02-17
DIAGNOSTIC CLASSIFICATION AND THE ENDORPHIN HYPOTHESIS OF
SCHIZOPHRENIA: INDIVIDUAL DIFFERENCES AND
PSYCHOPHARMACOLOGICAL STRATEGIES.
003167 03-08
TOWARD A BIOCHEMICAL CLASSIFICATION OF DEPRESSIVE-DISORDERS
IV: PRETREATMENT URINARY MHPG LEVELS AS PREDICTORS OF
ANTIDEPRESSANT RESPONSE TO IMIPRAMINE.
004406 04-09
THE CLASSIFICATION OF SLEEP-DISORDERS AND THE TREATMENT OF
VARIOUS FORMS OF SOMNAMBULISM.
004461 04-11

CLEARANCE
DELAYED CLEARANCE OF DIAZEPAM DUE TO CIMETIDINE.
000164 01-03
NORTRIPTYLINE AND ANTIPYRINE CLEARANCE IN RELATION TO
DEBRISOQUINE HYDROXYLATION IN MAN.
000754 01-13
VALPROIC-ACID DOSAGE AND PLASMA PROTEIN BINDING AND
CLEARANCE.
000755 01-13

CLEBOPRIDE
COMPARISON OF THE POTENCIES OF CLEBOPRIDE AND OTHER
SUBSTITUTED BENZAMIDE DRUGS ON ISOLATED GASTROINTESTINAL
TRACT OF THE GUINEA-PIG AND RAT.
003928 04-03

CLEFTS
FACIAL CLEFTS AMONG EPILEPTIC-PATIENTS.
003484 03-15

CLENBUTEROL
CLENBUTEROL, A CENTRAL BETA-ADRENOCEPTOR AGONIST.
000120 01-03

CLIMAX
THE BEHAVIOURAL-STATE DURING CLIMAX (HATCHING) IN THE
DOMESTIC-FOWL (GALLUS-DOMESTICUS).
001564 02-04

CLIMBING
THE MESOLIMBIC SYSTEM, DENERVATION AND THE CLIMBING RESPONSE
IN THE MOUSE.
000370 01-04
EFFECTS OF CHOLECYSTOKININ-OCTAPEPTIDE ON STRIATAL DOPAMINE
METABOLISM AND ON APOMORPHINE-INDUCED STEREOTYPED CAGE
CLIMBING IN MICE.
003031 03-04
ENHANCEMENT OF APOMORPHINE-INDUCED CLIMBING IN MICE BY
REVERSIBLE AND IRREVERSIBLE NARCOTIC ANTAGONIST DRUGS.
003068 03-04
USE OF THE INTRACEREBRAL INJECTION TECHNIQUE TO ELUCIDATE
MECHANISMS OF APOMORPHINE CLIMBING AND ITS ANTAGONISM IN
THE MOUSE.
004092 04-04

CLIMBING-BEHAVIOUR
EFFECT OF L HISTIDINE AND CHLORCYCLIZINE ON APOMORPHINE-INDUCED
CLIMBING-BEHAVIOUR AND METHAMPHETAMINE STEREOTYPY IN
MICE.
004147 04-04

CLINIC
NONCOOPERATION: AN EXAMINATION OF FACTORS LEADING TO
NONCOMPLIANCE IN A HYPERTENSION CLINIC.
002557 02-17
THE TREATMENT OF INSOMNIA THROUGH HOMEOPATHY IN A CLINIC.
004484 04-11

CLINICAL
CLINICAL COMPARISON OF OXYPROTHEPIN AND CLOTEPINE IN
SCHIZOPHRENIC-PATIENTS (CONTROLLED-STUDY).
000568 01-08
CLINICAL ASSESSMENT OF ONCE A DAY PHENOTHIAZINE
ADMINISTRATION.
000573 01-08
CLINICAL AND LABORATORY DIAGNOSTICS APPLICATIONS IN
DEPRESSION. (UNPUBLISHED PAPER).
000588 01-09
ON THE RELATIONSHIP OF NORTRIPTYLINE: AMITRIPTYLINE RATIO TO
CLINICAL IMPROVEMENT OF AMITRIPTYLINE TREATED DEPRESSIVE-
PATIENTS.
000599 01-09
CLINICAL AND BIOCHEMICAL-ACTION OF PIRACETAM (NOOTROPIL) IN
DRUG-RESISTANT DEPRESSION.
000600 01-09
PSYCHIATRIC-DISTURBANCE IN MENTALLY-HANDICAPPED-PATIENTS: A
PROSPECTIVE STUDY OF CURRENT CLINICAL USAGE OF DEPOT
FLUPHENAZINE IN HOSPITALS FOR THE MENTALLY-HANDICAPPED.
000668 01-11
SOCIAL AND CLINICAL SIGNIFICANCE OF DETERMINING THE BARBITURATE
LEVEL IN THE BLOOD SERUM OF PATIENTS TREATED WITH
ANTIEPILEPTIC-DRUGS.
000695 01-11
THE TREATMENT OF PARKINSONS-DISEASE USING A COMBINATION OF L-
DOPA AND DECARBOXYLASE INHIBITORS (CARBIDOPA, BENSERASIDE).
A CLINICAL AND BIOCHEMICAL COMPARATIVE INVESTIGATION.
000712 01-11
THE DOPAMINE-RADIORECEPTOR ASSAY -- A CLINICAL APPLICATION.
000904 01-16
ROTTING WITH THEIR RIGHTS ON: CONSTITUTIONAL THEORY AND
CLINICAL REALITY IN DRUG-REFUSAL BY PSYCHIATRIC-PATIENTS.
000911 01-17
TEXTBOOK OF CLINICAL PSYCHOPHARMACOLOGY.
000929 01-17
CLINICAL HANDBOOK OF ANTIPSYCHOTIC-DRUG THERAPY.
000961 01-17
TWENTY YEARS CLINICAL THERAPEUTIC EXPERIENCE WITH CALCIUM
GLUTAMATES EFFICACY.
000963 01-17
MONOAMINE-OXIDASE AND ITS INHIBITION: SOME CLINICAL
IMPLICATIONS.
000983 01-17
CRITERIA FOR CLINICAL DEVELOPMENT AND CLASSIFICATION OF
NOOTROPIC-DRUGS. AN EXAMPLE: PIRACETAM.
000988 01-17
BASIC AND CLINICAL NEUROBIOLOGICAL APPLICATIONS OF NEURONAL
(NSE) AND NONNEURONAL (NNE) ENOLASE. (UNPUBLISHED PAPER).
001041 02-01
SOME PHARMACOLOGICAL-ASPECTS AND BIOCHEMICAL-ASPECTS OF
TRH: EXPERIMENTAL AND CLINICAL DATA.
001189 02-03
POSSIBLE CLINICAL APPLICATIONS OF NOOTROPICS.
001890 02-07
ACTION OF TOFISOPAM ON THE ERGONOMIC VIGILANCE LEVEL. ITS
INTERACTION WITH THE EFFECTS OF ALCOHOL. CLINICAL
PHARMACOLOGICAL-STUDY.
001891 02-07
AMINEPTINE: CLINICAL REVIEW.
001896 02-07
CLINICAL ACTIVITY OF A NEW BENZODIAZEPINE: CLOXAZOLAM.
001904 02-07
CLINICAL STATE, PLASMA LEVELS OF HALOPERIDOL AND PROLACTIN:
001943 02-08
CLINICAL AND EEG CHANGES IN DEPRESSIVE-PATIENTS AFTER A SINGLE
INJECTION OF BETA ENDORPHIN.
001962 02-09
CLINICAL AND BIOCHEMICAL-DATA ON THE ACTION OF MAPROTILINE
AND CLOMIPRAMINE IN DEPRESSIVE-STATES (PRELIMINARY
OBSERVATION).
002032 02-09
FIRST CLINICAL IMPRESSIONS IN DAILY PRACTICE.
002046 02-09
DOUBLE-BLIND CLINICAL ASSESSMENT OF ALPRAZOLAM, A NEW
BENZODIAZEPINE DERIVATIVE, IN THE TREATMENT OF MODERATE TO
SEVERE ANXIETY.
002070 02-10
CLINICAL PROCESSES AND CENTRAL DOPAMINERGIC-ACTIVITY IN
PSYCHOTIC-DISORDERS.
002098 02-11
THE USE AND MISUSE OF SLEEPING-PILLS: A CLINICAL GUIDE.
002150 02-11
CEEG STUDY ON PATIENTS UNDER THE PSYCHIATRIC-DRUG TREATMENT;
THE CORRELATION BETWEEN EEG ALTERATION AND CLINICAL
EVOLUTION.
002165 02-11

TREATMENT OF MYOCLONUS WITH L 5 HYDROXYTRYPTOPHAN AND
CARBIDOPA: CLINICAL, ELECTROPHYSIOLOGICAL, AND BIOCHEMICAL-
OBSERVATIONS.
002180 02-11
CLINICAL USE OF SULPIRIDE IN ITALY.
002187 02-11
ON THE CLINICAL PHARMACOKINETICS OF THIORIDAZINE AND ITS
METABOLITES.
002207 02-13
CLINICAL EVIDENCE FOR MULTIPLE DOPAMINE-RECEPTORS IN MAN.
002264 02-13
CLINICAL NEUROPHYSIOLOGICAL ASPECTS OF PSYCHOPATHOLOGICAL-
CONDITIONS.
002274 02-13
CLINICAL COMPARABILITY OF PSYCHOTROPIC-DRUGS.
002526 02-17
ALIVAL: NEW CLINICAL APPLICATIONS, STUDIES IN PROGRESS, AND NEW
POSSIBILITIES.
002530 02-17
CLINICAL NEUROPHARMACOLOGY.
002567 02-17
REGULATION OF NEUROTRANSMISSION THROUGH PRESYNAPTIC-
RECEPTORS AND OTHER MECHANISMS: POSSIBLE CLINICAL RELEVANCE
AND THERAPEUTIC POTENTIAL.
002569 02-16
LIMITS, VALUE AND PERSPECTIVES OF THE PSYCHIATRIC-DIAGNOSIS IN
CLINICAL PSYCHOPHARMACOLOGY.
002631 02-17
REPEATED ANTIDEPRESSANT TREATMENTS INDUCE A LONG-LASTING
DOPAMINE-AUTORECEPTOR SUBSENSITIVITY: IS DAILY TREATMENT
NECESSARY FOR CLINICAL EFFICACY?
002659 03-03
CORRELATION BETWEEN ANTIAVOIDANCE ACTIVITIES OF ANTIPSYCHOTIC-
DRUGS IN RATS AND DAILY CLINICAL DOSES.
003032 03-04
RAPIDITY OF CLINICAL ANTIDEPRESSANT RESPONSE TO IMIPRAMINE.
(UNPUBLISHED PAPER).
003164 03-07
DIFFERENCES IN THE CLINICAL ACTION OF SOME NEUROLEPTIC-DRUGS.
003204 03-08
TREATMENT OF ORGANIC-BRAIN-DISTURBANCES IN ELDERLY-PATIENTS. A
CLINICAL DOUBLE-BLIND STUDY WITH MACROMOLECULAR ORGAN
LYSATES (CYTOPLASMATIC THERAPY ACCORDING TO THEURER).
003327 03-11
A CLINICAL, CONTROLLED-STUDY OF L ALPHA ACETYLMETHADOL IN THE
TREATMENT OF NARCOTIC ADDICTION.
003335 03-11
CLINICAL PHARMACOKINETICS IN NEWBORNS AND INFANTS: AGE-
RELATED DIFFERENCES AND THERAPEUTIC IMPLICATIONS.
003343 03-11
CLINICAL SIGNIFICANCE OF PYRIDOXINE ADMINISTRATION IN L-DOPA
THERAPY OF PARKINSONISM.
003345 03-11
PHENYTOIN: PHARMACOKINETICS AND CLINICAL THERAPEUTICS.
003353 03-11
CLINICAL PHARMACOKINETICS OF OXAZEPAM AND LORAZEPAM.
003410 03-13
SPINOCEREBELLAR DEGENERATION WITH PARKINSONIAN FEATURES: A
CLINICAL AND PATHOLOGICAL REPORT.
003436 03-13
TREATMENT OF HUNTINGTON-DISEASE WITH GAMMA ACETYLENIC-
GABA, AN IRREVERSIBLE INHIBITOR OF GABA-TRANSAMINASE:
INCREASED CSF GABA AND HOMOCARNOSINE WITHOUT CLINICAL
AMELIORATION.
003458 03-14
EFFECTS OF GRADUAL DECREASE AND DISCONTINUATION OF
NEUROLEPTICS ON CLINICAL CONDITION AND TARDIVE-DYSKINESIA.
003469 03-15
LECITHIN ADMINISTRATION IN TARDIVE-DYSKINESIA: CLINICAL AND
BIOMEDICAL-CORRELATES.
003496 03-15
THE CLINICAL DYNAMICS OF TETRAETHYL-LEAD POISONING.
003500 03-15
SEVERE WITHDRAWAL-SYNDROME AFTER CESSATION OF
BENZODIAZEPINE TREATMENT: SIX CLINICAL CASES.
003505 03-15
TIME-COURSE OF CLINICAL CHEMICAL PARAMETERS UNDER LONG-TERM
LITHIUM TREATMENT.
003515 03-15
CLINICAL USE OF THE ANTIPSYCHOTICS.
003607 03-17
ACCURACY OF PATIENT INTERVIEWS AND ESTIMATES BY CLINICAL STAFF
IN DETERMINING MEDICATION COMPLIANCE.
003618 03-17
SECOND-GENERATION ANTIDEPRESSANTS: A CLINICAL
PHARMACOTHERAPEUTIC RESEARCH STRATEGY.
003632 03-17
PHARMACOLOGICAL-BASES OF PSYCHONEUROENDOCRINOLOGY:
PRECLINICAL ASSESSMENT OF CLINICAL FACTS.
003735 04-03

PROLACTIN RELEASING POTENCIES OF ANTIPSYCHOTIC AND RELATED
NONANTIPSYCHOTIC COMPOUNDS IN FEMALE RATS: RELATION TO
CLINICAL POTENCIES.
003830 04-03
THE EFFECT OF ADENOSINE AND GUANOSINE ON THE CONTENT OF
SEROTONIN AND CATECHOLAMINES IN THE BRAIN IN THE
RESTORATION PERIOD FOLLOWING EXPERIMENTAL CLINICAL DEATH.
003882 04-03
CLINICAL AND BIOCHEMICAL-CORRELATIONS IN ABRUPT
DISCONTINUATION OF PSYCHOPHARMACOTHERAPY.
004330 04-08
HALOPERIDOL AND DROPERIDOL TREATMENT IN SCHIZOPHRENICS:
CLINICAL APPLICATION OF THE PROLACTIN MODEL.
004332 04-08
THE USE OF CLINICAL AND PHARMACOKINETIC CRITERIA IN FORECASTING
THE EFFICACY OF THERAPY IN SCHIZOPHRENIA.
004335 04-08
A CLINICAL AND PHARMACODYNAMIC EVALUATION OF SULPIRIDE.
004338 04-08
LONG-TERM NEUROLEPTIC TREATMENT OF CHRONIC SCHIZOPHRENIC-
PATIENTS: CLINICAL AND BIOCHEMICAL-EFFECTS OF WITHDRAWAL.
004344 04-08
CLINICAL DEPRESSIONS: DIAGNOSTIC AND THERAPEUTIC CHALLENGES.
004350 04-09
CLINICAL SIGNIFICANCE OF THE ERYTHROPLASMATIC RATIO OF LITHIUM.
004357 04-09
CLINICAL NEUROPHYSIOLOGICAL PROPERTIES OF ANTIDEPRESSANTS.
004373 04-09
CLINICAL RESULTS OBTAINED WITH THE USE OF LYSONEURO IN
DEPRESSIVE-SYNDROMES.
004397 04-09
CLINICAL USE OF A NEW BENZODIAZEPINE, PRAZEPAM.
004421 04-10
ARE THE ENKEPHALINS INVOLVED IN PARKINSONS-DISEASE? CLINICAL
AND NEUROENDOCRINE RESPONSES TO NALOXONE ADMINISTRATION.
004431 04-11
MEASUREMENTS OF NERVE CONDUCTION VELOCITY DURING DECREASING
TOXIC DIPHENYLHYDANTOIN LEVELS AND THE BEGINNING OF
CARBAMAZEPINE MEDICATION: A CLINICAL NEUROPHYSIOLOGICAL
REPORT.
004441 04-11
CLINICAL APPLICATION OF ANTIANDROGENS IN PSYCHIATRY.
004457 04-11
CLINICAL PHARMACOKINETICS OF CHLORDIAZEPOXIDE IN PATIENTS WITH
ALCOHOLIC HEPATITIS.
004473 04-11
CLINICAL PHARMACOKINETICS OF BENZODIAZEPINES.
004524 04-13
TREATMENT OF NARCOLEPSY AND SLEEP-APNEA WITH GAMMA
HYDROXYBUTYRATE: A CLINICAL AND POLYSOMNOGRAPHIC CASE-
STUDY.
004571 04-14
EFFECTS OF NEUROLEPTIC ADJUSTMENT ON CLINICAL CONDITION AND
TARDIVE-DYSKINESIA IN SCHIZOPHRENIC-PATIENTS.
004595 04-15
CLINICAL STRATEGIES FOR ANTIPSYCHOTIC-DRUG TREATMENT, TARDIVE-
DYSKINESIA, AND THE TRAINING OF RESEARCH PSYCHIATRISTS.
004603 04-15
CLINICAL AND PRECLINICAL EXPERIENCE WITH CHOLINE-CHLORIDE IN
HUNTINGTONS-DISEASE AND TARDIVE-DYSKINESIA: UNANSWERED
QUESTIONS.
004604 04-15
EPILEPTOGENIC PROPERTIES OF ENFLURANE AND THEIR CLINICAL
INTERPRETATION.
004609 04-15
ACUTE PHENCYCLIDINE (PCP) INTOXICATION: QUANTITATIVE URINE
LEVELS AND CLINICAL MANAGEMENT.
004665 04-15
SALIVA BENZODIAZEPINE LEVELS AND CLINICAL OUTCOME IN
DETOXIFYING ALCOHOLIC-PATIENTS.
004671 04-16
THERAPEUTIC MONITORING OF PLASMA CONCENTRATIONS OF TRICYCLIC-
ANTIDEPRESSANTS: PERSPECTIVE OF THE CLINICAL LABORATORY.
004681 04-16
THE USE OF CLINICAL KINETIC DATA IN TREATMENT WITH
ANTIDEPRESSANT-DRUGS.
004686 04-16

CLINICAL-ASPECTS
SOME CLINICAL-ASPECTS AND METABOLIC-ASPECTS OF PROPRANOLOL IN
CHRONIC SCHIZOPHRENIA.
001926 02-08
CLINICAL-ASPECTS OF ANXIETY AND ITS THERAPY.
002089 02-10
TREATMENT OF DYSKINETIC AND DYSTONIC-DISORDERS WITH CF-25-
397: CLINICAL-ASPECTS AND PHARMACOLOGICAL ASPECTS.
002121 02-11
CLINICAL-ASPECTS OF LITHIUM EFFLUX FROM ERYTHROCYTES.
002228 02-13

CLINICAL-ASPECTS ON PROLACTIN RESPONSE TO NEUROLEPTIC-DRUGS.
002590 02-17
THE NEUROPHYSIOLOGICAL AND CLINICAL-ASPECTS OF PAIN.
003457 03-14
CLINICAL-ASPECTS OF DYSKINESIA.
003461 03-15

CLINICAL-CORRELATION
CLINICAL-CORRELATION, BIOCHEMICAL-CORRELATION, AND
PSYCHOPHARMACOLOGICAL-CORRELATION IN PATIENTS WITH
DEPRESSIVE-SYMPTOMATOLOGY.
002018 02-09

CLINICAL-EFFECT
AMITRIPTYLINE PLASMA CONCENTRATION AND CLINICAL-EFFECT: A
WORLD-HEALTH-ORGANIZATION COLLABORATIVE-STUDY.
001976 02-09
SERUM CONCENTRATION AND CLINICAL-EFFECT OF ANTIEPILEPTICS.
003315 03-11
HYPERVENTILATION-SYNDROME AND BETA-RECEPTOR FUNCTION --
CLINICAL-EFFECT OF BETA BLOCKER UPON THE SYNDROME.
004459 04-11

CLINICAL-EFFECTIVENESS
TWENTY YEARS HALOPERIDOL: CLINICAL-EFFECTIVENESS AND
THEORETICAL IMPLICATIONS.
000938 01-17

CLINICAL-EFFECTS
A REEXAMINATION OF THE CLINICAL-EFFECTS OF IMIPRAMINE AND
AMITRIPTYLINE IN DEPRESSIVE-ILLNESS.
000579 01-09
A COMPARATIVE-STUDY ON THE CLINICAL-EFFECTS OF FLUNITRAZEPAM
AND LORAZEPAM.
000702 01-11
CLOMIPRAMINE: PLASMA LEVELS AND CLINICAL-EFFECTS.
002033 02-09
HUNTINGTONS-DISEASE: CLINICAL-EFFECTS OF A SHORT-TERM
TREATMENT WITH PIMOZIDE.
002091 02-11
CARBAMAZEPINE THERAPY IN TRIGEMINAL-NEURALGIA: CLINICAL-
EFFECTS IN RELATION TO PLASMA CONCENTRATION.
002181 02-11
A CONTROLLED DOUBLE-BLIND STUDY OF HALOPERIDOL VERSUS
THIORIDAZINE IN THE TREATMENT OF RESTLESS MENTALLY-
SUBNORMAL-PATIENTS: SERUM LEVELS AND CLINICAL-EFFECTS.
002185 02-11
PLASMA DELTA9 TETRAHYDROCANNABINOL CONCENTRATIONS AND
CLINICAL-EFFECTS AFTER ORAL AND INTRAVENOUS ADMINISTRATION
AND SMOKING.
002201 02-12
RELATIONSHIP BETWEEN BLOOD CONCENTRATIONS AND CLINICAL-
EFFECTS OF A NEW ANTIDEPRESSANT MAPROTILINE.
003271 03-09
THE BIOLOGICAL-EFFECTS AND CLINICAL-EFFECTS OF ORAL MAGNESIUM
AND ASSOCIATED MAGNESIUM VITAMIN-B6 ADMINISTRATION ON
CERTAIN DISORDERS OBSERVED IN INFANTILE AUTISM.
003291 03-11
A COMPARATIVE-STUDY ON THE CLINICAL-EFFECTS OF RECTAL
DIAZEPAM AND PENTOBARBITAL ON SMALL CHILDREN. RELATIONSHIP
BETWEEN PLASMA LEVEL AND EFFECT.
003330 03-11
CLINICAL-EFFECTS OF BETA ENDORPHIN INFUSIONS.
004360 04-09

CLINICAL-EFFICACY
THE CLINICAL-EFFICACY OF CLOZAPINE AS COMPARED TO LABORATORY
PARAMETERS.
001955 02-08
EVALUATION OF THE CLINICAL-EFFICACY OF SINGLE-DAILY-DOSES OF
ANTIDEPRESSANTS.
001985 02-09
PHENOTHIAZINE PLASMA AND RED-BLOOD-CELL CONCENTRATIONS, THEIR
RELATIONSHIP TO SIDE-EFFECTS AND CLINICAL-EFFICACY.
002386 02-15
CLINICAL-EFFICACY OF THE NEW ANTIDEPRESSANT BUPROPION
(WELLBUTRIN).
003227 03-09

CLINICAL-EVALUATION
CLINICAL-EVALUATION OF THE EFFECTS OF MINAPRINE.
001899 02-07
AN ATTEMPT AT A CLINICAL-EVALUATION OF MINAPRINE.
001900 02-07
AN ATTEMPT TO MAKE A CLINICAL-EVALUATION OF MINAPRINE,
(CONTINUATION OF THE STUDY).
001901 02-07
BROMOCRIPTINE AND PARKINSONS-DISEASE: A 16-HOUR CLINICAL-
EVALUATION.
002127 02-11
TO THE CLINICAL-EVALUATION OF ANXIOLYTICS (TOFISOPAM).
002494 02-16
GUIDELINES FOR THE CLINICAL-EVALUATION OF ANALGESIC-DRUGS.
002584 02-17

CLINICAL-EVALUATION OF THE PROPHYLACTIC EFFECTIVENESS OF
PROLONGED LITHIUM-CARBONATE THERAPY IN ENDOGENOUS
DEPRESSIVE-SYNDROMES.
004404 04-09
A CLINICAL-EVALUATION OF THE EFFECTS OF A NEW PSYCHOTROPIC-
AGENT, MEXAZOLAM (CS-386) ON PSYCHOSOMATIC-DISEASES AND
NEUROSIS: A COMPARATIVE-STUDY WITH OXAZOLAM, USING THE
DOUBLE-BLIND METHOD.
004491 04-11
CLINICAL-EVALUATION OF BROMPERIDOL VERSUS HALOPERIDOL IN
PSYCHOTIC-PATIENTS.
004562 04-14

CLINICAL-EXPERIENCE
NOMIFENSIN IN THE TREATMENT OF ENDOGENOUS DEPRESSIONS.
CLINICAL-EXPERIENCE AND EEG FINDINGS.
000613 01-09
CLINICAL-EXPERIENCE WITH NOMIFENSINE.
000642 01-09
CLINICAL-EXPERIENCE WITH LOW-DOSES OF HALOPERIDOL IN THE
TREATMENT OF NEUROSES.
000654 01-10
CLINICAL-EXPERIENCE WITH PIRACETAM THERAPY IN GERONTOLOGY.
000686 01-11
TREATMENT OF TARDIVE-DYSKINESIA WITH OXYPERTINE -- PRELIMINARY
CLINICAL-EXPERIENCE AND A BRIEF REVIEW OF THE LITERATURE.
000692 01-11
TRIMIPRAMINE: TWENTY YEARS WORLDWIDE CLINICAL-EXPERIENCE.
000985 01-17
CLINICAL-EXPERIENCE WITH SECOND-GENERATION ANTIDEPRESSANTS IN
ENDOGENOUS DEPRESSIONS.
001975 02-09
CLINICAL-EXPERIENCE WITH LITHIUM-CARBONICUM-RETARD IN
PSYCHIATRY.
002000 02-09
CLINICAL-EXPERIENCE WITH SUBSTITUTED BENZAMIDES IN FRENCH-
SPEAKING COUNTRIES.
002036 02-09
CLINICAL-EXPERIENCE WITH PSYCHIATRIC-TREATMENT OF THE ELDERLY
INVOLVING THE USE OF PIRACETAM.
002188 02-11
CLINICAL-EXPERIENCE WITH RETARD DIBENZEPINE (NOVERIL-240) IN
ENDOGENOUS DEPRESSIONS ACCOMPANIED BY SYMPTOMS OF DRUG-
RESISTANCE.
003245 03-09

CLINICAL-IMPLICATIONS
STRESS AND HYPERTENSION: CLINICAL-IMPLICATIONS.
002307 02-13
PSYCHOTROPIC-DRUGS AND THE HEART: CLINICAL-IMPLICATIONS.
002425 02-15
CLINICAL-IMPLICATIONS OF ENZYME INDUCTION AND ENZYME
INHIBITION.
003621 03-17

CLINICAL-PAPERS
DISCUSSION OF CLINICAL-PAPERS ON LITHIUM TRANSPORT IN AFFECTIVE-
DISORDERS.
001987 02-09

CLINICAL-PHARMACOLOGY
OBSERVATIONS ON CLINICAL-PHARMACOLOGY.
000970 01-17
CLINICAL-PHARMACOLOGY.
002247 02-13
BENZODIAZEPINES: CLINICAL-PHARMACOLOGY AND THERAPEUTIC USE.
002521 02-17
DRUGS AND THE ELDERLY: PERSPECTIVES IN GERIATRIC CLINICAL-
PHARMACOLOGY.
002534 02-17
CLINICAL-PHARMACOLOGY: DRUG DEVELOPMENT.
002547 02-17
CLINICAL-PHARMACOLOGY OF MIXED AGONIST ANTAGONIST DRUGS.
003329 03-11
CLINICAL-PHARMACOLOGY: ADVERSE DRUG INTERACTIONS.
003399 03-13
CLINICAL-PHARMACOLOGY: ELIMINATION OF DRUGS.
003400 03-13
CLINICAL-PHARMACOLOGY: DRUG ABSORPTION.
004740 04-17

CLINICAL-PICTURE
GERIATRIC ASPECTS OF PARKINSONISM (CLINICAL-PICTURE,
PATHOLOGICAL MECHANISMS, AND MULTIPLE TREATMENT).
003643 03-17
CHANGES IN THE CLINICAL-PICTURE AND THE COURSE OF PSYCHOSES
DURING MASSIVE PSYCHOPHARMACOTHERAPY AND THE
SIGNIFICANCE OF THESE CHANGES FOR IMPROVEMENTS IN
PSYCHIATRIC-TREATMENT.
004699 04-17

CLINICAL-PRACTICE
THE REAL AND IDEAL MANAGEMENT OF STIMULANT DRUG-TREATMENT
FOR HYPERACTIVE-CHILDREN: RECENT FINDINGS AND A REPORT FROM
CLINICAL-PRACTICE.
000715 01-11
NOOTROPIC-DRUGS IN CLINICAL-PRACTICE.
000811 01-14
RELIEF OF PAIN IN CLINICAL-PRACTICE.
003613 03-17
AMITRIPTYLINE AND NORTRIPTYLINE PLASMA LEVELS MONITORING.
PERSPECTIVE IN CLINICAL-PRACTICE.
004675 04-16
CLINICAL-RESPONSE
CLINICAL-RESPONSE AND SERUM NEUROLEPTIC LEVELS IN CHILDHOOD-
SCHIZOPHRENIA. (UNPUBLISHED PAPER).
000566 01-08
VILOXAZINE PLASMA CONCENTRATIONS AND CLINICAL-RESPONSE.
000614 01-09
PLASMA LEVELS OF IMIPRAMINE (IMI) AND DESMETHYLIMIPRAMINE
(DMI) AND CLINICAL-RESPONSE IN PREPUBERTAL MAJOR DEPRESSIVE-
DISORDER: A PRELIMINARY REPORT.
000619 01-09
IMIPRAMINE TREATMENT OF PREPUBERTAL MAJOR DEPRESSIVE-
DISORDERS: PLASMA LEVELS AND CLINICAL-RESPONSE --
PRELIMINARY REPORT.
000620 01-09
URINARY MHPG AND CLINICAL-RESPONSE TO AMITRIPTYLINE IN
DEPRESSED-PATIENTS.
000631 01-09
INTERACTION BETWEEN AMITRIPTYLINE AND PHENOTHIAZINE IN MAN:
METABOLITE NORTRIPTYLINE AND THE CORRELATION WITH CLINICAL-
RESPONSE.
000640 01-09
AMITRIPTYLINE, NORTRIPTYLINE PLASMA LEVELS AND CLINICAL-
RESPONSE IN WOMEN WITH AFFECTIVE-DISORDERS.
000757 01-13
INTERINDIVIDUAL VARIATION OF CLINICAL-RESPONSE TO HALOPERIDOL.
001230 02-03
RELATIONSHIPS BETWEEN CHLORPROMAZINE CONCENTRATIONS IN
PLASMA AND CEREBROSPINAL-FLUID AND CLINICAL-RESPONSE AND
BIOCHEMICAL-RESPONSE IN PSYCHOTIC-PATIENTS.
001905 02-08
CLINICAL-RESPONSE, PLASMA LEVELS AND PHARMACOKINETICS OF
DESIPRAMINE IN DEPRESSED-INPATIENTS.
002002 02-09
AGE-RELATED FACTORS AFFECTING ANTIDEPRESSANT-DRUG METABOLISM
AND CLINICAL-RESPONSE.
002035 02-09
HIGH-LEVELS OF AMITRIPTYLINE AND CLINICAL-RESPONSE.
002266 02-13
NEUROLEPTIC SERUM LEVELS MEASURED BY RADIORECEPTOR ASSAY
AND CLINICAL-RESPONSE IN SCHIZOPHRENIC-PATIENTS.
003199 03-08
PLASMA LEVELS OF CHLORPROMAZINE AND CLINICAL-RESPONSE.
003201 03-08
CLINICAL-RESPONSE AND BLOOD LEVELS IN THE TREATMENT OF
DEPRESSION WITH A NEW ANTIDEPRESSANT-DRUG, AMOXAPINE.
004356 04-09
LITHIUM IN THE PROPHYLAXIS OF RECURRENT AFFECTIVE-DISORDERS
(EFFECTIVENESS OF LOW PLASMA LEVELS AND PREDICTORS TO
CLINICAL-RESPONSE).
004365 04-09
PHARMACOKINETICS AND CLINICAL-RESPONSE TO TRICYCLIC-
ANTIDEPRESSANTS.
004370 04-09
THE RELATIONSHIPS BETWEEN CLINICAL-RESPONSE,
PSYCHOPHYSIOLOGICAL-VARIABLES AND PLASMA LEVELS OF
AMITRIPTYLINE AND DIAZEPAM IN NEUROTIC-OUTPATIENTS.
004423 04-10
SINGLE-CASE STUDY OF CLINICAL-RESPONSE TO HIGH-DOSE ERGOT
ALKALOID TREATMENT FOR DEMENTIA. PRELIMINARY REPORT.
004493 04-11
PROLACTIN AND NEUROLEPTIC-DRUGS: A BIOCHEMICAL INDEX OF
CLINICAL-RESPONSE?
004539 04-13
PLASMA NOMIFENSINE CONCENTRATION: CARDIOLOGICAL EFFECTS AND
CLINICAL-RESPONSE.
004639 04-15
CLINICAL-REVIEW
CLINICAL-REVIEW OF BETA-BLOCKERS IN ANXIETY.
004464 04-11
CLINICAL-SCALE
TREATMENT OF ASTHENO-DEPRESSIVE-DISORDERS WITH MINAPRINE
(CANTOR). MULTICENTER-STUDY OF 248 CASES EVALUATED WITH THE
FATIGUE STUDY GROUPS NO. 4 CLINICAL-SCALE.
001980 02-09
CLINICAL-STUDIES
HYDERGINE: A REVIEW OF 26 CLINICAL-STUDIES.
000704 01-11

MINAPRINE-CHLOROHYDRATE: SURVEY OF THE FIRST CLINICAL-STUDIES
OF THE FOURTH STAGE.
001902 02-07
CLINICAL-STUDIES AND BIOLOGICAL-STUDIES OF L TRYPTOPHAN IN
DEPRESSION.
001977 02-09
EFFECT OF SODIUM-VALPROATE AND BACLOFEN IN TARDIVE-DYSKINESIA:
CLINICAL-STUDIES AND NEUROENDOCRINE-STUDIES.
002441 02-15
REVIEW OF CLINICAL-STUDIES WITH ERGOTS IN GERONTOLOGY.
002624 02-17
MANAGEMENT OF SCHIZOPHRENIA: LONG-TERM CLINICAL-STUDIES WITH
SPECIAL REFERENCE TO THE COMBINATION OF PSYCHOTHERAPY AND
DEPOT NEUROLEPTICS.
003183 03-08
CLINICAL-STUDY
CONTRIBUTION TO THE CLINICAL-STUDY OF CEREBRAL DOPAMINERGIC
MECHANISMS: THE ACTION OF PIRIBEDIL IN PSYCHIATRY. FIRST
RESULTS.
000616 01-09
TRANSIENT-EFFECT OF L TRYPTOPHAN IN PROGRESSIVE MYOCLONUS
EPILEPSY WITHOUT LAFORA-BODIES: CLINICAL-STUDY AND
ELECTROPHYSIOLOGICAL-STUDY.
000694 01-11
CLINICAL-STUDY OF VILOXAZINE.
001972 02-09
VILOXAZINE IN THE TREATMENT OF DEPRESSIVE-NEUROSIS: A
CONTROLLED CLINICAL-STUDY WITH DOXEPIN AND PLACEBO.
002080 02-10
CLASSIFICATION OF ENDORPHINS/ENKEPHALINS IN BRAIN PHYSIOLOGY
AND PATHOLOGY (BASED ON EEG AND CLINICAL-STUDY OF
SYNTHETICALLY-MODIFIED METHIONINE-ENKEPHALIN).
002286 02-13
A CLINICAL-STUDY AND ENDOCRINE-STUDY OF MESTEROLONE IN
SECONDARY IMPOTENCE.
002315 02-14
A DOUBLE-BLIND CROSSED CLINICAL-STUDY WITH A NEW
PSYCHOPHARMACEUTICAL: TIADIPONE (QM-6008), DIAZEPAM, AND
A PLACEBO.
003153 03-07
CLINICAL-STUDY OF MAPROTILINE IN THE TREATMENT OF DEPRESSIVE-
STATES: COMPILATION OF 1520 OBSERVATIONS.
003206 03-09
ANXIOUS-DEPRESSIVE-SYNDROME. CLINICAL-STUDY OF A NEW
BENZODIAZEPINE, PRAZEPAM.
004354 04-09
VILOXAZINE IN THE TREATMENT OF DEPRESSIVE-NEUROSIS: A PLACEBO
AND STANDARD (IMIPRAMINE) CONTROLLED CLINICAL-STUDY.
004392 04-09
CLINICAL-TESTING
CLINICAL-TESTING OF MINAPRINE ON ELDERLY SUBJECTS WITH THE
ASTHENIC-DEPRESSIVE-SYNDROMES.
002123 02-11
CLINICAL-TESTS
RESULTS OF CLINICAL-TESTS OF VILOXAZINE (VIVALAN ICI): PART OF A
MULTICLINICAL-STUDY.
002006 02-09
CLINICAL-TRIAL
CLINICAL-TRIAL OF OXYPROTHEPIN-DECANOATE.
000542 01-07
CLINICAL-TRIAL OF VILOXAZINE IN DEPRESSIVE-CONDITIONS.
000589 01-09
INITIAL, CLINICAL-TRIAL OF A NEW, SPECIFIC 5 HT REUPTAKE INHIBITOR,
CITALOPRAM (LU-10-171).
000591 01-09
A CLINICAL-TRIAL OF ZIMELIDINE IN DEPRESSION.
001992 02-09
CLINICAL-TRIAL OF PYRAZIDOL IN ENDOGENOUS DEPRESSIVE-STATES.
002021 02-09
CLOMIPRAMINE TREATMENT OF OBSESSIVE-COMPULSIVE-DISORDER: I. A
CONTROLLED CLINICAL-TRIAL.
002086 02-10
CLINICAL-TRIAL WITH AMANTADINE AND HYDERGINE IN ELDERLY-
PATIENTS.
002093 02-11
FREE DESCRIPTION OF DRUG-EFFECTS AS A METHOD OF CLINICAL-TRIAL,
PRESENTED BY THE EXAMPLE OF PENTOBARBITONE, PROMAZINE AND
THEIR COMBINATION.
002561 02-17
NOVEL ANTIDEPRESSANTS: A CLINICAL-TRIAL OF MIANSERIN.
003240 03-09
AN OPEN CLINICAL-TRIAL OF MIANSERIN.
003241 03-09
DO PSYCHOTHERAPY AND PHARMACOTHERAPY FOR DEPRESSION
CONFLICT? EMPIRICAL EVIDENCE FROM A CLINICAL-TRIAL.
003256 03-09
CLINICAL-TRIAL OF HALAZEPAM AND CLORAZEPATE: CONSIDERATIONS
OF A SINGLE-BEDTIME-DOSE.
003277 03-10

CLINICAL-TRIAL OF PSYCHOTHERAPIES IS UNDER WAY.
004378 04-09
A COMPARATIVE CLINICAL-TRIAL WITH THE TRANQUILIZER TRAZODONE AND THE TRICYCLIC-ANTIDEPRESSANT CLOMIPRAMINE.
004380 04-09
DO PSYCHOTHERAPY AND PHARMACOTHERAPY FOR DEPRESSION CONFLICT? EMPIRICAL EVIDENCE FROM A CLINICAL-TRIAL. (UNPUBLISHED PAPER).
004401 04-09
CONTROLLED CLINICAL-TRIAL OF NOMIFENSINE IN THE TREATMENT OF DEPRESSION.
004417 04-09
CLOPIPAZAN (SKF-69634), A NEW NEUROLEPTIC ESSENTIALLY FREE OF EXTRAPYRAMIDAL LIABILITY: QUANTITATIVE PHARMACOEEG AND OPEN LABEL CLINICAL-TRIAL.
004620 04-15

CLINICAL-TRIALS
CLONIDINE FOR OPIATE DETOXIFICATION: OUTPATIENT CLINICAL-TRIALS.
000731 01-11
CLINICAL-TRIALS WITH RUBIDIUM-CHLORIDE IN DEPRESSED-PATIENTS.
001893 02-07
CLINICAL-TRIALS OF DEPAKENE (VALPROIC-ACID) COADMINISTERED WITH OTHER ANTICONVULSANTS IN EPILEPTIC-PATIENTS.
002367 02-14
DESIGN ASPECTS OF CLINICAL-TRIALS WITH ERGOT ALKALOIDS: A COMPARISON OF TWO GERIATRIC BEHAVIORAL-RATING-SCALES.
002512 02-16
PSYCHOTROPIC-DRUG REGISTRATION IN THE SCANDINAVIAN-COUNTRIES: THE ROLE OF CLINICAL-TRIALS.
002550 02-17
COORDINATING CLINICAL-TRIALS IN PSYCHOPHARMACOLOGY: PLANNING, DOCUMENTATION, AND ANALYSIS.
002574 02-17
PREDICTION AND PROGNOSTIC FACTORS IN CLINICAL-TRIALS OF PSYCHOTROPIC-DRUGS.
002615 02-17
CLINICAL-TRIALS WITH NEW BICYCLIC AND TETRACYCLIC COMPOUNDS: ZIMELIDINE AND MAPROTILINE.
003213,03-09
CLINICAL-TRIALS WITH CLOBAZAM IN GERIATRICS.
003279 03-10
QUALITY OF REPORTS OF CLINICAL-TRIALS SUBMITTED BY THE DRUG INDUSTRY TO THE FINNISH AND SWEDISH CONTROL AUTHORITIES.
003599 03-17

CLINICAL-VARIABLES
RELATIONSHIPS AMONG BIOCHEMICAL-VARIABLES, CLINICAL-VARIABLES, AND PHARMACOKINETIC-VARIABLES IN NEUROLEPTIC TREATED SCHIZOPHRENIC-PATIENTS.
001946 02-08

CLINICALLY
DRUG-THERAPY IN ENDOGENOUS DEPRESSION WITH POSSIBLE PRIMARY GABA DEFICIENCY CLINICALLY DETECTED: 38 NEW CASES.
000584 01-09
CLINICALLY SIGNIFICANT SIDE-EFFECTS OF LITHIUM TREATMENT.
000893 01-15

CLINICIANt
PATIENT CHARACTERISTICS AND CLINICIAN ATTITUDES INFLUENCING THE PRESCRIBING OF BENZODIAZEPINES.
003598 03-17

CLINICIANS
PREDICTABILITY OF PHENYTOIN SERUM LEVELS BY NOMOGRAMS AND CLINICIANS.
000909 01-16
THE CLINICIANS ROLE IN PSYCHOPHARMACOLOGICAL-RESEARCH.
002563 02-17

CLINICOEPIDEMIOLOGICAL
TARDIVE-DYSKINESIA: CLINICOEPIDEMIOLOGICAL REVISION AND CONTRIBUTION.
003466 03-15

CLINICS
THE USE OF MINAPRINE IN CHILD-PSYCHIATRY IN HOSPITALS AND OUTPATIENT CLINICS.
002169 02-11

CLOBAZAM
PHARMACOLOGICAL ACTIVITIES OF CLOBAZAM AND DIAZEPAM IN THE RAT: RELATION TO DRUG BRAIN LEVELS.
000036 01-03
PECIES-DIFFERENCES IN CLOBAZAM METABOLISM AND ANTILEPTAZOL S EFFECT.
001157 02-03
TREATMENT OF ANXIOUS-DEPRESSED OUTPATIENTS WITH A FIXED COMBINATION (NOMIFENSINE/CLOBAZAM) IN COMPARISON TO A MONOSUBSTANCE (DOXEPINE).
002028 02-09
ADVANTAGE OF MONOTHERAPY WITH CLOBAZAM IN THE TREATMENT AND POSTTREATMENT OF ALCOHOLIC WITHDRAWAL.
002140 02-11
CLINICAL-TRIALS WITH CLOBAZAM IN GERIATRICS.
· 003279 03-10
ANTIEPILEPTIC-EFFECT OF CLOBAZAM IN LENNOX-GASTAUT-SYNDROME.
004479 04-11

CLOCK
THE CLOCK AND THE BLUE GUITAR: STUDIES OF HUMAN GROWTH-HORMONE SECRETION IN SLEEP AND WAKING. (UNPUBLISHED PAPER).
002346 02-14

CLOFELIN
THE EFFECT OF CLOFELIN ON THE BIOELECTRIC-ACTIVITY OF THE BRAIN.
001449 02-03
THE EFFECT OF ANTIDEPRESSANTS ON THE HYPOTENSIVE-EFFECT OF CLOFELIN IN RATS.
003934 04-03

CLOFIBRATE
EFFECTS OF ALBUMIN, AMINO-ACIDS, AND CLOFIBRATE ON THE UPTAKE OF TRYPTOPHAN BY THE RAT-BRAIN.
002673 03-03

CLOMIPHENE-CITRATE
INFERENCES DERIVED FROM ELECTROENCEPHALOGRAPHIC RESPONSES TO ACUTE ADMINISTRATION OF CLOMIPHENE-CITRATE IN MALE ALBINO-RATS.
000155 01-03

CLOMIPRAMIN
INFUSION OF MAPROTILIN AND CLOMIPRAMIN AND THEIR COMBINATION IN THE TREATMENT OF DEPRESSION.
002056 02-09

CLOMIPRAMINE
EXPERIMENTAL EVALUATION OF ANTIDEPRESSANT ACTIVITY OF CLOMIPRAMINE, A NEW TRICYCLIC-ANTIDEPRESSANT DRUG.
001068 02-02
EFFECTS OF AMITRIPTYLINE AND CLOMIPRAMINE IN THE ISOLATED, PERFUSED RABBIT HEART.
001852 02-05
OUR FIRST EXPERIENCE WITH CLOMIPRAMINE.
002008 02-09
CLINICAL AND BIOCHEMICAL-DATA ON THE ACTION OF MAPROTILINE AND CLOMIPRAMINE IN DEPRESSIVE-STATES (PRELIMINARY OBSERVATION).
002032 02-09
CLOMIPRAMINE: PLASMA LEVELS AND CLINICAL-EFFECTS.
002033 02-09
CLOMIPRAMINE TREATMENT OF OBSESSIVE-COMPULSIVE-DISORDER: I. A CONTROLLED CLINICAL-TRIAL.
002086 02-10
CLOMIPRAMINE AND DOXEPIN IN DEPRESSIVE-NEUROSIS: PLASMA LEVELS AND THERAPEUTIC RESPONSE.
002258 02-13
CLOMIPRAMINE TREATMENT OF OBSESSIVE-COMPULSIVE-DISORDER: II. BIOCHEMICAL-ASPECTS.
002300 02-13
DIFFERENTIAL-EFFECTS OF CLOMIPRAMINE AND CLORGYLINE ON THE SENSITIVITY OF CORTICAL NEURONS TO SEROTONIN: EFFECT OF CHRONIC-TREATMENT.
002847 03-03
PHARMACOKINETICS OF CLOMIPRAMINE IN DEPRESSIVE-PATIENTS.
003216 03-09
THE TREATMENT OF DEPRESSION USING CLOMIPRAMINE IN GENERAL-MEDICAL-PRACTICE: 48 CASES TREATED ON AN OUTPATIENT BASIS.
003268 03-09
A COMPARATIVE CLINICAL-TRIAL WITH THE TRANQUILIZER TRAZODONE AND THE TRICYCLIC-ANTIDEPRESSANT CLOMIPRAMINE.
004380 04-09

CLONAZEPAM
BEHAVIORAL-ANALYSIS OF AMYGDALOID KINDLING IN BEAGLE-DOGS AND THE EFFECTS OF CLONAZEPAM, DIAZEPAM, PHENOBARBITAL, DIPHENYLHYDANTOIN, AND FLUNARIZINE ON SEIZURE MANIFESTATION.
000496 01-04
CLONAZEPAM AND DITHIADEN IN HYPERKINETIC-CHILDREN.
000729 01-11
THE EFFECT OF CLONAZEPAM ON ATROPINE SPIKES IN THE LIMBIC-SYSTEM.
001274 02-03
COMPARISON OF CLONAZEPAM AND DIAZEPAM IN EXPERIMENTAL-STUDIES.
001815 02-04
INFLUENCE OF PHENYTOIN AND PHENOBARBITAL ON THE DISPOSITION OF A SINGLE-ORAL-DOSE OF CLONAZEPAM.
002248 02-13
CLONAZEPAM AND PHENOBARBITAL IN TARDIVE-DYSKINESIA.
003294 03-11
TREATMENT OF EPILEPSIES WITH CLONAZEPAM (ANTELEPSIN).
004481 04-11
A COMPARATIVE-STUDY OF INTRAVENOUS LORAZEPAM AND CLONAZEPAM IN STATUS-EPILEPTICUS.
004487 04-11

CLONIDINE
INHIBITION OF NEURONAL UPTAKE REDUCES THE PRESYNAPTIC EFFECTS OF CLONIDINE BUT NOT OF ALPHA METHYLNORADRENALINE ON THE STIMULATION-EVOKED RELEASE OF 3H NORADRENALINE FROM RAT OCCIPITAL-CORTEX SLICES.
000227 01-03

Subject Index

INTERACTION OF ANTIDEPRESSANTS WITH CLONIDINE ON RAT-BRAIN TOTAL 3 METHOXY-4-HYDROXYPHENYLGLYCOL.
000300 01-03

THE LOCOMOTOR-EFFECT OF CLONIDINE AND ITS INTERACTION WITH ALPHA FLUPENTHIXOL OR HALOPERIDOL IN THE DEVELOPING RAT.
000445 01-04

DISPLACEMENT OF (3H)CLONIDINE BINDING BY CLONIDINE ANALOGUES IN MEMBRANES FROM RAT-CEREBRAL-CORTEX.
000536 01-06

ANTIMANIC-EFFECT OF CLONIDINE.
000598 01-09

IATROGENIC OPIATE ADDICTION: SUCCESSFUL DETOXIFICATION WITH CLONIDINE.
000666 01-11

CLONIDINE IN TOURETTE-SYNDROME.
000672 01-11

CLONIDINE FOR OPIATE DETOXIFICATION: OUTPATIENT CLINICAL-TRIALS.
000731 01-11

RAPID OPIATE DETOXIFICATION WITH CLONIDINE AND NALOXONE.
000820 01-14

CLONIDINE FOR OUTPATIENT OPIATE DETOXIFICATION.
000827 01-14

OPIATES AND SPECIFIC RECEPTOR BINDING OF (3H)CLONIDINE.
001256 02-03

POSSIBLE INVOLVEMENT OF CYCLIC-AMP AND FRONTAL-CORTEX IN AMITRIPTYLINE MEDIATED SUPPRESSION OF THE HYPOTENSIVE-EFFECT OF CLONIDINE.
001259 02-03

CLONIDINE ON THE PRESSOR RESPONSE TO RAISED INTRACRANIAL PRESSURE.
001316 02-03

INHIBITION OF NEUROSYMPATHETIC CEREBROARTERIAL CONSTRICTION BY CLONIDINE IN CATS.
001431 02-03

CLONIDINE AMELIORATES GILLES-DE-LA-TOURETTE-SYNDROME.
002106 02-11

CLONIDINE AND PSYCHOPHYSICAL PAIN.
002366 02-14

RELATIONSHIPS BETWEEN STRUCTURE AND ALPHA-ADRENERGIC-RECEPTOR AFFINITY OF CLONIDINE AND AND SOME RELATED CYCLIC-AMIDINES.
002698 03-03

THE TETRACYCLIC-ANTIDEPRESSANT MIANSERIN: EVALUATION OF ITS BLOCKADE OF PRESYNAPTIC ALPHA-ADRENOCEPTORS IN A SELF-STIMULATION MODEL USING CLONIDINE.
003016 03-04

PROSTAGLANDINS, CLONIDINE AND SEXUAL-RECEPTIVITY IN THE GUINEA-PIG.
003017 03-04

CLONIDINE ANALGESIA AND SUPPRESSION OF OPERANT RESPONDING: DISSOCIATION OF MECHANISM.
003046 03-04

EFFICACY OF CLONIDINE IN OPIATE WITHDRAWAL: A STUDY OF THIRTY PATIENTS.
003317 03-11

CLONIDINE IN TOURETTE-SYNDROME.
003420 03-13

DELIRIUM SECONDARY TO CLONIDINE THERAPY.
003494 03-15

THE HYPOTHERMIC-EFFECTS OF CLONIDINE AND OTHER IMIDAZOLIDINES IN RELATION TO THEIR ABILITY TO ENTER THE CENTRAL-NERVOUS-SYSTEM IN MICE.
003933 04-03

DIFFERENTIAL-EFFECTS OF ALPHA METHYLDOPAMINE, CLONIDINE AND HYDRALAZINE ON NOREPINEPHRINE AND EPINEPHRINE SYNTHESIZING ENZYMES IN THE BRAINSTEM NUCLEI OF SPONTANEOUSLY HYPERTENSIVE-RATS.
003947 04-03

CLONIDINE AND THE PRIMATE LOCUS-COERULEUS: EVIDENCE SUGGESTING ANXIOLYTIC AND ANTIWITHDRAWAL EFFECTS. (UNPUBLISHED PAPER).
003982 04-03

MULTIPLE ALPHA2-NORADRENERGIC-RECEPTOR SITES IN RAT-BRAIN: SELECTIVE REGULATION OF HIGH-AFFINITY (3H)CLONIDINE BINDING BY GUANINE-NUCLEOTIDES AND DIVALENT-CATIONS.
003992 04-03

PRELIMINARY TRIAL OF CLONIDINE TREATMENT IN TWO PATIENTS SUFFERING FROM CHRONIC SCHIZOPHRENIA.
004320 04-08

CLONIDINE-INDUCED
SEROTONERGIC MECHANISMS OF CLONIDINE-INDUCED HYPOTHERMIA IN RATS.
002806 03-03

EFFECTS OF ACUTELY AND CHRONICALLY ADMINISTERED ANTIDEPRESSANTS ON THE CLONIDINE-INDUCED DECREASE IN RAT-BRAIN 3 METHOXY-4-HYDROXYPHENYLETHYLENEGLYCOL-SULPHATE CONTENT.
002908 03-03

CLONIDINE-INDUCED HYPERPHAGIA IN MONKEYS: EVIDENCE FOR ALPHA2-NORADRENERGIC-RECEPTOR MEDIATION.
004215 04-04

S-

AN INVESTIGATION OF SOME SIDE-EFFECTS IN 47 PSYCHOTIC-PATIENTS DURING TREATMENT WITH CLOZAPINE AND DISCONTINUING OF THE TREATMENT.
002424 02-15

TIME-COURSE OF CHRONIC HALOPERIDOL AND CLOZAPINE UPON OPERANT RATE AND DURATION.
002989 03-04

TREATMENT OF THERAPEUTICALLY-RESISTANT PARANOID SCHIZOPHRENIC-PATIENTS WITH FLUPHENAZINE DEPOT COMBINED WITH OTHER PSYCHOTROPIC-DRUGS AND CLOZAPINE.
003172 03-08

THE EFFECT OF SMALL DOSES OF HALOPERIDOL AND CLOZAPINE ON BEHAVIORAL SHIFTS IN CATS, ARISING AFTER CESSATION OF ELECTRICAL-STIMULATION OF THE CAUDATE-NUCLEUS.
004067 04-04

SOME EFFECTS OF CLOZAPINE ON PUNISHED-RESPONDING BY MICE AND SQUIRREL-MONKEYS.
004224 04-04

A CASE OF ACUTE AGRANULOCYTOSIS DURING TREATMENT WITH CLOZAPINE.
004642 04-15

CLUES
FAMILY-TREE GIVES CLUES TO TREATING PSYCHOSES.
002363 02-14

CLUSTER-HEADACHES
LITHIUM-CARBONATE IN THE TREATMENT OF CLUSTER-HEADACHES.
000670 01-11

CNS
AN IN VIVO MODEL FOR INVESTIGATING ALPHA1-RECEPTORS AND ALPHA2-RECEPTORS IN THE CNS: STUDIES WITH MIANSERIN.
000053 01-03

EFFECTS OF RESERPINE, PROPRANOLOL, AND AMINOPHYLLINE ON SEIZURE ACTIVITY AND CNS CYCLIC-NUCLEOTIDES.
000115 01-03

3H ETHYLKETOCYCLAZOCINE BINDING: LACK OF EVIDENCE FOR A SEPARATE KAPPA-RECEPTOR IN RAT CNS.
000128 01-03

SEROTONIN-SENSITIVE ADENYLATE-CYCLASE AND (3H)SEROTONIN BINDING-SITES IN THE CNS OF THE RAT -- I. KINETIC PARAMETERS AND PHARMACOLOGICAL-PROPERTIES.
000213 01-03

SEROTONIN-SENSITIVE ADENYLATE-CYCLASE AND (3H)SEROTONIN BINDING-SITES IN THE CNS OF THE RAT -- II. RESPECTIVE REGIONAL AND SUBCELLULAR DISTRIBUTIONS AND ONTOGENETIC DEVELOPMENTS.
000214 01-03

STEROID-HORMONES AND CNS ACTIVITY.
000794 01-13

RAPID DEVELOPMENT OF HYPERSENSITIVITY AND HYPOSENSITIVITY TO APOMORPHINE AND HALOPERIDOL: ROLE OF NOREPINEPHRINE-RECEPTOR MECHANISMS IN CNS.
001178 02-03

EFFECT OF PYRITINOL AND PIRACETAM ON CHANGES IN FREE AMMONIA LEVEL IN CNS TISSUE AFTER PARADOXICAL SLEEP-DEPRIVATION IN RATS.
001199 02-03

EFFECT OF REPEATED ELECTROCONVULSIVE-SHOCKS (ECS) ON SUBTHRESHOLD DOSES OF SOME CNS STIMULANTS.
001361 02-03

EFFECTS OF GUANINE-NUCLEOTIDES ON CNS NEUROPEPTIDE-RECEPTORS. (UNPUBLISHED PAPER).
001383 02-03

NEW EXPERIMENTAL TECHNIQUES IN THE PHARMACOLOGICAL EVALUATION OF CNS ACTING DRUGS.
001479 02-03

SIMILARITIES AND DISSIMILARITIES BETWEEN DOPAMINE AND NEUROLEPTIC-RECEPTORS: FURTHER EVIDENCE FOR TYPE-1 AND TYPE-2 DOPAMINE-RECEPTORS IN THE CNS.
001480 02-03

MULTIPLE CNS RECEPTOR INTERACTIONS OF ERGOT ALKALOIDS: AFFINITY AND INTRINSIC ACTIVITY ANALYSIS IN IN VITRO BINDING SYSTEMS.
001516 02-03

EFFECTS OF THE BETA-ADRENOCEPTOR BLOCKING-AGENT SOTALOL ON CNS: SLEEP, EEG, AND PSYCHOPHYSIOLOGICAL PARAMETERS.
001570 02-04

HEMODYNAMIC FAILURE INDUCED BY NARCOTIC AND TOXIC DOSES OF 12 CNS DEPRESSANTS IN INTACT AND PITHED RATS.
001855 02-05

INFLUENCE OF CICLAZINDOL ON MONOAMINE UPTAKE AND CNS FUNCTION IN NORMAL SUBJECTS.
002268 02-13

DEVELOPMENT AND USE OF PHARMACOLOGICAL-PROBES OF THE CNS IN MAN: EVIDENCE OF CHOLINERGIC ABNORMALITY IN PRIMARY AFFECTIVE-ILLNESS.
002506 02-16

SOME WAYS TO INCREASE CHANCES TO DISCOVER THE CNS DRUGS OF THE FUTURE.
002528 02-17

PHARMACOLOGICAL EVIDENCE ON THE SPECIALIZATION OF CNS MECHANISMS RESPONSIBLE FOR MOTOR ACT INHIBITION BY AVERSIVE EVENTS.
002671 03-03

NEUROCHEMICAL-CONSEQUENCES FOLLOWING ADMINISTRATION OF CNS STIMULANTS TO THE NEONATAL RAT.
002926 03-03

DO BENZODIAZEPINES BIND AT ADENOSINE UPTAKE SITES IN CNS?
002933 03-03

IMMUNODETECTION OF ACH-RECEPTOR IN THE CNS. (UNPUBLISHED PAPER).
003670 04-01

ACYLCYANAMIDES, ACYLUREA, AND VARIOUS SUBSTITUTED ARYLALLOPHANATES; EFFECT ON THE CNS.
003689 04-02

CNS EFFECTS OF CHOLINE ADMINISTRATION: EVIDENCE FOR TEMPORAL DEPENDENCE.
003996 04-03

THE EFFECTS OF THYROTROPIN-RELEASING-HORMONE ON CYCLIC-AMP ACCUMULATION IN RABBIT CEREBROCORTICAL TISSUE IN THE PRESENCE AND ABSENCE OF CNS DEPRESSANTS.
004010 04-03

N,N DIISOPROPYLTRYPTAMINE (DIPT) AND 5 METHOXYDIISOPROPYLTRYPTAMINE (5 MEO-DIPT). TWO ORALLY ACTIVE TRYPTAMINE ANALOGS WITH CNS ACTIVITY.
004310 04-07

CNS EFFECTS OF ISF-2522, A NEW NOOTROPIC (A PHASE I SAFETY AND CNS EFFICACY STUDY WITH QUANTITATIVE PHARMACOEEG AND PHARMACOPSYCHOLOGY).
004519 04-13

PATHOPHYSIOLOGICAL AND MORPHOLOGICAL CHANGES IN THE CNS DURING LONG-TERM ADMINISTRATION OF HALOPERIDOL.
004633 04-15

CNS-ACTING
EFFECTS OF ANALGESICS AND CNS-ACTING DRUGS ON STRUGGLING FOLLOWING REPETITIVE STIMULATION OF THE TAIL, AND FLEXOR REFLEX TO A SINGLE STIMULATION OF THE SCIATIC-NERVE IN RATS.
004148 04-04

CNV
CNV VARIATIONS INDUCED BY THE ADMINISTRATION OF DIAZEPAM, HALOPERIDOL, PHENELZINE AND D-AMPHETAMINE.
002355 02-14

COADMINISTERED
CLINICAL-TRIALS OF DEPAKENE (VALPROIC-ACID) COADMINISTERED WITH OTHER ANTICONVULSANTS IN EPILEPTIC-PATIENTS.
002367 02-14

COBALT
STUDIES ON GAMMA AMINOBUTYRIC-ACID TRANSPORT IN COBALT EXPERIMENTAL EPILEPSY IN THE RAT.
003990 04-03

COCA-EXTRACTS
THE ANOREXIC AND ACTOMETRIC EFFECTS OF COCAINE AND TWO COCA-EXTRACTS.
000344 01-04

COCA-LEAF
A CONTRIBUTION TO OUR KNOWLEDGE OF COCA-LEAF CONTENT SUBSTANCES.
001022 02-01

COCAINE
THE ANOREXIC AND ACTOMETRIC EFFECTS OF COCAINE AND TWO COCA-EXTRACTS.
000344 01-04

INHIBITION OF BEHAVIORAL-EFFECTS OF COCAINE BY ACTINOMYCIN-D IN RATS.
000346 01-04

CONSEQUENT EVENTS AS DETERMINANTS OF DRUG-EFFECTS ON SCHEDULE-CONTROLLED BEHAVIOR: MODIFICATION OF EFFECTS OF COCAINE AND D-AMPHETAMINE FOLLOWING CHRONIC AMPHETAMINE ADMINISTRATION.
000350 01-04

EVIDENCE THAT A PREFERRED SUBSTRATE FOR MONOAMINE-OXIDASE-B MEDIATES STIMULUS PROPERTIES OF MAO-INHIBITORS: A POSSIBLE ROLE FOR BETA PHENYLETHYLAMINE IN THE COCAINE CUE.
000363 01-04

PROGRESSIVE-RATIO AND FIXED-RATIO SCHEDULES OF COCAINE MAINTAINED RESPONDING IN BABOONS.
000395 01-04

ROTATIONAL-BEHAVIOR INDUCED BY COCAINE ANALOGS IN RATS WITH UNILATERAL 6 HYDROXYDOPAMINE LESIONS OF THE SUBSTANTIA-NIGRA: DEPENDENCE UPON DOPAMINE UPTAKE INHIBITION.
000404 01-04

A COMPARISON OF THE EFFECTS OF D-AMPHETAMINE, COCAINE, IMIPRAMINE AND PENTOBARBITAL ON LOCAL AND OVERALL RATES OF RESPONDING MAINTAINED UNDER A FOUR-COMPONENT MULTIPLE FIXED-INTERVAL SCHEDULE.
000508 01-04

PROLONGED EFFECTS OF COCAINE ON HIPPOCAMPAL ACTIVITY.
001338 02-03

Subject Index

DIFFERENTIAL-EFFECTS OF COCAINE ON LIMBIC EXCITABILITY.
001339 02-03

MOTOR-ACTIVITY AND ROTATIONAL-BEHAVIOR AFTER ANALOGS OF COCAINE: CORRELATION WITH DOPAMINE UPTAKE BLOCKADE.
001650 02-04

INTRAVENOUS SELF-ADMINISTRATION OF COCAINE AND NORCOCAINE BY DOGS.
001760 02-04

THE PHARMACOLOGICAL RELEVANCE OF THE COCAINE BINDING-SITE IN MOUSE-BRAIN.
001772 02-04

THE EFFECTS OF LITHIUM ON CHOICE BETWEEN COCAINE AND FOOD IN THE RHESUS-MONKEY.
001825 02-04

BEHAVIOR MAINTAINED BY INTRAVENOUS INJECTION OF CODEINE, COCAINE, AND ETORPHINE IN THE RHESUS-MACAQUE AND THE PIGTAIL-MACAQUE.
001828 02-04

COCAINE EFFECTS IN SLEEP-DEPRIVED HUMANS.
002323 02-14

COCAINE AND AMPHETAMINE ANTAGONIZE THE DECREASE OF NORADRENERGIC NEUROTRANSMISSION ELICITED BY OXYMETAZOLINE BUT POTENTIATE THE INHIBITION BY ALPHA METHYLNOREPINEPHRINE IN THE PERFUSED CAT SPLEEN.
002801 03-03

DISCRIMINATIVE-STIMULUS PROPERTIES OF COCAINE, NORCOCAINE, AND N ALLYLNORCOCAINE.
002954 03-04

INTERACTIONS OF DIAZEPAM AND COCAINE IN THE MORPHINE TREATED RAT. (PH.D. DISSERTATION).
003115 03-04

AMITRIPTYLINE PROVIDES LONG-LASTING IMMUNIZATION AGAINST SUDDEN CARDIAC DEATH FROM COCAINE.
003122 03-05

ANTAGONISM OF INTRAVENOUS COCAINE LETHALITY IN NONHUMAN PRIMATES.
003127 03-05

THE EFFECTS OF ELECTRIC-SHOCK ON RESPONDING MAINTAINED BY COCAINE IN RHESUS-MONKEYS.
004071 04-04

COCAINE AND SEIZURE PROTECTION IN MICE OF VARYING BRAIN WEIGHTS.
004103 04-04

SECOND-ORDER SCHEDULES OF INTRAMUSCULAR COCAINE INJECTION IN THE SQUIRREL-MONKEY: COMPARISONS WITH FOOD PRESENTATION AND EFFECTS OF D-AMPHETAMINE AND PROMAZINE.
004152 04-04

REWARD AND DETECTION THRESHOLDS FOR BRAIN-STIMULATION: DISSOCIATIVE-EFFECTS OF COCAINE.
004160 04-04

DISCRIMINATIVE-STIMULUS PROPERTIES OF COCAINE RELATED TO AN ANXIOGENIC ACTION.
004219 04-04

BEHAVIORAL-EFFECTS OF SELF-ADMINISTERED COCAINE: RESPONDING MAINTAINED ALTERNATELY BY COCAINE AND ELECTRIC-SHOCK IN SQUIRREL-MONKEYS.
004225 04-04

EFFECT OF COCAINE AND LIDOCAINE ON THE EXPRESSION OF KINDLED SEIZURES IN THE RAT.
004233 04-04

COCAINE-INDUCED
DRUG ENVIRONMENT INTERACTION: CONTEXT DEPENDENCY OF COCAINE-INDUCED BEHAVIORAL-SENSITIZATION.
002866 03-03

THE EFFECT OF AMYGDALA KINDLING ON SPONTANEOUS AND COCAINE-INDUCED MOTOR-ACTIVITY AND LIDOCAINE SEIZURES.
003067 03-04

COCAINE-REINFORCED
CHLORPROMAZINE EFFECTS ON COCAINE-REINFORCED RESPONDING IN RHESUS-MONKEYS: RECIPROCAL MODIFICATION OF RATE ALTERING EFFECTS OF THE DRUGS.
004133 04-04

COCHLEAR
THE EFFECT OF FRUSEMIDE PIRETANIDE AND BUMETANIDE ON COCHLEAR SUCCINIC-DEHYDROGENASE.
003757 04-03

CODEINE
BEHAVIOR MAINTAINED BY INTRAVENOUS INJECTION OF CODEINE, COCAINE, AND ETORPHINE IN THE RHESUS-MACAQUE AND THE PIGTAIL-MACAQUE.
001828 02-04

COMPARATIVE-STUDIES OF THE PHARMACOLOGICAL-EFFECTS OF THE D-ISOMERS AND L-ISOMERS OF CODEINE.
004084 04-04

GLC/TLC ANALYSIS OF CODEINE AND MORPHINE IN URINE VIA DERIVATIZATION TECHNIQUES.
004687 04-16

SIMULTANEOUS DETERMINATION OF MORPHINE AND CODEINE IN BLOOD BY USE OF SELECT ION-MONITORING AND DEUTERATED INTERNAL STANDARDS.
004690 04-16

MANAGEMENT OF SCHIZOPHRENIA: LONG-TERM CLINICAL-STUDIES WITH SPECIAL REFERENCE TO THE COMBINATION OF PSYCHOTHERAPY AND DEPOT NEUROLEPTICS.

003183 03-08

THE BEHAVIORAL-EFFECTS OF D-AMPHETAMINE ALONE AND IN COMBINATION WITH ACUTE AND CHRONIC MORPHINE TREATMENTS IN RATS.

003915 04-03

INHIBITORY-ACTION OF THE COMBINATION OF AMINOPYRINE AND SECOBARBITAL ON EEG ACTIVATION, NEOCORTICAL RECRUITING AND AUGMENTING RESPONSES IN RABBITS.

004022 04-03

NEUROLEPTIC TRICYCLIC-ANTIDEPRESSANT COMBINATION: PHARMACOLOGICAL-ASPECTS AND THERAPEUTIC INTEREST.

004501 04-13

ELECTRORETINOGRAPHY (ERG) AS A TOOL OF INVESTIGATION IN HUMAN PSYCHOPHARMACOLOGY. ELECTRORETINOGRAPHIC-CHANGES INDUCED BY A COMBINATION OF CARBIDOPA AND LEVODOPA.

004507 04-13

NEUROLOGICAL TOLERANCE OF LITHIUM AND PSYCHOTROPIC-DRUGS IN COMBINATION: 265 CASES.

004594 04-15

COMBINATIONS

POTENTIATION OF LETHALITY IN MICE BY COMBINATIONS OF PENTAZOCINE AND TRIPELENNAMINE.

000529 01-05

EFFECTS OF CHLORDIAZEPOXIDE MORPHINE COMBINATIONS ON SPONTANEOUS LOCOMOTOR-ACTIVITY IN THREE INBRED STRAINS OF MICE.

001766 02-04

BEHAVIOURAL-EFFECTS OF ACETYLSALICYLIC-ACID, PARACETAMOL, CAFFEINE, GUAIPHENESIN AND THEIR COMBINATIONS.

001805 02-04

NMR SPECTRAL STUDY OF PROTON TRANSFER IN AMITRIPTYLINE-HYDROCHLORIDE CHLORDIAZEPOXIDE-HYDROCHLORIDE COMBINATIONS IN DIPOLAR APROTIC SOLVENTS.

003654 04-01

SIDE-EFFECTS AND UNDESIRABLE COMBINATIONS OF PSYCHOTROPIC-MEDICATIONS.

004663 04-15

COMBINED

EFFECTS OF L-DOPA AND L 5 HYDROXYTRYPTOPHAN ON LOCOMOTOR-ACTIVITY OF THE RAT AFTER SELECTIVE OR COMBINED DESTRUCTION OF CENTRAL CATECHOLAMINE AND SEROTONIN NEURONS.

000466 01-04

COMBINED MONOAMINE-OXIDASE-INHIBITOR TRICYCLIC-ANTIDEPRESSANT TREATMENT: A PILOT-STUDY.

000644 01-09

DEMONSTRATION OF SUBSTANCE-P IN AORTIC NERVE AFFERENT FIBERS BY COMBINED USE OF FLOURESCENT RETROGRADE NEURONAL LABELING AND IMMUNOCYTOCHEMISTRY. (UNPUBLISHED PAPER).

001024 02-01

HEXAMETHONIUM MODIFICATION OF CARDIOVASCULAR ADJUSTMENTS DURING COMBINED STATIC DYNAMIC ARM EXERCISE IN MONKEYS.

001242 02-03

EFFECT OF CHLORPROMAZINE ON CELL PROLIFERATION IN THE DEVELOPING RAT-BRAIN. A COMBINED BIOCHEMICAL-STUDY AND MORPHOLOGICAL-STUDY.

001407 02-03

A COMBINED BEHAVIORAL-PHARMACOTHERAPY APPROACH TO OBSESSIVE-COMPULSIVE-DISORDERS.

002082 02-10

MEDICAL PSYCHOLOGICAL AND COMBINED THERAPY IN THE CASES OF ENURESIS: A COMPARATIVE-STUDY.

002175 02-11

THE EFFECTS OF COMBINED SEDATIVE AND ANXIOLYTIC-PREPARATIONS ON SUBJECTIVE ASPECTS OF SLEEP AND OBJECTIVE MEASURE OF AROUSAL AND PERFORMANCE THE MORNING FOLLOWING NOCTURNAL MEDICATION: II. REPEATED DOSES.

002331 02-14

A TOPOGRAPHIC LOCALIZATION OF ENKEPHALIN ON THE DOPAMINE NEURONS OF THE RAT SUBSTANTIA-NIGRA AND VENTRAL TEGMENTAL AREA DEMONSTRATED BY COMBINED HISTOFLUORESCENCE IMMUNOCYTOCHEMISTRY.

002639 03-01

COMBINED EFFECTS OF ALCOHOL AND LITHIUM ON BODY COMPOSITION IN THE RAT MODEL.

002928 03-03

SYNERGISM OF COMBINED LITHIUM NEUROLEPTIC THERAPY: A DOUBLE-BLIND, PLACEBO-CONTROLLED CASE-STUDY.

003165 03-08

LITHIUM COMBINED WITH NEUROLEPTICS IN CHRONIC SCHIZOPHRENIC-PATIENTS AND SCHIZOAFFECTIVE-PATIENTS.

003168 03-08

TREATMENT OF THERAPEUTICALLY-RESISTANT PARANOID SCHIZOPHRENIC-PATIENTS WITH FLUPHENAZINE DEPOT COMBINED WITH OTHER PSYCHOTROPIC-DRUGS AND CLOZAPINE.

003172 03-08

Subject Index

COMBINED ADMINISTRATION OF NIALAMIDE AND VILOXAZINE TO DEPRESSIVE-PATIENTS.
003232 03-09

SENILE-DEMENTIA: COMBINED PHARMACOLOGIC-TREATMENT AND PSYCHOLOGIC-TREATMENT.
003393 03-11

PHARMACOPSYCHOLOGICAL INVESTIGATIONS CONCERNING THE COMBINED EFFECTS OF DIPOTASSIUM-CLORAZEPATE AND ETHANOL.
003456 03-14

GAS-CHROMATOGRAPHY, MASS-SPECTROMETRY, AND COMBINED CHROMATOGRAPHY MASS-SPECTROMETRY.
004290 04-06

NEUROTROPIC-DRUGS AS COMEDICATION TO PSYCHOTROPICS: COMBINED ADMINISTRATION OF A NEUROTROPIC-DRUG AND A TETRACYCLIC-ANTIDEPRESSANT.
004396 04-09

A MODIFIED VERSION OF THE SIMULTANEOUS DISCONTINUATION OF PSYCHOTROPIC-DRUGS (COMBINED WITH THE ADMINISTRATION OF DIURETICS) AS A METHOD OF HALTING PROLONGED ATTACKS OF SCHIZOPHRENIA.
004584 04-14

COMBINING
THE BENEFITS AND RISKS OF COMBINING AN MAO-INHIBITOR AND A TRICYCLIC-ANTIDEPRESSANT.
003273 03-09

COMEDICATION
NEUROTROPIC-DRUGS AS COMEDICATION TO PSYCHOTROPICS: COMBINED ADMINISTRATION OF A NEUROTROPIC-DRUG AND A TETRACYCLIC-ANTIDEPRESSANT.
004396 04-09

COMMERCIALLY-AVAILABLE
FALSE LABELLING OF COMMERCIALLY-AVAILABLE 3H CATECHOLAMINES?
000535 01-06

COMMUNAL
COMMUNAL MEDICATION.
002595 02-17

COMMUNICATION
DISCUSSION: COMMUNICATION AND POLYPHARMACY: DRUGS AND THE ELDERLY.
000957 01-17

BRIEF COMMUNICATION: BEHAVIORAL RECOVERY AFTER TOLUENE EXPOSURE IN RATS.
002969 03-04

COMMUNITY-BASED
ANTIPSYCHOTIC-DRUGS IN COMMUNITY-BASED SHELTERED-CARE-HOMES.
002171 02-11

COMP-EEG
EEG, COMP-EEG, REO-EG AND PHARMACOLOGICAL-CORRELATES OF GERIATRICS.
002162 02-11

COMPARABILITY
CLINICAL COMPARABILITY OF PSYCHOTROPIC-DRUGS.
002526 02-17

COMPARATIVE
A COMPARATIVE EVALUATION OF DOTHIEPIN (PROTHIEDEN) AND IMIPRAMINE.
000583 01-09

COMPARATIVE ENZYME-INDUCING EFFECTS OF CHLORPROMAZINE AND FLUPHENAZINE THERAPIES IN PSYCHOTIC-PATIENTS.
000682 01-11

THE TREATMENT OF PARKINSONS-DISEASE USING A COMBINATION OF L-DOPA AND DECARBOXYLASE INHIBITORS (CARBIDOPA, BENSERASIDE). A CLINICAL AND BIOCHEMICAL COMPARATIVE INVESTIGATION.
000712 01-11

THE COMPARATIVE DISPOSITION OF NOMIFENSINE (MERITAL) IN THE PREGNANT AND NONPREGNANT RAT.
000853 01-15

COMPARATIVE ANXIOLYTIC AND HYPNOTIC-EFFECTS OF 3 BENZODIAZEPINES ON BABOONS.
001581 02-04

COMPARATIVE EXPERIMENT OF THE ANTIDEPRESSANT EFFECTS OF AMINEPTINE AND CHLORIMIPRAMINE.
002029 02-09

COMPARATIVE CROSS-STUDY ON THE EFFECTS OF AMINEPTINE AND MAPROTILINE.
002065 02-10

SELF-MEDICATION, ABANDONMENT, MANIPULATION, AND DEPENDENCE IN DRUG-THERAPY IN PSYCHOSOMATIC-ILLNESS: COMPARATIVE POLYCENTRIC RESEARCH ON VARIOUS PSYCHOTROPIC-DRUGS.
002189 02-11

COMPARATIVE PROTEIN BINDING OF DIAZEPAM AND DESMETHYLDIAZEPAM.
002206 02-13

A COMPARATIVE REVIEW OF THE PHARMACOLOGICAL AND TOXICOLOGICAL PROPERTIES OF DISULFIRAM AND CALCIUM-CARBIMIDE.
003522 03-15

COMPARATIVE ANALGESIC, BEHAVIORAL, AND DEPENDENCE PROPERTIES OF MORPHINE AND O

S-1

A COMPARATIVE-STUDY OF BROMOCRIPTINE AND LEVODOPA IN PARKINSONS-DISEASE.
002117 02-11

MEDICAL PSYCHOLOGICAL AND COMBINED THERAPY IN THE CASES OF ENURESIS: A COMPARATIVE-STUDY.
002175 02-11

COMPARATIVE-STUDY OF VARIATIONS IN PROLACTIN LEVELS DURING TREATMENT WITH ANTIPSYCHOTIC-DRUGS.
002412 02-15

COMPARATIVE-STUDY ON THE EFFECT OF MORPHINE AND THE OPIOID-LIKE PEPTIDES IN THE VAS-DEFERENS OF RODENTS: STRAIN AND SPECIES-DIFFERENCES, EVIDENCE FOR MULTIPLE OPIATE-RECEPTORS.
002757 03-03

A COMPARATIVE-STUDY OF THE PHARMACOLOGY OF INHIBITORS OF GABA METABOLISM.
003036 03-04

A COMPARATIVE-STUDY ON THE CLINICAL-EFFECTS OF RECTAL DIAZEPAM AND PENTOBARBITAL ON SMALL CHILDREN. RELATIONSHIP BETWEEN PLASMA LEVEL AND EFFECT.
003330 03-11

CARDIOVASCULAR-EFFECTS OF MIANSERIN -- A COMPARATIVE-STUDY WITH AMITRIPTYLINE AND A PLACEBO IN HEALTHY SUBJECTS.
003503 03-15

A COMPARATIVE-STUDY OF THE PHARMACOLOGICAL-PROPERTIES OF THE POSITIVE POTENTIAL RECORDED FROM THE SUPERIOR CERVICAL GANGLIA OF SEVERAL SPECIES.
003779 04-03

A COMPARATIVE-STUDY OF INTRAVENOUS LORAZEPAM AND CLONAZEPAM IN STATUS-EPILEPTICUS.
004487 04-11

A CLINICAL-EVALUATION OF THE EFFECTS OF A NEW PSYCHOTROPIC-AGENT, MEXAZOLAM (CS-386) ON PSYCHOSOMATIC-DISEASES AND NEUROSIS: A COMPARATIVE-STUDY WITH OXAZOLAM, USING THE DOUBLE-BLIND METHOD.
004491 04-11

COMPARATIVE-TRIAL

A DOUBLE-BLIND GROUP COMPARATIVE-TRIAL OF MIANSERIN AND DIAZEPAM IN DEPRESSED-OUTPATIENTS.
000592 01-09

SINGLE-DOSE VERSUS MULTIPLE-DOSE COMPARATIVE-TRIAL OF DESIPRAMINE-HYDROCHLORIDE: A DOUBLE-PLACEBO METHOD.
002059 02-10

COMPARED

ANTIDEPRESSANT PROPERTIES OF 2 4 ETHYL-2-PIPERAZINYL-4-PHENYLQUINOLINE-HCL (AD-1308) AND ITS MECHANISM-OF-ACTION AS COMPARED WITH TRICYCLIC-ANTIDEPRESSANTS.
000152 01-03

ANTIDEPRESSANT TREATMENT BY INTRAVENOUS ADMINISTRATION COMPARED TO PERORAL ADMINISTRATION: A DOUBLE-BLIND STUDY OF QUINUPRAMINE.
000552 01-08

ANXIOLYTIC EFFICACY OF ALPRAZOLAM COMPARED TO DIAZEPAM AND PLACEBO.
000648 01-10

COMPARED PROPERTIES OF CENTRAL AND PERIPHERAL BINDING-SITES FOR PHENCYCLIDINE.
001521 02-03

MALE RAT SEXUAL-BEHAVIOR COMPARED AFTER 6 OHDA AND ELECTROLYTIC LESIONS IN THE DORSAL NA BUNDLE REGION OF THE MIDBRAIN.
001593 02-04

OXYPROTHEPINE-DECANOATE COMPARED WITH FLUPHENAZINE-DECANOATE IN THE TREATMENT OF SCHIZOPHRENIA: PRELIMINARY-COMMUNICATION.
001934 02-08

THE CLINICAL-EFFICACY OF CLOZAPINE AS COMPARED TO LABORATORY PARAMETERS.
001955 02-08

KETAZOLAM COMPARED TO DIAZEPAM AND PLACEBO IN THE TREATMENT OF ANXIETY.
002074 02-10

LEVODOPA COMPARED WITH BROMOCRIPTINE IN THE TREATMENT OF PARKINSONS-DISEASE.
002406 02-15

THE ACTION OF BENZODIAZEPINES ON THE LIMBIC-SYSTEM COMPARED TO OTHER TRANQUILIZERS.
002731 03-03

THE ANTIDEPRESSANT ACTION OF SULPHO-ADENOSYL-L-METHIONINE (SAME) COMPARED WITH THAT OF CHLORIMIPRAMINE: HYPOTHETICAL INTERPRETATIONS OF THE MECHANISM-OF-ACTION.
003150 03-07

COMPARING

EFFICACY AND PATTERN VALENCE OF PSYCHOACTIVE-DRUGS: A NEW METHOD OF COMPARING DRUGS APPLIED TO IDENTICAL PATIENTS IN RANDOMIZED-ORDER.
000699 01-11

A DOUBLE-BLIND MULTICENTRE-TRIAL COMPARING THE EFFICACY AND SIDE-EFFECTS OF MIANSERIN AND CHLORIMIPRAMINE IN DEPRESSED-INPATIENTS AND DEPRESSED-OUTPATIENTS.
004395 04-09

COMPARISON

COMPARISON OF MIANSERIN WITH DESIPRAMINE, MAPROTILINE AND PHENTOLAMINE ON CARDIAC PRESYNAPTIC AND VASCULAR POSTSYNAPTIC ALPHA-ADRENOCEPTORS AND NORADRENALINE REUPTAKE IN PITHED NORMOTENSIVE-RATS.
000044 01-03

A COMPARISON OF HUMAN TACTILE STIMULUS VELOCITY DISCRIMINATION WITH THE ABILITY OF S-I CORTICAL NEURONS IN AWAKE RHESUS-MONKEYS TO SIGNAL THE SAME VELOCITY DIFFERENCES BEFORE AND AFTER NONANESTHETIC DOSES OF PENTOBARBITAL.
000055 01-03

COMPARISON OF THE EFFECTS OF THE ISOMERS OF AMPHETAMINE, METHYLPHENIDATE AND DEOXYPIPRADROL ON THE UPTAKE OF L (3H)NOREPINEPHRINE AND (3H)DOPAMINE BY SYNAPTIC VESICLES FROM RAT-WHOLE-BRAIN, STRIATUM AND HYPOTHALAMUS.
000091 01-03

ANTAGONISM OF INTRASTRIATAL AND INTRAVENOUS KAINIC-ACID BY 1 NUCIFERINE: COMPARISON WITH VARIOUS ANTICONVULSANTS AND GABAMIMETICS.
000188 01-03

COMPARISON OF BETA-ADRENERGIC-RECEPTOR SUBTYPES IN MAMMALIAN TISSUES.
000207 01-03

COMPARISON OF BLOOD AND BILE LEVELS OF OXYPROTHEPIN AND DOCLOXYTHEPIN IN RATS.
000242 01-03

(3H)QUINUCLIDINYL-BENZILATE BINDING TO MUSCARINIC-RECEPTORS AND (3H)WB-4101 BINDING TO ALPHA-ADRENERGIC-RECEPTORS IN RABBIT IRIS: COMPARISON OF RESULTS IN SLICES AND MICROSOMAL FRACTIONS.
000299 01-03

A COMPARISON OF RATES OF DEPLETION AND RECOVERY OF NORADRENALINE STORES OF PERIPHERAL AND CENTRAL NORADRENERGIC NEURONES AFTER RESERPINE ADMINISTRATION: IMPORTANCE OF NEURONAL ACTIVITY.
000314 01-03

CGP-6085-A, A NEW, SPECIFIC, INHIBITOR OF SEROTONIN UPTAKE: NEUROCHEMICAL CHARACTERIZATION AND COMPARISON WITH OTHER SEROTONIN UPTAKE BLOCKERS.
000316 01-03

GABAERGIC ACTIONS OF THIP IN VIVO AND IN VITRO: A COMPARISON WITH MUSCIMOL AND GABA.
000319 01-03

ANTINOCICEPTIVE COMPARISON OF QUIPAZINE AND MORPHINE.
000435 01-04

A COMPARISON OF THE EFFECTS OF D-AMPHETAMINE, COCAINE, IMIPRAMINE AND PENTOBARBITAL ON LOCAL AND OVERALL RATES OF RESPONDING MAINTAINED UNDER A FOUR-COMPONENT MULTIPLE FIXED-INTERVAL SCHEDULE.
000508 01-04

A COMPARISON OF THE CARDIOVASCULAR EFFECTS OF HALOPERIDOL, THIORIDAZINE AND CHLORPROMAZINE-HCL.
000512 01-05

STUDY OF VIGILANCE AFTER INGESTION OF ZOPICLONE IN COMPARISON WITH NITRAZEPAM AND PLACEBO. METHODOLOGY OF THE STUDY: SELF-EVALUATION QUESTIONNAIRE AND PSYCHOMETRIC-TESTS.
000543 01-07

COMPUTERIZED EEG IN THE COMPARISON OF OXYPROTHEPIN AND FLUPHENAZINE-DECANOATE.
000567 01-08

CLINICAL COMPARISON OF OXYPROTHEPIN AND CLOTEPINE IN SCHIZOPHRENIC-PATIENTS (CONTROLLED-STUDY).
000568 01-08

DOUBLE-BLIND COMPARISON OF HALOPERIDOL AND THIOTHIXENE WITH AFTERCARE TREATMENT EVALUATION IN PSYCHIATRIC-OUTPATIENTS WITH SCHIZOPHRENIA.
000574 01-08

COMPARISON OF SINGLE-DOSE PHARMACOKINETICS OF IMIPRAMINE AND MAPROTILINE IN THE ELDERLY.
000596 01-09

SINTAMIL IN THE TREATMENT OF DEPRESSION: A COMPARISON OF SINGLE VS. DIVIDED DOSE ADMINISTRATION.
000629 01-09

DOUBLE-BLIND COMPARISON OF KETAZOLAM, DIAZEPAM AND PLACEBO IN ONCE-A-DAY VS T.I.D. DOSING.
000660 01-11

COMPARISON OF SUSTAINED-RELEASE AND STANDARD METHYLPHENIDATE IN THE TREATMENT OF MINIMAL-BRAIN-DYSFUNCTION.
000732 01-11

COMPARISON OF CYSTEINE-SULPHINIC-ACID-DECARBOXYLASE (CSD) ISOENZYMES AND GLUTAMIC-ACID-DECARBOXYLASE (GAD) IN RAT: IS BRAIN CSD-I IDENTICAL WITH LIVER CSD AND BRAIN CSD-II WITH GAD? (UNPUBLISHED PAPER).
001048 02-01

COMPARISON OF HIGHLY-ACTIVE AND ACTIVITY DEPLETED HEPARIN BY CIRCULAR DICHROISM SPECTROSCOPY. (UNPUBLISHED PAPER).
001057 02-01

GAMMA AMINOBUTYRIC-ACID AGONISTS: AN IN VITRO COMPARISON BETWEEN DEPRESSION OF SPINAL SYNAPTIC ACTIVITY AND DEPOLARIZATION OF SPINAL ROOT FIBRES IN THE RAT.
001104 02-03

ON THE MECHANISM OF A DIFFERENT DRUG DISTRIBUTION DURING CONVULSIVE-SEIZURE IN COMPARISON TO ANESTHESIA.
001151 02-03

A COMPARISON OF STRIATAL AND MESOLIMBIC DOPAMINE FUNCTION IN THE RAT DURING 6-MONTH TRIFLUOPERAZINE ADMINISTRATION.
001174 02-03

A COMPARISON OF THE EFFECTS OF METHYLPHENIDATE AND AMPHETAMINE ON THE SIMULTANEOUS RELEASE OF RADIOLABELLED DOPAMINE AND P OR M TYRAMINE FROM RAT STRIATAL SLICES.
001207 02-03

COMPARISON OF THE EFFECTS OF CENTRAL ADMINISTRATION OF SERINE AND GLYCINE ON BODY-TEMPERATURE OF THE RABBIT.
001248 02-03

MORPHINE AND ELECTROACUPUNCTURE: COMPARISON OF THE EFFECTS ON THE CORTICAL EVOKED-RESPONSES AFTER TOOTH-PULP STIMULATION IN RATS.
001294 02-03

THE NEW ANTIDEPRESSANT PIRLINDOLE: A COMPARISON WITH IMIPRAMINE AND TRANYLCYPROMINE.
001360 02-03

COMPARISON OF BIOLOGICAL-ACTIVITY AND BEHAVIORAL-ACTIVITY OF ALPHA AND GAMMA MELANOCYTE-STIMULATING-HORMONES. (UNPUBLISHED PAPER).
001398 02-03

DOPAMINE-AUTORECEPTORS: PHARMACOLOGY, FUNCTION AND COMPARISON WITH POSTSYNAPTIC DOPAMINE-RECEPTORS.
001453 02-03

DOSE-DEPENDENT PHARMACOKINETICS OF ALPHA METHYL-P-TYROSINE (ALPHA MT) AND COMPARISON OF CATECHOLAMINE TURNOVER-RATES AFTER TWO DOSES OF ALPHA MT.
001532 02-03

ANALGESIC ACTION OF INTRATHECAL AND INTRACEREBRAL BETA ENDORPHIN IN RATS: COMPARISON WITH MORPHINE.
001691 02-04

A COMPARISON BETWEEN THE EFFECTS OF MORPHINE ON THE REWARDING AND AVERSIVE-PROPERTIES OF LATERAL HYPOTHALAMIC AND CENTRAL GRAY STIMULATION.
001771 02-04

COMPARISON OF CLONAZEPAM AND DIAZEPAM IN EXPERIMENTAL-STUDIES.
001815 02-04

COMPARISON OF OPIATE AGONISTS AND THEIR N ALLYL DERIVATIVES IN THE PRODUCTION OF PHYSICAL-DEPENDENCE IN THE RAT.
001841 02-05

COMPARISON OF THE CLASSICAL AND RETARDED FORM OF LITHIUM-CARBONATE.
001888 02-07

A COMPARISON OF HALOPERIDOL, LITHIUM-CARBONATE AND THEIR COMBINATION IN THE TREATMENT OF MANIA.
001990 02-09

COMPARISON OF THE EFFECTS OF LOFEPRAMINE AND MIANSERIN IN DEPRESSED-PATIENTS IN A DOUBLE-BLIND TRIAL.
001996 02-09

THE USE OF VILOXAZINE IN HOSPITALIZED DEPRESSED-PATIENTS: RANDOM COMPARISON WITH IMIPRAMINE IN A DOUBLE-BLIND TRIAL.
001998 02-09

TREATMENT OF ANXIOUS-DEPRESSED OUTPATIENTS WITH A FIXED COMBINATION (NOMIFENSINE/CLOBAZAM) IN COMPARISON TO A MONOSUBSTANCE (DOXEPINE).
002028 02-09

DOUBLE-BLIND COMPARISON OF KETAZOLAM AND PLACEBO USING ONCE-A-DAY DOSING.
002067 02-10

NOMIFENSINE IN THE TREATMENT OF OBSESSIVE-COMPULSIVE-NEUROSIS. THERAPEUTIC-EFFICACY AND TOLERABILITY IN COMPARISON TO IMIPRAMINE.
002078 02-10

A DOUBLE-BLIND PARALLEL GROUP COMPARISON OF SINGLE-BEDTIME-DOSES OF HALAZEPAM AND PLACEBO.
002079 02-10

COMPARISON OF NITRAZEPAM 5 MG WITH TRIAZOLAM 0.5 MG IN YOUNG PSYCHIATRIC INSOMNIAC-INPATIENTS.
002096 02-11

COMPARISON OF SCH-12679 AND THIORIDAZINE IN AGGRESSIVE MENTAL-RETARDATES.
002119 02-11

A COMPARISON OF BIPERIDEN-HYDROCHLORIDE (AKINETON) AND BENZHEXOL (ARTANE) IN THE TREATMENT OF DRUG-INDUCED PARKINSONISM.
002146 02-11

THE PERIPHERAL ANTICHOLINERGIC-ACTIVITY OF TRICYCLIC-ANTIDEPRESSANTS: COMPARISON OF AMITRIPTYLINE AND DESIPRAMINE IN HUMAN VOLUNTEERS.
002298 02-13

EFFECTS OF HIPPOCAMPAL BRAIN-DAMAGE ON AUDITORY AND VISUAL RECENT MEMORY: COMPARISON WITH MARIJUANA INTOXICATED SUBJECTS.
002320 02-14

AN EVALUATION OF MAPROTILINE INTRAVENOUS KINETICS AND COMPARISON OF TWO ORAL DOSES.
002497 02-16

DESIGN ASPECTS OF CLINICAL-TRIALS WITH ERGOT ALKALOIDS: A COMPARISON OF TWO GERIATRIC BEHAVIORAL-RATING-SCALES.
002512 02-16

COMPARISON OF DRUG PRESCRIPTIONS FOR PSYCHIATRIC-PATIENTS AFTER HOSPITAL DISCHARGE IN THE DISTRICTS TEPLICE AND UHERSKE-HRADISTE.
002518 02-17

UTILIZATION OF PSYCHOTROPIC-DRUGS. AN INTERNATIONAL COMPARISON.
002616 02-16

A COMPARISON OF THE CONTRACTILE RESPONSES OF THE RABBIT BASILAR AND PULMONARY-ARTERIES TO SYMPATHOMIMETIC AGONISTS: CHARACTERISTICS.
002670 03-03

A COMPARISON OF THE EFFECTS OF PENTOBARBITAL AND DIPHENYLHYDANTOIN ON THE GABA SENSITIVITY AND EXCITABILITY OF ADULT SENSORY GANGLION CELLS.
002692 03-03

A COMPARISON OF THE NEUROCHEMICAL-EFFECTS OF BUPRENORPHINE WITH THOSE OF MORPHINE AND HALOPERIDOL IN RATS.
002701 03-03

PULMONARY METABOLISM OF IMIPRAMINE IN THE RAT AND RABBIT: COMPARISON WITH HEPATIC METABOLISM.
002845 03-03

EFFECTS OF PROLONGED TREATMENT WITH LITHIUM AND TRICYCLIC-ANTIDEPRESSANTS ON DISCHARGE FREQUENCY, NOREPINEPHRINE RESPONSES AND BETA-RECEPTOR BINDING IN RAT-CEREBELLUM: ELECTROPHYSIOLOGICAL AND BIOCHEMICAL COMPARISON.
002884 03-03

A COMPARISON OF HUMAN MUSCARINIC CHOLINERGIC-RECEPTOR RESPONSE TO A NUMBER OF PSYCHOTROPICS UTILIZING THE RADIOLABELED ANTAGONIST, (3H) QUINUCLIDINYL-BENZILATE. (PH.D. DISSERTATION).
002918 03-03

A COMPARISON OF DOPAMINE-RECEPTOR BLOCKING ASSAY WITH PLASMA DRUG LEVELS OF HALOPERIDOL IN SCHIZOPHRENIC-PATIENTS.
003182 03-08

A DOUBLE-BLIND COMPARISON BETWEEN AMOXAPINE AND AMITRIPTYLINE IN DEPRESSED-INPATIENTS.
003234 03-09

LITHIUM AND IMIPRAMINE IN THE PROPHYLAXIS OF UNIPOLAR AND BIPOLAR-II DEPRESSION: A PROSPECTIVE, PLACEBO-CONTROLLED COMPARISON.
003252 03-09

COMPARISON OF ANXIETY REDUCING SUBSTANCES. (PH.D. DISSERTATION).
003278 03-10

COMPARISON OF STANDARD AND HOLTOR-MONITORED EKGS IN A PATIENT TREATED WITH SEVERAL ANTIDEPRESSANTS.
003304 03-11

DOUBLE-BLIND COMPARISON OF ALPRAZOLAM AND DIAZEPAM FOR SUBCHRONIC WITHDRAWAL FROM ALCOHOL.
003332 03-11

COMPARISON OF SODIUM-VALPROATE AND PHENYTOIN AS SINGLE DRUG-TREATMENT IN EPILEPSY.
003371 03-11

COMPARISON OF THE EFFECTS OF FOUR BENZODIAZEPINES ON FRAME OF MIND AND BEHAVIOR IN HEALTHY SUBJECTS.
003441 03-14

A COMPARISON OF THE EFFECTS OF MORPHINE-SULPHATE AND NITROUS-OXIDE ANALGESIA ON CHRONIC PAIN STATES IN MAN.
003442 03-14

QUANTITATION AND COMPARISON OF PHENOBARBITAL LEVELS IN THE PLASMA, SALIVA, AND CEREBROSPINAL-FLUID OF THE RAT, AND THE DEMONSTRATION OF AN ALTERATION OF DRUG PASSAGE BY ETHANOL.
003725 04-03

PREJUNCTIONAL ACTIONS OF PIRIBEDIL ON THE ISOLATED KIDNEY OF THE RABBIT: COMPARISON WITH APOMORPHINE.
003749 04-03

COMPARISON OF THE EFFECTS OF THE STEREOISOMERS OF FENFLURAMINE ON THE ACETYLCHOLINE CONTENT OF RAT STRIATUM, HIPPOCAMPUS AND NUCLEUS-ACCUMBENS.
003758 04-03

COMPARISON OF THE BINDING CHARACTERISTICS OF TRITIATED OPIATES AND OPIOID-PEPTIDES.
003802 04-03

COMPARISON OF THE EFFECT OF INTRAVENOUS ADMINISTRATION OF D LYSERGIC-ACID-DIETHYLAMIDE ON FREE AND MEMBRANE-BOUND POLYSOMES IN THE RABBIT BRAIN.
003831 04-03

COMPARISON OF THE POTENCIES OF CLEBOPRIDE AND OTHER SUBSTITUTED BENZAMIDE DRUGS ON ISOLATED GASTROINTESTINAL TRACT OF THE GUINEA-PIG AND RAT.
003928 04-03

IN VIVO INTRANEURONAL MAO-INHIBITION IN RAT-BRAIN SKF-64139, COMPARISON TO OTHER POTENT PNMT INHIBITORS.
003935 04-03

L ASPARTATE BINDING-SITES IN RAT-CEREBELLUM: A COMPARISON OF THE BINDING OF L (3H)ASPARTATE AND L (3H)GLUTAMATE TO SYNAPTIC MEMBRANES.
004000 04-03

A COMPARISON OF THE RESPONSES TO SOME DOPAMINE-RECEPTOR AGONISTS AND ANTAGONISTS IN THE ISOLATED PERFUSED RAT KIDNEY.
004054 04-03

A COMPARISON BETWEEN SOME BIOCHEMICAL-EFFECTS AND BEHAVIOURAL-EFFECTS PRODUCED BY NEUROLEPTICS.
004116 04-04

COMPARISON OF THE EFFECTS OF BETA ENDORPHIN AND MORPHINE ON EXPLORATORY-BEHAVIOUR AND SOCIOSEXUAL-BEHAVIOUR IN THE MALE RAT.
004178 04-04

5 HYDROXYTRYPTAMINE-LIKE PROPERTIES OF M CHLOROPHENYLPIPERAZINE: COMPARISON WITH QUIPAZINE.
004210 04-04

A DOUBLE-BLIND COMPARISON OF THREE DOSAGES OF FLUTROLINE (CP-36584) IN THE TREATMENT OF SCHIZOPHRENIA.
004333 04-08

TRAZODONE EFFICACY AND SAFETY IN ENDOGENOUS DEPRESSION: A DOUBLE-BLIND COMPARISON WITH IMIPRAMINE.
004346 04-09

VALUE OF PROPANIDID IN ELECTROCONVULSIVE-THERAPY (COMPARISON WITH THIOPENTONE).
004379 04-09

A COMPARISON OF TRAZODONE AND DOTHIEPIN IN DEPRESSION.
004394 04-09

COMPARISON OF PSYCHOTROPIC-DRUG, RESPONSE COST, AND PSYCHOTROPIC-DRUG PLUS RESPONSE COST PROCEDURES FOR CONTROLLING INSTITUTIONALIZED MENTALLY-RETARDED PERSONS.
004438 04-11

DRUG PREFERENCE IN HUMANS: DOUBLE-BLIND CHOICE COMPARISON OF PENTOBARBITAL, DIAZEPAM AND PLACEBO.
004566 04-14

A COMPARISON OF RADIOIMMUNOASSAY WITH SPECTROPHOTOMETRY FOR THE DETERMINATION OF PLASMA DIPHENYLHYDANTOIN CONCENTRATIONS.
004684 04-16

COMPARISON OF SPECTROFLUOROMETRIC AND GAS-CHROMATOGRAPHY/MASS-SPECTROMETRY PROCEDURES FOR THE QUANTITATION OF MORPHINE IN BLOOD AND BRAIN.
004692 04-16

COMPARISONS
EFFECTS OF CHRONIC NEUROLEPTIC TREATMENT ON TYROSINE-HYDROXYLASE IN DOPAMINERGIC TERMINALS: COMPARISONS BETWEEN DRUGS AND BRAIN REGIONS REVEALS DIFFERENT MECHANISMS OF TOLERANCE.
001243 02-03

COMPARISONS OF THE EFFECTS OF GUANETHIDINE, 6 HYDROXYDOPAMINE AND DIETHYLDITHIOCARBAMATE ON RETENTION OF PASSIVE-AVOIDANCE.
001742 02-04

ATTENUATION OF THE EFFECTS OF PUNISHMENT BY ETHANOL: COMPARISONS WITH CHLORDIAZEPOXIDE.
001813 02-04

SECOND-ORDER SCHEDULES OF INTRAMUSCULAR COCAINE INJECTION IN THE SQUIRREL-MONKEY: COMPARISONS WITH FOOD PRESENTATION AND EFFECTS OF D-AMPHETAMINE AND PROMAZINE.
004152 04-04

COMPARTMENTALIZAION
HA-966 EFFECTS ON STRIATAL DOPAMINE METABOLISM: IMPLICATIONS FOR DOPAMINE COMPARTMENTALIZAION.
001150 02-03

COMPARTMENTATION
COMPARTMENTATION OF CATECHOLAMINES IN RAT-BRAIN: EFFECTS OF AGONISTS AND ANTAGONISTS.
000125 01-03

COMPARTMENTS
EFFECTS OF PSYCHOTROPIC-DRUGS ON THE DISTRIBUTION OF 3H DOPAMINE INTO COMPARTMENTS OF RAT STRIATAL SYNAPTOSOMES AND ON SUBSEQUENT DEPOLARIZATION-INDUCED 3H DOPAMINE RELEASE.
000067 01-03

COMPETITION
EFFECTS OF MORPHINE WITHDRAWAL ON FOOD COMPETITION HIERARCHIES AND FIGHTING-BEHAVIOR IN RATS.
001632 02-04

COMPETITIVE
THE DOPAMINE-RECEPTOR ANTAGONIST DOMPERIDONE IS ALSO A COMPETITIVE ANTAGONIST AT ALPHA1-ADRENOCEPTORS.
003785 04-03

COMPILATION
CLINICAL-STUDY OF MAPROTILINE IN THE TREATMENT OF DEPRESSIVE-STATES: COMPILATION OF 1520 OBSERVATIONS.
003206 03-09

COMPLEXE-1656
COMPARATIVE-STUDY OF THE INDUCTIVE EFFECT OF TWO PSYCHOMODERATORS -- TETRABAMATE AND COMPLEXE-1656 -- AND OF PHENOBARBITAL ON LIVER MICROSOMAL ENZYMES IN RATS.
001874 02-06

COMPLEXES
ATP COMPLEXES WITH THE ATPASE INHIBITOR QUERCETIN.
000045 01-03

ISOLATION OF SELECTIVE 3H CHLORNALTREXAMINE BOUND COMPLEXES, POSSIBLE OPIOID-RECEPTOR COMPONENTS IN BRAINS OF MICE.
001162 02-03

MULTIPLE BENZODIAZEPINE-RECEPTOR COMPLEXES: SOME BENZODIAZEPINE RECOGNITION SITES ARE COUPLED TO GABA-RECEPTORS AND IONOPHORES.
001484 02-03

COMPLIANCE
THE LITHIUM RATIO AS A GUIDE TO PATIENT COMPLIANCE.
000940 01-17

ACCURACY OF PATIENT INTERVIEWS AND ESTIMATES BY CLINICAL STAFF IN DETERMINING MEDICATION COMPLIANCE.
003618 03-17

THE INFLUENCE OF PATIENT BELIEFS ON COMPLIANCE TO THERAPY FOR DIABETES-MELLITUS. (PH.D. DISSERTATION).
003631 03-17

PHENYTOIN THERAPY FOR EPILEPTIC-CHILDREN: EVALUATION OF SALIVARY AND PLASMA CONCENTRATIONS AND OF METHODS OF ASSESSING COMPLIANCE.
004495 04-11

THE NEGATIVE INFLUENCE OF FAMILIES ON COMPLIANCE.
004745 04-17

COMPLICATING
ILEUS COMPLICATING HALOPERIDOL THERAPY.
003511 03-15

COMPLICATIONS
COMPLICATIONS OF CHRONIC LEVODOPA THERAPY: LONG-TERM EFFICACY OF DRUG-HOLIDAY.
003502 03-15

COMPOSED
EVIDENCE FOR, AND LOCALIZATION OF, A UNITARY DOPAMINE-RECEPTOR COMPOSED OF COOPERATIVELY LINKED SUBUNIT BINDING-SITES IN RAT STRIATUM.
000186 01-03

UNITARY DOPAMINERGIC-RECEPTOR COMPOSED OF COOPERATIVELY LINKED AGONIST AND ANTAGONIST SUBUNIT BINDING-SITES.
001342 02-03

COMPOSITION
COMBINED EFFECTS OF ALCOHOL AND LITHIUM ON BODY COMPOSITION IN THE RAT MODEL.
002928 03-03

DRUG-INDUCED CHANGES IN THE COMPOSITION OF THE CEREBRAL FREE AMINO-ACID POOL.
004039 04-03

COMPOUND-48-80
COMPOUND-48-80 INHIBITS NEUROTENSIN-INDUCED HYPOTENSION IN RATS.
000243 01-03

COMPREHENSIVE
STUDIES ON THE COMPREHENSIVE MEDICAL TREATMENT OF PEPTIC-ULCERS (3) -- UTILIZATION OF TRANQUILIZERS IN THE TREATMENT OF GASTRIC-ULCERS.
000653 01-10

IS IT POSSIBLE TO SET UP ANY RULES FOR A COMPREHENSIVE TREATMENT OF DEPRESSIVE-STATES?
001997 02-09

SOME PRINCIPLES OF DIFFERENTIATED METABOLIC DRUG-TREATMENT IN COMPREHENSIVE THERAPY OF MENTAL-DISORDERS.
004433 04-11

CORRECTION OF HORMONAL ACTIVITY OF THE THYROID-GLAND AS A METHOD OF PATHOGENIC THERAPY IN A COMPREHENSIVE TREATMENT OF PATIENTS WITH TEMPORAL EPILEPSY.
004579 04-14

COMPRESSED
TOLERANCE IN A COMPRESSED GASTRORESISTANT FORM IN PSYCHIATRIC-PATIENTS.
003157 03-07

COMPUTED-TOMOGRAPHY
PROGRESSIVE SUPRANUCLEAR PALSY, COMPUTED-TOMOGRAPHY, AND RESPONSE TO ANTIPARKINSONIAN-DRUGS.
003322 03-11

COMPUTER
A COMPUTER OCULOGRAPHIC AND EEG DOUBLE-BLIND STUDY INCLUDING WELL-BEING FOR DETERMINING CHANGED VIGILANCE UNDER THERAPY WITH TIAPRIDE.
000751 01-13

COMPUTER-ANALYZED
DISCOVERY OF PSYCHOTROPIC-DRUGS BY MEANS OF COMPUTER-ANALYZED EEG.
002203 02-13

COMPUTER-ANALYZED EEG IN AMPHETAMINE RESPONSIVE HYPERACTIVE-CHILDREN.
003338 03-11

COMPUTER-ANALYZED ELECTROENCEPHALOGRAM TO PREDICT THE THERAPEUTIC OUTCOME IN SCHIZOPHRENIA.
004680 04-16

COMPUTERIZED
COMPUTERIZED EEG IN THE COMPARISON OF OXYPROTHEPIN AND FLUPHENAZINE-DECANOATE.
000567 01-08

COMPUTERIZED SLEEP EEG (CSEEG) IN PSYCHIATRY AND PSYCHOPHARMACOLOGY.
002614 02-17

EVALUATION OF DRUG EFFICACY IN DEMENTIA: A COMPUTERIZED COGNITIVE ASSESSMENT SYSTEM.
003557 03-16

COMPUTERIZED MONITORING OF PSYCHOTROPIC-DRUG ORDERS: SOME TRENDS AND REVELATIONS.
003566 03-16

COMPUTERIZED ANALYSIS OF SLEEP RECORDINGS APPLIED TO DRUG EVALUATION: MIDAZOLAM IN NORMAL SUBJECTS.
004564 04-14

COMPUTERIZED-AXIAL-TOMOGRAPHY
THERAPEUTIC PLASMA LEVELS OF SOME ANTICONVULSANTS IN FOCAL EPILEPSY IN RELATION TO COMPUTERIZED-AXIAL-TOMOGRAPHY.
004439 04-11

COMPUTERIZING
COMPUTERIZING THE MMPI IN THE STUDY OF A NEW PSYCHOTROPIC-AGENT: TIAPRIDE.
000585 01-09

COMT-A
COMT-A AND COMT-B: CATALYTIC DIFFERENCES AND ROLE OF DISULFIDE BOND .
003927 04-03

COMT-B
COMT-A AND COMT-B: CATALYTIC DIFFERENCES AND ROLE OF DISULFIDE BOND .
003927 04-03

CONCENTRATE
EFFECT OF PSYCHIATRIC-INTERVENTION ON USE OF ANTIHEMOPHILIC-FACTOR CONCENTRATE.
000945 01-17

CONCENTRATION
COMPARATIVE-EFFECTS OF P CHLOROAMPHETAMINE AND L P CHLOROPHENYLPIPERAZINE ON 5 HYDROXYINDOLE CONCENTRATION IN RAT-BRAIN.
000101 01-03

EFFECTS OF GAMMA ACETYLENIC-GABA AND GAMMA VINYL-GABA ON ELECTRICALLY-INDUCED SPINAL-CORD CONVULSIONS AND ON SPINAL-CORD GABA CONCENTRATION.
000145 01-03

REGULATION OF STRIATAL ACETYLCHOLINE CONCENTRATION BY D2 DOPAMINE-RECEPTORS.
000269 01-03

PATHOPHYSIOLOGICAL-STUDIES ON SCHIZOPHRENIA WITH SPECIAL REFERENCE TO HOMOVANILLIC-ACID CONCENTRATION IN CEREBROSPINAL-FLUID.
000271 01-03

LONG-TERM EFFECTS OF CONTINUOUS EXPOSURE TO AMPHETAMINE ON BRAIN DOPAMINE CONCENTRATION AND SYNAPTOSOMAL UPTAKE IN MICE.
000287 01-03

INTRA AND EXTRA ERYTHROCYTE LITHIUM-ION CONCENTRATION RATIOS IN MANIC-PATIENTS.
000627 01-09

PRACTICAL AND THEORETICAL ASPECTS OF PHENYTOIN ADMINISTRATION. I. RELATIONSHIP BETWEEN DOSE AND PLASMA CONCENTRATION.
000760 01-13

TRANSCULTURAL PHARMACOKINETIC STUDY ON LI CONCENTRATION IN PLASMA AND SALIVA.
000769 01-13

LEVORPHANOL: RADIOIMMUNOASSAY AND PLASMA CONCENTRATION PROFILES IN DOG AND MAN.
000898 01-16

DETERMINATION OF DOSE PLASMA CONCENTRATION RELATIONSHIP OF PHENOBARBITAL IN EPILEPTIC-PATIENTS BY A NEW SPECIFIC RADIOIMMUNOASSAY.
000902 01-16

EFFECT OF 2 P CHLOROPHENYL-CYCLOPROPYLAMINE ON 5 HYDROXYINDOLE CONCENTRATION AND MONOAMINE-OXIDASE ACTIVITY IN RAT-BRAIN.
001237 02-03

THE INFLUENCE OF EXTERNAL SODIUM AND POTASSIUM ON LITHIUM UPTAKE BY PRIMARY BRAIN CELL CULTURES AT THERAPEUTIC LITHIUM CONCENTRATION.
001300 02-03

CHANGE IN OVERINCLUSIVE THINKING OF SCHIZOPHRENIC-PATIENTS IS RELATED TO PLASMA PHENOTHIAZINE CONCENTRATION.
001941 02-08

AMITRIPTYLINE PLASMA CONCENTRATION AND CLINICAL-EFFECT: A WORLD-HEALTH-ORGANIZATION COLLABORATIVE-STUDY.
001976 02-09

CONCENTRATION OF SEROTONIN METABOLITES IN THE CEREBROSPINAL-FLUID FROM ALCOHOLICS BEFORE AND DURING SULFIRAM THERAPY.
002095 02-11

CARBAMAZEPINE THERAPY IN TRIGEMINAL-NEURALGIA: CLINICAL-EFFECTS IN RELATION TO PLASMA CONCENTRATION.
002181 02-11

THE EFFECTS OF ALCOHOL AND CAFFEINE ON CONCENTRATION TEST PERFORMANCE.
002337 02-14

CHILDHOOD-ENURESIS: II. PSYCHOPATHOLOGY, TRICYCLIC CONCENTRATION IN PLASMA, AND ANTIENURETIC-EFFECT.
002354 02-14

CHANGES IN NORADRENERGIC TRANSMISSION ALTER THE CONCENTRATION OF CYTOPLASMIC PROGESTIN-RECEPTORS IN HYPOTHALAMUS.
002842 03-03

CORRELATION OF (14C)MUSCIMOL CONCENTRATION IN RAT-BRAIN WITH ANTICONVULSANT ACTIVITY.
003045 03-04

SERUM CONCENTRATION AND CLINICAL-EFFECT OF ANTIEPILEPTICS.
003315 03-11

HUMAN BRAIN, PLASMA, AND CEREBROSPINAL-FLUID CONCENTRATION OF SODIUM-VALPROATE AFTER 72 HOURS OF THERAPY.
003433 03-13

EFFECTS OF MOLINDONE AND FLUPHENAZINE ON THE BRAIN CONCENTRATION OF SOME PHENOLIC AND CATECHOLIC AMINES IN THE MOUSE AND THE RAT.
003870 04-03

ON THE IMPORTANCE OF AGONIST CONCENTRATION GRADIENTS WITHIN ISOLATED TISSUES. INCREASED MAXIMAL RESPONSES OF RAT VASA-DEFERENTIA TO (-) NORADRENALINE AFTER BLOCKADE OF NEURONAL UPTAKE.
003879 04-03

THE INFLUENCE OF D-AMPHETAMINE ON RAT-BRAIN STRIATAL REDUCED BIOPTERIN CONCENTRATION.
003922 04-03

SERUM CONCENTRATION OF ANTICONVULSANTS. PHARMACOKINETIC FINDINGS AND THEIR PRACTICAL APPLICATION.
004443 04-11

USE OF PLASMA CONCENTRATION DETERMINATIONS.
004498 04-13

PLASMA NOMIFENSINE CONCENTRATION: CARDIOLOGICAL EFFECTS AND CLINICAL-RESPONSE.
004639 04-15

CONCENTRATIONS
TOLERANCE TO INCREASES IN STRIATAL ACETYLCHOLINE CONCENTRATIONS AFTER REPEATED ADMINISTRATION OF APOMORPHINE-DIPIVALOYL-ESTER.
000464 01-04

VILOXAZINE PLASMA CONCENTRATIONS AND CLINICAL-RESPONSE.
000614 01-09

EFFECT OF DIAZEPAM AND DESMETHYLDIAZEPAM IN SPASTICITY AND RIGIDITY: A QUANTITATIVE STUDY OF REFLEXES AND PLASMA CONCENTRATIONS.
000701 01-11

PLASMA CHLORPROMAZINE CONCENTRATIONS IN CHILDREN WITH BEHAVIORAL-DISORDERS AND MENTAL-ILLNESS.
000717 01-11

CONVERSION SCALES FOR COMMONLY REQUESTED SERUM CONCENTRATIONS OF DRUGS AND OTHER SUBSTANCES OF THERAPEUTIC AND TOXICOLOGICAL IMPORTANCE, AND OF HORMONES.
000759 01-13

NEUROLEPTIC-EFFECT ON DESIPRAMINE STEADY-STATE PLASMA CONCENTRATIONS.
000781 01-13

SERUM CONCENTRATIONS OF PHENOBARBITAL AND DIPHENYLHYDANTOIN IN SEVERE MENTALLY-HANDICAPPED AND PHYSICALLY-HANDICAPPED-PATIENTS.
000856 01-15

VALUE OF SALIVA SAMPLES IN MONITORING CARBAMAZEPINE CONCENTRATIONS IN EPILEPTIC-PATIENTS.
000903 01-16

BRAIN SEROTONIN AND 5 HYDROXYINDOLEACETIC-ACID CONCENTRATIONS AND SEROTONIN SYNTHESIS FOLLOWING TETRAHYDRO-BETA-CARBOLINE ADMINISTRATION IN MICE.
001152 02-03

PROSTAGLANDIN-E RELEASE BY RAT MEDIAL BASAL HYPOTHALAMUS IN VITRO. INHIBITION BY MELATONIN AT SUBMICROMOLAR CONCENTRATIONS.
001159 02-03

RELATIONSHIPS BETWEEN CHLORPROMAZINE CONCENTRATIONS IN PLASMA AND CEREBROSPINAL-FLUID AND CLINICAL-RESPONSE AND BIOCHEMICAL-RESPONSE IN PSYCHOTIC-PATIENTS.
001905 02-08

SERUM NEUROLEPTIC CONCENTRATIONS IN SCHIZOPHRENIA. (UNPUBLISHED PAPER).
001945 02-08

LONG-TERM MONITORING OF TRICYCLIC-ANTIDEPRESSANT PLASMA CONCENTRATIONS.
002014 02-09

PLASMA DELTA9 TETRAHYDROCANNABINOL CONCENTRATIONS AND CLINICAL-EFFECTS AFTER ORAL AND INTRAVENOUS ADMINISTRATION AND SMOKING.
002201 02-12

PHARMACOKINETIC BASIS FOR PREDICTING STEADY-STATE SERUM DRUG CONCENTRATIONS OF IMIPRAMINE FROM SINGLE-DOSE DATA.
002225 02-13

SALIVARY IMMUNOGLOBULIN CONCENTRATIONS IN PATIENTS WITH EPILEPSY TREATED WITH CARBAMAZEPINE.
002234 02-13

THYMOANALEPTIC TREATMENT CONTROL THROUGH MEASUREMENT OF PLASMA CONCENTRATIONS OF AMITRIPTYLINE AND ITS METABOLITE NORTRIPTYLINE.
002304 02-13

PHENOTHIAZINE PLASMA AND RED-BLOOD-CELL CONCENTRATIONS, THEIR RELATIONSHIP TO SIDE-EFFECTS AND CLINICAL-EFFICACY.
002386 02-15

CONCENTRATIONS OF CIS(Z) FLUPENTHIXOL IN MATERNAL SERUM, AMNIOTIC-FLUID, UMBILICAL-CORD-SERUM, AND MILK.
002423 02-15

MEASUREMENT OF PLASMA CONCENTRATIONS OF DRUGS AS A FEEDBACK CONTROL MECHANISM DURING DRUG-THERAPY.
002525 02-17

ENHANCEMENT OF ETORPHINE BRAIN CONCENTRATIONS AND CHANGES IN ETORPHINE NALOXONE PA2 VALUES IN MORPHINE PRETREATED MICE.
002800 03-03

BEHAVIOURAL-RESPONSES TO DRUGS RELEASING 5 HYDROXYTRYPTAMINE AND CATECHOLAMINES: EFFECTS OF TREATMENTS ALTERING PRECURSOR CONCENTRATIONS IN BRAIN.
002990 03-04

RELATIONSHIP BETWEEN BLOOD CONCENTRATIONS AND CLINICAL-EFFECTS OF A NEW ANTIDEPRESSANT MAPROTILINE.
003271 03-09

PHENYTOIN CONCENTRATIONS IN VENOUS VERSUS CAPILLARY BLOOD OF GERIATRIC-PATIENTS.
003381 03-11

EXCESSIVE PLASMA CONCENTRATIONS OF TRICYCLIC-ANTIDEPRESSANTS RESULTING FROM USUAL DOSES: A REPORT OF SIX CASES.
003479 03-15

RESPIRATORY-DISEASE AND NASAL IMMUNOGLOBULIN CONCENTRATIONS IN PHENYTOIN TREATED EPILEPTIC-PATIENTS.
003486 03-15

CEREBROSPINAL-FLUID CONCENTRATIONS OF THIORIDAZINE AND ITS MAIN METABOLITES IN PSYCHIATRIC-PATIENTS.
003569 03-16

CHLORPROMAZINE, HALOPERIDOL, METOCLOPRAMIDE AND DOMPERIDONE RELEASE PROLACTIN THROUGH DOPAMINE ANTAGONISM AT LOW CONCENTRATIONS BUT PARADOXICALLY INHIBIT PROLACTIN RELEASE AT HIGH-CONCENTRATIONS.
003731 04-03

BRAIN AND SERUM CALCIUM CONCENTRATIONS FOLLOWING ELECTROCONVULSIVE-SHOCK OR BICUCULLINE-INDUCED CONVULSIONS IN RATS.
003736 04-03

EVIDENCE TO SUGGEST THAT DOPAMINE-INDUCED INCREASE IN GABA CONCENTRATIONS IN CHICK BRAIN IS MEDIATED THROUGH CYCLIC-AMP.
003952 04-03

PHENYTOIN THERAPY FOR EPILEPTIC-CHILDREN: EVALUATION OF SALIVARY AND PLASMA CONCENTRATIONS AND OF METHODS OF ASSESSING COMPLIANCE.
004495 04-11

ERYTHROCYTE CHOLINE CONCENTRATIONS ARE ELEVATED IN MANIC-PATIENTS.
004521 04-13

CONCENTRATIONS AND KINETICS OF CARBAMAZEPINE IN WHOLE SALIVA, PAROTID SALIVA, SERUM ULTRAFILTRATE, AND SERUM.
004545 04-13

CONCENTRATIONS OF CHLORPROMAZINE AND TWO OF ITS ACTIVE METABOLITES IN PLASMA AND CEREBROSPINAL-FLUID OF PSYCHOTIC-PATIENTS TREATED WITH FIXED DRUG DOSES.
004559 04-13

THERAPEUTIC MONITORING OF PLASMA CONCENTRATIONS OF TRICYCLIC-ANTIDEPRESSANTS: PERSPECTIVE OF THE CLINICAL LABORATORY.
004681 04-16

MEASUREMENT OF NEUROLEPTIC CONCENTRATIONS BY GLC AND RADIORECEPTOR ASSAY.
004682 04-16

A COMPARISON OF RADIOIMMUNOASSAY WITH SPECTROPHOTOMETRY FOR THE DETERMINATION OF PLASMA DIPHENYLHYDANTOIN CONCENTRATIONS.
004684 04-16

DRUG CONCENTRATIONS IN NEUROPSYCHIATRY.
004735 04-17

CONCERNS
THE USE OF PSYCHOPHARMACOLOGICAL-PROCEDURES TO ANALYSE THE ONTOGENY OF LEARNING AND RETENTION: ISSUES AND CONCERNS.
000482 01-04

CONCUSSION
INFLUENCING BRAIN CONCUSSION BY NOOTROPIL.
000724 01-11

CONDENSATION
SYNTHESIS OF POTENTIAL ANTICONVULSANTS: CONDENSATION OF ISATINS WITH ACETONE AND RELATED KETONES.
003699 04-02

CONDITIONAL
EFFECTS OF PHENCYCLIDINE, PENTOBARBITAL, AND D-AMPHETAMINE ON THE ACQUISITION AND PERFORMANCE OF CONDITIONAL DISCRIMINATIONS IN MONKEYS.
001723 02-04

CONDITIONED
ENHANCED SUPPRESSION OF CONDITIONED AVOIDANCE RESPONSE BY HALOPERIDOL BUT NOT PHENOXYBENZAMINE IN RATS WITH BILATERAL PARAFASCICULAR LESIONS.
000334 01-04

NORADRENERGIC AGONISTS AND ANTAGONISTS: EFFECTS ON CONDITIONED FEAR AS MEASURED BY THE POTENTIATED STARTLE PARADIGM.
000372 01-04

THE EFFECTS OF PIPRADROL ON THE ACQUISITION OF RESPONDING WITH CONDITIONED REINFORCEMENT: A ROLE FOR SENSORY PRECONDITIONING.
001572 02-04

MODULATION OF CONDITIONED TASTE-AVERSION BY SODIUM-PENTOBARBITAL.
001596 02-04

EFFECTS OF DRUGS ON THE EFFECTIVENESS OF CONDITIONED STIMULI.
001608 02-04

PREEXPOSURE TO DELTA9 THC BLOCKS THC-INDUCED CONDITIONED TASTE-AVERSION IN RATS.
001618 02-04

EFFECT OF CHOLINE ON CONDITIONED FOOD MOTOR-REFLEXES IN CATS.
001731 02-04

CONDITIONED SUPPRESSION OF DRINKING: A MEASURE OF THE CR ELICITED BY A LITHIUM CONDITIONED FLAVOR.
001747 02-04

THE EFFECTS OF CHLORDIAZEPOXIDE-HCL ADMINISTRATION UPON PUNISHMENT AND CONDITIONED SUPPRESSION IN THE RAT.
001757 02-04

ACTH POTENTIATES MORPHINE-INDUCED CONDITIONED TASTE-AVERSION.
001781 02-04

THE RELATIONSHIP BETWEEN POSITIVE REINFORCEMENT AND CONDITIONED TASTE-AVERSION PRODUCED BY SELF-ADMINISTERED DRUGS. (PH.D. DISSERTATION).
001798 02-04

EFFECTS OF DESGLYCINAMIDE-LYSINE-VASOPRESSIN ON A CONDITIONED TASTE-AVERSION IN RATS.
001811 02-04

TEMPORAL AND ENVIRONMENTAL CUES IN CONDITIONED HYPOTHERMIA AND HYPERTHERMIA ASSOCIATED WITH MORPHINE.
002709 03-03

LITHIUM-CHLORIDE AND DELTA9 THC LEAD TO CONDITIONED AVERSIONS IN THE PIGEON.
003003 03-04

THE EFFECTS OF IMIPRAMINE TREATMENT ON THE UNCONDITIONED ALIMENTARY BEHAVIOR AND CLASSICAL CONDITIONED SALIVARY REACTIONS IN DOGS.
003030 03-04

THE PHARMACOLOGICAL ANALYSIS OF MONOAMINERGIC MECHANISMS OF THE MEDIAL HYPOTHALAMUS IN FOOD PROCURING CONDITIONED REFLEXES IN RATS.
003100 03-04

EFFECTS OF CHLORDIAZEPOXIDE AND D-AMPHETAMINE ON RESPONDING SUPPRESSED BY CONDITIONED PUNISHMENT.
003105 03-04

DOPAMINE DEPLETION BY 6 HYDROXYDOPAMINE PREVENTS CONDITIONED TASTE-AVERSION INDUCED BY METHYLAMPHETAMINE BUT NOT LITHIUM-CHLORIDE.
003110 03-04

THE USE OF CONDITIONED SUPPRESSION TO EVALUATE THE NATURE OF NEUROLEPTIC-INDUCED AVOIDANCE-DEFICITS.
004070 04-04

NALOXONE FAILS TO BLOCK AMPHETAMINE-INDUCED ANOREXIA AND CONDITIONED TASTE-AVERSION.
004121 04-04

CONDITIONED DRUG-EFFECTS OF D-AMPHETAMINE-INDUCED AND
MORPHINE-INDUCED MOTOR ACCELERATION IN MICE: EXPERIMENTAL
APPROACH FOR PLACEBO-EFFECT.
004128 04-04

EFFECTS OF SUBCHRONIC DESMETHYLIMIPRAMINE (DMI) TREATMENT OF
THE CLASSICALLY CONDITIONED EYEBLINK RESPONSE IN RABBITS.
004180 04-04

THE EFFECT OF THE NEW ANTIDEPRESSANT INKASAN ON THE
BIOELECTRICAL-ACTIVITY OF THE BRAIN AND ON CONDITIONED
REFLEXES.
004212 D4-04

CONDITIONING
POSTNATAL ALCOHOL EXPOSURE IN THE RAT: ITS EFFECTS ON
AVOIDANCE CONDITIONING, HEBB-WILLIAMS MAZE-PERFORMANCE,
MATERNAL-BEHAVIOR, AND PUP DEVELOPMENT.
001580 02-04

THE EFFECTS OF PIMOZIDE DURING PAIRING ON THE TRANSFER OF
CLASSICAL CONDITIONING TO AN OPERANT DISCRIMINATION.
002956 03-04

CONDITIONING AND RETENTION OF DEFENSIVE BURYING AS A FUNCTION
OF ELAVIL AND THORAZINE INJECTION.
002974 03-04

MODIFICATION OF MOTOR-ACTIVITY, PASSIVE-AVOIDANCE
CONDITIONING AND EVOKED-POTENTIALS BY MICROINJECTIONS OF
STRYCHNINE IN BOTH CAUDATE-NUCLEI IN CATS.
003101 03-04

PHOSPHODIESTERASE INHIBITORS FACILITATE MEMORY FOR PASSIVE-
AVOIDANCE CONDITIONING.
003109 03-04

OPIATE-EFFECTS IN THE AMYGDALA CENTRAL NUCLEUS ON HEART RATE
CONDITIONING IN RABBITS.
003798 04-03

CONDITIONING OF AN INTEROCEPTIVE DRUG STIMULUS TO DIFFERENT
EXTEROCEPTIVE CONTEXTS.
004142 04-04

CONDITIONS
INTERRELATIONS AMONG PRIOR EXPERIENCE AND CURRENT CONDITIONS
IN THE DETERMINATION OF BEHAVIOR AND THE EFFECTS OF DRUGS.
001715 02-04

THE EFFECT OF CONDITIONS INFLUENCING ENDOGENOUS
PROSTAGLANDINS ON THE ACTIVITY OF DELTA'
TETRAHYDROCANNABINOL.
002196 02-12

EFFECTS OF CAFFEINE ADMINISTRATION ON FOOD AND WATER
CONSUMPTION UNDER VARIOUS EXPERIMENTAL CONDITIONS.
003049 03-04

ACUTE PHARMACOTOXIC PSYCHOSES IN CHRONIC CEREBRAL
CONDITIONS.
003475 03-15

CONDUCTANCE
ABSENCE OF POTASSIUM CONDUCTANCE IN CENTRAL MYELINATED
AXONS.
000166 01-03

TWO CONDUCTANCE MECHANISMS ACTIVATED BY APPLICATIONS OF L
GLUTAMIC-ACID, L ASPARTIC-ACID, DL HOMOCYSTEIC-ACID, N
METHYL-D-ASPARTIC-ACID, AND DL KAINIC-ACID TO CULTURED
MAMMALIAN CENTRAL NEURONES.
001349 02-03

BILATERAL SKIN CONDUCTANCE AND THE PUPILLARY LIGHT DARK
REFLEX: MANIPULATION BY CHLORPROMAZINE, HALOPERIDOL,
SCOPOLAMINE, AND PLACEBO.
004544 04-13

CONDUCTION
MEASUREMENTS OF NERVE CONDUCTION VELOCITY DURING DECREASING
TOXIC DIPHENYLHYDANTOIN LEVELS AND THE BEGINNING OF
CARBAMAZEPINE MEDICATION: A CLINICAL NEUROPHYSIOLOGICAL
REPORT.
004441 04-11

CONFERENCE
ABSTRACTS OF THE ANNUAL GENERAL CONFERENCE OF THE EUROPEAN-
BRAIN-AND-BEHAVIOUR-SOCIETY, HELD AT LOUVAIN-LA-NEUVE,
BELGIUM, ON NOVEMBER 13-15TH, 1980.
003617 03-17

CONFERENCES
PSYCHOPHARMACOLOGY AFTER 20 YEARS OF CONFERENCES IN JESENIK.
003646 03-17

CONFIRMATION
CONFIRMATION BEHAVIOR OF PHENCYCLIDINES AND BIOLOGICAL-
ACTIVITY.
001031 02-01

BEHAVIORAL CONFIRMATION OF DIFFUSE NOXIOUS INHIBITORY
CONTROLS (DNIC) AND EVIDENCE FOR A ROLE OF ENDOGENOUS
OPIATES.
002791 03-03

MASS SCREENING AND CONFIRMATION OF DIAZEPAM IN URINE BY EMIT
THIN-LAYER-CHROMATOGRAPHY.
004672 04-16

CONFLICT
HOSTILITY CONFLICT AND REPORTING OF SIDE-EFFECTS BY PSYCHIATRIC-
OUTPATIENTS.
000840 01-15

DO PSYCHOTHERAPY AND PHARMACOTHERAPY FOR DEPRESSION
CONFLICT? EMPIRICAL EVIDENCE FROM A CLINICAL-TRIAL.
003256 03-09

DO PSYCHOTHERAPY AND PHARMACOTHERAPY FOR DEPRESSION
CONFLICT? EMPIRICAL EVIDENCE FROM A CLINICAL-TRIAL.
(UNPUBLISHED PAPER).
004401 04-09

CONFLICT-BEHAVIOR
AN INTERFERENCE REDUCTION THEORY OF THE EFFECTS OF ETHANOL ON
CONFLICT-BEHAVIOR.
001586 02-04

EFFECT OF SODIUM-DIPROPYLACETATE ON CONFLICT-BEHAVIOR IN RATS.
004192 D4-04

CONFLICT-SITUATION
CONFLICT-SITUATION BASED ON INTRACRANIAL SELF-STIMULATION
BEHAVIOR AND THE EFFECT OF BENZODIAZEPINES.
003004 03-04

CONFORMATION
DOPAMINE-RECEPTOR BLOCKADE BY IMIDOLINE AND ITS PROPOSED
ACTIVE CONFORMATION.
001687 02-04

CONFORMATIONALLY
CONFORMATIONALLY RESTRICTED PHENOTHIAZINE NEUROLEPTICS. 1. 3
DIMETHYLAMINO-TETRAHYDROAZEPINOPHENOTHIAZINE.
001359 02-03

CONFORMATIONALLY RESTRICTED TRICYCLIC-ANTIDEPRESSANTS. 1.
OCTAHYDRODIBENZAZEPINONAPHTHYRIDINES AS RIGID IMIPRAMINE
ANALOGUES.
001710 02-04

THE SYNTHESIS AND ACTIVITY OF CIS AND TRANS 2
AMINOMETHYLCYCLOPROPANECARBOXYLIC-ACID AS
CONFORMATIONALLY RESTRICTED ANALOGUES OF GABA.
002633 03-01

EFFECTS OF CONFORMATIONALLY RESTRAINED ANALOGUES OF
SEROTONIN ON ITS UPTAKE AND BINDING IN RAT-BRAIN.
003794 04-03

CONFORMATIONS
CONVULSANT AND ANTICONVULSANT BARBITURATES. 1. MOLECULAR
CONFORMATIONS FROM CLASSICAL POTENTIAL ENERGY
CALCULATIONS.
001029 02-01

TWO OR MORE CONFORMATIONS OF BENZODIAZEPINE-RECEPTORS
DEPENDING ON GABA-RECEPTORS AND'OTHER VARIABLES.
001139 02-03

CONFRONTATION
THE MYTHOLOGEM OF REVERSIBLE DEATH. THE ANALYTICAL
CONFRONTATION OF ENDOGENOUS DELIRIUM WITH DELUSIONS IN
PSYCHEDELIC-EXPERIENCES.
002200 02-12

CONFUSIONAL-STATE
PROLONGED CONFUSIONAL-STATE AND EEG SEIZURE ACTIVITY
FOLLOWING CONCURRENT ECT AND LITHIUM USE.
000895 01-15

CONGESTIVE
INTRAVENOUS QUINIDINE IN CONGESTIVE CARDIOMYOPATHY.
003352 03-11

CONJUGATE
TRANSFER OF LORAZEPAM AND ITS CONJUGATE ACROSS THE HUMAN
PLACENTA.
000774 01-13

DOPAMINE CONJUGATE IN CEREBROSPINAL-FLUID.
003432 03-13

CONJUGATED
PRESENCE OF CONJUGATED CATECHOLAMINES IN RAT-BRAIN: A NEW
METHOD OF ANALYSIS OF CATECHOLAMINE-SULFATES.
004286 04-06

CONJUGATES
ANTICANDIDAL-ACTIVITY OF PYRIMIDINE-PEPTIDE CONJUGATES.
001059 02-01

CONJUGATION
BETA DIETHYLAMINOETHYLDIPHENYLPROPYLACETATE (SKF-525-A) AND
2,4 DICHLORO-6-PHENYLPHENOXYETHYLAMINE-HBR (DPEA) INHIBITION
OF FATTY-ACID CONJUGATION TO 11 HYDROXY-DELTA9-
TETRAHYDROCANNABINOL BY THE RAT LIVER MICROSOMAL SYSTEM.
000179 01-03

CONJUNCTION
EFFECTS OF CYCLOHEXIMIDE ADMINISTERED IN CONJUNCTION WITH
NICOTINE ON RETENTION OF A PASSIVE-AVOIDANCE TASK IN MICE.
001791 02-04

CONNECTION
HALLUCINATORY AND DELUSIONAL-STATES IN CONNECTION WITH BLOOD-
PRESSURE AND EEG.
000814 01-14

VARIOUS FACTORS IN THE PATHOGENESIS OF PATHOLOGICAL REACTIONS
OBSERVED IN CONNECTION WITH THE ADMINISTRATION OF
PSYCHOTROPIC-DRUGS.
003532 03-15

CONSCIOUS
EFFECT OF INTRAVENTRICULAR INJECTIONS OF ALPHA AMINOSULFONIC-ACIDS ON THE CENTRAL-NERVOUS-SYSTEM OF CONSCIOUS MICE.
000009 01-02
EEG CHANGE IN THE CONSCIOUS RAT DURING IMMOBILITY INDUCED BY PSYCHOLOGICAL-STRESS.
001297 02-03
EFFECTS OF ALPHA-ADRENOCEPTOR STIMULATING DRUGS ON BARORECEPTOR REFLEXES IN CONSCIOUS CATS.
001514 02-03
ANTIARRHYTHMIC-ACTIVITY OF AMITRIPTYLINE ANALOGUES IN CONSCIOUS DOGS AFTER MYOCARDIAL-INFARCTION: CYPROHEPTADINIUM-METHIODIDE.
001534 02-03
COMPARATIVE-STUDY OF AGGRESSIVE-BEHAVIOUR AFTER INJECTION OF CHOLINOMIMETICS, ANTICHOLINESTERASES, NICOTINIC, AND MUSCARINIC GANGLIONIC STIMULANTS INTO THE CEREBRAL VENTRICLES OF CONSCIOUS CATS: FAILURE OF NICOTINIC-DRUGS TO EVOKE AGGRESSION.
001568 02-04
THE PHARMACOLOGY OF AGGRESSIVE-BEHAVIOURAL-PHENOMENA ELICITED BY MUSCARINE INJECTED INTO THE CEREBRAL VENTRICLES OF CONSCIOUS CATS.
001569 02-04
VASOPRESSIN STIMULATES RELEASE OF BETA LIPOTROPIN AND BETA ENDORPHIN IN CONSCIOUS RATS AS MEASURED BY RADIOIMMUNOASSAY OF UNEXTRACTED PLASMA.
003715 04-03
MODULATORY EFFECT OF BRAIN ACETYLCHOLINE ON REFLEX-INDUCED BRADYCARDIA AND TACHYCARDIA IN CONSCIOUS RATS.
003744 04-03
EFFECT OF AMPHETAMINE ON PLASMA CORTICOSTERONE IN THE CONSCIOUS RAT.
003888 04-03
CENTRAL CARDIOVASCULAR-EFFECTS AND BIOCHEMICAL-EFFECTS OF BACLOFEN IN THE CONSCIOUS RAT.
003965 04-03
HYPOTENSION ALTERS THE RELEASE OF CATECHOLAMINES IN THE HYPOTHALAMUS OF THE CONSCIOUS RABBIT.
003968 04-03

CONSCIOUSNESS
ELECTIVE ALTERATION OF THE STATE OF CONSCIOUSNESS SUBJECTED TO THE EFFECTS OF PSYCHOACTIVE-SUBSTANCES.
000994 01-17

CONSENT
A REVISED CHECKLIST TO OBTAIN CONSENT TO TREATMENT WITH MEDICATION.
000984 01-17
MISINFORMED CONSENT.
004326 04-08

CONSIDERATIONS
CONSIDERATIONS ON PSYCHOACTIVE-DRUGS.
002622 02-17
CONSIDERATIONS ON LONG-ACTING CHEMOTHERAPY: AN EXPERIENCE WITH FLUPHENAZINE-DECANOATE.
003173 03-08
NOMIFENSINE: CONSIDERATIONS ON A NEW NONTRICYCLIC-ANTIDEPRESSANT.
003222 03-09
CLINICAL-TRIAL OF HALAZEPAM AND CLORAZEPATE: CONSIDERATIONS OF A SINGLE-BEDTIME-DOSE.
003277 03-10

CONSTITUENT
A CONSTITUENT OF KHAT-LEAVES WITH AMPHETAMINE-LIKE RELEASING PROPERTIES.
001307 02-03

CONSTITUTIONAL
ROTTING WITH THEIR RIGHTS ON: CONSTITUTIONAL THEORY AND CLINICAL REALITY IN DRUG-REFUSAL BY PSYCHIATRIC-PATIENTS.
000911 01-17
THE CONSTITUTIONAL RIGHT-TO-REFUSE ANTIPSYCHOTIC-MEDICATIONS.
004496 04-12

CONSTRICTION
INHIBITION OF NEUROSYMPATHETIC CEREBROARTERIAL CONSTRICTION BY CLONIDINE IN CATS.
001431 02-03

CONSUMMATORY-BEHAVIOR
CHRONIC DELTA9 TETRAHYDROCANNABINOL IN RATS: EFFECT ON SOCIAL-INTERACTIONS, MOUSE-KILLING, MOTOR-ACTIVITY, CONSUMMATORY-BEHAVIOR, AND BODY-TEMPERATURE.
001722 02-04

CONSUMMATORY-BEHAVIORS
MORPHINE ANTAGONISTS AND CONSUMMATORY-BEHAVIORS.
004196 04-04

CONTACTS
BENZODIAZEPINE-RECEPTORS: AUTORADIOGRAPHICAL AND IMMUNOCYTOCHEMICAL EVIDENCE FOR THEIR LOCALIZATION IN REGIONS OF GABAERGIC SYNAPTIC CONTACTS.
002643 03-01

CONTAMINATION
STREET PCP SCENE: ISSUES ON SYNTHESIS AND CONTAMINATION.
000744 01-12

CONTEMPORARY
CONTEMPORARY PROBLEMS IN THE PHARMACOLOGICAL-TREATMENT OF PARKINSONISM.
004628 04-15

CONTEXT
DRUG ENVIRONMENT INTERACTION: CONTEXT DEPENDENCY OF COCAINE-INDUCED BEHAVIORAL-SENSITIZATION.
002866 03-03

CONTEXTS
CONDITIONING OF AN INTEROCEPTIVE DRUG STIMULUS TO DIFFERENT EXTEROCEPTIVE CONTEXTS.
004142 04-04

CONTINGENCY
BEHAVIORAL-EFFECTS OF DRUGS: THE ROLE OF THE STIMULUS REINFORCER CONTINGENCY. (PH.D. DISSERTATION).
001537 02-03

CONTINGENT
CAPACITIES OF ATTENTION, STRESS-RESISTANCE, AND SLOW CEREBRAL POTENTIALS: EFFECTS OF CARPIPRAMINE ON CONTINGENT NEGATIVE VARIATION WAVES AND P-300.
003451 03-14

CONTINUOUS-ACCESS
CONTINUOUS-ACCESS PHENCYCLIDINE SELF-ADMINISTRATION BY RHESUS-MONKEYS LEADING TO PHYSICAL-DEPENDENCE.
000341 01-04

CONTRACEPTIVE
PHENOBARBITONE INTERACTION WITH ORAL CONTRACEPTIVE STEROIDS IN THE RABBIT AND RAT.
001832 02-05

CONTRACEPTIVES
EFFECT OF IMIPRAMINE ON HEPATIC GAMMA GLUTAMYLTRANSFERASE IN FEMALE RATS. INTERACTION WITH CONTRACEPTIVES.
001507 02-03

CONTRACTILE
A COMPARISON OF THE CONTRACTILE RESPONSES OF THE RABBIT BASILAR AND PULMONARY-ARTERIES TO SYMPATHOMIMETIC AGONISTS: CHARACTERISTICS.
002670 03-03

CONTRACTION
CALCIUM ANTAGONISM OF THE INHIBITORY-EFFECTS OF FENTANYL ON THE CONTRACTION OF THE NICTITATING MEMBRANE IN CATS.
002876 03-03

CONTRACTIONS
CHARACTERISTICS OF OSCILLATORY CONTRACTIONS ELICITED BY NALOXONE IN ILEUM PREPARATION FROM MORPHINE-DEPENDENT GUINEA-PIGS.
001491 02-03

CONTRALATERAL
CONTRALATERAL CIRCLING-BEHAVIOUR INDUCED BY INTRANIGRAL INJECTION OF MORPHINE AND ENKEPHALIN ANALOGUE FK-33-824 IN RATS.
001669 02-04
CONTRALATERAL CIRCLING-BEHAVIOUR INDUCED BY INTRANIGRAL INJECTION OF TAURINE IN RATS.
001670 02-04

CONTRASTING-EFFECTS
TRICYCLIC-ANTIDEPRESSANT DRUGS AND INDIVIDUAL DIFFERENCES IN THE EXPLORATORY-ACTIVITY OF RATS: CONTRASTING-EFFECTS OF TERTIARY AND SECONDARY AMINE COMPOUNDS.
000401 01-04
AN OBSERVATIONAL METHOD FOR QUANTIFYING THE BEHAVIOURAL-EFFECTS OF DOPAMINE AGONISTS: CONTRASTING-EFFECTS OF D-AMPHETAMINE AND APOMORPHINE.
002484 02-16

CONTRIBUTE
EVIDENCE THAT THE OPIATE-RECEPTORS OF THE SUBSTANTIA-GELATINOSA CONTRIBUTE TO THE DEPRESSION, BY INTRAVENOUS MORPHINE, OF THE SPINAL TRANSMISSION OF IMPULSES IN UNMYELINATED PRIMARY AFFERENTS.
002767 03-03

CONTRIBUTED
THE POSSIBILITY THAT A COMPONENT OF MORPHINE-INDUCED ANALGESIA IS CONTRIBUTED INDIRECTLY VIA THE RELEASE OF ENDOGENOUS OPIOIDS.
000263 01-03

CONTRIBUTION
CONTRIBUTION TO THE CLINICAL-STUDY OF CEREBRAL DOPAMINERGIC MECHANISMS: THE ACTION OF PIRIBEDIL IN PSYCHIATRY. FIRST RESULTS.
000616 01-09
CONTRIBUTION TO STUDY OF CEREBRAL DOPAMINERGIC MECHANISMS: REALITY OF THE PROBLEM.
000782 01-13
A CONTRIBUTION TO OUR KNOWLEDGE OF COCA-LEAF CONTENT SUBSTANCES.
001022 02-01

Subject Index

THE CONTRIBUTION OF ALPHA1 ACID GLYCOPROTEIN, LIPOPROTEINS, AND ALBUMIN TO THE PLASMA BINDING OF PERAZINE, AMITRIPTYLINE, AND NORTRIPTYLINE IN HEALTHY MAN.
002214 02-13

CONTRIBUTION TO THE PHARMACOKINETICS AND METABOLISM OF OXYPROTHEPIN.
002279 02-13

CONFESSION OF A MELANCHOLIAC: CONTRIBUTION TO THE PROBLEM OF PROPHYLAXIS OF MANIC-DEPRESSIVE-PSYCHOSIS USING LITHIUM.
003267 03-09

TARDIVE-DYSKINESIA: CLINICOEPIDEMIOLOGICAL REVISION AND CONTRIBUTION.
003466 03-15

CONTRIBUTION OF SOCIAL FACTORS TO OPIATE-INDUCED ACTIVATION IN THE MOUSE.
004156 04-04

CONTRIBUTIONS
CONTRIBUTIONS OF INDIVIDUAL DIFFERENCES TO SUBJECTIVE INTOXICATION.
002202 02-12

CONTRIBUTORS
CONTRIBUTORS TO FEMALE USE OF PSYCHOPHARMACOLOGICAL-AGENTS: DISSERTATION).
000956 01-17

CONTROL
PLASMA LEVELS OF DIPHENYLHYDANTOIN AND THE CONTROL OF ADULT EPILEPTIC-SEIZURES: A CHILEAN EXPERIENCE.
000102 01-03

THE ROLE OF INTRANEURONAL 5 HT AND OF TRYPTOPHAN-HYDROXYLASE ACTIVATION IN THE CONTROL OF 5 HT SYNTHESIS IN RAT-BRAIN SLICES INCUBATED IN K-ENRICHED MEDIUM.
000123 01-03

ROLE OF DOPAMINE STORAGE FUNCTION IN THE CONTROL OF RAT STRIATAL TYROSINE-HYDROXYLASE ACTIVITY.
000201 01-03

THE EFFECT OF DELTA9 TETRAHYDROCANNABINOL ON THE POSITIVE AND NEGATIVE FEEDBACK CONTROL OF LUTEINIZING-HORMONE RELEASE.
000286 01-03

BEHAVIORAL-PHARMACOLOGY AND THE STIMULUS CONTROL OF BEHAVIOR.
000381 01-04

STIMULUS INTENSITY CONTROL IN DEPRESSION: A STUDY OF THE COMPARATIVE-EFFECT OF DOXEPIN AND AMITRIPTYLINE ON CORTICAL EVOKED-POTENTIALS.
000763 01-13

RAPID CONTROL OF ACUTE PATIENTS THROUGH THE ADMINISTRATION OF HALOPERIDOL.
000818 01-14

RESPONSIVENESS TO VASOACTIVE-AGENTS OF CEREBRAL-ARTERIES AND MESENTERIC-ARTERIES ISOLATED FROM CONTROL AND RESERPINE TREATED DOGS.
001273 02-03

INTERNEURONES ARE PROBABLY NOT INVOLVED IN THE PRESYNAPTIC DOPAMINERGIC CONTROL OF DOPAMINE RELEASE IN RABBIT CAUDATE-NUCLEUS.
001298 02-03

A PHARMACOLOGICAL ANALYSIS OF THE ROLE OF THE AMYGDALA IN THE CONTROL OF GONADOTROPIN AND PROLACTIN SECRETION.
001418 02-03

CENTRAL PHARMACOLOGICAL CONTROL OF CORTICOSTERONE SECRETION IN THE INTACT RAT. DEMONSTRATION OF CHOLINERGIC AND SEROTONINERGIC FACILITATORY AND ALPHA-ADRENERGIC INHIBITORY MECHANISMS.
001487 02-03

THE EFFECTS OF D LYSERGIC-ACID-DIETHYLAMIDE (LSD), 2,5 DIMETHOXY-4-METHYLAMPHETAMINE (DOM) AND D-AMPHETAMINE ON OPERANT-RESPONDING IN CONTROL AND 6 HYDROXYDOPAMINE TREATED RATS.
001595 02-04

ADRENERGIC MODULATION OF THE HYPOTHALAMIC CHOLINERGIC MECHANISM IN THE CONTROL OF EMOTIONAL DEFENSIVE-BEHAVIOR IN THE CAT.
001761 02-04

A TRIPEPTIDE FOR CONTROL OF SCHIZOPHRENIC-SYMPTOMS.
001919 02-08

THYMOANALEPTIC TREATMENT CONTROL THROUGH MEASUREMENT OF PLASMA CONCENTRATIONS OF AMITRIPTYLINE AND ITS METABOLITE NORTRIPTYLINE.
002304 02-13

INTRAVENOUS CHLORIMIPRAMINE AFFECTS REM CYCLE IN PATIENTS WITH EXCESSIVE DAYTIME SLEEPINESS AND CONTROL SUBJECTS.
002341 02-14

A SIMPLE SYSTEM FOR CONTROL OF THE CONTINUOUS PERFORMANCE TEST IN PSYCHOPHARMACOLOGICAL-RESEARCH.
002474 02-16

MEASUREMENT OF PLASMA CONCENTRATIONS OF DRUGS AS A FEEDBACK CONTROL MECHANISM DURING DRUG-THERAPY.
002525 02-17

GABAERGIC MECHANISMS IN THE CONTROL OF PRL AND GH RELEASE.
002690 03-03

CONTROLLED-COMPARISON OF MIANSERINE WITH IMIPRAMINE IN ENDOGENOUS DEPRESSIONS.
000634 01-09
CONTROLLED-COMPARISON OF THE THERAPEUTIC EFFECTS OF NATRIUM-OXYBUTYRATE AND OXAZEPAM.
000658 01-10
CONTROLLED-COMPARISON OF PERPHENAZINE WITH PERPHENAZINE IN SCHIZOPHRENIA: A METHODICAL-CHECK OF A DOUBLE-BLIND CROSS-OVER DESIGN.
001937 02-08
LONG-TERM CONTROLLED-COMPARISON OF INJECTION OXYPROTHEPIN AND FLUPHENAZINE-DECANOATES IN PSYCHOTICS IN REMISSION.
001949 02-08
THE USE OF CLOROTEPIN AND DIAZEPAM IN A COMPLEX THERAPY OF NEUROSES (CONTROLLED-COMPARISON).
002064 02-10
THERAPEUTIC EFFECT OF MIANSERINE AND IMIPRAMINE IN ENDOGENOUS DEPRESSIONS (CONTROLLED-COMPARISON).
003264 03-09

CONTROLLED-RELEASE
STEADY-STATE LITHIUM BLOOD LEVEL FLUCTUATIONS IN MAN FOLLOWING ADMINISTRATION OF A LITHIUM-CARBONATE CONVENTIONAL AND CONTROLLED-RELEASE DOSAGE FORM.
003151 03-07

CONTROLLED-STUDY
CLINICAL COMPARISON OF OXYPROTHEPIN AND CLOTEPINE IN SCHIZOPHRENIC-PATIENTS (CONTROLLED-STUDY).
000568 01-08
KETAZOLAM AND DIAZEPAM IN ANXIETY: A CONTROLLED-STUDY.
000655 01-10
DISCONTINUATION OF ORAL AND DEPOT FLUPHENAZINE IN SCHIZOPHRENIC-PATIENTS AFTER ONE YEAR OF CONTINUOUS MEDICATION: A CONTROLLED-STUDY.
001931 02-08
NOMIFENSINE IN THE TREATMENT OF ENDOGENOUS DEPRESSION. A CONTROLLED-STUDY VS. NORTRIPTYLINE.
001978 02-09
DOUBLE-BLIND CONTROLLED-STUDY: AMINEPTINE VERSUS TRIMIPRAMINE.
002051 02-09
PROPRANOLOL IN CHRONIC ANXIETY-DISORDERS: A CONTROLLED-STUDY.
002073 02-10
DOUBLE-BLIND CONTROLLED-STUDY ON THE PSYCHOLEPTIC-EFFECTS OF AMINEPTINE IN MENTALLY-HANDICAPPED CHILDREN WITHOUT PERSONALITY-PROBLEMS.
002116 02-11
CONTROLLED-STUDY WITH BROMAZEPAM AND CLOROTEPIN IN CHILD INSTABILITY.
002190 02-11
AMOXAPINE AND IMIPRAMINE IN THE TREATMENT OF DEPRESSED-OUTPATIENTS: A CONTROLLED-STUDY.
003254 03-09
A CLINICAL, CONTROLLED-STUDY OF L ALPHA ACETYLMETHADOL IN THE TREATMENT OF NARCOTIC ADDICTION.
003335 03-11
IMIPRAMINE TREATMENT OF BORDERLINE-CHILDREN: CASE-REPORTS WITH A CONTROLLED-STUDY.
003356 03-11
A CONTROLLED-STUDY OF L-DOPA IN SCHIZOPHRENIA WITH REFERENCE TO THE THEORY OF DOPAMINERGIC-RECEPTOR HYPERSENSITIVITY.
004312 04-08

CONTROLLED-SUBSTANCES-ACT
GUIDELINES FOR SCHEDULING DRUGS UNDER THE CONTROLLED-SUBSTANCES-ACT.
003606 03-17

CONTROLLED-TRIAL
ANTIDEPRESSIVE TREATMENT IN PARKINSONS-DISEASE: A CONTROLLED-TRIAL OF THE EFFECT OF NORTRIPTYLINE IN PATIENTS WITH PARKINSONS-DISEASE TREATED WITH L-DOPA.
000659 01-11
A CONTROLLED-TRIAL OF BEHAVIOR-MODIFICATION AND METHYLPHENIDATE IN HYPERACTIVE-CHILDREN.
000678 01-11
CONTROLLED-TRIAL OF BEHAVIOUR-THERAPY, PHARMACOTHERAPY, AND THEIR COMBINATION IN THE TREATMENT OF OBESITY.
000725 01-11
CONTROLLED-TRIAL OF SULPIRIDE IN CHRONIC SCHIZOPHRENIC-PATIENTS.
001914 02-08
ANXIETY AND SEDATION DURING A STRESSFUL-SITUATION AFTER SINGLE-DOSE OF DIAZEPAM VERSUS N DESMETHYLDIAZEPAM -- A CONTROLLED-TRIAL.
002329 02-14
A CONTROLLED-TRIAL OF OXYPERTINE IN TARDIVE-DYSKINESIA.
004611 04-15

CONTROLLING
BRAIN LOCATIONS CONTROLLING THE BEHAVIORAL-EFFECTS OF CHRONIC AMPHETAMINE INTOXICATION.
001653 02-04

COMPARISON OF PSYCHOTROPIC-DRUG, RESPONSE COST, AND PSYCHOTROPIC-DRUG PLUS RESPONSE COST PROCEDURES FOR CONTROLLING INSTITUTIONALIZED MENTALLY-RETARDED PERSONS.
004438 04-11

CONTROLS
DOES SYSTEMIC MORPHINE INCREASE DESCENDING INHIBITORY CONTROLS OF DORSAL-HORN NEURONES INVOLVED IN NOCICEPTION?
000175 01-03
ACTH4-10 AND MEMORY IN ECT TREATED PATIENTS AND UNTREATED CONTROLS. II. EFFECT ON RETRIEVAL.
001983 02-09
EVALUATION OF NOMIFENSINE IN THE TREATMENT OF GERIATRIC DEPRESSION USING PSYCHOMETRIC-TESTS AND PLASMA LEVEL CONTROLS.
002004 02-09
BEHAVIORAL CONFIRMATION OF DIFFUSE NOXIOUS INHIBITORY CONTROLS (DNIC) AND EVIDENCE FOR A ROLE OF ENDOGENOUS OPIATES.
002791 03-03
5 HYDROXYTRYPTAMINE CONTROLS ACH-RECEPTOR SENSITIVITY OF BULLFROG SYMPATHETIC GANGLION CELLS.
003710 04-03
PROLACTIN AND GROWTH-HORMONE STUDIES IN SCHIZOPHRENIC-PATIENTS AND NORMAL CONTROLS.
004538 04-13

CONVALESCING
SEXUAL-DIFFICULTIES AMONG CONVALESCING ALCOHOLICS: INTEREST IN PRAZEPAM TREATMENT IN 30 CASES.
003296 03-11

CONVERGENCES
CONVERGENCES AND DIVERGENCES BETWEEN BIOLOGICAL-PSYCHIATRY AND PSYCHOTHERAPY.
002536 02-17

CONVERGENT
CONVERGENT PROPERTIES AND CHEMICAL SENSITIVITY OF MIDBRAIN RETICULAR FORMATION NEURONS OF UNANESTHETIZED RABBITS.
003972 04-03

CONVERSATION
HUMAN SOCIAL CONVERSATION: EFFECTS OF ETHANOL, SECOBARBITAL AND CHLORPROMAZINE.
004582 04-14

CONVERSION
THE CONVERSION OF (3H)TRYPTOPHAN TO 5 (3H)HYDROXYTRYPTAMINE IN MOUSE-BRAIN FOLLOWING DEPLETION OF PHENYLALANINE AND TYROSINE.
000148 01-03
CONVERSION SCALES FOR COMMONLY REQUESTED SERUM CONCENTRATIONS OF DRUGS AND OTHER SUBSTANCES OF THERAPEUTIC AND TOXICOLOGICAL IMPORTANCE, AND OF HORMONES.
000759 01-13

CONVERTING
CAPTOPRIL GIVEN INTRACEREBROVENTRICULARLY, SUBCUTANEOUSLY OR BY GAVAGE INHIBITS ANGIOTENSIN CONVERTING ENZYME ACTIVITY IN THE RAT-BRAIN.
001614 02-04

CONVULSANT
REDUCTION OF GAMMA AMINOBUTYRIC-ACID-MEDIATED (GABA) TRANSMISSION BY A CONVULSANT BENZODIAZEPINE.
000015 01-02
SYSTEMIC DIPIPERIDINOETHANE MIMICS THE CONVULSANT AND NEUROTOXIC-ACTIONS OF KAINIC-ACID.
000222 01-03
CONVULSANT AND ANTICONVULSANT BARBITURATES. 1. MOLECULAR CONFORMATIONS FROM CLASSICAL POTENTIAL ENERGY CALCULATIONS.
001029 02-01
REPEATED ELECTROCONVULSIVE-SHOCK DOES NOT INCREASE THE SUSCEPTIBILITY OF RATS TO A CAGE CONVULSANT (ISOPROPYLBICYCLOPHOSPHATE).
001184 02-03
CONVULSANT AND ANTICONVULSANT-DRUG BINDING-SITES RELATED TO GABA REGULATED CHLORIDE ION-CHANNELS.
002848 03-03
KETAMINE: CONVULSANT OR ANTICONVULSANT?
003060 03-04
STIMULATION OF FRUCTOSEBIPHOSPHATASE ACTIVITY AND SYNTHESIS IN THE CEREBRAL-CORTEX OF RATS SUBMITTED TO THE CONVULSANT METHIONINE-SULFOXIMINE.
003838 04-03

CONVULSANT-AGENTS
REGULATION OF THE STATE OF PHOSPHORYLATION OF SPECIFIC NEURONAL PROTEINS IN MOUSE-BRAIN BY IN VIVO ADMINISTRATION OF ANESTHETIC AND CONVULSANT-AGENTS.
000291 01-03

CONVULSANT-EFFECT
ON THE MEASUREMENT IN RATS OF THE CONVULSANT-EFFECT OF DRUGS AND THE CHANGES WHICH FOLLOW ELECTROCONVULSIVE-SHOCK.
002444 02-15

Subject Index

CONVULSANT-EFFECTS
CONVULSANT-EFFECTS OF AMINOOXYACETIC-ACID DURING ONTOGENESIS IN RATS.
001439 02-03

CONVULSANTS
CONVULSANTS ANTAGONISE INHIBITION IN THE OLFACTORY-CORTEX SLICE.
001466 02-03
AMINOPHYLLINE AND IMIDAZOLE AS CONVULSANTS.
004232 04-04

CONVULSION
EFFECTS OF KINDLING OR BRAIN-STIMULATION ON PENTYLENETETRAZOL-INDUCED CONVULSION SUSCEPTIBILITY.
000037 01-03

CONVULSIONS
EFFECTS OF GAMMA ACETYLENIC-GABA AND GAMMA VINYL-GABA ON ELECTRICALLY-INDUCED SPINAL-CORD CONVULSIONS AND ON SPINAL-CORD GABA CONCENTRATION.
000145 01-03
INVOLVEMENT OF CENTRAL CHOLINOCEPTORS IN METRAZOL-INDUCED CONVULSIONS.
000247 01-03
PRODUCTION OF CONVULSIONS IN MICE BY THE COMBINATION OF METHIONINE AND HOMOCYSTEINE.
001233 02-03
EFFECT OF ERGOT DERIVATIVES ON POSTDECAPITATION CONVULSIONS.
001288 02-03
HOMOCYSTEINE-INDUCED CONVULSIONS: ENHANCEMENT BY VITAMIN-B6 AND INHIBITION BY HYDRAZINE.
002758 03-03
INCORPORATION OF N ACETYLMANNOSAMINE INTO RAT-BRAIN SUBCELLULAR GANGLIOSIDES: EFFECT OF PENTYLENETETRAZOL-INDUCED CONVULSIONS IN BRAIN GANGLIOSIDES.
002937 03-03
BRAIN AND SERUM CALCIUM CONCENTRATIONS FOLLOWING ELECTROCONVULSIVE-SHOCK OR BICUCULLINE-INDUCED CONVULSIONS IN RATS.
003736 04-03
PYRAZOLE EXACERBATES HANDLING-INDUCED CONVULSIONS IN MICE.
004094 04-04
BEHAVIORAL-PHARMACOLOGY OF TETRAHYDROCANNABINOL CONVULSIONS IN RABBITS.
004288 04-06

CONVULSIVE
EFFECTS OF ANTICONVULSANTS AND GLUTAMATE ANTAGONISTS ON THE CONVULSIVE ACTION OF KAINIC-ACID.
000288 01-03
LOCOMOTOR AND CONVULSIVE RESPONSES TO PICROTOXIN IN AMYGDALA KINDLED RATS.
000416 01-04
LOWERING OF THE CONVULSIVE THRESHOLD BY NONSTEROIDAL ANTIINFLAMMATORY-DRUGS.
002904 03-03
THE ROLE OF GABA-MEDIATED NEUROTRANSMISSION IN CONVULSIVE STATE .
003334 03-11
CONVULSIVE AND DRUG-THERAPIES OF DEPRESSION.
004366 04-09

CONVULSIVE-SEIZURE
ON THE MECHANISM OF A DIFFERENT DRUG DISTRIBUTION DURING CONVULSIVE-SEIZURE IN COMPARISON TO ANESTHESIA.
001151 02-03
ON SOME RELATIONSHIPS BETWEEN GABAERGIC AND 5 HT-ERGIC MECHANISMS IN PENTYLENETETRAZOL CONVULSIVE-SEIZURE REACTIONS.
004166 04-04

CONVULSIVE-SHOCK-TREATMENT
REDUCTION IN OPIATE ACTIVATION AFTER CHRONIC ELECTROCONVULSIVE-SHOCK -- POSSIBLE ROLE FOR ENDORPHINS IN THE BEHAVIORAL-EFFECTS OF CONVULSIVE-SHOCK-TREATMENT. (UNPUBLISHED PAPER).
004154 04-04

COOLING
THE EFFECT OF PHARMACOLOGICAL DESTRUCTION OF HYPOTHALAMIC MONOAMINERGIC STRUCTURES ON BODY-TEMPERATURE AND GAS-EXCHANGE DURING EXTREME COOLING.
004016 04-03

COOPERATIVE
EFFECTS OF DOPAMINERGIC AGONISTS AND ANTAGONISTS ON (3H)APOMORPHINE BINDING TO STRIATAL MEMBRANES: SULPIRIDE LACK OF INTERACTIONS WITH POSITIVE COOPERATIVE (3H)APOMORPHINE BINDING.
000099 01-03
COOPERATIVE PSYCHIATRIC-STUDY OF ALIVAL: PRELIMINARY RESULTS.
002045 02-09

COOPERATIVELY
EVIDENCE FOR, AND LOCALIZATION OF, A UNITARY DOPAMINE-RECEPTOR COMPOSED OF COOPERATIVELY LINKED SUBUNIT BINDING-SITES IN RAT STRIATUM.
000186 01-03

CORTICAL RECOVERY FROM EFFECTS OF MONOCULAR DEPRIVATION:
ACCELERATION WITH NOREPINEPHRINE AND SUPPRESSION WITH 6
HYDROXYDOPAMINE.
003024 03-04
CORTICAL CONTROL OF NEURALLY MEDIATED ARRHYTHMOGENIC-
PROPERTIES OF DESACETYLLANATOSIDE-C.
003124 03-05
CORTICAL EVOKED-POTENTIALS IN GILLES-DE-LA-TOURETTES-SYNDROME
-- A SINGLE CASE-STUDY.
003431 03-13
THYROXIN SENSITIVITY OF SENSORIMOTOR CORTICAL NEURONS AND THE
HYPOTHALAMIC VENTROMEDIAL NUCLEUS.
003713 04-03
THE EFFECT OF LONG-TERM CONCURRENT ADMINISTRATION OF
CHLORPROMAZINE AND LITHIUM ON THE STRIATAL AND FRONTAL
CORTICAL DOPAMINE METABOLISM IN RATS.
003788 04-03
INVESTIGATION OF ACTION OF ENKEPHALIN ON THE SPONTANEOUS AND
EVOKED RELEASE OF ACETYLCHOLINE FROM RAT CORTICAL AND
STRIATAL SLICES.
003862 04-03
CORRELATIONS BETWEEN NA-K-ATPASE ACTIVITY AND ACETYLCHOLINE
RELEASE IN RAT CORTICAL SYNAPTOSOMES.
003937 04-03
CORTICAL-CORRELATES
CORTICAL-CORRELATES OF VIGILANCE REGULATION AND THEIR USE IN
EVALUATING THE EFFECTS OF TREATMENT.
002147 02-11
CORTICOCEREBRAL
ACCELERATION OF DESIPRAMINE-INDUCED DECREASE OF RAT
CORTICOCEREBRAL BETA-ADRENERGIC-RECEPTORS BY YOHIMBINE.
000326 01-03
CORTICOSTERIODS
PLASMA CORTICOSTERIODS IN MANIA: THE EFFECTS OF PIMOZIDE.
004363 04-09
CORTICOSTEROID
SIDE-EFFECTS OF CORTICOSTEROID THERAPY: PSYCHIATRIC-ASPECTS.
003508 03-15
CORTICOSTEROIDS
THE EFFECT OF ANTIDEPRESSANTS ON L 5 HTP-INDUCED CHANGES IN RAT
PLASMA CORTICOSTEROIDS.
000170 01-03
RELATIONSHIPS BETWEEN PLASMA CORTICOSTEROIDS AND
BENZODIAZEPINES IN STRESS.
000176 01-03
BENZODIAZEPINES, STRESS AND RAT PLASMA CORTICOSTEROIDS: THE
ROLE OF INDOLEAMINES.
003034 03-04
CORTICOSTERONE
CHANGES IN PLASMA CORTICOSTERONE LEVELS AS A MEASURE OF
ACUTE DEPENDENCE UPON LEVORPHANOL IN RATS.
000085 01-03
THE SENSITIVITY OF THE RAT CORTICOSTERONE RESPONSE TO
ENVIRONMENTAL MANIPULATIONS AND TO CHRONIC
CHLORDIAZEPOXIDE TREATMENT.
000092 01-03
EFFECTS OF PERINATAL THYROXINE AND/OR CORTICOSTERONE
TREATMENT ON THE ONTOGENESIS OF HYPOTHALAMIC AND
MESENCEPHALIC NOREPINEPHRINE AND DOPAMINE CONTENT.
000180 01-03
LONG-TERM EFFECT OF NEUROLEPTICS ON CORTICOSTERONE
SEPTOHIPPOCAMPAL UPTAKE IN RATS.
001107 02-03
CORTICOSTERONE INCREASES THE SYNTHESIS OF A SOLUBLE PROTEIN IN
PITUITARY-GLANDS FROM ADRENALECTOMIZED MALE RATS WHICH
PRECIPITATES WITH ANTI-RAT GROWTH-HORMONE ANTISERUM.
(UNPUBLISHED PAPER).
001122 02-03
LEUCINE-ENKEPHALIN AND METHIONINE-ENKEPHALIN PRODUCE OPPOSING
EFFECTS ON PLASMA CORTICOSTERONE LEVELS IN ETHER-STRESSED
MICE.
001245 02-03
THE EFFECT OF REPEATED ELECTROCONVULSIVE-SHOCK ON
CORTICOSTERONE RESPONSES TO CENTRALLY-ACTING
PHARMACOLOGICAL STIMULI IN THE MALE RAT.
001486 02-03
CENTRAL PHARMACOLOGICAL CONTROL OF CORTICOSTERONE SECRETION
IN THE INTACT RAT. DEMONSTRATION OF CHOLINERGIC AND
SEROTONINERGIC FACILITATORY AND ALPHA-ADRENERGIC INHIBITORY
MECHANISMS.
001487 02-03
EFFECT OF BROMOCRIPTINE ON EXPLORATORY-ACTIVITY, BRAIN-
MONOAMINES AND PLASMA CORTICOSTERONE IN THE
NORMOTENSIVE-RATS, GENETICALLY HYPERTENSIVE-RATS AND/OR
HYPERTENSIVE OBESE RATS.
001635 02-04
BRAIN GLUCOCORTICOID-RECEPTOR: CORRELATION OF IN VIVO UPTAKE
OF CORTICOSTERONE WITH BEHAVIORAL-EVENTS, ENDOCRINE-EVENTS,
AND NEUROPHARMACOLOGICAL EVENTS.
002515 02-17

DIFFERENTIAL-EFFECTS OF CANNABINOID EXPOSURE AND STRESS ON
PLASMA PROLACTIN, GROWTH-HORMONE AND CORTICOSTERONE
LEVELS IN MALE MICE.
002695 03-03
INTRAVENTRICULAR CORTICOSTERONE INJECTION FACILITATES MEMORY
OF AN APPETITIVE DISCRIMINATIVE TASK IN MICE.
003051 03-04
EFFECT OF AMPHETAMINE ON PLASMA CORTICOSTERONE IN THE
CONSCIOUS RAT.
003888 04-03
CORTICOSTRIATAL
A NOVEL GABA-RECEPTOR MODULATES STIMULUS-INDUCED GLUTAMATE
RELEASE FROM CORTICOSTRIATAL TERMINALS.
001376 02-03
CORTICOTROPIN
EFFECT OF TREATMENT WITH SODIUM-VALPROATE AND DIAZEPAM ON
PLASMA CORTICOTROPIN IN NELSONS-SYNDROME.
004463 04-11
CORTISOL
THE EFFECT OF CORTISOL MICROIONOPHORETIC-APPLICATIONS ON THE
ACTIVITY OF HIPPOCAMPAL NEURONS IN UNRESTRAINED RABBITS.
001123 02-03
EFFECTS OF NALOXONE UPON PROLACTIN AND CORTISOL IN NORMAL
WOMEN.
002213 02-13
MOOD AND BEHAVIORAL-EFFECTS OF PHYSOSTIGMINE ON HUMANS ARE
ACCOMPANIED BY ELEVATIONS IN PLASMA BETA ENDORPHIN AND
CORTISOL.
002280 02-13
PSYCHOTROPIC-DRUGS DO NOT INTERFERE WITH RADIOLIGAND ASSAYS
FOR PROLACTIN, CORTISOL, AND GROWTH-HORMONE.
002511 02-16
TSH, HGH, HPR, AND CORTISOL RESPONSE TO TRH IN DEPRESSED-
PATIENTS.
004399 04-09
CORTISOL DYNAMICS AND DEXAMETHASONE PHARMACOKINETICS IN
PRIMARY ENDOGENOUS DEPRESSION: PRELIMINARY FINDINGS.
004403 04-09
COST
COMPARISON OF PSYCHOTROPIC-DRUG, RESPONSE COST, AND
PSYCHOTROPIC-DRUG PLUS RESPONSE COST PROCEDURES FOR
CONTROLLING INSTITUTIONALIZED MENTALLY-RETARDED PERSONS.
004438 04-11
COTARDS-SYNDROME
BETA ENDORPHIN IN COTARDS-SYNDROME.
003187 03-08
COUNT
THE SPECIFIC ACTIVITY OF PLATELET MONOAMINE-OXIDASE VARIES
WITH PLATELET COUNT DURING SEVERE EXERCISE AND
NORADRENALINE INFUSION.
004509 04-13
COUNTERACT
PLASMA LEVELS OF BETA ENDORPHIN UNDER CHRONIC NEUROLEPTIC
TREATMENT IN SCHIZOPHRENIC-PATIENTS: FAILURE OF NALOXONE TO
COUNTERACT CURATIVE EFFECTS OF NEUROLEPTIC-DRUGS.
004321 04-08
COUNTERTRANSPORT
NA-DEPENDENT LI COUNTERTRANSPORT AND THE LITHIUM DISTRIBUTION
ACROSS THE HUMAN ERYTHROCYTE MEMBRANE: INTRODUCTION.
002227 02-13
COUNTRIES
CLINICAL-EXPERIENCE WITH SUBSTITUTED BENZAMIDES IN FRENCH-
SPEAKING COUNTRIES.
002036 02-09
COUPLED
SUBSENSITIVITY OF THE NOREPINEPHRINE-RECEPTOR COUPLED
ADENYLATE-CYCLASE SYSTEM IN BRAIN: EFFECTS OF NISOXETINE
VERSUS FLUOXETINE.
000208 01-03
MULTIPLE BENZODIAZEPINE-RECEPTOR COMPLEXES: SOME
BENZODIAZEPINE RECOGNITION SITES ARE COUPLED TO GABA-
RECEPTORS AND IONOPHORES.
001484 02-03
FUNCTIONAL ASPECTS OF THE NOREPINEPHRINE-RECEPTOR COUPLED
ADENYLATE-CYCLASE SYSTEM IN THE CENTRAL-NERVOUS-SYSTEM.
001493 02-03
COUPLING
TOLERANCE TO BARBITURATE-INDUCED CENTRAL-NERVOUS-SYSTEM
DEPRESSION: INVOLVEMENT OF STIMULUS SECRETION COUPLING IN
DISCRETE BRAIN AREAS. (PH.D. DISSERTATION).
001213 02-03
COVALENTLY-BONDED
THIOLS LIBERATE COVALENTLY-BONDED FLAVIN FROM MONOAMINE-
OXIDASE. (UNPUBLISHED PAPER).
001060 02-01
COVARIANCE
COVARIANCE OF PLASMA FREE 3 METHOXY-4-
HYDROXYPHENETHYLENEGLYCOL AND DIASTOLIC BLOOD-PRESSURE.
003418 03-13

COVERT
COVERT DYSKINESIA IN AMBULATORY SCHIZOPHRENIA.
000836 01-15

COYOTE
EFFECT OF LITHIUM-CHLORIDE IN COYOTE PUP DIET.
001835 02-05

CPK
TWO CASES OF FORM-FRUSTE-DU-SYNDROME-MALIN WITH HIGH-LEVELS
OF SERUM CPK.
004636 04-15

CPZ
LOW ORAL CPZ BIOAVAILABILITY IN CHRONIC SCHIZOPHRENIA.
(UNPUBLISHED PAPER).
001938 02-08

CR
CONDITIONED SUPPRESSION OF DRINKING: A MEASURE OF THE CR
ELICITED BY A LITHIUM CONDITIONED FLAVOR.
001747 02-04

CRAB
MECHANICAL-CHANGES IN CRAB NERVE FIBERS DURING ACTION
POTENTIALS. (UNPUBLISHED PAPER).
001505 02-03

CREATININE
STRUCTURE-ACTIVITY RELATIONSHIPS IN THE EFFECTS OF PHENACEMIDE
ANALOGS ON SERUM CREATININE AND ANTICONVULSANT ACTIVITY.
000249 01-03

CREATIVE-PROCESS
PSYCHEDELIC-DRUGS AND THE CREATIVE-PROCESS.
002199 02-12

CRIME
VOLUNTARY INTOXICATION FROM PHENCYCLIDINE. WILL IT RAISE A
REASONABLE-DOUBT OF THE MENTAL-CAPACITY OF A PERSON
CHARGED WITH A CRIME REQUIRING SPECIFIC INTENT OR MENTAL-
STATE?.
000914 01-17

PCP AND VIOLENT CRIME: THE PEOPLE VS. PEACE.
000986 01-17

CRIMINAL
CYCLICAL CRIMINAL ACTS IN PREMENSTRUAL-SYNDROME.
000927 01-17

CRIMINALLY-INSANE-OFFENDERS
RECIDIVISM AND REHABILITATION RATES FOR 135 CRIMINALLY-INSANE-
OFFENDERS. (D.ED. DISSERTATION).
002514 02-17

CRITERIA
CRITERIA FOR CLINICAL DEVELOPMENT AND CLASSIFICATION OF
NOOTROPIC-DRUGS. AN EXAMPLE: PIRACETAM.
000988 01-17

PREDICTIVE CRITERIA FOR LITHIUM-SALTS ACTIVITY.
002619 02-17

AMINE UPTAKE INHIBITORS: CRITERIA OF SELECTIVITY.
003921 04-03

THE USE OF CLINICAL AND PHARMACOKINETIC CRITERIA IN FORECASTING
THE EFFICACY OF THERAPY IN SCHIZOPHRENIA.
004335 04-08

CROSS-OVER
MAINTENANCE-THERAPY WITH FLUPHENAZINE-DECANOATE AND
OXYPROTHEPINE-DECANOATE IN SCHIZOPHRENIC-PATIENTS -- A
DOUBLE-BLIND CROSS-OVER COMPARATIVE-STUDY.
001924 02-08

CONTROLLED-COMPARISON OF PERPHENAZINE WITH PERPHENAZINE IN
SCHIZOPHRENIA: A METHODICAL-CHECK OF A DOUBLE-BLIND CROSS-
OVER DESIGN.
001937 02-08

CROSS-OVER STUDY OF ZIMELIDINE AND DESIPRAMINE IN DEPRESSION:
EVIDENCE FOR AMINE SPECIFICITY.
003250 03-09

A DOUBLE-BLIND, PLACEBO-CONTROLLED, CROSS-OVER TRIAL OF
CARBAMAZEPINE IN OVERACTIVE, SEVERELY MENTALLY-
HANDICAPPED PATIENTS.
003365 03-11

CROSS-STUDY
COMPARATIVE CROSS-STUDY ON THE EFFECTS OF AMINEPTINE AND
MAPROTILINE.
002065 02-10

CROSS-TOLERANCE
CHLORDIAZEPOXIDE ANTINOCICEPTION: CROSS-TOLERANCE WITH
OPIATES AND WITH STRESS.
000348 01-04

TOLERANCE TO SUPPRESSIVE EFFECTS OF CHLORDIAZEPOXIDE ON
OPERANT-BEHAVIOR: LACK OF CROSS-TOLERANCE TO PENTOBARBITAL.
000356 01-04

CROSS-TOLERANCE OF DOPAMINE METABOLISM TO BACLOFEN, GAMMA
BUTYROLACTONE AND HA-966 IN THE STRIATUM AND OLFACTORY
TUBERCLE OF THE RAT.
002681 03-03

DEVELOPMENT OF TOLERANCE TO THE EXCITATORY EFFECT OF MORPHINE
AND CROSS-TOLERANCE TO THE INHIBITORY ACTION OF BETA
ENDORPHIN IN THE ISOLATED RAT VAS-DEFERENS.
002756 03-03

ELECTROENCEPHALOGRAPHIC AND BEHAVIORAL-TOLERANCE TO AND
CROSS-TOLERANCE BETWEEN D ALA2-METHIONINE-ENKEPHALINAMIDE
AND MORPHINE IN THE RAT.
004038 04-03

CROSSED
SENSITIVE DEPRESSANT EFFECT OF BENZODIAZEPINES ON THE CROSSED
EXTENSOR REFLEX IN CHLORALOSE ANESTHETIZED RATS.
003027 03-04

A DOUBLE-BLIND CROSSED CLINICAL-STUDY WITH A NEW
PSYCHOPHARMACEUTICAL: TIADIPONE (QM-6008), DIAZEPAM, AND
A PLACEBO.
003153 03-07

CROSSING
EFFECTS OF SINGLE-ORAL-DOSAGES OF STEROIDS ON HUMAN EEG
BASELINE CROSSING T-SCORES SHOWN BY MULTIVARIATE STATISTICS
AND STANDARD PROFILES.
002239 02-13

CROSSROADS
MIND/BRAIN IN THE AGE OF PSYCHOPHARMACOLOGY: A CROSSROADS
FOR MEDICINE AND MINISTRY.
003624 03-17

CROWDING
SOCIAL CROWDING ENHANCES AVERSIVENESS OF NALOXONE IN RATS.
004201 04-04

CRYSTAL
THE CRYSTAL AND MOLECULAR STRUCTURE OF THE ACETYLCHOLINE
ANTAGONIST DIMETHYLAMINOBUTYNYLCYCLOHEXYLHYDROXY 2
PHENYLACETATE HCL.
000003 01-01

THE CRYSTAL AND MOLECULAR STRUCTURE OF THE NEUROLEPTIC
PIMOZIDE-HYDROCHLORIDE, BISFLUOROPHENYL-
BUTYLPIPERIDYLBENZIMIDAZOLINONE-HCL.
001015 02-01

CS
ETHANOL AVERSION INDUCED BY PARENTERALLY ADMINISTERED
ETHANOL ACTING BOTH AS CS AND UCS.
001721 02-04

CSEEG
COMPUTERIZED SLEEP EEG (CSEEG) IN PSYCHIATRY AND
PSYCHOPHARMACOLOGY.
002614 02-17

CSF
PRELIMINARY-STUDIES ON CSF GAMMA AMINOBUTYRIC-ACID LEVELS IN
PSYCHIATRIC-PATIENTS BEFORE AND DURING TREATMENT WITH
DIFFERENT PSYCHOTROPIC-DRUGS.
001959 02-08

INCREASED CSF GAMMA AMINOBUTYRIC-ACID AFTER TREATMENT WITH
GAMMA VINYL-GABA.
002237 02-13

TREATMENT OF HUNTINGTON-DISEASE WITH GAMMA ACETYLENIC-
GABA, AN IRREVERSIBLE INHIBITOR OF GABA-TRANSAMINASE:
INCREASED CSF GABA AND HOMOCARNOSINE WITHOUT CLINICAL
AMELIORATION.
003458 03-14

CU-AMINE-OXIDASES
CU-AMINE-OXIDASES: STUDIES RELATED TO THE MECHANISM-OF-ACTION
OF BOVINE PLASMA AMINE-OXIDASE (UNPUBLISHED PAPER).
003680 04-01

CUE
EVIDENCE THAT A PREFERRED SUBSTRATE FOR MONOAMINE-OXIDASE-B
MEDIATES STIMULUS PROPERTIES OF MAO-INHIBITORS; A POSSIBLE
ROLE FOR BETA PHENYLETHYLAMINE IN THE COCAINE CUE.
000363 01-04

FACTORS REGULATING DRUG CUE SENSITIVITY: LIMITS OF
DISCRIMINABILITY AND THE ROLE OF A PROGRESSIVELY DECREASING
TRAINING DOSE IN FENTANYL SALINE DISCRIMINATION.
004088 04-04

CUES
TEMPORAL AND ENVIRONMENTAL CUES IN CONDITIONED HYPOTHERMIA
AND HYPERTHERMIA ASSOCIATED WITH MORPHINE.
002709 03-03

CULTIVATION
THE EFFECT OF CHLORPROMAZINE AND MAGEPTIL ON THE
PROLIFERATION OF PERIPHERAL BLOOD LYMPHOCYTES IN CULTIVATION
WITH PHYTOHEMAGGLUTININ.
004541 04-13

CULTURE
ENHANCED TRANSFER OF EXPERIMENTAL ALLERGIC-ENCEPHALOMYELITIS
WITH STRAIN-13 GUINEA-PIG LYMPH-NODE CELLS: REQUIREMENT FOR
CULTURE WITH SPECIFIC ANTIGEN AND ALLOGENIC PERITONEAL
EXUDATE CELLS. (UNPUBLISHED PAPER).
001201 02-03

STIMULATION OF THE PLASMA MEMBRANE ENZYME, 5' NUCLEOTIDASE,
BY ETHANOL EXPOSURE TO NEURAL CELLS IN CULTURE.
001499 02-03

EFFECTS OF LITHIUM ON MORPHOLOGICAL CHARACTERISTICS OF
DISSOCIATED BRAIN CELLS IN CULTURE.
002765 03-03

CULTURED

NALOXONE ANTAGONISM OF GABA-EVOKED MEMBRANE POLARIZATIONS IN CULTURED MOUSE SPINAL-CORD NEURONS.
000116 01-03

ANTICONVULSANT AND ANESTHETIC BARBITURATES: DIFFERENT POSTSYNAPTIC ACTIONS IN CULTURED MAMMALIAN NEURONS.
000194 01-03

(-)PENTOBARBITAL OPENS ION-CHANNELS OF LONG-DURATION IN CULTURED MOUSE SPINAL NEURONS.
000198 01-03

PSYCHOTROPIC-DRUGS AND HISTAMINE H1-RECEPTORS OF CULTURED MOUSE NEUROBLASTOMA CELLS.
000250 01-03

ADENOSINE REGULATES VIA TWO DIFFERENT TYPES OF RECEPTORS, THE ACCUMULATION OF CYCLIC-AMP IN CULTURED BRAIN CELLS.
000308 01-03

GABA SYNTHESIS BY CULTURED FIBROBLASTS OBTAINED FROM PERSONS WITH HUNTINGTONS-DISEASE.
000765 01-13

EXCITATORY ACTION OF OPIOID-PEPTIDES AND OPIATES ON CULTURED HIPPOCAMPAL PYRAMIDAL CELLS.
001241 02-03

TWO CONDUCTANCE MECHANISMS ACTIVATED BY APPLICATIONS OF L GLUTAMIC-ACID, L ASPARTIC-ACID, DL HOMOCYSTEIC-ACID, N METHYL-D-ASPARTIC-ACID, AND DL KAINIC-ACID TO CULTURED MAMMALIAN CENTRAL NEURONES.
001349 02-03

LITHIUM-ION ENTRY INTO CULTURED CELLS OF NEURAL ORIGIN.
001433 02-03

GABA ANALOGUES ACTIVATE CHANNELS OF DIFFERENT DURATION ON CULTURED MOUSE SPINAL NEURONS.
002665 03-03

TOXIC EFFECTS OF ALPHA AMINOADIPATE ON CULTURED CEREBELLAR CELLS.
002729 03-03

HISTAMINE ACTIONS ON ACTIVITY OF CULTURED HYPOTHALAMIC NEURONS; EVIDENCE FOR MEDIATION BY HISTAMINE H1-RECEPTORS AND H2-RECEPTORS.
002732 03-03

IDENTIFICATION OF TWO BENZODIAZEPINE BINDING-SITES ON CELLS CULTURED FROM RAT-CEREBRAL-CORTEX.
002820 03-03

EFFECTS OF D AMINOLAEVULINIC-ACID, PORPHOBILINOGEN, AMINO-ACIDS AND BARBITURATES ON CALCIUM ACCUMULATION BY CULTURED NEURONS.
002859 03-03

CULTURES

THE INFLUENCE OF EXTERNAL SODIUM AND POTASSIUM ON LITHIUM UPTAKE BY PRIMARY BRAIN CELL CULTURES AT THERAPEUTIC LITHIUM CONCENTRATION.
001300 02-03

HEPATOTOXICITY OF SODIUM-VALPROATE AND OTHER ANTICONVULSANTS IN RAT HEPATOCYTE CULTURES.
002422 02-15

NA-INDEPENDENT BINDING OF (3H)GABA AND (3H)MUSCIMOL TO SUBCELLULAR PARTICLES OF NEURAL PRIMARY CULTURES AND WHOLE BRAIN.
002699 03-03

DOXEPIN, A TRICYCLIC-ANTIDEPRESSANT, BINDS TO NORMAL, INTACT ASTROGLIAL CELLS IN CULTURES AND INHIBITS THE ISOPROTERENOL-INDUCED INCREASE IN CYCLIC-AMP PRODUCTION.
003836 04-03

THE INACTIVATION OF GAMMA AMINOBUTYRIC-ACID-TRANSAMINASE IN DISSOCIATED NEURONAL CULTURES FROM SPINAL-CORD.
003980 04-03

BENZODIAZEPINE-RECEPTORS ON PRIMARY CULTURES OF MOUSE ASTROCYTES.
004029 04-03

CUMULATIVE

CUMULATIVE DOSE RESPONSE-CURVES IN BEHAVIORAL-PHARMACOLOGY.
001883 02-06

CUMULATIVE AFTERDISCHARGE AS THE PRINCIPAL FACTOR IN THE ACQUISITION OF KINDLED SEIZURES.
002862 03-03

CUP

MODIFIED CUP TECHNIQUE FOR MICROESTIMATION OF THE RELEASE AND UPTAKE OF NEUROTRANSMITTERS IN BRAIN SLICES.
003147 03-06

CUPS

ACETYLCHOLINE AND AMINO-ACID NEUROTRANSMITTERS IN EPIDURAL CUPS OF FREELY-MOVING-RATS: EFFECT OF ACUTE AND CHRONIC-TREATMENT WITH ANTISCHIZOPHRENIC-DRUGS.
001386 02-03

CURATIVE

PLASMA LEVELS OF BETA ENDORPHIN UNDER CHRONIC NEUROLEPTIC TREATMENT IN SCHIZOPHRENIC-PATIENTS: FAILURE OF NALOXONE TO COUNTERACT CURATIVE EFFECTS OF NEUROLEPTIC-DRUGS.
004321 04-08

CURRENT-VIEWS

ACTION MECHANISMS OF INSULIN THERAPY IN PSYCHIATRY, AND CURRENT-VIEWS ON THESE MECHANISMS.
002553 02-17

CURVES

USE OF SURVIVAL CURVES IN ANALYSIS OF ANTIPSYCHOTIC RELAPSE-STUDIES.
002481 02-16

THE EFFECT OF DIPHENYLHYDANTOIN ON EEG CURVES IN EPILEPTICS.
004494 04-11

CUTANEOUS

CUTANEOUS REACTION TO LITHIUM-CARBONATE: A CASE-REPORT.
000872 01-15

DIFFERENCES IN CUTANEOUS SENSORY RESPONSE PROPERTIES OF SINGLE SOMATOSENSORY CORTICAL NEURONS IN AWAKE AND HALOTHANE ANESTHETIZED RATS.
002687 03-03

MORPHINE DEPRESSES DORSAL-HORN NEURON RESPONSES TO CONTROLLED NOXIOUS AND NONNOXIOUS CUTANEOUS STIMULATION.
003782 04-03

CYCLAZOCINE

EFFECTS OF MORPHINE, PENTAZOCINE AND CYCLAZOCINE ALONE AND IN COMBINATION WITH NALOXONE ON ELECTRIC-SHOCK TITRATION IN THE SQUIRREL-MONKEY.
001611 02-04

DISCRIMINATIVE-STIMULUS EFFECTS OF CYCLAZOCINE IN THE RAT.
004236 04-04

CYCLE

INTRAVENOUS CHLORIMIPRAMINE AFFECTS REM CYCLE IN PATIENTS WITH EXCESSIVE DAYTIME SLEEPINESS AND CONTROL SUBJECTS.
002341 02-14

EFFECTS OF REPEATED ADMINISTRATIONS OF DIHYDROERGOTOXINE (REDERGINE) ON THE SLEEP-WAKEFULNESS CYCLE IN THE CAT.
003703 04-02

CYCLIC

THE LONG-TERM-TREATMENT OF PERIODICAL AND CYCLIC DEPRESSIONS WITH FLUPENTHIXOL-DECANOATE.
000603 01-09

THE EFFECT OF DIAZEPAM ON CYCLIC EXCITABILITY CHANGES IN AN EPILEPTIC-FOCUS IN THE CORTEX OF THE MAJOR HEMISPHERES.
003984 04-03

CYCLIC-ADENOSINE-MONOPHOSPHATE

EFFECT OF NALOXONE, HALOPERIDOL AND PROPRANOLOL ON CYCLIC-ADENOSINE-MONOPHOSPHATE CONTENT OF RAT AMYGDALA.
000071 01-03

ACTION OF CYCLIC-ADENOSINE-MONOPHOSPHATE ON CENTRAL NEURONS.
002940 03-03

CYCLIC-AMIDINES

RELATIONSHIPS BETWEEN STRUCTURE AND ALPHA-ADRENERGIC-RECEPTOR AFFINITY OF CLONIDINE AND AND SOME RELATED CYCLIC-AMIDINES.
002698 03-03

CYCLIC-AMP

MECHANISM OF CHLORPROMAZINE ACTION ON PLASMA GLUCOSE AND CYCLIC-AMP LEVELS.
000211 01-03

ADENOSINE REGULATES VIA TWO DIFFERENT TYPES OF RECEPTORS, THE ACCUMULATION OF CYCLIC-AMP IN CULTURED BRAIN CELLS.
000308 01-03

CHOLERA-TOXIN-INDUCED EPILEPTOGENIC-FOCUS – SPECIAL REFERENCE TO CYCLIC-AMP METABOLISM AND EPILEPTOGENIC-FOCUS.
000522 01-05

CENTRAL LEVELS OF NORADRENALINE, 3 METHOXY-4-HYDROXYPHENYLETHYLENEGLYCOL AND CYCLIC-AMP IN THE RAT AFTER ACTIVATION OF LOCUS-COERULEUS NEURONS: INFLUENCE OF SINGLE AND REPEATED NEUROLEPTIC TREATMENT.
001095 02-03

POSSIBLE INVOLVEMENT OF CYCLIC-AMP AND FRONTAL-CORTEX IN AMITRIPTYLINE MEDIATED SUPPRESSION OF THE HYPOTENSIVE-EFFECT OF CLONIDINE.
001259 02-03

DEVELOPMENT OF AND RECOVERY FROM SUBSENSITIVITY OF THE NORADRENERGIC CYCLIC-AMP GENERATING SYSTEM IN BRAIN: EFFECT OF AMPHETAMINE FOLLOWING INHIBITION OF ITS AROMATIC HYDROXYLATION BY IPRINDOLE.
001353 02-03

BRAIN STRIATAL TYROSINE-HYDROXYLASE: ACTIVATION OF THE ENZYME BY CYCLIC-AMP INDEPENDENT PHOSPHORYLATION.
001423 02-03

CYCLIC-AMP IN PSYCHOSES AND THE EFFECT OF DRUGS.
002294 02-13

RELATIONSHIP BETWEEN THE ACTIONS OF CALCIUM-IONS, OPIOIDS, AND PROSTAGLANDIN-E1 ON THE LEVEL OF CYCLIC-AMP IN NEUROBLASTOMA-X GLIOMA HYBRID CELLS.
002677 03-03

ALPHA2-ADRENERGIC AMINES, ADENOSINE AND PROSTAGLANDINS INHIBIT LIPOLYSIS AND CYCLIC-AMP ACCUMULATION IN HAMSTER ADIPOCYTES IN THE ABSENCE OF EXTRACELLULAR SODIUM.
002728 03-03

INCREASE IN PLASMA CYCLIC-AMP LEVELS ELICITED BY NALOXONE IN MORPHINE-DEPENDENT MALE MICE.
002834 03-03

AGGRESSION ALTERING EFFECTS OF CYCLIC-AMP.
003021 03-04

PLASMA LEVEL OF CYCLIC-AMP AND MENTAL-DISEASES.
003170 03-08

DOPAMINERGIC MECHANISMS IN THE TELEOST RETINA. II. FACTORS AFFECTING THE ACCUMULATION OF CYCLIC-AMP IN PIECES OF INTACT CARP RETINA.
003776 04-03

DOXEPIN, A TRICYCLIC-ANTIDEPRESSANT, BINDS TO NORMAL, INTACT ASTROGLIAL CELLS IN CULTURES AND INHIBITS THE ISOPROTERENOL-INDUCED INCREASE IN CYCLIC-AMP PRODUCTION.
003836 04-03

CIRCADIAN-VARIATION OF CYCLIC-AMP IN THE RAT PINEAL-GLAND.
003938 04-03

EFFECTS OF ALPHA-ADRENERGIC AND BETA-ADRENERGIC BLOCKERS ON CHLORPROMAZINE-INDUCED ELEVATION OF PLASMA GLUCOSE AND CYCLIC-AMP IN FED MICE.
003946 04-03

ADENOSINE AND CYCLIC-AMP IN RAT-CEREBRAL-CORTICAL SLICES: EFFECTS OF ADENOSINE UPTAKE INHIBITORS AND ADENOSINE-DEAMINASE INHIBITORS.
003950 04-03

EVIDENCE TO SUGGEST THAT DOPAMINE-INDUCED INCREASE IN GABA CONCENTRATIONS IN CHICK BRAIN IS MEDIATED THROUGH CYCLIC-AMP.
003952 04-03

THE EFFECTS OF THYROTROPIN-RELEASING-HORMONE ON CYCLIC-AMP ACCUMULATION IN RABBIT CEREBROCORTICAL TISSUE IN THE PRESENCE AND ABSENCE OF CNS DEPRESSANTS.
004010 04-03

CYCLIC-AMP-INDUCED
CYCLIC-AMP-INDUCED CHANGES IN THE ELECTROENCEPHALOGRAM AND IN BEHAVIOR DURING MORPHINE-DEPENDENCE AND ABSTINENCE IN THE RAT.
003078 03-04

CYCLIC-AMP-PHOSPHODIESTERASE
DIHYDROXY AND TRIHYDROXY ANALOGS OF CHLORPROMAZINE INFLUENCE THE CENTRAL-ACTIVITY OF ADENYLATE-CYCLASE AND CYCLIC-AMP-PHOSPHODIESTERASE.
001405 02-03

RNA-POLYMERASE-II IN C6-GLIOMA CELLS: ALPHA AMANITIN BLOCKADE OF CYCLIC-AMP-PHOSPHODIESTERASE INDUCTION BY BETA-ADRENERGIC STIMULATION. (UNPUBLISHED PAPER).
003998 04-03

CYCLIC-GMP
KAINIC-ACID INDUCED LESION OF RAT RETINA: DIFFERENTIAL-EFFECT ON CYCLIC-GMP AND BENZODIAZEPINE-RECEPTORS AND GABA-RECEPTORS.
002743 03-03

INVOLVEMENT OF CALCIUM CHANNELS IN SHORT-TERM DESENSITIZATION OF MUSCARINIC-RECEPTOR MEDIATED CYCLIC-GMP FORMATION IN MOUSE NEUROBLASTOMA CELLS.
003783 04-03

GUANYLATE-CYCLASE -- CYCLIC-GMP IN MOUSE CEREBRAL-CORTEX AND CEREBELLUM: MODIFICATION BY ANTICONVULSANTS.
003956 04-03

DESENSITIZATION OF HISTAMINE H1-RECEPTOR-MEDIATED CYCLIC-GMP FORMATION IN MOUSE NEUROBLASTOMA CELLS.
004030 04-03

CYCLIC-GMP-DEPENDENT
DEMONSTRATION OF A MUSCARINIC-RECEPTOR-MEDIATED CYCLIC-GMP-DEPENDENT HYPERPOLARIZATION OF THE MEMBRANE POTENTIAL OF MOUSE NEUROBLASTOMA CELLS USING (3H)TETRAPHENYLPHOSPHONIUM.
004049 04-03

CYCLIC-GUANOSINE-MONOPHOSPHATE
THE EFFECTS OF OPIATES ON THE LEVELS OF CYCLIC-GUANOSINE-MONOPHOSPHATE IN DISCRETE AREAS OF THE RAT CENTRAL-NERVOUS-SYSTEM.
000220 01-03

CENTRAL BLOOD-PRESSURE EFFECTS OF GUANYLYLIMIDODIPHOSPHATE AND CYCLIC-GUANOSINE-MONOPHOSPHATE.
000266 01-03

PHENYTOIN INHIBITION OF CYCLIC-GUANOSINE-MONOPHOSPHATE (C-GMP) ACCUMULATION IN NEUROBLASTOMA CELLS BY CALCIUM-CHANNEL BLOCKADE.
004020 04-03

CYCLIC-GUANOSINE-PHOSPHATE
ETHANOL-INDUCED CHANGES IN CYCLIC-GUANOSINE-PHOSPHATE METABOLISM IN MOUSE VESTIBULAR REGION.
003784 04-03

CYCLIC-NUCLEOTIDE
CIRCADIAN-RHYTHM OF CYCLIC-NUCLEOTIDE AND GABA LEVELS IN THE RAT-BRAIN.
000049 01-03

RELATIONSHIPS BETWEEN SEIZURE ACTIVITY AND CYCLIC-NUCLEOTIDE LEVELS IN BRAIN.
000089 01-03

INHIBITORY-EFFECTS OF ANTICONVULSANT-DRUGS ON CYCLIC-NUCLEOTIDE ACCUMULATION IN BRAIN
000090 01-03

INTERACTION OF DOPAMINERGIC ERGOT DERIVATIVES WITH CYCLIC-NUCLEOTIDE SYSTEM.
001482 02-03

CYCLIC-NUCLEOTIDE-PHOSPHODIESTERASES
AN IMPROVED ASSAY OF CYCLIC-NUCLEOTIDE-PHOSPHODIESTERASES WITH QAE-SEPHADEX COLUMNS.
001860 02-06

CYCLIC-NUCLEOTIDES
EFFECTS OF RESERPINE, PROPRANOLOL, AND AMINOPHYLLINE ON SEIZURE ACTIVITY AND CNS CYCLIC-NUCLEOTIDES.
000115 01-03

RAT-BRAIN STEADY-STATE LEVELS OF CYCLIC-NUCLEOTIDES AS AN ENDPOINT OF LSD-LIKE HALLUCINOGEN EFFECTS. (PH.D. DISSERTATION).
001426 02-03

CYCLIC-NUCLEOTIDES AND THE CENTRAL-EFFECTS OF OPIATES: AN OVERVIEW OF CURRENT RESEARCH.
001445 02-03

EFFECT OF FLUPHENAZINE ON THE CIRCADIAN-EXCRETION OF CYCLIC-NUCLEOTIDES AND ELECTROLYTES IN THE URINE OF CHRONIC SCHIZOPHRENICS.
001927 02-08

CYCLIC-NUCLEOTIDES AND THE NERVOUS-SYSTEM.
004542 04-13

CYCLICAL
CYCLICAL CRIMINAL ACTS IN PREMENSTRUAL-SYNDROME.
000927 01-17

CYCLING
MAOI-INDUCED RAPID CYCLING BIPOLAR AFFECTIVE-DISORDER IN AN ADOLESCENT.
004637 04-15

CYCLO-LEU-GLY
THE EFFECT OF CYCLO-LEU-GLY ON CHEMICAL DENERVATION SUPERSENSITIVITY OF DOPAMINE-RECEPTORS INDUCED BY INTRACEREBROVENTRICULAR INJECTION OF 6 HYDROXYDOPAMINE IN MICE.
001435 02-03

INHIBITION OF NEUROLEPTIC-INDUCED DOPAMINE-RECEPTOR SUPERSENSITIVITY BY CYCLO-LEU-GLY.
001576 02-04

CYCLOHEXIMIDE
EFFECTS OF CYCLOHEXIMIDE ADMINISTERED IN CONJUNCTION WITH NICOTINE ON RETENTION OF A PASSIVE-AVOIDANCE TASK IN MICE.
001791 02-04

A QUANTITATIVE REGIONAL ANALYSIS OF PROTEIN SYNTHESIS INHIBITION IN THE RAT-BRAIN FOLLOWING LOCALIZED INJECTION OF CYCLOHEXIMIDE.
002780 03-03

CYCLOHEXYLADENOSINE
ADENOSINE-RECEPTORS IN RAT TESTES: LABELING WITH 3H CYCLOHEXYLADENOSINE.
002835 03-03

CYCLOHEXYLBARBITURATE
ON-COLUMN GAS-CHROMATOGRAPHIC-SYNTHESIS OF 1,3 DIALYKYL (C=1-10), BENZYL, AND CYCLOHEXYLBARBITURATE DERIVATIVES.
003656 04-01

CYCLOHEXYLPHENOXYAMIDOXIMES
CYCLOHEXYLPHENOXYAMIDOXIMES AND IMIDAZOLINES WITH ANTIDEPRESSIVE AND ALPHA-ADRENERGIC-ACTIVITY.
001051 02-01

CYCLOID
LITHIUM UPTAKE IN RED CELLS OF CYCLOID AND UNIPOLAR DYSTHYMIC-PATIENTS.
003258 03-09

CYCLOPHOSPHAMIDE-INDUCED
CYCLOPHOSPHAMIDE-INDUCED SPERMATOGENIC EFFECTS DETECTED IN THE F1-GENERATION BY BEHAVIORAL-TESTING.
003121 03-05

CYCLOPROPYL-N-ARYLALKYLAMINES
MECHANISM OF INACTIVATION OF MITOCHONDRIAL MONOAMINE-OXIDASE BY N CYCLOPROPYL-N-ARYLALKYLAMINES.
001055 02-01

MECHANISM OF INACTIVATION OF MITOCHONDRIAL MONOAMINE-OXIDASE BY N CYCLOPROPYL-N-ARYLALKYLAMINES.
001088 02-02

CYCLOPROPYLMETHYL
STEREOSPECIFIC INHIBITION OF DOPAMINE-SENSITIVE ADENYLATE-CYCLASE IN CARP RETINA BY THE ENANTIOMERS OF (/-) 1

CYCLOPROPYLMETHYL
TRIFLUOROMETHYLTHIODIBENZOCYCLOHEPTENYLIDENEPIPERIDINE.
003706 04-02

CYCLOSPASMOL
EFFECTS OF CYCLOSPASMOL UPON SENSORY PARAMETERS IN PATIENTS
RECOVERING FROM CEREBROVASCULAR-ACCIDENTS.
002360 02-14

CYCLOTHYMIC-PATIENTS
PROPHYLACTIC-EFFECT OF LITHIUM AGAINST DEPRESSION IN
CYCLOTHYMIC-PATIENTS: A LIFE-TABLE ANALYSIS.
004391 04-09

CYPROHEPTADINE
METERGOLINE AND CYPROHEPTADINE SUPPRESS PROLACTIN RELEASE BY
A NON-5-HYDROXYTRYPTAMINERGIC, NONDOPAMINERGIC
MECHANISM.
003732 04-03

CYPROHEPTADINIUM-METHIODIDE
ANTIARRHYTHMIC-ACTIVITY OF AMITRIPTYLINE ANALOGUES IN
CONSCIOUS DOGS AFTER MYOCARDIAL-INFARCTION:
CYPROHEPTADINIUM-METHIODIDE.
001534 02-03

CYPROTERONACETATE
CYPROTERONACETATE IN THE THERAPY OF SEXUAL-DEVIATIONS.
000735 01-11

CYSTEINE
MORPHOLOGICAL CHANGES IN RAT-BRAIN INDUCED BY L CYSTEINE
INJECTION IN NEWBORN ANIMALS.
002774 03-03

CYSTEINE-SULPHINIC-ACID-DECARBOXYLASE
COMPARISON OF CYSTEINE-SULPHINIC-ACID-DECARBOXYLASE (CSD)
ISOENZYMES AND GLUTAMIC-ACID-DECARBOXYLASE (GAD) IN RAT: IS
BRAIN CSD-I IDENTICAL WITH LIVER CSD AND BRAIN CSD-II WITH
GAD? (UNPUBLISHED PAPER).
001048 02-01

CYTOCHALASIN
THE EFFECT OF COLCHICINE AND CYTOCHALASIN B ON THE RELEASE OF
TAURINE FROM THE CHICK RETINA.
002856 03-03

CYTOCHROME-P-450
EFFECT OF CANNABIDIOL ON CYTOCHROME-P-450 AND HEXOBARBITAL
SLEEP-TIME.
002675 03-03

CYTOPLASMATIC
TREATMENT OF ORGANIC-BRAIN-DISTURBANCES IN ELDERLY-PATIENTS. A
CLINICAL DOUBLE-BLIND STUDY WITH MACROMOLECULAR ORGAN
LYSATES (CYTOPLASMATIC THERAPY ACCORDING TO THEURER).
003327 03-11

CYTOPLASMIC
CHANGES IN NORADRENERGIC TRANSMISSION ALTER THE
CONCENTRATION OF CYTOPLASMIC PROGESTIN-RECEPTORS IN
HYPOTHALAMUS.
002842 03-03

THE NA-K-ATPASE: A PLAUSIBLE TRIGGER FOR VOLTAGE-INDEPENDENT
RELEASE OF CYTOPLASMIC NEUROTRANSMITTERS.
003953 04-03

CYTOSKELETAL
SYNTHESIS OF CYTOSKELETAL PROTEINS IN BULK ISOLATED NEURONAL
PERIKARYA.
003672 04-01

CZECHOSLOVAK
21. ANNUAL CZECHOSLOVAK PSYCHOPHARMACOLOGICAL-MEETING.
000917 01-17

CZECHOSLOVAKIA
CONSUMPTION OF PSYCHOTROPIC-DRUGS IN CZECHOSLOVAKIA.
002542 02-17

C10DICHOL
ANTITREMOR ACTION OF C10DICHOL, A PERIPHERAL ACETYLCHOLINE
SYNTHESIS INHIBITOR.
004096 04-04

C6-GLIOMA
REGULATION BY A BETA-ADRENERGIC-RECEPTOR OF A CA-INDEPENDENT
ADENOSINE-CYCLIC-MONOPHOSPHATE-PHOSPHODIESTERASE IN C6-
GLIOMA CELLS. (UNPUBLISHED PAPER).
001403 02-03

RNA-POLYMERASE-II IN C6-GLIOMA CELLS: ALPHA AMANITIN BLOCKADE
OF CYCLIC-AMP-PHOSPHODIESTERASE INDUCTION BY BETA-
ADRENERGIC STIMULATION. (UNPUBLISHED PAPER).
003998 04-03

D-AMPHETAMINE
PRIOR AND ONGOING EXPERIENCE AS DETERMINANTS OF THE EFFECTS OF
D-AMPHETAMINE AND CHLORPROMAZINE ON PUNISHED-BEHAVIOR.
000339 01-04

CONSEQUENT EVENTS AS DETERMINANTS OF DRUG-EFFECTS ON
SCHEDULE-CONTROLLED BEHAVIOR: MODIFICATION OF EFFECTS OF
COCAINE AND D-AMPHETAMINE FOLLOWING CHRONIC AMPHETAMINE
ADMINISTRATION.
000350 01-04

EFFECTS OF ACUTE AND CHRONIC INTERACTIONS OF DIAZEPAM AND D-
AMPHETAMINE ON PUNISHED-BEHAVIOR OF RATS.
000386 01-04

TOLERANCE TO THE DISCRIMINATIVE-STIMULUS PROPERTIES OF D-AMPHETAMINE.
002953 03-04

INTERACTION AMONG D-AMPHETAMINE, SCOPOLAMINE AND GENOTYPE IN AVOIDANCE-BEHAVIOR OF RATS.
003082 03-04

EFFECTS OF CHLORDIAZEPOXIDE AND D-AMPHETAMINE ON RESPONDING SUPPRESSED BY CONDITIONED PUNISHMENT.
003105 03-04

THE HYPERACTIVE-CHILD-SYNDROME: PERIPHERAL SYMPATHETIC-NERVOUS-SYSTEM FUNCTION AND THE EFFECT OF D-AMPHETAMINE.
003340 03-11

DRUG PREFERENCE AND MOOD IN HUMANS: REPEATED ASSESSMENT OF D-AMPHETAMINE.
003445 03-14

MYOINOSITOL TURNOVER IN THE INTACT RAT-BRAIN: INCREASED PRODUCTION AFTER D-AMPHETAMINE.
003723 04-03

THE BEHAVIORAL-EFFECTS OF D-AMPHETAMINE ALONE AND IN COMBINATION WITH ACUTE AND CHRONIC MORPHINE TREATMENTS IN RATS.
003915 04-03

THE INFLUENCE OF D-AMPHETAMINE ON RAT-BRAIN STRIATAL REDUCED BIOPTERIN CONCENTRATION.
003922 04-03

APPARENT SEROTONERGIC MODULATION OF THE DOSE-DEPENDENT BIPHASIC RESPONSE OF NEOSTRIATAL NEURONS PRODUCED BY D-AMPHETAMINE.
003981 04-03

KINETIC STUDIES ON THE ENTRY OF D-AMPHETAMINE INTO THE CENTRAL-NERVOUS-SYSTEM: I. CEREBROSPINAL-FLUID.
004005 04-03

SECOND-ORDER SCHEDULES OF INTRAMUSCULAR COCAINE INJECTION IN THE SQUIRREL-MONKEY: COMPARISONS WITH FOOD PRESENTATION AND EFFECTS OF D-AMPHETAMINE AND PROMAZINE.
004152 04-04

SEX, PLASMA PROLACTIN AND PLASMA 3 METHOXY-4-HYDROXYPHENYLGLYCOL (MHPG) PREDICT HERITABLE D-AMPHETAMINE EXCITATION IN MAN. (UNPUBLISHED PAPER).
004565 04-14

D-AMPHETAMINE-INDUCED
EFFECTS OF PHENCYCLIDINE AND METHYLPHENIDATE ON D-AMPHETAMINE-INDUCED BEHAVIORS IN RESERPINE PRETREATED RATS.
001616 02-04

DISSOCIATION OF D-AMPHETAMINE-INDUCED LOCOMOTOR-ACTIVITY AND STEREOTYPED-BEHAVIOUR BY LESIONS OF THE SUPERIOR-COLLICULUS.
001755 02-04

CONDITIONED DRUG-EFFECTS OF D-AMPHETAMINE-INDUCED AND MORPHINE-INDUCED MOTOR ACCELERATION IN MICE: EXPERIMENTAL APPROACH FOR PLACEBO-EFFECT.
004128 04-04

D-AMPHETAMINES
CATS DEVELOP TOLERANCE TO D-AMPHETAMINES EFFECTS UPON LOCOMOTION AND STEREOTYPED-BEHAVIORS.
003018 03-04

D-ISOMERS
COMPARATIVE-STUDIES OF THE PHARMACOLOGICAL-EFFECTS OF THE D-ISOMERS AND L-ISOMERS OF CODEINE.
004084 04-04

D-1
INHIBITION OF DOPAMINE D-1 AND D-2 BINDING-SITES IN NEURONAL TISSUE BY ASCORBATE.
003876 04-03

D-2
THREE CLASSES OF DOPAMINE-RECEPTOR (D-2, D-3, D-4) IDENTIFIED BY BINDING STUDIES WITH 3H APOMORPHINE AND 3H DOMPERIDONE.
002900 03-03

INHIBITION OF DOPAMINE D-1 AND D-2 BINDING-SITES IN NEURONAL TISSUE BY ASCORBATE.
003876 04-03

D-3
THREE CLASSES OF DOPAMINE-RECEPTOR (D-2, D-3, D-4) IDENTIFIED BY BINDING STUDIES WITH 3H APOMORPHINE AND 3H DOMPERIDONE.
002900 03-03

D-4
THREE CLASSES OF DOPAMINE-RECEPTOR (D-2, D-3, D-4) IDENTIFIED BY BINDING STUDIES WITH 3H APOMORPHINE AND 3H DOMPERIDONE.
002900 03-03

DAILY
REPEATED TRICYCLICS INDUCE A PROGRESSIVE DOPAMINE-AUTORECEPTOR SUBSENSITIVITY INDEPENDENT OF DAILY DRUG-TREATMENT.
000047 01-03

CORRELATION BETWEEN DAILY FLUCTUATIONS OF CARBAMAZEPINE SERUM LEVELS AND INTERMITTENT SIDE-EFFECTS.
000851 01-15

LOG-DOSE/RESPONSE-CURVE FLATTENING IN RATS AFTER DAILY INJECTION OF OPIATES.
001387 02-03

THE INFLUENCE OF DAILY BIOLOGICAL-RHYTHMICITY ON THE HOMING-BEHAVIOR, PSYCHOPHARMACOLOGICAL RESPONSIVENESS, LEARNING AND RETENTION OF SUCKLING RATS. (PH.D. DISSERTATION).
001660 02-04

THE INFLUENCE OF SINGLE DAILY HEROIN INJECTIONS ON DRINKING-PATTERNS IN THE RAT.
001746 02-04

CORRELATION BETWEEN DAILY DOSAGE OF CHLORPROMAZINE AND SUBSEQUENT SUPERSENSITIVITY.
001845 02-05

FIRST CLINICAL IMPRESSIONS IN DAILY PRACTICE.
002046 02-09

REPEATED ANTIDEPRESSANT TREATMENTS INDUCE A LONG-LASTING DOPAMINE-AUTORECEPTOR SUBSENSITIVITY: IS DAILY TREATMENT NECESSARY FOR CLINICAL EFFICACY?
002659 03-03

CORRELATION BETWEEN ANTIAVOIDANCE ACTIVITIES OF ANTIPSYCHOTIC-DRUGS IN RATS AND DAILY CLINICAL DOSES.
003032 03-04

DAMAGE
INFLUENCE OF AMPHETAMINE AND PHENYLPROPANOLAMINE ON FOOD INTAKE, ACTIVITY, AND BODY-TEMPERATURE IN RATS WITH VENTROMEDIAL HYPOTHALAMIC OR DORSOLATERAL TEGMENTAL DAMAGE.
000322 01-03

FACILITATION OF RECOVERY BY PROPANTHELINE-BROMIDE AFTER LATERAL HYPOTHALAMIC DAMAGE.
000396 01-04

EFFECTS OF AMPHETAMINE AND PHENYLPROPANOLAMINE ON FOOD INTAKE IN RATS WITH VENTROMEDIAL HYPOTHALAMIC OR DORSOLATERAL TEGMENTAL DAMAGE.
001818 02-04

FLUORESCENCE HISTOCHEMISTRY INDICATES DAMAGE OF STRIATAL DOPAMINE NERVE TERMINALS IN RATS AFTER MULTIPLE DOSES OF METHAMPHETAMINE.
002812 03-03

BEHAVIORAL-CHANGES AND BIOCHEMICAL-CHANGES AFTER HIPPOCAMPAL DAMAGE. (PH.D. DISSERTATION).
003069 03-04

ON THE QUESTION OF PARENCHYMAL DAMAGE CAUSED BY LONG-TERM THERAPY WITH PSYCHOTROPICS IN ADOLESCENCE.
004626 04-15

DAMS
GABA-RECEPTORS AND BENZODIAZEPINE-RECEPTORS IN THE OFFSPRING OF DAMS RECEIVING DIAZEPAM: ONTOGENETIC-STUDIES.
001849 02-05

DANGER
ON THE DANGER OF USING PSYCHOPHARMACEUTICALS DURING PREGNANCY: CRITICAL REVIEW OF THE LITERATURE.
000833 01-15

DANGEROUS
DIURETICS ARE DANGEROUS WITH LITHIUM.
002420 02-15

RECENT DEVELOPMENTS IN LITHIUM TREATMENT: IS IT DANGEROUS FOR THE KIDNEY?
002465 02-15

DANITRACEN
INTERACTION OF P CHLOROPHENYLALANINE, MIANSERINE AND DANITRACEN WITH AMPHETAMINE.
004599 04-15

DARK
BILATERAL SKIN CONDUCTANCE AND THE PUPILLARY LIGHT DARK REFLEX: MANIPULATION BY CHLORPROMAZINE, HALOPERIDOL, SCOPOLAMINE, AND PLACEBO.
004544 04-13

DATA
PRELIMINARY DATA ON ETHOSUXIMIDE AND THE EPISODIC-DYSCONTROL-SYNDROME.
000539 01-07

ADVANTAGE OF PHARMACOKINETIC DATA DURING TREATMENT OF PSYCHOSES WITH HALOPERIDOL.
000577 01-08

PREDICTION OF THE VOLUME OF DISTRIBUTION FROM IN VITRO DATA AND USE FOR ESTIMATING THE ABSOLUTE EXTENT OF ABSORPTION.
000907 01-16

SOME PHARMACOLOGICAL-ASPECTS AND BIOCHEMICAL-ASPECTS OF TRH: EXPERIMENTAL AND CLINICAL DATA.
001189 02-03

NEW DATA ON THE USE OF ANTIDEPRESSANT-DRUGS.
001195 02-03

ATROPINE AND NATURAL SLEEP: ACTIVITY DATA OF THE STRIATUM IN RATS.
001551 02-03

ACUTE AND CHRONIC LSD EFFECTS ON RAT STARTLE: DATA SUPPORTING AN LSD RAT MODEL OF SCHIZOPHRENIA.
002194 02-12

PHARMACOKINETIC BASIS FOR PREDICTING STEADY-STATE SERUM DRUG CONCENTRATIONS OF IMIPRAMINE FROM SINGLE-DOSE DATA.
002225 02-13

Subject Index

KINETIC DATA ON THE INHIBITION OF HIGH-AFFINITY CHOLINE
TRANSPORT INTO RAT-FOREBRAIN SYNAPTOSOMES BY CHOLINE-LIKE
COMPOUNDS AND NITROGEN-MUSTARD ANALOGUES.
002879 03-03

STATISTICAL ANALYSES OF PHYSIOLOGIC DATA FROM FEMALE PATIENTS
WITH AN ENDOMORPHOUS DEPRESSIVE COURSE: A TRIAL,
INTERACTIONS BETWEEN PHYSIOLOGIC PARAMETERS, TEST JUNCTURES
IN THIS PHASE.
003251 03-09

USE OF CURRENTLY AVAILABLE DATA SOURCES TO ASSESS DRUG
SCHEDULING.
003594 03-17

PRACTICAL IMPLICATIONS OF MODERN PSYCHOPHARMACOLOGICAL
DATA.
003596 03-17

SINGLE-DOSE PHARMACOKINETIC DATA ON ZIMELIDINE IN DEPRESSED-
PATIENTS.
004385 04-09

THE USE OF CLINICAL KINETIC DATA IN TREATMENT WITH
ANTIDEPRESSANT-DRUGS.
004686 04-16

DATES
EFFECTS OF FETAL TREATMENT WITH METHYLAZOXYMETHANOL-ACETATE
AT VARIOUS GESTATIONAL DATES ON THE NEUROCHEMISTRY OF THE
ADULT NEOCORTEX OF THE RAT.
002770 03-03

DAY-HOSPITAL
PSYCHIATRIC-DRUG-STUDY. PART II. MENTAL-HYGIENE-CLINIC SURVEY,
DAY-TREATMENT-CENTER SURVEY, DAY-HOSPITAL SURVEY.
004716 04-17

DAY-TREATMENT-CENTER
PSYCHIATRIC-DRUG-STUDY. PART II. MENTAL-HYGIENE-CLINIC SURVEY,
DAY-TREATMENT-CENTER SURVEY, DAY-HOSPITAL SURVEY.
004716 04-17

DAYTIME
THE DIFFERENTIAL-EFFECTS OF SHORT-ACTING AND LONG-ACTING
BENZODIAZEPINES UPON NOCTURNAL SLEEP AND DAYTIME
PERFORMANCE.
000822 01-14

INTRAVENOUS CHLORIMIPRAMINE AFFECTS REM CYCLE IN PATIENTS
WITH EXCESSIVE DAYTIME SLEEPINESS AND CONTROL SUBJECTS.
002341 02-14

DAYTIME EFFECTS OF L TRYPTOPHAN.
003455 03-14

DDT
A POSSIBLE NEUROCHEMICAL BASIS OF THE CENTRAL STIMULATORY
EFFECTS OF PP'DDT.
004274 04-05

DEACYLATION
PHYSIOLOGIC AND PHARMACOLOGIC IMPLICATIONS IN THE
DEACYLATION OF PHOSPHATIDYLSERINE IN MICE.
002682 03-03

DEAE
DOSE-EFFECT OF DEAE ON SUBJECTIVE PROBLEMS, VERTIGO,
DEPRESSION, ASTHENIA, CEPHALALGIA, AND TONIC POSTURAL
ACTIVITY PROBLEMS RECORDED WITH STATOKINESIMETER IN
POSTCONCUSSIONAL-SYNDROME.
004472 04-11

DEAFNESS
A CASE OF REVERSIBLE PURE-WORD DEAFNESS DURING LITHIUM
TOXICITY.
003481 03-15

DEALING
EXPERIMENTATION WITH MINAPRINE IN DEALING WITH CERTAIN
SEXUAL-DISORDERS: IMPOTENCE OR FRIGIDITY.
002153 02-11

DEAMINATION
SPECIES-DIFFERENCES IN THE DEAMINATION OF DOPAMINE AND OTHER
SUBSTRATES FOR MONOAMINE-OXIDASE IN BRAIN.
002233 02-13

DEANOL
DIMETHYLAMINOETHANOL (DEANOL) METABOLISM IN RAT-BRAIN AND
ITS EFFECT ON ACETYLCHOLINE SYNTHESIS.
000150 01-03

ON THE THERAPY OF NEUROLEPTIC-INDUCED TARDIVE-DYSKINESIA WITH
DIMETHYLAMINOETHANOL (DEANOL).
004627 04-15

GAS-CHROMATOGRAPHY/MASS-SPECTROMETRY STABLE ISOTOPIC
ANALYSES FOR DEANOL, CHOLINE, AND THEIR ACETYLESTERS.
004683 04-16

DEATH
THE MYTHOLOGEM OF REVERSIBLE DEATH. THE ANALYTICAL
CONFRONTATION OF ENDOGENOUS DELIRIUM WITH DELUSIONS IN
PSYCHEDELIC-EXPERIENCES.
002200 02-12

AMITRIPTYLINE PROVIDES LONG-LASTING IMMUNIZATION AGAINST
SUDDEN CARDIAC DEATH FROM COCAINE.
003122 03-05

EXCEPTIONAL CASES OF DEATH CAUSED BY TRICYCLIC-ANTIDEPRESSANT
AGENTS.
003490 03-15

THE EFFECT OF PHRENOLON ON DELAYED REACTIONS IN LOWER
MONKEYS.
001640 02-04

EFFECTS OF THIORIDAZINE (MELLARIL) ON TITRATING DELAYED
MATCHING-TO-SAMPLE PERFORMANCE IN MENTALLY-RETARDED
ADULTS.
002471 02-15

EFFECTS OF THIORIDAZINE (MELLARIL) ON TITRATING DELAYED
MATCHING-TO-SAMPLE PERFORMANCE OF MENTALLY-RETARDED
ADULTS.
003392 03-11

CAFFEINE BLOCKS THE DELAYED K OUTWARD-CURRENT OF MOLLUSCAN
NEURONS.
003834 04-03

THE EFFECT OF THIOPROPERAZINE ON DELAYED REACTIONS IN LOWER
MONKEYS.
004125 04-04

DELIMITED
PSYCHIATRIC-ILLNESS AND USE OF PSYCHOTROPIC-DRUGS IN THE
GEOGRAPHICALLY DELIMITED POPULATION OF SAMSO, DENMARK.
004734 04-17

DELIRIUM
DELIRIUM: TREATMENT POSSIBILITIES.
002141 02-11

DELIRIUM OR PSYCHOSIS? DIAGNOSTIC USE OF THE SODIUM-
AMOBARBITAL INTERVIEW.
002167 02-11

THE MYTHOLOGEM OF REVERSIBLE DEATH. THE ANALYTICAL
CONFRONTATION OF ENDOGENOUS DELIRIUM WITH DELUSIONS IN
PSYCHEDELIC-EXPERIENCES.
002200 02-12

DIFFERENTIAL DIAGNOSIS OF CIMETIDINE-INDUCED DELIRIUM.
003488 03-15

DELIRIUM SECONDARY TO CLONIDINE THERAPY.
003494 03-15

DELIRIUM-TREMENS
FLUNITRAZEPAM IN THE TREATMENT OF DELIRIUM-TREMENS --
PRELIMINARY REPORT.
000719 01-11

PHYSOSTIGMINE FOR TREATMENT OF DELIRIUM-TREMENS.
003364 03-11

A COMPARATIVE EVALUATION OF THE EFFICACY OF SOME THERAPEUTIC
METHODS USED IN DELIRIUM-TREMENS.
004486 04-11

DELIVERY
AVAILABILITY OF ISOSORBIDE-DINITRATE, DIAZEPAM AND
CHLORMETHIAZOLE, FROM I.V. DELIVERY SYSTEMS.
003558 03-16

DELTA-FORMS
INTERCONVERTING MU AND DELTA-FORMS OF TYPE-1 OPIATE-RECEPTORS
IN THE RAT STRIATAL PATCHES.
003737 04-03

DELTA-RECEPTOR
METKEPHAMID, A SYSTEMICALLY ACTIVE ANALOG OF METHIONINE-
ENKEPHALIN WITH POTENT OPIOID DELTA-RECEPTOR ACTIVITY.
002720 03-03

DELTA-RECEPTORS
EFFECTS OF CHANGES IN THE STRUCTURE OF ENKEPHALINS AND OF
NARCOTIC ANALGESIC-DRUGS ON THEIR INTERACTIONS WITH MU-
RECEPTORS AND DELTA-RECEPTORS.
000168 01-03

DELUSIONAL
THREE CASES OF UNIPOLAR DELUSIONAL DEPRESSION RESPONSIVE TO L-
DOPA.
000628 01-09

DELUSIONAL-STATES
HALLUCINATORY AND DELUSIONAL-STATES IN CONNECTION WITH BLOOD-
PRESSURE AND EEG.
000814 01-14

DELUSIONS
THE MYTHOLOGEM OF REVERSIBLE DEATH. THE ANALYTICAL
CONFRONTATION OF ENDOGENOUS DELIRIUM WITH DELUSIONS IN
PSYCHEDELIC-EXPERIENCES.
002200 02-12

DEMENTIA
AGE, DEMENTIA, DYSKINESIAS, AND LITHIUM RESPONSE.
000594 01-09

NEUROLOGICAL-STUDY AND NEUROPSYCHOPHARMACOLOGY-STUDY ON
DEMENTIA.
001090 02-11

DRUG-INDUCED DEMENTIA.
002431 02-15

PHARMACOLOGIC AND THERAPEUTIC-PERSPECTIVES ON DEMENTIA: AN
EXPERIMENTAL APPROACH.
003065 03-04

DOPAMINE AND DEMENTIA. AN ANIMAL-MODEL WITH DESTRUCTION OF
THE MESOCORTICAL DOPAMINERGIC PATHWAY: A PRELIMINARY
STUDY.
003085 03-04

PHARMACOLOGIC CHARACTERIZATION AND LECITHIN TREATMENT OF A
PATIENT WITH SPONTANEOUS ORAL FACIAL DYSKINESIA AND
DEMENTIA.
003347 03-11
USE OF THA IN TREATMENT OF ALZHEIMER-LIKE DEMENTIA: PILOT-STUDY
IN TWELVE PATIENTS.
003377 03-11
LEVELS OF 5 HYDROXYINDOLEACETIC-ACID AND TRYPTOPHAN IN
LUMBAR CEREBROSPINAL-FLUID AND BLOOD OF PATIENTS WITH
DEMENTIA AND NORMAL PRESSURE HYDROCEPHALUS AFTER
TRYPTOPHAN ADMINISTRATION.
003419 03-13
EXTRAPYRAMIDAL-DISORDERS AND BORDERLINE-SYNDROMES:
EREDOATAXIAS AND DEMENTIA.
003518 03-15
EVALUATION OF DRUG EFFICACY IN DEMENTIA: A COMPUTERIZED
COGNITIVE ASSESSMENT SYSTEM.
003557 03-16
SINGLE-CASE STUDY OF CLINICAL-RESPONSE TO HIGH-DOSE ERGOT
ALKALOID TREATMENT FOR DEMENTIA. PRELIMINARY REPORT.
004493 04-11

DEMENTIAS
CHOLINE-BITARTRATE TREATMENT OF ALZHEIMER-TYPE DEMENTIAS.
000675 01-11

DEMETHYLASE
PLASMA IMIPRAMINE LEVELS AND DEMETHYLASE ACTIVITY IN THE
LIVER OF STRESSED ANIMALS.
002793 03-03

DEMETHYLATED
PHARMACODYNAMIC PROFILES OF L ALPHA ACETYLMETHADOL (LAAM)
AND ITS N DEMETHYLATED METABOLITES, NORLAAM AND
DINORLAAM, DURING SELF-ADMINISTRATION IN THE DEPENDENT RAT.
000505 01-04

DEMETHYLATION
CHANGES IN BRAIN N DEMETHYLATION AND OPIATE-RECEPTOR CONTENT
CORRELATE WITH ANALGESIC EFFECTIVENESS OF MORPHINE.
000400 01-04
INTERINDIVIDUAL DIFFERENCES IN AMITRIPTYLINE DEMETHYLATION.
002282 02-13

DEMETHYLCHLORIMIPRAMINE
TECHNIQUES FOR PLASMA PROTEIN BINDING OF
DEMETHYLCHLORIMIPRAMINE.
000897 01-16

DEMETRIN
THE TRANQUILIZER DEMETRIN (PRAZEPAM).
003331 03-11

DEMONSTRATION
DEMONSTRATION OF SUBSTANCE-P IN AORTIC NERVE AFFERENT FIBERS
BY COMBINED USE OF FLOURESCENT RETROGRADE NEURONAL
LABELING AND IMMUNOCYTOCHEMISTRY. (UNPUBLISHED PAPER).
001024 02-01
A DEMONSTRATION OF NALOXONE PRECIPITATED OPIATE WITHDRAWAL
ON SINGLE NEURONES IN THE MORPHINE-TOLERANT/DEPENDENT RAT-
BRAIN.
001234 02-03
CENTRAL PHARMACOLOGICAL CONTROL OF CORTICOSTERONE SECRETION
IN THE INTACT RAT. DEMONSTRATION OF CHOLINERGIC AND
SEROTONINERGIC FACILITATORY AND ALPHA-ADRENERGIC INHIBITORY
MECHANISMS.
001487 02-03
DEMONSTRATION AND CHARACTERIZATION OF AN ENDOGENOUS
INHIBITOR OF GABA-ENHANCED (3H) DIAZEPAM BINDING FROM
BOVINE CEREBRAL-CORTEX.
002645 03-01
QUANTITATION AND COMPARISON OF PHENOBARBITAL LEVELS IN THE
PLASMA, SALIVA, AND CEREBROSPINAL-FLUID OF THE RAT, AND THE
DEMONSTRATION OF AN ALTERATION OF DRUG PASSAGE BY
ETHANOL.
003725 04-03
DEMONSTRATION OF A MUSCARINIC-RECEPTOR-MEDIATED CYCLIC-GMP-
DEPENDENT HYPERPOLARIZATION OF THE MEMBRANE POTENTIAL OF
MOUSE NEUROBLASTOMA CELLS USING
(3H)TETRAPHENYLPHOSPHONIUM.
004049 04-03
BUPRENORPHINE: DEMONSTRATION OF PHYSICAL-DEPENDENCE LIABILITY.
004104 04-04

DEMYELINATION
THE PATHOGENESIS OF PRIMARY INTERNODAL DEMYELINATION
PRODUCED BY ACETYL-ETHYL-TETRAMETHYL-TETRALIN: EVIDENCE FOR
PRESERVED SCHWANN-CELL SOMAL FUNCTION.
002905 03-03

DENDRITIC
EFFECTS OF LEAD EXPOSURE DURING DEVELOPMENT ON NEOCORTICAL
DENDRITIC AND SYNAPTIC STRUCTURE.
000525 01-05
ELECTRON MICROSCOPIC STUDIES OF BRAIN SLICES: THE EFFECTS OF
HIGH-FREQUENCY STIMULATION ON DENDRITIC ULTRASTRUCTURE.
(UNPUBLISHED PAPER).
001036 02-01

STRAIN DEPENDENT EFFECTS OF KETAMINE ON LOCOMOTOR-ACTIVITY AND ANTINOCICEPTION IN MICE.

000382 01-04

PHARMACODYNAMIC PROFILES OF L ALPHA ACETYLMETHADOL (LAAM) AND ITS N DEMETHYLATED METABOLITES, NORLAAM AND DINORLAAM, DURING SELF-ADMINISTRATION IN THE DEPENDENT RAT.

000505 01-04

OPIOID DEPENDENT DUAL-REGULATION OF ADENYLATE-CYCLASE IN A CELL-FREE SYSTEM. (UNPUBLISHED PAPER).

001033 02-01

A DEMONSTRATION OF NALOXONE PRECIPITATED OPIATE WITHDRAWAL ON SINGLE NEURONES IN THE MORPHINE-TOLERANT/DEPENDENT RAT-BRAIN.

001234 02-03

AGE DEPENDENT CHANGES IN THE BETA ENDORPHIN CONTENT OF DISCRETE RAT-BRAIN NUCLEI.

002635 03-01

NEURONAL MATURATION IN MAMMALIAN CELL-CULTURE IS DEPENDENT ON SPONTANEOUS ELECTRICAL-ACTIVITY.

002669 03-03

THE RELATIONSHIP BETWEEN THE ACUTE BEHAVIORAL-EFFECTS OF NARCOTIC ANTAGONISTS AND THE NARCOTIC DEPENDENT STATE.

003106 03-04

THE EFFECT OF SODIUM-DIPROPYLACETATE ON GAMMA AMINOBUTYRIC-ACID DEPENDENT INHIBITION IN THE RAT-CORTEX AND SUBSTANTIA-NIGRA IN RELATION TO ITS ANTICONVULSANT ACTIVITY.

003880 04-03

SCHEDULE DEPENDENT CHANGE OF PUNISHED-RESPONDING AFTER DIAZEPAM IN RATS.

004165 04-04

EFFECTS OF NARCOTIC ABSTINENCE ON SCHEDULE-CONTROLLED BEHAVIOR IN DEPENDENT RATS.

004230 04-04

DEPENDING
TWO OR MORE CONFORMATIONS OF BENZODIAZEPINE-RECEPTORS DEPENDING ON GABA-RECEPTORS AND OTHER VARIABLES.

001139 02-03

DEPENDS
INVOLVEMENT OF DOPAMINE IN CIRCLING RESPONSES TO MUSCIMOL DEPENDS ON INTRANIGRAL SITE OF INJECTION.

004158 04-04

DEPLETED
COMPARISON OF HIGHLY-ACTIVE AND ACTIVITY DEPLETED HEPARIN BY CIRCULAR DICHROISM SPECTROSCOPY. (UNPUBLISHED PAPER).

001057 02-01

DEPLETES
INTRANIGRAL INJECTION OF CAPSAICIN ENHANCES MOTOR-ACTIVITY AND DEPLETES NIGRAL 5 HYDROXYTRYPTAMINE BUT NOT SUBSTANCE-P.

004100 04-04

DEPLETING
INFLUENCE OF MONOAMINE DEPLETING PHARMACOLOGIC-AGENTS ON LEVELS OF ACTIVITY IN CAIMAN-SCLEROPS. .

001810 02-04

DEPLETION
DEPLETION OF EPINEPHRINE IN RAT HYPOTHALAMUS BY RO-4-1284: INFLUENCE OF PARGYLINE AND HARMALINE.

000100 01-03

THE CONVERSION OF (3H)TRYPTOPHAN TO 5 (3H)HYDROXYTRYPTAMINE IN MOUSE-BRAIN FOLLOWING DEPLETION OF PHENYLALANINE AND TYROSINE.

000148 01-03

EFFECTS OF BRAIN-MONOAMINE DEPLETION ON THERMOREGULATORY RESPONSES OF RABBITS TO DIFFERENT HYPOTHALAMIC TEMPERATURES.

000190 01-03

GABA DEPLETION AND BEHAVIOURAL-CHANGES PRODUCED BY INTRAVENTRICULAR PUTRESCINE IN CHICKS.

000218 01-03

A COMPARISON OF RATES OF DEPLETION AND RECOVERY OF NORADRENALINE STORES OF PERIPHERAL AND CENTRAL NORADRENERGIC NEURONES AFTER RESERPINE ADMINISTRATION: IMPORTANCE OF NEURONAL ACTIVITY.

000314 01-03

INTRAVENTRICULAR 6 HYDROXYDOPAMINE IN THE NEWBORN RAT AND LOCOMOTOR RESPONSES TO DRUGS IN INFANCY: NO SUPPORT FOR THE DOPAMINE DEPLETION MODEL OF MINIMAL-BRAIN-DYSFUNCTION.

000448 01-04

THE EFFECT OF SEROTONIN DEPLETION ON THE DISCRIMINABILITY OF LSD.

000499 01-04

LITHIUM ANTAGONISM OF ETHANOL-INDUCED DEPLETION OF CEREBELLAR GUANOSINE-CYCLIC-MONOPHOSPHATE AND STIMULATION OF STRIATAL DOPAMINE RELEASE.

002242 02-13

DOPAMINE DEPLETION SLOWS RETINAL TRANSMISSION.

002708 03-03

GABA DEPLETION IN CHICK BRAINSTEM AFTER INTRAVENTRICULAR INJECTION OF CEFAZOLIN.

002762 03-03

NOREPINEPHRINE DEPLETION ALTERS CEREBRAL OXIDATIVE METABOLISM IN THE ACTIVE STATE.
002798 03-03

SUBSTANCE-P, HEXAPEPTIDE-PGLU6(SP6-11), ANALGESIA AND SEROTONIN DEPLETION.
003050 03-04

DOPAMINE DEPLETION BY 6 HYDROXYDOPAMINE PREVENTS CONDITIONED TASTE-AVERSION INDUCED BY METHYLAMPHETAMINE BUT NOT LITHIUM-CHLORIDE.
003110 03-04

EFFECTS OF TRICYCLIC-ANTIDEPRESSANTS ON TETRABENAZINE-INDUCED DEPLETION OF BRAIN MONOAMINES IN RATS. 1. NOREPINEPHRINE.
004062 04-03

DEPOLARIZATION
CHANGES IN PRIMARY AFFERENT DEPOLARIZATION AFTER ADMINISTRATION OF GAMMA ACETYLENIC-GAMMA-AMINOBUTYRIC-ACID (GAG), A GAMMA AMINOBUTYRIC-ACID-TRANSAMINASE (GABA-TRANSAMINASE) INHIBITOR.
000174 01-03

GAMMA AMINOBUTYRIC-ACID AGONISTS: AN IN VITRO COMPARISON BETWEEN DEPRESSION OF SPINAL SYNAPTIC ACTIVITY AND DEPOLARIZATION OF SPINAL ROOT FIBRES IN THE RAT.
001104 02-03

DEPOLARIZATION-INDUCED
EFFECTS OF PSYCHOTROPIC-DRUGS ON THE DISTRIBUTION OF 3H DOPAMINE INTO COMPARTMENTS OF RAT STRIATAL SYNAPTOSOMES AND ON SUBSEQUENT DEPOLARIZATION-INDUCED 3H DOPAMINE RELEASE.
000067 01-03

EFFECTS OF CHLORDIAZEPOXIDE ON DEPOLARIZATION-INDUCED CALCIUM INFLUX INTO SYNAPTOSOMES.
000183 01-03

DEPOLARIZING
THE EFFECTS OF A BENZODIAZEPINE ON THE HYPERPOLARIZING AND THE DEPOLARIZING RESPONSES OF HIPPOCAMPAL CELLS TO GABA.
002763 03-03

DEPOLARIZING-AGENTS
EPINEPHRINE IS RELEASED FROM HYPOTHALAMUS BY DEPOLARIZING-AGENTS AND AMPHETAMINE.
001155 02-03

RELATIVE ACTIVITIES OF SUBSTANCES RELATED TO 5 HYDROXYTRYPTAMINE AS DEPOLARIZING-AGENTS OF SUPERIOR CERVICAL GANGLION CELLS.
004047 04-03

DEPOT
PSYCHIATRIC-DISTURBANCE IN MENTALLY-HANDICAPPED-PATIENTS: A PROSPECTIVE STUDY OF CURRENT CLINICAL USAGE OF DEPOT FLUPHENAZINE IN HOSPITALS FOR THE MENTALLY-HANDICAPPED.
000668 01-11

MICROSCOPIC EVIDENCE OF LYMPHOGENIC ABSORPTION OF OIL IN HUMANS RECEIVING NEUROLEPTIC OILY DEPOT PREPARATIONS INTRAMUSCULARLY.
000890 01-15

DISCONTINUATION OF ORAL AND DEPOT FLUPHENAZINE IN SCHIZOPHRENIC-PATIENTS AFTER ONE YEAR OF CONTINUOUS MEDICATION: A CONTROLLED-STUDY.
001931 02-08

PLASMA FLUPHENAZINE LEVELS BY RADIOIMMUNOASSAY IN SCHIZOPHRENIC-PATIENTS TREATED WITH DEPOT INJECTIONS OF FLUPHENAZINE-DECANOATE.
002510 02-16

TWELVE YEARS EXPERIENCE WITH THE TOTAL USE OF DEPOT NEUROLEPTICS IN A DEFINED POPULATION.
002544 02-17

TREATMENT OF THERAPEUTICALLY-RESISTANT PARANOID SCHIZOPHRENIC-PATIENTS WITH FLUPHENAZINE DEPOT COMBINED WITH OTHER PSYCHOTROPIC-DRUGS AND CLOZAPINE.
003172 03-08

MANAGEMENT OF SCHIZOPHRENIA: LONG-TERM CLINICAL-STUDIES WITH SPECIAL REFERENCE TO THE COMBINATION OF PSYCHOTHERAPY AND DEPOT NEUROLEPTICS.
003183 03-08

A FOLLOWUP STUDY OF SCHIZOPHRENIC-OUTPATIENTS TREATED WITH DEPOT NEUROLEPTICS.
004342 04-08

DEPOT FLUPHENAZINE MAINTENANCE-TREATMENT AND ASSOCIATED WEIGHT CHANGES.
004635 04-15

RESULTS OF TREATMENT BY MODITEN DEPOT IN OUTPATIENTS-WARDS IN THE SOUTH MORAVIAN REGION.
004648 04-15

DEPRENIL
ANTIDEPRESSANT POTENTIATION OF 5 HYDROXYTRYPTOPHAN BY L DEPRENIL IN AFFECTIVE-ILLNESS.
000608 01-09

DEPRENYL
INHIBITION OF MONOAMINE-OXIDASE BY CLORGYLINE AND DEPRENYL IN CIRCUMVENTRICULAR STRUCTURES OF RAT-BRAIN.
000159 01-03

THE MONOAMINE-OXIDASE-INHIBITORS CLORGYLINE AND L DEPRENYL ALSO AFFECT THE UPTAKE OF DOPAMINE, NORADRENALINE AND SEROTONIN BY RAT-BRAIN SYNAPTOSOMAL PREPARATIONS.
000171 01-03

BIOCHEMICAL-MEASUREMENTS DURING (-)DEPRENYL TREATMENT OF PARKINSONISM.
000673 01-11

DEPRENYL IN THE MANAGEMENT OF RESPONSE FLUCTUATIONS IN PATIENTS WITH PARKINSONS-DISEASE ON LEVODOPA.
002358 02-14

THE EFFECT OF DEPRENYL, A SELECTIVE MONOAMINE-OXIDASE-B-INHIBITOR, ON SLEEP AND MOOD IN MAN.
002365 02-14

DEPRENYL IN PARKINSON-DISEASE.
003309 03-11

DEPRENYL DOES NOT CAUSE INSOMNIA IN PARKINSONIAN-PATIENTS.
004569 04-14

IS THE FAILURE OF (-)DEPRENYL, A SELECTIVE MONOAMINE-OXIDASE-B-INHIBITOR, TO ALLEVIATE DEPRESSION RELATED TO FREEDOM FROM THE CHEESE EFFECT?
004640 04-15

DEPRESSANT
CENTRAL DEPRESSANT EFFECTS OF CAERULEIN AND CHOLECYSTOKININ-OCTAPEPTIDE (CCK-8) DIFFER FROM THOSE OF DIAZEPAM AND HALOPERIDOL.
002652 03-02

GABA-RECEPTORS AND THE DEPRESSANT ACTION OF PENTOBARBITAL.
002666 03-03

SENSITIVE DEPRESSANT EFFECT OF BENZODIAZEPINES ON THE CROSSED EXTENSOR REFLEX IN CHLORALOSE ANESTHETIZED RATS.
003027 03-04

1 SUBSTITUTED BENZYLTETRAHYDROPYRIMIDONES; A SERIES WITH STIMULANT AND DEPRESSANT ACTIVITIES.
003687 04-02

4 AMINOPYRIDINE BLOCKADE OF NEURONAL DEPRESSANT RESPONSES TO ADENOSINE-TRIPHOSPHATE.
003963 04-03

DEPRESSANTS
HEMODYNAMIC FAILURE INDUCED BY NARCOTIC AND TOXIC DOSES OF 12 CNS DEPRESSANTS IN INTACT AND PITHED RATS.
001855 02-05

THE EFFECTS OF THYROTROPIN-RELEASING-HORMONE ON CYCLIC-AMP ACCUMULATION IN RABBIT CEREBROCORTICAL TISSUE IN THE PRESENCE AND ABSENCE OF CNS DEPRESSANTS.
004010 04-03

DEPRESSED
GLUCOSE OXIDATION IN THE VENTROMEDIAL HYPOTHALAMUS IS NOT AFFECTED BY INSULIN OR OUABAIN BUT DEPRESSED BY ALLOXAN TREATMENT.
001145 02-03

ELECTROMYOGRAPHIC-ASSESSMENT OF SPINAL REFLEXES IN EXPERIMENTALLY DEPRESSED DOGS TREATED WITH ANTIDEPRESSANTS.
001620 02-04

VILOXAZINE AND THE DEPRESSED SCHIZOPHRENIC -- METHODOLOGICAL-ISSUES.
003181 03-08

THE PHARMACOLOGICAL-TREATMENT OF SCHIZOAFFECTIVE-DISORDER DEPRESSED; A REVIEW OF THE LITERATURE.
003634 03-17

DECREASED 3H IMIPRAMINE BINDING IN DEPRESSED MALES AND FEMALES.
004349 04-09

DEPRESSED-CHILD
HYPOMANIC-REACTION TO AMITRIPTYLINE IN A DEPRESSED-CHILD.
002418 02-15

DEPRESSED-INPATIENTS
CLINICAL-RESPONSE, PLASMA LEVELS AND PHARMACOKINETICS OF DESIPRAMINE IN DEPRESSED-INPATIENTS.
002002 02-09

A DOUBLE-BLIND COMPARISON BETWEEN AMOXAPINE AND AMITRIPTYLINE IN DEPRESSED-INPATIENTS.
003234 03-09

A DOUBLE-BLIND MULTICENTRE-TRIAL COMPARING THE EFFICACY AND SIDE-EFFECTS OF MIANSERIN AND CHLORIMIPRAMINE IN DEPRESSED-INPATIENTS AND DEPRESSED-OUTPATIENTS.
004395 04-09

DEPRESSED-OUTPATIENTS
A DOUBLE-BLIND GROUP COMPARATIVE-TRIAL OF MIANSERIN AND DIAZEPAM IN DEPRESSED-OUTPATIENTS.
000592 01-09

CHRONIC MOOD-DISORDERS IN DEPRESSED-OUTPATIENTS: DIAGNOSIS AND RESPONSE TO PHARMACOTHERAPY.
000624 01-09

DEPRESSED-OUTPATIENTS TREATED WITH COGNITIVE-THERAPY OR PHARMACOTHERAPY: A ONE-YEAR FOLLOWUP.
003235 03-09

AMOXAPINE AND IMIPRAMINE IN THE TREATMENT OF DEPRESSED-OUTPATIENTS: A CONTROLLED-STUDY.
003254 03-09
DEPRESSED-OUTPATIENTS: RESULTS ONE YEAR AFTER TREATMENT WITH DRUGS AND/OR INTERPERSONAL PSYCHOTHERAPY.
003272 03-09
A DOUBLE-BLIND MULTICENTRE-TRIAL COMPARING THE EFFICACY AND SIDE-EFFECTS OF MIANSERIN AND CHLORIMIPRAMINE IN DEPRESSED-INPATIENTS AND DEPRESSED-OUTPATIENTS.
004395 04-09
PERSONALITY AS A PREDICTOR OF PSYCHOTHERAPY AND PHARMACOTHERAPY-OUTCOME FOR DEPRESSED-OUTPATIENTS. (UNPUBLISHED PAPER).
004418 04-09

DEPRESSED-PATIENT
TREATMENT OF TARDIVE-DYSKINESIA IN AN AGITATED, DEPRESSED-PATIENT.
002038 02-09

DEPRESSED-PATIENTS
PREDICTION OF STEADY-STATE PLASMA LEVELS OF AMITRIPTYLINE AND NORTRIPTYLINE FROM A SINGLE-DOSE 24-HR. LEVEL IN DEPRESSED-PATIENTS.
000582 01-09
URINARY MHPG AND CLINICAL-RESPONSE TO AMITRIPTYLINE IN DEPRESSED-PATIENTS.
000631 01-09
EFFICACY OF DESIPRAMINE IN ENDOGENOMORPHICALLY DEPRESSED-PATIENTS.
000632 01-09
CLINICAL-TRIALS WITH RUBIDIUM-CHLORIDE IN DEPRESSED-PATIENTS.
001893 02-07
COMPARISON OF THE EFFECTS OF LOFEPRAMINE AND MIANSERIN IN DEPRESSED-PATIENTS IN A DOUBLE-BLIND TRIAL.
001996 02-09
THE USE OF VILOXAZINE IN HOSPITALIZED DEPRESSED-PATIENTS: RANDOM COMPARISON WITH IMIPRAMINE IN A DOUBLE-BLIND TRIAL.
001998 02-09
TREATMENT OF THERAPY-RESISTANT DEPRESSED-PATIENTS WITH IV. INFUSIONS OF NOMIFENSINE CONTROLLED BY GALVANIC-SKIN-RESISTANCE.
002012 02-09
TARDIVE-DYSKINESIA IN DEPRESSED-PATIENTS: SUCCESSFUL THERAPY WITH ANTIDEPRESSANTS AND LITHIUM.
002037 02-09
CARDIOVASCULAR-EFFECTS OF AMITRIPTYLINE, MIANSERIN AND ZIMELIDINE IN DEPRESSED-PATIENTS.
002215 02-13
EFFICACY OF DESIPRAMINE IN MILDLY DEPRESSED-PATIENTS: A DOUBLE-BLIND, PLACEBO-CONTROLLED-TRIAL.
003262 03-09
BEHAVIORAL-EFFECTS AND BIOLOGICAL-EFFECTS OF ACUTE BETA ENDORPHIN INJECTION IN SCHIZOPHRENIC-PATIENTS AND DEPRESSED-PATIENTS.
003357 03-11
3H IMIPRAMINE BINDING IN HUMAN PLATELETS: DIMINUTION OF BINDING-SITES IN DEPRESSED-PATIENTS.
003427 03-13
MULTICENTRE-STUDY WITH VILOXAZINE (VIVALAN) IN DEPRESSED-PATIENTS.
004375 04-09
SINGLE-DOSE PHARMACOKINETIC DATA ON ZIMELIDINE IN DEPRESSED-PATIENTS.
004385 04-09
TSH, HGH, HPR, AND CORTISOL RESPONSE TO TRH IN DEPRESSED-PATIENTS.
004399 04-09

DEPRESSION
BLOCKADE OF METHAMPHETAMINE-INDUCED DEPRESSION OF TYROSINE-HYDROXYLASE BY GABA-TRANSAMINASE INHIBITORS.
000130 01-03
DIAZEPAM POTENTIATION OF PURINERGIC DEPRESSION OF CENTRAL NEURONS.
000233 01-03
REWARD SYSTEM DEPRESSION FOLLOWING CHRONIC AMPHETAMINE: ANTAGONISM BY HALOPERIDOL.
000342 01-04
POSTAMPHETAMINE DEPRESSION OF SELF-STIMULATION RESPONDING FROM THE SUBSTANTIA-NIGRA: REVERSAL BY TRICYCLIC-ANTIDEPRESSANTS.
000419 01-04
LITHIUM TREATMENT IN POSTPSYCHOTIC DEPRESSION.
000575 01-08
DRUG-THERAPY IN ENDOGENOUS DEPRESSION WITH POSSIBLE PRIMARY GABA DEFICIENCY CLINICALLY DETECTED: 38 NEW CASES.
000584 01-09
CLINICAL AND LABORATORY DIAGNOSTICS APPLICATIONS IN DEPRESSION. (UNPUBLISHED PAPER).
000588 01-09
CLINICAL AND BIOCHEMICAL-ACTION OF PIRACETAM (NOOTROPIL) IN DRUG-RESISTANT DEPRESSION.
000600 01-09

TREATMENT OF DEPRESSION IN THE MEDICALLY-ILL ELDERLY WITH METHYLPHENIDATE.
000602 01-09
PREDICTION OF LOFEPRAMINE RESPONSE IN DEPRESSION BASED ON RESPONSE TO PARTIAL SLEEP-DEPRIVATION.
000617 01-09
THREE CASES OF UNIPOLAR DELUSIONAL DEPRESSION RESPONSIVE TO L-DOPA.
000628 01-09
SINTAMIL IN THE TREATMENT OF DEPRESSION: A COMPARISON OF SINGLE VS. DIVIDED DOSE ADMINISTRATION.
000629 01-09
ANTIDEPRESSIVE TREATMENT AND MOOD-SWING-PATTERNS IN ENDOGENOUS DEPRESSION.
000633 01-09
DECREASED UPTAKE OF 5 HYDROXYTRYPTAMINE IN BLOOD-PLATELETS FROM PATIENTS WITH ENDOGENOUS DEPRESSION.
000637 01-09
STIMULUS INTENSITY CONTROL IN DEPRESSION: A STUDY OF THE COMPARATIVE-EFFECT OF DOXEPIN AND AMITRIPTYLINE ON CORTICAL EVOKED-POTENTIALS.
000763 01-13
DEXAMETHASONE-SUPPRESSION-TESTS IN DEPRESSION AND RESPONSE TO TREATMENT.
000899 01-16
MONOAMINES AND DEPRESSION: AN INTERIM REPORT. I. SEROTONIN AND SEROTONIN PRECURSORS.
000996 01-17
DEPRESSION IN THE ELDERLY: RESEARCH DIRECTIONS IN PSYCHOPATHOLOGY, EPIDEMIOLOGY, AND TREATMENT.
000998 01-17
GAMMA AMINOBUTYRIC-ACID AGONISTS: AN IN VITRO COMPARISON BETWEEN DEPRESSION OF SPINAL SYNAPTIC ACTIVITY AND DEPOLARIZATION OF SPINAL ROOT FIBRES IN THE RAT.
001104 02-03
DEPRESSION AND FACILITATION OF SYNAPTIC RESPONSES IN CAT DORSAL-HORN BY SUBSTANCE-P ADMINISTERED INTO SUBSTANTIA-GELATINOSA.
001191 02-03
TOLERANCE TO BARBITURATE-INDUCED CENTRAL-NERVOUS-SYSTEM DEPRESSION: INVOLVEMENT OF STIMULUS SECRETION COUPLING IN DISCRETE BRAIN AREAS. (PH.D. DISSERTATION).
001213 02-03
AMINOPHYLLINE AND THEOPHYLLINE DERIVATIVES AS ANTAGONISTS OF NEURONAL DEPRESSION BY ADENOSINE: A MICROIONTOPHORETIC-STUDY.
001410 02-03
BIOCHEMICAL-STUDY OF THE ANIMAL-MODEL DEPRESSION INDUCED BY TETRABENAZINE.
001506 02-03
EFFECTS OF CHRONIC AMPHETAMINE OR RESERPINE ON SELF-STIMULATION RESPONDING: ANIMAL-MODEL OF DEPRESSION?
001699 02-04
PRESYNAPTIC AND POSTSYNAPTIC SEROTONERGIC MANIPULATIONS IN AN ANIMAL-MODEL OF DEPRESSION.
001730 02-04
RESULTS OF A SURVEY ON THE PRESENT TREATMENT OF DEPRESSION IN SPAIN.
001963 02-09
NOMIFENSINE IN THE TREATMENT OF VARIOUS TYPES OF DEPRESSION.
001968 02-09
DEXAMETHASONE-SUPPRESSION-TEST IDENTIFIES SUBTYPES OF DEPRESSION WHICH RESPOND TO DIFFERENT ANTIDEPRESSANTS.
001971 02-09
CLINICAL-STUDIES AND BIOLOGICAL-STUDIES OF L TRYPTOPHAN IN DEPRESSION.
001977 02-09
NOMIFENSINE IN THE TREATMENT OF ENDOGENOUS DEPRESSION. A CONTROLLED-STUDY VS. NORTRIPTYLINE.
001978 02-09
ENDOGENOUS DEPRESSION AND IMIPRAMINE LEVELS IN THE BLOOD.
001979 02-09
DEPRESSION: HOW TO RATIONALISE DRUG-THERAPY.
001988 02-09
A CLINICAL-TRIAL OF ZIMELIDINE IN DEPRESSION.
001992 02-09
TRAZODONE IN THE TREATMENT OF NEUROTIC DEPRESSION.
001994 02-09
AN OVERVIEW OF SEVENTEEN YEARS OF EXPERIENCE WITH DOTHIEPIN IN THE TREATMENT OF DEPRESSION IN EUROPE.
001995 02-09
EVALUATION OF NOMIFENSINE IN THE TREATMENT OF GERIATRIC DEPRESSION USING PSYCHOMETRIC-TESTS AND PLASMA LEVEL CONTROLS.
002004 02-09
INFUSION THERAPY IN THERAPY-RESISTANT DEPRESSION.
002007 02-09
LONG-TERM-TREATMENT OF DEPRESSION WITH ISOCARBOXAZIDE.
002011 02-09

D PHENYLALANINE IN ENDOGENOUS DEPRESSION.
002017 02-09
THE PHARMACOTHERAPY OF MAJOR DEPRESSIVE-SYNDROME. PART 1:
TREATMENT OF ACUTE DEPRESSION.
002044 02-09
INFUSION OF MAPROTILIN AND CLOMIPRAMIN AND THEIR COMBINATION
IN THE TREATMENT OF DEPRESSION.
002056 02-09
PHARMACOTHERAPY OF DEPRESSION IN THE ELDERLY.
002144 02-11
THE RELATIVE EFFICACY OF COGNITIVE-THERAPY AND CHEMOTHERAPY
FOR THE TREATMENT OF DEPRESSION AMONG THE RETIRED ELDERLY.
(PH.D. DISSERTATION).
002148 02-11
ENDOCRINE CHANGES AND BEHAVIORAL-CHANGES IN DEPRESSION AFTER
THYROTROPIN-RELEASING-HORMONE (TRH): ALTERATION BY
PRETREATMENT WITH THYROID-HORMONES.
002259 02-13
DOPA AND DOPAMINE AGONISTS IN DEPRESSION.
002310 02-13
L HTP AND THE SEROTONIN HYPOTHESIS: THEIR MEANING FOR
TREATMENT OF DEPRESSION.
002326 02-14
THEOPHYLLINE AND DEPRESSION.
002439 02-15
SUBTYPES OF DEPRESSION BASED ON EXCRETION OF MHPG AND
RESPONSE TO NORTRIPTYLINE.
002488 02-16
HETEROGENEOUS DEPRESSION OF GLUCOSE UTILIZATION IN THE
CAUDATE-NUCLEUS BY GABA AGONISTS.
002640 03-01
NONSEROTONERGIC DEPRESSION OF SPINAL MONOSYNAPTIC REFLEX
TRANSMISSION BY 5 HYDROXYTRYPTOPHAN.
002745 03-03
DEPRESSION OF VENTRAL ROOT DORSAL ROOT POTENTIAL BY DL ALPHA
AMINOADIPATE IN FROG SPINAL-CORD.
002755 03-03
EVIDENCE THAT THE OPIATE-RECEPTORS OF THE SUBSTANTIA-
GELATINOSA CONTRIBUTE TO THE DEPRESSION, BY INTRAVENOUS
MORPHINE, OF THE SPINAL TRANSMISSION OF IMPULSES IN
UNMYELINATED PRIMARY AFFERENTS.
002767 03-03
ROLE OF MONOAMINERGIC SYSTEMS IN MORPHINE-INDUCED
RESPIRATORY DEPRESSION.
002827 03-03
NEUROTRANSMITTERS AND DEPRESSION: TOO MUCH, TOO LITTLE, TOO
UNSTABLE -- OR NOT UNSTABLE ENOUGH?
002931 03-03
DEPRESSION OF RESERPINE-INDUCED MUSCULAR RIGIDITY IN RATS AFTER
ADMINISTRATION OF LISURIDE INTO THE SPINAL SUBARACHNOID
SPACE.
002962 03-04
THE DEXAMETHASONE-SUPPRESSION-TEST IN THE IDENTIFICATION OF
SUBTYPES OF DEPRESSION DIFFERENTIALLY RESPONSIVE TO
ANTIDEPRESSANTS.
003211 03-09
PROTOCOLS FOR THE USE OF PSYCHOACTIVE-DRUGS -- PART II:
PROTOCOL FOR THE TREATMENT OF DEPRESSION WITH TRICYCLIC-
ANTIDEPRESSANTS.
003214 03-09
AMOXAPINE AND AMITRIPTYLINE IN THE OUTPATIENT TREATMENT OF
ENDOGENOUS DEPRESSION.
003217 03-09
METHADONE AND MORPHINE IN DEPRESSION.
003220 03-09
SYNAPTIC AND BEHAVIOURAL-ACTIONS OF ANTIDEPRESSANT-DRUGS:
FURTHER THOUGHTS ON THE IMPLICATIONS FOR THEORIES OF
DEPRESSION.
003229 03-09
SLEEP AND TREATMENT PREDICTION IN ENDOGENOUS DEPRESSION.
003236 03-09
DEPRESSION SUBTYPES AFFECT THE STEADY-STATE PLASMA LEVELS AND
THERAPEUTIC-EFFICACY OF AMITRIPTYLINE AND NORTRIPTYLINE.
003244 03-09
PHENELZINE AND AMITRIPTYLINE IN NEUROTIC DEPRESSION.
(UNPUBLISHED PAPER).
003248 03-09
EFFECTS OF PHENELZINE AND AMITRIPTYLINE ON DEPRESSION.
003249 03-09
CROSS-OVER STUDY OF ZIMELIDINE AND DESIPRAMINE IN DEPRESSION:
EVIDENCE FOR AMINE SPECIFICITY.
003250 03-09
LITHIUM AND IMIPRAMINE IN THE PROPHYLAXIS OF UNIPOLAR AND
BIPOLAR-II DEPRESSION: A PROSPECTIVE, PLACEBO-CONTROLLED
COMPARISON.
003252 03-09
BEHAVIORAL-PREDICTORS OF AMITRIPTYLINE RESPONSE IN DEPRESSION.
003253 03-09
DO PSYCHOTHERAPY AND PHARMACOTHERAPY FOR DEPRESSION
CONFLICT? EMPIRICAL EVIDENCE FROM A CLINICAL-TRIAL.
003256 03-09

THE TREATMENT OF DEPRESSION USING CLOMIPRAMINE IN GENERAL-
MEDICAL-PRACTICE: 48 CASES TREATED ON AN OUTPATIENT BASIS.
003268 03-09
MANAGEMENT OF DEPRESSION WITH SEROTONIN PRECURSORS.
003269 03-09
MAPROTILINE VERSUS IMIPRAMINE AND PLACEBO IN NEUROTIC
DEPRESSION.
003287 03-10
NEUROENDOCRINOLOGY OF DEPRESSION -- A DISCUSSION.
003402 03-13
HIGH-AFFINITY 3H IMIPRAMINE BINDING: A NEW BIOLOGICAL TOOL FOR
STUDIES IN DEPRESSION.
003610 03-17
SPREADING DEPRESSION INDUCED BY MICROINJECTION OF ENKEPHALINS
INTO THE HIPPOCAMPUS AND NEOCORTEX.
004015 04-03
CANNABINOID-INDUCED ENHANCEMENT AND DEPRESSION OF CAT
MONOSYNAPTIC REFLEXES.
004040 04-03
RESPIRATORY DEPRESSION PRODUCED BY DIAZEPAM IN CATS: EFFECT OF
ANESTHESIA.
004272 04-05
POTENTIATION OF THE MORPHINE-INDUCED RESPIRATORY RATE
DEPRESSION BY CAPTOPRIL.
004275 04-05
TRAZODONE EFFICACY AND SAFETY IN ENDOGENOUS DEPRESSION: A
DOUBLE-BLIND COMPARISON WITH IMIPRAMINE.
004346 04-09
PHARMACOTHERAPY FOR DEPRESSION.
004351 04-09
RECEPTORS, ADENYLATE-CYCLASE, DEPRESSION, AND LITHIUM.
004353 04-09
CLINICAL-RESPONSE AND BLOOD LEVELS IN THE TREATMENT OF
DEPRESSION WITH A NEW ANTIDEPRESSANT-DRUG, AMOXAPINE.
004356 04-09
(3H) IMIPRAMINE BINDING IN HUMAN PLATELETS: A NEW
BIOCHEMICAL-PARAMETER IN DEPRESSION.
004358 04-09
A NEUROENDOCRINE-STUDY OF ADRENOCEPTOR FUNCTION IN
ENDOGENOUS DEPRESSION.
004362 04-09
PERIPHERAL SEROTONERGIC AND ADRENERGIC RESPONSES IN
DEPRESSION.
004364 04-09
CONVULSIVE AND DRUG-THERAPIES OF DEPRESSION.
004366 04-09
LONG-TERM-TREATMENT FOR DEPRESSION.
004372 04-09
CHOLINERGIC MECHANISMS IN MANIA AND DEPRESSION: QUESTIONS OF
SPECIFICITY.
004374 04-09
GUIDELINES ON THE DIAGNOSIS AND TREATMENT OF DEPRESSION.
004376 04-09
TREATMENT OF DEPRESSION WITH AN MAO-INHIBITOR FOLLOWED BY 5
HTP -- AN UNFINISHED RESEARCH PROJECT.
004377 04-09
CEREBROSPINAL-FLUID VALUES OF HVA AND 5 HIAA IN PATIENTS WITH
ENDOGENOUS DEPRESSION DURING THE COURSE OF TREATMENT.
004382 04-09
AN EVALUATION OF TRAZODONE IN THE TREATMENT OF DEPRESSION.
004386 04-09
THE NOSOLOGICAL INDEPENDENCE OF INVOLUTIONAL DEPRESSION AND
ITS DYNAMICS DURING PSYCHOPHARMACOTHERAPY.
004389 04-09
PROPHYLACTIC-EFFECT OF LITHIUM AGAINST DEPRESSION IN
CYCLOTHYMIC-PATIENTS: A LIFE-TABLE ANALYSIS.
004391 04-09
A COMPARISON OF TRAZODONE AND DOTHIEPIN IN DEPRESSION.
004394 04-09
DO PSYCHOTHERAPY AND PHARMACOTHERAPY FOR DEPRESSION
CONFLICT? EMPIRICAL EVIDENCE FROM A CLINICAL-TRIAL.
(UNPUBLISHED PAPER).
004401 04-09
CORTISOL DYNAMICS AND DEXAMETHASONE PHARMACOKINETICS IN
PRIMARY ENDOGENOUS DEPRESSION: PRELIMINARY FINDINGS.
004403 04-09
NEUROENDOCRINE DISTURBANCE IN DEPRESSION.
004405 04-09
ELECTROCARDIOGRAM-CHANGES AND PLASMA DESIPRAMINE LEVELS
DURING TREATMENT OF DEPRESSION.
004411 04-09
PHARMACOTHERAPY AND PSYCHOTHERAPY FOR AMBULATORY
DEPRESSION: EFFICACY AND CHOICES.
004413 04-09
TRAZODONE IN DEPRESSION.
004414 04-09
CONTROLLED CLINICAL-TRIAL OF NOMIFENSINE IN THE TREATMENT OF
DEPRESSION.
004417 04-09

DOSE-EFFECT OF DEAE ON SUBJECTIVE PROBLEMS, VERTIGO, DEPRESSION, ASTHENIA, CEPHALALGIA, AND TONIC POSTURAL ACTIVITY PROBLEMS RECORDED WITH STATOKINESIMETER IN POSTCONCUSSIONAL-SYNDROME.
004472 04-11

THE ACTIVITY OF BLOOD-PLATELET MONOAMINE-OXIDASE IN ENDOGENOUS DEPRESSION.
004547 04-13

IS THE FAILURE OF (-)DEPRENYL, A SELECTIVE MONOAMINE-OXIDASE-B-INHIBITOR, TO ALLEVIATE DEPRESSION RELATED TO FREEDOM FROM THE CHEESE EFFECT?
004640 04-15

DEPRESSIONS
STUDY OF INTRAVENOUS AMITRIPTYLINE IN ACUTE DEPRESSIONS.
000581 01-09

THE LONG-TERM-TREATMENT OF PERIODICAL AND CYCLIC DEPRESSIONS WITH FLUPENTHIXOL-DECANOATE.
000603 01-09

NOMIFENSIN IN THE TREATMENT OF ENDOGENOUS DEPRESSIONS. CLINICAL-EXPERIENCE AND EEG FINDINGS.
000613 01-09

CONTROLLED-COMPARISON OF MIANSERINE WITH IMIPRAMINE IN ENDOGENOUS DEPRESSIONS.
000634 01-09

TRAZODONE IN DEPRESSIONS.
000643 01-09

CLINICAL-EXPERIENCE WITH SECOND-GENERATION ANTIDEPRESSANTS IN ENDOGENOUS DEPRESSIONS.
001975 02-09

THE CORRELATION OF CATECHOLAMINE AND ADRENERGIC PARAMETERS WITH DRUG-THERAPY OF NEUROTIC AND ENDOGENOUS DEPRESSIONS.
002047 02-09

PYRAZIDOL IN THE TREATMENT OF DEPRESSIONS.
002055 02-09

IATROGENIC DEPRESSIONS.
002388 02-15

CLINICAL-EXPERIENCE WITH RETARD DIBENZEPINE (NOVERIL-240) IN ENDOGENOUS DEPRESSIONS ACCOMPANIED BY SYMPTOMS OF DRUG-RESISTANCE.
003245 03-09

THERAPEUTIC EFFECT OF MIANSERINE AND IMIPRAMINE IN ENDOGENOUS DEPRESSIONS (CONTROLLED-COMPARISON).
003264 03-09

THERAPEUTICS (I) -- PHARMACOLOGICAL-TREATMENT OF DEPRESSIONS.
003270 03-09

CLINICAL DEPRESSIONS: DIAGNOSTIC AND THERAPEUTIC CHALLENGES.
004350 04-09

ACTIVITY OF BROMAZEPAM AND LORAZEPAM IN NEUROTIC DEPRESSIONS.
004384 04-09

DEPRESSIVE
THE RELATIVE PROPHYLACTIC EFFICACY OF LITHIUM AGAINST MANIC AND DEPRESSIVE RECURRENCES IN BIPOLAR-PATIENTS.
002040 02-09

STATISTICAL ANALYSES OF PHYSIOLOGIC DATA FROM FEMALE PATIENTS WITH AN ENDOMORPHOUS DEPRESSIVE COURSE: A TRIAL, INTERACTIONS BETWEEN PHYSIOLOGIC PARAMETERS, TEST JUNCTURES IN THIS PHASE.
003251 03-09

DEPRESSIVE-CONDITIONS
CLINICAL-TRIAL OF VILOXAZINE IN DEPRESSIVE-CONDITIONS.
000589 01-09

THE TREATMENT OF DEPRESSIVE-CONDITIONS WITH NOMIFENSINE.
000609 01-09

VARIATIONS IN URINARY EXCRETION OF 3 METHOXY-4-HYDROXYPHENYLGLYCOL-SULFATE IN DEPRESSIVE-CONDITIONS.
002013 02-09

TREATMENT OF DEPRESSIVE-CONDITIONS IN THE ELDERLY.
003578 03-17

DEPRESSIVE-DISORDER
PLASMA LEVELS OF IMIPRAMINE (IMI) AND DESMETHYLIMIPRAMINE (DMI) AND CLINICAL-RESPONSE IN PREPUBERTAL MAJOR DEPRESSIVE-DISORDER: A PRELIMINARY REPORT.
000619 01-09

DEPRESSIVE-DISORDERS
IMIPRAMINE TREATMENT OF PREPUBERTAL MAJOR DEPRESSIVE-DISORDERS: PLASMA LEVELS AND CLINICAL-RESPONSE -- PRELIMINARY REPORT.
000620 01-09

PROLACTIN CHANGES IN MAJOR DEPRESSIVE-DISORDERS.
000752 01-13

TOWARD A BIOCHEMICAL CLASSIFICATION OF DEPRESSIVE-DISORDERS IV: PRETREATMENT URINARY MHPG LEVELS AS PREDICTORS OF ANTIDEPRESSANT RESPONSE TO IMIPRAMINE.
004406 04-09

DEPRESSIVE-ILLNESS
A REEXAMINATION OF THE CLINICAL-EFFECTS OF IMIPRAMINE AND AMITRIPTYLINE IN DEPRESSIVE-ILLNESS.
000579 01-09

GROWTH-HORMONE AFTER TRH IN WOMEN WITH DEPRESSIVE-ILLNESS.
000606 01-09

THE PHARMACOTHERAPY OF MAJOR DEPRESSIVE-SYNDROME. PART 2: PROPHYLAXIS OF RECURRENT DEPRESSIVE-ILLNESS.
002043 02-09

DEPRESSIVE-NEUROSIS
VILOXAZINE IN THE TREATMENT OF DEPRESSIVE-NEUROSIS: A CONTROLLED CLINICAL-STUDY WITH DOXEPIN AND PLACEBO.
002080 02-10

CLOMIPRAMINE AND DOXEPIN IN DEPRESSIVE-NEUROSIS: PLASMA LEVELS AND THERAPEUTIC RESPONSE.
002258 02-13

VILOXAZINE IN THE TREATMENT OF DEPRESSIVE-NEUROSIS: A PLACEBO AND STANDARD (IMIPRAMINE) CONTROLLED CLINICAL-STUDY.
004392 04-09

DEPRESSIVE-PATIENTS
COMPARATIVE-STUDY OF THE CARDIOTOXICITY OF AMITRIPTYLINE AND MAPROTILINE IN DEPRESSIVE-PATIENTS.
000595 01-09

ON THE RELATIONSHIP OF NORTRIPTYLINE: AMITRIPTYLINE RATIO TO CLINICAL IMPROVEMENT OF AMITRIPTYLINE TREATED DEPRESSIVE-PATIENTS.
000599 01-09

A PRELIMINARY STUDY ON DETERMINATION OF THE OPTIMUM OPIPRAMOL DOSAGE IN DEPRESSIVE-PATIENTS.
000601 01-09

CLINICAL AND EEG CHANGES IN DEPRESSIVE-PATIENTS AFTER A SINGLE INJECTION OF BETA ENDORPHIN.
001962 02-09

EFFECTS OF ANTIDEPRESSANTS ON PITUITARY HORMONAL SECRETIONS IN HEALTHY TEST SUBJECTS, NEUROTIC-PATIENTS, AND ENDOGENOUS DEPRESSIVE-PATIENTS.
002009 02-09

OUTPATIENT CARE OF DEPRESSIVE-PATIENTS WITH MIANSERIN.
002041 02-09

PHARMACOKINETICS OF CLOMIPRAMINE IN DEPRESSIVE-PATIENTS.
003216 03-09

COMBINED ADMINISTRATION OF NIALAMIDE AND VILOXAZINE TO DEPRESSIVE-PATIENTS.
003232 03-09

DEPRESSIVE-STATES
OUR EXPERIENCE WITH MAPROTILIN TREATMENT OF DEPRESSIVE-STATES.
000623 01-09

VILOXAZINE IN THE TREATMENT OF DEPRESSIVE-STATES.
000626 01-09

STUDY OF MAPROTILINE IN OUTPATIENT TREATMENT OF DEPRESSIVE-STATES BY THE GENERAL-PRACTITIONER: ADVANTAGE OF SINGLE-NIGHTLY-DOSE.
001961 02-09

VARIATIONS IN PSYCHOPHYSIOLOGICAL ACTIVATION RESPONSES IN DEPRESSIVE-STATES.
001965 02-09

IS IT POSSIBLE TO SET UP ANY RULES FOR A COMPREHENSIVE TREATMENT OF DEPRESSIVE-STATES?
001997 02-09

THE IMPORTANCE OF AMINEPTINE IN THE TREATMENT OF NONPSYCHOTIC DEPRESSIVE-STATES IN THE ELDERLY.
001999 02-09

LARGE-DOSES OF DIBENZEPINE NOVERIL IN THE TREATMENT OF DEPRESSIVE-STATES.
002020 02-09

CLINICAL-TRIAL OF PYRAZIDOL IN ENDOGENOUS DEPRESSIVE-STATES.
002021 02-09

CLINICAL AND BIOCHEMICAL-DATA ON THE ACTION OF MAPROTILINE AND CLOMIPRAMINE IN DEPRESSIVE-STATES (PRELIMINARY OBSERVATION).
002032 02-09

AN OPEN-STUDY OF MAPROTILINE 75MG IN THE TREATMENT OF DEPRESSIVE-STATES.
003152 03-07

CLINICAL-STUDY OF MAPROTILINE IN THE TREATMENT OF DEPRESSIVE-STATES: COMPILATION OF 1520 OBSERVATIONS.
003206 03-09

DEPRESSIVE-SYMPTOMATOLOGY
CLINICAL-CORRELATION, BIOCHEMICAL-CORRELATION, AND PSYCHOPHARMACOLOGICAL-CORRELATION IN PATIENTS WITH DEPRESSIVE-SYMPTOMATOLOGY.
002018 02-09

PHYSOSTIGMINE INDUCTION OF DEPRESSIVE-SYMPTOMATOLOGY IN NORMAL HUMAN SUBJECTS.
003255 03-09

DEPRESSIVE-SYMPTOMS
IMIPRAMINE AND EEG SLEEP IN CHILDREN WITH DEPRESSIVE-SYMPTOMS.
002339 02-14

DEPRESSIVE-SYNDROME
PSYCHOTROPIC-DRUGS AND DEPRESSIVE-SYNDROME IN SCHIZOPHRENIA.
000569 01-08

A CASE-REPORT OF CIMETIDINE-INDUCED DEPRESSIVE-SYNDROME.
000839 01-15

THE PHARMACOTHERAPY OF MAJOR DEPRESSIVE-SYNDROME. PART 2: PROPHYLAXIS OF RECURRENT DEPRESSIVE-ILLNESS.
002043 02-09
THE PHARMACOTHERAPY OF MAJOR DEPRESSIVE-SYNDROME. PART 1: TREATMENT OF ACUTE DEPRESSION.
002044 02-09

DEPRESSIVE-SYNDROMES
THE USEFULNESS OF THE ERYTHROCYTE LITHIUM INDEX IN THE EVALUATION OF DISORDERS OF ION-TRANSFER IN PATIENTS WITH DEPRESSIVE-SYNDROMES.
000625 01-09
CLINICAL RESULTS OBTAINED WITH THE USE OF LYSONEURO IN DEPRESSIVE-SYNDROMES.
000425 01-09
CLINICAL RESULTS OBTAINED WITH THE USE OF LYSONEURO IN DEPRESSIVE-SYNDROMES.
004397 04-09
CLINICAL-EVALUATION OF THE PROPHYLACTIC EFFECTIVENESS OF PROLONGED LITHIUM-CARBONATE THERAPY IN ENDOGENOUS DEPRESSIVE-SYNDROMES.
004404 04-09
VARIATIONS IN URINARY LEVELS OF 3 METHOXY-4-HYDROXYPHENYLGLYCOL-SULFATE IN PATIENTS WITH DEPRESSIVE-SYNDROMES.
004533 04-13
THE ACTIVITY OF ERYTHROCYTE CATECHOL-O-METHYLTRANSFERASE IN ENDOGENOUS DEPRESSIVE-SYNDROMES.
004546 04-13
THE ACTIVITY OF DOPAMINE-BETA-HYDROXYLASE IN THE PLASMA OF PATIENTS WITH ENDOGENOUS DEPRESSIVE-SYNDROMES.
004548 04-13

DEPRESSIVES
AN INVERSE CORRELATION BETWEEN SERUM LEVELS OF DESMETHYLIMIPRAMINE AND MELATONIN-LIKE IMMUNOREACTIVITY IN DMI RESPONSIVE DEPRESSIVES.
003228 03-09
THE THERAPEUTIC PROFILE OF MIANSERIN IN MILD ELDERLY DEPRESSIVES.
003297 03-11

DEPRESSOR
FAILURE OF ISOPRENALINE AND BETA-RECEPTOR BLOCKING-DRUGS TO MODIFY DEPRESSOR RESPONSE AND BRADYCARDIA INDUCED BY ELECTRICAL-STIMULATION OF THE ANTERIOR HYPOTHALAMUS OF CATS.
000520 01-05

DEPRIVATION
ROLE OF INTRACORTICAL INHIBITION IN DEPRIVATION AMBLYOPIA: REVERSAL BY MICROIONTOPHORETIC BICUCULLINE.
002684 03-03
CORTICAL RECOVERY FROM EFFECTS OF MONOCULAR DEPRIVATION: ACCELERATION WITH NOREPINEPHRINE AND SUPPRESSION WITH 6 HYDROXYDOPAMINE.
003024 03-04
CHANGES OF RESPONSE TO DOPAMINERGIC DRUGS IN RATS SUBMITTED TO REM SLEEP DEPRIVATION.
004239 04-04

DEPRIVED
NALOXONE: EFFECTS ON FOOD AND WATER CONSUMPTION IN THE NONDEPRIVED AND DEPRIVED RAT.
001599 02-04
DIFFERENTIAL-EFFECTS OF MORPHINE ON FOOD AND WATER INTAKE IN FOOD DEPRIVED AND FREELY-FEEDING RATS.
001765 02-04
NALOXONE SUPPRESSES FOOD/WATER CONSUMPTION IN THE DEPRIVED CAT.
004114 04-04
PHARMACOKINETIC-STUDY OF APOMORPHINE-INDUCED STEREOTYPY IN FOOD DEPRIVED RATS.
004247 04-04

DERIVATIVE
FLUORINATED ANALOGUES OF THE TRICYCLIC NEUROLEPTICS: 2,3 DIFLUORO DERIVATIVE OF CLOROTEPIN.
000001 01-01
THE USE OF THIOPROPERAZINE, A PHENOTHIAZINE DERIVATIVE, AS A LIGAND FOR NEUROLEPTIC-RECEPTORS -- I. IN VITRO STUDIES.
001133 02-03
THE USE OF THIOPROPERAZINE, A PHENOTHIAZINE DERIVATIVE, AS A LIGAND FOR NEUROLEPTIC-RECEPTORS -- II. IN VIVO STUDIES.
001137 02-03
SLEEP PROFILE AND ULTRADIAN SLEEP PERIODICITY IN HUMANS UNDER THE INFLUENCE OF A BUTYROPHENONE DERIVATIVE: I. SLEEP CORRECTION IN SUBJECTS WITH OLIGOSYMPTOMATIC SLEEP-DISORDERS.
001869 02-06
DOUBLE-BLIND CLINICAL ASSESSMENT OF ALPRAZOLAM, A NEW BENZODIAZEPINE DERIVATIVE, IN THE TREATMENT OF MODERATE TO SEVERE ANXIETY.
002070 02-10
DU-24565, A QUIPAZINE DERIVATIVE, A POTENT SELECTIVE SEROTONIN UPTAKE INHIBITOR.
002651 03-02
SYNTHESIS AND STRUCTURE-ACTIVITY RELATIONSHIP OF A PYRIMIDOPYRIMIDINE DERIVATIVE WITH ANTIDEPRESSANT ACTIVITY.
003653 04-01

A STEROID DERIVATIVE, R-5135, ANTAGONIZES THE GABA/BENZODIAZEPINE-RECEPTOR INTERACTION.
003851 04-03

DERIVATIVES
N TETRAHYDROFURYLALKYL AND N ALKOXYALKYL DERIVATIVES OF (-) NORMETAZOCINE, COMPOUNDS WITH DIFFERENTIATED OPIOID ACTION PROFILES.
000013 01-02
EFFECTS OF PHENOTHIAZINE DERIVATIVES AND RELATED COMPOUNDS ON TYROSINE-AMINOTRANSFERASE ACTIVITY.
000018 01-03
ANORECTIC-EFFECT OF LISURIDE AND OTHER ERGOT DERIVATIVES IN THE RAT.
000042 01-03
INHIBITION OF BRAIN SYNAPTOSOMAL UPTAKE OF CHOLINE BY SOME 2 CARBOXAMIDOSTRYCHNINE DERIVATIVES WITH MUSCLE-RELAXANT PROPERTIES.
000084 01-03
DIAZEPAM IN COMBINATION WITH TACRINE DERIVATIVES ANTAGONIZES BEHAVIOURAL-EFFECTS OF ANTICHOLINERGIC PSYCHOTOMIMETICS IN RATS.
000420 01-04
STRUCTURE-ACTIVITY RELATIONSHIP OF PHENCYCLIDINE DERIVATIVES.
001030 02-01
THE EFFECT OF PHENELZINE AND SOME OF ITS PARA HALOGENATED DERIVATIVES ON THE LEVELS OF BRAIN TYRAMINE AND OCTOPAMINE IN THE MOUSE.
001077 02-02
SYNTHESIS AND PHARMACOLOGY OF 2 AMINO-3-ETHOXYCARBONYL-4-PHENYLTHIOPHENE DERIVATIVES.
001083 02-02
SYNTHESIS AND ANXIOLYTIC-ACTIVITY OF A SERIES OF PYRAZINOBENZODIAZEPINE DERIVATIVES.
001089 02-02
DERIVATIVES OF 11 1 PIPERAZINYL-5H-PYRROLOBENZODIAZEPINE AS CENTRAL-NERVOUS-SYSTEM AGENTS.
001093 02-02
ADAPTIVE CHANGES OF THE STRIATAL DOPAMINE SYSTEM INDUCED BY REPEATED ADMINISTRATION OF NEUROLEPTICS AND ERGOT DERIVATIVES.
001156 02-03
NEUROPHYSIOLOGICAL-STUDY OF TWO O ANISAMIDE DERIVATIVES: SULPIRIDE AND SULTOPRIDE.
001170 02-03
EFFECT OF ERGOT DERIVATIVES ON POSTDECAPITATION CONVULSIONS.
001288 02-03
REGIONAL RELEASE OF (3H)ADENOSINE DERIVATIVES FROM RAT-BRAIN IN VIVO: EFFECT OF EXCITATORY AMINO-ACIDS, OPIATE AGONISTS, AND BENZODIAZEPINES.
001303 02-03
AMINOPHYLLINE AND THEOPHYLLINE DERIVATIVES AS ANTAGONISTS OF NEURONAL DEPRESSION BY ADENOSINE: A MICROIONTOPHORETIC-STUDY.
001410 02-03
INTERACTION OF DOPAMINERGIC ERGOT DERIVATIVES WITH CYCLIC-NUCLEOTIDE SYSTEM.
001482 02-03
PHENCYCLIDINE (PCP) AND DERIVATIVES: PHARMACOLOGY AND STRUCTURE-ACTIVITY RELATIONSHIPS.
001706 02-04
COMPARISON OF OPIATE AGONISTS AND THEIR N ALLYL DERIVATIVES IN THE PRODUCTION OF PHYSICAL-DEPENDENCE IN THE RAT.
001841 02-05
NEUROPSYCHOPHARMACOLOGICAL-STUDIES ON SOME BENZAMIDE DERIVATIVES.
002220 02-13
NEUROPHARMACOLOGY OF SYNTHETIC ERGOT DERIVATIVES IN MAN.
002429 02-15
CENTRAL DOPAMINERGIC-EFFECTS OF ERGOLINE DERIVATIVES.
002540 02-17
ON-COLUMN GAS-CHROMATOGRAPHIC-SYNTHESIS OF 1,3 DIALKYL (C=1-10), BENZYL, AND CYCLOHEXYLBARBITURATE DERIVATIVES.
003656 04-01
GAS-CHROMATOGRAPHIC-PROPERTIES OF 1,3 DIALKYLBARBITURATE DERIVATIVES.
003658 04-01
SPECTRA OF RADICAL CATIONS OF PHENOTHIAZINE DERIVATIVES IN SOLUTION AND SOLID STATE.
003673 04-01
SYNTHESIS AND BIOCHEMICAL AND PHARMACOLOGIC PROPERTIES OF ANALOGUES AND DERIVATIVES OF P CHLOROPHENYLALANINE.
003691 04-02
SYNTHESIS AND PHARMACOLOGICAL ACTIVITY OF SOME 2 IMINO-3-ALKYLTHIAZOLINE DERIVATIVES.
003698 04-02
MULTIPLE BENZODIAZEPINE-RECEPTORS: EVIDENCE OF A DISSOCIATION BETWEEN ANTICONFLICT AND ANTICONVULSANT PROPERTIES BY PK-8165 AND PK-9084 (TWO QUINOLINE DERIVATIVES).
003898 04-03

DESIPRAMINE

COMPARISON OF MIANSERIN WITH DESIPRAMINE, MAPROTILINE AND
PHENTOLAMINE ON CARDIAC PRESYNAPTIC AND VASCULAR
POSTSYNAPTIC ALPHA-ADRENOCEPTORS AND NORADRENALINE
REUPTAKE IN PITHED NORMOTENSIVE-RATS.
000044 01-03

FUNCTIONAL EVIDENCE FOR SUBSENSITIVITY OF NORADRENERGIC-
ALPHA2-RECEPTORS AFTER CHRONIC DESIPRAMINE TREATMENT.
000283 01-03

EFFICACY OF DESIPRAMINE IN ENDOGENOMORPHICALLY DEPRESSED-
PATIENTS.
000632 01-09

NEUROLEPTIC-EFFECT ON DESIPRAMINE STEADY-STATE PLASMA
CONCENTRATIONS.
000781 01-13

DESIPRAMINE: CARDIOVASCULAR EFFECTS AND PLASMA LEVELS.
000884 01-15

THE TIME-COURSE OF NORADRENERGIC PRESYNAPTIC AND
POSTSYNAPTIC ACTIVITY DURING CHRONIC DESIPRAMINE
TREATMENT.
001289 02-03

EFFECTS OF DESIPRAMINE AND YOHIMBINE ON ALPHA2-ADRENOCEPTOR
AND BETA-ADRENOCEPTOR SENSITIVITY.
001305 02-03

INTERACTION OF TRIAZOLAM WITH DESIPRAMINE: EFFECTS OF SINGLE
AND REPEATED TREATMENT ON CERTAIN PHARMACOLOGIC-
RESPONSES AND BRAIN CATECHOLAMINE LEVELS.
001323 02-03

EFFECTS OF NOMIFENSINE AND DESIPRAMINE ON THE SEQUELAE OF
INTRACEREBRALLY INJECTED 6 OHDA AND 5,6 DHT.
001522 02-03

CLINICAL-RESPONSE, PLASMA LEVELS AND PHARMACOKINETICS OF
DESIPRAMINE IN DEPRESSED-INPATIENTS.
002002 02-09

PLASMA DESIPRAMINE LEVELS AFTER SINGLE-DOSAGE AND AT STEADY-
STATE IN OUTPATIENTS.
002039 02-09

THE PERIPHERAL ANTICHOLINERGIC-ACTIVITY OF TRICYCLIC-
ANTIDEPRESSANTS: COMPARISON OF AMITRIPTYLINE AND
DESIPRAMINE IN HUMAN VOLUNTEERS.
002298 02-13

DIFFERENTIAL-EFFECT OF CHRONIC DESIPRAMINE AND AMITRIPTYLINE
TREATMENT ON RAT-BRAIN ADRENERGIC AND SEROTONERGIC-
RECEPTORS.
002914 03-03

DESIPRAMINE AND 2 HYDROXYDESIPRAMINE PHARMACOKINETICS IN
NORMAL VOLUNTEERS.
003154 03-07

CROSS-OVER STUDY OF ZIMELIDINE AND DESIPRAMINE IN DEPRESSION:
EVIDENCE FOR AMINE SPECIFICITY.
003250 03-09

EFFICACY OF DESIPRAMINE IN MILDLY DEPRESSED-PATIENTS: A DOUBLE-
BLIND, PLACEBO-CONTROLLED-TRIAL.
003262 03-09

ELECTROCARDIOGRAM-CHANGES AND PLASMA DESIPRAMINE LEVELS
DURING TREATMENT OF DEPRESSION.
004411 04-09

BLOCKADE BY IMIPRAMINE OR DESIPRAMINE OF PANIC-INDUCED BY
SODIUM-LACTATE.
004427 04-10

ANTICHOLINERGIC-EFFECTS AND PLASMA DESIPRAMINE LEVELS.
004550 04-13

DESIPRAMINE-HYDROCHLORIDE

SINGLE-DOSE VERSUS MULTIPLE-DOSE COMPARATIVE-TRIAL OF
DESIPRAMINE-HYDROCHLORIDE: A DOUBLE-PLACEBO METHOD.
002059 02-10

DESIPRAMINE-INDUCED

ACCELERATION OF DESIPRAMINE-INDUCED DECREASE OF RAT
CORTICOCEREBRAL BETA-ADRENERGIC-RECEPTORS BY YOHIMBINE.
000326 01-03

DESMETHYL

KINETICS AND NEUROPSYCHOLOGIC-EFFECTS OF IV DIAZEPAM IN THE
PRESENCE AND ABSENCE OF ITS ACTIVE N DESMETHYL METABOLITE IN
HUMANS.
002229 02-13

DESMETHYLATED-COMPOUND

INFLUENCE OF A CHRONIC NEW POTENTIAL ANTIDEPRESSANT,
DIMETHYLAMINOPROPYL-5-METHYL-3-PHENYL-1H-INDAZOLE (FS-32)
AND ITS N DESMETHYLATED-COMPOUND (FS-97): TREATMENT ON
MONOAMINERGIC-RECEPTOR SENSITIVITY IN THE RAT-BRAIN.
002787 03-03

DESMETHYLDIAZEPAM

EFFECT OF DIAZEPAM AND DESMETHYLDIAZEPAM IN SPASTICITY AND
RIGIDITY: A QUANTITATIVE STUDY OF REFLEXES AND PLASMA
CONCENTRATIONS.
000701 01-11

COMPARATIVE PROTEIN BINDING OF DIAZEPAM AND
DESMETHYLDIAZEPAM.
002206 02-13

Subject Index

INFLUENCE OF CIMETIDINE ON THE PHARMACOKINETICS OF
DESMETHYLDIAZEPAM AND OXAZEPAM.
002249 02-13

ANXIETY AND SEDATION DURING A STRESSFUL-SITUATION AFTER SINGLE-
DOSE OF DIAZEPAM VERSUS N DESMETHYLDIAZEPAM -- A
CONTROLLED-TRIAL.
002329 02-14

DESMETHYLDIAZEPAM KINETICS IN THE ELDERLY AFTER ORAL
PRAZEPAM.
004432 04-11

DESMETHYLDOXEPIN
RADIOIMMUNOASSAY FOR TOTAL DOXEPIN AND N DESMETHYLDOXEPIN
IN PLASMA.
002499 02-16

PLASMA LEVELS OF THE CIS-ISOMERS AND TRANS-ISOMERS OF DOXEPIN
AND DESMETHYLDOXEPIN AFTER ADMINISTRATION OF DOXEPIN TO
PATIENTS.
004355 04-09

DESMETHYLIMIPRAMINE
ABILITY OF AGED RATS TO ALTER BETA-ADRENERGIC-RECEPTORS OF
BRAIN IN RESPONSE TO REPEATED ADMINISTRATION OF RESERPINE
AND DESMETHYLIMIPRAMINE.
000113 01-03

STUDIES ON THE PUTATIVE ANTICHOLINERGIC-EFFECTS OF
DESMETHYLIMIPRAMINE.
000228 01-03

EFFECT OF DESMETHYLIMIPRAMINE ON THE KINETICS OF
CHLORPHENTERMINE ACCUMULATION IN ISOLATED PERFUSED RAT
LUNG.
000524 01-05

PLASMA LEVELS OF IMIPRAMINE (IMI) AND DESMETHYLIMIPRAMINE
(DMI) AND CLINICAL-RESPONSE IN PREPUBERTAL MAJOR DEPRESSIVE-
DISORDER: A PRELIMINARY REPORT.
000619 01-09

AN INVERSE CORRELATION BETWEEN SERUM LEVELS OF
DESMETHYLIMIPRAMINE AND MELATONIN-LIKE IMMUNOREACTIVITY
IN DMI RESPONSIVE DEPRESSIVES.
003228 03-09

EFFECT OF DESMETHYLIMIPRAMINE ON TISSUE DISTRIBUTION AND
ANORECTIC-ACTIVITY OF CHLORPHENTERMINE IN RATS.
004179 04-04

EFFECTS OF SUBCHRONIC DESMETHYLIMIPRAMINE (DMI) TREATMENT OF
THE CLASSICALLY CONDITIONED EYEBLINK RESPONSE IN RABBITS.
004180 04-04

DESMETHYLMETHSUXIMIDE
ELECTRON-CAPTURE GAS-LIQUID-CHROMATOGRAPHIC-DETERMINATION
OF ETHOSUXIMIDE AND DESMETHYLMETHSUXIMIDE IN PLASMA OR
SERUM.
000538 01-06

DESORPTION
DIFFERENTIAL BINDING OF CHLORPROMAZINE TO HUMAN BLOOD CELLS:
APPLICATION OF THE HYGROSCOPIC DESORPTION METHOD.
003556 03-16

DESTROYS
EXPOSURE OF MITOCHONDRIAL OUTER MEMBRANES TO NEURAMINIDASE
SELECTIVELY DESTROYS MONOAMINE-OXIDASE-A ACTIVITY.
001286 02-03

DESTRUCTION
EFFECTS OF L-DOPA AND L 5 HYDROXYTRYPTOPHAN ON LOCOMOTOR-
ACTIVITY OF THE RAT AFTER SELECTIVE OR COMBINED DESTRUCTION
OF CENTRAL CATECHOLAMINE AND SEROTONIN NEURONS.
000466 01-04

EFFECT OF SELECTIVE DESTRUCTION OF SEROTONERGIC NEURONS IN
NUCLEUS-RAPHE-MAGNUS ON MORPHINE-INDUCED ANTINOCICEPTION.
001724 02-04

DORSAL TEGMENTAL BUNDLE DESTRUCTION: EFFECTS ON OPERANT-
BEHAVIOR, BRAIN CATECHOLAMINE LEVELS, AND BEHAVIORAL-
SUPPRESSION PRODUCED BY ADRENERGIC AGONISTS.
001726 02-04

DOPAMINE AND DEMENTIA. AN ANIMAL-MODEL WITH DESTRUCTION OF
THE MESOCORTICAL DOPAMINERGIC PATHWAY: A PRELIMINARY
STUDY.
003085 03-04

BEHAVIORAL AND REGIONAL NEUROCHEMICAL SEQUELAE OF
HIPPOCAMPAL DESTRUCTION IN THE RAT.
003721 04-03

SENSORY NEUROTOXINS: CHEMICALLY-INDUCED SELECTIVE DESTRUCTION
OF PRIMARY SENSORY NEURONS.
003859 04-03

THE EFFECT OF PHARMACOLOGICAL DESTRUCTION OF HYPOTHALAMIC
MONOAMINERGIC STRUCTURES ON BODY-TEMPERATURE AND GAS-
EXCHANGE DURING EXTREME COOLING.
004016 04-03

DESTRUCTION OF 5 HYDROXYTRYPTAMINERGIC NEURONS AND THE
DYNAMICS OF DOPAMINE IN NUCLEUS-ACCUMBENS SEPTI AND OTHER
FOREBRAIN REGIONS OF THE RAT.
004171 04-04

DOPAMINE-RECEPTOR CHANGES FOLLOWING DESTRUCTION OF THE
NIGROSTRIATAL PATHWAY: LACK OF A RELATIONSHIP TO
ROTATIONAL-BEHAVIOR.
004229 04-04

DETERMINATION OF PHARMACODYNAMICS OF PSYCHOTROPIC-DRUGS BY PSYCHOMETRIC-ANALYSIS.
001895 02-07

MIANSERIN: DETERMINATION OF THERAPEUTIC DOSE RANGE.
002026 02-09

METHOD FOR THE DETERMINATION OF TRYPTOPHAN IN SERUM AND CEREBROSPINAL-FLUID.
002208 02-13

A METHOD FOR THE DETERMINATION OF AMITRIPTYLINE AND ITS METABOLITES NORTRIPTYLINE, 10 HYDROXYAMITRIPTYLINE, AND 10 HYDROXYNORTRIPTYLINE IN HUMAN PLASMA USING STABLE ISOTOPE DILUTION AND GAS-CHROMATOGRAPHY CHEMICAL-IONIZATION MASS-SPECTROMETRY.
002486 02-16

DETERMINATION OF TRICYCLIC-ANTIDEPRESSANTS AND TETRACYCLIC-ANTIDEPRESSANTS AND OF THEIR METABOLIC PRODUCTS IN BIOLOGICAL FLUIDS.
002498 02-16

A RAPID GAS-LIQUID-CHROMATOGRAPHY METHOD FOR SIMULTANEOUS DETERMINATION OF VARIOUS ANTICONVULSANTS.
002501 02-16

DETERMINATION OF GABA LEVELS BY A (3H)MUSCIMOL RADIORECEPTOR ASSAY.
003135 03-06

SIMULTANEOUS DETERMINATION OF FEMTOMOLE QUANTITIES OF 5 HYDROXYTRYPTOPHAN, SEROTONIN AND 5 HYDROXYINDOLEACETIC-ACID IN BRAIN USING HPLC WITH ELECTROCHEMICAL-DETECTION.
003139 03-06

THERAPEUTIC INTEREST OF BLOOD LEVELS DETERMINATION FOR ANTIDEPRESSANTS: METHODOLOGICAL APPROACH.
003571 03-16

A RAPID AND SIMPLE METHOD FOR THE DETERMINATION OF PICOGRAM LEVELS OF 3 METHOXYTYRAMINE IN BRAIN TISSUE USING LIQUID-CHROMATOGRAPHY WITH ELECTROCHEMICAL DETECTION.
003674 04-01

A SIMPLE DETERMINATION OF SEROTONIN, 5 HYDROXYINDOLEACETIC-ACID AND 5 HYDROXYTRYPTOPHAN-DECARBOXYLASE ACTIVITY IN RAT-BRAIN AREAS AND PARALLEL CORRELATION AMONG THE LEVELS.
004301 04-06

RAPID DETERMINATION OF CHLORPROMAZINE-HCL AND TWO OXIDATION PRODUCTS IN VARIOUS PHARMACEUTICAL SAMPLES USING HIGH-PERFORMANCE LIQUID-CHROMATOGRAPHY AND FLUORESCENCE DETECTION.
004302 04-06

DETERMINATION OF PICOMOLE AMOUNTS OF DOPAMINE, NORADRENALINE, 3,4 DIHYDROXYPHENYLALANINE, 3,4 DIHYDROXYPHENYLACETIC-ACID, HOMOVANILLIC-ACID, AND 5 HYDROXYINDOLEACETIC-ACID IN NERVOUS-TISSUE AFTER ONE-STEP PURIFICATION ON SEPHADEX-G-10, USING HIGH.
004305 04-06

EFFECTS OF RO-11-2465, A NEW PSYCHOTROPIC-AGENT ON THE UPTAKE OF SEROTONIN BY HUMAN PLATELETS -- IN VITRO DETERMINATION OF THE IC50.
004532 04-13

A COMPARISON OF RADIOIMMUNOASSAY WITH SPECTROPHOTOMETRY FOR THE DETERMINATION OF PLASMA DIPHENYLHYDANTOIN CONCENTRATIONS.
004684 04-16

SIMULTANEOUS DETERMINATION OF MORPHINE AND CODEINE IN BLOOD BY USE OF SELECT ION-MONITORING AND DEUTERATED INTERNAL STANDARDS.
004690 04-16

DETERMINATIONS
USE OF PLASMA CONCENTRATION DETERMINATIONS.
004498 04-13

KINETICS AND BIOTRANSFORMATION OF LORMETAZEPAM: II. RADIOIMMUNOLOGIC DETERMINATIONS IN PLASMA AND URINE OF YOUNG AND ELDERLY SUBJECTS: FIRST-PASS EFFECT.
004516 04-13

DETOXIFICATION
IATROGENIC OPIATE ADDICTION: SUCCESSFUL DETOXIFICATION WITH CLONIDINE.
000666 01-11

CLONIDINE FOR OPIATE DETOXIFICATION: OUTPATIENT CLINICAL-TRIALS.
000731 01-11

RAPID OPIATE DETOXIFICATION WITH CLONIDINE AND NALOXONE.
000820 01-14

CLONIDINE FOR OUTPATIENT OPIATE DETOXIFICATION.
000827 01-14

DETOXIFYING
SALIVA BENZODIAZEPINE LEVELS AND CLINICAL OUTCOME IN DETOXIFYING ALCOHOLIC-PATIENTS.
004671 04-16

DEUTERATED
SIMULTANEOUS DETERMINATION OF MORPHINE AND CODEINE IN BLOOD BY USE OF SELECT ION-MONITORING AND DEUTERATED INTERNAL STANDARDS.
004690 04-16

DEUTERIUM
NOREPINEPHRINE METABOLISM IN MAN USING DEUTERIUM LABELLING: 4 HYDROXY-3-METHOXYMANDELIC-ACID.
004534 04-13

DEVELOPED
A STUDY ON MENTAL-SYMPTOMS DEVELOPED DURING THE TREATMENT OF PARKINSONS-DISEASE.
004618 04-15

DEVELOPING
LOCALIZATION OF ALPHA BUNGAROTOXIN BINDING-SITES IN SYNAPSES OF THE DEVELOPING CHICK RETINA.
000065 01-03

EFFECTS OF APOMORPHINE ON ESCAPE PERFORMANCE AND ACTIVITY IN DEVELOPING RAT PUPS TREATED WITH 6 HYDROXYDOPAMINE (6 OHDA).
000426 01-04

THE LOCOMOTOR-EFFECT OF CLONIDINE AND ITS INTERACTION WITH ALPHA FLUPENTHIXOL OR HALOPERIDOL IN THE DEVELOPING RAT.
000445 01-04

EFFECT OF CHLORPROMAZINE ON CELL PROLIFERATION IN THE DEVELOPING RAT-BRAIN. A COMBINED BIOCHEMICAL-STUDY AND MORPHOLOGICAL-STUDY.
001407 02-03

HYPERACTIVITY IN DEVELOPING RATS: SEX-DIFFERENCES IN 6 HYDROXYDOPAMINE AND AMPHETAMINE EFFECTS.
002970 03-04

EFFECT OF AMPHETAMINE ON THE METABOLISM AND INCORPORATION OF (3H) THYMIDINE INTO DNA OF DEVELOPING RAT-BRAIN.
003729 04-03

THE EFFECTS OF CHRONIC METHYLPHENIDATE TREATMENT ON GROWTH AND ENDOCRINE FUNCTION IN THE DEVELOPING RAT.
003811 04-03

EFFECT OF NEONATAL HYDROCORTISONE TREATMENT ON BRAIN-MONOAMINES IN DEVELOPING RATS.
003893 04-03

THE INSENSITIVITY OF DEVELOPING BENZODIAZEPINE-RECEPTORS TO CHRONIC-TREATMENT WITH DIAZEPAM, GABA AND MUSCIMOL IN BRAIN CELL-CULTURES.
004002 04-03

DEVELOPMENT
REDUCTION OF OPIATE BINDING TO BRAINSTEM SLICES ASSOCIATED WITH THE DEVELOPMENT OF TOLERANCE TO MORPHINE IN RATS.
000066 01-03

PHENYLACETATE AND BRAIN-DYSFUNCTION IN EXPERIMENTAL PHENYLKETONURIA: SYNAPTIC DEVELOPMENT.
000191 01-03

EFFECTS OF 6 HYDROXYDOPAMINE AND AMPHETAMINE ON RAT MOTHERING-BEHAVIOR AND OFFSPRING DEVELOPMENT.
000452 01-04

CHRONIC ADMINISTRATION OF HALOPERIDOL DURING DEVELOPMENT: BEHAVIORAL-EFFECTS AND PSYCHOPHARMACOLOGICAL-EFFECTS.
000481 01-04

INTERACTIVE-EFFECTS OF NUTRITION AND CANNABIS UPON RAT PERINATAL DEVELOPMENT.
000513 01-05

EFFECTS OF LEAD EXPOSURE DURING DEVELOPMENT ON NEOCORTICAL DENDRITIC AND SYNAPTIC STRUCTURE.
000525 01-05

CRITERIA FOR CLINICAL DEVELOPMENT AND CLASSIFICATION OF NOOTROPIC-DRUGS. AN EXAMPLE: PIRACETAM.
000988 01-17

PRESYNAPTIC DOPAMINE-RECEPTORS: INSENSITIVITY TO KAINIC-ACID AND THE DEVELOPMENT OF SUPERSENSITIVITY FOLLOWING CHRONIC HALOPERIDOL.
001117 02-03

RAPID DEVELOPMENT OF HYPERSENSITIVITY AND HYPOSENSITIVITY TO APOMORPHINE AND HALOPERIDOL: ROLE OF NOREPINEPHRINE-RECEPTOR MECHANISMS IN CNS.
001178 02-03

EVOKED-POTENTIAL CHANGES IN THE SUPERIOR-COLLICULUS PARALLEL THE LESION-INDUCED DEVELOPMENT OF GROOMING REFLEXES IN THE CAT. (PH.D. DISSERTATION).
001179 02-03

DEVELOPMENT OF ACUTE OPIOID-TOLERANCE AND DEPENDENCE IN RAT STRIATAL NEURONES.
001235 02-03

EFFECTS OF MALNUTRITION AND QUIPAZINE ON RAT-CEREBRAL-CORTEX ATPASE ACTIVITY DURING DEVELOPMENT.
001276 02-03

BIPHASIC ACTIVITY OF MEMBRANE-BOUND ENZYMES IN BRAIN MITOCHONDRIA AND SYNAPTOSOMES DURING THE DEVELOPMENT OF TOLERANCE TO AND PHYSICAL-DEPENDENCE ON CHRONIC MORPHINE ADMINISTRATION TO RATS.
001285 02-03

EFFECTS OF PAVLOVIAN-CONDITIONING AND MIF-1 ON THE DEVELOPMENT OF MORPHINE-TOLERANCE IN RATS.
001327 02-03

DEVELOPMENT OF AND RECOVERY FROM SUBSENSITIVITY OF THE NORADRENERGIC CYCLIC-AMP GENERATING SYSTEM IN BRAIN: EFFECT

Subject Index

OF AMPHETAMINE FOLLOWING INHIBITION OF ITS AROMATIC
HYDROXYLATION BY IPRINDOLE.
　　　　　　　　　　　　001353 02-03

CHRONIC ADMINISTRATION OF HALOPERIDOL DURING DEVELOPMENT:
LATER PSYCHOPHARMACOLOGICAL RESPONSES TO APOMORPHINE
AND ARECOLINE.
　　　　　　　　　　　　001470 02-03

GLUCOCORTICOIDS AS A REGULATORY FACTOR FOR BRAIN TRYPTOPHAN-
HYDROXYLASE DURING DEVELOPMENT.
　　　　　　　　　　　　001500 02-03

POSTNATAL ALCOHOL EXPOSURE IN THE RAT: ITS EFFECTS ON
AVOIDANCE CONDITIONING, HEBB-WILLIAMS MAZE-PERFORMANCE,
MATERNAL-BEHAVIOR, AND PUP DEVELOPMENT.
　　　　　　　　　　　　001580 02-04

TOLERANCE DEVELOPMENT TO PHENCYCLIDINE BY CHRONIC
ADMINISTRATION.
　　　　　　　　　　　　001619 02-04

BEHAVIORAL-EFFECTS OF HASHISH IN MICE: II. NURSING-BEHAVIOR AND
DEVELOPMENT OF THE SUCKLINGS.
　　　　　　　　　　　　001626 02-04

EFFECTS OF RESERPINE AND AMPHETAMINE ON THE DEVELOPMENT OF
HYPERACTIVITY IN MATERNALLY-DEPRIVED RAT PUPS.
　　　　　　　　　　　　001654 02-04

EXPERIMENTAL DEPENDENCE ON BARBITURATES: II. RELATIONSHIP
BETWEEN DRUG LEVELS IN SERUM AND BRAIN AND THE
DEVELOPMENT OF DEPENDENCE IN RATS.
　　　　　　　　　　　　001800 02-04

THE DEVELOPMENT OF PROGENY IN CASES OF ANTENATAL EXPOSURE TO
PHENAZEPAM.
　　　　　　　　　　　　001854 02-05

THE ROLE OF FOLATE DEFICIENCY IN THE DEVELOPMENT OF PERIPHERAL
NEUROPATHY CAUSED BY ANTICONVULSANTS.
　　　　　　　　　　　　002402 02-15

NEUROLEPTIC-INDUCED REINNERVATION SPROUTING IN THE CENTRAL-
NERVOUS-SYSTEM (A MODEL FOR THE DEVELOPMENT OF TARDIVE-
DYSKINESIA AND SUPERSENSITIVITY PSYCHOSIS).
　　　　　　　　　　　　002459 02-15

DEVELOPMENT AND USE OF PHARMACOLOGICAL-PROBES OF THE CNS IN
MAN: EVIDENCE OF CHOLINERGIC ABNORMALITY IN PRIMARY
AFFECTIVE-ILLNESS.
　　　　　　　　　　　　002506 02-16

CLINICAL-PHARMACOLOGY: DRUG DEVELOPMENT.
　　　　　　　　　　　　002547 02-17

NEW DEVELOPMENT IN ANTIDEPRESSANT MEDICATION -- A REVIEW.
　　　　　　　　　　　　002558 02-17

BENZODIAZEPINE-RECEPTORS IN CHICK RETINA: DEVELOPMENT AND
CELLULAR LOCALIZATION.
　　　　　　　　　　　　002655 03-03

DEVELOPMENT OF TOLERANCE TO THE EXCITATORY EFFECT OF MORPHINE
AND CROSS-TOLERANCE TO THE INHIBITORY ACTION OF BETA
ENDORPHIN IN THE ISOLATED RAT VAS-DEFERENS.
　　　　　　　　　　　　002756 03-03

DEVELOPMENT OF ACUTE TOLERANCE TO THE EFFECTS OF NALOXONE ON
THE HYPOTHALAMIC PITUITARY LUTEINIZING-HORMONE AXIS IN THE
MALE RAT.
　　　　　　　　　　　　002853 03-03

EFFECTS OF ISOPROTERENOL ON THE DEVELOPMENT OF BETA-
ADRENERGIC-RECEPTORS IN BRAIN CELL AGGREGATES.
　　　　　　　　　　　　002932 03-03

SUPPRESSION OF ACTIVE SLEEP BY CHRONIC-TREATMENT WITH
CHLORIMIPRAMINE DURING EARLY POSTNATAL DEVELOPMENT:
EFFECTS UPON ADULT SLEEP AND BEHAVIOR IN THE RAT.
　　　　　　　　　　　　003056 03-04

DIFFERENTIATION OF OPIATE-RECEPTORS IN THE BRAIN BY THE SELECTIVE
DEVELOPMENT OF TOLERANCE.
　　　　　　　　　　　　003088 03-04

DIFFERENCE IN THE DEVELOPMENT OF TOLERANCE TO MORPHINE AND D
ALA2-METHIONINE-ENKEPHALIN IN C57 BL/6J AND DBA/2J MICE.
　　　　　　　　　　　　003126 03-05

PRELIMINARY-FINDINGS WITH REGARD TO RISK-FACTORS IN THE
DEVELOPMENT OF TARDIVE-DYSKINESIA.
　　　　　　　　　　　　003501 03-15

THE NECESSITY OF PSYCHOPHARMACOLOGY IN THE DEVELOPMENT OF
PSYCHIATRY.
　　　　　　　　　　　　003575 03-17

NERVE GROWTH-FACTOR STIMULATES DEVELOPMENT OF SUBSTANCE-P
IN THE EMBRYONIC SPINAL-CORD.
　　　　　　　　　　　　003881 04-03

CENTRAL DOPAMINERGIC NEURONS DURING DEVELOPMENT OF GENETIC
AND DOCA-SALT HYPERTENSION IN THE RAT.
　　　　　　　　　　　　003899 04-03

EFFECT OF PRENATAL NEUROLEPTIC TREATMENT ON MEMBRANE
RECEPTOR DEVELOPMENT IN THE BRAIN.
　　　　　　　　　　　　003989 04-03

ONTOGENY OF HISTAMINERGIC NEUROTRANSMISSION IN THE RAT-
BRAIN: CONCOMITANT DEVELOPMENT OF NEURONAL HISTAMINE, H1-
RECEPTORS, AND H1-RECEPTOR-MEDIATED STIMULATION OF
PHOSPHOLIPID TURNOVER.
　　　　　　　　　　　　004021 04-03

DIFFERENTIAL DIAGNOSIS AND TREATMENT OF PANIC ATTACKS AND
PHOBIC-STATES.
004424 04-10

DIAGNOSTIC
DIAGNOSTIC AND PROGNOSTIC SIGNIFICANCE OF
ELECTROENCEPHALOGRAPHY WITH INTRAVENOUS DIAZEPAM IN
EPILEPSY.
000696 01-11
PCP ABUSE: DIAGNOSTIC AND PSYCHOPHARMACOLOGICAL-TREATMENT
APPROACHES.
000746 01-12
DIAGNOSTIC CLASSIFICATION AND THE ENDORPHIN HYPOTHESIS OF
SCHIZOPHRENIA: INDIVIDUAL DIFFERENCES AND
PSYCHOPHARMACOLOGICAL STRATEGIES. (UNPUBLISHED PAPER).
001910 02-08
DELIRIUM OR PSYCHOSIS? DIAGNOSTIC USE OF THE SODIUM-
AMOBARBITAL INTERVIEW.
002167 02-11
DIAGNOSTIC CLASSIFICATION AND THE ENDORPHIN HYPOTHESIS OF
SCHIZOPHRENIA: INDIVIDUAL DIFFERENCES AND
PSYCHOPHARMACOLOGICAL STRATEGIES.
003167 03-08
CLINICAL DEPRESSIONS: DIAGNOSTIC AND THERAPEUTIC CHALLENGES.
004350 04-09
BLOOD LEVEL MEASUREMENTS OF TRICYCLIC DRUGS AS A DIAGNOSTIC
TOOL.
004368 D4-09

DIAGNOSTICS
CLINICAL AND LABORATORY DIAGNOSTICS APPLICATIONS IN
DEPRESSION. (UNPUBLISHED PAPER).
000588 01-09
THE USE OF SENSORY INTEGRATIVE DIAGNOSTICS TO PREDICT
HYPERACTIVE-CHILDRENS RESPONSIVENESS TO METHYLPHENIDATE
(RITALIN) AND PEMOLINE (CYLERT). (PH.D. DISSERTATION).
002133 02-11

DIALKYL-4-PYRAZOLIDINOLS
SYNTHESIS OF PHENYLURETHANS OF 1,2 DIALKYL-4-PYRAZOLIDINOLS AS
ANTICONVULSANT-AGENTS.
003695 04-02

DIALKYLBARBITURATE
GAS-CHROMATOGRAPHIC-PROPERTIES OF 1,3 DIALKYLBARBITURATE
DERIVATIVES.
003658 04-01

DIALYKYL
ON-COLUMN GAS-CHROMATOGRAPHIC-SYNTHESIS OF 1,3 DIALYKYL
(C=1-10), BENZYL, AND CYCLOHEXYLBARBITURATE DERIVATIVES.
003656 04-01

DIALYSIS
ORAL ALUMINUM AND NEUROPSYCHOLOGICAL FUNCTIONING: A STUDY
OF DIALYSIS PATIENTS RECEIVING ALUMINUM-HYDROXIDE GELS.
002283 02-13

DIAMINODIPHENOXYBUTANE
RETINOTOXIC-EFFECTS OF DIAMINODIPHENOXYBUTANE IN RATS.
000444 01-04

DIAPHRAGM
DIPHENYLHYDANTOIN-INDUCED BLOCK OF THE RAT PHRENIC-NERVE
DIAPHRAGM PREPARATION PRETREATED WITH P
HYDROXYMERCURIBENZOATE.
002749 03-03
OXOTREMORINE DOES NOT ENHANCE ACETYLCHOLINE RELEASE FROM
RAT DIAPHRAGM PREPARATIONS.
003819 04-03

DIASTEREOMERS
FUNCTIONAL CHARACTERIZATION OF CENTRAL ALPHA-ADRENOCEPTORS
BY. YOHIMBINE DIASTEREOMERS.
002748 03-03

DIASTOLIC
COVARIANCE OF PLASMA FREE 3 METHOXY-4-
HYDROXYPHENETHYLENEGLYCOL AND DIASTOLIC BLOOD-PRESSURE.
003418 03-13

DIAZEPAM
ANALYSIS FOR DIAZEPAM AND NORDIAZEPAM BY ELECTRON-CAPTURE
GAS-CHROMATOGRAPHY AND BY LIQUID-CHROMATOGRAPHY.
000006 01-01
PHARMACOLOGICAL ACTIVITIES OF CLOBAZAM AND DIAZEPAM IN THE
RAT: RELATION TO DRUG BRAIN LEVELS.
000036 01-03
THE EFFECT OF DIAZEPAM ON TENSION AND ELECTROLYTE DISTRIBUTION
IN FROG MUSCLE.
000069 01-03
ENTRY OF DIAZEPAM AND ITS MAJOR METABOLITE INTO
CEREBROSPINAL-FLUID.
000114 01-03
THE EFFECT OF DIAZEPAM ON EEG CHANGES FOLLOWING INTRASEPTAL
ADMINISTRATION OF ATROPINE.
000127 01-03
A PROBABLE SITE-OF-ACTION OF DIAZEPAM IN RAT CEREBELLAR GABA
SYSTEM.
000151 01-03

137

DELAYED CLEARANCE OF DIAZEPAM DUE TO CIMETIDINE.
000164 01-03
INTERACTION OF DIAZEPAM WITH SYNAPTIC TRANSMISSION IN THE IN VITRO RAT HIPPOCAMPUS.
000178 01-03
DIAZEPAM POTENTIATION OF PURINERGIC DEPRESSION OF CENTRAL NEURONS.
000233 01-03
PENTOBARBITAL POTENTIATES GABA-ENHANCED (3H) DIAZEPAM BINDING TO BENZODIAZEPINE-RECEPTORS.
000275 01-03
PROPERTIES OF (3H)DIAZEPAM BINDING-SITES ON RAT BLOOD-PLATELETS.
000317 01-03
INHIBITION OF (3H)DIAZEPAM BINDING TO RAT-BRAIN CORTICAL SYNAPTOSOMAL MEMBRANES BY ADENOSINE UPTAKE BLOCKERS.
000330 01-03
EFFECTS OF CHLORDIAZEPOXIDE AND DIAZEPAM ON FEEDING PERFORMANCE IN A FOOD PREFERENCE TEST.
000367 01-04
EFFECTS OF ACUTE AND CHRONIC INTERACTIONS OF DIAZEPAM AND D-AMPHETAMINE ON PUNISHED-BEHAVIOR OF RATS.
000386 01-04
THE INTERACTION OF ANTICHOLINESTERASES AND DIAZEPAM IN THE TREATMENT OF ANTICHOLINERGIC-SYNDROME IN DOGS.
000389 01-04
DIAZEPAM IN COMBINATION WITH TACRINE DERIVATIVES ANTAGONIZES BEHAVIOURAL-EFFECTS OF ANTICHOLINERGIC PSYCHOTOMIMETICS IN RATS.
000420 01-04
CORRELATION BETWEEN BENZODIAZEPINE-RECEPTOR OCCUPATION AND ANTICONVULSANT EFFECTS OF DIAZEPAM.
000450 01-04
IMPROVEMENT OF RESTITUTION FROM CEREBRAL ISCHEMIA IN HYPERGLYCEMIC RATS BY PENTOBARBITAL OR DIAZEPAM.
000475 01-04
BICUCULLINE ANTAGONIZES EFFECTS OF DIAZEPAM ON AGGRESSIVE AND TIMID-BEHAVIOUR IN MICE.
000485 01-04
BEHAVIORAL-ANALYSIS OF AMYGDALOID KINDLING IN BEAGLE-DOGS AND THE EFFECTS OF CLONAZEPAM, DIAZEPAM, PHENOBARBITAL, DIPHENYLHYDANTOIN, AND FLUNARIZINE ON SEIZURE MANIFESTATION.
000496 01-04
A DOUBLE-BLIND GROUP COMPARATIVE-TRIAL OF MIANSERIN AND DIAZEPAM IN DEPRESSED-OUTPATIENTS.
000592 01-09
ANXIOLYTIC EFFICACY OF ALPRAZOLAM COMPARED TO DIAZEPAM AND PLACEBO.
000648 01-10
KETAZOLAM AND DIAZEPAM IN ANXIETY: A CONTROLLED-STUDY.
000655 01-10
DOUBLE-BLIND COMPARISON OF KETAZOLAM, DIAZEPAM AND PLACEBO IN ONCE-A-DAY VS T.I.D. DOSING.
000660 01-11
DIAGNOSTIC AND PROGNOSTIC SIGNIFICANCE OF ELECTROENCEPHALOGRAPHY WITH INTRAVENOUS DIAZEPAM IN EPILEPSY.
000696 01-11
EFFECT OF DIAZEPAM AND DESMETHYLDIAZEPAM IN SPASTICITY AND RIGIDITY: A QUANTITATIVE STUDY OF REFLEXES AND PLASMA CONCENTRATIONS.
000701 01-11
INTERSUBJECT AND INTRASUBJECT VARIATION IN DIAZEPAM FREE FRACTION.
000747 01-13
PHARMACODYNAMICS AND PHARMACOKINETICS OF DIAZEPAM IN AN ABUSER.
000867 01-15
EFFECTS OF GABA AND DIAZEPAM ON 3H SEROTONIN RELEASE FROM HIPPOCAMPAL SYNAPTOSOMES.
001116 02-03
ETHANOL ENHANCES (3H)DIAZEPAM BINDING AT THE BENZODIAZEPINE GABA-RECEPTOR IONOPHORE COMPLEX.
001154 02-03
THE EFFECT OF EMOTIONAL-STRESS AND DIAZEPAM ON MONOAMINE METABOLITES IN THE CEREBROSPINAL-FLUID OF CATS. (PH.D. DISSERTATION).
001260 02-03
EVIDENCE FOR AN ENDOGENOUS COMPOUND INTERFERING WITH 3H DIAZEPAM BINDING TO RAT-BRAIN MEMBRANES.
001308 02-03
ETHYL-BETA-CARBOLINE-3-CARBOXYLATE ANTAGONISES THE EFFECT OF DIAZEPAM ON A FUNCTIONAL GABA-RECEPTOR.
001378 02-03
THE PROCONVULSANT AND DIAZEPAM REVERSING EFFECTS OF ETHYL-BETA-CARBOLINE-3-CARBOXYLATE.
001399 02-03

EFFECTS OF DIAZEPAM ON ADENOSINE AND ACETYLCHOLINE RELEASE FROM RAT-CEREBRAL-CORTEX; FURTHER EVIDENCE FOR A PURINERGIC MECHANISM IN ACTION OF DIAZEPAM.
001414 02-03
EVIDENCE FOR INVOLVEMENT OF DOPAMINE IN THE ACTION OF DIAZEPAM: POTENTIATION OF HALOPERIDOL AND CHLORPROMAZINE ACTION IN THE BRAIN.
001428 02-03
A STUDY OF A GLIAL GAMMA AMINOBUTYRIC-ACID SYSTEM: ITS REGULATION, FUNCTION AND THE EFFECTS OF DIAZEPAM. (PH.D. DISSERTATION).
001524 02-03
CHRONIC-TREATMENT WITH VALIUM (DIAZEPAM) FAILS TO AFFECT THE REPRODUCTIVE SYSTEM OF THE MALE RAT.
001535 02-03
VESTIBULO-OCULAR REFLEXES IN RABBITS: REDUCTION BY INTRAVENOUS INJECTION OF DIAZEPAM.
001566 02-04
EFFECT OF P CHLOROPHENYLALANINE ON DIAZEPAM WITHDRAWAL SIGNS IN RATS.
001797 02-04
COMPARISON OF CLONAZEPAM AND DIAZEPAM IN EXPERIMENTAL-STUDIES.
001815 02-04
GABA-RECEPTORS AND BENZODIAZEPINE-RECEPTORS IN THE OFFSPRING OF DAMS RECEIVING DIAZEPAM: ONTOGENETIC-STUDIES.
001849 02-05
HIGH-DOSE DIAZEPAM IN SCHIZOPHRENIA.
001909 02-08
THE USE OF CLOROTEPIN AND DIAZEPAM IN A COMPLEX THERAPY OF NEUROSES (CONTROLLED-COMPARISON).
002064 02-10
KETAZOLAM COMPARED TO DIAZEPAM AND PLACEBO IN THE TREATMENT OF ANXIETY.
002074 02-10
COMPARATIVE PROTEIN BINDING OF DIAZEPAM AND DESMETHYLDIAZEPAM.
002206 02-13
KINETICS AND NEUROPSYCHOLOGIC-EFFECTS OF IV DIAZEPAM IN THE PRESENCE AND ABSENCE OF ITS ACTIVE N DESMETHYL METABOLITE IN HUMANS.
002229 02-13
HEMODYNAMIC AND CEREBRAL METABOLIC-STUDY OF DIAZEPAM IN NEUROSURGICAL-RESUSCITATION.
002231 02-13
ANXIETY AND SEDATION DURING A STRESSFUL-SITUATION AFTER SINGLE-DOSE OF DIAZEPAM VERSUS N DESMETHYLDIAZEPAM -- A CONTROLLED-TRIAL.
002329 02-14
DRUG PREFERENCE AND MOOD IN HUMANS: DIAZEPAM.
002334 02-14
CNV VARIATIONS INDUCED BY THE ADMINISTRATION OF DIAZEPAM, HALOPERIDOL, PHENELZINE AND D-AMPHETAMINE.
002355 02-14
ACCIDENTAL INTRAARTERIAL INJECTION OF DIAZEPAM.
002598 02-17
DEMONSTRATION AND CHARACTERIZATION OF AN ENDOGENOUS INHIBITOR OF GABA-ENHANCED (3H) DIAZEPAM BINDING FROM BOVINE CEREBRAL-CORTEX.
002645 03-01
CENTRAL DEPRESSANT EFFECTS OF CAERULEIN AND CHOLECYSTOKININ-OCTAPEPTIDE (CCK-8) DIFFER FROM THOSE OF DIAZEPAM AND HALOPERIDOL.
002652 03-02
ETHYL-BETA-CARBOLINE-3-CARBOXYLATE ANTAGONIZES DIAZEPAM ACTIVITY.
002915 03-03
ELECTRICAL-ACTIVITY AND NA-K-ATPASE LEVEL IN THE PENICILLIN-INDUCED EPILEPTOGENIC-FOCUS OF THE RAT-BRAIN-CORTEX, AND THE EFFECT OF DIAZEPAM.
003070 03-04
INTERACTIONS OF DIAZEPAM AND COCAINE IN THE MORPHINE TREATED RAT. (PH.D. DISSERTATION).
003115 03-04
A DOUBLE-BLIND CROSSED CLINICAL-STUDY WITH A NEW PSYCHOPHARMACEUTICAL: TIADIPONE (QM-6008), DIAZEPAM, AND A PLACEBO.
003153 03-07
A COMPARATIVE-STUDY ON THE CLINICAL-EFFECTS OF RECTAL DIAZEPAM AND PENTOBARBITAL ON SMALL CHILDREN. RELATIONSHIP BETWEEN PLASMA LEVEL AND EFFECT.
003330 03-11
DOUBLE-BLIND COMPARISON OF ALPRAZOLAM AND DIAZEPAM FOR SUBCHRONIC WITHDRAWAL FROM ALCOHOL.
003332 03-11
THE REPLICABILITY OF THE PSYCHOPHYSIOLOGICAL-EFFECTS OF DIAZEPAM.
003413 03-13

DIAZEPAM AS TUMOUR PROMOTER.
003495 03-15
ABSENCE OF EFFECT OF DIAZEPAM ON TUMOURS.
003497 03-15
CA DIAZEPAM LINK? NO SCIENTIFIC TAKERS SO FAR.
003519 03-15
AVAILABILITY OF ISOSORBIDE-DINITRATE, DIAZEPAM AND
CHLORMETHIAZOLE, FROM I.V. DELIVERY SYSTEMS.
003558 03-16
DIAZEPAM ANXIOLYTIC-ACTIVITY IN HIPPOCAMPUS.
003743 04-03
INHIBITION OF (3H)DIAZEPAM BINDING BY AN ENDOGENOUS FRACTION
FROM RAT-BRAIN SYNAPTOSOMES.
003768 04-03
REGIONAL CHANGES IN (3H)DIAZEPAM BINDING IN THE BRAINS OF MICE
AFTER REMOVAL OF THE OLFACTORY-BULBS.
003844 04-03
EFFECT OF DIAZEPAM ON STRESS-INDUCED CHANGES IN BRAIN
HISTAMINE.
003932 04-03
THE EFFECT OF DIAZEPAM ON CYCLIC EXCITABILITY CHANGES IN AN
EPILEPTIC-FOCUS IN THE CORTEX OF THE MAJOR HEMISPHERES.
003984 04-03
THE INSENSITIVITY OF DEVELOPING BENZODIAZEPINE-RECEPTORS TO
CHRONIC-TREATMENT WITH DIAZEPAM, GABA AND MUSCIMOL IN
BRAIN CELL-CULTURES.
004002 04-03
SCHEDULE DEPENDENT CHANGE OF PUNISHED-RESPONDING AFTER
DIAZEPAM IN RATS.
004165 04-04
3 HYDROXYMETHYL-BETA-CARBOLINE ANTAGONIZES SOME
PHARMACOLOGIC ACTIONS OF DIAZEPAM.
004221 04-04
POTENTIATION OF THE EFFECTS OF ADENOSINE ON ISOLATED CARDIAC-
MUSCLE AND SMOOTH-MUSCLE BY DIAZEPAM.
004266 04-05
RESPIRATORY DEPRESSION PRODUCED BY DIAZEPAM IN CATS: EFFECT OF
ANESTHESIA.
004272 04-05
THE RELATIONSHIPS BETWEEN CLINICAL-RESPONSE,
PSYCHOPHYSIOLOGICAL-VARIABLES AND PLASMA LEVELS OF
AMITRIPTYLINE AND DIAZEPAM IN NEUROTIC-OUTPATIENTS.
004423 04-10
A DOUBLE-BLIND TRIAL: THE USE OF OXPRENOLOL AND DIAZEPAM IN
ANXIETY.
004428 04-10
EFFECT OF TREATMENT WITH SODIUM-VALPROATE AND DIAZEPAM ON
PLASMA CORTICOTROPIN IN NELSONS-SYNDROME.
004463 04-11
PROMETHAZINE AND DIAZEPAM POTENTIATE THE HALOPERIDOL-INDUCED
PROLACTIN RESPONSES.
004499 04-13
INTRAVENOUS DIAZEPAM AND ORAL ETHANOL INTERACTION.
004552 04-13
DRUG PREFERENCE IN HUMANS: DOUBLE-BLIND CHOICE COMPARISON OF
PENTOBARBITAL, DIAZEPAM AND PLACEBO.
004566 04-14
CASE-REPORT OF UNUSUAL DIAZEPAM ABSTINENCE-SYNDROME.
004643 04-15
MASS SCREENING AND CONFIRMATION OF DIAZEPAM IN URINE BY EMIT
THIN-LAYER-CHROMATOGRAPHY.
004672 04-16
DIAZEPAM-INDUCED
DIFFERENTIAL-EFFECTS OF NALOXONE AGAINST THE DIAZEPAM-INDUCED
RELEASE OF BEHAVIOR IN MICE IN THREE AVERSIVE-SITUATIONS.
000480 01-04
INTERACTION BETWEEN PURINE AND BENZODIAZEPINE: INOSINE
REVERSES DIAZEPAM-INDUCED STIMULATION OF MOUSE
EXPLORATORY-BEHAVIOR.
002972 03-04
DIAZEPAM-INDUCED ATAXIA IN TROTTING SQUIRREL-MONKEYS.
004138 04-04
DIAZEPAM-RECEPTOR
CHANGES IN MOUSE-BRAIN DIAZEPAM-RECEPTOR BINDING AFTER
PHENOBARBITAL ADMINISTRATION.
000281 01-03
DIAZEPINES
COMPARATIVE-STUDY OF SLEEP AND STATE ON AWAKENING WITH TWO
HYPNOTIC DIAZEPINES.
000817 01-14
DIBENZAZEPINES
THE EFFECT OF DIBENZAZEPINES (TRICYCLIC-ANTIDEPRESSANTS) ON
CEREBRAL CAPILLARY PERMEABILITY IN THE RAT IN VIVO.
003974 04-03
DIBENZEPINE
LARGE-DOSES OF DIBENZEPINE NOVERIL IN THE TREATMENT OF
DEPRESSIVE-STATES.
002020 02-09

CLINICAL-EXPERIENCE WITH RETARD DIBENZEPINE (NOVERIL-240) IN
ENDOGENOUS DEPRESSIONS ACCOMPANIED BY SYMPTOMS OF DRUG-
RESISTANCE.
003245 03-09
DIBUTYRYL-C-AMP
FACILITATION OF LORDOSIS BEHAVIOR IN THE OVARIECTOMIZED
ESTROGEN-PRIMED RAT BY DIBUTYRYL-C-AMP.
002957 03-04
DIBUTYRYL-CYCLIC-AMP
CATECHOLAMINE AND 5 HYDROXYTRYPTAMINE SYNTHESIS AND
METABOLISM FOLLOWING INTRACEREBROVENTRICULAR INJECTION OF
DIBUTYRYL-CYCLIC-AMP.
003769 04-03
DIBUTYRYL-CYCLIC-GUANOSINE-MONOPHOSPHATE
INHIBITION OF THE ACTION OF CHOLECYSTOKININ-OCTAPEPTIDE ON THE
GUINEA-PIG ILEUM MYENTERIC PLEXUS BY DIBUTYRYL-CYCLIC-
GUANOSINE-MONOPHOSPHATE.
001291 02-03
DICHLORO-6-PHENYLPHENOXYETHYLAMINE-HBR
BETA DIETHYLAMINOETHYLDIPHENYLPROPYLACETATE (SKF-525-A) AND
2,4 DICHLORO-6-PHENYLPHENOXYETHYLAMINE-HBR (DPEA) INHIBITION
OF FATTY-ACID CONJUGATION TO 11 HYDROXY-DELTA9-
TETRAHYDROCANNABINOL BY THE RAT LIVER MICROSOMAL SYSTEM.
000179 01-03
DICHLOROBENZYL-TETRAHYDROPYRIMIDONE
PHARMACOLOGY OF 1 DICHLOROBENZYL-TETRAHYDROPYRIMIDONE, A
NOVEL ANTIDEPRESSANT COMPOUND WITH ANTIANXIETY ACTIVITY.
003688 04-02
DICHOTIC
LATERALIZED DEFICITS AND DRUG INFLUENCES ON THE DICHOTIC
LISTENING OF SCHIZOPHRENIC-PATIENTS.
003443 03-14
DICHROISM
COMPARISON OF HIGHLY-ACTIVE AND ACTIVITY DEPLETED HEPARIN BY
CIRCULAR DICHROISM SPECTROSCOPY. (UNPUBLISHED PAPER).
001057 02-01
DIET
EFFECT OF LITHIUM-CHLORIDE IN COYOTE PUP DIET.
001835 02-05
SUBCUTANEOUS SILASTIC IMPLANTS: MAINTENANCE OF HIGH BLOOD
ETHANOL LEVELS IN RATS DRINKING A LIQUID DIET.
001865 02-06
DIETARY
FUNCTIONAL AND STRUCTURAL CONSEQUENCES OF LONG-TERM DIETARY
L-DOPA TREATMENT IN MICE.
000257 01-03
EFFECTS OF CHRONIC DIETARY LITHIUM ON ACTIVITY AND REGULATION
OF NA-K-ADENOSINE-TRIPHOSPHATASE IN RAT-BRAIN.
000297 01-03
DIETARY PROTEIN INTAKE INFLUENCES THE ANTIHYPERTENSIVE POTENCY
OF METHYLDOPA IN SPONTANEOUSLY HYPERTENSIVE-RATS.
004025 04-03
SUSTAINED DECREASE IN FAT CONSUMPTION PRODUCED BY
AMPHETAMINE IN RATS MAINTAINED ON A DIETARY SELF-SELECTION
REGIME.
004150 04-04
DIETETIC
DRUG AND DIETETIC THERAPIES FOR HYPERKINETIC-CHILDREN. (PH.D.
DISSERTATION).
003576 03-17
DIETHYLAMINOETHYLDIPHENYLPROPYLACETATE
BETA DIETHYLAMINOETHYLDIPHENYLPROPYLACETATE (SKF-525-A) AND
2,4 DICHLORO-6-PHENYLPHENOXYETHYLAMINE-HBR (DPEA) INHIBITION
OF FATTY-ACID CONJUGATION TO 11 HYDROXY-DELTA9-
TETRAHYDROCANNABINOL BY THE RAT LIVER MICROSOMAL SYSTEM.
000179 01-03
DIETHYLDITHIOCARBAMATE
COMPARISONS OF THE EFFECTS OF GUANETHIDINE, 6
HYDROXYDOPAMINE AND DIETHYLDITHIOCARBAMATE ON RETENTION
OF PASSIVE-AVOIDANCE.
001742 02-04
DIETHYLSTILBESTROL
COMPARATIVE-STUDY OF PROPHYLACTIC LITHIUM AND
DIETHYLSTILBESTROL IN SEXUAL-DEVIANTS.
000663 01-11
DIFENAMIZOLE
NEUROCHEMICAL-STUDIES OF AN ANALGESIC, 1,3 DIPHENYL-5-2-
DIMETHYLAMINOPROPIONAMIDE-PYRAZOLE (DIFENAMIZOLE).
002771 03-03
DIFFERENTIAL
DIFFERENTIAL REGULATION OF MUSCARINIC AGONIST BINDING-SITES
FOLLOWING CHRONIC CHOLINESTERASE INHIBITION.
000279 01-03
DIFFERENTIAL SENSITIVITY OF HYPOTHALAMIC DOPAMINERGIC AND
NORADRENERGIC NEURONES TO PHARMACOLOGICAL MANIPULATION.
001310 02-03
DIFFERENTIAL DOPAMINERGIC FUNCTION IN YOUNG AND OLD FEMALE
RATS AS MEASURED BY THREE BEHAVIORS.
001683 02-04

THE ROLE OF DIFFERENTIAL BLOCKADE OF ALPHA-ADRENERGIC AGONISTS IN CHLORPROMAZINE-INDUCED HYPOTENSION.
001851 02-05

THE DIFFERENTIAL DOSE-EFFECTS OF METHYLPHENIDATE ON HYPERACTIVE-CHILDREN AND THEIR MOTHERS. (PH.D. DISSERTATION).
002143 02-11

MIDBRAIN DOPAMINE NEURONS: DIFFERENTIAL RESPONSES TO AMPHETAMINE ISOMERS.
002680 03-03

DIFFERENTIAL REGULATION BY GUANINE-NUCLEOTIDES OF OPIATE AGONIST AND ANTAGONIST RECEPTOR INTERACTIONS.
002688 03-03

DIFFERENTIAL LOSS OF BIOLOGICAL-ACTIVITY OF THE ENKEPHALINS INDUCED BY CURRENT.
002783 03-03

(3H)MIANSERIN: DIFFERENTIAL LABELING OF SEROTONIN AND HISTAMINE-RECEPTORS IN RAT-BRAIN.
002860 03-03

DIFFERENTIAL REVERSAL BY SCOPOLAMINE AND THIP OF THE ANTISTEREOTYPIC AND CATALEPTIC-EFFECTS OF NEUROLEPTICS.
002948 03-04

THE DIFFERENTIAL NEUROCHEMICAL-BASES OF THE BEHAVIOURS ELICITED BY SEROTONERGIC-AGENTS AND BY THE COMBINATION OF A MONOAMINE-OXIDASE-INHIBITOR AND L-DOPA.
002976 03-04

DIFFERENTIAL ACTIONS OF CLASSICAL AND ATYPICAL ANTIPSYCHOTIC-DRUGS ON SPONTANEOUS NEURONAL ACTIVITY IN THE AMYGDALOID COMPLEX.
003131 03-05

DIFFERENTIAL DIAGNOSIS OF CIMETIDINE-INDUCED DELIRIUM.
003488 03-15

DIFFERENTIAL BINDING OF CHLORPROMAZINE TO HUMAN BLOOD CELLS: APPLICATION OF THE HYGROSCOPIC DESORPTION METHOD.
003556 03-16

PRESYNAPTIC AND POSTSYNAPTIC STRIATAL DOPAMINE-RECEPTORS: DIFFERENTIAL SENSITIVITY TO APOMORPHINE INHIBITION OF (3H)DOPAMINE AND (14C)GABA RELEASE IN VITRO
003741 04-03

DIFFERENTIAL TOLERANCE TO THE EFFECTS OF MORPHINE ON EVOKED ACTIVITY IN THE HIPPOCAMPAL SLICE.
003760 04-03

ACTION OF ENKEPHALIN ANALOGUES AND MORPHINE ON BRAIN ACETYLCHOLINE RELEASE: DIFFERENTIAL REVERSAL BY NALOXONE AND AN OPIATE-PENTAPEPTIDE.
003863 04-03

DIFFERENTIAL INHIBITION OF ALPHA1-ADRENOCEPTOR AND ALPHA2-ADRENOCEPTOR MEDIATED PRESSOR RESPONSES IN PITHED RATS.
004057 04-03

DIFFERENTIAL DIAGNOSIS AND TREATMENT OF PANIC ATTACKS AND PHOBIC-STATES.
004424 04-10

DIFFERENTIAL-EFFECT
KAINIC-ACID INDUCED LESION OF RAT RETINA: DIFFERENTIAL-EFFECT ON CYCLIC-GMP AND BENZODIAZEPINE-RECEPTORS AND GABA-RECEPTORS.
002743 03-03

DIFFERENTIAL-EFFECT OF CHRONIC DESIPRAMINE AND AMITRIPTYLINE TREATMENT ON RAT-BRAIN ADRENERGIC AND SEROTONERGIC-RECEPTORS.
002914 03-03

POTENTIATION OF BARBITURATE HYPNOSIS BY PROBENECID: DIFFERENTIAL-EFFECT IN TOLERANT ANIMALS.
003038 03-04

DIFFERENTIAL-EFFECTS
DIFFERENTIAL-EFFECTS OF N DIPROPYLACETATE AND AMINOOXYACETIC-ACID ON GAMMA AMINOBUTYRIC-ACID LEVELS IN DISCRETE AREAS OF RAT-BRAIN.
000140 01-03

A FURTHER CHARACTERIZATION OF THE DIFFERENTIAL-EFFECTS OF LEUCINE-ENKEPHALIN, METHIONINE-ENKEPHALIN AND THEIR ANALOGS ON MORPHINE-INDUCED ANALGESIA.
000311 01-03

DIFFERENTIAL-EFFECTS OF METHYLPHENIDATE ON SIGNALLED AND NONSIGNALLED REINFORCEMENT.
000380 01-04

DIFFERENTIAL-EFFECTS OF NALOXONE AGAINST THE DIAZEPAM-INDUCED RELEASE OF BEHAVIOR IN RATS IN THREE AVERSIVE-SITUATIONS.
000480 01-04

PRINCIPAL AND DIFFERENTIAL-EFFECTS OF HALOPERIDOL AND PLACEBO TREATMENTS UPON SPEECH DISFLUENCIES IN STUTTERERS.
000713 01-11

DIFFERENTIAL-EFFECTS ON BENZODIAZEPINE DISPOSITION BY DISULFIRAM AND ETHANOL.
000789 01-13

THE DIFFERENTIAL-EFFECTS OF SHORT-ACTING AND LONG-ACTING BENZODIAZEPINES UPON NOCTURNAL SLEEP AND DAYTIME PERFORMANCE.
000822 01-14

DIFFERENTIAL-EFFECTS OF COCAINE ON LIMBIC EXCITABILITY.
001339 02-03

DIFFERENTIAL-EFFECTS OF VARIOUS STIMULI ON AVP LEVELS IN BLOOD AND CEREBROSPINAL-FLUID.
001370 02-03

DIFFERENTIAL-EFFECTS OF SYSTEMIC VERSUS INTRACRANIAL INJECTION OF OPIATES ON CENTRAL, OROFACIAL AND LOWER BODY NOCICEPTION: SOMATOTYPY IN BULBAR ANALGESIA SYSTEMS.
001446 02-03

DIFFERENTIAL-EFFECTS OF IMIPRAMINE IN RATS AS A FUNCTION OF DRL SCHEDULE VALUE.
001714 02-04

DIFFERENTIAL-EFFECTS OF MORPHINE ON FOOD AND WATER INTAKE IN FOOD DEPRIVED AND FREELY-FEEDING RATS.
001765 02-04

DIFFERENTIAL-EFFECTS OF AMPHETAMINE AND NEUROLEPTICS ON NEGATIVE VS. POSITIVE SYMPTOMS IN SCHIZOPHRENIA.
001906 02-08

ANTIPSYCHOTIC-DRUGS: DIFFERENTIAL-EFFECTS ON DOPAMINE NEURONS IN BASAL GANGLIA AND MESOCORTEX FOLLOWING CHRONIC ADMINISTRATION IN HUMAN AND NONHUMAN PRIMATES.
002285 02-13

DIFFERENTIAL-EFFECTS OF KAINIC-ACID ON BENZODIAZEPINE-RECEPTORS, GABA-RECEPTORS, AND GABA-MODULIN IN THE CEREBELLAR-CORTEX.
002477 02-16

DIFFERENTIAL-EFFECTS OF PHARMACOLOGICAL-AGENTS ACTING ON MONOAMINERGIC SYSTEMS ON DRUG-INDUCED ANOREXIA.
002533 02-17

DIFFERENTIAL-EFFECTS OF CANNABINOID EXPOSURE AND STRESS ON PLASMA PROLACTIN, GROWTH-HORMONE AND CORTICOSTERONE LEVELS IN MALE MICE.
002695 03-03

DIFFERENTIAL-EFFECTS OF CLOMIPRAMINE AND CLORGYLINE ON THE SENSITIVITY OF CORTICAL NEURONS TO SEROTONIN: EFFECT OF CHRONIC-TREATMENT.
002847 03-03

DIFFERENTIAL-EFFECTS OF SHORT-TERM AND LONG-TERM LITHIUM ON TRYPTOPHAN UPTAKE AND SEROTONERGIC FUNCTION IN CAT BRAIN.
002911 03-03

DIFFERENTIAL-EFFECTS OF POTASSIUM ON THE POTENCY OF DIFFERENT OPIOIDS IN THE MOUSE VAS-DEFERENS.
002935 03-03

DIFFERENTIAL-EFFECTS OF ELECTROCONVULSIVE-SHOCK AND ANTIDEPRESSANT-DRUGS ON SEROTONIN2-RECEPTORS IN RAT-BRAIN.
003878 04-03

DIFFERENTIAL-EFFECTS OF PENTOBARBITAL AND ETHER ON THE SYNAPTIC TRANSMISSION OF THE HIPPOCAMPAL-CA1-REGION IN THE RAT.
003903 04-03

DIFFERENTIAL-EFFECTS OF ALPHA METHYLDOPAMINE, CLONIDINE AND HYDRALAZINE ON NOREPINEPHRINE AND EPINEPHRINE SYNTHESIZING ENZYMES IN THE BRAINSTEM NUCLEI OF SPONTANEOUSLY HYPERTENSIVE-RATS.
003947 04-03

DIFFERENTIAL-EFFECTS OF SEVERAL DOPAMINE UPTAKE INHIBITORS AND RELEASING-AGENTS ON LOCOMOTOR-ACTIVITY IN NORMAL AND IN RESERPINIZED MICE.
004130 04-04

DIFFERENTIAL-REINFORCEMENT-OF-LOW-RATES
THE EFFECTS OF TRICYCLIC-ANTIDEPRESSANTS ON PERFORMANCE UNDER A DIFFERENTIAL-REINFORCEMENT-OF-LOW-RATES SCHEDULE IN RATS.
004175 04-04

DIFFERENTIATE
MINI-SYMPOSIUM: III. SIMPLE IN VIVO TESTS THAT DIFFERENTIATE PROTOTYPE AGONISTS AT OPIATE-RECEPTORS.
004289 04-06

DIFFERENTIATED
N TETRAHYDROFURYLALKYL AND N ALKOXYALKYL DERIVATIVES OF (-) NORMETAZOCINE, COMPOUNDS WITH DIFFERENTIATED OPIOID ACTION PROFILES.
000013 01-02

QUESTIONS OF DIFFERENTIATED TREATMENT FOR EPILEPTIC-PATIENTS.
003605 03-17

SOME PRINCIPLES OF DIFFERENTIATED METABOLIC DRUG-TREATMENT IN COMPREHENSIVE THERAPY OF MENTAL-DISORDERS.
004433 04-11

DIFFERENTIATES
CATION REGULATION DIFFERENTIATES SPECIFIC BINDING OF (3H)SULPIRIDE AND (3H)SPIPERONE TO RAT STRIATAL PREPARATIONS.
004032 04-03

DIFFERENTIATION
BETA-ADRENOCEPTOR ANTAGONISTS: STUDIES ON BEHAVIOUR (DELAYED DIFFERENTIATION) IN THE MONKEY (MACACA-MULATTA).
000440 01-04

DIFFERENTIATION OF KAINATE AND QUISQUALATE-RECEPTORS IN THE CAT SPINAL-CORD BY SELECTIVE ANTAGONISMS WITH GAMMA D(AND L) GLUTAMYLGLYCINE.
002696 03-03

DIFFERENTIATION OF OPIATE-RECEPTORS IN THE BRAIN BY THE SELECTIVE DEVELOPMENT OF TOLERANCE.
003088 03-04

PHARMACOLOGICAL DIFFERENTIATION OF PRESYNAPTIC INHIBITORY
ALPHA-ADRENOCEPTORS AND OPIATE-RECEPTORS IN THE CAT
NICTITATING MEMBRANE.
003777 04-03
MINI-SYMPOSIUM. I. THE IN VIVO DIFFERENTIATION OF OPIATE-
RECEPTORS: INTRODUCTION.
004697 04-17

DIFFUSE
BEHAVIORAL CONFIRMATION OF DIFFUSE NOXIOUS INHIBITORY
CONTROLS (DNIC) AND EVIDENCE FOR A ROLE OF ENDOGENOUS
OPIATES.
002791 03-03

DIFLUORO
FLUORINATED ANALOGUES OF THE TRICYCLIC NEUROLEPTICS: 2,3
DIFLUORO DERIVATIVE OF CLOROTEPIN.
000001 01-01

DIFLUOROMETHYL-DOPA
IRREVERSIBLE INHIBITION OF AROMATIC-L-AMINO-ACID-DECARBOXYLASE
BY ALPHA DIFLUOROMETHYL-DOPA AND METABOLISM OF THE
INHIBITOR.
000248 01-03

DIFLUOROPHENYLSALICYLIC-ACID
ANALGESIC ACTIVITY OF DIFLUNISAL (MK-647; 5 2,4
DIFLUOROPHENYLSALICYLIC-ACID) IN RATS WITH HYPERALGESIA
INDUCED BY FREUNDS-ADJUVANT.
000502 01-04

DIGITOXIN
NONINTERACTION OF DIGITOXIN AND QUINIDINE.
000968 01-17

DIGOXIN
SUBJECTIVE ASSESSMENT OF SEXUAL-DYSFUNCTION OF PATIENTS ON
LONG-TERM ADMINISTRATION OF DIGOXIN.
002443 02-15
EFFECT OF DOSE ON BIOAVAILABILITY OF ORAL DIGOXIN.
003161 03-07

DIHYDRO-6-PHENYL-1H-S-TRIAZOLOBENZODIAZEPIN-1-ONES
2,4 DIHYDRO-6-PHENYL-1H-S-TRIAZOLOBENZODIAZEPIN-1-ONES WITH
ANTIANXIETY AND ANTIDEPRESSANT ACTIVITY.
001075 02-02

DIHYDROALPRENOLOL
DOWN REGULATION OF DIHYDROALPRENOLOL AND IMIPRAMINE
BINDING-SITES IN BRAIN OF RATS REPEATEDLY TREATED WITH
IMIPRAMINE.
001317 02-03

DIHYDROCAPSAICIN
EXCITATORY EFFECTS OF DIHYDROCAPSAICIN ON NOCICEPTIVE NEURONS
IN THE MEDIAL THALAMUS.
003714 04-03

DIHYDROERGOCRISTINE
INHIBITION OF SULPIRIDE-INDUCED PROLACTIN SECRETION BY
DIHYDROERGOCRISTINE IN MAN.
002277 02-13

DIHYDROERGOCRYPTINE
CHARACTERIZATION BY (3H)DIHYDROERGOCRYPTINE BINDING OF
ALPHA-ADRENERGIC-RECEPTORS IN NEUROBLASTOMA X GLIOMA
HYBRID CELLS.
003823 04-03

DIHYDROERGOTAMINE
DRUG-INDUCED ARTERIAL HYPOTENSION IN PSYCHIATRIC-PATIENTS
TREATED WITH DIHYDROERGOTAMINE.
001950 02-08

DIHYDROERGOTOXINE
NEUROPHARMACOLOGY OF BROMOCRIPTINE AND DIHYDROERGOTOXINE
(HYDERGINE).
001346 02-03
EFFECTS OF REPEATED ADMINISTRATIONS OF DIHYDROERGOTOXINE
(REDERGINE) ON THE SLEEP-WAKEFULNESS CYCLE IN THE CAT.
003703 04-02
CATECHOLAMINE TURNOVER IN RAT-CEREBRAL-CORTEX AND CAUDATE
FOLLOWING REPEATED TREATMENT WITH DIHYDROERGOTOXINE.
003765 04-03

DIHYDROMORPHINE
LOCALIZATION OF NALOXONE SENSITIVE (3H)DIHYDROMORPHINE
BINDING-SITES WITHIN THE HIPPOCAMPUS OF THE RAT.
001368 02-03
ALTERATIONS IN DIHYDROMORPHINE BINDING IN CEREBRAL
HEMISPHERES OF AGED MALE RATS.
003936 04-03

DIHYDROPICROTOXININ
SOLUBILIZATION OF THE DIHYDROPICROTOXININ BINDING-SITES.
001192 02-03
INTERACTION OF STEREOISOMERS OF BARBITURATES WITH (3H)ALPHA
DIHYDROPICROTOXININ BINDING-SITES.
004036 04-03

DIHYDROXY
DIHYDROXY AND TRIHYDROXY ANALOGS OF CHLORPROMAZINE
INFLUENCE THE CENTRAL-ACTIVITY OF ADENYLATE-CYCLASE AND
CYCLIC-AMP-PHOSPHODIESTERASE.
001405 02-03

DIHYDROXYNOMIFENSINE
EFFECTS OF 3',4' DIHYDROXYNOMIFENSINE ON THE DOPAMINE
VASCULAR RECEPTOR.
003890 04-03

DIHYDROXYPHENYLACETIC-ACID
DOPAMINE, NORADRENALINE AND 3,4 DIHYDROXYPHENYLACETIC-ACID
(DOPAC) LEVELS OF INDIVIDUAL BRAIN NUCLEI, EFFECTS OF
HALOPERIDOL AND PARGYLINE.
003792 04-03
DETERMINATION OF PICOMOLE AMOUNTS OF DOPAMINE,
NORADRENALINE, 3,4 DIHYDROXYPHENYLALANINE, 3,4
DIHYDROXYPHENYLACETIC-ACID, HOMOVANILLIC-ACID, AND 5
HYDROXYINDOLEACETIC-ACID IN NERVOUS-TISSUE AFTER ONE-STEP
PURIFICATION ON SEPHADEX-G-10, USING HIGH.
004305 04-06

DIHYDROXYPHENYLALANINE
AUTORADIOGRAPHIC STUDIES ON DISTRIBUTION OF L-3,4
DIHYDROXYPHENYLALANINE (L-DOPA) 14C AND L 5
HYDROXYTRYPTOPHAN (L 5 HTP) 14C IN THE CAT BRAIN.
003941 04-03
DETERMINATION OF PICOMOLE AMOUNTS OF DOPAMINE,
NORADRENALINE, 3,4 DIHYDROXYPHENYLALANINE, 3,4
DIHYDROXYPHENYLACETIC-ACID, HOMOVANILLIC-ACID, AND 5
HYDROXYINDOLEACETIC-ACID IN NERVOUS-TISSUE AFTER ONE-STEP
PURIFICATION ON SEPHADEX-G-10, USING HIGH.
004305 04-06

DIHYDROXYPHENYLETHYLENE-GLYCOL-SULFATE
EFFECTS OF MORPHINE AND OTHER CENTRALLY-ACTING DRUGS ON 3,4
DIHYDROXYPHENYLETHYLENE-GLYCOL-SULFATE (DOPEG-SO4) IN RAT-
BRAIN.
000136 01-03

DIHYDROXYPHENYLETHYLENEGLYCOL
POSTMORTEM STABILITY OF BRAIN 3 METHOXY-4-
HYDROXYPHENYLETHYLENEGLYCOL AND 3,4
DIHYDROXYPHENYLETHYLENEGLYCOL IN THE RAT AND MOUSE.
004048 04-03

DIHYDROXYTRYPTAMINE
UNILATERAL 5,7 DIHYDROXYTRYPTAMINE LESIONS OF THE DORSAL
RAPHE NUCLEUS (DRN) AND RAT ROTATIONAL-BEHAVIOUR.
001578 02-04
5,7 DIHYDROXYTRYPTAMINE LESIONS OF THE AMYGDALA REDUCE
AMPHETAMINE-INDUCED AND APOMORPHINE-INDUCED STEREOTYPED-
BEHAVIOUR IN THE RAT.
001589 02-04
THE EFFECTS OF INTRAVENTRICULAR 6 HYDROXYDOPAMINE AND 5,6
DIHYDROXYTRYPTAMINE ON MORPHINE-INDUCED LOCOMOTOR-
STIMULATION.
001784 02-04
DENERVATION SUPERSENSITIVITY TO 5 HYDROXYTRYPTOPHAN IN RATS
FOLLOWING SPINAL TRANSECTION AND 5,7 DIHYDROXYTRYPTAMINE
INJECTION.
003722 04-03

DIHYDROXYTRYPTAMINE-INDUCED
5,7 DIHYDROXYTRYPTAMINE-INDUCED MOUSE-KILLING AND
BEHAVIORAL-REVERSAL WITH VENTRICULAR ADMINISTRATION OF
SEROTONIN IN RATS.
001562 02-04

DIISOPROPYLTRYPTAMINE
N,N DIISOPROPYLTRYPTAMINE (DIPT) AND 5
METHOXYDIISOPROPYLTRYPTAMINE (5 MEO-DIPT). TWO ORALLY
ACTIVE TRYPTAMINE ANALOGS WITH CNS ACTIVITY.
004310 04-07

DIKETOPIPERAZINE
HISTIDYL-PROLINE DIKETOPIPERAZINE DECREASES FOOD INTAKE IN RATS.
004181 04-04

DILATION
CONSISTENT UNMASKING OF DOPAMINE-INDUCED DILATION OF THE
CANINE FEMORAL VASCULAR BED.
003911 04-03

DILATOR
DIRECT EVIDENCE AGAINST ACETYLCHOLINE AS THE DILATOR
TRANSMITTER IN THE CAT CEREBRAL-ARTERY.
001336 02-03

DILTIAZEM
TREATMENT OF UNSTABLE ANGINA BY DILTIAZEM.
004307 04-07

DILUTION
A METHOD FOR THE DETERMINATION OF AMITRIPTYLINE AND ITS
METABOLITES NORTRIPTYLINE, 10 HYDROXYAMITRIPTYLINE, AND 10
HYDROXYNORTRIPTYLINE IN HUMAN PLASMA USING STABLE ISOTOPE
DILUTION AND GAS-CHROMATOGRAPHY CHEMICAL-IONIZATION
MASS-SPECTROMETRY.
002486 02-16

DIMENSIONS
SOME OBSERVATIONS ON THE PSYCHOLOGICAL DIMENSIONS OF
PLACEBO-EFFECTS.
003573 03-17

DIMETHOXY-4-ALKYLPHENYLISOPROPYLAMINES
DOM AND RELATED 2,5 DIMETHOXY-4-ALKYLPHENYLISOPROPYLAMINES:
BEHAVIORAL AND SEROTONIN-RECEPTOR PROPERTIES.
003690 04-02
DIMETHOXY-4-METHYLAMPHETAMINE
ENHANCEMENT OF THE BEHAVIORAL-EFFECTS OF 2,5 DIMETHOXY-4-
METHYLAMPHETAMINE (DOM) BY PRETREATMENT WITH P
CHLOROPHENYLALANINE.
000364 01-04
THE EFFECTS OF D LYSERGIC-ACID-DIETHYLAMIDE (LSD), 2,5
DIMETHOXY-4-METHYLAMPHETAMINE (DOM) AND D-AMPHETAMINE
ON OPERANT-RESPONDING IN CONTROL AND 6 HYDROXYDOPAMINE
TREATED RATS.
001595 02-04
THE EFFECTS OF 2,5 DIMETHOXY-4-METHYLAMPHETAMINE (DOM) ON
OPERANT-BEHAVIOR: INTERACTIONS WITH OTHER NEUROACTIVE-
AGENTS.
004089 04-04
DIMETHOXYMETHYL-PHENOBARBITAL
METABOLISM OF DIMETHOXYMETHYL-PHENOBARBITAL (ETEROBARB) IN
PATIENTS WITH EPILEPSY.
002235 02-13
DIMETHYL-M-TYRAMINE
THE ROLE OF DOPAMINE IN THE HYPERMOTILITY INDUCED BY H-77-77
(4,ALPHA DIMETHYL-M-TYRAMINE) IN MICE.
001762 02-04
DIMETHYLAMINO-TETRAHYDROAZEPINOPHENOTHIAZINE
CONFORMATIONALLY RESTRICTED PHENOTHIAZINE NEUROLEPTICS. 1. 3
DIMETHYLAMINO-TETRAHYDROAZEPINOPHENOTHIAZINE.
001359 02-03
DIMETHYLAMINOBUTYNYLCYCLOHEXYLHYDROXY
THE CRYSTAL AND MOLECULAR STRUCTURE OF THE ACETYLCHOLINE
ANTAGONIST DIMETHYLAMINOBUTYNYLCYCLOHEXYLHYDROXY 2
PHENYLACETATE HCL.
000003 01-01
DIMETHYLAMINOPROPYL-5-METHYL-3-PHENYL-1H-INDAZOLE
PHARMACOLOGICAL-STUDIES ON A NEW THYMOLEPTIC
ANTIDEPRESSANT. DIMETHYLAMINOPROPYL-5-METHYL-3-PHENYL-1H-
INDAZOLE (FS-32).
001659 02-04
INFLUENCE OF A CHRONIC NEW POTENTIAL ANTIDEPRESSANT,
DIMETHYLAMINOPROPYL-5-METHYL-3-PHENYL-1H-INDAZOLE (FS-32)
AND ITS N DESMETHYLATED-COMPOUND (FS-97): TREATMENT ON
MONOAMINERGIC-RECEPTOR SENSITIVITY IN THE RAT-BRAIN.
002787 03-03
DIMETHYLTRYPTAMINE
BEHAVIOURAL-CHANGES INDUCED BY N,N DIMETHYLTRYPTAMINE IN
RODENTS.
000413 01-04
DIMETHYLTRYPTAMINES
STUDIES ON SEVERAL 7 SUBSTITUTED N,N DIMETHYLTRYPTAMINES.
001020 02-01
DIMINISHES
PIRACETAM DIMINISHES HIPPOCAMPAL ACETYLCHOLINE LEVELS IN RATS.
002934 03-03
DIMINUTION
3H IMIPRAMINE BINDING IN HUMAN PLATELETS: DIMINUTION OF
BINDING-SITES IN DEPRESSED-PATIENTS.
003427 03-13
DINORLAAM
PHARMACODYNAMIC PROFILES OF L ALPHA ACETYLMETHADOL (LAAM)
AND ITS N DEMETHYLATED METABOLITES, NORLAAM AND
DINORLAAM, DURING SELF-ADMINISTRATION IN THE DEPENDENT RAT.
000505 01-04
DIPHENYL-5,2-DIMETHYLAMINOPROPIONAMIDE-PYRAZOLE
NEUROCHEMICAL-STUDIES OF AN ANALGESIC, 1,3 DIPHENYL-5-2-
DIMETHYLAMINOPROPIONAMIDE-PYRAZOLE (DIFENAMIZOLE).
002771 03-03
DIPHENYLHYDANTOIN
PLASMA LEVELS OF DIPHENYLHYDANTOIN AND THE CONTROL OF ADULT
EPILEPTIC-SEIZURES: A CHILEAN EXPERIENCE.
000102 01-03
EFFECT OF DOPAMINERGIC AND GABAERGIC DRUGS GIVEN ALONE OR IN
COMBINATION ON THE ANTICONVULSANT ACTION OF PHENOBARBITAL
AND DIPHENYLHYDANTOIN IN THE ELECTROSHOCK-TEST IN MICE.
000163 01-03
EFFECTS OF DIPHENYLHYDANTOIN ON SPONTANEOUS MOTOR-ACTIVITY.
000284 01-03
BEHAVIORAL-ANALYSIS OF AMYGDALOID KINDLING IN BEAGLE-DOGS
AND THE EFFECTS OF CLONAZEPAM, DIAZEPAM, PHENOBARBITAL,
DIPHENYLHYDANTOIN, AND FLUNARIZINE ON SEIZURE
MANIFESTATION.
000496 01-04
SERUM CONCENTRATIONS OF PHENOBARBITAL AND
DIPHENYLHYDANTOIN IN SEVERE MENTALLY-HANDICAPPED AND
PHYSICALLY-HANDICAPPED-PATIENTS.
000856 01-15
PHOSPHORYLATION OF THE MEMBRANE-BOUND ACETYLCHOLINE-
RECEPTOR: INHIBITION BY DIPHENYLHYDANTOIN.
001257 02-03

CRITICAL PERIODS FOR DIPHENYLHYDANTOIN AND PHENOBARBITAL
ADMINISTRATION DURING GESTATION.
001630 02-04
PERINATAL EFFECTS OF PSYCHOTROPIC-DRUGS: THE ANTICONVULSANT-
DRUG DIPHENYLHYDANTOIN. (UNPUBLISHED PAPER).
001842 02-05
INTERRELATION AT PLASMATIC LEVEL BETWEEN ANTIEPILEPTIC-DRUGS
AND LIPIDS. ITS IMPLICATIONS IN THE EFFICIENCY OF TREATMENT IN
EPILEPSY. I. CHANGES INDUCED BY PHENOBARBITAL OR/AND
DIPHENYLHYDANTOIN IN SERUM LIPIDS.
002281 02-13
PAROXYSTIC-DYSKINESIAS DURING TREATMENT WITH
DIPHENYLHYDANTOIN.
002319 02-14
A COMPARISON OF THE EFFECTS OF PENTOBARBITAL AND
DIPHENYLHYDANTOIN ON THE GABA SENSITIVITY AND EXCITABILITY
OF ADULT SENSORY GANGLION CELLS.
002692 03-03
DIPHENYLHYDANTOIN REDUCES THE OUTWARD-CURRENT OF THE ACTION
POTENTIAL IN APLYSIA.
002805 03-03
CHANGES IN REGIONAL BRAIN LEVELS OF AMINO-ACID PUTATIVE
NEUROTRANSMITTERS AFTER PROLONGED TREATMENT WITH THE
ANTICONVULSANT-DRUGS DIPHENYLHYDANTOIN, PHENOBARBITONE,
SODIUM-VALPROATE, ETHOSUXIMIDE, AND SULTHIAME IN THE RAT.
003961 04-03
EFFECTS OF WITHDRAWAL FROM LONG-TERM DIPHENYLHYDANTOIN
TREATMENT ON AUDIOGENIC-SEIZURES AND MAXIMAL
ELECTROSHOCK-INDUCED SEIZURES IN RATS.
004101 04-04
MEASUREMENTS OF NERVE CONDUCTION VELOCITY DURING DECREASING
TOXIC DIPHENYLHYDANTOIN LEVELS AND THE BEGINNING OF
CARBAMAZEPINE MEDICATION: A CLINICAL NEUROPHYSIOLOGICAL
REPORT.
004441 04-11
THE EFFECT OF DIPHENYLHYDANTOIN ON EEG CURVES IN EPILEPTICS.
004494 04-11
TRANSIENT HYPERKINESIA AFTER A SINGLE INTRAVENOUS PERFUSION OF
DIPHENYLHYDANTOIN: REPORT OF A CASE ASSOCIATED WITH
NONTOXIC PLASMA LEVELS OF DIPHENYLHYDANTOIN.
004638 04-15
A COMPARISON OF RADIOIMMUNOASSAY WITH SPECTROPHOTOMETRY
FOR THE DETERMINATION OF PLASMA DIPHENYLHYDANTOIN
CONCENTRATIONS.
004684 04-16
DIPHENYLHYDANTOIN-INDUCED
DIPHENYLHYDANTOIN-INDUCED BLOCK OF THE RAT PHRENIC-NERVE
DIAPHRAGM PREPARATION PRETREATED WITH P
HYDROXYMERCURIBENZOATE.
002749 03-03
DIPIPERIDINOETHANE
SYSTEMIC DIPIPERIDINOETHANE MIMICS THE CONVULSANT AND
NEUROTOXIC-ACTIONS OF KAINIC-ACID.
000222 01-03
LESIONS OF AMYGDALA, PYRIFORM CORTEX AND OTHER BRAIN
STRUCTURES DUE TO DIPIPERIDINOETHANE INTOXICATION.
004273 04-05
DIPOLAR
NMR SPECTRAL STUDY OF PROTON TRANSFER IN AMITRIPTYLINE-
HYDROCHLORIDE CHLORDIAZEPOXIDE-HYDROCHLORIDE COMBINATIONS
IN DIPOLAR APROTIC SOLVENTS.
003654 04-01
DIPOTASSIUM-CHLORAZEPATE
PHARMACOPSYCHOLOGICAL INVESTIGATION OF CHANGES IN MOOD
INDUCED BY DIPOTASSIUM-CHLORAZEPATE WITH AND WITHOUT
SIMULTANEOUS ALCOHOL ADMINISTRATION.
000825 01-14
PHARMACOKINETICS OF DIPOTASSIUM-CHLORAZEPATE IN PATIENTS
AFTER REPEATED 50MG ORAL DOSES.
002211 02-13
DIPOTASSIUM-CLORAZEPATE
PHARMACOPSYCHOLOGICAL INVESTIGATIONS CONCERNING THE
COMBINED EFFECTS OF DIPOTASSIUM-CLORAZEPATE AND ETHANOL.
003456 03-14
DIPROPYL-ADTN
ACTIVATION OF PRESYNAPTIC ALPHA NORADRENALINE-RECEPTORS IN
RAT-BRAIN BY THE POTENT DOPAMINE-MIMETIC N,N DIPROPYL-ADTN.
001390 02-03
DIPROPYLACETAMIDE
EEG AND ANTICONVULSANT EFFECTS OF DIPROPYLACETIC-ACID AND
DIPROPYLACETAMIDE IN THE BABOON PAPIO-PAPIO.
001210 02-03
DIPROPYLACETATE
DIFFERENTIAL-EFFECTS OF N DIPROPYLACETATE AND AMINOOXYACETIC-
ACID ON GAMMA AMINOBUTYRIC-ACID LEVELS IN DISCRETE AREAS
OF RAT-BRAIN.
000140 01-03

DIPROPYLACETATE-INDUCED
DIPROPYLACETATE-INDUCED ABSTINENCE-BEHAVIOUR AS A POSSIBLE CORRELATE OF INCREASED GABAERGIC ACTIVITY IN THE RAT.
001606 02-04

DIPROPYLACETIC-ACID
EEG AND ANTICONVULSANT EFFECTS OF DIPROPYLACETIC-ACID AND DIPROPYLACETAMIDE IN THE BABOON PAPIO-PAPIO.
001210 02-03
INFLUENCE OF DIPROPYLACETIC-ACID ON THALAMOCORTICAL RESPONSES IN RATS.
001419 02-03

DIPSOGENIC-EFFECT
DIPSOGENIC-EFFECT OF L 5 HYDROXYTRYPTOPHAN IN RATS.
001623 02-04

DIRECTIONALITY
POSTURAL ASYMMETRY AND DIRECTIONALITY OF ROTATION IN RATS.
001729 02-04
DOES POSTURAL ASYMMETRY INDICATE DIRECTIONALITY OF ROTATION IN RATS: ROLE OF SEX AND HANDLING.
003061 03-04

DIRECTIONS
DEPRESSION IN THE ELDERLY: RESEARCH DIRECTIONS IN PSYCHOPATHOLOGY, EPIDEMIOLOGY, AND TREATMENT.
000998 01-17

DISADVANTAGES
ADVANTAGES AND DISADVANTAGES OF PROLONGED USE OF NEUROLEPTICS.
003470 03-15

DISAGGREGATION
AMPHETAMINE STEREOTYPIES AND POLYRIBOSOMAL DISAGGREGATION IN RATS: EFFECTS OF ADRENERGIC AND SEROTONERGIC BLOCKING-AGENTS.
001531 02-03

DISCHARGE
CORRECTION BY PROPRANOLOL OF THE ABNORMAL ADRENALINE DISCHARGE INDUCED BY EMOTIONAL-STRESS IN CEREBRAL HEMORRHAGE PATIENTS.
002295 02-13
COMPARISON OF DRUG PRESCRIPTIONS FOR PSYCHIATRIC-PATIENTS AFTER HOSPITAL DISCHARGE IN THE DISTRICTS TEPLICE AND UHERSKE-HRADISTE.
002518 02-17
EFFECTS OF PROLONGED TREATMENT WITH LITHIUM AND TRICYCLIC-ANTIDEPRESSANTS ON DISCHARGE FREQUENCY, NOREPINEPHRINE RESPONSES AND BETA-RECEPTOR BINDING IN RAT-CEREBELLUM: ELECTROPHYSIOLOGICAL AND BIOCHEMICAL COMPARISON.
002884 03-03
EFFECTS OF ACUTE AND CHRONIC AMPHETAMINE TREATMENT ON PURKINJE NEURON DISCHARGE IN RAT CEREBELLUM.
003793 04-03
EFFECT OF MEDIAN RAPHE STIMULATION ON HIPPOCAMPAL SEIZURE DISCHARGE INDUCED BY CARBACHOL IN THE RABBIT.
003951 04-03

DISCHARGED
FOLLOWUP TREATMENT AND AFTERCARE OF DISCHARGED SCHIZOPHRENIC-PATIENTS.
000944 01-17

DISCHARGES
INHIBITORY ACTIONS OF TAUROCYAMINE, HYPOTAURINE, HOMOTAURINE, TAURINE AND GABA ON SPIKE DISCHARGES OF PURKINJE-CELLS, AND LOCALIZATION OF SENSITIVE SITES, IN GUINEA-PIG CEREBELLAR SLICES.
002846 03-03
ANTIPEROXIDANT PRETREATMENT AND IRON-INDUCED EPILEPTIFORM DISCHARGES IN THE RAT: EEG AND HISTOPATHOLOGIC STUDIES.
002930 03-03

DISCONTINUATION
DISCONTINUATION OF ORAL AND DEPOT FLUPHENAZINE IN SCHIZOPHRENIC-PATIENTS AFTER ONE YEAR OF CONTINUOUS MEDICATION: A CONTROLLED-STUDY.
001931 02-08
PANIC-ANXIETY AFTER ABRUPT DISCONTINUATION OF AMITRIPTYLINE.
003223 03-09
EFFECTS OF GRADUAL DECREASE AND DISCONTINUATION OF NEUROLEPTICS ON CLINICAL CONDITION AND TARDIVE-DYSKINESIA.
003469 03-15
DISCONTINUATION OF ANTIPSYCHOTIC-DRUG THERAPY.
003514 03-15
CLINICAL AND BIOCHEMICAL-CORRELATIONS IN ABRUPT DISCONTINUATION OF PSYCHOPHARMACOTHERAPY.
004330 04-08
A MODIFIED VERSION OF THE SIMULTANEOUS DISCONTINUATION OF PSYCHOTROPIC-DRUGS (COMBINED WITH THE ADMINISTRATION OF DIURETICS) AS A METHOD OF HALTING PROLONGED ATTACKS OF SCHIZOPHRENIA.
004584 04-14

DISCONTINUING
AN INVESTIGATION OF SOME SIDE-EFFECTS IN 47 PSYCHOTIC-PATIENTS DURING TREATMENT WITH CLOZAPINE AND DISCONTINUING OF THE TREATMENT.
002424 02-15

DISCRETE
DIFFERENTIAL-EFFECTS OF N DIPROPYLACETATE AND AMINOOXYACETIC-ACID ON GAMMA AMINOBUTYRIC-ACID LEVELS IN DISCRETE AREAS OF RAT-BRAIN.
000140 01-03
THE EFFECTS OF OPIATES ON THE LEVELS OF CYCLIC-GUANOSINE-MONOPHOSPHATE IN DISCRETE AREAS OF THE RAT CENTRAL-NERVOUS-SYSTEM.
000220 01-03
BIOCHEMICAL-LOCALIZATION AND CHARACTERIZATION OF BOMBESIN-LIKE-PEPTIDES IN DISCRETE REGIONS OF RAT-BRAIN. (UNPUBLISHED PAPER).
001046 02-01
TOLERANCE TO BARBITURATE-INDUCED CENTRAL-NERVOUS-SYSTEM DEPRESSION: INVOLVEMENT OF STIMULUS SECRETION COUPLING IN DISCRETE BRAIN AREAS. (PH.D. DISSERTATION).
001213 02-03
CHOLECYSTOKININ-PEPTIDES PRODUCE MARKED REDUCTION OF DOPAMINE TURNOVER IN DISCRETE AREAS IN THE RAT-BRAIN FOLLOWING INTERAVENTRICULAR INJECTION.
001239 02-03
AGE DEPENDENT CHANGES IN THE BETA ENDORPHIN CONTENT OF DISCRETE RAT-BRAIN NUCLEI.
002635 03-01
MONOAMINE-OXIDASE-B ACTIVITIES TOWARD BETA PHENYLETHYLAMINE IN DISCRETE HYPOTHALAMIC AND CIRCUMVENTRICULAR NUCLEI OF THE RAT.
002781 03-03
INFLUENCE OF ESTROGEN AND PROGESTERONE ON GLUTAMIC-ACID-DECARBOXYLASE ACTIVITY IN DISCRETE REGIONS OF RAT-BRAIN.
002927 03-03

DISCRIMINABILITY
THE EFFECT OF SEROTONIN DEPLETION ON THE DISCRIMINABILITY OF LSD.
000499 01-04
FACTORS REGULATING DRUG CUE SENSITIVITY: LIMITS OF DISCRIMINABILITY AND THE ROLE OF A PROGRESSIVELY DECREASING TRAINING DOSE IN FENTANYL SALINE DISCRIMINATION.
004088 04-04

DISCRIMINANT
DRUG-VARIABLES IN THE ETIOLOGY OF TARDIVE-DYSKINESIA: APPLICATION OF DISCRIMINANT FUNCTION ANALYSIS.
000844 01-15
RESPONDERS AND NONRESPONDERS TO CHLORDIAZEPOXIDE AND PLACEBO: A DISCRIMINANT FUNCTION ANALYSIS.
002482 02-16
RESPONDERS AND NONRESPONDERS TO CHLORDIAZEPOXIDE AND PLACEBO. A DISCRIMINANT FUNCTION ANALYSIS. (UNPUBLISHED PAPER).
004420 04-10

DISCRIMINATE
USING PROFILES OF SACCHARIN AND WATER DRINKING TO DETECT AND DISCRIMINATE ACTIONS OF DRUGS AND TOXICANTS.
000503 01-04

DISCRIMINATED
MORPHINE EFFECTS UPON DISCRIMINATED APPROACH AND DISCRIMINATED AVOIDANCE IN RATS: ANTAGONISM BY NALOXONE.
000338 01-04

DISCRIMINATION
A COMPARISON OF HUMAN TACTILE STIMULUS VELOCITY DISCRIMINATION WITH THE ABILITY OF S-I CORTICAL NEURONS IN AWAKE RHESUS-MONKEYS TO SIGNAL THE SAME VELOCITY DIFFERENCES BEFORE AND AFTER NONANESTHETIC DOSES OF PENTOBARBITAL.
000055 01-03
INVESTIGATION OF NARCOTICS AND ANTITUSSIVES USING DRUG DISCRIMINATION TECHNIQUES.
000447 01-04
DRUGS AND THE DISCRIMINATION OF DURATION.
001561 02-04
EFFECTS OF MORPHINE, D-AMPHETAMINE, AND PENTOBARBITAL ON SHOCK AND LIGHT DISCRIMINATION PERFORMANCE IN RATS.
001639 02-04
THE EFFECT OF MORPHINE, PIMOZIDE AND NALOXONE ON DISCRIMINATION BY RATS IN A SHOCK-ESCAPE-TEST.
001700 02-04
GO-HERE-GO-THERE PERFORMANCE AFTER AMPHETAMINE: THE IMPORTANCE OF THE RESPONSE REQUIREMENT IN SUCCESSIVE DISCRIMINATION.
001759 02-04
LACK OF EFFECT OF CHOLINE AND NARCOTIC ANTAGONISTS UPON APOMORPHINE DISCRIMINATION.
001770 02-04
EFFECTS OF PIMOZIDE ON ACCURACY OF PERFORMANCE AND DISTRIBUTION OF CORRECT RESPONDING ON A SIMULTANEOUS DISCRIMINATION TASK IN THE RAT.
001806 02-04

DISCRIMINATION OF FUNCTIONALLY HETEROGENEOUS RECEPTOR
SUBPOPULATIONS: ANTIPSYCHOTIC AND ANTIDOPAMINERGIC
PROPERTIES OF METOCLOPRAMIDE.
002877 03-03

THE EFFECTS OF PIMOZIDE DURING PAIRING ON THE TRANSFER OF
CLASSICAL CONDITIONING TO AN OPERANT DISCRIMINATION.
002956 03-04

EXTENDED SCHEDULE TRANSFER OF ETHANOL DISCRIMINATION.
003087 03-04

FACTORS REGULATING DRUG CUE SENSITIVITY: LIMITS OF
DISCRIMINABILITY AND THE ROLE OF A PROGRESSIVELY DECREASING
TRAINING DOSE IN FENTANYL SALINE DISCRIMINATION.
004088 04-04

METHADONE-INDUCED ATTENUATION OF THE EFFECTS OF DELTA9
TETRAHYDROCANNABINOL ON TEMPORAL DISCRIMINATION IN
PIGEONS.
004095 04-04

DISCRIMINATION OF ELECTRIC-SHOCK: EFFECTS OF SOME OPIOID AND
NONOPIOID DRUGS.
004106 04-04

A SIGNAL-DETECTION-ANALYSIS OF MORPHINE EFFECTS ON THE
RESPONSE BIAS OF RATS IN A TWO-SHOCK DISCRIMINATION TASK.
004124 04-04

NARCOTIC DISCRIMINATION IN PIGEONS.
004132 04-04

RAPID ACQUISITION OF A TWO-DRUG DISCRIMINATION: TIME OF DAY
EFFECT UPON SALINE STATE.
004214 04-04

METHYLMERCURY-INDUCED CHANGES IN OPERANT DISCRIMINATION BY
THE PIGEON.
004271 04-05

DISCRIMINATIONS
EFFECTS OF PHENCYCLIDINE, PENTOBARBITAL, AND D-AMPHETAMINE ON
THE ACQUISITION AND PERFORMANCE OF CONDITIONAL
DISCRIMINATIONS IN MONKEYS.
001723 02-04

DISCRIMINATIVE
REINFORCING, DISCRIMINATIVE AND ACTIVATING PROPERTIES OF
AMPHETAMINE.
000804 01-14

THE EFFECTS OF OPIATE ANTAGONISTS ON THE DISCRIMINATIVE
STIMULUS PROPERTIES OF ETHANOL.
002947 03-04

INTRAVENTRICULAR CORTICOSTERONE INJECTION FACILITATES MEMORY
OF AN APPETITIVE DISCRIMINATIVE TASK IN MICE.
003051 03-04

DISCRIMINATIVE RESPONSE CONTROL BY NALOXONE IN MORPHINE
PRETREATED RATS.
003053 03-04

PHENCYCLIDINE-LIKE DISCRIMINATIVE EFFECTS OF OPIOIDS IN THE RAT.
004136 04-04

AVOIDANCE ENHANCEMENT AND DISCRIMINATIVE RESPONSE CONTROL
BY ANXIOLYTICS WITH DRUGS ACTING ON THE GABA SYSTEM.
004193 04-04

DISCRIMINATIVE-STIMULUS
DISCRIMINATIVE-STIMULUS EFFECTS OF NALTREXONE IN THE MORPHINE-
DEPENDENT RAT.
000391 01-04

LSD-25 AS A DISCRIMINATIVE-STIMULUS FOR RESPONSE SELECTION BY
PIGEONS.
000412 01-04

DISCRIMINATIVE-STIMULUS EFFECTS OF PENTOBARBITAL IN PIGEONS.
001651 02-04

DELTA9 THC AS A DISCRIMINATIVE-STIMULUS IN RATS AND PIGEONS:
GENERALIZATION TO THC METABOLITES AND SP-111.
001666 02-04

DISCRIMINATIVE-STIMULUS EFFECTS OF PROTOTYPE OPIATE-RECEPTOR
AGONISTS IN MONKEYS.
001803 02-04

TOLERANCE TO THE DISCRIMINATIVE-STIMULUS PROPERTIES OF D-
AMPHETAMINE.
002953 03-04

DISCRIMINATIVE-STIMULUS PROPERTIES OF COCAINE, NORCOCAINE, AND
N ALLYLNORCOCAINE.
002954 03-04

DISCRIMINATIVE-STIMULUS PROPERTIES OF PHENCYCLIDINE AND FIVE
ANALOGUES IN THE SQUIRREL-MONKEY.
002961 03-04

INFLUENCE OF MORPHINE ON THE DISCRIMINATIVE-STIMULUS
PROPERTIES OF REWARDING LATERAL HYPOTHALAMIC STIMULATION.
(PH.D. DISSERTATION).
003041 03-04

DISCRIMINATIVE-STIMULUS EFFECTS OF ETORPHINE IN RHESUS-
MONKEYS.
004134 04-04

DISCRIMINATIVE-STIMULUS PROPERTIES OF COCAINE RELATED TO AN
ANXIOGENIC ACTION.
004219 04-04

DISCRIMINATIVE-STIMULUS EFFECTS OF CYCLAZOCINE IN THE RAT.
004236 04-04

DISCRIMINATIVE-STIMULUS PROPERTIES OF THE HALLUCINOGENIC-AGENT
DOM.
004260 04-04

MINI-SYMPOSIUM. IV. DISCRIMINATIVE-STIMULUS EFFECTS OF
NARCOTICS: EVIDENCE FOR MULTIPLE RECEPTOR-MEDIATED ACTIONS.
004719 04-17

DISEASE-INDUCED
DISEASE-INDUCED CHANGES IN THE PLASMA BINDING OF BASIC DRUGS.
000975 01-17

DISFLUENCIES
PRINCIPAL AND DIFFERENTIAL-EFFECTS OF HALOPERIDOL AND PLACEBO
TREATMENTS UPON SPEECH DISFLUENCIES IN STUTTERERS.
000713 01-11

DISINHIBITING-AGENT
PERSPECTIVES ON PRAZINIL (CARPIPRAMINE): A DISINHIBITING-AGENT
WITH NO NEUROLEPTIC ACTIVITY. A REVIEW OF 38 CASES.
003149 03-07

DISINHIBITION
DISINHIBITION OF BEHAVIOR BY ANTIANXIETY-DRUGS.
002403 02-15

AMMONIA AND DISINHIBITION IN CAT MOTOR-CORTEX BY AMMONIUM-
ACETATE, MONOFLUOROACETATE AND INSULIN-INDUCED
HYPOGLYCEMIA.
004276 04-05

DISINHIBITORS
METHODOLOGICAL-CONSIDERATIONS CONCERNING THE PRESCRIPTION
AND USE OF SO CALLED DISINHIBITORS.
002571 02-17

DISINHIBITORY
CARPIPRAMINE: A DISINHIBITORY DRUG COMPOUND IN CHRONIC
SCHIZOPHRENIA.
003192 03-08

DISORDERS
THE USEFULNESS OF THE ERYTHROCYTE LITHIUM INDEX IN THE
EVALUATION OF DISORDERS OF ION-TRANSFER IN PATIENTS WITH
DEPRESSIVE-SYNDROMES.
000625 01-09

BRAIN FUNCTION IN OLD-AGE: EVALUATION OF CHANGES AND
DISORDERS.
000684 01-11

DISORDERS OF SMOOTH-PURSUIT EYE-MOVEMENTS IN SCHIZOPHRENICS
AND THE EFFECT OF NEUROLEPTICS IN THERAPEUTIC DOSES.
001912 02-08

DRUG-INDUCED DISORDERS OF THE URINARY TRACT.
002393 02-15

DRUG-INDUCED DISORDERS OF THE EYE.
002396 02-15

DRUG-INDUCED DISORDERS OF THE LIVER.
002397 02-15

DRUG-INDUCED DISORDERS OF MUSCLE.
002435 02-15

THE BIOLOGICAL-EFFECTS AND CLINICAL-EFFECTS OF ORAL MAGNESIUM
AND ASSOCIATED MAGNESIUM VITAMIN-B6 ADMINISTRATION ON
CERTAIN DISORDERS OBSERVED IN INFANTILE AUTISM.
003291 03-11

DISORIENTATION
AGITATION, DISORIENTATION, AND HALLUCINATIONS IN PATIENTS ON
CIMETIDINE: A REPORT OF THREE CASES AND LITERATURE REVIEW.
000896 01-15

DISPENSER
A DRUG DISPENSER TO MEASURE INDIVIDUAL DRINKING IN RAT
COLONIES.
000530 01-06

DISPOSITION
DISPOSITION OF VALPROIC-ACID IN THE RAT: DOSE-DEPENDENT
METABOLISM, DISTRIBUTION, ENTEROHEPATIC RECIRCULATION AND
CHOLERETIC-EFFECT.
000073 01-03

EFFECTS OF UREA ON HEXOBARBITAL AND ANTIPYRINE DISPOSITION IN
RATS.
000307 01-03

DIFFERENTIAL-EFFECTS ON BENZODIAZEPINE DISPOSITION BY DISULFIRAM
AND ETHANOL.
000789 01-13

CHLORDIAZEPOXIDE AND OXAZEPAM DISPOSITION IN CIRRHOSIS.
000790 01-13

THE COMPARATIVE DISPOSITION OF NOMIFENSINE (MERITAL) IN THE
PREGNANT AND NONPREGNANT RAT.
000853 01-15

DISPOSITION OF (3H) PHENCYCLIDINE IN THE RAT AFTER SINGLE-DOSES
AND MULTIPLE-DOSES.
001375 02-03

EFFECTS OF ANTICONVULSANTS AND METHOTREXATE ON CALCIUM
DISPOSITION.
001840 02-05

DISPOSITION AND ACTIVITY OF BETA-ADRENOCEPTOR ANTAGONISTS IN
THE RAT USING AN EX VIVO RECEPTOR BINDING ASSAY.
001878 02-06

INFLUENCE OF PHENYTOIN AND PHENOBARBITAL ON THE DISPOSITION OF A SINGLE-ORAL-DOSE OF CLONAZEPAM.
002248 02-13

DISPOSITION AND PHARMACOLOGICAL-EFFECTS OF M CHLOROPHENYLPIPERAZINE IN RATS.
002995 03-04

DISPOSITION OF METHADONE IN THE OVINE MATERNAL FETAL UNIT.
004027 04-03

DISRUPTION
DISRUPTION OF SELECTIVE ATTENTION BY APOMORPHINE, BUT NOT AMPHETAMINE, IN THE MONGOLIAN-GERBIL.
000358 01-04

DISRUPTION OF 5 HYDROXYTRYPTAMINERGIC NEURONAL FUNCTION BLOCKS THE ACTION OF MORPHINE ON TUBEROINFUNDIBULAR DOPAMINERGIC NEURONS.
002700 03-03

DISRUPTION OF AUTOSHAPED RESPONDING TO A SIGNAL OF BRAIN-STIMULATION REWARD BY NEUROLEPTIC-DRUGS.
004199 04-04

DISRUPTIVE
NALOXONE POTENTIATES THE DISRUPTIVE EFFECTS OF MESCALINE ON OPERANT-RESPONDING IN THE RAT.
000365 01-04

DISSIMILAR
DISSIMILAR EFFECTS OF NICOTINAMIDE AND INOSINE, PUTATIVE ENDOGENOUS LIGANDS OF THE BENZODIAZEPINE-RECEPTORS, ON PENTYLENETETRAZOL SEIZURES IN FOUR STRAINS OF MICE.
000173 01-03

DISSIMILARITIES
SIMILARITIES AND DISSIMILARITIES BETWEEN DOPAMINE AND NEUROLEPTIC-RECEPTORS: FURTHER EVIDENCE FOR TYPE-1 AND TYPE-2 DOPAMINE-RECEPTORS IN THE CNS.
001480 02-03

DISSOCIATION
DISSOCIATION OF THE STRYCHNINE EFFECT ON VISUAL-MEMORY AND VERBAL-MEMORY IN ORGANIC-PSYCHOSYNDROMES.
000816 01-14

BETA ENDORPHIN: DISSOCIATION OF RECEPTOR BINDING-ACTIVITY FROM ANALGESIC POTENCY.
001081 02-02

DISSOCIATION OF D-AMPHETAMINE-INDUCED LOCOMOTOR-ACTIVITY AND STEREOTYPED-BEHAVIOUR BY LESIONS OF THE SUPERIOR-COLLICULUS.
001755 02-04

DISSOCIATION OF THE STRYCHNINE EFFECT ON VISUAL-MEMORY AND VERBAL-MEMORY IN ORGANIC-PSYCHOSYNDROMES.
002155 02-11

CLONIDINE ANALGESIA AND SUPPRESSION OF OPERANT RESPONDING: DISSOCIATION OF MECHANISM.
003046 03-04

DISSOCIATION BETWEEN FREE AND BOUND PHENYTOIN LEVELS IN PRESENCE OF SODIUM-VALPROATE.
003367 03-11

MULTIPLE BENZODIAZEPINE-RECEPTORS: EVIDENCE OF A DISSOCIATION BETWEEN ANTICONFLICT AND ANTICONVULSANT PROPERTIES BY PK-8165 AND PK-9084 (TWO QUINOLINE DERIVATIVES).
003898 04-03

DISSOCIATIVE-EFFECTS
REWARD AND DETECTION THRESHOLDS FOR BRAIN-STIMULATION: DISSOCIATIVE-EFFECTS OF COCAINE.
004160 04-04

DISSOCIATIVE-SYNDROMES
THE USE OF A MORPHINE ANTAGONIST (NALOXONE) IN THE TREATMENT OF DISSOCIATIVE-SYNDROMES.
003194 03-08

DISTRESS
ASCENDING ENDORPHIN INHIBITION OF DISTRESS VOCALIZATION.
003011 03-04

DISTRIBUTION
(3H) 2 AMINODIHYDROXYTETRAHYDRONAPHTHALENE (ADTN): REGIONAL DISTRIBUTION AND IN VIVO BINDING AFTER ACUTE AND CHRONIC DRUG-TREATMENT.
000052 01-03

EFFECTS OF PSYCHOTROPIC-DRUGS ON THE DISTRIBUTION OF 3H DOPAMINE INTO COMPARTMENTS OF RAT STRIATAL SYNAPTOSOMES AND ON SUBSEQUENT DEPOLARIZATION-INDUCED 3H DOPAMINE RELEASE.
000067 01-03

THE EFFECT OF DIAZEPAM ON TENSION AND ELECTROLYTE DISTRIBUTION IN FROG MUSCLE.
000069 01-03

DISPOSITION OF VALPROIC-ACID IN THE RAT: DOSE-DEPENDENT METABOLISM, DISTRIBUTION, ENTEROHEPATIC RECIRCULATION AND CHOLERETIC-EFFECT.
000073 01-03

STUDIES ON THE DISTRIBUTION OF 14C SULPIRIDE AND ITS METABOLITES IN THE RAT AND GUINEA-PIG.
000078 01-03

DISTRIBUTION AND EXCRETION IN THE RAT AND MONKEY OF (82BR) BROMOCRIPTINE.
000196 01-03

REGIONAL DISTRIBUTION AND BIOCHEMICAL-PROPERTIES OF 125I TYRB-SUBSTANCE-P BINDING-SITES IN SYNAPTIC VESICLES.
000259 01-03

DISTRIBUTION OF 14C PHENYTOIN IN RAT PURKINJE-CELLS, CEREBELLAR AND CEREBRAL NEURONAL TISSUE AFTER A SINGLE INTRAPERITONEAL INJECTION.
000261 01-03

PREDICTION OF THE VOLUME OF DISTRIBUTION FROM IN VITRO DATA AND USE FOR ESTIMATING THE ABSOLUTE EXTENT OF ABSORPTION.
000907 01-16

ON THE MECHANISM OF A DIFFERENT DRUG DISTRIBUTION DURING CONVULSIVE-SEIZURE IN COMPARISON TO ANESTHESIA.
001151 02-03

EFFECTS OF PIMOZIDE ON ACCURACY OF PERFORMANCE AND DISTRIBUTION OF CORRECT RESPONDING ON A SIMULTANEOUS DISCRIMINATION TASK IN THE RAT.
001806 02-04

NA-DEPENDENT LI COUNTERTRANSPORT AND THE LITHIUM DISTRIBUTION ACROSS THE HUMAN ERYTHROCYTE MEMBRANE: INTRODUCTION.
002227 02-13

COMPARATIVE-STUDIES ON THE METABOLISM AND THE DISTRIBUTION OF SULPIRIDE AND SULTOPRIDE.
002240 02-13

QUANTITATIVE STUDY OF THE DISTRIBUTION OF LITHIUM IN THE MOUSE-BRAIN FOR VARIOUS DOSES OF LITHIUM GIVEN TO THE ANIMAL.
002299 02-13

THE DISTRIBUTION OF CHLORPROMAZINE BETWEEN PLASMA AND ERYTHROCYTES.
002496 02-16

DISTRIBUTION OF MEMBRANE GLYCOPROTEINS AMONG THE ORGANELLES OF A SINGLE IDENTIFIED NEURON OF APLYSIA. II. ISOLATION AND CHARACTERIZATION OF A GLYCOPROTEIN ASSOCIATED WITH VESICLES.
002657 03-03

BETA-ADRENERGIC-RECEPTOR SUBTYPES: PROPERTIES, DISTRIBUTION, AND REGULATION.
002829 03-03

LAMINAR DISTRIBUTION OF PUTATIVE NEUROTRANSMITTER AMINO-ACIDS AND LIGAND BINDING-SITES IN THE DOG OLFACTORY-BULB.
002836 03-03

DOPAMINERGIC AGONIST AND ANTAGONIST EFFECTS ON STRIATAL TYROSINE-HYDROXYLASE DISTRIBUTION.
002898 03-03

DISTRIBUTION OF CESIUM IN THE ORGANISM AND ITS EFFECT ON THE NUCLEOTIDE METABOLISM ENZYMES.
003696 04-02

AUTORADIOGRAPHIC STUDIES ON DISTRIBUTION OF L-3,4 DIHYDROXYPHENYLALANINE (L-DOPA) 14C AND L 5 HYDROXYTRYPTOPHAN (L 5 HTP) 14C IN THE CAT BRAIN.
003941 04-03

REGIONAL DISTRIBUTION OF (3H)IMIPRAMINE BINDING IN RAT-BRAIN.
003955 04-03

THE EFFECT OF P CHLOROPHENYLALANINE ON THE DISTRIBUTION OF BIOGENIC-AMINES IN THE BRAIN, AND ON MEMORY IN RATS.
004068 04-04

EFFECT OF DESMETHYLIMIPRAMINE ON TISSUE DISTRIBUTION AND ANORECTIC-ACTIVITY OF CHLORPHENTERMINE IN RATS.
004179 04-04

DISTRIBUTIONS
SEROTONIN-SENSITIVE ADENYLATE-CYCLASE AND (3H)SEROTONIN BINDING-SITES IN THE CNS OF THE RAT -- II. RESPECTIVE REGIONAL AND SUBCELLULAR DISTRIBUTIONS AND ONTOGENETIC DEVELOPMENTS.
000214 01-03

EXTRAHYPOTHALAMIC DISTRIBUTIONS AND FUNCTIONS OF HYPOTHALAMIC PEPTIDE-HORMONES. (UNPUBLISHED PAPER).
001211 02-03

DISTRICTS
COMPARISON OF DRUG PRESCRIPTIONS FOR PSYCHIATRIC-PATIENTS AFTER HOSPITAL DISCHARGE IN THE DISTRICTS TEPLICE AND UHERSKE-HRADISTE.
002518 02-17

DISTURBANCE
NEUROENDOCRINE DISTURBANCE IN DEPRESSION.
004405 04-09

DISTURBANCES
BIOLOGICAL-RHYTHM DISTURBANCES IN AFFECTIVE-ILLNESS.
002628 02-17

DISTURBED
AMPHETAMINIL IN THE TREATMENT OF DISTURBED ERECTION POTENCY.
002129 02-11

DOES P CHLOROPHENYLALANINE PRODUCE DISTURBED WAKING, DISTURBED SLEEP OR ACTIVATION BY PONTO-GENICULO-OCCIPITAL WAVES IN CATS?
003704 04-02

DISTURBED-BEHAVIOUR
DISTURBED-BEHAVIOUR INDUCED BY HIGH-DOSE ANTIPSYCHOTIC-DRUGS.
002375 02-15

Subject Index

DISULFIDE
SYNTHESIS AND BIOLOGICAL-ACTIVITY OF HUMAN BETA ENDORPHIN ANALOGS WITH DISULFIDE BRIDGES.
003655 04-01
COMT-A AND COMT-B: CATALYTIC DIFFERENCES AND ROLE OF DISULFIDE BONDS.
003927 04-03

DISULFIRAM
INHIBITION OF ALCOHOL-DEHYDROGENASE BY DISULFIRAM; POSSIBLE RELATION TO THE DISULFIRAM ETHANOL REACTION.
000270 01-03
DIFFERENTIAL-EFFECTS ON BENZODIAZEPINE DISPOSITION BY DISULFIRAM AND ETHANOL.
000789 01-13
METHADONE DISULFIRAM INTERACTION DURING METHADONE MAINTENANCE.
000796 01-13
DISULFIRAM ENCEPHALOPATHY AS A CAUSE OF THE CATATONIA-SYNDROME.
000894 01-15
EXPERIMENTAL-STUDIES ON HEPATOTOXICITY OF DISULFIRAM.
001844 02-05
A COMPARATIVE REVIEW OF THE PHARMACOLOGICAL AND TOXICOLOGICAL PROPERTIES OF DISULFIRAM AND CALCIUM-CARBIMIDE.
003522 03-15
DISULFIRAM AND NOCTURNAL PENILE-TUMESCENCE IN THE CHRONIC ALCOHOLIC.
004556 04-13

DITHIADEN
CLONAZEPAM AND DITHIADEN IN HYPERKINETIC-CHILDREN.
000729 01-11

DIURETICS
DIURETICS ARE DANGEROUS WITH LITHIUM.
002420 02-15
A MODIFIED VERSION OF THE SIMULTANEOUS DISCONTINUATION OF PSYCHOTROPIC-DRUGS (COMBINED WITH THE ADMINISTRATION OF DIURETICS) AS A METHOD OF HALTING PROLONGED ATTACKS OF SCHIZOPHRENIA.
004584 04-14

DIURNAL
DIURNAL GROWTH-HORMONE RESPONSES TO DEXTROAMPHETAMINE IN NORMAL YOUNG MEN AND POSTMENOPAUSAL-WOMEN.
003411 03-13
EFFECT OF LITHIUM ON REACTION-TIME — A STUDY OF DIURNAL VARIATIONS.
004607 04-15

DIVALENT-CATION
ALPHA2-ADRENOCEPTORS IN RAT-BRAIN: THE DIVALENT-CATION SITE.
001246 02-03

DIVALENT-CATIONS
MULTIPLE ALPHA2-NORADRENERGIC-RECEPTOR SITES IN RAT-BRAIN: SELECTIVE REGULATION OF HIGH-AFFINITY (3H)CLONIDINE BINDING BY GUANINE-NUCLEOTIDES AND DIVALENT-CATIONS.
003992 04-03

DIVERGENCES
CONVERGENCES AND DIVERGENCES BETWEEN BIOLOGICAL-PSYCHIATRY AND PSYCHOTHERAPY.
002536 02-17

DIVERGENT
DIVERGENT RESERPINE EFFECTS ON AMFONELIC-ACID AND AMPHETAMINE STIMULATION OF SYNAPTOSOMAL DOPAMINE FORMATION FROM PHENYLALANINE.
001113 02-03

DIVIDED
SINTAMIL IN THE TREATMENT OF DEPRESSION: A COMPARISON OF SINGLE VS. DIVIDED DOSE ADMINISTRATION.
000629 01-09
THERAPEUTIC-EFFICACY OF DOXEPIN IN DIVIDED AND SINGLE-DOSE REGIME.
003259 03-09

DMI
PLASMA LEVELS OF IMIPRAMINE (IMI) AND DESMETHYLIMIPRAMINE (DMI) AND CLINICAL-RESPONSE IN PREPUBERTAL MAJOR DEPRESSIVE-DISORDER: A PRELIMINARY REPORT.
000619 01-09
INFERENTIAL CHANGES AFTER CHRONIC-TREATMENTS WITH LI, DMI, OR ETHANOL DETECTED BY ELECTROPHYSIOLOGICAL-CORRELATES.
001136 02-03
AN INVERSE CORRELATION BETWEEN SERUM LEVELS OF DESMETHYLIMIPRAMINE AND MELATONIN-LIKE IMMUNOREACTIVITY IN DMI RESPONSIVE DEPRESSIVES.
003228 03-09
EFFECTS OF SUBCHRONIC DESMETHYLIMIPRAMINE (DMI) TREATMENT OF THE CLASSICALLY CONDITIONED EYEBLINK RESPONSE IN RABBITS.
004180 04-04
SUBCHRONIC-TREATMENT WITH THE TRICYCLIC-ANTIDEPRESSANT DMI INCREASES ISOLATION-INDUCED FIGHTING IN RATS.
004252 04-04

ANTIARRHYTHMIC-ACTIVITY OF AMITRIPTYLINE ANALOGUES IN
CONSCIOUS DOGS AFTER MYOCARDIAL-INFARCTION:
CYPROHEPTADINIUM-METHIODIDE.
001534 02-03

INFLUENCE OF IMIPRAMINE AND PARGYLINE ON THE
ARRHYTHMOGENICITY OF EPINEPHRINE DURING HALOTHANE,
ENFLURANE OR METHOXYFLURANE ANESTHESIA IN DOGS.
001539 02-03

ELECTROMYOGRAPHIC-ASSESSMENT OF SPINAL REFLEXES IN
EXPERIMENTALLY DEPRESSED DOGS TREATED WITH
ANTIDEPRESSANTS.
001620 02-04

GENETIC AND EXPERIMENTAL FACTORS AFFECTING THE PARADOXICAL-
EFFECTS OF AMPHETAMINE IN DOGS.
001704 02-04

INTRAVENOUS SELF-ADMINISTRATION OF COCAINE AND NORCOCAINE BY
DOGS.
001760 02-04

THE EFFECTS OF IMIPRAMINE TREATMENT ON THE UNCONDITIONED
ALIMENTARY BEHAVIOR AND CLASSICAL CONDITIONED SALIVARY
REACTIONS IN DOGS.
003030 03-04

CENTRAL HYPOTENSIVE-EFFECT OF GAMMA AMINOBUTYRIC-ACID IN
ANESTHETIZED DOGS.
003772 04-03

BETA-ADRENERGIC INFLUENCE ON CARDIAC DYNAMICS DURING SHOCK-
AVOIDANCE IN DOGS.
003813 04-03

EFFECT OF MORPHINE AND NALOXONE ON LEU-ENKEPHALIN-LIKE
IMMUNOREACTIVITY IN DOGS.
003894 04-03

DOSAGE FORM DESIGN FOR IMPROVEMENT OF BIOAVAILABILITY OF
LEVODOPA III: INFLUENCE OF DOSE ON PHARMACOKINETIC BEHAVIOR
OF LEVODOPA IN DOGS AND PARKINSONIAN-PATIENTS.
004551 04-13

DOM
ENHANCEMENT OF THE BEHAVIORAL-EFFECTS OF 2,5 DIMETHOXY-4-
METHYLAMPHETAMINE (DOM) BY PRETREATMENT WITH P
CHLOROPHENYLALANINE.
000364 01-04

THE EFFECTS OF D LYSERGIC-ACID-DIETHYLAMIDE (LSD), 2,5
DIMETHOXY-4-METHYLAMPHETAMINE (DOM) AND D-AMPHETAMINE
ON OPERANT-RESPONDING IN CONTROL AND 6 HYDROXYDOPAMINE
TREATED RATS.
001595 02-04

DOM AND RELATED 2,5 DIMETHOXY-4-ALKYLPHENYLISOPROPYLAMINES:
BEHAVIORAL AND SEROTONIN-RECEPTOR PROPERTIES.
003690 04-02

THE EFFECTS OF 2,5 DIMETHOXY-4-METHYLAMPHETAMINE (DOM) ON
OPERANT-BEHAVIOR: INTERACTIONS WITH OTHER NEUROACTIVE-
AGENTS.
004089 04-04

DISCRIMINATIVE-STIMULUS PROPERTIES OF THE HALLUCINOGENIC-AGENT
DOM.
004260 04-04

DOMESTIC
TONIC IMMOBILITY IN DOMESTIC FOWL: POSSIBLE INTERACTION OF
SEROTONERGIC AND DOPAMINERGIC MECHANISMS.
004246 04-04

DOMESTIC-FOWL
THE BEHAVIOURAL-STATE DURING CLIMAX (HATCHING) IN THE
DOMESTIC-FOWL (GALLUS-DOMESTICUS).
001564 02-04

DOMPERIDONE
THREE CLASSES OF DOPAMINE-RECEPTOR (D-2, D-3, D-4) IDENTIFIED BY
BINDING STUDIES WITH 3H APOMORPHINE AND 3H DOMPERIDONE.
002900 03-03

CHLORPROMAZINE, HALOPERIDOL, METOCLOPRAMIDE AND
DOMPERIDONE RELEASE PROLACTIN THROUGH DOPAMINE
ANTAGONISM AT LOW CONCENTRATIONS BUT PARADOXICALLY
INHIBIT PROLACTIN RELEASE AT HIGH-CONCENTRATIONS.
003731 04-03

THE DOPAMINE-RECEPTOR ANTAGONIST DOMPERIDONE IS ALSO A
COMPETITIVE ANTAGONIST AT ALPHA1-ADRENOCEPTORS.
003785 04-03

DOPA
DOPA AND DOPAMINE AGONISTS IN DEPRESSION.
002310 02-13

OPPOSITE EFFECTS OF NALOXONE ON SUBSTANCE-P-INDUCED IN BRAIN
DOPA SYNTHESIS AND IN LOCOMOTOR-ACTIVITY IN RATS.
003799 04-03

DOPA-DECARBOXYLASE
COMPARATIVE-STUDIES OF L-DOPA ALONE AND COMBINATION WITH A
PERIPHERAL DOPA-DECARBOXYLASE INHIBITOR, BENSERAZIDE-HCL, ON
PARKINSONS-DISEASE -- PART II: PHARMACOKINETIC-STUDY.
002309 02-13

THE INTERACTION OF 2,3,4 TRIHYDROXYBENZYLHYDRAZINE WITH
DOPA-DECARBOXYLASE FROM PIG KIDNEY.
002925 03-03

DOPAC
STRIATAL DOPAC LEVELS AS A PREDICTOR OF ANTIPSYCHOTIC-EFFICACY.
001533 02-03

DOPAMINE, NORADRENALINE AND 3,4 DIHYDROXYPHENYLACETIC-ACID
(DOPAC) LEVELS OF INDIVIDUAL BRAIN NUCLEI, EFFECTS OF
HALOPERIDOL AND PARGYLINE.
003792 04-03

DOPAMINE
ARYLDIALKENYLPIPERAZINES AS SELECTIVE AND VERY POTENT
INHIBITORS OF DOPAMINE UPTAKE.
000005 01-01

ANTIHISTAMINE EFFECT ON SYNAPTOSOMAL UPTAKE OF SEROTONIN,
NOREPINEPHRINE AND DOPAMINE.
000035 01-03

DOPAMINE, ACETYLCHOLINE, AND GABA EFFECTS IN ACUTE DYSTONIA IN
PRIMATES.
000043 01-03

REPEATED TRICYCLIC-ANTIDEPRESSANTS INDUCE A PROGRESSIVE SWITCH
IN THE ELECTROPHYSIOLOGICAL RESPONSE OF DOPAMINE NEURONS TO
AUTORECEPTOR STIMULATION.
000046 01-03

THE INFLUENCE OF BENZOCTAMINE ON DOPAMINE AND NOREPINEPHRINE
CONTENTS OF THE SUBSTANTIA-NIGRA AND ON THE MUSCLE STRETCH
REFLEX OF THE CAT.
000054 01-03

EFFECTS OF PSYCHOTROPIC-DRUGS ON THE DISTRIBUTION OF 3H
DOPAMINE INTO COMPARTMENTS OF RAT STRIATAL SYNAPTOSOMES
AND ON SUBSEQUENT DEPOLARIZATION-INDUCED 3H DOPAMINE
RELEASE.
000067 01-03

COMPARISON OF THE EFFECTS OF THE ISOMERS OF AMPHETAMINE,
METHYLPHENIDATE AND DEOXYPIPRADROL ON THE UPTAKE OF L
(3H)NOREPINEPHRINE AND (3H)DOPAMINE BY SYNAPTIC VESICLES
FROM RAT-WHOLE-BRAIN, STRIATUM AND HYPOTHALAMUS.
000091 01-03

THE EFFECTS OF TWO ANALOGS OF DOPAMINE ON GANGLIONIC
TRANSMISSION IN THE SYMPATHETIC-NERVOUS-SYSTEM.
000162 01-03

THE MONOAMINE-OXIDASE-INHIBITORS CLORGYLINE AND L DEPRENYL
ALSO AFFECT THE UPTAKE OF DOPAMINE, NORADRENALINE AND
SEROTONIN BY RAT-BRAIN SYNAPTOSOMAL PREPARATIONS.
000171 01-03

EFFECTS OF PERINATAL THYROXINE AND/OR CORTICOSTERONE
TREATMENT ON THE ONTOGENESIS OF HYPOTHALAMIC AND
MESENCEPHALIC NOREPINEPHRINE AND DOPAMINE CONTENT.
000180 01-03

ROLE OF DOPAMINE STORAGE FUNCTION IN THE CONTROL OF RAT
STRIATAL TYROSINE-HYDROXYLASE ACTIVITY.
000201 01-03

ACUTE AND CHRONIC EFFECTS OF NEUROLEPTICS AND ACUTE EFFECTS OF
APOMORPHINE AND AMPHETAMINE ON DOPAMINE TURNOVER IN
CORPUS-STRIATUM AND SUBSTANTIA-NIGRA OF THE RAT-BRAIN.
000215 01-03

EFFECTS OF DES-TYR-GAMMA-ENDORPHIN ON DOPAMINE RELEASE FROM
VARIOUS RAT-BRAIN REGIONS IN VITRO.
000264 01-03

LONG-TERM EFFECTS OF CONTINUOUS EXPOSURE TO AMPHETAMINE ON
BRAIN DOPAMINE CONCENTRATION AND SYNAPTOSOMAL UPTAKE IN
MICE.
000287 01-03

THE EFFECT OF A NEW FLUORINATED TRICYCLIC NEUROLEPTIC-DRUG
ISOFLOXYTHEPIN ON THE RAT STRIATAL DOPAMINE METABOLISM.
000306 01-03

ANALYSIS OF THE ACTIVATION OF DOPAMINE METABOLISM BY A
SEROTONIN UPTAKE INHIBITOR.
000315 01-03

SELECTIVE STORAGE IN VIVO OF 5,6 ADTN IN DOPAMINE RICH AREAS OF
THE RAT-BRAIN.
000324 01-03

MESOLIMBICOCORTICAL DOPAMINE TERMINAL-FIELDS ARE NECESSARY
FOR NORMAL LOCOMOTOR AND INVESTIGATORY EXPLORATION IN
RATS.
000383 01-04

RELATIONSHIPS BETWEEN SELECTIVE DENERVATION OF DOPAMINE
TERMINAL-FIELDS IN THE ANTERIOR-FOREBRAIN AND BEHAVIORAL-
RESPONSES TO AMPHETAMINE AND APOMORPHINE.
000404 01-04

ROTATIONAL-BEHAVIOR INDUCED BY COCAINE ANALOGS IN RATS WITH
UNILATERAL 6 HYDROXYDOPAMINE LESIONS OF THE SUBSTANTIA-
NIGRA: DEPENDENCE UPON DOPAMINE UPTAKE INHIBITION.
000448 01-04

INTRAVENTRICULAR 6 HYDROXYDOPAMINE IN THE NEWBORN RAT AND
LOCOMOTOR RESPONSES TO DRUGS IN INFANCY: NO SUPPORT FOR
THE DOPAMINE DEPLETION MODEL OF MINIMAL-BRAIN-DYSFUNCTION.
000448 01-04

SEX-DIFFERENCES IN AMPHETAMINE-ELICITED ROTATIONAL-BEHAVIOR
AND THE LATERALIZATION OF STRIATAL DOPAMINE IN RATS.
000459 01-04

PSYCHIATRIC MANIFESTATIONS INDUCED BY DOPAMINE PRECURSORS OR DOPAMINE AGONISTS.
000865 01-15

TETRAHYDRO-BETA-CARBOLINES AND CORRESPONDING TRYPTAMINES: IN VITRO INHIBITION OF SEROTONIN AND DOPAMINE UPTAKE BY HUMAN BLOOD-PLATELETS.
001067 02-02

TETRAHYDRO-BETA-CARBOLINES AND CORRESPONDING TRYPTAMINES: IN VITRO INHIBITION OF SEROTONIN, DOPAMINE AND NORADRENALINE UPTAKE IN RAT-BRAIN SYNAPTOSOMES.
001078 02-02

EFFECTS OF CHRONIC-TREATMENT WITH L SULPIRIDE AND HALOPERIDOL ON CENTRAL DOPAMINE TURNOVER EVALUATED IN DOPAMINE CELL BODY AND NERVE TERMINAL-RICH AREAS.
001096 02-03

INCREASED METABOLISM OF DOPAMINE AND SEROTONIN INDUCED IN FOREBRAIN AREAS BY ETORPHINE MICROINJECTION IN PERIAQUEDUCTAL GRAY.
001103 02-03

BIPHASIC RESPONSIVENESS OF RAT PIAL-ARTERIOLES TO DOPAMINE: DIRECT OBSERVATIONS ON THE MICROCIRCULATION.
001105 02-03

DIVERGENT RESERPINE EFFECTS ON AMFONELIC-ACID AND AMPHETAMINE STIMULATION OF SYNAPTOSOMAL DOPAMINE FORMATION FROM PHENYLALANINE.
001113 02-03

CHLOROETHYLNORAPOMORPHINE, A PROPOSED LONG-ACTING DOPAMINE ANTAGONIST: INTERACTIONS WITH DOPAMINE-RECEPTORS OF MAMMALIAN FOREBRAIN IN VITRO.
001114 02-03

DOPAMINE SYNTHESIS: TOLERANCE TO HALOPERIDOL AND SUPERSENSITIVITY TO APOMORPHINE DEPEND ON PRESYNAPTIC-RECEPTORS.
001129 02-03

DOPAMINE HYPOACTIVITY MEASURED BY IN VIVO VOLTAMMETRY.
001149 02-03

HA-966 EFFECTS ON STRIATAL DOPAMINE METABOLISM: IMPLICATIONS FOR DOPAMINE COMPARTMENTALIZAION.
001150 02-03

ADAPTIVE CHANGES OF THE STRIATAL DOPAMINE SYSTEM INDUCED BY REPEATED ADMINISTRATION OF NEUROLEPTICS AND ERGOT DERIVATIVES.
001156 02-03

DOPAMINE BIOSYNTHESIS IS REGULATED BY THE AMINE NEWLY RECAPTURED BY DOPAMINERGIC NERVE-ENDINGS.
001163 02-03

ALTERATIONS IN BASAL FIRING-RATE AND AUTORECEPTOR SENSITIVITY OF DOPAMINE NEURONS IN THE SUBSTANTIA-NIGRA FOLLOWING ACUTE AND EXTENDED EXPOSURE TO ESTROGEN.
001167 02-03

DOPAMINERGIC-SUPERSENSITIVITY: INFLUENCE OF DOPAMINE AGONISTS AND DRUGS USED FOR THE TREATMENT OF TARDIVE-DYSKINESIA.
001169 02-03

A COMPARISON OF STRIATAL AND MESOLIMBIC DOPAMINE FUNCTION IN THE RAT DURING 6-MONTH TRIFLUOPERAZINE ADMINISTRATION.
001174 02-03

CHANGES IN CEREBRAL DOPAMINE FUNCTION INDUCED BY A YEARS ADMINISTRATION OF TRIFLUOPERAZINE OR THIORIDAZINE AND THEIR SUBSEQUENT WITHDRAWAL.
001175 02-03

A COMPARISON OF THE EFFECTS OF METHYLPHENIDATE AND AMPHETAMINE ON THE SIMULTANEOUS RELEASE OF RADIOLABELLED DOPAMINE AND P OR M TYRAMINE FROM RAT STRIATAL SLICES.
001207 02-03

EFFECT OF MOXESTROL ON HALOPERIDOL-INDUCED CHANGES IN STRIATAL ACETYLCHOLINE LEVELS AND DOPAMINE TURNOVER.
001218 02-03

CHOLECYSTOKININ-PEPTIDES PRODUCE MARKED REDUCTION OF DOPAMINE TURNOVER IN DISCRETE AREAS IN THE RAT-BRAIN FOLLOWING INTERAVENTRICULAR INJECTION.
001239 02-03

THE AFFINITIES OF ERGOT COMPOUNDS FOR DOPAMINE AGONIST AND DOPAMINE ANTAGONIST RECEPTOR SITES.
001254 02-03

ANTAGONISM OF THE RENAL VASODILATOR ACTIVITY OF DOPAMINE BY METOCLOPRAMIDE.
001265 02-03

FURTHER EVIDENCE FOR THE EXISTENCE OF MULTIPLE RECEPTORS FOR DOPAMINE IN THE CENTRAL-NERVOUS-SYSTEM.
001296 02-03

INTERNEURONES ARE PROBABLY NOT INVOLVED IN THE PRESYNAPTIC DOPAMINERGIC CONTROL OF DOPAMINE RELEASE IN RABBIT CAUDATE-NUCLEUS.
001298 02-03

THE HYPERKINETIC-SYNDROME FOLLOWING LONG-TERM HALOPERIDOL TREATMENT: INVOLVEMENT OF DOPAMINE AND NORADRENALINE.
001299 02-03

STEREOSELECTIVE ACTIONS OF SUBSTITUTED BENZAMIDE DRUGS ON CEREBRAL DOPAMINE MECHANISMS.
001301 02-03

ENDOGENOUS GUANYL-NUCLEOTIDES: COMPONENTS OF THE STRIATUM WHICH CONFER DOPAMINE SENSITIVITY TO ADENYLATE-CYCLASE.
001313 02-03

DRUG-INDUCED RELEASE OF DOPAMINE FROM CORPUS-STRIATUM. (PH.D. DISSERTATION).
001343 02-03

THE EFFECT OF CARBIDINE ON DOPAMINE TURNOVER IN THE CORPUS-STRIATUM OF THE BRAINS OF RATS.
001352 02-03

DOPAMINE-SENSITIVE ADENYLATE-CYCLASE AND DOPAMINE/ NEUROLEPTIC-RECEPTOR BINDING: EFFECT OF NEUROLEPTIC-DRUGS.
001358 02-03

EVIDENCE FOR INVOLVEMENT OF DOPAMINE IN THE ACTION OF DIAZEPAM: POTENTIATION OF HALOPERIDOL AND CHLORPROMAZINE ACTION IN THE BRAIN.
001428 02-03

EFFECT OF REPEATED TREATMENT WITH NEUROLEPTICS ON DOPAMINE METABOLISM IN CELL BODIES AND TERMINALS OF DOPAMINERGIC-SYSTEMS IN THE RAT-BRAIN.
001464 02-03

EFFECT OF MELANOSTATIN AND THYROLIBERIN ON THE BIOSYNTHESIS AND RELEASE OF DOPAMINE BY RAT-BRAIN STRIATAL P2-FRACTIONS.
001472 02-03

SIMILARITIES AND DISSIMILARITIES BETWEEN DOPAMINE AND NEUROLEPTIC-RECEPTORS: FURTHER EVIDENCE FOR TYPE-1 AND TYPE-2 DOPAMINE-RECEPTORS IN THE CNS.
001480 02-03

DETECTION OF MULTIPLE RECEPTORS FOR DOPAMINE.
001481 02-03

LONG-TERM APPLICATION OF HALOPERIDOL: EFFECT OF ANTICHOLINERGIC TREATMENT ON THE RATE OF DOPAMINE SYNTHESIS.
001490 02-03

EVIDENCE THAT NORADRENALINE MODULATES THE INCREASE IN STRIATAL DOPAMINE METABOLISM INDUCED BY MUSCARINIC-RECEPTOR STIMULATION.
001518 02-03

EVALUATION OF THE EFFECT OF DRUGS ON DOPAMINE METABOLISM IN THE RAT SUPERIOR-CERVICAL-GANGLION BY HPLC WITH ELECTROCHEMICAL-DETECTION.
001530 02-03

MOTOR-ACTIVITY AND ROTATIONAL-BEHAVIOR AFTER ANALOGS OF COCAINE: CORRELATION WITH DOPAMINE UPTAKE BLOCKADE.
001650 02-04

PHENCYCLIDINE AS AN INDIRECT DOPAMINE AGONIST.
001719 02-04

EFFECT OF APOMORPHINE ON MORPHINE-INDUCED LOCOMOTOR-ACTIVITY AND INCREASE IN DOPAMINE TURNOVER IN RATS.
001728 02-04

STEREOTYPED-BEHAVIOUR AND ELECTROCORTICAL-CHANGES AFTER INTRACEREBRAL MICROINFUSION OF DOPAMINE AND APOMORPHINE IN FOWLS.
001734 02-04

THE ROLE OF DOPAMINE IN THE HYPERMOTILITY INDUCED BY H-77-77 (4,ALPHA DIMETHYL-M-TYRAMINE) IN MICE.
001762 02-04

CIRCLING PRODUCED BY SEROTONIN AND DOPAMINE AGONISTS IN RAPHE LESIONED RATS: A SEROTONIN MODEL.
001783 02-04

ON THE USE OF OPERANT-BEHAVIOR TO STUDY THE NEUROPSYCHOPHARMACOLOGY OF OPIATES WITH SPECIAL REFERENCE TO MORPHINE AND ITS RELATIONSHIP TO DOPAMINE IN THE CENTRAL-NERVOUS-SYSTEM.
001790 02-04

BEHAVIORAL-EFFECTS OF DOPAMINE AGONISTS ACROSS THE ESTROUS-CYCLE IN RATS.
001792 02-04

EFFECT OF NICKEL ON THE LEVELS OF DOPAMINE, NORADRENALINE AND SEROTONIN IN DIFFERENT REGIONS OF THE RAT-BRAIN.
001831 02-05

CEREBRAL VENTRICLES AND DOPAMINE IN SCHIZOPHRENIA. (UNPUBLISHED PAPER).
001928 02-08

PHENYLETHYLAMINE, DOPAMINE AND NOREPINEPHRINE IN SCHIZOPHRENIA. (UNPUBLISHED PAPER).
001957 02-08

ANTIPSYCHOTIC-PROPERTIES AND ANTIDYSKINETIC-PROPERTIES OF ERGOT DOPAMINE AGONISTS.
002178 02-11

SPECIES-DIFFERENCES IN THE DEAMINATION OF DOPAMINE AND OTHER SUBSTRATES FOR MONOAMINE-OXIDASE IN BRAIN.
002233 02-13

LITHIUM ANTAGONISM OF ETHANOL-INDUCED DEPLETION OF CEREBELLAR GUANOSINE-CYCLIC-MONOPHOSPHATE AND STIMULATION OF STRIATAL DOPAMINE RELEASE.
002242 02-13

ANTIPSYCHOTIC-DRUGS: DIFFERENTIAL-EFFECTS ON DOPAMINE NEURONS IN BASAL GANGLIA AND MESOCORTEX FOLLOWING CHRONIC ADMINISTRATION IN HUMAN AND NONHUMAN PRIMATES.
002285 02-13

DOPA AND DOPAMINE AGONISTS IN DEPRESSION.
002310 02-13

SHORT-TERM AND LONG-TERM EFFECTS ON GABA AND DOPAMINE NEURONS DURING TREATMENT WITH SULPIRIDE.
002311 02-13

DOPAMINE ANTAGONIST AND AGONIST TREATMENT OF TARDIVE-DYSKINESIA.
002377 02-15

CHANGES IN CEREBRAL DOPAMINE METABOLISM AND RECEPTORS DURING ONE-YEAR NEUROLEPTIC ADMINISTRATION AND SUBSEQUENT WITHDRAWAL: RELEVANCE TO BRAIN-BIOCHEMISTRY IN SCHIZOPHRENIA.
002390 02-15

AN OBSERVATIONAL METHOD FOR QUANTIFYING THE BEHAVIOURAL-EFFECTS OF DOPAMINE AGONISTS: CONTRASTING-EFFECTS OF D-AMPHETAMINE AND APOMORPHINE.
002484 02-16

PLASMA LEVODOPA, DOPAMINE AND THERAPEUTIC RESPONSE FOLLOWING LEVODOPA THERAPY OF PARKINSONIAN-PATIENTS.
002504 02-16

A TOPOGRAPHIC LOCALIZATION OF ENKEPHALIN ON THE DOPAMINE NEURONS OF THE RAT SUBSTANTIA-NIGRA AND VENTRAL TEGMENTAL AREA DEMONSTRATED BY COMBINED HISTOFLUORESCENCE IMMUNOCYTOCHEMISTRY.
002639 03-01

PHENYLETHYLAMINE EFFECTS ON DOPAMINE SYNTHESIS. STRUCTURE-ACTIVITY RELATIONSHIPS.
002649 03-02

MIDBRAIN DOPAMINE NEURONS: DIFFERENTIAL RESPONSES TO AMPHETAMINE ISOMERS.
002680 03-03

CROSS-TOLERANCE OF DOPAMINE METABOLISM TO BACLOFEN, GAMMA BUTYROLACTONE AND HA-966 IN THE STRIATUM AND OLFACTORY TUBERCLE OF THE RAT.
002681 03-03

DOPAMINE AS A POSSIBLE NEUROTRANSMITTER IN THE SPINAL-CORD.
002705 03-03

METHYLPHENIDATE-LIKE STIMULANTS IN VITRO RELEASE (3H)TYRAMINES BUT NOT (14C)DOPAMINE.
002706 03-03

DOPAMINE DEPLETION SLOWS RETINAL TRANSMISSION.
002708 03-03

EFFECT OF MAZINDOL ON BRAIN DOPAMINE TURNOVER IN SPIPERONE TREATED RATS.
002726 03-03

GABA-RECEPTORS AND BENZODIAZEPINE-RECEPTORS. STUDIES ON THEIR LOCALIZATION IN THE HIPPOCAMPUS AND THEIR INTERACTION WITH CENTRAL DOPAMINE NEURONS IN THE RAT-BRAIN.
002727 03-03

THE PRESYNAPTIC STIMULATING EFFECT OF ACETYLCHOLINE ON DOPAMINE RELEASE IS SUPPRESSED DURING ACTIVATION OF NIGROSTRIATAL DOPAMINERGIC NEURONS IN THE CAT.
002733 03-03

MODULATION BY ENDOGENOUS DOPAMINE OF THE RELEASE OF ACETYLCHOLINE IN THE CAUDATE-NUCLEUS OF THE RABBIT.
002751 03-03

THE EFFECT OF PHENCYCLIDINE ON DOPAMINE METABOLISM IN THE MOUSE-BRAIN.
002766 03-03

GABA ANTAGONISTS ENHANCE DOPAMINE TURNOVER IN THE RAT RETINA IN VIVO.
002772 03-03

LEVONANTRADOL, A POTENT CANNABINOID RELATED ANALGESIC, ANTAGONIZES HALOPERIDOL-INDUCED ACTIVATION OF STRIATAL DOPAMINE SYNTHESIS.
002786 03-03

NEUROLEPTIC-INDUCED ACUTE DYSTONIC REACTIONS MAY BE DUE TO ENHANCED DOPAMINE RELEASE ON TO SUPERSENSITIVE POSTSYNAPTIC-RECEPTORS.
002789 03-03

FLUORESCENCE HISTOCHEMISTRY INDICATES DAMAGE OF STRIATAL DOPAMINE NERVE TERMINALS IN RATS AFTER MULTIPLE DOSES OF METHAMPHETAMINE.
002812 03-03

PROPERTIES OF DOPAMINE AGONIST AND ANTAGONIST BINDING-SITES IN MAMMALIAN RETINA.
002814 03-03

EFFECT OF DOPAMINE ON ACTIVATION OF RAT STRIATAL ADENYLATE-CYCLASE BY FREE MG2 AND GUANYL-NUCLEOTIDES.
002825 03-03

NOREPINEPHRINE AND DOPAMINE CEREBRAL LEVELS AFTER CHRONIC-TREATMENT WITH NOMIFENSINE.
002872 03-03

ACUTE ACTION OF NOMIFENSINE ON NOREPINEPHRINE AND DOPAMINE LEVELS IN THE RAT-BRAIN.
002873 03-03

BIPHASIC-EFFECTS AND OPPOSITE-EFFECTS OF DOPAMINE AND APOMORPHINE ON ENDOGENOUS GABA RELEASE IN THE RAT SUBSTANTIA-NIGRA.
002923 03-03

SPINAL MODULATION OF THE ACOUSTIC STARTLE RESPONSE: THE ROLE OF NOREPINEPHRINE, SEROTONIN AND DOPAMINE.
002950 03-04

ESTROGEN POTENTIATES THE STEREOTYPY INDUCED BY DOPAMINE AGONISTS IN THE RAT.
002968 03-04

EFFECTS OF ACUTE OR CHRONIC ADMINISTRATION OF LOW-DOSES OF A DOPAMINE AGONIST ON DRINKING AND LOCOMOTOR-ACTIVITY IN THE RAT. ·
002982 03-04

THE ROLE OF CALCIUM AND DOPAMINE MEMBRANE CARRIER IN MEDIATING THE BEHAVIORAL-EFFECTS AND BIOCHEMICAL-EFFECTS OF AMPHETAMINE. (PH.D. DISSERTATION).
002996 03-04

EFFECTS OF CHOLECYSTOKININ-OCTAPEPTIDE ON STRIATAL DOPAMINE METABOLISM AND ON APOMORPHINE-INDUCED STEREOTYPED CAGE CLIMBING IN MICE.
003031 03-04

AN INVOLVEMENT OF DOPAMINE IN HIGHER-ORDER CHOICE MECHANISMS IN THE MONKEY.
003072 03-04

DOPAMINE AND DEMENTIA. AN ANIMAL-MODEL WITH DESTRUCTION OF THE MESOCORTICAL DOPAMINERGIC PATHWAY; A PRELIMINARY STUDY.
003085 03-04

DOPAMINE DEPLETION BY 6 HYDROXYDOPAMINE PREVENTS CONDITIONED TASTE-AVERSION INDUCED BY METHYLAMPHETAMINE BUT NOT LITHIUM-CHLORIDE.
003110 03-04

ABNORMAL TRANSMETHYLATION REACTION DURING THE METABOLISM OF DOPAMINE, TRYPTAMINE, AND SEROTONIN, AND SCHIZOPHRENIC-SYMPTOMS: A CRITICAL REVIEW.
003404 03-13

DOPAMINE CONJUGATE IN CEREBROSPINAL-FLUID.
003432 03-13

ALTERATIONS IN CEREBROSPINAL-FLUID DOPAMINE METABOLITES FOLLOWING PHYSOSTIGMINE INFUSION.
003477 03-15

CHLORPROMAZINE, HALOPERIDOL, METOCLOPRAMIDE AND DOMPERIDONE RELEASE PROLACTIN THROUGH DOPAMINE ANTAGONISM AT LOW CONCENTRATIONS BUT PARADOXICALLY INHIBIT PROLACTIN RELEASE AT HIGH-CONCENTRATIONS.
003731 04-03

DOPAMINE METABOLITES IN CAUDATE AND CORTEX AFTER LITHIUM AND HALOPERIDOL. (UNPUBLISHED PAPER).
003738 04-03

PRESYNAPTIC AND POSTSYNAPTIC STRIATAL DOPAMINE-RECEPTORS: DIFFERENTIAL SENSITIVITY TO APOMORPHINE INHIBITION OF (3H)DOPAMINE AND (14C)GABA RELEASE IN VITRO.
003741 04-03

GABA-ENHANCEMENT OF (3H)DOPAMINE RELEASE FROM SLICES OF RAT STRIATUM: DEPENDENCE ON SLICE SIZE.
003786 04-03

THE EFFECT OF LONG-TERM CONCURRENT ADMINISTRATION OF CHLORPROMAZINE AND LITHIUM ON THE STRIATAL AND FRONTAL CORTICAL DOPAMINE METABOLISM IN RATS.
003788 04-03

DOPAMINE, NORADRENALINE AND 3,4 DIHYDROXYPHENYLACETIC-ACID (DOPAC) LEVELS OF INDIVIDUAL BRAIN NUCLEI, EFFECTS OF HALOPERIDOL AND PARGYLINE.
003792 04-03

COMPARATIVE-EFFECTS OF AMANTADINE AND AMFONELIC-ACID ON DOPAMINE METABOLISM IN RAT-BRAIN.
003796 04-03

DOPAMINE INHIBITS BURST-FIRING OF NEUROSECRETORY CELL R-15 IN APLYSIA-CALIFORNICA: ESTABLISHMENT OF A DOSE-RESPONSE RELATIONSHIP. ·
003806 04-03

PRESYNAPTIC MODULATION OF SYNAPTIC TRANSMISSION IN HELIX-POMATIA: THE EFFECTS OF SEROTONIN AND DOPAMINE ANTAGONISTS.
003869 04-03

INCREASED MESOLIMBIC DOPAMINE BINDING FOLLOWING CHRONIC HALOPERIDOL TREATMENT.
003872 04-03

SOME BARBITURATES ENHANCE THE EFFECT OF MUSCIMOL ON DOPAMINE TURNOVER IN THE RAT RETINA.
003873 04-03

INHIBITION OF DOPAMINE D-1 AND D-2 BINDING-SITES IN NEURONAL TISSUE BY ASCORBATE.
003876 04-03

EFFECTS OF 3',4' DIHYDROXYNOMIFENSINE ON THE DOPAMINE VASCULAR RECEPTOR.
003890 04-03

PHENYLETHYLAMINE EFFECTS ON DOPAMINE SYNTHESIS: STRUCTURE-
ACTIVITY RELATIONSHIPS. (UNPUBLISHED PAPER).
003959 04-03

EFFECTS OF IN VIVO AMPHETAMINE ADMINISTRATION ON DOPAMINE
SYNTHESIS REGULATION IN RAT-BRAIN STRIATAL SYNAPTOSOMES.
(UNPUBLISHED PAPER).
003960 04-03

WHY DOES SULPIRIDE NOT BLOCK THE EFFECT OF DOPAMINE ON THE
DOPAMINE-SENSITIVE ADENYLATE-CYCLASE?
004055 04-03

EFFECTS OF A HIGH-DOSE TREATMENT OF METHAMPHETAMINE ON
CAUDATE DOPAMINE AND ANOREXIA IN RATS.
004073 04-04

EFFECTS OF DOPAMINE, APOMORPHINE, GAMMA HYDROXYBUTYRIC-
ACID, HALOPERIDOL AND PIMOZIDE ON REFLEX BRADYCARDIA IN
RATS.
004085 04-04

GENETIC VARIATIONS IN MIDBRAIN DOPAMINE CELL NUMBER: PARALLEL
WITH DIFFERENCES IN RESPONSES TO DOPAMINERGIC AGONISTS AND
IN NATURALISTIC BEHAVIORS MEDIATED BY CENTRAL DOPAMINERGIC-
SYSTEMS. (UNPUBLISHED PAPER).
004112 04-04

THE EFFECT OF DOPAMINE UPTAKE BLOCKING-AGENTS ON THE
AMPHETAMINE-INDUCED CIRCLING-BEHAVIOR IN MICE WITH
UNILATERAL NIGROSTRIATAL LESIONS.
004117 04-04

IS DOPAMINE ANTAGONISM A REQUISITE OF NEUROLEPTIC ACTIVITY?
004122 04-04

THE RELATIONSHIP BETWEEN LOSS OF DOPAMINE NERVE TERMINALS,
STRIATAL (3H)SPIROPERIDOL BINDING AND ROTATIONAL-BEHAVIOR IN
UNILATERALLY 6 HYDROXYDOPAMINE LESIONED RATS.
004129 04-04

DIFFERENTIAL-EFFECTS OF SEVERAL DOPAMINE UPTAKE INHIBITORS AND
RELEASING-AGENTS ON LOCOMOTOR-ACTIVITY IN NORMAL AND IN
RESERPINIZED MICE.
004130 04-04

INVOLVEMENT OF DOPAMINE IN CIRCLING RESPONSES TO MUSCIMOL
DEPENDS ON INTRANIGRAL SITE OF INJECTION.
004158 04-04

DESTRUCTION OF 5 HYDROXYTRYPTAMINERGIC NEURONS AND THE
DYNAMICS OF DOPAMINE IN NUCLEUS-ACCUMBENS SEPTI AND OTHER
FOREBRAIN REGIONS OF THE RAT.
004171 04-04

AVOIDANCE RESPONSE IN RATS AFTER INJECTION OF DOPAMINE INTO
THE NEOSTRIATUM.
004255 04-04

ANTAGONISM OF DOPAMINE SUPERSENSITIVITY BY ESTROGEN:
NEUROCHEMICAL-STUDIES IN AN ANIMAL-MODEL OF TARDIVE-
DYSKINESIA.
004268 04-05

DETERMINATION OF PICOMOLE AMOUNTS OF DOPAMINE,
NORADRENALINE, 3,4 DIHYDROXYPHENYLALANINE, 3,4
DIHYDROXYPHENYLACETIC-ACID, HOMOVANILLIC-ACID, AND 5
HYDROXYINDOLEACETIC-ACID IN NERVOUS-TISSUE AFTER ONE-STEP
PURIFICATION ON SEPHADEX-G-10, USING HIGH.
004305 04-06

DOPAMINE AND 5 HT SUPERSENSITIVITY IN NONORGANIC CENTRAL PAIN
AND IN MORPHINE ABSTINENCE: FORTUITOUS OR REAL ANALOGY?
004553 04-13

DOPAMINE-ACTIVATED
DOPAMINE-ACTIVATED ADENYLATE-CYCLASE OF SPINAL-CORD:
SUPERSENSITIVITY FOLLOWING TRANSECTION OF THE CORD.
003800 04-03

DOPAMINE-AUTORECEPTOR
REPEATED TRICYCLICS INDUCE A PROGRESSIVE DOPAMINE-
AUTORECEPTOR SUBSENSITIVITY INDEPENDENT OF DAILY DRUG-
TREATMENT.
000047 01-03

REPEATED ANTIDEPRESSANT TREATMENTS INDUCE A LONG-LASTING
DOPAMINE-AUTORECEPTOR SUBSENSITIVITY: IS DAILY TREATMENT
NECESSARY FOR CLINICAL EFFICACY?
002659 03-03

DOPAMINE-AUTORECEPTORS
TRICYCLIC-ANTIDEPRESSANTS INDUCE SUBSENSITIVITY OF PRESYNAPTIC
DOPAMINE-AUTORECEPTORS.
000048 01-03

DOPAMINE-AUTORECEPTORS: PHARMACOLOGY, FUNCTION AND
COMPARISON WITH POSTSYNAPTIC DOPAMINE-RECEPTORS.
001453 02-03

PHYSIOLOGICAL SIGNIFICANCE OF DOPAMINE-AUTORECEPTORS AS
STUDIED FOLLOWING THEIR SELECTIVE BLOCKADE BY MOLINDONE.
004065 04-04

DOPAMINE-BETA-HYDROXYLASE
DOPAMINE-BETA-HYDROXYLASE: A MODULATOR OF BETA-ADRENERGIC-
RECEPTOR ACTIVITY.
000302 01-03

DOPAMINE-BETA-HYDROXYLASE ACTIVITY AND NORADRENALINE
CONTENT IN PIAL-ARTERIES OF CAT AND GOAT.
001357 02-03

METHODOLOGICAL-ISSUES IN SPINAL-FLUID STUDIES OF SCHIZOPHRENIA:
THE CASE OF NOREPINEPHRINE AND DOPAMINE-BETA-HYDROXYLASE.
(UNPUBLISHED PAPER).
001952 02-08

PURIFICATION AND CHARACTERIZATION OF RAT PHEOCHROMOCYTOMA
DOPAMINE-BETA-HYDROXYLASE.
003664 04-01

REDUCTION IN THE LEVEL OF IMMUNOTITRATABLE DOPAMINE-BETA-
HYDROXYLASE AFTER CHRONIC ADMINISTRATION OF L-DOPA OR
ALPHA METHYLDOPA.
003764 04-03

RESERPINE EFFECT ON THE AXONAL TRANSPORT OF DOPAMINE-BETA-
HYDROXYLASE AND TYROSINE-HYDROXYLASE IN RAT-BRAIN.
003904 04-03

PLASMA DOPAMINE-BETA-HYDROXYLASE ACTIVITY IN CHRONIC
SCHIZOPHRENIC-PATIENTS TESTED WITH SINGLE-DOSE OF 2 BROMO-
ALPHA-ERGOCRIPTINE (PARLODEL).
004343 04-08

NORMAL PLASMA DOPAMINE-BETA-HYDROXYLASE IN NONTREATED AND
TREATED PARKINSON-PATIENTS.
004471 04-11

THE ACTIVITY OF DOPAMINE-BETA-HYDROXYLASE IN THE PLASMA OF
PATIENTS WITH ENDOGENOUS DEPRESSIVE-SYNDROMES.
004548 04-13

DOPAMINE-DEPENDENT
THE ROLE OF 5 HYDROXYTRYPTAMINE IN DOPAMINE-DEPENDENT
STEREOTYPED-BEHAVIOUR.
002966 03-04

DOPAMINE-DEPENDENT HYPERACTIVITY IN THE FOLLOWING
MANIPULATION OF GABA MECHANISMS IN THE REGION OF THE
NUCLEUS-ACCUMBENS.
003976 04-03

DOPAMINE-EVOKED
ALPHA FLUPENTHIXOL: AN ANTAGONIST OF DOPAMINE-EVOKED FLUID
SECRETION BY AN INSECT SALIVARY-GLAND PREPARATION.
000031 01-03

DOPAMINE-INDUCED
CONSISTENT UNMASKING OF DOPAMINE-INDUCED DILATION OF THE
CANINE FEMORAL VASCULAR BED.
003911 D4-03

EVIDENCE TO SUGGEST THAT DOPAMINE-INDUCED INCREASE IN GABA
CONCENTRATIONS IN CHICK BRAIN IS MEDIATED THROUGH CYCLIC-
AMP.
003952 04-03

DOPAMINE-MEDIATED
ACTIONS OF TETRAHYDRONORHARMANE (TETRAHYDRO-BETA-
CARBOLINE) ON 5 HYDROXYTRYPTAMINE AND DOPAMINE-MEDIATED
MECHANISMS.
002854 03-03

EFFECT OF ACUTE AND CHRONIC TRIIODOTHYRONINE (T3)
ADMINISTRATION TO RATS ON CENTRAL 5 HT AND DOPAMINE-
MEDIATED BEHAVIOURAL-RESPONSES AND RELATED BRAIN-
BIOCHEMISTRY.
002951 03-04

DOPAMINE-MIMETIC
ACTIVATION OF PRESYNAPTIC ALPHA NORADRENALINE-RECEPTORS IN
RAT-BRAIN BY THE POTENT DOPAMINE-MIMETIC N,N DIPROPYL-ADTN.
001390 02-03

DOPAMINE-RADIORECEPTOR
THE DOPAMINE-RADIORECEPTOR ASSAY – A CLINICAL APPLICATION.
000904 01-16

DOPAMINE-RECEPTOR
CHRONIC HIGH-DOSE PROPRANOLOL DOES NOT INCREASE DOPAMINE-
RECEPTOR NUMBER.
000083 01-03

HYPOPHYSECTOMY PREVENTS THE STRIATAL DOPAMINE-RECEPTOR
SUPERSENSITIVITY PRODUCED BY CHRONIC HALOPERIDOL TREATMENT.
000132 01-03

EVIDENCE FOR, AND LOCALIZATION OF, A UNITARY DOPAMINE-
RECEPTOR COMPOSED OF COOPERATIVELY LINKED SUBUNIT BINDING-
SITES IN RAT STRIATUM.
000186 01-03

IN VITRO ACETYLCHOLINE RELEASE FROM RAT CAUDATE-NUCLEUS AS A
NEW MODEL FOR TESTING DRUGS WITH DOPAMINE-RECEPTOR
ACTIVITY.
000289 01-03

REDUCTION OF FOOD INTAKE BY PIRIBEDIL IN THE RAT: RELATION TO
DOPAMINE-RECEPTOR STIMULATION.
000355 01-04

POSTSWIM GROOMING IN MICE INHIBITED BY DOPAMINE-RECEPTOR
ANTAGONISTS AND BY CANNABINOIDS.
000359 01-04

INCREASED DOPAMINE-RECEPTOR BINDING IN THE STRIATUM OF RATS
AFTER LONG-TERM ISOLATION.
000398 01-04

N ALKYLATED 2 AMINOTETRALINS: CENTRAL DOPAMINE-RECEPTOR
STIMULATING ACTIVITY.
000399 01-04

EXTINCTION AND DOPAMINE-RECEPTOR BLOCKADE AFTER INTERMITTENT REINFORCEMENT TRAINING: FAILURE TO OBSERVE FUNCTIONAL EQUIVALENCE.
000490 01-04

TRANSIENT ABOLITION OF GENERALIZED PHOTOSENSITIVE EPILEPTIC-DISCHARGE IN HUMANS BY APOMORPHINE, A DOPAMINE-RECEPTOR AGONIST.
000714 01-11

DOPAMINE-RECEPTOR: ISOLATION, PURIFICATION, AND REGULATION.
001011 02-01

NO EVIDENCE FOR INCREASED DOPAMINE-RECEPTOR BINDING IN SUPERRESPONSIVE MICE AFTER A SINGLE-DOSE OF NEUROLEPTICS.
001292 02-03

DOPAMINE-RECEPTOR BLOCKADE IN RAT-BRAIN AFTER ACUTE AND SUBCHRONIC-TREATMENT WITH TRICYCLIC-ANTIDEPRESSANTS.
001314 02-03

THE PITUITARY DOPAMINE-RECEPTOR.
001324 02-03

DOPAMINE-RECEPTOR: FROM SYNAPTIC MEMBRANES TO SOLUBILIZATION.
001326 02-03

EFFECTS OF HALOPERIDOL, A DOPAMINE-RECEPTOR ANTAGONIST, ON A DELAYED TYPE HYPERSENSITIVITY REACTION TO 1 CHLORODINITROBENZENE IN MICE.
001473 02-03

INHIBITION OF NEUROLEPTIC-INDUCED DOPAMINE-RECEPTOR SUPERSENSITIVITY BY CYCLO-LEU-GLY.
001576 02-04

DOPAMINE-RECEPTOR BLOCKADE BY IMIDOLINE AND ITS PROPOSED ACTIVE CONFORMATION.
001687 02-04

CHRONIC NEUROLEPTIC TREATMENT AND DOPAMINE-RECEPTOR REGULATION.
001837 02-05

APOMORPHINE HYPOTHERMIA: AN INDEX OF CENTRAL DOPAMINE-RECEPTOR FUNCTION IN MAN.
002221 02-13

NEUROCHEMICAL EVIDENCE AND BEHAVIORAL-EVIDENCE FOR A SELECTIVE PRESYNAPTIC DOPAMINE-RECEPTOR AGONIST.
002236 02-13

PERGOLIDE, A POTENT LONG-ACTING DOPAMINE-RECEPTOR AGONIST.
002257 02-13

DURING ONE YEARS NEUROLEPTIC TREATMENT IN RATS STRIATAL DOPAMINE-RECEPTOR BLOCKADE DECREASES BUT SERUM PROLACTIN LEVELS REMAIN ELEVATED.
002707 03-03

DOPAMINE-RECEPTOR SUPERSENSITIVITY IN THE CORPUS-STRIATUM FOLLOWING CHRONIC ELEVATION OF BRAIN GAMMA AMINOBUTYRIC-ACID.
002716 03-03

KAINATE LESION DISSOCIATES STRIATAL DOPAMINE-RECEPTOR RADIOLIGAND BINDING-SITES.
002803 03-03

LOCALIZATION OF GABA-RECEPTOR AND DOPAMINE-RECEPTOR SITES IN RETINAL GLIAL CELLS USING DL ALPHA AMINOADIPIC-ACID.
002828 03-03

THREE CLASSES OF DOPAMINE-RECEPTOR (D-2, D-3, D-4) IDENTIFIED BY BINDING STUDIES WITH 3H APOMORPHINE AND 3H DOMPERIDONE.
002900 03-03

A COMPARISON OF DOPAMINE-RECEPTOR BLOCKING ASSAY WITH PLASMA DRUG LEVELS OF HALOPERIDOL IN SCHIZOPHRENIC-PATIENTS.
003182 03-08

NEUROLEPTIC MALIGNANT-SYNDROME: A PATHOGENETIC ROLE FOR DOPAMINE-RECEPTOR BLOCKADE?
003492 03-15

THE DOPAMINE-RECEPTOR: ISOLATION, PURIFICATION AND REGULATION.
003660 04-01

DOPAMINE-RECEPTOR PURIFICATION AND CHARACTERIZATION. (UNPUBLISHED PAPER).
003661 04-01

THE DOPAMINE-RECEPTOR ANTAGONIST DOMPERIDONE IS ALSO A COMPETITIVE ANTAGONIST AT ALPHA1-ADRENOCEPTORS.
003785 04-03

RESPONSE OF STRIATONIGRAL SUBSTANCE-P SYSTEMS TO A DOPAMINE-RECEPTOR AGONIST AND ANTAGONIST.
003826 04-03

THE DOPAMINE-RECEPTOR COMPLEX: BIOCHEMICAL-CONSEQUENCES OF SUPERSENSITIVITY INDUCED BY TREATMENT WITH 6 HYDROXYDOPAMINE OR MORPHINE.
003958 04-03

DOPAMINE-RECEPTOR BINDING IN BOVINE INTERMEDIATE LOBE PITUITARY MEMBRANES.
004003 04-03

A COMPARISON OF THE RESPONSES TO SOME DOPAMINE-RECEPTOR AGONISTS AND ANTAGONISTS IN THE ISOLATED PERFUSED RAT KIDNEY.
004054 04-03

RELEVANCE OF DOPAMINE-RECEPTOR BINDING STUDIES FOR EVALUATION OF ANTIPARKINSONIAN-DRUGS.
004120 04-04

DOPAMINE-RECEPTOR CHANGES FOLLOWING DESTRUCTION OF THE NIGROSTRIATAL PATHWAY: LACK OF A RELATIONSHIP TO ROTATIONAL-BEHAVIOR.
004229 04-04

LITHIUM EFFECTS ON HALOPERIDOL-INDUCED PRESYNAPTIC AND POSTSYNAPTIC DOPAMINE-RECEPTOR SUPERSENSITIVITY.
004244 04-04

THE EFFECT OF THE DOPAMINE-RECEPTOR BLOCKING-DRUG PIMOZIDE ON THE STIMULANT AND ANORECTIC-ACTIONS OF DEXTROAMPHETAMINE IN MAN.
004580 04-14

DOPAMINE-RECEPTORS

EVIDENCE FOR AN IRREVERSIBLE INTERACTION OF BROMOCRYPTINE WITH CENTRAL DOPAMINE-RECEPTORS.
000023 01-03

REGULATION OF STRIATAL ACETYLCHOLINE CONCENTRATION BY D2 DOPAMINE-RECEPTORS.
000269 01-03

SODIUM-DEPENDENT INTERACTION OF BENZAMIDES WITH DOPAMINE-RECEPTORS.
000285 01-03

DOPAMINE-RECEPTORS AND SCHIZOPHRENIA: DRUG-EFFECT OR ILLNESS?
000564 01-08

METOCLOPRAMIDE AND SULPIRIDE AS SELECTIVE BLOCKING-AGENTS PRESYNAPTIC AND POSTSYNAPTIC DOPAMINE-RECEPTORS.
001102 02-03

DOPAMINE-RECEPTORS IN RAT-FRONTAL-CORTEX: PHARMACOLOGICAL-PROPERTIES IN VIVO AND IN VITRO.
001112 02-03

CHLOROETHYLNORAPOMORPHINE, A PROPOSED LONG-ACTING DOPAMINE ANTAGONIST: INTERACTIONS WITH DOPAMINE-RECEPTORS OF MAMMALIAN FOREBRAIN IN VITRO.
001114 02-03

PRESYNAPTIC DOPAMINE-RECEPTORS: INSENSITIVITY TO KAINIC-ACID AND THE DEVELOPMENT OF SUPERSENSITIVITY FOLLOWING CHRONIC HALOPERIDOL.
001117 02-03

IN VIVO (3H)SPIPERONE BINDING TO THE RAT HIPPOCAMPAL FORMATION: INVOLVEMENT OF DOPAMINE-RECEPTORS.
001131 02-03

CENTRAL-NERVOUS-SYSTEM DOPAMINE-RECEPTORS.
001185 02-03

RADIOLIGAND BINDING STUDIES: EVIDENCE FOR MULTIPLE DOPAMINE-RECEPTORS.
001186 02-03

PERIPHERAL PRESYNAPTIC AND POSTSYNAPTIC DOPAMINE-RECEPTORS: ARE THEY DIFFERENT FROM DOPAMINE-RECEPTORS IN THE CENTRAL-NERVOUS-SYSTEM.
001252 02-03

ATTEMPTS TO DEVELOP SUPERSENSITIVITY OR SUBSENSITIVITY RETINAL DOPAMINE-RECEPTORS AFTER VARIOUS TREATMENTS WITH ANTAGONISTS OR AGONISTS.
001350 02-03

MODIFICATION OF DOPAMINE-RECEPTORS IN BRAIN BY CONTINUOUS AMPHETAMINE ADMINISTRATIONS TO RATS.
001395 02-03

PRESYNAPTIC DOPAMINE-RECEPTORS IN STRIATAL NERVE-ENDINGS: ABSENCE OF HALOPERIDOL-INDUCED SUPERSENSITIVITY.
001424 02-03

THE EFFECT OF CYCLO-LEU-GLY ON CHEMICAL DENERVATION SUPERSENSITIVITY OF DOPAMINE-RECEPTORS INDUCED BY INTRACEREBROVENTRICULAR INJECTION OF 6 HYDROXYDOPAMINE IN MICE.
001435 02-03

DOPAMINE-AUTORECEPTORS: PHARMACOLOGY, FUNCTION AND COMPARISON WITH POSTSYNAPTIC DOPAMINE-RECEPTORS.
001453 02-03

SIMILARITIES AND DISSIMILARITIES BETWEEN DOPAMINE AND NEUROLEPTIC-RECEPTORS: FURTHER EVIDENCE FOR TYPE-1 AND TYPE-2 DOPAMINE-RECEPTORS IN THE CNS.
001480 02-03

HIGH-AFFINITY DOPAMINE-RECEPTORS (D3) IN RAT-BRAIN.
001509 02-03

RADIORECEPTOR LABELING OF PRESYNAPTIC AND POSTSYNAPTIC DOPAMINE-RECEPTORS.
001511 02-03

BINDING OF (3H)PERGOLIDE-MESYLATE TO DOPAMINE-RECEPTORS OF MAMMALIAN BRAINS.
001538 02-03

NEUROLEPTIC/DOPAMINE-RECEPTORS: ELEVATION AND REVERSAL.
001847 02-05

NEUROLEPTICS AND DOPAMINE-RECEPTORS, THERAPEUTIC IMPLICATIONS.
001942 02-08

CLINICAL EVIDENCE FOR MULTIPLE DOPAMINE-RECEPTORS IN MAN.
002264 02-13

DRUG-EFFECTS ON PRESYNAPTIC AND POSTSYNAPTIC DOPAMINE-RECEPTORS.
002372 02-15

SIMILARITIES BETWEEN THE BINDING OF 3H PIFLUTIXOL AND 3H FLUPENTIXOL TO RAT STRIATAL DOPAMINE-RECEPTORS IN VITRO.
002760 03-03
REGULATION BY CATIONS OF (3H)SPIROPERIDOL BINDING ASSOCIATED WITH DOPAMINE-RECEPTORS OF RAT-BRAIN.
002922 03-03
DOPAMINE-RECEPTORS, NEUROLEPTICS, AND SCHIZOPHRENIA.
003197 03-08
PRESYNAPTIC AND POSTSYNAPTIC STRIATAL DOPAMINE-RECEPTORS: DIFFERENTIAL SENSITIVITY TO APOMORPHINE INHIBITION OF (3H)DOPAMINE AND (14C)GABA RELEASE IN VITRO.
003741 04-03
SOLUBILIZATION OF NEUROLEPTIC/DOPAMINE-RECEPTORS OF HUMAN BRAIN STRIATUM.
003767 04-03
DOPAMINE-RECEPTORS IN SUBCELLULAR FRACTIONS FROM BOVINE CAUDATE: ENRICHMENT OF (3H)SPIPERONE BINDING IN A POSTSYNAPTIC MEMBRANE FRACTION.
003948 04-03
MODULATION OF DOPAMINE-RECEPTORS BY OPIATES. (UNPUBLISHED PAPER).
003949 04-03
CHRONIC NEUROLEPTIC TREATMENT SPECIFICALLY ALTERS THE NUMBER OF DOPAMINE-RECEPTORS IN RAT-BRAIN.
004033 04-03
BRAIN DOPAMINE-RECEPTORS.
004741 04-17
DOPAMINE-SENSITIVE
DOPAMINE-SENSITIVE ADENYLATE-CYCLASE AND RECEPTOR BINDING-ACTIVITIES FOLLOWING ACUTE AND CHRONIC NEUROLEPTIC-DRUG TREATMENT. (UNPUBLISHED PAPER).
001172 02-03
DOPAMINE-SENSITIVE ADENYLATE-CYCLASE AND DOPAMINE/ NEUROLEPTIC-RECEPTOR BINDING: EFFECT OF NEUROLEPTIC-DRUGS.
001358 02-03
STEREOSPECIFIC INHIBITION OF DOPAMINE-SENSITIVE ADENYLATE-CYCLASE IN CARP RETINA BY THE ENANTIOMERS OF (/-) 1 CYCLOPROPYLMETHYL TRIFLUOROMETHYLTHIODIBENZOCYCLOHEPTENYLIDENEPIPERIDINE.
003706 04-02
STIMULATORY ACTION OF LISURIDE ON DOPAMINE-SENSITIVE ADENYLATE-CYCLASE IN THE RAT STRIATAL HOMOGENATE.
003718 04-03
DOPAMINERGIC MECHANISMS IN THE TELEOST RETINA. I. DOPAMINE-SENSITIVE ADENYLATE-CYCLASE IN HOMOGENATES OF CARP RETINA; EFFECTS OF AGONISTS, ANTAGONISTS AND ERGOTS.
004051 04-03
WHY DOES SULPIRIDE NOT BLOCK THE EFFECT OF DOPAMINE ON THE DOPAMINE-SENSITIVE ADENYLATE-CYCLASE?
004055 04-03
DOPAMINERGIC
PRODRUGS OF SOME DOPAMINERGIC 2 AMINOTETRALINS: A REVIEW OF THEIR SYNTHESES AND NEUROCHEMICAL PROFILES.
000004 01-01
EFFECTS OF DOPAMINERGIC AGONISTS AND ANTAGONISTS ON (3H)APOMORPHINE BINDING TO STRIATAL MEMBRANES; SULPIRIDE LACK OF INTERACTIONS WITH POSITIVE COOPERATIVE (3H)APOMORPHINE BINDING.
000099 01-03
EFFECT OF DOPAMINERGIC AND GABAERGIC DRUGS GIVEN ALONE OR IN COMBINATION ON THE ANTICONVULSANT ACTION OF PHENOBARBITAL AND DIPHENYLHYDANTOIN IN THE ELECTROSHOCK-TEST IN MICE.
000163 01-03
DECARBOXYLATION OF EXOGENOUS L-DOPA IN RAT STRIATUM AFTER LESIONS OF THE DOPAMINERGIC NIGROSTRIATAL NEURONS: THE ROLE OF STRIATAL CAPILLARIES.
000202 01-03
STRIATAL DOPAMINERGIC ACTIVITY DURING WITHDRAWAL FROM CHRONIC NEUROLEPTIC TREATMENT IN RATS.
000203 01-03
EFFECTS OF ALPHA CHLORALOSE ON THE ACTIVITY OF THE NIGROSTRIATAL DOPAMINERGIC SYSTEM IN THE CAT.
000217 01-03
INTRAVENOUS GABA AGONIST ADMINISTRATION STIMULATES FIRING OF A10 DOPAMINERGIC NEURONS.
000320 01-03
EFFECT OF PICROTOXIN AND NIPECOTIC-ACID ON INHIBITORY RESPONSE OF DOPAMINERGIC NEURONS IN THE VENTRAL TEGMENTAL AREA TO STIMULATION OF THE NUCLEUS-ACCUMBENS.
000331 01-03
ROLE OF BRAIN DOPAMINERGIC MECHANISMS IN RODENT AGGRESSIVE-BEHAVIOR: INFLUENCE OF (OR -)N N PROPYLNORAPOMORPHINE ON THREE EXPERIMENTAL MODELS.
000340 01-04
EFFECTS OF DOPAMINERGIC AND CHOLINERGIC-DRUGS, NALOXONE AND L PROLYL-LEUCYL-GLYCINAMIDE ON LSD-INDUCED CATALEPSY.
000360 01-04
DIFFERENT DOPAMINERGIC MECHANISMS FOR AMFONELIC-ACID, AMPHETAMINE AND APOMORPHINE.
000465 01-04

NALOXONE OVERCOMES THE DOPAMINERGIC, EEG, AND BEHAVIORAL-EFFECTS OF GAMMA HYDROXYBUTYRATE.
000478 01-04
CONTRIBUTION TO THE CLINICAL-STUDY OF CEREBRAL DOPAMINERGIC MECHANISMS: THE ACTION OF PIRIBEDIL IN PSYCHIATRY. FIRST RESULTS.
000616 01-09
BROMOCRIPTINE AND DOPAMINERGIC FUNCTION IN HUNTINGTON-DISEASE.
000700 01-11
DOPAMINERGIC FACTORS IN HUMAN PROLACTIN REGULATION: A PITUITARY MODEL FOR THE STUDY OF A NEUROENDOCRINE SYSTEM IN MAN.
000776 01-13
CONTRIBUTION TO STUDY OF CEREBRAL DOPAMINERGIC MECHANISMS: REALITY OF THE PROBLEM.
000782 01-13
DOPAMINE BIOSYNTHESIS IS REGULATED BY THE AMINE NEWLY RECAPTURED BY DOPAMINERGIC NERVE-ENDINGS.
001163 02-03
GLYCINE ENHANCEMENT OF CAUDATE NEURONAL ACTIVITIES: RELATIONSHIP WITH THE DOPAMINERGIC NIGROSTRIATAL PATHWAY.
001225 02-03
EFFECTS OF CHRONIC NEUROLEPTIC TREATMENT ON TYROSINE-HYDROXYLASE IN DOPAMINERGIC TERMINALS: COMPARISONS BETWEEN DRUGS AND BRAIN REGIONS REVEALS DIFFERENT MECHANISMS OF TOLERANCE.
001243 02-03
ROLE OF CALMODULIN IN DOPAMINERGIC TRANSMISSION. (UNPUBLISHED PAPER).
001270 02-03
INTERNEURONES ARE PROBABLY NOT INVOLVED IN THE PRESYNAPTIC DOPAMINERGIC CONTROL OF DOPAMINE RELEASE IN RABBIT CAUDATE-NUCLEUS.
001298 02-03
DIFFERENTIAL SENSITIVITY OF HYPOTHALAMIC DOPAMINERGIC AND NORADRENERGIC NEURONES TO PHARMACOLOGICAL MANIPULATION.
001310 02-03
LONG-TERM EFFECTS OF HALOPERIDOL, CLOZAPINE, AND METHADONE ON RAT STRIATAL CHOLINERGIC AND DOPAMINERGIC DYNAMICS.
001325 02-03
SHORT-TERM AND LONG-TERM EFFECTS OF METHAMPHETAMINE ON BIOGENIC-AMINE METABOLISM IN EXTRASTRIATAL DOPAMINERGIC NUCLEI.
001384 02-03
PRESYNAPTIC AND POSTSYNAPTIC MECHANISMS IN HALOPERIDOL-INDUCED SENSITIZATION TO DOPAMINERGIC AGONISTS.
001392 02-03
INTERACTION OF DOPAMINERGIC ERGOT DERIVATIVES WITH CYCLIC-NUCLEOTIDE SYSTEM.
001482 02-03
DENERVATION IN THE DOPAMINERGIC MESOLIMBIC SYSTEM: FUNCTIONAL CHANGES FOLLOWED USING (-)N N PROPYLNORAPOMORPHINE DEPEND ON THE BASAL ACTIVITY LEVELS OF RATS.
001603 02-04
INTERACTION OF CHOLINERGIC AND DOPAMINERGIC INFLUENCES ON YAWNING-BEHAVIOR.
001656 02-04
DOPAMINERGIC INVOLVEMENT IN ATTENTION A NOVEL ANIMAL-MODEL.
001678 02-04
DIFFERENTIAL DOPAMINERGIC FUNCTION IN YOUNG AND OLD FEMALE RATS AS MEASURED BY THREE BEHAVIORS.
001683 02-04
THE EFFECT OF SOME STRUCTURAL GABA ANALOGUES ON THE SEROTONIN AND DOPAMINERGIC MECHANISMS.
001736 02-04
DYSKINESIA INDUCED BY LONG-TERM-TREATMENT WITH ANTIPSYCHOTIC-DRUGS: INVOLVEMENT OF PRESYNAPTIC AND POSTSYNAPTIC DOPAMINERGIC MECHANISMS.
001839 02-05
THE USE OF BROMOCRIPTINE FOR TESTING CENTRAL DOPAMINERGIC REACTIVITY.
002205 02-13
THE HYPOTHALAMIC DOPAMINERGIC REGULATION OF PROLACTIN: A MODEL FOR THE STUDY OF NEUROHORMONAL MECHANISMS IN MAN.
002568 02-17
DOPAMINERGIC ABNORMALITIES IN POSTMORTEM SCHIZOPHRENIC BRAIN.
002575 02-17
DISRUPTION OF 5 HYDROXYTRYPTAMINERGIC NEURONAL FUNCTION BLOCKS THE ACTION OF MORPHINE ON TUBEROINFUNDIBULAR DOPAMINERGIC NEURONS.
002700 03-03
THE PRESYNAPTIC STIMULATING EFFECT OF ACETYLCHOLINE ON DOPAMINE RELEASE IS SUPPRESSED DURING ACTIVATION OF NIGROSTRIATAL DOPAMINERGIC NEURONS IN THE CAT.
002733 03-03

DOPAMINERGIC INVOLVEMENT IN THE HYPERALGESIC EFFECT OF NOMIFENSINE.
002736 03-03

BASAL GANGLIA DOPAMINERGIC CONTROL OF SENSORIMOTOR FUNCTIONS RELATED TO MOTIVATED BEHAVIOR.
002815 03-03

IN VIVO VOLTAMMETRIC INVESTIGATIONS INTO THE ACTION OF HA-966 ON CENTRAL DOPAMINERGIC NEURONS.
002832 03-03

GLUCOSE SUPPRESSES BASAL FIRING AND HALOPERIDOL-INDUCED INCREASES IN THE FIRING-RATE OF CENTRAL DOPAMINERGIC NEURONS.
002880 03-03

DOPAMINERGIC AGONIST AND ANTAGONIST EFFECTS ON STRIATAL TYROSINE-HYDROXYLASE DISTRIBUTION.
002898 03-03

CHOLINERGIC, DOPAMINERGIC, NORADRENERGIC, OR GLUTAMINERGIC STIMULATION VENTRAL TO THE ANTERIOR SEPTUM DOES NOT SPECIFICALLY SUPPRESS DEFENSIVE-BEHAVIOR.
002945 03-04

INJECTIONS OF DOPAMINERGIC, CHOLINERGIC, SEROTONINERGIC AND GABAERGIC DRUGS INTO THE NUCLEUS-ACCUMBENS: EFFECTS ON LOCOMOTOR-ACTIVITY IN THE RAT.
003019 03-04

DOPAMINE AND DEMENTIA. AN ANIMAL-MODEL WITH DESTRUCTION OF THE MESOCORTICAL DOPAMINERGIC PATHWAY: A PRELIMINARY STUDY.
003085 03-04

DOPAMINERGIC AND GABAERGIC ASPECTS OF TARDIVE-DYSKINESIA.
003302 03-11

DOPAMINERGIC MECHANISMS IN THE TELEOST RETINA. II. FACTORS AFFECTING THE ACCUMULATION OF CYCLIC-AMP IN PIECES OF INTACT CARP RETINA.
003776 04-03

RELATIONSHIP BETWEEN THE PRESENCE OF DOPAMINERGIC NEURONS AND GABA-RECEPTORS IN SUBSTANTIA-NIGRA: EFFECTS OF LESIONS.
003797 04-03

INFLUENCE OF THE DOPAMINERGIC AGONISTS BROMOCRIPTINE, PIRIBEDIL AND NOMIFENSINE ON THE SYMPATHETIC NEURAL TRANSMISSION IN THE NICTITATING MEMBRANE OF THE CAT.
003822 04-03

STUDIES ON AXONAL TRANSPORT IN DOPAMINERGIC NEURONS: EFFECT OF NEUROPHARMACOLOGIC LESIONS.
003858 04-03

CHANGE IN CATECHOLAMINE SENSITIVE NA-K-ATPASE ACTIVITY IN THE RAT STRIATUM MICROSOMES FOLLOWING ELECTROLYTIC OR 6 HYDROXYDOPAMINE-INDUCED LESIONS OF DOPAMINERGIC NEURONS.
003871 04-03

CENTRAL DOPAMINERGIC NEURONS DURING DEVELOPMENT OF GENETIC AND DOCA-SALT HYPERTENSION IN THE RAT.
003899 04-03

EFFECTS OF METHAMPHETAMINE ON BLOOD FLOW IN THE CAUDATE-PUTAMEN AFTER LESIONS OF THE NIGROSTRIATAL DOPAMINERGIC BUNDLE IN THE RAT.
003910 04-03

DOPAMINERGIC MECHANISMS IN THE TELEOST RETINA. I. DOPAMINE-SENSITIVE ADENYLATE-CYCLASE IN HOMOGENATES OF CARP RETINA; EFFECTS OF AGONISTS, ANTAGONISTS AND ERGOTS.
004051 04-03

ACTIONS OF MU, KAPPA, SIGMA, DELTA AND AGONIST/ANTAGONIST OPIATES ON STRIATAL DOPAMINERGIC FUNCTION.
004053 04-03

EFFECTS OF DOPAMINERGIC DRUGS ON PHENCYCLIDINE-INDUCED BEHAVIOR IN THE RAT.
004083 04-04

GENETIC VARIATIONS IN MIDBRAIN DOPAMINE CELL NUMBER: PARALLEL WITH DIFFERENCES IN RESPONSES TO DOPAMINERGIC AGONISTS AND IN NATURALISTIC BEHAVIORS MEDIATED BY CENTRAL DOPAMINERGIC-SYSTEMS. (UNPUBLISHED PAPER).
004112 04-04

RELATION BETWEEN BRAIN CATECHOLAMINE-RECEPTORS AND DOPAMINERGIC STEREOTYPY IN RAT STRAINS.
004131 04-04

DOPAMINERGIC AGONISTS DIFFERENTIALLY AFFECT OPEN-FIELD ACTIVITY OF RATS WITH A10 LESIONS.
004135 04-04

DOPAMINERGIC NEURONS OF SPINAL-CORD: A POSSIBLE SITE FOR THE ACTION OF NEUROLEPTIC-DRUGS.
004188 04-04

GENOTYPIC INFLUENCES ON STRIATAL DOPAMINERGIC REGULATION IN MICE.
004217 04-04

CHANGES OF RESPONSE TO DOPAMINERGIC DRUGS IN RATS SUBMITTED TO REM SLEEP DEPRIVATION.
004239 04-04

TONIC IMMOBILITY IN DOMESTIC FOWL: POSSIBLE INTERACTION OF SEROTONERGIC AND DOPAMINERGIC MECHANISMS.
004246 04-04

IN NORMAL YOUNG MEN ACUTE DOPAMINERGIC BLOCKADE DOES NOT IMPAIR FREE WATER EXCRETION FOLLOWING A STANDARD WATER LOAD.
004600 04-15

DOPAMINERGIC-ACTIVITY
ROLE OF THE NEOSTRIATAL DOPAMINERGIC-ACTIVITY IN SEQUENCING AND SELECTING BEHAVIOURAL-STRATEGIES: FACILITATION OF PROCESSES INVOLVED IN SELECTING THE BEST STRATEGY IN A STRESSFUL-SITUATION.
000366 01-04

MORPHINE-DEPENDENCE AND DOPAMINERGIC-ACTIVITY: TESTS OF CIRCLING RESPONSES IN RATS WITH UNILATERAL NIGRAL LESIONS.
001641 02-04

CLINICAL PROCESSES AND CENTRAL DOPAMINERGIC-ACTIVITY IN PSYCHOTIC-DISORDERS.
002098 02-11

THE EFFECT OF ALTERED DOPAMINERGIC-ACTIVITY ON FOOD INTAKE IN THE RAT: EVIDENCE FOR AN OPTIMAL LEVEL OF DOPAMINERGIC-ACTIVITY FOR BEHAVIOR.
002632 02-17

DOPAMINERGIC-AGENT
A NEW DOPAMINERGIC-AGENT IN CURRENT PSYCHIATRIC-PRACTICE.
003156 03-07

DOPAMINERGIC-AGENTS
THE EFFECTS OF DOPAMINERGIC-AGENTS ON THE LOCOMOTOR-ACTIVITY OF RATS AFTER HIGH-DOSES OF METHYLAMPHETAMINE.
000427 01-04

DOPAMINERGIC-EFFECTS
CENTRAL DOPAMINERGIC-EFFECTS OF ERGOLINE DERIVATIVES.
002540 02-17

DOPAMINERGIC-RECEPTOR
MODIFICATION OF DOPAMINERGIC-RECEPTOR SENSITIVITY IN RAT-BRAIN AFTER AMYGDALOID KINDLING.
000106 01-03

EFFECTS OF LISURIDE ON BODY-TEMPERATURE OF RATS AND RABBITS: RELATION TO MICROSOMAL BIOTRANSFORMATION AND DOPAMINERGIC-RECEPTOR STIMULATION.
001161 02-03

UNITARY DOPAMINERGIC-RECEPTOR COMPOSED OF COOPERATIVELY LINKED AGONIST AND ANTAGONIST SUBUNIT BINDING-SITES.
001342 02-03

EFFECTS OF CHLORPROMAZINE ON DOPAMINERGIC-RECEPTOR FUNCTIONS IN RAT-BRAIN -- DIFFERENCE OF THE RESPONSE OF SEVERAL DOPAMINERGIC-SYSTEMS AFTER CHRONIC ADMINISTRATION.
002773 03-03

AN ENHANCED SENSITIVITY OF MUSCARINIC CHOLINERGIC-RECEPTOR ASSOCIATED WITH DOPAMINERGIC-RECEPTOR SUBSENSITIVITY AFTER CHRONIC ANTIDEPRESSANT TREATMENT.
002788 03-03

A CONTROLLED-STUDY OF L-DOPA IN SCHIZOPHRENIA WITH REFERENCE TO THE THEORY OF DOPAMINERGIC-RECEPTOR HYPERSENSITIVITY.
004312 04-08

DOPAMINERGIC-RECEPTORS
SELECTIVE INFLUENCE OF ERGOT ALKALOIDS ON CORTICAL AND STRIATAL DOPAMINERGIC-RECEPTORS AND SEROTONERGIC-RECEPTORS.
001447 02-03

EFFECT OF LONG-TERM-TREATMENT WITH HALOPERIDOL AND SULPIRIDE ON DIFFERENT TYPES OF DOPAMINERGIC-RECEPTORS.
001512 02-03

EVIDENCE FOR THERMOREGULATORY DOPAMINERGIC-RECEPTORS LOCATED IN THE PREOPTICUS-MEDIALIS-NUCLEUS OF THE RAT HYPOTHALAMUS.
003754 04-03

EFFECTS OF ACUTE AND CHRONIC ADMINISTRATION OF PHENCYCLIDINE ON DOPAMINERGIC-RECEPTORS IN RAT STRIATUM.
003901 04-03

DOPAMINERGIC-SUPERSENSITIVITY
DOPAMINERGIC-SUPERSENSITIVITY: INFLUENCE OF DOPAMINE AGONISTS AND DRUGS USED FOR THE TREATMENT OF TARDIVE-DYSKINESIA.
001169 02-03

STUDIES ON THE SPECIFICITY AND REVERSAL OF NEUROLEPTIC-INDUCED DOPAMINERGIC-SUPERSENSITIVITY. (PH.D. DISSERTATION).
001469 02-03

REDUCTION OF DOPAMINERGIC-SUPERSENSITIVITY BY A SINGLE-DOSE OF AMPHETAMINE.
001642 02-04

EFFECTS OF AGE ON DOPAMINERGIC-SUPERSENSITIVITY INDUCED BY CHRONIC FLUPHENAZINE.
003940 04-03

DOPAMINERGIC-SYSTEM
ACUTE AND CHRONIC HALOPERIDOL TREATMENT: EFFECTS ON NIGROSTRIATAL DOPAMINERGIC-SYSTEM ACTIVITY.
001153 02-03

CHRONOLOGY OF EXTRAPYRAMIDAL-EFFECTS OF NEUROLEPTIC-DRUGS AND THE NIGROSTRIATAL DOPAMINERGIC-SYSTEM.
002449 02-15

NEUROLEPTICS: ACTIVATION OR INHIBITION OF THE DOPAMINERGIC-SYSTEM?
003424 03-13

DOPAMINERGIC-SYSTEMS
DOPAMINERGIC-SYSTEMS AND SPEECH FLUENCY.
000821 01-14
INFLUENCE OF DOPAMINERGIC-SYSTEMS ON THE LATERAL HABENULAR NUCLEUS OF THE RAT.
001365 02-03
EFFECT OF REPEATED TREATMENT WITH NEUROLEPTICS ON DOPAMINE METABOLISM IN CELL BODIES AND TERMINALS OF DOPAMINERGIC-SYSTEMS IN THE RAT-BRAIN.
001464 02-03
TOLERANCE TO FLUPHENAZINE AND SUPERSENSITIVITY TO APOMORPHINE IN CENTRAL DOPAMINERGIC-SYSTEMS AFTER CHRONIC FLUPHENAZINE-DECANOATE TREATMENT.
001820 02-04
POSSIBLE INVOLVEMENT OF BRAIN DOPAMINERGIC-SYSTEMS IN THE EXPRESSION OF EMOTIONS IN DREAMS.
002325 02-14
EFFECTS OF CHLORPROMAZINE ON DOPAMINERGIC-RECEPTOR FUNCTIONS IN RAT-BRAIN -- DIFFERENCE OF THE RESPONSE OF SEVERAL DOPAMINERGIC-SYSTEMS AFTER CHRONIC ADMINISTRATION.
002773 03-03
GENETIC VARIATIONS IN MIDBRAIN DOPAMINE CELL NUMBER: PARALLEL WITH DIFFERENCES IN RESPONSES TO DOPAMINERGIC AGONISTS AND IN NATURALISTIC BEHAVIORS MEDIATED BY CENTRAL DOPAMINERGIC-SYSTEMS. (UNPUBLISHED PAPER).
004112 04-04

DORSAL-HORN
THE EFFECTS OF MORPHINE ON THE ACTIVITY OF CERTAIN DORSAL-HORN NEURONS OF THE SPINAL-CORD INVOLVED IN NOCICEPTIVE PROCESSES.
000028 01-03
DOES SYSTEMIC MORPHINE INCREASE DESCENDING INHIBITORY CONTROLS OF DORSAL-HORN NEURONES INVOLVED IN NOCICEPTION?
000175 01-03
DEPRESSION AND FACILITATION OF SYNAPTIC RESPONSES IN CAT DORSAL-HORN BY SUBSTANCE-P ADMINISTERED INTO SUBSTANTIA-GELATINOSA.
001191 02-03
THE STEREOSPECIFIC EFFECT OF NALOXONE ON RAT DORSAL-HORN NEURONES: INHIBITION IN SUPERFICIAL LAMINAE AND EXCITATION IN DEEPER LAMINAE.
001226 02-03
SUPRASPINAL INHIBITION OF THE EXCITATION OF DORSAL-HORN NEURONES BY IMPULSES IN UNMYELINATED PRIMARY AFFERENTS: LACK OF EFFECT BY STRYCHNINE AND BICUCULLINE.
003778 04-03
MORPHINE DEPRESSES DORSAL-HORN NEURON RESPONSES TO CONTROLLED NOXIOUS AND NONNOXIOUS CUTANEOUS STIMULATION.
003782 04-03

DORSOLATERAL
INFLUENCE OF AMPHETAMINE AND PHENYLPROPANOLAMINE ON FOOD INTAKE, ACTIVITY, AND BODY-TEMPERATURE IN RATS WITH VENTROMEDIAL HYPOTHALAMIC OR DORSOLATERAL TEGMENTAL DAMAGE.
000322 01-03
EFFECTS OF AMPHETAMINE AND PHENYLPROPANOLAMINE ON FOOD INTAKE IN RATS WITH VENTROMEDIAL HYPOTHALAMIC OR DORSOLATERAL TEGMENTAL DAMAGE.
001818 02-04
EFFECTS OF DORSOLATERAL TEGMENTAL LESIONS ON AMPHETAMINE-INDUCED AND LITHIUM-INDUCED TASTE-AVERSIONS.
003114 03-04

DOSAGE
DRUG RESPONSE DIFFERENCES OF HIGH AND STANDARD DOSAGE OF FLUPHENAZINE-DECANOATE IN RELATION TO SCHIZOPHRENIC-SYMPTOMS.
000562 01-08
A PRELIMINARY STUDY ON DETERMINATION OF THE OPTIMUM OPIPRAMOL DOSAGE IN DEPRESSIVE-PATIENTS.
000601 01-09
VALPROIC-ACID DOSAGE AND PLASMA PROTEIN BINDING AND CLEARANCE.
000755 01-13
INTRAMUSCULAR HALOPERIDOL-DECANOATE FOR NEUROLEPTIC MAINTENANCE-THERAPY: EFFICACY, DOSAGE SCHEDULE AND PLASMA LEVELS: AN OPEN MULTICENTER-STUDY.
000758 01-13
CORRELATION BETWEEN DAILY DOSAGE OF CHLORPROMAZINE AND SUBSEQUENT SUPERSENSITIVITY.
001845 02-05
PREDICTION OF DOSAGE OF LITHIUM-CARBONATE: USE OF A STANDARD PREDICTIVE METHOD.
001991 02-09
A NEW DOSAGE SCHEDULE FOR PIMOZIDE IN THE ACUTE STABILIZATION AND MAINTENANCE-TREATMENT OF PSYCHOSIS.
002022 02-09
EUHYPNOS-FORTE, HIGH-DOSE TEMAZEPAM FOR RESISTANT INSOMNIA: POSTMARKETING SURVEILLANCE IN 10,057 PATIENTS UNRESPONSIVE TO CONVENTIONAL HYPNOTIC DOSAGE.
002324 02-14

EEG ASSESSMENTS OF DOSAGE AND SLEEP PROFILES FOR A HYPNOTIC-DRUG OF THE TRIAZOLOTHIENODIACEPINE SERIES.
002338 02-14
INFUSIONS INTO THE OCULOMOTOR NUCLEUS OR NERVE: A METHOD OF ESTIMATING THE DOSAGE AT WHICH TRANSMITTER ANTAGONISTS INFUSED INTRACRANIALLY PRODUCE NONSPECIFIC BLOCKING OF NEURAL ACTIVITY.
003134 03-06
STEADY-STATE LITHIUM BLOOD LEVEL FLUCTUATIONS IN MAN FOLLOWING ADMINISTRATION OF A LITHIUM-CARBONATE CONVENTIONAL AND CONTROLLED-RELEASE DOSAGE FORM.
003151 03-07
DOSAGE OF INTRATUMORAL LITHIUM (CEREBRAL GLIOBLASTOMA): ON A FAILURE OF TREATMENT OF MANIC-DEPRESSIVE-PSYCHOSIS.
003226 03-09
NATURAL AND THERAPEUTIC ENVIRONMENTAL INDICATORS OF MAINTENANCE DOSAGE REQUIREMENTS.
003561 03-16
DOSAGE FORM DESIGN FOR IMPROVEMENT OF BIOAVAILABILITY OF LEVODOPA III: INFLUENCE OF DOSE ON PHARMACOKINETIC BEHAVIOR OF LEVODOPA IN DOGS AND PARKINSONIAN-PATIENTS.
004551 04-13

DOSAGES
A DOUBLE-BLIND COMPARISON OF THREE DOSAGES OF FLUTROLINE (CP-36584) IN THE TREATMENT OF SCHIZOPHRENIA.
004333 04-08

DOSE
FIRST DOSE BEHAVIORAL-TOLERANCE TO PHENCYCLIDINE ON FOOD REWARDED BAR-PRESSING-BEHAVIOR IN THE RAT.
000462 01-04
DOSE AND PHYSICAL-DEPENDENCE AS FACTORS IN THE SELF-ADMINISTRATION OF MORPHINE BY RATS.
000497 01-04
WHAT IS THE BEST MAINTENANCE DOSE OF NEUROLEPTICS IN SCHIZOPHRENIA?
000547 01-08
SINTAMIL IN THE TREATMENT OF DEPRESSION: A COMPARISON OF SINGLE VS. DIVIDED DOSE ADMINISTRATION.
000629 01-09
PRACTICAL AND THEORETICAL ASPECTS OF PHENYTOIN ADMINISTRATION. I. RELATIONSHIP BETWEEN DOSE AND PLASMA CONCENTRATION.
000760 01-13
EFFECT OF DOSE ON PHENYTOIN ABSORPTION.
000773 01-13
DETERMINATION OF DOSE PLASMA CONCENTRATION RELATIONSHIP OF PHENOBARBITAL IN EPILEPTIC-PATIENTS BY A NEW SPECIFIC RADIOIMMUNOASSAY.
000902 01-16
CUMULATIVE DOSE RESPONSE-CURVES IN BEHAVIORAL-PHARMACOLOGY.
001883 02-06
MIANSERIN: DETERMINATION OF THERAPEUTIC DOSE RANGE.
002026 02-09
DOSE SIZE AND INTERDOSE INTERVAL EFFECTS ON MORPHINE-TOLERANCE IN THE RAT. (PH.D. DISSERTATION).
003090 03-04
EFFECT OF DOSE ON BIOAVAILABILITY OF ORAL DIGOXIN.
003161 03-07
PROGNOSIS IN SCHIZOPHRENIA: INDIVIDUAL DIFFERENCES IN PSYCHOLOGICAL RESPONSE TO A TEST DOSE OF ANTIPSYCHOTIC-DRUG AND THEIR RELATIONSHIP TO BLOOD AND SALIVA LEVELS AND TREATMENT OUTCOME.
003189 03-08
FACTORS REGULATING DRUG CUE SENSITIVITY: LIMITS OF DISCRIMINABILITY AND THE ROLE OF A PROGRESSIVELY DECREASING TRAINING DOSE IN FENTANYL SALINE DISCRIMINATION.
004088 04-04
DOSAGE FORM DESIGN FOR IMPROVEMENT OF BIOAVAILABILITY OF LEVODOPA III: INFLUENCE OF DOSE ON PHARMACOKINETIC BEHAVIOR OF LEVODOPA IN DOGS AND PARKINSONIAN-PATIENTS.
004551 04-13

DOSE-DEPENDENT
DISPOSITION OF VALPROIC-ACID IN THE RAT: DOSE-DEPENDENT METABOLISM, DISTRIBUTION, ENTEROHEPATIC RECIRCULATION AND CHOLERETIC-EFFECT.
000073 01-03
STEREOSPECIFIC, DOSE-DEPENDENT ANTAGONISM BY NALOXONE OF NONOPIATE BEHAVIOR IN MICE.
000411 01-04
DOSE-DEPENDENT, AMPHETAMINE-INDUCED CHANGES IN PERMEABILITY OF THE BLOOD-BRAIN-BARRIER OF NORMOTENSIVE-RATS AND SPONTANEOUSLY HYPERTENSIVE-RATS.
001197 02-03
DOSE-DEPENDENT PHARMACOKINETICS OF ALPHA METHYL-P-TYROSINE (ALPHA MT) AND COMPARISON OF CATECHOLAMINE TURNOVER-RATES AFTER TWO DOSES OF ALPHA MT.
001532 02-03

APPARENT SEROTONERGIC MODULATION OF THE DOSE-DEPENDENT BIPHASIC RESPONSE OF NEOSTRIATAL NEURONS PRODUCED BY D-AMPHETAMINE.
003981 04-03

DOSE-EFFECT
DOSE-EFFECT OF DEAE ON SUBJECTIVE PROBLEMS, VERTIGO, DEPRESSION, ASTHENIA, CEPHALALGIA, AND TONIC POSTURAL ACTIVITY PROBLEMS RECORDED WITH STATOKINESIMETER IN POSTCONCUSSIONAL-SYNDROME.
004472 04-11

DOSE-EFFECTS
THE DIFFERENTIAL DOSE-EFFECTS OF METHYLPHENIDATE ON HYPERACTIVE-CHILDREN AND THEIR MOTHERS. (PH.D. DISSERTATION).
002143 02-11

DOSE-EFFECTS OF SECOBARBITAL IN A STERNBERG MEMORY SCANNING TASK.
003460 03-14

DOSE-RELATED
UNUSUAL DOSE-RELATED EFFECT OF AN ENDORPHIN ANALOG IN A COMPLEX MAZE.
001674 02-04

LITHIUM INDUCES DOSE-RELATED INCREASES AND DECREASES IN ACTIVITY LEVELS IN THE RAT.
004079 04-04

DOSE-RESPONSE
FLASH-EVOKED AFTERDISCHARGE IN RAT AS A MODEL OF THE ABSENCE SEIZURE: DOSE-RESPONSE STUDIES WITH THERAPEUTIC DRUGS.
000160 01-03

MODULATION OF APOMORPHINE-INDUCED STEREOTYPY BY ESTROGEN: TIME-COURSE AND DOSE-RESPONSE.
001636 02-04

AMPHETAMINE AND MATERNAL-BEHAVIOR; DOSE-RESPONSE RELATIONSHIPS.
001752 02-04

DOSE-RESPONSE STUDY OF THE PRECIPITATED ABSTINENCE-SYNDROME FOR MORPHINE: SYSTEMIC VS PERIAQUEDUCTAL GRAY NALOXONE. (PH.D. DISSERTATION).
002979 03-04

AN IMPROVED MODEL OF INTRASPECIFIC AGGRESSION: DOSE-RESPONSE ANALYSIS OF APOMORPHINE-INDUCED-FIGHTING AND STEREOTYPY IN THE RAT.
002983 03-04

DOSE-RESPONSE RELATIONSHIP BETWEEN NALOXONE INJECTIONS AND INTAKE OF SUCROSE SOLUTION.
003118 03-04

DOPAMINE INHIBITS BURST-FIRING OF NEUROSECRETORY CELL R-15 IN APLYSIA-CALIFORNICA: ESTABLISHMENT OF A DOSE-RESPONSE RELATIONSHIP.
003806 04-03

DOSES
A COMPARISON OF HUMAN TACTILE STIMULUS VELOCITY DISCRIMINATION WITH THE ABILITY OF S-I CORTICAL NEURONS IN AWAKE RHESUS-MONKEYS TO SIGNAL THE SAME VELOCITY DIFFERENCES BEFORE AND AFTER NONANESTHETIC DOSES OF PENTOBARBITAL.
000055 01-03

CONTROLLED-COMPARISON OF MEDIUM AND HIGH CLOROTEPIN DOSES IN CHRONIC SCHIZOPHRENIA.
000548 01-08

THE EFFECT OF SMALL AND MODERATE DOSES OF D-AMPHETAMINE ON HUNGER, MOOD, AND AROUSAL IN MAN.
000807 01-14

PERSPECTIVE ON ADEQUATE INDIVIDUALIZED DRUG DOSES.
000959 01-17

EFFECT OF REPEATED ELECTROCONVULSIVE-SHOCKS (ECS) ON SUBTHRESHOLD DOSES OF SOME CNS STIMULANTS.
001361 02-03

DECREASED BENZODIAZEPINE-RECEPTOR DENSITY IN RAT-CEREBELLUM FOLLOWING NEUROTOXIC DOSES OF PHENYTOIN.
001373 02-03

EFFECT OF ANTINOCICEPTIVE DOSES OF OXOTREMORINE ON MOUSE-BRAIN ACETYLCHOLINE TURNOVER-RATE.
001513 02-03

DOSE-DEPENDENT PHARMACOKINETICS OF ALPHA METHYL-P-TYROSINE (ALPHA MT) AND COMPARISON OF CATECHOLAMINE TURNOVER-RATES AFTER TWO DOSES OF ALPHA MT.
001532 02-03

HEMODYNAMIC FAILURE INDUCED BY NARCOTIC AND TOXIC DOSES OF 12 CNS DEPRESSANTS IN INTACT AND PITHED RATS.
001855 02-05

DISORDERS OF SMOOTH-PURSUIT EYE-MOVEMENTS IN SCHIZOPHRENICS AND THE EFFECT OF NEUROLEPTICS IN THERAPEUTIC DOSES.
001912 02-08

PHARMACOKINETICS OF DIPOTASSIUM-CHLORAZEPATE IN PATIENTS AFTER REPEATED 50MG ORAL DOSES.
002211 02-13

QUANTITATIVE STUDY OF THE DISTRIBUTION OF LITHIUM IN THE MOUSE-BRAIN FOR VARIOUS DOSES OF LITHIUM GIVEN TO THE ANIMAL.
002299 02-13

THE EFFECTS OF COMBINED SEDATIVE AND ANXIOLYTIC-PREPARATIONS ON SUBJECTIVE ASPECTS OF SLEEP AND OBJECTIVE MEASURE OF AROUSAL AND PERFORMANCE THE MORNING FOLLOWING NOCTURNAL MEDICATION: II. REPEATED DOSES.
002331 02-14

CARDIOVASCULAR-EFFECTS OF THERAPEUTIC DOSES OF TRICYCLIC-ANTIDEPRESSANTS: IMPORTANCE OF BLOOD LEVEL MONITORING.
002456 02-15

AN EVALUATION OF MAPROTILINE INTRAVENOUS KINETICS AND COMPARISON OF TWO ORAL DOSES.
002497 02-16

FLUORESCENCE HISTOCHEMISTRY INDICATES DAMAGE OF STRIATAL DOPAMINE NERVE TERMINALS IN RATS AFTER MULTIPLE DOSES OF METHAMPHETAMINE.
002812 03-03

SINGLE OR REPEATED ADMINISTRATION OF SMALL DOSES OF APOMORPHINE ON WATER INTAKE AND ACTIVITY IN WATER-DEPRIVED RATS.
002981 03-04

CORRELATION BETWEEN ANTIAVOIDANCE ACTIVITIES OF ANTIPSYCHOTIC-DRUGS IN RATS AND DAILY CLINICAL DOSES.
003032 03-04

2,4,5 TRICHLOROPHENOXYACETIC-ACID CAUSES BEHAVIORAL-EFFECTS IN CHICKENS AT ENVIRONMENTALLY RELEVANT DOSES.
003079 03-04

EXCESSIVE PLASMA CONCENTRATIONS OF TRICYCLIC-ANTIDEPRESSANTS RESULTING FROM USUAL DOSES: A REPORT OF SIX CASES.
003479 03-15

LONG-TERM EFFECTS OF MULTIPLE DOSES OF METHAMPHETAMINE ON TRYPTOPHAN-HYDROXYLASE AND TYROSINE-HYDROXYLASE ACTIVITY IN RAT-BRAIN.
003850 04-03

THE EFFECT OF SMALL DOSES OF HALOPERIDOL AND CLOZAPINE ON BEHAVIORAL SHIFTS IN CATS, ARISING AFTER CESSATION OF ELECTRICAL-STIMULATION OF THE CAUDATE-NUCLEUS.
004067 04-04

AGE-SPECIFIC DOSES OF LORMETAZEPAM AS A NIGHT SEDATIVE IN CASES OF CHRONIC SLEEP-DISTURBANCE.
004309 04-07

PHARMACOKINETICS OF CLOXAZOLAM IN MAN AFTER SINGLE AND MULTIPLE ORAL DOSES.
004530 04-13

CONCENTRATIONS OF CHLORPROMAZINE AND TWO OF ITS ACTIVE METABOLITES IN PLASMA AND CEREBROSPINAL-FLUID OF PSYCHOTIC-PATIENTS TREATED WITH FIXED DRUG DOSES.
004559 04-13

DOSING
DOUBLE-BLIND COMPARISON OF KETAZOLAM, DIAZEPAM AND PLACEBO IN ONCE-A-DAY VS T.I.D. DOSING.
000660 01-11

DOUBLE-BLIND COMPARISON OF KETAZOLAM AND PLACEBO USING ONCE-A-DAY DOSING.
002067 02-10

SINGLE POINT ESTIMATION OF PHENYTOIN DOSING REQUIREMENT.
003562 03-16

DOTHIEPIN
A COMPARATIVE EVALUATION OF DOTHIEPIN (PROTHIEDEN) AND IMIPRAMINE.
000583 01-09

AN OVERVIEW OF SEVENTEEN YEARS OF EXPERIENCE WITH DOTHIEPIN IN THE TREATMENT OF DEPRESSION IN EUROPE.
001995 02-09

A COMPARISON OF TRAZODONE AND DOTHIEPIN IN DEPRESSION.
004394 04-09

DOUBLE-BLIND
ANTIDEPRESSANT TREATMENT BY INTRAVENOUS ADMINISTRATION COMPARED TO PERORAL ADMINISTRATION: A DOUBLE-BLIND STUDY OF QUINUPRAMINE.
000552 01-08

DOUBLE-BLIND COMPARISON OF HALOPERIDOL AND THIOTHIXENE WITH AFTERCARE TREATMENT EVALUATION IN PSYCHIATRIC-OUTPATIENTS WITH SCHIZOPHRENIA.
000574 01-08

A DOUBLE-BLIND GROUP COMPARATIVE-TRIAL OF MIANSERIN AND DIAZEPAM IN DEPRESSED-OUTPATIENTS.
000592 01-09

DOUBLE-BLIND COMPARISON OF KETAZOLAM, DIAZEPAM AND PLACEBO IN ONCE-A-DAY VS T.I.D. DOSING.
000660 01-11

PSYCHOPATHOMETRIC DOUBLE-BLIND COURSE STUDY WITH NICERGOLINE VERSUS PLACEBO IN GERIATRIC-PATIENTS WITH TRANSIENT-SYNDROMES.
000665 01-11

A COMPUTER OCULOGRAPHIC AND EEG DOUBLE-BLIND STUDY INCLUDING WELL-BEING FOR DETERMINING CHANGED VIGILANCE UNDER THERAPY WITH TIAPRIDE.
000751 01-13

MAINTENANCE-THERAPY WITH FLUPHENAZINE-DECANOATE AND OXYPROTHEPINE-DECANOATE IN SCHIZOPHRENIC-PATIENTS – A DOUBLE-BLIND CROSS-OVER COMPARATIVE-STUDY.
001924 02-08

CONTROLLED-COMPARISON OF PERPHENAZINE WITH PERPHENAZINE IN SCHIZOPHRENIA: A METHODICAL-CHECK OF A DOUBLE-BLIND CROSS-OVER DESIGN.
001937 02-08

COMPARISON OF THE EFFECTS OF LOFEPRAMINE AND MIANSERIN IN DEPRESSED-PATIENTS IN A DOUBLE-BLIND TRIAL.
.001996 02-09

THE USE OF VILOXAZINE IN HOSPITALIZED DEPRESSED-PATIENTS: RANDOM COMPARISON WITH IMIPRAMINE IN A DOUBLE-BLIND TRIAL.
001998 02-09

ANTIDEPRESSANT ACTION OF AMINEPTINE: CONTROLLED DOUBLE-BLIND STUDY.
002030 02-09

DOUBLE-BLIND CONTROLLED EXPERIMENT: AMINEPTINE VERSUS AMITRIPTYLINE USING THE HAMILTON-DEPRESSION-RATING-SCALE.
002050 02-09

DOUBLE-BLIND CONTROLLED-STUDY: AMINEPTINE VERSUS TRIMIPRAMINE.
002051 02-09

DOUBLE-BLIND COMPARISON OF KETAZOLAM AND PLACEBO USING ONCE-A-DAY DOSING.
002067 02-10

DOUBLE-BLIND CLINICAL ASSESSMENT OF ALPRAZOLAM, A NEW BENZODIAZEPINE DERIVATIVE, IN THE TREATMENT OF MODERATE TO SEVERE ANXIETY.
002070 02-10

A DOUBLE-BLIND PARALLEL GROUP COMPARISON OF SINGLE-BEDTIME-DOSES OF HALAZEPAM AND PLACEBO.
002079 02-10

DOUBLE-BLIND CONTROLLED-STUDY ON THE PSYCHOLEPTIC-EFFECTS OF AMINEPTINE IN MENTALLY-HANDICAPPED CHILDREN WITHOUT PERSONALITY-PROBLEMS.
002116 02-11

NOMIFENSINE AS CONCOMITANT THERAPY IN THE TREATMENT OF PARKINSON-PATIENTS. A DOUBLE-BLIND PLACEBO-CONTROLLED-STUDY.
002130 02-11

A DOUBLE-BLIND STUDY WITH ORG-GB-94 IN PREMENOPAUSAL-WOMEN.
002173 02-11

A CONTROLLED DOUBLE-BLIND STUDY OF HALOPERIDOL VERSUS THIORIDAZINE IN THE TREATMENT OF RESTLESS MENTALLY-SUBNORMAL-PATIENTS: SERUM LEVELS AND CLINICAL-EFFECTS.
002185 02-11

DOUBLE-BLIND EVALUATION OF REINFORCING AND ANORECTIC-ACTIONS OF WEIGHT-CONTROL MEDICATIONS: INTERACTION OF PHARMACOLOGICAL-TREATMENT AND BEHAVIORAL-TREATMENTS.
002314 02-14

FACTORS DETERMINING PATIENT TENURE ON A 3-YEAR DOUBLE-BLIND INVESTIGATION OF PIMOZIDE VERSUS FLUPHENAZINE-HCL.
002513 02-17

A DOUBLE-BLIND CROSSED CLINICAL-STUDY WITH A NEW PSYCHOPHARMACEUTICAL: TIADIPONE (QM-6008), DIAZEPAM, AND A PLACEBO.
003153 03-07

SYNERGISM OF COMBINED LITHIUM NEUROLEPTIC THERAPY: A DOUBLE-BLIND, PLACEBO-CONTROLLED CASE-STUDY.
003165 03-08

PIPERIDONE IN CHRONIC SCHIZOPHRENIC-PATIENTS: A CONTROLLED DOUBLE-BLIND STUDY.
003184 03-08

DOUBLE-BLIND STUDY OF MIANSERIN AND AMITRIPTYLINE.
003231 03-09

PROPHYLACTIC LITHIUM WITH AND WITHOUT IMIPRAMINE FOR BIPOLAR-I-PATIENTS: A DOUBLE-BLIND STUDY.
003233 03-09

A DOUBLE-BLIND COMPARISON BETWEEN AMOXAPINE AND AMITRIPTYLINE IN DEPRESSED-INPATIENTS.
003234 03-09

EFFICACY OF DESIPRAMINE IN MILDLY DEPRESSED-PATIENTS: A DOUBLE-BLIND, PLACEBO-CONTROLLED-TRIAL.
003262 03-09

ANALYSIS OF SINGLE-BLIND, DOUBLE-BLIND PROCEDURES, MAINTENANCE OF PLACEBO-EFFECTS, AND DRUG-INDUCED DYSKINESIA WITH MENTALLY-RETARDED PERSONS -- BRIEF REPORT.
003298 03-11

A DOUBLE-BLIND, PLACEBO-CONTROLLED-STUDY OF PIRACETAM IN ELDERLY PSYCHIATRIC-PATIENTS.
003305 03-11

TREATMENT OF ORGANIC-BRAIN-DISTURBANCES IN ELDERLY-PATIENTS. A CLINICAL DOUBLE-BLIND STUDY WITH MACROMOLECULAR ORGAN LYSATES (CYTOPLASMATIC THERAPY ACCORDING TO THEURER).
003327 03-11

DOUBLE-BLIND COMPARISON OF ALPRAZOLAM AND DIAZEPAM FOR SUBCHRONIC WITHDRAWAL FROM ALCOHOL.
003332 03-11

A DOUBLE-BLIND, PLACEBO-CONTROLLED, CROSS-OVER TRIAL OF CARBAMAZEPINE IN OVERACTIVE, SEVERELY MENTALLY-HANDICAPPED PATIENTS.
003365 03-11

PSYCHOTROPIC-DRUG-INDUCED CHANGES IN AUDITORY AVERAGED EVOKED-POTENTIALS: RESULTS OF A DOUBLE-BLIND TRIAL USING AN OBJECTIVE FULLY AUTOMATED AEP ANALYSIS METHOD.
003412 03-13

DES-TYROSYL-GAMMA-ENDORPHIN IN SCHIZOPHRENIA: A DOUBLE-BLIND TRIAL IN 13 PATIENTS.
004322 04-08

A DOUBLE-BLIND COMPARISON OF THREE DOSAGES OF FLUTROLINE (CP-36584) IN THE TREATMENT OF SCHIZOPHRENIA.
004333 04-08

TRAZODONE EFFICACY AND SAFETY IN ENDOGENOUS DEPRESSION: A DOUBLE-BLIND COMPARISON WITH IMIPRAMINE.
004346 04-09

A PRELIMINARY DOUBLE-BLIND STUDY ON THE EFFICACY OF CARBAMAZEPINE IN PROPHYLAXIS OF MANIC-DEPRESSIVE-ILLNESS.
004388 04-09

A DOUBLE-BLIND MULTICENTRE-TRIAL COMPARING THE EFFICACY AND SIDE-EFFECTS OF MIANSERIN AND CHLORIMIPRAMINE IN DEPRESSED-INPATIENTS AND DEPRESSED-OUTPATIENTS.
004395 04-09

A DOUBLE-BLIND TRIAL: THE USE OF OXPRENOLOL AND DIAZEPAM IN ANXIETY.
004428 04-10

ANALYSIS OF SINGLE-BLIND AND DOUBLE-BLIND PROCEDURES, MAINTENANCE OF PLACEBO-EFFECTS AND DRUG-INDUCED DYSKINESIA WITH MENTALLY-RETARDED PERSON.
004437 04-11

THE EFFICACY OF PIRACETAM IN VERTIGO: A DOUBLE-BLIND STUDY IN PATIENTS WITH VERTIGO OF CENTRAL ORIGIN.
004478 04-11

A CLINICAL-EVALUATION OF THE EFFECTS OF A NEW PSYCHOTROPIC-AGENT, MEXAZOLAM (CS-386) ON PSYCHOSOMATIC-DISEASES AND NEUROSIS: A COMPARATIVE-STUDY WITH OXAZOLAM, USING THE DOUBLE-BLIND METHOD.
004491 04-11

DRUG PREFERENCE IN HUMANS: DOUBLE-BLIND CHOICE COMPARISON OF PENTOBARBITAL, DIAZEPAM AND PLACEBO.
004566 04-14

DOUBLE-PLACEBO
SINGLE-DOSE VERSUS MULTIPLE-DOSE COMPARATIVE-TRIAL OF DESIPRAMINE-HYDROCHLORIDE: A DOUBLE-PLACEBO METHOD.
002059 02-10

DOWN-SYNDROME
PHAGOCYTIC FUNCTION IN DOWN-SYNDROME – I. CHEMOTAXIS.
003401 03-13

DOWNS-SYNDROME
5 HYDROXYTRYPTOPHAN AND PYRIDOXINE: THEIR EFFECTS IN YOUNG CHILDREN WITH DOWNS-SYNDROME.
002161 02-11

A STUDY OF GAMMA AMINOBUTYRIC-ACID UPTAKE IN NORMAL AND DOWNS-SYNDROME PLATELETS.
003787 04-03

DOXEPIN
STIMULUS INTENSITY CONTROL IN DEPRESSION: A STUDY OF THE COMPARATIVE-EFFECT OF DOXEPIN AND AMITRIPTYLINE ON CORTICAL EVOKED-POTENTIALS.
000763 01-13

VILOXAZINE IN THE TREATMENT OF DEPRESSIVE-NEUROSIS: A CONTROLLED CLINICAL-STUDY WITH DOXEPIN AND PLACEBO.
002080 02-10

EFFECT OF DOXEPIN ON SEROTONIN METABOLISM IN RAT-BRAIN AND SEROTONIN UPTAKE BY HUMAN BLOOD-PLATELETS.
002243 02-13

CLOMIPRAMINE AND DOXEPIN IN DEPRESSIVE-NEUROSIS: PLASMA LEVELS AND THERAPEUTIC RESPONSE.
002258 02-13

SINGLE-DOSE PHARMACOKINETICS OF DOXEPIN IN HEALTHY VOLUNTEERS.
002303 02-13

RADIOIMMUNOASSAY FOR TOTAL DOXEPIN AND N DESMETHYLDOXEPIN IN PLASMA.
002499 02-16

THERAPEUTIC-EFFICACY OF DOXEPIN IN DIVIDED AND SINGLE-DOSE REGIME.
003259 03-09

DOXEPIN, A TRICYCLIC-ANTIDEPRESSANT, BINDS TO NORMAL, INTACT ASTROGLIAL CELLS IN CULTURES AND INHIBITS THE ISOPROTERENOL-INDUCED INCREASE IN CYCLIC-AMP PRODUCTION.
003836 04-03

PLASMA LEVELS OF THE CIS-ISOMERS AND TRANS-ISOMERS OF DOXEPIN AND DESMETHYLDOXEPIN AFTER ADMINISTRATION OF DOXEPIN TO PATIENTS.
004355 04-09

DOXEPIN PLASMA LEVELS AND ANXIOLYTIC RESPONSE.
004477 04-11

EFFECT OF THE CATECHOLAMINE-DEPLETING-AGENT 1 PHENYL-2-
THIAZOLYL-2-THIOUREA (U-14-624) ON DRUG METABOLISM IN THE
RAT.
000280 01-03

INFLUENCE OF GLUCOSE (IN VIVO OR IN VITRO) ON DURATION OF
NARCOTIC ANALGESICS AND ON THE KINETICS OF DRUG METABOLISM.
000292 01-03

INVESTIGATION OF NARCOTICS AND ANTITUSSIVES USING DRUG
DISCRIMINATION TECHNIQUES.
000447 01-04

A DRUG DISPENSER TO MEASURE INDIVIDUAL DRINKING IN RAT
COLONIES.
000530 01-06

DRUG AND SEIZURE IDENTIFICATION BY AUDIO-SPECTROMETRY. (PH.D.
DISSERTATION).
000532 01-06

DRUG RESPONSE DIFFERENCES OF HIGH AND STANDARD DOSAGE OF
FLUPHENAZINE-DECANOATE IN RELATION TO SCHIZOPHRENIC-
SYMPTOMS.
000562 01-08

TRICYCLIC-ANTIDEPRESSANT DRUG TOLERANCE IN ORIENTAL AND
OCCIDENTAL POPULATIONS.
000590 01-09

THE PCP PSYCHOSIS: PROLONGED INTOXICATION OR DRUG PRECIPITATED
FUNCTIONAL ILLNESS?
000739 01-12

DRUG SENSITIVE ECTO-ATPASE IN HUMAN LEUKOCYTES.
000779 01-13

HOW TO SUCCESSFULLY CHANGE A PATIENT FROM ONE DRUG TO
ANOTHER.
000913 01-17

AN ASSESSMENT PROGRAM TO REDUCE DRUG USE WITH THE
MENTALLY-RETARDED.
000937 01-17

HAZARDS OF DRUG USE AMONG THE ELDERLY.
000953 01-17

PERSPECTIVE ON ADEQUATE INDIVIDUALIZED DRUG DOSES.
000959 01-17

A NOTE ON PATTERNS OF DRUG PRESCRIBING IN A RESIDENTIAL-CENTER
FOR THE INTELLECTUALLY-HANDICAPPED.
000982 01-17

EXPERIMENTAL EVALUATION OF ANTIDEPRESSANT ACTIVITY OF
CLOMIPRAMINE, A NEW TRICYCLIC-ANTIDEPRESSANT DRUG.
001068 02-02

DRUG INTERFERENCE ON SOME BIOCHEMICAL-PARAMETERS OF RAT-
CEREBRAL-CORTEX DURING POSTISCHEMIC RECOVERY.
001126 02-03

ON THE MECHANISM OF A DIFFERENT DRUG DISTRIBUTION DURING
CONVULSIVE-SEIZURE IN COMPARISON TO ANESTHESIA.
001151 02-03

PROCEDURES FOR REDUCING DRUG INTAKE: NONHUMAN STUDIES.
001753 02-04

EXPERIMENTAL DEPENDENCE ON BARBITURATES: II. RELATIONSHIP
BETWEEN DRUG LEVELS IN SERUM AND BRAIN AND THE
DEVELOPMENT OF DEPENDENCE IN RATS.
001800 02-04

ELECTROLYTIC MICROINFUSION TRANSDUCER SYSTEM: AN ALTERNATIVE
METHOD OF INTRACRANIAL DRUG APPLICATION.
001861 02-06

METOCLOPRAMIDE: ANTIPSYCHOTIC-EFFICACY OF A DRUG LACKING
POTENCY IN RECEPTOR MODELS.
001948 02-08

PHARMACOKINETIC BASIS FOR PREDICTING STEADY-STATE SERUM DRUG
CONCENTRATIONS OF IMIPRAMINE FROM SINGLE-DOSE DATA.
002225 02-13

EFFECTS OF CAFFEINE ON PLASMA FREE FATTY-ACIDS, URINARY
CATECHOLAMINES, AND DRUG BINDING.
002272 02-13

DRUG PREFERENCE AND MOOD IN HUMANS: DIAZEPAM.
002334 02-14

DRUG PREFERENCE AND MOOD IN HUMANS: D-AMPHETAMINE.
002335 02-14

EARLY-ACTIVITY-STUDIES AND INTENSIVE DRUG EVALUATIONS OF NEW
PSYCHOPHARMACOLOGIC-AGENTS.
002348 02-14

SUBJECTIVE DRUG-EFFECTS AND DRUG PREFERENCE IN HEALTHY
VOLUNTEERS AS A MODEL OF A DRUGS REINFORCING EFFECTS:
STUDIES ON NOMIFENSINE, AMPHETAMINE AND PLACEBO.
002362 02-14

TREATMENT OF IATROGENIC DRUG DEPENDENCE IN THE GENERAL-
HOSPITAL.
002460 02-15

DRUG CONTENT OF THE MOTHERS-MILK.
002461 02-15

COMPARISON OF DRUG PRESCRIPTIONS FOR PSYCHIATRIC-PATIENTS
AFTER HOSPITAL DISCHARGE IN THE DISTRICTS TEPLICE AND UHERSKE-
HRADISTE.
002518 02-17

Subject Index

CLINICAL-PHARMACOLOGY: DRUG DEVELOPMENT.
002547 02-17

STRUCTURE OF VARIABILITY AND CORRELATION IN LEARNING AFTER DRUG ADMINISTRATION.
002562 02-17

INAPPROPRIATE ADH SECRETION: THE ROLE OF DRUG RECHALLENGE.
002629 02-17

DRUG ENVIRONMENT INTERACTION: CONTEXT DEPENDENCY OF COCAINE-INDUCED BEHAVIORAL-SENSITIZATION.
002866 03-03

DRUG REGIMENS FACILITATING AGGRESSION: BEHAVIOR, AMINE, AND RECEPTOR ALTERATIONS.
002987 03-04

LITHIUM DRUG INTERACTIONS ALTERING THE INTRACELLULAR LITHIUM LEVEL: AN IN VITRO STUDY.
003142 03-06

A COMPARISON OF-DOPAMINE-RECEPTOR BLOCKING ASSAY WITH PLASMA DRUG LEVELS OF HALOPERIDOL IN SCHIZOPHRENIC-PATIENTS.
003182 03-08

CARPIPRAMINE: A DISINHIBITORY DRUG COMPOUND IN CHRONIC SCHIZOPHRENIA.
003192 03-08

METHODOLOGY OF OUTPATIENT DRUG RESEARCH. (UNPUBLISHED PAPER).
003282 03-10

CLINICAL-PHARMACOLOGY: ADVERSE DRUG INTERACTIONS.
003399 03-13

LATERALIZED DEFICITS AND DRUG INFLUENCES ON THE DICHOTIC LISTENING OF SCHIZOPHRENIC-PATIENTS.
003443 03-14

DRUG PREFERENCE AND MOOD IN HUMANS: REPEATED ASSESSMENT OF D-AMPHETAMINE.
003445 03-14

HOW TO TREAT AND PREVENT DRUG TOXICITY.
003541 03-15

EFFECTS OF PENTAZOCINE AND NALORPHINE ON MOTILITY IN CHRONICALLY MORPHINE TREATED RATS: A POTENTIAL SUBSTITUTION TEST TO DETECT THE NARCOTIC CHARACTER OF A DRUG.
003555 03-16

EVALUATION OF DRUG EFFICACY IN DEMENTIA: A COMPUTERIZED COGNITIVE ASSESSMENT SYSTEM.
003557 03-16

DRUG AND DIETETIC THERAPIES FOR HYPERKINETIC-CHILDREN. (PH.D. DISSERTATION).
003576 03-17

GUIDELINES EMPLOYED BY THE FOOD-AND-DRUG-ADMINISTRATION IN DRUG SCHEDULING.
003586 03-17

DRUG DEPENDENCE: REFLECTIONS ON AND ANALYSIS OF AN EXPERIENCE IN THE PROVINCE OF RIGGIO-EMILIA.
003591 03-17

AN ANALYSIS OF DRUG DECISIONS IN A STATE PSYCHIATRIC-HOSPITAL.
003593 03-17

USE OF CURRENTLY AVAILABLE DATA SOURCES TO ASSESS DRUG SCHEDULING.
003594 03-17

QUALITY OF REPORTS OF CLINICAL-TRIALS SUBMITTED BY THE DRUG INDUSTRY TO THE FINNISH AND SWEDISH CONTROL AUTHORITIES.
003599 03-17

IMPACT OF DRUG SCHEDULING ON UTILIZATION.
003601 03-17

ACTION ON THE EMOTIONALLY-REINFORCED BRAIN SYSTEM AS A MEANS OF TREATING ALCOHOLISM AND DRUG ADDICTION PATHOGENETICALLY.
003641 03-17

HEPATIC-DISEASE AND DRUG PHARMACOKINETICS.
003650 03-17

QUANTITATION AND COMPARISON OF PHENOBARBITAL LEVELS IN THE PLASMA, SALIVA, AND CEREBROSPINAL-FLUID OF THE RAT, AND THE DEMONSTRATION OF AN ALTERATION OF DRUG PASSAGE BY ETHANOL.
003725 04-03

AGE-DEPENDENT MODIFICATION OF DRUG INTERFERENCE ON THE ENZYMATIC ACTIVITIES OF THE RAT-BRAIN.
003730 04-03

FACTORS REGULATING DRUG CUE SENSITIVITY: LIMITS OF DISCRIMINABILITY AND THE ROLE OF A PROGRESSIVELY DECREASING TRAINING DOSE IN FENTANYL SALINE DISCRIMINATION.
004088 04-04

CONDITIONING OF AN INTEROCEPTIVE DRUG STIMULUS TO DIFFERENT EXTEROCEPTIVE CONTEXTS.
004142 04-04

BARBITURATE-DEPENDENCE AND DRUG PREFERENCE.
004235 04-04

LACK OF SPECIFICITY OF AN ANIMAL BEHAVIOR MODEL FOR HALLUCINOGENIC DRUG ACTION.
004250 04-04

AUTORADIOGRAPHIC LOCALIZATION OF DRUG AND NEUROTRANSMITTER-RECEPTORS IN THE BRAIN.
004292 04-06

S-1

DRUG-INDUCED RELEASE OF DOPAMINE FROM CORPUS-STRIATUM.
(PH.D. DISSERTATION).
001343 02-03
DRUG-INDUCED ELEVATION OF GABA AFTER INTRACEREBRAL
MICROINJECTION: SITE OF ANTICONVULSANT ACTION.
001627 02-04
IMIPRAMINE NORMALIZES NATURALLY OCCURRING AND DRUG-INDUCED
DIFFERENCES IN THE EXPLORATORY-ACTIVITY OF RATS.
001646 02-04
GABA AGONISTS DISSOCIATE STRIATAL UNIT ACTIVITY FROM DRUG-
INDUCED STEREOTYPED-BEHAVIOUR.
001716 02-04
SUPERSENSITIVITY TO APOMORPHINE IN EXPERIMENTALLY-INDUCED
HYPOKINESIA AND DRUG-INDUCED MODIFICATIONS OF THE
APOMORPHINE RESPONSE.
001814 02-04
DRUG-INDUCED ARTERIAL HYPOTENSION IN PSYCHIATRIC-PATIENTS
TREATED WITH DIHYDROERGOTAMINE.
001950 02-08
A COMPARISON OF BIPERIDEN-HYDROCHLORIDE (AKINETON) AND
BENZHEXOL (ARTANE) IN THE TREATMENT OF DRUG-INDUCED
PARKINSONISM.
002146 02-11
DRUG-INDUCED DISORDERS OF THE URINARY TRACT.
002393 02-15
DRUG-INDUCED DISORDERS OF THE EYE.
002396 02-15
DRUG-INDUCED DISORDERS OF THE LIVER.
002397 02-15
CASE 3: ASSESSMENT AND TREATMENT OF DRUG-INDUCED TREMOR.
002407 02-15
DRUG-INDUCED DEMENTIA.
002431 02-15
DRUG-INDUCED DISORDERS OF MUSCLE.
002435 02-15
DIFFERENTIAL-EFFECTS OF PHARMACOLOGICAL-AGENTS ACTING ON
MONOAMINERGIC SYSTEMS ON DRUG-INDUCED ANOREXIA.
002533 02-17
AN ANALYSIS OF SPECIFICITY OF DRUG-INDUCED CHANGES IN DRUG-
REINFORCED RESPONDING. (PH.D. DISSERTATION).
003010 03-04
DRUG-INDUCED STIMULUS CONTROL AND THE CONCEPT OF BREAKING-
POINT: LSD AND QUIPAZINE.
003116 03-04
ANALYSIS OF SINGLE-BLIND, DOUBLE-BLIND PROCEDURES, MAINTENANCE
OF PLACEBO-EFFECTS, AND DRUG-INDUCED DYSKINESIA WITH
MENTALLY-RETARDED PERSONS -- BRIEF REPORT.
003298 03-11
DRUG-INDUCED CHANGES IN THE COMPOSITION OF THE CEREBRAL FREE
AMINO-ACID POOL.
004039 04-03
MODIFICATION OF DRUG-INDUCED CATATONIA AND TREMORS BY
QUIPAZINE IN RATS AND MICE.
004164 04-04
THE ROLE OF NIGRAL PROJECTIONS TO THE THALAMUS IN DRUG-
INDUCED CIRCLING-BEHAVIOUR IN THE RAT.
004205 04-04
ANALYSIS OF SINGLE-BLIND AND DOUBLE-BLIND PROCEDURES,
MAINTENANCE OF PLACEBO-EFFECTS AND DRUG-INDUCED DYSKINESIA
WITH MENTALLY-RETARDED PERSON.
004437 04-11
DRUG-INDUCED ALTERATIONS OF THE HYPOTHALAMUS HYPOPHYSIS
AXIS.
004535 04-13
DRUG-INDUCED PSYCHOSIS AND SCHIZOPHRENIA IN ADOLESCENTS.
004596 04-15
TARDIVE-DYSKINESIA AND OTHER DRUG-INDUCED MOVEMENT-
DISORDERS AMONG HANDICAPPED CHILDREN AND YOUTH.
004614 04-15

UG-INTERACTIONS
TRICYCLIC-ANTIDEPRESSANT DRUG-INTERACTIONS WITH HISTAMINE AND
ALPHA-ADRENERGIC-RECEPTORS.
000791 01-13
DRUG-INTERACTIONS IN PSYCHOPHARMACOLOGY
000915 01-17
DRUG-INTERACTIONS IN EPILEPSY.
003622 03-17
DRUG-INTERACTIONS OF AMITRIPTYLINE AND NORTRIPTYLINE WITH
WARFARIN IN THE RAT.
003912 04-03

UG-RECEPTORS
GABA-RECEPTOR ASSOCIATED DRUG-RECEPTORS.
002893 03-03

UG-REFUSAL
ROTTING WITH THEIR RIGHTS ON: CONSTITUTIONAL THEORY AND
CLINICAL REALITY IN DRUG-REFUSAL BY PSYCHIATRIC-PATIENTS.
000911 01-17

UG-REINFORCED
AN ANALYSIS OF SPECIFICITY OF DRUG-INDUCED CHANGES IN DRUG-
REINFORCED RESPONDING. (PH.D. DISSERTATION).
003010 03-04

DRUG-RESISTANCE
CLINICAL-EXPERIENCE WITH RETARD DIBENZEPINE (NOVERIL-240) IN
ENDOGENOUS DEPRESSIONS ACCOMPANIED BY SYMPTOMS OF DRUG-
RESISTANCE.
003245 03-09

DRUG-RESISTANT
CLINICAL AND BIOCHEMICAL-ACTION OF PIRACETAM (NOOTROPIL) IN
DRUG-RESISTANT DEPRESSION.
000600 01-09

DRUG-STUDIES
ANIMAL ACTIVITY MONITOR FOR CHRONIC DRUG-STUDIES.
(UNPUBLISHED PAPER).
001794 02-04

DRUG-THERAPIES
CONVULSIVE AND DRUG-THERAPIES OF DEPRESSION.
004366 04-09

DRUG-THERAPY
DRUG-THERAPY IN ENDOGENOUS DEPRESSION WITH POSSIBLE PRIMARY
GABA DEFICIENCY CLINICALLY DETECTED: 38 NEW CASES.
000584 01-09
THE PSYCHODYNAMIC-APPROACH TO DRUG-THERAPY.
000969 01-17
DEPRESSION: HOW TO RATIONALISE DRUG-THERAPY.
001988 02-09
THE CORRELATION OF CATECHOLAMINE AND ADRENERGIC PARAMETERS
WITH DRUG-THERAPY OF NEUROTIC AND ENDOGENOUS DEPRESSIONS.
002047 02-09
SELF-MEDICATION, ABANDONMENT, MANIPULATION, AND DEPENDENCE
IN DRUG-THERAPY IN PSYCHOSOMATIC-ILLNESS: COMPARATIVE
POLYCENTRIC RESEARCH ON VARIOUS PSYCHOTROPIC-DRUGS.
002189 02-11
MEASUREMENT OF PLASMA CONCENTRATIONS OF DRUGS AS A
FEEDBACK CONTROL MECHANISM DURING DRUG-THERAPY.
002525 02-17
TRANSFER FROM MULTIPLE TO SINGLE ANTIEPILEPTIC DRUG-THERAPY.
003316 03-11
RELAPSE AFTER SHORT-TERM DRUG-THERAPY IN NEUROTIC-
OUTPATIENTS.
004400 04-09
DRUG-THERAPY FOR HYPERACTIVITY: TREATMENT PROCEDURES IN
NATURAL SETTINGS.
004449 04-11
PROBLEMS REMAIN IN REVIEWS OF MEDICAID FINANCED DRUG-THERAPY
IN NURSING-HOMES.
004736 04-17

DRUG-TREATMENT
REPEATED TRICYCLICS INDUCE A PROGRESSIVE DOPAMINE-
AUTORECEPTOR SUBSENSITIVITY INDEPENDENT OF DAILY DRUG-
TREATMENT.
000047 01-03
(3H) 2 AMINODIHYDROXYTETRAHYDRONAPHTHALENE (ADTN):
REGIONAL DISTRIBUTION AND IN VIVO BINDING AFTER ACUTE AND
CHRONIC DRUG-TREATMENT.
000052 01-03
A NEW DRUG-TREATMENT FOR PREMENSTRUAL EXACERBATION OF
SCHIZOPHRENIA.
000553 01-08
THE REAL AND IDEAL MANAGEMENT OF STIMULANT DRUG-TREATMENT
OR HYPERACTIVE-CHILDREN: RECENT FINDINGS AND A REPORT FROM
CLINICAL-PRACTICE.
000715 01-11
PROBLEMS OF DRUG-TREATMENT OF MENTAL-DISORDERS.
002623 02-17
ELECTROPHYSIOLOGIC ASSESSMENT OF RECEPTOR CHANGES FOLLOWING
CHRONIC DRUG-TREATMENT.
003136 03-06
DRUG-TREATMENT OF THE PHOBIC-ANXIETY-SYNDROME.
003280 03-10
COMPARISON OF SODIUM-VALPROATE AND PHENYTOIN AS SINGLE
DRUG-TREATMENT IN EPILEPSY.
003371 03-11
ATTENTION DEFICIT-DISORDER (MINIMAL-BRAIN-DYSFUNCTION) IN
ADULTS: A REPLICATION STUDY OF DIAGNOSIS AND DRUG-
TREATMENT.
003389 03-11
TRICYCLIC-ANTIDEPRESSANT DRUG-TREATMENT DECREASES ALPHA2-
ADRENORECEPTORS ON HUMAN PLATELET MEMBRANES.
003408 03-13
AUDITORY BRAINSTEM EVOKED-RESPONSES IN HOSPITALIZED-PATIENTS
UNDERGOING DRUG-TREATMENT OR ECT.
003430 03-13
PSYCHIATRIC-SYNDROMES AND DRUG-TREATMENT.
003608 03-17
CHRONIC DRUG-TREATMENT OF THE CHRONICALLY-ILL: BENEFITS AND
RISKS.
003625 03-17
ALPHA2-ADRENORECEPTORS IN RAT-BRAIN ARE DECREASED AFTER
LONG-TERM TRICYCLIC-ANTIDEPRESSANT DRUG-TREATMENT.
004008 04-03

SOME PRINCIPLES OF DIFFERENTIATED METABOLIC DRUG-TREATMENT IN COMPREHENSIVE THERAPY OF MENTAL-DISORDERS.
004433 04-11
PREVALENCE OF DRUG-TREATMENT FOR HYPERACTIVITY AND OTHER CHILDHOOD BEHAVIOR-DISORDERS.
004713 04-17
PSYCHOSOCIAL-ASPECTS OF DRUG-TREATMENT FOR HYPERACTIVITY.
004714 04-17

DRUG-VARIABLES
DRUG-VARIABLES IN THE ETIOLOGY OF TARDIVE-DYSKINESIA: APPLICATION OF DISCRIMINANT FUNCTION ANALYSIS.
000844 01-15

DRUGS
EFFECTS OF MORPHINE AND OTHER CENTRALLY-ACTING DRUGS ON 3,4 DIHYDROXYPHENYLETHYLENE-GLYCOL-SULFATE (DOPEG-SO4) IN RAT-BRAIN.
000136 01-03
FLASH-EVOKED AFTERDISCHARGE IN RAT AS A MODEL OF THE ABSENCE SEIZURE: DOSE-RESPONSE STUDIES WITH THERAPEUTIC DRUGS.
000160 01-03
EFFECT OF DOPAMINERGIC AND GABAERGIC DRUGS GIVEN ALONE OR IN COMBINATION ON THE ANTICONVULSANT ACTION OF PHENOBARBITAL AND DIPHENYLHYDANTOIN IN THE ELECTROSHOCK-TEST IN MICE.
000163 01-03
IN VITRO ACETYLCHOLINE RELEASE FROM RAT CAUDATE-NUCLEUS AS A NEW MODEL FOR TESTING DRUGS WITH DOPAMINE-RECEPTOR ACTIVITY.
000289 01-03
TRICYCLIC-ANTIDEPRESSANT DRUGS AND INDIVIDUAL DIFFERENCES IN THE EXPLORATORY-ACTIVITY OF RATS: CONTRASTING-EFFECTS OF TERTIARY AND SECONDARY AMINE COMPOUNDS.
000401 01-04
BEHAVIORAL-EFFECTS AND ELECTROCORTICAL-EFFECTS AFTER INTRASTRIATAL CEFAZOLIN IN RATS ARE ANTAGONIZED BY DRUGS ENHANCING GABAERGIC TRANSMISSION.
000443 01-04
INTRAVENTRICULAR 6 HYDROXYDOPAMINE IN THE NEWBORN RAT AND LOCOMOTOR RESPONSES TO DRUGS IN INFANCY: NO SUPPORT FOR THE DOPAMINE DEPLETION MODEL OF MINIMAL-BRAIN-DYSFUNCTION.
000448 01-04
USING PROFILES OF SACCHARIN AND WATER DRINKING TO DETECT AND DISCRIMINATE ACTIONS OF DRUGS AND TOXICANTS.
000503 01-04
EFFECTS OF AGE AND OTHER DRUGS ON BENZODIAZEPINE KINETICS.
000681 01-11
EFFICACY AND PATTERN VALENCE OF PSYCHOACTIVE-DRUGS: A NEW METHOD OF COMPARING DRUGS APPLIED TO IDENTICAL PATIENTS IN RANDOMIZED-ORDER.
000699 01-11
CONVERSION SCALES FOR COMMONLY REQUESTED SERUM CONCENTRATIONS OF DRUGS AND OTHER SUBSTANCES OF THERAPEUTIC AND TOXICOLOGICAL IMPORTANCE, AND OF HORMONES.
000759 01-13
EFFECT OF DRUGS ON LEARNING AND MEMORY PROCESSES IN SIMPLE BEHAVIORAL-TESTS.
000809 01-14
DRUGS AND SEXUAL-FUNCTION.
000852 01-15
DRUGS FOR SENILE-DEMENTIA.
000947 01-17
DISCUSSION: COMMUNICATION AND POLYPHARMACY: DRUGS AND THE ELDERLY.
000957 01-17
DISEASE-INDUCED CHANGES IN THE PLASMA BINDING OF BASIC DRUGS.
000975 01-17
ALTERATION OF PROLACTIN SECRETION BY CENTRALLY-ACTING DRUGS.
001127 02-03
DOPAMINERGIC-SUPERSENSITIVITY: INFLUENCE OF DOPAMINE AGONISTS AND DRUGS USED FOR THE TREATMENT OF TARDIVE-DYSKINESIA.
001169 02-03
INFLUENCE OF DRUGS AFFECTING THE PITUITARY ADRENAL AXIS ON CHROMAFFIN CELLS.
001183 02-03
STUDIES ON THIORIDAZINE AND MESORIDAZINE METABOLISM. II. IN VIVO METABOLISM OF TRITIATED DRUGS IN RHESUS-MONKEYS.
001229 02-03
CENTRAL MONOAMINE SYNAPSES AS SITES OF ACTION FOR ERGOT DRUGS.
001238 02-03
EFFECTS OF CHRONIC NEUROLEPTIC TREATMENT ON TYROSINE-HYDROXYLASE IN DOPAMINERGIC TERMINALS: COMPARISONS BETWEEN DRUGS AND BRAIN REGIONS REVEALS DIFFERENT MECHANISMS OF TOLERANCE.
001243 02-03
STEREOSELECTIVE ACTIONS OF SUBSTITUTED BENZAMIDE DRUGS ON CEREBRAL DOPAMINE MECHANISMS.
001301 02-03
ADRENERGIC NONSPECIFIC POTENTIATION OF YOHIMBINE TOXICITY IN MICE BY ANTIDEPRESSANTS AND RELATED DRUGS AND

ANTIYOHIMBINE ACTION OF ANTIADRENERGIC AND SEROTONERGIC DRUGS.
001330 02-03
NEW EXPERIMENTAL TECHNIQUES IN THE PHARMACOLOGICAL EVALUATION OF CNS ACTING DRUGS.
001479 02-03
EFFECTS OF ALPHA-ADRENOCEPTOR STIMULATING DRUGS ON BARORECEPTOR REFLEXES IN CONSCIOUS CATS.
001514 02-03
EVALUATION OF THE EFFECT OF DRUGS ON DOPAMINE METABOLISM IN THE RAT SUPERIOR-CERVICAL-GANGLION BY HPLC WITH ELECTROCHEMICAL-DETECTION.
001530 02-03
BEHAVIORAL-EFFECTS OF DRUGS: THE ROLE OF THE STIMULUS REINFORCER CONTINGENCY. (PH.D. DISSERTATION).
001537 02-03
THE EFFECT OF NALOXONE ON THE ACTIVATION OF EMOTIONALLY POSITIVE REACTION PRODUCED BY DRUGS WITH A DEPENDENCE LIABILITY.
001556 02-03
DRUGS AND THE DISCRIMINATION OF DURATION.
001561 02-04
EFFECTS OF DRUGS ON THE EFFECTIVENESS OF CONDITIONED STIMULI.
001608 02-04
A SIGNAL-DETECTION-ANALYSIS OF CENTRALLY-ACTIVE DRUGS IN MICE.
001631 02-04
INTERACTIONS BETWEEN NALTREXONE AND NONOPIATE DRUGS EVALUATED BY SCHEDULE-CONTROLLED BEHAVIOR.
001645 02-04
INTERRELATIONS AMONG PRIOR EXPERIENCE AND CURRENT CONDITIONS IN THE DETERMINATION OF BEHAVIOR AND THE EFFECTS OF DRUGS.
001715 02-04
CHANGES OF PHYSICAL MORPHINE-DEPENDENCE IN RATS CHRONICALLY TREATED WITH DRUGS ACTING ON BRAIN 5 HYDROXYTRYPTAMINE.
001764 02-04
THE RELATIONSHIP BETWEEN POSITIVE REINFORCEMENT AND CONDITIONED TASTE-AVERSION PRODUCED BY SELF-ADMINISTERED DRUGS. (PH.D. DISSERTATION).
001798 02-04
PRESYNAPTIC ALPHA-ADRENOCEPTORS AND THE ACTION OF TRICYCLIC-ANTIDEPRESSANT DRUGS IN BEHAVIOURAL-DESPAIR IN RATS.
001829 02-04
THE USE OF SOCIAL-INTERACTION AS A METHOD FOR DETECTING ANXIOLYTIC-ACTIVITY OF CHLORDIAZEPOXIDE-LIKE DRUGS.
001866 02-06
TWO NEW DRUGS MAY PICK UP WHERE L-DOPA LEAVES OFF.
001897 02-07
THE PLACE OF SURVECTOR AMONG THE VARIOUS DRUGS USED IN TREATMENT OF MOOD-DISORDERS.
001969 02-09
DRUGS AND THE SPECIAL-CHILD.
002107 02-11
O METHOXYBENZAMIDES: RELATIONSHIPS BETWEEN STRUCTURE-ACTIVITY, AND PHARMACOKINETICS OF THESE DRUGS.
002246 02-13
CYCLIC-AMP IN PSYCHOSES AND THE EFFECT OF DRUGS.
002294 02-13
NOOTROPIC-DRUGS AND RELATED DRUGS INTERACTING WITH THE INTEGRATIVE ACTIVITY OF THE BRAIN.
002327 02-14
VIGILANCE IMPAIRING DRUGS: ANALYSIS OF SUBJECTIVE RESPONSES.
002332 02-14
SUBJECTIVE DRUG-EFFECTS AND DRUG PREFERENCE IN HEALTHY VOLUNTEERS AS A MODEL OF A DRUGS REINFORCING EFFECTS: STUDIES ON NOMIFENSINE, AMPHETAMINE AND PLACEBO.
002362 02-14
APPROACHES TO THE PROBLEM OF PREVENTING HAZARDS OF LONG-TERM NEUROLEPTIC TREATMENT AND OF AVOIDING UNNECESSARY DRUGS.
002426 02-15
ON THE MEASUREMENT IN RATS OF THE CONVULSANT-EFFECT OF DRUGS AND THE CHANGES WHICH FOLLOW ELECTROCONVULSIVE-SHOCK.
002444 02-15
DRUGS IN THE ELDERLY.
002451 02-15
PHYSICAL AND PHYSIOLOGICAL CHARACTERISTICS OF MICROPRESSURE EJECTION OF DRUGS FROM MULTIBARRELED PIPETTES.
002502 02-16
MEASUREMENT OF PLASMA CONCENTRATIONS OF DRUGS AS A FEEDBACK CONTROL MECHANISM DURING DRUG-THERAPY.
002525 02-17
SOME WAYS TO INCREASE CHANCES TO DISCOVER THE CNS DRUGS OF THE FUTURE.
002528 02-17
CHANGES IN BODY-TEMPERATURE AFTER ADMINISTRATION OF ADRENERGIC AND SEROTONERGIC-AGENTS AND RELATED DRUGS INCLUDING ANTIDEPRESSANTS.
002532 02-17

DRUGS AND THE ELDERLY: PERSPECTIVES IN GERIATRIC CLINICAL-PHARMACOLOGY.
002534 02-17
CLASSIFICATION OF DRUGS AND PATIENTS TO ACHIEVE MAXIMUM THERAPEUTIC RESPONSE.
002560 02-17
DRUGS OF THE FUTURE.
002572 02-17
NEUROPSYCHIATRIC SIDE-EFFECTS OF DRUGS IN THE ELDERLY. VOL. 9, AGING.
002573 02-17
DRUGS AND THE AGED.
002593 02-17
BEHAVIOURAL-RESPONSES TO DRUGS RELEASING 5 HYDROXYTRYPTAMINE AND CATECHOLAMINES: EFFECTS OF TREATMENTS ALTERING PRECURSOR CONCENTRATIONS IN BRAIN.
002990 03-04
INJECTIONS OF DOPAMINERGIC, CHOLINERGIC, SEROTONINERGIC AND GABAERGIC DRUGS INTO THE NUCLEUS-ACCUMBENS: EFFECTS ON LOCOMOTOR-ACTIVITY IN THE RAT.
003019 03-04
ENHANCEMENT OF APOMORPHINE-INDUCED CLIMBING IN MICE BY REVERSIBLE AND IRREVERSIBLE NARCOTIC ANTAGONIST DRUGS.
003068 03-04
ERGOT DRUGS SUPPRESS PLASMA PROLACTIN AND LACTATION BUT NOT AGGRESSION IN PARTURIENT MICE.
003159 03-07
DEPRESSED-OUTPATIENTS: RESULTS ONE YEAR AFTER TREATMENT WITH DRUGS AND/OR INTERPERSONAL PSYCHOTHERAPY.
003272 03-09
A NOTE ON THE PARADOXICAL-EFFECT OF STIMULANTS ON HYPERACTIVITY WITH REFERENCE TO THE RATE DEPENDENCY EFFECT OF DRUGS.
003320 03-11
CLINICAL-PHARMACOLOGY OF MIXED AGONIST ANTAGONIST DRUGS.
003329 03-11
CLINICAL-PHARMACOLOGY: ELIMINATION OF DRUGS.
003400 03-13
CAN DRUGS HALT MEMORY LOSS?
003447 03-14
NEUROPSYCHOLOGICAL-CORRELATES OF ASTHMA: EFFECT OF HYPOXIA OR DRUGS?
003482 03-15
RECEPTOR ADAPTATIONS TO CENTRALLY ACTING DRUGS.
003585 03-17
GUIDELINES FOR SCHEDULING DRUGS UNDER THE CONTROLLED-SUBSTANCES-ACT.
003606 03-17
INCREASE OF C-GMP AND ACCUMULATION OF 45CA2 EVOKED BY DRUGS ACTING ON SODIUM OR POTASSIUM CHANNELS.
003709 04-03
ACTION OF DRUGS ON THE CEREBELLAR ELECTRICAL-ACTIVITIES.
003804 04-03
COMPARISON OF THE POTENCIES OF CLEBOPRIDE AND OTHER SUBSTITUTED BENZAMIDE DRUGS ON ISOLATED GASTROINTESTINAL TRACT OF THE GUINEA-PIG AND RAT.
003928 04-03
EFFECT OF CHRONIC-TREATMENT WITH TRICYCLIC-ANTIDEPRESSANT DRUGS ON IDENTIFIED BRAIN NORADRENERGIC AND SEROTONERGIC NEURONS.
004026 04-03
EFFECTS ON THE PINNA-REFLEX OF DRUGS ACTING AT ALPHA-ADRENOCEPTORS.
004078 04-04
EFFECTS OF DOPAMINERGIC DRUGS ON PHENCYCLIDINE-INDUCED BEHAVIOR IN THE RAT.
004083 04-04
DISCRIMINATION OF ELECTRIC-SHOCK: EFFECTS OF SOME OPIOID AND NONOPIOID DRUGS.
004106 04-04
A STUDY OF THE EFFECT OF NEUROPHARMACOLOGICAL DRUGS ON THE FUNCTIONAL ACTIVITY OF RAT-BRAIN.
004107 04-04
CHLORPROMAZINE EFFECTS ON COCAINE-REINFORCED RESPONDING IN RHESUS-MONKEYS: RECIPROCAL MODIFICATION OF RATE ALTERING EFFECTS OF THE DRUGS.
004133 04-04
EFFECTS OF ANALGESICS AND CNS-ACTING DRUGS ON STRUGGLING FOLLOWING REPETITIVE STIMULATION OF THE TAIL, AND FLEXOR REFLEX TO A SINGLE STIMULATION OF THE SCIATIC-NERVE IN RATS.
004148 04-04
AVOIDANCE ENHANCEMENT AND DISCRIMINATIVE RESPONSE CONTROL BY ANXIOLYTICS WITH DRUGS ACTING ON THE GABA SYSTEM.
004193 04-04
CHANGES OF RESPONSE TO DOPAMINERGIC DRUGS IN RATS SUBMITTED TO REM SLEEP DEPRIVATION.
004239 04-04
THE SIMULTANEOUS INFUSION OF DRUGS VIA THE LEFT AND RIGHT VERTEBRAL-ARTERY OF THE CAT; A MODIFIED ANIMAL-MODEL FOR

THE STUDY OF POSSIBLE CENTRAL-ACTIONS OF DRUGS UPON THE LOWER BRAINSTEM.
004297 04-06
AN IMPROVED PNEUMATIC SYRINGE FOR SELF-ADMINISTRATION OF DRUGS BY RATS.
004304 04-06
DRUGS AND SCHIZOPHRENIA.
004314 04-08
BLOOD LEVEL MEASUREMENTS OF TRICYCLIC DRUGS AS A DIAGNOSTIC TOOL.
004368 04-09
INTERACTIONS BETWEEN ANTIDEPRESSANTS AND OTHER DRUGS.
004371 04-09
ACUTE EFFECT OF DRUGS UPON MEMORY OF PATIENTS WITH SENILE-DEMENTIA.
004561 04-14
PERSONALITY AND DRUGS IN VISUAL FIGURAL AFTEREFFECTS.
004581 04-14
IMPURITIES IN DRUGS V: MEPROBAMATE.
004631 04-15
DRUGS AND RENAL-DISEASE.
004645 04-15
THE USE OF EVENT-RELATED SLOW POTENTIALS OF THE BRAIN AS AN OBJECTIVE METHOD TO STUDY THE EFFECTS OF CENTRALLY ACTING DRUGS.
004669 04-16
SYMPATHOMIMETIC-AMINES AND TRICYCLIC-ANTIDEPRESSANT DRUGS.
004678 04-16
A MULTIVARIATE ANALYSIS OF THE INFRARED SPECTRA OF DRUGS OF ABUSE.
004688 04-16
DRUGS, ALCOHOL AND SEX.
004706 04-17
DRUGS, TRANSMITTERS AND HORMONES, AND MATING-BEHAVIOR.
004721 04-17

DRYNESS
TREATMENT OF DRUG-INDUCED DRYNESS OF MOUTH IN PSYCHIATRIC-PATIENTS -- A CONTROLLED-COMPARATIVE-STUDY.
000799 01-13

DSIP
THERMOREGULATORY AND LOCOMOTOR-EFFECTS OF DSIP: PARADOXICAL-INTERACTION WITH D-AMPHETAMINE.
001827 02-04

DU-24565
DU-24565, A QUIPAZINE DERIVATIVE, A POTENT SELECTIVE SEROTONIN UPTAKE INHIBITOR.
002651 03-02

DUAL-ACTION
A REFORMULATION OF THE DUAL-ACTION MODEL OF OPIOID DEPENDENCE: OPIOID-SPECIFIC NEURONAL KINDLING.
003645 03-17

DUAL-ACTIONS
PENTOBARBITAL: DUAL-ACTIONS TO INCREASE BRAIN BENZODIAZEPINE-RECEPTOR AFFINITY.
002896 03-03

DUAL-EFFECTS
DUAL-EFFECTS OF MESCALINE: THE TRANSMETHYLATION HYPOTHESIS REVISITED.
001584 02-04

DUAL-MECHANISM
EXCITATORY AND INHIBITORY-EFFECTS OF OPIATES IN THE RAT VAS-DEFERENS: A DUAL-MECHANISM OF OPIATE ACTION.
000143 01-03

DUAL-REGULATION
OPIOID DEPENDENT DUAL-REGULATION OF ADENYLATE-CYCLASE IN A CELL-FREE SYSTEM. (UNPUBLISHED PAPER).
001033 01-01

DUCKS
LONG-TERM EFFECTS OF TESTOSTERONE INJECTIONS ON THE SOCIAL-BEHAVIOUR OF MALE DUCKS AND THEIR PHYSIOLOGICAL-CORRELATES.
001565 02-04

DUPLICATION
NALOXONE REVERSIBLE DUPLICATION BY LANTHANUM OF OPIATE ANALGESIA EFFECTS ON OROFACIAL, LOWER BODY AND CENTRAL NOCICEPTION.
003028 03-04

DURATION
INFLUENCE OF GLUCOSE (IN VIVO OR IN VITRO) ON DURATION OF NARCOTIC ANALGESICS AND ON THE KINETICS OF DRUG METABOLISM.
000292 01-03
FACTORS INFLUENCING SEIZURE DURATION AND NUMBER OF SEIZURES APPLIED IN UNILATERAL ELECTROCONVULSIVE-THERAPY: ANESTHETICS AND BENZODIAZEPINES.
000792 01-13
DRUGS AND THE DISCRIMINATION OF DURATION.
001561 02-04
INTERACTIONS OF CHLORDIAZEPOXIDE AND ANORECTIC-AGENTS ON RATE AND DURATION PARAMETERS OF FEEDING IN THE RAT.
001600 02-04

Subject Index

GABA ANALOGUES ACTIVATE CHANNELS OF DIFFERENT DURATION ON CULTURED MOUSE SPINAL NEURONS.
002665 03-03

TIME-COURSE OF CHRONIC HALOPERIDOL AND CLOZAPINE UPON OPERANT RATE AND DURATION.
002989 03-04

CHRONIC EFFECTS OF NEUROLEPTICS HAVING HIGH OR LOW INCIDENCE OF EXTRAPYRAMIDAL SIDE-EFFECTS UPON FORCE, DURATION AND RATE OF OPERANT-RESPONSE IN RATS. (PH.D. DISSERTATION).
003125 03-05

EFFECTS OF PAIN, MORPHINE AND NALOXONE ON THE DURATION OF ANIMAL HYPNOSIS.
004081 04-04

LITHIUM ELIMINATION HALF-LIFE AND DURATION OF THERAPY.
004369 04-09

DYNAMIC

HEXAMETHONIUM MODIFICATION OF CARDIOVASCULAR ADJUSTMENTS DURING COMBINED STATIC DYNAMIC ARM EXERCISE IN MONKEYS.
001242 02-03

DYNAMICS

DYNAMICS OF ENDOGENOUS CATECHOLAMINE RELEASE FROM BRAIN FRAGMENTS OF MALE AND FEMALE RATS.
001121 02-03

MARIJUANA AND CHOLINERGIC DYNAMICS. (UNPUBLISHED PAPER).
001166 02-03

LONG-TERM EFFECTS OF HALOPERIDOL, CLOZAPINE, AND METHADONE ON RAT STRIATAL CHOLINERGIC AND DOPAMINERGIC DYNAMICS.
001325 02-03

DYNAMICS AND PROSPECTS OF THE PSYCHOTHERAPY AND PSYCHOPHARMACOTHERAPY RELATIONSHIP.
002594 02-17

THE CLINICAL DYNAMICS OF TETRAETHYL-LEAD POISONING.
003500 03-15

BETA-ADRENERGIC INFLUENCE ON CARDIAC DYNAMICS DURING SHOCK-AVOIDANCE IN DOGS.
003813 04-03

THE DYNAMICS OF SYSTEMIC VENOUS, ARTERIAL, AND CEREBROSPINAL-FLUID PRESSURE UNDER I.V. ADMINISTRATION OF POLYETHYLENE-GLYCOL.
004045 04-03

DESTRUCTION OF 5 HYDROXYTRYPTAMINERGIC NEURONS AND THE DYNAMICS OF DOPAMINE IN NUCLEUS-ACCUMBENS SEPTI AND OTHER FOREBRAIN REGIONS OF THE RAT.
004171 04-04

THE NOSOLOGICAL INDEPENDENCE OF INVOLUTIONAL DEPRESSION AND ITS DYNAMICS DURING PSYCHOPHARMACOTHERAPY.
004389 04-09

CORTISOL DYNAMICS AND DEXAMETHASONE PHARMACOKINETICS IN PRIMARY ENDOGENOUS DEPRESSION: PRELIMINARY FINDINGS.
004403 04-09

DYNORPHIN

SODIUM-CHLORIDE INHIBITION DECREASES LEVELS OF IMMUNOREACTIVE DYNORPHIN IN THE NEUROINTERMEDIATE PITUITARY OF RATS.
001283 02-03

DYNORPHIN: A POSSIBLE MODULATORY PEPTIDE ON MORPHINE OR BETA ENDORPHIN ANALGESIA IN MOUSE.
002994 03-04

DYSFUNCTIONS

DYSFUNCTIONS OF CHOLINERGIC PROCESSES IN SCHIZOPHRENIA.
002611 02-17

DYSKINESIA

ORAL DYSKINESIA IN BRAIN-DAMAGED RATS WITHDRAWN FROM A NEUROLEPTIC: IMPLICATION FOR MODELS OF TARDIVE-DYSKINESIA.
000393 01-04

IMPROVEMENT OF L-DOPA-INDUCED DYSKINESIA AND OF ON-OFF-PHENOMENON BY BROMOCRIPTINE.
000813 01-14

SPONTANEOUS DYSKINESIA IN THE ELDERLY AND TARDIVE-DYSKINESIA FROM NEUROLEPTICS. A SURVEY OF 270 ELDERLY-PATIENTS.
000834 01-15

COVERT DYSKINESIA IN AMBULATORY SCHIZOPHRENIA.
000836 01-15

DYSKINESIA INDUCED BY LONG-TERM-TREATMENT WITH ANTIPSYCHOTIC-DRUGS: INVOLVEMENT OF PRESYNAPTIC AND POSTSYNAPTIC DOPAMINERGIC MECHANISMS.
001839 02-05

THE TREATMENT OF BUCCOLINGUOFACIAL DYSKINESIA IN THE ELDERLY: THE CHOICE OF A NEUROLEPTIC-AGENT.
002223 02-13

CARBAMAZEPINE-INDUCED OROFACIAL DYSKINESIA.
002415 02-15

EXPERIMENTAL-STUDIES ON L-DOPA-INDUCED DYSKINESIA.
003129 03-05

ANALYSIS OF SINGLE-BLIND, DOUBLE-BLIND PROCEDURES, MAINTENANCE OF PLACEBO-EFFECTS, AND DRUG-INDUCED DYSKINESIA WITH MENTALLY-RETARDED PERSONS — BRIEF REPORT.
003298 03-11

PHARMACOLOGIC CHARACTERIZATION AND LECITHIN TREATMENT OF A PATIENT WITH SPONTANEOUS ORAL FACIAL DYSKINESIA AND DEMENTIA.
003347 03-11

ACUTE AND CHRONIC OPIATE-EFFECTS ON SINGLE UNITS AND EEG OF
MEDIAL THALAMUS AND HIPPOCAMPUS: A LATENCY ANALYSIS.
001344 02-03

RELATIONSHIP BETWEEN SERUM LEVELS AND FAST EEG ACTIVITIES IN
RATS BY A SINGLE ADMINISTRATION OF PHENOBARBITAL.
001462 02-03

EFFECTS OF THE BETA-ADRENOCEPTOR BLOCKING-AGENT SOTALOL ON
CNS: SLEEP, EEG, AND PSYCHOPHYSIOLOGICAL PARAMETERS.
001570 02-04

CLINICAL AND EEG CHANGES IN DEPRESSIVE-PATIENTS AFTER A SINGLE
INJECTION OF BETA ENDORPHIN.
001962 02-09

EEG CHANGES IN CHILDREN WITH TREATED PHENYLKETONURIA AFTER
PHENYLALANINE LOAD.
002115 02-11

THE RELATIONSHIP OF ALPHA AND DELTA EEG FREQUENCIES TO PAIN
AND MOOD IN FIBROSITIS-PATIENTS TREATED WITH CHLORPROMAZINE
AND L TRYPTOPHAN.
002152 02-11

EEG, COMP-EEG, REO-EG AND PHARMACOLOGICAL-CORRELATES OF
GERIATRICS.
002162 02-11

CEEG STUDY ON PATIENTS UNDER THE PSYCHIATRIC-DRUG TREATMENT;
THE CORRELATION BETWEEN EEG ALTERATION AND CLINICAL
EVOLUTION.
002165 02-11

ANTIHYPOXIDOTIC-DRUGS AND NOOTROPIC-DRUGS: PROOF OF THEIR
ENCEPHALOTROPIC AND PHARMACODYNAMIC PROPERTIES BY
ENCEPHALOTROPIC AND PHARMACODYNAMIC PROPERTIES BY
QUANTITATIVE EEG INVESTIGATIONS.
002166 02-11

DISCOVERY OF PSYCHOTROPIC-DRUGS BY MEANS OF COMPUTER-
ANALYZED EEG.
002203 02-13

EFFECTS OF SINGLE-ORAL-DOSAGES OF STEROIDS ON HUMAN EEG
BASELINE CROSSING T-SCORES SHOWN BY MULTIVARIATE STATISTICS
AND STANDARD PROFILES.
002239 02-13

CLASSIFICATION OF ENDORPHINS/ENKEPHALINS IN BRAIN PHYSIOLOGY
AND PATHOLOGY (BASED ON EEG AND CLINICAL-STUDY OF
SYNTHETICALLY-MODIFIED METHIONINE-ENKEPHALIN).
002286 02-13

CORRELATIONS BETWEEN PLASMA LEVELS OF ANTIEPILEPTIC-DRUGS AND
EEG INTENSIVE MONITORING.
002288 02-13

EEG ASSESSMENTS OF DOSAGE AND SLEEP PROFILES FOR A HYPNOTIC-
DRUG OF THE TRIAZOLOTHIENODIACEPINE SERIES.
002338 02-14

IMIPRAMINE AND EEG SLEEP IN CHILDREN WITH DEPRESSIVE-
SYMPTOMS.
002339 02-14

COMPUTERIZED SLEEP EEG (CSEEG) IN PSYCHIATRY AND
PSYCHOPHARMACOLOGY.
002614 02-17

SUPPRESSION OF AMPHETAMINE-INDUCED EEG AROUSAL IN THE
HIPPOCAMPUS OF HALOPERIDOL TREATED RABBITS.
002683 03-03

ANTIPEROXIDANT PRETREATMENT AND IRON-INDUCED EPILEPTIFORM
DISCHARGES IN THE RAT: EEG AND HISTOPATHOLOGIC STUDIES.
002930 03-03

EFFECT OF P CHLOROPHENYLALANINE AND TRYPTOPHAN ON SLEEP, EEG
AND MOTOR-ACTIVITY IN THE RAT.
002958 03-04

COMPUTER-ANALYZED EEG IN AMPHETAMINE RESPONSIVE
HYPERACTIVE-CHILDREN.
003338 03-11

EFFECT OF PIRACETAM ON EEG SPECTRA OF BOYS WITH LEARNING-
DISORDERS.
003383 03-11

ON THE EVALUATION OF A PROVOCATIVE EEG METHOD USING
MEDICATION IN THE DIAGNOSIS OF ORGANIC-BRAIN-SEIZURES IN
CHILDHOOD, WITH SPECIAL EMPHASIS ON SLEEP INDUCTION THROUGH
MEDICATION.
003387 03-11

STUDY OF THE EFFECTS OF PC-63-14 ON THE QUANTIFIED EEG.
003403 03-13

CORRELATED STUDY OF THE EFFECTS OF SE-5023 IN AN HYPOXIC
ATMOSPHERE ON QUANTIFIED EEG, VIGILANCE, MEMORY, AND
MOOD.
003440 03-14

INHIBITORY-ACTION OF THE COMBINATION OF AMINOPYRINE AND
SECOBARBITAL ON EEG ACTIVATION, NEOCORTICAL RECRUITING AND
AUGMENTING RESPONSES IN RABBITS.
004022 04-03

THE EFFECT OF DIPHENYLHYDANTOIN ON EEG CURVES IN EPILEPTICS.
004494 04-11

Subject Index

EFFECTIVENESS

CHANGES IN BRAIN N DEMETHYLATION AND OPIATE-RECEPTOR CONTENT CORRELATE WITH ANALGESIC EFFECTIVENESS OF MORPHINE.
000400 01-04

EFFECTS OF DRUGS ON THE EFFECTIVENESS OF CONDITIONED STIMULI.
001608 02-04

CEREBRAL SENESCENCE AND ITS PSYCHIC-MANIFESTATIONS. THE EFFECTIVENESS OF DEBRUMYL.
002105 02-11

TESTOSTERONE POTENTIATION OF THE EFFECTIVENESS OF ACTH1-24 ON THE INDUCTION OF THE STRETCH-YAWNING-SYNDROME (SYS) IN MALE GUINEA-PIGS.
003074 03-04

EVALUATION OF THE RELATIVE EFFECTIVENESS OF METHYLPHENIDATE AND COGNITIVE BEHAVIOR-MODIFICATION IN THE TREATMENT OF KINDERGARTEN-AGED HYPERACTIVE-CHILDREN.
003306 03-11

THE EFFECTIVENESS OF IMIPRAMINE IN THE TREATMENT OF ENURESIS: THE SIGNIFICANCE OF TYPE OF ENURESIS AND REPORTED LEVEL OF SLEEP. (PH.D. DISSERTATION).
003337 03-11

LITHIUM IN THE PROPHYLAXIS OF RECURRENT AFFECTIVE-DISORDERS (EFFECTIVENESS OF LOW PLASMA LEVELS AND PREDICTORS TO CLINICAL-RESPONSE).
004365 04-09

CLINICAL-EVALUATION OF THE PROPHYLACTIC EFFECTIVENESS OF PROLONGED LITHIUM-CARBONATE THERAPY IN ENDOGENOUS DEPRESSIVE-SYNDROMES.
004404 04-09

EFFECTOR

D PROPOXYPHENE ACTS DIFFERENTLY FROM MORPHINE ON OPIOID-RECEPTOR EFFECTOR MECHANISMS.
003062 03-04

EFFICACY

SINGLE-DOSE PHARMACOKINETICS AND ANTICONVULSANT EFFICACY OF PRIMIDONE IN MICE.
000177 01-03

EFFICACY OF DESIPRAMINE IN ENDOGENOMORPHICALLY DEPRESSED-PATIENTS.
000632 01-09

ANXIOLYTIC EFFICACY OF ALPRAZOLAM COMPARED TO DIAZEPAM AND PLACEBO.
000648 01-10

LONG-TERM EFFICACY OF BROMOCRIPTINE IN PARKINSONS-DISEASE.
000698 01-11

EFFICACY AND PATTERN VALENCE OF PSYCHOACTIVE-DRUGS: A NEW METHOD OF COMPARING DRUGS APPLIED TO IDENTICAL PATIENTS IN RANDOMIZED-ORDER.
000699 01-11

INTRAMUSCULAR HALOPERIDOL-DECANOATE FOR NEUROLEPTIC MAINTENANCE-THERAPY: EFFICACY, DOSAGE SCHEDULE AND PLASMA LEVELS: AN OPEN MULTICENTER-STUDY.
000758 01-13

TWENTY YEARS CLINICAL THERAPEUTIC EXPERIENCE WITH CALCIUM GLUTAMATES EFFICACY.
000963 01-17

PLASMA LEVELS AND THERAPEUTIC EFFICACY OF FLUPHENAZINE-HCL AND FLUPHENAZINE-DECANOATE.
001913 02-08

THE RELATIVE PROPHYLACTIC EFFICACY OF LITHIUM AGAINST MANIC AND DEPRESSIVE RECURRENCES IN BIPOLAR-PATIENTS.
002040 02-09

EFFICACY AND SIDE-EFFECTS OF LORAZEPAM, OXAZEPAM, AND TEMAZEPAM AS SLEEPING-AIDS IN PSYCHOGERIATRIC-INPATIENTS.
002076 02-10

EFFICACY AND SIDE-EFFECTS OF CHLORAL-HYDRATE AND TRYPTOPHAN AS SLEEPING-AIDS IN PSYCHOGERIATRIC-PATIENTS.
002077 02-10

THE RELATIVE EFFICACY OF COGNITIVE-THERAPY AND CHEMOTHERAPY FOR THE TREATMENT OF DEPRESSION AMONG THE RETIRED ELDERLY. (PH.D. DISSERTATION).
002148 02-11

THE EFFICACY OF TRIAZOLAM AND CHLORAL-HYDRATE IN GERIATRIC INSOMNIACS.
002160 02-11

LITHIUM: PROBLEMS OF APPLICATION, TOLERANCE, AND EFFICACY.
002434 02-15

REPEATED ANTIDEPRESSANT TREATMENTS INDUCE A LONG-LASTING DOPAMINE-AUTORECEPTOR SUBSENSITIVITY: IS DAILY TREATMENT NECESSARY FOR CLINICAL EFFICACY?
002659 03-03

EFFICACY OF DESIPRAMINE IN MILDLY DEPRESSED-PATIENTS: A DOUBLE-BLIND, PLACEBO-CONTROLLED-TRIAL.
003262 03-09

EFFICACY OF CLONIDINE IN OPIATE WITHDRAWAL: A STUDY OF THIRTY PATIENTS.
003317 03-11

EFFICACY OF LITHIUM IN TREATING MOOD-DISORDER OCCURRING AFTER BRAINSTEM INJURY.
003354 03-11

PAVING THE WAY TO SAFE PRESCRIBING FOR THE ELDERLY.
000999 01-17
THE IMPORTANCE OF AMINEPTINE IN THE TREATMENT OF NONPSYCHOTIC
DEPRESSIVE-STATES IN THE ELDERLY.
001999 02-09
CLINICAL-TESTING OF MINAPRINE ON ELDERLY SUBJECTS WITH THE
ASTHENIC-DEPRESSIVE-SYNDROMES.
002123 02-11
PHARMACOTHERAPY OF DEPRESSION IN THE ELDERLY.
002144 02-11
THE RELATIVE EFFICACY OF COGNITIVE-THERAPY AND CHEMOTHERAPY
FOR THE TREATMENT OF DEPRESSION AMONG THE RETIRED ELDERLY.
(PH.D. DISSERTATION).
002148 02-11
TREATMENTS FOR SLEEP-WAKE-DISORDERS IN THE ELDERLY.
002157 02-11
PIRIBEDIL IN ELDERLY PSYCHIATRIC-PATIENTS.
002170 02-11
PHARMACOKINETICS OF NORTRIPTYLINE IN ELDERLY VOLUNTEERS.
002184 02-11
CLINICAL-EXPERIENCE WITH PSYCHIATRIC-TREATMENT OF THE ELDERLY
INVOLVING THE USE OF PIRACETAM.
002188 02-11
THE TREATMENT OF BUCCOLINGUOFACIAL DYSKINESIA IN THE ELDERLY:
THE CHOICE OF A NEUROLEPTIC-AGENT.
002223 02-13
PNEUMONIA AND PSYCHOTROPIC-DRUG USE IN ELDERLY PSYCHIATRIC-
PATIENTS.
002391 02-15
DRUGS IN THE ELDERLY.
002451 02-15
DRUGS AND THE ELDERLY: PERSPECTIVES IN GERIATRIC CLINICAL-
PHARMACOLOGY.
002534 02-17
NEUROPSYCHIATRIC SIDE-EFFECTS OF DRUGS IN THE ELDERLY. VOL. 9,
AGING.
002573 02-17
THE THERAPEUTIC PROFILE OF MIANSERIN IN MILD ELDERLY
DEPRESSIVES.
003297 03-11
A DOUBLE-BLIND, PLACEBO-CONTROLLED-STUDY OF PIRACETAM IN
ELDERLY PSYCHIATRIC-PATIENTS.
003305 03-11
PHARMACOKINETICS OF AMITRIPTYLINE, IMIPRAMINE, AND
MAPROTILINE IN THE ELDERLY.
003324 03-11
TREATMENT OF DEPRESSIVE-CONDITIONS IN THE ELDERLY.
003578 03-17
DESMETHYLDIAZEPAM KINETICS IN THE ELDERLY AFTER ORAL
PRAZEPAM.
004432 04-11
KINETICS AND BIOTRANSFORMATION OF LORMETAZEPAM: II.
RADIOIMMUNOLOGIC DETERMINATIONS IN PLASMA AND URINE OF
YOUNG AND ELDERLY SUBJECTS: FIRST-PASS EFFECT.
004516 04-13
ELDERLY-PATIENTS
SPONTANEOUS DYSKINESIA IN THE ELDERLY AND TARDIVE-DYSKINESIA
FROM NEUROLEPTICS. A SURVEY OF 270 ELDERLY-PATIENTS.
000834 01-15
PSYCHOTROPIC-DRUGS AND POLYPHARMACY IN ELDERLY-PATIENTS IN A
GENERAL-HOSPITAL.
000981 01-17
CLINICAL-TRIAL WITH AMANTADINE AND HYDERGINE IN ELDERLY-
PATIENTS.
002093 02-11
TREATMENT OF ORGANIC-BRAIN-DISTURBANCES IN ELDERLY-PATIENTS. A
CLINICAL DOUBLE-BLIND STUDY WITH MACROMOLECULAR ORGAN
LYSATES (CYTOPLASMATIC THERAPY ACCORDING TO THEURER).
003327 03-11
THE ROLE OF PSYCHOPHARMACOTHERAPY IN THE TREATMENT OF
ELDERLY-PATIENTS WITH ORGANIC-MENTAL-SYNDROMES.
003368 03-11
ELECTIVE
ELECTIVE ALTERATION OF THE STATE OF CONSCIOUSNESS SUBJECTED TO
THE EFFECTS OF PSYCHOACTIVE-SUBSTANCES.
000994 01-17
ELECTRIC-SHOCK
NALORPHINES EFFECT UNDER SEVERAL SCHEDULES OF ELECTRIC-SHOCK
TITRATION.
000379 01-04
EFFECTS OF MORPHINE, PENTAZOCINE AND CYCLAZOCINE ALONE AND IN
COMBINATION WITH NALOXONE ON ELECTRIC-SHOCK TITRATION IN
THE SQUIRREL-MONKEY.
001611 02-04
THE EFFECTS OF ELECTRIC-SHOCK ON RESPONDING MAINTAINED BY
COCAINE IN RHESUS-MONKEYS.
004071 04-04
DISCRIMINATION OF ELECTRIC-SHOCK: EFFECTS OF SOME OPIOID AND
NONOPIOID DRUGS.
004106 04-04

BEHAVIORAL-EFFECTS OF SELF-ADMINISTERED COCAINE: RESPONDING
MAINTAINED ALTERNATELY BY COCAINE AND ELECTRIC-SHOCK IN
SQUIRREL-MONKEYS.
004225 04-04
ELECTRIC-STIMULATION
EFFECTS OF METHYSERGIDE AND NALOXONE ON ANALGESIA INDUCED BY
THE PERIPHERAL ELECTRIC-STIMULATION IN MICE.
003093 03-04
ELECTRICAL
THE EFFECTS OF THIORIDAZINE ON ELECTRICAL AND ISCHEMIC
VENTRICULAR FIBRILLATION IN THE DOG HEART IN SITU.
002697 03-03
ELECTRICAL-ACTIVITIES
ACTION OF DRUGS ON THE CEREBELLAR ELECTRICAL-ACTIVITIES.
003804 04-03
ELECTRICAL-ACTIVITY
EFFECTS OF HEMICHOLINIUM-3 AND CHOLINE ON HIPPOCAMPAL
ELECTRICAL-ACTIVITY DURING IMMOBILITY VS. MOVEMENT.
001438 02-03
NEURONAL MATURATION IN MAMMALIAN CELL-CULTURE IS DEPENDENT
ON SPONTANEOUS ELECTRICAL-ACTIVITY.
002669 03-03
ELECTRICAL-ACTIVITY AND NA-K-ATPASE LEVEL IN THE PENICILLIN-
INDUCED EPILEPTOGENIC-FOCUS OF THE RAT-BRAIN-CORTEX, AND THE
EFFECT OF DIAZEPAM.
003070 03-04
EFFECTS OF ENKEPHALIN, MORPHINE, AND NALOXONE ON THE
ELECTRICAL-ACTIVITY OF THE IN VITRO HIPPOCAMPAL SLICE
PREPARATION.
003918 04-03
EFFECTS OF A SHORT-ACTING BENZODIAZEPINE ON BRAIN ELECTRICAL-
ACTIVITY DURING SLEEP.
004568 04-14
ELECTRICAL-STIMULATION
FAILURE OF ISOPRENALINE AND BETA-RECEPTOR BLOCKING-DRUGS TO
MODIFY DEPRESSOR RESPONSE AND BRADYCARDIA INDUCED BY
ELECTRICAL-STIMULATION OF THE ANTERIOR HYPOTHALAMUS OF
CATS.
000520 01-05
FACTORS INFLUENCING THE RELEASE OF LABELLED GAMMA
AMINOBUTYRIC-ACID AND ACETYLCHOLINE EVOKED BY ELECTRICAL-
STIMULATION WITH ALTERNATING POLARITY FROM RAT CORTICAL
SLICES.
001130 02-03
RETROGRADE AMNESIA PRODUCED BY ELECTRICAL-STIMULATION OF THE
AMYGDALA: ATTENUATION WITH ADRENERGIC ANTAGONISTS.
(UNPUBLISHED PAPER).
001488 02-03
·EFFECTS OF ELECTROLYTIC AND 6 HYDROXYDOPAMINE LESIONS OF THE
LATERAL HYPOTHALAMUS ON ROTATION EVOKED BY ELECTRICAL-
STIMULATION OF THE SUBSTANTIA-NIGRA IN RATS.
003081 03-04
EVIDENCE FOR INVOLVEMENT OF SEPARATE MECHANISMS IN THE
PRODUCTION OF ANALGESIA BY ELECTRICAL-STIMULATION OF THE
NUCLEUS-RETICULARIS-PARAGIGANTOCELLULARIS AND NUCLEUS-
RAPHE-MAGNUS IN THE RAT.
003083 03-04
THE EFFECT OF ELECTRICAL-STIMULATION OF THE LOCUS-COERULEUS AND
INTRAPERITONEAL INJECTION OF CERTAIN PHARMACOLOGICAL
SUBSTANCES ON THE THRESHOLD OF HIPPOCAMPAL
AFTERDISCHARGES.
003885 04-03
PRESSOR EFFECTS OF ELECTRICAL-STIMULATION OF THE DORSAL AND
MEDIAN RAPHE NUCLEI IN ANESTHETIZED RATS.
003892 04-03
THE EFFECT OF SMALL DOSES OF HALOPERIDOL AND CLOZAPINE ON
BEHAVIORAL SHIFTS IN CATS, ARISING AFTER CESSATION OF
ELECTRICAL-STIMULATION OF THE CAUDATE-NUCLEUS.
004067 04-04
RETROGRADE AMNESIA PRODUCED BY ELECTRICAL-STIMULATION OF THE
AMYGDALA: ATTENUATION WITH ADRENERGIC ANTAGONISTS.
004231 04-04
ELECTRICALLY-INDUCED
EFFECTS OF GAMMA ACETYLENIC-GABA AND GAMMA VINYL-GABA ON
ELECTRICALLY-INDUCED SPINAL-CORD CONVULSIONS AND ON SPINAL-
CORD GABA CONCENTRATION.
000145 01-03
THE EFFECTS OF RESERPINE, IPRONIAZID AND L-DOPA ON ELECTRICALLY-
INDUCED SPINAL-CORD SEIZURES.
000146 01-03
EFFECTS OF NOREPINEPHRINE AND 5 HYDROXYTRYPTAMINE REUPTAKE
INHIBITORS ON ELECTRICALLY-INDUCED SPINAL-CORD SEIZURES IN
RATS.
004144 04-04
EFFECTS OF FLUOXETINE ON ELECTRICALLY-INDUCED SPINAL-CORD
SEIZURES IN RATS.
004145 04-04

Subject Index

ELECTROACUPUNCTURE
MORPHINE AND ELECTROACUPUNCTURE: COMPARISON OF THE EFFECTS
ON THE CORTICAL EVOKED-RESPONSES AFTER TOOTH-PULP
STIMULATION IN RATS.
001294 02-03

ELECTROCARDIOGRAM
FOLLOWUP STUDY ON THE INFLUENCE OF AN ANTIPSYCHOTIC-DRUG
(PROPERICIAZINE) ON LIVER FUNCTION, ELECTROCARDIOGRAM AND
ELECTROENCEPHALOGRAM.
000639 01-09

ELECTROCARDIOGRAM-CHANGES
ELECTROCARDIOGRAM-CHANGES AND PLASMA DESIPRAMINE LEVELS
DURING TREATMENT OF DEPRESSION.
004411 04-09

ELECTROCARDIOGRAPHIC-CHANGES
ELECTROCARDIOGRAPHIC-CHANGES DURING LITHIUM TREATMENT.
000881 01-15
ELECTROCARDIOGRAPHIC-CHANGES IN RATS DURING CHRONIC-
TREATMENT WITH ANTIDEPRESSANT AND NEUROLEPTIC-DRUGS.
004284 04-05

ELECTROCHEMICAL
A RAPID AND SIMPLE METHOD FOR THE DETERMINATION OF PICOGRAM
LEVELS OF 3 METHOXYTYRAMINE IN BRAIN TISSUE USING LIQUID-
CHROMATOGRAPHY WITH ELECTROCHEMICAL DETECTION.
003674 04-01

ELECTROCHEMICAL-DETECTION
HYPOTHALAMIC CATECHOLAMINE BIOSYNTHESIS IN VITRO AS
MEASURED BY LIQUID-CHROMATOGRAPHY AND ELECTROCHEMICAL-
DETECTION.
000537 01-06
EVALUATION OF THE EFFECT OF DRUGS ON DOPAMINE METABOLISM IN
THE RAT SUPERIOR-CERVICAL-GANGLION BY HPLC WITH
ELECTROCHEMICAL-DETECTION.
001530 02-03
SIMULTANEOUS DETERMINATION OF FEMTOMOLE QUANTITIES OF 5
HYDROXYTRYPTOPHAN, SEROTONIN AND 5 HYDROXYINDOLEACETIC-
ACID IN BRAIN USING HPLC WITH ELECTROCHEMICAL-DETECTION.
003139 03-06

ELECTROCHEMICAL-METHOD
AN AUTOMATED ELECTROCHEMICAL-METHOD FOR IN VIVO MONITORING
OF CATECHOLAMINE RELEASE.
001873 02-06

ELECTROCONVULSIVE-SHOCK
REPEATED ELECTROCONVULSIVE-SHOCK DOES NOT INCREASE THE
SUSCEPTIBILITY OF RATS TO A CAGE CONVULSANT
(ISOPROPYLBICYCLOPHOSPHATE).
001184 02-03
EFFECT OF SINGLE AND REPEATED ELECTROCONVULSIVE-SHOCK ON
SEROTONERGIC SYSTEM IN RAT-BRAIN — I. METABOLIC-STUDIES.
001332 02-03
THE EFFECT OF REPEATED ELECTROCONVULSIVE-SHOCK ON
CORTICOSTERONE RESPONSES TO CENTRALLY-ACTING
PHARMACOLOGICAL STIMULI IN THE MALE RAT.
001486 02-03
EFFECT OF SINGLE AND REPEATED ELECTROCONVULSIVE-SHOCK ON
SEROTONERGIC SYSTEM IN RAT-BRAIN — II. BEHAVIOURAL-STUDIES.
001697 02-04
ON THE MEASUREMENT IN RATS OF THE CONVULSANT-EFFECT OF DRUGS
AND THE CHANGES WHICH FOLLOW ELECTROCONVULSIVE-SHOCK.
002444 02-15
BRAIN AND SERUM CALCIUM CONCENTRATIONS FOLLOWING
ELECTROCONVULSIVE-SHOCK OR BICUCULLINE-INDUCED CONVULSIONS
IN RATS.
003736 04-03
DIFFERENTIAL-EFFECTS OF ELECTROCONVULSIVE-SHOCK AND
ANTIDEPRESSANT-DRUGS ON SEROTONIN2-RECEPTORS IN RAT-BRAIN.
003878 04-03
REDUCTION IN OPIATE ACTIVATION AFTER CHRONIC
ELECTROCONVULSIVE-SHOCK -- POSSIBLE ROLE FOR ENDORPHINS IN
THE BEHAVIORAL-EFFECTS OF CONVULSIVE-SHOCK-TREATMENT.
(UNPUBLISHED PAPER).
004154 04-04

ELECTROCONVULSIVE-SHOCKS
EFFECT OF REPEATED ELECTROCONVULSIVE-SHOCKS (ECS) ON·
SUBTHRESHOLD DOSES OF SOME CNS STIMULANTS.
001361 02-03

ELECTROCONVULSIVE-THERAPY
FACTORS INFLUENCING SEIZURE DURATION AND NUMBER OF SEIZURES
APPLIED IN UNILATERAL ELECTROCONVULSIVE-THERAPY: ANESTHETICS
AND BENZODIAZEPINES.
000792 01-13
ADMINISTRATION OF FLUNITRAZEPAM IN ELECTROCONVULSIVE-
THERAPY.
004319 04-08
VALUE OF PROPANIDID IN ELECTROCONVULSIVE-THERAPY (COMPARISON
WITH THIOPENTONE).
004379 04-09

ELECTROENCEPHALOGRAPHY
DIAGNOSTIC AND PROGNOSTIC SIGNIFICANCE OF
ELECTROENCEPHALOGRAPHY WITH INTRAVENOUS DIAZEPAM IN
EPILEPSY.
000696 01-11

ELECTROLYTE
THE EFFECT OF DIAZEPAM ON TENSION AND ELECTROLYTE DISTRIBUTION
IN FROG MUSCLE.
000069 01-03

ELECTROLYTE-DISTURBANCES
TREATMENT OF UNDERNUTRITION AND ELECTROLYTE-DISTURBANCES IN
ANOREXIA-NERVOSA.
004531 04-13

ELECTROLYTES
EFFECT OF FLUPHENAZINE ON THE CIRCADIAN-EXCRETION OF CYCLIC-
NUCLEOTIDES AND ELECTROLYTES IN THE URINE OF CHRONIC
SCHIZOPHRENICS.
001927 02-08

ELECTROLYTIC
MALE RAT SEXUAL-BEHAVIOR COMPARED AFTER 6 OHOA AND
ELECTROLYTIC LESIONS IN THE DORSAL NA BUNDLE REGION OF THE
MIDBRAIN.
001593 02-04
ELECTROLYTIC MICROINFUSION TRANSDUCER SYSTEM: AN ALTERNATIVE
METHOD OF INTRACRANIAL DRUG APPLICATION.
001861 02-06
EFFECTS OF ELECTROLYTIC AND 6 HYDROXYDOPAMINE LESIONS OF THE
LATERAL HYPOTHALAMUS ON ROTATION EVOKED BY ELECTRICAL-
STIMULATION OF THE SUBSTANTIA-NIGRA IN RATS.
003081 03-04
CHANGE IN CATECHOLAMINE SENSITIVE NA-K-ATPASE ACTIVITY IN THE
RAT STRIATUM MICROSOMES FOLLOWING ELECTROLYTIC OR 6
HYDROXYDOPAMINE-INDUCED LESIONS OF DOPAMINERGIC NEURONS.
003871 04-03

ELECTROMYOGRAPHIC-ASSESSMENT
ELECTROMYOGRAPHIC-ASSESSMENT OF SPINAL REFLEXES IN
EXPERIMENTALLY DEPRESSED DOGS TREATED WITH
ANTIDEPRESSANTS.
001620 02-04

ELECTROMYOGRAPHIC-METHOD
AN ELECTROMYOGRAPHIC-METHOD FOR THE ASSESSMENT OF
NALOXONE-INDUCED ABSTINENCE IN MORPHINE-DEPENDENT RATS.
000433 01-04

ELECTRON
ELECTRON PROBE MICROANALYSIS OF CALCIUM AND PHOSPHORUS IN
DENSE-BODIES ISOLATED FROM HUMAN PLATELETS. (UNPUBLISHED
PAPER).
001014 02-01
ELECTRON MICROSCOPIC STUDIES OF BRAIN SLICES: THE EFFECTS OF
HIGH-FREQUENCY STIMULATION ON DENDRITIC ULTRASTRUCTURE.
(UNPUBLISHED PAPER).
001036 02-01
A METHOD FOR MEASUREMENT OF TRANYLCYPROMINE IN RAT-BRAIN
REGIONS USING GAS-CHROMATOGRAPHY WITH ELECTRON CAPTURE
DETECTION.
003137 03-06

ELECTRON-CAPTURE
ANALYSIS FOR DIAZEPAM AND NORDIAZEPAM BY ELECTRON-CAPTURE
GAS-CHROMATOGRAPHY AND BY LIQUID-CHROMATOGRAPHY.
000006 01-01
ELECTRON-CAPTURE GAS-LIQUID-CHROMATOGRAPHIC-DETERMINATION
OF ETHOSUXIMIDE AND DESMETHYLMETHSUXIMIDE IN PLASMA OR
SERUM.
000538 01-06

ELECTRONYSTAGMOGRAPHY
PROGRESSIVE SUPRANUCLEAR PALSY: PNEUMOENCEPHALOGRAPHY,
ELECTRONYSTAGMOGRAPHY AND TREATMENT WITH METHYSERGIDE.
003355 03-11

ELECTROPHYSIOLOGIC
ELECTROPHYSIOLOGIC ASSESSMENT OF RECEPTOR CHANGES FOLLOWING
CHRONIC DRUG-TREATMENT.
003136 03-06

ELECTROPHYSIOLOGICAL
REPEATED TRICYCLIC-ANTIDEPRESSANTS INDUCE A PROGRESSIVE SWITCH
IN THE ELECTROPHYSIOLOGICAL RESPONSE OF DOPAMINE NEURONS TO
AUTORECEPTOR STIMULATION.
000046 01-03
ELECTROPHYSIOLOGICAL ACTIONS OF BENZODIAZEPINES.
000107 01-03
AGE-RELATED ELECTROPHYSIOLOGICAL CHANGES IN RAT-CEREBELLUM.
000197 01-03
TREATMENT OF MYOCLONUS WITH L 5 HYDROXYTRYPTOPHAN AND
CARBIDOPA: CLINICAL, ELECTROPHYSIOLOGICAL, AND BIOCHEMICAL-
OBSERVATIONS.
002180 02-11
EFFECTS OF PROLONGED TREATMENT WITH LITHIUM AND TRICYCLIC-
ANTIDEPRESSANTS ON DISCHARGE FREQUENCY, NOREPINEPHRINE
RESPONSES AND BETA-RECEPTOR BINDING IN RAT-CEREBELLUM:
ELECTROPHYSIOLOGICAL AND BIOCHEMICAL COMPARISON.
002884 03-03

ELECTROPHYSIOLOGICAL EVIDENCE FOR PRESYNAPTIC ACTIONS OF
PHENCYCLIDINE ON NORADRENERGIC TRANSMISSION IN RAT
CEREBELLUM.
003926 04-03
AN ELECTROPHYSIOLOGICAL MODEL OF GABA-MEDIATED
NEUROTRANSMISSION.
003929 04-03
CATECHOLAMINE MODULATION OF ENKEPHALIN-INDUCED
ELECTROPHYSIOLOGICAL RESPONSES IN CEREBRAL-CORTEX.
003957 04-03
ELECTROPHYSIOLOGICAL AND PSYCHOLOGICAL CHANGES INDUCED BY
STEROID-HORMONES IN MEN AND WOMEN.
004500 04-13

ELECTROPHYSIOLOGICAL-CHANGES
ELECTROPHYSIOLOGICAL-CHANGES AT A CENTRAL NORADRENERGIC
SYNAPSE DURING THALLIUM TOXICOSIS.
001848 02-05

ELECTROPHYSIOLOGICAL-CORRELATES
INFERENTIAL CHANGES AFTER CHRONIC-TREATMENTS WITH LI, DMI, OR
ETHANOL DETECTED BY ELECTROPHYSIOLOGICAL-CORRELATES.
001136 02-03

ELECTROPHYSIOLOGICAL-EFFECTS
THE ELECTROPHYSIOLOGICAL-EFFECTS OF ENKEPHALIN AND
PHENCYCLIDINE IN THE RAT CENTRAL-NERVOUS-SYSTEM. (PH.D.
DISSERTATION).
001406 02-03
BEHAVIORAL-EFFECTS AND ELECTROPHYSIOLOGICAL-EFFECTS OF OPIOID-
PEPTIDES IN CATS.
001612 02-04
ELECTROPHYSIOLOGICAL-EFFECTS OF IMIPRAMINE ON BOVINE
VENTRICULAR-MUSCLE AND PURKINJE-FIBRES.
003988 04-03

ELECTROPHYSIOLOGICAL-STUDIES
ANTIANXIETY-AGENTS AND SYNAPTIC TRANSMISSION IN THE BRAIN:
ELECTROPHYSIOLOGICAL-STUDIES. (PH.D. DISSERTATION).
002840 03-03

ELECTROPHYSIOLOGICAL-STUDY
TRANSIENT-EFFECT OF L TRYPTOPHAN IN PROGRESSIVE MYOCLONUS
EPILEPSY WITHOUT LAFORA-BODIES: CLINICAL-STUDY AND
ELECTROPHYSIOLOGICAL-STUDY.
000694 01-11

ELECTRORETINOGRAM
THE ELECTRORETINOGRAM IN PARKINSONS-DISEASE.
001295 02-03
CHANGES OF ELECTRORETINOGRAM AND NEUROCHEMICAL ASPECTS OF
GABAERGIC NEURONS OF RETINA AFTER INTRAOCULAR INJECTION OF
KAINIC-ACID IN RATS.
003807 04-03

ELECTRORETINOGRAPHIC-CHANGES
ELECTRORETINOGRAPHIC-CHANGES IN PATIENTS WITH PARKINSONISM
TREATED WITH VARIOUS CLASSES OF ANTIPARKINSONIAN-DRUGS.
000674 01-11
ELECTRORETINOGRAPHY (ERG) AS A TOOL OF INVESTIGATION IN HUMAN
PSYCHOPHARMACOLOGY. ELECTRORETINOGRAPHIC-CHANGES INDUCED
BY A COMBINATION OF CARBIDOPA AND LEVODOPA.
004507 04-13

ELECTRORETINOGRAPHY
ELECTRORETINOGRAPHY (ERG) AS A TOOL OF INVESTIGATION IN HUMAN
PSYCHOPHARMACOLOGY. ELECTRORETINOGRAPHIC-CHANGES INDUCED
BY A COMBINATION OF CARBIDOPA AND LEVODOPA.
004507 04-13

ELECTROSHOCK-INDUCED
EFFECTS OF WITHDRAWAL FROM LONG-TERM DIPHENYLHYDANTOIN
TREATMENT ON AUDIOGENIC-SEIZURES AND MAXIMAL
ELECTROSHOCK-INDUCED SEIZURES IN RATS.
004101 04-04

ELECTROSHOCK-TEST
EFFECT OF DOPAMINERGIC AND GABAERGIC DRUGS GIVEN ALONE OR IN
COMBINATION ON THE ANTICONVULSANT ACTION OF PHENOBARBITAL
AND DIPHENYLHYDANTOIN IN THE ELECTROSHOCK-TEST IN MICE.
000163 01-03

ELECTROSHOCK-TREATMENT
PROTECTIVE ACTION OF L 5 HYDROXYTRYPTOPHAN L GLUTAMATE
(MADE-1932) DURING ELECTROSHOCK-TREATMENT (ECT).
003043 03-04

ELEMENTARY
PREVALENCE OF HYPERACTIVITY AND RELATED TREATMENTS AMONG
ELEMENTARY SCHOOL CHILDREN.
004469 04-11

ELIMINATION
SHORT-TERM ETHANOL ADMINISTRATION IMPAIRS THE ELIMINATION OF
CHLORDIAZEPOXIDE (LIBRIUM) IN MAN.
002224 02-13
INFLUENCE OF PSYCHOTROPIC-DRUGS ON THE URINARY ELIMINATION OF
LITHIUM.
002895 03-03
CLINICAL-PHARMACOLOGY: ELIMINATION OF DRUGS.
003400 03-13

Subject Index

EFFECTS OF INDOMETHACIN AND METHYLPREDNISOLONE ON RENAL
ELIMINATION OF LITHIUM IN THE RAT.
004270 04-05

LITHIUM ELIMINATION HALF-LIFE AND DURATION OF THERAPY.
004369 04-09

EMBRYONIC
EFFECTS OF SOME NOOTROPIC-DRUGS UPON THE EMBRYONIC
MORPHOGENETIC SYSTEMS.
000144 01-03

NERVE GROWTH-FACTOR STIMULATES DEVELOPMENT OF SUBSTANCE-P
IN THE EMBRYONIC SPINAL-CORD.
003881 04-03

EMBRYOS
MATERNAL GLUCOCORTICOID-HORMONES INFLUENCE
NEUROTRANSMITTER PHENOTYPIC EXPRESSION IN EMBRYOS.
000149 01-03

EMD-28422
INCREASED BENZODIAZEPINE-RECEPTOR NUMBER ELICITED IN VITRO BY A
NOVEL PURINE, EMD-28422.
001475 02-03

EMERGENCIES
EMERGENCIES IN MANIC-DEPRESSIVE-PSYCHOSES.
003540 03-15

EMG-RECORDED
OPIOID-RECEPTORS IN THE CAUDATE-NUCLEUS CAN MEDIATE EMG-
RECORDED RIGIDITY IN RATS.
001649 02-04

EMIT
CARBAMAZEPINE-EPOXIDE DETERMINED BY EMIT CARBAMAZEPINE
REAGENT.
000533 01-06

MASS SCREENING AND CONFIRMATION OF DIAZEPAM IN URINE BY EMIT
THIN-LAYER-CHROMATOGRAPHY.
004672 04-16

EMOTIONAL
ADRENERGIC MODULATION OF THE HYPOTHALAMIC CHOLINERGIC
MECHANISM IN THE CONTROL OF EMOTIONAL DEFENSIVE-BEHAVIOR IN
THE CAT.
001761 02-04

THE ROLE OF OPIATE-RECEPTORS OF DIFFERENT BRAIN REGIONS IN
DETERMINING THE EMOTIONAL REACTIONS OF RATS.
004017 04-03

EMOTIONAL-BEHAVIOR
LONG-LASTING EFFECTS OF CHRONIC ADMINISTRATION OF
HALLUCINOGENIC-DRUGS ON RAT SOCIAL AND EMOTIONAL-BEHAVIOR.
(PH.D. DISSERTATION).
003029 03-04

EMOTIONAL-DISORDERS
EMOTIONAL-DISORDERS IN CHILDREN AND ADOLESCENTS: MEDICAL AND
PSYCHOLOGICAL APPROACHES TO TREATMENT.
004743 04-17

EMOTIONAL-STRESS
THE EFFECT OF EMOTIONAL-STRESS AND DIAZEPAM ON MONOAMINE
METABOLITES IN THE CEREBROSPINAL-FLUID OF CATS. (PH.D.
DISSERTATION).
001260 02-03

CORRECTION BY PROPRANOLOL OF THE ABNORMAL ADRENALINE
DISCHARGE INDUCED BY EMOTIONAL-STRESS IN CEREBRAL
HEMORRHAGE PATIENTS.
002295 02-13

EMOTIONALLY
THE EFFECT OF NALOXONE ON THE ACTIVATION OF EMOTIONALLY
POSITIVE REACTION PRODUCED BY DRUGS WITH A DEPENDENCE
LIABILITY.
001556 02-03

EMOTIONALLY-REINFORCED
ACTION ON THE EMOTIONALLY-REINFORCED BRAIN SYSTEM AS A MEANS
OF TREATING ALCOHOLISM AND DRUG ADDICTION
PATHOGENETICALLY.
003641 03-17

EMOTIONS
POSSIBLE INVOLVEMENT OF BRAIN DOPAMINERGIC-SYSTEMS IN THE
EXPRESSION OF EMOTIONS IN DREAMS.
002325 02-14

EMOTIVE
THE BEHAVIOR OF RATS IN THE OPEN-FIELD WITHOUT STRESS, UNDER
ACUTE AND PERSISTING INFLUENCE OF IMIPRAMINE AND
TRANYLCYPROMINE AS WELL AS ON THE INDIVIDUAL REACTION TYPE
(EMOTIVE AND NONEMOTIVE).
001624 02-04

EMPIRICAL
TOLERANCE TO DEXTROAMPHETAMINE-SULFATE IN HYPERACTIVE-
CHILDREN: ASSESSMENT USING AN EMPIRICAL NEUROPSYCHOLOGICAL
PARADIGM -- A PILOT-STUDY.
002126 02-11

DO PSYCHOTHERAPY AND PHARMACOTHERAPY FOR DEPRESSION
CONFLICT? EMPIRICAL EVIDENCE FROM A CLINICAL-TRIAL.
003256 03-09

BRAIN-SPECIFIC BENZODIAZEPINE-RECEPTORS AND PUTATIVE
ENDOGENOUS BENZODIAZEPINE-LIKE COMPOUNDS.
000225 01-03

THE POSSIBILITY THAT A COMPONENT OF MORPHINE-INDUCED
ANALGESIA IS CONTRIBUTED INDIRECTLY VIA THE RELEASE OF
ENDOGENOUS OPIOIDS.
000263 01-03

PURINES AS ENDOGENOUS LIGANDS OF THE BENZODIAZEPINE-RECEPTOR.
000276 01-03

DRUG-THERAPY IN ENDOGENOUS DEPRESSION WITH POSSIBLE PRIMARY
GABA DEFICIENCY CLINICALLY DETECTED: 38 NEW CASES.
000584 01-09

NOMIFENSIN IN THE TREATMENT OF ENDOGENOUS DEPRESSIONS.
CLINICAL-EXPERIENCE AND EEG FINDINGS.
000613 01-09

ANTIDEPRESSIVE TREATMENT AND MOOD-SWING-PATTERNS IN
ENDOGENOUS DEPRESSION.
000633 01-09

CONTROLLED-COMPARISON OF MIANSERINE WITH IMIPRAMINE IN
ENDOGENOUS DEPRESSIONS.
000634 01-09

DECREASED UPTAKE OF 5 HYDROXYTRYPTAMINE IN BLOOD-PLATELETS
FROM PATIENTS WITH ENDOGENOUS DEPRESSION.
000637 01-09

DYNAMICS OF ENDOGENOUS CATECHOLAMINE RELEASE FROM BRAIN
FRAGMENTS OF MALE AND FEMALE RATS.
001121 02-03

EVIDENCE FOR AN ENDOGENOUS COMPOUND INTERFERING WITH 3H
DIAZEPAM BINDING TO RAT-BRAIN MEMBRANES.
001308 02-03

ENDOGENOUS GUANYL-NUCLEOTIDES: COMPONENTS OF THE STRIATUM
WHICH CONFER DOPAMINE SENSITIVITY TO ADENYLATE-CYCLASE.
001313 02-03

ASCORBIC-ACID, AN ENDOGENOUS FACTOR REQUIRED FOR
ACETYLCHOLINE RELEASE FROM THE SYNAPTIC VESICLES.
001322 02-03

BENZODIAZEPINE-RECEPTOR: LOCALIZATION BY PHOTOAFFINITY
LABELING AND ISOLATION OF A POSSIBLE ENDOGENOUS LIGAND.
001381 02-03

1 METHYL-BETA-CARBOLINE (HARMANE), A POTENT ENDOGENOUS
INHIBITOR OF BENZODIAZEPINE-RECEPTOR BINDING.
001440 02-03

CLINICAL-EXPERIENCE WITH SECOND-GENERATION ANTIDEPRESSANTS IN
ENDOGENOUS DEPRESSIONS.
001975 02-09

NOMIFENSINE IN THE TREATMENT OF ENDOGENOUS DEPRESSION. A
CONTROLLED-STUDY VS. NORTRIPTYLINE.
001978 02-09

ENDOGENOUS DEPRESSION AND IMIPRAMINE LEVELS IN THE BLOOD.
001979 02-09

EFFECTS OF ANTIDEPRESSANTS ON PITUITARY HORMONAL SECRETIONS IN
HEALTHY TEST SUBJECTS, NEUROTIC-PATIENTS, AND ENDOGENOUS
DEPRESSIVE-PATIENTS.
002009 02-09

D PHENYLALANINE IN ENDOGENOUS DEPRESSION.
002017 02-09

CLINICAL-TRIAL OF PYRAZIDOL IN ENDOGENOUS DEPRESSIVE-STATES.
002021 02-09

THE CORRELATION OF CATECHOLAMINE AND ADRENERGIC PARAMETERS
WITH DRUG-THERAPY OF NEUROTIC AND ENDOGENOUS DEPRESSIONS.
002047 02-09

PHENYLALANINE LEVELS IN ENDOGENOUS PSYCHOSES.
002049 02-09

THE EFFECT OF CONDITIONS INFLUENCING ENDOGENOUS
PROSTAGLANDINS ON THE ACTIVITY OF DELTA'
TETRAHYDROCANNABINOL.
002196 02-12

THE MYTHOLOGEM OF REVERSIBLE DEATH. THE ANALYTICAL
CONFRONTATION OF ENDOGENOUS DELIRIUM WITH DELUSIONS IN
PSYCHEDELIC-EXPERIENCES.
002200 02-12

PURSUING THE ACTIONS OF PSYCHOTROPIC-DRUGS: RECEPTOR SITES
AND ENDOGENOUS CEREBRAL PROGRAMMES.
002578 02-17

THE REGULATION OF BENZODIAZEPINE RECOGNITION SITES BY
ENDOGENOUS MODULATORS.
002642 03-01

DEMONSTRATION AND CHARACTERIZATION OF AN ENDOGENOUS
INHIBITOR OF GABA-ENHANCED (3H) DIAZEPAM BINDING FROM
BOVINE CEREBRAL-CORTEX.
002645 03-01

MODULATION BY ENDOGENOUS DOPAMINE OF THE RELEASE OF
ACETYLCHOLINE IN THE CAUDATE-NUCLEUS OF THE RABBIT.
002751 03-03

BEHAVIORAL CONFIRMATION OF DIFFUSE NOXIOUS INHIBITORY
CONTROLS (DNIC) AND EVIDENCE FOR A ROLE OF ENDOGENOUS
OPIATES.
002791 03-03

BIPHASIC-EFFECTS AND OPPOSITE-EFFECTS OF DOPAMINE AND
APOMORPHINE ON ENDOGENOUS GABA RELEASE IN THE RAT
SUBSTANTIA-NIGRA.
002923 03-03

BLOCKADE OF ENDOGENOUS OPIATES REDUCES ACTIVITY IN THE RAT.
003111 03-04

AMOXAPINE AND AMITRIPTYLINE IN THE OUTPATIENT TREATMENT OF
ENDOGENOUS DEPRESSION.
003217 03-09

SLEEP AND TREATMENT PREDICTION IN ENDOGENOUS DEPRESSION.
003236 03-09

CLINICAL-EXPERIENCE WITH RETARD DIBENZEPINE (NOVERIL-240) IN
ENDOGENOUS DEPRESSIONS ACCOMPANIED BY SYMPTOMS OF DRUG-
RESISTANCE.
003245 03-09

THERAPEUTIC EFFECT OF MIANSERINE AND IMIPRAMINE IN ENDOGENOUS
DEPRESSIONS (CONTROLLED-COMPARISON).
003264 03-09

ON THE INTENSIVE TREATMENT OF ENDOGENOUS PSYCHOSES.
003384 03-11

ENDOGENOUS LIGANDS FOR BENZODIAZEPINE-RECEPTORS.
003615 03-17

INHIBITION OF (3H)DIAZEPAM BINDING BY AN ENDOGENOUS FRACTION
FROM RAT-BRAIN SYNAPTOSOMES.
003768 04-03

POSSIBLE ROLE OF AN ENDOGENOUS OPIATE IN THE CARDIOVASCULAR-
EFFECTS OF CENTRAL ALPHA-ADRENOCEPTOR STIMULATION IN
SPONTANEOUSLY HYPERTENSIVE-RATS.
003791 04-03

SEXUAL-BEHAVIOR DECREASES PAIN SENSITIVITY AND STIMULATES
ENDOGENOUS OPIOIDS IN MALE RATS.
004234 04-04

TRAZODONE EFFICACY AND SAFETY IN ENDOGENOUS DEPRESSION: A
DOUBLE-BLIND COMPARISON WITH IMIPRAMINE.
004346 04-09

A NEUROENDOCRINE-STUDY OF ADRENOCEPTOR FUNCTION IN
ENDOGENOUS DEPRESSION.
004362 04-09

THE EFFECT OF NALOXONE ON THE CONDITION OF PATIENTS WITH
ENDOGENOUS PSYCHOSES.
004381 04-09

CEREBROSPINAL-FLUID VALUES OF HVA AND 5 HIAA IN PATIENTS WITH
ENDOGENOUS DEPRESSION DURING THE COURSE OF TREATMENT.
004382 04-09

COMPARATIVE CHARACTERISTICS OF THE PROPHYLACTIC PROPERTIES OF
SHORT-TERM AND LONG-ACTING LITHIUM-CARBONATE PREPARATIONS
IN ENDOGENOUS AFFECTIVE-PSYCHOSES.
004390 04-09

CORTISOL DYNAMICS AND DEXAMETHASONE PHARMACOKINETICS IN
PRIMARY ENDOGENOUS DEPRESSION: PRELIMINARY FINDINGS.
004403 04-09

CLINICAL-EVALUATION OF THE PROPHYLACTIC EFFECTIVENESS OF
PROLONGED LITHIUM-CARBONATE THERAPY IN ENDOGENOUS
DEPRESSIVE-SYNDROMES.
004404 04-09

THE ACTIVITY OF ERYTHROCYTE CATECHOL-O-METHYLTRANSFERASE IN
ENDOGENOUS DEPRESSIVE-SYNDROMES.
004546 04-13

THE ACTIVITY OF BLOOD-PLATELET MONOAMINE-OXIDASE IN
ENDOGENOUS DEPRESSION.
004547 04-13

THE ACTIVITY OF DOPAMINE-BETA-HYDROXYLASE IN THE PLASMA OF
PATIENTS WITH ENDOGENOUS DEPRESSIVE-SYNDROMES.
004548 04-13

ENDOGENOUSLY-INDUCED
ENDORPHIN-INDUCED HYPERTHERMIA: CHARACTERIZATION OF THE
EXOGENOUSLY-INDUCED AND ENDOGENOUSLY-INDUCED EFFECTS.
000029 01-03

ENDOMORPHOUS
STATISTICAL ANALYSES OF PHYSIOLOGIC DATA FROM FEMALE PATIENTS
WITH AN ENDOMORPHOUS DEPRESSIVE COURSE: A TRIAL,
INTERACTIONS BETWEEN PHYSIOLOGIC PARAMETERS, TEST JUNCTURES
IN THIS PHASE.
003251 03-09

ENDORPHIN
STUDIES ON THE HYPERTHERMIC-RESPONSE OF BETA ENDORPHIN IN
MICE.
000137 01-03

METHIONINE-ENKEPHALIN ANTAGONISM AND ENDORPHIN POTENTIATION
OF NARCOTIC-INDUCED ANALGESIA.
000357 01-04

EFFECT OF BETA ENDORPHIN AND NALOXONE ON ACQUISITION,
MEMORY, AND RETRIEVAL OF SHUTTLE AVOIDANCE AND
HABITUATION LEARNING IN RATS.
000410 01-04

EFFECTS OF MORPHINE, BETA ENDORPHIN AND NALOXONE ON
CATECHOLAMINE LEVELS AND SEXUAL-BEHAVIOR IN THE MALE RAT.
000430 01-04

Subject Index

BETA ENDORPHIN AND ANALOGS: 360 MHZ PROTON NMR SPECTROSCOPY.
001028 02-01

CHEMISTRY OF BETA ENDORPHIN.
001038 02-01

BETA ENDORPHIN: DISSOCIATION OF RECEPTOR BINDING-ACTIVITY FROM ANALGESIC POTENCY.
001081 02-02

EVIDENCE THAT VASOPRESSIN IS INVOLVED IN THE ISOPRENALINE-INDUCED BETA ENDORPHIN RELEASE.
001319 02-03

ALTERED LEVELS OF BETA ENDORPHIN FRAGMENTS AFTER CHRONIC MORPHINE TREATMENT OF GUINEA-PIG ILEUM IN VITRO AND IN VIVO.
001404 02-03

NERVE CELL CALCIUM AS A MESSENGER FOR OPIATE AND ENDORPHIN ACTIONS.
001450 02-03

THE SHORT-TERM AND LONG-TERM EFFECTS OF BETA ENDORPHIN ON THE OPIATE ABSTINENCE-SYNDROME IN RATS.
001643 02-04

EFFECTS OF A LOW-DOSE AND A HIGH-DOSE OF BETA ENDORPHIN ON ACQUISITION AND RETENTION IN THE RAT.
001663 02-04

BETA ENDORPHIN CAUSES RETROGRADE AMNESIA AND IS RELEASED FROM THE RAT-BRAIN BY VARIOUS FORMS OF TRAINING AND STIMULATION.
001664 02-04

UNUSUAL DOSE-RELATED EFFECT OF AN ENDORPHIN ANALOG IN A COMPLEX MAZE.
001674 02-04

ANALGESIC ACTION OF INTRATHECAL AND INTRACEREBRAL BETA ENDORPHIN IN RATS: COMPARISON WITH MORPHINE.
001691 02-04

DIAGNOSTIC CLASSIFICATION AND THE ENDORPHIN HYPOTHESIS OF SCHIZOPHRENIA: INDIVIDUAL DIFFERENCES AND PSYCHOPHARMACOLOGICAL STRATEGIES. (UNPUBLISHED PAPER).
001910 02-08

CLINICAL AND EEG CHANGES IN DEPRESSIVE-PATIENTS AFTER A SINGLE INJECTION OF BETA ENDORPHIN.
001962 02-09

MOOD AND BEHAVIORAL-EFFECTS OF PHYSOSTIGMINE ON HUMANS ARE ACCOMPANIED BY ELEVATIONS IN PLASMA BETA ENDORPHIN AND CORTISOL.
002280 02-13

ENDORPHIN OPIATE INTERACTIONS WITH NEUROENDOCRINE SYSTEMS.
002552 02-17

AGE DEPENDENT CHANGES IN THE BETA ENDORPHIN CONTENT OF DISCRETE RAT-BRAIN NUCLEI.
002635 03-01

DEVELOPMENT OF TOLERANCE TO THE EXCITATORY EFFECT OF MORPHINE AND CROSS-TOLERANCE TO THE INHIBITORY ACTION OF BETA ENDORPHIN IN THE ISOLATED RAT VAS-DEFERENS.
002756 03-03

DYNORPHIN: A POSSIBLE MODULATORY PEPTIDE ON MORPHINE OR BETA ENDORPHIN ANALGESIA IN MOUSE.
002994 03-04

ASCENDING ENDORPHIN INHIBITION OF DISTRESS VOCALIZATION.
003011 03-04

MULTIDIMENSIONAL ANALYSES OF BEHAVIOR IN MICE TREATED WITH ALPHA ENDORPHIN.
003020 03-04

ENHANCEMENT OF ETHANOL-INDUCED SEDATION AND HYPOTHERMIA BY CENTRALLY ADMINISTERED NEUROTENSIN, BETA ENDORPHIN AND BOMBESIN.
003037 03-04

DIAGNOSTIC CLASSIFICATION AND THE ENDORPHIN HYPOTHESIS OF SCHIZOPHRENIA: INDIVIDUAL DIFFERENCES AND PSYCHOPHARMACOLOGICAL STRATEGIES.
003167 03-08

BETA ENDORPHIN LEVELS IN THE CEREBROSPINAL-FLUID OF SCHIZOPHRENICS.
003176 03-08

BETA ENDORPHIN IN COTARDS-SYNDROME.
003187 03-08

BETA ENDORPHIN AND SCHIZOPHRENIA.
003193 03-08

ENDORPHIN RESEARCH IN SCHIZOPHRENIC-PSYCHOSES.
003200 03-08

BEHAVIORAL-EFFECTS AND BIOLOGICAL-EFFECTS OF ACUTE BETA ENDORPHIN INJECTION IN SCHIZOPHRENIC-PATIENTS AND DEPRESSED-PATIENTS.
003357 03-11

SYNTHESIS AND BIOLOGICAL-ACTIVITY OF HUMAN BETA ENDORPHIN ANALOGS WITH DISULFIDE BRIDGES.
003655 04-01

VASOPRESSIN STIMULATES RELEASE OF BETA LIPOTROPIN AND BETA ENDORPHIN IN CONSCIOUS RATS AS MEASURED BY RADIOIMMUNOASSAY OF UNEXTRACTED PLASMA.
003715 04-03

ENDPOINT
RAT-BRAIN STEADY-STATE LEVELS OF CYCLIC-NUCLEOTIDES AS AN ENDPOINT OF LSD-LIKE HALLUCINOGEN EFFECTS. (PH.D. DISSERTATION).
001426 02-03

ENERGY
CONVULSANT AND ANTICONVULSANT BARBITURATES. 1. MOLECULAR CONFORMATIONS FROM CLASSICAL POTENTIAL ENERGY CALCULATIONS.
001029 02-01
ENERGY RESERVES AND SOUND-INDUCED SEIZURES. (UNPUBLISHED PAPER).
001467 02-03
NEURONAL ACTIVITY AND ENERGY METABOLISM: A SUMMARY OF A SYMPOSIUM. (UNPUBLISHED PAPER).
002308 02-13
THE EFFECT OF PROPYLNORANTIFEIN ON BEHAVIORAL-REACTIONS, ADRENOCORTICAL ACTIVITY, AND ENERGY METABOLISM IN THE ANIMAL BRAIN.
004075 04-04
EFFECT OF INORGANIC LEAD ON RAT-BRAIN MITOCHONDRIAL RESPIRATION AND ENERGY PRODUCTION.
004267 04-05

ENFLURANE
INFLUENCE OF IMIPRAMINE AND PARGYLINE ON THE ARRHYTHMOGENICITY OF EPINEPHRINE DURING HALOTHANE, ENFLURANE OR METHOXYFLURANE ANESTHESIA IN DOGS.
001539 02-03
EPILEPTOGENIC PROPERTIES OF ENFLURANE AND THEIR CLINICAL INTERPRETATION.
004609 04-15

ENGLAND
THE HLA-SYSTEM AND SCHIZOPHRENIA IN ENGLAND.
001933 02-08

ENKEPHALIN
ENKEPHALIN LEVELS DECREASE IN RAT STRIATUM DURING MORPHINE ABSTINENCE.
000027 01-03
EFFECTS OF ENKEPHALIN ANALOGUE AND NALOXONE ON CAT SPINAL-CORD DORSAL ROOT POTENTIALS.
000236 01-03
APPLICATION OF A SYNTHETIC ENKEPHALIN ANALOGUE DURING HEROIN WITHDRAWAL.
000685 01-11
THE ELECTROPHYSIOLOGICAL-EFFECTS OF ENKEPHALIN AND PHENCYCLIDINE IN THE RAT CENTRAL-NERVOUS-SYSTEM. (PH.D. DISSERTATION).
001406 02-03
ACTIONS OF ENKEPHALIN, MU AND PARTIAL AGONIST ANALGESICS ON ACETYLCHOLINE TURNOVER IN RAT-BRAIN.
001541 02-03
CONTRALATERAL CIRCLING-BEHAVIOUR INDUCED BY INTRANIGRAL INJECTION OF MORPHINE AND ENKEPHALIN ANALOGUE FK-33-824 IN RATS.
001669 02-04
BIPHASIC-EFFECTS OF A POTENT ENKEPHALIN ANALOGUE D MET2-PRO5-ENKEPHALINAMIDE AND MORPHINE ON LOCOMOTOR-ACTIVITY IN MICE.
001799 02-04
A TOPOGRAPHIC LOCALIZATION OF ENKEPHALIN ON THE DOPAMINE NEURONS OF THE RAT SUBSTANTIA-NIGRA AND VENTRAL TEGMENTAL AREA DEMONSTRATED BY COMBINED HISTOFLUORESCENCE IMMUNOCYTOCHEMISTRY.
002639 03-01
THE EFFECT OF BARBITURATES ON THE DEGRADATION OF ENKEPHALIN BY BRAIN ENZYMES.
002656 03-03
ENKEPHALIN ANALOGS AND PHYSICAL-DEPENDENCE.
003572 03-16
SYNTHESIS AND PHARMACOLOGICAL-STUDY OF SOME ENKEPHALIN ANALOGS IN RELATION TO THE PLURALITY OF OPIATE-RECEPTORS.
003682 04-02
INVESTIGATION OF ACTION OF ENKEPHALIN ON THE SPONTANEOUS AND EVOKED RELEASE OF ACETYLCHOLINE FROM RAT CORTICAL AND STRIATAL SLICES.
003862 04-03
ACTION OF ENKEPHALIN ANALOGUES AND MORPHINE ON BRAIN ACETYLCHOLINE RELEASE: DIFFERENTIAL REVERSAL BY NALOXONE AND AN OPIATE-PENTAPEPTIDE.
003863 04-03
CHARACTERIZATION OF ENKEPHALIN RELEASE FROM RAT STRIATUM.
003909 04-03
EFFECTS OF ENKEPHALIN, MORPHINE, AND NALOXONE ON THE ELECTRICAL-ACTIVITY OF THE IN VITRO HIPPOCAMPAL SLICE PREPARATION.
003918 04-03

ENKEPHALIN-CONTAINING
IMMUNOHISTOCHEMICAL LOCALIZATION OF LEUCINE-ENKEPHALIN IN THE SPINAL-CORD OF THE CAT: ENKEPHALIN-CONTAINING MARGINAL NEURONS AND PAIN MODULATION.
002638 03-01

ENKEPHALIN-INDUCED
CATECHOLAMINE MODULATION OF ENKEPHALIN-INDUCED ELECTROPHYSIOLOGICAL RESPONSES IN CEREBRAL-CORTEX.
003957 04-03

ENKEPHALIN-LIKE
ENKEPHALIN-LIKE CHARACTER AND ANALGESIA.
002650 03-02

ENKEPHALIN-RECEPTOR
ENKEPHALIN-RECEPTOR IN THE RABBIT ILEUM.
000221 01-03

ENKEPHALINERGIC
EFFECTS OF LONG-TERM ADMINISTRATION OF ANTIPSYCHOTIC-DRUGS ON ENKEPHALINERGIC NEURONS.
001284 02-03

ENKEPHALINS
ENKEPHALINS PRESYNAPTICALLY INHIBIT CHOLINERGIC TRANSMISSION IN SYMPATHETIC GANGLIA.
000167 01-03
EFFECTS OF CHANGES IN THE STRUCTURE OF ENKEPHALINS AND OF NARCOTIC ANALGESIC-DRUGS ON THEIR INTERACTIONS WITH MU-RECEPTORS AND DELTA-RECEPTORS.
000168 01-03
COMPARATIVE-EFFECTS OF SOMATOSTATIN AND ENKEPHALINS ON THE GUINEA-PIG ILEUM AND THE RAT VAS-DEFERENS.
001302 02-03
OPIATE AND PEPTIDE INTERACTION: EFFECT OF ENKEPHALINS ON MORPHINE ANALGESIA.
001698 02-04
ESTIMATING IN VIVO THE TURNOVER-RATE OF BRAIN ENKEPHALINS.
001884 02-06
CLASSIFICATION OF ENDORPHINS/ENKEPHALINS IN BRAIN PHYSIOLOGY AND PATHOLOGY (BASED ON EEG AND CLINICAL-STUDY OF SYNTHETICALLY-MODIFIED METHIONINE-ENKEPHALIN).
002286 02-13
HISTOCHEMICAL LOCALIZATION OF OPIATE-RECEPTORS AND THE ENKEPHALINS.
002566 02-17
NEUROBIOLOGY AND NEUROPHARMACOLOGY OF THE ENKEPHALINS.
002580 02-17
MOLECULAR ACTIONS OF OPIATES: HISTORICAL OVERVIEW AND NEW FINDINGS ON OPIATE-RECEPTOR INTERACTIONS WITH ENKEPHALINS AND GUANYL-NUCLEOTIDES.
002613 02-17
DIFFERENTIAL LOSS OF BIOLOGICAL-ACTIVITY OF THE ENKEPHALINS INDUCED BY CURRENT.
002783 03-03
POTENT TETRAPEPTIDE ENKEPHALINS.
003684 04-02
SPREADING DEPRESSION INDUCED BY MICROINJECTION OF ENKEPHALINS INTO THE HIPPOCAMPUS AND NEOCORTEX.
004015 04-03
ARE THE ENKEPHALINS INVOLVED IN PARKINSONS-DISEASE? CLINICAL AND NEUROENDOCRINE RESPONSES TO NALOXONE ADMINISTRATION.
004431 04-11

ENOLASE
THE ETIOLOGY OF TOXIC PERIPHERAL NEUROPATHIES: IN VITRO EFFECTS OF ACRYLAMIDE AND 2,5 HEXANEDIONE ON BRAIN ENOLASE AND OTHER GLYCOLYTIC ENZYMES.
000131 01-03
BASIC AND CLINICAL NEUROBIOLOGICAL APPLICATIONS OF NEURONAL (NSE) AND NONNEURONAL (NNE) ENOLASE. (UNPUBLISHED PAPER).
001041 02-01

ENOLASES
BIOCHEMICAL AND IMMUNOLOGICAL PROPERTIES OF THE MOUSE BRAIN ENOLASES PURIFIED BY A SIMPLE METHOD.
003668 04-01

ENRICHMENT
DOPAMINE-RECEPTORS IN SUBCELLULAR FRACTIONS FROM BOVINE CAUDATE: ENRICHMENT OF (3H)SPIPERONE BINDING IN A POSTSYNAPTIC MEMBRANE FRACTION.
003948 04-03

ENTERIC-COATED
MEAL-DEPENDENT ABSORPTION OF ENTERIC-COATED SODIUM-VALPROATE.
000777 01-13

ENTEROHEPATIC
DISPOSITION OF VALPROIC-ACID IN THE RAT: DOSE-DEPENDENT METABOLISM, DISTRIBUTION, ENTEROHEPATIC RECIRCULATION AND CHOLERETIC-EFFECT.
000073 01-03

ENURESIS
MEDICAL PSYCHOLOGICAL AND COMBINED THERAPY IN THE CASES OF ENURESIS: A COMPARATIVE-STUDY.
002175 02-11
THE EFFECTIVENESS OF IMIPRAMINE IN THE TREATMENT OF ENURESIS: THE SIGNIFICANCE OF TYPE OF ENURESIS AND REPORTED LEVEL OF SLEEP. (PH.D. DISSERTATION).
003337 03-11

Subject Index

ENVIRONMENT
ESR STUDIES OF BOVINE PLASMA AMINE-OXIDASE: PROBING OF THE ENVIRONMENT ABOUT THE SUBSTRATE LIBERATED SULFHYDRYL GROUPS IN THE ACTIVE SITE. (UNPUBLISHED PAPER).
001066 02-01
ERGOTISM IN A PSYCHIATRIC ENVIRONMENT ASSOCIATED WITH ERYTHROMYCIN-DIHYDROERGOTAMINE-PROPIONATE. AN OBSERVATION.
002379 02-15
SURGICAL MANIPULATION OF THE UTERINE ENVIRONMENT OF RAT FETUSES.
002478 02-16
DRUG ENVIRONMENT INTERACTION: CONTEXT DEPENDENCY OF COCAINE-INDUCED BEHAVIORAL-SENSITIZATION.
002866 03-03
DEBATE: THERAPEUTIC TRIALS IN A NATURAL ENVIRONMENT.
003635 03-17

ENVIRONMENTAL
THE SENSITIVITY OF THE RAT CORTICOSTERONE RESPONSE TO ENVIRONMENTAL MANIPULATIONS AND TO CHRONIC CHLORDIAZEPOXIDE TREATMENT.
000092 01-03
TEMPORAL AND ENVIRONMENTAL CUES IN CONDITIONED HYPOTHERMIA AND HYPERTHERMIA ASSOCIATED WITH MORPHINE.
002709 03-03
BIOCHEMICAL-EFFECTS AND BEHAVIORAL-EFFECTS OF ACUTE ETHANOL IN RATS AT DIFFERENT ENVIRONMENTAL TEMPERATURES.
002864 03-03
ENVIRONMENTAL MODULATION OF ANALGESIC TOLERANCE INDUCED BY MORPHINE PELLETS.
002944 03-04
NATURAL AND THERAPEUTIC ENVIRONMENTAL INDICATORS OF MAINTENANCE DOSAGE REQUIREMENTS.
003561 03-16

ENVIRONMENTALLY
2,4,5 TRICHLOROPHENOXYACETIC-ACID CAUSES BEHAVIORAL-EFFECTS IN CHICKENS AT ENVIRONMENTALLY RELEVANT DOSES.
003079 03-04

ENZYMATIC
ENZYMATIC CARBOXYMETHYLATION OF THE NICOTINIC ACETYLCHOLINE-RECEPTOR. (UNPUBLISHED PAPER).
001318 02-03
NEUROLEPTIC ACTION ON HEPATIC ENZYMATIC ACTIVITY.
002849 03-03
AGE-DEPENDENT MODIFICATION OF DRUG INTERFERENCE ON THE ENZYMATIC ACTIVITIES OF THE RAT-BRAIN.
003730 04-03

ENZYME
ENZYME INDUCING EFFECTS OF PHENOBARBITAL ON NITRAZEPAM METABOLISM IN DOGS.
000086 01-03
BRAIN STRIATAL TYROSINE-HYDROXYLASE: ACTIVATION OF THE ENZYME BY CYCLIC-AMP INDEPENDENT PHOSPHORYLATION.
001423 02-03
STIMULATION OF THE PLASMA MEMBRANE ENZYME, 5' NUCLEOTIDASE, BY ETHANOL EXPOSURE TO NEURAL CELLS IN CULTURE.
001499 02-03
CAPTOPRIL GIVEN INTRACEREBROVENTRICULARLY, SUBCUTANEOUSLY OR BY GAVAGE INHIBITS ANGIOTENSIN CONVERTING ENZYME ACTIVITY IN THE RAT-BRAIN.
001614 02-04
CLINICAL-IMPLICATIONS OF ENZYME INDUCTION AND ENZYME INHIBITION.
003621 03-17

ENZYME-INDUCING
COMPARATIVE ENZYME-INDUCING EFFECTS OF CHLORPROMAZINE AND FLUPHENAZINE THERAPIES IN PSYCHOTIC-PATIENTS.
000682 01-11

ENZYMES
THE ETIOLOGY OF TOXIC PERIPHERAL NEUROPATHIES: IN VITRO EFFECTS OF ACRYLAMIDE AND 2,5 HEXANEDIONE ON BRAIN ENOLASE AND OTHER GLYCOLYTIC ENZYMES.
000131 01-03
EFFECTS OF ACUTE AND CHRONIC PHENCYCLIDINE ON NEUROTRANSMITTER ENZYMES IN RAT-BRAIN.
000134 01-03
BIPHASIC ACTIVITY OF MEMBRANE-BOUND ENZYMES IN BRAIN MITOCHONDRIA AND SYNAPTOSOMES DURING THE DEVELOPMENT OF TOLERANCE TO AND PHYSICAL-DEPENDENCE ON CHRONIC MORPHINE ADMINISTRATION TO RATS.
001285 02-03
COMPARATIVE-STUDY OF THE INDUCTIVE EFFECT OF TWO PSYCHOMODERATORS -- TETRABAMATE AND COMPLEXE-1656 -- AND OF PHENOBARBITAL ON LIVER MICROSOMAL ENZYMES IN RATS.
001874 02-06
IMMUNOCYTOCHEMICAL LOCALIZATION OF CATECHOLAMINE SYNTHESIZING ENZYMES AND NEUROPEPTIDES IN AREA POSTREMA AND MEDIAL NUCLEUS-TRACTUS-SOLITARIUS OF RAT-BRAIN.
002634 03-01

SALIVARY IMMUNOGLOBULIN CONCENTRATIONS IN PATIENTS WITH
EPILEPSY TREATED WITH CARBAMAZEPINE.
                                                        002234 02-13
METABOLISM OF DIMETHOXYMETHYL-PHENOBARBITAL (ETEROBARB) IN
PATIENTS WITH EPILEPSY.
                                                        002235 02-13
INTERRELATION AT PLASMATIC LEVEL BETWEEN ANTIEPILEPTIC-DRUGS
AND LIPIDS. ITS IMPLICATIONS IN THE EFFICIENCY OF TREATMENT IN
EPILEPSY. I. CHANGES INDUCED BY PHENOBARBITAL OR/AND
DIPHENYLHYDANTOIN IN SERUM LIPIDS.
                                                        002281 02-13
THE QUESTION OF MINIMUM-DOSES OF ANTICONVULSANTS IN THE
TREATMENT OF EPILEPSY.
                                                        002306 02-13
EPILEPSY: NEUROTRANSMITTER, BEHAVIOUR AND PREGNANCY.
                                                        002466 02-15
EFFECTS OF D-AMPHETAMINE AND APOMORPHINE IN A NEW ANIMAL-
MODEL OF PETIT-MAL EPILEPSY.
                                                        002493 02-16
RECENT ADVANCES IN THE TREATMENT OF EPILEPSY.
                                                        003307 03-11
A PROSPECTIVE RANDOMISED-TRIAL ON THE EFFECT OF MONITORING
PLASMA ANTICONVULSANT LEVELS IN EPILEPSY.
                                                        003314 03-11
EPILEPSY AND CHRONIC CHAGAS-DISEASE.
                                                        003328 03-11
NALOXONE AND FOCAL EPILEPSY: A STUDY WITH DEPTH ELECTRODES.
                                                        003341 03-11
MONOTHERAPY OR POLYTHERAPY FOR EPILEPSY?
                                                        003366 03-11
COMPARISON OF SODIUM-VALPROATE AND PHENYTOIN AS SINGLE
DRUG-TREATMENT IN EPILEPSY.
                                                        003371 03-11
EPILEPSY IN ADULTS.
                                                        003375 03-11
INTENSIVE MONITORING IN REFRACTORY EPILEPSY.
                                                        003378 03-11
DRUG-INTERACTIONS IN EPILEPSY.
                                                        003622 03-17
STUDIES ON GAMMA AMINOBUTYRIC-ACID TRANSPORT IN COBALT
EXPERIMENTAL EPILEPSY IN THE RAT.
                                                        003990 04-03
THERAPEUTIC PLASMA LEVELS OF SOME ANTICONVULSANTS IN FOCAL
EPILEPSY IN RELATION TO COMPUTERIZED-AXIAL-TOMOGRAPHY.
                                                        004439 04-11
STOPPING MEDICATION IN CHILDREN WITH EPILEPSY.
                                                        004447 04-11
INFLUENCE OF CARBAMAZEPINE ON SERUM THYROXINE AND
TRIIODOTHYRONINE IN PATIENTS WITH EPILEPSY.
                                                        004488 04-11
CORRECTION OF HORMONAL ACTIVITY OF THE THYROID-GLAND AS A
METHOD OF PATHOGENIC THERAPY IN A COMPREHENSIVE TREATMENT
OF PATIENTS WITH TEMPORAL EPILEPSY.
                                                        004579 04-14
A CASE OF PETIT-MAL EPILEPSY AGGRAVATED BY LITHIUM.
                                                        004641 04-15
THE PROGNOSIS OF EPILEPSY AND THE STRATEGY FOR TERMINATING
ANTIEPILEPTIC THERAPY.
                                                        004724 04-17

EPILEPSY-PRONE
EFFECT OF RO-4-1284 ON AUDIOGENIC-SEIZURE SUSCEPTIBILITY AND
INTENSITY IN EPILEPSY-PRONE RATS.
                                                        003865 04-03

EPILEPTIC-CHILDREN
PHENYTOIN THERAPY FOR EPILEPTIC-CHILDREN: EVALUATION OF
SALIVARY AND PLASMA CONCENTRATIONS AND OF METHODS OF
ASSESSING COMPLIANCE.
                                                        004495 04-11

EPILEPTIC-DISCHARGE
TRANSIENT ABOLITION OF GENERALIZED PHOTOSENSITIVE EPILEPTIC-
DISCHARGE IN HUMANS BY APOMORPHINE, A DOPAMINE-RECEPTOR
AGONIST.
                                                        000714 01-11

EPILEPTIC-FOCI
NEURONAL ACTIVITY IN CHRONIC FERRIC-CHLORIDE EPILEPTIC-FOCI IN
CATS AND MONKEY.
                                                        000172 01-03

EPILEPTIC-FOCUS
THE EFFECT OF DIAZEPAM ON CYCLIC EXCITABILITY CHANGES IN AN
EPILEPTIC-FOCUS IN THE CORTEX OF THE MAJOR HEMISPHERES.
                                                        003984 04-03

EPILEPTIC-PATIENTS
CHRONIC ADMINISTRATION OF CANNABIDIOL TO HEALTHY VOLUNTEERS
AND EPILEPTIC-PATIENTS.
                                                        000669 01-11
CARBAMAZEPINE INTOXICATION DUE TO TRIACETYLOLEANDOMYCIN
ADMINISTRATION IN EPILEPTIC-PATIENTS.
                                                        000873 01-15
DETERMINATION OF DOSE PLASMA CONCENTRATION RELATIONSHIP OF
PHENOBARBITAL IN EPILEPTIC-PATIENTS BY A NEW SPECIFIC
RADIOIMMUNOASSAY.
                                                        000902 01-16
VALUE OF SALIVA SAMPLES IN MONITORING CARBAMAZEPINE
CONCENTRATIONS IN EPILEPTIC-PATIENTS.
                                                        000903 01-16
CLINICAL-TRIALS OF DEPAKENE (VALPROIC-ACID) COADMINISTERED WITH
OTHER ANTICONVULSANTS IN EPILEPTIC-PATIENTS.
                                                        002367 02-14
THE THERAPEUTIC ACTIVITY OF TRYPTOPHAN AND ITS EFFECT ON
SEROTONIN METABOLISM IN EPILEPTIC-PATIENTS.
                                                        003289 03-11
ON THE ANTICONVULSANT BLOOD LEVEL IN THERAPY-RESISTANT
EPILEPTIC-PATIENTS.
                                                        003300 03-11
FACIAL CLEFTS AMONG EPILEPTIC-PATIENTS.
                                                        003484 03-15
RESPIRATORY-DISEASE AND NASAL IMMUNOGLOBULIN
CONCENTRATIONS IN PHENYTOIN TREATED EPILEPTIC-PATIENTS.
                                                        003486 03-15
QUESTIONS OF DIFFERENTIATED TREATMENT FOR EPILEPTIC-PATIENTS.
                                                        003605 03-17
MECHANISM OF VALPROATE PHENOBARBITAL INTERACTION IN EPILEPTIC-
PATIENTS.
                                                        004522 04-13
NEUROLOGICAL-COMPLICATIONS DUE TO THE PHARMACOLOGICAL-
TREATMENT OF EPILEPTIC-PATIENTS.
                                                        004593 04-15

EPILEPTIC-PSYCHOSES
PATHOMORPHOSIS OF CHRONIC EPILEPTIC-PSYCHOSES.
                                                        003209 03-09

EPILEPTIC-SEIZURES
PLASMA LEVELS OF DIPHENYLHYDANTOIN AND THE CONTROL OF ADULT
EPILEPTIC-SEIZURES: A CHILEAN EXPERIENCE.
                                                        000102 01-03
POLYPHARMACY REGIMEN AS AN EXACERBATING RISK IN THERAPY-
RESISTANT EPILEPTIC-SEIZURES AND BEHAVIORAL-DISORDERS.
                                                        004720 04-17

EPILEPTIC-SUBJECTS
QUANTITATIVE ASSESSMENT OF SMOOTH-PURSUIT EYE-MOVEMENTS IN
HEALTHY AND EPILEPTIC-SUBJECTS.
                                                        002376 02-15

EPILEPTICS
PLASMA HDL CHOLESTEROL AND GROWTH-HORMONE IN EPILEPTICS
TREATED WITH ANTICONVULSANTS.
                                                        002260 02-13
BIOCHEMICAL-STUDIES OF HUMAN EPILEPTICS DURING ANTICONVULSANT
THERAPY.
                                                        004490 04-11
THE EFFECT OF DIPHENYLHYDANTOIN ON EEG CURVES IN EPILEPTICS.
                                                        004494 04-11

EPILEPTIFORM
SEIZURES AND RELATED EPILEPTIFORM ACTIVITY IN HIPPOCAMPUS
TRANSPLANTED TO THE ANTERIOR-CHAMBER OF THE EYE:
MODULATION BY CHOLINERGIC AND ADRENERGIC INPUT.
                                                        000095 01-03
ANTIPEROXIDANT PRETREATMENT AND IRON-INDUCED EPILEPTIFORM
DISCHARGES IN THE RAT: EEG AND HISTOPATHOLOGIC STUDIES.
                                                        002930 03-03

EPILEPTOGENIC
THE METABOLISM OF 5 HYDROXYTRYPTAMINE IN THE METHIONINE-
SULFOXIMINE EPILEPTOGENIC RAT-BRAIN.
                                                        002887 03-03
EPILEPTOGENIC PROPERTIES OF ENFLURANE AND THEIR CLINICAL
INTERPRETATION.
                                                        004609 04-15

EPILEPTOGENIC-EFFECT
ANTICONVULSANTS SPECIFIC FOR PETIT-MAL ANTAGONIZE
EPILEPTOGENIC-EFFECT OF LEUCINE-ENKEPHALIN.
                                                        000477 01-04

EPILEPTOGENIC-FOCUS
CHOLERA-TOXIN-INDUCED EPILEPTOGENIC-FOCUS -- SPECIAL REFERENCE
TO CYCLIC-AMP METABOLISM AND EPILEPTOGENIC-FOCUS.
                                                        000522 01-05
ELECTRICAL-ACTIVITY AND NA-K-ATPASE LEVEL IN THE PENICILLIN-
INDUCED EPILEPTOGENIC-FOCUS OF THE RAT-BRAIN-CORTEX, AND THE
EFFECT OF DIAZEPAM.
                                                        003070 03-04

EPINEPHRINE
DEPLETION OF EPINEPHRINE IN RAT HYPOTHALAMUS BY RO-4-1284:
INFLUENCE OF PARGYLINE AND HARMALINE.
                                                        000100 01-03
RELEASE OF ARACHIDONIC-ACID FROM ADRENAL CHROMAFFIN CELL-
CULTURES DURING SECRETION OF EPINEPHRINE. (UNPUBLISHED
PAPER).
                                                        001027 02-01

Subject Index

INHIBITORS OF PHENYLETHANOLAMINE-N-METHYLTRANSFERASE AND EPINEPHRINE BIOSYNTHESIS. 2. 1,2,3,4 TETRAHYDROISOQUINOLINE-7-SULFONANILIDES.
001069 02-02

EPINEPHRINE IS RELEASED FROM HYPOTHALAMUS BY DEPOLARIZING-AGENTS AND AMPHETAMINE.
001155 02-03

INFLUENCE OF IMIPRAMINE AND PARGYLINE ON THE ARRHYTHMOGENICITY OF EPINEPHRINE DURING HALOTHANE, ENFLURANE OR METHOXYFLURANE ANESTHESIA IN DOGS.
001539 02-03

EFFECTS OF AN EPINEPHRINE SYNTHESIS INHIBITOR, SKF-64139, ON THE SECRETION OF LUTEINIZING-HORMONE IN OVARIECTOMIZED FEMALE RATS.
002693 03-03

DIFFERENTIAL-EFFECTS OF ALPHA METHYLDOPAMINE, CLONIDINE AND HYDRALAZINE ON NOREPINEPHRINE AND EPINEPHRINE SYNTHESIZING ENZYMES IN THE BRAINSTEM NUCLEI OF SPONTANEOUSLY HYPERTENSIVE-RATS.
003947 04-03

EPISODIC-DYSCONTROL-SYNDROME
PRELIMINARY DATA ON ETHOSUXIMIDE AND THE EPISODIC-DYSCONTROL-SYNDROME.
000539 01-07

EQUIVALENCE
EXTINCTION AND DOPAMINE-RECEPTOR BLOCKADE AFTER INTERMITTENT REINFORCEMENT TRAINING: FAILURE TO OBSERVE FUNCTIONAL EQUIVALENCE.
000490 01-04

ERECTION
AMPHETAMINIL IN THE TREATMENT OF DISTURBED ERECTION POTENCY.
002129 02-11

EREDOATAXIAS
EXTRAPYRAMIDAL-DISORDERS AND BORDERLINE-SYNDROMES: EREDOATAXIAS AND DEMENTIA.
003518 03-15

ERGADYL
ATTEMPT AT PSYCHOLOGICAL UNDERSTANDING AND TREATMENT OF PSYCHOLOGICAL ASTHENIA AND ASTHENO-DEPRESSIVE-SYNDROMES USING ERGADYL.
001974 02-09

ERGOLINE
CENTRAL DOPAMINERGIC-EFFECTS OF ERGOLINE DERIVATIVES.
002540 02-17

ERGONOMIC
ACTION OF TOFISOPAM ON THE ERGONOMIC VIGILANCE LEVEL. ITS INTERACTION WITH THE EFFECTS OF ALCOHOL. CLINICAL PHARMACOLOGICAL-STUDY.
001891 02-07

ERGOPEPTINES
THE MOLECULAR ARCHITECTURE OF ERGOPEPTINES: A BASIS FOR BIOLOGICAL-INTERACTION.
001527 02-03

ERGOT
ANORECTIC-EFFECT OF LISURIDE AND OTHER ERGOT DERIVATIVES IN THE RAT.
000042 01-03

ADAPTIVE CHANGES OF THE STRIATAL DOPAMINE SYSTEM INDUCED BY REPEATED ADMINISTRATION OF NEUROLEPTICS AND ERGOT DERIVATIVES.
001156 02-03

CENTRAL MONOAMINE SYNAPSES AS SITES OF ACTION FOR ERGOT DRUGS.
001238 02-03

THE AFFINITIES OF ERGOT COMPOUNDS FOR DOPAMINE AGONIST AND DOPAMINE ANTAGONIST RECEPTOR SITES.
001254 02-03

EFFECT OF ERGOT DERIVATIVES ON POSTDECAPITATION CONVULSIONS.
001288 02-03

SELECTIVE INFLUENCE OF ERGOT ALKALOIDS ON CORTICAL AND STRIATAL DOPAMINERGIC-RECEPTORS AND SEROTONERGIC-RECEPTORS.
001447 02-03

INTERACTION OF DOPAMINERGIC ERGOT DERIVATIVES WITH CYCLIC-NUCLEOTIDE SYSTEM.
001482 02-03

ERGOT AND CATECHOLAMINE POTENCIES AT CATECHOLAMINE-RECEPTORS.
001510 02-03

MULTIPLE CNS RECEPTOR INTERACTIONS OF ERGOT ALKALOIDS; AFFINITY AND INTRINSIC ACTIVITY ANALYSIS IN IN VITRO BINDING SYSTEMS.
001516 02-03

ANTIPSYCHOTIC-PROPERTIES AND ANTIDYSKINETIC-PROPERTIES OF ERGOT DOPAMINE AGONISTS.
002178 02-11

CHARACTERIZATION OF ERGOT AND NONERGOT SEROTONIN ANTAGONISTS BY PROLACTIN AND GROWTH-HORMONE PROFILES DURING WAKEFULNESS AND SLEEP.
002217 02-13

NEUROPHARMACOLOGY OF SYNTHETIC ERGOT DERIVATIVES IN MAN.
002429 02-15

ESCAPE-BEHAVIOR
CHOLINE REVERSES NALOXONE-INDUCED DECREASES IN HIPPOCAMPAL ACETYLCHOLINE CONTENT AND SUPPRESSES ESCAPE-BEHAVIOR IN OPIATE-DEPENDENT RATS.
004076 04-04

ESERINE
BEHAVIOR-DEPENDENT EVOKED-POTENTIALS IN THE HIPPOCAMPAL-CA1 REGION OF THE RAT. II. EFFECTS OF ESERINE, ATROPINE, ETHER AND PENTOBARBITAL.
000184 01-03

ESEROLINE
INHIBITION OF (3H)NALOXONE BINDING IN HOMOGENATES OF RAT-BRAIN BY ESEROLINE, A DRUG, WITH ANALGESIC ACTIVITY, RELATED TO PHYSOSTIGMINE.
000104 01-03

ESR
ESR STUDIES OF SPIN LABELLED BOVINE LIVER MONOAMINE-OXIDASE-B. (UNPUBLISHED PAPER).
001065 02-01
ESR STUDIES OF BOVINE PLASMA AMINE-OXIDASE: PROBING OF THE ENVIRONMENT ABOUT THE SUBSTRATE LIBERATED SULFHYDRYL GROUPS IN THE ACTIVE SITE. (UNPUBLISHED PAPER).
001066 02-01

ESSENTIALLY
CLOPIPAZAN (SKF-69634), A NEW NEUROLEPTIC ESSENTIALLY FREE OF EXTRAPYRAMIDAL LIABILITY: QUANTITATIVE PHARMACOEEG AND OPEN LABEL CLINICAL-TRIAL.
004620 04-15

ESTERASE
NEUROTOXIC ESTERASE IN HUMAN NERVOUS-TISSUE.
003510 03-15

ESTROGEN
ALTERATIONS IN BASAL FIRING-RATE AND AUTORECEPTOR SENSITIVITY OF DOPAMINE NEURONS IN THE SUBSTANTIA-NIGRA FOLLOWING ACUTE AND EXTENDED EXPOSURE TO ESTROGEN.
001167 02-03
MODULATION OF APOMORPHINE-INDUCED STEREOTYPY BY ESTROGEN: TIME-COURSE AND DOSE-RESPONSE.
001636 02-04
INFLUENCE OF ESTROGEN AND PROGESTERONE ON GLUTAMIC-ACID-DECARBOXYLASE ACTIVITY IN DISCRETE REGIONS OF RAT-BRAIN.
002927 03-03
ESTROGEN POTENTIATES THE STEREOTYPY INDUCED BY DOPAMINE AGONISTS IN THE RAT.
002968 03-04
EFFECTS OF NEONATAL TESTOSTERONE AND ESTROGEN ON OPEN-FIELD BEHAVIOUR IN RATS.
003098 03-04
ANTAGONISM OF DOPAMINE SUPERSENSITIVITY BY ESTROGEN: NEUROCHEMICAL-STUDIES IN AN ANIMAL-MODEL OF TARDIVE-DYSKINESIA.
004268 04-05
THE EFFECTS OF ESTROGEN THERAPY ON THE SEX-LIFE OF POSTMENOPAUSAL-WOMEN.
004573 04-14

ESTROGEN-PRIMED
ATTEMPTS TO REINSTATE LORDOSIS REFLEX IN ESTROGEN-PRIMED SPINAL FEMALE RATS WITH MONOAMINE AGONISTS.
000421 01-04
FACILITATION OF LORDOSIS BEHAVIOR IN THE OVARIECTOMIZED ESTROGEN-PRIMED RAT BY DIBUTYRYL-C-AMP.
002957 03-04

ESTROGENS
BEHAVIORAL-EFFECTS OF ETHYNYL ESTROGENS IN THE FEMALE RAT.
000483 01-04
ANTIDOPAMINERGIC EFFECT OF ESTROGENS AT THE STRIATAL LEVEL.
003789 04-03

ESTROUS-CYCLE
BEHAVIORAL-EFFECTS OF DOPAMINE AGONISTS ACROSS THE ESTROUS-CYCLE IN RATS.
001792 02-04

ESTROUS-CYCLES
THE EFFECTS OF PROGESTERONE ON THE CIRCADIAN-CYCLES AND ESTROUS-CYCLES IN THE RAT. (PH.D. DISSERTATION).
001111 02-03

ETEROBARB
METABOLISM OF DIMETHOXYMETHYL-PHENOBARBITAL (ETEROBARB) IN PATIENTS WITH EPILEPSY.
002235 02-13

ETHANOL
ENHANCEMENT OF RAT-BRAIN METABOLISM OF A TRYPTOPHAN LOAD BY CHRONIC ETHANOL ADMINISTRATION.
000022 01-03
THE EFFECT OF PROPRANOLOL ON THE ELECTROENCEPHALOGRAM IN NORMAL AND ETHANOL DEPENDENT RATS.
000126 01-03
INHIBITION OF ALCOHOL-DEHYDROGENASE BY DISULFIRAM: POSSIBLE RELATION TO THE DISULFIRAM ETHANOL REACTION.
000270 01-03

CARDIOVASCULAR RESPONSE TO THE INTERACTION OF ETHANOL AND SOME BENZODIAZEPINES IN RATS.
000332 01-03
JOINT-EFFECTS OF D-AMPHETAMINE AND ETHANOL OR PENTOBARBITAL IN PIGEONS.
000403 01-04
IMPAIRMENT OF AVOIDANCE-BEHAVIOR FOLLOWING SHORT-TERM INGESTION OF ETHANOL, TERTIARY BUTANOL, OR PENTOBARBITAL IN MICE.
000479 01-04
DIFFERENTIAL-EFFECTS ON BENZODIAZEPINE DISPOSITION BY DISULFIRAM AND ETHANOL.
000789 01-13
INFERENTIAL CHANGES AFTER CHRONIC-TREATMENTS WITH LI, DMI, OR ETHANOL DETECTED BY ELECTROPHYSIOLOGICAL-CORRELATES.
001136 02-03
ETHANOL ENHANCES (3H)DIAZEPAM BINDING AT THE BENZODIAZEPINE GABA-RECEPTOR IONOPHORE COMPLEX.
001154 02-03
INTERACTION-STUDIES BETWEEN NARCOTIC ANALGESICS, NARCOTIC ANTAGONISTS AND ETHANOL: STUDIES DURING ACUTE AND CHRONIC-TREATMENT AND WITHDRAWAL STATES IN RATS AND MICE. (PH.D. DISSERTATION).
001165 02-03
INTERACTION STUDIES OF ETHANOL AND PSYCHOTROPIC-DRUGS IN RODENTS: POSSIBLE INVOLVEMENT OF ADENOSINE-TRIPHOSPHATASES.
001281 02-03
ALPHA-ADRENORECEPTOR MEDIATED ALTERATION OF ETHANOL EFFECTS ON NA-K-ATPASE OF RAT NEURONAL MEMBRANES.
001425 02-03
STIMULATION OF THE PLASMA MEMBRANE ENZYME, 5' NUCLEOTIDASE, BY ETHANOL EXPOSURE TO NEURAL CELLS IN CULTURE.
001499 02-03
TOLERANCE TO ETHANOL-INDUCED IMPAIRMENT OF WATER-ESCAPE IN RATS BRED FOR ETHANOL SENSITIVITY.
001567 02-04
AN INTERFERENCE REDUCTION THEORY OF THE EFFECTS OF ETHANOL ON CONFLICT-BEHAVIOR.
001586 02-04
ETHANOL-INDUCED ANALGESIA IN RATS SELECTIVELY BRED FOR ETHANOL SENSITIVITY.
001625 02-04
THE EXCITATORY COMPONENT OF ETHANOL IN MICE: A CHRONIC STUDY.
001712 02-04
ETHANOL AVERSION INDUCED BY PARENTERALLY ADMINISTERED ETHANOL ACTING BOTH AS CS AND UCS.
001721 02-04
PENTYLENETETRAZOL SEIZURE THRESHOLD: A QUANTITATIVE MEASURE OF ETHANOL DEPENDENCE IN RATS.
001750 02-04
THE EFFECTS OF ETHANOL, PHENOBARBITAL, AND BACLOFEN ON ETHANOL WITHDRAWAL IN THE RHESUS-MONKEY.
001802 02-04
ATTENUATION OF THE EFFECTS OF PUNISHMENT BY ETHANOL: COMPARISONS WITH CHLORDIAZEPOXIDE.
001813 02-04
SUBCUTANEOUS SILASTIC IMPLANTS: MAINTENANCE OF HIGH BLOOD ETHANOL LEVELS IN RATS DRINKING A LIQUID DIET.
001865 02-06
INTERCANNABINOID AND CANNABINOID ETHANOL INTERACTIONS AND THEIR EFFECTS ON HUMAN PERFORMANCE.
002193 02-12
SHORT-TERM ETHANOL ADMINISTRATION IMPAIRS THE ELIMINATION OF CHLORDIAZEPOXIDE (LIBRIUM) IN MAN.
002224 02-13
SEX-DIFFERENCES IN THE EFFECTS OF LOW-DOSES OF ETHANOL ON HUMAN REACTION-TIME.
002361 02-14
ADRENAL-HORMONES AND ETHANOL INGESTION IN C57BL/CRGL AND C3H/CRGL/2 MICE.
002739 03-03
BIOCHEMICAL-EFFECTS AND BEHAVIORAL-EFFECTS OF ACUTE ETHANOL IN RATS AT DIFFERENT ENVIRONMENTAL TEMPERATURES.
002864 03-03
THE EFFECTS OF OPIATE ANTAGONISTS ON THE DISCRIMINATIVE STIMULUS PROPERTIES OF ETHANOL.
002947 03-04
EXTENDED SCHEDULE TRANSFER OF ETHANOL DISCRIMINATION.
003087 03-04
PHARMACOPSYCHOLOGICAL INVESTIGATIONS CONCERNING THE COMBINED EFFECTS OF DIPOTASSIUM-CLORAZEPATE AND ETHANOL.
003456 03-14
QUANTITATION AND COMPARISON OF PHENOBARBITAL LEVELS IN THE PLASMA, SALIVA, AND CEREBROSPINAL-FLUID OF THE RAT, AND THE DEMONSTRATION OF AN ALTERATION OF DRUG PASSAGE BY ETHANOL.
003725 04-03

EFFECTS OF PENTOBARBITAL AND ETHANOL UPON SINGLE NEURON
ACTIVITY IN THE PRIMARY SOMATOSENSORY CORTEX OF THE RHESUS-
MONKEY.
003755 04-03
INHIBITION OF SYNAPTOSOMAL CALCIUM UPTAKE BY ETHANOL.
003827 04-03
EFFECT OF P CHLOROPHENYLALANINE ON THE ACQUISITION OF
TOLERANCE TO THE HYPNOTIC-EFFECTS OF PENTOBARBITAL, BARBITAL,
AND ETHANOL.
003883 04-03
THE EFFECT OF PRENATAL EXPOSURE TO ETHANOL OR OPIATES ON BRAIN
CATECHOLAMINE ACTIVITY.
003939 04-03
EFFECTS OF ETHANOL ON ACETYLCHOLINE AND ADENOSINE EFFLUX FROM
THE IN VIVO RAT-CEREBRAL-CORTEX.
003969 04-03
EFFECTS OF ETHANOL ADMINISTRATION AND WITHDRAWAL ON
NEUROTRANSMITTER-RECEPTOR SYSTEMS IN C57 MICE.
003979 04-03
THE EFFECTS OF ACUTE AND CHRONIC ETHANOL ADMINISTRATION AND
ITS WITHDRAWAL ON GAMMA AMINOBUTYRIC-ACID-RECEPTOR
BINDING IN RAT-BRAIN.
004035 04-03
ALTERATIONS IN GAMMA AMINOBUTYRIC-ACID-RECEPTOR SENSITIVITY
FOLLOWING ACUTE AND CHRONIC ETHANOL TREATMENTS.
004037 04-03
SELECTIVE EFFECT OF ETHANOL ON THE VESTIBULAR NUCLEUS NEURONS
IN THE CAT.
004139 04-04
ETHANOL SEDATIVE HYPNOTIC-INTERACTIONS: IN VITRO STUDIES ON NA-
K-ACTIVATED ADENOSINE-TRIPHOSPHATASE.
004269 04-05
INTRAVENOUS DIAZEPAM AND ORAL ETHANOL INTERACTION.
004552 04-13
HUMAN SOCIAL CONVERSATION: EFFECTS OF ETHANOL, SECOBARBITAL
AND CHLORPROMAZINE.
004582 04-14

ETHANOL-INDUCED
ANTAGONISTIC-EFFECTS OF PROPRANOLOL UPON ETHANOL-INDUCED
NARCOSIS IN MICE.
000439 01-04
TOLERANCE TO ETHANOL-INDUCED IMPAIRMENT OF WATER-ESCAPE IN
RATS BRED FOR ETHANOL SENSITIVITY.
001567 02-04
ETHANOL-INDUCED ANALGESIA IN RATS SELECTIVELY BRED FOR ETHANOL
SENSITIVITY.
001625 02-04
LITHIUM ANTAGONISM OF ETHANOL-INDUCED DEPLETION OF CEREBELLAR
GUANOSINE-CYCLIC-MONOPHOSPHATE AND STIMULATION OF
STRIATAL DOPAMINE RELEASE.
002242 02-13
ENHANCEMENT OF ETHANOL-INDUCED SEDATION AND HYPOTHERMIA BY
CENTRALLY ADMINISTERED NEUROTENSIN, BETA ENDORPHIN AND
BOMBESIN.
003037 03-04
ANTAGONISM OF ETHANOL-INDUCED DECREASE IN LH BY P
CHLOROPHENYLALANINE: LACK OF CORRELATION WITH ALTERED
SEROTONERGIC MECHANISMS.
003748 04-03
ETHANOL-INDUCED CHANGES IN CYCLIC-GUANOSINE-PHOSPHATE
METABOLISM IN MOUSE VESTIBULAR REGION.
003784 04-03

ETHER
BEHAVIOR-DEPENDENT EVOKED-POTENTIALS IN THE HIPPOCAMPAL-CA1
REGION OF THE RAT. II. EFFECTS OF ESERINE, ATROPINE, ETHER AND
PENTOBARBITAL.
000184 01-03
DIFFERENTIAL-EFFECTS OF PENTOBARBITAL AND ETHER ON THE SYNAPTIC
TRANSMISSION OF THE HIPPOCAMPAL-CA1-REGION IN THE RAT.
003903 04-03

ETHER-STRESSED
LEUCINE-ENKEPHALIN AND METHIONINE-ENKEPHALIN PRODUCE OPPOSING
EFFECTS ON PLASMA CORTICOSTERONE LEVELS IN ETHER-STRESSED
MICE.
001245 02-03

ETHOSUXIMIDE
ELECTRON-CAPTURE GAS-LIQUID-CHROMATOGRAPHIC-DETERMINATION
OF ETHOSUXIMIDE AND DESMETHYLMETHSUXIMIDE IN PLASMA OR
SERUM.
000538 01-06
PRELIMINARY DATA ON ETHOSUXIMIDE AND THE EPISODIC-DYSCONTROL-
SYNDROME.
000539 01-07
CHANGES IN REGIONAL BRAIN LEVELS OF AMINO-ACID PUTATIVE
NEUROTRANSMITTERS AFTER PROLONGED TREATMENT WITH THE
ANTICONVULSANT-DRUGS DIPHENYLHYDANTOIN, PHENOBARBITONE,
SODIUM-VALPROATE, ETHOSUXIMIDE, AND SULTHIAME IN THE RAT.
003961 04-03

ETHYL-ALCOHOL
OPIATE-RECEPTORS AND SLEEP. II. EFFECTS OF MICROINJECTIONS OF
ETHYL-ALCOHOL AND PENTOBARBITAL IN THE MEDIAN THALAMUS,

PERIAQUEDUCTAL GRAY MATTER AND NUCLEUS-TRACTUS-SOLITARIUS
OF THE RABBIT.
002917 03-03

ETHYL-BETA-CARBOLINE-CARBOXYLATE
ETHYL-BETA-CARBOLINE-CARBOXYLATE LOWERS SEIZURE THRESHOLD
AND ANTAGONIZES FLURAZEPAM-INDUCED SEDATION IN RATS.
002971 03-04

ETHYL-BETA-CARBOLINE-3-CARBOXYLATE
ETHYL-BETA-CARBOLINE-3-CARBOXYLATE ANTAGONISES THE EFFECT OF
DIAZEPAM ON A FUNCTIONAL GABA-RECEPTOR.
001378 02-03
THE PROCONVULSANT AND DIAZEPAM REVERSING EFFECTS OF ETHYL-
BETA-CARBOLINE-3-CARBOXYLATE.
001399 02-03
ETHYL-BETA-CARBOLINE-3-CARBOXYLATE ANTAGONIZES DIAZEPAM
ACTIVITY.
002915 03-03

ETHYL-2-PIPERAZINYL-4-PHENYLQUINOLINE-HCL
ANTIDEPRESSANT PROPERTIES OF 2 4 ETHYL-2-PIPERAZINYL-4-
PHENYLQUINOLINE-HCL (AD-1308) AND ITS MECHANISM-OF-ACTION
AS COMPARED WITH TRICYCLIC-ANTIDEPRESSANTS.
000152 01-03

ETHYLKETOCYCLAZOCINE
HIGH-AFFINITY BINDING OF 3H ETHYLKETOCYCLAZOCINE TO RAT-BRAIN
HOMOGENATE.
000124 01-03
3H ETHYLKETOCYCLAZOCINE BINDING: LACK OF EVIDENCE FOR A
SEPARATE KAPPA-RECEPTOR IN RAT CNS.
000128 01-03
EFFECTS OF CENTRALLY-ADMINISTERED PENTAZOCINE AND
ETHYLKETOCYCLAZOCINE ON THERMOREGULATION IN THE CAT.
000361 01-04
SPECIFIC, HIGH-AFFINITY (3H)ETHYLKETOCYCLAZOCINE BINDING IN RAT
CENTRAL-NERVOUS-SYSTEM: LACK OF EVIDENCE FOR KAPPA-
RECEPTORS.
003840 04-03

ETHYNYL
BEHAVIORAL-EFFECTS OF ETHYNYL ESTROGENS IN THE FEMALE RAT.
000483 01-04

ETIOLOGY
THE ETIOLOGY OF TOXIC PERIPHERAL NEUROPATHIES: IN VITRO EFFECTS
OF ACRYLAMIDE AND 2,5 HEXANEDIONE ON BRAIN ENOLASE AND
OTHER GLYCOLYTIC ENZYMES.
000131 01-03
DRUG-VARIABLES IN THE ETIOLOGY OF TARDIVE-DYSKINESIA:
APPLICATION OF DISCRIMINANT FUNCTION ANALYSIS.
000844 01-15
NEUROLEPTIC-INDUCED ELEVATIONS IN SERUM PROLACTIN LEVELS:
ETIOLOGY AND SIGNIFICANCE.
003190 03-08
THE TREATMENT AND ETIOLOGY OF TICS AND TOURETTE-SYNDROME.
003372 03-11

ETOMIDATE
NEUROPHYSIOLOGICAL-EFFECTS OF ETOMIDATE, A NEW SHORT-ACTING
HYPNOTIC.
002263 02-13

ETORPHINE
TIME-COURSE OF ETORPHINE LEVELS IN TISSUES OF OPIATE-TOLERANT
AND NONTOLERANT RATS.
000301 01-03
INCREASED METABOLISM OF DOPAMINE AND SEROTONIN INDUCED IN
FOREBRAIN AREAS BY ETORPHINE MICROINJECTION IN
PERIAQUEDUCTAL GRAY.
001103 02-03
BEHAVIOR MAINTAINED BY INTRAVENOUS INJECTION OF CODEINE,
COCAINE, AND ETORPHINE IN THE RHESUS-MACAQUE AND THE
PIGTAIL-MACAQUE.
001828 02-04
ENHANCEMENT OF ETORPHINE BRAIN CONCENTRATIONS AND CHANGES
IN ETORPHINE NALOXONE PA2 VALUES IN MORPHINE PRETREATED
MICE.
002800 03-03
A NEUROANATOMICAL-STUDY OF ANALGESIA AND CATATONIA INDUCED
BY ETORPHINE IN THE RAT. (PH.D. DISSERTATION).
003102 03-04
DISCRIMINATIVE-STIMULUS EFFECTS OF ETORPHINE IN RHESUS-
MONKEYS.
004134 04-04

EUROPE
AN OVERVIEW OF SEVENTEEN YEARS OF EXPERIENCE WITH DOTHIEPIN IN
THE TREATMENT OF DEPRESSION IN EUROPE.
001995 02-09

EUROPEAN-BRAIN-AND-BEHAVIOUR-SOCIETY
ABSTRACTS OF THE ANNUAL GENERAL CONFERENCE OF THE EUROPEAN-
BRAIN-AND-BEHAVIOUR-SOCIETY, HELD AT LOUVAIN-LA-NEUVE,
BELGIUM, ON NOVEMBER 13-15TH, 1980.
003617 03-17

EVALUATE
THE USE OF CONDITIONED SUPPRESSION TO EVALUATE THE NATURE OF NEUROLEPTIC-INDUCED AVOIDANCE-DEFICITS.
004070 04-04

EVALUATED
IN VIVO OCCUPATION OF CEREBRAL HISTAMINE H1-RECEPTORS EVALUATED WITH 3H MEPYRAMINE MAY PREDICT SEDATIVE PROPERTIES OF PSYCHOTROPIC-DRUGS.
000241 01-03

EFFECTS OF CHRONIC-TREATMENT WITH L SULPIRIDE AND HALOPERIDOL ON CENTRAL DOPAMINE TURNOVER EVALUATED IN DOPAMINE CELL BODY AND NERVE TERMINAL-RICH AREAS.
001096 02-03

INTERACTIONS BETWEEN NALTREXONE AND NONOPIATE DRUGS EVALUATED BY SCHEDULE-CONTROLLED BEHAVIOR.
001645 02-04

TREATMENT OF ASTHENO-DEPRESSIVE-DISORDERS WITH MINAPRINE (CANTOR). MULTICENTER-STUDY OF 248 CASES EVALUATED WITH THE FATIGUE STUDY GROUPS NO. 4 CLINICAL-SCALE.
001980 02-09

ASPIRIN ANALGESIA EVALUATED BY EVENT-RELATED POTENTIALS IN MAN: POSSIBLE CENTRAL-ACTION IN BRAIN.
002195 02-12

STUDY ON THE EFFECTS OF L 5 HTP ON THE STAGES OF SLEEP IN MAN AS EVALUATED BY USING SLEEP-DEPRIVATION.
003450 03-14

INTERACTIONS BETWEEN NARCOTIC AGONISTS, PARTIAL AGONISTS AND ANTAGONISTS EVALUATED BY SCHEDULE-CONTROLLED BEHAVIOR.
004127 04-04

EVALUATING
CORTICAL-CORRELATES OF VIGILANCE REGULATION AND THEIR USE IN EVALUATING THE EFFECTS OF TREATMENT.
002147 02-11

EVALUATION
DOUBLE-BLIND COMPARISON OF HALOPERIDOL AND THIOTHIXENE WITH AFTERCARE TREATMENT EVALUATION IN PSYCHIATRIC-OUTPATIENTS WITH SCHIZOPHRENIA.
000574 01-08

A COMPARATIVE EVALUATION OF DOTHIEPIN (PROTHIEDEN) AND IMIPRAMINE.
000583 01-09

THE USEFULNESS OF THE ERYTHROCYTE LITHIUM INDEX IN THE EVALUATION OF DISORDERS OF ION-TRANSFER IN PATIENTS WITH DEPRESSIVE-SYNDROMES.
000625 01-09

PRELIMINARY EVALUATION OF THE EFFECTS OF DEPAKINE IN EPILEPSY.
000664 01-11

BRAIN FUNCTION IN OLD-AGE: EVALUATION OF CHANGES AND DISORDERS.
000684 01-11

EVALUATION OF CLORAZEPATE (TRANXENE) AS AN ANTICONVULSANT -- A PILOT-STUDY.
000728 01-11

EXPERIMENTAL EVALUATION OF ANTIDEPRESSANT ACTIVITY OF CLOMIPRAMINE, A NEW TRICYCLIC-ANTIDEPRESSANT DRUG.
001068 02-02

NEW EXPERIMENTAL TECHNIQUES IN THE PHARMACOLOGICAL EVALUATION OF CNS ACTING DRUGS.
001479 02-03

EVALUATION OF THE EFFECT OF DRUGS ON DOPAMINE METABOLISM IN THE RAT SUPERIOR-CERVICAL-GANGLION BY HPLC WITH ELECTROCHEMICAL-DETECTION.
001530 02-03

P CHLOROAMPHETAMINE: EVALUATION OF A BRAIN METABOLITE.
001779 02-04

EVALUATION OF THE CLINICAL-EFFICACY OF SINGLE-DAILY-DOSES OF ANTIDEPRESSANTS.
001985 02-09

EVALUATION OF NOMIFENSINE IN THE TREATMENT OF GERIATRIC DEPRESSION USING PSYCHOMETRIC-TESTS AND PLASMA LEVEL CONTROLS.
002004 02-09

EVALUATION OF SYMPTOMATIC TREATMENT OF HYPERACTIVE-BEHAVIOR BY STIMULANT-DRUGS.
002134 02-11

QUINACRINE AND SEROTONIN BINDING BY SYNTHETIC MODELS FOR HUMAN PLATELET DENSE-BODIES: EVALUATION OF THE ROLE OF BINDING IN AMINE STORAGE. (UNPUBLISHED PAPER).
002219 02-13

DOUBLE-BLIND EVALUATION OF REINFORCING AND ANORECTIC-ACTIONS OF WEIGHT-CONTROL MEDICATIONS: INTERACTION OF PHARMACOLOGICAL-TREATMENT AND BEHAVIORAL-TREATMENTS.
002314 02-14

AN EVALUATION OF MAPROTILINE INTRAVENOUS KINETICS AND COMPARISON OF TWO ORAL DOSES.
002497 02-16

A CRITICAL EVALUATION OF THE USE OF TOXINS FROM DENDROASPIS VIRIDIS TO BLOCK NICOTINIC RESPONSES AT CENTRAL AND GANGLIONIC SYNAPSES.
002870 03-03

THE TETRACYCLIC-ANTIDEPRESSANT MIANSERIN: EVALUATION OF ITS BLOCKADE OF PRESYNAPTIC ALPHA-ADRENOCEPTORS IN A SELF-STIMULATION MODEL USING CLONIDINE.
003016 03-04

EVALUATION OF THE RELATIVE EFFECTIVENESS OF METHYLPHENIDATE AND COGNITIVE BEHAVIOR-MODIFICATION IN THE TREATMENT OF KINDERGARTEN-AGED HYPERACTIVE-CHILDREN.
003306 03-11

ON THE EVALUATION OF A PROVOCATIVE EEG METHOD USING MEDICATION IN THE DIAGNOSIS OF ORGANIC-BRAIN-SEIZURES IN CHILDHOOD, WITH SPECIAL EMPHASIS ON SLEEP INDUCTION THROUGH MEDICATION.
003387 03-11

EVALUATION OF DRUG EFFICACY IN DEMENTIA: A COMPUTERIZED COGNITIVE ASSESSMENT SYSTEM.
003557 03-16

BIOLOGICAL EVALUATION OF A TRH ANALOGUE WITH A MODIFIED PROLINE RESIDUE.
003662 04-01

FLUORESCENT PROBES OF ALPHA-ADRENERGIC AND BETA-ADRENERGIC AND OPIATE-RECEPTORS: BIOCHEMICAL AND HISTOCHEMICAL EVALUATION.
003685 04-02

OPIATE MECHANISMS: EVALUATION OF RESEARCH INVOLVING NEURONAL ACTION POTENTIALS.
003886 04-03

AN EVALUATION OF THE MECHANISM BY WHICH SEROTONERGIC ACTIVATION DEPRESSES RESPIRATION.
003917 04-03

RELEVANCE OF DOPAMINE-RECEPTOR BINDING STUDIES FOR EVALUATION OF ANTIPARKINSONIAN-DRUGS.
004120 04-04

NARCOTIC-REINFORCED RESPONDING: A RAPID EVALUATION PROCEDURE.
004253 04-04

A CLINICAL AND PHARMACODYNAMIC EVALUATION OF SULPIRIDE.
004338 04-08

EVALUATION OF LITHIUM RESPONSE: PSYCHOMETRIC-FINDINGS.
004348 04-09

AN EVALUATION OF TRAZODONE IN THE TREATMENT OF DEPRESSION.
004386 04-09

AN EVALUATION OF THE USEFULNESS OF THE ACYLASE TEST IN NEUROLEPTIC TREATMENT.
004426 04-10

A COMPARATIVE EVALUATION OF THE EFFICACY OF SOME THERAPEUTIC METHODS USED IN DELIRIUM-TREMENS.
004486 04-11

PHENYTOIN THERAPY FOR EPILEPTIC-CHILDREN: EVALUATION OF SALIVARY AND PLASMA CONCENTRATIONS AND OF METHODS OF ASSESSING COMPLIANCE.
004495 04-11

A COMPARATIVE EVALUATION OF THE USEFULNESS OF PSYCHOPHYSIOLOGICAL-TESTS DURING VARIOUS LEVELS OF ACTIVATION OF THE CENTRAL-NERVOUS-SYSTEM.
004543 04-13

COMPUTERIZED ANALYSIS OF SLEEP RECORDINGS APPLIED TO DRUG EVALUATION: MIDAZOLAM IN NORMAL SUBJECTS.
004564 04-14

AN EVALUATION OF THE ANTIANXIETY ACTION AND SIDE-EFFECTS OF PROPRANOLOL.
004660 04-15

EVALUATIONS
EARLY-ACTIVITY-STUDIES AND INTENSIVE DRUG EVALUATIONS OF NEW PSYCHOPHARMACOLOGIC-AGENTS.
002348 02-14

EVALUATIONS OF LOXAPINE-SUCCINATE IN THE AMBULATORY TREATMENT OF ACUTE SCHIZOPHRENIC-EPISODES.
004345 04-08

EVENT-RELATED
ASPIRIN ANALGESIA EVALUATED BY EVENT-RELATED POTENTIALS IN MAN: POSSIBLE CENTRAL-ACTION IN BRAIN.
002195 02-12

EVENT-RELATED POTENTIAL CHANGES WITH MORPHINE IN NONADDICTED HUMANS.
004512 04-13

THE USE OF EVENT-RELATED SLOW POTENTIALS OF THE BRAIN AS AN OBJECTIVE METHOD TO STUDY THE EFFECTS OF CENTRALLY ACTING DRUGS.
004669 04-16

EVIDENCE
EVIDENCE FOR AN IRREVERSIBLE INTERACTION OF BROMOCRYPTINE WITH CENTRAL DOPAMINE-RECEPTORS.
000023 01-03

SUPPRESSION OF SEROTONERGIC NEURONAL FIRING BY ALPHA-ADRENOCEPTOR ANTAGONISTS: EVIDENCE AGAINST GABA MEDIATION.
000024 01-03

EVIDENCE FOR A RECEPTOR SUPERSENSITIVITY FOLLOWING IMPAIRMENT OF CENTRAL SEROTONERGIC ACTIVITY IN THE RABBIT.
000041 01-03

3H ETHYLKETOCYCLAZOCINE BINDING: LACK OF EVIDENCE FOR A
SEPARATE KAPPA-RECEPTOR IN RAT CNS.
000128 01-03
EVIDENCE FOR A GABAERGIC NIGROTHALAMIC PATHWAY IN THE RAT: I.
BEHAVIOURAL-STUDIES AND BIOCHEMICAL-STUDIES.
000158 01-03
EVIDENCE FOR, AND LOCALIZATION OF, A UNITARY DOPAMINE-
RECEPTOR COMPOSED OF COOPERATIVELY LINKED SUBUNIT BINDING-
SITES IN RAT STRIATUM.
000186 01-03
EVIDENCE FOR A DIRECT INHIBITORY-EFFECT OF MORPHINE ON THE
SECRETION OF POSTERIOR PITUITARY-HORMONES.
000193 01-03
BLOCKADE OF STRIATAL NEURONE RESPONSES TO MORPHINE BY
AMINOPHYLLINE: EVIDENCE FOR ADENOSINE MEDIATION OF OPIATE
ACTION.
000229 01-03
THE EFFECT OF MORPHINE ON PURINE AND ACETYLCHOLINE RELEASE
FROM RAT-CEREBRAL-CORTEX: EVIDENCE FOR A PURINERGIC
COMPONENT IN MORPHINES ACTION.
000234 01-03
EVIDENCE OF A DIRECT ACTION OF ANGIOTENSIN-II ON NEURONES IN THE
SEPTUM AND IN THE MEDIAL PREOPTIC-AREA.
000272 01-03
FUNCTIONAL EVIDENCE FOR SUBSENSITIVITY OF NORADRENERGIC-
ALPHA2-RECEPTORS AFTER CHRONIC DESIPRAMINE TREATMENT.
000283 01-03
EVIDENCE THAT A PREFERRED SUBSTRATE FOR MONOAMINE-OXIDASE-B
MEDIATES STIMULUS PROPERTIES OF MAO-INHIBITORS. A POSSIBLE
ROLE FOR BETA PHENYLETHYLAMINE IN THE COCAINE CUE.
000363 01-04
CHRONIC AMPHETAMINE ADMINISTRATION TO CATS: BEHAVIORAL-
EVIDENCE AND NEUROCHEMICAL EVIDENCE FOR DECREASED CENTRAL
SEROTONERGIC FUNCTION.
000491 01-04
MICROSCOPIC EVIDENCE OF LYMPHOGENIC ABSORPTION OF OIL IN
HUMANS RECEIVING NEUROLEPTIC OILY DEPOT PREPARATIONS
INTRAMUSCULARLY.
000890 01-15
A STUDY OF ANTIPSYCHOTIC-DRUG USE IN NURSING-HOMES:
EPIDEMIOLOGIC EVIDENCE SUGGESTING MISUSE.
000979 01-17
RIA AND HPLC EVIDENCE FOR THE PRESENCE OF METHIONINE-
ENKEPHALIN AND CHOLECYSTOKININ IN THE NEURAL RETINA OF
SEVERAL VERTEBRATE SPECIES. (UNPUBLISHED PAPER).
001017 02-01
REGULATION OF HIPPOCAMPAL GLUTAMATE-RECEPTORS: EVIDENCE FOR
THE INVOLVEMENT OF A CALCIUM-ACTIVATED PROTEASE.
001120 02-03
RADIOLIGAND BINDING STUDIES: EVIDENCE FOR MULTIPLE DOPAMINE-
RECEPTORS.
001186 02-03
MORPHINE AND SUPRASPINAL INHIBITION OF SPINAL NEURONES:
EVIDENCE THAT MORPHINE DECREASES TONIC DESCENDING INHIBITION
IN THE ANESTHETIZED CAT.
001203 02-03
PHARMACOLOGICAL EVIDENCE AND BIOCHEMICAL-EVIDENCE FOR AN
INTERACTION BETWEEN THE BENZODIAZEPINE AND GABA-RECEPTORS.
001261 02-03
EVIDENCE SUGGESTING A TRANSMITTER OR NEUROMODULATORY ROLE
FOR SUBSTANCE-P AT THE FIRST SYNAPSE OF THE BARORECEPTOR
REFLEX.
001264 02-03
NO EVIDENCE FOR INCREASED DOPAMINE-RECEPTOR BINDING IN
SUPERRESPONSIVE MICE AFTER A SINGLE-DOSE OF NEUROLEPTICS.
001292 02-03
FURTHER EVIDENCE FOR THE EXISTENCE OF MULTIPLE RECEPTORS FOR
DOPAMINE IN THE CENTRAL-NERVOUS-SYSTEM.
001296 02-03
EVIDENCE FOR AN ENDOGENOUS COMPOUND INTERFERING WITH 3H
DIAZEPAM BINDING TO RAT-BRAIN MEMBRANES.
001308 02-03
EVIDENCE THAT VASOPRESSIN IS INVOLVED IN THE ISOPRENALINE-
INDUCED BETA ENDORPHIN RELEASE.
001319 02-03
DIRECT EVIDENCE AGAINST ACETYLCHOLINE AS THE DILATOR
TRANSMITTER IN THE CAT CEREBRAL-ARTERY.
001336 02-03
EFFECTS OF DIAZEPAM ON ADENOSINE AND ACETYLCHOLINE RELEASE
FROM RAT-CEREBRAL-CORTEX: FURTHER EVIDENCE FOR A PURINERGIC
MECHANISM IN ACTION OF DIAZEPAM.
001414 02-03
THYROTROPIN-RELEASING-HORMONE: NEUROCHEMICAL EVIDENCE FOR
THE POTENTIATION OF IMIPRAMINE EFFECTS ON THE METABOLISM
AND UPTAKE OF BRAIN CATECHOLAMINES.
001427 02-03
EVIDENCE FOR INVOLVEMENT OF DOPAMINE IN THE ACTION OF
DIAZEPAM: POTENTIATION OF HALOPERIDOL AND CHLORPROMAZINE
ACTION IN THE BRAIN.
001428 02-03

SIMILARITIES AND DISSIMILARITIES BETWEEN DOPAMINE AND
NEUROLEPTIC-RECEPTORS: FURTHER EVIDENCE FOR TYPE-1 AND TYPE-2
DOPAMINE-RECEPTORS IN THE CNS.
001480 02-03
LITHIUM EFFECTS ON HIGH-AFFINITY TRYPTOPHAN UPTAKE: EVIDENCE
AGAINST A STABILIZATION MECHANISM.
001496 02-03
PHARMACOLOGICAL EVIDENCE OF A POSSIBLE TRYPTAMINERGIC
REGULATION OF OPIATE-RECEPTORS BY USING INDALPINE, A SELECTIVE
5 HT UPTAKE INHIBITOR.
001517 02-03
EVIDENCE THAT NORADRENALINE MODULATES THE INCREASE IN
STRIATAL DOPAMINE METABOLISM INDUCED BY MUSCARINIC-
RECEPTOR STIMULATION.
001518 02-03
Y-MAZE BEHAVIOR AFTER AN ANALOG OF ACTH4-9, EVIDENCE FOR AN
ATTENTIONAL-ALTERATION.
001676 02-04
EFFECTS OF BRANCHED-CHAIN FATTY-ACIDS ON GABA DEGRADATION
AND BEHAVIOR: FURTHER EVIDENCE FOR A ROLE OF GABA IN QUASI-
MORPHINE ABSTINENCE-BEHAVIOR.
001809 02-04
NEUROCHEMICAL EVIDENCE AND BEHAVIORAL-EVIDENCE FOR A
SELECTIVE PRESYNAPTIC DOPAMINE-RECEPTOR AGONIST.
002236 02-13
CLINICAL EVIDENCE FOR MULTIPLE DOPAMINE-RECEPTORS IN MAN.
002264 02-13
DEVELOPMENT AND USE OF PHARMACOLOGICAL-PROBES OF THE CNS IN
MAN: EVIDENCE OF CHOLINERGIC ABNORMALITY IN PRIMARY
AFFECTIVE-ILLNESS.
002506 02-16
EVIDENCE THAT IT IS POSSIBLE TO CAUSE ANOREXIA BY INCREASING
RELEASE AND/OR DIRECTLY STIMULATING POSTSYNAPTIC SEROTONIN-
RECEPTORS IN THE BRAIN.
002602 02-17
THE EFFECT OF ALTERED DOPAMINERGIC-ACTIVITY ON FOOD INTAKE IN
THE RAT: EVIDENCE FOR AN OPTIMAL LEVEL OF DOPAMINERGIC-
ACTIVITY FOR BEHAVIOR.
002632 02-17
BENZODIAZEPINE-RECEPTORS: AUTORADIOGRAPHICAL AND
IMMUNOCYTOCHEMICAL EVIDENCE FOR THEIR LOCALIZATION IN
REGIONS OF GABAERGIC SYNAPTIC CONTACTS.
002643 03-01
PHARMACOLOGICAL EVIDENCE ON THE SPECIALIZATION OF CNS
MECHANISMS RESPONSIBLE FOR MOTOR ACT INHIBITION BY AVERSIVE
EVENTS.
002671 03-03
EVIDENCE FOR A TONIC GABAERGIC CONTROL OF SEROTONIN NEURONS
IN THE MEDIAN RAPHE NUCLEUS.
002719 03-03
HISTAMINE ACTIONS ON ACTIVITY OF CULTURED HYPOTHALAMIC
NEURONS: EVIDENCE FOR MEDIATION BY HISTAMINE H1-RECEPTORS
AND H2-RECEPTORS.
002732 03-03
COMPARATIVE-STUDY ON THE EFFECT OF MORPHINE AND THE OPIOID-
LIKE PEPTIDES IN THE VAS-DEFERENS OF RODENTS: STRAIN AND
SPECIES-DIFFERENCES, EVIDENCE FOR MULTIPLE OPIATE-RECEPTORS.
002757 03-03
EVIDENCE THAT THE OPIATE-RECEPTORS OF THE SUBSTANTIA-
GELATINOSA CONTRIBUTE TO THE DEPRESSION, BY INTRAVENOUS
MORPHINE, OF THE SPINAL TRANSMISSION OF IMPULSES IN
UNMYELINATED PRIMARY AFFERENTS.
002767 03-03
BEHAVIORAL CONFIRMATION OF DIFFUSE NOXIOUS INHIBITORY
CONTROLS (DNIC) AND EVIDENCE FOR A ROLE OF ENDOGENOUS
OPIATES.
002791 03-03
EVIDENCE FOR THE PRESENCE OF TWO TYPES OF MONOAMINE-OXIDASE
IN RABBIT CHOROID PLEXUS AND THEIR ROLE IN BREAKDOWN OF
AMINES INFLUENCING CEREBROSPINAL-FLUID FORMATION.
002807 03-03
PHARMACOLOGIC EVIDENCE FOR A TONIC MUSCARINIC INHIBITORY
INPUT TO THE EDINGER-WESTPHAL NUCLEUS IN THE DOG.
002889 03-03
THE PATHOGENESIS OF PRIMARY INTERNODAL DEMYELINATION
PRODUCED BY ACETYL-ETHYL-TETRAMETHYL-TETRALIN: EVIDENCE FOR
PRESERVED SCHWANN-CELL SOMAL FUNCTION.
002905 03-03
PHARMACOLOGICAL EVIDENCE FOR CATECHOLAMINE INVOLVEMENT IN
ANIMAL AGGRESSION.
003052 03-04
EVIDENCE FOR INVOLVEMENT OF SEPARATE MECHANISMS IN THE
PRODUCTION OF ANALGESIA BY ELECTRICAL-STIMULATION OF THE
NUCLEUS-RETICULARIS-PARAGIGANTOCELLULARIS AND NUCLEUS-
RAPHE-MAGNUS IN THE RAT.
003083 03-04
PHARMACOLOGICAL EVIDENCE FOR CATECHOLAMINE INVOLVEMENT IN
ANIMAL AGGRESSION.
003140 03-06

CROSS-OVER STUDY OF ZIMELIDINE AND DESIPRAMINE IN DEPRESSION:
EVIDENCE FOR AMINE SPECIFICITY.
003250 03-09
DO PSYCHOTHERAPY AND PHARMACOTHERAPY FOR DEPRESSION
CONFLICT? EMPIRICAL EVIDENCE FROM A CLINICAL-TRIAL.
003256 03-09
PHYSOSTIGMINE IN TOURETTE-SYNDROME: EVIDENCE FOR CHOLINERGIC
UNDERACTIVITY.
003286 03-10
PLASMA FREE AND TOTAL TRYPTOPHAN, BLOOD SEROTONIN, AND THE
HYPERACTIVITY-SYNDROME: NO EVIDENCE FOR THE SEROTONIN
DEFICIENCY HYPOTHESIS.
003312 03-11
EVIDENCE TO SUPPORT EARLY LEVODOPA THERAPY IN PARKINSON-
DISEASE.
003336 03-11
THE URBAN EPIDEMIC OF PHENCYCLIDINE USE: LABORATORY EVIDENCE
FROM A PUBLIC PSYCHIATRIC-HOSPITAL INPATIENT-SERVICE.
003554 03-16
EVIDENCE FOR THERMOREGULATORY DOPAMINERGIC-RECEPTORS
LOCATED IN THE PREOPTICUS-MEDIALIS-NUCLEUS OF THE RAT
HYPOTHALAMUS.
003754 04-03
SPECIFIC, HIGH-AFFINITY (3H)ETHYLKETOCYCLAZOCINE BINDING IN RAT
CENTRAL-NERVOUS-SYSTEM: LACK OF EVIDENCE FOR KAPPA-
RECEPTORS.
003840 04-03
MULTIPLE BENZODIAZEPINE-RECEPTORS: EVIDENCE OF A DISSOCIATION
BETWEEN ANTICONFLICT AND ANTICONVULSANT PROPERTIES BY PK-
8165 AND PK-9084 (TWO QUINOLINE DERIVATIVES).
003898 04-03
OPIOID BINDING PROPERTIES OF BRAIN AND PERIPHERAL TISSUES:
EVIDENCE FOR HETEROGENEITY IN OPIOID LIGAND BINDING SITES.
003902 04-03
ELECTROPHYSIOLOGICAL EVIDENCE FOR PRESYNAPTIC ACTIONS OF
PHENCYCLIDINE ON NORADRENERGIC TRANSMISSION IN RAT
CEREBELLUM.
003926 04-03
EVIDENCE TO SUGGEST THAT DOPAMINE-INDUCED INCREASE IN GABA
CONCENTRATIONS IN CHICK BRAIN IS MEDIATED THROUGH CYCLIC-
AMP.
003952 04-03
CLONIDINE AND THE PRIMATE LOCUS-COERULEUS: EVIDENCE SUGGESTING
ANXIOLYTIC AND ANTIWITHDRAWAL EFFECTS. (UNPUBLISHED PAPER).
003982 04-03
CNS EFFECTS OF CHOLINE ADMINISTRATION: EVIDENCE FOR TEMPORAL
DEPENDENCE.
003996 04-03
EVIDENCE THAT THERE ARE SUBCELLULAR POOLS OF NOREPINEPHRINE
AND THAT THERE IS FLUX OF NOREPINEPHRINE BETWEEN THESE
POOLS.
004004 04-03
IN VIVO EVIDENCE FOR GABAERGIC CONTROL OF SEROTONIN RELEASE IN
THE CAT SUBSTANTIA-NIGRA.
004011 04-03
CORE TEMPERATURE CHANGES FOLLOWING ADMINISTRATION OF
NALOXONE AND NALTREXONE TO RATS EXPOSED TO HOT AND COLD
AMBIENT TEMPERATURES. EVIDENCE FOR THE PHYSIOLOGICAL ROLE
OF ENDORPHINS IN HOT AND COLD ACCLIMATIZATION.
004034 04-03
ROTATIONAL-BEHAVIOUR ELICITED BY 5 HT IN THE RAT: EVIDENCE FOR
AN INHIBITORY ROLE OF 5 HT IN THE SUBSTANTIA-NIGRA AND
CORPUS-STRIATUM.
004141 04-04
EVIDENCE FOR SEDATIVE EFFECTS OF LOW-DOSES OF MORPHINE IN MICE
INVOLVING RECEPTORS INSENSITIVE TO NALOXONE.
004173 04-04
CLONIDINE-INDUCED HYPERPHAGIA IN MONKEYS: EVIDENCE FOR
ALPHA2-NORADRENERGIC-RECEPTOR MEDIATION.
004215 04-04
DO PSYCHOTHERAPY AND PHARMACOTHERAPY FOR DEPRESSION
CONFLICT? EMPIRICAL EVIDENCE FROM A CLINICAL-TRIAL.
(UNPUBLISHED PAPER).
004401 04-09
MINI-SYMPOSIUM. IV. DISCRIMINATIVE-STIMULUS EFFECTS OF
NARCOTICS: EVIDENCE FOR MULTIPLE RECEPTOR-MEDIATED ACTIONS.
004719 04-17

EVIL
MEDICATION: A NECESSARY EVIL?
002549 02-17

EVOKE
COMPARATIVE-STUDY OF AGGRESSIVE-BEHAVIOUR AFTER INJECTION OF
CHOLINOMIMETICS, ANTICHOLINESTERASES, NICOTINIC, AND
MUSCARINIC GANGLIONIC STIMULANTS INTO THE CEREBRAL
VENTRICLES OF CONSCIOUS CATS: FAILURE OF NICOTINIC-DRUGS TO
EVOKE AGGRESSION.
001568 02-04

EVOKED
SUPPRESSION OF EVOKED AND SPONTANEOUS RELEASE OF
NEUROTRANSMITTERS IN VIVO BY MORPHINE.
000058 01-03

PRESSURE REVERSAL OF THE EFFECT OF URETHANE ON THE EVOKED
SOMATOSENSORY CORTICAL RESPONSE IN THE RAT.
001106 02-03
FACTORS INFLUENCING THE RELEASE OF LABELLED GAMMA
AMINOBUTYRIC-ACID AND ACETYLCHOLINE EVOKED BY ELECTRICAL-
STIMULATION WITH ALTERNATING POLARITY FROM RAT CORTICAL
SLICES.
001130 02-03
SUBSTANCE-P, MORPHINE AND METHIONINE-ENKEPHALIN: EFFECTS ON
SPONTANEOUS AND EVOKED NEURONAL FIRING IN THE NUCLEUS-
RETICULARIS-GIGANTOCELLULARIS OF THE RAT.
001267 02-03
EFFECTS OF ELECTROLYTIC AND 6 HYDROXYDOPAMINE LESIONS OF THE
LATERAL HYPOTHALAMUS ON ROTATION EVOKED BY ELECTRICAL-
STIMULATION OF THE SUBSTANTIA-NIGRA IN RATS.
003081 03-04
INCREASE OF C-GMP AND ACCUMULATION OF 45CA2 EVOKED BY DRUGS
ACTING ON SODIUM OR POTASSIUM CHANNELS.
003709 04-03
DIFFERENTIAL TOLERANCE TO THE EFFECTS OF MORPHINE ON EVOKED
ACTIVITY IN THE HIPPOCAMPAL SLICE.
003760 04-03
MORPHINE AND METHIONINE-ENKEPHALIN: DIFFERENT EFFECTS ON
SPONTANEOUS AND EVOKED NEURONAL FIRING IN THE
MESENCEPHALIC RETICULAR FORMATION OF THE RAT.
003849 04-03
INVESTIGATION OF ACTION OF ENKEPHALIN ON THE SPONTANEOUS AND
EVOKED RELEASE OF ACETYLCHOLINE FROM RAT CORTICAL AND
STRIATAL SLICES.
003862 04-03
INFLUENCE OF CALCIUM ON NORADRENALINE RELEASE EVOKED BY 5
HYDROXYTRYPTAMINE, TYRAMINE AND POTASSIUM FROM GOAT
PIAL-ARTERIES.
003925 04-03

EVOKED-POTENTIAL
EVOKED-POTENTIAL CHANGES IN THE SUPERIOR-COLLICULUS PARALLEL
THE LESION-INDUCED DEVELOPMENT OF GROOMING REFLEXES IN THE
CAT. (PH.D. DISSERTATION).
001179 02-03
EVOKED-POTENTIAL STUDIES OF PORCINE CALCITONIN IN RABBITS.
002936 03-03
CEREBRAL EVOKED-POTENTIAL CHANGES PRODUCED BY TREATMENT
WITH LITHIUM-CARBONATE.
003263 03-09

EVOKED-POTENTIALS
BEHAVIOR-DEPENDENT EVOKED-POTENTIALS IN THE HIPPOCAMPAL-CA1
REGION OF THE RAT. II. EFFECTS OF ESERINE, ATROPINE, ETHER AND
PENTOBARBITAL.
000184 01-03
BRAINSTEM AUDITORY EVOKED-POTENTIALS AND MYELIN CHANGES IN
TRIETHYLTIN-INDUCED EDEMA IN YOUNG ADULT RATS.
000509 01-05
STIMULUS INTENSITY CONTROL IN DEPRESSION: A STUDY OF THE
COMPARATIVE-EFFECT OF DOXEPIN AND AMITRIPTYLINE ON CORTICAL
EVOKED-POTENTIALS.
000763 01-13
EFFECTS OF MORPHINE ON EVOKED-POTENTIALS RECORDED FROM THE
AMYGDALA BY TOOTH-PULP STIMULATION IN CATS.
001379 02-03
EFFECT OF OPIATES AND OPIATE ANTAGONISTS ON SOMATOSENSORY
EVOKED-POTENTIALS IN PATIENTS WITH SCHIZOPHRENIA AND
NORMAL ADULTS.
002222 02-13
EFFECTS OF LITHIUM ON EVOKED-POTENTIALS AND PERFORMANCE
DURING SUSTAINED ATTENTION.
002419 02-15
MODIFICATION OF MOTOR-ACTIVITY, PASSIVE-AVOIDANCE
CONDITIONING AND EVOKED-POTENTIALS BY MICROINJECTIONS OF
STRYCHNINE IN BOTH CAUDATE-NUCLEI IN CATS.
003101 03-04
PSYCHOTROPIC-DRUG-INDUCED CHANGES IN AUDITORY AVERAGED
EVOKED-POTENTIALS: RESULTS OF A DOUBLE-BLIND TRIAL USING AN
OBJECTIVE FULLY AUTOMATED AEP ANALYSIS METHOD.
003412 03-13
CORTICAL EVOKED-POTENTIALS IN GILLES-DE-LA-TOURETTES-SYNDROME
-- A SINGLE CASE-STUDY.
003431 03-13
ALTERATIONS OF EVOKED-POTENTIALS LINK RESEARCH IN ATTENTION-
DYSFUNCTION TO PEPTIDE RESPONSE SYMPTOMS OF SCHIZOPHRENIA.
004316 04-08
APOMORPHINE, HALOPERIDOL AND THE AVERAGE EVOKED-POTENTIALS
IN NORMAL HUMAN VOLUNTEERS.
004549 04-13

EVOKED-RESPONSE
THE BRAINSTEM AUDITORY EVOKED-RESPONSE AS A TOOL IN
NEUROBEHAVIORAL TOXICOLOGY AND MEDICINE.
004277 04-05

EVOKED-RESPONSES
MORPHINE AND ELECTROACUPUNCTURE: COMPARISON OF THE EFFECTS
ON THE CORTICAL EVOKED-RESPONSES AFTER TOOTH-PULP
STIMULATION IN RATS.
001294 02-03
AUDITORY BRAINSTEM EVOKED-RESPONSES IN HOSPITALIZED-PATIENTS
UNDERGOING DRUG-TREATMENT OR ECT.
003430 03-13
THE EFFECT OF CHOLINERGIC SUBSTANCES ON NOCICEPTIVE EVOKED-
RESPONSES IN SPECIFIC NUCLEI OF THE THALAMUS.
003770 04-03
THE EFFECT OF NOOTROPIL ON THE TRANSCALLOSAL AND PRIMARY
EVOKED-RESPONSES OF THE CAT CEREBRAL-CORTEX.
003780 04-03

EVOLUTION
CEEG STUDY ON PATIENTS UNDER THE PSYCHIATRIC-DRUG TREATMENT;
THE CORRELATION BETWEEN EEG ALTERATION AND CLINICAL
EVOLUTION.
002165 02-11
MINI-SYMPOSIUM: II. MULTIPLE OPIOID-RECEPTORS. A LITTLE ABOUT
THEIR HISTORY AND SOME IMPLICATIONS RELATED TO EVOLUTION.
004728 04-17

EVOLVING
MANIA: AN EVOLVING CONCEPT.
001966 02-09

EXACERBATE
DO STIMULANTS PROVOKE, CAUSE, OR EXACERBATE TICS AND
TOURETTE-SYNDROME?
004485 04-11

EXACERBATES
PYRAZOLE EXACERBATES HANDLING-INDUCED CONVULSIONS IN MICE.
004094 04-04

EXACERBATING
POLYPHARMACY REGIMEN AS AN EXACERBATING RISK IN THERAPY-
RESISTANT EPILEPTIC-SEIZURES AND BEHAVIORAL-DISORDERS.
004720 04-17

EXACERBATION
A NEW DRUG-TREATMENT FOR PREMENSTRUAL EXACERBATION OF
SCHIZOPHRENIA.
000553 01-08

EXAMINATION
THE EFFECT OF BETADRENOL ON EXAMINATION ANXIETY.
000650 01-10
AN EXAMINATION OF FACTORS INFLUENCING ADRENERGIC
TRANSMISSION IN THE PITHED RAT, WITH SPECIAL REFERENCE TO
NORADRENALINE UPTAKE MECHANISMS AND POSTJUNCTIONAL
ALPHA-ADRENOCEPTORS.
001196 02-03
NONCOOPERATION: AN EXAMINATION OF FACTORS LEADING TO
NONCOMPLIANCE IN A HYPERTENSION CLINIC.
002557 02-17
OXIDATION OF BETA PHENYLETHYLAMINE BY BOTH TYPES OF
MONOAMINE-OXIDASE: EXAMINATION OF ENZYMES IN BRAIN AND
LIVER MITOCHONDRIA OF EIGHT SPECIES.
004024 04-03

EXCESSES
PSYCHOMOTOR STIMULANTS AS ACTIVATORS OF NORMAL AND
PATHOLOGICAL-BEHAVIOR: IMPLICATIONS FOR THE EXCESSES IN
MANIA. (UNPUBLISHED PAPER).
002353 02-14

EXCESSIVE
SYSTEMIC   ND INTRAVENTRICULAR PROLACTIN INDUCES EXCESSIVE
GROOMING.
000378 01-04
INTRAVENOUS CHLORIMIPRAMINE AFFECTS REM CYCLE IN PATIENTS
WITH EXCESSIVE DAYTIME SLEEPINESS AND CONTROL SUBJECTS.
002341 02-14
EXCESSIVE PLASMA CONCENTRATIONS OF TRICYCLIC-ANTIDEPRESSANTS
RESULTING FROM USUAL DOSES: A REPORT OF SIX CASES.
003479 03-15

EXCITABILITY
DIFFERENTIAL-EFFECTS OF COCAINE ON LIMBIC EXCITABILITY.
001339 02-03
SUBACUTE CANNABINOID TREATMENT: ANTICONVULSANT ACTIVITY AND
WITHDRAWAL EXCITABILITY IN MICE.
001671 02-04
A COMPARISON OF THE EFFECTS OF PENTOBARBITAL AND
DIPHENYLHYDANTOIN ON THE GABA SENSITIVITY AND EXCITABILITY
OF ADULT SENSORY GANGLION CELLS.
002692 03-03
NYSTAGMIC RESPONSES OF HIPPOCAMPAL ORIGIN WITH REFERENCE TO
EXCITABILITY OF CHOLINERGIC AND ADRENERGIC COMPONENTS
INVOLVED IN THE HIPPOCAMPUS OF RABBITS.
003842 04-03
THE EFFECT OF PSYCHOSTIMULANTS ON CHANGES IN THE EXCITABILITY
OF THE VISUAL CEREBRAL-CORTEX.
003919 04-03
THE EFFECT OF DIAZEPAM ON CYCLIC EXCITABILITY CHANGES IN AN
EPILEPTIC-FOCUS IN THE CORTEX OF THE MAJOR HEMISPHERES.
003984 04-03

EXCITANT
PHARMACOLOGICAL ANTAGONISTS OF EXCITANT AMINO-ACID ACTION.
003587 03-17
BACLOFEN: STEREOSELECTIVE INHIBITION OF EXCITANT AMINO-ACID
RELEASE.
003867 04-03

EXCITATION
THE STEREOSPECIFIC EFFECT OF NALOXONE ON RAT DORSAL-HORN
NEURONES: INHIBITION IN SUPERFICIAL LAMINAE AND EXCITATION IN
DEEPER LAMINAE.
001226 02-03
INTRINSIC CHOLINERGIC EXCITATION IN THE RAT NEOSTRIATUM:
NICOTINIC AND MUSCARINIC-RECEPTORS.
001374 02-03
THE EFFECTS OF 5 HT UPTAKE AND MAO-INHIBITORS ON L 5 HTP-
INDUCED EXCITATION IN RATS.
001740 02-04
POTENTIATION OF L GLUTAMATE AND L ASPARTATE EXCITATION OF CAT
SPINAL NEURONES BY THE STEREOISOMERS OF THREO-3-
HYDROXYASPARTATE.
002768 03-03
SUPRASPINAL INHIBITION OF THE EXCITATION OF DORSAL-HORN
NEURONES BY IMPULSES IN UNMYELINATED PRIMARY AFFERENTS:
LACK OF EFFECT BY STRYCHNINE AND BICUCULLINE.
003778 04-03
INSEPARABILITY OF ACETYLCHOLINESTERASE AND NERVE EXCITATION.
003875 04-03
SEX, PLASMA PROLACTIN AND PLASMA 3 METHOXY-4-
HYDROXYPHENYLGLYCOL (MHPG) PREDICT HERITABLE D-
AMPHETAMINE EXCITATION IN MAN. (UNPUBLISHED PAPER).
004565 04-14

EXCITATORY
EXCITATORY AND INHIBITORY-EFFECTS OF OPIATES IN THE RAT VAS-
DEFERENS: A DUAL-MECHANISM OF OPIATE ACTION.
000143 01-03
OPIATE-RECEPTORS MAY MEDIATE THE SUPPRESSIVE BUT NOT THE
EXCITATORY ACTION OF ACTH ON MOTOR-ACTIVITY IN RATS.
000337 01-04
CENTRAL EXCITATORY ACTIONS OF FLURAZEPAM.
000526 01-05
EXCITATORY ACTION OF OPIOID-PEPTIDES AND OPIATES ON CULTURED
HIPPOCAMPAL PYRAMIDAL CELLS.
001241 02-03
REGIONAL RELEASE OF (3H)ADENOSINE DERIVATIVES FROM RAT-BRAIN
IN VIVO: EFFECT OF EXCITATORY AMINO-ACIDS, OPIATE AGONISTS,
AND BENZODIAZEPINES.
001303 02-03
5 METHOXYDIMETHYLTRYPTAMINE: SPINAL-CORD AND BRAINSTEM
MEDIATION OF EXCITATORY EFFECTS ON ACOUSTIC STARTLE.
001605 02-04
THE EXCITATORY COMPONENT OF ETHANOL IN MICE: A CHRONIC STUDY.
001712 02-04
THE EXCITATORY ACTION OF ACETYLCHOLINE ON HIPPOCAMPAL
NEURONES OF THE GUINEA-PIG AND RAT MAINTAINED IN VITRO.
002704 03-03
EFFECT OF ANTICONVULSANT-DRUGS ON INHIBITORY AND EXCITATORY
PATHWAYS.
002724 03-03
DEVELOPMENT OF TOLERANCE TO THE EXCITATORY EFFECT OF MORPHINE
AND CROSS-TOLERANCE TO THE INHIBITORY ACTION OF BETA
ENDORPHIN IN THE ISOLATED RAT VAS-DEFERENS.
002756 03-03
THE INTERACTION BETWEEN BARBITURATE ANESTHETICS AND
EXCITATORY AMINO-ACID RESPONSES ON CAT SPINAL NEURONES.
002799 03-03
EXCITATORY AND INHIBITORY-ACTIONS OF IBOTENIC-ACID ON FROG
SPINAL MOTONEURONES IN VITRO.
002841 03-03
EXCITATORY AMINO-ACID TRANSMITTERS.
003648 03-17
EXCITATORY EFFECTS OF DIHYDROCAPSAICIN ON NOCICEPTIVE NEURONS
IN THE MEDIAL THALAMUS.
003714 04-03
EFFECTS OF BARBITURATES ON INHIBITORY AND EXCITATORY RESPONSES
TO APPLIED NEUROTRANSMITTERS IN APLYSIA.
003762 04-03
THE EXCITATORY EFFECT OF ATROPINE ON THE NEURONS OF THE FROG
SYMPATHETIC GANGLIA.
004041 04-03

EXCITEMENT
PSYCHOTIC EXCITEMENT IN MEDICAL-EMERGENCIES.
004480 04-11

EXCRETION
OXAZEPAM-ESTERS. 2. CORRELATION OF HYDROPHOBICITY WITH SERUM
BINDING, BRAIN PENETRATION, AND EXCRETION.
000011 01-02
INCREASED URINARY EXCRETION OF CATECHOLAMINES AND THEIR
METABOLITES IN STREPTOZOTOCIN DIABETIC RAT.
000154 01-03

DISTRIBUTION AND EXCRETION IN THE RAT AND MONKEY OF (82BR) BROMOCRIPTINE.
000196 01-03
VARIATIONS IN URINARY EXCRETION OF 3 METHOXY-4-HYDROXYPHENYLGLYCOL-SULFATE IN DEPRESSIVE-CONDITIONS.
002013 02-09
SUBTYPES OF DEPRESSION BASED ON EXCRETION OF MHPG AND RESPONSE TO NORTRIPTYLINE.
002488 02-16
EXCRETION OF NORTRIPTYLINE INTO SALIVA.
003435 03-13
HYPERVENTILATION-SYNDROME, TREATMENT WITH L TRYPTOPHAN AND PYRIDOXINE; PREDICTIVE VALUES OF XANTHURENIC-ACID EXCRETION.
004456 04-11
CONSISTENCY IN CATECHOLAMINE EXCRETION IN LABORATORY AND NATURAL SETTINGS: CORRELATIONAL AND VARIANCE COMPONENTS ANALYSES.
004508 04-13
IN NORMAL YOUNG MEN ACUTE DOPAMINERGIC BLOCKADE DOES NOT IMPAIR FREE WATER EXCRETION FOLLOWING A STANDARD WATER LOAD.
004600 04-15

EXECUTION
SELECTIVE EFFECTS OF BARBITURATE AND AMPHETAMINE ON INFORMATION-PROCESSING AND RESPONSE EXECUTION.
004563 04-14

EXERCISE
HEXAMETHONIUM MODIFICATION OF CARDIOVASCULAR ADJUSTMENTS DURING COMBINED STATIC DYNAMIC ARM EXERCISE IN MONKEYS.
001242 02-03
THE SPECIFIC ACTIVITY OF PLATELET MONOAMINE-OXIDASE VARIES WITH PLATELET COUNT DURING SEVERE EXERCISE AND NORADRENALINE INFUSION.
004509 04-13

EXERTS
MORPHINE EXERTS TESTOSTERONE-LIKE EFFECTS IN THE HYPOTHALAMUS OF THE CASTRATED MALE RAT.
000051 01-03

EXHIBITIONISM
THE EFFECT OF ASSERTIVENESS TRAINING, PROVERA AND SEX OF THERAPIST IN THE TREATMENT OF GENITAL EXHIBITIONISM.
000697 01-11

EXISTENCE
FURTHER EVIDENCE FOR THE EXISTENCE OF MULTIPLE RECEPTORS FOR DOPAMINE IN THE CENTRAL-NERVOUS-SYSTEM.
001296 02-03

EXOGENOUS
DECARBOXYLATION OF EXOGENOUS L-DOPA IN RAT STRIATUM AFTER LESIONS OF THE DOPAMINERGIC NIGROSTRIATAL NEURONS: THE ROLE OF STRIATAL CAPILLARIES.
000202 01-03

EXOGENOUSLY-INDUCED
ENDORPHIN-INDUCED HYPERTHERMIA: CHARACTERIZATION OF THE EXOGENOUSLY-INDUCED AND ENDOGENOUSLY-INDUCED EFFECTS.
000029 01-03

EXOSECRETORY
THE EFFECT OF SEROTONIN ON THE EXOSECRETORY ACTION OF THE PANCREAS.
004043 04-03

EXPERIENCE
PLASMA LEVELS OF DIPHENYLHYDANTOIN AND THE CONTROL OF ADULT EPILEPTIC-SEIZURES; A CHILEAN EXPERIENCE.
000102 01-03
PRIOR AND ONGOING EXPERIENCE AS DETERMINANTS OF THE EFFECTS OF D-AMPHETAMINE AND CHLORPROMAZINE ON PUNISHED-BEHAVIOR.
000339 01-04
OUR EXPERIENCE WITH PIRACETAM (NOOTROPIL-UCB) TREATMENT IN CHILDREN FROM HIGH-RISK PREGNANCIES WITH SUBSEQUENT MINIMAL-BRAIN-DYSFUNCTION.
000544 01-07
OXYPROTHEPIN-DECANOATE INJECTIONS: EXPERIENCE WITH A LONG-TERM-TREATMENT OF SCHIZOPHRENIC-PSYCHOSES.
000576 01-08
OUR EXPERIENCE WITH MAPROTILIN TREATMENT OF DEPRESSIVE-STATES.
000623 01-09
OUR EXPERIENCE WITH TOFISOPAM (GRANDAXIN-EGYPT).
000647 01-10
EXPERIENCE WITH FLUSPIRILENE IN GERONTOPSYCHIATRY.
000691 01-11
TWENTY YEARS CLINICAL THERAPEUTIC EXPERIENCE WITH CALCIUM GLUTAMATES EFFICACY.
000963 01-17
INTERRELATIONS AMONG PRIOR EXPERIENCE AND CURRENT CONDITIONS IN THE DETERMINATION OF BEHAVIOR AND THE EFFECTS OF DRUGS.
001715 02-04
EXPERIENCE WITH OXYPROTHEPINE-DECANOATE IN THE MAINTENANCE-THERAPY OF SCHIZOPHRENIA.
001925 02-08
AN OVERVIEW OF SEVENTEEN YEARS OF EXPERIENCE WITH DOTHIEPIN IN THE TREATMENT OF DEPRESSION IN EUROPE.
001995 02-09

OUR FIRST EXPERIENCE WITH CLOMIPRAMINE.
002008 02-09
TWELVE YEARS EXPERIENCE WITH THE TOTAL USE OF DEPOT NEUROLEPTICS IN A DEFINED POPULATION.
002544 02-17
CONSIDERATIONS ON LONG-ACTING CHEMOTHERAPY: AN EXPERIENCE WITH FLUPHENAZINE-DECANOATE.
003173 03-08
EXPERIENCE IN USING THE HORMONES OF THE HYPOPHYSIS POSTERIOR LOBE IN MEMORY-DISTURBANCES OF VARYING GENESES.
003438 03-14
DRUG DEPENDENCE: REFLECTIONS ON AND ANALYSIS OF AN EXPERIENCE IN THE PROVINCE OF RIGGIO-EMILIA.
003591 03-17
CLINICAL AND PRECLINICAL EXPERIENCE WITH CHOLINE-CHLORIDE IN HUNTINGTONS-DISEASE AND TARDIVE-DYSKINESIA: UNANSWERED QUESTIONS.
004604 04-15

EXPERIENCED
NEUROLEPTIC TREATMENT AS EXPERIENCED BY A PSYCHIATRIST.
004613 04-15

EXPERIENCES
FURTHER EXPERIENCES WITH LOW-DOSES OF BROMOCRIPTINE IN PARKINSONS-DISEASE.
002401 02-15

EXPERIMENT
PLASMA CHLORPROMAZINE SERUM PROLACTIN RELATIONSHIP IN A SINGLE-DOSE EXPERIMENT.
000761 01-13
COMPARATIVE EXPERIMENT OF THE ANTIDEPRESSANT EFFECTS OF AMINEPTINE AND CHLORIMIPRAMINE.
002029 02-09
DOUBLE-BLIND CONTROLLED EXPERIMENT: AMINEPTINE VERSUS AMITRIPTYLINE USING THE HAMILTON-DEPRESSION-RATING-SCALE.
002050 02-09

EXPERIMENTAL
THE PARADOXICAL-EFFECT OF LIDOCAINE ON AN EXPERIMENTAL MODEL OF EPILEPSY.
000039 01-03
INFLUENCE OF PYRITHIOXINE ON EXPERIMENTAL HYPOXIA IN RATS.
000077 01-03
PHENYLACETATE AND BRAIN-DYSFUNCTION IN EXPERIMENTAL PHENYLKETONURIA: SYNAPTIC DEVELOPMENT.
000191 01-03
ROLE OF BRAIN DOPAMINERGIC MECHANISMS IN RODENT AGGRESSIVE-BEHAVIOR: INFLUENCE OF (OR -)N N PROPYLNORAPOMORPHINE ON THREE EXPERIMENTAL MODELS.
000340 01-04
PHENYLACETATE AND THE ENDURING BEHAVIORAL-DEFICIT IN EXPERIMENTAL PHENYLKETONURIA.
000388 01-04
ANTAGONISM BY CLASSICAL ANTIEPILEPTICS AND SODIUM-VALPROATE OF CEFAZOLIN-INDUCED EXPERIMENTAL EPILEPSY IN RATS.
000442 01-04
EXPERIMENTAL DYSTONIA INDUCED BY QUATERNARY CHLORPROMAZINE.
000461 01-04
ASSESSMENT OF ADRENERGIC-RECEPTORS IN VIVO IN EXPERIMENTAL ANIMALS AND MAN. (UNPUBLISHED PAPER).
001034 02-01
EXPERIMENTAL EVALUATION OF ANTIDEPRESSANT ACTIVITY OF CLOMIPRAMINE, A NEW TRICYCLIC-ANTIDEPRESSANT DRUG.
001068 02-02
AMOXAPINE IN EXPERIMENTAL PSYCHOPHARMACOLOGY: A NEUROLEPTIC OR AN ANTIDEPRESSANT?
001070 02-02
SOME PHARMACOLOGICAL-ASPECTS AND BIOCHEMICAL-ASPECTS OF TRH: EXPERIMENTAL AND CLINICAL DATA.
001189 02-03
ENHANCED TRANSFER OF EXPERIMENTAL ALLERGIC-ENCEPHALOMYELITIS WITH STRAIN-13 GUINEA-PIG LYMPH-NODE CELLS: REQUIREMENT FOR CULTURE WITH SPECIFIC ANTIGEN AND ALLOGENIC PERITONEAL EXUDATE CELLS. (UNPUBLISHED PAPER).
001201 02-03
ENHANCED TRANSFER OF EXPERIMENTAL ALLERGIC-ENCEPHALOMYELITIS WITH LEWIS-RAT LYMPH-NODE CELLS. (UNPUBLISHED PAPER).
001434 02-03
NEW EXPERIMENTAL TECHNIQUES IN THE PHARMACOLOGICAL EVALUATION OF CNS ACTING DRUGS.
001479 02-03
EFFECTS OF EXPERIMENTAL HYPOTHYROIDISM ON LEARNING IN RATS.
001587 02-04
GENETIC AND EXPERIMENTAL FACTORS AFFECTING THE PARADOXICAL-EFFECTS OF AMPHETAMINE IN DOGS.
001704 02-04
EXPERIMENTAL DEPENDENCE ON BARBITURATES: II. RELATIONSHIP BETWEEN DRUG LEVELS IN SERUM AND BRAIN AND THE DEVELOPMENT OF DEPENDENCE IN RATS.
001800 02-04

CENTRAL SEROTONIN-RECEPTOR SENSITIVITY IN RATS WITH
EXPERIMENTAL ALLERGIC-ENCEPHALOMYELITIS.
001821 02-04

EFFECTS OF CAFFEINE ADMINISTRATION ON FOOD AND WATER
CONSUMPTION UNDER VARIOUS EXPERIMENTAL CONDITIONS.
003049 03-04

PHARMACOLOGIC AND THERAPEUTIC-PERSPECTIVES ON DEMENTIA: AN
EXPERIMENTAL APPROACH.
003065 03-04

BEHAVIORAL-TEST FOR DETECTION OF SUBCLINICAL BRAIN-DAMAGE: AN
EXPERIMENTAL MODEL.
003120 03-04

PLACEBO-EFFECT: FROM CONTROL TO EXPERIMENTAL CONDITION.
003195 03-08

THE EFFECT OF ADENOSINE AND GUANOSINE ON THE CONTENT OF
SEROTONIN AND CATECHOLAMINES IN THE BRAIN IN THE
RESTORATION PERIOD FOLLOWING EXPERIMENTAL CLINICAL DEATH.
003882 04-03

STUDIES ON GAMMA AMINOBUTYRIC-ACID TRANSPORT IN COBALT
EXPERIMENTAL EPILEPSY IN THE RAT.
003990 04-03

CONDITIONED DRUG-EFFECTS OF D-AMPHETAMINE-INDUCED AND
MORPHINE-INDUCED MOTOR ACCELERATION IN MICE: EXPERIMENTAL
APPROACH FOR PLACEBO-EFFECT.
004128 04-04

ANALGESIC AND OTHER PHARMACOLOGICAL ACTIVITIES OF A NEW
NARCOTIC ANTAGONIST ANALGESIC (-) 1 3
METHYLBUTENYLHYDROXYPHENYLPHENYLETHYLPIPERAZINE AND ITS
ENANTIOMORPH IN EXPERIMENTAL ANIMALS.
004185 04-04

EXPERIMENTAL-EFFECTS
SOME EXPERIMENTAL-EFFECTS WITH TRAZODONE.
000105 01-03

EXPERIMENTAL-STUDIES
COMPARISON OF CLONAZEPAM AND DIAZEPAM IN EXPERIMENTAL-
STUDIES.
001815 02-04

EXPERIMENTAL-STUDIES ON HEPATOTOXICITY OF DISULFIRAM.
001844 02-05

EXPERIMENTAL-STUDIES ON L-DOPA-INDUCED DYSKINESIA.
003129 03-05

EXPERIMENTAL-STUDY
PHENOBARBITONE AND SODIUM-VALPROATE INTERACTION: AN
EXPERIMENTAL-STUDY.
001371 02-03

AN EXPERIMENTAL-STUDY OF THE NEUROTROPIC-ACTION OF LITHIUM-
OXYBUTYRATE.
001705 02-04

THE COMPLEX SPECIFIC PATHOGENETIC THERAPY OF THE STEREOTYPIC-
BEHAVIOR-SYNDROME (AN EXPERIMENTAL-STUDY).
004162 04-04

EXPERIMENTALLY
ELECTROMYOGRAPHIC-ASSESSMENT OF SPINAL REFLEXES IN
EXPERIMENTALLY DEPRESSED DOGS TREATED WITH
ANTIDEPRESSANTS.
001620 02-04

CAN THE ANTIDEPRESSIVE PROPERTIES OF LITHIUM BE DETERMINED
EXPERIMENTALLY?
003089 03-04

EXPERIMENTALLY-INDUCED
SUPERSENSITIVITY TO APOMORPHINE IN EXPERIMENTALLY-INDUCED
HYPOKINESIA AND DRUG-INDUCED MODIFICATIONS OF THE
APOMORPHINE RESPONSE.
001814 02-04

EXPERIMENTATION
EXPERIMENTATION WITH MINAPRINE IN DEALING WITH CERTAIN
SEXUAL-DISORDERS: IMPOTENCE OR FRIGIDITY.
002153 02-11

EXPERIMENTATION WITH MINAPRINE IN CHILD-PSYCHIATRY.
002344 02-14

EXPERIMENTER
EFFECTS OF EXPERIMENTER AND TEST LOCATION NOVELTY ON
NONSPECIFIC ACTIVITY IN RATS AND ITS MODIFICATION BY
METHAMPHETAMINE.
000409 01-04

EXPERIMENTS
A MICROCOMPUTER SYSTEM FOR THE CONTROL OF BEHAVIORAL
EXPERIMENTS.
004287 04-06

EXPLORATION
MESOLIMBICOCORTICAL DOPAMINE TERMINAL-FIELDS ARE NECESSARY
FOR NORMAL LOCOMOTOR AND INVESTIGATORY EXPLORATION IN
RATS.
000383 01-04

EXPLORATION AND MOTOR-ACTIVITY AFTER INTRAVENTRICULAR ACTH,
MORPHINE AND NALOXONE.
002991 03-04

SAME OR DIFFERENT? AN EXPLORATION OF THE BEHAVIORAL-EFFECTS OF
BENZAMIDES.
004207 04-04

EXPLORATORY-ACTIVITY
TRICYCLIC-ANTIDEPRESSANT DRUGS AND INDIVIDUAL DIFFERENCES IN
THE EXPLORATORY-ACTIVITY OF RATS: CONTRASTING-EFFECTS OF
TERTIARY AND SECONDARY AMINE COMPOUNDS.
000401 01-04

NALOXONE REDUCES SOCIAL-ACTIVITY AND EXPLORATORY-ACTIVITY IN
THE RAT.
001617 02-04

EFFECT OF BROMOCRIPTINE ON EXPLORATORY-ACTIVITY, BRAIN-
MONOAMINES AND PLASMA CORTICOSTERONE IN THE
NORMOTENSIVE-RATS, GENETICALLY HYPERTENSIVE-RATS AND/OR
HYPERTENSIVE OBESE RATS.
001635 02-04

IMIPRAMINE NORMALIZES NATURALLY OCCURRING AND DRUG-INDUCED
DIFFERENCES IN THE EXPLORATORY-ACTIVITY OF RATS.
001646 02-04

EXPLORATORY-BEHAVIOR
BIPHASIC-EFFECTS OF THYROTROPIN-RELEASING-HORMONE ON
EXPLORATORY-BEHAVIOR IN MICE.
001808 02-04

INTERACTION BETWEEN PURINE AND BENZODIAZEPINE: INOSINE
REVERSES DIAZEPAM-INDUCED STIMULATION OF MOUSE
EXPLORATORY-BEHAVIOR.
002972 03-04

EFFECTS OF SCOPOLAMINE, PILOCARPINE, AND OXOTREMORINE ON THE
EXPLORATORY-BEHAVIOR OF TWO PSYCHOGENETICALLY SELECTED
LINES OF RATS IN A COMPLEX MAZE.
003042 03-04

EXPLORATORY-BEHAVIOUR
COMPARISON OF THE EFFECTS OF BETA ENDORPHIN AND MORPHINE ON
EXPLORATORY-BEHAVIOUR AND SOCIOSEXUAL-BEHAVIOUR IN THE
MALE RAT.
004178 04-04

EXPLORE
BENZODIAZEPINES: A TOOL TO EXPLORE THE BIOCHEMICAL-BASIS AND
NEUROPHYSIOLOGICAL-BASIS OF ANXIETY.
000397 01-04

EXPLOSIVE
HEROIN, BUT NOT LEVORPHANOL, PRODUCES EXPLOSIVE MOTOR-
BEHAVIOR IN NALOXONE TREATED RATS.
001579 02-04

EXPOSED
PLASMA CATECHOLAMINES IN RATS EXPOSED TO COLD: EFFECTS OF
GANGLIONIC AND ADRENORECEPTOR BLOCKADE.
002863 03-03

CORE TEMPERATURE CHANGES FOLLOWING ADMINISTRATION OF
NALOXONE AND NALTREXONE TO RATS EXPOSED TO HOT AND COLD
AMBIENT TEMPERATURES. EVIDENCE FOR THE PHYSIOLOGICAL ROLE
OF ENDORPHINS IN HOT AND COLD ACCLIMATIZATION.
004034 04-03

EXPOSURE
LONG-TERM EFFECTS OF CONTINUOUS EXPOSURE TO AMPHETAMINE ON
BRAIN DOPAMINE CONCENTRATION AND SYNAPTOSOMAL UPTAKE IN
MICE.
000287 01-03

DELAYED MAZE-LEARNING IN RATS AFTER PRENATAL EXPOSURE TO
CLORAZEPATE.
000521 01-05

EFFECTS OF LEAD EXPOSURE DURING DEVELOPMENT ON NEOCORTICAL
DENDRITIC AND SYNAPTIC STRUCTURE.
000525 01-05

GLIAL CELL EFFECTS OF SUBACUTE FORMIC-ACID VAPOUR EXPOSURE.
000527 01-05

ALTERATIONS IN BASAL FIRING-RATE AND AUTORECEPTOR SENSITIVITY
OF DOPAMINE NEURONS IN THE SUBSTANTIA-NIGRA FOLLOWING
ACUTE AND EXTENDED EXPOSURE TO ESTROGEN.
001167 02-03

EXPOSURE OF MITOCHONDRIAL OUTER MEMBRANES TO NEURAMINIDASE
SELECTIVELY DESTROYS MONOAMINE-OXIDASE-A ACTIVITY.
001286 02-03

STIMULATION OF THE PLASMA MEMBRANE ENZYME, 5' NUCLEOTIDASE,
BY ETHANOL EXPOSURE TO NEURAL CELLS IN CULTURE.
001499 02-03

POSTNATAL ALCOHOL EXPOSURE IN THE RAT: ITS EFFECTS ON
AVOIDANCE CONDITIONING, HEBB-WILLIAMS MAZE-PERFORMANCE,
MATERNAL-BEHAVIOR, AND PUP DEVELOPMENT.
001580 02-04

ENHANCED LATERAL HYPOTHALAMIC SELF-STIMULATION RESPONDING
AFTER CHRONIC EXPOSURE TO AMPHETAMINE.
001688 02-04

THE DEVELOPMENT OF PROGENY IN CASES OF ANTENATAL EXPOSURE TO
PHENAZEPAM.
001854 02-05

DIFFERENTIAL-EFFECTS OF CANNABINOID EXPOSURE AND STRESS ON
PLASMA PROLACTIN, GROWTH-HORMONE AND CORTICOSTERONE
LEVELS IN MALE MICE.
002695 03-03

BRIEF COMMUNICATION: BEHAVIORAL RECOVERY AFTER TOLUENE
EXPOSURE IN RATS.
                                                    002969 03-04
PHENELZINE AND EXPOSURE IN THE TREATMENT OF PHOBIAS.
                                                    003285 03-10
PRENATAL EXPOSURE TO SYNTHETIC PROGESTINS INCREASES POTENTIAL
FOR AGGRESSION IN HUMANS.
                                                    003527 03-15
THE EFFECT OF PRENATAL EXPOSURE TO ETHANOL OR OPIATES ON BRAIN
CATECHOLAMINE ACTIVITY.
                                                    003939 04-03
NEUROTRANSMITTER-RECEPTORS IN BRAIN REGIONS OF ACRYLAMIDE
TREATED RATS. I: EFFECTS OF A SINGLE EXPOSURE TO ACRYLAMIDE.
                                                    004264 04-05
NEUROTRANSMITTER-RECEPTORS IN BRAIN REGIONS OF ACRYLAMIDE
TREATED RATS. II: EFFECTS OF EXTENDED EXPOSURE TO ACRYLAMIDE.
                                                    004265 04-05

EXPRESSION
MATERNAL GLUCOCORTICOID-HORMONES INFLUENCE
NEUROTRANSMITTER PHENOTYPIC EXPRESSION IN EMBRYOS.
                                                    000149 01-03
POSSIBLE INVOLVEMENT OF BRAIN DOPAMINERGIC-SYSTEMS IN THE
EXPRESSION OF EMOTIONS IN DREAMS.
                                                    002325 02-14
EFFECT OF COCAINE AND LIDOCAINE ON THE EXPRESSION OF KINDLED
SEIZURES IN THE RAT.
                                                    004233 04-04

EXTENSION
DELTA9 THC IN PIGEONS: A REPLICATION AND EXTENSION.
                                                    000394 01-04

EXTENSOR
SENSITIVE DEPRESSANT EFFECT OF BENZODIAZEPINES ON THE CROSSED
EXTENSOR REFLEX IN CHLORALOSE ANESTHETIZED RATS.
                                                    003027 04-04

EXTENT
PREDICTION OF THE VOLUME OF DISTRIBUTION FROM IN VITRO DATA
AND USE FOR ESTIMATING THE ABSOLUTE EXTENT OF ABSORPTION.
                                                    000907 01-16

EXTERNAL
THE INFLUENCE OF EXTERNAL SODIUM AND POTASSIUM ON LITHIUM
UPTAKE BY PRIMARY BRAIN CELL CULTURES AT THERAPEUTIC LITHIUM
CONCENTRATION.
                                                    001300 02-03

EXTEROCEPTIVE
CONDITIONING OF AN INTEROCEPTIVE DRUG STIMULUS TO DIFFERENT
EXTEROCEPTIVE CONTEXTS.
                                                    004142 04-04

EXTINCTION
THE USE OF EXTINCTION TO INVESTIGATE THE NATURE OF NEUROLEPTIC-
INDUCED AVOIDANCE-DEFICITS.
                                                    000345 01-04
EXTINCTION AND DOPAMINE-RECEPTOR BLOCKADE AFTER INTERMITTENT
REINFORCEMENT TRAINING: FAILURE TO OBSERVE FUNCTIONAL
EQUIVALENCE.
                                                    000490 01-04
ACCELERATED EXTINCTION AFTER POSTTRIAL HALOTHANE ANESTHESIA IN
RATS: AN AVERSIVE-EFFECT.
                                                    003001 03-04

EXTRACELLULAR
ALPHA2-ADRENERGIC AMINES, ADENOSINE AND PROSTAGLANDINS
INHIBIT LIPOLYSIS AND CYCLIC-AMP ACCUMULATION IN HAMSTER
ADIPOCYTES IN THE ABSENCE OF EXTRACELLULAR SODIUM.
                                                    002728 03-03

EXTRACTION
EFFECTS OF RATE OF BLOOD FLOW ON FRACTIONAL EXTRACTION AND ON
UPTAKE OF INFUSED NORADRENALINE BY BROWN ADIPOSE TISSUE IN
VIVO.
                                                    001231 02-03

EXTRACTS
METABOLISM OF 3H NORADRENALINE RELEASED FROM ISOLATED RAT
HYPOTHALAMUS BY EXTRACTS OF BLACK-WIDOW-SPIDER GLANDS.
                                                    000223 01-03
ASSAYING GABA-MODULIN ACTIVITY IN BRAIN EXTRACTS: RESOLUTION
OF INHERENT DIFFICULTIES. (UNPUBLISHED PAPER).
                                                    001045 02-01

EXTRAHYPOTHALAMIC
EXTRAHYPOTHALAMIC DISTRIBUTIONS AND FUNCTIONS OF
HYPOTHALAMIC PEPTIDE-HORMONES. (UNPUBLISHED PAPER).
                                                    001211 02-03

EXTRAPORTAL
ABSORPTION OF 14C LABELED METHADONE BY PORTAL AND
EXTRAPORTAL VENOUS CIRCULATIONS FOLLOWING INTRAPERITONEAL
AND INTRODUODENAL ADMINISTRATION.
                                                    000094 01-03

EXTRAPYRAMIDAL
PROLACTIN RESPONSE AND EXTRAPYRAMIDAL SIDE-EFFECTS DURING
PROPRANOLOL AND NEUROLEPTIC-DRUGS TREATMENT IN CHRONIC
SCHIZOPHRENIC-PATIENTS.
                                                    000841 01-15

NEUROLOGICAL SIDE-EFFECTS OF LITHIUM: ORGANIC-BRAIN-SYNDROME,
SEIZURES, EXTRAPYRAMIDAL SIDE-EFFECTS, AND EEG CHANGES.
                                                    000847 01-15
THE OCCURRENCE OF TARDIVE EXTRAPYRAMIDAL SYMPTOMS IN
SCHIZOPHRENIC-PATIENTS UNDERGOING PROLONGED NEUROLEPTIC
TREATMENT.
                                                    000885 01-15
EFFECT OF THE NEW GAMMA AMINOBUTYRIC-ACID AGONIST SL-76-002
ON STRIATAL ACETYLCHOLINE: RELATION TO NEUROLEPTIC-INDUCED
EXTRAPYRAMIDAL ALTERATIONS.
                                                    001119 02-03
USE OF LARGE-SINGLE-DOSES OF BROMOCRIPTINE IN SCHIZOPHRENIC-
PATIENTS WITH ELEVATED SERUM PROLACTIN LEVELS AND
EXTRAPYRAMIDAL SIDE-EFFECTS ASSOCIATED WITH NEUROLEPTIC
TREATMENT.
                                                    001944 02-08
PIRACETAM ACTION IN NEUROLEPTIC-INDUCED EXTRAPYRAMIDAL SIDE-
EFFECTS.
                                                    002132 02-11
PROPRANOLOL (INDERAL) FOR TARDIVE-DYSKINESIA AND
EXTRAPYRAMIDAL SIDE-EFFECTS FROM NEUROLEPTICS: POSSIBLE
INVOLVEMENT OF BETA-ADRENERGIC MECHANISMS.
                                                    002470 02-15
CHRONIC EFFECTS OF NEUROLEPTICS HAVING HIGH OR LOW INCIDENCE
OF EXTRAPYRAMIDAL SIDE-EFFECTS UPON FORCE, DURATION AND
RATE OF OPERANT-RESPONSE IN RATS. (PH.D. DISSERTATION).
                                                    003125 03-05
EXTRAPYRAMIDAL REACTION OF FLUPHENAZINE POTENTIATED BY
THYROTOXICOSIS.
                                                    003551 03-15
CORRECTION OF THE EXTRAPYRAMIDAL NEUROLEPTIC-SYNDROME BY
TRYPTOPHAN AND THE TIME-COURSE OF ITS CONTENT IN THE BLOOD
OF PATIENTS.
                                                    004434 04-11
CLOPIPAZAN (SKF-69634), A NEW NEUROLEPTIC ESSENTIALLY FREE OF
EXTRAPYRAMIDAL LIABILITY: QUANTITATIVE PHARMACOEEG AND
OPEN LABEL CLINICAL-TRIAL.
                                                    004620 04-15

EXTRAPYRAMIDAL-DISORDERS
A BIOCHEMICAL-STUDY OF LUMBAR CEREBROSPINAL-FLUID IN
EXTRAPYRAMIDAL-DISORDERS.
                                                    002186 02-11
EXTRAPYRAMIDAL-DISORDERS AND BORDERLINE-SYNDROMES:
EREDOATAXIAS AND DEMENTIA.
                                                    003518 03-15

EXTRAPYRAMIDAL-EFFECTS
CHRONOLOGY OF EXTRAPYRAMIDAL-EFFECTS OF NEUROLEPTIC-DRUGS
AND THE NIGROSTRIATAL DOPAMINERGIC-SYSTEM.
                                                    002449 02-15

EXTRAPYRAMIDAL-SYNDROMES
A TRIAL TREATMENT WITH TIAPRIDE FOR SOME EXTRAPYRAMIDAL-
SYNDROMES CAUSED BY NEUROLEPTIC-AGENTS.
                                                    003553 03-15

EXTRASTRIATAL
SHORT-TERM AND LONG-TERM EFFECTS OF METHAMPHETAMINE ON
BIOGENIC-AMINE METABOLISM IN EXTRASTRIATAL DOPAMINERGIC
NUCLEI.
                                                    001384 02-03

EXTRASYSTOLE
EFFECT OF AMITRIPTYLINE ANTIDOTES ON REPETITIVE EXTRASYSTOLE
THESHOLD.
                                                    001856 02-05

EXUDATE
ENHANCED TRANSFER OF EXPERIMENTAL ALLERGIC-ENCEPHALOMYELITIS
WITH STRAIN-13 GUINEA-PIG LYMPH-NODE CELLS: REQUIREMENT FOR
CULTURE WITH SPECIFIC ANTIGEN AND ALLOGENIC PERITONEAL
EXUDATE CELLS. (UNPUBLISHED PAPER).
                                                    001201 02-03

EYE
SEIZURES AND RELATED EPILEPTIFORM ACTIVITY IN HIPPOCAMPUS
TRANSPLANTED TO THE ANTERIOR-CHAMBER OF THE EYE:
MODULATION BY CHOLINERGIC AND ADRENERGIC INPUT.
                                                    000095 01-03
EYE BLINKS. (UNPUBLISHED PAPER).
                                                    001672 02-04
DRUG-INDUCED DISORDERS OF THE EYE.
                                                    002396 02-15

EYE-MOVEMENTS
DISORDERS OF SMOOTH-PURSUIT EYE-MOVEMENTS IN SCHIZOPHRENICS
AND THE EFFECT OF NEUROLEPTICS IN THERAPEUTIC DOSES.
                                                    001912 02-08
QUANTITATIVE ASSESSMENT OF SMOOTH-PURSUIT EYE-MOVEMENTS IN
HEALTHY AND EPILEPTIC-SUBJECTS.
                                                    002376 02-15
SMOOTH-PURSUIT EYE-MOVEMENTS: EFFECTS OF ALCOHOL AND
CHLORAL-HYDRATE.
                                                    003448 03-14

EYEBLINK
EFFECTS OF SUBCHRONIC DESMETHYLIMIPRAMINE (DMI) TREATMENT OF
THE CLASSICALLY CONDITIONED EYEBLINK RESPONSE IN RABBITS.
004180 04-04

FACIAL
DENERVATION SUPERSENSITIVITY TO SEROTONIN IN THE FACIAL
NUCLEUS.
001364 02-03
PHARMACOLOGIC CHARACTERIZATION AND LECITHIN TREATMENT OF A
PATIENT WITH SPONTANEOUS ORAL FACIAL DYSKINESIA AND
DEMENTIA.
003347 03-11
FACIAL CLEFTS AMONG EPILEPTIC-PATIENTS.
003484 03-15

FACT-SHEET
FACT-SHEET: TOURETTE-SYNDROME.
004474 04-11

FACTOR
ASCORBIC-ACID, AN ENDOGENOUS FACTOR REQUIRED FOR
ACETYLCHOLINE RELEASE FROM THE SYNAPTIC VESICLES.
001322 02-03
GLUCOCORTICOIDS AS A REGULATORY FACTOR FOR BRAIN TRYPTOPHAN-
HYDROXYLASE DURING DEVELOPMENT.
001500 02-03
CUMULATIVE AFTERDISCHARGE AS THE PRINCIPAL FACTOR IN THE
ACQUISITION OF KINDLED SEIZURES.
002862 03-03

FACTORIAL
STUDY ON THE STABILITY OF THE FACTORIAL STRUCTURE OF THE AMP
SYSTEM DURING TREATMENT.
004696 04-16

FACTS
PHARMACOLOGICAL-BASES OF PSYCHONEUROENDOCRINOLOGY:
PRECLINICAL ASSESSMENT OF CLINICAL FACTS.
003735 04-03

FAILS
CHRONIC-TREATMENT WITH VALIUM (DIAZEPAM) FAILS TO AFFECT THE
REPRODUCTIVE SYSTEM OF THE MALE RAT.
001535 02-03
NALOXONE FAILS TO BLOCK AMPHETAMINE-INDUCED ANOREXIA AND
CONDITIONED TASTE-AVERSION.
004121 04-04

FAILURE
A STATE-DEPENDENT FAILURE OF RATS TO MAXIMIZE REWARDS.
000392 01-04
EXTINCTION AND DOPAMINE-RECEPTOR BLOCKADE AFTER INTERMITTENT
REINFORCEMENT TRAINING: FAILURE TO OBSERVE FUNCTIONAL
EQUIVALENCE.
000490 01-04
FAILURE OF CLORAZEPATE TO CAUSE MALFORMATIONS OR FETAL
WASTAGE IN THE RAT.
000514 01-05
FAILURE OF ISOPRENALINE AND BETA-RECEPTOR BLOCKING-DRUGS TO
MODIFY DEPRESSOR RESPONSE AND BRADYCARDIA INDUCED BY
ELECTRICAL-STIMULATION OF THE ANTERIOR HYPOTHALAMUS OF
CATS.
000520 01-05
FAILURE OF NALOXONE TO REVERSE CATALEPSY ASSOCIATED WITH
SCHIZOPHRENIA: A CASE-REPORT.
000560 01-08
COMPARATIVE-STUDY OF AGGRESSIVE-BEHAVIOUR AFTER INJECTION OF
CHOLINOMIMETICS, ANTICHOLINESTERASES, NICOTINIC, AND
MUSCARINIC GANGLIONIC STIMULANTS INTO THE CEREBRAL
VENTRICLES OF CONSCIOUS CATS: FAILURE OF NICOTINIC-DRUGS TO
EVOKE AGGRESSION.
001568 02-04
HEMODYNAMIC FAILURE INDUCED BY NARCOTIC AND TOXIC DOSES OF
12 CNS DEPRESSANTS IN INTACT AND PITHED RATS.
001855 02-05
FAILURE OF NALOXONE TO REDUCE MANIC-SYMPTOMS.
001984 02-09
ANTIDEPRESSIVES IN RENAL FAILURE.
002284 02-13
FAILURE OF LITHIUM TREATMENT IN ESTABLISHED TARDIVE-DYSKINESIA.
002432 02-15
FAILURE TO FIND SEX-DIFFERENCES IN TESTOSTERONE ACTIVATED
AGGRESSION IN TWO STRAINS OF RATS.
003107 03-04
DOSAGE OF INTRATUMORAL LITHIUM (CEREBRAL GLIOBLASTOMA): ON A
FAILURE OF TREATMENT OF MANIC-DEPRESSIVE-PSYCHOSIS.
003226 03-09
PLASMA LEVELS OF BETA ENDORPHIN UNDER CHRONIC NEUROLEPTIC
TREATMENT IN SCHIZOPHRENIC-PATIENTS: FAILURE OF NALOXONE TO
COUNTERACT CURATIVE EFFECTS OF NEUROLEPTIC-DRUGS.
004321 04-08
IS THE FAILURE OF (-)DEPRENYL, A SELECTIVE MONOAMINE-OXIDASE-B-
INHIBITOR, TO ALLEVIATE DEPRESSION RELATED TO FREEDOM FROM
THE CHEESE EFFECT?
004640 04-15

FALSE
FALSE LABELLING OF COMMERCIALLY-AVAILABLE 3H CATECHOLAMINES?
000535 01-06

FAMILIAL
FAMILIAL OCCURRENCE OF TARDIVE-DYSKINESIA.
003548 03-15

FAMILIES
THE NEGATIVE INFLUENCE OF FAMILIES ON COMPLIANCE.
004745 04-17

FAMILY-TREE
FAMILY-TREE GIVES CLUES TO TREATING PSYCHOSES.
002363 02-14

FAST-ACTIVITY
MONOAMINE REPLACEMENT AFTER RESERPINE: CATECHOLAMINERGIC
AGONISTS RESTORE MOTOR-ACTIVITY BUT PHENYLETHYLAMINE
RESTORES ATROPINE-RESISTANT NEOCORTICAL LOW VOLTAGE FAST-
ACTIVITY.
000309 01-03
RESERPINE ABOLISHES MOVEMENT CORRELATED ATROPINE-RESISTANT
NEOCORTICAL LOW VOLTAGE FAST-ACTIVITY.
000310 01-03

FAT
SUSTAINED DECREASE IN FAT CONSUMPTION PRODUCED BY
AMPHETAMINE IN RATS MAINTAINED ON A DIETARY SELF-SELECTION
REGIME.
004150 04-04

FATALITIES
LOXAPINE FATALITIES.
004650 04-15

FATIGUE
TREATMENT OF ASTHENO-DEPRESSIVE-DISORDERS WITH MINAPRINE
(CANTOR). MULTICENTER-STUDY OF 248 CASES EVALUATED WITH THE
FATIGUE STUDY GROUPS NO. 4 CLINICAL-SCALE.
001980 02-09

FATTY-ACID
BETA DIETHYLAMINOETHYLDIPHENYLPROPYLACETATE (SKF-525-A) AND
2,4 DICHLORO-6-PHENYLPHENOXYETHYLAMINE-HBR (DPEA) INHIBITION
OF FATTY-ACID CONJUGATION TO 11 HYDROXY-DELTA9-
TETRAHYDROCANNABINOL BY THE RAT LIVER MICROSOMAL SYSTEM.
000179 01-03

FATTY-ACIDS
THE MECHANISM OF EFFECT OF NEUROPHARMACOLOGICAL-DRUGS. VI:
EFFECT OF NORADRENALINE AND 5 HYDROXYTRYPTAMINE ON BRAIN
FREE FATTY-ACIDS.
000274 01-03
THE EFFECTS OF PIRACETAM ON FREE FATTY-ACIDS IN THE BRAIN.
001474 02-03
EFFECTS OF BRANCHED-CHAIN FATTY-ACIDS ON GABA DEGRADATION
AND BEHAVIOR: FURTHER EVIDENCE FOR A ROLE OF GABA IN QUASI-
MORPHINE ABSTINENCE-BEHAVIOR.
001809 02-04
EFFECTS OF CAFFEINE ON PLASMA FREE FATTY-ACIDS, URINARY
CATECHOLAMINES, AND DRUG BINDING.
002272 02-13

FD-1
EFFECTS OF 1,3 BIS-TETRAHYDRO-2-FURANYL-5-
FLUOROPYRIMIDINEDIONE (FD-1) ON THE CENTRAL-NERVOUS-SYSTEM:
1. EFFECTS OF MONOAMINES IN THE BRAIN.
001857 02-05

FDA
FDA CLIPS PSYCHODRUG PIONEERS IND WINGS.
003160 03-07

FEAR
NORADRENERGIC AGONISTS AND ANTAGONISTS: EFFECTS ON
CONDITIONED FEAR AS MEASURED BY THE POTENTIATED STARTLE
PARADIGM.
000372 01-04
EFFECT OF ANTIANXIETY-DRUGS ON FEAR AND STRESS.
000801 01-14
AMYGDALA OPIATE-SENSITIVE MECHANISMS INFLUENCE FEAR
MOTIVATED RESPONSES AND MEMORY PROCESSES FOR AVERSIVE-
EXPERIENCES. (UNPUBLISHED PAPER).
001628 02-04

FEATURE
HOSTILITY PRODUCTION AS A COMMON FEATURE OF ANTIANXIETY-
AGENT ACTION.
004654 04-15

FEATURES
SPINOCEREBELLAR DEGENERATION WITH PARKINSONIAN FEATURES: A
CLINICAL AND PATHOLOGICAL REPORT.
003436 03-13

FEDERAL-COURT
FEDERAL-COURT UPHOLDS RIGHT-TO-REFUSE PSYCHOTROPIC-DRUGS,
ORDERS IMPROVEMENTS AT LIMA-STATE-HOSPITAL.
002583 02-17

FEEDBACK
THE EFFECT OF DELTA9 TETRAHYDROCANNABINOL ON THE POSITIVE AND
NEGATIVE FEEDBACK CONTROL OF LUTEINIZING-HORMONE RELEASE.
000286 01-03

MEASUREMENT OF PLASMA CONCENTRATIONS OF DRUGS AS A
FEEDBACK CONTROL MECHANISM DURING DRUG-THERAPY.
002525 02-17

FEEDING
EFFECTS OF CHLORDIAZEPOXIDE AND DIAZEPAM ON FEEDING
PERFORMANCE IN A FOOD PREFERENCE TEST.
000367 01-04

EFFECTS OF ACUTE OR CHRONIC ADMINISTRATION OF
CHLORDIAZEPOXIDE ON FEEDING PARAMETERS USING TWO FOOD
TEXTURES IN THE RAT.
000368 01-04

BODY-WEIGHT, FEEDING, AND DRINKING-BEHAVIORS IN RATS WITH
KAINIC-ACID-INDUCED LESIONS OF STRIATAL NEURONS -- WITH A
NOTE ON BODY-WEIGHT SYMPTOMATOLOGY IN HUNTINGTONS-
DISEASE.
000463 01-04

EFFECTS OF SPIPERONE ALONE AND IN COMBINATION WITH ANORECTIC-
AGENTS ON FEEDING PARAMETERS IN THE RAT.
001598 02-04

INTERACTIONS OF CHLORDIAZEPOXIDE AND ANORECTIC-AGENTS ON RATE
AND DURATION PARAMETERS OF FEEDING IN THE RAT.
001600 02-04

THE EFFECTS OF PARA CHLOROAMPHETAMINE ON FENFLURAMINE
ANOREXIA IN AD LIBITUM AND STIMULATION-INDUCED FEEDING IN
THE RAT.
001823 02-04

BEHAVIOURAL-ANALYSIS OF FEEDING: IMPLICATIONS FOR THE
PHARMACOLOGICAL MANIPULATION OF FOOD INTAKE IN ANIMALS
AND MAN.
002527 02-17

OPERANT FEEDING AND DRINKING IN PIGS FOLLOWING
INTRACEREBROVENTRICULAR INJECTION OF SYNTHETIC
CHOLECYSTOKININ-OCTAPEPTIDE.
003064 03-04

NALOXONE SUPPRESSES FEEDING AND DRINKING BUT NOT WHEEL
RUNNING IN RATS.
004080 04-04

FEELINGS
EFFECTS OF ATENOLOL AND PROPRANOLOL ON HUMAN PERFORMANCE
AND SUBJECTIVE FEELINGS.
002340 02-14

FEMALE
THE EFFECTS OF GONADECTOMY AND HYPOPHYSECTOMY ON THE
METABOLISM OF IMIPRAMINE AND LIDOCAINE BY THE LIVER OF MALE
AND FEMALE RATS.
000273 01-03

ATTEMPTS TO REINSTATE LORDOSIS REFLEX IN ESTROGEN-PRIMED
SPINAL FEMALE RATS WITH MONOAMINE AGONISTS.
000421 01-04

BEHAVIORAL-EFFECTS OF ETHYNYL ESTROGENS IN THE FEMALE RAT.
000483 01-04

PHENCYCLIDINE: EFFECTS OF CHRONIC ADMINISTRATION IN THE FEMALE
MOUSE ON GESTATION, MATERNAL-BEHAVIOR, AND THE NEONATES.
000517 01-05

CONTRIBUTORS TO FEMALE USE OF PSYCHOPHARMACOLOGICAL-AGENTS:
DISSERTATION).
000956 01-17

DYNAMICS OF ENDOGENOUS CATECHOLAMINE RELEASE FROM BRAIN
FRAGMENTS OF MALE AND FEMALE RATS.
001121 02-03

EFFECT OF IMIPRAMINE ON HEPATIC GAMMA GLUTAMYLTRANSFERASE
IN FEMALE RATS. INTERACTION WITH CONTRACEPTIVES.
001507 02-03

DIFFERENTIAL DOPAMINERGIC FUNCTION IN YOUNG AND OLD FEMALE
RATS AS MEASURED BY THREE BEHAVIORS.
001683 02-04

EFFECTS OF NEONATAL 6 HYDROXYDOPA ON BEHAVIOR IN FEMALE
RATS.
001717 02-04

OPIATE ANTAGONISTS AND FEMALE FUNCTIONING. (UNPUBLISHED
PAPER).
001735 02-04

THROMBOCYTOSIS IN THE OFFSPRING OF FEMALE MICE RECEIVING DL
METHADONE.
001836 02-05

EFFECTS OF AN EPINEPHRINE SYNTHESIS INHIBITOR, SKF-64139, ON THE
SECRETION OF LUTEINIZING-HORMONE IN OVARIECTOMIZED FEMALE
RATS.
002693 03-03

VASOTOCIN, PROSTAGLANDIN, AND FEMALE REPRODUCTIVE BEHAVIOR
IN THE FROG, RANA-PIPIENS.
002978 03-04

STATISTICAL ANALYSES OF PHYSIOLOGIC DATA FROM FEMALE PATIENTS
WITH AN ENDOMORPHOUS DEPRESSIVE COURSE: A TRIAL.
INTERACTIONS BETWEEN PHYSIOLOGIC PARAMETERS, TEST JUNCTURES
IN THIS PHASE.
003251 03-09

PROLACTIN RELEASING POTENCIES OF ANTIPSYCHOTIC AND RELATED
NONANTIPSYCHOTIC COMPOUNDS IN FEMALE RATS: RELATION TO
CLINICAL POTENCIES.
003830 04-03

PHARMACOTHERAPY AND FEMALE SEXUALITY.
004483 04-11

PRAZEPAM METABOLISM IN FEMALE SUBJECTS.
004504 04-13

FEMALES
DECREASED 3H IMIPRAMINE BINDING IN DEPRESSED MALES AND
FEMALES.
004349 04-09

FEMORAL
CONSISTENT UNMASKING OF DOPAMINE-INDUCED DILATION OF THE
CANINE FEMORAL VASCULAR BED.
003911 04-03

FEMTOMOLE
SIMULTANEOUS DETERMINATION OF FEMTOMOLE QUANTITIES OF 5
HYDROXYTRYPTOPHAN, SEROTONIN AND 5 HYDROXYINDOLEACETIC-
ACID IN BRAIN USING HPLC WITH ELECTROCHEMICAL-DETECTION.
003139 03-06

FENCAMFAMINE
ACUTE EFFECT OF BENZOCTAMINE (10 MG), SODIUM-
HYDROXYBUTYRATE (2 G) AND FENCAMFAMINE (10 MG) ON VERBAL-
ASSOCIATIONS.
000806 01-14

FENFLURAMINE
THE EFFECTS OF PARA CHLOROAMPHETAMINE ON FENFLURAMINE
ANOREXIA IN AD LIBITUM AND STIMULATION-INDUCED FEEDING IN
THE RAT.
001823 02-04

FENFLURAMINE POTENTIATION OF ANTIHYPERTENSIVE-EFFECTS OF
THIAZIDES.
002138 02-11

COMPARISON OF THE EFFECTS OF THE STEREOISOMERS OF
FENFLURAMINE ON THE ACETYLCHOLINE CONTENT OF RAT STRIATUM,
HIPPOCAMPUS AND NUCLEUS-ACCUMBENS.
003758 04-03

HABITUATION OF THE THE HEAD-POKE RESPONSE: EFFECTS OF AN
AMPHETAMINE BARBITURATE MIXTURE, PLG AND FENFLURAMINE.
004159 04-04

FENIL-ISOPROPIL-AMINA-SULFATE
BETTA-SPLENDENS MAZE-BEHAVIOR UNDER THE INFLUENCE OF THE BETA
FENIL-ISOPROPIL-AMINA-SULFATE.
001558 02-04

FENTANYL
CALCIUM ANTAGONISM OF THE INHIBITORY-EFFECTS OF FENTANYL ON
THE CONTRACTION OF THE NICTITATING MEMBRANE IN CATS.
002876 03-03

FACTORS REGULATING DRUG CUE SENSITIVITY: LIMITS OF
DISCRIMINABILITY AND THE ROLE OF A PROGRESSIVELY DECREASING
TRAINING DOSE IN FENTANYL SALINE DISCRIMINATION.
004088 04-04

FERRIC-CHLORIDE
NEURONAL ACTIVITY IN CHRONIC FERRIC-CHLORIDE EPILEPTIC-FOCI IN
CATS AND MONKEY.
000172 01-03

FETAL
FUNCTIONAL HYPERINNERVATION OF CEREBRAL-CORTEX BY
NORADRENERGIC NEURONS RESULTS FROM FETAL LESIONS: PARALLELS
WITH SCHIZOPHRENIA.
000059 01-03

REDUCTION OF FETAL RAT SPINAL-CORD VOLUME FOLLOWING
MATERNAL MORPHINE INJECTION.
000161 01-03

FAILURE OF CLORAZEPATE TO CAUSE MALFORMATIONS OR FETAL
WASTAGE IN THE RAT.
000514 01-05

TERATOGENICITY OF IMIPRAMINE AND AMITRIPTYLINE IN FETAL
HAMSTERS.
002410 02-15

MULTIINSTITUTIONAL-STUDY ON THE TERATOGENICITY OF FETAL
TOXICITY OF ANTIEPILEPTIC-DRUGS: A REPORT OF A COLLABORATIVE-
STUDY GROUP IN JAPAN.
002442 02-15

EFFECTS OF FETAL TREATMENT WITH METHYLAZOXYMETHANOL-ACETATE
AT VARIOUS GESTATIONAL DATES ON THE NEUROCHEMISTRY OF THE
ADULT NEOCORTEX OF THE RAT.
002770 03-03

DISPOSITION OF METHADONE IN THE OVINE MATERNAL FETAL UNIT.
004027 04-03

FETUSES
SURGICAL MANIPULATION OF THE UTERINE ENVIRONMENT OF RAT
FETUSES.
002478 02-16

FEVER
CENTRAL ADMINISTRATION OF SERINE CAUSES HYPOTHERMIA AND
INHIBITS FEVER IN RABBITS.
001247 02-03

THE ROLE OF PROTEIN SYNTHESIS IN THE HYPOTHALAMIC MECHANISM
MEDIATING PYROGEN FEVER.
001454 02-03

FI-RESPONDING
EFFECTS OF PSYCHOTROPIC-DRUGS ON FI-RESPONDING AND ADJUNCTIVE DRINKING IN RATS.
001693 02-04

FIBERS
DEMONSTRATION OF SUBSTANCE-P IN AORTIC NERVE AFFERENT FIBERS BY COMBINED USE OF FLOURESCENT RETROGRADE NEURONAL LABELING AND IMMUNOCYTOCHEMISTRY. (UNPUBLISHED PAPER).
001024 02-01
MECHANICAL-CHANGES IN CRAB NERVE FIBERS DURING ACTION POTENTIALS. (UNPUBLISHED PAPER).
001505 02-03
ULTRASTRUCTURAL LOCALIZATION OF MONOAMINES IN NERVE FIBERS OF THE PINEAL-GLAND IN GOLDEN HAMSTERS.
003666 04-01

FIBRES
GAMMA AMINOBUTYRIC-ACID AGONISTS: AN IN VITRO COMPARISON BETWEEN DEPRESSION OF SPINAL SYNAPTIC ACTIVITY AND DEPOLARIZATION OF SPINAL ROOT FIBRES IN THE RAT.
001104 02-03

FIBRILLATION
PROTECTIVE EFFECT OF PRENYLAMINE AGAINST VULNERABILITY TO VENTRICULAR FIBRILLATION IN THE NORMAL AND ISCHEMIC CANINE MYOCARDIUM.
000265 01-03
THE EFFECTS OF THIORIDAZINE ON ELECTRICAL AND ISCHEMIC VENTRICULAR FIBRILLATION IN THE DOG HEART IN SITU.
002697 03-03

FIBROBLASTS
GABA SYNTHESIS BY CULTURED FIBROBLASTS OBTAINED FROM PERSONS WITH HUNTINGTONS-DISEASE.
000765 01-13

FIBROSITIS-PATIENTS
THE RELATIONSHIP OF ALPHA AND DELTA EEG FREQUENCIES TO PAIN AND MOOD IN FIBROSITIS-PATIENTS TREATED WITH CHLORPROMAZINE AND L TRYPTOPHAN.
002152 02-11

FIGHTING
SELECTIVE INHIBITION BY NICOTINE OF SHOCK-INDUCED FIGHTING IN THE RAT.
002984 03-04
SUBCHRONIC-TREATMENT WITH THE TRICYCLIC-ANTIDEPRESSANT DMI INCREASES ISOLATION-INDUCED FIGHTING IN RATS.
004252 04-04

FIGHTING-BEHAVIOR
EFFECTS OF MORPHINE WITHDRAWAL ON FOOD COMPETITION HIERARCHIES AND FIGHTING-BEHAVIOR IN RATS.
001632 02-04

FIGURAL
PERSONALITY AND DRUGS IN VISUAL FIGURAL AFTEREFFECTS.
004581 04-14

FILTRATION
GLOMERULAR FILTRATION RATE AND CALCIUM METABOLISM IN LONG-TERM LITHIUM TREATMENT.
003542 03-15

FINNISH
QUALITY OF REPORTS OF CLINICAL-TRIALS SUBMITTED BY THE DRUG INDUSTRY TO THE FINNISH AND SWEDISH CONTROL AUTHORITIES.
003599 03-17

FIRING
SUPPRESSION OF SEROTONERGIC NEURONAL FIRING BY ALPHA-ADRENOCEPTOR ANTAGONISTS: EVIDENCE AGAINST GABA MEDIATION.
000024 01-03
INTRAVENOUS GABA AGONIST ADMINISTRATION STIMULATES FIRING OF A10 DOPAMINERGIC NEURONS.
000320 01-03
SUBSTANCE-P, MORPHINE AND METHIONINE-ENKEPHALIN: EFFECTS ON SPONTANEOUS AND EVOKED NEURONAL FIRING IN THE NUCLEUS-RETICULARIS-GIGANTOCELLULARIS OF THE RAT.
001267 02-03
LONG-TERM DECREASES IN SPONTANEOUS FIRING OF CAUDATE NEURONS INDUCED BY AMPHETAMINE IN CATS.
001340 02-03
GLUCOSE SUPPRESSES BASAL FIRING AND HALOPERIDOL-INDUCED INCREASES IN THE FIRING-RATE OF CENTRAL DOPAMINERGIC NEURONS.
002880 03-03
MORPHINE AND METHIONINE-ENKEPHALIN: DIFFERENT EFFECTS ON SPONTANEOUS AND EVOKED NEURONAL FIRING IN THE MESENCEPHALIC RETICULAR FORMATION OF THE RAT.
003849 04-03

FIRING-RATE
ALTERATIONS IN BASAL FIRING-RATE AND AUTORECEPTOR SENSITIVITY OF DOPAMINE NEURONS IN THE SUBSTANTIA-NIGRA FOLLOWING ACUTE AND EXTENDED EXPOSURE TO ESTROGEN.
001167 02-03
GLUCOSE SUPPRESSES BASAL FIRING AND HALOPERIDOL-INDUCED INCREASES IN THE FIRING-RATE OF CENTRAL DOPAMINERGIC NEURONS.
002880 03-03

FIRST-PASS
THE EFFECT OF MONOAMINE-OXIDASE-INHIBITORS ON FIRST-PASS METABOLISM OF TYRAMINE IN DOG INTESTINE.
000141 01-03
KINETICS AND BIOTRANSFORMATION OF LORMETAZEPAM: II. RADIOIMMUNOLOGIC DETERMINATIONS IN PLASMA AND URINE OF YOUNG AND ELDERLY SUBJECTS: FIRST-PASS EFFECT.
004516 04-13

FISH
BOMBESIN ALTERS BEHAVIORAL THERMOREGULATION IN FISH.
003026 03-04

FIXED-INTERVAL
A COMPARISON OF THE EFFECTS OF D-AMPHETAMINE, COCAINE, IMIPRAMINE AND PENTOBARBITAL ON LOCAL AND OVERALL RATES OF RESPONDING MAINTAINED UNDER A FOUR-COMPONENT MULTIPLE FIXED-INTERVAL SCHEDULE.
000508 01-04
THE EFFECTS OF DELTA9 TETRAHYDROCANNABINOL ALONE AND IN COMBINATION WITH CANNABIDIOL ON FIXED-INTERVAL PERFORMANCE IN RHESUS-MONKEYS.
001582 02-04

FIXED-RATIO
PROGRESSIVE-RATIO AND FIXED-RATIO SCHEDULES OF COCAINE MAINTAINED RESPONDING IN BABOONS.
000395 01-04
FIXED-RATIO SCHEDULES OF FOOD PRESENTATION AND STIMULUS-SHOCK TERMINATION: EFFECTS OF D-AMPHETAMINE, MORPHINE, AND CLOZAPINE.
000431 01-04

FK-33-824
CONTRALATERAL CIRCLING-BEHAVIOUR INDUCED BY INTRANIGRAL INJECTION OF MORPHINE AND ENKEPHALIN ANALOGUE FK-33-824 IN RATS.
001669 02-04

FLA-63
THE EFFECT OF FLA-63 ON PENTOBARBITONE-INDUCED SLEEP IN THE CHICK.
001741 02-04

FLAME-IONIZATION
DETERMINATION OF VALPROIC-ACID BY FLAME-IONIZATION GAS-LIQUID-CHROMATOGRAPHY.
000906 01-16

FLASH-EVOKED
FLASH-EVOKED AFTERDISCHARGE IN RAT AS A MODEL OF THE ABSENCE SEIZURE: DOSE-RESPONSE STUDIES WITH THERAPEUTIC DRUGS.
000160 01-03
POWER SPECTRAL ANALYSIS OF THE FLASH-EVOKED AFTERDISCHARGE.
003133 03-06

FLATTENING
LOG-DOSE/RESPONSE-CURVE FLATTENING IN RATS AFTER DAILY INJECTION OF OPIATES.
001387 02-03

FLAVIN
THIOLS LIBERATE COVALENTLY-BONDED FLAVIN FROM MONOAMINE-OXIDASE. (UNPUBLISHED PAPER).
001060 02-01

FLAVOR
CONDITIONED SUPPRESSION OF DRINKING: A MEASURE OF THE CR ELICITED BY A LITHIUM CONDITIONED FLAVOR.
001747 02-04

FLEXOR
EFFECTS OF ANALGESICS AND CNS-ACTING DRUGS ON STRUGGLING FOLLOWING REPETITIVE STIMULATION OF THE TAIL, AND FLEXOR REFLEX TO A SINGLE STIMULATION OF THE SCIATIC-NERVE IN RATS.
004148 04-04

FLICKER
PSYCHOACTIVE-DRUG QUANTIFICATION BY VISUAL FLICKER SENSITIVITY MEASUREMENT. (PH.D. DISSERTATION).
002485 02-16

FLORA
INHIBITION OF MONOAMINE-OXIDASE BY FURAZOLIDONE IN THE CHICKEN AND THE INFLUENCE OF THE ALIMENTARY FLORA THEREON.
003711 04-03

FLOURESCENT
DEMONSTRATION OF SUBSTANCE-P IN AORTIC NERVE AFFERENT FIBERS BY COMBINED USE OF FLOURESCENT RETROGRADE NEURONAL LABELING AND IMMUNOCYTOCHEMISTRY. (UNPUBLISHED PAPER).
001024 02-01

FLOW
PARASYMPATHOMIMETIC-INFLUENCE OF CARBACHOL ON LOCAL CEREBRAL BLOOD FLOW IN THE RABBIT BY A DIRECT VASODILATOR ACTION AND AN INHIBITION OF THE SYMPATHETIC MEDIATED VASOCONSTRICTION.
001109 02-03
EFFECT OF PAPAVERINE ON REGIONAL CEREBRAL BLOOD FLOW AND SMALL VESSEL BLOOD CONTENT.
001177 02-03

FLUORESCENCE
FLUORESCENCE HISTOCHEMISTRY INDICATES DAMAGE OF STRIATAL
DOPAMINE NERVE TERMINALS IN RATS AFTER MULTIPLE DOSES OF
METHAMPHETAMINE.
002812 03-03
RAPID DETERMINATION OF CHLORPROMAZINE-HCL AND TWO OXIDATION
PRODUCTS IN VARIOUS PHARMACEUTICAL SAMPLES USING HIGH-
PERFORMANCE LIQUID-CHROMATOGRAPHY AND FLUORESCENCE
DETECTION.
004302 04-06

FLUORESCENT
FLUORESCENT PROBES OF ALPHA-ADRENERGIC AND BETA-ADRENERGIC
AND OPIATE-RECEPTORS: BIOCHEMICAL AND HISTOCHEMICAL
EVALUATION.
003685 04-02

FLUORIDE
CEREBRAL FLUORIDE IN MANIA AND THE EFFECT OF LITHIUM: A
HYPOTHESIS.
004715 04-17

FLUORINATED
FLUORINATED ANALOGUES OF THE TRICYCLIC NEUROLEPTICS: 2,3
DIFLUORO DERIVATIVE OF CLOROTEPIN.
000001 01-01
THE EFFECT OF A NEW FLUORINATED TRICYCLIC NEUROLEPTIC-DRUG
ISOFLOXYTHEPIN ON THE RAT STRIATAL DOPAMINE METABOLISM.
000306 01-03

FLUORO-5-FLUOROPHENYL-2-FLUOROPHENYL
FLUORO-5-FLUOROPHENYL-2-FLUOROPHENYL 4
HYDROXYBUTYLHEXAHYDROPYRIDOINDOLE-HCL, A NEW POTENT
NEUROLEPTIC.
001092 02-02

FLUOROAMINOMETHYLPHENOLS
SYNTHESIS AND GABA-RECEPTOR BINDING-ACTIVITY OF TWO
FLUOROAMINOMETHYLPHENOLS.
003693 04-02

FLUOROTRYPTOPHAN
() 6 FLUOROTRYPTOPHAN, AN INHIBITOR OF TRYPTOPHAN-
HYDROXYLASE: SLEEP AND WAKEFULNESS IN THE RAT.
004189 04-04

FLUOXETINE
EFFECTS OF CHRONIC FLUOXETINE ADMINISTRATION ON SEROTONIN
METABOLISM.
000138 01-03
SUBSENSITIVITY OF THE NOREPINEPHRINE-RECEPTOR COUPLED
ADENYLATE-CYCLASE SYSTEM IN BRAIN: EFFECTS OF NISOXETINE
VERSUS FLUOXETINE.
000208 01-03
THE INABILITY OF CHRONIC FLUOXETINE TO POTENTIATE A SEROTONIN
MEDIATED EFFECT.
000293 01-03
EFFECTS OF LILLY-110140 (FLUOXETINE) ON SELF-STIMULATION
BEHAVIOR IN THE DORSAL AND VENTRAL REGIONS OF THE LATERAL
HYPOTHALAMUS IN THE MOUSE.
001590 02-04
EFFECT OF QUIPAZINE AND FLUOXETINE ON ANALGESIC-INDUCED
CATALEPSY AND ANTINOCICEPTION IN THE RAT.
001709 02-04
EFFECTS OF FLUOXETINE ON ELECTRICALLY-INDUCED SPINAL-CORD
SEIZURES IN RATS.
004145 04-04

FLUPENTHIXOL
ALPHA FLUPENTHIXOL: AN ANTAGONIST OF DOPAMINE-EVOKED FLUID
SECRETION BY AN INSECT SALIVARY-GLAND PREPARATION.
000031 01-03
CHARACTERISTICS OF 3H CIS FLUPENTHIXOL BINDING TO CALF BRAIN
MEMBRANES.
000062 01-03
THE LOCOMOTOR-EFFECT OF CLONIDINE AND ITS INTERACTION WITH
ALPHA FLUPENTHIXOL OR HALOPERIDOL IN THE DEVELOPING RAT.
000445 01-04
CONCENTRATIONS OF CIS(Z) FLUPENTHIXOL IN MATERNAL SERUM,
AMNIOTIC-FLUID, UMBILICAL-CORD-SERUM, AND MILK.
002423 02-15
SEQUELAE OF 6 MONTHS CONTINUOUS ADMINISTRATION OF CIS(Z)- AND
TRANS(E) FLUPENTHIXOL IN THE RAT.
004282 04-05

FLUPENTHIXOL-DECANOATE
THE LONG-TERM-TREATMENT OF PERIODICAL AND CYCLIC DEPRESSIONS
WITH FLUPENTHIXOL-DECANOATE.
000603 01-09

FLUPENTIXOL
SIMILARITIES BETWEEN THE BINDING OF 3H PIFLUTIXOL AND 3H
FLUPENTIXOL TO RAT STRIATAL DOPAMINE-RECEPTORS IN VITRO.
002760 03-03

FLUPHENAZINE
PSYCHIATRIC-DISTURBANCE IN MENTALLY-HANDICAPPED-PATIENTS: A
PROSPECTIVE STUDY OF CURRENT CLINICAL USAGE OF DEPOT
FLUPHENAZINE IN HOSPITALS FOR THE MENTALLY-HANDICAPPED.
000668 01-11

COMPARATIVE ENZYME-INDUCING EFFECTS OF CHLORPROMAZINE AND FLUPHENAZINE THERAPIES IN PSYCHOTIC-PATIENTS.
000682 01-11
RADIOIMMUNOASSAY FOR FLUPHENAZINE IN HUMAN PLASMA.
000905 01-16
TOLERANCE TO FLUPHENAZINE AND SUPERSENSITIVITY TO APOMORPHINE IN CENTRAL DOPAMINERGIC-SYSTEMS AFTER CHRONIC FLUPHENAZINE-DECANOATE TREATMENT.
001820 02-04
EFFECT OF FLUPHENAZINE ON THE CIRCADIAN-EXCRETION OF CYCLIC-NUCLEOTIDES AND ELECTROLYTES IN THE URINE OF CHRONIC SCHIZOPHRENICS.
001927 02-08
DISCONTINUATION OF ORAL AND DEPOT FLUPHENAZINE IN SCHIZOPHRENIC-PATIENTS AFTER ONE YEAR OF CONTINUOUS MEDICATION: A CONTROLLED-STUDY.
001931 02-08
PLASMA FLUPHENAZINE AND PROLACTIN LEVELS IN SCHIZOPHRENIC-PATIENTS DURING TREATMENT WITH LOW-DOSES AND HIGH-DOSES OF FLUPHENAZINE-ENANTHATE.
001956 02-08
MEASUREMENT OF FLUPHENAZINE BY GAS-CHROMATOGRAPHY IN HUMAN PLASMA AND RED-BLOOD-CELLS.
002491 02-16
PLASMA FLUPHENAZINE LEVELS BY RADIOIMMUNOASSAY IN SCHIZOPHRENIC-PATIENTS TREATED WITH DEPOT INJECTIONS OF FLUPHENAZINE-DECANOATE.
002510 02-16
TREATMENT OF THERAPEUTICALLY-RESISTANT PARANOID SCHIZOPHRENIC-PATIENTS WITH FLUPHENAZINE DEPOT COMBINED WITH OTHER PSYCHOTROPIC-DRUGS AND CLOZAPINE.
003172 03-08
EXTRAPYRAMIDAL REACTION OF FLUPHENAZINE POTENTIATED BY THYROTOXICOSIS.
003551 03-15
FLUPHENAZINE, TRIFLUOPERAZINE AND PERPHENAZINE IN VACUTAINERS.
003565 03-16
EFFECTS OF MOLINDONE AND FLUPHENAZINE ON THE BRAIN CONCENTRATION OF SOME PHENOLIC AND CATECHOLIC AMINES IN THE MOUSE AND THE RAT.
003870 04-03
EFFECTS OF AGE ON DOPAMINERGIC-SUPERSENSITIVITY INDUCED BY CHRONIC FLUPHENAZINE.
003940 04-03
BEHAVIOR OF RATS AND MICE ADMINISTERED ACTIVE METABOLITES OF FLUPHENAZINE, 7 HYDROXYFLUPHENAZINE AND FLUPHENAZINE-SULFOXIDE.
004256 04-04
DEPOT FLUPHENAZINE MAINTENANCE-TREATMENT AND ASSOCIATED WEIGHT CHANGES.
004635 04-15

FLUPHENAZINE-DECANOATE
DRUG RESPONSE DIFFERENCES OF HIGH AND STANDARD DOSAGE OF FLUPHENAZINE-DECANOATE IN RELATION TO SCHIZOPHRENIC-SYMPTOMS.
000562 01-08
COMPUTERIZED EEG IN THE COMPARISON OF OXYPROTHEPIN AND FLUPHENAZINE-DECANOATE.
000567 01-08
EMERGENCE OF APOMORPHINE-INDUCED VACUOUS CHEWING DURING 6 MONTHS CONTINUOUS TREATMENT WITH FLUPHENAZINE-DECANOATE.
001817 02-04
TOLERANCE TO FLUPHENAZINE AND SUPERSENSITIVITY TO APOMORPHINE IN CENTRAL DOPAMINERGIC-SYSTEMS AFTER CHRONIC FLUPHENAZINE-DECANOATE TREATMENT.
001820 02-04
PLASMA LEVELS AND THERAPEUTIC EFFICACY OF FLUPHENAZINE-HCL AND FLUPHENAZINE-DECANOATE.
001913 02-08
MAINTENANCE-THERAPY WITH FLUPHENAZINE-DECANOATE AND OXYPROTHEPINE-DECANOATE IN SCHIZOPHRENIC-PATIENTS -- A DOUBLE-BLIND CROSS-OVER COMPARATIVE-STUDY.
001924 02-08
METHODOLOGY AND RESULTS OF A LONG-TERM STUDY OF LONG-ACTING NEUROLEPTICS: PIPOTHIAZINE-PALMITATE AND FLUPHENAZINE-DECANOATE.
001929 02-08
INTERMITTENT PIMOZIDE VERSUS FLUPHENAZINE-DECANOATE AS MAINTENANCE-THERAPY IN CHRONIC SCHIZOPHRENIA.
001932 02-08
OXYPROTHEPINE-DECANOATE COMPARED WITH FLUPHENAZINE-DECANOATE IN THE TREATMENT OF SCHIZOPHRENIA: PRELIMINARY-COMMUNICATION.
001934 02-08
STUDY OF PROLACTIN VARIATIONS IN PSYCHIATRIC-PATIENTS TREATED WITH FLUPHENAZINE-DECANOATE.
002226 02-13
PLASMA FLUPHENAZINE LEVELS BY RADIOIMMUNOASSAY IN SCHIZOPHRENIC-PATIENTS TREATED WITH DEPOT INJECTIONS OF FLUPHENAZINE-DECANOATE.
002510 02-16

CONSIDERATIONS ON LONG-ACTING CHEMOTHERAPY: AN EXPERIENCE WITH FLUPHENAZINE-DECANOATE.
003173 03-08
THE PROLACTIN RESPONSE IN PATIENTS RECEIVING NEUROLEPTIC THERAPY. THE EFFECT OF FLUPHENAZINE-DECANOATE.
004318 04-08
THE COURSE OF LONG-TERM-TREATMENT WITH FLUPHENAZINE-DECANOATE (DAPOTUM-D).
004605 04-15

FLUPHENAZINE-DECANOATES
LONG-TERM CONTROLLED-COMPARISON OF INJECTION OXYPROTHEPIN AND FLUPHENAZINE-DECANOATES IN PSYCHOTICS IN REMISSION.
001949 02-08

FLUPHENAZINE-ENANTHATE
PLASMA FLUPHENAZINE AND PROLACTIN LEVELS IN SCHIZOPHRENIC-PATIENTS DURING TREATMENT WITH LOW-DOSES AND HIGH-DOSES OF FLUPHENAZINE-ENANTHATE.
001956 02-08

FLUPHENAZINE-HCL
PLASMA LEVELS AND THERAPEUTIC EFFICACY OF FLUPHENAZINE-HCL AND FLUPHENAZINE-DECANOATE.
001913 02-08
FACTORS DETERMINING PATIENT TENURE ON A 3-YEAR DOUBLE-BLIND INVESTIGATION OF PIMOZIDE VERSUS FLUPHENAZINE-HCL.
002513 02-17
INVESTIGATION INTO THE EFFECT OF FLUPHENAZINE-HCL (LYORODIN) IN CHILDREN WITH BEHAVIORAL-DISORDERS BY MEANS OF PSYCHOPHYSIOLOGICAL PARAMETERS.
003344 03-11

FLUPHENAZINE-SULFOXIDE
BEHAVIOR OF RATS AND MICE ADMINISTERED ACTIVE METABOLITES OF FLUPHENAZINE, 7 HYDROXYFLUPHENAZINE AND FLUPHENAZINE-SULFOXIDE.
004256 04-04

FLURAZEPAM
FLURAZEPAM EFFECTS ON METHYLPHENIDATE-INDUCED STEREOTYPED-BEHAVIOR.
000455 01-04
CENTRAL EXCITATORY ACTIONS OF FLURAZEPAM.
000526 01-05
INDIVIDUAL VARIATIONS IN THE EFFECTS OF FLURAZEPAM, CLORAZEPATE, L-DOPA AND THYROTROPIN-RELEASING-HORMONE ON REM SLEEP IN MAN.
002349 02-14
THE EFFECTS OF FLURAZEPAM, LORAZEPAM, AND TRIAZOLAM ON SLEEP AND MEMORY.
002357 02-14
EFFECT OF FLURAZEPAM, PENTOBARBITAL, AND CAFFEINE ON AROUSAL THRESHOLD.
003439 03-14
AUDITORY AROUSAL THRESHOLDS OF GOOD SLEEPERS AND POOR SLEEPERS WITH AND WITHOUT FLURAZEPAM.
003446 03-14

FLURAZEPAM-INDUCED
ETHYL-BETA-CARBOLINE-CARBOXYLATE LOWERS SEIZURE THRESHOLD AND ANTAGONIZES FLURAZEPAM-INDUCED SEDATION IN RATS.
002971 03-04
FLURAZEPAM-INDUCED SLEEP-APNEA-SYNDROME IN A PATIENT WITH INSOMNIA AND MILD SLEEP-RELATED RESPIRATORY CHANGES.
004729 04-17

FLUSPIRILENE
EXPERIENCE WITH FLUSPIRILENE IN GERONTOPSYCHIATRY.
000691 01-11
FLUSPIRILENE (IMAP) IN THE TREATMENT OF PSYCHOSOMATIC-COMPLAINTS IN HYPOCHONDRIACAL-PATIENTS.
002072 02-10
MAINTENANCE-TREATMENT WITH SEMIDEPOTE NEUROLEPTIC FLUSPIRILENE.
002151 02-11

FLUTROLINE
EEG AND BEHAVIORAL-PROFILE OF FLUTROLINE (CP-36-584), A NOVEL ANTIPSYCHOTIC-DRUG.
001071 02-02
A DOUBLE-BLIND COMPARISON OF THREE DOSAGES OF FLUTROLINE (CP-36584) IN THE TREATMENT OF SCHIZOPHRENIA.
004333 04-08

FLUVOXAMINE
FLUVOXAMINE AS AN ANTIDEPRESSANT-DRUG
003775 04-03

FLUX
EVIDENCE THAT THERE ARE SUBCELLULAR POOLS OF NOREPINEPHRINE AND THAT THERE IS FLUX OF NOREPINEPHRINE BETWEEN THESE POOLS.
004004 04-03

FLUXES
GABA FLUXES IN PRESYNAPTIC NERVE-ENDINGS FROM IMMATURE RATS.
000185 01-03

THE EFFECT OF ACETYLCHOLINE RELEASE ON CHOLINE FLUXES IN
ISOLATED SYNAPTIC TERMINALS.
                                                            003924 04-03
FOCAL
NALOXONE AND FOCAL EPILEPSY: A STUDY WITH DEPTH ELECTRODES.
                                                            003341 03-11
THERAPEUTIC PLASMA LEVELS OF SOME ANTICONVULSANTS IN FOCAL
EPILEPSY IN RELATION TO COMPUTERIZED-AXIAL-TOMOGRAPHY.
                                                            004439 04-11
FOLATE
THE ROLE OF FOLATE DEFICIENCY IN THE DEVELOPMENT OF PERIPHERAL
NEUROPATHY CAUSED BY ANTICONVULSANTS.
                                                            002402 02-15
FOLLICLE-STIMULATING-HORMONE
EFFECTS OF MORPHINE AND NALOXONE ON PHASIC RELEASE OF
LUTEINIZING-HORMONE AND FOLLICLE-STIMULATING-HORMONE
(40849).
                                                            000298 01-03
FOLLOWUP
FOLLOWUP STUDY ON THE INFLUENCE OF AN ANTIPSYCHOTIC-DRUG
(PROPERICIAZINE) ON LIVER FUNCTION, ELECTROCARDIOGRAM AND
ELECTROENCEPHALOGRAM.
                                                            000639 01-09
THE LONG-TERM RESULTS OF STEREOTAXIC SURGERY AND L-DOPA
THERAPY IN PATIENTS WITH PARKINSONS-DISEASE: A 10-YEAR
FOLLOWUP STUDY.
                                                            000693 01-11
FOLLOWUP TREATMENT AND AFTERCARE OF DISCHARGED
SCHIZOPHRENIC-PATIENTS.
                                                            000944 01-17
LEVODOPA AND PRESYMPTOMATIC DETECTION OF HUNTINGTONS-
DISEASE -- EIGHT-YEAR FOLLOWUP.
                                                            000950 01-17
A TEN YEAR FOLLOWUP OF LITHIUM-CARBONATE TREATMENT OF MANIC-
DEPRESSIVE-ILLNESS: PRELIMINARY-RESULTS.
                                                            002053 02-09
DEPRESSED-OUTPATIENTS TREATED WITH COGNITIVE-THERAPY OR
PHARMACOTHERAPY: A ONE-YEAR FOLLOWUP.
                                                            003235 03-09
THE USE OF PHARMACOKINETICS IN THE FOLLOWUP OF PSYCHIATRIC-
PATIENTS.
                                                            003616 03-17
A TWELVE-YEAR FOLLOWUP OF THE NIMH-PRB HIGH-DOSE
CHLORPROMAZINE STUDY OF CHRONIC SCHIZOPHRENICS --
IMPLICATIONS FOR DEINSTITUTIONALIZATION. (UNPUBLISHED PAPER).
                                                            004323 04-08
A FOLLOWUP STUDY OF SCHIZOPHRENIC-OUTPATIENTS TREATED WITH
DEPOT NEUROLEPTICS.
                                                            004342 04-08
HYPERACTIVES AS YOUNG ADULTS: PROSPECTIVE TEN-YEAR FOLLOWUP.
                                                            004454 04-11
FOOD
INFLUENCE OF AMPHETAMINE AND PHENYLPROPANOLAMINE ON FOOD
INTAKE, ACTIVITY, AND BODY-TEMPERATURE IN RATS WITH
VENTROMEDIAL HYPOTHALAMIC OR DORSOLATERAL TEGMENTAL
DAMAGE.
                                                            000322 01-03
REDUCTION OF FOOD INTAKE BY PIRIBEDIL IN THE RAT: RELATION TO
DOPAMINE-RECEPTOR STIMULATION.
                                                            000355 01-04
EFFECTS OF CHLORDIAZEPOXIDE AND DIAZEPAM ON FEEDING
PERFORMANCE IN A FOOD PREFERENCE TEST.
                                                            000367 01-04
EFFECTS OF ACUTE OR CHRONIC ADMINISTRATION OF
CHLORDIAZEPOXIDE ON FEEDING PARAMETERS USING TWO FOOD
TEXTURES IN THE RAT.
                                                            000368 01-04
FIXED-RATIO SCHEDULES OF FOOD PRESENTATION AND STIMULUS-SHOCK
TERMINATION: EFFECTS OF D-AMPHETAMINE, MORPHINE, AND
CLOZAPINE.
                                                            000431 01-04
FIRST DOSE BEHAVIORAL-TOLERANCE TO PHENCYCLIDINE ON FOOD
REWARDED BAR-PRESSING-BEHAVIOR IN THE RAT.
                                                            000462 01-04
PHENOBARBITAL EFFECTS ON WEIGHT-GAIN AND CIRCADIAN-CYCLING OF
FOOD INTAKE AND BODY-TEMPERATURE.
                                                            001409 02-03
NALOXONE: EFFECTS ON FOOD AND WATER CONSUMPTION IN THE
NONDEPRIVED AND DEPRIVED RAT.
                                                            001599 02-04
EFFECTS OF MORPHINE WITHDRAWAL ON FOOD COMPETITION
HIERARCHIES AND FIGHTING-BEHAVIOR IN RATS.
                                                            001632 02-04
EFFECT OF CHOLINE ON CONDITIONED FOOD MOTOR-REFLEXES IN CATS.
                                                            001731 02-04
DIFFERENTIAL-EFFECTS OF MORPHINE ON FOOD AND WATER INTAKE IN
FOOD DEPRIVED AND FREELY-FEEDING RATS.
                                                            001765 02-04

EFFECTS OF AMPHETAMINE AND PHENYLPROPANOLAMINE ON FOOD
INTAKE IN RATS WITH VENTROMEDIAL HYPOTHALAMIC OR
DORSOLATERAL TEGMENTAL DAMAGE.
                                                            001818 02-04
THE EFFECTS OF LITHIUM ON CHOICE BETWEEN COCAINE AND FOOD IN
THE RHESUS-MONKEY.
                                                            001825 02-04
BEHAVIOURAL-ANALYSIS OF FEEDING: IMPLICATIONS FOR THE
PHARMACOLOGICAL MANIPULATION OF FOOD INTAKE IN ANIMALS
AND MAN.
                                                            002527 02-17
THE EFFECT OF ALTERED DOPAMINERGIC-ACTIVITY ON FOOD INTAKE IN
THE RAT: EVIDENCE FOR AN OPTIMAL LEVEL OF DOPAMINERGIC-
ACTIVITY FOR BEHAVIOR.
                                                            002632 02-17
EFFECTS OF CAFFEINE ADMINISTRATION ON FOOD AND WATER
CONSUMPTION UNDER VARIOUS EXPERIMENTAL CONDITIONS.
                                                            003049 03-04
THE EFFECTS OF OPIATE ANTAGONISTS ON FOOD INTAKE ARE
STEREOSPECIFIC.
                                                            003080 03-04
THE PHARMACOLOGICAL ANALYSIS OF MONOAMINERGIC MECHANISMS
OF THE MEDIAL HYPOTHALAMUS IN FOOD PROCURING CONDITIONED
REFLEXES IN RATS.
                                                            003100 03-04
NEUROLEPTICS: INTERACTIONS WITH FOOD -- CHEMICAL AND
PHARMACODYNAMIC STUDIES ON THE INTERACTIONS OF COFFEE AND
TEA.
                                                            003612 03-17
FOOD PREFERENCE FOLLOWING ACUTE OR CHRONIC CHLORDIAZEPOXIDE
ADMINISTRATION: TOLERANCE TO AN ANTINEOPHOBIC ACTION.
                                                            004090 04-04
SUSTAINED INTRACEREBROVENTRICULAR INFUSION OF BRAIN FUELS
REDUCES BODY-WEIGHT AND FOOD INTAKE IN RATS.
                                                            004098 04-04
NALOXONE SUPPRESSES FOOD/WATER CONSUMPTION IN THE DEPRIVED
CAT.
                                                            004114 04-04
CHOICE BETWEEN FOOD AND HEROIN: EFFECTS OF MORPHINE,
NALOXONE, AND SECOBARBITAL.
                                                            004123 04-04
THE SITE OF ACTION OF NALOXONE IN SUPPRESSING FOOD AND WATER
INTAKE IN RATS.
                                                            004146 04-04
SECOND-ORDER SCHEDULES OF INTRAMUSCULAR COCAINE INJECTION IN
THE SQUIRREL-MONKEY: COMPARISONS WITH FOOD PRESENTATION
AND EFFECTS OF D-AMPHETAMINE AND PROMAZINE.
                                                            004152 04-04
HISTIDYL-PROLINE DIKETOPIPERAZINE DECREASES FOOD INTAKE IN RATS.
                                                            004181 04-04
PHARMACOKINETIC-STUDY OF APOMORPHINE-INDUCED STEREOTYPY IN
FOOD DEPRIVED RATS.
                                                            004247 04-04
FOOD-AND-DRUG-ADMINISTRATION
GUIDELINES EMPLOYED BY THE FOOD-AND-DRUG-ADMINISTRATION IN
DRUG SCHEDULING.
                                                            003586 03-17
FOOTSHOCK
SELECTIVE SENSITIZATION INDUCED BY LITHIUM MALAISE AND
FOOTSHOCK IN RATS.
                                                            003055 03-04
FOOTSHOCK ANALGESIA: PREVENTION BY BEHAVIOURAL-MANIPULATION
BUT NOT BY NALOXONE.
                                                            003073 03-04
FORCIBLE
MADNESS AND MEDICINE: THE FORCIBLE ADMINISTRATION OF
PSYCHOTROPIC-DRUGS.
                                                            002523 02-17
FOREBRAIN
INCREASED METABOLISM OF DOPAMINE AND SEROTONIN INDUCED IN
FOREBRAIN AREAS BY ETORPHINE MICROINJECTION IN
PERIAQUEDUCTAL GRAY.
                                                            001103 02-03
CHLOROETHYLNORAPOMORPHINE, A PROPOSED LONG-ACTING
DOPAMINE ANTAGONIST: INTERACTIONS WITH DOPAMINE-RECEPTORS
OF MAMMALIAN FOREBRAIN IN VITRO.
                                                            001114 02-03
DESTRUCTION OF 5 HYDROXYTRYPTAMINERGIC NEURONS AND THE
DYNAMICS OF DOPAMINE IN NUCLEUS-ACCUMBENS SEPTI AND OTHER
FOREBRAIN REGIONS OF THE RAT.
                                                            004171 04-04
FORECASTING
THE USE OF CLINICAL AND PHARMACOKINETIC CRITERIA IN FORECASTING
THE EFFICACY OF THERAPY IN SCHIZOPHRENIA.
                                                            004335 04-08
FORENSIC
THE NEUROLOGICAL FORENSIC ASPECTS OF THALLIUM POISONING.
                                                            002438 02-15

FORGETTING
AMYLOBARBITONE AND FORGETTING.
                                                    001763 02-04

FORM-FRUSTE-DU-SYNDROME-MALIN
TWO CASES OF FORM-FRUSTE-DU-SYNDROME-MALIN WITH HIGH-LEVELS
OF SERUM CPK.
                                                    004636 04-15

FORMATION
SYNERGISTIC ACTIONS OF PROPANTHELINE-BROMIDE WITH CIMETIDINE
AND THIOPROPAZATE-HYDROCHLORIDE IN THE PREVENTION OF
STRESS-ULCER FORMATION IN RATS.
                                                    000064 01-03
BRADYKININ-RECEPTOR STIMULATION OF C-AMP INVOLVES
PHOSPHOLIPID METHYLATION, CA-FLUX, PHOSPHOLIPASE-A2
ACTIVATION AND PROSTAGLANDIN FORMATION. (UNPUBLISHED
PAPER).
                                                    001002 02-01
DIVERGENT RESERPINE EFFECTS ON AMFONELIC-ACID AND
AMPHETAMINE STIMULATION OF SYNAPTOSOMAL DOPAMINE
FORMATION FROM PHENYLALANINE.
                                                    001113 02-03
IN VIVO (3H)SPIPERONE BINDING TO THE RAT HIPPOCAMPAL
FORMATION: INVOLVEMENT OF DOPAMINE-RECEPTORS.
                                                    001131 02-03
STRYCHNINE EFFECTS ON THE SENSORY RESPONSE PATTERNS OF
RETICULAR FORMATION NEURONS.
                                                    001219 02-03
THE EFFECTS OF NOREPINEPHRINE PERFUSION OF THE MESENCEPHALIC
RETICULAR FORMATION ON BEHAVIOR IN THE RAT: INTERACTION
WITH SEVERAL NEUROLEPTIC-DRUGS ON A MEASURE OF SUSTAINED
ATTENTION. (PH.D. DISSERTATION).
                                                    001563 02-04
EFFECTS OF SOCIAL-ISOLATION ON MEMORY FORMATION.
                                                    001607 02-04
EVIDENCE FOR THE PRESENCE OF TWO TYPES OF MONOAMINE-OXIDASE
IN RABBIT CHOROID PLEXUS AND THEIR ROLE IN BREAKDOWN OF
AMINES INFLUENCING CEREBROSPINAL-FLUID FORMATION.
                                                    002807 03-03
INVOLVEMENT OF CAUDATE-NUCLEUS, AMYGDALA OR RETICULAR
FORMATION IN NEUROLEPTIC AND NARCOTIC CATALEPSY.
                                                    002986 03-04
INVOLVEMENT OF CALCIUM CHANNELS IN SHORT-TERM
DESENSITIZATION OF MUSCARINIC-RECEPTOR MEDIATED CYCLIC-GMP
FORMATION IN MOUSE NEUROBLASTOMA CELLS.
                                                    003783 04-03
MORPHINE AND METHIONINE-ENKEPHALIN: DIFFERENT EFFECTS ON
SPONTANEOUS AND EVOKED NEURONAL FIRING IN THE
MESENCEPHALIC RETICULAR FORMATION OF THE RAT.
                                                    003849 04-03
CONVERGENT PROPERTIES AND CHEMICAL SENSITIVITY OF MIDBRAIN
RETICULAR FORMATION NEURONS OF UNANESTHETIZED RABBITS.
                                                    003972 04-03
DESENSITIZATION OF HISTAMINE H1-RECEPTOR-MEDIATED CYCLIC-GMP
FORMATION IN MOUSE NEUROBLASTOMA CELLS.
                                                    004030 04-03
THE ROLE OF RETICULOSEPTAL INPUTS IN THE FORMATION OF DIFFERENT
TYPES OF SENSORY REACTIONS OF THE HIPPOCAMPAL NEURONS.
                                                    004510 04-13
PHARMACOLOGICAL MODULATION OF FORMATION OF LONG-TERM
MEMORY.
                                                    004578 04-14

FORMIC-ACID
GLIAL CELL EFFECTS OF SUBACUTE FORMIC-ACID VAPOUR EXPOSURE.
                                                    000527 01-05

FORMULATIONS
SIMULTANEOUS HIGH-PERFORMANCE LIQUID-CHROMATOGRAPHIC-
DETERMINATION OF AMITRIPTYLINE-HYDROCHLORIDE IN TWO-
COMPONENT TABLET FORMULATIONS.
                                                    004673 04-16

FORNIX
FORNIX LESION PREVENTS AN ORGANOPHOSPHATE-INDUCED DECREASE
IN MUSCARINIC-RECEPTOR LEVEL IN RAT HIPPOCAMPUS.
                                                    001833 02-05

FORNIX-FIMBRIA
HIPPOCAMPAL SEROTONIN REUPTAKE AND NOCTURNAL LOCOMOTOR-
ACTIVITY AFTER MICROINJECTIONS OF 5,7 DHT IN THE FORNIX-
FIMBRIA.
                                                    002929 03-03

FOUR-COMPONENT
A COMPARISON OF THE EFFECTS OF D-AMPHETAMINE, COCAINE,
IMIPRAMINE AND PENTOBARBITAL ON LOCAL AND OVERALL RATES OF
RESPONDING MAINTAINED UNDER A FOUR-COMPONENT MULTIPLE
FIXED-INTERVAL SCHEDULE.
                                                    000508 01-04

FOWL
ENHANCED BEHAVIOURAL-EFFECTS, ELECTROCORTICAL-EFFECTS AND
HYPERTHERMIC-EFFECTS OF SEROTONIN-LIKE AGENTS AFTER
IMPAIRMENT OF SEROTONIN TRANSMISSION IN FOWL BRAIN.
                                                    001733 02-04

TONIC IMMOBILITY IN DOMESTIC FOWL: POSSIBLE INTERACTION OF
SEROTONERGIC AND DOPAMINERGIC MECHANISMS.
                                                    004246 04-04

FOWLS
STEREOTYPED-BEHAVIOUR AND ELECTROCORTICAL-CHANGES AFTER
INTRACEREBRAL MICROINFUSION OF DOPAMINE AND APOMORPHINE
IN FOWLS.
                                                    001734 02-04
CENTRAL-EFFECTS OF SUBSTANCE-P IN FOWLS.
                                                    003075 03-04

FRACTION
(3H)5 HT BINDING-SITES AND 5 HT-SENSITIVE ADENYLATE-CYCLASE IN
GLIAL CELL MEMBRANE FRACTION.
                                                    000093 01-03
INTERSUBJECT AND INTRASUBJECT VARIATION IN DIAZEPAM FREE
FRACTION.
                                                    000747 01-13
FURTHER CHARACTERIZATION OF THE BINDING OF SUBSTANCE-P TO A
FRACTION FROM RABBIT BRAIN ENRICHED IN SYNAPTIC MEMBRANES.
                                                    001394 02-03
TRIAL OF A PEPTIDE FRACTION OF ACTH (ACTH4-10) IN THE ALCOHOLIC
BRAIN-DAMAGE-SYNDROME.
                                                    002318 02-14
INHIBITION OF (3H)DIAZEPAM BINDING BY AN ENDOGENOUS FRACTION
FROM RAT-BRAIN SYNAPTOSOMES.
                                                    003768 04-03
DOPAMINE-RECEPTORS IN SUBCELLULAR FRACTIONS FROM BOVINE
CAUDATE: ENRICHMENT OF (3H)SPIPERONE BINDING IN A
POSTSYNAPTIC MEMBRANE FRACTION.
                                                    003948 04-03
THE HIGH-AFFINITY CHOLINE UPTAKE SYSTEM WITH RESPECT TO THE
MUSCARINIC-RECEPTORS USING A SYNAPTOSOMAL FRACTION
ABUNDANT IN PRESYNAPTIC MEMBRANES.
                                                    004028 04-03

FRACTIONAL
EFFECTS OF RATE OF BLOOD FLOW ON FRACTIONAL EXTRACTION AND ON
UPTAKE OF INFUSED NORADRENALINE BY BROWN ADIPOSE TISSUE IN
VIVO.
                                                    001231 02-03

FRACTIONS
3H IMIPRAMINE BINDING IN NEURONAL AND GLIAL FRACTIONS OF
HORSE STRIATUM.
                                                    000033 01-03
(3H)QUINUCLIDINYL-BENZILATE BINDING TO MUSCARINIC-RECEPTORS
AND (3H)WB-4101 BINDING TO ALPHA-ADRENERGIC-RECEPTORS IN
RABBIT IRIS: COMPARISON OF RESULTS IN SLICES AND MICROSOMAL
FRACTIONS.
                                                    000299 01-03
NEWLY SYNTHESIZED CHOLECYSTOKININ IN SUBCELLULAR FRACTIONS OF
THE RAT-BRAIN.
                                                    003805 04-03
EFFECT OF INHIBITORS OF GABA-AMINOTRANSFERASE ON THE
METABOLISM OF GABA IN BRAIN TISSUE AND SYNAPTOSOMAL
FRACTIONS.
                                                    003914 04-03
DOPAMINE-RECEPTORS IN SUBCELLULAR FRACTIONS FROM BOVINE
CAUDATE: ENRICHMENT OF (3H)SPIPERONE BINDING IN A
POSTSYNAPTIC MEMBRANE FRACTION.
                                                    003948 04-03

FRAGILE
FRAGILE SITES IN HUMAN CHROMOSOMES I. THE EFFECT OF METHIONINE
ON THE XQ-FRAGILE-SITE.
                                                    004515 04-13

FRAGMENT
PAPAIN-DERIVED FRAGMENT IIC TETANUS-TOXIN: ITS BINDING TO
ISOLATED SYNAPTIC MEMBRANES AND RETROGRADE AXONAL
TRANSPORT.
                                                    003734 04-03

FRAGMENTS
DYNAMICS OF ENDOGENOUS CATECHOLAMINE RELEASE FROM BRAIN
FRAGMENTS OF MALE AND FEMALE RATS.
                                                    001121 02-03
ALTERED LEVELS OF BETA ENDORPHIN FRAGMENTS AFTER CHRONIC
MORPHINE TREATMENT OF GUINEA-PIG ILEUM IN VITRO AND IN VIVO.
                                                    001404 02-03
THE EFFECT OF NEUROPEPTIDE FRAGMENTS OF ADRENOCORTICOTROPIN
AND VASOPRESSIN ON BEHAVIORAL-ACTIVITY IN RATS.
                                                    001812 02-04
NEUROTENSIN RELEASE BY RAT HYPOTHALAMIC FRAGMENTS IN VITRO.
                                                    003920 04-03

FRAME
COMPARISON OF THE EFFECTS OF FOUR BENZODIAZEPINES ON FRAME OF
MIND AND BEHAVIOR IN HEALTHY SUBJECTS.
                                                    003441 03-14

FREE
THE MECHANISM OF EFFECT OF NEUROPHARMACOLOGICAL-DRUGS. VI:
EFFECT OF NORADRENALINE AND 5 HYDROXYTRYPTAMINE ON BRAIN
FREE FATTY-ACIDS.
                                                    000274 01-03

INTERSUBJECT AND INTRASUBJECT VARIATION IN DIAZEPAM FREE
FRACTION.
000747 01-13
EFFECT OF PYRITINOL AND PIRACETAM ON CHANGES IN FREE AMMONIA
LEVEL IN CNS TISSUE AFTER PARADOXICAL SLEEP-DEPRIVATION IN
RATS.
001199 02-03
LITHIUM-INDUCED CHANGES IN THE BRAIN LEVELS OF FREE AMINO-ACIDS
IN STRESS-EXPOSED RATS.
001217 02-03
THE EFFECTS OF PIRACETAM ON FREE FATTY-ACIDS IN THE BRAIN.
001474 02-03
EFFECTS OF CAFFEINE ON PLASMA FREE FATTY-ACIDS, URINARY
CATECHOLAMINES, AND DRUG BINDING.
002272 02-13
FREE DESCRIPTION OF DRUG-EFFECTS AS A METHOD OF CLINICAL-TRIAL,
PRESENTED BY THE EXAMPLE OF PENTOBARBITONE, PROMAZINE AND
THEIR COMBINATION.
002561 02-17
EFFECT OF DOPAMINE ON ACTIVATION OF RAT STRIATAL ADENYLATE-
CYCLASE BY FREE MG2 AND GUANYL-NUCLEOTIDES.
002825 03-03
PLASMA FREE AND TOTAL TRYPTOPHAN, BLOOD SEROTONIN, AND THE
HYPERACTIVITY-SYNDROME: NO EVIDENCE FOR THE SEROTONIN
DEFICIENCY HYPOTHESIS.
003312 03-11
DISSOCIATION BETWEEN FREE AND BOUND PHENYTOIN LEVELS IN
PRESENCE OF SODIUM-VALPROATE.
003367 03-11
COVARIANCE OF PLASMA FREE 3 METHOXY-4-
HYDROXYPHENETHYLENEGLYCOL AND DIASTOLIC BLOOD-PRESSURE.
003418 03-13
COMPARISON OF THE EFFECT OF INTRAVENOUS ADMINISTRATION OF D
LYSERGIC-ACID-DIETHYLAMIDE ON FREE AND MEMBRANE-BOUND
POLYSOMES IN THE RABBIT BRAIN.
003831 04-03
CELL-FREE TRANSLATION OF FREE AND MEMBRANE-BOUND POLYSOMES
AND POLYADENYLATED MRNA FROM RABBIT BRAIN FOLLOWING
ADMINISTRATION OF D LYSERGIC-ACID-DIETHYLAMIDE IN VIVO.
003832 04-03
DRUG-INDUCED CHANGES IN THE COMPOSITION OF THE CEREBRAL FREE
AMINO-ACID POOL.
004039 04-03
IN NORMAL YOUNG MEN ACUTE DOPAMINERGIC BLOCKADE DOES NOT
IMPAIR FREE WATER EXCRETION FOLLOWING A STANDARD WATER
LOAD.
004600 04-15
CLOPIPAZAN (SKF-69634), A NEW NEUROLEPTIC ESSENTIALLY FREE OF
EXTRAPYRAMIDAL LIABILITY: QUANTITATIVE PHARMACOEEG AND
OPEN LABEL CLINICAL-TRIAL.
004620 04-15

FREEDOM
IS THE FAILURE OF (-)DEPRENYL, A SELECTIVE MONOAMINE-OXIDASE-B-
INHIBITOR, TO ALLEVIATE DEPRESSION RELATED TO FREEDOM FROM
THE CHEESE EFFECT?
004640 04-15

FREELY-FEEDING
DIFFERENTIAL-EFFECTS OF MORPHINE ON FOOD AND WATER INTAKE IN
FOOD DEPRIVED AND FREELY-FEEDING RATS.
001765 02-04

FREELY-MOVING-RATS
EFFECTS OF CHRONIC ADMINISTRATION OF DELTA9
TETRAHYDROCANNABINOL ON THE CARDIOVASCULAR SYSTEM, AND
PRESSOR AND BEHAVIORAL-RESPONSES TO BRAIN-STIMULATION IN
FREELY-MOVING-RATS.
000417 01-04
ACETYLCHOLINE AND AMINO-ACID NEUROTRANSMITTERS IN EPIDURAL
CUPS OF FREELY-MOVING-RATS: EFFECT OF ACUTE AND CHRONIC-
TREATMENT WITH ANTISCHIZOPHRENIC-DRUGS.
001386 02-03

FRENCH
PRINCIPLES OF FRENCH PHARMACOCLINICAL-CLASSIFICATION.
001892 02-07

FRENCH-GUIANA
PSYCHOTOMIMETIC USE OF TOBACCO IN SURINAM AND FRENCH-
GUIANA.
002592 02-17

FRENCH-SPEAKING
CLINICAL-EXPERIENCE WITH SUBSTITUTED BENZAMIDES IN FRENCH-
SPEAKING COUNTRIES.
002036 02-09

FREQUENCIES
THE RELATIONSHIP OF ALPHA AND DELTA EEG FREQUENCIES TO PAIN
AND MOOD IN FIBROSITIS-PATIENTS TREATED WITH CHLORPROMAZINE
AND L TRYPTOPHAN.
002152 02-11

FREQUENCY
AFFECTIVE-EPISODE FREQUENCY AND LITHIUM THERAPY.
000587 01-09

THE QUANTITATIVE MEASUREMENT OF CHANGES IN EEG FREQUENCY
SPECTRA PRODUCED IN THE CAT BY SEDATIVE HYPNOTICS AND
NEUROLEPTICS.
001220 02-03
EFFECTS OF PROLONGED TREATMENT WITH LITHIUM AND TRICYCLIC-
ANTIDEPRESSANTS ON DISCHARGE FREQUENCY, NOREPINEPHRINE
RESPONSES AND BETA-RECEPTOR BINDING IN RAT-CEREBELLUM:
ELECTROPHYSIOLOGICAL AND BIOCHEMICAL COMPARISON.
002884 03-03

FREUNDS-ADJUVANT
ANALGESIC ACTIVITY OF DIFLUNISAL (MK-647; 5 2,4
DIFLUOROPHENYLSALICYLIC-ACID) IN RATS WITH HYPERALGESIA
INDUCED BY FREUNDS-ADJUVANT.
000502 01-04

FRIGIDITY
EXPERIMENTATION WITH MINAPRINE IN DEALING WITH CERTAIN
SEXUAL-DISORDERS: IMPOTENCE OR FRIGIDITY.
002153 02-11

FROG
THE EFFECT OF DIAZEPAM ON TENSION AND ELECTROLYTE DISTRIBUTION
IN FROG MUSCLE.
000069 01-03
CHARACTERIZATION OF LRF-LIKE IMMUNOREACTIVITY IN THE FROG
SYMPATHETIC GANGLIA: NONIDENTITY WITH LRF-DECAPEPTIDE.
(UNPUBLISHED PAPER).
001018 02-01
THE EFFECTS OF SUBSTITUTED BENZAMIDES ON FROG RECTUS-
ABDOMINIS.
001228 02-03
DEPRESSION OF VENTRAL ROOT DORSAL ROOT POTENTIAL BY DL ALPHA
AMINOADIPATE IN FROG SPINAL-CORD.
002755 03-03
EXCITATORY AND INHIBITORY-ACTIONS OF IBOTENIC-ACID ON FROG
SPINAL MOTONEURONES IN VITRO.
002841 03-03
THE NEUROLATHYROGEN, BETA N OXALYL-L-ALPHA-BETA-
DIAMINOPROPIONIC-ACID, IS A POTENT AGONIST AT GLUTAMATE
PREFERRING RECEPTORS IN THE FROG SPINAL-CORD.
002858 03-03
VASOTOCIN, PROSTAGLANDIN, AND FEMALE REPRODUCTIVE BEHAVIOR
IN THE FROG, RANA-PIPIENS.
002978 03-04
THE EXCITATORY EFFECT OF ATROPINE ON THE NEURONS OF THE FROG
SYMPATHETIC GANGLIA.
004041 04-03

FRONTAL
THE EFFECT OF LONG-TERM CONCURRENT ADMINISTRATION OF
CHLORPROMAZINE AND LITHIUM ON THE STRIATAL AND FRONTAL
CORTICAL DOPAMINE METABOLISM IN RATS.
003788 04-03
ALPHA1-ADRENOCEPTORS AND ALPHA2-ADRENOCEPTORS IN RAT-
CEREBRAL-CORTEX: EFFECT OF FRONTAL LOBOTOMY.
003944 04-03

FRONTAL-CEREBRAL-CORTEX
THE EFFECTS OF LITHIUM ON MYOINOSITOL LEVELS IN LAYERS OF
FRONTAL-CEREBRAL-CORTEX, IN CEREBELLUM, AND IN CORPUS-
CALLOSUM OF THE RAT.
003712 04-03

FRONTAL-CORTEX
DOES (3H)SPIROPERIDOL LABEL A 5 HT-RECEPTOR IN THE FRONTAL-
CORTEX OF THE RAT?.
000206 01-03
SEROTONIN-RECEPTORS IN HIPPOCAMPUS AND FRONTAL-CORTEX.
000268 01-03
POSSIBLE INVOLVEMENT OF CYCLIC-AMP AND FRONTAL-CORTEX IN
AMITRIPTYLINE MEDIATED SUPPRESSION OF THE HYPOTENSIVE-EFFECT
OF CLONIDINE.
001259 02-03

FRUCTOSEBIPHOSPHATASE
STIMULATION OF FRUCTOSEBIPHOSPHATASE ACTIVITY AND SYNTHESIS
IN THE CEREBRAL-CORTEX OF RATS SUBMITTED TO THE CONVULSANT
METHIONINE-SULFOXIMINE.
003838 04-03

FRUSEMIDE
THE EFFECT OF FRUSEMIDE PIRETANIDE AND BUMETANIDE ON COCHLEAR
SUCCINIC-DEHYDROGENASE.
003757 04-03

FS-32
PHARMACOLOGICAL-STUDIES ON A NEW THYMOLEPTIC
ANTIDEPRESSANT. DIMETHYLAMINOPROPYL-5-METHYL-3-PHENYL-1H-
INDAZOLE (FS-32).
001659 02-04
INFLUENCE OF A CHRONIC NEW POTENTIAL ANTIDEPRESSANT,
DIMETHYLAMINOPROPYL-5-METHYL-3-PHENYL-1H-INDAZOLE (FS-32)
AND ITS N DESMETHYLATED-COMPOUND (FS-97): TREATMENT ON
MONOAMINERGIC-RECEPTOR SENSITIVITY IN THE RAT-BRAIN.
002787 03-03

FS-97
INFLUENCE OF A CHRONIC NEW POTENTIAL ANTIDEPRESSANT, DIMETHYLAMINOPROPYL-5-METHYL-3-PHENYL-1H-INDAZOLE (FS-32) AND ITS N DESMETHYLATED-COMPOUND (FS-97): TREATMENT ON MONOAMINERGIC-RECEPTOR SENSITIVITY IN THE RAT-BRAIN.
002787 03-03

FUCOSE
EFFECT OF L FUCOSE ON BRAIN PROTEIN METABOLISM AND RETENTION OF A LEARNED-BEHAVIOR IN RATS.
001819 02-04

FUELS
SUSTAINED INTRACEREBROVENTRICULAR INFUSION OF BRAIN FUELS REDUCES BODY-WEIGHT AND FOOD INTAKE IN RATS.
004098 04-04

FUNCTION
ROLE OF DOPAMINE STORAGE FUNCTION IN THE CONTROL OF RAT STRIATAL TYROSINE-HYDROXYLASE ACTIVITY.
000201 01-03

POSTINGESTION INTERFERENCE WITH BRAIN FUNCTION PREVENTS ATTENUATION OF NEOPHOBIA IN RATS.
000352 01-04

CHRONIC AMPHETAMINE ADMINISTRATION TO CATS: BEHAVIORAL-EVIDENCE AND NEUROCHEMICAL EVIDENCE FOR DECREASED CENTRAL SEROTONERGIC FUNCTION.
000491 01-04

FOLLOWUP STUDY ON THE INFLUENCE OF AN ANTIPSYCHOTIC-DRUG (PROPERICIAZINE) ON LIVER FUNCTION, ELECTROCARDIOGRAM AND ELECTROENCEPHALOGRAM.
000639 01-09

BRAIN FUNCTION IN OLD-AGE: EVALUATION OF CHANGES AND DISORDERS.
000684 01-11

BROMOCRIPTINE AND DOPAMINERGIC FUNCTION IN HUNTINGTON-DISEASE.
000700 01-11

MEMORY AND COGNITIVE FUNCTION IN THE ELDERLY: A PRELIMINARY-TRIAL OF PHYSOSTIGMINE.
000802 01-14

RENAL FUNCTION AND BIOPSY IN PATIENTS ON LITHIUM THERAPY.
000830 01-15

RENAL FUNCTION IN LITHIUM AND NONLITHIUM TREATED PATIENTS WITH AFFECTIVE-DISORDERS.
000837 01-15

DRUG-VARIABLES IN THE ETIOLOGY OF TARDIVE-DYSKINESIA: APPLICATION OF DISCRIMINANT FUNCTION ANALYSIS.
000844 01-15

RESIDUAL-EFFECTS OF TEMAZEPAM AND OTHER HYPNOTIC-COMPOUNDS ON COGNITIVE FUNCTION.
000879 01-15

A COMPARISON OF STRIATAL AND MESOLIMBIC DOPAMINE FUNCTION IN THE RAT DURING 6-MONTH TRIFLUOPERAZINE ADMINISTRATION.
001174 02-03

CHANGES IN CEREBRAL DOPAMINE FUNCTION INDUCED BY A YEARS ADMINISTRATION OF TRIFLUOPERAZINE OR THIORIDAZINE AND THEIR SUBSEQUENT WITHDRAWAL.
001175 02-03

EFFECTS OF CENTRALLY-ADMINISTERED AND SYSTEMICALLY ADMINISTERED L TYROSINE AND L LEUCINE ON OVARIAN FUNCTION IN THE OLD RAT.
001180 02-03

DRUG-INDUCED ALTERATIONS IN NEUROTRANSMITTER-RECEPTOR BINDING AND FUNCTION.
001215 02-03

THE EFFECT OF GABAMIMETICS ON NEUROTRANSMITTER-RECEPTOR BINDING AND FUNCTION IN RAT-BRAIN. (PH.D. DISSERTATION).
001221 02-03

INFLUENCE OF MORPHINE ON MEMBRANE TURNOVER AND FUNCTION.
001280 02-03

EFFECTS OF DIFFERENT MONOAMINE-OXIDASE-INHIBITORS ON RESPIRATORY ACTIVITY IN RATS WITH CHRONICALLY IMPAIRED CENTRAL SEROTONERGIC FUNCTION.
001389 02-03

DOPAMINE-AUTORECEPTORS: PHARMACOLOGY, FUNCTION AND COMPARISON WITH POSTSYNAPTIC DOPAMINE-RECEPTORS.
001453 02-03

A STUDY OF A GLIAL GAMMA AMINOBUTYRIC-ACID SYSTEM: ITS REGULATION, FUNCTION AND THE EFFECTS OF DIAZEPAM. (PH.D. DISSERTATION).
001524 02-03

DIFFERENTIAL DOPAMINERGIC FUNCTION IN YOUNG AND OLD FEMALE RATS AS MEASURED BY THREE BEHAVIORS.
001683 02-04

DIFFERENTIAL-EFFECTS OF IMIPRAMINE IN RATS AS A FUNCTION OF DRL SCHEDULE VALUE.
001714 02-04

PATHOPHYSIOLOGIC-IMPACT OF CENTRAL CATECHOLAMINERGIC FUNCTION IN SCHIZOPHRENIA AND SCHIZOPHRENIA-LIKE PSYCHOSES.
002174 02-11

APOMORPHINE HYPOTHERMIA: AN INDEX OF CENTRAL DOPAMINE-RECEPTOR FUNCTION IN MAN.
002221 02-13

EFFECT OF PSYCHOTROPIC-DRUGS ON NEUROENDOCRINE FUNCTION.
002265 02-13

INFLUENCE OF CICLAZINDOL ON MONOAMINE UPTAKE AND CNS FUNCTION IN NORMAL SUBJECTS.
002268 02-13

LITHIUM AND RENAL FUNCTION.
002416 02-15

RESPONDERS AND NONRESPONDERS TO CHLORDIAZEPOXIDE AND PLACEBO: A DISCRIMINANT FUNCTION ANALYSIS.
002482 02-16

PLACEBO, MEDICINE AND PAIN, OR THE RELATIVE FUNCTION OF MEDICATION IN THE TREATMENT OF PAIN.
002577 02-17

DISRUPTION OF 5 HYDROXYTRYPTAMINERGIC NEURONAL FUNCTION BLOCKS THE ACTION OF MORPHINE ON TUBEROINFUNDIBULAR DOPAMINERGIC NEURONS.
002700 03-03

CANNABIS-SATIVA: EFFECTS ON BRAIN FUNCTION AND ULTRASTRUCTURE IN RHESUS-MONKEYS.
002747 03-03

CENTRAL AND PERIPHERAL CATECHOLAMINE FUNCTION IN LEARNING AND MEMORY PROCESSES.
002823 03-03

INFLUENCE OF PSYCHOACTIVE AND NONPSYCHOACTIVE CANNABINOIDS ON CHROMATIN STRUCTURE AND FUNCTION IN HUMAN CELLS.
002831 03-03

THE PATHOGENESIS OF PRIMARY INTERNODAL DEMYELINATION PRODUCED BY ACETYL-ETHYL-TETRAMETHYL-TETRALIN: EVIDENCE FOR PRESERVED SCHWANN-CELL SOMAL FUNCTION.
002905 03-03

DIFFERENTIAL-EFFECTS OF SHORT-TERM AND LONG-TERM LITHIUM ON TRYPTOPHAN UPTAKE AND SEROTONERGIC FUNCTION IN CAT BRAIN.
002911 03-03

CONDITIONING AND RETENTION OF DEFENSIVE BURYING AS A FUNCTION OF ELAVIL AND THORAZINE INJECTION.
002974 03-04

EFFECT OF SODIUM-VALPROATE ON MOTOR FUNCTION REGULATED BY THE ACTIVATION OF GABA-RECEPTORS.
003033 03-04

THE HYPERACTIVE-CHILD-SYNDROME: PERIPHERAL SYMPATHETIC-NERVOUS-SYSTEM FUNCTION AND THE EFFECT OF D-AMPHETAMINE.
003340 03-11

PHAGOCYTIC FUNCTION IN DOWN-SYNDROME – I. CHEMOTAXIS.
003401 03-13

HABITUATION OF ELECTRODERMAL AND RESPIRATORY RESPONSES TO VISUAL STIMULI AS A FUNCTION OF PERSONALITY DIFFERENCES IN AFFECT LEVEL.
003414 03-13

BIOLOGICAL-EFFECTS OF CHLORPROMAZINE IN CHRONIC SCHIZOPHRENICS. II. WITH REFERENCE TO SYMPATHETIC NEURONAL FUNCTION.
003416 03-13

THE EFFECTS OF CHRONIC METHYLPHENIDATE TREATMENT ON GROWTH AND ENDOCRINE FUNCTION IN THE DEVELOPING RAT.
003811 04-03

ACTIONS OF MU, KAPPA, SIGMA, DELTA AND AGONIST/ANTAGONIST OPIATES ON STRIATAL DOPAMINERGIC FUNCTION.
004053 04-03

EFFECTS OF ANISOMYCIN ON RETENTION OF THE PASSIVE-AVOIDANCE HABIT AS A FUNCTION OF AGE.
004097 04-04

ACTH-LIKE PEPTIDES, PITUITARY ADRENOCORTICAL FUNCTION AND AVOIDANCE-BEHAVIOR.
004109 04-04

A NEUROENDOCRINE-STUDY OF ADRENOCEPTOR FUNCTION IN ENDOGENOUS DEPRESSION.
004362 04-09

ALTERATIONS IN NORADRENERGIC FUNCTION DURING CLORGYLINE TREATMENT.
004393 04-09

RESPONDERS AND NONRESPONDERS TO CHLORDIAZEPOXIDE AND PLACEBO. A DISCRIMINANT FUNCTION ANALYSIS. (UNPUBLISHED PAPER).
004420 04-10

HYPERVENTILATION-SYNDROME AND BETA-RECEPTOR FUNCTION – CLINICAL-EFFECT OF BETA BLOCKER UPON THE SYNDROME.
004459 04-11

KIDNEY FUNCTION IN PATIENTS WITH AFFECTIVE-DISORDERS WITH AND WITHOUT LITHIUM THERAPY.
004664 04-15

DOWN REGULATION OF NORADRENERGIC-RECEPTOR FUNCTION BY ANTIDEPRESSANT-DRUGS: FUNCTIONAL SIGNIFICANCE AND DISTINCTION FROM ANTIPSYCHOTIC-DRUGS. (UNPUBLISHED PAPER).
004746 04-17

FUNCTIONAL
FUNCTIONAL HYPERINNERVATION OF CEREBRAL-CORTEX BY NORADRENERGIC NEURONS RESULTS FROM FETAL LESIONS: PARALLELS WITH SCHIZOPHRENIA.
000059 01-03

FUNCTIONAL AND STRUCTURAL CONSEQUENCES OF LONG-TERM DIETARY
L-DOPA TREATMENT IN MICE.
000257 01-03
FUNCTIONAL EVIDENCE FOR SUBSENSITIVITY OF NORADRENERGIC-
ALPHA2-RECEPTORS AFTER CHRONIC DESIPRAMINE TREATMENT.
000283 01-03
REINNERVATION OF THE DENERVATED STRIATUM BY SUBSTANTIA-NIGRA
TRANSPLANTS: FUNCTIONAL CONSEQUENCES AS REVEALED BY
PHARMACOLOGICAL AND SENSORIMOTOR TESTING.
000347 01-04
EXTINCTION AND DOPAMINE-RECEPTOR BLOCKADE AFTER INTERMITTENT
REINFORCEMENT TRAINING: FAILURE TO OBSERVE FUNCTIONAL
EQUIVALENCE.
000490 01-04
THE PCP PSYCHOSIS: PROLONGED INTOXICATION OR DRUG PRECIPITATED
FUNCTIONAL ILLNESS?
000739 01-12
PSYCHOPHARMACOLOGICAL AND PSYCHOTHERAPEUTIC-APPROACHES TO
THE TREATMENT OF FUNCTIONAL PSYCHOSES.
000977 01-17
ETHYL-BETA-CARBOLINE-3-CARBOXYLATE ANTAGONISES THE EFFECT OF
DIAZEPAM ON A FUNCTIONAL GABA-RECEPTOR.
001378 02-03
HUMAN PLATELET 5 HT-RECEPTORS: CHARACTERISATION AND
FUNCTIONAL ASSOCIATION.
001412 02-03
FUNCTIONAL ASPECTS OF THE NOREPINEPHRINE-RECEPTOR COUPLED
ADENYLATE-CYCLASE SYSTEM IN THE CENTRAL-NERVOUS-SYSTEM.
001493 02-03
FUNCTIONAL ORGANIZATION OF THE CAUDATE-NUCLEUS AFTER
ADMINISTRATION OF CARBACHOL.
001495 02-03
DENERVATION IN THE DOPAMINERGIC MESOLIMBIC SYSTEM:
FUNCTIONAL CHANGES FOLLOWED USING (-)N N
PROPYLNORAPOMORPHINE DEPEND ON THE BASAL ACTIVITY LEVELS
OF RATS.
001603 02-04
THE STRIATONIGRAL GABA PATHWAY: FUNCTIONAL AND
NEUROCHEMICAL CHARACTERISTICS IN RATS WITH UNILATERAL
STRIATAL KAINIC-ACID LESIONS.
001816 02-04
FUNCTIONAL CHARACTERIZATION OF CENTRAL ALPHA-ADRENOCEPTORS
BY YOHIMBINE DIASTEREOMERS.
002748 03-03
THE FUNCTIONAL IMPORTANCE OF INCREASED BRAIN TRYPTOPHAN IN
THE SEROTONERGIC RESPONSE TO RESTRAINT STRESS.
002779 03-03
A STUDY OF THE EFFECT OF NEUROPHARMACOLOGICAL DRUGS ON THE
FUNCTIONAL ACTIVITY OF RAT-BRAIN.
004107 04-04
DOWN REGULATION OF NORADRENERGIC-RECEPTOR FUNCTION BY
ANTIDEPRESSANT-DRUGS: FUNCTIONAL SIGNIFICANCE AND
DISTINCTION FROM ANTIPSYCHOTIC-DRUGS. (UNPUBLISHED PAPER).
004746 04-17
NOTES ON PHARMACOTHERAPY OF FUNCTIONAL PSYCHOSES.
004748 04-17

FUNCTIONALLY
DISCRIMINATION OF FUNCTIONALLY HETEROGENEOUS RECEPTOR
SUBPOPULATIONS: ANTIPSYCHOTIC AND ANTIDOPAMINERGIC
PROPERTIES OF METOCLOPRAMIDE.
002877 03-03

FUNCTIONING
EFFECTS OF THIORIDAZINE ON THE COGNITIVE FUNCTIONING OF A
HYPOTONIC SCHIZOPHRENIC-BOY.
000557 01-08
OPIATE ANTAGONISTS AND FEMALE FUNCTIONING. (UNPUBLISHED
PAPER).
001735 02-04
ORAL ALUMINUM AND NEUROPSYCHOLOGICAL FUNCTIONING: A STUDY
OF DIALYSIS PATIENTS RECEIVING ALUMINUM-HYDROXIDE GELS.
002283 02-13
BLOOD-PRESSURE AND COGNITIVE FUNCTIONING.
004492 04-11

FUNCTIONS
EFFECTS OF LITHIUM-CARBONATE ON MEMORY AND OTHER COGNITIVE
FUNCTIONS.
000824 01-14
EXTRAHYPOTHALAMIC DISTRIBUTIONS AND FUNCTIONS OF
HYPOTHALAMIC PEPTIDE-HORMONES. (UNPUBLISHED PAPER).
001211 02-03
EFFECTS OF CHLORPROMAZINE ON DOPAMINERGIC-RECEPTOR FUNCTIONS
IN RAT-BRAIN -- DIFFERENCE OF THE RESPONSE OF SEVERAL
DOPAMINERGIC-SYSTEMS AFTER CHRONIC ADMINISTRATION.
002773 03-03
BASAL GANGLIA DOPAMINERGIC CONTROL OF SENSORIMOTOR
FUNCTIONS RELATED TO MOTIVATED BEHAVIOR.
002815 03-03
EFFECTS OF VASOPRESSIN ON HUMAN MEMORY FUNCTIONS.
003388 03-11

THE EFFECTS OF THEOPHYLLINE AND CAFFEINE ON THERMOREGULATORY
FUNCTIONS OF RATS AT DIFFERENT AMBIENT TEMPERATURES.
003907 04-03

FUNDAMENTAL
FUNDAMENTAL MECHANISMS UNDERLYING ALTERED BEHAVIOR
FOLLOWING CHRONIC ADMINISTRATION OF PSYCHOMOTOR
STIMULANTS.
002711 03-03

FUNGAL
ACTIONS OF TREMORGENIC FUNGAL TOXINS ON NEUROTRANSMITTER
RELEASE.
002843 03-03

FURAZOLIDONE
INHIBITION OF MONOAMINE-OXIDASE BY FURAZOLIDONE IN THE
CHICKEN AND THE INFLUENCE OF THE ALIMENTARY FLORA THEREON.
003711 04-03

F1-GENERATION
CYCLOPHOSPHAMIDE-INDUCED SPERMATOGENIC EFFECTS DETECTED IN
THE F1-GENERATION BY BEHAVIORAL-TESTING.
003121 03-05

GABA
REDUCTION OF GAMMA AMINOBUTYRIC-ACID-MEDIATED (GABA)
TRANSMISSION BY A CONVULSANT BENZODIAZEPINE.
000015 01-02
SUPPRESSION OF SEROTONERGIC NEURONAL FIRING BY ALPHA-
ADRENOCEPTOR ANTAGONISTS: EVIDENCE AGAINST GABA
MEDIATION.
000024 01-03
INFLUENCE OF CELLULAR-TRANSPORT ON THE INTERACTION OF AMINO-
ACIDS WITH GAMMA AMINOBUTYRIC-ACID-RECEPTORS (GABA) IN THE
ISOLATED OLFACTORY-CORTEX OF THE GUINEA-PIG.
000034 01-03
EFFECT OF AMINOOXYACETIC-ACID (AOAA) ON GABA LEVELS IN SOME
PARTS OF THE RAT-BRAIN.
000040 01-03
DOPAMINE, ACETYLCHOLINE, AND GABA EFFECTS IN ACUTE DYSTONIA IN
PRIMATES.
000043 01-03
CIRCADIAN-RHYTHM OF CYCLIC-NUCLEOTIDE AND GABA LEVELS IN THE
RAT-BRAIN.
000049 01-03
RELATIONSHIP OF ANTICONFLICT ACTIVITY OF BENZODIAZEPINES TO
BRAIN RECEPTOR BINDING, SEROTONIN, AND GABA.
000057 01-03
GABA BENZODIAZEPINE INTERACTIONS: PHYSIOLOGICAL,
PHARMACOLOGICAL AND DEVELOPMENTAL ASPECTS.
000103 01-03
EFFECTS OF GAMMA ACETYLENIC-GABA AND GAMMA VINYL-GABA ON
ELECTRICALLY-INDUCED SPINAL-CORD CONVULSIONS AND ON SPINAL-
CORD GABA CONCENTRATION.
000145 01-03
A PROBABLE SITE-OF-ACTION OF DIAZEPAM IN RAT CEREBELLAR GABA
SYSTEM.
000151 01-03
GABA INHIBITION OF 3H GLYCINE RELEASE FROM SLICES OF RAT
SUBSTANTIA-NIGRA IN VITRO.
000157 01-03
GABA FLUXES IN PRESYNAPTIC NERVE-ENDINGS FROM IMMATURE RATS.
000185 01-03
GABA DEPLETION AND BEHAVIOURAL-CHANGES PRODUCED BY
INTRAVENTRICULAR PUTRESCINE IN CHICKS.
000218 01-03
EFFECT OF GABA ANALOGUES ON BLOOD-PRESSURE AND CENTRAL GABA
METABOLISM IN THE RAT.
000231 01-03
GABAERGIC ACTIONS OF THIP IN VIVO AND IN VITRO: A COMPARISON
WITH MUSCIMOL AND GABA.
000319 01-03
INTRAVENOUS GABA AGONIST ADMINISTRATION STIMULATES FIRING OF
A10 DOPAMINERGIC NEURONS.
000320 01-03
ROTATION INDUCED BY INTRANIGRAL INJECTIONS OF GABA AGONISTS
AND ANTAGONISTS: ZONE-SPECIFIC EFFECTS.
000422 01-04
LOCOMOTOR-ACTIVITY ELICITED BY INJECTIONS OF PICROTOXIN INTO THE
VENTRAL TEGMENTAL AREA IS ATTENUATED BY INJECTIONS OF GABA
INTO THE GLOBUS-PALLIDUS.
000436 01-04
DRUG-THERAPY IN ENDOGENOUS DEPRESSION WITH POSSIBLE PRIMARY
GABA DEFICIENCY CLINICALLY DETECTED: 38 NEW CASES.
000584 01-09
GABA LEVELS IN HUMAN CEREBROSPINAL-FLUID: ALTERATIONS IN
PSYCHIATRIC-DISORDERS. (UNPUBLISHED PAPER).
000764 01-13
GABA SYNTHESIS BY CULTURED FIBROBLASTS OBTAINED FROM PERSONS
WITH HUNTINGTONS-DISEASE.
000765 01-13

THE REGULATION OF GABA-RECEPTORS AS A POSSIBLE MECHANISM FOR
GABA 1,4 BENZODIAZEPINE INTERACTIONS. (UNPUBLISHED PAPER).
001012 02-01
GABA AGONISTS AND UPTAKE INHIBITORS DESIGNED AS AGENTS WITH
IRREVERSIBLE ACTIONS.
001079 02-02
EFFECTS OF GABA AND DIAZEPAM ON 3H SEROTONIN RELEASE FROM
HIPPOCAMPAL SYNAPTOSOMES.
001116 02-03
INHIBITION BY ARYLSULPHATASE A OF NA-INDEPENDENT (3H) GABA
AND (3H) MUSCIMOL BINDING TO BOVINE CEREBELLAR SYNAPTIC
MEMBRANES.
001208 02-03
EFFECT OF GABA AGONIST AND ANTAGONISTS ON CARDIOVASCULAR
AND SYMPATHETIC RESPONSES IN SHR AND WKY RATS.
(UNPUBLISHED PAPER).
001224 02-03
GABA-MODULIN REGULATES SOLUBILIZED BENZODIAZEPINE AND GABA
RECOGNITION SITES. (UNPUBLISHED PAPER).
001263 02-03
GABA FACILITATION BY NORADRENALINE SHOWED SUPER-SENSITIVITY IN
CEREBELLUM AFTER 6 HYDROXYDOPAMINE.
001382 02-03
IN VIVO CHANGES IN THE GABA CONTENT OF NERVE-ENDINGS
(SYNAPTOSOMES) INDUCED BY INHIBITORS OF GABA UPTAKE.
001540 02-03
DRUG-INDUCED ELEVATION OF GABA AFTER INTRACEREBRAL
MICROINJECTION: SITE OF ANTICONVULSANT ACTION.
001627 02-04
ACTIVATION AND LATERALIZATION OF SENSORIMOTOR FIELD FOR
PERIORAL BITING-REFLEX BY INTRANIGRAL GABA AGONIST AND BY
SYSTEMIC APOMORPHINE IN THE RAT.
001657 02-04
GABA AGONISTS DISSOCIATE STRIATAL UNIT ACTIVITY FROM DRUG-
INDUCED STEREOTYPED-BEHAVIOUR.
001716 02-04
THE EFFECT OF SOME STRUCTURAL GABA ANALOGUES ON THE
SEROTONIN AND DOPAMINERGIC MECHANISMS.
001736 02-04
MOTOR-DEPRESSION AND HEAD-TWITCHES INDUCED BY IP INJECTION OF
GABA.
001788 02-04
EFFECTS OF BRANCHED-CHAIN FATTY-ACIDS ON GABA DEGRADATION
AND BEHAVIOR: FURTHER EVIDENCE FOR A ROLE OF GABA IN QUASI-
MORPHINE ABSTINENCE-BEHAVIOR.
001809 02-04
THE STRIATONIGRAL GABA PATHWAY: FUNCTIONAL AND
NEUROCHEMICAL CHARACTERISTICS IN RATS WITH UNILATERAL
STRIATAL KAINIC-ACID LESIONS.
001816 02-04
STUDIES ON GABA RELEASE IN VIVO USING A SIMPLE METHOD FOR
PERFUSION OF THE FOURTH VENTRICLE OF THE RAT.
001881 02-06
CEREBROSPINAL-FLUID GABA IN PSYCHOTIC-DISORDERS.
002097 02-11
BENZODIAZEPINE-RECEPTORS: THE EFFECT OF GABA ON THEIR
CHARACTERISTICS IN HUMAN BRAIN AND THEIR ALTERATION IN
HUNTINGTONS-DISEASE.
002163 02-11
SHORT-TERM AND LONG-TERM EFFECTS ON GABA AND DOPAMINE
NEURONS DURING TREATMENT WITH SULPIRIDE.
002311 02-13
TARDIVE-HYPERKINESIA. EFFECTS OF SULPIRIDE AND GABA SYSTEM
AGONISTS.
002405 02-15
THE SYNTHESIS AND ACTIVITY OF CIS AND TRANS 2
AMINOMETHYLCYCLOPROPANECARBOXYLIC-ACID AS
CONFORMATIONALLY RESTRICTED ANALOGUES OF GABA.
002633 03-01
HETEROGENEOUS DEPRESSION OF GLUCOSE UTILIZATION IN THE
CAUDATE-NUCLEUS BY GABA AGONISTS.
002640 03-01
PIPERIDINE-4-SULPHONIC-ACID, A NEW SPECIFIC GABA AGONIST.
002647 03-02
GABA ANALOGUES ACTIVATE CHANNELS OF DIFFERENT DURATION ON
CULTURED MOUSE SPINAL NEURONS.
002665 03-03
SENSITIVITY OF IDENTIFIED MEDIAL HYPOTHALAMIC NEURONS TO GABA,
GLYCINE AND RELATED AMINO-ACIDS: INFLUENCE OF BICUCULLINE,
PICROTOXIN AND STRYCHNINE ON SYNAPTIC INHIBITION.
002674 03-03
A COMPARISON OF THE EFFECTS OF PENTOBARBITAL AND
DIPHENYLHYDANTOIN ON THE GABA SENSITIVITY AND EXCITABILITY
OF ADULT SENSORY GANGLION CELLS.
002692 03-03
NA-INDEPENDENT BINDING OF (3H)GABA AND (3H)MUSCIMOL TO
SUBCELLULAR PARTICLES OF NEURAL PRIMARY CULTURES AND WHOLE
BRAIN.
002699 03-03

CHRONOLOGY OF NEUROCHEMICAL ALTERATIONS INDUCED BY GABA
AGONIST ADMINISTRATION.
002713 03-03
GABA DEPLETION IN CHICK BRAINSTEM AFTER INTRAVENTRICULAR
INJECTION OF CEFAZOLIN.
002762 03-03
THE EFFECTS OF A BENZODIAZEPINE ON THE HYPERPOLARIZING AND THE
DEPOLARIZING RESPONSES OF HIPPOCAMPAL CELLS TO GABA.
002763 03-03
GABA ANTAGONISTS ENHANCE DOPAMINE TURNOVER IN THE RAT
RETINA IN VIVO.
002772 03-03
MODULATION BY PICROTOXIN AND IPTBO OF 3H FLUNITRAZEPAM
BINDING TO THE GABA/BENZODIAZEPINE-RECEPTOR COMPLEX OF RAT-
CEREBELLUM.
002775 03-03
THE EFFECT OF SPECIFIC BRAIN LESIONS ON THE HIGH-AFFINITY BINDING
OF GABA IN THE SUBSTANTIA-NIGRA.
002795 03-03
GABA AGONISTS AS ANTIEPILEPTIC-AGENTS.
002826 03-03
INHIBITORY ACTIONS OF TAUROCYAMINE, HYPOTAURINE,
HOMOTAURINE, TAURINE AND GABA ON SPIKE DISCHARGES OF
PURKINJE-CELLS, AND LOCALIZATION OF SENSITIVE SITES, IN GUINEA-
PIG CEREBELLAR SLICES.
002846 03-03
CONVULSANT AND ANTICONVULSANT-DRUG BINDING-SITES RELATED TO
GABA REGULATED CHLORIDE ION-CHANNELS.
002848 03-03
GABA AND BACLOFEN POTENTIATE THE K-EVOKED RELEASE OF
METHIONINE-ENKEPHALIN FROM RAT STRIATAL SLICES.
002882 03-03
ACTION OF PYRAZOLOPYRIDINES AS MODULATORS OF
(3H)FLUNITRAZEPAM BINDING TO THE GABA/BENZODIAZEPINE-
RECEPTOR COMPLEX OF THE CEREBELLUM.
002909 03-03
BIPHASIC-EFFECTS AND OPPOSITE-EFFECTS OF DOPAMINE AND
APOMORPHINE ON ENDOGENOUS GABA RELEASE IN THE RAT
SUBSTANTIA-NIGRA.
002923 03-03
A COMPARATIVE-STUDY OF THE PHARMACOLOGY OF INHIBITORS OF
GABA METABOLISM.
003036 03-04
DETERMINATION OF GABA LEVELS BY A (3H)MUSCIMOL RADIORECEPTOR
ASSAY.
003135 03-06
GABA AND SCHIZOPHRENIA: STUDY OF THE ACTION OF A GABAERGIC
ANTAGONIST. PROGABIDE OR SL-76-002.
003175 03-08
THE EFFECT OF SODIUM-VALPROATE ON MANIA: THE GABA HYPOTHESIS
OF AFFECTIVE-DISORDERS.
003218 03-09
ON A POSSIBLE ROLE OF GABA IN MANIA. THERAPEUTIC-EFFICACY OF
SODIUM-VALPROATE.
003219 03-09
TREATMENT OF HUNTINGTON-DISEASE WITH GAMMA ACETYLENIC-
GABA, AN IRREVERSIBLE INHIBITOR OF GABA-TRANSAMINASE:
INCREASED CSF GABA AND HOMOCARNOSINE WITHOUT CLINICAL
AMELIORATION.
003458 03-14
PRESYNAPTIC AND POSTSYNAPTIC STRIATAL DOPAMINE-RECEPTORS:
DIFFERENTIAL SENSITIVITY TO APOMORPHINE INHIBITION OF
(3H)DOPAMINE AND (14C)GABA RELEASE IN VITRO.
003741 04-03
3H BACLOFEN AND 3H GABA BIND TO BICUCULLINE INSENSITIVE GABAB
SITES IN RAT-BRAIN.
003839 04-03
A STEROID DERIVATIVE, R-5135, ANTAGONIZES THE GABA/
BENZODIAZEPINE-RECEPTOR INTERACTION.
003851 04-03
SENSITIVITY TO GABA OF NEURONS OF THE DORSAL AND VENTRAL
LATERAL GENICULATE NUCLEI IN THE RAT.
003877 04-03
EFFECT OF INHIBITORS OF GABA-AMINOTRANSFERASE ON THE
METABOLISM OF GABA IN BRAIN TISSUE AND SYNAPTOSOMAL
FRACTIONS.
003914 04-03
EVIDENCE TO SUGGEST THAT DOPAMINE-INDUCED INCREASE IN GABA
CONCENTRATIONS IN CHICK BRAIN IS MEDIATED THROUGH CYCLIC-
AMP.
003952 04-03
DOPAMINE-DEPENDENT HYPERACTIVITY IN THE FOLLOWING
MANIPULATION OF GABA MECHANISMS IN THE REGION OF THE
NUCLEUS-ACCUMBENS.
003976 04-03
THE INSENSITIVITY OF DEVELOPING BENZODIAZEPINE-RECEPTORS TO
CHRONIC-TREATMENT WITH DIAZEPAM, GABA AND MUSCIMOL IN
BRAIN CELL-CULTURES.
004002 04-03

IN VITRO MODULATION BY AVERMECTIN-B1A OF THE GABA/
BENZODIAZEPINE-RECEPTOR COMPLEX OF RAT-CEREBELLUM.
004023 04-03
AVOIDANCE ENHANCEMENT AND DISCRIMINATIVE RESPONSE CONTROL
BY ANXIOLYTICS WITH DRUGS ACTING ON THE GABA SYSTEM.
004193 04-04
GABA-AMINOTRANSFERASE
COMPARATIVE-STUDY OF THE INHIBITION OF GABA-AMINOTRANSFERASE
BY DIFFERENT ANTICONVULSANT-DRUGS.
000192 01-03
EFFECT OF INHIBITORS OF GABA-AMINOTRANSFERASE ON THE
METABOLISM OF GABA IN BRAIN TISSUE AND SYNAPTOSOMAL
FRACTIONS.
003914 04-03
GABA-AUTORECEPTORS
GABA-AUTORECEPTORS: STRUCTURE-ACTIVITY RELATIONSHIPS FOR
AGONISTS.
002678 03-03
GABA-CHLORIDE
THE BENZODIAZEPINE GABA-CHLORIDE IONOPHORE-RECEPTOR COMPLEX:
COMMON SITE OF MINOR-TRANQUILIZER ACTION.
002857 03-03
GABA-ENHANCED
PENTOBARBITAL POTENTIATES GABA-ENHANCED (3H) DIAZEPAM
BINDING TO BENZODIAZEPINE-RECEPTORS.
000275 01-03
DEMONSTRATION AND CHARACTERIZATION OF AN ENDOGENOUS
INHIBITOR OF GABA-ENHANCED (3H) DIAZEPAM BINDING FROM
BOVINE CEREBRAL-CORTEX.
002645 03-01
GABA-ENHANCEMENT
GABA-ENHANCEMENT OF (3H)DOPAMINE RELEASE FROM SLICES OF RAT
STRIATUM: DEPENDENCE ON SLICE SIZE.
003786 04-03
GABA-EVOKED
NALOXONE ANTAGONISM OF GABA-EVOKED MEMBRANE
POLARIZATIONS IN CULTURED MOUSE SPINAL-CORD NEURONS.
000116 01-03
GABA-MEDIATED
BARBITURATE ENHANCEMENT OF GABA-MEDIATED INHIBITION AND
ACTIVATION OF CHLORIDE ION-CONDUCTANCE: CORRELATION WITH
ANTICONVULSANT AND ANESTHETIC ACTIONS.
002885 03-03
THE ROLE OF GABA-MEDIATED NEUROTRANSMISSION IN CONVULSIVE
STATES.
003334 03-11
AN ELECTROPHYSIOLOGICAL MODEL OF GABA-MEDIATED
NEUROTRANSMISSION.
003929 04-03
GABA-MODULIN
ASSAYING GABA-MODULIN ACTIVITY IN BRAIN EXTRACTS: RESOLUTION
OF INHERENT DIFFICULTIES. (UNPUBLISHED PAPER).
001045 02-01
GABA-MODULIN REGULATES SOLUBILIZED BENZODIAZEPINE AND GABA
RECOGNITION SITES. (UNPUBLISHED PAPER).
001263 02-03
DIFFERENTIAL-EFFECTS OF KAINIC-ACID ON BENZODIAZEPINE-RECEPTORS,
GABA-RECEPTORS, AND GABA-MODULIN IN THE CEREBELLAR-CORTEX.
002477 02-16
GABA-RECEPTOR
CHARACTERIZATION OF 3H GABA-RECEPTOR BINDING TO RAT-BRAIN
SYNAPTOSOMAL MEMBRANES; EFFECT OF NONGABAERGIC
COMPOUNDS.
000139 01-03
ETHANOL ENHANCES (3H)DIAZEPAM BINDING AT THE BENZODIAZEPINE
GABA-RECEPTOR IONOPHORE COMPLEX.
001154 02-03
A NOVEL GABA-RECEPTOR MODULATES STIMULUS-INDUCED GLUTAMATE
RELEASE FROM CORTICOSTRIATAL TERMINALS.
001376 02-03
BENZODIAZEPINES MODIFY THE AGONIST RESPONSES AT A PRESYNAPTIC
GABA-RECEPTOR.
001377 02-03
ETHYL-BETA-CARBOLINE-3-CARBOXYLATE ANTAGONISES THE EFFECT OF
DIAZEPAM ON A FUNCTIONAL GABA-RECEPTOR.
001378 02-03
THE EFFECTS OF ACUTE AND CHRONIC MORPHINE ADMINISTRATION ON
GABA-RECEPTOR BINDING.
002301 02-13
LOCALIZATION OF GABA-RECEPTOR AND DOPAMINE-RECEPTOR SITES IN
RETINAL GLIAL CELLS USING DL ALPHA AMINOADIPIC-ACID.
002828 03-03
GABA-RECEPTOR ASSOCIATED DRUG-RECEPTORS.
002893 03-03
SYNTHESIS AND GABA-RECEPTOR BINDING-ACTIVITY OF TWO
FLUOROAMINOMETHYLPHENOLS.
003693 04-02
ROLE OF THE ANTERIOR PITUITARY GABA-RECEPTOR IN THE CONTROL OF
PROLACTIN RELEASE.
003809 04-03

EFFECTS OF HALOPEMIDE ON GABA-RECEPTOR BINDING, UPTAKE AND
RELEASE.
003913 04-03
SPECIFIC GABA-RECEPTOR AGONISTS AND UPTAKE INHIBITORS: DESIGN,
DEVELOPMENT AND STRUCTURE-ACTIVITY STUDIES.
004725 04-17
GABA-RECEPTORS
THE REGULATION OF GABA-RECEPTORS AS A POSSIBLE MECHANISM FOR
GABA 1,4 BENZODIAZEPINE INTERACTIONS. (UNPUBLISHED PAPER).
001012 02-01
TWO OR MORE CONFORMATIONS OF BENZODIAZEPINE-RECEPTORS
DEPENDING ON GABA-RECEPTORS AND OTHER VARIABLES.
001139 02-03
PHARMACOLOGICAL EVIDENCE AND BIOCHEMICAL-EVIDENCE FOR AN
INTERACTION BETWEEN THE BENZODIAZEPINE AND GABA-RECEPTORS.
001261 02-03
MULTIPLE BENZODIAZEPINE-RECEPTOR COMPLEXES: SOME
BENZODIAZEPINE RECOGNITION SITES ARE COUPLED TO GABA-
RECEPTORS AND IONOPHORES.
001484 02-03
GABA-RECEPTORS AND BENZODIAZEPINE-RECEPTORS IN THE OFFSPRING
OF DAMS RECEIVING DIAZEPAM: ONTOGENETIC-STUDIES.
001849 02-05
DIFFERENTIAL-EFFECTS OF KAINIC-ACID ON BENZODIAZEPINE-RECEPTORS,
GABA-RECEPTORS, AND GABA-MODULIN IN THE CEREBELLAR-CORTEX.
002477 02-16
RADIOHISTOCHEMICAL STUDIES OF BENZODIAZEPINE AND GABA-
RECEPTORS AND THEIR INTERACTIONS.
002644 03-01
GABA-RECEPTORS AND THE DEPRESSANT ACTION OF PENTOBARBITAL.
002666 03-03
EFFECT OF PICROTOXIN ON BENZODIAZEPINE-RECEPTORS AND GABA-
RECEPTORS WITH REFERENCE TO THE EFFECT OF CHLORIDE ION.
002725 03-03
GABA-RECEPTORS AND BENZODIAZEPINE-RECEPTORS. STUDIES ON THEIR
LOCALIZATION IN THE HIPPOCAMPUS AND THEIR INTERACTION WITH
CENTRAL DOPAMINE NEURONS IN THE RAT-BRAIN.
002727 03-03
BENZODIAZEPINE RECOGNITION SITES ON GABA-RECEPTORS.
002730 03-03
ANTERIOR PITUITARY GABA-RECEPTORS AND THEIR REGULATION OF
PROLACTIN SECRETION.
002738 03-03
KAINIC-ACID INDUCED LESION OF RAT RETINA: DIFFERENTIAL-EFFECT ON
CYCLIC-GMP AND BENZODIAZEPINE-RECEPTORS AND GABA-
RECEPTORS.
002743 03-03
BARBITURATES AND GABA-RECEPTORS.
002769 03-03
GABA-RECEPTORS AS SUPRAMOLECULAR UNITS.
002819 03-03
GABA-RECEPTORS REGULATE THE AFFINITIES OF ANIONS REQUIRED FOR
BRAIN SPECIFIC BENZODIAZEPINE BINDING.
002903 03-03
EFFECT OF SODIUM-VALPROATE ON MOTOR FUNCTION REGULATED BY
THE ACTIVATION OF GABA-RECEPTORS.
003033 03-04
RELATIONSHIP BETWEEN THE PRESENCE OF DOPAMINERGIC NEURONS
AND GABA-RECEPTORS IN SUBSTANTIA-NIGRA: EFFECTS OF LESIONS.
003797 04-03
GABA-STIMULATED
CHARACTERIZATION OF GABA-STIMULATED BENZODIAZEPINE-RECEPTOR
BINDING.
001309 02-03
GABA-TRANSAMINASE
BLOCKADE OF METHAMPHETAMINE-INDUCED DEPRESSION OF TYROSINE-
HYDROXYLASE BY GABA-TRANSAMINASE INHIBITORS.
000130 01-03
CHANGES IN PRIMARY AFFERENT DEPOLARIZATION AFTER
ADMINISTRATION OF GAMMA ACETYLENIC-GAMMA-AMINOBUTYRIC-
ACID (GAG), A GAMMA AMINOBUTYRIC-ACID-TRANSAMINASE
(GABA-TRANSAMINASE) INHIBITOR.
000174 01-03
TREATMENT OF HUNTINGTON-DISEASE WITH GAMMA ACETYLENIC-
GABA, AN IRREVERSIBLE INHIBITOR OF GABA-TRANSAMINASE:
INCREASED CSF GABA AND HOMOCARNOSINE WITHOUT CLINICAL
AMELIORATION.
003458 03-14
THE PHARMACOLOGY OF GABA-TRANSAMINASE INHIBITORS.
003620 03-17
GABAB
3H BACLOFEN AND 3H GABA BIND TO BICUCULLINE INSENSITIVE GABAB
SITES IN RAT-BRAIN.
003839 04-03
GABAERGIC
EVIDENCE FOR A GABAERGIC NIGROTHALAMIC PATHWAY IN THE RAT: I.
BEHAVIOURAL-STUDIES AND BIOCHEMICAL-STUDIES.
000158 01-03

Subject Index

EFFECT OF DOPAMINERGIC AND GABAERGIC DRUGS GIVEN ALONE OR IN COMBINATION ON THE ANTICONVULSANT ACTION OF PHENOBARBITAL AND DIPHENYLHYDANTOIN IN THE ELECTROSHOCK-TEST IN MICE.
000163 01-03

GABAERGIC ACTIONS OF THIP IN VIVO AND IN VITRO: A COMPARISON WITH MUSCIMOL AND GABA.
000319 01-03

BEHAVIORAL-EFFECTS AND ELECTROCORTICAL-EFFECTS AFTER INTRASTRIATAL CEFAZOLIN IN RATS ARE ANTAGONIZED BY DRUGS ENHANCING GABAERGIC TRANSMISSION.
000443 01-04

THE INFLUENCE OF GABAERGIC SUBSTANCES ON THE EFFECTS OF STIMULATION OF THE CAUDATE-NUCLEUS AND AMPHETAMINE STEREOTYPY IN CATS.
000489 01-04

MODIFICATION OF GABAERGIC ACTIVITY AND THYROTROPIN SECRETION IN MALE RATS.
001362 02-03

DIPROPYLACETATE-INDUCED ABSTINENCE-BEHAVIOUR AS A POSSIBLE CORRELATE OF INCREASED GABAERGIC ACTIVITY IN THE RAT.
001606 02-04

INVOLVEMENT OF CHOLINERGIC AND GABAERGIC SYSTEMS IN SCHIZOPHRENIA.
001907 02-08

BENZODIAZEPINE-RECEPTORS: AUTORADIOGRAPHICAL AND IMMUNOCYTOCHEMICAL EVIDENCE FOR THEIR LOCALIZATION IN REGIONS OF GABAERGIC SYNAPTIC CONTACTS.
002643 03-01

GABAERGIC MECHANISMS IN THE CONTROL OF PRL AND GH RELEASE.
002690 03-03

EVIDENCE FOR A TONIC GABAERGIC CONTROL OF SEROTONIN NEURONS IN THE MEDIAN RAPHE NUCLEUS.
002719 03-03

INJECTIONS OF DOPAMINERGIC, CHOLINERGIC, SEROTONINERGIC AND GABAERGIC DRUGS INTO THE NUCLEUS-ACCUMBENS: EFFECTS ON LOCOMOTOR-ACTIVITY IN THE RAT.
003019 03-04

GABA AND SCHIZOPHRENIA: STUDY OF THE ACTION OF A GABAERGIC ANTAGONIST. PROGABIDE OR SL-76-002.
003175 03-08

DOPAMINERGIC AND GABAERGIC ASPECTS OF TARDIVE-DYSKINESIA.
003302 03-11

CHANGES OF ELECTRORETINOGRAM AND NEUROCHEMICAL ASPECTS OF GABAERGIC NEURONS OF RETINA AFTER INTRAOCULAR INJECTION OF KAINIC-ACID IN RATS.
003807 04-03

IN VIVO EVIDENCE FOR GABAERGIC CONTROL OF SEROTONIN RELEASE IN THE CAT SUBSTANTIA-NIGRA.
004011 04-03

ON SOME RELATIONSHIPS BETWEEN GABAERGIC AND 5 HT-ERGIC MECHANISMS IN PENTYLENETETRAZOL CONVULSIVE-SEIZURE REACTIONS.
004166 04-04

GABAMIMETIC
ANALGESIC PROPERTIES OF THE GABAMIMETIC THIP.
003013 03-04

GABAMIMETICS
ANTAGONISM OF INTRASTRIATAL AND INTRAVENOUS KAINIC-ACID BY 1 NUCIFERINE: COMPARISON WITH VARIOUS ANTICONVULSANTS AND GABAMIMETICS.
000188 01-03

THE EFFECT OF GABAMIMETICS ON NEUROTRANSMITTER-RECEPTOR BINDING AND FUNCTION IN RAT-BRAIN. (PH.D. DISSERTATION).
001221 02-03

BIPHASIC-EFFECTS OF DIRECT, BUT NOT INDIRECT, GABAMIMETICS AND ANTAGONISTS ON HALOPERIDOL-INDUCED CATALEPSY.
001826 02-04

GAD
PRODUCTION OF A SPECIFIC ANTISERUM TO RAT-BRAIN GLUTAMIC-ACID-DECARBOXYLASE (GAD) BY INJECTION OF AN ANTIGEN ANTIBODY COMPLEX. (UNPUBLISHED PAPER).
001047 02-01

COMPARISON OF CYSTEINE-SULPHINIC-ACIO-DECARBOXYLASE (CSD) ISOENZYMES AND GLUTAMIC-ACID-DECARBOXYLASE (GAD) IN RAT: IS BRAIN CSD-I IDENTICAL WITH LIVER CSD AND BRAIN CSD-II WITH GAD? (UNPUBLISHED PAPER).
001048 02-01

DECREASE OF GAD IMMUNOREACTIVE NERVE TERMINALS IN THE SUBSTANTIA-NIGRA AFTER KAINIC-ACID LESION OF THE STRIATUM. (UNPUBLISHED PAPER).
001400 02-03

GALACTORRHEA
THE EFFECT OF AMANTADINE ON PROLACTIN LEVELS AND GALACTORRHEA ON NEUROLEPTIC TREATED PATIENTS.
003373 03-11

GALLUS-DOMESTICUS
THE BEHAVIOURAL-STATE DURING CLIMAX (HATCHING) IN THE DOMESTIC-FOWL (GALLUS-DOMESTICUS).
001564 02-04

GANGLIOSIDE
ABNORMAL MATURATION OF CEREBRAL-CORTEX AND BEHAVIORAL-
DEFICIT IN ADULT RATS AFTER NEONATAL ADMINISTRATION OF
ANTIBODIES TO GANGLIOSIDE.
003025 03-04

GANGLIOSIDES
INCORPORATION OF N ACETYLMANNOSAMINE INTO RAT-BRAIN
SUBCELLULAR GANGLIOSIDES: EFFECT OF PENTYLENETETRAZOL-
INDUCED CONVULSIONS IN BRAIN GANGLIOSIDES.
002937 03-03

BEHAVIOURAL-CHANGES IN ADULT RATS FOLLOWING ADMINISTRATION
OF ANTIBODIES AGAINST BRAIN GANGLIOSIDES.
003071 03-04

GAS-CHROMATOGRAPHIC-PROPERTIES
GAS-CHROMATOGRAPHIC-PROPERTIES OF 1,3 DIALKYLBARBITURATE
DERIVATIVES.
003658 04-01

GAS-CHROMATOGRAPHIC-SYNTHESIS
ON-COLUMN GAS-CHROMATOGRAPHIC-SYNTHESIS OF 1,3 DIALYKYL
(C=1-10), BENZYL, AND CYCLOHEXYLBARBITURATE DERIVATIVES.
003656 04-01

GAS-CHROMATOGRAPHY
ANALYSIS FOR DIAZEPAM AND NORDIAZEPAM BY ELECTRON-CAPTURE
GAS-CHROMATOGRAPHY AND BY LIQUID-CHROMATOGRAPHY.
000006 01-01

QUANTITATIVE ANALYSIS OF 6 HYDROXYMELATONIN IN HUMAN URINE
BY GAS-CHROMATOGRAPHY NEGATIVE CHEMICAL-IONIZATION MASS-
SPECTROMETRY. (UNPUBLISHED PAPER).
001058 02-01

A METHOD FOR THE DETERMINATION OF AMITRIPTYLINE AND ITS
METABOLITES NORTRIPTYLINE, 10 HYDROXYAMITRIPTYLINE, AND 10
HYDROXYNORTRIPTYLINE IN HUMAN PLASMA USING STABLE ISOTOPE
DILUTION AND GAS-CHROMATOGRAPHY CHEMICAL-IONIZATION
MASS-SPECTROMETRY.
002486 02-16

MEASUREMENT OF FLUPHENAZINE BY GAS-CHROMATOGRAPHY IN
HUMAN PLASMA AND RED-BLOOD-CELLS.
002491 02-16

A METHOD FOR MEASUREMENT OF TRANYLCYPROMINE IN RAT-BRAIN
REGIONS USING GAS-CHROMATOGRAPHY WITH ELECTRON CAPTURE
DETECTION.
003137 03-06

GAS-CHROMATOGRAPHY, MASS-SPECTROMETRY, AND COMBINED
CHROMATOGRAPHY MASS-SPECTROMETRY.
004290 04-03

RAT-BRAIN AND PLASMA NOREPINEPHRINE GLYCOL METABOLITES
DETERMINED BY GAS-CHROMATOGRAPHY MASS-
FRAGMENTOGRAPHY.
004303 04-06

GAS-CHROMATOGRAPHY/MASS-SPECTROMETRY STABLE ISOTOPIC
ANALYSES FOR DEANOL, CHOLINE, AND THEIR ACETYLESTERS.
004683 04-16

COMPARISON OF SPECTROFLUOROMETRIC AND GAS-
CHROMATOGRAPHY/MASS-SPECTROMETRY PROCEDURES FOR THE
QUANTITATION OF MORPHINE IN BLOOD AND BRAIN.
004692 04-16

GAS-EXCHANGE
THE EFFECT OF PHARMACOLOGICAL DESTRUCTION OF HYPOTHALAMIC
MONOAMINERGIC STRUCTURES ON BODY-TEMPERATURE AND GAS-
EXCHANGE DURING EXTREME COOLING.
004016 04-03

GAS-LIQUID-CHROMATOGRAPHIC-DETERMINATION
ELECTRON-CAPTURE GAS-LIQUID-CHROMATOGRAPHIC-DETERMINATION
OF ETHOSUXIMIDE AND DESMETHYLMETHSUXIMIDE IN PLASMA OR
SERUM.
000538 01-06

GAS-LIQUID-CHROMATOGRAPHY
DETERMINATION OF VALPROIC-ACID BY FLAME-IONIZATION GAS-LIQUID-
CHROMATOGRAPHY.
000906 01-16

A RAPID GAS-LIQUID-CHROMATOGRAPHY METHOD FOR SIMULTANEOUS
DETERMINATION OF VARIOUS ANTICONVULSANTS.
002501 02-16

SIMULTANEOUS ADMINISTRATION OF FIVE ANTIEPILEPTIC-DRUGS IN
PLASMA THROUGH GAS-LIQUID-CHROMATOGRAPHY.
003563 03-16

GASTRIC
GASTRIC AND PYLORIC MOTOR-RESPONSE TO SYMPATHETIC-NERVE
STIMULATION AFTER CHEMICAL SYMPATHECTOMY. (UNPUBLISHED
PAPER).
001337 02-03

APHAGIA, GASTRIC PATHOLOGY, HYPERTHERMIA, AND SENSORIMOTOR-
DYSFUNCTIONS FOLLOWING LATERAL HYPOTHALAMIC LESIONS:
EFFECTS OF INSULIN PRETREATMENTS.
001638 02-04

INHIBITION OF PENTAGASTRIN-STIMULATED AND OVERNIGHT GASTRIC
SECRETION BY LM24056, A NEW PHENOTHIAZINE DERIVED
ANTISECRETORY DRUG.
004306 04-07

GASTRIC-ULCERS
STUDIES ON THE COMPREHENSIVE MEDICAL TREATMENT OF PEPTIC-
ULCERS (3) -- UTILIZATION OF TRANQUILIZERS IN THE TREATMENT OF
GASTRIC-ULCERS.
000653 01-10

GASTRIN
ON CORRELATION OF BEHAVIORAL-REACTIONS AND NEURONAL ACTIVITY
IN THE HYPOTHALAMUS UNDER SUBCUTANEOUS GASTRIN INJECTION.
002892 03-03

GASTROINTESTINAL
COMPARISON OF THE POTENCIES OF CLEBOPRIDE AND OTHER
SUBSTITUTED BENZAMIDE DRUGS ON ISOLATED GASTROINTESTINAL
TRACT OF THE GUINEA-PIG AND RAT.
003928 04-03

GASTRORESISTANT
TOLERANCE IN A COMPRESSED GASTRORESISTANT FORM IN
PSYCHIATRIC-PATIENTS.
003157 03-07

GAVAGE
CAPTOPRIL GIVEN INTRACEREBROVENTRICULARLY, SUBCUTANEOUSLY OR
BY GAVAGE INHIBITS ANGIOTENSIN CONVERTING ENZYME ACTIVITY
IN THE RAT-BRAIN.
001614 02-04

GENE
ENHANCED RESPONSES TO OPIATES PRODUCED BY A SINGLE GENE
SUBSTITUTION IN THE MOUSE.
001677 02-04

GENERAL-ACTIVITY
EFFECTS OF AN ACTH4-9 RELATED PEPTIDE UPON INTRACRANIAL SELF-
STIMULATION AND GENERAL-ACTIVITY IN THE RAT.
001679 02-04

GENERAL-HOSPITAL
PSYCHOTROPIC-DRUGS AND POLYPHARMACY IN ELDERLY-PATIENTS IN A
GENERAL-HOSPITAL.
000981 01-17.

TREATMENT OF IATROGENIC DRUG DEPENDENCE IN THE GENERAL-
HOSPITAL.
002460 02-15

PSYCHOTROPIC-DRUG USE AND POLYPHARMACY IN A GENERAL-
HOSPITAL.
003369 03-11

GENERAL-MEDICAL-PRACTICE
THE TREATMENT OF DEPRESSION USING CLOMIPRAMINE IN GENERAL-
MEDICAL-PRACTICE: 48 CASES TREATED ON AN OUTPATIENT BASIS.
003268 03-09

GENERAL-PRACTICE
PROGNOSTIC FACTORS DETERMINING RESPONSE TO ANTIDEPRESSANT-
DRUGS IN PSYCHIATRIC-OUTPATIENTS AND GENERAL-PRACTICE.
000638 01-09

MAPROTILINE ADMINISTERED IN A SINGLE-DAILY-DOSE IN GENERAL-
PRACTICE.
002027 02-09

JOB-SATISFACTION IN GENERAL-PRACTICE: IMPLICATIONS FOR
PRESCRIBING.
002579 02-17

GENERAL-PRACTITIONER
STUDY OF MAPROTILINE IN OUTPATIENT TREATMENT OF DEPRESSIVE-
STATES BY THE GENERAL-PRACTITIONER: ADVANTAGE OF SINGLE-
NIGHTLY-DOSE.
001961 02-09

GENERAL-PRACTITIONERS
DIFFICULTIES ENCOUNTERED DURING A CONTROLLED STUDY OF A NEW
HYPNOTIC-DRUG (TRIAZOLAM) BY A GROUP OF GENERAL-
PRACTITIONERS.
003155 03-07

GENERATING
DEVELOPMENT OF AND RECOVERY FROM SUBSENSITIVITY OF THE
NORADRENERGIC CYCLIC-AMP GENERATING SYSTEM IN BRAIN: EFFECT
OF AMPHETAMINE FOLLOWING INHIBITION OF ITS AROMATIC
HYDROXYLATION BY IPRINDOLE.
001353 02-03

GENERATION
HALOTHANE EFFECT ON C-AMP GENERATION AND HYDROLYSIS IN RAT-
BRAIN.
000305 01-03

GENERATORS
IDENTICAL RESPONSES OF THE TWO HIPPOCAMPAL THETA GENERATORS
TO PHYSIOLOGICAL AND PHARMACOLOGICAL ACTIVATION.
002792 03-03

GENESES
EXPERIENCE IN USING THE HORMONES OF THE HYPOPHYSIS POSTERIOR
LOBE IN MEMORY-DISTURBANCES OF VARYING GENESES.
003438 03-14

GENESIS
CEREBELLAR GRANULE CELL GENESIS IN THE HYDROCORTISONE TREATED
RAT.
000030 01-03

Subject Index

GENETIC
ON THE GENETIC SIDE-EFFECTS OF PSYCHOTROPIC-SUBSTANCES: I. PSYCHOPHARMACEUTICALS, NARCOTICS, AND ANTICONVULSANT.
000845 01-15
VITAMIN RESPONSIVE GENETIC ABNORMALITIES. (UNPUBLISHED PAPER).
001388 02-03
BIOGENIC-AMINES AND NEUROPEPTIDES PLAY A ROLE IN THE CENTRAL-REGULATION OF GENETIC HYPERTENSION. (UNPUBLISHED PAPER).
001455 02-03
CENTRAL BIOGENIC-AMINES AND NEUROPEPTIDES IN GENETIC HYPERTENSION. (UNPUBLISHED PAPER).
001456 02-03
SPONTANEOUSLY (GENETIC) HYPERTENSIVE-RATS PRESENT A NALOXONE SENSITIVE DECREASE IN PAIN SENSITIVITY. (UNPUBLISHED PAPER).
001457 02-03
CENTRAL AMINERGIC AND PEPTIDERGIC MECHANISMS IN SPONTANEOUSLY (GENETIC) HYPERTENSIVE-RATS. (UNPUBLISHED PAPER).
001459 02-03
GENETIC AND EXPERIMENTAL FACTORS AFFECTING THE PARADOXICAL-EFFECTS OF AMPHETAMINE IN DOGS.
001704 02-04
CENTRAL DOPAMINERGIC NEURONS DURING DEVELOPMENT OF GENETIC AND DOCA-SALT HYPERTENSION IN THE RAT.
003899 04-03
GENETIC VARIATIONS IN MIDBRAIN DOPAMINE CELL NUMBER: PARALLEL WITH DIFFERENCES IN RESPONSES TO DOPAMINERGIC AGONISTS AND IN NATURALISTIC BEHAVIORS MEDIATED BY CENTRAL DOPAMINERGIC-SYSTEMS. (UNPUBLISHED PAPER).
004112 04-04

GENETICALLY
EFFECT OF BROMOCRIPTINE ON EXPLORATORY-ACTIVITY, BRAIN-MONOAMINES AND PLASMA CORTICOSTERONE IN THE NORMOTENSIVE-RATS, GENETICALLY HYPERTENSIVE-RATS AND/OR HYPERTENSIVE OBESE RATS.
001635 02-04
NEUROCHEMICAL-EFFECTS AND BEHAVIORAL-EFFECTS OF CHRONIC D-AMPHETAMINE TREATMENT IN GENETICALLY OBESE (OBOB) MICE. (PH.D. DISSERTATION).
001739 02-04

GENICULATE
SENSITIVITY TO GABA OF NEURONS OF THE DORSAL AND VENTRAL LATERAL GENICULATE NUCLEI IN THE RAT.
003877 04-03

GENITAL
THE EFFECT OF ASSERTIVENESS TRAINING, PROVERA AND SEX OF THERAPIST IN THE TREATMENT OF GENITAL EXHIBITIONISM.
000697 01-11
STUDY OF LITHIUM LEVELS IN THE SERUM AND GENITAL ORGANS OF MALE RATS.
001494 02-03

GENOTYPE
THE INFLUENCE OF GENOTYPE AND SEX ON BEHAVIORAL-SENSITIVITY TO NICOTINE IN MICE.
001648 02-04
INTERACTION AMONG D-AMPHETAMINE, SCOPOLAMINE AND GENOTYPE IN AVOIDANCE-BEHAVIOR OF RATS.
003082 03-04

GENOTYPIC
GENOTYPIC INFLUENCES ON STRIATAL DOPAMINERGIC REGULATION IN MICE.
004217 04-04

GEOGRAPHICALLY
PSYCHIATRIC-ILLNESS AND USE OF PSYCHOTROPIC-DRUGS IN THE GEOGRAPHICALLY DELIMITED POPULATION OF SAMSO, DENMARK.
004734 04-17

GERBILS
NEUROPHARMACOLOGICAL ANALYSIS OF HANDLING-INDUCED SEIZURES IN GERBILS.
001876 02-06

GERIATRIC
EVALUATION OF NOMIFENSINE IN THE TREATMENT OF GERIATRIC DEPRESSION USING PSYCHOMETRIC-TESTS AND PLASMA LEVEL CONTROLS.
002004 02-09
THE EFFICACY OF TRIAZOLAM AND CHLORAL-HYDRATE IN GERIATRIC INSOMNIACS.
002160 02-11
DESIGN ASPECTS OF CLINICAL-TRIALS WITH ERGOT ALKALOIDS: A COMPARISON OF TWO GERIATRIC BEHAVIORAL-RATING-SCALES.
002512 02-16
DRUGS AND THE ELDERLY: PERSPECTIVES IN GERIATRIC CLINICAL-PHARMACOLOGY.
002534 02-17
GERIATRIC PSYCHOPHARMACOLOGY.
002582 02-17
GERIATRIC ASPECTS OF PARKINSONISM (CLINICAL-PICTURE, PATHOLOGICAL MECHANISMS, AND MULTIPLE TREATMENT).
003643 03-17

GLC/TLC ANALYSIS OF CODEINE AND MORPHINE IN URINE VIA DERIVATIZATION TECHNIQUES.
004687 04-16

GLIAL
3H IMIPRAMINE BINDING IN NEURONAL AND GLIAL FRACTIONS OF HORSE STRIATUM.
000033 01-03

(3H)5 HT BINDING-SITES AND 5 HT-SENSITIVE ADENYLATE-CYCLASE IN GLIAL CELL MEMBRANE FRACTION.
000093 01-03

GLIAL CELL EFFECTS OF SUBACUTE FORMIC-ACID VAPOUR EXPOSURE.
000527 01-05

A STUDY OF A GLIAL GAMMA AMINOBUTYRIC-ACID SYSTEM: ITS REGULATION, FUNCTION AND THE EFFECTS OF DIAZEPAM. (PH.D. DISSERTATION).
001524 02-03

LOCALIZATION OF GABA-RECEPTOR AND DOPAMINE-RECEPTOR SITES IN RETINAL GLIAL CELLS USING DL ALPHA AMINOADIPIC-ACID.
002828 03-03

GLIOBLASTOMA
DOSAGE OF INTRATUMORAL LITHIUM (CEREBRAL GLIOBLASTOMA): ON A FAILURE OF TREATMENT OF MANIC-DEPRESSIVE-PSYCHOSIS.
003226 03-09

GLIOMA
RELATIONSHIP BETWEEN THE ACTIONS OF CALCIUM-IONS, OPIOIDS, AND PROSTAGLANDIN-E1 ON THE LEVEL OF CYCLIC-AMP IN NEUROBLASTOMA-X GLIOMA HYBRID CELLS.
002677 03-03

CHARACTERIZATION BY (3H)DIHYDROERGOCRYPTINE BINDING OF ALPHA-ADRENERGIC-RECEPTORS IN NEUROBLASTOMA X GLIOMA HYBRID CELLS.
003823 04-03

OPIOIDS, NORADRENALINE AND GTP ANALOGS INHIBIT CHOLERA-TOXIN ACTIVATED ADENYLATE-CYCLASE IN NEUROBLASTOMA-X GLIOMA HYBRID CELLS.
003975 04-03

GLOBUS-PALLIDUS
LOCOMOTOR-ACTIVITY ELICITED BY INJECTIONS OF PICROTOXIN INTO THE VENTRAL TEGMENTAL AREA IS ATTENUATED BY INJECTIONS OF GABA INTO THE GLOBUS-PALLIDUS.
000436 01-04

GLOMERULAR
SELECTIVE NEUROTOXIC-ACTION OF CAPSAICIN ON GLOMERULAR C-TYPE TERMINALS IN RAT SUBSTANTIA-GELATINOSA.
003143 03-06

GLOMERULAR FILTRATION RATE AND CALCIUM METABOLISM IN LONG-TERM LITHIUM TREATMENT.
003542 03-15

GLOWINSKIS
NEUROLEPTIC ACTIVITY: A SUMMARY OF PROFESSOR JACQUES GLOWINSKIS PRESENTATION.
003628 03-17

GLUCOCORTICOID-HORMONES
MATERNAL GLUCOCORTICOID-HORMONES INFLUENCE NEUROTRANSMITTER PHENOTYPIC EXPRESSION IN EMBRYOS.
000149 01-03

GLUCOCORTICOID-RECEPTOR
BRAIN GLUCOCORTICOID-RECEPTOR: CORRELATION OF IN VIVO UPTAKE OF CORTICOSTERONE WITH BEHAVIORAL-EVENTS, ENDOCRINE-EVENTS, AND NEUROPHARMACOLOGICAL EVENTS.
002515 02-17

GLUCOCORTICOIDS
GLUCOCORTICOIDS AS A REGULATORY FACTOR FOR BRAIN TRYPTOPHAN-HYDROXYLASE DURING DEVELOPMENT.
001500 02-03

ROLE OF ADRENERGIC BLOCKING-AGENTS AND GLUCOCORTICOIDS ON THE REGULATION OF PITUITARY OPIOID-PEPTIDES LEVELS.
003801 04-03

GLUCOPRIVATION
INCREASED HUNGER AND THIRST DURING GLUCOPRIVATION IN HUMANS.
000828 01-14

GLUCOSAMINE
THE EFFECT OF LITHIUM ON THE INCORPORATION OF 3H GLUCOSAMINE INTO GLYCOPEPTIDES AND THE TRANSFORMATION OF 3H GLUCOSAMINE INTO SIALIC-ACID IN RAT-BRAIN.
001209 02-03

GLUCOSE
MECHANISM OF CHLORPROMAZINE ACTION ON PLASMA GLUCOSE AND CYCLIC-AMP LEVELS.
000211 01-03

INFLUENCE OF GLUCOSE (IN VIVO OR IN VITRO) ON DURATION OF NARCOTIC ANALGESICS AND ON THE KINETICS OF DRUG METABOLISM.
000292 01-03

IMPAIRED GLUCOSE TOLERANCE IN LONG-TERM LITHIUM TREATED PATIENTS.
000611 01-09

GLUCOSE OXIDATION IN THE VENTROMEDIAL HYPOTHALAMUS IS NOT AFFECTED BY INSULIN OR OUABAIN BUT DEPRESSED BY ALLOXAN TREATMENT.
001145 02-03

LOCAL CEREBRAL GLUCOSE UTILIZATION (LCGU) IN RAT-BRAIN DURING HYPOXEMIA. (UNPUBLISHED PAPER).
001380 02-03

REGIONAL CHANGES IN BRAIN GLUCOSE UTILIZATION IN RATS GIVEN A PYRETHROID INSECTICIDE.
001838 02-05

THEORY, PROCEDURE, AND APPLICATIONS OF THE RADIOACTIVE DEOXYGLUCOSE METHOD FOR THE MEASUREMENT OF LOCAL GLUCOSE UTILIZATION IN THE CENTRAL-NERVOUS-SYSTEM. (UNPUBLISHED PAPER).
001877 02-06

HETEROGENEOUS DEPRESSION OF GLUCOSE UTILIZATION IN THE CAUDATE-NUCLEUS BY GABA AGONISTS.
002640 03-01

GLUCOSE SUPPRESSES BASAL FIRING AND HALOPERIDOL-INDUCED INCREASES IN THE FIRING-RATE OF CENTRAL DOPAMINERGIC NEURONS.
002880 03-03

EFFECTS OF ALPHA-ADRENERGIC AND BETA-ADRENERGIC BLOCKERS ON CHLORPROMAZINE-INDUCED ELEVATION OF PLASMA GLUCOSE AND CYCLIC-AMP IN FED MICE.
003946 04-03

EFFECTS OF A SINGLE-THERAPEUTIC-DOSE OF GLYCEROL ON CEREBRAL METABOLISM IN THE BRAINS OF YOUNG MICE: POSSIBLE INCREASE IN BRAIN GLUCOSE TRANSPORT AND GLUCOSE UTILIZATION.
004281 04-05

INTERACTION OF CHLORPROMAZINE WITH THE TRANSPORT SYSTEM OF GLUCOSE IN HUMAN ERYTHROCYTES.
004529 04-13

GLUCOSE-6-PHOSPHATASE
EFFECTS OF ANIMAL AGE AND PHENOBARBITAL ON RAT LIVER GLUCOSE-6-PHOSPHATASE ACTIVITY.
003997 04-03

GLUTAMATE
EFFECTS OF ANTICONVULSANTS AND GLUTAMATE ANTAGONISTS ON THE CONVULSIVE ACTION OF KAINIC-ACID.
000288 01-03

A NOVEL GABA-RECEPTOR MODULATES STIMULUS-INDUCED GLUTAMATE RELEASE FROM CORTICOSTRIATAL TERMINALS.
001376 02-03

POTENTIATION OF L GLUTAMATE AND L ASPARTATE EXCITATION OF CAT SPINAL NEURONES BY THE STEREOISOMERS OF THREO-3-HYDROXYASPARTATE.
002768 03-03

THE NEUROLATHYROGEN, BETA N OXALYL-L-ALPHA-BETA-DIAMINOPROPIONIC-ACID, IS A POTENT AGONIST AT GLUTAMATE PREFERRING RECEPTORS IN THE FROG SPINAL-CORD.
002858 03-03

EFFECTS OF PROTEIN AND MEMBRANE MODIFYING AGENTS ON THE BINDING OF L (3H)GLUTAMATE TO CEREBELLAR SYNAPTIC MEMBRANES.
002888 03-03

THE EFFECTS OF ACETYLCHOLINE AND GLUTAMATE ON SEPTAL NEURONS IN VITRO.
002941 03-03

PROTECTIVE ACTION OF L 5 HYDROXYTRYPTOPHAN L GLUTAMATE (MADE-1932) DURING ELECTROSHOCK-TREATMENT (ECT).
003043 03-04

CHARACTERIZATION OF TWO (3H)GLUTAMATE BINDING-SITES IN RAT HIPPOCAMPAL MEMBRANES.
003726 04-03

THE HUMAN PLATELET AS A MODEL FOR THE GLUTAMATERGIC NEURON: PLATELET UPTAKE OF L GLUTAMATE.
003923 04-03

L ASPARTATE BINDING-SITES IN RAT-CEREBELLUM: A COMPARISON OF THE BINDING OF L (3H)ASPARTATE AND L (3H)GLUTAMATE TO SYNAPTIC MEMBRANES.
004000 04-03

HYPERACTIVITY FOLLOWING INJECTION OF A GLUTAMATE AGONIST AND 6,7 ADTN INTO RAT NUCLEUS-ACCUMBENS AND ITS INHIBITION BY THIP.
004066 04-04

GLUTAMATE-RECEPTORS
NUCIFERINE AND CENTRAL GLUTAMATE-RECEPTORS.
000063 01-03

REGULATION OF HIPPOCAMPAL GLUTAMATE-RECEPTORS: EVIDENCE FOR THE INVOLVEMENT OF A CALCIUM-ACTIVATED PROTEASE.
001120 02-03

GLUTAMATERGIC
THE HUMAN PLATELET AS A MODEL FOR THE GLUTAMATERGIC NEURON: PLATELET UPTAKE OF L GLUTAMATE.
003923 04-03

GLUTAMATES
TWENTY YEARS CLINICAL THERAPEUTIC EXPERIENCE WITH CALCIUM GLUTAMATES EFFICACY.
000963 01-17

GLUTAMIC-ACID
TWO CONDUCTANCE MECHANISMS ACTIVATED BY APPLICATIONS OF L GLUTAMIC-ACID, L ASPARTIC-ACID, DL HOMOCYSTEIC-ACID, N

Subject Index

METHYL-D-ASPARTIC-ACID, AND DL KAINIC-ACID TO CULTURED
MAMMALIAN CENTRAL NEURONES.
001349 02-03

IBOTENIC-ACID ANALOGUES AS INHIBITORS OF (3H)GLUTAMIC-ACID
BINDING TO CEREBELLAR MEMBRANES.
003848 04-03

GLUTAMIC-ACID-DECARBOXYLASE
PRODUCTION OF A SPECIFIC ANTISERUM TO RAT-BRAIN GLUTAMIC-ACID-
DECARBOXYLASE (GAD) BY INJECTION OF AN ANTIGEN ANTIBODY
COMPLEX. (UNPUBLISHED PAPER).
001047 02-01

COMPARISON OF CYSTEINE-SULPHINIC-ACID-DECARBOXYLASE (CSD)
ISOENZYMES AND GLUTAMIC-ACID-DECARBOXYLASE (GAD) IN RAT: IS
BRAIN CSD-I IDENTICAL WITH LIVER CSD AND BRAIN CSD-II WITH
GAD? (UNPUBLISHED PAPER).
001048 02-01

INFLUENCE OF ESTROGEN AND PROGESTERONE ON GLUTAMIC-ACID-
DECARBOXYLASE ACTIVITY IN DISCRETE REGIONS OF RAT-BRAIN.
002927 03-03

GLUTAMIC-ACID-DIETHYL-ESTER
IMPAIRMENT OF INSTRUMENTAL LEARNING IN RATS BY GLUTAMIC-
ACID-DIETHYL-ESTER.
002993 03-04

GLUTAMINERGIC
CHOLINERGIC, DOPAMINERGIC, NORADRENERGIC, OR GLUTAMINERGIC
STIMULATION VENTRAL TO THE ANTERIOR SEPTUM DOES NOT
SPECIFICALLY SUPPRESS DEFENSIVE-BEHAVIOR.
002945 03-04

GLUTAMYLGLYCINE
DIFFERENTIATION OF KAINATE AND QUISQUALATE-RECEPTORS IN THE
CAT SPINAL-CORD BY SELECTIVE ANTAGONISMS WITH GAMMA
D(AND L) GLUTAMYLGLYCINE.
002696 03-03

GLUTAMYLTRANSFERASE
EFFECT OF IMIPRAMINE ON HEPATIC GAMMA GLUTAMYLTRANSFERASE
IN FEMALE RATS. INTERACTION WITH CONTRACEPTIVES.
001507 02-03

GLUTARIMIDE
REDUCTION OF BARBITURATE ANESTHESIA BY NEW GLUTARIMIDE
COMPOUNDS IN MICE.
001748 02-04

GLYCEMIC-RESPONSE
MECHANISMS OF CHLORPROMAZINE AND CHLORPROMAZINE ISOSTERES
ON THE GLYCEMIC-RESPONSE IN MICE. (PH.D. DISSERTATION).
001525 02-03

GLYCEROL
EFFECTS OF A SINGLE-THERAPEUTIC-DOSE OF GLYCEROL ON CEREBRAL
METABOLISM IN THE BRAINS OF YOUNG MICE: POSSIBLE INCREASE IN
BRAIN GLUCOSE TRANSPORT AND GLUCOSE UTILIZATION.
004281 04-05

GLYCINE
GABA INHIBITION OF 3H GLYCINE RELEASE FROM SLICES OF RAT
SUBSTANTIA-NIGRA IN VITRO.
000157 01-03

GLYCINE ENHANCEMENT OF CAUDATE NEURONAL ACTIVITIES:
RELATIONSHIP WITH THE DOPAMINERGIC NIGROSTRIATAL PATHWAY.
001225 02-03

COMPARISON OF THE EFFECTS OF CENTRAL ADMINISTRATION OF SERINE
AND GLYCINE ON BODY-TEMPERATURE OF THE RABBIT.
001248 02-03

LOCALIZATION OF SENSITIVE SITES TO TAURINE, GAMMA
AMINOBUTYRIC-ACID, GLYCINE AND BETA ALANINE IN THE
MOLECULAR LAYER OF GUINEA-PIG CEREBELLAR SLICES.
001402 02-03

GLYCINE, ACETYLCHOLINE, AND SEROTONIN: NEUROTRANSMITTERS OR
NEUROMODULATORS?
002271 02-13

SENSITIVITY OF IDENTIFIED MEDIAL HYPOTHALAMIC NEURONS TO GABA,
GLYCINE AND RELATED AMINO-ACIDS; INFLUENCE OF BICUCULLINE,
PICROTOXIN AND STRYCHNINE ON SYNAPTIC INHIBITION.
002674 03-03

INHIBITION OF VASOPRESSIN RELEASE TO CAROTID OCCLUSION BY
GAMMA AMINOBUTYRIC-ACID AND GLYCINE.
002715 03-03

EFFECT OF LITHIUM ON GLYCINE LEVELS IN PATIENTS WITH AFFECTIVE-
DISORDERS.
004606 04-15

GLYCOL
RAT-BRAIN AND PLASMA NOREPINEPHRINE GLYCOL METABOLITES
DETERMINED BY GAS-CHROMATOGRAPHY MASS-
FRAGMENTOGRAPHY.
004303 04-06

GLYCOLYTIC
THE ETIOLOGY OF TOXIC PERIPHERAL NEUROPATHIES: IN VITRO EFFECTS
OF ACRYLAMIDE AND 2,5 HEXANEDIONE ON BRAIN ENOLASE AND
OTHER GLYCOLYTIC ENZYMES.
000131 01-03

GRAY

MORPHINE INJECTIONS INTO THE PERIAQUEDUCTAL PERIVENTRICULAR GRAY ATTENUATE SEPTAL HYPERREACTIVITY.
000390 01-04

INCREASED METABOLISM OF DOPAMINE AND SEROTONIN INDUCED IN FOREBRAIN AREAS BY ETORPHINE MICROINJECTION IN PERIAQUEDUCTAL GRAY.
001103 02-03

A COMPARISON BETWEEN THE EFFECTS OF MORPHINE ON THE REWARDING AND AVERSIVE-PROPERTIES OF LATERAL HYPOTHALAMIC AND CENTRAL GRAY STIMULATION.
001771 02-04

OPIATE-RECEPTORS AND SLEEP. II. EFFECTS OF MICROINJECTIONS OF ETHYL-ALCOHOL AND PENTOBARBITAL IN THE MEDIAN THALAMUS, PERIAQUEDUCTAL GRAY MATTER AND NUCLEUS-TRACTUS-SOLITARIUS OF THE RABBIT.
002917 03-03

DOSE-RESPONSE STUDY OF THE PRECIPITATED ABSTINENCE-SYNDROME FOR MORPHINE: SYSTEMIC VS PERIAQUEDUCTAL GRAY NALOXONE. (PH.D. DISSERTATION).
002979 03-04

GREY

EFFECT OF CHRONIC MORPHINE TREATMENT ON THE INTERACTION BETWEEN THE PERIAQUEDUCTAL GREY AND THE NUCLEUS-RAPHE-MAGNUS OF THE RAT.
003727 04-03

GROOMING

POSTSWIM GROOMING IN MICE INHIBITED BY DOPAMINE-RECEPTOR ANTAGONISTS AND BY CANNABINOIDS.
000359 01-04

SYSTEMIC AND INTRAVENTRICULAR PROLACTIN INDUCES EXCESSIVE GROOMING.
000378 01-04

EVOKED-POTENTIAL CHANGES IN THE SUPERIOR-COLLICULUS PARALLEL THE LESION-INDUCED DEVELOPMENT OF GROOMING REFLEXES IN THE CAT. (PH.D. DISSERTATION).
001179 02-03

ACTH-INDUCED GROOMING INVOLVES HIGH-AFFINITY OPIATE-RECEPTORS.
· 002985 03-04

GROUP

A DOUBLE-BLIND GROUP COMPARATIVE-TRIAL OF MIANSERIN AND DIAZEPAM IN DEPRESSED-OUTPATIENTS.
000592 01-09

A DOUBLE-BLIND PARALLEL GROUP COMPARISON OF SINGLE-BEDTIME-DOSES OF HALAZEPAM AND PLACEBO.
002079 02-10

MULTIINSTITUTIONAL-STUDY ON THE TERATOGENICITY AND FETAL TOXICITY OF ANTIEPILEPTIC-DRUGS: A REPORT OF A COLLABORATIVE-STUDY GROUP IN JAPAN.
002442 02-15

DIFFICULTIES ENCOUNTERED DURING A CONTROLLED STUDY OF A NEW HYPNOTIC-DRUG (TRIAZOLAM) BY A GROUP OF GENERAL-PRACTITIONERS.
003155 03-07

GROUP VERSUS INDIVIDUAL COGNITIVE-THERAPY: A PILOT-STUDY.
003257 03-09

EFFECT OF THE POSITION OF THE PHENOLIC GROUP IN MORPHINANS ON THEIR AFFINITY FOR OPIATE-RECEPTOR BINDING.
003702 04-02

GROUPS

ESR STUDIES OF BOVINE PLASMA AMINE-OXIDASE: PROBING OF THE ENVIRONMENT ABOUT THE SUBSTRATE LIBERATED SULFHYDRYL GROUPS IN THE ACTIVE SITE. (UNPUBLISHED PAPER).
001066 02-01

TREATMENT OF ASTHENO-DEPRESSIVE-DISORDERS WITH MINAPRINE (CANTOR). MULTICENTER-STUDY OF 248 CASES EVALUATED WITH THE FATIGUE STUDY GROUPS NO. 4 CLINICAL-SCALE.
001980 02-09

A RESEARCH PARADIGM TO INVESTIGATE THE EFFECT OF MANIPULATION ON SOCIAL-BEHAVIOR IN GROUPS.
003007 03-04

MEDICATION GROUPS FOR PSYCHIATRIC-PATIENTS.
003582 03-17

GROWTH

INHIBITION OF GROWTH IN YOUNG MICE TREATED WITH PENTAZOCINE: REVERSAL BY NALTREXONE.
000318 01-03

STRETCH-INDUCED MYOTUBE GROWTH CORRELATES WITH NA-PUMP ACTIVATION. (UNPUBLISHED PAPER).
002087 02-10

THE EFFECTS OF CHRONIC METHYLPHENIDATE TREATMENT ON GROWTH AND ENDOCRINE FUNCTION IN THE DEVELOPING RAT.
003811 04-03

ACTIVITY AND CATCH-UP GROWTH IN HYPOTHYROID RATS.
004190 04-04

GROWTH-FACTOR

NERVE GROWTH-FACTOR STIMULATES DEVELOPMENT OF SUBSTANCE-P IN THE EMBRYONIC SPINAL-CORD.
003881 04-03

GROWTH-HORMONE

ADMINISTRATION OF ANTISOMATOSTATIN SERUM TO RATS REVERSES THE INHIBITION OF PULSATILE GROWTH-HORMONE SECRETION PRODUCED BY INJECTION OF METERGOLINE BUT NOT YOHIMBINE. (UNPUBLISHED PAPER).
000019 01-03

L TRYPTOPHAN INJECTION ENHANCES PULSATILE GROWTH-HORMONE SECRETION IN THE RAT. (UNPUBLISHED PAPER).
000020 01-03

MORPHINE ACTS THROUGH ALPHA-ADRENERGIC AND SEROTONINERGIC NEURONS TO STIMULATE GROWTH-HORMONE SECRETION IN THE DOG.
000088 01-03

EFFECTS OF NORADRENERGIC AGONISTS AND ANTAGONISTS ON GROWTH-HORMONE SECRETION UNDER GAMMA HYDROXYBUTYRATE NARCOANALGESIA IN THE RAT.
000262 01-03

GROWTH-HORMONE AFTER TRH IN WOMEN WITH DEPRESSIVE-ILLNESS.
000606 01-09

GROWTH-HORMONE (GH) RELEASE FOLLOWING THYROTROPIN-RELEASING-HORMONE (TRH) INJECTION IN MANIC-PATIENTS RECEIVING LITHIUM-CARBONATE.
000645 01-09

CORTICOSTERONE INCREASES THE SYNTHESIS OF A SOLUBLE PROTEIN IN PITUITARY-GLANDS FROM ADRENALECTOMIZED MALE RATS WHICH PRECIPITATES WITH ANTI-RAT GROWTH-HORMONE ANTISERUM. (UNPUBLISHED PAPER).
001122 02-03

INFLUENCE OF NOMIFENSINE ON GROWTH-HORMONE, PROLACTIN, LUTEINISING-HORMONE AND THYREOTROPIN IN HEALTHY SUBJECTS AND HYPERPROLACTINAEMIC-PATIENTS.
002137 02-11

CHARACTERIZATION OF ERGOT AND NONERGOT SEROTONIN ANTAGONISTS BY PROLACTIN AND GROWTH-HORMONE PROFILES DURING WAKEFULNESS AND SLEEP.
002217 02-13

EFFECT OF L TRYPTOPHAN ON APOMORPHINE-INDUCED GROWTH-HORMONE SECRETION IN NORMAL SUBJECTS.
002253 02-13

PLASMA HDL CHOLESTEROL AND GROWTH-HORMONE IN EPILEPTICS TREATED WITH ANTICONVULSANTS.
002260 02-13

THE CLOCK AND THE BLUE GUITAR: STUDIES OF HUMAN GROWTH-HORMONE SECRETION IN SLEEP AND WAKING. (UNPUBLISHED PAPER).
002346 02-14

PSYCHOTROPIC-DRUGS DO NOT INTERFERE WITH RADIOLIGAND ASSAYS FOR PROLACTIN, CORTISOL, AND GROWTH-HORMONE.
002511 02-16

EFFECTS OF ELECTROCONVULSIVE-TREATMENT ON GROWTH-HORMONE SECRETION INDUCED BY MONOAMINE-RECEPTOR AGONISTS IN RESERPINE PRETREATED RATS.
002664 03-03

DIFFERENTIAL-EFFECTS OF CANNABINOID EXPOSURE AND STRESS ON PLASMA PROLACTIN, GROWTH-HORMONE AND CORTICOSTERONE LEVELS IN MALE MICE.
002695 03-03

EFFECT OF GROWTH-HORMONE ON MEMORY IN MICE.
003014 03-04

DIURNAL GROWTH-HORMONE RESPONSES TO DEXTROAMPHETAMINE IN NORMAL YOUNG MEN AND POSTMENOPAUSAL-WOMEN.
003411 03-13

LYMPHOCYTE MONOAMINE-OXIDASE AND PLASMA PROLACTIN AND GROWTH-HORMONE IN TARDIVE-DYSKINESIA.
003499 03-15

DIFFERENT EFFECTS OF TRICYCLIC-ANTIDEPRESSANTS AND TETRACYCLIC-ANTIDEPRESSANTS ON THE RELEASE OF TSH, PROLACTIN, AND GROWTH-HORMONE AFTER ADMINISTRATION OF THYROSTIMULATING-RELEASING-HORMONE IN MANIC-DEPRESSIVES.
004407 04-09

PROLACTIN AND GROWTH-HORMONE STUDIES IN SCHIZOPHRENIC-PATIENTS AND NORMAL CONTROLS.
004538 04-13

GTP

A HIGH-AFFINITY GTP BINDING-SITE IN RAT-BRAIN. (UNPUBLISHED PAPER).
001442 02-03

STIMULATION OF ADENYLATE-CYCLASE IN RAT STRIATUM BY PERGOLIDE: INFLUENCE OF GTP.
001448 02-03

OPIOIDS, NORADRENALINE AND GTP ANALOGS INHIBIT CHOLERA-TOXIN ACTIVATED ADENYLATE-CYCLASE IN NEUROBLASTOMA-X GLIOMA HYBRID CELLS.
003975 04-03

GUAIPHENESIN

BEHAVIOURAL-EFFECTS OF ACETYLSALICYLIC-ACID, PARACETAMOL, CAFFEINE, GUAIPHENESIN AND THEIR COMBINATIONS.
001805 02-04

GUANETHIDINE
COMPARISONS OF THE EFFECTS OF GUANETHIDINE, 6 HYDROXYDOPAMINE AND DIETHYLDITHIOCARBAMATE ON RETENTION OF PASSIVE-AVOIDANCE.
001742 02-04
THE IMPORTANCE OF CATECHOLAMINE UPTAKE INHIBITION IN THE REVERSAL OF GUANETHIDINE BLOCKADE OF ADRENERGIC NEURONS.
003900 04-03

GUANINE-NUCLEOTIDES
GUANINE-NUCLEOTIDES INHIBIT BINDING OF AGONISTS AND ANTAGONISTS TO SOLUBLE OPIATE-RECEPTORS. (UNPUBLISHED PAPER).
001035 02-01
EFFECTS OF GUANINE-NUCLEOTIDES ON CNS NEUROPEPTIDE-RECEPTORS. (UNPUBLISHED PAPER).
001383 02-03
DIFFERENTIAL REGULATION BY GUANINE-NUCLEOTIDES OF OPIATE AGONIST AND ANTAGONIST RECEPTOR INTERACTIONS.
002688 03-03
MULTIPLE ALPHA2-NORADRENERGIC-RECEPTOR SITES IN RAT-BRAIN: SELECTIVE REGULATION OF HIGH-AFFINITY (3H)CLONIDINE BINDING BY GUANINE-NUCLEOTIDES AND DIVALENT-CATIONS.
003992 04-03

GUANOSINE
THE EFFECT OF ADENOSINE AND GUANOSINE ON THE CONTENT OF SEROTONIN AND CATECHOLAMINES IN THE BRAIN IN THE RESTORATION PERIOD FOLLOWING EXPERIMENTAL CLINICAL DEATH.
003882 04-03

GUANOSINE-CYCLIC-MONOPHOSPHATE
LITHIUM ANTAGONISM OF ETHANOL-INDUCED DEPLETION OF CEREBELLAR GUANOSINE-CYCLIC-MONOPHOSPHATE AND STIMULATION OF STRIATAL DOPAMINE RELEASE.
002242 02-13

GUANOSINE-NUCLEOTIDES
THE EFFECT OF GUANOSINE-NUCLEOTIDES ON (3H)SULPIRIDE BINDING TO RAT STRIATAL MEMBRANES.
002722 03-03

GUANYL-NUCLEOTIDES
ENDOGENOUS GUANYL-NUCLEOTIDES: COMPONENTS OF THE STRIATUM WHICH CONFER DOPAMINE SENSITIVITY TO ADENYLATE-CYCLASE.
001313 02-03
MOLECULAR ACTIONS OF OPIATES: HISTORICAL OVERVIEW AND NEW FINDINGS ON OPIATE-RECEPTOR INTERACTIONS WITH ENKEPHALINS AND GUANYL-NUCLEOTIDES.
002613 02-17
EFFECT OF DOPAMINE ON ACTIVATION OF RAT STRIATAL ADENYLATE-CYCLASE BY FREE MG2 AND GUANYL-NUCLEOTIDES.
002825 03-03

GUANYLATE-CYCLASE
GUANYLATE-CYCLASE -- CYCLIC-GMP IN MOUSE CEREBRAL-CORTEX AND CEREBELLUM: MODIFICATION BY ANTICONVULSANTS.
003956 04-03

GUANYLYLIMIDODIPHOSPHATE
CENTRAL BLOOD-PRESSURE EFFECTS OF GUANYLYLIMIDODIPHOSPHATE AND CYCLIC-GUANOSINE-MONOPHOSPHATE.
000266 01-03

GUIDE
THE LITHIUM RATIO AS A GUIDE TO PATIENT COMPLIANCE.
000940 01-17
PHARMACOMANOMETRIC-STUDIES OF COLONIC MOTILITY AS A GUIDE TO THE CHEMOTHERAPY OF SCHIZOPHRENIA.
001930 02-08
THE USE AND MISUSE OF SLEEPING-PILLS: A CLINICAL GUIDE.
002150 02-11
LITHIUM TREATMENT OF MANIC-DEPRESSIVE-ILLNESS. A PRACTICAL GUIDE.
004408 04-09

GUIDELINES
GUIDELINES FOR THE CLINICAL-EVALUATION OF ANALGESIC-DRUGS.
002584 02-17
GUIDELINES EMPLOYED BY THE FOOD-AND-DRUG-ADMINISTRATION IN DRUG SCHEDULING.
003586 03-17
GUIDELINES FOR SCHEDULING DRUGS UNDER THE CONTROLLED-SUBSTANCES-ACT.
003606 03-17
GUIDELINES ON THE DIAGNOSIS AND TREATMENT OF DEPRESSION.
004376 04-09

GUINEA-PIG
INFLUENCE OF CELLULAR-TRANSPORT ON THE INTERACTION OF AMINO-ACIDS WITH GAMMA AMINOBUTYRIC-ACID-RECEPTORS (GABA) IN THE ISOLATED OLFACTORY-CORTEX OF THE GUINEA-PIG.
000034 01-03
HIGH-AFFINITY BINDING OF THE ANTITUSSIVE DEXTROMETHORPHAN IN GUINEA-PIG BRAIN.
000061 01-03
STUDIES ON THE DISTRIBUTION OF 14C SULPIRIDE AND ITS METABOLITES IN THE RAT AND GUINEA-PIG.
000078 01-03

ACTIONS OF CHLORPROMAZINE, HALOPERIDOL AND PIMOZIDE ON LIPID METABOLISM IN GUINEA-PIG BRAIN SLICES.
000129 01-03
EFFECT OF CHRONIC-TREATMENT WITH ANTIDEPRESSANTS ON BETA-ADRENERGIC-RECEPTOR BINDING IN GUINEA-PIG BRAIN.
000135 01-03
MET-ENKEPHALIN-ARG6-PHE7 INTERACTS WITH THE KAPPA-RECEPTORS ON GUINEA-PIG ILEUM.
001110 02-03
ENHANCED TRANSFER OF EXPERIMENTAL ALLERGIC-ENCEPHALOMYELITIS WITH STRAIN-13 GUINEA-PIG LYMPH-NODE CELLS: REQUIREMENT FOR CULTURE WITH SPECIFIC ANTIGEN AND ALLOGENIC PERITONEAL EXUDATE CELLS. (UNPUBLISHED PAPER).
001201 02-03
PERSISTENT EFFECTS OF HIGH-CONCENTRATIONS OF CHLORPROMAZINE ON 3H PROPYLBENZILYLCHOLINE-MUSTARD BINDING TO MUSCARINIC-RECEPTORS IN GUINEA-PIG INTESTINAL-MUSCLE STRIPS.
001266 02-03
INHIBITION OF THE ACTION OF CHOLECYSTOKININ-OCTAPEPTIDE ON THE GUINEA-PIG ILEUM MYENTERIC PLEXUS BY DIBUTYRYL-CYCLIC-GUANOSINE-MONOPHOSPHATE.
001291 02-03
COMPARATIVE-EFFECTS OF SOMATOSTATIN AND ENKEPHALINS ON THE GUINEA-PIG ILEUM AND THE RAT VAS-DEFERENS.
001302 02-03
INHIBITORY ACTION OF ADENOSINE ON SYNAPTIC TRANSMISSION IN THE HIPPOCAMPUS OF THE GUINEA-PIG IN VITRO.
001401 02-03
LOCALIZATION OF SENSITIVE SITES TO TAURINE, GAMMA AMINOBUTYRIC-ACID, GLYCINE AND BETA ALANINE IN THE MOLECULAR LAYER OF GUINEA-PIG CEREBELLAR SLICES.
001402 02-03
ALTERED LEVELS OF BETA ENDORPHIN FRAGMENTS AFTER CHRONIC MORPHINE TREATMENT OF GUINEA-PIG ILEUM IN VITRO AND IN VIVO.
001404 02-03
THE EXCITATORY ACTION OF ACETYLCHOLINE ON HIPPOCAMPAL NEURONES OF THE GUINEA-PIG AND RAT MAINTAINED IN VITRO.
002704 03-03
EFFECTS OF NEOMYCIN ON CALCIUM AND POLYPHOSPHOINOSITIDE METABOLISM OF GUINEA-PIG SYNAPTOSOMES.
002741 03-03
INHIBITORY ACTIONS OF TAUROCYAMINE, HYPOTAURINE, HOMOTAURINE, TAURINE AND GABA ON SPIKE DISCHARGES OF PURKINJE-CELLS, AND LOCALIZATION OF SENSITIVE SITES, IN GUINEA-PIG CEREBELLAR SLICES.
002846 03-03
PROSTAGLANDINS, CLONIDINE AND SEXUAL-RECEPTIVITY IN THE GUINEA-PIG.
003017 03-04
COMPARISON OF THE POTENCIES OF CLEBOPRIDE AND OTHER SUBSTITUTED BENZAMIDE DRUGS ON ISOLATED GASTROINTESTINAL TRACT OF THE GUINEA-PIG AND RAT.
003928 04-03
PROPERTIES OF A CDP-DIGLYCERIDE-HYDROLASE FROM GUINEA-PIG BRAIN.
003987 04-03
THE EFFECT OF CHRONIC LEVODOPA ON HALOPERIDOL-INDUCED BEHAVIORAL-SUPERSENSITIVITY IN THE GUINEA-PIG.
004249 04-04

GUINEA-PIGS
AMPHETAMINE-INDUCED HYPERSENSITIVITY IN GUINEA-PIGS.
000498 01-04
OBSERVATIONS ON CHLORALOSE-INDUCED MYOCLONUS IN GUINEA-PIGS.
001164 02-03
CHARACTERISTICS OF OSCILLATORY CONTRACTIONS ELICITED BY NALOXONE IN ILEUM PREPARATION FROM MORPHINE-DEPENDENT GUINEA-PIGS.
001491 02-03
TESTOSTERONE POTENTIATION OF THE EFFECTIVENESS OF ACTH1-24 ON THE INDUCTION OF THE STRETCH-YAWNING-SYNDROME (SYS) IN MALE GUINEA-PIGS.
003074 03-04

GUITAR
THE CLOCK AND THE BLUE GUITAR: STUDIES OF HUMAN GROWTH-HORMONE SECRETION IN SLEEP AND WAKING. (UNPUBLISHED PAPER).
002346 02-14

GUT
SEROTONIN PARTICIPATION IN GUT WITHDRAWAL FROM OPIATES.
000109 01-03

H-REFLEX
DES-TYROSINE-GAMMA-ENDORPHIN: H-REFLEX RESPONSE SIMILAR TO NEUROLEPTICS.
004540 04-13

HA-966
HA-966 EFFECTS ON STRIATAL DOPAMINE METABOLISM: IMPLICATIONS FOR DOPAMINE COMPARTMENTALIZAION.
001150 02-03

CROSS-TOLERANCE OF DOPAMINE METABOLISM TO BACLOFEN, GAMMA
BUTYROLACTONE AND HA-966 IN THE STRIATUM AND OLFACTORY
TUBERCLE OF THE RAT.
002681 03-03

IN VIVO VOLTAMMETRIC INVESTIGATIONS INTO THE ACTION OF HA-966
ON CENTRAL DOPAMINERGIC NEURONS.
002832 03-03

HABENULAR
INFLUENCE OF DOPAMINERGIC-SYSTEMS ON THE LATERAL HABENULAR
NUCLEUS OF THE RAT.
001365 02-03

HABENULO-INTERPEDUNCULAR
ANESTHETICS AND THE HABENULO-INTERPEDUNCULAR SYSTEM:
SELECTIVE SPARING OF METABOLIC ACTIVITY.
003833 04-03

HABIT
THE SMOKING HABIT AND PSYCHOPHARMACOLOGICAL-EFFECTS OF
NICOTINE.
003577 03-17

EFFECTS OF ANISOMYCIN ON RETENTION OF THE PASSIVE-AVOIDANCE
HABIT AS A FUNCTION OF AGE.
004097 04-04

HABITS
SMOKING AND VIGILANCE: THE EFFECTS OF TOBACCO SMOKING ON CFF
AS RELATED TO PERSONALITY AND SMOKING HABITS.
002368 02-14

HABITUATION
EFFECT OF BETA ENDORPHIN AND NALOXONE ON ACQUISITION,
MEMORY, AND RETRIEVAL OF SHUTTLE AVOIDANCE AND
HABITUATION LEARNING IN RATS.
000410 01-04

EFFECT OF PROPRANOLOL AND PHENOTHIAZINES ON ELECTRODERMAL
ORIENTING AND HABITUATION IN SCHIZOPHRENIA.
003174 03-08

HABITUATION OF ELECTRODERMAL AND RESPIRATORY RESPONSES TO
VISUAL STIMULI AS A FUNCTION OF PERSONALITY DIFFERENCES IN
AFFECT LEVEL.
003414 03-13

HABITUATION OF THE THE HEAD-POKE RESPONSE: EFFECTS OF AN
AMPHETAMINE BARBITURATE MIXTURE, PLG AND FENFLURAMINE.
004159 04-04

HAIR-LOSS
LITHIUM AND HAIR-LOSS. (UNPUBLISHED PAPER).
002005 02-09

HALAZEPAM
A DOUBLE-BLIND PARALLEL GROUP COMPARISON OF SINGLE-BEDTIME-
DOSES OF HALAZEPAM AND PLACEBO.
002079 02-10

CLINICAL-TRIAL OF HALAZEPAM AND CLORAZEPATE: CONSIDERATIONS
OF A SINGLE-BEDTIME-DOSE.
003277 03-10

HALF-LIFE
LITHIUM ELIMINATION HALF-LIFE AND DURATION OF THERAPY.
004369 04-09

HALLUCINATIONS
CIMETIDINE TOXICITY MANIFESTED AS PARANOIA AND
HALLUCINATIONS.
000829 01-15

HYPNAGOGIC AND HYPNOPOMPIC HALLUCINATIONS DURING
AMITRIPTYLINE TREATMENT.
000850 01-15

AN OLD SIDE-EFFECT REVISITED: VISUAL HALLUCINATIONS.
000886 01-15

AGITATION, DISORIENTATION, AND HALLUCINATIONS IN PATIENTS ON
CIMETIDINE: A REPORT OF THREE CASES AND LITERATURE REVIEW.
000896 01-15

HALLUCINATORY
HALLUCINATORY AND DELUSIONAL-STATES IN CONNECTION WITH BLOOD-
PRESSURE AND EEG.
000814 01-14

ANIMAL-MODEL OF PSYCHOSIS: HALLUCINATORY BEHAVIORS IN
MONKEYS DURING THE LATE STAGE OF CONTINUOUS AMPHETAMINE
INTOXICATION.
002988 03-04

HALLUCINOGEN
RAT-BRAIN STEADY-STATE LEVELS OF CYCLIC-NUCLEOTIDES AS AN
ENDPOINT OF LSD-LIKE HALLUCINOGEN EFFECTS. (PH.D.
DISSERTATION).
001426 02-03

HALLUCINOGENIC
ENTHEOGENIC (HALLUCINOGENIC) EFFECTS OF METHYLERGONOVINE.
000742 01-12

THE WORLD OF HALLUCINOGENIC PLANTS.
003396 03-12

LACK OF SPECIFICITY OF AN ANIMAL BEHAVIOR MODEL FOR
HALLUCINOGENIC DRUG ACTION.
004250 04-04

HALLUCINOGENIC-AGENT
DISCRIMINATIVE-STIMULUS PROPERTIES OF THE HALLUCINOGENIC-AGENT
DOM.
004260 04-04

HALLUCINOGENIC-DRUGS
LONG-LASTING EFFECTS OF CHRONIC ADMINISTRATION OF
HALLUCINOGENIC-DRUGS ON RAT SOCIAL AND EMOTIONAL-BEHAVIOR.
(PH.D. DISSERTATION).
003029 03-04

THE ROLE OF CENTRAL SEROTONERGIC MECHANISMS ON HEAD-TWITCH
AND BACKWARD LOCOMOTION INDUCED BY HALLUCINOGENIC-DRUGS.
003397 03-12

HALLUCINOGENS
HALLUCINOGENS.
002587 02-17

A COMMON MECHANISM FOR LYSERGIC-ACID, INDOLEALKYLAMINE AND
PHENETHYLAMINE HALLUCINOGENS: SEROTONERGIC MEDIATION OF
BEHAVIORAL-EFFECTS IN RATS.
004007 04-03

HALOGENATED
THE EFFECT OF PHENELZINE AND SOME OF ITS PARA HALOGENATED
DERIVATIVES ON THE LEVELS OF BRAIN TYRAMINE AND OCTOPAMINE
IN THE MOUSE.
001077 02-02

HALOPEMIDE
EFFECTS OF HALOPEMIDE ON POTASSIUM-INDUCED RELEASE OF
RADIOLABELED NEUROTRANSMITTERS FROM RAT CEREBROCORTICAL
SLICES IN VITRO.
001347 02-03

EFFECTS OF HALOPEMIDE ON GABA-RECEPTOR BINDING, UPTAKE AND
RELEASE.
003913 04-03

HALOPERIDOL
STEREOSPECIFIC BINDING OF 3H HALOPERIDOL IN RAT DORSAL SPINAL-
CORD.
000070 01-03

EFFECT OF NALOXONE, HALOPERIDOL AND PROPRANOLOL ON CYCLIC-
ADENOSINE-MONOPHOSPHATE CONTENT OF RAT AMYGDALA.
000071 01-03

INCORPORATION OF 4.5 3H LEUCINE INTO THE LIMBIC-SYSTEM OF ICR
MICE AS A LONG-TERM EFFECT OF HALOPERIDOL APPLICATION.
000118 01-03

ACTIONS OF CHLORPROMAZINE, HALOPERIDOL AND PIMOZIDE ON LIPID
METABOLISM IN GUINEA-PIG BRAIN SLICES.
000129 01-03

HYPOPHYSECTOMY PREVENTS THE STRIATAL DOPAMINE-RECEPTOR
SUPERSENSITIVITY PRODUCED BY CHRONIC HALOPERIDOL TREATMENT.
000132 01-03

EFFECTS OF CHRONIC HALOPERIDOL ON CAUDATE 3H SPIROPERIDOL
BINDING IN LESIONED RATS.
000255 01-03

ENHANCED SUPPRESSION OF CONDITIONED AVOIDANCE RESPONSE BY
HALOPERIDOL BUT NOT PHENOXYBENZAMINE IN RATS WITH
BILATERAL PARAFASCICULAR LESIONS.
000334 01-04

REWARD SYSTEM DEPRESSION FOLLOWING CHRONIC AMPHETAMINE:
ANTAGONISM BY HALOPERIDOL.
000342 01-04

MORPHINE VERSUS HALOPERIDOL CATALEPSY IN THE RAT: A
BEHAVIORAL-ANALYSIS OF POSTURAL SUPPORT MECHANISMS.
000376 01-04

ANTINOCICEPTIVE-EFFECT OF MORPHINE, OPIOID ANALGESICS AND
HALOPERIDOL INJECTED INTO THE CAUDATE-NUCLEUS OF THE RAT.
000414 01-04

EFFECTS OF THE POTENTIAL NEUROLEPTIC-PEPTIDE DES-TYR1-GAMMA-
ENDORPHIN AND HALOPERIDOL ON APOMORPHINE-INDUCED
BEHAVIOURAL-SYNDROMES IN RATS AND MICE.
000441 01-04

THE LOCOMOTOR-EFFECT OF CLONIDINE AND ITS INTERACTION WITH
ALPHA FLUPENTHIXOL OR HALOPERIDOL IN THE DEVELOPING RAT.
000445 01-04

CHRONIC ADMINISTRATION OF HALOPERIDOL DURING DEVELOPMENT:
BEHAVIORAL-EFFECTS AND PSYCHOPHARMACOLOGICAL-EFFECTS.
000481 01-04

EFFECT OF MORPHINE IN COMBINATION WITH CHLORPROMAZINE AND
HALOPERIDOL ON OPERANT-BEHAVIOR.
000486 01-04

A COMPARISON OF THE CARDIOVASCULAR EFFECTS OF HALOPERIDOL,
THIORIDAZINE AND CHLORPROMAZINE-HCL.
000512 01-05

INFLUENCE OF ROUTE-OF-ADMINISTRATION ON HALOPERIDOL PLASMA
LEVELS IN PSYCHOTIC-PATIENTS.
000549 01-08

EFFECTS OF TRIFLUOPERAZINE, CHLORPROMAZINE, AND HALOPERIDOL
UPON TEMPORAL INFORMATION-PROCESSING BY SCHIZOPHRENIC-
PATIENTS.
000554 01-08

DOUBLE-BLIND COMPARISON OF HALOPERIDOL AND THIOTHIXENE WITH
AFTERCARE TREATMENT EVALUATION IN PSYCHIATRIC-OUTPATIENTS
WITH SCHIZOPHRENIA.
000574 01-08

ADVANTAGE OF PHARMACOKINETIC DATA DURING TREATMENT OF PSYCHOSES WITH HALOPERIDOL.
000577 01-08

CLINICAL-EXPERIENCE WITH LOW-DOSES OF HALOPERIDOL IN THE TREATMENT OF NEUROSES.
000454 01-10

PRINCIPAL AND DIFFERENTIAL-EFFECTS OF HALOPERIDOL AND PLACEBO TREATMENTS UPON SPEECH DISFLUENCIES IN STUTTERERS.
000713 01-11

PSYCHOPHARMACOLOGY OF HALOPERIDOL.
000771 01-13

THE ULTRASTRUCTURAL CHANGES OF SYNAPSES IN RAT FOLLOWING LONG-TERM ADMINISTRATION OF THE NEUROLEPTICS RESERPINE AND HALOPERIDOL.
000795 01-13

RAPID CONTROL OF ACUTE PATIENTS THROUGH THE ADMINISTRATION OF HALOPERIDOL.
000818 01-14

TWENTY YEARS HALOPERIDOL: CLINICAL-EFFECTIVENESS AND THEORETICAL IMPLICATIONS.
000938 01-17

EFFECTS OF CHRONIC-TREATMENT WITH L SULPIRIDE AND HALOPERIDOL ON CENTRAL DOPAMINE TURNOVER EVALUATED IN DOPAMINE CELL BODY AND NERVE TERMINAL-RICH AREAS.
001096 02-03

PRESYNAPTIC DOPAMINE-RECEPTORS: INSENSITIVITY TO KAINIC-ACID AND THE DEVELOPMENT OF SUPERSENSITIVITY FOLLOWING CHRONIC HALOPERIDOL.
001117 02-03

DOPAMINE SYNTHESIS: TOLERANCE TO HALOPERIDOL AND SUPERSENSITIVITY TO APOMORPHINE DEPEND ON PRESYNAPTIC-RECEPTORS.
001129 02-03

ACUTE AND CHRONIC HALOPERIDOL TREATMENT: EFFECTS ON NIGROSTRIATAL DOPAMINERGIC-SYSTEM ACTIVITY.
001153 02-03

RAPID DEVELOPMENT OF HYPERSENSITIVITY AND HYPOSENSITIVITY TO APOMORPHINE AND HALOPERIDOL: ROLE OF NOREPINEPHRINE-RECEPTOR MECHANISMS IN CNS.
001178 02-03

LONG-TERM HALOPERIDOL TREATMENT OF MICE: A CHANGE IN BETA-ADRENERGIC-RECEPTOR RESPONSIVENESS.
001206 02-03

INTERINDIVIDUAL VARIATION OF CLINICAL-RESPONSE TO HALOPERIDOL.
001230 02-03

EFFECTS OF CHRONIC-TREATMENT WITH L SULPIRIDE AND HALOPERIDOL ON CENTRAL MONOAMINERGIC MECHANISMS.
001240 02-03

THE HYPERKINETIC-SYNDROME FOLLOWING LONG-TERM HALOPERIDOL TREATMENT: INVOLVEMENT OF DOPAMINE AND NORADRENALINE.
001299 02-03

LONG-TERM EFFECTS OF HALOPERIDOL, CLOZAPINE, AND METHADONE ON RAT STRIATAL CHOLINERGIC AND DOPAMINERGIC DYNAMICS.
001325 02-03

LONG-TERM HALOPERIDOL TREATMENT AND FACTORS EFFECTING THE ACTIVITY OF STRIATAL TYROSINE-HYDROXYLASE.
001348 02-03

BEHAVIORAL-CORRELATES AND BIOCHEMICAL-CORRELATES AFTER HALOPERIDOL AND CLOZAPINE LONG-TERM-TREATMENT.
001422 02-03

EVIDENCE FOR INVOLVEMENT OF DOPAMINE IN THE ACTION OF DIAZEPAM: POTENTIATION OF HALOPERIDOL AND CHLORPROMAZINE ACTION IN THE BRAIN.
001428 02-03

EFFECTS OF HALOPERIDOL AND D-AMPHETAMINE ON IN VIVO 3H SPIROPERIDOL BINDING IN THE RAT-FOREBRAIN.
001461 02-03

CHRONIC ADMINISTRATION OF HALOPERIDOL DURING DEVELOPMENT: LATER PSYCHOPHARMACOLOGICAL RESPONSES TO APOMORPHINE AND ARECOLINE.
001470 02-03

EFFECTS OF HALOPERIDOL, A DOPAMINE-RECEPTOR ANTAGONIST, ON A DELAYED TYPE HYPERSENSITIVITY REACTION TO 1 CHLORODINITROBENZENE IN MICE.
001473 02-03

LONG-TERM APPLICATION OF HALOPERIDOL: EFFECT OF ANTICHOLINERGIC TREATMENT ON THE RATE OF DOPAMINE SYNTHESIS.
001490 02-03

EFFECT OF LONG-TERM-TREATMENT WITH HALOPERIDOL AND SULPIRIDE ON DIFFERENT TYPES OF DOPAMINERGIC-RECEPTORS.
001512 02-03

NEUROLEPTIC TREATMENT FOR A SUBSTANTIAL PROPORTION OF ADULT LIFE: BEHAVIOURAL-SEQUELAE OF 9 MONTHS HALOPERIDOL ADMINISTRATION.
001858 02-05

CLINICAL STATE, PLASMA LEVELS OF HALOPERIDOL AND PROLACTIN:
001943 02-08

A COMPARISON OF HALOPERIDOL, LITHIUM-CARBONATE AND THEIR COMBINATION IN THE TREATMENT OF MANIA.
001990 02-09

A CONTROLLED DOUBLE-BLIND STUDY OF HALOPERIDOL VERSUS THIORIDAZINE IN THE TREATMENT OF RESTLESS MENTALLY-SUBNORMAL-PATIENTS: SERUM LEVELS AND CLINICAL-EFFECTS.
002185 02-11

THE EFFECT OF BENZTROPINE-MESYLATE ON THE PROLACTIN RESPONSE TO HALOPERIDOL.
002238 02-13

HALOPERIDOL PLASMA LEVEL MONITORING IN PSYCHIATRIC-PATIENTS.
002267 02-13

CNV VARIATIONS INDUCED BY THE ADMINISTRATION OF DIAZEPAM, HALOPERIDOL, PHENELZINE AND D-AMPHETAMINE.
002355 02-14

HALOPERIDOL STIMULATION OF PROLACTIN SECRETION: HOW MANY BLOOD SAMPLES ARE NEEDED TO DEFINE THE HORMONE RESPONSE?
002505 02-16

SPONTANEOUS ACTIVITY AND APOMORPHINE STEREOTYPY DURING AND AFTER WITHDRAWAL FROM 3 1/2 MONTHS CONTINUOUS ADMINISTRATION OF HALOPERIDOL: SOME METHODOLOGICAL-ISSUES.
002509 02-16

HALOPERIDOL UPDATE: 1958-1980.
002517 02-17

THERAPEUTIC PROFILE OF HALOPERIDOL.
002603 02-17

CENTRAL DEPRESSANT EFFECTS OF CAERULEIN AND CHOLECYSTOKININ-OCTAPEPTIDE (CCK-8) DIFFER FROM THOSE OF DIAZEPAM AND HALOPERIDOL.
002652 03-02

APOMORPHINE HALOPERIDOL INTERACTIONS: DIFFERENT TYPES OF ANTAGONISM IN CORTICAL AND SUBCORTICAL BRAIN REGIONS.
002662 03-03

SUPPRESSION OF AMPHETAMINE-INDUCED EEG AROUSAL IN THE HIPPOCAMPUS OF HALOPERIDOL TREATED RABBITS.
002683 03-03

A COMPARISON OF THE NEUROCHEMICAL-EFFECTS OF BUPRENORPHINE WITH THOSE OF MORPHINE AND HALOPERIDOL IN RATS.
002701 03-03

CHARACTERIZATION OF HALOPERIDOL MEDIATED EFFECTS ON RAT STRIATAL TYROSINE-HYDROXYLASE.
002867 03-03

INCREASED AMPHETAMINE STEREOTYPY AND LONGER HALOPERIDOL CATALEPSY IN SPONTANEOUSLY HYPERTENSIVE-RATS.
002891 03-03

TIME-COURSE OF CHRONIC HALOPERIDOL AND CLOZAPINE UPON OPERANT RATE AND DURATION.
002989 03-04

A COMPARISON OF DOPAMINE-RECEPTOR BLOCKING ASSAY WITH PLASMA DRUG LEVELS OF HALOPERIDOL IN SCHIZOPHRENIC-PATIENTS.
003182 03-08

RAPID TREATMENT OF ACUTE PSYCHOTIC-SYMPTOMS WITH HIGH-DOSE AND LOW-DOSE HALOPERIDOL: BEHAVIORAL-CONSIDERATIONS.
003346 03-11

EFFECTS OF LITHIUM-CARBONATE AND HALOPERIDOL ON COGNITION IN AGGRESSIVE, HOSPITALIZED SCHOOL-AGE CHILDREN.
003360 03-11

EFFECTS OF LITHIUM-CARBONATE AND HALOPERIDOL ON COGNITION IN AGGRESSIVE HOSPITALIZED SCHOOL-AGE CHILDREN.
003361 03-11

HALOPERIDOL — ITS USE IN CHILDREN.
003370 03-11

SERUM HALOPERIDOL LEVELS IN GILLES-DE-LA-TOURETTE-SYNDROME.
003374 03-11

ILEUS COMPLICATING HALOPERIDOL THERAPY.
003511 03-15

MEASUREMENT OF HALOPERIDOL IN HUMAN PLASMA USING REVERSED PHASE HIGH-PERFORMANCE LIQUID-CHROMATOGRAPHY. (UNPUBLISHED PAPER).
003667 04-01

CHLORPROMAZINE, HALOPERIDOL, METOCLOPRAMIDE AND DOMPERIDONE RELEASE PROLACTIN THROUGH DOPAMINE ANTAGONISM AT LOW CONCENTRATIONS BUT PARADOXICALLY INHIBIT PROLACTIN RELEASE AT HIGH-CONCENTRATIONS.
003731 04-03

DOPAMINE METABOLITES IN CAUDATE AND CORTEX AFTER LITHIUM AND HALOPERIDOL. (UNPUBLISHED PAPER).
003738 04-03

DOPAMINE, NORADRENALINE AND 3,4 DIHYDROXYPHENYLACETIC-ACID (DOPAC) LEVELS OF INDIVIDUAL BRAIN NUCLEI, EFFECTS OF HALOPERIDOL AND PARGYLINE.
003792 04-03

INCREASED MESOLIMBIC DOPAMINE BINDING FOLLOWING CHRONIC HALOPERIDOL TREATMENT.
003872 04-03

THE EFFECT OF SMALL DOSES OF HALOPERIDOL AND CLOZAPINE ON BEHAVIORAL SHIFTS IN CATS, ARISING AFTER CESSATION OF ELECTRICAL-STIMULATION OF THE CAUDATE-NUCLEUS.
004067 04-04

EFFECTS OF DOPAMINE, APOMORPHINE, GAMMA HYDROXYBUTYRIC-
ACID, HALOPERIDOL AND PIMOZIDE ON REFLEX BRADYCARDIA IN
RATS.
004085 04-04

AN ANALYSIS OF VISUAL OBJECT REVERSAL LEARNING IN THE
MARMOSET AFTER AMPHETAMINE AND HALOPERIDOL.
004208 04-04

HALOPERIDOL AND DROPERIDOL TREATMENT IN SCHIZOPHRENICS:
CLINICAL APPLICATION OF THE PROLACTIN MODEL.
004332 04-08

MOBILIZATION OF REFRACTORY CHRONIC SCHIZOPHRENICS WITH
HALOPERIDOL.
004337 04-08

· BILATERAL SKIN CONDUCTANCE AND THE PUPILLARY LIGHT DARK
REFLEX: MANIPULATION BY CHLORPROMAZINE, HALOPERIDOL,
SCOPOLAMINE, AND PLACEBO.
004544 04-13

APOMORPHINE, HALOPERIDOL AND THE AVERAGE EVOKED-POTENTIALS
IN NORMAL HUMAN VOLUNTEERS.
004549 04-13

CLINICAL-EVALUATION OF BROMPERIDOL VERSUS HALOPERIDOL IN
PSYCHOTIC-PATIENTS.
004562 04-14

PATHOPHYSIOLOGICAL AND MORPHOLOGICAL CHANGES IN THE CNS
DURING LONG-TERM ADMINISTRATION OF HALOPERIDOL.
004633 04-15

APOMORPHINE-INDUCED STEREOTYPY IN MATURE AND SENESCENT RATS
FOLLOWING CESSATION OF CHRONIC HALOPERIDOL TREATMENT.
004651 04-15

HALOPERIDOL-DECANOATE
INTRAMUSCULAR HALOPERIDOL-DECANOATE FOR NEUROLEPTIC
MAINTENANCE-THERAPY: EFFICACY, DOSAGE SCHEDULE AND PLASMA
LEVELS; AN OPEN MULTICENTER-STUDY.
000758 01-13

HALOPERIDOL-HYDROBROMIDE
THE STRUCTURE OF HALOPERIDOL-HYDROBROMIDE (CHLOROPHENYL-4-
HYDROXYPIPERIDINE-4-FLUOROBUTYROPHENONE HBR).
000002 01-01

HALOPERIDOL-INDUCED
EFFECT OF MOXESTROL ON HALOPERIDOL-INDUCED CHANGES IN
STRIATAL ACETYLCHOLINE LEVELS AND DOPAMINE TURNOVER.
001218 02-03

PRESYNAPTIC AND POSTSYNAPTIC MECHANISMS IN HALOPERIDOL-
INDUCED SENSITIZATION TO DOPAMINERGIC AGONISTS.
001392 02-03

PRESYNAPTIC DOPAMINE-RECEPTORS IN STRIATAL NERVE-ENDINGS:
ABSENCE OF HALOPERIDOL-INDUCED SUPERSENSITIVITY.
001424 02-03

BIPHASIC-EFFECTS OF DIRECT, BUT NOT INDIRECT, GABAMIMETICS AND
ANTAGONISTS ON HALOPERIDOL-INDUCED CATALEPSY.
001826 02-04

HALOPERIDOL-INDUCED TARDIVE-DYSKINESIA IN A CHILD WITH GILLES-
DE-LA-TOURETTES-DISEASE.
002437 02-15

LEVONANTRADOL, A POTENT CANNABINOID RELATED ANALGESIC,
ANTAGONIZES HALOPERIDOL-INDUCED ACTIVATION OF STRIATAL
DOPAMINE SYNTHESIS.
002786 03-03

GLUCOSE SUPPRESSES BASAL FIRING AND HALOPERIDOL-INDUCED
INCREASES IN THE FIRING-RATE OF CENTRAL DOPAMINERGIC
NEURONS.
002880 03-03

LITHIUM EFFECTS ON HALOPERIDOL-INDUCED PRESYNAPTIC AND
POSTSYNAPTIC DOPAMINE-RECEPTOR SUPERSENSITIVITY.
004244 04-04

THE EFFECT OF CHRONIC LEVODOPA ON HALOPERIDOL-INDUCED
BEHAVIORAL-SUPERSENSITIVITY IN THE GUINEA-PIG.
004249 04-04

PROMETHAZINE AND DIAZEPAM POTENTIATE THE HALOPERIDOL-INDUCED
PROLACTIN RESPONSES.
004499 04-13

ı **HALOTHANE**
INTRACELLULAR REDOX STATES UNDER HALOTHANE AND BARBITURATE
ANESTHESIA IN NORMAL, ISCHEMIC, AND ANOXIC MONKEY BRAIN.
000295 01-03

HALOTHANE EFFECT ON C-AMP GENERATION AND HYDROLYSIS IN RAT-
BRAIN.
000305 01-03

INFLUENCE OF IMIPRAMINE AND PARGYLINE ON THE
ARRHYTHMOGENICITY OF EPINEPHRINE DURING HALOTHANE,
ENFLURANE OR METHOXYFLURANE ANESTHESIA IN DOGS.
001539 02-03

DIFFERENCES IN CUTANEOUS SENSORY RESPONSE PROPERTIES OF SINGLE
SOMATOSENSORY CORTICAL NEURONS IN AWAKE AND HALOTHANE
ANESTHETIZED RATS.
002687 03-03

ACCELERATED EXTINCTION AFTER POSTTRIAL HALOTHANE ANESTHESIA IN
RATS: AN AVERSIVE-EFFECT.
003001 03-04

HALOTHANE ACCUMULATION IN RAT-BRAIN AND LIVER.
003774 04-03

HALT
CAN DRUGS HALT MEMORY LOSS?
003447 03-14

HALTING
A MODIFIED VERSION OF THE SIMULTANEOUS DISCONTINUATION OF
PSYCHOTROPIC-DRUGS (COMBINED WITH THE ADMINISTRATION OF
DIURETICS) AS A METHOD OF HALTING PROLONGED ATTACKS OF
SCHIZOPHRENIA.
004584 04-14

HAMILTON-DEPRESSION-RATING-SCALE
DOUBLE-BLIND CONTROLLED EXPERIMENT: AMINEPTINE VERSUS
AMITRIPTYLINE USING THE HAMILTON-DEPRESSION-RATING-SCALE.
002050 02-09

HAMSTER
ALPHA2-ADRENERGIC AMINES, ADENOSINE AND PROSTAGLANDINS
INHIBIT LIPOLYSIS AND CYCLIC-AMP ACCUMULATION IN HAMSTER
ADIPOCYTES IN THE ABSENCE OF EXTRACELLULAR SODIUM.
002728 03-03

EFFECT OF 6 HYDROXYDOPAMINE ON THE FINE STRUCTURE OF THE
HAMSTER PINEAL-GLAND.
003747 04-03

METHADONE REDUCES SEXUAL-PERFORMANCE AND SEXUAL-
MOTIVATION IN THE MALE SYRIAN GOLDEN HAMSTER.
004183 04-04

HAMSTERS
TERATOGENICITY OF IMIPRAMINE AND AMITRIPTYLINE IN FETAL
HAMSTERS.
002410 02-15

PINEAL-GLAND AND MELATONIN INFLUENCE ON CHRONIC ALCOHOL
CONSUMPTION BY HAMSTERS.
003076 03-04

ULTRASTRUCTURAL LOCALIZATION OF MONOAMINES IN NERVE FIBERS
OF THE PINEAL-GLAND IN GOLDEN HAMSTERS.
003666 04-01

HANDBOOK
HANDBOOK OF LITHIUM THERAPY.
000597 01-09

CLINICAL HANDBOOK OF ANTIPSYCHOTIC-DRUG THERAPY.
000961 01-17

HANDEDNESS
HANDEDNESS IN RATS: BLOCKADE OF REACHING-BEHAVIOR BY
UNILATERAL 6 OHDA INJECTIONS INTO SUBSTANTIA-NIGRA AND
CAUDATE-NUCLEUS.
001778 02-04

HANDICAPPED
TARDIVE-DYSKINESIA AND OTHER DRUG-INDUCED MOVEMENT-
DISORDERS AMONG HANDICAPPED CHILDREN AND YOUTH.
004614 04-15

HANDLING
HANDLING IN INFANCY, TASTE-AVERSION, AND BRAIN LATERALITY IN
RATS.
000375 01-04

DOES POSTURAL ASYMMETRY INDICATE DIRECTIONALITY OF ROTATION
.. IN RATS: ROLE OF SEX AND HANDLING.
003061 03-04

HANDLING-INDUCED
NEUROPHARMACOLOGICAL ANALYSIS OF HANDLING-INDUCED SEIZURES
IN GERBILS.
001876 02-06

PYRAZOLE EXACERBATES HANDLING-INDUCED CONVULSIONS IN MICE.
004094 04-04

HANDLING-INDUCED SEIZURES AND ROTATIONAL-BEHAVIOR IN THE
MONGOLIAN-GERBIL.
004216 04-04

HARMALINE
DEPLETION OF EPINEPHRINE IN RAT HYPOTHALAMUS BY RO-4-1284:
INFLUENCE OF PARGYLINE AND HARMALINE.
000100 01-03

A NEW APPROACH TO THE ASSESSMENT OF THE POTENCY OF
REVERSIBLE MONOAMINE-OXIDASE-INHIBITORS IN VIVO, AND ITS
APPLICATION TO D-AMPHETAMINE, P METHOXYAMPHETAMINE AND
HARMALINE.
000900 01-16

HARMALINE-INDUCED
HARMALINE-INDUCED TREMOR: THE BENZODIAZEPINE-RECEPTOR AS A
SITE-OF-ACTION.
001436 02-03

HARMANE
1 METHYL-BETA-CARBOLINE (HARMANE), A POTENT ENDOGENOUS
INHIBITOR OF BENZODIAZEPINE-RECEPTOR BINDING.
001440 02-03

BENZODIAZEPINE ANTAGONISM BY HARMANE AND OTHER BETA
CARBOLINES IN VITRO AND IN VIVO.
004211 04-04

HASHISH
BEHAVIORAL-EFFECTS OF HASHISH IN MICE: II. NURSING-BEHAVIOR AND
DEVELOPMENT OF THE SUCKLINGS.
001626 02-04

BEHAVIORAL-EFFECTS OF HASHISH IN MICE: III. SOCIAL-INTERACTIONS BETWEEN TWO RESIDENTS AND AN INTRUDER MALE.
001776 02-04

BEHAVIORAL-EFFECTS OF HASHISH IN MICE: I. SOCIAL-INTERACTIONS AND NEST-BUILDING-BEHAVIOR OF MALES.
001777 02-04

HATCHING
THE BEHAVIOURAL-STATE DURING CLIMAX (HATCHING) IN THE DOMESTIC-FOWL (GALLUS-DOMESTICUS).
001564 02-04

HAZARDS
HAZARDS OF DRUG USE AMONG THE ELDERLY.
000953 01-17

APPROACHES TO THE PROBLEM OF PREVENTING HAZARDS OF LONG-TERM NEUROLEPTIC TREATMENT AND OF AVOIDING UNNECESSARY DRUGS.
002426 02-15

SOME HAZARDS OF LITHIUM USE.
003498 03-15

HDL
PLASMA HDL CHOLESTEROL AND GROWTH-HORMONE IN EPILEPTICS TREATED WITH ANTICONVULSANTS.
002260 02-13

HEAD-POKE
HABITUATION OF THE THE HEAD-POKE RESPONSE: EFFECTS OF AN AMPHETAMINE BARBITURATE MIXTURE, PLG AND FENFLURAMINE.
004159 04-04

HEAD-SHAKING-BEHAVIOR
THE INVOLVEMENT OF SEROTONERGIC NEURONS IN THE CENTRAL-NERVOUS-SYSTEM AS THE POSSIBLE MECHANISM FOR SLOW HEAD-SHAKING-BEHAVIOR INDUCED BY METHAMPHETAMINE IN RATS.
000408 01-04

HEAD-TURNING
EFFECTS OF INTRAPALLIDAL OPIATE-RECEPTOR AGONISTS ON STRIATALLY-EVOKED HEAD-TURNING.
001785 02-04

HEAD-TWITCH
THE ROLE OF CENTRAL SEROTONERGIC MECHANISMS ON HEAD-TWITCH AND BACKWARD LOCOMOTION INDUCED BY HALLUCINOGENIC-DRUGS.
003397 03-12

HEAD-TWITCHES
MOTOR-DEPRESSION AND HEAD-TWITCHES INDUCED BY IP INJECTION OF GABA.
001788 02-04

HEADACHES
TOFISOPAM IN PSEUDONEURASTHENIA WITH HEADACHES.
002075 02-10

HEADS
QUINUCLIDINYL BENZILATE BINDING IN HOUSEFLY HEADS AND RAT-BRAIN.
003868 04-03

HEALTH-CARE-SERVICES
AIRCRAFT NOISE AND MENTAL-HEALTH: II. USE OF MEDICINES AND HEALTH-CARE-SERVICES.
003647 03-17

HEALTHY
CHRONIC ADMINISTRATION OF CANNABIDIOL TO HEALTHY VOLUNTEERS AND EPILEPTIC-PATIENTS.
000669 01-11

THE INFLUENCE OF LITHIUM-CARBONATE ON MOOD AND PERFORMANCE IN HEALTHY SUBJECTS.
000711 01-11

EEG AND PSYCHOEXPERIMENTAL-STUDIES IN HEALTHY SUBJECTS ON LITHIUM MEDICATION.
000768 01-13

THE EEG EFFECTS OF THYROTROPIN-RELEASING-HORMONE IN HEALTHY SUBJECTS AND CHRONIC SCHIZOPHRENICS.
000770 01-13

EFFECTS OF ANTIDEPRESSANTS ON PITUITARY HORMONAL SECRETIONS IN HEALTHY TEST SUBJECTS, NEUROTIC-PATIENTS, AND ENDOGENOUS DEPRESSIVE-PATIENTS.
002009 02-09

INFLUENCE OF NOMIFENSINE ON GROWTH-HORMONE, PROLACTIN, LUTEINISING-HORMONE AND THYREOTROPIN IN HEALTHY SUBJECTS AND HYPERPROLACTINAEMIC-PATIENTS.
002137 02-11

THE CONTRIBUTION OF ALPHA1 ACID GLYCOPROTEIN, LIPOPROTEINS, AND ALBUMIN TO THE PLASMA BINDING OF PERAZINE, AMITRIPTYLINE, AND NORTRIPTYLINE IN HEALTHY MAN.
002214 02-13

LEVELS OF MINERAL-ELEMENTS IN THE SERUM AND SALIVA OF HEALTHY MALE VOLUNTEERS AFTER A SINGLE-DOSE OF LI2CO3.
002297 02-13

SINGLE-DOSE PHARMACOKINETICS OF DOXEPIN IN HEALTHY VOLUNTEERS.
002303 02-13

SUBJECTIVE DRUG-EFFECTS AND DRUG PREFERENCE IN HEALTHY VOLUNTEERS AS A MODEL OF A DRUGS REINFORCING EFFECTS: STUDIES ON NOMIFENSINE, AMPHETAMINE AND PLACEBO.
002362 02-14

HEMODIALYSATE
BIOCHEMICAL-CHARACTERIZATION AND PHARMACOLOGICAL
CHARACTERIZATION OF A PEPTIDE FROM THE HEMODIALYSATE OF
PSYCHOTIC-PATIENTS.
001049 02-01

HEMODIALYSIS
LITHIUM KINETICS DURING HEMODIALYSIS IN A PATIENT WITH LITHIUM
POISONING.
003524 03-15

HEMODYNAMIC
CORRELATIONS BETWEEN HEMODYNAMIC PARAMETERS OF THE LIVER
AND NOREPINEPHRINE RELEASE UPON HEPATIC-NERVE STIMULATION IN
THE DOG.
001547 02-03
HEMODYNAMIC FAILURE INDUCED BY NARCOTIC AND TOXIC DOSES OF
12 CNS DEPRESSANTS IN INTACT AND PITHED RATS.
001855 02-05
HEMODYNAMIC AND CEREBRAL METABOLIC-STUDY OF DIAZEPAM IN
NEUROSURGICAL-RESUSCITATION.
002231 02-13

HEMOPERFUSION
HEMOPERFUSION FOR CHRONIC SCHIZOPHRENIA: PRELIMINARY
PSYCHIATRIC RESULTS.
003180 03-08

HEMORRHAGE
EFFECT OF PROSTAGLANDINS ON PLASMA CATECHOLAMINES, HEART
AND BLOOD-PRESSURE RESPONSES TO HEMORRHAGE. (UNPUBLISHED
PAPER).
001223 02-03
CORRECTION BY PROPRANOLOL OF THE ABNORMAL ADRENALINE
DISCHARGE INDUCED BY EMOTIONAL-STRESS IN CEREBRAL
HEMORRHAGE PATIENTS.
002295 02-13

HEPARIN
COMPARISON OF HIGHLY-ACTIVE AND ACTIVITY DEPLETED HEPARIN BY
CIRCULAR DICHROISM SPECTROSCOPY. (UNPUBLISHED PAPER).
001057 02-01

HEPATIC
EFFECT OF IMIPRAMINE ON HEPATIC GAMMA GLUTAMYLTRANSFERASE
IN FEMALE RATS. INTERACTION WITH CONTRACEPTIVES.
001507 02-03
EFFECT OF CHRONIC ADMINISTRATION OF PHENCYCLIDINE ON HEPATIC
MIXED-FUNCTION OXIDASES IN THE MOUSE.
002753 03-03
PULMONARY METABOLISM OF IMIPRAMINE IN THE RAT AND RABBIT:
COMPARISON WITH HEPATIC METABOLISM.
002845 03-03
NEUROLEPTIC ACTION ON HEPATIC ENZYMATIC ACTIVITY.
002849 03-03
SAFETY OF ANTICONVULSANTS IN HEPATIC PORPHYRIAS.
003132 03-05
HEPATIC SIDE-EFFECTS OF ANTIDEPRESSANT MEDICATIONS.
003523 03-15

HEPATIC-DISEASE
HEPATIC-DISEASE AND DRUG PHARMACOKINETICS.
003650 03-17

HEPATIC-NERVE
CORRELATIONS BETWEEN HEMODYNAMIC PARAMETERS OF THE LIVER
AND NOREPINEPHRINE RELEASE UPON HEPATIC-NERVE STIMULATION IN
THE DOG.
001547 02-03

HEPATITIS
CLINICAL PHARMACOKINETICS OF CHLORDIAZEPOXIDE IN PATIENTS WITH
ALCOHOLIC HEPATITIS.
004473 04-11

HEPATOCYTE
HEPATOTOXICITY OF SODIUM-VALPROATE AND OTHER
ANTICONVULSANTS IN RAT HEPATOCYTE CULTURES.
002422 02-15

HEPATOTOXICITY
EXPERIMENTAL-STUDIES ON HEPATOTOXICITY OF DISULFIRAM.
001844 02-05
HEPATOTOXICITY OF SODIUM-VALPROATE AND OTHER
ANTICONVULSANTS IN RAT HEPATOCYTE CULTURES.
002422 02-15

HERITABLE
SEX, PLASMA PROLACTIN AND PLASMA 3 METHOXY-4-
HYDROXYPHENYLGLYCOL (MHPG) PREDICT HERITABLE D-
AMPHETAMINE EXCITATION IN MAN. (UNPUBLISHED PAPER).
004565 04-14

HEROIN
REVERSAL OF SCHEDULE-INDUCED SELF-INJECTION OF HEROIN BY
NALOXONE.
000446 01-04
APPLICATION OF A SYNTHETIC ENKEPHALIN ANALOGUE DURING HEROIN
WITHDRAWAL.
000685 01-11
HEROIN, BUT NOT LEVORPHANOL, PRODUCES EXPLOSIVE MOTOR-
BEHAVIOR IN NALOXONE TREATED RATS.
001579 02-04

THE INFLUENCE OF SINGLE DAILY HEROIN INJECTIONS ON DRINKING-
PATTERNS IN THE RAT.
001746 02-04
SMALL-DOSE INTRAVENOUS HEROIN FACILITATES HYPOTHALAMIC SELF-
STIMULATION WITHOUT RESPONSE SUPPRESSION IN RATS.
002999 03-04
OPERANT ANALYSIS OF HUMAN HEROIN SELF-ADMINISTRATION AND THE
EFFECTS OF NALTREXONE.
003449 03-14
CHOICE BETWEEN FOOD AND HEROIN: EFFECTS OF MORPHINE,
NALOXONE, AND SECOBARBITAL.
004123 04-04
METHADONE TREATMENT OF HEROIN ADDICTS IN SWITZERLAND.
004452 04-11
SUPPRESSION OF MORPHINE ABSTINENCE IN HEROIN ADDICTS BY BETA
ENDORPHIN.
004489 04-11

HETEROGENEITY
OPIOID BINDING PROPERTIES OF BRAIN AND PERIPHERAL TISSUES:
EVIDENCE FOR HETEROGENEITY IN OPIOID LIGAND BINDING SITES.
003902 04-03
BENZODIAZEPINE-RECEPTOR: HETEROGENEITY IN RABBIT BRAIN.
004060 04-03

HETEROGENEOUS
HETEROGENEOUS DEPRESSION OF GLUCOSE UTILIZATION IN THE
CAUDATE-NUCLEUS BY GABA AGONISTS.
002640 03-01
DISCRIMINATION OF FUNCTIONALLY HETEROGENEOUS RECEPTOR
SUBPOPULATIONS: ANTIPSYCHOTIC AND ANTIDOPAMINERGIC
PROPERTIES OF METOCLOPRAMIDE.
002877 03-03

HEXAHYDROMETHYL-1H-PYRAZINOCARBAZOL-HCL
PHARMACOLOGICAL-PROPERTIES OF 2,3,3A,4,5,6 HEXAHYDROMETHYL-
1H-PYRAZINOCARBAZOL-HCL (PIRLINDOLE), A NEW ANTIDEPRESSANT.
004174 04-04

HEXAMETHONIUM
HEXAMETHONIUM MODIFICATION OF CARDIOVASCULAR ADJUSTMENTS
DURING COMBINED STATIC DYNAMIC ARM EXERCISE IN MONKEYS.
001242 02-03

HEXANEDIONE
THE ETIOLOGY OF TOXIC PERIPHERAL NEUROPATHIES: IN VITRO EFFECTS
OF ACRYLAMIDE AND 2,5 HEXANEDIONE ON BRAIN ENOLASE AND
OTHER GLYCOLYTIC ENZYMES.
000131 01-03

HEXAPEPTIDE-PGLU6
SUBSTANCE-P, HEXAPEPTIDE-PGLU6(SP6-11), ANALGESIA AND
SEROTONIN DEPLETION.
003050 03-04

HEXOBARBITAL
EFFECTS OF UREA ON HEXOBARBITAL AND ANTIPYRINE DISPOSITION IN
RATS.
000307 01-03
METABOLIC-STUDIES AND PSYCHOPHYSIOLOGIC-STUDIES OF
— CANNABIDIOL HEXOBARBITAL INTERACTION.
002209 02-13
EFFECT OF CANNABIDIOL ON CYTOCHROME-P-450 AND HEXOBARBITAL
SLEEP-TIME.
002675 03-03

HEXOBARBITAL-INDUCED
EFFECTS OF CHOLECYSTOKININ-LIKE PEPTIDES ON REARING-ACTIVITY AND
HEXOBARBITAL-INDUCED SLEEP.
000507 01-04
ENHANCEMENT OF HEXOBARBITAL-INDUCED SLEEP BY LYSINE AND ITS
METABOLITES.
002967 03-04

HGH
TSH, HGH, HPR, AND CORTISOL RESPONSE TO TRH IN DEPRESSED-
PATIENTS.
004399 04-09

HIAA
CEREBROSPINAL-FLUID VALUES OF HVA AND 5 HIAA IN PATIENTS WITH
ENDOGENOUS DEPRESSION DURING THE COURSE OF TREATMENT.
004382 04-09

HIERARCHIES
EFFECTS OF MORPHINE WITHDRAWAL ON FOOD COMPETITION
HIERARCHIES AND FIGHTING-BEHAVIOR IN RATS.
001632 02-04
OPIATE-RECEPTOR GRADIENTS IN MONKEY CEREBRAL-CORTEX:
CORRESPONDENCE WITH SENSORY PROCESSING HIERARCHIES.
002641 03-01

HIERARCHY
THE INTEGRITY OF THE SOCIAL HIERARCHY IN MICE FOLLOWING
ADMINISTRATION OF PSYCHOTROPIC-DRUGS.
004202 04-04

HIGH
CONTROLLED-COMPARISON OF MEDIUM AND HIGH CLOROTEPIN DOSES
IN CHRONIC SCHIZOPHRENIA.
000548 01-08

DRUG RESPONSE DIFFERENCES OF HIGH AND STANDARD DOSAGE OF FLUPHENAZINE-DECANOATE IN RELATION TO SCHIZOPHRENIC-SYMPTOMS.
000562 01-08

HIGH AND VERY HIGH-DOSAGE ANTIPSYCHOTICS: A CRITICAL REVIEW.
000662 01-11

BRAIN-MONOAMINES AND THE HIGH PRESSURE NEUROLOGICAL-SYNDROME.
001686 02-04

SUBCUTANEOUS SILASTIC IMPLANTS: MAINTENANCE OF HIGH BLOOD ETHANOL LEVELS IN RATS DRINKING A LIQUID DIET.
001865 02-06

CHRONIC EFFECTS OF NEUROLEPTICS HAVING HIGH OR LOW INCIDENCE OF EXTRAPYRAMIDAL SIDE-EFFECTS UPON FORCE, DURATION AND RATE OF OPERANT-RESPONSE IN RATS. (PH.D. DISSERTATION).
003125 03-05

DETERMINATION OF PICOMOLE AMOUNTS OF DOPAMINE, NORADRENALINE, 3,4 DIHYDROXYPHENYLALANINE, 3,4 DIHYDROXYPHENYLACETIC-ACID, HOMOVANILLIC-ACID, AND 5 HYDROXYINDOLEACETIC-ACID IN NERVOUS-TISSUE AFTER ONE-STEP PURIFICATION ON SEPHADEX-G-10, USING HIGH.
004305 04-06

HIGH-AFFINITY
INHIBITION OF HIGH-AFFINITY CHOLINE UPTAKE: STRUCTURE-ACTIVITY STUDIES.
000026 01-03

HIGH-AFFINITY BINDING OF THE ANTITUSSIVE DEXTROMETHORPHAN TO GUINEA-PIG BRAIN.
000061 01-03

HIGH-AFFINITY BINDING OF 3H ETHYLKETOCYCLAZOCINE TO RAT-BRAIN HOMOGENATE.
000124 01-03

HIGH-AFFINITY BINDING OF (3H)MIANSERIN TO RAT-CEREBRAL-CORTEX.
001204 02-03

A HIGH-AFFINITY GTP BINDING-SITE IN RAT-BRAIN. (UNPUBLISHED PAPER).
001442 02-03

LITHIUM EFFECTS ON HIGH-AFFINITY TRYPTOPHAN UPTAKE: EVIDENCE AGAINST A STABILIZATION MECHANISM.
001496 02-03

HIGH-AFFINITY DOPAMINE-RECEPTORS (D3) IN RAT-BRAIN.
001509 02-03

MU-RECEPTORS AND DELTA OPIATE-RECEPTORS: CORRELATION WITH HIGH-AFFINITY AND LOW AFFINITY OPIATE BINDING-SITES.
001554 02-03

HIGH-AFFINITY BINDING OF TRICYCLIC-ANTIDEPRESSANTS TO HISTAMINE H1-RECEPTORS: FACT AND ARTIFACT.
001880 02-06

THE EFFECT OF SPECIFIC BRAIN LESIONS ON THE HIGH-AFFINITY BINDING OF GABA IN THE SUBSTANTIA-NIGRA.
002795 03-03

HIGH-AFFINITY RENAL (3H)FLUNITRAZEPAM BINDING: CHARACTERIZATION, LOCALIZATION, AND ALTERATION IN HYPERTENSION.
002874 03-03

KINETIC DATA ON THE INHIBITION OF HIGH-AFFINITY CHOLINE TRANSPORT INTO RAT-FOREBRAIN SYNAPTOSOMES BY CHOLINE-LIKE COMPOUNDS AND NITROGEN-MUSTARD ANALOGUES.
002879 03-03

ACTH-INDUCED GROOMING INVOLVES HIGH-AFFINITY OPIATE-RECEPTORS.
002985 03-04

HIGH-AFFINITY 3H IMIPRAMINE BINDING: A NEW BIOLOGICAL TOOL FOR STUDIES IN DEPRESSION.
003610 03-17

SPECIFIC, HIGH-AFFINITY (3H)ETHYLKETOCYCLAZOCINE BINDING IN RAT CENTRAL-NERVOUS-SYSTEM: LACK OF EVIDENCE FOR KAPPA-RECEPTORS.
003840 04-03

EFFECTS OF DELTA9 TETRAHYDROCANNABINOL AND CANNABIDIOL ON SODIUM-DEPENDENT HIGH-AFFINITY CHOLINE UPTAKE IN THE RAT HIPPOCAMPUS.
003908 04-03

DOES HIGH-AFFINITY (3H) IMIPRAMINE BINDING LABEL SEROTONIN REUPTAKE SITES IN BRAIN AND PLATELET?
003962 04-03

HIGH-AFFINITY BINDING-SITES FOR A SOMATOSTATIN-28 ANALOG IN RAT-BRAIN.
003985 04-03

MULTIPLE ALPHA2-NORADRENERGIC-RECEPTOR SITES IN RAT-BRAIN: SELECTIVE REGULATION OF HIGH-AFFINITY (3H)CLONIDINE BINDING BY GUANINE-NUCLEOTIDES AND DIVALENT-CATIONS.
003992 04-03

PROPERTIES OF THE OPTICAL-ISOMERS AND METABOLITES OF KETAMINE ON THE HIGH-AFFINITY TRANSPORT AND CATABOLISM OF MONOAMINES.
004009 04-03

THE HIGH-AFFINITY CHOLINE UPTAKE SYSTEM WITH RESPECT TO THE MUSCARINIC-RECEPTORS USING A SYNAPTOSOMAL FRACTION ABUNDANT IN PRESYNAPTIC MEMBRANES.
004028 04-03

HIGH-AVOIDANCE
REGIONAL 5 HT ANALYSIS IN ROMAN HIGH-AVOIDANCE AND LOW-AVOIDANCE RATS FOLLOWING MAO-INHIBITION.
001202 02-03

BRAIN MUSCARINIC CHOLINERGIC-RECEPTOR BINDING IN ROMAN HIGH-AVOIDANCE AND LOW-AVOIDANCE RATS.
002852 03-03

HIGH-CONCENTRATIONS
PERSISTENT EFFECTS OF HIGH-CONCENTRATIONS OF CHLORPROMAZINE ON 3H PROPYLBENZILYLCHOLINE-MUSTARD BINDING TO MUSCARINIC-RECEPTORS IN GUINEA-PIG INTESTINAL-MUSCLE STRIPS.
001266 02-03

CHLORPROMAZINE, HALOPERIDOL, METOCLOPRAMIDE AND DOMPERIDONE RELEASE PROLACTIN THROUGH DOPAMINE ANTAGONISM AT LOW CONCENTRATIONS BUT PARADOXICALLY INHIBIT PROLACTIN RELEASE AT HIGH-CONCENTRATIONS.
003731 04-03

HIGH-DOSAGE
HIGH AND VERY HIGH-DOSAGE ANTIPSYCHOTICS: A CRITICAL REVIEW.
000662 01-11

EFFECTS OF HIGH-DOSAGE LISURIDE-HYDROGEN-MALEATE (LHM) IN PARKINSON-SYNDROME.
004460 04-11

HIGH-DOSAGES
NEUROLEPTICS ADMINISTERED IN HIGH-DOSAGES.
003185 03-08

HIGH-DOSE
CHRONIC HIGH-DOSE PROPRANOLOL DOES NOT INCREASE DOPAMINE-RECEPTOR NUMBER.
000083 01-03

EFFECTS OF A LOW-DOSE AND A HIGH-DOSE OF BETA ENDORPHIN ON ACQUISITION AND RETENTION IN THE RAT.
001663 02-04

HIGH-DOSE DIAZEPAM IN SCHIZOPHRENIA.
001909 02-08

EUHYPNOS-FORTE, HIGH-DOSE TEMAZEPAM FOR RESISTANT INSOMNIA: POSTMARKETING SURVEILLANCE IN 10,057 PATIENTS UNRESPONSIVE TO CONVENTIONAL HYPNOTIC DOSAGE.
002324 02-14

DISTURBED-BEHAVIOUR INDUCED BY HIGH-DOSE ANTIPSYCHOTIC-DRUGS.
002375 02-15

RAPID TREATMENT OF ACUTE PSYCHOTIC-SYMPTOMS WITH HIGH-DOSE AND LOW-DOSE HALOPERIDOL: BEHAVIORAL-CONSIDERATIONS.
003346 03-11

EFFECTS OF A HIGH-DOSE TREATMENT OF METHAMPHETAMINE ON CAUDATE DOPAMINE AND ANOREXIA IN RATS.
004073 04-04

INTRATHECAL HIGH-DOSE MORPHINE PRODUCES HYPERALGESIA IN THE RAT.
004254 04-04

A TWELVE-YEAR FOLLOWUP OF THE NIMH-PRB HIGH-DOSE CHLORPROMAZINE STUDY OF CHRONIC SCHIZOPHRENICS — IMPLICATIONS FOR DEINSTITUTIONALIZATION. (UNPUBLISHED PAPER).
004323 04-08

SINGLE-CASE STUDY OF CLINICAL-RESPONSE TO HIGH-DOSE ERGOT ALKALOID TREATMENT FOR DEMENTIA. PRELIMINARY REPORT.
004493 04-11

HIGH-DOSES
THE EFFECTS OF DOPAMINERGIC-AGENTS ON THE LOCOMOTOR-ACTIVITY OF RATS AFTER HIGH-DOSES OF METHYLAMPHETAMINE.
000427 01-04

BEHAVIORAL-DEPRESSION AND ITS NEUROCHEMICAL-CORRELATES AT HIGH-DOSES OF D-AMPHETAMINE IN RATS.
001601 02-04

PSYCHOPHARMACOLOGICAL-EFFECTS OF LOW-DOSES AND HIGH-DOSES OF APOMORPHINE DURING ONTOGENY.
001774 02-04

LONG-TERM APPLICATION OF HIGH-DOSES OF CLOROTEPIN TO CHRONIC SCHIZOPHRENIC-PATIENTS.
001908 02-08

PLASMA FLUPHENAZINE AND PROLACTIN LEVELS IN SCHIZOPHRENIC-PATIENTS DURING TREATMENT WITH LOW-DOSES AND HIGH-DOSES OF FLUPHENAZINE-ENANTHATE.
001956 02-08

HIGH-FREQUENCY
ELECTRON MICROSCOPIC STUDIES OF BRAIN SLICES: THE EFFECTS OF HIGH-FREQUENCY STIMULATION ON DENDRITIC ULTRASTRUCTURE. (UNPUBLISHED PAPER).
001036 02-01

HIGH-LEVELS
HIGH-LEVELS OF AMITRIPTYLINE AND CLINICAL-RESPONSE.
002266 02-13

TWO CASES OF FORM-FRUSTE-DU-SYNDROME-MALIN WITH HIGH-LEVELS OF SERUM CPK.
004636 04-15

HIGH-PERFORMANCE
3 CHLORO-4-PHENYLSUCCINIMIDOBENZENESULFONAMIDE (GS-385), A NEW ANTICONVULSANT: ITS QUANTITATIVE DETERMINATION,

PHARMACOKINETICS AND METABOLISM USING HIGH-PERFORMANCE LIQUID-CHROMATOGRAPHY.
000705 01-11

MEASUREMENT OF HALOPERIDOL IN HUMAN PLASMA USING REVERSED PHASE HIGH-PERFORMANCE LIQUID-CHROMATOGRAPHY. (UNPUBLISHED PAPER).
003667 04-01

HIGH-PERFORMANCE LIQUID-CHROMATOGRAPHY IN THE NEUROSCIENCES: METHODOLOGY.
004285 04-06

HIGH-PERFORMANCE LIQUID-CHROMATOGRAPHY IN THE NEUROSCIENCES: APPLICATIONS.
004296 04-06

RAPID DETERMINATION OF CHLORPROMAZINE-HCL AND TWO OXIDATION PRODUCTS IN VARIOUS PHARMACEUTICAL SAMPLES USING HIGH-PERFORMANCE LIQUID-CHROMATOGRAPHY AND FLUORESCENCE DETECTION.
004302 04-06

SIMULTANEOUS HIGH-PERFORMANCE LIQUID-CHROMATOGRAPHIC-DETERMINATION OF AMITRIPTYLINE-HYDROCHLORIDE IN TWO-COMPONENT TABLET FORMULATIONS.
004673 04-16

HIGH-RISK
OUR EXPERIENCE WITH PIRACETAM (NOOTROPIL-UCB) TREATMENT IN CHILDREN FROM HIGH-RISK PREGNANCIES WITH SUBSEQUENT MINIMAL-BRAIN-DYSFUNCTION.
000544 01-07

STRATEGY FOR THE STUDY OF PATIENTS AT HIGH-RISK FOR TARDIVE-DYSKINESIA.
000858 01-15

HIGH-SENSITIVITY
HIGH-SENSITIVITY NEGATIVE CHEMICAL-IONIZATION MASS-SPECTRAL-ANALYSIS OF BIOGENIC-AMINES AND METABOLITES. (UNPUBLISHED PAPER).
001042 02-01

HIGHER-ORDER
AN INVOLVEMENT OF DOPAMINE IN HIGHER-ORDER CHOICE MECHANISMS IN THE MONKEY.
003072 03-04

HIGHLIGHTS
HISTORICAL-PERSPECTIVES AND CURRENT HIGHLIGHTS ON LITHIUM TREATMENT IN MANIC-DEPRESSIVE-ILLNESS.
003224 03-09

HIGHLY-ACTIVE
COMPARISON OF HIGHLY-ACTIVE AND ACTIVITY DEPLETED HEPARIN BY CIRCULAR DICHROISM SPECTROSCOPY. (UNPUBLISHED PAPER).
001057 02-01

HIPPOCAMPAL
5 HT BLOCKADE AND THE STIMULANT-EFFECTS OF D-AMPHETAMINE AND L-AMPHETAMINE: NO INTERACTION IN SELF-STIMULATION OF PREFRONTAL-CORTEX, HYPOTHALAMUS, OR DORSAL TEGMENTUM. UNEXPECTED LETHALITY IN HIPPOCAMPAL SITES.
000387 01-04

EFFECTS OF GABA AND DIAZEPAM ON 3H SEROTONIN RELEASE FROM HIPPOCAMPAL SYNAPTOSOMES.
001116 02-03

REGULATION OF HIPPOCAMPAL GLUTAMATE-RECEPTORS: EVIDENCE FOR THE INVOLVEMENT OF A CALCIUM-ACTIVATED PROTEASE.
001120 02-03

THE EFFECT OF CORTISOL MICROIONOPHORETIC-APPLICATIONS ON THE ACTIVITY OF HIPPOCAMPAL NEURONS IN UNRESTRAINED RABBITS.
001123 02-03

IN VIVO (3H)SPIPERONE BINDING TO THE RAT HIPPOCAMPAL FORMATION: INVOLVEMENT OF DOPAMINE-RECEPTORS.
001131 02-03

EXCITATORY ACTION OF OPIOID-PEPTIDES AND OPIATES ON CULTURED HIPPOCAMPAL PYRAMIDAL CELLS.
001241 02-03

PROLONGED EFFECTS OF COCAINE ON HIPPOCAMPAL ACTIVITY.
001338 02-03

EFFECTS OF HEMICHOLINIUM-3 AND CHOLINE ON HIPPOCAMPAL ELECTRICAL-ACTIVITY DURING IMMOBILITY VS. MOVEMENT.
001438 02-03

EFFECTS OF HIPPOCAMPAL BRAIN-DAMAGE ON AUDITORY AND VISUAL RECENT MEMORY: COMPARISON WITH MARIJUANA INTOXICATED SUBJECTS.
002320 02-14 ·

THE EXCITATORY ACTION OF ACETYLCHOLINE ON HIPPOCAMPAL NEURONES OF THE GUINEA-PIG AND RAT MAINTAINED IN VITRO.
002704 03-03 ⟩

THE EFFECTS OF A BENZODIAZEPINE ON THE HYPERPOLARIZING AND THE DEPOLARIZING RESPONSES OF HIPPOCAMPAL CELLS TO GABA.
002763 03-03

IDENTICAL RESPONSES OF THE TWO HIPPOCAMPAL THETA GENERATORS TO PHYSIOLOGICAL AND PHARMACOLOGICAL ACTIVATION.
002792 03-03

A STUDY ON EFFECTS OF ANTIEPILEPTIC-DRUGS UPON THE HIPPOCAMPAL AFTERDISCHARGE.
002844 03-03

HIPPOCAMPAL SEROTONIN REUPTAKE AND NOCTURNAL LOCOMOTOR-ACTIVITY AFTER MICROINJECTIONS OF 5,7 DHT IN THE FORNIX-FIMBRIA.
002929 03-03

PIRACETAM DIMINISHES HIPPOCAMPAL ACETYLCHOLINE LEVELS IN RATS.
002934 03-03

BEHAVIORAL-CHANGES AND BIOCHEMICAL-CHANGES AFTER HIPPOCAMPAL DAMAGE. (PH.D. DISSERTATION).
003069 03-04

BEHAVIORAL AND REGIONAL NEUROCHEMICAL SEQUELAE OF HIPPOCAMPAL DESTRUCTION IN THE RAT.
003721 04-03

CHARACTERIZATION OF TWO (3H)GLUTAMATE BINDING-SITES IN RAT HIPPOCAMPAL MEMBRANES.
003726 04-03

ACETYLCHOLINE-INDUCED MODULATION OF HIPPOCAMPAL PYRAMIDAL NEURONS.
003728 04-03

DIFFERENTIAL TOLERANCE TO THE EFFECTS OF MORPHINE ON EVOKED ACTIVITY IN THE HIPPOCAMPAL SLICE.
003760 04-03

HIPPOCAMPAL SLOW ACTIVITY: TWO INPUT SYSTEMS? (UNPUBLISHED PAPER).
003812 04-03

NYSTAGMIC RESPONSES OF HIPPOCAMPAL ORIGIN WITH REFERENCE TO EXCITABILITY OF CHOLINERGIC AND ADRENERGIC COMPONENTS INVOLVED IN THE HIPPOCAMPUS OF RABBITS.
003842 04-03

THE EFFECT OF ELECTRICAL-STIMULATION OF THE LOCUS-COERULEUS AND INTRAPERITONEAL INJECTION OF CERTAIN PHARMACOLOGICAL SUBSTANCES ON THE THRESHOLD OF HIPPOCAMPAL AFTERDISCHARGES.
003885 04-03

EFFECTS OF ENKEPHALIN, MORPHINE, AND NALOXONE ON THE ELECTRICAL-ACTIVITY OF THE IN VITRO HIPPOCAMPAL SLICE PREPARATION.
003918 04-03

EFFECT OF MEDIAN RAPHE STIMULATION ON HIPPOCAMPAL SEIZURE DISCHARGE INDUCED BY CARBACHOL IN THE RABBIT.
003951 04-03

CHOLINE REVERSES NALOXONE-INDUCED DECREASES IN HIPPOCAMPAL ACETYLCHOLINE CONTENT AND SUPPRESSES ESCAPE-BEHAVIOR IN OPIATE-DEPENDENT RATS.
004076 04-04

HIPPOCAMPAL INVOLVEMENT IN THE PHARMACOLOGIC INDUCTION OF WITHDRAWAL-LIKE BEHAVIORS.
004140 04-04

THE ROLE OF RETICULOSEPTAL INPUTS IN THE FORMATION OF DIFFERENT TYPES OF SENSORY REACTIONS OF THE HIPPOCAMPAL NEURONS.
004510 04-13

HIPPOCAMPAL-CA1
BEHAVIOR-DEPENDENT EVOKED-POTENTIALS IN THE HIPPOCAMPAL-CA1 REGION OF THE RAT. II. EFFECTS OF ESERINE, ATROPINE, ETHER AND PENTOBARBITAL.
000184 01-03

HIPPOCAMPAL-CA1-REGION
DIFFERENTIAL-EFFECTS OF PENTOBARBITAL AND ETHER ON THE SYNAPTIC TRANSMISSION OF THE HIPPOCAMPAL-CA1-REGION IN THE RAT.
003903 04-03

HIPPOCAMPOCORTICAL
INFLUENCE OF CARBAMAZEPINE ON THALAMOCORTICAL AND HIPPOCAMPOCORTICAL SELF-SUSTAINED AFTERDISCHARGES IN RATS.
001356 02-03

HIPPOCAMPUS
MONOAMINERGIC DENERVATION OF THE RAT HIPPOCAMPUS: MICROIONTOPHORETIC STUDIES OF PRESYNAPTIC AND POSTSYNAPTIC SUPERSENSITIVITY TO NOREPINEPHRINE AND SEROTONIN.
000068 01-03

ADENINE-NUCLEOTIDES AND SYNAPTIC TRANSMISSION IN THE IN VITRO RAT HIPPOCAMPUS.
000080 01-03

SEIZURES AND RELATED EPILEPTIFORM ACTIVITY IN HIPPOCAMPUS TRANSPLANTED TO THE ANTERIOR-CHAMBER OF THE EYE: MODULATION BY CHOLINERGIC AND ADRENERGIC INPUT.
000095 01-03

INTERACTION OF DIAZEPAM WITH SYNAPTIC TRANSMISSION IN THE IN VITRO RAT HIPPOCAMPUS.
000178 01-03

SEROTONIN-RECEPTORS IN HIPPOCAMPUS AND FRONTAL-CORTEX.
000268 01-03

ACUTE AND CHRONIC OPIATE-EFFECTS ON SINGLE UNITS AND EEG OF MEDIAL THALAMUS AND HIPPOCAMPUS: A LATENCY ANALYSIS.
001344 02-03

LOCALIZATION OF NALOXONE SENSITIVE (3H)DIHYDROMORPHINE BINDING-SITES WITHIN THE HIPPOCAMPUS OF THE RAT.
001368 02-03

INHIBITORY ACTION OF ADENOSINE ON SYNAPTIC TRANSMISSION IN THE HIPPOCAMPUS OF THE GUINEA-PIG IN VITRO.
001401 02-03

Subject Index

FORNIX LESION PREVENTS AN ORGANOPHOSPHATE-INDUCED DECREASE IN MUSCARINIC-RECEPTOR LEVEL IN RAT HIPPOCAMPUS.
001833 02-05

SUPPRESSION OF AMPHETAMINE-INDUCED EEG AROUSAL IN THE HIPPOCAMPUS OF HALOPERIDOL TREATED RABBITS.
002683 03-03

GABA-RECEPTORS AND BENZODIAZEPINE-RECEPTORS. STUDIES ON THEIR LOCALIZATION IN THE HIPPOCAMPUS AND THEIR INTERACTION WITH CENTRAL DOPAMINE NEURONS IN THE RAT-BRAIN.
002727 03-03

EFFECTS OF PHENYTOIN ON PYRAMIDAL NEURONS OF THE RAT HIPPOCAMPUS.
002750 03-03

SOMATOSTATIN FACILITATES THE SEROTONIN RELEASE FROM RAT-CEREBRAL-CORTEX, HIPPOCAMPUS, AND HYPOTHALAMUS SLICES.
002913 03-03

DIAZEPAM ANXIOLYTIC-ACTIVITY IN HIPPOCAMPUS.
003743 04-03

COMPARISON OF THE EFFECTS OF THE STEREOISOMERS OF FENFLURAMINE ON THE ACETYLCHOLINE CONTENT OF RAT STRIATUM, HIPPOCAMPUS AND NUCLEUS-ACCUMBENS.
003758 04-03

NYSTAGMIC RESPONSES OF HIPPOCAMPAL ORIGIN WITH REFERENCE TO EXCITABILITY OF CHOLINERGIC AND ADRENERGIC COMPONENTS INVOLVED IN THE HIPPOCAMPUS OF RABBITS.
003842 04-03

EFFECTS OF DELTA9 TETRAHYDROCANNABINOL AND CANNABIDIOL ON SODIUM-DEPENDENT HIGH-AFFINITY CHOLINE UPTAKE IN THE RAT HIPPOCAMPUS.
003908 04-03

SPREADING DEPRESSION INDUCED BY MICROINJECTION OF ENKEPHALINS INTO THE HIPPOCAMPUS AND NEOCORTEX.
004015 04-03

EFFECTS OF 3 SULFAMOYLMETHYL-BENZISOXAZOLE (AD-810) AND SOME ANTIEPILEPTICS ON THE KINDLED SEIZURES IN THE NEOCORTEX, HIPPOCAMPUS AND AMYGDALA IN RATS.
004149 04-04

HISTAMINE

HISTAMINE H1-RECEPTORS LABELED IN VIVO: ANTIDEPRESSANT AND ANTIHISTAMINE INTERACTIONS.
000074 01-03

HISTAMINE AND PSYCHOTROPIC-DRUGS.
000112 01-03

IN VIVO OCCUPATION OF CEREBRAL HISTAMINE H1-RECEPTORS EVALUATED WITH 3H MEPYRAMINE MAY PREDICT SEDATIVE PROPERTIES OF PSYCHOTROPIC-DRUGS.
000241 01-03

PSYCHOTROPIC-DRUGS AND HISTAMINE H1-RECEPTORS OF CULTURED MOUSE NEUROBLASTOMA CELLS.
000250 01-03

TRICYCLIC-ANTIDEPRESSANT DRUG-INTERACTIONS WITH HISTAMINE AND ALPHA-ADRENERGIC-RECEPTORS.
000791 01-13

IGE MEDIATED HISTAMINE RELEASE IN RAT BASOPHILIC LEUKEMIA CELLS: RECEPTOR ACTIVATED PHOSPHOLIPID METHYLATION, CA-FLUX AND RELEASE OF ARACHIDONIC-ACID. (UNPUBLISHED PAPER).
001188 02-03

INDIRECT ADRENERGIC EFFECT OF HISTAMINE IN CAT CEREBRAL-ARTERIES.
001355 02-03

INTERACTION OF HISTAMINE H2-RECEPTOR BLOCKING-DRUGS WITH THE NORADRENERGIC SYSTEM IN RAT-BRAIN AND HEART.
001397 02-03

SOME CENTRAL-EFFECTS OF IMPROMIDINE, A POTENT AGONIST OF HISTAMINE H2-RECEPTORS.
001417 02-03

PSYCHOTROPIC-DRUG BLOCKADE OF HISTAMINE H1-RECEPTORS.
001432 02-03

NEGLIGIBLE AFFINITY OF HISTAMINE H2-RECEPTOR ANTAGONISTS FOR CENTRAL ALPHA1-ADRENOCEPTORS.
001508 02-03

HIGH-AFFINITY BINDING OF TRICYCLIC-ANTIDEPRESSANTS TO HISTAMINE H1-RECEPTORS: FACT AND ARTIFACT.
001880 02-06

HISTAMINE ACTIONS ON ACTIVITY OF CULTURED HYPOTHALAMIC NEURONS: EVIDENCE FOR MEDIATION BY HISTAMINE H1-RECEPTORS AND H2-RECEPTORS.
002732 03-03

DECREASED CEREBRAL CATABOLISM OF (3H)HISTAMINE IN VIVO AFTER S ADENOSYLMETHIONINE ADMINISTRATION.
002883 03-03

H2-RECEPTORS MEDIATE INCREASES IN PERMEABILITY OF THE BLOOD-BRAIN-BARRIER DURING ARTERIAL HISTAMINE INFUSION.
003817 04-03

EFFECT OF DIAZEPAM ON STRESS-INDUCED CHANGES IN BRAIN HISTAMINE.
003932 04-03

TRICYCLIC-ANTIDEPRESSANTS AND HISTAMINE H1-RECEPTORS.
003986 04-03

ONTOGENY OF HISTAMINERGIC NEUROTRANSMISSION IN THE RAT-BRAIN: CONCOMITANT DEVELOPMENT OF NEURONAL HISTAMINE, H1-

THE HISTORY OF RECENT DEVELOPMENTS IN PSYCHIATRY.
000939 01-17

HISTORY AND PHARMACOLOGY OF MINAPRINE.
002270 02-13

LONG-TERM CHANGES IN AIMS RATINGS AND THEIR RELATION TO
MEDICATION HISTORY.
003537 03-15

THE HISTORY OF PSYCHOTROPIC-DRUGS.
003609 03-17

MINI-SYMPOSIUM: II. MULTIPLE OPIOID-RECEPTORS. A LITTLE ABOUT
THEIR HISTORY AND SOME IMPLICATIONS RELATED TO EVOLUTION.
004728 04-17

HLA-SYSTEM
THE HLA-SYSTEM AND SCHIZOPHRENIA IN ENGLAND.
001933 02-08

HLA-SYSTEM AND PSYCHOPHARMACOLOGY.
002293 02-13

HOLEBOARD
EFFECTS OF SEROTONERGIC LESIONS ON INVESTIGATORY RESPONDING BY
RATS IN A HOLEBOARD.
001634 02-04

HOLTOR-MONITORED
COMPARISON OF STANDARD AND HOLTOR-MONITORED EKGS IN A
PATIENT TREATED WITH SEVERAL ANTIDEPRESSANTS.
003304 03-11

HOMEOPATHY
THE TREATMENT OF INSOMNIA THROUGH HOMEOPATHY IN A CLINIC.
004484 04-11

HOMING-BEHAVIOR
THE INFLUENCE OF DAILY BIOLOGICAL-RHYTHMICITY ON THE HOMING-
BEHAVIOR, PSYCHOPHARMACOLOGICAL RESPONSIVENESS, LEARNING
AND RETENTION OF SUCKLING RATS. (PH.D. DISSERTATION).
001660 02-04

HOMOCARNOSINE
TREATMENT OF HUNTINGTON-DISEASE WITH GAMMA ACETYLENIC-
GABA, AN IRREVERSIBLE INHIBITOR OF GABA-TRANSAMINASE:
INCREASED CSF GABA AND HOMOCARNOSINE WITHOUT CLINICAL
AMELIORATION.
003458 03-14

HOMOCYSTEIC-ACID
TWO CONDUCTANCE MECHANISMS ACTIVATED BY APPLICATIONS OF L
GLUTAMIC-ACID, L ASPARTIC-ACID, DL HOMOCYSTEIC-ACID, N
METHYL-D-ASPARTIC-ACID, AND DL KAINIC-ACID TO CULTURED
MAMMALIAN CENTRAL NEURONES.
001349 02-03

HOMOCYSTEINE
PRODUCTION OF CONVULSIONS IN MICE BY THE COMBINATION OF
METHIONINE AND HOMOCYSTEINE.
001233 02-03

HOMOCYSTEINE-INDUCED
HOMOCYSTEINE-INDUCED CONVULSIONS: ENHANCEMENT BY VITAMIN-B6
AND INHIBITION BY HYDRAZINE.
002758 03-03

HOMOGENATE
HIGH-AFFINITY BINDING OF 3H ETHYLKETOCYCLAZOCINE TO RAT-BRAIN
HOMOGENATE.
000124 01-03

STIMULATORY ACTION OF LISURIDE ON DOPAMINE-SENSITIVE
ADENYLATE-CYCLASE IN THE RAT STRIATAL HOMOGENATE.
003718 04-03

HOMOGENATES
INHIBITION OF (3H)NALOXONE BINDING IN HOMOGENATES OF RAT-
BRAIN BY ESEROLINE, A DRUG, WITH ANALGESIC ACTIVITY, RELATED
TO PHYSOSTIGMINE.
000104 01-03

DOPAMINERGIC MECHANISMS IN THE TELEOST RETINA. I. DOPAMINE-
SENSITIVE ADENYLATE-CYCLASE IN HOMOGENATES OF CARP RETINA;
EFFECTS OF AGONISTS, ANTAGONISTS AND ERGOTS.
004051 04-03

HOMOTAURINE
INHIBITORY ACTIONS OF TAUROCYAMINE, HYPOTAURINE,
HOMOTAURINE, TAURINE AND GABA ON SPIKE DISCHARGES OF
PURKINJE-CELLS, AND LOCALIZATION OF SENSITIVE SITES, IN GUINEA-
PIG CEREBELLAR SLICES.
002846 03-03

HOMOVANILLIC-ACID
PATHOPHYSIOLOGICAL-STUDIES ON SCHIZOPHRENIA WITH SPECIAL
REFERENCE TO HOMOVANILLIC-ACID CONCENTRATION IN
CEREBROSPINAL-FLUID.
000271 01-03

EFFECTS OF TIAPRIDE ON HOMOVANILLIC-ACID LEVELS IN HUMAN
CEREBROSPINAL-FLUID DRAWN AT PNEUMOENCEPHALOGRAPHY.
001483 02-03

DETERMINATION OF PICOMOLE AMOUNTS OF DOPAMINE,
NORADRENALINE, 3,4 DIHYDROXYPHENYLALANINE, 3,4
DIHYDROXYPHENYLACETIC-ACID, HOMOVANILLIC-ACID, AND 5
HYDROXYINDOLEACETIC-ACID IN NERVOUS-TISSUE AFTER ONE-STEP
PURIFICATION ON SEPHADEX-G-10, USING HIGH.
004305 04-06

CEREBROSPINAL-FLUID HOMOVANILLIC-ACID PATTERNS DURING
NEUROLEPTIC TREATMENT. (UNPUBLISHED PAPER).
004502 04-13

HORIZONTAL
CHANGES IN THE HORIZONTAL VESTIBULO-OCULAR REFLEX OF THE
RHESUS-MONKEY WITH BEHAVIORAL AND PHARMACOLOGICAL
ALERTING.
002997 03-04

HORMONAL
EFFECTS OF ANTIDEPRESSANTS ON PITUITARY HORMONAL SECRETIONS IN
HEALTHY TEST SUBJECTS, NEUROTIC-PATIENTS, AND ENDOGENOUS
DEPRESSIVE-PATIENTS.
002009 02-09

HORMONAL ABNORMALITIES IN ANOREXIA-NERVOSA (AN).
002099 02-11

HORMONAL STIMULATION AFTER INJECTION OF THYROTROPHIN-
RELEASING-FACTOR (TRF) AND ACTH1-24 IN PATIENTS FOLLOWING
CHRONIC-TREATMENT WITH NEUROLEPTICS: PRELIMINARY-STUDY.
004505 04-13

CORRECTION OF HORMONAL ACTIVITY OF THE THYROID-GLAND AS A
METHOD OF PATHOGENIC THERAPY IN A COMPREHENSIVE TREATMENT
OF PATIENTS WITH TEMPORAL EPILEPSY.
004579 04-14

HORMONAL-EFFECTS
SHORT-TERM HORMONAL-EFFECTS OF NALOXONE IN MAN.
000798 01-13

HORMONE
HORMONE LEVELS IN ACUTE SCHIZOPHRENIA WITH AND WITHOUT
NEUROLEPTIC-MEDICATION.
001923 02-08

HALOPERIDOL STIMULATION OF PROLACTIN SECRETION: HOW MANY
BLOOD SAMPLES ARE NEEDED TO DEFINE THE HORMONE RESPONSE?
002505 02-16

HORMONES
CONVERSION SCALES FOR COMMONLY REQUESTED SERUM
CONCENTRATIONS OF DRUGS AND OTHER SUBSTANCES OF
THERAPEUTIC AND TOXICOLOGICAL IMPORTANCE, AND OF
HORMONES.
000759 01-13

EXPERIENCE IN USING THE HORMONES OF THE HYPOPHYSIS POSTERIOR
LOBE IN MEMORY-DISTURBANCES OF VARYING GENESES.
003438 03-14

DRUGS, TRANSMITTERS AND HORMONES, AND MATING-BEHAVIOR.
004721 04-17

HORSE
3H IMIPRAMINE BINDING IN NEURONAL AND GLIAL FRACTIONS OF
HORSE STRIATUM.
000033 01-03

HORSERADISH-PEROXIDASE
A NEW METHOD FOR APPLICATION OF HORSERADISH-PEROXIDASE INTO
A RESTRICTED AREA OF THE BRAIN.
003141 03-06

HOSPITAL
HOSPITAL AND OUTPATIENT CARE FOR PSYCHOTIC-PATIENTS DURING THE
LAST THREE DECADES: SUBSEQUENT HOSPITAL AND OUTPATIENT
TREATMENT OF PSYCHOTIC-PATIENTS HOSPITALIZED FOR THE FIRST
TIME IN 1949-50, 1959-60 OR 1969-70.
000571 01-08

COMPARISON OF DRUG PRESCRIPTIONS FOR PSYCHIATRIC-PATIENTS
AFTER HOSPITAL DISCHARGE IN THE DISTRICTS TEPLICE AND UHERSKE-
HRADISTE.
002518 02-17

HOSPITALIZED
HOSPITAL AND OUTPATIENT CARE FOR PSYCHOTIC-PATIENTS DURING THE
LAST THREE DECADES: SUBSEQUENT HOSPITAL AND OUTPATIENT
TREATMENT OF PSYCHOTIC-PATIENTS HOSPITALIZED FOR THE FIRST
TIME IN 1949-50, 1959-60 OR 1969-70.
000571 01-08

THE USE OF VILOXAZINE IN HOSPITALIZED DEPRESSED-PATIENTS:
RANDOM COMPARISON WITH IMIPRAMINE IN A DOUBLE-BLIND TRIAL.
001998 02-09

ORIENTATIONAL TESTING OF CHLORPROMAZINE-HCL ON HOSPITALIZED
MENTAL-PATIENTS.
002131 02-11

MOLINDONE-HYDROCHLORIDE IN THE TREATMENT OF AGGRESSIVE,
HOSPITALIZED CHILDREN.
003321 03-11

EFFECTS OF LITHIUM-CARBONATE AND HALOPERIDOL ON COGNITION IN
AGGRESSIVE, HOSPITALIZED SCHOOL-AGE CHILDREN.
003360 03-11

EFFECTS OF LITHIUM-CARBONATE AND HALOPERIDOL ON COGNITION IN
AGGRESSIVE HOSPITALIZED SCHOOL-AGE CHILDREN.
003361 03-11

THE EFFECTS OF NEUROLEPTIC-DRUGS ON THE SOCIAL INTERACTIONS OF
HOSPITALIZED PSYCHOTIC-PATIENTS.
004577 04-14

HOSPITALIZED-PATIENTS
AUDITORY BRAINSTEM EVOKED-RESPONSES IN HOSPITALIZED-PATIENTS UNDERGOING DRUG-TREATMENT OR ECT.
003430 03-13

HOSPITALS
PSYCHIATRIC-DISTURBANCE IN MENTALLY-HANDICAPPED-PATIENTS: A PROSPECTIVE STUDY OF CURRENT CLINICAL USAGE OF DEPOT FLUPHENAZINE IN HOSPITALS FOR THE MENTALLY-HANDICAPPED.
000668 01-11
THE USE OF MINAPRINE IN CHILD-PSYCHIATRY IN HOSPITALS AND OUTPATIENT CLINICS.
002169 02-11

HOSTILITY
HOSTILITY CONFLICT AND REPORTING OF SIDE-EFFECTS BY PSYCHIATRIC-OUTPATIENTS.
000840 01-15
HOSTILITY PRODUCTION AS A COMMON FEATURE OF ANTIANXIETY-AGENT ACTION.
004654 04-15

HOT
CORE TEMPERATURE CHANGES FOLLOWING ADMINISTRATION OF NALOXONE AND NALTREXONE TO RATS EXPOSED TO HOT AND COLD AMBIENT TEMPERATURES. EVIDENCE FOR THE PHYSIOLOGICAL ROLE OF ENDORPHINS IN HOT AND COLD ACCLIMATIZATION.
004034 04-03

HOUSEFLY
QUINUCLIDINYL BENZILATE BINDING IN HOUSEFLY HEADS AND RAT-BRAIN.
003868 04-03

HPLC
AN HPLC AND RIA ANALYSIS OF THE CHOLECYSTOKININ-PEPTIDES IN RAT-BRAIN. (UNPUBLISHED PAPER).
001004 02-01
HPLC SEPARATION OF CHOLECYSTOKININ-PEPTIDES -- TWO SYSTEMS. (UNPUBLISHED PAPER).
001005 02-01
RIA AND HPLC EVIDENCE FOR THE PRESENCE OF METHIONINE-ENKEPHALIN AND CHOLECYSTOKININ IN THE NEURAL RETINA OF SEVERAL VERTEBRATE SPECIES. (UNPUBLISHED PAPER).
001017 02-01
EVALUATION OF THE EFFECT OF DRUGS ON DOPAMINE METABOLISM IN THE RAT SUPERIOR-CERVICAL-GANGLION BY HPLC WITH ELECTROCHEMICAL-DETECTION.
001530 02-03
SIMULTANEOUS DETERMINATION OF FEMTOMOLE QUANTITIES OF 5 HYDROXYTRYPTOPHAN, SEROTONIN AND 5 HYDROXYINDOLEACETIC-ACID IN BRAIN USING HPLC WITH ELECTROCHEMICAL-DETECTION.
003139 03-06

HPR
TSH, HGH, HPR, AND CORTISOL RESPONSE TO TRH IN DEPRESSED-PATIENTS.
004399 04-09

HT
(3H)5 HT BINDING-SITES AND 5 HT-SENSITIVE ADENYLATE-CYCLASE IN GLIAL CELL MEMBRANE FRACTION.
000093 01-03
THE ROLE OF INTRANEURONAL 5 HT AND OF TRYPTOPHAN-HYDROXYLASE ACTIVATION IN THE CONTROL OF 5 HT SYNTHESIS IN RAT-BRAIN SLICES INCUBATED IN K-ENRICHED MEDIUM.
000123 01-03
5 HT BLOCKADE AND THE STIMULANT-EFFECTS OF D-AMPHETAMINE AND L-AMPHETAMINE: NO INTERACTION IN SELF-STIMULATION OF PREFRONTAL-CORTEX, HYPOTHALAMUS, OR DORSAL TEGMENTUM. UNEXPECTED LETHALITY IN HIPPOCAMPAL SITES.
000387 01-04
INITIAL, CLINICAL-TRIAL OF A NEW, SPECIFIC 5 HT REUPTAKE INHIBITOR, CITALOPRAM (LU-10-171).
000591 01-09
REGIONAL 5 HT ANALYSIS IN ROMAN HIGH-AVOIDANCE AND LOW-AVOIDANCE RATS FOLLOWING MAO-INHIBITION.
001202 02-03
PHARMACOLOGICAL EVIDENCE OF A POSSIBLE TRYPTAMINERGIC REGULATION OF OPIATE-RECEPTORS BY USING INDALPINE, A SELECTIVE 5 HT UPTAKE INHIBITOR.
001517 02-03
THE EFFECTS OF 5 HT UPTAKE AND MAO-INHIBITORS ON L 5 HTP-INDUCED EXCITATION IN RATS.
001740 02-04
EFFECT OF ACUTE AND CHRONIC TRIIODOTHYRONINE (T3) ADMINISTRATION TO RATS ON CENTRAL 5 HT AND DOPAMINE-MEDIATED BEHAVIOURAL-RESPONSES AND RELATED BRAIN-BIOCHEMISTRY.
002951 03-04
ROTATIONAL-BEHAVIOUR ELICITED BY 5 HT IN THE RAT: EVIDENCE FOR AN INHIBITORY ROLE OF 5 HT IN THE SUBSTANTIA-NIGRA AND CORPUS-STRIATUM.
004141 04-04
DOPAMINE AND 5 HT SUPERSENSITIVITY IN NONORGANIC CENTRAL PAIN AND IN MORPHINE ABSTINENCE: FORTUITOUS OR REAL ANALOGY?
004553 04-13

HT-ERGIC
ON SOME RELATIONSHIPS BETWEEN GABAERGIC AND 5 HT-ERGIC MECHANISMS IN PENTYLENETETRAZOL CONVULSIVE-SEIZURE REACTIONS.
004166 04-04

HT-RECEPTOR
DOES (3H)SPIROPERIDOL LABEL A 5 HT-RECEPTOR IN THE FRONTAL-CORTEX OF THE RAT?.
000206 01-03
THE INFLUENCE OF 5 HT-RECEPTOR BLOCKING-AGENTS ON THE BEHAVIORAL-EFFECTS OF ANALGESICS IN RATS.
000429 01-04

HT-RECEPTORS
HUMAN PLATELET 5 HT-RECEPTORS: CHARACTERISATION AND FUNCTIONAL ASSOCIATION.
001412 02-03

HT-SENSITIVE
(3H)5 HT BINDING-SITES AND 5 HT-SENSITIVE ADENYLATE-CYCLASE IN GLIAL CELL MEMBRANE FRACTION.
000093 01-03

HTP
OPEN-STUDY OF L 5 HTP IN MELANCHOLIC-DEPRESSED-PATIENTS OVER 50 YEARS OF AGE.
002016 02-09
L HTP AND THE SEROTONIN HYPOTHESIS: THEIR MEANING FOR TREATMENT OF DEPRESSION.
002326 02-14
STUDY ON THE EFFECTS OF L 5 HTP ON THE STAGES OF SLEEP IN MAN AS EVALUATED BY USING SLEEP-DEPRIVATION.
003450 03-14
AUTORADIOGRAPHIC STUDIES ON DISTRIBUTION OF L-3,4 DIHYDROXYPHENYLALANINE (L-DOPA) 14C AND L 5 HYDROXYTRYPTOPHAN (L 5 HTP) 14C IN THE CAT BRAIN.
003941 04-03
TREATMENT OF DEPRESSION WITH AN MAO-INHIBITOR FOLLOWED BY 5 HTP -- AN UNFINISHED RESEARCH PROJECT.
004377 04-09

HTP-INDUCED
THE EFFECT OF ANTIDEPRESSANTS ON L 5 HTP-INDUCED CHANGES IN RAT PLASMA CORTICOSTEROIDS.
000170 01-03
THE EFFECTS OF 5 HT UPTAKE AND MAO-INHIBITORS ON L 5 HTP-INDUCED EXCITATION IN RATS.
001740 02-04

HT2
REGULATION OF SEROTONIN2-RECEPTORS (5 HT2) LABELED WITH (3H)SPIROPERIDOL BY CHRONIC-TREATMENT WITH THE ANTIDEPRESSANT AMITRIPTYLINE.
003964 04-03

HT2-RECEPTORS
RECEPTOR BINDING PROFILE OF R-41-468, A NOVEL ANTAGONIST AT 5 HT2-RECEPTORS.
002648 03-02

HUMAN
A COMPARISON OF HUMAN TACTILE STIMULUS VELOCITY DISCRIMINATION WITH THE ABILITY OF S-I CORTICAL NEURONS IN AWAKE RHESUS-MONKEYS TO SIGNAL THE SAME VELOCITY DIFFERENCES BEFORE AND AFTER NONANESTHETIC DOSES OF PENTOBARBITAL.
000055 01-03
IN VITRO EFFECT OF PHENCYCLIDINE AND OTHER PSYCHOMOTOR STIMULANTS ON SEROTONIN UPTAKE IN HUMAN PLATELETS.
000750 01-13
GABA LEVELS IN HUMAN CEREBROSPINAL-FLUID: ALTERATIONS IN PSYCHIATRIC-DISORDERS. (UNPUBLISHED PAPER).
000764 01-13
TRANSFER OF LORAZEPAM AND ITS CONJUGATE ACROSS THE HUMAN PLACENTA.
000774 01-13
DOPAMINERGIC FACTORS IN HUMAN PROLACTIN REGULATION: A PITUITARY MODEL FOR THE STUDY OF A NEUROENDOCRINE SYSTEM IN MAN.
000776 01-13
DRUG SENSITIVE ECTO-ATPASE IN HUMAN LEUKOCYTES.
000779 01-13
RADIOIMMUNOASSAY FOR FLUPHENAZINE IN HUMAN PLASMA.
000905 01-16
CHOLINERGIC ASPECTS OF TARDIVE-DYSKINESIA: HUMAN AND ANIMAL STUDIES.
000928 01-17
EFFECT OF NEUROLEPTIC-DRUGS ON LITHIUM UPTAKE BY THE HUMAN ERYTHROCYTE.
000973 01-17
PREPARATION AND CHARACTERIZATION OF SYNTHETIC MODELS FOR THE DENSE-BODIES OF HUMAN PLATELETS. (UNPUBLISHED PAPER).
001013 02-01

ELECTRON PROBE MICROANALYSIS OF CALCIUM AND PHOSPHORUS IN DENSE-BODIES ISOLATED FROM HUMAN PLATELETS. (UNPUBLISHED PAPER).
001014 02-01

QUANTITATIVE ANALYSIS OF 6 HYDROXYMELATONIN IN HUMAN URINE BY GAS-CHROMATOGRAPHY NEGATIVE CHEMICAL-IONIZATION MASS-SPECTROMETRY. (UNPUBLISHED PAPER).
001058 02-01

TETRAHYDRO-BETA-CARBOLINES AND CORRESPONDING TRYPTAMINES: IN VITRO INHIBITION OF SEROTONIN AND DOPAMINE UPTAKE BY HUMAN BLOOD-PLATELETS.
001067 02-02

HUMAN PLATELET 5 HT-RECEPTORS: CHARACTERISATION AND FUNCTIONAL ASSOCIATION.
001412 02-03

EFFECTS OF TIAPRIDE ON HOMOVANILLIC-ACID LEVELS IN HUMAN CEREBROSPINAL-FLUID DRAWN AT PNEUMOENCEPHALOGRAPHY.
001483 02-03

EFFECTS OF ORAL CHOLINE ON HUMAN COMPLEX PARTIAL SEIZURES.
002149 02-11

BENZODIAZEPINE-RECEPTORS: THE EFFECT OF GABA ON THEIR CHARACTERISTICS IN HUMAN BRAIN AND THEIR ALTERATION IN HUNTINGTONS-DISEASE.
002163 02-11

INTERCANNABINOID AND CANNABINOID ETHANOL INTERACTIONS AND THEIR EFFECTS ON HUMAN PERFORMANCE.
002193 02-12

QUINACRINE AND SEROTONIN BINDING BY SYNTHETIC MODELS FOR HUMAN PLATELET DENSE-BODIES: EVALUATION OF THE ROLE OF BINDING IN AMINE STORAGE. (UNPUBLISHED PAPER).
002219 02-13

NA-DEPENDENT LI COUNTERTRANSPORT AND THE LITHIUM DISTRIBUTION ACROSS THE HUMAN ERYTHROCYTE MEMBRANE: INTRODUCTION.
002227 02-13

EFFECTS OF SINGLE-ORAL-DOSAGES OF STEROIDS ON HUMAN EEG BASELINE CROSSING T-SCORES SHOWN BY MULTIVARIATE STATISTICS AND STANDARD PROFILES.
002239 02-13

ASPIRIN AND HUMAN SLEEP.
002241 02-13

EFFECT OF DOXEPIN ON SEROTONIN METABOLISM IN RAT-BRAIN AND SEROTONIN UPTAKE BY HUMAN BLOOD-PLATELETS.
002243 02-13

SPECIFIC 3H IMIPRAMINE BINDING IN HUMAN PLATELETS: INFLUENCE OF AGE AND SEX.
002254 02-13

ANTIPSYCHOTIC-DRUGS: DIFFERENTIAL-EFFECTS ON DOPAMINE NEURONS IN BASAL GANGLIA AND MESOCORTEX FOLLOWING CHRONIC ADMINISTRATION IN HUMAN AND NONHUMAN PRIMATES.
002285 02-13

THE PERIPHERAL ANTICHOLINERGIC-ACTIVITY OF TRICYCLIC-ANTIDEPRESSANTS: COMPARISON OF AMITRIPTYLINE AND DESIPRAMINE IN HUMAN VOLUNTEERS.
002298 02-13

HUMAN MEMORY AND THE EFFECTS OF PHYSOSTIGMINE AND CHOLINE-CHLORIDE.
002317 02-14

INFLUENCE OF OXYTOCIN ON HUMAN MEMORY PROCESSES.
002322 02-14

EFFECTS OF ATENOLOL AND PROPRANOLOL ON HUMAN PERFORMANCE AND SUBJECTIVE FEELINGS.
002340 02-14

THE CLOCK AND THE BLUE GUITAR: STUDIES OF HUMAN GROWTH-HORMONE SECRETION IN SLEEP AND WAKING. (UNPUBLISHED PAPER).
002346 02-14

SEX-DIFFERENCES IN THE EFFECTS OF LOW-DOSES OF ETHANOL ON HUMAN REACTION-TIME.
002361 02-14

A METHOD FOR THE DETERMINATION OF AMITRIPTYLINE AND ITS METABOLITES NORTRIPTYLINE, 10 HYDROXYAMITRIPTYLINE, AND 10 HYDROXYNORTRIPTYLINE IN HUMAN PLASMA USING STABLE ISOTOPE DILUTION AND GAS-CHROMATOGRAPHY CHEMICAL-IONIZATION MASS-SPECTROMETRY.
002486 02-16

MEASUREMENT OF FLUPHENAZINE BY GAS-CHROMATOGRAPHY IN HUMAN PLASMA AND RED-BLOOD-CELLS.
002491 02-16

INFLUENCE OF PSYCHOACTIVE AND NONPSYCHOACTIVE CANNABINOIDS ON CELL PROLIFERATION AND MACROMOLECULAR BIOSYNTHESIS IN HUMAN CELLS.
002830 03-03

INFLUENCE OF PSYCHOACTIVE AND NONPSYCHOACTIVE CANNABINOIDS ON CHROMATIN STRUCTURE AND FUNCTION IN HUMAN CELLS.
002831 03-03

A COMPARISON OF HUMAN MUSCARINIC CHOLINERGIC-RECEPTOR RESPONSE TO A NUMBER OF PSYCHOTROPICS UTILIZING THE RADIOLABELED ANTAGONIST, (3H) QUINUCLIDINYL-BENZILATE. (PH.D. DISSERTATION).
002918 03-03

INCREASES IN TESTOSTERONE LEVELS AND IN COPULATORY-BEHAVIOR OF MALE RHESUS-MONKEYS FOLLOWING TREATMENT WITH HUMAN CHORIONIC GONADOTROPHIN.
003012 03-04

PHYSOSTIGMINE INDUCTION OF DEPRESSIVE-SYMPTOMATOLOGY IN NORMAL HUMAN SUBJECTS.
003255 03-09

EFFECTS OF VASOPRESSIN ON HUMAN MEMORY FUNCTIONS.
003388 03-11

NONGENETIC FACTORS AFFECTING HUMAN PLATELET MONOAMINE-OXIDASE.
003407 03-13

TRICYCLIC-ANTIDEPRESSANT DRUG-TREATMENT DECREASES ALPHA2-ADRENORECEPTORS ON HUMAN PLATELET MEMBRANES.
003408 03-13

PSYCHOSOMATIC-STRESS AND LIPOPEROXIDES OF HUMAN PLATELET RICH PLASMA.
003423 03-13

3H IMIPRAMINE BINDING IN HUMAN PLATELETS: DIMINUTION OF BINDING-SITES IN DEPRESSED-PATIENTS.
003427 03-13

HUMAN BRAIN, PLASMA, AND CEREBROSPINAL-FLUID CONCENTRATION OF SODIUM-VALPROATE AFTER 72 HOURS OF THERAPY.
003433 03-13

OPERANT ANALYSIS OF HUMAN HEROIN SELF-ADMINISTRATION AND THE EFFECTS OF NALTREXONE.
003449 03-14

NEUROTOXIC ESTERASE IN HUMAN NERVOUS-TISSUE.
003510 03-15

DIFFERENTIAL BINDING OF CHLORPROMAZINE TO HUMAN BLOOD-CELLS: APPLICATION OF THE HYGROSCOPIC DESORPTION METHOD.
003556 03-16

SYNTHESIS AND BIOLOGICAL-ACTIVITY OF HUMAN BETA ENDORPHIN ANALOGS WITH DISULFIDE BRIDGES.
003655 04-01

A SELECTED ION-MONITORING ASSAY FOR BIOGENIC-AMINE METABOLITES AND PROBENECID, IN HUMAN LUMBAR CEREBROSPINAL-FLUID.
003663 04-01

MEASUREMENT OF HALOPERIDOL IN HUMAN PLASMA USING REVERSED PHASE HIGH-PERFORMANCE LIQUID-CHROMATOGRAPHY. (UNPUBLISHED PAPER).
003667 04-01

PARTIAL PURIFICATION OF ACID SPHINGOMYELINASE FROM NORMAL AND PATHOLOGICAL (M. NIEMANN-PICK TYPE C) HUMAN BRAIN.
003671 04-01

SOLUBILIZATION OF NEUROLEPTIC/DOPAMINE-RECEPTORS OF HUMAN BRAIN STRIATUM.
003767 04-03

THE HUMAN PLATELET AS A MODEL FOR THE GLUTAMATERGIC NEURON: PLATELET UPTAKE OF L GLUTAMATE.
003923 04-03

LIBERATION OF CATECHOLAMINES AND 5 HYDROXYTRYPTAMINE FROM HUMAN BLOOD-PLATELETS.
003967 04-03

(3H) IMIPRAMINE BINDING IN HUMAN PLATELETS: A NEW BIOCHEMICAL-PARAMETER IN DEPRESSION.
004358 04-09

BIOCHEMICAL-STUDIES OF HUMAN EPILEPTICS DURING ANTICONVULSANT THERAPY.
004490 04-11

ELECTRORETINOGRAPHY (ERG) AS A TOOL OF INVESTIGATION IN HUMAN PSYCHOPHARMACOLOGY. ELECTRORETINOGRAPHIC-CHANGES INDUCED BY A COMBINATION OF CARBIDOPA AND LEVODOPA.
004507 04-13

FRAGILE SITES IN HUMAN CHROMOSOMES I. THE EFFECT OF METHIONINE ON THE XQ-FRAGILE-SITE.
004515 04-13

INTERACTION OF CHLORPROMAZINE WITH THE TRANSPORT SYSTEM OF GLUCOSE IN HUMAN ERYTHROCYTES.
004529 04-13

EFFECTS OF RO-11-2465, A NEW PSYCHOTROPIC-AGENT ON THE UPTAKE OF SEROTONIN BY HUMAN PLATELETS -- IN VITRO DETERMINATION OF THE IC50.
004532 04-13

APOMORPHINE, HALOPERIDOL AND THE AVERAGE EVOKED-POTENTIALS IN NORMAL HUMAN VOLUNTEERS.
004549 04-13

HUMAN SOCIAL CONVERSATION: EFFECTS OF ETHANOL, SECOBARBITAL AND CHLORPROMAZINE.
004582 04-14

CHLORPROMAZINE ANALYSIS IN HUMAN PLASMA. (UNPUBLISHED PAPER).
004591 04-15

HUMAN PLATELET ALPHA2-ADRENERGIC-RECEPTORS: LABELING WITH 3H YOHIMBINE, A SELECTIVE ANTAGONIST LIGAND.
004676 04-16

HUMANS
TRANSIENT ABOLITION OF GENERALIZED PHOTOSENSITIVE EPILEPTIC-
DISCHARGE IN HUMANS BY APOMORPHINE, A DOPAMINE-RECEPTOR
AGONIST.
000714 01-11
EFFECT OF LITHIUM-CARBONATE ON CIRCADIAN-PERIODICITY IN
HUMANS.
000772 01-13
INCREASED HUNGER AND THIRST DURING GLUCOPRIVATION IN HUMANS.
000828 01-14
MICROSCOPIC EVIDENCE OF LYMPHOGENIC ABSORPTION OF OIL IN
HUMANS RECEIVING NEUROLEPTIC OILY DEPOT PREPARATIONS
INTRAMUSCULARLY.
000890 01-15
SLEEP PROFILE AND ULTRADIAN SLEEP PERIODICITY IN HUMANS UNDER
THE INFLUENCE OF A BUTYROPHENONE DERIVATIVE: I. SLEEP
CORRECTION IN SUBJECTS WITH OLIGOSYMPTOMATIC SLEEP-
DISORDERS.
001869 02-06
KINETICS AND NEUROPSYCHOLOGIC-EFFECTS OF IV DIAZEPAM IN THE
PRESENCE AND ABSENCE OF ITS ACTIVE N DESMETHYL METABOLITE IN
HUMANS.
002229 02-13
MOOD AND BEHAVIORAL-EFFECTS OF PHYSOSTIGMINE ON HUMANS ARE
ACCOMPANIED BY ELEVATIONS IN PLASMA BETA ENDORPHIN AND
CORTISOL.
002280 02-13
COCAINE EFFECTS IN SLEEP-DEPRIVED HUMANS.
002323 02-14
DRUG PREFERENCE AND MOOD IN HUMANS: DIAZEPAM.
002334 02-14
DRUG PREFERENCE AND MOOD IN HUMANS: D-AMPHETAMINE.
002335 02-14
PHARMACOKINETICS AND BIOAVAILABILITY OF CHLORDIAZEPOXIDE IN
HUMANS.
002564 02-17
A PRIMATE ANALOGUE OF AMPHETAMINE-INDUCED BEHAVIORS IN
HUMANS.
003006 03-04
DRUG PREFERENCE AND MOOD IN HUMANS: REPEATED ASSESSMENT OF
D-AMPHETAMINE.
003445 03-14
EFFECTS OF DEXTROAMPHETAMINE-SULFATE ON REPEATED ACQUISITION-
BEHAVIOR AND MOOD IN HUMANS: A PRELIMINARY REPORT.
003459 03-14
PRENATAL EXPOSURE TO SYNTHETIC PROGESTINS INCREASES POTENTIAL
FOR AGGRESSION IN HUMANS.
003527 03-15
EVENT-RELATED POTENTIAL CHANGES WITH MORPHINE IN NONADDICTED
HUMANS.
004512 04-13
LITHIUM EFFECTS ON CITRATE METABOLISM IN HUMANS AND RATS.
004537 04-13
DRUG PREFERENCE IN HUMANS: DOUBLE-BLIND CHOICE COMPARISON OF
PENTOBARBITAL, DIAZEPAM AND PLACEBO.
004566 04-14

HUNGARIAN
ABSENCE OF SEVERE TARDIVE-DYSKINESIA IN HUNGARIAN
SCHIZOPHRENIC-OUTPATIENTS.
002404 02-15
TARDIVE-DYSKINESIA ON HUNGARIAN PSYCHIATRIC-WARDS.
002447 02-15

HUNGER
THE EFFECT OF SMALL AND MODERATE DOSES OF D-AMPHETAMINE ON
HUNGER, MOOD, AND AROUSAL IN MAN.
000807 01-14
INCREASED HUNGER AND THIRST DURING GLUCOPRIVATION IN HUMANS.
000828 01-14

HUNTINGTON-DISEASE
BROMOCRIPTINE AND DOPAMINERGIC FUNCTION IN HUNTINGTON-
DISEASE.
000700 01-11
TREATMENT OF HUNTINGTON-DISEASE WITH GAMMA ACETYLENIC-
GABA, AN IRREVERSIBLE INHIBITOR OF GABA-TRANSAMINASE:
INCREASED CSF GABA AND HOMOCARNOSINE WITHOUT CLINICAL
AMELIORATION.
003458 03-14

HUNTINGTONS-CHOREA
PLATELET AGGREGATION, 5 HYDROXYTRYPTAMINE UPTAKE AND
RELEASE IN HUNTINGTONS-CHOREA.
002112 02-11

HUNTINGTONS-DISEASE
BODY-WEIGHT, FEEDING, AND DRINKING-BEHAVIORS IN RATS WITH
KAINIC-ACID-INDUCED LESIONS OF STRIATAL NEURONS -- WITH A
NOTE ON BODY-WEIGHT SYMPTOMATOLOGY IN HUNTINGTONS-
DISEASE.
000463 01-04
GABA SYNTHESIS BY CULTURED FIBROBLASTS OBTAINED FROM PERSONS
WITH HUNTINGTONS-DISEASE.
000765 01-13
LEVODOPA AND PRESYMPTOMATIC DETECTION OF HUNTINGTONS-
DISEASE -- EIGHT-YEAR FOLLOWUP.
000950 01-17
HUNTINGTONS-DISEASE: CLINICAL-EFFECTS OF A SHORT-TERM
TREATMENT WITH PIMOZIDE.
002091 02-11
BENZODIAZEPINE-RECEPTORS: THE EFFECT OF GABA ON THEIR
CHARACTERISTICS IN HUMAN BRAIN AND THEIR ALTERATION IN
HUNTINGTONS-DISEASE.
002163 02-11
EARLY DETECTION OF HUNTINGTONS-DISEASE. BLINK REFLEX AND
LEVODOPA LOAD IN PRESYMPTOMATIC AND INCIPIENT SUBJECTS.
003311 03-11
CHOLINOMIMETICS IN HUNTINGTONS-DISEASE.
004442 04-11
CLINICAL AND PRECLINICAL EXPERIENCE WITH CHOLINE-CHLORIDE IN
HUNTINGTONS-DISEASE AND TARDIVE-DYSKINESIA: UNANSWERED
QUESTIONS.
004604 04-15

HUSSER
THE TREATMENT OF CHRONIC SCHIZOPHRENIC-PATIENTS: AN INTERVIEW
WITH DR. J. HUSSER.
004328 04-08

HVA
CEREBROSPINAL-FLUID VALUES OF HVA AND 5 HIAA IN PATIENTS WITH
ENDOGENOUS DEPRESSION DURING THE COURSE OF TREATMENT.
004382 04-09

HYBRID
HYBRID PROTEINS USED TO STUDY THE MECHANISM OF TOXIN
ENTRANCE INTO CELLS. (UNPUBLISHED PAPER).
001063 02-01
PROSTACYCLIN-DEPENDENT ACTIVATION OF ADENYLATE-CYCLASE IN A
NEURONAL SOMATIC CELL HYBRID: PROSTANOID STRUCTURE-ACTIVITY
RELATIONSHIPS.
001132 02-03
RELATIONSHIP BETWEEN THE ACTIONS OF CALCIUM-IONS, OPIOIDS, AND
PROSTAGLANDIN-E1 ON THE LEVEL OF CYCLIC-AMP IN
NEUROBLASTOMA-X GLIOMA HYBRID CELLS.
002677 03-03
CHARACTERIZATION BY (3H)DIHYDROERGOCRYPTINE BINDING OF
ALPHA-ADRENERGIC-RECEPTORS IN NEUROBLASTOMA X GLIOMA
HYBRID CELLS.
003823 04-03
OPIOIDS, NORADRENALINE AND GTP ANALOGS INHIBIT CHOLERA-TOXIN
ACTIVATED ADENYLATE-CYCLASE IN NEUROBLASTOMA-X GLIOMA
HYBRID CELLS.
003975 04-03

HYDERGINE
HYDERGINE: A REVIEW OF 26 CLINICAL-STUDIES.
000704 01-11
NEUROPHARMACOLOGY OF BROMOCRIPTINE AND DIHYDROERGOTOXINE
(HYDERGINE).
001346 02-03
CLINICAL-TRIAL WITH AMANTADINE AND HYDERGINE IN ELDERLY-
PATIENTS.
002093 02-11

HYDIPHEN
THE PHARMACOLOGICAL CHARACTERISTICS OF THE TRANQUILIZING
EFFECT OF HYDIPHEN.
004261 04-04

HYDRALAZINE
BIOLOGIC-INTERACTION OF GAMMA-RADIATION WITH
PHENYLBUTAZONE, PHENYTOIN, OR HYDRALAZINE.
000518 01-05
INDUCTION OF HYPERSENSITIVITY OF BRAIN BY HYDRALAZINE
TREATMENT IN RATS.
003008 03-04
DIFFERENTIAL-EFFECTS OF ALPHA METHYLDOPAMINE, CLONIDINE AND
HYDRALAZINE ON NOREPINEPHRINE AND EPINEPHRINE SYNTHESIZING
ENZYMES IN THE BRAINSTEM NUCLEI OF SPONTANEOUSLY
HYPERTENSIVE-RATS.
003947 04-03

HYDRATE
PHARMACOLOGY OF 2 0 CHLOROBENZOYL-CHLORO-METHYL-NA-
GLYCYLGLYCINANILIDE HYDRATE (45-0088-S), A COMPOUND WITH
BENZODIAZEPINE-LIKE PROPERTIES.
003692 04-02

HYDRAZINE
HOMOCYSTEINE-INDUCED CONVULSIONS: ENHANCEMENT BY VITAMIN-B6
AND INHIBITION BY HYDRAZINE.
002758 03-03

HYDROCEPHALUS
LEVELS OF 5 HYDROXYINDOLEACETIC-ACID AND TRYPTOPHAN IN
LUMBAR CEREBROSPINAL-FLUID AND BLOOD OF PATIENTS WITH
DEMENTIA AND NORMAL PRESSURE HYDROCEPHALUS AFTER
TRYPTOPHAN ADMINISTRATION.
003419 03-13

HYDROCORTISONE
CEREBELLAR GRANULE CELL GENESIS IN THE HYDROCORTISONE TREATED RAT.
000030 01-03
REUPTAKE OF BIOGENIC AMINES BY BRAIN SLICES: EFFECT OF HYDROCORTISONE.
000187 01-03
EFFECT OF NEONATAL HYDROCORTISONE TREATMENT ON BRAIN-MONOAMINES IN DEVELOPING RATS.
003893 04-03

HYDROLYSIS
OXAZEPAM-ESTERS. 1. CORRELATION BETWEEN HYDROLYSIS RATES AND BRAIN APPEARANCE OF OXAZEPAM.
000010 01-02
HALOTHANE EFFECT ON C-AMP GENERATION AND HYDROLYSIS IN RAT-BRAIN.
000305 01-03

HYDROPHOBIC
IDENTIFICATION AND PARTIAL PURIFICATION OF A HYDROPHOBIC PROTEIN COMPONENT ASSOCIATED WITH (3H)SPIROPERIDOL BINDING-ACTIVITY. (UNPUBLISHED PAPER).
001007 02-01

HYDROPHOBICITY
OXAZEPAM-ESTERS. 2. CORRELATION OF HYDROPHOBICITY WITH SERUM BINDING, BRAIN PENETRATION, AND EXCRETION.
000011 01-02

HYDROXY-DELTA9-TETRAHYDROCANNABINOL
BETA DIETHYLAMINOETHYLDIPHENYLPROPYLACETATE (SKF-525-A) AND 2,4 DICHLORO-6-PHENYLPHENOXYYETHYLAMINE-HBR (DPEA) INHIBITION OF FATTY-ACID CONJUGATION TO 11 HYDROXY-DELTA9-TETRAHYDROCANNABINOL BY THE RAT LIVER MICROSOMAL SYSTEM.
000179 01-03

HYDROXY-3-METHOXYMANDELIC-ACID
NOREPINEPHRINE METABOLISM IN MAN USING DEUTERIUM LABELLING: 4 HYDROXY-3-METHOXYMANDELIC-ACID.
004534 04-13

HYDROXYAMITRIPTYLINE
A METHOD FOR THE DETERMINATION OF AMITRIPTYLINE AND ITS METABOLITES NORTRIPTYLINE, 10 HYDROXYAMITRIPTYLINE, AND 10 HYDROXYNORTRIPTYLINE IN HUMAN PLASMA USING STABLE ISOTOPE DILUTION AND GAS-CHROMATOGRAPHY CHEMICAL-IONIZATION MASS-SPECTROMETRY.
002486 02-16

HYDROXYBUTYLHEXAHYDROPYRIDOINDOLE-HCL
FLUORO-5-FLUOROPHENYL-2-FLUOROPHENYL 4 HYDROXYBUTYLHEXAHYDROPYRIDOINDOLE-HCL, A NEW POTENT NEUROLEPTIC.
001092 02-02

HYDROXYBUTYRATE
EFFECTS OF NORADRENERGIC AGONISTS AND ANTAGONISTS ON GROWTH-HORMONE SECRETION UNDER GAMMA HYDROXYBUTYRATE NARCOANALGESIA IN THE RAT.
000262 01-03
HYPERSYNCHRONOUS-ACTIVITY ELICITED BY GAMMA HYDROXYBUTYRATE DURING ONTOGENESIS IN RATS.
000460 01-04
NALOXONE OVERCOMES THE DOPAMINERGIC, EEG, AND BEHAVIORAL-EFFECTS OF GAMMA HYDROXYBUTYRATE.
000478 01-04
TREATMENT OF NARCOLEPSY AND SLEEP-APNEA WITH GAMMA HYDROXYBUTYRATE: A CLINICAL AND POLYSOMNOGRAPHIC CASE-STUDY.
004571 04-14

HYDROXYBUTYRIC-ACID
EFFECTS OF GAMMA HYDROXYBUTYRIC-ACID ON METABOLIC, RESPIRATORY AND VASOMOTOR ACTIVITIES AND BODY-TEMPERATURE IN RATS.
000189 01-03
GAMMA HYDROXYBUTYRIC-ACID AS HYPNOTIC.
000541 01-07
REGIONAL AND SUBCELLULAR LOCALIZATION IN RAT-BRAIN OF THE ENZYMES THAT CAN SYNTHESIZE GAMMA HYDROXYBUTYRIC-ACID.
003675 04-01
EFFECTS OF DOPAMINE, APOMORPHINE, GAMMA HYDROXYBUTYRIC-ACID, HALOPERIDOL AND PIMOZIDE ON REFLEX BRADYCARDIA IN RATS.
004085 04-04

HYDROXYCITRATE
INHIBITION OF THE SYNTHESIS OF ACETYLCHOLINE IN RAT-BRAIN SLICES BY (-) HYDROXYCITRATE AND CITRATE.
004044 04-03

HYDROXYDESIPRAMINE
DESIPRAMINE AND 2 HYDROXYDESIPRAMINE PHARMACOKINETICS IN NORMAL VOLUNTEERS.
003154 03-07

HYDROXYDOPA
EFFECTS OF NEONATAL 6 HYDROXYDOPA ON BEHAVIOR IN FEMALE RATS.
001717 02-04

DEVELOPMENTAL-CHANGE IN REARING RESPONSE TO ATROPINE IN RATS TREATED WITH 6 HYDROXYDOPA.
004191 04-04

HYDROXYDOPAMINE
ROTATIONAL-BEHAVIOR INDUCED BY COCAINE ANALOGS IN RATS WITH UNILATERAL 6-HYDROXYDOPAMINE LESIONS OF THE SUBSTANTIA-NIGRA: DEPENDENCE UPON DOPAMINE UPTAKE INHIBITION.
000404 01-04
EFFECTS OF APOMORPHINE ON ESCAPE PERFORMANCE AND ACTIVITY IN DEVELOPING RAT PUPS TREATED WITH 6 HYDROXYDOPAMINE (6 OHDA).
000426 01-04
INTRAVENTRICULAR 6 HYDROXYDOPAMINE IN THE NEWBORN RAT AND LOCOMOTOR RESPONSES TO DRUGS IN INFANCY: NO SUPPORT FOR THE DOPAMINE DEPLETION MODEL OF MINIMAL-BRAIN-DYSFUNCTION.
000448 01-04
EFFECTS OF 6 HYDROXYDOPAMINE AND AMPHETAMINE ON RAT MOTHERING-BEHAVIOR AND OFFSPRING DEVELOPMENT.
000452 01-04
GABA FACILITATION BY NORADRENALINE SHOWED SUPERSENSITIVITY IN CEREBELLUM AFTER 6 HYDROXYDOPAMINE.
001382 02-03
THE EFFECT OF CYCLO-LEU-GLY ON CHEMICAL DENERVATION SUPERSENSITIVITY OF DOPAMINE-RECEPTORS INDUCED BY INTRACEREBROVENTRICULAR INJECTION OF 6 HYDROXYDOPAMINE IN MICE.
001435 02-03
CENTRAL-ACTIONS OF NOREPINEPHRINE, PHENTOLAMINE AND 6 HYDROXYDOPAMINE IN SPONTANEOUSLY HYPERTENSIVE-RATS.
001553 02-03
THE EFFECTS OF D LYSERGIC-ACID-DIETHYLAMIDE (LSD), 2,5 DIMETHOXY-4-METHYLAMPHETAMINE (DOM) AND D-AMPHETAMINE ON OPERANT-RESPONDING IN CONTROL AND 6 HYDROXYDOPAMINE TREATED RATS.
001595 02-04
PERIPHERAL 6 HYDROXYDOPAMINE ADMINISTRATION IN THE RABBIT (ORYCTOLAGUS-CUNICULUS): EFFECTS ON PAVLOVIAN-CONDITIONING.
001668 02-04
COMPARISONS OF THE EFFECTS OF GUANETHIDINE, 6 HYDROXYDOPAMINE AND DIETHYLDITHIOCARBAMATE ON RETENTION OF PASSIVE-AVOIDANCE.
001742 02-04
THE EFFECTS OF INTRAVENTRICULAR 6 HYDROXYDOPAMINE AND 5,6 DIHYDROXYTRYPTAMINE ON MORPHINE-INDUCED LOCOMOTOR-STIMULATION.
001784 02-04
EFFECT OF 6 HYDROXYDOPAMINE LESIONS OF THE MEDIAL PREFRONTAL-CORTEX ON NEUROTRANSMITTER SYSTEMS IN SUBCORTICAL SITES IN THE RAT.
002869 03-03
HYPERACTIVITY IN DEVELOPING RATS: SEX-DIFFERENCES IN 6 HYDROXYDOPAMINE AND AMPHETAMINE EFFECTS.
002970 03-04
CORTICAL RECOVERY FROM EFFECTS OF MONOCULAR DEPRIVATION: ACCELERATION WITH NOREPINEPHRINE AND SUPPRESSION WITH 6 HYDROXYDOPAMINE.
003024 03-04
EFFECTS OF ELECTROLYTIC AND 6 HYDROXYDOPAMINE LESIONS OF THE LATERAL HYPOTHALAMUS ON ROTATION EVOKED BY ELECTRICAL-STIMULATION OF THE SUBSTANTIA-NIGRA IN RATS.
003081 03-04
DOPAMINE DEPLETION BY 6 HYDROXYDOPAMINE PREVENTS CONDITIONED TASTE-AVERSION INDUCED BY METHYLAMPHETAMINE BUT NOT LITHIUM-CHLORIDE.
003110 03-04
EFFECT OF 6 HYDROXYDOPAMINE ON THE FINE STRUCTURE OF THE HAMSTER PINEAL-GLAND.
003747 04-03
THE DOPAMINE-RECEPTOR COMPLEX: BIOCHEMICAL-CONSEQUENCES OF SUPERSENSITIVITY INDUCED BY TREATMENT WITH 6 HYDROXYDOPAMINE OR MORPHINE.
003958 04-03
THE RELATIONSHIP BETWEEN LOSS OF DOPAMINE NERVE TERMINALS, STRIATAL (3H)SPIROPERIDOL BINDING AND ROTATIONAL-BEHAVIOR IN UNILATERALLY 6 HYDROXYDOPAMINE LESIONED RATS.
004129 04-04
CATECHOLAMINE SEROTONIN INTERACTION EFFECTS ON ACTIVITY IN RATS NEONATALLY TREATED WITH 6 HYDROXYDOPAMINE.
004194 04-04
THE INFLUENCE OF UNILATERAL 6 HYDROXYDOPAMINE LESIONS OF THE SUBSTANTIA-NIGRA IN THE ABSENCE OF THE TELENCEPHALON.
004197 04-04

HYDROXYDOPAMINE-INDUCED
CHANGE IN CATECHOLAMINE SENSITIVE NA-K-ATPASE ACTIVITY IN THE RAT STRIATUM MICROSOMES FOLLOWING ELECTROLYTIC OR 6 HYDROXYDOPAMINE-INDUCED LESIONS OF DOPAMINERGIC NEURONS.
003871 04-03

HYDROXYFLUPHENAZINE
BEHAVIOR OF RATS AND MICE ADMINISTERED ACTIVE METABOLITES OF
FLUPHENAZINE, 7 HYDROXYFLUPHENAZINE AND FLUPHENAZINE-
SULFOXIDE.
004256 04-04

HYDROXYINDOLE
COMPARATIVE-EFFECTS OF P CHLOROAMPHETAMINE AND L P
CHLOROPHENYLPIPERAZINE ON 5 HYDROXYINDOLE CONCENTRATION IN
RAT-BRAIN.
000101 01-03
EFFECT OF 2 P CHLOROPHENYL-CYCLOPROPYLAMINE ON 5
HYDROXYINDOLE CONCENTRATION AND MONOAMINE-OXIDASE
ACTIVITY IN RAT-BRAIN.
001237 02-03

HYDROXYINDOLEACETIC-ACID
BRAIN SEROTONIN AND 5 HYDROXYINDOLEACETIC-ACID
CONCENTRATIONS AND SEROTONIN SYNTHESIS FOLLOWING
TETRAHYDRO-BETA-CARBOLINE ADMINISTRATION IN MICE.
001152 02-03
THE EFFECT OF MORPHINE ON THE CONTENT OF SEROTONIN, 5
HYDROXYINDOLEACETIC-ACID AND SUBSTANCE-P IN THE NUCLEI
RAPHE-MAGNUS AND RETICULARIS-GIGANTOCELLULARIS.
001328 02-03
SIMULTANEOUS DETERMINATION OF FEMTOMOLE QUANTITIES OF 5
HYDROXYTRYPTOPHAN, SEROTONIN AND 5 HYDROXYINDOLEACETIC-
ACID IN BRAIN USING HPLC WITH ELECTROCHEMICAL-DETECTION.
003139 03-06
LEVELS OF 5 HYDROXYINDOLEACETIC-ACID AND TRYPTOPHAN IN
LUMBAR CEREBROSPINAL-FLUID AND BLOOD OF PATIENTS WITH
DEMENTIA AND NORMAL PRESSURE HYDROCEPHALUS AFTER
TRYPTOPHAN ADMINISTRATION.
003419 03-13
A SIMPLE DETERMINATION OF SEROTONIN, 5 HYDROXYINDOLEACETIC-
ACID AND 5 HYDROXYTRYPTOPHAN-DECARBOXYLASE ACTIVITY IN
RAT-BRAIN AREAS AND PARALLEL CORRELATION AMONG THE LEVELS.
004301 04-06
DETERMINATION OF PICOMOLE AMOUNTS OF DOPAMINE,
NORADRENALINE, 3,4 DIHYDROXYPHENYLALANINE, 3,4
DIHYDROXYPHENYLACETIC-ACID, HOMOVANILLIC-ACID, AND 5
HYDROXYINDOLEACETIC-ACID IN NERVOUS-TISSUE AFTER ONE-STEP
PURIFICATION ON SEPHADEX-G-10, USING HIGH.
004305 04-06

HYDROXYINDOLES
A SPECIFIC AND SENSITIVE MICROASSAY FOR HYDROXYINDOLES IN
BIOLOGICAL-MATERIAL -- APPLICATION FOR CEREBRAL MICROVESSELS,
BRAIN, AND PINEAL-ORGAN OF THE RAT.
002503 02-16

HYDROXYLATION
NORTRIPTYLINE AND ANTIPYRINE CLEARANCE IN RELATION TO
· DEBRISOQUINE HYDROXYLATION IN MAN.
000754 01-13
DEVELOPMENT OF AND RECOVERY FROM SUBSENSITIVITY OF THE
NORADRENERGIC CYCLIC-AMP GENERATING SYSTEM IN BRAIN: EFFECT
OF AMPHETAMINE FOLLOWING INHIBITION OF ITS AROMATIC
HYDROXYLATION BY IPRINDOLE.
001353 02-03

HYDROXYMELATONIN
QUANTITATIVE ANALYSIS OF 6 HYDROXYMELATONIN IN HUMAN URINE
BY GAS-CHROMATOGRAPHY NEGATIVE CHEMICAL-IONIZATION MASS-
SPECTROMETRY. (UNPUBLISHED PAPER). ·
001058 02-01

HYDROXYMERCURIBENZOATE
DIPHENYLHYDANTOIN-INDUCED BLOCK OF THE RAT PHRENIC-NERVE
DIAPHRAGM PREPARATION PRETREATED WITH P
HYDROXYMERCURIBENZOATE.
002749 03-03

HYDROXYMETHYL-BETA-CARBOLINE
3 HYDROXYMETHYL-BETA-CARBOLINE ANTAGONIZES SOME
PHARMACOLOGIC ACTIONS OF DIAZEPAM.
004221 04-04

HYDROXYNORTRIPTYLINE
A METHOD FOR THE DETERMINATION OF AMITRIPTYLINE AND ITS
METABOLITES NORTRIPTYLINE, 10 HYDROXYAMITRIPTYLINE, AND 10
HYDROXYNORTRIPTYLINE IN HUMAN PLASMA USING STABLE ISOTOPE
DILUTION AND GAS-CHROMATOGRAPHY CHEMICAL-IONIZATION
MASS-SPECTROMETRY.
· 002486 02-16

HYDROXYTRYPTAMINE
EFFECT OF ACUTE ADMINISTRATION OF MORPHINE ON NEWLY
SYNTHESIZED 5 HYDROXYTRYPTAMINE IN SPINAL-CORD OF THE RAT.
000110 01-03
ALPHA-ADRENOCEPTOR-MEDIATED MODULATION OF 5
HYDROXYTRYPTAMINE RELEASE FROM RAT-BRAIN-CORTEX SLICES.
000111 01-03
THE CONVERSION OF (3H)TRYPTOPHAN TO 5 (3H)HYDROXYTRYPTAMINE
IN MOUSE-BRAIN FOLLOWING DEPLETION OF PHENYLALANINE AND
TYROSINE.
000148 01-03

(3H)ACETYLCHOLINE AND (3H)5 HYDROXYTRYPTAMINE RELEASE FROM
RAT-MIDBRAIN SLICES AND THE EFFECTS OF CALCIUM AND
PHENOBARBITAL.
000251 01-03
THE MECHANISM OF EFFECT OF NEUROPHARMACOLOGICAL-DRUGS. VI:
EFFECT OF NORADRENALINE AND 5 HYDROXYTRYPTAMINE ON BRAIN
FREE FATTY-ACIDS.
000274 01-03
DECREASED UPTAKE OF 5 HYDROXYTRYPTAMINE IN BLOOD-PLATELETS
FROM PATIENTS WITH ENDOGENOUS DEPRESSION.
000637 01-09
TRYPTOPHOL-INDUCED CHANGE IN BRAIN 5 HYDROXYTRYPTAMINE
METABOLISM.
001236 02-03
SEROTONIN-RECEPTOR MEDIATED MODULATION OF CA-DEPENDENT 5
HYDROXYTRYPTAMINE RELEASE FROM NEURONES OF THE RAT-BRAIN-
CORTEX.
001258 02-03
CHARACTERIZATION AND RADIOAUTOGRAPHY OF (3H)LSD BINDING BY
RAT-BRAIN SLICES IN VITRO: THE EFFECT OF 5 HYDROXYTRYPTAMINE.
001369 02-03
NEURONAL TRANSPORT OF 5 HYDROXYTRYPTAMINE.
001451 02-03
ROLE OF BRAIN CATECHOLAMINES AND 5 HYDROXYTRYPTAMINE IN
MORPHINE-INDUCED TEMPERATURE CHANGES IN NORMAL AND
TOLERANT RATS AND MICE.
001476 02-03
CHANGES OF PHYSICAL MORPHINE-DEPENDENCE IN RATS CHRONICALLY
TREATED WITH DRUGS ACTING ON BRAIN 5 HYDROXYTRYPTAMINE.
001764 02-04
THE IONIZATION OF 5 HYDROXYTRYPTAMINE AND RELATED
COMPOUNDS AND AN APPRAISAL OF METHODS FOR THE ESTIMATION
OF ZWITTERION CONSTANTS.
001859 02-06
PLATELET AGGREGATION, 5 HYDROXYTRYPTAMINE UPTAKE AND
RELEASE IN HUNTINGTONS-CHOREA.
002112 02-11
PHENOTHIAZINE ACTION ON CEREBRAL 5 HYDROXYTRYPTAMINE.
002850 03-03
LONG-ACTING ANTIPSYCHOTIC-DRUGS AND CEREBRAL 5
HYDROXYTRYPTAMINE.
002851 03-03
ACTIONS OF TETRAHYDRONORHARMANE (TETRAHYDRO-BETA-
CARBOLINE) ON 5 HYDROXYTRYPTAMINE AND DOPAMINE-MEDIATED
MECHANISMS.
002854 03-03
THE METABOLISM OF 5 HYDROXYTRYPTAMINE IN THE METHIONINE-
SULFOXIMINE EPILEPTOGENIC RAT-BRAIN.
002887 03-03
THE ROLE OF 5 HYDROXYTRYPTAMINE IN DOPAMINE-DEPENDENT
STEREOTYPED-BEHAVIOUR.
002966 03-04
BEHAVIOURAL-RESPONSES TO DRUGS RELEASING 5
HYDROXYTRYPTAMINE AND CATECHOLAMINES: EFFECTS OF
TREATMENTS ALTERING PRECURSOR CONCENTRATIONS IN BRAIN.
002990 03-04
5 HYDROXYTRYPTAMINE CONTROLS ACH-RECEPTOR SENSITIVITY OF
BULLFROG SYMPATHETIC GANGLION CELLS.
003710 04-03
INTERACTIONS BETWEEN A MONOFLUORINATED ANALOGUE OF P
CHLOROAMPHETAMINE AND 5 HYDROXYTRYPTAMINE IN BRAIN.
003719 04-03
CATECHOLAMINE AND 5 HYDROXYTRYPTAMINE SYNTHESIS AND
METABOLISM FOLLOWING INTRACEREBROVENTRICULAR INJECTION OF
DIBUTYRYL-CYCLIC-AMP.
003769 04-03
EFFECTS OF PHENYTOIN ON MOUSE CEREBELLAR 5 HYDROXYTRYPTAMINE
AND NOREPINEPHRINE.
003795 04-03
PRESYNAPTIC REGULATION OF THE RELEASE OF ACETYLCHOLINE BY 5
HYDROXYTRYPTAMINE.
003843 04-03
INFLUENCE OF CALCIUM ON NORADRENALINE RELEASE EVOKED BY 5
HYDROXYTRYPTAMINE, TYRAMINE AND POTASSIUM FROM GOAT
PIAL-ARTERIES.
003925 04-03
EFFECTS OF 5 HYDROXYTRYPTAMINE ON CENTRAL NEURONES
ANTAGONIZED BY BICUCULLINE AND PICROTOXIN.
003931 04-03
LIBERATION OF CATECHOLAMINES AND 5 HYDROXYTRYPTAMINE FROM
HUMAN BLOOD-PLATELETS.
003967 04-03
EFFECT OF IMIPRAMINE ON CENTRAL 5 HYDROXYTRYPTAMINE
TURNOVER AND METABOLISM IN RATS.
003999 04-03
RELATIVE ACTIVITIES OF SUBSTANCES RELATED TO 5
HYDROXYTRYPTAMINE AS DEPOLARIZING-AGENTS OF SUPERIOR
CERVICAL GANGLION CELLS.
004047 04-03

INTRANIGRAL INJECTION OF CAPSAICIN ENHANCES MOTOR-ACTIVITY
AND DEPLETES NIGRAL 5 HYDROXYTRYPTAMINE BUT NOT SUBSTANCE-
P.
                                                        004100 04-04
ATTENUATION OF PETHIDINE-INDUCED ANTINOCICEPTION BY ZIMELIDINE,
AN INHIBITOR OF 5 HYDROXYTRYPTAMINE REUPTAKE.
                                                        004118 04-04
EFFECTS OF NOREPINEPHRINE AND 5 HYDROXYTRYPTAMINE REUPTAKE
INHIBITORS ON ELECTRICALLY-INDUCED SPINAL-CORD SEIZURES IN
RATS.
                                                        004144 04-04

HYDROXYTRYPTAMINE-INDUCED
METERGOLINE ANTAGONISM OF 5 HYDROXYTRYPTAMINE-INDUCED
ACTIVATION OF RAT-CEREBRAL-CORTICAL NA-K-ATPASE.
                                                        000329 01-03
ENHANCEMENT OF 5 HYDROXYTRYPTAMINE-INDUCED BEHAVIORAL-
EFFECTS FOLLOWING CHRONIC ADMINISTRATION OF ANTIDEPRESSANT-
DRUGS.
                                                        001667 02-04

HYDROXYTRYPTAMINE-LIKE
5 HYDROXYTRYPTAMINE-LIKE PROPERTIES OF M
CHLOROPHENYLPIPERAZINE: COMPARISON WITH QUIPAZINE.
                                                        004210 04-04

HYDROXYTRYPTAMINE-RECEPTORS
ANTAGONISM OF 5 HYDROXYTRYPTAMINE-RECEPTORS BY QUIPAZINE.
                                                        001329 02-03

HYDROXYTRYPTAMINERGIC
DISRUPTION OF 5 HYDROXYTRYPTAMINERGIC NEURONAL FUNCTION
BLOCKS THE ACTION OF MORPHINE ON TUBEROINFUNDIBULAR
DOPAMINERGIC NEURONS.
                                                        002700 03-03
DESTRUCTION OF 5 HYDROXYTRYPTAMINERGIC NEURONS AND THE
DYNAMICS OF DOPAMINE IN NUCLEUS-ACCUMBENS SEPTI AND OTHER
FOREBRAIN REGIONS OF THE RAT.
                                                        004171 04-04

HYDROXYTRYPTOPHAN
REVERSAL OF PARA CHLOROPHENYLALANINE-INDUCED INSOMNIA BY 5
HYDROXYTRYPTOPHAN IN THE RAT.
                                                        000423 01-04
EFFECTS OF L-DOPA AND L 5 HYDROXYTRYPTOPHAN ON LOCOMOTOR-
ACTIVITY OF THE RAT AFTER SELECTIVE OR COMBINED DESTRUCTION
OF CENTRAL CATECHOLAMINE AND SEROTONIN NEURONS.
                                                        000466 01-04
ANTIDEPRESSANT POTENTIATION OF 5 HYDROXYTRYPTOPHAN BY L
DEPRENIL IN AFFECTIVE-ILLNESS.
                                                        000608 01-09
DIPSOGENIC-EFFECT OF L 5 HYDROXYTRYPTOPHAN IN RATS.
                                                        001623 02-04
5 HYDROXYTRYPTOPHAN AND PYRIDOXINE: THEIR EFFECTS IN YOUNG
CHILDREN WITH DOWNS-SYNDROME.
                                                        002161 02-11
TREATMENT OF MYOCLONUS WITH L 5 HYDROXYTRYPTOPHAN AND
CARBIDOPA: CLINICAL, ELECTROPHYSIOLOGICAL, AND BIOCHEMICAL-
OBSERVATIONS.
                                                        002180 02-11
BIOAVAILABILITY AND RELATED PHARMACOKINETICS IN MAN OF
ORALLY ADMINISTERED L 5 HYDROXYTRYPTOPHAN IN STEADY-STATE.
                                                        002261 02-13
NONSEROTONERGIC DEPRESSION OF SPINAL MONOSYNAPTIC REFLEX
TRANSMISSION BY 5 HYDROXYTRYPTOPHAN.
                                                        002745 03-03
PROTECTIVE ACTION OF L 5 HYDROXYTRYPTOPHAN L GLUTAMATE
(MADE-1932) DURING ELECTROSHOCK-TREATMENT (ECT).
                                                        003043 03-04
SIMULTANEOUS DETERMINATION OF FEMTOMOLE QUANTITIES OF 5
HYDROXYTRYPTOPHAN, SEROTONIN AND 5 HYDROXYINDOLEACETIC-
ACID IN BRAIN USING HPLC WITH ELECTROCHEMICAL-DETECTION.
                                                        003139 03-06
DENERVATION SUPERSENSITIVITY TO 5 HYDROXYTRYPTOPHAN IN RATS
FOLLOWING SPINAL TRANSECTION AND 5,7 DIHYDROXYTRYPTAMINE
INJECTION.
                                                        003722 04-03
AUTORADIOGRAPHIC STUDIES ON DISTRIBUTION OF L-3,4
DIHYDROXYPHENYLALANINE (L-DOPA) 14C AND L 5
HYDROXYTRYPTOPHAN (L 5 HTP) 14C IN THE CAT BRAIN.
                                                        003941 04-03

HYDROXYTRYPTOPHAN-DECARBOXYLASE
A SIMPLE DETERMINATION OF SEROTONIN, 5 HYDROXYINDOLEACETIC-
ACID AND 5 HYDROXYTRYPTOPHAN-DECARBOXYLASE ACTIVITY IN
RAT-BRAIN AREAS AND PARALLEL CORRELATION AMONG THE LEVELS.
                                                        004301 04-06

HYDROXYTRYPTOPHAN-INDUCED
L 5 HYDROXYTRYPTOPHAN-INDUCED DRINKING IN RATS: POSSIBLE
MECHANISMS FOR INDUCTION.
                                                        004237 04-04

HYGROSCOPIC
DIFFERENTIAL BINDING OF CHLORPROMAZINE TO HUMAN BLOOD CELLS:
APPLICATION OF THE HYGROSCOPIC DESORPTION METHOD.
                                                        003556 03-16

HYPERACTIVE
EFFECTS OF METHYLPHENIDATE ON SELECTIVE AND SUSTAINED
ATTENTION IN HYPERACTIVE, READING-DISABLED, AND PRESUMABLY
ATTENTION-DISORDERED BOYS.
                                                        002118 02-11
THE INFLUENCE OF METHYLPHENIDATE ON SPONTANEOUS AUTONOMIC-
ACTIVITY AND BEHAVIOR IN CHILDREN DIAGNOSED AS HYPERACTIVE.
                                                        003363 03-11

HYPERACTIVE-BEHAVIOR
EVALUATION OF SYMPTOMATIC TREATMENT OF HYPERACTIVE-BEHAVIOR
BY STIMULANT-DRUGS.
                                                        002134 02-11

HYPERACTIVE-BOYS
DEXTROAMPHETAMINE: COGNITIVE AND BEHAVIORAL-EFFECTS IN
NORMAL AND HYPERACTIVE-BOYS AND NORMAL ADULT MALES.
                                                        000716 01-11
EFFECTS OF METHYLPHENIDATE ON OPERANT-RESPONDING IN
HYPERACTIVE-BOYS. (PH.D. DISSERTATION).
                                                        002191 02-11

HYPERACTIVE-CHILD
PSYCHOACTIVE-DRUG-EFFECTS IN A HYPERACTIVE-CHILD: A CASE-STUDY
ANALYSIS OF BEHAVIOR-CHANGE AND TEACHER ATTENTION.
                                                        002313 02-14

HYPERACTIVE-CHILD-SYNDROME
THE HYPERACTIVE-CHILD-SYNDROME: PERIPHERAL SYMPATHETIC-
NERVOUS-SYSTEM FUNCTION AND THE EFFECT OF D-AMPHETAMINE.
                                                        003340 03-11

HYPERACTIVE-CHILDREN
A CONTROLLED-TRIAL OF BEHAVIOR-MODIFICATION AND
METHYLPHENIDATE IN HYPERACTIVE-CHILDREN.
                                                        000678 01-11
THE REAL AND IDEAL MANAGEMENT OF STIMULANT DRUG-TREATMENT
FOR HYPERACTIVE-CHILDREN: RECENT FINDINGS AND A REPORT FROM
CLINICAL-PRACTICE.
                                                        000715 01-11
THE PARENT CHILD INTERACTIONS OF HYPERACTIVE-CHILDREN AND THEIR
MODIFICATION BY STIMULANT-DRUGS.
                                                        002092 02-11
PREDICTING THE RESPONSE OF HYPERACTIVE-CHILDREN TO RITALIN: AN
EMPIRICAL-STUDY.
                                                        002120 02-11
TOLERANCE TO DEXTROAMPHETAMINE-SULFATE IN HYPERACTIVE-
CHILDREN: ASSESSMENT USING AN EMPIRICAL NEUROPSYCHOLOGICAL
PARADIGM -- A PILOT-STUDY.
                                                        002126 02-11
THE DIFFERENTIAL DOSE-EFFECTS OF METHYLPHENIDATE ON
HYPERACTIVE-CHILDREN AND THEIR MOTHERS. (PH.D.
DISSERTATION).
                                                        002143 02-11
EFFECTS OF AMPHETAMINE ON VIGILANCE PERFORMANCE IN NORMAL
AND HYPERACTIVE-CHILDREN.
                                                        002359 02-14
EVALUATION OF THE RELATIVE EFFECTIVENESS OF METHYLPHENIDATE
AND COGNITIVE BEHAVIOR-MODIFICATION IN THE TREATMENT OF
KINDERGARTEN-AGED HYPERACTIVE-CHILDREN.
                                                        003306 03-11
COMPUTER-ANALYZED EEG IN AMPHETAMINE RESPONSIVE
HYPERACTIVE-CHILDREN.
                                                        003338 03-11
PREDICTING STIMULANT-EFFECTIVENESS IN HYPERACTIVE-CHILDREN WITH
A REPEATABLE NEUROPSYCHOLOGICAL-BATTERY: A PRELIMINARY-
STUDY.
                                                        004453 04-11

HYPERACTIVE-CHILDRENS
THE USE OF SENSORY INTEGRATIVE DIAGNOSTICS TO PREDICT
HYPERACTIVE-CHILDRENS RESPONSIVENESS TO METHYLPHENIDATE
(RITALIN) AND PEMOLINE (CYLERT). (PH.D. DISSERTATION).
                                                        002133 02-11

HYPERACTIVES
HYPERACTIVES AS YOUNG ADULTS: PROSPECTIVE TEN-YEAR FOLLOWUP.
                                                        004454 04-11

HYPERACTIVITY
EFFECTS OF RESERPINE AND AMPHETAMINE ON THE DEVELOPMENT OF
HYPERACTIVITY IN MATERNALLY-DEPRIVED RAT PUPS.
                                                        001654 02-04
HYPERACTIVITY IN DEVELOPING RATS: SEX-DIFFERENCES IN 6
HYDROXYDOPAMINE AND AMPHETAMINE EFFECTS.
                                                        002970 03-04
A NOTE ON THE PARADOXICAL-EFFECT OF STIMULANTS ON
HYPERACTIVITY WITH REFERENCE TO THE RATE DEPENDENCY EFFECT
OF DRUGS.
                                                        003320 03-11
AUTONOMIC-EFFECTS OF DEXTROAMPHETAMINE IN NORMAL MEN:
IMPLICATIONS FOR HYPERACTIVITY AND SCHIZOPHRENIA.
                                                        003437 03-13
DOPAMINE-DEPENDENT HYPERACTIVITY IN THE FOLLOWING
MANIPULATION OF GABA MECHANISMS IN THE REGION OF THE
NUCLEUS-ACCUMBENS.
                                                        003976 04-03

HYPERACTIVITY FOLLOWING INJECTION OF A GLUTAMATE AGONIST AND
6,7 ADTN INTO RAT NUCLEUS-ACCUMBENS AND ITS INHIBITION BY
THIP.
004066 04-04
CENTRAL AND PERIPHERAL EFFECTS OF LITHIUM ON AMPHETAMINE-
INDUCED HYPERACTIVITY IN RATS.
004223 04-04
DRUG-THERAPY FOR HYPERACTIVITY: TREATMENT PROCEDURES IN
NATURAL SETTINGS.
004449 04-11
PREVALENCE OF HYPERACTIVITY AND RELATED TREATMENTS AMONG
ELEMENTARY SCHOOL CHILDREN.
004469 04-11
PREVALENCE OF DRUG-TREATMENT FOR HYPERACTIVITY AND OTHER
CHILDHOOD BEHAVIOR-DISORDERS.
004713 04-17
PSYCHOSOCIAL-ASPECTS OF DRUG-TREATMENT FOR HYPERACTIVITY.
004714 04-17

HYPERACTIVITY-SYNDROME
PLASMA FREE AND TOTAL TRYPTOPHAN, BLOOD SEROTONIN, AND THE
HYPERACTIVITY-SYNDROME: NO EVIDENCE FOR THE SEROTONIN
DEFICIENCY HYPOTHESIS.
003312 03-11

HYPERALGESIA
REPEATED ADMINISTRATION OF NALTREXONE PRODUCES TOLERANCE TO
NALOXONE-INDUCED HYPERALGESIA.
000453 01-04
ANALGESIC ACTIVITY OF DIFLUNISAL (MK-647; 5 2,4
DIFLUOROPHENYLSALICYLIC-ACID) IN RATS WITH HYPERALGESIA
INDUCED BY FREUNDS-ADJUVANT.
000502 01-04
INTRATHECAL HIGH-DOSE MORPHINE PRODUCES HYPERALGESIA IN THE
RAT.
004254 04-04

HYPERALGESIC
DOPAMINERGIC INVOLVEMENT IN THE HYPERALGESIC EFFECT OF
NOMIFENSINE.
002736 03-03

HYPERCALCEMIA
THIAZIDE-INDUCED HYPERCALCEMIA IN A MANIC-DEPRESSIVE-PATIENT.
000843 01-15
RENAL IMPAIRMENT, HYPERCALCEMIA, AND LITHIUM THERAPY.
003473 03-15

HYPERGLYCEMIA
BETA ENDORPHIN-INDUCED HYPERGLYCEMIA IS MEDIATED BY INCREASED
CENTRAL SYMPATHETIC OUTFLOW TO ADRENAL-MEDULLA.
002924 03-03
INTRAVENTRICULAR CHOLECYSTOKININ-OCTAPEPTIDE PRODUCES
HYPERGLYCEMIA IN RATS.
003943 04-03

HYPERGLYCEMIC
IMPROVEMENT OF RESTITUTION FROM CEREBRAL ISCHEMIA IN
HYPERGLYCEMIC RATS BY PENTOBARBITAL OR DIAZEPAM.
000475 01-04

HYPERINNERVATION
FUNCTIONAL HYPERINNERVATION OF CEREBRAL-CORTEX BY
NORADRENERGIC NEURONS RESULTS FROM FETAL LESIONS: PARALLELS
WITH SCHIZOPHRENIA.
000059 01-03

HYPERKINESIA
TRANSIENT HYPERKINESIA AFTER A SINGLE INTRAVENOUS PERFUSION OF
DIPHENYLHYDANTOIN: REPORT OF A CASE ASSOCIATED WITH
NONTOXIC PLASMA LEVELS OF DIPHENYLHYDANTOIN.
004638 04-15

HYPERKINESIS
ADVERSE-REACTIONS TO MEDICATIONS PRESCRIBED FOR HYPERKINESIS.
(PH.D. DISSERTATION).
002411 02-15

HYPERKINETIC
INTERACTION OF PSYCHOPHARMALOGIC-FACTORS AND PSYCHOSOCIAL-
FACTORS IN THE TREATMENT OF ANIMAL-MODELS OF
HYPOINHIBITORY (HYPERKINETIC) BEHAVIOR.
001602 02-04

HYPERKINETIC-BOYS
PREDICTORS OF ADOLESCENT HEIGHT AND WEIGHT IN HYPERKINETIC-
BOYS TREATED WITH METHYLPHENIDATE.
003509 03-15

HYPERKINETIC-CHILDREN
CLONAZEPAM AND DITHIADEN IN HYPERKINETIC-CHILDREN.
000729 01-11
EFFECTS OF METHYLPHENIDATE-HYDROCHLORIDE ON REPEATED
ACQUISITION-BEHAVIOR IN HYPERKINETIC-CHILDREN. (PH.D.
DISSERTATION).
003386 03-11
DRUG AND DIETETIC THERAPIES FOR HYPERKINETIC-CHILDREN. (PH.D.
DISSERTATION).
003576 03-17

HYPERKINETIC-SYNDROME
MINIMAL-BRAIN-DYSFUNCTION -- HYPERKINETIC-SYNDROME.
000730 01-11

NONCOOPERATION: AN EXAMINATION OF FACTORS LEADING TO NONCOMPLIANCE IN A HYPERTENSION CLINIC.

002557 02-17

HIGH-AFFINITY RENAL (3H)FLUNITRAZEPAM BINDING: CHARACTERIZATION, LOCALIZATION, AND ALTERATION IN HYPERTENSION.

002874 03-03

INTERMITTENT DECORTICATION AND PROGRESSIVE HYPERTHERMIA, HYPERTENSION AND TACHYCARDIA FOLLOWING METHYLGLUCAMINE IOTHALAMATE VENTRICULOGRAM.

003520 03-15

CENTRAL DOPAMINERGIC NEURONS DURING DEVELOPMENT OF GENETIC AND DOCA-SALT HYPERTENSION IN THE RAT.

003899 04-03

HYPERTENSIVE
EFFECT OF BROMOCRIPTINE ON EXPLORATORY-ACTIVITY, BRAIN-MONOAMINES AND PLASMA CORTICOSTERONE IN THE NORMOTENSIVE-RATS, GENETICALLY HYPERTENSIVE-RATS AND/OR HYPERTENSIVE OBESE RATS.

001635 02-04

HYPERTENSIVE-PATIENTS
THE EFFECT OF BETA-ADRENERGIC-RECEPTOR BLOCKING-DRUGS ON CEREBRAL BLOOD FLOW IN HYPERTENSIVE-PATIENTS.

002071 02-10

HYPERTENSIVE-RAT
PRESSOR EFFECTS OF DORSAL RAPHE STIMULATION AND INTRAHYPOTHALAMIC APPLICATION OF SEROTONIN IN THE SPONTANEOUSLY HYPERTENSIVE-RAT.

003117 03-04

HYPERTENSIVE-RATS
TYROSINE ADMINISTRATION REDUCES BLOOD-PRESSURE AND ENHANCES BRAIN NOREPINEPHRINE RELEASE IN SPONTANEOUSLY HYPERTENSIVE-RATS.

000296 01-03

DOSE-DEPENDENT, AMPHETAMINE-INDUCED CHANGES IN PERMEABILITY OF THE BLOOD-BRAIN-BARRIER OF NORMOTENSIVE-RATS AND SPONTANEOUSLY HYPERTENSIVE-RATS.

001197 02-03

INCREASED RENAL NEUROLEPTIC BINDING IN SPONTANEOUSLY HYPERTENSIVE-RATS.

001444 02-03

SPONTANEOUSLY (GENETIC) HYPERTENSIVE-RATS PRESENT A NALOXONE SENSITIVE DECREASE IN PAIN SENSITIVITY. (UNPUBLISHED PAPER).

001457 02-03

INCREASED ADRENALINE, BETA-ADRENERGIC-RECEPTOR STIMULATION AND PHOSPHOLIPID METHYLATION IN PINEAL-GLAND OF SPONTANEOUSLY HYPERTENSIVE-RATS. (UNPUBLISHED PAPER).

001458 02-03

CENTRAL AMINERGIC AND PEPTIDERGIC MECHANISMS IN SPONTANEOUSLY (GENETIC) HYPERTENSIVE-RATS. (UNPUBLISHED PAPER).

001459 02-03

CENTRAL-ACTIONS OF NOREPINEPHRINE, PHENTOLAMINE AND 6 HYDROXYDOPAMINE IN SPONTANEOUSLY HYPERTENSIVE-RATS.

001553 02-03

EFFECT OF BROMOCRIPTINE ON EXPLORATORY-ACTIVITY, BRAIN-MONOAMINES AND PLASMA CORTICOSTERONE IN THE NORMOTENSIVE-RATS, GENETICALLY HYPERTENSIVE-RATS AND/OR HYPERTENSIVE OBESE RATS.

001635 02-04

SELF-STIMULATION REACTION IN NORMOTENSIVE-RATS AND HYPERTENSIVE-RATS.

002663 03-03

INCREASED AMPHETAMINE STEREOTYPY AND LONGER HALOPERIDOL CATALEPSY IN SPONTANEOUSLY HYPERTENSIVE-RATS.

002891 03-03

POSSIBLE ROLE OF AN ENDOGENOUS OPIATE IN THE CARDIOVASCULAR-EFFECTS OF CENTRAL ALPHA-ADRENOCEPTOR STIMULATION IN SPONTANEOUSLY HYPERTENSIVE-RATS.

003791 04-03

DIFFERENTIAL-EFFECTS OF ALPHA METHYLDOPAMINE, CLONIDINE AND HYDRALAZINE ON NOREPINEPHRINE AND EPINEPHRINE SYNTHESIZING ENZYMES IN THE BRAINSTEM NUCLEI OF SPONTANEOUSLY HYPERTENSIVE-RATS.

003947 04-03

DIETARY PROTEIN INTAKE INFLUENCES THE ANTIHYPERTENSIVE POTENCY OF METHYLDOPA IN SPONTANEOUSLY HYPERTENSIVE-RATS.

004025 04-03

HYPERTHERMIA
ENDORPHIN-INDUCED HYPERTHERMIA: CHARACTERIZATION OF THE EXOGENOUSLY-INDUCED AND ENDOGENOUSLY-INDUCED EFFECTS.

000029 01-03

APHAGIA, GASTRIC PATHOLOGY, HYPERTHERMIA, AND SENSORIMOTOR-DYSFUNCTIONS FOLLOWING LATERAL HYPOTHALAMIC LESIONS: EFFECTS OF INSULIN PRETREATMENT.

001638 02-04

TEMPORAL AND ENVIRONMENTAL CUES IN CONDITIONED HYPOTHERMIA AND HYPERTHERMIA ASSOCIATED WITH MORPHINE.

002709 03-03

SELECTIVE EFFECTS OF LSD AND HYPERTHERMIA ON THE SYNTHESIS OF SYNAPTIC PROTEINS AND GLYCOPROTEINS.

002721 03-03

INTERMITTENT DECORTICATION AND PROGRESSIVE HYPERTHERMIA, HYPERTENSION AND TACHYCARDIA FOLLOWING METHYLGLUCAMINE IOTHALAMATE VENTRICULOGRAM.

003520 03-15

HYPERTHERMIC-DOSE
PROSTAGLANDINS IN THE BRAIN OF RATS GIVEN, ACUTELY, AND CHRONICALLY, A HYPERTHERMIC-DOSE OF MET-ENKEPHALIN.

001468 02-03

HYPERTHERMIC-EFFECTS
ENHANCED BEHAVIOURAL-EFFECTS, ELECTROCORTICAL-EFFECTS AND HYPERTHERMIC-EFFECTS OF SEROTONIN-LIKE AGENTS AFTER IMPAIRMENT OF SEROTONIN TRANSMISSION IN FOWL BRAIN.

001733 02-04

HYPERTHERMIC-RESPONSE
STUDIES ON THE HYPERTHERMIC-RESPONSE OF BETA ENDORPHIN IN MICE.

000137 01-03

HYPERTHERMIC-RESPONSE TO (-) CATHINONE, AN ALKALOID OF CATHA-EDULIS (KHAT).

003694 04-02

HYPERVENTILATION-SYNDROME
HYPERVENTILATION-SYNDROME, TREATMENT WITH L TRYPTOPHAN AND PYRIDOXINE; PREDICTIVE VALUES OF XANTHURENIC-ACID EXCRETION.

004456 04-11

HYPERVENTILATION-SYNDROME AND BETA-RECEPTOR FUNCTION -- CLINICAL-EFFECT OF BETA BLOCKER UPON THE SYNDROME.

004459 04-11

HYPNAGOGIC
HYPNAGOGIC AND HYPNOPOMPIC HALLUCINATIONS DURING AMITRIPTYLINE TREATMENT.

000850 01-15

HYPNOPOMPIC
HYPNAGOGIC AND HYPNOPOMPIC HALLUCINATIONS DURING AMITRIPTYLINE TREATMENT.

000850 01-15

HYPNOSEDATIVE
INTRAVENOUS PHENOBARBITAL THERAPY IN BARBITURATE AND OTHER HYPNOSEDATIVE WITHDRAWAL REACTIONS: A KINETIC APPROACH.

000703 01-11

HYPNOSIS
POTENTIATION OF BARBITURATE HYPNOSIS BY PROBENECID: DIFFERENTIAL-EFFECT IN TOLERANT ANIMALS.

003038 03-04

EFFECTS OF PAIN, MORPHINE AND NALOXONE ON THE DURATION OF ANIMAL HYPNOSIS.

004081 04-04

HYPNOTIC
GAMMA HYDROXYBUTYRIC-ACID AS HYPNOTIC.

000541 01-07

COMPARATIVE-STUDY OF SLEEP AND STATE ON AWAKENING WITH TWO HYPNOTIC DIAZEPINES.

000817 01-14

NEUROPHYSIOLOGICAL-EFFECTS OF ETOMIDATE, A NEW SHORT-ACTING HYPNOTIC.

002263 02-13

EUHYPNOS-FORTE, HIGH-DOSE TEMAZEPAM FOR RESISTANT INSOMNIA: POSTMARKETING SURVEILLANCE IN 10,057 PATIENTS UNRESPONSIVE TO CONVENTIONAL HYPNOTIC DOSAGE.

002324 02-14

HYPNOTIC ACTION OF FLUNITRAZEPAM (ROCHES ROIPNOL) IN PATIENTS WITH SEVERE PSYCHIATRIC-DISORDERS.

003295 03-11

HYPNOTIC-COMPOUNDS
RESIDUAL-EFFECTS OF TEMAZEPAM AND OTHER HYPNOTIC-COMPOUNDS ON COGNITIVE FUNCTION.

000879 01-15

HYPNOTIC-DRUG
PHARMACOLOGICAL-PROPERTIES OF TAGLUTIMIDE, A NEW SEDATIVE HYPNOTIC-DRUG.

001087 02-02

EEG ASSESSMENTS OF DOSAGE AND SLEEP PROFILES FOR A HYPNOTIC- . DRUG OF THE TRIAZOLOTHIENODIACEPINE SERIES.

002338 02-14

DIFFICULTIES ENCOUNTERED DURING A CONTROLLED STUDY OF A NEW HYPNOTIC-DRUG (TRIAZOLAM) BY A GROUP OF GENERAL- . PRACTITIONERS.

003155 03-07

HYPNOTIC-DRUGS
HYPNOTIC-DRUGS AND TREATMENT OF INSOMNIA.

003350 03-11

HYPNOTIC-EFFECTS
COMPARATIVE ANXIOLYTIC AND HYPNOTIC-EFFECTS OF 3 BENZODIAZEPINES ON BABOONS.

001581 02-04

EFFECT OF P CHLOROPHENYLALANINE ON THE ACQUISITION OF TOLERANCE TO THE HYPNOTIC-EFFECTS OF PENTOBARBITAL, BARBITAL, AND ETHANOL.
003883 04-03

HYPNOTIC-INTERACTIONS
ETHANOL SEDATIVE HYPNOTIC-INTERACTIONS: IN VITRO STUDIES ON NA-K-ACTIVATED ADENOSINE-TRIPHOSPHATASE.
004269 04-05

HYPNOTICA
THE TWO SURVIVAL CASES OF ALPHA-PATTERN COMA CAUSED BY LARGE AMOUNTS OF HYPNOTICA AND NEUROLEPTICA.
004608 04-15

HYPNOTICS
THE QUANTITATIVE MEASUREMENT OF CHANGES IN EEG FREQUENCY SPECTRA PRODUCED IN THE CAT BY SEDATIVE HYPNOTICS AND NEUROLEPTICS.
001220 02-03

HYPNOTIZABILITY
HYPNOTIZABILITY AND PSYCHOACTIVE-MEDICATION.
000823 01-14

HYPOACTIVITY
DOPAMINE HYPOACTIVITY MEASURED BY IN VIVO VOLTAMMETRY.
001149 02-03
LITHIUM AMELIORATION OF RESERPINE-INDUCED HYPOACTIVITY IN RATS.
004167 04-04

HYPOALGESIA
HYPOALGESIA INDUCED BY MICROINJECTION OF A NOREPINEPHRINE ANTAGONIST IN THE RAPHE-MAGNUS: REVERSAL BY INTRATHECAL ADMINISTRATION OF A SEROTONIN ANTAGONIST.
000121 01-03
HYPOALGESIA FOLLOWING MICROINJECTION OF NORADRENERGIC ANTAGONISTS IN THE NUCLEUS-RAPHE-MAGNUS.
000122 01-03

HYPOBARIC
EFFECT OF TABERNANTHINE ON THE TURNOVER TIME OF BRAIN CATECHOLAMINES IN NORMAL AND HYPOBARIC HYPOXIC RATS.
001187 02-03

HYPOCHONDRIACAL
THE PROBLEM OF PSYCHOPHARMACOTHERAPY OF SLOWLY PROGRESSIVE HYPOCHONDRIACAL SCHIZOPHRENIA.
004340 04-08

HYPOCHONDRIACAL-PATIENTS
FLUSPIRILENE (IMAP) IN THE TREATMENT OF PSYCHOSOMATIC-COMPLAINTS IN HYPOCHONDRIACAL-PATIENTS.
002072 02-10

HYPOGLYCEMIA
AMMONIA AND DISINHIBITION IN CAT MOTOR-CORTEX BY AMMONIUM-ACETATE, MONOFLUOROACETATE AND INSULIN-INDUCED HYPOGLYCEMIA.
004276 04-05

HYPOGLYCEMIC
EFFECTS OF BICUCULLINE-INDUCED SEIZURES ON CEREBRAL METABOLISM AND CIRCULATION OF RATS RENDERED HYPOGLYCEMIC BY STARVATION.
001134 02-03

HYPOINHIBITORY
INTERACTION OF PSYCHOPHARMALOGIC-FACTORS AND PSYCHOSOCIAL-FACTORS IN THE TREATMENT OF ANIMAL-MODELS OF HYPOINHIBITORY (HYPERKINETIC) BEHAVIOR.
001602 02-04

HYPOKINESIA
SUPERSENSITIVITY TO APOMORPHINE IN EXPERIMENTALLY-INDUCED HYPOKINESIA AND DRUG-INDUCED MODIFICATIONS OF THE APOMORPHINE RESPONSE.
001814 02-04

HYPOMANIA
HYPOMANIA AND TRICYCLIC-ANTIDEPRESSANT CHOICE.
000545 01-07
HYPOMANIA AS A STABLE STATE: LITHIUM PROPHYLAXIS IN TWO PATIENTS.
003212 03-09
HYPOMANIA AND MANIA AFTER WITHDRAWAL OF TRICYCLIC-ANTIDEPRESSANTS.
003243 03-09

HYPOMANIC-REACTION
HYPOMANIC-REACTION TO AMITRIPTYLINE IN A DEPRESSED-CHILD.
002418 02-15

HYPOPHYSECTOMY
HYPOPHYSECTOMY PREVENTS THE STRIATAL DOPAMINE-RECEPTOR SUPERSENSITIVITY PRODUCED BY CHRONIC HALOPERIDOL TREATMENT.
000132 01-03
THE EFFECTS OF GONADECTOMY AND HYPOPHYSECTOMY ON THE METABOLISM OF IMIPRAMINE AND LIDOCAINE BY THE LIVER OF MALE AND FEMALE RATS.
000273 01-03
HYPOPHYSECTOMY INCREASES THE SENSITIVITY OF RATS TO NALOXONE-INDUCED HYPOTHERMIA.
002710 03-03

HYPOPHYSIS
EXPERIENCE IN USING THE HORMONES OF THE HYPOPHYSIS POSTERIOR LOBE IN MEMORY-DISTURBANCES OF VARYING GENESES.
003438 03-14
DRUG-INDUCED ALTERATIONS OF THE HYPOTHALAMUS HYPOPHYSIS AXIS.
004535 04-13

HYPOSENSITIVITY
RAPID DEVELOPMENT OF HYPERSENSITIVITY AND HYPOSENSITIVITY TO APOMORPHINE AND HALOPERIDOL: ROLE OF NOREPINEPHRINE-RECEPTOR MECHANISMS IN CNS.
001178 02-03

HYPOTAURINE
INHIBITORY ACTIONS OF TAUROCYAMINE, HYPOTAURINE, HOMOTAURINE, TAURINE AND GABA ON SPIKE DISCHARGES OF PURKINJE-CELLS, AND LOCALIZATION OF SENSITIVE SITES, IN GUINEA-PIG CEREBELLAR SLICES.
002846 03-03

HYPOTENSION
COMPOUND-48-80 INHIBITS NEUROTENSIN-INDUCED HYPOTENSION IN RATS.
000243 01-03
THE ROLE OF DIFFERENTIAL BLOCKADE OF ALPHA-ADRENERGIC AGONISTS IN CHLORPROMAZINE-INDUCED HYPOTENSION.
001851 02-05
DRUG-INDUCED ARTERIAL HYPOTENSION IN PSYCHIATRIC-PATIENTS TREATED WITH DIHYDROERGOTAMINE.
001950 02-08
TREATMENT OF PSYCHOTROPIC-CAUSED ORTHOSTATIC HYPOTENSION.
002428 02-15
HYPOTENSION ALTERS THE RELEASE OF CATECHOLAMINES IN THE HYPOTHALAMUS OF THE CONSCIOUS RABBIT.
003968 04-03

HYPOTENSION-SYNDROMES
PHARMACOLOGIC DISTINCTION OF DIFFERENT ORTHOSTATIC HYPOTENSION-SYNDROMES.
003362 03-11

HYPOTENSIVE-ACTION
THE HYPOTENSIVE-ACTION OF 3 DEAZAADENOSINE.
001415 02-03

HYPOTENSIVE-EFFECT
POSSIBLE INVOLVEMENT OF CYCLIC-AMP AND FRONTAL-CORTEX IN AMITRIPTYLINE MEDIATED SUPPRESSION OF THE HYPOTENSIVE-EFFECT OF CLONIDINE.
001259 02-03
THE HYPOTENSIVE-EFFECT OF CENTRALLY-ADMINISTERED TYROSINE.
001548 02-03
CENTRAL HYPOTENSIVE-EFFECT OF GAMMA AMINOBUTYRIC-ACID IN ANESTHETIZED DOGS.
003772 04-03
THE EFFECT OF ANTIDEPRESSANTS ON THE HYPOTENSIVE-EFFECT OF CLOFELIN IN RATS.
003934 04-03

HYPOTHALAMIC
EFFECTS OF PERINATAL THYROXINE AND/OR CORTICOSTERONE TREATMENT ON THE ONTOGENESIS OF HYPOTHALAMIC AND MESENCEPHALIC NOREPINEPHRINE AND DOPAMINE CONTENT.
000180 01-03
EFFECTS OF BRAIN-MONOAMINE DEPLETION ON THERMOREGULATORY RESPONSES OF RABBITS TO DIFFERENT HYPOTHALAMIC TEMPERATURES.
000190 01-03
RELEASE OF GONADOTROPIN-RELEASING-HORMONE BY VERATRINE IN A HYPOTHALAMIC PITUITARY COINCUBATION.
000237 01-03
INFLUENCE OF AMPHETAMINE AND PHENYLPROPANOLAMINE ON FOOD INTAKE, ACTIVITY, AND BODY-TEMPERATURE IN RATS WITH VENTROMEDIAL HYPOTHALAMIC OR DORSOLATERAL TEGMENTAL DAMAGE.
000322 01-03
FACILITATION OF RECOVERY BY PROPANTHELINE-BROMIDE AFTER LATERAL HYPOTHALAMIC DAMAGE.
000396 01-04
HYPOTHALAMIC CATECHOLAMINE BIOSYNTHESIS IN VITRO AS MEASURED BY LIQUID-CHROMATOGRAPHY AND ELECTROCHEMICAL-DETECTION.
000537 01-06
THE IDENTITY AND HYPOTHALAMIC ORIGIN OF CHOLECYSTOKININ IN RAT-BRAIN AND POSTERIOR PITUITARY AND ITS POSSIBLE ROLE IN REGULATION OF NEUROSECRETION. (UNPUBLISHED PAPER).
001003 02-01
EXTRAHYPOTHALAMIC DISTRIBUTIONS AND FUNCTIONS OF HYPOTHALAMIC PEPTIDE-HORMONES. (UNPUBLISHED PAPER).
001211 02-03
SYSTEMIC INSULIN DECREASES LATERAL HYPOTHALAMIC UNIT ACTIVITY.
001275 02-03
DIFFERENTIAL SENSITIVITY OF HYPOTHALAMIC DOPAMINERGIC AND NORADRENERGIC NEURONES TO PHARMACOLOGICAL MANIPULATION.
001310 02-03

THE ROLE OF PROTEIN SYNTHESIS IN THE HYPOTHALAMIC MECHANISM MEDIATING PYROGEN FEVER.
0001454 02-03

APHAGIA, GASTRIC PATHOLOGY, HYPERTHERMIA, AND SENSORIMOTOR-DYSFUNCTIONS FOLLOWING LATERAL HYPOTHALAMIC LESIONS: EFFECTS OF INSULIN PRETREATMENTS.
001638 02-04

ENHANCED LATERAL HYPOTHALAMIC SELF-STIMULATION RESPONDING AFTER CHRONIC EXPOSURE TO AMPHETAMINE.
001688 02-04

SELF-ADMINISTRATION OF D ALA2-MET-ENKEPHALINAMIDE AT HYPOTHALAMIC SELF-STIMULATION SITES.
001738 02-04

ADRENERGIC MODULATION OF THE HYPOTHALAMIC CHOLINERGIC MECHANISM IN THE CONTROL OF EMOTIONAL DEFENSIVE-BEHAVIOR IN THE CAT.
001761 02-04

A COMPARISON BETWEEN THE EFFECTS OF MORPHINE ON THE REWARDING AND AVERSIVE-PROPERTIES OF LATERAL HYPOTHALAMIC AND CENTRAL GRAY STIMULATION.
001771 02-04

EFFECTS OF AMPHETAMINE AND PHENYLPROPANOLAMINE ON FOOD INTAKE IN RATS WITH VENTROMEDIAL HYPOTHALAMIC OR DORSOLATERAL TEGMENTAL DAMAGE.
001818 02-04

APOMORPHINE: SELECTIVE INHIBITION OF THE AVERSIVE COMPONENT OF LATERAL HYPOTHALAMIC SELF-STIMULATION.
002476 02-16

THE HYPOTHALAMIC DOPAMINERGIC REGULATION OF PROLACTIN: A MODEL FOR THE STUDY OF NEUROHORMONAL MECHANISMS IN MAN.
002568 02-17

SENSITIVITY OF IDENTIFIED MEDIAL HYPOTHALAMIC NEURONS TO GABA, GLYCINE AND RELATED AMINO-ACIDS; INFLUENCE OF BICUCULLINE, PICROTOXIN AND STRYCHNINE ON SYNAPTIC INHIBITION.
002674 03-03

HISTAMINE ACTIONS ON ACTIVITY OF CULTURED HYPOTHALAMIC NEURONS: EVIDENCE FOR MEDIATION BY HISTAMINE H1-RECEPTORS AND H2-RECEPTORS.
002732 03-03

MONOAMINE-OXIDASE-B ACTIVITIES TOWARD BETA PHENYLETHYLAMINE IN DISCRETE HYPOTHALAMIC AND CIRCUMVENTRICULAR NUCLEI OF THE RAT.
002781 03-03

DEVELOPMENT OF ACUTE TOLERANCE TO THE EFFECTS OF NALOXONE ON THE HYPOTHALAMIC PITUITARY LUTEINIZING-HORMONE AXIS IN THE MALE RAT.
002853 03-03

SMALL-DOSE INTRAVENOUS HEROIN FACILITATES HYPOTHALAMIC SELF-STIMULATION WITHOUT RESPONSE SUPPRESSION IN RATS.
002999 03-04

INFLUENCE OF MORPHINE ON THE DISCRIMINATIVE-STIMULUS PROPERTIES OF REWARDING LATERAL HYPOTHALAMIC STIMULATION. (PH.D. DISSERTATION).
003041 03-04

THYROXIN SENSITIVITY OF SENSORIMOTOR CORTICAL NEURONS AND THE HYPOTHALAMIC VENTROMEDIAL NUCLEUS.
003713 04-03

UNIMPAIRED QUININE METABOLISM IN RATS WITH VENTROMEDIAL HYPOTHALAMIC LESIONS.
003821 04-03

CATECHOLAMINE SYNTHESIS REGULATION IN HYPOTHALAMIC SYNAPTOSOMES. (UNPUBLISHED PAPER).
003829 04-03

SUBSTANCE-P INCREASES HYPOTHALAMIC BLOOD FLOW VIA AN INDIRECT ADRENERGIC CHOLINERGIC INTERACTION.
003887 04-03

NEUROTENSIN RELEASE BY RAT HYPOTHALAMIC FRAGMENTS IN VITRO.
003920 04-03

NEUROTRANSMITTER CONTROL OF HYPOTHALAMIC PITUITARY THYROID-FUNCTION IN RATS.
003942 04-03

EFFECTS OF CANNABINOIDS ON CATECHOLAMINE UPTAKE AND RELEASE IN HYPOTHALAMIC AND STRIATAL SYNAPTOSOMES.
003970 04-03

THE EFFECT OF PHARMACOLOGICAL DESTRUCTION OF HYPOTHALAMIC MONOAMINERGIC STRUCTURES ON BODY-TEMPERATURE AND GAS-EXCHANGE DURING EXTREME COOLING.
004016 04-03

HYPOTHALAMUS

MORPHINE EXERTS TESTOSTERONE-LIKE EFFECTS IN THE HYPOTHALAMUS OF THE CASTRATED MALE RAT.
000051 01-03

COMPARISON OF THE EFFECTS OF THE ISOMERS OF AMPHETAMINE, METHYLPHENIDATE AND DEOXYPIPRADROL ON THE UPTAKE OF L (3H)NOREPINEPHRINE AND (3H)DOPAMINE BY SYNAPTIC VESICLES FROM RAT-WHOLE-BRAIN, STRIATUM AND HYPOTHALAMUS.
000091 01-03

DEPLETION OF EPINEPHRINE IN RAT HYPOTHALAMUS BY RO-4-1284 INFLUENCE OF PARGYLINE AND HARMALINE.
000100 01-03

METABOLISM OF 3H NORADRENALINE RELEASED FROM ISOLATED RAT HYPOTHALAMUS BY EXTRACTS OF BLACK-WIDOW-SPIDER GLANDS.
000223 01-03

5 HT BLOCKADE AND THE STIMULANT-EFFECTS OF D-AMPHETAMINE AND L-AMPHETAMINE: NO INTERACTION IN SELF-STIMULATION OF PREFRONTAL-CORTEX, HYPOTHALAMUS, OR DORSAL TEGMENTUM. UNEXPECTED LETHALITY IN HIPPOCAMPAL SITES.
000387 01-04

FAILURE OF ISOPRENALINE AND BETA-RECEPTOR BLOCKING-DRUGS TO MODIFY DEPRESSOR RESPONSE AND BRADYCARDIA INDUCED BY ELECTRICAL-STIMULATION OF THE ANTERIOR HYPOTHALAMUS OF CATS.
000520 01-05

GLUCOSE OXIDATION IN THE VENTROMEDIAL HYPOTHALAMUS IS NOT AFFECTED BY INSULIN OR OUABAIN BUT DEPRESSED BY ALLOXAN TREATMENT.
001145 02-03

EPINEPHRINE IS RELEASED FROM HYPOTHALAMUS BY DEPOLARIZING-AGENTS AND AMPHETAMINE.
001155 02-03

PROSTAGLANDIN-E RELEASE BY RAT MEDIAL BASAL HYPOTHALAMUS IN VITRO. INHIBITION BY MELATONIN AT SUBMICROMOLAR CONCENTRATIONS.
001159 02-03

THE EFFECTS OF BOMBESIN INJECTED INTO THE ANTERIOR AND POSTERIOR HYPOTHALAMUS ON BODY-TEMPERATURE AND OXYGEN CONSUMPTION.
001544 02-03

INFLUENCE OF CHRONIC ALCOHOL INTOXICATION ON CIRCADIAN-RHYTHM OF NEUROSECRETORY CENTERS OF RAT HYPOTHALAMUS.
001549 02-03

EFFECTS OF LILLY-110140 (FLUOXETINE) ON SELF-STIMULATION BEHAVIOR IN THE DORSAL AND VENTRAL REGIONS OF THE LATERAL HYPOTHALAMUS IN THE MOUSE.
001590 02-04

PRESYNAPTIC REGULATION OF THE RELEASE OF CATECHOLAMINES IN THE CAT HYPOTHALAMUS.
002737 03-03

TEMPORAL PATTERNING OF NEURONAL ACTIVITY DURING THERMAL AND NEUROCHEMICAL STIMULATION OF THE PREOPTIC/ANTERIOR HYPOTHALAMUS OF THE AWAKE RABBIT.
002818 03-03

A BARBITURATE-EVOKED INTENSIFICATION OF POSTSYNAPTIC INHIBITION IN THE PREOPTIC OVULATORY TRIGGER REGION OF THE HYPOTHALAMUS.
002839 03-03

CHARACTERIZATION AND QUANTITATION OF ALPHA-ADRENERGIC-RECEPTOR SUBTYPES IN RAT HYPOTHALAMUS.
002842 03-03

CHANGES IN NORADRENERGIC TRANSMISSION ALTER THE CONCENTRATION OF CYTOPLASMIC PROGESTIN-RECEPTORS IN HYPOTHALAMUS.
002892 03-03

ON CORRELATION OF BEHAVIORAL-REACTIONS AND NEURONAL ACTIVITY IN THE HYPOTHALAMUS UNDER SUBCUTANEOUS GASTRIN INJECTION.
002913 03-03

SOMATOSTATIN FACILITATES THE SEROTONIN RELEASE FROM RAT-CEREBRAL-CORTEX, HIPPOCAMPUS, AND HYPOTHALAMUS SLICES.
002919 03-03

MEPACRINE TREATMENT PREVENTS IMMOBILIZATION-INDUCED DESENSITIZATION OF BETA-ADRENERGIC-RECEPTORS IN RAT HYPOTHALAMUS AND BRAINSTEM.
003044 03-04

TRH INCREASES LOCOMOTOR-ACTIVITY IN RATS AFTER IN.'ECTION INTO THE HYPOTHALAMUS.
003081 03-04

EFFECTS OF ELECTROLYTIC AND 6 HYDROXYDOPAMINE LESIONS OF THE LATERAL HYPOTHALAMUS ON ROTATION EVOKED BY ELECTRICAL-STIMULATION OF THE SUBSTANTIA-NIGRA IN RATS.
003100 03-04

THE PHARMACOLOGICAL ANALYSIS OF MONOAMINERGIC MECHANISMS OF THE MEDIAL HYPOTHALAMUS IN FOOD PROCURING CONDITIONED REFLEXES IN RATS.
003754 04-03

EVIDENCE FOR THERMOREGULATORY DOPAMINERGIC-RECEPTORS LOCATED IN THE PREOPTICUS-MEDIALIS-NUCLEUS OF THE RAT HYPOTHALAMUS.
003773 04-03

SELECTIVE MODIFICATION BY OPIATES OF NEURONAL ACTIVITY OF THE MEDIAL BASAL HYPOTHALAMUS.
003968 04-03

HYPOTENSION ALTERS THE RELEASE OF CATECHOLAMINES IN THE HYPOTHALAMUS OF THE CONSCIOUS RABBIT.
004535 04-13

DRUG-INDUCED ALTERATIONS OF THE HYPOTHALAMUS HYPOPHYSIS AXIS.
004535 04-13

HYPOTHERMIA
CENTRAL ADMINISTRATION OF SERINE CAUSES HYPOTHERMIA AND
INHIBITS FEVER IN RABBITS.
001247 02-03
APOMORPHINE HYPOTHERMIA: AN INDEX OF CENTRAL DOPAMINE-
RECEPTOR FUNCTION IN MAN.
002221 02-13
TEMPORAL AND ENVIRONMENTAL CUES IN CONDITIONED HYPOTHERMIA
AND HYPERTHERMIA ASSOCIATED WITH MORPHINE.
002709 03-03
HYPOPHYSECTOMY INCREASES THE SENSITIVITY OF RATS TO NALOXONE-
INDUCED HYPOTHERMIA.
002710 03-03
SEROTONERGIC MECHANISMS OF CLONIDINE-INDUCED HYPOTHERMIA IN
RATS.
002806 03-03
EFFECTS OF MORPHINE AND NALORPHINE ON KAINIC-ACID-INDUCED
HYPOTHERMIA IN RATS.
002921 03-03
ENHANCEMENT OF ETHANOL-INDUCED SEDATION AND HYPOTHERMIA BY
CENTRALLY ADMINISTERED NEUROTENSIN, BETA ENDORPHIN AND
BOMBESIN.
003037 03-04

HYPOTHERMIC-EFFECTS
THE HYPOTHERMIC-EFFECTS OF CLONIDINE AND OTHER IMIDAZOLIDINES
IN RELATION TO THEIR ABILITY TO ENTER THE CENTRAL-NERVOUS-
SYSTEM IN MICE.
003933 04-03
THE EFFECTS OF PEPTIDES ON TOLERANCE TO THE CATALEPTIC-EFFECTS
AND HYPOTHERMIC-EFFECTS OF MORPHINE IN THE RAT.
004072 04-04

HYPOTHESES
LITHIUM AND MANIA: HYPOTHESES.
001986 02-09

HYPOTHESIS
DUAL-EFFECTS OF MESCALINE: THE TRANSMETHYLATION HYPOTHESIS
REVISITED.
001584 02-04
DIAGNOSTIC CLASSIFICATION AND THE ENDORPHIN HYPOTHESIS OF
SCHIZOPHRENIA: INDIVIDUAL DIFFERENCES AND
PSYCHOPHARMACOLOGICAL STRATEGIES. (UNPUBLISHED PAPER).
001910 02-08
L HTP AND THE SEROTONIN HYPOTHESIS: THEIR MEANING FOR
TREATMENT OF DEPRESSION.
002326 02-14
DIAGNOSTIC CLASSIFICATION AND THE ENDORPHIN HYPOTHESIS OF
SCHIZOPHRENIA: INDIVIDUAL DIFFERENCES AND
PSYCHOPHARMACOLOGICAL STRATEGIES.
003167 03-08
THE EFFECT OF SODIUM-VALPROATE ON MANIA: THE GABA HYPOTHESIS
OF AFFECTIVE-DISORDERS.
003218 03-09
PLASMA FREE AND TOTAL TRYPTOPHAN, BLOOD SEROTONIN, AND THE
HYPERACTIVITY-SYNDROME: NO EVIDENCE FOR THE SEROTONIN
DEFICIENCY HYPOTHESIS.
003312 03-11
CEREBRAL FLUORIDE IN MANIA AND THE EFFECT OF LITHIUM: A
HYPOTHESIS.
004715 04-17

HYPOTHETICAL
THE ANTIDEPRESSANT ACTION OF SULPHO-ADENOSYL-L-METHIONINE
(SAME) COMPARED WITH THAT OF CHLORIMIPRAMINE:
HYPOTHETICAL INTERPRETATIONS OF THE MECHANISM-OF-ACTION.
003150 03-07

HYPOTHYROID
ACTIVITY AND CATCH-UP GROWTH IN HYPOTHYROID RATS.
004190 04-04

HYPOTHYROID-PATIENTS
THYROID-INDUCED MANIA IN HYPOTHYROID-PATIENTS.
000857 01-15

HYPOTHYROIDISM
EFFECTS OF EXPERIMENTAL HYPOTHYROIDISM ON LEARNING IN RATS.
001587 02-04

HYPOTONIC
EFFECTS OF THIORIDAZINE ON THE COGNITIVE FUNCTIONING OF A
HYPOTONIC SCHIZOPHRENIC-BOY.
000557 01-08

HYPOVOLEMIA
RENIN AND ALDOSTERONE SECRETIONS DURING HYPOVOLEMIA IN RATS:
RELATION TO NACL INTAKE.
000484 01-04

HYPOXEMIA
LOCAL CEREBRAL GLUCOSE UTILIZATION (LCGU) IN RAT-BRAIN DURING
HYPOXEMIA. (UNPUBLISHED PAPER).
001380 02-03
NA-GAMMA-HYDROXYBUTYRATE IN CEREBRAL PROTECTION DURING
SEVERE HYPOXEMIA IN THE RAT.
003895 04-03

HYPOXIA
INFLUENCE OF PYRITHIOXINE ON EXPERIMENTAL HYPOXIA IN RATS.
000077 01-03
SUBCELLULAR REACTION OF THE BRAIN TO HYPOXIA.
001354 02-03
NEUROPSYCHOLOGICAL-CORRELATES OF ASTHMA: EFFECT OF HYPOXIA
OR DRUGS?
003482 03-15

HYSTERIA
BROMISM, HYSTERIA AND NARCOLEPSY.
002472 02-15
ON THE USE OF CERTAIN PHARMACOLOGICAL CATEGORIES IN HYSTERIA.
004347 04-09
POSSIBILITIES OF PATHOGENETIC THERAPY OF HYSTERIA.
004429 04-10

H1-RECEPTOR
HISTAMINE AS A PUNISHER IN SQUIRREL-MONKEYS: EFFECTS OF
PENTOBARBITAL, CHLORDIAZEPOXIDE AND H1-RECEPTOR AND H2-
RECEPTOR ANTAGONISTS ON BEHAVIOR AND CARDIOVASCULAR
RESPONSE.
004119 04-04

H1-RECEPTOR-MEDIATED
ONTOGENY OF HISTAMINERGIC NEUROTRANSMISSION IN THE RAT-
BRAIN: CONCOMITANT DEVELOPMENT OF NEURONAL HISTAMINE, H1-
RECEPTORS, AND H1-RECEPTOR-MEDIATED STIMULATION OF
PHOSPHOLIPID TURNOVER.
004021 04-03
DESENSITIZATION OF HISTAMINE H1-RECEPTOR-MEDIATED CYCLIC-GMP
FORMATION IN MOUSE NEUROBLASTOMA CELLS.
004030 04-03

H1-RECEPTORS
HISTAMINE H1-RECEPTORS LABELED IN VIVO: ANTIDEPRESSANT AND
ANTIHISTAMINE INTERACTIONS.
000074 01-03
IN VIVO OCCUPATION OF CEREBRAL HISTAMINE H1-RECEPTORS
EVALUATED WITH 3H MEPYRAMINE MAY PREDICT SEDATIVE
PROPERTIES OF PSYCHOTROPIC-DRUGS.
000241 01-03
PSYCHOTROPIC-DRUGS AND HISTAMINE H1-RECEPTORS OF CULTURED
MOUSE NEUROBLASTOMA CELLS.
000250 01-03
PSYCHOTROPIC-DRUG BLOCKADE OF HISTAMINE H1-RECEPTORS.
001432 02-03
HIGH-AFFINITY BINDING OF TRICYCLIC-ANTIDEPRESSANTS TO HISTAMINE
H1-RECEPTORS: FACT AND ARTIFACT.
001880 02-06
HISTAMINE ACTIONS ON ACTIVITY OF CULTURED HYPOTHALAMIC
NEURONS: EVIDENCE FOR MEDIATION BY HISTAMINE H1-RECEPTORS
AND H2-RECEPTORS.
002732 03-03
TRICYCLIC-ANTIDEPRESSANTS AND HISTAMINE H1-RECEPTORS.
003986 04-03
ONTOGENY OF HISTAMINERGIC NEUROTRANSMISSION IN THE RAT-
BRAIN: CONCOMITANT DEVELOPMENT OF NEURONAL HISTAMINE, H1-
RECEPTORS, AND H1-RECEPTOR-MEDIATED STIMULATION OF
PHOSPHOLIPID TURNOVER.
004021 04-03
PSYCHOTHERAPEUTIC-DRUGS, HISTAMINE H1-RECEPTORS AND
MUSCARINIC ACETYLCHOLINE-RECEPTORS.
004737 04-17

H2-RECEPTOR
INTERACTION OF HISTAMINE H2-RECEPTOR BLOCKING-DRUGS WITH THE
NORADRENERGIC SYSTEM IN RAT-BRAIN AND HEART.
001397 02-03
NEGLIGIBLE AFFINITY OF HISTAMINE H2-RECEPTOR ANTAGONISTS FOR
CENTRAL ALPHA1-ADRENOCEPTORS.
001508 02-03
HISTAMINE AS A PUNISHER IN SQUIRREL-MONKEYS: EFFECTS OF
PENTOBARBITAL, CHLORDIAZEPOXIDE AND H1-RECEPTOR AND H2-
RECEPTOR ANTAGONISTS ON BEHAVIOR AND CARDIOVASCULAR
RESPONSE.
004119 04-04

H2-RECEPTORS
SOME CENTRAL-EFFECTS OF IMPROMIDINE, A POTENT AGONIST OF
HISTAMINE H2-RECEPTORS.
001417 02-03
HISTAMINE ACTIONS ON ACTIVITY OF CULTURED HYPOTHALAMIC
NEURONS: EVIDENCE FOR MEDIATION BY HISTAMINE H1-RECEPTORS
AND H2-RECEPTORS.
002732 03-03
H2-RECEPTORS MEDIATE INCREASES IN PERMEABILITY OF THE BLOOD-
BRAIN-BARRIER DURING ARTERIAL HISTAMINE INFUSION.
003817 04-03

IATROGENIC
IATROGENIC OPIATE ADDICTION: SUCCESSFUL DETOXIFICATION WITH
CLONIDINE.
000666 01-11
IATROGENIC DEPRESSIONS.
002388 02-15
TREATMENT OF IATROGENIC DRUG DEPENDENCE IN THE GENERAL-
HOSPITAL.
002460 02-15

IBOTENIC-ACID

EXCITATORY AND INHIBITORY-ACTIONS OF IBOTENIC-ACID ON FROG SPINAL MOTONEURONES IN VITRO.
002841 03-03

IBOTENIC-ACID ANALOGUES AS INHIBITORS OF (3H)GLUTAMIC-ACID BINDING TO CEREBELLAR MEMBRANES.
003848 04-03

IBUPROFEN

INTERACTION OF INDOMETHACIN AND IBUPROFEN WITH LITHIUM IN MANIC-PATIENTS UNDER A STEADY-STATE LITHIUM LEVEL.
000622 01-09

IC50

EFFECTS OF RO-11-2465, A NEW PSYCHOTROPIC-AGENT ON THE UPTAKE OF SEROTONIN BY HUMAN PLATELETS -- IN VITRO DETERMINATION OF THE IC50.
004532 04-13

IDEAL

THE REAL AND IDEAL MANAGEMENT OF STIMULANT DRUG-TREATMENT FOR HYPERACTIVE-CHILDREN: RECENT FINDINGS AND A REPORT FROM CLINICAL-PRACTICE.
000715 01-11

IDENTICAL

EFFICACY AND PATTERN VALENCE OF PSYCHOACTIVE-DRUGS: A NEW METHOD OF COMPARING DRUGS APPLIED TO IDENTICAL PATIENTS IN RANDOMIZED-ORDER.
000699 01-11

COMPARISON OF CYSTEINE-SULPHINIC-ACID-DECARBOXYLASE (CSD) ISOENZYMES AND GLUTAMIC-ACID-DECARBOXYLASE (GAD) IN RAT: IS BRAIN CSD-I IDENTICAL WITH LIVER CSD AND BRAIN CSD-II WITH GAD? (UNPUBLISHED PAPER).
001048 02-01

IDENTICAL RESPONSES OF THE TWO HIPPOCAMPAL THETA GENERATORS TO PHYSIOLOGICAL AND PHARMACOLOGICAL ACTIVATION.
002792 03-03

IDENTIFICATION

DRUG AND SEIZURE IDENTIFICATION BY AUDIO-SPECTROMETRY. (PH.D. DISSERTATION).
000532 01-06

IDENTIFICATION OF A SUBGROUP OF TARDIVE-DYSKINESIA PATIENTS BY PHARMACOLOGIC-PROBES.
000708 01-11

IDENTIFICATION AND PARTIAL PURIFICATION OF A HYDROPHOBIC PROTEIN COMPONENT ASSOCIATED WITH (3H)SPIROPERIDOL BINDING-ACTIVITY. (UNPUBLISHED PAPER).
001007 02-01

IDENTIFICATION AND QUANTIFICATION OF 1,2,3,4 TETRAHYDRO-BETA-CARBOLINE, 2 METHYL-TETRAHYDRO-BETA-CARBOLINE, AND 6 METHOXY-TETRAHYDRO-BETA-CARBOLINE AS IN VIVO CONSTITUENTS OF RAT-BRAIN AND ADRENAL-GLAND.
002636 03-01

IDENTIFICATION OF TWO BENZODIAZEPINE BINDING-SITES ON CELLS CULTURED FROM RAT-CEREBRAL-CORTEX.
002820 03-03

THE DEXAMETHASONE-SUPPRESSION-TEST IN THE IDENTIFICATION OF SUBTYPES OF DEPRESSION DIFFERENTIALLY RESPONSIVE TO ANTIDEPRESSANTS.
003211 03-09

IDENTIFIED

DISTRIBUTION OF MEMBRANE GLYCOPROTEINS AMONG THE ORGANELLES OF A SINGLE IDENTIFIED NEURON OF APLYSIA. II. ISOLATION AND CHARACTERIZATION OF A GLYCOPROTEIN ASSOCIATED WITH VESICLES.
002657 03-03

SENSITIVITY OF IDENTIFIED MEDIAL HYPOTHALAMIC NEURONS TO GABA, GLYCINE AND RELATED AMINO-ACIDS; INFLUENCE OF BICUCULLINE, PICROTOXIN AND STRYCHNINE ON SYNAPTIC INHIBITION.
002674 03-03

THREE CLASSES OF DOPAMINE-RECEPTOR (D-2, D-3, D-4) IDENTIFIED BY BINDING STUDIES WITH 3H APOMORPHINE AND 3H DOMPERIDONE.
002900 03-03

EFFECT OF CHRONIC-TREATMENT WITH TRICYCLIC-ANTIDEPRESSANT DRUGS ON IDENTIFIED BRAIN NORADRENERGIC AND SEROTONERGIC NEURONS.
004026 04-03

IDENTIFIES

DEXAMETHASONE-SUPPRESSION-TEST IDENTIFIES SUBTYPES OF DEPRESSION WHICH RESPOND TO DIFFERENT ANTIDEPRESSANTS.
001971 02-09

IDENTITY

THE IDENTITY AND HYPOTHALAMIC ORIGIN OF CHOLECYSTOKININ IN RAT-BRAIN AND POSTERIOR PITUITARY AND ITS POSSIBLE ROLE IN REGULATION OF NEUROSECRETION. (UNPUBLISHED PAPER).
001003 02-01

IDIOPATHIC

ABNORMAL REGULATION OF PROLACTIN RELEASE IN IDIOPATHIC PARKINSONS-DISEASE.
002255 02-13

A NEUROPHARMACOLOGICAL-STUDY AND NEUROENDOCRINE-STUDY ON IDIOPATHIC AND CHRONIC PHARMACOLOGICAL PARKINSONISM.
002371 02-15

IGE

IGE MEDIATED HISTAMINE RELEASE IN RAT BASOPHILIC LEUKEMIA CELLS: RECEPTOR ACTIVATED PHOSPHOLIPID METHYLATION, CA-FLUX AND RELEASE OF ARACHIDONIC-ACID. (UNPUBLISHED PAPER).
001188 02-03

ILEUM

ENKEPHALIN-RECEPTOR IN THE RABBIT ILEUM.
000221 01-03

MET-ENKEPHALIN-ARG6-PHE7 INTERACTS WITH THE KAPPA-RECEPTORS ON GUINEA-PIG ILEUM.
001110 02-03

INHIBITION OF THE ACTION OF CHOLECYSTOKININ-OCTAPEPTIDE ON THE GUINEA-PIG ILEUM MYENTERIC PLEXUS BY DIBUTYRYL-CYCLIC-GUANOSINE-MONOPHOSPHATE.
001291 02-03

COMPARATIVE-EFFECTS OF SOMATOSTATIN AND ENKEPHALINS ON THE GUINEA-PIG ILEUM AND THE RAT VAS-DEFERENS.
001302 02-03

ALTERED LEVELS OF BETA ENDORPHIN FRAGMENTS AFTER CHRONIC MORPHINE TREATMENT OF GUINEA-PIG ILEUM IN VITRO AND IN VIVO.
001404 02-03

CHARACTERISTICS OF OSCILLATORY CONTRACTIONS ELICITED BY NALOXONE IN ILEUM PREPARATION FROM MORPHINE-DEPENDENT GUINEA-PIGS.
001491 02-03

ILEUS

ILEUS COMPLICATING HALOPERIDOL THERAPY.
003511 03-15

ILLNESS

DOPAMINE-RECEPTORS AND SCHIZOPHRENIA: DRUG-EFFECT OR ILLNESS?
000564 01-08

THE PCP PSYCHOSIS: PROLONGED INTOXICATION OR DRUG PRECIPITATED FUNCTIONAL ILLNESS?
000739 01-12

IMAGING

SPECIFIC IN VIVO BINDING OF 77BR P BROMOSPIROPERIDOL IN RAT-BRAIN: A POTENTIAL TOOL FOR GAMMA-RAY IMAGING.
004293 04-06

IMIDAZOLE

AMINOPHYLLINE AND IMIDAZOLE AS CONVULSANTS.
004232 04-04

IMIDAZOLIDINES

THE HYPOTHERMIC-EFFECTS OF CLONIDINE AND OTHER IMIDAZOLIDINES IN RELATION TO THEIR ABILITY TO ENTER THE CENTRAL-NERVOUS-SYSTEM IN MICE.
003933 04-03

IMIDAZOLINES

CYCLOHEXYLPHENOXYAMIDOXIMES AND IMIDAZOLINES WITH ANTIDEPRESSIVE AND ALPHA-ADRENERGIC-ACTIVITY.
001051 02-01

IMIDOLINE

DOPAMINE-RECEPTOR BLOCKADE BY IMIDOLINE AND ITS PROPOSED ACTIVE CONFORMATION.
001687 02-04

IMINO-3-ALKYLTHIAZOLINE

SYNTHESIS AND PHARMACOLOGICAL ACTIVITY OF SOME 2 IMINO-3-ALKYLTHIAZOLINE DERIVATIVES.
003698 04-02

IMINODIBENZYLS

POSSIBLE MODE OF ACTION OF NEUROPSYCHIATRIC-AGENTS: PHENOTHIAZINES AND IMINODIBENZYLS.
001271 02-03

IMIPRAMINE

3H IMIPRAMINE BINDING IN NEURONAL AND GLIAL FRACTIONS OF HORSE STRIATUM.
000033 01-03

CENTRAL NORADRENERGIC ADAPTATION TO LONG-TERM-TREATMENT WITH IMIPRAMINE IN RHESUS-MONKEYS.
000182 01-03

IMIPRAMINE AFFECTS AUTONOMIC-CONTROL OF SINOATRIAL RATE IN ISOLATED RIGHT ATRIAL PREPARATIONS.
000195 01-03

THE EFFECTS OF GONADECTOMY AND HYPOPHYSECTOMY ON THE METABOLISM OF IMIPRAMINE AND LIDOCAINE BY THE LIVER OF MALE AND FEMALE RATS.
000273 01-03

IMIPRAMINE AND REM SLEEP: CHOLINERGIC MEDIATION IN ANIMALS.
000406 01-04

A COMPARISON OF THE EFFECTS OF D-AMPHETAMINE, COCAINE, IMIPRAMINE AND PENTOBARBITAL ON LOCAL AND OVERALL RATES OF RESPONDING MAINTAINED UNDER A FOUR-COMPONENT MULTIPLE FIXED-INTERVAL SCHEDULE.
000508 01-04

A REEXAMINATION OF THE CLINICAL-EFFECTS OF IMIPRAMINE AND AMITRIPTYLINE IN DEPRESSIVE-ILLNESS.
000579 01-09

A COMPARATIVE EVALUATION OF DOTHIEPIN (PROTHIEDEN) AND IMIPRAMINE.
000583 01-09

Subject Index

COMPARISON OF SINGLE-DOSE PHARMACOKINETICS OF IMIPRAMINE
AND MAPROTILINE IN THE ELDERLY.
000596 01-09

PLASMA LEVELS OF IMIPRAMINE (IMI) AND DESMETHYLIMIPRAMINE
(DMI) AND CLINICAL-RESPONSE IN PREPUBERTAL MAJOR DEPRESSIVE-
DISORDER: A PRELIMINARY REPORT.
000619 01-09

IMIPRAMINE TREATMENT OF PREPUBERTAL MAJOR DEPRESSIVE-
DISORDERS: PLASMA LEVELS AND CLINICAL-RESPONSE --
PRELIMINARY REPORT.
000620 01-09

D-AMPHETAMINE AS A PREDICTOR FOR RESPONSE TO IMIPRAMINE AND
AMITRIPTYLINE.
000621 01-09

CONTROLLED-COMPARISON OF MIANSERINE WITH IMIPRAMINE IN
ENDOGENOUS DEPRESSIONS.
000634 01-09

MHPG AS A PREDICTOR OF ANTIDEPRESSANT RESPONSE TO IMIPRAMINE
AND MAPROTILINE.
000787 01-13

RESPONSES TO TYRAMINE AND NOREPINEPHRINE AFTER IMIPRAMINE
AND TRAZODONE.
000864 01-15

LONG-TERM ADMINISTRATION OF ATROPINE, IMIPRAMINE, AND
VILOXAZINE ALTERS RESPONSIVENESS OF RAT-CORTICAL-NEURONES
TO ACETYLCHOLINE.
001306 02-03

DOWN REGULATION OF DIHYDROALPRENOLOL AND IMIPRAMINE
BINDING-SITES IN BRAIN OF RATS REPEATEDLY TREATED WITH
IMIPRAMINE.
001317 02-03

THE NEW ANTIDEPRESSANT PIRLINDOLE: A COMPARISON WITH
IMIPRAMINE AND TRANYLCYPROMINE.
001360 02-03

THYROTROPIN-RELEASING-HORMONE: NEUROCHEMICAL EVIDENCE FOR
THE POTENTIATION OF IMIPRAMINE EFFECTS ON THE METABOLISM
AND UPTAKE OF BRAIN CATECHOLAMINES.
001427 02-03

EFFECT OF IMIPRAMINE ON HEPATIC GAMMA GLUTAMYLTRANSFERASE
IN FEMALE RATS. INTERACTION WITH CONTRACEPTIVES.
001507 02-03

INFLUENCE OF IMIPRAMINE AND PARGYLINE ON THE
ARRHYTHMOGENICITY OF EPINEPHRINE DURING HALOTHANE,
ENFLURANE OR METHOXYFLURANE ANESTHESIA IN DOGS.
001539 02-03

THE BEHAVIOR OF RATS IN THE OPEN-FIELD WITHOUT STRESS, UNDER
ACUTE AND PERSISTING INFLUENCE OF IMIPRAMINE AND
TRANYLCYPROMINE AS WELL AS ON THE INDIVIDUAL REACTION TYPE
(EMOTIVE AND NONEMOTIVE).
001624 02-04

IMIPRAMINE NORMALIZES NATURALLY OCCURRING AND DRUG-INDUCED
DIFFERENCES IN THE EXPLORATORY-ACTIVITY OF RATS.
001646 02-04

CONFORMATIONALLY RESTRICTED TRICYCLIC-ANTIDEPRESSANTS. 1.
OCTAHYDRODIBENZAZEPINONAPHTHYRIDINES AS RIGID IMIPRAMINE
ANALOGUES.
001710 02-04

DIFFERENTIAL-EFFECTS OF IMIPRAMINE IN RATS AS A FUNCTION OF DRL
SCHEDULE VALUE.
001714 02-04

REVERSAL OF LEARNED-HELPLESSNESS BY IMIPRAMINE.
001751 02-04

ENDOGENOUS DEPRESSION AND IMIPRAMINE LEVELS IN THE BLOOD.
001979 02-09

THE USE OF VILOXAZINE IN HOSPITALIZED DEPRESSED-PATIENTS:
RANDOM COMPARISON WITH IMIPRAMINE IN A DOUBLE-BLIND TRIAL.
001998 02-09

NOMIFENSINE IN THE TREATMENT OF OBSESSIVE-COMPULSIVE-NEUROSIS.
THERAPEUTIC-EFFICACY AND TOLERABILITY IN COMPARISON TO
IMIPRAMINE.
002078 02-10

PHARMACOKINETIC BASIS FOR PREDICTING STEADY-STATE SERUM DRUG
CONCENTRATIONS OF IMIPRAMINE FROM SINGLE-DOSE DATA.
002225 02-13

SPECIFIC 3H IMIPRAMINE BINDING IN HUMAN PLATELETS: INFLUENCE OF
AGE AND SEX.
002254 02-13

IMIPRAMINE AND EEG SLEEP IN CHILDREN WITH DEPRESSIVE-
SYMPTOMS.
002339 02-14

EFFECTS OF IMIPRAMINE ON LEFT VENTRICULAR PERFORMANCE IN
CHILDREN.
002385 02-15

TERATOGENICITY OF IMIPRAMINE AND AMITRIPTYLINE IN FETAL
HAMSTERS.
002410 02-15

IMIPRAMINE: EFFECT OF OVARIAN STEROIDS ON MODIFICATIONS IN
SEROTONIN-RECEPTOR BINDING.
002778 03-03

IMITATION
IMITATION, SOCIAL FACILITATION, AND THE EFFECTS OF ACTH4-10 ON RATS BAR-PRESSING-BEHAVIOR.
003009 03-04

IMMATURE
GABA FLUXES IN PRESYNAPTIC NERVE-ENDINGS FROM IMMATURE RATS.
000185 01-03

IMMOBILITY
EEG CHANGE IN THE CONSCIOUS RAT DURING IMMOBILITY INDUCED BY PSYCHOLOGICAL-STRESS.
001297 02-03

EFFECTS OF HEMICHOLINIUM-3 AND CHOLINE ON HIPPOCAMPAL ELECTRICAL-ACTIVITY DURING IMMOBILITY VS. MOVEMENT.
001438 02-03

THE EFFECTS OF TRYPTOPHAN AND MANIPULATIONS OF SEROTONERGIC-RECEPTORS ON TONIC IMMOBILITY IN CHICKENS.
004245 04-04

TONIC IMMOBILITY IN DOMESTIC FOWL: POSSIBLE INTERACTION OF SEROTONERGIC AND DOPAMINERGIC MECHANISMS.
004246 04-04

IMMOBILIZATION
DESENSITIZATION OF ADRENOCEPTORS AFTER IMMOBILIZATION STRESS OR REPEATED INJECTION OF ISOPROTERENOL IN RATS. (UNPUBLISHED PAPER).
001546 02-03

IMMOBILIZATION-INDUCED
MEPACRINE TREATMENT PREVENTS IMMOBILIZATION-INDUCED DESENSITIZATION OF BETA-ADRENERGIC-RECEPTORS IN RAT HYPOTHALAMUS AND BRAINSTEM.
002919 03-03

IMMUNIZATION
AMITRIPTYLINE PROVIDES LONG-LASTING IMMUNIZATION AGAINST SUDDEN CARDIAC DEATH FROM COCAINE.
003122 03-05

NEUTRALIZATION OF THE EFFECT OF DELTA9 TETRAHYDROCANNABINOL ON BARBITURATE SLEEPING-TIME BY SPECIFIC ACTIVE IMMUNIZATION.
003803 04-03

IMMUNOCYTOCHEMICAL
IMMUNOCYTOCHEMICAL LOCALIZATION OF CATECHOLAMINE SYNTHESIZING ENZYMES AND NEUROPEPTIDES IN AREA POSTREMA AND MEDIAL NUCLEUS-TRACTUS-SOLITARIUS OF RAT-BRAIN.
002634 03-01

BENZODIAZEPINE-RECEPTORS: AUTORADIOGRAPHICAL AND IMMUNOCYTOCHEMICAL EVIDENCE FOR THEIR LOCALIZATION IN REGIONS OF GABAERGIC SYNAPTIC CONTACTS.
002643 03-01

IMMUNOCYTOCHEMISTRY
DEMONSTRATION OF SUBSTANCE-P IN AORTIC NERVE AFFERENT FIBERS BY COMBINED USE OF FLOURESCENT RETROGRADE NEURONAL LABELING AND IMMUNOCYTOCHEMISTRY. (UNPUBLISHED PAPER).
001024 02-01

A TOPOGRAPHIC LOCALIZATION OF ENKEPHALIN ON THE DOPAMINE NEURONS OF THE RAT SUBSTANTIA-NIGRA AND VENTRAL TEGMENTAL AREA DEMONSTRATED BY COMBINED HISTOFLUORESCENCE IMMUNOCYTOCHEMISTRY.
002639 03-01

IMMUNODETECTION
IMMUNODETECTION OF ACH-RECEPTOR IN THE CNS. (UNPUBLISHED PAPER).
003670 04-01

IMMUNOGLOBULIN
SALIVARY IMMUNOGLOBULIN CONCENTRATIONS IN PATIENTS WITH EPILEPSY TREATED WITH CARBAMAZEPINE.
002234 02-13

RESPIRATORY-DISEASE AND NASAL IMMUNOGLOBULIN CONCENTRATIONS IN PHENYTOIN TREATED EPILEPTIC-PATIENTS.
003486 03-15

PROSPECTS FOR THE TREATMENT OF POSTENCEPHALITIC PARKINSONISM WITH ANTILYMPHOCYTIC IMMUNOGLOBULIN.
004572 04-14

IMMUNOHISTOCHEMICAL
IMMUNOHISTOCHEMICAL LOCALIZATION OF LEUCINE-ENKEPHALIN IN THE SPINAL-CORD OF THE CAT: ENKEPHALIN-CONTAINING MARGINAL NEURONS AND PAIN MODULATION.
002638 03-01

IMMUNOLOGICAL
BIOCHEMICAL AND IMMUNOLOGICAL PROPERTIES OF THE MOUSE BRAIN ENOLASES PURIFIED BY A SIMPLE METHOD.
003668 04-01

IMMUNOLOGICAL COMPONENTS IN SCHIZOPHRENIA.
004324 04-08

IMMUNOREACTIVE
SODIUM-CHLORIDE INHIBITION DECREASES LEVELS OF IMMUNOREACTIVE DYNORPHIN IN THE NEUROINTERMEDIATE PITUITARY OF RATS.
001283 02-03

DECREASE OF GAD IMMUNOREACTIVE NERVE TERMINALS IN THE SUBSTANTIA-NIGRA AFTER KAINIC-ACID LESION OF THE STRIATUM. (UNPUBLISHED PAPER).
001400 02-03

IMMUNOREACTIVE CALCITONIN IN CEREBROSPINAL-FLUID OF MAN.
002637 03-01

IMMUNOREACTIVITY
CHARACTERIZATION OF LRF-LIKE IMMUNOREACTIVITY IN THE FROG SYMPATHETIC GANGLIA: NONIDENTITY WITH LRF-DECAPEPTIDE. (UNPUBLISHED PAPER).
001018 02-01

AN INVERSE CORRELATION BETWEEN SERUM LEVELS OF DESMETHYLIMIPRAMINE AND MELATONIN-LIKE IMMUNOREACTIVITY IN DMI RESPONSIVE DEPRESSIVES.
003228 03-09

EFFECT OF MORPHINE AND NALOXONE ON LEU-ENKEPHALIN-LIKE IMMUNOREACTIVITY IN DOGS.
003894 04-03

IMMUNOSTIMULANT
THE IMMUNOSTIMULANT ANTINEOPLASTIC ACTION OF SOME PSYCHOTROPIC-DRUGS OF THE SYDNONIMINE SERIES.
001520 02-03

IMMUNOSTIMULANTS
SYNTHETIC IMMUNOSTIMULANTS DERIVED FROM THE BACTERIAL CELL WALL.
001080 02-02

IMMUNOTITRATABLE
REDUCTION IN THE LEVEL OF IMMUNOTITRATABLE DOPAMINE-BETA-HYDROXYLASE AFTER CHRONIC ADMINISTRATION OF L-DOPA OR ALPHA METHYLDOPA.
003764 04-03

IMPAIR
IN NORMAL YOUNG MEN ACUTE DOPAMINERGIC BLOCKADE DOES NOT IMPAIR FREE WATER EXCRETION FOLLOWING A STANDARD WATER LOAD.
004600 04-15

IMPAIRED
IMPAIRED GLUCOSE TOLERANCE IN LONG-TERM LITHIUM TREATED PATIENTS.
000611 01-09

EFFECTS OF DIFFERENT MONOAMINE-OXIDASE-INHIBITORS ON RESPIRATORY ACTIVITY IN RATS WITH CHRONICALLY IMPAIRED CENTRAL SEROTONERGIC FUNCTION.
001389 02-03

IMPAIRING
VIGILANCE IMPAIRING DRUGS: ANALYSIS OF SUBJECTIVE RESPONSES.
002332 02-14

IMPAIRMENT
EVIDENCE FOR A RECEPTOR SUPERSENSITIVITY FOLLOWING IMPAIRMENT OF CENTRAL SEROTONERGIC ACTIVITY IN THE RABBIT.
000041 01-03

IMPAIRMENT OF AVOIDANCE-BEHAVIOR FOLLOWING SHORT-TERM INGESTION OF ETHANOL, TERTIARY BUTANOL, OR PENTOBARBITAL IN MICE.
000479 01-04

TOLERANCE TO ETHANOL-INDUCED IMPAIRMENT OF WATER-ESCAPE IN RATS BRED FOR ETHANOL SENSITIVITY.
001567 02-04

ENHANCED BEHAVIOURAL-EFFECTS, ELECTROCORTICAL-EFFECTS AND HYPERTHERMIC-EFFECTS OF SEROTONIN-LIKE AGENTS AFTER IMPAIRMENT OF SEROTONIN TRANSMISSION IN FOWL BRAIN.
001733 02-04

IMPAIRMENT OF INSTRUMENTAL LEARNING IN RATS BY GLUTAMIC-ACID-DIETHYL-ESTER.
002993 03-04

RENAL IMPAIRMENT, HYPERCALCEMIA, AND LITHIUM THERAPY.
003473 03-15

IMPAIRS
SHORT-TERM ETHANOL ADMINISTRATION IMPAIRS THE ELIMINATION OF CHLORDIAZEPOXIDE (LIBRIUM) IN MAN.
002224 02-13

IMPLANTATION
ASSESSMENT OF TOLERANCE TO AND PHYSICAL-DEPENDENCE ON PENTOBARBITAL, INDUCED BY MULTIPLE PELLET IMPLANTATION.
000385 01-04

IMPLANTS
SUBCUTANEOUS SILASTIC IMPLANTS: MAINTENANCE OF HIGH BLOOD ETHANOL LEVELS IN RATS DRINKING A LIQUID DIET.
001865 02-06

IMPOTENCE
EXPERIMENTATION WITH MINAPRINE IN DEALING WITH CERTAIN SEXUAL-DISORDERS: IMPOTENCE OR FRIGIDITY.
002153 02-11

A CLINICAL-STUDY AND ENDOCRINE-STUDY OF MESTEROLONE IN SECONDARY IMPOTENCE.
002315 02-14

IMPRESSIONS
FIRST CLINICAL IMPRESSIONS IN DAILY PRACTICE.
002046 02-09

IMPROMIDINE
SOME CENTRAL-EFFECTS OF IMPROMIDINE, A POTENT AGONIST OF HISTAMINE H2-RECEPTORS.
001417 02-03

Subject Index

IMPROVEMENTS
FEDERAL-COURT UPHOLDS RIGHT-TO-REFUSE PSYCHOTROPIC-DRUGS,
ORDERS IMPROVEMENTS AT LIMA-STATE-HOSPITAL.
002583 02-17

CHANGES IN THE CLINICAL-PICTURE AND THE COURSE OF PSYCHOSES
DURING MASSIVE PSYCHOPHARMACOTHERAPY AND THE
SIGNIFICANCE OF THESE CHANGES FOR IMPROVEMENTS IN
PSYCHIATRIC-TREATMENT.
004699 04-17

IMPULSE
AMPHETAMINE-INDUCED MOTILITY AND NIGROSTRIATAL IMPULSE FLOW.
003005 03-04

IMPULSES
EVIDENCE THAT THE OPIATE-RECEPTORS OF THE SUBSTANTIA-
GELATINOSA CONTRIBUTE TO THE DEPRESSION, BY INTRAVENOUS
MORPHINE, OF THE SPINAL TRANSMISSION OF IMPULSES IN
UNMYELINATED PRIMARY AFFERENTS.
002767 03-03

SUPRASPINAL INHIBITION OF THE EXCITATION OF DORSAL-HORN
NEURONES BY IMPULSES IN UNMYELINATED PRIMARY AFFERENTS:
LACK OF EFFECT BY STRYCHNINE AND BICUCULLINE.
003778 04-03

IMPURITIES
IMPURITIES IN DRUGS V: MEPROBAMATE.
004631 04-15

INABILITY
THE INABILITY OF CHRONIC FLUOXETINE TO POTENTIATE A SEROTONIN
MEDIATED EFFECT.
000293 01-03

THE INABILITY OF CHRONIC MIANSERIN TO BLOCK CENTRAL ALPHA2-
ADRENOCEPTORS.
001492 02-03

INACTIVATION
REVERSIBLE INACTIVATION OF RAPHE-MAGNUS NEURONS: EFFECTS ON
NOCICEPTIVE THRESHOLD AND MORPHINE-INDUCED ANALGESIA.
000240 01-03

MECHANISM OF INACTIVATION OF MITOCHONDRIAL MONOAMINE-
OXIDASE BY N CYCLOPROPYL-N-ARYLALKYLAMINES.
001055 02-01

MECHANISM OF INACTIVATION OF MITOCHONDRIAL MONOAMINE-
OXIDASE BY N CYCLOPROPYL-N-ARYLALKYLAMINES.
001088 02-02

THE INACTIVATION OF GAMMA AMINOBUTYRIC-ACID-TRANSAMINASE IN
DISSOCIATED NEURONAL CULTURES FROM SPINAL-CORD.
003980 04-03

INBRED
DIFFERENCES IN GAMMA AMINOBUTYRIC-ACID-RECEPTOR SENSITIVITY IN
INBRED STRAINS OF MICE.
000303 01-03

EFFECTS OF CHLORDIAZEPOXIDE MORPHINE COMBINATIONS ON
SPONTANEOUS LOCOMOTOR-ACTIVITY IN THREE INBRED STRAINS OF
MICE.
001766 02-04

EFFECTS OF MORPHINE AND CHLORDIAZEPOXIDE ON AVOIDANCE-
BEHAVIOUR IN TWO INBRED STRAINS OF MICE.
002973 03-04

INCIDENCE
CHRONIC EFFECTS OF NEUROLEPTICS HAVING HIGH OR LOW INCIDENCE
OF EXTRAPYRAMIDAL SIDE-EFFECTS UPON FORCE, DURATION AND
RATE OF OPERANT-RESPONSE IN RATS. (PH.D. DISSERTATION).
003125 03-05

LITHIUM AND THE CHANGING INCIDENCE OF MANIA.
003265 03-09

INCIPIENT
EARLY DETECTION OF HUNTINGTONS-DISEASE. BLINK REFLEX AND
LEVODOPA LOAD IN PRESYMPTOMATIC AND INCIPIENT SUBJECTS.
003311 03-11

INCUBATED
THE ROLE OF INTRANEURONAL 5 HT AND OF TRYPTOPHAN-
HYDROXYLASE ACTIVATION IN THE CONTROL OF 5 HT SYNTHESIS IN
RAT-BRAIN SLICES INCUBATED IN K-ENRICHED MEDIUM.
000123 01-03

IND
FDA CLIPS PSYCHODRUG PIONEERS IND WINGS.
003160 03-07

INDALPINE
PHARMACOLOGICAL EVIDENCE OF A POSSIBLE TRYPTAMINERGIC
REGULATION OF OPIATE-RECEPTORS BY USING INDALPINE, A SELECTIVE
5 HT UPTAKE INHIBITOR.
001517 02-03

INDEPENDENCE
THE NOSOLOGICAL INDEPENDENCE OF INVOLUTIONAL DEPRESSION AND
ITS DYNAMICS DURING PSYCHOPHARMACOTHERAPY.
004389 04-09

INDEPENDENT
REPEATED TRICYCLICS INDUCE A PROGRESSIVE DOPAMINE-
AUTORECEPTOR SUBSENSITIVITY INDEPENDENT OF DAILY DRUG-
TREATMENT.
000047 01-03

S

PROGNOSIS IN SCHIZOPHRENIA: INDIVIDUAL DIFFERENCES IN PSYCHOLOGICAL RESPONSE TO A TEST DOSE OF ANTIPSYCHOTIC-DRUG AND THEIR RELATIONSHIP TO BLOOD AND SALIVA LEVELS AND TREATMENT OUTCOME.
003189 03-08
GROUP VERSUS INDIVIDUAL COGNITIVE-THERAPY: A PILOT-STUDY.
003257 03-09
DOPAMINE, NORADRENALINE AND 3,4 DIHYDROXYPHENYLACETIC-ACID (DOPAC) LEVELS OF INDIVIDUAL BRAIN NUCLEI, EFFECTS OF HALOPERIDOL AND PARGYLINE.
003792 04-03
INDIVIDUAL DIFFERENCES IN EFFECTS OF TRICYCLIC-ANTIDEPRESSANTS AND ANTICHOLINERGIC-DRUGS ON OPERANT-BEHAVIOR IN THE SQUIRREL-MONKEY.
004176 04-04

INDIVIDUALIZATION
INDIVIDUALIZATION OF PHENYTOIN THERAPY.
002495 02-16

INDIVIDUALIZED
PERSPECTIVE ON ADEQUATE INDIVIDUALIZED DRUG DOSES.
000959 01-17

INDOL-3-YLMETHYLPIPERID-4-YL-3-BENZOYLUREA
BEHAVIOURAL AND NEUROCHEMICAL PROPERTIES OF 1 1 INDOL-3-YLMETHYLPIPERID-4-YL-3-BENZOYLUREA (WY-25093) IN RODENTS.
003686 04-02

INDOLEALKYLAMINE
A COMMON MECHANISM FOR LYSERGIC-ACID, INDOLEALKYLAMINE AND PHENETHYLAMINE HALLUCINOGENS: SEROTONERGIC MEDIATION OF BEHAVIORAL-EFFECTS IN RATS.
004007 04-03

INDOLEAMINE-N-METHYLTRANSFERASE
EFFECT OF NEUROLEPTICS ON INDOLEAMINE-N-METHYLTRANSFERASE ACTIVITY AND BRAIN METABOLISM OF BUFOTENIN.
002735 03-03

INDOLEAMINES
MASS-SPECTROMETRIC-ASSAYS OF INDOLEAMINES. (UNPUBLISHED PAPER).
001043 02-01
BENZODIAZEPINES, STRESS AND RAT PLASMA CORTICOSTEROIDS: THE ROLE OF INDOLEAMINES.
003034 03-04

INDOMETHACIN
INTERACTION OF INDOMETHACIN AND IBUPROFEN WITH LITHIUM IN MANIC-PATIENTS UNDER A STEADY-STATE LITHIUM LEVEL.
000622 01-09
EFFECT OF PROSTAGLANDIN-E1 AND ITS BIOSYNTHESIS INHIBITOR INDOMETHACIN ON DRINKING IN THE RAT.
001749 02-04
EFFECTS OF INDOMETHACIN AND METHYLPREDNISOLONE ON RENAL ELIMINATION OF LITHIUM IN THE RAT.
004270 04-05

INDORAMIN
CENTRAL SYMPATHETIC REACTIVITY INHIBITED BY INDORAMIN.
001193 02-03

INDUCE
REPEATED TRICYCLIC-ANTIDEPRESSANTS INDUCE A PROGRESSIVE SWITCH IN THE ELECTROPHYSIOLOGICAL RESPONSE OF DOPAMINE NEURONS TO AUTORECEPTOR STIMULATION.
000046 01-03
REPEATED TRICYCLICS INDUCE A PROGRESSIVE DOPAMINE-AUTORECEPTOR SUBSENSITIVITY INDEPENDENT OF DAILY DRUG-TREATMENT.
000047 01-03
TRICYCLIC-ANTIDEPRESSANTS INDUCE SUBSENSITIVITY OF PRESYNAPTIC DOPAMINE-AUTORECEPTORS.
000048 01-03
REPEATED ANTIDEPRESSANT TREATMENTS INDUCE A LONG-LASTING DOPAMINE-AUTORECEPTOR SUBSENSITIVITY: IS DAILY TREATMENT NECESSARY FOR CLINICAL EFFICACY?
002659 03-03

INDUCED
COMPARATIVE-STUDY OF ANALGESIA INDUCED BY N VAL5-ENKEPHALIN AND PRO5-ENKEPHALIN ANALOGS.
000021 01-03
HYPOALGESIA INDUCED BY MICROINJECTION OF A NOREPINEPHRINE ANTAGONIST IN THE RAPHE-MAGNUS: REVERSAL BY INTRATHECAL ADMINISTRATION OF A SEROTONIN ANTAGONIST.
000121 01-03
ASSESSMENT OF TOLERANCE TO AND PHYSICAL-DEPENDENCE ON PENTOBARBITAL, INDUCED BY MULTIPLE PELLET IMPLANTATION.
000385 01-04
ROTATIONAL-BEHAVIOR INDUCED BY COCAINE ANALOGS IN RATS WITH UNILATERAL 6 HYDROXYDOPAMINE LESIONS OF THE SUBSTANTIA-NIGRA: DEPENDENCE UPON DOPAMINE UPTAKE INHIBITION.
000404 01-04
THE INVOLVEMENT OF SEROTONERGIC NEURONS IN THE CENTRAL-NERVOUS-SYSTEM AS THE POSSIBLE MECHANISM FOR SLOW HEAD-SHAKING-BEHAVIOR INDUCED BY METHAMPHETAMINE IN RATS.
000408 01-04

BEHAVIOURAL-CHANGES INDUCED BY N,N DIMETHYLTRYPTAMINE IN RODENTS.
000413 01-04
CIRCLING-BEHAVIOUR INDUCED BY INTRANIGRAL INJECTION OF BACLOFEN IN RATS.
000415 01-04
ROTATION INDUCED BY INTRANIGRAL INJECTIONS OF GABA AGONISTS AND ANTAGONISTS: ZONE-SPECIFIC EFFECTS.
000422 01-04
MAPPING OF DYSKINETIC-MOVEMENTS INDUCED BY LOCAL APPLICATION OF PICROTOXIN OR () GAMMA ACETYLENIC-GABA ON THE RAT MOTOR-CORTEX.
000458 01-04
EXPERIMENTAL DYSTONIA INDUCED BY QUATERNARY CHLORPROMAZINE.
000461 01-04
NOREPINEPHRINE UPTAKE INHIBITORS AS BIOCHEMICALLY-SELECTIVE AND BEHAVIORALLY-SELECTIVE ANTAGONISTS OF THE LOCOMOTOR-STIMULATION INDUCED BY INDIRECTLY ACTING SYMPATHOMIMETIC-AMINES IN MICE.
000492 01-04
ANALGESIC ACTIVITY OF DIFLUNISAL (MK-647, 5 2,4 DIFLUOROPHENYLSALICYLIC-ACID) IN RATS WITH HYPERALGESIA INDUCED BY FREUNDS-ADJUVANT.
000502 01-04
FAILURE OF ISOPRENALINE AND BETA-RECEPTOR BLOCKING-DRUGS TO MODIFY DEPRESSOR RESPONSE AND BRADYCARDIA INDUCED BY ELECTRICAL-STIMULATION OF THE ANTERIOR HYPOTHALAMUS OF CATS.
000520 01-05
PHARMACOPSYCHOLOGICAL INVESTIGATION OF CHANGES IN MOOD INDUCED BY DIPOTASSIUM-CHLORAZEPATE WITH AND WITHOUT SIMULTANEOUS ALCOHOL ADMINISTRATION.
000825 01-14
PSYCHIATRIC MANIFESTATIONS INDUCED BY DOPAMINE PRECURSORS OR DOPAMINE AGONISTS.
000865 01-15
INCREASED METABOLISM OF DOPAMINE AND SEROTONIN INDUCED IN FOREBRAIN AREAS BY ETORPHINE MICROINJECTION IN PERIAQUEDUCTAL GRAY.
001103 02-03
ADAPTIVE CHANGES OF THE STRIATAL DOPAMINE SYSTEM INDUCED BY REPEATED ADMINISTRATION OF NEUROLEPTICS AND ERGOT DERIVATIVES.
001156 02-03
CHANGES IN CEREBRAL DOPAMINE FUNCTION INDUCED BY A YEARS ADMINISTRATION OF TRIFLUOPERAZINE OR THIORIDAZINE AND THEIR SUBSEQUENT WITHDRAWAL.
001175 02-03
EEG CHANGE IN THE CONSCIOUS RAT DURING IMMOBILITY INDUCED BY PSYCHOLOGICAL-STRESS.
001297 02-03
LONG-TERM DECREASES IN SPONTANEOUS FIRING OF CAUDATE NEURONS INDUCED BY AMPHETAMINE IN CATS.
001340 02-03
THE EFFECT OF CYCLO-LEU-GLY ON CHEMICAL DENERVATION SUPERSENSITIVITY OF DOPAMINE-RECEPTORS INDUCED BY INTRACEREBROVENTRICULAR INJECTION OF 6 HYDROXYDOPAMINE IN MICE.
001435 02-03
BIOCHEMICAL-STUDY OF THE ANIMAL-MODEL DEPRESSION INDUCED BY TETRABENAZINE.
001506 02-03
EVIDENCE THAT NORADRENALINE MODULATES THE INCREASE IN STRIATAL DOPAMINE METABOLISM INDUCED BY MUSCARINIC-RECEPTOR STIMULATION.
001518 02-03
IN VIVO CHANGES IN THE GABA CONTENT OF NERVE-ENDINGS (SYNAPTOSOMES) INDUCED BY INHIBITORS OF GABA UPTAKE.
001540 02-03
INFLUENCE OF THYROTROPIN-RELEASING-HORMONE AND HISTIDYL-PROLINE-DIKETOPIPERAZINE ON SPONTANEOUS LOCOMOTOR-ACTIVITY AND ANALGESIA INDUCED BY DELTA9 TETRAHYDROCANNABINOL IN THE MOUSE.
001575 02-04
BRAIN CATECHOLAMINES MODIFICATIONS. THE EFFECTS ON MEMORY FACILITATION INDUCED BY OXOTREMORINE IN MICE.
001658 02-04
CONTRALATERAL CIRCLING-BEHAVIOUR INDUCED BY INTRANIGRAL INJECTION OF MORPHINE AND ENKEPHALIN ANALOGUE FK-33-824 IN RATS.
001669 02-04
CONTRALATERAL CIRCLING-BEHAVIOUR INDUCED BY INTRANIGRAL INJECTION OF TAURINE IN RATS.
001670 02-04
OPIATE ANTAGONISTS AND LONG-TERM ANALGESIC REACTION INDUCED BY INESCAPABLE SHOCK IN RATS.
001707 02-04

Subject Index

ETHANOL AVERSION INDUCED BY PARENTERALLY ADMINISTERED ETHANOL ACTING BOTH AS CS AND UCS.
001721 02-04

THE ROLE OF DOPAMINE IN THE HYPERMOTILITY INDUCED BY H-77-77 (4,ALPHA DIMETHYL-M-TYRAMINE) IN MICE.
001762 02-04

MOTOR-DEPRESSION AND HEAD-TWITCHES INDUCED BY IP INJECTION OF GABA.
001788 02-04

THE EFFECT OF ASPIRIN AND PARACETAMOL ON THE INCREASED NALOXONE POTENCY INDUCED BY MORPHINE PRETREATMENT.
001824 02-04

DYSKINESIA INDUCED BY LONG-TERM-TREATMENT WITH ANTIPSYCHOTIC-DRUGS: INVOLVEMENT OF PRESYNAPTIC AND POSTSYNAPTIC DOPAMINERGIC MECHANISMS.
001839 02-05

HEMODYNAMIC FAILURE INDUCED BY NARCOTIC AND TOXIC DOSES OF 12 CNS DEPRESSANTS IN INTACT AND PITHED RATS.
001855 02-05

INTERRELATION AT PLASMATIC LEVEL BETWEEN ANTIEPILEPTIC-DRUGS AND LIPIDS. ITS IMPLICATIONS IN THE EFFICIENCY OF TREATMENT IN EPILEPSY. I. CHANGES INDUCED BY PHENOBARBITAL OR/AND DIPHENYLHYDANTOIN IN SERUM LIPIDS.
002281 02-13

CORRECTION BY PROPRANOLOL OF THE ABNORMAL ADRENALINE DISCHARGE INDUCED BY EMOTIONAL-STRESS IN CEREBRAL HEMORRHAGE PATIENTS.
002295 02-13

CNV VARIATIONS INDUCED BY THE ADMINISTRATION OF DIAZEPAM, HALOPERIDOL, PHENELZINE AND D-AMPHETAMINE.
002355 02-14

DISTURBED-BEHAVIOUR INDUCED BY HIGH-DOSE ANTIPSYCHOTIC-DRUGS.
002375 02-15

PARADOXICAL AKINESIA INDUCED BY ANTIDEPRESSANT-DRUGS.
002378 02-15

CHOREIC-MOVEMENTS INDUCED BY THE USE OF METHADONE.
002467 02-15

PHASIC ACTIVITY INDUCED BY P CHLOROPHENYLALANINE IN THE AUDITORY PATHWAY.
002661 03-03

EFFECTS OF ELECTROCONVULSIVE-TREATMENT ON GROWTH-HORMONE SECRETION INDUCED BY MONOAMINE-RECEPTOR AGONISTS IN RESERPINE PRETREATED RATS.
002664 03-03

CHRONOLOGY OF NEUROCHEMICAL ALTERATIONS INDUCED BY GABA AGONIST ADMINISTRATION.
002713 03-03

KAINIC-ACID INDUCED LESION OF RAT RETINA: DIFFERENTIAL-EFFECT ON CYCLIC-GMP AND BENZODIAZEPINE-RECEPTORS AND GABA-RECEPTORS.
002743 03-03

MORPHOLOGICAL CHANGES IN RAT-BRAIN INDUCED BY L CYSTEINE INJECTION IN NEWBORN ANIMALS.
002774 03-03

DIFFERENTIAL LOSS OF BIOLOGICAL-ACTIVITY OF THE ENKEPHALINS INDUCED BY CURRENT.
002783 03-03

NALOXONE EFFECTS ON THE BLOOD-PRESSURE RESPONSE INDUCED BY THIN-FIBER MUSCULAR AFFERENTS.
002794 03-03

ENVIRONMENTAL MODULATION OF ANALGESIC TOLERANCE INDUCED BY MORPHINE PELLETS.
002944 03-04

ESTROGEN POTENTIATES THE STEREOTYPY INDUCED BY DOPAMINE AGONISTS IN THE RAT.
002968 03-04

PHARMACOLOGICAL CHARACTERIZATION OF SCRATCHING-BEHAVIOUR INDUCED BY INTRACRANIAL INJECTION OF SUBSTANCE-P AND SOMATOSTATIN.
002980 03-04

SELECTIVE SENSITIZATION INDUCED BY LITHIUM MALAISE AND FOOTSHOCK IN RATS.
003055 03-04

EFFECTS OF METHYSERGIDE AND NALOXONE ON ANALGESIA INDUCED BY THE PERIPHERAL ELECTRIC-STIMULATION IN MICE.
003093 03-04

CENTRALLY INDUCED CARDIOVASCULAR AND SYMPATHETIC-NERVE RESPONSES TO BRADYKININ IN RATS.
003099 03-04

A NEUROANATOMICAL-STUDY OF ANALGESIA AND CATATONIA INDUCED BY ETORPHINE IN THE RAT. (PH.D. DISSERTATION).
003102 03-04

DOPAMINE DEPLETION BY 6 HYDROXYDOPAMINE PREVENTS CONDITIONED TASTE-AVERSION INDUCED BY METHYLAMPHETAMINE BUT NOT LITHIUM-CHLORIDE.
003110 03-04

AGGRESSIVE-BEHAVIOR INDUCED BY APOMORPHINE IN RATS SUBMITTED TO FOUR STRESSFUL-SITUATIONS.
003163 03-07

SORPTION OF CHLORMETHIAZOLE BY INTRAVENOUS INFUSION GIVING SETS.
002508 02-16

REVERSAL OF NORADRENALINE DENERVATION-INDUCED INCREASE OF BETA-ADRENORECEPTOR BINDING IN RAT NEOCORTEX BY NORADRENALINE INFUSION.
002672 03-03

ALTERATIONS IN CEREBROSPINAL-FLUID DOPAMINE METABOLITES FOLLOWING PHYSOSTIGMINE INFUSION.
003477 03-15

H2-RECEPTORS MEDIATE INCREASES IN PERMEABILITY OF THE BLOOD-BRAIN-BARRIER DURING ARTERIAL HISTAMINE INFUSION.
003817 04-03

SUSTAINED INTRACEREBROVENTRICULAR INFUSION OF BRAIN FUELS REDUCES BODY-WEIGHT AND FOOD INTAKE IN RATS.
004098 04-04

THE SIMULTANEOUS INFUSION OF DRUGS VIA THE LEFT AND RIGHT VERTEBRAL-ARTERY OF THE CAT; A MODIFIED ANIMAL-MODEL FOR THE STUDY OF POSSIBLE CENTRAL-ACTIONS OF DRUGS UPON THE LOWER BRAINSTEM.
004297 04-06

THE SPECIFIC ACTIVITY OF PLATELET MONOAMINE-OXIDASE VARIES WITH PLATELET COUNT DURING SEVERE EXERCISE AND NORADRENALINE INFUSION.
004509 04-13

INFUSIONS
TREATMENT OF THERAPY-RESISTANT DEPRESSED-PATIENTS WITH IV. INFUSIONS OF NOMIFENSINE CONTROLLED BY GALVANIC-SKIN-RESISTANCE.
002012 02-09

INFUSIONS INTO THE OCULOMOTOR NUCLEUS OR NERVE: A METHOD OF ESTIMATING THE DOSAGE AT WHICH TRANSMITTER ANTAGONISTS INFUSED INTRACRANIALLY PRODUCE NONSPECIFIC BLOCKING OF NEURAL ACTIVITY.
003134 03-06

CLINICAL-EFFECTS OF BETA ENDORPHIN INFUSIONS.
004360 04-09

INGESTION
ACUTE CHANGES IN BRAIN TRYPTOPHAN AND SEROTONIN FOLLOWING CARBOHYDRATE OR PROTEIN INGESTION BY DIABETIC RATS. (UNPUBLISHED PAPER).
000060 01-03

IMPAIRMENT OF AVOIDANCE-BEHAVIOR FOLLOWING SHORT-TERM INGESTION OF ETHANOL, TERTIARY BUTANOL, OR PENTOBARBITAL IN MICE.
000479 01-04

STUDY OF VIGILANCE AFTER INGESTION OF ZOPICLONE IN COMPARISON WITH NITRAZEPAM AND PLACEBO. METHODOLOGY OF THE STUDY: SELF-EVALUATION QUESTIONNAIRE AND PSYCHOMETRIC-TESTS.
000543 01-07

ADRENAL-HORMONES AND ETHANOL INGESTION IN C57BL/CRGL AND C3H/CRGL/2 MICE.
002739 03-03

NICOTINE INGESTION REDUCES ELEVATED BLOOD-PRESSURES IN RATS AND SQUIRREL-MONKEYS.
002759 03-03

INGESTIONAL
INTERFERENCE WITH INGESTIONAL AVERSION LEARNING PRODUCED BY PREEXPOSURE TO THE UNCONDITIONED-STIMULUS: ASSOCIATIVE-ASPECTS AND NONASSOCIATIVE-ASPECTS.
001610 02-04

INHIBIT
ENKEPHALINS PRESYNAPTICALLY INHIBIT CHOLINERGIC TRANSMISSION IN SYMPATHETIC GANGLIA.
000167 01-03

GUANINE-NUCLEOTIDES INHIBIT BINDING OF AGONISTS AND ANTAGONISTS TO SOLUBLE OPIATE-RECEPTORS. (UNPUBLISHED PAPER).
001035 02-01

ALPHA2-ADRENERGIC AMINES, ADENOSINE AND PROSTAGLANDINS INHIBIT LIPOLYSIS AND CYCLIC-AMP ACCUMULATION IN HAMSTER ADIPOCYTES IN THE ABSENCE OF EXTRACELLULAR SODIUM.
002728 03-03

CHLORPROMAZINE, HALOPERIDOL, METOCLOPRAMIDE AND DOMPERIDONE RELEASE PROLACTIN THROUGH DOPAMINE ANTAGONISM AT LOW CONCENTRATIONS BUT PARADOXICALLY INHIBIT PROLACTIN RELEASE AT HIGH-CONCENTRATIONS.
003731 04-03

OPIOIDS, NORADRENALINE AND GTP ANALOGS INHIBIT CHOLERA-TOXIN ACTIVATED ADENYLATE-CYCLASE IN NEUROBLASTOMA-X GLIOMA HYBRID CELLS.
003975 04-03

INHIBITED
POSTSWIM GROOMING IN MICE INHIBITED BY DOPAMINE-RECEPTOR ANTAGONISTS AND BY CANNABINOIDS.
000359 01-04

CENTRAL SYMPATHETIC REACTIVITY INHIBITED BY INDORAMIN.
001193 02-03

Subject Index

INHIBITION

ADMINISTRATION OF ANTISOMATOSTATIN SERUM TO RATS REVERSES THE INHIBITION OF PULSATILE GROWTH-HORMONE SECRETION PRODUCED BY INJECTION OF METERGOLINE BUT NOT YOHIMBINE. (UNPUBLISHED PAPER).
000019 01-03

MATURATION OF SYMPATHETIC NEUROTRANSMISSION IN THE RAT HEART. III. DEVELOPMENTAL-CHANGES IN RESERPINE INHIBITION OF NOREPINEPHRINE UPTAKE INTO ISOLATED SYNAPTIC VESICLES.
000025 01-03

INHIBITION OF HIGH-AFFINITY CHOLINE UPTAKE: STRUCTURE-ACTIVITY STUDIES.
000026 01-03

INHIBITION OF BRAIN SYNAPTOSOMAL UPTAKE OF CHOLINE BY SOME 2 CARBOXAMIDOSTRYCHNINE DERIVATIVES WITH MUSCLE-RELAXANT PROPERTIES.
000084 01-03

INHIBITION OF (3H)NALOXONE BINDING IN HOMOGENATES OF RAT-BRAIN BY ESEROLINE, A DRUG, WITH ANALGESIC ACTIVITY, RELATED TO PHYSOSTIGMINE.
000104 01-03

GABA INHIBITION OF 3H GLYCINE RELEASE FROM SLICES OF RAT SUBSTANTIA-NIGRA IN VITRO.
000157 01-03

INHIBITION OF MONOAMINE-OXIDASE BY CLORGYLINE AND DEPRENYL IN CIRCUMVENTRICULAR STRUCTURES OF RAT-BRAIN.
000159 01-03

BETA DIETHYLAMINOETHYLDIPHENYLPROPYLACETATE (SKF-525-A) AND 2,4 DICHLORO-6-PHENYLPHENOXYETHYLAMINE-HBR (DPEA) INHIBITION OF FATTY-ACID CONJUGATION TO 11 HYDROXY-DELTA9-TETRAHYDROCANNABINOL BY THE RAT LIVER MICROSOMAL SYSTEM.
000179 01-03

COMPARATIVE-STUDY OF THE INHIBITION OF GABA-AMINOTRANSFERASE BY DIFFERENT ANTICONVULSANT-DRUGS.
000192 01-03

INHIBITION OF IN VIVO 3H SPIPERONE BINDING BY THE PROPOSED ANTIPSYCHOTIC DES-TYR1-GAMMA-ENDORPHIN.
000226 01-03

INHIBITION OF NEURONAL UPTAKE REDUCES THE PRESYNAPTIC EFFECTS OF CLONIDINE BUT NOT OF ALPHA METHYLNORADRENALINE ON THE STIMULATION-EVOKED RELEASE OF 3H NORADRENALINE FROM RAT OCCIPITAL-CORTEX SLICES.
000227 01-03

IRREVERSIBLE INHIBITION OF AROMATIC-L-AMINO-ACID-DECARBOXYLASE BY ALPHA DIFLUOROMETHYL-DOPA AND METABOLISM OF THE INHIBITOR.
000248 01-03

MICROIONTOPHORETIC STUDIES ON NORADRENERGIC INHIBITION FROM LOCUS-COERULEUS OF SPINAL TRIGEMINAL-NUCLEUS NEURONS.
000260 01-03

INHIBITION OF ALCOHOL-DEHYDROGENASE BY DISULFIRAM; POSSIBLE RELATION TO THE DISULFIRAM ETHANOL REACTION.
000270 01-03

DIFFERENTIAL REGULATION OF MUSCARINIC AGONIST BINDING-SITES FOLLOWING CHRONIC CHOLINESTERASE INHIBITION.
000279 01-03

INHIBITION OF GROWTH IN YOUNG MICE TREATED WITH PENTAZOCINE: REVERSAL BY NALTREXONE.
000318 01-03

INHIBITION OF (3H)DIAZEPAM BINDING TO RAT-BRAIN CORTICAL SYNAPTOSOMAL MEMBRANES BY ADENOSINE UPTAKE BLOCKERS.
000330 01-03

INHIBITION OF BEHAVIORAL-EFFECTS OF COCAINE BY ACTINOMYCIN-D IN RATS.
000346 01-04

ROTATIONAL-BEHAVIOR INDUCED BY COCAINE ANALOGS IN RATS WITH UNILATERAL 6 HYDROXYDOPAMINE LESIONS OF THE SUBSTANTIA-NIGRA: DEPENDENCE UPON DOPAMINE UPTAKE INHIBITION.
000404 01-04

SELECTIVE INHIBITION OF MESOLIMBIC BEHAVIORAL-SUPERSENSITIVITY BY NALOXONE.
000467 01-04

MONOAMINE-OXIDASE AND ITS INHIBITION: SOME CLINICAL IMPLICATIONS.
000983 01-17

IRREVERSIBLE INHIBITION OF S ADENOSYLHOMOCYSTEINE-HYDROLASE BY NUCLEOSIDE ANALOGS. (UNPUBLISHED PAPER).
001010 02-01

TETRAHYDRO-BETA-CARBOLINES AND CORRESPONDING TRYPTAMINES: IN VITRO INHIBITION OF SEROTONIN AND DOPAMINE UPTAKE BY HUMAN BLOOD-PLATELETS.
001067 02-02

TETRAHYDRO-BETA-CARBOLINES AND CORRESPONDING TRYPTAMINES: IN VITRO INHIBITION OF SEROTONIN, DOPAMINE AND NORADRENALINE UPTAKE IN RAT-BRAIN SYNAPTOSOMES.
001078 02-02

INHIBITION BY LOCAL ANESTHETICS, PHENTOLAMINE AND PROPRANOLOL OF (3H)QUINUCLIDINYL-BENZYLATE BINDING TO CENTRAL MUSCARINIC-RECEPTORS.
001097 02-03

HOMOCYSTEINE-INDUCED CONVULSIONS: ENHANCEMENT BY VITAMIN-B6 AND INHIBITION BY HYDRAZINE.
002758 03-03

A QUANTITATIVE REGIONAL ANALYSIS OF PROTEIN SYNTHESIS INHIBITION IN THE RAT-BRAIN FOLLOWING LOCALIZED INJECTION OF CYCLOHEXIMIDE.
002780 03-03

COCAINE AND AMPHETAMINE ANTAGONIZE THE DECREASE OF NORADRENERGIC NEUROTRANSMISSION ELICITED BY OXYMETAZOLINE BUT POTENTIATE THE INHIBITION BY ALPHA METHYLNOREPINEPHRINE IN THE PERFUSED CAT SPLEEN.
002801 03-03

A BARBITURATE-EVOKED INTENSIFICATION OF POSTSYNAPTIC INHIBITION IN THE PREOPTIC OVULATORY TRIGGER REGION OF THE HYPOTHALAMUS.
002818 03-03

INHIBITION OF GAMMA AMINOBUTYRIC-ACID-TRANSAMINASE WITH 6 AMINONICOTINAMIDE IN REGIONS OF THE RAT-BRAIN.
002868 03-03

KINETIC DATA ON THE INHIBITION OF HIGH-AFFINITY CHOLINE TRANSPORT INTO RAT-FOREBRAIN SYNAPTOSOMES BY CHOLINE-LIKE COMPOUNDS AND NITROGEN-MUSTARD ANALOGUES.
002879 03-03

BARBITURATE ENHANCEMENT OF GABA-MEDIATED INHIBITION AND ACTIVATION OF CHLORIDE ION-CONDUCTANCE: CORRELATION WITH ANTICONVULSANT AND ANESTHETIC ACTIONS.
002885 03-03

SELECTIVE INHIBITION BY NICOTINE OF SHOCK-INDUCED FIGHTING IN THE RAT.
002984 03-04

ASCENDING ENDORPHIN INHIBITION OF DISTRESS VOCALIZATION.
003011 03-04

INHIBITION OF AGGRESSIVE-BEHAVIOR IN RHESUS-MONKEYS BY BUSPIRONE.
003103 03-04

NEUROLEPTICS: ACTIVATION OR INHIBITION OF THE DOPAMINERGIC-SYSTEM?
003424 03-13

CLINICAL-IMPLICATIONS OF ENZYME INDUCTION AND ENZYME INHIBITION.
003621 03-17

STEREOSPECIFIC INHIBITION OF DOPAMINE-SENSITIVE ADENYLATE-CYCLASE IN CARP RETINA BY THE ENANTIOMERS OF (/-) 1 CYCLOPROPYLMETHYL TRIFLUOROMETHYLTHIODIBENZOCYCLOHEPTENYLIDENEPIPERIDINE.
003706 04-02

INHIBITION OF MONOAMINE-OXIDASE BY FURAZOLIDONE IN THE CHICKEN AND THE INFLUENCE OF THE ALIMENTARY FLORA THEREON.
003711 04-03

PRESYNAPTIC AND POSTSYNAPTIC STRIATAL DOPAMINE-RECEPTORS: DIFFERENTIAL SENSITIVITY TO APOMORPHINE INHIBITION OF (3H)DOPAMINE AND (14C)GABA RELEASE IN VITRO.
003741 04-03

INHIBITION OF (3H)DIAZEPAM BINDING BY AN ENDOGENOUS FRACTION FROM RAT-BRAIN SYNAPTOSOMES.
003768 04-03

NONCOMPETITIVE AMINE UPTAKE INHIBITION BY THE NEW ANTIDEPRESSANT PRIDEFINE.
003771 04-03

SUPRASPINAL INHIBITION OF THE EXCITATION OF DORSAL-HORN NEURONES BY IMPULSES IN UNMYELINATED PRIMARY AFFERENTS: LACK OF EFFECT BY STRYCHNINE AND BICUCULLINE.
003778 04-03

INHIBITION OF SYNAPTOSOMAL CALCIUM UPTAKE BY ETHANOL.
003827 04-03

INHIBITION OF AMINOPEPTIDASE AND ACETYLCHOLINESTERASE BY PUROMYCIN AND PUROMYCIN ANALOGS.
003835 04-03

BACLOFEN: STEREOSELECTIVE INHIBITION OF EXCITANT AMINO-ACID RELEASE.
003867 04-03

CHARACTERISTICS OF THE INHIBITION OF RAT-BRAIN MONOAMINE-OXIDASE IN VITRO BY MD780515.
003874 04-03

INHIBITION OF DOPAMINE D-1 AND D-2 BINDING-SITES IN NEURONAL TISSUE BY ASCORBATE.
003876 04-03

THE EFFECT OF SODIUM-DIPROPYLACETATE ON GAMMA AMINOBUTYRIC-ACID DEPENDENT INHIBITION IN THE RAT-CORTEX AND SUBSTANTIA-NIGRA IN RELATION TO ITS ANTICONVULSANT ACTIVITY.
003880 04-03

THE IMPORTANCE OF CATECHOLAMINE UPTAKE INHIBITION IN THE REVERSAL OF GUANETHIDINE BLOCKADE OF ADRENERGIC NEURONS.
003900 04-03

INHIBITION OE LYSOSOMAL LIPASES BY CHLORPROMAZINE: A POSSIBLE MECHANISMS OF STABILIZATION.
003993 04-03

PHENYTOIN INHIBITION OF CYCLIC-GUANOSINE-MONOPHOSPHATE (C-GMP) ACCUMULATION IN NEUROBLASTOMA CELLS BY CALCIUM-CHANNEL BLOCKADE.
004020 04-03

INHIBITION BY CAFFEINE OF CALCIUM UPTAKE BY BRAIN MICROSOMAL VESICLES.
004042 04-03

INHIBITION OF THE SYNTHESIS OF ACETYLCHOLINE IN RAT-BRAIN SLICES BY (-) HYDROXYCITRATE AND CITRATE.
004044 04-03

DIFFERENTIAL INHIBITION OF ALPHA1-ADRENOCEPTOR AND ALPHA2-ADRENOCEPTOR MEDIATED PRESSOR RESPONSES IN PITHED RATS.
004057 04-03

HYPERACTIVITY FOLLOWING INJECTION OF A GLUTAMATE AGONIST AND 6,7 ADTN INTO RAT NUCLEUS-ACCUMBENS AND ITS INHIBITION BY THIP.
004066 04-04

SUPPRESSION OF ALCOHOL DRINKING WITH BRAIN ALDEHYDE-DEHYDROGENASE INHIBITION.
004220 04-04

INHIBITION OF PENTAGASTRIN-STIMULATED AND OVERNIGHT GASTRIC SECRETION BY LM24056, A NEW PHENOTHIAZINE DERIVED ANTISECRETORY DRUG.
004306 04-07

THE ANTIDEPRESSANT EFFECTS OF TRAZODONE AND INHIBITION OF PLATELET SEROTONIN REUPTAKE.
004383 04-09

INHIBITOR

ATP COMPLEXES WITH THE ATPASE INHIBITOR QUERCETIN.
000045 01-01

CHANGES IN PRIMARY AFFERENT DEPOLARIZATION AFTER ADMINISTRATION OF GAMMA ACETYLENIC-GAMMA-AMINOBUTYRIC-ACID (GAG), A GAMMA AMINOBUTYRIC-ACID-TRANSAMINASE (GABA-TRANSAMINASE) INHIBITOR.
000174 01-01

IRREVERSIBLE INHIBITION OF AROMATIC-L-AMINO-ACID-DECARBOXYLASE BY ALPHA DIFLUOROMETHYL-DOPA AND METABOLISM OF THE INHIBITOR.
000248 01-03

ANALYSIS OF THE ACTIVATION OF DOPAMINE METABOLISM BY A SEROTONIN UPTAKE INHIBITOR.
000315 01-03

CGP-6085-A, A NEW, SPECIFIC, INHIBITOR OF SEROTONIN UPTAKE: NEUROCHEMICAL CHARACTERIZATION AND COMPARISON WITH OTHER SEROTONIN UPTAKE BLOCKERS.
000316 01-03

INITIAL, CLINICAL-TRIAL OF A NEW, SPECIFIC 5 HT REUPTAKE INHIBITOR, CITALOPRAM (LU-10-171).
000591 01-09

THE BLOCKADE OF ALPHA2-ADRENOCEPTORS BY THE PNMT INHIBITOR SKF-64139.
001255 02-03

1 METHYL-BETA-CARBOLINE (HARMANE), A POTENT ENDOGENOUS INHIBITOR OF BENZODIAZEPINE-RECEPTOR BINDING.
001440 02-03

PHARMACOLOGICAL EVIDENCE OF A POSSIBLE TRYPTAMINERGIC REGULATION OF OPIATE-RECEPTORS BY USING INDALPINE, A SELECTIVE 5 HT UPTAKE INHIBITOR.
001517 02-03

EFFECT OF PROSTAGLANDIN-E1 AND ITS BIOSYNTHESIS INHIBITOR INDOMETHACIN ON DRINKING IN THE RAT.
001749 02-04

AN INHIBITOR OF OPIOID-PEPTIDE DEGRADATION PRODUCES ANALGESIA IN MICE.
001780 02-04

CHANGES IN THE AUGMENTER REDUCER TENDENCY AND IN PAIN MEASURES AS A RESULT OF TREATMENT WITH A SEROTONIN REUPTAKE INHIBITOR ZIMELIDINE.
002305 02-13

COMPARATIVE-STUDIES OF L-DOPA ALONE AND COMBINATION WITH A PERIPHERAL DOPA-DECARBOXYLASE INHIBITOR, BENSERAZIDE-HCL, ON PARKINSONS-DISEASE -- PART II: PHARMACOKINETIC-STUDY.
002309 02-13

DEMONSTRATION AND CHARACTERIZATION OF AN ENDOGENOUS INHIBITOR OF GABA-ENHANCED (3H) DIAZEPAM BINDING FROM BOVINE CEREBRAL-CORTEX.
002645 03-01

DU-24565, A QUIPAZINE DERIVATIVE, A POTENT SELECTIVE SEROTONIN UPTAKE INHIBITOR.
002651 03-02

EFFECTS OF AN EPINEPHRINE SYNTHESIS INHIBITOR, SKF-64139, ON THE SECRETION OF LUTEINIZING-HORMONE IN OVARIECTOMIZED FEMALE RATS.
002693 03-03

TREATMENT OF HUNTINGTON-DISEASE WITH GAMMA ACETYLENIC-GABA, AN IRREVERSIBLE INHIBITOR OF GABA-TRANSAMINASE: INCREASED CSF GABA AND HOMOCARNOSINE WITHOUT CLINICAL AMELIORATION.
003458 03-14

ANTITREMOR ACTION OF C10DICHOL, A PERIPHERAL ACETYLCHOLINE SYNTHESIS INHIBITOR.
004096 04-04

ANORECTIC-PROPERTIES OF A NEW LONG ACTING SEROTONIN UPTAKE
INHIBITOR.
004105 04-04
ATTENUATION OF PETHIDINE-INDUCED ANTINOCICEPTION BY ZIMELIDINE,
AN INHIBITOR OF 5 HYDROXYTRYPTAMINE REUPTAKE.
004118 04-04
() 6 FLUOROTRYPTOPHAN, AN INHIBITOR OF TRYPTOPHAN-
HYDROXYLASE: SLEEP AND WAKEFULNESS IN THE RAT.
004189 04-04

INHIBITORS
ARYLDIALKENYLPIPERAZINES AS SELECTIVE AND VERY POTENT
INHIBITORS OF DOPAMINE UPTAKE.
000005 01-01
BLOCKADE OF METHAMPHETAMINE-INDUCED DEPRESSION OF TYROSINE-
HYDROXYLASE BY GABA-TRANSAMINASE INHIBITORS.
000130 01-03
IN VIVO EFFECT OF PROTEASE INHIBITORS IN DENERVATION ATROPHY.
000290 01-03
NOREPINEPHRINE UPTAKE INHIBITORS AS BIOCHEMICALLY-SELECTIVE
AND BEHAVIORALLY-SELECTIVE ANTAGONISTS OF THE LOCOMOTOR-
STIMULATION INDUCED BY INDIRECTLY ACTING SYMPATHOMIMETIC-
AMINES IN MICE.
000492 01-04
COMPARATIVE-STUDIES OF MAO-A AND MAO-B INHIBITORS IN MAN.
000612 01-09
THE TREATMENT OF PARKINSONS-DISEASE USING A COMBINATION OF L-
DOPA AND DECARBOXYLASE INHIBITORS (CARBIDOPA, BENSERASIDE).
A CLINICAL AND BIOCHEMICAL COMPARATIVE INVESTIGATION.
000712 01-11
ADENOSINE ANALOGS AS SUBSTRATES AND INHIBITORS OF S
ADENOSYLHOMOCYSTEINE-HYDROLASE. (UNPUBLISHED PAPER).
001021 02-01
INHIBITORS OF PHENYLETHANOLAMINE-N-METHYLTRANSFERASE AND
EPINEPHRINE BIOSYNTHESIS. 2. 1,2,3,4 TETRAHYDROISOQUINOLINE-7-
SULFONANILIDES.
001069 02-02
GABA AGONISTS AND UPTAKE INHIBITORS DESIGNED AS AGENTS WITH
IRREVERSIBLE ACTIONS.
001079 02-02
IN VIVO CHANGES IN THE GABA CONTENT OF NERVE-ENDINGS
(SYNAPTOSOMES) INDUCED BY INHIBITORS OF GABA UPTAKE.
001540 02-03
A COMPARATIVE-STUDY OF THE PHARMACOLOGY OF INHIBITORS OF
GABA METABOLISM.
003036 03-04
PHOSPHODIESTERASE INHIBITORS FACILITATE MEMORY FOR PASSIVE-
AVOIDANCE CONDITIONING.
003109 03-04
THE PHARMACOLOGY OF GABA-TRANSAMINASE INHIBITORS.
003620 03-17
IBOTENIC-ACID ANALOGUES AS INHIBITORS OF (3H)GLUTAMIC-ACID
BINDING TO CEREBELLAR MEMBRANES.
003848 04-03
EFFECT OF INHIBITORS OF GABA-AMINOTRANSFERASE ON THE
METABOLISM OF GABA IN BRAIN TISSUE AND SYNAPTOSOMAL
FRACTIONS.
003914 04-03
AMINE UPTAKE INHIBITORS: CRITERIA OF SELECTIVITY.
003921 04-03
IN VIVO INTRANEURONAL MAO-INHIBITION IN RAT-BRAIN SKF-64139,
COMPARISON TO OTHER POTENT PNMT INHIBITORS.
003935 04-03
ADENOSINE AND CYCLIC-AMP IN RAT-CEREBRAL-CORTICAL SLICES:
EFFECTS OF ADENOSINE UPTAKE INHIBITORS AND ADENOSINE-
DEAMINASE INHIBITORS.
003950 04-03
DIFFERENTIAL-EFFECTS OF SEVERAL DOPAMINE UPTAKE INHIBITORS AND
RELEASING-AGENTS ON LOCOMOTOR-ACTIVITY IN NORMAL AND IN
RESERPINIZED MICE.
004130 04-04
EFFECTS OF NOREPINEPHRINE AND 5 HYDROXYTRYPTAMINE REUPTAKE
INHIBITORS ON ELECTRICALLY-INDUCED SPINAL-CORD SEIZURES IN
RATS.
004144 04-04
SPECIFIC GABA-RECEPTOR AGONISTS AND UPTAKE INHIBITORS: DESIGN,
DEVELOPMENT AND STRUCTURE-ACTIVITY STUDIES.
004725 04-17

INHIBITORY
DOES SYSTEMIC MORPHINE INCREASE DESCENDING INHIBITORY
CONTROLS OF DORSAL-HORN NEURONES INVOLVED IN NOCICEPTION?
000175 01-03
EFFECT OF PICROTOXIN AND NIPECOTIC-ACID ON INHIBITORY RESPONSE
OF DOPAMINERGIC NEURONS IN THE VENTRAL TEGMENTAL AREA TO
STIMULATION OF THE NUCLEUS-ACCUMBENS.
000331 01-03
INHIBITORY ACTION OF MORPHINE ON THE RELEASE OF A BRADYKININ-
LIKE SUBSTANCE AFTER SCIATIC-NERVE STIMULATION.
001293 02-03
INHIBITORY ACTION OF ADENOSINE ON SYNAPTIC TRANSMISSION IN THE
HIPPOCAMPUS OF THE GUINEA-PIG IN VITRO.
001401 02-03

INITIAL

INITIAL, CLINICAL-TRIAL OF A NEW, SPECIFIC 5 HT REUPTAKE INHIBITOR, CITALOPRAM (LU-10-171).

000591 01-09

INITIAL PRESCRIPTION OF PSYCHOTROPIC-MEDICATIONS FOR ADOLESCENTS IN A MEDICAL/PROFESSIONAL INSTITUTE, AND THE ROLE OF THE PSYCHIATRIST IN A MEDICAL/PROFESSIONAL INSTITUTE.

002621 02-17

SENILE-DEMENTIA IN ITS STILL GUIDABLE INITIAL PHASE.

004698 04-17

INJECTABLE

ANTIDEPRESSANT ACTION OF INJECTABLE 1694.

001960 02-09

USE OF INJECTABLE LORAZEPAM IN ALCOHOL WITHDRAWAL.

002176 02-11

INJECTED

ANTINOCICEPTIVE-EFFECT OF MORPHINE, OPIOID ANALGESICS AND HALOPERIDOL INJECTED INTO THE CAUDATE-NUCLEUS OF THE RAT.

000414 01-04

EFFECTS OF NOMIFENSINE AND DESIPRAMINE ON THE SEQUELAE OF INTRACEREBRALLY INJECTED 6 OHDA AND 5,6 DHT.

001522 02-03

THE EFFECTS OF BOMBESIN INJECTED INTO THE ANTERIOR AND POSTERIOR HYPOTHALAMUS ON BODY-TEMPERATURE AND OXYGEN CONSUMPTION.

001544 02-03

THE PHARMACOLOGY OF AGGRESSIVE-BEHAVIOURAL-PHENOMENA ELICITED BY MUSCARINE INJECTED INTO THE CEREBRAL VENTRICLES OF CONSCIOUS CATS.

001569 02-04

CENTRAL-ACTION OF INTRAVENTRICULARLY INJECTED MIDODRINE IN RATS.

001684 02-04

INJECTION

ADMINISTRATION OF ANTISOMATOSTATIN SERUM TO RATS REVERSES THE INHIBITION OF PULSATILE GROWTH-HORMONE SECRETION PRODUCED BY INJECTION OF METERGOLINE BUT NOT YOHIMBINE. (UNPUBLISHED PAPER).

000019 01-03

L TRYPTOPHAN INJECTION ENHANCES PULSATILE GROWTH-HORMONE SECRETION IN THE RAT. (UNPUBLISHED PAPER).

000020 01-03

CORTICAL NEUROCHEMICAL CHANGES AFTER INTRASTRIATAL INJECTION OF KAINIC-ACID.

000133 01-03

REDUCTION OF FETAL RAT SPINAL-CORD VOLUME FOLLOWING MATERNAL MORPHINE INJECTION.

000161 01-03

DISTRIBUTION OF 14C PHENYTOIN IN RAT PURKINJE-CELLS, CEREBELLAR AND CEREBRAL NEURONAL TISSUE AFTER A SINGLE INTRAPERITONEAL INJECTION.

000261 01-03

CIRCLING-BEHAVIOUR INDUCED BY INTRANIGRAL INJECTION OF BACLOFEN IN RATS.

000415 01-04

INTRACRANIAL INJECTION PARAMETERS WHICH AFFECT ANGIOTENSIN-II-INDUCED DRINKING.

000534 01-06

GROWTH-HORMONE (GH) RELEASE FOLLOWING THYROTROPIN-RELEASING-HORMONE (TRH) INJECTION IN MANIC-PATIENTS RECEIVING LITHIUM-CARBONATE.

000645 01-09

PRODUCTION OF A SPECIFIC ANTISERUM TO RAT-BRAIN GLUTAMIC-ACID-DECARBOXYLASE (GAD) BY INJECTION OF AN ANTIGEN ANTIBODY COMPLEX. (UNPUBLISHED PAPER).

001047 02-01

CHOLECYSTOKININ-PEPTIDES PRODUCE MARKED REDUCTION OF DOPAMINE TURNOVER IN DISCRETE AREAS IN THE RAT-BRAIN FOLLOWING INTERAVENTRICULAR INJECTION.

001239 02-03

LOG-DOSE/RESPONSE-CURVE FLATTENING IN RATS AFTER DAILY INJECTION OF OPIATES.

001387 02-03

THE EFFECT OF CYCLO-LEU-GLY ON CHEMICAL DENERVATION SUPERSENSITIVITY OF DOPAMINE-RECEPTORS INDUCED BY INTRACEREBROVENTRICULAR INJECTION OF 6 HYDROXYDOPAMINE IN MICE.

001435 02-03

DIFFERENTIAL-EFFECTS OF SYSTEMIC VERSUS INTRACRANIAL INJECTION OF OPIATES ON CENTRAL, OROFACIAL AND LOWER BODY NOCICEPTION: SOMATOTYPY IN BULBAR ANALGESIA SYSTEMS.

001446 02-03

DESENSITIZATION OF ADRENOCEPTORS AFTER IMMOBILIZATION STRESS OR REPEATED INJECTION OF ISOPROTERENOL IN RATS. (UNPUBLISHED PAPER).

001546 02-03

VESTIBULO-OCULAR REFLEXES IN RABBITS: REDUCTION BY INTRAVENOUS INJECTION OF DIAZEPAM.

001566 02-04

COMPARATIVE-STUDY OF AGGRESSIVE-BEHAVIOUR AFTER INJECTION OF CHOLINOMIMETICS, ANTICHOLINESTERASES, NICOTINIC, AND

MUSCARINIC GANGLIONIC STIMULANTS INTO THE CEREBRAL VENTRICLES OF CONSCIOUS CATS: FAILURE OF NICOTINIC-DRUGS TO EVOKE AGGRESSION.

001568 02-04

DIFFERENT BEHAVIORAL-EFFECTS FOLLOWING INTRACEREBRAL, INTRACEREBROVENTRICULAR OR INTRAPERITONEAL INJECTION OF NALOXONE IN THE RAT.

001665 02-04

CONTRALATERAL CIRCLING-BEHAVIOUR INDUCED BY INTRANIGRAL INJECTION OF MORPHINE AND ENKEPHALIN ANALOGUE FK-33-824 IN RATS.

001669 02-04

CONTRALATERAL CIRCLING-BEHAVIOUR INDUCED BY INTRANIGRAL INJECTION OF TAURINE IN RATS.

001670 02-04

MOTOR-DEPRESSION AND HEAD-TWITCHES INDUCED BY IP INJECTION OF GABA.

001788 02-04

BEHAVIOR MAINTAINED BY INTRAVENOUS INJECTION OF CODEINE, COCAINE, AND ETORPHINE IN THE RHESUS-MACAQUE AND THE PIGTAIL-MACAQUE.

001828 02-04

LOCAL AND DISTANT NEURONAL DEGENERATION FOLLOWING INTRASTRIATAL INJECTION OF KAINIC-ACID.

001885 02-06

LONG-TERM CONTROLLED-COMPARISON OF INJECTION OXYPROTHEPIN AND FLUPHENAZINE-DECANOATES IN PSYCHOTICS IN REMISSION.

001949 02-08

CLINICAL AND EEG CHANGES IN DEPRESSIVE-PATIENTS AFTER A SINGLE INJECTION OF BETA ENDORPHIN.

001962 02-09

THE TSH RESPONSE TO TRH INJECTION IN PSYCHIATRIC-PATIENTS: A REVIEW.

002145 02-11

ACCIDENTAL INTRAARTERIAL INJECTION OF DIAZEPAM.

002598 02-17

GABA DEPLETION IN CHICK BRAINSTEM AFTER INTRAVENTRICULAR INJECTION OF CEFAZOLIN.

002762 03-03

MORPHOLOGICAL CHANGES IN RAT-BRAIN INDUCED BY L CYSTEINE INJECTION IN NEWBORN ANIMALS.

002774 03-03

A QUANTITATIVE REGIONAL ANALYSIS OF PROTEIN SYNTHESIS INHIBITION IN THE RAT-BRAIN FOLLOWING LOCALIZED INJECTION OF CYCLOHEXIMIDE.

002780 03-03

ON CORRELATION OF BEHAVIORAL-REACTIONS AND NEURONAL ACTIVITY IN THE HYPOTHALAMUS UNDER SUBCUTANEOUS GASTRIN INJECTION.

002892 03-03

CONDITIONING AND RETENTION OF DEFENSIVE BURYING AS A FUNCTION OF ELAVIL AND THORAZINE INJECTION.

002974 03-04

PHARMACOLOGICAL CHARACTERIZATION OF SCRATCHING-BEHAVIOUR INDUCED BY INTRACRANIAL INJECTION OF SUBSTANCE-P AND SOMATOSTATIN.

002980 03-04

SEIZURES ELICITED BY SUBCUTANEOUS INJECTION OF METRAZOL DURING ONTOGENESIS IN RATS.

003039 03-04

TRH INCREASES LOCOMOTOR-ACTIVITY IN RATS AFTER INJECTION INTO THE HYPOTHALAMUS.

003044 03-04

INTRAVENTRICULAR CORTICOSTERONE INJECTION FACILITATES MEMORY OF AN APPETITIVE DISCRIMINATIVE TASK IN MICE.

003051 03-04

OPERANT FEEDING AND DRINKING IN PIGS FOLLOWING INTRACEREBROVENTRICULAR INJECTION OF SYNTHETIC CHOLECYSTOKININ-OCTAPEPTIDE.

003064 03-04

INCREASES IN SKIN-RESISTANCE OF WHITE RATS FOLLOWING SCOPOLAMINE INJECTION.

003138 03-06

BEHAVIORAL-EFFECTS AND BIOLOGICAL-EFFECTS OF ACUTE BETA ENDORPHIN INJECTION IN SCHIZOPHRENIC-PATIENTS AND DEPRESSED-PATIENTS.

003357 03-11

DENERVATION SUPERSENSITIVITY TO 5 HYDROXYTRYPTOPHAN IN RATS FOLLOWING SPINAL TRANSECTION AND 5,7 DIHYDROXYTRYPTAMINE INJECTION.

003722 04-03

CATECHOLAMINE AND 5 HYDROXYTRYPTAMINE SYNTHESIS AND METABOLISM FOLLOWING INTRACEREBROVENTRICULAR INJECTION OF DIBUTYRYL-CYCLIC-AMP.

003769 04-03

CHANGES OF ELECTRORETINOGRAM AND NEUROCHEMICAL ASPECTS OF GABAERGIC NEURONS OF RETINA AFTER INTRAOCULAR INJECTION OF KAINIC-ACID IN RATS.

003807 04-03

THE EFFECT OF ELECTRICAL-STIMULATION OF THE LOCUS-COERULEUS AND INTRAPERITONEAL INJECTION OF CERTAIN PHARMACOLOGICAL SUBSTANCES ON THE THRESHOLD OF HIPPOCAMPAL AFTERDISCHARGES.
003885 04-03

HYPERACTIVITY FOLLOWING INJECTION OF A GLUTAMATE AGONIST AND 6,7 ADTN INTO RAT NUCLEUS-ACCUMBENS AND ITS INHIBITION BY THIP.
004066 04-04

USE OF THE INTRACEREBRAL INJECTION TECHNIQUE TO ELUCIDATE MECHANISMS OF APOMORPHINE CLIMBING AND ITS ANTAGONISM IN THE MOUSE.
004092 04-04

INTRANIGRAL INJECTION OF CAPSAICIN ENHANCES MOTOR-ACTIVITY AND DEPLETES NIGRAL 5 HYDROXYTRYPTAMINE BUT NOT SUBSTANCE-P.
004100 04-04

SECOND-ORDER SCHEDULES OF INTRAMUSCULAR COCAINE INJECTION IN THE SQUIRREL-MONKEY: COMPARISONS WITH FOOD PRESENTATION AND EFFECTS OF D-AMPHETAMINE AND PROMAZINE.
004152 04-04

INVOLVEMENT OF DOPAMINE IN CIRCLING RESPONSES TO MUSCIMOL DEPENDS ON INTRANIGRAL SITE OF INJECTION.
004158 04-04

AVOIDANCE RESPONSE IN RATS AFTER INJECTION OF DOPAMINE INTO THE NEOSTRIATUM.
004255 04-04

HORMONAL STIMULATION AFTER INJECTION OF THYROTROPHIN-RELEASING-FACTOR (TRF) AND ACTH1-24 IN PATIENTS FOLLOWING CHRONIC-TREATMENT WITH NEUROLEPTICS: PRELIMINARY-STUDY.
004505 04-13

INJECTIONS
EFFECT OF INTRAVENTRICULAR INJECTIONS OF ALPHA AMINOSULFONIC-ACIDS ON THE CENTRAL-NERVOUS-SYSTEM OF CONSCIOUS MICE.
000009 01-02

WATER INTAKE AND TIME-COURSE OF DRINKING AFTER SINGLE OR REPEATED CHLORDIAZEPOXIDE INJECTIONS.
000369 01-04

MORPHINE INJECTIONS INTO THE PERIAQUEDUCTAL PERIVENTRICULAR GRAY ATTENUATE SEPTAL HYPERREACTIVITY.
000390 01-04

ROTATION INDUCED BY INTRANIGRAL INJECTIONS OF GABA AGONISTS AND ANTAGONISTS: ZONE-SPECIFIC EFFECTS.
000422 01-04

LOCOMOTOR-ACTIVITY ELICITED BY INJECTIONS OF PICROTOXIN INTO THE VENTRAL TEGMENTAL AREA IS ATTENUATED BY INJECTIONS OF GABA INTO THE GLOBUS-PALLIDUS.
000436 01-04

OXYPROTHEPIN-DECANOATE INJECTIONS: EXPERIENCE WITH A LONG-TERM-TREATMENT OF SCHIZOPHRENIC-PSYCHOSES.
000576 01-08

LONG-TERM EFFECTS OF TESTOSTERONE INJECTIONS ON THE SOCIAL-BEHAVIOUR OF MALE DUCKS AND THEIR PHYSIOLOGICAL-CORRELATES.
001565 02-04

BEHAVIOURAL-RESPONSES TO STEREOTACTICALLY CONTROLLED INJECTIONS OF MONOAMINE NEUROTRANSMITTERS INTO THE ACCUMBENS AND CAUDATE-PUTAMEN NUCLEI.
001708 02-04

THE INFLUENCE OF SINGLE DAILY HEROIN INJECTIONS ON DRINKING-PATTERNS IN THE RAT.
001746 02-04

HANDEDNESS IN RATS: BLOCKADE OF REACHING-BEHAVIOR BY UNILATERAL 6 OHDA INJECTIONS INTO SUBSTANTIA-NIGRA AND CAUDATE-NUCLEUS.
001778 02-04

PLASMA FLUPHENAZINE LEVELS BY RADIOIMMUNOASSAY IN SCHIZOPHRENIC-PATIENTS TREATED WITH DEPOT INJECTIONS OF FLUPHENAZINE-DECANOATE.
002510 02-16

THE EFFECTS OF INJECTIONS OF BOMBESIN INTO THE CEREBRAL VENTRICLES ON BEHAVIORAL THERMOREGULATION.
002952 03-04

INJECTIONS OF DOPAMINERGIC, CHOLINERGIC, SEROTONINERGIC AND GABAERGIC DRUGS INTO THE NUCLEUS-ACCUMBENS: EFFECTS ON LOCOMOTOR-ACTIVITY IN THE RAT.
003019 03-04

DOSE-RESPONSE RELATIONSHIP BETWEEN NALOXONE INJECTIONS AND INTAKE OF SUCROSE SOLUTION.
003118 03-04

OPIATE-DEPENDENCE FOLLOWING ACUTE INJECTIONS OF MORPHINE AND NALOXONE: THE ASSESSMENT OF VARIOUS WITHDRAWAL SIGNS.
004209 04-04

INJURY
OPIATE ANTAGONIST IMPROVES NEUROLOGIC RECOVERY AFTER SPINAL INJURY.
002714 03-03

EFFICACY OF LITHIUM IN TREATING MOOD-DISORDER OCCURRING AFTER BRAINSTEM INJURY.
003354 03-11

INSEPARABILITY
INSEPARABILITY OF ACETYLCHOLINESTERASE AND NERVE EXCITATION.
003875 04-03
INSOMNIA
REVERSAL OF PARA CHLOROPHENYLALANINE-INDUCED INSOMNIA BY 5 HYDROXYTRYPTOPHAN IN THE RAT.
000423 01-04
RATIONAL USE OF BENZODIAZEPINES FOR ANXIETY AND INSOMNIA.
002063 02-10
EUHYPNOS-FORTE, HIGH-DOSE TEMAZEPAM FOR RESISTANT INSOMNIA: POSTMARKETING SURVEILLANCE IN 10,057 PATIENTS UNRESPONSIVE TO CONVENTIONAL HYPNOTIC DOSAGE.
002324 02-14
HYPNOTIC-DRUGS AND TREATMENT OF INSOMNIA.
003350 03-11
FLUNITRAZEPAM IN THE TREATMENT OF INSOMNIA: A STUDY OF 50 PSYCHIATRIC-PATIENTS.
003444 03-14
THE TREATMENT OF INSOMNIA THROUGH HOMEOPATHY IN A CLINIC.
004484 04-11
DEPRENYL DOES NOT CAUSE INSOMNIA IN PARKINSONIAN-PATIENTS.
004569 04-14
FLURAZEPAM-INDUCED SLEEP-APNEA-SYNDROME IN A PATIENT WITH INSOMNIA AND MILD SLEEP-RELATED RESPIRATORY CHANGES.
004729 04-17
INSOMNIAC-INPATIENTS
COMPARISON OF NITRAZEPAM 5 MG WITH TRIAZOLAM 0.5 MG IN YOUNG PSYCHIATRIC INSOMNIAC-INPATIENTS.
002096 02-11
INSOMNIACS
CHRONIC USE OF TRIAZOLAM: THE EFFECTS ON THE SLEEP PATTERNS OF INSOMNIACS.
000710 01-11
THE EFFICACY OF TRIAZOLAM AND CHLORAL-HYDRATE IN GERIATRIC INSOMNIACS.
002160 02-11
INSTABILITY
CONTROLLED-STUDY WITH BROMAZEPAM AND CLOROTEPIN IN CHILD INSTABILITY.
002190 02-11
INSTITUTE
INITIAL PRESCRIPTION OF PSYCHOTROPIC-MEDICATIONS FOR ADOLESCENTS IN A MEDICAL/PROFESSIONAL INSTITUTE, AND THE ROLE OF THE PSYCHIATRIST IN A MEDICAL/PROFESSIONAL INSTITUTE.
002621 02-17
INSTITUTIONALIZED
COMPARISON OF PSYCHOTROPIC-DRUG, RESPONSE COST, AND PSYCHOTROPIC-DRUG PLUS RESPONSE COST PROCEDURES FOR CONTROLLING INSTITUTIONALIZED MENTALLY-RETARDED PERSONS.
004438 04-11
INSTRUMENTAL
IMPAIRMENT OF INSTRUMENTAL LEARNING IN RATS BY GLUTAMIC-ACID-DIETHYL-ESTER.
002993 03-04
INSUFFICIENT
THERAPEUTIC TREATMENT OF INSUFFICIENT PERFORMANCE IN CEREBROVASCULAR-DISEASES.
004718 04-17
INSULIN
GLUCOSE OXIDATION IN THE VENTROMEDIAL HYPOTHALAMUS IS NOT AFFECTED BY INSULIN OR OUABAIN BUT DEPRESSED BY ALLOXAN TREATMENT.
001145 02-03
SYSTEMIC INSULIN DECREASES LATERAL HYPOTHALAMIC UNIT ACTIVITY.
001275 02-03
APHAGIA, GASTRIC PATHOLOGY, HYPERTHERMIA, AND SENSORIMOTOR-DYSFUNCTIONS FOLLOWING LATERAL HYPOTHALAMIC LESIONS: EFFECTS OF INSULIN PRETREATMENTS.
001638 02-04
ACTION MECHANISMS OF INSULIN THERAPY IN PSYCHIATRY, AND CURRENT-VIEWS ON THESE MECHANISMS.
002553 02-17
INSULIN-INDUCED
AMMONIA AND DISINHIBITION IN CAT MOTOR-CORTEX BY AMMONIUM-ACETATE, MONOFLUOROACETATE AND INSULIN-INDUCED HYPOGLYCEMIA.
004276 04-05
INTAKE
INFLUENCE OF AMPHETAMINE AND PHENYLPROPANOLAMINE ON FOOD INTAKE, ACTIVITY, AND BODY-TEMPERATURE IN RATS WITH VENTROMEDIAL HYPOTHALAMIC OR DORSOLATERAL TEGMENTAL DAMAGE.
000322 01-03
REDUCTION OF FOOD INTAKE BY PIRIBEDIL IN THE RAT: RELATION TO DOPAMINE-RECEPTOR STIMULATION.
000355 01-04
WATER INTAKE AND TIME-COURSE OF DRINKING AFTER SINGLE OR REPEATED CHLORDIAZEPOXIDE INJECTIONS.
000369 01-04

RENIN AND ALDOSTERONE SECRETIONS DURING HYPOVOLEMIA IN RATS: RELATION TO NACL INTAKE.
000484 01-04
PHENOBARBITAL EFFECTS ON WEIGHT-GAIN AND CIRCADIAN-CYCLING OF FOOD INTAKE AND BODY-TEMPERATURE.
001409 02-03
PROCEDURES FOR REDUCING DRUG INTAKE: NONHUMAN STUDIES.
001753 02-04
DIFFERENTIAL-EFFECTS OF MORPHINE ON FOOD AND WATER INTAKE IN FOOD DEPRIVED AND FREELY-FEEDING RATS.
001765 02-04
EFFECTS OF AMPHETAMINE AND PHENYLPROPANOLAMINE ON FOOD INTAKE IN RATS WITH VENTROMEDIAL HYPOTHALAMIC OR DORSOLATERAL TEGMENTAL DAMAGE.
001818 02-04
BEHAVIOURAL-ANALYSIS OF FEEDING: IMPLICATIONS FOR THE PHARMACOLOGICAL MANIPULATION OF FOOD INTAKE IN ANIMALS AND MAN.
002527 02-17
PATTERNS OF USE IN THE INTAKE OF ORAL MEDICATION.
002591 02-17
THE EFFECT OF ALTERED DOPAMINERGIC-ACTIVITY ON FOOD INTAKE IN THE RAT: EVIDENCE FOR AN OPTIMAL LEVEL OF DOPAMINERGIC-ACTIVITY FOR BEHAVIOR.
002632 02-17
SINGLE OR REPEATED ADMINISTRATION OF SMALL DOSES OF APOMORPHINE ON WATER INTAKE AND ACTIVITY IN WATER-DEPRIVED RATS.
002981 03-04
THE EFFECTS OF OPIATE ANTAGONISTS ON FOOD INTAKE ARE STEREOSPECIFIC.
003080 03-04
DOSE-RESPONSE RELATIONSHIP BETWEEN NALOXONE INJECTIONS AND INTAKE OF SUCROSE SOLUTION.
003118 03-04
DIETARY PROTEIN INTAKE INFLUENCES THE ANTIHYPERTENSIVE POTENCY OF METHYLDOPA IN SPONTANEOUSLY HYPERTENSIVE-RATS.
004025 04-03
SUSTAINED INTRACEREBROVENTRICULAR INFUSION OF BRAIN FUELS REDUCES BODY-WEIGHT AND FOOD INTAKE IN RATS.
004098 04-04
THE SITE OF ACTION OF NALOXONE IN SUPPRESSING FOOD AND WATER INTAKE IN RATS.
004146 04-04
HISTIDYL-PROLINE DIKETOPIPERAZINE DECREASES FOOD INTAKE IN RATS.
004181 04-04
INTEGRATIVE
THE USE OF SENSORY INTEGRATIVE DIAGNOSTICS TO PREDICT HYPERACTIVE-CHILDRENS RESPONSIVENESS TO METHYLPHENIDATE (RITALIN) AND PEMOLINE (CYLERT). (PH.D. DISSERTATION).
002133 02-11
NOOTROPIC-DRUGS AND RELATED DRUGS INTERACTING WITH THE INTEGRATIVE ACTIVITY OF THE BRAIN.
002327 02-14
INTEGRITY
THE INTEGRITY OF THE SOCIAL HIERARCHY IN MICE FOLLOWING ADMINISTRATION OF PSYCHOTROPIC-DRUGS.
004202 04-04
INTELLECTUALLY-HANDICAPPED
A NOTE ON PATTERNS OF DRUG PRESCRIBING IN A RESIDENTIAL-CENTER FOR THE INTELLECTUALLY-HANDICAPPED.
000982 01-17
INTELLIGENCE
BEHAVIOR AND LEARNING DIFFICULTIES IN CHILDREN OF NORMAL INTELLIGENCE BORN TO ALCOHOLIC MOTHERS.
004658 04-15
INTENSIFICATION
A BARBITURATE-EVOKED INTENSIFICATION OF POSTSYNAPTIC INHIBITION IN THE PREOPTIC OVULATORY TRIGGER REGION OF THE HYPOTHALAMUS.
002818 03-03
INTERACTING
NOOTROPIC-DRUGS AND RELATED DRUGS INTERACTING WITH THE INTEGRATIVE ACTIVITY OF THE BRAIN.
002327 02-14
INTERACTION
EVIDENCE FOR AN IRREVERSIBLE INTERACTION OF BROMOCRIPTINE WITH CENTRAL DOPAMINE-RECEPTORS.
000023 01-03
INFLUENCE OF CELLULAR-TRANSPORT ON THE INTERACTION OF AMINO-ACIDS WITH GAMMA AMINOBUTYRIC-ACID-RECEPTORS (GABA) IN THE ISOLATED OLFACTORY-CORTEX OF THE GUINEA-PIG.
000034 01-03
INTERACTION OF DIAZEPAM WITH SYNAPTIC TRANSMISSION IN THE IN VITRO RAT HIPPOCAMPUS.
000178 01-03
SODIUM-DEPENDENT INTERACTION OF BENZAMIDES WITH DOPAMINE-RECEPTORS.
000285 01-03

INTERACTION OF ANTIDEPRESSANTS WITH CLONIDINE ON RAT-BRAIN
TOTAL 3 METHOXY-4-HYDROXYPHENYLGLYCOL.
000300 01-03
CARDIOVASCULAR RESPONSE TO THE INTERACTION OF ETHANOL AND
SOME BENZODIAZEPINES IN RATS.
000332 01-03
EFFECTS OF L AND D AMINO-ACIDS ON ANALGESIA AND LOCOMOTOR-
ACTIVITY OF MICE: THEIR INTERACTION WITH MORPHINE.
000336 01-04
5 HT BLOCKADE AND THE STIMULANT-EFFECTS OF D-AMPHETAMINE AND
L-AMPHETAMINE: NO INTERACTION IN SELF-STIMULATION OF
PREFRONTAL-CORTEX, HYPOTHALAMUS, OR DORSAL TEGMENTUM.
UNEXPECTED LETHALITY IN HIPPOCAMPAL SITES.
000387 01-04
THE INTERACTION OF ANTICHOLINESTERASES AND DIAZEPAM IN THE
TREATMENT OF ANTICHOLINERGIC-SYNDROME IN DOGS.
000389 01-04
THE LOCOMOTOR-EFFECT OF CLONIDINE AND ITS INTERACTION WITH
ALPHA FLUPENTHIXOL OR HALOPERIDOL IN THE DEVELOPING RAT.
000445 01-04
INTERACTION OF INDOMETHACIN AND IBUPROFEN WITH LITHIUM IN
MANIC-PATIENTS UNDER A STEADY-STATE LITHIUM LEVEL.
000622 01-09
INTERACTION BETWEEN AMITRIPTYLINE AND PHENOTHIAZINE IN MAN:
METABOLITE NORTRIPTYLINE AND THE CORRELATION WITH CLINICAL-
RESPONSE.
000640 01-09
METHADONE DISULFIRAM INTERACTION DURING METHADONE
MAINTENANCE.
000796 01-13
INTERACTION OF BIOGENIC-AMINE SYSTEMS IN BRAIN. (UNPUBLISHED
PAPER).
001141 02-03
PHARMACOLOGICAL EVIDENCE AND BIOCHEMICAL-EVIDENCE FOR AN
INTERACTION BETWEEN THE BENZODIAZEPINE AND GABA-RECEPTORS.
001261 02-03
INTERACTION STUDIES OF ETHANOL AND PSYCHOTROPIC-DRUGS IN
RODENTS: POSSIBLE INVOLVEMENT OF ADENOSINE-TRIPHOSPHATASES.
001281 02-03
BENZODIAZEPINE BINDING IN CHICKEN RETINA AND ITS INTERACTION
WITH GAMMA AMINOBUTYRIC-ACID.
001287 02-03
INTERACTION OF TRIAZOLAM WITH DESIPRAMINE: EFFECTS OF SINGLE
AND REPEATED TREATMENT ON CERTAIN PHARMACOLOGIC-
RESPONSES AND BRAIN CATECHOLAMINE LEVELS.
001323 02-03
PHENOBARBITONE AND SODIUM-VALPROATE INTERACTION: AN
EXPERIMENTAL-STUDY.
001371 02-03
INTERACTION OF HISTAMINE H2-RECEPTOR BLOCKING-DRUGS WITH THE
NORADRENERGIC SYSTEM IN RAT-BRAIN AND HEART.
001397 02-03
INTERACTION OF DOPAMINERGIC ERGOT DERIVATIVES WITH CYCLIC-
NUCLEOTIDE SYSTEM.
001482 02-03
EFFECT OF IMIPRAMINE ON HEPATIC GAMMA GLUTAMYLTRANSFERASE
IN FEMALE RATS. INTERACTION WITH CONTRACEPTIVES.
001507 02-03
THE EFFECTS OF NOREPINEPHRINE PERFUSION OF THE MESENCEPHALIC
RETICULAR FORMATION ON BEHAVIOR IN THE RAT: INTERACTION
WITH SEVERAL NEUROLEPTIC-DRUGS ON A MEASURE OF SUSTAINED
ATTENTION. (PH.D. DISSERTATION).
001563 02-04
INTERACTION OF PSYCHOPHARMACOLOGIC-FACTORS AND PSYCHOSOCIAL-
FACTORS IN THE TREATMENT OF ANIMAL-MODELS OF
HYPOINHIBITORY (HYPERKINETIC) BEHAVIOR.
001602 02-04
INTERACTION OF CHOLINERGIC AND DOPAMINERGIC INFLUENCES ON
YAWNING-BEHAVIOR.
001656 02-04
OPIATE AND PEPTIDE INTERACTION: EFFECT OF ENKEPHALINS ON
MORPHINE ANALGESIA.
001698 02-04
INVESTIGATIONS ON THE INTERACTION OF THYROTROPIN-RELEASING-
HORMONE (TRH) AND MK-771 WITH CENTRAL NORADRENERGIC
MECHANISMS.
001701 02-04
INTERACTION OF PROSTAGLANDINS AND THE EFFECTS OF MORPHINE AND
AMPHETAMINE IN RATS. (PH.D. DISSERTATION).
001732 02-04
PHENOBARBITONE INTERACTION WITH ORAL CONTRACEPTIVE STEROIDS
IN THE RABBIT AND RAT.
001832 02-05
ACTION OF TOFISOPAM ON THE ERGONOMIC VIGILANCE LEVEL. ITS
INTERACTION WITH THE EFFECTS OF ALCOHOL. CLINICAL
PHARMACOLOGICAL-STUDY.
001891 02-07
PHARMACOKINETIC INTERACTION BETWEEN PROPRANOLOL AND
CHLORPROMAZINE IN SCHIZOPHRENIC-PATIENTS.
001940 02-08

METABOLIC-STUDIES AND PSYCHOPHYSIOLOGIC-STUDIES OF
CANNABIDIOL HEXOBARBITAL INTERACTION.
002209 02-13
INTERACTION BETWEEN PHENYTOIN AND VALPROIC-ACID: PLASMA
PROTEIN BINDING AND METABOLIC-EFFECTS.
002276 02-13
DOUBLE-BLIND EVALUATION OF REINFORCING AND ANORECTIC-ACTIONS
OF WEIGHT-CONTROL MEDICATIONS: INTERACTION OF
PHARMACOLOGICAL-TREATMENT AND BEHAVIORAL-TREATMENTS.
002314 02-14
GABA-RECEPTORS AND BENZODIAZEPINE-RECEPTORS. STUDIES ON THEIR
LOCALIZATION IN THE HIPPOCAMPUS AND THEIR INTERACTION WITH
CENTRAL DOPAMINE NEURONS IN THE RAT-BRAIN.
002727 03-03
PHENYTOIN VALPROIC-ACID INTERACTION IN RHESUS-MONKEY.
002785 03-03
INTERACTION OF CHLORDIAZEPOXIDE AND SODIUM-VALPROATE IN THE
NUCLEUS-ACCUMBENS OF THE RAT.
002796 03-03
THE INTERACTION BETWEEN BARBITURATE ANESTHETICS AND
EXCITATORY AMINO-ACID RESPONSES ON CAT SPINAL NEURONES.
002799 03-03
DRUG ENVIRONMENT INTERACTION: CONTEXT DEPENDENCY OF COCAINE-
INDUCED BEHAVIORAL-SENSITIZATION.
002866 03-03
INTERACTION BETWEEN THE EFFECTS OF STRESS AND MORPHINE ON
BODY-TEMPERATURE IN RATS.
002906 03-03
THE INTERACTION OF 2,3,4 TRIHYDROXYBENZYLHYDRAZINE WITH
DOPA-DECARBOXYLASE FROM PIG KIDNEY.
002925 03-03
INTERACTION BETWEEN PURINE AND BENZODIAZEPINE: INOSINE
REVERSES DIAZEPAM-INDUCED STIMULATION OF MOUSE
EXPLORATORY-BEHAVIOR.
002972 03-04
INTERACTION AMONG D-AMPHETAMINE, SCOPOLAMINE AND GENOTYPE
IN AVOIDANCE-BEHAVIOR OF RATS.
003082 03-04
EFFECT OF CHRONIC MORPHINE TREATMENT ON THE INTERACTION
BETWEEN THE PERIAQUEDUCTAL GREY AND THE NUCLEUS-RAPHE-
MAGNUS OF THE RAT.
003727 04-03
INTERACTION OF THE TRICYCLIC-ANTIDEPRESSANT AMITRIPTYLINE WITH
PREJUNCTIONAL ALPHA AND MUSCARINIC-RECEPTORS IN THE DOG
SAPHENOUS VEIN.
003756 04-03
A STEROID DERIVATIVE, R-5135, ANTAGONIZES THE GABA/
BENZODIAZEPINE-RECEPTOR INTERACTION.
003851 04-03
THE INTERACTION OF TRAZODONE WITH RAT-BRAIN MUSCARINIC-
CHOLINOCEPTORS.
003855 04-03
SUBSTANCE-P INCREASES HYPOTHALAMIC BLOOD FLOW VIA AN
INDIRECT ADRENERGIC CHOLINERGIC INTERACTION.
003887 04-03
THE INTERACTION OF AMINE LOCAL ANESTHETICS WITH MUSCARINIC-
RECEPTORS.
004031 04-03
INTERACTION OF STEREOISOMERS OF BARBITURATES WITH (3H)ALPHA
DIHYDROPICROTOXININ BINDING-SITES.
004036 04-03
CATECHOLAMINE SEROTONIN INTERACTION EFFECTS ON ACTIVITY IN
RATS NEONATALLY TREATED WITH 6 HYDROXYDOPAMINE.
004194 04-04
TONIC IMMOBILITY IN DOMESTIC FOWL: POSSIBLE INTERACTION OF
SEROTONERGIC AND DOPAMINERGIC MECHANISMS.
004246 04-04
RECENT STUDIES ON INTERACTION BETWEEN OPIOID-PEPTIDES AND THEIR
RECEPTORS.
004300 04-06
THE INTERACTION OF PSYCHOPHARMACOLOGY AND PSYCHOANALYSIS IN
THE BORDERLINE-PATIENT.
004430 04-10
MECHANISM OF VALPROATE PHENOBARBITAL INTERACTION IN EPILEPTIC-
PATIENTS.
004522 04-13
INTERACTION OF CHLORPROMAZINE WITH THE TRANSPORT SYSTEM OF
GLUCOSE IN HUMAN ERYTHROCYTES.
004529 04-13
INTRAVENOUS DIAZEPAM AND ORAL ETHANOL INTERACTION.
004552 04-13
KINETICS OF A CARBAMAZEPINE-ETHOSUXIMIDE INTERACTION.
004558 04-13
INTERACTION OF P CHLOROPHENYLALANINE, MIANSERINE AND
DANITRACEN WITH AMPHETAMINE.
004599 04-15

INTERACTION-STUDIES
INTERACTION-STUDIES BETWEEN NARCOTIC ANALGESICS, NARCOTIC
ANTAGONISTS AND ETHANOL: STUDIES DURING ACUTE AND CHRONIC-

TREATMENT AND WITHDRAWAL STATES IN RATS AND MICE. (PH.D. DISSERTATION).
001165 02-03

INTERACTIONS
HISTAMINE H1-RECEPTORS LABELED IN VIVO: ANTIDEPRESSANT AND ANTIHISTAMINE INTERACTIONS.
000074 01-03
EFFECTS OF DOPAMINERGIC AGONISTS AND ANTAGONISTS ON (3H)APOMORPHINE BINDING TO STRIATAL MEMBRANES: SULPIRIDE LACK OF INTERACTIONS WITH POSITIVE COOPERATIVE (3H)APOMORPHINE BINDING.
000099 01-03
GABA BENZODIAZEPINE INTERACTIONS: PHYSIOLOGICAL, PHARMACOLOGICAL AND DEVELOPMENTAL ASPECTS.
000103 01-03
EFFECTS OF CHANGES IN THE STRUCTURE OF ENKEPHALINS AND OF NARCOTIC ANALGESIC-DRUGS ON THEIR INTERACTIONS WITH MU-RECEPTORS AND DELTA-RECEPTORS.
000168 01-03
INTERACTIONS OF NOREPINEPHRINE WITH PURKINJE-CELL RESPONSES TO PUTATIVE AMINO-ACID NEUROTRANSMITTERS APPLIED BY MICROIONTOPHORESIS.
000209 01-03
INTERACTIONS OF OXYPERTINE WITH RAT-BRAIN MONOAMINE-RECEPTORS.
000212 01-03
EFFECTS OF ACUTE AND CHRONIC INTERACTIONS OF DIAZEPAM AND D-AMPHETAMINE ON PUNISHED-BEHAVIOR OF RATS.
000386 01-04
ALBUMIN BINDING INTERACTIONS OF SODIUM-VALPROATE.
000762 01-13
THE REGULATION OF GABA-RECEPTORS AS A POSSIBLE MECHANISM FOR GABA 1,4 BENZODIAZEPINE INTERACTIONS. (UNPUBLISHED PAPER).
001012 02-01
INTERACTIONS OF NEUROPEPTIDES WITH CHOLINERGIC SEPTOHIPPOCAMPAL PATHWAY: INDICATION FOR A POSSIBLE TRANSSYNAPTIC REGULATION. (UNPUBLISHED PAPER).
001062 02-01
CHLOROETHYLNORAPOMORPHINE, A PROPOSED LONG-ACTING DOPAMINE ANTAGONIST: INTERACTIONS WITH DOPAMINE-RECEPTORS OF MAMMALIAN FOREBRAIN IN VITRO.
001114 02-03
REGULATION OF RECEPTOR BINDING INTERACTIONS OF 125I ANGIOTENSIN-II AND 125I SARCOSINE1-LEUCINE8-ANGIOTENSIN-II, AN ANGIOTENSIN ANTAGONIST, BY SODIUM-ION.
001124 02-03
RECEPTOR BINDING INTERACTIONS OF THE ANGIOTENSIN-II ANTAGONIST, 125I SARCOSINE1-LEUCINE8-ANGIOTENSIN-II, WITH MAMMALIAN BRAIN AND PERIPHERAL TISSUES.
001125 02-03
OPIATE INTERACTIONS WITH CHOLINERGIC NEURONS.
001198 02-03
INTERACTIONS BETWEEN MORPHINE AND THE OPIOID-LIKE PEPTIDES IN THE RAT VAS-DEFERENS.
001290 02-03
PINEAL INTERACTIONS WITH THE CENTRAL-NERVOUS-SYSTEM: NEUROENDOCRINE IMPLICATIONS. (PH.D. DISSERTATION).
001341 02-03
MULTIPLE CNS RECEPTOR INTERACTIONS OF ERGOT ALKALOIDS: AFFINITY AND INTRINSIC ACTIVITY ANALYSIS IN IN VITRO BINDING SYSTEMS.
001516 02-03
INTERACTIONS OF CHLORDIAZEPOXIDE AND ANORECTIC-AGENTS ON RATE AND DURATION PARAMETERS OF FEEDING IN THE RAT.
001600 02-04
INTERACTIONS BETWEEN NALTREXONE AND NONOPIATE DRUGS EVALUATED BY SCHEDULE-CONTROLLED BEHAVIOR.
001645 02-04
THE PARENT CHILD INTERACTIONS OF HYPERACTIVE-CHILDREN AND THEIR MODIFICATION BY STIMULANT-DRUGS.
002092 02-11
INTERCANNABINOID AND CANNABINOID ETHANOL INTERACTIONS AND THEIR EFFECTS ON HUMAN PERFORMANCE.
002193 02-12
PSYCHOTHERAPEUTIC-DRUGS: IMPORTANT ADVERSE-REACTIONS AND INTERACTIONS.
002383 02-15
ENDORPHIN OPIATE INTERACTIONS WITH NEUROENDOCRINE SYSTEMS.
002552 02-17
MOLECULAR ACTIONS OF OPIATES: HISTORICAL OVERVIEW AND NEW FINDINGS ON OPIATE-RECEPTOR INTERACTIONS WITH ENKEPHALINS AND GUANYL-NUCLEOTIDES.
002613 02-17
RADIOHISTOCHEMICAL STUDIES OF BENZODIAZEPINE AND GABA-RECEPTORS AND THEIR INTERACTIONS.
002644 03-01
INTERACTIONS OF TRICYCLIC-ANTIDEPRESSANTS WITH A SYNAPTIC ION-CHANNEL.
002660 03-03
APOMORPHINE HALOPERIDOL INTERACTIONS: DIFFERENT TYPES OF ANTAGONISM IN CORTICAL AND SUBCORTICAL BRAIN REGIONS.
002662 03-03

DIFFERENTIAL REGULATION BY GUANINE-NUCLEOTIDES OF OPIATE AGONIST AND ANTAGONIST RECEPTOR INTERACTIONS.
002688 03-03
INTERACTIONS OF NARCOTICS WITH SYNAPTOSOMAL CALCIUM TRANSPORT.
002712 03-03
KAINIC-ACID AND NEUROTRANSMITTER INTERACTIONS IN THE BASAL GANGLIA.
002824 03-03
INTERACTIONS OF DIAZEPAM AND COCAINE IN THE MORPHINE TREATED RAT. (PH.D. DISSERTATION).
003115 03-04
LITHIUM DRUG INTERACTIONS ALTERING THE INTRACELLULAR LITHIUM LEVEL: AN IN VITRO STUDY.
003142 03-06
STATISTICAL ANALYSES OF PHYSIOLOGIC DATA FROM FEMALE PATIENTS WITH AN ENDOMORPHOUS DEPRESSIVE COURSE: A TRIAL, INTERACTIONS BETWEEN PHYSIOLOGIC PARAMETERS, TEST JUNCTURES IN THIS PHASE.
003251 03-09
CLINICAL-PHARMACOLOGY: ADVERSE DRUG INTERACTIONS.
003399 03-13
NEUROLEPTICS: INTERACTIONS WITH FOOD -- CHEMICAL AND PHARMACODYNAMIC STUDIES ON THE INTERACTIONS OF COFFEE AND TEA.
003612 03-17
INTERACTIONS BETWEEN ALCOHOL AND MEDICATIONS.
003629 03-17
INTERACTIONS BETWEEN A MONOFLUORINATED ANALOGUE OF P CHLOROAMPHETAMINE AND 5 HYDROXYTRYPTAMINE IN BRAIN.
003719 04-03
INTERACTIONS BETWEEN CHLORPROMAZINE AND SOME OF ITS METABOLITES.
004001 04-03
MODULATORY INTERACTIONS BETWEEN NOREPINEPHRINE AND TAURINE, BETA ALANINE, GAMMA AMINOBUTYRIC-ACID AND MUSCIMOL APPLIED IONTOPHORETICALLY TO CEREBELLAR PURKINJE-CELLS.
004058 04-03
THE EFFECTS OF 2,5 DIMETHOXY-4-METHYLAMPHETAMINE (DOM) ON OPERANT-BEHAVIOR: INTERACTIONS WITH OTHER NEUROACTIVE-AGENTS.
004089 04-04
INTERACTIONS BETWEEN NARCOTIC AGONISTS, PARTIAL AGONISTS AND ANTAGONISTS EVALUATED BY SCHEDULE-CONTROLLED BEHAVIOR.
004127 04-04
THE EFFECTS OF NEFOPAM ON BLOOD ACID BASE STATUS IN THE RABBIT: INTERACTIONS WITH MORPHINE IN THE MOUSE AND RABBIT.
004279 04-05
INTERACTIONS BETWEEN ANTIDEPRESSANTS AND OTHER DRUGS.
004371 04-09
THE EFFECTS OF NEUROLEPTIC-DRUGS ON THE SOCIAL INTERACTIONS OF HOSPITALIZED PSYCHOTIC-PATIENTS.
004577 04-14

INTERACTIVE-EFFECTS
INTERACTIVE-EFFECTS OF NUTRITION AND CANNABIS UPON RAT PERINATAL DEVELOPMENT.
000513 01-05

INTERAVENTRICULAR
CHOLECYSTOKININ-PEPTIDES PRODUCE MARKED REDUCTION OF DOPAMINE TURNOVER IN DISCRETE AREAS IN THE RAT-BRAIN FOLLOWING INTERAVENTRICULAR INJECTION.
001239 02-03

INTERCANNABINOID
INTERCANNABINOID AND CANNABINOID ETHANOL INTERACTIONS AND THEIR EFFECTS ON HUMAN PERFORMANCE.
002193 02-12

INTERCONVERTING
INTERCONVERTING MU AND DELTA-FORMS OF TYPE-1 OPIATE-RECEPTORS IN THE RAT STRIATAL PATCHES.
003737 04-03

INTERDOSE
DOSE SIZE AND INTERDOSE INTERVAL EFFECTS ON MORPHINE-TOLERANCE IN THE RAT. (PH.D. DISSERTATION).
003090 03-04

INTEREST
THE INTEREST OF THE STIMULATING EFFECT OF CARPIPRAMINE IN PSYCHOSOMATIC-MEDICINE.
002061 02-10
SEXUAL-DIFFICULTIES AMONG CONVALESCING ALCOHOLICS: INTEREST IN PRAZEPAM TREATMENT IN 30 CASES.
003296 03-11
THERAPEUTIC INTEREST OF BLOOD LEVELS DETERMINATION FOR ANTIDEPRESSANTS: METHODOLOGICAL APPROACH.
003571 03-16
NEUROLEPTIC TRICYCLIC-ANTIDEPRESSANT COMBINATION: PHARMACOLOGICAL-ASPECTS AND THERAPEUTIC INTEREST.
004501 04-13

INTERFACES
INTERFACES OF PSYCHOPHARMACOLOGY AND CARDIOLOGY -- PART
TWO.
003529 03-15
INTERFACES OF PSYCHOPHARMACOLOGY AND CARDIOLOGY -- PART
ONE.
003530 03-15

INTERFERENCE
POSTINGESTION INTERFERENCE WITH BRAIN FUNCTION PREVENTS
ATTENUATION OF NEOPHOBIA IN RATS.
000352 01-04
DRUG INTERFERENCE ON SOME BIOCHEMICAL-PARAMETERS OF RAT-
CEREBRAL-CORTEX DURING POSTISCHEMIC RECOVERY.
001126 02-03
AN INTERFERENCE REDUCTION THEORY OF THE EFFECTS OF ETHANOL ON
CONFLICT-BEHAVIOR.
001586 02-04
INTERFERENCE WITH INGESTIONAL AVERSION LEARNING PRODUCED BY
PREEXPOSURE TO THE UNCONDITIONED-STIMULUS: ASSOCIATIVE-
ASPECTS AND NONASSOCIATIVE-ASPECTS.
001610 02-04
AGE-DEPENDENT MODIFICATION OF DRUG INTERFERENCE ON THE
ENZYMATIC ACTIVITIES OF THE RAT-BRAIN.
003730 04-03

INTERICTAL
ACTIVATION OF CORTICAL CIRCUITS DURING INTERICTAL SPIKES.
000056 01-03

INTERINDIVIDUAL
INTERINDIVIDUAL VARIATION OF CLINICAL-RESPONSE TO HALOPERIDOL.
001230 02-03
INTERINDIVIDUAL DIFFERENCES IN AMITRIPTYLINE DEMETHYLATION.
002282 02-13

INTERMEDIATE
LONG-TERM-TREATMENT OF RATS WITH MORPHINE DECREASES IN VITRO
BIOSYNTHESIS IN AND RELEASE OF BETA ENDORPHIN FROM
INTERMEDIATE/POSTERIOR LOBES OF PITUITARY.
003846 04-03
DOPAMINE-RECEPTOR BINDING IN BOVINE INTERMEDIATE LOBE
PITUITARY MEMBRANES.
004003 04-03

INTERMEDIATES
ANTICONVULSANT PROPERTIES OF SELECTED PYRROLOPYRIMIDINEDIONES
AND INTERMEDIATES.
003700 04-02

INTERMITTENT
EXTINCTION AND DOPAMINE-RECEPTOR BLOCKADE AFTER INTERMITTENT
REINFORCEMENT TRAINING: FAILURE TO OBSERVE FUNCTIONAL
EQUIVALENCE.
000490 01-04
CORRELATION BETWEEN DAILY FLUCTUATIONS OF CARBAMAZEPINE
SERUM LEVELS AND INTERMITTENT SIDE-EFFECTS.
000851 01-15
INTERMITTENT PIMOZIDE VERSUS FLUPHENAZINE-DECANOATE AS
MAINTENANCE-THERAPY IN CHRONIC SCHIZOPHRENIA.
001932 02-08
INTERMITTENT DECORTICATION AND PROGRESSIVE HYPERTHERMIA,
HYPERTENSION AND TACHYCARDIA FOLLOWING METHYLGLUCAMINE
IOTHALAMATE VENTRICULOGRAM.
003520 03-15

INTERNAL
GLC MASS-SPECTROMETRIC-DETERMINATION OF MAPROTILINE AND ITS
MAJOR METABOLITE USING STABLE ISOTOPE-LABELED ANALOG AS
INTERNAL STANDARD.
004291 04-06
SIMULTANEOUS DETERMINATION OF MORPHINE AND CODEINE IN BLOOD
BY USE OF SELECT ION-MONITORING AND DEUTERATED INTERNAL
STANDARDS.
004690 04-16

INTERNEURONES
INTERNEURONES ARE PROBABLY NOT INVOLVED IN THE PRESYNAPTIC
DOPAMINERGIC CONTROL OF DOPAMINE RELEASE IN RABBIT
CAUDATE-NUCLEUS.
001298 02-03

INTERNODAL
THE PATHOGENESIS OF PRIMARY INTERNODAL DEMYELINATION
PRODUCED BY ACETYL-ETHYL-TETRAMETHYL-TETRALIN: EVIDENCE FOR
PRESERVED SCHWANN-CELL SOMAL FUNCTION.
002905 03-03

INTEROCEPTIVE
CONDITIONING OF AN INTEROCEPTIVE DRUG STIMULUS TO DIFFERENT
EXTEROCEPTIVE CONTEXTS.
004142 04-04

INTERPERSONAL
EFFECTS OF TRICYCLIC-ANTIDEPRESSANTS ON INTERPERSONAL LEARNING.
003225 03-09
DEPRESSED-OUTPATIENTS: RESULTS ONE YEAR AFTER TREATMENT WITH
DRUGS AND/OR INTERPERSONAL PSYCHOTHERAPY.
003272 03-09

INTERPRETATION
EPILEPTOGENIC PROPERTIES OF ENFLURANE AND THEIR CLINICAL
INTERPRETATION.
004609 04-15

INTERPRETATIONS
THE ANTIDEPRESSANT ACTION OF SULPHO-ADENOSYL-L-METHIONINE
(SAME) COMPARED WITH THAT OF CHLORIMIPRAMINE
HYPOTHETICAL INTERPRETATIONS OF THE MECHANISM-OF-ACTION.
003150 03-07

INTERRELATION
INTERRELATION AT PLASMATIC LEVEL BETWEEN ANTIEPILEPTIC-DRUGS
AND LIPIDS. ITS IMPLICATIONS IN THE EFFICIENCY OF TREATMENT IN
EPILEPSY. I. CHANGES INDUCED BY PHENOBARBITAL OR/AND
DIPHENYLHYDANTOIN IN SERUM LIPIDS.
002281 02-13

INTERRELATIONS
INTERRELATIONS AMONG PRIOR EXPERIENCE AND CURRENT CONDITIONS
IN THE DETERMINATION OF BEHAVIOR AND THE EFFECTS OF DRUGS.
001715 02-04

INTERSTITIAL
THE ROLE OF LITHIUM IN THE PRODUCTION OF INTERSTITIAL NEPHRITIS:
A CASE-HISTORY.
004655 04-15

INTERSUBJECT
INTERSUBJECT AND INTRASUBJECT VARIATION IN DIAZEPAM FREE
FRACTION.
000747 01-13

INTERVAL
DOSE SIZE AND INTERDOSE INTERVAL EFFECTS ON MORPHINE-TOLERANCE
IN THE RAT. (PH.D. DISSERTATION).
003090 03-04

INTERVIEW
DELIRIUM OR PSYCHOSIS? DIAGNOSTIC USE OF THE SODIUM-
AMOBARBITAL INTERVIEW.
002167 02-11
THE TREATMENT OF CHRONIC SCHIZOPHRENIC-PATIENTS: AN INTERVIEW
WITH DR. J. HUSSER.
004328 04-08

INTERVIEWS
ACCURACY OF PATIENT INTERVIEWS AND ESTIMATES BY CLINICAL STAFF
IN DETERMINING MEDICATION COMPLIANCE.
003618 03-17

INTESTINAL
STIMULATION OF RETINAL ADENYLATE-CYCLASE BY VASOACTIVE
INTESTINAL PEPTIDE (VIP).
002811 03-03

INTESTINAL-MUSCLE
PERSISTENT EFFECTS OF HIGH-CONCENTRATIONS OF CHLORPROMAZINE
ON 3H PROPYLBENZILYLCHOLINE-MUSTARD BINDING TO MUSCARINIC-
RECEPTORS IN GUINEA-PIG INTESTINAL-MUSCLE STRIPS.
001266 02-03

INTESTINE
THE EFFECT OF MONOAMINE-OXIDASE-INHIBITORS ON FIRST-PASS
METABOLISM OF TYRAMINE IN DOG INTESTINE.
000141 01-03

INTOXICATED
EFFECTS OF HIPPOCAMPAL BRAIN-DAMAGE ON AUDITORY AND VISUAL
RECENT MEMORY: COMPARISON WITH MARIJUANA INTOXICATED
SUBJECTS.
002320 02-14

INTOXICATION
THE PCP PSYCHOSIS: PROLONGED INTOXICATION OR DRUG PRECIPITATED
FUNCTIONAL ILLNESS?
000739 01-12
REVERSAL BY PHENYTOIN OF CARBAMAZEPINE-INDUCED WATER
INTOXICATION: A PHARMACOKINETIC-INTERACTION.
000783 01-13
APPLICATION OF A RADIOIMMUNOASSAY SCREENING-TEST FOR
DETECTION AND MANAGEMENT OF PHENCYCLIDINE INTOXICATION.
000859 01-15
INTOXICATION ASSOCIATED WITH LITHIUM AND ECT.
000870 01-15
CARBAMAZEPINE INTOXICATION DUE TO TRIACETYLOLEANDOMYCIN
ADMINISTRATION IN EPILEPTIC-PATIENTS.
000873 01-15
VOLUNTARY INTOXICATION FROM PHENCYCLIDINE. WILL IT RAISE A
REASONABLE-DOUBT OF THE MENTAL-CAPACITY OF A PERSON
CHARGED WITH A CRIME REQUIRING SPECIFIC INTENT OR MENTAL-
STATE?.
000914 01-17
INFLUENCE OF CHRONIC ALCOHOL INTOXICATION ON CIRCADIAN-RHYTHM
OF NEUROSECRETORY CENTERS OF RAT HYPOTHALAMUS.
001549 02-03
BRAIN LOCATIONS CONTROLLING THE BEHAVIORAL-EFFECTS OF CHRONIC
AMPHETAMINE INTOXICATION.
001653 02-04
CONTRIBUTIONS OF INDIVIDUAL DIFFERENCES TO SUBJECTIVE
INTOXICATION.
002202 02-12

REGIONAL CEREBRAL BLOOD FLOW IN A CASE OF AMPHETAMINE INTOXICATION.
002210 02-13

ANTECEDENTS OF SELF-INDUCED WATER INTOXICATION: A PRELIMINARY-REPORT.
002414 02-15

BRADYCARDIA, PERSISTENT DIABETES-INSIPIDUS, AND TARDIVE-DYSKINESIA WITH LITHIUM INTOXICATION.
002427 02-15

ANIMAL-MODEL OF PSYCHOSIS: HALLUCINATORY BEHAVIORS IN MONKEYS DURING THE LATE STAGE OF CONTINUOUS AMPHETAMINE INTOXICATION.
002988 03-04

PRUSSIAN-BLUE: SPECIFIC TREATMENT OF THALLIUM, ARSENIC, INDUSTRIAL-SOLVENT INTOXICATION, AND OTHER POLYNEUROPATHOLOGIES. A POSSIBLE ANTIPSYCHOTIC-AGENT.
003348 03-11

PHENCYCLIDINE (PCP) INTOXICATION: DIAGNOSIS IN STAGES AND ALGORITHMS OF TREATMENT.
003525 03-15

PERIPHERAL NEUROPATHY DUE TO LITHIUM INTOXICATION.
003544 03-15

LESIONS OF AMYGDALA, PYRIFORM CORTEX AND OTHER BRAIN STRUCTURES DUE TO DIPIPERIDINOETHANE INTOXICATION.
004273 04-05

ACUTE PHENCYCLIDINE (PCP) INTOXICATION: QUANTITATIVE URINE LEVELS AND CLINICAL MANAGEMENT.
004665 04-15

INTRAARTERIAL
ACCIDENTAL INTRAARTERIAL INJECTION OF DIAZEPAM.
002598 02-17

INTRAAXONAL
THE EFFECT OF CHRONIC NICOTINE AND WITHDRAWAL ON INTRAAXONAL TRANSPORT OF ACETYLCHOLINE AND RELATED ENZYMES IN SCIATIC-NERVE OF THE RAT.
'003897 04-03

INTRACELLULAR
AN INTRACELLULAR OPIATE-RECEPTOR.
000278 01-03

INTRACELLULAR REDOX STATES UNDER HALOTHANE AND BARBITURATE ANESTHESIA IN NORMAL, ISCHEMIC, AND ANOXIC MONKEY BRAIN.
000295 01-03

INTRACELLULAR OBSERVATIONS ON THE EFFECTS OF MUSCARINIC AGONISTS ON RAT SYMPATHETIC NEURONES.
001143 02-03

PERSISTENT EFFECTS OF CHRONIC ADMINISTRATION OF LSD ON INTRACELLULAR SEROTONIN CONTENT IN RAT-MIDBRAIN.
001333 02-03

THE IN VITRO BRAIN SLICE AS A USEFUL NEUROPHYSIOLOGICAL PREPARATION FOR INTRACELLULAR RECORDING.
001864 02-06

LITHIUM DRUG INTERACTIONS ALTERING THE INTRACELLULAR LITHIUM LEVEL: AN IN VITRO STUDY.
003142 03-06

INTRACELLULAR LITHIUM: ITS VALUE IN THE PREDICTION OF A POSITIVE RESPONSE TO LITHIUM.
003382 03-11

INTRACEREBRAL
DRUG-INDUCED ELEVATION OF GABA AFTER INTRACEREBRAL MICROINJECTION: SITE OF ANTICONVULSANT ACTION.
001627 02-04

DIFFERENT BEHAVIORAL-EFFECTS FOLLOWING INTRACEREBRAL, INTRACEREBROVENTRICULAR OR INTRAPERITONEAL INJECTION OF NALOXONE IN THE RAT.
001665 02-04

ANALGESIC ACTION OF INTRATHECAL AND INTRACEREBRAL BETA ENDORPHIN IN RATS: COMPARISON WITH MORPHINE.
001691 02-04

STEREOTYPED-BEHAVIOUR AND ELECTROCORTICAL-CHANGES AFTER INTRACEREBRAL MICROINFUSION OF DOPAMINE AND APOMORPHINE IN FOWLS.
001734 02-04

USE OF THE INTRACEREBRAL INJECTION TECHNIQUE TO ELUCIDATE MECHANISMS OF APOMORPHINE CLIMBING AND ITS ANTAGONISM IN THE MOUSE.
004092 04-04

INTRACEREBRAL SUBSTANCE-P IN MICE: BEHAVIORAL-EFFECTS AND NARCOTIC-AGENTS.
004218 04-04

INTRACEREBRALLY
EFFECTS OF NOMIFENSINE AND DESIPRAMINE ON THE SEQUELAE OF INTRACEREBRALLY INJECTED 6 OHDA AND 5,6 DHT.
001522 02-03

INTRACEREBROVENTRICULAR
THE EFFECT OF CYCLO-LEU-GLY ON CHEMICAL DENERVATION SUPERSENSITIVITY OF DOPAMINE-RECEPTORS INDUCED BY INTRACEREBROVENTRICULAR INJECTION OF 6 HYDROXYDOPAMINE IN MICE.
001435 02-03

DIFFERENT BEHAVIORAL-EFFECTS FOLLOWING INTRACEREBRAL, INTRACEREBROVENTRICULAR OR INTRAPERITONEAL INJECTION OF NALOXONE IN THE RAT.
001665 02-04

OPERANT FEEDING AND DRINKING IN PIGS FOLLOWING INTRACEREBROVENTRICULAR INJECTION OF SYNTHETIC CHOLECYSTOKININ-OCTAPEPTIDE.
003064 03-04

CATECHOLAMINE AND 5 HYDROXYTRYPTAMINE SYNTHESIS AND METABOLISM FOLLOWING INTRACEREBROVENTRICULAR INJECTION OF DIBUTYRYL-CYCLIC-AMP.
003769 04-03

SUSTAINED INTRACEREBROVENTRICULAR INFUSION OF BRAIN FUELS REDUCES BODY-WEIGHT AND FOOD INTAKE IN RATS.
004098 04-04

INTRACEREBROVENTRICULARLY
CAPTOPRIL GIVEN INTRACEREBROVENTRICULARLY, SUBCUTANEOUSLY OR BY GAVAGE INHIBITS ANGIOTENSIN CONVERTING ENZYME ACTIVITY IN THE RAT-BRAIN.
001614 02-04

THE ANTINOCICEPTIVE-EFFECT OF INTRACEREBROVENTRICULARLY ADMINISTERED PROSTAGLANDIN-E1 IN THE RAT.
001769 02-04

INTRACORTICAL
ROLE OF INTRACORTICAL INHIBITION IN DEPRIVATION AMBLYOPIA: REVERSAL BY MICROIONTOPHORETIC BICUCULLINE.
002684 03-03

INTRACRANIAL
INTRACRANIAL INJECTION PARAMETERS WHICH AFFECT ANGIOTENSIN-II-INDUCED DRINKING.
000534 01-06

CLONIDINE ON THE PRESSOR RESPONSE TO RAISED INTRACRANIAL PRESSURE.
001316 02-03

DIFFERENTIAL-EFFECTS OF SYSTEMIC VERSUS INTRACRANIAL INJECTION OF OPIATES ON CENTRAL, OROFACIAL AND LOWER BODY NOCICEPTION: SOMATOTYPY IN BULBAR ANALGESIA SYSTEMS.
001446 02-03

EFFECTS OF AN ACTH4-9 RELATED PEPTIDE UPON INTRACRANIAL SELF-STIMULATION AND GENERAL-ACTIVITY IN THE RAT.
001679 02-04

ELECTROLYTIC MICROINFUSION TRANSDUCER SYSTEM: AN ALTERNATIVE METHOD OF INTRACRANIAL DRUG APPLICATION.
001861 02-06

INTRACRANIAL SELF-ADMINISTRATION OF MORPHINE INTO THE VENTRAL TEGMENTAL AREA IN RATS.
002960 03-04

PHARMACOLOGICAL CHARACTERIZATION OF SCRATCHING-BEHAVIOUR INDUCED BY INTRACRANIAL INJECTION OF SUBSTANCE-P AND SOMATOSTATIN.
002980 03-04

CONFLICT-SITUATION BASED ON INTRACRANIAL SELF-STIMULATION BEHAVIOR AND THE EFFECT OF BENZODIAZEPINES.
003004 03-04

INTRACRANIAL-STIMULATION
ADDICTIVE-AGENTS AND INTRACRANIAL-STIMULATION (ICS): MORPHINE, NALOXONE, AND PRESSING FOR AMYGDALOID ICS.
000371 01-04

INTRACRANIALLY
INFUSIONS INTO THE OCULOMOTOR NUCLEUS OR NERVE: A METHOD OF ESTIMATING THE DOSAGE AT WHICH TRANSMITTER ANTAGONISTS INFUSED INTRACRANIALLY PRODUCE NONSPECIFIC BLOCKING OF NEURAL ACTIVITY.
003134 03-06

INTRAHYPOTHALAMIC
INTRAHYPOTHALAMIC MICROINJECTIONS OF NORADRENALINE WITH AND WITHOUT INDUCTION OF THE ALIMENTARY DRIVE AS A REWARD IN A T-MAZE LEARNING IN RATS.
001604 02-04

PRESSOR EFFECTS OF DORSAL RAPHE STIMULATION AND INTRAHYPOTHALAMIC APPLICATION OF SEROTONIN IN THE SPONTANEOUSLY HYPERTENSIVE-RAT.
003117 03-04

INTRAMUSCULAR
INTRAMUSCULAR HALOPERIDOL-DECANOATE FOR NEUROLEPTIC MAINTENANCE-THERAPY: EFFICACY, DOSAGE SCHEDULE AND PLASMA LEVELS: AN OPEN MULTICENTER-STUDY.
000758 01-13

ABSCESSES FOLLOWING PROLONGED INTRAMUSCULAR ADMINISTRATION OF PERPHENAZINE-ENANTATE.
000888 01-15

SECOND-ORDER SCHEDULES OF INTRAMUSCULAR COCAINE INJECTION IN THE SQUIRREL-MONKEY: COMPARISONS WITH FOOD PRESENTATION AND EFFECTS OF D-AMPHETAMINE AND PROMAZINE.
004152 04-04

Subject Index

ANTAGONISM OF INTRAVENOUS COCAINE LETHALITY IN NONHUMAN PRIMATES.
003127 03-05

INTRAVENOUS QUINIDINE IN CONGESTIVE CARDIOMYOPATHY.
003352 03-11

INTRAVENOUS VALPROATE: EFFECTS ON PLASMA AND SALIVA PHENYTOIN LEVELS.
003359 03-11

INTRAVENOUS LORAZEPAM TO PREVENT NAUSEA AND VOMITING ASSOCIATED WITH CANCER CHEMOTHERAPY.
003614 03-17

EFFECT OF INTRAVENOUS ADMINISTRATION OF D LYSERGIC-ACID-DIETHYLAMIDE ON SUBSEQUENT PROTEIN SYNTHESIS IN A CELL-FREE SYSTEM DERIVED FROM BRAIN.
003761 04-03

COMPARISON OF THE EFFECT OF INTRAVENOUS ADMINISTRATION OF D LYSERGIC-ACID-DIETHYLAMIDE ON FREE AND MEMBRANE-BOUND POLYSOMES IN THE RABBIT BRAIN.
003831 04-03

A COMPARATIVE-STUDY OF INTRAVENOUS LORAZEPAM AND CLONAZEPAM IN STATUS-EPILEPTICUS.
004487 04-11

INTRAVENOUS DIAZEPAM AND ORAL ETHANOL INTERACTION.
004552 04-13

TRANSIENT HYPERKINESIA AFTER A SINGLE INTRAVENOUS PERFUSION OF DIPHENYLHYDANTOIN: REPORT OF A CASE ASSOCIATED WITH NONTOXIC PLASMA LEVELS OF DIPHENYLHYDANTOIN.
004638 04-15

INTRAVENTRICULAR
EFFECT OF INTRAVENTRICULAR INJECTIONS OF ALPHA AMINOSULFONIC-ACIDS ON THE CENTRAL-NERVOUS-SYSTEM OF CONSCIOUS MICE.
000009 01-02

GABA DEPLETION AND BEHAVIOURAL-CHANGES PRODUCED BY INTRAVENTRICULAR PUTRESCINE IN CHICKS.
000218 01-03

EFFECTS OF SYSTEMIC AND INTRAVENTRICULAR ADMINISTRATION OF CANNABINOIDS ON SCHEDULE-CONTROLLED RESPONDING IN THE SQUIRREL-MONKEY.
000354 01-04

SYSTEMIC AND INTRAVENTRICULAR PROLACTIN INDUCES EXCESSIVE GROOMING.
000378 01-04

INTRAVENTRICULAR 6 HYDROXYDOPAMINE IN THE NEWBORN RAT AND LOCOMOTOR RESPONSES TO DRUGS IN INFANCY: NO SUPPORT FOR THE DOPAMINE DEPLETION MODEL OF MINIMAL-BRAIN-DYSFUNCTION.
000448 01-04

THE EFFECTS OF INTRAVENTRICULAR 6 HYDROXYDOPAMINE AND 5,6 DIHYDROXYTRYPTAMINE ON MORPHINE-INDUCED LOCOMOTOR-STIMULATION.
001784 02-04

GABA DEPLETION IN CHICK BRAINSTEM AFTER INTRAVENTRICULAR INJECTION OF CEFAZOLIN.
002762 03-03

EXPLORATION AND MOTOR-ACTIVITY AFTER INTRAVENTRICULAR ACTH, MORPHINE AND NALOXONE.
002991 03-04

INTRAVENTRICULAR CORTICOSTERONE INJECTION FACILITATES MEMORY OF AN APPETITIVE DISCRIMINATIVE TASK IN MICE.
003051 03-04

INTRAVENTRICULAR CHOLECYSTOKININ-OCTAPEPTIDE PRODUCES HYPERGLYCEMIA IN RATS.
003943 04-03

ANALGESIA FOLLOWING INTRAVENTRICULAR ADMINISTRATION OF 2 DEOXY-D-GLUCOSE.
004074 04-04

INTRAVENTRICULARLY
CENTRAL-ACTION OF INTRAVENTRICULARLY INJECTED MIDODRINE IN RATS.
001684 02-04

INTRINSIC
INTRINSIC CHOLINERGIC EXCITATION IN THE RAT NEOSTRIATUM: NICOTINIC AND MUSCARINIC-RECEPTORS.
001374 02-03

MULTIPLE CNS RECEPTOR INTERACTIONS OF ERGOT ALKALOIDS: AFFINITY AND INTRINSIC ACTIVITY ANALYSIS IN IN VITRO BINDING SYSTEMS.
001516 02-03

INTRODUODENAL
ABSORPTION OF 14C LABELED METHADONE BY PORTAL AND EXTRAPORTAL VENOUS CIRCULATIONS FOLLOWING INTRAPERITONEAL AND INTRODUODENAL ADMINISTRATION.
000094 01-03

INTROVERSION
INTROVERSION AND SEVERITY OF THE BENZODIAZEPINE WITHDRAWAL.
000923 01-17

INTRUDER
BEHAVIORAL-EFFECTS OF HASHISH IN MICE: III. SOCIAL-INTERACTIONS BETWEEN TWO RESIDENTS AND AN INTRUDER MALE.
001776 02-04

INVERSE
AN INVERSE CORRELATION BETWEEN SERUM LEVELS OF DESMETHYLIMIPRAMINE AND MELATONIN-LIKE IMMUNOREACTIVITY IN DMI RESPONSIVE DEPRESSIVES.
003228 03-09

INVESTIGATE
THE USE OF EXTINCTION TO INVESTIGATE THE NATURE OF NEUROLEPTIC-INDUCED AVOIDANCE-DEFICITS.
000345 01-04

A RESEARCH PARADIGM TO INVESTIGATE THE EFFECT OF MANIPULATION ON SOCIAL-BEHAVIOR IN GROUPS.
003007 03-04

INVESTIGATING
AN IN VIVO MODEL FOR INVESTIGATING ALPHA1-RECEPTORS AND ALPHA2-RECEPTORS IN THE CNS: STUDIES WITH MIANSERIN.
000053 01-03

INVESTIGATORY
MESOLIMBICOCORTICAL DOPAMINE TERMINAL-FIELDS ARE NECESSARY FOR NORMAL LOCOMOTOR AND INVESTIGATORY EXPLORATION IN RATS.
000383 01-04

EFFECTS OF SEROTONERGIC LESIONS ON INVESTIGATORY RESPONDING BY RATS IN A HOLEBOARD.
001634 02-04

INVOLUNTARY-MOVEMENTS
THE EFFECTS OF CHOLINERGIC-DRUGS ON THE INVOLUNTARY-MOVEMENTS OF TARDIVE-DYSKINESIA.
000726 01-11

PREVALENCE OF PERSISTENT ABNORMAL INVOLUNTARY-MOVEMENTS AMONG PATIENTS IN A NIGERIAN LONG-STAY PSYCHIATRIC UNIT.
004334 04-08

INVOLUNTARY-PATIENTS
THE RIGHTS OF INVOLUNTARY-PATIENTS TO REFUSE PHARMACOTHERAPY: WHAT IS REASONABLE?
004730 04-17

INVOLUTIONAL
THE NOSOLOGICAL INDEPENDENCE OF INVOLUTIONAL DEPRESSION AND ITS DYNAMICS DURING PSYCHOPHARMACOTHERAPY.
004389 04-09

ION-CHANNEL
INTERACTIONS OF TRICYCLIC-ANTIDEPRESSANTS WITH A SYNAPTIC ION-CHANNEL.
002660 03-03

ION-CHANNELS
(-)PENTOBARBITAL OPENS ION-CHANNELS OF LONG-DURATION IN CULTURED MOUSE SPINAL NEURONS.
000198 01-03

CONVULSANT AND ANTICONVULSANT-DRUG BINDING-SITES RELATED TO GABA REGULATED CHLORIDE ION-CHANNELS.
002848 03-03

ION-CONDUCTANCE
BARBITURATE ENHANCEMENT OF GABA-MEDIATED INHIBITION AND ACTIVATION OF CHLORIDE ION-CONDUCTANCE: CORRELATION WITH ANTICONVULSANT AND ANESTHETIC ACTIONS.
002885 03-03

ION-MONITORING
A SELECTED ION-MONITORING ASSAY FOR BIOGENIC-AMINE METABOLITES AND PROBENECID, IN HUMAN LUMBAR CEREBROSPINAL-FLUID.
003663 04-01

A QUANTITATIVE PROBE FOR BIOLOGICAL-PSYCHIATRY: SELECTED ION-MONITORING.
004685 04-16

SIMULTANEOUS DETERMINATION OF MORPHINE AND CODEINE IN BLOOD BY USE OF SELECT ION-MONITORING AND DEUTERATED INTERNAL STANDARDS.
004690 04-16

ION-TRANSFER
THE USEFULNESS OF THE ERYTHROCYTE LITHIUM INDEX IN THE EVALUATION OF DISORDERS OF ION-TRANSFER IN PATIENTS WITH DEPRESSIVE-SYNDROMES.
000625 01-09

IONIZATION
THE IONIZATION OF 5 HYDROXYTRYPTAMINE AND RELATED COMPOUNDS AND AN APPRAISAL OF METHODS FOR THE ESTIMATION OF ZWITTERION CONSTANTS.
001859 02-06

IONOPHORE
ETHANOL ENHANCES (3H)DIAZEPAM BINDING AT THE BENZODIAZEPINE GABA-RECEPTOR IONOPHORE COMPLEX.
001154 02-03

IONOPHORE-RECEPTOR
THE BENZODIAZEPINE GABA-CHLORIDE IONOPHORE-RECEPTOR COMPLEX: COMMON SITE OF MINOR-TRANQUILIZER ACTION.
002857 03-03

IONOPHORES
MULTIPLE BENZODIAZEPINE-RECEPTOR COMPLEXES: SOME
BENZODIAZEPINE RECOGNITION SITES ARE COUPLED TO GABA-
RECEPTORS AND IONOPHORES.
001484 02-03

IONOPHORESIS
IONOPHORESIS -- PROGRESS AND PITFALLS.
003144 03-06

IONTOPHORESIS
QUANTIFICATION OF NORADRENALINE IONTOPHORESIS.
002475 02-16

IONTOPHORESIS OF KAINIC-ACID.
004294 04-06

IONTOPHORETIC
THE PHYSICS OF IONTOPHORETIC PIPETTES.
004299 04-06

IONTOPHORETICALLY
MODULATORY INTERACTIONS BETWEEN NOREPINEPHRINE AND TAURINE,
BETA ALANINE, GAMMA AMINOBUTYRIC-ACID AND MUSCIMOL
APPLIED IONTOPHORETICALLY TO CEREBELLAR PURKINJE-CELLS.
004058 04-03

IOTHALAMATE
INTERMITTENT DECORTICATION AND PROGRESSIVE HYPERTHERMIA,
HYPERTENSION AND TACHYCARDIA FOLLOWING METHYLGLUCAMINE
IOTHALAMATE VENTRICULOGRAM.
003520 03-15

IP
MOTOR-DEPRESSION AND HEAD-TWITCHES INDUCED BY IP INJECTION OF
GABA.
001788 02-04

IPRINDOLE
DEVELOPMENT OF AND RECOVERY FROM SUBSENSITIVITY OF THE
NORADRENERGIC CYCLIC-AMP GENERATING SYSTEM IN BRAIN: EFFECT
OF AMPHETAMINE FOLLOWING INHIBITION OF ITS AROMATIC
HYDROXYLATION BY IPRINDOLE.
001353 02-03

IPRONIAZID
THE EFFECTS OF RESERPINE, IPRONIAZID AND L-DOPA ON ELECTRICALLY-
INDUCED SPINAL-CORD SEIZURES.
000146 01-03

IPTBO
MODULATION BY PICROTOXIN AND IPTBO OF 3H FLUNITRAZEPAM
BINDING TO THE GABA/BENZODIAZEPINE-RECEPTOR COMPLEX OF RAT-
CEREBELLUM.
002775 03-03

IRAZEPINE
IN VIVO EFFECTS OF TWO NOVEL ALKYLATING BENZODIAZEPINES,
IRAZEPINE AND KENAZEPINE,
004251 04-04

IRIS
(3H)QUINUCLIDINYL-BENZILATE BINDING TO MUSCARINIC-RECEPTORS
AND (3H)WB-4101 BINDING TO ALPHA-ADRENERGIC-RECEPTORS IN
RABBIT IRIS: COMPARISON OF RESULTS IN SLICES AND MICROSOMAL
FRACTIONS.
000299 01-03

OPIATE-RECEPTORS IN THE RABBIT IRIS.
001200 02-03

IRON
SEX-DIFFERENCE IN BRAIN IRON. (UNPUBLISHED PAPER).
001278 02-03

TOXICITY OF OXYGEN IN IRON RICH AREAS OF RAT-BRAIN.
(UNPUBLISHED PAPER).
001498 02-03

IRON-INDUCED
ANTIPEROXIDANT PRETREATMENT AND IRON-INDUCED EPILEPTIFORM
DISCHARGES IN THE RAT: EEG AND HISTOPATHOLOGIC STUDIES.
002930 03-03

IRREVERSIBLE
EVIDENCE FOR AN IRREVERSIBLE INTERACTION OF BROMOCRYPTINE
WITH CENTRAL DOPAMINE-RECEPTORS.
000223 01-03

IRREVERSIBLE INHIBITION OF AROMATIC-L-AMINO-ACID-DECARBOXYLASE
BY ALPHA DIFLUOROMETHYL-DOPA AND METABOLISM OF THE
INHIBITOR.
000248 01-03

IRREVERSIBLE INHIBITION OF S ADENOSYLHOMOCYSTEINE-HYDROLASE BY
NUCLEOSIDE ANALOGS. (UNPUBLISHED PAPER).
001010 02-01

GABA AGONISTS AND UPTAKE INHIBITORS DESIGNED AS AGENTS WITH
IRREVERSIBLE ACTIONS.
001079 02-02

PATHOPHYSIOLOGICAL-ASPECTS OF REVERSIBLE AND IRREVERSIBLE
TARDIVE-DYSKINESIA.
002124 02-11

ENHANCEMENT OF APOMORPHINE-INDUCED CLIMBING IN MICE BY
REVERSIBLE AND IRREVERSIBLE NARCOTIC ANTAGONIST DRUGS.
003068 03-04

TREATMENT OF HUNTINGTON-DISEASE WITH GAMMA ACETYLENIC-
GABA, AN IRREVERSIBLE INHIBITOR OF GABA-TRANSAMINASE:

INCREASED CSF GABA AND HOMOCARNOSINE WITHOUT CLINICAL
AMELIORATION.
003458 03-14

ISATINS
SYNTHESIS OF POTENTIAL ANTICONVULSANTS: CONDENSATION OF
ISATINS WITH ACETONE AND RELATED KETONES.
003699 04-02

ISCHEMIA
IMPROVEMENT OF RESTITUTION FROM CEREBRAL ISCHEMIA IN
HYPERGLYCEMIC RATS BY PENTOBARBITAL OR DIAZEPAM.
000475 01-04

ISCHEMIC
PROTECTIVE EFFECT OF PRENYLAMINE AGAINST VULNERABILITY TO
VENTRICULAR FIBRILLATION IN THE NORMAL AND ISCHEMIC CANINE
MYOCARDIUM.
000265 01-03

INTRACELLULAR REDOX STATES UNDER HALOTHANE AND BARBITURATE
ANESTHESIA IN NORMAL, ISCHEMIC, AND ANOXIC MONKEY BRAIN.
000295 01-03

ALTERATION OF PHARMACOKINETIC PARAMETERS FOR PENTOBARBITAL
BY ISCHEMIC STROKE AND REVERSION TO NORMAL BY
DEXAMETHASONE TREATMENT.
000321 01-03

THE EFFECTS OF THIORIDAZINE ON ELECTRICAL AND ISCHEMIC
VENTRICULAR FIBRILLATION IN THE DOG HEART IN SITU.
002697 03-03

ISF-2522I
CNS EFFECTS OF ISF-2522. A NEW NOOTROPIC (A PHASE I SAFETY AND
CNS EFFICACY STUDY WITH QUANTITATIVE PHARMACOEEG AND
PHARMACOPSYCHOLOGY).
004519 04-13

ISOCARBOXAZIDE
LONG-TERM-TREATMENT OF DEPRESSION WITH ISOCARBOXAZIDE.
002011 02-09

ISOENZYMES
COMPARISON OF CYSTEINE-SULPHINIC-ACID-DECARBOXYLASE (CSD)
ISOENZYMES AND GLUTAMIC-ACID-DECARBOXYLASE (GAD) IN RAT: IS
BRAIN CSD-I IDENTICAL WITH LIVER CSD AND BRAIN CSD-II WITH
GAD? (UNPUBLISHED PAPER).
001048 02-01

ISOFLOXYTHEPIN
THE EFFECT OF A NEW FLUORINATED TRICYCLIC NEUROLEPTIC-DRUG
ISOFLOXYTHEPIN ON THE RAT STRIATAL DOPAMINE METABOLISM.
000306 01-03

KINETICS OF CENTRAL-ACTIONS OF ISOFLOXYTHEPIN, AN ORAL
NEUROLEPTIC-DRUG WITH PROLONGED ACTION IN RODENTS.
001720 02-04

ISOLATED
MATURATION OF SYMPATHETIC NEUROTRANSMISSION IN THE RAT
HEART. III. DEVELOPMENTAL-CHANGES IN RESERPINE INHIBITION OF
NOREPINEPHRINE UPTAKE INTO ISOLATED SYNAPTIC VESICLES.
000025 01-03

INFLUENCE OF CELLULAR-TRANSPORT ON THE INTERACTION OF AMINO-
ACIDS WITH GAMMA AMINOBUTYRIC-ACID-RECEPTORS (GABA) IN THE
ISOLATED OLFACTORY-CORTEX OF THE GUINEA-PIG.
000034 01-03

IMIPRAMINE AFFECTS AUTONOMIC-CONTROL OF SINOATRIAL RATE IN
ISOLATED RIGHT ATRIAL PREPARATIONS.
000195 01-03

1-M CHLOROPHENYLPIPERAZINE: A METABOLITE OF TRAZODONE
ISOLATED FROM RAT URINE.
000204 01-03

REACTIVITY OF ISOLATED CANINE CEREBRAL-ARTERIES TO ADENINE-
NUCLEOTIDES AND ADENOSINE.
000210 01-03

METABOLISM OF 3H NORADRENALINE RELEASED FROM ISOLATED RAT
HYPOTHALAMUS BY EXTRACTS OF BLACK-WIDOW-SPIDER GLANDS.
000223 01-03

EFFECT OF DESMETHYLIMIPRAMINE ON THE KINETICS OF
CHLORPHENTERMINE ACCUMULATION IN ISOLATED PERFUSED RAT
LUNG.
000524 01-05

ELECTRON PROBE MICROANALYSIS OF CALCIUM AND PHOSPHORUS IN
DENSE-BODIES ISOLATED FROM HUMAN PLATELETS. (UNPUBLISHED
PAPER).
001014 02-01

ACUTE AND CHRONIC EFFECTS OF MORPHINE ON TRANSMEMBRANE
POTENTIAL AND ON SHORT-CIRCUIT CURRENT IN ISOLATED TOAD
SKIN: APPARENT MORPHINE-DEPENDENCE.
001176 02-03

RESPONSIVENESS TO VASOACTIVE-AGENTS OF CEREBRAL-ARTERIES AND
MESENTERIC-ARTERIES ISOLATED FROM CONTROL AND RESERPINE
TREATED DOGS.
001273 02-03

EFFECTS OF AMITRIPTYLINE AND CLOMIPRAMINE IN THE ISOLATED,
PERFUSED RABBIT HEART.
001852 02-05

MEASUREMENT OF THE MEMBRANE POTENTIAL OF ISOLATED NERVE
TERMINALS BY THE LIPOPHILIC CATION
(3H)TRIPHENYLMETHYLPHOSPHONIUM-BROMIDE.
002746 03-03

DEVELOPMENT OF TOLERANCE TO THE EXCITATORY EFFECT OF MORPHINE
AND CROSS-TOLERANCE TO THE INHIBITORY ACTION OF BETA
ENDORPHIN IN THE ISOLATED RAT VAS-DEFERENS.
002756 03-03

THE EFFECT OF MONOAMINES ON MOTONEURONS IN THE ISOLATED RAT
SPINAL-CORD.
002790 03-03

EFFECTS OF BENSERAZIDE AND CARBIDOPA ON THE METABOLISM OF L
TRYPTOPHAN BY ISOLATED RAT LIVER CELLS.
002899 03-03

CHARACTERIZATION OF THE ISOLATED PERFUSED MOUSE-BRAIN AS A
SYSTEM FOR NEUROCHEMICAL-STUDIES.
003146 03-06

SYNTHESIS OF CYTOSKELETAL PROTEINS IN BULK ISOLATED NEURONAL
PERIKARYA.
003672 04-01

PAPAIN-DERIVED FRAGMENT IIC TETANUS-TOXIN: ITS BINDING TO
ISOLATED SYNAPTIC MEMBRANES AND RETROGRADE AXONAL
TRANSPORT.
003734 04-03

PREJUNCTIONAL ACTIONS OF PIRIBEDIL ON THE ISOLATED KIDNEY OF THE
RABBIT: COMPARISON WITH APOMORPHINE.
003749 04-03

UPTAKE OF RADIOCALCIUM BY NERVE-ENDINGS ISOLATED FROM RAT-
BRAIN: KINETIC STUDIES.
003814 04-03

UPTAKE OF RADIOCALCIUM BY NERVE-ENDINGS ISOLATED FROM RAT-
BRAIN: PHARMACOLOGICAL-STUDIES.
003815 04-03

ACCUMULATION OF AMANTADINE BY ISOLATED CHROMAFFIN
GRANULES.
003866 04-03

ON THE IMPORTANCE OF AGONIST CONCENTRATION GRADIENTS WITHIN
ISOLATED TISSUES. INCREASED MAXIMAL RESPONSES OF RAT VASA-
DEFERENTIA TO (-) NORADRENALINE AFTER BLOCKADE OF NEURONAL
UPTAKE.
003879 04-03

THE EFFECT OF ACETYLCHOLINE RELEASE ON CHOLINE FLUXES IN
ISOLATED SYNAPTIC TERMINALS.
003924 04-03

COMPARISON OF THE POTENCIES OF CLEBOPRIDE AND OTHER
SUBSTITUTED BENZAMIDE DRUGS ON ISOLATED GASTROINTESTINAL
TRACT OF THE GUINEA-PIG AND RAT.
003928 04-03

A COMPARISON OF THE RESPONSES TO SOME DOPAMINE-RECEPTOR
AGONISTS AND ANTAGONISTS IN THE ISOLATED PERFUSED RAT
KIDNEY.
004054 04-03

POTENTIATION OF THE EFFECTS OF ADENOSINE ON ISOLATED CARDIAC-
MUSCLE AND SMOOTH-MUSCLE BY DIAZEPAM.
004266 04-05

ISOLATION
INCREASED DOPAMINE-RECEPTOR BINDING IN THE STRIATUM OF RATS
AFTER LONG-TERM ISOLATION.
000398 01-04

DOPAMINE-RECEPTOR: ISOLATION, PURIFICATION, AND REGULATION.
001011 02-01

ISOLATION OF PSYCHOACTIVE CANNABINOID PRECURSORS FROM
CANNABIS OF SOVIET PROVENIENCE GROWN IN MISSISSIPPI.
001023 02-01

ISOLATION OF SELECTIVE 3H CHLORNALTREXAMINE BOUND COMPLEXES,
POSSIBLE OPIOID-RECEPTOR COMPONENTS IN BRAINS OF MICE.
001162 02-03

ISOLATION INCREASES THE RESPONSES TO BETA-ADRENERGIC
STIMULATION IN MICE.
001232 02-03

BENZODIAZEPINE-RECEPTOR: LOCALIZATION BY PHOTOAFFINITY
LABELING AND ISOLATION OF A POSSIBLE ENDOGENOUS LIGAND.
001381 02-03

DISTRIBUTION OF MEMBRANE GLYCOPROTEINS AMONG THE ORGANELLES
OF A SINGLE IDENTIFIED NEURON OF APLYSIA. II. ISOLATION AND
CHARACTERIZATION OF A GLYCOPROTEIN ASSOCIATED WITH
VESICLES.
002657 03-03

THE DOPAMINE-RECEPTOR: ISOLATION, PURIFICATION AND REGULATION.
003660 04-01

ISOLATION-INDUCED
EFFECTS OF SODIUM-DIPROPYLACETATE, MUSCIMOL-HYDROBROMIDE
AND (R,S) NIPECOTIC-ACID-AMIDE ON ISOLATION-INDUCED
AGGRESSIVE-BEHAVIOR IN MICE.
001756 02-04

SUBCHRONIC-TREATMENT WITH THE TRICYCLIC-ANTIDEPRESSANT DMI
INCREASES ISOLATION-INDUCED FIGHTING IN RATS.
004252 04-04

ISOLE
SPECIFIC AND NONSPECIFIC MULTIPLE UNIT ACTIVITIES DURING
PENTYLENETETRAZOL SEIZURES. I. ANIMALS WITH ENCEPHALE ISOLE.
004046 04-03

ISOMER
POSSIBLE MECHANISMS OF EFFECT OF ACTH4-10 AND ITS ANALOG,
CONTAINING D ISOMER OF PHENYLALANINE, ON BEHAVIOR.
002949 03-04

ISOMERIZATION
ISOMERIZATION OF THE MUSCARINIC-RECEPTOR ANTAGONIST COMPLEX.
003860 04-03

ISOMERS
COMPARISON OF THE EFFECTS OF THE ISOMERS OF AMPHETAMINE,
METHYLPHENIDATE AND DEOXYPIPRADROL ON THE UPTAKE OF L
(3H)NOREPINEPHRINE AND (3H)DOPAMINE BY SYNAPTIC VESICLES
FROM RAT-WHOLE-BRAIN, STRIATUM AND HYPOTHALAMUS.
000091 01-03

MIDBRAIN DOPAMINE NEURONS: DIFFERENTIAL RESPONSES TO
AMPHETAMINE ISOMERS.
002680 03-03

RELATIVE POTENCY OF AMPHETAMINE ISOMERS IN CAUSING THE
SEROTONIN BEHAVIORAL-SYNDROME IN RATS.
003094 03-04

THE EFFECT OF PROPRANOLOL AND ITS ISOMERS ON PURKINJE
NEURONES IN RAT CEREBELLUM.
004059 04-03

ISOPRENALIN
SPONTANEOUS MOTOR-ACTIVITY IN RATS GIVEN REPEATEDLY BETA-
SYMPATHOMIMETICS -- ISOPRENALIN AND SALBUTAMOL.
001804 02-04

ISOPRENALINE
FAILURE OF ISOPRENALINE AND BETA-RECEPTOR BLOCKING-DRUGS TO
MODIFY DEPRESSOR RESPONSE AND BRADYCARDIA INDUCED BY
ELECTRICAL-STIMULATION OF THE ANTERIOR HYPOTHALAMUS OF
CATS.
000520 01-05

ISOPRENALINE-INDUCED
EVIDENCE THAT VASOPRESSIN IS INVOLVED IN THE ISOPRENALINE-
INDUCED BETA ENDORPHIN RELEASE.
001319 02-03

ISOPRINOSINE
ISOPRINOSINE IN SUBACUTE SCLEROSING PANENCEPHALITIS.
000687 01-11

ISOPROPYLBICYCLOPHOSPHATE
REPEATED ELECTROCONVULSIVE-SHOCK DOES NOT INCREASE THE
SUSCEPTIBILITY OF RATS TO A CAGE CONVULSANT
(ISOPROPYLBICYCLOPHOSPHATE).
001184 02-03

ISOPROTERENOL
EFFECT OF ISOPROTERENOL ON CEREBRAL CIRCULATION IN DOGS.
000199 01-03

THE REGULATION OF CARDIAC MUSCARINIC CHOLINERGIC-RECEPTORS BY
ISOPROTERENOL.
001441 02-03

DESENSITIZATION OF ADRENOCEPTORS AFTER IMMOBILIZATION STRESS
OR REPEATED INJECTION OF ISOPROTERENOL IN RATS. (UNPUBLISHED
PAPER).
001546 02-03

EFFECTS OF ISOPROTERENOL ON THE DEVELOPMENT OF BETA-
ADRENERGIC-RECEPTORS IN BRAIN CELL AGGREGATES.
002932 03-03

ISOPROTERENOL-INDUCED
DOXEPIN, A TRICYCLIC-ANTIDEPRESSANT, BINDS TO NORMAL, INTACT
ASTROGLIAL CELLS IN CULTURES AND INHIBITS THE ISOPROTERENOL-
INDUCED INCREASE IN CYCLIC-AMP PRODUCTION.
003836 04-03

ISOSORBIDE-DINITRATE
AVAILABILITY OF ISOSORBIDE-DINITRATE, DIAZEPAM AND
CHLORMETHIAZOLE, FROM I.V. DELIVERY SYSTEMS.
003558 03-16

ISOSTERES
MECHANISMS OF CHLORPROMAZINE AND CHLORPROMAZINE ISOSTERES
ON THE GLYCEMIC-RESPONSE IN MICE. (PH.D. DISSERTATION).
001525 02-03

ISOTOPE
A METHOD FOR THE DETERMINATION OF AMITRIPTYLINE AND ITS
METABOLITES NORTRIPTYLINE, 10 HYDROXYAMITRIPTYLINE, AND 10
HYDROXYNORTRIPTYLINE IN HUMAN PLASMA USING STABLE ISOTOPE
DILUTION AND GAS-CHROMATOGRAPHY CHEMICAL-IONIZATION
MASS-SPECTROMETRY.
002486 02-16

ISOTOPE-LABELED
GLC MASS-SPECTROMETRIC-DETERMINATION OF MAPROTILINE AND ITS
MAJOR METABOLITE USING STABLE ISOTOPE-LABELED ANALOG AS
INTERNAL STANDARD.
004291 04-06

ISOTOPES
STABLE ISOTOPES USED IN STUDIES OF METRIFONATE.
003847 04-03

ISOTOPIC
GAS-CHROMATOGRAPHY/MASS-SPECTROMETRY STABLE ISOTOPIC
ANALYSES FOR DEANOL, CHOLINE, AND THEIR ACETYLESTERS.
004683 04-16

ITALY
CLINICAL USE OF SULPIRIDE IN ITALY.
002187 02-11
PSYCHOTROPIC-DRUGS AND PSYCHIATRIC-HOSPITAL ADMISSIONS IN
VERONA, ITALY.
004717 04-17

JAIL
THE USE OF MINOR-TRANQUILIZERS WITH JAIL INMATES.
003308 03-11

JAPAN
MULTIINSTITUTIONAL-STUDY ON THE TERATOGENICITY AND FETAL
TOXICITY OF ANTIEPILEPTIC-DRUGS: A REPORT OF A COLLABORATIVE-
STUDY GROUP IN JAPAN.
002442 02-15

JAW
SENSORY AND ASSOCIATIVE-EFFECTS OF LSD ON CLASSICAL APPETITIVE-
CONDITIONING OF THE RABBIT JAW MOVEMENT RESPONSE.
001637 02-04

JEJUNAL-FLUID
OPIATE-RECEPTOR MEDIATED INHIBITION OF RAT JEJUNAL-FLUID
SECRETION.
001334 02-03

JESENIK
PSYCHOPHARMACOLOGY AFTER 20 YEARS OF CONFERENCES IN JESENIK.
003646 03-17

JOB-SATISFACTION
JOB-SATISFACTION IN GENERAL-PRACTICE: IMPLICATIONS FOR
PRESCRIBING.
002579 02-17

JOINT-EFFECTS
JOINT-EFFECTS OF D-AMPHETAMINE AND ETHANOL OR PENTOBARBITAL
IN PIGEONS.
000403 01-04

JUDGMENTS
PUBLIC JUDGMENTS ON THE IMPORTANCE OF VALIUM INFORMATION.
003590 03-17

JUMPING
REDUCTION IN THE NUMBER OF SEROTONIN-RECEPTORS IN THE
BRAINSTEM OF MORPHINE-DEPENDENT RATS: RELATION TO BLOCKADE
OF NALOXONE PRECIPITATED JUMPING BY SEROTONIN AGONISTS.
000258 01-03

JUNCTURES
STATISTICAL ANALYSES OF PHYSIOLOGIC DATA FROM FEMALE PATIENTS
WITH AN ENDOMORPHOUS DEPRESSIVE COURSE: A TRIAL,
INTERACTIONS BETWEEN PHYSIOLOGIC PARAMETERS, TEST JUNCTURES
IN THIS PHASE.
003251 03-09

JUVENILE
IN UTERO ALCOHOL HEIGHTENS JUVENILE REACTIVITY.
000510 01-05

K
CAFFEINE BLOCKS THE DELAYED K OUTWARD-CURRENT OF MOLLUSCAN
NEURONS.
003834 04-03

K-ENRICHED
THE ROLE OF INTRANEURONAL 5 HT AND OF TRYPTOPHAN-
HYDROXYLASE ACTIVATION IN THE CONTROL OF 5 HT SYNTHESIS IN
RAT-BRAIN SLICES INCUBATED IN K-ENRICHED MEDIUM.
000123 01-03

K-EVOKED
GABA AND BACLOFEN POTENTIATE THE K-EVOKED RELEASE OF
METHIONINE-ENKEPHALIN FROM RAT STRIATAL SLICES.
002882 03-03

KAINATE
DIFFERENTIATION OF KAINATE AND QUISQUALATE-RECEPTORS IN THE
CAT SPINAL-CORD BY SELECTIVE ANTAGONISMS WITH GAMMA
D(AND L) GLUTAMYLGLYCINE.
002696 03-03
KAINATE LESION DISSOCIATES STRIATAL DOPAMINE-RECEPTOR
RADIOLIGAND BINDING-SITES.
002803 03-03

KAINIC-ACID
CORTICAL NEUROCHEMICAL CHANGES AFTER INTRASTRIATAL INJECTION
OF KAINIC-ACID.
000133 01-03
ANTAGONISM OF INTRASTRIATAL AND INTRAVENOUS KAINIC-ACID BY 1
NUCIFERINE: COMPARISON WITH VARIOUS ANTICONVULSANTS AND
GABAMIMETICS.
000188 01-03
SYSTEMIC DIPIPERIDINOETHANE MIMICS THE CONVULSANT AND
NEUROTOXIC-ACTIONS OF KAINIC-ACID.
000222 01-03
EFFECTS OF ANTICONVULSANTS AND GLUTAMATE ANTAGONISTS ON THE
CONVULSIVE ACTION OF KAINIC-ACID.
000288 01-03

PRESYNAPTIC DOPAMINE-RECEPTORS: INSENSITIVITY TO KAINIC-ACID
AND THE DEVELOPMENT OF SUPERSENSITIVITY FOLLOWING CHRONIC
HALOPERIDOL.
001117 02-03
TWO CONDUCTANCE MECHANISMS ACTIVATED BY APPLICATIONS OF L
GLUTAMIC-ACID, L ASPARTIC-ACID, DL HOMOCYSTEIC-ACID, N
METHYL-D-ASPARTIC-ACID, AND DL KAINIC-ACID TO CULTURED
MAMMALIAN CENTRAL NEURONES.
001349 02-03
DECREASE OF GAD IMMUNOREACTIVE NERVE TERMINALS IN THE
SUBSTANTIA-NIGRA AFTER KAINIC-ACID LESION OF THE STRIATUM.
(UNPUBLISHED PAPER).
001400 02-03
EFFECTS OF KAINIC-ACID ON BODY-TEMPERATURE OF RATS: ROLE OF
CATECHOLAMINERGIC AND SEROTONERGIC SYSTEMS.
001515 02-03
THE STRIATONIGRAL GABA PATHWAY: FUNCTIONAL AND
NEUROCHEMICAL CHARACTERISTICS IN RATS WITH UNILATERAL
STRIATAL KAINIC-ACID LESIONS.
001816 02-04
LOCAL AND DISTANT NEURONAL DEGENERATION FOLLOWING
INTRASTRIATAL INJECTION OF KAINIC-ACID.
001885 02-06
DIFFERENTIAL-EFFECTS OF KAINIC-ACID ON BENZODIAZEPINE-RECEPTORS,
GABA-RECEPTORS, AND GABA-MODULIN IN THE CEREBELLAR-CORTEX.
002477 02-16
EFFECT OF KAINIC-ACID LESIONS ON MUSCARINIC AGONIST RECEPTOR
SUBTYPES IN RAT STRIATUM.
002679 03-03
KAINIC-ACID INDUCED LESION OF RAT RETINA: DIFFERENTIAL-EFFECT ON
CYCLIC-GMP AND BENZODIAZEPINE-RECEPTORS AND GABA-
RECEPTORS.
002743 03-03
KAINIC-ACID AND NEUROTRANSMITTER INTERACTIONS IN THE BASAL
GANGLIA.
002824 03-03
KAINIC-ACID NEUROTOXICITY AND SEIZURES.
002939 03-03
CHANGES OF ELECTRORETINOGRAM AND NEUROCHEMICAL ASPECTS OF
GABAERGIC NEURONS OF RETINA AFTER INTRAOCULAR INJECTION OF
KAINIC-ACID IN RATS.
003807 04-03
IONTOPHORESIS OF KAINIC-ACID.
004294 04-06

KAINIC-ACID-INDUCED
BODY-WEIGHT, FEEDING, AND DRINKING-BEHAVIORS IN RATS WITH
KAINIC-ACID-INDUCED LESIONS OF STRIATAL NEURONS -- WITH A
NOTE ON BODY-WEIGHT SYMPTOMATOLOGY IN HUNTINGTONS-
DISEASE.
000463 01-04
KAINIC-ACID-INDUCED WET-DOG-SHAKES IN RATS: THE RELATION TO
CENTRAL NEUROTRANSMITTERS.
001685 02-04
EFFECTS OF MORPHINE AND NALORPHINE ON KAINIC-ACID-INDUCED
HYPOTHERMIA IN RATS.
002921 03-03

KAPPA-RECEPTOR
3H ETHYLKETOCYCLAZOCINE BINDING: LACK OF EVIDENCE FOR A
SEPARATE KAPPA-RECEPTOR IN RAT CNS.
000128 01-03

KAPPA-RECEPTORS
MET-ENKEPHALIN-ARG6-PHE7 INTERACTS WITH THE KAPPA-RECEPTORS
ON GUINEA-PIG ILEUM.
001110 02-03
SPECIFIC, HIGH-AFFINITY (3H)ETHYLKETOCYCLAZOCINE BINDING IN RAT
CENTRAL-NERVOUS-SYSTEM: LACK OF EVIDENCE FOR KAPPA-
RECEPTORS.
003840 04-03

KENAZEPINE
IN VIVO EFFECTS OF TWO NOVEL ALKYLATING BENZODIAZEPINE,
IRAZEPINE AND KENAZEPINE,
004251 04-04

KETAMINE
STRAIN DEPENDENT EFFECTS OF KETAMINE ON LOCOMOTOR-ACTIVITY
AND ANTINOCICEPTION IN MICE.
000382 01-04
KETAMINE: CONVULSANT OR ANTICONVULSANT?
003060 03-04
CHANGES IN GAMMA AMINOBUTYRIC-ACID SHUNT ENZYMES IN
REGIONS OF RAT-BRAIN WITH KETAMINE ANESTHESIA.
003891 04-03
PROPERTIES OF THE OPTICAL-ISOMERS AND METABOLITES OF KETAMINE
ON THE HIGH-AFFINITY TRANSPORT AND CATABOLISM OF
MONOAMINES.
004009 04-03

KETAZOLAM
KETAZOLAM AND DIAZEPAM IN ANXIETY: A CONTROLLED-STUDY.
000655 01-10

DOUBLE-BLIND COMPARISON OF KETAZOLAM, DIAZEPAM AND PLACEBO IN ONCE-A-DAY VS T.I.D. DOSING.
000660 01-11

DOUBLE-BLIND COMPARISON OF KETAZOLAM AND PLACEBO USING ONCE-A-DAY DOSING.
002067 02-10

KETAZOLAM COMPARED TO DIAZEPAM AND PLACEBO IN THE TREATMENT OF ANXIETY.
002074 02-10

KETONES

SYNTHESIS OF POTENTIAL ANTICONVULSANTS: CONDENSATION OF ISATINS WITH ACETONE AND RELATED KETONES.
003699 04-02

KHAT

RELATIVE POTENCIES OF TWO PHENYLALKYLAMINES FOUND IN THE ABUSED PLANT CATHA-EDULIS, KHAT.
001084 02-02

HYPERTHERMIC-RESPONSE TO (-) CATHINONE, AN ALKALOID OF CATHA-EDULIS (KHAT).
003694 04-02

KHAT-LEAVES

A CONSTITUENT OF KHAT-LEAVES WITH AMPHETAMINE-LIKE RELEASING PROPERTIES.
001307 02-03

KIDNEY

LITHIUM AND THE KIDNEY.
002244 02-13

RECENT DEVELOPMENTS IN LITHIUM TREATMENT: IS IT DANGEROUS FOR THE KIDNEY?
002465 02-15

THE INTERACTION OF 2,3,4 TRIHYDROXYBENZYLHYDRAZINE WITH DOPA-DECARBOXYLASE FROM PIG KIDNEY.
002925 03-03

LITHIUM PROPHYLAXIS AND THE KIDNEY.
003463 03-15

LITHIUM-CARBONATE AND THE KIDNEY.
003478 03-15

LITHIUM AND THE KIDNEY SCARE.
003534 03-15

PREJUNCTIONAL ACTIONS OF PIRIBEDIL ON THE ISOLATED KIDNEY OF THE RABBIT: COMPARISON WITH APOMORPHINE.
003749 04-03

A COMPARISON OF THE RESPONSES TO SOME DOPAMINE-RECEPTOR AGONISTS AND ANTAGONISTS IN THE ISOLATED PERFUSED RAT KIDNEY.
004054 04-03

KIDNEY FUNCTION IN PATIENTS WITH AFFECTIVE-DISORDERS WITH AND WITHOUT LITHIUM THERAPY.
004664 04-15

KIDS

ASTHMA THERAPY MAY UNDERCUT KIDS AT SCHOOL.
004475 04-11

KINDERGARTEN-AGED

EVALUATION OF THE RELATIVE EFFECTIVENESS OF METHYLPHENIDATE AND COGNITIVE BEHAVIOR-MODIFICATION IN THE TREATMENT OF KINDERGARTEN-AGED HYPERACTIVE-CHILDREN.
003306 03-11

KINDLED

LOCOMOTOR AND CONVULSIVE RESPONSES TO PICROTOXIN IN AMYGDALA KINDLED RATS.
000416 01-04

BARBITURATE SERUM LEVELS AND PROTECTION AGAINST KINDLED AMYGDALOID SEIZURES IN THE RAT.
001559 02-04

PHARMACOLOGICAL MODIFICATION OF AMYGDALOID KINDLED SEIZURES.
001588 02-04

THE ANTICONVULSANT PROPERTIES OF MELATONIN ON KINDLED SEIZURES IN RATS.
002653 03-03

CUMULATIVE AFTERDISCHARGE AS THE PRINCIPAL FACTOR IN THE ACQUISITION OF KINDLED SEIZURES.
002862 03-03

VALPROIC-ACID SERUM LEVELS AND PROTECTION AGAINST KINDLED AMYGDALOID SEIZURES IN THE RAT.
002946 03-04

THE EFFECTS OF VARIOUS ANESTHETICS ON AMYGDALOID KINDLED SEIZURES.
002959 03-04

EFFECTS OF 3 SULFAMOYLMETHYL-BENZISOXAZOLE (AD-810) AND SOME ANTIEPILEPTICS ON THE KINDLED SEIZURES IN THE NEOCORTEX, HIPPOCAMPUS AND AMYGDALA IN RATS.
004149 04-04

SEROTONERGIC MECHANISM IN SEIZURES KINDLED FROM THE RABBIT AMYGDALA.
004227 04-04

EFFECT OF COCAINE AND LIDOCAINE ON THE EXPRESSION OF KINDLED SEIZURES IN THE RAT.
004233 04-04

KINDLING

EFFECTS OF KINDLING OR BRAIN-STIMULATION ON PENTYLENETETRAZOL-INDUCED CONVULSION SUSCEPTIBILITY.
000037 01-03

MODIFICATION OF DOPAMINERGIC-RECEPTOR SENSITIVITY IN RAT-BRAIN AFTER AMYGDALOID KINDLING.
000106 01-03

THE ROLE OF BIOGENIC-AMINES IN AMYGDALAR KINDLING. I. LOCAL AMYGDALAR AFTERDISCHARGE.
000327 01-03

BEHAVIORAL-ANALYSIS OF AMYGDALOID KINDLING IN BEAGLE-DOGS AND THE EFFECTS OF CLONAZEPAM, DIAZEPAM, PHENOBARBITAL, DIPHENYLHYDANTOIN, AND FLUNARIZINE ON SEIZURE MANIFESTATION.
000496 01-04

NALOXONE FACILITATES AMYGDALOID KINDLING IN RATS.
001644 02-04

CHRONOLOGICAL ELECTROENCEPHALOGRAPHIC AND NEUROPHARMACOLOGICAL-STUDY IN CORTICAL KINDLING RABBITS.
002761 03-03

THE EFFECT OF AMYGDALA KINDLING ON SPONTANEOUS AND COCAINE-INDUCED MOTOR-ACTIVITY AND LIDOCAINE SEIZURES.
003067 03-04

A REFORMULATION OF THE DUAL-ACTION MODEL OF OPIOID DEPENDENCE: OPIOID-SPECIFIC NEURONAL KINDLING.
003645 03-17

KINETIC

SEROTONIN-SENSITIVE ADENYLATE-CYCLASE AND (3H)SEROTONIN BINDING-SITES IN THE CNS OF THE RAT -- I. KINETIC PARAMETERS AND PHARMACOLOGICAL-PROPERTIES.
000213 01-03

INTRAVENOUS PHENOBARBITAL THERAPY IN BARBITURATE AND OTHER HYPNOSEDATIVE WITHDRAWAL REACTIONS: A KINETIC APPROACH.
000703 01-11

KINETIC DATA ON THE INHIBITION OF HIGH-AFFINITY CHOLINE TRANSPORT INTO RAT-FOREBRAIN SYNAPTOSOMES BY CHOLINE-LIKE COMPOUNDS AND NITROGEN-MUSTARD ANALOGUES.
002879 03-03

PHYSICAL AND KINETIC PROPERTIES OF CHOLINE-ACETYL-TRANSFERASE FROM RAT AND BOVINE BRAIN.
003676 04-01

UPTAKE OF RADIOCALCIUM BY NERVE-ENDINGS ISOLATED FROM RAT-BRAIN: KINETIC STUDIES.
003814 04-03

STUDIES ON THE KINETIC PROPERTIES OF TRYPTOPHAN-HYDROXYLASE OF RABBIT MESENCEPHALON AND PONS-MEDULLA: EFFECT OF LONG-TERM-TREATMENT WITH NEUROLEPTICS AND ANTIDEPRESSANTS.
003852 04-03

KINETIC STUDIES ON THE ENTRY OF D-AMPHETAMINE INTO THE CENTRAL-NERVOUS-SYSTEM: I. CEREBROSPINAL-FLUID.
004005 04-03

THE USE OF CLINICAL KINETIC DATA IN TREATMENT WITH ANTIDEPRESSANT-DRUGS.
004686 04-16

KINETICS

NONLINEAR REGRESSION ANALYSIS OF NOREPINEPHRINE RESPONSE KINETICS IN CEREBRAL VASCULATURE.
000256 01-03

INFLUENCE OF GLUCOSE (IN VIVO OR IN VITRO) ON DURATION OF NARCOTIC ANALGESICS AND ON THE KINETICS OF DRUG METABOLISM.
000292 01-03

EFFECT OF DESMETHYLIMIPRAMINE ON THE KINETICS OF CHLORPHENTERMINE ACCUMULATION IN ISOLATED PERFUSED RAT LUNG.
000524 01-05

EFFECTS OF AGE AND OTHER DRUGS ON BENZODIAZEPINE KINETICS.
000681 01-11

LORAZEPAM KINETICS IN THE ELDERLY.
000766 01-13

EFFECTS OF THREE ANTIBIOTICS ON THEOPHYLLINE KINETICS.
000784 01-13

THE INFLUENCE OF PENTIFYLLINE AND THEOPHYLLINE ON REACTION KINETICS OF CATECHOLAMINE STIMULATED ATPASE FROM RAT-BRAIN.
001052 02-01

KINETICS OF CENTRAL-ACTIONS OF ISOFLOXYTHEPIN, AN ORAL NEUROLEPTIC-DRUG WITH PROLONGED ACTION IN RODENTS.
001720 02-04

PHENYTOIN KINETICS IN CHILDREN.
002113 02-11

BIOAVAILABILITY AND KINETICS OF MAPROTILINE.
002204 02-13

KINETICS AND NEUROPSYCHOLOGIC-EFFECTS OF IV DIAZEPAM IN THE PRESENCE AND ABSENCE OF ITS ACTIVE N DESMETHYL METABOLITE IN HUMANS.
002229 02-13

FACTORS INFLUENCING NORTRIPTYLINE STEADY-STATE KINETICS: PLASMA AND SALIVA LEVELS.
002251 02-13

AN EVALUATION OF MAPROTILINE INTRAVENOUS KINETICS AND
COMPARISON OF TWO ORAL DOSES.
002497 02-16
LITHIUM KINETICS DURING HEMODIALYSIS IN A PATIENT WITH LITHIUM
POISONING.
003524 03-15
ON THE KINETICS OF IMIPRAMINE AND RELATED ANTIDEPRESSANTS.
003945 04-03
DESMETHYLDIAZEPAM KINETICS IN THE ELDERLY AFTER ORAL
PRAZEPAM.
004432 04-11
EFFECT OF NOREPINEPHRINE UPTAKE BLOCKERS ON NOREPINEPHRINE
KINETICS.
004506 04-13
KINETICS AND BIOTRANSFORMATION OF LORMETAZEPAM: II.
RADIOIMMUNOLOGIC DETERMINATIONS IN PLASMA AND URINE OF
YOUNG AND ELDERLY SUBJECTS: FIRST-PASS EFFECT.
004516 04-13
CONCENTRATIONS AND KINETICS OF CARBAMAZEPINE IN WHOLE
SALIVA, PAROTID SALIVA, SERUM ULTRAFILTRATE, AND SERUM.
004545 04-13
KINETICS OF A CARBAMAZEPINE-ETHOSUXIMIDE INTERACTION.
004558 04-13
THE KINETICS OF PSYCHIATRIC-DRUGS.
004739 04-17

KLEINE-LEVIN-SYNDROME
LITHIUM TREATMENT OF THE KLEINE-LEVIN-SYNDROME.
003390 03-11

KNOWLEDGE
A CONTRIBUTION TO OUR KNOWLEDGE OF COCA-LEAF CONTENT
SUBSTANCES.
001022 02-01

KUGELBERG-WELANDER
THE USE OF LITHIUM-CARBONATE FOR TREATING KUGELBERG-WELANDER
SPINAL AMYOTROPHY PATIENTS.
003326 03-11

L-AMPHETAMINE
5 HT BLOCKADE AND THE STIMULANT-EFFECTS OF D-AMPHETAMINE AND
L-AMPHETAMINE: NO INTERACTION IN SELF-STIMULATION OF
PREFRONTAL-CORTEX, HYPOTHALAMUS, OR DORSAL TEGMENTUM.
UNEXPECTED LETHALITY IN HIPPOCAMPAL SITES.
000387 01-04

L-DOPA
THE EFFECTS OF RESERPINE, IPRONIAZID AND L-DOPA ON ELECTRICALLY-
INDUCED SPINAL-CORD SEIZURES.
000146 01-03
DECARBOXYLATION OF EXOGENOUS L-DOPA IN RAT STRIATUM AFTER
LESIONS OF THE DOPAMINERGIC NIGROSTRIATAL NEURONS: THE ROLE
OF STRIATAL CAPILLARIES.
000202 01-03
FUNCTIONAL AND STRUCTURAL CONSEQUENCES OF LONG-TERM DIETARY
L-DOPA TREATMENT IN MICE.
000257 01-03
EFFECTS OF L-DOPA AND L 5 HYDROXYTRYPTOPHAN ON LOCOMOTOR-
ACTIVITY OF THE RAT AFTER SELECTIVE OR COMBINED DESTRUCTION
OF CENTRAL CATECHOLAMINE AND SEROTONIN NEURONS.
000466 01-04
THREE CASES OF UNIPOLAR DELUSIONAL DEPRESSION RESPONSIVE TO L-
DOPA.
000628 01-09
ANTIDEPRESSIVE TREATMENT IN PARKINSONS-DISEASE: A CONTROLLED-
TRIAL OF THE EFFECT OF NORTRIPTYLINE IN PATIENTS WITH
PARKINSONS-DISEASE TREATED WITH L-DOPA.
000659 01-11
THE LONG-TERM RESULTS OF STEREOTAXIC SURGERY AND L-DOPA
THERAPY IN PATIENTS WITH PARKINSONS-DISEASE: A 10-YEAR
FOLLOWUP STUDY.
000693 01-11
THE TREATMENT OF PARKINSONS-DISEASE USING A COMBINATION OF L-
DOPA AND DECARBOXYLASE INHIBITORS (CARBIDOPA, BENSERASIDE).
A CLINICAL AND BIOCHEMICAL COMPARATIVE INVESTIGATION.
000712 01-11
L-DOPA ENHANCES ACQUISITION OF AN INHIBITORY AVOIDANCE
RESPONSE.
001711 02-04
TWO NEW DRUGS MAY PICK UP WHERE L-DOPA LEAVES OFF.
001897 02-07
COMPARATIVE-STUDIES OF L-DOPA ALONE AND COMBINATION WITH A
PERIPHERAL DOPA-DECARBOXYLASE INHIBITOR, BENSERAZIDE-HCL, ON
PARKINSONS-DISEASE – PART II: PHARMACOKINETIC-STUDY.
002309 02-13
INDIVIDUAL VARIATIONS IN THE EFFECTS OF FLURAZEPAM,
CLORAZEPATE, L-DOPA AND THYROTROPIN-RELEASING-HORMONE ON
REM SLEEP IN MAN.
002349 02-14
THE DIFFERENTIAL NEUROCHEMICAL-BASES OF THE BEHAVIOURS ELICITED
BY SEROTONERGIC-AGENTS AND BY THE COMBINATION OF A
MONOAMINE-OXIDASE-INHIBITOR AND L-DOPA.
002976 03-04

CLINICAL SIGNIFICANCE OF PYRIDOXINE ADMINISTRATION IN L-DOPA
THERAPY OF PARKINSONISM.
003345 03-11
REDUCTION IN THE LEVEL OF IMMUNOTITRATABLE DOPAMINE-BETA-
HYDROXYLASE AFTER CHRONIC ADMINISTRATION OF L-DOPA OR
ALPHA METHYLDOPA.
003764 D4-03
PHARMACOLOGICAL DIFFERENCE OF L-DOPA, APOMORPHINE, AND
BROMOCRIPTINE AGAINST METOCLOPRAMIDE.
003790 04-03
AUTORADIOGRAPHIC STUDIES ON DISTRIBUTION OF L-3,4
DIHYDROXYPHENYLALANINE (L-DOPA) 14C AND L 5
HYDROXYTRYPTOPHAN (L 5 HTP) 14C IN THE CAT BRAIN.
003941 04-03
DECREASE OF NORADRENALINE O METHYLATION IN RAT-BRAIN INDUCED
BY L-DOPA. REVERSAL EFFECT OF S ADENOSYL-L-METHIONINE.
004019 04-03
EFFECTS OF NARCOTIC ANTAGONISTS ON L-DOPA REVERSAL OF
RESERPINE-INDUCED CATALEPSY AND BLEPHAROPTOSIS IN MICE.
004186 04-04
A CONTROLLED-STUDY OF L-DOPA IN SCHIZOPHRENIA WITH REFERENCE
TO THE THEORY OF DOPAMINERGIC-RECEPTOR HYPERSENSITIVITY.
004312 04-08
ASSESSING L-DOPA THERAPY FOR PARKINSONS.
004465 04-11
PROBLEMS OF TREATING DEFORMING MYODYSTONIA WITH L-DOPA,
AND PREDICTION OF ITS THERAPEUTIC EFFECT.
004536 04-13

L-DOPA-INDUCED
IMPROVEMENT OF L-DOPA-INDUCED DYSKINESIA AND OF ON-OFF-
PHENOMENON BY BROMOCRIPTINE.
000813 01-14
EXPERIMENTAL-STUDIES ON L-DOPA-INDUCED DYSKINESIA.
003129 03-05
STUDIES ON THE MECHANISMS OF L-DOPA-INDUCED SALIVARY
SECRETION.
003130 03-05

L-DOPAS
L-DOPAS MECHANISM-OF-ACTION IN PARKINSONS-DISEASE.
003323 03-11

L-ISOMERS
COMPARATIVE-STUDIES OF THE PHARMACOLOGICAL-EFFECTS OF THE D-
ISOMERS AND L-ISOMERS OF CODEINE.
004084 04-03

LABEL
DOES (3H)SPIROPERIDOL LABEL A 5 HT-RECEPTOR IN THE FRONTAL-
CORTEX OF THE RAT?.
000206 01-03
DOES HIGH-AFFINITY (3H) IMIPRAMINE BINDING LABEL SEROTONIN
REUPTAKE SITES IN BRAIN AND PLATELET?
003962 04-03
BACLOFEN IN THE TREATMENT OF TARDIVE-DYSKINESIA: OPEN LABEL
STUDY.
004619 04-15
CLOPIPAZAN (SKF-69634), A NEW NEUROLEPTIC ESSENTIALLY FREE OF
EXTRAPYRAMIDAL LIABILITY: QUANTITATIVE PHARMACOEEG AND
OPEN LABEL CLINICAL-TRIAL.
004620 04-15

LABELED
HISTAMINE H1-RECEPTORS LABELED IN VIVO: ANTIDEPRESSANT AND
ANTIHISTAMINE INTERACTIONS.
000074 01-03
ABSORPTION OF 14C LABELED METHADONE BY PORTAL AND
EXTRAPORTAL VENOUS CIRCULATIONS FOLLOWING INTRAPERITONEAL
AND INTRODUODENAL ADMINISTRATION.
000094 01-03
REGULATION OF SEROTONIN2-RECEPTORS (5 HT2) LABELED WITH
(3H)SPIROPERIDOL BY CHRONIC-TREATMENT WITH THE
ANTIDEPRESSANT AMITRIPTYLINE.
003964 04-03

LABELING
DEMONSTRATION OF SUBSTANCE-P IN AORTIC NERVE AFFERENT FIBERS
BY COMBINED USE OF FLOURESCENT RETROGRADE NEURONAL
LABELING AND IMMUNOCYTOCHEMISTRY. (UNPUBLISHED PAPER).
001024 02-01
BENZODIAZEPINE-RECEPTOR: LOCALIZATION BY PHOTOAFFINITY
LABELING AND ISOLATION OF A POSSIBLE ENDOGENOUS LIGAND.
001381 02-03
RADIORECEPTOR LABELING OF PRESYNAPTIC AND POSTSYNAPTIC
DOPAMINE-RECEPTORS.
001511 02-03
ADENOSINE-RECEPTORS IN RAT TESTES: LABELING WITH 3H
CYCLOHEXYLADENOSINE.
002835 03-03
(3H)MIANSERIN: DIFFERENTIAL LABELING OF SEROTONIN AND
HISTAMINE-RECEPTORS IN RAT-BRAIN.
002860 03-03

HUMAN PLATELET ALPHA2-ADRENERGIC-RECEPTORS: LABELING WITH 3H YOHIMBINE, A SELECTIVE ANTAGONIST LIGAND.
004676 04-16

LABELLED
ESR STUDIES OF SPIN LABELLED BOVINE LIVER MONOAMINE-OXIDASE-B. (UNPUBLISHED PAPER).
001065 02-01
FACTORS INFLUENCING THE RELEASE OF LABELLED GAMMA AMINOBUTYRIC-ACID AND ACETYLCHOLINE EVOKED BY ELECTRICAL-STIMULATION WITH ALTERNATING POLARITY FROM RAT CORTICAL SLICES.
001130 02-03
INDICATIONS FOR A BRAIN UPTAKE OF LABELLED VASOPRESSIN AND OCYTOCIN AND THE PROBLEM OF THE BLOOD-BRAIN-BARRIER.
003669 04-01

LABELLING
FALSE LABELLING OF COMMERCIALLY-AVAILABLE 3H CATECHOLAMINES?
000535 01-06
NOREPINEPHRINE METABOLISM IN MAN USING DEUTERIUM LABELLING: 4 HYDROXY-3-METHOXYMANDELIC-ACID.
004534 04-13

LABORATORY
TESTOSTERONE AND PERSISTENCE OF SOCIAL INVESTIGATION IN LABORATORY RATS.
000488 01-04
CLINICAL AND LABORATORY DIAGNOSTICS APPLICATIONS IN DEPRESSION. (UNPUBLISHED PAPER).
000588 01-09
THE CLINICAL-EFFICACY OF CLOZAPINE AS COMPARED TO LABORATORY PARAMETERS.
001955 02-08
THE URBAN EPIDEMIC OF PHENCYCLIDINE USE: LABORATORY EVIDENCE FROM A PUBLIC PSYCHIATRIC-HOSPITAL INPATIENT-SERVICE.
003554 03-16
CONSISTENCY IN CATECHOLAMINE EXCRETION IN LABORATORY AND NATURAL SETTINGS: CORRELATIONAL AND VARIANCE COMPONENTS ANALYSES.
004508 04-13
EFFECTS OF SUPIDIMIDE (CG-3033) ON OBJECTIVE AND SUBJECTIVE SLEEP PARAMETERS (A SLEEP LABORATORY STUDY).
004567 04-14
THERAPEUTIC MONITORING OF PLASMA CONCENTRATIONS OF TRICYCLIC-ANTIDEPRESSANTS: PERSPECTIVE OF THE CLINICAL LABORATORY.
004681 04-16

LACTATION
ERGOT DRUGS SUPPRESS PLASMA PROLACTIN AND LACTATION BUT NOT AGGRESSION IN PARTURIENT MICE.
003159 03-07

LACTIC-ACIDEMIA
REVERSIBLE ALEXIA, MITOCHONDRIAL MYOPATHY, AND LACTIC-ACIDEMIA.
000723 01-11

LAFORA-BODIES
TRANSIENT-EFFECT OF L TRYPTOPHAN IN PROGRESSIVE MYOCLONUS EPILEPSY WITHOUT LAFORA-BODIES: CLINICAL-STUDY AND ELECTROPHYSIOLOGICAL-STUDY.
000694 01-11

LAMINAE
THE STEREOSPECIFIC EFFECT OF NALOXONE ON RAT DORSAL-HORN NEURONES; INHIBITION IN SUPERFICIAL LAMINAE AND EXCITATION IN DEEPER LAMINAE.
001226 02-03

LAMINAR
LAMINAR DISTRIBUTION OF PUTATIVE NEUROTRANSMITTER AMINO-ACIDS AND LIGAND BINDING-SITES IN THE DOG OLFACTORY-BULB.
002836 03-03

LANTHANUM
NALOXONE REVERSIBLE DUPLICATION BY LANTHANUM OF OPIATE ANALGESIA EFFECTS ON OROFACIAL, LOWER BODY AND CENTRAL NOCICEPTION.
003028 03-04

LARGE-DOSES
LARGE-DOSES OF VITAMINS AND BEHAVIORAL-CONSEQUENCES. (PH.D. DISSERTATION).
001633 02-04
LARGE-DOSES OF DIBENZEPINE NOVERIL IN THE TREATMENT OF DEPRESSIVE-STATES.
002020 02-09

LARGE-SINGLE-DOSES
USE OF LARGE-SINGLE-DOSES OF BROMOCRIPTINE IN SCHIZOPHRENIC-PATIENTS WITH ELEVATED SERUM PROLACTIN LEVELS AND EXTRAPYRAMIDAL SIDE-EFFECTS ASSOCIATED WITH NEUROLEPTIC TREATMENT.
001944 02-08

LARYNGEAL-EFFECTS
LARYNGEAL-EFFECTS OF SEROTONIN IN RABBITS.
001501 02-03

LATENCY
PROLONGATION OF THE EJACULATION LATENCY IN THE MALE RAT BY THIORIDAZINE AND CHLORIMIPRAMINE.
000335 01-04

A STUDY OF THE QUANTAL (ALL-OR-NONE) CHANGE IN REFLEX LATENCY PRODUCED BY OPIATE ANALGESICS.
000425 01-04
ACUTE AND CHRONIC OPIATE-EFFECTS ON SINGLE UNITS AND EEG OF MEDIAL THALAMUS AND HIPPOCAMPUS; A LATENCY ANALYSIS.
001344 02-03

LATENT
SELF-STIMULATION AND LOCOMOTOR CHANGES INDICATING LATENT ANTICHOLINERGIC-ACTIVITY BY AN ATYPICAL NEUROLEPTIC (THIORIDAZINE).
003560 03-16

LATERAL
FACILITATION OF RECOVERY BY PROPANTHELINE-BROMIDE AFTER LATERAL HYPOTHALAMIC DAMAGE.
000396 01-04
SYSTEMIC INSULIN DECREASES LATERAL HYPOTHALAMIC UNIT ACTIVITY.
001275 02-03
INFLUENCE OF DOPAMINERGIC-SYSTEMS ON THE LATERAL HABENULAR NUCLEUS OF THE RAT.
001365 02-03
EFFECTS OF LILLY-110140 (FLUOXETINE) ON SELF-STIMULATION BEHAVIOR IN THE DORSAL AND VENTRAL REGIONS OF THE LATERAL HYPOTHALAMUS IN THE MOUSE.
001590 02-04
APHAGIA, GASTRIC PATHOLOGY, HYPERTHERMIA, AND SENSORIMOTOR-DYSFUNCTIONS FOLLOWING LATERAL HYPOTHALAMIC LESIONS: EFFECTS OF INSULIN PRETREATMENTS.
001638 02-04
ENHANCED LATERAL HYPOTHALAMIC SELF-STIMULATION RESPONDING AFTER CHRONIC EXPOSURE TO AMPHETAMINE.
001688 02-04
A COMPARISON BETWEEN THE EFFECTS OF MORPHINE ON THE REWARDING AND AVERSIVE-PROPERTIES OF LATERAL HYPOTHALAMIC AND CENTRAL GRAY STIMULATION.
001771 02-04
APOMORPHINE; SELECTIVE INHIBITION OF THE AVERSIVE COMPONENT OF LATERAL HYPOTHALAMIC SELF-STIMULATION.
002476 02-16
INFLUENCE OF MORPHINE ON THE DISCRIMINATIVE-STIMULUS PROPERTIES OF REWARDING LATERAL HYPOTHALAMIC STIMULATION. (PH.D. DISSERTATION).
003041 03-04
EFFECTS OF ELECTROLYTIC AND 6 HYDROXYDOPAMINE LESIONS OF THE LATERAL HYPOTHALAMUS ON ROTATION EVOKED BY ELECTRICAL-STIMULATION OF THE SUBSTANTIA-NIGRA IN RATS.
003081 03-04
SENSITIVITY TO GABA OF NEURONS OF THE DORSAL AND VENTRAL LATERAL GENICULATE NUCLEI IN THE RAT.
003877 04-03

LATERALITY
HANDLING IN INFANCY, TASTE-AVERSION, AND BRAIN LATERALITY IN RATS.
000375 01-04

LATERALIZATION
SEX-DIFFERENCES IN AMPHETAMINE-ELICITED ROTATIONAL-BEHAVIOR AND THE LATERALIZATION OF STRIATAL DOPAMINE IN RATS.
000459 01-04
ACTIVATION AND LATERALIZATION OF SENSORIMOTOR FIELD FOR PERIORAL BITING-REFLEX BY INTRANIGRAL GABA AGONIST AND BY SYSTEMIC APOMORPHINE IN THE RAT.
001657 02-04

LATERALIZED
LATERALIZED DEFICITS AND DRUG INFLUENCES ON THE DICHOTIC LISTENING OF SCHIZOPHRENIC-PATIENTS.
003443 03-14

LAYERS
THE EFFECTS OF LITHIUM ON MYOINOSITOL LEVELS IN LAYERS OF FRONTAL-CEREBRAL-CORTEX, IN CEREBELLUM, AND IN CORPUS-CALLOSUM OF THE RAT.
003712 04-03

LCGU
LOCAL CEREBRAL GLUCOSE UTILIZATION (LCGU) IN RAT-BRAIN DURING HYPOXEMIA. (UNPUBLISHED PAPER).
001380 02-03

LD50
EFFECT OF AGE AND ROUTE-OF-ADMINISTRATION ON LD50 OF LITHIUM-CHLORIDE IN THE RAT.
001413 02-03

LEAD
EFFECTS OF LEAD ON MOVEMENT OF ALBUMIN INTO BRAIN.
000076 01-03
EFFECTS OF LEAD EXPOSURE DURING DEVELOPMENT ON NEOCORTICAL DENDRITIC AND SYNAPTIC STRUCTURE.
000525 01-05
LITHIUM-CHLORIDE AND DELTA9 THC LEAD TO CONDITIONED AVERSIONS IN THE PIGEON.
003003 03-04

EFFECT OF INORGANIC LEAD ON RAT-BRAIN MITOCHONDRIAL
RESPIRATION AND ENERGY PRODUCTION.
004267 04-05

LEARNED-BEHAVIOR
EFFECT OF L FUCOSE ON BRAIN PROTEIN METABOLISM AND RETENTION
OF A LEARNED-BEHAVIOR IN RATS.
001819 02-04

LEARNED-FEAR
ACTH MEDIATION OF LEARNED-FEAR: BLOCKADE BY NALOXONE AND
NALTREXONE.
001597 02-04

LEARNED-HELPLESSNESS
REVERSAL OF LEARNED-HELPLESSNESS BY IMIPRAMINE.
001751 02-04

NEUROCHEMICAL BASIS OF THE ACTION OF ANTIDEPRESSANTS ON
LEARNED-HELPLESSNESS.
001775 02-04

LEARNING
EFFECT OF BETA ENDORPHIN AND NALOXONE ON ACQUISITION,
MEMORY, AND RETRIEVAL OF SHUTTLE AVOIDANCE AND
HABITUATION LEARNING IN RATS.
000410 01-04

THE USE OF PSYCHOPHARMACOLOGICAL-PROCEDURES TO ANALYSE THE
ONTOGENY OF LEARNING AND RETENTION: ISSUES AND CONCERNS.
000482 01-04

INFLUENCE OF PYRITHIOXINE, MECLOPHENOXATE AND PIRACETAM ON
THE LEARNING PROCESS IN MAN.
000805 01-14

EFFECT OF DRUGS ON LEARNING AND MEMORY PROCESSES IN SIMPLE
BEHAVIORAL-TESTS.
000809 01-14

EFFECTS OF METHYLPHENIDATE ON LEARNING A BEGINNING READING
VOCABULARY BY NORMAL ADULTS.
000812 01-14

THE INFLUENCE OF NOOTROPIC-DRUGS ON LEARNING AND MEMORY OF
DEFENSE REACTIONS.
000815 01-14

SEROTONINMIMETIC AND ANTIDEPRESSANT-DRUGS ON PASSIVE-
AVOIDANCE LEARNING BY OLFACTORY BULBECTOMISED RATS.
001585 02-04

EFFECTS OF EXPERIMENTAL HYPOTHYROIDISM ON LEARNING IN RATS.
001587 02-04

INTRAHYPOTHALAMIC MICROINJECTIONS OF NORADRENALINE WITH AND
WITHOUT INDUCTION OF THE ALIMENTARY DRIVE AS A REWARD IN A
T-MAZE LEARNING IN RATS.
001604 02-04

INTERFERENCE WITH INGESTIONAL AVERSION LEARNING PRODUCED BY
PREEXPOSURE TO THE UNCONDITIONED-STIMULUS: ASSOCIATIVE-
ASPECTS AND NONASSOCIATIVE-ASPECTS.
001610 02-04

TWO-WAY AVOIDANCE LEARNING UNDER THE INFLUENCE OF NOOTROPIC-
DRUGS.
001647 02-04

THE INFLUENCE OF DAILY BIOLOGICAL-RHYTHMICITY ON THE HOMING-
BEHAVIOR, PSYCHOPHARMACOLOGICAL RESPONSIVENESS, LEARNING
AND RETENTION OF SUCKLING RATS. (PH.D. DISSERTATION).
001660 02-04

PIRACETAM EFFECT ON LEARNING AND MEMORY IN RATS.
001689 02-04

STRUCTURE OF VARIABILITY AND CORRELATION IN LEARNING AFTER
DRUG ADMINISTRATION.
002562 02-17

CENTRAL AND PERIPHERAL CATECHOLAMINE FUNCTION IN LEARNING
AND MEMORY PROCESSES.
002823 03-03

BRAIN MECHANISMS OF LEARNING.
002916 03-03

IMPAIRMENT OF INSTRUMENTAL LEARNING IN RATS BY GLUTAMIC-
ACID-DIETHYL-ESTER.
002993 03-04

EFFECTS OF TRICYCLIC-ANTIDEPRESSANTS ON INTERPERSONAL LEARNING.
003225 03-09

AN ANALYSIS OF VISUAL OBJECT REVERSAL LEARNING IN THE
MARMOSET AFTER AMPHETAMINE AND HALOPERIDOL.
004208 04-04

BEHAVIOR AND LEARNING DIFFICULTIES IN CHILDREN OF NORMAL
INTELLIGENCE BORN TO ALCOHOLIC MOTHERS.
004658 04-15

LEARNING-ABILITY
INFLUENCE OF NICERGOLINE ON MOLECULAR BIOLOGICAL PROCESSES IN
THE BRAIN AND LEARNING-ABILITY OF THE RAT.
000449 01-04

LEARNING-DISABILITIES
UNDERSTANDING AND USE OF CHEMOTHERAPY BY LEARNING-
DISABILITIES AND BEHAVIOR-DISORDERS TEACHERS.
000965 01-17

LEARNING-DISORDERS
EFFECT OF PIRACETAM ON EEG SPECTRA OF BOYS WITH LEARNING-
DISORDERS.
003383 03-11

LECITHIN
LECITHIN IN THE TREATMENT OF TARDIVE-DYSKINESIA.
002380 02-15

USE OF CHOLINE AND LECITHIN IN THE TREATMENT OF TARDIVE-
DYSKINESIA.
002473 02-15

LECITHIN AND MEMORY TRAINING IN ALZHEIMERS-DISEASE. (PH.D.
DISSERTATION).
003299 03-11

PHARMACOLOGIC CHARACTERIZATION AND LECITHIN TREATMENT OF A
PATIENT WITH SPONTANEOUS ORAL FACIAL DYSKINESIA AND
DEMENTIA.
003347 03-11

THE EFFECTS OF LECITHIN ON MEMORY IN PATIENTS WITH SENILE-
DEMENTIA OF THE ALZHEIMERS-TYPE.
003385 03-11

LECITHIN ADMINISTRATION IN TARDIVE-DYSKINESIA: CLINICAL AND
BIOMEDICAL-CORRELATES.
003496 03-15

LECITHIN FOR THE TREATMENT OF TARDIVE-DYSKINESIA.
004612 04-15

LECTINS
DEVELOPMENTALLY REGULATED LECTINS IN SLIME MOULDS AND CHICK
TISSUES -- ARE THEY CELL ADHESION MOLECULES?
003724 04-03

LEEDS-SLEEP-EVALUATION-QUESTIONNAIRE
THE LEEDS-SLEEP-EVALUATION-QUESTIONNAIRE IN
PSYCHOPHARMACOLOGICAL-INVESTIGATIONS -- A REVIEW.
002351 02-14

LEFT
EFFECTS OF IMIPRAMINE ON LEFT VENTRICULAR PERFORMANCE IN
CHILDREN.
002385 02-15

THE SIMULTANEOUS INFUSION OF DRUGS VIA THE LEFT AND RIGHT
VERTEBRAL-ARTERY OF THE CAT; A MODIFIED ANIMAL-MODEL FOR
THE STUDY OF POSSIBLE CENTRAL-ACTIONS OF DRUGS UPON THE
LOWER BRAINSTEM.
004297 04-06

LEGAL
MEDICAL AND LEGAL IMPLICATIONS OF SIDE-EFFECTS FROM
NEUROLEPTIC-DRUGS. A ROUND-TABLE DISCUSSION.
003471 03-15

LENNOX-GASTAUT-SYNDROME
ANTICONVULSANT-INDUCED STATUS-EPILEPTICUS IN LENNOX-GASTAUT-
SYNDROME.
003467 03-15

ANTIEPILEPTIC-EFFECT OF CLOBAZAM IN LENNOX-GASTAUT-SYNDROME.
004479 04-11

LEPTINOTARSIN
RELEASE OF ACETYLCHOLINE FROM RAT-BRAIN SYNAPTOSOMES
STIMULATED WITH LEPTINOTARSIN, A NEW NEUROTOXIN.
003148 03-06

LERGOTRILE
PSYCHIATRIC-EFFECTS OF BROMOCRIPTINE AND LERGOTRILE IN
PARKINSONIAN-PATIENTS.
002453 02-15

LESCH-NYHANS-SYNDROME
BEHAVIORAL-STUDIES AND NEUROCHEMICAL-STUDIES OF LESCH-NYHANS-
SYNDROME.
001743 02-04

SEROTONERGIC APPROACHES TO THE MODIFICATION OF BEHAVIOR IN
THE LESCH-NYHANS-SYNDROME.
004576 04-14

LESION
ABSENCE OF LITHIUM-INDUCED TASTE-AVERSION AFTER AREA-POSTREMA
LESION.
000456 01-04

DECREASE OF GAD IMMUNOREACTIVE NERVE TERMINALS IN THE
SUBSTANTIA-NIGRA AFTER KAINIC-ACID LESION OF THE STRIATUM.
(UNPUBLISHED PAPER).
001400 02-03

FORNIX LESION PREVENTS AN ORGANOPHOSPHATE-INDUCED DECREASE
IN MUSCARINIC-RECEPTOR LEVEL IN RAT HIPPOCAMPUS.
001833 02-05

KAINIC-ACID INDUCED LESION OF RAT RETINA: DIFFERENTIAL-EFFECT ON
CYCLIC-GMP AND BENZODIAZEPINE-RECEPTORS AND GABA-
RECEPTORS.
002743 03-03

KAINATE LESION DISSOCIATES STRIATAL DOPAMINE-RECEPTOR
RADIOLIGAND BINDING-SITES.
002803 03-03

LESION-INDUCED
EVOKED-POTENTIAL CHANGES IN THE SUPERIOR-COLLICULUS PARALLEL
THE LESION-INDUCED DEVELOPMENT OF GROOMING REFLEXES IN THE
CAT. (PH.D. DISSERTATION).
001179 02-03

LESIONED
EFFECTS OF CHRONIC HALOPERIDOL ON CAUDATE 3H SPIROPERIDOL
BINDING IN LESIONED RATS.
000255 01-03
CIRCLING PRODUCED BY SEROTONIN AND DOPAMINE AGONISTS IN
RAPHE LESIONED RATS: A SEROTONIN MODEL.
001783 02-04
THE RELATIONSHIP BETWEEN LOSS OF DOPAMINE NERVE TERMINALS,
STRIATAL (3H)SPIROPERIDOL BINDING AND ROTATIONAL-BEHAVIOR IN
UNILATERALLY 6 HYDROXYDOPAMINE LESIONED RATS.
004129 04-04

LESIONING
A MODEL FOR PSYCHONEUROENDOCRINE INVESTIGATION: SPECIFIC
CHEMICAL LESIONING OF THE MEDIAN-EMINENCE.
001478 02-03

LESIONS
FUNCTIONAL HYPERINNERVATION OF CEREBRAL-CORTEX BY
NORADRENERGIC NEURONS RESULTS FROM FETAL LESIONS: PARALLELS
WITH SCHIZOPHRENIA.
000059 01-03
DECARBOXYLATION OF EXOGENOUS L-DOPA IN RAT STRIATUM AFTER
LESIONS OF THE DOPAMINERGIC NIGROSTRIATAL NEURONS; THE ROLE
OF STRIATAL CAPILLARIES.
000202 01-03
ENHANCED SUPPRESSION OF CONDITIONED AVOIDANCE RESPONSE BY
HALOPERIDOL BUT NOT PHENOXYBENZAMINE IN RATS WITH
BILATERAL PARAFASCICULAR LESIONS.
000334 01-04
ROTATIONAL-BEHAVIOR INDUCED BY COCAINE ANALOGS IN RATS WITH
UNILATERAL 6 HYDROXYDOPAMINE LESIONS OF THE SUBSTANTIA-
NIGRA: DEPENDENCE UPON DOPAMINE UPTAKE INHIBITION.
000404 01-04
BODY-WEIGHT, FEEDING, AND DRINKING-BEHAVIORS IN RATS WITH
KAINIC-ACID-INDUCED LESIONS OF STRIATAL NEURONS -- WITH A
NOTE ON BODY-WEIGHT SYMPTOMATOLOGY IN HUNTINGTONS-
DISEASE.
000463 01-04
EFFECTS OF RAPHE-MAGNUS AND RAPHE-PALLIDUS LESIONS ON
MORPHINE-INDUCED ANALGESIA AND SPINAL-CORD MONOAMINES.
001420 02-03
UNILATERAL 5,7 DIHYDROXYTRYPTAMINE LESIONS OF THE DORSAL
RAPHE NUCLEUS (DRN) AND RAT ROTATIONAL-BEHAVIOUR.
001578 02-04
5,7 DIHYDROXYTRYPTAMINE LESIONS OF THE AMYGDALA REDUCE
AMPHETAMINE-INDUCED AND APOMORPHINE-INDUCED STEREOTYPED-
BEHAVIOUR IN THE RAT.
001589 02-04
MALE RAT SEXUAL-BEHAVIOR COMPARED AFTER 6 OHDA AND
ELECTROLYTIC LESIONS IN THE DORSAL NA BUNDLE REGION OF THE
MIDBRAIN.
001593 02-04
MODULATION OF OPIATE-RECEPTOR BINDING IN STRIATUM AND
AMYGDALA BY SELECTIVE MESENCEPHALIC LESIONS.
001629 02-04
EFFECTS OF SEROTONERGIC LESIONS ON INVESTIGATORY RESPONDING BY
RATS IN A HOLEBOARD.
001634 02-04
APHAGIA, GASTRIC PATHOLOGY, HYPERTHERMIA, AND SENSORIMOTOR-
DYSFUNCTIONS FOLLOWING LATERAL HYPOTHALAMIC LESIONS:
EFFECTS OF INSULIN PRETREATMENTS.
001638 02-04
MORPHINE-DEPENDENCE AND DOPAMINERGIC-ACTIVITY: TESTS OF
CIRCLING RESPONSES IN RATS WITH UNILATERAL NIGRAL LESIONS.
001641 02-04
THE INFLUENCE OF ANTERIOR NEOSTRIATAL LESIONS ON THE
BEHAVIOURAL-EFFECTS OF SPIROPERIDOL IN RATS.
001702 02-04
DISSOCIATION OF D-AMPHETAMINE-INDUCED LOCOMOTOR-ACTIVITY AND
STEREOTYPED-BEHAVIOUR BY LESIONS OF THE SUPERIOR-COLLICULUS.
001755 02-04
THE STRIATONIGRAL GABA PATHWAY: FUNCTIONAL AND
NEUROCHEMICAL CHARACTERISTICS IN RATS WITH UNILATERAL
STRIATAL KAINIC-ACID LESIONS.
001816 02-04
EFFECT OF KAINIC-ACID LESIONS ON MUSCARINIC AGONIST RECEPTOR
SUBTYPES IN RAT STRIATUM.
002679 03-03
THE EFFECT OF SPECIFIC BRAIN LESIONS ON THE HIGH-AFFINITY BINDING
OF GABA IN THE SUBSTANTIA-NIGRA.
002795 03-03
EFFECT OF 6 HYDROXYDOPAMINE LESIONS OF THE MEDIAL PREFRONTAL-
CORTEX ON NEUROTRANSMITTER SYSTEMS IN SUBCORTICAL SITES IN
THE RAT.
002869 03-04
EFFECTS OF ELECTROLYTIC AND 6 HYDROXYDOPAMINE LESIONS OF THE
LATERAL HYPOTHALAMUS ON ROTATION EVOKED BY ELECTRICAL-
STIMULATION OF THE SUBSTANTIA-NIGRA IN RATS.
003081 03-04
EFFECTS OF DORSOLATERAL TEGMENTAL LESIONS ON AMPHETAMINE-
INDUCED AND LITHIUM-INDUCED TASTE-AVERSIONS.
003114 03-04

RELATIONSHIP BETWEEN THE PRESENCE OF DOPAMINERGIC NEURONS
AND GABA-RECEPTORS IN SUBSTANTIA-NIGRA: EFFECTS OF LESIONS.
003797 04-03
UNIMPAIRED QUININE METABOLISM IN RATS WITH VENTROMEDIAL
HYPOTHALAMIC LESIONS.
003821 04-03
STUDIES ON AXONAL TRANSPORT IN DOPAMINERGIC NEURONS: EFFECT
OF NEUROPHARMACOLOGIC LESIONS.
003858 04-03
CHANGE IN CATECHOLAMINE SENSITIVE NA-K-ATPASE ACTIVITY IN THE
RAT STRIATUM MICROSOMES FOLLOWING ELECTROLYTIC OR 6
HYDROXYDOPAMINE-INDUCED LESIONS OF DOPAMINERGIC NEURONS.
003871 04-03
EFFECTS OF METHAMPHETAMINE ON BLOOD FLOW IN THE CAUDATE-
PUTAMEN AFTER LESIONS OF THE NIGROSTRIATAL DOPAMINERGIC
BUNDLE IN THE RAT.
003910 04-03
THE EFFECT OF DOPAMINE UPTAKE BLOCKING-AGENTS ON THE
AMPHETAMINE-INDUCED CIRCLING-BEHAVIOR IN MICE WITH
UNILATERAL NIGROSTRIATAL LESIONS.
004117 04-04
DOPAMINERGIC AGONISTS DIFFERENTIALLY AFFECT OPEN-FIELD ACTIVITY
OF RATS WITH A10 LESIONS.
004135 04-04
THE INFLUENCE OF UNILATERAL 6 HYDROXYDOPAMINE LESIONS OF THE
SUBSTANTIA-NIGRA IN THE ABSENCE OF THE TELENCEPHALON.
004197 04-04
LESIONS OF AMYGDALA, PYRIFORM CORTEX AND OTHER BRAIN
STRUCTURES DUE TO DIPIPERIDINOETHANE INTOXICATION.
004273 04-05

LETHAL
LETHAL SELF-ADMINISTRATION OF MORPHINE BY RATS.
000343 01-04

LETHALITY
5 HT BLOCKADE AND THE STIMULANT-EFFECTS OF D-AMPHETAMINE AND
L-AMPHETAMINE: NO INTERACTION IN SELF-STIMULATION OF
PREFRONTAL-CORTEX, HYPOTHALAMUS, OR DORSAL TEGMENTUM.
UNEXPECTED LETHALITY IN HIPPOCAMPAL SITES.
000387 01-04
POSSIBLE MECHANISM FOR THE ENHANCED LETHALITY OF MORPHINE IN
AGGREGATED MICE.
000437 01-04
POTENTIATION OF LETHALITY IN MICE BY COMBINATIONS OF
PENTAZOCINE AND TRIPELENNAMINE.
000529 01-05
ANTAGONISM OF INTRAVENOUS COCAINE LETHALITY IN NONHUMAN
PRIMATES.
003127 03-05

LEU-ENKEPHALIN-LIKE
EFFECT OF MORPHINE AND NALOXONE ON LEU-ENKEPHALIN-LIKE
IMMUNOREACTIVITY IN DOGS.
003894 04-03

LEUCINE
INCORPORATION OF 4.5 3H LEUCINE INTO THE LIMBIC-SYSTEM OF ICR
MICE AS A LONG-TERM EFFECT OF HALOPERIDOL APPLICATION.
000118 01-03
EFFECTS OF CENTRALLY-ADMINISTERED AND SYSTEMICALLY
ADMINISTERED L TYROSINE AND L LEUCINE ON OVARIAN FUNCTION IN
THE OLD RAT.
001180 02-03

LEUCINE-ENKEPHALIN
A FURTHER CHARACTERIZATION OF THE DIFFERENTIAL-EFFECTS OF
LEUCINE-ENKEPHALIN, METHIONINE-ENKEPHALIN AND THEIR ANALOGS
ON MORPHINE-INDUCED ANALGESIA.
000311 01-03
ANTICONVULSANTS SPECIFIC FOR PETIT-MAL ANTAGONIZE
EPILEPTOGENIC-EFFECT OF LEUCINE-ENKEPHALIN.
000477 01-04
LEUCINE-ENKEPHALIN AND METHIONINE-ENKEPHALIN PRODUCE OPPOSING
EFFECTS ON PLASMA CORTICOSTERONE LEVELS IN ETHER-STRESSED
MICE.
001245 02-03
IMMUNOHISTOCHEMICAL LOCALIZATION OF LEUCINE-ENKEPHALIN IN THE
SPINAL-CORD OF THE CAT: ENKEPHALIN-CONTAINING MARGINAL
NEURONS AND PAIN MODULATION.
002638 03-01

LEUKEMIA
IGE MEDIATED HISTAMINE RELEASE IN RAT BASOPHILIC LEUKEMIA
CELLS: RECEPTOR ACTIVATED PHOSPHOLIPID METHYLATION, CA-FLUX
AND RELEASE OF ARACHIDONIC-ACID. (UNPUBLISHED PAPER).
001188 02-03

LEUKOCYTE
AN ATTEMPT TO ASSESS THE EFFECT OF LITHIUM ON THE NEUTROPHIL
LEUKOCYTE SYSTEM IN AFFECTIVE-PSYCHOSIS.
004416 04-09

LEUKOCYTES
DRUG SENSITIVE ECTO-ATPASE IN HUMAN LEUKOCYTES.
000779 01-13

LEUKOPENIC-DISORDERS
LITHIUM-SALTS IN LEUKOPENIC-DISORDERS.
001000 01-17

LEVER-PRESSING
PIMOZIDE ATTENUATES LEVER-PRESSING FOR WATER REINFORCEMENT IN
RATS.
003000 03-04

LEVODOPA
LEVODOPA AND PRESYMPTOMATIC DETECTION OF HUNTINGTONS-
DISEASE – EIGHT-YEAR FOLLOWUP.
000950 01-17

A COMPARATIVE-STUDY OF BROMOCRIPTINE AND LEVODOPA IN
PARKINSONS-DISEASE.
002117 02-11

INCREASED RATIO OF CARBIDOPA TO LEVODOPA IN TREATMENT OF
PARKINSONS-DISEASE.
002182 02-11

DEPRENYL IN THE MANAGEMENT OF RESPONSE FLUCTUATIONS IN
PATIENTS WITH PARKINSONS-DISEASE ON LEVODOPA.
002358 02-14

LEVODOPA COMPARED WITH BROMOCRIPTINE IN THE TREATMENT OF
PARKINSONS-DISEASE.
002406 02-15

PLASMA LEVODOPA, DOPAMINE AND THERAPEUTIC RESPONSE
FOLLOWING LEVODOPA THERAPY OF PARKINSONIAN-PATIENTS.
002504 02-16

EARLY DETECTION OF HUNTINGTONS-DISEASE. BLINK REFLEX AND
LEVODOPA LOAD IN PRESYMPTOMATIC AND INCIPIENT SUBJECTS.
003311 03-11

EVIDENCE TO SUPPORT EARLY LEVODOPA THERAPY IN PARKINSON-
DISEASE.
003336 03-11

ABSORPTION OF LEVODOPA AFTER RECTAL ADMINISTRATION.
003406 03-13

COMPLICATIONS OF CHRONIC LEVODOPA THERAPY: LONG-TERM
EFFICACY OF DRUG-HOLIDAY.
003502 03-15

THE EFFECT OF CHRONIC LEVODOPA ON HALOPERIDOL-INDUCED
BEHAVIORAL-SUPERSENSITIVITY IN THE GUINEA-PIG.
004249 04-04

LEVODOPA: LONG-TERM IMPACT ON PARKINSONS-DISEASE.
004476 04-11

ELECTRORETINOGRAPHY (ERG) AS A TOOL OF INVESTIGATION IN HUMAN
PSYCHOPHARMACOLOGY. ELECTRORETINOGRAPHIC-CHANGES INDUCED
BY A COMBINATION OF CARBIDOPA AND LEVODOPA.
004507 04-13

DOSAGE FORM DESIGN FOR IMPROVEMENT OF BIOAVAILABILITY OF
LEVODOPA III: INFLUENCE OF DOSE ON PHARMACOKINETIC BEHAVIOR
OF LEVODOPA IN DOGS AND PARKINSONIAN-PATIENTS.
004551 04-13

ELECTROENCEPHALOGRAPHIC CHANGE IN PARKINSONIAN-PATIENTS
TREATED WITH LEVODOPA CARBIDOPA.
004557 04-13

LEVOMEPROMAZINE
AN UNUSUAL CASE OF THIORIDAZINE AND LEVOMEPROMAZINE
DEPENDENCE.
004634 04-15

LEVONANTRADOL
LEVONANTRADOL, A POTENT CANNABINOID RELATED ANALGESIC,
ANTAGONIZES HALOPERIDOL-INDUCED ACTIVATION OF STRIATAL
DOPAMINE SYNTHESIS.
002786 03-03

LEVORPHANOL
CHANGES IN PLASMA CORTICOSTERONE LEVELS AS A MEASURE OF
ACUTE DEPENDENCE UPON LEVORPHANOL IN RATS.
000085 01-03

LEVORPHANOL: RADIOIMMUNOASSAY AND PLASMA CONCENTRATION
PROFILES IN DOG AND MAN.
000898 01-16

HEROIN, BUT NOT LEVORPHANOL, PRODUCES EXPLOSIVE MOTOR-
BEHAVIOR IN NALOXONE TREATED RATS.
001579 02-04

LEWIS-RAT
ENHANCED TRANSFER OF EXPERIMENTAL ALLERGIC-ENCEPHALOMYELITIS
WITH LEWIS-RAT LYMPH-NODE CELLS. (UNPUBLISHED PAPER).
001434 02-03

LH
BASAL AND STIMULATED LEVELS OF PROLACTIN, TSH AND LH IN SERUM
OF CHRONIC SCHIZOPHRENIC-PATIENTS, LONG-TERM TREATED WITH
NEUROLEPTICS.
001935 02-08

BASAL AND STIMULATED LEVELS OF PROLACTIN, TSH, AND LH IN SERUM
OF CHRONIC SCHIZOPHRENIC-PATIENTS LONG-TERM TREATED WITH
NEUROLEPTICS: RELATIONS TO PSYCHOPATHOLOGY.
001936 02-08

LACK OF CORRELATION BETWEEN NALOXONE-INDUCED CHANGES IN
SEXUAL-BEHAVIOR AND SERUM LH IN MALE RATS.
002821 03-03

ANTAGONISM OF ETHANOL-INDUCED DECREASE IN LH BY P
CHLOROPHENYLALANINE: LACK OF CORRELATION WITH ALTERED
SEROTONERGIC MECHANISMS.
003748 04-03

LHRH
BODY-WEIGHT AND RESPONSES TO LHRH INFUSION IN ANOREXIA-
NERVOSA.
002062 02-10

LI
TRANSCULTURAL PHARMACOKINETIC STUDY ON LI CONCENTRATION IN
PLASMA AND SALIVA.
000769 01-13

INFERENTIAL CHANGES AFTER CHRONIC-TREATMENTS WITH LI, DMI, OR
ETHANOL DETECTED BY ELECTROPHYSIOLOGICAL-CORRELATES.
001136 02-03

LI
NA-DEPENDENT LI COUNTERTRANSPORT AND THE LITHIUM DISTRIBUTION
ACROSS THE HUMAN ERYTHROCYTE MEMBRANE: INTRODUCTION.
002227 02-13

LIABILITY
THE EFFECT OF NALOXONE ON THE ACTIVATION OF EMOTIONALLY
POSITIVE REACTION PRODUCED BY DRUGS WITH A DEPENDENCE
LIABILITY.
001556 02-03

RELAPSE TO NARCOTIC SELF-ADMINISTRATION IN MORPHINE
POSTADDICT RATS: A POSSIBLE MODEL FOR PREDICTING ABUSE
LIABILITY OF NARCOTIC-DRUGS. (PH.D. DISSERTATION).
003097 03-04

BUPRENORPHINE: DEMONSTRATION OF PHYSICAL-DEPENDENCE LIABILITY.
004104 04-04

CLOPIPAZAN (SKF-69634), A NEW NEUROLEPTIC ESSENTIALLY FREE OF
EXTRAPYRAMIDAL LIABILITY: QUANTITATIVE PHARMACOEEG AND
OPEN LABEL CLINICAL-TRIAL.
004620 04-15

LIABLE
TARDIVE-DYSKINESIA AND LITHIUM ASSOCIATED NEPHROPATHY: ARE
YOU LIABLE?
000846 01-15

LIBERATE
THIOLS LIBERATE COVALENTLY-BONDED FLAVIN FROM MONOAMINE-
OXIDASE. (UNPUBLISHED PAPER).
001060 02-01

LIBERATED
ESR STUDIES OF BOVINE PLASMA AMINE-OXIDASE: PROBING OF THE
ENVIRONMENT ABOUT THE SUBSTRATE LIBERATED SULFHYDRYL
GROUPS IN THE ACTIVE SITE. (UNPUBLISHED PAPER).
001066 02-01

LIBERATION
LIBERATION OF CATECHOLAMINES AND 5 HYDROXYTRYPTAMINE FROM
HUMAN BLOOD-PLATELETS.
003967 04-03

LIBRIUM
SHORT-TERM ETHANOL ADMINISTRATION IMPAIRS THE ELIMINATION OF
CHLORDIAZEPOXIDE (LIBRIUM) IN MAN.
002224 02-13

LICL
CHARACTERISTIC HYPERPYREXIA INDUCED BY LICL AND
TRANYLCYPROMINE IN RATS.
004278 04-05

LIDOCAINE
THE PARADOXICAL-EFFECT OF LIDOCAINE ON AN EXPERIMENTAL MODEL
OF EPILEPSY.
000039 01-03

THE EFFECTS OF GONADECTOMY AND HYPOPHYSECTOMY ON THE
METABOLISM OF IMIPRAMINE AND LIDOCAINE BY THE LIVER OF MALE
AND FEMALE RATS.
000273 01-03

THE EFFECT OF AMYGDALA KINDLING ON SPONTANEOUS AND COCAINE-
INDUCED MOTOR-ACTIVITY AND LIDOCAINE SEIZURES.
003067 03-04

EFFECT OF COCAINE AND LIDOCAINE ON THE EXPRESSION OF KINDLED
SEIZURES IN THE RAT.
004233 04-04

LIFE
NEUROLEPTIC TREATMENT FOR A SUBSTANTIAL PROPORTION OF ADULT
LIFE: BEHAVIOURAL-SEQUELAE OF 9 MONTHS HALOPERIDOL
ADMINISTRATION.
001858 02-05

LIFE EVENTS AND RESPONSE TO ANTIDEPRESSANTS.
003238 03-09

LIFE-TABLE
PROPHYLACTIC-EFFECT OF LITHIUM AGAINST DEPRESSION IN
CYCLOTHYMIC-PATIENTS: A LIFE-TABLE ANALYSIS.
004391 04-09

LIGAND
THE USE OF THIOPROPERAZINE, A PHENOTHIAZINE DERIVATIVE, AS A
LIGAND FOR NEUROLEPTIC-RECEPTORS – I. IN VITRO STUDIES.
001133 02-03

THE USE OF THIOPROPERAZINE, A PHENOTHIAZINE DERIVATIVE, AS A
LIGAND FOR NEUROLEPTIC-RECEPTORS -- II. IN VIVO STUDIES.
001137 02-03

BENZODIAZEPINE-RECEPTOR: LOCALIZATION BY PHOTOAFFINITY
LABELING AND ISOLATION OF A POSSIBLE ENDOGENOUS LIGAND.
001381 02-03

ASCORBATE DECREASES LIGAND BINDING TO NEUROTRANSMITTER-
RECEPTORS.
002804 03-03

LAMINAR DISTRIBUTION OF PUTATIVE NEUROTRANSMITTER AMINO-
ACIDS AND LIGAND BINDING-SITES IN THE DOG OLFACTORY-BULB.
002836 03-03

(3H)METERGOLINE: A NEW LIGAND OF SEROTONIN-RECEPTORS IN THE
RAT-BRAIN.
003825 04-03

OPIOID BINDING PROPERTIES OF BRAIN AND PERIPHERAL TISSUES:
EVIDENCE FOR HETEROGENEITY IN OPIOID LIGAND BINDING SITES.
003902 04-03

HUMAN PLATELET ALPHA2-ADRENERGIC-RECEPTORS: LABELING WITH 3H
YOHIMBINE, A SELECTIVE ANTAGONIST LIGAND.
004676 04-16

LIGANDS

DISSIMILAR EFFECTS OF NICOTINAMIDE AND INOSINE, PUTATIVE
ENDOGENOUS LIGANDS OF THE BENZODIAZEPINE-RECEPTORS, ON
PENTYLENETETRAZOL SEIZURES IN FOUR STRAINS OF MICE.
000173 01-03

PURINES AS ENDOGENOUS LIGANDS OF THE BENZODIAZEPINE-RECEPTOR.
000276 01-03

CHANGES IN ALPHA-ADRENERGIC-RECEPTORS IN RAT-BRAIN IN VITRO BY
PREINCUBATION WITH ALPHA-ADRENERGIC LIGANDS.
001272 02-03

ENDOGENOUS LIGANDS FOR BENZODIAZEPINE-RECEPTORS.
003615 03-17

LIGHT

EFFECTS OF MORPHINE, D-AMPHETAMINE, AND PENTOBARBITAL ON
SHOCK AND LIGHT DISCRIMINATION PERFORMANCE IN RATS.
001639 02-04

NEUROTENSIN-RECEPTOR LOCALIZATION BY LIGHT MICROSCOPIC
AUTORADIOGRAPHY IN RAT-BRAIN.
002938 03-03

BILATERAL SKIN CONDUCTANCE AND THE PUPILLARY LIGHT,DARK
REFLEX: MANIPULATION BY CHLORPROMAZINE, HALOPERIDOL,
SCOPOLAMINE, AND PLACEBO.
004544 04-13

LIMA-STATE-HOSPITAL

FEDERAL-COURT UPHOLDS RIGHT-TO-REFUSE PSYCHOTROPIC-DRUGS,
ORDERS IMPROVEMENTS AT LIMA-STATE-HOSPITAL.
002583 02-17

LIMBIC

DIFFERENTIAL-EFFECTS OF COCAINE ON LIMBIC EXCITABILITY.
001339 02-03

POSSIBLE LIMBIC SITES OF ACTION OF ANTIANXIETY-DRUGS.
002069 02-10

LIMBIC-SYSTEM

INCORPORATION OF 4.5 3H LEUCINE INTO THE LIMBIC-SYSTEM OF ICR
MICE AS A LONG-TERM EFFECT OF HALOPERIDOL APPLICATION.
000118 01-03

ANATOMICOPHYSIOLOGICAL AND NEUROCHEMICAL-STUDY OF THE
LIMBIC-SYSTEM: EFFECT OF NOMIFENSINE.
001160 02-03

THE EFFECT OF CLONAZEPAM ON ATROPINE SPIKES IN THE LIMBIC-
SYSTEM.
001274 02-03

LSD-INDUCED ULTRASTRUCTURAL MODIFICATIONS OF LIMBIC-SYSTEM
NUCLEI AND OTHER CEREBRAL ZONES.
002198 02-12

THE ACTION OF BENZODIAZEPINES ON THE LIMBIC-SYSTEM COMPARED
TO OTHER TRANQUILIZERS.
002731 03-03

LIMIT

CASE-REPORT: USING ATTRIBUTION THEORY TO LIMIT NEED FOR
NEUROLEPTIC-MEDICINE.
000559 01-08

LIMITS

LIMITS, VALUE AND PERSPECTIVES OF THE PSYCHIATRIC-DIAGNOSIS IN
CLINICAL PSYCHOPHARMACOLOGY.
002631 02-17

FACTORS REGULATING DRUG CUE SENSITIVITY: LIMITS OF
DISCRIMINABILITY AND THE ROLE OF A PROGRESSIVELY DECREASING
TRAINING DOSE IN FENTANYL SALINE DISCRIMINATION.
004088 04-04

LINE

INHIBITION OF CHEMOTAXIS BY S 3 DEAZAADENOSYLHOMOCYSTEINE IN
A MOUSE MACROPHAGE CELL LINE. (UNPUBLISHED PAPER).
001100 02-03

LINK

CA DIAZEPAM LINK? NO SCIENTIFIC TAKERS SO FAR.
003519 03-15

ALTERATIONS OF EVOKED-POTENTIALS LINK RESEARCH IN ATTENTION-
DYSFUNCTION TO PEPTIDE RESPONSE SYMPTOMS OF SCHIZOPHRENIA.
004316 04-08

LINKED

EVIDENCE FOR, AND LOCALIZATION OF, A UNITARY DOPAMINE-
RECEPTOR COMPOSED OF COOPERATIVELY LINKED SUBUNIT BINDING-
SITES IN RAT STRIATUM.
000186 01-03

ANTI-THY-1-2 MONOCLONAL ANTIBODY LINKED TO RICIN IS A POTENT
CELL TYPE SPECIFIC TOXIN. (UNPUBLISHED PAPER).
001064 02-01

UNITARY DOPAMINERGIC-RECEPTOR COMPOSED OF COOPERATIVELY
LINKED AGONIST AND ANTAGONIST SUBUNIT BINDING-SITES.
001342 02-03

LIPASES

INHIBITION OF LYSOSOMAL LIPASES BY CHLORPROMAZINE: A POSSIBLE
MECHANISMS OF STABILIZATION.
003993 04-03

LIPID

ACTIONS OF CHLORPROMAZINE, HALOPERIDOL AND PIMOZIDE ON LIPID
METABOLISM IN GUINEA-PIG BRAIN SLICES.
000129 01-03

LIPIDS

INTERRELATION AT PLASMATIC LEVEL BETWEEN ANTIEPILEPTIC-DRUGS
AND LIPIDS. ITS IMPLICATIONS IN THE EFFICIENCY OF TREATMENT IN
EPILEPSY. I. CHANGES INDUCED BY PHENOBARBITAL OR/AND
DIPHENYLHYDANTOIN IN SERUM LIPIDS.
002281 02-13

LIPOLYSIS

ALPHA2-ADRENERGIC AMINES, ADENOSINE AND PROSTAGLANDINS
INHIBIT LIPOLYSIS AND CYCLIC-AMP ACCUMULATION IN HAMSTER
ADIPOCYTES IN THE ABSENCE OF EXTRACELLULAR SODIUM.
002728 03-03

NALOXONE IN THE TREATMENT OF ANOREXIA-NERVOSA: EFFECT ON
WEIGHT-GAIN AND LIPOLYSIS.
003342 03-11

LIPOPEROXIDES

PSYCHOSOMATIC-STRESS AND LIPOPEROXIDES OF HUMAN PLATELET
RICH PLASMA.
003423 03-13

LIPOPHILIC

MEASUREMENT OF THE MEMBRANE POTENTIAL OF ISOLATED NERVE
TERMINALS BY THE LIPOPHILIC CATION
(3H)TRIPHENYLMETHYLPHOSPHONIUM-BROMIDE.
002746 03-03

LIPOPROTEINS

THE CONTRIBUTION OF ALPHA1 ACID GLYCOPROTEIN, LIPOPROTEINS,
AND ALBUMIN TO THE PLASMA BINDING OF PERAZINE,
AMITRIPTYLINE, AND NORTRIPTYLINE IN HEALTHY MAN.
002214 02-13

LIPOSOMES

PARTITIONING AND EFFLUX OF PHENOTHIAZINES FROM LIPOSOMES.
000007 01-02

PASSAGE THROUGH THE BLOOD-BRAIN-BARRIER OF THYROTROPIN-
RELEASING-HORMONE ENCAPSULATED IN LIPOSOMES.
004298 04-06

LIPOTROPIN

VASOPRESSIN STIMULATES RELEASE OF BETA LIPOTROPIN AND BETA
ENDORPHIN IN CONSCIOUS RATS AS MEASURED BY
RADIOIMMUNOASSAY OF UNEXTRACTED PLASMA.
003715 04-03

LIQUID

SUBCUTANEOUS SILASTIC IMPLANTS: MAINTENANCEOF HIGH BLOOD
ETHANOL LEVELS IN RATS DRINKING A LIQUID DIE .
001865 02-06

LIQUID-CHROMATOGRAPHIC-DETERMINATION

SIMULTANEOUS HIGH-PERFORMANCE LIQUID-CHROMATOGRAPHIC-
DETERMINATION OF AMITRIPTYLINE-HYDROCHLORIDE IN TWO-
COMPONENT TABLET FORMULATIONS.
004673 04-16

LIQUID-CHROMATOGRAPHY

ANALYSIS FOR DIAZEPAM AND NORDIAZEPAM BY ELECTRON-CAPTURE
GAS-CHROMATOGRAPHY AND BY LIQUID-CHROMATOGRAPHY.
000006 01-01

HYPOTHALAMIC CATECHOLAMINE BIOSYNTHESIS IN VITRO AS
MEASURED BY LIQUID-CHROMATOGRAPHY AND ELECTROCHEMICAL-
DETECTION.
000537 01-06

3 CHLORO-4-PHENYLSUCCINIMIDOBENZENESULFONAMIDE (GS-385), A
NEW ANTICONVULSANT: ITS QUANTITATIVE DETERMINATION,
PHARMACOKINETICS AND METABOLISM USING HIGH-PERFORMANCE
LIQUID-CHROMATOGRAPHY.
000705 01-11

MEASUREMENT OF HALOPERIDOL IN HUMAN PLASMA USING REVERSED
PHASE HIGH-PERFORMANCE LIQUID-CHROMATOGRAPHY.
(UNPUBLISHED PAPER).
003667 04-01

A RAPID AND SIMPLE METHOD FOR THE DETERMINATION OF PICOGRAM
LEVELS OF 3 METHOXYTYRAMINE IN BRAIN TISSUE USING LIQUID-
CHROMATOGRAPHY WITH ELECTROCHEMICAL DETECTION.
003674 04-01

Subject Index

HIGH-PERFORMANCE LIQUID-CHROMATOGRAPHY IN THE
NEUROSCIENCES: METHODOLOGY.
004285 04-06

HIGH-PERFORMANCE LIQUID-CHROMATOGRAPHY IN THE
NEUROSCIENCES: APPLICATIONS.
004296 04-06

RAPID DETERMINATION OF CHLORPROMAZINE-HCL AND TWO OXIDATION
PRODUCTS IN VARIOUS PHARMACEUTICAL SAMPLES USING HIGH-
PERFORMANCE LIQUID-CHROMATOGRAPHY AND FLUORESCENCE
DETECTION.
004302 04-06

LIQUOR

MORPHINE ANALGESIA FOLLOWING ITS INFUSION INTO DIFFERENT
LIQUOR SPACES IN RAT-BRAIN.
001429 02-03

LISTENING

LATERALIZED DEFICITS AND DRUG INFLUENCES ON THE DICHOTIC
LISTENING OF SCHIZOPHRENIC-PATIENTS.
003443 03-14

LISURIDE

ANORECTIC-EFFECT OF LISURIDE AND OTHER ERGOT DERIVATIVES IN THE
RAT.
000042 01-03

EFFECTS OF LISURIDE ON BODY-TEMPERATURE OF RATS AND RABBITS:
RELATION TO MICROSOMAL BIOTRANSFORMATION AND
DOPAMINERGIC-RECEPTOR STIMULATION.
001161 02-03

LISURIDE IN THE TREATMENT OF PARKINSONISM.
002168 02-11

DEPRESSION OF RESERPINE-INDUCED MUSCULAR RIGIDITY IN RATS AFTER
ADMINISTRATION OF LISURIDE INTO THE SPINAL SUBARACHNOID
SPACE.
002962 03-04

LISURIDE IN PARKINSONISM.
003319 03-11

LISURIDE IN PARKINSONISM.
003422 03-13

STIMULATORY ACTION OF LISURIDE ON DOPAMINE-SENSITIVE
ADENYLATE-CYCLASE IN THE RAT STRIATAL HOMOGENATE.
003718 04-03

LISURIDE-HYDROGEN-MALEATE

EFFECTS OF HIGH-DOSAGE LISURIDE-HYDROGEN-MALEATE (LHM) IN
PARKINSON-SYNDROME.
004460 04-11

LITHIOTHERAPY

ADHERENCE TO LITHIOTHERAPY.
002507 02-16

LITHIUM

LITHIUM LEVELS IN BLOOD-PLATELETS, SERUM, RED-BLOOD-CELLS AND
BRAIN REGIONS IN RATS GIVEN ACUTE OR CHRONIC LITHIUM-SALT
TREATMENTS.
000082 01-03

LITHIUM REDUCES THE NUMBER OF ACETYLCHOLINE-RECEPTORS IN
SKELETAL-MUSCLE.
000232 01-03

THE ACUTE AND CHRONIC EFFECT OF LITHIUM ON SERUM TESTOSTERONE
IN RATS.
000238 01-03

EFFECTS OF CHRONIC DIETARY LITHIUM ON ACTIVITY AND REGULATION
OF NA-K-ADENOSINE-TRIPHOSPHATASE IN RAT-BRAIN.
000297 01-03

LITHIUM: EFFECTS ON SEROTONIN-RECEPTORS IN RAT-BRAIN.
000304 01-03

LITHIUM RESPONSE IN GOOD PROGNOSIS SCHIZOPHRENIA.
000555 01-08

LITHIUM TREATMENT IN POSTPSYCHOTIC DEPRESSION.
000575 01-08

AFFECTIVE-EPISODE FREQUENCY AND LITHIUM THERAPY.
000587 01-09

EEG IN PATIENTS TREATED WITH LITHIUM.
000593 01-09

AGE, DEMENTIA, DYSKINESIAS, AND LITHIUM RESPONSE.
000594 01-09

HANDBOOK OF LITHIUM THERAPY.
000597 01-09

COGNITIVE AND AFFECTIVE-FUNCTIONS IN PATIENTS WITH AFFECTIVE-
DISORDERS TREATED WITH LITHIUM: AN ASSESSMENT BY
QUESTIONNAIRE.
000604 01-09

LITHIUM LEVEL IN SOME BIOLOGICAL FLUIDS AT ITS PROPHYLACTIC
THERAPEUTIC APPLICATION.
000605 01-09

IMPAIRED GLUCOSE TOLERANCE IN LONG-TERM LITHIUM TREATED
PATIENTS.
000611 01-09

INTERACTION OF INDOMETHACIN AND IBUPROFEN WITH LITHIUM IN
MANIC-PATIENTS UNDER A STEADY-STATE LITHIUM LEVEL.
000622 01-09

CONDITIONED SUPPRESSION OF DRINKING: A MEASURE OF THE CR ELICITED BY A LITHIUM CONDITIONED FLAVOR.
001747 02-04

THE EFFECTS OF LITHIUM ON CHOICE BETWEEN COCAINE AND FOOD IN THE RHESUS-MONKEY.
001825 02-04

ENDOCRINE-EFFECTS OF LITHIUM IN MANIC-DEPRESSIVE-PATIENTS.
001970 02-09

LITHIUM AND MANIA: HYPOTHESES.
001986 02-09

DISCUSSION OF CLINICAL-PAPERS ON LITHIUM TRANSPORT IN AFFECTIVE-DISORDERS.
001987 02-09

LITHIUM AND HAIR-LOSS. (UNPUBLISHED PAPER).
002005 02-09

RAPID RECURRENCE OF MANIA FOLLOWING LITHIUM WITHDRAWAL.
002010 02-09

LITHIUM TRANSPORT STUDIES IN AFFECTIVE-DISORDERS.
002024 02-09

SENSITIZATION AND OSCILLATION FOLLOWING REPEATED STIMULATION: RELATIONSHIP TO AFFECTIVE-ILLNESS AND ITS TREATMENT WITH LITHIUM AND CARBAMAZEPINE.
002031 02-09

TARDIVE-DYSKINESIA IN DEPRESSED-PATIENTS: SUCCESSFUL THERAPY WITH ANTIDEPRESSANTS AND LITHIUM.
002037 02-09

THE RELATIVE PROPHYLACTIC EFFICACY OF LITHIUM AGAINST MANIC AND DEPRESSIVE RECURRENCES IN BIPOLAR-PATIENTS.
002040 02-09

EFFECT OF LITHIUM ON POTASSIUM AND CALCIUM IN SERUM, ERYTHOCYTES AND IN URINE.
002054 02-09

PHARMACODYNAMIC ASPECTS OF LONG-TERM PROPHYLACTIC LITHIUM.
002212 02-13

NA-DEPENDENT LI COUNTERTRANSPORT AND THE LITHIUM DISTRIBUTION ACROSS THE HUMAN ERYTHROCYTE MEMBRANE: INTRODUCTION.
002227 02-13

CLINICAL-ASPECTS OF LITHIUM EFFLUX FROM ERYTHROCYTES.
002228 02-13

LITHIUM ANTAGONISM OF ETHANOL-INDUCED DEPLETION OF CEREBELLAR GUANOSINE-CYCLIC-MONOPHOSPHATE AND STIMULATION OF STRIATAL DOPAMINE RELEASE.
002242 02-13

LITHIUM AND THE KIDNEY.
002244 02-13

ABNORMALITIES OF LITHIUM TRANSPORT IN PATIENTS WITH AFFECTIVE-DISORDERS.
002269 02-13

QUANTITATIVE STUDY OF THE DISTRIBUTION OF LITHIUM IN THE MOUSE-BRAIN FOR VARIOUS DOSES OF LITHIUM GIVEN TO THE ANIMAL.
002299 02-13

LITHIUM THERAPY IN AGGRESSIVE MENTALLY-SUBNORMAL-PATIENTS.
002316 02-14

AN UNUSUAL SIDE-EFFECT OF LITHIUM.
002381 02-15

LITHIUM AND RENAL FUNCTION.
002416 02-15

EFFECTS OF LITHIUM ON EVOKED-POTENTIALS AND PERFORMANCE DURING SUSTAINED ATTENTION.
002419 02-15

DIURETICS ARE DANGEROUS WITH LITHIUM.
002420 02-15

BRADYCARDIA, PERSISTENT DIABETES-INSIPIDUS, AND TARDIVE-DYSKINESIA WITH LITHIUM INTOXICATION.
002427 02-15

FAILURE OF LITHIUM TREATMENT IN ESTABLISHED TARDIVE-DYSKINESIA.
002432 02-15

LITHIUM: PROBLEMS OF APPLICATION, TOLERANCE, AND EFFICACY.
002434 02-15

UPDATE ON LITHIUM: 1979-1980.
002450 02-15

NEUROTOXICITY OF LITHIUM. I.
002452 02-15

LITHIUM IN 1979.
002457 02-15

RECENT DEVELOPMENTS IN LITHIUM TREATMENT: IS IT DANGEROUS FOR THE KIDNEY?
002465 02-15

EFFECTS OF LITHIUM, AND LITHIUM AND ALCOHOL ADMINISTRATION ON NA-K-ATPASE.
002744 03-03

EFFECTS OF LITHIUM ON MORPHOLOGICAL CHARACTERISTICS OF DISSOCIATED BRAIN CELLS IN CULTURE.
002765 03-03

LITHIUM, ASSIMILATION OF NUTRIENTS AND REPRODUCTION. (UNPUBLISHED PAPER).
002777 03-03

EFFECTS OF PROLONGED TREATMENT WITH LITHIUM AND TRICYCLIC-ANTIDEPRESSANTS ON DISCHARGE FREQUENCY, NOREPINEPHRINE RESPONSES AND BETA-RECEPTOR BINDING IN RAT-CEREBELLUM: ELECTROPHYSIOLOGICAL AND BIOCHEMICAL COMPARISON.
002884 03-03

INFLUENCE OF PSYCHOTROPIC-DRUGS ON THE URINARY ELIMINATION OF LITHIUM.
002895 03-03

DIFFERENTIAL-EFFECTS OF SHORT-TERM AND LONG-TERM LITHIUM ON TRYPTOPHAN UPTAKE AND SEROTONERGIC FUNCTION IN CAT BRAIN.
002911 03-03

COMBINED EFFECTS OF ALCOHOL AND LITHIUM ON BODY COMPOSITION IN THE RAT MODEL.
002928 03-03

LITHIUM AND PORCINE AGGRESSION.
003048 03-04

SELECTIVE SENSITIZATION INDUCED BY LITHIUM MALAISE AND FOOTSHOCK IN RATS.
003055 03-04

CAN THE ANTIDEPRESSIVE PROPERTIES OF LITHIUM BE DETERMINED EXPERIMENTALLY?
003089 03-04

LITHIUM DRUG INTERACTIONS ALTERING THE INTRACELLULAR LITHIUM LEVEL: AN IN VITRO STUDY.
003142 03-06

STEADY-STATE LITHIUM BLOOD LEVEL FLUCTUATIONS IN MAN FOLLOWING ADMINISTRATION OF A LITHIUM-CARBONATE CONVENTIONAL AND CONTROLLED-RELEASE DOSAGE FORM.
003151 03-07

SYNERGISM OF COMBINED LITHIUM NEUROLEPTIC THERAPY: A DOUBLE-BLIND, PLACEBO-CONTROLLED CASE-STUDY.
003165 03-08

LITHIUM COMBINED WITH NEUROLEPTICS IN CHRONIC SCHIZOPHRENIC-PATIENTS AND SCHIZOAFFECTIVE-PATIENTS.
003168 03-08

LATE RESULTS OF LITHIUM TREATMENT OF ADOLESCENTS WITH ATTACK LIKE SCHIZOPHRENIA.
003177 03-08

CORRELATIONS BETWEEN LITHIUM LEVELS IN CEREBROSPINAL-FLUID AND LITHIUM LEVELS IN BLOOD PLASMA AND ERYTHROCYTES.
003210 03-09

HYPOMANIA AS A STABLE STATE: LITHIUM PROPHYLAXIS IN TWO PATIENTS.
003212 03-09

LITHIUM EFFECT ON PARATHYROID-HORMONE.
003215 03-09

HISTORICAL-PERSPECTIVES AND CURRENT HIGHLIGHTS ON LITHIUM TREATMENT IN MANIC-DEPRESSIVE-ILLNESS.
003224 03-09

DOSAGE OF INTRATUMORAL LITHIUM (CEREBRAL GLIOBLASTOMA): ON A FAILURE OF TREATMENT OF MANIC-DEPRESSIVE-PSYCHOSIS.
003226 03-09

PROPHYLACTIC LITHIUM WITH AND WITHOUT IMIPRAMINE FOR BIPOLAR-I-PATIENTS: A DOUBLE-BLIND STUDY.
003233 03-09

LITHIUM IN CHILDREN OF LITHIUM RESPONDING PARENTS.
003242 03-09

LITHIUM: A BIOPSYCHOSOCIAL-PERSPECTIVE.
003247 03-09

LITHIUM AND IMIPRAMINE IN THE PROPHYLAXIS OF UNIPOLAR AND BIPOLAR-II DEPRESSION: A PROSPECTIVE, PLACEBO-CONTROLLED COMPARISON.
003252 03-09

LITHIUM UPTAKE IN RED CELLS OF CYCLOID AND UNIPOLAR DYSTHYMIC-PATIENTS.
003258 03-09

LITHIUM IN 1978.
003261 03-09

LITHIUM AND THE CHANGING INCIDENCE OF MANIA.
003265 03-09

EFFECT OF LITHIUM ON PROLACTIN RESPONSES TO THYROTROPIN-RELEASING-HORMONE IN PATIENTS WITH MANIC-STATE.
003266 03-09

CONFESSION OF A MELANCHOLIAC: CONTRIBUTION TO THE PROBLEM OF PROPHYLAXIS OF MANIC-DEPRESSIVE-PSYCHOSIS USING LITHIUM.
003267 03-09

THE EFFECT OF WITHDRAWAL FROM PROLONGED PROPHYLACTIC TREATMENT WITH LITHIUM.
003339 03-11

EFFICACY OF LITHIUM IN TREATING MOOD-DISORDER OCCURRING AFTER BRAINSTEM INJURY.
003354 03-11

INTRACELLULAR LITHIUM: ITS VALUE IN THE PREDICTION OF A POSITIVE RESPONSE TO LITHIUM.
003382 03-11

LITHIUM TREATMENT OF THE KLEINE-LEVIN-SYNDROME.
003390 03-11

DERMATOLOGIC MANIFESTATIONS OF LITHIUM: A REVIEW.
003462 03-15

LITHIUM PROPHYLAXIS AND THE KIDNEY.
003463 03-15

RENAL IMPAIRMENT, HYPERCALCEMIA, AND LITHIUM THERAPY.
003473 03-15

Subject Index

A CASE OF REVERSIBLE PURE-WORD DEAFNESS DURING LITHIUM TOXICITY.
003481 03-15

HYPERPARATHYROIDISM IN ASSOCIATION WITH LITHIUM THERAPY.
003489 03-15

SOME HAZARDS OF LITHIUM USE.
003498 03-15

LITHIUM THERAPY AND THYROID-FUNCTION: A LONG-TERM STUDY.
003504 03-15

TIME-COURSE OF CLINICAL CHEMICAL PARAMETERS UNDER LONG-TERM LITHIUM TREATMENT.
003515 03-15

LITHIUM KINETICS DURING HEMODIALYSIS IN A PATIENT WITH LITHIUM POISONING.
003524 03-15

LITHIUM AND MARIJUANA.
003526 03-15

LITHIUM NEUROTOXICITY AT THERAPEUTIC LEVELS: A CASE-REPORT.
003533 03-15

LITHIUM AND THE KIDNEY SCARE.
003534 03-15

GLOMERULAR FILTRATION RATE AND CALCIUM METABOLISM IN LONG-TERM LITHIUM TREATMENT.
003542 03-15

PERIPHERAL NEUROPATHY DUE TO LITHIUM INTOXICATION.
003544 03-15

RENAL SIDE-EFFECTS OF LITHIUM: THE IMPORTANCE OF THE SERUM LITHIUM LEVEL.
003547 03-15

BIBLIOGRAPHY ON THE BIOLOGY AND PHARMACOLOGY OF LITHIUM.
003630 03-17

LITHIUM AND MANIA.
003640 03-17

EFFECT OF LOW-DOSE LITHIUM ADMINISTRATION AND SUBSEQUENT WITHDRAWAL ON BIOGENIC-AMINES IN RAT-BRAIN.
003708 04-03

THE EFFECTS OF LITHIUM ON MYOINOSITOL LEVELS IN LAYERS OF FRONTAL-CEREBRAL-CORTEX, IN CEREBELLUM, AND IN CORPUS-CALLOSUM OF THE RAT.
003712 04-03

DOPAMINE METABOLITES IN CAUDATE AND CORTEX AFTER LITHIUM AND HALOPERIDOL. (UNPUBLISHED PAPER).
003738 04-03

THE EFFECT OF LONG-TERM CONCURRENT ADMINISTRATION OF CHLORPROMAZINE AND LITHIUM ON THE STRIATAL AND FRONTAL CORTICAL DOPAMINE METABOLISM IN RATS.
003788 04-03

LITHIUM INDUCES DOSE-RELATED INCREASES AND DECREASES IN ACTIVITY LEVELS IN THE RAT.
004079 04-04

EFFECTS OF LITHIUM ON BEHAVIOUR AND CENTRAL MONOAMINES.
004110 04-04

LITHIUM AMELIORATION OF RESERPINE-INDUCED HYPOACTIVITY IN RATS.
004167 04-04

LITHIUM AND MOTOR-ACTIVITY OF ANIMALS: EFFECTS AND POSSIBLE MECHANISM-OF-ACTION.
004222 04-04

CENTRAL AND PERIPHERAL EFFECTS OF LITHIUM ON AMPHETAMINE-INDUCED HYPERACTIVITY IN RATS.
004223 04-04

LITHIUM EFFECTS ON HALOPERIDOL-INDUCED PRESYNAPTIC AND POSTSYNAPTIC DOPAMINE-RECEPTOR SUPERSENSITIVITY.
004244 04-04

EFFECTS OF INDOMETHACIN AND METHYLPREDNISOLONE ON RENAL ELIMINATION OF LITHIUM IN THE RAT.
004270 04-05

EVALUATION OF LITHIUM RESPONSE: PSYCHOMETRIC-FINDINGS.
004348 04-09

RECEPTORS, ADENYLATE-CYCLASE, DEPRESSION, AND LITHIUM.
004353 04-09

CLINICAL SIGNIFICANCE OF THE ERYTHROPLASMATIC RATIO OF LITHIUM.
004357 04-09

LITHIUM IN THE PROPHYLAXIS OF RECURRENT AFFECTIVE-DISORDERS (EFFECTIVENESS OF LOW PLASMA LEVELS AND PREDICTORS TO CLINICAL-RESPONSE).
004365 04-09

LITHIUM USE IN AFFECTIVE-DISORDERS.
004367 04-09

LITHIUM ELIMINATION HALF-LIFE AND DURATION OF THERAPY.
004369 04-09

PROPHYLACTIC-EFFECT OF LITHIUM AGAINST DEPRESSION IN CYCLOTHYMIC-PATIENTS: A LIFE-TABLE ANALYSIS.
004391 04-09

LITHIUM TREATMENT OF MANIC-DEPRESSIVE-ILLNESS. A PRACTICAL GUIDE.
004408 04-09

LITHIUM AND AGGRESSIVE-BEHAVIOR.
004409 04-09

AN ATTEMPT TO ASSESS THE EFFECT OF LITHIUM ON THE NEUTROPHIL LEUKOCYTE SYSTEM IN AFFECTIVE-PSYCHOSIS.
004416 04-09

EFFECTS OF LITHIUM-CARBONATE AND HALOPERIDOL ON COGNITION IN AGGRESSIVE, HOSPITALIZED SCHOOL-AGE CHILDREN.
003360 03-11

EFFECTS OF LITHIUM-CARBONATE AND HALOPERIDOL ON COGNITION IN AGGRESSIVE HOSPITALIZED SCHOOL-AGE CHILDREN.
003361 03-11

THE MANAGEMENT OF CHRONIC BEHAVIOR-DISORDERS IN MENTALLY-RETARDED ADULTS WITH LITHIUM-CARBONATE.
003376 03-11

LITHIUM-CARBONATE AND THE KIDNEY.
003478 03-15

COMPARATIVE CHARACTERISTICS OF THE PROPHYLACTIC PROPERTIES OF SHORT-TERM AND LONG-ACTING LITHIUM-CARBONATE PREPARATIONS IN ENDOGENOUS AFFECTIVE-PSYCHOSES.
004390 04-09

CLINICAL-EVALUATION OF THE PROPHYLACTIC EFFECTIVENESS OF PROLONGED LITHIUM-CARBONATE THERAPY IN ENDOGENOUS DEPRESSIVE-SYNDROMES.
004404 04-09

UNWANTED EFFECTS OF LITHIUM-CARBONATE USED IN THE PREVENTION OF RELAPSES OF AFFECTIVE-ILLNESS.
004625 04-15

LITHIUM-CARBONATE IN THE TREATMENT OF MOVEMENT-DISORDERS. A CRITICAL REVIEW.
004668 04-15

LITHIUM-CARBONICUM-RETARD
CLINICAL-EXPERIENCE WITH LITHIUM-CARBONICUM-RETARD IN PSYCHIATRY.
002000 02-09

LITHIUM-CHLORIDE
EFFECT OF AGE AND ROUTE-OF-ADMINISTRATION ON LD50 OF LITHIUM-CHLORIDE IN THE RAT.
001413 02-03

EFFECT OF LITHIUM-CHLORIDE IN COYOTE PUP DIET.
001835 02-05

LITHIUM-CHLORIDE AND DELTA9 THC LEAD TO CONDITIONED AVERSIONS IN THE PIGEON.
003003 03-04

DOPAMINE DEPLETION BY 6 HYDROXYDOPAMINE PREVENTS CONDITIONED TASTE-AVERSION INDUCED BY METHYLAMPHETAMINE BUT NOT LITHIUM-CHLORIDE.
003110 03-04

LITHIUM-HYDROXYBUTYRATE
THE EFFECT OF LITHIUM-HYDROXYBUTYRATE ON THE BIOELECTRICAL-ACTIVITY OF THE CORTEX AND SOME SUBCORTICAL STRUCTURES OF THE RABBIT BRAIN.
003994 04-03

LITHIUM-INDUCED
ABSENCE OF LITHIUM-INDUCED TASTE-AVERSION AFTER AREA-POSTREMA LESION.
000456 01-04

LITHIUM-INDUCED COGWHEEL RIGIDITY: TREATMENT WITH AMANTADINE.
000748 01-13

LITHIUM-INDUCED CHANGES IN THE BRAIN LEVELS OF FREE AMINO-ACIDS IN STRESS-EXPOSED RATS.
001217 02-03

ATTENUATION OF THE LITHIUM-INDUCED DIABETES-INSIPIDUS-LIKE SYNDROME BY AMILORIDE IN RATS.
002717 03-03

EFFECTS OF DORSOLATERAL TEGMENTAL LESIONS ON AMPHETAMINE-INDUCED AND LITHIUM-INDUCED TASTE-AVERSIONS.
003114 03-04

LITHIUM-ION
INTRA AND EXTRA ERYTHROCYTE LITHIUM-ION CONCENTRATION RATIOS IN MANIC-PATIENTS.
000627 01-09

LITHIUM-ION ENTRY INTO CULTURED CELLS OF NEURAL ORIGIN.
001433 02-03

THE LITHIUM-ION: IS IT SPECIFIC FOR MANIA?
002516 02-16

LITHIUM-OXYBUTYRATE
AN EXPERIMENTAL-STUDY OF THE NEUROTROPIC-ACTION OF LITHIUM-OXYBUTYRATE.
001705 02-04

LITHIUM-PUMP
LITHIUM-PUMP REPRESSION AS AN INDICATOR OF PROPHYLACTIC RESPONSE.
001989 02-09

THE REPRESSION OF THE LITHIUM-PUMP AS AN INDICATOR OF RESPONSE TO PROPHYLACTIC TREATMENT.
003221 03-09

LITHIUM-SALT
LITHIUM LEVELS IN BLOOD-PLATELETS, SERUM, RED-BLOOD-CELLS AND BRAIN REGIONS IN RATS GIVEN ACUTE OR CHRONIC LITHIUM-SALT TREATMENTS.
000082 01-03

LITHIUM-SALTS
THE INFLUENCE OF LITHIUM-SALTS AND ANTIDEPRESSANT MEDICATION ON SERUM PROLACTIN LEVEL.
000780 01-13

LITHIUM-SALTS IN LEUKOPENIC-DISORDERS.
001000 01-17

MOTOR-LEARNING ABILITIES IN SUBJECTS TREATED WITH LITHIUM-SALTS AND TRICYCLIC-ANTIDEPRESSANTS.
002058 02-09

PREDICTIVE CRITERIA FOR LITHIUM-SALTS ACTIVITY.
002619 02-17

LIVER
BETA DIETHYLAMINOETHYLDIPHENYLPROPYLACETATE (SKF-525-A) AND 2,4 DICHLORO-6-PHENYLPHENOXYETHYLAMINE-HBR (DPEA) INHIBITION OF FATTY-ACID CONJUGATION TO 11 HYDROXY-DELTA9-TETRAHYDROCANNABINOL BY THE RAT LIVER MICROSOMAL SYSTEM.
000179 01-03

THE EFFECTS OF GONADECTOMY AND HYPOPHYSECTOMY ON THE METABOLISM OF IMIPRAMINE AND LIDOCAINE BY THE LIVER OF MALE AND FEMALE RATS.
000273 01-03

FOLLOWUP STUDY ON THE INFLUENCE OF AN ANTIPSYCHOTIC-DRUG (PROPERICIAZINE) ON LIVER FUNCTION, ELECTROCARDIOGRAM AND ELECTROENCEPHALOGRAM.
000639 01-09

COMPARISON OF CYSTEINE-SULPHINIC-ACID-DECARBOXYLASE (CSD) ISOENZYMES AND GLUTAMIC-ACID-DECARBOXYLASE (GAD) IN RAT: IS BRAIN CSD-I IDENTICAL WITH LIVER CSD AND BRAIN CSD-II WITH GAD? (UNPUBLISHED PAPER).
001048 02-01

ESR STUDIES OF SPIN LABELLED BOVINE LIVER MONOAMINE-OXIDASE-B. (UNPUBLISHED PAPER).
001065 02-01

CORRELATIONS BETWEEN HEMODYNAMIC PARAMETERS OF THE LIVER AND NOREPINEPHRINE RELEASE UPON HEPATIC-NERVE STIMULATION IN THE DOG.
001547 02-03

COMPARATIVE-STUDY OF THE INDUCTIVE EFFECT OF TWO PSYCHOMODERATORS -- TETRABAMATE AND COMPLEXE-1656 -- AND OF PHENOBARBITAL ON LIVER MICROSOMAL ENZYMES IN RATS.
001874 02-06

DRUG-INDUCED DISORDERS OF THE LIVER.
002397 02-15

PLASMA IMIPRAMINE LEVELS AND DEMETHYLASE ACTIVITY IN THE LIVER OF STRESSED ANIMALS.
002793 03-03

EFFECTS OF BENSERAZIDE AND CARBIDOPA ON THE METABOLISM OF L TRYPTOPHAN BY ISOLATED RAT LIVER CELLS.
002899 03-03

HALOTHANE ACCUMULATION IN RAT-BRAIN AND LIVER.
003774 04-03

EFFECTS OF ANIMAL AGE AND PHENOBARBITAL ON RAT LIVER GLUCOSE-6-PHOSPHATASE ACTIVITY.
003997 04-03

OXIDATION OF BETA PHENYLETHYLAMINE BY BOTH TYPES OF MONOAMINE-OXIDASE: EXAMINATION OF ENZYMES IN BRAIN AND LIVER MITOCHONDRIA OF EIGHT SPECIES.
004024 04-03

LI2CO3
LEVELS OF MINERAL-ELEMENTS IN THE SERUM AND SALIVA OF HEALTHY MALE VOLUNTEERS AFTER A SINGLE-DOSE OF LI2CO3.
002297 02-13

LM24056
INHIBITION OF PENTAGASTRIN-STIMULATED AND OVERNIGHT GASTRIC SECRETION BY LM24056, A NEW PHENOTHIAZINE DERIVED ANTISECRETORY DRUG.
004306 04-07

LOAD
ENHANCEMENT OF RAT-BRAIN METABOLISM OF A TRYPTOPHAN LOAD BY CHRONIC ETHANOL ADMINISTRATION.
000022 01-03

EEG CHANGES IN CHILDREN WITH TREATED PHENYLKETONURIA AFTER PHENYLALANINE LOAD.
002115 02-11

EARLY DETECTION OF HUNTINGTONS-DISEASE. BLINK REFLEX AND LEVODOPA LOAD IN PRESYMPTOMATIC AND INCIPIENT SUBJECTS.
003311 03-11

IN NORMAL YOUNG MEN ACUTE DOPAMINERGIC BLOCKADE DOES NOT IMPAIR FREE WATER EXCRETION FOLLOWING A STANDARD WATER LOAD.
004600 04-15

LOADED
CENTRAL-EFFECTS OF ANGIOTENSIN-II IN WATER AND SALINE LOADED RATS.
003845 04-03

LOBE
EXPERIENCE IN USING THE HORMONES OF THE HYPOPHYSIS POSTERIOR LOBE IN MEMORY-DISTURBANCES OF VARYING GENESES.
003438 03-14

DOPAMINE-RECEPTOR BINDING IN BOVINE INTERMEDIATE LOBE PITUITARY MEMBRANES.
004003 04-03

Subject Index

LOBES
LONG-TERM-TREATMENT OF RATS WITH MORPHINE DECREASES IN VITRO
BIOSYNTHESIS IN AND RELEASE OF BETA ENDORPHIN FROM
INTERMEDIATE/POSTERIOR LOBES OF PITUITARY.
003846 04-03

LOBOTOMY
ALPHA1-ADRENOCEPTORS AND ALPHA2-ADRENOCEPTORS IN RAT-
CEREBRAL-CORTEX: EFFECT OF FRONTAL LOBOTOMY.
003944 04-03

LOCAL
THE ROLE OF BIOGENIC-AMINES IN AMYGDALAR KINDLING. I. LOCAL
AMYGDALAR AFTERDISCHARGE.
000327 01-03

MAPPING OF DYSKINETIC-MOVEMENTS INDUCED BY LOCAL APPLICATION
OF PICROTOXIN OR () GAMMA ACETYLENIC-GABA ON THE RAT
MOTOR-CORTEX.
000458 01-04

A COMPARISON OF THE EFFECTS OF D-AMPHETAMINE, COCAINE,
IMIPRAMINE AND PENTOBARBITAL ON LOCAL AND OVERALL RATES OF
RESPONDING MAINTAINED UNDER A FOUR-COMPONENT MULTIPLE
FIXED-INTERVAL SCHEDULE.
000508 01-04

INHIBITION BY LOCAL ANESTHETICS, PHENTOLAMINE AND PROPRANOLOL
OF (3H)QUINUCLYDINYL-BENZYLATE BINDING TO CENTRAL
MUSCARINIC-RECEPTORS.
001097 02-03

PARASYMPATHOMIMETIC-INFLUENCE OF CARBACHOL ON LOCAL
CEREBRAL BLOOD FLOW IN THE RABBIT BY A DIRECT VASODILATOR
ACTION AND AN INHIBITION OF THE SYMPATHETIC MEDIATED
VASOCONSTRICTION.
001109 02-03

LOCAL CEREBRAL GLUCOSE UTILIZATION (LCGU) IN RAT-BRAIN DURING
HYPOXEMIA. (UNPUBLISHED PAPER).
001380 02-03

THEORY, PROCEDURE, AND APPLICATIONS OF THE RADIOACTIVE
DEOXYGLUCOSE METHOD FOR THE MEASUREMENT OF LOCAL GLUCOSE
UTILIZATION IN THE CENTRAL-NERVOUS-SYSTEM. (UNPUBLISHED
PAPER).
001877 02-06

LOCAL AND DISTANT NEURONAL DEGENERATION FOLLOWING
INTRASTRIATAL INJECTION OF KAINIC-ACID.
001885 02-06

THE INTERACTION OF AMINE LOCAL ANESTHETICS WITH MUSCARINIC-
RECEPTORS.
004031 04-03

LOCALISATION
NEURONAL LOCALISATION OF BENZODIAZEPINE-RECEPTORS IN
CEREBELLUM.
003739 04-03

LOCALIZATION
LOCALIZATION OF ALPHA BUNGAROTOXIN BINDING-SITES IN SYNAPSES
OF THE DEVELOPING CHICK RETINA.
000065 01-03

CALCIUM LOCALIZATION IN THE SYMPATHETIC GANGLION OF THE
BULLFROG AND EFFECTS OF CAFFEINE.
000098 01-03

EVIDENCE FOR, AND LOCALIZATION OF, A UNITARY DOPAMINE-
RECEPTOR COMPOSED OF COOPERATIVELY LINKED SUBUNIT BINDING-
SITES IN RAT STRIATUM.
000186 01-03

LOCALIZATION OF NALOXONE SENSITIVE (3H)DIHYDROMORPHINE
BINDING-SITES WITHIN THE HIPPOCAMPUS OF THE RAT.
001368 02-03

BENZODIAZEPINE-RECEPTOR: LOCALIZATION BY PHOTOAFFINITY
LABELING AND ISOLATION OF A POSSIBLE ENDOGENOUS LIGAND.
001381 02-03

LOCALIZATION OF SENSITIVE SITES TO TAURINE, GAMMA
AMINOBUTYRIC-ACID, GLYCINE AND BETA ALANINE IN THE
MOLECULAR LAYER OF GUINEA-PIG CEREBELLAR SLICES.
001402 02-03

HISTOCHEMICAL LOCALIZATION OF OPIATE-RECEPTORS AND THE
ENKEPHALINS.
002566 02-17

IMMUNOCYTOCHEMICAL LOCALIZATION OF CATECHOLAMINE
SYNTHESIZING ENZYMES AND NEUROPEPTIDES IN AREA POSTREMA
AND MEDIAL NUCLEUS-TRACTUS-SOLITARIUS OF RAT-BRAIN.
002634 03-01

IMMUNOHISTOCHEMICAL LOCALIZATION OF LEUCINE-ENKEPHALIN IN THE
SPINAL-CORD OF THE CAT: ENKEPHALIN-CONTAINING MARGINAL
NEURONS AND PAIN MODULATION.
002638 03-01

A TOPOGRAPHIC LOCALIZATION OF ENKEPHALIN ON THE DOPAMINE
NEURONS OF THE RAT SUBSTANTIA-NIGRA AND VENTRAL TEGMENTAL
AREA DEMONSTRATED BY COMBINED HISTOFLUORESCENCE
IMMUNOCYTOCHEMISTRY.
002639 03-01

BENZODIAZEPINE-RECEPTORS: AUTORADIOGRAPHICAL AND
IMMUNOCYTOCHEMICAL EVIDENCE FOR THEIR LOCALIZATION IN
REGIONS OF GABAERGIC SYNAPTIC CONTACTS.
002643 03-01

LOCOMOTOR-ACTIVITY ELICITED BY INJECTIONS OF PICROTOXIN INTO THE VENTRAL TEGMENTAL AREA IS ATTENUATED BY INJECTIONS OF GABA INTO THE GLOBUS-PALLIDUS.
000436 01-04

EFFECTS OF L-DOPA AND L 5 HYDROXYTRYPTOPHAN ON LOCOMOTOR-ACTIVITY OF THE RAT AFTER SELECTIVE OR COMBINED DESTRUCTION OF CENTRAL CATECHOLAMINE AND SEROTONIN NEURONS.
000466 01-04

INFLUENCE OF THYROTROPIN-RELEASING-HORMONE AND HISTIDYL-PROLINE-DIKETOPIPERAZINE ON SPONTANEOUS LOCOMOTOR-ACTIVITY AND ANALGESIA INDUCED BY DELTA9 TETRAHYDROCANNABINOL IN THE MOUSE.
001575 02-04

EFFECT OF APOMORPHINE ON MORPHINE-INDUCED DECREASE IN LOCOMOTOR-ACTIVITY AND INCREASE IN DOPAMINE TURNOVER IN RATS.
001728 02-04

DISSOCIATION OF D-AMPHETAMINE-INDUCED LOCOMOTOR-ACTIVITY AND STEREOTYPED-BEHAVIOUR BY LESIONS OF THE SUPERIOR-COLLICULUS.
001755 02-04

EFFECTS OF CHLORDIAZEPOXIDE MORPHINE COMBINATIONS ON SPONTANEOUS LOCOMOTOR-ACTIVITY IN THREE INBRED STRAINS OF MICE.
001766 02-04

BIPHASIC-EFFECTS OF A POTENT ENKEPHALIN ANALOGUE D MET2-PRO5-ENKEPHALINAMIDE AND MORPHINE ON LOCOMOTOR-ACTIVITY IN MICE.
001799 02-04

HIPPOCAMPAL SEROTONIN REUPTAKE AND NOCTURNAL LOCOMOTOR-ACTIVITY AFTER MICROINJECTIONS OF 5,7 DHT IN THE FORNIX-FIMBRIA.
002929 03-03

EFFECTS OF ACUTE OR CHRONIC ADMINISTRATION OF LOW-DOSES OF A DOPAMINE AGONIST ON DRINKING AND LOCOMOTOR-ACTIVITY IN THE RAT.
002982 03-04

INJECTIONS OF DOPAMINERGIC, CHOLINERGIC, SEROTONINERGIC AND GABAERGIC DRUGS INTO THE NUCLEUS-ACCUMBENS: EFFECTS ON LOCOMOTOR-ACTIVITY IN THE RAT.
003019 03-04

TRH INCREASES LOCOMOTOR-ACTIVITY IN RATS AFTER INJECTION INTO THE HYPOTHALAMUS.
003044 03-04

OPPOSITE EFFECTS OF NALOXONE ON SUBSTANCE-P-INDUCED IN BRAIN DOPA SYNTHESIS AND IN LOCOMOTOR-ACTIVITY IN RATS.
003799 04-03

LOCOMOTOR-ACTIVITY IN MORPHINE-DEPENDENT AND POSTDEPENDENT RATS.
004077 04-04

DIFFERENTIAL-EFFECTS OF SEVERAL DOPAMINE UPTAKE INHIBITORS AND RELEASING-AGENTS ON LOCOMOTOR-ACTIVITY IN NORMAL AND IN RESERPINIZED MICE.
004130 04-04

THE EFFECTS OF P CHLOROAMPHETAMINE ADMINISTRATION ON LOCOMOTOR-ACTIVITY AND SEROTONIN IN NEONATAL AND ADULT RATS. (UNPUBLISHED PAPER).
004169 04-04

LOCOMOTOR-EFFECT
THE LOCOMOTOR-EFFECT OF CLONIDINE AND ITS INTERACTION WITH ALPHA FLUPENTHIXOL OR HALOPERIDOL IN THE DEVELOPING RAT.
000445 01-04

LOCOMOTOR-EFFECTS
THERMOREGULATORY AND LOCOMOTOR-EFFECTS OF DSIP; PARADOXICAL-INTERACTION WITH D-AMPHETAMINE.
001827 02-04

LOCOMOTOR-STIMULATION
NOREPINEPHRINE UPTAKE INHIBITORS AS BIOCHEMICALLY-SELECTIVE AND BEHAVIORALLY-SELECTIVE ANTAGONISTS OF THE LOCOMOTOR-STIMULATION INDUCED BY INDIRECTLY ACTING SYMPATHOMIMETIC-AMINES IN MICE.
000492 01-04

INFLUENCE OF BENZODIAZEPINE TRANQUILIZERS ON AMPHETAMINE-INDUCED LOCOMOTOR-STIMULATION IN MICE.
001767 02-04

INFLUENCE OF BENZODIAZEPINE TRANQUILIZERS ON SCOPOLAMINE-INDUCED LOCOMOTOR-STIMULATION IN MICE.
001768 02-04

THE EFFECTS OF INTRAVENTRICULAR 6 HYDROXYDOPAMINE AND 5,6 DIHYDROXYTRYPTAMINE ON MORPHINE-INDUCED LOCOMOTOR-STIMULATION.
001784 02-04

EFFECTS OF PROPRANOLOL ON THE LOCOMOTOR-STIMULATION INDUCED BY ACTIVATION OF POSTSYNAPTIC CATECHOLAMINE-RECEPTORS.
004126 04-04

LOCUS
THE ALBINO LOCUS PRODUCES ABNORMAL RESPONSES TO OPIATES IN THE MOUSE.
001675 02-04

LOCUS-COERULEUS
MICROIONTOPHORETIC STUDIES ON NORADRENERGIC INHIBITION FROM LOCUS-COERULEUS OF SPINAL TRIGEMINAL-NUCLEUS NEURONS.
000260 01-03

CENTRAL LEVELS OF NORADRENALINE, 3 METHOXY-4-HYDROXYPHENYLETHYLENEGLYCOL AND CYCLIC-AMP IN THE RAT AFTER ACTIVATION OF LOCUS-COERULEUS NEURONS: INFLUENCE OF SINGLE AND REPEATED NEUROLEPTIC TREATMENT.
001095 02-03

OPIATES AND OPIOID-PEPTIDES HYPERPOLARIZE LOCUS-COERULEUS NEURONS IN VITRO.
001408 02-03

THE NEUROANATOMY AND PHARMACOLOGY OF THE NUCLEUS LOCUS-COERULEUS. (UNPUBLISHED PAPER).
003810 04-03

THE EFFECT OF ELECTRICAL-STIMULATION OF THE LOCUS-COERULEUS AND INTRAPERITONEAL INJECTION OF CERTAIN PHARMACOLOGICAL SUBSTANCES ON THE THRESHOLD OF HIPPOCAMPAL AFTERDISCHARGES.
003885 04-03

CLONIDINE AND THE PRIMATE LOCUS-COERULEUS: EVIDENCE SUGGESTING ANXIOLYTIC AND ANTIWITHDRAWAL EFFECTS. (UNPUBLISHED PAPER).
003982 04-03

LOFEPRAMINE
PREDICTION OF LOFEPRAMINE RESPONSE IN DEPRESSION BASED ON RESPONSE TO PARTIAL SLEEP-DEPRIVATION.
000617 01-09

COMPARISON OF THE EFFECTS OF LOFEPRAMINE AND MIANSERIN IN DEPRESSED-PATIENTS IN A DOUBLE-BLIND TRIAL.
001996 02-09

THE PHARMACOLOGICAL PROFILE OF LOFEPRAMINE, A NEW ANTIDEPRESSANT-DRUG.
004006 04-03

LOG-DOSE
LOG-DOSE/RESPONSE-CURVE FLATTENING IN RATS AFTER DAILY INJECTION OF OPIATES.
001387 02-03

LONG-ACTING
THE PLACE OF LONG-ACTING NEUROLEPTICS IN THE TREATMENT OF SCHIZOPHRENIA.
000563 01-08

THE DIFFERENTIAL-EFFECTS OF SHORT-ACTING AND LONG-ACTING BENZODIAZEPINES UPON NOCTURNAL SLEEP AND DAYTIME PERFORMANCE.
000822 01-14

PHARMACOKINETICS OF BENZODIAZEPINES: SHORT-ACTING VERSUS LONG-ACTING.
000920 01-17

CHLOROETHYLNORAPOMORPHINE, A PROPOSED LONG-ACTING DOPAMINE ANTAGONIST: INTERACTIONS WITH DOPAMINE-RECEPTORS OF MAMMALIAN FOREBRAIN IN VITRO.
001114 02-03

METHODOLOGY AND RESULTS OF A LONG-TERM STUDY OF LONG-ACTING NEUROLEPTICS: PIPOTHIAZINE-PALMITATE AND FLUPHENAZINE-DECANOATE.
001929 02-08

PERGOLIDE, A POTENT LONG-ACTING DOPAMINE-RECEPTOR AGONIST.
002257 02-13

MALIGNANT-HYPERTHERMIC-SYNDROMES IN THE COURSE OF TREATMENT WITH LONG-ACTING NEUROLEPTICS.
002430 02-15

LONG-ACTING ANTIPSYCHOTIC-DRUGS.
002519 02-17

PRESENT INDICATIONS OF LONG-ACTING NEUROLEPTICS.
002576 02-17

LONG-ACTING ANTIPSYCHOTIC-DRUGS AND CEREBRAL 5 HYDROXYTRYPTAMINE.
002851 03-03

CONSIDERATIONS ON LONG-ACTING CHEMOTHERAPY: AN EXPERIENCE WITH FLUPHENAZINE-DECANOATE.
003173 03-08

NALOXAZONE, A LONG-ACTING OPIATE ANTAGONIST: EFFECTS ON ANALGESIA IN INTACT ANIMALS AND ON OPIATE-RECEPTOR BINDING IN VITRO.
004198 04-04

COMPARATIVE CHARACTERISTICS OF THE PROPHYLACTIC PROPERTIES OF SHORT-TERM AND LONG-ACTING LITHIUM-CARBONATE PREPARATIONS IN ENDOGENOUS AFFECTIVE-PSYCHOSES.
004390 04-09

LONG-DURATION
(-)PENTOBARBITAL OPENS ION-CHANNELS OF LONG-DURATION IN CULTURED MOUSE SPINAL NEURONS.
000198 01-03

LONG-EVANS-RATS
RAT PUP-KILLING AND MATERNAL-BEHAVIOR IN MALE LONG-EVANS-RATS: PRENATAL STIMULATION AND POSTNATAL TESTOSTERONE.
003054 03-04

Subject Index

LONG-LASTING

REPEATED ANTIDEPRESSANT TREATMENTS INDUCE A LONG-LASTING DOPAMINE-AUTORECEPTOR SUBSENSITIVITY: IS DAILY TREATMENT NECESSARY FOR CLINICAL EFFICACY?
002659 03-03

LONG-LASTING EFFECTS OF CHRONIC ADMINISTRATION OF HALLUCINOGENIC-DRUGS ON RAT SOCIAL AND EMOTIONAL-BEHAVIOR. (PH.D. DISSERTATION).
003029 03-04

AMITRIPTYLINE PROVIDES LONG-LASTING IMMUNIZATION AGAINST SUDDEN CARDIAC DEATH FROM COCAINE.
003122 03-05

LONG-STAY

PREVALENCE OF PERSISTENT ABNORMAL INVOLUNTARY-MOVEMENTS AMONG PATIENTS IN A NIGERIAN LONG-STAY PSYCHIATRIC UNIT.
004334 04-08

LONG-TERM

INCORPORATION OF 4.5 3H LEUCINE INTO THE LIMBIC-SYSTEM OF ICR MICE AS A LONG-TERM EFFECT OF HALOPERIDOL APPLICATION.
000118 01-03

LONG-TERM ANTIDEPRESSANT TREATMENT DECREASES SPIROPERIDOL-LABELED SEROTONIN-RECEPTOR BINDING.
000230 01-03

LONG-TERM ANTIDEPRESSANT TREATMENT: ALTERATIONS IN CEREBRAL CAPILLARY PERMEABILITY.
000239 01-03

FUNCTIONAL AND STRUCTURAL CONSEQUENCES OF LONG-TERM DIETARY L-DOPA TREATMENT IN MICE.
000257 01-03

LONG-TERM EFFECTS OF CONTINUOUS EXPOSURE TO AMPHETAMINE ON BRAIN DOPAMINE CONCENTRATION AND SYNAPTOSOMAL UPTAKE IN MICE.
000287 01-03

THE LONG-TERM REGULATION OF GANGLIONIC TYROSINE-HYDROXYLASE BY PREGANGLIONIC NERVE ACTIVITY.
000333 01-03

INCREASED DOPAMINE-RECEPTOR BINDING IN THE STRIATUM OF RATS AFTER LONG-TERM ISOLATION.
000398 01-04

IMPAIRED GLUCOSE TOLERANCE IN LONG-TERM LITHIUM TREATED PATIENTS.
000611 01-09

THE LONG-TERM RESULTS OF STEREOTAXIC SURGERY AND L-DOPA THERAPY IN PATIENTS WITH PARKINSONS-DISEASE: A 10-YEAR FOLLOWUP STUDY.
000693 01-11

LONG-TERM EFFICACY OF BROMOCRIPTINE IN PARKINSONS-DISEASE.
000698 01-11

METHODOLOGICAL REMARKS ON LONG-TERM LITHIUM TREATMENT.
000749 01-13

THE AUTOINDUCTION OF CARBAMAZEPINE DURING LONG-TERM THERAPY.
000785 01-13

THE ULTRASTRUCTURAL CHANGES OF SYNAPSES IN RAT FOLLOWING LONG-TERM ADMINISTRATION OF THE NEUROLEPTICS RESERPINE AND HALOPERIDOL.
000795 01-13

BILATERAL PAPILLOEDEMA IN LONG-TERM THERAPY WITH LITHIUM-CARBONATE.
000878 01-15

TARDIVE TOURETTE-SYNDROME IN AN AUTISTIC-PATIENT AFTER LONG-TERM NEUROLEPTIC ADMINISTRATION.
000887 01-15

ENDOCRINOLOGICAL CHANGES IN PATIENTS WITH SEXUAL-DYSFUNCTION UNDER LONG-TERM NEUROLEPTIC TREATMENT.
000912 01-17

LONG-TERM EFFECT OF NEUROLEPTICS ON CORTICOSTERONE SEPTOHIPPOCAMPAL UPTAKE IN RATS.
001107 02-03

LONG-TERM HALOPERIDOL TREATMENT OF MICE: A CHANGE IN BETA-ADRENERGIC-RECEPTOR RESPONSIVENESS.
001206 02-03

EFFECTS OF LONG-TERM ADMINISTRATION OF ANTIPSYCHOTIC-DRUGS ON ENKEPHALINERGIC NEURONS.
001284 02-03

THE HYPERKINETIC-SYNDROME FOLLOWING LONG-TERM HALOPERIDOL TREATMENT: INVOLVEMENT OF DOPAMINE AND NORADRENALINE.
001299 02-03

LONG-TERM ADMINISTRATION OF ATROPINE, IMIPRAMINE, AND VILOXAZINE ALTERS RESPONSIVENESS OF RAT-CORTICAL-NEURONES TO ACETYLCHOLINE.
001306 02-03

LONG-TERM EFFECTS OF HALOPERIDOL, CLOZAPINE, AND METHADONE ON RAT STRIATAL CHOLINERGIC AND DOPAMINERGIC DYNAMICS.
001325 02-03

LONG-TERM DECREASES IN SPONTANEOUS FIRING OF CAUDATE NEURONS INDUCED BY AMPHETAMINE IN CATS.
001340 02-03

LONG-TERM HALOPERIDOL TREATMENT AND FACTORS EFFECTING THE ACTIVITY OF STRIATAL TYROSINE-HYDROXYLASE.
001348 02-03

TIME-COURSE OF CLINICAL CHEMICAL PARAMETERS UNDER LONG-TERM LITHIUM TREATMENT.
003515 03-15
LONG-TERM CHANGES IN AIMS RATINGS AND THEIR RELATION TO MEDICATION HISTORY.
003537 03-15
GLOMERULAR FILTRATION RATE AND CALCIUM METABOLISM IN LONG-TERM LITHIUM TREATMENT.
003542 03-15
THE EFFECT OF LONG-TERM CONCURRENT ADMINISTRATION OF CHLORPROMAZINE AND LITHIUM ON THE STRIATAL AND FRONTAL CORTICAL DOPAMINE METABOLISM IN RATS.
003788 04-03
LONG-TERM EFFECTS OF MULTIPLE DOSES OF METHAMPHETAMINE ON TRYPTOPHAN-HYDROXYLASE AND TYROSINE-HYDROXYLASE ACTIVITY IN RAT-BRAIN.
003850 04-03
ALPHA2-ADRENORECEPTORS IN RAT-BRAIN ARE DECREASED AFTER LONG-TERM TRICYCLIC-ANTIDEPRESSANT DRUG-TREATMENT.
004008 04-03
EFFECTS OF WITHDRAWAL FROM LONG-TERM DIPHENYLHYDANTOIN TREATMENT ON AUDIOGENIC-SEIZURES AND MAXIMAL ELECTROSHOCK-INDUCED SEIZURES IN RATS.
004101 04-04
THE EFFECT OF LONG-TERM MAINTENANCE-THERAPY ON SCHIZOPHRENIC-PATIENTS USING SOMATOTHERAPEUTIC MEASURES.
004325 04-08
LONG-TERM NEUROLEPTIC TREATMENT OF CHRONIC SCHIZOPHRENIC-PATIENTS: CLINICAL AND BIOCHEMICAL-EFFECTS OF WITHDRAWAL.
004344 04-08
LEVODOPA: LONG-TERM IMPACT ON PARKINSONS-DISEASE.
004476 04-11
PHARMACOLOGICAL MODULATION OF FORMATION OF LONG-TERM MEMORY.
004578 04-14
LONG-TERM USE AND ABUSE OF BENZODIAZEPINES.
004598 04-15
ON THE QUESTION OF PARENCHYMAL DAMAGE CAUSED BY LONG-TERM THERAPY WITH PSYCHOTROPICS IN ADOLESCENCE.
004626 04-15
PATHOPHYSIOLOGICAL AND MORPHOLOGICAL CHANGES IN THE CNS DURING LONG-TERM ADMINISTRATION OF HALOPERIDOL.
004633 04-15

LONG-TERM-TREATMENT
CENTRAL NORADRENERGIC ADAPTATION TO LONG-TERM-TREATMENT WITH IMIPRAMINE IN RHESUS-MONKEYS.
000182 01-03
OXYPROTHEPIN-DECANOATE INJECTIONS: EXPERIENCE WITH A LONG-TERM-TREATMENT OF SCHIZOPHRENIC-PSYCHOSES.
000576 01-08
THE LONG-TERM-TREATMENT OF PERIODICAL AND CYCLIC DEPRESSIONS WITH FLUPENTHIXOL-DECANOATE.
000603 01-09
BEHAVIORAL-CORRELATES AND BIOCHEMICAL-CORRELATES AFTER HALOPERIDOL AND CLOZAPINE LONG-TERM-TREATMENT.
001422 02-03
EFFECT OF LONG-TERM-TREATMENT WITH HALOPERIDOL AND SULPIRIDE ON DIFFERENT TYPES OF DOPAMINERGIC-RECEPTORS.
001512 02-03
BEHAVIORAL-CONSEQUENCES OF LONG-TERM-TREATMENT WITH NEUROLEPTIC-DRUGS.
001661 02-04
APPARENT TOLERANCE TO SOME ASPECTS OF AMPHETAMINE STEREOTYPY WITH LONG-TERM-TREATMENT.
001758 02-04
DYSKINESIA INDUCED BY LONG-TERM-TREATMENT WITH ANTIPSYCHOTIC-DRUGS: INVOLVEMENT OF PRESYNAPTIC AND POSTSYNAPTIC DOPAMINERGIC MECHANISMS.
001839 02-05
LONG-TERM-TREATMENT OF DEPRESSION WITH ISOCARBOXAZIDE.
002011 02-09
LONG-TERM-TREATMENT WITH NEUROLEPTIC-AGENTS: ADAPTATION PHENOMENA AND THEIR SIGNIFICANCE WITH REGARD TO SCHIZOPHRENIC-SYMPTOMATOLOGY AND SIDE-EFFECTS.
002370 02-15
AMITRIPTYLINE: LONG-TERM-TREATMENT ELEVATES ALPHA-ADRENERGIC AND MUSCARINIC-RECEPTOR BINDING IN MOUSE-BRAIN.
002875 03-03
ACCELERATED METABOLISM OF PROBENECID DURING LONG-TERM-TREATMENT OF RATS WITH ANTICONVULSANT-DRUGS: EFFECT ON CENTRAL SEROTONIN TURNOVER STUDIES.
002890 03-03
LONG-TERM-TREATMENT OF SCHIZOPHRENIA.
003171 03-08
LONG-TERM-TREATMENT OF RATS WITH MORPHINE DECREASES IN VITRO BIOSYNTHESIS IN AND RELEASE OF BETA ENDORPHIN FROM INTERMEDIATE/POSTERIOR LOBES OF PITUITARY.
003846 04-03

STUDIES ON THE KINETIC PROPERTIES OF TRYPTOPHAN-HYDROXYLASE OF RABBIT MESENCEPHALON AND PONS-MEDULLA: EFFECT OF LONG-TERM-TREATMENT WITH NEUROLEPTICS AND ANTIDEPRESSANTS.
003852 04-03
LONG-TERM-TREATMENT FOR DEPRESSION.
004372 04-09
THE COURSE OF LONG-TERM-TREATMENT WITH FLUPHENAZINE-DECANOATE (DAPOTUM-D).
004605 04-15

LOOK
LOOK AND OLD-AGE.
000930 01-17
EFFECTS OF CHLORPROMAZINE ON ESCAPE AND AVOIDANCE RESPONSES: A CLOSER LOOK.
004226 04-04

LOPERAMIDE
ABUSE POTENTIAL OF LOPERAMIDE.
002413 02-15

LOPIRAZEPAM
CLASSIFICATION AND ASSESSMENT OF CEREBRAL BIOAVAILABILITY OF LOPIRAZEPAM (D-12524) BY QUANTITATIVE EEG AND PSYCHOMETRIC-ANALYSIS
000720 01-11

LORAZEPAM
A COMPARATIVE-STUDY ON THE CLINICAL-EFFECTS OF FLUNITRAZEPAM AND LORAZEPAM.
000702 01-11
LORAZEPAM KINETICS IN THE ELDERLY.
000766 01-13
TRANSFER OF LORAZEPAM AND ITS CONJUGATE ACROSS THE HUMAN PLACENTA.
000774 01-13
PHARMACOKINETIC-STUDY OF LORAZEPAM OVERDOSAGE.
000831 01-15
A CASE-REPORT OF LORAZEPAM WITHDRAWAL.
000889 01-15
EFFICACY AND SIDE-EFFECTS OF LORAZEPAM, OXAZEPAM, AND TEMAZEPAM AS SLEEPING-AIDS IN PSYCHOGERIATRIC-INPATIENTS.
002076 02-10
USE OF INJECTABLE LORAZEPAM IN ALCOHOL WITHDRAWAL.
002176 02-11
THE EFFECTS OF FLURAZEPAM, LORAZEPAM, AND TRIAZOLAM ON SLEEP AND MEMORY.
002357 02-14
CLINICAL PHARMACOKINETICS OF OXAZEPAM AND LORAZEPAM.
003410 03-13
EFFECT OF MATERNAL LORAZEPAM ON THE NEONATE.
003549 03-15
INTRAVENOUS LORAZEPAM TO PREVENT NAUSEA AND VOMITING ASSOCIATED WITH CANCER CHEMOTHERAPY.
003614 03-17
ACTIVITY OF BROMAZEPAM AND LORAZEPAM IN NEUROTIC DEPRESSIONS.
004384 04-09
A COMPARATIVE-STUDY OF INTRAVENOUS LORAZEPAM AND CLONAZEPAM IN STATUS-EPILEPTICUS.
004487 04-11

LORDOSIS
ATTEMPTS TO REINSTATE LORDOSIS REFLEX IN ESTROGEN-PRIMED SPINAL FEMALE RATS WITH MONOAMINE AGONISTS.
000421 01-04
FACILITATION OF LORDOSIS BEHAVIOR IN THE OVARIECTOMIZED ESTROGEN-PRIMED RAT BY DIBUTYRYL-C-AMP.
002957 03-04
EFFECTS OF ACUTE CENTRAL AND PERIPHERAL ACTH1-24 ADMINISTRATION ON LORDOSIS BEHAVIOR.
002975 03-04

LORMETAZEPAM
AGE-SPECIFIC DOSES OF LORMETAZEPAM AS A NIGHT SEDATIVE IN CASES OF CHRONIC SLEEP-DISTURBANCE.
004309 04-07
KINETICS AND BIOTRANSFORMATION OF LORMETAZEPAM: II. RADIOIMMUNOLOGIC DETERMINATIONS IN PLASMA AND URINE OF YOUNG AND ELDERLY SUBJECTS: FIRST-PASS EFFECT.
004516 04-13

LOSS
BENZODIAZEPINES CAUSE SMALL LOSS OF BODY-WEIGHT.
002446 02-15
DIFFERENTIAL LOSS OF BIOLOGICAL-ACTIVITY OF THE ENKEPHALINS INDUCED BY CURRENT.
002783 03-03
CAN DRUGS HALT MEMORY LOSS?
003447 03-14
THE RELATIONSHIP BETWEEN LOSS OF DOPAMINE NERVE TERMINALS, STRIATAL (3H)SPIROPERIDOL BINDING AND ROTATIONAL-BEHAVIOR IN UNILATERALLY 6 HYDROXYDOPAMINE LESIONED RATS.
004129 04-04

LOUVAIN-LA-NEUVE
ABSTRACTS OF THE ANNUAL GENERAL CONFERENCE OF THE EUROPEAN-BRAIN-AND-BEHAVIOUR-SOCIETY, HELD AT LOUVAIN-LA-NEUVE, BELGIUM, ON NOVEMBER 13-15TH, 1980.
003617 03-17

LOW
MONOAMINE REPLACEMENT AFTER RESERPINE: CATECHOLAMINERGIC AGONISTS RESTORE MOTOR-ACTIVITY BUT PHENYLETHYLAMINE RESTORES ATROPINE-RESISTANT NEOCORTICAL LOW VOLTAGE FAST-ACTIVITY.
000309 01-03
RESERPINE ABOLISHES MOVEMENT CORRELATED ATROPINE-RESISTANT NEOCORTICAL LOW VOLTAGE FAST-ACTIVITY.
000310 01-03
MU-RECEPTORS AND DELTA OPIATE-RECEPTORS: CORRELATION WITH HIGH-AFFINITY AND LOW AFFINITY OPIATE BINDING-SITES.
001554 02-03
LOW ORAL CPZ BIOAVAILABILITY IN CHRONIC SCHIZOPHRENIA. (UNPUBLISHED PAPER).
001938 02-08
CHRONIC EFFECTS OF NEUROLEPTICS HAVING HIGH OR LOW INCIDENCE OF EXTRAPYRAMIDAL SIDE-EFFECTS UPON FORCE, DURATION AND RATE OF OPERANT-RESPONSE IN RATS. (PH.D. DISSERTATION).
003125 03-05
LOW SERUM PROLACTIN AND EARLY RELAPSE FOLLOWING NEUROLEPTIC WITHDRAWAL.
003166 03-08
CHLORPROMAZINE, HALOPERIDOL, METOCLOPRAMIDE AND DOMPERIDONE RELEASE PROLACTIN THROUGH DOPAMINE ANTAGONISM AT LOW CONCENTRATIONS BUT PARADOXICALLY INHIBIT PROLACTIN RELEASE AT HIGH-CONCENTRATIONS.
003731 04-03
LITHIUM IN THE PROPHYLAXIS OF RECURRENT AFFECTIVE-DISORDERS (EFFECTIVENESS OF LOW PLASMA LEVELS AND PREDICTORS TO CLINICAL-RESPONSE).
004365 04-09

LOW-AVOIDANCE
REGIONAL 5 HT ANALYSIS IN ROMAN HIGH-AVOIDANCE AND LOW-AVOIDANCE RATS FOLLOWING MAO-INHIBITION.
001202 02-03
BRAIN MUSCARINIC CHOLINERGIC-RECEPTOR BINDING IN ROMAN HIGH-AVOIDANCE AND LOW-AVOIDANCE RATS.
002852 03-03

LOW-DOSAGES
ON THE EFFECTS OF SULTOPRIDE ADMINISTERED IN LOW-DOSAGES TO OLDER CHILDREN AND ADOLESCENTS.
003230 03-09

LOW-DOSE
EFFECTS OF A LOW-DOSE AND A HIGH-DOSE OF BETA ENDORPHIN ON ACQUISITION AND RETENTION IN THE RAT.
001663 02-04
RAPID TREATMENT OF ACUTE PSYCHOTIC-SYMPTOMS WITH HIGH-DOSE AND LOW-DOSE HALOPERIDOL: BEHAVIORAL-CONSIDERATIONS.
003346 03-11
EFFECT OF LOW-DOSE LITHIUM ADMINISTRATION AND SUBSEQUENT WITHDRAWAL ON BIOGENIC-AMINES IN RAT-BRAIN.
003708 04-03

LOW-DOSES
CLINICAL-EXPERIENCE WITH LOW-DOSES OF HALOPERIDOL IN THE TREATMENT OF NEUROSES.
000654 01-10
PSYCHOPHARMACOLOGICAL-EFFECTS OF LOW-DOSES AND HIGH-DOSES OF APOMORPHINE DURING ONTOGENY.
001774 02-04
PLASMA FLUPHENAZINE AND PROLACTIN LEVELS IN SCHIZOPHRENIC-PATIENTS DURING TREATMENT WITH LOW-DOSES AND HIGH-DOSES OF FLUPHENAZINE-ENANTHATE.
001956 02-08
SEX-DIFFERENCES IN THE EFFECTS OF LOW-DOSES OF ETHANOL ON HUMAN REACTION-TIME.
002361 02-14
TARDIVE-DYSKINESIA FOLLOWING LOW-DOSES OF PIPERACETAZINE.
002399 02-15
FURTHER EXPERIENCES WITH LOW-DOSES OF BROMOCRIPTINE IN PARKINSONS-DISEASE.
002401 02-15
EFFECTS OF ACUTE OR CHRONIC ADMINISTRATION OF LOW-DOSES OF A DOPAMINE AGONIST ON DRINKING AND LOCOMOTOR-ACTIVITY IN THE RAT.
002982 03-04
EVIDENCE FOR SEDATIVE EFFECTS OF LOW-DOSES OF MORPHINE IN MICE INVOLVING RECEPTORS INSENSITIVE TO NALOXONE.
004173 04-04

LOWERING
LOWERING OF THE CONVULSIVE THRESHOLD BY NONSTEROIDAL ANTIINFLAMMATORY-DRUGS.
002904 03-03

LOXAPINE
THE PLACE OF LOXAPINE — A NEW NEUROLEPTIC-DRUG.
001886 02-07

LOXAPINE FATALITIES.
004650 04-15

LOXAPINE-SUCCINATE
LOXAPINE-SUCCINATE: A NEW NEUROLEPTIC-DRUG.
000551 01-08
EVALUATIONS OF LOXAPINE-SUCCINATE IN THE AMBULATORY TREATMENT OF ACUTE SCHIZOPHRENIC-EPISODES.
004345 04-08

LRF-DECAPEPTIDE
CHARACTERIZATION OF LRF-LIKE IMMUNOREACTIVITY IN THE FROG SYMPATHETIC GANGLIA: NONIDENTITY WITH LRF-DECAPEPTIDE. (UNPUBLISHED PAPER).
001018 02-01

LRF-LIKE
CHARACTERIZATION OF LRF-LIKE IMMUNOREACTIVITY IN THE FROG SYMPATHETIC GANGLIA: NONIDENTITY WITH LRF-DECAPEPTIDE. (UNPUBLISHED PAPER).
001018 02-01

LSD
DECREASED SPIROPERIDOL AND LSD BINDING IN RAT-BRAIN AFTER CONTINUOUS AMPHETAMINE.
000216 01-03
THE EFFECT OF SEROTONIN DEPLETION ON THE DISCRIMINABILITY OF LSD.
000499 01-04
THE EFFECTS OF LSD AND SOME ANALOGUES ON THE RESPONSES OF SINGLE CORTICAL NEURONS OF THE CAT TO OPTICAL-STIMULATION.
000738 01-12
PERSISTENT EFFECTS OF CHRONIC ADMINISTRATION OF LSD ON INTRACELLULAR SEROTONIN CONTENT IN RAT-MIDBRAIN.
001333 02-03
CHARACTERIZATION AND RADIOAUTOGRAPHY OF (3H)LSD BINDING BY RAT-BRAIN SLICES IN VITRO: THE EFFECT OF 5 HYDROXYTRYPTAMINE.
001369 02-03
THE EFFECTS OF D LYSERGIC-ACID-DIETHYLAMIDE (LSD), 2,5 DIMETHOXY-4-METHYLAMPHETAMINE (DOM) AND D-AMPHETAMINE ON OPERANT-RESPONDING IN CONTROL AND 6 HYDROXYDOPAMINE TREATED RATS.
001595 02-04
SENSORY AND ASSOCIATIVE-EFFECTS OF LSD ON CLASSICAL APPETITIVE-CONDITIONING OF THE RABBIT JAW MOVEMENT RESPONSE.
001637 02-04
AN ANALYSIS OF SOME PERCEPTUAL-EFFECTS OF MORPHINE, CHLORPROMAZINE, AND LSD.
001652 02-04
ACUTE AND CHRONIC LSD EFFECTS ON RAT STARTLE: DATA SUPPORTING AN LSD RAT MODEL OF SCHIZOPHRENIA.
002194 02-12
SELECTIVE EFFECTS OF LSD AND HYPERTHERMIA ON THE SYNTHESIS OF SYNAPTIC PROTEINS AND GLYCOPROTEINS.
002721 03-03
DRUG-INDUCED STIMULUS CONTROL AND THE CONCEPT OF BREAKING-POINT: LSD AND QUIPAZINE.
003116 03-04
LSD, PSYCHOTOGENIC PROCEDURES AND BRAIN NEUROHUMORS. (UNPUBLISHED PAPER).
004448 04-11
LSD: MY PROBLEM CHILD.
004497 04-12

LSD-INDUCED
EFFECTS OF DOPAMINERGIC AND CHOLINERGIC-DRUGS, NALOXONE AND L PROLYL-LEUCYL-GLYCINAMIDE ON LSD-INDUCED CATALEPSY.
000360 01-04
LSD-INDUCED ULTRASTRUCTURAL MODIFICATIONS OF LIMBIC-SYSTEM NUCLEI AND OTHER CEREBRAL ZONES.
002198 02-12

LSD-LIKE
RAT-BRAIN STEADY-STATE LEVELS OF CYCLIC-NUCLEOTIDES AS AN ENDPOINT OF LSD-LIKE HALLUCINOGEN EFFECTS. (PH.D. DISSERTATION).
001426 02-03

LSD-25
LSD-25 AS A DISCRIMINATIVE-STIMULUS FOR RESPONSE SELECTION BY PIGEONS.
000412 01-04

LUMBAR
A BIOCHEMICAL-STUDY OF LUMBAR CEREBROSPINAL-FLUID IN EXTRAPYRAMIDAL-DISORDERS.
002186 02-11
LEVELS OF 5 HYDROXYINDOLEACETIC-ACID AND TRYPTOPHAN IN LUMBAR CEREBROSPINAL-FLUID AND BLOOD OF PATIENTS WITH DEMENTIA AND NORMAL PRESSURE HYDROCEPHALUS AFTER TRYPTOPHAN ADMINISTRATION.
003419 03-13
A SELECTED ION-MONITORING ASSAY FOR BIOGENIC-AMINE METABOLITES AND PROBENECID, IN HUMAN LUMBAR CEREBROSPINAL-FLUID.
003663 04-01

LUNG
EFFECT OF DESMETHYLIMIPRAMINE ON THE KINETICS OF CHLORPHENTERMINE ACCUMULATION IN ISOLATED PERFUSED RAT LUNG.
000524 01-05

LUPUS-ERYTHEMATOSUS
ACETYLATOR PHENOTYPE AND LUPUS-ERYTHEMATOSUS.
003545 03-15

LUPUS-LIKE-ILLNESS
LUPUS-LIKE-ILLNESS ASSOCIATED WITH CHLORPROMAZINE.
002408 02-15

LUTEINISING-HORMONE
INFLUENCE OF NOMIFENSINE ON GROWTH-HORMONE, PROLACTIN, LUTEINISING-HORMONE AND THYREOTROPIN IN HEALTHY SUBJECTS AND HYPERPROLACTINAEMIC-PATIENTS.
002137 02-11

LUTEINIZING-HORMONE
THE EFFECT OF DELTA9 TETRAHYDROCANNABINOL ON THE POSITIVE AND NEGATIVE FEEDBACK CONTROL OF LUTEINIZING-HORMONE RELEASE.
000286 01-03

EFFECTS OF MORPHINE AND NALOXONE ON PHASIC RELEASE OF LUTEINIZING-HORMONE AND FOLLICLE-STIMULATING-HORMONE (40849).
000298 01-03

EFFECTS OF AN EPINEPHRINE SYNTHESIS INHIBITOR, SKF-64139, ON THE SECRETION OF LUTEINIZING-HORMONE IN OVARIECTOMIZED FEMALE RATS.
002693 03-03

DEVELOPMENT OF ACUTE TOLERANCE TO THE EFFECTS OF NALOXONE ON THE HYPOTHALAMIC PITUITARY LUTEINIZING-HORMONE AXIS IN THE MALE RAT.
002853 03-03

LYMPH-NODE
ENHANCED TRANSFER OF EXPERIMENTAL ALLERGIC-ENCEPHALOMYELITIS WITH STRAIN-13 GUINEA-PIG-LYMPH-NODE CELLS: REQUIREMENT FOR CULTURE WITH SPECIFIC ANTIGEN AND ALLOGENIC PERITONEAL EXUDATE CELLS. (UNPUBLISHED PAPER).
001201 02-03

ENHANCED TRANSFER OF EXPERIMENTAL ALLERGIC-ENCEPHALOMYELITIS WITH LEWIS-RAT LYMPH-NODE CELLS. (UNPUBLISHED PAPER).
001434 02-03

LYMPHOCYTE
LYMPHOCYTE MONOAMINE-OXIDASE AND PLASMA PROLACTIN AND GROWTH-HORMONE IN TARDIVE-DYSKINESIA.
003499 03-15

LYMPHOCYTES
THE EFFECT OF CHLORPROMAZINE AND MAGEPTIL ON THE PROLIFERATION OF PERIPHERAL BLOOD LYMPHOCYTES IN CULTIVATION WITH PHYTOHEMAGGLUTININ.
004541 04-13

LYMPHOGENIC
MICROSCOPIC EVIDENCE OF LYMPHOGENIC ABSORPTION OF OIL IN HUMANS RECEIVING NEUROLEPTIC OILY DEPOT PREPARATIONS INTRAMUSCULARLY.
000890 01-15

LYSATES
TREATMENT OF ORGANIC-BRAIN-DISTURBANCES IN ELDERLY-PATIENTS. A CLINICAL DOUBLE-BLIND STUDY WITH MACROMOLECULAR ORGAN LYSATES (CYTOPLASMATIC THERAPY ACCORDING TO THEURER).
003327 03-11

LYSED
EFFECT OF MORPHINE ON CALCIUM UPTAKE BY LYSED SYNAPTOSOMES.
000117 01-03

LYSERGIC-ACID
A COMMON MECHANISM FOR LYSERGIC-ACID, INDOLEALKYLAMINE AND PHENETHYLAMINE HALLUCINOGENS: SEROTONERGIC MEDIATION OF BEHAVIORAL-EFFECTS IN RATS.
004007 04-03

LYSERGIC-ACID-DIETHYLAMIDE
LYSERGIC-ACID-DIETHYLAMIDE: MORPHOLOGICAL-STUDY OF ITS EFFECT ON SYNAPSES.
001315 02-03

THE EFFECTS OF D LYSERGIC-ACID-DIETHYLAMIDE (LSD), 2,5 DIMETHOXY-4-METHYLAMPHETAMINE (DOM) AND D-AMPHETAMINE ON OPERANT-RESPONDING IN CONTROL AND 6 HYDROXYDOPAMINE TREATED RATS.
001595 02-04

EFFECT OF INTRAVENOUS ADMINISTRATION OF D LYSERGIC-ACID-DIETHYLAMIDE ON SUBSEQUENT PROTEIN SYNTHESIS IN A CELL-FREE SYSTEM DERIVED FROM BRAIN.
003761 04-03

COMPARISON OF THE EFFECT OF INTRAVENOUS ADMINISTRATION OF D LYSERGIC-ACID-DIETHYLAMIDE ON FREE AND MEMBRANE-BOUND POLYSOMS IN THE RABBIT BRAIN.
003831 04-03

CELL-FREE TRANSLATION OF FREE AND MEMBRANE-BOUND POLYSOMES AND POLYADENYLATED MRNA FROM RABBIT BRAIN FOLLOWING ADMINISTRATION OF D LYSERGIC-ACID-DIETHYLAMIDE IN VIVO.
003832 04-03

LYSINE
ENHANCEMENT OF HEXOBARBITAL-INDUCED SLEEP BY LYSINE AND ITS METABOLITES.
002967 03-04

BLOCKADE BY L LYSINE OF NONNARCOTIC ANALGESICS.
003857 04-03

LYSINE-VASOPRESSIN
USE OF LYSINE-VASOPRESSIN IN THE TREATMENT OF POSTTRAUMATIC AMNESIA.
004583 04-14

LYSONEURO
CLINICAL RESULTS OBTAINED WITH THE USE OF LYSONEURO IN DEPRESSIVE-SYNDROMES.
004397 04-09

LYSOSOMAL
INHIBITION OF LYSOSOMAL LIPASES BY CHLORPROMAZINE: A POSSIBLE MECHANISMS OF STABILIZATION.
003993 04-03

LYTIC-EFFECTS
MECHANISM OF MEMBRANE STABILIZING AND LYTIC-EFFECTS OF TRICYCLIC-ANTIDEPRESSANTS.
004283 04-05

MACACA-MULATTA
BETA-ADRENOCEPTOR ANTAGONISTS: STUDIES ON BEHAVIOUR (DELAYED DIFFERENTIATION) IN THE MONKEY (MACACA-MULATTA).
000440 01-04

SYNCHRONIZATION OF EEG ACTIVITY OF MALE RHESUS-MONKEYS MACACA-MULATTA TREATED WITH OVOCYCLIN.
001312 02-03

EFFECTS OF METHAQUALONE ON SOCIAL-BEHAVIOR IN MONKEYS (MACACA-MULATTA).
001594 02-04

MACROMOLECULAR
INFLUENCE OF PSYCHOACTIVE AND NONPSYCHOACTIVE CANNABINOIDS ON CELL PROLIFERATION AND MACROMOLECULAR BIOSYNTHESIS IN HUMAN CELLS.
002830 03-03

TREATMENT OF ORGANIC-BRAIN-DISTURBANCES IN ELDERLY-PATIENTS. A CLINICAL DOUBLE-BLIND STUDY WITH MACROMOLECULAR ORGAN LYSATES (CYTOPLASMATIC THERAPY ACCORDING TO THEURER).
003327 03-11

MACROMOLECULE
EFFECT OF OPIATES ON MACROMOLECULE BIOSYNTHESIS.
001335 02-03

MACROPHAGE
CHEMOTAXIS BY MOUSE MACROPHAGE CELL LINES. (UNPUBLISHED PAPER).
001099 02-03

INHIBITION OF CHEMOTAXIS BY S 3 DEAZAADENOSYLHOMOCYSTEINE IN A MOUSE MACROPHAGE CELL LINE. (UNPUBLISHED PAPER).
001100 02-03

MACROPHAGES
PROTEIN ABNORMALITIES IN MACROPHAGES BEARING ASBESTOS. (UNPUBLISHED PAPER).
001037 02-01

MADE-1932
PROTECTIVE ACTION OF L 5 HYDROXYTRYPTOPHAN L GLUTAMATE (MADE-1932) DURING ELECTROSHOCK-TREATMENT (ECT).
003043 03-04

MADNESS
MADNESS AND MEDICINE: THE FORCIBLE ADMINISTRATION OF PSYCHOTROPIC-DRUGS.
002523 02-17

MAGEPTIL
THE EFFECT OF CHLORPROMAZINE AND MAGEPTIL ON THE PROLIFERATION OF PERIPHERAL BLOOD LYMPHOCYTES IN CULTIVATION WITH PHYTOHEMAGGLUTININ.
004541 04-13

MAGNESIUM
THE BIOLOGICAL-EFFECTS AND CLINICAL-EFFECTS OF ORAL MAGNESIUM AND ASSOCIATED MAGNESIUM VITAMIN-B6 ADMINISTRATION ON CERTAIN DISORDERS OBSERVED IN INFANTILE AUTISM.
003291 03-11

MAGNITUDE
POSSIBLE INFLUENCE OF OPIOID NORMETABOLITES ON THE ONSET, MAGNITUDE AND QUALITY OF THE OPIOID ABSTINENCE-SYNDROME.
004610 04-15

MAINTENANCE
WHAT IS THE BEST MAINTENANCE DOSE OF NEUROLEPTICS IN SCHIZOPHRENIA?
000547 01-08

METHADONE DISULFIRAM INTERACTION DURING METHADONE MAINTENANCE.
000796 01-13

SUBCUTANEOUS SILASTIC IMPLANTS: MAINTENANCE OF HIGH BLOOD ETHANOL LEVELS IN RATS DRINKING A LIQUID DIET.
001865 02-06

THE CHANGE OF BLOOD PROLACTIN LEVEL DUE TO THE WITHDRAWAL OF
MAINTENANCE NEUROLEPTICS.
002559 02-17

ANALYSIS OF SINGLE-BLIND, DOUBLE-BLIND PROCEDURES, MAINTENANCE
OF PLACEBO-EFFECTS, AND DRUG-INDUCED DYSKINESIA WITH
MENTALLY-RETARDED PERSONS -- BRIEF REPORT.
003298 03-11

DYSTONIC REACTION DURING MAINTENANCE ANTIPSYCHOTIC THERAPY.
003485 03-15

NATURAL AND THERAPEUTIC ENVIRONMENTAL INDICATORS OF
MAINTENANCE DOSAGE REQUIREMENTS.
003561 03-16

ANALYSIS OF SINGLE-BLIND AND DOUBLE-BLIND PROCEDURES,
MAINTENANCE OF PLACEBO-EFFECTS AND DRUG-INDUCED DYSKINESIA
WITH MENTALLY-RETARDED PERSON.
004437 04-11

MAINTENANCE-THERAPY
INTRAMUSCULAR HALOPERIDOL-DECANOATE FOR NEUROLEPTIC
MAINTENANCE-THERAPY: EFFICACY, DOSAGE SCHEDULE AND PLASMA
LEVELS: AN OPEN MULTICENTER-STUDY.
000758 01-13

MAINTENANCE-THERAPY WITH FLUPHENAZINE-DECANOATE AND
OXYPROTHEPINE-DECANOATE IN SCHIZOPHRENIC-PATIENTS – A
DOUBLE-BLIND CROSS-OVER COMPARATIVE-STUDY.
001924 02-08

EXPERIENCE WITH OXYPROTHEPINE-DECANOATE IN THE MAINTENANCE-
THERAPY OF SCHIZOPHRENIA.
001925 02-08

INTERMITTENT PIMOZIDE VERSUS FLUPHENAZINE-DECANOATE AS
MAINTENANCE-THERAPY IN CHRONIC SCHIZOPHRENIA.
001932 02-08

THE EFFECT OF LONG-TERM MAINTENANCE-THERAPY ON SCHIZOPHRENIC-
PATIENTS USING SOMATOTHERAPEUTIC MEASURES.
004325 04-08

MAINTENANCE-TREATMENT
A NEW DOSAGE SCHEDULE FOR PIMOZIDE IN THE ACUTE STABILIZATION
AND MAINTENANCE-TREATMENT OF PSYCHOSIS.
002022 02-09

MAINTENANCE-TREATMENT WITH SEMIDEPOTE NEUROLEPTIC
FLUSPIRILENE.
002151 02-11

DEPOT FLUPHENAZINE MAINTENANCE-TREATMENT AND ASSOCIATED
WEIGHT CHANGES.
004635 04-15

MAJOR-TRANQUILIZERS
MAJOR-TRANQUILIZERS AND HEART-DISEASE: TO USE OR NOT TO USE.
000866 01-15

MAJOR-TRANQUILLIZERS
MAJOR-TRANQUILLIZERS IN PSYCHIATRY.
000987 01-17

MALAISE
SELECTIVE SENSITIZATION INDUCED BY LITHIUM MALAISE AND
FOOTSHOCK IN RATS.
003055 03-04

MALE
MORPHINE EXERTS TESTOSTERONE-LIKE EFFECTS IN THE HYPOTHALAMUS
OF THE CASTRATED MALE RAT.
000051 01-03

INFERENCES DERIVED FROM ELECTROENCEPHALOGRAPHIC RESPONSES TO
ACUTE ADMINISTRATION OF CLOMIPHENE-CITRATE IN MALE ALBINO-
RATS.
000155 01-03

THE EFFECTS OF GONADECTOMY AND HYPOPHYSECTOMY ON THE
METABOLISM OF IMIPRAMINE AND LIDOCAINE BY THE LIVER OF MALE
AND FEMALE RATS.
000273 01-03

PROLONGATION OF THE EJACULATION LATENCY IN THE MALE RAT BY
THIORIDAZINE AND CHLORIMIPRAMINE.
000335 01-04

EFFECTS OF MORPHINE, BETA ENDORPHIN AND NALOXONE ON
CATECHOLAMINE LEVELS AND SEXUAL-BEHAVIOR IN THE MALE RAT.
000430 01-04

SEXUAL-BEHAVIOUR OF MORPHINE-DEPENDENT AND ABSTINENT MALE
RATS.
000438 01-04

DYNAMICS OF ENDOGENOUS CATECHOLAMINE RELEASE FROM BRAIN
FRAGMENTS OF MALE AND FEMALE RATS.
001121 02-03

CORTICOSTERONE INCREASES THE SYNTHESIS OF A SOLUBLE PROTEIN IN
PITUITARY-GLANDS FROM ADRENALECTOMIZED MALE RATS WHICH
PRECIPITATES WITH ANTI-RAT GROWTH-HORMONE ANTISERUM.
(UNPUBLISHED PAPER).
001122 02-03

EFFECT OF AMINOOXYACETIC-ACID AND BICUCULLINE ON PROLACTIN
RELEASE IN CASTRATED MALE RATS.
001194 02-03

SYNCHRONIZATION OF EEG ACTIVITY OF MALE RHESUS-MONKEYS
MACACA-MULATTA TREATED WITH OVOCYCLIN.
001312 02-03

THE EFFECT OF SMALL AND MODERATE DOSES OF D-AMPHETAMINE ON HUNGER, MOOD, AND AROUSAL IN MAN.
000807 01-14

LEVORPHANOL: RADIOIMMUNOASSAY AND PLASMA CONCENTRATION PROFILES IN DOG AND MAN.
000898 01-16

ASSESSMENT OF ADRENERGIC-RECEPTORS IN VIVO IN EXPERIMENTAL ANIMALS AND MAN. (UNPUBLISHED PAPER).
001034 02-01

BIOCHEMICAL-EFFECTS OF ZIMELIDINE IN MAN.
001967 02-09

ASPIRIN ANALGESIA EVALUATED BY EVENT-RELATED POTENTIALS IN MAN: POSSIBLE CENTRAL-ACTION IN BRAIN.
002195 02-12

THE CONTRIBUTION OF ALPHA1 ACID GLYCOPROTEIN, LIPOPROTEINS, AND ALBUMIN TO THE PLASMA BINDING OF PERAZINE, AMITRIPTYLINE, AND NORTRIPTYLINE IN HEALTHY MAN.
002214 02-13

APOMORPHINE HYPOTHERMIA: AN INDEX OF CENTRAL DOPAMINE-RECEPTOR FUNCTION IN MAN.
002221 02-13

SHORT-TERM ETHANOL ADMINISTRATION IMPAIRS THE ELIMINATION OF CHLORDIAZEPOXIDE (LIBRIUM) IN MAN.
002224 02-13

TELE-METHYLHISTAMINE IS A SPECIFIC MAO-B SUBSTRATE IN MAN.
002230 02-13

BIOAVAILABILITY AND RELATED PHARMACOKINETICS IN MAN OF ORALLY ADMINISTERED L 5 HYDROXYTRYPTOPHAN IN STEADY-STATE.
002261 02-13

CLINICAL EVIDENCE FOR MULTIPLE DOPAMINE-RECEPTORS IN MAN.
002264 02-13

INHIBITION OF SULPIRIDE-INDUCED PROLACTIN SECRETION BY DIHYDROERGOCRISTINE IN MAN.
002277 02-13

THE PHARMACOKINETICS OF BROMOCRIPTINE IN MAN.
002291 02-13

INDIVIDUAL VARIATIONS IN THE EFFECTS OF FLURAZEPAM, CLORAZEPATE, L-DOPA AND THYROTROPIN-RELEASING-HORMONE ON REM SLEEP IN MAN.
002349 02-14

THE EFFECT OF DEPRENYL, A SELECTIVE MONOAMINE-OXIDASE-B-INHIBITOR, ON SLEEP AND MOOD IN MAN.
002365 02-14

NEUROPHARMACOLOGY OF SYNTHETIC ERGOT DERIVATIVES IN MAN.
002429 02-15

DEVELOPMENT AND USE OF PHARMACOLOGICAL-PROBES OF THE CNS IN MAN: EVIDENCE OF CHOLINERGIC ABNORMALITY IN PRIMARY AFFECTIVE-ILLNESS.
002506 02-16

BEHAVIOURAL-ANALYSIS OF FEEDING: IMPLICATIONS FOR THE PHARMACOLOGICAL MANIPULATION OF FOOD INTAKE IN ANIMALS AND MAN.
002527 02-17

THE HYPOTHALAMIC DOPAMINERGIC REGULATION OF PROLACTIN: A MODEL FOR THE STUDY OF NEUROHORMONAL MECHANISMS IN MAN.
002568 02-17

PSYCHOPHARMACOLOGY OF ANORECTIC-DRUGS IN MAN.
002607 02-17

IMMUNOREACTIVE CALCITONIN IN CEREBROSPINAL-FLUID OF MAN.
002637 03-01

STEADY-STATE LITHIUM BLOOD LEVEL FLUCTUATIONS IN MAN FOLLOWING ADMINISTRATION OF A LITHIUM-CARBONATE CONVENTIONAL AND CONTROLLED-RELEASE DOSAGE FORM.
003151 03-07

EFFECT OF A PSYCHOACTIVE-DRUG, TRAZODONE, ON PROLACTIN SECRETION IN MAN.
003425 03-13

A COMPARISON OF THE EFFECTS OF MORPHINE-SULPHATE AND NITROUS-OXIDE ANALGESIA ON CHRONIC PAIN STATES IN MAN.
003442 03-14

STUDY ON THE EFFECTS OF L 5 HTP ON THE STAGES OF SLEEP IN MAN AS EVALUATED BY USING SLEEP-DEPRIVATION.
003450 03-14

POSITRON-TOMOGRAPHY. A NEW METHOD FOR IN VIVO BRAIN STUDIES OF BENZODIAZEPINE, IN ANIMAL AND IN MAN.
003564 03-16

PHARMACOKINETIC-STUDY IN MAN OF THE CH-757 PREPARATION.
004440 04-11

PHARMACOKINETICS OF CLOXAZOLAM IN MAN AFTER SINGLE AND MULTIPLE ORAL DOSES.
004530 04-13

NOREPINEPHRINE METABOLISM IN MAN USING DEUTERIUM LABELLING: 4 HYDROXY-3-METHOXYMANDELIC-ACID.
004534 04-13

THE PHARMACOKINETICS OF MIDAZOLAM IN MAN.
004555 04-13

SEX, PLASMA PROLACTIN AND PLASMA 3 METHOXY-4-HYDROXYPHENYLGLYCOL (MHPG) PREDICT HERITABLE D-AMPHETAMINE EXCITATION IN MAN. (UNPUBLISHED PAPER).
004565 04-14

A SYNTHETIC ACTH4-9 ANALOGUE (ORGANON-2766) AND SLEEP IN HEALTHY MAN.
004574 04-14

THE EFFECT OF THE DOPAMINE-RECEPTOR BLOCKING-DRUG PIMOZIDE ON THE STIMULANT AND ANORECTIC-ACTIONS OF DEXTROAMPHETAMINE IN MAN.
004580 04-14

MANAGEMENT
ACUTE MANAGEMENT OF THE VIOLENT AGGRESSIVE-PATIENT.
000586 01-09

THE REAL AND IDEAL MANAGEMENT OF STIMULANT DRUG-TREATMENT FOR HYPERACTIVE-CHILDREN: RECENT FINDINGS AND A REPORT FROM CLINICAL-PRACTICE.
000715 01-11

APPLICATION OF A RADIOIMMUNOASSAY SCREENING-TEST FOR DETECTION AND MANAGEMENT OF PHENCYCLIDINE INTOXICATION.
000859 01-15

DEPRENYL IN THE MANAGEMENT OF RESPONSE FLUCTUATIONS IN PATIENTS WITH PARKINSONS-DISEASE ON LEVODOPA.
002358 02-14

TARDIVE-DYSKINESIA: RECOGNITION, MANAGEMENT, AND PREVENTION.
002392 02-15

MONOAMINE-OXIDASE-INHIBITORS: PRESCRIPTION AND PATIENT MANAGEMENT.
002454 02-15

DRUG-HOLIDAY AND MANAGEMENT OF PARKINSON-DISEASE.
002468 02-15

MANAGEMENT OF SCHIZOPHRENIA: LONG-TERM CLINICAL-STUDIES WITH SPECIAL REFERENCE TO THE COMBINATION OF PSYCHOTHERAPY AND DEPOT NEUROLEPTICS.
003183 03-08

MANAGEMENT OF DEPRESSION WITH SEROTONIN PRECURSORS.
003269 03-09

THE MANAGEMENT OF CHRONIC BEHAVIOR-DISORDERS IN MENTALLY-RETARDED ADULTS WITH LITHIUM-CARBONATE.
003376 03-11

ACUTE PHENCYCLIDINE (PCP) INTOXICATION: QUANTITATIVE URINE LEVELS AND CLINICAL MANAGEMENT.
004665 04-15

MANAGING
PARAPROFESSIONAL AND PROFESSIONAL TEAMWORK AND TRAINING IN MANAGING PCP AND OTHER DRUG-ABUSE PROBLEMS.
000924 01-17

MANGANESE
MENTAL-DISTURBANCES IN CHRONIC MANGANESE POISONING.
004621 04-15

MANIA
THYROID-INDUCED MANIA IN HYPOTHYROID-PATIENTS.
000857 01-15

MANIA: AN EVOLVING CONCEPT.
001966 02-09

LITHIUM AND MANIA: HYPOTHESES.
001986 02-09

A COMPARISON OF HALOPERIDOL, LITHIUM-CARBONATE AND THEIR COMBINATION IN THE TREATMENT OF MANIA.
001990 02-09

RAPID RECURRENCE OF MANIA FOLLOWING LITHIUM WITHDRAWAL.
002010 02-09

PSYCHOMOTOR STIMULANTS AS ACTIVATORS OF NORMAL AND PATHOLOGICAL-BEHAVIOR: IMPLICATIONS FOR THE EXCESSES IN MANIA. (UNPUBLISHED PAPER).
002353 02-14

THE LITHIUM-ION: IS IT SPECIFIC FOR MANIA?
002516 02-16

THE EFFECT OF SODIUM-VALPROATE ON MANIA: THE GABA HYPOTHESIS OF AFFECTIVE-DISORDERS.
003218 03-09

ON A POSSIBLE ROLE OF GABA IN MANIA. THERAPEUTIC-EFFICACY OF SODIUM-VALPROATE.
003219 03-09

HYPOMANIA AND MANIA AFTER WITHDRAWAL OF TRICYCLIC-ANTIDEPRESSANTS.
003243 03-09

IS MANIA OVERDIAGNOSED?: THE THREE COMMON PITFALLS IN DIAGNOSING MANIC-DEPRESSIVE-ILLNESS.
003260 03-09

LITHIUM AND THE CHANGING INCIDENCE OF MANIA.
003265 03-09

LITHIUM AND MANIA.
003640 03-17

CHANGES IN BLOOD PLASMA OSMOLALITY AND STATES OF MANIA.
004352 04-09

PLASMA CORTICOSTERIODS IN MANIA: THE EFFECTS OF PIMOZIDE.
004363 04-09

CHOLINERGIC MECHANISMS IN MANIA AND DEPRESSION: QUESTIONS OF SPECIFICITY.
004374 D4-09

TRICYCLIC-ANTIDEPRESSANT-INDUCED MANIA.
004656 04-15

CHOLINOMIMETICS IN MANIA, SCHIZOPHRENIA, AND MEMORY-DISORDERS.
004703 04-17

CEREBRAL FLUORIDE IN MANIA AND THE EFFECT OF LITHIUM: A HYPOTHESIS.
004715 04-17

MANIC
THE RELATIVE PROPHYLACTIC EFFICACY OF LITHIUM AGAINST MANIC AND DEPRESSIVE RECURRENCES IN BIPOLAR-PATIENTS.
002040 02-09

MANIC-DEPRESSIVE-ILLNESS
PSYCHOBIOLOGICAL-RESEARCH IN MANIC-DEPRESSIVE-ILLNESS. (UNPUBLISHED PAPER).
001973 02-09

A TEN YEAR FOLLOWUP OF LITHIUM-CARBONATE TREATMENT OF MANIC-DEPRESSIVE-ILLNESS: PRELIMINARY-RESULTS.
002053 02-09

HISTORICAL-PERSPECTIVES AND CURRENT HIGHLIGHTS ON LITHIUM TREATMENT IN MANIC-DEPRESSIVE-ILLNESS.
003224 03-09

IS MANIA OVERDIAGNOSED?: THE THREE COMMON PITFALLS IN DIAGNOSING MANIC-DEPRESSIVE-ILLNESS.
003260 03-09

A PRELIMINARY DOUBLE-BLIND STUDY ON THE EFFICACY OF CARBAMAZEPINE IN PROPHYLAXIS OF MANIC-DEPRESSIVE-ILLNESS.
004388 04-09

LITHIUM TREATMENT OF MANIC-DEPRESSIVE-ILLNESS. A PRACTICAL GUIDE.
004408 04-09

MANIC-DEPRESSIVE-PATIENT
THIAZIDE-INDUCED HYPERCALCEMIA IN A MANIC-DEPRESSIVE-PATIENT.
000843 01-15

MANIC-DEPRESSIVE-PATIENTS
ENDOCRINE-EFFECTS OF LITHIUM IN MANIC-DEPRESSIVE-PATIENTS.
001970 02-09

MANIC-DEPRESSIVE-PSYCHOSES
EMERGENCIES IN MANIC-DEPRESSIVE-PSYCHOSES.
003540 03-15

MANIC-DEPRESSIVE-PSYCHOSIS
DOSAGE OF INTRATUMORAL LITHIUM (CEREBRAL GLIOBLASTOMA): ON A FAILURE OF TREATMENT OF MANIC-DEPRESSIVE-PSYCHOSIS.
003226 03-09

CONFESSION OF A MELANCHOLIAC: CONTRIBUTION TO THE PROBLEM OF PROPHYLAXIS OF MANIC-DEPRESSIVE-PSYCHOSIS USING LITHIUM.
003267 03-09

MANIC-DEPRESSIVES
DIFFERENT EFFECTS OF TRICYCLIC-ANTIDEPRESSANTS AND TETRACYCLIC-ANTIDEPRESSANTS ON THE RELEASE OF TSH, PROLACTIN, AND GROWTH-HORMONE AFTER ADMINISTRATION OF THYROSTIMULATING-RELEASING-HORMONE IN MANIC-DEPRESSIVES.
004407 04-09

MANIC-MELANCHOLIC-DISORDERS
BIOLOGY OF MANIC-MELANCHOLIC-DISORDERS.
000978 01-17

MANIC-PATIENTS
INTERACTION OF INDOMETHACIN AND IBUPROFEN WITH LITHIUM IN MANIC-PATIENTS UNDER A STEADY-STATE LITHIUM LEVEL.
000622 01-09

INTRA AND EXTRA ERYTHROCYTE LITHIUM-ION CONCENTRATION RATIOS IN MANIC-PATIENTS.
000627 01-09

GROWTH-HORMONE (GH) RELEASE FOLLOWING THYROTROPIN-RELEASING-HORMONE (TRH) INJECTION IN MANIC-PATIENTS RECEIVING LITHIUM-CARBONATE.
000645 01-09

ERYTHROCYTE CHOLINE CONCENTRATIONS ARE ELEVATED IN MANIC-PATIENTS.
004521 04-13

MANIC-PSYCHOSIS
MANIC-PSYCHOSIS FOLLOWING RAPID WITHDRAWAL FROM BACLOFEN.
000832 01-15

MANIC-STATE
EFFECT OF LITHIUM ON PROLACTIN RESPONSES TO THYROTROPIN-RELEASING-HORMONE IN PATIENTS WITH MANIC-STATE.
003266 03-09

MANIC-STATE INDUCED BY SALBUTAMOL TAKEN ORALLY
004622 04-15

MANIC-SYMPTOMS
FAILURE OF NALOXONE TO REDUCE MANIC-SYMPTOMS.
001984 02-09

MANIFESTATION
BEHAVIORAL-ANALYSIS OF AMYGDALOID KINDLING IN BEAGLE-DOGS AND THE EFFECTS OF CLONAZEPAM, DIAZEPAM, PHENOBARBITAL, DIPHENYLHYDANTOIN, AND FLUNARIZINE ON SEIZURE MANIFESTATION.
000496 01-04

MANIFESTATIONS
PSYCHIATRIC MANIFESTATIONS INDUCED BY DOPAMINE PRECURSORS OR DOPAMINE AGONISTS.
000865 01-15
DERMATOLOGIC MANIFESTATIONS OF LITHIUM: A REVIEW.
003462 03-15
MANIFESTED
CIMETIDINE TOXICITY MANIFESTED AS PARANOIA AND HALLUCINATIONS.
000829 01-15
MANIPULATION
DIFFERENTIAL SENSITIVITY OF HYPOTHALAMIC DOPAMINERGIC AND NORADRENERGIC NEURONES TO PHARMACOLOGICAL MANIPULATION.
001310 02-03
SELF-MEDICATION, ABANDONMENT, MANIPULATION, AND DEPENDENCE IN DRUG-THERAPY IN PSYCHOSOMATIC-ILLNESS: COMPARATIVE POLYCENTRIC RESEARCH ON VARIOUS PSYCHOTROPIC-DRUGS.
002189 02-11
SURGICAL MANIPULATION OF THE UTERINE ENVIRONMENT OF RAT FETUSES.
002478 02-16
BEHAVIOURAL-ANALYSIS OF FEEDING: IMPLICATIONS FOR THE PHARMACOLOGICAL MANIPULATION OF FOOD INTAKE IN ANIMALS AND MAN.
002527 02-17
A RESEARCH PARADIGM TO INVESTIGATE THE EFFECT OF MANIPULATION ON SOCIAL-BEHAVIOR IN GROUPS.
003007 03-04
PHARMACOLOGIC MANIPULATION OF BRAIN AND PITUITARY ENDORPHIN CONTENT AND RELEASE.
003837 04-03
DOPAMINE-DEPENDENT HYPERACTIVITY IN THE FOLLOWING MANIPULATION OF GABA MECHANISMS IN THE REGION OF THE NUCLEUS-ACCUMBENS.
003976 04-03
BILATERAL SKIN CONDUCTANCE AND THE PUPILLARY LIGHT DARK REFLEX: MANIPULATION BY CHLORPROMAZINE, HALOPERIDOL, SCOPOLAMINE, AND PLACEBO.
004544 04-13
MANIPULATIONS
THE SENSITIVITY OF THE RAT CORTICOSTERONE RESPONSE TO ENVIRONMENTAL MANIPULATIONS AND TO CHRONIC CHLORDIAZEPOXIDE TREATMENT.
000092 01-03
PRESYNAPTIC AND POSTSYNAPTIC SEROTONERGIC MANIPULATIONS IN AN ANIMAL-MODEL OF DEPRESSION.
001730 02-04
THE EFFECTS OF TRYPTOPHAN AND MANIPULATIONS OF SEROTONERGIC-RECEPTORS ON TONIC IMMOBILITY IN CHICKENS.
004245 04-04
MAO-A
COMPARATIVE-STUDIES OF MAO-A AND MAO-B INHIBITORS IN MAN.
000612 01-09
MAO-B
COMPARATIVE-STUDIES OF MAO-A AND MAO-B INHIBITORS IN MAN.
000612 01-09
TELE-METHYLHISTAMINE IS A SPECIFIC MAO-B SUBSTRATE IN MAN.
002230 02-13
MAO-INHIBITION
REGIONAL 5 HT ANALYSIS IN ROMAN HIGH-AVOIDANCE AND LOW-AVOIDANCE RATS FOLLOWING MAO-INHIBITION.
001202 02-03
MAO-INHIBITORS AND PLATELET MAO-INHIBITION.
001993 02-09
IN VIVO INTRANEURONAL MAO-INHIBITION IN RAT-BRAIN SKF-64139, COMPARISON TO OTHER POTENT PNMT INHIBITORS.
003935 04-03
MAO-INHIBITOR
THE BENEFITS AND RISKS OF COMBINING AN MAO-INHIBITOR AND A TRICYCLIC-ANTIDEPRESSANT.
003273 03-09
TREATMENT OF DEPRESSION WITH AN MAO-INHIBITOR FOLLOWED BY 5 HTP -- AN UNFINISHED RESEARCH PROJECT.
004377 04-09
MAO-INHIBITORS
EVIDENCE THAT A PREFERRED SUBSTRATE FOR MONOAMINE-OXIDASE-B MEDIATES STIMULUS PROPERTIES OF MAO-INHIBITORS: A POSSIBLE ROLE FOR BETA PHENYLETHYLAMINE IN THE COCAINE CUE.
000363 01-04
THE EFFECTS OF 5 HT UPTAKE AND MAO-INHIBITORS ON L 5 HTP-INDUCED EXCITATION IN RATS.
001740 02-04
MAO-INHIBITORS AND PLATELET MAO-INHIBITION.
001993 02-09
MAOI-INDUCED
MAOI-INDUCED RAPID CYCLING BIPOLAR AFFECTIVE-DISORDER IN AN ADOLESCENT.
004637 04-15

MAPPING
MAPPING OF DYSKINETIC-MOVEMENTS INDUCED BY LOCAL APPLICATION OF PICROTOXIN OR () GAMMA ACETYLENIC-GABA ON THE RAT MOTOR-CORTEX.
000458 01-04
ANATOMOBIOCHEMICAL MAPPING OF THE BRAIN: NEUROPSYCHIATRIC-CORRELATIONS.
002630 02-17
MAPROTILIN
OUR EXPERIENCE WITH MAPROTILIN TREATMENT OF DEPRESSIVE- ATES.
000628T01-09
INFUSION OF MAPROTILIN AND CLOMIPRAMIN AND THEIR COMBINATION IN THE TREATMENT OF DEPRESSION.
002056 02-09
MAPROTILINE
COMPARISON OF MIANSERIN WITH DESIPRAMINE, MAPROTILINE AND PHENTOLAMINE ON CARDIAC PRESYNAPTIC AND VASCULAR POSTSYNAPTIC ALPHA-ADRENOCEPTORS AND NORADRENALINE REUPTAKE IN PITHED NORMOTENSIVE-RATS.
000044 01-03
COMPARATIVE-STUDY OF THE CARDIOTOXICITY OF AMITRIPTYLINE AND MAPROTILINE IN DEPRESSIVE-PATIENTS.
000595 01-09
COMPARISON OF SINGLE-DOSE PHARMACOKINETICS OF IMIPRAMINE AND MAPROTILINE IN THE ELDERLY.
000596 01-09
MHPG AS A PREDICTOR OF ANTIDEPRESSANT RESPONSE TO IMIPRAMINE AND MAPROTILINE.
000787 01-13
STUDY OF MAPROTILINE IN OUTPATIENT TREATMENT OF DEPRESSIVE-STATES BY THE GENERAL-PRACTITIONER: ADVANTAGE OF SINGLE-NIGHTLY-DOSE.
001961 02-09
MAPROTILINE ADMINISTERED IN A SINGLE-DAILY-DOSE IN GENERAL-PRACTICE.
002027 02-09
CLINICAL AND BIOCHEMICAL-DATA ON THE ACTION OF MAPROTILINE AND CLOMIPRAMINE IN DEPRESSIVE-STATES (PRELIMINARY OBSERVATION).
002032 02-09
COMPARATIVE CROSS-STUDY ON THE EFFECTS OF AMINEPTINE AND MAPROTILINE.
002065 02-10
BIOAVAILABILITY AND KINETICS OF MAPROTILINE.
002204 02-13
AN EVALUATION OF MAPROTILINE INTRAVENOUS KINETICS AND COMPARISON OF TWO ORAL DOSES.
002497 02-16
AN OPEN-STUDY OF MAPROTILINE 75MG IN THE TREATMENT OF DEPRESSIVE-STATES.
003152 03-07
CLINICAL-STUDY OF MAPROTILINE IN THE TREATMENT OF DEPRESSIVE-STATES: COMPILATION OF 1520 OBSERVATIONS.
003206 03-09
CLINICAL-TRIALS WITH NEW BICYCLIC AND TETRACYCLIC COMPOUNDS: ZIMELIDINE AND MAPROTILINE.
003213 03-09
RELATIONSHIP BETWEEN BLOOD CONCENTRATIONS AND CLINICAL-EFFECTS OF A NEW ANTIDEPRESSANT MAPROTILINE.
003271 03-09
MAPROTILINE VERSUS IMIPRAMINE AND PLACEBO IN NEUROTIC DEPRESSION.
003287 03-10
PHARMACOKINETICS OF AMITRIPTYLINE, IMIPRAMINE, AND MAPROTILINE IN THE ELDERLY.
003324 03-11
GLC MASS-SPECTROMETRIC-DETERMINATION OF MAPROTILINE AND ITS MAJOR METABOLITE USING STABLE ISOTOPE-LABELED ANALOG AS INTERNAL STANDARD.
004291 04-06
MAPROTILINE, NOMIFENSINE, MIANSERIN, ZIMELIDINE: A REVIEW OF ANTIDEPRESSANT EFFICACY IN INPATIENTS.
004731 04-17
MARGINAL
IMMUNOHISTOCHEMICAL LOCALIZATION OF LEUCINE-ENKEPHALIN IN THE SPINAL-CORD OF THE CAT: ENKEPHALIN-CONTAINING MARGINAL NEURONS AND PAIN MODULATION.
002638 03-01
MARIHUANA
THERAPEUTIC ASPECTS OF MARIHUANA.
000667 01-11
EFFECTS OF MARIHUANA ON PREGNANT RATS AND THEIR OFFSPRING.
001830 02-05
MEMORY: THE EFFECTS OF ALCOHOL AND OF MARIHUANA.
004570 04-14
MARIJUANA
MARIJUANA: A REVIEW OF MEDICAL RESEARCH WITH IMPLICATIONS FOR ADOLESCENTS.
000871 01-15

MARIJUANA AND CHOLINERGIC DYNAMICS. (UNPUBLISHED PAPER).
001166 02-03
EFFECTS OF HIPPOCAMPAL BRAIN-DAMAGE ON AUDITORY AND VISUAL
RECENT MEMORY: COMPARISON WITH MARIJUANA INTOXICATED
SUBJECTS.
002320 02-14
LITHIUM AND MARIJUANA.
003526 03-15

MARKED
CHOLECYSTOKININ-PEPTIDES PRODUCE MARKED REDUCTION OF
DOPAMINE TURNOVER IN DISCRETE AREAS IN THE RAT-BRAIN
FOLLOWING INTERAVENTRICULAR INJECTION.
001239 02-03

MARMOSET
AN ANALYSIS OF VISUAL OBJECT REVERSAL LEARNING IN THE
MARMOSET AFTER AMPHETAMINE AND HALOPERIDOL.
004208 04-04

MASS-FRAGMENTOGRAPHY
RAT-BRAIN AND PLASMA NOREPINEPHRINE GLYCOL METABOLITES
DETERMINED BY GAS-CHROMATOGRAPHY MASS-
FRAGMENTOGRAPHY.
004303 04-06

MASS-SPECTRAL-ANALYSIS
HIGH-SENSITIVITY NEGATIVE CHEMICAL-IONIZATION MASS-SPECTRAL-
ANALYSIS OF BIOGENIC-AMINES AND METABOLITES. (UNPUBLISHED
PAPER).
001042 02-01

MASS-SPECTROMETRIC-ASSAYS
MASS-SPECTROMETRIC-ASSAYS OF INDOLEAMINES. (UNPUBLISHED
PAPER).
001043 02-01

MASS-SPECTROMETRIC-DETERMINATION
GLC MASS-SPECTROMETRIC-DETERMINATION OF MAPROTILINE AND ITS
MAJOR METABOLITE USING STABLE ISOTOPE-LABELED ANALOG AS
INTERNAL STANDARD.
004291 04-06

MASS-SPECTROMETRY
QUANTITATIVE ANALYSIS OF 6 HYDROXYMELATONIN IN HUMAN URINE
BY GAS-CHROMATOGRAPHY NEGATIVE CHEMICAL-IONIZATION MASS-
SPECTROMETRY. (UNPUBLISHED PAPER).
001058 02-01
A METHOD FOR THE DETERMINATION OF AMITRIPTYLINE AND ITS
METABOLITES NORTRIPTYLINE, 10 HYDROXYAMITRIPTYLINE, AND 10
HYDROXYNORTRIPTYLINE IN HUMAN PLASMA USING STABLE ISOTOPE
DILUTION AND GAS-CHROMATOGRAPHY CHEMICAL-IONIZATION
MASS-SPECTROMETRY.
002486 02-16
GAS-CHROMATOGRAPHY, MASS-SPECTROMETRY, AND COMBINED
CHROMATOGRAPHY MASS-SPECTROMETRY.
004290 04-06
GAS-CHROMATOGRAPHY/MASS-SPECTROMETRY STABLE ISOTOPIC
ANALYSES FOR DEANOL, CHOLINE, AND THEIR ACETYLESTERS.
004683 04-16
COMPARISON OF SPECTROFLUOROMETRIC AND GAS-
CHROMATOGRAPHY/MASS-SPECTROMETRY PROCEDURES FOR THE
QUANTITATION OF MORPHINE IN BLOOD AND BRAIN.
004692 04-16

MASTECTOMY
PSYCHIATRIC MORBIDITY AND PHYSICAL TOXICITY ASSOCIATED WITH
ADJUVANT CHEMOTHERAPY AFTER MASTECTOMY.
002433 02-15

MATCHING-TO-SAMPLE
EFFECTS OF THIORIDAZINE (MELLARIL) ON TITRATING DELAYED
MATCHING-TO-SAMPLE PERFORMANCE IN MENTALLY-RETARDED
ADULTS.
002471 02-15
EFFECTS OF THIORIDAZINE (MELLARIL) ON TITRATING DELAYED
MATCHING-TO-SAMPLE PERFORMANCE OF MENTALLY-RETARDED
ADULTS.
003392 03-11

MATERNAL
MATERNAL GLUCOCORTICOID-HORMONES INFLUENCE
NEUROTRANSMITTER PHENOTYPIC EXPRESSION IN EMBRYOS.
000149 01-03
REDUCTION OF FETAL RAT SPINAL-CORD VOLUME FOLLOWING
MATERNAL MORPHINE INJECTION.
000161 01-03
CONCENTRATIONS OF CIS(Z) FLUPENTHIXOL IN MATERNAL SERUM,
AMNIOTIC-FLUID, UMBILICAL-CORD-SERUM, AND MILK.
002423 02-15
EFFECT OF MATERNAL LORAZEPAM ON THE NEONATE.
003549 03-15
DISPOSITION OF METHADONE IN THE OVINE MATERNAL FETAL UNIT.
004027 04-03

MATERNAL-BEHAVIOR
PHENCYCLIDINE: EFFECTS OF CHRONIC ADMINISTRATION IN THE FEMALE
MOUSE ON GESTATION, MATERNAL-BEHAVIOR, AND THE NEONATES.
000517 01-05

POSTNATAL ALCOHOL EXPOSURE IN THE RAT: ITS EFFECTS ON
AVOIDANCE CONDITIONING, HEBB-WILLIAMS MAZE-PERFORMANCE,
MATERNAL-BEHAVIOR, AND PUP DEVELOPMENT.
001580 02-04
AMPHETAMINE AND MATERNAL-BEHAVIOR: DOSE-RESPONSE
RELATIONSHIPS.
001752 02-04
RAT PUP-KILLING AND MATERNAL-BEHAVIOR IN MALE LONG-EVANS-
RATS: PRENATAL STIMULATION AND POSTNATAL TESTOSTERONE.
003054 03-04

MATERNALLY-DEPRIVED
EFFECTS OF RESERPINE AND AMPHETAMINE ON THE DEVELOPMENT OF
HYPERACTIVITY IN MATERNALLY-DEPRIVED RAT PUPS.
001654 02-04

MATERNITY-BLUES
PROSPECTIVE-TRIAL OF L TRYPTOPHAN IN MATERNITY-BLUES.
000683 01-11

MATING-BEHAVIOR
DRUGS, TRANSMITTERS AND HORMONES, AND MATING-BEHAVIOR.
004721 04-17

MATURATION
MATURATION OF SYMPATHETIC NEUROTRANSMISSION IN THE RAT
HEART. III. DEVELOPMENTAL-CHANGES IN RESERPINE INHIBITION OF
NOREPINEPHRINE UPTAKE INTO ISOLATED SYNAPTIC VESICLES.
000025 01-03
NEURONAL MATURATION IN MAMMALIAN CELL-CULTURE IS DEPENDENT
ON SPONTANEOUS ELECTRICAL-ACTIVITY.
002669 03-03
MATURATION OF SYMPATHETIC NEUROTRANSMISSION IN THE RAT
HEART. VII. SUPPRESSION OF SYMPATHETIC RESPONSES BY
DEXAMETHASONE.
002802 03-03
ABNORMAL MATURATION OF CEREBRAL-CORTEX AND BEHAVIORAL-
DEFICIT IN ADULT RATS AFTER NEONATAL ADMINISTRATION OF
ANTIBODIES TO GANGLIOSIDE.
003025 03-04

MATURE
APOMORPHINE-INDUCED STEREOTYPY IN MATURE AND SENESCENT RATS
FOLLOWING CESSATION OF CHRONIC HALOPERIDOL TREATMENT.
004651 04-15

MAXIMIZE
A STATE-DEPENDENT FAILURE OF RATS TO MAXIMIZE REWARDS.
000392 01-04

MAXIMUM
CLASSIFICATION OF DRUGS AND PATIENTS TO ACHIEVE MAXIMUM
THERAPEUTIC RESPONSE.
002560 02-17

MAZE
UNUSUAL DOSE-RELATED EFFECT OF AN ENDORPHIN ANALOG IN A
COMPLEX MAZE.
001674 02-04
EFFECTS OF SCOPOLAMINE, PILOCARPINE, AND OXOTREMORINE ON THE
EXPLORATORY-BEHAVIOR OF TWO PSYCHOGENETICALLY SELECTED
LINES OF RATS IN A COMPLEX MAZE.
003042 03-04

MAZE-BEHAVIOR
BETTA-SPLENDENS MAZE-BEHAVIOR UNDER THE INFLUENCE OF THE BETA
FENIL-ISOPROPIL-AMINA-SULFATE.
001558 02-04

MAZE-LEARNING
DELAYED MAZE-LEARNING IN RATS AFTER PRENATAL EXPOSURE TO
CLORAZEPATE.
000521 01-05

MAZE-PERFORMANCE
POSTNATAL ALCOHOL EXPOSURE IN THE RAT: ITS EFFECTS ON
AVOIDANCE CONDITIONING, HEBB-WILLIAMS MAZE-PERFORMANCE,
MATERNAL-BEHAVIOR, AND PUP DEVELOPMENT.
001580 02-04
NEONATAL ADMINISTRATION OF MET-ENKEPHALIN FACILITATES MAZE-
PERFORMANCE OF ADULT RATS.
001673 02-04

MAZINDOL
EFFECT OF MAZINDOL ON BRAIN DOPAMINE TURNOVER IN SPIPERONE
TREATED RATS.
002726 03-03

MD780515
CHARACTERISTICS OF THE INHIBITION OF RAT-BRAIN MONOAMINE-
OXIDASE IN VITRO BY MD780515.
003874 04-03

MEAL
METABOLIC-CORRELATES OF THE EFFECTS OF 2 DEOXY-D-GLUCOSE ON
MEAL SIZE AND POST MEAL SATIETY IN RATS.
003035 03-04

MEAL-DEPENDENT
MEAL-DEPENDENT ABSORPTION OF ENTERIC-COATED SODIUM-
VALPROATE.
000777 01-13

MEANING

L HTP AND THE SEROTONIN HYPOTHESIS: THEIR MEANING FOR
TREATMENT OF DEPRESSION.
002326 02-14

CHARACTER AND MEANING OF QUASI-MORPHINE WITHDRAWAL
PHENOMENA ELICITED BY METHYLXANTHINES.
004087 04-04

MEASUREMENTS

BLOOD LEVEL MEASUREMENTS OF TRICYCLIC DRUGS AS A DIAGNOSTIC
TOOL.
004368 04-09

MEASUREMENTS OF NERVE CONDUCTION VELOCITY DURING DECREASING
TOXIC DIPHENYLHYDANTOIN LEVELS AND THE BEGINNING OF
CARBAMAZEPINE MEDICATION: A CLINICAL NEUROPHYSIOLOGICAL
REPORT.
004441 04-11

MEBICAR

THE EFFECT OF MEBICAR ON THE CONDITION OF ANIMALS UNDER
CERTAIN EXTREME CIRCUMSTANCES.
004262 04-04

MECHANICAL-CHANGES

MECHANICAL-CHANGES IN CRAB NERVE FIBERS DURING ACTION
POTENTIALS. (UNPUBLISHED PAPER).
001505 02-03

MECHANISM

MECHANISM OF CHLORPROMAZINE ACTION ON PLASMA GLUCOSE AND
CYCLIC-AMP LEVELS.
000211 01-03

THE MECHANISM OF EFFECT OF NEUROPHARMACOLOGICAL-DRUGS. VI:
EFFECT OF NORADRENALINE AND 5 HYDROXYTRYPTAMINE ON BRAIN
FREE FATTY-ACIDS.
000274 01-03

THE INVOLVEMENT OF SEROTONERGIC NEURONS IN THE CENTRAL-
NERVOUS-SYSTEM AS THE POSSIBLE MECHANISM FOR SLOW HEAD-
SHAKING-BEHAVIOR INDUCED BY METHAMPHETAMINE IN RATS.
000408 01-04

POSSIBLE MECHANISM FOR THE ENHANCED LETHALITY OF MORPHINE IN
AGGREGATED MICE.
000437 01-04

ON THE MECHANISM OF THERAPEUTIC ACTIONS OF PSYCHOTROPIC-
DRUGS.
000964 01-17

THE REGULATION OF GABA-RECEPTORS AS A POSSIBLE MECHANISM FOR
GABA 1,4 BENZODIAZEPINE INTERACTIONS. (UNPUBLISHED PAPER).
001012 02-01

MECHANISM OF INACTIVATION OF MITOCHONDRIAL MONOAMINE-
OXIDASE BY N CYCLOPROPYL-N-ARYLALKYLAMINES.
001055 02-01

HYBRID PROTEINS USED TO STUDY THE MECHANISM OF TOXIN
ENTRANCE INTO CELLS. (UNPUBLISHED PAPER).
001063 02-01

MECHANISM OF INACTIVATION OF MITOCHONDRIAL MONOAMINE-
OXIDASE BY N CYCLOPROPYL-N-ARYLALKYLAMINES.
001088 02-02

ON THE MECHANISM OF A DIFFERENT DRUG DISTRIBUTION DURING
CONVULSIVE-SEIZURE IN COMPARISON TO ANESTHESIA.
001151 02-03

EFFECTS OF DIAZEPAM ON ADENOSINE AND ACETYLCHOLINE RELEASE
FROM RAT-CEREBRAL-CORTEX: FURTHER EVIDENCE FOR A PURINERGIC
MECHANISM IN ACTION OF DIAZEPAM.
001414 02-03

THE ROLE OF PROTEIN SYNTHESIS IN THE HYPOTHALAMIC MECHANISM
MEDIATING PYROGEN FEVER.
001454 02-03

LITHIUM EFFECTS ON HIGH-AFFINITY TRYPTOPHAN UPTAKE: EVIDENCE
AGAINST A STABILIZATION MECHANISM.
001496 02-03

ADRENERGIC MODULATION OF THE HYPOTHALAMIC CHOLINERGIC
MECHANISM IN THE CONTROL OF EMOTIONAL DEFENSIVE-BEHAVIOR IN
THE CAT.
001761 02-04

MEASUREMENT OF PLASMA CONCENTRATIONS OF DRUGS AS A
FEEDBACK CONTROL MECHANISM DURING DRUG-THERAPY.
002525 02-17

CLONIDINE ANALGESIA AND SUPPRESSION OF OPERANT RESPONDING:
DISSOCIATION OF MECHANISM.
003046 03-04

METERGOLINE AND CYPROHEPTADINE SUPPRESS PROLACTIN RELEASE BY
A NON-5-HYDROXYTRYPTAMINERGIC, NONDOPAMINERGIC
MECHANISM.
003732 04-03

AN EVALUATION OF THE MECHANISM BY WHICH SEROTONERGIC
ACTIVATION DEPRESSES RESPIRATION.
003917 04-03

A COMMON MECHANISM FOR LYSERGIC-ACID, INDOLEALKYLAMINE AND
PHENETHYLAMINE HALLUCINOGENS: SEROTONERGIC MEDIATION OF
BEHAVIORAL-EFFECTS IN RATS.
004007 04-03

SEROTONERGIC MECHANISM IN SEIZURES KINDLED FROM THE RABBIT
AMYGDALA.
004227 04-04

MECHANISM OF MEMBRANE STABILIZING AND LYTIC-EFFECTS OF
TRICYCLIC-ANTIDEPRESSANTS.
004283 04-05

MECHANISM OF LITHIUM INCLUDED ELEVATION IN RED-BLOOD-CELL
CHOLINE CONTENT: AN IN VITRO ANALYSIS.
004511 04-13

A MECHANISM FOR THE ACCUMULATION OF CHOLINE IN ERYTHROCYTES
DURING TREATMENT WITH LITHIUM.
004520 04-13

MECHANISM OF VALPROATE PHENOBARBITAL INTERACTION IN EPILEPTIC-
PATIENTS.
004522 04-13

MECHANISM-OF-ACTION

ANTIDEPRESSANT PROPERTIES OF 2 4 ETHYL-2-PIPERAZINYL-4-
PHENYLQUINOLINE-HCL (AD-1308) AND ITS MECHANISM-OF-ACTION
AS COMPARED WITH TRICYCLIC-ANTIDEPRESSANTS.
000152 01-03

MECHANISM-OF-ACTION OF THE BENZODIAZEPINES: BEHAVIORAL-
ASPECT.
000468 01-04

THE MECHANISM-OF-ACTION OF DELTA9 TETRAHYDROCANNABINOL ON
BODY-TEMPERATURE IN MICE.
001190 02-03

ON THE MECHANISM-OF-ACTION OF 2 AMINO-4-METHYLPYRIDINE, A
MORPHINE-LIKE ANALGESIC.
001574 02-04

ON THE PROPOSED MECHANISM-OF-ACTION OF ANTIDEPRESSANTS.
002256 02-13

RECENT INVESTIGATIONS ON THE MECHANISM-OF-ACTION OF
NOMIFENSINE.
002289 02-13

MECHANISM-OF-ACTION OF BENZODIAZEPINES.
002302 02-13

THE ANTIDEPRESSANT ACTION OF SULPHO-ADENOSYL-L-METHIONINE
(SAME) COMPARED WITH THAT OF CHLORIMIPRAMINE:
HYPOTHETICAL INTERPRETATIONS OF THE MECHANISM-OF-ACTION.
003150 03-07

L-DOPAS MECHANISM-OF-ACTION IN PARKINSONS-DISEASE.
003323 03-11

MECHANISM-OF-ACTION OF BARBITURATES.
003600 03-17

CU-AMINE-OXIDASES: STUDIES RELATED TO THE MECHANISM-OF-ACTION
OF BOVINE PLASMA AMINE-OXIDASE (UNPUBLISHED PAPER).
003680 04-01

STUDIES ON THE MECHANISM-OF-ACTION OF AVERMECTIN-B1A:
STIMULATION OF RELEASE OF GAMMA AMINOBUTYRIC-ACID FROM
BRAIN SYNAPTOSOMES.
003973 04-03

LITHIUM AND MOTOR-ACTIVITY OF ANIMALS: EFFECTS AND POSSIBLE
MECHANISM-OF-ACTION.
004222 04-04

MECHANISMS

ROLE OF BRAIN DOPAMINERGIC MECHANISMS IN RODENT AGGRESSIVE-
BEHAVIOR: INFLUENCE OF (OR -)N N PROPYLNORAPOMORPHINE ON
THREE EXPERIMENTAL MODELS.
000340 01-04

CHOLINERGIC MECHANISMS AND CATAPLEXY IN DOGS.
000374 01-04

MORPHINE VERSUS HALOPERIDOL CATALEPSY IN THE RAT: A
BEHAVIORAL-ANALYSIS OF POSTURAL SUPPORT MECHANISMS.
000376 01-04

DIFFERENT DOPAMINERGIC MECHANISMS FOR AMFONELIC-ACID,
AMPHETAMINE AND APOMORPHINE.
000465 01-04

CHOLINERGIC MECHANISMS IN SCENT-MARKING-BEHAVIOR BY
MONGOLIAN-GERBILS (MERIONES-UNGUICULATUS).
000504 01-04

CONTRIBUTION TO THE CLINICAL-STUDY OF CEREBRAL DOPAMINERGIC
MECHANISMS: THE ACTION OF PIRIBEDIL IN PSYCHIATRY. FIRST
RESULTS.
000616 01-09

CONTRIBUTION TO STUDY OF CEREBRAL DOPAMINERGIC MECHANISMS:
REALITY OF THE PROBLEM.
000782 01-13

MECHANISMS OF PAIN AND ANALGESIC COMPOUNDS.
000916 01-17

NEUROCHEMICAL MECHANISMS OF OPIATES AND ENDORPHINS.
000958 01-17

OPIOID MECHANISMS IN REGULATION OF CEREBRAL MONOAMINES IN
VIVO.
001098 02-03

RAPID DEVELOPMENT OF HYPERSENSITIVITY AND HYPOSENSITIVITY TO
APOMORPHINE AND HALOPERIDOL: ROLE OF NOREPINEPHRINE-
RECEPTOR MECHANISMS IN CNS.
001178 02-03

AN EXAMINATION OF FACTORS INFLUENCING ADRENERGIC
TRANSMISSION IN THE PITHED RAT, WITH SPECIAL REFERENCE TO

NORADRENALINE UPTAKE MECHANISMS AND POSTJUNCTIONAL
ALPHA-ADRENOCEPTORS.
001196 02-03
MECHANISMS INVOLVED IN CENTRAL-EFFECTS OF PROSTAGLANDIN-
F2ALPHA. (UNPUBLISHED PAPER).
001222 02-03
EFFECTS OF CHRONIC-TREATMENT WITH L SULPIRIDE AND HALOPERIDOL
ON CENTRAL MONOAMINERGIC MECHANISMS.
001240 02-03
EFFECTS OF CHRONIC NEUROLEPTIC TREATMENT ON TYROSINE-
HYDROXYLASE IN DOPAMINERGIC TERMINALS: COMPARISONS
BETWEEN DRUGS AND BRAIN REGIONS REVEALS DIFFERENT
MECHANISMS OF TOLERANCE.
001243 02-03
STEREOSELECTIVE ACTIONS OF SUBSTITUTED BENZAMIDE DRUGS ON
CEREBRAL DOPAMINE MECHANISMS.
001301 02-03
CERTAIN MECHANISMS OF THE ACTION OF PSYCHOTROPIC-DRUGS ON
TRANSPORT ATPASES.
001331 02-03
TWO CONDUCTANCE MECHANISMS ACTIVATED BY APPLICATIONS OF L
GLUTAMIC-ACID, L ASPARTIC-ACID, DL HOMOCYSTEIC-ACID, N
METHYL-D-ASPARTIC-ACID, AND DL KAINIC-ACID TO CULTURED
MAMMALIAN CENTRAL NEURONES.
001349 02-03
EFFECTS OF NEUROLEPTICS ON NEUROENDOCRINE MECHANISMS FOR
GONADOTROPIN SECRETION.
001391 02-03
PRESYNAPTIC AND POSTSYNAPTIC MECHANISMS IN HALOPERIDOL-
INDUCED SENSITIZATION TO DOPAMINERGIC AGONISTS.
001392 02-03
CENTRAL AMINERGIC AND PEPTIDERGIC MECHANISMS IN
SPONTANEOUSLY (GENETIC) HYPERTENSIVE-RATS. (UNPUBLISHED
PAPER).
001459 02-03
CENTRAL PHARMACOLOGICAL CONTROL OF CORTICOSTERONE SECRETION
IN THE INTACT RAT. DEMONSTRATION OF CHOLINERGIC AND
SEROTONINERGIC FACILITATORY AND ALPHA-ADRENERGIC INHIBITORY
MECHANISMS.
001487 02-03
MECHANISMS OF CHLORPROMAZINE AND CHLORPROMAZINE ISOSTERES
ON THE GLYCEMIC-RESPONSE IN MICE. (PH.D. DISSERTATION).
001525 02-03
THE PHARMACOLOGY OF CATECHOLAMINE INVOLVEMENT IN THE
NEURAL MECHANISMS OF REWARD.
001526 02-03
AMYGDALA OPIATE-SENSITIVE MECHANISMS INFLUENCE FEAR
MOTIVATED RESPONSES AND MEMORY PROCESSES FOR AVERSIVE-
EXPERIENCES. (UNPUBLISHED PAPER).
001628 02-04
INVESTIGATIONS ON THE INTERACTION OF THYROTROPIN-RELEASING-
HORMONE (TRH) AND MK-771 WITH CENTRAL NORADRENERGIC
MECHANISMS.
001701 02-04
THE EFFECT OF SOME STRUCTURAL GABA ANALOGUES ON THE
SEROTONIN AND DOPAMINERGIC MECHANISMS.
001736 02-04
DYSKINESIA INDUCED BY LONG-TERM-TREATMENT WITH
ANTIPSYCHOTIC-DRUGS: INVOLVEMENT OF PRESYNAPTIC AND
POSTSYNAPTIC DOPAMINERGIC MECHANISMS.
001839 02-05
MECHANISMS OF ACTION OF THE ANTIDEPRESSANTS.
002218 02-13
MECHANISMS OF OPIATE ANALGESIA AND THE ROLE OF ENDORPHINS IN
PAIN SUPPRESSION. (UNPUBLISHED PAPER).
002275 02-13
REFLECTIONS ON ACTION MECHANISMS OF PSYCHOTROPIC-
MEDICATIONS.
002296 02-13
PROPRANOLOL (INDERAL) FOR TARDIVE-DYSKINESIA AND
EXTRAPYRAMIDAL SIDE-EFFECTS FROM NEUROLEPTICS: POSSIBLE
INVOLVEMENT OF BETA-ADRENERGIC MECHANISMS.
002470 02-15
ACTION MECHANISMS OF INSULIN-THERAPY IN PSYCHIATRY, AND
CURRENT-VIEWS ON THESE MECHANISMS.
002553 02-17
THE HYPOTHALAMIC DOPAMINERGIC REGULATION OF PROLACTIN: A
MODEL FOR THE STUDY OF NEUROHORMONAL MECHANISMS IN MAN.
002568 02-17
REGULATION OF NEUROTRANSMISSION THROUGH PRESYNAPTIC-
RECEPTORS AND OTHER MECHANISMS: POSSIBLE CLINICAL RELEVANCE
AND THERAPEUTIC POTENTIAL.
002569 02-16
PHARMACOLOGICAL EVIDENCE ON THE SPECIALIZATION OF CNS
MECHANISMS RESPONSIBLE FOR MOTOR ACT INHIBITION BY AVERSIVE
EVENTS.
002671 03-03
GABAERGIC MECHANISMS IN THE CONTROL OF PRL AND GH RELEASE.
002690 03-03

FUNDAMENTAL MECHANISMS UNDERLYING ALTERED BEHAVIOR
FOLLOWING CHRONIC ADMINISTRATION OF PSYCHOMOTOR
STIMULANTS.
002711 03-03
SEROTONERGIC MECHANISMS OF CLONIDINE-INDUCED HYPOTHERMIA IN
RATS.
002806 03-03
ACTIONS OF TETRAHYDRONORHARMANE (TETRAHYDRO-BETA-
CARBOLINE) ON 5 HYDROXYTRYPTAMINE AND DOPAMINE-MEDIATED
MECHANISMS.
002854 03-03
A REEVALUATION OF THE MECHANISMS UNDERLYING SIMPLE CELL
ORIENTATION SELECTIVITY.
002894 03-03
BRAIN MECHANISMS OF LEARNING.
002916 03-03
POSSIBLE MECHANISMS OF EFFECT OF ACTH4-10 AND ITS ANALOG,
CONTAINING D ISOMER OF PHENYLALANINE, ON BEHAVIOR.
002949 03-04
D PROPOXYPHENE ACTS DIFFERENTLY FROM MORPHINE ON OPIOID-
RECEPTOR EFFECTOR MECHANISMS.
003062 03-04
AN INVOLVEMENT OF DOPAMINE IN HIGHER-ORDER CHOICE
MECHANISMS IN THE MONKEY.
003072 03-04
EVIDENCE FOR INVOLVEMENT OF SEPARATE MECHANISMS IN THE
PRODUCTION OF ANALGESIA BY ELECTRICAL-STIMULATION OF THE
NUCLEUS-RETICULARIS-PARAGIGANTOCELLULARIS AND NUCLEUS-
RAPHE-MAGNUS IN THE RAT.
003083 03-04
THE PHARMACOLOGICAL ANALYSIS OF MONOAMINERGIC MECHANISMS
OF THE MEDIAL HYPOTHALAMUS IN FOOD PROCURING CONDITIONED
REFLEXES IN RATS.
003100 03-04
STUDIES ON THE MECHANISMS OF L-DOPA-INDUCED SALIVARY
SECRETION.
003130 03-05
THE ROLE OF CENTRAL SEROTONERGIC MECHANISMS ON HEAD-TWITCH
AND BACKWARD LOCOMOTION INDUCED BY HALLUCINOGENIC-DRUGS.
003397 03-12
GERIATRIC ASPECTS OF PARKINSONISM (CLINICAL-PICTURE,
PATHOLOGICAL MECHANISMS, AND MULTIPLE TREATMENT).
003643 03-17
ANTAGONISM OF ETHANOL-INDUCED DECREASE IN LH BY P
CHLOROPHENYLALANINE: LACK OF CORRELATION WITH ALTERED
SEROTONERGIC MECHANISMS.
003748 04-03
DOPAMINERGIC MECHANISMS IN THE TELEOST RETINA. II. FACTORS
AFFECTING THE ACCUMULATION OF CYCLIC-AMP IN PIECES OF INTACT
CARP RETINA.
003776 04-03
COMPARATIVE-EFFECTS OF SUBSTITUTED PHENYLETHYLAMINES ON BRAIN
SEROTONERGIC MECHANISMS.
003854 04-03
FURTHER ANALYSIS OF THE MECHANISMS OF ACTION OF
BATRACHOTOXIN ON THE MEMBRANE OF MYELINATED NERVE.
003884 04-03
OPIATE MECHANISMS: EVALUATION OF RESEARCH INVOLVING
NEURONAL ACTION POTENTIALS.
003886 04-03
DOPAMINE-DEPENDENT HYPERACTIVITY IN THE FOLLOWING
MANIPULATION OF GABA MECHANISMS IN THE REGION OF THE
NUCLEUS-ACCUMBENS.
003976 04-03
INHIBITION OF LYSOSOMAL LIPASES BY CHLORPROMAZINE: A POSSIBLE
MECHANISMS OF STABILIZATION.
003993 04-03
DOPAMINERGIC MECHANISMS IN THE TELEOST RETINA. I. DOPAMINE-
SENSITIVE ADENYLATE-CYCLASE IN HOMOGENATES OF CARP RETINA:
EFFECTS OF AGONISTS, ANTAGONISTS AND ERGOTS.
004051 04-03
USE OF THE INTRACEREBRAL INJECTION TECHNIQUE TO ELUCIDATE
MECHANISMS OF APOMORPHINE CLIMBING AND ITS ANTAGONISM IN
THE MOUSE.
004092 04-04
ON SOME RELATIONSHIPS BETWEEN GABAERGIC AND 5 HT-ERGIC
MECHANISMS IN PENTYLENETETRAZOL CONVULSIVE-SEIZURE
REACTIONS.
004166 04-04
L 5 HYDROXYTRYPTOPHAN-INDUCED DRINKING IN RATS: POSSIBLE
MECHANISMS FOR INDUCTION.
004237 04-04
TONIC IMMOBILITY IN DOMESTIC FOWL: POSSIBLE INTERACTION OF
SEROTONERGIC AND DOPAMINERGIC MECHANISMS.
004246 04-04
CHOLINERGIC MECHANISMS IN MANIA AND DEPRESSION: QUESTIONS OF
SPECIFICITY.
004374 04-09

OPIOID DEPENDENCE: MECHANISMS AND TREATMENT.
004587 04-14
MECHANISMS AND PHARMACOLOGICAL IMPLICATIONS OF ALTERING CALMODULIN ACTIVITY.
004751 04-17

MECLOPHENOXATE
INFLUENCE OF PYRITHIOXINE, MECLOPHENOXATE AND PIRACETAM ON THE LEARNING PROCESS IN MAN.
000805 01-14

MEDIAN
EVIDENCE FOR A TONIC GABAERGIC CONTROL OF SEROTONIN NEURONS IN THE MEDIAN RAPHE NUCLEUS.
002719 03-03
OPIATE-RECEPTORS AND SLEEP. II. EFFECTS OF MICROINJECTIONS OF ETHYL-ALCOHOL AND PENTOBARBITAL IN THE MEDIAN THALAMUS, PERIAQUEDUCTAL GRAY MATTER AND NUCLEUS-TRACTUS-SOLITARIUS OF THE RABBIT.
002917 03-03
PRESSOR EFFECTS OF ELECTRICAL-STIMULATION OF THE DORSAL AND MEDIAN RAPHE NUCLEI IN ANESTHETIZED RATS.
003892 04-03
EFFECT OF MEDIAN RAPHE STIMULATION ON HIPPOCAMPAL SEIZURE DISCHARGE INDUCED BY CARBACHOL IN THE RABBIT.
003951 04-03

MEDIAN-EMINENCE
A MODEL FOR PSYCHONEUROENDOCRINE INVESTIGATION: SPECIFIC CHEMICAL LESIONING OF THE MEDIAN-EMINENCE.
001478 02-03

MEDICAID
PROBLEMS REMAIN IN REVIEWS OF MEDICAID FINANCED DRUG-THERAPY IN NURSING-HOMES.
004736 04-17

MEDICAL
STUDIES ON THE COMPREHENSIVE MEDICAL TREATMENT OF PEPTIC-ULCERS (3) -- UTILIZATION OF TRANQUILIZERS IN THE TREATMENT OF GASTRIC-ULCERS.
000653 01-10
THE ROLE OF CHOLINERGIC-SUPERSENSITIVITY IN THE MEDICAL SYMPTOMS ASSOCIATED WITH WITHDRAWAL OF ANTIPSYCHOTIC-DRUGS.
000869 01-15
MARIJUANA: A REVIEW OF MEDICAL RESEARCH WITH IMPLICATIONS FOR ADOLESCENTS.
000871 01-15
MEDICAL AND PSYCHIATRIC-COMPLICATIONS OF PENTAZOCINE AND TRIPELENNAMINE ABUSE.
000955 01-17
MEDICAL PSYCHOLOGICAL AND COMBINED THERAPY IN THE CASES OF ENURESIS: A COMPARATIVE-STUDY.
002175 02-11
INITIAL PRESCRIPTION OF PSYCHOTROPIC-MEDICATIONS FOR ADOLESCENTS IN A MEDICAL/PROFESSIONAL INSTITUTE, AND THE ROLE OF THE PSYCHIATRIST IN A MEDICAL/PROFESSIONAL INSTITUTE.
002621 02-17
MEDICAL AND LEGAL IMPLICATIONS OF SIDE-EFFECTS FROM NEUROLEPTIC-DRUGS. A ROUND-TABLE DISCUSSION.
003471 03-15
EMOTIONAL-DISORDERS IN CHILDREN AND ADOLESCENTS: MEDICAL AND PSYCHOLOGICAL APPROACHES TO TREATMENT.
004743 04-17

MEDICAL-EMERGENCIES
PSYCHOTIC EXCITEMENT IN MEDICAL-EMERGENCIES.
004480 04-11

MEDICAL-MODEL
HOW APPROPRIATE IS A MEDICAL-MODEL IN PSYCHIATRIC-PRACTICE?
002531 02-17

MEDICALLY-ILL
TREATMENT OF DEPRESSION IN THE MEDICALLY-ILL ELDERLY WITH METHYLPHENIDATE.
000602 01-09

MEDICATION
CHILDREN ON MEDICATION: A PRIMER FOR SCHOOL PERSONNEL.
000676 01-11
EEG AND PSYCHOEXPERIMENTAL-STUDIES IN HEALTHY SUBJECTS ON LITHIUM MEDICATION.
000768 01-13
THE INFLUENCE OF LITHIUM-SALTS AND ANTIDEPRESSANT MEDICATION ON SERUM PROLACTIN LEVEL.
000780 01-13
MEDICATION USE AND DEATHS ATTRIBUTED TO ASPHYXIA AMONG PSYCHIATRIC-PATIENTS.
000838 01-15
A REVISED CHECKLIST TO OBTAIN CONSENT TO TREATMENT WITH MEDICATION.
000984 01-17
DISCONTINUATION OF ORAL AND DEPOT FLUPHENAZINE IN SCHIZOPHRENIC-PATIENTS AFTER ONE YEAR OF CONTINUOUS MEDICATION: A CONTROLLED-STUDY.
001931 02-08

THERAPEUTIC RESULTS IN A PSYCHOGERIATRIC-WARD AFTER CHANGE OF MEDICATION.
002136 02-11
THE EFFECTS OF COMBINED SEDATIVE AND ANXIOLYTIC-PREPARATIONS ON SUBJECTIVE ASPECTS OF SLEEP AND OBJECTIVE MEASURE OF AROUSAL AND PERFORMANCE THE MORNING FOLLOWING NOCTURNAL MEDICATION: II. REPEATED DOSES.
002331 02-14
MEDICATION AND PREGNANCY.
002424 02-17
MEDICATION: A NECESSARY EVIL?
002549 02-17
NEW DEVELOPMENT IN ANTIDEPRESSANT MEDICATION -- A REVIEW.
002558 02-17
PLACEBO, MEDICINE AND PAIN, OR THE RELATIVE FUNCTION OF MEDICATION IN THE TREATMENT OF PAIN.
002577 02-17
PATTERNS OF USE IN THE INTAKE OF ORAL MEDICATION.
002591 02-17
COMMUNAL MEDICATION.
002595 02-17
THE NEED FOR CONTINUOUS USE OF ANTIPARKINSONIAN MEDICATION WITH CHRONIC SCHIZOPHRENIC-PATIENTS RECEIVING LONG-TERM NEUROLEPTIC THERAPY.
003186 03-08
ON THE EVALUATION OF A PROVOCATIVE EEG METHOD USING MEDICATION IN THE DIAGNOSIS OF ORGANIC-BRAIN-SEIZURES IN CHILDHOOD, WITH SPECIAL EMPHASIS ON SLEEP INDUCTION THROUGH MEDICATION.
003387 03-11
LONG-TERM CHANGES IN AIMS RATINGS AND THEIR RELATION TO MEDICATION HISTORY.
003537 03-15
MEDICATION GROUPS FOR PSYCHIATRIC-PATIENTS.
003582 03-17
THE MEDICATION SEMINAR AND PRIMARY CARE EDUCATION.
003592 03-17
ACCURACY OF PATIENT INTERVIEWS AND ESTIMATES BY CLINICAL STAFF IN DETERMINING MEDICATION COMPLIANCE.
003618 03-17
WIDOWS AND WIDOWERS AND THEIR MEDICATION USE: NURSING IMPLICATIONS.
003626 03-17
MEASUREMENTS OF NERVE CONDUCTION VELOCITY DURING DECREASING TOXIC DIPHENYLHYDANTOIN LEVELS AND THE BEGINNING OF CARBAMAZEPINE MEDICATION: A CLINICAL NEUROPHYSIOLOGICAL REPORT.
004441 04-11
STOPPING MEDICATION IN CHILDREN WITH EPILEPSY.
004447 04-11

MEDICATIONS
DOUBLE-BLIND EVALUATION OF REINFORCING AND ANORECTIC-ACTIONS OF WEIGHT-CONTROL MEDICATIONS: INTERACTION OF PHARMACOLOGICAL-TREATMENT AND BEHAVIORAL-TREATMENTS.
002314 02-14
EDEMAS AND MYOCLONIES IN A PATIENT WITH PARKINSONS-DISEASE TREATED BY AMANTADINE: PROBLEM WITH ASSOCIATED MEDICATIONS.
002389 02-15
ADVERSE-REACTIONS TO MEDICATIONS PRESCRIBED FOR HYPERKINESIS. (PH.D. DISSERTATION).
002411 02-15
HEPATIC SIDE-EFFECTS OF ANTIDEPRESSANT MEDICATIONS.
003523 03-15
INTERACTIONS BETWEEN ALCOHOL AND MEDICATIONS.
003629 03-17

MEDICINE
THE RATIONAL USE OF MUSCLE-RELAXANTS IN REHABILITATION MEDICINE.
000943 01-17
THE PRESENT STATUS OF THE BENZODIAZEPINES IN PSYCHIATRY AND MEDICINE.
000954 01-17
MADNESS AND MEDICINE: THE FORCIBLE ADMINISTRATION OF PSYCHOTROPIC-DRUGS.
002523 02-17
PLACEBO, MEDICINE AND PAIN, OR THE RELATIVE FUNCTION OF MEDICATION IN THE TREATMENT OF PAIN.
002577 02-17
PHENCYCLIDINE-HCL: A CHALLENGE TO MEDICINE.
003395 03-12
MIND/BRAIN IN THE AGE OF PSYCHOPHARMACOLOGY: A CROSSROADS FOR MEDICINE AND MINISTRY.
003624 03-17
THE BRAINSTEM AUDITORY EVOKED-RESPONSE AS A TOOL IN NEUROBEHAVIORAL TOXICOLOGY AND MEDICINE.
004277 04-05

MEDICINES
AIRCRAFT NOISE AND MENTAL-HEALTH: II. USE OF MEDICINES AND
HEALTH-CARE-SERVICES.
003647 03-17
UNDESIRABLE EFFECTS OF MEDICINES: A REVIEW OF SEVERAL
PUBLICATIONS ISSUED FROM 1977-1979.
004632 04-15

MEDIUM
THE ROLE OF INTRANEURONAL 5 HT AND OF TRYPTOPHAN-
HYDROXYLASE ACTIVATION IN THE CONTROL OF 5 HT SYNTHESIS IN
RAT-BRAIN SLICES INCUBATED IN K-ENRICHED MEDIUM.
000123 01-03
CONTROLLED-COMPARISON OF MEDIUM AND HIGH CLOROTEPIN DOSES
IN CHRONIC SCHIZOPHRENIA.
000548 01-08

MEDROXYPROGESTERONE
MEDROXYPROGESTERONE TREATMENT OF OBSTRUCTIVE SLEEP-APNEA.
002128 02-11

MEDROXYPROGESTERONE-ACETATE
TREATMENT OF SEX-OFFENDERS WITH MEDROXYPROGESTERONE-
ACETATE.
004450 04-11

MELANCHOLIA
STANDARDIZATION OF THE DEXAMETHASONE-SUPPRESSION-TEST FOR
THE DIAGNOSIS OF MELANCHOLIA. (UNPUBLISHED PAPER).
004359 04-09

MELANCHOLIAC
CONFESSION OF A MELANCHOLIAC: CONTRIBUTION TO THE PROBLEM OF
PROPHYLAXIS OF MANIC-DEPRESSIVE-PSYCHOSIS USING LITHIUM.
003267 03-09

MELANCHOLIC-DEPRESSED-PATIENTS
OPEN-STUDY OF L 5 HTP IN MELANCHOLIC-DEPRESSED-PATIENTS OVER
50 YEARS OF AGE.
002016 02-09

MELANOCORTICOTROPIC-HORMONES
EFFECT OF NICOTINE ON IN VIVO SECRETION OF MELANOCORTICOTROPIC-
HORMONES IN THE RAT.
003759 04-03

MELANOCYTE-STIMULATING-HORMONE
STUDIES ON THE EFFECT OF ALPHA MELANOCYTE-STIMULATING-
HORMONE AND RELATED PEPTIDES ON THE ACCUMULATION OF P
AMINOHIPPURIC-ACID IN RENAL CORTICAL SLICES. (UNPUBLISHED
PAPER).
001372 02-03

MELANOCYTE-STIMULATING-HORMONES
COMPARISON OF BIOLOGICAL-ACTIVITY AND BEHAVIORAL-ACTIVITY OF
ALPHA AND GAMMA MELANOCYTE-STIMULATING-HORMONES.
(UNPUBLISHED PAPER).
001398 02-03

MELANOSTATIN
EFFECT OF MELANOSTATIN AND THYROLIBERIN ON THE BIOSYNTHESIS
AND RELEASE OF DOPAMINE BY RAT-BRAIN STRIATAL P2-FRACTIONS.
001472 02-03

MELATONIN
EFFECTS OF MELATONIN AND PROPRANOLOL ON SLEEP OF THE RAT.
000432 01-04
PROSTAGLANDIN-E RELEASE BY RAT MEDIAL BASAL HYPOTHALAMUS IN
VITRO. INHIBITION BY MELATONIN AT SUBMICROMOLAR
CONCENTRATIONS.
001159 02-03
THE ANTICONVULSANT PROPERTIES OF MELATONIN ON KINDLED
SEIZURES IN RATS.
002653 03-03
PINEAL-GLAND AND MELATONIN INFLUENCE ON CHRONIC ALCOHOL
CONSUMPTION BY HAMSTERS.
003076 03-04

MELATONIN-LIKE
AN INVERSE CORRELATION BETWEEN SERUM LEVELS OF
DESMETHYLIMIPRAMINE AND MELATONIN-LIKE IMMUNOREACTIVITY
IN DMI RESPONSIVE DEPRESSIVES.
003228 03-09

MELLARIL
EFFECTS OF THIORIDAZINE (MELLARIL) ON TITRATING DELAYED
MATCHING-TO-SAMPLE PERFORMANCE IN MENTALLY-RETARDED
ADULTS.
002471 02-15
EFFECTS OF THIORIDAZINE (MELLARIL) ON TITRATING DELAYED
MATCHING-TO-SAMPLE PERFORMANCE OF MENTALLY-RETARDED
ADULTS.
003392 03-11

MEMBERS
THE ACUTE AND CHRONIC EFFECT OF 5 METHOXYTRYPTAMINE ON
SELECTED MEMBERS OF A PRIMATE SOCIAL-COLONY.
001073 02-02

MEMBRANE
(3H)5 HT BINDING-SITES AND 5 HT-SENSITIVE ADENYLATE-CYCLASE IN
GLIAL CELL MEMBRANE FRACTION.
000093 01-03
NALOXONE ANTAGONISM OF GABA-EVOKED MEMBRANE
POLARIZATIONS IN CULTURED MOUSE SPINAL-CORD NEURONS.
000116 01-03

INFLUENCE OF MORPHINE ON MEMBRANE TURNOVER AND FUNCTION.
001280 02-03
STIMULATION OF THE PLASMA MEMBRANE ENZYME, 5' NUCLEOTIDASE,
BY ETHANOL EXPOSURE TO NEURAL CELLS IN CULTURE.
001499 02-03
NA-DEPENDENT LI COUNTERTRANSPORT AND THE LITHIUM DISTRIBUTION
ACROSS THE HUMAN ERYTHROCYTE MEMBRANE: INTRODUCTION.
002227 02-13
DISTRIBUTION OF MEMBRANE GLYCOPROTEINS AMONG THE ORGANELLES
OF A SINGLE IDENTIFIED NEURON OF APLYSIA. II. ISOLATION AND
CHARACTERIZATION OF A GLYCOPROTEIN ASSOCIATED WITH
VESICLES.
002657 03-03
MEASUREMENT OF THE MEMBRANE POTENTIAL OF ISOLATED NERVE
TERMINALS BY THE LIPOPHILIC CATION
(3H)TRIPHENYLMETHYLPHOSPHONIUM-BROMIDE.
002746 03-03
CALCIUM ANTAGONISM OF THE INHIBITORY-EFFECTS OF FENTANYL ON
THE CONTRACTION OF THE NICTITATING MEMBRANE IN CATS.
002876 03-03
EFFECTS OF PROTEIN AND MEMBRANE MODIFYING AGENTS ON THE
BINDING OF L (3H)GLUTAMATE TO CEREBELLAR SYNAPTIC
MEMBRANES.
002888 03-03
THE ROLE OF CALCIUM AND DOPAMINE MEMBRANE CARRIER IN
MEDIATING THE BEHAVIORAL-EFFECTS AND BIOCHEMICAL-EFFECTS OF
AMPHETAMINE. (PH.D. DISSERTATION).
002996 03-04
PHARMACOLOGICAL DIFFERENTIATION OF PRESYNAPTIC INHIBITORY
ALPHA-ADRENOCEPTORS AND OPIATE-RECEPTORS IN THE CAT
NICTITATING MEMBRANE.
003777 04-03
INFLUENCE OF THE DOPAMINERGIC AGONISTS BROMOCRIPTINE, PIRIBEDIL
AND NOMIFENSINE ON THE SYMPATHETIC NEURAL TRANSMISSION IN
THE NICTITATING MEMBRANE OF THE CAT.
003822 04-03
FURTHER ANALYSIS OF THE MECHANISMS OF ACTION OF
BATRACHOTOXIN ON THE MEMBRANE OF MYELINATED NERVE.
003884 04-03
DOPAMINE-RECEPTORS IN SUBCELLULAR FRACTIONS FROM BOVINE
CAUDATE: ENRICHMENT OF (3H)SPIPERONE BINDING IN A
POSTSYNAPTIC MEMBRANE FRACTION.
003948 04-03
EFFECT OF PRENATAL NEUROLEPTIC TREATMENT ON MEMBRANE
RECEPTOR DEVELOPMENT IN THE BRAIN.
003989 04-03
DEMONSTRATION OF A MUSCARINIC-RECEPTOR-MEDIATED CYCLIC-GMP-
DEPENDENT HYPERPOLARIZATION OF THE MEMBRANE POTENTIAL OF
MOUSE NEUROBLASTOMA CELLS USING
(3H)TETRAPHENYLPHOSPHONIUM.
004049 04-03
MECHANISM OF MEMBRANE STABILIZING AND LYTIC-EFFECTS OF
TRICYCLIC-ANTIDEPRESSANTS.
004283 04-05

MEMBRANE-BOUND
PHOSPHORYLATION OF THE MEMBRANE-BOUND ACETYLCHOLINE-
RECEPTOR: INHIBITION BY DIPHENYLHYDANTOIN.
001257 02-03
BIPHASIC ACTIVITY OF MEMBRANE-BOUND ENZYMES IN BRAIN
MITOCHONDRIA AND SYNAPTOSOMES DURING THE DEVELOPMENT OF
TOLERANCE TO AND PHYSICAL-DEPENDENCE ON CHRONIC MORPHINE
ADMINISTRATION TO RATS.
001285 02-03
COMPARISON OF THE EFFECT OF INTRAVENOUS ADMINISTRATION OF D
LYSERGIC-ACID-DIETHYLAMIDE ON FREE AND MEMBRANE-BOUND
POLYSOMES IN THE RABBIT BRAIN.
003831 04-03
CELL-FREE TRANSLATION OF FREE AND MEMBRANE-BOUND POLYSOMES
AND POLYADENYLATED MRNA FROM RABBIT BRAIN FOLLOWING
ADMINISTRATION OF D LYSERGIC-ACID-DIETHYLAMIDE IN VIVO.
003832 04-03

MEMBRANES
CHARACTERISTICS OF 3H CIS FLUPENTHIXOL BINDING TO CALF BRAIN
MEMBRANES.
000062 01-03
EFFECTS OF DOPAMINERGIC AGONISTS AND ANTAGONISTS ON
(3H)APOMORPHINE BINDING TO STRIATAL MEMBRANES: SULPIRIDE
LACK OF INTERACTIONS WITH POSITIVE COOPERATIVE
(3H)APOMORPHINE BINDING.
000099 01-03
CHARACTERIZATION OF 3H DOPAMINE-RECEPTOR BINDING TO RAT-BRAIN
SYNAPTOSOMAL MEMBRANES: EFFECT OF NONGABAERGIC
COMPOUNDS.
000139 01-03
ACTION OF BARBITURATES ON ACTIVITY OF ACETYLCHOLINESTERASE
FROM SYNAPTOSOMAL MEMBRANES.
000224 01-03
STEREOSPECIFIC NICOTINE-RECEPTORS ON RAT-BRAIN MEMBRANES.
000254 01-03

BIOCHEMICAL-PROPERTIES OF SPIPERONE BINDING TO RAT-BRAIN MEMBRANES.
000294 01-03

INHIBITION OF (3H)DIAZEPAM BINDING TO RAT-BRAIN CORTICAL SYNAPTOSOMAL MEMBRANES BY ADENOSINE UPTAKE BLOCKERS.
000330 01-03

DISPLACEMENT OF (3H)CLONIDINE BINDING BY CLONIDINE ANALOGUES IN MEMBRANES FROM RAT-CEREBRAL-CORTEX.
000536 01-06

OPIATE-RECEPTORS IN MEMBRANES AND IN SOLUTION. (UNPUBLISHED PAPER).
001032 02-01

INHIBITION BY ARYLSULPHATASE A OF NA-INDEPENDENT (3H) GABA AND (3H) MUSCIMOL BINDING TO BOVINE CEREBELLAR SYNAPTIC MEMBRANES.
001208 02-03

CALMODULIN RELEASE FROM STRIATAL MEMBRANES AFTER ACUTE AND CHRONIC TREATMENT WITH BUTACLAMOL.
001249 02-03

EXPOSURE OF MITOCHONDRIAL OUTER MEMBRANES TO NEURAMINIDASE SELECTIVELY DESTROYS MONOAMINE-OXIDASE-A ACTIVITY.
001286 02-03

EVIDENCE FOR AN ENDOGENOUS COMPOUND INTERFERING WITH 3H DIAZEPAM BINDING TO RAT-BRAIN MEMBRANES.
001308 02-03

DOPAMINE-RECEPTOR: FROM SYNAPTIC MEMBRANES TO SOLUBILIZATION.
001326 02-03

FURTHER CHARACTERIZATION OF THE BINDING OF SUBSTANCE-P TO A FRACTION FROM RABBIT BRAIN ENRICHED IN SYNAPTIC MEMBRANES.
001394 02-03

ALPHA-ADRENORECEPTOR MEDIATED ALTERATION OF ETHANOL EFFECTS ON NA-K-ATPASE OF RAT NEURONAL MEMBRANES.
001425 02-03

BINDING OF PHENCYCLIDINE TO RAT-BRAIN MEMBRANES: TECHNICAL-ASPECT.
001882 02-06

THE EFFECT OF GUANOSINE-NUCLEOTIDES ON (3H)SULPIRIDE BINDING TO RAT STRIATAL MEMBRANES.
002722 03-03

EFFECTS OF PROTEIN AND MEMBRANE MODIFYING AGENTS ON THE BINDING OF L (3H)GLUTAMATE TO CEREBELLAR SYNAPTIC MEMBRANES.
002888 03-03

TRICYCLIC-ANTIDEPRESSANT DRUG-TREATMENT DECREASES ALPHA2-ADRENORECEPTORS ON HUMAN PLATELET MEMBRANES.
003408 03-13

CHARACTERIZATION OF TWO (3H)GLUTAMATE BINDING-SITES IN RAT HIPPOCAMPAL MEMBRANES.
003726 04-03

PAPAIN-DERIVED FRAGMENT IIC TETANUS-TOXIN: ITS BINDING TO ISOLATED SYNAPTIC MEMBRANES AND RETROGRADE AXONAL TRANSPORT.
003734 04-03

IBOTENIC-ACID ANALOGUES AS INHIBITORS OF (3H)GLUTAMIC-ACID BINDING TO CEREBELLAR MEMBRANES.
003848 04-03

BINDING OF (3H) MUSCIMOL, A POTENT GAMMA AMINOBUTYRIC-ACID-RECEPTOR AGONIST, TO MEMBRANES OF THE BOVINE RETINA.
003954 04-03

L ASPARTATE BINDING-SITES IN RAT-CEREBELLUM: A COMPARISON OF THE BINDING OF L (3H)ASPARTATE AND L (3H)GLUTAMATE TO SYNAPTIC MEMBRANES.
004000 04-03

DOPAMINE-RECEPTOR BINDING IN BOVINE INTERMEDIATE LOBE PITUITARY MEMBRANES.
004003 04-03

THE HIGH-AFFINITY CHOLINE UPTAKE SYSTEM WITH RESPECT TO THE MUSCARINIC-RECEPTORS USING A SYNAPTOSOMAL FRACTION ABUNDANT IN PRESYNAPTIC MEMBRANES.
004028 04-03

MEMORY

EFFECT OF BETA ENDORPHIN AND NALOXONE ON ACQUISITION, MEMORY, AND RETRIEVAL OF SHUTTLE AVOIDANCE AND HABITUATION LEARNING IN RATS.
000410 01-04

AROUSAL AND SHORT-TERM MEMORY: EFFECTS OF CAFFEINE AND TRIAL SPACING ON DELAYED ALTERNATION PERFORMANCE.
000487 01-04

MEMORY AND COGNITIVE FUNCTION IN THE ELDERLY: A PRELIMINARY-TRIAL OF PHYSOSTIGMINE.
000802 01-14

PIRACETAM AND RETRIEVAL OF MEMORY IN YOUNG RATS.
000803 01-14

EFFECT OF DRUGS ON LEARNING AND MEMORY PROCESSES IN SIMPLE BEHAVIORAL-TESTS.
000809 01-14

THE INFLUENCE OF NOOTROPIC-DRUGS ON LEARNING AND MEMORY OF DEFENSE REACTIONS.
000815 01-14

EFFECTS OF LITHIUM-CARBONATE ON MEMORY AND OTHER COGNITIVE FUNCTIONS.
000824 01-14

ACTH MODULATION OF MEMORY STORAGE PROCESSING. (UNPUBLISHED PAPER).
001250 02-03

PERIPHERAL CATECHOLAMINES AND MEMORY MODULATION. (UNPUBLISHED PAPER).
001251 02-03

ROLE OF NEUROTRANSMITTERS AND PROTEIN SYNTHESIS IN SHORT-TERM AND LONG-TERM MEMORY.
001573 02-04

EFFECTS OF SOCIAL-ISOLATION ON MEMORY FORMATION.
001607 02-04

AMYGDALA OPIATE-SENSITIVE MECHANISMS INFLUENCE FEAR MOTIVATED RESPONSES AND MEMORY PROCESSES FOR AVERSIVE-EXPERIENCES. (UNPUBLISHED PAPER).
001628 02-04

BRAIN CATECHOLAMINES MODIFICATIONS. THE EFFECTS ON MEMORY FACILITATION INDUCED BY OXOTREMORINE IN MICE.
001658 02-04

PIRACETAM EFFECT ON LEARNING AND MEMORY IN RATS.
001689 02-04

ACTH4-10 AND MEMORY IN ECT TREATED AND UNTREATED PATIENTS. I. EFFECT ON CONSOLIDATION.
001982 02-09

ACTH4-10 AND MEMORY IN ECT TREATED PATIENTS AND UNTREATED CONTROLS. II. EFFECT ON RETRIEVAL.
001983 02-09

HUMAN MEMORY AND THE EFFECTS OF PHYSOSTIGMINE AND CHOLINE-CHLORIDE.
002317 02-14

EFFECTS OF HIPPOCAMPAL BRAIN-DAMAGE ON AUDITORY AND VISUAL RECENT MEMORY: COMPARISON WITH MARIJUANA INTOXICATED SUBJECTS.
002320 02-14

INFLUENCE OF OXYTOCIN ON HUMAN MEMORY PROCESSES.
002322 02-14

ADRENALINE: A SECRET AGENT IN MEMORY.
002345 02-14

THE EFFECTS OF FLURAZEPAM, LORAZEPAM, AND TRIAZOLAM ON SLEEP AND MEMORY.
002357 02-14

CENTRAL AND PERIPHERAL CATECHOLAMINE FUNCTION IN LEARNING AND MEMORY PROCESSES.
002823 03-03

A PSYCHOPHARMACOLOGICAL APPROACH TO MEMORY PROCESSING.
002901 03-03

EFFECT OF PHENTOLAMINE ADMINISTRATION INTO THE AMYGDALA COMPLEX OF RATS ON TIME-DEPENDENT MEMORY PROCESSES.
002998 03-04

EFFECT OF GROWTH-HORMONE ON MEMORY IN MICE.
003014 03-04

INTRAVENTRICULAR CORTICOSTERONE INJECTION FACILITATES MEMORY OF AN APPETITIVE DISCRIMINATIVE TASK IN MICE.
003051 03-04

PHOSPHODIESTERASE INHIBITORS FACILITATE MEMORY FOR PASSIVE-AVOIDANCE CONDITIONING.
003109 03-04

LECITHIN AND MEMORY TRAINING IN ALZHEIMERS-DISEASE. (PH.D. DISSERTATION).
003299 03-11

THE EFFECTS OF LECITHIN ON MEMORY IN PATIENTS WITH SENILE-DEMENTIA OF THE ALZHEIMERS-TYPE.
003385 03-11

EFFECTS OF VASOPRESSIN ON HUMAN MEMORY FUNCTIONS.
003388 03-11

CORRELATED STUDY OF THE EFFECTS OF SE-5023 IN AN HYPOXIC ATMOSPHERE ON QUANTIFIED EEG, VIGILANCE, MEMORY, AND MOOD.
003440 03-14

CAN DRUGS HALT MEMORY LOSS?
003447 03-14

EFFECTS OF CHOLINERGIC-DRUGS ON MEMORY IN ALZHEIMERS-DISEASE.
003454 03-14

DOSE-EFFECTS OF SECOBARBITAL IN A STERNBERG MEMORY SCANNING TASK.
003460 03-14

THE PHARMACOLOGY OF MEMORY: A NEUROBIOLOGICAL-PERSPECTIVE.
003636 03-17

THE EFFECT OF P CHLOROPHENYLALANINE ON THE DISTRIBUTION OF BIOGENIC-AMINES IN THE BRAIN, AND ON MEMORY IN RATS.
004068 04-04

THE EFFECTS OF COLCHICINE AND VINBLASTINE ON MEMORY IN CHICKS.
004069 04-04

MEMORY, OPIATE-RECEPTORS, AND AGING.
004143 04-04

OPIATE MODULATION OF MEMORY. (UNPUBLISHED PAPER).
004177 04-04

Subject Index

ACUTE EFFECT OF DRUGS UPON MEMORY OF PATIENTS WITH SENILE-
DEMENTIA.
004561 04-14

MEMORY: THE EFFECTS OF ALCOHOL AND OF MARIHUANA.
004570 04-14

PHARMACOLOGICAL MODULATION OF FORMATION OF LONG-TERM
MEMORY.
004578 04-14

VARIOUS ASPECTS OF THE EFFECT OF ANTICONVULSANT-DRUGS ON
MEMORY.
004602 04-15

MEMORY-DISORDERS
CHOLINOMIMETICS IN MANIA, SCHIZOPHRENIA, AND MEMORY-
DISORDERS.
004703 04-17

MEMORY-DISTURBANCES
ON A CASE OF MEMORY-DISTURBANCES TREATED WITH VASOPRESSIN.
003301 03-11

EXPERIENCE IN USING THE HORMONES OF THE HYPOPHYSIS POSTERIOR
LOBE IN MEMORY-DISTURBANCES OF VARYING GENESES.
003438 03-14

MEN
DIURNAL GROWTH-HORMONE RESPONSES TO DEXTROAMPHETAMINE IN
NORMAL YOUNG MEN AND POSTMENOPAUSAL-WOMEN.
003411 03-13

AUTONOMIC-EFFECTS OF DEXTROAMPHETAMINE IN NORMAL MEN:
IMPLICATIONS FOR HYPERACTIVITY AND SCHIZOPHRENIA.
003437 03-13

ELECTROPHYSIOLOGICAL AND PSYCHOLOGICAL CHANGES INDUCED BY
STEROID-HORMONES IN MEN AND WOMEN.
004500 04-13

IN NORMAL YOUNG MEN ACUTE DOPAMINERGIC BLOCKADE DOES NOT
IMPAIR FREE WATER EXCRETION FOLLOWING A STANDARD WATER
LOAD.
004600 04-15

MENTAL-CAPACITY
VOLUNTARY INTOXICATION FROM PHENCYCLIDINE. WILL IT RAISE A
REASONABLE-DOUBT OF THE MENTAL-CAPACITY OF A PERSON
CHARGED WITH A CRIME REQUIRING SPECIFIC INTENT OR MENTAL-
STATE?.
000914 01-17

MENTAL-DISEASES
PLASMA LEVEL OF CYCLIC-AMP AND MENTAL-DISEASES.
003170 03-08

MENTAL-DISORDERS
ERGOTS IN THE TREATMENT OF MENTAL-DISORDERS OF OLD-AGE.
002545 02-17

PROBLEMS OF DRUG-TREATMENT OF MENTAL-DISORDERS.
002623 02-17

SOME PRINCIPLES OF DIFFERENTIATED METABOLIC DRUG-TREATMENT IN
COMPREHENSIVE THERAPY OF MENTAL-DISORDERS.
004433 04-11

MENTAL-DISTURBANCES
MENTAL-DISTURBANCES IN CHRONIC MANGANESE POISONING.
004621 04-15

MENTAL-HEALTH
PSYCHOPHARMACOLOGY -- AN AREA OF RESEARCH TO IMPROVE
MENTAL-HEALTH CARE.
002586 02-17

AIRCRAFT NOISE AND MENTAL-HEALTH: II. USE OF MEDICINES AND
HEALTH-CARE-SERVICES.
003647 03-17

MENTAL-HYGIENE-CLINIC
PSYCHIATRIC-DRUG-STUDY. PART II. MENTAL-HYGIENE-CLINIC SURVEY,
DAY-TREATMENT-CENTER SURVEY, DAY-HOSPITAL SURVEY.
004716 04-17

MENTAL-ILLNESS
PLASMA CHLORPROMAZINE CONCENTRATIONS IN CHILDREN WITH
BEHAVIORAL-DISORDERS AND MENTAL-ILLNESS.
000717 01-11

OBSERVATIONS ABOUT STATES OF MENTAL-ILLNESS AS ILLUMINATED BY
THEIR RESPONSE TO PHARMACEUTIC-AGENTS.
000972 01-17

POSSIBLE ROLE OF THE THYMUS-GLAND IN MENTAL-ILLNESS.
002273 02-13

MENTAL-ILLNESSES
BRAIN CATECHOLAMINES, MENTAL-ILLNESSES, AGING AND SENILE-
DEMENTIA: BIOCHEMICAL-CONSIDERATIONS AND PHARMACOLOGICAL-
CONSIDERATIONS.
001550 02-03

ENDORPHINS IN MENTAL-ILLNESSES, AND PARTICULARLY IN
SCHIZOPHRENIA.
003203 03-08

MENTAL-PATIENTS
ORIENTATIONAL TESTING OF CHLORPROMAZINE-HCL ON HOSPITALIZED
MENTAL-PATIENTS.
002131 02-11

MENTAL-RETARDATES
COMPARISON OF SCH-12679 AND THIORIDAZINE IN AGGRESSIVE
MENTAL-RETARDATES.
002119 02-11

MESTEROLONE
A CLINICAL-STUDY AND ENDOCRINE-STUDY OF MESTEROLONE IN
SECONDARY IMPOTENCE.
002315 02-14

MET-ENKEPHALIN
PROSTAGLANDINS IN THE BRAIN OF RATS GIVEN, ACUTELY, AND
CHRONICALLY, A HYPERTHERMIC-DOSE OF MET-ENKEPHALIN.
001468 02-03
NEONATAL ADMINISTRATION OF MET-ENKEPHALIN FACILITATES MAZE-
PERFORMANCE OF ADULT RATS.
001673 02-04

MET-ENKEPHALIN-ARG6-PHE7
MET-ENKEPHALIN-ARG6-PHE7 INTERACTS WITH THE KAPPA-RECEPTORS
ON GUINEA-PIG ILEUM.
001110 02-03

METABOLIC
EFFECTS OF GAMMA HYDROXYBUTYRIC-ACID ON METABOLIC,
RESPIRATORY AND VASOMOTOR ACTIVITIES AND BODY-
TEMPERATURE IN RATS.
000189 01-03
SWIMMING CAPACITY OF MICE AFTER PROLONGED TREATMENT WITH
PSYCHOSTIMULANTS: II. EFFECT OF METHAMPHETAMINE ON
SWIMMING PERFORMANCE AND AVAILABILITY OF METABOLIC
SUBSTRATES.
001613 02-04
DETERMINATION OF TRICYCLIC-ANTIDEPRESSANTS AND TETRACYCLIC-
ANTIDEPRESSANTS AND OF THEIR METABOLIC PRODUCTS IN
BIOLOGICAL FLUIDS.
002498 02-16
BEHAVIORAL AND METABOLIC ALTERATIONS IN PROGENY OF
METHADONE-TREATED RATS. (PH.D. DISSERTATION).
003113 03-04
ANESTHETICS AND THE HABENULO-INTERPEDUNCULAR SYSTEM:
SELECTIVE SPARING OF METABOLIC ACTIVITY.
003833 04-03
METABOLIC AND SYMPATHOADRENAL ABNORMALITIES IN THE OBESE
ZUCKER RAT: EFFECT OF CHRONIC PHENOXYBENZAMINE TREATMENT.
003905 04-03
SOME PRINCIPLES OF DIFFERENTIATED METABOLIC DRUG-TREATMENT IN
COMPREHENSIVE THERAPY OF MENTAL-DISORDERS.
004433 04-11

METABOLIC-ASPECTS
SOME CLINICAL-ASPECTS AND METABOLIC-ASPECTS OF PROPRANOLOL IN
CHRONIC SCHIZOPHRENIA.
001926 02-08

METABOLIC-CORRELATES
METABOLIC-CORRELATES OF THE EFFECTS OF 2 DEOXY-D-GLUCOSE ON
MEAL SIZE AND POST MEAL SATIETY IN RATS.
003035 03-04

METABOLIC-EFFECTS
CEREBRAL CIRCULATORY AND METABOLIC-EFFECTS OF PIRIBEDIL.
000200 01-03
INTERACTION BETWEEN PHENYTOIN AND VALPROIC-ACID: PLASMA
PROTEIN BINDING AND METABOLIC-EFFECTS.
002276 02-13

METABOLIC-STUDIES
EFFECT OF SINGLE AND REPEATED ELECTROCONVULSIVE-SHOCK ON
SEROTONERGIC SYSTEM IN RAT-BRAIN -- I. METABOLIC-STUDIES.
001332 02-03
METABOLIC-STUDIES AND PSYCHOPHYSIOLOGIC-STUDIES OF
CANNABIDIOL HEXOBARBITAL INTERACTION.
002209 02-13

METABOLIC-STUDY
HEMODYNAMIC AND CEREBRAL METABOLIC-STUDY OF DIAZEPAM IN
NEUROSURGICAL-RESUSCITATION.
002231 02-13

METABOLISM
ENHANCEMENT OF RAT-BRAIN METABOLISM OF A TRYPTOPHAN LOAD
BY CHRONIC ETHANOL ADMINISTRATION.
000022 01-03
DISPOSITION OF VALPROIC-ACID IN THE RAT: DOSE-DEPENDENT
METABOLISM, DISTRIBUTION, ENTEROHEPATIC RECIRCULATION AND
CHOLERETIC-EFFECT.
000073 01-03
ENZYME INDUCING EFFECTS OF PHENOBARBITAL ON NITRAZEPAM
METABOLISM IN DOGS.
000086 01-03
ACTIONS OF CHLORPROMAZINE, HALOPERIDOL AND PIMOZIDE ON LIPID
METABOLISM IN GUINEA-PIG BRAIN SLICES.
000129 01-03
EFFECTS OF CHRONIC FLUOXETINE ADMINISTRATION ON SEROTONIN
METABOLISM.
000138 01-03
THE EFFECT OF MONOAMINE-OXIDASE-INHIBITORS ON FIRST-PASS
METABOLISM OF TYRAMINE IN DOG INTESTINE.
000141 01-03
DIMETHYLAMINOETHANOL (DEANOL) METABOLISM IN RAT-BRAIN AND
ITS EFFECT ON ACETYLCHOLINE SYNTHESIS.
000150 01-03

273

MONOAMINE-OXIDASE-INHIBITION AND BRAIN-AMINE METABOLISM
AFTER ORAL TREATMENT WITH TOLOXATONE IN THE RAT.
000156 01-03

PHARMACOKINETICS AND METABOLISM OF
CHLORODIMETHYLAMINOETHOXYDIBENZOTHIEPINE (ZOTEPINE) IN RAT,
MOUSE, DOG AND MAN.
000219 01-03

METABOLISM OF 3H NORADRENALINE RELEASED FROM ISOLATED RAT
HYPOTHALAMUS BY EXTRACTS OF BLACK-WIDOW-SPIDER GLANDS.
000223 01-03

EFFECT OF GABA ANALOGUES ON BLOOD-PRESSURE AND CENTRAL GABA
METABOLISM IN THE RAT.
000231 01-03

IRREVERSIBLE INHIBITION OF AROMATIC-L-AMINO-ACID-DECARBOXYLASE
BY ALPHA DIFLUOROMETHYL-DOPA AND METABOLISM OF THE
INHIBITOR.
000248 01-03

THE EFFECTS OF GONADECTOMY AND HYPOPHYSECTOMY ON THE
METABOLISM OF IMIPRAMINE AND LIDOCAINE BY THE LIVER OF MALE
AND FEMALE RATS.
000273 01-03

EFFECT OF THE CATECHOLAMINE-DEPLETING-AGENT 1 PHENYL-2-
THIAZOLYL-2-THIOUREA (U-14-624) ON DRUG METABOLISM IN THE
RAT.
000280 01-03

INFLUENCE OF GLUCOSE (IN VIVO OR IN VITRO) ON DURATION OF
NARCOTIC ANALGESICS AND ON THE KINETICS OF DRUG METABOLISM.
000292 01-03

THE EFFECT OF A NEW FLUORINATED TRICYCLIC NEUROLEPTIC-DRUG
ISOFLOXYTHEPIN ON THE RAT STRIATAL DOPAMINE METABOLISM.
000306 01-03

ANALYSIS OF THE ACTIVATION OF DOPAMINE METABOLISM BY A
SEROTONIN UPTAKE INHIBITOR.
000315 01-03

RELATIONSHIP BETWEEN DELTA9 TETRAHYDROCANNABINOL-INDUCED
MOUSE-KILLING-BEHAVIOR ON THE RAT AND THE METABOLISM OF
MONOAMINES IN THE BRAIN, PARTICULARLY THE OLFACTORY-BULB.
000472 01-04

CHOLERA-TOXIN-INDUCED EPILEPTOGENIC-FOCUS — SPECIAL REFERENCE
TO CYCLIC-AMP METABOLISM AND EPILEPTOGENIC-FOCUS.
000522 01-05

3 CHLORO-4-PHENYLSUCCINIMIDOBENZENESULFONAMIDE (GS-385), A
NEW ANTICONVULSANT: ITS QUANTITATIVE DETERMINATION,
PHARMACOKINETICS AND METABOLISM USING HIGH-PERFORMANCE
LIQUID-CHROMATOGRAPHY.
000705 01-11

INCREASED METABOLISM OF DOPAMINE AND SEROTONIN INDUCED IN
FOREBRAIN AREAS BY ETORPHINE MICROINJECTION IN
PERIAQUEDUCTAL GRAY.
001103 02-03

PHOSPHOLIPID METABOLISM, CALCIUM-FLUX AND THE RECEPTOR-
MEDIATED INDUCTION OF CHEMOTAXIS IN RABBIT NEUTROPHILS.
(UNPUBLISHED PAPER).
001118 02-03

EFFECTS OF BICUCULLINE-INDUCED SEIZURES ON CEREBRAL METABOLISM
AND CIRCULATION OF RATS RENDERED HYPOGLYCEMIC BY
STARVATION.
001134 02-03

HA-966 EFFECTS ON STRIATAL DOPAMINE METABOLISM: IMPLICATIONS
FOR DOPAMINE COMPARTMENTALIZAION.
001150 02-03

SPECIES-DIFFERENCES IN CLOBAZAM METABOLISM AND ANTILEPTAZOL
EFFECT.
001157 02-03

STUDIES ON THIORIDAZINE AND MESORIDAZINE METABOLISM. II. IN
VIVO METABOLISM OF TRITIATED DRUGS IN RHESUS-MONKEYS.
001229 02-03

TRYPTOPHOL-INDUCED CHANGE IN BRAIN 5 HYDROXYTRYPTAMINE
METABOLISM.
001236 02-03

SHORT-TERM AND LONG-TERM EFFECTS OF METHAMPHETAMINE ON
BIOGENIC-AMINE METABOLISM IN EXTRASTRIATAL DOPAMINERGIC
NUCLEI.
001384 02-03

THE EFFECT OF SODIUM-SALICYLATE ON CEREBRAL BLOOD FLOW AND
METABOLISM.
001416 02-03

THYROTROPIN-RELEASING-HORMONE: NEUROCHEMICAL EVIDENCE FOR
THE POTENTIATION OF IMIPRAMINE EFFECTS ON THE METABOLISM
AND UPTAKE OF BRAIN CATECHOLAMINES.
001427 02-03

EFFECT OF REPEATED TREATMENT WITH NEUROLEPTICS ON DOPAMINE
METABOLISM IN CELL BODIES AND TERMINALS OF DOPAMINERGIC-
SYSTEMS IN THE RAT-BRAIN.
001464 02-03

EVIDENCE THAT NORADRENALINE MODULATES THE INCREASE IN
STRIATAL DOPAMINE METABOLISM INDUCED BY MUSCARINIC-
RECEPTOR STIMULATION.
001518 02-03

EVALUATION OF THE EFFECT OF DRUGS ON DOPAMINE METABOLISM IN
THE RAT SUPERIOR-CERVICAL-GANGLION BY HPLC WITH
ELECTROCHEMICAL-DETECTION.
001530 02-03

EFFECT OF L FUCOSE ON BRAIN PROTEIN METABOLISM AND RETENTION
OF A LEARNED-BEHAVIOR IN RATS.
001819 02-04

STUDIES ON THIORIDAZINE AND MESORIDAZINE METABOLISM. I.
PROTEIN BINDING.
001867 02-06

AGE-RELATED FACTORS AFFECTING ANTIDEPRESSANT-DRUG METABOLISM
AND CLINICAL-RESPONSE.
002035 02-09

METABOLISM OF DIMETHOXYMETHYL-PHENOBARBITAL (ETEROBARB) IN
PATIENTS WITH EPILEPSY.
002235 02-13

COMPARATIVE-STUDIES ON THE METABOLISM AND THE DISTRIBUTION OF
SULPIRIDE AND SULTOPRIDE.
002240 02-13

EFFECT OF DOXEPIN ON SEROTONIN METABOLISM IN RAT-BRAIN AND
SEROTONIN UPTAKE BY HUMAN BLOOD-PLATELETS.
002243 02-13

TOXICOLOGY — PHARMACOLOGY — METABOLISM.
002252 02-13

CONTRIBUTION TO THE PHARMACOKINETICS AND METABOLISM OF
OXYPROTHEPIN.
002279 02-13

NEURONAL ACTIVITY AND ENERGY METABOLISM: A SUMMARY OF A
SYMPOSIUM. (UNPUBLISHED PAPER).
002308 02-13

CHANGES IN CEREBRAL DOPAMINE METABOLISM AND RECEPTORS
DURING ONE-YEAR NEUROLEPTIC ADMINISTRATION AND SUBSEQUENT
WITHDRAWAL: RELEVANCE TO BRAIN-BIOCHEMISTRY IN
SCHIZOPHRENIA.
002390 02-15

STUDY OF METABOLISM AND BLOOD LEVELS OF ANTIDEPRESSANTS:
TOWARDS A RATIONALIZATION OF THEIR THERAPEUTIC USE.
002625 02-17

CROSS-TOLERANCE OF DOPAMINE METABOLISM TO BACLOFEN, GAMMA
BUTYROLACTONE AND HA-966 IN THE STRIATUM AND OLFACTORY
TUBERCLE OF THE RAT.
002681 03-03

EFFECT OF NEUROLEPTICS ON INDOLEAMINE-N-METHYLTRANSFERASE
ACTIVITY AND BRAIN METABOLISM OF BUFOTENIN.
002735 03-03

EFFECTS OF NEOMYCIN ON CALCIUM AND POLYPHOSPHOINOSITIDE
METABOLISM OF GUINEA-PIG SYNAPTOSOMES.
002741 03-03

THE EFFECTS OF D-AMPHETAMINE AND POTASSIUM ON SEROTONIN
RELEASE AND METABOLISM IN RAT-CEREBRAL-CORTEX TISSUE.
002754 03-03

THE EFFECT OF PHENCYCLIDINE ON DOPAMINE METABOLISM IN THE
MOUSE-BRAIN.
002766 03-03

NOREPINEPHRINE DEPLETION ALTERS CEREBRAL OXIDATIVE METABOLISM
IN THE ACTIVE STATE.
002798 03-03

PULMONARY METABOLISM OF IMIPRAMINE IN THE RAT AND RABBIT:
COMPARISON WITH HEPATIC METABOLISM.
002845 03-03

MULTIPLE EFFECTS OF REPEATED ADMINISTRATION OF GAMMA
ACETYLENIC-GABA ON RAT-BRAIN METABOLISM.
002878 03-03

THE METABOLISM OF 5 HYDROXYTRYPTAMINE IN THE METHIONINE-
SULFOXIMINE EPILEPTOGENIC RAT-BRAIN.
002887 03-03

ACCELERATED METABOLISM OF PROBENECID DURING LONG-TERM-
TREATMENT OF RATS WITH ANTICONVULSANT-DRUGS: EFFECT ON
CENTRAL SEROTONIN TURNOVER STUDIES.
002890 03-03

EFFECTS OF BENSERAZIDE AND CARBIDOPA ON THE METABOLISM OF L
TRYPTOPHAN BY ISOLATED RAT LIVER CELLS.
002899 03-03

EFFECTS OF CHOLECYSTOKININ-OCTAPEPTIDE ON STRIATAL DOPAMINE
METABOLISM AND ON APOMORPHINE-INDUCED STEREOTYPED CAGE
CLIMBING IN MICE.
003031 03-04

A COMPARATIVE-STUDY OF THE PHARMACOLOGY OF INHIBITORS OF
GABA METABOLISM.
003036 03-04

THE THERAPEUTIC ACTIVITY OF TRYPTOPHAN AND ITS EFFECT ON
SEROTONIN METABOLISM IN EPILEPTIC-PATIENTS.
003289 03-11

THE EFFECTS OF PHENYTOIN ON PHENOBARBITONE AND PRIMIDONE
METABOLISM.
003333 03-11

ABNORMAL TRANSMETHYLATION REACTION DURING THE METABOLISM OF DOPAMINE, TRYPTAMINE, AND SEROTONIN, AND SCHIZOPHRENIC-SYMPTOMS: A CRITICAL REVIEW.
003404 03-13

GLOMERULAR FILTRATION RATE AND CALCIUM METABOLISM IN LONG-TERM LITHIUM TREATMENT.
003542 03-15

DISTRIBUTION OF CESIUM IN THE ORGANISM AND ITS EFFECT ON THE NUCLEOTIDE METABOLISM ENZYMES.
003696 04-02

EFFECT OF AMPHETAMINE ON THE METABOLISM AND INCORPORATION OF (3H) THYMIDINE INTO DNA OF DEVELOPING RAT-BRAIN.
003729 04-03

THE EFFECTS OF ANTIDEPRESSANTS ON THE RETENTION AND METABOLISM OF (3H) NOREPINEPHRINE IN RAT-BRAIN SLICES.
003763 04-03

CATECHOLAMINE AND 5 HYDROXYTRYPTAMINE SYNTHESIS AND METABOLISM FOLLOWING INTRACEREBROVENTRICULAR INJECTION OF DIBUTYRYL-CYCLIC-AMP.
003769 04-03

ETHANOL-INDUCED CHANGES IN CYCLIC-GUANOSINE-PHOSPHATE METABOLISM IN MOUSE VESTIBULAR REGION.
003784 04-03

THE EFFECT OF LONG-TERM CONCURRENT ADMINISTRATION OF CHLORPROMAZINE AND LITHIUM ON THE STRIATAL AND FRONTAL CORTICAL DOPAMINE METABOLISM IN RATS.
003788 04-03

COMPARATIVE-EFFECTS OF AMANTADINE AND AMFONELIC-ACID ON DOPAMINE METABOLISM IN RAT-BRAIN.
003796 04-03

ALTERATIONS OF ACETYLCHOLINE AND CHOLINE METABOLISM IN MAMMALIAN PREPARATIONS TREATED WITH BETA BUNGAROTOXIN.
003820 04-03

UNIMPAIRED QUININE METABOLISM IN RATS WITH VENTROMEDIAL HYPOTHALAMIC LESIONS.
003821 04-03

EFFECT OF INHIBITORS OF GABA-AMINOTRANSFERASE ON THE METABOLISM OF GABA IN BRAIN TISSUE AND SYNAPTOSOMAL FRACTIONS.
003914 04-03

EFFECT OF IMIPRAMINE ON CENTRAL 5 HYDROXYTRYPTAMINE TURNOVER AND METABOLISM IN RATS.
003999 04-03

THE EFFECT OF PROPYLNORANTIFEIN ON BEHAVIORAL-REACTIONS, ADRENOCORTICAL ACTIVITY, AND ENERGY METABOLISM IN THE ANIMAL BRAIN.
004075 04-04

EFFECT OF PRENATAL PHENYTOIN ADMINISTRATION ON BRAIN TRYPTOPHAN METABOLISM OF RAT OFFSPRING DURING THE PREWEANING PERIOD.
004108 04-04

EFFECTS OF A SINGLE-THERAPEUTIC-DOSE OF GLYCEROL ON CEREBRAL METABOLISM IN THE BRAINS OF YOUNG MICE: POSSIBLE INCREASE IN BRAIN GLUCOSE TRANSPORT AND GLUCOSE UTILIZATION.
004281 04-05

PRAZEPAM METABOLISM IN FEMALE SUBJECTS.
004504 04-13

NOREPINEPHRINE METABOLISM IN MAN USING DEUTERIUM LABELLING: 4 HYDROXY-3-METHOXYMANDELIC-ACID.
004534 04-13

LITHIUM EFFECTS ON CITRATE METABOLISM IN HUMANS AND RATS.
004537 04-13

CATECHOLAMINE METABOLISM IN A PSYCHOACTIVE CACTUS.
004722 04-17

METABOLITE
ENTRY OF DIAZEPAM AND ITS MAJOR METABOLITE INTO CEREBROSPINAL-FLUID.
000114 01-03

1-M CHLOROPHENYLPIPERAZINE: A METABOLITE OF TRAZODONE ISOLATED FROM RAT URINE.
000204 01-03

INTERACTION BETWEEN AMITRIPTYLINE AND PHENOTHIAZINE IN MAN: METABOLITE NORTRIPTYLINE AND THE CORRELATION WITH CLINICAL-RESPONSE.
000640 01-09

P CHLOROAMPHETAMINE: EVALUATION OF A BRAIN METABOLITE.
001779 02-04

KINETICS AND NEUROPSYCHOLOGIC-EFFECTS OF IV DIAZEPAM IN THE PRESENCE AND ABSENCE OF ITS ACTIVE N DESMETHYL METABOLITE IN HUMANS.
002229 02-13

THYMOANALEPTIC TREATMENT CONTROL THROUGH MEASUREMENT OF PLASMA CONCENTRATIONS OF AMITRIPTYLINE AND ITS METABOLITE NORTRIPTYLINE.
002304 02-13

ALPHA METHYLEPINEPHRINE, A METHYLDOPA METABOLITE THAT BINDS TO ALPHA-RECEPTORS IN RAT-BRAIN.
002734 03-03

GLC MASS-SPECTROMETRIC-DETERMINATION OF MAPROTILINE AND ITS MAJOR METABOLITE USING STABLE ISOTOPE-LABELED ANALOG AS INTERNAL STANDARD.
004291 04-06

METABOLITES
STUDIES ON THE DISTRIBUTION OF 14C SULPIRIDE AND ITS METABOLITES IN THE RAT AND GUINEA-PIG.
000078 01-03

PHARMACOKINETICS OF PRIMIDONE AND ITS ACTIVE METABOLITES IN THE DOG.
000097 01-03

INCREASED URINARY EXCRETION OF CATECHOLAMINES AND THEIR METABOLITES IN STREPTOZOTOCIN DIABETIC RAT.
000154 01-03

PHARMACODYNAMIC PROFILES OF L ALPHA ACETYLMETHADOL (LAAM) AND ITS N DEMETHYLATED METABOLITES, NORLAAM AND DINORLAAM, DURING SELF-ADMINISTRATION IN THE DEPENDENT RAT.
000505 01-04

HIGH-SENSITIVITY NEGATIVE CHEMICAL-IONIZATION MASS-SPECTRAL-ANALYSIS OF BIOGENIC-AMINES AND METABOLITES. (UNPUBLISHED PAPER).
001042 02-01

THE EFFECT OF EMOTIONAL-STRESS AND DIAZEPAM ON MONOAMINE METABOLITES IN THE CEREBROSPINAL-FLUID OF CATS. (PH.D. DISSERTATION).
001260 02-03

DELTA9 THC AS A DISCRIMINATIVE-STIMULUS IN RATS AND PIGEONS: GENERALIZATION TO THC METABOLITES AND SP-111.
001666 02-04

PLASMA AND BRAIN LEVELS OF DELTA6 THC AND SEVEN MONOOXYGENATED METABOLITES CORRELATED TO THE CATALEPTIC-EFFECT IN THE MOUSE.
001737 02-04

CONCENTRATION OF SEROTONIN METABOLITES IN THE CEREBROSPINAL-FLUID FROM ALCOHOLICS BEFORE AND DURING SULFIRAM THERAPY.
002095 02-11

ON THE CLINICAL PHARMACOKINETICS OF THIORIDAZINE AND ITS METABOLITES.
002207 02-13

A METHOD FOR THE DETERMINATION OF AMITRIPTYLINE AND ITS METABOLITES NORTRIPTYLINE, 10 HYDROXYAMITRIPTYLINE, AND 10 HYDROXYNORTRIPTYLINE IN HUMAN PLASMA USING STABLE ISOTOPE DILUTION AND GAS-CHROMATOGRAPHY CHEMICAL-IONIZATION MASS-SPECTROMETRY.
002486 02-16

ENHANCEMENT OF HEXOBARBITAL-INDUCED SLEEP BY LYSINE AND ITS METABOLITES.
002967 03-04

ALTERATIONS IN CEREBROSPINAL-FLUID DOPAMINE METABOLITES FOLLOWING PHYSOSTIGMINE INFUSION.
003477 03-15

CEREBROSPINAL-FLUID CONCENTRATIONS OF THIORIDAZINE AND ITS MAIN METABOLITES IN PSYCHIATRIC-PATIENTS.
003569 03-16

A SELECTED ION-MONITORING ASSAY FOR BIOGENIC-AMINE METABOLITES AND PROBENECID, IN HUMAN LUMBAR CEREBROSPINAL-FLUID.
003663 04-01

DOPAMINE METABOLITES IN CAUDATE AND CORTEX AFTER LITHIUM AND HALOPERIDOL. (UNPUBLISHED PAPER).
003738 04-03

INTERACTIONS BETWEEN CHLORPROMAZINE AND SOME OF ITS METABOLITES.
004001 04-03

PROPERTIES OF THE OPTICAL-ISOMERS AND METABOLITES OF KETAMINE ON THE HIGH-AFFINITY TRANSPORT AND CATABOLISM OF MONOAMINES.
004009 04-03

ANTICONVULSANT ACTIVITY OF METABOLITES OF VALPROIC-ACID.
004168 04-04

BEHAVIOR OF RATS AND MICE ADMINISTERED ACTIVE METABOLITES OF FLUPHENAZINE, 7 HYDROXYFLUPHENAZINE AND FLUPHENAZINE-SULFOXIDE.
004256 04-04

RAT-BRAIN AND PLASMA NOREPINEPHRINE GLYCOL METABOLITES DETERMINED BY GAS-CHROMATOGRAPHY MASS-FRAGMENTOGRAPHY.
004303 04-06

CONCENTRATIONS OF CHLORPROMAZINE AND TWO OF ITS ACTIVE METABOLITES IN PLASMA AND CEREBROSPINAL-FLUID OF PSYCHOTIC-PATIENTS TREATED WITH FIXED DRUG DOSES.
004559 04-13

METERGOLINE
ADMINISTRATION OF ANTISOMATOSTATIN SERUM TO RATS REVERSES THE INHIBITION OF PULSATILE GROWTH-HORMONE SECRETION PRODUCED BY INJECTION OF METERGOLINE BUT NOT YOHIMBINE. (UNPUBLISHED PAPER).
000019 01-03

METERGOLINE ANTAGONISM OF 5 HYDROXYTRYPTAMINE-INDUCED
ACTIVATION OF RAT-CEREBRAL-CORTICAL NA-K-ATPASE.
000329 01-03
METERGOLINE AND CYPROHEPTADINE SUPPRESS PROLACTIN RELEASE BY
A NON-5-HYDROXYTRYPTAMINERGIC, NONDOPAMINERGIC
MECHANISM.
003732 04-03
(3H)METERGOLINE: A NEW LIGAND OF SEROTONIN-RECEPTORS IN THE
RAT-BRAIN.
003825 04-03

METHADONE
ABSORPTION OF 14C-LABELED METHADONE BY PORTAL AND
EXTRAPORTAL VENOUS CIRCULATIONS FOLLOWING INTRAPERITONEAL
AND INTRODUODENAL ADMINISTRATION.
000094 01-03
METHADONE DISULFIRAM INTERACTION DURING METHADONE
MAINTENANCE.
000796 01-13
LONG-TERM EFFECTS OF HALOPERIDOL, CLOZAPINE, AND METHADONE
ON RAT STRIATAL CHOLINERGIC AND DOPAMINERGIC DYNAMICS.
001325 02-03
EFFECTS OF PRENATAL METHADONE ON RAT-BRAIN CATECHOLAMINES.
001367 02-03
FACILITATION OF SELF-STIMULATION IN RATS BY METHADONE.
001795 02-04
THROMBOCYTOSIS IN THE OFFSPRING OF FEMALE MICE RECEIVING DL
METHADONE.
001836 02-05
CHOREIC-MOVEMENTS INDUCED BY THE USE OF METHADONE.
002467 02-15
BEHAVIORAL-EFFECTS OF METHADONE IN SCHIZOPHRENIC-PATIENTS.
003178 03-08
METHADONE AND MORPHINE IN DEPRESSION.
003220 03-09
DISPOSITION OF METHADONE IN THE OVINE MATERNAL FETAL UNIT.
004027 04-03
METHADONE REDUCES SEXUAL-PERFORMANCE AND SEXUAL-
MOTIVATION IN THE MALE SYRIAN GOLDEN HAMSTER.
004183 04-04
METHADONE TREATMENT OF HEROIN ADDICTS IN SWITZERLAND.
004452 04-11
METHADONE USE IN PATIENTS WITH CHRONIC RENAL-DISEASE.
004467 04-11

METHADONE-CHLORHYDRATE
THE TREATMENT OF OPIATE ADDICTION USING METHADONE-
CHLORHYDRATE.
002600 02-17

METHADONE-INDUCED
METHADONE-INDUCED ATTENUATION OF THE EFFECTS OF DELTA9
TETRAHYDROCANNABINOL ON TEMPORAL DISCRIMINATION IN
PIGEONS.
004095 04-04

METHADONE-TREATED
BEHAVIORAL AND METABOLIC ALTERATIONS IN PROGENY OF
METHADONE-TREATED RATS. (PH.D. DISSERTATION).
003113 03-04

METHAMPHETAMINE
THE INVOLVEMENT OF SEROTONERGIC NEURONS IN THE CENTRAL-
NERVOUS-SYSTEM AS THE POSSIBLE MECHANISM FOR SLOW HEAD-
SHAKING-BEHAVIOR INDUCED BY METHAMPHETAMINE IN RATS.
000408 01-04
EFFECTS OF EXPERIMENTER AND TEST LOCATION NOVELTY ON
NONSPECIFIC ACTIVITY IN RATS AND ITS MODIFICATION BY
METHAMPHETAMINE.
000409 01-04
SHORT-TERM AND LONG-TERM EFFECTS OF METHAMPHETAMINE ON
BIOGENIC-AMINE METABOLISM IN EXTRASTRIATAL DOPAMINERGIC
NUCLEI.
001384 02-03
SWIMMING CAPACITY OF MICE AFTER PROLONGED TREATMENT WITH
PSYCHOSTIMULANTS: II. EFFECT OF METHAMPHETAMINE ON
SWIMMING PERFORMANCE AND AVAILABILITY OF METABOLIC
SUBSTRATES.
001613 02-04
FLUORESCENCE HISTOCHEMISTRY INDICATES DAMAGE OF STRIATAL
DOPAMINE NERVE TERMINALS IN RATS AFTER MULTIPLE DOSES OF
METHAMPHETAMINE.
002812 03-03
METHAMPHETAMINE AND TIME ESTIMATION.
003040 03-04
LONG-TERM EFFECTS OF MULTIPLE DOSES OF METHAMPHETAMINE ON
TRYPTOPHAN-HYDROXYLASE AND TYROSINE-HYDROXYLASE ACTIVITY
IN RAT-BRAIN.
003850 04-03
EFFECTS OF METHAMPHETAMINE ON BLOOD FLOW IN THE CAUDATE-
PUTAMEN AFTER LESIONS OF THE NIGROSTRIATAL DOPAMINERGIC
BUNDLE IN THE RAT.
003910 04-03
EFFECTS OF A HIGH-DOSE TREATMENT OF METHAMPHETAMINE ON
CAUDATE DOPAMINE AND ANOREXIA IN RATS.
004073 04-04

EFFECT OF L HISTIDINE AND CHLORCYCLIZINE ON APOMORPHINE-INDUCED
CLIMBING-BEHAVIOUR AND METHAMPHETAMINE STEREOTYPY IN
MICE.
004147 04-04

METHAMPHETAMINE-INDUCED
BLOCKADE OF METHAMPHETAMINE-INDUCED DEPRESSION OF TYROSINE-
HYDROXYLASE BY GABA-TRANSAMINASE INHIBITORS.
000130 01-03

METHAQUALONE
EFFECTS OF METHAQUALONE ON SOCIAL-BEHAVIOR IN MONKEYS
(MACACA-MULATTA).
001594 02-04
ACUTE EFFECT OF CLOROTEPIN (0.5MG AND 1.0MG) AND
METHAQUALONE (300MG) ON VERBAL-ASSOCIATIONS.
002333 02-14
METHAQUALONE RIA STRUCTURE VERSUS REACTIVITY.
003657 04-01

METHIONINE
PRODUCTION OF CONVULSIONS IN MICE BY THE COMBINATION OF
METHIONINE AND HOMOCYSTEINE.
001233 02-03
FRAGILE SITES IN HUMAN CHROMOSOMES I. THE EFFECT OF METHIONINE
ON THE XQ-FRAGILE-SITE.
004515 04-13

METHIONINE-ENKEPHALIN
A FURTHER CHARACTERIZATION OF THE DIFFERENTIAL-EFFECTS OF
LEUCINE-ENKEPHALIN, METHIONINE-ENKEPHALIN AND THEIR ANALOGS
ON MORPHINE-INDUCED ANALGESIA.
000311 01-03
METHIONINE-ENKEPHALIN ANTAGONISM AND ENDORPHIN POTENTIATION
OF NARCOTIC-INDUCED ANALGESIA.
000357 01-04
RIA AND HPLC EVIDENCE FOR THE PRESENCE OF METHIONINE-
ENKEPHALIN AND CHOLECYSTOKININ IN THE NEURAL RETINA OF
SEVERAL VERTEBRATE SPECIES. (UNPUBLISHED PAPER).
001017 02-01
LEUCINE-ENKEPHALIN AND METHIONINE-ENKEPHALIN PRODUCE OPPOSING
EFFECTS ON PLASMA CORTICOSTERONE LEVELS IN ETHER-STRESSED
MICE.
001245 02-03
SUBSTANCE-P, MORPHINE AND METHIONINE-ENKEPHALIN: EFFECTS ON
SPONTANEOUS AND EVOKED NEURONAL FIRING IN THE NUCLEUS-
RETICULARIS-GIGANTOCELLULARIS OF THE RAT.
001267 02-03
CLASSIFICATION OF ENDORPHINS/ENKEPHALINS IN BRAIN PHYSIOLOGY
AND PATHOLOGY (BASED ON EEG AND CLINICAL-STUDY OF
SYNTHETICALLY-MODIFIED METHIONINE-ENKEPHALIN).
002286 02-13
METKEPHAMID, A SYSTEMICALLY ACTIVE ANALOG OF METHIONINE-
ENKEPHALIN WITH POTENT OPIOID DELTA-RECEPTOR ACTIVITY.
002720 03-03
GABA AND BACLOFEN POTENTIATE THE K-EVOKED RELEASE OF
METHIONINE-ENKEPHALIN FROM RAT STRIATAL SLICES.
002882 03-03
MORPHINE AND METHIONINE-ENKEPHALIN: DIFFERENT EFFECTS ON
SPONTANEOUS AND EVOKED NEURONAL FIRING IN THE
MESENCEPHALIC RETICULAR FORMATION OF THE RAT.
003849 04-03

METHIONINE-SULFOXIMINE
THE METABOLISM OF 5 HYDROXYTRYPTAMINE IN THE METHIONINE-
SULFOXIMINE EPILEPTOGENIC RAT-BRAIN.
002887 03-03
STIMULATION OF FRUCTOSEBIPHOSPHATASE ACTIVITY AND SYNTHESIS
IN THE CEREBRAL-CORTEX OF RATS SUBMITTED TO THE CONVULSANT
METHIONINE-SULFOXIMINE.
003838 04-03

METHOD
EFFICACY AND PATTERN VALENCE OF PSYCHOACTIVE-DRUGS: A NEW
METHOD OF COMPARING DRUGS APPLIED TO IDENTICAL PATIENTS IN
RANDOMIZED-ORDER.
000699 01-11
ELECTROLYTIC MICROINFUSION TRANSDUCER SYSTEM: AN ALTERNATIVE
METHOD OF INTRACRANIAL DRUG APPLICATION.
001861 02-06
THE USE OF SOCIAL-INTERACTION AS A METHOD FOR DETECTING
ANXIOLYTIC-ACTIVITY OF CHLORDIAZEPOXIDE-LIKE DRUGS.
001866 02-06
THEORY, PROCEDURE, AND APPLICATIONS OF THE RADIOACTIVE
DEOXYGLUCOSE METHOD FOR THE MEASUREMENT OF LOCAL GLUCOSE
UTILIZATION IN THE CENTRAL-NERVOUS-SYSTEM. (UNPUBLISHED
PAPER).
001877 02-06
STUDIES ON GABA RELEASE IN VIVO USING A SIMPLE METHOD FOR
PERFUSION OF THE FOURTH VENTRICLE OF THE RAT.
001881 02-06
PREDICTION OF DOSAGE OF LITHIUM-CARBONATE: USE OF A STANDARD
PREDICTIVE METHOD.
001991 02-09

SINGLE-DOSE VERSUS MULTIPLE-DOSE COMPARATIVE-TRIAL OF DESIPRAMINE-HYDROCHLORIDE: A DOUBLE-PLACEBO METHOD.
002059 02-10

METHOD FOR THE DETERMINATION OF TRYPTOPHAN IN SERUM AND CEREBROSPINAL-FLUID.
002208 02-13

AN OBSERVATIONAL METHOD FOR QUANTIFYING THE BEHAVIOURAL-EFFECTS OF DOPAMINE AGONISTS: CONTRASTING-EFFECTS OF D-AMPHETAMINE AND APOMORPHINE.
002484 02-16

A METHOD FOR THE DETERMINATION OF AMITRIPTYLINE AND ITS METABOLITES NORTRIPTYLINE, 10 HYDROXYAMITRIPTYLINE, AND 10 HYDROXYNORTRIPTYLINE IN HUMAN PLASMA USING STABLE ISOTOPE DILUTION AND GAS-CHROMATOGRAPHY CHEMICAL-IONIZATION MASS-SPECTROMETRY.
002486 02-16

AN AUTOMATED METHOD FOR STUDYING STEREOTYPED GNAWING.
002500 02-16

A RAPID GAS-LIQUID-CHROMATOGRAPHY METHOD FOR SIMULTANEOUS DETERMINATION OF VARIOUS ANTICONVULSANTS.
002501 02-16

FREE DESCRIPTION OF DRUG-EFFECTS AS A METHOD OF CLINICAL-TRIAL, PRESENTED BY THE EXAMPLE OF PENTOBARBITONE, PROMAZINE AND THEIR COMBINATION.
002561 02-17

INFUSIONS INTO THE OCULOMOTOR NUCLEUS OR NERVE: A METHOD OF ESTIMATING THE DOSAGE AT WHICH TRANSMITTER ANTAGONISTS INFUSED INTRACRANIALLY PRODUCE NONSPECIFIC BLOCKING OF NEURAL ACTIVITY.
003134 03-06

A METHOD FOR MEASUREMENT OF TRANYLCYPROMINE IN RAT-BRAIN REGIONS USING GAS-CHROMATOGRAPHY WITH ELECTRON CAPTURE DETECTION.
003137 03-06

A NEW METHOD FOR APPLICATION OF HORSERADISH-PEROXIDASE INTO A RESTRICTED AREA OF THE BRAIN.
003141 03-06

ON THE EVALUATION OF A PROVOCATIVE EEG METHOD USING MEDICATION IN THE DIAGNOSIS OF ORGANIC-BRAIN-SEIZURES IN CHILDHOOD, WITH SPECIAL EMPHASIS ON SLEEP INDUCTION THROUGH MEDICATION.
003387 03-11

PSYCHOTROPIC-DRUG-INDUCED CHANGES IN AUDITORY AVERAGED EVOKED-POTENTIALS: RESULTS OF A DOUBLE-BLIND TRIAL USING AN OBJECTIVE FULLY AUTOMATED AEP ANALYSIS METHOD.
003412 03-13

DIFFERENTIAL BINDING OF CHLORPROMAZINE TO HUMAN BLOOD CELLS: APPLICATION OF THE HYGROSCOPIC DESORPTION METHOD.
003556 03-16

FIRST RESULTS OF AN ORIGINAL METHOD FOR MEASURING BLOOD LEVELS OF ANTIDEPRESSANTS (AMITRIPTYLINE AND NORTRIPTYLINE).
003559 03-16

POSITRON-TOMOGRAPHY. A NEW METHOD FOR IN VIVO BRAIN STUDIES OF BENZODIAZEPINE, IN ANIMAL AND IN MAN.
003564 03-16

BIOCHEMICAL AND IMMUNOLOGICAL PROPERTIES OF THE MOUSE BRAIN ENOLASES PURIFIED BY A SIMPLE METHOD.
003668 04-01

A RAPID AND SIMPLE METHOD FOR THE DETERMINATION OF PICOGRAM LEVELS OF 3 METHOXYTYRAMINE IN BRAIN TISSUE USING LIQUID-CHROMATOGRAPHY WITH ELECTROCHEMICAL DETECTION.
003674 04-01

PRESENCE OF CONJUGATED CATECHOLAMINES IN RAT-BRAIN: A NEW METHOD OF ANALYSIS OF CATECHOLAMINE-SULFATES.
004286 04-06

A SIMPLE HISTOCHEMICAL SCREENING METHOD FOR AMINE UPTAKE.
004295 04-06

A CLINICAL-EVALUATION OF THE EFFECTS OF A NEW PSYCHOTROPIC-AGENT, MEXAZOLAM (CS-386) ON PSYCHOSOMATIC-DISEASES AND NEUROSIS: A COMPARATIVE-STUDY WITH OXAZOLAM, USING THE DOUBLE-BLIND METHOD.
004491 04-11

CORRECTION OF HORMONAL ACTIVITY OF THE THYROID-GLAND AS A METHOD OF PATHOGENIC THERAPY IN A COMPREHENSIVE TREATMENT OF PATIENTS WITH TEMPORAL EPILEPSY.
004579 04-14

A MODIFIED VERSION OF THE SIMULTANEOUS DISCONTINUATION OF PSYCHOTROPIC-DRUGS (COMBINED WITH THE ADMINISTRATION OF DIURETICS) AS A METHOD OF HALTING PROLONGED ATTACKS OF SCHIZOPHRENIA.
004584 04-14

THE USE OF EVENT-RELATED SLOW POTENTIALS OF THE BRAIN AS AN OBJECTIVE METHOD TO STUDY THE EFFECTS OF CENTRALLY ACTING DRUGS.
004669 04-16

METHODICAL-CHECK
CONTROLLED-COMPARISON OF PERPHENAZINE WITH PERPHENAZINE IN SCHIZOPHRENIA: A METHODICAL-CHECK OF A DOUBLE-BLIND CROSS-OVER DESIGN.
001937 02-08

METHODOLOGICAL
METHODOLOGICAL REMARKS ON LONG-TERM LITHIUM TREATMENT.
000749 01-13

SOME METHODOLOGICAL WAYS OF MONITORING THE EFFECTS OF PSYCHOTHERAPEUTIC-DRUGS.
003567 03-16

THERAPEUTIC INTEREST OF BLOOD LEVELS DETERMINATION FOR ANTIDEPRESSANTS: METHODOLOGICAL APPROACH.
003571 03-16

METHODOLOGICAL-CONSIDERATIONS
METHODS AND METHODOLOGICAL-CONSIDERATIONS IN MEASURING ANTIANXIETY-EFFECTS OF TRANQUILIZING-DRUGS.
002537 02-17

METHODOLOGICAL-CONSIDERATIONS CONCERNING THE PRESCRIPTION AND USE OF SO CALLED DISINHIBITORS.
002571 02-17

METHODOLOGICAL-ISSUES
METHODOLOGICAL-ISSUES IN SPINAL-FLUID STUDIES OF SCHIZOPHRENIA: THE CASE OF NOREPINEPHRINE AND DOPAMINE-BETA-HYDROXYLASE. (UNPUBLISHED PAPER).
001952 02-08

SPONTANEOUS ACTIVITY AND APOMORPHINE STEREOTYPY DURING AND AFTER WITHDRAWAL FROM 3 1/2 MONTHS CONTINUOUS ADMINISTRATION OF HALOPERIDOL: SOME METHODOLOGICAL-ISSUES.
002509 02-16

VILOXAZINE AND THE DEPRESSED SCHIZOPHRENIC -- METHODOLOGICAL-ISSUES.
003181 03-08

METHODOLOGICAL-PROBLEM
SIDE-EFFECTS OF BETA-ADRENERGIC BLOCKING-DRUGS: A METHODOLOGICAL-PROBLEM.
002395 02-15

METHODOLOGIES
PHYSICO-CHEMICAL METHODOLOGIES IN PSYCHIATRIC-RESEARCH.
004679 04-16

METHODOLOGY
STUDY OF VIGILANCE AFTER INGESTION OF ZOPICLONE IN COMPARISON WITH NITRAZEPAM AND PLACEBO. METHODOLOGY OF THE STUDY: SELF-EVALUATION QUESTIONNAIRE AND PSYCHOMETRIC-TESTS.
000543 01-07

METHODOLOGY AND RESULTS OF A LONG-TERM STUDY OF LONG-ACTING NEUROLEPTICS: PIPOTHIAZINE-PALMITATE AND FLUPHENAZINE-DECANOATE.
001929 02-08

METHODOLOGY OF OUTPATIENT DRUG RESEARCH. (UNPUBLISHED PAPER).
003282 03-10

HIGH-PERFORMANCE LIQUID-CHROMATOGRAPHY IN THE NEUROSCIENCES: METHODOLOGY.
004285 04-06

METHODS
THE IONIZATION OF 5 HYDROXYTRYPTAMINE AND RELATED COMPOUNDS AND AN APPRAISAL OF METHODS FOR THE ESTIMATION OF ZWITTERION CONSTANTS.
001859 02-06

METHODS OF MULTICENTER-TRIALS IN PSYCHIATRY -- PART I: REVIEW.
002483 02-16

METHODS AND METHODOLOGICAL-CONSIDERATIONS IN MEASURING ANTIANXIETY-EFFECTS OF TRANQUILIZING-DRUGS.
002537 02-17

A COMPARATIVE EVALUATION OF THE EFFICACY OF SOME THERAPEUTIC METHODS USED IN DELIRIUM-TREMENS.
004486 04-11

PHENYTOIN THERAPY FOR EPILEPTIC-CHILDREN: EVALUATION OF SALIVARY AND PLASMA CONCENTRATIONS AND OF METHODS OF ASSESSING COMPLIANCE.
004495 04-11

METHOTREXATE
EFFECTS OF ANTICONVULSANTS AND METHOTREXATE ON CALCIUM DISPOSITION.
001840 02-05

METHOXY-TETRAHYDRO-BETA-CARBOLINE
IDENTIFICATION AND QUANTIFICATION OF 1,2,3,4 TETRAHYDRO-BETA-CARBOLINE, 2 METHYL-TETRAHYDRO-BETA-CARBOLINE, AND 6 METHOXY-TETRAHYDRO-BETA-CARBOLINE AS IN VIVO CONSTITUENTS OF RAT-BRAIN AND ADRENAL-GLAND.
002636 03-01

METHOXY-4-HYDROXYPHENETHYLENEGLYCOL
COVARIANCE OF PLASMA FREE 3 METHOXY-4-HYDROXYPHENETHYLENEGLYCOL AND DIASTOLIC BLOOD-PRESSURE.
003418 03-13

METHOXY-4-HYDROXYPHENYLETHYLENEGLYCOL
CENTRAL LEVELS OF NORADRENALINE, 3 METHOXY-4-HYDROXYPHENYLETHYLENEGLYCOL AND CYCLIC-AMP IN THE RAT AFTER ACTIVATION OF LOCUS-COERULEUS NEURONS: INFLUENCE OF SINGLE AND REPEATED NEUROLEPTIC TREATMENT.
001095 02-03

SPECIFIC AND SENSITIVE RADIOIMMUNOASSAY FOR 3 METHOXY-4-HYDROXYPHENYLETHYLENEGLYCOL (MOPEG).
002776 03-03

POSTMORTEM STABILITY OF BRAIN 3 METHOXY-4-HYDROXYPHENYLETHYLENEGLYCOL AND 3,4 DIHYDROXYPHENYLETHYLENEGLYCOL IN THE RAT AND MOUSE.
004048 04-03

METHOXY-4-HYDROXYPHENYLETHYLENEGLYCOL-SULPHATE
EFFECTS OF ACUTELY AND CHRONICALLY ADMINISTERED ANTIDEPRESSANTS ON THE CLONIDINE-INDUCED DECREASE IN RAT-BRAIN 3 METHOXY-4-HYDROXYPHENYLETHYLENEGLYCOL-SULPHATE CONTENT.
002908 03-03

METHOXY-4-HYDROXYPHENYLGLYCOL
INTERACTION OF ANTIDEPRESSANTS WITH CLONIDINE ON RAT-BRAIN TOTAL 3 METHOXY-4-HYDROXYPHENYLGLYCOL.
000300 01-03

SEX, PLASMA PROLACTIN AND PLASMA 3 METHOXY-4-HYDROXYPHENYLGLYCOL (MHPG) PREDICT HERITABLE D-AMPHETAMINE EXCITATION IN MAN. (UNPUBLISHED PAPER).
004565 04-14

METHOXY-4-HYDROXYPHENYLGLYCOL-SULFATE
VARIATIONS IN URINARY EXCRETION OF 3 METHOXY-4-HYDROXYPHENYLGLYCOL-SULFATE IN DEPRESSIVE-CONDITIONS.
002013 02-09

VARIATIONS IN URINARY LEVELS OF 3 METHOXY-4-HYDROXYPHENYLGLYCOL-SULFATE IN PATIENTS WITH DEPRESSIVE-SYNDROMES.
004533 04-13

METHOXYAMPHETAMINE
A NEW APPROACH TO THE ASSESSMENT OF THE POTENCY OF REVERSIBLE MONOAMINE-OXIDASE-INHIBITORS IN VIVO, AND ITS APPLICATION TO D-AMPHETAMINE, P METHOXYAMPHETAMINE AND HARMALINE.
000900 01-16

METHOXYBENZAMIDES
O METHOXYBENZAMIDES: RELATIONSHIPS BETWEEN STRUCTURE-ACTIVITY, AND PHARMACOKINETICS OF THESE DRUGS.
002246 02-13

METHOXYDIISOPROPYLTRYPTAMINE
N,N DIISOPROPYLTRYPTAMINE (DIPT) AND 5 METHOXYDIISOPROPYLTRYPTAMINE (5 MEO-DIPT). TWO ORALLY ACTIVE TRYPTAMINE ANALOGS WITH CNS ACTIVITY.
004310 04-07

METHOXYDIMETHYLTRYPTAMINE
5 METHOXYDIMETHYLTRYPTAMINE: SPINAL-CORD AND BRAINSTEM MEDIATION OF EXCITATORY EFFECTS ON ACOUSTIC STARTLE.
001605 02-04

METHOXYFLURANE
INFLUENCE OF IMIPRAMINE AND PARGYLINE ON THE ARRHYTHMOGENICITY OF EPINEPHRINE DURING HALOTHANE, ENFLURANE OR METHOXYFLURANE ANESTHESIA IN DOGS.
001539 02-03

METHOXYLPHENYLCARBAMOYLDIETHYLAMINOPROPIOPHENONEOXIME
COMPARATIVE ANALGESIC, BEHAVIORAL, AND DEPENDENCE PROPERTIES OF MORPHINE AND O METHOXYLPHENYLCARBAMOYLDIETHYLAMINOPROPIOPHENONEOXIME HCL.
003707 04-02

METHOXYTRYPTAMINE
THE ACUTE AND CHRONIC EFFECT OF 5 METHOXYTRYPTAMINE ON SELECTED MEMBERS OF A PRIMATE SOCIAL-COLONY.
001073 02-02

METHOXYTYRAMINE
A RAPID AND SIMPLE METHOD FOR THE DETERMINATION OF PICOGRAM LEVELS OF 3 METHOXYTYRAMINE IN BRAIN TISSUE USING LIQUID-CHROMATOGRAPHY WITH ELECTROCHEMICAL DETECTION.
003674 04-01

METHYL-BETA-CARBOLINE
1 METHYL-BETA-CARBOLINE (HARMANE), A POTENT ENDOGENOUS INHIBITOR OF BENZODIAZEPINE-RECEPTOR BINDING.
001440 02-03

METHYL-D-ASPARTIC-ACID
TWO CONDUCTANCE MECHANISMS ACTIVATED BY APPLICATIONS OF L GLUTAMIC-ACID, L ASPARTIC-ACID, DL HOMOCYSTEIC-ACID, N METHYL-D-ASPARTIC-ACID, AND DL KAINIC-ACID TO CULTURED MAMMALIAN CENTRAL NEURONES.
001349 02-03

METHYL-P-TYROSINE
DOSE-DEPENDENT PHARMACOKINETICS OF ALPHA METHYL-P-TYROSINE (ALPHA MT) AND COMPARISON OF CATECHOLAMINE TURNOVER-RATES AFTER TWO DOSES OF ALPHA MT.
001532 02-03

METHYL-TETRAHYDRO-BETA-CARBOLINE
IDENTIFICATION AND QUANTIFICATION OF 1,2,3,4 TETRAHYDRO-BETA-CARBOLINE, 2 METHYL-TETRAHYDRO-BETA-CARBOLINE, AND 6 METHOXY-TETRAHYDRO-BETA-CARBOLINE AS IN VIVO CONSTITUENTS OF RAT-BRAIN AND ADRENAL-GLAND.
002636 03-01

METHYLAMPHETAMINE
THE EFFECTS OF DOPAMINERGIC-AGENTS ON THE LOCOMOTOR-ACTIVITY OF RATS AFTER HIGH-DOSES OF METHYLAMPHETAMINE.
000427 01-04

DOPAMINE DEPLETION BY 6 HYDROXYDOPAMINE PREVENTS CONDITIONED TASTE-AVERSION INDUCED BY METHYLAMPHETAMINE BUT NOT LITHIUM-CHLORIDE.
003110 03-04

METHYLATION
PHOSPHOLIPID METHYLATION AND TRANSMEMBRANE SIGNALLING. (UNPUBLISHED PAPER).
001001 02-01

BRADYKININ-RECEPTOR STIMULATION OF C-AMP INVOLVES PHOSPHOLIPID METHYLATION, CA-FLUX, PHOSPHOLIPASE-A2 ACTIVATION AND PROSTAGLANDIN FORMATION. (UNPUBLISHED PAPER).
001002 02-01

IGE MEDIATED HISTAMINE RELEASE IN RAT BASOPHILIC LEUKEMIA CELLS: RECEPTOR ACTIVATED PHOSPHOLIPID METHYLATION, CA-FLUX AND RELEASE OF ARACHIDONIC-ACID. (UNPUBLISHED PAPER).
001188 02-03

PHOSPHOLIPID METHYLATION: A BIOCHEMICAL-EVENT OF SIGNAL TRANSDUCTION. (UNPUBLISHED PAPER).
001279 02-03

INCREASED ADRENALINE, BETA-ADRENERGIC-RECEPTOR STIMULATION AND PHOSPHOLIPID METHYLATION IN PINEAL-GLAND OF SPONTANEOUSLY HYPERTENSIVE-RATS. (UNPUBLISHED PAPER).
001458 02-03

DECREASE OF NORADRENALINE O METHYLATION IN RAT-BRAIN INDUCED BY L-DOPA. REVERSAL EFFECT OF S ADENOSYL-L-METHIONINE.
004019 04-03

METHYLAZOXYMETHANOL-ACETATE
EFFECTS OF FETAL TREATMENT WITH METHYLAZOXYMETHANOL-ACETATE AT VARIOUS GESTATIONAL DATES ON THE NEUROCHEMISTRY OF THE ADULT NEOCORTEX OF THE RAT.
002770 03-03

METHYLBUTENYLHYDROXYPHENYLPHENYLETHYLPIPERAZINE
ANALGESIC AND OTHER PHARMACOLOGICAL ACTIVITIES OF A NEW NARCOTIC ANTAGONIST ANALGESIC (-) 1 3 METHYLBUTENYLHYDROXYPHENYLPHENYLETHYLPIPERAZINE AND ITS ENANTIOMORPH IN EXPERIMENTAL ANIMALS.
004185 04-04

METHYLDOPA
METHYLDOPA PRODUCES CENTRAL INHIBITION OF PARASYMPATHETIC-ACTIVITY IN THE CAT.
001321 02-03

ALPHA METHYLEPINEPHRINE, A METHYLDOPA METABOLITE THAT BINDS TO ALPHA-RECEPTORS IN RAT-BRAIN.
002734 03-03

REDUCTION IN THE LEVEL OF IMMUNOTITRATABLE DOPAMINE-BETA-HYDROXYLASE AFTER CHRONIC ADMINISTRATION OF L-DOPA OR ALPHA METHYLDOPA.
003764 04-03

DIETARY PROTEIN INTAKE INFLUENCES THE ANTIHYPERTENSIVE POTENCY OF METHYLDOPA IN SPONTANEOUSLY HYPERTENSIVE-RATS.
004025 04-03

METHYLDOPAMINE
DIFFERENTIAL-EFFECTS OF ALPHA METHYLDOPAMINE, CLONIDINE AND HYDRALAZINE ON NOREPINEPHRINE AND EPINEPHRINE SYNTHESIZING ENZYMES IN THE BRAINSTEM NUCLEI OF SPONTANEOUSLY HYPERTENSIVE-RATS.
003947 04-03

METHYLENEDIOXYAMPHETAMINE
CENTRALLY ACTIVE N SUBSTITUTED ANALOGS OF 3,4 METHYLENEDIOXYPHENYLISOPROPYLAMINE (3,4 METHYLENEDIOXYAMPHETAMINE).
003683 04-02

METHYLENEDIOXYPHENYLISOPROPYLAMINE
CENTRALLY ACTIVE N SUBSTITUTED ANALOGS OF 3,4 METHYLENEDIOXYPHENYLISOPROPYLAMINE (3,4 METHYLENEDIOXYAMPHETAMINE).
003683 04-02

METHYLEPINEPHRINE
ALPHA METHYLEPINEPHRINE, A METHYLDOPA METABOLITE THAT BINDS TO ALPHA-RECEPTORS IN RAT-BRAIN.
002734 03-03

METHYLERGONOVINE
ENTHEOGENIC (HALLUCINOGENIC) EFFECTS OF METHYLERGONOVINE.
000742 01-12

METHYLGLUCAMINE
INTERMITTENT DECORTICATION AND PROGRESSIVE HYPERTHERMIA, HYPERTENSION AND TACHYCARDIA FOLLOWING METHYLGLUCAMINE IOTHALAMATE VENTRICULOGRAM.
003520 03-15

METHYLMERCURY
RESEARCH STRATEGIES FOR ASSESSING THE EFFECTS OF METHYLMERCURY ON BEHAVIOR.
003128 03-05

METHYLMERCURY-INDUCED
METHYLMERCURY-INDUCED CHANGES IN OPERANT DISCRIMINATION BY
THE PIGEON.
004271 04-05

METHYLNORADRENALINE
INHIBITION OF NEURONAL UPTAKE REDUCES THE PRESYNAPTIC EFFECTS
OF CLONIDINE BUT NOT OF ALPHA METHYLNORADRENALINE ON THE
STIMULATION-EVOKED RELEASE OF 3H NORADRENALINE FROM RAT
OCCIPITAL-CORTEX SLICES.
000227 01-03

METHYLNOREPINEPHRINE
COCAINE AND AMPHETAMINE ANTAGONIZE THE DECREASE OF
NORADRENERGIC NEUROTRANSMISSION ELICITED BY OXYMETAZOLINE
BUT POTENTIATE THE INHIBITION BY ALPHA METHYLNOREPINEPHRINE
IN THE PERFUSED CAT SPLEEN.
002801 03-03

METHYLPHENIDATE
COMPARISON OF THE EFFECTS OF THE ISOMERS OF AMPHETAMINE,
METHYLPHENIDATE AND DEOXYPIPRADROL ON THE UPTAKE OF L
(3H)NOREPINEPHRINE AND (3H)DOPAMINE BY SYNAPTIC VESICLES
FROM RAT-WHOLE-BRAIN, STRIATUM AND HYPOTHALAMUS.
000091 01-03

DIFFERENTIAL-EFFECTS OF METHYLPHENIDATE ON SIGNALLED AND
NONSIGNALLED REINFORCEMENT.
000380 01-04

THE EFFECTS OF THE METHYLPHENIDATE AND D-AMPHETAMINE RELATED
TO ROUTE-OF-ADMINISTRATION.
000476 01-04

TREATMENT OF DEPRESSION IN THE MEDICALLY-ILL ELDERLY WITH
METHYLPHENIDATE.
000602 01-09

A CONTROLLED-TRIAL OF BEHAVIOR-MODIFICATION AND
METHYLPHENIDATE IN HYPERACTIVE-CHILDREN.
000678 01-11

COMPARISON OF SUSTAINED-RELEASE AND STANDARD
METHYLPHENIDATE IN THE TREATMENT OF MINIMAL-BRAIN-
DYSFUNCTION.
000732 01-11

EFFECTS OF METHYLPHENIDATE ON LEARNING A BEGINNING READING
VOCABULARY BY NORMAL ADULTS.
000812 01-14

A COMPARISON OF THE EFFECTS OF METHYLPHENIDATE AND
AMPHETAMINE ON THE SIMULTANEOUS RELEASE OF RADIOLABELLED
DOPAMINE AND P OR M TYRAMINE FROM RAT STRIATAL SLICES.
001207 02-03

EFFECTS OF PHENCYCLIDINE AND METHYLPHENIDATE ON D-
AMPHETAMINE-INDUCED BEHAVIORS IN RESERPINE PRETREATED RATS.
001616 02-04

EFFECTS OF METHYLPHENIDATE ON SELECTIVE AND SUSTAINED
ATTENTION IN HYPERACTIVE, READING-DISABLED, AND PRESUMABLY
ATTENTION-DISORDERED BOYS.
002118 02-11

THE USE OF SENSORY INTEGRATIVE DIAGNOSTICS TO PREDICT
HYPERACTIVE-CHILDRENS RESPONSIVENESS TO METHYLPHENIDATE
(RITALIN) AND PEMOLINE (CYLERT). (PH.D. DISSERTATION).
002133 02-11

THE DIFFERENTIAL DOSE-EFFECTS OF METHYLPHENIDATE ON
HYPERACTIVE-CHILDREN AND THEIR MOTHERS. (PH.D.
DISSERTATION).
002143 02-11

EFFECTS OF METHYLPHENIDATE ON OPERANT-RESPONDING IN
HYPERACTIVE-BOYS. (PH.D. DISSERTATION).
002191 02-11

EVALUATION OF THE RELATIVE EFFECTIVENESS OF METHYLPHENIDATE
AND COGNITIVE BEHAVIOR-MODIFICATION IN THE TREATMENT OF
KINDERGARTEN-AGED HYPERACTIVE-CHILDREN.
003306 03-11

THE INFLUENCE OF METHYLPHENIDATE ON SPONTANEOUS AUTONOMIC-
ACTIVITY AND BEHAVIOR IN CHILDREN DIAGNOSED AS HYPERACTIVE.
003363 03-11

PREDICTORS OF ADOLESCENT HEIGHT AND WEIGHT IN HYPERKINETIC-
BOYS TREATED WITH METHYLPHENIDATE.
003509 03-15

THE EFFECTS OF CHRONIC METHYLPHENIDATE TREATMENT ON GROWTH
AND ENDOCRINE FUNCTION IN THE DEVELOPING RAT.
003811 04-03

METHYLPHENIDATE-HYDROCHLORIDE
EFFECTS OF METHYLPHENIDATE-HYDROCHLORIDE ON REPEATED
ACQUISITION-BEHAVIOR IN HYPERKINETIC-CHILDREN. (PH.D.
DISSERTATION).
003386 03-11

METHYLPHENIDATE-INDUCED
FLURAZEPAM EFFECTS ON METHYLPHENIDATE-INDUCED STEREOTYPED-
BEHAVIOR.
000455 01-04

METHYLPHENIDATE-LIKE
METHYLPHENIDATE-LIKE STIMULANTS IN VITRO RELEASE (3H)TYRAMINES
BUT NOT (14C)DOPAMINE.
002706 03-03

METHYLPHENYLALANINE
EFFECT OF ALPHA METHYLPHENYLALANINE AND PHENYLALANINE ON
BRAIN POLYRIBOSOMES AND PROTEIN SYNTHESIS.
003733 04-03

METHYLPREDNISOLONE
EFFECTS OF INDOMETHACIN AND METHYLPREDNISOLONE ON RENAL
ELIMINATION OF LITHIUM IN THE RAT.
004270 04-05

METHYLTRANSFERASES
DIFFERENCES IN ACTIVITY IN CEREBRAL METHYLTRANSFERASES AND
MONOAMINE-OXIDASES BETWEEN AUDIOGENIC-SEIZURE SUSCEPTIBLE
AND RESISTANT MICE AND DEERMICE.
000377 01-04

METHYLXANTHINES
METHYLXANTHINES MODULATE ADENOSINE RELEASE FROM SLICES OF
CEREBRAL-CORTEX.
002907 03-03

ADENOSINE-RECEPTORS IN THE CENTRAL-NERVOUS-SYSTEM:
RELATIONSHIP TO THE CENTRAL-ACTIONS OF METHYLXANTHINES.
003766 04-03

CHARACTER AND MEANING OF QUASI-MORPHINE WITHDRAWAL
PHENOMENA ELICITED BY METHYLXANTHINES.
004087 04-04

METHYSERGIDE
METHYSERGIDE AND SUPRASPINAL INHIBITION OF THE SPINAL
TRANSMISSION OF NOCICEPTIVE INFORMATION IN THE ANESTHETIZED
CAT.
002740 03-03

EFFECTS OF METHYSERGIDE AND NALOXONE ON ANALGESIA INDUCED BY
THE PERIPHERAL ELECTRIC-STIMULATION IN MICE.
003093 03-04

PROGRESSIVE SUPRANUCLEAR PALSY: PNEUMOENCEPHALOGRAPHY,
ELECTRONYSTAGMOGRAPHY AND TREATMENT WITH METHYSERGIDE.
003355 03-11

METKEPHAMID
METKEPHAMID, A SYSTEMICALLY ACTIVE ANALOG OF METHIONINE-
ENKEPHALIN WITH POTENT OPIOID DELTA-RECEPTOR ACTIVITY.
002720 03-03

METOCLOPRAMIDE
METOCLOPRAMIDE AND SULPIRIDE AS SELECTIVE BLOCKING-AGENTS
PRESYNAPTIC AND POSTSYNAPTIC DOPAMINE-RECEPTORS.
001102 02-03

ANTAGONISM OF THE RENAL VASODILATOR ACTIVITY OF DOPAMINE BY
METOCLOPRAMIDE.
001265 02-03

METOCLOPRAMIDE: ANTIPSYCHOTIC-EFFICACY OF A DRUG LACKING
POTENCY IN RECEPTOR MODELS.
001948 02-08

DISCRIMINATION OF FUNCTIONALLY HETEROGENEOUS RECEPTOR
SUBPOPULATIONS: ANTIPSYCHOTIC AND ANTIDOPAMINERGIC
PROPERTIES OF METOCLOPRAMIDE.
002877 03-03

CHLORPROMAZINE, HALOPERIDOL, METOCLOPRAMIDE AND
DOMPERIDONE RELEASE PROLACTIN THROUGH DOPAMINE
ANTAGONISM AT LOW CONCENTRATIONS BUT PARADOXICALLY
INHIBIT PROLACTIN RELEASE AT HIGH-CONCENTRATIONS.
003731 04-03

PHARMACOLOGICAL DIFFERENCE OF L-DOPA, APOMORPHINE, AND
BROMOCRIPTINE AGAINST METOCLOPRAMIDE.
003790 04-03

METRAZOL
SEIZURES ELICITED BY SUBCUTANEOUS INJECTION OF METRAZOL DURING
ONTOGENESIS IN RATS.
003039 03-04

ELECTROCORTICOGRAPHIC ACTIVITY ELICITED BY METRAZOL DURING
ONTOGENESIS IN RATS.
004064 04-03

METRAZOL-INDUCED
INVOLVEMENT OF CENTRAL CHOLINOCEPTORS IN METRAZOL-INDUCED
CONVULSIONS.
000247 01-03

METRIFONATE
STABLE ISOTOPES USED IN STUDIES OF METRIFONATE.
003847 04-03

MET2-PRO5-ENKEPHALINAMIDE
BIPHASIC-EFFECTS OF A POTENT ENKEPHALIN ANALOGUE D MET2-PRO5-
ENKEPHALINAMIDE AND MORPHINE ON LOCOMOTOR-ACTIVITY IN
MICE.
001799 02-04

MEXAZOLAM
A CLINICAL-EVALUATION OF THE EFFECTS OF A NEW PSYCHOTROPIC-
AGENT, MEXAZOLAM (CS-386) ON PSYCHOSOMATIC-DISEASES AND
NEUROSIS: A COMPARATIVE-STUDY WITH OXAZOLAM, USING THE
DOUBLE-BLIND METHOD.
004491 04-11

MG2
EFFECT OF DOPAMINE ON ACTIVATION OF RAT STRIATAL ADENYLATE-
CYCLASE BY FREE MG2 AND GUANYL-NUCLEOTIDES.
002825 03-03

MHPG
URINARY MHPG AND CLINICAL-RESPONSE TO AMITRIPTYLINE IN
DEPRESSED-PATIENTS.
000631 01-09
MHPG AS A PREDICTOR OF ANTIDEPRESSANT RESPONSE TO IMIPRAMINE
AND MAPROTILINE.
000787 01-13
SUBTYPES OF DEPRESSION BASED ON EXCRETION OF MHPG AND
RESPONSE TO NORTRIPTYLINE.
002488 02-16
TOWARD A BIOCHEMICAL CLASSIFICATION OF DEPRESSIVE-DISORDERS
IV: PRETREATMENT URINARY MHPG LEVELS AS PREDICTORS OF
ANTIDEPRESSANT RESPONSE TO IMIPRAMINE.
004406 04-09
SEX, PLASMA PROLACTIN AND PLASMA 3 METHOXY-4-
HYDROXYPHENYLGLYCOL (MHPG) PREDICT HERITABLE D-
AMPHETAMINE EXCITATION IN MAN. (UNPUBLISHED PAPER).
004565 04-14

MIANSERIN
COMPARISON OF MIANSERIN WITH DESIPRAMINE, MAPROTILINE AND
PHENTOLAMINE ON CARDIAC PRESYNAPTIC AND VASCULAR
POSTSYNAPTIC ALPHA-ADRENOCEPTORS AND NORADRENALINE
REUPTAKE IN PITHED NORMOTENSIVE-RATS.
000044 01-03
AN IN VIVO MODEL FOR INVESTIGATING ALPHA1-RECEPTORS AND
ALPHA2-RECEPTORS IN THE CNS: STUDIES WITH MIANSERIN.
000053 01-03
EFFECT OF MIANSERIN ON NORADRENERGIC TRANSMISSION IN THE RAT
ANOCOCCYGEUS-MUSCLE.
000075 01-03
3H MIANSERIN BINDING IN CALF CAUDATE: POSSIBLE INVOLVEMENT OF
SEROTONIN-RECEPTORS IN ANTIDEPRESSANT-DRUG ACTION.
000325 01-03
A DOUBLE-BLIND GROUP COMPARATIVE-TRIAL OF MIANSERIN AND
DIAZEPAM IN DEPRESSED-OUTPATIENTS.
000592 01-09
HIGH-AFFINITY BINDING OF (3H)MIANSERIN TO RAT-CEREBRAL-CORTEX.
001204 02-03
MIANSERIN: DIRECT ACTIVATION OF BRAIN NOREPINEPHRINE NEURONS
BY BLOCKING ALPHA2-RECEPTORS.
001214 02-03
THE INABILITY OF CHRONIC MIANSERIN TO BLOCK CENTRAL ALPHA2-
ADRENOCEPTORS.
001492 02-03
COMPARISON OF THE EFFECTS OF LOFEPRAMINE AND MIANSERIN IN
DEPRESSED-PATIENTS IN A DOUBLE-BLIND TRIAL.
001996 02-09
MIANSERIN: DETERMINATION OF THERAPEUTIC DOSE RANGE.
002026 02-09
OUTPATIENT CARE OF DEPRESSIVE-PATIENTS WITH MIANSERIN.
002041 02-09
CARDIOVASCULAR-EFFECTS OF AMITRIPTYLINE, MIANSERIN AND
ZIMELIDINE IN DEPRESSED-PATIENTS.
002215 02-13
CARDIOVASCULAR-EFFECTS OF MIANSERIN AND AMITRIPTYLINE IN
HEALTHY VOLUNTEERS.
002469 02-15
(3H)MIANSERIN: DIFFERENTIAL LABELING OF SEROTONIN AND
HISTAMINE-RECEPTORS IN RAT-BRAIN.
002860 03-03
THE TETRACYCLIC-ANTIDEPRESSANT MIANSERIN: EVALUATION OF ITS
BLOCKADE OF PRESYNAPTIC ALPHA-ADRENOCEPTORS IN A SELF-
STIMULATION MODEL USING CLONIDINE.
003016 03-04
THERAPEUTIC TRIAL OF A NEW ANTIDEPRESSANT: MIANSERIN.
003208 03-09
DOUBLE-BLIND STUDY OF MIANSERIN AND AMITRIPTYLINE.
003231 03-09
NOVEL ANTIDEPRESSANTS: A CLINICAL-TRIAL OF MIANSERIN.
003240 03-09
AN OPEN CLINICAL-TRIAL OF MIANSERIN.
003241 03-09
THE THERAPEUTIC PROFILE OF MIANSERIN IN MILD ELDERLY
DEPRESSIVES.
003297 03-11
CARDIOVASCULAR-EFFECTS OF MIANSERIN -- A COMPARATIVE-STUDY
WITH AMITRIPTYLINE AND A PLACEBO IN HEALTHY SUBJECTS.
003503 03-15
MIANSERIN: A POSSIBLE CAUSE OF NEUTROPENIA AND
AGRANULOCYTOSIS.
003517 03-15
SUPERSENSITIVITY OF CENTRAL NORADRENERGIC PRESYNAPTIC-
AUTORECEPTORS FOLLOWING CHRONIC-TREATMENT WITH THE
ANTIDEPRESSANT MIANSERIN.
003745 04-03
A DOUBLE-BLIND MULTICENTRE-TRIAL COMPARING THE EFFICACY AND
SIDE-EFFECTS OF MIANSERIN AND CHLORIMIPRAMINE IN DEPRESSED-
INPATIENTS AND DEPRESSED-OUTPATIENTS.
004395 04-09

MAPROTILINE, NOMIFENSINE, MIANSERIN, ZIMELIDINE: A REVIEW OF
ANTIDEPRESSANT EFFICACY IN INPATIENTS.
004731 04-17
MIANSERINE
CONTROLLED-COMPARISON OF MIANSERINE WITH IMIPRAMINE IN
ENDOGENOUS DEPRESSIONS.
000634 01-09
THERAPEUTIC EFFECT OF MIANSERINE AND IMIPRAMINE IN ENDOGENOUS
DEPRESSIONS (CONTROLLED-COMPARISON).
003264 03-09
INTERACTION OF P CHLOROPHENYLALANINE, MIANSERINE AND
DANITRACEN WITH AMPHETAMINE.
004599 04-15
MICROANALYSIS
ELECTRON PROBE MICROANALYSIS OF CALCIUM AND PHOSPHORUS IN
DENSE-BODIES ISOLATED FROM HUMAN PLATELETS. (UNPUBLISHED
PAPER).
001014 02-01
MICROASSAY
A SPECIFIC AND SENSITIVE MICROASSAY FOR HYDROXYINDOLES IN
BIOLOGICAL-MATERIAL -- APPLICATION FOR CEREBRAL MICROVESSELS,
BRAIN, AND PINEAL-ORGAN OF THE RAT.
002503 02-16
MICROCIRCULATION
BIPHASIC RESPONSIVENESS OF RAT PIAL-ARTERIOLES TO DOPAMINE:
DIRECT OBSERVATIONS ON THE MICROCIRCULATION.
001105 02-03
MICROCOMPUTER
A MICROCOMPUTER SYSTEM FOR THE CONTROL OF BEHAVIORAL
EXPERIMENTS.
004287 04-06
MICROESTIMATION
MODIFIED CUP TECHNIQUE FOR MICROESTIMATION OF THE RELEASE AND
UPTAKE OF NEUROTRANSMITTERS IN BRAIN SLICES.
003147 03-06
MICROINFUSION
STEREOTYPED-BEHAVIOUR AND ELECTROCORTICAL-CHANGES AFTER
INTRACEREBRAL MICROINFUSION OF DOPAMINE AND APOMORPHINE
IN FOWLS.
001734 02-04
ELECTROLYTIC MICROINFUSION TRANSDUCER SYSTEM: AN ALTERNATIVE
METHOD OF INTRACRANIAL DRUG APPLICATION.
001861 02-06
MICROINJECTION
HYPOALGESIA INDUCED BY MICROINJECTION OF A NOREPINEPHRINE
ANTAGONIST IN THE RAPHE-MAGNUS: REVERSAL BY INTRATHECAL
ADMINISTRATION OF A SEROTONIN ANTAGONIST.
000121 01-03
HYPOALGESIA FOLLOWING MICROINJECTION OF NORADRENERGIC
ANTAGONISTS IN THE NUCLEUS-RAPHE-MAGNUS.
000122 01-03
INCREASED METABOLISM OF DOPAMINE AND SEROTONIN INDUCED IN
FOREBRAIN AREAS BY ETORPHINE MICROINJECTION IN
PERIAQUEDUCTAL GRAY.
001103 02-03
DRUG-INDUCED ELEVATION OF GABA AFTER INTRACEREBRAL
MICROINJECTION: SITE OF ANTICONVULSANT ACTION.
001627 02-04
SPREADING DEPRESSION INDUCED BY MICROINJECTION OF ENKEPHALINS
INTO THE HIPPOCAMPUS AND NEOCORTEX.
004015 04-03
MICROINJECTIONS
INTRAHYPOTHALAMIC MICROINJECTIONS OF NORADRENALINE WITH AND
WITHOUT INDUCTION OF THE ALIMENTARY DRIVE AS A REWARD IN A
T-MAZE LEARNING IN RATS.
001604 02-04
OPIATE-RECEPTORS AND SLEEP. II. EFFECTS OF MICROINJECTIONS OF
ETHYL-ALCOHOL AND PENTOBARBITAL IN THE MEDIAN THALAMUS,
PERIAQUEDUCTAL GRAY MATTER AND NUCLEUS-TRACTUS-SOLITARIUS
OF THE RABBIT.
002917 03-03
HIPPOCAMPAL SEROTONIN REUPTAKE AND NOCTURNAL LOCOMOTOR-
ACTIVITY AFTER MICROINJECTIONS OF 5,7 DHT IN THE FORNIX-
FIMBRIA.
002929 03-03
MODIFICATION OF MOTOR-ACTIVITY, PASSIVE-AVOIDANCE
CONDITIONING AND EVOKED-POTENTIALS BY MICROINJECTIONS OF
STRYCHNINE IN BOTH CAUDATE-NUCLEI IN CATS.
003101 03-04
MICROIONOPHORETIC-APPLICATIONS
THE EFFECT OF CORTISOL MICROIONOPHORETIC-APPLICATIONS ON THE
ACTIVITY OF HIPPOCAMPAL NEURONS IN UNRESTRAINED RABBITS.
001123 02-03
MICROIONTOPHORESIS
INTERACTIONS OF NOREPINEPHRINE WITH PURKINJE-CELL RESPONSES TO
PUTATIVE AMINO-ACID NEUROTRANSMITTERS APPLIED BY
MICROIONTOPHORESIS.
000209 01-03

MICROIONTOPHORETIC
MONOAMINERGIC DENERVATION OF THE RAT HIPPOCAMPUS:
MICROIONTOPHORETIC STUDIES OF PRESYNAPTIC AND POSTSYNAPTIC
SUPERSENSITIVITY TO NOREPINEPHRINE AND SEROTONIN.
000068 01-03
MICROIONTOPHORETIC STUDIES ON NORADRENERGIC INHIBITION FROM
LOCUS-COERULEUS OF SPINAL TRIGEMINAL-NUCLEUS NEURONS.
000260 01-03
ROLE OF INTRACORTICAL INHIBITION IN DEPRIVATION AMBLYOPIA:
REVERSAL BY MICROIONTOPHORETIC BICUCULLINE.
002684 03-03

MICROIONTOPHORETIC-STUDY
EFFECT OF CHRONIC TRICYCLIC-ANTIDEPRESSANT TREATMENT ON THE
SEROTONINERGIC-AUTORECEPTOR: A MICROIONTOPHORETIC-STUDY IN
THE RAT.
001135 02-03
AMINOPHYLLINE AND THEOPHYLLINE DERIVATIVES AS ANTAGONISTS OF
NEURONAL DEPRESSION BY ADENOSINE: A MICROIONTOPHORETIC-
STUDY.
001410 02-03

MICROPRESSURE
PHYSICAL AND PHYSIOLOGICAL CHARACTERISTICS OF MICROPRESSURE
EJECTION OF DRUGS FROM MULTIBARRELED PIPETTES.
002502 02-16

MICROPROPERTIES
MICROPROPERTIES OF OPERANT-BEHAVIOR AS ASPECTS OF TOXICITY.
004666 04-15

MICROSCOPIC
MICROSCOPIC EVIDENCE OF LYMPHOGENIC ABSORPTION OF OIL IN
HUMANS RECEIVING NEUROLEPTIC OILY DEPOT PREPARATIONS
INTRAMUSCULARLY.
000890 01-15
ELECTRON MICROSCOPIC STUDIES OF BRAIN SLICES: THE EFFECTS OF
HIGH-FREQUENCY STIMULATION ON DENDRITIC ULTRASTRUCTURE.
(UNPUBLISHED PAPER).
001036 02-01
NEUROTENSIN-RECEPTOR LOCALIZATION BY LIGHT MICROSCOPIC
AUTORADIOGRAPHY IN RAT-BRAIN.
002938 03-03

MICROSOMAL
BETA DIETHYLAMINOETHYLDIPHENYLPROPYLACETATE (SKF-525-A) AND
2,4 DICHLORO-6-PHENYLPHENOXYETHYLAMINE-HBR (DPEA) INHIBITION
OF FATTY-ACID CONJUGATION TO 11 HYDROXY-DELTA9-
TETRAHYDROCANNABINOL BY THE RAT LIVER MICROSOMAL SYSTEM.
000179 01-03
(3H)QUINUCLIDINYL-BENZILATE BINDING TO MUSCARINIC-RECEPTORS
AND (3H)WB-4101 BINDING TO ALPHA-ADRENERGIC-RECEPTORS IN
RABBIT IRIS: COMPARISON OF RESULTS IN SLICES AND MICROSOMAL
FRACTIONS.
000299 01-03
EFFECTS OF LISURIDE ON BODY-TEMPERATURE OF RATS AND RABBITS:
RELATION TO MICROSOMAL BIOTRANSFORMATION AND
DOPAMINERGIC-RECEPTOR STIMULATION.
001161 02-03
COMPARATIVE-STUDY OF THE INDUCTIVE EFFECT OF TWO
PSYCHOMODERATORS -- TETRABAMATE AND COMPLEXE-1656 -- AND
OF PHENOBARBITAL ON LIVER MICROSOMAL ENZYMES IN RATS.
001874 02-06
INHIBITION BY CAFFEINE OF CALCIUM UPTAKE BY BRAIN MICROSOMAL
VESICLES.
004042 04-03

MICROSOMES
CHANGE IN CATECHOLAMINE SENSITIVE NA-K-ATPASE ACTIVITY IN THE
RAT STRIATUM MICROSOMES FOLLOWING ELECTROLYTIC OR 6
HYDROXYDOPAMINE-INDUCED LESIONS OF DOPAMINERGIC NEURONS.
003871 04-03

MICROVESSELS
A SPECIFIC AND SENSITIVE MICROASSAY FOR HYDROXYINDOLES IN
BIOLOGICAL-MATERIAL -- APPLICATION FOR CEREBRAL MICROVESSELS,
BRAIN, AND PINEAL-ORGAN OF THE RAT.
002503 02-16

MIDAZOLAM
THE PHARMACOKINETICS OF MIDAZOLAM IN MAN.
004555 04-13
COMPUTERIZED ANALYSIS OF SLEEP RECORDINGS APPLIED TO DRUG
EVALUATION: MIDAZOLAM IN NORMAL SUBJECTS.
004564 04-14

MIDBRAIN
ON THE NEUROCHEMICAL BASIS OF SELF-STIMULATION WITH MIDBRAIN
RAPHE ELECTRODE PLACEMENTS.
000373 01-04
MALE RAT SEXUAL-BEHAVIOR COMPARED AFTER 6 OHDA AND
ELECTROLYTIC LESIONS IN THE DORSAL NA BUNDLE REGION OF THE
MIDBRAIN.
001593 02-04
MIDBRAIN DOPAMINE NEURONS: DIFFERENTIAL RESPONSES TO
AMPHETAMINE ISOMERS.
002680 03-03
CONVERGENT PROPERTIES AND CHEMICAL SENSITIVITY OF MIDBRAIN
RETICULAR FORMATION NEURONS OF UNANESTHETIZED RABBITS.
003972 04-03

GENETIC VARIATIONS IN MIDBRAIN DOPAMINE CELL NUMBER: PARALLEL
WITH DIFFERENCES IN RESPONSES TO DOPAMINERGIC AGONISTS AND
IN NATURALISTIC BEHAVIORS MEDIATED BY CENTRAL DOPAMINERGIC-
SYSTEMS. (UNPUBLISHED PAPER).
004112 04-04

MIDODRINE
CENTRAL-ACTION OF INTRAVENTRICULARLY INJECTED MIDODRINE IN
RATS.
001684 02-04

MIDWEST
EPIDEMIOLOGY OF PCP ABUSE: THE MIDWEST PERSPECTIVE.
000740 01-12

MIF-1
NALOXONE-LIKE ACTIONS OF MIF-1 DO NOT REQUIRE THE PRESENCE OF
THE PITUITARY.
001311 02-03
EFFECTS OF PAVLOVIAN-CONDITIONING AND MIF-1 ON THE
DEVELOPMENT OF MORPHINE-TOLERANCE IN RATS.
001327 02-03

MIGRAINE
PHARMACOLOGY OF MIGRAINE.
003623 03-17

MILK
CONCENTRATIONS OF CIS(Z) FLUPENTHIXOL IN MATERNAL SERUM,
AMNIOTIC-FLUID, UMBILICAL-CORD-SERUM, AND MILK.
002423 02-15

MIMICKING
NEUROLEPTIC-INDUCED SYNDROME MIMICKING MYASTHENIA-GRAVIS.
003474 03-15

MIMICS
SYSTEMIC DIPIPERIDINOETHANE MIMICS THE CONVULSANT AND
NEUROTOXIC-ACTIONS OF KAINIC-ACID.
000222 01-03

MINAPRINE
MINAPRINE AND INHIBITION.
001887 02-07
TRIAL WITH MINAPRINE IN SUBJECTS WITH PSYCHIATRIC-DISORDERS.
001889 02-07
CLINICAL-EVALUATION OF THE EFFECTS OF MINAPRINE.
001899 02-07
AN ATTEMPT AT A CLINICAL-EVALUATION OF MINAPRINE.
001900 02-07
AN ATTEMPT TO MAKE A CLINICAL-EVALUATION OF MINAPRINE,
(CONTINUATION OF THE STUDY).
001901 02-07
TREATMENT OF ASTHENO-DEPRESSIVE-DISORDERS WITH MINAPRINE
(CANTOR). MULTICENTER-STUDY OF 248 CASES EVALUATED WITH THE
FATIGUE STUDY GROUPS NO. 4 CLINICAL-SCALE.
001980 02-09
CLINICAL-TESTING OF MINAPRINE ON ELDERLY SUBJECTS WITH THE
ASTHENIC-DEPRESSIVE-SYNDROMES.
002123 02-11
MINAPRINE IN SEVERE PSYCHOPATHOLOGY: STUDY OF 20 CASES.
002135 02-11
EXPERIMENTATION WITH MINAPRINE IN DEALING WITH CERTAIN
SEXUAL-DISORDERS: IMPOTENCE OR FRIGIDITY.
002153 02-11
THE USE OF MINAPRINE IN CHILD-PSYCHIATRY IN HOSPITALS AND
OUTPATIENT CLINICS.
002169 02-11
HISTORY AND PHARMACOLOGY OF MINAPRINE.
002270 02-13
EXPERIMENTATION WITH MINAPRINE IN CHILD-PSYCHIATRY.
002344 02-14
POLYGRAPHIC-STUDY OF NIGHT SLEEP UNDER THE EFFECTS OF
MINAPRINE.
003313 03-11

MINAPRINE-CHLOROHYDRATE
MINAPRINE-CHLOROHYDRATE: SURVEY OF THE FIRST CLINICAL-STUDIES
OF THE FOURTH STAGE.
001902 02-07

MIND
COMPARISON OF THE EFFECTS OF FOUR BENZODIAZEPINES ON FRAME OF
MIND AND BEHAVIOR IN HEALTHY SUBJECTS.
003441 03-14
MIND/BRAIN IN THE AGE OF PSYCHOPHARMACOLOGY: A CROSSROADS
FOR MEDICINE AND MINISTRY.
003624 03-17

MINERAL-ELEMENTS
LEVELS OF MINERAL-ELEMENTS IN THE SERUM AND SALIVA OF HEALTHY
MALE VOLUNTEERS AFTER A SINGLE-DOSE OF LI2CO3.
002297 02-13

MINI-MULT
PSYCHOTHERAPEUTIC-DRUG RECOMMENDATIONS BASED ON THE MINI-
MULT.
002606 02-17

MINI-SYMPOSIUM
MINI-SYMPOSIUM: III. SIMPLE IN VIVO TESTS THAT DIFFERENTIATE PROTOTYPE AGONISTS AT OPIATE-RECEPTORS.
004289 D4-06
MINI-SYMPOSIUM. I. THE IN VIVO DIFFERENTIATION OF OPIATE-RECEPTORS: INTRODUCTION.
004697 04-17
MINI-SYMPOSIUM. IV. DISCRIMINATIVE-STIMULUS EFFECTS OF NARCOTICS: EVIDENCE FOR MULTIPLE RECEPTOR-MEDIATED ACTIONS.
004719 04-17
MINI-SYMPOSIUM: II. MULTIPLE OPIOID-RECEPTORS. A LITTLE ABOUT THEIR HISTORY AND SOME IMPLICATIONS RELATED TO EVOLUTION.
004728 04-17

MINIMAL-BRAIN-DYSFUNCTION
INTRAVENTRICULAR 6 HYDROXYDOPAMINE IN THE NEWBORN RAT AND LOCOMOTOR RESPONSES TO DRUGS IN INFANCY: NO SUPPORT FOR THE DOPAMINE DEPLETION MODEL OF MINIMAL-BRAIN-DYSFUNCTION.
000448 01-04
OUR EXPERIENCE WITH PIRACETAM (NOOTROPIL-UCB) TREATMENT IN CHILDREN FROM HIGH-RISK PREGNANCIES WITH SUBSEQUENT MINIMAL-BRAIN-DYSFUNCTION.
000544 01-07
MINIMAL-BRAIN-DYSFUNCTION -- HYPERKINETIC-SYNDROME.
000730 01-11
COMPARISON OF SUSTAINED-RELEASE AND STANDARD METHYLPHENIDATE IN THE TREATMENT OF MINIMAL-BRAIN-DYSFUNCTION.
000732 01-11
ATTENTION DEFICIT-DISORDER (MINIMAL-BRAIN-DYSFUNCTION) IN ADULTS: A REPLICATION STUDY OF DIAGNOSIS AND DRUG-TREATMENT.
003389 03-11

MINIMUM-DOSES
THE QUESTION OF MINIMUM-DOSES OF ANTICONVULSANTS IN THE TREATMENT OF EPILEPSY.
002306 02-13

MINIREVIEW
TRANYLCYPROMINE STEREOISOMERS, MONOAMINERGIC NEUROTRANSMISSION AND BEHAVIOR. A MINIREVIEW.
000016 01-02

MINISTRY
MIND/BRAIN IN THE AGE OF PSYCHOPHARMACOLOGY: A CROSSROADS FOR MEDICINE AND MINISTRY.
003624 03-17

MINOR-TRANQUILIZER
THE BENZODIAZEPINE GABA-CHLORIDE IONOPHORE-RECEPTOR COMPLEX: COMMON SITE OF MINOR-TRANQUILIZER ACTION.
002857 03-03

MINOR-TRANQUILIZERS
THE USE OF MINOR-TRANQUILIZERS WITH JAIL INMATES.
003308 03-11

MISINFORMED
MISINFORMED CONSENT.
004326 04-08

MISONIDAZOLE
ACETYLCHOLINESTERASE AND CHOLINESTERASE ACTIVITIES IN THE MOUSE CEREBELLUM FOLLOWING MISONIDAZOLE TREATMENT.
003123 03-05

MISSISSIPPI
ISOLATION OF PSYCHOACTIVE CANNABINOID PRECURSORS FROM CANNABIS OF SOVIET PROVENIENCE GROWN IN MISSISSIPPI.
001023 02-01

MISUSE
A STUDY OF ANTIPSYCHOTIC-DRUG USE IN NURSING-HOMES: EPIDEMIOLOGIC EVIDENCE SUGGESTING MISUSE.
000979 01-17
THE USE AND MISUSE OF SLEEPING-PILLS: A CLINICAL GUIDE.
002150 02-11

MITOCHONDRIA
CHANGE IN PYRUVATE-DEHYDROGENASE ACTIVITY INFLUENCE PYRUVATE SUPPORTED CALCIUM ACCUMULATION BY BRAIN MITOCHONDRIA. (UNPUBLISHED PAPER).
001147 02-03
BIPHASIC ACTIVITY OF MEMBRANE-BOUND ENZYMES IN BRAIN MITOCHONDRIA AND SYNAPTOSOMES DURING THE DEVELOPMENT OF TOLERANCE TO AND PHYSICAL-DEPENDENCE ON CHRONIC MORPHINE ADMINISTRATION TO RATS.
001285 02-03
OXIDATION OF BETA PHENYLETHYLAMINE BY BOTH TYPES OF MONOAMINE-OXIDASE: EXAMINATION OF ENZYMES IN BRAIN AND LIVER MITOCHONDRIA OF EIGHT SPECIES.
004024 04-03

MITOCHONDRIAL
REVERSIBLE ALEXIA, MITOCHONDRIAL MYOPATHY, AND LACTIC-ACIDEMIA.
000723 01-11
MECHANISM OF INACTIVATION OF MITOCHONDRIAL MONOAMINE-OXIDASE BY N CYCLOPROPYL-N-ARYLALKYLAMINES.
001055 02-01

MECHANISM OF INACTIVATION OF MITOCHONDRIAL MONOAMINE-OXIDASE BY N CYCLOPROPYL-N-ARYLALKYLAMINES.
001088 02-02
EXPOSURE OF MITOCHONDRIAL OUTER MEMBRANES TO NEURAMINIDASE SELECTIVELY DESTROYS MONOAMINE-OXIDASE-A ACTIVITY.
001286 02-03
EFFECT OF INORGANIC LEAD ON RAT-BRAIN MITOCHONDRIAL RESPIRATION AND ENERGY PRODUCTION.
004267 04-05

MITRAL-VALVE
EFFECT OF SODIUM-LACTATE ON PATIENTS WITH PANIC-DISORDER AND MITRAL-VALVE PROLAPSE.
003409 03-13
ARRHYTHMIA INDUCED BY A TRICYCLIC-ANTIDEPRESSANT IN A PATIENT WITH UNDIAGNOSED MITRAL-VALVE PROLAPSE.
003521 03-15

MIXED-FUNCTION
EFFECT OF CHRONIC ADMINISTRATION OF PHENCYCLIDINE ON HEPATIC MIXED-FUNCTION OXIDASES IN THE MOUSE.
002753 03-03

MIXTURE
HABITUATION OF THE THE HEAD-POKE RESPONSE: EFFECTS OF AN AMPHETAMINE BARBITURATE MIXTURE, PLG AND FENFLURAMINE.
004159 04-04
CHARACTERISTICS OF THE STIMULUS PRODUCED BY THE MIXTURE OF CANNABIDIOL WITH DELTA9 TETRAHYDROCANNABINOL.
004263 04-04

MK-771
INVESTIGATIONS ON THE INTERACTION OF THYROTROPIN-RELEASING-HORMONE (TRH) AND MK-771 WITH CENTRAL NORADRENERGIC MECHANISMS.
001701 02-04

MMPI
COMPUTERIZING THE MMPI IN THE STUDY OF A NEW PSYCHOTROPIC-AGENT: TIAPRIDE.
000585 01-09
MMPI PREDICTION OF IMIPRAMINE RESPONSE: A REPLICATION STUDY.
003570 03-16

MOBILIZATION
MOBILIZATION OF REFRACTORY CHRONIC SCHIZOPHRENICS WITH HALOPERIDOL.
004337 04-08

MODEL
THE PARADOXICAL-EFFECT OF LIDOCAINE ON AN EXPERIMENTAL MODEL OF EPILEPSY.
000039 01-03
AN IN VIVO MODEL FOR INVESTIGATING ALPHA1-RECEPTORS AND ALPHA2-RECEPTORS IN THE CNS: STUDIES WITH MIANSERIN.
000053 01-03
FLASH-EVOKED AFTERDISCHARGE IN RAT AS A MODEL OF THE ABSENCE SEIZURE: DOSE-RESPONSE STUDIES WITH THERAPEUTIC DRUGS.
000160 01-03
IN VITRO ACETYLCHOLINE RELEASE FROM RAT CAUDATE-NUCLEUS AS A NEW MODEL FOR TESTING DRUGS WITH DOPAMINE-RECEPTOR ACTIVITY.
000289 01-03
INTRAVENTRICULAR 6 HYDROXYDOPAMINE IN THE NEWBORN RAT AND LOCOMOTOR RESPONSES TO DRUGS IN INFANCY: NO SUPPORT FOR THE DOPAMINE DEPLETION MODEL OF MINIMAL-BRAIN-DYSFUNCTION.
000448 01-04
DOPAMINERGIC FACTORS IN HUMAN PROLACTIN REGULATION: A PITUITARY MODEL FOR THE STUDY OF A NEUROENDOCRINE SYSTEM IN MAN.
000776 01-13
A MODEL FOR PSYCHONEUROENDOCRINE INVESTIGATION: SPECIFIC CHEMICAL LESIONING OF THE MEDIAN-EMINENCE.
001478 02-03
CIRCLING PRODUCED BY SEROTONIN AND DOPAMINE AGONISTS IN RAPHE LESIONED RATS: A SEROTONIN MODEL.
001783 02-04
ACUTE AND CHRONIC LSD EFFECTS ON RAT STARTLE: DATA SUPPORTING AN LSD RAT MODEL OF SCHIZOPHRENIA.
002194 02-12
SUBJECTIVE DRUG-EFFECTS AND DRUG PREFERENCE IN HEALTHY VOLUNTEERS AS A MODEL OF A DRUGS REINFORCING EFFECTS: STUDIES ON NOMIFENSINE, AMPHETAMINE AND PLACEBO.
002362 02-14
NEUROLEPTIC-INDUCED REINNERVATION SPROUTING IN THE CENTRAL-NERVOUS-SYSTEM (A MODEL FOR THE DEVELOPMENT OF TARDIVE-DYSKINESIA AND SUPERSENSITIVITY PSYCHOSIS).
002459 02-15
A NOVEL PSYCHOMETRIC-TEST MODEL APPLYING TAILORED TESTING FOR ECONOMIC AND EFFICIENT COLLECTION OF PSYCHOPHARMACOLOGICAL-EFFECTS.
002479 02-16
THE HYPOTHALAMIC DOPAMINERGIC REGULATION OF PROLACTIN: A MODEL FOR THE STUDY OF NEUROHORMONAL MECHANISMS IN MAN.
002568 02-17

A POSSIBLE ECOPHARMACOGENETIC MODEL IN NEUROPSYCHOPHARMACOLOGY ASPECTS IN ALCOHOLISM AND PHARMACODEPENDENCE.
002596 02-17

COMBINED EFFECTS OF ALCOHOL AND LITHIUM ON BODY COMPOSITION IN THE RAT MODEL.
002928 03-03

AN IMPROVED MODEL OF INTRASPECIFIC AGGRESSION: DOSE-RESPONSE ANALYSIS OF APOMORPHINE-INDUCED-FIGHTING AND STEREOTYPY IN THE RAT.
002983 03-04

THE TETRACYCLIC-ANTIDEPRESSANT MIANSERIN: EVALUATION OF ITS BLOCKADE OF PRESYNAPTIC ALPHA-ADRENOCEPTORS IN A SELF-STIMULATION MODEL USING CLONIDINE.
003016 03-04

A TEST OF A NEUROTRANSMITTER MODEL OF THE AFFECTIVE-DISORDERS. (PH.D. DISSERTATION).
003063 03-04

RELAPSE TO NARCOTIC SELF-ADMINISTRATION IN MORPHINE POSTADDICT RATS: A POSSIBLE MODEL FOR PREDICTING ABUSE LIABILITY OF NARCOTIC-DRUGS. (PH.D. DISSERTATION).
003097 03-04

BEHAVIORAL-TEST FOR DETECTION OF SUBCLINICAL BRAIN-DAMAGE: AN EXPERIMENTAL MODEL.
003120 03-04

A REFORMULATION OF THE DUAL-ACTION MODEL OF OPIOID DEPENDENCE: OPIOID-SPECIFIC NEURONAL KINDLING.
003645 03-17

THE HUMAN PLATELET AS A MODEL FOR THE GLUTAMATERGIC NEURON: PLATELET UPTAKE OF L GLUTAMATE.
003923 04-03

AN ELECTROPHYSIOLOGICAL MODEL OF GABA-MEDIATED NEUROTRANSMISSION.
003929 04-03

THE STEREOTYPED-BEHAVIOR-SYNDROME: A NEW MODEL AND PROPOSED THERAPY.
004163 04-04

LACK OF SPECIFICITY OF AN ANIMAL BEHAVIOR MODEL FOR HALLUCINOGENIC DRUG ACTION.
004250 04-04

HALOPERIDOL AND DROPERIDOL TREATMENT IN SCHIZOPHRENICS: CLINICAL APPLICATION OF THE PROLACTIN MODEL.
004332 04-08

MODELS

ROLE OF BRAIN DOPAMINERGIC MECHANISMS IN RODENT AGGRESSIVE-BEHAVIOR: INFLUENCE OF (OR -)N N PROPYLNORAPOMORPHINE ON THREE EXPERIMENTAL MODELS.
000340 01-04

ORAL DYSKINESIA IN BRAIN-DAMAGED RATS WITHDRAWN FROM A NEUROLEPTIC: IMPLICATION FOR MODELS OF TARDIVE-DYSKINESIA.
000393 01-04

PREPARATION AND CHARACTERIZATION OF SYNTHETIC MODELS FOR THE DENSE-BODIES OF HUMAN PLATELETS. (UNPUBLISHED PAPER).
001013 02-01

METOCLOPRAMIDE: ANTIPSYCHOTIC-EFFICACY OF A DRUG LACKING POTENCY IN RECEPTOR MODELS.
001948 02-08

QUINACRINE AND SEROTONIN BINDING BY SYNTHETIC MODELS FOR HUMAN PLATELET DENSE-BODIES: EVALUATION OF THE ROLE OF BINDING IN AMINE STORAGE. (UNPUBLISHED PAPER).
002219 02-13

THE VALIDITY OF MODELS IN PSYCHOPHARMACOLOGY.
003633 03-17

MODERN-VIEWS

MODERN-VIEWS ON THE PRINCIPLES OF THE PHARMACOLOGICAL-TREATMENT OF EPILEPSY.
000931 01-17

MODIFICATION

MODIFICATION OF DOPAMINERGIC-RECEPTOR SENSITIVITY IN RAT-BRAIN AFTER AMYGDALOID KINDLING.
000106 01-03

CONSEQUENT EVENTS AS DETERMINANTS OF DRUG-EFFECTS ON SCHEDULE-CONTROLLED BEHAVIOR: MODIFICATION OF EFFECTS OF COCAINE AND D-AMPHETAMINE FOLLOWING CHRONIC AMPHETAMINE ADMINISTRATION.
000350 01-04

MODIFICATION OF THE PROLINE RESIDUE OF TRH ENHANCES BIOLOGICAL-ACTIVITY AND INHIBITS DEGRADATION.
000351 01-04

RATS REACTIONS TO A PREDATOR: MODIFICATION BY CHLORDIAZEPOXIDE.
000353 01-04

EFFECTS OF EXPERIMENTER AND TEST LOCATION NOVELTY ON NONSPECIFIC ACTIVITY IN RATS AND ITS MODIFICATION BY METHAMPHETAMINE.
000409 01-04

HEXAMETHONIUM MODIFICATION OF CARDIOVASCULAR ADJUSTMENTS DURING COMBINED STATIC DYNAMIC ARM EXERCISE IN MONKEYS.
001242 02-03

MODIFICATION OF GABAERGIC ACTIVITY AND THYROTROPIN SECRETION IN MALE RATS.
001362 02-03

MODIFICATION OF DOPAMINE-RECEPTORS IN BRAIN BY CONTINUOUS AMPHETAMINE ADMINISTRATIONS TO RATS.
001395 02-03

SHORT-TERM AND LONG-TERM MODIFICATION OF SKELETAL-MUSCLE SODIUM-PUMP ACTIVITY AND MUSCLE PROTEIN TURNOVER. (UNPUBLISHED PAPER).
001519 02-03

PHARMACOLOGICAL MODIFICATION OF AMYGDALOID KINDLED SEIZURES.
001588 02-04

THE PARENT CHILD INTERACTIONS OF HYPERACTIVE-CHILDREN AND THEIR MODIFICATION BY STIMULANT-DRUGS.
002092 02-11

MODIFICATION OF MOTOR-ACTIVITY, PASSIVE-AVOIDANCE CONDITIONING AND EVOKED-POTENTIALS BY MICROINJECTIONS OF STRYCHNINE IN BOTH CAUDATE-NUCLEI IN CATS.
003101 03-04

AGE-DEPENDENT MODIFICATION OF DRUG INTERFERENCE ON THE ENZYMATIC ACTIVITIES OF THE RAT-BRAIN.
003730 04-03

SELECTIVE MODIFICATION BY OPIATES OF NEURONAL ACTIVITY OF THE MEDIAL BASAL HYPOTHALAMUS.
003773 04-03

GUANYLATE-CYCLASE -- CYCLIC-GMP IN MOUSE CEREBRAL-CORTEX AND CEREBELLUM: MODIFICATION BY ANTICONVULSANTS.
003956 04-03

CHLORPROMAZINE EFFECTS ON COCAINE-REINFORCED RESPONDING IN RHESUS-MONKEYS: RECIPROCAL MODIFICATION OF RATE ALTERING EFFECTS OF THE DRUGS.
004133 04-04

MODIFICATION OF DRUG-INDUCED CATATONIA AND TREMORS BY QUIPAZINE IN RATS AND MICE.
004164 04-04

SEROTONERGIC APPROACHES TO THE MODIFICATION OF BEHAVIOR IN THE LESCH-NYHANS-SYNDROME.
004576 04-14

MODIFICATIONS

BRAIN CATECHOLAMINES MODIFICATIONS. THE EFFECTS ON MEMORY FACILITATION INDUCED BY OXOTREMORINE IN MICE.
001658 02-04

SUPERSENSITIVITY TO APOMORPHINE IN EXPERIMENTALLY-INDUCED HYPOKINESIA AND DRUG-INDUCED MODIFICATIONS OF THE APOMORPHINE RESPONSE.
001814 02-04

LSD-INDUCED ULTRASTRUCTURAL MODIFICATIONS OF LIMBIC-SYSTEM NUCLEI AND OTHER CEREBRAL ZONES.
002198 02-12

IMIPRAMINE: EFFECT OF OVARIAN STEROIDS ON MODIFICATIONS IN SEROTONIN-RECEPTOR BINDING.
002778 03-03

MODIFYING

NEUROPHARMACOLOGICAL-AGENTS MODIFYING ENDOTOXIN-INDUCED CHANGES IN MICE.
001543 02-03

EFFECTS OF PROTEIN AND MEMBRANE MODIFYING AGENTS ON THE BINDING OF L (3H)GLUTAMATE TO CEREBELLAR SYNAPTIC MEMBRANES.
002888 03-03

ON MONOAMINERGIC-INTERACTION WITH BEHAVIOUR MODIFYING PEPTIDE-HORMONES.
004700 04-17

MODITEN

RESULTS OF TREATMENT BY MODITEN DEPOT IN OUTPATIENTS-WARDS IN THE SOUTH MORAVIAN REGION.
004648 04-15

MOLECULAR

THE CRYSTAL AND MOLECULAR STRUCTURE OF THE ACETYLCHOLINE ANTAGONIST DIMETHYLAMINOBUTYNYLCYCLOHEXYLHYDROXY 2 PHENYLACETATE HCL.
000003 01-01

INFLUENCE OF NICERGOLINE ON MOLECULAR BIOLOGICAL PROCESSES IN THE BRAIN AND LEARNING-ABILITY OF THE RAT.
000449 01-04

THE CRYSTAL AND MOLECULAR STRUCTURE OF THE NEUROLEPTIC PIMOZIDE-HYDROCHLORIDE, BISFLUOROPHENYL-BUTYLPIPERIDYLBENZIMIDAZOLINONE-HCL.
001015 02-01

CONVULSANT AND ANTICONVULSANT BARBITURATES. 1. MOLECULAR CONFORMATIONS FROM CLASSICAL POTENTIAL ENERGY CALCULATIONS.
001029 02-01

LOCALIZATION OF SENSITIVE SITES TO TAURINE, GAMMA AMINOBUTYRIC-ACID, GLYCINE AND BETA ALANINE IN THE MOLECULAR LAYER OF GUINEA-PIG CEREBELLAR SLICES.
001402 02-03

THE MOLECULAR ARCHITECTURE OF ERGOPEPTINES: A BASIS FOR
BIOLOGICAL-INTERACTION.
001527 02-03

MOLECULAR ACTIONS OF OPIATES: HISTORICAL OVERVIEW AND NEW
FINDINGS ON OPIATE-RECEPTOR INTERACTIONS WITH ENKEPHALINS
AND GUANYL-NUCLEOTIDES.
002613 02-17

MOLECULES
DEVELOPMENTALLY REGULATED LECTINS IN SLIME MOULDS AND CHICK
TISSUES -- ARE THEY CELL ADHESION MOLECULES?
003724 04-03

MOLINDONE
EFFECTS OF MOLINDONE AND FLUPHENAZINE ON THE BRAIN
CONCENTRATION OF SOME PHENOLIC AND CATECHOLIC AMINES IN THE
MOUSE AND THE RAT.
003870 04-03

PHYSIOLOGICAL SIGNIFICANCE OF DOPAMINE-AUTORECEPTORS AS
STUDIED FOLLOWING THEIR SELECTIVE BLOCKADE BY MOLINDONE.
004065 04-04

MOLINDONE-HYDROCHLORIDE
MOLINDONE-HYDROCHLORIDE IN THE TREATMENT OF AGGRESSIVE,
HOSPITALIZED CHILDREN.
003321 03-11

MOLLUSCAN
CAFFEINE BLOCKS THE DELAYED K OUTWARD-CURRENT OF MOLLUSCAN
NEURONS.
003834 04-03

MONGOLIAN-GERBIL
DISRUPTION OF SELECTIVE ATTENTION BY APOMORPHINE, BUT NOT
AMPHETAMINE, IN THE MONGOLIAN-GERBIL.
000358 01-04

BRAIN BENZODIAZEPINE-RECEPTORS AND THEIR RAPID CHANGES AFTER
SEIZURES IN THE MONGOLIAN-GERBIL.
003717 04-03

HANDLING-INDUCED SEIZURES AND ROTATIONAL-BEHAVIOR IN THE
MONGOLIAN-GERBIL.
004216 04-04

MONGOLIAN-GERBILS
CHOLINERGIC MECHANISMS IN SCENT-MARKING-BEHAVIOR IN
MONGOLIAN-GERBILS (MERIONES-UNGUICULATUS).
000504 01-04

MONITOR
ANIMAL ACTIVITY MONITOR FOR CHRONIC DRUG-STUDIES.
(UNPUBLISHED PAPER).
001794 02-04

MONITORING
VALUE OF SALIVA SAMPLES IN MONITORING CARBAMAZEPINE
CONCENTRATIONS IN EPILEPTIC-PATIENTS.
000903 01-16

AN AUTOMATED ELECTROCHEMICAL-METHOD FOR IN VIVO MONITORING
OF CATECHOLAMINE RELEASE.
001873 02-06

LONG-TERM MONITORING OF TRICYCLIC-ANTIDEPRESSANT PLASMA
CONCENTRATIONS.
002014 02-09

HALOPERIDOL PLASMA LEVEL MONITORING IN PSYCHIATRIC-PATIENTS.
002267 02-13

CORRELATIONS BETWEEN PLASMA LEVELS OF ANTIEPILEPTIC-DRUGS AND
EEG INTENSIVE MONITORING.
002288 02-13

CARDIOVASCULAR-EFFECTS OF THERAPEUTIC DOSES OF TRICYCLIC-
ANTIDEPRESSANTS: IMPORTANCE OF BLOOD LEVEL MONITORING.
002456 02-15

A PROSPECTIVE RANDOMISED-TRIAL ON THE EFFECT OF MONITORING
PLASMA ANTICONVULSANT LEVELS IN EPILEPSY.
003314 03-11

INTENSIVE MONITORING IN REFRACTORY EPILEPSY.
003378 03-11

COMPUTERIZED MONITORING OF PSYCHOTROPIC-DRUG ORDERS: SOME
TRENDS AND REVELATIONS.
003566 03-16

SOME METHODOLOGICAL WAYS OF MONITORING THE EFFECTS OF
PSYCHOTHERAPEUTIC-DRUGS.
003567 03-16

AMITRIPTYLINE AND NORTRIPTYLINE PLASMA LEVELS MONITORING.
PERSPECTIVE IN CLINICAL-PRACTICE.
004675 04-16

THERAPEUTIC MONITORING OF PLASMA CONCENTRATIONS OF TRICYCLIC-
ANTIDEPRESSANTS: PERSPECTIVE OF THE CLINICAL LABORATORY.
004681 04-16

MONKEY
NEURONAL ACTIVITY IN CHRONIC FERRIC-CHLORIDE EPILEPTIC-FOCI IN
CATS AND MONKEY.
000172 01-03

DISTRIBUTION AND EXCRETION IN THE RAT AND MONKEY OF (82BR)
BROMOCRIPTINE.
000196 01-03

INTRACELLULAR REDOX STATES UNDER HALOTHANE AND BARBITURATE
ANESTHESIA IN NORMAL, ISCHEMIC, AND ANOXIC MONKEY BRAIN.
000295 01-03

BETA-ADRENOCEPTOR ANTAGONISTS: STUDIES ON BEHAVIOUR (DELAYED
DIFFERENTIATION) IN THE MONKEY (MACACA-MULATTA).
000440 01-04

OPIATE-RECEPTOR GRADIENTS IN MONKEY CEREBRAL-CORTEX:
CORRESPONDENCE WITH SENSORY PROCESSING HIERARCHIES.
002641 03-01

AN INVOLVEMENT OF DOPAMINE IN HIGHER-ORDER CHOICE
MECHANISMS IN THE MONKEY.
003072 03-04

MORPHINE-LIKE STIMULUS EFFECTS IN THE MONKEY: OPIOIDS WITH
ANTAGONIST PROPERTIES.
003086 03-04

MONKEYS
BIOCHEMICAL-STUDIES AFTER CHRONIC ADMINISTRATION OF
NEUROLEPTICS TO MONKEYS.
000523 01-05

HEXAMETHONIUM MODIFICATION OF CARDIOVASCULAR ADJUSTMENTS
DURING COMBINED STATIC DYNAMIC ARM EXERCISE IN MONKEYS.
001242 02-03

EFFECTS OF METHAQUALONE ON SOCIAL-BEHAVIOR IN MONKEYS
(MACACA-MULATTA).
001594 02-04

THE EFFECT OF PHRENOLON ON DELAYED REACTIONS IN LOWER
MONKEYS.
001640 02-04

EFFECTS OF PHENCYCLIDINE, PENTOBARBITAL, AND D-AMPHETAMINE ON
THE ACQUISITION AND PERFORMANCE OF CONDITIONAL
DISCRIMINATIONS IN MONKEYS.
001723 02-04

DISCRIMINATIVE-STIMULUS EFFECTS OF PROTOTYPE OPIATE-RECEPTOR
AGONISTS IN MONKEYS.
001803 02-04

ANIMAL-MODEL OF PSYCHOSIS: HALLUCINATORY BEHAVIORS IN
MONKEYS DURING THE LATE STAGE OF CONTINUOUS AMPHETAMINE
INTOXICATION.
002988 03-04

THE EFFECT OF THIOPROPERAZINE ON DELAYED REACTIONS IN LOWER
MONKEYS.
004125 04-04

CLONIDINE-INDUCED HYPERPHAGIA IN MONKEYS: EVIDENCE FOR
ALPHA2-NORADRENERGIC-RECEPTOR MEDIATION.
004215 04-04

MONOAMINE
MONOAMINE REPLACEMENT AFTER RESERPINE: CATECHOLAMINERGIC
AGONISTS RESTORE MOTOR-ACTIVITY BUT PHENYLETHYLAMINE
RESTORES ATROPINE-RESISTANT NEOCORTICAL LOW VOLTAGE FAST-
ACTIVITY.
000309 01-03

ATTEMPTS TO REINSTATE LORDOSIS REFLEX IN ESTROGEN-PRIMED
SPINAL FEMALE RATS WITH MONOAMINE AGONISTS.
000421 01-04

FURTHER STUDIES ON THE INHIBITION OF MONOAMINE SYNTHESIS BY
MONOFLUOROMETHYLDOPA.
001128 02-03

CENTRAL MONOAMINE SYNAPSES AS SITES OF ACTION FOR ERGOT
DRUGS.
001238 02-03

THE EFFECT OF EMOTIONAL-STRESS AND DIAZEPAM ON MONOAMINE
METABOLITES IN THE CEREBROSPINAL-FLUID OF CATS. (PH.D.
DISSERTATION).
001260 02-03

EFFECT OF QUIPAZINE ON BRAINSTEM MONOAMINE NEURONS
HISTOFLUORESCENCE STUDIES.
001477 02-03

BEHAVIOURAL-RESPONSES TO STEREOTACTICALLY CONTROLLED
INJECTIONS OF MONOAMINE NEUROTRANSMITTERS INTO THE
ACCUMBENS AND CAUDATE-PUTAMEN NUCLEI.
001708 02-04

INFLUENCE OF MONOAMINE DEPLETING PHARMACOLOGIC-AGENTS ON
LEVELS OF ACTIVITY IN CAIMAN-SCLEROPS.
001810 02-04

INFLUENCE OF CICLAZINDOL ON MONOAMINE UPTAKE AND CNS
FUNCTION IN NORMAL SUBJECTS.
002268 02-13

MONOAMINE-OXIDASE
INHIBITION OF MONOAMINE-OXIDASE BY CLORGYLINE AND DEPRENYL IN
CIRCUMVENTRICULAR STRUCTURES OF RAT-BRAIN.
000159 01-03

MONOAMINE-OXIDASE AND ITS INHIBITION: SOME CLINICAL
IMPLICATIONS.
000983 01-17

MECHANISM OF INACTIVATION OF MITOCHONDRIAL MONOAMINE-
OXIDASE BY N CYCLOPROPYL-N-ARYLALKYLAMINES.
001055 02-01

THIOLS LIBERATE COVALENTLY-BONDED FLAVIN FROM MONOAMINE-
OXIDASE. (UNPUBLISHED PAPER).
001060 02-01

MECHANISM OF INACTIVATION OF MITOCHONDRIAL MONOAMINE-OXIDASE BY N CYCLOPROPYL-N-ARYLALKYLAMINES.
001088 02-02

EFFECT OF 2 P CHLOROPHENYL-CYCLOPROPYLAMINE ON 5 HYDROXYINDOLE CONCENTRATION AND MONOAMINE-OXIDASE ACTIVITY IN RAT-BRAIN.
001237 02-03

MONOAMINE-OXIDASE, PHENYLETHYLAMINE, NOREPINEPHRINE AND SCHIZOPHRENIA. (UNPUBLISHED PAPER).
001958 02-08

SPECIES-DIFFERENCES IN THE DEAMINATION OF DOPAMINE AND OTHER SUBSTRATES FOR MONOAMINE-OXIDASE IN BRAIN.
002233 02-13

EVIDENCE FOR THE PRESENCE OF TWO TYPES OF MONOAMINE-OXIDASE IN RABBIT CHOROID PLEXUS AND THEIR ROLE IN BREAKDOWN OF AMINES INFLUENCING CEREBROSPINAL-FLUID FORMATION.
002807 03-03

A PROBABLE NEUROLEPTIC-EFFECT ON PLATELET MONOAMINE-OXIDASE IN CHRONIC SCHIZOPHRENIC-PATIENTS.
003169 03-08

NONGENETIC FACTORS AFFECTING HUMAN PLATELET MONOAMINE-OXIDASE.
003407 03-13

LYMPHOCYTE MONOAMINE-OXIDASE AND PLASMA PROLACTIN AND GROWTH-HORMONE IN TARDIVE-DYSKINESIA.
003499 03-15

INHIBITION OF MONOAMINE-OXIDASE BY FURAZOLIDONE IN THE CHICKEN AND THE INFLUENCE OF THE ALIMENTARY FLORA THEREON.
003711 04-03

CHARACTERISTICS OF THE INHIBITION OF RAT-BRAIN MONOAMINE-OXIDASE IN VITRO BY MD780515.
003874 04-03

OXIDATION OF BETA PHENYLETHYLAMINE BY BOTH TYPES OF MONOAMINE-OXIDASE: EXAMINATION OF ENZYMES IN BRAIN AND LIVER MITOCHONDRIA OF EIGHT SPECIES.
004024 04-03

THE SPECIFIC ACTIVITY OF PLATELET MONOAMINE-OXIDASE VARIES WITH PLATELET COUNT DURING SEVERE EXERCISE AND NORADRENALINE INFUSION.
004509 04-13

THE ACTIVITY OF BLOOD-PLATELET MONOAMINE-OXIDASE IN ENDOGENOUS DEPRESSION.
004547 04-13

MONOAMINE-OXIDASE-A
EXPOSURE OF MITOCHONDRIAL OUTER MEMBRANES TO NEURAMINIDASE SELECTIVELY DESTROYS MONOAMINE-OXIDASE-A ACTIVITY.
001286 02-03

MONOAMINE-OXIDASE-B
EVIDENCE THAT A PREFERRED SUBSTRATE FOR MONOAMINE-OXIDASE-B MEDIATES STIMULUS PROPERTIES OF MAO-INHIBITORS: A POSSIBLE ROLE FOR BETA PHENYLETHYLAMINE IN THE COCAINE CUE.
000363 01-04

ESR STUDIES OF SPIN LABELLED BOVINE LIVER MONOAMINE-OXIDASE-B. (UNPUBLISHED PAPER).
001065 02-01

MONOAMINE-OXIDASE-B ACTIVITIES TOWARD BETA PHENYLETHYLAMINE IN DISCRETE HYPOTHALAMIC AND CIRCUMVENTRICULAR NUCLEI OF THE RAT.
002781 03-03

MONOAMINE-OXIDASE-B-INHIBITOR
THE EFFECT OF DEPRENYL, A SELECTIVE MONOAMINE-OXIDASE-B-INHIBITOR, ON SLEEP AND MOOD IN MAN.
002365 02-14

IS THE FAILURE OF (-)DEPRENYL, A SELECTIVE MONOAMINE-OXIDASE-B-INHIBITOR, TO ALLEVIATE DEPRESSION RELATED TO FREEDOM FROM THE CHEESE EFFECT?
004640 04-15

MONOAMINE-OXIDASE-INHIBITION
NEUROTRANSMITTER RELATED ADAPTATION IN THE CENTRAL-NERVOUS-SYSTEM FOLLOWING CHRONIC MONOAMINE-OXIDASE-INHIBITION.
000038 01-03

MONOAMINE-OXIDASE-INHIBITION AND BRAIN-AMINE METABOLISM AFTER ORAL TREATMENT WITH TOLOXATONE IN THE RAT.
000156 01-03

MONOAMINE-OXIDASE-INHIBITOR
COMBINED MONOAMINE-OXIDASE-INHIBITOR TRICYCLIC-ANTIDEPRESSANT TREATMENT: A PILOT-STUDY.
000644 01-09

THE DIFFERENTIAL NEUROCHEMICAL-BASES OF THE BEHAVIOURS ELICITED BY SEROTONERGIC-AGENTS AND BY THE COMBINATION OF A MONOAMINE-OXIDASE-INHIBITOR AND L-DOPA.
002976 03-04

MONOAMINE-OXIDASE-INHIBITORS
CORRELATION BETWEEN MONOAMINE-OXIDASE-INHIBITORS AND ANTICONVULSANTS.
000081 01-03

THE EFFECT OF MONOAMINE-OXIDASE-INHIBITORS ON FIRST-PASS METABOLISM OF TYRAMINE IN DOG INTESTINE.
000141 01-03

THE MONOAMINE-OXIDASE-INHIBITORS CLORGYLINE AND L DEPRENYL ALSO AFFECT THE UPTAKE OF DOPAMINE, NORADRENALINE AND SEROTONIN BY RAT-BRAIN SYNAPTOSOMAL PREPARATIONS.
000171 01-03

A NEW APPROACH TO THE ASSESSMENT OF THE POTENCY OF REVERSIBLE MONOAMINE-OXIDASE-INHIBITORS IN VIVO, AND ITS APPLICATION TO D-AMPHETAMINE, P METHOXYAMPHETAMINE AND HARMALINE.
000900 01-16

EFFECTS OF DIFFERENT MONOAMINE-OXIDASE-INHIBITORS ON RESPIRATORY ACTIVITY IN RATS WITH CHRONICALLY IMPAIRED CENTRAL SEROTONERGIC FUNCTION.
001389 02-03

DECREASE IN (3H) SEROTONIN BINDING IN RAT-BRAIN PRODUCED BY THE REPEATED ADMINISTRATION OF EITHER MONOAMINE-OXIDASE-INHIBITORS ON CENTRALLY-ACTING SEROTONIN AGONISTS.
001463 02-03

MONOAMINE-OXIDASE-INHIBITORS: PRESCRIPTION AND PATIENT MANAGEMENT.
002454 02-15

MONOAMINE-OXIDASES
DIFFERENCES IN ACTIVITY IN CEREBRAL METHYLTRANSFERASES AND MONOAMINE-OXIDASES BETWEEN AUDIOGENIC-SEIZURE SUSCEPTIBLE AND RESISTANT MICE AND DEERMICE.
000377 01-04

MONOAMINE-RECEPTOR
EFFECTS OF ELECTROCONVULSIVE-TREATMENT ON GROWTH-HORMONE SECRETION INDUCED BY MONOAMINE-RECEPTOR AGONISTS IN RESERPINE PRETREATED RATS.
002664 03-03

MONOAMINE-RECEPTORS
INTERACTIONS OF OXYPERTINE WITH RAT-BRAIN MONOAMINE-RECEPTORS.
000212 01-03

MONOAMINERGIC
TRANYLCYPROMINE STEREOISOMERS, MONOAMINERGIC NEUROTRANSMISSION AND BEHAVIOR. A MINIREVIEW.
000016 01-02

MONOAMINERGIC DENERVATION OF THE RAT HIPPOCAMPUS: MICROIONTOPHORETIC STUDIES OF PRESYNAPTIC AND POSTSYNAPTIC SUPERSENSITIVITY TO NOREPINEPHRINE AND SEROTONIN.
000068 01-03

EFFECTS OF CHRONIC-TREATMENT WITH L SULPIRIDE AND HALOPERIDOL ON CENTRAL MONOAMINERGIC MECHANISMS.
001240 02-03

NEUROPEPTIDES AND MONOAMINERGIC NEUROTRANSMITTERS: THEIR RELATION TO PAIN.
001497 02-03

DIFFERENTIAL-EFFECTS OF PHARMACOLOGICAL-AGENTS ACTING ON MONOAMINERGIC SYSTEMS ON DRUG-INDUCED ANOREXIA.
002533 02-17

ROLE OF MONOAMINERGIC SYSTEMS IN MORPHINE-INDUCED RESPIRATORY DEPRESSION.
002827 03-03

THE PHARMACOLOGICAL ANALYSIS OF MONOAMINERGIC MECHANISMS OF THE MEDIAL HYPOTHALAMUS IN FOOD PROCURING CONDITIONED REFLEXES IN RATS.
003100 03-04

THE EFFECT OF PHARMACOLOGICAL DESTRUCTION OF HYPOTHALAMIC MONOAMINERGIC STRUCTURES ON BODY-TEMPERATURE AND GAS-EXCHANGE DURING EXTREME COOLING.
004016 04-03

MONOAMINERGIC-INTERACTION
ON MONOAMINERGIC-INTERACTION WITH BEHAVIOUR MODIFYING PEPTIDE-HORMONES.
004700 04-17

MONOAMINERGIC-RECEPTOR
INFLUENCE OF A CHRONIC NEW POTENTIAL ANTIDEPRESSANT, DIMETHYLAMINOPROPYL-5-METHYL-3-PHENYL-1H-INDAZOLE (FS-32) AND ITS N DESMETHYLATED-COMPOUND (FS-97): TREATMENT ON MONOAMINERGIC-RECEPTOR SENSITIVITY IN THE RAT-BRAIN.
002787 03-03

MONOAMINES
RELATION BETWEEN THE EFFECTS OF ANTIDEPRESSANT-DRUGS ON THE UPTAKE OF MONOAMINES AND ON THE SPONTANEOUS ACTIVITY OF CENTRAL NEURONS.
000267 01-03

RELATIONSHIP BETWEEN DELTA9 TETRAHYDROCANNABINOL-INDUCED MOUSE-KILLING-BEHAVIOR ON THE RAT AND THE METABOLISM OF MONOAMINES IN THE BRAIN, PARTICULARLY THE OLFACTORY-BULB.
000472 01-04

MONOAMINES AND DEPRESSION: AN INTERIM REPORT. I. SEROTONIN AND SEROTONIN PRECURSORS.
000996 01-17

OPIOID MECHANISMS IN REGULATION OF CEREBRAL MONOAMINES IN VIVO.
001098 02-03

EFFECT OF LITHIUM ON STRESS-INDUCED CHANGES IN THE BRAIN LEVELS
OF MONOAMINES IN RATS.
001216 02-03
EFFECTS OF RAPHE-MAGNUS AND RAPHE-PALLIDUS LESIONS ON
MORPHINE-INDUCED ANALGESIA AND SPINAL-CORD MONOAMINES.
001420 02-03
EFFECTS OF 1,3 BIS-TETRAHYDRO-2-FURANYL-5-
FLUOROPYRIMIDINEDIONE (FD-1) ON THE CENTRAL-NERVOUS-SYSTEM:
1. EFFECTS OF MONOAMINES IN THE BRAIN.
001857 02-05
MONOAMINES, EPILEPSY AND SCHIZOPHRENIA.
002183 02-11
EFFECTS OF 4 AMINOPYRIDINE ON THE TURNOVER OF MONOAMINES IN
THE CENTRAL-NERVOUS-SYSTEM OF THE RAT.
002658 03-03
THE EFFECT OF MONOAMINES ON MOTONEURONS OF THE ISOLATED RAT
SPINAL-CORD.
002790 03-03
ULTRASTRUCTURAL LOCALIZATION OF MONOAMINES IN NERVE FIBERS
OF THE PINEAL-GLAND IN GOLDEN HAMSTERS.
003666 04-01
PROPERTIES OF THE OPTICAL-ISOMERS AND METABOLITES OF KETAMINE
ON THE HIGH-AFFINITY TRANSPORT AND CATABOLISM OF
MONOAMINES.
004009 04-03
EFFECTS OF TRICYCLIC-ANTIDEPRESSANTS ON TETRABENAZINE-INDUCED
DEPLETION OF BRAIN MONOAMINES IN RATS. 1. NOREPINEPHRINE.
004062 04-03
EFFECTS OF LITHIUM ON BEHAVIOUR AND CENTRAL MONOAMINES.
004110 04-04

MONOCLONAL
ANTI-THY-1-2 MONOCLONAL ANTIBODY LINKED TO RICIN IS A POTENT
CELL TYPE SPECIFIC TOXIN. (UNPUBLISHED PAPER).
001064 02-01

MONOCULAR
CORTICAL RECOVERY FROM EFFECTS OF MONOCULAR DEPRIVATION:
ACCELERATION WITH NOREPINEPHRINE AND SUPPRESSION WITH 6
HYDROXYDOPAMINE.
003024 03-04

MONOFLUORINATED
INTERACTIONS BETWEEN A MONOFLUORINATED ANALOGUE OF P
CHLOROAMPHETAMINE AND 5 HYDROXYTRYPTAMINE IN BRAIN.
003719 04-03

MONOFLUOROACETATE
AMMONIA AND DISINHIBITION IN CAT MOTOR-CORTEX BY AMMONIUM-
ACETATE, MONOFLUOROACETATE AND INSULIN-INDUCED
HYPOGLYCEMIA.
004276 04-05

MONOFLUOROMETHYLDOPA
FURTHER STUDIES ON THE INHIBITION OF MONOAMINE SYNTHESIS BY
MONOFLUOROMETHYLDOPA.
001128 02-03

MONOMETHYLHYDRAZINE
RELATION OF MONOMETHYLHYDRAZINE (MMH) SEIZURE THRESHOLDS
TO AFTERDISCHARGE THRESHOLDS WITH AMYGDALOID STIMULATION
IN CATS.
000474 01-04

MONOOXYGENATED
PLASMA AND BRAIN LEVELS OF DELTA6 THC AND SEVEN
MONOOXYGENATED METABOLITES CORRELATED TO THE CATALEPTIC-
EFFECT IN THE MOUSE.
001737 02-04

MONOSODIUM-GLUTAMATE
MONOSODIUM-GLUTAMATE: INCREASED NEUROTOXICITY AFTER
REMOVAL OF NEURONAL REUPTAKE SITES.
003889 04-03

MONOSUBSTANCE
TREATMENT OF ANXIOUS-DEPRESSED OUTPATIENTS WITH A FIXED
COMBINATION (NOMIFENSINE/CLOBAZAM) IN COMPARISON TO A
MONOSUBSTANCE (DOXEPINE).
002028 02-09

MONOSYNAPTIC
NONSEROTONERGIC DEPRESSION OF SPINAL MONOSYNAPTIC REFLEX
TRANSMISSION BY 5 HYDROXYTRYPTOPHAN.
002745 03-03
CANNABINOID-INDUCED ENHANCEMENT AND DEPRESSION OF CAT
MONOSYNAPTIC REFLEXES.
004040 04-03

MONOTHERAPY
ADVANTAGE OF MONOTHERAPY WITH CLOBAZAM IN THE TREATMENT
AND POSTTREATMENT OF ALCOHOLIC WITHDRAWAL.
002140 02-11
MONOTHERAPY OR POLYTHERAPY FOR EPILEPSY?
003366 03-11

MOOD
THE INFLUENCE OF LITHIUM-CARBONATE ON MOOD AND PERFORMANCE
IN HEALTHY SUBJECTS.
000711 01-11
THE EFFECT OF SMALL AND MODERATE DOSES OF D-AMPHETAMINE ON
HUNGER, MOOD, AND AROUSAL IN MAN.
000807 01-14

PHARMACOPSYCHOLOGICAL INVESTIGATION OF CHANGES IN MOOD
INDUCED BY DIPOTASSIUM-CHLORAZEPATE WITH AND WITHOUT
SIMULTANEOUS ALCOHOL ADMINISTRATION.
000825 01-14
THE RELATIONSHIP OF ALPHA AND DELTA EEG FREQUENCIES TO PAIN
AND MOOD IN FIBROSITIS-PATIENTS TREATED WITH CHLORPROMAZINE
AND L TRYPTOPHAN.
002152 02-11
MOOD AND BEHAVIORAL-EFFECTS OF PHYSOSTIGMINE ON HUMANS ARE
ACCOMPANIED BY ELEVATIONS IN PLASMA BETA ENDORPHIN AND
CORTISOL.
002280 02-13
DRUG PREFERENCE AND MOOD IN HUMANS: DIAZEPAM.
002334 02-14
DRUG PREFERENCE AND MOOD IN HUMANS: D-AMPHETAMINE.
002335 02-14
THE EFFECT OF DEPRENYL, A SELECTIVE MONOAMINE-OXIDASE-B-
INHIBITOR, ON SLEEP AND MOOD IN MAN.
002365 02-14
CORRELATED STUDY OF THE EFFECTS OF SE-5023 IN AN HYPOXIC
ATMOSPHERE ON QUANTIFIED EEG, VIGILANCE, MEMORY, AND
MOOD.
003440 03-14
DRUG PREFERENCE AND MOOD IN HUMANS: REPEATED ASSESSMENT OF
D-AMPHETAMINE.
003445 03-14
EFFECTS OF DEXTROAMPHETAMINE-SULFATE ON REPEATED ACQUISITION-
BEHAVIOR AND MOOD IN HUMANS: A PRELIMINARY REPORT.
003459 03-14
ON THE RELATIONSHIP BETWEEN MEASURES OBTAINED BY VIDEO-
ANALYSIS OF NONVERBAL-BEHAVIOR AND SELF-RATING OF MOOD.
004410 04-09
THE EFFECT OF FIVE TRICYCLIC-ANTIDEPRESSANTS ON SALIVARY FLOW
AND MOOD IN HEALTHY VOLUNTEERS.
004560 04-14

MOOD-DISORDER
EFFICACY OF LITHIUM IN TREATING MOOD-DISORDER OCCURRING AFTER
BRAINSTEM INJURY.
003354 03-11

MOOD-DISORDERS
CHRONIC MOOD-DISORDERS IN DEPRESSED-OUTPATIENTS: DIAGNOSIS
AND RESPONSE TO PHARMACOTHERAPY.
000624 01-09
THE PLACE OF SURVECTOR AMONG THE VARIOUS DRUGS USED IN
TREATMENT OF MOOD-DISORDERS.
001969 02-09

MOOD-SWING-PATTERNS
ANTIDEPRESSIVE TREATMENT AND MOOD-SWING-PATTERNS IN
ENDOGENOUS DEPRESSION.
000633 01-09

MORAVIAN
RESULTS OF TREATMENT BY MODITEN DEPOT IN OUTPATIENTS-WARDS IN
THE SOUTH MORAVIAN REGION.
004648 04-15

MORBIDITY
PSYCHIATRIC MORBIDITY AND PHYSICAL TOXICITY ASSOCIATED WITH
ADJUVANT CHEMOTHERAPY AFTER MASTECTOMY.
002433 02-15

MORPHICEPTIN
MORPHICEPTIN (NH4-TYR-PRO-PHE-PRO-CONH2): A POTENT AND
SPECIFIC AGONIST FOR MORPHINE MU-RECEPTORS.
003746 04-03

MORPHINANS
EFFECT OF THE POSITION OF THE PHENOLIC GROUP IN MORPHINANS ON
THEIR AFFINITY FOR OPIATE-RECEPTOR BINDING.
003702 04-02

MORPHINE
ENKEPHALIN LEVELS DECREASE IN RAT STRIATUM DURING MORPHINE
ABSTINENCE.
000027 01-03
THE EFFECTS OF MORPHINE ON THE ACTIVITY OF CERTAIN DORSAL-HORN
NEURONS OF THE SPINAL-CORD INVOLVED IN NOCICEPTIVE PROCESSES.
000028 01-03
MORPHINE EXERTS TESTOSTERONE-LIKE EFFECTS IN THE HYPOTHALAMUS
OF THE CASTRATED MALE RAT.
000051 01-03
SUPPRESSION OF EVOKED AND SPONTANEOUS RELEASE OF
NEUROTRANSMITTERS IN VIVO BY MORPHINE.
000058 01-03
REDUCTION OF OPIATE BINDING TO BRAINSTEM SLICES ASSOCIATED
WITH THE DEVELOPMENT OF TOLERANCE TO MORPHINE IN RATS.
000066 01-03
MORPHINE ACTS THROUGH ALPHA-ADRENERGIC AND SEROTONINERGIC
NEURONS TO STIMULATE GROWTH-HORMONE SECRETION IN THE DOG.
000088 01-03
EFFECT OF ACUTE ADMINISTRATION OF MORPHINE ON NEWLY
SYNTHESIZED 5 HYDROXYTRYPTAMINE IN SPINAL-CORD OF THE RAT.
000110 01-03

EFFECT OF MORPHINE ON CALCIUM UPTAKE BY LYSED SYNAPTOSOMES.
000117 01-03

EFFECTS OF MORPHINE AND OTHER CENTRALLY-ACTING DRUGS ON 3,4 DIHYDROXYPHENYLETHYLENE-GLYCOL-SULFATE (DOPEG-SO4) IN RAT-BRAIN.
000136 01-03

REDUCTION OF FETAL RAT SPINAL-CORD VOLUME FOLLOWING MATERNAL MORPHINE INJECTION.
000161 01-03

THE RELATIONSHIP BETWEEN MORPHINE, ASPARTIC-ACID AND L ASPARAGINASE IN RATS.
000169 01-03

DOES SYSTEMIC MORPHINE INCREASE DESCENDING INHIBITORY CONTROLS OF DORSAL-HORN NEURONES INVOLVED IN NOCICEPTION?
000175 01-03

EVIDENCE FOR A DIRECT INHIBITORY-EFFECT OF MORPHINE ON THE SECRETION OF POSTERIOR PITUITARY-HORMONES.
000193 01-03

BLOCKADE OF STRIATAL NEURONE RESPONSES TO MORPHINE BY AMINOPHYLLINE: EVIDENCE FOR ADENOSINE MEDIATION OF OPIATE ACTION.
000229 01-03

THE EFFECT OF MORPHINE ON PURINE AND ACETYLCHOLINE RELEASE FROM RAT-CEREBRAL-CORTEX: EVIDENCE FOR A PURINERGIC COMPONENT IN MORPHINES ACTION.
000234 01-03

REDUCTION OF VOLUNTARY MORPHINE CONSUMPTION FOLLOWING TREATMENT WITH ZIMELIDINE.
000253 01-03

EFFECTS OF MORPHINE AND NALOXONE ON PHASIC RELEASE OF LUTEINIZING-HORMONE AND FOLLICLE-STIMULATING-HORMONE (40849).
000298 01-03

EFFECTS OF L AND D AMINO-ACIDS ON ANALGESIA AND LOCOMOTOR-ACTIVITY OF MICE: THEIR INTERACTION WITH MORPHINE.
000336 01-04

MORPHINE EFFECTS UPON DISCRIMINATED APPROACH AND DISCRIMINATED AVOIDANCE IN RATS: ANTAGONISM BY NALOXONE.
000338 01-04

LETHAL SELF-ADMINISTRATION OF MORPHINE BY RATS.
000343 01-04

ADDICTIVE-AGENTS AND INTRACRANIAL-STIMULATION (ICS): MORPHINE, NALOXONE, AND PRESSING FOR AMYGDALOID ICS.
000371 01-04

MORPHINE VERSUS HALOPERIDOL CATALEPSY IN THE RAT: A BEHAVIORAL-ANALYSIS OF POSTURAL SUPPORT MECHANISMS.
000376 01-04

MORPHINE INJECTIONS INTO THE PERIAQUEDUCTAL PERIVENTRICULAR GRAY ATTENUATE SEPTAL HYPERREACTIVITY.
000390 01-04

CHANGES IN BRAIN N DEMETHYLATION AND OPIATE-RECEPTOR CONTENT CORRELATE WITH ANALGESIC EFFECTIVENESS OF MORPHINE.
000400 01-04

ANTINOCICEPTIVE-EFFECT OF MORPHINE, OPIOID ANALGESICS AND HALOPERIDOL INJECTED INTO THE CAUDATE-NUCLEUS OF THE RAT.
000414 01-04

EFFECTS OF MORPHINE, BETA ENDORPHIN AND NALOXONE ON CATECHOLAMINE LEVELS AND SEXUAL-BEHAVIOR IN THE MALE RAT.
000430 01-04

FIXED-RATIO SCHEDULES OF FOOD PRESENTATION AND STIMULUS-SHOCK TERMINATION: EFFECTS OF D-AMPHETAMINE, MORPHINE, AND CLOZAPINE.
000431 01-04

ANTINOCICEPTIVE COMPARISON OF QUIPAZINE AND MORPHINE.
000435 01-04

POSSIBLE MECHANISM FOR THE ENHANCED LETHALITY OF MORPHINE IN AGGREGATED MICE.
000437 01-04

MORPHINE ENHANCES ADENOSINE RELEASE FROM THE IN VIVO RAT-CEREBRAL-CORTEX.
000451 01-04

REWARDING AND AVERSIVE-EFFECTS OF MORPHINE: TEMPORAL AND PHARMACOLOGICAL-PROPERTIES.
000470 01-04

EFFECT OF MORPHINE IN COMBINATION WITH CHLORPROMAZINE AND HALOPERIDOL ON OPERANT-BEHAVIOR.
000486 01-04

PROCONVULSANT AND ANTICONVULSANT ACTION OF MORPHINE IN RATS.
000494 01-04

DOSE AND PHYSICAL-DEPENDENCE AS FACTORS IN THE SELF-ADMINISTRATION OF MORPHINE BY RATS.
000497 01-04

MORPHINE TREATMENT AT DIFFERENT INFANT AGES: INFLUENCE ON LATER MORPHINE EFFECTS IN RATS. (PH.D. DISSERTATION).
000511 01-05

THE ANALGESIC AND RESPIRATORY EFFECTS OF MEPTAZINOL, MORPHINE AND PENTAZOCINE IN THE RAT.
000516 01-05

ACUTE AND CHRONIC EFFECTS OF MORPHINE ON TRANSMEMBRANE POTENTIAL AND ON SHORT-CIRCUIT CURRENT IN ISOLATED TOAD SKIN: APPARENT MORPHINE-DEPENDENCE.
001176 02-03

MORPHINE AND SUPRASPINAL INHIBITION OF SPINAL NEURONES: EVIDENCE THAT MORPHINE DECREASES TONIC DESCENDING INHIBITION IN THE ANESTHETIZED CAT.
001203 02-03

SUBSTANCE-P, MORPHINE AND METHIONINE-ENKEPHALIN: EFFECTS ON SPONTANEOUS AND EVOKED NEURONAL FIRING IN THE NUCLEUS-RETICULARIS-GIGANTOCELLULARIS OF THE RAT.
001267 02-03

INFLUENCE OF MORPHINE ON MEMBRANE TURNOVER AND FUNCTION.
001280 02-03

BIPHASIC ACTIVITY OF MEMBRANE-BOUND ENZYMES IN BRAIN MITOCHONDRIA AND SYNAPTOSOMES DURING THE DEVELOPMENT OF TOLERANCE TO AND PHYSICAL-DEPENDENCE ON CHRONIC MORPHINE ADMINISTRATION TO RATS.
001285 02-03

INTERACTIONS BETWEEN MORPHINE AND THE OPIOID-LIKE PEPTIDES IN THE RAT VAS-DEFERENS.
001290 02-03

INHIBITORY ACTION OF MORPHINE ON THE RELEASE OF A BRADYKININ-LIKE SUBSTANCE AFTER SCIATIC-NERVE STIMULATION.
001293 02-03

MORPHINE AND ELECTROACUPUNCTURE: COMPARISON OF THE EFFECTS ON THE CORTICAL EVOKED-RESPONSES AFTER TOOTH-PULP STIMULATION IN RATS.
001294 02-03

THE EFFECT OF MORPHINE ON THE CONTENT OF SEROTONIN, 5 HYDROXYINDOLEACETIC-ACID AND SUBSTANCE-P IN THE NUCLEI RAPHE-MAGNUS AND RETICULARIS-GIGANTOCELLULARIS.
001328 02-03

AGE-RELATED CHANGES IN BODY-TEMPERATURE RESPONSES TO MORPHINE IN RATS.
001366 02-03

EFFECTS OF MORPHINE ON EVOKED-POTENTIALS RECORDED FROM THE AMYGDALA BY TOOTH-PULP STIMULATION IN CATS.
001379 02-03

SUPPRESSIVE EFFECT OF MORPHINE ON SERUM GONADOTROPIN LEVELS IN CASTRATED RATS.
001393 02-03

ALTERED LEVELS OF BETA ENDORPHIN FRAGMENTS AFTER CHRONIC MORPHINE TREATMENT OF GUINEA-PIG ILEUM IN VITRO AND IN VIVO.
001404 02-03

MORPHINE ANALGESIA FOLLOWING ITS INFUSION INTO DIFFERENT LIQUOR SPACES IN RAT-BRAIN.
001429 02-03

EFFECTS OF MORPHINE, PENTAZOCINE AND CYCLAZOCINE ALONE AND IN COMBINATION WITH NALOXONE ON ELECTRIC-SHOCK TITRATION IN THE SQUIRREL-MONKEY.
001611 02-04

EFFECTS OF MORPHINE WITHDRAWAL ON FOOD COMPETITION HIERARCHIES AND FIGHTING-BEHAVIOR IN RATS.
001632 02-04

EFFECTS OF MORPHINE, D-AMPHETAMINE, AND PENTOBARBITAL ON SHOCK AND LIGHT DISCRIMINATION PERFORMANCE IN RATS.
001639 02-04

AN ANALYSIS OF SOME PERCEPTUAL-EFFECTS OF MORPHINE, CHLORPROMAZINE, AND LSD.
001652 02-04

CONTRALATERAL CIRCLING-BEHAVIOUR INDUCED BY INTRANIGRAL INJECTION OF MORPHINE AND ENKEPHALIN ANALOGUE FK-33-824 IN RATS.
001669 02-04

ANALGESIC ACTION OF INTRATHECAL AND INTRACEREBRAL BETA ENDORPHIN IN RATS: COMPARISON WITH MORPHINE.
001691 02-04

MORPHINE ANALGESIA AFTER INTRATHECAL ADMINISTRATION OF A NARCOTIC AGONIST, CHLOROXYMORPHAMINE AND ANTAGONIST, CHLORNALTREXAMINE.
001695 02-04

OPIATE AND PEPTIDE INTERACTION: EFFECT OF ENKEPHALINS ON MORPHINE ANALGESIA.
001698 02-04

THE EFFECT OF MORPHINE, PIMOZIDE AND NALOXONE ON DISCRIMINATION BY RATS IN A SHOCK-ESCAPE-TEST.
001700 02-04

INTERACTION OF PROSTAGLANDINS AND THE EFFECTS OF MORPHINE AND AMPHETAMINE IN RATS. (PH.D. DISSERTATION).
001732 02-04

BRIEF SOCIAL-ISOLATION, PAIN RESPONSIVITY, AND MORPHINE ANALGESIA IN YOUNG RATS.
001744 02-04

DIFFERENTIAL-EFFECTS OF MORPHINE ON FOOD AND WATER INTAKE IN FOOD DEPRIVED AND FREELY-FEEDING RATS.
001765 02-04

EFFECTS OF CHLORDIAZEPOXIDE MORPHINE COMBINATIONS ON SPONTANEOUS LOCOMOTOR-ACTIVITY IN THREE INBRED STRAINS OF MICE.
001766 02-04

A COMPARISON BETWEEN THE EFFECTS OF MORPHINE ON THE REWARDING AND AVERSIVE-PROPERTIES OF LATERAL HYPOTHALAMIC AND CENTRAL GRAY STIMULATION.
001771 02-04

ON THE USE OF OPERANT-BEHAVIOR TO STUDY THE NEUROPSYCHOPHARMACOLOGY OF OPIATES WITH SPECIAL REFERENCE TO MORPHINE AND ITS RELATIONSHIP TO DOPAMINE IN THE CENTRAL-NERVOUS-SYSTEM.
001790 02-04

BIPHASIC-EFFECTS OF A POTENT ENKEPHALIN ANALOGUE D MET2-PRO5-ENKEPHALINAMIDE AND MORPHINE ON LOCOMOTOR-ACTIVITY IN MICE.
001799 02-04

THE EFFECT OF ASPIRIN AND PARACETAMOL ON THE INCREASED NALOXONE POTENCY INDUCED BY MORPHINE PRETREATMENT.
001824 02-04

INTRATHECAL MORPHINE IN MICE: A NEW TECHNIQUE.
001868 02-06

THE EFFECTS OF ACUTE AND CHRONIC MORPHINE ADMINISTRATION ON GABA-RECEPTOR BINDING.
002301 02-13

DISRUPTION OF 5 HYDROXYTRYPTAMINERGIC NEURONAL FUNCTION BLOCKS THE ACTION OF MORPHINE ON TUBEROINFUNDIBULAR DOPAMINERGIC NEURONS.
002700 03-03

A COMPARISON OF THE NEUROCHEMICAL-EFFECTS OF BUPRENORPHINE WITH THOSE OF MORPHINE AND HALOPERIDOL IN RATS.
002701 03-03

TEMPORAL AND ENVIRONMENTAL CUES IN CONDITIONED HYPOTHERMIA AND HYPERTHERMIA ASSOCIATED WITH MORPHINE.
002709 03-03

THE PARTICIPATION OF SUBSTANTIA-NIGRA ZONA-COMPACTA AND ZONA-RETICULATA NEURONS IN MORPHINE SUPPRESSION OF CAUDATE SPONTANEOUS NEURONAL ACTIVITIES IN THE RAT.
002718 03-03

DEVELOPMENT OF TOLERANCE TO THE EXCITATORY EFFECT OF MORPHINE AND CROSS-TOLERANCE TO THE INHIBITORY ACTION OF BETA ENDORPHIN IN THE ISOLATED RAT VAS-DEFERENS.
002756 03-03

COMPARATIVE-STUDY ON THE EFFECT OF MORPHINE AND THE OPIOID-LIKE PEPTIDES IN THE VAS-DEFERENS OF RODENTS: STRAIN AND SPECIES-DIFFERENCES, EVIDENCE FOR MULTIPLE OPIATE-RECEPTORS.
002757 03-03

EVIDENCE THAT THE OPIATE-RECEPTORS OF THE SUBSTANTIA-GELATINOSA CONTRIBUTE TO THE DEPRESSION, BY INTRAVENOUS MORPHINE, OF THE SPINAL TRANSMISSION OF IMPULSES IN UNMYELINATED PRIMARY AFFERENTS.
002767 03-03

ENHANCEMENT OF ETORPHINE BRAIN CONCENTRATIONS AND CHANGES IN ETORPHINE NALOXONE PA2 VALUES IN MORPHINE PRETREATED MICE.
002800 03-03

REDUCED TOLERANCE TO MORPHINE THERMOREGULATORY-EFFECTS IN SENESCENT RATS.
002822 03-03

ANTINOCICEPTIVE ACTION OF MORPHINE AND PENTAZOCINE ON UNIT ACTIVITY IN THE NUCLEUS-CENTRALIS-LATERALIS, NUCLEUS-VENTRALIS-LATERALIS AND NEARBY STRUCTURES OF THE CAT.
002837 03-03

MORPHINE WITHDRAWAL CAUSES SUBSENSITIVITY OF ADRENERGIC-RECEPTOR RESPONSE.
002838 03-03

INTERACTION BETWEEN THE EFFECTS OF STRESS AND MORPHINE ON BODY-TEMPERATURE IN RATS.
002906 03-03

EFFECTS OF MORPHINE AND NALORPHINE ON KAINIC-ACID-INDUCED HYPOTHERMIA IN RATS.
002921 03-03

ANALGESIC TOLERANCE PRODUCED BY MORPHINE PELLETS IS FACILITATED BY ANALGESIC TESTING.
002943 03-04

ENVIRONMENTAL MODULATION OF ANALGESIC TOLERANCE INDUCED BY MORPHINE PELLETS.
002944 03-04

INTRACRANIAL SELF-ADMINISTRATION OF MORPHINE INTO THE VENTRAL TEGMENTAL AREA IN RATS.
002960 03-04

EFFECTS OF MORPHINE AND CHLORDIAZEPOXIDE ON AVOIDANCE-BEHAVIOUR IN TWO INBRED STRAINS OF MICE.
002973 03-04

DOSE-RESPONSE STUDY OF THE PRECIPITATED ABSTINENCE-SYNDROME FOR MORPHINE: SYSTEMIC VS PERIAQUEDUCTAL GRAY NALOXONE. (PH.D. DISSERTATION).
002979 03-04

EXPLORATION AND MOTOR-ACTIVITY AFTER INTRAVENTRICULAR ACTH, MORPHINE AND NALOXONE.
002991 03-04

DYNORPHIN: A POSSIBLE MODULATORY PEPTIDE ON MORPHINE OR BETA ENDORPHIN ANALGESIA IN MOUSE.
002994 03-04

INFLUENCE OF MORPHINE ON THE DISCRIMINATIVE-STIMULUS PROPERTIES OF REWARDING LATERAL HYPOTHALAMIC STIMULATION. (PH.D. DISSERTATION).
003041 03-04

DISCRIMINATIVE RESPONSE CONTROL BY NALOXONE IN MORPHINE PRETREATED RATS.
003053 03-04

D PROPOXYPHENE ACTS DIFFERENTLY FROM MORPHINE ON OPIOID-RECEPTOR EFFECTOR MECHANISMS.
003062 03-04

RELAPSE TO NARCOTIC SELF-ADMINISTRATION IN MORPHINE POSTADDICT RATS: A POSSIBLE MODEL FOR PREDICTING ABUSE LIABILITY OF NARCOTIC-DRUGS. (PH.D. DISSERTATION).
003097 03-04

INTERACTIONS OF DIAZEPAM AND COCAINE IN THE MORPHINE TREATED RAT. (PH.D. DISSERTATION).
003115 03-04

DIFFERENCE IN THE DEVELOPMENT OF TOLERANCE TO MORPHINE AND D ALA2-METHIONINE-ENKEPHALIN IN C57 BL/6J AND DBA/2J MICE.
003126 03-05

THE USE OF A MORPHINE ANTAGONIST (NALOXONE) IN THE TREATMENT OF DISSOCIATIVE-SYNDROMES.
003194 03-08

METHADONE AND MORPHINE IN DEPRESSION.
003220 03-09

EFFECTS OF PENTAZOCINE AND NALORPHINE ON MOTILITY IN CHRONICALLY MORPHINE TREATED RATS: A POTENTIAL SUBSTITUTION TEST TO DETECT THE NARCOTIC CHARACTER OF A DRUG.
003555 03-16

COMPARATIVE ANALGESIC, BEHAVIORAL, AND DEPENDENCE PROPERTIES OF MORPHINE AND O METHOXYLPHENYLCARBAMOYLDIETHYLAMINOPROPIOPHENONEOXIME HCL.
003707 04-02

EFFECT OF CHRONIC MORPHINE TREATMENT ON THE INTERACTION BETWEEN THE PERIAQUEDUCTAL GREY AND THE NUCLEUS-RAPHE-MAGNUS OF THE RAT.
003727 04-03

MORPHICEPTIN (NH4-TYR-PRO-PHE-PRO-CONH2): A POTENT AND SPECIFIC AGONIST FOR MORPHINE MU-RECEPTORS.
003746 04-03

DIFFERENTIAL TOLERANCE TO THE EFFECTS OF MORPHINE ON EVOKED ACTIVITY IN THE HIPPOCAMPAL SLICE.
003760 04-03

MORPHINE DEPRESSES DORSAL-HORN NEURON RESPONSES TO CONTROLLED NOXIOUS AND NONNOXIOUS CUTANEOUS STIMULATION.
003782 04-03

LONG-TERM-TREATMENT OF RATS WITH MORPHINE DECREASES IN VITRO BIOSYNTHESIS IN AND RELEASE OF BETA ENDORPHIN FROM INTERMEDIATE/POSTERIOR LOBES OF PITUITARY.
003846 04-03

MORPHINE AND METHIONINE-ENKEPHALIN: DIFFERENT EFFECTS ON SPONTANEOUS AND EVOKED NEURONAL FIRING IN THE MESENCEPHALIC RETICULAR FORMATION OF THE RAT.
003849 04-03

ACTION OF ENKEPHALIN ANALOGUES AND MORPHINE ON BRAIN ACETYLCHOLINE RELEASE: DIFFERENTIAL REVERSAL BY NALOXONE AND AN OPIATE-PENTAPEPTIDE.
003863 04-03

EFFECTS OF MORPHINE AND CAFFEINE ON ADENOSINE RELEASE FROM RAT-CEREBRAL-CORTEX: IS CAFFEINE A MORPHINE ANTAGONIST.
003864 04-03

EFFECT OF MORPHINE AND NALOXONE ON LEU-ENKEPHALIN-LIKE IMMUNOREACTIVITY IN DOGS.
003894 04-03

THE BEHAVIORAL-EFFECTS OF D-AMPHETAMINE ALONE AND IN COMBINATION WITH ACUTE AND CHRONIC MORPHINE TREATMENTS IN RATS.
003915 04-03

EFFECTS OF ENKEPHALIN, MORPHINE, AND NALOXONE ON THE ELECTRICAL-ACTIVITY OF THE IN VITRO HIPPOCAMPAL SLICE PREPARATION.
003918 04-03

THE DOPAMINE-RECEPTOR COMPLEX: BIOCHEMICAL-CONSEQUENCES OF SUPERSENSITIVITY INDUCED BY TREATMENT WITH 6 HYDROXYDOPAMINE OR MORPHINE.
003958 04-03

ELECTROENCEPHALOGRAPHIC AND BEHAVIORAL-TOLERANCE TO AND CROSS-TOLERANCE BETWEEN D ALA2-METHIONINE-ENKEPHALINAMIDE AND MORPHINE IN THE RAT.
004038 04-03

THE EFFECTS OF PEPTIDES ON TOLERANCE TO THE CATALEPTIC-EFFECTS AND HYPOTHERMIC-EFFECTS OF MORPHINE IN THE RAT.
004072 04-04

EFFECTS OF PAIN, MORPHINE AND NALOXONE ON THE DURATION OF ANIMAL HYPNOSIS.
004081 04-04

CHOICE BETWEEN FOOD AND HEROIN: EFFECTS OF MORPHINE, NALOXONE, AND SECOBARBITAL.
004123 04-04

A SIGNAL-DETECTION-ANALYSIS OF MORPHINE EFFECTS ON THE RESPONSE BIAS OF RATS IN A TWO-SHOCK DISCRIMINATION TASK.
004124 04-04

EFFECTS OF LEVO ALPHA ACETYLMETHADOL (LAAM) ON MORPHINE SELF-ADMINISTRATION IN THE RAT.
004170 04-04

EVIDENCE FOR SEDATIVE EFFECTS OF LOW-DOSES OF MORPHINE IN MICE INVOLVING RECEPTORS INSENSITIVE TO NALOXONE.
004173 04-04

COMPARISON OF THE EFFECTS OF BETA ENDORPHIN AND MORPHINE ON EXPLORATORY-BEHAVIOUR AND SOCIOSEXUAL-BEHAVIOUR IN THE MALE RAT.
004178 04-04

MORPHINE DIFFERENTIALLY AFFECTS VENTRAL TEGMENTAL AND SUBSTANTIA-NIGRA BRAIN REWARD THRESHOLDS.
004187 04-04

MORPHINE ANTAGONISTS AND CONSUMMATORY-BEHAVIORS.
004196 04-04

OPIATE-DEPENDENCE FOLLOWING ACUTE INJECTIONS OF MORPHINE AND NALOXONE: THE ASSESSMENT OF VARIOUS WITHDRAWAL SIGNS.
004209 04-04

ANTAGONISM BY PHENOXYBENZAMINE AND PENTAZOCINE OF THE ANTINOCICEPTIVE-EFFECTS OF MORPHINE IN THE SPINAL-CORD.
004213 04-04

PHARMACOLOGICAL-ASPECTS OF SHAKING-BEHAVIOR PRODUCED BY TRH, AG-3-5, AND MORPHINE WITHDRAWAL.
004248 04-04

INTRATHECAL HIGH-DOSE MORPHINE PRODUCES HYPERALGESIA IN THE RAT.
004254 04-04

EATING-BEHAVIOR REVEALS RATS PREFERENCE FOR MORPHINE.
004257 04-04

ORAL SELF-ADMINISTRATION OF MORPHINE IN RATS.
004258 04-04

MORPHINE CHALLENGES IN LEVO ALPHA ACETYLMETHADOL (LAAM) POSTADDICT RATS.
004259 04-04

THE EFFECTS OF NEFOPAM ON BLOOD ACID BASE STATUS IN THE RABBIT: INTERACTIONS WITH MORPHINE IN THE MOUSE AND RABBIT.
004279 04-05

SUPPRESSION OF MORPHINE ABSTINENCE IN HEROIN ADDICTS BY BETA ENDORPHIN.
004489 04-11

EVENT-RELATED POTENTIAL CHANGES WITH MORPHINE IN NONADDICTED HUMANS.
004512 04-13

DOPAMINE AND 5 HT SUPERSENSITIVITY IN NONORGANIC CENTRAL PAIN AND IN MORPHINE ABSTINENCE: FORTUITOUS OR REAL ANALOGY?
004553 04-13

GLC/TLC ANALYSIS OF CODEINE AND MORPHINE IN URINE VIA DERIVATIZATION TECHNIQUES.
004687 04-16

SIMULTANEOUS DETERMINATION OF MORPHINE AND CODEINE IN BLOOD BY USE OF SELECT ION-MONITORING AND DEUTERATED INTERNAL STANDARDS.
004690 04-16

COMPARISON OF SPECTROFLUOROMETRIC AND GAS-CHROMATOGRAPHY/MASS-SPECTROMETRY PROCEDURES FOR THE QUANTITATION OF MORPHINE IN BLOOD AND BRAIN.
004692 04-16

MORPHINE-DEPENDENCE
ACUTE AND CHRONIC EFFECTS OF MORPHINE ON TRANSMEMBRANE POTENTIAL AND ON SHORT-CIRCUIT CURRENT IN ISOLATED TOAD SKIN: APPARENT MORPHINE-DEPENDENCE.
001176 02-03

MORPHINE-DEPENDENCE AND DOPAMINERGIC-ACTIVITY: TESTS OF CIRCLING RESPONSES IN RATS WITH UNILATERAL NIGRAL LESIONS.
001641 02-04

CHANGES OF PHYSICAL MORPHINE-DEPENDENCE IN RATS CHRONICALLY TREATED WITH DRUGS ACTING ON BRAIN 5 HYDROXYTRYPTAMINE.
001764 02-04

CYCLIC-AMP-INDUCED CHANGES IN THE ELECTROENCEPHALOGRAM AND IN BEHAVIOR DURING MORPHINE-DEPENDENCE AND ABSTINENCE IN THE RAT.
003078 03-04

MORPHINE-DEPENDENT
REDUCTION IN THE NUMBER OF SEROTONIN-RECEPTORS IN THE BRAINSTEM OF MORPHINE-DEPENDENT RATS: RELATION TO BLOCKADE OF NALOXONE PRECIPITATED JUMPING BY SEROTONIN AGONISTS.
000258 01-03

SCHEDULE-CONTROLLED BEHAVIOR IN THE MORPHINE-DEPENDENT AND POSTDEPENDENT RAT.
000349 01-04

DISCRIMINATIVE-STIMULUS EFFECTS OF NALTREXONE IN THE MORPHINE-DEPENDENT RAT.
000391 01-04

AN ELECTROMYOGRAPHIC-METHOD FOR THE ASSESSMENT OF NALOXONE-INDUCED ABSTINENCE IN MORPHINE-DEPENDENT RATS.
000433 01-04

SEXUAL-BEHAVIOUR OF MORPHINE-DEPENDENT AND ABSTINENT MALE RATS.
000438 01-04

NORADRENALINE RELEASE FROM SLICES OF THE THALAMUS OF NORMAL AND MORPHINE-DEPENDENT RATS.
001142 02-03

CHARACTERISTICS OF OSCILLATORY CONTRACTIONS ELICITED BY NALOXONE IN ILEUM PREPARATION FROM MORPHINE-DEPENDENT GUINEA-PIGS.
001491 02-03

INCREASE IN PLASMA CYCLIC-AMP LEVELS ELICITED BY NALOXONE IN MORPHINE-DEPENDENT MALE MICE.
002834 03-03

LOCOMOTOR-ACTIVITY IN MORPHINE-DEPENDENT AND POSTDEPENDENT RATS.
004077 04-04

MORPHINE-INDUCED
REVERSIBLE INACTIVATION OF RAPHE-MAGNUS NEURONS: EFFECTS ON NOCICEPTIVE THRESHOLD AND MORPHINE-INDUCED ANALGESIA.
000240 01-03

THE POSSIBILITY THAT A COMPONENT OF MORPHINE-INDUCED ANALGESIA IS CONTRIBUTED INDIRECTLY VIA THE RELEASE OF ENDOGENOUS OPIOIDS.
000263 01-03

A FURTHER CHARACTERIZATION OF THE DIFFERENTIAL-EFFECTS OF LEUCINE-ENKEPHALIN, METHIONINE-ENKEPHALIN AND THEIR ANALOGS ON MORPHINE-INDUCED ANALGESIA.
000311 01-03

EFFECTS OF RAPHE-MAGNUS AND RAPHE-PALLIDUS LESIONS ON MORPHINE-INDUCED ANALGESIA AND SPINAL-CORD MONOAMINES.
001420 02-03

ROLE OF BRAIN CATECHOLAMINES AND 5 HYDROXYTRYPTAMINE IN MORPHINE-INDUCED TEMPERATURE CHANGES IN NORMAL AND TOLERANT RATS AND MICE.
001476 02-03

EFFECT OF SELECTIVE DESTRUCTION OF SEROTONERGIC NEURONS IN NUCLEUS-RAPHE-MAGNUS ON MORPHINE-INDUCED ANTINOCICEPTION.
001724 02-04

EFFECT OF APOMORPHINE ON MORPHINE-INDUCED DECREASE IN LOCOMOTOR-ACTIVITY AND INCREASE IN DOPAMINE TURNOVER IN RATS.
001728 02-04

ACTH POTENTIATES MORPHINE-INDUCED CONDITIONED TASTE-AVERSION.
001781 02-04

THE EFFECTS OF INTRAVENTRICULAR 6 HYDROXYDOPAMINE AND 5,6 DIHYDROXYTRYPTAMINE ON MORPHINE-INDUCED LOCOMOTOR-STIMULATION.
001784 02-04

EPIDURAL MORPHINE-INDUCED CATATONIA.
002400 02-15

ROLE OF MONOAMINERGIC SYSTEMS IN MORPHINE-INDUCED RESPIRATORY DEPRESSION.
002827 03-03

CONDITIONED DRUG-EFFECTS OF D-AMPHETAMINE-INDUCED AND MORPHINE-INDUCED MOTOR ACCELERATION IN MICE: EXPERIMENTAL APPROACH FOR PLACEBO-EFFECT.
004128 04-04

POTENTIATION OF THE MORPHINE-INDUCED RESPIRATORY RATE DEPRESSION BY CAPTOPRIL.
004275 04-05

MORPHINE-LIKE
ON THE MECHANISM-OF-ACTION OF 2 AMINO-4-METHYLPYRIDINE, A MORPHINE-LIKE ANALGESIC.
001574 02-04

MORPHINE-LIKE STIMULUS EFFECTS IN THE MONKEY: OPIOIDS WITH ANTAGONIST PROPERTIES.
003086 03-04

MORPHINE-SULPHATE
A COMPARISON OF THE EFFECTS OF MORPHINE-SULPHATE AND NITROUS-OXIDE ANALGESIA ON CHRONIC PAIN STATES IN MAN.
003442 03-14

MORPHINE-TOLERANCE
EFFECTS OF PAVLOVIAN-CONDITIONING AND MIF-1 ON THE DEVELOPMENT OF MORPHINE-TOLERANCE IN RATS.
001327 02-03

DOSE SIZE AND INTERDOSE INTERVAL EFFECTS ON MORPHINE-TOLERANCE IN THE RAT. (PH.D. DISSERTATION).
003090 03-04

MORPHINE-TOLERANT
A DEMONSTRATION OF NALOXONE PRECIPITATED OPIATE WITHDRAWAL ON SINGLE NEURONES IN THE MORPHINE-TOLERANT/DEPENDENT RAT-BRAIN.
001234 02-03

MORPHINES
THE EFFECT OF MORPHINE ON PURINE AND ACETYLCHOLINE RELEASE
FROM RAT-CEREBRAL-CORTEX: EVIDENCE FOR A PURINERGIC
COMPONENT IN MORPHINES ACTION.
000234 01-03

MORPHINOMIMETICS
STEREOCHEMICAL ANATOMY OF MORPHINOMIMETICS.
002197 02-12

MORPHOGENETIC
EFFECTS OF SOME NOOTROPIC-DRUGS UPON THE EMBRYONIC
MORPHOGENETIC SYSTEMS.
000144 01-03

MORPHOLOGICAL
EFFECTS OF LITHIUM ON MORPHOLOGICAL CHARACTERISTICS OF
DISSOCIATED BRAIN CELLS IN CULTURE.
002765 03-03

MORPHOLOGICAL CHANGES IN RAT-BRAIN INDUCED BY L CYSTEINE
INJECTION IN NEWBORN ANIMALS.
002774 03-03

PATHOPHYSIOLOGICAL AND MORPHOLOGICAL CHANGES IN THE CNS
DURING LONG-TERM ADMINISTRATION OF HALOPERIDOL.
004633 04-15

MORPHOLOGICAL-STUDY
LYSERGIC-ACID-DIETHYLAMIDE: MORPHOLOGICAL-STUDY OF ITS EFFECT
ON SYNAPSES.
001315 02-03

EFFECT OF CHLORPROMAZINE ON CELL PROLIFERATION IN THE
DEVELOPING RAT-BRAIN. A COMBINED BIOCHEMICAL-STUDY AND
MORPHOLOGICAL-STUDY.
001407 02-03

MOTHERING-BEHAVIOR
EFFECTS OF 6 HYDROXYDOPAMINE AND AMPHETAMINE ON RAT
MOTHERING-BEHAVIOR AND OFFSPRING DEVELOPMENT.
000452 01-04

MOTHERS
INCREASED MESOLIMBIC 3H SPIROPERIDOL BINDING IN 4 WEEK OLD
OFFSPRING OF NURSING RAT MOTHERS TREATED WITH PENFLURIDOL.
000087 01-03

THE DIFFERENTIAL DOSE-EFFECTS OF METHYLPHENIDATE ON
HYPERACTIVE-CHILDREN AND THEIR MOTHERS. (PH.D.
DISSERTATION).
002143 02-11

BEHAVIOR AND LEARNING DIFFICULTIES IN CHILDREN OF NORMAL
INTELLIGENCE BORN TO ALCOHOLIC MOTHERS.
004658 04-15

MOTHERS-MILK
DRUG CONTENT OF THE MOTHERS-MILK.
002461 02-15

MOTILITY
PHARMACOMANOMETRIC-STUDIES OF COLONIC MOTILITY AS A GUIDE
TO THE CHEMOTHERAPY OF SCHIZOPHRENIA.
001930 02-08

AMPHETAMINE-INDUCED MOTILITY AND NIGROSTRIATAL IMPULSE FLOW.
003005 03-04

EFFECTS OF PENTAZOCINE AND NALORPHINE ON MOTILITY IN
CHRONICALLY MORPHINE TREATED RATS: A POTENTIAL SUBSTITUTION
TEST TO DETECT THE NARCOTIC CHARACTER OF A DRUG.
003555 03-16

MOTIVATED
AMYGDALA OPIATE-SENSITIVE MECHANISMS INFLUENCE FEAR
MOTIVATED RESPONSES AND MEMORY PROCESSES FOR AVERSIVE-
EXPERIENCES. (UNPUBLISHED PAPER).
001628 02-04

BASAL GANGLIA DOPAMINERGIC CONTROL OF SENSORIMOTOR
FUNCTIONS RELATED TO MOTIVATED BEHAVIOR.
002815 03-03

MOTONEURONES
EXCITATORY AND INHIBITORY-ACTIONS OF IBOTENIC-ACID ON FROG
SPINAL MOTONEURONES IN VITRO.
002841 03-03

MOTONEURONS
THE EFFECT OF MONOAMINES ON MOTONEURONS OF THE ISOLATED RAT
SPINAL-CORD.
002790 03-03

VOLTAGE CLAMP STUDY OF CAT SPINAL MOTONEURONS DURING
STRYCHNINE-INDUCED SEIZURES.
002886 03-03

MOTOR
PHARMACOLOGICAL EVIDENCE ON THE SPECIALIZATION OF CNS
MECHANISMS RESPONSIBLE FOR MOTOR ACT INHIBITION BY AVERSIVE
EVENTS.
002671 03-03

EFFECT OF SODIUM-VALPROATE ON MOTOR FUNCTION REGULATED BY
THE ACTIVATION OF GABA-RECEPTORS.
003033 03-04

CONDITIONED DRUG-EFFECTS OF D-AMPHETAMINE-INDUCED AND
MORPHINE-INDUCED MOTOR ACCELERATION IN MICE: EXPERIMENTAL
APPROACH FOR PLACEBO-EFFECT.
004128 04-04

MOTOR-ACTIVITY
EFFECTS OF DIPHENYLHYDANTOIN ON SPONTANEOUS MOTOR-ACTIVITY.
000284 01-03

MONOAMINE REPLACEMENT AFTER RESERPINE: CATECHOLAMINERGIC
AGONISTS RESTORE MOTOR-ACTIVITY BUT PHENYLETHYLAMINE
RESTORES ATROPINE-RESISTANT NEOCORTICAL LOW VOLTAGE FAST-
ACTIVITY.
000309 01-03

OPIATE-RECEPTORS MAY MEDIATE THE SUPPRESSIVE BUT NOT THE
EXCITATORY ACTION OF ACTH ON MOTOR-ACTIVITY IN RATS.
000337 01-04

EFFECTS OF THIORIDAZINE ON APOMORPHINE-ELICITED STEREOTYPIC-
BEHAVIOR AND MOTOR-ACTIVITY.
000424 01-04

N PENTYLAMINE: EFFECT ON MOTOR-ACTIVITY OF MICE.
000500 01-04

MOTOR-ACTIVITY AND ROTATIONAL-BEHAVIOR AFTER ANALOGS OF
COCAINE: CORRELATION WITH DOPAMINE UPTAKE BLOCKADE.
001650 02-04

CHRONIC DELTA9 TETRAHYDROCANNABINOL IN RATS: EFFECT ON
SOCIAL-INTERACTIONS, MOUSE-KILLING, MOTOR-ACTIVITY,
CONSUMMATORY-BEHAVIOR, AND BODY-TEMPERATURE.
001722 02-04

SPONTANEOUS MOTOR-ACTIVITY IN RATS GIVEN REPEATEDLY BETA-
SYMPATHOMIMETICS — ISOPRENALINE AND SALBUTAMOL.
001804 02-04

EFFECT OF P CHLOROPHENYLALANINE AND TRYPTOPHAN ON SLEEP, EEG
AND MOTOR-ACTIVITY IN THE RAT.
002958 03-04

EXPLORATION AND MOTOR-ACTIVITY AFTER INTRAVENTRICULAR ACTH,
MORPHINE AND NALOXONE.
002991 03-04

THE EFFECT OF AMYGDALA KINDLING ON SPONTANEOUS AND COCAINE-
INDUCED MOTOR-ACTIVITY AND LIDOCAINE SEIZURES.
003067 03-04

MODIFICATION OF MOTOR-ACTIVITY, PASSIVE-AVOIDANCE
CONDITIONING AND EVOKED-POTENTIALS BY MICROINJECTIONS OF
STRYCHNINE IN BOTH CAUDATE-NUCLEI IN CATS.
003101 03-04

INTRANIGRAL INJECTION OF CAPSAICIN ENHANCES MOTOR-ACTIVITY
AND DEPLETES NIGRAL 5 HYDROXYTRYPTAMINE BUT NOT SUBSTANCE-
P.
004100 04-04

LITHIUM AND MOTOR-ACTIVITY OF ANIMALS: EFFECTS AND POSSIBLE
MECHANISM-OF-ACTION.
004222 04-04

MOTOR-BEHAVIOR
HEROIN, BUT NOT LEVORPHANOL, PRODUCES EXPLOSIVE MOTOR-
BEHAVIOR IN NALOXONE TREATED RATS.
001579 02-04

MOTOR-CORTEX
MAPPING OF DYSKINETIC-MOVEMENTS INDUCED BY LOCAL APPLICATION
OF PICROTOXIN OR () GAMMA ACETYLENIC-GABA ON THE RAT
MOTOR-CORTEX.
000458 01-04

AMMONIA AND DISINHIBITION IN CAT MOTOR-CORTEX BY AMMONIUM-
ACETATE, MONOFLUOROACETATE AND INSULIN-INDUCED
HYPOGLYCEMIA.
004276 04-05

MOTOR-DEPRESSION
MOTOR-DEPRESSION AND HEAD-TWITCHES INDUCED BY IP INJECTION OF
GABA.
001788 02-04

MOTOR-EFFECTS
MOTOR-EFFECTS OF SEROTONIN IN THE CENTRAL-NERVOUS-SYSTEM.
000941 01-17

MOTOR-LEARNING
MOTOR-LEARNING ABILITIES IN SUBJECTS TREATED WITH LITHIUM-SALTS
AND TRICYCLIC-ANTIDEPRESSANTS.
002058 02-09

MOTOR-REFLEXES
EFFECT OF CHOLINE ON CONDITIONED FOOD MOTOR-REFLEXES IN CATS.
001731 02-04

MOTOR-RESPONSE
GASTRIC AND PYLORIC MOTOR-RESPONSE TO SYMPATHETIC-NERVE
STIMULATION AFTER CHEMICAL SYMPATHECTOMY. (UNPUBLISHED
PAPER).
001337 02-03

MOULDS
DEVELOPMENTALLY REGULATED LECTINS IN SLIME MOULDS AND CHICK
TISSUES — ARE THEY CELL ADHESION MOLECULES?
003724 04-03

MOUSE-BRAIN
THE CONVERSION OF (3H)TRYPTOPHAN TO 5 (3H)HYDROXYTRYPTAMINE
IN MOUSE-BRAIN FOLLOWING DEPLETION OF PHENYLALANINE AND
TYROSINE.
000148 01-03

CHANGES IN MOUSE-BRAIN DIAZEPAM-RECEPTOR BINDING AFTER
PHENOBARBITAL ADMINISTRATION.
000281 01-03
REGULATION OF THE STATE OF PHOSPHORYLATION OF SPECIFIC
NEURONAL PROTEINS IN MOUSE-BRAIN BY IN VIVO ADMINISTRATION
OF ANESTHETIC AND CONVULSANT-AGENTS.
000291 01-03
UPTAKE OF PIPERIDINE AND PIPECOLIC-ACID BY SYNAPTOSOMES FROM
MOUSE-BRAIN.
001396 02-03
EFFECT OF ANTINOCICEPTIVE DOSES OF OXOTREMORINE ON MOUSE-
BRAIN ACETYLCHOLINE TURNOVER-RATE.
001513 02-03
THE PHARMACOLOGICAL RELEVANCE OF THE COCAINE BINDING-SITE IN
MOUSE-BRAIN.
001772 02-04
QUANTITATIVE STUDY OF THE DISTRIBUTION OF LITHIUM IN THE MOUSE-
BRAIN FOR VARIOUS DOSES OF LITHIUM GIVEN TO THE ANIMAL.
002299 02-13
THE EFFECT OF PHENCYCLIDINE ON DOPAMINE METABOLISM IN THE
MOUSE-BRAIN.
002766 03-03
AMITRIPTYLINE: LONG-TERM-TREATMENT ELEVATES ALPHA-ADRENERGIC
AND MUSCARINIC-RECEPTOR BINDING IN MOUSE-BRAIN.
002875 03-03
CHARACTERIZATION OF THE ISOLATED PERFUSED MOUSE-BRAIN AS A
SYSTEM FOR NEUROCHEMICAL-STUDIES.
003146 03-06

MOUSE-KILLING
5,7 DIHYDROXYTRYPTAMINE-INDUCED MOUSE-KILLING AND
BEHAVIORAL-REVERSAL WITH VENTRICULAR ADMINISTRATION OF
SEROTONIN IN RATS.
001562 02-04
CHRONIC DELTA9 TETRAHYDROCANNABINOL IN RATS: EFFECT ON
SOCIAL-INTERACTIONS, MOUSE-KILLING, MOTOR-ACTIVITY,
CONSUMMATORY-BEHAVIOR, AND BODY-TEMPERATURE.
001722 02-04

MOUSE-KILLING-BEHAVIOR
RELATIONSHIP BETWEEN DELTA9 TETRAHYDROCANNABINOL-INDUCED
MOUSE-KILLING-BEHAVIOR ON THE RAT AND THE METABOLISM OF
MONOAMINES IN THE BRAIN, PARTICULARLY THE OLFACTORY-BULB.
000472 01-04

MOUTH
TREATMENT OF DRUG-INDUCED DRYNESS OF MOUTH IN PSYCHIATRIC-
PATIENTS — A CONTROLLED-COMPARATIVE-STUDY.
000799 01-13

MOVEMENT
EFFECTS OF LEAD ON MOVEMENT OF ALBUMIN INTO BRAIN.
000076 01-03
RESERPINE ABOLISHES MOVEMENT CORRELATED ATROPINE-RESISTANT
NEOCORTICAL LOW VOLTAGE FAST-ACTIVITY.
000310 01-03
EFFECTS OF HEMICHOLINIUM-3 AND CHOLINE ON HIPPOCAMPAL
ELECTRICAL-ACTIVITY DURING IMMOBILITY VS. MOVEMENT.
001438 02-03
SENSORY AND ASSOCIATIVE-EFFECTS OF LSD ON CLASSICAL APPETITIVE-
CONDITIONING OF THE RABBIT JAW MOVEMENT RESPONSE.
001637 02-04

MOVEMENT-DISORDERS
TARDIVE-DYSKINESIA AND OTHER MOVEMENT-DISORDERS IN CHILDREN
TREATED WITH PSYCHOTROPIC-DRUGS.
000849 01-15
EFFECTS OF CHOLINE CONTAINING COMPOUNDS ON TARDIVE-DYSKINESIA
AND OTHER MOVEMENT-DISORDERS.
000942 01-17
TARDIVE-DYSKINESIA AND OTHER DRUG-INDUCED MOVEMENT-
DISORDERS AMONG HANDICAPPED CHILDREN AND YOUTH.
004614 04-15
LITHIUM-CARBONATE IN THE TREATMENT OF MOVEMENT-DISORDERS. A
CRITICAL REVIEW.
004668 04-15

MOVEMENTS
ABNORMAL MOVEMENTS INDUCED BY PSYCHOTROPIC-DRUGS.
004652 04-15

MOXESTROL
EFFECT OF MOXESTROL ON HALOPERIDOL-INDUCED CHANGES IN
STRIATAL ACETYLCHOLINE LEVELS AND DOPAMINE TURNOVER.
001218 02-03

MRNA
CELL-FREE TRANSLATION OF FREE AND MEMBRANE-BOUND POLYSOMES
AND POLYADENYLATED MRNA FROM RABBIT BRAIN FOLLOWING
ADMINISTRATION OF D LYSERGIC-ACID-DIETHYLAMIDE IN VIVO.
003832 04-03

MU
ACTIONS OF ENKEPHALIN, MU AND PARTIAL AGONIST ANALGESICS ON
ACETYLCHOLINE TURNOVER IN RAT-BRAIN.
001541 02-03
INTERCONVERTING MU AND DELTA-FORMS OF TYPE-1 OPIATE-RECEPTORS
IN THE RAT STRIATAL PATCHES.
003737 04-03

ACTIONS OF MU, KAPPA, SIGMA, DELTA AND AGONIST/ANTAGONIST
OPIATES ON STRIATAL DOPAMINERGIC FUNCTION.
004053 04-03

MU-RECEPTORS
EFFECTS OF CHANGES IN THE STRUCTURE OF ENKEPHALINS AND OF
NARCOTIC ANALGESIC-DRUGS ON THEIR INTERACTIONS WITH MU-
RECEPTORS AND DELTA-RECEPTORS.
000168 01-03
MU-RECEPTORS AND DELTA OPIATE-RECEPTORS: CORRELATION WITH
HIGH-AFFINITY AND LOW AFFINITY-OPIATE BINDING-SITES.
001554 02-03
MORPHICEPTIN (NH4-TYR-PRO-PHE-PRO-CONH2): A POTENT AND
SPECIFIC AGONIST FOR MORPHINE MU-RECEPTORS.
003746 04-03

MULTIBARRELED
PHYSICAL AND PHYSIOLOGICAL CHARACTERISTICS OF MICROPRESSURE
EJECTION OF DRUGS FROM MULTIBARRELED PIPETTES.
002502 02-16

MULTICENTER-STUDY
INTRAMUSCULAR HALOPERIDOL-DECANOATE FOR NEUROLEPTIC
MAINTENANCE-THERAPY: EFFICACY, DOSAGE SCHEDULE AND PLASMA
LEVELS: AN OPEN MULTICENTER-STUDY.
000758 01-13
TREATMENT OF ASTHENO-DEPRESSIVE-DISORDERS WITH MINAPRINE
(CANTOR). MULTICENTER-STUDY OF 248 CASES EVALUATED WITH THE
FATIGUE STUDY GROUPS NO. 4 CLINICAL-SCALE.
001980 02-09

MULTICENTER-TRIAL
FACTORS WHICH AFFECT ANTIDEPRESSANT-DRUG RESPONSE IN A
MULTICENTER-TRIAL.
003239 03-09

MULTICENTER-TRIALS
METHODS OF MULTICENTER-TRIALS IN PSYCHIATRY -- PART I: REVIEW.
002483 02-16

MULTICENTRE-STUDY
MULTICENTRE-STUDY WITH VILOXAZINE (VIVALAN) IN DEPRESSED-
PATIENTS.
004375 04-09

MULTICENTRE-TRIAL
A DOUBLE-BLIND MULTICENTRE-TRIAL COMPARING THE EFFICACY AND
SIDE-EFFECTS OF MIANSERIN AND CHLORIMIPRAMINE IN DEPRESSED-
INPATIENTS AND DEPRESSED-OUTPATIENTS.
004395 04-09

MULTICLINICAL-STUDY
RESULTS OF CLINICAL-TESTS OF VILOXAZINE (VIVALAN ICI): PART OF A
MULTICLINICAL-STUDY.
002006 02-09

MULTIDIMENSIONAL
MULTIDIMENSIONAL ANALYSES OF BEHAVIOR IN MICE TREATED WITH
ALPHA ENDORPHIN.
003020 03-04
A SYMPTOM-PROFILE-ANALYSIS OF ANTIPSYCHOTIC-DRUG TREATMENT:
NONPARAMETRIC MULTIDIMENSIONAL TECHNIQUE.
003196 03-08

MULTIINSTITUTIONAL-STUDY
MULTIINSTITUTIONAL-STUDY ON THE TERATOGENICITY AND FETAL
TOXICITY OF ANTIEPILEPTIC-DRUGS: A REPORT OF A COLLABORATIVE-
STUDY GROUP IN JAPAN.
002442 02-15

MULTIPLE-DOSE
SINGLE-DOSE VERSUS MULTIPLE-DOSE COMPARATIVE-TRIAL OF
DESIPRAMINE-HYDROCHLORIDE: A DOUBLE-PLACEBO METHOD.
002059 02-10

MULTIPLE-DOSES
DISPOSITION OF (3H) PHENCYCLIDINE IN THE RAT AFTER SINGLE-DOSES
AND MULTIPLE-DOSES.
001375 02-03

MULTIPLE-SCHEDULE
INFLUENCE OF INTRAVENOUS SELF-ADMINISTERED PSYCHOMOTOR
STIMULANTS ON PERFORMANCE OF RHESUS-MONKEYS IN A MULTIPLE-
SCHEDULE PARADIGM.
001655 02-04

MULTIVARIATE
ASSESSMENT OF MULTIVARIATE RELATIONSHIPS IN REACTIVITY OF
PATIENTS RECEIVING LITHIUM THERAPY.
000819 01-14
MULTIVARIATE APPROACHES APPLIED TO STUDIES OF NOREPINEPHRINE
AND SEROTONIN UPTAKE.
001460 02-03
EFFECTS OF SINGLE-ORAL-DOSAGES OF STEROIDS ON HUMAN EEG
BASELINE CROSSING T-SCORES SHOWN BY MULTIVARIATE STATISTICS
AND STANDARD PROFILES.
002239 02-13
A MULTIVARIATE ANALYSIS OF THE INFRARED SPECTRA OF DRUGS OF
ABUSE.
004688 04-16

MURINE
NEURONAL LOCALIZATION OF BENZODIAZEPINE-RECEPTORS IN THE
MURINE CEREBELLUM.
000902 03-03

MUSCARINE
THE PHARMACOLOGY OF AGGRESSIVE-BEHAVIOURAL-PHENOMENA
ELICITED BY MUSCARINE INJECTED INTO THE CEREBRAL VENTRICLES OF
CONSCIOUS CATS.
001569 02-04

MUSCARINIC
DIFFERENTIAL REGULATION OF MUSCARINIC AGONIST BINDING-SITES
FOLLOWING CHRONIC CHOLINESTERASE INHIBITION.
000279 01-03
INTRACELLULAR OBSERVATIONS ON THE EFFECTS OF MUSCARINIC
AGONISTS ON RAT SYMPATHETIC NEURONES.
001143 02-03
THE BINDING OF SOME ANTIDEPRESSANT-DRUGS TO BRAIN MUSCARINIC
ACETYLCHOLINE-RECEPTORS.
001253 02-03
THE REGULATION OF CARDIAC MUSCARINIC CHOLINERGIC-RECEPTORS BY
ISOPROTERENOL.
001441 02-03
COMPARATIVE-STUDY OF AGGRESSIVE-BEHAVIOUR AFTER INJECTION OF
CHOLINOMIMETICS, ANTICHOLINESTERASES, NICOTINIC, AND
MUSCARINIC GANGLIONIC STIMULANTS INTO THE CEREBRAL
VENTRICLES OF CONSCIOUS CATS: FAILURE OF NICOTINIC-DRUGS TO
EVOKE AGGRESSION.
001568 02-04
MUSCARINIC ACETYLCHOLINE-RECEPTOR. (UNPUBLISHED PAPER).
002667 03-03
EFFECT OF KAINIC-ACID LESIONS ON MUSCARINIC AGONIST RECEPTOR
SUBTYPES IN RAT STRIATUM.
002679 03-03
AN ENHANCED SENSITIVITY OF MUSCARINIC CHOLINERGIC-RECEPTOR
ASSOCIATED WITH DOPAMINERGIC-RECEPTOR SUBSENSITIVITY AFTER
CHRONIC ANTIDEPRESSANT TREATMENT.
002788 03-03
BRAIN MUSCARINIC CHOLINERGIC-RECEPTOR BINDING IN ROMAN HIGH-
AVOIDANCE AND LOW-AVOIDANCE RATS.
002852 03-03
PHARMACOLOGIC EVIDENCE FOR A TONIC MUSCARINIC INHIBITORY
INPUT TO THE EDINGER-WESTPHAL NUCLEUS IN THE DOG.
002889 03-03
A COMPARISON OF HUMAN MUSCARINIC CHOLINERGIC-RECEPTOR
RESPONSE TO A NUMBER OF PSYCHOTROPICS UTILIZING THE
RADIOLABELED ANTAGONIST, (3H) QUINUCLIDINYL-BENZILATE. (PH.D.
DISSERTATION).
002918 03-03
POSSIBLE MUSCARINIC CHOLINERGIC MEDIATION OF PATTERNED
AGGRESSIVE REFLEXES IN THE CAT.
004153 04-04
PSYCHOTHERAPEUTIC-DRUGS, HISTAMINE H1-RECEPTORS AND
MUSCARINIC ACETYLCHOLINE-RECEPTORS.
004737 04-17

MUSCARINIC-CHOLINOCEPTOR
CHRONIC SYMPATHETIC DENERVATION INCREASES MUSCARINIC-
CHOLINOCEPTOR BINDING IN THE RAT SUBMAXILLARY-GLAND.
000235 01-03

MUSCARINIC-CHOLINOCEPTORS
THE INTERACTION OF TRAZODONE WITH RAT-BRAIN MUSCARINIC-
CHOLINOCEPTORS.
003855 04-03

MUSCARINIC-RECEPTOR
THE EFFECTS OF MUSCARINIC-RECEPTOR BLOCKERS ON THE TURNOVER-
RATE OF ACETYLCHOLINE IN VARIOUS REGIONS OF THE RAT-BRAIN.
000328 01-03
INCREASED MUSCARINIC-RECEPTOR BINDING IN RAT-FOREBRAIN AFTER
SCOPOLAMINE.
001351 02-03
EVIDENCE THAT NORADRENALINE MODULATES THE INCREASE IN
STRIATAL DOPAMINE METABOLISM INDUCED BY MUSCARINIC-
RECEPTOR STIMULATION.
001518 02-03
FORNIX LESION PREVENTS AN ORGANOPHOSPHATE-INDUCED DECREASE
IN MUSCARINIC-RECEPTOR LEVEL IN RAT HIPPOCAMPUS.
001833 02-05
AMITRIPTYLINE: LONG-TERM-TREATMENT ELEVATES ALPHA-ADRENERGIC
AND MUSCARINIC-RECEPTOR BINDING IN MOUSE-BRAIN.
002875 03-03
INVOLVEMENT OF CALCIUM CHANNELS IN SHORT-TERM
DESENSITIZATION OF MUSCARINIC-RECEPTOR MEDIATED CYCLIC-GMP
FORMATION IN MOUSE NEUROBLASTOMA CELLS.
003783 04-03
ISOMERIZATION OF THE MUSCARINIC-RECEPTOR ANTAGONIST COMPLEX.
003860 04-03
MUSCARINIC-RECEPTOR: MULTIPLE SITES OR UNITARY CONCEPT?
003896 04-03

MUSCARINIC-RECEPTOR-MEDIATED
DEMONSTRATION OF A MUSCARINIC-RECEPTOR-MEDIATED CYCLIC-GMP-
DEPENDENT HYPERPOLARIZATION OF THE MEMBRANE POTENTIAL OF

MOUSE NEUROBLASTOMA CELLS USING
(3H)TETRAPHENYLPHOSPHONIUM.
004049 04-03

MUSCARINIC-RECEPTORS
(3H)QUINUCLIDINYL-BENZILATE BINDING TO MUSCARINIC-RECEPTORS
AND (3H)WB-4101 BINDING TO ALPHA-ADRENERGIC-RECEPTORS IN
RABBIT IRIS: COMPARISON OF RESULTS IN SLICES AND MICROSOMAL
FRACTIONS.
000299 01-03
INHIBITION BY LOCAL ANESTHETICS, PHENTOLAMINE AND PROPRANOLOL
OF (3H)QUINUCLIDINYL-BENZYLATE BINDING TO CENTRAL
MUSCARINIC-RECEPTORS.
001097 02-03
MUSCARINIC-RECEPTORS IN RAT SYMPATHETIC GANGLIA.
001144 02-03
PERSISTENT EFFECTS OF HIGH-CONCENTRATIONS OF CHLORPROMAZINE
ON 3H PROPYLBENZILYLCHOLINE-MUSTARD BINDING TO MUSCARINIC-
RECEPTORS IN GUINEA-PIG INTESTINAL-MUSCLE STRIPS.
001266 02-03
INTRINSIC CHOLINERGIC EXCITATION IN THE RAT NEOSTRIATUM:
NICOTINIC AND MUSCARINIC-RECEPTORS.
001374 02-03
INTERACTION OF THE TRICYCLIC-ANTIDEPRESSANT AMITRIPTYLINE WITH
PREJUNCTIONAL ALPHA AND MUSCARINIC-RECEPTORS IN THE DOG
SAPHENOUS VEIN.
003756 04-03
THE HIGH-AFFINITY CHOLINE UPTAKE SYSTEM WITH RESPECT TO THE
MUSCARINIC-RECEPTORS USING A SYNAPTOSOMAL FRACTION
ABUNDANT IN PRESYNAPTIC MEMBRANES.
004028 04-03
THE INTERACTION OF AMINE LOCAL ANESTHETICS WITH MUSCARINIC-
RECEPTORS.
004031 04-03

MUSCIMOL
GABAERGIC ACTIONS OF THIP IN VIVO AND IN VITRO: A COMPARISON
WITH MUSCIMOL AND GABA.
000319 01-03
INHIBITION BY ARYLSULPHATASE A OF NA-INDEPENDENT (3H) GABA
AND (3H) MUSCIMOL BINDING TO BOVINE CEREBELLAR SYNAPTIC
MEMBRANES.
001208 02-03
PHYSIOLOGICAL-STUDIES AND BEHAVIORAL-STUDIES WITH MUSCIMOL.
002538 02-17
NA-INDEPENDENT BINDING OF (3H)GABA AND (3H)MUSCIMOL TO
SUBCELLULAR PARTICLES OF NEURAL PRIMARY CULTURES AND WHOLE
BRAIN.
002699 03-03
CORRELATION OF (14C)MUSCIMOL CONCENTRATION IN RAT-BRAIN WITH
ANTICONVULSANT ACTIVITY.
003045 03-04
DETERMINATION OF GABA LEVELS BY A (3H)MUSCIMOL RADIORECEPTOR
ASSAY.
003135 03-06
SOME BARBITURATES ENHANCE THE EFFECT OF MUSCIMOL ON
DOPAMINE TURNOVER IN THE RAT RETINA.
003873 04-03
BINDING OF (3H) MUSCIMOL, A POTENT GAMMA AMINOBUTYRIC-ACID-
RECEPTOR AGONIST, TO MEMBRANES OF THE BOVINE RETINA.
003954 04-03
THE INSENSITIVITY OF DEVELOPING BENZODIAZEPINE-RECEPTORS TO
CHRONIC-TREATMENT WITH DIAZEPAM, GABA AND MUSCIMOL IN
BRAIN CELL-CULTURES.
004002 04-03
MODULATORY INTERACTIONS BETWEEN NOREPINEPHRINE AND TAURINE,
BETA ALANINE, GAMMA AMINOBUTYRIC-ACID AND MUSCIMOL
APPLIED IONTOPHORETICALLY TO CEREBELLAR PURKINJE-CELLS.
004058 04-03
INVOLVEMENT OF DOPAMINE IN CIRCLING RESPONSES TO MUSCIMOL
DEPENDS ON INTRANIGRAL SITE OF INJECTION.
004158 04-04

MUSCIMOL-HYDROBROMIDE
EFFECTS OF SODIUM-DIPROPYLACETATE, MUSCIMOL-HYDROBROMIDE
AND (R,S) NIPECOTIC-ACID-AMIDE ON ISOLATION-INDUCED
AGGRESSIVE-BEHAVIOR IN MICE.
001756 02-04

MUSCLE
THE INFLUENCE OF BENZOCTAMINE ON DOPAMINE AND NOREPINEPHRINE
CONTENTS OF THE SUBSTANTIA-NIGRA AND ON THE MUSCLE STRETCH
REFLEX OF THE CAT.
000054 01-03
THE EFFECT OF DIAZEPAM ON TENSION AND ELECTROLYTE DISTRIBUTION
IN FROG MUSCLE.
000069 01-03
SHORT-TERM AND LONG-TERM MODIFICATION OF SKELETAL-MUSCLE
SODIUM-PUMP ACTIVITY AND MUSCLE PROTEIN TURNOVER.
(UNPUBLISHED PAPER).
001519 02-03
DRUG-INDUCED DISORDERS OF MUSCLE.
002435 02-15

MUSCLE-RELAXANT
INHIBITION OF BRAIN SYNAPTOSOMAL UPTAKE OF CHOLINE BY SOME 2 CARBOXAMIDOSTRYCHNINE DERIVATIVES WITH MUSCLE-RELAXANT PROPERTIES.
000084 01-03
THE SITE OF ACTION OF MUSCLE-RELAXANT PURINE NUCLEOSIDES.
003742 04-03

MUSCLE-RELAXANTS
THE RATIONAL USE OF MUSCLE-RELAXANTS IN REHABILITATION MEDICINE.
000943 01-17

MUSCULAR
NALOXONE EFFECTS ON THE BLOOD-PRESSURE RESPONSE INDUCED BY THIN-FIBER MUSCULAR AFFERENTS.
002794 03-03
DEPRESSION OF RESERPINE-INDUCED MUSCULAR RIGIDITY IN RATS AFTER ADMINISTRATION OF LISURIDE INTO THE SPINAL SUBARACHNOID SPACE.
002962 03-04

MUTAGENIC
IS LITHIUM MUTAGENIC IN MAN?
000753 01-13

MYASTHENIA-GRAVIS
NEUROLEPTIC-INDUCED SYNDROME MIMICKING MYASTHENIA-GRAVIS.
003474 03-15

MYELIN
BRAINSTEM AUDITORY EVOKED-POTENTIALS AND MYELIN CHANGES IN TRIETHYLTIN-INDUCED EDEMA IN YOUNG ADULT RATS.
000509 01-05
CHARACTERIZATION OF THE BASIC PROTEINS FROM RODENT PERIPHERAL-NERVOUS-SYSTEM MYELIN.
003665 04-01

MYELINATED
ABSENCE OF POTASSIUM CONDUCTANCE IN CENTRAL MYELINATED AXONS.
000166 01-03
FURTHER ANALYSIS OF THE MECHANISMS OF ACTION OF BATRACHOTOXIN ON THE MEMBRANE OF MYELINATED NERVE.
003884 04-03

MYENTERIC
INHIBITION OF THE ACTION OF CHOLECYSTOKININ-OCTAPEPTIDE ON THE GUINEA-PIG ILEUM MYENTERIC PLEXUS BY DIBUTYRYL-CYCLIC-GUANOSINE-MONOPHOSPHATE.
001291 02-03

MYOCARDIAL-INFARCTION
ANTIARRHYTHMIC-ACTIVITY OF AMITRIPTYLINE ANALOGUES IN CONSCIOUS DOGS AFTER MYOCARDIAL-INFARCTION: CYPROHEPTADINIUM-METHIODIDE.
001534 02-03

MYOCARDIUM
PROTECTIVE EFFECT OF PRENYLAMINE AGAINST VULNERABILITY TO VENTRICULAR FIBRILLATION IN THE NORMAL AND ISCHEMIC CANINE MYOCARDIUM.
000265 01-03

MYOCLONIES
EDEMAS AND MYOCLONIES IN A PATIENT WITH PARKINSONS-DISEASE TREATED BY AMANTADINE: PROBLEM WITH ASSOCIATED MEDICATIONS.
002389 02-15

MYOCLONUS
TRANSIENT-EFFECT OF L TRYPTOPHAN IN PROGRESSIVE MYOCLONUS EPILEPSY WITHOUT LAFORA-BODIES: CLINICAL-STUDY AND ELECTROPHYSIOLOGICAL-STUDY.
000694 01-11
OBSERVATIONS ON CHLORALOSE-INDUCED MYOCLONUS IN GUINEA-PIGS.
001164 02-03
TREATMENT OF MYOCLONUS WITH L 5 HYDROXYTRYPTOPHAN AND CARBIDOPA: CLINICAL, ELECTROPHYSIOLOGICAL, AND BIOCHEMICAL-OBSERVATIONS.
002180 02-11

MYODYSTONIA
PROBLEMS OF TREATING DEFORMING MYODYSTONIA WITH L-DOPA, AND PREDICTION OF ITS THERAPEUTIC EFFECT.
004536 04-13

MYOINOSITOL
THE EFFECTS OF LITHIUM ON MYOINOSITOL LEVELS IN LAYERS OF FRONTAL-CEREBRAL-CORTEX, IN CEREBELLUM, AND IN CORPUS-CALLOSUM OF THE RAT.
003712 04-03
MYOINOSITOL TURNOVER IN THE INTACT RAT-BRAIN: INCREASED PRODUCTION AFTER D-AMPHETAMINE.
003723 04-03

MYOPATHY
REVERSIBLE ALEXIA, MITOCHONDRIAL MYOPATHY, AND LACTIC-ACIDEMIA.
000723 01-11

MYOTUBE
STRETCH-INDUCED MYOTUBE GROWTH CORRELATES WITH NA-PUMP ACTIVATION. (UNPUBLISHED PAPER).
002087 02-10

MYTH
THE STIMULANT-EFFECT OF NEUROLEPTICS: MYTH OR REALITY?
000362 01-04

MYTHOLOGEM
THE MYTHOLOGEM OF REVERSIBLE DEATH. THE ANALYTICAL CONFRONTATION OF ENDOGENOUS DELIRIUM WITH DELUSIONS IN PSYCHEDELIC-EXPERIENCES.
002200 02-12

N-4
SYNTHESIS AND PHARMACOLOGICAL PROPERTIES OF N-4 1 AZETIDINYLBUTYNYL 2 PYRROLIDONE, A HIGHLY POTENT OXOTREMORINE-LIKE-AGENT.
003701 04-02

NA
MALE RAT SEXUAL-BEHAVIOR COMPARED AFTER 6 OHDA AND ELECTROLYTIC LESIONS IN THE DORSAL NA BUNDLE REGION OF THE MIDBRAIN.
001593 02-04

NA-DEPENDENT
NA-DEPENDENT LI COUNTERTRANSPORT AND THE LITHIUM DISTRIBUTION ACROSS THE HUMAN ERYTHROCYTE MEMBRANE: INTRODUCTION.
002227 02-13

NA-INDEPENDENT
NA-INDEPENDENT BINDING OF (3H)GABA AND (3H)MUSCIMOL TO SUBCELLULAR PARTICLES OF NEURAL PRIMARY CULTURES AND WHOLE BRAIN.
002699 03-03

NA-K-ADENOSINE-TRIPHOSPHATASE
EFFECTS OF CHRONIC DIETARY LITHIUM ON ACTIVITY AND REGULATION OF NA-K-ADENOSINE-TRIPHOSPHATASE IN RAT-BRAIN.
000297 01-03
NORADRENERGIC STIMULATION IN VIVO INCREASES NA-K-ADENOSINE-TRIPHOSPHATASE ACTIVITY.
002910 03-03

NA-K-ATPASE
METERGOLINE ANTAGONISM OF 5 HYDROXYTRYPTAMINE-INDUCED ACTIVATION OF RAT-CEREBRAL-CORTICAL NA-K-ATPASE.
000329 01-03
ALPHA-ADRENORECEPTOR MEDIATED ALTERATION OF ETHANOL EFFECTS ON NA-K-ATPASE OF RAT NEURONAL MEMBRANES.
001425 02-03
CHANGE IN CATECHOLAMINE SENSITIVE NA-K-ATPASE ACTIVITY IN THE RAT STRIATUM MICROSOMES FOLLOWING ELECTROLYTIC OR 6 HYDROXYDOPAMINE-INDUCED LESIONS OF DOPAMINERGIC NEURONS.
003871 04-03
CORRELATIONS BETWEEN NA-K-ATPASE ACTIVITY AND ACETYLCHOLINE RELEASE IN RAT CORTICAL SYNAPTOSOMES.
003937 04-03
THE NA-K-ATPASE: A PLAUSIBLE TRIGGER FOR VOLTAGE-INDEPENDENT RELEASE OF CYTOPLASMIC NEUROTRANSMITTERS.
003953 04-03

NA-GAMMA-HYDROXYBUTYRATE
NA-GAMMA-HYDROXYBUTYRATE IN CEREBRAL PROTECTION DURING SEVERE HYPOXEMIA IN THE RAT.
003895 04-03

NA-INDEPENDENT
INHIBITION BY ARYLSULPHATASE A OF NA-INDEPENDENT (3H) GABA AND (3H) MUSCIMOL BINDING TO BOVINE CEREBELLAR SYNAPTIC MEMBRANES.
001208 02-03

NA-K
THE EFFECT OF NORADRENALINE ON NA-K TRANSPORT IN RAT-CEREBRAL-CORTICAL SLICES.
004056 04-03

NA-K-ACTIVATED
ETHANOL SEDATIVE HYPNOTIC-INTERACTIONS: IN VITRO STUDIES ON NA-K-ACTIVATED ADENOSINE-TRIPHOSPHATASE.
004269 04-05

NA-K-ATPASE
EFFECTS OF LITHIUM, AND LITHIUM AND ALCOHOL ADMINISTRATION ON NA-K-ATPASE.
002744 03-03
ELECTRICAL-ACTIVITY AND NA-K-ATPASE LEVEL IN THE PENICILLIN-INDUCED EPILEPTOGENIC-FOCUS OF THE RAT-BRAIN-CORTEX, AND THE EFFECT OF DIAZEPAM.
003070 03-04

NA-PUMP
STRETCH-INDUCED MYOTUBE GROWTH CORRELATES WITH NA-PUMP ACTIVATION. (UNPUBLISHED PAPER).
002087 02-10

NABILONE
A SINGLE-DOSE STUDY OF NABILONE, A SYNTHETIC CANNABINOID.
002328 02-14

NACL
RENIN AND ALDOSTERONE SECRETIONS DURING HYPOVOLEMIA IN RATS: RELATION TO NACL INTAKE.
000484 01-04

NALORPHINE
EFFECTS OF MORPHINE AND NALORPHINE ON KAINIC-ACID-INDUCED HYPOTHERMIA IN RATS.
002921 03-03
EFFECTS OF PENTAZOCINE AND NALORPHINE ON MOTILITY IN CHRONICALLY MORPHINE TREATED RATS: A POTENTIAL SUBSTITUTION TEST TO DETECT THE NARCOTIC CHARACTER OF A DRUG.
003555 03-16

NALORPHINES
NALORPHINES EFFECT UNDER SEVERAL SCHEDULES OF ELECTRIC-SHOCK TITRATION.
000379 01-04

NALOXAZONE
NALOXAZONE, A LONG-ACTING OPIATE ANTAGONIST: EFFECTS ON ANALGESIA IN INTACT ANIMALS AND ON OPIATE-RECEPTOR BINDING IN VITRO.
004198 04-04

NALOXONE
EFFECT OF NALOXONE, HALOPERIDOL AND PROPRANOLOL ON CYCLIC-ADENOSINE-MONOPHOSPHATE CONTENT OF RAT AMYGDALA.
000071 01-03
INHIBITION OF (3H)NALOXONE BINDING IN HOMOGENATES OF RAT-BRAIN BY ESEROLINE, A DRUG, WITH ANALGESIC ACTIVITY, RELATED TO PHYSOSTIGMINE.
000104 01-03
NALOXONE ANTAGONISM OF GABA-EVOKED MEMBRANE POLARIZATIONS IN CULTURED MOUSE SPINAL-CORD NEURONS.
000116 01-03
NALOXONE PROMOTES STIMULUS-EVOKED VASOPRESSIN RELEASE IN VIVO.
000165 01-03
EFFECTS OF ENKEPHALIN ANALOGUE AND NALOXONE ON CAT SPINAL-CORD DORSAL ROOT POTENTIALS.
000236 01-03
REDUCTION IN THE NUMBER OF SEROTONIN-RECEPTORS IN THE BRAINSTEM OF MORPHINE-DEPENDENT RATS: RELATION TO BLOCKADE OF NALOXONE PRECIPITATED JUMPING BY SEROTONIN AGONISTS.
000258 01-03
EFFECTS OF MORPHINE AND NALOXONE ON PHASIC RELEASE OF LUTEINIZING-HORMONE AND FOLLICLE-STIMULATING-HORMONE (40849).
000298 01-03
MORPHINE EFFECTS UPON DISCRIMINATED APPROACH AND DISCRIMINATED AVOIDANCE IN RATS: ANTAGONISM BY NALOXONE.
000338 01-04
EFFECTS OF DOPAMINERGIC AND CHOLINERGIC-DRUGS, NALOXONE AND L PROLYL-LEUCYL-GLYCINAMIDE ON LSD-INDUCED CATALEPSY.
000360 01-04
NALOXONE POTENTIATES THE DISRUPTIVE EFFECTS OF MESCALINE ON OPERANT-RESPONDING IN THE RAT.
000365 01-04
ADDICTIVE-AGENTS AND INTRACRANIAL-STIMULATION (ICS): MORPHINE, NALOXONE, AND PRESSING FOR AMYGDALOID ICS.
000371 01-04
NALOXONE REVERSIBLE EFFECTS OF D ALA2-MET5-ENKEPHALINAMIDE-INDUCED BEHAVIORAL-ACTIVITY IN RATS.
000402 01-04
EFFECT OF BETA ENDORPHIN AND NALOXONE ON ACQUISITION, MEMORY, AND RETRIEVAL OF SHUTTLE AVOIDANCE AND HABITUATION LEARNING IN RATS.
000410 01-04
STEREOSPECIFIC, DOSE-DEPENDENT ANTAGONISM BY NALOXONE OF NONOPIATE BEHAVIOR IN MICE.
000411 01-04
EFFECTS OF MORPHINE, BETA ENDORPHIN AND NALOXONE ON CATECHOLAMINE LEVELS AND SEXUAL-BEHAVIOR IN THE MALE RAT.
000430 01-04
REVERSAL OF SCHEDULE-INDUCED SELF-INJECTION OF HEROIN BY NALOXONE.
000446 01-04
SELECTIVE INHIBITION OF MESOLIMBIC BEHAVIORAL-SUPERSENSITIVITY BY NALOXONE.
000467 01-04
NALOXONE OVERCOMES THE DOPAMINERGIC, EEG, AND BEHAVIORAL-EFFECTS OF GAMMA HYDROXYBUTYRATE.
000478 01-04
DIFFERENTIAL-EFFECTS OF NALOXONE AGAINST THE DIAZEPAM-INDUCED RELEASE OF BEHAVIOR IN RATS IN THREE AVERSIVE-SITUATIONS.
000480 01-04
FAILURE OF NALOXONE TO REVERSE CATALEPSY ASSOCIATED WITH SCHIZOPHRENIA: A CASE-REPORT.
000560 01-08
SHORT-TERM HORMONAL-EFFECTS OF NALOXONE IN MAN.
000798 01-13
NALOXONE REDUCES CIGARETTE SMOKING.
000808 01-14
RAPID OPIATE DETOXIFICATION WITH CLONIDINE AND NALOXONE.
000820 01-14

THE STEREOSPECIFIC EFFECT OF NALOXONE ON RAT DORSAL-HORN NEURONES; INHIBITION IN SUPERFICIAL LAMINAE AND EXCITATION IN DEEPER LAMINAE.
001226 02-03
A DEMONSTRATION OF NALOXONE PRECIPITATED OPIATE WITHDRAWAL ON SINGLE NEURONES IN THE MORPHINE-TOLERANT/DEPENDENT RAT-BRAIN.
001234 02-03
LOCALIZATION OF NALOXONE SENSITIVE (3H)DIHYDROMORPHINE BINDING-SITES WITHIN THE HIPPOCAMPUS OF THE RAT.
001368 02-03
SPONTANEOUSLY (GENETIC) HYPERTENSIVE-RATS PRESENT A NALOXONE SENSITIVE DECREASE IN PAIN SENSITIVITY. (UNPUBLISHED PAPER).
001457 02-03
CHARACTERISTICS OF OSCILLATORY CONTRACTIONS ELICITED BY NALOXONE IN ILEUM PREPARATION FROM MORPHINE-DEPENDENT GUINEA-PIGS.
001491 02-03
THE EFFECT OF NALOXONE ON THE ACTIVATION OF EMOTIONALLY POSITIVE REACTION PRODUCED BY DRUGS WITH A DEPENDENCE LIABILITY.
001556 02-03
HEROIN, BUT NOT LEVORPHANOL, PRODUCES EXPLOSIVE MOTOR-BEHAVIOR IN NALOXONE TREATED RATS.
001579 02-04
ACTH MEDIATION OF LEARNED-FEAR: BLOCKADE BY NALOXONE AND NALTREXONE.
001597 02-04
NALOXONE: EFFECTS ON FOOD AND WATER CONSUMPTION IN THE NONDEPRIVED AND DEPRIVED RAT.
001599 02-04
EFFECTS OF MORPHINE, PENTAZOCINE AND CYCLAZOCINE ALONE AND IN COMBINATION WITH NALOXONE ON ELECTRIC-SHOCK TITRATION IN THE SQUIRREL-MONKEY.
001611 02-04
NALOXONE PRETREATMENT ENHANCES SHOCK-ELICITED AGGRESSION.
001615 02-04
NALOXONE REDUCES SOCIAL-ACTIVITY AND EXPLORATORY-ACTIVITY IN THE RAT.
001617 02-04
NALOXONE FACILITATES AMYGDALOID KINDLING IN RATS.
001644 02-04
DIFFERENT BEHAVIORAL-EFFECTS FOLLOWING INTRACEREBRAL, INTRACEREBROVENTRICULAR OR INTRAPERITONEAL INJECTION OF NALOXONE IN THE RAT.
001665 02-04
THE EFFECT OF MORPHINE, PIMOZIDE AND NALOXONE ON DISCRIMINATION BY RATS IN A SHOCK-ESCAPE-TEST.
001700 02-04
ANTAGONISM OF 2 DEOXY-D-GLUCOSE-INDUCED HYPERPHAGIA BY NALOXONE: POSSIBLE INVOLVEMENT OF ENDORPHINS.
001773 02-04
NALOXONE AND SHUTTLEBOX SELF-STIMULATION IN THE RAT.
001793 02-04
THE EFFECT OF ASPIRIN AND PARACETAMOL ON THE INCREASED NALOXONE POTENCY INDUCED BY MORPHINE PRETREATMENT.
001824 02-04
ON A POSSIBLE ROLE OF ENDORPHINS IN PSYCHIATRIC-DISORDERS – ACTIONS OF NALOXONE IN PSYCHIATRIC-PATIENTS.
001917 02-08
FAILURE OF NALOXONE TO REDUCE MANIC-SYMPTOMS.
001984 02-09
EFFECTS OF NALOXONE UPON PROLACTIN AND CORTISOL IN NORMAL WOMEN.
002213 02-13
NALOXONE EFFECTS ON THE BLOOD-PRESSURE RESPONSE INDUCED BY THIN-FIBER MUSCULAR AFFERENTS.
002794 03-03
ENHANCEMENT OF ETORPHINE BRAIN CONCENTRATIONS AND CHANGES IN ETORPHINE NALOXONE PA2 VALUES IN MORPHINE PRETREATED MICE.
002800 03-03
NALOXONE REVERSAL OF THE PENTOBARBITAL-INDUCED BLOCKADE OF OVULATION IN THE RAT.
002817 03-03
INCREASE IN PLASMA CYCLIC-AMP LEVELS ELICITED BY NALOXONE IN MORPHINE-DEPENDENT MALE MICE.
002834 03-03
DEVELOPMENT OF ACUTE TOLERANCE TO THE EFFECTS OF NALOXONE ON THE HYPOTHALAMIC PITUITARY LUTEINIZING-HORMONE AXIS IN THE MALE RAT.
002853 03-03
SUPPRESSION OF SERUM PROLACTIN BY NALOXONE BUT NOT BY ANTI-BETA-ENDORPHIN ANTISERUM IN STRESSED AND UNSTRESSED RATS.
002871 03-03
POTENTIATION OF APOMORPHINE AND D-AMPHETAMINE EFFECTS BY NALOXONE.
002942 03-04

SUPPRESSION OF DRINKING BY NALOXONE IN THE RAT: A FURTHER
CHARACTERIZATION.
002963 03-04
DOSE-RESPONSE STUDY OF THE PRECIPITATED ABSTINENCE-SYNDROME
FOR MORPHINE: SYSTEMIC VS PERIAQUEDUCTAL GRAY NALOXONE.
(PH.D. DISSERTATION).
002979 03-04
EXPLORATION AND MOTOR-ACTIVITY AFTER INTRAVENTRICULAR ACTH,
MORPHINE AND NALOXONE.
002991 03-04
NALOXONE REVERSIBLE DUPLICATION BY LANTHANUM OF OPIATE
ANALGESIA EFFECTS ON OROFACIAL, LOWER BODY AND CENTRAL
NOCICEPTION.
003028 03-04
DISCRIMINATIVE RESPONSE CONTROL BY NALOXONE IN MORPHINE
PRETREATED RATS.
003053 03-04
EFFECTS OF CHRONIC NALOXONE TREATMENT ON BRAIN-STIMULATION
REWARD.
003066 03-04
FOOTSHOCK ANALGESIA: PREVENTION BY BEHAVIOURAL-MANIPULATION
BUT NOT BY NALOXONE.
003073 03-04
COPULATORY-BEHAVIOR AND SEXUAL-REFLEXES OF MALE RATS TREATED
WITH NALOXONE.
003077 03-04
EFFECTS OF METHYSERGIDE AND NALOXONE ON ANALGESIA INDUCED BY
THE PERIPHERAL ELECTRIC-STIMULATION IN MICE.
003093 03-04
DOSE-RESPONSE RELATIONSHIP BETWEEN NALOXONE INJECTIONS AND
INTAKE OF SUCROSE SOLUTION.
003118 03-04
THE USE OF A MORPHINE ANTAGONIST (NALOXONE) IN THE TREATMENT
OF DISSOCIATIVE-SYNDROMES.
003194 03-08
NALOXONE AND FOCAL EPILEPSY: A STUDY WITH DEPTH ELECTRODES.
003341 03-11
NALOXONE IN THE TREATMENT OF ANOREXIA-NERVOSA: EFFECT ON
WEIGHT-GAIN AND LIPOLYSIS.
003342 03-11
OPPOSITE EFFECTS OF NALOXONE ON SUBSTANCE-P-INDUCED IN BRAIN
DOPA SYNTHESIS AND IN LOCOMOTOR-ACTIVITY IN RATS.
003799 04-03
ACTION OF ENKEPHALIN ANALOGUES AND MORPHINE ON BRAIN
ACETYLCHOLINE RELEASE: DIFFERENTIAL REVERSAL BY NALOXONE AND
AN OPIATE-PENTAPEPTIDE.
003863 04-03
EFFECT OF MORPHINE AND NALOXONE ON LEU-ENKEPHALIN-LIKE
IMMUNOREACTIVITY IN DOGS.
003894 04-03
EFFECTS OF ENKEPHALIN, MORPHINE, AND NALOXONE ON THE
ELECTRICAL-ACTIVITY OF THE IN VITRO HIPPOCAMPAL SLICE
PREPARATION.
003918 04-03
CORE TEMPERATURE CHANGES FOLLOWING ADMINISTRATION OF
NALOXONE AND NALTREXONE TO RATS EXPOSED TO HOT AND COLD
AMBIENT TEMPERATURES. EVIDENCE FOR THE PHYSIOLOGICAL ROLE
OF ENDORPHINS IN HOT AND COLD ACCLIMATIZATION.
004034 04-03
NALOXONE SUPPRESSES FEEDING AND DRINKING BUT NOT WHEEL
RUNNING IN RATS.
004080 04-04
EFFECTS OF PAIN, MORPHINE AND NALOXONE ON THE DURATION OF
ANIMAL HYPNOSIS.
004081 04-04
NALOXONE SUPPRESSES FOOD/WATER CONSUMPTION IN THE DEPRIVED
CAT.
004114 04-04
NALOXONE FAILS TO BLOCK AMPHETAMINE-INDUCED ANOREXIA AND
CONDITIONED TASTE-AVERSION.
004121 04-04
CHOICE BETWEEN FOOD AND HEROIN: EFFECTS OF MORPHINE,
NALOXONE, AND SECOBARBITAL.
004123 04-04
THE SITE OF ACTION OF NALOXONE IN SUPPRESSING FOOD AND WATER
INTAKE IN RATS.
004146 04-04
EVIDENCE FOR SEDATIVE EFFECTS OF LOW-DOSES OF MORPHINE IN MICE
INVOLVING RECEPTORS INSENSITIVE TO NALOXONE.
004173 04-04
SOCIAL CROWDING ENHANCES AVERSIVENESS OF NALOXONE IN RATS.
004201 04-04
OPIATE-DEPENDENCE FOLLOWING ACUTE INJECTIONS OF MORPHINE AND
NALOXONE: THE ASSESSMENT OF VARIOUS WITHDRAWAL SIGNS.
004209 04-04
PLASMA LEVELS OF BETA ENDORPHIN UNDER CHRONIC NEUROLEPTIC
TREATMENT IN SCHIZOPHRENIC-PATIENTS: FAILURE OF NALOXONE TO
COUNTERACT CURATIVE EFFECTS OF NEUROLEPTIC-DRUGS.
004321 04-08

THE EFFECT OF NALOXONE ON THE CONDITION OF PATIENTS WITH
ENDOGENOUS PSYCHOSES.
004381 04-09
ARE THE ENKEPHALINS INVOLVED IN PARKINSONS-DISEASE? CLINICAL
AND NEUROENDOCRINE RESPONSES TO NALOXONE ADMINISTRATION.
004431 04-11

NALOXONE-INDUCED
AN ELECTROMYOGRAPHIC-METHOD FOR THE ASSESSMENT OF
NALOXONE-INDUCED ABSTINENCE IN MORPHINE-DEPENDENT RATS.
000433 01-04
REPEATED ADMINISTRATION OF NALTREXONE PRODUCES TOLERANCE TO
NALOXONE-INDUCED HYPERALGESIA.
000453 01-04
HYPOPHYSECTOMY INCREASES THE SENSITIVITY OF RATS TO NALOXONE-
INDUCED HYPOTHERMIA.
002710 03-03
LACK OF CORRELATION BETWEEN NALOXONE-INDUCED CHANGES IN
SEXUAL-BEHAVIOR AND SERUM LH IN MALE RATS.
002821 03-03
CHOLINE REVERSES NALOXONE-INDUCED DECREASES IN HIPPOCAMPAL
ACETYLCHOLINE CONTENT AND SUPPRESSES ESCAPE-BEHAVIOR IN
OPIATE-DEPENDENT RATS.
004076 04-04

NALOXONE-LIKE
NALOXONE-LIKE ACTIONS OF MIF-1 DO NOT REQUIRE THE PRESENCE OF
THE PITUITARY.
001311 02-03

NALTREXONE
INHIBITION OF GROWTH IN YOUNG MICE TREATED WITH PENTAZOCINE:
REVERSAL BY NALTREXONE.
000318 01-03
DISCRIMINATIVE-STIMULUS EFFECTS OF NALTREXONE IN THE MORPHINE-
DEPENDENT RAT.
000391 01-04
REPEATED ADMINISTRATION OF NALTREXONE PRODUCES TOLERANCE TO
NALOXONE-INDUCED HYPERALGESIA.
000453 01-04
ACTH MEDIATION OF LEARNED-FEAR: BLOCKADE BY NALOXONE AND
NALTREXONE.
001597 02-04
INTERACTIONS BETWEEN NALTREXONE AND NONOPIATE DRUGS
EVALUATED BY SCHEDULE-CONTROLLED BEHAVIOR.
001645 02-04
BEHAVIOURAL-EFFECTS AND ENDOCRINE-EFFECTS OF NALTREXONE IN
MALE TALAPOIN-MONKEYS.
001718 02-04
OPERANT ANALYSIS OF HUMAN HEROIN SELF-ADMINISTRATION AND THE
EFFECTS OF NALTREXONE.
003449 03-14
CORE TEMPERATURE CHANGES FOLLOWING ADMINISTRATION OF
NALOXONE AND NALTREXONE TO RATS EXPOSED TO HOT AND COLD
AMBIENT TEMPERATURES. EVIDENCE FOR THE PHYSIOLOGICAL ROLE
OF ENDORPHINS IN HOT AND COLD ACCLIMATIZATION.
004034 04-03

NARCOANALGESIA
EFFECTS OF NORADRENERGIC AGONISTS AND ANTAGONISTS ON
GROWTH-HORMONE SECRETION UNDER GAMMA HYDROXYBUTYRATE
NARCOANALGESIA IN THE RAT.
000262 01-03

NARCOLEPSY
BROMISM, HYSTERIA AND NARCOLEPSY.
002472 02-15
TREATMENT OF NARCOLEPSY AND SLEEP-APNEA WITH GAMMA
HYDROXYBUTYRATE: A CLINICAL AND POLYSOMNOGRAPHIC CASE-
STUDY.
004571 04-14

NARCOSIS
ANTAGONISTIC-EFFECTS OF PROPRANOLOL UPON ETHANOL-INDUCED
NARCOSIS IN MICE.
000439 01-04

NARCOTIC
EFFECTS OF CHANGES IN THE STRUCTURE OF ENKEPHALINS AND OF
NARCOTIC ANALGESIC-DRUGS ON THEIR INTERACTIONS WITH MU-
RECEPTORS AND DELTA-RECEPTORS.
000168 01-03
INFLUENCE OF GLUCOSE (IN VIVO OR IN VITRO) ON DURATION OF
NARCOTIC ANALGESICS AND ON THE KINETICS OF DRUG METABOLISM.
000292 01-03
TARDIVE-DYSKINESIA RESULTING FROM CHRONIC NARCOTIC
TREATMENT.
000922 01-17
INTERACTION-STUDIES BETWEEN NARCOTIC ANALGESICS, NARCOTIC
ANTAGONISTS AND ETHANOL: STUDIES DURING ACUTE AND CHRONIC-
TREATMENT AND WITHDRAWAL STATES IN RATS AND MICE. (PH.D.
DISSERTATION).
001165 02-03
A PROPOSED MODE OF ACTION FOR NARCOTIC AGONISTS AND
ANTAGONISTS.
001168 02-03

Subject Index

THE EFFECT OF PSYCHOTROPIC-SUBSTANCES AND NARCOTIC ANALGESIC-DRUGS ON 14C NORADRENALINE UPTAKE BY SYNAPTOSOMES OF THE CEREBRAL-CORTEX OF RATS.
001363 02-03

NARCOTIC ANTAGONIST PRECIPITATED ABSTINENCE: RELATIONSHIP TO WITHDRAWAL INDUCING BENZAZOCINES. (PH.D. DISSERTATION).
001518 02-03

NARCOTIC ANALGESICS AND STEREOTYPED-BEHAVIOUR IN MICE.
001694 02-04

MORPHINE ANALGESIA AFTER INTRATHECAL ADMINISTRATION OF A NARCOTIC AGONIST, CHLOROXYMORPHAMINE AND ANTAGONIST, CHLORNALTREXAMINE.
001695 02-04

LACK OF EFFECT OF CHOLINE AND NARCOTIC ANTAGONISTS UPON APOMORPHINE DISCRIMINATION.
001770 02-04

HEMODYNAMIC FAILURE INDUCED BY NARCOTIC AND TOXIC DOSES OF 12 CNS DEPRESSANTS IN INTACT AND PITHED RATS.
001855 02-05

INVOLVEMENT OF CAUDATE-NUCLEUS, AMYGDALA OR RETICULAR FORMATION IN NEUROLEPTIC AND NARCOTIC CATALEPSY.
002986 03-04

ENHANCEMENT OF APOMORPHINE-INDUCED CLIMBING IN MICE BY REVERSIBLE AND IRREVERSIBLE NARCOTIC ANTAGONIST DRUGS.
003068 03-04

RELAPSE TO NARCOTIC SELF-ADMINISTRATION IN MORPHINE POSTADDICT RATS: A POSSIBLE MODEL FOR PREDICTING ABUSE LIABILITY OF NARCOTIC-DRUGS. (PH.D. DISSERTATION).
003097 03-04

THE RELATIONSHIP BETWEEN THE ACUTE BEHAVIORAL-EFFECTS OF NARCOTIC ANTAGONISTS AND THE NARCOTIC DEPENDENT STATE.
003106 03-04

A CLINICAL, CONTROLLED-STUDY OF L ALPHA ACETYLMETHADOL IN THE TREATMENT OF NARCOTIC ADDICTION.
003335 03-11

EFFECTS OF PENTAZOCINE AND NALORPHINE ON MOTILITY IN CHRONICALLY MORPHINE TREATED RATS: A POTENTIAL SUBSTITUTION TEST TO DETECT THE NARCOTIC CHARACTER OF A DRUG.
003555 03-16

PHARMACOLOGICAL-STUDIES WITH AN ALKYLATING NARCOTIC AGONIST, CHLOROXYMORPHAMINE, AND ANTAGONIST, CHLORNALTREXAMINE.
004082 04-04

INTERACTIONS BETWEEN NARCOTIC AGONISTS, PARTIAL AGONISTS AND ANTAGONISTS EVALUATED BY SCHEDULE-CONTROLLED BEHAVIOR.
004127 04-04

NARCOTIC DISCRIMINATION IN PIGEONS.
004132 04-04

ANALGESIC AND OTHER PHARMACOLOGICAL ACTIVITIES OF A NEW NARCOTIC ANTAGONIST ANALGESIC (-) 1 3 METHYLBUTENYLHYDROXYPHENYLPHENYLETHYLPIPERAZINE AND ITS ENANTIOMORPH IN EXPERIMENTAL ANIMALS.
004185 04-04

EFFECTS OF NARCOTIC ANTAGONISTS ON L-DOPA REVERSAL OF RESERPINE-INDUCED CATALEPSY AND BLEPHAROPTOSIS IN MICE.
004186 04-04

EFFECTS OF NARCOTIC ABSTINENCE ON SCHEDULE-CONTROLLED BEHAVIOR IN DEPENDENT RATS.
004230 04-04

NARCOTIC-AGENTS
INFLUENCE OF NARCOTIC-AGENTS ON TEMPERATURE REGULATION.
001108 02-03

INTRACEREBRAL SUBSTANCE-P IN MICE: BEHAVIORAL-EFFECTS AND NARCOTIC-AGENTS.
004218 04-04

NARCOTIC-DRUGS
RELAPSE TO NARCOTIC SELF-ADMINISTRATION IN MORPHINE POSTADDICT RATS: A POSSIBLE MODEL FOR PREDICTING ABUSE LIABILITY OF NARCOTIC-DRUGS. (PH.D. DISSERTATION).
003097 03-04

NARCOTIC-INDUCED
METHIONINE-ENKEPHALIN ANTAGONISM AND ENDORPHIN POTENTIATION OF NARCOTIC-INDUCED ANALGESIA.
000357 01-04

NARCOTIC-REINFORCED
NARCOTIC-REINFORCED RESPONDING: A RAPID EVALUATION PROCEDURE.
004253 04-04

NARCOTICS
INVESTIGATION OF NARCOTICS AND ANTITUSSIVES USING DRUG DISCRIMINATION TECHNIQUES.
000447 01-04

ON THE GENETIC SIDE-EFFECTS OF PSYCHOTROPIC-SUBSTANCES: I. PSYCHOPHARMACEUTICALS, NARCOTICS, AND ANTICONVULSANT.
000845 01-15

INTERACTIONS OF NARCOTICS WITH SYNAPTOSOMAL CALCIUM TRANSPORT.
002712 03-03

MINI-SYMPOSIUM. IV. DISCRIMINATIVE-STIMULUS EFFECTS OF NARCOTICS: EVIDENCE FOR MULTIPLE RECEPTOR-MEDIATED ACTIONS.
004719 04-17

EFFECTS OF 3 SULFAMOYLMETHYL-BENZISOXAZOLE (AD-810) AND SOME ANTIEPILEPTICS ON THE KINDLED SEIZURES IN THE NEOCORTEX, HIPPOCAMPUS AND AMYGDALA IN RATS.
004149 04-04

NEOCORTICAL
MONOAMINE REPLACEMENT AFTER RESERPINE: CATECHOLAMINERGIC AGONISTS RESTORE MOTOR-ACTIVITY BUT PHENYLETHYLAMINE RESTORES ATROPINE-RESISTANT NEOCORTICAL LOW VOLTAGE FAST-ACTIVITY.
000309 01-03

RESERPINE ABOLISHES MOVEMENT CORRELATED ATROPINE-RESISTANT NEOCORTICAL LOW VOLTAGE FAST-ACTIVITY.
000310 01-03

EFFECTS OF LEAD EXPOSURE DURING DEVELOPMENT ON NEOCORTICAL DENDRITIC AND SYNAPTIC STRUCTURE.
000525 01-05

INHIBITORY-ACTION OF THE COMBINATION OF AMINOPYRINE AND SECOBARBITAL ON EEG ACTIVATION, NEOCORTICAL RECRUITING AND AUGMENTING RESPONSES IN RABBITS.
004022 04-03

NEOMYCIN
EFFECTS OF NEOMYCIN ON CALCIUM AND POLYPHOSPHOINOSITIDE METABOLISM OF GUINEA-PIG SYNAPTOSOMES.
002741 03-03

NEONATAL
NEONATAL ADMINISTRATION OF MET-ENKEPHALIN FACILITATES MAZE-PERFORMANCE OF ADULT RATS.
001673 02-04

EFFECTS OF NEONATAL 6 HYDROXYDOPA ON BEHAVIOR IN FEMALE RATS.
001717 02-04

NEUROCHEMICAL-CONSEQUENCES FOLLOWING ADMINISTRATION OF CNS STIMULANTS TO THE NEONATAL RAT.
002926 03-03

ABNORMAL MATURATION OF CEREBRAL-CORTEX AND BEHAVIORAL-DEFICIT IN ADULT RATS AFTER NEONATAL ADMINISTRATION OF ANTIBODIES TO GANGLIOSIDE.
003025 03-04

EFFECTS OF NEONATAL TESTOSTERONE AND ESTROGEN ON OPEN-FIELD BEHAVIOUR IN RATS.
003098 03-04

EFFECT OF NEONATAL HYDROCORTISONE TREATMENT ON BRAIN-MONOAMINES IN DEVELOPING RATS.
003893 04-03

THE EFFECTS OF P CHLOROAMPHETAMINE ADMINISTRATION ON LOCOMOTOR-ACTIVITY AND SEROTONIN IN NEONATAL AND ADULT RATS. (UNPUBLISHED PAPER).
004169 04-04

NEONATALLY
CATECHOLAMINE SEROTONIN INTERACTION EFFECTS ON ACTIVITY IN RATS NEONATALLY TREATED WITH 6 HYDROXYDOPAMINE.
004194 04-04

NEONATE
EFFECT OF MATERNAL LORAZEPAM ON THE NEONATE.
003549 03-15

NEONATES
PHENCYCLIDINE: EFFECTS OF CHRONIC ADMINISTRATION IN THE FEMALE MOUSE ON GESTATION, MATERNAL-BEHAVIOR, AND THE NEONATES.
000517 01-05

NEOPHOBIA
POSTINGESTION INTERFERENCE WITH BRAIN FUNCTION PREVENTS ATTENTUATION OF NEOPHOBIA IN RATS.
000352 01-04

NEOSTRIATAL
ROLE OF THE NEOSTRIATAL DOPAMINERGIC-ACTIVITY IN SEQUENCING AND SELECTING BEHAVIOURAL-STRATEGIES: FACILITATION OF PROCESSES INVOLVED IN SELECTING THE BEST STRATEGY IN A STRESSFUL-SITUATION.
000366 01-04

THE INFLUENCE OF ANTERIOR NEOSTRIATAL LESIONS ON THE BEHAVIOURAL-EFFECTS OF SPIROPERIDOL IN RATS.
001702 02-04

APPARENT SEROTONERGIC MODULATION OF THE DOSE-DEPENDENT BIPHASIC RESPONSE OF NEOSTRIATAL NEURONS PRODUCED BY D-AMPHETAMINE.
003981 04-03

NEOSTRIATUM
OPPOSITE EFFECTS OF D-AMPHETAMINE ON SPONTANEOUS NEURONAL ACTIVITY IN THE NEOSTRIATUM AND NUCLEUS-ACCUMBENS.
000454 01-04

INTRINSIC CHOLINERGIC EXCITATION IN THE RAT NEOSTRIATUM: NICOTINIC AND MUSCARINIC-RECEPTORS.
001374 02-03

AVOIDANCE RESPONSE IN RATS AFTER INJECTION OF DOPAMINE INTO THE NEOSTRIATUM.
004255 04-04

NEPHRITIS
THE ROLE OF LITHIUM IN THE PRODUCTION OF INTERSTITIAL NEPHRITIS: A CASE-HISTORY.
004655 04-15

NEPHROPATHY
TARDIVE-DYSKINESIA AND LITHIUM ASSOCIATED NEPHROPATHY: ARE YOU LIABLE?
000846 01-15

NERVE
THE LONG-TERM REGULATION OF GANGLIONIC TYROSINE-HYDROXYLASE BY PREGANGLIONIC NERVE ACTIVITY.
000333 01-03

DEMONSTRATION OF SUBSTANCE-P IN AORTIC NERVE AFFERENT FIBERS BY COMBINED USE OF FLOURESCENT RETROGRADE NEURONAL LABELING AND IMMUNOCYTOCHEMISTRY. (UNPUBLISHED PAPER).
001024 02-01

EFFECTS OF CHRONIC-TREATMENT WITH L SULPIRIDE AND HALOPERIDOL ON CENTRAL DOPAMINE TURNOVER EVALUATED IN DOPAMINE CELL BODY AND NERVE TERMINAL-RICH AREAS.
001096 02-03

DECREASE OF GAD IMMUNOREACTIVE NERVE TERMINALS IN THE SUBSTANTIA-NIGRA AFTER KAINIC-ACID LESION OF THE STRIATUM. (UNPUBLISHED PAPER).
001400 02-03

NERVE CELL CALCIUM AS A MESSENGER FOR OPIATE AND ENDORPHIN ACTIONS.
001450 02-03

MECHANICAL-CHANGES IN CRAB NERVE FIBERS DURING ACTION POTENTIALS. (UNPUBLISHED PAPER).
001505 02-03

MEASUREMENT OF THE MEMBRANE POTENTIAL OF ISOLATED NERVE TERMINALS BY THE LIPOPHILIC CATION (3H)TRIPHENYLMETHYLPHOSPHONIUM-BROMIDE.
002746 03-03

FLUORESCENCE HISTOCHEMISTRY INDICATES DAMAGE OF STRIATAL DOPAMINE NERVE TERMINALS IN RATS AFTER MULTIPLE DOSES OF METHAMPHETAMINE.
002812 03-03

INFUSIONS INTO THE OCULOMOTOR NUCLEUS OR NERVE: A METHOD OF ESTIMATING THE DOSAGE AT WHICH TRANSMITTER ANTAGONISTS INFUSED INTRACRANIALLY PRODUCE NONSPECIFIC BLOCKING OF NEURAL ACTIVITY.
003134 03-06

ULTRASTRUCTURAL LOCALIZATION OF MONOAMINES IN NERVE FIBERS OF THE PINEAL-GLAND IN GOLDEN HAMSTERS.
003666 04-01

INSEPARABILITY OF ACETYLCHOLINESTERASE AND NERVE EXCITATION.
003875 04-03

NERVE GROWTH-FACTOR STIMULATES DEVELOPMENT OF SUBSTANCE-P IN THE EMBRYONIC SPINAL-CORD.
003881 04-03

FURTHER ANALYSIS OF THE MECHANISMS OF ACTION OF BATRACHOTOXIN ON THE MEMBRANE OF MYELINATED NERVE.
003884 04-03

THE RELATIONSHIP BETWEEN LOSS OF DOPAMINE NERVE TERMINALS, STRIATAL (3H)SPIROPERIDOL BINDING AND ROTATIONAL-BEHAVIOR IN UNILATERALLY 6 HYDROXYDOPAMINE LESIONED RATS.
004129 04-04

MEASUREMENTS OF NERVE CONDUCTION VELOCITY DURING DECREASING TOXIC DIPHENYLHYDANTOIN LEVELS AND THE BEGINNING OF CARBAMAZEPINE MEDICATION: A CLINICAL NEUROPHYSIOLOGICAL REPORT.
004441 04-11

NERVE-ENDINGS
GABA FLUXES IN PRESYNAPTIC NERVE-ENDINGS FROM IMMATURE RATS.
000185 01-03

DOPAMINE BIOSYNTHESIS IS REGULATED BY THE AMINE NEWLY RECAPTURED BY DOPAMINERGIC NERVE-ENDINGS.
001163 02-03

PRESYNAPTIC DOPAMINE-RECEPTORS IN STRIATAL NERVE-ENDINGS: ABSENCE OF HALOPERIDOL-INDUCED SUPERSENSITIVITY.
001424 02-03

IN VIVO CHANGES IN THE GABA CONTENT OF NERVE-ENDINGS (SYNAPTOSOMES) INDUCED BY INHIBITORS OF GABA UPTAKE.
001540 02-03,

UPTAKE OF RADIOCALCIUM BY NERVE-ENDINGS ISOLATED FROM RAT-BRAIN: KINETIC STUDIES.
003814 04-03

UPTAKE OF RADIOCALCIUM BY NERVE-ENDINGS ISOLATED FROM RAT-BRAIN: PHARMACOLOGICAL-STUDIES.
003815 04-03

NERVES
PILLS FOR NERVES.
000652 01-10

NERVOUS-SYSTEM
CYCLIC-NUCLEOTIDES AND THE NERVOUS-SYSTEM.
004542 04-13

NERVOUS-TISSUE
NEUROTOXIC ESTERASE IN HUMAN NERVOUS-TISSUE.
003510 03-15

DETERMINATION OF PICOMOLE AMOUNTS OF DOPAMINE, NORADRENALINE, 3,4 DIHYDROXYPHENYLALANINE, 3,4 DIHYDROXYPHENYLACETIC-ACID, HOMOVANILLIC-ACID, AND 5

HYDROXYINDOLEACETIC-ACID IN NERVOUS-TISSUE AFTER ONE-STEP PURIFICATION ON SEPHADEX-G-10, USING HIGH.
004305 04-06

NEST-BUILDING-BEHAVIOR
BEHAVIORAL-EFFECTS OF HASHISH IN MICE: I. SOCIAL-INTERACTIONS AND NEST-BUILDING-BEHAVIOR OF MALES.
001777 02-04

NEURAL
RIA AND HPLC EVIDENCE FOR THE PRESENCE OF METHIONINE-ENKEPHALIN AND CHOLECYSTOKININ IN THE NEURAL RETINA OF SEVERAL VERTEBRATE SPECIES. (UNPUBLISHED PAPER).
001017 02-01
LITHIUM-ION ENTRY INTO CULTURED CELLS OF NEURAL ORIGIN.
001433 02-03
STIMULATION OF THE PLASMA MEMBRANE ENZYME, 5' NUCLEOTIDASE, BY ETHANOL EXPOSURE TO NEURAL CELLS IN CULTURE.
001499 02-03
THE PHARMACOLOGY OF CATECHOLAMINE INVOLVEMENT IN THE NEURAL MECHANISMS OF REWARD.
001526 02-03
NA-INDEPENDENT BINDING OF (3H)GABA AND (3H)MUSCIMOL TO SUBCELLULAR PARTICLES OF NEURAL PRIMARY CULTURES AND WHOLE BRAIN.
002699 03-03
INFUSIONS INTO THE OCULOMOTOR NUCLEUS OR NERVE: A METHOD OF ESTIMATING THE DOSAGE AT WHICH TRANSMITTER ANTAGONISTS INFUSED INTRACRANIALLY PRODUCE NONSPECIFIC BLOCKING OF NEURAL ACTIVITY.
003134 03-06
INFLUENCE OF THE DOPAMINERGIC AGONISTS BROMOCRIPTINE, PIRIBEDIL AND NOMIFENSINE ON THE SYMPATHETIC NEURAL TRANSMISSION IN THE NICTITATING MEMBRANE OF THE CAT.
003822 04-03

NEURALLY
CORTICAL CONTROL OF NEURALLY MEDIATED ARRHYTHMOGENIC-PROPERTIES OF DESACETYLLANATOSIDE-C.
003124 03-05

NEURAMINIDASE
EXPOSURE OF MITOCHONDRIAL OUTER MEMBRANES TO NEURAMINIDASE SELECTIVELY DESTROYS MONOAMINE-OXIDASE-A ACTIVITY.
001286 02-03

NEUROACTIVE-AGENTS
THE EFFECTS OF 2,5 DIMETHOXY-4-METHYLAMPHETAMINE (DOM) ON OPERANT-BEHAVIOR: INTERACTIONS WITH OTHER NEUROACTIVE-AGENTS.
004089 04-04

NEUROANATOMICAL-STUDY
A NEUROANATOMICAL-STUDY OF ANALGESIA AND CATATONIA INDUCED BY ETORPHINE IN THE RAT. (PH.D. DISSERTATION).
003102 03-04

NEUROANATOMY
SATIETY CENTER NEUROANATOMY. (UNPUBLISHED PAPER).
003678 04-01
THE NEUROANATOMY AND PHARMACOLOGY OF THE NUCLEUS LOCUS-COERULEUS. (UNPUBLISHED PAPER).
003810 04-03

NEUROBEHAVIORAL
THE BRAINSTEM AUDITORY EVOKED-RESPONSE AS A TOOL IN NEUROBEHAVIORAL TOXICOLOGY AND MEDICINE.
004277 04-05

NEUROBIOLOGICAL
BASIC AND CLINICAL NEUROBIOLOGICAL APPLICATIONS OF NEURONAL (NSE) AND NONNEURONAL (NNE) ENOLASE. (UNPUBLISHED PAPER).
001041 02-01

NEUROBIOLOGICAL-PERSPECTIVE
THE PHARMACOLOGY OF MEMORY: A NEUROBIOLOGICAL-PERSPECTIVE.
003636 03-17

NEUROBIOLOGY
PEPTIDES IN NEUROBIOLOGY: AN OVERVIEW. (UNPUBLISHED PAPER).
001008 02-01
NEUROBIOLOGY AND NEUROPHARMACOLOGY OF THE ENKEPHALINS.
002580 02-17

NEUROBLASTOMA
PSYCHOTROPIC-DRUGS AND HISTAMINE H1-RECEPTORS OF CULTURED MOUSE NEUROBLASTOMA CELLS.
000250 01-03
INVOLVEMENT OF CALCIUM CHANNELS IN SHORT-TERM DESENSITIZATION OF MUSCARINIC-RECEPTOR MEDIATED CYCLIC-GMP FORMATION IN MOUSE NEUROBLASTOMA CELLS.
003783 04-03
CHARACTERIZATION BY (3H)DIHYDROERGOCRYPTINE BINDING OF ALPHA-ADRENERGIC-RECEPTORS IN NEUROBLASTOMA X GLIOMA HYBRID CELLS.
003823 04-03
PHENYTOIN INHIBITION OF CYCLIC-GUANOSINE-MONOPHOSPHATE (C-GMP) ACCUMULATION IN NEUROBLASTOMA CELLS BY CALCIUM-CHANNEL BLOCKADE.
004020 04-03
DESENSITIZATION OF HISTAMINE H1-RECEPTOR-MEDIATED CYCLIC-GMP FORMATION IN MOUSE NEUROBLASTOMA CELLS.
004030 04-03

DEMONSTRATION OF A MUSCARINIC-RECEPTOR-MEDIATED CYCLIC-GMP-DEPENDENT HYPERPOLARIZATION OF THE MEMBRANE POTENTIAL OF MOUSE NEUROBLASTOMA CELLS USING (3H)TETRAPHENYLPHOSPHONIUM.
004049 04-03

NEUROBLASTOMA-X
RELATIONSHIP BETWEEN THE ACTIONS OF CALCIUM-IONS, OPIOIDS, AND PROSTAGLANDIN-E1 ON THE LEVEL OF CYCLIC-AMP IN NEUROBLASTOMA-X GLIOMA HYBRID CELLS.
002677 03-03
OPIOIDS, NORADRENALINE AND GTP ANALOGS INHIBIT CHOLERA-TOXIN ACTIVATED ADENYLATE-CYCLASE IN NEUROBLASTOMA-X GLIOMA HYBRID CELLS.
003975 04-03

NEUROCHEMICAL
PRODRUGS OF SOME DOPAMINERGIC 2 AMINOTETRALINS: A REVIEW OF THEIR SYNTHESES AND NEUROCHEMICAL PROFILES.
000004 01-01
CORTICAL NEUROCHEMICAL CHANGES AFTER INTRASTRIATAL INJECTION OF KAINIC-ACID.
000133 01-03
CGP-6085-A, A NEW, SPECIFIC, INHIBITOR OF SEROTONIN UPTAKE: NEUROCHEMICAL CHARACTERIZATION AND COMPARISON WITH OTHER SEROTONIN UPTAKE BLOCKERS.
000316 01-03
ON THE NEUROCHEMICAL BASIS OF SELF-STIMULATION WITH MIDBRAIN RAPHE ELECTRODE PLACEMENTS.
000373 01-04
CHRONIC AMPHETAMINE ADMINISTRATION TO CATS: BEHAVIORAL-EVIDENCE AND NEUROCHEMICAL EVIDENCE FOR DECREASED CENTRAL SEROTONERGIC FUNCTION.
000491 01-04
NEUROCHEMICAL MECHANISMS OF OPIATES AND ENDORPHINS.
000958 01-17
NEUROPHARMACOLOGICAL AND NEUROCHEMICAL APPROACHES TO PRECLINICAL-EVALUATION OF NEUROLEPTICS.
001094 02-02
THYROTROPIN-RELEASING-HORMONE: NEUROCHEMICAL EVIDENCE FOR THE POTENTIATION OF IMIPRAMINE EFFECTS ON THE METABOLISM AND UPTAKE OF BRAIN CATECHOLAMINES.
001427 02-03
NEUROCHEMICAL BASIS OF THE ACTION OF ANTIDEPRESSANTS ON LEARNED-HELPLESSNESS.
001775 02-04
THE STRIATONIGRAL GABA PATHWAY: FUNCTIONAL AND NEUROCHEMICAL CHARACTERISTICS IN RATS WITH UNILATERAL STRIATAL KAINIC-ACID LESIONS.
001816 02-04
NEUROCHEMICAL EVIDENCE AND BEHAVIORAL-EVIDENCE FOR A SELECTIVE PRESYNAPTIC DOPAMINE-RECEPTOR AGONIST.
002236 02-13
CHRONOLOGY OF NEUROCHEMICAL ALTERATIONS INDUCED BY GABA AGONIST ADMINISTRATION.
002713 03-03
TEMPORAL PATTERNING OF NEURONAL ACTIVITY DURING THERMAL AND NEUROCHEMICAL STIMULATION OF THE PREOPTIC/ANTERIOR HYPOTHALAMUS OF THE AWAKE RABBIT.
002737 03-03
RECENT REVIEWS OF BIOCHEMICAL, NEUROCHEMICAL, AND PHARMACOLOGICAL TOPICS.
003649 03-17
BEHAVIOURAL AND NEUROCHEMICAL PROPERTIES OF 1 1 INDOL-3-YLMETHYLPIPERID-4-YL-3-BENZOYLUREA (WY-25093) IN RODENTS.
003686 04-02
BEHAVIORAL AND REGIONAL NEUROCHEMICAL SEQUELAE OF HIPPOCAMPAL DESTRUCTION IN THE RAT.
003721 04-03
CHANGES OF ELECTRORETINOGRAM AND NEUROCHEMICAL ASPECTS OF GABAERGIC NEURONS OF RETINA AFTER INTRAOCULAR INJECTION OF KAINIC-ACID IN RATS.
003807 04-03
A POSSIBLE NEUROCHEMICAL BASIS OF THE CENTRAL STIMULATORY EFFECTS OF PP'DDT.
004274 04-05

NEUROCHEMICAL-BASES
THE DIFFERENTIAL NEUROCHEMICAL-BASES OF THE BEHAVIOURS ELICITED BY SEROTONERGIC-AGENTS AND BY THE COMBINATION OF A MONOAMINE-OXIDASE-INHIBITOR AND L-DOPA.
002976 03-04

NEUROCHEMICAL-CONSEQUENCES
NEUROCHEMICAL-CONSEQUENCES FOLLOWING ADMINISTRATION OF CNS STIMULANTS TO THE NEONATAL RAT.
002926 03-03

NEUROCHEMICAL-CORRELATES
BEHAVIORAL-DEPRESSION AND ITS NEUROCHEMICAL-CORRELATES AT HIGH-DOSES OF D-AMPHETAMINE IN RATS.
001601 02-04

NEUROCHEMICAL-EFFECTS
NEUROCHEMICAL-EFFECTS AND BEHAVIORAL-EFFECTS OF CHRONIC D-AMPHETAMINE TREATMENT IN GENETICALLY OBESE (OBOB) MICE. (PH.D. DISSERTATION).
001739 02-04
A COMPARISON OF THE NEUROCHEMICAL-EFFECTS OF BUPRENORPHINE WITH THOSE OF MORPHINE AND HALOPERIDOL IN RATS.
002701 03-03
A REEVALUATION OF THE NEUROCHEMICAL-EFFECTS AND ANTINOCICEPTIVE-EFFECTS OF INTRATHECAL CAPSAICIN IN THE RAT.
004184 04-04
NEUROCHEMICAL-PHARMACOLOGY
NEUROCHEMICAL-PHARMACOLOGY AND BIOCHEMICAL-PHARMACOLOGY.
003639 03-17
NEUROCHEMICAL-STUDIES
BEHAVIORAL-STUDIES AND NEUROCHEMICAL-STUDIES OF LESCH-NYHANS-SYNDROME.
001743 02-04
NEUROCHEMICAL-STUDIES OF AN ANALGESIC, 1,3 DIPHENYL-5-2-DIMETHYLAMINOPROPIONAMIDE-PYRAZOLE (DIFENAMIZOLE).
002771 03-03
CHARACTERIZATION OF THE ISOLATED PERFUSED MOUSE-BRAIN AS A SYSTEM FOR NEUROCHEMICAL-STUDIES.
003146 03-06
ANTAGONISM OF DOPAMINE SUPERSENSITIVITY BY ESTROGEN: NEUROCHEMICAL-STUDIES IN AN ANIMAL-MODEL OF TARDIVE-DYSKINESIA.
004268 04-05
NEUROCHEMICAL-STUDY
ANATOMICOPHYSIOLOGICAL AND NEUROCHEMICAL-STUDY OF THE LIMBIC-SYSTEM: EFFECT OF NOMIFENSINE.
001160 02-03
NEUROCHEMISTRY
EFFECTS OF FETAL TREATMENT WITH METHYLAZOXYMETHANOL-ACETATE AT VARIOUS GESTATIONAL DATES ON THE NEUROCHEMISTRY OF THE ADULT NEOCORTEX OF THE RAT.
002770 03-03
ESSAYS IN NEUROCHEMISTRY AND NEUROPHARMACOLOGY.
003652 03-17
NEUROENDOCRINE
DOPAMINERGIC FACTORS IN HUMAN PROLACTIN REGULATION: A PITUITARY MODEL FOR THE STUDY OF A NEUROENDOCRINE SYSTEM IN MAN.
000776 01-13
PINEAL INTERACTIONS WITH THE CENTRAL-NERVOUS-SYSTEM: NEUROENDOCRINE IMPLICATIONS. (PH.D. DISSERTATION).
001341 02-03
EFFECTS OF NEUROLEPTICS ON NEUROENDOCRINE MECHANISMS FOR GONADOTROPIN SECRETION.
001391 02-03
EFFECT OF PSYCHOTROPIC-DRUGS ON NEUROENDOCRINE FUNCTION.
002265 02-13
ENDORPHIN OPIATE INTERACTIONS WITH NEUROENDOCRINE SYSTEMS.
002552 02-17
NEUROENDOCRINE APPROACHES TO PSYCHONEUROPHARMACOLOGIC-RESEARCH.
003426 03-13
NEUROENDOCRINE DISTURBANCE IN DEPRESSION.
004405 04-09
ARE THE ENKEPHALINS INVOLVED IN PARKINSONS-DISEASE? CLINICAL AND NEUROENDOCRINE RESPONSES TO NALOXONE ADMINISTRATION.
004431 04-11
BIOCHEMICAL AND NEUROENDOCRINE APPROACHES TO A MALIGNANT-SYNDROME OF NEUROLEPTIC.
004589 04-15
NEUROENDOCRINE-STUDIES
EFFECT OF SODIUM-VALPROATE AND BACLOFEN IN TARDIVE-DYSKINESIA; CLINICAL-STUDIES AND NEUROENDOCRINE-STUDIES.
002441 02-15
NEUROENDOCRINE-STUDY
A NEUROENDOCRINE-STUDY OF SUPERSENSITIVITY IN TARDIVE-DYSKINESIA.
000908 01-16
A NEUROPHARMACOLOGICAL-STUDY AND NEUROENDOCRINE-STUDY ON IDIOPATHIC AND CHRONIC PHARMACOLOGICAL PARKINSONISM.
002371 02-15
A NEUROENDOCRINE-STUDY OF ADRENOCEPTOR FUNCTION IN ENDOGENOUS DEPRESSION.
004362 04-09
NEUROENDOCRINE-TESTS
NEUROENDOCRINE-TESTS DURING TREATMENT WITH NEUROLEPTIC-DRUGS: I. PLASMA PROLACTIN RESPONSE TO CHLORPROMAZINE CHALLENGE.
004329 04-08
NEUROENDOCRINOLOGY
NEUROENDOCRINOLOGY OF DEPRESSION — A DISCUSSION.
003402 03-13
NEUROHORMONAL
THE HYPOTHALAMIC DOPAMINERGIC REGULATION OF PROLACTIN: A MODEL FOR THE STUDY OF NEUROHORMONAL MECHANISMS IN MAN.
002568 02-17

NEUROHUMORS
LSD, PSYCHOTOGENIC PROCEDURES AND BRAIN NEUROHUMORS. (UNPUBLISHED PAPER).
004448 04-11
NEUROINTERMEDIATE
SODIUM-CHLORIDE INHIBITION DECREASES LEVELS OF IMMUNOREACTIVE DYNORPHIN IN THE NEUROINTERMEDIATE PITUITARY OF RATS.
001283 02-03
NEUROLATHYROGEN
THE NEUROLATHYROGEN, BETA N OXALYL-L-ALPHA-BETA-DIAMINOPROPIONIC-ACID, IS A POTENT AGONIST AT GLUTAMATE PREFERRING RECEPTORS IN THE FROG SPINAL-CORD.
002858 03-03
NEUROLEPTIC
STRIATAL DOPAMINERGIC ACTIVITY DURING WITHDRAWAL FROM CHRONIC NEUROLEPTIC TREATMENT IN RATS.
000203 01-03
ORAL DYSKINESIA IN BRAIN-DAMAGED RATS WITHDRAWN FROM A NEUROLEPTIC: IMPLICATION FOR MODELS OF TARDIVE-DYSKINESIA.
000393 01-04
NEUROLEPTIC AND THYMOLEPTIC TREATMENT OF PSYCHOTIC-OUTPATIENTS.
000556 01-08
CLINICAL-RESPONSE AND SERUM NEUROLEPTIC LEVELS IN CHILDHOOD-SCHIZOPHRENIA. (UNPUBLISHED PAPER).
000566 01-08
INTRAMUSCULAR HALOPERIDOL-DECANOATE FOR NEUROLEPTIC MAINTENANCE-THERAPY: EFFICACY, DOSAGE SCHEDULE AND PLASMA LEVELS: AN OPEN MULTICENTER-STUDY.
000758 01-13
THE OCCURRENCE OF TARDIVE EXTRAPYRAMIDAL SYMPTOMS IN SCHIZOPHRENIC-PATIENTS UNDERGOING PROLONGED NEUROLEPTIC TREATMENT.
000885 01-15
TARDIVE TOURETTE-SYNDROME IN AN AUTISTIC-PATIENT AFTER LONG-TERM NEUROLEPTIC ADMINISTRATION.
000887 01-15
MICROSCOPIC EVIDENCE OF LYMPHOGENIC ABSORPTION OF OIL IN HUMANS RECEIVING NEUROLEPTIC OILY DEPOT PREPARATIONS INTRAMUSCULARLY.
000890 01-15
ENDOCRINOLOGICAL CHANGES IN PATIENTS WITH SEXUAL-DYSFUNCTION UNDER LONG-TERM NEUROLEPTIC TREATMENT.
000912 01-17
THE CRYSTAL AND MOLECULAR STRUCTURE OF THE NEUROLEPTIC PIMOZIDE-HYDROCHLORIDE, BISFLUOROPHENYL-BUTYLPIPERIDYLBENZIMIDAZOLINONE-HCL.
001015 02-01
AMOXAPINE IN EXPERIMENTAL PSYCHOPHARMACOLOGY: A NEUROLEPTIC OR AN ANTIDEPRESSANT?
001070 02-02
FLUORO-5-FLUOROPHENYL-2-FLUOROPHENYL 4 HYDROXYBUTYLHEXAHYDROPYRIDOINDOLE-HCL, A NEW POTENT NEUROLEPTIC.
001092 02-02
CENTRAL LEVELS OF NORADRENALINE, 3 METHOXY-4-HYDROXYPHENYLETHYLENEGLYCOL AND CYCLIC-AMP IN THE RAT AFTER ACTIVATION OF LOCUS-COERULEUS NEURONS: INFLUENCE OF SINGLE AND REPEATED NEUROLEPTIC TREATMENT.
001095 02-03
EFFECTS OF CHRONIC NEUROLEPTIC TREATMENT ON TYROSINE-HYDROXYLASE IN DOPAMINERGIC TERMINALS: COMPARISONS BETWEEN DRUGS AND BRAIN REGIONS REVEALS DIFFERENT MECHANISMS OF TOLERANCE.
001243 02-03
PERINATAL NEUROLEPTIC ACTIONS -- DEVELOPMENTAL RESULTS. (UNPUBLISHED PAPER).
001277 02-03
INCREASED RENAL NEUROLEPTIC BINDING IN SPONTANEOUSLY HYPERTENSIVE-RATS.
001444 02-03
THE ROLE OF GAMMA AMINOBUTYRIC-ACID IN ACUTE AND CHRONIC NEUROLEPTIC ACTION.
001465 02-03
BRAIN-MONOAMINES IN THE RHESUS-MONKEY DURING LONG-TERM NEUROLEPTIC ADMINISTRATION.
001471 02-03
CHRONIC NEUROLEPTIC TREATMENT AND DOPAMINE-RECEPTOR REGULATION.
001837 02-05
3H APOMORPHINE-RECEPTORS IN VARIOUS RAT-BRAIN REGIONS: A STUDY OF SPECIFIC AND NONSPECIFIC BINDING AND THE INFLUENCE OF CHRONIC NEUROLEPTIC TREATMENT.
001846 02-05
NEUROLEPTIC/DOPAMINE-RECEPTORS: ELEVATION AND REVERSAL.
001847 02-05

NEUROLEPTIC TREATMENT FOR A SUBSTANTIAL PROPORTION OF ADULT LIFE: BEHAVIOURAL-SEQUELAE OF 9 MONTHS HALOPERIDOL ADMINISTRATION.
001858 02-05

USE OF LARGE-SINGLE-DOSES OF BROMOCRIPTINE IN SCHIZOPHRENIC-PATIENTS WITH ELEVATED SERUM PROLACTIN LEVELS AND EXTRAPYRAMIDAL SIDE-EFFECTS ASSOCIATED WITH NEUROLEPTIC TREATMENT.
001944 02-08

SERUM NEUROLEPTIC CONCENTRATIONS IN SCHIZOPHRENIA. (UNPUBLISHED PAPER).
001945 02-08

RELATIONSHIPS AMONG BIOCHEMICAL-VARIABLES, CLINICAL-VARIABLES, AND PHARMACOKINETIC-VARIABLES IN NEUROLEPTIC TREATED SCHIZOPHRENIC-PATIENTS.
001946 02-08

MAINTENANCE-TREATMENT WITH SEMIDEPOTE NEUROLEPTIC FLUSPIRILENE.
002151 02-11

CHANGES IN CEREBRAL DOPAMINE METABOLISM AND RECEPTORS DURING ONE-YEAR NEUROLEPTIC ADMINISTRATION AND SUBSEQUENT WITHDRAWAL: RELEVANCE TO BRAIN-BIOCHEMISTRY IN SCHIZOPHRENIA.
002390 02-15

APPROACHES TO THE PROBLEM OF PREVENTING HAZARDS OF LONG-TERM NEUROLEPTIC TREATMENT AND OF AVOIDING UNNECESSARY DRUGS.
002426 02-15

NEUROLEPTIC BLOOD LEVELS AND THERAPEUTIC EFFECT.
002480 02-16

RELATIONSHIP BETWEEN STRUCTURE AND NEUROLEPTIC ACTIVITY: PHARMACOPHORE AND PHARMACOKINETICS.
002492 02-16

DURING ONE YEARS NEUROLEPTIC TREATMENT IN RATS STRIATAL DOPAMINE-RECEPTOR BLOCKADE DECREASES BUT SERUM PROLACTIN LEVELS REMAIN ELEVATED.
002707 03-03

NEUROLEPTIC ACTION ON HEPATIC ENZYMATIC ACTIVITY.
002849 03-03

INVOLVEMENT OF CAUDATE-NUCLEUS, AMYGDALA OR RETICULAR FORMATION IN NEUROLEPTIC AND NARCOTIC CATALEPSY.
002986 03-04

PERSPECTIVES ON PRAZINIL (CARPIPRAMINE): A DISINHIBITING-AGENT WITH NO NEUROLEPTIC ACTIVITY. A REVIEW OF 38 CASES.
003149 03-07

SYNERGISM OF COMBINED LITHIUM NEUROLEPTIC THERAPY: A DOUBLE-BLIND, PLACEBO-CONTROLLED CASE-STUDY.
003165 03-08

LOW SERUM PROLACTIN AND EARLY RELAPSE FOLLOWING NEUROLEPTIC WITHDRAWAL.
003166 03-08

THE NEED FOR CONTINUOUS USE OF ANTIPARKINSONIAN MEDICATION WITH CHRONIC SCHIZOPHRENIC-PATIENTS RECEIVING LONG-TERM NEUROLEPTIC THERAPY.
003186 03-08

NEUROLEPTIC SERUM LEVELS MEASURED BY RADIORECEPTOR ASSAY AND CLINICAL-RESPONSE IN SCHIZOPHRENIC-PATIENTS.
003199 03-08

CHANGES IN THE PSYCHOPATHOLOGY OF PSYCHOSIS DUE TO NEUROLEPTIC TREATMENT.
003281 03-10

THE EFFECT OF AMANTADINE ON PROLACTIN LEVELS AND GALACTORRHEA ON NEUROLEPTIC TREATED PATIENTS.
003373 03-11

NEUROLEPTIC MALIGNANT-SYNDROME: A PATHOGENETIC ROLE FOR DOPAMINE-RECEPTOR BLOCKADE?
003492 03-15

CHOLINERGIC REBOUND IN NEUROLEPTIC WITHDRAWAL-SYNDROMES.
003506 03-15

ON SENSORY-DISTURBANCES OCCURRING DURING NEUROLEPTIC THERAPY.
003531 03-15

SELF-STIMULATION AND LOCOMOTOR CHANGES INDICATING LATENT ANTICHOLINERGIC-ACTIVITY BY AN ATYPICAL NEUROLEPTIC (THIORIDAZINE).
003560 03-16

NEUROLEPTIC ACTIVITY: A SUMMARY OF PROFESSOR JACQUES GLOWINSKIS PRESENTATION.
003628 03-17

SOLUBILIZATION OF NEUROLEPTIC/DOPAMINE-RECEPTORS OF HUMAN BRAIN STRIATUM.
003767 04-03

EFFECT OF PRENATAL NEUROLEPTIC TREATMENT ON MEMBRANE RECEPTOR DEVELOPMENT IN THE BRAIN.
003989 04-03

CHRONIC NEUROLEPTIC TREATMENT SPECIFICALLY ALTERS THE NUMBER OF DOPAMINE-RECEPTORS IN RAT-BRAIN.
004033 04-03

IS DOPAMINE ANTAGONISM A REQUISITE OF NEUROLEPTIC ACTIVITY?
004122 04-04

BEHAVIORAL AND BIOCHEMICAL-STUDIES OF THE SCOPOLAMINE-INDUCED REVERSAL OF NEUROLEPTIC ACTIVITY.
004195 04-04

THE PROLACTIN RESPONSE IN PATIENTS RECEIVING NEUROLEPTIC THERAPY. THE EFFECT OF FLUPHENAZINE-DECANOATE.
004318 04-08

PLASMA LEVELS OF BETA ENDORPHIN UNDER CHRONIC NEUROLEPTIC TREATMENT IN SCHIZOPHRENIC-PATIENTS: FAILURE OF NALOXONE TO COUNTERACT CURATIVE EFFECTS OF NEUROLEPTIC-DRUGS.
004321 04-08

LONG-TERM NEUROLEPTIC TREATMENT OF CHRONIC SCHIZOPHRENIC-PATIENTS: CLINICAL AND BIOCHEMICAL-EFFECTS OF WITHDRAWAL.
004344 04-08

AN EVALUATION OF THE USEFULNESS OF THE ACYLASE TEST IN NEUROLEPTIC TREATMENT.
004426 04-10

NEUROLEPTIC TRICYCLIC-ANTIDEPRESSANT COMBINATION: PHARMACOLOGICAL-ASPECTS AND THERAPEUTIC INTEREST.
004501 04-13

CEREBROSPINAL-FLUID HOMOVANILLIC-ACID PATTERNS DURING NEUROLEPTIC TREATMENT. (UNPUBLISHED PAPER).
004502 04-13

BIOCHEMICAL AND NEUROENDOCRINE APPROACHES TO A MALIGNANT-SYNDROME OF NEUROLEPTIC.
004589 04-15

EFFECTS OF NEUROLEPTIC ADJUSTMENT ON CLINICAL CONDITION AND TARDIVE-DYSKINESIA IN SCHIZOPHRENIC-PATIENTS.
004595 04-15

NEUROLEPTIC TREATMENT AS EXPERIENCED BY A PSYCHIATRIST.
004613 04-15

CLOPIPAZAN (SKF-69634), A NEW NEUROLEPTIC ESSENTIALLY FREE OF EXTRAPYRAMIDAL LIABILITY: QUANTITATIVE PHARMACOEEG AND OPEN LABEL CLINICAL-TRIAL.
004620 04-15

MEASUREMENT OF NEUROLEPTIC CONCENTRATIONS BY GLC AND RADIORECEPTOR ASSAY.
004682 04-16

NEUROLEPTIC-AGENT

THE TREATMENT OF BUCCOLINGUOFACIAL DYSKINESIA IN THE ELDERLY: THE CHOICE OF A NEUROLEPTIC-AGENT.
002223 02-13

NEUROLEPTIC-AGENTS

SYNTHESIS OF SOME 5 PHENYLHEXAHYDROAZEPINOINDOLES AS POTENTIAL NEUROLEPTIC-AGENTS.
001019 02-01

LONG-TERM-TREATMENT WITH NEUROLEPTIC-AGENTS: ADAPTATION PHENOMENA AND THEIR SIGNIFICANCE WITH REGARD TO SCHIZOPHRENIC-SYMPTOMATOLOGY AND SIDE-EFFECTS.
002370 02-15

A TRIAL TREATMENT WITH TIAPRIDE FOR SOME EXTRAPYRAMIDAL-SYNDROMES CAUSED BY NEUROLEPTIC-AGENTS.
003553 03-15

NEUROLEPTIC-DRUG

THE EFFECT OF A NEW FLUORINATED TRICYCLIC NEUROLEPTIC-DRUG ISOFLOXYTHEPIN ON THE RAT STRIATAL DOPAMINE METABOLISM.
000306 01-03

PHARMACOLOGICAL-STUDY OF CHLORODIMETHYLAMINOETHOXYDIBENZOTHIEPINE (ZOTEPINE), A NEW NEUROLEPTIC-DRUG.
000493 01-04

TOXICOLOGICAL AND TERATOLOGICAL STUDIES OF CHLORODIMETHYLAMINOETHOXYDIBENZOTHIEPINE (ZOTEPINE), A NEW NEUROLEPTIC-DRUG.
000515 01-05

LOXAPINE-SUCCINATE: A NEW NEUROLEPTIC-DRUG.
000551 01-08

DOPAMINE-SENSITIVE ADENYLATE-CYCLASE AND RECEPTOR BINDING-ACTIVITIES FOLLOWING ACUTE AND CHRONIC NEUROLEPTIC-DRUG TREATMENT. (UNPUBLISHED PAPER).
001172 02-03

KINETICS OF CENTRAL-ACTIONS OF ISOFLOXYTHEPIN, AN ORAL NEUROLEPTIC-DRUG WITH PROLONGED ACTION IN RODENTS.
001720 02-04

THE PLACE OF LOXAPINE — A NEW NEUROLEPTIC-DRUG.
001886 02-07

NEUROLEPTIC-DRUGS

PROLACTIN RESPONSE AND EXTRAPYRAMIDAL SIDE-EFFECTS DURING PROPRANOLOL AND NEUROLEPTIC-DRUGS TREATMENT IN CHRONIC SCHIZOPHRENIC-PATIENTS.
000841 01-15

EFFECT OF NEUROLEPTIC-DRUGS ON LITHIUM UPTAKE BY THE HUMAN ERYTHROCYTE.
000973 01-17

DOPAMINE-SENSITIVE ADENYLATE-CYCLASE AND DOPAMINE/ NEUROLEPTIC-RECEPTOR BINDING: EFFECT OF NEUROLEPTIC-DRUGS.
001358 02-03

THE EFFECTS OF NOREPINEPHRINE PERFUSION OF THE MESENCEPHALIC RETICULAR FORMATION ON BEHAVIOR IN THE RAT: INTERACTION

WITH SEVERAL NEUROLEPTIC-DRUGS ON A MEASURE OF SUSTAINED ATTENTION. (PH.D. DISSERTATION).
001563 02-04

BEHAVIORAL-CONSEQUENCES OF LONG-TERM-TREATMENT WITH NEUROLEPTIC-DRUGS.
001661 02-04

THE PHOTOCHEMICAL-STABILITY OF CIS-ISOMERS AND TRANS-ISOMERS OF TRICYCLIC NEUROLEPTIC-DRUGS.
001872 02-06

TARDIVE-DYSKINESIA FROM NEUROLEPTIC-DRUGS: REVIEW OF THE LITERATURE.
002398 02-15

THE INFLUENCE OF NEUROLEPTIC-DRUGS ON PROLACTIN SECRETION IN CHILDREN.
002409 02-15

CHRONOLOGY OF EXTRAPYRAMIDAL-EFFECTS OF NEUROLEPTIC-DRUGS AND THE NIGROSTRIATAL DOPAMINERGIC-SYSTEM.
002449 02-15

CLINICAL-ASPECTS ON PROLACTIN RESPONSE TO NEUROLEPTIC-DRUGS.
002590 02-17

ENHANCEMENT OF NORADRENALINE RELEASE FROM RAT-CEREBRAL-CORTEX BY NEUROLEPTIC-DRUGS.
002742 03-03

DIFFERENCES IN THE CLINICAL ACTION OF SOME NEUROLEPTIC-DRUGS.
003204 03-08

MEDICAL AND LEGAL IMPLICATIONS OF SIDE-EFFECTS FROM NEUROLEPTIC-DRUGS. A ROUND-TABLE DISCUSSION.
003471 03-15

DOPAMINERGIC NEURONS OF SPINAL-CORD: A POSSIBLE SITE FOR THE ACTION OF NEUROLEPTIC-DRUGS.
004188 04-04

DISRUPTION OF AUTOSHAPED RESPONDING TO A SIGNAL OF BRAIN-STIMULATION REWARD BY NEUROLEPTIC-DRUGS.
004199 04-04

ELECTROCARDIOGRAPHIC-CHANGES IN RATS DURING CHRONIC-TREATMENT WITH ANTIDEPRESSANT AND NEUROLEPTIC-DRUGS.
004284 04-05

PLASMA LEVELS OF BETA ENDORPHIN UNDER CHRONIC NEUROLEPTIC TREATMENT IN SCHIZOPHRENIC-PATIENTS: FAILURE OF NALOXONE TO COUNTERACT CURATIVE EFFECTS OF NEUROLEPTIC-DRUGS.
004321 04-08

NEUROENDOCRINE-TESTS DURING TREATMENT WITH NEUROLEPTIC-DRUGS: I. PLASMA PROLACTIN RESPONSE TO CHLORPROMAZINE CHALLENGE.
004329 04-08

THE EFFECT OF AN INTENSIVE COURSE OF NEUROLEPTIC-DRUGS ON SCHIZOPHRENIC-PATIENTS AND THEIR SUBSEQUENT COURSE FOLLOWING THE CESSATION OF ALL NEUROLEPTIC-MEDICATION.
004341 04-08

CHANGES IN PSYCHOPATHOLOGIC SYMPTOMS DURING 20 DAYS OF TREATMENT WITH ANTIDEPRESSANTS AND NEUROLEPTIC-DRUGS.
004415 04-09

PROLACTIN AND NEUROLEPTIC-DRUGS: A BIOCHEMICAL INDEX OF CLINICAL-RESPONSE?
004539 04-13

THE EFFECTS OF NEUROLEPTIC-DRUGS ON THE SOCIAL INTERACTIONS OF HOSPITALIZED PSYCHOTIC-PATIENTS.
004577 04-14

NEUROLEPTIC-EFFECT
NEUROLEPTIC-EFFECT ON DESIPRAMINE STEADY-STATE PLASMA CONCENTRATIONS.
000781 01-13

A PROBABLE NEUROLEPTIC-EFFECT ON PLATELET MONOAMINE-OXIDASE IN CHRONIC SCHIZOPHRENIC-PATIENTS.
003169 03-08

NEUROLEPTIC-EFFECTS
SUSTAINED GAMMA AMINOBUTYRIC-ACID-RECEPTOR STIMULATION AND CHRONIC NEUROLEPTIC-EFFECTS.
001345 02-03

NEUROLEPTIC-INDUCED
THE USE OF EXTINCTION TO INVESTIGATE THE NATURE OF NEUROLEPTIC-INDUCED AVOIDANCE-DEFICITS.
000345 01-04

NEUROLEPTIC-INDUCED TARDIVE-DYSKINESIA: RECENT PATHOPHYSIOLOGICAL-DATA, THERAPEUTIC TRIALS.
000842 01-15

EFFECT OF THE NEW GAMMA AMINOBUTYRIC-ACID AGONIST SL-76-002 ON STRIATAL ACETYLCHOLINE: RELATION TO NEUROLEPTIC-INDUCED EXTRAPYRAMIDAL ALTERATIONS.
001119 02-03

STUDIES ON THE SPECIFICITY AND REVERSAL OF NEUROLEPTIC-INDUCED DOPAMINERGIC-SUPERSENSITIVITY. (PH.D. DISSERTATION).
001469 02-03

INHIBITION OF NEUROLEPTIC-INDUCED DOPAMINE-RECEPTOR SUPERSENSITIVITY BY CYCLO-LEU-GLY.
001576 02-04

ANTICHOLINERGICS PROMOTE NEUROLEPTIC-INDUCED TARDIVE-DYSKINESIA.
001834 02-05

PIRACETAM ACTION IN NEUROLEPTIC-INDUCED EXTRAPYRAMIDAL SIDE-EFFECTS.
002132 02-11

NEUROLEPTIC-INDUCED TARDIVE-DYSKINESIAS.
002382 02-15

NEUROLEPTIC-INDUCED REINNERVATION SPROUTING IN THE CENTRAL-NERVOUS-SYSTEM (A MODEL FOR THE DEVELOPMENT OF TARDIVE-DYSKINESIA AND SUPERSENSITIVITY PSYCHOSIS).
002459 02-15

NEUROLEPTIC-INDUCED ACUTE DYSTONIC REACTIONS MAY BE DUE TO ENHANCED DOPAMINE RELEASE ON TO SUPERSENSITIVE POSTSYNAPTIC-RECEPTORS.
002789 03-03

NEUROLEPTIC-INDUCED ELEVATIONS IN SERUM PROLACTIN LEVELS: ETIOLOGY AND SIGNIFICANCE.
003190 03-08

NEUROLEPTIC-INDUCED SYNDROME MIMICKING MYASTHENIA-GRAVIS.
003474 03-15

THE DIAGNOSIS AND TREATMENT OF NEUROLEPTIC-INDUCED PARKINSONISM.
003493 03-15

THE USE OF CONDITIONED SUPPRESSION TO EVALUATE THE NATURE OF NEUROLEPTIC-INDUCED AVOIDANCE-DEFICITS.
004070 04-04

ON THE THERAPY OF NEUROLEPTIC-INDUCED TARDIVE-DYSKINESIA WITH DIMETHYLAMINOETHANOL (DEANOL).
004627 04-15

NEUROLEPTIC-MEDICATION
TIME-COURSE OF THE ANTIPSYCHOTIC-EFFECT IN SCHIZOPHRENIA AND SOME CHANGES IN POSTMORTEM BRAIN AND THEIR RELATION TO NEUROLEPTIC-MEDICATION.
001911 02-08

HORMONE LEVELS IN ACUTE SCHIZOPHRENIA WITH AND WITHOUT NEUROLEPTIC-MEDICATION.
001923 02-08

PHENYLKETONURIA: THE INADVISABILITY OF NEUROLEPTIC-MEDICATION.
003380 03-11

THE EFFECT OF AN INTENSIVE COURSE OF NEUROLEPTIC-DRUGS ON SCHIZOPHRENIC-PATIENTS AND THEIR SUBSEQUENT COURSE FOLLOWING THE CESSATION OF ALL NEUROLEPTIC-MEDICATION.
004341 04-08

NEUROLEPTIC-MEDICINE
CASE-REPORT: USING ATTRIBUTION THEORY TO LIMIT NEED FOR NEUROLEPTIC-MEDICINE.
000559 01-08

NEUROLEPTIC-PEPTIDE
EFFECTS OF THE POTENTIAL NEUROLEPTIC-PEPTIDE DES-TYR1-GAMMA-ENDORPHIN AND HALOPERIDOL ON APOMORPHINE-INDUCED BEHAVIOURAL-SYNDROMES IN RATS AND MICE.
000441 01-04

NEUROLEPTIC-RECEPTOR
DOPAMINE-SENSITIVE ADENYLATE-CYCLASE AND DOPAMINE/NEUROLEPTIC-RECEPTOR BINDING: EFFECT OF NEUROLEPTIC-DRUGS.
001358 02-03

NEUROLEPTIC-RECEPTORS
THE USE OF THIOPROPERAZINE, A PHENOTHIAZINE DERIVATIVE, AS A LIGAND FOR NEUROLEPTIC-RECEPTORS -- I. IN VITRO STUDIES.
001133 02-03

THE USE OF THIOPROPERAZINE, A PHENOTHIAZINE DERIVATIVE, AS A LIGAND FOR NEUROLEPTIC-RECEPTORS -- II. IN VIVO STUDIES.
001137 02-03

SIMILARITIES AND DISSIMILARITIES BETWEEN DOPAMINE AND NEUROLEPTIC-RECEPTORS: FURTHER EVIDENCE FOR TYPE-1 AND TYPE-2 DOPAMINE-RECEPTORS IN THE CNS.
001480 02-03

NEUROLEPTIC-SYNDROME
CORRECTION OF THE EXTRAPYRAMIDAL NEUROLEPTIC-SYNDROME BY TRYPTOPHAN AND THE TIME-COURSE OF ITS CONTENT IN THE BLOOD OF PATIENTS.
004434 04-11

NEUROLEPTICA
THE TWO SURVIVAL CASES OF ALPHA-PATTERN COMA CAUSED BY LARGE AMOUNTS OF HYPNOTICA AND NEUROLEPTICA.
004608 04-15

NEUROLEPTICS
FLUORINATED ANALOGUES OF THE TRICYCLIC NEUROLEPTICS: 2,3 DIFLUORO DERIVATIVE OF CLOROTEPIN.
000001 01-01

ACUTE AND CHRONIC EFFECTS OF NEUROLEPTICS AND ACUTE EFFECTS OF APOMORPHINE AND AMPHETAMINE ON DOPAMINE TURNOVER IN CORPUS-STRIATUM AND SUBSTANTIA-NIGRA OF THE RAT-BRAIN.
000215 01-03

CHANGES IN OPIATE ACTIVITY OF RAT PITUITARY FOLLOWING ACUTE ADMINISTRATION OF NEUROLEPTICS.
000282 01-03

THE STIMULANT-EFFECT OF NEUROLEPTICS: MYTH OR REALITY?
000362 01-04

BIOCHEMICAL-STUDIES AFTER CHRONIC ADMINISTRATION OF NEUROLEPTICS TO MONKEYS.
000523 01-05

WHAT IS THE BEST MAINTENANCE DOSE OF NEUROLEPTICS IN SCHIZOPHRENIA?
000547 01-08

THE PLACE OF LONG-ACTING NEUROLEPTICS IN THE TREATMENT OF SCHIZOPHRENIA.
000563 01-08

THE ULTRASTRUCTURAL CHANGES OF SYNAPSES IN RAT FOLLOWING LONG-TERM ADMINISTRATION OF THE NEUROLEPTICS RESERPINE AND HALOPERIDOL.
000795 01-13

SPONTANEOUS DYSKINESIA IN THE ELDERLY AND TARDIVE-DYSKINESIA FROM NEUROLEPTICS. A SURVEY OF 270 ELDERLY-PATIENTS.
000834 01-15

NEUROLEPTICS AND NEUROTRANSMITTER-RECEPTORS.
000980 01-17

NEUROPHARMACOLOGICAL AND NEUROCHEMICAL APPROACHES TO PRECLINICAL-EVALUATION OF NEUROLEPTICS.
001094 02-02

LONG-TERM EFFECT OF NEUROLEPTICS ON CORTICOSTERONE SEPTOHIPPOCAMPAL UPTAKE IN RATS.
001107 02-03

ADAPTIVE CHANGES OF THE STRIATAL DOPAMINE SYSTEM INDUCED BY REPEATED ADMINISTRATION OF NEUROLEPTICS AND ERGOT DERIVATIVES.
001156 02-03

THE QUANTITATIVE MEASUREMENT OF CHANGES IN EEG FREQUENCY SPECTRA PRODUCED IN THE CAT BY SEDATIVE HYPNOTICS AND NEUROLEPTICS.
001220 02-03

NO EVIDENCE FOR INCREASED DOPAMINE-RECEPTOR BINDING IN SUPERRESPONSIVE MICE AFTER A SINGLE-DOSE OF NEUROLEPTICS.
001292 02-03

CONFORMATIONALLY RESTRICTED PHENOTHIAZINE NEUROLEPTICS. 1. 3 DIMETHYLAMINO-TETRAHYDROAZEPINOPHENOTHIAZINE.
001359 02-03

EFFECTS OF NEUROLEPTICS ON NEUROENDOCRINE MECHANISMS FOR GONADOTROPIN SECRETION.
001391 02-03

EFFECT OF REPEATED TREATMENT WITH NEUROLEPTICS ON DOPAMINE METABOLISM IN CELL BODIES AND TERMINALS OF DOPAMINERGIC-SYSTEMS IN THE RAT-BRAIN.
001464 02-03

MODULATION OF BETA-ADRENERGIC-RECEPTORS AND CALMODULIN FOLLOWING ACUTE AND CHRONIC-TREATMENT WITH NEUROLEPTICS.
001529 02-03

BEHAVIORAL-EFFECTS, ANTIDOPAMINERGIC-EFFECTS, AND PROHYPNOTIC-EFFECTS OF NEUROLEPTICS DURING AND AFTER PROLONGED TREATMENT.
001577 02-04

10 PIPERAZINYL-4H-THIENOBENZODIAZEPINES AS POTENTIAL NEUROLEPTICS.
001591 02-04

4 PIPERAZINYL-10H-THIENOBENZODIAZEPINES AS POTENTIAL NEUROLEPTICS.
001592 02-04

DIFFERENTIAL-EFFECTS OF AMPHETAMINE AND NEUROLEPTICS ON NEGATIVE VS. POSITIVE SYMPTOMS IN SCHIZOPHRENIA.
001906 02-08

DISORDERS OF SMOOTH-PURSUIT EYE-MOVEMENTS IN SCHIZOPHRENICS AND THE EFFECT OF NEUROLEPTICS IN THERAPEUTIC DOSES.
001912 02-08

METHODOLOGY AND RESULTS OF A LONG-TERM STUDY OF LONG-ACTING NEUROLEPTICS: PIPOTHIAZINE-PALMITATE AND FLUPHENAZINE-DECANOATE.
001929 02-08

BASAL AND STIMULATED LEVELS OF PROLACTIN, TSH AND LH IN SERUM OF CHRONIC SCHIZOPHRENIC-PATIENTS, LONG-TERM TREATED WITH NEUROLEPTICS.
001935 02-08

BASAL AND STIMULATED LEVELS OF PROLACTIN, TSH, AND LH IN SERUM OF CHRONIC SCHIZOPHRENIC-PATIENTS LONG-TERM TREATED WITH NEUROLEPTICS: RELATIONS TO PSYCHOPATHOLOGY.
001936 02-08

NEUROLEPTICS AND DOPAMINE-RECEPTORS, THERAPEUTIC IMPLICATIONS.
001942 02-08

THE ASSOCIATION OF RETARD NEUROLEPTICS TO OTHER NEUROLEPTICS IN THE REHABILITATION OF PSYCHOTIC-PATIENTS.
002108 02-11

MALIGNANT-HYPERTHERMIC-SYNDROMES IN THE COURSE OF TREATMENT WITH LONG-ACTING NEUROLEPTICS.
002430 02-15

PROPRANOLOL (INDERAL) FOR TARDIVE-DYSKINESIA AND EXTRAPYRAMIDAL SIDE-EFFECTS FROM NEUROLEPTICS: POSSIBLE INVOLVEMENT OF BETA-ADRENERGIC MECHANISMS.
002470 02-15

TWELVE YEARS EXPERIENCE WITH THE TOTAL USE OF DEPOT NEUROLEPTICS IN A DEFINED POPULATION.
002544 02-17

THE CHANGE OF BLOOD PROLACTIN LEVEL DUE TO THE WITHDRAWAL OF MAINTENANCE NEUROLEPTICS.
002559 02-17

PRESENT INDICATIONS OF LONG-ACTING NEUROLEPTICS.
002576 02-17

NEUROLEPTICS IN 1978.
002626 02-17

EFFECT OF NEUROLEPTICS ON INDOLEAMINE-N-METHYLTRANSFERASE ACTIVITY AND BRAIN METABOLISM OF BUFOTENIN.
002735 03-03

DIFFERENTIAL REVERSAL BY SCOPOLAMINE AND THIP OF THE ANTISTEREOTYPIC AND CATALEPTIC-EFFECTS OF NEUROLEPTICS.
002948 03-04

CHRONIC EFFECTS OF NEUROLEPTICS HAVING HIGH OR LOW INCIDENCE OF EXTRAPYRAMIDAL SIDE-EFFECTS UPON FORCE, DURATION AND RATE OF OPERANT-RESPONSE IN RATS. (PH.D. DISSERTATION).
003125 03-05

LITHIUM COMBINED WITH NEUROLEPTICS IN CHRONIC SCHIZOPHRENIC-PATIENTS AND SCHIZOAFFECTIVE-PATIENTS.
003168 03-08

MANAGEMENT OF SCHIZOPHRENIA: LONG-TERM CLINICAL-STUDIES WITH SPECIAL REFERENCE TO THE COMBINATION OF PSYCHOTHERAPY AND DEPOT NEUROLEPTICS.
003183 03-08

NEUROLEPTICS ADMINISTERED IN HIGH-DOSAGES.
003185 03-08

DOPAMINE-RECEPTORS, NEUROLEPTICS, AND SCHIZOPHRENIA.
003197 03-08

NEUROLEPTICS: ACTIVATION OR INHIBITION OF THE DOPAMINERGIC-SYSTEM?
003424 03-13

EFFECTS OF GRADUAL DECREASE AND DISCONTINUATION OF NEUROLEPTICS ON CLINICAL CONDITION AND TARDIVE-DYSKINESIA.
003469 03-15

ADVANTAGES AND DISADVANTAGES OF PROLONGED USE OF NEUROLEPTICS.
003470 03-15

NEUROLEPTICS: INTERACTIONS WITH FOOD – CHEMICAL AND PHARMACODYNAMIC STUDIES ON THE INTERACTIONS OF COFFEE AND TEA.
003612 03-17

INCREASE OF NEUROTENSIN CONTENT ELICITED BY NEUROLEPTICS IN NUCLEUS-ACCUMBENS.
003808 04-03

STUDIES ON THE KINETIC PROPERTIES OF TRYPTOPHAN-HYDROXYLASE OF RABBIT MESENCEPHALON AND PONS-MEDULLA; EFFECT OF LONG-TERM-TREATMENT WITH NEUROLEPTICS AND ANTIDEPRESSANTS.
003852 04-03

THE EFFECT OF TYPICAL AND ATYPICAL NEUROLEPTICS ON BINDING OF (3H)SPIROPERIDOL IN CALF CAUDATE.
003906 04-03

PRESYNAPTIC AND POSTSYNAPTIC ALPHA-ADRENOCEPTOR ANTAGONISM BY NEUROLEPTICS IN VIVO.
003966 04-03

CLASSICAL NEUROLEPTICS AND DECONDITIONING ACTIVITY AFTER SINGLE OR REPEATED TREATMENTS: ROLE OF DIFFERENT CEREBRAL NEUROTRANSMITTERS.
004115 04-04

A COMPARISON BETWEEN SOME BIOCHEMICAL-EFFECTS AND BEHAVIOURAL-EFFECTS PRODUCED BY NEUROLEPTICS.
004116 04-04

A FOLLOWUP STUDY OF SCHIZOPHRENIC-OUTPATIENTS TREATED WITH DEPOT NEUROLEPTICS.
004342 04-08

HORMONAL STIMULATION AFTER INJECTION OF THYROTROPHIN-RELEASING-FACTOR (TRF) AND ACTH1-24 IN PATIENTS FOLLOWING CHRONIC-TREATMENT WITH NEUROLEPTICS: PRELIMINARY-STUDY.
004505 04-13

DES-TYROSINE-GAMMA-ENDORPHIN: H-REFLEX RESPONSE SIMILAR TO NEUROLEPTICS.
004540 04-13

NEUROLEPTICS AND THEIR SIDE-EFFECTS.
004590 04-15

RECEPTOR TECHNIQUES IN THE STUDY OF PLASMA LEVELS OF NEUROLEPTICS AND ANTIDEPRESSANT-DRUGS.
004694 04-16

NEUROLEPTICS IN 1979.
004749 04-17

NEUROLOGIC
OPIATE ANTAGONIST IMPROVES NEUROLOGIC RECOVERY AFTER SPINAL INJURY.
002714 03-03

NEUROLOGICAL
NEUROLOGICAL SIDE-EFFECTS OF LITHIUM: ORGANIC-BRAIN-SYNDROME, SEIZURES, EXTRAPYRAMIDAL SIDE-EFFECTS, AND EEG CHANGES.
000847 01-15

THE NEUROLOGICAL FORENSIC ASPECTS OF THALLIUM POISONING.
002438 02-15
NEUROLOGICAL TOLERANCE OF LITHIUM AND PSYCHOTROPIC-DRUGS IN
COMBINATION: 265 CASES.
004594 04-15

NEUROLOGICAL-COMPLICATIONS
DYSKINETIC AND NEUROLOGICAL-COMPLICATIONS IN CHILDREN TREATED
WITH PSYCHOTROPIC-MEDICATIONS.
000880 01-15
NEUROLOGICAL-COMPLICATIONS DUE TO THE PHARMACOLOGICAL-
TREATMENT OF EPILEPTIC-PATIENTS.
004593 04-15

NEUROLOGICAL-STUDY
NEUROLOGICAL-STUDY AND NEUROPSYCHOPHARMACOLOGY-STUDY ON
DEMENTIA.
001090 02-11

NEUROLOGICAL-SYNDROME
BRAIN-MONOAMINES AND THE HIGH PRESSURE NEUROLOGICAL-
SYNDROME.
001686 02-04

NEUROLOGY
CHILD-PSYCHIATRY AND PSYCHOPHARMACOTHERAPY IN GENERAL
PRACTICE, IN PEDIATRICS, AND IN NEUROLOGY.
003288 03-11
CHANGES IN AND CURRENT PROGRESS OF NEUROLOGY AND
PSYCHIATRY.
003550 03-15

NEUROMODULATORS
GLYCINE, ACETYLCHOLINE, AND SEROTONIN: NEUROTRANSMITTERS OR
NEUROMODULATORS?
002271 02-13

NEUROMODULATORY
EVIDENCE SUGGESTING A TRANSMITTER OR NEUROMODULATORY ROLE
FOR SUBSTANCE-P AT THE FIRST SYNAPSE OF THE BARORECEPTOR
REFLEX.
001264 02-03

NEURON
AUTOCORRELATION ANALYSIS OF SINGLE NEURON ACTIVITY AFTER
ADMINISTRATION OF PENTOBARBITAL.
001268 02-03
DISTRIBUTION OF MEMBRANE GLYCOPROTEINS AMONG THE ORGANELLES
OF A SINGLE IDENTIFIED NEURON OF APLYSIA. II. ISOLATION AND
CHARACTERIZATION OF A GLYCOPROTEIN ASSOCIATED WITH
VESICLES.
002657 03-03
EFFECTS OF PENTOBARBITAL AND ETHANOL UPON SINGLE NEURON
ACTIVITY IN THE PRIMARY SOMATOSENSORY CORTEX OF THE RHESUS-
MONKEY.
003755 04-03
MORPHINE DEPRESSES DORSAL-HORN NEURON RESPONSES TO
CONTROLLED NOXIOUS AND NONNOXIOUS CUTANEOUS STIMULATION.
003782 04-03
EFFECTS OF ACUTE AND CHRONIC AMPHETAMINE TREATMENT ON
PURKINJE NEURON DISCHARGE IN RAT CEREBELLUM.
003793 04-03
THE HUMAN PLATELET AS A MODEL FOR THE GLUTAMATERGIC NEURON:
PLATELET UPTAKE OF L GLUTAMATE.
003923 04-03

NEURONAL
SUPPRESSION OF SEROTONERGIC NEURONAL FIRING BY ALPHA-
ADRENOCEPTOR ANTAGONISTS: EVIDENCE AGAINST GABA
MEDIATION.
000024 01-03
3H IMIPRAMINE BINDING IN NEURONAL AND GLIAL FRACTIONS OF
HORSE STRIATUM.
000033 01-03
NEURONAL ACTIVITY IN CHRONIC FERRIC-CHLORIDE EPILEPTIC-FOCI IN
CATS AND MONKEY.
000172 01-03
INHIBITION OF NEURONAL UPTAKE REDUCES THE PRESYNAPTIC EFFECTS
OF CLONIDINE BUT NOT OF ALPHA METHYLNORADRENALINE ON THE
STIMULATION-EVOKED RELEASE OF 3H NORADRENALINE FROM RAT
OCCIPITAL-CORTEX SLICES.
000227 01-03
DISTRIBUTION OF 14C PHENYTOIN IN RAT PURKINJE-CELLS, CEREBELLAR
AND CEREBRAL NEURONAL TISSUE AFTER A SINGLE INTRAPERITONEAL
INJECTION.
000261 01-03
REGULATION OF THE STATE OF PHOSPHORYLATION OF SPECIFIC
NEURONAL PROTEINS IN MOUSE-BRAIN BY IN VIVO ADMINISTRATION
OF ANESTHETIC AND CONVULSANT-AGENTS.
000291 01-03
A COMPARISON OF RATES OF DEPLETION AND RECOVERY OF
NORADRENALINE STORES OF PERIPHERAL AND CENTRAL
NORADRENERGIC NEURONES AFTER RESERPINE ADMINISTRATION:
IMPORTANCE OF NEURONAL ACTIVITY.
000314 01-03
OPPOSITE EFFECTS OF D-AMPHETAMINE ON SPONTANEOUS NEURONAL
ACTIVITY IN THE NEOSTRIATUM AND NUCLEUS-ACCUMBENS.
000454 01-04

DEMONSTRATION OF SUBSTANCE-P IN AORTIC NERVE AFFERENT FIBERS
BY COMBINED USE OF FLOURESCENT RETROGRADE NEURONAL
LABELING AND IMMUNOCYTOCHEMISTRY. (UNPUBLISHED PAPER).
001024 02-01
BASIC AND CLINICAL NEUROBIOLOGICAL APPLICATIONS OF NEURONAL
(NSE) AND NONNEURONAL (NNE) ENOLASE. (UNPUBLISHED PAPER).
001041 02-01
REGULATION OF ACETYLCHOLINE RELEASE DURING INCREASED NEURONAL
ACTIVITY. (UNPUBLISHED PAPER).
001061 02-01
PROSTACYCLIN-DEPENDENT ACTIVATION OF ADENYLATE-CYCLASE IN A
NEURONAL SOMATIC CELL HYBRID: PROSTANOID STRUCTURE-ACTIVITY
RELATIONSHIPS.
001132 02-03
GLYCINE ENHANCEMENT OF CAUDATE NEURONAL ACTIVITIES:
RELATIONSHIP WITH THE DOPAMINERGIC NIGROSTRIATAL PATHWAY.
001225 02-03
SUBSTANCE-P, MORPHINE AND METHIONINE-ENKEPHALIN: EFFECTS ON
SPONTANEOUS AND EVOKED NEURONAL FIRING IN THE NUCLEUS-
RETICULARIS-GIGANTOCELLULARIS OF THE RAT.
001267 02-03
AMINOPHYLLINE AND THEOPHYLLINE DERIVATIVES AS ANTAGONISTS OF
NEURONAL DEPRESSION BY ADENOSINE: A MICROIONTOPHORETIC-
STUDY.
001410 02-03
ALPHA-ADRENORECEPTOR MEDIATED ALTERATION OF ETHANOL EFFECTS
ON NA-K-ATPASE OF RAT NEURONAL MEMBRANES.
001425 02-03
NEURONAL TRANSPORT OF 5 HYDROXYTRYPTAMINE.
001451 02-03
LOCAL AND DISTANT NEURONAL DEGENERATION FOLLOWING
INTRASTRIATAL INJECTION OF KAINIC-ACID.
001885 02-06
NEURONAL ACTIVITY AND ENERGY METABOLISM: A SUMMARY OF A
SYMPOSIUM. (UNPUBLISHED PAPER).
002308 02-13
NEURONAL MATURATION IN MAMMALIAN CELL-CULTURE IS DEPENDENT
ON SPONTANEOUS ELECTRICAL-ACTIVITY.
002669 03-03
DISRUPTION OF 5 HYDROXYTRYPTAMINERGIC NEURONAL FUNCTION
BLOCKS THE ACTION OF MORPHINE ON TUBEROINFUNDIBULAR
DOPAMINERGIC NEURONS.
002700 03-03
THE PARTICIPATION OF SUBSTANTIA-NIGRA ZONA-COMPACTA AND
ZONA-RETICULATA NEURONS IN MORPHINE SUPPRESSION OF CAUDATE
SPONTANEOUS NEURONAL ACTIVITIES IN THE RAT.
002718 03-03
TEMPORAL PATTERNING OF NEURONAL ACTIVITY DURING THERMAL AND
NEUROCHEMICAL STIMULATION OF THE PREOPTIC/ANTERIOR
HYPOTHALAMUS OF THE AWAKE RABBIT.
002737 03-03
ON CORRELATION OF BEHAVIORAL-REACTIONS AND NEURONAL ACTIVITY
IN THE HYPOTHALAMUS UNDER SUBCUTANEOUS GASTRIN INJECTION.
002892 03-03
NEURONAL LOCALIZATION OF BENZODIAZEPINE-RECEPTORS IN THE
MURINE CEREBELLUM.
002902 03-03
DIFFERENTIAL ACTIONS OF CLASSICAL AND ATYPICAL ANTIPSYCHOTIC-
DRUGS ON SPONTANEOUS NEURONAL ACTIVITY IN THE AMYGDALOID
COMPLEX.
003131 03-05
BIOLOGICAL-EFFECTS OF CHLORPROMAZINE IN CHRONIC
SCHIZOPHRENICS. II. WITH REFERENCE TO SYMPATHETIC NEURONAL
FUNCTION.
003416 03-13
A REFORMULATION OF THE DUAL-ACTION MODEL OF OPIOID
DEPENDENCE: OPIOID-SPECIFIC NEURONAL KINDLING.
003645 03-17
SYNTHESIS OF CYTOSKELETAL PROTEINS IN BULK ISOLATED NEURONAL
PERIKARYA.
003672 04-01
NEURONAL SENSITIVITY OF SOME BRAIN REGIONS TO ANGIOTENSIN-II IN
RABBITS.
003716 04-03
NEURONAL LOCALISATION OF BENZODIAZEPINE-RECEPTORS IN
CEREBELLUM.
003739 04-03
SELECTIVE MODIFICATION BY OPIATES OF NEURONAL ACTIVITY OF THE
MEDIAL BASAL HYPOTHALAMUS.
003773 04-03
MORPHINE AND METHIONINE-ENKEPHALIN: DIFFERENT EFFECTS ON
SPONTANEOUS AND EVOKED NEURONAL FIRING IN THE
MESENCEPHALIC RETICULAR FORMATION OF THE RAT.
003849 04-03
INHIBITION OF DOPAMINE D-1 AND D-2 BINDING-SITES IN NEURONAL
TISSUE BY ASCORBATE.
003876 04-03
ON THE IMPORTANCE OF AGONIST CONCENTRATION GRADIENTS WITHIN
ISOLATED TISSUES. INCREASED MAXIMAL RESPONSES OF RAT VASA-

ALTERATIONS IN BASAL FIRING-RATE AND AUTORECEPTOR SENSITIVITY OF DOPAMINE NEURONS IN THE SUBSTANTIA-NIGRA FOLLOWING ACUTE AND EXTENDED EXPOSURE TO ESTROGEN.
001167 02-03
OPIATE INTERACTIONS WITH CHOLINERGIC NEURONS.
001198 02-03
MIANSERIN: DIRECT ACTIVATION OF BRAIN NOREPINEPHRINE NEURONS BY BLOCKING ALPHA2-RECEPTORS.
001214 02-03
STRYCHNINE EFFECTS ON THE SENSORY RESPONSE PATTERNS OF RETICULAR FORMATION NEURONS.
001219 02-03
EFFECTS OF LONG-TERM ADMINISTRATION OF ANTIPSYCHOTIC-DRUGS ON ENKEPHALINERGIC NEURONS.
001284 02-03
LONG-TERM DECREASES IN SPONTANEOUS FIRING OF CAUDATE NEURONS INDUCED BY AMPHETAMINE IN CATS.
001340 02-03
OPIATES AND OPIOID-PEPTIDES HYPERPOLARIZE LOCUS-COERULEUS NEURONS IN VITRO.
001408 02-03
EFFECT OF QUIPAZINE ON BRAINSTEM MONOAMINE NEURONS HISTOFLUORESCENCE STUDIES.
001477 02-03
ENHANCED SENSITIVITY OF AMYGDALOID NEURONS TO SEROTONIN AND NOREPINEPHRINE AFTER CHRONIC ANTIDEPRESSANT TREATMENT.
001523 02-03
EFFECT OF SELECTIVE DESTRUCTION OF SEROTONERGIC NEURONS IN NUCLEUS-RAPHE-MAGNUS ON MORPHINE-INDUCED ANTINOCICEPTION.
001724 02-04
ANTIPSYCHOTIC-DRUGS: DIFFERENTIAL-EFFECTS ON DOPAMINE NEURONS IN BASAL GANGLIA AND MESOCORTEX FOLLOWING CHRONIC ADMINISTRATION IN HUMAN AND NONHUMAN PRIMATES.
002285 02-13
SHORT-TERM AND LONG-TERM EFFECTS ON GABA AND DOPAMINE NEURONS DURING TREATMENT WITH SULPIRIDE.
002311 02-13
IMMUNOHISTOCHEMICAL LOCALIZATION OF LEUCINE-ENKEPHALIN IN THE SPINAL-CORD OF THE CAT: ENKEPHALIN-CONTAINING MARGINAL NEURONS AND PAIN MODULATION.
002638 03-01
A TOPOGRAPHIC LOCALIZATION OF ENKEPHALIN ON THE DOPAMINE NEURONS OF THE RAT SUBSTANTIA-NIGRA AND VENTRAL TEGMENTAL AREA DEMONSTRATED BY COMBINED HISTOFLUORESCENCE IMMUNOCYTOCHEMISTRY.
002639 03-01
GABA ANALOGUES ACTIVATE CHANNELS OF DIFFERENT DURATION ON CULTURED MOUSE SPINAL NEURONS.
002665 03-03
SENSITIVITY OF IDENTIFIED MEDIAL HYPOTHALAMIC NEURONS TO GABA, GLYCINE AND RELATED AMINO-ACIDS; INFLUENCE OF BICUCULLINE, PICROTOXIN AND STRYCHNINE ON SYNAPTIC INHIBITION.
002674 03-03
MIDBRAIN DOPAMINE NEURONS: DIFFERENTIAL RESPONSES TO AMPHETAMINE ISOMERS.
002680 03-03
DIFFERENCES IN CUTANEOUS SENSORY RESPONSE PROPERTIES OF SINGLE SOMATOSENSORY CORTICAL NEURONS IN AWAKE AND HALOTHANE ANESTHETIZED RATS.
002687 03-03
DISRUPTION OF 5 HYDROXYTRYPTAMINERGIC NEURONAL FUNCTION BLOCKS THE ACTION OF MORPHINE ON TUBEROINFUNDIBULAR DOPAMINERGIC NEURONS.
002700 03-03
THE PARTICIPATION OF SUBSTANTIA-NIGRA ZONA-COMPACTA AND ZONA-RETICULATA NEURONS IN MORPHINE SUPPRESSION OF CAUDATE SPONTANEOUS NEURONAL ACTIVITIES IN THE RAT.
002718 03-03
EVIDENCE FOR A TONIC GABAERGIC CONTROL OF SEROTONIN NEURONS IN THE MEDIAN RAPHE NUCLEUS.
002719 03-03
GABA-RECEPTORS AND BENZODIAZEPINE-RECEPTORS. STUDIES ON THEIR LOCALIZATION IN THE HIPPOCAMPUS AND THEIR INTERACTION WITH CENTRAL DOPAMINE NEURONS IN THE RAT-BRAIN.
002727 03-03
HISTAMINE ACTIONS ON ACTIVITY OF CULTURED HYPOTHALAMIC NEURONS: EVIDENCE FOR MEDIATION BY HISTAMINE H1-RECEPTORS AND H2-RECEPTORS.
002732 03-03
THE PRESYNAPTIC STIMULATING EFFECT OF ACETYLCHOLINE ON DOPAMINE RELEASE IS SUPPRESSED DURING ACTIVATION OF NIGROSTRIATAL DOPAMINERGIC NEURONS IN THE CAT.
002733 03-03
EFFECTS OF PHENYTOIN ON PYRAMIDAL NEURONS OF THE RAT HIPPOCAMPUS.
002750 03-03
TRIMETHADIONE EFFECTS ON CHOLINERGIC RESPONSES IN APLYSIA NEURONS.
002782 03-03

IN VIVO VOLTAMMETRIC INVESTIGATIONS INTO THE ACTION OF HA-966 ON CENTRAL DOPAMINERGIC NEURONS.
002832 03-03
DIFFERENTIAL-EFFECTS OF CLOMIPRAMINE AND CLORGYLINE ON THE SENSITIVITY OF CORTICAL NEURONS TO SEROTONIN: EFFECT OF CHRONIC-TREATMENT.
002847 03-03
EFFECTS OF D AMINOLAEVULINIC-ACID, PORPHOBILINOGEN, AMINO-ACIDS AND BARBITURATES ON CALCIUM ACCUMULATION BY CULTURED NEURONS.
002859 03-03
GLUCOSE SUPPRESSES BASAL FIRING AND HALOPERIDOL-INDUCED INCREASES IN THE FIRING-RATE OF CENTRAL DOPAMINERGIC NEURONS.
002880 03-03
ACTION OF CYCLIC-ADENOSINE-MONOPHOSPHATE ON CENTRAL NEURONS.
002940 03-03
THE EFFECTS OF ACETYLCHOLINE AND GLUTAMATE ON SEPTAL NEURONS IN VITRO.
002941 03-03
THYROXIN SENSITIVITY OF SENSORIMOTOR CORTICAL NEURONS AND THE HYPOTHALAMIC VENTROMEDIAL NUCLEUS.
003713 04-03
EXCITATORY EFFECTS OF DIHYDROCAPSAICIN ON NOCICEPTIVE NEURONS IN THE MEDIAL THALAMUS.
003714 04-03
ACETYLCHOLINE-INDUCED MODULATION OF HIPPOCAMPAL PYRAMIDAL NEURONS.
003728 04-03
RELATIONSHIP BETWEEN THE PRESENCE OF DOPAMINERGIC NEURONS AND GABA-RECEPTORS IN SUBSTANTIA-NIGRA: EFFECTS OF LESIONS.
003797 04-03
CHANGES OF ELECTRORETINOGRAM AND NEUROCHEMICAL ASPECTS OF GABAERGIC NEURONS OF RETINA AFTER INTRAOCULAR INJECTION OF KAINIC-ACID IN RATS.
003807 04-03.
CAFFEINE BLOCKS THE DELAYED K OUTWARD-CURRENT OF MOLLUSCAN NEURONS.
003834 04-03
STUDIES ON AXONAL TRANSPORT IN DOPAMINERGIC NEURONS: EFFECT OF NEUROPHARMACOLOGIC LESIONS.
003858 04-03
SENSORY NEUROTOXINS: CHEMICALLY-INDUCED SELECTIVE DESTRUCTION OF PRIMARY SENSORY NEURONS.
003859 04-03
CHANGE IN CATECHOLAMINE SENSITIVE NA-K-ATPASE ACTIVITY IN THE RAT STRIATUM MICROSOMES FOLLOWING ELECTROLYTIC OR 6 HYDROXYDOPAMINE-INDUCED LESIONS OF DOPAMINERGIC NEURONS.
003871 04-03
SENSITIVITY TO GABA OF NEURONS OF THE DORSAL AND VENTRAL LATERAL GENICULATE NUCLEI IN THE RAT.
003877 04-03
CENTRAL DOPAMINERGIC NEURONS DURING DEVELOPMENT OF GENETIC AND DOCA-SALT HYPERTENSION IN THE RAT.
003899 04-03
THE IMPORTANCE OF CATECHOLAMINE UPTAKE INHIBITION IN THE REVERSAL OF GUANETHIDINE BLOCKADE OF ADRENERGIC NEURONS.
003900 04-03
CONVERGENT PROPERTIES AND CHEMICAL SENSITIVITY OF MIDBRAIN RETICULAR FORMATION NEURONS OF UNANESTHETIZED RABBITS.
003972 04-03
APPARENT SEROTONERGIC MODULATION OF THE DOSE-DEPENDENT BIPHASIC RESPONSE OF NEOSTRIATAL NEURONS PRODUCED BY D-AMPHETAMINE.
003981 04-03
EFFECTS OF ZIMELIDINE ON SEROTONINERGIC AND NORADRENERGIC NEURONS AFTER REPEATED ADMINISTRATION IN THE RAT.
003991 04-03
EFFECT OF CHRONIC-TREATMENT WITH TRICYCLIC-ANTIDEPRESSANT DRUGS ON IDENTIFIED BRAIN NORADRENERGIC AND SEROTONERGIC NEURONS.
004026 04-03
THE EXCITATORY EFFECT OF ATROPINE ON THE NEURONS OF THE FROG SYMPATHETIC GANGLIA.
004041 04-03
SELECTIVE EFFECT OF ETHANOL ON THE VESTIBULAR NUCLEUS NEURONS IN THE CAT.
004139 04-04
DESTRUCTION OF 5 HYDROXYTRYPTAMINERGIC NEURONS AND THE DYNAMICS OF DOPAMINE IN NUCLEUS-ACCUMBENS SEPTI AND OTHER FOREBRAIN REGIONS OF THE RAT.
004171 04-04
DOPAMINERGIC NEURONS OF SPINAL-CORD: A POSSIBLE SITE FOR THE ACTION OF NEUROLEPTIC-DRUGS.
004188 04-04
THE ROLE OF RETICULOSEPTAL INPUTS IN THE FORMATION OF DIFFERENT TYPES OF SENSORY REACTIONS OF THE HIPPOCAMPAL NEURONS.
004510 04-13

Subject Index

NEUROOTOLOGY
STUDIES ON THE TREATMENT AND DIAGNOSIS OF NEUROTIC VERTIGO
FROM THE VIEWPOINT OF NEUROOTOLOGY: OBSERVATION OF THE
BALANCE TEST FOR ANALYZING NEUROTIC VERTIGO.
004387 04-09

NEUROPATHIES
THE ETIOLOGY OF TOXIC PERIPHERAL NEUROPATHIES: IN VITRO EFFECTS
OF ACRYLAMIDE AND 2,5 HEXANEDIONE ON BRAIN ENOLASE AND
OTHER GLYCOLYTIC ENZYMES.
000131 01-03   NEU

NEUROPATHY
THE ROLE OF FOLATE DEFICIENCY IN THE DEVELOPMENT OF PERIPHERAL
NEUROPATHY CAUSED BY ANTICONVULSANTS.
002402 02-15

PERIPHERAL NEUROPATHY DUE TO LITHIUM INTOXICATION.
003544 03-15

NEUROPEPTIDE
THE EFFECT OF NEUROPEPTIDE FRAGMENTS OF ADRENOCORTICOTROPIN
AND VASOPRESSIN ON BEHAVIORAL-ACTIVITY IN RATS.
001812 02-04

NEUROPEPTIDE TREATMENT OF SOCIOPATHY: RESEARCH IN PROGRESS.
002369 02-14

NEUROPEPTIDE-RECEPTORS
EFFECTS OF GUANINE-NUCLEOTIDES ON CNS NEUROPEPTIDE-RECEPTORS.
(UNPUBLISHED PAPER).
001383 02-03   NEU

NEUROPEPTIDES
INTERACTIONS OF NEUROPEPTIDES WITH CHOLINERGIC
SEPTOHIPPOCAMPAL PATHWAY: INDICATION FOR A POSSIBLE
TRANSSYNAPTIC REGULATION. (UNPUBLISHED PAPER).
001062 02-01   NEU

BIOGENIC-AMINES AND NEUROPEPTIDES PLAY A ROLE IN THE CENTRAL-
REGULATION OF GENETIC HYPERTENSION. (UNPUBLISHED PAPER).
001455 02-03

CENTRAL BIOGENIC-AMINES AND NEUROPEPTIDES IN GENETIC
HYPERTENSION. (UNPUBLISHED PAPER).
001456 02-03   NEU

NEUROPEPTIDES AND MONOAMINERGIC NEUROTRANSMITTERS: THEIR
RELATION TO PAIN.
001497 02-03

PSYCHOSTIMULANTS AND NEUROPEPTIDES IN GEROPSYCHIATRY.
002125 02-11   NEU

IMMUNOCYTOCHEMICAL LOCALIZATION OF CATECHOLAMINE
SYNTHESIZING ENZYMES AND NEUROPEPTIDES IN AREA POSTREMA
AND MEDIAL NUCLEUS-TRACTUS-SOLITARIUS OF RAT-BRAIN.
002634 03-01   NEU

NEUROPHARMACOLOGIC
STUDIES ON AXONAL TRANSPORT IN DOPAMINERGIC NEURONS: EFFECT
OF NEUROPHARMACOLOGIC LESIONS.
003858 04-03   NEU

NEUROPHARMACOLOGICAL
NEUROPHARMACOLOGICAL AND NEUROCHEMICAL APPROACHES TO
PRECLINICAL-EVALUATION OF NEUROLEPTICS.
001094 02-02   NEU

NEUROPHARMACOLOGICAL ANALYSIS OF HANDLING-INDUCED SEIZURES
IN GERBILS.
001876 02-06   NEU

BRAIN GLUCOCORTICOID-RECEPTOR: CORRELATION OF IN VIVO UPTAKE
OF CORTICOSTERONE WITH BEHAVIORAL-EVENTS, ENDOCRINE-EVENTS,
AND NEUROPHARMACOLOGICAL EVENTS.
002515 02-17   NEU

A STUDY OF THE EFFECT OF NEUROPHARMACOLOGICAL DRUGS ON THE
FUNCTIONAL ACTIVITY OF RAT-BRAIN.
004107 04-04

NEUROPHARMACOLOGICAL-AGENTS
NEUROPHARMACOLOGICAL-AGENTS MODIFYING ENDOTOXIN-INDUCED
CHANGES IN MICE.
001543 02-03   NEU

NEUROPHARMACOLOGICAL-DRUGS
THE MECHANISM OF EFFECT OF NEUROPHARMACOLOGICAL-DRUGS. VI:
EFFECT OF NORADRENALINE AND 5 HYDROXYTRYPTAMINE ON BRAIN
FREE FATTY-ACIDS.
000274 01-03   NEU

NEUROPHARMACOLOGICAL-STUDIES
NEUROPHARMACOLOGICAL-STUDIES OF PHENCYCLIDINE-INDUCED
BEHAVIORAL-STIMULATION IN MICE.
001622 02-04

NEUROPHARMACOLOGICAL-STUDY
A NEUROPHARMACOLOGICAL-STUDY AND NEUROENDOCRINE-STUDY ON
IDIOPATHIC AND CHRONIC PHARMACOLOGICAL PARKINSONISM.
002371 02-15   NEU

CHRONOLOGICAL ELECTROENCEPHALOGRAPHIC AND
NEUROPHARMACOLOGICAL-STUDY IN CORTICAL KINDLING RABBITS.
002761 03-03   NEU

NEUROPHARMACOLOGY
NEUROPHARMACOLOGY OF BROMOCRIPTINE AND DIHYDROERGOTOXINE
(HYDERGINE).
001346 02-03

NEUROPHARMACOLOGY OF SYNTHETIC ERGOT DERIVATIVES IN MAN.
002429 02-15

A POSSIBLE ECOPHARMACOGENETIC MODEL IN NEUROPSYCHOPHARMACOLOGY ASPECTS IN ALCOHOLISM AND PHARMACODEPENDENCE.
002596 02-17

NEUROPSYCHOPHARMACOLOGY-STUDY
NEUROLOGICAL-STUDY AND NEUROPSYCHOPHARMACOLOGY-STUDY ON DEMENTIA.
001090 02-11

NEUROSCIENCES
HIGH-PERFORMANCE LIQUID-CHROMATOGRAPHY IN THE NEUROSCIENCES: METHODOLOGY.
004285 04-06

HIGH-PERFORMANCE LIQUID-CHROMATOGRAPHY IN THE NEUROSCIENCES: APPLICATIONS.
004296 04-06

NEUROSECRETION
THE IDENTITY AND HYPOTHALAMIC ORIGIN OF CHOLECYSTOKININ IN RAT-BRAIN AND POSTERIOR PITUITARY AND ITS POSSIBLE ROLE IN REGULATION OF NEUROSECRETION. (UNPUBLISHED PAPER).
001003 02-01

NEUROSECRETORY
INFLUENCE OF CHRONIC ALCOHOL INTOXICATION ON CIRCADIAN-RHYTHM OF NEUROSECRETORY CENTERS OF RAT HYPOTHALAMUS.
001549 02-03

DOPAMINE INHIBITS BURST-FIRING OF NEUROSECRETORY CELL R-15 IN APLYSIA-CALIFORNICA: ESTABLISHMENT OF A DOSE-RESPONSE RELATIONSHIP.
003806 04-03

NEUROSES
CLINICAL-EXPERIENCE WITH LOW-DOSES OF HALOPERIDOL IN THE TREATMENT OF NEUROSES.
000654 01-10

THE USE OF CLOROTEPIN AND DIAZEPAM IN A COMPLEX THERAPY OF NEUROSES (CONTROLLED-COMPARISON).
002064 02-10

PSYCHOPHARMACOLOGY OF NEUROSES.
003274 03-10

NEUROSIS
THERAPEUTIC APPLICATION OF PHYSOSTIGMINE IN NEUROSIS.
000651 01-10

A CLINICAL-EVALUATION OF THE EFFECTS OF A NEW PSYCHOTROPIC-AGENT, MEXAZOLAM (CS-386) ON PSYCHOSOMATIC-DISEASES AND NEUROSIS: A COMPARATIVE-STUDY WITH OXAZOLAM, USING THE DOUBLE-BLIND METHOD.
004491 04-11

NEUROSURGICAL-RESUSCITATION
HEMODYNAMIC AND CEREBRAL METABOLIC-STUDY OF DIAZEPAM IN NEUROSURGICAL-RESUSCITATION.
002231 02-13

NEUROSYMPATHETIC
INHIBITION OF NEUROSYMPATHETIC CEREBROARTERIAL CONSTRICTION BY CLONIDINE IN CATS.
001431 02-03

NEUROTENSIN
ENHANCEMENT OF ETHANOL-INDUCED SEDATION AND HYPOTHERMIA BY CENTRALLY ADMINISTERED NEUROTENSIN, BETA ENDORPHIN AND BOMBESIN.
003037 03-04

INCREASE OF NEUROTENSIN CONTENT ELICITED BY NEUROLEPTICS IN NUCLEUS-ACCUMBENS.
003808 04-03

NEUROTENSIN RELEASE BY RAT HYPOTHALAMIC FRAGMENTS IN VITRO.
003920 04-03

NEUROTENSIN BLOCKS CERTAIN AMPHETAMINE-INDUCED BEHAVIOURS.
004111 04-04

NEUROTENSIN-INDUCED
COMPOUND-48-80 INHIBITS NEUROTENSIN-INDUCED HYPOTENSION IN RATS.
000243 01-03

NEUROTENSIN-RECEPTOR
NEUROTENSIN-RECEPTOR LOCALIZATION BY LIGHT MICROSCOPIC AUTORADIOGRAPHY IN RAT-BRAIN.
002938 03-03

NEUROTIC
TRAZODONE IN THE TREATMENT OF NEUROTIC DEPRESSION.
001994 02-09

THE CORRELATION OF CATECHOLAMINE AND ADRENERGIC PARAMETERS WITH DRUG-THERAPY OF NEUROTIC AND ENDOGENOUS DEPRESSIONS.
002047 02-09

PHENELZINE AND AMITRIPTYLINE IN NEUROTIC DEPRESSION. (UNPUBLISHED PAPER).
003248 03-09

MAPROTILINE VERSUS IMIPRAMINE AND PLACEBO IN NEUROTIC DEPRESSION.
003287 03-10

ACTIVITY OF BROMAZEPAM AND LORAZEPAM IN NEUROTIC DEPRESSIONS.
004384 04-09

STUDIES ON THE TREATMENT AND DIAGNOSIS OF NEUROTIC VERTIGO FROM THE VIEWPOINT OF NEUROOTOLOGY: OBSERVATION OF THE BALANCE TEST FOR ANALYZING NEUROTIC VERTIGO.
004387 04-09

NEUROTIC-OUTPATIENTS
RELAPSE AFTER SHORT-TERM DRUG-THERAPY IN NEUROTIC-OUTPATIENTS.
004400 04-09

THE RELATIONSHIPS BETWEEN CLINICAL-RESPONSE, PSYCHOPHYSIOLOGICAL-VARIABLES AND PLASMA LEVELS OF AMITRIPTYLINE AND DIAZEPAM IN NEUROTIC-OUTPATIENTS.
004423 04-10

NEUROTIC-PATIENTS
EFFECTS OF ANTIDEPRESSANTS ON PITUITARY HORMONAL SECRETIONS IN HEALTHY TEST SUBJECTS, NEUROTIC-PATIENTS, AND ENDOGENOUS DEPRESSIVE-PATIENTS.
002009 02-09

PREDICTION OF RESPONSE TO TREATMENT WITH PHENELZINE IN NEUROTIC-PATIENTS.
002081 02-10

ALPRAZOLAM, A NEW TYPE ANXIOLYTIC IN NEUROTIC-PATIENTS: A PILOT-STUDY.
004422 04-10

NEUROTICS
PLACEBO REACTION IN NEUROTICS RATED WITH THE SCL-90 QUESTIONNAIRE.
000976 01-17

NEUROTOXIC
DECREASED BENZODIAZEPINE-RECEPTOR DENSITY IN RAT-CEREBELLUM FOLLOWING NEUROTOXIC DOSES OF PHENYTOIN.
001373 02-03

NEUROTOXIC ESTERASE IN HUMAN NERVOUS-TISSUE.
003510 03-15

NEUROTOXIC-ACTION
SELECTIVE NEUROTOXIC-ACTION OF CAPSAICIN ON GLOMERULAR C-TYPE TERMINALS IN RAT SUBSTANTIA-GELATINOSA.
003143 03-06

NEUROTOXIC-ACTIONS
SYSTEMIC DIPIPERIDINOETHANE MIMICS THE CONVULSANT AND NEUROTOXIC-ACTIONS OF KAINIC-ACID.
000222 01-03

NEUROTOXICITY
NEUROTOXICITY OF LITHIUM. II.
000883 01-15

NEUROTOXICITY OF LITHIUM. I.
002452 02-15

KAINIC-ACID NEUROTOXICITY AND SEIZURES.
002939 03-03

LITHIUM NEUROTOXICITY AT THERAPEUTIC LEVELS: A CASE-REPORT.
003533 03-15

MONOSODIUM-GLUTAMATE: INCREASED NEUROTOXICITY AFTER REMOVAL OF NEURONAL REUPTAKE SITES.
003889 04-03

NEUROTOXIN
RELEASE OF ACETYLCHOLINE FROM RAT-BRAIN SYNAPTOSOMES STIMULATED WITH LEPTINOTARSIN, A NEW NEUROTOXIN.
003148 03-06

NEUROTOXINS
THE EFFECTS OF ALPHA AND BETA NEUROTOXINS FROM THE VENOMS OF VARIOUS SNAKES ON TRANSMISSION IN AUTONOMIC GANGLIA.
003750 04-03

SENSORY NEUROTOXINS: CHEMICALLY-INDUCED SELECTIVE DESTRUCTION OF PRIMARY SENSORY NEURONS.
003859 04-03

NEUROTRANSMISSION
TRANYLCYPROMINE STEREOISOMERS, MONOAMINERGIC NEUROTRANSMISSION AND BEHAVIOR. A MINIREVIEW.
000016 01-02

MATURATION OF SYMPATHETIC NEUROTRANSMISSION IN THE RAT HEART. III. DEVELOPMENTAL-CHANGES IN RESERPINE INHIBITION OF NOREPINEPHRINE UPTAKE INTO ISOLATED SYNAPTIC VESICLES.
000025 01-03

REGULATION OF NEUROTRANSMISSION THROUGH PRESYNAPTIC-RECEPTORS AND OTHER MECHANISMS: POSSIBLE CLINICAL RELEVANCE AND THERAPEUTIC POTENTIAL.
002569 02-16

COCAINE AND AMPHETAMINE ANTAGONIZE THE DECREASE OF NORADRENERGIC NEUROTRANSMISSION ELICITED BY OXYMETAZOLINE BUT POTENTIATE THE INHIBITION BY ALPHA METHYLNOREPINEPHRINE IN THE PERFUSED CAT SPLEEN.
002801 03-03

MATURATION OF SYMPATHETIC NEUROTRANSMISSION IN THE RAT HEART. VII. SUPPRESSION OF SYMPATHETIC RESPONSES BY DEXAMETHASONE..
002802 03-03

THE ROLE OF GABA-MEDIATED NEUROTRANSMISSION IN CONVULSIVE STATES.
003334 03-11

AN ELECTROPHYSIOLOGICAL MODEL OF GABA-MEDIATED
NEUROTRANSMISSION.
003929 04-03

ONTOGENY OF HISTAMINERGIC NEUROTRANSMISSION IN THE RAT-
BRAIN: CONCOMITANT DEVELOPMENT OF NEURONAL HISTAMINE, H1-
RECEPTORS, AND H1-RECEPTOR-MEDIATED STIMULATION OF
PHOSPHOLIPID TURNOVER.
004021 04-03

NEUROTRANSMITTER
NEUROTRANSMITTER RELATED ADAPTATION IN THE CENTRAL-NERVOUS-
SYSTEM FOLLOWING CHRONIC MONOAMINE-OXIDASE-INHIBITION.
000038 01-03

EFFECTS OF ACUTE AND CHRONIC PHENCYCLIDINE ON
NEUROTRANSMITTER ENZYMES IN RAT-BRAIN.
000134 01-03

MATERNAL GLUCOCORTICOID-HORMONES INFLUENCE
NEUROTRANSMITTER PHENOTYPIC EXPRESSION IN EMBRYOS.
000149 01-03

EPILEPSY: NEUROTRANSMITTER, BEHAVIOUR AND PREGNANCY.
002466 02-15

DOPAMINE AS A POSSIBLE NEUROTRANSMITTER IN THE SPINAL-CORD.
002705 03-03

KAINIC-ACID AND NEUROTRANSMITTER INTERACTIONS IN THE BASAL
GANGLIA.
002824 03-03

LAMINAR DISTRIBUTION OF PUTATIVE NEUROTRANSMITTER AMINO-
ACIDS AND LIGAND BINDING-SITES IN THE DOG OLFACTORY-BULB.
002836 03-03

ACTIONS OF TREMORGENIC FUNGAL TOXINS ON NEUROTRANSMITTER
RELEASE.
002843 03-03

EFFECT OF 6 HYDROXYDOPAMINE LESIONS OF THE MEDIAL PREFRONTAL-
CORTEX ON NEUROTRANSMITTER SYSTEMS IN SUBCORTICAL SITES IN
THE RAT.
002869 03-03

A TEST OF A NEUROTRANSMITTER MODEL OF THE AFFECTIVE-DISORDERS.
(PH.D. DISSERTATION).
003063 03-04

NEUROTRANSMITTER CONTROL OF HYPOTHALAMIC PITUITARY THYROID-
FUNCTION IN RATS.
003942 04-03

BEHAVIORAL-EVIDENCE THAT SUBSTANCE-P MAY BE A SPINAL-CORD
SENSORY NEUROTRANSMITTER.
004200 04-04

NEUROTRANSMITTER-RECEPTOR
DRUG-INDUCED ALTERATIONS IN NEUROTRANSMITTER-RECEPTOR
BINDING AND FUNCTION.
001215 02-03

THE EFFECT OF GABAMIMETICS ON NEUROTRANSMITTER-RECEPTOR
BINDING AND FUNCTION IN RAT-BRAIN. (PH.D. DISSERTATION).
001221 02-03

EFFECTS OF ETHANOL ADMINISTRATION AND WITHDRAWAL ON
NEUROTRANSMITTER-RECEPTOR SYSTEMS IN C57 MICE.
003979 04-03

NEUROTRANSMITTER-RECEPTORS
NEUROLEPTICS AND NEUROTRANSMITTER-RECEPTORS.
000980 01-17

MULTIPLE NEUROTRANSMITTER-RECEPTORS.
000990 01-17

ANTIDEPRESSANT-DRUGS SLOW CIRCADIAN-RHYTHMS IN BEHAVIOR AND
BRAIN NEUROTRANSMITTER-RECEPTORS.
001536 02-03

ASCORBATE DECREASES LIGAND BINDING TO NEUROTRANSMITTER-
RECEPTORS.
002804 03-03

NEUROTRANSMITTER-RECEPTORS IN BRAIN REGIONS OF ACRYLAMIDE
TREATED RATS. I: EFFECTS OF A SINGLE EXPOSURE TO ACRYLAMIDE.
004264 04-05

NEUROTRANSMITTER-RECEPTORS IN BRAIN REGIONS OF ACRYLAMIDE
TREATED RATS. II: EFFECTS OF EXTENDED EXPOSURE TO ACRYLAMIDE.
004265 04-05

AUTORADIOGRAPHIC LOCALIZATION OF DRUG AND NEUROTRANSMITTER-
RECEPTORS IN THE BRAIN.
004292 04-06

NEUROTRANSMITTERS
SUPPRESSION OF EVOKED AND SPONTANEOUS RELEASE OF
NEUROTRANSMITTERS IN VIVO BY MORPHINE.
000058 01-03

INTERACTIONS OF NOREPINEPHRINE WITH PURKINJE-CELL RESPONSES TO
PUTATIVE AMINO-ACID NEUROTRANSMITTERS APPLIED BY
MICROIONTOPHORESIS.
000209 01-03

BENZODIAZEPINES AND NEUROTRANSMITTERS.
000925 01-17

EFFECTS OF HALOPEMIDE ON POTASSIUM-INDUCED RELEASE OF
RADIOLABELED NEUROTRANSMITTERS FROM RAT CEREBROCORTICAL
SLICES IN VITRO.
001347 02-03

ACETYLCHOLINE AND AMINO-ACID NEUROTRANSMITTERS IN EPIDURAL
CUPS OF FREELY-MOVING-RATS: EFFECT OF ACUTE AND CHRONIC-
TREATMENT WITH ANTISCHIZOPHRENIC-DRUGS.
001386 02-03

NEUROPEPTIDES AND MONOAMINERGIC NEUROTRANSMITTERS: THEIR
RELATION TO PAIN.
001497 02-03

ROLE OF NEUROTRANSMITTERS AND PROTEIN SYNTHESIS IN SHORT-
TERM AND LONG-TERM MEMORY.
001573 02-04

KAINIC-ACID-INDUCED WET-DOG-SHAKES IN RATS: THE RELATION TO
CENTRAL NEUROTRANSMITTERS.
001685 02-04

BEHAVIOURAL-RESPONSES TO STEREOTACTICALLY CONTROLLED
INJECTIONS OF MONOAMINE NEUROTRANSMITTERS INTO THE
ACCUMBENS AND CAUDATE-PUTAMEN NUCLEI.
001708 02-04

GLYCINE, ACETYLCHOLINE, AND SEROTONIN: NEUROTRANSMITTERS OR
NEUROMODULATORS?
002271 02-13

NEUROTRANSMITTERS AND DEPRESSION: TOO MUCH, TOO LITTLE, TOO
UNSTABLE — OR NOT UNSTABLE ENOUGH?
002931 03-03

A POSSIBLE ROLE FOR CATECHOLAMINE NEUROTRANSMITTERS IN THE
ANTICONVULSANT ACTIVITY OF CHLORDIAZEPOXIDE.
003119 03-04

MODIFIED CUP TECHNIQUE FOR MICROESTIMATION OF THE RELEASE AND
UPTAKE OF NEUROTRANSMITTERS IN BRAIN SLICES.
003147 03-06

EFFECTS OF BARBITURATES ON INHIBITORY AND EXCITATORY RESPONSES
TO APPLIED NEUROTRANSMITTERS IN APLYSIA.
003762 04-03

THE NA-K-ATPASE: A PLAUSIBLE TRIGGER FOR VOLTAGE-INDEPENDENT
RELEASE OF CYTOPLASMIC NEUROTRANSMITTERS.
003953 04-03

CHANGES IN REGIONAL BRAIN LEVELS OF AMINO-ACID PUTATIVE
NEUROTRANSMITTERS AFTER PROLONGED TREATMENT WITH THE
ANTICONVULSANT-DRUGS DIPHENYLHYDANTOIN, PHENOBARBITONE,
SODIUM-VALPROATE, ETHOSUXIMIDE, AND SULTHIAME IN THE RAT.
003961 04-03

CLASSICAL NEUROLEPTICS AND DECONDITIONING ACTIVITY AFTER SINGLE
OR REPEATED TREATMENTS: ROLE OF DIFFERENT CEREBRAL
NEUROTRANSMITTERS.
004115 04-04

NEUROTROPIC-ACTION
AN EXPERIMENTAL-STUDY OF THE NEUROTROPIC-ACTION OF LITHIUM-
OXYBUTYRATE.
001705 02-04

NEUROTROPIC-DRUG
NEUROTROPIC-DRUGS AS COMEDICATION TO PSYCHOTROPICS:
COMBINED ADMINISTRATION OF A NEUROTROPIC-DRUG AND A
TETRACYCLIC-ANTIDEPRESSANT.
004396 04-09

NEUROTROPIC-DRUGS
NEUROTROPIC-DRUGS AS COMEDICATION TO PSYCHOTROPICS:
COMBINED ADMINISTRATION OF A NEUROTROPIC-DRUG AND A
TETRACYCLIC-ANTIDEPRESSANT.
004396 04-09

NEUROVASCULAR-PHARMACOLOGY
THE NEUROVASCULAR-PHARMACOLOGY AND CARDIOVASCULAR-
PHARMACOLOGY OF RS-51324, A POTENTIAL ANTIDEPRESSANT.
001091 02-02

NEUTRAL
TRANSPORT OF NEUTRAL AMINO-ACIDS AT THE BLOOD-BRAIN-BARRIER.
002764 03-03

NEUTRALIZATION
NEUTRALIZATION OF THE EFFECT OF DELTA9 TETRAHYDROCANNABINOL
ON BARBITURATE SLEEPING-TIME BY SPECIFIC ACTIVE IMMUNIZATION.
003803 04-03

NEUTROPENIA
MIANSERIN: A POSSIBLE CAUSE OF NEUTROPENIA AND
AGRANULOCYTOSIS.
003517 03-15

NEUTROPHIL
AN ATTEMPT TO ASSESS THE EFFECT OF LITHIUM ON THE NEUTROPHIL
LEUKOCYTE SYSTEM IN AFFECTIVE-PSYCHOSIS.
004416 04-09

NEUTROPHILS
PHOSPHOLIPID METABOLISM, CALCIUM-FLUX AND THE RECEPTOR-
MEDIATED INDUCTION OF CHEMOTAXIS IN RABBIT NEUTROPHILS.
(UNPUBLISHED PAPER).
001118 02-03

NEWBORN
INTRAVENTRICULAR 6 HYDROXYDOPAMINE IN THE NEWBORN RAT AND
LOCOMOTOR RESPONSES TO DRUGS IN INFANCY: NO SUPPORT FOR
THE DOPAMINE DEPLETION MODEL OF MINIMAL-BRAIN-DYSFUNCTION.
000448 01-04

MORPHOLOGICAL CHANGES IN RAT-BRAIN INDUCED BY L CYSTEINE INJECTION IN NEWBORN ANIMALS.

002774 03-03

NEWBORNS
CLINICAL PHARMACOKINETICS IN NEWBORNS AND INFANTS: AGE-RELATED DIFFERENCES AND THERAPEUTIC IMPLICATIONS.

003343 03-11

NEWS
THERAPEUTIC NEWS.

004308 04-07

NIALAMIDE
COMBINED ADMINISTRATION OF NIALAMIDE AND VILOXAZINE TO DEPRESSIVE-PATIENTS.

003232 03-09

NICERGOLINE
INFLUENCE OF NICERGOLINE ON MOLECULAR BIOLOGICAL PROCESSES IN THE BRAIN AND LEARNING-ABILITY OF THE RAT.

000449 01-04

PSYCHOPATHOMETRIC DOUBLE-BLIND COURSE STUDY WITH NICERGOLINE VERSUS PLACEBO IN GERIATRIC-PATIENTS WITH TRANSIENT-SYNDROMES.

000665 01-11

DETERMINATION OF THE ENCEPHALOTROPIC, PSYCHOTROPIC AND PHARMACODYNAMIC PROPERTIES OF NICERGOLINE BY MEANS OF QUANTITATIVE PHARMACOELECTROENCEPHALOGRAPHY AND PSYCHOMETRIC-ANALYSES.

000788 01-13

NICKEL
EFFECT OF NICKEL ON THE LEVELS OF DOPAMINE, NORADRENALINE AND SEROTONIN IN DIFFERENT REGIONS OF THE RAT-BRAIN.

001831 02-05

NICOTINAMIDE
DISSIMILAR EFFECTS OF NICOTINAMIDE AND INOSINE, PUTATIVE ENDOGENOUS LIGANDS OF THE BENZODIAZEPINE-RECEPTORS, ON PENTYLENETETRAZOL SEIZURES IN FOUR STRAINS OF MICE.

000173 01-03

NICOTINE
STUDIES ON THE BIOCHEMICAL-EFFECTS AND BEHAVIOURAL-EFFECTS OF ORAL NICOTINE.

001115 02-03

THE INFLUENCE OF GENOTYPE AND SEX ON BEHAVIORAL-SENSITIVITY TO NICOTINE IN MICE.

001648 02-04

EFFECTS OF CYCLOHEXIMIDE ADMINISTERED IN CONJUNCTION WITH NICOTINE ON RETENTION OF A PASSIVE-AVOIDANCE TASK IN MICE.

001791 02-04

THE USE OF NICOTINE CHEWING-GUM AS AN AID TO STOPPING SMOKING.

002343 02-14

NICOTINE INGESTION REDUCES ELEVATED BLOOD-PRESSURES IN RATS AND SQUIRREL-MONKEYS.

002759 03-03

SELECTIVE INHIBITION BY NICOTINE OF SHOCK-INDUCED FIGHTING IN THE RAT.

002984 03-04

THE SMOKING HABIT AND PSYCHOPHARMACOLOGICAL-EFFECTS OF NICOTINE.

003577 03-17

EFFECT OF NICOTINE ON IN VIVO SECRETION OF MELANOCORTICOTROPIC-HORMONES IN THE RAT.

003759 04-03

THE EFFECT OF CHRONIC NICOTINE AND WITHDRAWAL ON INTRAAXONAL TRANSPORT OF ACETYLCHOLINE AND RELATED ENZYMES IN SCIATIC-NERVE OF THE RAT.

003897 04-03

THE ROLE OF NICOTINE IN THE BEHAVIORAL-ASPECTS OF CIGARETTE SMOKING.

004575 04-14

NICOTINE-RECEPTORS
STEREOSPECIFIC NICOTINE-RECEPTORS ON RAT-BRAIN MEMBRANES.

000254 01-03

NICOTINIC
ENZYMATIC CARBOXYMETHYLATION OF THE NICOTINIC ACETYLCHOLINE-RECEPTOR. (UNPUBLISHED PAPER).

001318 02-03

INTRINSIC CHOLINERGIC EXCITATION IN THE RAT NEOSTRIATUM: NICOTINIC AND MUSCARINIC-RECEPTORS.

001374 02-03

COMPARATIVE-STUDY OF AGGRESSIVE-BEHAVIOUR AFTER INJECTION OF CHOLINOMIMETICS, ANTICHOLINESTERASES, NICOTINIC, AND MUSCARINIC GANGLIONIC STIMULANTS INTO THE CEREBRAL VENTRICLES OF CONSCIOUS CATS: FAILURE OF NICOTINIC-DRUGS TO EVOKE AGGRESSION.

001568 02-04

A CRITICAL EVALUATION OF THE USE OF TOXINS FROM DENDROASPIS VIRIDIS TO BLOCK NICOTINIC RESPONSES AT CENTRAL AND GANGLIONIC SYNAPSES.

002870 03-03

NICOTINIC-DRUGS
COMPARATIVE-STUDY OF AGGRESSIVE-BEHAVIOUR AFTER INJECTION OF CHOLINOMIMETICS, ANTICHOLINESTERASES, NICOTINIC, AND

MUSCARINIC GANGLIONIC STIMULANTS INTO THE CEREBRAL VENTRICLES OF CONSCIOUS CATS: FAILURE OF NICOTINIC-DRUGS TO EVOKE AGGRESSION.

001568 02-04

NICTITATING
CALCIUM ANTAGONISM OF THE INHIBITORY-EFFECTS OF FENTANYL ON THE CONTRACTION OF THE NICTITATING MEMBRANE IN CATS.

002876 03-03

PHARMACOLOGICAL DIFFERENTIATION OF PRESYNAPTIC INHIBITORY ALPHA-ADRENOCEPTORS AND OPIATE-RECEPTORS IN THE CAT NICTITATING MEMBRANE.

003777 04-03

INFLUENCE OF THE DOPAMINERGIC AGONISTS BROMOCRIPTINE, PIRIBEDIL AND NOMIFENSINE ON THE SYMPATHETIC NEURAL TRANSMISSION IN THE NICTITATING MEMBRANE OF THE CAT.

003822 04-03

NIDA
PHENCYCLIDINE: A NIDA PERSPECTIVE.

000743 01-12

NIEMANN-PICK
PARTIAL PURIFICATION OF ACID SPHINGOMYELINASE FROM NORMAL AND PATHOLOGICAL (M. NIEMANN-PICK TYPE C) HUMAN BRAIN.

003671 04-01

NIGERIAN
PREVALENCE OF PERSISTENT ABNORMAL INVOLUNTARY-MOVEMENTS AMONG PATIENTS IN A NIGERIAN LONG-STAY PSYCHIATRIC UNIT.

004334 04-08

NIGHT
POLYGRAPHIC-STUDY OF NIGHT SLEEP UNDER THE EFFECTS OF MINAPRINE.

003313 03-11

AGE-SPECIFIC DOSES OF LORMETAZEPAM AS A NIGHT SEDATIVE IN CASES OF CHRONIC SLEEP-DISTURBANCE.

004309 04-07

NIGHT-TERRORS
SURVECTOR AND SLEEP-DISORDERS: SLEEP-WALKING, NIGHTMARES, AND NIGHT-TERRORS.

002110 02-11

NIGHTMARES
SURVECTOR AND SLEEP-DISORDERS: SLEEP-WALKING, NIGHTMARES, AND NIGHT-TERRORS.

002110 02-11

NIGRAL
MORPHINE-DEPENDENCE AND DOPAMINERGIC-ACTIVITY: TESTS OF CIRCLING RESPONSES IN RATS WITH UNILATERAL NIGRAL LESIONS.

001641 02-04

INTRANIGRAL INJECTION OF CAPSAICIN ENHANCES MOTOR-ACTIVITY AND DEPLETES NIGRAL 5 HYDROXYTRYPTAMINE BUT NOT SUBSTANCE-P.

004100 04-04

THE ROLE OF NIGRAL PROJECTIONS TO THE THALAMUS IN DRUG-INDUCED CIRCLING-BEHAVIOUR IN THE RAT.

004205 04-04

NIGROSTRIATAL
DECARBOXYLATION OF EXOGENOUS L-DOPA IN RAT STRIATUM AFTER LESIONS OF THE DOPAMINERGIC NIGROSTRIATAL NEURONS: THE ROLE OF STRIATAL CAPILLARIES.

000202 01-03

EFFECTS OF ALPHA CHLORALOSE ON THE ACTIVITY OF THE NIGROSTRIATAL DOPAMINERGIC SYSTEM IN THE CAT.

000217 01-03

ACUTE AND CHRONIC HALOPERIDOL TREATMENT: EFFECTS ON NIGROSTRIATAL DOPAMINERGIC-SYSTEM ACTIVITY.

001153 02-03

GLYCINE ENHANCEMENT OF CAUDATE NEURONAL ACTIVITIES: RELATIONSHIP WITH THE DOPAMINERGIC NIGROSTRIATAL PATHWAY.

001225 02-03

SUPERSENSITIVITY AND THE EFFECTS OF LONG-TERM AMPHETAMINE IN THE RAT NIGROSTRIATAL SYSTEM. (PH.D. DISSERTATION).

001485 02-03

CHRONOLOGY OF EXTRAPYRAMIDAL-EFFECTS OF NEUROLEPTIC-DRUGS AND THE NIGROSTRIATAL DOPAMINERGIC-SYSTEM.

002449 02-15

THE PRESYNAPTIC STIMULATING EFFECT OF ACETYLCHOLINE ON DOPAMINE RELEASE IS SUPPRESSED DURING ACTIVATION OF NIGROSTRIATAL DOPAMINERGIC NEURONS IN THE CAT.

002733 03-03

AMPHETAMINE-INDUCED MOTILITY AND NIGROSTRIATAL IMPULSE FLOW.

003005 03-04

EFFECTS OF METHAMPHETAMINE ON BLOOD FLOW IN THE CAUDATE-PUTAMEN AFTER LESIONS OF THE NIGROSTRIATAL DOPAMINERGIC BUNDLE IN THE RAT.

003910 04-03

THE EFFECT OF DOPAMINE UPTAKE BLOCKING-AGENTS ON THE AMPHETAMINE-INDUCED CIRCLING-BEHAVIOR IN MICE WITH UNILATERAL NIGROSTRIATAL LESIONS.

004117 04-04

DOPAMINE-RECEPTOR CHANGES FOLLOWING DESTRUCTION OF THE NIGROSTRIATAL PATHWAY: LACK OF A RELATIONSHIP TO ROTATIONAL-BEHAVIOR.
004229 04-04

NIGROTHALAMIC
EVIDENCE FOR A GABAERGIC NIGROTHALAMIC PATHWAY IN THE RAT: I. BEHAVIOURAL-STUDIES AND BIOCHEMICAL-STUDIES.
000158 01-03

NIMETAZEPAM
REVERSIBLE RING-OPENING REACTIONS OF NIMETAZEPAM AND NITRAZEPAM IN ACIDIC MEDIA AT BODY-TEMPERATURE.
004517 04-13

NIMH-PRB
A TWELVE-YEAR FOLLOWUP OF THE NIMH-PRB HIGH-DOSE CHLORPROMAZINE STUDY OF CHRONIC SCHIZOPHRENICS -- IMPLICATIONS FOR DEINSTITUTIONALIZATION. (UNPUBLISHED PAPER).
004323 04-08

NIPECOTIC-ACID
EFFECT OF PICROTOXIN AND NIPECOTIC-ACID ON INHIBITORY RESPONSE OF DOPAMINERGIC NEURONS IN THE VENTRAL TEGMENTAL AREA TO STIMULATION OF THE NUCLEUS-ACCUMBENS.
000331 01-03

NIPECOTIC-ACID-AMIDE
EFFECTS OF SODIUM-DIPROPYLACETATE, MUSCIMOL-HYDROBROMIDE AND (R,S) NIPECOTIC-ACID-AMIDE ON ISOLATION-INDUCED AGGRESSIVE-BEHAVIOR IN MICE.
001756 02-04

NISOXETINE
SUBSENSITIVITY OF THE NOREPINEPHRINE-RECEPTOR COUPLED ADENYLATE-CYCLASE SYSTEM IN BRAIN: EFFECTS OF NISOXETINE VERSUS FLUOXETINE.
000208 01-03

NITRAZEPAM
ENZYME INDUCING EFFECTS OF PHENOBARBITAL ON NITRAZEPAM METABOLISM IN DOGS.
000086 01-03
STUDY OF VIGILANCE AFTER INGESTION OF ZOPICLONE IN COMPARISON WITH NITRAZEPAM AND PLACEBO. METHODOLOGY OF THE STUDY: SELF-EVALUATION QUESTIONNAIRE AND PSYCHOMETRIC-TESTS.
000543 01-07
COMPARISON OF NITRAZEPAM 5 MG WITH TRIAZOLAM 0.5 MG IN YOUNG PSYCHIATRIC INSOMNIAC-INPATIENTS.
002096 02-11
THE EFFECTS OF TRIAZOLAM AND NITRAZEPAM ON SLEEP QUALITY, MORNING VIGILANCE, AND PSYCHOMOTOR PERFORMANCE.
002330 02-14
REVERSIBLE RING-OPENING REACTIONS OF NIMETAZEPAM AND NITRAZEPAM IN ACIDIC MEDIA AT BODY-TEMPERATURE.
004517 04-13

NITROGEN-MUSTARD
KINETIC DATA ON THE INHIBITION OF HIGH-AFFINITY CHOLINE TRANSPORT INTO RAT-FOREBRAIN SYNAPTOSOMES BY CHOLINE-LIKE COMPOUNDS AND NITROGEN-MUSTARD ANALOGUES.
002879 03-03

NITROUS-OXIDE
TOLERANCE OF MICE TO NITROUS-OXIDE.
000418 01-04
A COMPARISON OF THE EFFECTS OF MORPHINE-SULPHATE AND NITROUS-OXIDE ANALGESIA ON CHRONIC PAIN STATES IN MAN.
003442 03-14

NMR
BETA ENDORPHIN AND ANALOGS: 360 MHZ PROTON NMR SPECTROSCOPY.
001028 02-01
NMR SPECTRAL STUDY OF PROTON TRANSFER IN AMITRIPTYLINE-HYDROCHLORIDE CHLORDIAZEPOXIDE-HYDROCHLORIDE COMBINATIONS IN DIPOLAR APROTIC SOLVENTS.
003654 04-01

NOCICEPTION
DOES SYSTEMIC MORPHINE INCREASE DESCENDING INHIBITORY CONTROLS OF DORSAL-HORN NEURONES INVOLVED IN NOCICEPTION?
000175 01-03
DIFFERENTIAL-EFFECTS OF SYSTEMIC VERSUS INTRACRANIAL INJECTION OF OPIATES ON CENTRAL, OROFACIAL AND LOWER BODY NOCICEPTION: SOMATOTYPY IN BULBAR ANALGESIA SYSTEMS.
001446 02-03
NALOXONE REVERSIBLE DUPLICATION BY LANTHANUM OF OPIATE ANALGESIA EFFECTS ON OROFACIAL, LOWER BODY AND CENTRAL NOCICEPTION.
003028 03-04

NOCICEPTIVE
THE EFFECTS OF MORPHINE ON THE ACTIVITY OF CERTAIN DORSAL-HORN NEURONS OF THE SPINAL-CORD INVOLVED IN NOCICEPTIVE PROCESSES.
000028 01-03
REVERSIBLE INACTIVATION OF RAPHE-MAGNUS NEURONS: EFFECTS ON NOCICEPTIVE THRESHOLD AND MORPHINE-INDUCED ANALGESIA.
000240 01-03
METHYSERGIDE AND SUPRASPINAL INHIBITION OF THE SPINAL TRANSMISSION OF NOCICEPTIVE INFORMATION IN THE ANESTHETIZED CAT.
002740 03-03

EXCITATORY EFFECTS OF DIHYDROCAPSAICIN ON NOCICEPTIVE NEURONS IN THE MEDIAL THALAMUS.
003714 04-03
THE EFFECT OF CHOLINERGIC SUBSTANCES ON NOCICEPTIVE EVOKED-RESPONSES IN SPECIFIC NUCLEI OF THE THALAMUS.
003770 04-03

NOCTURNAL
THE DIFFERENTIAL-EFFECTS OF SHORT-ACTING AND LONG-ACTING BENZODIAZEPINES UPON NOCTURNAL SLEEP AND DAYTIME PERFORMANCE.
000822 01-14
THE EFFECTS OF COMBINED SEDATIVE AND ANXIOLYTIC-PREPARATIONS ON SUBJECTIVE ASPECTS OF SLEEP AND OBJECTIVE MEASURE OF AROUSAL AND PERFORMANCE THE MORNING FOLLOWING NOCTURNAL MEDICATION: II. REPEATED DOSES.
002331 02-14
THE EFFECT OF BUTOCTAMIDE-HYDROGEN-SUCCINATE ON NOCTURNAL SLEEP: ALL-NIGHT POLYGRAPHICAL-STUDIES.
002350 02-14
HIPPOCAMPAL SEROTONIN REUPTAKE AND NOCTURNAL LOCOMOTOR-ACTIVITY AFTER MICROINJECTIONS OF 5,7 DHT IN THE FORNIX-FIMBRIA.
002929 03-03
DISULFIRAM AND NOCTURNAL PENILE-TUMESCENCE IN THE CHRONIC ALCOHOLIC.
004556 04-13

NOISE
AIRCRAFT NOISE AND MENTAL-HEALTH: II. USE OF MEDICINES AND HEALTH-CARE-SERVICES.
003647 03-17

NOMIFENSIN
NOMIFENSIN IN THE TREATMENT OF ENDOGENOUS DEPRESSIONS. CLINICAL-EXPERIENCE AND EEG FINDINGS.
000613 01-09

NOMIFENSINE
THE TREATMENT OF DEPRESSIVE-CONDITIONS WITH NOMIFENSINE.
000609 01-09
CLINICAL-EXPERIENCE WITH NOMIFENSINE.
000642 01-09
THE COMPARATIVE DISPOSITION OF NOMIFENSINE (MERITAL) IN THE PREGNANT AND NONPREGNANT RAT.
000853 01-15
ANATOMICOPHYSIOLOGICAL AND NEUROCHEMICAL-STUDY OF THE LIMBIC-SYSTEM: EFFECT OF NOMIFENSINE.
001160 02-03
EFFECTS OF NOMIFENSINE AND DESIPRAMINE ON THE SEQUELAE OF INTRACEREBRALLY INJECTED 6 OHDA AND 5,6 DHT.
001522 02-03
NOMIFENSINE IN THE TREATMENT OF VARIOUS TYPES OF DEPRESSION.
001968 02-09
NOMIFENSINE IN THE TREATMENT OF ENDOGENOUS DEPRESSION. A CONTROLLED-STUDY VS. NORTRIPTYLINE.
001978 02-09
EVALUATION OF NOMIFENSINE IN THE TREATMENT OF GERIATRIC DEPRESSION USING PSYCHOMETRIC-TESTS AND PLASMA LEVEL CONTROLS.
002004 02-09
TREATMENT OF THERAPY-RESISTANT DEPRESSED-PATIENTS WITH IV. INFUSIONS OF NOMIFENSINE CONTROLLED BY GALVANIC-SKIN-RESISTANCE.
002012 02-09
PROFILE OF THE ANTIDEPRESSANT ACTION OF NOMIFENSINE.
002025 02-09
TREATMENT OF ANXIOUS-DEPRESSED OUTPATIENTS WITH A FIXED COMBINATION (NOMIFENSINE/CLOBAZAM) IN COMPARISON TO A MONOSUBSTANCE (DOXEPINE).
002028 02-09
NOMIFENSINE IN THE TREATMENT OF OBSESSIVE-COMPULSIVE-NEUROSIS. THERAPEUTIC-EFFICACY AND TOLERABILITY IN COMPARISON TO IMIPRAMINE.
002078 02-10
NOMIFENSINE AS CONCOMITANT THERAPY IN THE TREATMENT OF PARKINSON-PATIENTS. A DOUBLE-BLIND PLACEBO-CONTROLLED-STUDY.
002130 02-11
INFLUENCE OF NOMIFENSINE ON GROWTH-HORMONE, PROLACTIN, LUTEINISING-HORMONE AND THYREOTROPIN IN HEALTHY SUBJECTS AND HYPERPROLACTINAEMIC-PATIENTS.
002137 02-11
RECENT INVESTIGATIONS ON THE MECHANISM-OF-ACTION OF NOMIFENSINE.
002289 02-13
SUBJECTIVE DRUG-EFFECTS AND DRUG PREFERENCE IN HEALTHY VOLUNTEERS AS A MODEL OF A DRUGS REINFORCING EFFECTS: STUDIES ON NOMIFENSINE, AMPHETAMINE AND PLACEBO.
002362 02-14
DOPAMINERGIC INVOLVEMENT IN THE HYPERALGESIC EFFECT OF NOMIFENSINE.
002736 03-03

NOREPINEPHRINE AND DOPAMINE CEREBRAL LEVELS AFTER CHRONIC-TREATMENT WITH NOMIFENSINE.
002872 03-03

ACUTE ACTION OF NOMIFENSINE ON NOREPINEPHRINE AND DOPAMINE LEVELS IN THE RAT-BRAIN.
002873 03-03

NOMIFENSINE: CONSIDERATIONS ON A NEW NONTRICYCLIC-ANTIDEPRESSANT.
003222 03-09

INFLUENCE OF THE DOPAMINERGIC AGONISTS BROMOCRIPTINE, PIRIBEDIL AND NOMIFENSINE ON THE SYMPATHETIC NEURAL TRANSMISSION IN THE NICTITATING MEMBRANE OF THE CAT.
003822 04-03

CONTROLLED CLINICAL-TRIAL OF NOMIFENSINE IN THE TREATMENT OF DEPRESSION.
004417 04-09

PLASMA NOMIFENSINE CONCENTRATION: CARDIOLOGICAL EFFECTS AND CLINICAL-RESPONSE.
004639 04-15

MAPROTILINE, NOMIFENSINE, MIANSERIN, ZIMELIDINE: A REVIEW OF ANTIDEPRESSANT EFFICACY IN INPATIENTS.
004731 04-17

NOMOGRAMS
PREDICTABILITY OF PHENYTOIN SERUM LEVELS BY NOMOGRAMS AND CLINICIANS.
000909 01-16

NON-5-HYDROXYTRYPTAMINERGIC
METERGOLINE AND CYPROHEPTADINE SUPPRESS PROLACTIN RELEASE BY A NON-5-HYDROXYTRYPTAMINERGIC, NONDOPAMINERGIC MECHANISM.
003732 04-03

NONADDICTED
EVENT-RELATED POTENTIAL CHANGES WITH MORPHINE IN NONADDICTED HUMANS.
004512 04-13

NONANESTHETIC
A COMPARISON OF HUMAN TACTILE STIMULUS VELOCITY DISCRIMINATION WITH THE ABILITY OF S-I CORTICAL NEURONS IN AWAKE RHESUS-MONKEYS TO SIGNAL THE SAME VELOCITY DIFFERENCES BEFORE AND AFTER NONANESTHETIC DOSES OF PENTOBARBITAL.
000055 01-03

NONANTIPSYCHOTIC
PROLACTIN RELEASING POTENCIES OF ANTIPSYCHOTIC AND RELATED NONANTIPSYCHOTIC COMPOUNDS IN FEMALE RATS: RELATION TO CLINICAL POTENCIES.
003830 04-03

NONASSOCIATIVE-ASPECTS
INTERFERENCE WITH INGESTIONAL AVERSION LEARNING PRODUCED BY PREEXPOSURE TO THE UNCONDITIONED-STIMULUS: ASSOCIATIVE-ASPECTS AND NONASSOCIATIVE-ASPECTS.
001610 02-04

NONCOMPETITIVE
NONCOMPETITIVE AMINE UPTAKE INHIBITION BY THE NEW ANTIDEPRESSANT PRIDEFINE.
003771 04-03

NONCOMPLIANCE
NONCOOPERATION: AN EXAMINATION OF FACTORS LEADING TO NONCOMPLIANCE IN A HYPERTENSION CLINIC.
002557 02-17

NONCOOPERATION
NONCOOPERATION: AN EXAMINATION OF FACTORS LEADING TO NONCOMPLIANCE IN A HYPERTENSION CLINIC.
002557 02-17

NONDEPRIVED
NALOXONE: EFFECTS ON FOOD AND WATER CONSUMPTION IN THE NONDEPRIVED AND DEPRIVED RAT.
001599 02-04

NONDOPAMINERGIC
METERGOLINE AND CYPROHEPTADINE SUPPRESS PROLACTIN RELEASE BY A NON-5-HYDROXYTRYPTAMINERGIC, NONDOPAMINERGIC MECHANISM.
003732 04-03

NONEMOTIVE
THE BEHAVIOR OF RATS IN THE OPEN-FIELD WITHOUT STRESS, UNDER ACUTE AND PERSISTING INFLUENCE OF IMIPRAMINE AND TRANYLCYPROMINE AS WELL AS ON THE INDIVIDUAL REACTION TYPE (EMOTIVE AND NONEMOTIVE).
001624 02-04

NONERGOT
CHARACTERIZATION OF ERGOT AND NONERGOT SEROTONIN ANTAGONISTS BY PROLACTIN AND GROWTH-HORMONE PROFILES DURING WAKEFULNESS AND SLEEP.
002217 02-13

NONGABAERGIC
CHARACTERIZATION OF 3H GABA-RECEPTOR BINDING TO RAT-BRAIN SYNAPTOSOMAL MEMBRANES: EFFECT OF NONGABAERGIC COMPOUNDS.
000139 01-03

NONGENETIC
NONGENETIC FACTORS AFFECTING HUMAN PLATELET MONOAMINE-OXIDASE.
003407 03-13

NONHUMAN
PROCEDURES FOR REDUCING DRUG INTAKE: NONHUMAN STUDIES.
001753 02-04

ANTIPSYCHOTIC-DRUGS: DIFFERENTIAL-EFFECTS ON DOPAMINE NEURONS IN BASAL GANGLIA AND MESOCORTEX FOLLOWING CHRONIC ADMINISTRATION IN HUMAN AND NONHUMAN PRIMATES.
002285 02-13

ANTAGONISM OF INTRAVENOUS COCAINE LETHALITY IN NONHUMAN PRIMATES.
003127 03-05

NONIDENTITY
CHARACTERIZATION OF LRF-LIKE IMMUNOREACTIVITY IN THE FROG SYMPATHETIC GANGLIA: NONIDENTITY WITH LRF-DECAPEPTIDE. (UNPUBLISHED PAPER).
001018 02-01

NONINTERACTION
NONINTERACTION OF DIGITOXIN AND QUINIDINE.
000968 01-17

NONLINEAR
NONLINEAR REGRESSION ANALYSIS OF NOREPINEPHRINE RESPONSE KINETICS IN CEREBRAL VASCULATURE.
000256 01-03

NONLITHIUM
RENAL FUNCTION IN LITHIUM AND NONLITHIUM TREATED PATIENTS WITH AFFECTIVE-DISORDERS.
000837 01-15

NONNARCOTIC
BLOCKADE BY L LYSINE OF NONNARCOTIC ANALGESICS.
003857 04-03

NONNEURONAL
BASIC AND CLINICAL NEUROBIOLOGICAL APPLICATIONS OF NEURONAL (NSE) AND NONNEURONAL (NNE) ENOLASE. (UNPUBLISHED PAPER).
001041 02-01

NONNOXIOUS
MORPHINE DEPRESSES DORSAL-HORN NEURON RESPONSES TO CONTROLLED NOXIOUS AND NONNOXIOUS CUTANEOUS STIMULATION.
003782 04-03

NONOPIATE
STEREOSPECIFIC, DOSE-DEPENDENT ANTAGONISM BY NALOXONE OF NONOPIATE BEHAVIOR IN MICE.
000411 01-04

INTERACTIONS BETWEEN NALTREXONE AND NONOPIATE DRUGS EVALUATED BY SCHEDULE-CONTROLLED BEHAVIOR.
001645 02-04

NONOPIOID
DISCRIMINATION OF ELECTRIC-SHOCK: EFFECTS OF SOME OPIOID AND NONOPIOID DRUGS.
004106 04-04

NONORGANIC
DOPAMINE AND 5 HT SUPERSENSITIVITY IN NONORGANIC CENTRAL PAIN AND IN MORPHINE ABSTINENCE: FORTUITOUS OR REAL ANALOGY?
004553 04-13

NONPARAMETRIC
A SYMPTOM-PROFILE-ANALYSIS OF ANTIPSYCHOTIC-DRUG TREATMENT: NONPARAMETRIC MULTIDIMENSIONAL TECHNIQUE.
003196 03-08

NONPREGNANT
THE COMPARATIVE DISPOSITION OF NOMIFENSINE (MERITAL) IN THE PREGNANT AND NONPREGNANT RAT.
000853 01-15

NONPSYCHOACTIVE
INFLUENCE OF PSYCHOACTIVE AND NONPSYCHOACTIVE CANNABINOIDS ON CELL PROLIFERATION AND MACROMOLECULAR BIOSYNTHESIS IN HUMAN CELLS.
002830 03-03

INFLUENCE OF PSYCHOACTIVE AND NONPSYCHOACTIVE CANNABINOIDS ON CHROMATIN STRUCTURE AND FUNCTION IN HUMAN CELLS.
002831 03-03

NONPSYCHOTIC
THE IMPORTANCE OF AMINEPTINE IN THE TREATMENT OF NONPSYCHOTIC DEPRESSIVE-STATES IN THE ELDERLY.
001999 02-09

NONRESPONDERS
RESPONDERS AND NONRESPONDERS TO CHLORDIAZEPOXIDE AND PLACEBO: A DISCRIMINANT FUNCTION ANALYSIS.
002482 02-16

RESPONDERS AND NONRESPONDERS TO CHLORDIAZEPOXIDE AND PLACEBO. A DISCRIMINANT FUNCTION ANALYSIS. (UNPUBLISHED PAPER).
004420 04-10

NONSEROTONERGIC
NONSEROTONERGIC DEPRESSION OF SPINAL MONOSYNAPTIC REFLEX TRANSMISSION BY 5 HYDROXYTRYPTOPHAN.
002745 03-03

NONSIGNALLED
DIFFERENTIAL-EFFECTS OF METHYLPHENIDATE ON SIGNALLED AND
NONSIGNALLED REINFORCEMENT.
000380 01-04
NONSPECIFIC
EFFECTS OF EXPERIMENTER AND TEST LOCATION NOVELTY ON
NONSPECIFIC ACTIVITY IN RATS AND ITS MODIFICATION BY
METHAMPHETAMINE.
000409 01-04
ADRENERGIC NONSPECIFIC POTENTIATION OF YOHIMBINE TOXICITY IN
MICE BY ANTIDEPRESSANTS AND RELATED DRUGS AND
ANTIYOHIMBINE ACTION OF ANTIADRENERGIC AND SEROTONERGIC
DRUGS.
001330 02-03
3H APOMORPHINE-RECEPTORS IN VARIOUS RAT-BRAIN REGIONS: A
STUDY OF SPECIFIC AND NONSPECIFIC BINDING AND THE INFLUENCE OF
CHRONIC NEUROLEPTIC TREATMENT.
001846 02-05
INFUSIONS INTO THE OCULOMOTOR NUCLEUS OR NERVE: A METHOD OF
ESTIMATING THE DOSAGE AT WHICH TRANSMITTER ANTAGONISTS
INFUSED INTRACRANIALLY PRODUCE NONSPECIFIC BLOCKING OF
NEURAL ACTIVITY.
003134 03-06
SPECIFIC AND NONSPECIFIC MULTIPLE UNIT ACTIVITIES DURING
PENTYLENETETRAZOL SEIZURES. I. ANIMALS WITH ENCEPHALE ISOLE.
004046 04-03
NONSPECIFIC FACTORS IN DRUG-EFFECTS: PLACEBO PERSONALITY.
004704 04-17
NONSTEROIDAL
LOWERING OF THE CONVULSIVE THRESHOLD BY NONSTEROIDAL
ANTIINFLAMMATORY-DRUGS.
002904 03-03
NONTOLERANT
TIME-COURSE OF ETORPHINE LEVELS IN TISSUES OF OPIATE-TOLERANT
AND NONTOLERANT RATS.
000301 01-03
NONTOXIC
TRANSIENT HYPERKINESIA AFTER A SINGLE INTRAVENOUS PERFUSION OF
DIPHENYLHYDANTOIN: REPORT OF A CASE ASSOCIATED WITH
NONTOXIC PLASMA LEVELS OF DIPHENYLHYDANTOIN.
004638 04-15
NONTREATED
NORMAL PLASMA DOPAMINE-BETA-HYDROXYLASE IN NONTREATED AND
TREATED PARKINSON-PATIENTS.
004471 04-11
NONTRICYCLIC-ANTIDEPRESSANT
NOMIFENSINE: CONSIDERATIONS ON A NEW NONTRICYCLIC-
ANTIDEPRESSANT.
003222 03-09
NONVERBAL-BEHAVIOR
ON THE RELATIONSHIP BETWEEN MEASURES OBTAINED BY VIDEO-
ANALYSIS OF NONVERBAL-BEHAVIOR AND SELF-RATING OF MOOD.
004410 04-09
NOOTROPIC
CNS EFFECTS OF ISF-2522, A NEW NOOTROPIC (A PHASE I SAFETY AND
CNS EFFICACY STUDY WITH QUANTITATIVE PHARMACOEEG AND
PHARMACOPSYCHOLOGY).
004519 04-13
NOOTROPIC-DRUGS
EFFECTS OF SOME NOOTROPIC-DRUGS UPON THE EMBRYONIC
MORPHOGENETIC SYSTEMS.
000144 01-03
POSSIBILITIES OF INFLUENCE ON THE ORGANIC-PSYCHOSYNDROME WITH
NOOTROPIC-DRUGS IN CHRONIC ALCOHOLISM.
000707 01-11
PHARMACOLOGY OF NOOTROPIC-DRUGS.
000800 01-14
NOOTROPIC-DRUGS IN CLINICAL-PRACTICE.
000811 01-14
THE INFLUENCE OF NOOTROPIC-DRUGS ON LEARNING AND MEMORY OF
DEFENSE REACTIONS.
000815 01-14
CRITERIA FOR CLINICAL DEVELOPMENT AND CLASSIFICATION OF
NOOTROPIC-DRUGS. AN EXAMPLE: PIRACETAM.
000988 01-17
THE EFFECTS OF NOOTROPIC-DRUGS ON THE SUSCEPTIBILITY TO
AUDIOGENIC-SEIZURES IN RATS.
001571 02-04
TWO-WAY AVOIDANCE LEARNING UNDER THE INFLUENCE OF NOOTROPIC-
DRUGS.
001647 02-04
ANTIHYPOXIDOTIC-DRUGS AND NOOTROPIC-DRUGS: PROOF OF THEIR
ENCEPHALOTROPIC AND PHARMACODYNAMIC PROPERTIES BY
ENCEPHALOTROPIC AND PHARMACODYNAMIC PROPERTIES BY
QUANTITATIVE EEG INVESTIGATIONS.
002166 02-11
NOOTROPIC-DRUGS AND RELATED DRUGS INTERACTING WITH THE
INTEGRATIVE ACTIVITY OF THE BRAIN.
002327 02-14

NOOTROPICS
POSSIBLE CLINICAL APPLICATIONS OF NOOTROPICS.
001890 02-07
NOOTROPIL
CLINICAL AND BIOCHEMICAL-ACTION OF PIRACETAM (NOOTROPIL) IN
DRUG-RESISTANT DEPRESSION.
000600 01-09
INFLUENCING BRAIN CONCUSSION BY NOOTROPIL.
000724 01-11
THE EFFECT OF NOOTROPIL ON THE TRANSCALLOSAL AND PRIMARY
EVOKED-RESPONSES OF THE CAT CEREBRAL-CORTEX.
003780 04-03
NOOTROPIL-UCB
OUR EXPERIENCE WITH PIRACETAM (NOOTROPIL-UCB) TREATMENT IN
CHILDREN FROM HIGH-RISK PREGNANCIES WITH SUBSEQUENT
MINIMAL-BRAIN-DYSFUNCTION.
000544 01-07
NOOTROPYL
SOME THERAPEUTIC EFFECTS OF NOOTROPYL.
004458 04-11
NORADRENALINE
COMPARISON OF MIANSERIN WITH DESIPRAMINE, MAPROTILINE AND
PHENTOLAMINE ON CARDIAC PRESYNAPTIC AND VASCULAR
POSTSYNAPTIC ALPHA-ADRENOCEPTORS AND NORADRENALINE
REUPTAKE IN PITHED NORMOTENSIVE-RATS.
000044 01-03
THE MONOAMINE-OXIDASE-INHIBITORS CLORGYLINE AND L DEPRENYL
ALSO AFFECT THE UPTAKE OF DOPAMINE, NORADRENALINE AND
SEROTONIN BY RAT-BRAIN SYNAPTOSOMAL PREPARATIONS.
000171 01-03
METABOLISM OF 3H NORADRENALINE RELEASED FROM ISOLATED RAT
HYPOTHALAMUS BY EXTRACTS OF BLACK-WIDOW-SPIDER GLANDS.
000223 01-03
INHIBITION OF NEURONAL UPTAKE REDUCES THE PRESYNAPTIC EFFECTS
OF CLONIDINE BUT NOT OF ALPHA METHYLNORADRENALINE ON THE
STIMULATION-EVOKED RELEASE OF 3H NORADRENALINE FROM RAT
OCCIPITAL-CORTEX SLICES.
000227 01-03
THE MECHANISM OF EFFECT OF NEUROPHARMACOLOGICAL-DRUGS. VI:
EFFECT OF NORADRENALINE AND 5 HYDROXYTRYPTAMINE ON BRAIN
FREE FATTY-ACIDS.
000274 01-03
A COMPARISON OF RATES OF DEPLETION AND RECOVERY OF
NORADRENALINE STORES OF PERIPHERAL AND CENTRAL
NORADRENERGIC NEURONES AFTER RESERPINE ADMINISTRATION:
IMPORTANCE OF NEURONAL ACTIVITY.
000314 01-03
TETRAHYDRO-BETA-CARBOLINES AND CORRESPONDING TRYPTAMINES:
IN VITRO INHIBITION OF SEROTONIN, DOPAMINE AND
NORADRENALINE UPTAKE IN RAT-BRAIN SYNAPTOSOMES.
001078 02-02
CENTRAL LEVELS OF NORADRENALINE, 3 METHOXY-4-
HYDROXYPHENYLETHYLENEGLYCOL AND CYCLIC-AMP IN THE RAT
AFTER ACTIVATION OF LOCUS-COERULEUS NEURONS: INFLUENCE OF
SINGLE AND REPEATED NEUROLEPTIC TREATMENT.
001095 02-03
NORADRENALINE RELEASE FROM SLICES OF THE THALAMUS OF NORMAL
AND MORPHINE-DEPENDENT RATS.
001142 02-03
AN EXAMINATION OF FACTORS INFLUENCING ADRENERGIC
TRANSMISSION IN THE PITHED RAT, WITH SPECIAL REFERENCE TO
NORADRENALINE UPTAKE MECHANISMS AND POSTJUNCTIONAL
ALPHA-ADRENOCEPTORS.
001196 02-03
EFFECTS OF RATE OF BLOOD FLOW ON FRACTIONAL EXTRACTION AND ON
UPTAKE OF INFUSED NORADRENALINE BY BROWN ADIPOSE TISSUE IN
VIVO.
001231 02-03
THE HYPERKINETIC-SYNDROME FOLLOWING LONG-TERM HALOPERIDOL
TREATMENT: INVOLVEMENT OF DOPAMINE AND NORADRENALINE.
001299 02-03
DOPAMINE-BETA-HYDROXYLASE ACTIVITY AND NORADRENALINE
CONTENT IN PIAL-ARTERIES OF CAT AND GOAT.
001357 02-03
THE EFFECT OF PSYCHOTROPIC-SUBSTANCES AND NARCOTIC ANALGESIC-
DRUGS ON 14C NORADRENALINE UPTAKE BY SYNAPTOSOMES OF THE
CEREBRAL-CORTEX OF RATS.
001363 02-03
GABA FACILITATION BY NORADRENALINE SHOWED SUPERSENSITIVITY IN
CEREBELLUM AFTER 6 HYDROXYDOPAMINE.
001382 02-03
EVIDENCE THAT NORADRENALINE MODULATES THE INCREASE IN
STRIATAL DOPAMINE METABOLISM INDUCED BY MUSCARINIC-
RECEPTOR STIMULATION.
001518 02-03
INTRAHYPOTHALAMIC MICROINJECTIONS OF NORADRENALINE WITH AND
WITHOUT INDUCTION OF THE ALIMENTARY DRIVE AS A REWARD IN A
T-MAZE LEARNING IN RATS.
001604 02-04

EFFECT OF NICKEL ON THE LEVELS OF DOPAMINE, NORADRENALINE AND
SEROTONIN IN DIFFERENT REGIONS OF THE RAT-BRAIN.
001831 02-05
BLOOD LEVEL OF AMITRIPTYLINE, NORTRIPTYLINE, NORADRENALINE,
SEROTONIN AND THERAPEUTIC RESPONSE.
002057 02-09
QUANTIFICATION OF NORADRENALINE IONTOPHORESIS.
002475 02-16
REVERSAL OF NORADRENALINE DENERVATION-INDUCED INCREASE OF
BETA-ADRENORECEPTOR BINDING IN RAT NEOCORTEX BY
NORADRENALINE INFUSION.
002672 03-03
ENHANCEMENT OF NORADRENALINE RELEASE FROM RAT-CEREBRAL-
CORTEX BY NEUROLEPTIC-DRUGS.
002742 03-03
DOPAMINE, NORADRENALINE AND 3,4 DIHYDROXYPHENYLACETIC-ACID
(DOPAC) LEVELS OF INDIVIDUAL BRAIN NUCLEI, EFFECTS OF
HALOPERIDOL AND PARGYLINE.
003792 04-03
REGULATION OF NORADRENALINE OVERFLOW IN RAT-CEREBRAL-CORTEX
BY PROSTAGLANDIN-E2.
003841 04-03
ON THE IMPORTANCE OF AGONIST CONCENTRATION GRADIENTS WITHIN
ISOLATED TISSUES. INCREASED MAXIMAL RESPONSES OF RAT VASA-
DEFERENTIA TO (-) NORADRENALINE AFTER BLOCKADE OF NEURONAL
UPTAKE.
003879 04-03
INFLUENCE OF CALCIUM ON NORADRENALINE RELEASE EVOKED BY 5
HYDROXYTRYPTAMINE, TYRAMINE AND POTASSIUM FROM GOAT
PIAL-ARTERIES.
003925 04-03
OPIOIDS, NORADRENALINE AND GTP ANALOGS INHIBIT CHOLERA-TOXIN
ACTIVATED ADENYLATE-CYCLASE IN NEUROBLASTOMA-X GLIOMA
HYBRID CELLS.
003975 04-03
DECREASE OF NORADRENALINE O METHYLATION IN RAT-BRAIN INDUCED
BY L-DOPA. REVERSAL EFFECT OF S ADENOSYL-L-METHIONINE.
004019 04-03
THE EFFECT OF NORADRENALINE ON NA-K TRANSPORT IN RAT-CEREBRAL-
CORTICAL SLICES.
004056 04-03
DETERMINATION OF PICOMOLE AMOUNTS OF DOPAMINE,
NORADRENALINE, 3,4 DIHYDROXYPHENYLALANINE, 3,4
DIHYDROXYPHENYLACETIC-ACID, HOMOVANILLIC-ACID, AND 5
HYDROXYINDOLEACETIC-ACID IN NERVOUS-TISSUE AFTER ONE-STEP
PURIFICATION ON SEPHADEX-G-10, USING HIGH.
004305 04-06
THE SPECIFIC ACTIVITY OF PLATELET MONOAMINE-OXIDASE VARIES
WITH PLATELET COUNT DURING SEVERE EXERCISE AND
NORADRENALINE INFUSION.
004509 04-13

NORADRENALINE-RECEPTORS
ACTIVATION OF PRESYNAPTIC ALPHA NORADRENALINE-RECEPTORS IN
RAT-BRAIN BY THE POTENT DOPAMINE-MIMETIC N,N DIPROPYL-ADTN.
001390 02-03

NORADRENERGIC
FUNCTIONAL HYPERINNERVATION OF CEREBRAL-CORTEX BY
NORADRENERGIC NEURONS RESULTS FROM FETAL LESIONS: PARALLELS
WITH SCHIZOPHRENIA.
000059 01-03
EFFECT OF MIANSERIN ON NORADRENERGIC TRANSMISSION IN THE RAT
ANOCOCCYGEUS-MUSCLE.
000075 01-03
HYPOALGESIA FOLLOWING MICROINJECTION OF NORADRENERGIC
ANTAGONISTS IN THE NUCLEUS-RAPHE-MAGNUS.
000122 01-03
CENTRAL NORADRENERGIC ADAPTATION TO LONG-TERM-TREATMENT
WITH IMIPRAMINE IN RHESUS-MONKEYS.
000182 01-03
MICROIONTOPHORETIC STUDIES ON NORADRENERGIC INHIBITION FROM
LOCUS-COERULEUS OF SPINAL TRIGEMINAL-NUCLEUS NEURONS.
000260 01-03
EFFECTS OF NORADRENERGIC AGONISTS AND ANTAGONISTS ON
GROWTH-HORMONE SECRETION UNDER GAMMA HYDROXYBUTYRATE
NARCOANALGESIA IN THE RAT.
000262 01-03
A COMPARISON OF RATES OF DEPLETION AND RECOVERY OF
NORADRENALINE STORES OF PERIPHERAL AND CENTRAL
NORADRENERGIC NEURONES AFTER RESERPINE ADMINISTRATION:
IMPORTANCE OF NEURONAL ACTIVITY.
000314 01-03
NORADRENERGIC AGONISTS AND ANTAGONISTS: EFFECTS ON
CONDITIONED FEAR AS MEASURED BY THE POTENTIATED STARTLE
PARADIGM.
000372 01-04
THE TIME-COURSE OF NORADRENERGIC PRESYNAPTIC AND
POSTSYNAPTIC ACTIVITY DURING CHRONIC DESIPRAMINE TREATMENT.
001289 02-03
DIFFERENTIAL SENSITIVITY OF HYPOTHALAMIC DOPAMINERGIC AND
NORADRENERGIC NEURONES TO PHARMACOLOGICAL MANIPULATION.
001310 02-03

DEVELOPMENT OF AND RECOVERY FROM SUBSENSITIVITY OF THE
NORADRENERGIC CYCLIC-AMP GENERATING SYSTEM IN BRAIN. EFFECT
OF AMPHETAMINE FOLLOWING INHIBITION OF ITS AROMATIC
HYDROXYLATION BY IPRINDOLE.
001353 02-03
INTERACTION OF HISTAMINE H2-RECEPTOR BLOCKING-DRUGS WITH THE
NORADRENERGIC SYSTEM IN RAT-BRAIN AND HEART.
001397 02-03
INVESTIGATIONS ON THE INTERACTION OF THYROTROPIN-RELEASING-
HORMONE (TRH) AND MK-771 WITH CENTRAL NORADRENERGIC
MECHANISMS.
001701 02-04
ELECTROPHYSIOLOGICAL-CHANGES AT A CENTRAL NORADRENERGIC
SYNAPSE DURING THALLIUM TOXICOSIS.
001848 02-05
COCAINE AND AMPHETAMINE ANTAGONIZE THE DECREASE OF
NORADRENERGIC NEUROTRANSMISSION ELICITED BY OXYMETAZOLINE
BUT POTENTIATE THE INHIBITION BY ALPHA METHYLNOREPINEPHRINE
IN THE PERFUSED CAT SPLEEN.
002801 03-03
CHANGES IN NORADRENERGIC TRANSMISSION ALTER THE
CONCENTRATION OF CYTOPLASMIC PROGESTIN-RECEPTORS IN
HYPOTHALAMUS.
002842 03-03
NORADRENERGIC STIMULATION IN VIVO INCREASES NA-K-ADENOSINE-
TRIPHOSPHATASE ACTIVITY.
002910 03-03
CHOLINERGIC, DOPAMINERGIC, NORADRENERGIC, OR GLUTAMINERGIC
STIMULATION VENTRAL TO THE ANTERIOR SEPTUM DOES NOT
SPECIFICALLY SUPPRESS DEFENSIVE-BEHAVIOR.
002945 03-04
SUPERSENSITIVITY OF CENTRAL NORADRENERGIC PRESYNAPTIC-
AUTORECEPTORS FOLLOWING CHRONIC-TREATMENT WITH THE
ANTIDEPRESSANT MIANSERIN.
003745 04-03
ELECTROPHYSIOLOGICAL EVIDENCE FOR PRESYNAPTIC ACTIONS OF
PHENCYCLIDINE ON NORADRENERGIC TRANSMISSION IN RAT
CEREBELLUM.
003926 04-03
EFFECTS OF ZIMELIDINE ON SEROTONINERGIC AND NORADRENERGIC
NEURONS AFTER REPEATED ADMINISTRATION IN THE RAT.
003991 04-03
EFFECT OF CHRONIC-TREATMENT WITH TRICYCLIC-ANTIDEPRESSANT
DRUGS ON IDENTIFIED BRAIN NORADRENERGIC AND SEROTONERGIC
NEURONS.
004026 04-03
NORADRENERGIC INFLUENCES ON SOUND-INDUCED SEIZURES.
004137 04-04
ALTERATIONS IN NORADRENERGIC FUNCTION DURING CLORGYLINE
TREATMEN .
004393 04-09

NORADRENERGIC-ALPHA2-RECEPTORS
FUNCTIONAL EVIDENCE FOR SUBSENSITIVITY OF NORADRENERGIC-
ALPHA2-RECEPTORS AFTER CHRONIC DESIPRAMINE TREATMENT.
000283 01-03

NORADRENERGIC-RECEPTOR
DOWN REGULATION OF NORADRENERGIC-RECEPTOR FUNCTION BY
ANTIDEPRESSANT-DRUGS: FUNCTIONAL SIGNIFICANCE AND
DISTINCTION FROM ANTIPSYCHOTIC-DRUGS. (UNPUBLISHED PAPER).
004746 04-17

NORCOCAINE
INTRAVENOUS SELF-ADMINISTRATION OF COCAINE AND NORCOCAINE BY
DOGS.
001760 02-04
DISCRIMINATIVE-STIMULUS PROPERTIES OF COCAINE, NORCOCAINE, AND
N ALLYLNORCOCAINE.
002954 03-04
EFFECTS OF NORCOCAINE AND SOME NORCOCAINE DERIVATIVES ON
SCHEDULE-CONTROLLED BEHAVIOR OF PIGEONS AND SQUIRREL-
MONKEYS.
004012 04-03

NORDIAZEPAM
ANALYSIS FOR DIAZEPAM AND NORDIAZEPAM BY ELECTRON-CAPTURE
GAS-CHROMATOGRAPHY AND BY LIQUID-CHROMATOGRAPHY.
000006 01-01

NOREPINEPHRINE
MATURATION OF SYMPATHETIC NEUROTRANSMISSION IN THE RAT
HEART. III. DEVELOPMENTAL-CHANGES IN RESERPINE INHIBITION OF
NOREPINEPHRINE UPTAKE INTO ISOLATED SYNAPTIC VESICLES.
000025 01-03
ANTIHISTAMINE EFFECT ON SYNAPTOSOMAL UPTAKE OF SEROTONIN,
NOREPINEPHRINE AND DOPAMINE.
000035 01-03
THE INFLUENCE OF BENZOCTAMINE ON DOPAMINE AND NOREPINEPHRINE
CONTENTS OF THE SUBSTANTIA-NIGRA AND ON THE MUSCLE STRETCH
REFLEX OF THE CAT.
000054 01-03

MONOAMINERGIC DENERVATION OF THE RAT HIPPOCAMPUS: MICROIONTOPHORETIC STUDIES OF PRESYNAPTIC AND POSTSYNAPTIC SUPERSENSITIVITY TO NOREPINEPHRINE AND SEROTONIN.
000068 01-03
RELEASE OF ENDOGENOUS NOREPINEPHRINE FROM A RABBIT CEREBRAL-ARTERY.
000079 01-03
COMPARISON OF THE EFFECTS OF THE ISOMERS OF AMPHETAMINE, METHYLPHENIDATE AND DEOXYPIPRADROL ON THE UPTAKE OF L (3H)NOREPINEPHRINE AND (3H)DOPAMINE BY SYNAPTIC VESICLES FROM RAT-WHOLE-BRAIN, STRIATUM AND HYPOTHALAMUS.
000091 01-03
HYPOALGESIA INDUCED BY MICROINJECTION OF A NOREPINEPHRINE ANTAGONIST IN THE RAPHE-MAGNUS: REVERSAL BY INTRATHECAL ADMINISTRATION OF A SEROTONIN ANTAGONIST.
000121 01-03
EFFECTS OF PERINATAL THYROXINE AND/OR CORTICOSTERONE TREATMENT ON THE ONTOGENESIS OF HYPOTHALAMIC AND MESENCEPHALIC NOREPINEPHRINE AND DOPAMINE CONTENT.
000180 01-03
INTERACTIONS OF NOREPINEPHRINE WITH PURKINJE-CELL RESPONSES TO PUTATIVE AMINO-ACID NEUROTRANSMITTERS APPLIED BY MICROIONTOPHORESIS.
000209 01-03
NONLINEAR REGRESSION ANALYSIS OF NOREPINEPHRINE RESPONSE KINETICS IN CEREBRAL VASCULATURE.
000256 01-03
TYROSINE ADMINISTRATION REDUCES BLOOD-PRESSURE AND ENHANCES BRAIN NOREPINEPHRINE RELEASE IN SPONTANEOUSLY HYPERTENSIVE-RATS.
000296 01-03
ON THE CAPACITY OF PRESYNAPTIC ALPHA-RECEPTORS TO MODULATE NOREPINEPHRINE RELEASE FROM SLICES OF RAT NEOCORTEX AND THE AFFINITY OF SOME AGONISTS AND ANTAGONISTS FOR THESE RECEPTORS.
000323 01-03
NOREPINEPHRINE UPTAKE INHIBITORS AS BIOCHEMICALLY-SELECTIVE AND BEHAVIORALLY-SELECTIVE ANTAGONISTS OF THE LOCOMOTOR-STIMULATION INDUCED BY INDIRECTLY ACTING SYMPATHOMIMETIC-AMINES IN MICE.
000492 01-04
RESPONSES TO TYRAMINE AND NOREPINEPHRINE AFTER IMIPRAMINE AND TRAZODONE.
000864 01-15
MIANSERIN: DIRECT ACTIVATION OF BRAIN NOREPINEPHRINE NEURONS BY BLOCKING ALPHA2-RECEPTORS.
001214 02-03
MULTIVARIATE APPROACHES APPLIED TO STUDIES OF NOREPINEPHRINE AND SEROTONIN UPTAKE.
001460 02-03
ENHANCED SENSITIVITY OF AMYGDALOID NEURONS TO SEROTONIN AND NOREPINEPHRINE AFTER CHRONIC ANTIDEPRESSANT TREATMENT.
001523 02-03
CORRELATIONS BETWEEN HEMODYNAMIC PARAMETERS OF THE LIVER AND NOREPINEPHRINE RELEASE UPON HEPATIC-NERVE STIMULATION IN THE DOG.
001547 02-03
CENTRAL-ACTIONS OF NOREPINEPHRINE, PHENTOLAMINE AND 6 HYDROXYDOPAMINE IN SPONTANEOUSLY HYPERTENSIVE-RATS.
001553 02-03
THE EFFECTS OF NOREPINEPHRINE PERFUSION OF THE MESENCEPHALIC RETICULAR FORMATION ON BEHAVIOR IN THE RAT: INTERACTION WITH SEVERAL NEUROLEPTIC-DRUGS ON A MEASURE OF SUSTAINED ATTENTION. (PH.D. DISSERTATION).
001563 02-04
METHODOLOGICAL-ISSUES IN SPINAL-FLUID STUDIES OF SCHIZOPHRENIA: THE CASE OF NOREPINEPHRINE AND DOPAMINE-BETA-HYDROXYLASE. (UNPUBLISHED PAPER).
001952 02-08
PHENYLETHYLAMINE, DOPAMINE AND NOREPINEPHRINE IN SCHIZOPHRENIA. (UNPUBLISHED PAPER).
001957 02-08
MONOAMINE-OXIDASE, PHENYLETHYLAMINE, NOREPINEPHRINE AND SCHIZOPHRENIA. (UNPUBLISHED PAPER).
001958 02-08
EFFECT OF PIRIBEDIL (ET-495) ON PLASMA NOREPINEPHRINE: RELATIONSHIP TO ANTIDEPRESSANT RESPONSE.
002034 02-09
THE ROLE OF NOREPINEPHRINE IN AFFECTIVE-DISORDERS.
002278 02-13
CALCIUM-SENSITIVE ACCUMULATION OF NOREPINEPHRINE IN RAT-CEREBRAL-CORTEX.
002685 03-03
NOREPINEPHRINE DEPLETION ALTERS CEREBRAL OXIDATIVE METABOLISM IN THE ACTIVE STATE.
002798 03-03
NOREPINEPHRINE AND DOPAMINE CEREBRAL LEVELS AFTER CHRONIC-TREATMENT WITH NOMIFENSINE.
002872 03-03

ACUTE ACTION OF NOMIFENSINE ON NOREPINEPHRINE AND DOPAMINE LEVELS IN THE RAT-BRAIN.
002873 03-03
EFFECTS OF PROLONGED TREATMENT WITH LITHIUM AND TRICYCLIC-ANTIDEPRESSANTS ON DISCHARGE FREQUENCY, NOREPINEPHRINE RESPONSES AND BETA-RECEPTOR BINDING IN RAT-CEREBELLUM: ELECTROPHYSIOLOGICAL AND BIOCHEMICAL COMPARISON.
002884 03-03
STIMULATORY EFFECT OF SOMATOSTATIN ON NOREPINEPHRINE RELEASE FROM RAT-BRAIN-CORTEX SLICES.
002920 03-03
SPINAL MODULATION OF THE ACOUSTIC STARTLE RESPONSE: THE ROLE OF NOREPINEPHRINE, SEROTONIN AND DOPAMINE.
002950 03-04
CORTICAL RECOVERY FROM EFFECTS OF MONOCULAR DEPRIVATION: ACCELERATION WITH NOREPINEPHRINE AND SUPPRESSION WITH 6 HYDROXYDOPAMINE.
003024 03-04
THE EFFECTS OF ANTIDEPRESSANTS ON THE RETENTION AND METABOLISM OF (3H) NOREPINEPHRINE IN RAT-BRAIN SLICES.
003763 04-03
EFFECTS OF PHENYTOIN ON MOUSE CEREBELLAR 5 HYDROXYTRYPTAMINE AND NOREPINEPHRINE.
003795 04-03
DIFFERENTIAL-EFFECTS OF ALPHA METHYLDOPAMINE, CLONIDINE AND HYDRALAZINE ON NOREPINEPHRINE AND EPINEPHRINE SYNTHESIZING ENZYMES IN THE BRAINSTEM NUCLEI OF SPONTANEOUSLY HYPERTENSIVE-RATS.
003947 04-03
EVIDENCE THAT THERE ARE SUBCELLULAR POOLS OF NOREPINEPHRINE AND THAT THERE IS FLUX OF NOREPINEPHRINE BETWEEN THESE POOLS.
004004 04-03
MODULATORY INTERACTIONS BETWEEN NOREPINEPHRINE AND TAURINE, BETA ALANINE, GAMMA AMINOBUTYRIC-ACID AND MUSCIMOL APPLIED IONTOPHORETICALLY TO CEREBELLAR PURKINJE-CELLS.
004058 04-03
EFFECTS OF TRICYCLIC-ANTIDEPRESSANTS ON TETRABENAZINE-INDUCED DEPLETION OF BRAIN MONOAMINES IN RATS. 1. NOREPINEPHRINE.
004062 04-03
EFFECTS OF NOREPINEPHRINE AND 5 HYDROXYTRYPTAMINE REUPTAKE INHIBITORS ON ELECTRICALLY-INDUCED SPINAL-CORD SEIZURES IN RATS.
004144 04-04.
RAT-BRAIN AND PLASMA NOREPINEPHRINE GLYCOL METABOLITES DETERMINED BY GAS-CHROMATOGRAPHY MASS-FRAGMENTOGRAPHY.
004303 04-06
EFFECT OF NOREPINEPHRINE UPTAKE BLOCKERS ON NOREPINEPHRINE KINETICS.
004506 04-13
NOREPINEPHRINE METABOLISM IN MAN USING DEUTERIUM LABELLING: 4 HYDROXY-3-METHOXYMANDELIC-ACID.
004534 04-13

NOREPINEPHRINE-RECEPTOR
SUBSENSITIVITY OF THE NOREPINEPHRINE-RECEPTOR COUPLED ADENYLATE-CYCLASE SYSTEM IN BRAIN: EFFECTS OF NISOXETINE VERSUS FLUOXETINE.
000208 01-03
RAPID DEVELOPMENT OF HYPERSENSITIVITY AND HYPOSENSITIVITY TO APOMORPHINE AND HALOPERIDOL: ROLE OF NOREPINEPHRINE-RECEPTOR MECHANISMS IN CNS.
001178 02-03
FUNCTIONAL ASPECTS OF THE NOREPINEPHRINE-RECEPTOR COUPLED ADENYLATE-CYCLASE SYSTEM IN THE CENTRAL-NERVOUS-SYSTEM.
001493 02-03

NORLAAM
PHARMACODYNAMIC PROFILES OF L ALPHA ACETYLMETHADOL (LAAM) AND ITS N DEMETHYLATED METABOLITES, NORLAAM AND DINORLAAM, DURING SELF-ADMINISTRATION IN THE DEPENDENT RAT.
000505 01-04

NORMAL
THE EFFECT OF PROPRANOLOL ON THE ELECTROENCEPHALOGRAM IN NORMAL AND ETHANOL DEPENDENT RATS.
000126 01-03
PROTECTIVE EFFECT OF PRENYLAMINE AGAINST VULNERABILITY TO VENTRICULAR FIBRILLATION IN THE NORMAL AND ISCHEMIC CANINE MYOCARDIUM.
000265 01-03
INTRACELLULAR REDOX STATES UNDER HALOTHANE AND BARBITURATE ANESTHESIA IN NORMAL, ISCHEMIC, AND ANOXIC MONKEY BRAIN.
000295 01-03
ALTERATION OF PHARMACOKINETIC PARAMETERS FOR PENTOBARBITAL BY ISCHEMIC STROKE AND REVERSION TO NORMAL BY DEXAMETHASONE TREATMENT.
000321 01-03

MESOLIMBICOCORTICAL DOPAMINE TERMINAL-FIELDS ARE NECESSARY FOR NORMAL LOCOMOTOR AND INVESTIGATORY EXPLORATION IN RATS.
000383 01-04

DEXTROAMPHETAMINE: COGNITIVE AND BEHAVIORAL-EFFECTS IN NORMAL AND HYPERACTIVE-BOYS AND NORMAL ADULT MALES.
000716 01-11

PHARMACOKINETICS OF CHLORPROMAZINE IN NORMAL VOLUNTEERS.
000778 01-13

EFFECTS OF METHYLPHENIDATE ON LEARNING A BEGINNING READING VOCABULARY BY NORMAL ADULTS.
000812 01-14

NORADRENALINE RELEASE FROM SLICES OF THE THALAMUS OF NORMAL AND MORPHINE-DEPENDENT RATS.
001142 02-03

EFFECT OF TABERNANTHINE ON THE TURNOVER TIME OF BRAIN CATECHOLAMINES IN NORMAL AND HYPOBARIC HYPOXIC RATS.
001187 02-03

ROLE OF BRAIN CATECHOLAMINES AND 5 HYDROXYTRYPTAMINE IN MORPHINE-INDUCED TEMPERATURE CHANGES IN NORMAL AND TOLERANT RATS AND MICE.
001476 02-03

EFFECTS OF NALOXONE UPON PROLACTIN AND CORTISOL IN NORMAL WOMEN.
002213 02-13

EFFECT OF OPIATES AND OPIATE ANTAGONISTS ON SOMATOSENSORY EVOKED-POTENTIALS IN PATIENTS WITH SCHIZOPHRENIA AND NORMAL ADULTS.
002222 02-13

EFFECT OF L TRYPTOPHAN ON APOMORPHINE-INDUCED GROWTH-HORMONE SECRETION IN NORMAL SUBJECTS.
002253 02-13

INFLUENCE OF CICLAZINDOL ON MONOAMINE UPTAKE AND CNS FUNCTION IN NORMAL SUBJECTS.
002268 02-13

PSYCHOMOTOR STIMULANTS AS ACTIVATORS OF NORMAL AND PATHOLOGICAL-BEHAVIOR: IMPLICATIONS FOR THE EXCESSES IN MANIA. (UNPUBLISHED PAPER).
002353 02-14

EFFECTS OF AMPHETAMINE ON VIGILANCE PERFORMANCE IN NORMAL AND HYPERACTIVE-CHILDREN.
002359 02-14

AMPHETAMINE-INDUCED ROTATION IN NORMAL CATS.
003002 03-04

DESIPRAMINE AND 2 HYDROXYDESIPRAMINE PHARMACOKINETICS IN NORMAL VOLUNTEERS.
003154 03-07

PHYSOSTIGMINE INDUCTION OF DEPRESSIVE-SYMPTOMATOLOGY IN NORMAL HUMAN SUBJECTS.
003255 03-09

ACUTE EFFECTS OF CAFFEINE IN NORMAL PREPUBERTAL BOYS.
003310 03-11

DIURNAL GROWTH-HORMONE RESPONSES TO DEXTROAMPHETAMINE IN NORMAL YOUNG MEN AND POSTMENOPAUSAL-WOMEN.
003411 03-13

LEVELS OF 5 HYDROXYINDOLEACETIC-ACID AND TRYPTOPHAN IN LUMBAR CEREBROSPINAL-FLUID AND BLOOD OF PATIENTS WITH DEMENTIA AND NORMAL PRESSURE HYDROCEPHALUS AFTER TRYPTOPHAN ADMINISTRATION.
003419 03-13

AUTONOMIC-EFFECTS OF DEXTROAMPHETAMINE IN NORMAL MEN: IMPLICATIONS FOR HYPERACTIVITY AND SCHIZOPHRENIA.
003437 03-13

PARTIAL PURIFICATION OF ACID SPHINGOMYELINASE FROM NORMAL AND PATHOLOGICAL (M. NIEMANN-PICK TYPE C) HUMAN BRAIN.
003671 04-01

A STUDY OF GAMMA AMINOBUTYRIC-ACID UPTAKE IN NORMAL AND DOWNS-SYNDROME PLATELETS.
003787 04-03

DOXEPIN, A TRICYCLIC-ANTIDEPRESSANT, BINDS TO NORMAL, INTACT ASTROGLIAL CELLS IN CULTURES AND INHIBITS THE ISOPROTERENOL-INDUCED INCREASE IN CYCLIC-AMP PRODUCTION.
003836 04-03

DIFFERENTIAL-EFFECTS OF SEVERAL DOPAMINE UPTAKE INHIBITORS AND RELEASING-AGENTS ON LOCOMOTOR-ACTIVITY IN NORMAL AND IN RESERPINIZED MICE.
004130 04-04

NORMAL PLASMA DOPAMINE-BETA-HYDROXYLASE IN NONTREATED AND TREATED PARKINSON-PATIENTS.
004471 04-11

PROLACTIN AND GROWTH-HORMONE STUDIES IN SCHIZOPHRENIC-PATIENTS AND NORMAL CONTROLS.
004538 04-13

APOMORPHINE, HALOPERIDOL AND THE AVERAGE EVOKED-POTENTIALS IN NORMAL HUMAN VOLUNTEERS.
004549 04-13

COMPUTERIZED ANALYSIS OF SLEEP RECORDINGS APPLIED TO DRUG EVALUATION: MIDAZOLAM IN NORMAL SUBJECTS.
004564 04-14

IN NORMAL YOUNG MEN ACUTE DOPAMINERGIC BLOCKADE DOES NOT IMPAIR FREE WATER EXCRETION FOLLOWING A STANDARD WATER LOAD.
004600 04-15

BEHAVIOR AND LEARNING DIFFICULTIES IN CHILDREN OF NORMAL INTELLIGENCE BORN TO ALCOHOLIC MOTHERS.
004658 04-15

NORMALIZES
IMIPRAMINE NORMALIZES NATURALLY OCCURRING AND DRUG-INDUCED DIFFERENCES IN THE EXPLORATORY-ACTIVITY OF RATS.
001646 02-04

NORMETABOLITES
POSSIBLE INFLUENCE OF OPIOID NORMETABOLITES ON THE ONSET, MAGNITUDE AND QUALITY OF THE OPIOID ABSTINENCE-SYNDROME.
004610 04-15

NORMETAZOCINE
N TETRAHYDROFURYLALKYL AND N ALKOXYALKYL DERIVATIVES OF (-) NORMETAZOCINE, COMPOUNDS WITH DIFFERENTIATED OPIOID ACTION PROFILES.
000013 01-02

NORMOTENSIVE-RATS
COMPARISON OF MIANSERIN WITH DESIPRAMINE, MAPROTILINE AND PHENTOLAMINE ON CARDIAC PRESYNAPTIC AND VASCULAR POSTSYNAPTIC ALPHA-ADRENOCEPTORS AND NORADRENALINE REUPTAKE IN PITHED NORMOTENSIVE-RATS.
000044 01-03

DOSE-DEPENDENT, AMPHETAMINE-INDUCED CHANGES IN PERMEABILITY OF THE BLOOD-BRAIN-BARRIER OF NORMOTENSIVE-RATS AND SPONTANEOUSLY HYPERTENSIVE-RATS.
001197 02-03

EFFECT OF BROMOCRIPTINE ON EXPLORATORY-ACTIVITY, BRAIN-MONOAMINES AND PLASMA CORTICOSTERONE IN THE NORMOTENSIVE-RATS, GENETICALLY HYPERTENSIVE-RATS AND/OR HYPERTENSIVE OBESE RATS.
001635 02-04

SELF-STIMULATION REACTION IN NORMOTENSIVE-RATS AND HYPERTENSIVE-RATS.
002663 03-03

NORTRIPTYLINE
PREDICTION OF STEADY-STATE PLASMA LEVELS OF AMITRIPTYLINE AND NORTRIPTYLINE FROM A SINGLE-DOSE 24-HR. LEVEL IN DEPRESSED-PATIENTS.
000582 01-09

ON THE RELATIONSHIP OF NORTRIPTYLINE: AMITRIPTYLINE RATIO TO CLINICAL IMPROVEMENT OF AMITRIPTYLINE TREATED DEPRESSIVE-PATIENTS.
000599 01-09

INTERACTION BETWEEN AMITRIPTYLINE AND PHENOTHIAZINE IN MAN: METABOLITE NORTRIPTYLINE AND THE CORRELATION WITH CLINICAL-RESPONSE.
000640 01-09

ANTIDEPRESSIVE TREATMENT IN PARKINSONS-DISEASE: A CONTROLLED-TRIAL OF THE EFFECT OF NORTRIPTYLINE IN PATIENTS WITH PARKINSONS-DISEASE TREATED WITH L-DOPA.
000659 01-11

NORTRIPTYLINE AND ANTIPYRINE CLEARANCE IN RELATION TO DEBRISOQUINE HYDROXYLATION IN MAN.
000754 01-13

AMITRIPTYLINE, NORTRIPTYLINE PLASMA LEVELS AND CLINICAL-RESPONSE IN WOMEN WITH AFFECTIVE-DISORDERS.
000757 01-13

CARDIOVASCULAR EFFECTS OF NORTRIPTYLINE IN GERIATRIC-PATIENTS.
000882 01-15

NOMIFENSINE IN THE TREATMENT OF ENDOGENOUS DEPRESSION. A CONTROLLED-STUDY VS. NORTRIPTYLINE.
001978 02-09

BLOOD LEVEL OF AMITRIPTYLINE, NORTRIPTYLINE, NORADRENALINE, SEROTONIN AND THERAPEUTIC RESPONSE.
002057 02-09

PHARMACOKINETICS OF NORTRIPTYLINE IN ELDERLY VOLUNTEERS.
002184 02-11

THE CONTRIBUTION OF ALPHA1 ACID GLYCOPROTEIN, LIPOPROTEINS, AND ALBUMIN TO THE PLASMA BINDING OF PERAZINE, AMITRIPTYLINE, AND NORTRIPTYLINE IN HEALTHY MAN.
002214 02-13

FACTORS INFLUENCING NORTRIPTYLINE STEADY-STATE KINETICS: PLASMA AND SALIVA LEVELS.
002251 02-13

THYMOANALEPTIC TREATMENT CONTROL THROUGH MEASUREMENT OF PLASMA CONCENTRATIONS OF AMITRIPTYLINE AND ITS METABOLITE NORTRIPTYLINE.
002304 02-13

A METHOD FOR THE DETERMINATION OF AMITRIPTYLINE AND ITS METABOLITES NORTRIPTYLINE, 10 HYDROXYAMITRIPTYLINE, AND 10 HYDROXYNORTRIPTYLINE IN HUMAN PLASMA USING STABLE ISOTOPE DILUTION AND GAS-CHROMATOGRAPHY CHEMICAL-IONIZATION MASS-SPECTROMETRY.
002486 02-16

SUBTYPES OF DEPRESSION BASED ON EXCRETION OF MHPG AND RESPONSE TO NORTRIPTYLINE.
002488 02-16

DEPRESSION SUBTYPES AFFECT THE STEADY-STATE PLASMA LEVELS AND THERAPEUTIC-EFFICACY OF AMITRIPTYLINE AND NORTRIPTYLINE.
003244 03-09

TYRAMINE PRESSOR TEST AND CARDIOVASCULAR-EFFECTS OF CHLORIMIPRAMINE AND NORTRIPTYLINE IN HEALTHY VOLUNTEERS.
003428 03-13

EXCRETION OF NORTRIPTYLINE INTO SALIVA.
003435 03-13

FIRST RESULTS OF AN ORIGINAL-METHOD FOR MEASURING BLOOD LEVELS OF ANTIDEPRESSANTS (AMITRIPTYLINE AND NORTRIPTYLINE).
003559 03-16

DRUG-INTERACTIONS OF AMITRIPTYLINE AND NORTRIPTYLINE WITH WARFARIN IN THE RAT.
003912 04-03

AMITRIPTYLINE AND NORTRIPTYLINE PLASMA LEVELS MONITORING. PERSPECTIVE IN CLINICAL-PRACTICE.
004675 04-16

NOSE-POKE
TITRATION PROCEDURE WITH RATS USING A NOSE-POKE RESPONSE AND TAIL-SHOCK.
001862 02-06

NOSOLOGICAL
THE NOSOLOGICAL INDEPENDENCE OF INVOLUTIONAL DEPRESSION AND ITS DYNAMICS DURING PSYCHOPHARMACOTHERAPY.
004389 04-09

NOVELTY
EFFECTS OF EXPERIMENTER AND TEST LOCATION NOVELTY ON NONSPECIFIC ACTIVITY IN RATS AND ITS MODIFICATION BY METHAMPHETAMINE.
000409 01-04

NOXIOUS
BEHAVIORAL CONFIRMATION OF DIFFUSE NOXIOUS INHIBITORY CONTROLS (DNIC) AND EVIDENCE FOR A ROLE OF ENDOGENOUS OPIATES.
002791 03-03

MORPHINE DEPRESSES DORSAL-HORN NEURON RESPONSES TO CONTROLLED NOXIOUS AND NONNOXIOUS CUTANEOUS STIMULATION.
003782 04-03

NUCIFERINE
NUCIFERINE AND CENTRAL GLUTAMATE-RECEPTORS.
000063 01-03

ANTAGONISM OF INTRASTRIATAL AND INTRAVENOUS KAINIC-ACID BY 1 NUCIFERINE: COMPARISON WITH VARIOUS ANTICONVULSANTS AND GABAMIMETICS.
000188 01-03

NUCLEI
THE EFFECT OF MORPHINE ON THE CONTENT OF SEROTONIN, 5 HYDROXYINDOLEACETIC-ACID AND SUBSTANCE-P IN THE NUCLEI RAPHE-MAGNUS AND RETICULARIS-GIGANTOCELLULARIS.
001328 02-03

SHORT-TERM AND LONG-TERM EFFECTS OF METHAMPHETAMINE ON BIOGENIC-AMINE METABOLISM IN EXTRASTRIATAL DOPAMINERGIC NUCLEI.
001384 02-03

BEHAVIOURAL-RESPONSES TO STEREOTACTICALLY CONTROLLED INJECTIONS OF MONOAMINE NEUROTRANSMITTERS INTO THE ACCUMBENS AND CAUDATE-PUTAMEN NUCLEI.
001708 02-04

LSD-INDUCED ULTRASTRUCTURAL MODIFICATIONS OF LIMBIC-SYSTEM NUCLEI AND OTHER CEREBRAL ZONES.
002198 02-12

AGE DEPENDENT CHANGES IN THE BETA ENDORPHIN CONTENT OF DISCRETE RAT-BRAIN NUCLEI.
002635 03-01

MONOAMINE-OXIDASE-B ACTIVITIES TOWARD BETA PHENYLETHYLAMINE IN DISCRETE HYPOTHALAMIC AND CIRCUMVENTRICULAR NUCLEI OF THE RAT.
002781 03-03

PURIFICATION AND SUBUNIT STRUCTURE OF DNA-DEPENDENT RNA-POLYMERASE-BII FROM RAT-BRAIN NUCLEI.
003679 04-01

THE EFFECT OF CHOLINERGIC SUBSTANCES ON NOCICEPTIVE EVOKED-RESPONSES IN SPECIFIC NUCLEI OF THE THALAMUS.
003770 04-03

DOPAMINE, NORADRENALINE AND 3,4 DIHYDROXYPHENYLACETIC-ACID (DOPAC) LEVELS OF INDIVIDUAL BRAIN NUCLEI, EFFECTS OF HALOPERIDOL AND PARGYLINE.
003792 04-03

SENSITIVITY TO GABA OF NEURONS OF THE DORSAL AND VENTRAL LATERAL GENICULATE NUCLEI IN THE RAT.
003877 04-03

PRESSOR EFFECTS OF ELECTRICAL-STIMULATION OF THE DORSAL AND MEDIAN RAPHE NUCLEI IN ANESTHETIZED RATS.
003892 04-03

DIFFERENTIAL-EFFECTS OF ALPHA METHYLDOPAMINE, CLONIDINE AND HYDRALAZINE ON NOREPINEPHRINE AND EPINEPHRINE SYNTHESIZING

ENZYMES IN THE BRAINSTEM NUCLEI OF SPONTANEOUSLY HYPERTENSIVE-RATS.
003947 04-03

NUCLEOSIDE
IRREVERSIBLE INHIBITION OF S ADENOSYLHOMOCYSTEINE-HYDROLASE BY NUCLEOSIDE ANALOGS. (UNPUBLISHED PAPER).
001010 02-01

NUCLEOSIDES
THE SITE OF ACTION OF MUSCLE-RELAXANT PURINE NUCLEOSIDES.
003742 04-03

NUCLEOTIDASE
STIMULATION OF THE PLASMA MEMBRANE ENZYME, 5' NUCLEOTIDASE, BY ETHANOL EXPOSURE TO NEURAL CELLS IN CULTURE.
001499 02-03

NUCLEOTIDE
DISTRIBUTION OF CESIUM IN THE ORGANISM AND ITS EFFECT ON THE NUCLEOTIDE METABOLISM ENZYMES.
003696 04-02

NUCLEUS
THE INFLUENCE OF CHLORALOSE ANESTHESIA ON THE ACTIVITY OF RED NUCLEUS NEURONS IN CATS.
000245 01-03

DENERVATION SUPERSENSITIVITY TO SEROTONIN IN THE FACIAL NUCLEUS.
001364 02-03

INFLUENCE OF DOPAMINERGIC-SYSTEMS ON THE LATERAL HABENULAR NUCLEUS OF THE RAT.
001365 02-03

UNILATERAL 5,7 DIHYDROXYTRYPTAMINE LESIONS OF THE DORSAL RAPHE NUCLEUS (DRN) AND RAT ROTATIONAL-BEHAVIOUR.
001578 02-04

EVIDENCE FOR A TONIC GABAERGIC CONTROL OF SEROTONIN NEURONS IN THE MEDIAN RAPHE NUCLEUS.
002719 03-03

PHARMACOLOGIC EVIDENCE FOR A TONIC MUSCARINIC INHIBITORY INPUT TO THE EDINGER-WESTPHAL NUCLEUS IN THE DOG.
002889 03-03

INFUSIONS INTO THE OCULOMOTOR NUCLEUS OR NERVE: A METHOD OF ESTIMATING THE DOSAGE AT WHICH TRANSMITTER ANTAGONISTS INFUSED INTRACRANIALLY PRODUCE NONSPECIFIC BLOCKING OF NEURAL ACTIVITY.
003134 03-06

THYROXIN SENSITIVITY OF SENSORIMOTOR CORTICAL NEURONS AND THE HYPOTHALAMIC VENTROMEDIAL NUCLEUS.
003713 04-03

OPIATE-EFFECTS IN THE AMYGDALA CENTRAL NUCLEUS ON HEART RATE CONDITIONING IN RABBITS.
003798 04-03

THE NEUROANATOMY AND PHARMACOLOGY OF THE NUCLEUS LOCUS-COERULEUS. (UNPUBLISHED PAPER).
003810 04-03

SELECTIVE EFFECT OF ETHANOL ON THE VESTIBULAR NUCLEUS NEURONS IN THE CAT.
004139 04-04

NUCLEUS-ACCUMBENS
EFFECT OF PICROTOXIN AND NIPECOTIC-ACID ON INHIBITORY RESPONSE OF DOPAMINERGIC NEURONS IN THE VENTRAL TEGMENTAL AREA TO STIMULATION OF THE NUCLEUS-ACCUMBENS.
000331 01-03

OPPOSITE EFFECTS OF D-AMPHETAMINE ON SPONTANEOUS NEURONAL ACTIVITY IN THE NEOSTRIATUM AND NUCLEUS-ACCUMBENS.
000454 01-04

INTERACTION OF CHLORDIAZEPOXIDE AND SODIUM-VALPROATE IN THE NUCLEUS-ACCUMBENS OF THE RAT.
002796 03-03

INJECTIONS OF DOPAMINERGIC, CHOLINERGIC, SEROTONINERGIC AND GABAERGIC DRUGS INTO THE NUCLEUS-ACCUMBENS: EFFECTS ON LOCOMOTOR-ACTIVITY IN THE RAT.
003019 03-04

COMPARISON OF THE EFFECTS OF THE STEREOISOMERS OF FENFLURAMINE ON THE ACETYLCHOLINE CONTENT OF RAT STRIATUM, HIPPOCAMPUS AND NUCLEUS-ACCUMBENS.
003758 04-03

INCREASE OF NEUROTENSIN CONTENT ELICITED BY NEUROLEPTICS IN NUCLEUS-ACCUMBENS.
003808 04-03

DOPAMINE-DEPENDENT HYPERACTIVITY IN THE FOLLOWING MANIPULATION OF GABA MECHANISMS IN THE REGION OF THE NUCLEUS-ACCUMBENS.
003976 04-03

HYPERACTIVITY FOLLOWING INJECTION OF A GLUTAMATE AGONIST AND 6,7 ADTN INTO RAT NUCLEUS-ACCUMBENS AND ITS INHIBITION BY THIP.
004066 04-04

DESTRUCTION OF 5 HYDROXYTRYPTAMINERGIC NEURONS AND THE DYNAMICS OF DOPAMINE IN NUCLEUS-ACCUMBENS SEPTI AND OTHER FOREBRAIN REGIONS OF THE RAT.
004171 04-04

NUCLEUS-CENTRALIS-LATERALIS
ANTINOCICEPTIVE ACTION OF MORPHINE AND PENTAZOCINE ON UNIT ACTIVITY IN THE NUCLEUS-CENTRALIS-LATERALIS, NUCLEUS-VENTRALIS-LATERALIS AND NEARBY STRUCTURES OF THE CAT.
002837 03-03

NUCLEUS-RAPHE-MAGNUS
HYPOALGESIA FOLLOWING MICROINJECTION OF NORADRENERGIC ANTAGONISTS IN THE NUCLEUS-RAPHE-MAGNUS.
000122 01-03

EFFECT OF SELECTIVE DESTRUCTION OF SEROTONERGIC NEURONS IN NUCLEUS-RAPHE-MAGNUS ON MORPHINE-INDUCED ANTINOCICEPTION.
001724 02-04

EVIDENCE FOR INVOLVEMENT OF SEPARATE MECHANISMS IN THE PRODUCTION OF ANALGESIA BY ELECTRICAL-STIMULATION OF THE NUCLEUS-RETICULARIS-PARAGIGANTOCELLULARIS AND NUCLEUS-RAPHE-MAGNUS IN THE RAT.
003083 03-04

EFFECT OF CHRONIC MORPHINE TREATMENT ON THE INTERACTION BETWEEN THE PERIAQUEDUCTAL GREY AND THE NUCLEUS-RAPHE-MAGNUS OF THE RAT.
003727 04-03

NUCLEUS-RETICULARIS-GIGANTOCELLULARIS
SUBSTANCE-P, MORPHINE AND METHIONINE-ENKEPHALIN: EFFECTS ON SPONTANEOUS AND EVOKED NEURONAL FIRING IN THE NUCLEUS-RETICULARIS-GIGANTOCELLULARIS OF THE RAT.
001267 02-03

NUCLEUS-RETICULARIS-PARAGIGANTOCELLULARIS
EVIDENCE FOR INVOLVEMENT OF SEPARATE MECHANISMS IN THE PRODUCTION OF ANALGESIA BY ELECTRICAL-STIMULATION OF THE NUCLEUS-RETICULARIS-PARAGIGANTOCELLULARIS AND NUCLEUS-RAPHE-MAGNUS IN THE RAT.
003083 03-04

NUCLEUS-TRACTUS-SOLITARIUS
IMMUNOCYTOCHEMICAL LOCALIZATION OF CATECHOLAMINE SYNTHESIZING ENZYMES AND NEUROPEPTIDES IN AREA POSTREMA AND MEDIAL NUCLEUS-TRACTUS-SOLITARIUS OF RAT-BRAIN.
002634 03-01

OPIATE-RECEPTORS AND SLEEP. II. EFFECTS OF MICROINJECTIONS OF ETHYL-ALCOHOL AND PENTOBARBITAL IN THE MEDIAN THALAMUS, PERIAQUEDUCTAL GRAY MATTER AND NUCLEUS-TRACTUS-SOLITARIUS OF THE RABBIT.
002917 03-03

NUCLEUS-VENTRALIS-LATERALIS
ANTINOCICEPTIVE ACTION OF MORPHINE AND PENTAZOCINE ON UNIT ACTIVITY IN THE NUCLEUS-CENTRALIS-LATERALIS, NUCLEUS-VENTRALIS-LATERALIS AND NEARBY STRUCTURES OF THE CAT.
002837 03-03

NURSING
INCREASED MESOLIMBIC 3H SPIROPERIDOL BINDING IN 4 WEEK OLD OFFSPRING OF NURSING RAT MOTHERS TREATED WITH PENFLURIDOL.
000087 01-03

NURSING ASPECTS OF PSYCHOPHARMACOLOGY.
002618 02-17

WIDOWS AND WIDOWERS AND THEIR MEDICATION USE: NURSING IMPLICATIONS.
003626 03-17

NURSING-BEHAVIOR
BEHAVIORAL-EFFECTS OF HASHISH IN MICE: II. NURSING-BEHAVIOR AND DEVELOPMENT OF THE SUCKLINGS.
001626 02-04

NURSING-HOMES
A STUDY OF ANTIPSYCHOTIC-DRUG USE IN NURSING-HOMES: EPIDEMIOLOGIC EVIDENCE SUGGESTING MISUSE.
000979 01-17

PROBLEMS REMAIN IN REVIEWS OF MEDICAID FINANCED DRUG-THERAPY IN NURSING-HOMES.
004736 04-17

NUTRIENTS
LITHIUM, ASSIMILATION OF NUTRIENTS AND REPRODUCTION. (UNPUBLISHED PAPER).
002777 03-03

NUTRITION
INTERACTIVE-EFFECTS OF NUTRITION AND CANNABIS UPON RAT PERINATAL DEVELOPMENT.
000513 01-05

NYSTAGMIC
NYSTAGMIC RESPONSES OF HIPPOCAMPAL ORIGIN WITH REFERENCE TO EXCITABILITY OF CHOLINERGIC AND ADRENERGIC COMPONENTS INVOLVED IN THE HIPPOCAMPUS OF RABBITS.
003842 04-03

OBESE
EFFECT OF BROMOCRIPTINE ON EXPLORATORY-ACTIVITY, BRAIN-MONOAMINES AND PLASMA CORTICOSTERONE IN THE NORMOTENSIVE-RATS, GENETICALLY HYPERTENSIVE-RATS AND/OR HYPERTENSIVE OBESE RATS.
001635 02-04

NEUROCHEMICAL-EFFECTS AND BEHAVIORAL-EFFECTS OF CHRONIC D-AMPHETAMINE TREATMENT IN GENETICALLY OBESE (OBOB) MICE. (PH.D. DISSERTATION).
001739 02-04

METABOLIC AND SYMPATHOADRENAL ABNORMALITIES IN THE OBESE ZUCKER RAT: EFFECT OF CHRONIC PHENOXYBENZAMINE TREATMENT.
003905 04-03

OBESITY
CONTROLLED-TRIAL OF BEHAVIOUR-THERAPY, PHARMACOTHERAPY, AND THEIR COMBINATION IN THE TREATMENT OF OBESITY.
000725 01-11

OBJECT
AN ANALYSIS OF VISUAL OBJECT REVERSAL LEARNING IN THE MARMOSET AFTER AMPHETAMINE AND HALOPERIDOL.
004208 04-04

OBJECTIVE
AN OBJECTIVE CLASSIFICATION OF PSYCHOACTIVE-DRUGS.
001894 02-07

THE EFFECTS OF COMBINED SEDATIVE AND ANXIOLYTIC-PREPARATIONS ON SUBJECTIVE ASPECTS OF SLEEP AND OBJECTIVE MEASURE OF AROUSAL AND PERFORMANCE THE MORNING FOLLOWING NOCTURNAL MEDICATION: II. REPEATED DOSES.
002331 02-14

PSYCHOTROPIC-DRUG-INDUCED CHANGES IN AUDITORY AVERAGED EVOKED-POTENTIALS: RESULTS OF A DOUBLE-BLIND TRIAL USING AN OBJECTIVE FULLY AUTOMATED AEP ANALYSIS METHOD.
003412 03-13

EFFECTS OF SUPIDIMIDE (CG-3033) ON OBJECTIVE AND SUBJECTIVE SLEEP PARAMETERS (A SLEEP LABORATORY STUDY).
004567 04-14

THE USE OF EVENT-RELATED SLOW POTENTIALS OF THE BRAIN AS AN OBJECTIVE METHOD TO STUDY THE EFFECTS OF CENTRALLY ACTING DRUGS.
004669 04-16

OBSERVATION
CLINICAL AND BIOCHEMICAL-DATA ON THE ACTION OF MAPROTILINE AND CLOMIPRAMINE IN DEPRESSIVE-STATES (PRELIMINARY OBSERVATION).
002032 02-09

ERGOTISM IN A PSYCHIATRIC ENVIRONMENT ASSOCIATED WITH ERYTHROMYCIN-DIHYDROERGOTAMINE-PROPIONATE. AN OBSERVATION.
002379 02-15

STUDIES ON THE TREATMENT AND DIAGNOSIS OF NEUROTIC VERTIGO FROM THE VIEWPOINT OF NEUROOTOLOGY: OBSERVATION OF THE BALANCE TEST FOR ANALYZING NEUROTIC VERTIGO.
004387 04-09

OBSERVATIONAL
AN OBSERVATIONAL METHOD FOR QUANTIFYING THE BEHAVIOURAL-EFFECTS OF DOPAMINE AGONISTS: CONTRASTING-EFFECTS OF D-AMPHETAMINE AND APOMORPHINE.
002484 02-16

OBSERVATIONS
TARDIVE-DYSKINESIAS (OBSERVATIONS CONCERNING THREE CASES).
000861 01-15

OBSERVATIONS ON CLINICAL-PHARMACOLOGY.
000970 01-17

OBSERVATIONS ABOUT STATES OF MENTAL-ILLNESS AS ILLUMINATED BY THEIR RESPONSE TO PHARMACEUTIC-AGENTS.
000972 01-17

BIPHASIC RESPONSIVENESS OF RAT PIAL-ARTERIOLES TO DOPAMINE: DIRECT OBSERVATIONS ON THE MICROCIRCULATION.
001105 02-03

INTRACELLULAR OBSERVATIONS ON THE EFFECTS OF MUSCARINIC AGONISTS ON RAT SYMPATHETIC NEURONES.
001143 02-03

OBSERVATIONS ON CHLORALOSE-INDUCED MYOCLONUS IN GUINEA-PIGS.
001164 02-03

CLINICAL-STUDY OF MAPROTILINE IN THE TREATMENT OF DEPRESSIVE-STATES: COMPILATION OF 1520 OBSERVATIONS.
003206 03-09

OBSERVATIONS ON THE USE OF CITICOLINE IN DYSTHYMIC-PATIENTS.
003207 03-09

SOME OBSERVATIONS ON THE PSYCHOLOGICAL DIMENSIONS OF PLACEBO-EFFECTS.
003573 03-17

SOME OBSERVATIONS ON THE PHARMACOLOGICAL ACTIVITY OF MIF (PRO-LEU-GLY-NH2).
004240 04-04

OBSERVE
EXTINCTION AND DOPAMINE-RECEPTOR BLOCKADE AFTER INTERMITTENT REINFORCEMENT TRAINING: FAILURE TO OBSERVE FUNCTIONAL EQUIVALENCE.
000490 01-04

OBSERVED
THE BIOLOGICAL-EFFECTS AND CLINICAL-EFFECTS OF ORAL MAGNESIUM AND ASSOCIATED MAGNESIUM VITAMIN-B6 ADMINISTRATION ON CERTAIN DISORDERS OBSERVED IN INFANTILE AUTISM.
003291 03-11

VARIOUS FACTORS IN THE PATHOGENESIS OF PATHOLOGICAL REACTIONS OBSERVED IN CONNECTION WITH THE ADMINISTRATION OF PSYCHOTROPIC-DRUGS.
003532 03-15

OBSESSIVE-COMPULSIVE-DISORDER
CLOMIPRAMINE TREATMENT OF OBSESSIVE-COMPULSIVE-DISORDER: I. A
CONTROLLED CLINICAL-TRIAL.
002086 02-10
CLOMIPRAMINE TREATMENT OF OBSESSIVE-COMPULSIVE-DISORDER: II.
BIOCHEMICAL-ASPECTS.
002300 02-13

OBSESSIVE-COMPULSIVE-DISORDERS
BEHAVIORAL-TREATMENT AND PHARMACOLOGICAL-TREATMENT OF
OBSESSIVE-COMPULSIVE-DISORDERS.
000657 01-10
A COMBINED BEHAVIORAL-PHARMACOTHERAPY APPROACH TO
OBSESSIVE-COMPULSIVE-DISORDERS.
002082 02-10

OBSESSIVE-COMPULSIVE-NEUROSIS
AMITRIPTYLINE THERAPY OF OBSESSIVE-COMPULSIVE-NEUROSIS.
000656 01-10
NOMIFENSINE IN THE TREATMENT OF OBSESSIVE-COMPULSIVE-NEUROSIS.
THERAPEUTIC-EFFICACY AND TOLERABILITY IN COMPARISON TO
IMIPRAMINE.
002078 02-10

OBSESSIVE-SYMPTOM
OBSESSIVE-SYMPTOM RESPONSE TO BEHAVIOUR-THERAPY AND TO
ANTIDEPRESSANT-DRUGS.
002084 02-10

OBSTRUCTIVE
MEDROXYPROGESTERONE TREATMENT OF OBSTRUCTIVE SLEEP-APNEA.
002128 02-11

OCCIDENTAL
TRICYCLIC-ANTIDEPRESSANT DRUG TOLERANCE IN ORIENTAL AND
OCCIDENTAL POPULATIONS.
000590 01-09

OCCIPITAL-CORTEX
INHIBITION OF NEURONAL UPTAKE REDUCES THE PRESYNAPTIC EFFECTS
OF CLONIDINE BUT NOT OF ALPHA METHYLNORADRENALINE ON THE
STIMULATION-EVOKED RELEASE OF 3H NORADRENALINE FROM RAT
OCCIPITAL-CORTEX SLICES.
000227 01-03

OCCLUSION
INHIBITION OF VASOPRESSIN RELEASE TO CAROTID OCCLUSION BY
GAMMA AMINOBUTYRIC-ACID AND GLYCINE.
002715 03-03

OCCUPATION
IN VIVO OCCUPATION OF CEREBRAL HISTAMINE H1-RECEPTORS
EVALUATED WITH 3H MEPYRAMINE MAY PREDICT SEDATIVE
PROPERTIES OF PSYCHOTROPIC-DRUGS.
000241 01-03
CORRELATION BETWEEN BENZODIAZEPINE-RECEPTOR OCCUPATION AND
ANTICONVULSANT EFFECTS OF DIAZEPAM.
000450 01-04

OCTAHYDRODIBENZAZEPINONAPHTHYRIDINES
CONFORMATIONALLY RESTRICTED TRICYCLIC-ANTIDEPRESSANTS. 1.
OCTAHYDRODIBENZAZEPINONAPHTHYRIDINES AS RIGID IMIPRAMINE
ANALOGUES.
001710 02-04

OCTOPAMINE
THE EFFECT OF PHENELZINE AND SOME OF ITS PARA HALOGENATED
DERIVATIVES ON THE LEVELS OF BRAIN TYRAMINE AND OCTOPAMINE
IN THE MOUSE.
001077 02-02
BETA PHENYLETHYLAMINE, PHENYLETHANOLAMINE, TYRAMINE AND
OCTOPAMINE. (UNPUBLISHED PAPER).
002601 02-17

OCULAR-COMPLICATION
AN UNUSUAL OCULAR-COMPLICATION OF THIORIDAZINE.
000848 01-15

OCULOGRAPHIC
A COMPUTER OCULOGRAPHIC AND EEG DOUBLE-BLIND STUDY INCLUDING
WELL-BEING FOR DETERMINING CHANGED VIGILANCE UNDER THERAPY
WITH TIAPRIDE.
000751 01-13

OCULOMOTOR
INFUSIONS INTO THE OCULOMOTOR NUCLEUS OR NERVE: A METHOD OF
ESTIMATING THE DOSAGE AT WHICH TRANSMITTER ANTAGONISTS
INFUSED INTRACRANIALLY PRODUCE NONSPECIFIC BLOCKING OF
NEURAL ACTIVITY.
003134 03-06

OCYTOCIN
INDICATIONS FOR A BRAIN UPTAKE OF LABELLED VASOPRESSIN AND
OCYTOCIN AND THE PROBLEM OF THE BLOOD-BRAIN-BARRIER.
003669 04-01

OFFSPRING
INCREASED MESOLIMBIC 3H SPIROPERIDOL BINDING IN 4 WEEK OLD
OFFSPRING OF NURSING RAT MOTHERS TREATED WITH PENFLURIDOL.
000087 01-03
EFFECTS OF 6 HYDROXYDOPAMINE AND AMPHETAMINE ON RAT
MOTHERING-BEHAVIOR AND OFFSPRING DEVELOPMENT.
000452 01-04
EFFECTS OF MARIHUANA ON PREGNANT RATS AND THEIR OFFSPRING.
001830 02-05

THROMBOCYTOSIS IN THE OFFSPRING OF FEMALE MICE RECEIVING DL
METHADONE.
001836 02-05
GABA-RECEPTORS AND BENZODIAZEPINE-RECEPTORS IN THE OFFSPRING
OF DAMS RECEIVING DIAZEPAM: ONTOGENETIC-STUDIES.
001849 02-05
EFFECT OF PRENATAL PHENYTOIN ADMINISTRATION ON BRAIN
TRYPTOPHAN METABOLISM OF RAT OFFSPRING DURING THE
PREWEANING PERIOD.
004108 04-04

OHDA
EFFECTS OF APOMORPHINE ON ESCAPE PERFORMANCE AND ACTIVITY IN
DEVELOPING RAT PUPS TREATED WITH 6 HYDROXYDOPAMINE (6
OHDA).
000426 01-04
EFFECTS OF NOMIFENSINE AND DESIPRAMINE ON THE SEQUELAE OF
INTRACEREBRALLY INJECTED 6 OHDA AND 5,6 DHT.
001522 02-03
MALE RAT SEXUAL-BEHAVIOR COMPARED AFTER 6 OHDA AND
ELECTROLYTIC LESIONS IN THE DORSAL NA BUNDLE REGION OF THE
MIDBRAIN.
001593 02-04
HANDEDNESS IN RATS: BLOCKADE OF REACHING-BEHAVIOR BY
UNILATERAL 6 OHDA INJECTIONS INTO SUBSTANTIA-NIGRA AND
CAUDATE-NUCLEUS.
001778 02-04

OIL
MICROSCOPIC EVIDENCE OF LYMPHOGENIC ABSORPTION OF OIL IN
HUMANS RECEIVING NEUROLEPTIC OILY DEPOT PREPARATIONS
INTRAMUSCULARLY.
000890 01-15

OILY
MICROSCOPIC EVIDENCE OF LYMPHOGENIC ABSORPTION OF OIL IN
HUMANS RECEIVING NEUROLEPTIC OILY DEPOT PREPARATIONS
INTRAMUSCULARLY.
000890 01-15

OLD-AGE
BRAIN FUNCTION IN OLD-AGE: EVALUATION OF CHANGES AND
DISORDERS.
000684 01-11
LOOK AND OLD-AGE.
000930 01-17
ERGOTS IN THE TREATMENT OF MENTAL-DISORDERS OF OLD-AGE.
002545 02-17

OLFACTORY
SEROTONINMIMETIC AND ANTIDEPRESSANT-DRUGS ON PASSIVE-
AVOIDANCE LEARNING BY OLFACTORY BULBECTOMISED RATS.
001585 02-04
CROSS-TOLERANCE OF DOPAMINE METABOLISM TO BACLOFEN, GAMMA
BUTYROLACTONE AND HA-966 IN THE STRIATUM AND OLFACTORY
TUBERCLE OF THE RAT.
002681 03-03
SLEEP ELICITED BY OLFACTORY TUBERCLE STIMULATION AND THE EFFECT
OF ATROPINE.
002955 03-04

OLFACTORY-BULB
RELATIONSHIP BETWEEN DELTA9 TETRAHYDROCANNABINOL-INDUCED
MOUSE-KILLING-BEHAVIOR ON THE RAT AND THE METABOLISM OF
MONOAMINES IN THE BRAIN, PARTICULARLY THE OLFACTORY-BULB.
000472 01-04
LAMINAR DISTRIBUTION OF PUTATIVE NEUROTRANSMITTER AMINO-
ACIDS AND LIGAND BINDING-SITES IN THE DOG OLFACTORY-BULB.
002836 03-03

OLFACTORY-BULBECTOMY
EFFECTS OF OLFACTORY-BULBECTOMY AND PERIPHERALLY-INDUCED
ANOSMIA ON THERMOREGULATION IN THE RAT: SUSCEPTIBILITY TO
ANTIDEPRESSANT-DRUGS.
004113 04-04

OLFACTORY-BULBS
REGIONAL CHANGES IN (3H)DIAZEPAM BINDING IN THE BRAINS OF MICE
AFTER REMOVAL OF THE OLFACTORY-BULBS.
003844 04-03

OLFACTORY-CORTEX
INFLUENCE OF CELLULAR-TRANSPORT ON THE INTERACTION OF AMINO-
ACIDS WITH GAMMA AMINOBUTYRIC-ACID-RECEPTORS (GABA) IN THE
ISOLATED OLFACTORY-CORTEX OF THE GUINEA-PIG.
000034 01-03
CONVULSANTS ANTAGONISE INHIBITION IN THE OLFACTORY-CORTEX
SLICE.
001466 02-03

OLIGOPHRENICS
THERAPY AND SOCIAL ADAPTATION OF OLIGOPHRENICS (REVIEW OF THE
LITERATURE).
004444 04-11

OLIGOSYMPTOMATIC
SLEEP PROFILE AND ULTRADIAN SLEEP PERIODICITY IN HUMANS UNDER
THE INFLUENCE OF A BUTYROPHENONE DERIVATIVE: I. SLEEP

CORRECTION IN SUBJECTS WITH OLIGOSYMPTOMATIC SLEEP-DISORDERS.
001869 02-06

ON-COLUMN
ON-COLUMN GAS-CHROMATOGRAPHIC-SYNTHESIS OF 1,3 DIALYKYL (C=1-10), BENZYL, AND CYCLOHEXYLBARBITURATE DERIVATIVES.
003656 04-01

ON-OFF-PHENOMENON
IMPROVEMENT OF L-DOPA-INDUCED DYSKINESIA AND OF ON-OFF-PHENOMENON BY BROMOCRIPTINE.
000813 01-14

ONE-STEP
DETERMINATION OF PICOMOLE AMOUNTS OF DOPAMINE, NORADRENALINE, 3,4 DIHYDROXYPHENYLALANINE, 3,4 DIHYDROXYPHENYLACETIC-ACID, HOMOVANILLIC-ACID, AND 5 HYDROXYINDOLEACETIC-ACID IN NERVOUS-TISSUE AFTER ONE-STEP PURIFICATION ON SEPHADEX-G-10, USING HIGH.
004305 04-06

ONSET
BIPOLAR AFFECTIVE-PSYCHOSIS WITH ONSET BEFORE AGE 16 YEARS: REPORT OF 10 CASES.
002001 02-09
POSSIBLE INFLUENCE OF OPIOID NORMETABOLITES ON THE ONSET, MAGNITUDE AND QUALITY OF THE OPIOID ABSTINENCE-SYNDROME.
004610 04-15

ONTOGENESIS
EFFECTS OF PERINATAL THYROXINE AND/OR CORTICOSTERONE TREATMENT ON THE ONTOGENESIS OF HYPOTHALAMIC AND MESENCEPHALIC NOREPINEPHRINE AND DOPAMINE CONTENT.
000180 01-03
HYPERSYNCHRONOUS-ACTIVITY ELICITED BY GAMMA HYDROXYBUTYRATE DURING ONTOGENESIS IN RATS.
000460 01-04
CONVULSANT-EFFECTS OF AMINOOXYACETIC-ACID DURING ONTOGENESIS IN RATS.
001439 02-03
SEIZURES ELICITED BY SUBCUTANEOUS INJECTION OF METRAZOL DURING ONTOGENESIS IN RATS.
003039 03-04
ELECTROCORTICOGRAPHIC ACTIVITY ELICITED BY METRAZOL DURING ONTOGENESIS IN RATS.
004064 04-03

ONTOGENETIC
SEROTONIN-SENSITIVE ADENYLATE-CYCLASE AND (3H)SEROTONIN BINDING-SITES IN THE CNS OF THE RAT -- II. RESPECTIVE REGIONAL AND SUBCELLULAR DISTRIBUTIONS AND ONTOGENETIC DEVELOPMENTS.
000214 01-03

ONTOGENETIC-STUDIES
GABA-RECEPTORS AND BENZODIAZEPINE-RECEPTORS IN THE OFFSPRING OF DAMS RECEIVING DIAZEPAM: ONTOGENETIC-STUDIES.
001849 02-05

ONTOGENY
THE USE OF PSYCHOPHARMACOLOGICAL-PROCEDURES TO ANALYSE THE ONTOGENY OF LEARNING AND RETENTION: ISSUES AND CONCERNS.
000482 01-04
ONTOGENY OF MAMMALIAN CARDIAC ALPHA1-ADRENERGIC-RECEPTORS.
001545 02-03
PSYCHOPHARMACOLOGICAL-EFFECTS OF LOW-DOSES AND HIGH-DOSES OF APOMORPHINE DURING ONTOGENY.
001774 02-04
ONTOGENY OF HISTAMINERGIC NEUROTRANSMISSION IN THE RAT-BRAIN: CONCOMITANT DEVELOPMENT OF NEURONAL HISTAMINE, H1-RECEPTORS, AND H1-RECEPTOR-MEDIATED STIMULATION OF PHOSPHOLIPID TURNOVER.
004021 04-03

OPACITIES
OCCURRENCE OF CORNEAL OPACITIES IN RATS AFTER ACUTE ADMINISTRATION OF L ALPHA ACETYLMETHADOL.
001853 02-05

OPEN
INTRAMUSCULAR HALOPERIDOL-DECANOATE FOR NEUROLEPTIC MAINTENANCE-THERAPY: EFFICACY, DOSAGE SCHEDULE AND PLASMA LEVELS: AN OPEN MULTICENTER-STUDY.
000758 01-13
AN OPEN CLINICAL-TRIAL OF MIANSERIN.
003241 03-09
BACLOFEN IN THE TREATMENT OF TARDIVE-DYSKINESIA: OPEN LABEL STUDY.
004619 04-15
CLOPIPAZAN (SKF-69634), A NEW NEUROLEPTIC ESSENTIALLY FREE OF EXTRAPYRAMIDAL LIABILITY: QUANTITATIVE PHARMACOEEG AND OPEN LABEL CLINICAL-TRIAL.
004620 04-15

OPEN-FIELD
OPEN-FIELD PERFORMANCE OF RATS AFTER ENDOTOXIN TREATMENT.
000473 01-04
THE BEHAVIOR OF RATS IN THE OPEN-FIELD WITHOUT STRESS, UNDER ACUTE AND PERSISTING INFLUENCE OF IMIPRAMINE AND

TRANYLCYPROMINE AS WELL AS ON THE INDIVIDUAL REACTION TYPE (EMOTIVE AND NONEMOTIVE).
001624 02-04
EFFECTS OF NEONATAL TESTOSTERONE AND ESTROGEN ON OPEN-FIELD BEHAVIOUR IN RATS.
003098 03-04
DOPAMINERGIC AGONISTS DIFFERENTIALLY AFFECT OPEN-FIELD ACTIVITY OF RATS WITH A10 LESIONS.
004135 04-04

OPEN-STUDY
OPEN-STUDY OF L 5 HTP IN MELANCHOLIC-DEPRESSED-PATIENTS OVER 50 YEARS OF AGE.
002016 02-09
AN OPEN-STUDY OF MAPROTILINE 75MG IN THE TREATMENT OF DEPRESSIVE-STATES.
003152 03-07
A PRELIMINARY OPEN-STUDY OF THE USE OF AMINEPTINE IN THE DEFICIENT SYNDROME OF HEBEPHRENICS AND OF ADDICTS DURING WITHDRAWAL.
004445 04-11

OPENS
(-)PENTOBARBITAL OPENS ION-CHANNELS OF LONG-DURATION IN CULTURED MOUSE SPINAL NEURONS.
000198 01-03

OPERANT
EFFECTS OF APOMORPHINE ON ELICITED AND OPERANT PECKING IN PIGEONS.
001557 02-04
THE EFFECTS OF PIMOZIDE DURING PAIRING ON THE TRANSFER OF CLASSICAL CONDITIONING TO AN OPERANT DISCRIMINATION.
002956 03-04
TIME-COURSE OF CHRONIC HALOPERIDOL AND CLOZAPINE UPON OPERANT RATE AND DURATION.
002989 03-04
CLONIDINE ANALGESIA AND SUPPRESSION OF OPERANT RESPONDING: DISSOCIATION OF MECHANISM.
003046 03-04
OPERANT FEEDING AND DRINKING IN PIGS FOLLOWING INTRACEREBROVENTRICULAR INJECTION OF SYNTHETIC CHOLECYSTOKININ-OCTAPEPTIDE.
003064 03-04
OPERANT ANALYSIS OF HUMAN HEROIN SELF-ADMINISTRATION AND THE EFFECTS OF NALTREXONE.
003449 03-14
METHYLMERCURY-INDUCED CHANGES IN OPERANT DISCRIMINATION BY THE PIGEON.
004271 04-05

OPERANT-BEHAVIOR
TOLERANCE TO SUPPRESSIVE EFFECTS OF CHLORDIAZEPOXIDE ON OPERANT-BEHAVIOR: LACK OF CROSS-TOLERANCE TO PENTOBARBITAL.
000356 01-04
EFFECT OF MORPHINE IN COMBINATION WITH CHLORPROMAZINE AND HALOPERIDOL ON OPERANT-BEHAVIOR.
000486 01-04
DORSAL TEGMENTAL BUNDLE DESTRUCTION: EFFECTS ON OPERANT-BEHAVIOR, BRAIN CATECHOLAMINE LEVELS, AND BEHAVIORAL-SUPPRESSION PRODUCED BY ADRENERGIC AGONISTS.
001726 02-04
ON THE USE OF OPERANT-BEHAVIOR TO STUDY THE NEUROPSYCHOPHARMACOLOGY OF OPIATES WITH SPECIAL REFERENCE TO MORPHINE AND ITS RELATIONSHIP TO DOPAMINE IN THE CENTRAL-NERVOUS-SYSTEM.
001790 02-04
THE EFFECTS OF 2,5 DIMETHOXY-4-METHYLAMPHETAMINE (DOM) ON OPERANT-BEHAVIOR: INTERACTIONS WITH OTHER NEUROACTIVE-AGENTS.
004089 04-04
INDIVIDUAL DIFFERENCES IN EFFECTS OF TRICYCLIC-ANTIDEPRESSANTS AND ANTICHOLINERGIC-DRUGS ON OPERANT-BEHAVIOR IN THE SQUIRREL-MONKEY.
004176 04-04
MICROPROPERTIES OF OPERANT-BEHAVIOR AS ASPECTS OF TOXICITY.
004666 04-15

OPERANT-RESPONDING
NALOXONE POTENTIATES THE DISRUPTIVE EFFECTS OF MESCALINE ON OPERANT-RESPONDING IN THE RAT.
000365 01-04
THE EFFECTS OF D LYSERGIC-ACID-DIETHYLAMIDE (LSD), 2,5 DIMETHOXY-4-METHYLAMPHETAMINE (DOM) AND D-AMPHETAMINE ON OPERANT-RESPONDING IN CONTROL AND 6 HYDROXYDOPAMINE TREATED RATS.
001595 02-04
EFFECTS OF METHYLPHENIDATE ON OPERANT-RESPONDING IN HYPERACTIVE-BOYS. (PH.D. DISSERTATION).
002191 02-11

Subject Index

OPERANT-RESPONSE
CHRONIC EFFECTS OF NEUROLEPTICS HAVING HIGH OR LOW INCIDENCE OF EXTRAPYRAMIDAL SIDE-EFFECTS UPON FORCE, DURATION AND RATE OF OPERANT-RESPONSE IN RATS. (PH.D. DISSERTATION).
003125 03-05

OPERATIONS
DEPENDENCE OF THE AVFAIL EFFECT ON THE SEQUENCE OF TRAINING OPERATIONS.
001086 02-02

OPHTHALMOLOGICAL
OPHTHALMOLOGICAL SIDE-EFFECTS OF LITHIUM.
004615 04-15

OPIATE
REDUCTION OF OPIATE BINDING TO BRAINSTEM SLICES ASSOCIATED WITH THE DEVELOPMENT OF TOLERANCE TO MORPHINE IN RATS.
000066 01-03

EXCITATORY AND INHIBITORY-EFFECTS OF OPIATES IN THE RAT VAS-DEFERENS: A DUAL-MECHANISM OF OPIATE ACTION.
000143 01-03

BLOCKADE OF STRIATAL NEURONE RESPONSES TO MORPHINE BY AMINOPHYLLINE: EVIDENCE FOR ADENOSINE MEDIATION OF OPIATE ACTION.
000229 01-03

CHANGES IN OPIATE ACTIVITY OF RAT PITUITARY FOLLOWING ACUTE ADMINISTRATION OF NEUROLEPTICS.
000282 01-03

A STUDY OF THE QUANTAL (ALL-OR-NONE) CHANGE IN REFLEX LATENCY PRODUCED BY OPIATE ANALGESICS.
000425 01-04

IATROGENIC OPIATE ADDICTION: SUCCESSFUL DETOXIFICATION WITH CLONIDINE.
000666 01-11

CLONIDINE FOR OPIATE DETOXIFICATION: OUTPATIENT CLINICAL-TRIALS.
000731 01-11

RAPID OPIATE DETOXIFICATION WITH CLONIDINE AND NALOXONE.
000820 01-14

CLONIDINE FOR OUTPATIENT OPIATE DETOXIFICATION.
000827 01-14

ROLE OF PROTEIN-KINASES IN OPIATE ACTIONS IN BRAIN.
001173 02-03

OPIATE INTERACTIONS WITH CHOLINERGIC NEURONS.
001198 02-03

A DEMONSTRATION OF NALOXONE PRECIPITATED OPIATE WITHDRAWAL ON SINGLE NEURONES IN THE MORPHINE-TOLERANT/DEPENDENT RAT-BRAIN.
001234 02-03

REGIONAL RELEASE OF (3H)ADENOSINE DERIVATIVES FROM RAT-BRAIN IN VIVO: EFFECT OF EXCITATORY AMINO-ACIDS, OPIATE AGONISTS, AND BENZODIAZEPINES.
001303 02-03

NERVE CELL CALCIUM AS A MESSENGER FOR OPIATE AND ENDORPHIN ACTIONS.
001450 02-03

MU-RECEPTORS AND DELTA OPIATE-RECEPTORS: CORRELATION WITH HIGH-AFFINITY AND LOW AFFINITY OPIATE BINDING-SITES.
001554 02-03

THE SHORT-TERM AND LONG-TERM EFFECTS OF BETA ENDORPHIN ON THE OPIATE ABSTINENCE-SYNDROME IN RATS.
001643 02-04

OPIATE ACTIONS AND CATECHOLAMINES.
001662 02-04

STRESS-INDUCED FACILITATION OF OPIATE CATALEPSY IN THE RAT.
001680 02-04

OPIATE AND PEPTIDE INTERACTION: EFFECT OF ENKEPHALINS ON MORPHINE ANALGESIA.
001698 02-04

OPIATE ANTAGONISTS AND LONG-TERM ANALGESIC REACTION INDUCED BY INESCAPABLE SHOCK IN RATS.
001707 02-04

OPIATE ANTAGONISTS AND FEMALE FUNCTIONING. (UNPUBLISHED PAPER).
001735 02-04

COMPARISON OF OPIATE AGONISTS AND THEIR N ALLYL DERIVATIVES IN THE PRODUCTION OF PHYSICAL-DEPENDENCE IN THE RAT.
001841 02-05

EFFECT OF OPIATES AND OPIATE ANTAGONISTS ON SOMATOSENSORY EVOKED-POTENTIALS IN PATIENTS WITH SCHIZOPHRENIA AND NORMAL ADULTS.
002222 02-13

MECHANISMS OF OPIATE ANALGESIA AND THE ROLE OF ENDORPHINS IN PAIN SUPPRESSION. (UNPUBLISHED PAPER).
002275 02-13

ENDORPHIN OPIATE INTERACTIONS WITH NEUROENDOCRINE SYSTEMS.
002552 02-17

THE TREATMENT OF OPIATE ADDICTION USING METHADONE-CHLORHYDRATE.
002600 02-17

REVIEW AND OVERVIEW OF FOUR DECADES OF OPIATE RESEARCH.
002627 02-17

EFFECTS OF INTRAPALLIDAL OPIATE-RECEPTOR AGONISTS ON STRIATALLY-EVOKED HEAD-TURNING.
001785 02-04

DISCRIMINATIVE-STIMULUS EFFECTS OF PROTOTYPE OPIATE-RECEPTOR AGONISTS IN MONKEYS.
001803 02-04

MOLECULAR ACTIONS OF OPIATES: HISTORICAL OVERVIEW AND NEW FINDINGS ON OPIATE-RECEPTOR INTERACTIONS WITH ENKEPHALINS AND GUANYL-NUCLEOTIDES.
002613 02-17

OPIATE-RECEPTOR GRADIENTS IN MONKEY CEREBRAL-CORTEX: CORRESPONDENCE WITH SENSORY PROCESSING HIERARCHIES.
002641 03-01

EFFECT OF THE POSITION OF THE PHENOLIC GROUP IN MORPHINANS ON THEIR AFFINITY FOR OPIATE-RECEPTOR BINDING.
003702 04-02

NALOXAZONE, A LONG-ACTING OPIATE ANTAGONIST: EFFECTS ON ANALGESIA IN INTACT ANIMALS AND ON OPIATE-RECEPTOR BINDING IN VITRO.
004198 04-04

OPIATE-RECEPTORS

OPIATE-RECEPTORS MAY MEDIATE THE SUPPRESSIVE BUT NOT THE EXCITATORY ACTION OF ACTH ON MOTOR-ACTIVITY IN RATS.
000337 01-04

IN VITRO AUTORADIOGRAPHY OF OPIATE-RECEPTORS IN RAT-BRAIN SUGGESTS LOCI OF OPIATE-ERGIC PATHWAYS. (UNPUBLISHED PAPER).
001025 02-01

OPIATE-RECEPTORS IN MEMBRANES AND IN SOLUTION. (UNPUBLISHED PAPER).
001032 02-01

GUANINE-NUCLEOTIDES INHIBIT BINDING OF AGONISTS AND ANTAGONISTS TO SOLUBLE OPIATE-RECEPTORS. (UNPUBLISHED PAPER).
001035 02-01

BIOCHEMICAL-EVIDENCE FOR TYPE-1 AND TYPE-2 OPIATE-RECEPTORS. (UNPUBLISHED PAPER).
001050 02-01

SOLUBILIZATION OF ACTIVE OPIATE-RECEPTORS. (UNPUBLISHED PAPER).
001056 02-01

OPIATE-RECEPTORS IN THE RABBIT IRIS.
001200 02-03

PHARMACOLOGICAL EVIDENCE OF A POSSIBLE TRYPTAMINERGIC REGULATION OF OPIATE-RECEPTORS BY USING INDALPINE, A SELECTIVE 5 HT UPTAKE INHIBITOR.
001517 02-03

MU-RECEPTORS AND DELTA OPIATE-RECEPTORS: CORRELATION WITH HIGH-AFFINITY AND LOW AFFINITY OPIATE BINDING-SITES.
001554 02-03

FURTHER STUDIES ON OPIATE-RECEPTORS THAT MEDIATE ANTINOCICEPTION: TOOTH-PULP STIMULATION IN THE DOG.
001782 02-04

A CLASSIFICATION OF OPIATE-RECEPTORS THAT MEDIATE ANTINOCICEPTION IN ANIMALS.
001807 02-04

HISTOCHEMICAL LOCALIZATION OF OPIATE-RECEPTORS AND THE ENKEPHALINS.
002566 02-17

IN VITRO STUDIES OF OPIATE-RECEPTORS.
002609 02-17

OPIATE-RECEPTORS: PROBLEMS OF DEFINITION AND CHARACTERIZATION.
002620 02-17

COMPARATIVE-STUDY ON THE EFFECT OF MORPHINE AND THE OPIOID-LIKE PEPTIDES IN THE VAS-DEFERENS OF RODENTS: STRAIN AND SPECIES-DIFFERENCES, EVIDENCE FOR MULTIPLE OPIATE-RECEPTORS.
002757 03-03

EVIDENCE THAT THE OPIATE-RECEPTORS OF THE SUBSTANTIA-GELATINOSA CONTRIBUTE TO THE DEPRESSION, BY INTRAVENOUS MORPHINE, OF THE SPINAL TRANSMISSION OF IMPULSES IN UNMYELINATED PRIMARY AFFERENTS.
002767 03-03

OPIATE-RECEPTORS AND SLEEP. II. EFFECTS OF MICROINJECTIONS OF ETHYL-ALCOHOL AND PENTOBARBITAL IN THE MEDIAN THALAMUS, PERIAQUEDUCTAL GRAY MATTER AND NUCLEUS-TRACTUS-SOLITARIUS OF THE RABBIT.
002917 03-03

ACTH-INDUCED GROOMING INVOLVES HIGH-AFFINITY OPIATE-RECEPTORS.
002985 03-04

DIFFERENTIATION OF OPIATE-RECEPTORS IN THE BRAIN BY THE SELECTIVE DEVELOPMENT OF TOLERANCE.
003088 03-04

MULTIPLE OPIATE-RECEPTORS.
003581 03-17

SYNTHESIS AND PHARMACOLOGICAL-STUDY OF SOME ENKEPHALIN ANALOGS IN RELATION TO THE PLURALITY OF OPIATE-RECEPTORS.
003682 04-02

FLUORESCENT PROBES OF ALPHA-ADRENERGIC AND BETA-ADRENERGIC AND OPIATE-RECEPTORS: BIOCHEMICAL AND HISTOCHEMICAL EVALUATION.
003685 04-02

INTERCONVERTING MU AND DELTA-FORMS OF TYPE-1 OPIATE-RECEPTORS IN THE RAT STRIATAL PATCHES.
003737 04-03

PHARMACOLOGICAL DIFFERENTIATION OF PRESYNAPTIC INHIBITORY ALPHA-ADRENOCEPTORS AND OPIATE-RECEPTORS IN THE CAT NICTITATING MEMBRANE.
003777 04-03

THE ROLE OF OPIATE-RECEPTORS OF DIFFERENT BRAIN REGIONS IN DETERMINING THE EMOTIONAL REACTIONS OF RATS.
004017 04-03

MEMORY, OPIATE-RECEPTORS, AND AGING.
004143 04-04

MINI-SYMPOSIUM: III. SIMPLE IN VIVO TESTS THAT DIFFERENTIATE PROTOTYPE AGONISTS AT OPIATE-RECEPTORS.
004289 04-06

MINI-SYMPOSIUM. I. THE IN VIVO DIFFERENTIATION OF OPIATE-RECEPTORS: INTRODUCTION.
004697 04-17

OPIATE-SENSITIVE

AMYGDALA OPIATE-SENSITIVE MECHANISMS INFLUENCE FEAR MOTIVATED RESPONSES AND MEMORY PROCESSES FOR AVERSIVE-EXPERIENCES. (UNPUBLISHED PAPER).
001628 02-04

OPIATE-TOLERANT

TIME-COURSE OF ETORPHINE LEVELS IN TISSUES OF OPIATE-TOLERANT AND NONTOLERANT RATS.
000301 01-03

OPIATES

SEROTONIN PARTICIPATION IN GUT WITHDRAWAL FROM OPIATES.
000109 01-03

EXCITATORY AND INHIBITORY-EFFECTS OF OPIATES IN THE RAT VAS-DEFERENS: A DUAL-MECHANISM OF OPIATE ACTION.
000143 01-03

THE EFFECTS OF OPIATES ON THE LEVELS OF CYCLIC-GUANOSINE-MONOPHOSPHATE IN DISCRETE AREAS OF THE RAT CENTRAL-NERVOUS-SYSTEM.
000220 01-03

CHLORDIAZEPOXIDE ANTINOCICEPTION: CROSS-TOLERANCE WITH OPIATES AND WITH STRESS.
000348 01-04

THE OPIATES: TWO CENTURIES OF SCIENTIFIC-STUDY.
000952 01-17

NEUROCHEMICAL MECHANISMS OF OPIATES AND ENDORPHINS.
000958 01-17

EXCITATORY ACTION OF OPIOID-PEPTIDES AND OPIATES ON CULTURED HIPPOCAMPAL PYRAMIDAL CELLS.
001241 02-03

OPIATES AND SPECIFIC RECEPTOR BINDING OF (3H)CLONIDINE.
001256 02-03

EFFECT OF OPIATES ON MACROMOLECULE BIOSYNTHESIS.
001335 02-03

LOG-DOSE/RESPONSE-CURVE FLATTENING IN RATS AFTER DAILY INJECTION OF OPIATES.
001387 02-03

OPIATES AND OPIOID-PEPTIDES HYPERPOLARIZE LOCUS-COERULEUS NEURONS IN VITRO.
001408 02-03

CYCLIC-NUCLEOTIDES AND THE CENTRAL-EFFECTS OF OPIATES: AN OVERVIEW OF CURRENT RESEARCH.
001445 02-03

DIFFERENTIAL-EFFECTS OF SYSTEMIC VERSUS INTRACRANIAL INJECTION OF OPIATES ON CENTRAL, OROFACIAL AND LOWER BODY NOCICEPTION: SOMATOTYPY IN BULBAR ANALGESIA SYSTEMS.
001446 02-03

THE ALBINO LOCUS PRODUCES ABNORMAL RESPONSES TO OPIATES IN THE MOUSE.
001675 02-04

ENHANCED RESPONSES TO OPIATES PRODUCED BY A SINGLE GENE SUBSTITUTION IN THE MOUSE.
001677 02-04

ON THE USE OF OPERANT-BEHAVIOR TO STUDY THE NEUROPSYCHOPHARMACOLOGY OF OPIATES WITH SPECIAL REFERENCE TO MORPHINE AND ITS RELATIONSHIP TO DOPAMINE IN THE CENTRAL-NERVOUS-SYSTEM.
001790 02-04

EFFECT OF OPIATES AND OPIATE ANTAGONISTS ON SOMATOSENSORY EVOKED-POTENTIALS IN PATIENTS WITH SCHIZOPHRENIA AND NORMAL ADULTS.
002222 02-13

MOLECULAR ACTIONS OF OPIATES: HISTORICAL OVERVIEW AND NEW FINDINGS ON OPIATE-RECEPTOR INTERACTIONS WITH ENKEPHALINS AND GUANYL-NUCLEOTIDES.
002613 02-17

BEHAVIORAL CONFIRMATION OF DIFFUSE NOXIOUS INHIBITORY CONTROLS (DNIC) AND EVIDENCE FOR A ROLE OF ENDOGENOUS OPIATES.
002791 03-03

BLOCKADE OF ENDOGENOUS OPIATES REDUCES ACTIVITY IN THE RAT.
003111 03-04

RIA OPIATES: STRUCTURE VERSUS REACTIVITY.
003659 04-01

SELECTIVE MODIFICATION BY OPIATES OF NEURONAL ACTIVITY OF THE MEDIAL BASAL HYPOTHALAMUS.
003773 04-03

COMPARISON OF THE BINDING CHARACTERISTICS OF TRITIATED OPIATES AND OPIOID-PEPTIDES.
003802 04-03

THE EFFECT OF PRENATAL EXPOSURE TO ETHANOL OR OPIATES ON BRAIN CATECHOLAMINE ACTIVITY.
003939 04-03

MODULATION OF DOPAMINE-RECEPTORS BY OPIATES. (UNPUBLISHED PAPER).
003949 04-03

ACTIONS OF MU, KAPPA, SIGMA, DELTA AND AGONIST/ANTAGONIST OPIATES ON STRIATAL DOPAMINERGIC FUNCTION.
004053 04-03

OPIOID
N TETRAHYDROFURYLALKYL AND N ALKOXYALKYL DERIVATIVES OF (-) NORMETAZOCINE, COMPOUNDS WITH DIFFERENTIATED OPIOID ACTION PROFILES.
000013 01-02

ANTINOCICEPTIVE-EFFECT OF MORPHINE, OPIOID ANALGESICS AND HALOPERIDOL INJECTED INTO THE CAUDATE-NUCLEUS OF THE RAT.
000414 01-04

OPIOID DEPENDENT DUAL-REGULATION OF ADENYLATE-CYCLASE IN A CELL-FREE SYSTEM. (UNPUBLISHED PAPER).
001033 02-01

OPIOID MECHANISMS IN REGULATION OF CEREBRAL MONOAMINES IN VIVO.
001098 02-03

ROLES OF SEROTONIN AND GAMMA AMINOBUTYRIC-ACID IN OPIOID EFFECTS.
001140 02-03

OPIOID BLOCKADE AND SOCIAL-COMFORT IN CHICKS.
001745 02-04

METKEPHAMID, A SYSTEMICALLY ACTIVE ANALOG OF METHIONINE-ENKEPHALIN WITH POTENT OPIOID DELTA-RECEPTOR ACTIVITY.
002720 03-03

A REFORMULATION OF THE DUAL-ACTION MODEL OF OPIOID DEPENDENCE: OPIOID-SPECIFIC NEURONAL KINDLING.
003645 03-17

OPIOID ACTIVITIES OF BETA CASOMORPHINS.
003740 04-03

OPIOID BINDING PROPERTIES OF BRAIN AND PERIPHERAL TISSUES: EVIDENCE FOR HETEROGENEITY IN OPIOID LIGAND BINDING SITES.
003902 04-03

DISCRIMINATION OF ELECTRIC-SHOCK: EFFECTS OF SOME OPIOID AND NONOPIOID DRUGS.
004106 04-04

OPIOID DEPENDENCE: MECHANISMS AND TREATMENT.
004587 04-14

POSSIBLE INFLUENCE OF OPIOID NORMETABOLITES ON THE ONSET, MAGNITUDE AND QUALITY OF THE OPIOID ABSTINENCE-SYNDROME.
004610 04-15

OPIOID-LIKE
INTERACTIONS BETWEEN MORPHINE AND THE OPIOID-LIKE PEPTIDES IN THE RAT VAS-DEFERENS.
001290 02-03

COMPARATIVE-STUDY ON THE EFFECT OF MORPHINE AND THE OPIOID-LIKE PEPTIDES IN THE VAS-DEFERENS OF RODENTS: STRAIN AND SPECIES-DIFFERENCES, EVIDENCE FOR MULTIPLE OPIATE-RECEPTORS.
002757 03-03

OPIOID-PEPTIDE
AN INHIBITOR OF OPIOID-PEPTIDE DEGRADATION PRODUCES ANALGESIA IN MICE.
001780 02-04

OPIOID-PEPTIDES
EXCITATORY ACTION OF OPIOID-PEPTIDES AND OPIATES ON CULTURED HIPPOCAMPAL PYRAMIDAL CELLS.
001241 02-03

OPIATES AND OPIOID-PEPTIDES HYPERPOLARIZE LOCUS-COERULEUS NEURONS IN VITRO.
001408 02-03

BEHAVIORAL-EFFECTS AND ELECTROPHYSIOLOGICAL-EFFECTS OF OPIOID-PEPTIDES IN CATS.
001612 02-04

ROLE OF ADRENERGIC BLOCKING-AGENTS AND GLUCOCORTICOIDS ON THE REGULATION OF PITUITARY OPIOID-PEPTIDES LEVELS.
003801 04-03

COMPARISON OF THE BINDING CHARACTERISTICS OF TRITIATED OPIATES AND OPIOID-PEPTIDES.
003802 04-03

RECENT STUDIES ON INTERACTION BETWEEN OPIOID-PEPTIDES AND THEIR RECEPTORS.
004300 04-06

OPIOID-RECEPTOR
ISOLATION OF SELECTIVE 3H CHLORNALTREXAMINE BOUND COMPLEXES, POSSIBLE OPIOID-RECEPTOR COMPONENTS IN BRAINS OF MICE.
001162 02-03

D PROPOXYPHENE ACTS DIFFERENTLY FROM MORPHINE ON OPIOID-RECEPTOR EFFECTOR MECHANISMS.
003062 03-04

OPIOID-RECEPTORS
OPIOID-RECEPTORS IN THE CAUDATE-NUCLEUS CAN MEDIATE EMG-RECORDED RIGIDITY IN RATS.
001649 02-04

MINI-SYMPOSIUM: II. MULTIPLE OPIOID-RECEPTORS. A LITTLE ABOUT THEIR HISTORY AND SOME IMPLICATIONS RELATED TO EVOLUTION.
004728 04-17

OPIOID-SPECIFIC
A REFORMULATION OF THE DUAL-ACTION MODEL OF OPIOID DEPENDENCE: OPIOID-SPECIFIC NEURONAL KINDLING.
003645 03-17

OPIOID-TOLERANCE
DEVELOPMENT OF ACUTE OPIOID-TOLERANCE AND DEPENDENCE IN RAT STRIATAL NEURONES.
001235 02-03

OPIOIDS
THE POSSIBILITY THAT A COMPONENT OF MORPHINE-INDUCED ANALGESIA IS CONTRIBUTED INDIRECTLY VIA THE RELEASE OF ENDOGENOUS OPIOIDS.
000263 01-03

RELATIONSHIP BETWEEN THE ACTIONS OF CALCIUM-IONS, OPIOIDS, AND PROSTAGLANDIN-E1 ON THE LEVEL OF CYCLIC-AMP IN NEUROBLASTOMA-X GLIOMA HYBRID CELLS.
002677 03-03

DIFFERENTIAL-EFFECTS OF POTASSIUM ON THE POTENCY OF DIFFERENT OPIOIDS IN THE MOUSE VAS-DEFERENS.
002935 03-03

MORPHINE-LIKE STIMULUS EFFECTS IN THE MONKEY: OPIOIDS WITH ANTAGONIST PROPERTIES.
003086 03-04

OPIOIDS, NORADRENALINE AND GTP ANALOGS INHIBIT CHOLERA-TOXIN ACTIVATED ADENYLATE-CYCLASE IN NEUROBLASTOMA-X GLIOMA HYBRID CELLS.
003975 04-03

PHENCYCLIDINE-LIKE DISCRIMINATIVE EFFECTS OF OPIOIDS IN THE RAT.
004136 04-04

SEXUAL-BEHAVIOR DECREASES PAIN SENSITIVITY AND STIMULATES ENDOGENOUS OPIOIDS IN MALE RATS.
004234 04-04

OPIPRAMOL
A PRELIMINARY STUDY ON DETERMINATION OF THE OPTIMUM OPIPRAMOL DOSAGE IN DEPRESSIVE-PATIENTS.
000601 01-09

OPIUM
SIMILARITIES BETWEEN CANNABIS AND OPIUM.
002554 02-17

OPPOSITE-EFFECTS
BIPHASIC-EFFECTS AND OPPOSITE-EFFECTS OF DOPAMINE AND APOMORPHINE ON ENDOGENOUS GABA RELEASE IN THE RAT SUBSTANTIA-NIGRA.
002923 03-03

OPTICAL-ISOMERS
THE PHARMACOLOGICAL ACTION OF THE OPTICAL-ISOMERS OF SYDNOCARB.
003681 04-02

PROPERTIES OF THE OPTICAL-ISOMERS AND METABOLITES OF KETAMINE ON THE HIGH-AFFINITY TRANSPORT AND CATABOLISM OF MONOAMINES.
004009 04-03

OPTICAL-STIMULATION
THE EFFECTS OF LSD AND SOME ANALOGUES ON THE RESPONSES OF SINGLE CORTICAL NEURONS OF THE CAT TO OPTICAL-STIMULATION.
000738 01-12

ORDINAL
MILD, MODERATE, SEVERE — THE STATISTICAL ANALYSIS OF SHORT ORDINAL SCALES.
004677 04-16

ORG-GB-94
A DOUBLE-BLIND STUDY WITH ORG-GB-94 IN PREMENOPAUSAL-WOMEN.
002173 02-11

ORG-2766
INDUCTION OF ANALGESIA BY CENTRAL ADMINISTRATION OF ORG-2766, AN ANALOG OF ACTH4-9.
003112 03-04

ORGAN
TREATMENT OF ORGANIC-BRAIN-DISTURBANCES IN ELDERLY-PATIENTS. A CLINICAL DOUBLE-BLIND STUDY WITH MACROMOLECULAR ORGAN LYSATES (CYTOPLASMATIC THERAPY ACCORDING TO THEURER).
003327 03-11

ORGANELLES
DISTRIBUTION OF MEMBRANE GLYCOPROTEINS AMONG THE ORGANELLES OF A SINGLE IDENTIFIED NEURON OF APLYSIA. II. ISOLATION AND CHARACTERIZATION OF A GLYCOPROTEIN ASSOCIATED WITH VESICLES.
002657 03-03

ORGANIC-BRAIN-DISTURBANCES
TREATMENT OF ORGANIC-BRAIN-DISTURBANCES IN ELDERLY-PATIENTS. A CLINICAL DOUBLE-BLIND STUDY WITH MACROMOLECULAR ORGAN LYSATES (CYTOPLASMATIC THERAPY ACCORDING TO THEURER).
003327 03-11

ORGANIC-BRAIN-SEIZURES
ON THE EVALUATION OF A PROVOCATIVE EEG METHOD USING MEDICATION IN THE DIAGNOSIS OF ORGANIC-BRAIN-SEIZURES IN CHILDHOOD, WITH SPECIAL EMPHASIS ON SLEEP INDUCTION THROUGH MEDICATION.
003387 03-11

ORGANIC-BRAIN-SYNDROME
NEUROLOGICAL SIDE-EFFECTS OF LITHIUM: ORGANIC-BRAIN-SYNDROME, SEIZURES, EXTRAPYRAMIDAL SIDE-EFFECTS, AND EEG CHANGES.
000847 01-15

ORGANIC-MENTAL-SYNDROMES
THE ROLE OF PSYCHOPHARMACOTHERAPY IN THE TREATMENT OF ELDERLY-PATIENTS WITH ORGANIC-MENTAL-SYNDROMES.
003368 03-11

ORGANIC-PSYCHOSYNDROME
POSSIBILITIES OF INFLUENCE ON THE ORGANIC-PSYCHOSYNDROME WITH NOOTROPIC-DRUGS IN CHRONIC ALCOHOLISM.
000707 01-11

ORGANIC-PSYCHOSYNDROMES
DISSOCIATION OF THE STRYCHNINE EFFECT ON VISUAL-MEMORY AND VERBAL-MEMORY IN ORGANIC-PSYCHOSYNDROMES.
000816 01-14
DISSOCIATION OF THE STRYCHNINE EFFECT ON VISUAL-MEMORY AND VERBAL-MEMORY IN ORGANIC-PSYCHOSYNDROMES.
002155 02-11

ORGANISM
DISTRIBUTION OF CESIUM IN THE ORGANISM AND ITS EFFECT ON THE NUCLEOTIDE METABOLISM ENZYMES.
003696 04-02

ORGANIZATION
FUNCTIONAL ORGANIZATION OF THE CAUDATE-NUCLEUS AFTER ADMINISTRATION OF CARBACHOL.
001495 02-03

ORGANON-2766
A SYNTHETIC ACTH4-9 ANALOGUE (ORGANON-2766) AND SLEEP IN HEALTHY MAN.
004574 04-14

ORGANOPHOSPHATE-INDUCED
FORNIX LESION PREVENTS AN ORGANOPHOSPHATE-INDUCED DECREASE IN MUSCARINIC-RECEPTOR LEVEL IN RAT HIPPOCAMPUS.
001833 02-05

ORGANS
STUDY OF LITHIUM LEVELS IN THE SERUM AND GENITAL ORGANS OF MALE RATS.
001494 02-03
INFLUENCE OF CANNABIS AND DELTA9 TETRAHYDROCANNABINOL ON THE BIOCHEMISTRY OF THE MALE REPRODUCTIVE ORGANS.
002686 03-03

ORIENTAL
TRICYCLIC-ANTIDEPRESSANT DRUG TOLERANCE IN ORIENTAL AND OCCIDENTAL POPULATIONS.
000590 01-09

ORIENTATION
A REEVALUATION OF THE MECHANISMS UNDERLYING SIMPLE CELL ORIENTATION SELECTIVITY.
002894 03-03

ORIENTATIONAL
ORIENTATIONAL TESTING OF CHLORPROMAZINE-HCL ON HOSPITALIZED MENTAL-PATIENTS.
002131 02-11

ORIENTATIONS
THE RESEARCH FOR NEW ANTIDEPRESSANTS: PRESENT ORIENTATIONS.
002543 02-17

ORIENTING
EFFECT OF PROPRANOLOL AND PHENOTHIAZINES ON ELECTRODERMAL ORIENTING AND HABITUATION IN SCHIZOPHRENIA.
003174 03-08

ORIGIN
THE IDENTITY AND HYPOTHALAMIC ORIGIN OF CHOLECYSTOKININ IN RAT-BRAIN AND POSTERIOR PITUITARY AND ITS POSSIBLE ROLE IN REGULATION OF NEUROSECRETION. (UNPUBLISHED PAPER).
001003 02-01
LITHIUM-ION ENTRY INTO CULTURED CELLS OF NEURAL ORIGIN.
001433 02-03
NYSTAGMIC RESPONSES OF HIPPOCAMPAL ORIGIN WITH REFERENCE TO EXCITABILITY OF CHOLINERGIC AND ADRENERGIC COMPONENTS INVOLVED IN THE HIPPOCAMPUS OF RABBITS.
003842 04-03
THE EFFICACY OF PIRACETAM IN VERTIGO: A DOUBLE-BLIND STUDY IN PATIENTS WITH VERTIGO OF CENTRAL ORIGIN.
004478 04-11

ORIGINAL
FIRST RESULTS OF AN ORIGINAL METHOD FOR MEASURING BLOOD LEVELS OF ANTIDEPRESSANTS (AMITRIPTYLINE AND NORTRIPTYLINE).
003559 03-16

ORNITHINE-DECARBOXYLASE
EFFECT OF OXOTREMORINE ON ORNITHINE-DECARBOXYLASE ACTIVITY OF THE ADRENAL-GLAND IN RAT.
000246 01-03

OROFACIAL
DIFFERENTIAL-EFFECTS OF SYSTEMIC VERSUS INTRACRANIAL INJECTION OF OPIATES ON CENTRAL, OROFACIAL AND LOWER BODY NOCICEPTION: SOMATOTYPY IN BULBAR ANALGESIA SYSTEMS.
001446 02-03
CARBAMAZEPINE-INDUCED OROFACIAL DYSKINESIA.
002415 02-15
NALOXONE REVERSIBLE DUPLICATION BY LANTHANUM OF OPIATE ANALGESIA EFFECTS ON OROFACIAL, LOWER BODY AND CENTRAL NOCICEPTION.
003028 03-04

ORTHOSTATIC
TREATMENT OF PSYCHOTROPIC-CAUSED ORTHOSTATIC HYPOTENSION.
002428 02-15
PHARMACOLOGIC DISTINCTION OF DIFFERENT ORTHOSTATIC HYPOTENSION-SYNDROMES.
003362 03-11

ORYCTOLAGUS-CUNICULUS
PERIPHERAL AUTONOMIC-MECHANISMS AND PAVLOVIAN-CONDITIONING IN THE RABBIT (ORYCTOLAGUS-CUNICULUS).
001560 02-04
PERIPHERAL 6 HYDROXYDOPAMINE ADMINISTRATION IN THE RABBIT (ORYCTOLAGUS-CUNICULUS): EFFECTS ON PAVLOVIAN-CONDITIONING.
001668 02-04

OSCILLATION
SENSITIZATION AND OSCILLATION FOLLOWING REPEATED STIMULATION: RELATIONSHIP TO AFFECTIVE-ILLNESS AND ITS TREATMENT WITH LITHIUM AND CARBAMAZEPINE.
002031 02-09

OSCILLATORY
CHARACTERISTICS OF OSCILLATORY CONTRACTIONS ELICITED BY NALOXONE IN ILEUM PREPARATION FROM MORPHINE-DEPENDENT GUINEA-PIGS.
001491 02-03

OSMOLALITY
CHANGES IN BLOOD PLASMA OSMOLALITY AND STATES OF MANIA.
004352 04-09

OSTEOMALACIA
BIOCHEMICAL-EVIDENCE FOR OSTEOMALACIA WITH CARBAMAZEPINE THERAPY.
002445 02-15

OUABAIN
GLUCOSE OXIDATION IN THE VENTROMEDIAL HYPOTHALAMUS IS NOT AFFECTED BY INSULIN OR OUABAIN BUT DEPRESSED BY ALLOXAN TREATMENT.
001145 02-03

OUTCOME
PREDICTING OUTCOME OF ANTIPSYCHOTIC-DRUG TREATMENT FROM EARLY-RESPONSE.
000565 01-08
CHLORPROMAZINE LEVELS AND THE OUTCOME OF TREATMENT IN SCHIZOPHRENIC-PATIENTS.
003188 03-08
PROGNOSIS IN SCHIZOPHRENIA: INDIVIDUAL DIFFERENCES IN PSYCHOLOGICAL RESPONSE TO A TEST DOSE OF ANTIPSYCHOTIC-DRUG AND THEIR RELATIONSHIP TO BLOOD AND SALIVA LEVELS AND TREATMENT OUTCOME.
003189 03-08
PREDICTING OUTCOME FROM MEASURES OF ATTENTION AND AUTONOMIC-FUNCTIONING.
003205 03-08
SALIVA BENZODIAZEPINE LEVELS AND CLINICAL OUTCOME IN DETOXIFYING ALCOHOLIC-PATIENTS.
004671 04-16
COMPUTER-ANALYZED ELECTROENCEPHALOGRAM TO PREDICT THE THERAPEUTIC OUTCOME IN SCHIZOPHRENIA.
004680 04-16

OUTER
EXPOSURE OF MITOCHONDRIAL OUTER MEMBRANES TO NEURAMINIDASE SELECTIVELY DESTROYS MONOAMINE-OXIDASE-A ACTIVITY.
001286 02-03

OUTFLOW
BETA ENDORPHIN-INDUCED HYPERGLYCEMIA IS MEDIATED BY INCREASED CENTRAL SYMPATHETIC OUTFLOW TO ADRENAL-MEDULLA.
002924 03-03

OUTPATIENT
HOSPITAL AND OUTPATIENT CARE FOR PSYCHOTIC-PATIENTS DURING THE LAST THREE DECADES: SUBSEQUENT HOSPITAL AND OUTPATIENT TREATMENT OF PSYCHOTIC-PATIENTS HOSPITALIZED FOR THE FIRST TIME IN 1949-50, 1959-60 OR 1969-70.
000571 01-08
CLONIDINE FOR OPIATE DETOXIFICATION: OUTPATIENT CLINICAL-TRIALS.
000731 01-11
CLONIDINE FOR OUTPATIENT OPIATE DETOXIFICATION.
000827 01-14

OUTPATIENT TREATMENT ISSUES AND STRATEGIES FOR ACUTE AND
CHRONIC PCP ABUSERS.
                                                          000919 01-17
USE OF THE LITHIUM RESPONSE SCALE WITH AN OUTPATIENT
PSYCHIATRIC-SAMPLE.
                                                          000921 01-17
STUDY OF MAPROTILINE IN OUTPATIENT TREATMENT OF DEPRESSIVE-
STATES BY THE GENERAL-PRACTITIONER: ADVANTAGE OF SINGLE-
NIGHTLY-DOSE.
                                                          001961 02-09
OUTPATIENT CARE OF DEPRESSIVE-PATIENTS WITH MIANSERIN.
                                                          002041 02-09
ARCALION-200 PRESCRIBED AS A PSYCHIATRIC-DRUG AND
ANTIALCOHOLISM-DRUG ON AN OUTPATIENT AND INPATIENT BASIS.
                                                          002103 02-11
THE USE OF MINAPRINE IN CHILD-PSYCHIATRY IN HOSPITALS AND
OUTPATIENT CLINICS.
                                                          002169 02-11
AMOXAPINE AND AMITRIPTYLINE IN THE OUTPATIENT TREATMENT OF
ENDOGENOUS DEPRESSION.
                                                          003217 03-09
THE TREATMENT OF DEPRESSION USING CLOMIPRAMINE IN GENERAL-
MEDICAL-PRACTICE: 48 CASES TREATED ON AN OUTPATIENT BASIS.
                                                          003268 03-09
METHODOLOGY OF OUTPATIENT DRUG RESEARCH. (UNPUBLISHED
PAPER).
                                                          003282 03-10

OUTPATIENTS
TREATMENT OF ANXIOUS-DEPRESSED OUTPATIENTS WITH A FIXED
COMBINATION (NOMIFENSINE/CLOBAZAM) IN COMPARISON TO A
MONOSUBSTANCE (DOXEPINE).
                                                          002028 02-09
PLASMA DESIPRAMINE LEVELS AFTER SINGLE-DOSAGE AND AT STEADY-
STATE IN OUTPATIENTS.
                                                          002039 02-09

OUTPATIENTS-WARDS
RESULTS OF TREATMENT BY MODITEN DEPOT IN OUTPATIENTS-WARDS IN
THE SOUTH MORAVIAN REGION.
                                                          004648 04-15

OUTWARD-CURRENT
DIPHENYLHYDANTOIN REDUCES THE OUTWARD-CURRENT OF THE ACTION
POTENTIAL IN APLYSIA.
                                                          002805 03-03
CAFFEINE BLOCKS THE DELAYED K OUTWARD-CURRENT OF MOLLUSCAN
NEURONS.
                                                          003834 04-03

OVARIAN
EFFECTS OF CENTRALLY-ADMINISTERED AND SYSTEMICALLY
ADMINISTERED L TYROSINE AND L LEUCINE ON OVARIAN FUNCTION IN
THE OLD RAT.
                                                          001180 02-03
IMIPRAMINE: EFFECT OF OVARIAN STEROIDS ON MODIFICATIONS IN
SEROTONIN-RECEPTOR BINDING.
                                                          002778 03-03

OVARIECTOMIZED
EFFECTS OF AN EPINEPHRINE SYNTHESIS INHIBITOR, SKF-64139, ON THE
SECRETION OF LUTEINIZING-HORMONE IN OVARIECTOMIZED FEMALE
RATS.
                                                          002693 03-03
FACILITATION OF LORDOSIS BEHAVIOR IN THE OVARIECTOMIZED
ESTROGEN-PRIMED RAT BY DIBUTYRYL-C-AMP.
                                                          002957 03-04

OVERACTIVE
A DOUBLE-BLIND, PLACEBO-CONTROLLED, CROSS-OVER TRIAL OF
CARBAMAZEPINE IN OVERACTIVE, SEVERELY MENTALLY-
HANDICAPPED PATIENTS.
                                                          003365 03-11

OVERDIAGNOSED
IS MANIA OVERDIAGNOSED?: THE THREE COMMON PITFALLS IN
DIAGNOSING MANIC-DEPRESSIVE-ILLNESS.
                                                          003260 03-09

OVERDOSAGE
PHARMACOKINETIC-STUDY OF LORAZEPAM OVERDOSAGE.
                                                          000831 01-15
THE NEW ANTIDEPRESSANT PIRLINDOLE: ANTAGONISM OF ACUTE
OVERDOSAGE IN THE MOUSE.
                                                          001082 02-02
ACUTE OVERDOSAGE WITH FLUNITRAZEPAM.
                                                          003513 03-15

OVERDOSE
THA — A REVIEW OF THE LITERATURE AND ITS USE IN TREATMENT OF
FIVE OVERDOSE PATIENTS.
                                                          003539 03-15

OVEREATING
AMPHETAMINE-INDUCED OVEREATING AND OVERWEIGHT IN RATS.
                                                          003015 03-04

OVERFLOW
REGULATION OF NORADRENALINE OVERFLOW IN RAT-CEREBRAL-CORTEX
BY PROSTAGLANDIN-E2.
                                                          003841 04-03

OVERINCLUSIVE
CHANGE IN OVERINCLUSIVE THINKING OF SCHIZOPHRENIC-PATIENTS IS
RELATED TO PLASMA PHENOTHIAZINE CONCENTRATION.
                                                          001941 02-08

OVERNIGHT
INHIBITION OF PENTAGASTRIN-STIMULATED AND OVERNIGHT GASTRIC
SECRETION BY LM24056, A NEW PHENOTHIAZINE DERIVED
ANTISECRETORY DRUG.
                                                          004306 04-07

OVERVIEW
PEPTIDES IN NEUROBIOLOGY: AN OVERVIEW. (UNPUBLISHED PAPER).
                                                          001008 02-01
CYCLIC-NUCLEOTIDES AND THE CENTRAL-EFFECTS OF OPIATES: AN
OVERVIEW OF CURRENT RESEARCH.
                                                          001445 02-03
AN OVERVIEW OF SEVENTEEN YEARS OF EXPERIENCE WITH DOTHIEPIN IN
THE TREATMENT OF DEPRESSION IN EUROPE.
                                                          001995 02-09
MOLECULAR ACTIONS OF OPIATES: HISTORICAL OVERVIEW AND NEW
FINDINGS ON OPIATE-RECEPTOR INTERACTIONS WITH ENKEPHALINS
AND GUANYL-NUCLEOTIDES.
                                                          002613 02-17
REVIEW AND OVERVIEW OF FOUR DECADES OF OPIATE RESEARCH.
                                                          002627 02-17
DEPENDENCE ON TRANQUILIZERS (AN OVERVIEW WITH (CASE-STUDIES).
                                                          003580 03-17
AN OVERVIEW OF PHARMACOLOGIC-TREATMENT OF COGNITIVE DECLINE
IN THE AGED.
                                                          004482 04-11

OVERWEIGHT
AMPHETAMINE-INDUCED OVEREATING AND OVERWEIGHT IN RATS.
                                                          003015 03-04

OVINE
DISPOSITION OF METHADONE IN THE OVINE MATERNAL FETAL UNIT.
                                                          004027 04-03

OVOCYCLIN
SYNCHRONIZATION OF EEG ACTIVITY OF MALE RHESUS-MONKEYS
MACACA-MULATTA TREATED WITH OVOCYCLIN.
                                                          001312 02-03

OVULATION
NALOXONE REVERSAL OF THE PENTOBARBITAL-INDUCED BLOCKADE OF
OVULATION IN THE RAT.
                                                          002817 03-03

OVULATORY
A BARBITURATE-EVOKED INTENSIFICATION OF POSTSYNAPTIC INHIBITION
IN THE PREOPTIC OVULATORY TRIGGER REGION OF THE
HYPOTHALAMUS.
                                                          002818 03-03

OXALYL-L-ALPHA-BETA-DIAMINOPROPIONIC-ACID
THE NEUROLATHYROGEN, BETA N OXALYL-L-ALPHA-BETA-
DIAMINOPROPIONIC-ACID, IS A POTENT AGONIST AT GLUTAMATE
PREFERRING RECEPTORS IN THE FROG SPINAL-CORD.
                                                          002858 03-03

OXAZEPAM
OXAZEPAM-ESTERS. 1. CORRELATION BETWEEN HYDROLYSIS RATES AND
BRAIN APPEARANCE OF OXAZEPAM.
                                                          000010 01-02
CONTROLLED-COMPARISON OF THE THERAPEUTIC EFFECTS OF NATRIUM-
OXYBUTYRATE AND OXAZEPAM.
                                                          000658 01-10
CHLORDIAZEPOXIDE AND OXAZEPAM DISPOSITION IN CIRRHOSIS.
                                                          000790 01-13
EFFICACY AND SIDE-EFFECTS OF LORAZEPAM, OXAZEPAM, AND
TEMAZEPAM AS SLEEPING-AIDS IN PSYCHOGERIATRIC-INPATIENTS.
                                                          002076 02-10
INFLUENCE OF CIMETIDINE ON THE PHARMACOKINETICS OF
DESMETHYLDIAZEPAM AND OXAZEPAM.
                                                          002249 02-13
CLINICAL PHARMACOKINETICS OF OXAZEPAM AND LORAZEPAM.
                                                          003410 03-13

OXAZEPAM-ESTERS
OXAZEPAM-ESTERS. 1. CORRELATION BETWEEN HYDROLYSIS RATES AND
BRAIN APPEARANCE OF OXAZEPAM.
                                                          000010 01-02
OXAZEPAM-ESTERS. 2. CORRELATION OF HYDROPHOBICITY WITH SERUM
BINDING, BRAIN PENETRATION, AND EXCRETION.
                                                          000011 01-02

OXAZOLAM
A CLINICAL-EVALUATION OF THE EFFECTS OF A NEW PSYCHOTROPIC-
AGENT, MEXAZOLAM (CS-386) ON PSYCHOSOMATIC-DISEASES AND
NEUROSIS: A COMPARATIVE-STUDY WITH OXAZOLAM, USING THE
DOUBLE-BLIND METHOD.
                                                          004491 04-11

OXIDASES
EFFECT OF CHRONIC ADMINISTRATION OF PHENCYCLIDINE ON HEPATIC
MIXED-FUNCTION OXIDASES IN THE MOUSE.
                                                          002753 03-03

OXYPROTHEPIN-DECANOATE INJECTIONS: EXPERIENCE WITH A LONG-
TERM-TREATMENT OF SCHIZOPHRENIC-PSYCHOSES.
000576 01-08

OXYPROTHEPINE-DECANOATE
MAINTENANCE-THERAPY WITH FLUPHENAZINE-DECANOATE AND
OXYPROTHEPINE-DECANOATE IN SCHIZOPHRENIC-PATIENTS -- A
DOUBLE-BLIND CROSS-OVER COMPARATIVE-STUDY.
001924 02-08
EXPERIENCE WITH OXYPROTHEPINE-DECANOATE IN THE MAINTENANCE-
THERAPY OF SCHIZOPHRENIA.
001925 02-08
OXYPROTHEPINE-DECANOATE COMPARED WITH FLUPHENAZINE-
DECANOATE IN THE TREATMENT OF SCHIZOPHRENIA: PRELIMINARY-
COMMUNICATION.
001934 02-08

OXYTOCIN
INFLUENCE OF OXYTOCIN ON HUMAN MEMORY PROCESSES.
002322 02-14

P-300
CAPACITIES OF ATTENTION, STRESS-RESISTANCE, AND SLOW CEREBRAL
POTENTIALS: EFFECTS OF CARPIPRAMINE ON CONTINGENT NEGATIVE
VARIATION WAVES AND P-300.
003451 03-14

PACIFIC-ISLANDERS
PSYCHOPHARMACOLOGY FOR ASIAN-AMERICANS AND PACIFIC-
ISLANDERS.
000734 01-11

PACKET
TYRAMINE CONTENT OF CANNED AND PACKET SOUPS.
002394 02-15

PAIN
PAIN AND TRYPTOPHAN.
000775 01-13
MECHANISMS OF PAIN AND ANALGESIC COMPOUNDS.
000916 01-17
PSYCHOPHARMACOLOGY OF ANALGESIA AND PAIN. (UNPUBLISHED
PAPER).
001411 02-03
SPONTANEOUSLY (GENETIC) HYPERTENSIVE-RATS PRESENT A NALOXONE
SENSITIVE DECREASE IN PAIN SENSITIVITY. (UNPUBLISHED PAPER).
001457 02-03
NEUROPEPTIDES AND MONOAMINERGIC NEUROTRANSMITTERS: THEIR
RELATION TO PAIN.
001497 02-03
BRIEF SOCIAL-ISOLATION, PAIN RESPONSIVITY, AND MORPHINE
ANALGESIA IN YOUNG RATS.
001744 02-04
TREATMENT OF CHRONIC PAIN WITH ANTIDEPRESSANT-DRUGS.
002048 02-09
THE RELATIONSHIP OF ALPHA AND DELTA EEG FREQUENCIES TO PAIN
AND MOOD IN FIBROSITIS-PATIENTS TREATED WITH CHLORPROMAZINE
AND L TRYPTOPHAN.
002152 02-11
MECHANISMS OF OPIATE ANALGESIA AND THE ROLE OF ENDORPHINS IN
PAIN SUPPRESSION. (UNPUBLISHED PAPER).
002275 02-13
CHANGES IN THE AUGMENTER REDUCER TENDENCY AND IN PAIN
MEASURES AS A RESULT OF TREATMENT WITH A SEROTONIN
REUPTAKE INHIBITOR ZIMELIDINE.
002305 02-13
CLONIDINE AND PSYCHOPHYSICAL PAIN.
002366 02-14
PSYCHOPHARMACEUTICALS FOR TREATING PAIN.
002548 02-17
PLACEBO, MEDICINE AND PAIN, OR THE RELATIVE FUNCTION OF
MEDICATION IN THE TREATMENT OF PAIN.
002577 02-17
IMMUNOHISTOCHEMICAL LOCALIZATION OF LEUCINE-ENKEPHALIN IN THE
SPINAL-CORD OF THE CAT: ENKEPHALIN-CONTAINING MARGINAL
NEURONS AND PAIN MODULATION.
002638 03-01
A COMPARISON OF THE EFFECTS OF MORPHINE-SULPHATE AND NITROUS-
OXIDE ANALGESIA ON CHRONIC PAIN STATES IN MAN.
003442 03-14
THE NEUROPHYSIOLOGICAL AND CLINICAL-ASPECTS OF PAIN.
003457 03-14
RELIEF OF PAIN IN CLINICAL-PRACTICE.
003613 03-17
TREATMENT OF CANCER PAIN.
003619 03-17
EFFECTS OF PAIN, MORPHINE AND NALOXONE ON THE DURATION OF
ANIMAL HYPNOSIS.
004081 04-04
SEXUAL-BEHAVIOR DECREASES PAIN SENSITIVITY AND STIMULATES
ENDOGENOUS OPIOIDS IN MALE RATS.
004234 04-04
DOPAMINE AND 5 HT SUPERSENSITIVITY IN NONORGANIC CENTRAL PAIN
AND IN MORPHINE ABSTINENCE: FORTUITOUS OR REAL ANALOGY?
004553 04-13

PAIRING
THE EFFECTS OF PIMOZIDE DURING PAIRING ON THE TRANSFER OF
CLASSICAL CONDITIONING TO AN OPERANT DISCRIMINATION.
002956 03-04

PALSY
PROGRESSIVE SUPRANUCLEAR PALSY, COMPUTED-TOMOGRAPHY, AND
RESPONSE TO ANTIPARKINSONIAN-DRUGS.
003322 03-11
PROGRESSIVE SUPRANUCLEAR PALSY: PNEUMOENCEPHALOGRAPHY,
ELECTRONYSTAGMOGRAPHY AND TREATMENT WITH METHYSERGIDE.
003355 03-11

PANCREAS
THE EFFECT OF SEROTONIN ON THE EXOSECRETORY ACTION OF THE
PANCREAS.
004043 04-03

PANENCEPHALITIS
ISOPRINOSINE IN SUBACUTE SCLEROSING PANENCEPHALITIS.
000687 01-11
REVIEW OF 38 CASES OF SUBACUTE SCLEROSING PANENCEPHALITIS:
EFFECT OF AMANTADINE ON THE NATURAL COURSE OF THE DISEASE.
000718 01-11

PANIC
DIFFERENTIAL DIAGNOSIS AND TREATMENT OF PANIC ATTACKS AND
PHOBIC-STATES.
004424 04-10

PANIC-ANXIETY
PANIC-ANXIETY AFTER ABRUPT DISCONTINUATION OF AMITRIPTYLINE.
003223 03-09

PANIC-DISORDER
EFFECT OF SODIUM-LACTATE ON PATIENTS WITH PANIC-DISORDER AND
MITRAL-VALVE PROLAPSE.
003409 03-13

PANIC-INDUCED
BLOCKADE BY IMIPRAMINE OR DESIPRAMINE OF PANIC-INDUCED BY
SODIUM-LACTATE.
004427 04-10

PAPAIN-DERIVED
PAPAIN-DERIVED FRAGMENT IIC TETANUS-TOXIN: ITS BINDING TO
ISOLATED SYNAPTIC MEMBRANES AND RETROGRADE AXONAL
TRANSPORT.
003734 04-03

PAPAVERINE
EFFECT OF PAPAVERINE ON REGIONAL CEREBRAL BLOOD FLOW AND
SMALL VESSEL BLOOD CONTENT.
001177 02-03

PAPILLOEDEMA
BILATERAL PAPILLOEDEMA IN LONG-TERM THERAPY WITH LITHIUM-
CARBONATE.
000878 01-15

PAPIO-PAPIO
EEG AND ANTICONVULSANT EFFECTS OF DIPROPYLACETIC-ACID AND
DIPROPYLACETAMIDE IN THE BABOON PAPIO-PAPIO.
001210 02-03

PARACETAMOL
BEHAVIOURAL-EFFECTS OF ACETYLSALICYLIC-ACID, PARACETAMOL,
CAFFEINE, GUAIPHENESIN AND THEIR COMBINATIONS.
001805 02-04
THE EFFECT OF ASPIRIN AND PARACETAMOL ON THE INCREASED
NALOXONE POTENCY INDUCED BY MORPHINE PRETREATMENT.
001824 02-04

PARADIGM
NORADRENERGIC AGONISTS AND ANTAGONISTS: EFFECTS ON
CONDITIONED FEAR AS MEASURED BY THE POTENTIATED STARTLE
PARADIGM.
000372 01-04
INFLUENCE OF INTRAVENOUS SELF-ADMINISTERED PSYCHOMOTOR
STIMULANTS ON PERFORMANCE OF RHESUS-MONKEYS IN A MULTIPLE-
SCHEDULE PARADIGM.
001655 02-04
TOLERANCE TO DEXTROAMPHETAMINE-SULFATE IN HYPERACTIVE-
CHILDREN: ASSESSMENT USING AN EMPIRICAL NEUROPSYCHOLOGICAL
PARADIGM — A PILOT-STUDY.
002126 02-11
A RESEARCH PARADIGM TO INVESTIGATE THE EFFECT OF MANIPULATION
ON SOCIAL-BEHAVIOR IN GROUPS.
003007 03-04

PARADOXICAL
EFFECT OF PYRITINOL AND PIRACETAM ON CHANGES IN FREE AMMONIA
LEVEL IN CNS TISSUE AFTER PARADOXICAL SLEEP-DEPRIVATION IN
RATS.
001199 02-03
PARADOXICAL IMPROVEMENT FOLLOWING IV AMPHETAMINE IN
SCHIZOPHRENIA. (UNPUBLISHED PAPER).
001951 02-08
PARADOXICAL AKINESIA INDUCED BY ANTIDEPRESSANT-DRUGS.
002378 02-15

PARADOXICAL-EFFECT
THE PARADOXICAL-EFFECT OF LIDOCAINE ON AN EXPERIMENTAL MODEL
OF EPILEPSY.
000039 01-03

A NOTE ON THE PARADOXICAL-EFFECT OF STIMULANTS ON
HYPERACTIVITY WITH REFERENCE TO THE RATE DEPENDENCY EFFECT
OF DRUGS.
003320 03-11

PARADOXICAL-EFFECTS
GENETIC AND EXPERIMENTAL FACTORS AFFECTING THE PARADOXICAL-
EFFECTS OF AMPHETAMINE IN DOGS.
001704 02-04

PARADOXICAL-INTERACTION
THERMOREGULATORY AND LOCOMOTOR-EFFECTS OF DSIP:
PARADOXICAL-INTERACTION WITH D-AMPHETAMINE.
001827 02-04

PARADOXICAL-SLEEP
PRAZOSIN INCREASES PARADOXICAL-SLEEP.
000405 01-04

PARADOXICALLY
CHLORPROMAZINE, HALOPERIDOL, METOCLOPRAMIDE AND
DOMPERIDONE RELEASE PROLACTIN THROUGH DOPAMINE
ANTAGONISM AT LOW CONCENTRATIONS BUT PARADOXICALLY
INHIBIT PROLACTIN RELEASE AT HIGH-CONCENTRATIONS.
003731 04-03

PARAFASCICULAR
ENHANCED SUPPRESSION OF CONDITIONED AVOIDANCE RESPONSE BY
HALOPERIDOL BUT NOT PHENOXYBENZAMINE IN RATS WITH
BILATERAL PARAFASCICULAR LESIONS.
000334 01-04

PARALLEL
EVOKED-POTENTIAL CHANGES IN THE SUPERIOR-COLLICULUS PARALLEL
THE LESION-INDUCED DEVELOPMENT OF GROOMING REFLEXES IN THE
CAT. (PH.D. DISSERTATION).
001179 02-03
A DOUBLE-BLIND PARALLEL GROUP COMPARISON OF SINGLE-BEDTIME-
DOSES OF HALAZEPAM AND PLACEBO.
002079 02-10
GENETIC VARIATIONS IN MIDBRAIN DOPAMINE CELL NUMBER: PARALLEL
WITH DIFFERENCES IN RESPONSES TO DOPAMINERGIC AGONISTS AND
IN NATURALISTIC BEHAVIORS MEDIATED BY CENTRAL DOPAMINERGIC-
SYSTEMS. (UNPUBLISHED PAPER).
004112 04-04
A SIMPLE DETERMINATION OF SEROTONIN, 5 HYDROXYINDOLEACETIC-
ACID AND 5 HYDROXYTRYPTOPHAN-DECARBOXYLASE ACTIVITY IN
RAT-BRAIN AREAS AND PARALLEL CORRELATION AMONG THE LEVELS.
004301 04-06

PARALLELS
FUNCTIONAL HYPERINNERVATION OF CEREBRAL-CORTEX BY
NORADRENERGIC NEURONS RESULTS FROM FETAL LESIONS: PARALLELS
WITH SCHIZOPHRENIA.
000059 01-03

PARAMETERS
SEROTONIN-SENSITIVE ADENYLATE-CYCLASE AND (3H)SEROTONIN
BINDING-SITES IN THE CNS OF THE RAT — I. KINETIC PARAMETERS
AND PHARMACOLOGICAL-PROPERTIES.
000213 01-03
ALTERATION OF PHARMACOKINETIC PARAMETERS FOR PENTOBARBITAL
BY ISCHEMIC STROKE AND REVERSION TO NORMAL BY
DEXAMETHASONE TREATMENT.
000321 01-03
EFFECTS OF ACUTE OR CHRONIC ADMINISTRATION OF
CHLORDIAZEPOXIDE ON FEEDING PARAMETERS USING TWO FOOD
TEXTURES IN THE RAT.
000368 01-04
INTRACRANIAL INJECTION PARAMETERS WHICH AFFECT ANGIOTENSIN-II-
INDUCED DRINKING.
000534 01-06
CORRELATIONS BETWEEN HEMODYNAMIC PARAMETERS OF THE LIVER
AND NOREPINEPHRINE RELEASE UPON HEPATIC-NERVE STIMULATION IN
THE DOG.
001547 02-03
EFFECTS OF THE BETA-ADRENOCEPTOR BLOCKING-AGENT SOTALOL ON
CNS: SLEEP, EEG, AND PSYCHOPHYSIOLOGICAL PARAMETERS.
001570 02-04
EFFECTS OF SPIPERONE ALONE AND IN COMBINATION WITH ANORECTIC-
AGENTS ON FEEDING PARAMETERS IN THE RAT.
001598 02-04
INTERACTIONS OF CHLORDIAZEPOXIDE AND ANORECTIC-AGENTS ON RATE
AND DURATION PARAMETERS OF FEEDING IN THE RAT.
001600 02-04
THE CLINICAL-EFFICACY OF CLOZAPINE AS COMPARED TO LABORATORY
PARAMETERS.
001955 02-08
THE CORRELATION OF CATECHOLAMINE AND ADRENERGIC PARAMETERS
WITH DRUG-THERAPY OF NEUROTIC AND ENDOGENOUS DEPRESSIONS.
002047 02-09
EFFECTS OF CYCLOSPASMOL UPON SENSORY PARAMETERS IN PATIENTS
RECOVERING FROM CEREBROVASCULAR-ACCIDENTS.
002360 02-14
EFFECTS OF ANXIETY REDUCTION BY BEHAVIOURAL-TECHNIQUES AND
MEPROBAMATE ON CERTAIN PARAMETERS OF INFORMATION THEORY.
003108 03-04

STATISTICAL ANALYSES OF PHYSIOLOGIC DATA FROM FEMALE PATIENTS WITH AN ENDOMORPHOUS DEPRESSIVE COURSE: A TRIAL, INTERACTIONS BETWEEN PHYSIOLOGIC PARAMETERS, TEST JUNCTURES IN THIS PHASE.
003251 03-09

INVESTIGATION INTO THE EFFECT OF FLUPHENAZINE-HCL (LYORODIN) IN CHILDREN WITH BEHAVIORAL-DISORDERS BY MEANS OF PSYCHOPHYSIOLOGICAL PARAMETERS.
003344 03-11

TIME-COURSE OF CLINICAL CHEMICAL PARAMETERS UNDER LONG-TERM LITHIUM TREATMENT.
003515 03-15

EFFECTS OF SUPIDIMIDE (CG-3033) ON OBJECTIVE AND SUBJECTIVE SLEEP PARAMETERS (A SLEEP LABORATORY STUDY).
004567 04-14

PARANOIA
CIMETIDINE TOXICITY MANIFESTED AS PARANOIA AND HALLUCINATIONS.
000829 01-15

PARANOID
THE RELATIONSHIP BETWEEN THE THIORIDAZINE LEVEL IN THE PLASMA AND SYMPTOMS OF PARANOID SCHIZOPHRENIA.
000546 01-08

TREATMENT OF THERAPEUTICALLY-RESISTANT PARANOID SCHIZOPHRENIC-PATIENTS WITH FLUPHENAZINE DEPOT COMBINED WITH OTHER PSYCHOTROPIC-DRUGS AND CLOZAPINE.
003172 03-08

PARAPROFESSIONAL
PARAPROFESSIONAL AND PROFESSIONAL TEAMWORK AND TRAINING IN MANAGING PCP AND OTHER DRUG-ABUSE PROBLEMS.
000924 01-17

PARASYMPATHETIC-ACTIVITY
METHYLDOPA PRODUCES CENTRAL INHIBITION OF PARASYMPATHETIC-ACTIVITY IN THE CAT.
001321 02-03

PARASYMPATHOMIMETIC-INFLUENCE
PARASYMPATHOMIMETIC-INFLUENCE OF CARBACHOL ON LOCAL CEREBRAL BLOOD FLOW IN THE RABBIT BY A DIRECT VASODILATOR ACTION AND AN INHIBITION OF THE SYMPATHETIC MEDIATED VASOCONSTRICTION.
001109 02-03

PARATHYROID-HORMONE
LITHIUM EFFECT ON PARATHYROID-HORMONE.
003215 03-09

PARENCHYMAL
ON THE QUESTION OF PARENCHYMAL DAMAGE CAUSED BY LONG-TERM THERAPY WITH PSYCHOTROPICS IN ADOLESCENCE.
004626 04-15

PARENT
THE PARENT CHILD INTERACTIONS OF HYPERACTIVE-CHILDREN AND THEIR MODIFICATION BY STIMULANT-DRUGS.
002092 02-11

PARENTERAL
THE BIOAVAILABILITY OF ORAL AND PARENTERAL CHLORIMIPRAMINE (ANAFRANIL).
002232 02-13

PARENTERALLY
ETHANOL AVERSION INDUCED BY PARENTERALLY ADMINISTERED ETHANOL ACTING BOTH AS CS AND UCS.
001721 02-04

PARENTS
LITHIUM IN CHILDREN OF LITHIUM RESPONDING PARENTS.
003242 03-09

PARGYLINE
DEPLETION OF EPINEPHRINE IN RAT HYPOTHALAMUS BY RO-4-1284: INFLUENCE OF PARGYLINE AND HARMALINE.
000100 01-03

INFLUENCE OF IMIPRAMINE AND PARGYLINE ON THE ARRHYTHMOGENICITY OF EPINEPHRINE DURING HALOTHANE, ENFLURANE OR METHOXYFLURANE ANESTHESIA IN DOGS.
001539 02-03

DOPAMINE, NORADRENALINE AND 3,4 DIHYDROXYPHENYLACETIC-ACID (DOPAC) LEVELS OF INDIVIDUAL BRAIN NUCLEI, EFFECTS OF HALOPERIDOL AND PARGYLINE.
003792 04-03

PARKINSON-DISEASE
SINEMET AND THYROID-FUNCTION IN PARKINSON-DISEASE.
000733 01-11

DRUG-HOLIDAY AND MANAGEMENT OF PARKINSON-DISEASE.
002468 02-15

DEPRENYL IN PARKINSON-DISEASE.
003309 03-11

EVIDENCE TO SUPPORT EARLY LEVODOPA THERAPY IN PARKINSON-DISEASE.
003336 03-11

PARKINSON-PATIENTS
NOMIFENSINE AS CONCOMITANT THERAPY IN THE TREATMENT OF PARKINSON-PATIENTS. A DOUBLE-BLIND PLACEBO-CONTROLLED-STUDY.
002130 02-11

NORMAL PLASMA DOPAMINE-BETA-HYDROXYLASE IN NONTREATED AND TREATED PARKINSON-PATIENTS.
004471 04-11

PARKINSON-SYNDROME
EFFECTS OF HIGH-DOSAGE LISURIDE-HYDROGEN-MALEATE (LHM) IN PARKINSON-SYNDROME.
004460 04-11

PARKINSONIAN
SPINOCEREBELLAR DEGENERATION WITH PARKINSONIAN FEATURES: A CLINICAL AND PATHOLOGICAL REPORT.
003436 03-13

PARKINSONIAN-PATIENTS
PSYCHIATRIC-EFFECTS OF BROMOCRIPTINE AND LERGOTRILE IN PARKINSONIAN-PATIENTS.
002453 02-15

PLASMA LEVODOPA, DOPAMINE AND THERAPEUTIC RESPONSE FOLLOWING LEVODOPA THERAPY OF PARKINSONIAN-PATIENTS.
002504 02-16

DOSAGE FORM DESIGN FOR IMPROVEMENT OF BIOAVAILABILITY OF LEVODOPA III: INFLUENCE OF DOSE ON PHARMACOKINETIC BEHAVIOR OF LEVODOPA IN DOGS AND PARKINSONIAN-PATIENTS.
004551 04-13

ELECTROENCEPHALOGRAPHIC CHANGE IN PARKINSONIAN-PATIENTS TREATED WITH LEVODOPA CARBIDOPA.
004557 04-13

DEPRENYL DOES NOT CAUSE INSOMNIA IN PARKINSONIAN-PATIENTS.
004569 04-14

PARKINSONIAN-SYNDROME
TREATMENT OF PARKINSONIAN-SYNDROME WITH DEXETIMIDE.
002111 02-11

PARKINSONISM
BIOCHEMICAL-MEASUREMENTS DURING (-)DEPRENYL TREATMENT OF PARKINSONISM.
000673 01-11

ELECTRORETINOGRAPHIC-CHANGES IN PATIENTS WITH PARKINSONISM TREATED WITH VARIOUS CLASSES OF ANTIPARKINSONIAN-DRUGS.
000674 01-11

A COMPARISON OF BIPERIDEN-HYDROCHLORIDE (AKINETON) AND BENZHEXOL (ARTANE) IN THE TREATMENT OF DRUG-INDUCED PARKINSONISM.
002146 02-11

PARKINSONISM: IS YOUR TREATMENT APPROPRIATE?
002159 02-11

LISURIDE IN THE TREATMENT OF PARKINSONISM.
002168 02-11

A NEUROPHARMACOLOGICAL-STUDY AND NEUROENDOCRINE-STUDY ON IDIOPATHIC AND CHRONIC PHARMACOLOGICAL PARKINSONISM.
002371 02-15

PROGRESS IN THE PHARMACOTHERAPY OF PARKINSONISM.
002384 02-15

LISURIDE IN PARKINSONISM.
003319 03-11

CLINICAL SIGNIFICANCE OF PYRIDOXINE ADMINISTRATION IN L-DOPA THERAPY OF PARKINSONISM.
003345 03-11

LISURIDE IN PARKINSONISM.
003422 03-13

THE DIAGNOSIS AND TREATMENT OF NEUROLEPTIC-INDUCED PARKINSONISM.
003493 03-15

GERIATRIC ASPECTS OF PARKINSONISM (CLINICAL-PICTURE, PATHOLOGICAL MECHANISMS, AND MULTIPLE TREATMENT).
003643 03-17

PROSPECTS FOR THE TREATMENT OF POSTENCEPHALITIC PARKINSONISM WITH ANTILYMPHOCYTIC IMMUNOGLOBULIN.
004572 04-14

CONTEMPORARY PROBLEMS IN THE PHARMACOLOGICAL-TREATMENT OF PARKINSONISM.
004628 04-15

PARKINSONS
ASSESSING L-DOPA THERAPY FOR PARKINSONS.
004465 04-11

PARKINSONS-DISEASE
ANTIDEPRESSIVE TREATMENT IN PARKINSONS-DISEASE: A CONTROLLED-TRIAL OF THE EFFECT OF NORTRIPTYLINE IN PATIENTS WITH PARKINSONS-DISEASE TREATED WITH L-DOPA.
000659 01-11

VASOPRESSIN THERAPY IN PARKINSONS-DISEASE.
000689 01-11

THE LONG-TERM RESULTS OF STEREOTAXIC SURGERY AND L-DOPA THERAPY IN PATIENTS WITH PARKINSONS-DISEASE: A 10-YEAR FOLLOWUP STUDY.
000693 01-11

LONG-TERM EFFICACY OF BROMOCRIPTINE IN PARKINSONS-DISEASE.
000698 01-11

THE TREATMENT OF PARKINSONS-DISEASE USING A COMBINATION OF L-DOPA AND DECARBOXYLASE INHIBITORS (CARBIDOPA, BENSERASIDE). A CLINICAL AND BIOCHEMICAL COMPARATIVE INVESTIGATION.
000712 01-11

Subject Index

THE ELECTRORETINOGRAM IN PARKINSONS-DISEASE.
001295 02-03

A COMPARATIVE-STUDY OF BROMOCRIPTINE AND LEVODOPA IN PARKINSONS-DISEASE.
002117 02-11

BROMOCRIPTINE AND PARKINSONS-DISEASE: A 16-HOUR CLINICAL-EVALUATION.
002127 02-11

THE ROLE OF BROMOCRIPTINE IN THE TREATMENT OF PARKINSONS-DISEASE.
002177 02-11

INCREASED RATIO OF CARBIDOPA TO LEVODOPA IN TREATMENT OF PARKINSONS-DISEASE.
002182 02-11

ABNORMAL REGULATION OF PROLACTIN RELEASE IN IDIOPATHIC PARKINSONS-DISEASE.
002255 02-13

COMPARATIVE-STUDIES OF L-DOPA ALONE AND COMBINATION WITH A PERIPHERAL DOPA-DECARBOXYLASE INHIBITOR, BENSERAZIDE-HCL, ON PARKINSONS-DISEASE — PART II: PHARMACOKINETIC-STUDY.
002309 02-13

BROMOCRIPTINE IN PARKINSONS-DISEASE: REPORT ON 106 PATIENTS TREATED FOR UP TO 5 YEARS.
002342 02-14

DEPRENYL IN THE MANAGEMENT OF RESPONSE FLUCTUATIONS IN PATIENTS WITH PARKINSONS-DISEASE ON LEVODOPA.
002358 02-14

EDEMAS AND MYOCLONIES IN A PATIENT WITH PARKINSONS-DISEASE TREATED BY AMANTADINE: PROBLEM WITH ASSOCIATED MEDICATIONS.
002389 02-15

FURTHER EXPERIENCES WITH LOW-DOSES OF BROMOCRIPTINE IN PARKINSONS-DISEASE.
002401 02-15

LEVODOPA COMPARED WITH BROMOCRIPTINE IN THE TREATMENT OF PARKINSONS-DISEASE.
002406 02-15

L-DOPAS MECHANISM-OF-ACTION IN PARKINSONS-DISEASE.
003323 03-11

RECENT ADVANCES IN THE TREATMENT OF PARKINSONS-DISEASE.
003528 03-15

ARE THE ENKEPHALINS INVOLVED IN PARKINSONS-DISEASE? CLINICAL AND NEUROENDOCRINE RESPONSES TO NALOXONE ADMINISTRATION.
004431 04-11

LEVODOPA: LONG-TERM IMPACT ON PARKINSONS-DISEASE.
004476 04-11

A STUDY ON MENTAL-SYMPTOMS DEVELOPED DURING THE TREATMENT OF PARKINSONS-DISEASE.
004618 04-15

PAROTID
CONCENTRATIONS AND KINETICS OF CARBAMAZEPINE IN WHOLE SALIVA, PAROTID SALIVA, SERUM ULTRAFILTRATE, AND SERUM.
004545 04-13

PAROXYSTIC-DYSKINESIAS
PAROXYSTIC-DYSKINESIAS DURING TREATMENT WITH DIPHENYLHYDANTOIN.
002319 02-14

PARTICIPATION
SEROTONIN PARTICIPATION IN GUT WITHDRAWAL FROM OPIATES.
000109 01-03

THE PARTICIPATION OF SUBSTANTIA-NIGRA ZONA-COMPACTA AND ZONA-RETICULATA NEURONS IN MORPHINE SUPPRESSION OF CAUDATE SPONTANEOUS NEURONAL ACTIVITIES IN THE RAT.
002718 03-03

PARTICLES
NA-INDEPENDENT BINDING OF (3H)GABA AND (3H)MUSCIMOL TO SUBCELLULAR PARTICLES OF NEURAL PRIMARY CULTURES AND WHOLE BRAIN.
002699 03-03

PARTITIONING
PARTITIONING AND EFFLUX OF PHENOTHIAZINES FROM LIPOSOMES.
000007 01-02

PARTURIENT
ERGOT DRUGS SUPPRESS PLASMA PROLACTIN AND LACTATION BUT NOT AGGRESSION IN PARTURIENT MICE.
003159 03-07

PASSAGE
QUANTITATION AND COMPARISON OF PHENOBARBITAL LEVELS IN THE PLASMA, SALIVA, AND CEREBROSPINAL-FLUID OF THE RAT, AND THE DEMONSTRATION OF AN ALTERATION OF DRUG PASSAGE BY ETHANOL.
003725 04-03

PASSAGE THROUGH THE BLOOD-BRAIN-BARRIER OF THYROTROPIN-RELEASING-HORMONE ENCAPSULATED IN LIPOSOMES.
004298 04-06

PASSIVE-AVOIDANCE
SEROTONINMIMETIC AND ANTIDEPRESSANT-DRUGS ON PASSIVE-AVOIDANCE LEARNING BY OLFACTORY BULBECTOMISED RATS.
001585 02-04

S

PATHOMORPHOSIS
PATHOMORPHOSIS OF CHRONIC EPILEPTIC-PSYCHOSES.
003209 03-09
PECULIARITIES OF THE CEREBRAL PATHOMORPHOLOGY OF PATIENTS
WITH SCHIZOPHRENIA TREATED WITH PSYCHOTROPIC-DRUGS
(PHARMACOLOGICAL PATHOMORPHOSIS).
004528 04-13
THE DRUG PATHOMORPHOSIS OF SCHIZOPHRENIA.
004732 04-17
PATHOPHYSIOLOGIC-BASIS
PATHOPHYSIOLOGIC-BASIS OF TARDIVE-DYSKINESIA.
002373 02-15
PATHOPHYSIOLOGIC-IMPACT
PATHOPHYSIOLOGIC-IMPACT OF CENTRAL CATECHOLAMINERGIC
FUNCTION IN SCHIZOPHRENIA AND SCHIZOPHRENIA-LIKE PSYCHOSES.
002174 02-11
PATHOPHYSIOLOGICAL
PATHOPHYSIOLOGICAL AND MORPHOLOGICAL CHANGES IN THE CNS
DURING LONG-TERM ADMINISTRATION OF HALOPERIDOL.
004633 04-15
PATHOPHYSIOLOGICAL-ASPECTS
PATHOPHYSIOLOGICAL-ASPECTS OF REVERSIBLE AND IRREVERSIBLE
TARDIVE-DYSKINESIA.
002124 02-11
PATHOPHYSIOLOGICAL-DATA
NEUROLEPTIC-INDUCED TARDIVE-DYSKINESIA: RECENT
PATHOPHYSIOLOGICAL-DATA, THERAPEUTIC TRIALS.
000842 01-15
PATHOPHYSIOLOGICAL-STUDIES
PATHOPHYSIOLOGICAL-STUDIES ON SCHIZOPHRENIA WITH SPECIAL
REFERENCE TO HOMOVANILLIC-ACID CONCENTRATION IN
CEREBROSPINAL-FLUID.
000271 01-03
PATHWAY
EVIDENCE FOR A GABAERGIC NIGROTHALAMIC PATHWAY IN THE RAT: I.
BEHAVIOURAL-STUDIES AND BIOCHEMICAL-STUDIES.
000158 01-03
INTERACTIONS OF NEUROPEPTIDES WITH CHOLINERGIC
SEPTOHIPPOCAMPAL PATHWAY: INDICATION FOR A POSSIBLE
TRANSSYNAPTIC REGULATION. (UNPUBLISHED PAPER).
001062 02-01
GLYCINE ENHANCEMENT OF CAUDATE NEURONAL ACTIVITIES:
RELATIONSHIP WITH THE DOPAMINERGIC NIGROSTRIATAL PATHWAY.
001225 02-03
THE STRIATONIGRAL GABA PATHWAY: FUNCTIONAL AND
NEUROCHEMICAL CHARACTERISTICS IN RATS WITH UNILATERAL
STRIATAL KAINIC-ACID LESIONS.
001816 02-04
PHASIC ACTIVITY INDUCED BY P CHLOROPHENYLALANINE IN THE
AUDITORY PATHWAY.
002661 03-03
DOPAMINE AND DEMENTIA. AN ANIMAL-MODEL WITH DESTRUCTION OF
THE MESOCORTICAL DOPAMINERGIC PATHWAY: A PRELIMINARY
STUDY.
003085 03-04
DOPAMINE-RECEPTOR CHANGES FOLLOWING DESTRUCTION OF THE
NIGROSTRIATAL PATHWAY: LACK OF A RELATIONSHIP TO
ROTATIONAL-BEHAVIOR.
004229 04-04
PATHWAYS
IN VITRO AUTORADIOGRAPHY OF OPIATE-RECEPTORS IN RAT-BRAIN
SUGGESTS LOCI OF OPIATE-ERGIC PATHWAYS. (UNPUBLISHED PAPER).
001025 02-01
EFFECT OF ANTICONVULSANT-DRUGS ON INHIBITORY AND EXCITATORY
PATHWAYS.
002724 03-03
PATIENT
HOW TO SUCCESSFULLY CHANGE A PATIENT FROM ONE DRUG TO
ANOTHER.
000913 01-17
THE LITHIUM RATIO AS A GUIDE TO PATIENT COMPLIANCE.
000940 01-17
EDEMAS AND MYOCLONIES IN A PATIENT WITH PARKINSONS-DISEASE
TREATED BY AMANTADINE: PROBLEM WITH ASSOCIATED
MEDICATIONS.
002389 02-15
MONOAMINE-OXIDASE-INHIBITORS: PRESCRIPTION AND PATIENT
MANAGEMENT.
002454 02-15
FACTORS DETERMINING PATIENT TENURE ON A 3-YEAR DOUBLE-BLIND
INVESTIGATION OF PIMOZIDE VERSUS FLUPHENAZINE-HCL.
002513 02-17
COMPARISON OF STANDARD AND HOLTOR-MONITORED EKGS IN A
PATIENT TREATED WITH SEVERAL ANTIDEPRESSANTS.
003304 03-11
PHARMACOLOGIC CHARACTERIZATION AND LECITHIN TREATMENT OF A
PATIENT WITH SPONTANEOUS ORAL FACIAL DYSKINESIA AND
DEMENTIA.
003347 03-11

ARRHYTHMIA INDUCED BY A TRICYCLIC-ANTIDEPRESSANT IN A PATIENT
WITH UNDIAGNOSED MITRAL-VALVE PROLAPSE.
003521 03-15
LITHIUM KINETICS DURING HEMODIALYSIS IN A PATIENT WITH LITHIUM
POISONING.
003524 03-15
PATIENT CHARACTERISTICS AND CLINICIAN ATTITUDES INFLUENCING THE
PRESCRIBING OF BENZODIAZEPINES.
003598 03-17
ACCURACY OF PATIENT INTERVIEWS AND ESTIMATES BY CLINICAL STAFF
IN DETERMINING MEDICATION COMPLIANCE.
003618 03-17
THE INFLUENCE OF PATIENT BELIEFS ON COMPLIANCE TO THERAPY FOR
DIABETES-MELLITUS. (PH.D. DISSERTATION).
003631 03-17
FLURAZEPAM-INDUCED SLEEP-APNEA-SYNDROME IN A PATIENT WITH
INSOMNIA AND MILD SLEEP-RELATED RESPIRATORY CHANGES.
004729 04-17
PATIENTS
EEG IN PATIENTS TREATED WITH LITHIUM.
000593 01-09
COGNITIVE AND AFFECTIVE-FUNCTIONS IN PATIENTS WITH AFFECTIVE-
DISORDERS TREATED WITH LITHIUM: AN ASSESSMENT BY
QUESTIONNAIRE.
000604 01-09
IMPAIRED GLUCOSE TOLERANCE IN LONG-TERM LITHIUM TREATED
PATIENTS.
000611 01-09
THE USEFULNESS OF THE ERYTHROCYTE LITHIUM INDEX IN THE
EVALUATION OF DISORDERS OF ION-TRANSFER IN PATIENTS WITH
DEPRESSIVE-SYNDROMES.
000625 01-09
DECREASED UPTAKE OF 5 HYDROXYTRYPTAMINE IN BLOOD-PLATELETS
FROM PATIENTS WITH ENDOGENOUS DEPRESSION.
000637 01-09
ANTIDEPRESSIVE TREATMENT IN PARKINSONS-DISEASE: A CONTROLLED-
TRIAL OF THE EFFECT OF NORTRIPTYLINE IN PATIENTS WITH
PARKINSONS-DISEASE TREATED WITH L-DOPA.
000659 01-11
ELECTRORETINOGRAPHIC-CHANGES IN PATIENTS WITH PARKINSONISM
TREATED WITH VARIOUS CLASSES OF ANTIPARKINSONIAN-DRUGS.
000674 01-11
THE LONG-TERM RESULTS OF STEREOTAXIC SURGERY AND L-DOPA
THERAPY IN PATIENTS WITH PARKINSONS-DISEASE: A 10-YEAR
FOLLOWUP STUDY.
000693 01-11
SOCIAL AND CLINICAL SIGNIFICANCE OF DETERMINING THE BARBITURATE
LEVEL IN THE BLOOD SERUM OF PATIENTS TREATED WITH
ANTIEPILEPTIC-DRUGS.
000695 01-11
EFFICACY AND PATTERN VALENCE OF PSYCHOACTIVE-DRUGS: A NEW
METHOD OF COMPARING DRUGS APPLIED TO IDENTICAL PATIENTS IN
RANDOMIZED-ORDER.
000699 01-11
IDENTIFICATION OF A SUBGROUP OF TARDIVE-DYSKINESIA PATIENTS BY
PHARMACOLOGIC-PROBES.
000708 01-11
RAPID CONTROL OF ACUTE PATIENTS THROUGH THE ADMINISTRATION OF
HALOPERIDOL.
000818 01-14
ASSESSMENT OF MULTIVARIATE RELATIONSHIPS IN REACTIVITY OF
PATIENTS RECEIVING LITHIUM THERAPY.
000819 01-14
RENAL FUNCTION AND BIOPSY IN PATIENTS ON LITHIUM THERAPY.
000830 01-15
RENAL FUNCTION IN LITHIUM AND NONLITHIUM TREATED PATIENTS
WITH AFFECTIVE-DISORDERS.
000837 01-15
STRATEGY FOR THE STUDY OF PATIENTS AT HIGH-RISK FOR TARDIVE-
DYSKINESIA.
000858 01-15
AGITATION, DISORIENTATION, AND HALLUCINATIONS IN PATIENTS ON
CIMETIDINE: A REPORT OF THREE CASES AND LITERATURE REVIEW.
000896 01-15
ENDOCRINOLOGICAL CHANGES IN PATIENTS WITH SEXUAL-DYSFUNCTION
UNDER LONG-TERM NEUROLEPTIC TREATMENT.
000912 01-17
CONSIDER THIS ... PSYCHOTROPIC-MEDICATIONS AND THEIR EFFECTS ON
PATIENTS.
000967 01-17
ACTH4-10 AND MEMORY IN ECT TREATED AND UNTREATED PATIENTS. I.
EFFECT ON CONSOLIDATION.
001982 02-09
ACTH4-10 AND MEMORY IN ECT TREATED PATIENTS AND UNTREATED
CONTROLS. II. EFFECT ON RETRIEVAL.
001983 02-09
INCREASED VULNERABILITY TO CHOLINERGIC STIMULATION IN
AFFECTIVE-DISORDER PATIENTS.
002003 02-09

CLINICAL-CORRELATION, BIOCHEMICAL-CORRELATION, AND PSYCHOPHARMACOLOGICAL-CORRELATION IN PATIENTS WITH DEPRESSIVE-SYMPTOMATOLOGY.
002018 02-09

ELECTROENCEPHALOGRAPHIC-EFFECTS AND BEHAVIOURAL-EFFECTS OF SODIUM-VALPROATE IN PATIENTS WITH PHOTOSENSITIVE EPILEPSY. A SINGLE-DOSE TRIAL.
002154 02-11

CEEG STUDY ON PATIENTS UNDER THE PSYCHIATRIC-DRUG TREATMENT; THE CORRELATION BETWEEN EEG ALTERATION AND CLINICAL EVOLUTION.
002165 02-11

PHARMACOKINETICS OF DIPOTASSIUM-CHLORAZEPATE IN PATIENTS AFTER REPEATED 50MG ORAL DOSES.
002211 02-13

EFFECT OF OPIATES AND OPIATE ANTAGONISTS ON SOMATOSENSORY EVOKED-POTENTIALS IN PATIENTS WITH SCHIZOPHRENIA AND NORMAL ADULTS.
002222 02-13

SALIVARY IMMUNOGLOBULIN CONCENTRATIONS IN PATIENTS WITH EPILEPSY TREATED WITH CARBAMAZEPINE.
002234 02-13

METABOLISM OF DIMETHOXYMETHYL-PHENOBARBITAL (ETEROBARB) IN PATIENTS WITH EPILEPSY.
002235 02-13

ABNORMALITIES OF LITHIUM TRANSPORT IN PATIENTS WITH AFFECTIVE-DISORDERS.
002269 02-13

ORAL ALUMINUM AND NEUROPSYCHOLOGICAL FUNCTIONING: A STUDY OF DIALYSIS PATIENTS RECEIVING ALUMINUM-HYDROXIDE GELS.
002283 02-13

CORRECTION BY PROPRANOLOL OF THE ABNORMAL ADRENALINE DISCHARGE INDUCED BY EMOTIONAL-STRESS IN CEREBRAL HEMORRHAGE PATIENTS.
002295 02-13

EUHYPNOS-FORTE, HIGH-DOSE TEMAZEPAM FOR RESISTANT INSOMNIA: POSTMARKETING SURVEILLANCE IN 10,057 PATIENTS UNRESPONSIVE TO CONVENTIONAL HYPNOTIC DOSAGE.
002324 02-14

INTRAVENOUS CHLORIMIPRAMINE AFFECTS REM CYCLE IN PATIENTS WITH EXCESSIVE DAYTIME SLEEPINESS AND CONTROL SUBJECTS.
002341 02-14

BROMOCRIPTINE IN PARKINSONS-DISEASE: REPORT ON 106 PATIENTS TREATED FOR UP TO 5 YEARS.
002342 02-14

DEPRENYL IN THE MANAGEMENT OF RESPONSE FLUCTUATIONS IN PATIENTS WITH PARKINSONS-DISEASE ON LEVODOPA.
002358 02-14

EFFECTS OF CYCLOSPASMOL UPON SENSORY PARAMETERS IN PATIENTS RECOVERING FROM CEREBROVASCULAR-ACCIDENTS.
002360 02-14

SUBJECTIVE ASSESSMENT OF SEXUAL-DYSFUNCTION OF PATIENTS ON LONG-TERM ADMINISTRATION OF DIGOXIN.
002443 02-15

CLASSIFICATION OF DRUGS AND PATIENTS TO ACHIEVE MAXIMUM THERAPEUTIC RESPONSE.
002560 02-17

HYPOMANIA AS A STABLE STATE: LITHIUM PROPHYLAXIS IN TWO PATIENTS.
003212 03-09

STATISTICAL ANALYSES OF PHYSIOLOGIC DATA FROM FEMALE PATIENTS WITH AN ENDOMORPHOUS DEPRESSIVE COURSE: A TRIAL, INTERACTIONS BETWEEN PHYSIOLOGIC PARAMETERS, TEST JUNCTURES IN THIS PHASE.
003251 03-09

EFFECT OF LITHIUM ON PROLACTIN RESPONSES TO THYROTROPIN-RELEASING-HORMONE IN PATIENTS WITH MANIC-STATE.
003266 03-09

HYPNOTIC ACTION OF FLUNITRAZEPAM (ROCHES ROIPNOL) IN PATIENTS WITH SEVERE PSYCHIATRIC-DISORDERS.
003295 03-11

EFFICACY OF CLONIDINE IN OPIATE WITHDRAWAL: A STUDY OF THIRTY PATIENTS.
003317 03-11

THE USE OF LITHIUM-CARBONATE FOR TREATING KUGELBERG-WELANDER SPINAL AMYOTROPHY PATIENTS.
003326 03-11

A DOUBLE-BLIND, PLACEBO-CONTROLLED, CROSS-OVER TRIAL OF CARBAMAZEPINE IN OVERACTIVE, SEVERELY MENTALLY-HANDICAPPED PATIENTS.
003365 03-11

THE EFFECT OF AMANTADINE ON PROLACTIN LEVELS AND GALACTORRHEA ON NEUROLEPTIC TREATED PATIENTS.
003373 03-11

USE OF THA IN TREATMENT OF ALZHEIMER-LIKE DEMENTIA: PILOT-STUDY IN TWELVE PATIENTS.
003377 03-11

THE EFFECTS OF LECITHIN ON MEMORY IN PATIENTS WITH SENILE-DEMENTIA OF THE ALZHEIMERS-TYPE.
003385 03-11

PROPRANOLOL IN THE TREATMENT OF RAGE AND VIOLENT-BEHAVIOR IN PATIENTS WITH CHRONIC-BRAIN-SYNDROMES.
003394 03-11

EFFECT OF SODIUM-LACTATE ON PATIENTS WITH PANIC-DISORDER AND MITRAL-VALVE PROLAPSE.
003409 03-13

LEVELS OF 5 HYDROXYINDOLEACETIC-ACID AND TRYPTOPHAN IN LUMBAR CEREBROSPINAL-FLUID AND BLOOD OF PATIENTS WITH DEMENTIA AND NORMAL PRESSURE HYDROCEPHALUS AFTER TRYPTOPHAN ADMINISTRATION.
003419 03-13

THA -- A REVIEW OF THE LITERATURE AND ITS USE IN TREATMENT OF FIVE OVERDOSE PATIENTS.
003539 03-15

EFFECTS OF ANESTHESIA ON PATIENTS TAKING PSYCHOTROPIC-DRUGS.
003603 03-17

THE PROLACTIN RESPONSE IN PATIENTS RECEIVING NEUROLEPTIC THERAPY. THE EFFECT OF FLUPHENAZINE-DECANOATE.
004318 04-08

PRELIMINARY TRIAL OF CLONIDINE TREATMENT IN TWO PATIENTS SUFFERING FROM CHRONIC SCHIZOPHRENIA.
004320 04-08

DES-TYROSYL-GAMMA-ENDORPHIN IN SCHIZOPHRENIA: A DOUBLE-BLIND TRIAL IN 13 PATIENTS.
004322 04-08

PREVALENCE OF PERSISTENT ABNORMAL INVOLUNTARY-MOVEMENTS AMONG PATIENTS IN A NIGERIAN LONG-STAY PSYCHIATRIC UNIT.
004334 04-08

PLASMA LEVELS OF THE CIS-ISOMERS AND TRANS-ISOMERS OF DOXEPIN AND DESMETHYLDOXEPIN AFTER ADMINISTRATION OF DOXEPIN TO PATIENTS.
004355 04-09

THE EFFECT OF NALOXONE ON THE CONDITION OF PATIENTS WITH ENDOGENOUS PSYCHOSES.
004381 04-09

CEREBROSPINAL-FLUID VALUES OF HVA AND 5 HIAA IN PATIENTS WITH ENDOGENOUS DEPRESSION DURING THE COURSE OF TREATMENT.
004382 04-09

CORRECTION OF THE EXTRAPYRAMIDAL NEUROLEPTIC-SYNDROME BY TRYPTOPHAN AND THE TIME-COURSE OF ITS CONTENT IN THE BLOOD OF PATIENTS.
004434 04-11

METHADONE USE IN PATIENTS WITH CHRONIC RENAL-DISEASE.
004467 04-11

CLINICAL PHARMACOKINETICS OF CHLORDIAZEPOXIDE IN PATIENTS WITH ALCOHOLIC HEPATITIS.
004473 04-11

THE EFFICACY OF PIRACETAM IN VERTIGO: A DOUBLE-BLIND STUDY IN PATIENTS WITH VERTIGO OF CENTRAL ORIGIN.
004478 04-11

INFLUENCE OF CARBAMAZEPINE ON SERUM THYROXINE AND TRIIODOTHYRONINE IN PATIENTS WITH EPILEPSY.
004488 04-11

HORMONAL STIMULATION AFTER INJECTION OF THYROTROPHIN-RELEASING-FACTOR (TRF) AND ACTH1-24 IN PATIENTS FOLLOWING CHRONIC-TREATMENT WITH NEUROLEPTICS: PRELIMINARY-STUDY.
004505 04-13

PECULIARITIES OF THE CEREBRAL PATHOMORPHOLOGY OF PATIENTS WITH SCHIZOPHRENIA TREATED WITH PSYCHOTROPIC-DRUGS (PHARMACOLOGICAL PATHOMORPHOSIS).
004528 04-13

VARIATIONS IN URINARY LEVELS OF 3 METHOXY-4-HYDROXYPHENYLGLYCOL-SULFATE IN PATIENTS WITH DEPRESSIVE-SYNDROMES.
004533 04-13

THE ACTIVITY OF DOPAMINE-BETA-HYDROXYLASE IN THE PLASMA OF PATIENTS WITH ENDOGENOUS DEPRESSIVE-SYNDROMES.
004548 04-13

ACUTE EFFECT OF DRUGS UPON MEMORY OF PATIENTS WITH SENILE-DEMENTIA.
004561 04-14

CORRECTION OF HORMONAL ACTIVITY OF THE THYROID-GLAND AS A METHOD OF PATHOGENIC THERAPY IN A COMPREHENSIVE TREATMENT OF PATIENTS WITH TEMPORAL EPILEPSY.
004579 04-14

EFFECT OF LITHIUM ON GLYCINE LEVELS IN PATIENTS WITH AFFECTIVE-DISORDERS.
004606 04-15

KIDNEY FUNCTION IN PATIENTS WITH AFFECTIVE-DISORDERS WITH AND WITHOUT LITHIUM THERAPY.
004664 04-15

PATTERN
EFFICACY AND PATTERN VALENCE OF PSYCHOACTIVE-DRUGS: A NEW METHOD OF COMPARING DRUGS APPLIED TO IDENTICAL PATIENTS IN RANDOMIZED-ORDER.
000699 01-11

SENSORY PROCESSING, CARDIOVASCULAR REACTIVITY, AND THE TYPE A CORONARY-PRONE BEHAVIOR PATTERN.
003405 03-13

PATTERNED
POSSIBLE MUSCARINIC CHOLINERGIC MEDIATION OF PATTERNED
AGGRESSIVE REFLEXES IN THE CAT.
004153 04-04

PATTERNING
TEMPORAL PATTERNING OF NEURONAL ACTIVITY DURING THERMAL AND
NEUROCHEMICAL STIMULATION OF THE PREOPTIC/ANTERIOR
HYPOTHALAMUS OF THE AWAKE RABBIT.
002737 03-03

PATTERNS
CHRONIC USE OF TRIAZOLAM: THE EFFECTS ON THE SLEEP PATTERNS OF
INSOMNIACS.
000710 01-11

A NOTE ON PATTERNS OF DRUG PRESCRIBING IN A RESIDENTIAL-CENTER
FOR THE INTELLECTUALLY-HANDICAPPED.
000982 01-17

STRYCHNINE EFFECTS ON THE SENSORY RESPONSE PATTERNS OF
RETICULAR FORMATION NEURONS.
001219 02-03

SOME ODD PATTERNS OF PSYCHOTROPIC SELF-MEDICATION.
002565 02-17

PATTERNS OF USE IN THE INTAKE OF ORAL MEDICATION.
002591 02-17

CEREBROSPINAL-FLUID HOMOVANILLIC-ACID PATTERNS DURING
NEUROLEPTIC TREATMENT. (UNPUBLISHED PAPER).
004502 04-13

PAVING
PAVING THE WAY TO SAFE PRESCRIBING FOR THE ELDERLY.
000999 01-17

PAVLOVIAN-CONDITIONING
EFFECTS OF PAVLOVIAN-CONDITIONING AND MIF-1 ON THE
DEVELOPMENT OF MORPHINE-TOLERANCE IN RATS.
001327 02-03

PERIPHERAL AUTONOMIC-MECHANISMS AND PAVLOVIAN-CONDITIONING
IN THE RABBIT (ORYCTOLAGUS-CUNICULUS).
001560 02-04

PERIPHERAL 6 HYDROXYDOPAMINE ADMINISTRATION IN THE RABBIT
(ORYCTOLAGUS-CUNICULUS): EFFECTS ON PAVLOVIAN-CONDITIONING.
001668 02-04

PA2
ENHANCEMENT OF ETORPHINE BRAIN CONCENTRATIONS AND CHANGES
IN ETORPHINE NALOXONE PA2 VALUES IN MORPHINE PRETREATED
MICE.
002800 03-03

PC-63-14
STUDY OF THE EFFECTS OF PC-63-14 ON THE QUANTIFIED EEG.
003403 03-13

PCP
ISSUES FOR INPATIENT TREATMENT OF CHRONIC PCP ABUSE.
000736 01-12

HISTORY AND PHARMACOLOGY OF PCP AND PCP RELATED ANALOGS.
000737 01-12

THE PCP PSYCHOSIS: PROLONGED INTOXICATION OR DRUG PRECIPITATED
FUNCTIONAL ILLNESS?
000739 01-12

EPIDEMIOLOGY OF PCP ABUSE: THE MIDWEST PERSPECTIVE.
000740 01-12

THE EPIDEMIOLOGY OF PCP USE IN THE LATE 1970S.
000741 01-12

STREET PCP SCENE: ISSUES ON SYNTHESIS AND CONTAMINATION.
000744 01-12

PCP AND SEXUAL-DYSFUNCTION.
000745 01-12

PCP ABUSE: DIAGNOSTIC AND PSYCHOPHARMACOLOGICAL-TREATMENT
APPROACHES.
000746 01-12

OUTPATIENT TREATMENT ISSUES AND STRATEGIES FOR ACUTE AND
CHRONIC PCP ABUSERS.
000919 01-17

PARAPROFESSIONAL AND PROFESSIONAL TEAMWORK AND TRAINING IN
MANAGING PCP AND OTHER DRUG-ABUSE PROBLEMS.
000924 01-17

CHRONIC PHENCYCLIDINE (PCP) ABUSE: A PSYCHIATRIC-PERSPECTIVE.
000935 01-17

PCP AND VIOLENT CRIME: THE PEOPLE VS. PEACE.
000986 01-17

PHENCYCLIDINE (PCP) AND DERIVATIVES: PHARMACOLOGY AND
STRUCTURE-ACTIVITY RELATIONSHIPS.
001706 02-04

PHENCYCLIDINE (PCP) INTOXICATION: DIAGNOSIS IN STAGES AND
ALGORITHMS OF TREATMENT.
003525 03-15

ACUTE PHENCYCLIDINE (PCP) INTOXICATION: QUANTITATIVE URINE
LEVELS AND CLINICAL MANAGEMENT.
004665 04-15

PEACE
PCP AND VIOLENT CRIME: THE PEOPLE VS. PEACE.
000986 01-17

PECKING
EFFECTS OF APOMORPHINE ON ELICITED AND OPERANT PECKING IN
PIGEONS.
001557 02-04

PECKING-BEHAVIOR
APOMORPHINE: EFFECTS ON THE TIMING AND SEQUENCING OF PECKING-
BEHAVIOR IN CHICKS.
000428 01-04

PECULIARITIES
PHARMACOLOGICAL PECULIARITIES OF A BENZODIAZEPINE/ATARACTIC-
DRUG AND ITS THERAPEUTIC RELEVANCE: THE SPECIAL STATUS OF
CLORAZEPATE-DIPOTASSIUM (TRANXILIUM).
004527 04-13

PECULIARITIES OF THE CEREBRAL PATHOMORPHOLOGY OF PATIENTS
WITH SCHIZOPHRENIA TREATED WITH PSYCHOTROPIC-DRUGS
(PHARMACOLOGICAL PATHOMORPHOSIS).
004528 04-13

PEDIATRIC-PRACTICE
PSYCHOPHARMACEUTICALS IN PEDIATRIC-PRACTICE.
003491 03-15

PEDIATRIC-PSYCHOPHARMACOLOGY
CLASSIFICATION OF PSYCHOTROPIC-DRUGS IN PEDIATRIC-
PSYCHOPHARMACOLOGY.
001903 02-07

PEDIATRICS
CHILD-PSYCHIATRY AND PSYCHOPHARMACOTHERAPY IN GENERAL
PRACTICE, IN PEDIATRICS, AND IN NEUROLOGY.
003288 03-11

PELLET
ASSESSMENT OF TOLERANCE TO AND PHYSICAL-DEPENDENCE ON
PENTOBARBITAL, INDUCED BY MULTIPLE PELLET IMPLANTATION.
000385 01-04

A SILICONE PELLET FOR LONG-TERM CONTINUOUS ADMINISTRATION OF
AMPHETAMINE.
001875 02-06

PELLETS
ANALGESIC TOLERANCE PRODUCED BY MORPHINE PELLETS IS
FACILITATED BY ANALGESIC TESTING.
002943 03-04

ENVIRONMENTAL MODULATION OF ANALGESIC TOLERANCE INDUCED BY
MORPHINE PELLETS.
002944 03-04

PEMOLINE
THE USE OF SENSORY INTEGRATIVE DIAGNOSTICS TO PREDICT
HYPERACTIVE-CHILDRENS RESPONSIVENESS TO METHYLPHENIDATE
(RITALIN) AND PEMOLINE (CYLERT). (PH.D. DISSERTATION).
002133 02-11

GILLES-DE-LA-TOURETTES-DISORDER ASSOCIATED WITH PEMOLINE.
002436 02-15

PEMOLINE-INDUCED
PEMOLINE-INDUCED SELF-BITING IN RATS AND SELF-MUTILATION IN THE
DELANGE-SYNDROME.
001727 02-04

PEMOLINE-INDUCED CHOREA.
003516 03-15

PENETRATION
OXAZEPAM-ESTERS. 2. CORRELATION OF HYDROPHOBICITY WITH SERUM
BINDING, BRAIN PENETRATION, AND EXCRETION.
000011 01-02

PENFLURIDOL
INCREASED MESOLIMBIC 3H SPIROPERIDOL BINDING IN 4 WEEK OLD
OFFSPRING OF NURSING RAT MOTHERS TREATED WITH PENFLURIDOL.
000087 01-03

PLASMA PROLACTIN AND TESTOSTERONE DURING PENFLURIDOL
TREATMENT.
000874 01-15

PENFLURIDOL IN THE TREATMENT OF GILLES-DE-LA-TOURETTES-
SYNDROME.
002158 02-11

PENICILLIN-INDUCED
ELECTRICAL-ACTIVITY AND NA-K-ATPASE LEVEL IN THE PENICILLIN-
INDUCED EPILEPTOGENIC-FOCUS OF THE RAT-BRAIN-CORTEX, AND THE
EFFECT OF DIAZEPAM.
003070 03-04

PENILE-TUMESCENCE
DISULFIRAM AND NOCTURNAL PENILE-TUMESCENCE IN THE CHRONIC
ALCOHOLIC.
004556 04-13

PENTAGASTRIN-STIMULATED
INHIBITION OF PENTAGASTRIN-STIMULATED AND OVERNIGHT GASTRIC
SECRETION BY LM24056, A NEW PHENOTHIAZINE DERIVED
ANTISECRETORY DRUG.
004306 04-07

PENTAZOCINE
INHIBITION OF GROWTH IN YOUNG MICE TREATED WITH PENTAZOCINE:
REVERSAL BY NALTREXONE.
000318 01-03

EFFECTS OF CENTRALLY-ADMINISTERED PENTAZOCINE AND
ETHYLKETOCYCLAZOCINE ON THERMOREGULATION IN THE CAT.
000361 01-04

THE ANALGESIC AND RESPIRATORY EFFECTS OF MEPTAZINOL, MORPHINE
AND PENTAZOCINE IN THE RAT.
000516 01-05

POTENTIATION OF LETHALITY IN MICE BY COMBINATIONS OF PENTAZOCINE AND TRIPELENNAMINE.
000529 01-05

MEDICAL AND PSYCHIATRIC-COMPLICATIONS OF PENTAZOCINE AND TRIPELENNAMINE ABUSE.
000955 01-17

EFFECTS OF MORPHINE, PENTAZOCINE AND CYCLAZOCINE ALONE AND IN COMBINATION WITH NALOXONE ON ELECTRIC-SHOCK TITRATION IN THE SQUIRREL-MONKEY.
001611 02-04

ANTINOCICEPTIVE ACTION OF MORPHINE AND PENTAZOCINE ON UNIT ACTIVITY IN THE NUCLEUS-CENTRALIS-LATERALIS, NUCLEUS-VENTRALIS-LATERALIS AND NEARBY STRUCTURES OF THE CAT.
002837 03-03

EFFECTS OF PENTAZOCINE AND NALORPHINE ON MOTILITY IN CHRONICALLY MORPHINE TREATED RATS: A POTENTIAL SUBSTITUTION TEST TO DETECT THE NARCOTIC CHARACTER OF A DRUG.
003555 03-16

ANTAGONISM BY PHENOXYBENZAMINE AND PENTAZOCINE OF THE ANTINOCICEPTIVE-EFFECTS OF MORPHINE IN THE SPINAL-CORD.
004213 04-04

PENTIFYLLINE
THE INFLUENCE OF PENTIFYLLINE AND THEOPHYLLINE ON REACTION KINETICS OF CATECHOLAMINE STIMULATED ATPASE FROM RAT-BRAIN.
001052 02-01

PENTOBARBITAL
A COMPARISON OF HUMAN TACTILE STIMULUS VELOCITY DISCRIMINATION WITH THE ABILITY OF S-I CORTICAL NEURONS IN AWAKE RHESUS-MONKEYS TO SIGNAL THE SAME VELOCITY DIFFERENCES BEFORE AND AFTER NONANESTHETIC DOSES OF PENTOBARBITAL.
000055 01-03

BEHAVIOR-DEPENDENT EVOKED-POTENTIALS IN THE HIPPOCAMPAL-CA1 REGION OF THE RAT. II. EFFECTS OF ESERINE, ATROPINE, ETHER AND PENTOBARBITAL.
000184 01-03

(-)PENTOBARBITAL OPENS ION-CHANNELS OF LONG-DURATION IN CULTURED MOUSE SPINAL NEURONS.
000198 01-03

PENTOBARBITAL POTENTIATES GABA-ENHANCED (3H) DIAZEPAM BINDING TO BENZODIAZEPINE-RECEPTORS.
000275 01-03

ALTERATION OF PHARMACOKINETIC PARAMETERS FOR PENTOBARBITAL BY ISCHEMIC STROKE AND REVERSION TO NORMAL BY DEXAMETHASONE TREATMENT.
000321 01-03

TOLERANCE TO SUPPRESSIVE EFFECTS OF CHLORDIAZEPOXIDE ON OPERANT-BEHAVIOR: LACK OF CROSS-TOLERANCE TO PENTOBARBITAL.
000356 01-04

ASSESSMENT OF TOLERANCE TO AND PHYSICAL-DEPENDENCE ON PENTOBARBITAL, INDUCED BY MULTIPLE PELLET IMPLANTATION.
000385 01-04

JOINT-EFFECTS OF D-AMPHETAMINE AND ETHANOL OR PENTOBARBITAL IN PIGEONS.
000403 01-04

IMPROVEMENT OF RESTITUTION FROM CEREBRAL ISCHEMIA IN HYPERGLYCEMIC RATS BY PENTOBARBITAL OR DIAZEPAM.
000475 01-04

IMPAIRMENT OF AVOIDANCE-BEHAVIOR FOLLOWING SHORT-TERM INGESTION OF ETHANOL, TERTIARY BUTANOL, OR PENTOBARBITAL IN MICE.
000479 01-04

A COMPARISON OF THE EFFECTS OF D-AMPHETAMINE, COCAINE, IMIPRAMINE AND PENTOBARBITAL ON LOCAL AND OVERALL RATES OF RESPONDING MAINTAINED UNDER A FOUR-COMPONENT MULTIPLE FIXED-INTERVAL SCHEDULE.
000508 01-04

AUTOCORRELATION ANALYSIS OF SINGLE NEURON ACTIVITY AFTER ADMINISTRATION OF PENTOBARBITAL.
001268 02-03

EFFECTS OF MORPHINE, D-AMPHETAMINE, AND PENTOBARBITAL ON SHOCK AND LIGHT DISCRIMINATION PERFORMANCE IN RATS.
001639 02-04

DISCRIMINATIVE-STIMULUS EFFECTS OF PENTOBARBITAL IN PIGEONS.
001651 02-04

THE EFFECTS OF D-AMPHETAMINE, CHLORDIAZEPOXIDE, AND PENTOBARBITAL ON BEHAVIOR MAINTAINED BY ESCAPE FROM PUNISHMENT IN PIGEONS. (PH.D. DISSERTATION).
001713 02-04

EFFECTS OF PHENCYCLIDINE, PENTOBARBITAL, AND D-AMPHETAMINE ON THE ACQUISITION AND PERFORMANCE OF CONDITIONAL DISCRIMINATIONS IN MONKEYS.
001723 02-04

GABA-RECEPTORS AND THE DEPRESSANT ACTION OF PENTOBARBITAL.
002666 03-03

A COMPARISON OF THE EFFECTS OF PENTOBARBITAL AND DIPHENYLHYDANTOIN ON THE GABA SENSITIVITY AND EXCITABILITY OF ADULT SENSORY GANGLION CELLS.
002692 03-03

PENTOBARBITAL: DUAL-ACTIONS TO INCREASE BRAIN BENZODIAZEPINE-RECEPTOR AFFINITY.
002896 03-03

OPIATE-RECEPTORS AND SLEEP. II. EFFECTS OF MICROINJECTIONS OF ETHYL-ALCOHOL AND PENTOBARBITAL IN THE MEDIAN THALAMUS, PERIAQUEDUCTAL GRAY MATTER AND NUCLEUS-TRACTUS-SOLITARIUS OF THE RABBIT.
002917 03-03

A COMPARATIVE-STUDY ON THE CLINICAL-EFFECTS OF RECTAL DIAZEPAM AND PENTOBARBITAL ON SMALL CHILDREN. RELATIONSHIP BETWEEN PLASMA LEVEL AND EFFECT.
003330 03-11

EFFECT OF FLURAZEPAM, PENTOBARBITAL, AND CAFFEINE ON AROUSAL THRESHOLD.
003439 03-14

EFFECTS OF PENTOBARBITAL AND ETHANOL UPON SINGLE NEURON ACTIVITY IN THE PRIMARY SOMATOSENSORY CORTEX OF THE RHESUS-MONKEY.
003755 04-03

EFFECT OF P CHLOROPHENYLALANINE ON THE ACQUISITION OF TOLERANCE TO THE HYPNOTIC-EFFECTS OF PENTOBARBITAL, BARBITAL, AND ETHANOL.
003883 04-03

DIFFERENTIAL-EFFECTS OF PENTOBARBITAL AND ETHER ON THE SYNAPTIC TRANSMISSION OF THE HIPPOCAMPAL-CA1-REGION IN THE RAT.
003903 04-03

HISTAMINE AS A PUNISHER IN SQUIRREL-MONKEYS: EFFECTS OF PENTOBARBITAL, CHLORDIAZEPOXIDE AND H1-RECEPTOR AND H2-RECEPTOR ANTAGONISTS ON BEHAVIOR AND CARDIOVASCULAR RESPONSE.
004119 04-04

DRUG PREFERENCE IN HUMANS: DOUBLE-BLIND CHOICE COMPARISON OF PENTOBARBITAL, DIAZEPAM AND PLACEBO.
004566 04-14

PENTOBARBITAL-INDUCED
NALOXONE REVERSAL OF THE PENTOBARBITAL-INDUCED BLOCKADE OF OVULATION IN THE RAT.
002817 03-03

PENTOBARBITONE
FREE DESCRIPTION OF DRUG-EFFECTS AS A METHOD OF CLINICAL-TRIAL, PRESENTED BY THE EXAMPLE OF PENTOBARBITONE, PROMAZINE AND THEIR COMBINATION.
002561 02-17

PENTOBARBITONE-INDUCED
THE EFFECT OF FLA-63 ON PENTOBARBITONE-INDUCED SLEEP IN THE CHICK.
001741 02-04

PENTYLAMINE
N PENTYLAMINE: EFFECT ON MOTOR-ACTIVITY OF MICE.
000500 01-04

PENTYLENETETRAZOL
DISSIMILAR EFFECTS OF NICOTINAMIDE AND INOSINE, PUTATIVE ENDOGENOUS LIGANDS OF THE BENZODIAZEPINE-RECEPTORS, ON PENTYLENETETRAZOL SEIZURES IN FOUR STRAINS OF MICE.
000173 01-03

PENTYLENETETRAZOL SEIZURE THRESHOLD: A QUANTITATIVE MEASURE OF ETHANOL DEPENDENCE IN RATS.
001750 02-04

THE ANXIOMIMETIC PROPERTIES OF PENTYLENETETRAZOL IN THE RAT. (PH.D. DISSERTATION).
003092 03-04

SPECIFIC AND NONSPECIFIC MULTIPLE UNIT ACTIVITIES DURING PENTYLENETETRAZOL SEIZURES. I. ANIMALS WITH ENCEPHALE ISOLE.
004046 04-03

RELATIONSHIP BETWEEN PENTYLENETETRAZOL-INDUCED SEIZURES AND BRAIN PENTYLENETETRAZOL LEVELS IN MICE.
004061 04-03

ON SOME RELATIONSHIPS BETWEEN GABAERGIC AND 5 HT-ERGIC MECHANISMS IN PENTYLENETETRAZOL CONVULSIVE-SEIZURE REACTIONS.
004166 04-04

PENTYLENETETRAZOL-INDUCED
EFFECTS OF KINDLING OR BRAIN-STIMULATION ON PENTYLENETETRAZOL-INDUCED CONVULSION SUSCEPTIBILITY.
000037 01-03

INCORPORATION OF N ACETYLMANNOSAMINE INTO RAT-BRAIN SUBCELLULAR GANGLIOSIDES: EFFECT OF PENTYLENETETRAZOL-INDUCED CONVULSIONS IN BRAIN GANGLIOSIDES.
002937 03-03

RELATIONSHIP BETWEEN PENTYLENETETRAZOL-INDUCED SEIZURES AND BRAIN PENTYLENETETRAZOL LEVELS IN MICE.
004061 04-03

PEOPLE
PCP AND VIOLENT CRIME: THE PEOPLE VS. PEACE.
000986 01-17

PEPTIC-ULCERS
STUDIES ON THE COMPREHENSIVE MEDICAL TREATMENT OF PEPTIC-ULCERS (3) — UTILIZATION OF TRANQUILIZERS IN THE TREATMENT OF GASTRIC-ULCERS.
000653 01-10

PEPTIDE
BIOCHEMICAL-CHARACTERIZATION AND PHARMACOLOGICAL CHARACTERIZATION OF A PEPTIDE FROM THE HEMODIALYSATE OF PSYCHOTIC-PATIENTS.
001049 02-01
EFFECTS OF AN ACTH4-9 RELATED PEPTIDE UPON INTRACRANIAL SELF-STIMULATION AND GENERAL-ACTIVITY IN THE RAT.
001679 02-04
OPIATE AND PEPTIDE INTERACTION: EFFECT OF ENKEPHALINS ON MORPHINE ANALGESIA.
001698 02-04
TRIAL OF A PEPTIDE FRACTION OF ACTH (ACTH4-10) IN THE ALCOHOLIC BRAIN-DAMAGE-SYNDROME.
002318 02-14
STIMULATION OF RETINAL ADENYLATE-CYCLASE BY VASOACTIVE INTESTINAL PEPTIDE (VIP).
002811 03-03
DYNORPHIN: A POSSIBLE MODULATORY PEPTIDE ON MORPHINE OR BETA ENDORPHIN ANALGESIA IN MOUSE.
002994 03-04
ALTERATIONS OF EVOKED-POTENTIALS LINK RESEARCH IN ATTENTION-DYSFUNCTION TO PEPTIDE RESPONSE SYMPTOMS OF SCHIZOPHRENIA.
004316 04-08

PEPTIDE-HORMONES
EXTRAHYPOTHALAMIC DISTRIBUTIONS AND FUNCTIONS OF HYPOTHALAMIC PEPTIDE-HORMONES. (UNPUBLISHED PAPER).
001211 02-03
ON MONOAMINERGIC-INTERACTION WITH BEHAVIOUR MODIFYING PEPTIDE-HORMONES.
004700 04-17

PEPTIDERGIC
CENTRAL AMINERGIC AND PEPTIDERGIC MECHANISMS IN SPONTANEOUSLY (GENETIC) HYPERTENSIVE-RATS. (UNPUBLISHED PAPER).
001459 02-03

PEPTIDES
EFFECTS OF CHOLECYSTOKININ-LIKE PEPTIDES ON REARING ACTIVITY AND HEXOBARBITAL-INDUCED SLEEP.
000507 01-04
PEPTIDES IN NEUROBIOLOGY: AN OVERVIEW. (UNPUBLISHED PAPER).
001008 02-01
INTERACTIONS BETWEEN MORPHINE AND THE OPIOID-LIKE PEPTIDES IN THE RAT VAS-DEFERENS.
001290 02-03
STUDIES ON THE EFFECT OF ALPHA MELANOCYTE-STIMULATING-HORMONE AND RELATED PEPTIDES ON THE ACCUMULATION OF P AMINOHIPPURIC-ACID IN RENAL CORTICAL SLICES. (UNPUBLISHED PAPER).
001372 02-03
COMPARATIVE-STUDY ON THE EFFECT OF MORPHINE AND THE OPIOID-LIKE PEPTIDES IN THE VAS-DEFERENS OF RODENTS: STRAIN AND SPECIES-DIFFERENCES, EVIDENCE FOR MULTIPLE OPIATE-RECEPTORS.
002757 03-03
THE EFFECTS OF PEPTIDES ON TOLERANCE TO THE CATALEPTIC-EFFECTS AND HYPOTHERMIC-EFFECTS OF MORPHINE IN THE RAT.
004072 04-04
ACTH-LIKE PEPTIDES, PITUITARY ADRENOCORTICAL FUNCTION AND AVOIDANCE-BEHAVIOR.
004109 04-04

PERAZINE
THE CONTRIBUTION OF ALPHA1 ACID GLYCOPROTEIN, LIPOPROTEINS, AND ALBUMIN TO THE PLASMA BINDING OF PERAZINE, AMITRIPTYLINE, AND NORTRIPTYLINE IN HEALTHY MAN.
002214 02-13
BINDING OF PERAZINE TO ALPHA1 ACID GLYCOPROTEIN.
002290 02-13

PERCEPTUAL-EFFECTS
AN ANALYSIS OF SOME PERCEPTUAL-EFFECTS OF MORPHINE, CHLORPROMAZINE, AND LSD.
001652 02-04

PERFORMANCE
EFFECTS OF CHLORDIAZEPOXIDE AND DIAZEPAM ON FEEDING PERFORMANCE IN A FOOD PREFERENCE TEST.
000367 01-04
EFFECTS OF APOMORPHINE ON ESCAPE PERFORMANCE AND ACTIVITY IN DEVELOPING RAT PUPS TREATED WITH 6 HYDROXYDOPAMINE (6 OHDA).
000426 01-04
OPEN-FIELD PERFORMANCE OF RATS AFTER ENDOTOXIN TREATMENT.
000473 01-04
AROUSAL AND SHORT-TERM MEMORY: EFFECTS OF CAFFEINE AND TRIAL SPACING ON DELAYED ALTERNATION PERFORMANCE.
000487 01-04
THE INFLUENCE OF LITHIUM-CARBONATE ON MOOD AND PERFORMANCE IN HEALTHY SUBJECTS.
000711 01-11

THE DIFFERENTIAL-EFFECTS OF SHORT-ACTING AND LONG-ACTING BENZODIAZEPINES UPON NOCTURNAL SLEEP AND DAYTIME PERFORMANCE.
000822 01-14
THE EFFECTS OF DELTA9 TETRAHYDROCANNABINOL ALONE AND IN COMBINATION WITH CANNABIDIOL ON FIXED-INTERVAL PERFORMANCE IN RHESUS-MONKEYS.
001582 02-04
SWIMMING CAPACITY OF MICE AFTER PROLONGED TREATMENT WITH PSYCHOSTIMULANTS: II. EFFECT OF METHAMPHETAMINE ON SWIMMING PERFORMANCE AND AVAILABILITY OF METABOLIC SUBSTRATES.
001613 02-04
EFFECTS OF MORPHINE, D-AMPHETAMINE, AND PENTOBARBITAL ON SHOCK AND LIGHT DISCRIMINATION PERFORMANCE IN RATS.
001639 02-04
INFLUENCE OF INTRAVENOUS SELF-ADMINISTERED PSYCHOMOTOR STIMULANTS ON PERFORMANCE OF RHESUS-MONKEYS IN A MULTIPLE-SCHEDULE PARADIGM.
001655 02-04
EFFECTS OF PHENCYCLIDINE, PENTOBARBITAL, AND D-AMPHETAMINE ON THE ACQUISITION AND PERFORMANCE OF CONDITIONAL DISCRIMINATIONS IN MONKEYS.
001723 02-04
DRUG-EFFECTS ON THE PERFORMANCE OF PIGEONS UNDER A NEGATIVE AUTOMAINTENANCE-SCHEDULE.
001754 02-04
GO-HERE-GO-THERE PERFORMANCE AFTER AMPHETAMINE: THE IMPORTANCE OF THE RESPONSE REQUIREMENT IN SUCCESSIVE DISCRIMINATION.
001759 02-04
EFFECTS OF PIMOZIDE ON ACCURACY OF PERFORMANCE AND DISTRIBUTION OF CORRECT RESPONDING ON A SIMULTANEOUS DISCRIMINATION TASK IN THE RAT.
001806 02-04
INTERCANNABINOID AND CANNABINOID ETHANOL INTERACTIONS AND THEIR EFFECTS ON HUMAN PERFORMANCE.
002193 02-12
THE EFFECTS OF TRIAZOLAM AND NITRAZEPAM ON SLEEP QUALITY, MORNING VIGILANCE, AND PSYCHOMOTOR PERFORMANCE.
002330 02-14
THE EFFECTS OF COMBINED SEDATIVE AND ANXIOLYTIC-PREPARATIONS ON SUBJECTIVE ASPECTS OF SLEEP AND OBJECTIVE MEASURE OF AROUSAL AND PERFORMANCE THE MORNING FOLLOWING NOCTURNAL MEDICATION: II. REPEATED DOSES.
002331 02-14
PERSONALITY TRAIT AND ANTIANXIETY-DRUG EFFECTS ON PSYCHOMOTOR PERFORMANCE.
002336 02-14
THE EFFECTS OF ALCOHOL AND CAFFEINE ON CONCENTRATION TEST PERFORMANCE.
002337 02-14
EFFECTS OF ATENOLOL AND PROPRANOLOL ON HUMAN PERFORMANCE AND SUBJECTIVE FEELINGS.
002340 02-14
EFFECTS OF AMPHETAMINE ON VIGILANCE PERFORMANCE IN NORMAL AND HYPERACTIVE-CHILDREN.
002359 02-14
EFFECTS OF IMIPRAMINE ON LEFT VENTRICULAR PERFORMANCE IN CHILDREN.
002385 02-15
EFFECTS OF LITHIUM ON EVOKED-POTENTIALS AND PERFORMANCE DURING SUSTAINED ATTENTION.
002419 02-15
EFFECTS OF THIORIDAZINE (MELLARIL) ON TITRATING DELAYED MATCHING-TO-SAMPLE PERFORMANCE IN MENTALLY-RETARDED ADULTS.
002471 02-15
A SIMPLE SYSTEM FOR CONTROL OF THE CONTINUOUS PERFORMANCE TEST IN PSYCHOPHARMACOLOGICAL-RESEARCH.
002474 02-16
EFFECTS OF THIORIDAZINE (MELLARIL) ON TITRATING DELAYED MATCHING-TO-SAMPLE PERFORMANCE OF MENTALLY-RETARDED ADULTS.
003392 03-11
THE EFFECTS OF TRICYCLIC-ANTIDEPRESSANTS ON PERFORMANCE UNDER A DIFFERENTIAL-REINFORCEMENT-OF-LOW-RATES SCHEDULE IN RATS.
004175 04-04
THERAPEUTIC TREATMENT OF INSUFFICIENT PERFORMANCE IN CEREBROVASCULAR-DISEASES.
004718 04-17

PERFUSED
EFFECT OF DESMETHYLIMIPRAMINE ON THE KINETICS OF CHLORPHENTERMINE ACCUMULATION IN ISOLATED PERFUSED RAT LUNG.
000524 01-05
EFFECTS OF AMITRIPTYLINE AND CLOMIPRAMINE IN THE ISOLATED, PERFUSED RABBIT HEART.
001852 02-05

COCAINE AND AMPHETAMINE ANTAGONIZE THE DECREASE OF
NORADRENERGIC NEUROTRANSMISSION ELICITED BY OXYMETAZOLINE
BUT POTENTIATE THE INHIBITION BY ALPHA METHYLNOREPINEPHRINE
IN THE PERFUSED CAT SPLEEN.
002801 03-03

CHARACTERIZATION OF THE ISOLATED PERFUSED MOUSE-BRAIN AS A
SYSTEM FOR NEUROCHEMICAL-STUDIES.
003146 03-06

A COMPARISON OF THE RESPONSES TO SOME DOPAMINE-RECEPTOR
AGONISTS AND ANTAGONISTS IN THE ISOLATED PERFUSED RAT
KIDNEY.
004054 04-03

PERFUSION
THE EFFECTS OF NOREPINEPHRINE PERFUSION OF THE MESENCEPHALIC
RETICULAR FORMATION ON BEHAVIOR IN THE RAT: INTERACTION
WITH SEVERAL NEUROLEPTIC-DRUGS ON A MEASURE OF SUSTAINED
ATTENTION. (PH.D. DISSERTATION).
001563 02-04

STUDIES ON GABA RELEASE IN VIVO USING A SIMPLE METHOD FOR
PERFUSION OF THE FOURTH VENTRICLE OF THE RAT.
001881 02-06

TRANSIENT HYPERKINESIA AFTER A SINGLE INTRAVENOUS PERFUSION OF
DIPHENYLHYDANTOIN: REPORT OF A CASE ASSOCIATED WITH
NONTOXIC PLASMA LEVELS OF DIPHENYLHYDANTOIN.
004638 04-15

PERGOLIDE
STIMULATION OF ADENYLATE-CYCLASE IN RAT STRIATUM BY
PERGOLIDE: INFLUENCE OF GTP.
001448 02-03

PERGOLIDE, A POTENT LONG-ACTING DOPAMINE-RECEPTOR AGONIST.
002257 02-13

PERGOLIDE-MESYLATE
BINDING OF (3H)PERGOLIDE-MESYLATE TO DOPAMINE-RECEPTORS OF
MAMMALIAN BRAINS.
001538 02-03

PERIAQUEDUCTAL
MORPHINE INJECTIONS INTO THE PERIAQUEDUCTAL PERIVENTRICULAR
GRAY ATTENUATE SEPTAL HYPERREACTIVITY.
000390 01-04

INCREASED METABOLISM OF DOPAMINE AND SEROTONIN INDUCED IN
FOREBRAIN AREAS BY ETORPHINE MICROINJECTION IN
PERIAQUEDUCTAL GRAY.
001103 02-03

OPIATE-RECEPTORS AND SLEEP. II. EFFECTS OF MICROINJECTIONS OF
ETHYL-ALCOHOL AND PENTOBARBITAL IN THE MEDIAN THALAMUS,
PERIAQUEDUCTAL GRAY MATTER AND NUCLEUS-TRACTUS-SOLITARIUS
OF THE RABBIT.
002917 03-03

DOSE-RESPONSE STUDY OF THE PRECIPITATED ABSTINENCE-SYNDROME
FOR MORPHINE: SYSTEMIC VS PERIAQUEDUCTAL GRAY NALOXONE.
(PH.D. DISSERTATION).
002979 03-04

EFFECT OF CHRONIC MORPHINE TREATMENT ON THE INTERACTION
BETWEEN THE PERIAQUEDUCTAL GREY AND THE NUCLEUS-RAPHE-
MAGNUS OF THE RAT.
003727 04-03

PERIKARYA
SYNTHESIS OF CYTOSKELETAL PROTEINS IN BULK ISOLATED NEURONAL
PERIKARYA.
003672 04-01

PERINATAL
EFFECTS OF PERINATAL THYROXINE AND/OR CORTICOSTERONE
TREATMENT ON THE ONTOGENESIS OF HYPOTHALAMIC AND
MESENCEPHALIC NOREPINEPHRINE AND DOPAMINE CONTENT.
000180 01-03

INTERACTIVE-EFFECTS OF NUTRITION AND CANNABIS UPON RAT
PERINATAL DEVELOPMENT.
000513 01-05

PERINATAL NEUROLEPTIC ACTIONS -- DEVELOPMENTAL RESULTS.
(UNPUBLISHED PAPER).
001277 02-03

PERINATAL EFFECTS OF PSYCHOTROPIC-DRUGS: THE ANTICONVULSANT-
DRUG DIPHENYLHYDANTOIN. (UNPUBLISHED PAPER).
001842 02-05

PERIODICAL
THE LONG-TERM-TREATMENT OF PERIODICAL AND CYCLIC DEPRESSIONS
WITH FLUPENTHIXOL-DECANOATE.
000603 01-09

PERIODICITY
SLEEP PROFILE AND ULTRADIAN SLEEP PERIODICITY IN HUMANS UNDER
THE INFLUENCE OF A BUTYROPHENONE DERIVATIVE: I. SLEEP
CORRECTION IN SUBJECTS WITH OLIGOSYMPTOMATIC SLEEP-
DISORDERS.
001869 02-06

PERIODS
CRITICAL PERIODS FOR DIPHENYLHYDANTOIN AND PHENOBARBITAL
ADMINISTRATION DURING GESTATION.
001630 02-04

PERIORAL
ACTIVATION AND LATERALIZATION OF SENSORIMOTOR FIELD FOR
PERIORAL BITING-REFLEX BY INTRANIGRAL GABA AGONIST AND BY
SYSTEMIC APOMORPHINE IN THE RAT.
001657 02-04

PERIPHERAL
THE ETIOLOGY OF TOXIC PERIPHERAL NEUROPATHIES: IN VITRO EFFECTS
OF ACRYLAMIDE AND 2,5 HEXANEDIONE ON BRAIN ENOLASE AND
OTHER GLYCOLYTIC ENZYMES.
000131 01-03

A COMPARISON OF RATES OF DEPLETION AND RECOVERY OF
NORADRENALINE STORES OF PERIPHERAL AND CENTRAL
NORADRENERGIC NEURONES AFTER RESERPINE ADMINISTRATION:
IMPORTANCE OF NEURONAL ACTIVITY.
000314 01-03

PERIPHERAL ALPHA-ADRENERGIC-RECEPTOR SUBTYPES.
000901 01-16

RECEPTOR BINDING INTERACTIONS OF THE ANGIOTENSIN-II ANTAGONIST,
125I SARCOSINE1-LEUCINE8-ANGIOTENSIN-II, WITH MAMMALIAN
BRAIN AND PERIPHERAL TISSUES.
001125 02-03

PERIPHERAL CATECHOLAMINES AND MEMORY MODULATION.
(UNPUBLISHED PAPER).
001251 02-03

PERIPHERAL PRESYNAPTIC AND POSTSYNAPTIC DOPAMINE-RECEPTORS:
ARE THEY DIFFERENT FROM DOPAMINE-RECEPTORS IN THE CENTRAL-
NERVOUS-SYSTEM.
001252 02-03

COMPARED PROPERTIES OF CENTRAL AND PERIPHERAL BINDING-SITES
FOR PHENCYCLIDINE.
001521 02-03

PERIPHERAL AUTONOMIC-MECHANISMS AND PAVLOVIAN-CONDITIONING
IN THE RABBIT (ORYCTOLAGUS-CUNICULUS).
001560 02-04

PERIPHERAL 6 HYDROXYDOPAMINE ADMINISTRATION IN THE RABBIT
(ORYCTOLAGUS-CUNICULUS): EFFECTS ON PAVLOVIAN-CONDITIONING.
001668 02-04

THE PERIPHERAL ANTICHOLINERGIC-ACTIVITY OF TRICYCLIC-
ANTIDEPRESSANTS: COMPARISON OF AMITRIPTYLINE AND
DESIPRAMINE IN HUMAN VOLUNTEERS.
002298 02-13

COMPARATIVE-STUDIES OF L-DOPA ALONE AND COMBINATION WITH A
PERIPHERAL DOPA-DECARBOXYLASE INHIBITOR, BENSERAZIDE-HCL, ON
PARKINSONS-DISEASE -- PART II. PHARMACOKINETIC-STUDY.
002309 02-13

THE ROLE OF FOLATE DEFICIENCY IN THE DEVELOPMENT OF PERIPHERAL
NEUROPATHY CAUSED BY ANTICONVULSANTS.
002402 02-15

CENTRAL AND PERIPHERAL CATECHOLAMINE FUNCTION IN LEARNING
AND MEMORY PROCESSES.
002823 03-03

EFFECTS OF ACUTE CENTRAL AND PERIPHERAL ACTH1-24
ADMINISTRATION ON LORDOSIS BEHAVIOR.
002975 03-04

EFFECTS OF METHYSERGIDE AND NALOXONE ON ANALGESIA INDUCED BY
THE PERIPHERAL ELECTRIC-STIMULATION IN MICE.
003093 03-04

THE HYPERACTIVE-CHILD-SYNDROME: PERIPHERAL SYMPATHETIC-
NERVOUS-SYSTEM FUNCTION AND THE EFFECT OF D-AMPHETAMINE.
003340 03-11

PERIPHERAL NEUROPATHY DUE TO LITHIUM INTOXICATION.
003544 03-15

OPIOID BINDING PROPERTIES OF BRAIN AND PERIPHERAL TISSUES:
EVIDENCE FOR HETEROGENEITY IN OPIOID LIGAND BINDING SITES.
003902 04-03

ANTITREMOR ACTION OF C10DICHOL, A PERIPHERAL ACETYLCHOLINE
SYNTHESIS INHIBITOR.
004096 04-04

CENTRAL AND PERIPHERAL EFFECTS OF LITHIUM ON AMPHETAMINE-
INDUCED HYPERACTIVITY IN RATS.
004223 04-04

PERIPHERAL SEROTONERGIC AND ADRENERGIC RESPONSES IN
DEPRESSION.
004364 04-09

THE EFFECT OF CHLORPROMAZINE AND MAGEPTIL ON THE
PROLIFERATION OF PERIPHERAL BLOOD LYMPHOCYTES IN CULTIVATION
WITH PHYTOHEMAGGLUTININ.
004541 04-13

PERIPHERAL-CORRELATES
PERIPHERAL-CORRELATES OF SEROTONERGICALLY-INFLUENCED
BEHAVIORS IN VERVET-MONKEYS (CERCOPITHECUS-AETHIOPS-
SABAEUS).
004204 04-04

PERIPHERAL-NERVOUS-SYSTEM
CHARACTERIZATION OF THE BASIC PROTEINS FROM RODENT
PERIPHERAL-NERVOUS-SYSTEM MYELIN.
003665 04-01

PERIPHERALLY-INDUCED
EFFECTS OF OLFACTORY-BULBECTOMY AND PERIPHERALLY-INDUCED
ANOSMIA ON THERMOREGULATION IN THE RAT: SUSCEPTIBILITY TO
ANTIDEPRESSANT-DRUGS.
004113 04-04

PERITONEAL
ENHANCED TRANSFER OF EXPERIMENTAL ALLERGIC-ENCEPHALOMYELITIS
WITH STRAIN-13 GUINEA-PIG LYMPH-NODE CELLS: REQUIREMENT FOR
CULTURE WITH SPECIFIC ANTIGEN AND ALLOGENIC PERITONEAL
EXUDATE CELLS. (UNPUBLISHED PAPER).
001201 02-03

PERIVENTRICULAR
MORPHINE INJECTIONS INTO THE PERIAQUEDUCTAL PERIVENTRICULAR
GRAY ATTENUATE SEPTAL HYPERREACTIVITY.
000390 01-04

PERMEABILITY
LONG-TERM ANTIDEPRESSANT TREATMENT: ALTERATIONS IN CEREBRAL
CAPILLARY PERMEABILITY.
000239 01-03

DOSE-DEPENDENT, AMPHETAMINE-INDUCED CHANGES IN PERMEABILITY
OF THE BLOOD-BRAIN-BARRIER OF NORMOTENSIVE-RATS AND
SPONTANEOUSLY HYPERTENSIVE-RATS.
001197 02-03

H2-RECEPTORS MEDIATE INCREASES IN PERMEABILITY OF THE BLOOD-
BRAIN-BARRIER DURING ARTERIAL HISTAMINE INFUSION.
003817 04-03

THE EFFECT OF DIBENZAZEPINES (TRICYCLIC-ANTIDEPRESSANTS) ON
CEREBRAL CAPILLARY PERMEABILITY IN THE RAT IN VIVO.
003974 04-03

PERORAL
ANTIDEPRESSANT TREATMENT BY INTRAVENOUS ADMINISTRATION
COMPARED TO PERORAL ADMINISTRATION: A DOUBLE-BLIND STUDY
OF QUINUPRAMINE.
000552 01-08

PERPHENAZINE
CONTROLLED-COMPARISON OF PERPHENAZINE WITH PERPHENAZINE IN
SCHIZOPHRENIA: A METHODICAL-CHECK OF A DOUBLE-BLIND CROSS-
OVER DESIGN.
001937 02-08

FLUPHENAZINE, TRIFLUOPERAZINE AND PERPHENAZINE IN VACUTAINERS.
003565 03-16

PERPHENAZINE-ENANTATE
ABSCESSES FOLLOWING PROLONGED INTRAMUSCULAR ADMINISTRATION
OF PERPHENAZINE-ENANTATE.
000888 01-15

PERSON
VOLUNTARY INTOXICATION FROM PHENCYCLIDINE. WILL IT RAISE A
REASONABLE-DOUBT OF THE MENTAL-CAPACITY OF A PERSON
CHARGED WITH A CRIME REQUIRING SPECIFIC INTENT OR MENTAL-
STATE?.
000914 01-17

ANALYSIS OF SINGLE-BLIND AND DOUBLE-BLIND PROCEDURES,
MAINTENANCE OF PLACEBO-EFFECTS AND DRUG-INDUCED DYSKINESIA
WITH MENTALLY-RETARDED PERSON.
004437 04-11

PERSONALITY
PERSONALITY TRAIT AND ANTIANXIETY-DRUG EFFECTS ON
PSYCHOMOTOR PERFORMANCE.
002336 02-14

SMOKING AND VIGILANCE: THE EFFECTS OF TOBACCO SMOKING ON CFF
AS RELATED TO PERSONALITY AND SMOKING HABITS.
002368 02-14

HABITUATION OF ELECTRODERMAL AND RESPIRATORY RESPONSES TO
VISUAL STIMULI AS A FUNCTION OF PERSONALITY DIFFERENCES IN
AFFECT LEVEL.
003414 03-13

PERSONALITY AS A PREDICTOR OF PSYCHOTHERAPY AND
PHARMACOTHERAPY-OUTCOME FOR DEPRESSED-OUTPATIENTS.
(UNPUBLISHED PAPER).
004418 04-09

PERSONALITY AND DRUGS IN VISUAL FIGURAL AFTEREFFECTS.
004581 04-14

NONSPECIFIC FACTORS IN DRUG-EFFECTS: PLACEBO PERSONALITY.
004704 04-17

PERSONALITY-DISORDERS
PIMOZIDE IN THE TREATMENT OF SOME SOCIAL-MALADJUSTMENTS IN
PERSONALITY-DISORDERS.
002068 02-10

PERSONALITY-PROBLEMS
DOUBLE-BLIND CONTROLLED-STUDY ON THE PSYCHOLEPTIC-EFFECTS OF
AMINEPTINE IN MENTALLY-HANDICAPPED CHILDREN WITHOUT
PERSONALITY-PROBLEMS.
002116 02-11

PERSONNEL
CHILDREN ON MEDICATION: A PRIMER FOR SCHOOL PERSONNEL.
000676 01-11

PERSONS
GABA SYNTHESIS BY CULTURED FIBROBLASTS OBTAINED FROM PERSONS
WITH HUNTINGTONS-DISEASE.
000765 01-13

ANALYSIS OF SINGLE-BLIND, DOUBLE-BLIND PROCEDURES, MAINTENANCE
OF PLACEBO-EFFECTS, AND DRUG-INDUCED DYSKINESIA WITH
MENTALLY-RETARDED PERSONS -- BRIEF REPORT.
003298 03-11

COMPARISON OF PSYCHOTROPIC-DRUG, RESPONSE COST, AND
PSYCHOTROPIC-DRUG PLUS RESPONSE COST PROCEDURES FOR
CONTROLLING INSTITUTIONALIZED MENTALLY-RETARDED PERSONS.
004438 04-11

PERSPECTIVE
EPIDEMIOLOGY OF PCP ABUSE: THE MIDWEST PERSPECTIVE.
000740 01-12

PHENCYCLIDINE: A NIDA PERSPECTIVE.
000743 01-12

PERSPECTIVE ON ADEQUATE INDIVIDUALIZED DRUG DOSES.
000959 01-17

AMITRIPTYLINE AND NORTRIPTYLINE PLASMA LEVELS MONITORING.
PERSPECTIVE IN CLINICAL-PRACTICE.
004675 04-16

THERAPEUTIC MONITORING OF PLASMA CONCENTRATIONS OF TRICYCLIC-
ANTIDEPRESSANTS: PERSPECTIVE OF THE CLINICAL LABORATORY.
004681 04-16

PERSPECTIVES
DRUGS AND THE ELDERLY: PERSPECTIVES IN GERIATRIC CLINICAL-
PHARMACOLOGY.
002534 02-17

NEW PERSPECTIVES ON THE MODE OF ACTION OF ANTIDEPRESSANT-
DRUGS.
002617 02-17

LIMITS, VALUE AND PERSPECTIVES OF THE PSYCHIATRIC-DIAGNOSIS IN
CLINICAL PSYCHOPHARMACOLOGY.
002631 02-17

PERSPECTIVES ON PRAZINIL (CARPIPRAMINE): A DISINHIBITING-AGENT
WITH NO NEUROLEPTIC ACTIVITY. A REVIEW OF 38 CASES.
003149 03-07

PETHIDINE-INDUCED
ATTENUATION OF PETHIDINE-INDUCED ANTINOCICEPTION BY ZIMELIDINE,
AN INHIBITOR OF 5 HYDROXYTRYPTAMINE REUPTAKE.
004118 04-04

PETIT-MAL
ANTICONVULSANTS SPECIFIC FOR PETIT-MAL ANTAGONIZE
EPILEPTOGENIC-EFFECT OF LEUCINE-ENKEPHALIN.
000477 01-04

A PHARMACOLOGICAL INVESTIGATION OF AN ANIMAL-MODEL OF THE
PETIT-MAL SEIZURE. (PH.D. DISSERTATION).
001870 02-06

EFFECTS OF D-AMPHETAMINE AND APOMORPHINE IN A NEW ANIMAL-
MODEL OF PETIT-MAL EPILEPSY.
002493 02-16

A CASE OF PETIT-MAL EPILEPSY AGGRAVATED BY LITHIUM.
004641 04-15

PHAGOCYTIC
PHAGOCYTIC FUNCTION IN DOWN-SYNDROME -- I. CHEMOTAXIS.
003401 03-13

PHARMACEUTIC-AGENTS
PROBLEMS INVOLVED IN THE COMBINATION OF PHARMACEUTIC-AGENTS
WITH PSYCHOTHERAPY OR PSYCHOANALYSIS.
000971 01-17

OBSERVATIONS ABOUT STATES OF MENTAL-ILLNESS AS ILLUMINATED BY
THEIR RESPONSE TO PHARMACEUTIC-AGENTS.
000972 01-17

PHARMACEUTICAL
RAPID DETERMINATION OF CHLORPROMAZINE-HCL AND TWO OXIDATION
PRODUCTS IN VARIOUS PHARMACEUTICAL SAMPLES USING HIGH-
PERFORMANCE LIQUID-CHROMATOGRAPHY AND FLUORESCENCE
DETECTION.
004302 04-06

PHARMACOCLINICAL-CLASSIFICATION
PRINCIPLES OF FRENCH PHARMACOCLINICAL-CLASSIFICATION.
001892 02-07

PHARMACODEPENDENCE
A POSSIBLE ECOPHARMACOGENETIC MODEL IN
NEUROPSYCHOPHARMACOLOGY ASPECTS IN ALCOHOLISM AND
PHARMACODEPENDENCE.
002596 02-17

PHARMACODYNAMIC
PHARMACODYNAMIC PROFILES OF L ALPHA ACETYLMETHADOL (LAAM)
AND ITS N DEMETHYLATED METABOLITES, NORLAAM AND
DINORLAAM, DURING SELF-ADMINISTRATION IN THE DEPENDENT RAT.
000505 01-04

DETERMINATION OF THE ENCEPHALOTROPIC, PSYCHOTROPIC AND
PHARMACODYNAMIC PROPERTIES OF NICERGOLINE BY MEANS OF
QUANTITATIVE PHARMACOELECTROENCEPHALOGRAPHY AND
PSYCHOMETRIC-ANALYSES.
000788 01-13

ANTIHYPOXIDOTIC-DRUGS AND NOOTROPIC-DRUGS: PROOF OF THEIR
ENCEPHALOTROPIC AND PHARMACODYNAMIC PROPERTIES BY
ENCEPHALOTROPIC AND PHARMACODYNAMIC PROPERTIES BY
QUANTITATIVE EEG INVESTIGATIONS.
002166 02-11

PHARMACODYNAMIC ASPECTS OF LONG-TERM PROPHYLACTIC LITHIUM.
002212 02-13
NEUROLEPTICS; INTERACTIONS WITH FOOD -- CHEMICAL AND
PHARMACODYNAMIC STUDIES ON THE INTERACTIONS OF COFFEE AND
TEA.
003612 03-17
A CLINICAL AND PHARMACODYNAMIC EVALUATION OF SULPIRIDE.
004338 04-08

PHARMACODYNAMICS
PHARMACODYNAMICS AND PHARMACOKINETICS OF DIAZEPAM IN AN
ABUSER.
000867 01-15
DETERMINATION OF PHARMACODYNAMICS OF PSYCHOTROPIC-DRUGS BY
PSYCHOMETRIC-ANALYSIS.
001895 02-07

PHARMACOEEG
CNS EFFECTS OF ISF-2522, A NEW NOOTROPIC (A PHASE I SAFETY AND
CNS EFFICACY STUDY WITH QUANTITATIVE PHARMACOEEG AND
PHARMACOPSYCHOLOGY).
004519 04-13
CLOPIPAZAN (SKF-69634), A NEW NEUROLEPTIC ESSENTIALLY FREE OF
EXTRAPYRAMIDAL LIABILITY: QUANTITATIVE PHARMACOEEG AND
OPEN LABEL CLINICAL-TRIAL.
004620 04-15

PHARMACOELECTROENCEPHALOGRAPHY
DETERMINATION OF THE ENCEPHALOTROPIC, PSYCHOTROPIC AND
PHARMACODYNAMIC PROPERTIES OF NICERGOLINE BY MEANS OF
QUANTITATIVE PHARMACOELECTROENCEPHALOGRAPHY AND
PSYCHOMETRIC-ANALYSES.
000788 01-13

PHARMACOKINETIC
ALTERATION OF PHARMACOKINETIC PARAMETERS FOR PENTOBARBITAL
BY ISCHEMIC STROKE AND REVERSION TO NORMAL BY
DEXAMETHASONE TREATMENT.
000321 01-03
ADVANTAGE OF PHARMACOKINETIC DATA DURING TREATMENT OF
PSYCHOSES WITH HALOPERIDOL.
000577 01-08
TRANSCULTURAL PHARMACOKINETIC STUDY ON LI CONCENTRATION IN
PLASMA AND SALIVA.
000769 01-13
PHARMACOKINETIC INTERACTION BETWEEN PROPRANOLOL AND
CHLORPROMAZINE IN SCHIZOPHRENIC-PATIENTS.
001940 02-08
PHARMACOKINETIC BASIS FOR PREDICTING STEADY-STATE SERUM DRUG
CONCENTRATIONS OF IMIPRAMINE FROM SINGLE-DOSE DATA.
002225 02-13
PHARMACOKINETIC PROFILE OF VALPROIC-ACID IN RHESUS-MONKEYS
FOLLOWING SINGLE BOLUS AND CONSTANT RATE INTRAVENOUS
ADMINISTRATIONS.
002797 03-03
THE USE OF CLINICAL AND PHARMACOKINETIC CRITERIA IN FORECASTING
THE EFFICACY OF THERAPY IN SCHIZOPHRENIA.
004335 04-08
SINGLE-DOSE PHARMACOKINETIC DATA ON ZIMELIDINE IN DEPRESSED-
PATIENTS.
004385 04-09
SERUM CONCENTRATION OF ANTICONVULSANTS. PHARMACOKINETIC
FINDINGS AND THEIR PRACTICAL APPLICATION.
004443 04-11
DOSAGE FORM DESIGN FOR IMPROVEMENT OF BIOAVAILABILITY OF
LEVODOPA III: INFLUENCE OF DOSE ON PHARMACOKINETIC BEHAVIOR
OF LEVODOPA IN DOGS AND PARKINSONIAN-PATIENTS.
004551 04-13

PHARMACOKINETIC-BASES
USE OF ANTIDEPRESSANTS: PHARMACOKINETIC-BASES.
001981 02-09

PHARMACOKINETIC-INTERACTION
REVERSAL BY PHENYTOIN OF CARBAMAZEPINE-INDUCED WATER
INTOXICATION: A PHARMACOKINETIC-INTERACTION.
000783 01-13

PHARMACOKINETIC-STUDIES
PHARMACOKINETIC-STUDIES WITH CHOLINE-CHLORIDE: A PRELIMINARY
REPORT.
004514 04-13

PHARMACOKINETIC-STUDY
PHARMACOKINETIC-STUDY OF LORAZEPAM OVERDOSAGE.
000831 01-15
COMPARATIVE-STUDIES OF L-DOPA ALONE AND COMBINATION WITH A
PERIPHERAL DOPA-DECARBOXYLASE INHIBITOR, BENSERAZIDE-HCL, ON
PARKINSONS-DISEASE -- PART II: PHARMACOKINETIC-STUDY.
002309 02-13
PHARMACOKINETIC-STUDY OF APOMORPHINE-INDUCED STEREOTYPY IN
FOOD DEPRIVED RATS.
004247 04-04
PHARMACOKINETIC-STUDY IN MAN OF THE CH-757 PREPARATION.
004440 04-11

PHARMACOKINETIC-VARIABLES
RELATIONSHIPS AMONG BIOCHEMICAL-VARIABLES, CLINICAL-
VARIABLES, AND PHARMACOKINETIC-VARIABLES IN NEUROLEPTIC
TREATED SCHIZOPHRENIC-PATIENTS.
001946 02-08

PHARMACOKINETICS
PHARMACOKINETICS OF CARBAMAZEPINE IN THE DOG.
000096 01-03
PHARMACOKINETICS OF PRIMIDONE AND ITS ACTIVE METABOLITES IN
THE DOG.
000097 01-03
SINGLE-DOSE PHARMACOKINETICS AND ANTICONVULSANT EFFICACY OF
PRIMIDONE IN MICE.
000177 01-03
PHARMACOKINETICS AND METABOLISM OF
CHLORODIMETHYLAMINOETHOXYDIBENZOTHIEPINE (ZOTEPINE) IN RAT,
MOUSE, DOG AND MAN.
000219 01-03
COMPARISON OF SINGLE-DOSE PHARMACOKINETICS OF IMIPRAMINE
AND MAPROTILINE IN THE ELDERLY.
000596 01-09
3 CHLORO-4-PHENYLSUCCINIMIDOBENZENESULFONAMIDE (GS-385), A
NEW ANTICONVULSANT: ITS QUANTITATIVE DETERMINATION,
PHARMACOKINETICS AND METABOLISM USING HIGH-PERFORMANCE
LIQUID-CHROMATOGRAPHY.
000705 01-11
PHARMACOKINETICS OF CHLORPROMAZINE IN NORMAL VOLUNTEERS.
000778 01-13
PHARMACODYNAMICS AND PHARMACOKINETICS OF DIAZEPAM IN AN
ABUSER.
000867 01-15
PHARMACOKINETICS OF BENZODIAZEPINES: SHORT-ACTING VERSUS
LONG-ACTING.
000920 01-17
DOSE-DEPENDENT PHARMACOKINETICS OF ALPHA METHYL-P-TYROSINE
(ALPHA MT) AND COMPARISON OF CATECHOLAMINE TURNOVER-
RATES AFTER TWO DOSES OF ALPHA MT.
001532 02-03
CLINICAL-RESPONSE, PLASMA LEVELS AND PHARMACOKINETICS OF
DESIPRAMINE IN DEPRESSED-INPATIENTS.
002002 02-09
PHARMACOKINETICS OF NORTRIPTYLINE IN ELDERLY VOLUNTEERS.
002184 02-11
ON THE CLINICAL PHARMACOKINETICS OF THIORIDAZINE AND ITS
METABOLITES.
002207 02-13
PHARMACOKINETICS OF DIPOTASSIUM-CHLORAZEPATE IN PATIENTS
AFTER REPEATED 50MG ORAL DOSES.
002211 02-13
O METHOXYBENZAMIDES: RELATIONSHIPS BETWEEN STRUCTURE-
ACTIVITY, AND PHARMACOKINETICS OF THESE DRUGS.
002246 02-13
INFLUENCE OF CIMETIDINE ON THE PHARMACOKINETICS OF
DESMETHYLDIAZEPAM AND OXAZEPAM.
002249 02-13
BIOAVAILABILITY AND RELATED PHARMACOKINETICS IN MAN OF
ORALLY ADMINISTERED L 5 HYDROXYTRYPTOPHAN IN STEADY-STATE.
002261 02-13
CONTRIBUTION TO THE PHARMACOKINETICS AND METABOLISM OF
OXYPROTHEPIN.
002279 02-13
THE PHARMACOKINETICS OF BROMOCRIPTINE IN MAN.
002291 02-13
SINGLE-DOSE PHARMACOKINETICS OF DOXEPIN IN HEALTHY
VOLUNTEERS.
002303 02-13
RELATIONSHIP BETWEEN STRUCTURE AND NEUROLEPTIC ACTIVITY:
PHARMACOPHORE AND PHARMACOKINETICS.
002492 02-16
PHARMACOKINETICS AND PLASMA LEVELS OF POLYCYCLIC-
ANTIDEPRESSANTS: A GENERAL VIEW OF PRODUCTS.
002529 02-17
PHARMACOKINETICS AND BIOAVAILABILITY OF CHLORDIAZEPOXIDE IN
HUMANS.
002564 02-17
DESIPRAMINE AND 2 HYDROXYDESIPRAMINE PHARMACOKINETICS IN
NORMAL VOLUNTEERS.
003154 03-07
PHARMACOKINETICS OF CLOMIPRAMINE IN DEPRESSIVE-PATIENTS.
003216 03-09
PHARMACOKINETICS OF AMITRIPTYLINE, IMIPRAMINE, AND
MAPROTILINE IN THE ELDERLY.
003324 03-11
CLINICAL PHARMACOKINETICS IN NEWBORNS AND INFANTS: AGE-
RELATED DIFFERENCES AND THERAPEUTIC IMPLICATIONS.
003343 03-11
PHENYTOIN: PHARMACOKINETICS AND CLINICAL THERAPEUTICS.
003353 03-11

CLINICAL PHARMACOKINETICS OF OXAZEPAM AND LORAZEPAM.
003410 03-13
THE EFFECTS OF SALICYLATE ON THE PHARMACOKINETICS OF PHENYTOIN.
003421 03-13
THE USE OF PHARMACOKINETICS IN THE FOLLOWUP OF PSYCHIATRIC-PATIENTS.
003616 03-17
HEPATIC-DISEASE AND DRUG PHARMACOKINETICS.
003650 03-17
PHARMACOKINETICS AND CLINICAL-RESPONSE TO TRICYCLIC-ANTIDEPRESSANTS.
004370 04-09
CORTISOL DYNAMICS AND DEXAMETHASONE PHARMACOKINETICS IN PRIMARY ENDOGENOUS DEPRESSION: PRELIMINARY FINDINGS.
004403 04-09
CLINICAL PHARMACOKINETICS OF CHLORDIAZEPOXIDE IN PATIENTS WITH ALCOHOLIC HEPATITIS.
004473 04-11
CLINICAL PHARMACOKINETICS OF BENZODIAZEPINES.
004524 04-13
PHARMACOKINETICS OF CLOXAZOLAM IN MAN AFTER SINGLE AND MULTIPLE ORAL DOSES.
004530 04-13
THE PHARMACOKINETICS OF MIDAZOLAM IN MAN.
004555 04-13
PHARMACOKINETICS OF ANTICONVULSANT-DRUGS.
004738 04-17

PHARMACOLOGIC
PHYSIOLOGIC AND PHARMACOLOGIC IMPLICATIONS IN THE DEACYLATION OF PHOSPHATIDYLSERINE IN MICE.
002682 03-03
PHARMACOLOGIC APPROACHES TO THE TREATMENT OF SENILE-DEMENTIA.
002809 03-03
PHARMACOLOGIC EVIDENCE FOR A TONIC MUSCARINIC INHIBITORY INPUT TO THE EDINGER-WESTPHAL NUCLEUS IN THE DOG.
002889 03-03
PHARMACOLOGIC AND THERAPEUTIC-PERSPECTIVES ON DEMENTIA: AN EXPERIMENTAL APPROACH.
003065 03-04
PHARMACOLOGIC CHARACTERIZATION AND LECITHIN TREATMENT OF A PATIENT WITH SPONTANEOUS ORAL FACIAL DYSKINESIA AND DEMENTIA.
003347 03-11
PHARMACOLOGIC DISTINCTION OF DIFFERENT ORTHOSTATIC HYPOTENSION-SYNDROMES.
003362 03-11
SYNTHESIS AND BIOCHEMICAL AND PHARMACOLOGIC PROPERTIES OF ANALOGUES AND DERIVATIVES OF P CHLOROPHENYLALANINE.
003691 04-02
PHARMACOLOGIC MANIPULATION OF BRAIN AND PITUITARY ENDORPHIN CONTENT AND RELEASE.
003837 04-03
HIPPOCAMPAL INVOLVEMENT IN THE PHARMACOLOGIC INDUCTION OF WITHDRAWAL-LIKE BEHAVIORS.
004140 04-04
3 HYDROXYMETHYL-BETA-CARBOLINE ANTAGONIZES SOME PHARMACOLOGIC ACTIONS OF DIAZEPAM.
004221 04-04

PHARMACOLOGIC-AGENTS
INFLUENCE OF MONOAMINE DEPLETING PHARMACOLOGIC-AGENTS ON LEVELS OF ACTIVITY IN CAIMAN-SCLEROPS.
001810 02-04

PHARMACOLOGIC-EFFECTS
TOXICOLOGIC AND PHARMACOLOGIC-EFFECTS OF PHENCYCLIDINE-HCL IN THE DOG. (PH.D. DISSERTATION).
000519 01-05

PHARMACOLOGIC-PROBES
IDENTIFICATION OF A SUBGROUP OF TARDIVE-DYSKINESIA PATIENTS BY PHARMACOLOGIC-PROBES.
000708 01-11
PHARMACOLOGIC-PROBES INTO TARDIVE-DYSKINESIA.
002179 02-11

PHARMACOLOGIC-RESPONSES
INTERACTION OF TRIAZOLAM WITH DESIPRAMINE: EFFECTS OF SINGLE AND REPEATED TREATMENT ON CERTAIN PHARMACOLOGIC-RESPONSES AND BRAIN CATECHOLAMINE LEVELS.
001323 02-03

PHARMACOLOGIC-STUDIES
PHARMACOLOGIC-STUDIES OF TARDIVE-DYSKINESIA.
002387 02-15

PHARMACOLOGIC-TREATMENT
SENILE-DEMENTIA: COMBINED PHARMACOLOGIC-TREATMENT AND PSYCHOLOGIC-TREATMENT.
003393 03-11
AN OVERVIEW OF PHARMACOLOGIC-TREATMENT OF COGNITIVE DECLINE IN THE AGED.
004482 04-11

PHARMACOLOGICAL
3 SULFAMOYLMETHYL-1-2-BENZISOXAZOLE, A NEW TYPE OF ANTICONVULSANT-DRUG: PHARMACOLOGICAL PROFILE.
000012 01-02
PHARMACOLOGICAL ACTIVITIES OF CLOBAZAM AND DIAZEPAM IN THE RAT: RELATION TO DRUG BRAIN LEVELS.
000036 01-03
GABA BENZODIAZEPINE INTERACTIONS: PHYSIOLOGICAL, PHARMACOLOGICAL AND DEVELOPMENTAL ASPECTS.
000103 01-03
REINNERVATION OF THE DENERVATED STRIATUM BY SUBSTANTIA-NIGRA TRANSPLANTS: FUNCTIONAL CONSEQUENCES AS REVEALED BY PHARMACOLOGICAL AND SENSORIMOTOR TESTING.
000347 01-04
DECOMPOSITION OF PHARMACOLOGICAL ACTIVITY INDICES INTO MUTUALLY INDEPENDENT COMPONENTS USING PRINCIPAL COMPONENT ANALYSIS.
001039 02-01
BIOCHEMICAL-CHARACTERIZATION AND PHARMACOLOGICAL CHARACTERIZATION OF A PEPTIDE FROM THE HEMODIALYSATE OF PSYCHOTIC-PATIENTS.
001049 02-01
RECEPTOR PLASTICITY: BIOCHEMICAL-CORRELATES AND PHARMACOLOGICAL SIGNIFICANCE.
001181 02-03
PHARMACOLOGICAL EVIDENCE AND BIOCHEMICAL-EVIDENCE FOR AN INTERACTION BETWEEN THE BENZODIAZEPINE AND GABA-RECEPTORS.
001261 02-03
DIFFERENTIAL SENSITIVITY OF HYPOTHALAMIC DOPAMINERGIC AND NORADRENERGIC NEURONES TO PHARMACOLOGICAL MANIPULATION.
001310 02-03
A PHARMACOLOGICAL ANALYSIS OF THE ROLE OF THE AMYGDALA IN THE CONTROL OF GONADOTROPIN AND PROLACTIN SECRETION.
001418 02-03
NEW EXPERIMENTAL TECHNIQUES IN THE PHARMACOLOGICAL EVALUATION OF CNS ACTING DRUGS.
001479 02-03
THE EFFECT OF REPEATED ELECTROCONVULSIVE-SHOCK ON CORTICOSTERONE RESPONSES TO CENTRALLY-ACTING PHARMACOLOGICAL STIMULI IN THE MALE RAT.
001486 02-03
CENTRAL PHARMACOLOGICAL CONTROL OF CORTICOSTERONE SECRETION IN THE INTACT RAT. DEMONSTRATION OF CHOLINERGIC AND SEROTONINERGIC FACILITATORY AND ALPHA-ADRENERGIC INHIBITORY MECHANISMS.
001487 02-03
PHARMACOLOGICAL EVIDENCE OF A POSSIBLE TRYPTAMINERGIC REGULATION OF OPIATE-RECEPTORS BY USING INDALPINE, A SELECTIVE 5 HT UPTAKE INHIBITOR.
001517 02-03
PHARMACOLOGICAL MODIFICATION OF AMYGDALOID KINDLED SEIZURES.
001588 02-04
THE PHARMACOLOGICAL RELEVANCE OF THE COCAINE BINDING-SITE IN MOUSE-BRAIN.
001772 02-06
A PHARMACOLOGICAL INVESTIGATION OF AN ANIMAL-MODEL OF THE PETIT-MAL SEIZURE. (PH.D. DISSERTATION).
001870 02-07
AMINEPTINE, A NEW ANTIDEPRESSANT: PHARMACOLOGICAL REVIEW.
001898 02-07
TREATMENT OF DYSKINETIC AND DYSTONIC-DISORDERS WITH CF-25-397: CLINICAL-ASPECTS AND PHARMACOLOGICAL ASPECTS.
002121 02-11
PHARMACOLOGICAL REFLECTIONS ON O ANISAMIDES.
002292 02-13
A NEUROPHARMACOLOGICAL-STUDY AND NEUROENDOCRINE-STUDY ON IDIOPATHIC AND CHRONIC PHARMACOLOGICAL PARKINSONISM.
002371 02-15
BEHAVIOURAL-ANALYSIS OF FEEDING: IMPLICATIONS FOR THE PHARMACOLOGICAL MANIPULATION OF FOOD INTAKE IN ANIMALS AND MAN.
002527 02-17
PHARMACOLOGICAL EVIDENCE ON THE SPECIALIZATION OF CNS MECHANISMS RESPONSIBLE FOR MOTOR ACT INHIBITION BY AVERSIVE EVENTS.
002671 03-03
IDENTICAL RESPONSES OF THE TWO HIPPOCAMPAL THETA GENERATORS TO PHYSIOLOGICAL AND PHARMACOLOGICAL ACTIVATION.
002792 03-03
PHARMACOLOGICAL CHARACTERIZATION OF SCRATCHING-BEHAVIOUR INDUCED BY INTRACRANIAL INJECTION OF SUBSTANCE-P AND SOMATOSTATIN.
002980 03-04
CHANGES IN THE HORIZONTAL VESTIBULO-OCULAR REFLEX OF THE RHESUS-MONKEY WITH BEHAVIORAL AND PHARMACOLOGICAL ALERTING.
002997 03-04

PHARMACOLOGICAL EVIDENCE FOR CATECHOLAMINE INVOLVEMENT IN
ANIMAL AGGRESSION.
003052 03-04
THE PHARMACOLOGICAL ANALYSIS OF MONOAMINERGIC MECHANISMS
OF THE MEDIAL HYPOTHALAMUS IN FOOD PROCURING CONDITIONED
REFLEXES IN RATS.
003100 03-04
PHARMACOLOGICAL EVIDENCE FOR CATECHOLAMINE INVOLVEMENT IN
ANIMAL AGGRESSION.
003140 03-06
2 AMINO-4-PHOSPHONOBUTYRIC-ACID: A NEW PHARMACOLOGICAL
TOOL FOR RETINA RESEARCH.
003145 03-06
A COMPARATIVE REVIEW OF THE PHARMACOLOGICAL AND
TOXICOLOGICAL PROPERTIES OF DISULFIRAM AND CALCIUM-
CARBIMIDE.
003522 03-15
PHARMACOLOGICAL ANTAGONISTS OF EXCITANT AMINO-ACID ACTION.
003587 03-17
RECENT REVIEWS OF BIOCHEMICAL, NEUROCHEMICAL, AND
PHARMACOLOGICAL TOPICS.
003649 03-17
THE PHARMACOLOGICAL ACTION OF THE OPTICAL-ISOMERS OF
SYDNOCARB.
003681 04-02
SYNTHESIS AND PHARMACOLOGICAL ACTIVITY OF SOME 2 IMINO-3-
ALKYLTHIAZOLINE DERIVATIVES.
003698 04-02
SYNTHESIS AND PHARMACOLOGICAL PROPERTIES OF N-4 1
AZETIDINYLBUTYNYL 2 PYRROLIDONE, A HIGHLY POTENT
OXOTREMORINE-LIKE-AGENT.
003701 04-02
PHARMACOLOGICAL DIFFERENTIATION OF PRESYNAPTIC INHIBITORY
ALPHA-ADRENOCEPTORS AND OPIATE-RECEPTORS IN THE CAT
NICTITATING MEMBRANE.
003777 04-03
PHARMACOLOGICAL DIFFERENCE OF L-DOPA, APOMORPHINE, AND
BROMOCRIPTINE AGAINST METOCLOPRAMIDE.
003790 04-03
THE EFFECT OF ELECTRICAL-STIMULATION OF THE LOCUS-COERULEUS AND
INTRAPERITONEAL INJECTION OF CERTAIN PHARMACOLOGICAL
SUBSTANCES ON THE THRESHOLD OF HIPPOCAMPAL
AFTERDISCHARGES.
003885 04-03
THE PHARMACOLOGICAL PROFILE OF LOFEPRAMINE, A NEW
ANTIDEPRESSANT-DRUG.
004006 04-03
THE EFFECT OF PHARMACOLOGICAL DESTRUCTION OF HYPOTHALAMIC
MONOAMINERGIC STRUCTURES ON BODY-TEMPERATURE AND GAS-
EXCHANGE DURING EXTREME COOLING.
004016 04-03
PHARMACOLOGICAL REGULATION OF CALMODULIN.
004052 04-03
PHARMACOLOGICAL AND BIOCHEMICAL-PROPERTIES OF BRL-14342, A
NOVEL POTENTIAL ANTIDEPRESSANT-DRUG.
004086 04-04
ANALGESIC AND OTHER PHARMACOLOGICAL ACTIVITIES OF A NEW
NARCOTIC ANTAGONIST ANALGESIC (-) 1 3
METHYLBUTENYLHYDROXYPHENYLPHENYLETHYLPIPERAZINE AND ITS
ENANTIOMORPH IN EXPERIMENTAL ANIMALS.
004185 04-04
SOME OBSERVATIONS ON THE PHARMACOLOGICAL ACTIVITY OF MIF
(PRO-LEU-GLY-NH2).
004240 04-04
THE PHARMACOLOGICAL CHARACTERISTICS OF THE TRANQUILIZING
EFFECT OF HYDIPHEN.
004261 04-04
ON THE USE OF CERTAIN PHARMACOLOGICAL CATEGORIES IN HYSTERIA.
004347 04-09
PHARMACOLOGICAL INFLUENCE OF SEXUAL-FUNCTIONS IN ADOLESCENTS.
004436 04-11
PHARMACOLOGICAL PECULIARITIES OF A BENZODIAZEPINE/ATARACTIC-
DRUG AND ITS THERAPEUTIC RELEVANCE: THE SPECIAL STATUS OF
CLORAZEPATE-DIPOTASSIUM (TRANXILIUM).
004527 04-13
PECULIARITIES OF THE CEREBRAL PATHOMORPHOLOGY OF PATIENTS
WITH SCHIZOPHRENIA TREATED WITH PSYCHOTROPIC-DRUGS
(PHARMACOLOGICAL PATHOMORPHOSIS).
004528 04-13
PHARMACOLOGICAL MODULATION OF FORMATION OF LONG-TERM
MEMORY.
004578 04-14
MECHANISMS AND PHARMACOLOGICAL IMPLICATIONS OF ALTERING
CALMODULIN ACTIVITY.
004751 04-17

PHARMACOLOGICAL-AGENTS
DIFFERENTIAL-EFFECTS OF PHARMACOLOGICAL-AGENTS ACTING ON
MONOAMINERGIC SYSTEMS ON DRUG-INDUCED ANOREXIA.
002533 02-17

PHARMACOLOGICAL-ASPECTS
SOME PHARMACOLOGICAL-ASPECTS AND BIOCHEMICAL-ASPECTS OF
TRH: EXPERIMENTAL AND CLINICAL DATA.
001189 02-03
PHARMACOLOGICAL-ASPECTS OF SHAKING-BEHAVIOR PRODUCED BY
TRH, AG-3-5, AND MORPHINE WITHDRAWAL.
004248 04-04
NEUROLEPTIC TRICYCLIC-ANTIDEPRESSANT COMBINATION:
PHARMACOLOGICAL-ASPECTS AND THERAPEUTIC INTEREST.
004501 04-13

PHARMACOLOGICAL-BASES
PHARMACOLOGICAL-BASES OF PSYCHONEUROENDOCRINOLOGY:
PRECLINICAL ASSESSMENT OF CLINICAL FACTS.
003735 04-03

PHARMACOLOGICAL-CONSIDERATIONS
BRAIN CATECHOLAMINES, MENTAL-ILLNESSES, AGING AND SENILE-
DEMENTIA: BIOCHEMICAL-CONSIDERATIONS AND PHARMACOLOGICAL-
CONSIDERATIONS.
001550 02-03

PHARMACOLOGICAL-CORRELATES
EEG, COMP-EEG, REO-EG AND PHARMACOLOGICAL-CORRELATES OF
GERIATRICS.
002162 02-11

PHARMACOLOGICAL-EFFECTS
BIOCHEMICAL-CHARACTERIZATION OF THE RAT SYMPATHETIC
GANGLION: PHARMACOLOGICAL-EFFECTS OF RESERPINE ON
GANGLIONIC CATECHOLAMINES.
000153 01-03
DISPOSITION AND PHARMACOLOGICAL-EFFECTS OF M
CHLOROPHENYLPIPERAZINE IN RATS.
002995 03-04
COMPARATIVE-STUDIES OF THE PHARMACOLOGICAL-EFFECTS OF THE D-
ISOMERS AND L-ISOMERS OF CODEINE.
004084 04-04
ASPECTS OF PHARMACOLOGICAL-EFFECTS OF ANTIEPILEPTIC-DRUGS.
004462 04-11

PHARMACOLOGICAL-PROBES
DEVELOPMENT AND USE OF PHARMACOLOGICAL-PROBES OF THE CNS IN
MAN: EVIDENCE OF CHOLINERGIC ABNORMALITY IN PRIMARY
AFFECTIVE-ILLNESS.
002506 02-16

PHARMACOLOGICAL-PROPERTIES
SEROTONIN-SENSITIVE ADENYLATE-CYCLASE AND (3H)SEROTONIN
BINDING-SITES IN THE CNS OF THE RAT — I. KINETIC PARAMETERS
AND PHARMACOLOGICAL-PROPERTIES.
000213 01-03
REWARDING AND AVERSIVE-EFFECTS OF MORPHINE: TEMPORAL AND
PHARMACOLOGICAL-PROPERTIES.
000470 01-04
PHARMACOLOGICAL-PROPERTIES OF TAGLUTIMIDE, A NEW SEDATIVE
HYPNOTIC-DRUG.
001087 02-02
DOPAMINE-RECEPTORS IN RAT-FRONTAL-CORTEX: PHARMACOLOGICAL-
PROPERTIES IN VIVO AND IN VITRO.
001112 02-03
A COMPARATIVE-STUDY OF THE PHARMACOLOGICAL-PROPERTIES OF THE
POSITIVE POTENTIAL RECORDED FROM THE SUPERIOR CERVICAL
GANGLIA OF SEVERAL SPECIES.
003779 04-03
PHARMACOLOGICAL-PROPERTIES OF 2,3,3A,4,5,6 HEXAHYDROMETHYL-
1H-PYRAZINOCARBAZOL-HCL (PIRLINDOLE), A NEW ANTIDEPRESSANT.
004174 04-04
PHARMACOLOGICAL-PROPERTIES OF SOME SECOND-GENERATION
ANTIDEPRESSANT-DRUGS.
004726 04-17

PHARMACOLOGICAL-STUDIES
PHARMACOLOGICAL-STUDIES ON A NEW THYMOLEPTIC
ANTIDEPRESSANT. DIMETHYLAMINOPROPYL-5-METHYL-3-PHENYL-1H-
INDAZOLE (FS-32).
001659 02-04
PHARMACOLOGICAL-STUDIES ON STIMULATION PRODUCED ANALGESIA
IN MICE.
002964 03-04
PHARMACOLOGICAL-STUDIES OF TARDIVE-DYSKINESIA: IMPLICATIONS
FOR FUTURE RESEARCH.
003465 03-15
UPTAKE OF RADIOCALCIUM BY NERVE-ENDINGS ISOLATED FROM RAT-
BRAIN: PHARMACOLOGICAL-STUDIES.
003815 04-03
PHARMACOLOGICAL-STUDIES WITH AN ALKYLATING NARCOTIC
AGONIST, CHLOROXYMORPHAMINE, AND ANTAGONIST,
CHLORNALTREXAMINE.
004082 04-04

PHARMACOLOGICAL-STUDY
A PHARMACOLOGICAL-STUDY OF THE NEW SOVIET ANTIDEPRESSANT
INKASAN.
000008 01-02

PHARMACOLOGICAL-STUDY OF CHLORODIMETHYLAMINOETHOXYDIBENZOTHIEPINE (ZOTEPINE), A NEW NEUROLEPTIC-DRUG.
000493 01-04

ACTION OF TOFISOPAM ON THE ERGONOMIC VIGILANCE LEVEL. ITS INTERACTION WITH THE EFFECTS OF ALCOHOL. CLINICAL PHARMACOLOGICAL-STUDY.
001891 02-07

SYNTHESIS AND PHARMACOLOGICAL-STUDY OF SOME ENKEPHALIN ANALOGS IN RELATION TO THE PLURALITY OF OPIATE-RECEPTORS.
003682 04-02

PHARMACOLOGICAL-TREATMENT
BEHAVIORAL-TREATMENT AND PHARMACOLOGICAL-TREATMENT OF OBSESSIVE-COMPULSIVE-DISORDERS.
000657 01-10

MODERN-VIEWS ON THE PRINCIPLES OF THE PHARMACOLOGICAL-TREATMENT OF EPILEPSY.
000931 01-17

DOUBLE-BLIND EVALUATION OF REINFORCING AND ANORECTIC-ACTIONS OF WEIGHT-CONTROL MEDICATIONS: INTERACTION OF PHARMACOLOGICAL-TREATMENT AND BEHAVIORAL-TREATMENTS.
002314 02-14

THERAPEUTICS (I) -- PHARMACOLOGICAL-TREATMENT OF DEPRESSIONS.
003270 03-09

REFLECTIONS ON ANTIPSYCHOTIC CHEMOTHERAPY: THE BEGINNING OF PHARMACOLOGICAL-TREATMENT.
003292 03-11

THE PHARMACOLOGICAL-TREATMENT OF SCHIZOAFFECTIVE-DISORDER DEPRESSED; A REVIEW OF THE LITERATURE.
003634 03-17

PHOBIA: PSYCHOLOGICAL-TREATMENT AND PHARMACOLOGICAL-TREATMENT.
004425 04-10

NEUROLOGICAL-COMPLICATIONS DUE TO THE PHARMACOLOGICAL-TREATMENT OF EPILEPTIC-PATIENTS.
004593 04-15

CONTEMPORARY PROBLEMS IN THE PHARMACOLOGICAL-TREATMENT OF PARKINSONISM.
004628 04-15

PHARMACOLOGY
PHARMACOLOGY OF PHENETHYLAMINE TRACE AMINES IN THE DOG -- DISCUSSION.
000469 01-04

HISTORY AND PHARMACOLOGY OF PCP AND PCP RELATED ANALOGS.
000737 01-12

PHARMACOLOGY: CURRENT ANTIDEPRESSANTS.
000793 01-13

PHARMACOLOGY OF NOOTROPIC-DRUGS.
000800 01-14

PHARMACOLOGY: NEW ANTIDEPRESSANTS.
000936 01-17

SYNTHESIS AND PHARMACOLOGY OF 2 AMINO-3-ETHOXYCARBONYL-4-PHENYLTHIOPHENE DERIVATIVES.
001083 02-02

PHARMACOLOGY OF THE SURVECTOR.
001085 02-02

DOPAMINE-AUTORECEPTORS: PHARMACOLOGY, FUNCTION AND COMPARISON WITH POSTSYNAPTIC DOPAMINE-RECEPTORS.
001453 02-03

THE PHARMACOLOGY OF CATECHOLAMINE INVOLVEMENT IN THE NEURAL MECHANISMS OF REWARD.
001526 02-03

THE PHARMACOLOGY OF AGGRESSIVE-BEHAVIOURAL-PHENOMENA ELICITED BY MUSCARINE INJECTED INTO THE CEREBRAL VENTRICLES OF CONSCIOUS CATS.
001569 02-04

PHENCYCLIDINE (PCP) AND DERIVATIVES: PHARMACOLOGY AND STRUCTURE-ACTIVITY RELATIONSHIPS.
001706 02-04

TOXICOLOGY -- PHARMACOLOGY -- METABOLISM.
002252 02-13

HISTORY AND PHARMACOLOGY OF MINAPRINE.
002270 02-13

ADVANCES IN PHARMACOLOGY AND CHEMOTHERAPY.
002546 02-17

A COMPARATIVE-STUDY OF THE PHARMACOLOGY OF INHIBITORS OF GABA METABOLISM.
003036 03-04

ON THE PHYSIOLOGY AND PHARMACOLOGY OF ENDORPHINS.
003417 03-13

THE PHARMACOLOGY OF GABA-TRANSAMINASE INHIBITORS.
003620 03-17

PHARMACOLOGY OF MIGRAINE.
003623 03-17

BIBLIOGRAPHY ON THE BIOLOGY AND PHARMACOLOGY OF LITHIUM.
003630 03-17

THE PHARMACOLOGY OF MEMORY: A NEUROBIOLOGICAL-PERSPECTIVE.
003636 03-17

PHARMACOLOGY OF 1 DICHLOROBENZYL-TETRAHYDROPYRIMIDONE, A NOVEL ANTIDEPRESSANT COMPOUND WITH ANTIANXIETY ACTIVITY.
003688 04-02

PHARMACOLOGY OF 2 O CHLOROBENZOYL-CHLORO-METHYL-NA-GLYCYLGLYCINANILIDE HYDRATE (45-0088-S), A COMPOUND WITH BENZODIAZEPINE-LIKE PROPERTIES.
003692 04-02

THE NEUROANATOMY AND PHARMACOLOGY OF THE NUCLEUS LOCUS-COERULEUS. (UNPUBLISHED PAPER).
003810 04-03

SPINAL-CORD PHARMACOLOGY OF ADRENERGIC AGONIST-MEDIATED ANTINOCICEPTION.
004206 04-04

PHARMACOMANOMETRIC-STUDIES
PHARMACOMANOMETRIC-STUDIES OF COLONIC MOTILITY AS A GUIDE TO THE CHEMOTHERAPY OF SCHIZOPHRENIA.
001930 02-08

PHARMACOPHORE
RELATIONSHIP BETWEEN STRUCTURE AND NEUROLEPTIC ACTIVITY: PHARMACOPHORE AND PHARMACOKINETICS.
002492 02-16

PHARMACOPSYCHOLOGICAL
PHARMACOPSYCHOLOGICAL INVESTIGATION OF CHANGES IN MOOD INDUCED BY DIPOTASSIUM-CHLORAZEPATE WITH AND WITHOUT SIMULTANEOUS ALCOHOL ADMINISTRATION.
000825 01-14

PHARMACOPSYCHOLOGICAL INVESTIGATIONS CONCERNING THE COMBINED EFFECTS OF DIPOTASSIUM-CLORAZEPATE AND ETHANOL.
003456 03-14

PHARMACOPSYCHOLOGY
CNS EFFECTS OF ISF-2522, A NEW NOOTROPIC (A PHASE I SAFETY AND CNS EFFICACY STUDY WITH QUANTITATIVE PHARMACOEEG AND PHARMACOPSYCHOLOGY).
004519 04-13

PHARMACOTHERAPEUTIC
SECOND-GENERATION ANTIDEPRESSANTS: A CLINICAL PHARMACOTHERAPEUTIC RESEARCH STRATEGY.
003632 03-17

PHARMACOTHERAPY
CHRONIC MOOD-DISORDERS IN DEPRESSED-OUTPATIENTS: DIAGNOSIS AND RESPONSE TO PHARMACOTHERAPY.
000624 01-09

CONTROLLED-TRIAL OF BEHAVIOUR-THERAPY, PHARMACOTHERAPY, AND THEIR COMBINATION IN THE TREATMENT OF OBESITY.
000725 01-11

DISTINGUISHING SCHIZOPHRENIAS BY MEANS OF PHARMACOTHERAPY.
001947 02-08

THE PHARMACOTHERAPY OF MAJOR DEPRESSIVE-SYNDROME. PART 2: PROPHYLAXIS OF RECURRENT DEPRESSIVE-ILLNESS.
002043 02-09

THE PHARMACOTHERAPY OF MAJOR DEPRESSIVE-SYNDROME. PART 1: TREATMENT OF ACUTE DEPRESSION.
002044 02-09

PHARMACOTHERAPY OF DEPRESSION IN THE ELDERLY.
002144 02-11

PROGRESS IN THE PHARMACOTHERAPY OF PARKINSONISM.
002384 02-15

DEPRESSED-OUTPATIENTS TREATED WITH COGNITIVE-THERAPY OR PHARMACOTHERAPY: A ONE-YEAR FOLLOWUP.
003235 03-09

DO PSYCHOTHERAPY AND PHARMACOTHERAPY FOR DEPRESSION CONFLICT? EMPIRICAL EVIDENCE FROM A CLINICAL-TRIAL.
003256 03-09

PHARMACOTHERAPY FOR AGE-RELATED BEHAVIORAL-DEFICIENCIES.
003391 03-11

PHARMACOTHERAPY FOR DEPRESSION.
004351 04-09

DO PSYCHOTHERAPY AND PHARMACOTHERAPY FOR DEPRESSION CONFLICT? EMPIRICAL EVIDENCE FROM A CLINICAL-TRIAL. (UNPUBLISHED PAPER).
004401 04-09

PHARMACOTHERAPY AND PSYCHOTHERAPY FOR AMBULATORY DEPRESSION: EFFICACY AND CHOICES.
004413 04-09

PHARMACOTHERAPY OF SEXUAL-IMPOTENCE IN THE MALE.
004435 04-11

PHARMACOTHERAPY FOR SEXUAL-OFFENDERS: REVIEW OF THE ACTION OF ANTIANDROGENS WITH SPECIAL REFERENCE TO THEIR PSYCHIC-EFFECTS.
004455 04-11

PHARMACOTHERAPY AND FEMALE SEXUALITY.
004483 04-11

THE RIGHTS OF INVOLUNTARY-PATIENTS TO REFUSE PHARMACOTHERAPY: WHAT IS REASONABLE?
004730 04-17

NOTES ON PHARMACOTHERAPY OF FUNCTIONAL PSYCHOSES.
004748 04-17

PHARMACOTHERAPY-OUTCOME
PERSONALITY AS A PREDICTOR OF PSYCHOTHERAPY AND PHARMACOTHERAPY-OUTCOME FOR DEPRESSED-OUTPATIENTS. (UNPUBLISHED PAPER).
004418 04-09

PHARMACOTOXIC
ACUTE PHARMACOTOXIC PSYCHOSES IN CHRONIC CEREBRAL
CONDITIONS.
003475 03-15

PHASIC
EFFECTS OF MORPHINE AND NALOXONE ON PHASIC RELEASE OF
LUTEINIZING-HORMONE AND FOLLICLE-STIMULATING-HORMONE
(40849).
000298 01-03
PHASIC ACTIVITY INDUCED BY P CHLOROPHENYLALANINE IN THE
AUDITORY PATHWAY.
002661 03-03
CATECHOLAMINERGIC INVOLVEMENT IN PHASIC VERSUS TONIC
ELECTROCORTICAL AROUSAL.
002723 03-03

PHENACEMIDE
STRUCTURE-ACTIVITY RELATIONSHIPS IN THE EFFECTS OF PHENACEMIDE
ANALOGS ON SERUM CREATININE AND ANTICONVULSANT ACTIVITY.
000249 01-03

PHENAZEPAM
USE OF THE NEW TRANQUILIZER PHENAZEPAM IN PSYCHIATRIC-
PRACTICE.
000578 01-09
THE DEVELOPMENT OF PROGENY IN CASES OF ANTENATAL EXPOSURE TO
PHENAZEPAM.
001854 02-05
THE USE OF PHENAZEPAM IN THE TREATMENT OF PSYCHOTIC-PATIENTS.
003351 03-11

PHENCYCLIDINE
EFFECTS OF ACUTE AND CHRONIC PHENCYCLIDINE ON
NEUROTRANSMITTER ENZYMES IN RAT-BRAIN.
000134 01-03
CONTINUOUS-ACCESS PHENCYCLIDINE SELF-ADMINISTRATION BY RHESUS-
MONKEYS LEADING TO PHYSICAL-DEPENDENCE.
000341 01-04
FIRST DOSE BEHAVIORAL-TOLERANCE TO PHENCYCLIDINE ON FOOD
REWARDED BAR-PRESSING-BEHAVIOR IN THE RAT.
000462 01-04
PHENCYCLIDINE: EFFECTS OF CHRONIC ADMINISTRATION IN THE FEMALE
MOUSE ON GESTATION, MATERNAL-BEHAVIOR, AND THE NEONATES.
000517 01-05
PHENCYCLIDINE: A NIDA PERSPECTIVE.
000743 01-12
IN VITRO EFFECT OF PHENCYCLIDINE AND OTHER PSYCHOMOTOR
STIMULANTS ON SEROTONIN UPTAKE IN HUMAN PLATELETS.
000750 01-13
APPLICATION OF A RADIOIMMUNOASSAY SCREENING-TEST FOR
DETECTION AND MANAGEMENT OF PHENCYCLIDINE INTOXICATION.
000859 01-15
VOLUNTARY INTOXICATION FROM PHENCYCLIDINE. WILL IT RAISE A
REASONABLE-DOUBT OF THE MENTAL-CAPACITY OF A PERSON
CHARGED WITH A CRIME REQUIRING SPECIFIC INTENT OR MENTAL-
STATE?.
000914 01-17
CHRONIC PHENCYCLIDINE (PCP) ABUSE: A PSYCHIATRIC-PERSPECTIVE.
000935 01-17
STRUCTURE-ACTIVITY RELATIONSHIP OF PHENCYCLIDINE DERIVATIVES.
001030 02-01
THE DISCOVERY OF PHENCYCLIDINE.
001040 02-01
DISPOSITION OF (3H) PHENCYCLIDINE IN THE RAT AFTER SINGLE-DOSES
AND MULTIPLE-DOSES.
001375 02-03
THE ELECTROPHYSIOLOGICAL-EFFECTS OF ENKEPHALIN AND
PHENCYCLIDINE IN THE RAT CENTRAL-NERVOUS-SYSTEM. (PH.D.
DISSERTATION).
001406 02-03
COMPARED PROPERTIES OF CENTRAL AND PERIPHERAL BINDING-SITES
FOR PHENCYCLIDINE.
001521 02-03
(3H) PHENCYCLIDINE BINDING TO SPECIFIC BRAIN RECEPTOR SITES.
001555 02-03
EFFECTS OF PHENCYCLIDINE AND METHYLPHENIDATE ON D-
AMPHETAMINE-INDUCED BEHAVIORS IN RESERPINE PRETREATED RATS.
001616 02-04
TOLERANCE DEVELOPMENT TO PHENCYCLIDINE BY CHRONIC
ADMINISTRATION.
001619 02-04
PHENCYCLIDINE (PCP) AND DERIVATIVES: PHARMACOLOGY AND
STRUCTURE-ACTIVITY RELATIONSHIPS.
001706 02-04
PHENCYCLIDINE AS AN INDIRECT DOPAMINE AGONIST.
001719 02-04
EFFECTS OF PHENCYCLIDINE, PENTOBARBITAL, AND D-AMPHETAMINE ON
THE ACQUISITION AND PERFORMANCE OF CONDITIONAL
DISCRIMINATIONS IN MONKEYS.
001723 02-04
EFFECTS OF ACUTE VS. CHRONIC PHENCYCLIDINE ON BRAIN-
BIOCHEMISTRY AND BEHAVIOR.
001789 02-04

BINDING OF PHENCYCLIDINE TO RAT-BRAIN MEMBRANES: TECHNICAL-
ASPECT.
001882 02-06
EFFECT OF CHRONIC ADMINISTRATION OF PHENCYCLIDINE ON HEPATIC
MIXED-FUNCTION OXIDASES IN THE MOUSE.
002753 03-03
THE EFFECT OF PHENCYCLIDINE ON DOPAMINE METABOLISM IN THE
MOUSE-BRAIN.
002766 03-03
DISCRIMINATIVE-STIMULUS PROPERTIES OF PHENCYCLIDINE AND FIVE
ANALOGUES IN THE SQUIRREL-MONKEY.
002961 03-04
EFFECTS OF CHRONIC ADMINISTRATION OF PHENCYCLIDINE ON
STEREOTYPED-BEHAVIORS AND ATAXIC-BEHAVIORS IN THE RAT.
003095 03-04
PHENCYCLIDINE (PCP) INTOXICATION: DIAGNOSIS IN STAGES AND
ALGORITHMS OF TREATMENT.
003525 03-15
THE URBAN EPIDEMIC OF PHENCYCLIDINE USE: LABORATORY EVIDENCE
FROM A PUBLIC PSYCHIATRIC-HOSPITAL INPATIENT-SERVICE.
003554 03-16
EFFECTS OF ACUTE AND CHRONIC ADMINISTRATION OF PHENCYCLIDINE
ON DOPAMINERGIC-RECEPTORS IN RAT STRIATUM.
003901 04-03
ELECTROPHYSIOLOGICAL EVIDENCE FOR PRESYNAPTIC ACTIONS OF
PHENCYCLIDINE ON NORADRENERGIC TRANSMISSION IN RAT
CEREBELLUM.
003926 04-03
ACUTE PHENCYCLIDINE (PCP) INTOXICATION: QUANTITATIVE URINE
LEVELS AND CLINICAL MANAGEMENT.
004665 04-15

PHENCYCLIDINE-HCL
TOXICOLOGIC AND PHARMACOLOGIC-EFFECTS OF PHENCYCLIDINE-HCL IN
THE DOG. (PH.D. DISSERTATION).
000519 01-05
PHENCYCLIDINE-HCL: A CHALLENGE TO MEDICINE.
003395 03-12

PHENCYCLIDINE-INDUCED
PHENCYCLIDINE-INDUCED STIMULATION OF SYNAPTOSOMAL TYROSINE-
HYDROXYLASE ACTIVITY.
001304 02-03
NEUROPHARMACOLOGICAL-STUDIES OF PHENCYCLIDINE-INDUCED
BEHAVIORAL-STIMULATION IN MICE.
001622 02-04
EFFECTS OF DOPAMINERGIC DRUGS ON PHENCYCLIDINE-INDUCED
BEHAVIOR IN THE RAT.
004083 04-04

PHENCYCLIDINE-LIKE
PHENCYCLIDINE-LIKE DISCRIMINATIVE EFFECTS OF OPIOIDS IN THE RAT.
004136 04-04

PHENCYCLIDINES
CONFIRMATION BEHAVIOR OF PHENCYCLIDINES AND BIOLOGICAL-
ACTIVITY.
001031 02-01

PHENELZINE
THE EFFECT OF PHENELZINE AND SOME OF ITS PARA HALOGENATED
DERIVATIVES ON THE LEVELS OF BRAIN TYRAMINE AND OCTOPAMINE
IN THE MOUSE.
001077 02-02
PREDICTION OF RESPONSE TO TREATMENT WITH PHENELZINE IN
NEUROTIC-PATIENTS.
002081 02-10
CNV VARIATIONS INDUCED BY THE ADMINISTRATION OF DIAZEPAM,
HALOPERIDOL, PHENELZINE AND D-AMPHETAMINE.
002355 02-14
PHENELZINE AND AMITRIPTYLINE IN NEUROTIC DEPRESSION.
- (UNPUBLISHED PAPER).
003248 03-09
EFFECTS OF PHENELZINE AND AMITRIPTYLINE ON DEPRESSION.
003249 03-09
PHENELZINE AND EXPOSURE IN THE TREATMENT OF PHOBIAS.
003285 03-10
TREATMENT OF TRAUMATIC WAR-NEUROSIS WITH PHENELZINE.
003325 03-11
COMPARATIVE-EFFECTS OF PHENELZINE AND AMITRIPTYLINE: A
PLACEBO-CONTROLLED-TRIAL.
004402 04-09

PHENETHYLAMINE
PHARMACOLOGY OF PHENETHYLAMINE TRACE AMINES IN THE DOG —
DISCUSSION.
000469 01-04
SEROTONERGIC PROPERTIES OF BETA PHENETHYLAMINE IN RATS.
001787 02-04
A COMMON MECHANISM FOR LYSERGIC-ACID, INDOLEALKYLAMINE AND
PHENETHYLAMINE HALLUCINOGENS: SEROTONERGIC MEDIATION OF
BEHAVIORAL-EFFECTS IN RATS.
004007 04-03

PHENETHYLAMINES
SUBSTITUTED PHENETHYLAMINES AND ANOREXIA.
0002541 02-17

PHENOBARBITAL
ENZYME INDUCING EFFECTS OF PHENOBARBITAL ON NITRAZEPAM METABOLISM IN DOGS.
000086 01-03
EFFECT OF DOPAMINERGIC AND GABAERGIC DRUGS GIVEN ALONE OR IN COMBINATION ON THE ANTICONVULSANT ACTION OF PHENOBARBITAL AND DIPHENYLHYDANTOIN IN THE ELECTROSHOCK-TEST IN MICE.
000163 01-03
(3H)ACETYLCHOLINE AND (3H)5 HYDROXYTRYPTAMINE RELEASE FROM RAT-MIDBRAIN SLICES AND THE EFFECTS OF CALCIUM AND PHENOBARBITAL.
000251 01-03
CHANGES IN MOUSE-BRAIN DIAZEPAM-RECEPTOR BINDING AFTER PHENOBARBITAL ADMINISTRATION.
000281 01-03
BEHAVIORAL-ANALYSIS OF AMYGDALOID KINDLING IN BEAGLE-DOGS AND THE EFFECTS OF CLONAZEPAM, DIAZEPAM, PHENOBARBITAL, DIPHENYLHYDANTOIN, AND FLUNARIZINE ON SEIZURE MANIFESTATION.
000496 01-04
INTRAVENOUS PHENOBARBITAL THERAPY IN BARBITURATE AND OTHER HYPNOSEDATIVE WITHDRAWAL REACTIONS: A KINETIC APPROACH.
000703 01-11
SERUM CONCENTRATIONS OF PHENOBARBITAL AND DIPHENYLHYDANTOIN IN SEVERE MENTALLY-HANDICAPPED AND PHYSICALLY-HANDICAPPED-PATIENTS.
000856 01-15
DETERMINATION OF DOSE PLASMA CONCENTRATION RELATIONSHIP OF PHENOBARBITAL IN EPILEPTIC-PATIENTS BY A NEW SPECIFIC RADIOIMMUNOASSAY.
000902 01-16
PHENOBARBITAL EFFECTS ON WEIGHT-GAIN AND CIRCADIAN-CYCLING OF FOOD INTAKE AND BODY-TEMPERATURE.
001409 02-03
RELATIONSHIP BETWEEN SERUM LEVELS AND FAST EEG ACTIVITIES IN RATS BY A SINGLE ADMINISTRATION OF PHENOBARBITAL.
001462 02-03
CRITICAL PERIODS FOR DIPHENYLHYDANTOIN AND PHENOBARBITAL ADMINISTRATION DURING GESTATION.
001630 02-04
THE EFFECTS OF ETHANOL, PHENOBARBITAL, AND BACLOFEN ON ETHANOL WITHDRAWAL IN THE RHESUS-MONKEY.
001802 02-04
COMPARATIVE-STUDY OF THE INDUCTIVE EFFECT OF TWO PSYCHOMODERATORS -- TETRABAMATE AND COMPLEXE-1656 -- AND OF PHENOBARBITAL ON LIVER MICROSOMAL ENZYMES IN RATS.
001874 02-06
INFLUENCE OF PHENYTOIN AND PHENOBARBITAL ON THE DISPOSITION OF A SINGLE-ORAL-DOSE OF CLONAZEPAM.
002248 02-13
INTERRELATION AT PLASMATIC LEVEL BETWEEN ANTIEPILEPTIC-DRUGS AND LIPIDS. ITS IMPLICATIONS IN THE EFFICIENCY OF TREATMENT IN EPILEPSY. I. CHANGES INDUCED BY PHENOBARBITAL OR/AND DIPHENYLHYDANTOIN IN SERUM LIPIDS.
002281 02-13
IN VITRO CELLULAR ADAPTATION OF SEROTONERGIC PROCESSES AFTER CHRONIC CENTRAL PHENOBARBITAL ADMINISTRATION.
002813 03-03
CLONAZEPAM AND PHENOBARBITAL IN TARDIVE-DYSKINESIA.
003294 03-11
QUANTITATION AND COMPARISON OF PHENOBARBITAL LEVELS IN THE PLASMA, SALIVA, AND CEREBROSPINAL-FLUID OF THE RAT, AND THE DEMONSTRATION OF AN ALTERATION OF DRUG PASSAGE BY ETHANOL.
003725 04-03
EFFECTS OF ANIMAL AGE AND PHENOBARBITAL ON RAT LIVER GLUCOSE-6-PHOSPHATASE ACTIVITY.
003997 04-03
MECHANISM OF VALPROATE PHENOBARBITAL INTERACTION IN EPILEPTIC-PATIENTS.
004522 04-13

PHENOBARBITONE
PHENOBARBITONE AND SODIUM-VALPROATE INTERACTION: AN EXPERIMENTAL-STUDY.
001371 02-03
PHENOBARBITONE INTERACTION WITH ORAL CONTRACEPTIVE STEROIDS IN THE RABBIT AND RAT.
001832 02-05
THE EFFECTS OF PHENYTOIN ON PHENOBARBITONE AND PRIMIDONE METABOLISM.
003333 03-11
CHANGES IN REGIONAL BRAIN LEVELS OF AMINO-ACID PUTATIVE NEUROTRANSMITTERS AFTER PROLONGED TREATMENT WITH THE ANTICONVULSANT-DRUGS DIPHENYLHYDANTOIN, PHENOBARBITONE, SODIUM-VALPROATE, ETHOSUXIMIDE, AND SULTHIAME IN THE RAT.
003961 04-03

PHENOLIC
EFFECT OF THE POSITION OF THE PHENOLIC GROUP IN MORPHINANS ON THEIR AFFINITY FOR OPIATE-RECEPTOR BINDING.
003702 04-02
EFFECTS OF MOLINDONE AND FLUPHENAZINE ON THE BRAIN CONCENTRATION OF SOME PHENOLIC AND CATECHOLIC AMINES IN THE MOUSE AND THE RAT.
003870 04-03

PHENOMENA
LONG-TERM-TREATMENT WITH NEUROLEPTIC-AGENTS: ADAPTATION PHENOMENA AND THEIR SIGNIFICANCE WITH REGARD TO SCHIZOPHRENIC-SYMPTOMATOLOGY AND SIDE-EFFECTS.
002370 02-15
CHARACTER AND MEANING OF QUASI-MORPHINE WITHDRAWAL PHENOMENA ELICITED BY METHYLXANTHINES.
004087 04-04

PHENOTHIAZINE
EFFECT OF STRUCTURE ON PHENOTHIAZINE CATION RADICAL REACTIONS IN AQUEOUS BUFFERS.
000014 01-02
EFFECTS OF PHENOTHIAZINE DERIVATIVES AND RELATED COMPOUNDS ON TYROSINE-AMINOTRANSFERASE ACTIVITY.
000018 01-03
CLINICAL ASSESSMENT OF ONCE A DAY PHENOTHIAZINE ADMINISTRATION.
000573 01-08
INTERACTION BETWEEN AMITRIPTYLINE AND PHENOTHIAZINE IN MAN: METABOLITE NORTRIPTYLINE AND THE CORRELATION WITH CLINICAL-RESPONSE.
000640 01-09
THE USE OF THIOPROPERAZINE, A PHENOTHIAZINE DERIVATIVE, AS A LIGAND FOR NEUROLEPTIC-RECEPTORS -- I. IN VITRO STUDIES.
001133 02-03
THE USE OF THIOPROPERAZINE, A PHENOTHIAZINE DERIVATIVE, AS A LIGAND FOR NEUROLEPTIC-RECEPTORS -- II. IN VIVO STUDIES.
001137 02-03
CONFORMATIONALLY RESTRICTED PHENOTHIAZINE NEUROLEPTICS. 1. 3 DIMETHYLAMINO-TETRAHYDROAZEPINOPHENOTHIAZINE.
001359 02-03
CHANGE IN OVERINCLUSIVE THINKING OF SCHIZOPHRENIC-PATIENTS IS RELATED TO PLASMA PHENOTHIAZINE CONCENTRATION.
001941 02-08
PHENOTHIAZINE PLASMA AND RED-BLOOD-CELL CONCENTRATIONS, THEIR RELATIONSHIP TO SIDE-EFFECTS AND CLINICAL-EFFICACY.
002386 02-15
PHENOTHIAZINE ACTION ON CEREBRAL 5 HYDROXYTRYPTAMINE.
002850 03-03
INCREASED SERUM PROLACTIN LEVELS DURING PHENOTHIAZINE AND BUTYROPHENONE TREATMENT OF SIX POSTPARTUM WOMEN.
003318 03-11
SPECTRA OF RADICAL CATIONS OF PHENOTHIAZINE DERIVATIVES IN SOLUTION AND SOLID STATE.
003673 04-01
INHIBITION OF PENTAGASTRIN-STIMULATED AND OVERNIGHT GASTRIC SECRETION BY LM24056, A NEW PHENOTHIAZINE DERIVED ANTISECRETORY DRUG.
004306 04-07

PHENOTHIAZINES
PARTITIONING AND EFFLUX OF PHENOTHIAZINES FROM LIPOSOMES.
000007 01-02
POSSIBLE MODE OF ACTION OF NEUROPSYCHIATRIC-AGENTS: PHENOTHIAZINES AND IMINODIBENZYLS.
001271 02-03
EFFECT OF PROPRANOLOL AND PHENOTHIAZINES ON ELECTRODERMAL ORIENTING AND HABITUATION IN SCHIZOPHRENIA.
003174 03-08

PHENOTYPE
ACETYLATOR PHENOTYPE AND LUPUS-ERYTHEMATOSUS.
003545 03-15

PHENOTYPIC
MATERNAL GLUCOCORTICOID-HORMONES INFLUENCE NEUROTRANSMITTER PHENOTYPIC EXPRESSION IN EMBRYOS.
000149 01-03

PHENOXYBENZAMINE
ENHANCED SUPPRESSION OF CONDITIONED AVOIDANCE RESPONSE BY HALOPERIDOL BUT NOT PHENOXYBENZAMINE IN RATS WITH BILATERAL PARAFASCICULAR LESIONS.
000334 01-04
METABOLIC AND SYMPATHOADRENAL ABNORMALITIES IN THE OBESE ZUCKER RAT: EFFECT OF CHRONIC PHENOXYBENZAMINE TREATMENT.
003905 04-03
PHENOXYBENZAMINE AND BROMOCRIPTINE ATTENUATE NEED FOR REM SLEEP IN RATS.
004203 04-04
ANTAGONISM BY PHENOXYBENZAMINE AND PENTAZOCINE OF THE ANTINOCICEPTIVE-EFFECTS OF MORPHINE IN THE SPINAL-CORD.
004213 04-04

PHENTOLAMINE
COMPARISON OF MIANSERIN WITH DESIPRAMINE, MAPROTILINE AND PHENTOLAMINE ON CARDIAC PRESYNAPTIC AND VASCULAR POSTSYNAPTIC ALPHA-ADRENOCEPTORS AND NORADRENALINE REUPTAKE IN PITHED NORMOTENSIVE-RATS.
000044 01-03
INHIBITION BY LOCAL ANESTHETICS, PHENTOLAMINE AND PROPRANOLOL OF (3H)QUINUCLYDINYL-BENZYLATE BINDING TO CENTRAL MUSCARINIC-RECEPTORS.
001097 02-03
CENTRAL-ACTIONS OF NOREPINEPHRINE, PHENTOLAMINE AND 6 HYDROXYDOPAMINE IN SPONTANEOUSLY HYPERTENSIVE-RATS.
001553 02-03
EFFECT OF PHENTOLAMINE ADMINISTRATION INTO THE AMYGDALA COMPLEX OF RATS ON TIME-DEPENDENT MEMORY PROCESSES.
002998 03-04

PHENYL-2-THIAZOLYL-2-THIOUREA
EFFECT OF THE CATECHOLAMINE-DEPLETING-AGENT 1 PHENYL-2-THIAZOLYL-2-THIOUREA (U-14-624) ON DRUG METABOLISM IN THE RAT.
000280 01-03

PHENYLACETATE
THE CRYSTAL AND MOLECULAR STRUCTURE OF THE ACETYLCHOLINE ANTAGONIST DIMETHYLAMINOBUTYNYLCYCLOHEXYLHYDROXY 2 PHENYLACETATE HCL.
000003 01-01
PHENYLACETATE AND BRAIN-DYSFUNCTION IN EXPERIMENTAL PHENYLKETONURIA: SYNAPTIC DEVELOPMENT.
000191 01-03
PHENYLACETATE AND THE ENDURING BEHAVIORAL-DEFICIT IN EXPERIMENTAL PHENYLKETONURIA.
000388 01-04

PHENYLALANINE
THE CONVERSION OF (3H)TRYPTOPHAN TO 5 (3H)HYDROXYTRYPTAMINE IN MOUSE-BRAIN FOLLOWING DEPLETION OF PHENYLALANINE AND TYROSINE.
000148 01-03
DIVERGENT RESERPINE EFFECTS ON AMFONELIC-ACID AND AMPHETAMINE STIMULATION OF SYNAPTOSOMAL DOPAMINE FORMATION FROM PHENYLALANINE.
001113 02-03
D PHENYLALANINE IN ENDOGENOUS DEPRESSION.
002017 02-09
PHENYLALANINE LEVELS IN ENDOGENOUS PSYCHOSES.
002049 02-09
EEG CHANGES IN CHILDREN WITH TREATED PHENYLKETONURIA AFTER PHENYLALANINE LOAD.
002115 02-11
POSSIBLE MECHANISMS OF EFFECT OF ACTH4-10 AND ITS ANALOG, CONTAINING D ISOMER OF PHENYLALANINE, ON BEHAVIOR.
002949 03-04
EFFECT OF ALPHA METHYLPHENYLALANINE AND PHENYLALANINE ON BRAIN POLYRIBOSOMES AND PROTEIN SYNTHESIS.
003733 04-04

PHENYLALKYLAMINES
RELATIVE POTENCIES OF TWO PHENYLALKYLAMINES FOUND IN THE ABUSED PLANT CATHA-EDULIS, KHAT.
001084 02-02

PHENYLBUTAZONE
BIOLOGIC-INTERACTION OF GAMMA-RADIATION WITH PHENYLBUTAZONE, PHENYTOIN, OR HYDRALAZINE.
000518 01-05

PHENYLETHANOLAMINE
BETA PHENYLETHYLAMINE, PHENYLETHANOLAMINE, TYRAMINE AND OCTOPAMINE. (UNPUBLISHED PAPER).
002601 02-17

PHENYLETHANOLAMINE-N-METHYLTRANSFERASE
INHIBITORS OF PHENYLETHANOLAMINE-N-METHYLTRANSFERASE AND EPINEPHRINE BIOSYNTHESIS. 2. 1,2,3,4 TETRAHYDROISOQUINOLINE-7-SULFONANILIDES.
001069 02-02

PHENYLETHYLAMINE
MONOAMINE REPLACEMENT AFTER RESERPINE; CATECHOLAMINERGIC AGONISTS RESTORE MOTOR-ACTIVITY BUT PHENYLETHYLAMINE RESTORES ATROPINE-RESISTANT NEOCORTICAL LOW VOLTAGE FAST-ACTIVITY.
000309 01-03
EVIDENCE THAT A PREFERRED SUBSTRATE FOR MONOAMINE-OXIDASE-B MEDIATES STIMULUS PROPERTIES OF MAO-INHIBITORS; A POSSIBLE ROLE FOR BETA PHENYLETHYLAMINE IN THE COCAINE CUE.
000363 01-04
PHENYLETHYLAMINE, DOPAMINE AND NOREPINEPHRINE IN SCHIZOPHRENIA. (UNPUBLISHED PAPER).
001957 02-08
MONOAMINE-OXIDASE, PHENYLETHYLAMINE, NOREPINEPHRINE AND SCHIZOPHRENIA. (UNPUBLISHED PAPER).
001958 02-08
BETA PHENYLETHYLAMINE, PHENYLETHANOLAMINE, TYRAMINE AND OCTOPAMINE. (UNPUBLISHED PAPER).
002601 02-17

PHENYLETHYLAMINE EFFECTS ON DOPAMINE SYNTHESIS. STRUCTURE-ACTIVITY RELATIONSHIPS.
002649 03-02
MONOAMINE-OXIDASE-B ACTIVITIES TOWARD BETA PHENYLETHYLAMINE IN DISCRETE HYPOTHALAMIC AND CIRCUMVENTRICULAR NUCLEI OF THE RAT.
002781 03-03
PHENYLETHYLAMINE EFFECTS ON DOPAMINE SYNTHESIS: STRUCTURE-ACTIVITY RELATIONSHIPS. (UNPUBLISHED PAPER).
003959 04-03
BETA PHENYLETHYLAMINE REVERSAL OF CHLORPROMAZINE-INDUCED ACTIVATION OF STRIATAL TYROSINE-HYDROXYLASE AND CATALEPSY.
004018 04-03
OXIDATION OF BETA PHENYLETHYLAMINE BY BOTH TYPES OF MONOAMINE-OXIDASE: EXAMINATION OF ENZYMES IN BRAIN AND LIVER MITOCHONDRIA OF EIGHT SPECIES.
004024 04-03

PHENYLETHYLAMINES
COMPARATIVE-EFFECTS OF SUBSTITUTED PHENYLETHYLAMINES ON BRAIN SEROTONERGIC MECHANISMS.
003854 04-03

PHENYLHEXAHYDROAZEPINOINDOLES
SYNTHESIS OF SOME 5 PHENYLHEXAHYDROAZEPINOINDOLES AS POTENTIAL NEUROLEPTIC-AGENTS.
001019 02-01

PHENYLKETONURIA
PHENYLACETATE AND BRAIN-DYSFUNCTION IN EXPERIMENTAL PHENYLKETONURIA: SYNAPTIC DEVELOPMENT.
000191 01-03
PHENYLACETATE AND THE ENDURING BEHAVIORAL-DEFICIT IN EXPERIMENTAL PHENYLKETONURIA.
000388 01-04
EEG CHANGES IN CHILDREN WITH TREATED PHENYLKETONURIA AFTER PHENYLALANINE LOAD.
002115 02-11
PHENYLKETONURIA: THE INADVISABILITY OF NEUROLEPTIC-MEDICATION.
003380 03-11

PHENYLPROPANOLAMINE .
INFLUENCE OF AMPHETAMINE AND PHENYLPROPANOLAMINE ON FOOD INTAKE, ACTIVITY, AND BODY-TEMPERATURE IN RATS WITH VENTROMEDIAL HYPOTHALAMIC OR DORSOLATERAL TEGMENTAL DAMAGE.
000322 01-03
EFFECTS OF AMPHETAMINE AND PHENYLPROPANOLAMINE ON FOOD INTAKE IN RATS WITH VENTROMEDIAL HYPOTHALAMIC OR DORSOLATERAL TEGMENTAL DAMAGE.
001818 02-04
AMPHETAMINE-LIKE REACTIONS TO PHENYLPROPANOLAMINE.
003480 03-15

PHENYLURETHANS
SYNTHESIS OF PHENYLURETHANS OF 1,2 DIALKYL-4-PYRAZOLIDINOLS AS ANTICONVULSANT-AGENTS.
003695 04-02

PHENYTOIN
DISTRIBUTION OF 14C PHENYTOIN IN RAT PURKINJE-CELLS, CEREBELLAR AND CEREBRAL NEURONAL TISSUE AFTER A SINGLE INTRAPERITONEAL INJECTION.
000261 01-03
BIOLOGIC-INTERACTION OF GAMMA-RADIATION WITH PHENYLBUTAZONE, PHENYTOIN, OR HYDRALAZINE.
000518 01-05
VALPROIC-ACID AND PLASMA LEVELS OF PHENYTOIN.
000756 01-13
PRACTICAL AND THEORETICAL ASPECTS OF PHENYTOIN ADMINISTRATION. I. RELATIONSHIP BETWEEN DOSE AND PLASMA CONCENTRATION.
000760 01-13
EFFECT OF DOSE ON PHENYTOIN ABSORPTION.
000773 01-13
REVERSAL BY PHENYTOIN OF CARBAMAZEPINE-INDUCED WATER INTOXICATION: A PHARMACOKINETIC-INTERACTION.
000783 01-13
PREDICTABILITY OF PHENYTOIN SERUM LEVELS BY NOMOGRAMS AND CLINICIANS.
000909 01-16
DECREASED BENZODIAZEPINE-RECEPTOR DENSITY IN RAT-CEREBELLUM FOLLOWING NEUROTOXIC DOSES OF PHENYTOIN.
001373 02-03
PHENYTOIN KINETICS IN CHILDREN.
002113 02-11
INFLUENCE OF PHENYTOIN AND PHENOBARBITAL ON THE DISPOSITION OF A SINGLE-ORAL-DOSE OF CLONAZEPAM.
002248 02-13
INTERACTION BETWEEN PHENYTOIN AND VALPROIC-ACID: PLASMA PROTEIN BINDING AND METABOLIC-EFFECTS.
002276 02-13
INDIVIDUALIZATION OF PHENYTOIN THERAPY.
002495 02-16

EFFECTS OF PHENYTOIN ON PYRAMIDAL NEURONS OF THE RAT HIPPOCAMPUS.
002750 03-03

PHENYTOIN VALPROIC-ACID INTERACTION IN RHESUS-MONKEY.
002785 03-03

THE EFFECTS OF PHENYTOIN ON PHENOBARBITONE AND PRIMIDONE METABOLISM.
003333 03-11

PHENYTOIN: PHARMACOKINETICS AND CLINICAL THERAPEUTICS.
003353 03-11

INTRAVENOUS VALPROATE: EFFECTS ON PLASMA AND SALIVA PHENYTOIN LEVELS.
003359 03-11

DISSOCIATION BETWEEN FREE AND BOUND PHENYTOIN LEVELS IN PRESENCE OF SODIUM-VALPROATE.
003367 03-11

COMPARISON OF SODIUM-VALPROATE AND PHENYTOIN AS SINGLE DRUG-TREATMENT IN EPILEPSY.
003371 03-11

PHENYTOIN CONCENTRATIONS IN VENOUS VERSUS CAPILLARY BLOOD OF GERIATRIC-PATIENT.
003381 03-11

THE EFFECTS OF SALICYLATE ON THE PHARMACOKINETICS OF PHENYTOIN.
003421 03-13

RESPIRATORY-DISEASE AND NASAL IMMUNOGLOBULIN CONCENTRATIONS IN PHENYTOIN TREATED EPILEPTIC-PATIENTS.
003486 03-15

PHENYTOIN TOXICITY IN A BRAIN-DAMAGE ADOLESCENT: A CASE-REPORT.
003512 03-15

SINGLE POINT ESTIMATION OF PHENYTOIN DOSING REQUIREMENT.
003562 03-16

EFFECTS OF PHENYTOIN ON MOUSE CEREBELLAR 5 HYDROXYTRYPTAMINE AND NOREPINEPHRINE.
003795 04-03

PHENYTOIN INHIBITION OF CYCLIC-GUANOSINE-MONOPHOSPHATE (C-GMP) ACCUMULATION IN NEUROBLASTOMA CELLS BY CALCIUM-CHANNEL BLOCKADE.
004020 04-03

EFFECT OF PRENATAL PHENYTOIN ADMINISTRATION ON BRAIN TRYPTOPHAN METABOLISM OF RAT OFFSPRING DURING THE PREWEANING PERIOD.
004108 04-04

PHENYTOIN THERAPY FOR EPILEPTIC-CHILDREN: EVALUATION OF SALIVARY AND PLASMA CONCENTRATIONS AND OF METHODS OF ASSESSING COMPLIANCE.
004495 04-11

ANTIEPILEPTIC THERAPY WITH PHENYTOIN: WHICH IS THE OPTIMUM SERUM LEVEL?
004586 04-14

PHEOCHROMOCYTOMA
PURIFICATION AND CHARACTERIZATION OF RAT PHEOCHROMOCYTOMA DOPAMINE-BETA-HYDROXYLASE.
003664 04-01

PHOBIA
PHOBIA: PSYCHOLOGICAL-TREATMENT AND PHARMACOLOGICAL-TREATMENT.
004425 04-10

PHOBIAS
PHENELZINE AND EXPOSURE IN THE TREATMENT OF PHOBIAS.
003285 03-10

PHOBIC-ANXIETY
BEHAVIORAL-DESENSITIZATION OF PHOBIC-ANXIETY USING THIOPENTAL-SODIUM.
002352 02-14

PHOBIC-ANXIETY-SYNDROME
DRUG-TREATMENT OF THE PHOBIC-ANXIETY-SYNDROME.
003280 03-10

PHOBIC-STATES
DIFFERENTIAL DIAGNOSIS AND TREATMENT OF PANIC ATTACKS AND PHOBIC-STATES.
004424 04-10

PHOBIC-SUBJECTS
BEHAVIORAL-EFFECTS AND SUBJECTIVE-EFFECTS OF BETA-ADRENERGIC BLOCKADE IN PHOBIC-SUBJECTS.
002060 02-10

PHOSPHATIDYLSERINE
PHYSIOLOGIC AND PHARMACOLOGIC IMPLICATIONS IN THE DEACYLATION OF PHOSPHATIDYLSERINE IN MICE.
002682 03-03

PHOSPHODIESTERASE
PHOSPHODIESTERASE INHIBITORS FACILITATE MEMORY FOR PASSIVE-AVOIDANCE CONDITIONING.
003109 03-04

PHOSPHOLIPASE-A2
BRADYKININ-RECEPTOR STIMULATION OF C-AMP INVOLVES PHOSPHOLIPID METHYLATION, CA-FLUX, PHOSPHOLIPASE-A2 ACTIVATION AND PROSTAGLANDIN FORMATION. (UNPUBLISHED PAPER).
001002 02-01

PHOSPHOLIPID
PHOSPHOLIPID METHYLATION AND TRANSMEMBRANE SIGNALLING. (UNPUBLISHED PAPER).
001001 02-01

BRADYKININ-RECEPTOR STIMULATION OF C-AMP INVOLVES PHOSPHOLIPID METHYLATION, CA-FLUX, PHOSPHOLIPASE-A2 ACTIVATION AND PROSTAGLANDIN FORMATION. (UNPUBLISHED PAPER).
001002 02-01

PHOSPHOLIPID METABOLISM, CALCIUM-FLUX AND THE RECEPTOR-MEDIATED INDUCTION OF CHEMOTAXIS IN RABBIT NEUTROPHILS. (UNPUBLISHED PAPER).
001118 02-03

IGE MEDIATED HISTAMINE RELEASE IN RAT BASOPHILIC LEUKEMIA CELLS: RECEPTOR ACTIVATED PHOSPHOLIPID METHYLATION, CA-FLUX AND RELEASE OF ARACHIDONIC-ACID. (UNPUBLISHED PAPER).
001188 02-03

PHOSPHOLIPID METHYLATION: A BIOCHEMICAL-EVENT OF SIGNAL TRANSDUCTION. (UNPUBLISHED PAPER).
001279 02-03

INCREASED ADRENALINE, BETA-ADRENERGIC-RECEPTOR STIMULATION AND PHOSPHOLIPID METHYLATION IN PINEAL-GLAND OF SPONTANEOUSLY HYPERTENSIVE-RATS. (UNPUBLISHED PAPER).
001458 02-03

ONTOGENY OF HISTAMINERGIC NEUROTRANSMISSION IN THE RAT-BRAIN: CONCOMITANT DEVELOPMENT OF NEURONAL HISTAMINE, H1-RECEPTORS, AND H1-RECEPTOR-MEDIATED STIMULATION OF PHOSPHOLIPID TURNOVER.
004021 04-03

PHOSPHORUS
ELECTRON PROBE MICROANALYSIS OF CALCIUM AND PHOSPHORUS IN DENSE-BODIES ISOLATED FROM HUMAN PLATELETS. (UNPUBLISHED PAPER).
001014 02-01

PHOSPHORYLATION
REGULATION OF THE STATE OF PHOSPHORYLATION OF SPECIFIC NEURONAL PROTEINS IN MOUSE-BRAIN BY IN VIVO ADMINISTRATION OF ANESTHETIC AND CONVULSANT-AGENTS.
000291 01-03

PHOSPHORYLATION OF THE MEMBRANE-BOUND ACETYLCHOLINE-RECEPTOR: INHIBITION BY DIPHENYLHYDANTOIN.
001257 02-03

BRAIN STRIATAL TYROSINE-HYDROXYLASE: ACTIVATION OF THE ENZYME BY CYCLIC-AMP INDEPENDENT PHOSPHORYLATION.
001423 02-03

PHOTOAFFINITY
BENZODIAZEPINE-RECEPTOR: LOCALIZATION BY PHOTOAFFINITY LABELING AND ISOLATION OF A POSSIBLE ENDOGENOUS LIGAND.
001381 02-03

PHOTOCHEMICAL-STABILITY
THE PHOTOCHEMICAL-STABILITY OF CIS-ISOMERS AND TRANS-ISOMERS OF TRICYCLIC NEUROLEPTIC-DRUGS.
001872 02-06

PHOTOSENSITIVE
TRANSIENT ABOLITION OF GENERALIZED PHOTOSENSITIVE EPILEPTIC-DISCHARGE IN HUMANS BY APOMORPHINE, A DOPAMINE-RECEPTOR AGONIST.
000714 01-11

ELECTROENCEPHALOGRAPHIC-EFFECTS AND BEHAVIOURAL-EFFECTS OF SODIUM-VALPROATE IN PATIENTS WITH PHOTOSENSITIVE EPILEPSY. A SINGLE-DOSE TRIAL.
002154 02-11

THE EFFECT OF SODIUM-VALPROATE ON THE PHOTOSENSITIVE VEP.
004513 04-13

PHRENIC-NERVE
DIPHENYLHYDANTOIN-INDUCED BLOCK OF THE RAT PHRENIC-NERVE DIAPHRAGM PREPARATION PRETREATED WITH P HYDROXYMERCURIBENZOATE.
002749 03-03

PHRENOLON
THE EFFECT PHRENOLON ON DELAYED REACTIONS IN LOWER MONKEYS OF
001640 02-04

PHYSICAL
CHANGES OF PHYSICAL MORPHINE-DEPENDENCE IN RATS CHRONICALLY TREATED WITH DRUGS ACTING ON BRAIN 5 HYDROXYTRYPTAMINE.
001764 02-04

PSYCHIATRIC MORBIDITY AND PHYSICAL TOXICITY ASSOCIATED WITH ADJUVANT CHEMOTHERAPY AFTER MASTECTOMY.
002433 02-15

PHYSICAL AND PHYSIOLOGICAL CHARACTERISTICS OF MICROPRESSURE EJECTION OF DRUGS FROM MULTIBARRELED PIPETTES.
002502 02-16

PHYSICAL AND KINETIC PROPERTIES OF CHOLINE-ACETYL-TRANSFERASE FROM RAT AND BOVINE BRAIN.
003676 04-01

PHYSICAL-DEPENDENCE
CONTINUOUS-ACCESS PHENCYCLIDINE SELF-ADMINISTRATION BY RHESUS-MONKEYS LEADING TO PHYSICAL-DEPENDENCE.
000341 01-04
ASSESSMENT OF TOLERANCE TO AND PHYSICAL-DEPENDENCE ON PENTOBARBITAL, INDUCED BY MULTIPLE PELLET IMPLANTATION.
000385 01-04
DOSE AND PHYSICAL-DEPENDENCE AS FACTORS IN THE SELF-ADMINISTRATION OF MORPHINE BY RATS.
000497 01-04
BIPHASIC ACTIVITY OF MEMBRANE-BOUND ENZYMES IN BRAIN MITOCHONDRIA AND SYNAPTOSOMES DURING THE DEVELOPMENT OF TOLERANCE TO AND PHYSICAL-DEPENDENCE ON CHRONIC MORPHINE ADMINISTRATION TO RATS.
001285 02-03
COMPARISON OF OPIATE AGONISTS AND THEIR N ALLYL DERIVATIVES IN THE PRODUCTION OF PHYSICAL-DEPENDENCE IN THE RAT.
001841 02-05
ENKEPHALIN ANALOGS AND PHYSICAL-DEPENDENCE.
003572 03-16
BUPRENORPHINE: DEMONSTRATION OF PHYSICAL-DEPENDENCE LIABILITY.
004104 04-04

PHYSICALLY-HANDICAPPED-PATIENTS
SERUM CONCENTRATIONS OF PHENOBARBITAL AND DIPHENYLHYDANTOIN IN SEVERE MENTALLY-HANDICAPPED AND PHYSICALLY-HANDICAPPED-PATIENTS.
000856 01-15

PHYSICO-CHEMICAL
PHYSICO-CHEMICAL METHODOLOGIES IN PSYCHIATRIC-RESEARCH.
004679 04-16

PHYSICS
THE PHYSICS OF IONTOPHORETIC PIPETTES.
004299 04-06

PHYSIOLOGIC
PHYSIOLOGIC AND PHARMACOLOGIC IMPLICATIONS IN THE DEACYLATION OF PHOSPHATIDYLSERINE IN MICE.
002682 03-03
STATISTICAL ANALYSES OF PHYSIOLOGIC DATA FROM FEMALE PATIENTS WITH AN ENDOMORPHOUS DEPRESSIVE COURSE: A TRIAL, INTERACTIONS BETWEEN PHYSIOLOGIC PARAMETERS, TEST JUNCTURES IN THIS PHASE.
003251 03-09

PHYSIOLOGICAL
GABA BENZODIAZEPINE INTERACTIONS: PHYSIOLOGICAL, PHARMACOLOGICAL AND DEVELOPMENTAL ASPECTS.
000103 01-03
PHYSICAL AND PHYSIOLOGICAL CHARACTERISTICS OF MICROPRESSURE EJECTION OF DRUGS FROM MULTIBARRELED PIPETTES.
002502 02-16
IDENTICAL RESPONSES OF THE TWO HIPPOCAMPAL THETA GENERATORS TO PHYSIOLOGICAL AND PHARMACOLOGICAL ACTIVATION.
002792 03-03
CORE TEMPERATURE CHANGES FOLLOWING ADMINISTRATION OF NALOXONE AND NALTREXONE TO RATS EXPOSED TO HOT AND COLD AMBIENT TEMPERATURES. EVIDENCE FOR THE PHYSIOLOGICAL ROLE OF ENDORPHINS IN HOT AND COLD ACCLIMATIZATION.
004034 04-03
PHYSIOLOGICAL SIGNIFICANCE OF DOPAMINE-AUTORECEPTORS AS STUDIED FOLLOWING THEIR SELECTIVE BLOCKADE BY MOLINDONE.
004065 04-04
PHYSIOLOGICAL AND BEHAVIORAL APPROACHES TO THE STUDY OF THE QUASI-MORPHINE WITHDRAWAL-SYNDROME.
004242 04-04
MEPROBAMATE REDUCES ACCURACY OF PHYSIOLOGICAL DETECTION OF DECEPTION.
004585 04-14
BIOLOGICAL AND PHYSIOLOGICAL PREDICTORS OF DRUG RESPONSE. (UNPUBLISHED PAPER).
004708 04-17

PHYSIOLOGICAL-CORRELATES
LONG-TERM EFFECTS OF TESTOSTERONE INJECTIONS ON THE SOCIAL-BEHAVIOUR OF MALE DUCKS AND THEIR PHYSIOLOGICAL-CORRELATES.
001565 02-04

PHYSIOLOGICAL-STUDIES
PHYSIOLOGICAL-STUDIES AND BEHAVIORAL-STUDIES WITH MUSCIMOL.
002538 02-17

PHYSIOLOGY
CLASSIFICATION OF ENDORPHINS/ENKEPHALINS IN BRAIN PHYSIOLOGY AND PATHOLOGY (BASED ON EEG AND CLINICAL-STUDY OF SYNTHETICALLY-MODIFIED METHIONINE-ENKEPHALIN).
002286 02-13
ON THE PHYSIOLOGY AND PHARMACOLOGY OF ENDORPHINS.
003417 03-13

PHYSOSTIGMINE
INHIBITION OF (3H)NALOXONE BINDING IN HOMOGENATES OF RAT-BRAIN BY ESEROLINE, A DRUG, WITH ANALGESIC ACTIVITY, RELATED TO PHYSOSTIGMINE.
000104 01-03
THERAPEUTIC APPLICATION OF PHYSOSTIGMINE IN NEUROSIS.
000651 01-10
MEMORY AND COGNITIVE FUNCTION IN THE ELDERLY: A PRELIMINARY-TRIAL OF PHYSOSTIGMINE.
000802 01-14
MOOD AND BEHAVIORAL-EFFECTS OF PHYSOSTIGMINE ON HUMANS ARE ACCOMPANIED BY ELEVATIONS IN PLASMA BETA ENDORPHIN AND CORTISOL.
002280 02-13
HUMAN MEMORY AND THE EFFECTS OF PHYSOSTIGMINE AND CHOLINE-CHLORIDE.
002317 02-14
PHYSOSTIGMINE INDUCTION OF DEPRESSIVE-SYMPTOMATOLOGY IN NORMAL HUMAN SUBJECTS.
003255 03-09
PHYSOSTIGMINE IN TOURETTE-SYNDROME: EVIDENCE FOR CHOLINERGIC UNDERACTIVITY.
003286 03-10
PHYSOSTIGMINE FOR TREATMENT OF DELIRIUM-TREMENS.
003364 03-11
ALTERATIONS IN CEREBROSPINAL-FLUID DOPAMINE METABOLITES FOLLOWING PHYSOSTIGMINE INFUSION.
003477 03-15

PHYTOHEMAGGLUTININ
THE EFFECT OF CHLORPROMAZINE AND MAGEPTIL ON THE PROLIFERATION OF PERIPHERAL BLOOD LYMPHOCYTES IN CULTIVATION WITH PHYTOHEMAGGLUTININ.
004541 04-13

PIAL-ARTERIES
DOPAMINE-BETA-HYDROXYLASE ACTIVITY AND NORADRENALINE CONTENT IN PIAL-ARTERIES OF CAT AND GOAT.
001357 02-03
INFLUENCE OF CALCIUM ON NORADRENALINE RELEASE EVOKED BY 5 HYDROXYTRYPTAMINE, TYRAMINE AND POTASSIUM FROM GOAT PIAL-ARTERIES.
003925 04-03

PIAL-ARTERIOLES
BIPHASIC RESPONSIVENESS OF RAT PIAL-ARTERIOLES TO DOPAMINE: DIRECT OBSERVATIONS ON THE MICROCIRCULATION.
001105 02-03

PICK
TWO NEW DRUGS MAY PICK UP WHERE L-DOPA LEAVES OFF.
001897 02-07

PICOGRAM
A RAPID AND SIMPLE METHOD FOR THE DETERMINATION OF PICOGRAM LEVELS OF 3 METHOXYTYRAMINE IN BRAIN TISSUE USING LIQUID-CHROMATOGRAPHY WITH ELECTROCHEMICAL DETECTION.
003674 04-01

PICOMOLE
DETERMINATION OF PICOMOLE AMOUNTS OF DOPAMINE, NORADRENALINE, 3,4 DIHYDROXYPHENYLALANINE, 3,4 DIHYDROXYPHENYLACETIC-ACID, HOMOVANILLIC-ACID, AND 5 HYDROXYINDOLEACETIC-ACID IN NERVOUS-TISSUE AFTER ONE-STEP PURIFICATION ON SEPHADEX-G-10, USING HIGH.
004305 04-06

PICROTOXIN
EFFECT OF PICROTOXIN AND NIPECOTIC-ACID ON INHIBITORY RESPONSE OF DOPAMINERGIC NEURONS IN THE VENTRAL TEGMENTAL AREA TO STIMULATION OF THE NUCLEUS-ACCUMBENS.
000331 01-03
LOCOMOTOR AND CONVULSIVE RESPONSES TO PICROTOXIN IN AMYGDALA KINDLED RATS.
000416 01-04
LOCOMOTOR-ACTIVITY ELICITED BY INJECTIONS OF PICROTOXIN INTO THE VENTRAL TEGMENTAL AREA IS ATTENUATED BY INJECTIONS OF GABA INTO THE GLOBUS-PALLIDUS.
000436 01-04
MAPPING OF DYSKINETIC-MOVEMENTS INDUCED BY LOCAL APPLICATION OF PICROTOXIN OR () GAMMA ACETYLENIC-GABA ON THE RAT MOTOR-CORTEX.
000458 01-04
SENSITIVITY OF IDENTIFIED MEDIAL HYPOTHALAMIC NEURONS TO GABA, GLYCINE AND RELATED AMINO-ACIDS; INFLUENCE OF BICUCULLINE, PICROTOXIN AND STRYCHNINE ON SYNAPTIC INHIBITION.
002674 03-03
EFFECT OF PICROTOXIN ON BENZODIAZEPINE-RECEPTORS AND GABA-RECEPTORS WITH REFERENCE TO THE EFFECT OF CHLORIDE ION.
002725 03-03
MODULATION BY PICROTOXIN AND IPTBO OF 3H FLUNITRAZEPAM BINDING TO THE GABA/BENZODIAZEPINE-RECEPTOR COMPLEX OF RAT-CEREBELLUM.
002775 03-03
EFFECTS OF 5 HYDROXYTRYPTAMINE ON CENTRAL NEURONES ANTAGONIZED BY BICUCULLINE AND PICROTOXIN
003931 04-03

PIECES
DOPAMINERGIC MECHANISMS IN THE TELEOST RETINA. II. FACTORS AFFECTING THE ACCUMULATION OF CYCLIC-AMP IN PIECES OF INTACT CARP RETINA.
003776 04-03

PIFLUTIXOL
SIMILARITIES BETWEEN THE BINDING OF 3H PIFLUTIXOL AND 3H
FLUPENTIXOL TO RAT STRIATAL DOPAMINE-RECEPTORS IN VITRO.
002760 03-03

PIG
THE INTERACTION OF 2,3,4 TRIHYDROXYBENZYLHYDRAZINE WITH
DOPA-DECARBOXYLASE FROM PIG KIDNEY.
002925 03-03

PIGEON
LITHIUM-CHLORIDE AND DELTA9 THC LEAD TO CONDITIONED AVERSIONS
IN THE PIGEON.
003003 03-04

A CHARACTERIZATION OF THE BEHAVIORAL-EFFECTS OF LEVO ALPHA
ACETYLMETHADOL IN THE RAT AND IN THE PIGEON. (PH.D.
DISSERTATION).
003047 03-04

METHYLMERCURY-INDUCED CHANGES IN OPERANT DISCRIMINATION BY
THE PIGEON.
004271 04-05

PIGEONS
DELTA9 THC IN PIGEONS: A REPLICATION AND EXTENSION.
000394 01-04

JOINT-EFFECTS OF D-AMPHETAMINE AND ETHANOL OR PENTOBARBITAL
IN PIGEONS.
000403 01-04

LSD-25 AS A DISCRIMINATIVE-STIMULUS FOR RESPONSE SELECTION BY
PIGEONS.
000412 01-04

EFFECTS OF APOMORPHINE ON ELICITED AND OPERANT PECKING IN
PIGEONS.
001557 02-04

DISCRIMINATIVE-STIMULUS EFFECTS OF PENTOBARBITAL IN PIGEONS.
001651 02-04

DELTA9 THC AS A DISCRIMINATIVE-STIMULUS IN RATS AND PIGEONS:
GENERALIZATION TO THC METABOLITES AND SP-111.
001666 02-04

THE EFFECTS OF D-AMPHETAMINE, CHLORDIAZEPOXIDE, AND
PENTOBARBITAL ON BEHAVIOR MAINTAINED BY ESCAPE FROM
PUNISHMENT IN PIGEONS. (PH.D. DISSERTATION).
001713 02-04

DRUG-EFFECTS ON THE PERFORMANCE OF PIGEONS UNDER A NEGATIVE
AUTOMAINTENANCE-SCHEDULE.
001754 02-04

EFFECTS OF NORCOCAINE AND SOME NORCOCAINE DERIVATIVES ON
SCHEDULE-CONTROLLED BEHAVIOR OF PIGEONS AND SQUIRREL-
MONKEYS.
004012 04-03

METHADONE-INDUCED ATTENUATION OF THE EFFECTS OF DELTA9
TETRAHYDROCANNABINOL ON TEMPORAL DISCRIMINATION IN
PIGEONS.
004095 04-04

NARCOTIC DISCRIMINATION IN PIGEONS.
004132 04-04

PIGS
OPERANT FEEDING AND DRINKING IN PIGS FOLLOWING
INTRACEREBROVENTRICULAR INJECTION OF SYNTHETIC
CHOLECYSTOKININ-OCTAPEPTIDE.
003064 03-04

PIGTAIL-MACAQUE
BEHAVIOR MAINTAINED BY INTRAVENOUS INJECTION OF CODEINE,
COCAINE, AND ETORPHINE IN THE RHESUS-MACAQUE AND THE
PIGTAIL-MACAQUE.
001828 02-04

PILLS
PILLS FOR NERVES.
000652 01-10

PILOCARPINE
EFFECTS OF SCOPOLAMINE, PILOCARPINE, AND OXOTREMORINE ON THE
EXPLORATORY-BEHAVIOR OF TWO PSYCHOGENETICALLY SELECTED
LINES OF RATS IN A COMPLEX MAZE.
003042 03-04

PILOT-STUDY
COMBINED MONOAMINE-OXIDASE-INHIBITOR TRICYCLIC-
ANTIDEPRESSANT TREATMENT: A PILOT-STUDY.
000644 01-09

EVALUATION OF CLORAZEPATE (TRANXENE) AS AN ANTICONVULSANT --
A PILOT-STUDY.
000728 01-11

BACLOFEN IN TRIGEMINAL-NEURALGIA: ITS EFFECT ON THE SPINAL
TRIGEMINAL-NUCLEUS: A PILOT-STUDY.
002122 02-11

TOLERANCE TO DEXTROAMPHETAMINE-SULFATE IN HYPERACTIVE-
CHILDREN: ASSESSMENT USING AN EMPIRICAL NEUROPSYCHOLOGICAL
PARADIGM -- A PILOT-STUDY.
002126 02-11

GROUP VERSUS INDIVIDUAL COGNITIVE-THERAPY: A PILOT-STUDY.
003257 03-09

USE OF THA IN TREATMENT OF ALZHEIMER-LIKE DEMENTIA: PILOT-STUDY
IN TWELVE PATIENTS.
003377 03-11

ALPRAZOLAM, A NEW TYPE ANXIOLYTIC IN NEUROTIC-PATIENTS: A
PILOT-STUDY.
004422 04-10

PIMOZIDE
ACTIONS OF CHLORPROMAZINE, HALOPERIDOL AND PIMOZIDE ON LIPID
METABOLISM IN GUINEA-PIG BRAIN SLICES.
000129 01-03

BIPHASIC-EFFECTS OF PIMOZIDE ON SLEEP-WAKEFULNESS IN DOGS.
000495 01-04

THE EFFECT OF MORPHINE, PIMOZIDE AND NALOXONE ON
DISCRIMINATION BY RATS IN A SHOCK-ESCAPE-TEST.
001700 02-04

EFFECTS OF PIMOZIDE ON ACCURACY OF PERFORMANCE AND
DISTRIBUTION OF CORRECT RESPONDING ON A SIMULTANEOUS
DISCRIMINATION TASK IN THE RAT.
001806 02-04

INTERMITTENT PIMOZIDE VERSUS FLUPHENAZINE-DECANOATE AS
MAINTENANCE-THERAPY IN CHRONIC SCHIZOPHRENIA.
001932 02-08

A NEW DOSAGE SCHEDULE FOR PIMOZIDE IN THE ACUTE STABILIZATION
AND MAINTENANCE-TREATMENT OF PSYCHOSIS.
002022 02-09

PIMOZIDE IN THE TREATMENT OF SOME SOCIAL-MALADJUSTMENTS IN
PERSONALITY-DISORDERS.
002068 02-10

HUNTINGTONS-DISEASE: CLINICAL-EFFECTS OF A SHORT-TERM
TREATMENT WITH PIMOZIDE.
002091 02-11

USE OF PIMOZIDE (ORAP) IN CHILD-PSYCHIATRY.
002100 02-11

FACTORS DETERMINING PATIENT TENURE ON A 3-YEAR DOUBLE-BLIND
INVESTIGATION OF PIMOZIDE VERSUS FLUPHENAZINE-HCL.
002513 02-17

THE EFFECTS OF PIMOZIDE DURING PAIRING ON THE TRANSFER OF
CLASSICAL CONDITIONING TO AN OPERANT DISCRIMINATION.
002956 03-04

PIMOZIDE ATTENUATES LEVER-PRESSING FOR WATER REINFORCEMENT IN
RATS.
003000 03-04

EFFECTS OF DOPAMINE, APOMORPHINE, GAMMA HYDROXYBUTYRIC-
ACII , HALOPERIDOL AND PIMOZIDE ON REFLEX BRADYCARDIA IN
RATS.
004085 04-04

PLASMA CORTICOSTERIODS IN MANIA: THE EFFECTS OF PIMOZIDE.
004363 04-09

THE EFFECT OF THE DOPAMINE-RECEPTOR BLOCKING-DRUG PIMOZIDE ON
THE STIMULANT AND ANORECTIC-ACTIONS OF DEXTROAMPHETAMINE
IN MAN.
004580 04-14

PIMOZIDE-HYDROCHLORIDE
THE CRYSTAL AND MOLECULAR STRUCTURE OF THE NEUROLEPTIC
PIMOZIDE-HYDROCHLORIDE, BISFLUOROPHENYL-
BUTYLPIPERIDYLBENZIMIDAZOLINONE-HCL.
001015 02-01

PINEAL
PINEAL INTERACTIONS WITH THE CENTRAL-NERVOUS-SYSTEM:
NEUROENDOCRINE IMPLICATIONS. (PH.D. DISSERTATION).
001341 02-03

ADRENERGIC REGULATION OF THE REDUCTION IN ACETYL-COENZYME-
A:ARYLAMINE-N-ACETYLTRANSFERASE IN THE RAT PINEAL.
002654 03-03

PINEAL-GLAND
INCREASED ADRENALINE, BETA-ADRENERGIC-RECEPTOR STIMULATION
AND PHOSPHOLIPID METHYLATION IN PINEAL-GLAND OF
SPONTANEOUSLY HYPERTENSIVE-RATS: (UNPUBLISHED PAPER).
001458 02-03

PINEAL-GLAND. (UNPUBLISHED PAPER).
001552 02-03

PINEAL-GLAND AND MELATONIN INFLUENCE ON CHRONIC ALCOHOL
CONSUMPTION BY HAMSTERS.
003076 03-04

ULTRASTRUCTURAL LOCALIZATION OF MONOAMINES IN NERVE FIBERS
OF THE PINEAL-GLAND IN GOLDEN HAMSTERS.
003666 04-01

EFFECT OF 6 HYDROXYDOPAMINE ON THE FINE STRUCTURE OF THE
HAMSTER PINEAL-GLAND.
003747 04-03

CIRCADIAN-VARIATION OF CYCLIC-AMP IN THE RAT PINEAL-GLAND.
003938 04-03

PINEAL-ORGAN
A SPECIFIC AND SENSITIVE MICROASSAY FOR HYDROXYINDOLES IN
BIOLOGICAL-MATERIAL -- APPLICATION FOR CEREBRAL MICROVESSELS,
BRAIN, AND PINEAL-ORGAN OF THE RAT.
002503 02-16

PINNA-REFLEX
EFFECTS ON THE PINNA-REFLEX OF DRUGS ACTING AT ALPHA-
ADRENOCEPTORS.
004078 04-04

PIONEERS
FDA CLIPS PSYCHODRUG PIONEERS IND WINGS.
003160 03-07

PIPECOLIC-ACID
UPTAKE OF PIPERIDINE AND PIPECOLIC-ACID BY SYNAPTOSOMES FROM MOUSE-BRAIN.
001396 02-03

PIPERACETAZINE
TARDIVE-DYSKINESIA FOLLOWING LOW-DOSES OF PIPERACETAZINE.
002399 02-15

PIPERAZINYL-10H-THIENOBENZODIAZEPINES
4 PIPERAZINYL-10H-THIENOBENZODIAZEPINES AS POTENTIAL NEUROLEPTICS.
001592 02-04

PIPERAZINYL-4H-THIENOBENZODIAZEPINES
10 PIPERAZINYL-4H-THIENOBENZODIAZEPINES AS POTENTIAL NEUROLEPTICS.
001591 02-04

PIPERAZINYL-5H-PYRROLOBENZODIAZEPINE
DERIVATIVES OF 11 1 PIPERAZINYL-5H-PYRROLOBENZODIAZEPINE AS CENTRAL-NERVOUS-SYSTEM AGENTS.
001093 02-02

PIPERIDINE
UPTAKE OF PIPERIDINE AND PIPECOLIC-ACID BY SYNAPTOSOMES FROM MOUSE-BRAIN.
001396 02-03

PIPERIDINE-4-SULPHONIC-ACID
PIPERIDINE-4-SULPHONIC-ACID, A NEW SPECIFIC GABA AGONIST.
002647 03-02

PIPERIDONE
PIPERIDONE IN CHRONIC SCHIZOPHRENIC-PATIENTS: A CONTROLLED DOUBLE-BLIND STUDY.
003184 03-08

PIPETTES
PHYSICAL AND PHYSIOLOGICAL CHARACTERISTICS OF MICROPRESSURE EJECTION OF DRUGS FROM MULTIBARRELED PIPETTES.
002502 02-16

THE PHYSICS OF IONTOPHORETIC PIPETTES.
004299 04-06

PIPOTHIAZINE-PALMITATE
LONG-TERM EFFECTS OF PIPOTHIAZINE-PALMITATE.
001922 02-08

METHODOLOGY AND RESULTS OF A LONG-TERM STUDY OF LONG-ACTING NEUROLEPTICS: PIPOTHIAZINE-PALMITATE AND FLUPHENAZINE-DECANOATE.
001929 02-08

PIPRADROL
THE EFFECTS OF PIPRADROL ON THE ACQUISITION OF RESPONDING WITH CONDITIONED REINFORCEMENT: A ROLE FOR SENSORY PRECONDITIONING.
001572 02-04

PIRACETAM
OUR EXPERIENCE WITH PIRACETAM (NOOTROPIL-UCB) TREATMENT IN CHILDREN FROM HIGH-RISK PREGNANCIES WITH SUBSEQUENT MINIMAL-BRAIN-DYSFUNCTION.
000544 01-07

CLINICAL AND BIOCHEMICAL-ACTION OF PIRACETAM (NOOTROPIL) IN DRUG-RESISTANT DEPRESSION.
000600 01-09

CLINICAL-EXPERIENCE WITH PIRACETAM THERAPY IN GERONTOLOGY.
000686 01-11

PIRACETAM AND RETRIEVAL OF MEMORY IN YOUNG RATS.
000803 01-14

INFLUENCE OF PYRITHIOXINE, MECLOPHENOXATE AND PIRACETAM ON THE LEARNING PROCESS IN MAN.
000805 01-14

CRITERIA FOR CLINICAL DEVELOPMENT AND CLASSIFICATION OF NOOTROPIC-DRUGS. AN EXAMPLE: PIRACETAM.
000988 01-17

EFFECT OF PYRITINOL AND PIRACETAM ON CHANGES IN FREE AMMONIA LEVEL IN CNS TISSUE AFTER PARADOXICAL SLEEP-DEPRIVATION IN RATS. .
001199 02-03

THE EFFECTS OF PIRACETAM ON FREE FATTY-ACIDS IN THE BRAIN.
001474 02-03

PIRACETAM EFFECT ON LEARNING AND MEMORY IN RATS. .
001689 02-04

EFFECT OF PIRACETAM ON AGONISTIC-BEHAVIOUR IN MICE.
001796 02-04

PIRACETAM ACTION IN NEUROLEPTIC-INDUCED EXTRAPYRAMIDAL SIDE-EFFECTS.
002132 02-11

CLINICAL-EXPERIENCE WITH PSYCHIATRIC-TREATMENT OF THE ELDERLY INVOLVING THE USE OF PIRACETAM.
002188 02-11

PIRACETAM DIMINISHES HIPPOCAMPAL ACETYLCHOLINE LEVELS IN RATS.
002934 03-03

A DOUBLE-BLIND, PLACEBO-CONTROLLED-STUDY OF PIRACETAM IN ELDERLY PSYCHIATRIC-PATIENTS.
003305 03-11

EFFECT OF PIRACETAM ON EEG SPECTRA OF BOYS WITH LEARNING-DISORDERS.
003383 03-11

PIRACETAM ACTIVITY MAY DIFFER ACCORDING TO THE AGE OF THE RECIPIENT MOUSE.
003705 04-02

THE EFFICACY OF PIRACETAM IN VERTIGO: A DOUBLE-BLIND STUDY IN PATIENTS WITH VERTIGO OF CENTRAL ORIGIN.
004478 04-11

PIRETANIDE
THE EFFECT OF FRUSEMIDE PIRETANIDE AND BUMETANIDE ON COCHLEAR SUCCINIC-DEHYDROGENASE.
003757 04-03

PIRIBEDIL
CEREBRAL CIRCULATORY AND METABOLIC-EFFECTS OF PIRIBEDIL.
000200 01-03

REDUCTION OF FOOD INTAKE BY PIRIBEDIL IN THE RAT: RELATION TO DOPAMINE-RECEPTOR STIMULATION.
000355 01-04

CONTRIBUTION TO THE CLINICAL-STUDY OF CEREBRAL DOPAMINERGIC MECHANISMS: THE ACTION OF PIRIBEDIL IN PSYCHIATRY. FIRST RESULTS.
000616 01-09

AMPHETAMINE AND PIRIBEDIL IN AFFECTIVE-ILLNESS.
000618 01-09

EFFECT OF PIRIBEDIL (ET-495) ON PLASMA NOREPINEPHRINE: RELATIONSHIP TO ANTIDEPRESSANT RESPONSE.
002034 02-09

PIRIBEDIL IN ELDERLY PSYCHIATRIC-PATIENTS.
002170 02-11

PREJUNCTIONAL ACTIONS OF PIRIBEDIL ON THE ISOLATED KIDNEY OF THE RABBIT: COMPARISON WITH APOMORPHINE.
003749 04-03

INFLUENCE OF THE DOPAMINERGIC AGONISTS BROMOCRIPTINE, PIRIBEDIL AND NOMIFENSINE ON THE SYMPATHETIC NEURAL TRANSMISSION IN THE NICTITATING MEMBRANE OF THE CAT.
003822 04-03

PIRLINDOLE
THE NEW ANTIDEPRESSANT PIRLINDOLE: ANTAGONISM OF ACUTE OVERDOSAGE IN THE MOUSE.
001082 02-02

THE NEW ANTIDEPRESSANT PIRLINDOLE: A COMPARISON WITH IMIPRAMINE AND TRANYLCYPROMINE.
001360 02-03

PHARMACOLOGICAL-PROPERTIES OF 2,3,3A,4,5,6 HEXAHYDROMETHYL-1H-PYRAZINOCARBAZOL-HCL (PIRLINDOLE), A NEW ANTIDEPRESSANT.
004174 04-04

PITFALLS
IONOPHORESIS — PROGRESS AND PITFALLS.
003144 03-06

IS MANIA OVERDIAGNOSED?: THE THREE COMMON PITFALLS IN DIAGNOSING MANIC-DEPRESSIVE-ILLNESS.
003260 03-09

PITHED
COMPARISON OF MIANSERIN WITH DESIPRAMINE, MAPROTILINE AND PHENTOLAMINE ON CARDIAC PRESYNAPTIC AND VASCULAR POSTSYNAPTIC ALPHA-ADRENOCEPTORS AND NORADRENALINE REUPTAKE IN PITHED NORMOTENSIVE-RATS.
000044 01-03

AN EXAMINATION OF FACTORS INFLUENCING ADRENERGIC TRANSMISSION IN THE PITHED RAT, WITH SPECIAL REFERENCE TO NORADRENALINE UPTAKE MECHANISMS AND POSTJUNCTIONAL ALPHA-ADRENOCEPTORS.
001196 02-03

HEMODYNAMIC FAILURE INDUCED BY NARCOTIC AND TOXIC DOSES OF 12 CNS DEPRESSANTS IN INTACT AND PITHED RATS.
001855 02-05

DIFFERENTIAL INHIBITION OF ALPHA1-ADRENOCEPTOR AND ALPHA2-ADRENOCEPTOR MEDIATED PRESSOR RESPONSES IN PITHED RATS.
004057 04-05

PITUITARY
RELEASE OF GONADOTROPIN-RELEASING-HORMONE BY VERATRINE IN A HYPOTHALAMIC PITUITARY COINCUBATION.
000237 01-03

CHANGES IN OPIATE ACTIVITY OF RAT PITUITARY FOLLOWING ACUTE ADMINISTRATION OF NEUROLEPTICS.
000282 01-03

DOPAMINERGIC FACTORS IN HUMAN PROLACTIN REGULATION: A PITUITARY MODEL FOR THE STUDY OF A NEUROENDOCRINE SYSTEM IN MAN.
000776 01-13

THE IDENTITY AND HYPOTHALAMIC ORIGIN OF CHOLECYSTOKININ IN RAT-BRAIN AND POSTERIOR PITUITARY AND ITS POSSIBLE ROLE IN REGULATION OF NEUROSECRETION. (UNPUBLISHED PAPER).
001003 02-01

INFLUENCE OF DRUGS AFFECTING THE PITUITARY ADRENAL AXIS ON CHROMAFFIN CELLS.
001183 02-03

SODIUM-CHLORIDE INHIBITION DECREASES LEVELS OF IMMUNOREACTIVE DYNORPHIN IN THE NEUROINTERMEDIATE PITUITARY OF RATS.
001283 02-03

NALOXONE-LIKE ACTIONS OF MIF-1 DO NOT REQUIRE THE PRESENCE OF THE PITUITARY.
001311 02-03

THE PITUITARY DOPAMINE-RECEPTOR.
001324 02-03

EFFECTS OF ANTIDEPRESSANTS ON PITUITARY HORMONAL SECRETIONS IN HEALTHY TEST SUBJECTS, NEUROTIC-PATIENTS, AND ENDOGENOUS DEPRESSIVE-PATIENTS.
002009 02-09

ANTERIOR PITUITARY GABA-RECEPTORS AND THEIR REGULATION OF PROLACTIN SECRETION.
002738 03-03

DEVELOPMENT OF ACUTE TOLERANCE TO THE EFFECTS OF NALOXONE ON THE HYPOTHALAMIC PITUITARY LUTEINIZING-HORMONE AXIS IN THE MALE RAT.
002853 03-03

ROLE OF ADRENERGIC BLOCKING-AGENTS AND GLUCOCORTICOIDS ON THE REGULATION OF PITUITARY OPIOID-PEPTIDES LEVELS.
003801 04-03

ROLE OF THE ANTERIOR PITUITARY GABA-RECEPTOR IN THE CONTROL OF PROLACTIN RELEASE.
003809 04-03

PHARMACOLOGIC MANIPULATION OF BRAIN AND PITUITARY ENDORPHIN CONTENT AND RELEASE.
003837 04-03

LONG-TERM-TREATMENT OF RATS WITH MORPHINE DECREASES IN VITRO BIOSYNTHESIS IN AND RELEASE OF BETA ENDORPHIN FROM INTERMEDIATE/POSTERIOR LOBES OF PITUITARY.
003846 04-03

NEUROTRANSMITTER CONTROL OF HYPOTHALAMIC PITUITARY THYROID-FUNCTION IN RATS.
003942 04-03

DOPAMINE-RECEPTOR BINDING IN BOVINE INTERMEDIATE LOBE PITUITARY MEMBRANES.
004003 04-03

EFFECTS OF CAFFEINE ON ANTERIOR PITUITARY AND THYROID-FUNCTION IN THE RAT.
004014 04-03

ACTH-LIKE PEPTIDES, PITUITARY ADRENOCORTICAL FUNCTION AND AVOIDANCE-BEHAVIOR.
004109 04-04

PITUITARY-GLANDS
CORTICOSTERONE INCREASES THE SYNTHESIS OF A SOLUBLE PROTEIN IN PITUITARY-GLANDS FROM ADRENALECTOMIZED MALE RATS WHICH PRECIPITATES WITH ANTI-RAT GROWTH-HORMONE ANTISERUM. (UNPUBLISHED PAPER).
001122 02-03

THE DIRECT EFFECT OF RESERPINE IN VITRO ON PROLACTIN RELEASE FROM RAT ANTERIOR PITUITARY-GLANDS.
002810 03-03

PITUITARY-HORMONES
EVIDENCE FOR A DIRECT INHIBITORY-EFFECT OF MORPHINE ON THE SECRETION OF POSTERIOR PITUITARY-HORMONES.
000193 01-03

BIOSYNTHESIS OF POSTERIOR PITUITARY-HORMONES. (UNPUBLISHED PAPER).
001053 02-01

BIOSYNTHESIS, AXONAL TRANSPORT AND RELEASE OF POSTERIOR PITUITARY-HORMONES. (UNPUBLISHED PAPER).
001148 02-03

BIOLOGICAL-EFFECTS OF CHLORPROMAZINE IN CHRONIC SCHIZOPHRENICS. I. WITH REFERENCE TO PITUITARY-HORMONES.
003415 03-13

PK-8165
MULTIPLE BENZODIAZEPINE-RECEPTORS: EVIDENCE OF A DISSOCIATION BETWEEN ANTICONFLICT AND ANTICONVULSANT PROPERTIES BY PK-8165 AND PK-9084 (TWO QUINOLINE DERIVATIVES).
003898 04-03

PK-9084
MULTIPLE BENZODIAZEPINE-RECEPTORS: EVIDENCE OF A DISSOCIATION BETWEEN ANTICONFLICT AND ANTICONVULSANT PROPERTIES BY PK-8165 AND PK-9084 (TWO QUINOLINE DERIVATIVES).
003898 04-03

PLACEBO
STUDY OF VIGILANCE AFTER INGESTION OF ZOPICLONE IN COMPARISON WITH NITRAZEPAM AND PLACEBO. METHODOLOGY OF THE STUDY: SELF-EVALUATION QUESTIONNAIRE AND PSYCHOMETRIC-TESTS.
000543 01-07

ANXIOLYTIC EFFICACY OF ALPRAZOLAM COMPARED TO DIAZEPAM AND PLACEBO.
000648 01-10

TWO BASS-SCALE-FACTORS AND RESPONSE TO PLACEBO AND ANXIOLYTIC-DRUGS.
000649 01-10

DOUBLE-BLIND COMPARISON OF KETAZOLAM, DIAZEPAM AND PLACEBO IN ONCE-A-DAY VS T.I.D. DOSING.
000660 01-11

PSYCHOPATHOMETRIC DOUBLE-BLIND COURSE STUDY WITH NICERGOLINE VERSUS PLACEBO IN GERIATRIC-PATIENTS WITH TRANSIENT-SYNDROMES.
000665 01-11

PRINCIPAL AND DIFFERENTIAL-EFFECTS OF HALOPERIDOL AND PLACEBO TREATMENTS UPON SPEECH DISFLUENCIES IN STUTTERERS.
000713 01-11

PLACEBO REACTION IN NEUROTICS RATED WITH THE SCL-90 QUESTIONNAIRE.
000976 01-17

DOUBLE-BLIND COMPARISON OF KETAZOLAM AND PLACEBO USING ONCE-A-DAY DOSING.
002067 02-10

KETAZOLAM COMPARED TO DIAZEPAM AND PLACEBO IN THE TREATMENT OF ANXIETY.
002074 02-10

A DOUBLE-BLIND PARALLEL GROUP COMPARISON OF SINGLE-BEDTIME-DOSES OF HALAZEPAM AND PLACEBO.
002079 02-10

VILOXAZINE IN THE TREATMENT OF DEPRESSIVE-NEUROSIS: A CONTROLLED CLINICAL-STUDY WITH DOXEPIN AND PLACEBO.
002080 02-10

SUBJECTIVE DRUG-EFFECTS AND DRUG PREFERENCE IN HEALTHY VOLUNTEERS AS A MODEL OF A DRUGS REINFORCING EFFECTS: STUDIES ON NOMIFENSINE, AMPHETAMINE AND PLACEBO.
002362 02-14

RESPONDERS AND NONRESPONDERS TO CHLORDIAZEPOXIDE AND PLACEBO: A DISCRIMINANT FUNCTION ANALYSIS.
002482 02-16

PLACEBO, MEDICINE AND PAIN, OR THE RELATIVE FUNCTION OF MEDICATION IN THE TREATMENT OF PAIN.
002577 02-17

A DOUBLE-BLIND CROSSED CLINICAL-STUDY WITH A NEW PSYCHOPHARMACEUTICAL: TIADIPONE (QM-6008), DIAZEPAM, AND A PLACEBO.
003153 03-07

MAPROTILINE VERSUS IMIPRAMINE AND PLACEBO IN NEUROTIC DEPRESSION.
003287 03-10

CARDIOVASCULAR-EFFECTS OF MIANSERIN -- A COMPARATIVE-STUDY WITH AMITRIPTYLINE AND A PLACEBO IN HEALTHY SUBJECTS.
003503 03-15

THE PLACEBO CONCEPT.
003595 03-17

VILOXAZINE IN THE TREATMENT OF DEPRESSIVE-NEUROSIS: A PLACEBO AND STANDARD (IMIPRAMINE) CONTROLLED CLINICAL-STUDY.
004392 04-09

RESPONDERS AND NONRESPONDERS TO CHLORDIAZEPOXIDE AND PLACEBO. A DISCRIMINANT FUNCTION ANALYSIS. (UNPUBLISHED PAPER).
004420 04-10

BILATERAL SKIN CONDUCTANCE AND THE PUPILLARY LIGHT DARK REFLEX: MANIPULATION BY CHLORPROMAZINE, HALOPERIDOL, SCOPOLAMINE, AND PLACEBO.
004544 04-13

DRUG PREFERENCE IN HUMANS: DOUBLE-BLIND CHOICE COMPARISON OF PENTOBARBITAL, DIAZEPAM AND PLACEBO.
004566 04-14

NONSPECIFIC FACTORS IN DRUG-EFFECTS: PLACEBO PERSONALITY.
004704 04-17

PLACEBO-CONTROLLED
SYNERGISM OF COMBINED LITHIUM NEUROLEPTIC THERAPY: A DOUBLE-BLIND, PLACEBO-CONTROLLED CASE-STUDY.
003165 03-08

LITHIUM AND IMIPRAMINE IN THE PROPHYLAXIS OF UNIPOLAR AND BIPOLAR-II DEPRESSION: A PROSPECTIVE, PLACEBO-CONTROLLED COMPARISON.
003252 03-09

A DOUBLE-BLIND, PLACEBO-CONTROLLED, CROSS-OVER TRIAL OF CARBAMAZEPINE IN OVERACTIVE, SEVERELY MENTALLY-HANDICAPPED PATIENTS.
003365 03-11

PLACEBO-CONTROLLED-STUDY
NOMIFENSINE AS CONCOMITANT THERAPY IN THE TREATMENT OF PARKINSON-PATIENTS. A DOUBLE-BLIND PLACEBO-CONTROLLED-STUDY.
002130 02-11

A DOUBLE-BLIND, PLACEBO-CONTROLLED-STUDY OF PIRACETAM IN ELDERLY PSYCHIATRIC-PATIENTS.
003305 03-11

PLACEBO-CONTROLLED-TRIAL
EFFICACY OF DESIPRAMINE IN MILDLY DEPRESSED-PATIENTS: A DOUBLE-BLIND, PLACEBO-CONTROLLED-TRIAL.
003262 03-09

COMPARATIVE-EFFECTS OF PHENELZINE AND AMITRIPTYLINE: A PLACEBO-CONTROLLED-TRIAL.
004402 04-09

PLACEBO-EFFECT
PLACEBO-EFFECT: FROM CONTROL TO EXPERIMENTAL CONDITION.
003195 03-08
CONDITIONED DRUG-EFFECTS OF D-AMPHETAMINE-INDUCED AND
MORPHINE-INDUCED MOTOR ACCELERATION IN MICE: EXPERIMENTAL
APPROACH FOR PLACEBO-EFFECT.
004128 04-04

PLACEBO-EFFECTS
ANALYSIS OF SINGLE-BLIND, DOUBLE-BLIND PROCEDURES, MAINTENANCE
OF PLACEBO-EFFECTS, AND DRUG-INDUCED DYSKINESIA WITH
MENTALLY-RETARDED PERSONS -- BRIEF REPORT.
003298 03-11
SOME OBSERVATIONS ON THE PSYCHOLOGICAL DIMENSIONS OF
PLACEBO-EFFECTS.
003573 03-17
ANALYSIS OF SINGLE-BLIND AND DOUBLE-BLIND PROCEDURES,
MAINTENANCE OF PLACEBO-EFFECTS AND DRUG-INDUCED DYSKINESIA
WITH MENTALLY-RETARDED PERSON.
004437 04-11

PLACEMENTS
ON THE NEUROCHEMICAL BASIS OF SELF-STIMULATION WITH MIDBRAIN
RAPHE ELECTRODE PLACEMENTS.
000373 01-04

PLACENTA
TRANSFER OF LORAZEPAM AND ITS CONJUGATE ACROSS THE HUMAN
PLACENTA.
000774 01-13
SPECIFIC BINDING FOR OPIATE-LIKE-DRUGS IN THE PLACENTA.
000797 01-13

PLANT
RELATIVE POTENCIES OF TWO PHENYLALKYLAMINES FOUND IN THE
ABUSED PLANT CATHA-EDULIS, KHAT.
001084 02-02

PLANTS
THE WORLD OF HALLUCINOGENIC PLANTS.
003396 03-12

PLASMA
CHANGES IN PLASMA CORTICOSTERONE LEVELS AS A MEASURE OF
ACUTE DEPENDENCE UPON LEVORPHANOL IN RATS.
000085 01-03
PLASMA LEVELS OF DIPHENYLHYDANTOIN AND THE CONTROL OF ADULT
EPILEPTIC-SEIZURES: A CHILEAN EXPERIENCE.
000102 01-03
THE EFFECT OF ANTIDEPRESSANTS ON L 5 HTP-INDUCED CHANGES IN RAT
PLASMA CORTICOSTEROIDS.
000170 01-03
RELATIONSHIPS BETWEEN PLASMA CORTICOSTEROIDS AND
BENZODIAZEPINES IN STRESS.
000176 01-03
MECHANISM OF CHLORPROMAZINE ACTION ON PLASMA GLUCOSE AND
CYCLIC-AMP LEVELS.
000211 01-03
ELECTRON-CAPTURE GAS-LIQUID-CHROMATOGRAPHIC-DETERMINATION
OF ETHOSUXIMIDE AND DESMETHYLMETHSUXIMIDE IN PLASMA OR
SERUM.
000538 01-06
THE RELATIONSHIP BETWEEN THE THIORIDAZINE LEVEL IN THE PLASMA
AND SYMPTOMS OF PARANOID SCHIZOPHRENIA.
000546 01-08
INFLUENCE OF ROUTE-OF-ADMINISTRATION ON HALOPERIDOL PLASMA
LEVELS IN PSYCHOTIC-PATIENTS.
000549 01-08
PREDICTION OF STEADY-STATE PLASMA LEVELS OF AMITRIPTYLINE AND
NORTRIPTYLINE FROM A SINGLE-DOSE 24-HR. LEVEL IN DEPRESSED-
PATIENTS.
000582 01-09
VILOXAZINE PLASMA CONCENTRATIONS AND CLINICAL-RESPONSE.
000614 01-09
PLASMA LEVELS OF IMIPRAMINE (IMI) AND DESMETHYLIMIPRAMINE
(DMI) AND CLINICAL-RESPONSE IN PREPUBERTAL MAJOR DEPRESSIVE-
DISORDER: A PRELIMINARY REPORT.
000619 01-09
IMIPRAMINE TREATMENT OF PREPUBERTAL MAJOR DEPRESSIVE-
DISORDERS: PLASMA LEVELS AND CLINICAL-RESPONSE --
PRELIMINARY REPORT.
000620 01-09
LITHIUM TREATMENT IN AFFECTIVE-DISORDERS: THERAPEUTIC PLASMA
LEVEL.
000635 01-09
LITHIUM TREATMENT IN AFFECTIVE-DISORDERS FROM VIEWPOINT OF
TRANSCULTURAL PSYCHOPHARMACOLOGY: THERAPEUTIC PLASMA
LEVEL.
000636 01-09
TRICYCLIC-ANTIDEPRESSANTS: THERAPEUTIC PLASMA LEVEL.
000646 01-09
EFFECT OF DIAZEPAM AND DESMETHYLDIAZEPAM IN SPASTICITY AND
RIGIDITY: A QUANTITATIVE STUDY OF REFLEXES AND PLASMA
CONCENTRATIONS.
000701 01-11

PLASMA CHLORPROMAZINE CONCENTRATIONS IN CHILDREN WITH
BEHAVIORAL-DISORDERS AND MENTAL-ILLNESS.
000717 01-11
VALPROIC-ACID DOSAGE AND PLASMA PROTEIN BINDING AND
CLEARANCE.
000755 01-13
VALPROIC-ACID AND PLASMA LEVELS OF PHENYTOIN.
000756 01-13
AMITRIPTYLINE, NORTRIPTYLINE PLASMA LEVELS AND CLINICAL-
RESPONSE IN WOMEN WITH AFFECTIVE-DISORDERS.
000757 01-13
INTRAMUSCULAR HALOPERIDOL-DECANOATE FOR NEUROLEPTIC
MAINTENANCE-THERAPY: EFFICACY, DOSAGE SCHEDULE AND PLASMA
LEVELS: AN OPEN MULTICENTER-STUDY.
000758 01-13
PRACTICAL AND THEORETICAL ASPECTS OF PHENYTOIN
ADMINISTRATION. I. RELATIONSHIP BETWEEN DOSE AND PLASMA
CONCENTRATION.
000760 01-13
PLASMA CHLORPROMAZINE SERUM PROLACTIN RELATIONSHIP IN A
SINGLE-DOSE EXPERIMENT.
000761 01-13
TRANSCULTURAL PHARMACOKINETIC STUDY ON LI CONCENTRATION IN
PLASMA AND SALIVA.
000769 01-13
NEUROLEPTIC-EFFECT ON DESIPRAMINE STEADY-STATE PLASMA
CONCENTRATIONS.
000781 01-13
PLASMA AND SALIVA LEVELS OF CHLORPROMAZINE AND SUBJECTIVE
RESPONSE.
000826 01-14
PLASMA PROLACTIN AND TESTOSTERONE DURING PENFLURIDOL
TREATMENT.
000874 01-15
DESIPRAMINE: CARDIOVASCULAR EFFECTS AND PLASMA LEVELS.
000884 01-15
IMPORTANCE OF AKINESIA: PLASMA CHLORPROMAZINE AND PROLACTIN
LEVELS.
000891 01-15
TECHNIQUES FOR PLASMA PROTEIN BINDING OF
DEMETHYLCHLORIMIPRAMINE.
000897 01-16
LEVORPHANOL: RADIOIMMUNOASSAY AND PLASMA CONCENTRATION
PROFILES IN DOG AND MAN.
000898 01-16
DETERMINATION OF DOSE PLASMA CONCENTRATION RELATIONSHIP OF
PHENOBARBITAL IN EPILEPTIC-PATIENTS BY A NEW SPECIFIC
RADIOIMMUNOASSAY.
000902 01-16
RADIOIMMUNOASSAY FOR FLUPHENAZINE IN HUMAN PLASMA.
000905 01-16
DISEASE-INDUCED CHANGES IN THE PLASMA BINDING OF BASIC DRUGS.
000975 01-17
ESR STUDIES OF BOVINE PLASMA AMINE-OXIDASE: PROBING OF THE
ENVIRONMENT ABOUT THE SUBSTRATE LIBERATED SULFHYDRYL
GROUPS IN THE ACTIVE SITE. (UNPUBLISHED PAPER).
001066 02-01
EFFECT OF PROSTAGLANDINS ON PLASMA CATECHOLAMINES, HEART
AND BLOOD-PRESSURE RESPONSES TO HEMORRHAGE. (UNPUBLISHED
PAPER).
001223 02-03
LEUCINE-ENKEPHALIN AND METHIONINE-ENKEPHALIN PRODUCE OPPOSING
EFFECTS ON PLASMA CORTICOSTERONE LEVELS IN ETHER-STRESSED
MICE.
001245 02-03
STIMULATION OF THE PLASMA MEMBRANE ENZYME, 5' NUCLEOTIDASE,
BY ETHANOL EXPOSURE TO NEURAL CELLS IN CULTURE.
001499 02-03
EFFECT OF BROMOCRIPTINE ON EXPLORATORY-ACTIVITY, BRAIN-
MONOAMINES AND PLASMA CORTICOSTERONE IN THE
NORMOTENSIVE-RATS, GENETICALLY HYPERTENSIVE-RATS AND/OR
HYPERTENSIVE OBESE RATS.
001635 02-04
PLASMA AND BRAIN LEVELS OF DELTA6 THC AND SEVEN
MONOOXYGENATED METABOLITES CORRELATED TO THE CATALEPTIC-
EFFECT IN THE MOUSE.
001737 02-04
RELATIONSHIPS BETWEEN CHLORPROMAZINE CONCENTRATIONS IN
PLASMA AND CEREBROSPINAL-FLUID AND CLINICAL-RESPONSE AND
BIOCHEMICAL-RESPONSE IN PSYCHOTIC-PATIENTS.
001905 02-08
PLASMA LEVELS AND THERAPEUTIC EFFICACY OF FLUPHENAZINE-HCL
AND FLUPHENAZINE-DECANOATE.
001913 02-08
CHANGE IN OVERINCLUSIVE THINKING OF SCHIZOPHRENIC-PATIENTS IS
RELATED TO PLASMA PHENOTHIAZINE CONCENTRATION.
001941 02-08
CLINICAL STATE, PLASMA LEVELS OF HALOPERIDOL AND PROLACTIN:
001943 02-08

PLASMA FLUPHENAZINE AND PROLACTIN LEVELS IN SCHIZOPHRENIC-PATIENTS DURING TREATMENT WITH LOW-DOSES AND HIGH-DOSES OF FLUPHENAZINE-ENANTHATE.
001956 02-08

AMITRIPTYLINE PLASMA CONCENTRATION AND CLINICAL-EFFECT: A WORLD-HEALTH-ORGANIZATION COLLABORATIVE-STUDY.
001976 02-09

CLINICAL-RESPONSE, PLASMA LEVELS AND PHARMACOKINETICS OF DESIPRAMINE IN DEPRESSED-INPATIENTS.
002002 02-09

EVALUATION OF NOMIFENSINE IN THE TREATMENT OF GERIATRIC DEPRESSION USING PSYCHOMETRIC-TESTS AND PLASMA LEVEL CONTROLS.
002004 02-09

LONG-TERM MONITORING OF TRICYCLIC-ANTIDEPRESSANT PLASMA CONCENTRATIONS.
002014 02-09

CLOMIPRAMINE: PLASMA LEVELS AND CLINICAL-EFFECTS.
002033 02-09

EFFECT OF PIRIBEDIL (ET-495) ON PLASMA NOREPINEPHRINE: RELATIONSHIP TO ANTIDEPRESSANT RESPONSE.
002034 02-09

PLASMA DESIPRAMINE LEVELS AFTER SINGLE-DOSAGE AND AT STEADY-STATE IN OUTPATIENTS.
002039 02-09

CARBAMAZEPINE THERAPY IN TRIGEMINAL-NEURALGIA: CLINICAL-EFFECTS IN RELATION TO PLASMA CONCENTRATION.
002181 02-11

PLASMA DELTA9 TETRAHYDROCANNABINOL CONCENTRATIONS AND CLINICAL-EFFECTS AFTER ORAL AND INTRAVENOUS ADMINISTRATION AND SMOKING.
002201 02-12

THE CONTRIBUTION OF ALPHA1 ACID GLYCOPROTEIN, LIPOPROTEINS, AND ALBUMIN TO THE PLASMA BINDING OF PERAZINE, AMITRIPTYLINE, AND NORTRIPTYLINE IN HEALTHY MAN.
002214 02-13

FACTORS INFLUENCING NORTRIPTYLINE STEADY-STATE KINETICS: PLASMA AND SALIVA LEVELS.
002251 02-13

CLOMIPRAMINE AND DOXEPIN IN DEPRESSIVE-NEUROSIS: PLASMA LEVELS AND THERAPEUTIC RESPONSE.
002258 02-13

PLASMA HDL CHOLESTEROL AND GROWTH-HORMONE IN EPILEPTICS TREATED WITH ANTICONVULSANTS.
002260 02-13

HALOPERIDOL PLASMA LEVEL MONITORING IN PSYCHIATRIC-PATIENTS.
002267 02-13

EFFECTS OF CAFFEINE ON PLASMA FREE FATTY-ACIDS, URINARY CATECHOLAMINES, AND DRUG BINDING.
002272 02-13

INTERACTION BETWEEN PHENYTOIN AND VALPROIC-ACID: PLASMA PROTEIN BINDING AND METABOLIC-EFFECTS.
002276 02-13

MOOD AND BEHAVIORAL-EFFECTS OF PHYSOSTIGMINE ON HUMANS ARE ACCOMPANIED BY ELEVATIONS IN PLASMA BETA ENDORPHIN AND CORTISOL.
002280 02-13

CORRELATIONS BETWEEN PLASMA LEVELS OF ANTIEPILEPTIC-DRUGS AND EEG INTENSIVE MONITORING.
002288 02-13

THYMOANALEPTIC TREATMENT CONTROL THROUGH MEASUREMENT OF PLASMA CONCENTRATIONS OF AMITRIPTYLINE AND ITS METABOLITE NORTRIPTYLINE.
002304 02-13

CHILDHOOD-ENURESIS: II. PSYCHOPATHOLOGY, TRICYCLIC CONCENTRATION IN PLASMA, AND ANTIENURETIC-EFFECT.
002354 02-14

PHENOTHIAZINE PLASMA AND RED-BLOOD-CELL CONCENTRATIONS, THEIR RELATIONSHIP TO SIDE-EFFECTS AND CLINICAL-EFFICACY.
002386 02-15

A METHOD FOR THE DETERMINATION OF AMITRIPTYLINE AND ITS METABOLITES NORTRIPTYLINE, 10 HYDROXYAMITRIPTYLINE, AND 10 HYDROXYNORTRIPTYLINE IN HUMAN PLASMA USING STABLE ISOTOPE DILUTION AND GAS-CHROMATOGRAPHY CHEMICAL-IONIZATION MASS-SPECTROMETRY.
002486 02-16

MEASUREMENT OF FLUPHENAZINE BY GAS-CHROMATOGRAPHY IN HUMAN PLASMA AND RED-BLOOD-CELLS.
002491 02-16

THE DISTRIBUTION OF CHLORPROMAZINE BETWEEN PLASMA AND ERYTHROCYTES.
002496 02-16

RADIOIMMUNOASSAY FOR TOTAL DOXEPIN AND N DESMETHYLDOXEPIN IN PLASMA.
002499 02-16

PLASMA LEVODOPA, DOPAMINE AND THERAPEUTIC RESPONSE FOLLOWING LEVODOPA THERAPY OF PARKINSONIAN-PATIENTS.
002504 02-16

PLASMA FLUPHENAZINE LEVELS BY RADIOIMMUNOASSAY IN SCHIZOPHRENIC-PATIENTS TREATED WITH DEPOT INJECTIONS OF FLUPHENAZINE-DECANOATE.
002510 02-16

MEASUREMENT OF PLASMA CONCENTRATIONS OF DRUGS AS A FEEDBACK CONTROL MECHANISM DURING DRUG-THERAPY.
002525 02-17

PHARMACOKINETICS AND PLASMA LEVELS OF POLYCYCLIC-ANTIDEPRESSANTS: A GENERAL VIEW OF PRODUCTS.
002529 02-17

DIFFERENTIAL-EFFECTS OF CANNABINOID EXPOSURE AND STRESS ON PLASMA PROLACTIN, GROWTH-HORMONE AND CORTICOSTERONE LEVELS IN MALE MICE.
002695 03-03

PLASMA IMIPRAMINE LEVELS AND DEMETHYLASE ACTIVITY IN THE LIVER OF STRESSED ANIMALS.
002793 03-03

INCREASE IN PLASMA CYCLIC-AMP LEVELS ELICITED BY NALOXONE IN MORPHINE-DEPENDENT MALE MICE.
002834 03-03

PLASMA CATECHOLAMINES IN RATS EXPOSED TO COLD: EFFECTS OF GANGLIONIC AND ADRENORECEPTOR BLOCKADE.
002863 03-03

BENZODIAZEPINES, STRESS AND RAT PLASMA CORTICOSTEROIDS: THE ROLE OF INDOLEAMINES.
003034 03-04

ERGOT DRUGS SUPPRESS PLASMA PROLACTIN AND LACTATION BUT NOT AGGRESSION IN PARTURIENT MICE.
003159 03-07

PLASMA LEVEL OF CYCLIC-AMP AND MENTAL-DISEASES.
003170 03-08

A COMPARISON OF DOPAMINE-RECEPTOR BLOCKING ASSAY WITH PLASMA DRUG LEVELS OF HALOPERIDOL IN SCHIZOPHRENIC-PATIENTS.
003182 03-08

PLASMA LEVELS OF CHLORPROMAZINE AND CLINICAL-RESPONSE.
003201 03-08

CORRELATIONS BETWEEN LITHIUM LEVELS IN CEREBROSPINAL-FLUID AND LITHIUM LEVELS IN BLOOD PLASMA AND ERYTHROCYTES.
003210 03-09

DEPRESSION SUBTYPES AFFECT THE STEADY-STATE PLASMA LEVELS AND THERAPEUTIC-EFFICACY OF AMITRIPTYLINE AND NORTRIPTYLINE.
003244 03-09

RELEVANCY OF TRICYCLIC-ANTIDEPRESSANT PLASMA LEVELS.
003246 03-09

PLASMA FREE AND TOTAL TRYPTOPHAN, BLOOD SEROTONIN, AND THE HYPERACTIVITY-SYNDROME: NO EVIDENCE FOR THE SEROTONIN DEFICIENCY HYPOTHESIS.
003312 03-11

A PROSPECTIVE RANDOMISED-TRIAL ON THE EFFECT OF MONITORING PLASMA ANTICONVULSANT LEVELS IN EPILEPSY.
003314 03-11

A COMPARATIVE-STUDY ON THE CLINICAL-EFFECTS OF RECTAL DIAZEPAM AND PENTOBARBITAL ON SMALL CHILDREN. RELATIONSHIP BETWEEN PLASMA LEVEL AND EFFECT.
003330 03-11

INTRAVENOUS VALPROATE: EFFECTS ON PLASMA AND SALIVA PHENYTOIN LEVELS.
003359 03-11

COVARIANCE OF PLASMA FREE 3 METHOXY-4-HYDROXYPHENETHYLENEGLYCOL AND DIASTOLIC BLOOD-PRESSURE.
003418 03-13

PSYCHOSOMATIC-STRESS AND LIPOPEROXIDES OF HUMAN PLATELET RICH PLASMA.
003423 03-13

HUMAN BRAIN, PLASMA, AND CEREBROSPINAL-FLUID CONCENTRATION OF SODIUM-VALPROATE AFTER 72 HOURS OF THERAPY.
003433 03-13

EXCESSIVE PLASMA CONCENTRATIONS OF TRICYCLIC-ANTIDEPRESSANTS RESULTING FROM USUAL DOSES: A REPORT OF SIX CASES.
003479 03-15

LYMPHOCYTE MONOAMINE-OXIDASE AND PLASMA PROLACTIN AND GROWTH-HORMONE IN TARDIVE-DYSKINESIA.
003499 03-15

SIMULTANEOUS ADMINISTRATION OF FIVE ANTIEPILEPTIC-DRUGS IN PLASMA THROUGH GAS-LIQUID-CHROMATOGRAPHY.
003563 03-16

MEASUREMENT OF HALOPERIDOL IN HUMAN PLASMA USING REVERSED PHASE HIGH-PERFORMANCE LIQUID-CHROMATOGRAPHY. (UNPUBLISHED PAPER).
003667 04-01

CU-AMINE-OXIDASES: STUDIES RELATED TO THE MECHANISM-OF-ACTION OF BOVINE PLASMA AMINE-OXIDASE (UNPUBLISHED PAPER).
003680 04-01

VASOPRESSIN STIMULATES RELEASE OF BETA LIPOTROPIN AND BETA ENDORPHIN IN CONSCIOUS RATS AS MEASURED BY RADIOIMMUNOASSAY OF UNEXTRACTED PLASMA.
003715 04-03

QUANTITATION AND COMPARISON OF PHENOBARBITAL LEVELS IN THE PLASMA, SALIVA, AND CEREBROSPINAL-FLUID OF THE RAT, AND THE

DEMONSTRATION OF AN ALTERATION OF DRUG PASSAGE BY ETHANOL.
003725 04-03

EFFECT OF AMPHETAMINE ON PLASMA CORTICOSTERONE IN THE CONSCIOUS RAT.
003888 04-03

EFFECTS OF ALPHA-ADRENERGIC AND BETA-ADRENERGIC BLOCKERS ON CHLORPROMAZINE-INDUCED ELEVATION OF PLASMA GLUCOSE AND CYCLIC-AMP IN FED MICE.
003946 04-03

RAT-BRAIN AND PLASMA NOREPINEPHRINE GLYCOL METABOLITES DETERMINED BY GAS-CHROMATOGRAPHY MASS-FRAGMENTOGRAPHY.
004303 04-06

PLASMA LEVELS OF BETA ENDORPHIN UNDER CHRONIC NEUROLEPTIC TREATMENT IN SCHIZOPHRENIC-PATIENTS: FAILURE OF NALOXONE TO COUNTERACT CURATIVE EFFECTS OF NEUROLEPTIC-DRUGS.
004321 04-08

NEUROENDOCRINE-TESTS DURING TREATMENT WITH NEUROLEPTIC-DRUGS: I. PLASMA PROLACTIN RESPONSE TO CHLORPROMAZINE CHALLENGE.
004329 04-08

PLASMA DOPAMINE-BETA-HYDROXYLASE ACTIVITY IN CHRONIC SCHIZOPHRENIC-PATIENTS TESTED WITH SINGLE-DOSE OF 2 BROMO-ALPHA-ERGOCRIPTINE (PARLODEL).
004343 04-08

CHANGES IN BLOOD PLASMA OSMOLALITY AND STATES OF MANIA.
004352 04-09

PLASMA LEVELS OF THE CIS-ISOMERS AND TRANS-ISOMERS OF DOXEPIN AND DESMETHYLDOXEPIN AFTER ADMINISTRATION OF DOXEPIN TO PATIENTS.
004355 04-09

PLASMA CORTICOSTERIODS IN MANIA: THE EFFECTS OF PIMOZIDE.
004363 04-09

LITHIUM IN THE PROPHYLAXIS OF RECURRENT AFFECTIVE-DISORDERS (EFFECTIVENESS OF LOW PLASMA LEVELS AND PREDICTORS TO CLINICAL-RESPONSE).
004365 04-09

ELECTROCARDIOGRAM-CHANGES AND PLASMA DESIPRAMINE LEVELS DURING TREATMENT OF DEPRESSION.
004411 04-09

THE RELATIONSHIPS BETWEEN CLINICAL-RESPONSE, PSYCHOPHYSIOLOGICAL-VARIABLES AND PLASMA LEVELS OF AMITRIPTYLINE AND DIAZEPAM IN NEUROTIC-OUTPATIENTS.
004423 04-10

THERAPEUTIC PLASMA LEVELS OF SOME ANTICONVULSANTS IN FOCAL EPILEPSY IN RELATION TO COMPUTERIZED-AXIAL-TOMOGRAPHY.
004439 04-11

EFFECT OF TREATMENT WITH SODIUM-VALPROATE AND DIAZEPAM ON PLASMA CORTICOTROPIN IN NELSONS-SYNDROME.
004463 04-11

NORMAL PLASMA DOPAMINE-BETA-HYDROXYLASE IN NONTREATED AND TREATED PARKINSON-PATIENTS.
004471 04-11

DOXEPIN PLASMA LEVELS AND ANXIOLYTIC RESPONSE.
004477 04-11

PHENYTOIN THERAPY FOR EPILEPTIC-CHILDREN: EVALUATION OF SALIVARY AND PLASMA CONCENTRATIONS AND OF METHODS OF ASSESSING COMPLIANCE.
004495 04-11

USE OF PLASMA CONCENTRATION DETERMINATIONS.
004498 04-13

KINETICS AND BIOTRANSFORMATION OF LORMETAZEPAM: II. RADIOIMMUNOLOGIC DETERMINATIONS IN PLASMA AND URINE OF YOUNG AND ELDERLY SUBJECTS: FIRST-PASS EFFECT.
004516 04-13

VALPROIC-ACID IN CHILDHOOD-EPILEPSY: ANTICONVULSIVE EFFICACY IN RELATION TO ITS PLASMA LEVELS.
004525 04-13

THE ACTIVITY OF DOPAMINE-BETA-HYDROXYLASE IN THE PLASMA OF PATIENTS WITH ENDOGENOUS DEPRESSIVE-SYNDROMES.
004548 04-13

ANTICHOLINERGIC-EFFECTS AND PLASMA DESIPRAMINE LEVELS.
004550 04-13

CONCENTRATIONS OF CHLORPROMAZINE AND TWO OF ITS ACTIVE METABOLITES IN PLASMA AND CEREBROSPINAL-FLUID OF PSYCHOTIC-PATIENTS TREATED WITH FIXED DRUG DOSES.
004559 04-13

SEX, PLASMA PROLACTIN AND PLASMA 3 METHOXY-4-HYDROXYPHENYLGLYCOL (MHPG) PREDICT HERITABLE D-AMPHETAMINE EXCITATION IN MAN. (UNPUBLISHED PAPER).
004565 04-14

CHLORPROMAZINE ANALYSIS IN HUMAN PLASMA. (UNPUBLISHED PAPER).
004591 04-15

TRANSIENT HYPERKINESIA AFTER A SINGLE INTRAVENOUS PERFUSION OF DIPHENYLHYDANTOIN: REPORT OF A CASE ASSOCIATED WITH NONTOXIC PLASMA LEVELS OF DIPHENYLHYDANTOIN.
004638 04-15

PLASMA NOMIFENSINE CONCENTRATION: CARDIOLOGICAL EFFECTS AND CLINICAL-RESPONSE.
004639 04-15

AMITRIPTYLINE AND NORTRIPTYLINE PLASMA LEVELS MONITORING. PERSPECTIVE IN CLINICAL-PRACTICE.
004675 04-16

THERAPEUTIC MONITORING OF PLASMA CONCENTRATIONS OF TRICYCLIC-ANTIDEPRESSANTS: PERSPECTIVE OF THE CLINICAL LABORATORY.
004681 04-16

A COMPARISON OF RADIOIMMUNOASSAY WITH SPECTROPHOTOMETRY FOR THE DETERMINATION OF PLASMA DIPHENYLHYDANTOIN CONCENTRATIONS.
004684 04-16

RECEPTOR TECHNIQUES IN THE STUDY OF PLASMA LEVELS OF NEUROLEPTICS AND ANTIDEPRESSANT-DRUGS.
004694 04-16

PLASMATIC
INTERRELATION AT PLASMATIC LEVEL BETWEEN ANTIEPILEPTIC-DRUGS AND LIPIDS. ITS IMPLICATIONS IN THE EFFICIENCY OF TREATMENT IN EPILEPSY. I. CHANGES INDUCED BY PHENOBARBITAL OR/AND DIPHENYLHYDANTOIN IN SERUM LIPIDS.
002281 02-13

PLASTICITY
RECEPTOR PLASTICITY: BIOCHEMICAL-CORRELATES AND PHARMACOLOGICAL SIGNIFICANCE.
001181 02-03

A RADIOIMMUNOASSAY FOR EPENDYMINS BETA AND GAMMA: TWO GOLDFISH BRAIN PROTEINS INVOLVED IN BEHAVIORAL PLASTICITY.
003677 04-01

PLATELET
HUMAN PLATELET 5 HT-RECEPTORS: CHARACTERISATION AND FUNCTIONAL ASSOCIATION.
001412 02-03

MAO-INHIBITORS AND PLATELET MAO-INHIBITION.
001993 02-09

PLATELET AGGREGATION, 5 HYDROXYTRYPTAMINE UPTAKE AND RELEASE IN HUNTINGTONS-CHOREA.
002112 02-11

QUINACRINE AND SEROTONIN BINDING BY SYNTHETIC MODELS FOR HUMAN PLATELET DENSE-BODIES: EVALUATION OF THE ROLE OF BINDING IN AMINE STORAGE. (UNPUBLISHED PAPER).
002219 02-13

A PROBABLE NEUROLEPTIC-EFFECT ON PLATELET MONOAMINE-OXIDASE IN CHRONIC SCHIZOPHRENIC-PATIENTS.
003169 03-08

NONGENETIC FACTORS AFFECTING HUMAN PLATELET MONOAMINE-OXIDASE.
003407 03-13

TRICYCLIC-ANTIDEPRESSANT DRUG-TREATMENT DECREASES ALPHA2-ADRENORECEPTORS ON HUMAN PLATELET MEMBRANES.
003408 03-13

PSYCHOSOMATIC-STRESS AND LIPOPEROXIDES OF HUMAN PLATELET RICH PLASMA.
003423 03-13

THE HUMAN PLATELET AS A MODEL FOR THE GLUTAMATERGIC NEURON: PLATELET UPTAKE OF L GLUTAMATE.
003923 04-03

DOES HIGH-AFFINITY (3H) IMIPRAMINE BINDING LABEL SEROTONIN REUPTAKE SITES IN BRAIN AND PLATELET?
003962 04-03

THE ANTIDEPRESSANT EFFECTS OF TRAZODONE AND INHIBITION OF PLATELET SEROTONIN REUPTAKE.
004383 04-09

THE SPECIFIC ACTIVITY OF PLATELET MONOAMINE-OXIDASE VARIES WITH PLATELET COUNT DURING SEVERE EXERCISE AND NORADRENALINE INFUSION.
004509 04-13

SELECTIVE INHIBITORY-EFFECTS OF CHLORPROMAZINE AND IMIPRAMINE ON PLATELET AGGREGATION.
004518 04-13

HUMAN PLATELET ALPHA2-ADRENERGIC-RECEPTORS: LABELING WITH 3H YOHIMBINE, A SELECTIVE ANTAGONIST LIGAND.
004676 04-16

PLATELETS
IN VITRO EFFECT OF PHENCYCLIDINE AND OTHER PSYCHOMOTOR STIMULANTS ON SEROTONIN UPTAKE IN HUMAN PLATELETS.
000750 01-13

PREPARATION AND CHARACTERIZATION OF SYNTHETIC MODELS FOR THE DENSE-BODIES OF HUMAN PLATELETS. (UNPUBLISHED PAPER).
001013 02-01

ELECTRON PROBE MICROANALYSIS OF CALCIUM AND PHOSPHORUS IN DENSE-BODIES ISOLATED FROM HUMAN PLATELETS. (UNPUBLISHED PAPER).
001014 02-01

SPECIFIC 3H IMIPRAMINE BINDING IN HUMAN PLATELETS: INFLUENCE OF AGE AND SEX.
002254 02-13

3H IMIPRAMINE BINDING IN HUMAN PLATELETS: DIMINUTION OF BINDING-SITES IN DEPRESSED-PATIENTS.
003427 03-13

A STUDY OF GAMMA AMINOBUTYRIC-ACID UPTAKE IN NORMAL AND DOWNS-SYNDROME PLATELETS.
003787 04-03

(3H) IMIPRAMINE BINDING IN HUMAN PLATELETS: A NEW BIOCHEMICAL-PARAMETER IN DEPRESSION.
004358 04-09

EFFECTS OF RO-11-2465, A NEW PSYCHOTROPIC-AGENT ON THE UPTAKE OF SEROTONIN BY HUMAN PLATELETS -- IN VITRO DETERMINATION OF THE IC50.
004532 04-13

ANTIDEPRESSANTS AND THE SEROTONIN UPTAKE IN PLATELETS.
004727 04-17

PLAUSIBLE
THE NA-K-ATPASE: A PLAUSIBLE TRIGGER FOR VOLTAGE-INDEPENDENT RELEASE OF CYTOPLASMIC NEUROTRANSMITTERS.
003953 04-03

PLAY
BIOGENIC-AMINES AND NEUROPEPTIDES PLAY A ROLE IN THE CENTRAL-REGULATION OF GENETIC HYPERTENSION. (UNPUBLISHED PAPER).
001455 02-03

DOES RAPID-EYE-MOVEMENT SLEEP PLAY A ROLE IN BRAIN DEVELOPMENT?
004091 04-04

PLEXIFORM
BRAIN-SPECIFIC BENZODIAZEPINE-RECEPTORS ARE LOCALIZED IN THE INNER PLEXIFORM LAYER OF RAT RETINA.
000277 01-03

PLEXUS
INHIBITION OF THE ACTION OF CHOLECYSTOKININ-OCTAPEPTIDE ON THE GUINEA-PIG ILEUM MYENTERIC PLEXUS BY DIBUTYRYL-CYCLIC-GUANOSINE-MONOPHOSPHATE.
001291 02-03

EVIDENCE FOR THE PRESENCE OF TWO TYPES OF MONOAMINE-OXIDASE IN RABBIT CHOROID PLEXUS AND THEIR ROLE IN BREAKDOWN OF AMINES INFLUENCING CEREBROSPINAL-FLUID FORMATION.
002807 03-03

PLG
HABITUATION OF THE THE HEAD-POKE RESPONSE: EFFECTS OF AN AMPHETAMINE BARBITURATE MIXTURE, PLG AND FENFLURAMINE.
004159 04-04

PLURALITY
SYNTHESIS AND PHARMACOLOGICAL-STUDY OF SOME ENKEPHALIN ANALOGS IN RELATION TO THE PLURALITY OF OPIATE-RECEPTORS.
003682 04-02

PNEUMATIC
AN IMPROVED PNEUMATIC SYRINGE FOR SELF-ADMINISTRATION OF DRUGS BY RATS.
004304 04-06

PNEUMOENCEPHALOGRAPHY
EFFECTS OF TIAPRIDE ON HOMOVANILLIC-ACID LEVELS IN HUMAN CEREBROSPINAL-FLUID DRAWN AT PNEUMOENCEPHALOGRAPHY.
001483 02-03

PROGRESSIVE SUPRANUCLEAR PALSY: PNEUMOENCEPHALOGRAPHY, ELECTRONYSTAGMOGRAPHY AND TREATMENT WITH METHYSERGIDE.
003355 03-11

PNEUMONIA
PNEUMONIA AND PSYCHOTROPIC-DRUG USE IN ELDERLY PSYCHIATRIC-PATIENTS.
002391 02-15

PNMT
THE BLOCKADE OF ALPHA2-ADRENOCEPTORS BY THE PNMT INHIBITOR SKF-64139.
001255 02-03

IN VIVO INTRANEURONAL MAO-INHIBITION IN RAT-BRAIN SKF-64139, COMPARISON TO OTHER POTENT PNMT INHIBITORS.
003935 04-03

POINT
SINGLE POINT ESTIMATION OF PHENYTOIN DOSING REQUIREMENT.
003562 03-16

POISONING
ACUTE GENERALIZED POLYNEUROPATHY ACCOMPANYING LITHIUM POISONING.
000835 01-15

THE NEUROLOGICAL FORENSIC ASPECTS OF THALLIUM POISONING.
002438 02-15

PSYCHIATRIC-ASPECTS OF ACUTE POISONING WITH TRICYCLIC AND RELATED ANTIDEPRESSANTS -- 1980.
002458 02-15

THE CLINICAL DYNAMICS OF TETRAETHYL-LEAD POISONING.
003500 03-15

LITHIUM KINETICS DURING HEMODIALYSIS IN A PATIENT WITH LITHIUM POISONING.
003524 03-15

MENTAL-DISTURBANCES IN CHRONIC MANGANESE POISONING.
004621 04-15

POLARITY
FACTORS INFLUENCING THE RELEASE OF LABELLED GAMMA AMINOBUTYRIC-ACID AND ACETYLCHOLINE EVOKED BY ELECTRICAL-STIMULATION WITH ALTERNATING POLARITY FROM RAT CORTICAL SLICES.
001130 02-03

POLARIZATIONS
NALOXONE ANTAGONISM OF GABA-EVOKED MEMBRANE POLARIZATIONS IN CULTURED MOUSE SPINAL-CORD NEURONS.
000116 01-03

POLYADENYLATED
CELL-FREE TRANSLATION OF FREE AND MEMBRANE-BOUND POLYSOMES AND POLYADENYLATED MRNA FROM RABBIT BRAIN FOLLOWING ADMINISTRATION OF D LYSERGIC-ACID-DIETHYLAMIDE IN VIVO.
003832 04-03

POLYCENTRIC
SELF-MEDICATION, ABANDONMENT, MANIPULATION, AND DEPENDENCE IN DRUG-THERAPY IN PSYCHOSOMATIC-ILLNESS: COMPARATIVE POLYCENTRIC RESEARCH ON VARIOUS PSYCHOTROPIC-DRUGS.
002189 02-11

POLYCYCLIC-ANTIDEPRESSANTS
PHARMACOKINETICS AND PLASMA LEVELS OF POLYCYCLIC-ANTIDEPRESSANTS: A GENERAL VIEW OF PRODUCTS.
002529 02-17

POLYETHYLENE-GLYCOL
THE DYNAMICS OF SYSTEMIC VENOUS, ARTERIAL, AND CEREBROSPINAL-FLUID PRESSURE UNDER I.V. ADMINISTRATION OF POLYETHYLENE-GLYCOL.
004045 04-03

POLYGRAPHIC-STUDY
POLYGRAPHIC-STUDY OF NIGHT SLEEP UNDER THE EFFECTS OF MINAPRINE.
003313 03-11

POLYGRAPHICAL-STUDIES
THE EFFECT OF BUTOCTAMIDE-HYDROGEN-SUCCINATE ON NOCTURNAL SLEEP: ALL-NIGHT POLYGRAPHICAL-STUDIES.
002350 02-14

POLYNEUROPATHOLOGIES
PRUSSIAN-BLUE: SPECIFIC TREATMENT OF THALLIUM, ARSENIC, INDUSTRIAL-SOLVENT INTOXICATION, AND OTHER POLYNEUROPATHOLOGIES. A POSSIBLE ANTIPSYCHOTIC-AGENT.
003348 03-11

POLYNEUROPATHY
ACUTE GENERALIZED POLYNEUROPATHY ACCOMPANYING LITHIUM POISONING.
000835 01-15

POLYPHARMACY
DISCUSSION: COMMUNICATION AND POLYPHARMACY: DRUGS AND THE ELDERLY.
000957 01-17

PSYCHOTROPIC-DRUGS AND POLYPHARMACY IN ELDERLY-PATIENTS IN A GENERAL-HOSPITAL.
000981 01-17

PSYCHOTROPIC-DRUG USE AND POLYPHARMACY IN A GENERAL-HOSPITAL.
003369 03-11

POLYPHARMACY REGIMEN AS AN EXACERBATING RISK IN THERAPY-RESISTANT EPILEPTIC-SEIZURES AND BEHAVIORAL-DISORDERS.
004720 04-17

POLYPHOSPHOINOSITIDE
EFFECTS OF NEOMYCIN ON CALCIUM AND POLYPHOSPHOINOSITIDE METABOLISM OF GUINEA-PIG SYNAPTOSOMES.
002741 03-03

POLYRIBOSOMAL
AMPHETAMINE STEREOTYPIES AND POLYRIBOSOMAL DISAGGREGATION IN RATS: EFFECTS OF ADRENERGIC AND SEROTONERGIC BLOCKING-AGENTS.
001531 02-03

POLYRIBOSOMES
EFFECT OF ALPHA METHYLPHENYLALANINE AND PHENYLALANINE ON BRAIN POLYRIBOSOMES AND PROTEIN SYNTHESIS.
003733 04-03

POLYSOMES
COMPARISON OF THE EFFECT OF INTRAVENOUS ADMINISTRATION OF D LYSERGIC-ACID-DIETHYLAMIDE ON FREE AND MEMBRANE-BOUND POLYSOMES IN THE RABBIT BRAIN.
003831 04-03

CELL-FREE TRANSLATION OF FREE AND MEMBRANE-BOUND POLYSOMES AND POLYADENYLATED MRNA FROM RABBIT BRAIN FOLLOWING ADMINISTRATION OF D LYSERGIC-ACID-DIETHYLAMIDE IN VIVO.
003832 04-03

POLYSOMNOGRAPHIC
TREATMENT OF NARCOLEPSY AND SLEEP-APNEA WITH GAMMA HYDROXYBUTYRATE: A CLINICAL AND POLYSOMNOGRAPHIC CASE-STUDY.
004571 04-14

POLYTHERAPY
MONOTHERAPY OR POLYTHERAPY FOR EPILEPSY?
003366 03-11

PONS-MEDULLA
STUDIES ON THE KINETIC PROPERTIES OF TRYPTOPHAN-HYDROXYLASE OF RABBIT MESENCEPHALON AND PONS-MEDULLA: EFFECT OF LONG-TERM-TREATMENT WITH NEUROLEPTICS AND ANTIDEPRESSANTS.
003852 04-03

PONTO-GENICULO-OCCIPITAL
DOES P CHLOROPHENYLALANINE PRODUCE DISTURBED WAKING, DISTURBED SLEEP OR ACTIVATION BY PONTO-GENICULO-OCCIPITAL WAVES IN CATS?
003704 04-02

POPULATION
TWELVE YEARS EXPERIENCE WITH THE TOTAL USE OF DEPOT NEUROLEPTICS IN A DEFINED POPULATION.
002544 02-17

PSYCHOACTIVE-MEDICATION USE AND ABUSE AMONG AN ADULT RURAL POPULATION. (PH.D. DISSERTATION).
003627 03-17

PSYCHIATRIC-ILLNESS AND USE OF PSYCHOTROPIC-DRUGS IN THE GEOGRAPHICALLY DELIMITED POPULATION OF SAMSO, DENMARK.
004734 04-17

POPULATIONS
TRICYCLIC-ANTIDEPRESSANT DRUG TOLERANCE IN ORIENTAL AND OCCIDENTAL POPULATIONS.
000590 01-09

PORCINE
EVOKED-POTENTIAL STUDIES OF PORCINE CALCITONIN IN RABBITS.
002936 03-03

LITHIUM AND PORCINE AGGRESSION.
003048 03-04

PORPHOBILINOGEN
EFFECTS OF D AMINOLAEVULINIC-ACID, PORPHOBILINOGEN, AMINO-ACIDS AND BARBITURATES ON CALCIUM ACCUMULATION BY CULTURED NEURONS.
002859 03-03

PORPHYRIAS
SAFETY OF ANTICONVULSANTS IN HEPATIC PORPHYRIAS.
003132 03-05

PORTACAVAL
ORAL BIOAVAILABILITY OF APOMORPHINE IN THE RAT WITH A PORTACAVAL VENOUS ANASTOMOSIS.
001158 02-03

PORTAL
ABSORPTION OF 14C LABELED METHADONE BY PORTAL AND EXTRAPORTAL VENOUS CIRCULATIONS FOLLOWING INTRAPERITONEAL AND INTRODUODENAL ADMINISTRATION.
000094 01-03

POSITION
THE SYMPATHETIC-NERVOUS-SYSTEM AND HYPERTENSION: A POSITION PAPER. (UNPUBLISHED PAPER).
002250 02-13

RESPECTIVE POSITION OF ANTIDEPRESSANTS IN THERAPEUTICS.
002581 02-17

EFFECT OF THE POSITION OF THE PHENOLIC GROUP IN MORPHINANS ON THEIR AFFINITY FOR OPIATE-RECEPTOR BINDING.
003702 04-02

POSITIVE
EFFECTS OF DOPAMINERGIC AGONISTS AND ANTAGONISTS ON (3H)APOMORPHINE BINDING TO STRIATAL MEMBRANES: SULPIRIDE LACK OF INTERACTIONS WITH POSITIVE COOPERATIVE (3H)APOMORPHINE BINDING.
000099 01-03

THE EFFECT OF DELTA9 TETRAHYDROCANNABINOL ON THE POSITIVE AND NEGATIVE FEEDBACK CONTROL OF LUTEINIZING-HORMONE RELEASE.
000286 01-03

THE EFFECT OF NALOXONE ON THE ACTIVATION OF EMOTIONALLY POSITIVE REACTION PRODUCED BY DRUGS WITH A DEPENDENCE LIABILITY.
001556 02-03

THE RELATIONSHIP BETWEEN POSITIVE REINFORCEMENT AND CONDITIONED TASTE-AVERSION PRODUCED BY SELF-ADMINISTERED DRUGS. (PH.D. DISSERTATION).
001798 02-04

DIFFERENTIAL-EFFECTS OF AMPHETAMINE AND NEUROLEPTICS ON NEGATIVE VS. POSITIVE SYMPTOMS IN SCHIZOPHRENIA.
001906 02-08

INTRACELLULAR LITHIUM: ITS VALUE IN THE PREDICTION OF A POSITIVE RESPONSE TO LITHIUM.
003382 03-11

A COMPARATIVE-STUDY OF THE PHARMACOLOGICAL-PROPERTIES OF THE POSITIVE POTENTIAL RECORDED FROM THE SUPERIOR CERVICAL GANGLIA OF SEVERAL SPECIES.
003779 04-03

POSITRON-TOMOGRAPHY
POSITRON-TOMOGRAPHY. A NEW METHOD FOR IN VIVO BRAIN STUDIES OF BENZODIAZEPINE, IN ANIMAL AND IN MAN.
003564 03-16

POSTADDICT
RELAPSE TO NARCOTIC SELF-ADMINISTRATION IN MORPHINE POSTADDICT RATS: A POSSIBLE MODEL FOR PREDICTING ABUSE LIABILITY OF NARCOTIC-DRUGS. (PH.D. DISSERTATION).
003097 03-04

MORPHINE CHALLENGES IN LEVO ALPHA ACETYLMETHADOL (LAAM) POSTADDICT RATS.
004259 04-04

POSTAMPHETAMINE
POSTAMPHETAMINE DEPRESSION OF SELF-STIMULATION RESPONDING FROM THE SUBSTANTIA-NIGRA: REVERSAL BY TRICYCLIC-ANTIDEPRESSANTS.
000419 01-04

POSTCONCUSSIONAL-SYNDROME
DOSE-EFFECT OF DEAE ON SUBJECTIVE PROBLEMS, VERTIGO, DEPRESSION, ASTHENIA, CEPHALALGIA, AND TONIC POSTURAL ACTIVITY PROBLEMS RECORDED WITH STATOKINESIMETER IN POSTCONCUSSIONAL-SYNDROME.
004472 04-11

POSTDECAPITATION
EFFECT OF ERGOT DERIVATIVES ON POSTDECAPITATION CONVULSIONS.
001288 02-03

POSTDEPENDENT
SCHEDULE-CONTROLLED BEHAVIOR IN THE MORPHINE-DEPENDENT AND POSTDEPENDENT RAT.
000349 01-04

LOCOMOTOR-ACTIVITY IN MORPHINE-DEPENDENT AND POSTDEPENDENT RATS.
004077 04-04

POSTENCEPHALITIC
PROSPECTS FOR THE TREATMENT OF POSTENCEPHALITIC PARKINSONISM WITH ANTILYMPHOCYTIC IMMUNOGLOBULIN.
004572 04-14

POSTERIOR
EVIDENCE FOR A DIRECT INHIBITORY-EFFECT OF MORPHINE ON THE SECRETION OF POSTERIOR PITUITARY-HORMONES.
000193 01-03

THE IDENTITY AND HYPOTHALAMIC ORIGIN OF CHOLECYSTOKININ IN RAT-BRAIN AND POSTERIOR PITUITARY AND ITS POSSIBLE ROLE IN REGULATION OF NEUROSECRETION. (UNPUBLISHED PAPER).
001003 02-01

BIOSYNTHESIS OF POSTERIOR PITUITARY-HORMONES. (UNPUBLISHED PAPER).
001053 02-01

BIOSYNTHESIS, AXONAL TRANSPORT AND RELEASE OF POSTERIOR PITUITARY-HORMONES. (UNPUBLISHED PAPER).
001148 02-03

THE EFFECTS OF BOMBESIN INJECTED INTO THE ANTERIOR AND POSTERIOR HYPOTHALAMUS ON BODY-TEMPERATURE AND OXYGEN CONSUMPTION.
001544 02-03

EXPERIENCE IN USING THE HORMONES OF THE HYPOPHYSIS POSTERIOR LOBE IN MEMORY-DISTURBANCES OF VARYING GENESES.
003438 03-14

LONG-TERM-TREATMENT OF RATS WITH MORPHINE DECREASES IN VITRO BIOSYNTHESIS IN AND RELEASE OF BETA ENDORPHIN FROM INTERMEDIATE/POSTERIOR LOBES OF PITUITARY.
003846 04-03

POSTINGESTION
POSTINGESTION INTERFERENCE WITH BRAIN FUNCTION PREVENTS ATTENTUATION OF NEOPHOBIA IN RATS.
000352 01-04

POSTISCHEMIC
DRUG INTERFERENCE ON SOME BIOCHEMICAL-PARAMETERS OF RAT-CEREBRAL-CORTEX DURING POSTISCHEMIC RECOVERY.
001126 02-03

POSTJUNCTIONAL
AN EXAMINATION OF FACTORS INFLUENCING ADRENERGIC TRANSMISSION IN THE PITHED RAT, WITH SPECIAL REFERENCE TO NORADRENALINE UPTAKE MECHANISMS AND POSTJUNCTIONAL ALPHA-ADRENOCEPTORS.
001196 02-03

POSTMARKETING
EUHYPNOS-FORTE, HIGH-DOSE TEMAZEPAM FOR RESISTANT INSOMNIA: POSTMARKETING SURVEILLANCE IN 10,057 PATIENTS UNRESPONSIVE TO CONVENTIONAL HYPNOTIC DOSAGE.
002324 02-14

POSTMENOPAUSAL-WOMEN
DIURNAL GROWTH-HORMONE RESPONSES TO DEXTROAMPHETAMINE IN NORMAL YOUNG MEN AND POSTMENOPAUSAL-WOMEN.
003411 03-13

THE EFFECTS OF ESTROGEN THERAPY ON THE SEX-LIFE OF POSTMENOPAUSAL-WOMEN.
004573 04-14

POSTMORTEM
TIME-COURSE OF THE ANTIPSYCHOTIC-EFFECT IN SCHIZOPHRENIA AND SOME CHANGES IN POSTMORTEM BRAIN AND THEIR RELATION TO NEUROLEPTIC-MEDICATION.
001911 02-08

DOPAMINERGIC ABNORMALITIES IN POSTMORTEM SCHIZOPHRENIC BRAIN.
002575 02-17

POSTMORTEM STABILITY OF BRAIN 3 METHOXY-4-
HYDROXYPHENYLETHYLENEGLYCOL AND 3,4
DIHYDROXYPHENYLETHYLENEGLYCOL IN THE RAT AND MOUSE.
004048 04-03

POSTNATAL
POSTNATAL ALCOHOL EXPOSURE IN THE RAT: ITS EFFECTS ON
AVOIDANCE CONDITIONING, HEBB-WILLIAMS MAZE-PERFORMANCE,
MATERNAL-BEHAVIOR, AND PUP DEVELOPMENT.
001580 02-04
RAT PUP-KILLING AND MATERNAL-BEHAVIOR IN MALE LONG-EVANS-
RATS: PRENATAL STIMULATION AND POSTNATAL TESTOSTERONE.
003054 03-04
SUPPRESSION OF ACTIVE SLEEP BY CHRONIC-TREATMENT WITH
CHLORIMIPRAMINE DURING EARLY POSTNATAL DEVELOPMENT:
EFFECTS UPON ADULT SLEEP AND BEHAVIOR IN THE RAT.
003056 03-04

POSTPARTUM
INCREASED SERUM PROLACTIN LEVELS DURING PHENOTHIAZINE AND
BUTYROPHENONE TREATMENT OF SIX POSTPARTUM WOMEN.
003318 03-11

POSTPSYCHOTIC
LITHIUM TREATMENT IN POSTPSYCHOTIC DEPRESSION.
000575 01-08

POSTREMA
IMMUNOCYTOCHEMICAL LOCALIZATION OF CATECHOLAMINE
SYNTHESIZING ENZYMES AND NEUROPEPTIDES IN AREA POSTREMA
AND MEDIAL NUCLEUS-TRACTUS-SOLITARIUS OF RAT-BRAIN.
002634 03-01

POSTSWIM
POSTSWIM GROOMING IN MICE INHIBITED BY DOPAMINE-RECEPTOR
ANTAGONISTS AND BY CANNABINOIDS.
000359 01-04

POSTSYNAPTIC
COMPARISON OF MIANSERIN WITH DESIPRAMINE, MAPROTILINE AND
PHENTOLAMINE ON CARDIAC PRESYNAPTIC AND VASCULAR
POSTSYNAPTIC ALPHA-ADRENOCEPTORS AND NORADRENALINE
REUPTAKE IN PITHED NORMOTENSIVE-RATS.
000044 01-03
MONOAMINERGIC DENERVATION OF THE RAT HIPPOCAMPUS:
MICROIONTOPHORETIC STUDIES OF PRESYNAPTIC AND POSTSYNAPTIC
SUPERSENSITIVITY TO NOREPINEPHRINE AND SEROTONIN.
000068 01-03
THE EFFECTS OF BROMOCRIPTINE ON PRESYNAPTIC AND POSTSYNAPTIC
ALPHA-ADRENOCEPTORS IN THE MOUSE VAS-DEFERENS.
000108 01-03
ANTICONVULSANT AND ANESTHETIC BARBITURATES: DIFFERENT
POSTSYNAPTIC ACTIONS IN CULTURED MAMMALIAN NEURONS.
000194 01-03
METOCLOPRAMIDE AND SULPIRIDE AS SELECTIVE BLOCKING-AGENTS
PRESYNAPTIC AND POSTSYNAPTIC DOPAMINE-RECEPTORS.
001102 02-03
EFFECTS OF ALPHA-ADRENOCEPTOR AGONISTS AND ANTAGONISTS AND
OF ANTIDEPRESSANT-DRUGS ON PRESYNAPTIC AND POSTSYNAPTIC
ALPHA-ADRENOCEPTORS.
001146 02-03
PERIPHERAL PRESYNAPTIC AND POSTSYNAPTIC DOPAMINE-RECEPTORS:
ARE THEY DIFFERENT FROM DOPAMINE-RECEPTORS IN THE CENTRAL-
NERVOUS-SYSTEM.
001252 02-03
THE TIME-COURSE OF NORADRENERGIC PRESYNAPTIC AND
POSTSYNAPTIC ACTIVITY DURING CHRONIC DESIPRAMINE
TREATMENT.
001289 02-03
PRESYNAPTIC AND POSTSYNAPTIC MECHANISMS IN HALOPERIDOL-
INDUCED SENSITIZATION TO DOPAMINERGIC AGONISTS.
001392 02-03
DOPAMINE-AUTORECEPTORS: PHARMACOLOGY, FUNCTION AND
COMPARISON WITH POSTSYNAPTIC DOPAMINE-RECEPTORS.
001453 02-03
RADIORECEPTOR LABELING OF PRESYNAPTIC AND POSTSYNAPTIC
DOPAMINE-RECEPTORS.
001511 02-03
PRESYNAPTIC AND POSTSYNAPTIC SEROTONERGIC MANIPULATIONS IN
AN ANIMAL-MODEL OF DEPRESSION.
001730 02-04
DYSKINESIA INDUCED BY LONG-TERM-TREATMENT WITH
ANTIPSYCHOTIC-DRUGS: INVOLVEMENT OF PRESYNAPTIC AND
POSTSYNAPTIC DOPAMINERGIC MECHANISMS.
001839 02-05
DRUG-EFFECTS ON PRESYNAPTIC AND POSTSYNAPTIC DOPAMINE-
RECEPTORS.
002372 02-15
EVIDENCE THAT IT IS POSSIBLE TO CAUSE ANOREXIA BY INCREASING
RELEASE AND/OR DIRECTLY STIMULATING POSTSYNAPTIC SEROTONIN-
RECEPTORS IN THE BRAIN.
002602 02-17
A BARBITURATE-EVOKED INTENSIFICATION OF POSTSYNAPTIC INHIBITION
IN THE PREOPTIC OVULATORY TRIGGER REGION OF THE
HYPOTHALAMUS.
002818 03-03

PRESYNAPTIC AND POSTSYNAPTIC STRIATAL DOPAMINE-RECEPTORS:
DIFFERENTIAL SENSITIVITY TO APOMORPHINE INHIBITION OF
(3H)DOPAMINE AND (14C)GABA RELEASE IN VITRO.
003741 04-03
DOPAMINE-RECEPTORS IN SUBCELLULAR FRACTIONS FROM BOVINE
CAUDATE: ENRICHMENT OF (3H)SPIPERONE BINDING IN A
POSTSYNAPTIC MEMBRANE FRACTION.
003948 04-03
PRESYNAPTIC AND POSTSYNAPTIC ALPHA-ADRENOCEPTOR ANTAGONISM
BY NEUROLEPTICS IN VIVO.
003966 04-03
EFFECTS OF PROPRANOLOL ON THE LOCOMOTOR-STIMULATION INDUCED
BY ACTIVATION OF POSTSYNAPTIC CATECHOLAMINE-RECEPTORS.
004126 04-04
LITHIUM EFFECTS ON HALOPERIDOL-INDUCED PRESYNAPTIC AND
POSTSYNAPTIC DOPAMINE-RECEPTOR SUPERSENSITIVITY.
004244 04-04

POSTSYNAPTIC-RECEPTORS
NEUROLEPTIC-INDUCED ACUTE DYSTONIC REACTIONS MAY BE DUE TO
ENHANCED DOPAMINE RELEASE ON TO SUPERSENSITIVE
POSTSYNAPTIC-RECEPTORS.
002789 03-03

POSTTRAUMATIC
USE OF LYSINE-VASOPRESSIN IN THE TREATMENT OF POSTTRAUMATIC
AMNESIA.
004583 04-14

POSTTREATMENT
ADVANTAGE OF MONOTHERAPY WITH CLOBAZAM IN THE TREATMENT
AND POSTTREATMENT OF ALCOHOLIC WITHDRAWAL.
002140 02-11

POSTTRIAL
ACCELERATED EXTINCTION AFTER POSTTRIAL HALOTHANE ANESTHESIA IN
RATS: AN AVERSIVE-EFFECT.
003001 03-04

POSTURAL
MORPHINE VERSUS HALOPERIDOL CATALEPSY IN THE RAT: A
BEHAVIORAL-ANALYSIS OF POSTURAL SUPPORT MECHANISMS.
000376 01-04
POSTURAL ASYMMETRY AND DIRECTIONALITY OF ROTATION IN RATS.
001729 02-04
DOES POSTURAL ASYMMETRY INDICATE DIRECTIONALITY OF ROTATION
IN RATS: ROLE OF SEX AND HANDLING.
003061 03-04
DOSE-EFFECT OF DEAE ON SUBJECTIVE PROBLEMS, VERTIGO,
DEPRESSION, ASTHENIA, CEPHALALGIA, AND TONIC POSTURAL
ACTIVITY PROBLEMS RECORDED WITH STATOKINESIMETER IN
POSTCONCUSSIONAL-SYNDROME.
004472 04-11

POTASSIUM
ABSENCE OF POTASSIUM CONDUCTANCE IN CENTRAL MYELINATED
AXONS.
000166 01-03
THE INFLUENCE OF EXTERNAL SODIUM AND POTASSIUM ON LITHIUM
UPTAKE BY PRIMARY BRAIN CELL CULTURES AT THERAPEUTIC LITHIUM
CONCENTRATION.
001300 02-03
EFFECT OF LITHIUM ON POTASSIUM AND CALCIUM IN SERUM,
ERYTHROCYTES AND IN URINE.
002054 02-09
THE EFFECTS OF D-AMPHETAMINE AND POTASSIUM ON SEROTONIN
RELEASE AND METABOLISM IN RAT-CEREBRAL-CORTEX TISSUE.
002754 03-03
DIFFERENTIAL-EFFECTS OF POTASSIUM ON THE POTENCY OF DIFFERENT
OPIOIDS IN THE MOUSE VAS-DEFERENS.
002935 03-03
INCREASE OF C-GMP AND ACCUMULATION OF 45CA2 EVOKED BY DRUGS
ACTING ON SODIUM OR POTASSIUM CHANNELS.
003709 04-03
INFLUENCE OF CALCIUM ON NORADRENALINE RELEASE EVOKED BY 5
HYDROXYTRYPTAMINE, TYRAMINE AND POTASSIUM FROM GOAT
PIAL-ARTERIES.
003925 04-03

POTASSIUM-INDUCED
EFFECTS OF HALOPEMIDE ON POTASSIUM-INDUCED RELEASE OF
RADIOLABELED NEUROTRANSMITTERS FROM RAT CEREBROCORTICAL
SLICES IN VITRO.
001347 02-03

POTENCIES
RELATIVE POTENCIES OF TWO PHENYLALKYLAMINES FOUND IN THE
ABUSED PLANT CATHA-EDULIS, KHAT.
001084 02-02
ERGOT AND CATECHOLAMINE POTENCIES AT CATECHOLAMINE-
RECEPTORS.
001510 02-03
PROLACTIN RELEASING POTENCIES OF ANTIPSYCHOTIC AND RELATED
NONANTIPSYCHOTIC COMPOUNDS IN FEMALE RATS: RELATION TO
CLINICAL POTENCIES.
003830 04-03

COMPARISON OF THE POTENCIES OF CLEBOPRIDE AND OTHER SUBSTITUTED BENZAMIDE DRUGS ON ISOLATED GASTROINTESTINAL TRACT OF THE GUINEA-PIG AND RAT.
003928 04-03

POTENCY
A NEW APPROACH TO THE ASSESSMENT OF THE POTENCY OF REVERSIBLE MONOAMINE-OXIDASE-INHIBITORS IN VIVO, AND ITS APPLICATION TO D-AMPHETAMINE, P METHOXYAMPHETAMINE AND HARMALINE.
000900 01-16

BETA ENDORPHIN: DISSOCIATION OF RECEPTOR BINDING-ACTIVITY FROM ANALGESIC POTENCY.
001081 02-02

THE EFFECT OF ASPIRIN AND PARACETAMOL ON THE INCREASED NALOXONE POTENCY INDUCED BY MORPHINE PRETREATMENT.
001824 02-04

METOCLOPRAMIDE: ANTIPSYCHOTIC-EFFICACY OF A DRUG LACKING POTENCY IN RECEPTOR MODELS.
001948 02-08

AMPHETAMINIL IN THE TREATMENT OF DISTURBED ERECTION POTENCY.
002129 02-11

DIFFERENTIAL-EFFECTS OF POTASSIUM ON THE POTENCY OF DIFFERENT OPIOIDS IN THE MOUSE VAS-DEFERENS.
002935 03-03

RELATIVE POTENCY OF AMPHETAMINE ISOMERS IN CAUSING THE SEROTONIN BEHAVIORAL-SYNDROME IN RATS.
003094 03-04

DIETARY PROTEIN INTAKE INFLUENCES THE ANTIHYPERTENSIVE POTENCY OF METHYLDOPA IN SPONTANEOUSLY HYPERTENSIVE-RATS.
004025 04-03

POTENTIAL
EFFECTS OF THE POTENTIAL NEUROLEPTIC-PEPTIDE DES-TYR1-GAMMA-ENDORPHIN AND HALOPERIDOL ON APOMORPHINE-INDUCED BEHAVIOURAL-SYNDROMES IN RATS AND MICE.
000441 01-04

SYNTHESIS OF SOME 5 PHENYLHEXAHYDROAZEPINOINDOLES AS POTENTIAL NEUROLEPTIC-AGENTS.
001019 02-01

CONVULSANT AND ANTICONVULSANT BARBITURATES. 1. MOLECULAR CONFORMATIONS FROM CLASSICAL POTENTIAL ENERGY CALCULATIONS.
001029 02-01

6 SUBSTITUTED AMINO-4H-S-TRIAZOLOBENZODIAZEPINES AND 4 SUBSTITUTED AMINO-6H-S-TRIAZOLOBENZODIAZEPINES WITH POTENTIAL ANTIANXIETY ACTIVITY.
001076 02-02

THE NEUROVASCULAR-PHARMACOLOGY AND CARDIOVASCULAR-PHARMACOLOGY OF RS-51324, A POTENTIAL ANTIDEPRESSANT.
001091 02-02

ACUTE AND CHRONIC EFFECTS OF MORPHINE ON TRANSMEMBRANE POTENTIAL AND ON SHORT-CIRCUIT CURRENT IN ISOLATED TOAD SKIN: APPARENT MORPHINE-DEPENDENCE.
001176 02-03

10 PIPERAZINYL-4H-THIENOBENZODIAZEPINES AS POTENTIAL NEUROLEPTICS.
001591 02-04

4 PIPERAZINYL-10H-THIENOBENZODIAZEPINES AS POTENTIAL NEUROLEPTICS.
001592 02-04

ABUSE POTENTIAL OF LOPERAMIDE.
002413 02-15

REGULATION OF NEUROTRANSMISSION THROUGH PRESYNAPTIC-RECEPTORS AND OTHER MECHANISMS: POSSIBLE CLINICAL RELEVANCE AND THERAPEUTIC POTENTIAL.
002569 02-16

MEASUREMENT OF THE MEMBRANE POTENTIAL OF ISOLATED NERVE TERMINALS BY THE LIPOPHILIC CATION (3H)TRIPHENYLMETHYLPHOSPHONIUM-BROMIDE.
002746 03-03

DEPRESSION OF VENTRAL ROOT DORSAL ROOT POTENTIAL BY DL ALPHA AMINOADIPATE IN FROG SPINAL-CORD.
002755 03-03

INFLUENCE OF A CHRONIC NEW POTENTIAL ANTIDEPRESSANT, DIMETHYLAMINOPROPYL-5-METHYL-3-PHENYL-1H-INDAZOLE (FS-32) AND ITS N DESMETHYLATED-COMPOUND (FS-97): TREATMENT ON MONOAMINERGIC-RECEPTOR SENSITIVITY IN THE RAT-BRAIN.
002787 03-03

DIPHENYLHYDANTOIN REDUCES THE OUTWARD-CURRENT OF THE ACTION POTENTIAL IN APLYSIA.
002805 03-03

PRENATAL EXPOSURE TO SYNTHETIC PROGESTINS INCREASES POTENTIAL FOR AGGRESSION IN HUMANS.
003527 03-15

EFFECTS OF PENTAZOCINE AND NALORPHINE ON MOTILITY IN CHRONICALLY MORPHINE TREATED RATS: A POTENTIAL SUBSTITUTION TEST TO DETECT THE NARCOTIC CHARACTER OF A DRUG.
003555 03-16

SYNTHESIS OF POTENTIAL ANTICONVULSANTS: CONDENSATION OF ISATINS WITH ACETONE AND RELATED KETONES.
003699 04-02

A COMPARATIVE-STUDY OF THE PHARMACOLOGICAL-PROPERTIES OF THE POSITIVE POTENTIAL RECORDED FROM THE SUPERIOR CERVICAL GANGLIA OF SEVERAL SPECIES.
003779 04-03

DEMONSTRATION OF A MUSCARINIC-RECEPTOR-MEDIATED CYCLIC-GMP-DEPENDENT HYPERPOLARIZATION OF THE MEMBRANE POTENTIAL OF MOUSE NEUROBLASTOMA CELLS USING (3H)TETRAPHENYLPHOSPHONIUM.
004049 04-03

PHARMACOLOGICAL AND BIOCHEMICAL-PROPERTIES OF BRL-14342, A NOVEL POTENTIAL ANTIDEPRESSANT-DRUG.
004086 04-04

SPECIFIC IN VIVO BINDING OF 77BR P BROMOSPIROPERIDOL IN RAT-BRAIN: A POTENTIAL TOOL FOR GAMMA-RAY IMAGING.
004293 04-06

EVENT-RELATED POTENTIAL CHANGES WITH MORPHINE IN NONADDICTED HUMANS.
004512 04-13

POTENTIALS
EFFECTS OF ENKEPHALIN ANALOGUE AND NALOXONE ON CAT SPINAL-CORD DORSAL ROOT POTENTIALS.
000236 01-03

THE EFFECT OF CISMETHRIN ON THE RAT DORSAL ROOT POTENTIALS.
000528 01-05

MECHANICAL-CHANGES IN CRAB NERVE FIBERS DURING ACTION POTENTIALS. (UNPUBLISHED PAPER).
001505 02-03

ASPIRIN ANALGESIA EVALUATED BY EVENT-RELATED POTENTIALS IN MAN: POSSIBLE CENTRAL-ACTION IN BRAIN.
002195 02-12

CAPACITIES OF ATTENTION, STRESS-RESISTANCE, AND SLOW CEREBRAL POTENTIALS: EFFECTS OF CARPIPRAMINE ON CONTINGENT NEGATIVE VARIATION WAVES AND P-300.
003451 03-14

OPIATE MECHANISMS: EVALUATION OF RESEARCH INVOLVING NEURONAL ACTION POTENTIALS.
003886 04-03

THE USE OF EVENT-RELATED SLOW POTENTIALS OF THE BRAIN AS AN OBJECTIVE METHOD TO STUDY THE EFFECTS OF CENTRALLY ACTING DRUGS.
004669 04-16

POTENTIATE
THE INABILITY OF CHRONIC FLUOXETINE TO POTENTIATE A SEROTONIN MEDIATED EFFECT.
000293 01-03

COCAINE AND AMPHETAMINE ANTAGONIZE THE DECREASE OF NORADRENERGIC NEUROTRANSMISSION ELICITED BY OXYMETAZOLINE BUT POTENTIATE THE INHIBITION BY ALPHA METHYLNOREPINEPHRINE IN THE PERFUSED CAT SPLEEN.
002801 03-03

GABA AND BACLOFEN POTENTIATE THE K-EVOKED RELEASE OF METHIONINE-ENKEPHALIN FROM RAT STRIATAL SLICES.
002882 03-03

PROMETHAZINE AND DIAZEPAM POTENTIATE THE HALOPERIDOL-INDUCED PROLACTIN RESPONSES.
004499 04-13

POTENTIATED
NORADRENERGIC AGONISTS AND ANTAGONISTS: EFFECTS ON CONDITIONED FEAR AS MEASURED BY THE POTENTIATED STARTLE PARADIGM.
000372 01-04

EXTRAPYRAMIDAL REACTION OF FLUPHENAZINE POTENTIATED BY THYROTOXICOSIS.
003551 03-15

POTENTIATES
PENTOBARBITAL POTENTIATES GABA-ENHANCED (3H) DIAZEPAM BINDING TO BENZODIAZEPINE-RECEPTORS.
000275 01-03

NALOXONE POTENTIATES THE DISRUPTIVE EFFECTS OF MESCALINE ON OPERANT-RESPONDING IN THE RAT.
000365 01-04

ACTH POTENTIATES MORPHINE-INDUCED CONDITIONED TASTE-AVERSION.
001781 02-04

ESTROGEN POTENTIATES THE STEREOTYPY INDUCED BY DOPAMINE AGONISTS IN THE RAT.
002968 03-04

POTENTIATION
ACUTE VERSUS CHRONIC EFFECTS OF SEROTONIN UPTAKE BLOCKERS ON POTENTIATION OF THE SEROTONIN SYNDROME.
000050 01-03

DIAZEPAM POTENTIATION OF PURINERGIC DEPRESSION OF CENTRAL NEURONS.
000233 01-03

METHIONINE-ENKEPHALIN ANTAGONISM AND ENDORPHIN POTENTIATION OF NARCOTIC-INDUCED ANALGESIA.
000357 01-04

POTENTIATION OF LETHALITY IN MICE BY COMBINATIONS OF PENTAZOCINE AND TRIPELENNAMINE.
000529 01-05

PRECIPITATES
CORTICOSTERONE INCREASES THE SYNTHESIS OF A SOLUBLE PROTEIN IN
PITUITARY-GLANDS FROM ADRENALECTOMIZED MALE RATS WHICH
PRECIPITATES WITH ANTI-RAT GROWTH-HORMONE ANTISERUM.
(UNPUBLISHED PAPER).
001122 02-03

PRECLINICAL
PHARMACOLOGICAL-BASES OF PSYCHONEUROENDOCRINOLOGY:
PRECLINICAL ASSESSMENT OF CLINICAL FACTS.
003735 04-03
CLINICAL AND PRECLINICAL EXPERIENCE WITH CHOLINE-CHLORIDE IN
HUNTINGTONS-DISEASE AND TARDIVE-DYSKINESIA: UNANSWERED
QUESTIONS.
004604 04-15

PRECLINICAL-EVALUATION
NEUROPHARMACOLOGICAL AND NEUROCHEMICAL APPROACHES TO
PRECLINICAL-EVALUATION OF NEUROLEPTICS.
001094 02-02

PRECONDITIONING
THE EFFECTS OF PIPRADROL ON THE ACQUISITION OF RESPONDING WITH
CONDITIONED REINFORCEMENT: A ROLE FOR SENSORY
PRECONDITIONING.
001572 02-04

PRECURSOR
BEHAVIOURAL-RESPONSES TO DRUGS RELEASING 5
HYDROXYTRYPTAMINE AND CATECHOLAMINES: EFFECTS OF
TREATMENTS ALTERING PRECURSOR CONCENTRATIONS IN BRAIN.
002990 03-04

PRECURSORS
PSYCHIATRIC MANIFESTATIONS INDUCED BY DOPAMINE PRECURSORS OR
DOPAMINE AGONISTS.
000865 01-15
MONOAMINES AND DEPRESSION: AN INTERIM REPORT. I. SEROTONIN
AND SEROTONIN PRECURSORS.
000996 01-17
ISOLATION OF PSYCHOACTIVE CANNABINOID PRECURSORS FROM
CANNABIS OF SOVIET PROVENIENCE GROWN IN MISSISSIPPI.
001023 02-01
MANAGEMENT OF DEPRESSION WITH SEROTONIN PRECURSORS.
003269 03-09

PREDATOR
RATS REACTIONS TO A PREDATOR: MODIFICATION BY
CHLORDIAZEPOXIDE.
000353 01-04

PREDICTABILITY
PREDICTABILITY OF PHENYTOIN SERUM LEVELS BY NOMOGRAMS AND
CLINICIANS.
000909 01-16

PREDICTING
PREDICTING OUTCOME OF ANTIPSYCHOTIC-DRUG TREATMENT FROM
EARLY-RESPONSE.
000565 01-08
PREDICTING THE RESPONSE OF HYPERACTIVE-CHILDREN TO RITALIN: AN
EMPIRICAL-STUDY.
002120 02-11
PHARMACOKINETIC BASIS FOR PREDICTING STEADY-STATE SERUM DRUG
CONCENTRATIONS OF IMIPRAMINE FROM SINGLE-DOSE DATA.
002225 02-13
RELAPSE TO NARCOTIC SELF-ADMINISTRATION IN MORPHINE
POSTADDICT RATS: A POSSIBLE MODEL FOR PREDICTING ABUSE
LIABILITY OF NARCOTIC-DRUGS. (PH.D. DISSERTATION).
003097 03-04
PREDICTING OUTCOME FROM MEASURES OF ATTENTION AND
AUTONOMIC-FUNCTIONING.
003205 03-08
PREDICTING STIMULANT-EFFECTIVENESS IN HYPERACTIVE-CHILDREN WITH
A REPEATABLE NEUROPSYCHOLOGICAL-BATTERY: A PRELIMINARY-
STUDY.
004453 04-11

PREDICTIVE
PREDICTION OF DOSAGE OF LITHIUM-CARBONATE: USE OF A STANDARD
PREDICTIVE METHOD.
001991 02-09
PREDICTIVE CRITERIA FOR LITHIUM-SALTS ACTIVITY.
002619 02-17
HYPERVENTILATION-SYNDROME, TREATMENT WITH L TRYPTOPHAN AND
PYRIDOXINE; PREDICTIVE VALUES OF XANTHURENIC-ACID EXCRETION.
004456 04-11

PREDICTOR
D-AMPHETAMINE AS A PREDICTOR FOR RESPONSE TO IMIPRAMINE AND
AMITRIPTYLINE.
000621 01-09
MHPG AS A PREDICTOR OF ANTIDEPRESSANT RESPONSE TO IMIPRAMINE
AND MAPROTILINE.
000787 01-13
STRIATAL DOPAC LEVELS AS A PREDICTOR OF ANTIPSYCHOTIC-EFFICACY.
001533 02-03

PERSONALITY AS A PREDICTOR OF PSYCHOTHERAPY AND
PHARMACOTHERAPY-OUTCOME FOR DEPRESSED-OUTPATIENTS.
(UNPUBLISHED PAPER).
004418 04-09

PREDICTORS
PREDICTORS OF ADOLESCENT HEIGHT AND WEIGHT IN HYPERKINETIC-
BOYS TREATED WITH METHYLPHENIDATE.
003509 03-15
LITHIUM IN THE PROPHYLAXIS OF RECURRENT AFFECTIVE-DISORDERS
(EFFECTIVENESS OF LOW PLASMA LEVELS AND PREDICTORS TO
CLINICAL-RESPONSE).
004365 04-09
TOWARD A BIOCHEMICAL CLASSIFICATION OF DEPRESSIVE-DISORDERS
IV: PRETREATMENT URINARY MHPG LEVELS AS PREDICTORS OF
ANTIDEPRESSANT RESPONSE TO IMIPRAMINE.
004406 04-09
BIOLOGICAL AND PHYSIOLOGICAL PREDICTORS OF DRUG RESPONSE.
(UNPUBLISHED PAPER).
004708 04-17

PREEXPOSURE
INTERFERENCE WITH INGESTIONAL AVERSION LEARNING PRODUCED BY
PREEXPOSURE TO THE UNCONDITIONED-STIMULUS: ASSOCIATIVE-
ASPECTS AND NONASSOCIATIVE-ASPECTS.
001610 02-04
PREEXPOSURE TO DELTA9 THC BLOCKS THC-INDUCED CONDITIONED
TASTE-AVERSION IN RATS.
001618 02-04

PREFRONTAL-CORTEX
5 HT BLOCKADE AND THE STIMULANT-EFFECTS OF D-AMPHETAMINE AND
L-AMPHETAMINE: NO INTERACTION IN SELF-STIMULATION OF
PREFRONTAL-CORTEX, HYPOTHALAMUS, OR DORSAL TEGMENTUM.
UNEXPECTED LETHALITY IN HIPPOCAMPAL SITES.
000387 01-04
FACILITATION OF SELF-STIMULATION OF THE PREFRONTAL-CORTEX IN
RATS FOLLOWING CHRONIC ADMINISTRATION OF SPIROPERIDOL OR
AMPHETAMINE.
000457 01-04
EFFECT OF 6 HYDROXYDOPAMINE LESIONS OF THE MEDIAL PREFRONTAL-
CORTEX ON NEUROTRANSMITTER SYSTEMS IN SUBCORTICAL SITES IN
THE RAT.
002869 03-03

PREGANGLIONIC
THE LONG-TERM REGULATION OF GANGLIONIC TYROSINE-HYDROXYLASE
BY PREGANGLIONIC NERVE ACTIVITY.
000333 01-03

PREGNANCIES
OUR EXPERIENCE WITH PIRACETAM (NOOTROPIL-UCB) TREATMENT IN
CHILDREN FROM HIGH-RISK PREGNANCIES WITH SUBSEQUENT
MINIMAL-BRAIN-DYSFUNCTION.
000544 01-07

PREGNANCY
PREGNANCY AND EPILEPSY: SHOULD ANTICONVULSANT-DRUGS BE
CONTINUED?
000679 01-11
ON THE DANGER OF USING PSYCHOPHARMACEUTICALS DURING
PREGNANCY: CRITICAL REVIEW OF THE LITERATURE.
000833 01-15
MEDICATION AND PREGNANCY.
002424 02-17
PSYCHOPHARMACEUTICALS AND PREGNANCY: A REVIEW.
002462 02-15
EPILEPSY: NEUROTRANSMITTER, BEHAVIOUR AND PREGNANCY.
002466 02-15

PREGNANT
THE COMPARATIVE DISPOSITION OF NOMIFENSINE (MERITAL) IN THE
PREGNANT AND NONPREGNANT RAT.
000853 01-15
EFFECTS OF MARIHUANA ON PREGNANT RATS AND THEIR OFFSPRING.
001830 02-05

PREINCUBATION
CHANGES IN ALPHA-ADRENERGIC-RECEPTORS IN RAT-BRAIN IN VITRO BY
PREINCUBATION WITH ALPHA-ADRENERGIC LIGANDS.
001272 02-03
BENZODIAZEPINE-RECEPTORS: EFFECT OF TISSUE PREINCUBATION AT 37
DEGREES C.
004013 04-03

PREJUNCTIONAL
PREJUNCTIONAL ACTIONS OF PIRIBEDIL ON THE ISOLATED KIDNEY OF THE
RABBIT; COMPARISON WITH APOMORPHINE.
003749 04-03
INTERACTION OF THE TRICYCLIC-ANTIDEPRESSANT AMITRIPTYLINE WITH
PREJUNCTIONAL ALPHA AND MUSCARINIC-RECEPTORS IN THE DOG
SAPHENOUS VEIN.
003756 04-03

PRELIMINARY-COMMUNICATION
OXYPROTHEPINE-DECANOATE COMPARED WITH FLUPHENAZINE-
DECANOATE IN THE TREATMENT OF SCHIZOPHRENIA: PRELIMINARY-
COMMUNICATION.
001934 02-08

PRELIMINARY-FINDINGS
PRELIMINARY-FINDINGS WITH REGARD TO RISK-FACTORS IN THE
DEVELOPMENT OF TARDIVE-DYSKINESIA.
003501 03-15

PRELIMINARY-REPORT
ANTECEDENTS OF SELF-INDUCED WATER INTOXICATION: A PRELIMINARY-
REPORT.
002414 02-15

PRELIMINARY-RESULTS
A TEN YEAR FOLLOWUP OF LITHIUM-CARBONATE TREATMENT OF MANIC-
DEPRESSIVE-ILLNESS: PRELIMINARY-RESULTS.
002053 02-09

PRELIMINARY-STUDIES
PRELIMINARY-STUDIES ON CSF GAMMA AMINOBUTYRIC-ACID LEVELS IN
PSYCHIATRIC-PATIENTS BEFORE AND DURING TREATMENT WITH
DIFFERENT PSYCHOTROPIC-DRUGS.
001959 02-08

PRELIMINARY-STUDY
PREDICTING STIMULANT-EFFECTIVENESS IN HYPERACTIVE-CHILDREN WITH
A REPEATABLE NEUROPSYCHOLOGICAL-BATTERY: A PRELIMINARY-
STUDY.
004453 04-11
HORMONAL STIMULATION AFTER INJECTION OF THYROTROPHIN-
RELEASING-FACTOR (TRF) AND ACTH1-24 IN PATIENTS FOLLOWING
CHRONIC-TREATMENT WITH NEUROLEPTICS: PRELIMINARY-STUDY.
004505 04-13

PRELIMINARY-TRIAL
MEMORY AND COGNITIVE FUNCTION IN THE ELDERLY: A PRELIMINARY-
TRIAL OF PHYSOSTIGMINE.
000802 01-14

PREMATURE
BIOELECTRICAL-ACTIVITY OF THE RAT BRAIN AFTER PREMATURE
WEANING AND AFTER RNA ADMINISTRATION.
002865 03-03

PREMENOPAUSAL-WOMEN
A DOUBLE-BLIND STUDY WITH ORG-GB-94 IN PREMENOPAUSAL-WOMEN.
002173 02-11

PREMENSTRUAL
A NEW DRUG-TREATMENT FOR PREMENSTRUAL EXACERBATION OF
SCHIZOPHRENIA.
000553 01-08

PREMENSTRUAL-SYNDROME
CYCLICAL CRIMINAL ACTS IN PREMENSTRUAL-SYNDROME.
000927 01-17

PRENATAL
DELAYED MAZE-LEARNING IN RATS AFTER PRENATAL EXPOSURE TO
CLORAZEPATE.
000521 01-05
EFFECTS OF PRENATAL METHADONE ON RAT-BRAIN CATECHOLAMINES.
001367 02-03
RAT PUP-KILLING AND MATERNAL-BEHAVIOR IN MALE LONG-EVANS-
RATS: PRENATAL STIMULATION AND POSTNATAL TESTOSTERONE.
003054 03-04
PRENATAL EXPOSURE TO SYNTHETIC PROGESTINS INCREASES POTENTIAL
FOR AGGRESSION IN HUMANS.
003527 03-15
THE EFFECT OF PRENATAL EXPOSURE TO ETHANOL OR OPIATES ON BRAIN
CATECHOLAMINE ACTIVITY.
003939 04-03
EFFECT OF PRENATAL NEUROLEPTIC TREATMENT ON MEMBRANE
RECEPTOR DEVELOPMENT IN THE BRAIN.
003989 04-03
EFFECT OF PRENATAL PHENYTOIN ADMINISTRATION ON BRAIN
TRYPTOPHAN METABOLISM OF RAT OFFSPRING DURING THE
PREWEANING PERIOD.
004108 04-04

PRENYLAMINE
PROTECTIVE EFFECT OF PRENYLAMINE AGAINST VULNERABILITY TO
VENTRICULAR FIBRILLATION IN THE NORMAL AND ISCHEMIC CANINE
MYOCARDIUM.
000265 01-03

PREOPTIC
TEMPORAL PATTERNING OF NEURONAL ACTIVITY DURING THERMAL AND
NEUROCHEMICAL STIMULATION OF THE PREOPTIC/ANTERIOR
HYPOTHALAMUS OF THE AWAKE RABBIT.
002737 03-03
A BARBITURATE-EVOKED INTENSIFICATION OF POSTSYNAPTIC INHIBITION
IN THE PREOPTIC OVULATORY TRIGGER REGION OF THE
HYPOTHALAMUS.
002818 03-03

PREOPTIC-AREA
EVIDENCE OF A DIRECT ACTION OF ANGIOTENSIN-II ON NEURONES IN THE
SEPTUM AND IN THE MEDIAL PREOPTIC-AREA.
000272 01-03

PREOPTICUS-MEDIALIS-NUCLEUS
EVIDENCE FOR THERMOREGULATORY DOPAMINERGIC-RECEPTORS
LOCATED IN THE PREOPTICUS-MEDIALIS-NUCLEUS OF THE RAT
HYPOTHALAMUS.
003754 04-03

PREPUBERTAL
PLASMA LEVELS OF IMIPRAMINE (IMI) AND DESMETHYLIMIPRAMINE (DMI) AND CLINICAL-RESPONSE IN PREPUBERTAL MAJOR DEPRESSIVE-DISORDER: A PRELIMINARY REPORT.
000619 01-09
IMIPRAMINE TREATMENT OF PREPUBERTAL MAJOR DEPRESSIVE-DISORDERS: PLASMA LEVELS AND CLINICAL-RESPONSE -- PRELIMINARY REPORT.
000620 01-09
ACUTE EFFECTS OF CAFFEINE IN NORMAL PREPUBERTAL BOYS.
003310 03-11

PRESCRIBING
A NOTE ON PATTERNS OF DRUG PRESCRIBING IN A RESIDENTIAL-CENTER FOR THE INTELLECTUALLY-HANDICAPPED.
000982 01-17
PAVING THE WAY TO SAFE PRESCRIBING FOR THE ELDERLY.
000999 01-17
JOB-SATISFACTION IN GENERAL-PRACTICE: IMPLICATIONS FOR PRESCRIBING.
002579 02-17
PATIENT CHARACTERISTICS AND CLINICIAN ATTITUDES INFLUENCING THE PRESCRIBING OF BENZODIAZEPINES.
003598 03-17
WHAT IS STANDARD PRACTICE IN PRESCRIBING PSYCHOTROPICS?
003638 03-17

PRESCRIPTION
TRENDS IN THE PRESCRIPTION OF PSYCHOTROPIC-DRUGS (1970-1977) IN A STATE-HOSPITAL.
000926 01-17
MONOAMINE-OXIDASE-INHIBITORS: PRESCRIPTION AND PATIENT MANAGEMENT.
002454 02-15
METHODOLOGICAL-CONSIDERATIONS CONCERNING THE PRESCRIPTION AND USE OF SO CALLED DISINHIBITORS.
002571 02-17
INITIAL PRESCRIPTION OF PSYCHOTROPIC-MEDICATIONS FOR ADOLESCENTS IN A MEDICAL/PROFESSIONAL INSTITUTE, AND THE ROLE OF THE PSYCHIATRIST IN A MEDICAL/PROFESSIONAL INSTITUTE.
002621 02-17

PRESCRIPTIONS
COMPARISON OF DRUG PRESCRIPTIONS FOR PSYCHIATRIC-PATIENTS AFTER HOSPITAL DISCHARGE IN THE DISTRICTS TEPLICE AND UHERSKE-HRADISTE.
002518 02-17

PRESSOR
EFFECTS OF CHRONIC ADMINISTRATION OF DELTA9 TETRAHYDROCANNABINOL ON THE CARDIOVASCULAR SYSTEM, AND PRESSOR AND BEHAVIORAL-RESPONSES TO BRAIN-STIMULATION IN FREELY-MOVING-RATS.
000417 01-04
CLONIDINE ON THE PRESSOR RESPONSE TO RAISED INTRACRANIAL PRESSURE.
001316 02-03
EFFECTS OF DELTA9 TETRAHYDROCANNABINOL ON THE CARDIOVASCULAR-SYSTEM, AND PRESSOR AND BEHAVIORAL-RESPONSES TO BRAIN-STIMULATION IN RATS.
001681 02-04
PRESSOR EFFECTS OF DORSAL RAPHE STIMULATION AND INTRAHYPOTHALAMIC APPLICATION OF SEROTONIN IN THE SPONTANEOUSLY HYPERTENSIVE-RAT.
003117 03-04
TYRAMINE PRESSOR TEST AND CARDIOVASCULAR-EFFECTS OF CHLORIMIPRAMINE AND NORTRIPTYLINE IN HEALTHY VOLUNTEERS.
003428 03-13
PRESSOR EFFECTS OF ELECTRICAL-STIMULATION OF THE DORSAL AND MEDIAN RAPHE NUCLEI IN ANESTHETIZED RATS.
003892 04-03
DIFFERENTIAL INHIBITION OF ALPHA1-ADRENOCEPTOR AND ALPHA2-ADRENOCEPTOR MEDIATED PRESSOR RESPONSES IN PITHED RATS.
004057 04-03

PRESSURE
PRESSURE REVERSAL OF THE EFFECT OF URETHANE ON THE EVOKED SOMATOSENSORY CORTICAL RESPONSE IN THE RAT.
001106 02-03
CLONIDINE ON THE PRESSOR RESPONSE TO RAISED INTRACRANIAL PRESSURE.
001316 02-03
BRAIN-MONOAMINES AND THE HIGH PRESSURE NEUROLOGICAL-SYNDROME.
001686 02-04
LEVELS OF 5 HYDROXYINDOLEACETIC-ACID AND TRYPTOPHAN IN LUMBAR CEREBROSPINAL-FLUID AND BLOOD OF PATIENTS WITH DEMENTIA AND NORMAL PRESSURE HYDROCEPHALUS AFTER TRYPTOPHAN ADMINISTRATION.
003419 03-13
INTRAOCULAR PRESSURE CHANGES FOLLOWING MODIFIED ECT.
003536 03-15
THE DYNAMICS OF SYSTEMIC VENOUS, ARTERIAL, AND CEREBROSPINAL-FLUID PRESSURE UNDER I.V. ADMINISTRATION OF POLYETHYLENE-GLYCOL.
004045 04-03

PRESYMPTOMATIC
LEVODOPA AND PRESYMPTOMATIC DETECTION OF HUNTINGTONS-DISEASE -- EIGHT-YEAR FOLLOWUP.
000950 01-17
EARLY DETECTION OF HUNTINGTONS-DISEASE. BLINK REFLEX AND LEVODOPA LOAD IN PRESYMPTOMATIC AND INCIPIENT SUBJECTS.
003311 03-11

PRESYNAPTIC
COMPARISON OF MIANSERIN WITH DESIPRAMINE, MAPROTILINE AND PHENTOLAMINE ON CARDIAC PRESYNAPTIC AND VASCULAR POSTSYNAPTIC ALPHA-ADRENOCEPTORS AND NORADRENALINE REUPTAKE IN PITHED NORMOTENSIVE-RATS.
000044 01-03
TRICYCLIC-ANTIDEPRESSANTS INDUCE SUBSENSITIVITY OF PRESYNAPTIC DOPAMINE-AUTORECEPTORS.
000048 01-03
MONOAMINERGIC DENERVATION OF THE RAT HIPPOCAMPUS: MICROIONTOPHORETIC STUDIES OF PRESYNAPTIC AND POSTSYNAPTIC SUPERSENSITIVITY TO NOREPINEPHRINE AND SEROTONIN.
000068 01-03
THE EFFECTS OF BROMOCRIPTINE ON PRESYNAPTIC AND POSTSYNAPTIC ALPHA-ADRENOCEPTORS IN THE MOUSE VAS-DEFERENS.
000108 01-03
GABA FLUXES IN PRESYNAPTIC NERVE-ENDINGS FROM IMMATURE RATS.
000185 01-03
INHIBITION OF NEURONAL UPTAKE REDUCES THE PRESYNAPTIC EFFECTS OF CLONIDINE BUT NOT OF ALPHA METHYLNORADRENALINE ON THE STIMULATION-EVOKED RELEASE OF 3H NORADRENALINE FROM RAT OCCIPITAL-CORTEX SLICES.
000227 01-03
ON THE CAPACITY OF PRESYNAPTIC ALPHA-RECEPTORS TO MODULATE NOREPINEPHRINE RELEASE FROM SLICES OF RAT NEOCORTEX AND THE AFFINITY OF SOME AGONISTS AND ANTAGONISTS FOR THESE RECEPTORS.
000323 01-03
METOCLOPRAMIDE AND SULPIRIDE AS SELECTIVE BLOCKING-AGENTS PRESYNAPTIC AND POSTSYNAPTIC DOPAMINE-RECEPTORS.
001102 02-03
PRESYNAPTIC DOPAMINE-RECEPTORS: INSENSITIVITY TO KAINIC-ACID AND THE DEVELOPMENT OF SUPERSENSITIVITY FOLLOWING CHRONIC HALOPERIDOL.
001117 02-03
EFFECTS OF ALPHA-ADRENOCEPTOR AGONISTS AND ANTAGONISTS AND OF ANTIDEPRESSANT-DRUGS ON PRESYNAPTIC AND POSTSYNAPTIC ALPHA-ADRENOCEPTORS.
001146 02-03
PRESYNAPTIC ACTIONS OF 4 AMINOPYRIDINE AND GAMMA AMINOBUTYRIC-ACID ON RAT SYMPATHETIC GANGLIA IN VITRO.
001244 02-03
PERIPHERAL PRESYNAPTIC AND POSTSYNAPTIC DOPAMINE-RECEPTORS: ARE THEY DIFFERENT FROM DOPAMINE-RECEPTORS IN THE CENTRAL-NERVOUS-SYSTEM.
001252 02-03
THE TIME-COURSE OF NORADRENERGIC PRESYNAPTIC AND POSTSYNAPTIC ACTIVITY DURING CHRONIC DESIPRAMINE TREATMENT.
001289 02-03
INTERNEURONES ARE PROBABLY NOT INVOLVED IN THE PRESYNAPTIC DOPAMINERGIC CONTROL OF DOPAMINE RELEASE IN RABBIT CAUDATE-NUCLEUS.
001298 02-03
BENZODIAZEPINES MODIFY THE AGONIST RESPONSES AT A PRESYNAPTIC GABA-RECEPTOR.
001377 02-03
ACTIVATION OF PRESYNAPTIC ALPHA NORADRENALINE-RECEPTORS IN RAT-BRAIN BY THE POTENT DOPAMINE-MIMETIC N,N DIPROPYL-ADTN.
001390 02-03
PRESYNAPTIC AND POSTSYNAPTIC MECHANISMS IN HALOPERIDOL-INDUCED SENSITIZATION TO DOPAMINERGIC AGONISTS.
001392 02-03
PRESYNAPTIC DOPAMINE-RECEPTORS IN STRIATAL NERVE-ENDINGS: ABSENCE OF HALOPERIDOL-INDUCED SUPERSENSITIVITY.
001424 02-03
RADIORECEPTOR LABELING OF PRESYNAPTIC AND POSTSYNAPTIC DOPAMINE-RECEPTORS.
001511 02-03
PRESYNAPTIC AND POSTSYNAPTIC SEROTONERGIC MANIPULATIONS IN AN ANIMAL-MODEL OF DEPRESSION.
001730 02-04
PRESYNAPTIC ALPHA-ADRENOCEPTORS AND THE ACTION OF TRICYCLIC-ANTIDEPRESSANT DRUGS IN BEHAVIOURAL-DESPAIR IN RATS.
001829 02-04
DYSKINESIA INDUCED BY LONG-TERM-TREATMENT WITH ANTIPSYCHOTIC-DRUGS: INVOLVEMENT OF PRESYNAPTIC AND POSTSYNAPTIC DOPAMINERGIC MECHANISMS.
001839 02-05
NEUROCHEMICAL EVIDENCE AND BEHAVIORAL-EVIDENCE FOR A SELECTIVE PRESYNAPTIC DOPAMINE-RECEPTOR AGONIST.
002236 02-13

Subject Index

DRUG-EFFECTS ON PRESYNAPTIC AND POSTSYNAPTIC DOPAMINE-
RECEPTORS.
002372 02-15

PRESYNAPTIC REGULATION OF THE RELEASE OF CATECHOLAMINES IN THE
CAT HYPOTHALAMUS.
002703 03-03

THE PRESYNAPTIC STIMULATING EFFECT OF ACETYLCHOLINE ON
DOPAMINE RELEASE IS SUPPRESSED DURING ACTIVATION OF
NIGROSTRIATAL DOPAMINERGIC NEURONS IN THE CAT.
002733 03-03

THE TETRACYCLIC-ANTIDEPRESSANT MIANSERIN: EVALUATION OF ITS
BLOCKADE OF PRESYNAPTIC ALPHA-ADRENOCEPTORS IN A SELF-
STIMULATION MODEL USING CLONIDINE.
003016 03-04

PRESYNAPTIC AND POSTSYNAPTIC STRIATAL DOPAMINE-RECEPTORS:
DIFFERENTIAL SENSITIVITY TO APOMORPHINE INHIBITION OF
(3H)DOPAMINE AND (14C)GABA RELEASE IN VITRO.
003741 04-03

PHARMACOLOGICAL DIFFERENTIATION OF PRESYNAPTIC INHIBITORY
ALPHA-ADRENOCEPTORS AND OPIATE-RECEPTORS IN THE CAT
NICTITATING MEMBRANE.
003777 04-03

PRESYNAPTIC REGULATION OF THE RELEASE OF ACETYLCHOLINE BY 5
HYDROXYTRYPTAMINE.
003843 04-03

PRESYNAPTIC MODULATION OF SYNAPTIC TRANSMISSION IN HELIX-
POMATIA: THE EFFECTS OF SEROTONIN AND DOPAMINE
ANTAGONISTS.
003869 04-03

ELECTROPHYSIOLOGICAL EVIDENCE FOR PRESYNAPTIC ACTIONS OF
PHENCYCLIDINE ON NORADRENERGIC TRANSMISSION IN RAT
CEREBELLUM.
003926 04-03

PRESYNAPTIC AND POSTSYNAPTIC ALPHA-ADRENOCEPTOR ANTAGONISM
BY NEUROLEPTICS IN VIVO.
003966 04-03

THE HIGH-AFFINITY CHOLINE UPTAKE SYSTEM WITH RESPECT TO THE
MUSCARINIC-RECEPTORS USING A SYNAPTOSOMAL FRACTION
ABUNDANT IN PRESYNAPTIC MEMBRANES.
004028 04-03

LITHIUM EFFECTS ON HALOPERIDOL-INDUCED PRESYNAPTIC AND
POSTSYNAPTIC DOPAMINE-RECEPTOR SUPERSENSITIVITY.
004244 04-04

PRESYNAPTIC-AUTORECEPTORS
SUPERSENSITIVITY OF CENTRAL NORADRENERGIC PRESYNAPTIC-
AUTORECEPTORS FOLLOWING CHRONIC-TREATMENT WITH THE
ANTIDEPRESSANT MIANSERIN.
003745 04-03

PRESYNAPTIC-RECEPTORS
DOPAMINE SYNTHESIS: TOLERANCE TO HALOPERIDOL AND
SUPERSENSITIVITY TO APOMORPHINE DEPEND ON PRESYNAPTIC-
RECEPTORS.
001129 02-03

REGULATION OF NEUROTRANSMISSION THROUGH PRESYNAPTIC-
RECEPTORS AND OTHER MECHANISMS: POSSIBLE CLINICAL RELEVANCE
AND THERAPEUTIC POTENTIAL.
002569 02-16

PRESYNAPTIC-RECEPTORS.
003637 03-17

PRESYNAPTICALLY
ENKEPHALINS PRESYNAPTICALLY INHIBIT CHOLINERGIC TRANSMISSION
IN SYMPATHETIC GANGLIA.
000167 01-03

PRETREATED
EFFECTS OF PHENCYCLIDINE AND METHYLPHENIDATE ON D-
AMPHETAMINE-INDUCED BEHAVIORS IN RESERPINE PRETREATED RATS.
001616 02-04

EFFECTS OF ELECTROCONVULSIVE-TREATMENT ON GROWTH-HORMONE
SECRETION INDUCED BY MONOAMINE-RECEPTOR AGONISTS IN
RESERPINE PRETREATED RATS.
002664 03-03

DIPHENYLHYDANTOIN-INDUCED BLOCK OF THE RAT PHRENIC-NERVE
DIAPHRAGM PREPARATION PRETREATED WITH P
HYDROXYMERCURIBENZOATE.
002749 03-03

ENHANCEMENT OF ETORPHINE BRAIN CONCENTRATIONS AND CHANGES
IN ETORPHINE NALOXONE PA2 VALUES IN MORPHINE PRETREATED
MICE.
002800 03-03

DISCRIMINATIVE RESPONSE CONTROL BY NALOXONE IN MORPHINE
PRETREATED RATS.
003053 03-04

PRETREATMENT
ENHANCEMENT OF THE BEHAVIORAL-EFFECTS OF 2,5 DIMETHOXY-4-
METHYLAMPHETAMINE (DOM) BY PRETREATMENT WITH P
CHLOROPHENYLALANINE.
000364 01-04

NALOXONE PRETREATMENT ENHANCES SHOCK-ELICITED AGGRESSION.
001615 02-04

DEVELOPMENT AND USE OF PHARMACOLOGICAL-PROBES OF THE CNS IN MAN: EVIDENCE OF CHOLINERGIC ABNORMALITY IN PRIMARY AFFECTIVE-ILLNESS.
002506 02-16

NA-INDEPENDENT BINDING OF (3H)GABA AND (3H)MUSCIMOL TO SUBCELLULAR PARTICLES OF NEURAL PRIMARY CULTURES AND WHOLE BRAIN.
002699 03-03

EVIDENCE THAT THE OPIATE-RECEPTORS OF THE SUBSTANTIA-GELATINOSA CONTRIBUTE TO THE DEPRESSION, BY INTRAVENOUS MORPHINE, OF THE SPINAL TRANSMISSION OF IMPULSES IN UNMYELINATED PRIMARY AFFERENTS.
002767 03-03

THE PATHOGENESIS OF PRIMARY INTERNODAL DEMYELINATION PRODUCED BY ACETYL-ETHYL-TETRAMETHYL-TETRALIN: EVIDENCE FOR PRESERVED SCHWANN-CELL SOMAL FUNCTION.
002905 03-03

THE MEDICATION SEMINAR AND PRIMARY CARE EDUCATION.
003592 03-17

EFFECTS OF PENTOBARBITAL AND ETHANOL UPON SINGLE NEURON ACTIVITY IN THE PRIMARY SOMATOSENSORY CORTEX OF THE RHESUS-MONKEY.
003755 04-03

SUPRASPINAL INHIBITION OF THE EXCITATION OF DORSAL-HORN NEURONES BY IMPULSES IN UNMYELINATED PRIMARY AFFERENTS: LACK OF EFFECT BY STRYCHNINE AND BICUCULLINE.
003778 04-03

THE EFFECT OF NOOTROPIL ON THE TRANSCALLOSAL AND PRIMARY EVOKED-RESPONSES OF THE CAT CEREBRAL-CORTEX.
003780 04-03

SENSORY NEUROTOXINS: CHEMICALLY-INDUCED SELECTIVE DESTRUCTION OF PRIMARY SENSORY NEURONS.
003859 04-03

BENZODIAZEPINE-RECEPTORS ON PRIMARY CULTURES OF MOUSE ASTROCYTES.
004029 04-03

CORTISOL DYNAMICS AND DEXAMETHASONE PHARMACOKINETICS IN PRIMARY ENDOGENOUS DEPRESSION: PRELIMINARY FINDINGS.
004403 04-09

PRIMATE
THE ACUTE AND CHRONIC EFFECT OF 5 METHOXYTRYPTAMINE.ON SELECTED MEMBERS OF A PRIMATE SOCIAL-COLONY.
001073 02-02

A PRIMATE ANALOGUE OF AMPHETAMINE-INDUCED BEHAVIORS IN HUMANS.
003006 03-04

CLONIDINE AND THE PRIMATE LOCUS-COERULEUS: EVIDENCE SUGGESTING ANXIOLYTIC AND ANTIWITHDRAWAL EFFECTS. (UNPUBLISHED PAPER).
003982 04-03

PRIMATES
DOPAMINE, ACETYLCHOLINE, AND GABA EFFECTS IN ACUTE DYSTONIA IN PRIMATES.
000043 01-03

ANTIPSYCHOTIC-DRUGS: DIFFERENTIAL-EFFECTS ON DOPAMINE NEURONS IN BASAL GANGLIA AND MESOCORTEX FOLLOWING CHRONIC ADMINISTRATION IN HUMAN AND NONHUMAN PRIMATES.
002285 02-13

ANTAGONISM OF INTRAVENOUS COCAINE LETHALITY IN NONHUMAN PRIMATES.
003127 03-05

PRIMER
CHILDREN ON MEDICATION: A PRIMER FOR SCHOOL PERSONNEL.
000676 01-11

PRIMIDONE
PHARMACOKINETICS OF PRIMIDONE AND ITS ACTIVE METABOLITES IN THE DOG.
000097 01-03

SINGLE-DOSE PHARMACOKINETICS AND ANTICONVULSANT EFFICACY OF PRIMIDONE IN MICE.
000177 01-03

THE EFFECTS OF PHENYTOIN ON PHENOBARBITONE AND PRIMIDONE METABOLISM.
003333 03-11

PRINCIPLES
MODERN-VIEWS ON THE PRINCIPLES OF THE PHARMACOLOGICAL-TREATMENT OF EPILEPSY.
000931 01-17

PRINCIPLES OF FRENCH PHARMACOCLINICAL-CLASSIFICATION.
001892 02-07

SOME PRINCIPLES OF DIFFERENTIATED METABOLIC DRUG-TREATMENT IN COMPREHENSIVE THERAPY OF MENTAL-DISORDERS.
004433 04-11

PRL
GABAERGIC MECHANISMS IN THE CONTROL OF PRL AND GH RELEASE.
002690 03-03

PRO-LEU-GLY-NH2
SOME OBSERVATIONS ON THE PHARMACOLOGICAL ACTIVITY OF MIF (PRO-LEU-GLY-NH2).
004240 04-04

PROBE
ELECTRON PROBE MICROANALYSIS OF CALCIUM AND PHOSPHORUS IN DENSE-BODIES ISOLATED FROM HUMAN PLATELETS. (UNPUBLISHED PAPER).
001014 02-01

A QUANTITATIVE PROBE FOR BIOLOGICAL-PSYCHIATRY: SELECTED ION-MONITORING.
004685 04-16

PROBENECID
ACCELERATED METABOLISM OF PROBENECID DURING LONG-TERM-TREATMENT OF RATS WITH ANTICONVULSANT-DRUGS: EFFECT ON CENTRAL SEROTONIN TURNOVER STUDIES.
002890 03-03

POTENTIATION OF BARBITURATE HYPNOSIS BY PROBENECID: DIFFERENTIAL-EFFECT IN TOLERANT ANIMALS.
003038 03-04

A SELECTED ION-MONITORING ASSAY FOR BIOGENIC-AMINE METABOLITES AND PROBENECID, IN HUMAN LUMBAR CEREBROSPINAL-FLUID.
003663 04-01

PROBES
FLUORESCENT PROBES OF ALPHA-ADRENERGIC AND BETA-ADRENERGIC AND OPIATE-RECEPTORS: BIOCHEMICAL AND HISTOCHEMICAL EVALUATION.
003685 04-02

PROBING
ESR STUDIES OF BOVINE PLASMA AMINE-OXIDASE: PROBING OF THE ENVIRONMENT ABOUT THE SUBSTRATE LIBERATED SULFHYDRYL GROUPS IN THE ACTIVE SITE. (UNPUBLISHED PAPER).
001066 02-01

PROCEDURES
PROCEDURES FOR REDUCING DRUG INTAKE: NONHUMAN STUDIES.
001753 02-04

ANALYSIS OF SINGLE-BLIND, DOUBLE-BLIND PROCEDURES, MAINTENANCE OF PLACEBO-EFFECTS, AND DRUG-INDUCED DYSKINESIA IN MENTALLY-RETARDED PERSONS -- BRIEF REPORT.
003298 03-11

ANALYSIS OF SINGLE-BLIND AND DOUBLE-BLIND PROCEDURES, MAINTENANCE OF PLACEBO-EFFECTS AND DRUG-INDUCED DYSKINESIA WITH MENTALLY-RETARDED PERSON.
004437 04-11

COMPARISON OF PSYCHOTROPIC-DRUG, RESPONSE COST, AND PSYCHOTROPIC-DRUG PLUS RESPONSE COST PROCEDURES FOR CONTROLLING INSTITUTIONALIZED MENTALLY-RETARDED PERSONS.
004438 04-11

LSD, PSYCHOTOGENIC PROCEDURES AND BRAIN NEUROHUMORS. (UNPUBLISHED PAPER).
004448 04-11

DRUG-THERAPY FOR HYPERACTIVITY: TREATMENT PROCEDURES IN NATURAL SETTINGS.
004449 04-11

COMPARISON OF SPECTROFLUOROMETRIC AND GAS-CHROMATOGRAPHY/MASS-SPECTROMETRY PROCEDURES FOR THE QUANTITATION OF MORPHINE IN BLOOD AND BRAIN.
004692 04-16

PROCESSING
ACTH MODULATION OF MEMORY STORAGE PROCESSING. (UNPUBLISHED PAPER).
001250 02-03

OPIATE-RECEPTOR GRADIENTS IN MONKEY CEREBRAL-CORTEX: CORRESPONDENCE WITH SENSORY PROCESSING HIERARCHIES.
002641 03-01

A PSYCHOPHARMACOLOGICAL APPROACH TO MEMORY PROCESSING.
002901 03-03

SENSORY PROCESSING, CARDIOVASCULAR REACTIVITY, AND THE TYPE A CORONARY-PRONE BEHAVIOR PATTERN.
003405 03-13

PROCONVULSANT
PROCONVULSANT AND ANTICONVULSANT ACTION OF MORPHINE IN RATS.
000494 01-04

THE PROCONVULSANT AND DIAZEPAM REVERSING EFFECTS OF ETHYL-BETA-CARBOLINE-3-CARBOXYLATE.
001399 02-03

PROCURING
THE PHARMACOLOGICAL ANALYSIS OF MONOAMINERGIC MECHANISMS OF THE MEDIAL HYPOTHALAMUS IN FOOD PROCURING CONDITIONED REFLEXES IN RATS.
003100 03-04

PRODRUGS
PRODRUGS OF SOME DOPAMINERGIC 2 AMINOTETRALINS: A REVIEW OF THEIR SYNTHESES AND NEUROCHEMICAL PROFILES.
000004 01-01

PROFESSIONAL
PARAPROFESSIONAL AND PROFESSIONAL TEAMWORK AND TRAINING IN MANAGING PCP AND OTHER DRUG-ABUSE PROBLEMS.
000924 01-17

Subject Index

INITIAL PRESCRIPTION OF PSYCHOTROPIC-MEDICATIONS FOR
ADOLESCENTS IN A MEDICAL/PROFESSIONAL INSTITUTE, AND THE
ROLE OF THE PSYCHIATRIST IN A MEDICAL/PROFESSIONAL INSTITUTE.
002621 02-17

PROFESSOR
NEUROLEPTIC ACTIVITY: A SUMMARY OF PROFESSOR JACQUES
GLOWINSKIS PRESENTATION.
003628 03-17

PROFILE
3 SULFAMOYLMETHYL-1-2-BENZISOXAZOLE, A NEW TYPE OF
ANTICONVULSANT-DRUG: PHARMACOLOGICAL PROFILE.
000012 01-02

3 SULFAMOYLMETHYL-1-2-BENZISOXAZOLE, A NEW TYPE OF
ANTICONVULSANT-DRUG: ELECTROENCEPHALOGRAPHIC PROFILE.
000142 01-03

SLEEP PROFILE AND ULTRADIAN SLEEP PERIODICITY IN HUMANS UNDER
THE INFLUENCE OF A BUTYROPHENONE DERIVATIVE: I. SLEEP
CORRECTION IN SUBJECTS WITH OLIGOSYMPTOMATIC SLEEP-
DISORDERS.
001869 02-06

PROFILE OF THE ANTIDEPRESSANT ACTION OF NOMIFENSINE.
002025 02-09

THERAPEUTIC PROFILE OF HALOPERIDOL.
002603 02-17

RECEPTOR BINDING PROFILE OF R-41-468, A NOVEL ANTAGONIST AT 5
HT2-RECEPTORS.
002648 03-02

PHARMACOKINETIC PROFILE OF VALPROIC-ACID IN RHESUS-MONKEYS
FOLLOWING SINGLE BOLUS AND CONSTANT RATE INTRAVENOUS
ADMINISTRATIONS.
002797 03-03

THE THERAPEUTIC PROFILE OF MIANSERIN IN MILD ELDERLY
DEPRESSIVES.
003297 03-11

THE PHARMACOLOGICAL PROFILE OF LOFEPRAMINE, A NEW
ANTIDEPRESSANT-DRUG.
004006 04-03

PROFILES
PRODRUGS OF SOME DOPAMINERGIC 2 AMINOTETRALINS: A REVIEW OF
THEIR SYNTHESES AND NEUROCHEMICAL PROFILES.
000004 01-01

N TETRAHYDROFURYLALKYL AND N ALKOXYALKYL DERIVATIVES OF (-)
NORMETAZOCINE, COMPOUNDS WITH DIFFERENTIATED OPIOID ACTION
PROFILES.
000013 01-02

USING PROFILES OF SACCHARIN AND WATER DRINKING TO DETECT AND
DISCRIMINATE ACTIONS OF DRUGS AND TOXICANTS.
000503 01-04

PHARMACODYNAMIC PROFILES OF L ALPHA ACETYLMETHADOL (LAAM)
AND ITS N DEMETHYLATED METABOLITES, NORLAAM AND
DINORLAAM, DURING SELF-ADMINISTRATION IN THE DEPENDENT RAT.
000505 01-04

LEVORPHANOL: RADIOIMMUNOASSAY AND PLASMA CONCENTRATION
PROFILES IN DOG AND MAN.
000898 01-16

CHARACTERIZATION OF ERGOT AND NONERGOT SEROTONIN
ANTAGONISTS BY PROLACTIN AND GROWTH-HORMONE PROFILES
DURING WAKEFULNESS AND SLEEP.
002217 02-13

EFFECTS OF SINGLE-ORAL-DOSAGES OF STEROIDS ON HUMAN EEG
BASELINE CROSSING T-SCORES SHOWN BY MULTIVARIATE STATISTICS
AND STANDARD PROFILES.
002239 02-13

EEG ASSESSMENTS OF DOSAGE AND SLEEP PROFILES FOR A HYPNOTIC-
DRUG OF THE TRIAZOLOTHIENODIACEPINE SERIES.
002238 02-14

PROGABIDE
GABA AND SCHIZOPHRENIA: STUDY OF THE ACTION OF A GABAERGIC
ANTAGONIST. PROGABIDE OR SL-76-002.
003175 03-08

PROGENY
THE DEVELOPMENT OF PROGENY IN CASES OF ANTENATAL EXPOSURE TO
PHENAZEPAM.
001854 02-05

BEHAVIORAL AND METABOLIC ALTERATIONS IN PROGENY OF
METHADONE-TREATED RATS. (PH.D. DISSERTATION).
003113 03-04

PROGESTERONE
THE EFFECTS OF PROGESTERONE ON THE CIRCADIAN-CYCLES AND
ESTROUS-CYCLES IN THE RAT. (PH.D. DISSERTATION).
011111 02-03

INFLUENCE OF ESTROGEN AND PROGESTERONE ON GLUTAMIC-ACID-
DECARBOXYLASE ACTIVITY IN DISCRETE REGIONS OF RAT-BRAIN.
002927 03-03

PROGESTIN-RECEPTORS
CHANGES IN NORADRENERGIC TRANSMISSION ALTER THE
CONCENTRATION OF CYTOPLASMIC PROGESTIN-RECEPTORS IN .
HYPOTHALAMUS.
002842 03-03

S

DOPAMINERGIC FACTORS IN HUMAN PROLACTIN REGULATION: A PITUITARY MODEL FOR THE STUDY OF A NEUROENDOCRINE SYSTEM IN MAN.
000776 01-13

THE INFLUENCE OF LITHIUM-SALTS AND ANTIDEPRESSANT MEDICATION ON SERUM PROLACTIN LEVEL.
000780 01-13

PROLACTIN RESPONSE AND EXTRAPYRAMIDAL SIDE-EFFECTS DURING PROPRANOLOL AND NEUROLEPTIC-DRUGS TREATMENT IN CHRONIC SCHIZOPHRENIC-PATIENTS.
000841 01-15

PLASMA PROLACTIN AND TESTOSTERONE DURING PENFLURIDOL TREATMENT.
000874 01-15

IMPORTANCE OF AKINESIA: PLASMA CHLORPROMAZINE AND PROLACTIN LEVELS.
000891 01-15

EFFECT OF SEROTONIN ON PROLACTIN SECRETION IN VIVO.
001016 02-01

ALTERATION OF PROLACTIN SECRETION BY CENTRALLY-ACTING DRUGS.
001127 02-03

SERUM PROLACTIN DURING AGING AND THE EFFECTS OF ERGOTS.
001171 02-03

EFFECT OF AMINOOXYACETIC-ACID AND BICUCULLINE ON PROLACTIN RELEASE IN CASTRATED MALE RATS.
001194 02-03

A PHARMACOLOGICAL ANALYSIS OF THE ROLE OF THE AMYGDALA IN THE CONTROL OF GONADOTROPIN AND PROLACTIN SECRETION.
001418 02-03

EFFECT OF PROPRANOLOL TREATMENT ON SERUM PROLACTIN LEVEL IN SCHIZOPHRENIC-PATIENTS.
001916 02-08

BASAL AND STIMULATED LEVELS OF PROLACTIN, TSH AND LH IN SERUM OF CHRONIC SCHIZOPHRENIC-PATIENTS, LONG-TERM TREATED WITH NEUROLEPTICS.
001935 02-08

BASAL AND STIMULATED LEVELS OF PROLACTIN, TSH, AND LH IN SERUM OF CHRONIC SCHIZOPHRENIC-PATIENTS LONG-TERM TREATED WITH NEUROLEPTICS: RELATIONS TO PSYCHOPATHOLOGY.
001936 02-08

CLINICAL STATE, PLASMA LEVELS OF HALOPERIDOL AND PROLACTIN.
001943 02-08

USE OF LARGE-SINGLE-DOSES OF BROMOCRIPTINE IN SCHIZOPHRENIC-PATIENTS WITH ELEVATED SERUM PROLACTIN LEVELS AND EXTRAPYRAMIDAL SIDE-EFFECTS ASSOCIATED WITH NEUROLEPTIC TREATMENT.
001944 02-08

PLASMA FLUPHENAZINE AND PROLACTIN LEVELS IN SCHIZOPHRENIC-PATIENTS DURING TREATMENT WITH LOW-DOSES AND HIGH-DOSES OF FLUPHENAZINE-ENANTHATE.
001956 02-08

INFLUENCE OF NOMIFENSINE ON GROWTH-HORMONE, PROLACTIN, LUTEINISING-HORMONE AND THYREOTROPIN IN HEALTHY SUBJECTS AND HYPERPROLACTINAEMIC-PATIENTS.
002137 02-11

EFFECTS OF NALOXONE UPON PROLACTIN AND CORTISOL IN NORMAL WOMEN.
002213 02-13

CHARACTERIZATION OF ERGOT AND NONERGOT SEROTONIN ANTAGONISTS BY PROLACTIN AND GROWTH-HORMONE PROFILES DURING WAKEFULNESS AND SLEEP.
002217 02-13

STUDY OF PROLACTIN VARIATIONS IN PSYCHIATRIC-PATIENTS TREATED WITH FLUPHENAZINE-DECANOATE.
002226 02-13

THE EFFECT OF BENZTROPINE-MESYLATE ON THE PROLACTIN RESPONSE TO HALOPERIDOL.
002238 02-13

ABNORMAL REGULATION OF PROLACTIN RELEASE IN IDIOPATHIC PARKINSONS-DISEASE.
002255 02-13

INHIBITION OF SULPIRIDE-INDUCED PROLACTIN SECRETION BY DIHYDROERGOCRISTINE IN MAN.
002277 02-13

THE INFLUENCE OF NEUROLEPTIC-DRUGS ON PROLACTIN SECRETION IN CHILDREN.
002409 02-15

COMPARATIVE-STUDY OF VARIATIONS IN PROLACTIN LEVELS DURING TREATMENT WITH ANTIPSYCHOTIC-DRUGS.
002412 02-15

HALOPERIDOL STIMULATION OF PROLACTIN SECRETION: HOW MANY BLOOD SAMPLES ARE NEEDED TO DEFINE THE HORMONE RESPONSE?
002505 02-16

PSYCHOTROPIC-DRUGS DO NOT INTERFERE WITH RADIOLIGAND ASSAYS FOR PROLACTIN, CORTISOL, AND GROWTH-HORMONE.
002511 02-16

THE CHANGE OF BLOOD PROLACTIN LEVEL DUE TO THE WITHDRAWAL OF MAINTENANCE NEUROLEPTICS.
002559 02-17

THE HYPOTHALAMIC DOPAMINERGIC REGULATION OF PROLACTIN: A MODEL FOR THE STUDY OF NEUROHORMONAL MECHANISMS IN MAN.
002568 02-17

CLINICAL-ASPECTS ON PROLACTIN RESPONSE TO NEUROLEPTIC-DRUGS.
002590 02-17

DIFFERENTIAL-EFFECTS OF CANNABINOID EXPOSURE AND STRESS ON PLASMA PROLACTIN, GROWTH-HORMONE AND CORTICOSTERONE LEVELS IN MALE MICE.
002695 03-03

DURING ONE YEARS NEUROLEPTIC TREATMENT IN RATS STRIATAL DOPAMINE-RECEPTOR BLOCKADE DECREASES BUT SERUM PROLACTIN LEVELS REMAIN ELEVATED.
002707 03-03

ANTERIOR PITUITARY GABA-RECEPTORS AND THEIR REGULATION OF PROLACTIN SECRETION.
002738 03-03

THE DIRECT EFFECT OF RESERPINE IN VITRO ON PROLACTIN RELEASE FROM RAT ANTERIOR PITUITARY-GLANDS.
002810 03-03

SUPPRESSION OF SERUM PROLACTIN BY NALOXONE BUT NOT BY ANTI-BETA-ENDORPHIN ANTISERUM IN STRESSED AND UNSTRESSED RATS.
002871 03-03

ERGOT DRUGS SUPPRESS PLASMA PROLACTIN AND LACTATION BUT NOT AGGRESSION IN PARTURIENT MICE.
003159 03-07

LOW SERUM PROLACTIN AND EARLY RELAPSE FOLLOWING NEUROLEPTIC WITHDRAWAL.
003166 03-08

NEUROLEPTIC-INDUCED ELEVATIONS IN SERUM PROLACTIN LEVELS: ETIOLOGY AND SIGNIFICANCE.
003190 03-08

EFFECT OF LITHIUM ON PROLACTIN RESPONSES TO THYROTROPIN-RELEASING-HORMONE IN PATIENTS WITH MANIC-STATE.
003266 03-09

INCREASED SERUM PROLACTIN LEVELS DURING PHENOTHIAZINE AND BUTYROPHENONE TREATMENT OF SIX POSTPARTUM WOMEN.
003318 03-11

THE EFFECT OF AMANTADINE ON PROLACTIN LEVELS AND GALACTORRHEA ON NEUROLEPTIC TREATED PATIENTS.
003373 03-11

EFFECT OF A PSYCHOACTIVE-DRUG, TRAZODONE, ON PROLACTIN SECRETION IN MAN.
003425 03-13

LYMPHOCYTE MONOAMINE-OXIDASE AND PLASMA PROLACTIN AND GROWTH-HORMONE IN TARDIVE-DYSKINESIA.
003499 03-15

CHLORPROMAZINE, HALOPERIDOL, METOCLOPRAMIDE AND DOMPERIDONE RELEASE PROLACTIN THROUGH DOPAMINE ANTAGONISM AT LOW CONCENTRATIONS BUT PARADOXICALLY INHIBIT PROLACTIN RELEASE AT HIGH-CONCENTRATIONS.
003731 04-03

METERGOLINE AND CYPROHEPTADINE SUPPRESS PROLACTIN RELEASE BY A NON-5-HYDROXYTRYPTAMINERGIC, NONDOPAMINERGIC MECHANISM.
003732 04-03

ROLE OF THE ANTERIOR PITUITARY GABA-RECEPTOR IN THE CONTROL OF PROLACTIN RELEASE.
003809 04-03

PROLACTIN RELEASING POTENCIES OF ANTIPSYCHOTIC AND RELATED NONANTIPSYCHOTIC COMPOUNDS IN FEMALE RATS: RELATION TO CLINICAL POTENCIES.
003830 04-03

THE PROLACTIN RESPONSE IN PATIENTS RECEIVING NEUROLEPTIC THERAPY. THE EFFECT OF FLUPHENAZINE-DECANOATE.
004318 04-08

NEUROENDOCRINE-TESTS DURING TREATMENT WITH NEUROLEPTIC-DRUGS: I. PLASMA PROLACTIN RESPONSE TO CHLORPROMAZINE CHALLENGE.
004329 04-08

HALOPERIDOL AND DROPERIDOL-TREATMENT IN SCHIZOPHRENICS: CLINICAL APPLICATION OF THE PROLACTIN MODEL.
004332 04-08

DIFFERENT EFFECTS OF TRICYCLIC-ANTIDEPRESSANTS AND TETRACYCLIC-ANTIDEPRESSANTS ON THE RELEASE OF TSH, PROLACTIN, AND GROWTH-HORMONE AFTER ADMINISTRATION OF THYROSTIMULATING-RELEASING-HORMONE IN MANIC-DEPRESSIVES.
004407 04-09

PROMETHAZINE AND DIAZEPAM POTENTIATE THE HALOPERIDOL-INDUCED PROLACTIN RESPONSES.
004499 04-13

PROLACTIN AND GROWTH-HORMONE STUDIES IN SCHIZOPHRENIC-PATIENTS AND NORMAL CONTROLS.
004538 04-13

PROLACTIN AND NEUROLEPTIC-DRUGS: A BIOCHEMICAL INDEX OF CLINICAL-RESPONSE?
004539 04-13

SEX, PLASMA PROLACTIN AND PLASMA 3 METHOXY-4-
HYDROXYPHENYLGLYCOL (MHPG) PREDICT HERITABLE D-
AMPHETAMINE EXCITATION IN MAN. (UNPUBLISHED PAPER).
004565 04-14

PROLACTINAEMIA
BASAL PROLACTINAEMIA AND RESPONSES TO TRH AND SULPIRIDE IN
DIFFERENT CATEGORIES OF MALE SEXUAL-DYSFUNCTIONS.
004503 04-13

PROLAPSE
EFFECT OF SODIUM-LACTATE ON PATIENTS WITH PANIC-DISORDER AND
MITRAL-VALVE PROLAPSE.
003409 03-13
ARRHYTHMIA INDUCED BY A TRICYCLIC-ANTIDEPRESSANT IN A PATIENT
WITH UNDIAGNOSED MITRAL-VALVE PROLAPSE.
003521 03-15

PROLIFERATION
EFFECT OF CHLORPROMAZINE ON CELL PROLIFERATION IN THE
DEVELOPING RAT-BRAIN. A COMBINED BIOCHEMICAL-STUDY AND
MORPHOLOGICAL-STUDY.
001407 02-03
INFLUENCE OF PSYCHOACTIVE AND NONPSYCHOACTIVE CANNABINOIDS
ON CELL PROLIFERATION AND MACROMOLECULAR BIOSYNTHESIS IN
HUMAN CELLS.
002830 03-03
THE EFFECT OF CHLORPROMAZINE AND MAGEPTIL ON THE
PROLIFERATION OF PERIPHERAL BLOOD LYMPHOCYTES IN CULTIVATION
WITH PHYTOHEMAGGLUTININ.
004541 04-13

PROLINE
MODIFICATION OF THE PROLINE RESIDUE OF TRH ENHANCES BIOLOGICAL-   PRO
ACTIVITY AND INHIBITS DEGRADATION.
000351 01-04
BIOLOGICAL EVALUATION OF A TRH ANALOGUE WITH A MODIFIED   PRO
PROLINE RESIDUE.
003662 04-01

PROLONGATION
PROLONGATION OF THE EJACULATION LATENCY IN THE MALE RAT BY
THIORIDAZINE AND CHLORIMIPRAMINE.
000335 01-04

PROLYL-LEUCYL-GLYCINAMIDE
EFFECTS OF DOPAMINERGIC AND CHOLINERGIC-DRUGS, NALOXONE AND
L PROLYL-LEUCYL-GLYCINAMIDE ON LSD-INDUCED CATALEPSY.
000360 01-04

PROMAZINE
FREE DESCRIPTION OF DRUG-EFFECTS AS A METHOD OF CLINICAL-TRIAL,
PRESENTED BY THE EXAMPLE OF PENTOBARBITONE, PROMAZINE AND
THEIR COMBINATION.
002561 02-17
SECOND-ORDER SCHEDULES OF INTRAMUSCULAR COCAINE INJECTION IN
THE SQUIRREL-MONKEY: COMPARISONS WITH FOOD PRESENTATION
AND EFFECTS OF D-AMPHETAMINE AND PROMAZINE.
004152 04-04

PROMETHAZINE
PROMETHAZINE AND DIAZEPAM POTENTIATE THE HALOPERIDOL-INDUCED
PROLACTIN RESPONSES.
004499 04-13

PROMOTER
DIAZEPAM AS TUMOUR PROMOTER.
003495 03-15

PROMOTES
NALOXONE PROMOTES STIMULUS-EVOKED VASOPRESSIN RELEASE IN   ,   PRO
VIVO.
000165 01-03

PROOF
ANTIHYPOXIDOTIC-DRUGS AND NOOTROPIC-DRUGS: PROOF OF THEIR   PRO
ENCEPHALOTROPIC AND PHARMACODYNAMIC PROPERTIES BY
ENCEPHALOTROPIC AND PHARMACODYNAMIC PROPERTIES BY
QUANTITATIVE EEG INVESTIGATIONS.
002166 02-11   PRO

PROPANIDID
VALUE OF PROPANIDID IN ELECTROCONVULSIVE-THERAPY (COMPARISON
WITH THIOPENTONE).
004379 04-09

PROPANTHELINE-BROMIDE
SYNERGISTIC ACTIONS OF PROPANTHELINE-BROMIDE WITH CIMETIDINE
AND THIOPROPAZATE-HYDROCHLORIDE IN THE PREVENTION OF
STRESS-ULCER FORMATION IN RATS.
000064 01-03
FACILITATION OF RECOVERY BY PROPANTHELINE-BROMIDE AFTER
LATERAL HYPOTHALAMIC DAMAGE.
000396 01-04

PROPERICIAZINE
FOLLOWUP STUDY ON THE INFLUENCE OF AN ANTIPSYCHOTIC-DRUG
(PROPERICIAZINE) ON LIVER FUNCTION, ELECTROCARDIOGRAM AND
ELECTROENCEPHALOGRAM.
000639 01-09

PROPHYLACTIC
LITHIUM LEVEL IN SOME BIOLOGICAL FLUIDS AT ITS PROPHYLACTIC
THERAPEUTIC APPLICATION.
000605 01-09

PROLACTIN RESPONSE AND EXTRAPYRAMIDAL SIDE-EFFECTS DURING PROPRANOLOL AND NEUROLEPTIC-DRUGS TREATMENT IN CHRONIC SCHIZOPHRENIC-PATIENTS.
000841 01-15
INHIBITION BY LOCAL ANESTHETICS, PHENTOLAMINE AND PROPRANOLOL OF (3H)QUINUCLYDINYL-BENZYLATE BINDING TO CENTRAL MUSCARINIC-RECEPTORS.
001097 02-03
ANTIPSYCHOTIC-EFFECT OF PROPRANOLOL ON CHRONIC SCHIZOPHRENICS: STUDY OF A GRADUAL TREATMENT REGIMEN.
001915 02-08
EFFECT OF PROPRANOLOL TREATMENT ON SERUM PROLACTIN LEVEL IN SCHIZOPHRENIC-PATIENTS.
001916 02-08
DEXTRO PROPRANOLOL IN SCHIZOPHRENIA.
001921 02-08
SOME CLINICAL-ASPECTS AND METABOLIC-ASPECTS OF PROPRANOLOL IN CHRONIC SCHIZOPHRENIA.
001926 02-08
PROPRANOLOL IN SCHIZOPHRENIA — MORE GUESS THAN GAUSS.
001939 02-08
PHARMACOKINETIC INTERACTION BETWEEN PROPRANOLOL AND CHLORPROMAZINE IN SCHIZOPHRENIC-PATIENTS.
001940 02-08
PROPRANOLOL IN CHRONIC ANXIETY-DISORDERS: A CONTROLLED-STUDY.
002073 02-10
CORRECTION BY PROPRANOLOL OF THE ABNORMAL ADRENALINE DISCHARGE INDUCED BY EMOTIONAL-STRESS IN CEREBRAL HEMORRHAGE PATIENTS.
002295 02-13
EFFECTS OF ATENOLOL AND PROPRANOLOL ON HUMAN PERFORMANCE AND SUBJECTIVE FEELINGS.
002340 02-14
PROPRANOLOL (INDERAL) FOR TARDIVE-DYSKINESIA AND EXTRAPYRAMIDAL SIDE-EFFECTS FROM NEUROLEPTICS: POSSIBLE INVOLVEMENT OF BETA-ADRENERGIC MECHANISMS.
002470 02-15
EFFECT OF PROPRANOLOL AND PHENOTHIAZINES ON ELECTRODERMAL ORIENTING AND HABITUATION IN SCHIZOPHRENIA.
003174 03-08
PROPRANOLOL IN THE TREATMENT OF RAGE AND VIOLENT-BEHAVIOR IN PATIENTS WITH CHRONIC-BRAIN-SYNDROMES.
003394 03-11
BENZODIAZEPINE WITHDRAWAL SYMPTOMS AND PROPRANOLOL.
003543 03-15
THE EFFECT OF PROPRANOLOL AND ITS ISOMERS ON PURKINJE NEURONES IN RAT CEREBELLUM.
004059 04-03
EFFECTS OF PROPRANOLOL ON THE LOCOMOTOR-STIMULATION INDUCED BY ACTIVATION OF POSTSYNAPTIC CATECHOLAMINE-RECEPTORS.
004126 04-04
AN EVALUATION OF THE ANTIANXIETY ACTION AND SIDE-EFFECTS OF PROPRANOLOL.
004660 04-15

PROPYLBENZILYLCHOLINE-MUSTARD
PERSISTENT EFFECTS OF HIGH-CONCENTRATIONS OF CHLORPROMAZINE ON 3H PROPYLBENZILYLCHOLINE-MUSTARD BINDING TO MUSCARINIC-RECEPTORS IN GUINEA-PIG INTESTINAL-MUSCLE STRIPS.
001266 02-03

PROPYLNORANTIFEIN
THE EFFECT OF PROPYLNORANTIFEIN ON BEHAVIORAL-REACTIONS, ADRENOCORTICAL ACTIVITY, AND ENERGY METABOLISM IN THE ANIMAL BRAIN.
004075 04-04

PROPYLNORAPOMORPHINE
ROLE OF BRAIN DOPAMINERGIC MECHANISMS IN RODENT AGGRESSIVE-BEHAVIOR: INFLUENCE OF (OR -)N N PROPYLNORAPOMORPHINE ON THREE EXPERIMENTAL MODELS.
000340 01-04
DENERVATION IN THE DOPAMINERGIC MESOLIMBIC SYSTEM: FUNCTIONAL CHANGES FOLLOWED USING (-)N N PROPYLNORAPOMORPHINE DEPEND ON THE BASAL ACTIVITY LEVELS OF RATS.
001603 02-04
BEHAVIORAL-FACILITATION FOLLOWING CHRONIC ADMINISTRATION OF N N PROPYLNORAPOMORPHINE.
001822 02-04

PROSPECTIVE-TRIAL
PROSPECTIVE-TRIAL OF L TRYPTOPHAN IN MATERNITY-BLUES.
000683 01-11

PROSTACYCLIN-DEPENDENT
PROSTACYCLIN-DEPENDENT ACTIVATION OF ADENYLATE-CYCLASE IN A NEURONAL SOMATIC CELL HYBRID: PROSTANOID STRUCTURE-ACTIVITY RELATIONSHIPS.
001132 02-03

PROSTAGLANDIN
BRADYKININ-RECEPTOR STIMULATION OF C-AMP INVOLVES PHOSPHOLIPID METHYLATION, CA-FLUX, PHOSPHOLIPASE-A2 ACTIVATION AND PROSTAGLANDIN FORMATION. (UNPUBLISHED PAPER).
001002 02-01

VASOTOCIN, PROSTAGLANDIN, AND FEMALE REPRODUCTIVE BEHAVIOR IN THE FROG, RANA-PIPIENS.
002978 03-04

PROSTAGLANDIN-D2
EFFECT OF PROSTAGLANDIN-D2, PROSTAGLANDIN-E2 AND PROSTAGLANDIN-F2ALPHA ON CATECHOLAMINE RELEASE FROM SLICES OF RAT AND RABBIT BRAIN.
003983 04-03

PROSTAGLANDIN-E
PROSTAGLANDIN-E RELEASE BY RAT MEDIAL BASAL HYPOTHALAMUS IN VITRO. INHIBITION BY MELATONIN AT SUBMICROMOLAR CONCENTRATIONS.
001159 02-03

PROSTAGLANDIN-E1
INHIBITION OF ACH RELEASE BY PROSTAGLANDIN-E1 IN THE RABBIT SUPERIOR-CERVICAL-GANGLION.
001205 02-03
EFFECT OF PROSTAGLANDIN-E1 AND ITS BIOSYNTHESIS INHIBITOR INDOMETHACIN ON DRINKING IN THE RAT.
001749 02-04
THE ANTINOCICEPTIVE-EFFECT OF INTRACEREBROVENTRICULARLY ADMINISTERED PROSTAGLANDIN-E1 IN THE RAT.
001769 02-04
RELATIONSHIP BETWEEN THE ACTIONS OF CALCIUM-IONS, OPIOIDS, AND PROSTAGLANDIN-E1 ON THE LEVEL OF CYCLIC-AMP IN NEUROBLASTOMA-X GLIOMA HYBRID CELLS.
002677 03-03

PROSTAGLANDIN-E2
REGULATION OF NORADRENALINE OVERFLOW IN RAT-CEREBRAL-CORTEX BY PROSTAGLANDIN-E2.
003841 04-03
EFFECT OF PROSTAGLANDIN-D2, PROSTAGLANDIN-E2 AND PROSTAGLANDIN-F2ALPHA ON CATECHOLAMINE RELEASE FROM SLICES OF RAT AND RABBIT BRAIN.
003983 04-03

PROSTAGLANDIN-F2ALPHA
MECHANISMS INVOLVED IN CENTRAL-EFFECTS OF PROSTAGLANDIN-F2ALPHA. (UNPUBLISHED PAPER).
001222 02-03
EFFECT OF PROSTAGLANDIN-D2, PROSTAGLANDIN-E2 AND PROSTAGLANDIN-F2ALPHA ON CATECHOLAMINE RELEASE FROM SLICES OF RAT AND RABBIT BRAIN.
003983 04-03

PROSTAGLANDINS
EFFECT OF PROSTAGLANDINS ON PLASMA CATECHOLAMINES, HEART AND BLOOD-PRESSURE RESPONSES TO HEMORRHAGE. (UNPUBLISHED PAPER).
001223 02-03
PROSTAGLANDINS IN THE BRAIN OF RATS GIVEN, ACUTELY, AND CHRONICALLY, A HYPERTHERMIC-DOSE OF MET-ENKEPHALIN.
001468 02-03
INTERACTION OF PROSTAGLANDINS AND THE EFFECTS OF MORPHINE AND AMPHETAMINE IN RATS. (PH.D. DISSERTATION).
001732 02-04
THE EFFECT OF CONDITIONS INFLUENCING ENDOGENOUS PROSTAGLANDINS ON THE ACTIVITY OF DELTA' TETRAHYDROCANNABINOL.
002196 02-12
ALPHA2-ADRENERGIC AMINES, ADENOSINE AND PROSTAGLANDINS INHIBIT LIPOLYSIS AND CYCLIC-AMP ACCUMULATION IN HAMSTER ADIPOCYTES IN THE ABSENCE OF EXTRACELLULAR SODIUM.
002728 03-03
PROSTAGLANDINS, CLONIDINE AND SEXUAL-RECEPTIVITY IN THE GUINEA-PIG.
003017 03-04

PROSTANOID
PROSTACYCLIN-DEPENDENT ACTIVATION OF ADENYLATE-CYCLASE IN A NEURONAL SOMATIC CELL HYBRID: PROSTANOID STRUCTURE-ACTIVITY RELATIONSHIPS.
001132 02-03

PROTEASE
IN VIVO EFFECT OF PROTEASE INHIBITORS IN DENERVATION ATROPHY.
000290 01-03
REGULATION OF HIPPOCAMPAL GLUTAMATE-RECEPTORS: EVIDENCE FOR THE INVOLVEMENT OF A CALCIUM-ACTIVATED PROTEASE.
001120 02-03

PROTECTION
BARBITURATE SERUM LEVELS AND PROTECTION AGAINST KINDLED AMYGDALOID SEIZURES IN THE RAT.
001559 02-04
VALPROIC-ACID SERUM LEVELS AND PROTECTION AGAINST KINDLED AMYGDALOID SEIZURES IN THE RAT.
002946 03-04
NA-GAMMA-HYDROXYBUTYRATE IN CEREBRAL PROTECTION DURING SEVERE HYPOXEMIA IN THE RAT.
003895 04-03
COCAINE AND SEIZURE PROTECTION IN MICE OF VARYING BRAIN WEIGHTS.
004103 04-04

PROTECTIVE
PROTECTIVE EFFECT OF PRENYLAMINE AGAINST VULNERABILITY TO VENTRICULAR FIBRILLATION IN THE NORMAL AND ISCHEMIC CANINE MYOCARDIUM.
000265 01-03
PROTECTIVE ACTION OF L 5 HYDROXYTRYPTOPHAN L GLUTAMATE (MADE-1932) DURING ELECTROSHOCK-TREATMENT (ECT).
003043 03-04

PROTEIN
ACUTE CHANGES IN BRAIN TRYPTOPHAN AND SEROTONIN FOLLOWING CARBOHYDRATE OR PROTEIN INGESTION BY DIABETIC RATS. (UNPUBLISHED PAPER).
000060 01-03
VALPROIC-ACID DOSAGE AND PLASMA PROTEIN BINDING AND CLEARANCE.
000755 01-03
INFLUENCE OF DEXTROPROPOXYPHENE ON STEADY-STATE SERUM LEVELS AND PROTEIN BINDING OF THREE ANTIEPILEPTIC-DRUGS IN MAN.
000767 01-13
TECHNIQUES FOR PLASMA PROTEIN BINDING OF DEMETHYLCHLORIMIPRAMINE.
000897 01-16
IDENTIFICATION AND PARTIAL PURIFICATION OF A HYDROPHOBIC PROTEIN COMPONENT ASSOCIATED WITH (3H)SPIROPERIDOL BINDING-ACTIVITY. (UNPUBLISHED PAPER).
001007 02-01
PROTEIN ABNORMALITIES IN MACROPHAGES BEARING ASBESTOS. (UNPUBLISHED PAPER).
001037 02-01
CORTICOSTERONE INCREASES THE SYNTHESIS OF A SOLUBLE PROTEIN IN PITUITARY-GLANDS FROM ADRENALECTOMIZED MALE RATS WHICH PRECIPITATES WITH ANTI-RAT GROWTH-HORMONE ANTISERUM. (UNPUBLISHED PAPER).
001122 02-03
THE ROLE OF PROTEIN SYNTHESIS IN THE HYPOTHALAMIC MECHANISM MEDIATING PYROGEN FEVER.
001454 02-03
SHORT-TERM AND LONG-TERM MODIFICATION OF SKELETAL-MUSCLE SODIUM-PUMP ACTIVITY AND MUSCLE PROTEIN TURNOVER. (UNPUBLISHED PAPER).
001519 02-03
ROLE OF NEUROTRANSMITTERS AND PROTEIN SYNTHESIS IN SHORT-TERM AND LONG-TERM MEMORY.
001573 02-04
EFFECT OF L FUCOSE ON BRAIN PROTEIN METABOLISM AND RETENTION OF A LEARNED-BEHAVIOR IN RATS.
001819 02-04
STUDIES ON THIORIDAZINE AND MESORIDAZINE METABOLISM. I. PROTEIN BINDING.
001867 02-06
COMPARATIVE PROTEIN BINDING OF DIAZEPAM AND DESMETHYLDIAZEPAM.
002206 02-13
INTERACTION BETWEEN PHENYTOIN AND VALPROIC-ACID: PLASMA PROTEIN BINDING AND METABOLIC-EFFECTS.
002276 02-13
A QUANTITATIVE REGIONAL ANALYSIS OF PROTEIN SYNTHESIS INHIBITION IN THE RAT-BRAIN FOLLOWING LOCALIZED INJECTION OF CYCLOHEXIMIDE.
002780 03-03
EFFECTS OF PROTEIN AND MEMBRANE MODIFYING AGENTS ON THE BINDING OF L (3H)GLUTAMATE TO CEREBELLAR SYNAPTIC MEMBRANES.
002888 03-03
EFFECT OF ALPHA METHYLPHENYLALANINE AND PHENYLALANINE ON BRAIN POLYRIBOSOMES AND PROTEIN SYNTHESIS.
003733 04-03
EFFECT OF INTRAVENOUS ADMINISTRATION OF D LYSERGIC-ACID-DIETHYLAMIDE ON SUBSEQUENT PROTEIN SYNTHESIS IN A CELL-FREE SYSTEM DERIVED FROM BRAIN.
003761 04-03
DIETARY PROTEIN INTAKE INFLUENCES THE ANTIHYPERTENSIVE POTENCY OF METHYLDOPA IN SPONTANEOUSLY HYPERTENSIVE-RATS.
004025 04-03
PROTEIN BINDING OF CHLORPROMAZINE IN CEREBROSPINAL-FLUID AND SERUM.
004311 04-08

PROTEIN-KINASES
ROLE OF PROTEIN-KINASES IN OPIATE ACTIONS IN BRAIN.
001173 02-03

PROTEINS
REGULATION OF THE STATE OF PHOSPHORYLATION OF SPECIFIC NEURONAL PROTEINS IN MOUSE-BRAIN BY IN VIVO ADMINISTRATION OF ANESTHETIC AND CONVULSANT-AGENTS.
000291 01-03
HYBRID PROTEINS USED TO STUDY THE MECHANISM OF TOXIN ENTRANCE INTO CELLS. (UNPUBLISHED PAPER).
001063 02-01
SELECTIVE EFFECTS OF LSD AND HYPERTHERMIA ON THE SYNTHESIS OF SYNAPTIC PROTEINS AND GLYCOPROTEINS.
002721 03-03

CHARACTERIZATION OF THE BASIC PROTEINS FROM RODENT PERIPHERAL-NERVOUS-SYSTEM MYELIN.
003665 04-01
SYNTHESIS OF CYTOSKELETAL PROTEINS IN BULK ISOLATED NEURONAL PERIKARYA.
003672 04-01
A RADIOIMMUNOASSAY FOR EPENDYMINS BETA AND GAMMA: TWO GOLDFISH BRAIN PROTEINS INVOLVED IN BEHAVIORAL PLASTICITY.
003677 04-01

PROTOCOL
PROTOCOLS FOR THE USE OF PSYCHOACTIVE-DRUGS – PART I: PROTOCOL FOR THE TREATMENT OF PSYCHOSIS WITH ANTIPSYCHOTICS.
000949 01-17
PROTOCOLS FOR THE USE OF PSYCHOACTIVE-DRUGS – PART II: PROTOCOL FOR THE TREATMENT OF DEPRESSION WITH TRICYCLIC-ANTIDEPRESSANTS.
003214 03-09

PROTOCOLS
PROTOCOLS FOR THE USE OF PSYCHOACTIVE-DRUGS – PART I: PROTOCOL FOR THE TREATMENT OF PSYCHOSIS WITH ANTIPSYCHOTICS.
000949 01-17
PROTOCOLS FOR THE USE OF PSYCHOACTIVE-DRUGS – PART II: PROTOCOL FOR THE TREATMENT OF DEPRESSION WITH TRICYCLIC-ANTIDEPRESSANTS.
003214 03-09

PROTON
BETA ENDORPHIN AND ANALOGS: 360 MHZ PROTON NMR SPECTROSCOPY.
001028 02-01
NMR SPECTRAL STUDY OF PROTON TRANSFER IN AMITRIPTYLINE-HYDROCHLORIDE CHLORDIAZEPOXIDE-HYDROCHLORIDE COMBINATIONS IN DIPOLAR APROTIC SOLVENTS.
003654 04-01

PROTOTYPE
DISCRIMINATIVE-STIMULUS EFFECTS OF PROTOTYPE OPIATE-RECEPTOR AGONISTS IN MONKEYS.
001803 02-04
MINI-SYMPOSIUM: III. SIMPLE IN VIVO TESTS THAT DIFFERENTIATE PROTOTYPE AGONISTS AT OPIATE-RECEPTORS.
004289 04-06

PROVENIENCE
ISOLATION OF PSYCHOACTIVE CANNABINOID PRECURSORS FROM CANNABIS OF SOVIET PROVENIENCE GROWN IN MISSISSIPPI.
001023 02-01

PROVERA
THE EFFECT OF ASSERTIVENESS TRAINING, PROVERA AND SEX OF THERAPIST IN THE TREATMENT OF GENITAL EXHIBITIONISM.
000697 01-11

PROVOKE
DO STIMULANTS PROVOKE, CAUSE, OR EXACERBATE TICS AND TOURETTE-SYNDROME?
004485 04-11

PROS-ENKEPHALIN
COMPARATIVE-STUDY OF ANALGESIA INDUCED BY N VAL5-ENKEPHALIN AND PRO5-ENKEPHALIN ANALOGS.
000021 01-03

PRUSSIAN-BLUE
PRUSSIAN-BLUE: SPECIFIC TREATMENT OF THALLIUM, ARSENIC, INDUSTRIAL-SOLVENT INTOXICATION, AND OTHER POLYNEUROPATHOLOGIES. A POSSIBLE ANTIPSYCHOTIC-AGENT.
003348 03-11

PSEUDONEURASTHENIA
TOFISOPAM IN PSEUDONEURASTHENIA WITH HEADACHES.
002075 02-10

PSYCHEDELIC-DRUGS
PSYCHEDELIC-DRUGS AND THE CREATIVE-PROCESS.
002199 02-12

PSYCHEDELIC-EXPERIENCES
THE MYTHOLOGEM OF REVERSIBLE DEATH. THE ANALYTICAL CONFRONTATION OF ENDOGENOUS DELIRIUM WITH DELUSIONS IN PSYCHEDELIC-EXPERIENCES.
002200 02-12

PSYCHIATRIC
PSYCHIATRIC MANIFESTATIONS INDUCED BY DOPAMINE PRECURSORS OR DOPAMINE AGONISTS.
000865 01-15
COMPARISON OF NITRAZEPAM 5 MG WITH TRIAZOLAM 0.5 MG IN YOUNG PSYCHIATRIC INSOMNIAC-INPATIENTS.
002096 02-11
ERGOTISM IN A PSYCHIATRIC ENVIRONMENT ASSOCIATED WITH ERYTHROMYCIN-DIHYDROERGOTAMINE-PROPIONATE. AN OBSERVATION.
002379 02-15
PSYCHIATRIC MORBIDITY AND PHYSICAL TOXICITY ASSOCIATED WITH ADJUVANT CHEMOTHERAPY AFTER MASTECTOMY.
002433 02-15

PSYCHIATRIC IMPLICATIONS OF ANTICONVULSANT-DRUGS.
002463 02-15
MODERN CONCEPTS IN PSYCHIATRIC SURGERY.
002551 02-17
HEMOPERFUSION FOR CHRONIC SCHIZOPHRENIA: PRELIMINARY
PSYCHIATRIC RESULTS.
003180 03-08
PREVALENCE OF PERSISTENT ABNORMAL INVOLUNTARY-MOVEMENTS
AMONG PATIENTS IN A NIGERIAN LONG-STAY PSYCHIATRIC UNIT.
004334 04-08
PSYCHIATRIC USES OF BETA-BLOCKERS.
004709 04-17
PSYCHIATRIC-ASPECTS
PSYCHIATRIC-ASPECTS OF ACUTE POISONING WITH TRICYCLIC AND
RELATED ANTIDEPRESSANTS — 1980.
002458 02-15
SIDE-EFFECTS OF CORTICOSTEROID THERAPY: PSYCHIATRIC-ASPECTS.
003508 03-15
PSYCHIATRIC-COMPLICATIONS
MEDICAL AND PSYCHIATRIC-COMPLICATIONS OF PENTAZOCINE AND
TRIPELENNAMINE ABUSE.
000955 01-17
PSYCHIATRIC-DIAGNOSIS
LIMITS, VALUE AND PERSPECTIVES OF THE PSYCHIATRIC-DIAGNOSIS IN
CLINICAL PSYCHOPHARMACOLOGY.
002631 02-17
PSYCHIATRIC-DISORDERS
GABA LEVELS IN HUMAN CEREBROSPINAL-FLUID: ALTERATIONS IN
PSYCHIATRIC-DISORDERS. (UNPUBLISHED PAPER).
000764 01-13
ANIMAL-MODELS OF PSYCHIATRIC-DISORDERS.
001871 02-06
TRIAL WITH MINAPRINE IN SUBJECTS WITH PSYCHIATRIC-DISORDERS.
001889 02-07
ON A POSSIBLE ROLE OF ENDORPHINS IN PSYCHIATRIC-DISORDERS --
ACTIONS OF NALOXONE IN PSYCHIATRIC-PATIENTS.
001917 02-08
HYPNOTIC ACTION OF FLUNITRAZEPAM (ROCHES ROIPNOL) IN PATIENTS
WITH SEVERE PSYCHIATRIC-DISORDERS.
003295 03-11
PSYCHIATRIC-DISTURBANCE
PSYCHIATRIC-DISTURBANCE IN MENTALLY-HANDICAPPED-PATIENTS: A
PROSPECTIVE STUDY OF CURRENT CLINICAL USAGE OF DEPOT
FLUPHENAZINE IN HOSPITALS FOR THE MENTALLY-HANDICAPPED.
000668 01-11
PSYCHIATRIC-DRUG
ARCALION-200 PRESCRIBED AS A PSYCHIATRIC-DRUG AND
ANTIALCOHOLISM-DRUG ON AN OUTPATIENT AND INPATIENT BASIS.
002103 02-11
CEEG STUDY ON PATIENTS UNDER THE PSYCHIATRIC-DRUG TREATMENT:
THE CORRELATION BETWEEN EEG ALTERATION AND CLINICAL
EVOLUTION.
002165 02-11
PSYCHIATRIC-DRUG-STUDY
PSYCHIATRIC-DRUG-STUDY. PART II. MENTAL-HYGIENE-CLINIC SURVEY,
DAY-TREATMENT-CENTER SURVEY, DAY-HOSPITAL SURVEY.
004716 04-17
PSYCHIATRIC-DRUGS
THE USE OF PSYCHIATRIC-DRUGS FOR DECADES.
002555 02-17
THE KINETICS OF PSYCHIATRIC-DRUGS.
004739 04-17
PSYCHIATRIC-EFFECTS
PSYCHIATRIC-EFFECTS OF BROMOCRIPTINE AND LERGOTRILE IN
PARKINSONIAN-PATIENTS.
002453 02-15
PSYCHIATRIC-EMERGENCIES
PSYCHOPHARMACOLOGY IN PSYCHIATRIC-EMERGENCIES.
000933 01-17
PSYCHIATRIC-HOSPITAL
THE URBAN EPIDEMIC OF PHENCYCLIDINE USE: LABORATORY EVIDENCE
FROM A PUBLIC PSYCHIATRIC-HOSPITAL INPATIENT-SERVICE.
003554 03-16
AN ANALYSIS OF DRUG DECISIONS IN A STATE PSYCHIATRIC-HOSPITAL.
003593 03-17
PSYCHOTROPIC-DRUGS AND PSYCHIATRIC-HOSPITAL ADMISSIONS IN
VERONA, ITALY.
004717 04-17
PSYCHIATRIC-ILLNESS
PSYCHIATRIC-ILLNESS AND USE OF PSYCHOTROPIC-DRUGS IN THE
GEOGRAPHICALLY DELIMITED POPULATION OF SAMSO, DENMARK.
004734 04-17
PSYCHIATRIC-INPATIENTS
USE OF BENZODIAZEPINES IN PSYCHIATRIC-INPATIENTS.
000910 01-17
THE PREVALENCE OF PRESUMED TARDIVE-DYSKINESIA IN PSYCHIATRIC-
INPATIENTS AND PSYCHIATRIC-OUTPATIENTS.
002417 02-15
PSYCHIATRIC-INTERVENTION
EFFECT OF PSYCHIATRIC-INTERVENTION ON USE OF ANTIHEMOPHILIC-
FACTOR CONCENTRATE.
000945 01-17

PSYCHIATRIC-MOVEMENTS
PSYCHIATRIC-MOVEMENTS AND PSYCHOPHARMACOLOGY: BETWEEN
AFFECT AND REPRESENTATION.
003604 03-17
PSYCHIATRIC-OUTPATIENTS
DOUBLE-BLIND COMPARISON OF HALOPERIDOL AND THIOTHIXENE WITH
AFTERCARE TREATMENT EVALUATION IN PSYCHIATRIC-OUTPATIENTS
WITH SCHIZOPHRENIA.
000574 01-08
PROGNOSTIC FACTORS DETERMINING RESPONSE TO ANTIDEPRESSANT-
DRUGS IN PSYCHIATRIC-OUTPATIENTS AND GENERAL-PRACTICE.
000638 01-09
HOSTILITY CONFLICT AND REPORTING OF SIDE-EFFECTS BY PSYCHIATRIC-
OUTPATIENTS.
000840 01-15
THE PREVALENCE OF PRESUMED TARDIVE-DYSKINESIA IN PSYCHIATRIC-
INPATIENTS AND PSYCHIATRIC-OUTPATIENTS.
002417 02-15
PSYCHIATRIC-PATIENTS
ANXIETY AND THYROID-ACTIVITY IN PSYCHIATRIC-PATIENTS.
000786 01-13
TREATMENT OF DRUG-INDUCED DRYNESS OF MOUTH IN PSYCHIATRIC-
PATIENTS -- A CONTROLLED-COMPARATIVE-STUDY.
000799 01-13
MEDICATION USE AND DEATHS ATTRIBUTED TO ASPHYXIA AMONG
PSYCHIATRIC-PATIENTS.
000838 01-15
ROTTING WITH THEIR RIGHTS ON: CONSTITUTIONAL THEORY AND
CLINICAL REALITY IN DRUG-REFUSAL BY PSYCHIATRIC-PATIENTS.
000911 01-17
ON A POSSIBLE ROLE OF ENDORPHINS IN PSYCHIATRIC-PATIENTS --
ACTIONS OF NALOXONE IN PSYCHIATRIC-PATIENTS.
001917 02-08
DRUG-INDUCED ARTERIAL HYPOTENSION IN PSYCHIATRIC-PATIENTS
TREATED WITH DIHYDROERGOTAMINE.
001950 02-08
PRELIMINARY-STUDIES ON CSF GAMMA AMINOBUTYRIC-ACID LEVELS IN
PSYCHIATRIC-PATIENTS BEFORE AND DURING TREATMENT WITH
DIFFERENT PSYCHOTROPIC-DRUGS.
001959 02-08
THE TSH RESPONSE TO TRH INJECTION IN PSYCHIATRIC-PATIENTS: A
REVIEW.
002145 02-11
PIRIBEDIL IN ELDERLY PSYCHIATRIC-PATIENTS.
002170 02-11
STUDY OF PROLACTIN VARIATIONS IN PSYCHIATRIC-PATIENTS TREATED
WITH FLUPHENAZINE-DECANOATE.
002226 02-13
HALOPERIDOL PLASMA LEVEL MONITORING IN PSYCHIATRIC-PATIENTS.
002267 02-13
PNEUMONIA AND PSYCHOTROPIC-DRUG USE IN ELDERLY PSYCHIATRIC-
PATIENTS.
002391 02-15
COMPARISON OF DRUG PRESCRIPTIONS FOR PSYCHIATRIC-PATIENTS
AFTER HOSPITAL DISCHARGE IN THE DISTRICTS TEPLICE AND UHERSKE-
HRADISTE.
002518 02-17
TOLERANCE IN A COMPRESSED GASTRORESISTANT FORM IN
PSYCHIATRIC-PATIENTS.
003157 03-07
TOLERANCE STUDY IN PSYCHIATRIC-PATIENTS OF A NEW PREPARATION
OF SODIUM-DIPROPYLACETATE.
003158 03-07
A DOUBLE-BLIND, PLACEBO-CONTROLLED-STUDY OF PIRACETAM IN
ELDERLY PSYCHIATRIC-PATIENTS.
003305 03-11
FLUNITRAZEPAM IN THE TREATMENT OF INSOMNIA: A STUDY OF 50
PSYCHIATRIC-PATIENTS.
003444 03-14
CEREBROSPINAL-FLUID CONCENTRATIONS OF THIORIDAZINE AND ITS
MAIN METABOLITES IN PSYCHIATRIC-PATIENTS.
003569 03-16
MEDICATION GROUPS FOR PSYCHIATRIC-PATIENTS.
003582 03-17
THE USE OF PHARMACOKINETICS IN THE FOLLOWUP OF PSYCHIATRIC-
PATIENTS.
003616 03-17
PSYCHIATRIC-PERSPECTIVE
CHRONIC PHENCYCLIDINE (PCP) ABUSE: A PSYCHIATRIC-PERSPECTIVE.
000935 01-17
PSYCHIATRIC-PRACTICE
USE OF THE NEW TRANQUILIZER PHENAZEPAM IN PSYCHIATRIC-
PRACTICE.
000578 01-09
HOW APPROPRIATE IS A MEDICAL-MODEL IN PSYCHIATRIC-PRACTICE?
002531 02-17
ROUNDTABLE DISCUSSION: ALIVALS PLACE IN PSYCHIATRIC-PRACTICE.
002585 02-17

Subject Index

A NEW DOPAMINERGIC-AGENT IN CURRENT PSYCHIATRIC-PRACTICE.
003156 03-07

PSYCHIATRIC-RESEARCH
PHYSICO-CHEMICAL METHODOLOGIES IN PSYCHIATRIC-RESEARCH.
004679 04-16

PSYCHIATRIC-SAMPLE
USE OF THE LITHIUM RESPONSE SCALE WITH AN OUTPATIENT
PSYCHIATRIC-SAMPLE.
000921 01-17

PSYCHIATRIC-STUDY
COOPERATIVE PSYCHIATRIC-STUDY OF ALIVAL: PRELIMINARY RESULTS.
002045 02-09

PSYCHIATRIC-SYNDROMES
PSYCHIATRIC-SYNDROMES AND DRUG-TREATMENT.
003608 03-17

PSYCHIATRIC-TREATMENT
CLINICAL-EXPERIENCE WITH PSYCHIATRIC-TREATMENT OF THE ELDERLY
INVOLVING THE USE OF PIRACETAM.
002188 02-11

CHANGES IN THE CLINICAL-PICTURE AND THE COURSE OF PSYCHOSES
DURING MASSIVE PSYCHOPHARMACOTHERAPY AND THE
SIGNIFICANCE OF THESE CHANGES FOR IMPROVEMENTS IN
PSYCHIATRIC-TREATMENT.
004699 04-17

PSYCHIATRIC-WARDS
TARDIVE-DYSKINESIA ON HUNGARIAN PSYCHIATRIC-WARDS.
002447 02-15

PSYCHIATRIST
INITIAL PRESCRIPTION OF PSYCHOTROPIC-MEDICATIONS FOR
ADOLESCENTS IN A MEDICAL/PROFESSIONAL INSTITUTE, AND THE
ROLE OF THE PSYCHIATRIST IN A MEDICAL/PROFESSIONAL INSTITUTE.
002621 02-17

NEUROLEPTIC TREATMENT AS EXPERIENCED BY A PSYCHIATRIST.
004613 04-15

PSYCHIATRISTS
CLINICAL STRATEGIES FOR ANTIPSYCHOTIC-DRUG TREATMENT, TARDIVE-
DYSKINESIA, AND THE TRAINING OF RESEARCH PSYCHIATRISTS.
004603 04-15

PSYCHIATRY
CONTRIBUTION TO THE CLINICAL-STUDY OF CEREBRAL DOPAMINERGIC
MECHANISMS: THE ACTION OF PIRIBEDIL IN PSYCHIATRY. FIRST
RESULTS.
000616 01-09

THE HISTORY OF RECENT DEVELOPMENTS IN PSYCHIATRY.
000939 01-17

THE PRESENT STATUS OF THE BENZODIAZEPINES IN PSYCHIATRY AND
MEDICINE.
000954 01-17

MAJOR-TRANQUILLIZERS IN PSYCHIATRY.
000987 01-17

CLINICAL-EXPERIENCE WITH LITHIUM-CARBONICUM-RETARD IN
PSYCHIATRY.
002000 02-09

BETA-BLOCKERS IN PSYCHIATRY.
002109 02-11

BEHAVIORAL-DISTURBANCES IN PSYCHIATRY: A THERAPEUTIC
APPROACH.
002321 02-14

METHODS OF MULTICENTER-TRIALS IN PSYCHIATRY -- PART I: REVIEW.
002483 02-16

ACTION MECHANISMS OF INSULIN THERAPY IN PSYCHIATRY, AND
CURRENT-VIEWS ON THESE MECHANISMS.
002553 02-17

COMPUTERIZED SLEEP EEG (CSEEG) IN PSYCHIATRY AND
PSYCHOPHARMACOLOGY.
002614 02-17

CHANGES IN AND CURRENT PROGRESS OF NEUROLOGY AND
PSYCHIATRY.
003550 03-15

THE NECESSITY OF PSYCHOPHARMACOLOGY IN THE DEVELOPMENT OF
PSYCHIATRY.
003575 03-17

THE USE OF ANTIDEPRESSANTS IN PSYCHIATRY.
003597 03-17

CLINICAL APPLICATION OF ANTIANDROGENS IN PSYCHIATRY.
004457 04-11

CURRENT TRENDS IN TREATMENT IN PSYCHIATRY.
004747 04-17

PSYCHIC-EFFECTS
PHARMACOTHERAPY FOR SEXUAL-OFFENDERS: REVIEW OF THE ACTION
OF ANTIANDROGENS WITH SPECIAL REFERENCE TO THEIR PSYCHIC-
EFFECTS.
004455 04-11

PSYCHIC-MANIFESTATIONS
CEREBRAL SENESCENCE AND ITS PSYCHIC-MANIFESTATIONS. THE
EFFECTIVENESS OF DEBRUMYL.
002105 02-11

PSYCHOACTIVE
ISOLATION OF PSYCHOACTIVE CANNABINOID PRECURSORS FROM
CANNABIS OF SOVIET PROVENIENCE GROWN IN MISSISSIPPI.
001023 02-01

PSYCHOGERIATRIC-WARD
THERAPEUTIC RESULTS IN A PSYCHOGERIATRIC-WARD AFTER CHANGE OF MEDICATION.
002136 02-11

PSYCHOLEPTIC-DRUGS
ANTAGONISTIC-EFFECTS OF PSYCHOLEPTIC-DRUGS ON STRESS-INDUCED ANALGESIA.
001609 02-04

PSYCHOLEPTIC-EFFECTS
DOUBLE-BLIND CONTROLLED-STUDY ON THE PSYCHOLEPTIC-EFFECTS OF AMINEPTINE IN MENTALLY-HANDICAPPED CHILDREN WITHOUT PERSONALITY-PROBLEMS.
002116 02-11

PSYCHOLOGIC-TREATMENT
SENILE-DEMENTIA: COMBINED PHARMACOLOGIC-TREATMENT AND PSYCHOLOGIC-TREATMENT.
003393 03-11

PSYCHOLOGICAL
ATTEMPT AT PSYCHOLOGICAL UNDERSTANDING AND TREATMENT OF PSYCHOLOGICAL ASTHENIA AND ASTHENO-DEPRESSIVE-SYNDROMES USING ERGADYL.
001974 02-09
MEDICAL PSYCHOLOGICAL AND COMBINED THERAPY IN THE CASES OF ENURESIS: A COMPARATIVE-STUDY.
002175 02-11
PROGNOSIS IN SCHIZOPHRENIA: INDIVIDUAL DIFFERENCES IN PSYCHOLOGICAL RESPONSE TO A TEST DOSE OF ANTIPSYCHOTIC-DRUG AND THEIR RELATIONSHIP TO BLOOD AND SALIVA LEVELS AND TREATMENT OUTCOME.
003189 03-08
SOME OBSERVATIONS ON THE PSYCHOLOGICAL DIMENSIONS OF PLACEBO-EFFECTS.
003573 03-17
ELECTROPHYSIOLOGICAL AND PSYCHOLOGICAL CHANGES INDUCED BY STEROID-HORMONES IN MEN AND WOMEN.
004500 04-13
EMOTIONAL-DISORDERS IN CHILDREN AND ADOLESCENTS: MEDICAL AND PSYCHOLOGICAL APPROACHES TO TREATMENT.
004743 04-17

PSYCHOLOGICAL-STRESS
EEG CHANGE IN THE CONSCIOUS RAT DURING IMMOBILITY INDUCED BY PSYCHOLOGICAL-STRESS.
001297 02-03

PSYCHOLOGICAL-TREATMENT
PHOBIA: PSYCHOLOGICAL-TREATMENT AND PHARMACOLOGICAL-TREATMENT.
004425 04-10

PSYCHOLOGICAL-VIEW
A PSYCHOLOGICAL-VIEW ON PROBLEMS AND CONCEPTS OF LITHIUM RESEARCH.
000810 01-14

PSYCHOMETRIC-ANALYSES
DETERMINATION OF THE ENCEPHALOTROPIC, PSYCHOTROPIC AND PHARMACODYNAMIC PROPERTIES OF NICERGOLINE BY MEANS OF QUANTITATIVE PHARMACOELECTROENCEPHALOGRAPHY AND PSYCHOMETRIC-ANALYSES.
000788 01-13

PSYCHOMETRIC-ANALYSIS
CLASSIFICATION AND ASSESSMENT OF CEREBRAL BIOAVAILABILITY OF LOPIRAZEPAM (D-12524) BY QUANTITATIVE EEG AND PSYCHOMETRIC-ANALYSIS.
000720 01-11
DETERMINATION OF PHARMACODYNAMICS OF PSYCHOTROPIC-DRUGS BY PSYCHOMETRIC-ANALYSIS.
001895 02-07

PSYCHOMETRIC-FINDINGS
EVALUATION OF LITHIUM RESPONSE: PSYCHOMETRIC-FINDINGS.
004348 04-09

PSYCHOMETRIC-TEST
A NOVEL PSYCHOMETRIC-TEST MODEL APPLYING TAILORED TESTING FOR ECONOMIC AND EFFICIENT COLLECTION OF PSYCHOPHARMACOLOGICAL-EFFECTS.
002479 02-16

PSYCHOMETRIC-TESTS
STUDY OF VIGILANCE AFTER INGESTION OF ZOPICLONE IN COMPARISON WITH NITRAZEPAM AND PLACEBO. METHODOLOGY OF THE STUDY: SELF-EVALUATION QUESTIONNAIRE AND PSYCHOMETRIC-TESTS.
000543 01-07
EVALUATION OF NOMIFENSINE IN THE TREATMENT OF GERIATRIC DEPRESSION USING PSYCHOMETRIC-TESTS AND PLASMA LEVEL CONTROLS.
002004 02-09

PSYCHOMODERATORS
COMPARATIVE-STUDY OF THE INDUCTIVE EFFECT OF TWO PSYCHOMODERATORS -- TETRABAMATE AND COMPLEXE-1656 -- AND OF PHENOBARBITAL ON LIVER MICROSOMAL ENZYMES IN RATS.
001874 02-06

PSYCHOMOTOR
IN VITRO EFFECT OF PHENCYCLIDINE AND OTHER PSYCHOMOTOR STIMULANTS ON SEROTONIN UPTAKE IN HUMAN PLATELETS.
000750 01-13

INFLUENCE OF INTRAVENOUS SELF-ADMINISTERED PSYCHOMOTOR STIMULANTS ON PERFORMANCE OF RHESUS-MONKEYS IN A MULTIPLE-SCHEDULE PARADIGM.
001655 02-04
THE EFFECTS OF TRIAZOLAM AND NITRAZEPAM ON SLEEP QUALITY, MORNING VIGILANCE, AND PSYCHOMOTOR PERFORMANCE.
002330 02-14
PERSONALITY TRAIT AND ANTIANXIETY-DRUG EFFECTS ON PSYCHOMOTOR PERFORMANCE.
002336 02-14
PSYCHOMOTOR STIMULANTS AS ACTIVATORS OF NORMAL AND PATHOLOGICAL-BEHAVIOR: IMPLICATIONS FOR THE EXCESSES IN MANIA. (UNPUBLISHED PAPER).
002353 02-14
FUNDAMENTAL MECHANISMS UNDERLYING ALTERED BEHAVIOR FOLLOWING CHRONIC ADMINISTRATION OF PSYCHOMOTOR STIMULANTS.
002711 03-03
SEXUAL-EFFECTS OF ANTIDEPRESSANTS AND PSYCHOMOTOR STIMULANT-DRUGS.
004646 04-15

PSYCHONEUROENDOCRINE
A MODEL FOR PSYCHONEUROENDOCRINE INVESTIGATION: SPECIFIC CHEMICAL LESIONING OF THE MEDIAN-EMINENCE.
001478 02-03

PSYCHONEUROENDOCRINOLOGY
PSYCHONEUROENDOCRINOLOGY AND ABNORMAL-BEHAVIOR.
002347 02-14
PHARMACOLOGICAL-BASES OF PSYCHONEUROENDOCRINOLOGY: PRECLINICAL ASSESSMENT OF CLINICAL FACTS.
003735 04-03

PSYCHONEUROPHARMACOLOGIC-RESEARCH
NEUROENDOCRINE APPROACHES TO PSYCHONEUROPHARMACOLOGIC-RESEARCH.
003426 03-13

PSYCHOPATHOLOGIC
CHANGES IN PSYCHOPATHOLOGIC SYMPTOMS DURING 20 DAYS OF TREATMENT WITH ANTIDEPRESSANTS AND NEUROLEPTIC-DRUGS.
004415 04-09

PSYCHOPATHOLOGICAL-CONDITIONS
CLINICAL NEUROPHYSIOLOGICAL ASPECTS OF PSYCHOPATHOLOGICAL-CONDITIONS.
002274 02-13

PSYCHOPATHOLOGICAL-FINDINGS
CORRELATIONS BETWEEN VISUAL-EVOKED-POTENTIALS AND PSYCHOPATHOLOGICAL-FINDINGS IN SCHIZOPHRENIC-PATIENTS UNDER TREATMENT WITH VARIOUS PSYCHOPHARMACOLOGICAL-DRUGS.
004315 04-08

PSYCHOPATHOLOGY
DEPRESSION IN THE ELDERLY: RESEARCH DIRECTIONS IN PSYCHOPATHOLOGY, EPIDEMIOLOGY, AND TREATMENT.
000998 01-17
BASAL AND STIMULATED LEVELS OF PROLACTIN, TSH, AND LH IN SERUM OF CHRONIC SCHIZOPHRENIC-PATIENTS LONG-TERM TREATED WITH NEUROLEPTICS: RELATIONS TO PSYCHOPATHOLOGY.
001936 02-08
MINAPRINE IN SEVERE PSYCHOPATHOLOGY: STUDY OF 20 CASES.
002135 02-11
CHILDHOOD-ENURESIS: II. PSYCHOPATHOLOGY, TRICYCLIC CONCENTRATION IN PLASMA, AND ANTIENURETIC-EFFECT.
002354 02-14
CHANGES IN THE PSYCHOPATHOLOGY OF PSYCHOSIS DUE TO NEUROLEPTIC TREATMENT.
003281 03-10
ALCOHOL WITHDRAWAL USING TIAPRIDE: QUANTITATIVE PSYCHOPATHOLOGY.
003293 03-11
ENDORPHINS IN PSYCHOPATHOLOGY.
004313 04-08
PSYCHOPATHOLOGY AND ENDORPHINS.
004317 04-08
PSYCHOTROPIC-DRUGS AND THEIR RELATIONSHIP WITH PSYCHOPATHOLOGY OF AFFECTIVE-DISORDERS.
004361 04-09

PSYCHOPATHOMETRIC
PSYCHOPATHOMETRIC DOUBLE-BLIND COURSE STUDY WITH NICERGOLINE VERSUS PLACEBO IN GERIATRIC-PATIENTS WITH TRANSIENT-SYNDROMES.
000665 01-11

PSYCHOPHARMACEUTICAL
A DOUBLE-BLIND CROSSED CLINICAL-STUDY WITH A NEW PSYCHOPHARMACEUTICAL: TIADIPONE (QM-6008), DIAZEPAM, AND A PLACEBO.
003153 03-07

PSYCHOPHARMACEUTICAL-THERAPY
PSYCHOPHARMACEUTICAL-THERAPY TO CALM DRIVE, ACTIVITY, AND RESTLESSNESS IN CHILDHOOD.
002604 02-17

Subject Index

PSYCHOPHARMACEUTICALS   PSY
ON THE DANGER OF USING PSYCHOPHARMACEUTICALS DURING
PREGNANCY: CRITICAL REVIEW OF THE LITERATURE.
000833 01-15
ON THE GENETIC SIDE-EFFECTS OF PSYCHOTROPIC-SUBSTANCES: I.
PSYCHOPHARMACEUTICALS, NARCOTICS, AND ANTICONVULSANT.
000845 01-15   PSY
PSYCHOPHARMACEUTICALS AND PREGNANCY: A REVIEW.
002462 02-15
PSYCHOPHARMACEUTICALS -- A PROBLEM FOR PSYCHOTHERAPISTS?   PSY
002535 02-17
PSYCHOPHARMACEUTICALS FOR TREATING PAIN.
002548 02-17
EFFECTS OF PSYCHOPHARMACEUTICALS ON DRIVING CAPACITY.   PSY
003453 03-14
PSYCHOPHARMACEUTICALS IN PEDIATRIC-PRACTICE.
003491 03-15

PSYCHOPHARMACOLOGIC-AGENTS
EARLY-ACTIVITY-STUDIES AND INTENSIVE DRUG EVALUATIONS OF NEW
PSYCHOPHARMACOLOGIC-AGENTS.
002348 02-14

PSYCHOPHARMACOLOGICAL
PSYCHOPHARMACOLOGICAL AND PSYCHOTHERAPEUTIC-APPROACHES TO
THE TREATMENT OF FUNCTIONAL PSYCHOSES.
000977 01-17
CHRONIC ADMINISTRATION OF HALOPERIDOL DURING DEVELOPMENT:
LATER PSYCHOPHARMACOLOGICAL RESPONSES TO APOMORPHINE
AND ARECOLINE.
001470 02-03
THE INFLUENCE OF DAILY BIOLOGICAL-RHYTHMICITY ON THE HOMING-
BEHAVIOR, PSYCHOPHARMACOLOGICAL RESPONSIVENESS, LEARNING
AND RETENTION OF SUCKLING RATS. (PH.D. DISSERTATION).
001660 02-04
DIAGNOSTIC CLASSIFICATION AND THE ENDORPHIN HYPOTHESIS OF
SCHIZOPHRENIA: INDIVIDUAL DIFFERENCES AND
PSYCHOPHARMACOLOGICAL STRATEGIES. (UNPUBLISHED PAPER).
001910 02-08
A PSYCHOPHARMACOLOGICAL APPROACH TO MEMORY PROCESSING.
002901 03-03
DIAGNOSTIC CLASSIFICATION AND THE ENDORPHIN HYPOTHESIS OF
SCHIZOPHRENIA: INDIVIDUAL DIFFERENCES AND
PSYCHOPHARMACOLOGICAL STRATEGIES.
003167 03-08
PRACTICAL IMPLICATIONS OF MODERN PSYCHOPHARMACOLOGICAL
DATA.
003596 03-17
PSYCHOPHARMACOLOGICAL AND SOCIAL ASPECTS OF SCHIZOPHRENIA:
RECENT DEVELOPMENTS.
004336 04-08

PSYCHOPHARMACOLOGICAL-AGENTS
CONTRIBUTORS TO FEMALE USE OF PSYCHOPHARMACOLOGICAL-AGENTS:
DISSERTATION).
000956 01-17

PSYCHOPHARMACOLOGICAL-CORRELATION
CLINICAL-CORRELATION, BIOCHEMICAL-CORRELATION, AND
PSYCHOPHARMACOLOGICAL-CORRELATION IN PATIENTS WITH
DEPRESSIVE-SYMPTOMATOLOGY.
002018 02-09

PSYCHOPHARMACOLOGICAL-DRUGS
CORRELATIONS BETWEEN VISUAL-EVOKED-POTENTIALS AND
PSYCHOPATHOLOGICAL-FINDINGS IN SCHIZOPHRENIC-PATIENTS UNDER
TREATMENT WITH VARIOUS PSYCHOPHARMACOLOGICAL-DRUGS.
004315 04-08

PSYCHOPHARMACOLOGICAL-EFFECTS
CHRONIC ADMINISTRATION OF HALOPERIDOL DURING DEVELOPMENT:
BEHAVIORAL-EFFECTS AND PSYCHOPHARMACOLOGICAL-EFFECTS.
000481 01-04
PSYCHOPHARMACOLOGICAL-EFFECTS OF LOW-DOSES AND HIGH-DOSES
OF APOMORPHINE DURING ONTOGENY.
001774 02-04
A NOVEL PSYCHOMETRIC-TEST MODEL APPLYING TAILORED TESTING FOR
ECONOMIC AND EFFICIENT COLLECTION OF
PSYCHOPHARMACOLOGICAL-EFFECTS.
002479 02-16
THE SMOKING HABIT AND PSYCHOPHARMACOLOGICAL-EFFECTS OF
NICOTINE.
003577 03-17

PSYCHOPHARMACOLOGICAL-INVESTIGATIONS
THE LEEDS-SLEEP-EVALUATION-QUESTIONNAIRE IN
PSYCHOPHARMACOLOGICAL-INVESTIGATIONS — A REVIEW.
002351 02-14

PSYCHOPHARMACOLOGICAL-MEETING
21. ANNUAL CZECHOSLOVAK PSYCHOPHARMACOLOGICAL-MEETING.
000917 01-17

PSYCHOPHARMACOLOGICAL-PROCEDURES
THE USE OF PSYCHOPHARMACOLOGICAL-PROCEDURES TO ANALYSE THE
ONTOGENY OF LEARNING AND RETENTION: ISSUES AND CONCERNS.
000482 01-04

PSYCHIATRIC-MOVEMENTS AND PSYCHOPHARMACOLOGY: BETWEEN AFFECT AND REPRESENTATION.
003604 03-17

MIND/BRAIN IN THE AGE OF PSYCHOPHARMACOLOGY: A CROSSROADS FOR MEDICINE AND MINISTRY.
003624 03-17

THE VALIDITY OF MODELS IN PSYCHOPHARMACOLOGY.
003633 03-17

PSYCHOPHARMACOLOGY AFTER 20 YEARS OF CONFERENCES IN JESENIK.
003646 03-17

PROGRESS IN PSYCHOPHARMACOLOGY.
004398 04-09

THE INTERACTION OF PSYCHOPHARMACOLOGY AND PSYCHOANALYSIS IN THE BORDERLINE-PATIENT.
004430 04-10

CHILD PSYCHOPHARMACOLOGY.
004470 04-11

ELECTRORETINOGRAPHY (ERG) AS A TOOL OF INVESTIGATION IN HUMAN PSYCHOPHARMACOLOGY. ELECTRORETINOGRAPHIC-CHANGES INDUCED BY A COMBINATION OF CARBIDOPA AND LEVODOPA.
004507 04-13

DEVELOPMENT OF PSYCHOPHARMACOLOGY.
004667 04-15

ON THE USE OF REPEATED MEASURES DESIGNS IN PSYCHOPHARMACOLOGY.
004695 04-16

PSYCHOPHARMACOLOGY FOR THE AGED.
004701 04-17

PSYCHOPHARMACOLOGY OF AGING.
004710 04-17

PSYCHOPHARMACOLOGY AND PSYCHOTHERAPY IN THE TREATMENT OF ANXIETY.
004712 04-17

PSYCHOPHARMACOTHERAPY
DYNAMICS AND PROSPECTS OF THE PSYCHOTHERAPY AND PSYCHOPHARMACOTHERAPY RELATIONSHIP.
002594 02-17

CHILD-PSYCHIATRY AND PSYCHOPHARMACOTHERAPY IN GENERAL PRACTICE, IN PEDIATRICS, AND IN NEUROLOGY.
003288 03-11

THE ROLE OF PSYCHOTHERAPY AND PSYCHOPHARMACOTHERAPY IN THE TREATMENT OF ELDERLY-PATIENTS WITH ORGANIC-MENTAL-SYNDROMES.
003368 03-11

CLINICAL AND BIOCHEMICAL-CORRELATIONS IN ABRUPT DISCONTINUATION OF PSYCHOPHARMACOTHERAPY.
004330 04-08

THE PROBLEM OF PSYCHOPHARMACOTHERAPY OF SLOWLY PROGRESSIVE HYPOCHONDRIACAL SCHIZOPHRENIA.
004340 04-08

THE NOSOLOGICAL INDEPENDENCE OF INVOLUTIONAL DEPRESSION AND ITS DYNAMICS DURING PSYCHOPHARMACOTHERAPY.
004389 04-09

PSYCHOPHARMACOTHERAPY OF SEXUAL-DISORDERS IN THE AGED.
004466 04-11

CHANGES IN THE CLINICAL-PICTURE AND THE COURSE OF PSYCHOSES DURING MASSIVE PSYCHOPHARMACOTHERAPY AND THE SIGNIFICANCE OF THESE CHANGES FOR IMPROVEMENTS IN PSYCHIATRIC-TREATMENT.
004699 04-17

PSYCHOPHARMACOTHERAPY: THE PRESENT STATE AND THE DEVELOPMENT OF TRENDS.
004723 04-17

PSYCHOPHARMALOGIC-FACTORS
INTERACTION OF PSYCHOPHARMALOGIC-FACTORS AND PSYCHOSOCIAL-FACTORS IN THE TREATMENT OF ANIMAL-MODELS OF HYPOINHIBITORY (HYPERKINETIC) BEHAVIOR.
001602 02-04

PSYCHOPHYSICAL
CLONIDINE AND PSYCHOPHYSICAL PAIN.
002366 02-14

PSYCHOPHYSIOLOGIC-STUDIES
METABOLIC-STUDIES AND PSYCHOPHYSIOLOGIC-STUDIES OF CANNABIDIOL HEXOBARBITAL INTERACTION.
002209 02-13

PSYCHOPHYSIOLOGICAL
EFFECTS OF THE BETA-ADRENOCEPTOR BLOCKING-AGENT SOTALOL ON CNS; SLEEP, EEG, AND PSYCHOPHYSIOLOGICAL PARAMETERS.
001570 02-04

VARIATIONS IN PSYCHOPHYSIOLOGICAL ACTIVATION RESPONSES IN DEPRESSIVE-STATES.
001965 02-09

INVESTIGATION INTO THE EFFECT OF FLUPHENAZINE-HCL (LYORODIN) IN CHILDREN WITH BEHAVIORAL-DISORDERS BY MEANS OF PSYCHOPHYSIOLOGICAL PARAMETERS.
003344 03-11

PSYCHOPHYSIOLOGICAL-EFFECTS
THE REPLICABILITY OF THE PSYCHOPHYSIOLOGICAL-EFFECTS OF DIAZEPAM.
003413 03-13

PSYCHOPHYSIOLOGICAL-TESTS
A COMPARATIVE EVALUATION OF THE USEFULNESS OF PSYCHOPHYSIOLOGICAL-TESTS DURING VARIOUS LEVELS OF ACTIVATION OF THE CENTRAL-NERVOUS-SYSTEM.
004543 04-13

PSYCHOPHYSIOLOGICAL-VARIABLES
THE RELATIONSHIPS BETWEEN CLINICAL-RESPONSE, PSYCHOPHYSIOLOGICAL-VARIABLES AND PLASMA LEVELS OF AMITRIPTYLINE AND DIAZEPAM IN NEUROTIC-OUTPATIENTS.
004423 04-10

PSYCHOSES
ADVANTAGE OF PHARMACOKINETIC DATA DURING TREATMENT OF PSYCHOSES WITH HALOPERIDOL.
000577 01-08

PSYCHOPHARMACOLOGICAL AND PSYCHOTHERAPEUTIC-APPROACHES TO THE TREATMENT OF FUNCTIONAL PSYCHOSES.
000977 01-17

PHENYLALANINE LEVELS IN ENDOGENOUS PSYCHOSES.
002049 02-09

PATHOPHYSIOLOGIC-IMPACT OF CENTRAL CATECHOLAMINERGIC FUNCTION IN SCHIZOPHRENIA AND SCHIZOPHRENIA-LIKE PSYCHOSES.
002174 02-11

CYCLIC-AMP IN PSYCHOSES AND THE EFFECT OF DRUGS.
002294 02-13

FAMILY-TREE GIVES CLUES TO TREATING PSYCHOSES.
002363 02-14

ON THE INTENSIVE TREATMENT OF ENDOGENOUS PSYCHOSES.
003384 03-11

ACUTE PHARMACOTOXIC PSYCHOSES IN CHRONIC CEREBRAL CONDITIONS.
003475 03-15

THE EFFECT OF NALOXONE ON THE CONDITION OF PATIENTS WITH ENDOGENOUS PSYCHOSES.
004381 04-09

CHANGES IN THE CLINICAL-PICTURE AND THE COURSE OF PSYCHOSES DURING MASSIVE PSYCHOPHARMACOTHERAPY AND THE SIGNIFICANCE OF THESE CHANGES FOR IMPROVEMENTS IN PSYCHIATRIC-TREATMENT.
004699 04-17

NOTES ON PHARMACOTHERAPY OF FUNCTIONAL PSYCHOSES.
004748 04-17

PSYCHOSIS
THE PCP PSYCHOSIS: PROLONGED INTOXICATION OR DRUG PRECIPITATED FUNCTIONAL ILLNESS?
000739 01-12

PROTOCOLS FOR THE USE OF PSYCHOACTIVE-DRUGS -- PART I: PROTOCOL FOR THE TREATMENT OF PSYCHOSIS WITH ANTIPSYCHOTICS.
000949 01-17

A NEW DOSAGE SCHEDULE FOR PIMOZIDE IN THE ACUTE STABILIZATION AND MAINTENANCE-TREATMENT OF PSYCHOSIS.
002022 02-09

DELIRIUM OR PSYCHOSIS? DIAGNOSTIC USE OF THE SODIUM-AMOBARBITAL INTERVIEW.
002167 02-11

NEUROLEPTIC-INDUCED REINNERVATION SPROUTING IN THE CENTRAL-NERVOUS-SYSTEM (A MODEL FOR THE DEVELOPMENT OF TARDIVE-DYSKINESIA AND SUPERSENSITIVITY PSYCHOSIS).
002459 02-15

ANIMAL-MODEL OF PSYCHOSIS: HALLUCINATORY BEHAVIORS IN MONKEYS DURING THE LATE STAGE OF CONTINUOUS AMPHETAMINE INTOXICATION.
002988 03-04

CHANGES IN THE PSYCHOPATHOLOGY OF PSYCHOSIS DUE TO NEUROLEPTIC TREATMENT.
003281 03-10

TOXIC PSYCHOSIS FOLLOWING USE OF QUINACRINE.
003507 03-15

DRUG-INDUCED PSYCHOSIS AND SCHIZOPHRENIA IN ADOLESCENTS.
004596 04-15

PSYCHOSOCIAL-ASPECTS
PSYCHOSOCIAL-ASPECTS OF DRUG-TREATMENT FOR HYPERACTIVITY.
004714 04-17

PSYCHOSOCIAL-FACTORS
INTERACTION OF PSYCHOPHARMALOGIC-FACTORS AND PSYCHOSOCIAL-FACTORS IN THE TREATMENT OF ANIMAL-MODELS OF HYPOINHIBITORY (HYPERKINETIC) BEHAVIOR.
001602 02-04

PSYCHOSOMATIC-COMPLAINTS
FLUSPIRILENE (IMAP) IN THE TREATMENT OF PSYCHOSOMATIC-COMPLAINTS IN HYPOCHONDRIACAL-PATIENTS.
002072 02-10

PSYCHOSOMATIC-DISEASES
A CLINICAL-EVALUATION OF THE EFFECTS OF A NEW PSYCHOTROPIC-AGENT, MEXAZOLAM (CS-386) ON PSYCHOSOMATIC-DISEASES AND NEUROSIS: A COMPARATIVE-STUDY WITH OXAZOLAM, USING THE DOUBLE-BLIND METHOD.
004491 04-11

Subject Index

PSYCHOSOMATIC-ILLNESS
SELF-MEDICATION, ABANDONMENT, MANIPULATION, AND DEPENDENCE
IN DRUG-THERAPY IN PSYCHOSOMATIC-ILLNESS: COMPARATIVE
POLYCENTRIC RESEARCH ON VARIOUS PSYCHOTROPIC-DRUGS.
002189 02-11

PSYCHOSOMATIC-MEDICINE
THE INTEREST OF THE STIMULATING EFFECT OF CARPIPRAMINE IN
PSYCHOSOMATIC-MEDICINE.
002061 02-10

PSYCHOSOMATIC-STRESS
PSYCHOSOMATIC-STRESS AND LIPOPEROXIDES OF HUMAN PLATELET
RICH PLASMA.
003423 03-13

PSYCHOSOMATICS
COGNITION AND PSYCHOSOMATICS.
002312 02-14

PSYCHOSTIMULANTS
SWIMMING CAPACITY OF MICE AFTER PROLONGED TREATMENT WITH
PSYCHOSTIMULANTS: II. EFFECT OF METHAMPHETAMINE ON
SWIMMING PERFORMANCE AND AVAILABILITY OF METABOLIC
SUBSTRATES.
001613 02-04
PSYCHOSTIMULANTS AND NEUROPEPTIDES IN GEROPSYCHIATRY.
002125 02-11
THE EFFECT OF PSYCHOSTIMULANTS ON CHANGES IN THE EXCITABILITY
OF THE VISUAL CEREBRAL-CORTEX.
003919 04-03

PSYCHOTHERAPEUTIC-APPROACHES
PSYCHOPHARMACOLOGICAL AND PSYCHOTHERAPEUTIC-APPROACHES TO
THE TREATMENT OF FUNCTIONAL PSYCHOSES.
000977 01-17

PSYCHOTHERAPEUTIC-DRUG
PSYCHOTHERAPEUTIC-DRUG RECOMMENDATIONS BASED ON THE MINI-
MULT.
002606 02-17

PSYCHOTHERAPEUTIC-DRUGS
PSYCHOTHERAPEUTIC-DRUGS: IMPORTANT ADVERSE-REACTIONS AND
INTERACTIONS.
002383 02-15
SOME METHODOLOGICAL WAYS OF MONITORING THE EFFECTS OF
PSYCHOTHERAPEUTIC-DRUGS.
003567 03-16
PSYCHOTHERAPEUTIC-DRUGS, HISTAMINE H1-RECEPTORS AND
MUSCARINIC ACETYLCHOLINE-RECEPTORS.
004737 04-17

PSYCHOTHERAPIES
CLINICAL-TRIAL OF PSYCHOTHERAPIES IS UNDER WAY.
004378 D4-09

PSYCHOTHERAPISTS
PSYCHOPHARMACEUTICALS -- A PROBLEM FOR PSYCHOTHERAPISTS?
002535 02-17

PSYCHOTHERAPY
PROBLEMS INVOLVED IN THE COMBINATION OF PHARMACEUTIC-AGENTS
WITH PSYCHOTHERAPY OR PSYCHOANALYSIS.
000971 01-17
PSYCHOTHERAPY AND DYSPNOEA.
002164 02-11
CONVERGENCES AND DIVERGENCES BETWEEN BIOLOGICAL-PSYCHIATRY
AND PSYCHOTHERAPY.
002536 02-17
DYNAMICS AND PROSPECTS OF THE PSYCHOTHERAPY AND
PSYCHOPHARMACOTHERAPY RELATIONSHIP.
002594 02-17
MANAGEMENT OF SCHIZOPHRENIA: LONG-TERM CLINICAL-STUDIES WITH
SPECIAL REFERENCE TO THE COMBINATION OF PSYCHOTHERAPY AND
DEPOT NEUROLEPTICS.
003183 03-08
DO PSYCHOTHERAPY AND PHARMACOTHERAPY FOR DEPRESSION
CONFLICT? EMPIRICAL EVIDENCE FROM A CLINICAL-TRIAL.
003256 03-09
DEPRESSED-OUTPATIENTS: RESULTS ONE YEAR AFTER TREATMENT WITH
DRUGS AND/OR INTERPERSONAL PSYCHOTHERAPY.
003272 03-09
EFFECTS OF ALTHESIN IN PSYCHOTHERAPY OF SCHIZOPHRENICS:
PRELIMINARY REPORT.
004331 04-08
DO PSYCHOTHERAPY AND PHARMACOTHERAPY FOR DEPRESSION
CONFLICT? EMPIRICAL EVIDENCE FROM A CLINICAL-TRIAL.
(UNPUBLISHED PAPER).
004401 04-09
PHARMACOTHERAPY AND PSYCHOTHERAPY FOR AMBULATORY
DEPRESSION: EFFICACY AND CHOICES.
004413 04-09
PERSONALITY AS A PREDICTOR OF PSYCHOTHERAPY AND
PHARMACOTHERAPY-OUTCOME FOR DEPRESSED-OUTPATIENTS.
(UNPUBLISHED PAPER).
004418 04-09
PSYCHOPHARMACOLOGY AND PSYCHOTHERAPY IN THE TREATMENT OF
ANXIETY.
004712 04-17

PSYCHOTROPIC-ACTION
PSYCHOTROPIC-ACTION OF THYROTROPIN-RELEASING-HORMONE.
002023 02-09

PSYCHOTROPIC-AGENT
COMPUTERIZING THE MMPI IN THE STUDY OF A NEW PSYCHOTROPIC-AGENT: TIAPRIDE.
000585 01-09

A CLINICAL-EVALUATION OF THE EFFECTS OF A NEW PSYCHOTROPIC-AGENT, MEXAZOLAM (CS-386) ON PSYCHOSOMATIC-DISEASES AND NEUROSIS: A COMPARATIVE-STUDY WITH OXAZOLAM, USING THE DOUBLE-BLIND METHOD.
004491 04-11

EFFECTS OF RO-11-2465, A NEW PSYCHOTROPIC-AGENT ON THE UPTAKE OF SEROTONIN BY HUMAN PLATELETS -- IN VITRO DETERMINATION OF THE IC50.
004532 04-13

PSYCHOTROPIC-CAUSED
TREATMENT OF PSYCHOTROPIC-CAUSED ORTHOSTATIC HYPOTENSION.
002428 02-15

PSYCHOTROPIC-DRUG
PSYCHOTROPIC-DRUG BLOCKADE OF HISTAMINE H1-RECEPTORS.
001432 02-03

PNEUMONIA AND PSYCHOTROPIC-DRUG USE IN ELDERLY PSYCHIATRIC-PATIENTS.
002391 02-15

PSYCHOTROPIC-DRUG REGISTRATION IN THE SCANDINAVIAN-COUNTRIES: THE ROLE OF CLINICAL-TRIALS.
002550 02-17

PSYCHOTROPIC-DRUG USE AND POLYPHARMACY IN A GENERAL-HOSPITAL.
003369 03-11

COMPUTERIZED MONITORING OF PSYCHOTROPIC-DRUG ORDERS: SOME TRENDS AND REVELATIONS.
003566 03-16

SEX-DIFFERENCES IN PSYCHOTROPIC-DRUG USE.
003589 03-17

COMPARISON OF PSYCHOTROPIC-DRUG, RESPONSE COST, AND PSYCHOTROPIC-DRUG PLUS RESPONSE COST PROCEDURES FOR CONTROLLING INSTITUTIONALIZED MENTALLY-RETARDED PERSONS.
004438 04-11

PSYCHOTROPIC-DRUG-INDUCED
PSYCHOTROPIC-DRUG-INDUCED CHANGES IN AUDITORY AVERAGED EVOKED-POTENTIALS: RESULTS OF A DOUBLE-BLIND TRIAL USING AN OBJECTIVE FULLY AUTOMATED AEP ANALYSIS METHOD.
003412 03-13

PSYCHOTROPIC-DRUGS
EFFECTS OF PSYCHOTROPIC-DRUGS ON THE DISTRIBUTION OF 3H DOPAMINE INTO COMPARTMENTS OF RAT STRIATAL SYNAPTOSOMES AND ON SUBSEQUENT DEPOLARIZATION-INDUCED 3H DOPAMINE RELEASE.
000067 01-03

HISTAMINE AND PSYCHOTROPIC-DRUGS.
000112 01-03

IN VIVO OCCUPATION OF CEREBRAL HISTAMINE H1-RECEPTORS EVALUATED WITH 3H MEPYRAMINE MAY PREDICT SEDATIVE PROPERTIES OF PSYCHOTROPIC-DRUGS.
000241 01-03

PSYCHOTROPIC-DRUGS AND HISTAMINE H1-RECEPTORS OF CULTURED MOUSE NEUROBLASTOMA CELLS.
000250 01-03

PSYCHOTROPIC-DRUGS AND DEPRESSIVE-SYNDROME IN SCHIZOPHRENIA.
000569 01-08

TARDIVE-DYSKINESIA AND OTHER MOVEMENT-DISORDERS IN CHILDREN TREATED WITH PSYCHOTROPIC-DRUGS.
000849 01-15

TRENDS IN THE PRESCRIPTION OF PSYCHOTROPIC-DRUGS (1970-1977) IN A STATE-HOSPITAL.
000926 01-17

ON THE MECHANISM OF THERAPEUTIC ACTIONS OF PSYCHOTROPIC-DRUGS.
000964 01-17

PSYCHOTROPIC-DRUGS AND POLYPHARMACY IN ELDERLY-PATIENTS IN A GENERAL-HOSPITAL.
000981 01-17

WHO PRESCRIBES PSYCHOTROPIC-DRUGS.
000993 01-17

INTERACTION STUDIES OF ETHANOL AND PSYCHOTROPIC-DRUGS IN RODENTS: POSSIBLE INVOLVEMENT OF ADENOSINE-TRIPHOSPHATASES.
001281 02-03

CERTAIN MECHANISMS OF THE ACTION OF PSYCHOTROPIC-DRUGS ON TRANSPORT ATPASES.
001331 02-03

THE IMMUNOSTIMULANT ANTINEOPLASTIC ACTION OF SOME PSYCHOTROPIC-DRUGS OF THE SYDNONIMINE SERIES.
001520 02-03

EFFECTS OF PSYCHOTROPIC-DRUGS ON FI-RESPONDING AND ADJUNCTIVE DRINKING IN RATS.
001693 02-04

PERINATAL EFFECTS OF PSYCHOTROPIC-DRUGS: THE ANTICONVULSANT-DRUG DIPHENYLHYDANTOIN. (UNPUBLISHED PAPER).
001842 02-05

DETERMINATION OF PHARMACODYNAMICS OF PSYCHOTROPIC-DRUGS BY PSYCHOMETRIC-ANALYSIS.
001895 02-07

CLASSIFICATION OF PSYCHOTROPIC-DRUGS IN PEDIATRIC-PSYCHOPHARMACOLOGY.
001903 02-07

PRELIMINARY-STUDIES ON CSF GAMMA AMINOBUTYRIC-ACID LEVELS IN PSYCHIATRIC-PATIENTS BEFORE AND DURING TREATMENT WITH DIFFERENT PSYCHOTROPIC-DRUGS.
001959 02-08

SELF-MEDICATION, ABANDONMENT, MANIPULATION, AND DEPENDENCE IN DRUG-THERAPY IN PSYCHOSOMATIC-ILLNESS: COMPARATIVE POLYCENTRIC RESEARCH ON VARIOUS PSYCHOTROPIC-DRUGS.
002189 02-11

DISCOVERY OF PSYCHOTROPIC-DRUGS BY MEANS OF COMPUTER-ANALYZED EEG.
002203 02-13

EFFECT OF PSYCHOTROPIC-DRUGS ON NEUROENDOCRINE FUNCTION.
002265 02-13

PSYCHOTROPIC-DRUGS AND THE HEART: CLINICAL-IMPLICATIONS.
002425 02-15

PSYCHOTROPIC-DRUGS DO NOT INTERFERE WITH RADIOLIGAND ASSAYS FOR PROLACTIN, CORTISOL, AND GROWTH-HORMONE.
002511 02-16

MADNESS AND MEDICINE: THE FORCIBLE ADMINISTRATION OF PSYCHOTROPIC-DRUGS.
002523 02-17

CLINICAL COMPARABILITY OF PSYCHOTROPIC-DRUGS.
002526 02-17

CONSUMPTION OF PSYCHOTROPIC-DRUGS IN CZECHOSLOVAKIA.
002542 02-17

PURSUING THE ACTIONS OF PSYCHOTROPIC-DRUGS: RECEPTOR SITES AND ENDOGENOUS CEREBRAL PROGRAMMES.
002578 02-17

FEDERAL-COURT UPHOLDS RIGHT-TO-REFUSE PSYCHOTROPIC-DRUGS, ORDERS IMPROVEMENTS AT LIMA-STATE-HOSPITAL.
002583 02-17

CLASSIFICATION AND PSYCHOTROPIC-DRUGS.
002605 02-17

PREDICTION AND PROGNOSTIC FACTORS IN CLINICAL-TRIALS OF PSYCHOTROPIC-DRUGS.
002615 02-17

UTILIZATION OF PSYCHOTROPIC-DRUGS. AN INTERNATIONAL COMPARISON.
002616 02-16

INFLUENCE OF PSYCHOTROPIC-DRUGS ON THE URINARY ELIMINATION OF LITHIUM.
002895 03-03

TREATMENT OF THERAPEUTICALLY-RESISTANT PARANOID SCHIZOPHRENIC-PATIENTS WITH FLUPHENAZINE DEPOT COMBINED WITH OTHER PSYCHOTROPIC-DRUGS AND CLOZAPINE.
003172 03-08

VARIOUS FACTORS IN THE PATHOGENESIS OF PATHOLOGICAL REACTIONS OBSERVED IN CONNECTION WITH THE ADMINISTRATION OF PSYCHOTROPIC-DRUGS.
003532 03-15

TIME-BLIND ANALYSIS AND OTHER VIDEO-STRATEGIES IN PHASE II TRIALS OF PSYCHOTROPIC-DRUGS.
003568 03-16

EFFECTS OF ANESTHESIA ON PATIENTS TAKING PSYCHOTROPIC-DRUGS.
003603 03-17

THE HISTORY OF PSYCHOTROPIC-DRUGS.
003609 03-17

THE INTEGRITY OF THE SOCIAL HIERARCHY IN MICE FOLLOWING ADMINISTRATION OF PSYCHOTROPIC-DRUGS.
004202 04-04

PSYCHOTROPIC-DRUGS AND THEIR RELATIONSHIP WITH PSYCHOPATHOLOGY OF AFFECTIVE-DISORDERS.
004361 04-09

PECULIARITIES OF THE CEREBRAL PATHOMORPHOLOGY OF PATIENTS WITH SCHIZOPHRENIA TREATED WITH PSYCHOTROPIC-DRUGS (PHARMACOLOGICAL PATHOMORPHOSIS).
004528 04-13

A MODIFIED VERSION OF THE SIMULTANEOUS DISCONTINUATION OF PSYCHOTROPIC-DRUGS (COMBINED WITH THE ADMINISTRATION OF DIURETICS) AS A METHOD OF HALTING PROLONGED ATTACKS OF SCHIZOPHRENIA.
004584 04-14

NEUROLOGICAL TOLERANCE OF LITHIUM AND PSYCHOTROPIC-DRUGS IN COMBINATION: 265 CASES.
004594 04-15

ABNORMAL MOVEMENTS INDUCED BY PSYCHOTROPIC-DRUGS.
004652 04-15

PSYCHOTROPIC-DRUGS AND PSYCHIATRIC-HOSPITAL ADMISSIONS IN VERONA, ITALY.
004717 04-17

PSYCHIATRIC-ILLNESS AND USE OF PSYCHOTROPIC-DRUGS IN THE GEOGRAPHICALLY DELIMITED POPULATION OF SAMSO, DENMARK.
004734 04-17

PSYCHOTROPIC-MEDICATION
THE EFFECTS OF PSYCHOTROPIC-MEDICATION ON COGNITIVE CONTROL MEASURES. (PH.D. DISSERTATION).
004523 04-13

PSYCHOTROPIC-MEDICATIONS
DYSKINETIC AND NEUROLOGICAL-COMPLICATIONS IN CHILDREN TREATED WITH PSYCHOTROPIC-MEDICATIONS.
000880 01-15
CONSIDER THIS ... PSYCHOTROPIC-MEDICATIONS AND THEIR EFFECTS ON PATIENTS.
000967 01-17
PREDICTION OF RESPONSE TO PSYCHOTROPIC-MEDICATIONS.
002216 02-13
REFLECTIONS ON ACTION MECHANISMS OF PSYCHOTROPIC-MEDICATIONS.
002296 02-13
INITIAL PRESCRIPTION OF PSYCHOTROPIC-MEDICATIONS FOR ADOLESCENTS IN A MEDICAL/PROFESSIONAL INSTITUTE, AND THE ROLE OF THE PSYCHIATRIST IN A MEDICAL/PROFESSIONAL INSTITUTE.
002621 02-17
PSYCHOTROPIC-MEDICATIONS AND GLAUCOMA.
004647 04-15
SIDE-EFFECTS AND UNDESIRABLE COMBINATIONS OF PSYCHOTROPIC-MEDICATIONS.
004663 04-15

PSYCHOTROPIC-SUBSTANCES
ON THE GENETIC SIDE-EFFECTS OF PSYCHOTROPIC-SUBSTANCES: I. PSYCHOPHARMACEUTICALS, NARCOTICS, AND ANTICONVULSANT.
000845 01-15
THE EFFECT OF PSYCHOTROPIC-SUBSTANCES AND NARCOTIC ANALGESIC-DRUGS ON 14C NORADRENALINE UPTAKE BY SYNAPTOSOMES OF THE CEREBRAL-CORTEX OF RATS.
001363 02-03

PSYCHOTROPICS
A COMPARISON OF HUMAN MUSCARINIC CHOLINERGIC-RECEPTOR RESPONSE TO A NUMBER OF PSYCHOTROPICS UTILIZING THE RADIOLABELED ANTAGONIST, (3H) QUINUCLIDINYL-BENZILATE. (PH.D. DISSERTATION).
002918 03-03
WHAT IS STANDARD PRACTICE IN PRESCRIBING PSYCHOTROPICS?
003638 03-17
NEUROTROPIC-DRUGS AS COMEDICATION TO PSYCHOTROPICS: COMBINED ADMINISTRATION OF A NEUROTROPIC-DRUG AND A TETRACYCLIC-ANTIDEPRESSANT.
004396 04-09
ON THE QUESTION OF PARENCHYMAL DAMAGE CAUSED BY LONG-TERM THERAPY WITH PSYCHOTROPICS IN ADOLESCENCE.
004626 04-15

PSYCHPHARMACOTHERAPY
THE STATE OF THE ADRENERGIC AND CHOLINERGIC SYSTEMS IN SCHIZOPHRENIC-PATIENTS DURING PSYCHPHARMACOTHERAPY.
004526 04-13

PUBLIC
THE URBAN EPIDEMIC OF PHENCYCLIDINE USE: LABORATORY EVIDENCE FROM A PUBLIC PSYCHIATRIC-HOSPITAL INPATIENT-SERVICE.
003554 03-16
PUBLIC JUDGMENTS ON THE IMPORTANCE OF VALIUM INFORMATION.
003590 03-17

PUBLICATIONS
UNDESIRABLE EFFECTS OF MEDICINES: A REVIEW OF SEVERAL PUBLICATIONS ISSUED FROM 1977-1979.
004632 04-15

PULMONARY
PULMONARY METABOLISM OF IMIPRAMINE IN THE RAT AND RABBIT: COMPARISON WITH HEPATIC METABOLISM.
002845 03-03

PULMONARY-ARTERIES
A COMPARISON OF THE CONTRACTILE RESPONSES OF THE RABBIT BASILAR AND PULMONARY-ARTERIES TO SYMPATHOMIMETIC AGONISTS: CHARACTERISTICS.
002670 03-03

PULSATILE
ADMINISTRATION OF ANTISOMATOSTATIN SERUM TO RATS REVERSES THE INHIBITION OF PULSATILE GROWTH-HORMONE SECRETION PRODUCED BY INJECTION OF METERGOLINE BUT NOT YOHIMBINE. (UNPUBLISHED PAPER).
000019 01-03
L TRYPTOPHAN INJECTION ENHANCES PULSATILE GROWTH-HORMONE SECRETION IN THE RAT. (UNPUBLISHED PAPER).
000020 01-03

PULVINAR
SELECTIVE SYNAPTIC ANTAGONISM BY ATROPINE AND ALPHA AMINOADIPATE OF PULVINAR AND CORTICAL AFFERENTS TO THE SUPRASYLVIAN VISUAL AREA (CLARE-BISHOP AREA).
002752 03-03

PUNISHED-BEHAVIOR
PRIOR AND ONGOING EXPERIENCE AS DETERMINANTS OF THE EFFECTS OF D-AMPHETAMINE AND CHLORPROMAZINE ON PUNISHED-BEHAVIOR.
000339 01-04

EFFECTS OF ACUTE AND CHRONIC INTERACTIONS OF DIAZEPAM AND D-AMPHETAMINE ON PUNISHED-BEHAVIOR OF RATS.
000386 01-04

PUNISHED-RESPONDING
SCHEDULE DEPENDENT CHANGE OF PUNISHED-RESPONDING AFTER DIAZEPAM IN RATS.
004165 04-04
SOME EFFECTS OF CLOZAPINE ON PUNISHED-RESPONDING BY MICE AND SQUIRREL-MONKEYS.
004224 04-04

PUNISHER
HISTAMINE AS A PUNISHER IN SQUIRREL-MONKEYS: EFFECTS OF PENTOBARBITAL, CHLORDIAZEPOXIDE AND H1-RECEPTOR AND H2-RECEPTOR ANTAGONISTS ON BEHAVIOR AND CARDIOVASCULAR RESPONSE.
004119 04-04

PUNISHMENT
THE EFFECTS OF D-AMPHETAMINE, CHLORDIAZEPOXIDE, AND PENTOBARBITAL ON BEHAVIOR MAINTAINED BY ESCAPE FROM PUNISHMENT IN PIGEONS. (PH.D. DISSERTATION).
001713 02-04
THE EFFECTS OF CHLORDIAZEPOXIDE-HCL ADMINISTRATION UPON PUNISHMENT AND CONDITIONED SUPPRESSION IN THE RAT.
001757 02-04
ATTENUATION OF THE EFFECTS OF PUNISHMENT BY ETHANOL: COMPARISONS WITH CHLORDIAZEPOXIDE.
001813 02-04
EFFECTS OF CHLORDIAZEPOXIDE AND D-AMPHETAMINE ON RESPONDING SUPPRESSED BY CONDITIONED PUNISHMENT.
003105 03-04

PUP
POSTNATAL ALCOHOL EXPOSURE IN THE RAT: ITS EFFECTS ON AVOIDANCE CONDITIONING, HEBB-WILLIAMS MAZE-PERFORMANCE, MATERNAL-BEHAVIOR, AND PUP DEVELOPMENT.
001580 02-04
EFFECT OF LITHIUM-CHLORIDE IN COYOTE PUP DIET.
001835 02-05

PUP-KILLING
RAT PUP-KILLING AND MATERNAL-BEHAVIOR IN MALE LONG-EVANS-RATS: PRENATAL STIMULATION AND POSTNATAL TESTOSTERONE.
003054 03-04

PUPILLARY
BILATERAL SKIN CONDUCTANCE AND THE PUPILLARY LIGHT DARK REFLEX: MANIPULATION BY CHLORPROMAZINE, HALOPERIDOL, SCOPOLAMINE, AND PLACEBO.
004544 04-13

PUPS
EFFECTS OF APOMORPHINE ON ESCAPE PERFORMANCE AND ACTIVITY IN DEVELOPING RAT PUPS TREATED WITH 6 HYDROXYDOPAMINE (6 OHDA).
000426 01-04
EFFECTS OF RESERPINE AND AMPHETAMINE ON THE DEVELOPMENT OF HYPERACTIVITY IN MATERNALLY-DEPRIVED RAT PUPS.
001654 02-04

PURE-WORD
A CASE OF REVERSIBLE PURE-WORD DEAFNESS DURING LITHIUM TOXICITY.
003481 03-15

PURIFICATION
IDENTIFICATION AND PARTIAL PURIFICATION OF A HYDROPHOBIC PROTEIN COMPONENT ASSOCIATED WITH (3H)SPIROPERIDOL BINDING-ACTIVITY. (UNPUBLISHED PAPER).
001007 02-01
DOPAMINE-RECEPTOR: ISOLATION, PURIFICATION, AND REGULATION.
001011 02-01
THE DOPAMINE-RECEPTOR: ISOLATION, PURIFICATION AND REGULATION.
003660 04-01
DOPAMINE-RECEPTOR PURIFICATION AND CHARACTERIZATION. (UNPUBLISHED PAPER).
003661 04-01
PURIFICATION AND CHARACTERIZATION OF RAT PHEOCHROMOCYTOMA DOPAMINE-BETA-HYDROXYLASE.
003664 04-01
PARTIAL PURIFICATION OF ACID SPHINGOMYELINASE FROM NORMAL AND PATHOLOGICAL (M. NIEMANN-PICK TYPE C) HUMAN BRAIN.
003671 04-01
PURIFICATION AND SUBUNIT STRUCTURE OF DNA-DEPENDENT RNA-POLYMERASE-BII FROM RAT-BRAIN NUCLEI.
003679 04-01
DETERMINATION OF PICOMOLE AMOUNTS OF DOPAMINE, NORADRENALINE, 3,4 DIHYDROXYPHENYLALANINE, 3,4 DIHYDROXYPHENYLACETIC-ACID, HOMOVANILLIC-ACID, AND 5 HYDROXYINDOLEACETIC-ACID IN NERVOUS-TISSUE AFTER ONE-STEP PURIFICATION ON SEPHADEX-G-10, USING HIGH.
004305 04-06

PURIFIED
AFFINITY CHROMATOGRAPHY OF THE BETA-ADRENERGIC-RECEPTOR AND
CHARACTERIZATION OF ANTIBODIES RAISED AGAINST PURIFIED
RECEPTOR PREPARATIONS.
001009 02-01
BIOCHEMICAL AND IMMUNOLOGICAL PROPERTIES OF THE MOUSE BRAIN
ENOLASES PURIFIED BY A SIMPLE METHOD.
003668 04-01

PURINE
THE EFFECT OF MORPHINE ON PURINE AND ACETYLCHOLINE RELEASE
FROM RAT-CEREBRAL-CORTEX: EVIDENCE FOR A PURINERGIC
COMPONENT IN MORPHINES ACTION.
000234 01-03
INCREASED BENZODIAZEPINE-RECEPTOR NUMBER ELICITED IN VITRO BY A
NOVEL PURINE, EMD-28422.
001475 02-03
INTERACTION BETWEEN PURINE AND BENZODIAZEPINE: INOSINE
REVERSES DIAZEPAM-INDUCED STIMULATION OF MOUSE
EXPLORATORY-BEHAVIOR.
002972 03-04
THE SITE OF ACTION OF MUSCLE-RELAXANT PURINE NUCLEOSIDES.
003742 04-03

PURINERGIC
DIAZEPAM POTENTIATION OF PURINERGIC DEPRESSION OF CENTRAL
NEURONS.
000233 01-03
THE EFFECT OF MORPHINE ON PURINE AND ACETYLCHOLINE RELEASE
FROM RAT-CEREBRAL-CORTEX: EVIDENCE FOR A PURINERGIC
COMPONENT IN MORPHINES ACTION.
000234 01-03
EFFECTS OF DIAZEPAM ON ADENOSINE AND ACETYLCHOLINE RELEASE
FROM RAT-CEREBRAL-CORTEX: FURTHER EVIDENCE FOR A PURINERGIC
MECHANISM IN ACTION OF DIAZEPAM.
001414 02-03

PURINES
PURINES AS ENDOGENOUS LIGANDS OF THE BENZODIAZEPINE-RECEPTOR.
000276 01-03

PURKINJE
EFFECTS OF ACUTE AND CHRONIC AMPHETAMINE TREATMENT ON
PURKINJE NEURON DISCHARGE IN RAT CEREBELLUM.
003793 04-03
THE EFFECT OF PROPRANOLOL AND ITS ISOMERS ON PURKINJE
NEURONES IN RAT CEREBELLUM.
004059 04-03

PURKINJE-CELL
INTERACTIONS OF NOREPINEPHRINE WITH PURKINJE-CELL RESPONSES TO
PUTATIVE AMINO-ACID NEUROTRANSMITTERS APPLIED BY
MICROIONTOPHORESIS.
000209 01-03

PURKINJE-CELLS
DISTRIBUTION OF 14C PHENYTOIN IN RAT PURKINJE-CELLS, CEREBELLAR
AND CEREBRAL NEURONAL TISSUE AFTER A SINGLE INTRAPERITONEAL
INJECTION.
000261 01-03
INHIBITORY ACTIONS OF TAUROCYAMINE, HYPOTAURINE,
HOMOTAURINE, TAURINE AND GABA ON SPIKE DISCHARGES OF
PURKINJE-CELLS, AND LOCALIZATION OF SENSITIVE SITES, IN GUINEA-
PIG CEREBELLAR SLICES.
002846 03-03
MODULATORY INTERACTIONS BETWEEN NOREPINEPHRINE AND TAURINE,
BETA ALANINE, GAMMA AMINOBUTYRIC-ACID AND MUSCIMOL
APPLIED IONTOPHORETICALLY TO CEREBELLAR PURKINJE-CELLS.
004058 04-03

PURKINJE-FIBRES
ELECTROPHYSIOLOGICAL-EFFECTS OF IMIPRAMINE ON BOVINE
VENTRICULAR-MUSCLE AND PURKINJE-FIBRES.
003988 04-03

PUROMYCIN
INHIBITION OF AMINOPEPTIDASE AND ACETYLCHOLINESTERASE BY
PUROMYCIN AND PUROMYCIN ANALOGS.
003835 04-03

PUTATIVE
DISSIMILAR EFFECTS OF NICOTINAMIDE AND INOSINE, PUTATIVE
ENDOGENOUS LIGANDS OF THE BENZODIAZEPINE-RECEPTORS, ON
PENTYLENETETRAZOL SEIZURES IN FOUR STRAINS OF MICE.
000173 01-03
INTERACTIONS OF NOREPINEPHRINE WITH PURKINJE-CELL RESPONSES TO
PUTATIVE AMINO-ACID NEUROTRANSMITTERS APPLIED BY
MICROIONTOPHORESIS.
000209 01-03
BRAIN-SPECIFIC BENZODIAZEPINE-RECEPTORS AND PUTATIVE
ENDOGENOUS BENZODIAZEPINE-LIKE COMPOUNDS.
000225 01-03
STUDIES ON THE PUTATIVE ANTICHOLINERGIC-EFFECTS OF
DESMETHYLIMIPRAMINE.
000228 01-03
LAMINAR DISTRIBUTION OF PUTATIVE NEUROTRANSMITTER AMINO-
ACIDS AND LIGAND BINDING-SITES IN THE DOG OLFACTORY-BULB.
002836 03-03
CHANGES IN REGIONAL BRAIN LEVELS OF AMINO-ACID PUTATIVE
NEUROTRANSMITTERS AFTER PROLONGED TREATMENT WITH THE

ANTICONVULSANT-DRUGS DIPHENYLHYDANTOIN, PHENOBARBITONE,
SODIUM-VALPROATE, ETHOSUXIMIDE, AND SULTHIAME IN THE RAT.
003961 04-03

PUTRESCINE
GABA DEPLETION AND BEHAVIOURAL-CHANGES PRODUCED BY
INTRAVENTRICULAR PUTRESCINE IN CHICKS.
000218 01-03

PYLORIC
GASTRIC AND PYLORIC MOTOR-RESPONSE TO SYMPATHETIC-NERVE
STIMULATION AFTER CHEMICAL SYMPATHECTOMY. (UNPUBLISHED
PAPER).
001337 02-03

PYRAMIDAL
EXCITATORY ACTION OF OPIOID-PEPTIDES AND OPIATES ON CULTURED
HIPPOCAMPAL PYRAMIDAL CELLS.
001241 02-03
EFFECTS OF PHENYTOIN ON PYRAMIDAL NEURONS OF THE RAT
HIPPOCAMPUS.
002750 03-03
ACETYLCHOLINE-INDUCED MODULATION OF HIPPOCAMPAL PYRAMIDAL
NEURONS.
003728 04-03

PYRAZIDOL
CLINICAL-TRIAL OF PYRAZIDOL IN ENDOGENOUS DEPRESSIVE-STATES.
002021 02-09
PYRAZIDOL IN THE TREATMENT OF DEPRESSIONS.
002055 02-09

PYRAZINOBENZODIAZEPINE
SYNTHESIS AND ANXIOLYTIC-ACTIVITY OF A SERIES OF
PYRAZINOBENZODIAZEPINE DERIVATIVES.
001089 02-02

PYRAZOLE
PYRAZOLE EXACERBATES HANDLING-INDUCED CONVULSIONS IN MICE.
004094 04-04

PYRAZOLOPYRIDINES
ACTION OF PYRAZOLOPYRIDINES AS MODULATORS OF
(3H)FLUNITRAZEPAM BINDING TO THE GABA/BENZODIAZEPINE-
RECEPTOR COMPLEX OF THE CEREBELLUM.
002909 03-03

PYRETHROID
REGIONAL CHANGES IN BRAIN GLUCOSE UTILIZATION IN RATS GIVEN A
PYRETHROID INSECTICIDE.
001838 02-05

PYRIDOXINE
5 HYDROXYTRYPTOPHAN AND PYRIDOXINE: THEIR EFFECTS IN YOUNG
CHILDREN WITH DOWNS-SYNDROME.
002161 02-11
CLINICAL SIGNIFICANCE OF PYRIDOXINE ADMINISTRATION IN L-DOPA
THERAPY OF PARKINSONISM.
003345 03-11
HYPERVENTILATION-SYNDROME; TREATMENT WITH L TRYPTOPHAN AND
PYRIDOXINE; PREDICTIVE VALUES OF XANTHURENIC-ACID EXCRETION.
004456 04-11

PYRIFORM
LESIONS OF AMYGDALA, PYRIFORM CORTEX AND OTHER BRAIN
STRUCTURES DUE TO DIPIPERIDINOETHANE INTOXICATION.
004273 04-05

PYRIMIDINE-PEPTIDE
ANTICANDIDAL-ACTIVITY OF PYRIMIDINE-PEPTIDE CONJUGATES.
001059 02-01

PYRIMIDOPYRIMIDINE
SYNTHESIS AND STRUCTURE-ACTIVITY RELATIONSHIP OF A
PYRIMIDOPYRIMIDINE DERIVATIVE WITH ANTIDEPRESSANT ACTIVITY.
003653 04-01

PYRITHIOXINE
INFLUENCE OF PYRITHIOXINE ON EXPERIMENTAL HYPOXIA IN RATS.
000077 01-03
INFLUENCE OF PYRITHIOXINE, MECLOPHENOXATE AND PIRACETAM ON
THE LEARNING PROCESS IN MAN.
000805 01-14

PYRITINOL
PYRITINOL ADMINISTRATION AS PART OF EPILEPSY TREATMENT IN
CHILDREN.
000671 01-11
EFFECT OF PYRITINOL AND PIRACETAM ON CHANGES IN FREE AMMONIA
LEVEL IN CNS TISSUE AFTER PARADOXICAL SLEEP-DEPRIVATION IN
RATS.
001199 02-03

PYROGEN
THE ROLE OF PROTEIN SYNTHESIS IN THE HYPOTHALAMIC MECHANISM
MEDIATING PYROGEN FEVER.
001454 02-03

PYRROLIDONE
SYNTHESIS AND PHARMACOLOGICAL PROPERTIES OF N-4 1
AZETIDINYLBUTYNYL 2 PYRROLIDONE, A HIGHLY POTENT
OXOTREMORINE-LIKE-AGENT.
003701 04-02

Subject Index

PYRROLOPYRIMIDINEDIONES
ANTICONVULSANT PROPERTIES OF SELECTED PYRROLOPYRIMIDINEDIONES
AND INTERMEDIATES.
003700 04-02

PYRUVATE
CHANGE IN PYRUVATE-DEHYDROGENASE ACTIVITY INFLUENCE PYRUVATE
SUPPORTED CALCIUM ACCUMULATION BY BRAIN MITOCHONDRIA.
(UNPUBLISHED PAPER).
001147 02-03

PYRUVATE-DEHYDROGENASE
CHANGE IN PYRUVATE-DEHYDROGENASE ACTIVITY INFLUENCE PYRUVATE
SUPPORTED CALCIUM ACCUMULATION BY BRAIN MITOCHONDRIA.
(UNPUBLISHED PAPER).
001147 02-03

P2-FRACTIONS
EFFECT OF MELANOSTATIN AND THYROLIBERIN ON THE BIOSYNTHESIS
AND RELEASE OF DOPAMINE BY RAT-BRAIN STRIATAL P2-FRACTIONS.
001472 02-03

QAE-SEPHADEX
AN IMPROVED ASSAY OF CYCLIC-NUCLEOTIDE-PHOSPHODIESTERASES
WITH QAE-SEPHADEX COLUMNS.
001860 02-06

QM-6008
A DOUBLE-BLIND CROSSED CLINICAL-STUDY WITH A NEW
PSYCHOPHARMACEUTICAL: TIADIPONE (QM-6008), DIAZEPAM, AND
A PLACEBO.
003153 03-07

QUALITY
THE EFFECTS OF TRIAZOLAM AND NITRAZEPAM ON SLEEP QUALITY,
MORNING VIGILANCE, AND PSYCHOMOTOR PERFORMANCE.
002330 02-14

QUALITY OF REPORTS OF CLINICAL-TRIALS SUBMITTED TO THE DRUG
INDUSTRY TO THE FINNISH AND SWEDISH CONTROL AUTHORITIES.
003599 03-17

POSSIBLE INFLUENCE OF OPIOID NORMETABOLITES ON THE ONSET,
MAGNITUDE AND QUALITY OF THE OPIOID ABSTINENCE-SYNDROME.
004610 04-15

QUANTAL
A STUDY OF THE QUANTAL (ALL-OR-NONE) CHANGE IN REFLEX LATENCY
PRODUCED BY OPIATE ANALGESICS.
000425 01-04

QUANTIFICATION
QUANTIFICATION OF NORADRENALINE IONTOPHORESIS.
002475 02-16

PSYCHOACTIVE-DRUG QUANTIFICATION BY VISUAL FLICKER SENSITIVITY
MEASUREMENT. (PH.D. DISSERTATION).
002485 02-16

IDENTIFICATION AND QUANTIFICATION OF 1,2,3,4 TETRAHYDRO-BETA-
CARBOLINE, 2 METHYL-TETRAHYDRO-BETA-CARBOLINE, AND 6
METHOXY-TETRAHYDRO-BETA-CARBOLINE AS IN VIVO CONSTITUENTS
OF RAT-BRAIN AND ADRENAL-GLAND.
002636 03-01

QUANTIFIED
STUDY OF THE EFFECTS OF PC-63-14 ON THE QUANTIFIED EEG.
003403 03-13

CORRELATED STUDY OF THE EFFECTS OF SE-5023 IN AN HYPOXIC
ATMOSPHERE ON QUANTIFIED EEG, VIGILANCE, MEMORY, AND
MOOD.
003440 03-14

QUANTIFYING
AN OBSERVATIONAL METHOD FOR QUANTIFYING THE BEHAVIOURAL-
EFFECTS OF DOPAMINE AGONISTS: CONTRASTING-EFFECTS OF D-
AMPHETAMINE AND APOMORPHINE.
002484 02-16

QUANTITATION
CHARACTERIZATION AND QUANTITATION OF ALPHA-ADRENERGIC-
RECEPTOR SUBTYPES IN RAT HYPOTHALAMUS.
002839 03-03

QUANTITATION AND COMPARISON OF PHENOBARBITAL LEVELS IN THE
PLASMA, SALIVA, AND CEREBROSPINAL-FLUID OF THE RAT, AND THE
DEMONSTRATION OF AN ALTERATION OF DRUG PASSAGE BY
ETHANOL.
003725 04-03

COMPARISON OF SPECTROFLUOROMETRIC AND GAS-
CHROMATOGRAPHY/MASS-SPECTROMETRY PROCEDURES FOR THE
QUANTITATION OF MORPHINE IN BLOOD AND BRAIN.
004692 04-16

QUANTITATIVE
EFFECT OF DIAZEPAM AND DESMETHYLDIAZEPAM IN SPASTICITY AND
RIGIDITY: A QUANTITATIVE STUDY OF REFLEXES AND PLASMA
CONCENTRATIONS.
000701 01-11

3 CHLORO-4-PHENYLSUCCINIMIDOBENZENESULFONAMIDE (GS-385), A
NEW ANTICONVULSANT: ITS QUANTITATIVE DETERMINATION,
PHARMACOKINETICS AND METABOLISM USING HIGH-PERFORMANCE
LIQUID-CHROMATOGRAPHY.
000705 01-11

CLASSIFICATION AND ASSESSMENT OF CEREBRAL BIOAVAILABILITY OF
LOPIRAZEPAM (D-12524) BY QUANTITATIVE EEG AND
PSYCHOMETRIC-ANALYSIS.
000720 01-11

CHOLINERGIC MECHANISMS IN MANIA AND DEPRESSION: QUESTIONS OF
SPECIFICITY.
004374 04-09
CLINICAL AND PRECLINICAL EXPERIENCE WITH CHOLINE-CHLORIDE IN
HUNTINGTONS-DISEASE AND TARDIVE-DYSKINESIA: UNANSWERED
QUESTIONS.
004604 04-15

QUICKLY-MADE
QUICKLY-MADE CANNULA FOR REPEATED CEREBROSPINAL-FLUID
SAMPLING IN RATS.
001879 02-06

QUINACRINE
QUINACRINE AND SEROTONIN BINDING BY SYNTHETIC MODELS FOR
HUMAN PLATELET DENSE-BODIES: EVALUATION OF THE ROLE OF
BINDING IN AMINE STORAGE. (UNPUBLISHED PAPER).
002219 02-13
TOXIC PSYCHOSIS FOLLOWING USE OF QUINACRINE.
003507 03-15

QUINIDINE
NONINTERACTION OF DIGITOXIN AND QUINIDINE.
000968 01-17
INTRAVENOUS QUINIDINE IN CONGESTIVE CARDIOMYOPATHY.
003352 03-11

QUININE
UNIMPAIRED QUININE METABOLISM IN RATS WITH VENTROMEDIAL
HYPOTHALAMIC LESIONS.
003821 04-03

QUINOLINE
MULTIPLE BENZODIAZEPINE-RECEPTORS: EVIDENCE OF A DISSOCIATION
BETWEEN ANTICONFLICT AND ANTICONVULSANT PROPERTIES BY PK-
8165 AND PK-9084 (TWO QUINOLINE DERIVATIVES).
003898 04-03

QUINUCLIDINYL
QUINUCLIDINYL BENZILATE BINDING IN HOUSEFLY HEADS AND RAT-
BRAIN.
003868 04-03

QUINUCLIDINYL-BENZILATE
(3H)QUINUCLIDINYL-BENZILATE BINDING TO MUSCARINIC-RECEPTORS
AND (3H)WB-4101 BINDING TO ALPHA-ADRENERGIC-RECEPTORS IN
RABBIT IRIS: COMPARISON OF RESULTS IN SLICES AND MICROSOMAL
FRACTIONS.
000299 01-03
A COMPARISON OF HUMAN MUSCARINIC CHOLINERGIC-RECEPTOR
RESPONSE TO A NUMBER OF PSYCHOTROPICS UTILIZING THE
RADIOLABELED ANTAGONIST, (3H) QUINUCLIDINYL-BENZILATE. (PH.D.
DISSERTATION).
002918 03-03

QUINUCLYDINYL-BENZYLATE
INHIBITION BY LOCAL ANESTHETICS, PHENTOLAMINE AND PROPRANOLOL
OF (3H)QUINUCLYDINYL-BENZYLATE BINDING TO CENTRAL
MUSCARINIC-RECEPTORS.
001097 02-03

QUINUPRAMINE
ANTIDEPRESSANT TREATMENT BY INTRAVENOUS ADMINISTRATION
COMPARED TO PERORAL ADMINISTRATION: A DOUBLE-BLIND STUDY
OF QUINUPRAMINE.
000552 01-08

QUIPAZINE
ANTINOCICEPTIVE COMPARISON OF QUIPAZINE AND MORPHINE.
000435 01-04
EFFECTS OF MALNUTRITION AND QUIPAZINE ON RAT-CEREBRAL-CORTEX
ATPASE ACTIVITY DURING DEVELOPMENT.
001276 02-03
ANTAGONISM OF 5 HYDROXYTRYPTAMINE-RECEPTORS BY QUIPAZINE.
001329 02-03
EFFECT OF QUIPAZINE ON BRAINSTEM MONOAMINE NEURONS
HISTOFLUORESCENCE STUDIES.
001477 02-03
EFFECT OF QUIPAZINE AND FLUOXETINE ON ANALGESIC-INDUCED
CATALEPSY AND ANTINOCICEPTION IN THE RAT.
001709 02-04
DU-24565, A QUIPAZINE DERIVATIVE, A POTENT SELECTIVE SEROTONIN
UPTAKE INHIBITOR.
002651 03-02
DRUG-INDUCED STIMULUS CONTROL AND THE CONCEPT OF BREAKING-
POINT: LSD AND QUIPAZINE.
003116 03-04
MODIFICATION OF DRUG-INDUCED CATATONIA AND TREMORS BY
QUIPAZINE IN RATS AND MICE.
004164 04-04
5 HYDROXYTRYPTAMINE-LIKE PROPERTIES OF M
CHLOROPHENYLPIPERAZINE: COMPARISON WITH QUIPAZINE.
004210 04-04

QUISQUALATE-RECEPTORS
DIFFERENTIATION OF KAINATE AND QUISQUALATE-RECEPTORS IN THE
CAT SPINAL-CORD BY SELECTIVE ANTAGONISMS WITH GAMMA
D(AND L) GLUTAMYLGLYCINE.
002696 03-03

R-15
DOPAMINE INHIBITS BURST-FIRING OF NEUROSECRETORY CELL R-15 IN
APLYSIA-CALIFORNICA: ESTABLISHMENT OF A DOSE-RESPONSE
RELATIONSHIP.
003806 04-03

R-41-468
RECEPTOR BINDING PROFILE OF R-41-468, A NOVEL ANTAGONIST AT 5
HT2-RECEPTORS.
002648 03-02

R-5135
A STEROID DERIVATIVE, R-5135, ANTAGONIZES THE GABA/
BENZODIAZEPINE-RECEPTOR INTERACTION.
003851 04-03

RABBIT
EVIDENCE FOR A RECEPTOR SUPERSENSITIVITY FOLLOWING IMPAIRMENT
OF CENTRAL SEROTONERGIC ACTIVITY IN THE RABBIT.
000041 01-03
RELEASE OF ENDOGENOUS NOREPINEPHRINE FROM A RABBIT CEREBRAL-
ARTERY.
000079 01-03
ENKEPHALIN-RECEPTOR IN THE RABBIT ILEUM.
000221 01-03
(3H)QUINUCLIDINYL-BENZILATE BINDING TO MUSCARINIC-RECEPTORS
AND (3H)WB-4101 BINDING TO ALPHA-ADRENERGIC-RECEPTORS IN
RABBIT IRIS: COMPARISON OF RESULTS IN SLICES AND MICROSOMAL
FRACTIONS.
000299 01-03
PARASYMPATHOMIMETIC-INFLUENCE OF CARBACHOL ON LOCAL
CEREBRAL BLOOD FLOW IN THE RABBIT BY A DIRECT VASODILATOR
ACTION AND AN INHIBITION OF THE SYMPATHETIC MEDIATED
VASOCONSTRICTION.
001109 02-03
PHOSPHOLIPID METABOLISM, CALCIUM-FLUX AND THE RECEPTOR-
MEDIATED INDUCTION OF CHEMOTAXIS IN RABBIT NEUTROPHILS.
(UNPUBLISHED PAPER).
001118 02-03
OPIATE-RECEPTORS IN THE RABBIT IRIS.
001200 02-03
INHIBITION OF ACH RELEASE BY PROSTAGLANDIN-E1 IN THE RABBIT
SUPERIOR-CERVICAL-GANGLION.
001205 02-03
COMPARISON OF THE EFFECTS OF CENTRAL ADMINISTRATION OF SERINE
AND GLYCINE ON BODY-TEMPERATURE OF THE RABBIT.
001248 02-03
INTERNEURONES ARE PROBABLY NOT INVOLVED IN THE PRESYNAPTIC
DOPAMINERGIC CONTROL OF DOPAMINE RELEASE IN RABBIT
CAUDATE-NUCLEUS.
001298 02-03
FURTHER CHARACTERIZATION OF THE BINDING OF SUBSTANCE-P TO A
FRACTION FROM RABBIT BRAIN ENRICHED IN SYNAPTIC MEMBRANES.
001394 02-03
PERIPHERAL AUTONOMIC-MECHANISMS AND PAVLOVIAN-CONDITIONING
IN THE RABBIT (ORYCTOLAGUS-CUNICULUS).
001560 02-04
SENSORY AND ASSOCIATIVE-EFFECTS OF LSD ON CLASSICAL APPETITIVE-
CONDITIONING OF THE RABBIT JAW MOVEMENT RESPONSE.
001637 02-04
PERIPHERAL 6 HYDROXYDOPAMINE ADMINISTRATION IN THE RABBIT
(ORYCTOLAGUS-CUNICULUS): EFFECTS ON PAVLOVIAN-CONDITIONING.
001668 02-04
PHENOBARBITONE INTERACTION WITH ORAL CONTRACEPTIVE STEROIDS
IN THE RABBIT AND RAT.
001832 02-05
EFFECTS OF AMITRIPTYLINE AND CLOMIPRAMINE IN THE ISOLATED,
PERFUSED RABBIT HEART.
001852 02-05
A COMPARISON OF THE CONTRACTILE RESPONSES OF THE RABBIT
BASILAR AND PULMONARY-ARTERIES TO SYMPATHOMIMETIC
AGONISTS: CHARACTERISTICS.
002670 03-03
TEMPORAL PATTERNING OF NEURONAL ACTIVITY DURING THERMAL AND
NEUROCHEMICAL STIMULATION OF THE PREOPTIC/ANTERIOR
HYPOTHALAMUS OF THE AWAKE RABBIT.
002737 03-03
MODULATION BY ENDOGENOUS DOPAMINE OF THE RELEASE OF
ACETYLCHOLINE IN THE CAUDATE-NUCLEUS OF THE RABBIT.
002751 03-03
EVIDENCE FOR THE PRESENCE OF TWO TYPES OF MONOAMINE-OXIDASE
IN RABBIT CHOROID PLEXUS AND THEIR ROLE IN BREAKDOWN OF
AMINES INFLUENCING CEREBROSPINAL-FLUID FORMATION.
002807 03-03
PULMONARY METABOLISM OF IMIPRAMINE IN THE RAT AND RABBIT:
COMPARISON WITH HEPATIC METABOLISM.
002845 03-03
OPIATE-RECEPTORS AND SLEEP. II. EFFECTS OF MICROINJECTIONS OF
ETHYL-ALCOHOL AND PENTOBARBITAL IN THE MEDIAN THALAMUS,
PERIAQUEDUCTAL GRAY MATTER AND NUCLEUS-TRACTUS-SOLITARIUS
OF THE RABBIT.
002917 03-03

PREJUNCTIONAL ACTIONS OF PIRIBEDIL ON THE ISOLATED KIDNEY OF THE
RABBIT: COMPARISON WITH APOMORPHINE.
003749 04-03
COMPARISON OF THE EFFECT OF INTRAVENOUS ADMINISTRATION OF D
LYSERGIC-ACID-DIETHYLAMIDE ON FREE AND MEMBRANE-BOUND
POLYSOMES IN THE RABBIT BRAIN.
003831 04-03
CELL-FREE TRANSLATION OF FREE AND MEMBRANE-BOUND POLYSOMES
AND POLYADENYLATED MRNA FROM RABBIT BRAIN FOLLOWING
ADMINISTRATION OF D LYSERGIC-ACID-DIETHYLAMIDE IN VIVO.
003832 04-03
STUDIES ON THE KINETIC PROPERTIES OF TRYPTOPHAN-HYDROXYLASE OF
RABBIT MESENCEPHALON AND PONS-MEDULLA: EFFECT OF LONG-
TERM-TREATMENT WITH NEUROLEPTICS AND ANTIDEPRESSANTS.
003852 04-03
EFFECT OF MEDIAN RAPHE STIMULATION ON HIPPOCAMPAL SEIZURE
DISCHARGE INDUCED BY CARBACHOL IN THE RABBIT.
003951 04-03
HYPOTENSION ALTERS THE RELEASE OF CATECHOLAMINES IN THE
HYPOTHALAMUS OF THE CONSCIOUS RABBIT.
003968 04-03
EFFECT OF PROSTAGLANDIN-D2, PROSTAGLANDIN-E2 AND
PROSTAGLANDIN-F2ALPHA ON CATECHOLAMINE RELEASE FROM SLICES
OF RAT AND RABBIT BRAIN.
003983 04-03
THE EFFECT OF LITHIUM-HYDROXYBUTYRATE ON THE BIOELECTRICAL-
ACTIVITY OF THE CORTEX AND SOME SUBCORTICAL STRUCTURES OF
THE RABBIT BRAIN.
003994 04-03
THE EFFECTS OF THYROTROPIN-RELEASING-HORMONE ON CYCLIC-AMP
ACCUMULATION IN RABBIT CEREBROCORTICAL TISSUE IN THE
PRESENCE AND ABSENCE OF CNS DEPRESSANTS.
004010 04-03
BENZODIAZEPINE-RECEPTOR: HETEROGENEITY IN RABBIT BRAIN.
004060 04-03
SEROTONERGIC MECHANISM IN SEIZURES KINDLED FROM THE RABBIT
AMYGDALA.
004227 04-04
THE EFFECTS OF NEFOPAM ON BLOOD ACID BASE STATUS IN THE RABBIT:
INTERACTIONS WITH MORPHINE IN THE MOUSE AND RABBIT.
004279 04-05

RABBITS
EFFECTS OF BRAIN-MONOAMINE DEPLETION ON THERMOREGULATORY
RESPONSES OF RABBITS TO DIFFERENT HYPOTHALAMIC
TEMPERATURES.
000190 01-03
THE EFFECT OF CORTISOL MICROIONOPHORETIC-APPLICATIONS ON THE
ACTIVITY OF HIPPOCAMPAL NEURONS IN UNRESTRAINED RABBITS.
001123 02-03
EFFECTS OF LISURIDE ON BODY-TEMPERATURE OF RATS AND RABBITS:
RELATION TO MICROSOMAL BIOTRANSFORMATION AND
DOPAMINERGIC-RECEPTOR STIMULATION.
001161 02-03
CENTRAL ADMINISTRATION OF SERINE CAUSES HYPOTHERMIA AND
INHIBITS FEVER IN RABBITS.
001247 02-03
LARYNGEAL-EFFECTS OF SEROTONIN IN RABBITS.
001501 02-03
VESTIBULO-OCULAR REFLEXES IN RABBITS: REDUCTION BY INTRAVENOUS
INJECTION OF DIAZEPAM.
001566 02-04
SUPPRESSION OF AMPHETAMINE-INDUCED EEG AROUSAL IN THE
HIPPOCAMPUS OF HALOPERIDOL TREATED RABBITS.
002683 03-03
CHRONOLOGICAL ELECTROENCEPHALOGRAPHIC AND
NEUROPHARMACOLOGICAL-STUDY IN CORTICAL KINDLING RABBITS.
002761 03-03
EVOKED-POTENTIAL STUDIES OF PORCINE CALCITONIN IN RABBITS.
002936 03-03
NEURONAL SENSITIVITY OF SOME BRAIN REGIONS TO ANGIOTENSIN-II IN
RABBITS.
003716 04-03
OPIATE-EFFECTS IN THE AMYGDALA CENTRAL NUCLEUS ON HEART RATE
CONDITIONING IN RABBITS.
003798 04-03
NYSTAGMIC RESPONSES OF HIPPOCAMPAL ORIGIN WITH REFERENCE TO
EXCITABILITY OF CHOLINERGIC AND ADRENERGIC COMPONENTS
INVOLVED IN THE HIPPOCAMPUS OF RABBITS.
003842 04-03
CONVERGENT PROPERTIES AND CHEMICAL SENSITIVITY OF MIDBRAIN
RETICULAR FORMATION NEURONS OF UNANESTHETIZED RABBITS.
003972 04-03
INHIBITORY-ACTION OF THE COMBINATION OF AMINOPYRINE AND
SECOBARBITAL ON EEG ACTIVATION, NEOCORTICAL RECRUITING AND
AUGMENTING RESPONSES IN RABBITS.
004022 04-03
EFFECTS OF SUBCHRONIC DESMETHYLIMIPRAMINE (DMI) TREATMENT OF
THE CLASSICALLY CONDITIONED EYEBLINK RESPONSE IN RABBITS.
004180 04-04

BEHAVIORAL-PHARMACOLOGY OF TETRAHYDROCANNABINOL
CONVULSIONS IN RABBITS.
004288 04-06

RADICAL
EFFECT OF STRUCTURE ON PHENOTHIAZINE CATION RADICAL REACTIONS
IN AQUEOUS BUFFERS.
000014 01-02
SPECTRA OF RADICAL CATIONS OF PHENOTHIAZINE DERIVATIVES IN
SOLUTION AND SOLID STATE.
003673 04-01

RADIOACTIVE
THEORY, PROCEDURE, AND APPLICATIONS OF THE RADIOACTIVE
DEOXYGLUCOSE METHOD FOR THE MEASUREMENT OF LOCAL GLUCOSE
UTILIZATION IN THE CENTRAL-NERVOUS-SYSTEM. (UNPUBLISHED
PAPER).
001877 02-06

RADIOAUTOGRAPHY
CHARACTERIZATION AND RADIOAUTOGRAPHY OF (3H)LSD BINDING BY
RAT-BRAIN SLICES IN VITRO: THE EFFECT OF 5 HYDROXYTRYPTAMINE.
001369 02-03

RADIOCALCIUM
UPTAKE OF RADIOCALCIUM BY NERVE-ENDINGS ISOLATED FROM RAT-
BRAIN: KINETIC STUDIES.
003814 04-03
UPTAKE OF RADIOCALCIUM BY NERVE-ENDINGS ISOLATED FROM RAT-
BRAIN: PHARMACOLOGICAL-STUDIES.
003815 04-03

RADIOHISTOCHEMICAL
RADIOHISTOCHEMICAL STUDIES OF BENZODIAZEPINE AND GABA-
RECEPTORS AND THEIR INTERACTIONS.
002644 03-01

RADIOIMMUNOASSAY
APPLICATION OF A RADIOIMMUNOASSAY SCREENING-TEST FOR
DETECTION AND MANAGEMENT OF PHENCYCLIDINE INTOXICATION.
000859 01-15
LEVORPHANOL: RADIOIMMUNOASSAY AND PLASMA CONCENTRATION
PROFILES IN DOG AND MAN.
000898 01-16
DETERMINATION OF DOSE PLASMA CONCENTRATION RELATIONSHIP OF
PHENOBARBITAL IN EPILEPTIC-PATIENTS BY A NEW SPECIFIC
RADIOIMMUNOASSAY.
000902 01-16
RADIOIMMUNOASSAY FOR FLUPHENAZINE IN HUMAN PLASMA.
000905 01-16
RADIOIMMUNOASSAY FOR TOTAL DOXEPIN AND N DESMETHYLDOXEPIN
IN PLASMA.
002499 02-16
PLASMA FLUPHENAZINE LEVELS BY RADIOIMMUNOASSAY IN
SCHIZOPHRENIC-PATIENTS TREATED WITH DEPOT INJECTIONS OF
FLUPHENAZINE-DECANOATE.
002510 02-16
SPECIFIC AND SENSITIVE RADIOIMMUNOASSAY FOR 3 METHOXY-4-
HYDROXYPHENYLETHYLENEGLYCOL (MOPEG).
002776 03-03
A RADIOIMMUNOASSAY FOR EPENDYMINS BETA AND GAMMA: TWO
GOLDFISH BRAIN PROTEINS INVOLVED IN BEHAVIORAL PLASTICITY.
003677 04-01
VASOPRESSIN STIMULATES RELEASE OF BETA LIPOTROPIN AND BETA
ENDORPHIN IN CONSCIOUS RATS AS MEASURED BY
RADIOIMMUNOASSAY OF UNEXTRACTED PLASMA.
003715 04-03
RADIOIMMUNOASSAY OF TRICYCLIC-ANTIDEPRESSANTS.
004674 04-16
A COMPARISON OF RADIOIMMUNOASSAY WITH SPECTROPHOTOMETRY
FOR THE DETERMINATION OF PLASMA DIPHENYLHYDANTOIN
CONCENTRATIONS.
004684 04-16
SERUM LEVELS OF BUTORPHANOL BY RADIOIMMUNOASSAY.
004691 04-16
A SENSITIVE BENZODIAZEPINE RADIOIMMUNOASSAY OF BROAD
SPECIFICITY.
004693 04-16

RADIOIMMUNOLOGIC
KINETICS AND BIOTRANSFORMATION OF LORMETAZEPAM: II.
RADIOIMMUNOLOGIC DETERMINATIONS IN PLASMA AND URINE OF
YOUNG AND ELDERLY SUBJECTS: FIRST-PASS EFFECT.
004516 04-13

RADIOLABELED
EFFECTS OF HALOPEMIDE ON POTASSIUM-INDUCED RELEASE OF
RADIOLABELED NEUROTRANSMITTERS FROM RAT CEREBROCORTICAL
SLICES IN VITRO.
001347 02-03
A COMPARISON OF HUMAN MUSCARINIC CHOLINERGIC-RECEPTOR
RESPONSE TO A NUMBER OF PSYCHOTROPICS UTILIZING THE
RADIOLABELED ANTAGONIST, (3H) QUINUCLIDINYL-BENZILATE. (PH.D.
DISSERTATION).
002918 03-03

RADIOLABELLED
A COMPARISON OF THE EFFECTS OF METHYLPHENIDATE AND
AMPHETAMINE ON THE SIMULTANEOUS RELEASE OF RADIOLABELLED
DOPAMINE AND P OR M TYRAMINE FROM RAT STRIATAL SLICES.
001207 02-03

RADIOLIGAND
RADIOLIGAND BINDING STUDIES: EVIDENCE FOR MULTIPLE DOPAMINE-
RECEPTORS.
001186 02-03
PSYCHOTROPIC-DRUGS DO NOT INTERFERE WITH RADIOLIGAND ASSAYS
FOR PROLACTIN, CORTISOL, AND GROWTH-HORMONE.
002511 02-16
KAINATE LESION DISSOCIATES STRIATAL DOPAMINE-RECEPTOR
RADIOLIGAND BINDING-SITES.
002803 03-03

RADIORECEPTOR
RADIORECEPTOR LABELING OF PRESYNAPTIC AND POSTSYNAPTIC
DOPAMINE-RECEPTORS.
001511 02-03
DETERMINATION OF GABA LEVELS BY A (3H)MUSCIMOL RADIORECEPTOR
ASSAY.
003135 03-06
NEUROLEPTIC SERUM LEVELS MEASURED BY RADIORECEPTOR ASSAY
AND CLINICAL-RESPONSE IN SCHIZOPHRENIC-PATIENTS.
003199 03-08
MEASUREMENT OF NEUROLEPTIC CONCENTRATIONS BY GLC AND
RADIORECEPTOR ASSAY.
004682 04-16
A RAPID AND SENSITIVE RADIORECEPTOR ASSAY FOR TERTIARY AMINE
TRICYCLIC-ANTIDEPRESSANTS.
004689 04-16

RAGE
PROPRANOLOL IN THE TREATMENT OF RAGE AND VIOLENT-BEHAVIOR IN
PATIENTS WITH CHRONIC-BRAIN-SYNDROMES.
003394 03-11

RANA-PIPIENS
VASOTOCIN, PROSTAGLANDIN, AND FEMALE REPRODUCTIVE BEHAVIOR
IN THE FROG, RANA-PIPIENS.
002978 03-04

RANDOM
THE USE OF VILOXAZINE IN HOSPITALIZED DEPRESSED-PATIENTS:
RANDOM COMPARISON WITH IMIPRAMINE IN A DOUBLE-BLIND TRIAL.
001998 02-09

RANDOMISED-TRIAL
A PROSPECTIVE RANDOMISED-TRIAL ON THE EFFECT OF MONITORING
PLASMA ANTICONVULSANT LEVELS IN EPILEPSY.
003314 03-11

RANDOMIZED-ORDER
EFFICACY AND PATTERN VALENCE OF PSYCHOACTIVE-DRUGS: A NEW
METHOD OF COMPARING DRUGS APPLIED TO IDENTICAL PATIENTS IN
RANDOMIZED-ORDER.
000699 01-11

RAPHE-MAGNUS
HYPOALGESIA INDUCED BY MICROINJECTION OF A NOREPINEPHRINE
ANTAGONIST IN THE RAPHE-MAGNUS: REVERSAL BY INTRATHECAL
ADMINISTRATION OF A SEROTONIN ANTAGONIST.
000121 01-03
REVERSIBLE INACTIVATION OF RAPHE-MAGNUS NEURONS: EFFECTS ON
NOCICEPTIVE THRESHOLD AND MORPHINE-INDUCED ANALGESIA.
000240 01-03
THE EFFECT OF MORPHINE ON THE CONTENT OF SEROTONIN, 5
HYDROXYINDOLEACETIC-ACID AND SUBSTANCE-P IN THE NUCLEI
RAPHE-MAGNUS AND RETICULARIS-GIGANTOCELLULARIS.
001328 02-03
EFFECTS OF RAPHE-MAGNUS AND RAPHE-PALLIDUS LESIONS ON
MORPHINE-INDUCED ANALGESIA AND SPINAL-CORD MONOAMINES.
001420 02-03

RAPHE-PALLIDUS
EFFECTS OF RAPHE-MAGNUS AND RAPHE-PALLIDUS LESIONS ON
MORPHINE-INDUCED ANALGESIA AND SPINAL-CORD MONOAMINES.
001420 02-03

RAPID-EYE-MOVEMENT
DOES RAPID-EYE-MOVEMENT SLEEP PLAY A ROLE IN BRAIN
DEVELOPMENT?
004091 04-04

RAPIDITY
RAPIDITY OF CLINICAL ANTIDEPRESSANT RESPONSE TO IMIPRAMINE.
(UNPUBLISHED PAPER).
003164 03-07

RASHES
MITIGATING ACUTE SKIN RASHES AND NAUSEA FROM LITHIUM.
004661 04-15

RAT-BRAIN
ENHANCEMENT OF RAT-BRAIN METABOLISM OF A TRYPTOPHAN LOAD
BY CHRONIC ETHANOL ADMINISTRATION.
000022 01-03
EFFECT OF AMINOOXYACETIC-ACID (AOAA) ON GABA LEVELS IN SOME
PARTS OF THE RAT-BRAIN.
000040 01-03

CIRCADIAN-RHYTHM OF CYCLIC-NUCLEOTIDE AND GABA LEVELS IN THE
RAT-BRAIN.
000049 01-03
COMPARATIVE-EFFECTS OF P CHLOROAMPHETAMINE AND L P
CHLOROPHENYLPIPERAZINE ON 5 HYDROXYINDOLE CONCENTRATION IN
RAT-BRAIN.
000101 01-03
INHIBITION OF (3H)NALOXONE BINDING IN HOMOGENATES OF RAT-
BRAIN BY ESEROLINE, A DRUG, WITH ANALGESIC ACTIVITY, RELATED
TO PHYSOSTIGMINE.
000104 01-03
MODIFICATION OF DOPAMINERGIC-RECEPTOR SENSITIVITY IN RAT-BRAIN
AFTER AMYGDALOID KINDLING.
000106 01-03
THE ROLE OF INTRANEURONAL 5 HT AND OF TRYPTOPHAN-
HYDROXYLASE ACTIVATION IN THE CONTROL OF 5 HT SYNTHESIS IN
RAT-BRAIN SLICES INCUBATED IN K-ENRICHED MEDIUM.
000123 01-03
HIGH-AFFINITY BINDING OF 3H ETHYLKETOCYCLAZOCINE TO RAT-BRAIN
HOMOGENATE.
000124 01-03
COMPARTMENTATION OF CATECHOLAMINES IN RAT-BRAIN: EFFECTS OF
AGONISTS AND ANTAGONISTS.
000125 01-03
EFFECTS OF ACUTE AND CHRONIC PHENCYCLIDINE ON
NEUROTRANSMITTER ENZYMES IN RAT-BRAIN.
000134 01-03
EFFECTS OF MORPHINE AND OTHER CENTRALLY-ACTING DRUGS ON 3,4
DIHYDROXYPHENYLETHYLENE-GLYCOL-SULFATE (DOPEG-SO4) IN RAT-
BRAIN.
000136 01-03
CHARACTERIZATION OF 3H GABA-RECEPTOR BINDING TO RAT-BRAIN
SYNAPTOSOMAL MEMBRANES: EFFECT OF NONGABAERGIC
COMPOUNDS.
000139 01-03
DIFFERENTIAL-EFFECTS OF N DIPROPYLACETATE AND AMINOOXYACETIC-
ACID ON GAMMA AMINOBUTYRIC-ACID LEVELS IN DISCRETE AREAS
OF RAT-BRAIN.
000140 01-03
DIMETHYLAMINOETHANOL (DEANOL) METABOLISM IN RAT-BRAIN AND
ITS EFFECT ON ACETYLCHOLINE SYNTHESIS.
000150 01-03
INHIBITION OF MONOAMINE-OXIDASE BY CLORGYLINE AND DEPRENYL IN
CIRCUMVENTRICULAR STRUCTURES OF RAT-BRAIN.
000159 01-03
THE MONOAMINE-OXIDASE-INHIBITORS CLORGYLINE AND L DEPRENYL
ALSO AFFECT THE UPTAKE OF DOPAMINE, NORADRENALINE AND
SEROTONIN BY RAT-BRAIN SYNAPTOSOMAL PREPARATIONS.
000171 01-03
3H PRAZOSIN BINDS SPECIFICALLY TO ALPHA1-ADRENOCEPTORS IN RAT-
BRAIN.
000205 01-03
INTERACTIONS OF OXYPERTINE WITH RAT-BRAIN MONOAMINE-
RECEPTORS.
000212 01-03
ACUTE AND CHRONIC EFFECTS OF NEUROLEPTICS AND ACUTE EFFECTS OF
APOMORPHINE AND AMPHETAMINE ON DOPAMINE TURNOVER IN
CORPUS-STRIATUM AND SUBSTANTIA-NIGRA OF THE RAT-BRAIN.
000215 01-03
DECREASED SPIROPERIDOL AND LSD BINDING IN RAT-BRAIN AFTER
CONTINUOUS AMPHETAMINE.
000216 01-03
STEREOSPECIFIC NICOTINE-RECEPTORS ON RAT-BRAIN MEMBRANES.
000254 01-03
EFFECTS OF DES-TYR-GAMMA-ENDORPHIN ON DOPAMINE RELEASE FROM
VARIOUS RAT-BRAIN REGIONS IN VITRO.
000264 01-03
BIOCHEMICAL-PROPERTIES OF SPIPERONE BINDING TO RAT-BRAIN
MEMBRANES.
000294 01-03
EFFECTS OF CHRONIC DIETARY LITHIUM ON ACTIVITY AND REGULATION
OF NA-K-ADENOSINE-TRIPHOSPHATASE IN RAT-BRAIN.
000297 01-03
INTERACTION OF ANTIDEPRESSANTS WITH CLONIDINE ON RAT-BRAIN
TOTAL 3 METHOXY-4-HYDROXYPHENYLGLYCOL.
000300 01-03
LITHIUM: EFFECTS ON SEROTONIN-RECEPTORS IN RAT-BRAIN.
000304 01-03
HALOTHANE EFFECT ON C-AMP GENERATION AND HYDROLYSIS IN RAT-
BRAIN.
000305 01-03
ACTION OF THE ANTIDEPRESSANT PRIDEFINE (AHR-1118) ON BIOGENIC-
AMINES IN THE RAT-BRAIN.
000312 01-03
SELECTIVE STORAGE IN VIVO OF 5,6 ADTN IN DOPAMINE RICH AREAS OF
THE RAT-BRAIN.
000324 01-03

THE EFFECTS OF MUSCARINIC-RECEPTOR BLOCKERS ON THE TURNOVER-RATE OF ACETYLCHOLINE IN VARIOUS REGIONS OF THE RAT-BRAIN.
000328 01-03

INHIBITION OF (3H)DIAZEPAM BINDING TO RAT-BRAIN CORTICAL SYNAPTOSOMAL MEMBRANES BY ADENOSINE UPTAKE BLOCKERS.
000330 01-03

THE IDENTITY AND HYPOTHALAMIC ORIGIN OF CHOLECYSTOKININ IN RAT-BRAIN AND POSTERIOR PITUITARY AND ITS POSSIBLE ROLE IN REGULATION OF NEUROSECRETION. (UNPUBLISHED PAPER).
001003 02-01

AN HPLC AND RIA ANALYSIS OF THE CHOLECYSTOKININ-PEPTIDES IN RAT-BRAIN. (UNPUBLISHED PAPER).
001004 02-01

IN VITRO AUTORADIOGRAPHY OF OPIATE-RECEPTORS IN RAT-BRAIN SUGGESTS LOCI OF OPIATE-ERGIC PATHWAYS. (UNPUBLISHED PAPER).
001025 02-01

BIOCHEMICAL-LOCALIZATION AND CHARACTERIZATION OF BOMBESIN-LIKE-PEPTIDES IN DISCRETE REGIONS OF RAT-BRAIN. (UNPUBLISHED PAPER).
001046 02-01

PRODUCTION OF A SPECIFIC ANTISERUM TO RAT-BRAIN GLUTAMIC-ACID-DECARBOXYLASE (GAD) BY INJECTION OF AN ANTIGEN ANTIBODY COMPLEX. (UNPUBLISHED PAPER).
001047 02-01

THE INFLUENCE OF PENTIFYLLINE AND THEOPHYLLINE ON REACTION KINETICS OF CATECHOLAMINE STIMULATED ATPASE FROM RAT-BRAIN.
001052 02-01

TETRAHYDRO-BETA-CARBOLINES AND CORRESPONDING TRYPTAMINES: IN VITRO INHIBITION OF SEROTONIN, DOPAMINE AND NORADRENALINE UPTAKE IN RAT-BRAIN SYNAPTOSOMES.
001078 02-02

THE EFFECT OF LITHIUM ON THE INCORPORATION OF 3H GLUCOSAMINE INTO GLYCOPEPTIDES AND THE TRANSFORMATION OF 3H GLUCOSAMINE INTO SIALIC-ACID IN RAT-BRAIN.
001209 02-03

THE EFFECT OF GABAMIMETICS ON NEUROTRANSMITTER-RECEPTOR BINDING AND FUNCTION IN RAT-BRAIN. (PH.D. DISSERTATION).
001221 02-03

A DEMONSTRATION OF NALOXONE PRECIPITATED OPIATE WITHDRAWAL ON SINGLE NEURONES IN THE MORPHINE-TOLERANT/DEPENDENT RAT-BRAIN.
001234 02-03

EFFECT OF 2 P CHLOROPHENYL-CYCLOPROPYLAMINE ON 5 HYDROXYINDOLE CONCENTRATION AND MONOAMINE-OXIDASE ACTIVITY IN RAT-BRAIN.
001237 02-03

CHOLECYSTOKININ-PEPTIDES PRODUCE MARKED REDUCTION OF DOPAMINE TURNOVER IN DISCRETE AREAS IN THE RAT-BRAIN FOLLOWING INTERAVENTRICULAR INJECTION.
001239 02-03

ALPHA2-ADRENOCEPTORS IN RAT-BRAIN: THE DIVALENT-CATION SITE.
001246 02-03

MULTIPLE RECEPTORS FOR SEROTONIN IN THE RAT-BRAIN.
001269 02-03

CHANGES IN ALPHA-ADRENERGIC-RECEPTORS IN RAT-BRAIN IN VITRO BY PREINCUBATION WITH ALPHA-ADRENERGIC LIGANDS.
001272 02-03

REGIONAL RELEASE OF (3H)ADENOSINE DERIVATIVES FROM RAT-BRAIN IN VIVO: EFFECT OF EXCITATORY AMINO-ACIDS, OPIATE AGONISTS, AND BENZODIAZEPINES.
001303 02-03

EVIDENCE FOR AN ENDOGENOUS COMPOUND INTERFERING WITH 3H DIAZEPAM BINDING TO RAT-BRAIN MEMBRANES.
001308 02-03

DOPAMINE-RECEPTOR BLOCKADE IN RAT-BRAIN AFTER ACUTE AND SUBCHRONIC-TREATMENT WITH TRICYCLIC-ANTIDEPRESSANTS.
001314 02-03

ABUNDANCE AND LOCATION OF 125I SALMON CALCITONIN BINDING-SITE IN RAT-BRAIN.
001320 02-03

EFFECT OF SINGLE AND REPEATED ELECTROCONVULSIVE-SHOCK ON SEROTONERGIC SYSTEM IN RAT-BRAIN -- I. METABOLIC-STUDIES.
001332 02-03

EFFECTS OF PRENATAL METHADONE ON RAT-BRAIN CATECHOLAMINES.
001367 02-03

CHARACTERIZATION AND RADIOAUTOGRAPHY OF (3H)LSD BINDING BY RAT-BRAIN SLICES IN VITRO: THE EFFECT OF 5 HYDROXYTRYPTAMINE.
001369 02-03

LOCAL CEREBRAL GLUCOSE UTILIZATION (LCGU) IN RAT-BRAIN DURING HYPOXEMIA. (UNPUBLISHED PAPER).
001380 02-03

ACTIVATION OF PRESYNAPTIC ALPHA NORADRENALINE-RECEPTORS IN RAT-BRAIN BY THE POTENT DOPAMINE-MIMETIC N,N DIPROPYL-ADTN.
001390 02-03

INTERACTION OF HISTAMINE H2-RECEPTOR BLOCKING-DRUGS WITH THE NORADRENERGIC SYSTEM IN RAT-BRAIN AND HEART.
001397 02-03

EFFECT OF CHLORPROMAZINE ON CELL PROLIFERATION IN THE DEVELOPING RAT-BRAIN. A COMBINED BIOCHEMICAL-STUDY AND MORPHOLOGICAL-STUDY.
001407 02-03

RAT-BRAIN STEADY-STATE LEVELS OF CYCLIC-NUCLEOTIDES AS AN ENDPOINT OF LSD-LIKE HALLUCINOGEN EFFECTS. (PH.D. DISSERTATION).
001426 02-03

MORPHINE ANALGESIA FOLLOWING ITS INFUSION INTO DIFFERENT LIQUOR SPACES IN RAT-BRAIN.
001429 02-03

A HIGH-AFFINITY GTP BINDING-SITE IN RAT-BRAIN. (UNPUBLISHED PAPER).
001442 02-03

DECREASE IN (3H) SEROTONIN BINDING IN RAT-BRAIN PRODUCED BY THE REPEATED ADMINISTRATION OF EITHER MONOAMINE-OXIDASE-INHIBITORS ON CENTRALLY-ACTING SEROTONIN AGONISTS.
001463 02-03

EFFECT OF REPEATED TREATMENT WITH NEUROLEPTICS ON DOPAMINE METABOLISM IN CELL BODIES AND TERMINALS OF DOPAMINERGIC-SYSTEMS IN THE RAT-BRAIN.
001464 02-03

EFFECT OF MELANOSTATIN AND THYROLIBERIN ON THE BIOSYNTHESIS AND RELEASE OF DOPAMINE BY RAT-BRAIN STRIATAL P2-FRACTIONS.
001472 02-03

TOXICITY OF OXYGEN IN IRON RICH AREAS OF RAT-BRAIN. (UNPUBLISHED PAPER).
001498 02-03

HIGH-AFFINITY DOPAMINE-RECEPTORS (D3) IN RAT-BRAIN.
001509 02-03

ACTIONS OF ENKEPHALIN, MU AND PARTIAL AGONIST ANALGESICS ON ACETYLCHOLINE TURNOVER IN RAT-BRAIN.
001541 02-03

CAPTOPRIL GIVEN INTRACEREBROVENTRICULARLY, SUBCUTANEOUSLY OR BY GAVAGE INHIBITS ANGIOTENSIN CONVERTING ENZYME ACTIVITY IN THE RAT-BRAIN.
001614 02-04

BETA ENDORPHIN CAUSES RETROGRADE AMNESIA AND IS RELEASED FROM THE RAT-BRAIN BY VARIOUS FORMS OF TRAINING AND STIMULATION.
001664 02-04

EFFECT OF SINGLE AND REPEATED ELECTROCONVULSIVE-SHOCK ON SEROTONERGIC SYSTEM IN RAT-BRAIN -- II. BEHAVIOURAL-STUDIES.
001697 02-04

EFFECT OF NICKEL ON THE LEVELS OF DOPAMINE, NORADRENALINE AND SEROTONIN IN DIFFERENT REGIONS OF THE RAT-BRAIN.
001831 02-05

3H APOMORPHINE-RECEPTORS IN VARIOUS RAT-BRAIN REGIONS; A STUDY OF SPECIFIC AND NONSPECIFIC BINDING AND THE INFLUENCE OF CHRONIC NEUROLEPTIC TREATMENT.
001846 02-05

BINDING OF PHENCYCLIDINE TO RAT-BRAIN MEMBRANES: TECHNICAL-ASPECT.
001882 02-06

EFFECT OF DOXEPIN ON SEROTONIN METABOLISM IN RAT-BRAIN AND SEROTONIN UPTAKE BY HUMAN BLOOD-PLATELETS.
002243 02-13

IMMUNOCYTOCHEMICAL LOCALIZATION OF CATECHOLAMINE SYNTHESIZING ENZYMES AND NEUROPEPTIDES IN AREA POSTREMA AND MEDIAL NUCLEUS-TRACTUS-SOLITARIUS OF RAT-BRAIN.
002634 03-01

AGE DEPENDENT CHANGES IN THE BETA ENDORPHIN CONTENT OF DISCRETE RAT-BRAIN NUCLEI.
002635 03-01

IDENTIFICATION AND QUANTIFICATION OF 1,2,3,4 TETRAHYDRO-BETA-CARBOLINE, 2 METHYL-TETRAHYDRO-BETA-CARBOLINE, AND 6 METHOXY-TETRAHYDRO-BETA-CARBOLINE AS IN VIVO CONSTITUENTS OF RAT-BRAIN AND ADRENAL-GLAND.
002636 03-01

EFFECTS OF ALBUMIN, AMINO-ACIDS, AND CLOFIBRATE ON THE UPTAKE OF TRYPTOPHAN BY THE RAT-BRAIN.
002673 03-03

GABA-RECEPTORS AND BENZODIAZEPINE-RECEPTORS. STUDIES ON THEIR LOCALIZATION IN THE HIPPOCAMPUS AND THEIR INTERACTION WITH CENTRAL DOPAMINE NEURONS IN THE RAT-BRAIN.
002727 03-03

ALPHA METHYLEPINEPHRINE, A METHYLDOPA METABOLITE THAT BINDS TO ALPHA-RECEPTORS IN RAT-BRAIN.
002734 03-03

EFFECTS OF CHLORPROMAZINE ON DOPAMINERGIC-RECEPTOR FUNCTIONS IN RAT-BRAIN -- DIFFERENCE OF THE RESPONSE OF SEVERAL DOPAMINERGIC-SYSTEMS AFTER CHRONIC ADMINISTRATION.
002773 03-03

MORPHOLOGICAL CHANGES IN RAT-BRAIN INDUCED BY L CYSTEINE INJECTION IN NEWBORN ANIMALS.
002774 03-03

A QUANTITATIVE REGIONAL ANALYSIS OF PROTEIN SYNTHESIS INHIBITION IN THE RAT-BRAIN FOLLOWING LOCALIZED INJECTION OF CYCLOHEXIMIDE.
002780 03-03

INFLUENCE OF A CHRONIC NEW POTENTIAL ANTIDEPRESSANT, DIMETHYLAMINOPROPYL-5-METHYL-3-PHENYL-1H-INDAZOLE (FS-32)

AND ITS N DESMETHYLATED-COMPOUND (FS-97): TREATMENT ON MONOAMINERGIC-RECEPTOR SENSITIVITY IN THE RAT-BRAIN.
002787 03-03

(3H)MIANSERIN: DIFFERENTIAL LABELING OF SEROTONIN AND HISTAMINE-RECEPTORS IN RAT-BRAIN.
002860 03-03

INHIBITION OF GAMMA AMINOBUTYRIC-ACID-TRANSAMINASE WITH 6 AMINONICOTINAMIDE IN REGIONS OF THE RAT-BRAIN.
002868 03-03

ACUTE ACTION OF NOMIFENSINE ON NOREPINEPHRINE AND DOPAMINE LEVELS IN THE RAT-BRAIN.
002873 03-03

MULTIPLE EFFECTS OF REPEATED ADMINISTRATION OF GAMMA ACETYLENIC-GABA ON RAT-BRAIN METABOLISM.
002878 03-03

3H SEROTONIN BINDING-SITES IN RAT-BRAIN: EFFECTS OF REPEATED ADMINISTRATION OF ANTIDEPRESSANT-DRUGS. (PH.D. DISSERTATION).
002881 03-03

THE METABOLISM OF 5 HYDROXYTRYPTAMINE IN THE METHIONINE-SULFOXIMINE EPILEPTOGENIC RAT-BRAIN.
002887 03-03

EFFECTS OF ACUTELY AND CHRONICALLY ADMINISTERED ANTIDEPRESSANTS ON THE CLONIDINE-INDUCED DECREASE IN RAT-BRAIN 3 METHOXY-4-HYDROXYPHENYLETHYLENEGLYCOL-SULPHATE CONTENT.
002908 03-03

DIFFERENTIAL-EFFECT OF CHRONIC DESIPRAMINE AND AMITRIPTYLINE TREATMENT ON RAT-BRAIN ADRENERGIC AND SEROTONERGIC-RECEPTORS.
002914 03-03

REGULATION BY CATIONS OF (3H)SPIROPERIDOL BINDING ASSOCIATED WITH DOPAMINE-RECEPTORS OF RAT-BRAIN.
002922 03-03

INFLUENCE OF ESTROGEN AND PROGESTERONE ON GLUTAMIC-ACID-DECARBOXYLASE ACTIVITY IN DISCRETE REGIONS OF RAT-BRAIN.
002927 03-03

INCORPORATION OF N ACETYLMANNOSAMINE INTO RAT-BRAIN SUBCELLULAR GANGLIOSIDES: EFFECT OF PENTYLENETETRAZOL-INDUCED CONVULSIONS IN BRAIN GANGLIOSIDES.
002937 03-03

NEUROTENSIN-RECEPTOR LOCALIZATION BY LIGHT MICROSCOPIC AUTORADIOGRAPHY IN RAT-BRAIN.
002938 03-03

CORRELATION OF (14C)MUSCIMOL CONCENTRATION IN RAT-BRAIN WITH ANTICONVULSANT ACTIVITY.
003045 03-04

A METHOD FOR MEASUREMENT OF TRANYLCYPROMINE IN RAT-BRAIN REGIONS USING GAS-CHROMATOGRAPHY WITH ELECTRON CAPTURE DETECTION.
003137 03-06

RELEASE OF ACETYLCHOLINE FROM RAT-BRAIN SYNAPTOSOMES STIMULATED WITH LEPTINOTARSIN, A NEW NEUROTOXIN.
003148 03-06

REGIONAL AND SUBCELLULAR LOCALIZATION IN RAT-BRAIN OF THE ENZYMES THAT CAN SYNTHESIZE GAMMA HYDROXYBUTYRIC-ACID.
003675 04-01

PURIFICATION AND SUBUNIT STRUCTURE OF DNA-DEPENDENT RNA-POLYMERASE-BII FROM RAT-BRAIN NUCLEI.
003679 04-01

EFFECT OF LOW-DOSE LITHIUM ADMINISTRATION AND SUBSEQUENT WITHDRAWAL ON BIOGENIC-AMINES IN RAT-BRAIN.
003708 04-03

MYOINOSITOL TURNOVER IN THE INTACT RAT-BRAIN: INCREASED PRODUCTION AFTER D-AMPHETAMINE.
003723 04-03

EFFECT OF AMPHETAMINE ON THE METABOLISM AND INCORPORATION OF (3H) THYMIDINE INTO DNA OF DEVELOPING RAT-BRAIN.
003729 04-03

AGE-DEPENDENT MODIFICATION OF DRUG INTERFERENCE ON THE ENZYMATIC ACTIVITIES OF THE RAT-BRAIN.
003730 04-03

THE EFFECTS OF ANTIDEPRESSANTS ON THE RETENTION AND METABOLISM OF (3H) NOREPINEPHRINE IN RAT-BRAIN SLICES.
003763 04-03

INHIBITION OF (3H)DIAZEPAM BINDING BY AN ENDOGENOUS FRACTION FROM RAT-BRAIN SYNAPTOSOMES.
003768 04-03

HALOTHANE ACCUMULATION IN RAT-BRAIN AND LIVER.
003774 04-03

EFFECTS OF CONFORMATIONALLY RESTRAINED ANALOGUES OF SEROTONIN ON ITS UPTAKE AND BINDING IN RAT-BRAIN.
003794 04-03

COMPARATIVE-EFFECTS OF AMANTADINE AND AMFONELIC-ACID ON DOPAMINE METABOLISM IN RAT-BRAIN.
003796 04-03

NEWLY SYNTHESIZED CHOLECYSTOKININ IN SUBCELLULAR FRACTIONS OF THE RAT-BRAIN.
003805 04-03

UPTAKE OF RADIOCALCIUM BY NERVE-ENDINGS ISOLATED FROM RAT-BRAIN: KINETIC STUDIES.
003814 04-03

UPTAKE OF RADIOCALCIUM BY NERVE-ENDINGS ISOLATED FROM RAT-BRAIN: PHARMACOLOGICAL-STUDIES.
003815 04-03

(3H)METERGOLINE: A NEW LIGAND OF SEROTONIN-RECEPTORS IN THE RAT-BRAIN.
003825 04-03

3H BACLOFEN AND 3H GABA BIND TO BICUCULLINE INSENSITIVE GABAB SITES IN RAT-BRAIN.
003839 04-03

LONG-TERM EFFECTS OF MULTIPLE DOSES OF METHAMPHETAMINE ON TRYPTOPHAN-HYDROXYLASE AND TYROSINE-HYDROXYLASE ACTIVITY IN RAT-BRAIN.
003850 04-03

THE INTERACTION OF TRAZODONE WITH RAT-BRAIN MUSCARINIC-CHOLINOCEPTORS.
003855 04-03

QUINUCLIDINYL BENZILATE BINDING IN HOUSEFLY HEADS AND RAT-BRAIN.
003868 04-03

CHARACTERISTICS OF THE INHIBITION OF RAT-BRAIN MONOAMINE-OXIDASE IN VITRO BY MD780515.
003874 04-03

DIFFERENTIAL-EFFECTS OF ELECTROCONVULSIVE-SHOCK AND ANTIDEPRESSANT-DRUGS ON SEROTONIN2-RECEPTORS IN RAT-BRAIN.
003878 04-03

CHANGES IN GAMMA AMINOBUTYRIC-ACID SHUNT ENZYMES IN REGIONS OF RAT-BRAIN WITH KETAMINE ANESTHESIA.
003891 04-03

RESERPINE EFFECT ON THE AXONAL TRANSPORT OF DOPAMINE-BETA-HYDROXYLASE AND TYROSINE-HYDROXYLASE IN RAT-BRAIN.
003904 04-03

THE INFLUENCE OF D-AMPHETAMINE ON RAT-BRAIN STRIATAL REDUCED BIOPTERIN CONCENTRATION.
003922 04-03

IN VIVO INTRANEURONAL MAO-INHIBITION IN RAT-BRAIN SKF-64139, COMPARISON TO OTHER POTENT PNMT INHIBITORS.
003935 04-03

REGIONAL DISTRIBUTION OF (3H)IMIPRAMINE BINDING IN RAT-BRAIN.
003955 04-03

EFFECTS OF IN VIVO AMPHETAMINE ADMINISTRATION ON DOPAMINE SYNTHESIS REGULATION IN RAT-BRAIN STRIATAL SYNAPTOSOMES. (UNPUBLISHED PAPER).
003960 04-03

HIGH-AFFINITY BINDING-SITES FOR A SOMATOSTATIN-28 ANALOG IN RAT-BRAIN.
003985 04-03

MULTIPLE ALPHA2-NORADRENERGIC-RECEPTOR SITES IN RAT-BRAIN: SELECTIVE REGULATION OF HIGH-AFFINITY (3H)CLONIDINE BINDING BY GUANINE-NUCLEOTIDES AND DIVALENT-CATIONS.
003992 04-03

ALPHA2-ADRENORECEPTORS IN RAT-BRAIN ARE DECREASED AFTER LONG-TERM TRICYCLIC-ANTIDEPRESSANT DRUG-TREATMENT.
004008 04-03

DECREASE OF NORADRENALINE O METHYLATION IN RAT-BRAIN INDUCED BY L-DOPA. REVERSAL EFFECT OF S ADENOSYL-L-METHIONINE.
004019 04-03

ONTOGENY OF HISTAMINERGIC NEUROTRANSMISSION IN THE RAT-BRAIN: CONCOMITANT DEVELOPMENT OF NEURONAL HISTAMINE, H1-RECEPTORS, AND H1-RECEPTOR-MEDIATED STIMULATION OF PHOSPHOLIPID TURNOVER.
004021 04-03

CHRONIC NEUROLEPTIC TREATMENT SPECIFICALLY ALTERS THE NUMBER OF DOPAMINE-RECEPTORS IN RAT-BRAIN.
004033 04-03

THE EFFECTS OF ACUTE AND CHRONIC ETHANOL ADMINISTRATION AND ITS WITHDRAWAL ON GAMMA AMINOBUTYRIC-ACID-RECEPTOR BINDING IN RAT-BRAIN.
004035 04-03

INHIBITION OF THE SYNTHESIS OF ACETYLCHOLINE IN RAT-BRAIN SLICES BY (-) HYDROXYCITRATE AND CITRATE.
004044 04-03

DEVELOPMENTAL-CHANGE OF BETA-ADRENERGIC-RECEPTORS IN RAT-BRAIN.
004050 04-03

A STUDY OF THE EFFECT OF NEUROPHARMACOLOGICAL DRUGS ON THE FUNCTIONAL ACTIVITY OF RAT-BRAIN.
004107 04-04

EFFECT OF INORGANIC LEAD ON RAT-BRAIN MITOCHONDRIAL RESPIRATION AND ENERGY PRODUCTION.
004267 04-05

PRESENCE OF CONJUGATED CATECHOLAMINES IN RAT-BRAIN: A NEW METHOD OF ANALYSIS OF CATECHOLAMINE-SULFATES.
004286 04-06

SPECIFIC IN VIVO BINDING OF 77BR P BROMOSPIROPERIDOL IN RAT-BRAIN: A POTENTIAL TOOL FOR GAMMA-RAY IMAGING.
004293 04-06

A SIMPLE DETERMINATION OF SEROTONIN, 5 HYDROXYINDOLEACETIC-ACID AND 5 HYDROXYTRYPTOPHAN-DECARBOXYLASE ACTIVITY IN RAT-BRAIN AREAS AND PARALLEL CORRELATION AMONG THE LEVELS.
004301 04-06

RAT-BRAIN AND PLASMA NOREPINEPHRINE GLYCOL METABOLITES DETERMINED BY GAS-CHROMATOGRAPHY MASS-FRAGMENTOGRAPHY.
004303 04-06

RAT-BRAIN-CORTEX
ALPHA-ADRENOCEPTOR-MEDIATED MODULATION OF 5 HYDROXYTRYPTAMINE RELEASE FROM RAT-BRAIN-CORTEX SLICES.
000111 01-03

SEROTONIN-RECEPTOR MEDIATED MODULATION OF CA-DEPENDENT 5 HYDROXYTRYPTAMINE RELEASE FROM NEURONES OF THE RAT-BRAIN-CORTEX.
001258 02-03

STIMULATORY EFFECT OF SOMATOSTATIN ON NOREPINEPHRINE RELEASE FROM RAT-BRAIN-CORTEX SLICES.
002920 03-03

ELECTRICAL-ACTIVITY AND NA-K-ATPASE LEVEL IN THE PENICILLIN-INDUCED EPILEPTOGENIC-FOCUS OF THE RAT-BRAIN-CORTEX, AND THE EFFECT OF DIAZEPAM.
003070 03-04

RAT-CEREBELLUM
AGE-RELATED ELECTROPHYSIOLOGICAL CHANGES IN RAT-CEREBELLUM.
000197 01-03

DECREASED BENZODIAZEPINE-RECEPTOR DENSITY IN RAT-CEREBELLUM FOLLOWING NEUROTOXIC DOSES OF PHENYTOIN.
001373 02-03

MODULATION BY PICROTOXIN AND IPTBO OF 3H FLUNITRAZEPAM BINDING TO THE GABA/BENZODIAZEPINE-RECEPTOR COMPLEX OF RAT-CEREBELLUM.
002775 03-03

EFFECTS OF PROLONGED TREATMENT WITH LITHIUM AND TRICYCLIC-ANTIDEPRESSANTS ON DISCHARGE FREQUENCY, NOREPINEPHRINE RESPONSES AND BETA-RECEPTOR BINDING IN RAT-CEREBELLUM: ELECTROPHYSIOLOGICAL AND BIOCHEMICAL COMPARISON.
002884 03-03

L ASPARTATE BINDING-SITES IN RAT-CEREBELLUM: A COMPARISON OF THE BINDING OF L (3H)ASPARTATE AND L (3H)GLUTAMATE TO SYNAPTIC MEMBRANES.
004000 04-03

IN VITRO MODULATION BY AVERMECTIN-B1A OF THE GABA/ BENZODIAZEPINE-RECEPTOR COMPLEX OF RAT-CEREBELLUM.
004023 04-03

RAT-CEREBRAL-CORTEX
AGONIST-INDUCED CHANGES IN BETA-ADRENERGIC-RECEPTOR DENSITY AND RECEPTOR-MEDIATED RESPONSIVENESS IN SLICES OF RAT-CEREBRAL-CORTEX.
000072 01-03

THE EFFECT OF MORPHINE ON PURINE AND ACETYLCHOLINE RELEASE FROM RAT-CEREBRAL-CORTEX: EVIDENCE FOR A PURINERGIC COMPONENT IN MORPHINES ACTION.
000234 01-03

MORPHINE ENHANCES ADENOSINE RELEASE FROM THE IN VIVO RAT-CEREBRAL-CORTEX.
000451 01-04

DISPLACEMENT OF (3H)CLONIDINE BINDING BY CLONIDINE ANALOGUES IN MEMBRANES FROM RAT-CEREBRAL-CORTEX.
000536 01-06

DRUG INTERFERENCE ON SOME BIOCHEMICAL-PARAMETERS OF RAT-CEREBRAL-CORTEX DURING POSTISCHEMIC RECOVERY.
001126 02-03

HIGH-AFFINITY BINDING OF (3H)MIANSERIN TO RAT-CEREBRAL-CORTEX.
001204 02-03

EFFECTS OF MALNUTRITION AND QUIPAZINE ON RAT-CEREBRAL-CORTEX ATPASE ACTIVITY DURING DEVELOPMENT.
001276 02-03

EFFECTS OF DIAZEPAM ON ADENOSINE AND ACETYLCHOLINE RELEASE FROM RAT-CEREBRAL-CORTEX: FURTHER EVIDENCE FOR A PURINERGIC MECHANISM IN ACTION OF DIAZEPAM.
001414 02-03

CALCIUM-SENSITIVE ACCUMULATION OF NOREPINEPHRINE IN RAT-CEREBRAL-CORTEX.
002685 03-03

ENHANCEMENT OF NORADRENALINE RELEASE FROM RAT-CEREBRAL-CORTEX BY NEUROLEPTIC-DRUGS.
002742 03-03

THE EFFECTS OF D-AMPHETAMINE AND POTASSIUM ON SEROTONIN RELEASE AND METABOLISM IN RAT-CEREBRAL-CORTEX TISSUE.
002754 03-03

IDENTIFICATION OF TWO BENZODIAZEPINE BINDING-SITES ON CELLS CULTURED FROM RAT-CEREBRAL-CORTEX.
002820 03-03

SOMATOSTATIN FACILITATES THE SEROTONIN RELEASE FROM RAT-CEREBRAL-CORTEX, HIPPOCAMPUS, AND HYPOTHALAMUS SLICES.
002913 03-03

CATECHOLAMINE TURNOVER IN RAT-CEREBRAL-CORTEX AND CAUDATE FOLLOWING REPEATED TREATMENT WITH DIHYDROERGOTOXINE.
003765 04-03

REGULATION OF NORADRENALINE OVERFLOW IN RAT-CEREBRAL-CORTEX BY PROSTAGLANDIN-E2.
003841 04-03

THE UPTAKE OF CARNITINE BY SLICES OF RAT-CEREBRAL-CORTEX.
003853 04-03

EFFECTS OF MORPHINE AND CAFFEINE ON ADENOSINE RELEASE FROM RAT-CEREBRAL-CORTEX: IS CAFFEINE A MORPHINE ANTAGONIST.
003864 04-03

ALPHA1-ADRENOCEPTORS AND ALPHA2-ADRENOCEPTORS IN RAT-CEREBRAL-CORTEX: EFFECT OF FRONTAL LOBOTOMY.
003944 04-03

EFFECTS OF ETHANOL ON ACETYLCHOLINE AND ADENOSINE EFFLUX FROM THE IN VIVO RAT-CEREBRAL-CORTEX.
003969 04-03

RAT-CEREBRAL-CORTICAL
METERGOLINE ANTAGONISM OF 5 HYDROXYTRYPTAMINE-INDUCED ACTIVATION OF RAT-CEREBRAL-CORTICAL NA-K-ATPASE.
000329 01-03

ADENOSINE AND CYCLIC-AMP IN RAT-CEREBRAL-CORTICAL SLICES: EFFECTS OF ADENOSINE UPTAKE INHIBITORS AND ADENOSINE-DEAMINASE INHIBITORS.
003950 04-03

THE EFFECT OF NORADRENALINE ON NA-K TRANSPORT IN RAT-CEREBRAL-CORTICAL SLICES.
004056 04-03

RAT-CORTEX
THE EFFECT OF SODIUM-DIPROPYLACETATE ON GAMMA AMINOBUTYRIC-ACID DEPENDENT INHIBITION IN THE RAT-CORTEX AND SUBSTANTIA-NIGRA IN RELATION TO ITS ANTICONVULSANT ACTIVITY.
003880 04-03

RAT-CORTICAL-NEURONES
LONG-TERM ADMINISTRATION OF ATROPINE, IMIPRAMINE, AND VILOXAZINE ALTERS RESPONSIVENESS OF RAT-CORTICAL-NEURONES TO ACETYLCHOLINE.
001306 02-03

• **RAT-FOREBRAIN**
INCREASED MUSCARINIC-RECEPTOR BINDING IN RAT-FOREBRAIN AFTER SCOPOLAMINE.
001351 02-03

EFFECTS OF HALOPERIDOL AND D-AMPHETAMINE ON IN VIVO 3H SPIROPERIDOL BINDING IN THE RAT-FOREBRAIN.
001461 02-03

KINETIC DATA ON THE INHIBITION OF HIGH-AFFINITY CHOLINE TRANSPORT INTO RAT-FOREBRAIN SYNAPTOSOMES BY CHOLINE-LIKE COMPOUNDS AND NITROGEN-MUSTARD ANALOGUES.
002879 03-03

RAT-FRONTAL-CORTEX
DOPAMINE-RECEPTORS IN RAT-FRONTAL-CORTEX: PHARMACOLOGICAL-PROPERTIES IN VIVO AND IN VITRO.
001112 02-03

SOLUBILIZATION OF SEROTONIN-RECEPTORS FROM RAT-FRONTAL-CORTEX.
002489 02-16

RAT-MIDBRAIN
(3H)ACETYLCHOLINE AND (3H)5 HYDROXYTRYPTAMINE RELEASE FROM RAT-MIDBRAIN SLICES AND THE EFFECTS OF CALCIUM AND PHENOBARBITAL.
000251 01-03

PERSISTENT EFFECTS OF CHRONIC ADMINISTRATION OF LSD ON INTRACELLULAR SEROTONIN CONTENT IN RAT-MIDBRAIN.
001333 02-03

RAT-WHOLE-BRAIN
COMPARISON OF THE EFFECTS OF THE ISOMERS OF AMPHETAMINE, METHYLPHENIDATE AND DEOXYPIPRADROL ON THE UPTAKE OF L (3H)NOREPINEPHRINE AND (3H)DOPAMINE BY SYNAPTIC VESICLES FROM RAT-WHOLE-BRAIN, STRIATUM AND HYPOTHALAMUS.
000091 01-03

RATE
IMIPRAMINE AFFECTS AUTONOMIC-CONTROL OF SINOATRIAL RATE IN ISOLATED RIGHT ATRIAL PREPARATIONS.
000195 01-03

EFFECTS OF RATE OF BLOOD FLOW ON FRACTIONAL EXTRACTION AND ON UPTAKE OF INFUSED NORADRENALINE BY BROWN ADIPOSE TISSUE IN VIVO.
001231 02-03

LONG-TERM APPLICATION OF HALOPERIDOL: EFFECT OF ANTICHOLINERGIC TREATMENT ON THE RATE OF DOPAMINE SYNTHESIS.
001490 02-03

INTERACTIONS OF CHLORDIAZEPOXIDE AND ANORECTIC-AGENTS ON RATE AND DURATION PARAMETERS OF FEEDING IN THE RAT.
001600 02-04

PHARMACOKINETIC PROFILE OF VALPROIC-ACID IN RHESUS-MONKEYS FOLLOWING SINGLE BOLUS AND CONSTANT RATE INTRAVENOUS ADMINISTRATIONS.
002797 03-03

TIME-COURSE OF CHRONIC HALOPERIDOL AND CLOZAPINE UPON OPERANT RATE AND DURATION.
002989 03-04

CHRONIC EFFECTS OF NEUROLEPTICS HAVING HIGH OR LOW INCIDENCE
OF EXTRAPYRAMIDAL SIDE-EFFECTS UPON FORCE, DURATION AND
RATE OF OPERANT-RESPONSE IN RATS. (PH.D. DISSERTATION).
003125 03-05

A NOTE ON THE PARADOXICAL-EFFECT OF STIMULANTS ON
HYPERACTIVITY WITH REFERENCE TO THE RATE DEPENDENCY EFFECT
OF DRUGS.
003320 03-11

GLOMERULAR FILTRATION RATE AND CALCIUM METABOLISM IN LONG-
TERM LITHIUM TREATMENT.
003542 03-15

OPIATE-EFFECTS IN THE AMYGDALA CENTRAL NUCLEUS ON HEART RATE
CONDITIONING IN RABBITS.
003798 04-03

CHLORPROMAZINE EFFECTS ON COCAINE-REINFORCED RESPONDING IN
RHESUS-MONKEYS: RECIPROCAL MODIFICATION OF RATE ALTERING
EFFECTS OF THE DRUGS.
004133 04-04

POTENTIATION OF THE MORPHINE-INDUCED RESPIRATORY RATE
DEPRESSION BY CAPTOPRIL.
004275 04-05

RATED
PLACEBO REACTION IN NEUROTICS RATED WITH THE SCL-90
QUESTIONNAIRE.
000976 01-17

RATES
OXAZEPAM-ESTERS. 1. CORRELATION BETWEEN HYDROLYSIS RATES AND
BRAIN APPEARANCE OF OXAZEPAM.
000010 01-02

A COMPARISON OF RATES OF DEPLETION AND RECOVERY OF
NORADRENALINE STORES OF PERIPHERAL AND CENTRAL
NORADRENERGIC NEURONES AFTER RESERPINE ADMINISTRATION:
IMPORTANCE OF NEURONAL ACTIVITY.
000314 01-03

A COMPARISON OF THE EFFECTS OF D-AMPHETAMINE, COCAINE,
IMIPRAMINE AND PENTOBARBITAL ON LOCAL AND OVERALL RATES OF
RESPONDING MAINTAINED UNDER A FOUR-COMPONENT MULTIPLE
FIXED-INTERVAL SCHEDULE.
000508 01-04

RECIDIVISM AND REHABILITATION RATES FOR 135 CRIMINALLY-INSANE-
OFFENDERS. (D.ED. DISSERTATION).
002514 02-17

BLINK RATES AND RECEPTOR SUPERSENSITIVITY.
003022 03-04

DRUG-EFFECT ON BLINK RATES IN RHESUS-MONKEYS: PRELIMINARY
STUDIES.
003023 03-04

RATING
RATING OF ANTIDEPRESSANT ACTIVITY.
002487 02-16

RATINGS
LONG-TERM CHANGES IN AIMS RATINGS AND THEIR RELATION TO
MEDICATION HISTORY.
003537 03-15

RATIONALISE
DEPRESSION: HOW TO RATIONALISE DRUG-THERAPY.
001988 02-09

RATIONALIZATION
STUDY OF METABOLISM AND BLOOD LEVELS OF ANTIDEPRESSANTS:
TOWARDS A RATIONALIZATION OF THEIR THERAPEUTIC USE.
002625 02-17

REACHING-BEHAVIOR
HANDEDNESS IN RATS: BLOCKADE OF REACHING-BEHAVIOR BY
UNILATERAL 6 OHDA INJECTIONS INTO SUBSTANTIA-NIGRA AND
CAUDATE-NUCLEUS.
001778 02-04

REACTION
INHIBITION OF ALCOHOL-DEHYDROGENASE BY DISULFIRAM; POSSIBLE
RELATION TO THE DISULFIRAM ETHANOL REACTION.
000270 01-03

CUTANEOUS REACTION TO LITHIUM-CARBONATE: A CASE-REPORT.
000872 01-15

PLACEBO REACTION IN NEUROTICS RATED WITH THE SCL-90
QUESTIONNAIRE.
000976 01-17

THE INFLUENCE OF PENTIFYLLINE AND THEOPHYLLINE ON REACTION
KINETICS OF CATECHOLAMINE STIMULATED ATPASE FROM RAT-BRAIN.
001052 02-01

SUBCELLULAR REACTION OF THE BRAIN TO HYPOXIA.
001354 02-03

EFFECTS OF HALOPERIDOL, A DOPAMINE-RECEPTOR ANTAGONIST, ON A
DELAYED TYPE HYPERSENSITIVITY REACTION TO 1
CHLORODINITROBENZENE IN MICE.
001473 02-03

THE EFFECT OF NALOXONE ON THE ACTIVATION OF EMOTIONALLY
POSITIVE REACTION PRODUCED BY DRUGS WITH A DEPENDENCE
LIABILITY.
001556 02-03

THE BEHAVIOR OF RATS IN THE OPEN-FIELD WITHOUT STRESS, UNDER
ACUTE AND PERSISTING INFLUENCE OF IMIPRAMINE AND

TRANYLCYPROMINE AS WELL AS ON THE INDIVIDUAL REACTION TYPE
(EMOTIVE AND NONEMOTIVE).
001624 02-04

OPIATE ANTAGONISTS AND LONG-TERM ANALGESIC REACTION INDUCED
BY INESCAPABLE SHOCK IN RATS.
001707 02-04

SELF-STIMULATION REACTION IN NORMOTENSIVE-RATS AND
HYPERTENSIVE-RATS.
002663 03-03

ABNORMAL TRANSMETHYLATION REACTION DURING THE METABOLISM
OF DOPAMINE, TRYPTAMINE, AND SEROTONIN, AND SCHIZOPHRENIC-
SYMPTOMS: A CRITICAL REVIEW.
003404 03-13

DYSTONIC REACTION DURING MAINTENANCE ANTIPSYCHOTIC THERAPY.
003485 03-15

EXTRAPYRAMIDAL REACTION OF FLUPHENAZINE POTENTIATED BY
THYROTOXICOSIS.
003551 03-15

REACTION-TIME
SEX-DIFFERENCES IN THE EFFECTS OF LOW-DOSES OF ETHANOL ON
HUMAN REACTION-TIME.
002361 02-14

EFFECT OF LITHIUM ON REACTION-TIME -- A STUDY OF DIURNAL
VARIATIONS.
004607 04-15

REACTIONS
EFFECT OF STRUCTURE ON PHENOTHIAZINE CATION RADICAL REACTIONS
IN AQUEOUS BUFFERS.
000014 01-02

RATS REACTIONS TO A PREDATOR: MODIFICATION BY
CHLORDIAZEPOXIDE.
000353 01-04

INTRAVENOUS PHENOBARBITAL THERAPY IN BARBITURATE AND OTHER
HYPNOSEDATIVE WITHDRAWAL REACTIONS: A KINETIC APPROACH.
000703 01-11

THE INFLUENCE OF NOOTROPIC-DRUGS ON LEARNING AND MEMORY OF
DEFENSE REACTIONS.
000815 01-14

THE EFFECT OF PHRENOLON ON DELAYED REACTIONS IN LOWER
MONKEYS.
001640 02-04

NEUROLEPTIC-INDUCED ACUTE DYSTONIC REACTIONS MAY BE DUE TO
ENHANCED DOPAMINE RELEASE ON TO SUPERSENSITIVE
POSTSYNAPTIC-RECEPTORS.
002789 03-03

THE EFFECTS OF IMIPRAMINE TREATMENT ON THE UNCONDITIONED
ALIMENTARY BEHAVIOR AND CLASSICAL CONDITIONED SALIVARY
REACTIONS IN DOGS.
003030 03-04

AMPHETAMINE-LIKE REACTIONS TO PHENYLPROPANOLAMINE.
003480 03-15

VARIOUS FACTORS IN THE PATHOGENESIS OF PATHOLOGICAL REACTIONS
OBSERVED IN CONNECTION WITH THE ADMINISTRATION OF
PSYCHOTROPIC-DRUGS.
003532 03-15

THE ROLE OF OPIATE-RECEPTORS OF DIFFERENT BRAIN REGIONS IN
DETERMINING THE EMOTIONAL REACTIONS OF RATS.
004017 04-03

THE EFFECT OF THIOPROPERAZINE ON DELAYED REACTIONS IN LOWER
MONKEYS.
004125 04-04

ON SOME RELATIONSHIPS BETWEEN GABAERGIC AND 5 HT-ERGIC
MECHANISMS IN PENTYLENETETRAZOL CONVULSIVE-SEIZURE
REACTIONS.
004166 04-04

THE ROLE OF RETICULOSEPTAL INPUTS IN THE FORMATION OF DIFFERENT
TYPES OF SENSORY REACTIONS OF THE HIPPOCAMPAL NEURONS.
004510 04-13

REVERSIBLE RING-OPENING REACTIONS OF NIMETAZEPAM AND
NITRAZEPAM IN ACIDIC MEDIA AT BODY-TEMPERATURE.
004517 04-13

REACTIVITY
REACTIVITY OF ISOLATED CANINE CEREBRAL-ARTERIES TO ADENINE-
NUCLEOTIDES AND ADENOSINE.
000210 01-03

IN UTERO ALCOHOL HEIGHTENS JUVENILE REACTIVITY.
000510 01-05

ASSESSMENT OF MULTIVARIATE RELATIONSHIPS IN REACTIVITY OF
PATIENTS RECEIVING LITHIUM THERAPY.
000819 01-14

CENTRAL SYMPATHETIC REACTIVITY INHIBITED BY INDORAMIN.
001193 02-03

THE USE OF BROMOCRIPTINE FOR TESTING CENTRAL DOPAMINERGIC
REACTIVITY.
002205 02-13

SENSORY PROCESSING, CARDIOVASCULAR REACTIVITY, AND THE TYPE A
CORONARY-PRONE BEHAVIOR PATTERN.
003405 03-13

METHAQUALONE RIA STRUCTURE VERSUS REACTIVITY.
003657 04-01

RIA OPIATES: STRUCTURE VERSUS REACTIVITY.
003659 04-01

READING
EFFECTS OF METHYLPHENIDATE ON LEARNING A BEGINNING READING VOCABULARY BY NORMAL ADULTS.
000812 01-14

READING-DISABLED
EFFECTS OF METHYLPHENIDATE ON SELECTIVE AND SUSTAINED ATTENTION IN HYPERACTIVE, READING-DISABLED, AND PRESUMABLY ATTENTION-DISORDERED BOYS.
002118 02-11

REAGENT
CARBAMAZEPINE-EPOXIDE DETERMINED BY EMIT CARBAMAZEPINE REAGENT.
000533 01-06

REALITY
THE STIMULANT-EFFECT OF NEUROLEPTICS: MYTH OR REALITY?
000362 01-04

CONTRIBUTION TO STUDY OF CEREBRAL DOPAMINERGIC MECHANISMS: REALITY OF THE PROBLEM.
000782 01-13

ROTTING WITH THEIR RIGHTS ON: CONSTITUTIONAL THEORY AND CLINICAL REALITY IN DRUG-REFUSAL BY PSYCHIATRIC-PATIENTS.
000911 01-17

REARING
EFFECTS OF CHOLECYSTOKININ-LIKE PEPTIDES ON REARING ACTIVITY AND HEXOBARBITAL-INDUCED SLEEP.
000507 01-04

DEVELOPMENTAL-CHANGE IN REARING RESPONSE TO ATROPINE IN RATS TREATED WITH 6 HYDROXYDOPA.
004191 04-04

REASONABLE
THE RIGHTS OF INVOLUNTARY-PATIENTS TO REFUSE PHARMACOTHERAPY: WHAT IS REASONABLE?
004730 04-17

REASONABLE-DOUBT
VOLUNTARY INTOXICATION FROM PHENCYCLIDINE. WILL IT RAISE A REASONABLE-DOUBT OF THE MENTAL-CAPACITY OF A PERSON CHARGED WITH A CRIME REQUIRING SPECIFIC INTENT OR MENTAL-STATE?.
000914 01-17

REASSESSMENT
BENZODIAZEPINES IN SCHIZOPHRENIA: A NEED FOR REASSESSMENT.
004733 04-17

REBOUND
CAFFEINE PRODUCES REM SLEEP REBOUND IN RATS.
000244 01-03

CHOLINERGIC REBOUND IN NEUROLEPTIC WITHDRAWAL-SYNDROMES.
003506 03-15

RECEPTOR
EVIDENCE FOR A RECEPTOR SUPERSENSITIVITY FOLLOWING IMPAIRMENT OF CENTRAL SEROTONERGIC ACTIVITY IN THE RABBIT.
000041 01-03

RELATIONSHIP OF ANTICONFLICT ACTIVITY OF BENZODIAZEPINES TO BRAIN RECEPTOR BINDING, SEROTONIN, AND GABA.
000057 01-03

AFFINITY CHROMATOGRAPHY OF THE BETA-ADRENERGIC-RECEPTOR AND CHARACTERIZATION OF ANTIBODIES RAISED AGAINST PURIFIED RECEPTOR PREPARATIONS.
001009 02-01

BETA ENDORPHIN: DISSOCIATION OF RECEPTOR BINDING-ACTIVITY FROM ANALGESIC POTENCY.
001081 02-02

REGULATION OF RECEPTOR BINDING INTERACTIONS OF 125I ANGIOTENSIN-II AND 125I SARCOSINE1-LEUCINE8-ANGIOTENSIN-II, AN ANGIOTENSIN ANTAGONIST, BY SODIUM-ION.
001124 02-03

RECEPTOR BINDING INTERACTIONS OF THE ANGIOTENSIN-II ANTAGONIST, 125I SARCOSINE1-LEUCINE8-ANGIOTENSIN-II, WITH MAMMALIAN BRAIN AND PERIPHERAL TISSUES.
001125 02-03

DOPAMINE-SENSITIVE ADENYLATE-CYCLASE AND RECEPTOR BINDING-ACTIVITIES FOLLOWING ACUTE AND CHRONIC NEUROLEPTIC-DRUG TREATMENT. (UNPUBLISHED PAPER).
001172 02-03

RECEPTOR PLASTICITY: BIOCHEMICAL-CORRELATES AND PHARMACOLOGICAL SIGNIFICANCE.
001181 02-03

IGE MEDIATED HISTAMINE RELEASE IN RAT BASOPHILIC LEUKEMIA CELLS: RECEPTOR ACTIVATED PHOSPHOLIPID METHYLATION, CA-FLUX AND RELEASE OF ARACHIDONIC-ACID. (UNPUBLISHED PAPER).
001188 02-03

THE AFFINITIES OF ERGOT COMPOUNDS FOR DOPAMINE AGONIST AND DOPAMINE ANTAGONIST RECEPTOR SITES.
001254 02-03

OPIATES AND SPECIFIC RECEPTOR BINDING OF (3H)CLONIDINE.
001256 02-03

MULTIPLE CNS RECEPTOR INTERACTIONS OF ERGOT ALKALOIDS: AFFINITY AND INTRINSIC ACTIVITY ANALYSIS IN IN VITRO BINDING SYSTEMS.
001516 02-03

(3H) PHENCYCLIDINE BINDING TO SPECIFIC BRAIN RECEPTOR SITES.
001555 02-03

DISPOSITION AND ACTIVITY OF BETA-ADRENOCEPTOR ANTAGONISTS IN THE RAT USING AN EX VIVO RECEPTOR BINDING ASSAY.
001878 02-06

METOCLOPRAMIDE: ANTIPSYCHOTIC-EFFICACY OF A DRUG LACKING POTENCY IN RECEPTOR MODELS.
001948 02-08

PURSUING THE ACTIONS OF PSYCHOTROPIC-DRUGS: RECEPTOR SITES AND ENDOGENOUS CEREBRAL PROGRAMMES.
002578 02-17

RECEPTOR BINDING PROFILE OF R-41-468, A NOVEL ANTAGONIST AT 5 HT2-RECEPTORS.
002648 03-02

EFFECT OF KAINIC-ACID LESIONS ON MUSCARINIC AGONIST RECEPTOR SUBTYPES IN RAT STRIATUM.
002679 03-03

DIFFERENTIAL REGULATION BY GUANINE-NUCLEOTIDES OF OPIATE AGONIST AND ANTAGONIST RECEPTOR INTERACTIONS.
002688 03-03

TWO DISTINCT SEROTONIN-RECEPTORS: REGIONAL VARIATIONS IN RECEPTOR BINDING IN MAMMALIAN BRAIN.
002861 03-03

DISCRIMINATION OF FUNCTIONALLY HETEROGENEOUS RECEPTOR SUBPOPULATIONS: ANTIPSYCHOTIC AND ANTIDOPAMINERGIC PROPERTIES OF METOCLOPRAMIDE.
002877 03-03

DRUG REGIMENS FACILITATING AGGRESSION: BEHAVIOR, AMINE, AND RECEPTOR ALTERATIONS.
002987 03-04

BLINK RATES AND RECEPTOR SUPERSENSITIVITY.
003022 03-04

ELECTROPHYSIOLOGIC ASSESSMENT OF RECEPTOR CHANGES FOLLOWING CHRONIC DRUG-TREATMENT.
003136 03-06

RECEPTOR ADAPTATIONS TO CENTRALLY ACTING DRUGS.
003585 03-17

STRUCTURE-ACTIVITY AND RECEPTOR BINDING OF ANTAGONIST ANALGESICS.
003611 03-17

EFFECTS OF 3',4' DIHYDROXYNOMIFENSINE ON THE DOPAMINE VASCULAR RECEPTOR.
003890 04-03

EFFECT OF PRENATAL NEUROLEPTIC TREATMENT ON MEMBRANE RECEPTOR DEVELOPMENT IN THE BRAIN.
003989 04-03

RECEPTOR TECHNIQUES IN THE STUDY OF PLASMA LEVELS OF NEUROLEPTICS AND ANTIDEPRESSANT-DRUGS.
004694 04-16

RECEPTOR-MEDIATED
AGONIST-INDUCED CHANGES IN BETA-ADRENERGIC-RECEPTOR DENSITY AND RECEPTOR-MEDIATED RESPONSIVENESS IN SLICES OF RAT-CEREBRAL-CORTEX.
000072 01-03

PHOSPHOLIPID METABOLISM, CALCIUM-FLUX AND THE RECEPTOR-MEDIATED INDUCTION OF CHEMOTAXIS IN RABBIT NEUTROPHILS. (UNPUBLISHED PAPER).
001118 02-03

MINI-SYMPOSIUM. IV. DISCRIMINATIVE-STIMULUS EFFECTS OF NARCOTICS: EVIDENCE FOR MULTIPLE RECEPTOR-MEDIATED ACTIONS.
004719 04-17

RECEPTORS
ADENOSINE REGULATES VIA TWO DIFFERENT TYPES OF RECEPTORS, THE ACCUMULATION OF CYCLIC-AMP IN CULTURED BRAIN CELLS.
000308 01-03

ON THE CAPACITY OF PRESYNAPTIC ALPHA-RECEPTORS TO MODULATE NOREPINEPHRINE RELEASE FROM SLICES OF RAT NEOCORTEX AND THE AFFINITY OF SOME AGONISTS AND ANTAGONISTS FOR THESE RECEPTORS.
000323 01-03

MULTIPLE RECEPTORS FOR SEROTONIN IN THE RAT-BRAIN.
001269 02-03

FURTHER EVIDENCE FOR THE EXISTENCE OF MULTIPLE RECEPTORS FOR DOPAMINE IN THE CENTRAL-NERVOUS-SYSTEM.
001296 02-03

DETECTION OF MULTIPLE RECEPTORS FOR DOPAMINE.
001481 02-03

CHANGES IN CEREBRAL DOPAMINE METABOLISM AND RECEPTORS DURING ONE-YEAR NEUROLEPTIC ADMINISTRATION AND SUBSEQUENT WITHDRAWAL: RELEVANCE TO BRAIN-BIOCHEMISTRY IN SCHIZOPHRENIA.
002390 02-15

THE NEUROLATHYROGEN, BETA N OXALYL-L-ALPHA-BETA-DIAMINOPROPIONIC-ACID, IS A POTENT AGONIST AT GLUTAMATE PREFERRING RECEPTORS IN THE FROG SPINAL-CORD.
002858 03-03

EFFECTS OF ANTIDEPRESSANT-DRUGS ON DIFFERENT RECEPTORS IN THE BRAIN.
003824 04-03

EVIDENCE FOR SEDATIVE EFFECTS OF LOW-DOSES OF MORPHINE IN MICE INVOLVING RECEPTORS INSENSITIVE TO NALOXONE.
004173 04-04

RECENT STUDIES ON INTERACTION BETWEEN OPIOID-PEPTIDES AND THEIR RECEPTORS.
004300 04-06

RECEPTORS, ADENYLATE-CYCLASE, DÉPRESSION, AND LITHIUM.
004353 04-09

RECHALLENGE
INAPPROPRIATE ADH SECRETION: THE ROLE OF DRUG RECHALLENGE.
002629 02-17

RECIDIVISM
RECIDIVISM AND REHABILITATION RATES FOR 135 CRIMINALLY-INSANE-OFFENDERS. (D.ED. DISSERTATION).
002514 02-17

RECIPIENT
PIRACETAM ACTIVITY MAY DIFFER ACCORDING TO THE AGE OF THE RECIPIENT MOUSE.
003705 04-02

RECIRCULATION
DISPOSITION OF VALPROIC-ACID IN THE RAT: DOSE-DEPENDENT METABOLISM, DISTRIBUTION, ENTEROHEPATIC RECIRCULATION AND CHOLERETIC-EFFECT.
000073 01-03

RECLASSIFICATION
RECLASSIFICATION OF THE TARDIVE-DYSKINESIA SYNDROME.
002374 02-15

RECOGNITION
GABA-MODULIN REGULATES SOLUBILIZED BENZODIAZEPINE AND GABA RECOGNITION SITES. (UNPUBLISHED PAPER).
001263 02-03

MULTIPLE BENZODIAZEPINE-RECEPTOR COMPLEXES: SOME BENZODIAZEPINE RECOGNITION SITES ARE COUPLED TO GABA-RECEPTORS AND IONOPHORES.
001484 02-03

TARDIVE-DYSKINESIA: RECOGNITION, MANAGEMENT, AND PREVENTION.
002392 02-15

THE REGULATION OF BENZODIAZEPINE RECOGNITION SITES BY ENDOGENOUS MODULATORS.
002642 03-01

BENZODIAZEPINE RECOGNITION SITES ON GABA-RECEPTORS.
002730 03-03

RECONCEPTUALIZED
ANXIETY RECONCEPTUALIZED.
000951 01-17

RECORDING
THE IN VITRO BRAIN SLICE AS A USEFUL NEUROPHYSIOLOGICAL PREPARATION FOR INTRACELLULAR RECORDING.
001864 02-06

RECORDINGS
COMPUTERIZED ANALYSIS OF SLEEP RECORDINGS APPLIED TO DRUG EVALUATION: MIDAZOLAM IN NORMAL SUBJECTS.
004564 04-14

RECOVERING
EFFECTS OF CYCLOSPASMOL UPON SENSORY PARAMETERS IN PATIENTS RECOVERING FROM CEREBROVASCULAR-ACCIDENTS.
002360 02-14

RECOVERY
A COMPARISON OF RATES OF DEPLETION AND RECOVERY OF NORADRENALINE STORES OF PERIPHERAL AND CENTRAL NORADRENERGIC NEURONES AFTER RESERPINE ADMINISTRATION: IMPORTANCE OF NEURONAL ACTIVITY.
000314 01-03

FACILITATION OF RECOVERY BY PROPANTHELINE-BROMIDE AFTER LATERAL HYPOTHALAMIC DAMAGE.
000396 01-04

DRUG INTERFERENCE ON SOME BIOCHEMICAL-PARAMETERS OF RAT-CEREBRAL-CORTEX DURING POSTISCHEMIC RECOVERY.
001126 02-03

DEVELOPMENT OF AND RECOVERY FROM SUBSENSITIVITY OF THE NORADRENERGIC CYCLIC-AMP GENERATING SYSTEM IN BRAIN: EFFECT OF AMPHETAMINE FOLLOWING INHIBITION OF ITS AROMATIC HYDROXYLATION BY IPRINDOLE.
001353 02-03

CHANGES IN PREVALENCE, SEVERITY, AND RECOVERY IN TARDIVE-DYSKINESIA WITH AGE.
002455 02-15

OPIATE ANTAGONIST IMPROVES NEUROLOGIC RECOVERY AFTER SPINAL INJURY.
002714 03-03

BRIEF COMMUNICATION: BEHAVIORAL RECOVERY AFTER TOLUENE EXPOSURE IN RATS.
002969 03-04

CORTICAL RECOVERY FROM EFFECTS OF MONOCULAR DEPRIVATION: ACCELERATION WITH NOREPINEPHRINE AND SUPPRESSION WITH 6 HYDROXYDOPAMINE.
003024 03-04

TARDIVE-DYSKINESIA: TWO-YEAR RECOVERY.
003535 03-15

RECRUITING
INHIBITORY-ACTION OF THE COMBINATION OF AMINOPYRINE AND SECOBARBITAL ON EEG ACTIVATION, NEOCORTICAL RECRUITING AND AUGMENTING RESPONSES IN RABBITS.
004022 04-03

RECTUS-ABDOMINIS
THE EFFECTS OF SUBSTITUTED BENZAMIDES ON FROG RECTUS-ABDOMINIS.
001228 02-03

RECURRENCE
RAPID RECURRENCE OF MANIA FOLLOWING LITHIUM WITHDRAWAL.
002010 02-09

RECURRENCES
THE RELATIVE PROPHYLACTIC EFFICACY OF LITHIUM AGAINST MANIC AND DEPRESSIVE RECURRENCES IN BIPOLAR-PATIENTS.
002040 02-09

RECURRENT
THE PHARMACOTHERAPY OF MAJOR DEPRESSIVE-SYNDROME. PART 2: PROPHYLAXIS OF RECURRENT DEPRESSIVE-ILLNESS.
002043 02-09

LITHIUM IN THE PROPHYLAXIS OF RECURRENT AFFECTIVE-DISORDERS (EFFECTIVENESS OF LOW PLASMA LEVELS AND PREDICTORS TO CLINICAL-RESPONSE).
004365 04-09

RECYCLES
5' TRIPHOSPHATE RECYCLES INDEPENDENTLY OF ACETYLCHOLINE IN CHOLINERGIC SYNAPTIC VESICLES.
004063 04-03

RED-BLOOD-CELL
PHENOTHIAZINE PLASMA AND RED-BLOOD-CELL CONCENTRATIONS, THEIR RELATIONSHIP TO SIDE-EFFECTS AND CLINICAL-EFFICACY.
002386 02-15

MECHANISM OF LITHIUM INCLUDED ELEVATION IN RED-BLOOD-CELL CHOLINE CONTENT: AN IN VITRO ANALYSIS.
004511 04-13

RED-BLOOD-CELLS
LITHIUM LEVELS IN BLOOD-PLATELETS, SERUM, RED-BLOOD-CELLS AND BRAIN REGIONS IN RATS GIVEN ACUTE OR CHRONIC LITHIUM-SALT TREATMENTS.
000082 01-03

THE EFFLUX OF LITHIUM FROM RED-BLOOD-CELLS AND THE EFFECT OF LITHIUM PROPHYLAXIS.
000630 01-09

MEASUREMENT OF FLUPHENAZINE BY GAS-CHROMATOGRAPHY IN HUMAN PLASMA AND RED-BLOOD-CELLS.
002491 02-16

REDERGINE
EFFECTS OF REPEATED ADMINISTRATIONS OF DIHYDROERGOTOXINE (REDERGINE) ON THE SLEEP-WAKEFULNESS CYCLE IN THE CAT.
003703 04-02

REDOX
INTRACELLULAR REDOX STATES UNDER HALOTHANE AND BARBITURATE ANESTHESIA IN NORMAL, ISCHEMIC, AND ANOXIC MONKEY BRAIN.
000295 01-03

REDUCER
CHANGES IN THE AUGMENTER REDUCER TENDENCY AND IN PAIN MEASURES AS A RESULT OF TREATMENT WITH A SEROTONIN REUPTAKE INHIBITOR ZIMELIDINE.
002305 02-13

REDUCING
PROCEDURES FOR REDUCING DRUG INTAKE: NONHUMAN STUDIES.
001753 02-04

COMPARISON OF ANXIETY REDUCING SUBSTANCES. (PH.D. DISSERTATION).
003278 03-10

REDUCTION
REDUCTION OF GAMMA AMINOBUTYRIC-ACID-MEDIATED (GABA) TRANSMISSION BY A CONVULSANT BENZODIAZEPINE.
000015 01-02

REDUCTION OF OPIATE BINDING TO BRAINSTEM SLICES ASSOCIATED WITH THE DEVELOPMENT OF TOLERANCE TO MORPHINE IN RATS.
000066 01-03

REDUCTION OF FETAL RAT SPINAL-CORD VOLUME FOLLOWING MATERNAL MORPHINE INJECTION.
000161 01-03

REDUCTION OF VOLUNTARY MORPHINE CONSUMPTION FOLLOWING TREATMENT WITH ZIMELIDINE.
000253 01-03

REDUCTION IN THE NUMBER OF SEROTONIN-RECEPTORS IN THE BRAINSTEM OF MORPHINE-DEPENDENT RATS: RELATION TO BLOCKADE OF NALOXONE PRECIPITATED JUMPING BY SEROTONIN AGONISTS.
000258 01-03

REDUCTION OF FOOD INTAKE BY PIRIBEDIL IN THE RAT: RELATION TO DOPAMINE-RECEPTOR STIMULATION.
000355 01-04

CHOLECYSTOKININ-PEPTIDES PRODUCE MARKED REDUCTION OF
DOPAMINE TURNOVER IN DISCRETE AREAS IN THE RAT-BRAIN
FOLLOWING INTERAVENTRICULAR INJECTION.
                                                    001239 02-03
VESTIBULO-OCULAR REFLEXES IN RABBITS: REDUCTION BY INTRAVENOUS
INJECTION OF DIAZEPAM.
                                                    001566 02-04
AN INTERFERENCE REDUCTION THEORY OF THE EFFECTS OF ETHANOL ON
CONFLICT-BEHAVIOR.
                                                    001586 02-04
REDUCTION OF DOPAMINERGIC-SUPERSENSITIVITY BY A SINGLE-DOSE OF
AMPHETAMINE.
                                                    001642 02-04
SELECTIVE REDUCTION BY DEXAMETHASONE OF STRESS RELATED
HYPERPHAGIAS.
                                                    001703 02-04
REDUCTION OF BARBITURATE ANESTHESIA BY NEW GLUTARIMIDE
COMPOUNDS IN MICE.
                                                    001748 02-04
ADRENERGIC REGULATION OF THE REDUCTION IN ACETYL-COENZYME-
A:ARYLAMINE-N-ACETYLTRANSFERASE IN THE RAT PINEAL.
                                                    002654 03-03
EFFECTS OF ANXIETY REDUCTION BY BEHAVIOURAL-TECHNIQUES AND
MEPROBAMATE ON CERTAIN PARAMETERS OF INFORMATION THEORY.
                                                    003108 03-04
REDUCTION IN THE LEVEL OF IMMUNOTITRATABLE DOPAMINE-BETA-
HYDROXYLASE AFTER CHRONIC ADMINISTRATION OF L-DOPA OR
ALPHA METHYLDOPA.
                                                    003764 04-03
REDUCTION IN OPIATE ACTIVATION AFTER CHRONIC
ELECTROCONVULSIVE-SHOCK -- POSSIBLE ROLE FOR ENDORPHINS IN
THE BEHAVIORAL-EFFECTS OF CONVULSIVE-SHOCK-TREATMENT.
(UNPUBLISHED PAPER).
                                                    004154 04-04

REEVALUATION
A REEVALUATION OF THE MECHANISMS UNDERLYING SIMPLE CELL
ORIENTATION SELECTIVITY.
                                                    002894 03-03
A REEVALUATION OF THE NEUROCHEMICAL-EFFECTS AND
ANTINOCICEPTIVE-EFFECTS OF INTRATHECAL CAPSAICIN IN THE RAT.
                                                    004184 04-04

REEXAMINATION
A REEXAMINATION OF THE CLINICAL-EFFECTS OF IMIPRAMINE AND
AMITRIPTYLINE IN DEPRESSIVE-ILLNESS.
                                                    000579 01-09

REFLEX
THE INFLUENCE OF BENZOCTAMINE ON DOPAMINE AND NOREPINEPHRINE
CONTENTS OF THE SUBSTANTIA-NIGRA AND ON THE MUSCLE STRETCH
REFLEX OF THE CAT.
                                                    000054 01-03
ATTEMPTS TO REINSTATE LORDOSIS REFLEX IN ESTROGEN-PRIMED
SPINAL FEMALE RATS WITH MONOAMINE AGONISTS.
                                                    000421 01-04
A STUDY OF THE QUANTAL (ALL-OR-NONE) CHANGE IN REFLEX LATENCY
PRODUCED BY OPIATE ANALGESICS.
                                                    000425 01-04
EVIDENCE SUGGESTING A TRANSMITTER OR NEUROMODULATORY ROLE
FOR SUBSTANCE-P AT THE FIRST SYNAPSE OF THE BARORECEPTOR
REFLEX.
                                                    001264 02-03
NONSEROTONERGIC DEPRESSION OF SPINAL MONOSYNAPTIC REFLEX
TRANSMISSION BY 5 HYDROXYTRYPTOPHAN.
                                                    002745 03-03
CHANGES IN THE HORIZONTAL VESTIBULO-OCULAR REFLEX OF THE
RHESUS-MONKEY WITH BEHAVIORAL AND PHARMACOLOGICAL
ALERTING.
                                                    002997 03-04
SENSITIVE DEPRESSANT EFFECT OF BENZODIAZEPINES ON THE CROSSED
EXTENSOR REFLEX IN CHLORALOSE ANESTHETIZED RATS.
                                                    003027 03-04
EARLY DETECTION OF HUNTINGTONS-DISEASE. BLINK REFLEX AND
LEVODOPA LOAD IN PRESYMPTOMATIC AND INCIPIENT SUBJECTS.
                                                    003311 03-11
EFFECTS OF DOPAMINE, APOMORPHINE, GAMMA HYDROXYBUTYRIC-
ACID, HALOPERIDOL AND PIMOZIDE ON REFLEX BRADYCARDIA IN
RATS.
                                                    004085 04-04
EFFECTS OF ANALGESICS AND CNS-ACTING DRUGS ON STRUGGLING
FOLLOWING REPETITIVE STIMULATION OF THE TAIL, AND FLEXOR
REFLEX TO A SINGLE STIMULATION OF THE SCIATIC-NERVE IN RATS.
                                                    004148 04-04
BILATERAL SKIN CONDUCTANCE AND THE PUPILLARY LIGHT DARK
REFLEX: MANIPULATION BY CHLORPROMAZINE, HALOPERIDOL,
SCOPOLAMINE, AND PLACEBO.
                                                    004544 04-13

REFLEX-INDUCED
MODULATORY EFFECT OF BRAIN ACETYLCHOLINE ON REFLEX-INDUCED
BRADYCARDIA AND TACHYCARDIA IN CONSCIOUS RATS.
                                                    003744 04-03

REFLEXES
EFFECT OF DIAZEPAM AND DESMETHYLDIAZEPAM IN SPASTICITY AND
RIGIDITY: A QUANTITATIVE STUDY OF REFLEXES AND PLASMA
CONCENTRATIONS.
                                                    000701 01-11
EVOKED-POTENTIAL CHANGES IN THE SUPERIOR-COLLICULUS PARALLEL
THE LESION-INDUCED DEVELOPMENT OF GROOMING REFLEXES IN THE
CAT. (PH.D. DISSERTATION).
                                                    001179 02-03
EFFECTS OF ALPHA-ADRENOCEPTOR STIMULATING DRUGS ON
BARORECEPTOR REFLEXES IN CONSCIOUS CATS.
                                                    001514 02-03
VESTIBULO-OCULAR REFLEXES IN RABBITS: REDUCTION BY INTRAVENOUS
INJECTION OF DIAZEPAM.
                                                    001566 02-04
ELECTROMYOGRAPHIC-ASSESSMENT OF SPINAL REFLEXES IN
EXPERIMENTALLY DEPRESSED DOGS TREATED WITH
ANTIDEPRESSANTS.
                                                    001620 02-04
THE PHARMACOLOGICAL ANALYSIS OF MONOAMINERGIC MECHANISMS
OF THE MEDIAL HYPOTHALAMUS IN FOOD PROCURING CONDITIONED
REFLEXES IN RATS.
                                                    003100 03-04
CANNABINOID-INDUCED ENHANCEMENT AND DEPRESSION OF CAT
MONOSYNAPTIC REFLEXES.
                                                    004040 04-03
POSSIBLE MUSCARINIC CHOLINERGIC MEDIATION OF PATTERNED
AGGRESSIVE REFLEXES IN THE CAT.
                                                    004153 04-04
THE EFFECT OF THE NEW ANTIDEPRESSANT INKASAN ON THE
BIOELECTRICAL-ACTIVITY OF THE BRAIN AND ON CONDITIONED
REFLEXES.
                                                    004212 04-04

REFORMULATION
A REFORMULATION OF THE DUAL-ACTION MODEL OF OPIOID
DEPENDENCE: OPIOID-SPECIFIC NEURONAL KINDLING.
                                                    003645 03-17

REFRACTORY
INTENSIVE MONITORING IN REFRACTORY EPILEPSY.
                                                    003378 03-11
MOBILIZATION OF REFRACTORY CHRONIC SCHIZOPHRENICS WITH
HALOPERIDOL.
                                                    004337 04-08

REFUSE
THE RIGHTS OF INVOLUNTARY-PATIENTS TO REFUSE
PHARMACOTHERAPY: WHAT IS REASONABLE?
                                                    004730 04-17

REGARD
LONG-TERM-TREATMENT WITH NEUROLEPTIC-AGENTS: ADAPTATION
PHENOMENA AND THEIR SIGNIFICANCE WITH REGARD TO
SCHIZOPHRENIC-SYMPTOMATOLOGY AND SIDE-EFFECTS.
                                                    002370 02-15
PRELIMINARY-FINDINGS WITH REGARD TO RISK-FACTORS IN THE
DEVELOPMENT OF TARDIVE-DYSKINESIA.
                                                    003501 03-15

REGIME
THERAPEUTIC-EFFICACY OF DOXEPIN IN DIVIDED AND SINGLE-DOSE
REGIME.
                                                    003259 03-09
SUSTAINED DECREASE IN FAT CONSUMPTION PRODUCED BY
AMPHETAMINE IN RATS MAINTAINED ON A DIETARY SELF-SELECTION
REGIME.
                                                    004150 04-04

REGIMEN
ANTIPSYCHOTIC-EFFECT OF PROPRANOLOL ON CHRONIC
SCHIZOPHRENICS: STUDY OF A GRADUAL TREATMENT REGIMEN.
                                                    001915 02-08
POLYPHARMACY REGIMEN AS AN EXACERBATING RISK IN THERAPY-
RESISTANT EPILEPTIC-SEIZURES AND BEHAVIORAL-DISORDERS.
                                                    004720 04-17

REGIMENS
DRUG REGIMENS FACILITATING AGGRESSION: BEHAVIOR, AMINE, AND
RECEPTOR ALTERATIONS.
                                                    002987 03-04

REGISTRATION
PSYCHOTROPIC-DRUG REGISTRATION IN THE SCANDINAVIAN-COUNTRIES:
THE ROLE OF CLINICAL-TRIALS.
                                                    002550 02-17

REGRESSION
NONLINEAR REGRESSION ANALYSIS OF NOREPINEPHRINE RESPONSE
KINETICS IN CEREBRAL VASCULATURE.
                                                    000256 01-01

REGULATION
REGULATION OF STRIATAL ACETYLCHOLINE CONCENTRATION BY D2
DOPAMINE-RECEPTORS.
                                                    000269 01-03
DIFFERENTIAL REGULATION OF MUSCARINIC AGONIST BINDING-SITES
FOLLOWING CHRONIC CHOLINESTERASE INHIBITION.
                                                    000279 01-03

REGULATION OF THE STATE OF PHOSPHORYLATION OF SPECIFIC
NEURONAL PROTEINS IN MOUSE-BRAIN BY IN VIVO ADMINISTRATION
OF ANESTHETIC AND CONVULSANT-AGENTS.
000291 01-03
EFFECTS OF CHRONIC DIETARY LITHIUM ON ACTIVITY AND REGULATION
OF NA-K-ADENOSINE-TRIPHOSPHATASE IN RAT-BRAIN.
000297 01-03
THE LONG-TERM REGULATION OF GANGLIONIC TYROSINE-HYDROXYLASE
BY PREGANGLIONIC NERVE ACTIVITY.
000333 01-03
DOPAMINERGIC FACTORS IN HUMAN PROLACTIN REGULATION: A
PITUITARY MODEL FOR THE STUDY OF A NEUROENDOCRINE SYSTEM IN
MAN.
000776 01-13
THE IDENTITY AND HYPOTHALAMIC ORIGIN OF CHOLECYSTOKININ IN
RAT-BRAIN AND POSTERIOR PITUITARY AND ITS POSSIBLE ROLE IN
REGULATION OF NEUROSECRETION. (UNPUBLISHED PAPER).
001003 02-01
DOPAMINE-RECEPTOR: ISOLATION, PURIFICATION, AND REGULATION.
001011 02-01
THE REGULATION OF GABA-RECEPTORS AS A POSSIBLE MECHANISM FOR
GABA 1,4 BENZODIAZEPINE INTERACTIONS. (UNPUBLISHED PAPER).
001012 02-01
REGULATION OF ACETYLCHOLINE RELEASE DURING INCREASED NEURONAL
ACTIVITY. (UNPUBLISHED PAPER).
001061 02-01
INTERACTIONS OF NEUROPEPTIDES WITH CHOLINERGIC
SEPTOHIPPOCAMPAL PATHWAY: INDICATION FOR A POSSIBLE
TRANSSYNAPTIC REGULATION. (UNPUBLISHED PAPER).
001062 02-01
OPIOID MECHANISMS IN REGULATION OF CEREBRAL MONOAMINES IN
VIVO.
001098 02-03
INFLUENCE OF NARCOTIC-AGENTS ON TEMPERATURE REGULATION.
001108 02-03
REGULATION OF HIPPOCAMPAL GLUTAMATE-RECEPTORS: EVIDENCE FOR
THE INVOLVEMENT OF A CALCIUM-ACTIVATED PROTEASE.
001120 02-03
REGULATION OF RECEPTOR BINDING INTERACTIONS OF 125I
ANGIOTENSIN-II AND 125I SARCOSINE1-LEUCINE8-ANGIOTENSIN-II, AN
ANGIOTENSIN ANTAGONIST, BY SODIUM-ION.
001124 02-03
REGULATION OF CHOLINERGIC TRANSMISSION IN ADRENAL-MEDULLA.
(UNPUBLISHED PAPER).
001182 02-03
REGULATION OF TYROSINE-HYDROXYLASE AFTER CHRONIC-TREATMENT
WITH CLASSIC AND ATYPICAL ANTISCHIZOPHRENIC-DRUGS.
001262 02-03
DOWN REGULATION OF DIHYDROALPRENOLOL AND IMIPRAMINE
BINDING-SITES IN BRAIN OF RATS REPEATEDLY TREATED WITH
IMIPRAMINE.
001317 02-03
REGULATION BY A BETA-ADRENERGIC-RECEPTOR OF A CA-INDEPENDENT
ADENOSINE-CYCLIC-MONOPHOSPHATE-PHOSPHODIESTERASE IN C6-
GLIOMA CELLS. (UNPUBLISHED PAPER).
001403 02-03
THE REGULATION OF CARDIAC MUSCARINIC CHOLINERGIC-RECEPTORS BY
ISOPROTERENOL.
001441 02-03
PHARMACOLOGICAL EVIDENCE OF A POSSIBLE TRYPTAMINERGIC
REGULATION OF OPIATE-RECEPTORS BY USING INDALPINE, A SELECTIVE
5 HT UPTAKE INHIBITOR.
001517 02-03
A STUDY OF A GLIAL GAMMA AMINOBUTYRIC-ACID SYSTEM: ITS
REGULATION, FUNCTION AND THE EFFECTS OF DIAZEPAM. (PH.D.
DISSERTATION).
001524 02-03
CHRONIC NEUROLEPTIC TREATMENT AND DOPAMINE-RECEPTOR
REGULATION.
001837 02-05
CORTICAL-CORRELATES OF VIGILANCE REGULATION AND THEIR USE IN
EVALUATING THE EFFECTS OF TREATMENT.
002147 02-11
ABNORMAL REGULATION OF PROLACTIN RELEASE IN IDIOPATHIC
PARKINSONS-DISEASE.
002255 02-13
THE HYPOTHALAMIC DOPAMINERGIC REGULATION OF PROLACTIN: A
MODEL FOR THE STUDY OF NEUROHORMONAL MECHANISMS IN MAN.
002568 02-17
REGULATION OF NEUROTRANSMISSION THROUGH PRESYNAPTIC-
RECEPTORS AND OTHER MECHANISMS: POSSIBLE CLINICAL RELEVANCE
AND THERAPEUTIC POTENTIAL.
002569 02-16
THE REGULATION OF BENZODIAZEPINE RECOGNITION SITES BY
ENDOGENOUS MODULATORS.
002642 03-01
ADRENERGIC REGULATION OF THE REDUCTION IN ACETYL-COENZYME-
A:ARYLAMINE-N-ACETYLTRANSFERASE IN THE RAT PINEAL.
002654 03-03

DIFFERENTIAL REGULATION BY GUANINE-NUCLEOTIDES OF OPIATE
AGONIST AND ANTAGONIST RECEPTOR INTERACTIONS.
002688 03-03
PRESYNAPTIC REGULATION OF THE RELEASE OF CATECHOLAMINES IN THE
CAT HYPOTHALAMUS.
002703 03-03
ANTERIOR PITUITARY GABA-RECEPTORS AND THEIR REGULATION OF
PROLACTIN SECRETION.
002738 03-03
BETA-ADRENERGIC-RECEPTOR SUBTYPES: PROPERTIES, DISTRIBUTION,
AND REGULATION.
002829 03-03
REGULATION BY CATIONS OF (3H)SPIROPERIDOL BINDING ASSOCIATED
WITH DOPAMINE-RECEPTORS OF RAT-BRAIN.
002922 03-03
THE DOPAMINE-RECEPTOR: ISOLATION, PURIFICATION AND REGULATION.
003660 04-01
ROLE OF ADRENERGIC BLOCKING-AGENTS AND GLUCOCORTICOIDS ON
THE REGULATION OF PITUITARY OPIOID-PEPTIDES LEVELS.
003801 04-03
REGULATION OF ALPHA1-ADRENOCEPTORS IN THE CEREBRAL-CORTEX OF
THE RAT BY THYROID-HORMONES.
003816 04-03
REGULATION OF BIOGENESIS OF PSYCHOTOMIMETIC AMINES.
(UNPUBLISHED PAPER).
003818 04-03
CATECHOLAMINE SYNTHESIS REGULATION IN HYPOTHALAMIC
SYNAPTOSOMES. (UNPUBLISHED PAPER).
003829 04-03
REGULATION OF NORADRENALINE OVERFLOW IN RAT-CEREBRAL-CORTEX
BY PROSTAGLANDIN-E2.
003841 04-03
PRESYNAPTIC REGULATION OF THE RELEASE OF ACETYLCHOLINE BY 5
HYDROXYTRYPTAMINE.
003843 04-03
EFFECTS OF IN VIVO AMPHETAMINE ADMINISTRATION ON DOPAMINE
SYNTHESIS REGULATION IN RAT-BRAIN STRIATAL SYNAPTOSOMES.
(UNPUBLISHED PAPER).
003960 04-03
REGULATION OF SEROTONIN2-RECEPTORS (5 HT2) LABELED WITH
(3H)SPIROPERIDOL BY CHRONIC-TREATMENT WITH THE
ANTIDEPRESSANT AMITRIPTYLINE.
003964 04-03
MULTIPLE ALPHA2-NORADRENERGIC-RECEPTOR SITES IN RAT-BRAIN:
SELECTIVE REGULATION OF HIGH-AFFINITY (3H)CLONIDINE BINDING BY
GUANINE-NUCLEOTIDES AND DIVALENT-CATIONS.
003992 04-03
CATION REGULATION DIFFERENTIATES SPECIFIC BINDING OF
(3H)SULPIRIDE AND (3H)SPIPERONE TO RAT STRIATAL PREPARATIONS.
004032 04-03
PHARMACOLOGICAL REGULATION OF CALMODULIN.
004052 04-03
GENOTYPIC INFLUENCES ON STRIATAL DOPAMINERGIC REGULATION IN
MICE.
004217 04-04
DOWN REGULATION OF NORADRENERGIC-RECEPTOR FUNCTION BY
ANTIDEPRESSANT-DRUGS: FUNCTIONAL SIGNIFICANCE AND
DISTINCTION FROM ANTIPSYCHOTIC-DRUGS. (UNPUBLISHED PAPER).
004746 04-17

REGULATORY
GLUCOCORTICOIDS AS A REGULATORY FACTOR FOR BRAIN TRYPTOPHAN-
HYDROXYLASE DURING DEVELOPMENT.
001500 02-03

REHABILITATION
THE RATIONAL USE OF MUSCLE-RELAXANTS IN REHABILITATION
MEDICINE.
000943 01-17
THE ASSOCIATION OF RETARD NEUROLEPTICS TO OTHER NEUROLEPTICS
IN THE REHABILITATION OF PSYCHOTIC-PATIENTS.
002108 02-11
RECIDIVISM AND REHABILITATION RATES FOR 135 CRIMINALLY-INSANE-
OFFENDERS. (D.ED. DISSERTATION).
002514 02;17

REINFORCEMENT
DIFFERENTIAL-EFFECTS OF METHYLPHENIDATE ON SIGNALLED AND
NONSIGNALLED REINFORCEMENT.
000380 01-04
EXTINCTION AND DOPAMINE-RECEPTOR BLOCKADE AFTER INTERMITTENT
REINFORCEMENT TRAINING: FAILURE TO OBSERVE FUNCTIONAL
EQUIVALENCE.
000490 01-04
THE EFFECTS OF PIPRADROL ON THE ACQUISITION OF RESPONDING WITH
CONDITIONED REINFORCEMENT: A ROLE FOR SENSORY
PRECONDITIONING.
001572 02-04
THE RELATIONSHIP BETWEEN POSITIVE REINFORCEMENT AND
CONDITIONED TASTE-AVERSION PRODUCED BY SELF-ADMINISTERED
DRUGS. (PH.D. DISSERTATION).
001798 02-04

PIMOZIDE ATTENUATES LEVER-PRESSING FOR WATER REINFORCEMENT IN RATS.
000000 03-04

REINFORCER
BEHAVIORAL-EFFECTS OF DRUGS: THE ROLE OF THE STIMULUS REINFORCER CONTINGENCY. (PH.D. DISSERTATION).
001537 02-03

REINFORCING
REINFORCING, DISCRIMINATIVE AND ACTIVATING PROPERTIES OF AMPHETAMINE.
000804 01-14
DOUBLE-BLIND EVALUATION OF REINFORCING AND ANORECTIC-ACTIONS OF WEIGHT-CONTROL MEDICATIONS: INTERACTION OF PHARMACOLOGICAL-TREATMENT AND BEHAVIORAL-TREATMENTS.
002314 02-14
SUBJECTIVE DRUG-EFFECTS AND DRUG PREFERENCE IN HEALTHY VOLUNTEERS AS A MODEL OF A DRUGS REINFORCING EFFECTS: STUDIES ON NOMIFENSINE, AMPHETAMINE AND PLACEBO.
002362 02-14

REINNERVATION
REINNERVATION OF THE DENERVATED STRIATUM BY SUBSTANTIA-NIGRA TRANSPLANTS: FUNCTIONAL CONSEQUENCES AS REVEALED BY PHARMACOLOGICAL AND SENSORIMOTOR TESTING.
000347 01-04
NEUROLEPTIC-INDUCED REINNERVATION SPROUTING IN THE CENTRAL-NERVOUS-SYSTEM (A MODEL FOR THE DEVELOPMENT OF TARDIVE-DYSKINESIA AND SUPERSENSITIVITY PSYCHOSIS).
002459 02-15

RELAPSE
RELAPSE TO NARCOTIC SELF-ADMINISTRATION IN MORPHINE POSTADDICT RATS: A POSSIBLE MODEL FOR PREDICTING ABUSE LIABILITY OF NARCOTIC-DRUGS. (PH.D. DISSERTATION).
003097 03-04
LOW SERUM PROLACTIN AND EARLY RELAPSE FOLLOWING NEUROLEPTIC WITHDRAWAL.
003166 03-08
THE EFFECTS OF A DRUG-HOLIDAY ON RELAPSE AND TARDIVE-DYSKINESIA IN CHRONIC-SCHIZOPHRENICS.
003487 03-15
RELAPSE AFTER SHORT-TERM DRUG-THERAPY IN NEUROTIC-OUTPATIENTS.
004400 04-09

RELAPSE-STUDIES
USE OF SURVIVAL CURVES IN ANALYSIS OF ANTIPSYCHOTIC RELAPSE-STUDIES.
002481 02-16

RELAPSES
UNWANTED EFFECTS OF LITHIUM-CARBONATE USED IN THE PREVENTION OF RELAPSES OF AFFECTIVE-ILLNESS.
004625 04-15

RELEASE
SUPPRESSION OF EVOKED AND SPONTANEOUS RELEASE OF NEUROTRANSMITTERS IN VIVO BY MORPHINE.
000058 01-03
EFFECTS OF PSYCHOTROPIC-DRUGS ON THE DISTRIBUTION OF 3H DOPAMINE INTO COMPARTMENTS OF RAT STRIATAL SYNAPTOSOMES AND ON SUBSEQUENT DEPOLARIZATION-INDUCED 3H DOPAMINE RELEASE.
000067 01-03
RELEASE OF ENDOGENOUS NOREPINEPHRINE FROM A RABBIT CEREBRAL-ARTERY.
000079 01-03
ALPHA-ADRENOCEPTOR-MEDIATED MODULATION OF 5 HYDROXYTRYPTAMINE RELEASE FROM RAT-BRAIN-CORTEX SLICES.
000111 01-03
GABA INHIBITION OF 3H GLYCINE RELEASE FROM SLICES OF RAT SUBSTANTIA-NIGRA IN VITRO.
000157 01-03
NALOXONE PROMOTES STIMULUS-EVOKED VASOPRESSIN RELEASE IN VIVO.
000165 01-03
INHIBITION OF NEURONAL UPTAKE REDUCES THE PRESYNAPTIC EFFECTS OF CLONIDINE BUT NOT OF ALPHA METHYLNORADRENALINE ON THE STIMULATION-EVOKED RELEASE OF 3H NORADRENALINE FROM RAT OCCIPITAL-CORTEX SLICES.
000227 01-03
THE EFFECT OF MORPHINE ON PURINE AND ACETYLCHOLINE RELEASE FROM RAT-CEREBRAL-CORTEX: EVIDENCE FOR A PURINERGIC COMPONENT IN MORPHINES ACTION.
000234 01-03
RELEASE OF GONADOTROPIN-RELEASING-HORMONE BY VERATRINE IN A HYPOTHALAMIC PITUITARY COINCUBATION.
000237 01-03
(3H)ACETYLCHOLINE AND (3H)5 HYDROXYTRYPTAMINE RELEASE FROM RAT-MIDBRAIN SLICES AND THE EFFECTS OF CALCIUM AND PHENOBARBITAL.
000251 01-03
THE POSSIBILITY THAT A COMPONENT OF MORPHINE-INDUCED ANALGESIA IS CONTRIBUTED INDIRECTLY VIA THE RELEASE OF ENDOGENOUS OPIOIDS. '
000263 01-03

EFFECTS OF DES-TYR-GAMMA-ENDORPHIN ON DOPAMINE RELEASE FROM VARIOUS RAT-BRAIN REGIONS IN VITRO.
000264 01-03
THE EFFECT OF DELTA9 TETRAHYDROCANNABINOL ON THE POSITIVE AND NEGATIVE FEEDBACK CONTROL OF LUTEINIZING-HORMONE RELEASE.
000286 01-03
IN VITRO ACETYLCHOLINE RELEASE FROM RAT CAUDATE-NUCLEUS AS A NEW MODEL FOR TESTING DRUGS WITH DOPAMINE-RECEPTOR ACTIVITY.
000289 01-03
TYROSINE ADMINISTRATION REDUCES BLOOD-PRESSURE AND ENHANCES BRAIN NOREPINEPHRINE RELEASE IN SPONTANEOUSLY HYPERTENSIVE-RATS.
000296 01-03
EFFECTS OF MORPHINE AND NALOXONE ON PHASIC RELEASE OF LUTEINIZING-HORMONE AND FOLLICLE-STIMULATING-HORMONE (40849).
000298 01-03
ON THE CAPACITY OF PRESYNAPTIC ALPHA-RECEPTORS TO MODULATE NOREPINEPHRINE RELEASE FROM SLICES OF RAT NEOCORTEX AND THE AFFINITY OF SOME AGONISTS AND ANTAGONISTS FOR THESE RECEPTORS.
000323 01-03
MORPHINE ENHANCES ADENOSINE RELEASE FROM THE IN VIVO RAT-CEREBRAL-CORTEX.
000451 01-04
DIFFERENTIAL-EFFECTS OF NALOXONE AGAINST THE DIAZEPAM-INDUCED RELEASE OF BEHAVIOR IN RATS IN THREE AVERSIVE-SITUATIONS.
000480 01-04
GROWTH-HORMONE (GH) RELEASE FOLLOWING THYROTROPIN-RELEASING-HORMONE (TRH) INJECTION IN MANIC-PATIENTS RECEIVING LITHIUM-CARBONATE.
000645 01-09
THE RELEASE OF CATECHOLAMINES FROM ADRENERGIC NEURONS.
000974 01-17
RELEASE OF ARACHIDONIC-ACID FROM ADRENAL CHROMAFFIN CELL-CULTURES DURING SECRETION OF EPINEPHRINE. (UNPUBLISHED PAPER).
001027 02-01
REGULATION OF ACETYLCHOLINE RELEASE DURING INCREASED NEURONAL ACTIVITY. (UNPUBLISHED PAPER).
001061 02-01
EFFECTS OF GABA AND DIAZEPAM ON 3H SEROTONIN RELEASE FROM HIPPOCAMPAL SYNAPTOSOMES.
001116 02-03
DYNAMICS OF ENDOGENOUS CATECHOLAMINE RELEASE FROM BRAIN FRAGMENTS OF MALE AND FEMALE RATS.
001121 02-03
FACTORS INFLUENCING THE RELEASE OF LABELLED GAMMA AMINOBUTYRIC-ACID AND ACETYLCHOLINE EVOKED BY ELECTRICAL-STIMULATION WITH ALTERNATING POLARITY FROM RAT CORTICAL SLICES.
001130 02-03
NORADRENALINE RELEASE FROM SLICES OF THE THALAMUS OF NORMAL AND MORPHINE-DEPENDENT RATS.
001142 02-03
BIOSYNTHESIS, AXONAL TRANSPORT AND RELEASE OF POSTERIOR PITUITARY-HORMONES. (UNPUBLISHED PAPER).
001148 02-03
PROSTAGLANDIN-E RELEASE BY RAT MEDIAL BASAL HYPOTHALAMUS IN VITRO. INHIBITION BY MELATONIN AT SUBMICROMOLAR CONCENTRATIONS.
001159 02-03
IGE MEDIATED HISTAMINE RELEASE IN RAT BASOPHILIC LEUKEMIA CELLS: RECEPTOR ACTIVATED PHOSPHOLIPID METHYLATION, CA-FLUX AND RELEASE OF ARACHIDONIC-ACID. (UNPUBLISHED PAPER).
001188 02-03
EFFECT OF AMINOOXYACETIC-ACID AND BICUCULLINE ON PROLACTIN RELEASE IN CASTRATED MALE RATS.
001194 02-03
INHIBITION OF ACH RELEASE BY PROSTAGLANDIN-E1 IN THE RABBIT SUPERIOR-CERVICAL-GANGLION.
001205 02-03
A COMPARISON OF THE EFFECTS OF METHYLPHENIDATE AND AMPHETAMINE ON THE SIMULTANEOUS RELEASE OF RADIOLABELLED DOPAMINE AND P OR M TYRAMINE FROM RAT STRIATAL SLICES.
001207 02-03
CALMODULIN RELEASE FROM STRIATAL MEMBRANES AFTER ACUTE AND CHRONIC TREATMENT WITH BUTACLAMOL.
001249 02-03
SEROTONIN-RECEPTOR MEDIATED MODULATION OF CA-DEPENDENT 5 HYDROXYTRYPTAMINE RELEASE FROM NEURONES OF THE RAT-BRAIN-CORTEX.
001258 02-03
INHIBITORY ACTION OF MORPHINE ON THE RELEASE OF A BRADYKININ-LIKE SUBSTANCE AFTER SCIATIC-NERVE STIMULATION.
001293 02-03

INTERNEURONES ARE PROBABLY NOT INVOLVED IN THE PRESYNAPTIC DOPAMINERGIC CONTROL OF DOPAMINE RELEASE IN RABBIT CAUDATE-NUCLEUS.
001298 02-03

• REGIONAL RELEASE OF (3H)ADENOSINE DERIVATIVES FROM RAT-BRAIN IN VIVO: EFFECT OF EXCITATORY AMINO-ACIDS, OPIATE AGONISTS, AND BENZODIAZEPINES.
001303 02-03

EVIDENCE THAT VASOPRESSIN IS INVOLVED IN THE ISOPRENALINE-INDUCED BETA ENDORPHIN RELEASE.
001319 02-03

ASCORBIC-ACID, AN ENDOGENOUS FACTOR REQUIRED FOR ACETYLCHOLINE RELEASE FROM THE SYNAPTIC VESICLES.
001322 02-03

DRUG-INDUCED RELEASE OF DOPAMINE FROM CORPUS-STRIATUM. (PH.D. DISSERTATION).
001343 02-03

EFFECTS OF HALOPEMIDE ON POTASSIUM-INDUCED RELEASE OF RADIOLABELED NEUROTRANSMITTERS FROM RAT CEREBROCORTICAL SLICES IN VITRO.
001347 02-03

A NOVEL GABA-RECEPTOR MODULATES STIMULUS-INDUCED GLUTAMATE RELEASE FROM CORTICOSTRIATAL TERMINALS.
001376 02-03

EFFECTS OF DIAZEPAM ON ADENOSINE AND ACETYLCHOLINE RELEASE FROM RAT-CEREBRAL-CORTEX: FURTHER EVIDENCE FOR A PURINERGIC MECHANISM IN ACTION OF DIAZEPAM.
001414 02-03

EFFECT OF MELANOSTATIN AND THYROLIBERIN ON THE BIOSYNTHESIS AND RELEASE OF DOPAMINE BY RAT-BRAIN STRIATAL P2-FRACTIONS.
001472 02-03

CORRELATIONS BETWEEN HEMODYNAMIC PARAMETERS OF THE LIVER AND NOREPINEPHRINE RELEASE UPON HEPATIC-NERVE STIMULATION IN THE DOG.
001547 02-03

AN AUTOMATED ELECTROCHEMICAL-METHOD FOR IN VIVO MONITORING OF CATECHOLAMINE RELEASE.
001873 02-06

STUDIES ON GABA RELEASE IN VIVO USING A SIMPLE METHOD FOR PERFUSION OF THE FOURTH VENTRICLE OF THE RAT.
001881 02-06

PLATELET AGGREGATION, 5 HYDROXYTRYPTAMINE UPTAKE AND RELEASE IN HUNTINGTONS-CHOREA.
002112 02-11

LITHIUM ANTAGONISM OF ETHANOL-INDUCED DEPLETION OF CEREBELLAR GUANOSINE-CYCLIC-MONOPHOSPHATE AND STIMULATION OF STRIATAL DOPAMINE RELEASE.
002242 02-13

ABNORMAL REGULATION OF PROLACTIN RELEASE IN IDIOPATHIC PARKINSONS-DISEASE.
002255 02-13

EVIDENCE THAT IT IS POSSIBLE TO CAUSE ANOREXIA BY INCREASING RELEASE AND/OR DIRECTLY STIMULATING POSTSYNAPTIC SEROTONIN-RECEPTORS IN THE BRAIN.
002602 02-17

SEX-DIFFERENCES IN THE AMPHETAMINE STIMULATED RELEASE OF CATECHOLAMINES FROM RAT STRIATAL TISSUE IN VITRO.
002668 03-03

GABAERGIC MECHANISMS IN THE CONTROL OF PRL AND GH RELEASE.
002690 03-03

EFFECT OF TETANUS TOXIN ON TRANSMITTER RELEASE FROM THE SUBSTANTIA-NIGRA AND STRIATUM IN VITRO.
002691 03-03

PRESYNAPTIC REGULATION OF THE RELEASE OF CATECHOLAMINES IN THE CAT HYPOTHALAMUS.
002703 03-03

METHYLPHENIDATE-LIKE STIMULANTS IN VITRO RELEASE (3H)TYRAMINES BUT NOT (14C)DOPAMINE.
002706 03-03

INHIBITION OF VASOPRESSIN RELEASE TO CAROTID OCCLUSION BY GAMMA AMINOBUTYRIC-ACID AND GLYCINE.
002715 03-03

THE PRESYNAPTIC STIMULATING EFFECT OF ACETYLCHOLINE ON DOPAMINE RELEASE IS SUPPRESSED DURING ACTIVATION OF NIGROSTRIATAL DOPAMINERGIC NEURONS IN THE CAT.
002733 03-03

ENHANCEMENT OF NORADRENALINE RELEASE FROM RAT-CEREBRAL-CORTEX BY NEUROLEPTIC-DRUGS.
002742 03-03

MODULATION BY ENDOGENOUS DOPAMINE OF THE RELEASE OF ACETYLCHOLINE IN THE CAUDATE-NUCLEUS OF THE RABBIT.
002751 03-03

THE EFFECTS OF D-AMPHETAMINE AND POTASSIUM ON SEROTONIN RELEASE AND METABOLISM IN RAT-CEREBRAL-CORTEX TISSUE.
002754 03-03

NEUROLEPTIC-INDUCED ACUTE DYSTONIC REACTIONS MAY BE DUE TO ENHANCED DOPAMINE RELEASE ON TO SUPERSENSITIVE POSTSYNAPTIC-RECEPTORS.
002789 03-03

THE DIRECT EFFECT OF RESERPINE IN VITRO ON PROLACTIN RELEASE FROM RAT ANTERIOR PITUITARY-GLANDS.
002810 03-03

ACTIONS OF TREMORGENIC FUNGAL TOXINS ON NEUROTRANSMITTER RELEASE.
002843 03-03

THE EFFECT OF COLCHICINE AND CYTOCHALASIN B ON THE RELEASE OF TAURINE FROM THE CHICK RETINA.
002856 03-03

GABA AND BACLOFEN POTENTIATE THE K-EVOKED RELEASE OF METHIONINE-ENKEPHALIN FROM RAT STRIATAL SLICES.
002882 03-03

ACTIONS OF BETA BUNGAROTOXIN ON AMINO-ACID TRANSMITTER RELEASE.
002897 03-03

METHYLXANTHINES MODULATE ADENOSINE RELEASE FROM SLICES OF CEREBRAL-CORTEX.
002907 03-03

SOMATOSTATIN FACILITATES THE SEROTONIN RELEASE FROM RAT-CEREBRAL-CORTEX, HIPPOCAMPUS, AND HYPOTHALAMUS SLICES.
002913 03-03

STIMULATORY EFFECT OF SOMATOSTATIN ON NOREPINEPHRINE RELEASE FROM RAT-BRAIN-CORTEX SLICES.
002920 03-03

BIPHASIC-EFFECTS AND OPPOSITE-EFFECTS OF DOPAMINE AND APOMORPHINE ON ENDOGENOUS GABA RELEASE IN THE RAT SUBSTANTIA-NIGRA.
002923 03-03

MODIFIED CUP TECHNIQUE FOR MICROESTIMATION OF THE RELEASE AND UPTAKE OF NEUROTRANSMITTERS IN BRAIN SLICES.
003147 03-06

RELEASE OF ACETYLCHOLINE FROM RAT-BRAIN SYNAPTOSOMES STIMULATED WITH LEPTINOTARSIN, A NEW NEUROTOXIN.
003148 03-06

VASOPRESSIN STIMULATES RELEASE OF BETA LIPOTROPIN AND BETA ENDORPHIN IN CONSCIOUS RATS AS MEASURED BY RADIOIMMUNOASSAY OF UNEXTRACTED PLASMA.
003715 04-03

CHLORPROMAZINE, HALOPERIDOL, METOCLOPRAMIDE AND DOMPERIDONE RELEASE PROLACTIN THROUGH DOPAMINE ANTAGONISM AT LOW CONCENTRATIONS BUT PARADOXICALLY INHIBIT PROLACTIN RELEASE AT HIGH-CONCENTRATIONS.
003731 04-03

METERGOLINE AND CYPROHEPTADINE SUPPRESS PROLACTIN RELEASE BY A NON-5-HYDROXYTRYPTAMINERGIC, NONDOPAMINERGIC MECHANISM.
003732 04-03

PRESYNAPTIC AND POSTSYNAPTIC STRIATAL DOPAMINE-RECEPTORS: DIFFERENTIAL SENSITIVITY TO APOMORPHINE INHIBITION OF (3H)DOPAMINE AND (14C)GABA RELEASE IN VITRO.
003741 04-03

GABA-ENHANCEMENT OF (3H)DOPAMINE RELEASE FROM SLICES OF RAT STRIATUM: DEPENDENCE ON SLICE SIZE.
003786 04-03

ROLE OF THE ANTERIOR PITUITARY GABA-RECEPTOR IN THE CONTROL OF PROLACTIN RELEASE.
003809 04-03

OXOTREMORINE DOES NOT ENHANCE ACETYLCHOLINE RELEASE FROM RAT DIAPHRAGM PREPARATIONS.
003819 04-03

PHARMACOLOGIC MANIPULATION OF BRAIN AND PITUITARY ENDORPHIN CONTENT AND RELEASE.
003837 04-03

PRESYNAPTIC REGULATION OF THE RELEASE OF ACETYLCHOLINE BY 5 HYDROXYTRYPTAMINE.
003843 04-03

LONG-TERM-TREATMENT OF RATS WITH MORPHINE DECREASES IN VITRO BIOSYNTHESIS IN AND RELEASE OF BETA ENDORPHIN FROM INTERMEDIATE/POSTERIOR LOBES OF PITUITARY.
003846 04-03

INVESTIGATION OF ACTION OF ENKEPHALIN ON THE SPONTANEOUS AND EVOKED RELEASE OF ACETYLCHOLINE FROM RAT CORTICAL AND STRIATAL SLICES.
003862 04-03

ACTION OF ENKEPHALIN ANALOGUES AND MORPHINE ON BRAIN ACETYLCHOLINE RELEASE: DIFFERENTIAL REVERSAL BY NALOXONE AND AN OPIATE-PENTAPEPTIDE.
003863 04-03

EFFECTS OF MORPHINE AND CAFFEINE ON ADENOSINE RELEASE FROM RAT-CEREBRAL-CORTEX: IS CAFFEINE A MORPHINE ANTAGONIST.
003864 04-03

BACLOFEN: STEREOSELECTIVE INHIBITION OF EXCITANT AMINO-ACID RELEASE.
003867 04-03

CHARACTERIZATION OF ENKEPHALIN RELEASE FROM RAT STRIATUM.
003909 04-03

EFFECTS OF HALOPEMIDE ON GABA-RECEPTOR BINDING, UPTAKE AND RELEASE.
003913 04-03

Subject Index

NEUROTENSIN RELEASE BY RAT HYPOTHALAMIC FRAGMENTS IN VITRO.
003920 04-03

THE EFFECT OF ACETYLCHOLINE RELEASE ON CHOLINE FLUXES IN
ISOLATED SYNAPTIC TERMINALS.
003924 04-03

INFLUENCE OF CALCIUM ON NORADRENALINE RELEASE EVOKED BY 5
HYDROXYTRYPTAMINE, TYRAMINE AND POTASSIUM FROM GOAT
PIAL-ARTERIES.
003925 04-03

CORRELATIONS BETWEEN NA-K-ATPASE ACTIVITY AND ACETYLCHOLINE
RELEASE IN RAT CORTICAL SYNAPTOSOMES.
003937 04-03

THE NA-K-ATPASE: A PLAUSIBLE TRIGGER FOR VOLTAGE-INDEPENDENT
RELEASE OF CYTOPLASMIC NEUROTRANSMITTERS.
003953 04-03

HYPOTENSION ALTERS THE RELEASE OF CATECHOLAMINES IN THE
HYPOTHALAMUS OF THE CONSCIOUS RABBIT.
003968 04-03

EFFECTS OF CANNABINOIDS ON CATECHOLAMINE UPTAKE AND RELEASE
IN HYPOTHALAMIC AND STRIATAL SYNAPTOSOMES.
003970 04-03

STUDIES ON THE MECHANISM-OF-ACTION OF AVERMECTIN-B1A:
STIMULATION OF RELEASE OF GAMMA AMINOBUTYRIC-ACID FROM
BRAIN SYNAPTOSOMES.
003973 04-03

EFFECT OF PROSTAGLANDIN-D2, PROSTAGLANDIN-E2 AND
PROSTAGLANDIN-F2ALPHA ON CATECHOLAMINE RELEASE FROM SLICES
OF RAT AND RABBIT BRAIN.
003983 04-03

IN VIVO EVIDENCE FOR GABAERGIC CONTROL OF SEROTONIN RELEASE IN
THE CAT SUBSTANTIA-NIGRA.
004011 04-03

DIFFERENT EFFECTS OF TRICYCLIC-ANTIDEPRESSANTS AND TETRACYCLIC-
ANTIDEPRESSANTS ON THE RELEASE OF TSH, PROLACTIN, AND
GROWTH-HORMONE AFTER ADMINISTRATION OF THYROSTIMULATING-
RELEASING-HORMONE IN MANIC-DEPRESSIVES.
004407 04-09

RELEASING
A CONSTITUENT OF KHAT-LEAVES WITH AMPHETAMINE-LIKE RELEASING
PROPERTIES.
001307 02-03

BEHAVIOURAL-RESPONSES TO DRUGS RELEASING 5
HYDROXYTRYPTAMINE AND CATECHOLAMINES: EFFECTS OF
TREATMENTS ALTERING PRECURSOR CONCENTRATIONS IN BRAIN.
002990 03-04

PROLACTIN RELEASING POTENCIES OF ANTIPSYCHOTIC AND RELATED
NONANTIPSYCHOTIC COMPOUNDS IN FEMALE RATS: RELATION TO
CLINICAL POTENCIES.
003830 04-03

RELEASING-AGENTS
DIFFERENTIAL-EFFECTS OF SEVERAL DOPAMINE UPTAKE INHIBITORS AND
RELEASING-AGENTS ON LOCOMOTOR-ACTIVITY IN NORMAL AND IN
RESERPINIZED MICE.
004130 04-04

RELIEF
RELIEF OF PAIN IN CLINICAL-PRACTICE.
003613 03-17

REM
CAFFEINE PRODUCES REM SLEEP REBOUND IN RATS.
000244 01-03

IMIPRAMINE AND REM SLEEP: CHOLINERGIC MEDIATION IN ANIMALS.
000406 01-04

INTRAVENOUS CHLORIMIPRAMINE AFFECTS REM CYCLE IN PATIENTS
WITH EXCESSIVE DAYTIME SLEEPINESS AND CONTROL SUBJECTS.
002341 02-14

INDIVIDUAL VARIATIONS IN THE EFFECTS OF FLURAZEPAM,
CLORAZEPATE, L-DOPA AND THYROTROPIN-RELEASING-HORMONE ON
REM SLEEP IN MAN.
002349 02-14

PHENOXYBENZAMINE AND BROMOCRIPTINE ATTENUATE NEED FOR REM
SLEEP IN RATS.
004203 04-04

CHANGES OF RESPONSE TO DOPAMINERGIC DRUGS IN RATS SUBMITTED
TO REM SLEEP DEPRIVATION.
004239 04-04

REMISSION
LONG-TERM CONTROLLED-COMPARISON OF INJECTION OXYPROTHEPIN
AND FLUPHENAZINE-DECANOATES IN PSYCHOTICS IN REMISSION.
001949 02-08

RENAL
RENAL FUNCTION AND BIOPSY IN PATIENTS ON LITHIUM THERAPY.
000830 01-15

RENAL FUNCTION IN LITHIUM AND NONLITHIUM TREATED PATIENTS
WITH AFFECTIVE-DISORDERS.
000837 01-15

ANTAGONISM OF THE RENAL VASODILATOR ACTIVITY OF DOPAMINE BY
METOCLOPRAMIDE.
001265 02-03

STUDIES ON THE EFFECT OF ALPHA MELANOCYTE-STIMULATING-
HORMONE AND RELATED PEPTIDES ON THE ACCUMULATION OF P

VASOTOCIN, PROSTAGLANDIN, AND FEMALE REPRODUCTIVE BEHAVIOR IN THE FROG, RANA-PIPIENS.
002978 03-04

RESEARCH
A PSYCHOLOGICAL-VIEW ON PROBLEMS AND CONCEPTS OF LITHIUM RESEARCH.
000810 01-14

MARIJUANA: A REVIEW OF MEDICAL RESEARCH WITH IMPLICATIONS FOR ADOLESCENTS.
000871 01-15

TARDIVE-DYSKINESIA: RESEARCH & TREATMENT.
000934 01-17

DEPRESSION IN THE ELDERLY: RESEARCH DIRECTIONS IN PSYCHOPATHOLOGY, EPIDEMIOLOGY, AND TREATMENT.
000998 01-17

CYCLIC-NUCLEOTIDES AND THE CENTRAL-EFFECTS OF OPIATES: AN OVERVIEW OF CURRENT RESEARCH.
001445 02-03

THE LONG-TERM TREATMENT WITH BENZODIAZEPINES: SUGGESTIONS FOR FURTHER RESEARCH.
002085 02-10

SELF-MEDICATION, ABANDONMENT, MANIPULATION, AND DEPENDENCE IN DRUG-THERAPY IN PSYCHOSOMATIC-ILLNESS: COMPARATIVE POLYCENTRIC RESEARCH ON VARIOUS PSYCHOTROPIC-DRUGS.
002189 02-11

NEUROPEPTIDE TREATMENT OF SOCIOPATHY: RESEARCH IN PROGRESS.
002369 02-14

THE RESEARCH FOR NEW ANTIDEPRESSANTS: PRESENT ORIENTATIONS.
002543 02-17

PSYCHOPHARMACOLOGY — AN AREA OF RESEARCH TO IMPROVE MENTAL-HEALTH CARE.
002586 02-17

REVIEW AND OVERVIEW OF FOUR DECADES OF OPIATE RESEARCH.
002627 02-17

A RESEARCH PARADIGM TO INVESTIGATE THE EFFECT OF MANIPULATION ON SOCIAL-BEHAVIOR IN GROUPS.
003007 03-04

RESEARCH STRATEGIES FOR ASSESSING THE EFFECTS OF METHYLMERCURY ON BEHAVIOR.
003128 03-05

2 AMINO-4-PHOSPHONOBUTYRIC-ACID: A NEW PHARMACOLOGICAL TOOL FOR RETINA RESEARCH.
003145 03-06

ENDORPHIN RESEARCH IN SCHIZOPHRENIC-PSYCHOSES.
003200 03-08

METHODOLOGY OF OUTPATIENT DRUG RESEARCH. (UNPUBLISHED PAPER).
003282 03-10

PHARMACOLOGICAL-STUDIES OF TARDIVE-DYSKINESIA: IMPLICATIONS FOR FUTURE RESEARCH.
003465 03-15

SECOND-GENERATION ANTIDEPRESSANTS: A CLINICAL PHARMACOTHERAPEUTIC RESEARCH STRATEGY.
003632 03-17

OPIATE MECHANISMS: EVALUATION OF RESEARCH INVOLVING NEURONAL ACTION POTENTIALS.
003886 04-03

ALTERATIONS OF EVOKED-POTENTIALS LINK RESEARCH IN ATTENTION-DYSFUNCTION TO PEPTIDE RESPONSE SYMPTOMS OF SCHIZOPHRENIA.
004316 04-08

TREATMENT OF DEPRESSION WITH AN MAO-INHIBITOR FOLLOWED BY 5 HTP — AN UNFINISHED RESEARCH PROJECT.
004377 04-09

CLINICAL STRATEGIES FOR ANTIPSYCHOTIC-DRUG TREATMENT, TARDIVE-DYSKINESIA, AND THE TRAINING OF RESEARCH PSYCHIATRISTS.
004603 04-15

NEW BIOLOGICAL RESEARCH RELEVANT TO ANXIETY.
004705 04-17

RESERPINE
MATURATION OF SYMPATHETIC NEUROTRANSMISSION IN THE RAT HEART. III. DEVELOPMENTAL-CHANGES IN RESERPINE INHIBITION OF NOREPINEPHRINE UPTAKE INTO ISOLATED SYNAPTIC VESICLES.
000025 01-03

ABILITY OF AGED RATS TO ALTER BETA-ADRENERGIC-RECEPTORS OF BRAIN IN RESPONSE TO REPEATED ADMINISTRATION OF RESERPINE AND DESMETHYLIMIPRAMINE.
000113 01-03

EFFECTS OF RESERPINE, PROPRANOLOL, AND AMINOPHYLLINE ON SEIZURE ACTIVITY AND CNS CYCLIC-NUCLEOTIDES.
000115 01-03

THE EFFECTS OF RESERPINE, IPRONIAZID AND L-DOPA ON ELECTRICALLY-INDUCED SPINAL-CORD SEIZURES.
000146 01-03

BIOCHEMICAL-CHARACTERIZATION OF THE RAT SYMPATHETIC GANGLION: PHARMACOLOGICAL-EFFECTS OF RESERPINE ON GANGLIONIC CATECHOLAMINES.
000153 01-03

MONOAMINE REPLACEMENT AFTER RESERPINE: CATECHOLAMINERGIC AGONISTS RESTORE MOTOR-ACTIVITY BUT PHENYLETHYLAMINE

RESTORES ATROPINE-RESISTANT NEOCORTICAL LOW VOLTAGE FAST-ACTIVITY.
000309 01-03

RESERPINE ABOLISHES MOVEMENT CORRELATED ATROPINE-RESISTANT NEOCORTICAL LOW VOLTAGE FAST-ACTIVITY.
000310 01-03

A COMPARISON OF RATES OF DEPLETION AND RECOVERY OF NORADRENALINE STORES OF PERIPHERAL AND CENTRAL NORADRENERGIC NEURONES AFTER RESERPINE ADMINISTRATION: IMPORTANCE OF NEURONAL ACTIVITY.
000314 01-03

THE ULTRASTRUCTURAL CHANGES OF SYNAPSES IN RAT FOLLOWING LONG-TERM ADMINISTRATION OF THE NEUROLEPTICS RESERPINE AND HALOPERIDOL.
000795 01-13

DIVERGENT RESERPINE EFFECTS ON AMFONELIC-ACID AND AMPHETAMINE STIMULATION OF SYNAPTOSOMAL DOPAMINE FORMATION FROM PHENYLALANINE.
001113 02-03

RESPONSIVENESS TO VASOACTIVE-AGENTS OF CEREBRAL-ARTERIES AND MESENTERIC-ARTERIES ISOLATED FROM CONTROL AND RESERPINE TREATED DOGS.
001273 02-03

EFFECTS OF PHENCYCLIDINE AND METHYLPHENIDATE ON D-AMPHETAMINE-INDUCED BEHAVIORS IN RESERPINE PRETREATED RATS.
001616 02-04

EFFECTS OF RESERPINE AND AMPHETAMINE ON THE DEVELOPMENT OF HYPERACTIVITY IN MATERNALLY-DEPRIVED RAT PUPS.
001654 02-04

EFFECTS OF CHRONIC AMPHETAMINE OR RESERPINE ON SELF-STIMULATION RESPONDING: ANIMAL-MODEL OF DEPRESSION?
001699 02-04

EFFECTS OF ELECTROCONVULSIVE-TREATMENT ON GROWTH-HORMONE SECRETION INDUCED BY MONOAMINE-RECEPTOR AGONISTS IN RESERPINE PRETREATED RATS.
002664 03-03

THE DIRECT EFFECT OF RESERPINE IN VITRO ON PROLACTIN RELEASE FROM RAT ANTERIOR PITUITARY-GLANDS.
002810 03-03

RESERPINE EFFECT ON THE AXONAL TRANSPORT OF DOPAMINE-BETA-HYDROXYLASE AND TYROSINE-HYDROXYLASE IN RAT-BRAIN.
003904 04-03

RESERPINE-INDUCED
DEPRESSION OF RESERPINE-INDUCED MUSCULAR RIGIDITY IN RATS AFTER ADMINISTRATION OF LISURIDE INTO THE SPINAL SUBARACHNOID SPACE.
002962 03-04

LITHIUM AMELIORATION OF RESERPINE-INDUCED HYPOACTIVITY IN RATS.
004167 04-04

EFFECTS OF NARCOTIC ANTAGONISTS ON L-DOPA REVERSAL OF RESERPINE-INDUCED CATALEPSY AND BLEPHAROPTOSIS IN MICE.
004186 04-04

RESERPINIZED
DIFFERENTIAL-EFFECTS OF SEVERAL DOPAMINE UPTAKE INHIBITORS AND RELEASING-AGENTS ON LOCOMOTOR-ACTIVITY IN NORMAL AND IN RESERPINIZED MICE.
004130 04-04

RESERVES
ENERGY RESERVES AND SOUND-INDUCED SEIZURES. (UNPUBLISHED PAPER).
001467 02-03

RESIDENTIAL-CENTER
A NOTE ON PATTERNS OF DRUG PRESCRIBING IN A RESIDENTIAL-CENTER FOR THE INTELLECTUALLY-HANDICAPPED.
000982 01-17

RESIDENTS
BEHAVIORAL-EFFECTS OF HASHISH IN MICE: III. SOCIAL-INTERACTIONS BETWEEN TWO RESIDENTS AND AN INTRUDER MALE.
001776 02-04

RESIDUAL-EFFECTS
RESIDUAL-EFFECTS OF TEMAZEPAM AND OTHER HYPNOTIC-COMPOUNDS ON COGNITIVE FUNCTION.
000879 01-15

RESIDUE
MODIFICATION OF THE PROLINE RESIDUE OF TRH ENHANCES BIOLOGICAL-ACTIVITY AND INHIBITS DEGRADATION.
000351 01-04

BIOLOGICAL EVALUATION OF A TRH ANALOGUE WITH A MODIFIED PROLINE RESIDUE.
003662 04-01

RESISTANT
DIFFERENCES IN ACTIVITY IN CEREBRAL METHYLTRANSFERASES AND MONOAMINE-OXIDASES BETWEEN AUDIOGENIC-SEIZURE SUSCEPTIBLE AND RESISTANT MICE AND DEERMICE.
000377 01-04

EUHYPNOS-FORTE, HIGH-DOSE TEMAZEPAM FOR RESISTANT INSOMNIA:
POSTMARKETING SURVEILLANCE IN 10,057 PATIENTS UNRESPONSIVE
. TO CONVENTIONAL HYPNOTIC DOSAGE.
                                                                002324 02-14
RESOLUTION
ASSAYING GABA-MODULIN ACTIVITY IN BRAIN EXTRACTS: RESOLUTION
OF INHERENT DIFFICULTIES. (UNPUBLISHED PAPER).
                                                                001045 02-01
RESPECTIVE
SEROTONIN-SENSITIVE ADENYLATE-CYCLASE AND (3H)SEROTONIN
BINDING-SITES IN THE CNS OF THE RAT -- II. RESPECTIVE REGIONAL
AND SUBCELLULAR DISTRIBUTIONS AND ONTOGENETIC
DEVELOPMENTS.
                                                                000214 01-03
RESPECTIVE POSITION OF ANTIDEPRESSANTS IN THERAPEUTICS.
                                                                002581 02-17
RESPIRATION
AN EVALUATION OF THE MECHANISM BY WHICH SEROTONERGIC
ACTIVATION DEPRESSES RESPIRATION.
                                                                003917 04-03
EFFECT OF INORGANIC LEAD ON RAT-BRAIN MITOCHONDRIAL
RESPIRATION AND ENERGY PRODUCTION.
                                                                004267 04-05
RESPIRATORY
EFFECTS OF GAMMA HYDROXYBUTYRIC-ACID ON METABOLIC,
RESPIRATORY AND VASOMOTOR ACTIVITIES AND BODY-
TEMPERATURE IN RATS.
                                                                000189 01-03
THE ANALGESIC AND RESPIRATORY EFFECTS OF MEPTAZINOL, MORPHINE
AND PENTAZOCINE IN THE RAT.
                                                                000516 01-05
EFFECTS OF DIFFERENT MONOAMINE-OXIDASE-INHIBITORS ON
RESPIRATORY ACTIVITY IN RATS WITH CHRONICALLY IMPAIRED
CENTRAL SEROTONERGIC FUNCTION.
                                                                001389 02-03
INFLUENCE OF RESPIRATORY STRESS AND HYPERTENSION UPON THE
BLOOD-BRAIN-BARRIER.
                                                                001437 02-03
ROLE OF MONOAMINERGIC SYSTEMS IN MORPHINE-INDUCED
RESPIRATORY DEPRESSION.
                                                                002827 03-03
HABITUATION OF ELECTRODERMAL AND RESPIRATORY RESPONSES TO
VISUAL STIMULI AS A FUNCTION OF PERSONALITY DIFFERENCES IN
AFFECT LEVEL.
                                                                003414 03-13
OPIATE SYSTEM INFLUENCES CENTRAL RESPIRATORY CHEMOSENSORS.
                                                                003971 04-03
RESPIRATORY DEPRESSION PRODUCED BY DIAZEPAM IN CATS: EFFECT OF
ANESTHESIA.
                                                                004272 04-05
POTENTIATION OF THE MORPHINE-INDUCED RESPIRATORY RATE
DEPRESSION BY CAPTOPRIL.
                                                                004275 04-05
FLURAZEPAM-INDUCED SLEEP-APNEA-SYNDROME IN A PATIENT WITH
INSOMNIA AND MILD SLEEP-RELATED RESPIRATORY CHANGES.
                                                                004729 04-17
RESPIRATORY-DISEASE
RESPIRATORY-DISEASE AND NASAL IMMUNOGLOBULIN
CONCENTRATIONS IN PHENYTOIN TREATED EPILEPTIC-PATIENTS.
                                                                003486 03-15
RESPONDERS
THE SELECTION OF LITHIUM RESPONDERS.
                                                                000997 01-17
RESPONDERS AND NONRESPONDERS TO CHLORDIAZEPOXIDE AND
PLACEBO: A DISCRIMINANT FUNCTION ANALYSIS.
                                                                002482 02-16
RESPONDERS AND NONRESPONDERS TO CHLORDIAZEPOXIDE AND
PLACEBO. A DISCRIMINANT FUNCTION ANALYSIS. (UNPUBLISHED
PAPER).
                                                                004420 04-10
RESPONSE-CURVE
LOG-DOSE/RESPONSE-CURVE FLATTENING IN RATS AFTER DAILY
INJECTION OF OPIATES.
                                                                001387 02-03
RESPONSE-CURVES
CUMULATIVE DOSE RESPONSE-CURVES IN BEHAVIORAL-
PHARMACOLOGY.
                                                                001883 02-06
RESPONSIVITY
BRIEF SOCIAL-ISOLATION, PAIN RESPONSIVITY, AND MORPHINE
ANALGESIA IN YOUNG RATS.
                                                                001744 02-04
RESTITUTION
IMPROVEMENT OF RESTITUTION FROM CEREBRAL ISCHEMIA IN
HYPERGLYCEMIC RATS BY PENTOBARBITAL OR DIAZEPAM.
                                                                000475 01-04
RESTLESS
A CONTROLLED DOUBLE-BLIND STUDY OF HALOPERIDOL VERSUS
THIORIDAZINE IN THE TREATMENT OF RESTLESS MENTALLY-
SUBNORMAL-PATIENTS: SERUM LEVELS AND CLINICAL-EFFECTS.
                                                                002185 02-11

RESTLESSNESS
PSYCHOPHARMACEUTICAL-THERAPY TO CALM DRIVE, ACTIVITY, AND
RESTLESSNESS IN CHILDHOOD.
                                                                002604 02-17
RESTORATION
THE EFFECT OF ADENOSINE AND GUANOSINE ON THE CONTENT OF
SEROTONIN AND CATECHOLAMINES IN THE BRAIN IN THE
RESTORATION PERIOD FOLLOWING EXPERIMENTAL CLINICAL DEATH.
                                                                003882 04-03
RESTRAINED
EFFECTS OF CONFORMATIONALLY RESTRAINED ANALOGUES OF
SEROTONIN ON ITS UPTAKE AND BINDING IN RAT-BRAIN.
                                                                003794 04-03
RESTRAINT
THE FUNCTIONAL IMPORTANCE OF INCREASED BRAIN TRYPTOPHAN IN
THE SEROTONERGIC RESPONSE TO RESTRAINT STRESS.
                                                                002779 03-03
RESTRICTED
CONFORMATIONALLY RESTRICTED PHENOTHIAZINE NEUROLEPTICS. 1. 3
DIMETHYLAMINO-TETRAHYDROAZEPINOPHENOTHIAZINE.
                                                                001359 02-03
CONFORMATIONALLY RESTRICTED TRICYCLIC-ANTIDEPRESSANTS. 1.
OCTAHYDRODIBENZAZEPINONAPHTHYRIDINES AS RIGID IMIPRAMINE
ANALOGUES.
                                                                001710 02-04
THE SYNTHESIS AND ACTIVITY OF CIS AND TRANS 2
AMINOMETHYLCYCLOPROPANECARBOXYLIC-ACID AS
CONFORMATIONALLY RESTRICTED ANALOGUES OF GABA.
                                                                002633 03-01
A NEW METHOD FOR APPLICATION OF HORSERADISH-PEROXIDASE INTO
A RESTRICTED AREA OF THE BRAIN.
                                                                003141 03-06
RETARD
THE ASSOCIATION OF RETARD NEUROLEPTICS TO OTHER NEUROLEPTICS
IN THE REHABILITATION OF PSYCHOTIC-PATIENTS.
                                                                002108 02-11
CLINICAL-EXPERIENCE WITH RETARD DIBENZEPINE (NOVERIL-240) IN
ENDOGENOUS DEPRESSIONS ACCOMPANIED BY SYMPTOMS OF DRUG-
RESISTANCE.
                                                                003245 03-09
RETARDED
COMPARISON OF THE CLASSICAL AND RETARDED FORM OF LITHIUM-
CARBONATE.
                                                                001888 02-07
RETENTION
THE USE OF PSYCHOPHARMACOLOGICAL-PROCEDURES TO ANALYSE THE
ONTOGENY OF LEARNING AND RETENTION: ISSUES AND CONCERNS.
                                                                000482 01-04
THE INFLUENCE OF DAILY BIOLOGICAL-RHYTHMICITY ON THE HOMING-
BEHAVIOR, PSYCHOPHARMACOLOGICAL RESPONSIVENESS, LEARNING
AND RETENTION OF SUCKLING RATS. (PH.D. DISSERTATION).
                                                                001660 02-04
EFFECTS OF A LOW-DOSE AND A HIGH-DOSE OF BETA ENDORPHIN ON
ACQUISITION AND RETENTION IN THE RAT.
                                                                001663 02-04
COMPARISONS OF THE EFFECTS OF GUANETHIDINE, 6
HYDROXYDOPAMINE AND DIETHYLDITHIOCARBAMATE ON RETENTION
OF PASSIVE-AVOIDANCE.
                                                                001742 02-04
EFFECTS OF CYCLOHEXIMIDE ADMINISTERED IN CONJUNCTION WITH
NICOTINE ON RETENTION OF A PASSIVE-AVOIDANCE TASK IN MICE.
                                                                001791 02-04
EFFECT OF L FUCOSE ON BRAIN PROTEIN METABOLISM AND RETENTION
OF A LEARNED-BEHAVIOR IN RATS.
                                                                001819 02-04
CONDITIONING AND RETENTION OF DEFENSIVE BURYING AS A FUNCTION
OF ELAVIL AND THORAZINE INJECTION.
                                                                002974 03-04
THE EFFECTS OF ANTIDEPRESSANTS ON THE RETENTION AND
METABOLISM OF (3H) NOREPINEPHRINE IN RAT-BRAIN SLICES.
                                                                003763 04-03
EFFECTS OF ANISOMYCIN ON RETENTION OF THE PASSIVE-AVOIDANCE
HABIT AS A FUNCTION OF AGE.
                                                                004097 04-04
RETICULAR
STRYCHNINE EFFECTS ON THE SENSORY RESPONSE PATTERNS OF
RETICULAR FORMATION NEURONS.
                                                                001219 02-03
THE EFFECTS OF NOREPINEPHRINE PERFUSION OF THE MESENCEPHALIC
RETICULAR FORMATION ON BEHAVIOR IN THE RAT: INTERACTION
WITH SEVERAL NEUROLEPTIC-DRUGS ON A MEASURE OF SUSTAINED
ATTENTION. (PH.D. DISSERTATION).
                                                                001563 02-04
INVOLVEMENT OF CAUDATE-NUCLEUS, AMYGDALA OR RETICULAR
. FORMATION IN NEUROLEPTIC AND NARCOTIC CATALEPSY.
                                                                002986 03-04

MORPHINE AND METHIONINE-ENKEPHALIN: DIFFERENT EFFECTS ON SPONTANEOUS AND EVOKED NEURONAL FIRING IN THE MESENCEPHALIC RETICULAR FORMATION OF THE RAT.
003849 04-03

CONVERGENT PROPERTIES AND CHEMICAL SENSITIVITY OF MIDBRAIN RETICULAR FORMATION NEURONS OF UNANESTHETIZED RABBITS.
003972 04-03

RETICULARIS-GIGANTOCELLULARIS
THE EFFECT OF MORPHINE ON THE CONTENT OF SEROTONIN, 5 HYDROXYINDOLEACETIC-ACID AND SUBSTANCE-P IN THE NUCLEI RAPHE-MAGNUS AND RETICULARIS-GIGANTOCELLULARIS.
001328 02-03

RETICULOSEPTAL
THE ROLE OF RETICULOSEPTAL INPUTS IN THE FORMATION OF DIFFERENT TYPES OF SENSORY REACTIONS OF THE HIPPOCAMPAL NEURONS.
004510 04-13

RETINA
LOCALIZATION OF ALPHA BUNGAROTOXIN BINDING-SITES IN SYNAPSES OF THE DEVELOPING CHICK RETINA.
000065 01-03

BRAIN-SPECIFIC BENZODIAZEPINE-RECEPTORS ARE LOCALIZED IN THE INNER PLEXIFORM LAYER OF RAT RETINA.
000277 01-03

RIA AND HPLC EVIDENCE FOR THE PRESENCE OF METHIONINE-ENKEPHALIN AND CHOLECYSTOKININ IN THE NEURAL RETINA OF SEVERAL VERTEBRATE SPECIES. (UNPUBLISHED PAPER).
001017 02-01

BENZODIAZEPINE BINDING IN CHICKEN RETINA AND ITS INTERACTION WITH GAMMA AMINOBUTYRIC-ACID.
001287 02-03

BENZODIAZEPINE-RECEPTORS IN CHICK RETINA: DEVELOPMENT AND CELLULAR LOCALIZATION.
002655 03-03

KAINIC-ACID INDUCED LESION OF RAT RETINA: DIFFERENTIAL-EFFECT ON CYCLIC-GMP AND BENZODIAZEPINE-RECEPTORS AND GABA-RECEPTORS.
002743 03-03

GABA ANTAGONISTS ENHANCE DOPAMINE TURNOVER IN THE RAT RETINA IN VIVO.
002772 03-03

PROPERTIES OF DOPAMINE AGONIST AND ANTAGONIST BINDING-SITES IN MAMMALIAN RETINA.
002814 03-03

THE EFFECT OF COLCHICINE AND CYTOCHALASIN B ON THE RELEASE OF TAURINE FROM THE CHICK RETINA.
002856 03-03

2 AMINO-4-PHOSPHONOBUTYRIC-ACID: A NEW PHARMACOLOGICAL TOOL FOR RETINA RESEARCH.
003145 03-06

STEREOSPECIFIC INHIBITION OF DOPAMINE-SENSITIVE ADENYLATE-CYCLASE IN CARP RETINA BY THE ENANTIOMERS OF (/-) 1 CYCLOPROPYLMETHYL TRIFLUOROMETHYLTHIODIBENZOCYCLOHEPTENYLIDENEPIPERIDINE.
003706 04-02

DOPAMINERGIC MECHANISMS IN THE TELEOST RETINA. II. FACTORS AFFECTING THE ACCUMULATION OF CYCLIC-AMP IN PIECES OF INTACT CARP RETINA.
003776 04-03

CHANGES IN ELECTRORETINOGRAM AND NEUROCHEMICAL ASPECTS OF GABAERGIC NEURONS OF RETINA AFTER INTRAOCULAR INJECTION OF KAINIC-ACID IN RATS.
003807 04-03

SOME BARBITURATES ENHANCE THE EFFECT OF MUSCIMOL ON DOPAMINE TURNOVER IN THE RAT RETINA.
003873 04-03

BINDING OF (3H) MUSCIMOL, A POTENT GAMMA AMINOBUTYRIC-ACID-RECEPTOR AGONIST, TO MEMBRANES OF THE BOVINE RETINA.
003954 04-03

DOPAMINERGIC MECHANISMS IN THE TELEOST RETINA. I. DOPAMINE-SENSITIVE ADENYLATE-CYCLASE IN HOMOGENATES OF CARP RETINA, EFFECTS OF AGONISTS, ANTAGONISTS AND ERGOTS.
004051 04-03

RETINAL
RETINAL TOXICITY OF MAM-ACETATE IS DEVELOPMENTALLY SPECIFIC. (UNPUBLISHED PAPER).
001212 02-03

ATTEMPTS TO DEVELOP SUPERSENSITIVITY OR SUBSENSITIVITY RETINAL DOPAMINE-RECEPTORS AFTER VARIOUS TREATMENTS WITH ANTAGONISTS OR AGONISTS.
001350 02-03

DOPAMINE DEPLETION SLOWS RETINAL TRANSMISSION.
002708 03-03

STIMULATION OF RETINAL ADENYLATE-CYCLASE BY VASOACTIVE INTESTINAL PEPTIDE (VIP).
002811 03-03

LOCALIZATION OF GABA-RECEPTOR AND DOPAMINE-RECEPTOR SITES IN RETINAL GLIAL CELLS USING DL ALPHA AMINOADIPIC-ACID.
002828 03-03

RETINOTOXIC-EFFECTS
RETINOTOXIC-EFFECTS OF DIAMINODIPHENOXYBUTANE IN RATS.
000444 01-04

RETIRED
THE RELATIVE EFFICACY OF COGNITIVE-THERAPY AND CHEMOTHERAPY FOR THE TREATMENT OF DEPRESSION AMONG THE RETIRED ELDERLY. (PH.D. DISSERTATION).
002148 02-11

RETRIEVAL
EFFECT OF BETA ENDORPHIN AND NALOXONE ON ACQUISITION, MEMORY, AND RETRIEVAL OF SHUTTLE AVOIDANCE AND HABITUATION LEARNING IN RATS.
000410 01-04

PIRACETAM AND RETRIEVAL OF MEMORY IN YOUNG RATS.
000803 01-14

ACTH4-10 AND MEMORY IN ECT TREATED PATIENTS AND UNTREATED CONTROLS. II. EFFECT ON RETRIEVAL.
001983 02-09

RETROGRADE
DEMONSTRATION OF SUBSTANCE-P IN AORTIC NERVE AFFERENT FIBERS BY COMBINED USE OF FLOURESCENT RETROGRADE NEURONAL LABELING AND IMMUNOCYTOCHEMISTRY. (UNPUBLISHED PAPER).
001024 02-01

RETROGRADE AMNESIA PRODUCED BY ELECTRICAL-STIMULATION OF THE AMYGDALA: ATTENUATION WITH ADRENERGIC ANTAGONISTS. (UNPUBLISHED PAPER).
001488 02-03

BETA ENDORPHIN CAUSES RETROGRADE AMNESIA AND IS RELEASED FROM THE RAT-BRAIN BY VARIOUS FORMS OF TRAINING AND STIMULATION.
001664 02-04

PAPAIN-DERIVED FRAGMENT IIC TETANUS-TOXIN: ITS BINDING TO ISOLATED SYNAPTIC MEMBRANES AND RETROGRADE AXONAL TRANSPORT.
003734 04-03

RETROGRADE AMNESIA PRODUCED BY ELECTRICAL-STIMULATION OF THE AMYGDALA: ATTENUATION WITH ADRENERGIC ANTAGONISTS.
004231 04-04

REUPTAKE
COMPARISON OF MIANSERIN WITH DESIPRAMINE, MAPROTILINE AND PHENTOLAMINE ON CARDIAC PRESYNAPTIC AND VASCULAR POSTSYNAPTIC ALPHA-ADRENOCEPTORS AND NORADRENALINE REUPTAKE IN PITHED NORMOTENSIVE-RATS.
000044 01-03

REUPTAKE OF BIOGENIC-AMINES BY BRAIN SLICES: EFFECT OF HYDROCORTISONE.
000187 01-03

INITIAL, CLINICAL-TRIAL OF A NEW, SPECIFIC 5 HT REUPTAKE INHIBITOR, CITALOPRAM (LU-10-171).
000591 01-09

CHANGES IN THE AUGMENTER REDUCER TENDENCY AND IN PAIN MEASURES AS A RESULT OF TREATMENT WITH A SEROTONIN REUPTAKE INHIBITOR ZIMELIDINE.
002305 02-13

HIPPOCAMPAL SEROTONIN REUPTAKE AND NOCTURNAL LOCOMOTOR-ACTIVITY AFTER MICROINJECTIONS OF 5,7 DHT IN THE FORNIX-FIMBRIA.
002929 03-03

MONOSODIUM-GLUTAMATE: INCREASED NEUROTOXICITY AFTER REMOVAL OF NEURONAL REUPTAKE SITES.
003889 04-03

DOES HIGH-AFFINITY (3H) IMIPRAMINE BINDING LABEL SEROTONIN REUPTAKE SITES IN BRAIN AND PLATELET?
003962 04-03

ATTENUATION OF PETHIDINE-INDUCED ANTINOCICEPTION BY ZIMELIDINE, AN INHIBITOR OF 5 HYDROXYTRYPTAMINE REUPTAKE.
004118 04-04

EFFECTS OF NOREPINEPHRINE AND 5 HYDROXYTRYPTAMINE REUPTAKE INHIBITORS ON ELECTRICALLY-INDUCED SPINAL-CORD SEIZURES IN RATS.
004144 04-04

THE ANTIDEPRESSANT EFFECTS OF TRAZODONE AND INHIBITION OF PLATELET SEROTONIN REUPTAKE.
004383 04-09

REVELATIONS
COMPUTERIZED MONITORING OF PSYCHOTROPIC-DRUG ORDERS: SOME TRENDS AND REVELATIONS.
003566 03-16

REVERSAL
HYPOALGESIA INDUCED BY MICROINJECTION OF A NOREPINEPHRINE ANTAGONIST IN THE RAPHE-MAGNUS: REVERSAL BY INTRATHECAL ADMINISTRATION OF A SEROTONIN ANTAGONIST.
000121 01-03

INHIBITION OF GROWTH IN YOUNG MICE TREATED WITH PENTAZOCINE: REVERSAL BY NALTREXONE.
000318 01-03

POSTAMPHETAMINE DEPRESSION OF SELF-STIMULATION RESPONDING FROM THE SUBSTANTIA-NIGRA: REVERSAL BY TRICYCLIC-ANTIDEPRESSANTS.
000419 01-04

Subject Index

REVERSAL OF PARA CHLOROPHENYLALANINE-INDUCED INSOMNIA BY 5 HYDROXYTRYPTOPHAN IN THE RAT.
000423 01-04

REVERSAL OF SCHEDULE-INDUCED SELF-INJECTION OF HEROIN BY NALOXONE.
000446 01-04

REVERSAL BY PHENYTOIN OF CARBAMAZEPINE-INDUCED WATER INTOXICATION: A PHARMACOKINETIC-INTERACTION.
000783 01-13

PRESSURE REVERSAL OF THE EFFECT OF URETHANE ON THE EVOKED SOMATOSENSORY CORTICAL RESPONSE IN THE RAT.
001106 02-03

STUDIES ON THE SPECIFICITY AND REVERSAL OF NEUROLEPTIC-INDUCED DOPAMINERGIC-SUPERSENSITIVITY. (PH.D. DISSERTATION).
001469 02-03

REVERSAL OF LEARNED-HELPLESSNESS BY IMIPRAMINE.
001751 02-04

NEUROLEPTIC/DOPAMINE-RECEPTORS: ELEVATION AND REVERSAL.
001847 02-05

REVERSAL OF NORADRENALINE DENERVATION-INDUCED INCREASE OF BETA-ADRENORECEPTOR BINDING IN RAT NEOCORTEX BY NORADRENALINE INFUSION.
002672 03-03

ROLE OF INTRACORTICAL INHIBITION IN DEPRIVATION AMBLYOPIA: REVERSAL BY MICROIONTOPHORETIC BICUCULLINE.
002684 03-03

NALOXONE REVERSAL OF THE PENTOBARBITAL-INDUCED BLOCKADE OF OVULATION IN THE RAT.
002817 03-03

DIFFERENTIAL REVERSAL BY SCOPOLAMINE AND THIP OF THE ANTISTEREOTYPIC AND CATALEPTIC-EFFECTS OF NEUROLEPTICS.
002948 03-04

ACTION OF ENKEPHALIN ANALOGUES AND MORPHINE ON BRAIN ACETYLCHOLINE RELEASE: DIFFERENTIAL REVERSAL BY NALOXONE AND AN OPIATE-PENTAPEPTIDE.
003863 04-03

THE IMPORTANCE OF CATECHOLAMINE UPTAKE INHIBITION IN THE REVERSAL OF GUANETHIDINE BLOCKADE OF ADRENERGIC NEURONS.
003900 04-03

BETA PHENYLETHYLAMINE REVERSAL OF CHLORPROMAZINE-INDUCED ACTIVATION OF STRIATAL TYROSINE-HYDROXYLASE AND CATALEPSY.
004018 04-03

DECREASE OF NORADRENALINE O METHYLATION IN RAT-BRAIN INDUCED BY L-DOPA. REVERSAL EFFECT OF S ADENOSYL-L-METHIONINE.
004019 04-03

EFFECTS OF NARCOTIC ANTAGONISTS ON L-DOPA REVERSAL OF RESERPINE-INDUCED CATALEPSY AND BLEPHAROPTOSIS IN MICE.
004186 04-04

BEHAVIORAL AND BIOCHEMICAL-STUDIES OF THE SCOPOLAMINE-INDUCED REVERSAL OF NEUROLEPTIC ACTIVITY.
004195 04-04

AN ANALYSIS OF VISUAL OBJECT REVERSAL LEARNING IN THE MARMOSET AFTER AMPHETAMINE AND HALOPERIDOL.
004208 04-04

REVERSE

FAILURE OF NALOXONE TO REVERSE CATALEPSY ASSOCIATED WITH SCHIZOPHRENIA: A CASE-REPORT.
000560 01-08

SEPARATION OF BARBITURATES USING REVERSE PHASE THIN-LAYER-CHROMATOGRAPHY.
004670 04-16

REVERSIBILITY

REVERSIBILITY OF TARDIVE-DYSKINESIA.
000854 01-15

REVERSIBLE

REVERSIBLE INACTIVATION OF RAPHE-MAGNUS NEURONS: EFFECTS ON NOCICEPTIVE THRESHOLD AND MORPHINE-INDUCED ANALGESIA.
000240 01-03

NALOXONE REVERSIBLE EFFECTS OF D ALA2-MET5-ENKEPHALINAMIDE-INDUCED BEHAVIORAL-ACTIVITY IN RATS.
000402 01-04

REVERSIBLE ALEXIA, MITOCHONDRIAL MYOPATHY, AND LACTIC-ACIDEMIA.
000723 01-11

A NEW APPROACH TO THE ASSESSMENT OF THE POTENCY OF REVERSIBLE MONOAMINE-OXIDASE-INHIBITORS IN VIVO, AND ITS APPLICATION TO D-AMPHETAMINE, P METHOXYAMPHETAMINE AND HARMALINE.
000900 01-16

PATHOPHYSIOLOGICAL-ASPECTS OF REVERSIBLE AND IRREVERSIBLE TARDIVE-DYSKINESIA.
002124 02-11

THE MYTHOLOGEM OF REVERSIBLE DEATH. THE ANALYTICAL CONFRONTATION OF ENDOGENOUS DELIRIUM WITH DELUSIONS IN PSYCHEDELIC-EXPERIENCES.
002200 02-12

NALOXONE REVERSIBLE DUPLICATION BY LANTHANUM OF OPIATE ANALGESIA EFFECTS ON OROFACIAL, LOWER BODY AND CENTRAL NOCICEPTION.
003028 03-04

THE EFFECTS OF ETHANOL, PHENOBARBITAL, AND BACLOFEN ON
ETHANOL WITHDRAWAL IN THE RHESUS-MONKEY.
001802 02-04
THE EFFECTS OF LITHIUM ON CHOICE BETWEEN COCAINE AND FOOD IN
THE RHESUS-MONKEY.
001825 02-04
PHENYTOIN VALPROIC-ACID INTERACTION IN RHESUS-MONKEY.
002785 03-03
CHANGES IN THE HORIZONTAL VESTIBULO-OCULAR REFLEX OF THE
RHESUS-MONKEY WITH BEHAVIORAL AND PHARMACOLOGICAL
ALERTING.
002997 03-04
EFFECTS OF PENTOBARBITAL AND ETHANOL UPON SINGLE NEURON
ACTIVITY IN THE PRIMARY SOMATOSENSORY CORTEX OF THE RHESUS-
MONKEY.
003755 04-03

RHESUS-MONKEYS
A COMPARISON OF HUMAN TACTILE STIMULUS VELOCITY
DISCRIMINATION WITH THE ABILITY OF S-I CORTICAL NEURONS IN
AWAKE RHESUS-MONKEYS TO SIGNAL THE SAME VELOCITY
DIFFERENCES BEFORE AND AFTER NONANESTHETIC DOSES OF
PENTOBARBITAL.
000055 01-03
CENTRAL NORADRENERGIC ADAPTATION TO LONG-TERM-TREATMENT
WITH IMIPRAMINE IN RHESUS-MONKEYS.
000182 01-03
CONTINUOUS-ACCESS PHENCYCLIDINE SELF-ADMINISTRATION BY RHESUS-
MONKEYS LEADING TO PHYSICAL-DEPENDENCE.
000341 01-04
STUDIES ON THIORIDAZINE AND MESORIDAZINE METABOLISM. II. IN
VIVO METABOLISM OF TRITIATED DRUGS IN RHESUS-MONKEYS.
001229 02-03
SYNCHRONIZATION OF EEG ACTIVITY OF MALE RHESUS-MONKEYS
MACACA-MULATTA TREATED WITH OVOCYCLIN.
001312 02-03
THE EFFECTS OF DELTA9 TETRAHYDROCANNABINOL ALONE AND IN
COMBINATION WITH CANNABIDIOL ON FIXED-INTERVAL
PERFORMANCE IN RHESUS-MONKEYS.
001582 02-04
AN ABSTINENCE-SYNDROME FOLLOWING CHRONIC ADMINISTRATION OF
DELTA9 TETRAHYDROCANNABINOL IN RHESUS-MONKEYS.
001621 02-04
INFLUENCE OF INTRAVENOUS SELF-ADMINISTERED PSYCHOMOTOR
STIMULANTS ON PERFORMANCE OF RHESUS-MONKEYS IN A MULTIPLE-
SCHEDULE PARADIGM.
001655 02-04
LONG-TERM CHLORPROMAZINE IN RHESUS-MONKEYS: PRODUCTION OF
DYSKINESIAS AND CHANGES IN SOCIAL-BEHAVIOR.
001850 02-05
CANNABIS-SATIVA: EFFECTS ON BRAIN FUNCTION AND ULTRASTRUCTURE
IN RHESUS-MONKEYS.
002747 03-03
PHARMACOKINETIC PROFILE OF VALPROIC-ACID IN RHESUS-MONKEYS
FOLLOWING SINGLE BOLUS AND CONSTANT RATE INTRAVENOUS
ADMINISTRATIONS.
002797 03-03
INCREASES IN TESTOSTERONE LEVELS AND IN COPULATORY-BEHAVIOR OF
MALE RHESUS-MONKEYS FOLLOWING TREATMENT WITH HUMAN
CHORIONIC GONADOTROPHIN.
003012 03-04
DRUG-EFFECT ON BLINK RATES IN RHESUS-MONKEYS: PRELIMINARY
STUDIES.
003023 03-04
INHIBITION OF AGGRESSIVE-BEHAVIOR IN RHESUS-MONKEYS BY
BUSPIRONE.
003103 03-04
THE EFFECTS OF ELECTRIC-SHOCK ON RESPONDING MAINTAINED BY
COCAINE IN RHESUS-MONKEYS.
004071 04-04
CHLORPROMAZINE EFFECTS ON COCAINE-REINFORCED RESPONDING IN
RHESUS-MONKEYS: RECIPROCAL MODIFICATION OF RATE ALTERING
EFFECTS OF THE DRUGS.
004133 04-04
DISCRIMINATIVE-STIMULUS EFFECTS OF ETORPHINE IN RHESUS-
MONKEYS.
004134 04-04

RIA
AN HPLC AND RIA ANALYSIS OF THE CHOLECYSTOKININ-PEPTIDES IN
RAT-BRAIN. (UNPUBLISHED PAPER).
001004 02-01
RIA AND HPLC EVIDENCE FOR THE PRESENCE OF METHIONINE-
ENKEPHALIN AND CHOLECYSTOKININ IN THE NEURAL RETINA OF
SEVERAL VERTEBRATE SPECIES. (UNPUBLISHED PAPER).
001017 02-01
METHAQUALONE RIA STRUCTURE VERSUS REACTIVITY.
003657 04-01
RIA OPIATES: STRUCTURE VERSUS REACTIVITY.
003659 04-01

RICIN
ANTI-THY-1-2 MONOCLONAL ANTIBODY LINKED TO RICIN IS A POTENT
CELL TYPE SPECIFIC TOXIN. (UNPUBLISHED PAPER).
001064 02-01

RIGGIO-EMILIA
DRUG DEPENDENCE: REFLECTIONS ON AND ANALYSIS OF AN EXPERIENCE
IN THE PROVINCE OF RIGGIO-EMILIA.
003591 03-17

RIGHT
IMIPRAMINE AFFECTS AUTONOMIC-CONTROL OF SINOATRIAL RATE IN
ISOLATED RIGHT ATRIAL PREPARATIONS.
000195 01-03
THE SIMULTANEOUS INFUSION OF DRUGS VIA THE LEFT AND RIGHT
VERTEBRAL-ARTERY OF THE CAT; A MODIFIED ANIMAL-MODEL FOR
THE STUDY OF POSSIBLE CENTRAL-ACTIONS OF DRUGS UPON THE
LOWER BRAINSTEM.
004297 04-06

RIGHT-TO-REFUSE
FEDERAL-COURT UPHOLDS RIGHT-TO-REFUSE PSYCHOTROPIC-DRUGS,
ORDERS IMPROVEMENTS AT LIMA-STATE-HOSPITAL.
002583 02-17
THE CONSTITUTIONAL RIGHT-TO-REFUSE ANTIPSYCHOTIC-MEDICATIONS.
004496 04-12

RIGHTS
ROTTING WITH THEIR RIGHTS ON: CONSTITUTIONAL THEORY AND
CLINICAL REALITY IN DRUG-REFUSAL BY PSYCHIATRIC-PATIENTS.
000911 01-17
THE RIGHTS OF INVOLUNTARY-PATIENTS TO REFUSE
PHARMACOTHERAPY: WHAT IS REASONABLE?
004730 04-17

RIGID
CONFORMATIONALLY RESTRICTED TRICYCLIC-ANTIDEPRESSANTS. 1.
OCTAHYDRODIBENZAZEPINONAPHTHYRIDINES AS RIGID IMIPRAMINE
ANALOGUES.
001710 02-04

RIGIDITY
EFFECT OF DIAZEPAM AND DESMETHYLDIAZEPAM IN SPASTICITY AND
RIGIDITY: A QUANTITATIVE STUDY OF REFLEXES AND PLASMA
CONCENTRATIONS.
000701 01-11
LITHIUM-INDUCED COGWHEEL RIGIDITY: TREATMENT WITH
AMANTADINE.
000748 01-13
OPIOID-RECEPTORS IN THE CAUDATE-NUCLEUS CAN MEDIATE EMG-
RECORDED RIGIDITY IN RATS.
001649 02-04
DEPRESSION OF RESERPINE-INDUCED MUSCULAR RIGIDITY IN RATS AFTER
ADMINISTRATION OF LISURIDE INTO THE SPINAL SUBARACHNOID
SPACE.
002962 03-04

RING-OPENING
REVERSIBLE RING-OPENING REACTIONS OF NIMETAZEPAM AND
NITRAZEPAM IN ACIDIC MEDIA AT BODY-TEMPERATURE.
004517 04-13

RISK
POLYPHARMACY REGIMEN AS AN EXACERBATING RISK IN THERAPY-
RESISTANT EPILEPTIC-SEIZURES AND BEHAVIORAL-DISORDERS.
004720 04-17

RISK-FACTORS
PRELIMINARY-FINDINGS WITH REGARD TO RISK-FACTORS IN THE
DEVELOPMENT OF TARDIVE-DYSKINESIA.
003501 03-15

RISKS
THE BENEFITS AND RISKS OF COMBINING AN MAO-INHIBITOR AND A
TRICYCLIC-ANTIDEPRESSANT.
003273 03-09
CHRONIC DRUG-TREATMENT OF THE CHRONICALLY-ILL: BENEFITS AND
RISKS.
003625 03-17

RITALIN
PREDICTING THE RESPONSE OF HYPERACTIVE-CHILDREN TO RITALIN: AN
EMPIRICAL-STUDY.
002120 02-11
THE USE OF SENSORY INTEGRATIVE DIAGNOSTICS TO PREDICT
HYPERACTIVE-CHILDRENS RESPONSIVENESS TO METHYLPHENIDATE
(RITALIN) AND PEMOLINE (CYLERT). (PH.D. DISSERTATION).
002133 02-11

RNA
BIOELECTRICAL-ACTIVITY OF THE RAT BRAIN AFTER PREMATURE
WEANING AND AFTER RNA ADMINISTRATION.
002865 03-03

RNA-POLYMERASE-BII
PURIFICATION AND SUBUNIT STRUCTURE OF DNA-DEPENDENT RNA-
POLYMERASE-BII FROM RAT-BRAIN NUCLEI:
003679 04-01

RNA-POLYMERASE-II
RNA-POLYMERASE-II IN C6-GLIOMA CELLS: ALPHA AMANITIN BLOCKADE OF CYCLIC-AMP-PHOSPHODIESTERASE INDUCTION BY BETA-ADRENERGIC STIMULATION. (UNPUBLISHED PAPER).
003998 D4-03

RO-11-2465
EFFECTS OF RO-11-2465, A NEW PSYCHOTROPIC-AGENT ON THE UPTAKE OF SEROTONIN BY HUMAN PLATELETS -- IN VITRO DETERMINATION OF THE IC50.
004532 04-13

RO-4-1284
DEPLETION OF EPINEPHRINE IN RAT HYPOTHALAMUS BY RO-4-1284: INFLUENCE OF PARGYLINE AND HARMALINE.
000100 01-03
EFFECT OF RO-4-1284 ON AUDIOGENIC-SEIZURE SUSCEPTIBILITY AND INTENSITY IN EPILEPSY-PRONE RATS.
003865 04-03

RODENT
ROLE OF BRAIN DOPAMINERGIC MECHANISMS IN RODENT AGGRESSIVE-BEHAVIOR: INFLUENCE OF (OR -)N N PROPYLNORAPOMORPHINE ON THREE EXPERIMENTAL MODELS.
000340 01-04
CHARACTERIZATION OF THE BASIC PROTEINS FROM RODENT PERIPHERAL-NERVOUS-SYSTEM MYELIN.
003665 04-01

RODENTS
BEHAVIORAL-CHANGES INDUCED BY N,N DIMETHYLTRYPTAMINE IN RODENTS.
000413 01-04
INTERACTION STUDIES OF ETHANOL AND PSYCHOTROPIC-DRUGS IN RODENTS: POSSIBLE INVOLVEMENT OF ADENOSINE-TRIPHOSPHATASES.
001281 02-03
KINETICS OF CENTRAL-ACTIONS-OF ISOFLOXYTHEPIN, AN ORAL NEUROLEPTIC-DRUG WITH PROLONGED ACTION IN RODENTS.
001720 02-04
COMPARATIVE-STUDY ON THE EFFECT OF MORPHINE AND THE OPIOID-LIKE PEPTIDES IN THE VAS-DEFERENS OF RODENTS: STRAIN AND SPECIES-DIFFERENCES, EVIDENCE FOR MULTIPLE OPIATE-RECEPTORS.
002757 03-03
BEHAVIOURAL AND NEUROCHEMICAL PROPERTIES OF 1 1 INDOL-3-YLMETHYLPIPERID-4-YL-3-BENZOYLUREA (WY-25093) IN RODENTS.
003686 04-02

ROMAN
REGIONAL 5 HT ANALYSIS IN ROMAN HIGH-AVOIDANCE AND LOW-AVOIDANCE RATS FOLLOWING MAO-INHIBITION.
001202 02-03
BRAIN MUSCARINIC CHOLINERGIC-RECEPTOR BINDING IN ROMAN HIGH-AVOIDANCE AND LOW-AVOIDANCE RATS.
002852 03-03

ROOT
EFFECTS OF ENKEPHALIN ANALOGUE AND NALOXONE ON CAT SPINAL-CORD DORSAL ROOT POTENTIALS.
000236 01-03
THE EFFECT OF CISMETHRIN ON THE RAT DORSAL ROOT POTENTIALS.
000528 01-05
GAMMA AMINOBUTYRIC-ACID AGONISTS: AN IN VITRO COMPARISON BETWEEN DEPRESSION OF SPINAL SYNAPTIC ACTIVITY AND DEPOLARIZATION OF SPINAL ROOT FIBRES IN THE RAT.
001104 02-03
DEPRESSION OF VENTRAL ROOT DORSAL ROOT POTENTIAL BY DL ALPHA AMINOADIPATE IN FROG SPINAL-CORD.
002755 03-03

ROTATION
ROTATION INDUCED BY INTRANIGRAL INJECTIONS OF GABA AGONISTS AND ANTAGONISTS: ZONE-SPECIFIC EFFECTS.
000422 01-04
POSTURAL ASYMMETRY AND DIRECTIONALITY OF ROTATION IN RATS.
001729 02-04
AMPHETAMINE-INDUCED ROTATION IN NORMAL CATS.
003002 03-04
DOES POSTURAL ASYMMETRY INDICATE DIRECTIONALITY OF ROTATION IN RATS: ROLE OF SEX AND HANDLING.
003061 03-04
EFFECTS OF ELECTROLYTIC AND 6 HYDROXYDOPAMINE LESIONS OF THE LATERAL HYPOTHALAMUS ON ROTATION EVOKED BY ELECTRICAL-STIMULATION OF THE SUBSTANTIA-NIGRA IN RATS.
003081 03-04

ROTATIONAL-BEHAVIOR
ROTATIONAL-BEHAVIOR INDUCED BY COCAINE ANALOGS IN RATS WITH UNILATERAL 6 HYDROXYDOPAMINE LESIONS OF THE SUBSTANTIA-NIGRA: DEPENDENCE UPON DOPAMINE UPTAKE INHIBITION.
000404 01-04
SEX-DIFFERENCES IN AMPHETAMINE-ELICITED ROTATIONAL-BEHAVIOR AND THE LATERALIZATION OF STRIATAL DOPAMINE IN RATS.
000459 01-04
MOTOR-ACTIVITY AND ROTATIONAL-BEHAVIOR AFTER ANALOGS OF COCAINE: CORRELATION WITH DOPAMINE UPTAKE BLOCKADE.
001650 02-04

THE RELATIONSHIP BETWEEN LOSS OF DOPAMINE NERVE TERMINALS, STRIATAL (3H)SPIROPERIDOL BINDING AND ROTATIONAL-BEHAVIOR IN UNILATERALLY 6 HYDROXYDOPAMINE LESIONED RATS.
004129 04-04
HANDLING-INDUCED SEIZURES AND ROTATIONAL-BEHAVIOR IN THE MONGOLIAN-GERBIL.
004216 04-04
DOPAMINE-RECEPTOR CHANGES FOLLOWING DESTRUCTION OF THE NIGROSTRIATAL PATHWAY: LACK OF A RELATIONSHIP TO ROTATIONAL-BEHAVIOR.
004229 04-04

ROTATIONAL-BEHAVIOUR
UNILATERAL 5,7 DIHYDROXYTRYPTAMINE LESIONS OF THE DORSAL RAPHE NUCLEUS (DRN) AND RAT ROTATIONAL-BEHAVIOUR.
001578 02-04
ROTATIONAL-BEHAVIOUR ELICITED BY 5 HT IN THE RAT: EVIDENCE FOR AN INHIBITORY ROLE OF 5 HT IN THE SUBSTANTIA-NIGRA AND CORPUS-STRIATUM.
004141 04-04

ROUTE-OF-ADMINISTRATION
THE EFFECTS OF THE METHYLPHENIDATE AND D-AMPHETAMINE RELATED TO ROUTE-OF-ADMINISTRATION.
000476 01-04
INFLUENCE OF ROUTE-OF-ADMINISTRATION ON HALOPERIDOL PLASMA LEVELS IN PSYCHOTIC-PATIENTS.
000549 01-08
EFFECT OF AGE AND ROUTE-OF-ADMINISTRATION ON LD50 OF LITHIUM-CHLORIDE IN THE RAT.
001413 02-03

RS-51324
THE NEUROVASCULAR-PHARMACOLOGY AND CARDIOVASCULAR-PHARMACOLOGY OF RS-51324, A POTENTIAL ANTIDEPRESSANT.
001091 02-02

RUBIDIUM-CHLORIDE
CLINICAL-TRIALS WITH RUBIDIUM-CHLORIDE IN DEPRESSED-PATIENTS.
001893 02-07

RUNNING
NALOXONE SUPPRESSES FEEDING AND DRINKING BUT NOT WHEEL RUNNING IN RATS.
004080 04-04

RURAL
PSYCHOACTIVE-MEDICATION USE AND ABUSE AMONG AN ADULT RURAL POPULATION. (PH.D. DISSERTATION).
003627 03-17

RX-336-M
RX-336-M, A NEW CHEMICAL TOOL IN THE ANALYSIS OF THE QUASI-MORPHINE WITHDRAWAL-SYNDROME.
004093 04-04

S-I
A COMPARISON OF HUMAN TACTILE STIMULUS VELOCITY DISCRIMINATION WITH THE ABILITY OF S-I CORTICAL NEURONS IN AWAKE RHESUS-MONKEYS TO SIGNAL THE SAME VELOCITY DIFFERENCES BEFORE AND AFTER NONANESTHETIC DOSES OF PENTOBARBITAL.
000055 01-03

SACCHARIN
USING PROFILES OF SACCHARIN AND WATER DRINKING TO DETECT AND DISCRIMINATE ACTIONS OF DRUGS AND TOXICANTS.
000503 01-04

SAFE
PAVING THE WAY TO SAFE PRESCRIBING FOR THE ELDERLY.
000999 01-17

SAFETY
SAFETY OF ANTICONVULSANTS IN HEPATIC PORPHYRIAS.
003132 03-05
TRAZODONE EFFICACY AND SAFETY IN ENDOGENOUS DEPRESSION: A DOUBLE-BLIND COMPARISON WITH IMIPRAMINE.
004346 04-09
CNS EFFECTS OF ISF-2522, A NEW NOOTROPIC (A PHASE I SAFETY AND CNS EFFICACY STUDY WITH QUANTITATIVE PHARMACOEEG AND PHARMACOPSYCHOLOGY).
004519 04-13

SALBUTAMOL
SPONTANEOUS MOTOR-ACTIVITY IN RATS GIVEN REPEATEDLY BETA-SYMPATHOMIMETICS -- ISOPRENALIN AND SALBUTAMOL.
001804 02-04
MANIC-STATE INDUCED BY SALBUTAMOL TAKEN ORALLY.
004622 04-15

SALICYLATE
THE EFFECTS OF SALICYLATE ON THE PHARMACOKINETICS OF PHENYTOIN.
003421 03-13

SALINE
CENTRAL-EFFECTS OF ANGIOTENSIN-II IN WATER AND SALINE LOADED RATS.
003845 04-03

FACTORS REGULATING DRUG CUE SENSITIVITY: LIMITS OF DISCRIMINABILITY AND THE ROLE OF A PROGRESSIVELY DECREASING TRAINING DOSE IN FENTANYL SALINE DISCRIMINATION.
004088 04-04
RAPID ACQUISITION OF A TWO-DRUG DISCRIMINATION: TIME OF DAY EFFECT UPON SALINE STATE.
004214 04-04

SALIVA
TRANSCULTURAL PHARMACOKINETIC STUDY ON LI CONCENTRATION IN PLASMA AND SALIVA.
000769 01-13
PLASMA AND SALIVA LEVELS OF CHLORPROMAZINE AND SUBJECTIVE RESPONSE.
000826 01-14
VALUE OF SALIVA SAMPLES IN MONITORING CARBAMAZEPINE CONCENTRATIONS IN EPILEPTIC-PATIENTS.
000903 01-16
FACTORS INFLUENCING NORTRIPTYLINE STEADY-STATE KINETICS: PLASMA AND SALIVA LEVELS.
002251 02-13
LEVELS OF MINERAL-ELEMENTS IN THE SERUM AND SALIVA OF HEALTHY MALE VOLUNTEERS AFTER A SINGLE-DOSE OF LI2CO3.
002297 02-13
PROGNOSIS IN SCHIZOPHRENIA: INDIVIDUAL DIFFERENCES IN PSYCHOLOGICAL RESPONSE TO A TEST DOSE OF ANTIPSYCHOTIC-DRUG AND THEIR RELATIONSHIP TO BLOOD AND SALIVA LEVELS AND TREATMENT OUTCOME.
003189 03-08
INTRAVENOUS VALPROATE: EFFECTS ON PLASMA AND SALIVA PHENYTOIN LEVELS.
003359 03-11
EXCRETION OF NORTRIPTYLINE INTO SALIVA.
003435 03-13
QUANTITATION AND COMPARISON OF PHENOBARBITAL LEVELS IN THE PLASMA, SALIVA, AND CEREBROSPINAL-FLUID OF THE RAT, AND THE DEMONSTRATION OF AN ALTERATION OF DRUG PASSAGE BY ETHANOL.
003725 04-03
CONCENTRATIONS AND KINETICS OF CARBAMAZEPINE IN WHOLE SALIVA, PAROTID SALIVA, SERUM ULTRAFILTRATE, AND SERUM.
004545 04-13
SALIVA BENZODIAZEPINE LEVELS AND CLINICAL OUTCOME IN DETOXIFYING ALCOHOLIC-PATIENTS.
004671 04-16

SALIVARY
SALIVARY IMMUNOGLOBULIN CONCENTRATIONS IN PATIENTS WITH EPILEPSY TREATED WITH CARBAMAZEPINE.
002234 02-13
THE EFFECTS OF IMIPRAMINE TREATMENT ON THE UNCONDITIONED ALIMENTARY BEHAVIOR AND CLASSICAL CONDITIONED SALIVARY REACTIONS IN DOGS.
003030 03-04
STUDIES ON THE MECHANISMS OF L-DOPA-INDUCED SALIVARY SECRETION.
003130 03-05
PHENYTOIN THERAPY FOR EPILEPTIC-CHILDREN: EVALUATION OF SALIVARY AND PLASMA CONCENTRATIONS AND OF METHODS OF ASSESSING COMPLIANCE.
004495 04-11
THE EFFECT OF FIVE TRICYCLIC-ANTIDEPRESSANTS ON SALIVARY FLOW AND MOOD IN HEALTHY VOLUNTEERS.
004560 04-14

SALIVARY-GLAND
ALPHA FLUPENTHIXOL: AN ANTAGONIST OF DOPAMINE-EVOKED FLUID SECRETION BY AN INSECT SALIVARY-GLAND PREPARATION.
000031 01-03

SALMON
ABUNDANCE AND LOCATION OF 125I SALMON CALCITONIN BINDING-SITE IN RAT-BRAIN.
001320 02-03

SALT
RENAL BENZODIAZEPINE BINDING INCREASES DURING DEOXYCORTICOSTERONE/SALT HYPERTENSION IN RATS.
001430 02-03

SAMPLES
VALUE OF SALIVA SAMPLES IN MONITORING CARBAMAZEPINE CONCENTRATIONS IN EPILEPTIC-PATIENTS.
000903 01-16
HALOPERIDOL STIMULATION OF PROLACTIN SECRETION: HOW MANY BLOOD SAMPLES ARE NEEDED TO DEFINE THE HORMONE RESPONSE?
002505 02-16
RAPID DETERMINATION OF CHLORPROMAZINE-HCL AND TWO OXIDATION PRODUCTS IN VARIOUS PHARMACEUTICAL SAMPLES USING HIGH-PERFORMANCE LIQUID-CHROMATOGRAPHY AND FLUORESCENCE DETECTION.
004302 04-06

SAMPLING
QUICKLY-MADE CANNULA FOR REPEATED CEREBROSPINAL-FLUID SAMPLING IN RATS.
001879 02-06

SAMSO
PSYCHIATRIC-ILLNESS AND USE OF PSYCHOTROPIC-DRUGS IN THE GEOGRAPHICALLY DELIMITED POPULATION OF SAMSO, DENMARK.
004734 04-17

SAPHENOUS
INTERACTION OF THE TRICYCLIC-ANTIDEPRESSANT AMITRIPTYLINE WITH PREJUNCTIONAL ALPHA AND MUSCARINIC-RECEPTORS IN THE DOG SAPHENOUS VEIN.
003756 04-03

SARCOSINE1-LEUCINE8-ANGIOTENSIN-II
REGULATION OF RECEPTOR BINDING INTERACTIONS OF 125I ANGIOTENSIN-II AND 125I SARCOSINE1-LEUCINE8-ANGIOTENSIN-II, AN ANGIOTENSIN ANTAGONIST, BY SODIUM-ION.
001124 02-03
RECEPTOR BINDING INTERACTIONS OF THE ANGIOTENSIN-II ANTAGONIST, 125I SARCOSINE1-LEUCINE8-ANGIOTENSIN-II, WITH MAMMALIAN BRAIN AND PERIPHERAL TISSUES.
001125 02-03

SATIETY
METABOLIC-CORRELATES OF THE EFFECTS OF 2 DEOXY-D-GLUCOSE ON MEAL SIZE AND POST MEAL SATIETY IN RATS.
003035 03-04
SATIETY CENTER NEUROANATOMY. (UNPUBLISHED PAPER).
003678 04-01

SATYRIASIS
SATYRIASIS: A CASE-STUDY.
000709 01-11

SCALE
USE OF THE LITHIUM RESPONSE SCALE WITH AN OUTPATIENT PSYCHIATRIC-SAMPLE.
000921 01-17

SCALES
CONVERSION SCALES FOR COMMONLY REQUESTED SERUM CONCENTRATIONS OF DRUGS AND OTHER SUBSTANCES OF THERAPEUTIC AND TOXICOLOGICAL IMPORTANCE, AND OF HORMONES.
000759 01-13
MILD, MODERATE, SEVERE -- THE STATISTICAL ANALYSIS OF SHORT ORDINAL SCALES.
004677 04-16

SCANDINAVIAN-COUNTRIES
PSYCHOTROPIC-DRUG REGISTRATION IN THE SCANDINAVIAN-COUNTRIES: THE ROLE OF CLINICAL-TRIALS.
002550 02-17

SCANNING
DOSE-EFFECTS OF SECOBARBITAL IN A STERNBERG MEMORY SCANNING TASK.
003460 03-14

SCARE
LITHIUM AND THE KIDNEY SCARE.
003534 03-15

SCENE
STREET PCP SCENE: ISSUES ON SYNTHESIS AND CONTAMINATION.
000744 01-12

SCENT-MARKING-BEHAVIOR
CHOLINERGIC MECHANISMS IN SCENT-MARKING-BEHAVIOR BY MONGOLIAN-GERBILS (MERIONES-UNGUICULATUS).
000504 01-04

SCH-12679
COMPARISON OF SCH-12679 AND THIORIDAZINE IN AGGRESSIVE MENTAL-RETARDATES.
002119 02-11

SCHEDULE
A COMPARISON OF THE EFFECTS OF D-AMPHETAMINE, COCAINE, IMIPRAMINE AND PENTOBARBITAL ON LOCAL AND OVERALL RATES OF RESPONDING MAINTAINED UNDER A FOUR-COMPONENT MULTIPLE FIXED-INTERVAL SCHEDULE.
000508 01-04
INTRAMUSCULAR HALOPERIDOL-DECANOATE FOR NEUROLEPTIC MAINTENANCE-THERAPY: EFFICACY, DOSAGE SCHEDULE AND PLASMA LEVELS: AN OPEN MULTICENTER-STUDY.
000758 01-13
DIFFERENTIAL-EFFECTS OF IMIPRAMINE IN RATS AS A FUNCTION OF DRL SCHEDULE VALUE.
001714 02-04
A NEW DOSAGE SCHEDULE FOR PIMOZIDE IN THE ACUTE STABILIZATION AND MAINTENANCE-TREATMENT OF PSYCHOSIS.
002022 02-09
EXTENDED SCHEDULE TRANSFER OF ETHANOL DISCRIMINATION.
003087 03-04
SCHEDULE DEPENDENT CHANGE OF PUNISHED-RESPONDING AFTER DIAZEPAM IN RATS.
004165 04-04
THE EFFECTS OF TRICYCLIC-ANTIDEPRESSANTS ON PERFORMANCE UNDER A DIFFERENTIAL-REINFORCEMENT-OF-LOW-RATES SCHEDULE IN RATS.
004175 04-04

SCHEDULE-CONTROLLED
SCHEDULE-CONTROLLED BEHAVIOR IN THE MORPHINE-DEPENDENT AND POSTDEPENDENT RAT.
000349 01-04
CONSEQUENT EVENTS AS DETERMINANTS OF DRUG-EFFECTS ON SCHEDULE-CONTROLLED BEHAVIOR: MODIFICATION OF EFFECTS OF COCAINE AND D-AMPHETAMINE FOLLOWING CHRONIC AMPHETAMINE ADMINISTRATION.
000350 01-04
EFFECTS OF SYSTEMIC AND INTRAVENTRICULAR ADMINISTRATION OF CANNABINOIDS ON SCHEDULE-CONTROLLED RESPONDING IN THE SQUIRREL-MONKEY.
000354 01-04
INTERACTIONS BETWEEN NALTREXONE AND NONOPIATE DRUGS EVALUATED BY SCHEDULE-CONTROLLED BEHAVIOR.
001645 02-04
EFFECTS OF NORCOCAINE AND SOME NORCOCAINE DERIVATIVES ON SCHEDULE-CONTROLLED BEHAVIOR OF PIGEONS AND SQUIRREL-MONKEYS.
004012 04-03
INTERACTIONS BETWEEN NARCOTIC AGONISTS, PARTIAL AGONISTS AND ANTAGONISTS EVALUATED BY SCHEDULE-CONTROLLED BEHAVIOR.
004127 04-04
EFFECTS OF NARCOTIC ABSTINENCE ON SCHEDULE-CONTROLLED BEHAVIOR IN DEPENDENT RATS.
004230 04-04

SCHEDULE-INDUCED
REVERSAL OF SCHEDULE-INDUCED SELF-INJECTION OF HEROIN BY NALOXONE.
000446 01-04
DRUG-EFFECTS ON SCHEDULE-INDUCED BEHAVIORS. (PH.D. DISSERTATION).
001786 02-04

SCHEDULES
NALORPHINES EFFECT UNDER SEVERAL SCHEDULES OF ELECTRIC-SHOCK TITRATION.
000379 01-04
PROGRESSIVE-RATIO AND FIXED-RATIO SCHEDULES OF COCAINE MAINTAINED RESPONDING IN BABOONS.
000395 01-04
FIXED-RATIO SCHEDULES OF FOOD PRESENTATION AND STIMULUS-SHOCK TERMINATION: EFFECTS OF D-AMPHETAMINE, MORPHINE, AND CLOZAPINE.
000431 01-04
SECOND-ORDER SCHEDULES OF INTRAMUSCULAR COCAINE INJECTION IN THE SQUIRREL-MONKEY: COMPARISONS WITH FOOD PRESENTATION AND EFFECTS OF D-AMPHETAMINE AND PROMAZINE.
004152 04-04

SCHEDULING
GUIDELINES EMPLOYED BY THE FOOD-AND-DRUG-ADMINISTRATION IN DRUG SCHEDULING.
003586 03-17
USE OF CURRENTLY AVAILABLE DATA SOURCES TO ASSESS DRUG SCHEDULING.
003594 03-17
IMPACT OF DRUG SCHEDULING ON UTILIZATION.
003601 03-17
GUIDELINES FOR SCHEDULING DRUGS UNDER THE CONTROLLED-SUBSTANCES-ACT.
003606 03-17

SCHIZOAFFECTIVE-DISORDER
THE PHARMACOLOGICAL-TREATMENT OF SCHIZOAFFECTIVE-DISORDER DEPRESSED; A REVIEW OF THE LITERATURE.
003634 03-17

SCHIZOAFFECTIVE-PATIENTS
LITHIUM COMBINED WITH NEUROLEPTICS IN CHRONIC SCHIZOPHRENIC-PATIENTS AND SCHIZOAFFECTIVE-PATIENTS.
003168 03-08

SCHIZOAFFECTIVE-PSYCHOSES
THE TREATMENT OF SCHIZOAFFECTIVE-PSYCHOSES WITH LITHIUM-CARBONATE.
000607 01-09

SCHIZOPHRENIA
FUNCTIONAL HYPERINNERVATION OF CEREBRAL-CORTEX BY NORADRENERGIC NEURONS RESULTS FROM FETAL LESIONS: PARALLELS WITH SCHIZOPHRENIA.
000059 01-03
PATHOPHYSIOLOGICAL-STUDIES ON SCHIZOPHRENIA WITH SPECIAL REFERENCE TO HOMOVANILLIC-ACID CONCENTRATION IN CEREBROSPINAL-FLUID.
000271 01-03
THE RELATIONSHIP BETWEEN THE THIORIDAZINE LEVEL IN THE PLASMA AND SYMPTOMS OF PARANOID SCHIZOPHRENIA.
000546 01-08
WHAT IS THE BEST MAINTENANCE DOSE OF NEUROLEPTICS IN SCHIZOPHRENIA?
000547 01-08
CONTROLLED-COMPARISON OF MEDIUM AND HIGH CLOROTEPIN DOSES IN CHRONIC SCHIZOPHRENIA.
000548 01-08

A NEW DRUG-TREATMENT FOR PREMENSTRUAL EXACERBATION OF SCHIZOPHRENIA.
000553 01-08
LITHIUM RESPONSE IN GOOD PROGNOSIS SCHIZOPHRENIA.
000555 01-08
FAILURE OF NALOXONE TO REVERSE CATALEPSY ASSOCIATED WITH SCHIZOPHRENIA: A CASE-REPORT.
000560 01-08
SODIUM-VALPROATE IN SCHIZOPHRENIA: SOME BIOCHEMICAL-CORRELATES.
000561 01-08
THE PLACE OF LONG-ACTING NEUROLEPTICS IN THE TREATMENT OF SCHIZOPHRENIA.
000563 01-08
DOPAMINE-RECEPTORS AND SCHIZOPHRENIA: DRUG-EFFECT OR ILLNESS?
000564 01-08
PSYCHOTROPIC-DRUGS AND DEPRESSIVE-SYNDROME IN SCHIZOPHRENIA.
000569 01-08
DOUBLE-BLIND COMPARISON OF HALOPERIDOL AND THIOTHIXENE WITH AFTERCARE TREATMENT EVALUATION IN PSYCHIATRIC-OUTPATIENTS WITH SCHIZOPHRENIA.
000574 01-08
COVERT DYSKINESIA IN AMBULATORY SCHIZOPHRENIA.
000836 01-15
DIFFERENTIAL-EFFECTS OF AMPHETAMINE AND NEUROLEPTICS ON NEGATIVE VS. POSITIVE SYMPTOMS IN SCHIZOPHRENIA.
001906 02-08
INVOLVEMENT OF CHOLINERGIC AND GABAERGIC SYSTEMS IN SCHIZOPHRENIA.
001907 02-08
HIGH-DOSE DIAZEPAM IN SCHIZOPHRENIA.
001909 02-08
DIAGNOSTIC CLASSIFICATION AND THE ENDORPHIN HYPOTHESIS OF SCHIZOPHRENIA: INDIVIDUAL DIFFERENCES AND PSYCHOPHARMACOLOGICAL STRATEGIES. (UNPUBLISHED PAPER).
001910 02-08
TIME-COURSE OF THE ANTIPSYCHOTIC-EFFECT IN SCHIZOPHRENIA AND SOME CHANGES IN POSTMORTEM BRAIN AND THEIR RELATION TO NEUROLEPTIC-MEDICATION.
001911 02-08
DES-TYR1-GAMMA-ENDORPHIN IN SCHIZOPHRENIA.
001918 02-08
DEXTRO PROPRANOLOL IN SCHIZOPHRENIA.
001921 02-08
HORMONE LEVELS IN ACUTE SCHIZOPHRENIA WITH AND WITHOUT NEUROLEPTIC-MEDICATION.
001923 02-08
EXPERIENCE WITH OXYPROTHEPINE-DECANOATE IN THE MAINTENANCE-THERAPY OF SCHIZOPHRENIA.
001925 02-08
SOME CLINICAL-ASPECTS AND METABOLIC-ASPECTS OF PROPRANOLOL IN CHRONIC SCHIZOPHRENIA.
001926 02-08
CEREBRAL VENTRICLES AND DOPAMINE IN SCHIZOPHRENIA. (UNPUBLISHED PAPER).
001928 02-08
PHARMACOMANOMETRIC-STUDIES OF COLONIC MOTILITY AS A GUIDE TO THE CHEMOTHERAPY OF SCHIZOPHRENIA.
001930 02-08
INTERMITTENT PIMOZIDE VERSUS FLUPHENAZINE-DECANOATE AS MAINTENANCE-THERAPY IN CHRONIC SCHIZOPHRENIA.
001932 02-08
THE HLA-SYSTEM AND SCHIZOPHRENIA IN ENGLAND.
001933 02-08
OXYPROTHEPINE-DECANOATE COMPARED WITH FLUPHENAZINE-DECANOATE IN THE TREATMENT OF SCHIZOPHRENIA: PRELIMINARY-COMMUNICATION.
001934 02-08
CONTROLLED-COMPARISON OF PERPHENAZINE WITH PERPHENAZINE IN SCHIZOPHRENIA: A METHODICAL-CHECK OF A DOUBLE-BLIND CROSS-OVER DESIGN.
001937 02-08
LOW ORAL CPZ BIOAVAILABILITY IN CHRONIC SCHIZOPHRENIA. (UNPUBLISHED PAPER).
001938 02-08
PROPRANOLOL IN SCHIZOPHRENIA — MORE GUESS THAN GAUSS.
001939 02-08
SERUM NEUROLEPTIC CONCENTRATIONS IN SCHIZOPHRENIA. (UNPUBLISHED PAPER).
001945 02-08
PARADOXICAL IMPROVEMENT FOLLOWING IV AMPHETAMINE IN SCHIZOPHRENIA. (UNPUBLISHED PAPER).
001951 02-08
METHODOLOGICAL-ISSUES IN SPINAL-FLUID STUDIES OF SCHIZOPHRENIA: THE CASE OF NOREPINEPHRINE AND DOPAMINE-BETA-HYDROXYLASE. (UNPUBLISHED PAPER).
001952 02-08

ANTIPSYCHOTIC-EFFECT OF GAMMA-TYPE ENDORPHINS IN
SCHIZOPHRENIA.
001953 02-08

VASOPRESSIN AND SCHIZOPHRENIA.
001954 02-08

PHENYLETHYLAMINE, DOPAMINE AND NOREPINEPHRINE IN
SCHIZOPHRENIA. (UNPUBLISHED PAPER).
001957 02-08

MONOAMINE-OXIDASE, PHENYLETHYLAMINE, NOREPINEPHRINE AND
SCHIZOPHRENIA. (UNPUBLISHED PAPER).
001958 02-08

PATHOPHYSIOLOGIC-IMPACT OF CENTRAL CATECHOLAMINERGIC
FUNCTION IN SCHIZOPHRENIA AND SCHIZOPHRENIA-LIKE PSYCHOSES.
002174 02-11

MONOAMINES, EPILEPSY AND SCHIZOPHRENIA.
002183 02-11

ACUTE AND CHRONIC LSD EFFECTS ON RAT STARTLE: DATA SUPPORTING
AN LSD RAT MODEL OF SCHIZOPHRENIA.
002194 02-12

EFFECT OF OPIATES AND OPIATE ANTAGONISTS ON SOMATOSENSORY
EVOKED-POTENTIALS IN PATIENTS WITH SCHIZOPHRENIA AND
NORMAL ADULTS.
002222 02-13

CHANGES IN CEREBRAL DOPAMINE METABOLISM AND RECEPTORS
DURING ONE-YEAR NEUROLEPTIC ADMINISTRATION AND SUBSEQUENT
WITHDRAWAL: RELEVANCE TO BRAIN-BIOCHEMISTRY IN
SCHIZOPHRENIA.
002390 02-15

DYSFUNCTIONS OF CHOLINERGIC PROCESSES IN SCHIZOPHRENIA.
002611 02-17

DIAGNOSTIC CLASSIFICATION AND THE ENDORPHIN HYPOTHESIS OF
SCHIZOPHRENIA: INDIVIDUAL DIFFERENCES AND
PSYCHOPHARMACOLOGICAL STRATEGIES.
003167 03-08

LONG-TERM-TREATMENT OF SCHIZOPHRENIA.
003171 03-08

EFFECT OF PROPRANOLOL AND PHENOTHIAZINES ON ELECTRODERMAL
ORIENTING AND HABITUATION IN SCHIZOPHRENIA.
003174 03-08

GABA AND SCHIZOPHRENIA: STUDY OF THE ACTION OF A GABAERGIC
ANTAGONIST. PROGABIDE OR SL-76-002.
003175 03-08

LATE RESULTS OF LITHIUM TREATMENT OF ADOLESCENTS WITH ATTACK
LIKE SCHIZOPHRENIA.
003177 03-08

HEMOPERFUSION FOR CHRONIC SCHIZOPHRENIA: PRELIMINARY
PSYCHIATRIC RESULTS.
003180 03-08

MANAGEMENT OF SCHIZOPHRENIA: LONG-TERM CLINICAL-STUDIES WITH
SPECIAL REFERENCE TO THE COMBINATION OF PSYCHOTHERAPY AND
DEPOT NEUROLEPTICS.
003183 03-08

PROGNOSIS IN SCHIZOPHRENIA: INDIVIDUAL DIFFERENCES IN
PSYCHOLOGICAL RESPONSE TO A TEST DOSE OF ANTIPSYCHOTIC-DRUG
AND THEIR RELATIONSHIP TO BLOOD AND SALIVA LEVELS AND
TREATMENT OUTCOME.
003189 03-08

CARPIPRAMINE: A DISINHIBITORY DRUG COMPOUND IN CHRONIC
SCHIZOPHRENIA.
003192 03-08

BETA ENDORPHIN AND SCHIZOPHRENIA.
003193 03-08

DOPAMINE-RECEPTORS, NEUROLEPTICS, AND SCHIZOPHRENIA.
003197 03-08

ENDORPHINS IN MENTAL-ILLNESSES, AND PARTICULARLY IN
SCHIZOPHRENIA.
003203 03-08

AUTONOMIC-EFFECTS OF DEXTROAMPHETAMINE IN NORMAL MEN:
IMPLICATIONS FOR HYPERACTIVITY AND SCHIZOPHRENIA.
003437 03-13

A CONTROLLED-STUDY OF L-DOPA IN SCHIZOPHRENIA WITH REFERENCE
TO THE THEORY OF DOPAMINERGIC-RECEPTOR HYPERSENSITIVITY.
004312 04-08

DRUGS AND SCHIZOPHRENIA.
004314 04-08

ALTERATIONS OF EVOKED-POTENTIALS LINK RESEARCH IN ATTENTION-
DYSFUNCTION TO PEPTIDE RESPONSE SYMPTOMS OF SCHIZOPHRENIA.
004316 04-08

PRELIMINARY TRIAL OF CLONIDINE TREATMENT IN TWO PATIENTS
SUFFERING FROM CHRONIC SCHIZOPHRENIA.
004320 04-08

DES-TYROSYL-GAMMA-ENDORPHIN IN SCHIZOPHRENIA: A DOUBLE-BLIND
TRIAL IN 13 PATIENTS.
004322 04-08

IMMUNOLOGICAL COMPONENTS IN SCHIZOPHRENIA.
004324 04-08

APOMORPHINE IN SCHIZOPHRENIA.
004327 04-08

A DOUBLE-BLIND COMPARISON OF THREE DOSAGES OF FLUTROLINE (CP-
36584) IN THE TREATMENT OF SCHIZOPHRENIA.
004333 04-08

THE USE OF CLINICAL AND PHARMACOKINETIC CRITERIA IN FORECASTING
THE EFFICACY OF THERAPY IN SCHIZOPHRENIA.
004335 04-08

PSYCHOPHARMACOLOGICAL AND SOCIAL ASPECTS OF SCHIZOPHRENIA:
RECENT DEVELOPMENTS.
004336 04-08

THE PROBLEM OF PSYCHOPHARMACOTHERAPY OF SLOWLY PROGRESSIVE
HYPOCHONDRIACAL SCHIZOPHRENIA.
004340 04-08

PECULIARITIES OF THE CEREBRAL PATHOMORPHOLOGY OF PATIENTS
WITH SCHIZOPHRENIA TREATED WITH PSYCHOTROPIC-DRUGS
(PHARMACOLOGICAL PATHOMORPHOSIS).
004528 04-13

A MODIFIED VERSION OF THE SIMULTANEOUS DISCONTINUATION OF
PSYCHOTROPIC-DRUGS (COMBINED WITH THE ADMINISTRATION OF
DIURETICS) AS A METHOD OF HALTING PROLONGED ATTACKS OF
SCHIZOPHRENIA.
004584 04-14

DRUG-INDUCED PSYCHOSIS AND SCHIZOPHRENIA IN ADOLESCENTS.
004596 04-15

COMPUTER-ANALYZED ELECTROENCEPHALOGRAM TO PREDICT THE
THERAPEUTIC OUTCOME IN SCHIZOPHRENIA.
004680 04-16

CHOLINOMIMETICS IN MANIA, SCHIZOPHRENIA, AND MEMORY-
DISORDERS.
004703 04-17

THE DRUG PATHOMORPHOSIS OF SCHIZOPHRENIA.
004732 04-17

BENZODIAZEPINES IN SCHIZOPHRENIA: A NEED FOR REASSESSMENT.
004733 04-17

SCHIZOPHRENIA-LIKE
PATHOPHYSIOLOGIC-IMPACT OF CENTRAL CATECHOLAMINERGIC
FUNCTION IN SCHIZOPHRENIA AND SCHIZOPHRENIA-LIKE PSYCHOSES.
002174 02-11

SCHIZOPHRENIAS
DISTINGUISHING SCHIZOPHRENIAS BY MEANS OF PHARMACOTHERAPY.
001947 02-08

SCHIZOPHRENIC
DOPAMINERGIC ABNORMALITIES IN POSTMORTEM SCHIZOPHRENIC
BRAIN.
002575 02-17

VILOXAZINE AND THE DEPRESSED SCHIZOPHRENIC -- METHODOLOGICAL-
ISSUES.
003181 03-08

SCHIZOPHRENIC-BOY
EFFECTS OF THIORIDAZINE ON THE COGNITIVE FUNCTIONING OF A
HYPOTONIC SCHIZOPHRENIC-BOY.
000557 01-08

SCHIZOPHRENIC-EPISODES
EVALUATIONS OF LOXAPINE-SUCCINATE IN THE AMBULATORY
TREATMENT OF ACUTE SCHIZOPHRENIC-EPISODES.
004345 04-08

SCHIZOPHRENIC-OUTPATIENTS
ABSENCE OF SEVERE TARDIVE-DYSKINESIA IN HUNGARIAN
SCHIZOPHRENIC-OUTPATIENTS.
002404 02-15

TARDIVE-DYSKINESIA IN SCHIZOPHRENIC-OUTPATIENTS: PREVALENCE
AND SIGNIFICANT VARIABLES.
003483 03-15

A FOLLOWUP STUDY OF SCHIZOPHRENIC-OUTPATIENTS TREATED WITH
DEPOT NEUROLEPTICS.
004342 04-08

SCHIZOPHRENIC-PATIENTS
STUDY ON VISUALLY-EVOKED-POTENTIALS IN SCHIZOPHRENIC-PATIENTS
IN SULPIRIDE THERAPY.
000550 01-08

EFFECTS OF TRIFLUOPERAZINE, CHLORPROMAZINE, AND HALOPERIDOL
UPON TEMPORAL INFORMATION-PROCESSING BY SCHIZOPHRENIC-
PATIENTS.
000554 01-08

THE EFFECT OF THIORIDAZINE ON PROLACTIN LEVELS IN ACUTELY
SCHIZOPHRENIC-PATIENTS: CHALLENGE-DOSE AND STEADY-STATE
LEVELS.
000558 01-08

CLINICAL COMPARISON OF OXYPROTHEPIN AND CLOTEPINE IN
SCHIZOPHRENIC-PATIENTS (CONTROLLED-STUDY).
000568 01-08

PROLACTIN AND SOMATOTROPIN RESPONSES TO TRH IN SCHIZOPHRENIC-
PATIENTS.
000570 01-08

PROLACTIN RESPONSE AND EXTRAPYRAMIDAL SIDE-EFFECTS DURING
PROPRANOLOL AND NEUROLEPTIC-DRUGS TREATMENT IN CHRONIC
SCHIZOPHRENIC-PATIENTS.
000841 01-15

THE OCCURRENCE OF TARDIVE EXTRAPYRAMIDAL SYMPTOMS IN
SCHIZOPHRENIC-PATIENTS UNDERGOING PROLONGED NEUROLEPTIC
TREATMENT.
000885 01-15

FOLLOWUP TREATMENT AND AFTERCARE OF DISCHARGED
SCHIZOPHRENIC-PATIENTS.
000944 01-17
LONG-TERM APPLICATION OF HIGH-DOSES OF CLOROTEPIN TO CHRONIC
SCHIZOPHRENIC-PATIENTS.
001908 02-08
CONTROLLED-TRIAL OF SULPIRIDE IN CHRONIC SCHIZOPHRENIC-PATIENTS.
001914 02-08
EFFECT OF PROPRANOLOL TREATMENT ON SERUM PROLACTIN LEVEL IN
SCHIZOPHRENIC-PATIENTS.
001916 02-08
MAINTENANCE-THERAPY WITH FLUPHENAZINE-DECANOATE AND
OXYPROTHEPINE-DECANOATE IN SCHIZOPHRENIC-PATIENTS — A
DOUBLE-BLIND CROSS-OVER COMPARATIVE-STUDY.
001924 02-08
DISCONTINUATION OF ORAL AND DEPOT FLUPHENAZINE IN
SCHIZOPHRENIC-PATIENTS AFTER ONE YEAR OF CONTINUOUS
MEDICATION: A CONTROLLED-STUDY.
001931 02-08
BASAL AND STIMULATED LEVELS OF PROLACTIN, TSH AND LH IN SERUM
OF CHRONIC SCHIZOPHRENIC-PATIENTS, LONG-TERM TREATED WITH
NEUROLEPTICS.
001935 02-08
BASAL AND STIMULATED LEVELS OF PROLACTIN, TSH, AND LH IN SERUM
OF CHRONIC SCHIZOPHRENIC-PATIENTS LONG-TERM TREATED WITH
NEUROLEPTICS: RELATIONS TO PSYCHOPATHOLOGY.
001936 02-08
PHARMACOKINETIC INTERACTION BETWEEN PROPRANOLOL AND
CHLORPROMAZINE IN SCHIZOPHRENIC-PATIENTS.
001940 02-08
CHANGE IN OVERINCLUSIVE THINKING OF SCHIZOPHRENIC-PATIENTS IS
RELATED TO PLASMA PHENOTHIAZINE CONCENTRATION.
001941 02-08
USE OF LARGE-SINGLE-DOSES OF BROMOCRIPTINE IN SCHIZOPHRENIC-
PATIENTS WITH ELEVATED SERUM PROLACTIN LEVELS AND
EXTRAPYRAMIDAL SIDE-EFFECTS ASSOCIATED WITH NEUROLEPTIC
TREATMENT.
001944 02-08
RELATIONSHIPS AMONG BIOCHEMICAL-VARIABLES, CLINICAL-
VARIABLES, AND PHARMACOKINETIC-VARIABLES IN NEUROLEPTIC
TREATED SCHIZOPHRENIC-PATIENTS.
001946 02-08
PLASMA FLUPHENAZINE AND PROLACTIN LEVELS IN SCHIZOPHRENIC-
PATIENTS DURING TREATMENT WITH LOW-DOSES AND HIGH-DOSES OF
FLUPHENAZINE-ENANTHATE.
001956 02-08
PLASMA FLUPHENAZINE LEVELS BY RADIOIMMUNOASSAY IN
SCHIZOPHRENIC-PATIENTS TREATED WITH DEPOT INJECTIONS OF
FLUPHENAZINE-DECANOATE.
002510 02-16
LITHIUM COMBINED WITH NEUROLEPTICS IN CHRONIC SCHIZOPHRENIC-
PATIENTS AND SCHIZOAFFECTIVE-PATIENTS.
003168 03-08
A PROBABLE NEUROLEPTIC-EFFECT ON PLATELET MONOAMINE-OXIDASE
IN CHRONIC SCHIZOPHRENIC-PATIENTS.
003169 03-08
TREATMENT OF THERAPEUTICALLY-RESISTANT PARANOID
SCHIZOPHRENIC-PATIENTS WITH FLUPHENAZINE DEPOT COMBINED
WITH OTHER PSYCHOTROPIC-DRUGS AND CLOZAPINE.
003172 03-08
BEHAVIORAL-EFFECTS OF METHADONE IN SCHIZOPHRENIC-PATIENTS.
003178 03-08
A COMPARISON OF DOPAMINE-RECEPTOR BLOCKING ASSAY WITH
PLASMA DRUG LEVELS OF HALOPERIDOL IN SCHIZOPHRENIC-PATIENTS.
003182 03-08
PIPERIDONE IN CHRONIC SCHIZOPHRENIC-PATIENTS: A CONTROLLED
DOUBLE-BLIND STUDY.
003184 03-08
THE NEED FOR CONTINUOUS USE OF ANTIPARKINSONIAN MEDICATION
WITH CHRONIC SCHIZOPHRENIC-PATIENTS RECEIVING LONG-TERM
NEUROLEPTIC THERAPY.
003186 03-08
CHLORPROMAZINE LEVELS AND THE OUTCOME OF TREATMENT IN
SCHIZOPHRENIC-PATIENTS.
003188 03-08
NEUROLEPTIC SERUM LEVELS MEASURED BY RADIORECEPTOR ASSAY
AND CLINICAL-RESPONSE IN SCHIZOPHRENIC-PATIENTS.
003199 03-08
BEHAVIORAL-EFFECTS AND BIOLOGICAL-EFFECTS OF ACUTE BETA
ENDORPHIN INJECTION IN SCHIZOPHRENIC-PATIENTS AND DEPRESSED-
PATIENTS.
003357 03-11
LATERALIZED DEFICITS AND DRUG INFLUENCES ON THE DICHOTIC
LISTENING OF SCHIZOPHRENIC-PATIENTS.
003443 03-14
CORRELATIONS BETWEEN VISUAL-EVOKED-POTENTIALS AND
PSYCHOPATHOLOGICAL-FINDINGS IN SCHIZOPHRENIC-PATIENTS UNDER
TREATMENT WITH VARIOUS PSYCHOPHARMACOLOGICAL-DRUGS.
004315 04-08

PLASMA LEVELS OF BETA ENDORPHIN UNDER CHRONIC NEUROLEPTIC
TREATMENT IN SCHIZOPHRENIC-PATIENTS: FAILURE OF NALOXONE TO
COUNTERACT CURATIVE EFFECTS OF NEUROLEPTIC-DRUGS.
004321 04-08
THE EFFECT OF LONG-TERM MAINTENANCE-THERAPY ON SCHIZOPHRENIC-
PATIENTS USING SOMATOTHERAPEUTIC MEASURES.
004325 04-08
THE TREATMENT OF CHRONIC SCHIZOPHRENIC-PATIENTS: AN INTERVIEW
WITH DR. J. HUSSER.
004328 04-08
THE USE OF SODIUM-NUCLEINATE IN THE TREATMENT OF
SCHIZOPHRENIC-PATIENTS.
004339 04-08
THE EFFECT OF AN INTENSIVE COURSE OF NEUROLEPTIC-DRUGS ON
SCHIZOPHRENIC-PATIENTS AND THEIR SUBSEQUENT COURSE
FOLLOWING THE CESSATION OF ALL NEUROLEPTIC-MEDICATION.
004341 04-08
PLASMA DOPAMINE-BETA-HYDROXYLASE ACTIVITY IN CHRONIC
SCHIZOPHRENIC-PATIENTS TESTED WITH SINGLE-DOSE OF 2 BROMO-
ALPHA-ERGOCRIPTINE (PARLODEL).
004343 04-08
LONG-TERM NEUROLEPTIC TREATMENT OF CHRONIC SCHIZOPHRENIC-
PATIENTS: CLINICAL AND BIOCHEMICAL-EFFECTS OF WITHDRAWAL.
004344 04-08
THE STATE OF THE ADRENERGIC AND CHOLINERGIC SYSTEMS IN
SCHIZOPHRENIC-PATIENTS DURING PSYCHPHARMACOTHERAPY.
004526 04-13
PROLACTIN AND GROWTH-HORMONE STUDIES IN SCHIZOPHRENIC-
PATIENTS AND NORMAL CONTROLS.
004538 04-13
EFFECTS OF NEUROLEPTIC ADJUSTMENT ON CLINICAL CONDITION AND
TARDIVE-DYSKINESIA IN SCHIZOPHRENIC-PATIENTS.
004595 04-15

SCHIZOPHRENIC-PSYCHOSES
OXYPROTHEPIN-DECANOATE INJECTIONS: EXPERIENCE WITH A LONG-
TERM-TREATMENT OF SCHIZOPHRENIC-PSYCHOSES.
000576 01-08
DIAGNOSIS AND TREATMENT OF ACUTE SCHIZOPHRENIC-PSYCHOSES.
003191 03-08
ENDORPHIN RESEARCH IN SCHIZOPHRENIC-PSYCHOSES.
003200 03-08

SCHIZOPHRENIC-SYMPTOMATOLOGY
LONG-TERM-TREATMENT WITH NEUROLEPTIC-AGENTS: ADAPTATION
PHENOMENA AND THEIR SIGNIFICANCE WITH REGARD TO
SCHIZOPHRENIC-SYMPTOMATOLOGY AND SIDE-EFFECTS.
002370 02-15

SCHIZOPHRENIC-SYMPTOMS
DRUG RESPONSE DIFFERENCES OF HIGH AND STANDARD DOSAGE OF
FLUPHENAZINE-DECANOATE IN RELATION TO SCHIZOPHRENIC-
SYMPTOMS.
000562 01-08
APOMORPHINE REDUCES SCHIZOPHRENIC-SYMPTOMS.
000572 01-08
A TRIPEPTIDE FOR CONTROL OF SCHIZOPHRENIC-SYMPTOMS.
001919 02-08
ABNORMAL TRANSMETHYLATION REACTION DURING THE METABOLISM
OF DOPAMINE, TRYPTAMINE, AND SEROTONIN, AND SCHIZOPHRENIC-
SYMPTOMS: A CRITICAL REVIEW.
003404 03-13

SCHIZOPHRENICS
THE EEG EFFECTS OF THYROTROPIN-RELEASING-HORMONE IN HEALTHY
SUBJECTS AND CHRONIC SCHIZOPHRENICS.
000770 01-13
DISORDERS OF SMOOTH-PURSUIT EYE-MOVEMENTS IN SCHIZOPHRENICS
AND THE EFFECT OF NEUROLEPTICS IN THERAPEUTIC DOSES.
001912 02-08
ANTIPSYCHOTIC-EFFECT OF PROPRANOLOL ON CHRONIC
SCHIZOPHRENICS: STUDY OF A GRADUAL TREATMENT REGIMEN.
001915 02-08
EFFECT OF FLUPHENAZINE ON THE CIRCADIAN-EXCRETION OF CYCLIC-
NUCLEOTIDES AND ELECTROLYTES IN THE URINE OF CHRONIC
SCHIZOPHRENICS.
001927 02-08
BETA ENDORPHIN LEVELS IN THE CEREBROSPINAL-FLUID OF
SCHIZOPHRENICS.
003176 03-08
BIOLOGICAL-EFFECTS OF CHLORPROMAZINE IN CHRONIC
SCHIZOPHRENICS. III. THE MUTUAL RELATION OF EACH INDEX.
003179 03-08
DES-TYR-GAMMA-ENDORPHIN ADMINISTRATION IN CHRONIC
SCHIZOPHRENICS: A PRELIMINARY REPORT.
003198 03-08
BIOLOGICAL-EFFECTS OF CHLORPROMAZINE IN CHRONIC
SCHIZOPHRENICS. I. WITH REFERENCE TO PITUITARY-HORMONES.
003415 03-13
BIOLOGICAL-EFFECTS OF CHLORPROMAZINE IN CHRONIC
SCHIZOPHRENICS. II. WITH REFERENCE TO SYMPATHETIC NEURONAL
FUNCTION.
003416 03-13

A TWELVE-YEAR FOLLOWUP OF THE NIMH-PRB HIGH-DOSE CHLORPROMAZINE STUDY OF CHRONIC SCHIZOPHRENICS -- IMPLICATIONS FOR DEINSTITUTIONALIZATION. (UNPUBLISHED PAPER).
004323 04-08

EFFECTS OF ALTHESIN IN PSYCHOTHERAPY OF SCHIZOPHRENICS: PRELIMINARY REPORT.
004331 04-08

HALOPERIDOL AND DROPERIDOL TREATMENT IN SCHIZOPHRENICS: CLINICAL APPLICATION OF THE PROLACTIN MODEL.
004332 04-08

MOBILIZATION OF REFRACTORY CHRONIC SCHIZOPHRENICS WITH HALOPERIDOL.
004337 04-08

SCHOOL
CHILDREN ON MEDICATION: A PRIMER FOR SCHOOL PERSONNEL.
000676 01-11

PREVALENCE OF HYPERACTIVITY AND RELATED TREATMENTS AMONG ELEMENTARY SCHOOL CHILDREN.
004469 04-11

ASTHMA THERAPY MAY UNDERCUT KIDS AT SCHOOL.
004475 04-11

SCHOOL-AGE
EFFECTS OF LITHIUM-CARBONATE AND HALOPERIDOL ON COGNITION IN AGGRESSIVE, HOSPITALIZED SCHOOL-AGE CHILDREN.
003360 03-11

EFFECTS OF LITHIUM-CARBONATE AND HALOPERIDOL ON COGNITION IN AGGRESSIVE HOSPITALIZED SCHOOL-AGE CHILDREN.
003361 03-11

SCHWANN-CELL
THE PATHOGENESIS OF PRIMARY INTERNODAL DEMYELINATION PRODUCED BY ACETYL-ETHYL-TETRAMETHYL-TETRALIN: EVIDENCE FOR PRESERVED SCHWANN-CELL SOMAL FUNCTION.
002905 03-03

SCIATIC-NERVE
INHIBITORY ACTION OF MORPHINE ON THE RELEASE OF A BRADYKININ-LIKE SUBSTANCE AFTER SCIATIC-NERVE STIMULATION.
001293 02-03

THE EFFECT OF CHRONIC NICOTINE AND WITHDRAWAL ON INTRAAXONAL TRANSPORT OF ACETYLCHOLINE AND RELATED ENZYMES IN SCIATIC-NERVE OF THE RAT.
003897 04-03

EFFECTS OF ANALGESICS AND CNS-ACTING DRUGS ON STRUGGLING FOLLOWING REPETITIVE STIMULATION OF THE TAIL, AND FLEXOR REFLEX TO A SINGLE STIMULATION OF THE SCIATIC-NERVE IN RATS.
004148 04-04

SCIENTIFIC
CA DIAZEPAM LINK? NO SCIENTIFIC TAKERS SO FAR.
003519 03-15

SCIENTIFIC-STUDY
THE OPIATES: TWO CENTURIES OF SCIENTIFIC-STUDY.
000952 01-17

SCL-90
PLACEBO REACTION IN NEUROTICS RATED WITH THE SCL-90 QUESTIONNAIRE.
000976 01-17

SCLEROSING
ISOPRINOSINE IN SUBACUTE SCLEROSING PANENCEPHALITIS.
000687 01-11

REVIEW OF 38 CASES OF SUBACUTE SCLEROSING PANENCEPHALITIS: EFFECT OF AMANTADINE ON THE NATURAL COURSE OF THE DISEASE.
000718 01-11

SCOPOLAMINE
INCREASED MUSCARINIC-RECEPTOR BINDING IN RAT-FOREBRAIN AFTER SCOPOLAMINE.
001351 02-03

EFFECTS OF SCOPOLAMINE ON AGONISTIC-BEHAVIOUR IN MICE.
001690 02-04

DIFFERENTIAL REVERSAL BY SCOPOLAMINE AND THIP OF THE ANTISTEREOTYPIC AND CATALEPTIC-EFFECTS OF NEUROLEPTICS.
002948 03-04

EFFECTS OF SCOPOLAMINE, PILOCARPINE, AND OXOTREMORINE ON THE EXPLORATORY-BEHAVIOR OF TWO PSYCHOGENETICALLY SELECTED LINES OF RATS IN A COMPLEX MAZE.
003042 03-04

INTERACTION AMONG D-AMPHETAMINE, SCOPOLAMINE AND GENOTYPE IN AVOIDANCE-BEHAVIOR OF RATS.
003082 03-04

INCREASES IN SKIN-RESISTANCE OF WHITE RATS FOLLOWING SCOPOLAMINE INJECTION.
003138 03-06

SCOPOLAMINE IN CHOLINOLYTIC TREATMENT.
004468 04-11

BILATERAL SKIN CONDUCTANCE AND THE PUPILLARY LIGHT DARK REFLEX: MANIPULATION BY CHLORPROMAZINE, HALOPERIDOL, SCOPOLAMINE, AND PLACEBO.
004544 04-13

SCOPOLAMINE-INDUCED
INFLUENCE OF BENZODIAZEPINE TRANQUILIZERS ON SCOPOLAMINE-INDUCED LOCOMOTOR-STIMULATION IN MICE.
001768 02-04

TIME-DEPENDENT CHANGES IN ANTEROGRADE SCOPOLAMINE-INDUCED AMNESIA IN RATS.
004182 04-04

BEHAVIORAL AND BIOCHEMICAL-STUDIES OF THE SCOPOLAMINE-INDUCED REVERSAL OF NEUROLEPTIC ACTIVITY.
004195 04-04

SCRATCHING-BEHAVIOUR
PHARMACOLOGICAL CHARACTERIZATION OF SCRATCHING-BEHAVIOUR INDUCED BY INTRACRANIAL INJECTION OF SUBSTANCE-P AND SOMATOSTATIN.
002980 03-04

SCREENING
A SIMPLE HISTOCHEMICAL SCREENING METHOD FOR AMINE UPTAKE.
004295 04-06

MASS SCREENING AND CONFIRMATION OF DIAZEPAM IN URINE BY EMIT THIN-LAYER-CHROMATOGRAPHY.
004672 04-16

SCREENING-TEST
APPLICATION OF A RADIOIMMUNOASSAY SCREENING-TEST FOR DETECTION AND MANAGEMENT OF PHENCYCLIDINE INTOXICATION.
000859 01-15

OXOTREMORINE BEHAVIOURAL-EFFECTS AS A SCREENING-TEST IN MICE.
001072 02-02

SE-5023
CORRELATED STUDY OF THE EFFECTS OF SE-5023 IN AN HYPOXIC ATMOSPHERE ON QUANTIFIED EEG, VIGILANCE, MEMORY, AND MOOD.
003440 03-14

SECOBARBITAL
DOSE-EFFECTS OF SECOBARBITAL IN A STERNBERG MEMORY SCANNING TASK.
003460 03-14

INHIBITORY-ACTION OF THE COMBINATION OF AMINOPYRINE AND SECOBARBITAL ON EEG ACTIVATION, NEOCORTICAL RECRUITING AND AUGMENTING RESPONSES IN RABBITS.
004022 04-03

CHOICE BETWEEN FOOD AND HEROIN: EFFECTS OF MORPHINE, NALOXONE, AND SECOBARBITAL.
004123 04-04

HUMAN SOCIAL CONVERSATION: EFFECTS OF ETHANOL, SECOBARBITAL AND CHLORPROMAZINE.
004582 04-14

SECOND-GENERATION
CLINICAL-EXPERIENCE WITH SECOND-GENERATION ANTIDEPRESSANTS IN ENDOGENOUS DEPRESSIONS.
001975 02-09

SECOND-GENERATION ANTIDEPRESSANTS
002042 02-09

SECOND-GENERATION ANTIDEPRESSANTS: A CLINICAL PHARMACOTHERAPEUTIC RESEARCH STRATEGY.
003632 03-17

PHARMACOLOGICAL-PROPERTIES OF SOME SECOND-GENERATION ANTIDEPRESSANT-DRUGS.
004726 04-17

SECOND-ORDER
SECOND-ORDER SCHEDULES OF INTRAMUSCULAR COCAINE INJECTION IN THE SQUIRREL-MONKEY: COMPARISONS WITH FOOD PRESENTATION AND EFFECTS OF D-AMPHETAMINE AND PROMAZINE.
004152 04-04

SECRET
ADRENALINE: A SECRET AGENT IN MEMORY.
002345 02-14

SECRETION
ADMINISTRATION OF ANTISOMATOSTATIN SERUM TO RATS REVERSES THE INHIBITION OF PULSATILE GROWTH-HORMONE SECRETION PRODUCED BY INJECTION OF METERGOLINE BUT NOT YOHIMBINE. (UNPUBLISHED PAPER).
000019 01-03

L TRYPTOPHAN INJECTION ENHANCES PULSATILE GROWTH-HORMONE SECRETION IN THE RAT. (UNPUBLISHED PAPER).
000020 01-03

ALPHA FLUPENTHIXOL: AN ANTAGONIST OF DOPAMINE-EVOKED FLUID SECRETION BY AN INSECT SALIVARY-GLAND PREPARATION.
000031 01-03

MORPHINE ACTS THROUGH ALPHA-ADRENERGIC AND SEROTONINERGIC NEURONS TO STIMULATE GROWTH-HORMONE SECRETION IN THE DOG.
000088 01-03

EVIDENCE FOR A DIRECT INHIBITORY-EFFECT OF MORPHINE ON THE SECRETION OF POSTERIOR PITUITARY-HORMONES.
000193 01-03

EFFECTS OF NORADRENERGIC AGONISTS AND ANTAGONISTS ON GROWTH-HORMONE SECRETION UNDER GAMMA HYDROXYBUTYRATE NARCOANALGESIA IN THE RAT.
000262 01-03

EFFECT OF SEROTONIN ON PROLACTIN SECRETION IN VIVO.
001016 02-01

RELEASE OF ARACHIDONIC-ACID FROM ADRENAL CHROMAFFIN CELL-CULTURES DURING SECRETION OF EPINEPHRINE. (UNPUBLISHED PAPER).
001027 02-01

ALTERATION OF PROLACTIN SECRETION BY CENTRALLY-ACTING DRUGS.
001127 02-03

TOLERANCE TO BARBITURATE-INDUCED CENTRAL-NERVOUS-SYSTEM DEPRESSION: INVOLVEMENT OF STIMULUS SECRETION COUPLING IN DISCRETE BRAIN AREAS. (PH.D. DISSERTATION).
001213 02-03

OPIATE-RECEPTOR MEDIATED INHIBITION OF RAT JEJUNAL-FLUID SECRETION.
001334 02-03

MODIFICATION OF GABAERGIC ACTIVITY AND THYROTROPIN SECRETION IN MALE RATS.
001362 02-03

EFFECTS OF NEUROLEPTICS ON NEUROENDOCRINE MECHANISMS FOR GONADOTROPIN SECRETION.
001391 02-03

A PHARMACOLOGICAL ANALYSIS OF THE ROLE OF THE AMYGDALA IN THE CONTROL OF GONADOTROPIN AND PROLACTIN SECRETION.
001418 02-03

CENTRAL PHARMACOLOGICAL CONTROL OF CORTICOSTERONE SECRETION IN THE INTACT RAT. DEMONSTRATION OF CHOLINERGIC AND SEROTONINERGIC FACILITATORY AND ALPHA-ADRENERGIC INHIBITORY MECHANISMS.
001487 02-03

EFFECT OF L TRYPTOPHAN ON APOMORPHINE-INDUCED GROWTH-HORMONE SECRETION IN NORMAL SUBJECTS.
002253 02-13

INHIBITION OF SULPIRIDE-INDUCED PROLACTIN SECRETION BY DIHYDROERGOCRISTINE IN MAN.
002277 02-13

THE CLOCK AND THE BLUE GUITAR: STUDIES OF HUMAN GROWTH-HORMONE SECRETION IN SLEEP AND WAKING. (UNPUBLISHED PAPER).
002346 02-14

THE INFLUENCE OF NEUROLEPTIC-DRUGS ON PROLACTIN SECRETION IN CHILDREN.
002409 02-15

HALOPERIDOL STIMULATION OF PROLACTIN SECRETION: HOW MANY BLOOD SAMPLES ARE NEEDED TO DEFINE THE HORMONE RESPONSE?
002505 02-16

INAPPROPRIATE ADH SECRETION: THE ROLE OF DRUG RECHALLENGE.
002629 02-17

EFFECTS OF ELECTROCONVULSIVE-TREATMENT ON GROWTH-HORMONE SECRETION INDUCED BY MONOAMINE-RECEPTOR AGONISTS IN RESERPINE PRETREATED RATS.
002664 03-03

EFFECTS OF AN EPINEPHRINE SYNTHESIS INHIBITOR, SKF-64139, ON THE SECRETION OF LUTEINIZING-HORMONE IN OVARIECTOMIZED FEMALE RATS.
002693 03-03

ANTERIOR PITUITARY GABA-RECEPTORS AND THEIR REGULATION OF PROLACTIN SECRETION.
002738 03-03

STUDIES ON THE MECHANISMS OF L-DOPA-INDUCED SALIVARY SECRETION.
003130 03-05

EFFECT OF A PSYCHOACTIVE-DRUG, TRAZODONE, ON PROLACTIN SECRETION IN MAN.
003425 03-13

EFFECT OF NICOTINE ON IN VIVO SECRETION OF MELANOCORTICOTROPIC-HORMONES IN THE RAT.
003759 04-03

INHIBITION OF PENTAGASTRIN-STIMULATED AND OVERNIGHT GASTRIC SECRETION BY LM24056, A NEW PHENOTHIAZINE DERIVED ANTISECRETORY DRUG.
004306 04-07

SECRETIONS
RENIN AND ALDOSTERONE SECRETIONS DURING HYPOVOLEMIA IN RATS: RELATION TO NACL INTAKE.
000484 01-04

EFFECTS OF ANTIDEPRESSANTS ON PITUITARY HORMONAL SECRETIONS IN HEALTHY TEST SUBJECTS, NEUROTIC-PATIENTS, AND ENDOGENOUS DEPRESSIVE-PATIENTS.
002009 02-09

SEDATION
ANXIETY AND SEDATION DURING A STRESSFUL-SITUATION AFTER SINGLE-DOSE OF DIAZEPAM VERSUS N DESMETHYLDIAZEPAM -- A CONTROLLED-TRIAL.
002329 02-14

ETHYL-BETA-CARBOLINE-CARBOXYLATE LOWERS SEIZURE THRESHOLD AND ANTAGONIZES FLURAZEPAM-INDUCED SEDATION IN RATS.
002971 03-04

ENHANCEMENT OF ETHANOL-INDUCED SEDATION AND HYPOTHERMIA BY CENTRALLY ADMINISTERED NEUROTENSIN, BETA ENDORPHIN AND BOMBESIN.
003037 03-04

SEDATIVE
IN VIVO OCCUPATION OF CEREBRAL HISTAMINE H1-RECEPTORS EVALUATED WITH 3H MEPYRAMINE MAY PREDICT SEDATIVE PROPERTIES OF PSYCHOTROPIC-DRUGS.
000241 01-03

PHARMACOLOGICAL-PROPERTIES OF TAGLUTIMIDE, A NEW SEDATIVE HYPNOTIC-DRUG.
001087 02-02

THE QUANTITATIVE MEASUREMENT OF CHANGES IN EEG FREQUENCY SPECTRA PRODUCED IN THE CAT BY SEDATIVE HYPNOTICS AND NEUROLEPTICS.
001220 02-03

THE EFFECTS OF COMBINED SEDATIVE AND ANXIOLYTIC-PREPARATIONS ON SUBJECTIVE ASPECTS OF SLEEP AND OBJECTIVE MEASURE OF AROUSAL AND PERFORMANCE THE MORNING FOLLOWING NOCTURNAL MEDICATION: II. REPEATED DOSES.
002331 02-14

EVIDENCE FOR SEDATIVE EFFECTS OF LOW-DOSES OF MORPHINE IN MICE INVOLVING RECEPTORS INSENSITIVE TO NALOXONE.
004173 04-04

ETHANOL SEDATIVE HYPNOTIC-INTERACTIONS: IN VITRO STUDIES ON NA-K-ACTIVATED ADENOSINE-TRIPHOSPHATASE.
004269 04-05

AGE-SPECIFIC DOSES OF LORMETAZEPAM AS A NIGHT SEDATIVE IN CASES OF CHRONIC SLEEP-DISTURBANCE.
004309 04-07

SEIZURE
RELATIONSHIPS BETWEEN SEIZURE ACTIVITY AND CYCLIC-NUCLEOTIDE LEVELS IN BRAIN.
000089 01-03

EFFECTS OF RESERPINE, PROPRANOLOL, AND AMINOPHYLLINE ON SEIZURE ACTIVITY AND CNS CYCLIC-NUCLEOTIDES.
000115 01-03

FLASH-EVOKED AFTERDISCHARGE IN RAT AS A MODEL OF THE ABSENCE SEIZURE: DOSE-RESPONSE STUDIES WITH THERAPEUTIC DRUGS.
000160 01-03

RELATION OF MONOMETHYLHYDRAZINE (MMH) SEIZURE THRESHOLDS TO AFTERDISCHARGE THRESHOLDS WITH AMYGDALOID STIMULATION IN CATS.
000474 01-04

BEHAVIORAL-ANALYSIS OF AMYGDALOID KINDLING IN BEAGLE-DOGS AND THE EFFECTS OF CLONAZEPAM, DIAZEPAM, PHENOBARBITAL, DIPHENYLHYDANTOIN, AND FLUNARIZINE ON SEIZURE MANIFESTATION.
000496 01-04

DRUG AND SEIZURE IDENTIFICATION BY AUDIO-SPECTROMETRY. (PH.D. DISSERTATION).
000532 01-06

FACTORS INFLUENCING SEIZURE DURATION AND NUMBER OF SEIZURES APPLIED IN UNILATERAL ELECTROCONVULSIVE-THERAPY: ANESTHETICS AND BENZODIAZEPINES.
000792 01-13

PROLONGED CONFUSIONAL-STATE AND EEG SEIZURE ACTIVITY FOLLOWING CONCURRENT ECT AND LITHIUM USE.
000895 01-15

PENTYLENETETRAZOL SEIZURE THRESHOLD: A QUANTITATIVE MEASURE OF ETHANOL DEPENDENCE IN RATS.
001750 02-04

A PHARMACOLOGICAL INVESTIGATION OF AN ANIMAL-MODEL OF THE PETIT-MAL SEIZURE. (PH.D. DISSERTATION).
001870 02-06

BEHAVIORAL-INTERVENTION FOR SELF-STIMULATORY, ATTENDING AND SEIZURE BEHAVIOR IN A CEREBRAL-PALSIED-CHILD.
002104 02-11

ETHYL-BETA-CARBOLINE-CARBOXYLATE LOWERS SEIZURE THRESHOLD AND ANTAGONIZES FLURAZEPAM-INDUCED SEDATION IN RATS.
002971 03-04

EFFECT OF MEDIAN RAPHE STIMULATION ON HIPPOCAMPAL SEIZURE DISCHARGE INDUCED BY CARBACHOL IN THE RABBIT.
003951 04-03

COCAINE AND SEIZURE PROTECTION IN MICE OF VARYING BRAIN WEIGHTS.
004103 04-04

NEW ANTIDEPRESSANT-DRUGS AND THE SEIZURE THRESHOLD.
004662 04-15

SEIZURES
SEIZURES AND RELATED EPILEPTIFORM ACTIVITY IN HIPPOCAMPUS TRANSPLANTED TO THE ANTERIOR-CHAMBER OF THE EYE: MODULATION BY CHOLINERGIC AND ADRENERGIC INPUT.
000095 01-03

THE EFFECTS OF RESERPINE, IPRONIAZID AND L-DOPA ON ELECTRICALLY-INDUCED SPINAL-CORD SEIZURES.
000146 01-03

DISSIMILAR EFFECTS OF NICOTINAMIDE AND INOSINE, PUTATIVE ENDOGENOUS LIGANDS OF THE BENZODIAZEPINE-RECEPTORS, ON PENTYLENETETRAZOL SEIZURES IN FOUR STRAINS OF MICE.
000173 01-03

FACTORS INFLUENCING SEIZURE DURATION AND NUMBER OF SEIZURES APPLIED IN UNILATERAL ELECTROCONVULSIVE-THERAPY: ANESTHETICS AND BENZODIAZEPINES.
000792 01-13
NEUROLOGICAL SIDE-EFFECTS OF LITHIUM: ORGANIC-BRAIN-SYNDROME, SEIZURES, EXTRAPYRAMIDAL SIDE-EFFECTS, AND EEG CHANGES.
000847 01-15
SEIZURES DURING TRICYCLIC THERAPY.
000868 01-15
EFFECTS OF BICUCULLINE-INDUCED SEIZURES ON CEREBRAL METABOLISM AND CIRCULATION OF RATS RENDERED HYPOGLYCEMIC BY STARVATION.
001134 02-03
ENERGY RESERVES AND SOUND-INDUCED SEIZURES. (UNPUBLISHED PAPER).
001467 02-03
BARBITURATE SERUM LEVELS AND PROTECTION AGAINST KINDLED AMYGDALOID SEIZURES IN THE RAT.
001559 02-04
PHARMACOLOGICAL MODIFICATION OF AMYGDALOID KINDLED SEIZURES.
001588 02-04
NEUROPHARMACOLOGICAL ANALYSIS OF HANDLING-INDUCED SEIZURES IN GERBILS.
001876 02-06
EFFECTS OF ORAL CHOLINE ON HUMAN COMPLEX PARTIAL SEIZURES.
002149 02-11
THE ANTICONVULSANT PROPERTIES OF MELATONIN ON KINDLED SEIZURES IN RATS.
002653 03-03
CAFFEINE-INDUCED AND AMINOPHYLLINE-INDUCED SEIZURES.
002689 03-03
CUMULATIVE AFTERDISCHARGE AS THE PRINCIPAL FACTOR IN THE ACQUISITION OF KINDLED SEIZURES.
002862 03-03
VOLTAGE CLAMP STUDY OF CAT SPINAL MOTONEURONS DURING STRYCHNINE-INDUCED SEIZURES.
002886 03-03
KAINIC-ACID NEUROTOXICITY AND SEIZURES.
002939 03-03
VALPROIC-ACID SERUM LEVELS AND PROTECTION AGAINST KINDLED AMYGDALOID SEIZURES IN THE RAT.
002946 03-04
THE EFFECTS OF VARIOUS ANESTHETICS ON AMYGDALOID KINDLED SEIZURES.
002959 03-04
SEIZURES ELICITED BY SUBCUTANEOUS INJECTION OF METRAZOL DURING ONTOGENESIS IN RATS.
003039 03-04
THE EFFECT OF AMYGDALA KINDLING ON SPONTANEOUS AND COCAINE-INDUCED MOTOR-ACTIVITY AND LIDOCAINE SEIZURES.
003067 03-04
BRAIN BENZODIAZEPINE-RECEPTORS AND THEIR RAPID CHANGES AFTER SEIZURES IN THE MONGOLIAN-GERBIL.
003717 04-03
SPECIFIC AND NONSPECIFIC MULTIPLE UNIT ACTIVITIES DURING PENTYLENETETRAZOL SEIZURES. I. ANIMALS WITH ENCEPHALE ISOLE.
004046 04-03
RELATIONSHIP BETWEEN PENTYLENETETRAZOL-INDUCED SEIZURES AND BRAIN PENTYLENETETRAZOL LEVELS IN MICE.
004061 04-03
EFFECTS OF WITHDRAWAL FROM LONG-TERM DIPHENYLHYDANTOIN TREATMENT ON AUDIOGENIC-SEIZURES AND MAXIMAL ELECTROSHOCK-INDUCED SEIZURES IN RATS.
004101 04-04
NORADRENERGIC INFLUENCES ON SOUND-INDUCED SEIZURES.
004137 04-04
EFFECTS OF NOREPINEPHRINE AND 5 HYDROXYTRYPTAMINE REUPTAKE INHIBITORS ON ELECTRICALLY-INDUCED SPINAL-CORD SEIZURES IN RATS.
004144 04-04
EFFECTS OF FLUOXETINE ON ELECTRICALLY-INDUCED SPINAL-CORD SEIZURES IN RATS.
004145 04-04
EFFECTS OF 3 SULFAMOYLMETHYL-BENZISOXAZOLE (AD-810) AND SOME ANTIEPILEPTICS ON THE KINDLED SEIZURES IN THE NEOCORTEX, HIPPOCAMPUS AND AMYGDALA IN RATS.
004149 04-04
EFFECT OF GAMMA VINYL-GABA ON BICUCULLINE-INDUCED SEIZURES.
004157 04-04
THE BENZODIAZEPINES AND INOSINE ANTAGONIZE CAFFEINE-INDUCED SEIZURES.
004172 04-04
HANDLING-INDUCED SEIZURES AND ROTATIONAL-BEHAVIOR IN THE MONGOLIAN-GERBIL.
004216 04-04
SEROTONERGIC MECHANISM IN SEIZURES KINDLED FROM THE RABBIT AMYGDALA.
004227 04-04

EFFECT OF COCAINE AND LIDOCAINE ON THE EXPRESSION OF KINDLED SEIZURES IN THE RAT.
004233 04-04

SELECTING
ROLE OF THE NEOSTRIATAL DOPAMINERGIC-ACTIVITY IN SEQUENCING AND SELECTING BEHAVIOURAL-STRATEGIES: FACILITATION OF PROCESSES INVOLVED IN SELECTING THE BEST STRATEGY IN A STRESSFUL-SITUATION.
000366 01-04

SELECTION
LSD-25 AS A DISCRIMINATIVE-STIMULUS FOR RESPONSE SELECTION BY PIGEONS.
000412 01-04
THE SELECTION OF LITHIUM RESPONDERS.
000997 01-17

SELECTIVE
ARYLDIALKENYLPIPERAZINES AS SELECTIVE AND VERY POTENT INHIBITORS OF DOPAMINE UPTAKE.
000005 01-01
SELECTIVE STORAGE IN VIVO OF 5,6 ADTN IN DOPAMINE RICH AREAS OF THE RAT-BRAIN.
000324 01-03
DISRUPTION OF SELECTIVE ATTENTION BY APOMORPHINE, BUT NOT AMPHETAMINE, IN THE MONGOLIAN-GERBIL.
000358 01-04
RELATIONSHIPS BETWEEN SELECTIVE DENERVATION OF DOPAMINE TERMINAL-FIELDS IN THE ANTERIOR-FOREBRAIN AND BEHAVIORAL-RESPONSES TO AMPHETAMINE AND APOMORPHINE.
000384 01-04
EFFECTS OF L-DOPA AND L 5 HYDROXYTRYPTOPHAN ON LOCOMOTOR-ACTIVITY OF THE RAT AFTER SELECTIVE OR COMBINED DESTRUCTION OF CENTRAL CATECHOLAMINE AND SEROTONIN NEURONS.
000466 01-04
SELECTIVE INHIBITION OF MESOLIMBIC BEHAVIORAL-SUPERSENSITIVITY BY NALOXONE.
000467 01-04
METOCLOPRAMIDE AND SULPIRIDE AS SELECTIVE BLOCKING-AGENTS PRESYNAPTIC AND POSTSYNAPTIC DOPAMINE-RECEPTORS.
001102 02-03
ISOLATION OF SELECTIVE 3H CHLORNALTREXAMINE BOUND COMPLEXES, POSSIBLE OPIOID-RECEPTOR COMPONENTS IN BRAINS OF MICE.
001162 02-03
SELECTIVE INFLUENCE OF ERGOT ALKALOIDS ON CORTICAL AND STRIATAL DOPAMINERGIC-RECEPTORS AND SEROTONERGIC-RECEPTORS.
001447 02-03
PHARMACOLOGICAL EVIDENCE OF A POSSIBLE TRYPTAMINERGIC REGULATION OF OPIATE-RECEPTORS BY USING INDALPINE, A SELECTIVE 5 HT UPTAKE INHIBITOR.
001517 02-03
MODULATION OF OPIATE-RECEPTOR BINDING IN STRIATUM AND AMYGDALA BY SELECTIVE MESENCEPHALIC LESIONS.
001629 02-04
SELECTIVE REDUCTION BY DEXAMETHASONE OF STRESS RELATED HYPERPHAGIAS.
001703 02-04
EFFECT OF SELECTIVE DESTRUCTION OF SEROTONERGIC NEURONS IN NUCLEUS-RAPHE-MAGNUS ON MORPHINE-INDUCED ANTINOCICEPTION.
001724 02-04
EFFECTS OF METHYLPHENIDATE ON SELECTIVE AND SUSTAINED ATTENTION IN HYPERACTIVE, READING-DISABLED, AND PRESUMABLY ATTENTION-DISORDERED BOYS.
002118 02-11
NEUROCHEMICAL EVIDENCE AND BEHAVIORAL-EVIDENCE FOR A SELECTIVE PRESYNAPTIC DOPAMINE-RECEPTOR AGONIST.
002236 02-13
THE EFFECT OF DEPRENYL, A SELECTIVE MONOAMINE-OXIDASE-B-INHIBITOR, ON SLEEP AND MOOD IN MAN.
002365 02-14
APOMORPHINE: SELECTIVE INHIBITION OF THE AVERSIVE COMPONENT OF LATERAL HYPOTHALAMIC SELF-STIMULATION.
002476 02-16
SELECTIVE ANTAGONISTS OF BENZODIAZEPINES.
002646 03-02
DU-24565, A QUIPAZINE DERIVATIVE, A POTENT SELECTIVE SEROTONIN UPTAKE INHIBITOR.
002651 03-02
DIFFERENTIATION OF KAINATE AND QUISQUALATE-RECEPTORS IN THE CAT SPINAL-CORD BY SELECTIVE ANTAGONISMS WITH GAMMA D(AND L) GLUTAMYLGLYCINE.
002696 03-03
SELECTIVE EFFECTS OF LSD AND HYPERTHERMIA ON THE SYNTHESIS OF SYNAPTIC PROTEINS AND GLYCOPROTEINS.
002721 03-03
SELECTIVE SYNAPTIC ANTAGONISM BY ATROPINE AND ALPHA AMINOADIPATE OF PULVINAR AND CORTICAL AFFERENTS TO THE SUPRASYLVIAN VISUAL AREA (CLARE-BISHOP AREA).
002752 03-03

SELECTIVE INHIBITION BY NICOTINE OF SHOCK-INDUCED FIGHTING IN THE RAT.
002984 03-04

SELECTIVE SENSITIZATION INDUCED BY LITHIUM MALAISE AND FOOTSHOCK IN RATS.
003055 03-04

DIFFERENTIATION OF OPIATE-RECEPTORS IN THE BRAIN BY THE SELECTIVE DEVELOPMENT OF TOLERANCE.
003088 03-04

SELECTIVE NEUROTOXIC-ACTION OF CAPSAICIN ON GLOMERULAR C-TYPE TERMINALS IN RAT SUBSTANTIA-GELATINOSA.
003143 03-06

SELECTIVE MODIFICATION BY OPIATES OF NEURONAL ACTIVITY OF THE MEDIAL BASAL HYPOTHALAMUS.
003773 04-03

ANESTHETICS AND THE HABENULO-INTERPEDUNCULAR SYSTEM: SELECTIVE SPARING OF METABOLIC ACTIVITY.
003833 04-03

SENSORY NEUROTOXINS: CHEMICALLY-INDUCED SELECTIVE DESTRUCTION OF PRIMARY SENSORY NEURONS.
003859 04-03

MULTIPLE ALPHA2-NORADRENERGIC-RECEPTOR SITES IN RAT-BRAIN: SELECTIVE REGULATION OF HIGH-AFFINITY (3H)CLONIDINE BINDING BY GUANINE-NUCLEOTIDES AND DIVALENT-CATIONS.
003992 04-03

PHYSIOLOGICAL SIGNIFICANCE OF DOPAMINE-AUTORECEPTORS AS STUDIED FOLLOWING THEIR SELECTIVE BLOCKADE BY MOLINDONE.
004065 04-04

SELECTIVE EFFECT OF ETHANOL ON THE VESTIBULAR NUCLEUS NEURONS IN THE CAT.
004139 04-04

SELECTIVE INHIBITORY-EFFECTS OF CHLORPROMAZINE AND IMIPRAMINE ON PLATELET AGGREGATION.
004518 04-13

SELECTIVE EFFECTS OF BARBITURATE AND AMPHETAMINE ON INFORMATION-PROCESSING AND RESPONSE EXECUTION.
004563 04-14

IS THE FAILURE OF (-)DEPRENYL, A SELECTIVE MONOAMINE-OXIDASE-B-INHIBITOR, TO ALLEVIATE DEPRESSION RELATED TO FREEDOM FROM THE CHEESE EFFECT?
004640 04-15

HUMAN PLATELET ALPHA2-ADRENERGIC-RECEPTORS: LABELING WITH 3H YOHIMBINE, A SELECTIVE ANTAGONIST LIGAND.
004676 04-16

SELECTIVITY
A REEVALUATION OF THE MECHANISMS UNDERLYING SIMPLE CELL ORIENTATION SELECTIVITY.
002894 03-03

AMINE UPTAKE INHIBITORS: CRITERIA OF SELECTIVITY.
003921 04-03

SELF-ADMINISTERED
INFLUENCE OF INTRAVENOUS SELF-ADMINISTERED PSYCHOMOTOR STIMULANTS ON PERFORMANCE OF RHESUS-MONKEYS IN A MULTIPLE-SCHEDULE PARADIGM.
001655 02-04

THE RELATIONSHIP BETWEEN POSITIVE REINFORCEMENT AND CONDITIONED TASTE-AVERSION PRODUCED BY SELF-ADMINISTERED DRUGS.*(PH.D. DISSERTATION).
001798 02-04

BEHAVIORAL-EFFECTS OF SELF-ADMINISTERED COCAINE: RESPONDING MAINTAINED ALTERNATELY BY COCAINE AND ELECTRIC-SHOCK IN SQUIRREL-MONKEYS.
004225 04-04

SELF-ADMINISTRATION
CONTINUOUS-ACCESS PHENCYCLIDINE SELF-ADMINISTRATION BY RHESUS-MONKEYS LEADING TO PHYSICAL-DEPENDENCE.
000341 01-04

LETHAL SELF-ADMINISTRATION OF MORPHINE BY RATS.
000343 01-04

DOSE AND PHYSICAL-DEPENDENCE AS FACTORS IN THE SELF-ADMINISTRATION OF MORPHINE BY RATS.
000497 01-04

PHARMACODYNAMIC PROFILES OF L ALPHA ACETYLMETHADOL (LAAM) AND ITS N DEMETHYLATED METABOLITES, NORLAAM AND DINORLAAM, DURING SELF-ADMINISTRATION IN THE DEPENDENT RAT.
000505 01-04

SELF-ADMINISTRATION OF D-AMPHETAMINE AND AMINERGIC SYSTEMS IN THE RAT.
001696 02-04

SELF-ADMINISTRATION OF D ALA2-MET-ENKEPHALINAMIDE AT HYPOTHALAMIC SELF-STIMULATION SITES.
001738 02-04

INTRAVENOUS SELF-ADMINISTRATION OF COCAINE AND NORCOCAINE BY DOGS.
001760 02-04

INTRACRANIAL SELF-ADMINISTRATION OF MORPHINE INTO THE VENTRAL TEGMENTAL AREA IN RATS.
002960 03-04

RELAPSE TO NARCOTIC SELF-ADMINISTRATION IN MORPHINE POSTADDICT RATS: A POSSIBLE MODEL FOR PREDICTING ABUSE LIABILITY OF NARCOTIC-DRUGS. (PH.D. DISSERTATION).
003097 03-04

OPERANT ANALYSIS OF HUMAN HEROIN SELF-ADMINISTRATION AND THE EFFECTS OF NALTREXONE.
003449 03-14

EFFECTS OF LEVO ALPHA ACETYLMETHADOL (LAAM) ON MORPHINE SELF-ADMINISTRATION IN THE RAT.
004170 04-04

ORAL SELF-ADMINISTRATION OF MORPHINE IN RATS.
004258 04-04

AN IMPROVED PNEUMATIC SYRINGE FOR SELF-ADMINISTRATION OF DRUGS BY RATS.
004304 04-06

SELF-BITING
PEMOLINE-INDUCED SELF-BITING IN RATS AND SELF-MUTILATION IN THE DELANGE-SYNDROME.
001727 02-04

SELF-EVALUATION
STUDY OF VIGILANCE AFTER INGESTION OF ZOPICLONE IN COMPARISON WITH NITRAZEPAM AND PLACEBO. METHODOLOGY OF THE STUDY: SELF-EVALUATION QUESTIONNAIRE AND PSYCHOMETRIC-TESTS.
000543 01-07

SELF-INDUCED
ANTECEDENTS OF SELF-INDUCED WATER INTOXICATION: A PRELIMINARY-REPORT.
002414 02-15

SELF-INJECTION
REVERSAL OF SCHEDULE-INDUCED SELF-INJECTION OF HEROIN BY NALOXONE.
000446 01-04

EFFECTS OF BODY-WEIGHT LEVELS ON CANNABIS SELF-INJECTION.
001801 02-04

SELF-INJURY
SELF-INJURY IN SUBNORMAL-PATIENTS.
003452 03-14

SELF-MEDICATION
SELF-MEDICATION, ABANDONMENT, MANIPULATION, AND DEPENDENCE IN DRUG-THERAPY IN PSYCHOSOMATIC-ILLNESS. COMPARATIVE POLYCENTRIC RESEARCH ON VARIOUS PSYCHOTROPIC-DRUGS.
002189 02-11

SOME ODD PATTERNS OF PSYCHOTROPIC SELF-MEDICATION.
002565 02-17

SELF-MEDICATION.
003574 03-17

SELF-MUTILATION
PEMOLINE-INDUCED SELF-BITING IN RATS AND SELF-MUTILATION IN THE DELANGE-SYNDROME.
001727 02-04

SELF-RATING
ON THE RELATIONSHIP BETWEEN MEASURES OBTAINED BY VIDEO-ANALYSIS OF NONVERBAL-BEHAVIOR AND SELF-RATING OF MOOD.
004410 04-09

SELF-SELECTION
SUSTAINED DECREASE IN FAT CONSUMPTION PRODUCED BY AMPHETAMINE IN RATS MAINTAINED ON A DIETARY SELF-SELECTION REGIME.
004150 04-04

SELF-STIMULATION
ON THE NEUROCHEMICAL BASIS OF SELF-STIMULATION WITH MIDBRAIN RAPHE ELECTRODE PLACEMENTS.
000373 01-04

5 HT BLOCKADE AND THE STIMULANT-EFFECTS OF D-AMPHETAMINE AND L-AMPHETAMINE: NO INTERACTION IN SELF-STIMULATION OF PREFRONTAL-CORTEX, HYPOTHALAMUS, OR DORSAL TEGMENTUM. UNEXPECTED LETHALITY IN HIPPOCAMPAL SITES.
000387 01-04

POSTAMPHETAMINE DEPRESSION OF SELF-STIMULATION RESPONDING FROM THE SUBSTANTIA-NIGRA: REVERSAL BY TRICYCLIC-ANTIDEPRESSANTS.
000419 01-04

FACILITATION OF SELF-STIMULATION OF THE PREFRONTAL-CORTEX IN RATS FOLLOWING CHRONIC ADMINISTRATION OF SPIROPERIDOL OR AMPHETAMINE.
000457 01-04

EFFECTS OF LILLY-110140 (FLUOXETINE) ON SELF-STIMULATION BEHAVIOR IN THE DORSAL AND VENTRAL REGIONS OF THE LATERAL HYPOTHALAMUS IN THE MOUSE.
001590 02-04

EFFECTS OF AN ACTH4-9 RELATED PEPTIDE UPON INTRACRANIAL SELF-STIMULATION AND GENERAL-ACTIVITY IN THE RAT.
001679 02-04

ENHANCED LATERAL HYPOTHALAMIC SELF-STIMULATION RESPONDING AFTER CHRONIC EXPOSURE TO AMPHETAMINE.
001688 02-04

EFFECTS OF CHRONIC AMPHETAMINE OR RESERPINE ON SELF-STIMULATION RESPONDING: ANIMAL-MODEL OF DEPRESSION?
001699 02-04

SELF-ADMINISTRATION OF D ALA2-MET-ENKEPHALINAMIDE AT
HYPOTHALAMIC SELF-STIMULATION SITES.
001738 02-04
NALOXONE AND SHUTTLEBOX SELF-STIMULATION IN THE RAT.
001793 02-04
FACILITATION OF SELF-STIMULATION IN RATS BY METHADONE.
001795 02-04
APOMORPHINE: SELECTIVE INHIBITION OF THE AVERSIVE COMPONENT OF
LATERAL HYPOTHALAMIC SELF-STIMULATION.
002476 02-16
SELF-STIMULATION REACTION IN NORMOTENSIVE-RATS AND
HYPERTENSIVE-RATS.
002663 03-03
SMALL-DOSE INTRAVENOUS HEROIN FACILITATES HYPOTHALAMIC SELF-
STIMULATION WITHOUT RESPONSE SUPPRESSION IN RATS.
002999 03-04
CONFLICT-SITUATION BASED ON INTRACRANIAL SELF-STIMULATION
BEHAVIOR AND THE EFFECT OF BENZODIAZEPINES.
003004 03-04
THE TETRACYCLIC-ANTIDEPRESSANT MIANSERIN: EVALUATION OF ITS
BLOCKADE OF PRESYNAPTIC ALPHA-ADRENOCEPTORS IN A SELF-
STIMULATION MODEL USING CLONIDINE.
003016 03-04
SELF-STIMULATION AND LOCOMOTOR CHANGES INDICATING LATENT
ANTICHOLINERGIC-ACTIVITY BY AN ATYPICAL NEUROLEPTIC
(THIORIDAZINE).
003560 03-16

SELF-STIMULATORY
BEHAVIORAL-INTERVENTION FOR SELF-STIMULATORY, ATTENDING AND
SEIZURE BEHAVIOR IN A CEREBRAL-PALSIED-CHILD.
002104 02-11

SELF-SUSTAINED
INFLUENCE OF CARBAMAZEPINE ON THALAMOCORTICAL AND
HIPPOCAMPOCORTICAL SELF-SUSTAINED AFTERDISCHARGES IN RATS.
001356 02-03

SEMIDEPOTE
MAINTENANCE-TREATMENT WITH SEMIDEPOTE NEUROLEPTIC
FLUSPIRILENE.
002151 02-11

SEMINAR
THE MEDICATION SEMINAR AND PRIMARY CARE EDUCATION.
003592 03-17

SENESCENCE
CEREBRAL SENESCENCE AND ITS PSYCHIC-MANIFESTATIONS. THE
EFFECTIVENESS OF DEBRUMYL.
002105 02-11

SENESCENT
REDUCED TOLERANCE TO MORPHINE THERMOREGULATORY-EFFECTS IN
SENESCENT RATS.
002822 03-03
APOMORPHINE-INDUCED STEREOTYPY IN MATURE AND SENESCENT RATS
FOLLOWING CESSATION OF CHRONIC HALOPERIDOL TREATMENT.
004651 04-15

SENILE-DEMENTIA
DRUGS FOR SENILE-DEMENTIA.
000947 01-17
BRAIN CATECHOLAMINES, MENTAL-ILLNESSES, AGING AND SENILE-
DEMENTIA: BIOCHEMICAL-CONSIDERATIONS AND PHARMACOLOGICAL-
CONSIDERATIONS.
001550 02-03
PHARMACOLOGIC APPROACHES TO THE TREATMENT OF SENILE-
DEMENTIA.
002809 03-03
THE EFFECTS OF LECITHIN ON MEMORY IN PATIENTS WITH SENILE-
DEMENTIA OF THE ALZHEIMERS-TYPE.
003385 03-11
SENILE-DEMENTIA: COMBINED PHARMACOLOGIC-TREATMENT AND
PSYCHOLOGIC-TREATMENT.
003393 03-11
ACUTE EFFECT OF DRUGS UPON MEMORY OF PATIENTS WITH SENILE-
DEMENTIA.
004561 04-14
SENILE-DEMENTIA IN ITS STILL GUIDABLE INITIAL PHASE.
004698 04-17

SENSITIVE
DRUG SENSITIVE ECTO-ATPASE IN HUMAN LEUKOCYTES.
000779 01-13
LOCALIZATION OF NALOXONE SENSITIVE (3H)DIHYDROMORPHINE
BINDING-SITES WITHIN THE HIPPOCAMPUS OF THE RAT.
001368 02-03
LOCALIZATION OF SENSITIVE SITES TO TAURINE, GAMMA
AMINOBUTYRIC-ACID, GLYCINE AND BETA ALANINE IN THE
MOLECULAR LAYER OF GUINEA-PIG CEREBELLAR SLICES.
001402 02-03
SPONTANEOUSLY (GENETIC) HYPERTENSIVE-RATS PRESENT A NALOXONE
SENSITIVE DECREASE IN PAIN SENSITIVITY. (UNPUBLISHED PAPER).
001457 02-03
A SPECIFIC AND SENSITIVE MICROASSAY FOR HYDROXYINDOLES IN
BIOLOGICAL-MATERIAL -- APPLICATION FOR CEREBRAL MICROVESSELS,
BRAIN, AND PINEAL-ORGAN OF THE RAT.
002503 02-16

SPECIFIC AND SENSITIVE RADIOIMMUNOASSAY FOR 3 METHOXY-4-
HYDROXYPHENYLETHYLENEGLYCOL (MOPEG).
002776 03-03
INHIBITORY ACTIONS OF TAUROCYAMINE, HYPOTAURINE,
HOMOTAURINE, TAURINE AND GABA ON SPIKE DISCHARGES OF
PURKINJE-CELLS, AND LOCALIZATION OF SENSITIVE SITES, IN GUINEA-
PIG CEREBELLAR SLICES.
002846 03-03
SENSITIVE DEPRESSANT EFFECT OF BENZODIAZEPINES ON THE CROSSED
EXTENSOR REFLEX IN CHLORALOSE ANESTHETIZED RATS.
003027 03-04
CHANGE IN CATECHOLAMINE SENSITIVE NA-K-ATPASE ACTIVITY IN THE
RAT STRIATUM MICROSOMES FOLLOWING ELECTROLYTIC OR 6
HYDROXYDOPAMINE-INDUCED LESIONS OF DOPAMINERGIC NEURONS.
003871 04-03
A RAPID AND SENSITIVE RADIORECEPTOR ASSAY FOR TERTIARY AMINE
TRICYCLIC-ANTIDEPRESSANTS.
004689 04-16
A SENSITIVE BENZODIAZEPINE RADIOIMMUNOASSAY OF BROAD
SPECIFICITY.
004693 04-16

SENSITIVITY
THE SENSITIVITY OF THE RAT CORTICOSTERONE RESPONSE TO
ENVIRONMENTAL MANIPULATIONS AND TO CHRONIC
CHLORDIAZEPOXIDE TREATMENT.
000092 01-03
MODIFICATION OF DOPAMINERGIC-RECEPTOR SENSITIVITY IN RAT-BRAIN
AFTER AMYGDALOID KINDLING.
000106 01-03
DIFFERENCES IN GAMMA AMINOBUTYRIC-ACID-RECEPTOR SENSITIVITY IN
INBRED STRAINS OF MICE.
000303 01-03
ALTERATIONS IN BASAL FIRING-RATE AND AUTORECEPTOR SENSITIVITY
OF DOPAMINE NEURONS IN THE SUBSTANTIA-NIGRA FOLLOWING
ACUTE AND EXTENDED EXPOSURE TO ESTROGEN.
001167 02-03
EFFECTS OF DESIPRAMINE AND YOHIMBINE ON ALPHA2-ADRENOCEPTOR
AND BETA-ADRENOCEPTOR SENSITIVITY.
001305 02-03
DIFFERENTIAL SENSITIVITY OF HYPOTHALAMIC DOPAMINERGIC AND
NORADRENERGIC NEURONES TO PHARMACOLOGICAL MANIPULATION.
001310 02-03
ENDOGENOUS GUANYL-NUCLEOTIDES: COMPONENTS OF THE STRIATUM
WHICH CONFER DOPAMINE SENSITIVITY TO ADENYLATE-CYCLASE.
001313 02-03
SPONTANEOUSLY (GENETIC) HYPERTENSIVE-RATS PRESENT A NALOXONE
SENSITIVE DECREASE IN PAIN SENSITIVITY. (UNPUBLISHED PAPER).
001457 02-03
ENHANCED SENSITIVITY OF AMYGDALOID NEURONS TO SEROTONIN AND
NOREPINEPHRINE AFTER CHRONIC ANTIDEPRESSANT TREATMENT.
001523 02-03
TOLERANCE TO ETHANOL-INDUCED IMPAIRMENT OF WATER-ESCAPE IN
RATS BRED FOR ETHANOL SENSITIVITY.
001567 02-04
ETHANOL-INDUCED ANALGESIA IN RATS SELECTIVELY BRED FOR ETHANOL
SENSITIVITY.
001625 02-04
CENTRAL SEROTONIN-RECEPTOR SENSITIVITY IN RATS WITH
EXPERIMENTAL ALLERGIC-ENCEPHALOMYELITIS.
001821 02-04
PSYCHOACTIVE-DRUG QUANTIFICATION BY VISUAL FLICKER SENSITIVITY
MEASUREMENT. (PH.D. DISSERTATION).
002485 02-16
SENSITIVITY OF IDENTIFIED MEDIAL HYPOTHALAMIC NEURONS TO GABA,
GLYCINE AND RELATED AMINO-ACIDS; INFLUENCE OF BICUCULLINE,
PICROTOXIN AND STRYCHNINE ON SYNAPTIC INHIBITION.
002674 03-03
A COMPARISON OF THE EFFECTS OF PENTOBARBITAL AND
DIPHENYLHYDANTOIN ON THE GABA SENSITIVITY AND EXCITABILITY
OF ADULT SENSORY GANGLION CELLS.
002692 03-03
HYPOPHYSECTOMY INCREASES THE SENSITIVITY OF RATS TO NALOXONE-
INDUCED HYPOTHERMIA.
002710 03-03
INFLUENCE OF A CHRONIC NEW POTENTIAL ANTIDEPRESSANT,
DIMETHYLAMINOPROPYL-5-METHYL-3-PHENYL-1H-INDAZOLE (FS-32)
AND ITS N DESMETHYLATED-COMPOUND (FS-97): TREATMENT ON
MONOAMINERGIC-RECEPTOR SENSITIVITY IN THE RAT-BRAIN.
002787 03-03
AN ENHANCED SENSITIVITY OF MUSCARINIC CHOLINERGIC-RECEPTOR
ASSOCIATED WITH DOPAMINERGIC-RECEPTOR SUBSENSITIVITY AFTER
CHRONIC ANTIDEPRESSANT TREATMENT.
002788 03-03
L HISTIDINE; EFFECTS ON SENSITIVITY OF CAT SPINAL NEURONES TO
AMINO-ACIDS.
002808 03-03

Subject Index

DIFFERENTIAL-EFFECTS OF CLOMIPRAMINE AND CLORGYLINE ON THE SENSITIVITY OF CORTICAL NEURONS TO SEROTONIN: EFFECT OF CHRONIC-TREATMENT.
002847 03-03

5 HYDROXYTRYPTAMINE CONTROLS ACH-RECEPTOR SENSITIVITY OF BULLFROG SYMPATHETIC GANGLION CELLS.
003710 04-03

THYROXIN SENSITIVITY OF SENSORIMOTOR CORTICAL NEURONS AND THE HYPOTHALAMIC VENTROMEDIAL NUCLEUS.
003713 04-03

NEURONAL SENSITIVITY OF SOME BRAIN REGIONS TO ANGIOTENSIN-II IN RABBITS.
003716 04-03

PRESYNAPTIC AND POSTSYNAPTIC STRIATAL DOPAMINE-RECEPTORS: DIFFERENTIAL SENSITIVITY TO APOMORPHINE INHIBITION OF (3H)DOPAMINE AND (14C)GABA RELEASE IN VITRO.
003741 04-03

SENSITIVITY TO GABA OF NEURONS OF THE DORSAL AND VENTRAL LATERAL GENICULATE NUCLEI IN THE RAT.
003877 04-03

CONVERGENT PROPERTIES AND CHEMICAL SENSITIVITY OF MIDBRAIN RETICULAR FORMATION NEURONS OF UNANESTHETIZED RABBITS.
003972 04-03

ALTERATIONS IN GAMMA AMINOBUTYRIC-ACID-RECEPTOR SENSITIVITY FOLLOWING ACUTE AND CHRONIC ETHANOL TREATMENTS.
004037 04-03

FACTORS REGULATING DRUG CUE SENSITIVITY: LIMITS OF DISCRIMINABILITY AND THE ROLE OF A PROGRESSIVELY DECREASING TRAINING DOSE IN FENTANYL SALINE DISCRIMINATION.
004088 04-04

SEXUAL-BEHAVIOR DECREASES PAIN SENSITIVITY AND STIMULATES ENDOGENOUS OPIOIDS IN MALE RATS.
004234 04-04

SENSITIZATION
PRESYNAPTIC AND POSTSYNAPTIC MECHANISMS IN HALOPERIDOL-INDUCED SENSITIZATION TO DOPAMINERGIC AGONISTS.
001392 02-03

SENSITIZATION AND OSCILLATION FOLLOWING REPEATED STIMULATION: RELATIONSHIP TO AFFECTIVE-ILLNESS AND ITS TREATMENT WITH LITHIUM AND CARBAMAZEPINE.
002031 02-09

SELECTIVE SENSITIZATION INDUCED BY LITHIUM MALAISE AND FOOTSHOCK IN RATS.
003055 03-04

SENSORIMOTOR
REINNERVATION OF THE DENERVATED STRIATUM BY SUBSTANTIA-NIGRA TRANSPLANTS: FUNCTIONAL CONSEQUENCES AS REVEALED BY PHARMACOLOGICAL AND SENSORIMOTOR TESTING.
000347 01-04

ACTIVATION AND LATERALIZATION OF SENSORIMOTOR FIELD FOR PERIORAL BITING-REFLEX BY INTRANIGRAL GABA AGONIST AND BY SYSTEMIC APOMORPHINE IN THE RAT.
001657 02-04

BASAL GANGLIA DOPAMINERGIC CONTROL OF SENSORIMOTOR FUNCTIONS RELATED TO MOTIVATED BEHAVIOR.
002815 03-03

THYROXIN SENSITIVITY OF SENSORIMOTOR CORTICAL NEURONS AND THE HYPOTHALAMIC VENTROMEDIAL NUCLEUS.
003713 D4-03

SENSORIMOTOR-DYSFUNCTIONS
APHAGIA, GASTRIC PATHOLOGY, HYPERTHERMIA, AND SENSORIMOTOR-DYSFUNCTIONS FOLLOWING LATERAL HYPOTHALAMIC LESIONS: EFFECTS OF INSULIN PRETREATMENTS.
001638 02-04

SENSORY
STRYCHNINE EFFECTS ON THE SENSORY RESPONSE PATTERNS OF RETICULAR FORMATION NEURONS.
001219 02-03

THE EFFECTS OF PIPRADROL ON THE ACQUISITION OF RESPONDING WITH CONDITIONED REINFORCEMENT: A ROLE FOR SENSORY PRECONDITIONING.
001572 02-04

SENSORY AND ASSOCIATIVE-EFFECTS OF LSD ON CLASSICAL APPETITIVE-CONDITIONING OF THE RABBIT JAW MOVEMENT RESPONSE.
001637 02-04

THE USE OF SENSORY INTEGRATIVE DIAGNOSTICS TO PREDICT HYPERACTIVE-CHILDRENS RESPONSIVENESS TO METHYLPHENIDATE (RITALIN) AND PEMOLINE (CYLERT). (PH.D. DISSERTATION).
002133 02-11

EFFECTS OF CYCLOSPASMOL UPON SENSORY PARAMETERS IN PATIENTS RECOVERING FROM CEREBROVASCULAR-ACCIDENTS.
002360 02-14

OPIATE-RECEPTOR GRADIENTS IN MONKEY CEREBRAL-CORTEX: CORRESPONDENCE WITH SENSORY PROCESSING HIERARCHIES.
002641 03-01

DIFFERENCES IN CUTANEOUS SENSORY RESPONSE PROPERTIES OF SINGLE SOMATOSENSORY CORTICAL NEURONS IN AWAKE AND HALOTHANE ANESTHETIZED RATS.
002687 03-03

SERINE
CENTRAL ADMINISTRATION OF SERINE CAUSES HYPOTHERMIA AND INHIBITS FEVER IN RABBITS.
001247 02-03
COMPARISON OF THE EFFECTS OF CENTRAL ADMINISTRATION OF SERINE AND GLYCINE ON BODY-TEMPERATURE OF THE RABBIT.
001248 02-03

SEROTONERGIC
SUPPRESSION OF SEROTONERGIC NEURONAL FIRING BY ALPHA-ADRENOCEPTOR ANTAGONISTS: EVIDENCE AGAINST GABA MEDIATION.
000024 01-03
EVIDENCE FOR A RECEPTOR SUPERSENSITIVITY FOLLOWING IMPAIRMENT OF CENTRAL SEROTONERGIC ACTIVITY IN THE RABBIT.
000041 01-03
THE INVOLVEMENT OF SEROTONERGIC NEURONS IN THE CENTRAL-NERVOUS-SYSTEM AS THE POSSIBLE MECHANISM FOR SLOW HEAD-SHAKING-BEHAVIOR INDUCED BY METHAMPHETAMINE IN RATS.
000408 01-04
CHRONIC AMPHETAMINE ADMINISTRATION TO CATS: BEHAVIORAL-EVIDENCE AND NEUROCHEMICAL EVIDENCE FOR DECREASED CENTRAL SEROTONERGIC FUNCTION.
000491 01-04
ADRENERGIC NONSPECIFIC POTENTIATION OF YOHIMBINE TOXICITY IN MICE BY ANTIDEPRESSANTS AND RELATED DRUGS AND ANTIYOHIMBINE ACTION OF ANTIADRENERGIC AND SEROTONERGIC DRUGS.
001330 02-03
EFFECT OF SINGLE AND REPEATED ELECTROCONVULSIVE-SHOCK ON SEROTONERGIC SYSTEM IN RAT-BRAIN -- I. METABOLIC-STUDIES.
001332 02-03
SEROTONERGIC AND CATECHOLAMINERGIC INFLUENCE ON THYROID-FUNCTION IN THE VERVET-MONKEY.
001385 02-03
EFFECTS OF DIFFERENT MONOAMINE-OXIDASE-INHIBITORS ON RESPIRATORY ACTIVITY IN RATS WITH CHRONICALLY IMPAIRED CENTRAL SEROTONERGIC FUNCTION.
001389 02-03
EFFECTS OF KAINIC-ACID ON BODY-TEMPERATURE OF RATS: ROLE OF CATECHOLAMINERGIC AND SEROTONERGIC SYSTEMS.
001515 02-03
AMPHETAMINE STEREOTYPIES AND POLYRIBOSOMAL DISAGGREGATION IN RATS: EFFECTS OF ADRENERGIC AND SEROTONERGIC BLOCKING-AGENTS.
001531 02-03
EFFECTS OF SEROTONERGIC LESIONS ON INVESTIGATORY RESPONDING BY RATS IN A HOLEBOARD.
001634 02-04
EFFECT OF SINGLE AND REPEATED ELECTROCONVULSIVE-SHOCK ON SEROTONERGIC SYSTEM IN RAT-BRAIN -- II. BEHAVIOURAL-STUDIES.
001697 02-04
EFFECT OF SELECTIVE DESTRUCTION OF SEROTONERGIC NEURONS IN NUCLEUS-RAPHE-MAGNUS ON MORPHINE-INDUCED ANTINOCICEPTION.
001724 02-04
PRESYNAPTIC AND POSTSYNAPTIC SEROTONERGIC MANIPULATIONS IN AN ANIMAL-MODEL OF DEPRESSION.
001730 02-04
SEROTONERGIC PROPERTIES OF BETA PHENETHYLAMINE IN RATS.
001787 02-04
THE FUNCTIONAL IMPORTANCE OF INCREASED BRAIN TRYPTOPHAN IN THE SEROTONERGIC RESPONSE TO RESTRAINT STRESS.
002779 03-03
SEROTONERGIC MECHANISMS OF CLONIDINE-INDUCED HYPOTHERMIA IN RATS.
002806 03-03
IN VITRO CELLULAR ADAPTATION OF SEROTONERGIC PROCESSES AFTER CHRONIC CENTRAL PHENOBARBITAL ADMINISTRATION.
002813 03-03
DIFFERENTIAL-EFFECTS OF SHORT-TERM AND LONG-TERM LITHIUM ON TRYPTOPHAN UPTAKE AND SEROTONERGIC FUNCTION IN CAT BRAIN.
002911 03-03
THE ROLE OF CENTRAL SEROTONERGIC MECHANISMS ON HEAD-TWITCH AND BACKWARD LOCOMOTION INDUCED BY HALLUCINOGENIC-DRUGS.
003397 03-12
ANTAGONISM OF ETHANOL-INDUCED DECREASE IN LH BY P CHLOROPHENYLALANINE: LACK OF CORRELATION WITH ALTERED SEROTONERGIC MECHANISMS.
003748 04-03
COMPARATIVE-EFFECTS OF SUBSTITUTED PHENYLETHYLAMINES ON BRAIN SEROTONERGIC MECHANISMS.
003854 04-03
AN EVALUATION OF THE MECHANISM BY WHICH SEROTONERGIC ACTIVATION DEPRESSES RESPIRATION.
003917 04-03
APPARENT SEROTONERGIC MODULATION OF THE DOSE-DEPENDENT BIPHASIC RESPONSE OF NEOSTRIATAL NEURONS PRODUCED BY D-AMPHETAMINE.
003981 04-03

A COMMON MECHANISM FOR LYSERGIC-ACID, INDOLEALKYLAMINE AND PHENETHYLAMINE HALLUCINOGENS: SEROTONERGIC MEDIATION OF BEHAVIORAL-EFFECTS IN RATS.
004007 04-03
EFFECT OF CHRONIC-TREATMENT WITH TRICYCLIC-ANTIDEPRESSANT DRUGS ON IDENTIFIED BRAIN NORADRENERGIC AND SEROTONERGIC NEURONS.
004026 04-03
SEROTONERGIC MECHANISM IN SEIZURES KINDLED FROM THE RABBIT AMYGDALA.
004227 04-04
TONIC IMMOBILITY IN DOMESTIC FOWL: POSSIBLE INTERACTION OF SEROTONERGIC AND DOPAMINERGIC MECHANISMS.
004246 D4-04
PERIPHERAL SEROTONERGIC AND ADRENERGIC RESPONSES IN DEPRESSION.
004364 04-09
SEROTONERGIC APPROACHES TO THE MODIFICATION OF BEHAVIOR IN THE LESCH-NYHANS-SYNDROME.
004576 04-14

SEROTONERGIC-AGENTS
CHANGES IN BODY-TEMPERATURE AFTER ADMINISTRATION OF ADRENERGIC AND SEROTONERGIC-AGENTS AND RELATED DRUGS INCLUDING ANTIDEPRESSANTS.
002532 02-17
THE DIFFERENTIAL NEUROCHEMICAL-BASES OF THE BEHAVIOURS ELICITED BY SEROTONERGIC-AGENTS AND BY THE COMBINATION OF A MONOAMINE-OXIDASE-INHIBITOR AND L-DOPA.
002976 03-04

SEROTONERGIC-RECEPTORS
SELECTIVE INFLUENCE OF ERGOT ALKALOIDS ON CORTICAL AND STRIATAL DOPAMINERGIC-RECEPTORS AND SEROTONERGIC-RECEPTORS.
001447 02-03
DIFFERENTIAL-EFFECT OF CHRONIC DESIPRAMINE AND AMITRIPTYLINE TREATMENT ON RAT-BRAIN ADRENERGIC AND SEROTONERGIC-RECEPTORS.
002914 03-03
THE EFFECTS OF TRYPTOPHAN AND MANIPULATIONS OF SEROTONERGIC-RECEPTORS ON TONIC IMMOBILITY IN CHICKENS.
004245 04-04

SEROTONERGICALLY-INFLUENCED
PERIPHERAL-CORRELATES OF SEROTONERGICALLY-INFLUENCED BEHAVIORS IN VERVET-MONKEYS (CERCOPITHECUS-AETHIOPS-SABAEUS).
004204 04-04

SEROTONIN
ANTIHISTAMINE EFFECT ON SYNAPTOSOMAL UPTAKE OF SEROTONIN, NOREPINEPHRINE AND DOPAMINE.
000035 01-03
ACUTE VERSUS CHRONIC EFFECTS OF SEROTONIN UPTAKE BLOCKERS ON POTENTIATION OF THE SEROTONIN SYNDROME.
000050 01-03
RELATIONSHIP OF ANTICONFLICT ACTIVITY OF BENZODIAZEPINES TO BRAIN RECEPTOR BINDING, SEROTONIN, AND GABA.
000057 01-03
ACUTE CHANGES IN BRAIN TRYPTOPHAN AND SEROTONIN FOLLOWING CARBOHYDRATE OR PROTEIN INGESTION BY DIABETIC RATS. (UNPUBLISHED PAPER).
000060 01-03
MONOAMINERGIC DENERVATION OF THE RAT HIPPOCAMPUS: MICROIONTOPHORETIC STUDIES OF PRESYNAPTIC AND POSTSYNAPTIC SUPERSENSITIVITY TO NOREPINEPHRINE AND SEROTONIN.
000068 01-03
SEROTONIN PARTICIPATION IN GUT WITHDRAWAL FROM OPIATES.
000109 01-03
HYPOALGESIA INDUCED BY MICROINJECTION OF A NOREPINEPHRINE ANTAGONIST IN THE RAPHE-MAGNUS: REVERSAL BY INTRATHECAL ADMINISTRATION OF A SEROTONIN ANTAGONIST.
000121 01-03
EFFECTS OF CHRONIC FLUOXETINE ADMINISTRATION ON SEROTONIN METABOLISM.
000138 01-03
THE MONOAMINE-OXIDASE-INHIBITORS CLORGYLINE AND L DEPRENYL ALSO AFFECT THE UPTAKE OF DOPAMINE, NORADRENALINE AND SEROTONIN BY RAT-BRAIN SYNAPTOSOMAL PREPARATIONS.
000171 01-03
SEROTONIN-SENSITIVE ADENYLATE-CYCLASE AND (3H)SEROTONIN BINDING-SITES IN THE CNS OF THE RAT -- I. KINETIC PARAMETERS AND PHARMACOLOGICAL-PROPERTIES.
000213 01-03
SEROTONIN-SENSITIVE ADENYLATE-CYCLASE AND (3H)SEROTONIN BINDING-SITES IN THE CNS OF THE RAT -- II. RESPECTIVE REGIONAL AND SUBCELLULAR DISTRIBUTIONS AND ONTOGENETIC DEVELOPMENTS.
000214 01-03
REDUCTION IN THE NUMBER OF SEROTONIN-RECEPTORS IN THE BRAINSTEM OF MORPHINE-DEPENDENT RATS: RELATION TO BLOCKADE OF NALOXONE PRECIPITATED JUMPING BY SEROTONIN AGONISTS.
000258 01-03

THE INABILITY OF CHRONIC FLUOXETINE TO POTENTIATE A SEROTONIN MEDIATED EFFECT. 000293 01-03

ANALYSIS OF THE ACTIVATION OF DOPAMINE METABOLISM BY A SEROTONIN UPTAKE INHIBITOR. 000315 01-03

CGP-6085-A, A NEW, SPECIFIC, INHIBITOR OF SEROTONIN UPTAKE: NEUROCHEMICAL CHARACTERIZATION AND COMPARISON WITH OTHER SEROTONIN UPTAKE BLOCKERS. 000316 01-03

EFFECTS OF L-DOPA AND L 5 HYDROXYTRYPTOPHAN ON LOCOMOTOR-ACTIVITY OF THE RAT AFTER SELECTIVE OR COMBINED DESTRUCTION OF CENTRAL CATECHOLAMINE AND SEROTONIN NEURONS. 000466 01-04

THE EFFECT OF SEROTONIN DEPLETION ON THE DISCRIMINABILITY OF LSD. 000499 01-04

IN VITRO EFFECT OF PHENCYCLIDINE AND OTHER PSYCHOMOTOR STIMULANTS ON SEROTONIN UPTAKE IN HUMAN PLATELETS. 000750 01-13

MOTOR-EFFECTS OF SEROTONIN IN THE CENTRAL-NERVOUS-SYSTEM. 000941 01-17

MONOAMINES AND DEPRESSION: AN INTERIM REPORT. I. SEROTONIN AND SEROTONIN PRECURSORS. 000996 01-17

EFFECT OF SEROTONIN ON PROLACTIN SECRETION IN VIVO. 001016 02-01

TETRAHYDRO-BETA-CARBOLINES AND CORRESPONDING TRYPTAMINES: IN VITRO INHIBITION OF SEROTONIN AND DOPAMINE UPTAKE BY HUMAN BLOOD-PLATELETS. 001067 02-02

TETRAHYDRO-BETA-CARBOLINES AND CORRESPONDING TRYPTAMINES: IN VITRO INHIBITION OF SEROTONIN, DOPAMINE AND NORADRENALINE UPTAKE IN RAT-BRAIN SYNAPTOSOMES. 001078 02-02

INCREASED METABOLISM OF DOPAMINE AND SEROTONIN INDUCED IN FOREBRAIN AREAS BY ETORPHINE MICROINJECTION IN PERIAQUEDUCTAL GRAY. 001103 02-02

EFFECTS OF GABA AND DIAZEPAM ON 3H SEROTONIN RELEASE FROM HIPPOCAMPAL SYNAPTOSOMES. 001116 02-03

ROLES OF SEROTONIN AND GAMMA AMINOBUTYRIC-ACID IN OPIOID EFFECTS. 001140 02-03

BRAIN SEROTONIN AND 5 HYDROXYINDOLEACETIC-ACID CONCENTRATIONS AND SEROTONIN SYNTHESIS FOLLOWING TETRAHYDRO-BETA-CARBOLINE ADMINISTRATION IN MICE. 001152 02-03

MULTIPLE RECEPTORS FOR SEROTONIN IN THE RAT-BRAIN. 001269 02-03

THE EFFECT OF MORPHINE ON THE CONTENT OF SEROTONIN, 5 HYDROXYINDOLEACETIC-ACID AND SUBSTANCE-P IN THE NUCLEI RAPHE-MAGNUS AND RETICULARIS-GIGANTOCELLULARIS. 001328 02-03

PERSISTENT EFFECTS OF CHRONIC ADMINISTRATION OF LSD ON INTRACELLULAR SEROTONIN CONTENT IN RAT-MIDBRAIN. 001333 02-03

DENERVATION SUPERSENSITIVITY TO SEROTONIN IN THE FACIAL NUCLEUS. 001364 02-03

MULTIVARIATE APPROACHES APPLIED TO STUDIES OF NOREPINEPHRINE AND SEROTONIN UPTAKE. 001460 02-03

DECREASE IN (3H) SEROTONIN BINDING IN RAT-BRAIN PRODUCED BY THE REPEATED ADMINISTRATION OF EITHER MONOAMINE-OXIDASE-INHIBITORS ON CENTRALLY-ACTING SEROTONIN AGONISTS. 001463 02-03

LARYNGEAL-EFFECTS OF SEROTONIN IN RABBITS. 001501 02-03

ENHANCED SENSITIVITY OF AMYGDALOID NEURONS TO SEROTONIN AND NOREPINEPHRINE AFTER CHRONIC ANTIDEPRESSANT TREATMENT. 001523 02-03

5,7 DIHYDROXYTRYPTAMINE-INDUCED MOUSE-KILLING AND BEHAVIORAL-REVERSAL WITH VENTRICULAR ADMINISTRATION OF SEROTONIN IN RATS. 001562 02-04

ENHANCED BEHAVIOURAL-EFFECTS, ELECTROCORTICAL-EFFECTS AND HYPERTHERMIC-EFFECTS OF SEROTONIN-LIKE AGENTS AFTER IMPAIRMENT OF SEROTONIN TRANSMISSION IN FOWL BRAIN. 001733 02-04

THE EFFECT OF SOME STRUCTURAL GABA ANALOGUES ON THE SEROTONIN AND DOPAMINERGIC MECHANISMS. 001736 02-04

CIRCLING PRODUCED BY SEROTONIN AND DOPAMINE AGONISTS IN RAPHE LESIONED RATS: A SEROTONIN MODEL. 001783 02-04

EFFECT OF NICKEL ON THE LEVELS OF DOPAMINE, NORADRENALINE AND SEROTONIN IN DIFFERENT REGIONS OF THE RAT-BRAIN. 001831 02-05

BLOOD LEVEL OF AMITRIPTYLINE, NORTRIPTYLINE, NORADRENALINE, SEROTONIN AND THERAPEUTIC RESPONSE. 002057 02-09

CONCENTRATION OF SEROTONIN METABOLITES IN THE CEREBROSPINAL-FLUID FROM ALCOHOLICS BEFORE AND DURING SULFIRAM THERAPY. 002095 02-11

CHARACTERIZATION OF ERGOT AND NONERGOT SEROTONIN ANTAGONISTS BY PROLACTIN AND GROWTH-HORMONE PROFILES DURING WAKEFULNESS AND SLEEP. 002217 02-13

QUINACRINE AND SEROTONIN BINDING BY SYNTHETIC MODELS FOR HUMAN PLATELET DENSE-BODIES: EVALUATION OF THE ROLE OF BINDING IN AMINE STORAGE. (UNPUBLISHED PAPER). 002219 02-13

EFFECT OF DOXEPIN ON SEROTONIN METABOLISM IN RAT-BRAIN AND SEROTONIN UPTAKE BY HUMAN BLOOD-PLATELETS. 002243 02-13

GLYCINE, ACETYLCHOLINE, AND SEROTONIN: NEUROTRANSMITTERS OR NEUROMODULATORS? 002271 02-13

CHANGES IN THE AUGMENTER REDUCER TENDENCY AND IN PAIN MEASURES AS A RESULT OF TREATMENT WITH A SEROTONIN REUPTAKE INHIBITOR ZIMELIDINE. 002305 02-13

L HTP AND THE SEROTONIN HYPOTHESIS: THEIR MEANING FOR TREATMENT OF DEPRESSION. 002326 02-14

DU-24565, A QUIPAZINE DERIVATIVE, A POTENT SELECTIVE SEROTONIN UPTAKE INHIBITOR. 002651 03-02

EVIDENCE FOR A TONIC GABAERGIC CONTROL OF SEROTONIN NEURONS IN THE MEDIAN RAPHE NUCLEUS. 002719 03-03

THE EFFECTS OF D-AMPHETAMINE AND POTASSIUM ON SEROTONIN RELEASE AND METABOLISM IN RAT-CEREBRAL-CORTEX. 002754 03-03

DIFFERENTIAL-EFFECTS OF CLOMIPRAMINE AND CLORGYLINE ON THE SENSITIVITY OF CORTICAL NEURONS TO SEROTONIN: EFFECT OF CHRONIC-TREATMENT. 002847 03-03

(3H)MIANSERIN: DIFFERENTIAL LABELING OF SEROTONIN AND HISTAMINE-RECEPTORS IN RAT-BRAIN. 002860 03-03

3H SEROTONIN BINDING-SITES IN RAT-BRAIN: EFFECTS OF REPEATED ADMINISTRATION OF ANTIDEPRESSANT-DRUGS. (PH.D. DISSERTATION). 002881 03-03

ACCELERATED METABOLISM OF PROBENECID DURING LONG-TERM-TREATMENT OF RATS WITH ANTICONVULSANT-DRUGS: EFFECT ON CENTRAL SEROTONIN TURNOVER STUDIES. 002890 03-03

SOMATOSTATIN FACILITATES THE SEROTONIN RELEASE FROM RAT-CEREBRAL-CORTEX, HIPPOCAMPUS, AND HYPOTHALAMUS SLICES. 002913 03-03

HIPPOCAMPAL SEROTONIN REUPTAKE AND NOCTURNAL LOCOMOTOR-ACTIVITY AFTER MICROINJECTIONS OF 5,7 DHT IN THE FORNIX-FIMBRIA. 002929 03-03

SPINAL MODULATION OF THE ACOUSTIC STARTLE RESPONSE: THE ROLE OF NOREPINEPHRINE, SEROTONIN AND DOPAMINE. 002950 03-04

SUBSTANCE-P, HEXAPEPTIDE-PGLU6(SP6-11), ANALGESIA AND SEROTONIN DEPLETION. 003050 03-04

RELATIVE POTENCY OF AMPHETAMINE ISOMERS IN CAUSING THE SEROTONIN BEHAVIORAL-SYNDROME IN RATS. 003094 03-04

PRESSOR EFFECTS OF DORSAL RAPHE STIMI''ATION AND INTRAHYPOTHALAMIC APPLICATION OF SEROTONIN IN THE SPONTANEOUSLY HYPERTENSIVE-RAT. 003117 03-04

SIMULTANEOUS DETERMINATION OF FEMTOMOLE QUANTITIES OF 5 HYDROXYTRYPTOPHAN, SEROTONIN AND 5 HYDROXYINDOLEACETIC-ACID IN BRAIN USING HPLC WITH ELECTROCHEMICAL-DETECTION. 003139 03-06

MANAGEMENT OF DEPRESSION WITH SEROTONIN PRECURSORS. 003269 03-09

THE THERAPEUTIC ACTIVITY OF TRYPTOPHAN AND ITS EFFECT ON SEROTONIN METABOLISM IN EPILEPTIC-PATIENTS. 003289 03-11

PLASMA FREE AND TOTAL TRYPTOPHAN, BLOOD SEROTONIN, AND THE HYPERACTIVITY-SYNDROME: NO EVIDENCE FOR THE SEROTONIN DEFICIENCY HYPOTHESIS. 003312 03-11

ABNORMAL TRANSMETHYLATION REACTION DURING THE METABOLISM OF DOPAMINE, TRYPTAMINE, AND SEROTONIN, AND SCHIZOPHRENIC-SYMPTOMS: A CRITICAL REVIEW. 003404 03-13

EFFECTS OF CONFORMATIONALLY RESTRAINED ANALOGUES OF SEROTONIN ON ITS UPTAKE AND BINDING IN RAT-BRAIN.
003794 04-03

PRESYNAPTIC MODULATION OF SYNAPTIC TRANSMISSION IN HELIX-POMATIA: THE EFFECTS OF SEROTONIN AND DOPAMINE ANTAGONISTS.
003869 04-03

THE EFFECT OF ADENOSINE AND GUANOSINE ON THE CONTENT OF SEROTONIN AND CATECHOLAMINES IN THE BRAIN IN THE RESTORATION PERIOD FOLLOWING EXPERIMENTAL CLINICAL DEATH.
003882 04-03

DOES HIGH-AFFINITY (3H) IMIPRAMINE BINDING LABEL SEROTONIN REUPTAKE SITES IN BRAIN AND PLATELET?
003962 04-03

IN VIVO EVIDENCE FOR GABAERGIC CONTROL OF SEROTONIN RELEASE IN THE CAT SUBSTANTIA-NIGRA.
004011 04-03

THE EFFECT OF SEROTONIN ON THE EXOSECRETORY ACTION OF THE PANCREAS.
004043 04-03

ANORECTIC-PROPERTIES OF A NEW LONG ACTING SEROTONIN UPTAKE INHIBITOR.
004105 04-04

THE EFFECTS OF P CHLOROAMPHETAMINE ADMINISTRATION ON LOCOMOTOR-ACTIVITY AND SEROTONIN IN NEONATAL AND ADULT RATS. (UNPUBLISHED PAPER).
004169 04-04

CATECHOLAMINE SEROTONIN INTERACTION EFFECTS ON ACTIVITY IN RATS NEONATALLY TREATED WITH 6 HYDROXYDOPAMINE.
004194 04-04

A SIMPLE DETERMINATION OF SEROTONIN, 5 HYDROXYINDOLEACETIC-ACID AND 5 HYDROXYTRYPTOPHAN-DECARBOXYLASE ACTIVITY IN RAT-BRAIN AREAS AND PARALLEL CORRELATION AMONG THE LEVELS.
004301 04-06

THE ANTIDEPRESSANT EFFECTS OF TRAZODONE AND INHIBITION OF PLATELET SEROTONIN REUPTAKE.
004383 04-09

EFFECTS OF RO-11-2465, A NEW PSYCHOTROPIC-AGENT ON THE UPTAKE OF SEROTONIN BY HUMAN PLATELETS -- IN VITRO DETERMINATION OF THE IC50.
004532 04-13

ANTIDEPRESSANTS AND THE SEROTONIN UPTAKE IN PLATELETS.
004727 04-17

SEROTONIN-LIKE
ENHANCED BEHAVIOURAL-EFFECTS, ELECTROCORTICAL-EFFECTS AND HYPERTHERMIC-EFFECTS OF SEROTONIN-LIKE AGENTS AFTER IMPAIRMENT OF SEROTONIN TRANSMISSION IN FOWL BRAIN.
001733 02-04

SEROTONIN-RECEPTOR
LONG-TERM ANTIDEPRESSANT TREATMENT DECREASES SPIROPERIDOL-LABELED SEROTONIN-RECEPTOR BINDING.
000230 01-03

SEROTONIN-RECEPTOR MEDIATED MODULATION OF CA-DEPENDENT 5 HYDROXYTRYPTAMINE RELEASE FROM NEURONES OF THE RAT-BRAIN-CORTEX.
001258 02-03

CENTRAL SEROTONIN-RECEPTOR SENSITIVITY IN RATS WITH EXPERIMENTAL ALLERGIC-ENCEPHALOMYELITIS.
001821 02-04

IMIPRAMINE: EFFECT OF OVARIAN STEROIDS ON MODIFICATIONS IN SEROTONIN-RECEPTOR BINDING.
002778 03-03

DOM AND RELATED 2,5 DIMETHOXY-4-ALKYLPHENYLISOPROPYLAMINES: BEHAVIORAL AND SEROTONIN-RECEPTOR PROPERTIES.
003690 04-02

SEROTONIN-RECEPTORS
REDUCTION IN THE NUMBER OF SEROTONIN-RECEPTORS IN THE BRAINSTEM OF MORPHINE-DEPENDENT RATS: RELATION TO BLOCKADE OF NALOXONE PRECIPITATED JUMPING BY SEROTONIN AGONISTS.
000258 01-03

SEROTONIN-RECEPTORS IN HIPPOCAMPUS AND FRONTAL-CORTEX.
000268 01-03

LITHIUM: EFFECTS ON SEROTONIN-RECEPTORS IN RAT-BRAIN.
000304 01-03

3H MIANSERIN BINDING IN CALF CAUDATE: POSSIBLE INVOLVEMENT OF SEROTONIN-RECEPTORS IN ANTIDEPRESSANT-DRUG ACTION.
000325 01-03

SOLUBILIZATION OF SEROTONIN-RECEPTORS FROM RAT-FRONTAL-CORTEX.
002489 02-16

EVIDENCE THAT IT IS POSSIBLE TO CAUSE ANOREXIA BY INCREASING RELEASE AND/OR DIRECTLY STIMULATING POSTSYNAPTIC SEROTONIN-RECEPTORS IN THE BRAIN.
002602 02-17

TWO DISTINCT SEROTONIN-RECEPTORS: REGIONAL VARIATIONS IN RECEPTOR BINDING IN MAMMALIAN BRAIN.
002861 03-03

(3H)METERGOLINE: A NEW LIGAND OF SEROTONIN-RECEPTORS IN THE RAT-BRAIN.
003825 04-03

SEROTONIN-SENSITIVE
SEROTONIN-SENSITIVE ADENYLATE-CYCLASE AND (3H)SEROTONIN BINDING-SITES IN THE CNS OF THE RAT -- I. KINETIC PARAMETERS AND PHARMACOLOGICAL-PROPERTIES.
000213 01-03

SEROTONIN-SENSITIVE ADENYLATE-CYCLASE AND (3H)SEROTONIN BINDING-SITES IN THE CNS OF THE RAT -- II. RESPECTIVE REGIONAL AND SUBCELLULAR DISTRIBUTIONS AND ONTOGENETIC DEVELOPMENTS.
000214 01-03

SEROTONINERGIC
MORPHINE ACTS THROUGH ALPHA-ADRENERGIC AND SEROTONINERGIC NEURONS TO STIMULATE GROWTH-HORMONE SECRETION IN THE DOG.
000088 01-03

STRUCTURAL REQUIREMENTS FOR UPTAKE INTO SEROTONINERGIC NEURONES.
001452 02-03

CENTRAL PHARMACOLOGICAL CONTROL OF CORTICOSTERONE SECRETION IN THE INTACT RAT. DEMONSTRATION OF CHOLINERGIC AND SEROTONINERGIC FACILITATORY AND ALPHA-ADRENERGIC INHIBITORY MECHANISMS.
001487 02-03

INJECTIONS OF DOPAMINERGIC, CHOLINERGIC, SEROTONINERGIC AND GABAERGIC DRUGS INTO THE NUCLEUS-ACCUMBENS: EFFECTS ON LOCOMOTOR-ACTIVITY IN THE RAT.
003019 03-04

EFFECTS OF ZIMELIDINE ON SEROTONINERGIC AND NORADRENERGIC NEURONS AFTER REPEATED ADMINISTRATION IN THE RAT.
003991 04-03

SEROTONINERGIC-AUTORECEPTOR
EFFECT OF CHRONIC TRICYCLIC-ANTIDEPRESSANT TREATMENT ON THE SEROTONINERGIC-AUTORECEPTOR: A MICROIONTOPHORETIC-STUDY IN THE RAT.
001135 02-03

SEROTONINMIMETIC
SEROTONINMIMETIC AND ANTIDEPRESSANT-DRUGS ON PASSIVE-AVOIDANCE LEARNING IN OLFACTORY BULBECTOMISED RATS.
001585 02-04

SEROTONIN2-RECEPTORS
DIFFERENTIAL-EFFECTS OF ELECTROCONVULSIVE-SHOCK AND ANTIDEPRESSANT-DRUGS ON SEROTONIN2-RECEPTORS IN RAT-BRAIN.
003878 04-03

REGULATION OF SEROTONIN2-RECEPTORS (5 HT2) LABELED WITH (3H)SPIROPERIDOL BY CHRONIC-TREATMENT WITH THE ANTIDEPRESSANT AMITRIPTYLINE.
003964 04-03

SERUM
OXAZEPAM-ESTERS. 2. CORRELATION OF HYDROPHOBICITY WITH SERUM BINDING, BRAIN PENETRATION, AND EXCRETION.
000011 01-02

ADMINISTRATION OF ANTISOMATOSTATIN SERUM TO RATS REVERSES THE INHIBITION OF PULSATILE GROWTH-HORMONE SECRETION PRODUCED BY INJECTION OF METERGOLINE BUT NOT YOHIMBINE. (UNPUBLISHED PAPER).
000019 01-03

LITHIUM LEVELS IN BLOOD-PLATELETS, SERUM, RED-BLOOD-CELLS AND BRAIN REGIONS IN RATS GIVEN ACUTE OR CHRONIC LITHIUM-SALT TREATMENTS.
000082 01-03

THE ACUTE AND CHRONIC EFFECT OF LITHIUM ON SERUM TESTOSTERONE IN RATS.
000238 01-03

STRUCTURE-ACTIVITY RELATIONSHIPS IN THE EFFECTS OF PHENACEMIDE ANALOGS ON SERUM CREATININE AND ANTICONVULSANT ACTIVITY.
000249 01-03

ELECTRON-CAPTURE GAS-LIQUID-CHROMATOGRAPHIC-DETERMINATION OF ETHOSUXIMIDE AND DESMETHYLMETHSUXIMIDE IN PLASMA OR SERUM.
000538 01-06

CLINICAL-RESPONSE AND SERUM NEUROLEPTIC LEVELS IN CHILDHOOD-SCHIZOPHRENIA. (UNPUBLISHED PAPER).
000566 01-08

SOCIAL AND CLINICAL SIGNIFICANCE OF DETERMINING THE BARBITURATE LEVEL IN THE BLOOD SERUM OF PATIENTS TREATED WITH ANTIEPILEPTIC-DRUGS.
000695 01-11

CONVERSION SCALES FOR COMMONLY REQUESTED SERUM CONCENTRATIONS OF DRUGS AND OTHER SUBSTANCES OF THERAPEUTIC AND TOXICOLOGICAL IMPORTANCE, AND OF HORMONES.
000759 01-13

PLASMA CHLORPROMAZINE SERUM PROLACTIN RELATIONSHIP IN A SINGLE-DOSE EXPERIMENT.
000761 01-13

INFLUENCE OF DEXTROPROPOXYPHENE ON STEADY-STATE SERUM LEVELS AND PROTEIN BINDING OF THREE ANTIEPILEPTIC-DRUGS IN MAN.
000767 01-13

THE INFLUENCE OF LITHIUM-SALTS AND ANTIDEPRESSANT MEDICATION ON SERUM PROLACTIN LEVEL.
000780 01-13

CORRELATION BETWEEN DAILY FLUCTUATIONS OF CARBAMAZEPINE SERUM LEVELS AND INTERMITTENT SIDE-EFFECTS.
000851 01-15

SERUM CONCENTRATIONS OF PHENOBARBITAL AND DIPHENYLHYDANTOIN IN SEVERE MENTALLY-HANDICAPPED AND PHYSICALLY-HANDICAPPED-PATIENTS.
000856 01-15

PREDICTABILITY OF PHENYTOIN SERUM LEVELS BY NOMOGRAMS AND CLINICIANS.
000909 01-16

SERUM PROLACTIN DURING AGING AND THE EFFECTS OF ERGOTS.
001171 02-03

SUPPRESSIVE EFFECT OF MORPHINE ON SERUM GONADOTROPIN LEVELS IN CASTRATED RATS.
001393 02-03

RELATIONSHIP BETWEEN SERUM LEVELS AND FAST EEG ACTIVITIES IN RATS BY A SINGLE ADMINISTRATION OF PHENOBARBITAL.
001462 02-03

STUDY OF LITHIUM LEVELS IN THE SERUM AND GENITAL ORGANS OF MALE RATS.
001494 02-03

BARBITURATE SERUM LEVELS AND PROTECTION AGAINST KINDLED AMYGDALOID SEIZURES IN THE RAT.
001559 02-04

EXPERIMENTAL DEPENDENCE ON BARBITURATES: II. RELATIONSHIP BETWEEN DRUG LEVELS IN SERUM AND BRAIN AND THE DEVELOPMENT OF DEPENDENCE IN RATS.
001800 02-04

EFFECT OF PROPRANOLOL TREATMENT ON SERUM PROLACTIN LEVEL IN SCHIZOPHRENIC-PATIENTS.
001916 02-08

BASAL AND STIMULATED LEVELS OF PROLACTIN, TSH AND LH IN SERUM OF CHRONIC SCHIZOPHRENIC-PATIENTS, LONG-TERM TREATED WITH NEUROLEPTICS.
001935 02-08

BASAL AND STIMULATED LEVELS OF PROLACTIN, TSH, AND LH IN SERUM OF CHRONIC SCHIZOPHRENIC-PATIENTS LONG-TERM TREATED WITH NEUROLEPTICS: RELATIONS TO PSYCHOPATHOLOGY.
001936 02-08

USE OF LARGE-SINGLE-DOSES OF BROMOCRIPTINE IN SCHIZOPHRENIC-PATIENTS WITH ELEVATED SERUM PROLACTIN LEVELS AND EXTRAPYRAMIDAL SIDE-EFFECTS ASSOCIATED WITH NEUROLEPTIC TREATMENT.
001944 02-08

SERUM NEUROLEPTIC CONCENTRATIONS IN SCHIZOPHRENIA. (UNPUBLISHED PAPER).
001945 02-08

EFFECT OF LITHIUM ON POTASSIUM AND CALCIUM IN SERUM, ERYTHOCYTES AND IN URINE.
002054 02-09

A CONTROLLED DOUBLE-BLIND STUDY OF HALOPERIDOL VERSUS THIORIDAZINE IN THE TREATMENT OF RESTLESS MENTALLY-SUBNORMAL-PATIENTS: SERUM LEVELS AND CLINICAL-EFFECTS.
002185 02-11

METHOD FOR THE DETERMINATION OF TRYPTOPHAN IN SERUM AND CEREBROSPINAL-FLUID.
002208 02-13

PHARMACOKINETIC BASIS FOR PREDICTING STEADY-STATE SERUM DRUG CONCENTRATIONS OF IMIPRAMINE FROM SINGLE-DOSE DATA.
002225 02-13

INTERRELATION AT PLASMATIC LEVEL BETWEEN ANTIEPILEPTIC-DRUGS AND LIPIDS. ITS IMPLICATIONS IN THE EFFICIENCY OF TREATMENT IN EPILEPSY. I. CHANGES INDUCED BY PHENOBARBITAL OR/AND DIPHENYLHYDANTOIN IN SERUM LIPIDS.
002281 02-13

LEVELS OF MINERAL-ELEMENTS IN THE SERUM AND SALIVA OF HEALTHY MALE VOLUNTEERS AFTER A SINGLE-DOSE OF LI2CO3.
002297 02-13

CONCENTRATIONS OF CIS(Z) FLUPENTHIXOL IN MATERNAL SERUM, AMNIOTIC-FLUID, UMBILICAL-CORD-SERUM, AND MILK.
002423 02-15

DURING ONE YEARS NEUROLEPTIC TREATMENT IN RATS STRIATAL DOPAMINE-RECEPTOR BLOCKADE DECREASES BUT SERUM PROLACTIN LEVELS REMAIN ELEVATED.
002707 03-03

LACK OF CORRELATION BETWEEN NALOXONE-INDUCED CHANGES IN SEXUAL-BEHAVIOR AND SERUM LH IN MALE RATS.
002821 03-03

SUPPRESSION OF SERUM PROLACTIN BY NALOXONE BUT NOT BY ANTI-BETA-ENDORPHIN ANTISERUM IN STRESSED AND UNSTRESSED RATS.
002871 03-03

VALPROIC-ACID SERUM LEVELS AND PROTECTION AGAINST KINDLED AMYGDALOID SEIZURES IN THE RAT.
002946 03-04

LOW SERUM PROLACTIN AND EARLY RELAPSE FOLLOWING NEUROLEPTIC WITHDRAWAL.
003166 03-08

NEUROLEPTIC-INDUCED ELEVATIONS IN SERUM PROLACTIN LEVELS: ETIOLOGY AND SIGNIFICANCE.
003190 03-08

NEUROLEPTIC SERUM LEVELS MEASURED BY RADIORECEPTOR ASSAY AND CLINICAL-RESPONSE IN SCHIZOPHRENIC-PATIENTS.
003199 03-08

AN INVERSE CORRELATION BETWEEN SERUM LEVELS OF DESMETHYLIMIPRAMINE AND MELATONIN-LIKE IMMUNOREACTIVITY IN DMI RESPONSIVE DEPRESSIVES.
003228 03-09

SERUM CONCENTRATION AND CLINICAL-EFFECT OF ANTIEPILEPTICS.
003315 03-11

INCREASED SERUM PROLACTIN LEVELS DURING PHENOTHIAZINE AND BUTYROPHENONE TREATMENT OF SIX POSTPARTUM WOMEN.
003318 03-11

SERUM HALOPERIDOL LEVELS IN GILLES-DE-LA-TOURETTE-SYNDROME.
003374 03-11

RENAL SIDE-EFFECTS OF LITHIUM: THE IMPORTANCE OF THE SERUM LITHIUM LEVEL.
003547 03-15

BRAIN AND SERUM CALCIUM CONCENTRATIONS FOLLOWING ELECTROCONVULSIVE-SHOCK OR BICUCULLINE-INDUCED CONVULSIONS IN RATS.
003736 04-03

PROTEIN BINDING OF CHLORPROMAZINE IN CEREBROSPINAL-FLUID AND SERUM.
004311 04-08

SERUM CONCENTRATION OF ANTICONVULSANTS. PHARMACOKINETIC FINDINGS AND THEIR PRACTICAL APPLICATION.
004443 04-11

INFLUENCE OF CARBAMAZEPINE ON SERUM THYROXINE AND TRIIODOTHYRONINE IN PATIENTS WITH EPILEPSY.
004488 04-11

CONCENTRATIONS AND KINETICS OF CARBAMAZEPINE IN WHOLE SALIVA, PAROTID SALIVA, SERUM ULTRAFILTRATE, AND SERUM.
004545 04-13

ANTIEPILEPTIC THERAPY WITH PHENYTOIN: WHICH IS THE OPTIMUM SERUM LEVEL?
004586 04-14

TWO CASES OF FORM-FRUSTE-DU-SYNDROME-MALIN WITH HIGH-LEVELS OF SERUM CPK.
004636 04-15

SERUM LEVELS OF BUTORPHANOL BY RADIOIMMUNOASSAY.
004691 04-16

SEVERE
SERUM CONCENTRATIONS OF PHENOBARBITAL AND DIPHENYLHYDANTOIN IN SEVERE MENTALLY-HANDICAPPED AND PHYSICALLY-HANDICAPPED-PATIENTS.
000856 01-15

DOUBLE-BLIND CLINICAL ASSESSMENT OF ALPRAZOLAM, A NEW BENZODIAZEPINE DERIVATIVE, IN THE TREATMENT OF MODERATE TO SEVERE ANXIETY.
002070 02-10

MINAPRINE IN SEVERE PSYCHOPATHOLOGY: STUDY OF 20 CASES.
002135 02-11

ABSENCE OF SEVERE TARDIVE-DYSKINESIA IN HUNGARIAN SCHIZOPHRENIC-OUTPATIENTS.
002404 02-15

HYPNOTIC ACTION OF FLUNITRAZEPAM (ROCHES ROIPNOL) IN PATIENTS WITH SEVERE PSYCHIATRIC-DISORDERS.
003295 03-11

SEVERE WITHDRAWAL-SYNDROME AFTER CESSATION OF BENZODIAZEPINE TREATMENT: SIX CLINICAL CASES.
003505 03-15

NA-GAMMA-HYDROXYBUTYRATE IN CEREBRAL PROTECTION DURING SEVERE HYPOXEMIA IN THE RAT.
003895 04-03

THE SPECIFIC ACTIVITY OF PLATELET MONOAMINE-OXIDASE VARIES WITH PLATELET COUNT DURING SEVERE EXERCISE AND NORADRENALINE INFUSION.
004509 04-13

MILD, MODERATE, SEVERE — THE STATISTICAL ANALYSIS OF SHORT ORDINAL SCALES.
004677 04-16

SEVERELY
A DOUBLE-BLIND, PLACEBO-CONTROLLED, CROSS-OVER TRIAL OF CARBAMAZEPINE IN OVERACTIVE, SEVERELY MENTALLY-HANDICAPPED PATIENTS.
003365 03-11

SEVERITY
INTROVERSION AND SEVERITY OF THE BENZODIAZEPINE WITHDRAWAL.
000923 01-17

CHANGES IN PREVALENCE, SEVERITY, AND RECOVERY IN TARDIVE-DYSKINESIA WITH AGE.
002455 02-15

SEX
THE EFFECT OF ASSERTIVENESS TRAINING, PROVERA AND SEX OF THERAPIST IN THE TREATMENT OF GENITAL EXHIBITIONISM.
000697 01-11

THE INFLUENCE OF GENOTYPE AND SEX ON BEHAVIORAL-SENSITIVITY TO
NICOTINE IN MICE.
001648 02-04
SPECIFIC 3H IMIPRAMINE BINDING IN HUMAN PLATELETS: INFLUENCE OF
AGE AND SEX.
002254 02-13
DOES POSTURAL ASYMMETRY INDICATE DIRECTIONALITY OF ROTATION
IN RATS: ROLE OF SEX AND HANDLING.
003061 03-04
SEX, PLASMA PROLACTIN AND PLASMA 3 METHOXY-4-
HYDROXYPHENYLGLYCOL (MHPG) PREDICT HERITABLE D-
AMPHETAMINE EXCITATION IN MAN. (UNPUBLISHED PAPER).
004565 04-14
DRUGS, ALCOHOL AND SEX.
004706 04-17

SEX-DIFFERENCE
SEX-DIFFERENCE IN BRAIN IRON. (UNPUBLISHED PAPER).
001278 02-03

SEX-DIFFERENCES
SEX-DIFFERENCES IN AMPHETAMINE-ELICITED ROTATIONAL-BEHAVIOR
AND THE LATERALIZATION OF STRIATAL DOPAMINE IN RATS.
000459 01-04
SEX-DIFFERENCES IN THE EFFECTS OF LOW-DOSES OF ETHANOL ON
HUMAN REACTION-TIME.
002361 02-14
SEX-DIFFERENCES IN THE AMPHETAMINE STIMULATED RELEASE OF
CATECHOLAMINES FROM RAT STRIATAL TISSUE IN VITRO.
002668 03-03
HYPERACTIVITY IN DEVELOPING RATS: SEX-DIFFERENCES IN 6
HYDROXYDOPAMINE AND AMPHETAMINE EFFECTS.
002970 03-04
GONADECTOMY AND SEX-DIFFERENCES IN THE BEHAVIORAL-RESPONSES
TO AMPHETAMINE AND APOMORPHINE OF RATS.
003084 03-04
FAILURE TO FIND SEX-DIFFERENCES IN TESTOSTERONE ACTIVATED
AGGRESSION IN TWO STRAINS OF RATS.
003107 03-04
SEX-DIFFERENCES IN PSYCHOTROPIC-DRUG USE.
003589 03-17

SEX-HORMONE
SEX-HORMONE INFLUENCES ON YAWNING-BEHAVIOR.
000407 01-04

SEX-LIFE
THE EFFECTS OF ESTROGEN THERAPY ON THE SEX-LIFE OF
POSTMENOPAUSAL-WOMEN.
004573 04-14

SEX-OFFENDERS
TREATMENT OF SEX-OFFENDERS WITH MEDROXYPROGESTERONE-
ACETATE.
004450 04-11

SEXUAL-BEHAVIOR
EFFECTS OF MORPHINE, BETA ENDORPHIN AND NALOXONE ON
CATECHOLAMINE LEVELS AND SEXUAL-BEHAVIOR IN THE MALE RAT.
000430 01-04
MALE RAT SEXUAL-BEHAVIOR COMPARED AFTER 6 OHDA AND
ELECTROLYTIC LESIONS IN THE DORSAL NA BUNDLE REGION OF THE
MIDBRAIN.
001593 02-04
LACK OF CORRELATION BETWEEN NALOXONE-INDUCED CHANGES IN
SEXUAL-BEHAVIOR AND SERUM LH IN MALE RATS.
002821 03-03
SEXUAL-BEHAVIOR DECREASES PAIN SENSITIVITY AND STIMULATES
ENDOGENOUS OPIOIDS IN MALE RATS.
004234 04-04
THE EFFECTS OF ANTIANXIETY AND ANTIPSYCHOTIC-DRUGS ON SEXUAL-
BEHAVIOR.
004657 04-15

SEXUAL-BEHAVIOUR
SEXUAL-BEHAVIOUR OF MORPHINE-DEPENDENT AND ABSTINENT MALE
RATS.
000438 01-04

SEXUAL-DEVIANTS
COMPARATIVE-STUDY OF PROPHYLACTIC LITHIUM AND
DIETHYLSTILBESTROL IN SEXUAL-DEVIANTS.
000663 01-11

SEXUAL-DEVIATIONS
CYPROTERONACETATE IN THE THERAPY OF SEXUAL-DEVIATIONS.
000735 01-11

SEXUAL-DIFFICULTIES
SEXUAL-DIFFICULTIES AMONG CONVALESCING ALCOHOLICS: INTEREST IN
PRAZEPAM TREATMENT IN 30 CASES.
003296 03-11

SEXUAL-DISORDERS
EXPERIMENTATION WITH MINAPRINE IN DEALING WITH CERTAIN
SEXUAL-DISORDERS: IMPOTENCE OR FRIGIDITY.
002153 02-11
PSYCHOPHARMACOTHERAPY OF SEXUAL-DISORDERS IN THE AGED.
004466 04-11

SEXUAL-DYSFUNCTION
PCP AND SEXUAL-DYSFUNCTION.
000745 01-12

ENDOCRINOLOGICAL CHANGES IN PATIENTS WITH SEXUAL-DYSFUNCTION
UNDER LONG-TERM NEUROLEPTIC TREATMENT.
000912 01-17
SUBJECTIVE ASSESSMENT OF SEXUAL-DYSFUNCTION OF PATIENTS ON
LONG-TERM ADMINISTRATION OF DIGOXIN.
002443 02-15

SEXUAL-DYSFUNCTIONS
BASAL PROLACTINAEMIA AND RESPONSES TO TRH AND SULPIRIDE IN
DIFFERENT CATEGORIES OF MALE SEXUAL-DYSFUNCTIONS.
004503 04-13

SEXUAL-EFFECTS
SEXUAL-EFFECTS OF ANTIDEPRESSANTS AND PSYCHOMOTOR STIMULANT-
DRUGS.
004646 04-15

SEXUAL-FUNCTION
DRUGS AND SEXUAL-FUNCTION.
000852 01-15

SEXUAL-FUNCTIONS
PHARMACOLOGICAL INFLUENCE OF SEXUAL-FUNCTIONS IN ADOLESCENTS.
004436 04-11

SEXUAL-IMPOTENCE
PHARMACOTHERAPY OF SEXUAL-IMPOTENCE IN THE MALE.
004435 04-11

SEXUAL-MOTIVATION
METHADONE REDUCES SEXUAL-PERFORMANCE AND SEXUAL-
MOTIVATION IN THE MALE SYRIAN GOLDEN HAMSTER.
004183 04-04

SEXUAL-OFFENDERS
PHARMACOTHERAPY FOR SEXUAL-OFFENDERS: REVIEW OF THE ACTION
OF ANTIANDROGENS WITH SPECIAL REFERENCE TO THEIR PSYCHIC-
EFFECTS.
004455 04-11

SEXUAL-PERFORMANCE
METHADONE REDUCES SEXUAL-PERFORMANCE AND SEXUAL-
MOTIVATION IN THE MALE SYRIAN GOLDEN HAMSTER.
004183 04-04

SEXUAL-RECEPTIVITY
PROSTAGLANDINS, CLONIDINE AND SEXUAL-RECEPTIVITY IN THE GUINEA-
PIG.
003017 03-04

SEXUAL-REFLEXES
COPULATORY-BEHAVIOR AND SEXUAL-REFLEXES OF MALE RATS TREATED
WITH NALOXONE.
003077 03-04

SEXUALITY
PHARMACOTHERAPY AND FEMALE SEXUALITY.
004483 04-11

SHAKING-BEHAVIOR
PHARMACOLOGICAL-ASPECTS OF SHAKING-BEHAVIOR PRODUCED BY
TRH, AG-3-5, AND MORPHINE WITHDRAWAL.
004248 04-04

SHELTERED-CARE-HOMES
ANTIPSYCHOTIC-DRUGS IN COMMUNITY-BASED SHELTERED-CARE-HOMES.
002171 02-11

SHIFTS
THE EFFECT OF SMALL DOSES OF HALOPERIDOL AND CLOZAPINE ON
BEHAVIORAL SHIFTS IN CATS, ARISING AFTER CESSATION OF
ELECTRICAL-STIMULATION OF THE CAUDATE-NUCLEUS.
004067 04-04

SHOCK
CHANGES OF ACTH, STH, TSH AND PROLACTIN LEVELS IN ENDOTOXIN
SHOCK IN RATS.
000119 01-03
EFFECTS OF MORPHINE, D-AMPHETAMINE, AND PENTOBARBITAL ON
SHOCK AND LIGHT DISCRIMINATION PERFORMANCE IN RATS.
001639 02-04
OPIATE ANTAGONISTS AND LONG-TERM ANALGESIC REACTION INDUCED
BY INESCAPABLE SHOCK IN RATS.
001707 02-04

SHOCK-AVOIDANCE
BETA-ADRENERGIC INFLUENCE ON CARDIAC DYNAMICS DURING SHOCK-
AVOIDANCE IN DOGS.
003813 04-03

SHOCK-ELICITED
NALOXONE PRETREATMENT ENHANCES SHOCK-ELICITED AGGRESSION.
001615 02-04

SHOCK-ESCAPE-TEST
THE EFFECT OF MORPHINE, PIMOZIDE AND NALOXONE ON
DISCRIMINATION BY RATS IN A SHOCK-ESCAPE-TEST.
001700 02-04

SHOCK-INDUCED
SELECTIVE INHIBITION BY NICOTINE OF SHOCK-INDUCED FIGHTING IN THE
RAT.
002984 03-04
FACILITATED SHOCK-INDUCED AGGRESSION AFTER CHRONIC-TREATMENT
WITH ANTIDEPRESSANT-DRUGS IN THE RAT.
003058 03-04

SHOCK-INDUCED-FIGHTING
SHOCK-INDUCED-FIGHTING (SIF): PSYCHOPHARMACOLOGICAL-STUDIES.
003091 03-04

SHORT
MILD, MODERATE, SEVERE — THE STATISTICAL ANALYSIS OF SHORT ORDINAL SCALES.
004677 04-16

SHORT-ACTING
THE DIFFERENTIAL-EFFECTS OF SHORT-ACTING AND LONG-ACTING BENZODIAZEPINES UPON NOCTURNAL SLEEP AND DAYTIME PERFORMANCE.
000822 01-14

PHARMACOKINETICS OF BENZODIAZEPINES: SHORT-ACTING VERSUS LONG-ACTING.
000920 01-17

NEUROPHYSIOLOGICAL-EFFECTS OF ETOMIDATE, A NEW SHORT-ACTING HYPNOTIC.
002263 02-13

EFFECTS OF A SHORT-ACTING BENZODIAZEPINE ON BRAIN ELECTRICAL-ACTIVITY DURING SLEEP.
004568 04-14

SHORT-CIRCUIT
ACUTE AND CHRONIC EFFECTS OF MORPHINE ON TRANSMEMBRANE POTENTIAL AND ON SHORT-CIRCUIT CURRENT IN ISOLATED TOAD SKIN: APPARENT MORPHINE-DEPENDENCE.
001176 02-03

SHORT-TERM
IMPAIRMENT OF AVOIDANCE-BEHAVIOR FOLLOWING SHORT-TERM INGESTION OF ETHANOL, TERTIARY BUTANOL, OR PENTOBARBITAL IN MICE.
000479 01-04

AROUSAL AND SHORT-TERM MEMORY: EFFECTS OF CAFFEINE AND TRIAL SPACING ON DELAYED ALTERNATION PERFORMANCE.
000487 01-04

SHORT-TERM HORMONAL-EFFECTS OF NALOXONE IN MAN.
000798 01-13

THE SHORT-TERM USE OF BENZODIAZEPINES.
000962 01-17

SHORT-TERM AND LONG-TERM EFFECTS OF METHAMPHETAMINE ON BIOGENIC-AMINE METABOLISM IN EXTRASTRIATAL DOPAMINERGIC NUCLEI.
001384 02-03

SHORT-TERM AND LONG-TERM MODIFICATION OF SKELETAL-MUSCLE SODIUM-PUMP ACTIVITY AND MUSCLE PROTEIN TURNOVER. (UNPUBLISHED PAPER).
001519 02-03

ROLE OF NEUROTRANSMITTERS AND PROTEIN SYNTHESIS IN SHORT-TERM AND LONG-TERM MEMORY.
001573 02-04

THE SHORT-TERM AND LONG-TERM EFFECTS OF BETA ENDORPHIN ON THE OPIATE ABSTINENCE-SYNDROME IN RATS.
001643 02-04

HUNTINGTONS-DISEASE: CLINICAL-EFFECTS OF A SHORT-TERM TREATMENT WITH PIMOZIDE.
002091 02-11

SHORT-TERM ETHANOL ADMINISTRATION IMPAIRS THE ELIMINATION OF CHLORDIAZEPOXIDE (LIBRIUM) IN MAN.
002224 02-13

SHORT-TERM AND LONG-TERM EFFECTS ON GABA AND DOPAMINE NEURONS DURING TREATMENT WITH SULPIRIDE.
002311 02-13

DIFFERENTIAL-EFFECTS OF SHORT-TERM AND LONG-TERM LITHIUM ON TRYPTOPHAN UPTAKE AND SEROTONERGIC FUNCTION IN CAT BRAIN.
002911 03-03

INVOLVEMENT OF CALCIUM CHANNELS IN SHORT-TERM DESENSITIZATION OF MUSCARINIC-RECEPTOR MEDIATED CYCLIC-GMP FORMATION IN MOUSE NEUROBLASTOMA CELLS.
003783 04-03

COMPARATIVE CHARACTERISTICS OF THE PROPHYLACTIC PROPERTIES OF SHORT-TERM AND LONG-ACTING LITHIUM-CARBONATE PREPARATIONS IN ENDOGENOUS AFFECTIVE-PSYCHOSES.
004390 04-09

RELAPSE AFTER SHORT-TERM DRUG-THERAPY IN NEUROTIC-OUTPATIENTS.
004400 04-09

SHUNT
CHANGES IN GAMMA AMINOBUTYRIC-ACID SHUNT ENZYMES IN REGIONS OF RAT-BRAIN WITH KETAMINE ANESTHESIA.
003891 04-03

SHUTTLE
EFFECT OF BETA ENDORPHIN AND NALOXONE ON ACQUISITION, MEMORY, AND RETRIEVAL OF SHUTTLE AVOIDANCE AND HABITUATION LEARNING IN RATS.
000410 01-04

SHUTTLEBOX
NALOXONE AND SHUTTLEBOX SELF-STIMULATION IN THE RAT.
001793 02-04

SIALIC-ACID
THE EFFECT OF LITHIUM ON THE INCORPORATION OF 3H GLUCOSAMINE INTO GLYCOPEPTIDES AND THE TRANSFORMATION OF 3H GLUCOSAMINE INTO SIALIC-ACID IN RAT-BRAIN.
001209 02-03

SIDE-EFFECT
AN OLD SIDE-EFFECT REVISITED: VISUAL HALLUCINATIONS.
000886 01-15

AN UNUSUAL SIDE-EFFECT OF LITHIUM.
002381 02-15

SIDE-EFFECTS
HOSTILITY CONFLICT AND REPORTING OF SIDE-EFFECTS BY PSYCHIATRIC-OUTPATIENTS.
000840 01-15

PROLACTIN RESPONSE AND EXTRAPYRAMIDAL SIDE-EFFECTS DURING PROPRANOLOL AND NEUROLEPTIC-DRUGS TREATMENT IN CHRONIC SCHIZOPHRENIC-PATIENTS.
000841 01-15

ON THE GENETIC SIDE-EFFECTS OF PSYCHOTROPIC-SUBSTANCES: I. PSYCHOPHARMACEUTICALS, NARCOTICS, AND ANTICONVULSANT.
000845 01-15

NEUROLOGICAL SIDE-EFFECTS OF LITHIUM: ORGANIC-BRAIN-SYNDROME, SEIZURES, EXTRAPYRAMIDAL SIDE-EFFECTS, AND EEG CHANGES.
000847 01-15

CORRELATION BETWEEN DAILY FLUCTUATIONS OF CARBAMAZEPINE SERUM LEVELS AND INTERMITTENT SIDE-EFFECTS.
000851 01-15

CLINICALLY SIGNIFICANT SIDE-EFFECTS OF LITHIUM TREATMENT.
000893 01-15

USE OF LARGE-SINGLE-DOSES OF BROMOCRIPTINE IN SCHIZOPHRENIC-PATIENTS WITH ELEVATED SERUM PROLACTIN LEVELS AND EXTRAPYRAMIDAL SIDE-EFFECTS ASSOCIATED WITH NEUROLEPTIC TREATMENT.
001944 02-08

EFFICACY AND SIDE-EFFECTS OF LORAZEPAM, OXAZEPAM, AND TEMAZEPAM AS SLEEPING-AIDS IN PSYCHOGERIATRIC-INPATIENTS.
002076 02-10

EFFICACY AND SIDE-EFFECTS OF CHLORAL-HYDRATE AND TRYPTOPHAN AS SLEEPING-AIDS IN PSYCHOGERIATRIC-PATIENTS.
002077 02-10

AN ATTEMPT TO TREAT THE SIDE-EFFECTS OF PSYCHOTROPIC THERAPY WITH BROMOCRIPTINE.
002094 02-11

PIRACETAM ACTION IN NEUROLEPTIC-INDUCED EXTRAPYRAMIDAL SIDE-EFFECTS.
002132 02-11

LONG-TERM-TREATMENT WITH NEUROLEPTIC-AGENTS: ADAPTATION PHENOMENA AND THEIR SIGNIFICANCE WITH REGARD TO SCHIZOPHRENIC-SYMPTOMATOLOGY AND SIDE-EFFECTS.
002370 02-15

PHENOTHIAZINE PLASMA AND RED-BLOOD-CELL CONCENTRATIONS, THEIR RELATIONSHIP TO SIDE-EFFECTS AND CLINICAL-EFFICACY.
002386 02-15

SIDE-EFFECTS OF BETA-ADRENERGIC BLOCKING-DRUGS: A METHODOLOGICAL-PROBLEM.
002395 02-15

AN INVESTIGATION OF SOME SIDE-EFFECTS IN 47 PSYCHOTIC-PATIENTS DURING TREATMENT WITH CLOZAPINE AND DISCONTINUING OF THE TREATMENT.
002424 02-15

PROPRANOLOL (INDERAL) FOR TARDIVE-DYSKINESIA AND EXTRAPYRAMIDAL SIDE-EFFECTS FROM NEUROLEPTICS: POSSIBLE INVOLVEMENT OF BETA-ADRENERGIC MECHANISMS.
002470 02-15

NEUROPSYCHIATRIC SIDE-EFFECTS OF DRUGS IN THE ELDERLY. VOL. 9, AGING.
002573 02-17

CHRONIC EFFECTS OF NEUROLEPTICS HAVING HIGH OR LOW INCIDENCE OF EXTRAPYRAMIDAL SIDE-EFFECTS UPON FORCE, DURATION AND RATE OF OPERANT-RESPONSE IN RATS. (PH.D. DISSERTATION).
003125 03-05

MEDICAL AND LEGAL IMPLICATIONS OF SIDE-EFFECTS FROM NEUROLEPTIC-DRUGS. A ROUND-TABLE DISCUSSION.
003471 03-15

SIDE-EFFECTS OF CORTICOSTEROID THERAPY: PSYCHIATRIC-ASPECTS.
003508 03-15

HEPATIC SIDE-EFFECTS OF ANTIDEPRESSANT MEDICATIONS.
003523 03-15

RENAL SIDE-EFFECTS OF LITHIUM: THE IMPORTANCE OF THE SERUM LITHIUM LEVEL.
003547 03-15

A DOUBLE-BLIND MULTICENTRE-TRIAL COMPARING THE EFFICACY AND SIDE-EFFECTS OF MIANSERIN AND CHLORIMIPRAMINE IN DEPRESSED-INPATIENTS AND DEPRESSED-OUTPATIENTS.
004395 04-09

NEUROLEPTICS AND THEIR SIDE-EFFECTS.
004590 04-15

OPHTHALMOLOGICAL SIDE-EFFECTS OF LITHIUM.
004615 04-15

AN EVALUATION OF THE ANTIANXIETY ACTION AND SIDE-EFFECTS OF PROPRANOLOL.
004660 04-15
SIDE-EFFECTS AND UNDESIRABLE COMBINATIONS OF PSYCHOTROPIC-MEDICATIONS.
004663 04-15

SIDMAN-AVOIDANCE
EFFECTS OF REPEATED ADMINISTRATION OF D-AMPHETAMINE ON SIDMAN-AVOIDANCE RESPONDING IN RATS.
001692 02-04

SIGMA
ACTIONS OF MU, KAPPA, SIGMA, DELTA AND AGONIST/ANTAGONIST OPIATES ON STRIATAL DOPAMINERGIC FUNCTION.
004053 04-03

SIGNAL
A COMPARISON OF HUMAN TACTILE STIMULUS VELOCITY DISCRIMINATION WITH THE ABILITY OF S-I CORTICAL NEURONS IN AWAKE RHESUS-MONKEYS TO SIGNAL THE SAME VELOCITY DIFFERENCES BEFORE AND AFTER NONANESTHETIC DOSES OF PENTOBARBITAL.
000055 01-03
BIOCHEMICAL-MECHANISM OF SIGNAL TRANSDUCTION ACROSS BIOMEMBRANES. (UNPUBLISHED PAPER).
001026 02-01
PHOSPHOLIPID METHYLATION: A BIOCHEMICAL-EVENT OF SIGNAL TRANSDUCTION. (UNPUBLISHED PAPER).
001279 02-03
DISRUPTION OF AUTOSHAPED RESPONDING TO A SIGNAL OF BRAIN-STIMULATION REWARD BY NEUROLEPTIC-DRUGS.
004199 04-04

SIGNAL-DETECTION-ANALYSIS
A SIGNAL-DETECTION-ANALYSIS OF CENTRALLY-ACTIVE DRUGS IN MICE.
001631 02-04
A SIGNAL-DETECTION-ANALYSIS OF MORPHINE EFFECTS ON THE RESPONSE BIAS OF RATS IN A TWO-SHOCK DISCRIMINATION TASK.
004124 04-04

SIGNALLED
DIFFERENTIAL-EFFECTS OF METHYLPHENIDATE ON SIGNALLED AND NONSIGNALLED REINFORCEMENT.
000380 01-04

SIGNALLING
PHOSPHOLIPID METHYLATION AND TRANSMEMBRANE SIGNALLING. (UNPUBLISHED PAPER).
001001 02-01

SILASTIC
SUBCUTANEOUS SILASTIC IMPLANTS: MAINTENANCE OF HIGH BLOOD ETHANOL LEVELS IN RATS DRINKING A LIQUID DIET.
001865 02-06

SILICONE
A SILICONE PELLET FOR LONG-TERM CONTINUOUS ADMINISTRATION OF AMPHETAMINE.
001875 02-06

SINEMET
SINEMET AND THYROID-FUNCTION IN PARKINSON-DISEASE.
000733 01-11

SINGLE
DISTRIBUTION OF 14C PHENYTOIN IN RAT PURKINJE-CELLS, CEREBELLAR AND CEREBRAL NEURONAL TISSUE AFTER A SINGLE INTRAPERITONEAL INJECTION.
000261 01-03
WATER INTAKE AND TIME-COURSE OF DRINKING AFTER SINGLE OR REPEATED CHLORDIAZEPOXIDE INJECTIONS.
000369 01-04
SINTAMIL IN THE TREATMENT OF DEPRESSION: A COMPARISON OF SINGLE VS. DIVIDED DOSE ADMINISTRATION.
000629 01-09
THE EFFECTS OF LSD AND SOME ANALOGUES ON THE RESPONSES OF SINGLE CORTICAL NEURONS OF THE CAT TO OPTICAL-STIMULATION.
000738 01-12
CENTRAL LEVELS OF NORADRENALINE, 3 METHOXY-4-HYDROXYPHENYLETHYLENEGLYCOL AND CYCLIC-AMP IN THE RAT AFTER ACTIVATION OF LOCUS-COERULEUS NEURONS: INFLUENCE OF SINGLE AND REPEATED NEUROLEPTIC TREATMENT.
001095 02-03
A DEMONSTRATION OF NALOXONE PRECIPITATED OPIATE WITHDRAWAL ON SINGLE NEURONES IN THE MORPHINE-TOLERANT/DEPENDENT RAT-BRAIN.
001234 02-03
AUTOCORRELATION ANALYSIS OF SINGLE NEURON ACTIVITY AFTER ADMINISTRATION OF PENTOBARBITAL.
001268 02-03
INTERACTION OF TRIAZOLAM WITH DESIPRAMINE: EFFECTS OF SINGLE AND REPEATED TREATMENT ON CERTAIN PHARMACOLOGIC-RESPONSES AND BRAIN CATECHOLAMINE LEVELS.
001323 02-03
EFFECT OF SINGLE AND REPEATED ELECTROCONVULSIVE-SHOCK ON SEROTONERGIC SYSTEM IN RAT-BRAIN -- I. METABOLIC-STUDIES.
001332 02-03
ACUTE AND CHRONIC OPIATE-EFFECTS ON SINGLE UNITS AND EEG OF MEDIAL THALAMUS AND HIPPOCAMPUS: A LATENCY ANALYSIS.
001344 02-03

RELATIONSHIP BETWEEN SERUM LEVELS AND FAST EEG ACTIVITIES IN RATS BY A SINGLE ADMINISTRATION OF PHENOBARBITAL.
001462 02-03
ENHANCED RESPONSES TO OPIATES PRODUCED BY A SINGLE GENE SUBSTITUTION IN THE MOUSE.
001677 02-04
EFFECT OF SINGLE AND REPEATED ELECTROCONVULSIVE-SHOCK ON SEROTONERGIC SYSTEM IN RAT-BRAIN -- II. BEHAVIOURAL-STUDIES.
001697 02-04
THE INFLUENCE OF SINGLE DAILY HEROIN INJECTIONS ON DRINKING-PATTERNS IN THE RAT.
001746 02-04
CLINICAL AND EEG CHANGES IN DEPRESSIVE-PATIENTS AFTER A SINGLE INJECTION OF BETA ENDORPHIN.
001962 02-09
DISTRIBUTION OF MEMBRANE GLYCOPROTEINS AMONG THE ORGANELLES OF A SINGLE IDENTIFIED NEURON OF APLYSIA. II. ISOLATION AND CHARACTERIZATION OF A GLYCOPROTEIN ASSOCIATED WITH VESICLES.
002657 03-03
DIFFERENCES IN CUTANEOUS SENSORY RESPONSE PROPERTIES OF SINGLE SOMATOSENSORY CORTICAL NEURONS IN AWAKE AND HALOTHANE ANESTHETIZED RATS.
002687 03-03
PHARMACOKINETIC PROFILE OF VALPROIC-ACID IN RHESUS-MONKEYS FOLLOWING SINGLE BOLUS AND CONSTANT RATE INTRAVENOUS ADMINISTRATIONS.
002797 03-03
SINGLE OR REPEATED ADMINISTRATION OF SMALL DOSES OF APOMORPHINE ON WATER INTAKE AND ACTIVITY IN WATER-DEPRIVED RATS.
002981 03-04
TRANSFER FROM MULTIPLE TO SINGLE ANTIEPILEPTIC DRUG-THERAPY.
003316 03-11
COMPARISON OF SODIUM-VALPROATE AND PHENYTOIN AS SINGLE DRUG-TREATMENT IN EPILEPSY.
003371 03-11
CORTICAL EVOKED-POTENTIALS IN GILLES-DE-LA-TOURETTES-SYNDROME -- A SINGLE CASE-STUDY.
003431 03-13
SINGLE POINT ESTIMATION OF PHENYTOIN DOSING REQUIREMENT.
003562 03-16
EFFECTS OF PENTOBARBITAL AND ETHANOL UPON SINGLE NEURON ACTIVITY IN THE PRIMARY SOMATOSENSORY CORTEX OF THE RHESUS-MONKEY.
003755 04-03
CLASSICAL NEUROLEPTICS AND DECONDITIONING ACTIVITY AFTER SINGLE OR REPEATED TREATMENTS: ROLE OF DIFFERENT CEREBRAL NEUROTRANSMITTERS.
004115 04-04
EFFECTS OF ANALGESICS AND CNS-ACTING DRUGS ON STRUGGLING FOLLOWING REPETITIVE STIMULATION OF THE TAIL, AND FLEXOR REFLEX TO A SINGLE STIMULATION OF THE SCIATIC-NERVE IN RATS.
004148 04-04
NEUROTRANSMITTER-RECEPTORS IN BRAIN REGIONS OF ACRYLAMIDE TREATED RATS. I: EFFECTS OF A SINGLE EXPOSURE TO ACRYLAMIDE.
004264 04-05
PHARMACOKINETICS OF CLOXAZOLAM IN MAN AFTER SINGLE AND MULTIPLE ORAL DOSES.
004530 04-13
TRANSIENT HYPERKINESIA AFTER A SINGLE INTRAVENOUS PERFUSION OF DIPHENYLHYDANTOIN: REPORT OF A CASE ASSOCIATED WITH NONTOXIC PLASMA LEVELS OF DIPHENYLHYDANTOIN.
004638 04-15

SINGLE-BEDTIME-DOSE
CLINICAL-TRIAL OF HALAZEPAM AND CLORAZEPATE: CONSIDERATIONS OF A SINGLE-BEDTIME-DOSE.
003277 03-10

SINGLE-BEDTIME-DOSES
A DOUBLE-BLIND PARALLEL GROUP COMPARISON OF SINGLE-BEDTIME-DOSES OF HALAZEPAM AND PLACEBO.
002079 02-10

SINGLE-BLIND
ANALYSIS OF SINGLE-BLIND, DOUBLE-BLIND PROCEDURES, MAINTENANCE OF PLACEBO-EFFECTS, AND DRUG-INDUCED DYSKINESIA WITH MENTALLY-RETARDED PERSONS -- BRIEF REPORT.
003298 03-11
ANALYSIS OF SINGLE-BLIND AND DOUBLE-BLIND PROCEDURES, MAINTENANCE OF PLACEBO-EFFECTS AND DRUG-INDUCED DYSKINESIA WITH MENTALLY-RETARDED PERSON.
004437 04-11

SINGLE-CASE
SINGLE-CASE STUDY OF CLINICAL-RESPONSE TO HIGH-DOSE ERGOT ALKALOID TREATMENT FOR DEMENTIA. PRELIMINARY REPORT.
004493 04-11

SINGLE-DAILY-DOSE
MAPROTILINE ADMINISTERED IN A SINGLE-DAILY-DOSE IN GENERAL-PRACTICE.
002027 02-09

Subject Index

SINGLE-DAILY-DOSES
EVALUATION OF THE CLINICAL-EFFICACY OF SINGLE-DAILY-DOSES OF
ANTIDEPRESSANTS.
001985 02-09

SINGLE-DOSAGE
PLASMA DESIPRAMINE LEVELS AFTER SINGLE-DOSAGE AND AT STEADY-
STATE IN OUTPATIENTS.
002039 02-09

SINGLE-DOSE
SINGLE-DOSE PHARMACOKINETICS AND ANTICONVULSANT EFFICACY OF
PRIMIDONE IN MICE.
000177 01-03

PREDICTION OF STEADY-STATE PLASMA LEVELS OF AMITRIPTYLINE AND
NORTRIPTYLINE FROM A SINGLE-DOSE 24-HR. LEVEL IN DEPRESSED-
PATIENTS.
000582 01-09

COMPARISON OF SINGLE-DOSE PHARMACOKINETICS OF IMIPRAMINE
AND MAPROTILINE IN THE ELDERLY.
000596 01-09

PLASMA CHLORPROMAZINE SERUM PROLACTIN RELATIONSHIP IN A
SINGLE-DOSE EXPERIMENT.
000761 01-13

NO EVIDENCE FOR INCREASED DOPAMINE-RECEPTOR BINDING IN
SUPERRESPONSIVE MICE AFTER A SINGLE-DOSE OF NEUROLEPTICS.
001292 02-03

REDUCTION OF DOPAMINERGIC-SUPERSENSITIVITY BY A SINGLE-DOSE OF
AMPHETAMINE.
001642 02-04

SINGLE-DOSE VERSUS MULTIPLE-DOSE COMPARATIVE-TRIAL OF
DESIPRAMINE-HYDROCHLORIDE: A DOUBLE-PLACEBO METHOD.
002059 02-10

ELECTROENCEPHALOGRAPHIC-EFFECTS AND BEHAVIOURAL-EFFECTS OF
SODIUM-VALPROATE IN PATIENTS WITH PHOTOSENSITIVE EPILEPSY. A
SINGLE-DOSE TRIAL.
002154 02-11

PHARMACOKINETIC BASIS FOR PREDICTING STEADY-STATE SERUM DRUG
CONCENTRATIONS OF IMIPRAMINE FROM SINGLE-DOSE DATA.
002225 02-13

LEVELS OF MINERAL-ELEMENTS IN THE SERUM AND SALIVA OF HEALTHY
MALE VOLUNTEERS AFTER A SINGLE-DOSE OF LI2CO3.
002297 02-13

SINGLE-DOSE PHARMACOKINETICS OF DOXEPIN IN HEALTHY
VOLUNTEERS.
002303 02-13

A SINGLE-DOSE STUDY OF NABILONE, A SYNTHETIC CANNABINOID.
002328 02-14

ANXIETY AND SEDATION DURING A STRESSFUL-SITUATION AFTER SINGLE-
DOSE OF DIAZEPAM VERSUS N DESMETHYLDIAZEPAM -- A
CONTROLLED-TRIAL.
002329 02-14

THERAPEUTIC-EFFICACY OF DOXEPIN IN DIVIDED AND SINGLE-DOSE
REGIME.
003259 03-09

PLASMA DOPAMINE-BETA-HYDROXYLASE ACTIVITY IN CHRONIC
SCHIZOPHRENIC-PATIENTS TESTED WITH SINGLE-DOSE OF 2 BROMO-
ALPHA-ERGOCRIPTINE (PARLODEL).
004343 04-08

SINGLE-DOSE PHARMACOKINETIC DATA ON ZIMELIDINE IN DEPRESSED-
PATIENTS.
004385 04-09

SINGLE-DOSES
DISPOSITION OF (3H) PHENCYCLIDINE IN THE RAT AFTER SINGLE-DOSES
AND MULTIPLE-DOSES.
001375 02-03

SINGLE-NIGHTLY-DOSE
STUDY OF MAPROTILINE IN OUTPATIENT TREATMENT OF DEPRESSIVE-
STATES BY THE GENERAL-PRACTITIONER: ADVANTAGE OF SINGLE-
NIGHTLY-DOSE.
001961 02-09

SINGLE-ORAL-DOSAGES
EFFECTS OF SINGLE-ORAL-DOSAGES OF STEROIDS ON HUMAN EEG
BASELINE CROSSING T-SCORES SHOWN BY MULTIVARIATE STATISTICS
AND STANDARD PROFILES.
002239 02-13

SINGLE-ORAL-DOSE
INFLUENCE OF PHENYTOIN AND PHENOBARBITAL ON THE DISPOSITION OF
A SINGLE-ORAL-DOSE OF CLONAZEPAM.
002248 02-13

SINGLE-THERAPEUTIC-DOSE
EFFECTS OF A SINGLE-THERAPEUTIC-DOSE OF GLYCEROL ON CEREBRAL
METABOLISM IN THE BRAINS OF YOUNG MICE: POSSIBLE INCREASE IN
BRAIN GLUCOSE TRANSPORT AND GLUCOSE UTILIZATION.
004281 04-05

SINOATRIAL
IMIPRAMINE AFFECTS AUTONOMIC-CONTROL OF SINOATRIAL RATE IN
ISOLATED RIGHT ATRIAL PREPARATIONS.
000195 01-03

SINTAMIL
SINTAMIL IN THE TREATMENT OF DEPRESSION: A COMPARISON OF
SINGLE VS. DIVIDED DOSE ADMINISTRATION.
000629 01-09

CHARACTERIZATION OF ERGOT AND NONERGOT SEROTONIN
ANTAGONISTS BY PROLACTIN AND GROWTH-HORMONE PROFILES
DURING WAKEFULNESS AND SLEEP.
002217 02-13
ASPIRIN AND HUMAN SLEEP.
002241 02-13
THE EFFECTS OF TRIAZOLAM AND NITRAZEPAM ON SLEEP QUALITY,
MORNING VIGILANCE, AND PSYCHOMOTOR PERFORMANCE.
002330 02-14
THE EFFECTS OF COMBINED SEDATIVE AND ANXIOLYTIC-PREPARATIONS
ON SUBJECTIVE ASPECTS OF SLEEP AND OBJECTIVE MEASURE OF
AROUSAL AND PERFORMANCE THE MORNING FOLLOWING NOCTURNAL
MEDICATION: II. REPEATED DOSES.
002331 02-14
EEG ASSESSMENTS OF DOSAGE AND SLEEP PROFILES FOR A HYPNOTIC-
DRUG OF THE TRIAZOLOTHIENODIACEPINE SERIES.
002338 02-14
IMIPRAMINE AND EEG SLEEP IN CHILDREN WITH DEPRESSIVE-
SYMPTOMS.
002339 02-14
THE CLOCK AND THE BLUE GUITAR: STUDIES OF HUMAN GROWTH-
HORMONE SECRETION IN SLEEP AND WAKING. (UNPUBLISHED PAPER).
002346 02-14
INDIVIDUAL VARIATIONS IN THE EFFECTS OF FLURAZEPAM,
CLORAZEPATE, L-DOPA AND THYROTROPIN-RELEASING-HORMONE ON
REM SLEEP IN MAN.
002349 02-14
THE EFFECT OF BUTOCTAMIDE-HYDROGEN-SUCCINATE ON NOCTURNAL
SLEEP: ALL-NIGHT POLYGRAPHICAL-STUDIES.
002350 02-14
THE EFFECTS OF FLURAZEPAM, LORAZEPAM, AND TRIAZOLAM ON SLEEP
AND MEMORY.
002357 02-14
THE EFFECT OF DEPRENYL, A SELECTIVE MONOAMINE-OXIDASE-B-
INHIBITOR, ON SLEEP AND MOOD IN MAN.
002365 02-14
COMPUTERIZED SLEEP EEG (CSEEG) IN PSYCHIATRY AND
PSYCHOPHARMACOLOGY.
002614 02-17
OPIATE-RECEPTORS AND SLEEP. II. EFFECTS OF MICROINJECTIONS OF
ETHYL-ALCOHOL AND PENTOBARBITAL IN THE MEDIAN THALAMUS,
PERIAQUEDUCTAL GRAY MATTER AND NUCLEUS-TRACTUS-SOLITARIUS
OF THE RABBIT.
002917 03-03
SLEEP ELICITED BY OLFACTORY TUBERCLE STIMULATION AND THE EFFECT
OF ATROPINE.
002955 03-04
EFFECT OF P CHLOROPHENYLALANINE AND TRYPTOPHAN ON SLEEP, EEG
AND MOTOR-ACTIVITY IN THE RAT.
002958 03-04
ENHANCEMENT OF HEXOBARBITAL-INDUCED SLEEP BY LYSINE AND ITS
METABOLITES.
002967 03-04
SUPPRESSION OF ACTIVE SLEEP BY CHRONIC-TREATMENT WITH
CHLORIMIPRAMINE DURING EARLY POSTNATAL DEVELOPMENT:
EFFECTS UPON ADULT SLEEP AND BEHAVIOR IN THE RAT.
003056 03-04
SLEEP AND TREATMENT PREDICTION IN ENDOGENOUS DEPRESSION.
003236 03-09
POLYGRAPHIC-STUDY OF NIGHT SLEEP UNDER THE EFFECTS OF
MINAPRINE.
003313 03-11
THE EFFECTIVENESS OF IMIPRAMINE IN THE TREATMENT OF ENURESIS:
THE SIGNIFICANCE OF TYPE OF ENURESIS AND REPORTED LEVEL OF
SLEEP. (PH.D. DISSERTATION).
003337 03-11
ON THE EVALUATION OF A PROVOCATIVE EEG METHOD USING
MEDICATION IN THE DIAGNOSIS OF ORGANIC-BRAIN-SEIZURES IN
CHILDHOOD, WITH SPECIAL EMPHASIS ON SLEEP INDUCTION THROUGH
MEDICATION.
003387 03-11
STUDY ON THE EFFECTS OF L 5 HTP ON THE STAGES OF SLEEP IN MAN AS
EVALUATED BY USING SLEEP-DEPRIVATION.
003450 03-14
DOES P CHLOROPHENYLALANINE PRODUCE DISTURBED WAKING,
DISTURBED SLEEP OR ACTIVATION BY PONTO-GENICULO-OCCIPITAL
WAVES IN CATS?
003704 04-02
DOES RAPID-EYE-MOVEMENT SLEEP PLAY A ROLE IN BRAIN
DEVELOPMENT?
004091 04-04
() 6 FLUOROTRYPTOPHAN, AN INHIBITOR OF TRYPTOPHAN-
HYDROXYLASE: SLEEP AND WAKEFULNESS IN THE RAT.
004189 04-04
PHENOXYBENZAMINE AND BROMOCRIPTINE ATTENUATE NEED FOR REM
SLEEP IN RATS.
004203 04-04
CHANGES OF RESPONSE TO DOPAMINERGIC DRUGS IN RATS SUBMITTED
TO REM SLEEP DEPRIVATION.
004239 04-04

COMPUTERIZED ANALYSIS OF SLEEP RECORDINGS APPLIED TO DRUG
EVALUATION: MIDAZOLAM IN NORMAL SUBJECTS.
004564 04-14
EFFECTS OF SUPIDIMIDE (CG-3033) ON OBJECTIVE AND SUBJECTIVE SLEEP
PARAMETERS (A SLEEP LABORATORY STUDY).
004567 04-14
EFFECTS OF A SHORT-ACTING BENZODIAZEPINE ON BRAIN ELECTRICAL-
ACTIVITY DURING SLEEP.
004568 04-14
A SYNTHETIC ACTH4-9 ANALOGUE (ORGANON-2766) AND SLEEP IN
HEALTHY MAN.
004574 04-14

SLEEP-APNEA
MEDROXYPROGESTERONE TREATMENT OF OBSTRUCTIVE SLEEP-APNEA.
002128 02-11
TREATMENT OF NARCOLEPSY AND SLEEP-APNEA WITH GAMMA
HYDROXYBUTYRATE: A CLINICAL AND POLYSOMNOGRAPHIC CASE-
STUDY.
004571 04-14

SLEEP-APNEA-SYNDROME
FLURAZEPAM-INDUCED SLEEP-APNEA-SYNDROME IN A PATIENT WITH
INSOMNIA AND MILD SLEEP-RELATED RESPIRATORY CHANGES.
004729 04-17

SLEEP-DEPRIVATION
PREDICTION OF LOFEPRAMINE RESPONSE IN DEPRESSION BASED ON
RESPONSE TO PARTIAL SLEEP-DEPRIVATION.
000617 01-09
EFFECT OF PYRITINOL AND PIRACETAM ON CHANGES IN FREE AMMONIA
LEVEL IN CNS TISSUE AFTER PARADOXICAL SLEEP-DEPRIVATION IN
RATS.
001199 02-03
STUDY ON THE EFFECTS OF L 5 HTP ON THE STAGES OF SLEEP IN MAN AS
EVALUATED BY USING SLEEP-DEPRIVATION.
003450 03-14

SLEEP-DEPRIVED
COCAINE EFFECTS IN SLEEP-DEPRIVED HUMANS.
002323 02-14

SLEEP-DISORDERS
SLEEP PROFILE AND ULTRADIAN SLEEP PERIODICITY IN HUMANS UNDER
THE INFLUENCE OF A BUTYROPHENONE DERIVATIVE: I. SLEEP
CORRECTION IN SUBJECTS WITH OLIGOSYMPTOMATIC SLEEP-
DISORDERS.
001869 02-06
SURVECTOR AND SLEEP-DISORDERS: SLEEP-WALKING, NIGHTMARES,
AND NIGHT-TERRORS.
002110 02-11
THE CLASSIFICATION OF SLEEP-DISORDERS AND THE TREATMENT OF
VARIOUS FORMS OF SOMNAMBULISM.
004461 04-11

SLEEP-DISTURBANCE
AGE-SPECIFIC DOSES OF LORMETAZEPAM AS A NIGHT SEDATIVE IN
CASES OF CHRONIC SLEEP-DISTURBANCE.
004309 04-07

SLEEP-RELATED
—FLURAZEPAM-INDUCED SLEEP-APNEA-SYNDROME IN A PATIENT WITH
INSOMNIA AND MILD SLEEP-RELATED RESPIRATORY CHANGES.
004729 04-17

SLEEP-TIME
EFFECT OF CANNABIDIOL ON CYTOCHROME-P-450 AND HEXOBARBITAL
SLEEP-TIME.
002675 03-03

SLEEP-WAKE-DISORDERS
TREATMENTS FOR SLEEP-WAKE-DISORDERS IN THE ELDERLY.
002157 02-11

SLEEP-WAKEFULNESS
BIPHASIC-EFFECTS OF PIMOZIDE ON SLEEP-WAKEFULNESS IN DOGS.
000495 01-04
EFFECTS OF REPEATED ADMINISTRATIONS OF DIHYDROERGOTOXINE
(REDERGINE) ON THE SLEEP-WAKEFULNESS CYCLE IN THE CAT.
003703 04-02

SLEEP-WALKING
SURVECTOR AND SLEEP-DISORDERS: SLEEP-WALKING, NIGHTMARES,
AND NIGHT-TERRORS.
002110 02-11

SLEEPERS
AUDITORY AROUSAL THRESHOLDS OF GOOD SLEEPERS AND POOR
SLEEPERS WITH AND WITHOUT FLURAZEPAM.
003446 03-14

SLEEPINESS
INTRAVENOUS CHLORIMIPRAMINE AFFECTS REM CYCLE IN PATIENTS
WITH EXCESSIVE DAYTIME SLEEPINESS AND CONTROL SUBJECTS.
002314 02-14

SLEEPING-AIDS
EFFICACY AND SIDE-EFFECTS OF LORAZEPAM, OXAZEPAM, AND
TEMAZEPAM AS SLEEPING-AIDS IN PSYCHOGERIATRIC-INPATIENTS.
002076 02-10
EFFICACY AND SIDE-EFFECTS OF CHLORAL-HYDRATE AND TRYPTOPHAN
AS SLEEPING-AIDS IN PSYCHOGERIATRIC-PATIENTS.
002077 02-10

SLEEPING-PILL
THE SLEEPING-PILL.
000946 01-17

SLEEPING-PILLS
THE USE AND MISUSE OF SLEEPING-PILLS: A CLINICAL GUIDE.
002150 02-11

SLEEPING-TIME
NEUTRALIZATION OF THE EFFECT OF DELTA9 TETRAHYDROCANNABINOL ON BARBITURATE SLEEPING-TIME BY SPECIFIC ACTIVE IMMUNIZATION.
003803 04-03

SLICE
CONVULSANTS ANTAGONISE INHIBITION IN THE OLFACTORY-CORTEX SLICE.
001466 02-03

THE IN VITRO BRAIN SLICE AS A USEFUL NEUROPHYSIOLOGICAL PREPARATION FOR INTRACELLULAR RECORDING.
001864 02-06

DIFFERENTIAL TOLERANCE TO THE EFFECTS OF MORPHINE ON EVOKED ACTIVITY IN THE HIPPOCAMPAL SLICE.
003760 04-03

GABA-ENHANCEMENT OF (3H)DOPAMINE RELEASE FROM SLICES OF RAT STRIATUM: DEPENDENCE ON SLICE SIZE.
003786 04-03

EFFECTS OF ENKEPHALIN, MORPHINE, AND NALOXONE ON THE ELECTRICAL-ACTIVITY OF THE IN VITRO HIPPOCAMPAL SLICE PREPARATION.
003918 04-03

SLICES
REDUCTION OF OPIATE BINDING TO BRAINSTEM SLICES ASSOCIATED WITH THE DEVELOPMENT OF TOLERANCE TO MORPHINE IN RATS.
000066 01-03

AGONIST-INDUCED CHANGES IN BETA-ADRENERGIC-RECEPTOR DENSITY AND RECEPTOR-MEDIATED RESPONSIVENESS IN SLICES OF RAT-CEREBRAL-CORTEX.
000072 01-03

ALPHA-ADRENOCEPTOR-MEDIATED MODULATION OF 5 HYDROXYTRYPTAMINE RELEASE FROM RAT-BRAIN-CORTEX SLICES.
000111 01-03

THE ROLE OF INTRANEURONAL 5 HT AND OF TRYPTOPHAN-HYDROXYLASE ACTIVATION IN THE CONTROL OF 5 HT SYNTHESIS IN RAT-BRAIN SLICES INCUBATED IN K-ENRICHED MEDIUM.
000123 01-03

ACTIONS OF CHLORPROMAZINE, HALOPERIDOL AND PIMOZIDE ON LIPID METABOLISM IN GUINEA-PIG BRAIN SLICES.
000129 01-03

GABA INHIBITION OF 3H GLYCINE RELEASE FROM SLICES OF RAT SUBSTANTIA-NIGRA IN VITRO.
000157 01-03

REUPTAKE OF BIOGENIC-AMINES BY BRAIN SLICES: EFFECT OF HYDROCORTISONE.
000187 01-03

INHIBITION OF NEURONAL UPTAKE REDUCES THE PRESYNAPTIC EFFECTS OF CLONIDINE BUT NOT OF ALPHA METHYLNORADRENALINE ON THE STIMULATION-EVOKED RELEASE OF 3H NORADRENALINE FROM RAT OCCIPITAL-CORTEX SLICES.
000227 01-03

(3H)ACETYLCHOLINE AND (3H)5 HYDROXYTRYPTAMINE RELEASE FROM RAT-MIDBRAIN SLICES AND THE EFFECTS OF CALCIUM AND PHENOBARBITAL.
000251 01-03

(3H)QUINUCLIDINYL-BENZILATE BINDING TO MUSCARINIC-RECEPTORS AND (3H)WB-4101 BINDING TO ALPHA-ADRENERGIC-RECEPTORS IN RABBIT IRIS: COMPARISON OF RESULTS IN SLICES AND MICROSOMAL FRACTIONS.
000299 01-03

ON THE CAPACITY OF PRESYNAPTIC ALPHA-RECEPTORS TO MODULATE NOREPINEPHRINE RELEASE FROM SLICES OF RAT NEOCORTEX AND THE AFFINITY OF SOME AGONISTS AND ANTAGONISTS FOR THESE RECEPTORS.
000323 01-03

ELECTRON MICROSCOPIC STUDIES OF BRAIN SLICES: THE EFFECTS OF HIGH-FREQUENCY STIMULATION ON DENDRITIC ULTRASTRUCTURE. (UNPUBLISHED PAPER).
001036 02-01

FACTORS INFLUENCING THE RELEASE OF LABELLED GAMMA AMINOBUTYRIC-ACID AND ACETYLCHOLINE EVOKED BY ELECTRICAL-STIMULATION WITH ALTERNATING POLARITY FROM RAT CORTICAL SLICES.
001130 02-03

NORADRENALINE RELEASE FROM SLICES OF THE THALAMUS OF NORMAL AND MORPHINE-DEPENDENT RATS.
001142 02-03

A COMPARISON OF THE EFFECTS OF METHYLPHENIDATE AND AMPHETAMINE ON THE SIMULTANEOUS RELEASE OF RADIOLABELLED DOPAMINE AND P OR M TYRAMINE FROM RAT STRIATAL SLICES.
001207 02-03

EFFECTS OF HALOPEMIDE ON POTASSIUM-INDUCED RELEASE OF RADIOLABELED NEUROTRANSMITTERS FROM RAT CEREBROCORTICAL SLICES IN VITRO.
001347 02-03

CHARACTERIZATION AND RADIOAUTOGRAPHY OF (3H)LSD BINDING BY RAT-BRAIN SLICES IN VITRO: THE EFFECT OF 5 HYDROXYTRYPTAMINE.
001369 02-03

STUDIES ON THE EFFECT OF ALPHA MELANOCYTE-STIMULATING-HORMONE AND RELATED PEPTIDES ON THE ACCUMULATION OF P AMINOHIPPURIC-ACID IN RENAL CORTICAL SLICES. (UNPUBLISHED PAPER).
001372 02-03

LOCALIZATION OF SENSITIVE SITES TO TAURINE, GAMMA AMINOBUTYRIC-ACID, GLYCINE AND BETA ALANINE IN THE MOLECULAR LAYER OF GUINEA-PIG CEREBELLAR SLICES.
001402 02-03

INHIBITORY ACTIONS OF TAUROCYAMINE, HYPOTAURINE, HOMOTAURINE, TAURINE AND GABA ON SPIKE DISCHARGES OF PURKINJE-CELLS, AND LOCALIZATION OF SENSITIVE SITES, IN GUINEA-PIG CEREBELLAR SLICES.
002846 03-03

GABA AND BACLOFEN POTENTIATE THE K-EVOKED RELEASE OF METHIONINE-ENKEPHALIN FROM RAT STRIATAL SLICES.
002882 03-03

METHYLXANTHINES MODULATE ADENOSINE RELEASE FROM SLICES OF CEREBRAL-CORTEX.
002907 03-03

SOMATOSTATIN FACILITATES THE SEROTONIN RELEASE FROM RAT-CEREBRAL-CORTEX, HIPPOCAMPUS, AND HYPOTHALAMUS SLICES.
002913 03-03

STIMULATORY EFFECT OF SOMATOSTATIN ON NOREPINEPHRINE RELEASE FROM RAT-BRAIN-CORTEX SLICES.
002920 03-03

MODIFIED CUP TECHNIQUE FOR MICROESTIMATION OF THE RELEASE AND UPTAKE OF NEUROTRANSMITTERS IN BRAIN SLICES.
003147 03-06

THE EFFECTS OF ANTIDEPRESSANTS ON THE RETENTION AND METABOLISM OF (3H) NOREPINEPHRINE IN RAT-BRAIN SLICES.
003763 04-03

GABA-ENHANCEMENT OF (3H)DOPAMINE RELEASE FROM SLICES OF RAT STRIATUM: DEPENDENCE ON SLICE SIZE.
003786 04-03

THE UPTAKE OF CARNITINE BY SLICES OF RAT-CEREBRAL-CORTEX.
003853 04-03

INVESTIGATION OF ACTION OF ENKEPHALIN ON THE SPONTANEOUS AND EVOKED RELEASE OF ACETYLCHOLINE FROM RAT CORTICAL AND STRIATAL SLICES.
003862 04-03

ADENOSINE AND CYCLIC-AMP IN RAT-CEREBRAL-CORTICAL SLICES: EFFECTS OF ADENOSINE UPTAKE INHIBITORS AND ADENOSINE-DEAMINASE INHIBITORS.
003950 04-03

EFFECT OF PROSTAGLANDIN-D2, PROSTAGLANDIN-E2 AND PROSTAGLANDIN-F2ALPHA ON CATECHOLAMINE RELEASE FROM SLICES OF RAT AND RABBIT BRAIN.
003983 04-03

INHIBITION OF THE SYNTHESIS OF ACETYLCHOLINE IN RAT-BRAIN SLICES BY (-) HYDROXYCITRATE AND CITRATE.
004044 04-03

THE EFFECT OF NORADRENALINE ON NA-K TRANSPORT IN RAT-CEREBRAL-CORTICAL SLICES.
004056 04-03

SLIME
DEVELOPMENTALLY REGULATED LECTINS IN SLIME MOULDS AND CHICK TISSUES – ARE THEY CELL ADHESION MOLECULES?
003724 04-03

SMALL-DOSE
SMALL-DOSE INTRAVENOUS HEROIN FACILITATES HYPOTHALAMIC SELF-STIMULATION WITHOUT RESPONSE SUPPRESSION IN RATS.
002999 03-04

SMOKING
NALOXONE REDUCES CIGARETTE SMOKING.
000808 01-14

PLASMA DELTA9 TETRAHYDROCANNABINOL CONCENTRATIONS AND CLINICAL-EFFECTS AFTER ORAL AND INTRAVENOUS ADMINISTRATION AND SMOKING.
002201 02-12

THE USE OF NICOTINE CHEWING-GUM AS AN AID TO STOPPING SMOKING.
002343 02-14

SMOKING AND VIGILANCE: THE EFFECTS OF TOBACCO SMOKING ON CFF AS RELATED TO PERSONALITY AND SMOKING HABITS.
002368 02-14

THE SMOKING HABIT AND PSYCHOPHARMACOLOGICAL-EFFECTS OF NICOTINE.
003577 03-17

THE ROLE OF NICOTINE IN THE BEHAVIORAL-ASPECTS OF CIGARETTE SMOKING.
004575 04-14

SMOOTH-MUSCLE
POTENTIATION OF THE EFFECTS OF ADENOSINE ON ISOLATED CARDIAC-MUSCLE AND SMOOTH-MUSCLE BY DIAZEPAM.
004266 04-05

SMOOTH-PURSUIT
DISORDERS OF SMOOTH-PURSUIT EYE-MOVEMENTS IN SCHIZOPHRENICS AND THE EFFECT OF NEUROLEPTICS IN THERAPEUTIC DOSES.
001912 02-08
QUANTITATIVE ASSESSMENT OF SMOOTH-PURSUIT EYE-MOVEMENTS IN HEALTHY AND EPILEPTIC-SUBJECTS.
002376 02-15
SMOOTH-PURSUIT EYE-MOVEMENTS: EFFECTS OF ALCOHOL AND CHLORAL-HYDRATE.
003448 03-14

SNAKES
THE EFFECTS OF ALPHA AND BETA NEUROTOXINS FROM THE VENOMS OF VARIOUS SNAKES ON TRANSMISSION IN AUTONOMIC GANGLIA.
003750 04-03

SOCIAL
TESTOSTERONE AND PERSISTENCE OF SOCIAL INVESTIGATION IN LABORATORY RATS.
000488 01-04
SOCIAL AND CLINICAL SIGNIFICANCE OF DETERMINING THE BARBITURATE LEVEL IN THE BLOOD SERUM OF PATIENTS TREATED WITH ANTIEPILEPTIC-DRUGS.
000695 01-11
IMITATION, SOCIAL FACILITATION, AND THE EFFECTS OF ACTH4-10 ON RATS BAR-PRESSING-BEHAVIOR.
003009 03-04
LONG-LASTING EFFECTS OF CHRONIC ADMINISTRATION OF HALLUCINOGENIC-DRUGS ON RAT SOCIAL AND EMOTIONAL-BEHAVIOR. (PH.D. DISSERTATION).
003029 03-04
CONTRIBUTION OF SOCIAL FACTORS TO OPIATE-INDUCED ACTIVATION IN THE MOUSE.
004156 04-04
SOCIAL CROWDING ENHANCES AVERSIVENESS OF NALOXONE IN RATS.
004201 04-04
THE INTEGRITY OF THE SOCIAL HIERARCHY IN MICE FOLLOWING ADMINISTRATION OF PSYCHOTROPIC-DRUGS.
004202 04-04
PSYCHOPHARMACOLOGICAL AND SOCIAL ASPECTS OF SCHIZOPHRENIA: RECENT DEVELOPMENTS.
004336 04-08
THERAPY AND SOCIAL ADAPTATION OF OLIGOPHRENICS (REVIEW OF THE LITERATURE).
004444 04-11
THE EFFECTS OF NEUROLEPTIC-DRUGS ON THE SOCIAL INTERACTIONS OF HOSPITALIZED PSYCHOTIC-PATIENTS.
004577 04-14
HUMAN SOCIAL CONVERSATION: EFFECTS OF ETHANOL, SECOBARBITAL AND CHLORPROMAZINE.
004582 04-14

SOCIAL-ACTIVITY
NALOXONE REDUCES SOCIAL-ACTIVITY AND EXPLORATORY-ACTIVITY IN THE RAT.
001617 02-04

SOCIAL-BEHAVIOR
EFFECTS OF METHAQUALONE ON SOCIAL-BEHAVIOR IN MONKEYS (MACACA-MULATTA).
001594 02-04
LONG-TERM CHLORPROMAZINE IN RHESUS-MONKEYS: PRODUCTION OF DYSKINESIAS AND CHANGES IN SOCIAL-BEHAVIOR.
001850 02-05
A RESEARCH PARADIGM TO INVESTIGATE THE EFFECT OF MANIPULATION ON SOCIAL-BEHAVIOR IN GROUPS.
003007 03-04

SOCIAL-BEHAVIOUR
LONG-TERM EFFECTS OF TESTOSTERONE INJECTIONS ON THE SOCIAL-BEHAVIOUR OF MALE DUCKS AND THEIR PHYSIOLOGICAL-CORRELATES.
001565 02-04

SOCIAL-COLONY
THE ACUTE AND CHRONIC EFFECT OF 5 METHOXYTRYPTAMINE ON SELECTED MEMBERS OF A PRIMATE SOCIAL-COLONY.
001073 02-02

SOCIAL-COMFORT
OPIOID BLOCKADE AND SOCIAL-COMFORT IN CHICKS.
001745 02-04

SOCIAL-INTERACTION
THE USE OF SOCIAL-INTERACTION AS A METHOD FOR DETECTING ANXIOLYTIC-ACTIVITY OF CHLORDIAZEPOXIDE-LIKE DRUGS.
001866 02-06

SOCIAL-INTERACTIONS
CHRONIC DELTA9 TETRAHYDROCANNABINOL IN RATS: EFFECT ON SOCIAL-INTERACTIONS, MOUSE-KILLING, MOTOR-ACTIVITY, CONSUMMATORY-BEHAVIOR, AND BODY-TEMPERATURE.
001722 02-04
BEHAVIORAL-EFFECTS OF HASHISH IN MICE: III. SOCIAL-INTERACTIONS BETWEEN TWO RESIDENTS AND AN INTRUDER MALE.
001776 02-04
BEHAVIORAL-EFFECTS OF HASHISH IN MICE: I. SOCIAL-INTERACTIONS AND NEST-BUILDING-BEHAVIOR OF MALES.
001777 02-04

SOCIAL-ISOLATION
EFFECTS OF SOCIAL-ISOLATION ON MEMORY FORMATION.
001607 02-04
BRIEF SOCIAL-ISOLATION, PAIN RESPONSIVITY, AND MORPHINE ANALGESIA IN YOUNG RATS.
001744 02-04

SOCIAL-MALADJUSTMENTS
PIMOZIDE IN THE TREATMENT OF SOME SOCIAL-MALADJUSTMENTS IN PERSONALITY-DISORDERS.
002068 02-10

SOCIAL-PSYCHIATRY
SOCIAL-PSYCHIATRY AND PSYCHOPHARMACOLOGY.
002612 02-17

SOCIOPATHY
NEUROPEPTIDE TREATMENT OF SOCIOPATHY: RESEARCH IN PROGRESS.
002369 02-14

SOCIOSEXUAL-BEHAVIOUR
COMPARISON OF THE EFFECTS OF BETA ENDORPHIN AND MORPHINE ON EXPLORATORY-BEHAVIOUR AND SOCIOSEXUAL-BEHAVIOUR IN THE MALE RAT.
004178 04-04

SODIUM
THE INFLUENCE OF EXTERNAL SODIUM AND POTASSIUM ON LITHIUM UPTAKE BY PRIMARY BRAIN CELL CULTURES AT THERAPEUTIC LITHIUM CONCENTRATION.
001300 02-03
ALPHA2-ADRENERGIC AMINES, ADENOSINE AND PROSTAGLANDINS INHIBIT LIPOLYSIS AND CYCLIC-AMP ACCUMULATION IN HAMSTER ADIPOCYTES IN THE ABSENCE OF EXTRACELLULAR SODIUM.
002728 03-03
INCREASE OF C-GMP AND ACCUMULATION OF 45CA2 EVOKED BY DRUGS ACTING ON SODIUM OR POTASSIUM CHANNELS.
003709 04-03

SODIUM-AMOBARBITAL
DELIRIUM OR PSYCHOSIS? DIAGNOSTIC USE OF THE SODIUM-AMOBARBITAL INTERVIEW.
002167 02-11

SODIUM-CHLORIDE
SODIUM-CHLORIDE INHIBITION DECREASES LEVELS OF IMMUNOREACTIVE DYNORPHIN IN THE NEUROINTERMEDIATE PITUITARY OF RATS.
001283 02-03

SODIUM-DEPENDENT
SODIUM-DEPENDENT INTERACTION OF BENZAMIDES WITH DOPAMINE-RECEPTORS.
000285 01-03
EFFECTS OF DELTA9 TETRAHYDROCANNABINOL AND CANNABIDIOL ON SODIUM-DEPENDENT HIGH-AFFINITY CHOLINE UPTAKE IN THE RAT HIPPOCAMPUS.
003908 04-03

SODIUM-DIPROPYLACETATE
EFFECTS OF SODIUM-DIPROPYLACETATE, MUSCIMOL-HYDROBROMIDE AND (R,S) NIPECOTIC-ACID-AMIDE ON ISOLATION-INDUCED AGGRESSIVE-BEHAVIOR IN MICE.
001756 02-04
TOLERANCE STUDY IN PSYCHIATRIC-PATIENTS OF A NEW PREPARATION OF SODIUM-DIPROPYLACETATE.
003158 03-07
THE EFFECT OF SODIUM-DIPROPYLACETATE ON GAMMA AMINOBUTYRIC-ACID DEPENDENT INHIB..ION IN THE RAT-CORTEX AND SUBSTANTIA-NIGRA IN RELATION TO ITS ANTICONVULSANT ACTIVITY.
003880 04-03
EFFECT OF SODIUM-DIPROPYLACETATE ON CONFLICT-BEHAVIOR IN RATS.
004192 04-04

SODIUM-HYDROXYBUTYRATE
ACUTE EFFECT OF BENZOCTAMINE (10 MG), SODIUM-HYDROXYBUTYRATE (2 G) AND FENCAMFAMINE (10 MG) ON VERBAL-ASSOCIATIONS.
000806 01-14

SODIUM-ION
REGULATION OF RECEPTOR BINDING INTERACTIONS OF 125I ANGIOTENSIN-II AND 125I SARCOSINE1-LEUCINE8-ANGIOTENSIN-II, AN ANGIOTENSIN ANTAGONIST; BY SODIUM-ION.
001124 02-03

SODIUM-LACTATE
EFFECT OF SODIUM-LACTATE ON PATIENTS WITH PANIC-DISORDER AND MITRAL-VALVE PROLAPSE.
003409 03-13
BLOCKADE BY IMIPRAMINE OR DESIPRAMINE OF PANIC-INDUCED BY SODIUM-LACTATE.
004427 04-10

SODIUM-NUCLEINATE
THE USE OF SODIUM-NUCLEINATE IN THE TREATMENT OF SCHIZOPHRENIC-PATIENTS.
004339 04-08

SODIUM-PENTOBARBITAL
MODULATION OF CONDITIONED TASTE-AVERSION BY SODIUM-PENTOBARBITAL.
001596 02-04

SODIUM-PUMP
SHORT-TERM AND LONG-TERM MODIFICATION OF SKELETAL-MUSCLE SODIUM-PUMP ACTIVITY AND MUSCLE PROTEIN TURNOVER. (UNPUBLISHED PAPER).
001519 02-03

SODIUM-SALICYLATE
THE EFFECT OF SODIUM-SALICYLATE ON CEREBRAL BLOOD FLOW AND METABOLISM.
001416 02-03

SODIUM-VALPROATE
ANTAGONISM BY CLASSICAL ANTIEPILEPTICS AND SODIUM-VALPROATE OF CEFAZOLIN-INDUCED EXPERIMENTAL EPILEPSY IN RATS.
000442 01-04

SODIUM-VALPROATE IN SCHIZOPHRENIA: SOME BIOCHEMICAL-CORRELATES.
000561 01-08

ALBUMIN BINDING INTERACTIONS OF SODIUM-VALPROATE.
000762 01-13

MEAL-DEPENDENT ABSORPTION OF ENTERIC-COATED SODIUM-VALPROATE.
000777 01-13

PHENOBARBITONE AND SODIUM-VALPROATE INTERACTION: AN EXPERIMENTAL-STUDY.
001371 02-03

SODIUM-VALPROATE IN THE TREATMENT OF ALCOHOL WITHDRAWAL-SYNDROME.
002139 02-11

ELECTROENCEPHALOGRAPHIC-EFFECTS AND BEHAVIOURAL-EFFECTS OF SODIUM-VALPROATE IN PATIENTS WITH PHOTOSENSITIVE EPILEPSY. A SINGLE-DOSE TRIAL.
002154 02-11

HEPATOTOXICITY OF SODIUM-VALPROATE AND OTHER ANTICONVULSANTS IN RAT HEPATOCYTE CULTURES.
002422 02-15

EFFECT OF SODIUM-VALPROATE AND BACLOFEN IN TARDIVE-DYSKINESIA: CLINICAL-STUDIES AND NEUROENDOCRINE-STUDIES.
002441 02-15

INTERACTION OF CHLORDIAZEPOXIDE AND SODIUM-VALPROATE IN THE NUCLEUS-ACCUMBENS OF THE RAT.
002796 03-03

EFFECT OF SODIUM-VALPROATE ON MOTOR FUNCTION REGULATED BY THE ACTIVATION OF GABA-RECEPTORS.
003033 03-04

THE EFFECT OF SODIUM-VALPROATE ON MANIA: THE GABA HYPOTHESIS OF AFFECTIVE-DISORDERS.
003218 03-09

ON A POSSIBLE ROLE OF GABA IN MANIA. THERAPEUTIC-EFFICACY OF SODIUM-VALPROATE.
003219 03-09

DISSOCIATION BETWEEN FREE AND BOUND PHENYTOIN LEVELS IN PRESENCE OF SODIUM-VALPROATE.
003367 03-11

COMPARISON OF SODIUM-VALPROATE AND PHENYTOIN AS SINGLE DRUG-TREATMENT IN EPILEPSY.
003371 03-11

HUMAN BRAIN, PLASMA, AND CEREBROSPINAL-FLUID CONCENTRATION OF SODIUM-VALPROATE AFTER 72 HOURS OF THERAPY.
003433 03-13

ASTERIXIS ASSOCIATED WITH SODIUM-VALPROATE.
003468 03-15

CHANGES IN REGIONAL BRAIN LEVELS OF AMINO-ACID PUTATIVE NEUROTRANSMITTERS AFTER PROLONGED TREATMENT WITH THE ANTICONVULSANT-DRUGS DIPHENYLHYDANTOIN, PHENOBARBITONE, SODIUM-VALPROATE, ETHOSUXIMIDE, AND SULTHIAME IN THE RAT.
003961 04-03

EFFECT OF TREATMENT WITH SODIUM-VALPROATE AND DIAZEPAM ON PLASMA CORTICOTROPIN IN NELSONS-SYNDROME.
004463 04-11

THE EFFECT OF SODIUM-VALPROATE ON THE PHOTOSENSITIVE VEP.
004513 04-13

SOLID
SPECTRA OF RADICAL CATIONS OF PHENOTHIAZINE DERIVATIVES IN SOLUTION AND SOLID STATE.
003673 04-01

SOLUBILIZATION
SOLUBILIZATION OF ACTIVE OPIATE-RECEPTORS. (UNPUBLISHED PAPER).
001056 02-01

SOLUBILIZATION OF THE DIHYDROPICROTOXININ BINDING-SITES.
001192 02-03

DOPAMINE-RECEPTOR: FROM SYNAPTIC MEMBRANES TO SOLUBILIZATION.
001326 02-03

SOLUBILIZATION OF SEROTONIN-RECEPTORS FROM RAT-FRONTAL-CORTEX.
002489 02-16

SOLUBILIZATION OF NEUROLEPTIC/DOPAMINE-RECEPTORS OF HUMAN BRAIN STRIATUM.
003767 04-03

SOLUBILIZED
GABA-MODULIN REGULATES SOLUBILIZED BENZODIAZEPINE AND GABA RECOGNITION SITES. (UNPUBLISHED PAPER).
001263 02-03

SOLUBLE
GUANINE-NUCLEOTIDES INHIBIT BINDING OF AGONISTS AND ANTAGONISTS TO SOLUBLE OPIATE-RECEPTORS. (UNPUBLISHED PAPER).
001035 02-01

CORTICOSTERONE INCREASES THE SYNTHESIS OF A SOLUBLE PROTEIN IN PITUITARY-GLANDS FROM ADRENALECTOMIZED MALE RATS WHICH PRECIPITATES WITH ANTI-RAT GROWTH-HORMONE ANTISERUM. (UNPUBLISHED PAPER).
001122 02-03

ACTIVATION OF SOLUBLE STRIATAL TYROSINE-HYDROXYLASE IN THE RAT BRAIN AFTER CDP-CHOLINE ADMINISTRATION.
002816 03-03

SOLUTION
OPIATE-RECEPTORS IN MEMBRANES AND IN SOLUTION. (UNPUBLISHED PAPER).
001032 02-01

DOSE-RESPONSE RELATIONSHIP BETWEEN NALOXONE INJECTIONS AND INTAKE OF SUCROSE SOLUTION.
003118 03-04

SPECTRA OF RADICAL CATIONS OF PHENOTHIAZINE DERIVATIVES IN SOLUTION AND SOLID STATE.
003673 04-01

SOLVENTS
NMR SPECTRAL STUDY OF PROTON TRANSFER IN AMITRIPTYLINE-HYDROCHLORIDE CHLORDIAZEPOXIDE-HYDROCHLORIDE COMBINATIONS IN DIPOLAR APROTIC SOLVENTS.
003654 04-01

SOMAL
THE PATHOGENESIS OF PRIMARY INTERNODAL DEMYELINATION PRODUCED BY ACETYL-ETHYL-TETRAMETHYL-TETRALIN: EVIDENCE FOR PRESERVED SCHWANN-CELL SOMAL FUNCTION.
002905 03-03

SOMATIC
PROSTACYCLIN-DEPENDENT ACTIVATION OF ADENYLATE-CYCLASE IN A NEURONAL SOMATIC CELL HYBRID: PROSTANOID STRUCTURE-ACTIVITY RELATIONSHIPS.
001132 02-03

SOMATOSENSORY
PRESSURE REVERSAL OF THE EFFECT OF URETHANE ON THE EVOKED SOMATOSENSORY CORTICAL RESPONSE IN THE RAT.
001106 02-03

EFFECT OF OPIATES AND OPIATE ANTAGONISTS ON SOMATOSENSORY EVOKED-POTENTIALS IN PATIENTS WITH SCHIZOPHRENIA AND NORMAL ADULTS.
002222 02-13

DIFFERENCES IN CUTANEOUS SENSORY RESPONSE PROPERTIES OF SINGLE SOMATOSENSORY CORTICAL NEURONS IN AWAKE AND HALOTHANE ANESTHETIZED RATS.
002687 03-03

EFFECTS OF PENTOBARBITAL AND ETHANOL UPON SINGLE NEURON ACTIVITY IN THE PRIMARY SOMATOSENSORY CORTEX OF THE RHESUS-MONKEY.
003755 04-03

SOMATOSTATIN
COMPARATIVE-EFFECTS OF SOMATOSTATIN AND ENKEPHALINS ON THE GUINEA-PIG ILEUM AND THE RAT VAS-DEFERENS.
001302 02-03

SOMATOSTATIN FACILITATES THE SEROTONIN RELEASE FROM RAT-CEREBRAL-CORTEX, HIPPOCAMPUS, AND HYPOTHALAMUS SLICES.
002913 03-03

STIMULATORY EFFECT OF SOMATOSTATIN ON NOREPINEPHRINE RELEASE FROM RAT-BRAIN-CORTEX SLICES.
002920 03-03

PHARMACOLOGICAL CHARACTERIZATION OF SCRATCHING-BEHAVIOUR INDUCED BY INTRACRANIAL INJECTION OF SUBSTANCE-P AND SOMATOSTATIN.
002980 03-04

SOMATOSTATIN-28
HIGH-AFFINITY BINDING-SITES FOR A SOMATOSTATIN-28 ANALOG IN RAT-BRAIN.
003985 04-03

SOMATOTHERAPEUTIC
THE EFFECT OF LONG-TERM MAINTENANCE-THERAPY ON SCHIZOPHRENIC-PATIENTS USING SOMATOTHERAPEUTIC MEASURES.
004325 04-08

SOMATOTROPIN
PROLACTIN AND SOMATOTROPIN RESPONSES TO TRH IN SCHIZOPHRENIC-PATIENTS.
000570 01-08

SOMATOTYPY
DIFFERENTIAL-EFFECTS OF SYSTEMIC VERSUS INTRACRANIAL INJECTION OF OPIATES ON CENTRAL, OROFACIAL AND LOWER BODY NOCICEPTION: SOMATOTYPY IN BULBAR ANALGESIA SYSTEMS.
001446 02-03

SOMNAMBULISM
THE CLASSIFICATION OF SLEEP-DISORDERS AND THE TREATMENT OF VARIOUS FORMS OF SOMNAMBULISM.
004461 04-11

SORPTION
SORPTION OF CHLORMETHIAZOLE BY INTRAVENOUS INFUSION GIVING SETS.
002508 02-16

SOTALOL
EFFECTS OF THE BETA-ADRENOCEPTOR BLOCKING-AGENT SOTALOL ON CNS: SLEEP, EEG, AND PSYCHOPHYSIOLOGICAL PARAMETERS.
001570 02-04

SOUND-INDUCED
ENERGY RESERVES AND SOUND-INDUCED SEIZURES. (UNPUBLISHED PAPER).
001467 02-03
NORADRENERGIC INFLUENCES ON SOUND-INDUCED SEIZURES.
004137 04-04

SOUPS
TYRAMINE CONTENT OF CANNED AND PACKET SOUPS.
002394 02-15

SOUTH
RESULTS OF TREATMENT BY MODITEN DEPOT IN OUTPATIENTS-WARDS IN THE SOUTH MORAVIAN REGION.
004648 04-15

SOVIET
A PHARMACOLOGICAL-STUDY OF THE NEW SOVIET ANTIDEPRESSANT INKASAN.
000008 01-02
ISOLATION OF PSYCHOACTIVE CANNABINOID PRECURSORS FROM CANNABIS OF SOVIET PROVENIENCE GROWN IN MISSISSIPPI.
001023 02-01

SP-111
DELTA9 THC AS A DISCRIMINATIVE-STIMULUS IN RATS AND PIGEONS: GENERALIZATION TO THC METABOLITES AND SP-111.
001666 02-04

SPACE
DEPRESSION OF RESERPINE-INDUCED MUSCULAR RIGIDITY IN RATS AFTER ADMINISTRATION OF LISURIDE INTO THE SPINAL SUBARACHNOID-SPACE.
002962 03-04

SPACES
MORPHINE ANALGESIA FOLLOWING ITS INFUSION INTO DIFFERENT LIQUOR SPACES IN RAT-BRAIN.
001429 02-03

SPACING
AROUSAL AND SHORT-TERM MEMORY: EFFECTS OF CAFFEINE AND TRIAL SPACING ON DELAYED ALTERNATION PERFORMANCE.
000487 01-04

SPAIN
RESULTS OF A SURVEY ON THE PRESENT TREATMENT OF DEPRESSION IN SPAIN.
001963 02-09

SPARING
ANESTHETICS AND THE HABENULO-INTERPEDUNCULAR SYSTEM: SELECTIVE SPARING OF METABOLIC ACTIVITY.
003833 04-03

SPASTICITY
EFFECT OF DIAZEPAM AND DESMETHYLDIAZEPAM IN SPASTICITY AND RIGIDITY: A QUANTITATIVE STUDY OF REFLEXES AND PLASMA CONCENTRATIONS.
000701 01-11

SPECIAL-CHILD
DRUGS AND THE SPECIAL-CHILD.
002107 02-11

SPECIALIZATION
PHARMACOLOGICAL EVIDENCE ON THE SPECIALIZATION OF CNS MECHANISMS RESPONSIBLE FOR MOTOR ACT INHIBITION BY AVERSIVE EVENTS.
002671 03-03

SPECIES
RIA AND HPLC EVIDENCE FOR THE PRESENCE OF METHIONINE-ENKEPHALIN AND CHOLECYSTOKININ IN THE NEURAL RETINA OF SEVERAL VERTEBRATE SPECIES. (UNPUBLISHED PAPER).
001017 02-01
A COMPARATIVE-STUDY OF THE PHARMACOLOGICAL-PROPERTIES OF THE POSITIVE POTENTIAL RECORDED FROM THE SUPERIOR CERVICAL GANGLIA OF SEVERAL SPECIES.
003779 04-03
OXIDATION OF BETA PHENYLETHYLAMINE BY BOTH TYPES OF MONOAMINE-OXIDASE: EXAMINATION OF ENZYMES IN BRAIN AND LIVER MITOCHONDRIA OF EIGHT SPECIES.
004024 04-03

SPECIES-DIFFERENCES
SPECIES-DIFFERENCES IN CLOBAZAM METABOLISM AND ANTILEPTAZOL EFFECT.
001157 02-03
SPECIES-DIFFERENCES IN THE DEAMINATION OF DOPAMINE AND OTHER SUBSTRATES FOR MONOAMINE-OXIDASE IN BRAIN.
002233 02-13

COMPARATIVE-STUDY ON THE EFFECT OF MORPHINE AND THE OPIOID-LIKE PEPTIDES IN THE VAS-DEFERENS OF RODENTS: STRAIN AND SPECIES-DIFFERENCES, EVIDENCE FOR MULTIPLE OPIATE-RECEPTORS.
002757 03-03

SPECIFICITY
STUDIES ON THE SPECIFICITY AND REVERSAL OF NEUROLEPTIC-INDUCED DOPAMINERGIC-SUPERSENSITIVITY. (PH.D. DISSERTATION).
001469 02-03
AN ANALYSIS-OF SPECIFICITY OF DRUG-INDUCED CHANGES IN DRUG-REINFORCED RESPONDING. (PH.D. DISSERTATION).
003010 03-04
CROSS-OVER STUDY OF ZIMELIDINE AND DESIPRAMINE IN DEPRESSION: EVIDENCE FOR AMINE SPECIFICITY.
003250 03-09
LACK OF SPECIFICITY OF AN ANIMAL BEHAVIOR MODEL FOR HALLUCINOGENIC DRUG ACTION.
004250 04-04
CHOLINERGIC MECHANISMS IN MANIA AND DEPRESSION: QUESTIONS OF SPECIFICITY.
004374 04-09
A SENSITIVE BENZODIAZEPINE RADIOIMMUNOASSAY OF BROAD SPECIFICITY.
004693 04-16

SPECTRA
THE QUANTITATIVE MEASUREMENT OF CHANGES IN EEG FREQUENCY SPECTRA PRODUCED IN THE CAT BY SEDATIVE HYPNOTICS AND NEUROLEPTICS.
001220 02-03
EFFECT OF PIRACETAM ON EEG SPECTRA OF BOYS WITH LEARNING-DISORDERS.
003383 03-11
SPECTRA OF RADICAL CATIONS OF PHENOTHIAZINE DERIVATIVES IN SOLUTION AND SOLID STATE.
003673 04-01
A MULTIVARIATE ANALYSIS OF THE INFRARED SPECTRA OF DRUGS OF ABUSE.
004688 04-16

SPECTRAL
POWER SPECTRAL ANALYSIS OF THE FLASH-EVOKED AFTERDISCHARGE.
003133 03-06
NMR SPECTRAL STUDY OF PROTON TRANSFER IN AMITRIPTYLINE-HYDROCHLORIDE CHLORDIAZEPOXIDE-HYDROCHLORIDE COMBINATIONS IN DIPOLAR APROTIC SOLVENTS.
003654 04-01

SPECTROFLUOROMETRIC
COMPARISON OF SPECTROFLUOROMETRIC AND GAS-CHROMATOGRAPHY/MASS-SPECTROMETRY PROCEDURES FOR THE QUANTITATION OF MORPHINE IN BLOOD AND BRAIN.
004692 04-16

SPECTROPHOTOMETRY
A COMPARISON OF RADIOIMMUNOASSAY WITH SPECTROPHOTOMETRY FOR THE DETERMINATION OF PLASMA DIPHENYLHYDANTOIN CONCENTRATIONS.
004684 04-16

SPECTROSCOPY
BETA ENDORPHIN AND ANALOGS: 360 MHZ PROTON NMR SPECTROSCOPY.
001028 02-01
COMPARISON OF HIGHLY-ACTIVE AND ACTIVITY DEPLETED HEPARIN BY CIRCULAR DICHROISM SPECTROSCOPY. (UNPUBLISHED PAPER).
001057 02-01

SPEECH
PRINCIPAL AND DIFFERENTIAL-EFFECTS OF HALOPERIDOL AND PLACEBO TREATMENTS UPON SPEECH DISFLUENCIES IN STUTTERERS.
000713 01-11
DOPAMINERGIC-SYSTEMS AND SPEECH FLUENCY.
000821 01-14

SPERMATOGENIC
CYCLOPHOSPHAMIDE-INDUCED SPERMATOGENIC EFFECTS DETECTED IN THE F1-GENERATION BY BEHAVIORAL-TESTING.
003121 03-05

SPHINGOMYELINASE
PARTIAL PURIFICATION OF ACID SPHINGOMYELINASE FROM NORMAL AND PATHOLOGICAL (M. NIEMANN-PICK TYPE C) HUMAN BRAIN.
003671 04-01

SPIKE
INHIBITORY ACTIONS OF TAUROCYAMINE, HYPOTAURINE, HOMOTAURINE, TAURINE AND GABA ON SPIKE DISCHARGES OF PURKINJE-CELLS, AND LOCALIZATION OF SENSITIVE SITES, IN GUINEA-PIG CEREBELLAR SLICES.
002846 03-03

SPIKES
ACTIVATION OF CORTICAL CIRCUITS DURING INTERICTAL SPIKES.
000056 01-03
THE EFFECT OF CLONAZEPAM ON ATROPINE SPIKES IN THE LIMBIC-SYSTEM.
001274 02-03

SPIN
ESR STUDIES OF SPIN LABELLED BOVINE LIVER MONOAMINE-OXIDASE-B. (UNPUBLISHED PAPER).
001065 02-01

SPINAL
(-)PENTOBARBITAL OPENS ION-CHANNELS OF LONG-DURATION IN CULTURED MOUSE SPINAL NEURONS.
000198 01-03
MICROIONTOPHORETIC STUDIES ON NORADRENERGIC INHIBITION FROM LOCUS-COERULEUS OF SPINAL TRIGEMINAL-NUCLEUS NEURONS.
000260 01-03
ATTEMPTS TO REINSTATE LORDOSIS REFLEX IN ESTROGEN-PRIMED SPINAL FEMALE RATS WITH MONOAMINE AGONISTS.
000421 01-04
GAMMA AMINOBUTYRIC-ACID AGONISTS: AN IN VITRO COMPARISON BETWEEN DEPRESSION OF SPINAL SYNAPTIC ACTIVITY AND DEPOLARIZATION OF SPINAL ROOT FIBRES IN THE RAT.
001104 02-03
MORPHINE AND SUPRASPINAL INHIBITION OF SPINAL NEURONES: EVIDENCE THAT MORPHINE DECREASES TONIC DESCENDING INHIBITION IN THE ANESTHETIZED CAT.
001203 02-03
ELECTROMYOGRAPHIC-ASSESSMENT OF SPINAL REFLEXES IN EXPERIMENTALLY DEPRESSED DOGS TREATED WITH ANTIDEPRESSANTS.
001620 02-04
BACLOFEN IN TRIGEMINAL-NEURALGIA: ITS EFFECT ON THE SPINAL TRIGEMINAL-NUCLEUS: A PILOT-STUDY.
002122 02-11
GABA ANALOGUES ACTIVATE CHANNELS OF DIFFERENT DURATION ON CULTURED MOUSE SPINAL NEURONS.
002665 03-03
OPIATE ANTAGONIST IMPROVES NEUROLOGIC RECOVERY AFTER SPINAL INJURY.
002714 03-03
METHYSERGIDE AND SUPRASPINAL INHIBITION OF THE SPINAL TRANSMISSION OF NOCICEPTIVE INFORMATION IN THE ANESTHETIZED CAT.
002740 03-03
NONSEROTONERGIC DEPRESSION OF SPINAL MONOSYNAPTIC REFLEX TRANSMISSION BY 5 HYDROXYTRYPTOPHAN.
002745 03-03
EVIDENCE THAT THE OPIATE-RECEPTORS OF THE SUBSTANTIA-GELATINOSA CONTRIBUTE TO THE DEPRESSION, BY INTRAVENOUS MORPHINE, OF THE SPINAL TRANSMISSION OF IMPULSES IN UNMYELINATED PRIMARY AFFERENTS.
002767 03-03
POTENTIATION OF L GLUTAMATE AND L ASPARTATE EXCITATION OF CAT SPINAL NEURONES BY THE STEREOISOMERS OF THREO-3-HYDROXYASPARTATE.
002768 03-03
THE INTERACTION BETWEEN BARBITURATE ANESTHETICS AND EXCITATORY AMINO-ACID RESPONSES ON CAT SPINAL NEURONES.
002799 03-03
L HISTIDINE: EFFECTS ON SENSITIVITY OF CAT SPINAL NEURONES TO AMINO-ACIDS.
002808 03-03
EXCITATORY AND INHIBITORY-ACTIONS OF IBOTENIC-ACID ON FROG SPINAL MOTONEURONES IN VITRO.
002841 03-03
VOLTAGE CLAMP STUDY OF CAT SPINAL MOTONEURONS DURING STRYCHNINE-INDUCED SEIZURES.
002886 03-03
SPINAL MODULATION OF THE ACOUSTIC STARTLE RESPONSE: THE ROLE OF NOREPINEPHRINE, SEROTONIN AND DOPAMINE.
002950 03-04
DEPRESSION OF RESERPINE-INDUCED MUSCULAR RIGIDITY IN RATS AFTER ADMINISTRATION OF LISURIDE INTO THE SPINAL SUBARACHNOID SPACE.
002962 03-04
THE USE OF LITHIUM-CARBONATE FOR TREATING KUGELBERG-WELANDER SPINAL AMYOTROPHY PATIENTS.
003326 03-11
DENERVATION SUPERSENSITIVITY TO 5 HYDROXYTRYPTOPHAN IN RATS FOLLOWING SPINAL TRANSECTION AND 5,7 DIHYDROXYTRYPTAMINE INJECTION.
003722 04-03

SPINAL-CORD
THE EFFECTS OF MORPHINE ON THE ACTIVITY OF CERTAIN DORSAL-HORN NEURONS OF THE SPINAL-CORD INVOLVED IN NOCICEPTIVE PROCESSES.
000028 01-03
STEREOSPECIFIC BINDING OF 3H HALOPERIDOL IN RAT DORSAL SPINAL-CORD.
000070 01-03
EFFECT OF ACUTE ADMINISTRATION OF MORPHINE ON NEWLY SYNTHESIZED 5 HYDROXYTRYPTAMINE IN SPINAL-CORD OF THE RAT.
000110 01-03
NALOXONE ANTAGONISM OF GABA-EVOKED MEMBRANE POLARIZATIONS IN CULTURED MOUSE SPINAL-CORD NEURONS.
000116 01-03

EFFECTS OF GAMMA ACETYLENIC-GABA AND GAMMA VINYL-GABA ON ELECTRICALLY-INDUCED SPINAL-CORD CONVULSIONS AND ON SPINAL-CORD GABA CONCENTRATION.
000145 01-03
THE EFFECTS OF RESERPINE, IPRONIAZID AND L-DOPA ON ELECTRICALLY-INDUCED SPINAL-CORD SEIZURES.
000146 01-03
REDUCTION OF FETAL RAT SPINAL-CORD VOLUME FOLLOWING MATERNAL MORPHINE INJECTION.
000161 01-03
EFFECTS OF ENKEPHALIN ANALOGUE AND NALOXONE ON CAT SPINAL-CORD DORSAL ROOT POTENTIALS.
000236 01-03
EFFECTS OF RAPHE-MAGNUS AND RAPHE-PALLIDUS LESIONS ON MORPHINE-INDUCED ANALGESIA AND SPINAL-CORD MONOAMINES.
001420 02-03
5 METHOXYDIMETHYLTRYPTAMINE: SPINAL-CORD AND BRAINSTEM MEDIATION OF EXCITATORY EFFECTS ON ACOUSTIC STARTLE.
001605 02-04
IMMUNOHISTOCHEMICAL LOCALIZATION OF LEUCINE-ENKEPHALIN IN THE SPINAL-CORD OF THE CAT: ENKEPHALIN-CONTAINING MARGINAL NEURONS AND PAIN MODULATION.
002638 03-01
DIFFERENTIATION OF KAINATE AND QUISQUALATE-RECEPTORS IN THE CAT SPINAL-CORD BY SELECTIVE ANTAGONISMS WITH GAMMA D(AND L) GLUTAMYLGLYCINE.
002696 03-03
DOPAMINE AS A POSSIBLE NEUROTRANSMITTER IN THE SPINAL-CORD.
002705 03-03
DEPRESSION OF VENTRAL ROOT DORSAL ROOT POTENTIAL BY DL ALPHA AMINOADIPATE IN FROG SPINAL-CORD.
002755 03-03
THE EFFECT OF MONOAMINES ON MOTONEURONS OF THE ISOLATED RAT SPINAL-CORD.
002790 03-03
THE NEUROLATHYROGEN, BETA N OXALYL-L-ALPHA-BETA-DIAMINOPROPIONIC-ACID, IS A POTENT AGONIST AT GLUTAMATE PREFERRING RECEPTORS IN THE FROG SPINAL-CORD.
002858 03-03
DOPAMINE-ACTIVATED ADENYLATE-CYCLASE OF SPINAL-CORD: SUPERSENSITIVITY FOLLOWING TRANSECTION OF THE CORD.
003800 04-03
NERVE GROWTH-FACTOR STIMULATES DEVELOPMENT OF SUBSTANCE-P IN THE EMBRYONIC SPINAL-CORD.
003881 04-03
THE INACTIVATION OF GAMMA AMINOBUTYRIC-ACID-TRANSAMINASE IN DISSOCIATED NEURONAL CULTURES FROM SPINAL-CORD.
003980 04-03
EFFECTS OF NOREPINEPHRINE AND 5 HYDROXYTRYPTAMINE REUPTAKE INHIBITORS ON ELECTRICALLY-INDUCED SPINAL-CORD SEIZURES IN RATS.
004144 04-04
EFFECTS OF FLUOXETINE ON ELECTRICALLY-INDUCED SPINAL-CORD SEIZURES IN RATS.
004145 04-04
DOPAMINERGIC NEURONS OF SPINAL-CORD: A POSSIBLE SITE FOR THE ACTION OF NEUROLEPTIC-DRUGS.
004188 04-04
BEHAVIORAL-EVIDENCE THAT SUBSTANCE-P MAY BE A SPINAL-CORD SENSORY NEUROTRANSMITTER.
004200 04-04
SPINAL-CORD PHARMACOLOGY OF ADRENERGIC AGONIST-MEDIATED ANTINOCICEPTION.
004206 04-04
ANTAGONISM BY PHENOXYBENZAMINE AND PENTAZOCINE OF THE ANTINOCICEPTIVE-EFFECTS OF MORPHINE IN THE SPINAL-CORD.
004213 04-04

SPINAL-FLUID
METHODOLOGICAL-ISSUES IN SPINAL-FLUID STUDIES OF SCHIZOPHRENIA: THE CASE OF NOREPINEPHRINE AND DOPAMINE-BETA-HYDROXYLASE. (UNPUBLISHED PAPER).
001952 02-08

SPINOCEREBELLAR
SPINOCEREBELLAR DEGENERATION WITH PARKINSONIAN FEATURES: A CLINICAL AND PATHOLOGICAL REPORT.
003436 03-13

SPIPERONE
INHIBITION OF IN VIVO 3H SPIPERONE BINDING BY THE PROPOSED ANTIPSYCHOTIC DES-TYR1-GAMMA-ENDORPHIN.
000226 01-03
BIOCHEMICAL-PROPERTIES OF SPIPERONE BINDING TO RAT-BRAIN MEMBRANES.
000294 01-03
IN VIVO (3H)SPIPERONE BINDING TO THE RAT HIPPOCAMPAL FORMATION: INVOLVEMENT OF DOPAMINE-RECEPTORS.
001131 02-03
EFFECTS OF SPIPERONE ALONE AND IN COMBINATION WITH ANORECTIC-AGENTS ON FEEDING PARAMETERS IN THE RAT.
001598 02-04

EFFECT OF MAZINDOL ON BRAIN DOPAMINE TURNOVER IN SPIPERONE TREATED RATS.
002726 03-03
EFFECT OF CHRONIC SULPIRIDE ON STRIATAL SPIPERONE BINDING.
003720 04-03
DOPAMINE-RECEPTORS IN SUBCELLULAR FRACTIONS FROM BOVINE CAUDATE: ENRICHMENT OF (3H)SPIPERONE BINDING IN A POSTSYNAPTIC MEMBRANE FRACTION.
003948 04-03
CATION REGULATION DIFFERENTIATES SPECIFIC BINDING OF (3H)SULPIRIDE AND (3H)SPIPERONE TO RAT STRIATAL PREPARATIONS.
004032 04-03

SPIROPERIDOL
INCREASED MESOLIMBIC 3H SPIROPERIDOL BINDING IN 4 WEEK OLD OFFSPRING OF NURSING RAT MOTHERS TREATED WITH PENFLURIDOL.
000087 01-03
DOES (3H)SPIROPERIDOL LABEL A 5 HT-RECEPTOR IN THE FRONTAL-CORTEX OF THE RAT?.
000206 01-03
DECREASED SPIROPERIDOL AND LSD BINDING IN RAT-BRAIN AFTER CONTINUOUS AMPHETAMINE.
000216 01-03
EFFECTS OF CHRONIC HALOPERIDOL ON CAUDATE 3H SPIROPERIDOL BINDING IN LESIONED RATS.
000255 01-03
FACILITATION OF SELF-STIMULATION OF THE PREFRONTAL-CORTEX IN RATS FOLLOWING CHRONIC ADMINISTRATION OF SPIROPERIDOL OR AMPHETAMINE.
000457 01-04
IDENTIFICATION AND PARTIAL PURIFICATION OF A HYDROPHOBIC PROTEIN COMPONENT ASSOCIATED WITH (3H)SPIROPERIDOL BINDING-ACTIVITY. (UNPUBLISHED PAPER).
001007 02-01
CHRONIC LITHIUM REDUCES (3H)SPIROPERIDOL BINDING IN RAT STRIATUM.
001443 02-03
EFFECTS OF HALOPERIDOL AND D-AMPHETAMINE ON IN VIVO 3H SPIROPERIDOL BINDING IN THE RAT-FOREBRAIN.
001461 02-03
THE INFLUENCE OF ANTERIOR NEOSTRIATAL LESIONS ON THE BEHAVIOURAL-EFFECTS OF SPIROPERIDOL IN RATS.
001702 02-04
REGULATION BY CATIONS OF (3H)SPIROPERIDOL BINDING ASSOCIATED WITH DOPAMINE-RECEPTORS OF RAT-BRAIN.
002922 03-03
THE EFFECT OF TYPICAL AND ATYPICAL NEUROLEPTICS ON BINDING OF (3H)SPIROPERIDOL IN CALF CAUDATE.
003906 04-03
REGULATION OF SEROTONIN2-RECEPTORS (5 HT2) LABELED WITH (3H)SPIROPERIDOL BY CHRONIC-TREATMENT WITH THE ANTIDEPRESSANT AMITRIPTYLINE.
003964 04-03
THE RELATIONSHIP BETWEEN LOSS OF DOPAMINE NERVE TERMINALS, STRIATAL (3H)SPIROPERIDOL BINDING AND ROTATIONAL-BEHAVIOR IN UNILATERALLY 6 HYDROXYDOPAMINE LESIONED RATS.
004129 04-04

SPIROPERIDOL-LABELED
LONG-TERM ANTIDEPRESSANT TREATMENT DECREASES SPIROPERIDOL-LABELED SEROTONIN-RECEPTOR BINDING.
000230 01-03

SPLEEN
COCAINE AND AMPHETAMINE ANTAGONIZE THE DECREASE OF NORADRENERGIC NEUROTRANSMISSION ELICITED BY OXYMETAZOLINE BUT POTENTIATE THE INHIBITION BY ALPHA METHYLNOREPINEPHRINE IN THE PERFUSED CAT SPLEEN.
002801 03-03

SPREADING
SPREADING DEPRESSION INDUCED BY MICROINJECTION OF ENKEPHALINS INTO THE HIPPOCAMPUS AND NEOCORTEX.
004015 04-04

SPROUTING
NEUROLEPTIC-INDUCED REINNERVATION SPROUTING IN THE CENTRAL-NERVOUS-SYSTEM (A MODEL FOR THE DEVELOPMENT OF TARDIVE-DYSKINESIA AND SUPERSENSITIVITY PSYCHOSIS).
002459 02-15

SP6-11
SUBSTANCE-P, HEXAPEPTIDE-PGLU6(SP6-11), ANALGESIA AND SEROTONIN DEPLETION.
003050 03-04

SQUIRREL-MONKEY
EFFECTS OF SYSTEMIC AND INTRAVENTRICULAR ADMINISTRATION OF CANNABINOIDS ON SCHEDULE-CONTROLLED RESPONDING IN THE SQUIRREL-MONKEY.
000354 01-04
EFFECTS OF MORPHINE, PENTAZOCINE AND CYCLAZOCINE ALONE AND IN COMBINATION WITH NALOXONE ON ELECTRIC-SHOCK TITRATION IN THE SQUIRREL-MONKEY.
001611 02-04
DISCRIMINATIVE-STIMULUS PROPERTIES OF PHENCYCLIDINE AND FIVE ANALOGUES IN THE SQUIRREL-MONKEY.
002961 03-04

SECOND-ORDER SCHEDULES OF INTRAMUSCULAR COCAINE INJECTION IN THE SQUIRREL-MONKEY: COMPARISONS WITH FOOD PRESENTATION AND EFFECTS OF D-AMPHETAMINE AND PROMAZINE.
004152 04-04
INDIVIDUAL DIFFERENCES IN EFFECTS OF TRICYCLIC-ANTIDEPRESSANTS AND ANTICHOLINERGIC-DRUGS ON OPERANT-BEHAVIOR IN THE SQUIRREL-MONKEY.
004176 04-04

SQUIRREL-MONKEYS
ACUTE AND CHRONIC EFFECTS OF DELTA9 TETRAHYDROCANNABINOL ON COMPLEX BEHAVIOR OF SQUIRREL-MONKEYS.
001583 02-04
NICOTINE INGESTION REDUCES ELEVATED BLOOD-PRESSURES IN RATS AND SQUIRREL-MONKEYS.
002759 03-03
EFFECTS OF NORCOCAINE AND SOME NORCOCAINE DERIVATIVES ON SCHEDULE-CONTROLLED BEHAVIOR OF PIGEONS AND SQUIRREL-MONKEYS.
004012 04-03
HISTAMINE AS A PUNISHER IN SQUIRREL-MONKEYS: EFFECTS OF PENTOBARBITAL, CHLORDIAZEPOXIDE AND H1-RECEPTOR AND H2-RECEPTOR ANTAGONISTS ON BEHAVIOR AND CARDIOVASCULAR RESPONSE.
004119 04-04
DIAZEPAM-INDUCED ATAXIA IN TROTTING SQUIRREL-MONKEYS.
004138 04-04
SOME EFFECTS OF CLOZAPINE ON PUNISHED-RESPONDING BY MICE AND SQUIRREL-MONKEYS.
004224 04-04
BEHAVIORAL-EFFECTS OF SELF-ADMINISTERED COCAINE: RESPONDING MAINTAINED ALTERNATELY BY COCAINE AND ELECTRIC-SHOCK IN SQUIRREL-MONKEYS.
004225 04-04

STABILITY
POSTMORTEM STABILITY OF BRAIN 3 METHOXY-4-HYDROXYPHENYLETHYLENEGLYCOL AND 3,4 DIHYDROXYPHENYLETHYLENEGLYCOL IN THE RAT AND MOUSE.
004048 04-03
STUDY ON THE STABILITY OF THE FACTORIAL STRUCTURE OF THE AMP SYSTEM DURING TREATMENT.
004696 04-16

STABILIZATION
LITHIUM EFFECTS ON HIGH-AFFINITY TRYPTOPHAN UPTAKE: EVIDENCE AGAINST A STABILIZATION MECHANISM.
001496 02-03
A NEW DOSAGE SCHEDULE FOR PIMOZIDE IN THE ACUTE STABILIZATION AND MAINTENANCE-TREATMENT OF PSYCHOSIS.
002022 02-09
INHIBITION OF LYSOSOMAL LIPASES BY CHLORPROMAZINE: A POSSIBLE MECHANISMS OF STABILIZATION.
003993 04-03

STABILIZING
MECHANISM OF MEMBRANE STABILIZING AND LYTIC-EFFECTS OF TRICYCLIC-ANTIDEPRESSANTS.
004283 04-05

STABLE
A METHOD FOR THE DETERMINATION OF AMITRIPTYLINE AND ITS METABOLITES NORTRIPTYLINE, 10 HYDROXYAMITRIPTYLINE, AND 10 HYDROXYNORTRIPTYLINE IN HUMAN PLASMA USING STABLE ISOTOPE DILUTION AND GAS-CHROMATOGRAPHY CHEMICAL-IONIZATION MASS-SPECTROMETRY.
002486 02-16
HYPOMANIA AS A STABLE STATE: LITHIUM PROPHYLAXIS IN TWO PATIENTS.
003212 03-09
STABLE ISOTOPES USED IN STUDIES OF METRIFONATE.
003847 04-03
GLC MASS-SPECTROMETRIC-DETERMINATION OF MAPROTILINE AND ITS MAJOR METABOLITE USING STABLE ISOTOPE-LABELED ANALOG AS INTERNAL STANDARD.
004291 04-06
GAS-CHROMATOGRAPHY/MASS-SPECTROMETRY STABLE ISOTOPIC ANALYSES FOR DEANOL, CHOLINE, AND THEIR ACETYLESTERS.
004683 04-16

STAFF
ACCURACY OF PATIENT INTERVIEWS AND ESTIMATES BY CLINICAL STAFF IN DETERMINING MEDICATION COMPLIANCE.
003618 03-17

STAGE
MINAPRINE-CHLOROHYDRATE: SURVEY OF THE FIRST CLINICAL-STUDIES OF THE FOURTH STAGE.
001902 02-07
ANIMAL-MODEL OF PSYCHOSIS: HALLUCINATORY BEHAVIORS IN MONKEYS DURING THE LATE STAGE OF CONTINUOUS AMPHETAMINE INTOXICATION.
002988 03-04

STAGES
STUDY ON THE EFFECTS OF L 5 HTP ON THE STAGES OF SLEEP IN MAN AS EVALUATED BY USING SLEEP-DEPRIVATION.
003450 03-14
PHENCYCLIDINE (PCP) INTOXICATION: DIAGNOSIS IN STAGES AND ALGORITHMS OF TREATMENT.
003525 03-15

STANDARDIZATION
STANDARDIZATION OF THE DEXAMETHASONE-SUPPRESSION-TEST FOR THE DIAGNOSIS OF MELANCHOLIA. (UNPUBLISHED PAPER).
004359 04-09

STANDARDS
SIMULTANEOUS DETERMINATION OF MORPHINE AND CODEINE IN BLOOD BY USE OF SELECT ION-MONITORING AND DEUTERATED INTERNAL STANDARDS.
004690 04-16

STARTLE
NORADRENERGIC AGONISTS AND ANTAGONISTS: EFFECTS ON CONDITIONED FEAR AS MEASURED BY THE POTENTIATED STARTLE PARADIGM.
000372 01-04
5 METHOXYDIMETHYLTRYPTAMINE: SPINAL-CORD AND BRAINSTEM MEDIATION OF EXCITATORY EFFECTS ON ACOUSTIC STARTLE.
001605 02-04
ACUTE AND CHRONIC LSD EFFECTS ON RAT STARTLE: DATA SUPPORTING AN LSD RAT MODEL OF SCHIZOPHRENIA.
002194 02-12
SPINAL MODULATION OF THE ACOUSTIC STARTLE RESPONSE: THE ROLE OF NOREPINEPHRINE, SEROTONIN AND DOPAMINE.
002950 03-04

STARVATION
EFFECTS OF BICUCULLINE-INDUCED SEIZURES ON CEREBRAL METABOLISM AND CIRCULATION OF RATS RENDERED HYPOGLYCEMIC BY STARVATION.
001134 02-03

STATE-DEPENDENT
A STATE-DEPENDENT FAILURE OF RATS TO MAXIMIZE REWARDS.
000392 01-04

STATE-HOSPITAL
TRENDS IN THE PRESCRIPTION OF PSYCHOTROPIC-DRUGS (1970-1977) IN A STATE-HOSPITAL.
000926 01-17

STATIC
HEXAMETHONIUM MODIFICATION OF CARDIOVASCULAR ADJUSTMENTS DURING COMBINED STATIC DYNAMIC ARM EXERCISE IN MONKEYS.
001242 02-03

STATISTICAL
STATISTICAL ANALYSES OF PHYSIOLOGIC DATA FROM FEMALE PATIENTS WITH AN ENDOMORPHOUS DEPRESSIVE COURSE: A TRIAL, INTERACTIONS BETWEEN PHYSIOLOGIC PARAMETERS, TEST JUNCTURES IN THIS PHASE.
003251 03-09
MILD, MODERATE, SEVERE — THE STATISTICAL ANALYSIS OF SHORT ORDINAL SCALES.
004677 04-16

STATISTICS
EFFECTS OF SINGLE-ORAL-DOSAGES OF STEROIDS ON HUMAN EEG BASELINE CROSSING T-SCORES SHOWN BY MULTIVARIATE STATISTICS AND STANDARD PROFILES.
002239 02-13

STATOKINESIMETER
DOSE-EFFECT OF DEAE ON SUBJECTIVE PROBLEMS, VERTIGO, DEPRESSION, ASTHENIA, CEPHALALGIA, AND TONIC POSTURAL ACTIVITY PROBLEMS RECORDED WITH STATOKINESIMETER IN POSTCONCUSSIONAL-SYNDROME.
004472 04-11

STATUS-EPILEPTICUS
RECTAL VALPROATE SYRUP AND STATUS-EPILEPTICUS.
000727 01-11
ANTICONVULSANT-INDUCED STATUS-EPILEPTICUS IN LENNOX-GASTAUT-SYNDROME.
003467 03-15
A COMPARATIVE-STUDY OF INTRAVENOUS LORAZEPAM AND CLONAZEPAM IN STATUS-EPILEPTICUS.
004487 04-11

STEADY-STATE
THE EFFECT OF THIORIDAZINE ON PROLACTIN LEVELS IN ACUTELY SCHIZOPHRENIC-PATIENTS: CHALLENGE-DOSE AND STEADY-STATE LEVELS.
000558 01-08
PREDICTION OF STEADY-STATE PLASMA LEVELS OF AMITRIPTYLINE AND NORTRIPTYLINE FROM A SINGLE-DOSE 24-HR. LEVEL IN DEPRESSED-PATIENTS.
000582 01-09
INTERACTION OF INDOMETHACIN AND IBUPROFEN WITH LITHIUM IN MANIC-PATIENTS UNDER A STEADY-STATE LITHIUM LEVEL.
000622 01-09
INFLUENCE OF DEXTROPROPOXYPHENE ON STEADY-STATE SERUM LEVELS AND PROTEIN BINDING OF THREE ANTIEPILEPTIC-DRUGS IN MAN.
000767 01-13

NEUROLEPTIC-EFFECT ON DESIPRAMINE STEADY-STATE PLASMA CONCENTRATIONS.
000781 01-13
RAT-BRAIN STEADY-STATE LEVELS OF CYCLIC-NUCLEOTIDES AS AN ENDPOINT OF LSD-LIKE HALLUCINOGEN EFFECTS. (PH.D. DISSERTATION).
001426 02-03
PLASMA DESIPRAMINE LEVELS AFTER SINGLE-DOSAGE AND AT STEADY-STATE IN OUTPATIENTS.
002039 02-09
PHARMACOKINETIC BASIS FOR PREDICTING STEADY-STATE SERUM DRUG CONCENTRATIONS OF IMIPRAMINE FROM SINGLE-DOSE DATA.
002225 02-13
FACTORS INFLUENCING NORTRIPTYLINE STEADY-STATE KINETICS: PLASMA AND SALIVA LEVELS.
002251 02-13
BIOAVAILABILITY AND RELATED PHARMACOKINETICS IN MAN OF ORALLY ADMINISTERED L 5 HYDROXYTRYPTOPHAN IN STEADY-STATE.
002261 02-13
STEADY-STATE LITHIUM BLOOD LEVEL FLUCTUATIONS IN MAN FOLLOWING ADMINISTRATION OF A LITHIUM-CARBONATE CONVENTIONAL AND CONTROLLED-RELEASE DOSAGE FORM.
003151 03-07
DEPRESSION SUBTYPES AFFECT THE STEADY-STATE PLASMA LEVELS AND THERAPEUTIC-EFFICACY OF AMITRIPTYLINE AND NORTRIPTYLINE.
003244 03-09

STEREOCHEMICAL
STEREOCHEMICAL ANATOMY OF MORPHINOMIMETICS.
002197 02-12

STEREOISOMERS
TRANYLCYPROMINE STEREOISOMERS, MONOAMINERGIC NEUROTRANSMISSION AND BEHAVIOR. A MINIREVIEW.
000016 01-02
POTENTIATION OF L GLUTAMATE AND L ASPARTATE EXCITATION OF CAT SPINAL NEURONES BY THE STEREOISOMERS OF THRED-3-HYDROXYASPARTATE.
002768 03-03
COMPARISON OF THE EFFECTS OF THE STEREOISOMERS OF FENFLURAMINE ON THE ACETYLCHOLINE CONTENT OF RAT STRIATUM, HIPPOCAMPUS AND NUCLEUS-ACCUMBENS.
004303 04-03
INTERACTION OF STEREOISOMERS OF BARBITURATES WITH (3H)ALPHA DIHYDROPICROTOXININ BINDING-SITES.
004036 04-03

STEREOSELECTIVE
STEREOSELECTIVE ACTIONS OF SUBSTITUTED BENZAMIDE DRUGS ON CEREBRAL DOPAMINE MECHANISMS.
001301 02-03
BACLOFEN: STEREOSELECTIVE INHIBITION OF EXCITANT AMINO-ACID RELEASE.
003867 04-03

STEREOSPECIFIC
STEREOSPECIFIC BINDING OF 3H HALOPERIDOL IN RAT DORSAL SPINAL-CORD.
000070 01-03
STEREOSPECIFIC NICOTINE-RECEPTORS ON RAT-BRAIN MEMBRANES.
000254 01-03
STEREOSPECIFIC, DOSE-DEPENDENT ANTAGONISM BY NALOXONE OF NONOPIATE BEHAVIOR IN MICE.
000411 01-04
THE STEREOSPECIFIC EFFECT OF NALOXONE ON RAT DORSAL-HORN NEURONES; INHIBITION IN SUPERFICIAL LAMINAE AND EXCITATION IN DEEPER LAMINAE.
001226 02-03
THE EFFECTS OF OPIATE ANTAGONISTS ON FOOD INTAKE ARE STEREOSPECIFIC.
003080 03-04
STEREOSPECIFIC INHIBITION OF DOPAMINE-SENSITIVE ADENYLATE-CYCLASE IN CARP RETINA BY THE ENANTIOMERS OF (/-) 1 CYCLOPROPYLMETHYL TRIFLUOROMETHYLTHIODIBENZOCYCLOHEPTENYLIDENEPIPERIDINE.
003706 04-02

STEREOTACTICALLY
BEHAVIOURAL-RESPONSES TO STEREOTACTICALLY CONTROLLED INJECTIONS OF MONOAMINE NEUROTRANSMITTERS INTO THE ACCUMBENS AND CAUDATE-PUTAMEN NUCLEI.
001708 02-04

STEREOTAXIC
THE LONG-TERM RESULTS OF STEREOTAXIC SURGERY AND L-DOPA THERAPY IN PATIENTS WITH PARKINSONS-DISEASE: A 10-YEAR FOLLOWUP STUDY.
000693 01-11

STEREOTYPED
AN AUTOMATED METHOD FOR STUDYING STEREOTYPED GNAWING.
002500 02-16
EFFECTS OF CHOLECYSTOKININ-OCTAPEPTIDE ON STRIATAL DOPAMINE METABOLISM AND ON APOMORPHINE-INDUCED STEREOTYPED CAGE CLIMBING IN MICE.
003031 03-04

STEREOTYPED-BEHAVIOR
FLURAZEPAM EFFECTS ON METHYLPHENIDATE-INDUCED STEREOTYPED-BEHAVIOR.
000455 01-04

STEREOTYPED-BEHAVIOR-SYNDROME
THE STEREOTYPED-BEHAVIOR-SYNDROME: A NEW MODEL AND PROPOSED THERAPY.
004163 04-04

STEREOTYPED-BEHAVIORS
CATS DEVELOP TOLERANCE TO D-AMPHETAMINES EFFECTS UPON LOCOMOTION AND STEREOTYPED-BEHAVIORS.
003018 03-04

EFFECTS OF CHRONIC ADMINISTRATION OF PHENCYCLIDINE ON STEREOTYPED-BEHAVIORS AND ATAXIC-BEHAVIORS IN THE RAT.
003095 03-04

STEREOTYPED-BEHAVIOUR
5,7 DIHYDROXYTRYPTAMINE LESIONS OF THE AMYGDALA REDUCE AMPHETAMINE-INDUCED AND APOMORPHINE-INDUCED STEREOTYPED-BEHAVIOUR IN THE RAT.
001589 02-04

NARCOTIC ANALGESICS AND STEREOTYPED-BEHAVIOUR IN MICE.
001694 02-04

GABA AGONISTS DISSOCIATE STRIATAL UNIT ACTIVITY FROM DRUG-INDUCED STEREOTYPED-BEHAVIOUR.
001716 02-04

STEREOTYPED-BEHAVIOUR AND ELECTROCORTICAL-CHANGES AFTER INTRACEREBRAL MICROINFUSION OF DOPAMINE AND APOMORPHINE IN FOWLS.
001734 02-04

DISSOCIATION OF D-AMPHETAMINE-INDUCED LOCOMOTOR-ACTIVITY AND STEREOTYPED-BEHAVIOUR BY LESIONS OF THE SUPERIOR-COLLICULUS.
001755 02-04

THE ROLE OF 5 HYDROXYTRYPTAMINE IN DOPAMINE-DEPENDENT STEREOTYPED-BEHAVIOUR.
002966 03-04

STEREOTYPIC-BEHAVIOR
EFFECTS OF THIORIDAZINE ON APOMORPHINE-ELICITED STEREOTYPIC-BEHAVIOR AND MOTOR-ACTIVITY.
000424 01-04

THE PATHOGENESIS OF STEREOTYPIC-BEHAVIOR.
004161 04-04

STEREOTYPIC-BEHAVIOR-SYNDROME
THE COMPLEX SPECIFIC PATHOGENETIC THERAPY OF THE STEREOTYPIC-BEHAVIOR-SYNDROME (AN EXPERIMENTAL-STUDY).
004162 04-04

STEREOTYPIES
AMPHETAMINE STEREOTYPIES AND POLYRIBOSOMAL DISAGGREGATION IN RATS: EFFECTS OF ADRENERGIC AND SEROTONERGIC BLOCKING-AGENTS.
001531 02-03

STEREOTYPY
THE INFLUENCE OF GABAERGIC SUBSTANCES ON THE EFFECTS OF STIMULATION OF THE CAUDATE-NUCLEUS AND AMPHETAMINE STEREOTYPY IN CATS.
000489 01-04

MODULATION OF APOMORPHINE-INDUCED STEREOTYPY BY ESTROGEN: TIME-COURSE AND DOSE-RESPONSE.
001636 02-04

APPARENT TOLERANCE TO SOME ASPECTS OF AMPHETAMINE STEREOTYPY WITH LONG-TERM-TREATMENT.
001758 02-04

SPONTANEOUS ACTIVITY AND APOMORPHINE STEREOTYPY DURING AND AFTER WITHDRAWAL FROM 3 1/2 MONTHS CONTINUOUS ADMINISTRATION OF HALOPERIDOL: SOME METHODOLOGICAL-ISSUES.
002509 02-16

INCREASED AMPHETAMINE STEREOTYPY AND LONGER HALOPERIDOL CATALEPSY IN SPONTANEOUSLY HYPERTENSIVE-RATS.
002891 03-03

ESTROGEN POTENTIATES THE STEREOTYPY INDUCED BY DOPAMINE AGONISTS IN THE RAT.
002968 03-04

AN IMPROVED MODEL OF INTRASPECIFIC AGGRESSION: DOSE-RESPONSE ANALYSIS OF APOMORPHINE-INDUCED-FIGHTING AND STEREOTYPY IN THE RAT.
002983 03-04

RELATION BETWEEN BRAIN CATECHOLAMINE-RECEPTORS AND DOPAMINERGIC STEREOTYPY IN RAT STRAINS.
004131 04-04

EFFECT OF L HISTIDINE AND CHLORCYCLIZINE ON APOMORPHINE-INDUCED CLIMBING-BEHAVIOUR AND METHAMPHETAMINE STEREOTYPY IN MICE.
004147 04-04

PHARMACOKINETIC-STUDY OF APOMORPHINE-INDUCED STEREOTYPY IN FOOD DEPRIVED RATS.
004247 04-04

APOMORPHINE-INDUCED STEREOTYPY IN MATURE AND SENESCENT RATS FOLLOWING CESSATION OF CHRONIC HALOPERIDOL TREATMENT.
004651 04-15

STERNBERG
DOSE-EFFECTS OF SECOBARBITAL IN A STERNBERG MEMORY SCANNING TASK.
003460 03-14

STEROID
A STEROID DERIVATIVE, R-5135, ANTAGONIZES THE GABA/BENZODIAZEPINE-RECEPTOR INTERACTION.
003851 04-03

STEROID-HORMONES
STEROID-HORMONES AND CNS ACTIVITY.
000794 01-13

ELECTROPHYSIOLOGICAL AND PSYCHOLOGICAL CHANGES INDUCED BY STEROID-HORMONES IN MEN AND WOMEN.
004500 04-13

STEROIDS
PHENOBARBITONE INTERACTION WITH ORAL CONTRACEPTIVE STEROIDS IN THE RABBIT AND RAT.
001832 02-05

EFFECTS OF SINGLE-ORAL-DOSAGES OF STEROIDS ON HUMAN EEG BASELINE CROSSING T-SCORES SHOWN BY MULTIVARIATE STATISTICS AND STANDARD PROFILES.
002239 02-13

IMIPRAMINE: EFFECT OF OVARIAN STEROIDS ON MODIFICATIONS IN SEROTONIN-RECEPTOR BINDING.
002778 03-03

STH
CHANGES OF ACTH, STH, TSH AND PROLACTIN LEVELS IN ENDOTOXIN SHOCK IN RATS.
000119 01-03

STIMULANT
THE REAL AND IDEAL MANAGEMENT OF STIMULANT DRUG-TREATMENT FOR HYPERACTIVE-CHILDREN: RECENT FINDINGS AND A REPORT FROM CLINICAL-PRACTICE.
000715 01-11

1 SUBSTITUTED BENZYLTETRAHYDROPYRIMIDONES: A SERIES WITH STIMULANT AND DEPRESSANT ACTIVITIES.
003687 04-02

THE EFFECT OF THE DOPAMINE-RECEPTOR BLOCKING-DRUG PIMOZIDE ON THE STIMULANT AND ANORECTIC-ACTIONS OF DEXTROAMPHETAMINE IN MAN.
004580 04-14

STIMULANT-DRUGS
THE PARENT CHILD INTERACTIONS OF HYPERACTIVE-CHILDREN AND THEIR MODIFICATION BY STIMULANT-DRUGS.
002092 02-11

EVALUATION OF SYMPTOMATIC TREATMENT OF HYPERACTIVE-BEHAVIOR BY STIMULANT-DRUGS.
002134 02-11

SEXUAL-EFFECTS OF ANTIDEPRESSANTS AND PSYCHOMOTOR STIMULANT-DRUGS.
004646 04-15

STIMULANT-EFFECT
THE STIMULANT-EFFECT OF NEUROLEPTICS: MYTH OR REALITY?
000362 01-04

STIMULANT-EFFECTIVENESS
PREDICTING STIMULANT-EFFECTIVENESS IN HYPERACTIVE-CHILDREN WITH A REPEATABLE NEUROPSYCHOLOGICAL-BATTERY: A PRELIMINARY-STUDY.
004453 04-11

STIMULANT-EFFECTS
5 HT BLOCKADE AND THE STIMULANT-EFFECTS OF D-AMPHETAMINE AND L-AMPHETAMINE: NO INTERACTION IN SELF-STIMULATION OF PREFRONTAL-CORTEX, HYPOTHALAMUS, OR DORSAL TEGMENTUM. UNEXPECTED LETHALITY IN HIPPOCAMPAL SITES.
000387 01-04

STIMULANTS
IN VITRO EFFECT OF PHENCYCLIDINE AND OTHER PSYCHOMOTOR STIMULANTS ON SEROTONIN UPTAKE IN HUMAN PLATELETS.
000750 01-13

EFFECT OF REPEATED ELECTROCONVULSIVE-SHOCKS (ECS) ON SUBTHRESHOLD DOSES OF SOME CNS STIMULANTS.
001361 02-03

COMPARATIVE-STUDY OF AGGRESSIVE-BEHAVIOUR AFTER INJECTION OF CHOLINOMIMETICS, ANTICHOLINESTERASES, NICOTINIC, AND MUSCARINIC GANGLIONIC STIMULANTS INTO THE CEREBRAL VENTRICLES OF CONSCIOUS CATS: FAILURE OF NICOTINIC-DRUGS TO EVOKE AGGRESSION.
001568 02-04

INFLUENCE OF INTRAVENOUS SELF-ADMINISTERED PSYCHOMOTOR STIMULANTS ON PERFORMANCE OF RHESUS-MONKEYS IN A MULTIPLE-SCHEDULE PARADIGM.
001655 02-04

PSYCHOMOTOR STIMULANTS AS ACTIVATORS OF NORMAL AND PATHOLOGICAL-BEHAVIOR: IMPLICATIONS FOR THE EXCESSES IN MANIA. (UNPUBLISHED PAPER).
002353 02-14

METHYLPHENIDATE-LIKE STIMULANTS IN VITRO RELEASE (3H)TYRAMINES BUT NOT (14C)DOPAMINE.
002706 03-03

FUNDAMENTAL MECHANISMS UNDERLYING ALTERED BEHAVIOR FOLLOWING CHRONIC ADMINISTRATION OF PSYCHOMOTOR STIMULANTS.
002711 03-03

NEUROCHEMICAL-CONSEQUENCES FOLLOWING ADMINISTRATION OF CNS STIMULANTS TO THE NEONATAL RAT.
002926 03-03

A NOTE ON THE PARADOXICAL-EFFECT OF STIMULANTS ON HYPERACTIVITY WITH REFERENCE TO THE RATE DEPENDENCY EFFECT OF DRUGS.
003320 03-11

DO STIMULANTS PROVOKE, CAUSE, OR EXACERBATE TICS AND TOURETTE-SYNDROME?
004485 04-11

STIMULATE
MORPHINE ACTS THROUGH ALPHA-ADRENERGIC AND SEROTONINERGIC NEURONS TO STIMULATE GROWTH-HORMONE SECRETION IN THE DOG.
000088 01-03

STIMULATED
THE INFLUENCE OF PENTIFYLLINE AND THEOPHYLLINE ON REACTION KINETICS OF CATECHOLAMINE STIMULATED ATPASE FROM RAT-BRAIN.
001052 02-01

BASAL AND STIMULATED LEVELS OF PROLACTIN, TSH AND LH IN SERUM OF CHRONIC SCHIZOPHRENIC-PATIENTS, LONG-TERM TREATED WITH NEUROLEPTICS.
001935 02-08

BASAL AND STIMULATED LEVELS OF PROLACTIN, TSH, AND LH IN SERUM OF CHRONIC SCHIZOPHRENIC-PATIENTS LONG-TERM TREATED WITH NEUROLEPTICS: RELATIONS TO PSYCHOPATHOLOGY.
001936 02-08

SEX-DIFFERENCES IN THE AMPHETAMINE STIMULATED RELEASE OF CATECHOLAMINES FROM RAT STRIATAL TISSUE IN VITRO.
002668 03-03

RELEASE OF ACETYLCHOLINE FROM RAT-BRAIN SYNAPTOSOMES STIMULATED WITH LEPTINOTARSIN, A NEW NEUROTOXIN.
003148 03-06

STIMULATES
INTRAVENOUS GABA AGONIST ADMINISTRATION STIMULATES FIRING OF A10 DOPAMINERGIC NEURONS.
000320 01-03

VASOPRESSIN STIMULATES RELEASE OF BETA LIPOTROPIN AND BETA ENDORPHIN IN CONSCIOUS RATS AS MEASURED BY RADIOIMMUNOASSAY OF UNEXTRACTED PLASMA.
003715 04-03

NERVE GROWTH-FACTOR STIMULATES DEVELOPMENT OF SUBSTANCE-P IN THE EMBRYONIC SPINAL-CORD.
003881 04-03

SEXUAL-BEHAVIOR DECREASES PAIN SENSITIVITY AND STIMULATES ENDOGENOUS OPIOIDS IN MALE RATS.
004234 04-04

STIMULATING
N ALKYLATED 2 AMINOTETRALINS: CENTRAL DOPAMINE-RECEPTOR STIMULATING ACTIVITY.
000399 01-04

EFFECTS OF ALPHA-ADRENOCEPTOR STIMULATING DRUGS ON BARORECEPTOR REFLEXES IN CONSCIOUS CATS.
001514 02-03

THE INTEREST OF THE STIMULATING EFFECT OF CARPIPRAMINE IN PSYCHOSOMATIC-MEDICINE.
002061 02-10

EVIDENCE THAT IT IS POSSIBLE TO CAUSE ANOREXIA BY INCREASING RELEASE AND/OR DIRECTLY STIMULATING POSTSYNAPTIC SEROTONIN-RECEPTORS IN THE BRAIN.
002602 02-17

THE PRESYNAPTIC STIMULATING EFFECT OF ACETYLCHOLINE ON DOPAMINE RELEASE IS SUPPRESSED DURING ACTIVATION OF NIGROSTRIATAL DOPAMINERGIC NEURONS IN THE CAT.
002733 03-03

THE STIMULATING EFFECT OF AMPHETAMINE ON THE VISUAL SYSTEM.
003398 03-13

STIMULATION
REPEATED TRICYCLIC-ANTIDEPRESSANTS INDUCE A PROGRESSIVE SWITCH IN THE ELECTROPHYSIOLOGICAL RESPONSE OF DOPAMINE NEURONS TO AUTORECEPTOR STIMULATION.
000046 01-03

EFFECT OF PICROTOXIN AND NIPECOTIC-ACID ON INHIBITORY RESPONSE OF DOPAMINERGIC NEURONS IN THE VENTRAL TEGMENTAL AREA TO STIMULATION OF THE NUCLEUS-ACCUMBENS.
000331 01-03

REDUCTION OF FOOD INTAKE BY PIRIBEDIL IN THE RAT: RELATION TO DOPAMINE-RECEPTOR STIMULATION.
000355 01-04

RELATION OF MONOMETHYLHYDRAZINE (MMH) SEIZURE THRESHOLDS TO AFTERDISCHARGE THRESHOLDS WITH AMYGDALOID STIMULATION IN CATS.
000474 01-04

THE INFLUENCE OF GABAERGIC SUBSTANCES ON THE EFFECTS OF STIMULATION OF THE CAUDATE-NUCLEUS AND AMPHETAMINE STEREOTYPY IN CATS.
000489 01-04

BRADYKININ-RECEPTOR STIMULATION OF C-AMP INVOLVES PHOSPHOLIPID METHYLATION, CA-FLUX, PHOSPHOLIPASE-A2 ACTIVATION AND PROSTAGLANDIN FORMATION. (UNPUBLISHED PAPER).
001002 02-01

ELECTRON MICROSCOPIC STUDIES OF BRAIN SLICES: THE EFFECTS OF HIGH-FREQUENCY STIMULATION ON DENDRITIC ULTRASTRUCTURE. (UNPUBLISHED PAPER).
001036 02-01

DIVERGENT RESERPINE EFFECTS ON AMFONELIC-ACID AND AMPHETAMINE STIMULATION OF SYNAPTOSOMAL DOPAMINE FORMATION FROM PHENYLALANINE.
001113 02-03

EFFECTS OF LISURIDE ON BODY-TEMPERATURE OF RATS AND RABBITS: RELATION TO MICROSOMAL BIOTRANSFORMATION AND DOPAMINERGIC-RECEPTOR STIMULATION.
001161 02-03

ISOLATION INCREASES THE RESPONSES TO BETA-ADRENERGIC STIMULATION IN MICE.
001232 02-03

INHIBITORY ACTION OF MORPHINE ON THE RELEASE OF A BRADYKININ-LIKE SUBSTANCE AFTER SCIATIC-NERVE STIMULATION.
001293 02-03

MORPHINE AND ELECTROACUPUNCTURE: COMPARISON OF THE EFFECTS ON THE CORTICAL EVOKED-RESPONSES AFTER TOOTH-PULP STIMULATION IN RATS.
001294 02-03

PHENCYCLIDINE-INDUCED STIMULATION OF SYNAPTOSOMAL TYROSINE-HYDROXYLASE ACTIVITY.
001304 02-03

GASTRIC AND PYLORIC MOTOR-RESPONSE TO SYMPATHETIC-NERVE STIMULATION AFTER CHEMICAL SYMPATHECTOMY. (UNPUBLISHED PAPER).
001337 02-03

SUSTAINED GAMMA AMINOBUTYRIC-ACID-RECEPTOR STIMULATION AND CHRONIC NEUROLEPTIC-EFFECTS.
001345 02-03

EFFECTS OF MORPHINE ON EVOKED-POTENTIALS RECORDED FROM THE AMYGDALA BY TOOTH-PULP STIMULATION IN CATS.
001379 02-03

STIMULATION OF ADENYLATE-CYCLASE IN RAT STRIATUM BY PERGOLIDE: INFLUENCE OF GTP.
001448 02-03

INCREASED ADRENALINE, BETA-ADRENERGIC-RECEPTOR STIMULATION AND PHOSPHOLIPID METHYLATION IN PINEAL-GLAND OF SPONTANEOUSLY HYPERTENSIVE-RATS. (UNPUBLISHED PAPER).
001458 02-03

STIMULATION OF THE PLASMA MEMBRANE ENZYME, 5' NUCLEOTIDASE, BY ETHANOL EXPOSURE TO NEURAL CELLS IN CULTURE.
001499 02-03

EVIDENCE THAT NORADRENALINE MODULATES THE INCREASE IN STRIATAL DOPAMINE METABOLISM INDUCED BY MUSCARINIC-RECEPTOR STIMULATION.
001518 02-03

CORRELATIONS BETWEEN HEMODYNAMIC PARAMETERS OF THE LIVER AND NOREPINEPHRINE RELEASE UPON HEPATIC-NERVE STIMULATION IN THE DOG.
001547 02-03

BETA ENDORPHIN CAUSES RETROGRADE AMNESIA AND IS RELEASED FROM THE RAT-BRAIN BY VARIOUS FORMS OF TRAINING AND STIMULATION.
001664 02-04

A COMPARISON BETWEEN THE EFFECTS OF MORPHINE ON THE REWARDING AND AVERSIVE-PROPERTIES OF LATERAL HYPOTHALAMIC AND CENTRAL GRAY STIMULATION.
001771 02-04

FURTHER STUDIES ON OPIATE-RECEPTORS THAT MEDIATE ANTINOCICEPTION: TOOTH-PULP STIMULATION IN THE DOG.
001782 02-04

INCREASED VULNERABILITY TO CHOLINERGIC STIMULATION IN AFFECTIVE-DISORDER PATIENTS.
002003 02-09

SENSITIZATION AND OSCILLATION FOLLOWING REPEATED STIMULATION: RELATIONSHIP TO AFFECTIVE-ILLNESS AND ITS TREATMENT WITH LITHIUM AND CARBAMAZEPINE.
002031 02-09

LITHIUM ANTAGONISM OF ETHANOL-INDUCED DEPLETION OF CEREBELLAR GUANOSINE-CYCLIC-MONOPHOSPHATE AND STIMULATION OF STRIATAL DOPAMINE RELEASE.
002242 02-13

HALOPERIDOL STIMULATION OF PROLACTIN SECRETION: HOW MANY BLOOD SAMPLES ARE NEEDED TO DEFINE THE HORMONE RESPONSE?
002505 02-16

TEMPORAL PATTERNING OF NEURONAL ACTIVITY DURING THERMAL AND NEUROCHEMICAL STIMULATION OF THE PREOPTIC/ANTERIOR HYPOTHALAMUS OF THE AWAKE RABBIT.
002737 03-03

STIMULATION OF RETINAL ADENYLATE-CYCLASE BY VASOACTIVE INTESTINAL PEPTIDE (VIP).
002811 03-03

NORADRENERGIC STIMULATION IN VIVO INCREASES NA-K-ADENOSINE-TRIPHOSPHATASE ACTIVITY.
002910 03-03

CHOLINERGIC, DOPAMINERGIC, NORADRENERGIC, OR GLUTAMINERGIC STIMULATION VENTRAL TO THE ANTERIOR SEPTUM DOES NOT SPECIFICALLY SUPPRESS DEFENSIVE-BEHAVIOR.
002945 03-04

SLEEP ELICITED BY OLFACTORY TUBERCLE STIMULATION AND THE EFFECT OF ATROPINE.
002955 03-04

PHARMACOLOGICAL-STUDIES ON STIMULATION PRODUCED ANALGESIA IN MICE.
002964 03-04

INTERACTION BETWEEN PURINE AND BENZODIAZEPINE: INOSINE REVERSES DIAZEPAM-INDUCED STIMULATION OF MOUSE EXPLORATORY-BEHAVIOR.
002972 03-04

INFLUENCE OF MORPHINE ON THE DISCRIMINATIVE-STIMULUS PROPERTIES OF REWARDING LATERAL HYPOTHALAMIC STIMULATION. (PH.D. DISSERTATION).
003041 03-04

RAT PUP-KILLING AND MATERNAL-BEHAVIOR IN MALE LONG-EVANS-RATS: PRENATAL STIMULATION AND POSTNATAL TESTOSTERONE.
003054 03-04

PRESSOR EFFECTS OF DORSAL RAPHE STIMULATION AND INTRAHYPOTHALAMIC APPLICATION OF SEROTONIN IN THE SPONTANEOUSLY HYPERTENSIVE-RAT.
003117 03-04

MORPHINE DEPRESSES DORSAL-HORN NEURON RESPONSES TO CONTROLLED NOXIOUS AND NONNOXIOUS CUTANEOUS STIMULATION.
003782 04-03

POSSIBLE ROLE OF AN ENDOGENOUS OPIATE IN THE CARDIOVASCULAR-EFFECTS OF CENTRAL ALPHA-ADRENOCEPTOR STIMULATION IN SPONTANEOUSLY HYPERTENSIVE-RATS.
003791 04-03

STIMULATION OF FRUCTOSEBIPHOSPHATASE ACTIVITY AND SYNTHESIS IN THE CEREBRAL-CORTEX OF RATS SUBMITTED TO THE CONVULSANT METHIONINE-SULFOXIMINE.
003838 04-03

EFFECT OF MEDIAN RAPHE STIMULATION ON HIPPOCAMPAL SEIZURE DISCHARGE INDUCED BY CARBACHOL IN THE RABBIT.
003951 04-03

STUDIES ON THE MECHANISM-OF-ACTION OF AVERMECTIN-B1A: STIMULATION OF RELEASE OF GAMMA AMINOBUTYRIC-ACID FROM BRAIN SYNAPTOSOMES.
003973 04-03

RNA-POLYMERASE-II IN C6-GLIOMA CELLS: ALPHA AMANITIN BLOCKADE OF CYCLIC-AMP-PHOSPHODIESTERASE INDUCTION BY BETA-ADRENERGIC STIMULATION. (UNPUBLISHED PAPER).
003998 04-03

ONTOGENY OF HISTAMINERGIC NEUROTRANSMISSION IN THE RAT-BRAIN: CONCOMITANT DEVELOPMENT OF NEURONAL HISTAMINE, H1-RECEPTORS, AND H1-RECEPTOR-MEDIATED STIMULATION OF PHOSPHOLIPID TURNOVER.
004021 04-03

EFFECTS OF ANALGESICS AND CNS-ACTING DRUGS ON STRUGGLING FOLLOWING REPETITIVE STIMULATION OF THE TAIL, AND FLEXOR REFLEX TO A SINGLE STIMULATION OF THE SCIATIC-NERVE IN RATS.
004148 04-04

HORMONAL STIMULATION AFTER INJECTION OF THYROTROPHIN-RELEASING-FACTOR (TRF) AND ACTH1-24 IN PATIENTS FOLLOWING CHRONIC-TREATMENT WITH NEUROLEPTICS: PRELIMINARY-STUDY.
004505 04-13

STIMULATION-EVOKED
INHIBITION OF NEURONAL UPTAKE REDUCES THE PRESYNAPTIC EFFECTS OF CLONIDINE BUT NOT OF ALPHA METHYLNORADRENALINE ON THE STIMULATION-EVOKED RELEASE OF 3H NORADRENALINE FROM RAT OCCIPITAL-CORTEX SLICES.
000227 01-03

STIMULATION-INDUCED
THE EFFECTS OF PARA CHLOROAMPHETAMINE ON FENFLURAMINE ANOREXIA IN AD LIBITUM AND STIMULATION-INDUCED FEEDING IN THE RAT.
001823 02-04

STIMULATORY
STIMULATORY EFFECT OF SOMATOSTATIN ON NOREPINEPHRINE RELEASE FROM RAT-BRAIN-CORTEX SLICES.
002920 03-03

STIMULATORY ACTION OF LISURIDE ON DOPAMINE-SENSITIVE ADENYLATE-CYCLASE IN THE RAT STRIATAL HOMOGENATE.
003718 04-04

A POSSIBLE NEUROCHEMICAL BASIS OF THE CENTRAL STIMULATORY EFFECTS OF PP'DDT.
004274 04-05

STIMULI
DIFFERENTIAL-EFFECTS OF VARIOUS STIMULI ON AVP LEVELS IN BLOOD AND CEREBROSPINAL-FLUID.
001370 02-03

THE EFFECT OF REPEATED ELECTROCONVULSIVE-SHOCK ON CORTICOSTERONE RESPONSES TO CENTRALLY-ACTING PHARMACOLOGICAL STIMULI IN THE MALE RAT.
001486 02-03

EFFECTS OF DRUGS ON THE EFFECTIVENESS OF CONDITIONED STIMULI.
001608 02-04

CANALIZATION OF AROUSAL IN THE PREWEANLING RAT: EFFECTS OF AMPHETAMINE ON AGGREGATION WITH SURROGATE STIMULI.
002965 03-04

HABITUATION OF ELECTRODERMAL AND RESPIRATORY RESPONSES TO VISUAL STIMULI AS A FUNCTION OF PERSONALITY DIFFERENCES IN AFFECT LEVEL.
003414 03-13

STIMULUS
A COMPARISON OF HUMAN TACTILE STIMULUS VELOCITY DISCRIMINATION WITH THE ABILITY OF S-I CORTICAL NEURONS IN AWAKE RHESUS-MONKEYS TO SIGNAL THE SAME VELOCITY DIFFERENCES BEFORE AND AFTER NONANESTHETIC DOSES OF PENTOBARBITAL.
000055 01-03

EVIDENCE THAT A PREFERRED SUBSTRATE FOR MONOAMINE-OXIDASE-B MEDIATES STIMULUS PROPERTIES OF MAO-INHIBITORS: A POSSIBLE ROLE FOR BETA PHENYLETHYLAMINE IN THE COCAINE CUE.
000363 01-04

BEHAVIORAL-PHARMACOLOGY AND THE STIMULUS CONTROL OF BEHAVIOR.
000381 01-04

STIMULUS INTENSITY CONTROL IN DEPRESSION: A STUDY OF THE COMPARATIVE-EFFECT OF DOXEPIN AND AMITRIPTYLINE ON CORTICAL EVOKED-POTENTIALS.
000763 01-13

TOLERANCE TO BARBITURATE-INDUCED CENTRAL-NERVOUS-SYSTEM DEPRESSION: INVOLVEMENT OF STIMULUS SECRETION COUPLING IN DISCRETE BRAIN AREAS. (PH.D. DISSERTATION).
001213 02-03

BEHAVIORAL-EFFECTS OF DRUGS: THE ROLE OF THE STIMULUS REINFORCER CONTINGENCY. (PH.D. DISSERTATION).
001537 02-03

THE EFFECTS OF OPIATE ANTAGONISTS ON THE DISCRIMINATIVE STIMULUS PROPERTIES OF ETHANOL.
002947 03-04

MORPHINE-LIKE STIMULUS EFFECTS IN THE MONKEY: OPIOIDS WITH ANTAGONIST PROPERTIES.
003086 03-04

DRUG-INDUCED STIMULUS CONTROL AND THE CONCEPT OF BREAKING-POINT: LSD AND QUIPAZINE.
003116 03-04

CONDITIONING OF AN INTEROCEPTIVE DRUG STIMULUS TO DIFFERENT EXTEROCEPTIVE CONTEXTS.
004142 04-04

CHARACTERISTICS OF THE STIMULUS PRODUCED BY THE MIXTURE OF CANNABIDIOL WITH DELTA9 TETRAHYDROCANNABINOL.
004263 04-04

STIMULUS-EVOKED
NALOXONE PROMOTES STIMULUS-EVOKED VASOPRESSIN RELEASE IN VIVO.
000165 01-03

STIMULUS-INDUCED
A NOVEL GABA-RECEPTOR MODULATES STIMULUS-INDUCED GLUTAMATE RELEASE FROM CORTICOSTRIATAL TERMINALS.
001376 02-03

STIMULUS-SHOCK
FIXED-RATIO SCHEDULES OF FOOD PRESENTATION AND STIMULUS-SHOCK TERMINATION: EFFECTS OF D-AMPHETAMINE, MORPHINE, AND CLOZAPINE.
000431 01-04

STOPPING
THE USE OF NICOTINE CHEWING-GUM AS AN AID TO STOPPING SMOKING.
002343 02-14

STOPPING MEDICATION IN CHILDREN WITH EPILEPSY.
004447 04-11

STORAGE
ROLE OF DOPAMINE STORAGE FUNCTION IN THE CONTROL OF RAT STRIATAL TYROSINE-HYDROXYLASE ACTIVITY.
000201 01-03

SELECTIVE STORAGE IN VIVO OF 5,6 ADTN IN DOPAMINE RICH AREAS OF THE RAT-BRAIN.
000324 01-03

ACTH MODULATION OF MEMORY STORAGE PROCESSING. (UNPUBLISHED PAPER).
001250 02-03

QUINACRINE AND SEROTONIN BINDING BY SYNTHETIC MODELS FOR HUMAN PLATELET DENSE-BODIES: EVALUATION OF THE ROLE OF BINDING IN AMINE STORAGE. (UNPUBLISHED PAPER).
002219 02-13

STORES
A COMPARISON OF RATES OF DEPLETION AND RECOVERY OF NORADRENALINE STORES OF PERIPHERAL AND CENTRAL

NORADRENERGIC NEURONES AFTER RESERPINE ADMINISTRATION:
IMPORTANCE OF NEURONAL ACTIVITY.
000314 01-03

STRAIN
AUDIOGENIC-SEIZURES: INCREASED BENZODIAZEPINE-RECEPTOR BINDING
IN A SUSCEPTIBLE STRAIN OF MICE.
000252 01-03
STRAIN DEPENDENT EFFECTS OF KETAMINE ON LOCOMOTOR-ACTIVITY
AND ANTINOCICEPTION IN MICE.
000382 01-04
COMPARATIVE-STUDY ON THE EFFECT OF MORPHINE AND THE OPIOID-
LIKE PEPTIDES IN THE VAS-DEFERENS OF RODENTS: STRAIN AND
SPECIES-DIFFERENCES, EVIDENCE FOR MULTIPLE OPIATE-RECEPTORS.
002757 03-03

STRAIN-13
ENHANCED TRANSFER OF EXPERIMENTAL ALLERGIC-ENCEPHALOMYELITIS
WITH STRAIN-13 GUINEA-PIG LYMPH-NODE CELLS: REQUIREMENT FOR
CULTURE WITH SPECIFIC ANTIGEN AND ALLOGENIC PERITONEAL
EXUDATE CELLS. (UNPUBLISHED PAPER).
001201 02-03

STRAINS
DISSIMILAR EFFECTS OF NICOTINAMIDE AND INOSINE, PUTATIVE
ENDOGENOUS LIGANDS OF THE BENZODIAZEPINE-RECEPTORS, ON
PENTYLENETETRAZOL SEIZURES IN FOUR STRAINS OF MICE.
000173 01-03
DIFFERENCES IN GAMMA AMINOBUTYRIC-ACID-RECEPTOR SENSITIVITY IN
INBRED STRAINS OF MICE.
000303 01-03
EFFECTS OF CHLORDIAZEPOXIDE MORPHINE COMBINATIONS ON
SPONTANEOUS LOCOMOTOR-ACTIVITY IN THREE INBRED STRAINS OF
MICE.
001766 02-04
EFFECTS OF MORPHINE AND CHLORDIAZEPOXIDE ON AVOIDANCE-
BEHAVIOUR IN TWO INBRED STRAINS OF MICE.
002973 03-04
FAILURE TO FIND SEX-DIFFERENCES IN TESTOSTERONE ACTIVATED
AGGRESSION IN TWO STRAINS OF RATS.
003107 03-04
RELATION BETWEEN BRAIN CATECHOLAMINE-RECEPTORS AND
DOPAMINERGIC STEREOTYPY IN RAT STRAINS.
004131 04-04
ACETYLCHOLINE TURNOVER AND AGGRESSION IN RELATED THREE
STRAINS OF MICE.
004151 04-04

STRATEGIES
OUTPATIENT TREATMENT ISSUES AND STRATEGIES FOR ACUTE AND
CHRONIC PCP ABUSERS.
000919 01-17
DIAGNOSTIC CLASSIFICATION AND THE ENDORPHIN HYPOTHESIS OF
SCHIZOPHRENIA: INDIVIDUAL DIFFERENCES AND
PSYCHOPHARMACOLOGICAL STRATEGIES. (UNPUBLISHED PAPER).
001910 02-08
RESEARCH STRATEGIES FOR ASSESSING THE EFFECTS OF
METHYLMERCURY ON BEHAVIOR.
003128 03-05
DIAGNOSTIC CLASSIFICATION AND THE ENDORPHIN HYPOTHESIS OF
SCHIZOPHRENIA: INDIVIDUAL DIFFERENCES AND
PSYCHOPHARMACOLOGICAL STRATEGIES.
003167 03-08
CURRENT BIOLOGIC STRATEGIES FOR ANXIETY.
003276 03-10
CLINICAL STRATEGIES FOR ANTIPSYCHOTIC-DRUG TREATMENT, TARDIVE-
DYSKINESIA, AND THE TRAINING OF RESEARCH PSYCHIATRISTS.
004603 04-15

STRATBGY
ROLE OF THE NEOSTRIATAL DOPAMINERGIC-ACTIVITY IN SEQUENCING
AND SELECTING BEHAVIOURAL-STRATEGIES: FACILITATION OF
PROCESSES INVOLVED IN SELECTING THE BEST STRATEGY IN A
STRESSFUL-SITUATION.
000366 01-04
STRATEGY FOR THE STUDY OF PATIENTS AT HIGH-RISK FOR TARDIVE-
DYSKINESIA.
000858 01-15
SECOND-GENERATION ANTIDEPRESSANTS: A CLINICAL
PHARMACOTHERAPEUTIC RESEARCH STRATEGY.
003632 03-17
THE PROGNOSIS OF EPILEPSY AND THE STRATEGY FOR TERMINATING
ANTIEPILEPTIC THERAPY.
004724 04-17

STREET
STREET PCP SCENE: ISSUES ON SYNTHESIS AND CONTAMINATION.
000744 01-12

STREPTOZOTOCIN
INCREASED URINARY EXCRETION OF CATECHOLAMINES AND THEIR
METABOLITES IN STREPTOZOTOCIN DIABETIC RAT.
000154 01-03

STRESS
RELATIONSHIPS BETWEEN PLASMA CORTICOSTEROIDS AND
BENZODIAZEPINES IN STRESS.
000176 01-03

CHLORDIAZEPOXIDE ANTINOCICEPTION: CROSS-TOLERANCE WITH
OPIATES AND WITH STRESS.
000348 01-04
EFFECT OF ANTIANXIETY-DRUGS ON FEAR AND STRESS.
000801 01-14
INFLUENCE OF RESPIRATORY STRESS AND HYPERTENSION UPON THE
BLOOD-BRAIN-BARRIER.
001437 02-03
DESENSITIZATION OF ADRENOCEPTORS AFTER IMMOBILIZATION STRESS
OR REPEATED INJECTION OF ISOPROTERENOL IN RATS. (UNPUBLISHED
PAPER).
001546 02-03
THE BEHAVIOR OF RATS IN THE OPEN-FIELD WITHOUT STRESS, UNDER
ACUTE AND PERSISTING INFLUENCE OF IMIPRAMINE AND
TRANYLCYPROMINE AS WELL AS ON THE INDIVIDUAL REACTION TYPE
(EMOTIVE AND NONEMOTIVE).
001624 02-04
SELECTIVE REDUCTION BY DEXAMETHASONE OF STRESS RELATED
HYPERPHAGIAS.
001703 02-04
STRESS AND HYPERTENSION: CLINICAL-IMPLICATIONS.
002307 02-13
DIFFERENTIAL-EFFECTS OF CANNABINOID EXPOSURE AND STRESS ON
PLASMA PROLACTIN, GROWTH-HORMONE AND CORTICOSTERONE
LEVELS IN MALE MICE.
002695 03-03
THE FUNCTIONAL IMPORTANCE OF INCREASED BRAIN TRYPTOPHAN IN
THE SEROTONERGIC RESPONSE TO RESTRAINT STRESS.
002779 03-03
INTERACTION BETWEEN THE EFFECTS OF STRESS AND MORPHINE ON
BODY-TEMPERATURE IN RATS.
002906 03-03
BENZODIAZEPINES, STRESS AND RAT PLASMA CORTICOSTEROIDS: THE
ROLE OF INDOLEAMINES.
003034 03-04

STRESS-EXPOSED
LITHIUM-INDUCED CHANGES IN THE BRAIN LEVELS OF FREE AMINO-ACIDS
IN STRESS-EXPOSED RATS.
001217 02-03

STRESS-INDUCED
EFFECT OF LITHIUM ON STRESS-INDUCED CHANGES IN THE BRAIN LEVELS
OF MONOAMINES IN RATS.
001216 02-03
ANTAGONISTIC-EFFECTS OF PSYCHOLEPTIC-DRUGS ON STRESS-INDUCED
ANALGESIA.
001609 02-04
STRESS-INDUCED FACILITATION OF OPIATE CATALEPSY IN THE RAT.
001680 02-04
SUBSTANCE-P SUPPRESSES STRESS-INDUCED EATING.
001725 02-04
BOMBESIN INHIBITS STRESS-INDUCED EATING.
003059 03-04
EFFECT OF DIAZEPAM ON STRESS-INDUCED CHANGES IN BRAIN
HISTAMINE.
003932 04-03

STRESS-MODULATED
STRESS-MODULATED ALTERATION OF BRAIN BIOGENIC-AMINES IN THE
RAT: EFFECTS OF L TRYPTOPHAN.
003978 04-03

STRESS-RESISTANCE
CAPACITIES OF ATTENTION, STRESS-RESISTANCE, AND SLOW CEREBRAL
POTENTIALS: EFFECTS OF CARPIPRAMINE ON CONTINGENT NEGATIVE
VARIATION WAVES AND P-300.
003451 03-14

STRESS-ULCER
SYNERGISTIC ACTIONS OF PROPANTHELINE-BROMIDE WITH CIMETIDINE
AND THIOPROPAZATE-HYDROCHLORIDE IN THE PREVENTION OF
STRESS-ULCER FORMATION IN RATS.
000064 01-03

STRESSED
PLASMA IMIPRAMINE LEVELS AND DEMETHYLASE ACTIVITY IN THE
LIVER OF STRESSED ANIMALS.
002793 03-03
SUPPRESSION OF SERUM PROLACTIN BY NALOXONE BUT NOT BY ANTI-
BETA-ENDORPHIN ANTISERUM IN STRESSED AND UNSTRESSED RATS.
002871 03-03

STRESSFUL-SITUATION
ROLE OF THE NEOSTRIATAL DOPAMINERGIC-ACTIVITY IN SEQUENCING
AND SELECTING BEHAVIOURAL-STRATEGIES: FACILITATION OF
PROCESSES INVOLVED IN SELECTING THE BEST STRATEGY IN A
STRESSFUL-SITUATION.
000366 01-04
ANXIETY AND SEDATION DURING A STRESSFUL-SITUATION AFTER SINGLE-
DOSE OF DIAZEPAM VERSUS N DESMETHYLDIAZEPAM — A
CONTROLLED-TRIAL.
002329 02-14

STRESSFUL-SITUATIONS
AGGRESSIVE-BEHAVIOR INDUCED BY APOMORPHINE IN RATS SUBMITTED TO FOUR STRESSFUL-SITUATIONS.
003163 03-07

STRETCH
THE INFLUENCE OF BENZOCTAMINE ON DOPAMINE AND NOREPINEPHRINE CONTENTS OF THE SUBSTANTIA-NIGRA AND ON THE MUSCLE STRETCH REFLEX OF THE CAT.
000054 01-03

STRETCH-INDUCED
STRETCH-INDUCED MYOTUBE GROWTH CORRELATES WITH NA-PUMP ACTIVATION. (UNPUBLISHED PAPER).
002087 02-10

STRETCH-YAWNING-SYNDROME
TESTOSTERONE POTENTIATION OF THE EFFECTIVENESS OF ACTH1-24 ON THE INDUCTION OF THE STRETCH-YAWNING-SYNDROME (SYS) IN MALE GUINEA-PIGS.
003074 03-04

STRIATAL
EFFECTS OF PSYCHOTROPIC-DRUGS ON THE DISTRIBUTION OF 3H DOPAMINE INTO COMPARTMENTS OF RAT STRIATAL SYNAPTOSOMES AND ON SUBSEQUENT DEPOLARIZATION-INDUCED 3H DOPAMINE RELEASE.
000067 01-03

EFFECTS OF DOPAMINERGIC AGONISTS AND ANTAGONISTS ON (3H)APOMORPHINE BINDING TO STRIATAL MEMBRANES; SULPIRIDE LACK OF INTERACTIONS WITH POSITIVE COOPERATIVE (3H)APOMORPHINE BINDING.
000099 01-03

HYPOPHYSECTOMY PREVENTS THE STRIATAL DOPAMINE-RECEPTOR SUPERSENSITIVITY PRODUCED BY CHRONIC HALOPERIDOL TREATMENT.
000132 01-03

ROLE OF DOPAMINE STORAGE FUNCTION IN THE CONTROL OF RAT STRIATAL TYROSINE-HYDROXYLASE ACTIVITY.
000201 01-03

DECARBOXYLATION OF EXOGENOUS L-DOPA IN RAT STRIATUM AFTER LESIONS OF THE DOPAMINERGIC NIGROSTRIATAL NEURONS; THE ROLE OF STRIATAL CAPILLARIES.
000202 01-03

STRIATAL DOPAMINERGIC ACTIVITY DURING WITHDRAWAL FROM CHRONIC NEUROLEPTIC TREATMENT IN RATS.
000203 01-03

BLOCKADE OF STRIATAL NEURONE RESPONSES TO MORPHINE BY AMINOPHYLLINE; EVIDENCE FOR ADENOSINE MEDIATION OF OPIATE ACTION.
000229 01-03

REGULATION OF STRIATAL ACETYLCHOLINE CONCENTRATION BY D2 DOPAMINE-RECEPTORS.
000269 01-03

THE EFFECT OF A NEW FLUORINATED TRICYCLIC NEUROLEPTIC-DRUG ISOFLOXYTHEPIN ON THE RAT STRIATAL DOPAMINE METABOLISM.
000306 01-03

SEX-DIFFERENCES IN AMPHETAMINE-ELICITED ROTATIONAL-BEHAVIOR AND THE LATERALIZATION OF STRIATAL DOPAMINE IN RATS.
000459 01-04

BODY-WEIGHT, FEEDING, AND DRINKING-BEHAVIORS IN RATS WITH KAINIC-ACID-INDUCED LESIONS OF STRIATAL NEURONS -- WITH A NOTE ON BODY-WEIGHT SYMPTOMATOLOGY IN HUNTINGTONS-DISEASE.
000463 01-04

TOLERANCE TO INCREASES IN STRIATAL ACETYLCHOLINE CONCENTRATIONS AFTER REPEATED ADMINISTRATION OF APOMORPHINE-DIPIVALOYL-ESTER.
000464 01-04

EFFECT OF THE NEW GAMMA AMINOBUTYRIC-ACID AGONIST SL-76-002 ON STRIATAL ACETYLCHOLINE; RELATION TO NEUROLEPTIC-INDUCED EXTRAPYRAMIDAL ALTERATIONS.
001119 02-03

HA-966 EFFECTS ON STRIATAL DOPAMINE METABOLISM; IMPLICATIONS FOR DOPAMINE COMPARTMENTALIZAION.
001150 02-03

ADAPTIVE CHANGES OF THE STRIATAL DOPAMINE SYSTEM INDUCED BY REPEATED ADMINISTRATION OF NEUROLEPTICS AND ERGOT DERIVATIVES.
001156 02-03

A COMPARISON OF STRIATAL AND MESOLIMBIC DOPAMINE FUNCTION IN THE RAT DURING 6-MONTH TRIFLUOPERAZINE ADMINISTRATION.
001174 02-03

A COMPARISON OF THE EFFECTS OF METHYLPHENIDATE AND AMPHETAMINE ON THE SIMULTANEOUS RELEASE OF RADIOLABELLED DOPAMINE AND P OR M TYRAMINE FROM RAT STRIATAL SLICES.
001207 02-03

EFFECT OF MOXESTROL ON HALOPERIDOL-INDUCED CHANGES IN STRIATAL ACETYLCHOLINE LEVELS AND DOPAMINE TURNOVER.
001218 02-03

DEVELOPMENT OF ACUTE OPIOID-TOLERANCE AND DEPENDENCE IN RAT STRIATAL NEURONES.
001235 02-03

CALMODULIN RELEASE FROM STRIATAL MEMBRANES AFTER ACUTE AND CHRONIC TREATMENT WITH BUTACLAMOL.
001249 02-03

LONG-TERM EFFECTS OF HALOPERIDOL, CLOZAPINE, AND METHADONE ON RAT STRIATAL CHOLINERGIC AND DOPAMINERGIC DYNAMICS.
001325 02-03

LONG-TERM HALOPERIDOL TREATMENT AND FACTORS EFFECTING THE ACTIVITY OF STRIATAL TYROSINE-HYDROXYLASE.
001348 02-03

BRAIN STRIATAL TYROSINE-HYDROXYLASE: ACTIVATION OF THE ENZYME BY CYCLIC-AMP INDEPENDENT PHOSPHORYLATION.
001423 02-03

PRESYNAPTIC DOPAMINE-RECEPTORS IN STRIATAL NERVE-ENDINGS: ABSENCE OF HALOPERIDOL-INDUCED SUPERSENSITIVITY.
001424 02-03

SELECTIVE INFLUENCE OF ERGOT ALKALOIDS ON CORTICAL AND STRIATAL DOPAMINERGIC-RECEPTORS AND SEROTONERGIC-RECEPTORS.
001447 02-03

EFFECT OF MELANOSTATIN AND THYROLIBERIN ON THE BIOSYNTHESIS AND RELEASE OF DOPAMINE BY RAT-BRAIN STRIATAL P2-FRACTIONS.
001472 02-03

EVIDENCE THAT NORADRENALINE MODULATES THE INCREASE IN STRIATAL DOPAMINE METABOLISM INDUCED BY MUSCARINIC-RECEPTOR STIMULATION.
001518 02-03

STRIATAL DOPAC LEVELS AS A PREDICTOR OF ANTIPSYCHOTIC-EFFICACY.
001533 02-03

GABA AGONISTS DISSOCIATE STRIATAL UNIT ACTIVITY FROM DRUG-INDUCED STEREOTYPED-BEHAVIOUR.
001716 02-04

THE STRIATONIGRAL GABA PATHWAY: FUNCTIONAL AND NEUROCHEMICAL CHARACTERISTICS IN RATS WITH UNILATERAL STRIATAL KAINIC-ACID LESIONS.
001816 02-04

LITHIUM ANTAGONISM OF ETHANOL-INDUCED DEPLETION OF CEREBELLAR GUANOSINE-CYCLIC-MONOPHOSPHATE AND STIMULATION OF STRIATAL DOPAMINE RELEASE.
002242 02-13

SEX-DIFFERENCES IN THE AMPHETAMINE STIMULATED RELEASE OF CATECHOLAMINES FROM RAT STRIATAL TISSUE IN VITRO.
002668 03-03

DURING ONE YEARS NEUROLEPTIC TREATMENT IN RATS STRIATAL DOPAMINE-RECEPTOR BLOCKADE DECREASES BUT SERUM PROLACTIN LEVELS REMAIN ELEVATED.
002707 03-03

THE EFFECT OF GUANOSINE-NUCLEOTIDES ON (3H)SULPIRIDE BINDING TO RAT STRIATAL MEMBRANES.
002722 03-03

SIMILARITIES BETWEEN THE BINDING OF 3H PIFLUTIXOL AND 3H FLUPENTIXOL TO RAT STRIATAL DOPAMINE-RECEPTORS IN VITRO.
002760 03-03

LEVONANTRADOL, A POTENT CANNABINOID RELATED ANALGESIC, ANTAGONIZES HALOPERIDOL-INDUCED ACTIVATION OF STRIATAL DOPAMINE SYNTHESIS.
002786 03-03

KAINATE LESION DISSOCIATES STRIATAL DOPAMINE-RECEPTOR RADIOLIGAND BINDING-SITES.
002803 03-03

FLUORESCENCE HISTOCHEMISTRY INDICATES DAMAGE OF STRIATAL DOPAMINE NERVE TERMINALS IN RATS AFTER MULTIPLE DOSES OF METHAMPHETAMINE.
002812 03-03

ACTIVATION OF SOLUBLE STRIATAL TYROSINE-HYDROXYLASE IN THE RAT BRAIN AFTER CDP-CHOLINE ADMINISTRATION.
002816 03-03

EFFECT OF DOPAMINE ON ACTIVATION OF RAT STRIATAL ADENYLATE-CYCLASE BY FREE MG2 AND GUANYL-NUCLEOTIDES.
002825 03-03

CHARACTERIZATION OF HALOPERIDOL MEDIATED EFFECTS ON RAT STRIATAL TYROSINE-HYDROXYLASE.
002867 03-03

GABA AND BACLOFEN POTENTIATE THE K-EVOKED RELEASE OF METHIONINE-ENKEPHALIN FROM RAT STRIATAL SLICES.
002882 03-03

DOPAMINERGIC AGONIST AND ANTAGONIST EFFECTS ON STRIATAL TYROSINE-HYDROXYLASE DISTRIBUTION.
002898 03-03

EFFECTS OF CHOLECYSTOKININ-OCTAPEPTIDE ON STRIATAL DOPAMINE METABOLISM AND ON APOMORPHINE-INDUCED STEREOTYPED CAGE CLIMBING IN MICE.
003031 03-04

STIMULATORY ACTION OF LISURIDE ON DOPAMINE-SENSITIVE ADENYLATE-CYCLASE IN THE RAT STRIATAL HOMOGENATE.
003718 04-03

EFFECT OF CHRONIC SULPIRIDE ON STRIATAL SPIPERONE BINDING.
003720 04-03

INTERCONVERTING MU AND DELTA-FORMS OF TYPE-1 OPIATE-RECEPTORS IN THE RAT STRIATAL PATCHES.
003737 04-03

PRESYNAPTIC AND POSTSYNAPTIC STRIATAL DOPAMINE-RECEPTORS:
DIFFERENTIAL SENSITIVITY TO APOMORPHINE INHIBITION OF
(3H)DOPAMINE AND (14C)GABA RELEASE IN VITRO.
003741 04-03

THE EFFECT OF LONG-TERM CONCURRENT ADMINISTRATION OF
CHLORPROMAZINE AND LITHIUM ON THE STRIATAL AND FRONTAL
CORTICAL DOPAMINE METABOLISM IN RATS.
003788 04-03

ANTIDOPAMINERGIC EFFECT OF ESTROGENS AT THE STRIATAL LEVEL.
003789 04-03

INVESTIGATION OF ACTION OF ENKEPHALIN ON THE SPONTANEOUS AND
EVOKED RELEASE OF ACETYLCHOLINE FROM RAT CORTICAL AND
STRIATAL SLICES.
003862 04-03

THE INFLUENCE OF D-AMPHETAMINE ON RAT-BRAIN STRIATAL REDUCED
BIOPTERIN CONCENTRATION.
003922 04-03

EFFECTS OF IN VIVO AMPHETAMINE ADMINISTRATION ON DOPAMINE
SYNTHESIS REGULATION IN RAT-BRAIN STRIATAL SYNAPTOSOMES.
(UNPUBLISHED PAPER).
003960 04-03

EFFECTS OF CANNABINOIDS ON CATECHOLAMINE UPTAKE AND RELEASE
IN HYPOTHALAMIC AND STRIATAL SYNAPTOSOMES.
003970 04-03

BETA PHENYLETHYLAMINE REVERSAL OF CHLORPROMAZINE-INDUCED
ACTIVATION OF STRIATAL TYROSINE-HYDROXYLASE AND CATALEPSY.
004018 04-03

CATION REGULATION DIFFERENTIATES SPECIFIC BINDING OF
(3H)SULPIRIDE AND (3H)SPIPERONE TO RAT STRIATAL PREPARATIONS.
004032 04-03

ACTIONS OF MU, KAPPA, SIGMA, DELTA AND AGONIST/ANTAGONIST
OPIATES ON STRIATAL DOPAMINERGIC FUNCTION.
004053 04-03

THE RELATIONSHIP BETWEEN LOSS OF DOPAMINE NERVE TERMINALS,
STRIATAL (3H)SPIROPERIDOL BINDING AND ROTATIONAL-BEHAVIOR IN
UNILATERALLY 6 HYDROXYDOPAMINE LESIONED RATS.
004129 04-04

GENOTYPIC INFLUENCES ON STRIATAL DOPAMINERGIC REGULATION IN
MICE.
004217 04-04

STRIATALLY-EVOKED
EFFECTS OF INTRAPALLIDAL OPIATE-RECEPTOR AGONISTS ON
STRIATALLY-EVOKED HEAD-TURNING.
001785 02-04

STRIATONIGRAL
THE STRIATONIGRAL GABA PATHWAY: FUNCTIONAL AND
NEUROCHEMICAL CHARACTERISTICS IN RATS WITH UNILATERAL
STRIATAL KAINIC-ACID LESIONS.
001816 02-04

RESPONSE OF STRIATONIGRAL SUBSTANCE-P SYSTEMS TO A DOPAMINE-
RECEPTOR AGONIST AND ANTAGONIST.
003826 04-03

STRIATUM
ENKEPHALIN LEVELS DECREASE IN RAT STRIATUM DURING MORPHINE
ABSTINENCE.
000027 01-03

3H IMIPRAMINE BINDING IN NEURONAL AND GLIAL FRACTIONS OF
HORSE STRIATUM.
000033 01-03

COMPARISON OF THE EFFECTS OF THE ISOMERS OF AMPHETAMINE,
METHYLPHENIDATE AND DEOXYPIPRADROL ON THE UPTAKE OF L
(3H)NOREPINEPHRINE AND (3H)DOPAMINE BY SYNAPTIC VESICLES
FROM RAT-WHOLE-BRAIN, STRIATUM AND HYPOTHALAMUS.
000091 01-03

EVIDENCE FOR, AND LOCALIZATION OF, A UNITARY DOPAMINE-
RECEPTOR COMPOSED OF COOPERATIVELY LINKED SUBUNIT BINDING-
SITES IN RAT STRIATUM.
000186 01-03

DECARBOXYLATION OF EXOGENOUS L-DOPA IN RAT STRIATUM AFTER
LESIONS OF THE DOPAMINERGIC NIGROSTRIATAL NEURONS: THE ROLE
OF STRIATAL CAPILLARIES.
000202 01-03

REINNERVATION OF THE DENERVATED STRIATUM BY SUBSTANTIA-NIGRA
TRANSPLANTS: FUNCTIONAL CONSEQUENCES AS REVEALED BY
PHARMACOLOGICAL AND SENSORIMOTOR TESTING.
000347 01-04

INCREASED DOPAMINE-RECEPTOR BINDING IN THE STRIATUM OF RATS
AFTER LONG-TERM ISOLATION.
000398 01-04

ENDOGENOUS GUANYL-NUCLEOTIDES: COMPONENTS OF THE STRIATUM
WHICH CONFER DOPAMINE SENSITIVITY TO ADENYLATE-CYCLASE.
001313 02-03

DECREASE OF GAD IMMUNOREACTIVE NERVE TERMINALS IN THE
SUBSTANTIA-NIGRA AFTER KAINIC-ACID LESION OF THE STRIATUM.
(UNPUBLISHED PAPER).
001400 02-03

CHRONIC LITHIUM REDUCES (3H)SPIROPERIDOL BINDING IN RAT
STRIATUM.
001443 02-03

RELATIONSHIPS BETWEEN STRUCTURE AND ALPHA-ADRENERGIC-RECEPTOR AFFINITY OF CLONIDINE AND AND SOME RELATED CYCLIC-AMIDINES.
002698 03-03
INFLUENCE OF PSYCHOACTIVE AND NONPSYCHOACTIVE CANNABINOIDS ON CHROMATIN STRUCTURE AND FUNCTION IN HUMAN CELLS.
002831 03-03
METHAQUALONE RIA STRUCTURE VERSUS REACTIVITY.
003657 04-01
RIA OPIATES: STRUCTURE VERSUS REACTIVITY.
003659 04-01
PURIFICATION AND SUBUNIT STRUCTURE OF DNA-DEPENDENT RNA-POLYMERASE-BII FROM RAT-BRAIN NUCLEI.
003679 04-01
EFFECT OF 6 HYDROXYDOPAMINE ON THE FINE STRUCTURE OF THE HAMSTER PINEAL-GLAND.
003747 04-03
STUDY ON THE STABILITY OF THE FACTORIAL STRUCTURE OF THE AMP SYSTEM DURING TREATMENT.
004696 04-16

STRUCTURE-ACTIVITY
INHIBITION OF HIGH-AFFINITY CHOLINE UPTAKE: STRUCTURE-ACTIVITY STUDIES.
000026 01-03
STRUCTURE-ACTIVITY RELATIONSHIPS IN THE EFFECTS OF PHENACEMIDE ANALOGS ON SERUM CREATININE AND ANTICONVULSANT ACTIVITY.
000249 01-03
STRUCTURE-ACTIVITY RELATIONSHIP OF PHENCYCLIDINE DERIVATIVES.
001030 02-01
PROSTACYCLIN-DEPENDENT ACTIVATION OF ADENYLATE-CYCLASE IN A NEURONAL SOMATIC CELL HYBRID: PROSTANOID STRUCTURE-ACTIVITY RELATIONSHIPS.
001132 02-03
STRUCTURE-ACTIVITY RELATIONSHIPS AMONG SOME D N ALKYLATED AMPHETAMINES.
001542 02-03
PHENCYCLIDINE (PCP) AND DERIVATIVES: PHARMACOLOGY AND STRUCTURE-ACTIVITY RELATIONSHIPS.
001706 02-04
O METHOXYBENZAMIDES: RELATIONSHIPS BETWEEN STRUCTURE-ACTIVITY, AND PHARMACOKINETICS OF THESE DRUGS.
002246 02-13
CHEMICAL STRUCTURE OF SURVECTOR. STRUCTURE-ACTIVITY RELATIONSHIP.
002262 02-13
PHENYLETHYLAMINE EFFECTS ON DOPAMINE SYNTHESIS. STRUCTURE-ACTIVITY RELATIONSHIPS.
002649 03-02
GABA-AUTORECEPTORS: STRUCTURE-ACTIVITY RELATIONSHIPS FOR AGONISTS.
002678 03-03
STRUCTURE-ACTIVITY AND RECEPTOR BINDING OF ANTAGONIST ANALGESICS.
003611 03-17
SYNTHESIS AND STRUCTURE-ACTIVITY RELATIONSHIP OF A PYRIMIDOPYRIMIDINE DERIVATIVE WITH ANTIDEPRESSANT ACTIVITY.
003653 04-01
PHENYLETHYLAMINE EFFECTS ON DOPAMINE SYNTHESIS: STRUCTURE-ACTIVITY RELATIONSHIPS. (UNPUBLISHED PAPER).
003959 04-03
SPECIFIC GABA-RECEPTOR AGONISTS AND UPTAKE INHIBITORS: DESIGN, DEVELOPMENT AND STRUCTURE-ACTIVITY STUDIES.
004725 04-17

STRUCTURES
INHIBITION OF MONOAMINE-OXIDASE BY CLORGYLINE AND DEPRENYL IN CIRCUMVENTRICULAR STRUCTURES OF RAT-BRAIN.
000159 01-03
ANTINOCICEPTIVE ACTION OF MORPHINE AND PENTAZOCINE ON UNIT ACTIVITY IN THE NUCLEUS-CENTRALIS-LATERALIS, NUCLEUS-VENTRALIS-LATERALIS AND NEARBY STRUCTURES OF THE CAT.
002837 03-03
THE EFFECT OF LITHIUM-HYDROXYBUTYRATE ON THE BIOELECTRICAL-ACTIVITY OF THE CORTEX AND SOME SUBCORTICAL STRUCTURES OF THE RABBIT BRAIN.
003994 04-03
THE EFFECT OF PHARMACOLOGICAL DESTRUCTION OF HYPOTHALAMIC MONOAMINERGIC STRUCTURES ON BODY-TEMPERATURE AND GAS-EXCHANGE DURING EXTREME COOLING.
004016 04-03
LESIONS OF AMYGDALA, PYRIFORM CORTEX AND OTHER BRAIN STRUCTURES DUE TO DIPIPERIDINOETHANE INTOXICATION.
004273 04-05

STRUGGLING
EFFECTS OF ANALGESICS AND CNS-ACTING DRUGS ON STRUGGLING FOLLOWING REPETITIVE STIMULATION OF THE TAIL, AND FLEXOR REFLEX TO A SINGLE STIMULATION OF THE SCIATIC-NERVE IN RATS.
004148 04-04

STRYCHNINE
DISSOCIATION OF THE STRYCHNINE EFFECT ON VISUAL-MEMORY AND VERBAL-MEMORY IN ORGANIC-PSYCHOSYNDROMES.
000816 01-14

STRYCHNINE EFFECTS ON THE SENSORY RESPONSE PATTERNS OF RETICULAR FORMATION NEURONS.
001219 02-03
DISSOCIATION OF THE STRYCHNINE EFFECT ON VISUAL-MEMORY AND VERBAL-MEMORY IN ORGANIC-PSYCHOSYNDROMES.
002155 02-11
INFLUENCE OF STRYCHNINE ON THE CONSOLIDATION PHASE OF VISUAL-MEMORY IN GERONTOPSYCHIATRIC-PATIENTS.
002156 02-11
SENSITIVITY OF IDENTIFIED MEDIAL HYPOTHALAMIC NEURONS TO GABA, GLYCINE AND RELATED AMINO-ACIDS: INFLUENCE OF BICUCULLINE, PICROTOXIN AND STRYCHNINE ON SYNAPTIC INHIBITION.
002674 03-03
MODIFICATION OF MOTOR-ACTIVITY, PASSIVE-AVOIDANCE CONDITIONING AND EVOKED-POTENTIALS BY MICROINJECTIONS OF STRYCHNINE IN BOTH CAUDATE-NUCLEI IN CATS.
003101 03-04
SUPRASPINAL INHIBITION OF THE EXCITATION OF DORSAL-HORN NEURONES BY IMPULSES IN UNMYELINATED PRIMARY AFFERENTS: LACK OF EFFECT BY STRYCHNINE AND BICUCULLINE.
003778 04-03

STRYCHNINE-INDUCED
VOLTAGE CLAMP STUDY OF CAT SPINAL MOTONEURONS DURING STRYCHNINE-INDUCED SEIZURES.
002886 03-03

STUTTERERS
PRINCIPAL AND DIFFERENTIAL-EFFECTS OF HALOPERIDOL AND PLACEBO TREATMENTS UPON SPEECH DISFLUENCIES IN STUTTERERS.
000713 01-11

STUTTERING
ADULT-ONSET STUTTERING TREATED WITH ANTICONVULSANTS.
003290 03-11

SUBACUTE
GLIAL CELL EFFECTS OF SUBACUTE FORMIC-ACID VAPOUR EXPOSURE.
000527 01-05
ISOPRINOSINE IN SUBACUTE SCLEROSING PANENCEPHALITIS.
000687 01-11
REVIEW OF 38 CASES OF SUBACUTE SCLEROSING PANENCEPHALITIS: EFFECT OF AMANTADINE ON THE NATURAL COURSE OF THE DISEASE.
000718 01-11
SUBACUTE CANNABINOID TREATMENT: ANTICONVULSANT ACTIVITY AND WITHDRAWAL EXCITABILITY IN MICE.
001671 02-04

SUBARACHNOID
DEPRESSION OF RESERPINE-INDUCED MUSCULAR RIGIDITY IN RATS AFTER ADMINISTRATION OF LISURIDE INTO THE SPINAL SUBARACHNOID SPACE.
002962 03-04

SUBCELLULAR
SEROTONIN-SENSITIVE ADENYLATE-CYCLASE AND (3H)SEROTONIN BINDING-SITES IN THE CNS OF THE RAT -- II. RESPECTIVE REGIONAL AND SUBCELLULAR DISTRIBUTIONS AND ONTOGENETIC DEVELOPMENTS.
000214 01-03
SUBCELLULAR REACTION OF THE BRAIN TO HYPOXIA.
001354 02-03
NA-INDEPENDENT BINDING OF (3H)GABA AND (3H)MUSCIMOL TO SUBCELLULAR PARTICLES OF NEURAL PRIMARY CULTURES AND WHOLE BRAIN.
002699 03-03
INCORPORATION OF N ACETYLMANNOSAMINE INTO RAT-BRAIN SUBCELLULAR GANGLIOSIDES: EFFECT OF PENTYLENETETRAZOL-INDUCED CONVULSIONS IN BRAIN GANGLIOSIDES.
002937 03-03
REGIONAL AND SUBCELLULAR LOCALIZATION IN RAT-BRAIN OF THE ENZYMES THAT CAN SYNTHESIZE GAMMA HYDROXYBUTYRIC-ACID.
003675 04-01
NEWLY SYNTHESIZED CHOLECYSTOKININ IN SUBCELLULAR FRACTIONS OF THE RAT-BRAIN.
003805 04-03
DOPAMINE-RECEPTORS IN SUBCELLULAR FRACTIONS FROM BOVINE CAUDATE: ENRICHMENT OF (3H)SPIPERONE BINDING IN A POSTSYNAPTIC MEMBRANE FRACTION.
003948 04-03
EVIDENCE THAT THERE ARE SUBCELLULAR POOLS OF NOREPINEPHRINE AND THAT THERE IS FLUX OF NOREPINEPHRINE BETWEEN THESE POOLS.
004004 04-03

SUBCHRONIC
DOUBLE-BLIND COMPARISON OF ALPRAZOLAM AND DIAZEPAM FOR SUBCHRONIC WITHDRAWAL FROM ALCOHOL.
003332 03-11
EFFECTS OF SUBCHRONIC DESMETHYLIMIPRAMINE (DMI) TREATMENT OF THE CLASSICALLY CONDITIONED EYEBLINK RESPONSE IN RABBITS.
004180 04-04

SUBCHRONIC-TREATMENT
ATTENUATION OF AMPHETAMINE ANOREXIA IN RATS FOLLOWING SUBCHRONIC-TREATMENT WITH A TRICYCLIC-ANTIDEPRESSANT.
000501 01-04

DOPAMINE-RECEPTOR BLOCKADE IN RAT-BRAIN AFTER ACUTE AND
SUBCHRONIC-TREATMENT WITH TRICYCLIC-ANTIDEPRESSANTS.
001314 02-03
SUBCHRONIC-TREATMENT WITH THE TRICYCLIC-ANTIDEPRESSANT DMI
INCREASES ISOLATION-INDUCED FIGHTING IN RATS.
004252 04-04

SUBCLINICAL
BEHAVIORAL-TEST FOR DETECTION OF SUBCLINICAL BRAIN-DAMAGE: AN
EXPERIMENTAL MODEL.
003120 03-04

SUBCORTICAL
APOMORPHINE HALOPERIDOL INTERACTIONS: DIFFERENT TYPES OF
ANTAGONISM IN CORTICAL AND SUBCORTICAL BRAIN REGIONS.
002662 03-03
EFFECT OF 6 HYDROXYDOPAMINE LESIONS OF THE MEDIAL PREFRONTAL-
CORTEX ON NEUROTRANSMITTER SYSTEMS IN SUBCORTICAL SITES IN
THE RAT.
002869 03-03
THE EFFECT OF LITHIUM-HYDROXYBUTYRATE ON THE BIOELECTRICAL-
ACTIVITY OF THE CORTEX AND SOME SUBCORTICAL STRUCTURES OF
THE RABBIT BRAIN.
003994 04-03

SUBCUTANEOUS
SUBCUTANEOUS SILASTIC IMPLANTS: MAINTENANCE OF HIGH BLOOD
ETHANOL LEVELS IN RATS DRINKING A LIQUID DIET.
001865 02-06
ON CORRELATION OF BEHAVIORAL-REACTIONS AND NEURONAL ACTIVITY
IN THE HYPOTHALAMUS UNDER SUBCUTANEOUS GASTRIN INJECTION.
002892 03-03
SEIZURES ELICITED BY SUBCUTANEOUS INJECTION OF METRAZOL DURING
ONTOGENESIS IN RATS.
003039 03-04

SUBCUTANEOUSLY
CAPTOPRIL GIVEN INTRACEREBROVENTRICULARLY, SUBCUTANEOUSLY OR
BY GAVAGE INHIBITS ANGIOTENSIN CONVERTING ENZYME ACTIVITY
IN THE RAT-BRAIN.
001614 02-04

SUBGROUP
IDENTIFICATION OF A SUBGROUP OF TARDIVE-DYSKINESIA PATIENTS BY
PHARMACOLOGIC-PROBES.
000708 01-11

SUBJECTIVE
PLASMA AND SALIVA LEVELS OF CHLORPROMAZINE AND SUBJECTIVE
RESPONSE.
000826 01-14
CONTRIBUTIONS OF INDIVIDUAL DIFFERENCES TO SUBJECTIVE
INTOXICATION.
002202 02-12
THE EFFECTS OF COMBINED SEDATIVE AND ANXIOLYTIC-PREPARATIONS
ON SUBJECTIVE ASPECTS OF SLEEP AND OBJECTIVE MEASURE OF
AROUSAL AND PERFORMANCE THE MORNING FOLLOWING NOCTURNAL
MEDICATION: II. REPEATED DOSES.
002331 02-14
VIGILANCE IMPAIRING DRUGS: ANALYSIS OF SUBJECTIVE RESPONSES.
002332 02-14
EFFECTS OF ATENOLOL AND PROPRANOLOL ON HUMAN PERFORMANCE
AND SUBJECTIVE FEELINGS.
002340 02-14
SUBJECTIVE DRUG-EFFECTS AND DRUG PREFERENCE IN HEALTHY
VOLUNTEERS AS A MODEL OF A DRUGS REINFORCING EFFECTS:
STUDIES ON NOMIFENSINE, AMPHETAMINE AND PLACEBO.
002362 02-14
SUBJECTIVE ASSESSMENT OF SEXUAL-DYSFUNCTION OF PATIENTS ON
LONG-TERM ADMINISTRATION OF DIGOXIN.
002443 02-15
SUBJECTIVE RESPONSE TO ANTIPSYCHOTIC-DRUGS.
003202 03-08
DOSE-EFFECT OF DEAE ON SUBJECTIVE PROBLEMS, VERTIGO,
DEPRESSION, ASTHENIA, CEPHALALGIA, AND TONIC POSTURAL
ACTIVITY PROBLEMS RECORDED WITH STATOKINESIMETER IN
POSTCONCUSSIONAL-SYNDROME.
004472 04-11
EFFECTS OF SUPIDIMIDE (CG-3033) ON OBJECTIVE AND SUBJECTIVE SLEEP
PARAMETERS (A SLEEP LABORATORY STUDY).
004567 04-14

SUBJECTIVE-EFFECTS
BEHAVIORAL-EFFECTS AND SUBJECTIVE-EFFECTS OF BETA-ADRENERGIC
BLOCKADE IN PHOBIC-SUBJECTS.
002060 02-10

SUBMAXILLARY-GLAND
CHRONIC SYMPATHETIC DENERVATION INCREASES MUSCARINIC-
CHOLINOCEPTOR BINDING IN THE RAT SUBMAXILLARY-GLAND.
000235 01-03

SUBMICROMOLAR
PROSTAGLANDIN-E RELEASE BY RAT MEDIAL BASAL HYPOTHALAMUS IN
VITRO. INHIBITION BY MELATONIN AT SUBMICROMOLAR
CONCENTRATIONS.
001159 02-03

SUBNORMAL-PATIENTS
SELF-INJURY IN SUBNORMAL-PATIENTS.
003452 03-14

SUBPOPULATIONS
DISCRIMINATION OF FUNCTIONALLY HETEROGENEOUS RECEPTOR
SUBPOPULATIONS: ANTIPSYCHOTIC AND ANTIDOPAMINERGIC
PROPERTIES OF METOCLOPRAMIDE.
002877 03-03

SUBSENSITIVITY
REPEATED TRICYCLICS INDUCE A PROGRESSIVE DOPAMINE-
AUTORECEPTOR SUBSENSITIVITY INDEPENDENT OF DAILY DRUG-
TREATMENT.
000047 01-03
TRICYCLIC-ANTIDEPRESSANTS INDUCE SUBSENSITIVITY OF PRESYNAPTIC
DOPAMINE-AUTORECEPTORS.
000048 01-03
SUBSENSITIVITY OF THE NOREPINEPHRINE-RECEPTOR COUPLED
ADENYLATE-CYCLASE SYSTEM IN BRAIN: EFFECTS OF NISOXETINE
VERSUS FLUOXETINE.
000208 01-03
FUNCTIONAL EVIDENCE FOR SUBSENSITIVITY OF NORADRENERGIC-
ALPHA2-RECEPTORS AFTER CHRONIC DESIPRAMINE TREATMENT.
000283 01-03
ATTEMPTS TO DEVELOP SUPERSENSITIVITY OR SUBSENSITIVITY RETINAL
DOPAMINE-RECEPTORS AFTER VARIOUS TREATMENTS WITH
ANTAGONISTS OR AGONISTS.
001350 02-03
DEVELOPMENT OF AND RECOVERY FROM SUBSENSITIVITY OF THE
NORADRENERGIC CYCLIC-AMP GENERATING SYSTEM IN BRAIN: EFFECT
OF AMPHETAMINE FOLLOWING INHIBITION OF ITS AROMATIC
HYDROXYLATION BY IPRINDOLE.
001353 02-03
REPEATED ANTIDEPRESSANT TREATMENTS INDUCE A LONG-LASTING
DOPAMINE-AUTORECEPTOR SUBSENSITIVITY: IS DAILY TREATMENT
NECESSARY FOR CLINICAL EFFICACY?
002659 03-03
AN ENHANCED SENSITIVITY OF MUSCARINIC CHOLINERGIC-RECEPTOR
ASSOCIATED WITH DOPAMINERGIC-RECEPTOR SUBSENSITIVITY AFTER
CHRONIC ANTIDEPRESSANT TREATMENT.
002788 03-03
MORPHINE WITHDRAWAL CAUSES SUBSENSITIVITY OF ADRENERGIC-
RECEPTOR RESPONSE.
002838 03-03

SUBSTANCE
INHIBITORY ACTION OF MORPHINE ON THE RELEASE OF A BRADYKININ-
LIKE SUBSTANCE AFTER SCIATIC-NERVE STIMULATION.
001293 02-03

SUBSTANCE-P
DEMONSTRATION OF SUBSTANCE-P IN AORTIC NERVE AFFERENT FIBERS
BY COMBINED USE OF FLOURESCENT RETROGRADE NEURONAL
LABELING AND IMMUNOCYTOCHEMISTRY. (UNPUBLISHED PAPER).
001024 02-01
DEPRESSION AND FACILITATION OF SYNAPTIC RESPONSES IN CAT
DORSAL-HORN BY SUBSTANCE-P ADMINISTERED INTO SUBSTANTIA-
GELATINOSA.
001191 02-03
EVIDENCE SUGGESTING A TRANSMITTER OR NEUROMODULATORY ROLE
FOR SUBSTANCE-P AT THE FIRST SYNAPSE OF THE BARORECEPTOR
REFLEX.
001264 02-03
SUBSTANCE-P, MORPHINE AND METHIONINE-ENKEPHALIN: EFFECTS ON
SPONTANEOUS AND EVOKED NEURONAL FIRING IN THE NUCLEUS-
RETICULARIS-GIGANTOCELLULARIS OF THE RAT.
001267 02-03
THE EFFECT OF MORPHINE ON THE CONTENT OF SEROTONIN, 5
HYDROXYINDOLEACETIC-ACID AND SUBSTANCE-P IN THE NUCLEI
RAPHE-MAGNUS AND RETICULARIS-GIGANTOCELLULARIS.
001328 02-03
FURTHER CHARACTERIZATION OF THE BINDING OF SUBSTANCE-P TO A
FRACTION FROM RABBIT BRAIN ENRICHED IN SYNAPTIC MEMBRANES.
001394 02-03
SUBSTANCE-P SUPPRESSES STRESS-INDUCED EATING.
001725 02-04
PHARMACOLOGICAL CHARACTERIZATION OF SCRATCHING-BEHAVIOUR
INDUCED BY INTRACRANIAL INJECTION OF SUBSTANCE-P AND
SOMATOSTATIN.
002980 03-04
SUBSTANCE-P, HEXAPEPTIDE-PGLU6(SP6-11), ANALGESIA AND
SEROTONIN DEPLETION.
003050 03-04
CENTRAL-EFFECTS OF SUBSTANCE-P IN FOWLS.
003075 03-04
RESPONSE OF STRIATONIGRAL SUBSTANCE-P SYSTEMS TO A DOPAMINE-
RECEPTOR AGONIST AND ANTAGONIST.
003826 04-03
NERVE GROWTH-FACTOR STIMULATES DEVELOPMENT OF SUBSTANCE-P
IN THE EMBRYONIC SPINAL-CORD.
003881 04-03
SUBSTANCE-P INCREASES HYPOTHALAMIC BLOOD FLOW VIA AN
INDIRECT ADRENERGIC CHOLINERGIC INTERACTION.
003887 04-03

INTRANIGRAL INJECTION OF CAPSAICIN ENHANCES MOTOR-ACTIVITY AND DEPLETES NIGRAL 5 HYDROXYTRYPTAMINE BUT NOT SUBSTANCE-P.
004100 04-04

BEHAVIORAL-EVIDENCE THAT SUBSTANCE-P MAY BE A SPINAL-CORD SENSORY NEUROTRANSMITTER.
004200 04-04

INTRACEREBRAL SUBSTANCE-P IN MICE: BEHAVIORAL-EFFECTS AND NARCOTIC-AGENTS.
004218 04-04

SUBSTANCE-P-INDUCED
OPPOSITE EFFECTS OF NALOXONE ON SUBSTANCE-P-INDUCED IN BRAIN DOPA SYNTHESIS AND IN LOCOMOTOR-ACTIVITY IN RATS.
003799 04-03

SUBSTANTIA-GELATINOSA
DEPRESSION AND FACILITATION OF SYNAPTIC RESPONSES IN CAT DORSAL-HORN BY SUBSTANCE-P ADMINISTERED INTO SUBSTANTIA-GELATINOSA.
001191 02-03

EVIDENCE THAT THE OPIATE-RECEPTORS OF THE SUBSTANTIA-GELATINOSA CONTRIBUTE TO THE DEPRESSION, BY INTRAVENOUS MORPHINE, OF THE SPINAL TRANSMISSION OF IMPULSES IN UNMYELINATED PRIMARY AFFERENTS.
002767 03-03

SELECTIVE NEUROTOXIC-ACTION OF CAPSAICIN ON GLOMERULAR C-TYPE TERMINALS IN RAT SUBSTANTIA-GELATINOSA.
003143 03-06

SUBSTANTIA-NIGRA
THE INFLUENCE OF BENZOCTAMINE ON DOPAMINE AND NOREPINEPHRINE CONTENTS OF THE SUBSTANTIA-NIGRA AND ON THE MUSCLE STRETCH REFLEX OF THE CAT.
000054 01-03

GABA INHIBITION OF 3H GLYCINE RELEASE FROM SLICES OF RAT SUBSTANTIA-NIGRA IN VITRO.
000157 01-03

ACUTE AND CHRONIC EFFECTS OF NEUROLEPTICS AND ACUTE EFFECTS OF APOMORPHINE AND AMPHETAMINE ON DOPAMINE TURNOVER IN CORPUS-STRIATUM AND SUBSTANTIA-NIGRA OF THE RAT-BRAIN.
000215 01-03

REINNERVATION OF THE DENERVATED STRIATUM BY SUBSTANTIA-NIGRA TRANSPLANTS: FUNCTIONAL CONSEQUENCES AS REVEALED BY PHARMACOLOGICAL AND SENSORIMOTOR TESTING.
000347 01-04

ROTATIONAL-BEHAVIOR INDUCED BY COCAINE ANALOGS IN RATS WITH UNILATERAL 6 HYDROXYDOPAMINE LESIONS OF THE SUBSTANTIA-NIGRA: DEPENDENCE UPON DOPAMINE UPTAKE INHIBITION.
000404 01-04

POSTAMPHETAMINE DEPRESSION OF SELF-STIMULATION RESPONDING FROM THE SUBSTANTIA-NIGRA: REVERSAL BY TRICYCLIC-ANTIDEPRESSANTS.
000419 01-04

ALTERATIONS IN BASAL FIRING-RATE AND AUTORECEPTOR SENSITIVITY OF DOPAMINE NEURONS IN THE SUBSTANTIA-NIGRA FOLLOWING ACUTE AND EXTENDED EXPOSURE TO ESTROGEN.
001167 02-03

DECREASE OF GAD IMMUNOREACTIVE NERVE TERMINALS IN THE SUBSTANTIA-NIGRA AFTER KAINIC-ACID LESION OF THE STRIATUM. (UNPUBLISHED PAPER).
001400 02-03

HANDEDNESS IN RATS: BLOCKADE OF REACHING-BEHAVIOR BY UNILATERAL 6 OHDA INJECTIONS INTO SUBSTANTIA-NIGRA AND CAUDATE-NUCLEUS.
001778 02-04

A TOPOGRAPHIC LOCALIZATION OF ENKEPHALIN ON THE DOPAMINE NEURONS OF THE RAT SUBSTANTIA-NIGRA AND VENTRAL TEGMENTAL AREA DEMONSTRATED BY COMBINED HISTOFLUORESCENCE IMMUNOCYTOCHEMISTRY.
002639 03-01

EFFECT OF TENTANUS TOXIN ON TRANSMITTER RELEASE FROM THE SUBSTANTIA-NIGRA AND STRIATUM IN VITRO.
002691 03-03

THE PARTICIPATION OF SUBSTANTIA-NIGRA ZONA-COMPACTA AND ZONA-RETICULATA NEURONS IN MORPHINE SUPPRESSION OF CAUDATE SPONTANEOUS NEURONAL ACTIVITIES IN THE RAT.
002718 03-03

THE EFFECT OF SPECIFIC BRAIN LESIONS ON THE HIGH-AFFINITY BINDING OF GABA IN THE SUBSTANTIA-NIGRA.
002795 03-03

BIPHASIC-EFFECTS AND OPPOSITE-EFFECTS OF DOPAMINE AND APOMORPHINE ON ENDOGENOUS GABA RELEASE IN THE RAT SUBSTANTIA-NIGRA.
002923 03-03

EFFECTS OF ELECTROLYTIC AND 6 HYDROXYDOPAMINE LESIONS OF THE LATERAL HYPOTHALAMUS ON ROTATION EVOKED BY ELECTRICAL-STIMULATION OF THE SUBSTANTIA-NIGRA IN RATS.
003081 03-04

RELATIONSHIP BETWEEN THE PRESENCE OF DOPAMINERGIC NEURONS AND GABA-RECEPTORS IN SUBSTANTIA-NIGRA: EFFECTS OF LESIONS.
003797 04-03

THE EFFECT OF SODIUM-DIPROPYLACETATE ON GAMMA AMINOBUTYRIC-ACID DEPENDENT INHIBITION IN THE RAT-CORTEX AND SUBSTANTIA-NIGRA IN RELATION TO ITS ANTICONVULSANT ACTIVITY.
003880 04-03

IN VIVO EVIDENCE FOR GABAERGIC CONTROL OF SEROTONIN RELEASE IN THE CAT SUBSTANTIA-NIGRA.
004011 04-03

ROTATIONAL-BEHAVIOUR ELICITED BY 5 HT IN THE RAT: EVIDENCE FOR AN INHIBITORY ROLE OF 5 HT IN THE SUBSTANTIA-NIGRA AND CORPUS-STRIATUM.
004141 04-04

MORPHINE DIFFERENTIALLY AFFECTS VENTRAL TEGMENTAL AND SUBSTANTIA-NIGRA BRAIN REWARD THRESHOLDS.
004187 04-04

THE INFLUENCE OF UNILATERAL 6 HYDROXYDOPAMINE LESIONS OF THE SUBSTANTIA-NIGRA IN THE ABSENCE OF THE TELENCEPHALON.
004197 04-04

SUBSTITUTED
STUDIES ON SEVERAL 7 SUBSTITUTED N,N DIMETHYLTRYPTAMINES.
001020 02-01

6 SUBSTITUTED AMINO-4H-S-TRIAZOLOBENZODIAZEPINES AND 4 SUBSTITUTED AMINO-6H-S-TRIAZOLOBENZODIAZEPINES WITH POTENTIAL ANTIANXIETY ACTIVITY.
001076 02-02

THE EFFECTS OF SUBSTITUTED BENZAMIDES ON FROG RECTUS-ABDOMINIS.
001228 02-03

STEREOSELECTIVE ACTIONS OF SUBSTITUTED BENZAMIDE DRUGS ON CEREBRAL DOPAMINE MECHANISMS.
001301 02-03

CLINICAL-EXPERIENCE WITH SUBSTITUTED BENZAMIDES IN FRENCH-SPEAKING COUNTRIES.
002036 02-09

SUBSTITUTED PHENETHYLAMINES AND ANOREXIA.
002541 02-17

CENTRALLY ACTIVE N SUBSTITUTED ANALOGS OF 3,4 METHYLENEDIOXYPHENYLISOPROPYLAMINE (3,4 METHYLENEDIOXYAMPHETAMINE).
003683 04-02

1 SUBSTITUTED BENZYLTETRAHYDROPYRIMIDONES: A SERIES WITH STIMULANT AND DEPRESSANT ACTIVITIES.
003687 04-02

ACYLCYANAMIDES, ACYLUREA, AND VARIOUS SUBSTITUTED ARYLALLOPHANATES; EFFECT ON THE CNS.
003689 04-02

COMPARATIVE-EFFECTS OF SUBSTITUTED PHENYLETHYLAMINES ON BRAIN SEROTONERGIC MECHANISMS.
003854 04-03

COMPARISON OF THE POTENCIES OF CLEBOPRIDE AND OTHER SUBSTITUTED BENZAMIDE DRUGS ON ISOLATED GASTROINTESTINAL TRACT OF THE GUINEA-PIG AND RAT.
003928 04-03

SUBSTITUTION
ENHANCED RESPONSES TO OPIATES PRODUCED BY A SINGLE GENE SUBSTITUTION IN THE MOUSE.
001677 02-04

EFFECTS OF PENTAZOCINE AND NALORPHINE ON MOTILITY IN CHRONICALLY MORPHINE TREATED RATS: A POTENTIAL SUBSTITUTION TEST TO DETECT THE NARCOTIC CHARACTER OF A DRUG.
003555 03-16

SUBSTRATE
EVIDENCE THAT A PREFERRED SUBSTRATE FOR MONOAMINE-OXIDASE-B MEDIATES STIMULUS PROPERTIES OF MAO-INHIBITORS: A POSSIBLE ROLE FOR BETA PHENYLETHYLAMINE IN THE COCAINE CUE.
000363 01-04

ESR STUDIES OF BOVINE PLASMA AMINE-OXIDASE: PROBING OF THE ENVIRONMENT ABOUT THE SUBSTRATE LIBERATED SULFHYDRYL GROUPS IN THE ACTIVE SITE. (UNPUBLISHED PAPER).
001066 02-01

TELE-METHYLHISTAMINE IS A SPECIFIC MAO-B SUBSTRATE IN MAN.
002230 02-13

SUBSTRATES
ADENOSINE ANALOGS AS SUBSTRATES AND INHIBITORS OF S ADENOSYLHOMOCYSTEINE-HYDROLASE. (UNPUBLISHED PAPER).
001021 02-01

SWIMMING CAPACITY OF MICE AFTER PROLONGED TREATMENT WITH PSYCHOSTIMULANTS: II. EFFECT OF METHAMPHETAMINE ON SWIMMING PERFORMANCE AND AVAILABILITY OF METABOLIC SUBSTRATES.
001613 02-04

SPECIES-DIFFERENCES IN THE DEAMINATION OF DOPAMINE AND OTHER SUBSTRATES FOR MONOAMINE-OXIDASE IN BRAIN.
002233 02-13

SUBSYNDROMES
SUBSYNDROMES OF TARDIVE-DYSKINESIA.
002421 02-15

SUBTHRESHOLD
EFFECT OF REPEATED ELECTROCONVULSIVE-SHOCKS (ECS) ON
SUBTHRESHOLD DOSES OF SOME CNS STIMULANTS.
001361 02-03

SUBTYPES
COMPARISON OF BETA-ADRENERGIC-RECEPTOR SUBTYPES IN
MAMMALIAN TISSUES.
000207 01-03

PERIPHERAL ALPHA-ADRENERGIC-RECEPTOR SUBTYPES.
000901 01-16

DEXAMETHASONE-SUPPRESSION-TEST IDENTIFIES SUBTYPES OF
DEPRESSION WHICH RESPOND TO DIFFERENT ANTIDEPRESSANTS.
001971 02-09

SUBTYPES OF DEPRESSION BASED ON EXCRETION OF MHPG AND
RESPONSE TO NORTRIPTYLINE.
002488 02-16

EFFECT OF KAINIC-ACID LESIONS ON MUSCARINIC AGONIST RECEPTOR
SUBTYPES IN RAT STRIATUM.
002679 03-03

BETA-ADRENERGIC-RECEPTOR SUBTYPES: PROPERTIES, DISTRIBUTION,
AND REGULATION.
002829 03-03

CHARACTERIZATION AND QUANTITATION OF ALPHA-ADRENERGIC-
RECEPTOR SUBTYPES IN RAT HYPOTHALAMUS.
002839 03-03

THE DEXAMETHASONE-SUPPRESSION-TEST IN THE IDENTIFICATION OF
SUBTYPES OF DEPRESSION DIFFERENTIALLY RESPONSIVE TO
ANTIDEPRESSANTS.
003211 03-09

DEPRESSION SUBTYPES AFFECT THE STEADY-STATE PLASMA LEVELS AND
THERAPEUTIC-EFFICACY OF AMITRIPTYLINE AND NORTRIPTYLINE.
003244 03-09

SUBUNIT
EVIDENCE FOR, AND LOCALIZATION OF, A UNITARY DOPAMINE-
RECEPTOR COMPOSED OF COOPERATIVELY LINKED SUBUNIT BINDING-
SITES IN RAT STRIATUM.
000186 01-03

UNITARY DOPAMINERGIC-RECEPTOR COMPOSED OF COOPERATIVELY
LINKED AGONIST AND ANTAGONIST SUBUNIT BINDING-SITES.
001342 02-03

PURIFICATION AND SUBUNIT STRUCTURE OF DNA-DEPENDENT RNA-
POLYMERASE-BII FROM RAT-BRAIN NUCLEI.
003679 04-01

SUCCINATE-DEHYDROGENASE
CHANGES IN THE CORTICAL ACTIVITY OF SUCCINATE-DEHYDROGENASE
UNDER THE INFLUENCE OF CHLORPROMAZINE (A HISTOCHEMICAL-
STUDY AND ELECTROCYTOCHEMICAL-STUDY).
002784 03-03

SUCCINIC-DEHYDROGENASE
THE EFFECT OF FRUSEMIDE PIRETANIDE AND BUMETANIDE ON COCHLEAR
SUCCINIC-DEHYDROGENASE.
003757 04-03

SUCKLING
THE INFLUENCE OF DAILY BIOLOGICAL-RHYTHMICITY ON THE HOMING-
BEHAVIOR, PSYCHOPHARMACOLOGICAL RESPONSIVENESS, LEARNING
AND RETENTION OF SUCKLING RATS. (PH.D. DISSERTATION).
001660 02-04

SUCKLINGS
BEHAVIORAL-EFFECTS OF HASHISH IN MICE: II. NURSING-BEHAVIOR AND
DEVELOPMENT OF THE SUCKLINGS.
001626 02-04

SUCROSE
DOSE-RESPONSE RELATIONSHIP BETWEEN NALOXONE INJECTIONS AND
INTAKE OF SUCROSE SOLUTION.
003118 03-04

SUDDEN
AMITRIPTYLINE PROVIDES LONG-LASTING IMMUNIZATION AGAINST
SUDDEN CARDIAC DEATH FROM COCAINE.
003122 03-05

SUFFERING
PRELIMINARY TRIAL OF CLONIDINE TREATMENT IN TWO PATIENTS
SUFFERING FROM CHRONIC SCHIZOPHRENIA.
004320 04-08

SULFAMOYLMETHYL-BENZISOXAZOLE
EFFECTS OF 3 SULFAMOYLMETHYL-BENZISOXAZOLE (AD-810) AND SOME
ANTIEPILEPTICS ON THE KINDLED SEIZURES IN THE NEOCORTEX,
HIPPOCAMPUS AND AMYGDALA IN RATS.
004149 04-04

SULFAMOYLMETHYL-1-2-BENZISOXAZOLE
3 SULFAMOYLMETHYL-1-2-BENZISOXAZOLE, A NEW TYPE OF
ANTICONVULSANT-DRUG: PHARMACOLOGICAL PROFILE.
000012 01-02

3 SULFAMOYLMETHYL-1-2-BENZISOXAZOLE, A NEW TYPE OF
ANTICONVULSANT-DRUG: ELECTROENCEPHALOGRAPHIC PROFILE.
000142 01-03

SULFHYDRYL
ESR STUDIES OF BOVINE PLASMA AMINE-OXIDASE; PROBING OF THE
ENVIRONMENT ABOUT THE SUBSTRATE LIBERATED SULFHYDRYL
GROUPS IN THE ACTIVE SITE. (UNPUBLISHED PAPER).
001066 02-01

SULFIRAM
CONCENTRATION OF SEROTONIN METABOLITES IN THE CEREBROSPINAL-
FLUID FROM ALCOHOLICS BEFORE AND DURING SULFIRAM THERAPY.
002095 02-11

SULPHO-ADENOSYL-L-METHIONINE
THE ANTIDEPRESSANT ACTION OF SULPHO-ADENOSYL-L-METHIONINE
(SAME) COMPARED WITH THAT OF CHLORIMIPRAMINE:
HYPOTHETICAL INTERPRETATIONS OF THE MECHANISM-OF-ACTION.
003150 03-07

SULPIRIDE
BIOAVAILABILITY OF 14C SULPIRIDE IN DOGS.
000017 01-03

STUDIES ON THE DISTRIBUTION OF 14C SULPIRIDE AND ITS METABOLITES
IN THE RAT AND GUINEA-PIG.
000078 01-03

EFFECTS OF DOPAMINERGIC AGONISTS AND ANTAGONISTS ON
(3H)APOMORPHINE BINDING TO STRIATAL MEMBRANES; SULPIRIDE
LACK OF INTERACTIONS WITH POSITIVE COOPERATIVE
(3H)APOMORPHINE BINDING.
000099 01-03

STUDY ON VISUALLY-EVOKED-POTENTIALS IN SCHIZOPHRENIC-PATIENTS
IN SULPIRIDE THERAPY.
000550 01-08

EFFECTS OF CHRONIC-TREATMENT WITH L SULPIRIDE AND HALOPERIDOL
ON CENTRAL DOPAMINE TURNOVER EVALUATED IN DOPAMINE CELL
BODY AND NERVE TERMINAL-RICH AREAS.
001096 02-03

BIOAVAILABILITY OF SULPIRIDE TABLET AND CAPSULE IN DOGS.
001101 02-03

METOCLOPRAMIDE AND SULPIRIDE AS SELECTIVE BLOCKING-AGENTS
PRESYNAPTIC AND POSTSYNAPTIC DOPAMINE-RECEPTORS.
001102 02-03

NEUROPHYSIOLOGICAL-STUDY OF TWO O ANISAMIDE DERIVATIVES:
SULPIRIDE AND SULTOPRIDE.
001170 02-03

EFFECTS OF CHRONIC-TREATMENT WITH L SULPIRIDE AND HALOPERIDOL
ON CENTRAL MONOAMINERGIC MECHANISMS.
001240 02-03

EFFECT OF LONG-TERM-TREATMENT WITH HALOPERIDOL AND SULPIRIDE
ON DIFFERENT TYPES OF DOPAMINERGIC-RECEPTORS.
001512 02-03

CONTROLLED-TRIAL OF SULPIRIDE IN CHRONIC SCHIZOPHRENIC-PATIENTS.
001914 02-08

CLINICAL USE OF SULPIRIDE IN ITALY.
002187 02-11

COMPARATIVE-STUDIES ON THE METABOLISM AND THE DISTRIBUTION OF
SULPIRIDE AND SULTOPRIDE.
002240 02-13

SHORT-TERM AND LONG-TERM EFFECTS ON GABA AND DOPAMINE
NEURONS DURING TREATMENT WITH SULPIRIDE.
002311 02-13

TARDIVE-HYPERKINESIA. EFFECTS OF SULPIRIDE AND GABA SYSTEM
AGONISTS.
002405 02-15

THE EFFECT OF GUANOSINE-NUCLEOTIDES ON (3H)SULPIRIDE BINDING TO
RAT STRIATAL MEMBRANES.
002722 03-03

EFFECT OF CHRONIC SULPIRIDE ON STRIATAL SPIPERONE BINDING.
003720 04-03

CATION REGULATION DIFFERENTIATES SPECIFIC BINDING OF
(3H)SULPIRIDE AND (3H)SPIPERONE TO RAT STRIATAL PREPARATIONS.
004032 04-03

WHY DOES SULPIRIDE NOT BLOCK THE EFFECT OF DOPAMINE ON THE
DOPAMINE-SENSITIVE ADENYLATE-CYCLASE?
004055 04-03

A CLINICAL AND PHARMACODYNAMIC EVALUATION OF SULPIRIDE.
004338 04-08

BASAL PROLACTINAEMIA AND RESPONSES TO TRH AND SULPIRIDE IN
DIFFERENT CATEGORIES OF MALE SEXUAL-DYSFUNCTIONS.
004503 04-13

SULPIRIDE-INDUCED
INHIBITION OF SULPIRIDE-INDUCED PROLACTIN SECRETION BY
DIHYDROERGOCRISTINE IN MAN.
002277 02-13

SULTHIAME
CHANGES IN REGIONAL BRAIN LEVELS OF AMINO-ACID PUTATIVE
NEUROTRANSMITTERS AFTER PROLONGED TREATMENT WITH THE
ANTICONVULSANT-DRUGS DIPHENYLHYDANTOIN, PHENOBARBITONE,
SODIUM-VALPROATE, ETHOSUXIMIDE, AND SULTHIAME IN THE RAT.
003961 04-03

SULTOPRIDE
NEUROPHYSIOLOGICAL-STUDY OF TWO O ANISAMIDE DERIVATIVES:
SULPIRIDE AND SULTOPRIDE.
001170 02-03

SULTOPRIDE (BARNETIL).
001920 02-08

COMPARATIVE-STUDIES ON THE METABOLISM AND THE DISTRIBUTION OF
SULPIRIDE AND SULTOPRIDE.
002240 02-13

ON THE EFFECTS OF SULTOPRIDE ADMINISTERED IN LOW-DOSAGES TO OLDER CHILDREN AND ADOLESCENTS.
003230 03-09

SUPERIOR
A COMPARATIVE-STUDY OF THE PHARMACOLOGICAL-PROPERTIES OF THE POSITIVE POTENTIAL RECORDED FROM THE SUPERIOR CERVICAL GANGLIA OF SEVERAL SPECIES.
003779 04-03

RELATIVE ACTIVITIES OF SUBSTANCES RELATED TO 5 HYDROXYTRYPTAMINE AS DEPOLARIZING-AGENTS OF SUPERIOR CERVICAL GANGLION CELLS.
004047 04-03

SUPERIOR-CERVICAL-GANGLION
INHIBITION OF ACH RELEASE BY PROSTAGLANDIN-E1 IN THE RABBIT SUPERIOR-CERVICAL-GANGLION.
001205 02-03

EVALUATION OF THE EFFECT OF DRUGS ON DOPAMINE METABOLISM IN THE RAT SUPERIOR-CERVICAL-GANGLION BY HPLC WITH ELECTROCHEMICAL-DETECTION.
001530 02-03

SUPERIOR-COLLICULUS
EVOKED-POTENTIAL CHANGES IN THE SUPERIOR-COLLICULUS PARALLEL THE LESION-INDUCED DEVELOPMENT OF GROOMING REFLEXES IN THE CAT. (PH.D. DISSERTATION).
001179 02-03

DISSOCIATION OF D-AMPHETAMINE-INDUCED LOCOMOTOR-ACTIVITY AND STEREOTYPED-BEHAVIOUR BY LESIONS OF THE SUPERIOR-COLLICULUS.
001755 02-04

SUPERRESPONSIVE
NO EVIDENCE FOR INCREASED DOPAMINE-RECEPTOR BINDING IN SUPERRESPONSIVE MICE AFTER A SINGLE-DOSE OF NEUROLEPTICS.
001292 02-03

SUPERSENSITIVE
NEUROLEPTIC-INDUCED ACUTE DYSTONIC REACTIONS MAY BE DUE TO ENHANCED DOPAMINE RELEASE ON TO SUPERSENSITIVE POSTSYNAPTIC-RECEPTORS.
002789 03-03

SUPERSENSITIVITY
EVIDENCE FOR A RECEPTOR SUPERSENSITIVITY FOLLOWING IMPAIRMENT OF CENTRAL SEROTONERGIC ACTIVITY IN THE RABBIT.
000041 01-03

MONOAMINERGIC DENERVATION OF THE RAT HIPPOCAMPUS: MICROIONTOPHORETIC STUDIES OF PRESYNAPTIC AND POSTSYNAPTIC SUPERSENSITIVITY TO NOREPINEPHRINE AND SEROTONIN.
000068 01-03

HYPOPHYSECTOMY PREVENTS THE STRIATAL DOPAMINE-RECEPTOR SUPERSENSITIVITY PRODUCED BY CHRONIC HALOPERIDOL TREATMENT.
000132 01-03

A NEUROENDOCRINE-STUDY OF SUPERSENSITIVITY IN TARDIVE-DYSKINESIA.
000908 01-16

PRESYNAPTIC DOPAMINE-RECEPTORS: INSENSITIVITY TO KAINIC-ACID AND THE DEVELOPMENT OF SUPERSENSITIVITY FOLLOWING CHRONIC HALOPERIDOL.
001117 02-03

DOPAMINE SYNTHESIS: TOLERANCE TO HALOPERIDOL AND SUPERSENSITIVITY TO APOMORPHINE DEPEND ON PRESYNAPTIC-RECEPTORS.
001129 02-03

ATTEMPTS TO DEVELOP SUPERSENSITIVITY OR SUBSENSITIVITY RETINAL DOPAMINE-RECEPTORS AFTER VARIOUS TREATMENTS WITH ANTAGONISTS OR AGONISTS.
001350 02-03

DENERVATION SUPERSENSITIVITY TO SEROTONIN IN THE FACIAL NUCLEUS.
001364 02-03

GABA FACILITATION BY NORADRENALINE SHOWED SUPERSENSITIVITY IN CEREBELLUM AFTER 6 HYDROXYDOPAMINE.
001382 02-03

PRESYNAPTIC DOPAMINE-RECEPTORS IN STRIATAL NERVE-ENDINGS: ABSENCE OF HALOPERIDOL-INDUCED SUPERSENSITIVITY.
001424 02-03

THE EFFECT OF CYCLO-LEU-GLY ON CHEMICAL DENERVATION SUPERSENSITIVITY OF DOPAMINE-RECEPTORS INDUCED BY INTRACEREBROVENTRICULAR INJECTION OF 6 HYDROXYDOPAMINE IN MICE.
001435 02-03

SUPERSENSITIVITY AND THE EFFECTS OF LONG-TERM AMPHETAMINE IN THE RAT NIGROSTRIATAL SYSTEM. (PH.D. DISSERTATION).
001485 02-03

INHIBITION OF NEUROLEPTIC-INDUCED DOPAMINE-RECEPTOR SUPERSENSITIVITY BY CYCLO-LEU-GLY.
001576 02-04

SUPERSENSITIVITY TO APOMORPHINE IN EXPERIMENTALLY-INDUCED HYPOKINESIA AND DRUG-INDUCED MODIFICATIONS OF THE APOMORPHINE RESPONSE.
001814 02-04

TOLERANCE TO FLUPHENAZINE AND SUPERSENSITIVITY TO APOMORPHINE IN CENTRAL DOPAMINERGIC-SYSTEMS AFTER CHRONIC FLUPHENAZINE-DECANOATE TREATMENT.
001820 02-04

CORRELATION BETWEEN DAILY DOSAGE OF CHLORPROMAZINE AND SUBSEQUENT SUPERSENSITIVITY.
001845 02-05

NEUROLEPTIC-INDUCED REINNERVATION SPROUTING IN THE CENTRAL-NERVOUS-SYSTEM (A MODEL FOR THE DEVELOPMENT OF TARDIVE-DYSKINESIA AND SUPERSENSITIVITY PSYCHOSIS).
002459 02-15

DOPAMINE-RECEPTOR SUPERSENSITIVITY IN THE CORPUS-STRIATUM FOLLOWING CHRONIC ELEVATION OF BRAIN GAMMA AMINOBUTYRIC-ACID.
002716 03-03

BLINK RATES AND RECEPTOR SUPERSENSITIVITY.
003022 03-04

SUPERSENSITIVITY TO THE BEHAVIORAL-EFFECTS OF OPIATE ANTAGONISTS.
003096 03-04

DENERVATION SUPERSENSITIVITY TO 5 HYDROXYTRYPTOPHAN IN RATS FOLLOWING SPINAL TRANSECTION AND 5,7 DIHYDROXYTRYPTAMINE INJECTION.
003722 04-03

SUPERSENSITIVITY OF CENTRAL NORADRENERGIC PRESYNAPTIC-AUTORECEPTORS FOLLOWING CHRONIC-TREATMENT WITH THE ANTIDEPRESSANT MIANSERIN.
003745 04-03

DOPAMINE-ACTIVATED ADENYLATE-CYCLASE OF SPINAL-CORD: SUPERSENSITIVITY FOLLOWING TRANSECTION OF THE CORD.
003800 04-03

THE DOPAMINE-RECEPTOR COMPLEX: BIOCHEMICAL-CONSEQUENCES OF SUPERSENSITIVITY INDUCED BY TREATMENT WITH 6 HYDROXYDOPAMINE OR MORPHINE.
003958 04-03

LITHIUM EFFECTS ON HALOPERIDOL-INDUCED PRESYNAPTIC AND POSTSYNAPTIC DOPAMINE-RECEPTOR SUPERSENSITIVITY.
004244 04-04

ANTAGONISM OF DOPAMINE SUPERSENSITIVITY BY ESTROGEN: NEUROCHEMICAL-STUDIES IN AN ANIMAL-MODEL OF TARDIVE-DYSKINESIA.
004268 04-05

DOPAMINE AND 5 HT SUPERSENSITIVITY IN NONORGANIC CENTRAL PAIN AND IN MORPHINE ABSTINENCE: FORTUITOUS OR REAL ANALOGY?
004553 04-13

SUPIDIMIDE
EFFECTS OF SUPIDIMIDE (CG-3033) ON OBJECTIVE AND SUBJECTIVE SLEEP PARAMETERS (A SLEEP LABORATORY STUDY).
004567 04-14

SUPPRESS
CHOLINERGIC, DOPAMINERGIC, NORADRENERGIC, OR GLUTAMINERGIC STIMULATION VENTRAL TO THE ANTERIOR SEPTUM DOES NOT SPECIFICALLY SUPPRESS DEFENSIVE-BEHAVIOR.
002945 03-04

ERGOT DRUGS SUPPRESS PLASMA PROLACTIN AND LACTATION BUT NOT AGGRESSION IN PARTURIENT MICE.
003159 03-07

METERGOLINE AND CYPROHEPTADINE SUPPRESS PROLACTIN RELEASE BY A NON-5-HYDROXYTRYPTAMINERGIC, NONDOPAMINERGIC MECHANISM.
003732 04-03

SUPPRESSED
ALCOHOL AND CHLORDIAZEPOXIDE INCREASE SUPPRESSED AGGRESSION IN MICE.
000434 01-04

THE PRESYNAPTIC STIMULATING EFFECT OF ACETYLCHOLINE ON DOPAMINE RELEASE IS SUPPRESSED DURING ACTIVATION OF NIGROSTRIATAL DOPAMINERGIC NEURONS IN THE CAT.
002733 03-03

EFFECTS OF CHLORDIAZEPOXIDE AND D-AMPHETAMINE ON RESPONDING SUPPRESSED BY CONDITIONED PUNISHMENT.
003105 03-03

SUPPRESSES
SUBSTANCE-P SUPPRESSES STRESS-INDUCED EATING.
001725 02-04

GLUCOSE SUPPRESSES BASAL FIRING AND HALOPERIDOL-INDUCED INCREASES IN THE FIRING-RATE OF CENTRAL DOPAMINERGIC NEURONS.
002880 03-03

CHOLINE REVERSES NALOXONE-INDUCED DECREASES IN HIPPOCAMPAL ACETYLCHOLINE CONTENT AND SUPPRESSES ESCAPE-BEHAVIOR IN OPIATE-DEPENDENT RATS.
004076 04-04

NALOXONE SUPPRESSES FEEDING AND DRINKING BUT NOT WHEEL RUNNING IN RATS.
004080 04-04

NALOXONE SUPPRESSES FOOD/WATER CONSUMPTION IN THE DEPRIVED CAT.
004114 04-04

SUPPRESSING
THE SITE OF ACTION OF NALOXONE IN SUPPRESSING FOOD AND WATER INTAKE IN RATS.
004146 04-04

SUPPRESSION

SUPPRESSION OF SEROTONERGIC NEURONAL FIRING BY ALPHA-ADRENOCEPTOR ANTAGONISTS: EVIDENCE AGAINST GABA MEDIATION.
000024 01-03

SUPPRESSION OF EVOKED AND SPONTANEOUS RELEASE OF NEUROTRANSMITTERS IN VIVO BY MORPHINE.
000058 01-03

ENHANCED SUPPRESSION OF CONDITIONED AVOIDANCE RESPONSE BY HALOPERIDOL BUT NOT PHENOXYBENZAMINE IN RATS WITH BILATERAL PARAFASCICULAR LESIONS.
000334 01-04

POSSIBLE INVOLVEMENT OF CYCLIC-AMP AND FRONTAL-CORTEX IN AMITRIPTYLINE MEDIATED SUPPRESSION OF THE HYPOTENSIVE-EFFECT OF CLONIDINE.
001259 02-03

CONDITIONED SUPPRESSION OF DRINKING: A MEASURE OF THE CR ELICITED BY A LITHIUM CONDITIONED FLAVOR.
001747 02-04

THE EFFECTS OF CHLORDIAZEPOXIDE-HCL ADMINISTRATION UPON PUNISHMENT AND CONDITIONED SUPPRESSION IN THE RAT.
001757 02-04

MECHANISMS OF OPIATE ANALGESIA AND THE ROLE OF ENDORPHINS IN PAIN SUPPRESSION. (UNPUBLISHED PAPER).
002275 02-13

SUPPRESSION OF AMPHETAMINE-INDUCED EEG AROUSAL IN THE HIPPOCAMPUS OF HALOPERIDOL TREATED RABBITS.
002683 03-03

THE PARTICIPATION OF SUBSTANTIA-NIGRA ZONA-COMPACTA AND ZONA-RETICULATA NEURONS IN MORPHINE SUPPRESSION OF CAUDATE SPONTANEOUS NEURONAL ACTIVITIES IN THE RAT.
002718 03-03

MATURATION OF SYMPATHETIC NEUROTRANSMISSION IN THE RAT HEART. VII. SUPPRESSION OF SYMPATHETIC RESPONSES BY DEXAMETHASONE.
002802 03-03

SUPPRESSION OF SERUM PROLACTIN BY NALOXONE BUT NOT BY ANTI-BETA-ENDORPHIN ANTISERUM IN STRESSED AND UNSTRESSED RATS.
002871 03-03

SUPPRESSION OF DRINKING BY NALOXONE IN THE RAT: A FURTHER CHARACTERIZATION.
002963 03-04

SMALL-DOSE INTRAVENOUS HEROIN FACILITATES HYPOTHALAMIC SELF-STIMULATION WITHOUT RESPONSE SUPPRESSION IN RATS.
002999 03-04

CORTICAL RECOVERY FROM EFFECTS OF MONOCULAR DEPRIVATION: ACCELERATION WITH NOREPINEPHRINE AND SUPPRESSION WITH 6 HYDROXYDOPAMINE.
003024 03-04

CLONIDINE ANALGESIA AND SUPPRESSION OF OPERANT RESPONDING: DISSOCIATION OF MECHANISM.
003046 03-04

SUPPRESSION OF ACTIVE SLEEP BY CHRONIC-TREATMENT WITH CHLORIMIPRAMINE DURING EARLY POSTNATAL DEVELOPMENT: EFFECTS UPON ADULT SLEEP AND BEHAVIOR IN THE RAT.
003056 03-04

THE USE OF CONDITIONED SUPPRESSION TO EVALUATE THE NATURE OF NEUROLEPTIC-INDUCED AVOIDANCE-DEFICITS.
004070 04-04

SUPPRESSION OF ALCOHOL DRINKING WITH BRAIN ALDEHYDE-DEHYDROGENASE INHIBITION.
004220 04-04

SUPPRESSION OF MORPHINE ABSTINENCE IN HEROIN ADDICTS BY BETA ENDORPHIN.
004489 04-11

SUPPRESSIVE

OPIATE-RECEPTORS MAY MEDIATE THE SUPPRESSIVE BUT NOT THE EXCITATORY ACTION OF ACTH ON MOTOR-ACTIVITY IN RATS.
000337 01-04

TOLERANCE TO SUPPRESSIVE EFFECTS OF CHLORDIAZEPOXIDE ON OPERANT-BEHAVIOR: LACK OF CROSS-TOLERANCE TO PENTOBARBITAL.
000356 01-04

SUPPRESSIVE EFFECT OF MORPHINE ON SERUM GONADOTROPIN LEVELS IN CASTRATED RATS.
001393 02-03

SUPRAMOLECULAR

GABA-RECEPTORS AS SUPRAMOLECULAR UNITS.
002819 03-03

SUPRANUCLEAR

PROGRESSIVE SUPRANUCLEAR PALSY, COMPUTED-TOMOGRAPHY, AND RESPONSE TO ANTIPARKINSONIAN-DRUGS.
003322 03-11

PROGRESSIVE SUPRANUCLEAR PALSY: PNEUMOENCEPHALOGRAPHY, ELECTRONYSTAGMOGRAPHY AND TREATMENT WITH METHYSERGIDE.
003355 03-11

SUPRASPINAL

MORPHINE AND SUPRASPINAL INHIBITION OF SPINAL NEURONES: EVIDENCE THAT MORPHINE DECREASES TONIC DESCENDING INHIBITION IN THE ANESTHETIZED CAT.
001203 02-03

METHYSERGIDE AND SUPRASPINAL INHIBITION OF THE SPINAL TRANSMISSION OF NOCICEPTIVE INFORMATION IN THE ANESTHETIZED CAT.
002740 03-03

SUPRASPINAL INHIBITION OF THE EXCITATION OF DORSAL-HORN NEURONES BY IMPULSES IN UNMYELINATED PRIMARY AFFERENTS: LACK OF EFFECT BY STRYCHNINE AND BICUCULLINE.
003778 04-03

SUPRASYLVIAN

SELECTIVE SYNAPTIC ANTAGONISM BY ATROPINE AND ALPHA AMINOADIPATE OF PULVINAR AND CORTICAL AFFERENTS TO THE SUPRASYLVIAN VISUAL AREA (CLARE-BISHOP AREA).
002752 03-03

SURGERY

THE LONG-TERM RESULTS OF STEREOTAXIC SURGERY AND L-DOPA THERAPY IN PATIENTS WITH PARKINSONS-DISEASE: A 10-YEAR FOLLOWUP STUDY.
000693 01-11

MODERN CONCEPTS IN PSYCHIATRIC SURGERY.
002551 02-17

SURGICAL

SURGICAL MANIPULATION OF THE UTERINE ENVIRONMENT OF RAT FETUSES.
002478 02-16

SURINAM

PSYCHOTOMIMETIC USE OF TOBACCO IN SURINAM AND FRENCH-GUIANA.
002592 02-17

SURROGATE

CANALIZATION OF AROUSAL IN THE PREWEANLING RAT: EFFECTS OF AMPHETAMINE ON AGGREGATION WITH SURROGATE STIMULI.
002965 03-04

SURVECTOR

PHARMACOLOGY OF THE SURVECTOR.
001085 02-02

THE PLACE OF SURVECTOR AMONG THE VARIOUS DRUGS USED IN TREATMENT OF MOOD-DISORDERS.
001969 02-09

INHIBITION AND APATHY: TREATMENT WITH SURVECTOR.
002066 02-10

SURVECTOR AND SLEEP-DISORDERS: SLEEP-WALKING, NIGHTMARES, AND NIGHT-TERRORS.
002110 02-11

CHEMICAL STRUCTURE OF SURVECTOR. STRUCTURE-ACTIVITY RELATIONSHIP.
002262 02-13

SURVEILLANCE

EUHYPNOS-FORTE, HIGH-DOSE TEMAZEPAM FOR RESISTANT INSOMNIA: POSTMARKETING SURVEILLANCE IN 10,057 PATIENTS UNRESPONSIVE TO CONVENTIONAL HYPNOTIC DOSAGE.
002324 02-14

SURVIVAL

USE OF SURVIVAL CURVES IN ANALYSIS OF ANTIPSYCHOTIC RELAPSE-STUDIES.
002481 02-16

THE TWO SURVIVAL CASES OF ALPHA-PATTERN COMA CAUSED BY LARGE AMOUNTS OF HYPNOTICA AND NEUROLEPTICA.
004608 04-15

SUSCEPTIBILITY

EFFECTS OF KINDLING OR BRAIN-STIMULATION ON PENTYLENETETRAZOL-INDUCED CONVULSION SUSCEPTIBILITY.
000037 01-03

REPEATED ELECTROCONVULSIVE-SHOCK DOES NOT INCREASE THE SUSCEPTIBILITY OF RATS TO A CAGE CONVULSANT (ISOPROPYLBICYCLOPHOSPHATE).
001184 02-03

THE EFFECTS OF NOOTROPIC-DRUGS ON THE SUSCEPTIBILITY TO AUDIOGENIC-SEIZURES IN RATS.
001571 02-04

EFFECT OF RO-4-1284 ON AUDIOGENIC-SEIZURE SUSCEPTIBILITY AND INTENSITY IN EPILEPSY-PRONE RATS.
003865 04-03

EFFECTS OF OLFACTORY-BULBECTOMY AND PERIPHERALLY-INDUCED ANOSMIA ON THERMOREGULATION IN THE RAT: SUSCEPTIBILITY TO ANTIDEPRESSANT-DRUGS.
004113 04-04

SUSCEPTIBLE

AUDIOGENIC-SEIZURES: INCREASED BENZODIAZEPINE-RECEPTOR BINDING IN A SUSCEPTIBLE STRAIN OF MICE.
000252 01-03

DIFFERENCES IN ACTIVITY IN CEREBRAL METHYLTRANSFERASES AND MONOAMINE-OXIDASES BETWEEN AUDIOGENIC-SEIZURE SUSCEPTIBLE AND RESISTANT MICE AND DEERMICE.
000377 01-04

SUSTAINED-RELEASE

COMPARISON OF SUSTAINED-RELEASE AND STANDARD METHYLPHENIDATE IN THE TREATMENT OF MINIMAL-BRAIN-DYSFUNCTION.
000732 01-11

SWEDISH
QUALITY OF REPORTS OF CLINICAL-TRIALS SUBMITTED BY THE DRUG INDUSTRY TO THE FINNISH AND SWEDISH CONTROL AUTHORITIES.
003599 03-17

SWIMMING
SWIMMING CAPACITY OF MICE AFTER PROLONGED TREATMENT WITH PSYCHOSTIMULANTS: II. EFFECT OF METHAMPHETAMINE ON SWIMMING PERFORMANCE AND AVAILABILITY OF METABOLIC SUBSTRATES.
001613 02-04

SWITCH
REPEATED TRICYCLIC-ANTIDEPRESSANTS INDUCE A PROGRESSIVE SWITCH IN THE ELECTROPHYSIOLOGICAL RESPONSE OF DOPAMINE NEURONS TO AUTORECEPTOR STIMULATION.
000046 01-03

SWITZERLAND
METHADONE TREATMENT OF HEROIN ADDICTS IN SWITZERLAND.
004452 04-11

SYDNOCARB
THE PHARMACOLOGICAL ACTION OF THE OPTICAL-ISOMERS OF SYDNOCARB.
003681 04-02

SYDNONIMINE
THE IMMUNOSTIMULANT ANTINEOPLASTIC ACTION OF SOME PSYCHOTROPIC-DRUGS OF THE SYDNONIMINE SERIES.
001520 02-03

SYMPATHECTOMY
GASTRIC AND PYLORIC MOTOR-RESPONSE TO SYMPATHETIC-NERVE STIMULATION AFTER CHEMICAL SYMPATHECTOMY. (UNPUBLISHED PAPER).
001337 02-03

SYMPATHETIC
MATURATION OF SYMPATHETIC NEUROTRANSMISSION IN THE RAT HEART. III. DEVELOPMENTAL-CHANGES IN RESERPINE INHIBITION OF NOREPINEPHRINE UPTAKE INTO ISOLATED SYNAPTIC VESICLES.
000025 01-03

CALCIUM LOCALIZATION IN THE SYMPATHETIC GANGLION OF THE BULLFROG AND EFFECTS OF CAFFEINE.
000098 01-03

BIOCHEMICAL-CHARACTERIZATION OF THE RAT SYMPATHETIC GANGLION: PHARMACOLOGICAL-EFFECTS OF RESERPINE ON GANGLIONIC CATECHOLAMINES.
000153 01-03

ENKEPHALINS PRESYNAPTICALLY INHIBIT CHOLINERGIC TRANSMISSION IN SYMPATHETIC GANGLIA.
000167 01-03

CHRONIC SYMPATHETIC DENERVATION INCREASES MUSCARINIC-CHOLINOCEPTOR BINDING IN THE RAT SUBMAXILLARY-GLAND.
000235 01-03

CHARACTERIZATION OF LRF-LIKE IMMUNOREACTIVITY IN THE FROG SYMPATHETIC GANGLIA: NONIDENTITY WITH LRF-DECAPEPTIDE. (UNPUBLISHED PAPER).
001018 02-01

PARASYMPATHOMIMETIC-INFLUENCE OF CARBACHOL ON LOCAL CEREBRAL BLOOD FLOW IN THE RABBIT BY A DIRECT VASODILATOR ACTION AND AN INHIBITION OF THE SYMPATHETIC MEDIATED VASOCONSTRICTION.
001109 02-03

INTRACELLULAR OBSERVATIONS ON THE EFFECTS OF MUSCARINIC AGONISTS ON RAT SYMPATHETIC NEURONES.
001143 02-03

MUSCARINIC-RECEPTORS IN RAT SYMPATHETIC GANGLIA.
001144 02-03

CENTRAL SYMPATHETIC REACTIVITY INHIBITED BY INDORAMIN.
001193 02-03

EFFECT OF GABA AGONIST AND ANTAGONISTS ON CARDIOVASCULAR AND SYMPATHETIC RESPONSES IN SHR AND WKY RATS. (UNPUBLISHED PAPER).
001224 02-03

PRESYNAPTIC ACTIONS OF 4 AMINOPYRIDINE AND GAMMA AMINOBUTYRIC-ACID ON RAT SYMPATHETIC GANGLIA IN VITRO.
001244 02-03

MATURATION OF SYMPATHETIC NEUROTRANSMISSION IN THE RAT HEART. VII. SUPPRESSION OF SYMPATHETIC RESPONSES BY DEXAMETHASONE.
002802 03-03

BETA ENDORPHIN-INDUCED HYPERGLYCEMIA IS MEDIATED BY INCREASED CENTRAL SYMPATHETIC OUTFLOW TO ADRENAL-MEDULLA.
002924 03-03

BIOLOGICAL-EFFECTS OF CHLORPROMAZINE IN CHRONIC SCHIZOPHRENICS. II. WITH REFERENCE TO SYMPATHETIC NEURONAL FUNCTION.
003416 03-13

5 HYDROXYTRYPTAMINE CONTROLS ACH-RECEPTOR SENSITIVITY OF BULLFROG SYMPATHETIC GANGLION CELLS.
003710 04-03

INFLUENCE OF THE DOPAMINERGIC AGONISTS BROMOCRIPTINE, PIRIBEDIL AND NOMIFENSINE ON THE SYMPATHETIC NEURAL TRANSMISSION IN THE NICTITATING MEMBRANE OF THE CAT.
003822 04-03

THE EXCITATORY EFFECT OF ATROPINE ON THE NEURONS OF THE FROG SYMPATHETIC GANGLIA.
004041 04-03

SYMPATHETIC-NERVE
GASTRIC AND PYLORIC MOTOR-RESPONSE TO SYMPATHETIC-NERVE STIMULATION AFTER CHEMICAL SYMPATHECTOMY. (UNPUBLISHED PAPER).
001337 02-03

CENTRALLY INDUCED CARDIOVASCULAR AND SYMPATHETIC-NERVE RESPONSES TO BRADYKININ IN RATS.
003099 03-04

SYMPATHETIC-NERVOUS-SYSTEM
THE EFFECTS OF TWO ANALOGS OF DOPAMINE ON GANGLIONIC TRANSMISSION IN THE SYMPATHETIC-NERVOUS-SYSTEM.
000162 01-03

THE SYMPATHETIC-NERVOUS-SYSTEM AND HYPERTENSION: A POSITION PAPER. (UNPUBLISHED PAPER).
002250 02-13

THE HYPERACTIVE-CHILD-SYNDROME: PERIPHERAL SYMPATHETIC-NERVOUS-SYSTEM FUNCTION AND THE EFFECT OF D-AMPHETAMINE.
003340 03-11

SYMPATHOADRENAL
METABOLIC AND SYMPATHOADRENAL ABNORMALITIES IN THE OBESE ZUCKER RAT: EFFECT OF CHRONIC PHENOXYBENZAMINE TREATMENT.
003905 04-03

SYMPATHOMIMETIC
A COMPARISON OF THE CONTRACTILE RESPONSES OF THE RABBIT BASILAR AND PULMONARY-ARTERIES TO SYMPATHOMIMETIC AGONISTS: CHARACTERISTICS.
002670 03-03

SYMPATHOMIMETIC-AMINES
NOREPINEPHRINE UPTAKE INHIBITORS AS BIOCHEMICALLY-SELECTIVE AND BEHAVIORALLY-SELECTIVE ANTAGONISTS OF THE LOCOMOTOR-STIMULATION INDUCED BY INDIRECTLY ACTING SYMPATHOMIMETIC-AMINES IN MICE.
000492 01-04

SYMPATHOMIMETIC-AMINES AND TRICYCLIC-ANTIDEPRESSANT DRUGS.
004678 04-16

SYMPTOM-PROFILE-ANALYSIS
A SYMPTOM-PROFILE-ANALYSIS OF ANTIPSYCHOTIC-DRUG TREATMENT: NONPARAMETRIC MULTIDIMENSIONAL TECHNIQUE.
003196 03-08

SYMPTOMATIC
EVALUATION OF SYMPTOMATIC TREATMENT OF HYPERACTIVE-BEHAVIOR BY STIMULANT-DRUGS.
002134 02-11

SYMPTOMATOLOGY
BODY-WEIGHT, FEEDING, AND DRINKING-BEHAVIORS IN RATS WITH KAINIC-ACID-INDUCED LESIONS OF STRIATAL NEURONS -- WITH A NOTE ON BODY-WEIGHT SYMPTOMATOLOGY IN HUNTINGTONS-DISEASE.
000463 01-04

SYMPTOMS
THE RELATIONSHIP BETWEEN THE THIORIDAZINE LEVEL IN THE PLASMA AND SYMPTOMS OF PARANOID SCHIZOPHRENIA.
000546 01-08

THE ROLE OF CHOLINERGIC-SUPERSENSITIVITY IN THE MEDICAL SYMPTOMS ASSOCIATED WITH WITHDRAWAL OF ANTIPSYCHOTIC-DRUGS.
000869 01-15

THE OCCURRENCE OF TARDIVE EXTRAPYRAMIDAL SYMPTOMS IN SCHIZOPHRENIC-PATIENTS UNDERGOING PROLONGED NEUROLEPTIC TREATMENT.
000885 01-15

DIFFERENTIAL-EFFECTS OF AMPHETAMINE AND NEUROLEPTICS ON NEGATIVE VS. POSITIVE SYMPTOMS IN SCHIZOPHRENIA.
001906 02-08

EFFECT OF TRICYCLIC-ANTIDEPRESSANTS ON INDIVIDUAL SYMPTOMS.
002052 02-09

CLINICAL-EXPERIENCE WITH RETARD DIBENZEPINE (NOVERIL-240) IN ENDOGENOUS DEPRESSIONS ACCOMPANIED BY SYMPTOMS OF DRUG-RESISTANCE.
003245 03-09

BENZODIAZEPINE WITHDRAWAL SYMPTOMS AND PROPRANOLOL.
003543 03-15

ALTERATIONS OF EVOKED-POTENTIALS LINK RESEARCH IN ATTENTION-DYSFUNCTION TO PEPTIDE RESPONSE SYMPTOMS OF SCHIZOPHRENIA.
004316 04-08

CHANGES IN PSYCHOPATHOLOGIC SYMPTOMS DURING 20 DAYS OF TREATMENT WITH ANTIDEPRESSANTS AND NEUROLEPTIC-DRUGS.
004415 04-09

WITHDRAWAL SYMPTOMS AFTER GRADUATED CESSATION OF IMIPRAMINE IN CHILDREN.
004630 04-15

ANOREXIA-NERVOSA. SYMPTOMS, COURSE AND POSSIBILITIES FOR TREATMENT.
004711 04-17

SYNAPSE
EVIDENCE SUGGESTING A TRANSMITTER OR NEUROMODULATORY ROLE FOR SUBSTANCE-P AT THE FIRST SYNAPSE OF THE BARORECEPTOR REFLEX.
001264 02-03

ELECTROPHYSIOLOGICAL-CHANGES AT A CENTRAL NORADRENERGIC SYNAPSE DURING THALLIUM TOXICOSIS.
001848 02-05

SYNAPSES
LOCALIZATION OF ALPHA BUNGAROTOXIN BINDING-SITES IN SYNAPSES OF THE DEVELOPING CHICK RETINA.
000065 01-03

THE ULTRASTRUCTURAL CHANGES OF SYNAPSES IN RAT FOLLOWING LONG-TERM ADMINISTRATION OF THE NEUROLEPTICS RESERPINE AND HALOPERIDOL.
000795 01-13

CENTRAL MONOAMINE SYNAPSES AS SITES OF ACTION FOR ERGOT DRUGS.
001238 02-03

LYSERGIC-ACID-DIETHYLAMIDE: MORPHOLOGICAL-STUDY OF ITS EFFECT ON SYNAPSES.
001315 02-03

A CRITICAL EVALUATION OF THE USE OF TOXINS FROM DENDROASPIS VIRIDIS TO BLOCK NICOTINIC RESPONSES AT CENTRAL AND GANGLIONIC SYNAPSES.
002870 03-03

SYNAPTIC
MATURATION OF SYMPATHETIC NEUROTRANSMISSION IN THE RAT HEART. III. DEVELOPMENTAL-CHANGES IN RESERPINE INHIBITION OF NOREPINEPHRINE UPTAKE INTO ISOLATED SYNAPTIC VESICLES.
000025 01-03

ADENINE-NUCLEOTIDES AND SYNAPTIC TRANSMISSION IN THE IN VITRO RAT HIPPOCAMPUS.
000080 01-03

COMPARISON OF THE EFFECTS OF THE ISOMERS OF AMPHETAMINE, METHYLPHENIDATE AND DEOXYPIPRADROL ON THE UPTAKE OF L (3H)NOREPINEPHRINE AND (3H)DOPAMINE BY SYNAPTIC VESICLES FROM RAT-WHOLE-BRAIN, STRIATUM AND HYPOTHALAMUS.
000091 01-03

INTERACTION OF DIAZEPAM WITH SYNAPTIC TRANSMISSION IN THE IN VITRO RAT HIPPOCAMPUS.
000178 01-03

PHENYLACETATE AND BRAIN-DYSFUNCTION IN EXPERIMENTAL PHENYLKETONURIA: SYNAPTIC DEVELOPMENT.
000191 01-03

REGIONAL DISTRIBUTION AND BIOCHEMICAL-PROPERTIES OF 125I TYR8-SUBSTANCE-P BINDING-SITES IN SYNAPTIC VESICLES.
000259 01-03

EFFECTS OF LEAD EXPOSURE DURING DEVELOPMENT ON NEOCORTICAL DENDRITIC AND SYNAPTIC STRUCTURE.
000525 01-05

GAMMA AMINOBUTYRIC-ACID AGONISTS: AN IN VITRO COMPARISON BETWEEN DEPRESSION OF SPINAL SYNAPTIC ACTIVITY AND DEPOLARIZATION OF SPINAL ROOT FIBRES IN THE RAT.
001104 02-03

DEPRESSION AND FACILITATION OF SYNAPTIC RESPONSES IN CAT DORSAL-HORN BY SUBSTANCE-P ADMINISTERED INTO SUBSTANTIA-GELATINOSA.
001191 02-03

INHIBITION BY ARYLSULPHATASE A OF NA-INDEPENDENT (3H) GABA AND (3H) MUSCIMOL BINDING TO BOVINE CEREBELLAR SYNAPTIC MEMBRANES.
001208 02-03

ASCORBIC-ACID, AN ENDOGENOUS FACTOR REQUIRED FOR ACETYLCHOLINE RELEASE FROM THE SYNAPTIC VESICLES.
001322 02-03

DOPAMINE-RECEPTOR: FROM SYNAPTIC MEMBRANES TO SOLUBILIZATION.
001326 02-03

FURTHER CHARACTERIZATION OF THE BINDING OF SUBSTANCE-P TO A FRACTION FROM RABBIT BRAIN ENRICHED IN SYNAPTIC MEMBRANES.
001394 02-03

INHIBITORY ACTION OF ADENOSINE ON SYNAPTIC TRANSMISSION IN THE HIPPOCAMPUS OF THE GUINEA-PIG IN VITRO.
001401 02-03

BENZODIAZEPINE-RECEPTORS: AUTORADIOGRAPHICAL AND IMMUNOCYTOCHEMICAL EVIDENCE FOR THEIR LOCALIZATION IN REGIONS OF GABAERGIC SYNAPTIC CONTACTS.
002643 03-01

INTERACTIONS OF TRICYCLIC-ANTIDEPRESSANTS WITH A SYNAPTIC ION-CHANNEL.
002660 03-03

SENSITIVITY OF IDENTIFIED MEDIAL HYPOTHALAMIC NEURONS TO GABA, GLYCINE AND RELATED AMINO-ACIDS: INFLUENCE OF BICUCULLINE, PICROTOXIN AND STRYCHNINE ON SYNAPTIC INHIBITION.
002674 03-03

SELECTIVE EFFECTS OF LSD AND HYPERTHERMIA ON THE SYNTHESIS OF SYNAPTIC PROTEINS AND GLYCOPROTEINS.
002721 03-03

SELECTIVE SYNAPTIC ANTAGONISM BY ATROPINE AND ALPHA AMINOADIPATE OF PULVINAR AND CORTICAL AFFERENTS TO THE SUPRASYLVIAN VISUAL AREA (CLARE-BISHOP AREA).
002752 03-03

ANTIANXIETY-AGENTS AND SYNAPTIC TRANSMISSION IN THE BRAIN: ELECTROPHYSIOLOGICAL-STUDIES. (PH.D. DISSERTATION).
002840 03-03

EFFECTS OF PROTEIN AND MEMBRANE MODIFYING AGENTS ON THE BINDING OF L (3H)GLUTAMATE TO CEREBELLAR SYNAPTIC MEMBRANES.
002888 03-03

CALMODULIN: ITS ROLE IN SYNAPTIC TRANSMISSION.
003162 03-07

SYNAPTIC AND BEHAVIOURAL-ACTIONS OF ANTIDEPRESSANT-DRUGS: FURTHER THOUGHTS ON THE IMPLICATIONS FOR THEORIES OF DEPRESSION.
003229 03-09

PAPAIN-DERIVED FRAGMENT IIC TETANUS-TOXIN: ITS BINDING TO ISOLATED SYNAPTIC MEMBRANES AND RETROGRADE AXONAL TRANSPORT.
003734 04-03

PRESYNAPTIC MODULATION OF SYNAPTIC TRANSMISSION IN HELIX-POMATIA: THE EFFECTS OF SEROTONIN AND DOPAMINE ANTAGONISTS.
003869 04-03

DIFFERENTIAL-EFFECTS OF PENTOBARBITAL AND ETHER ON THE SYNAPTIC TRANSMISSION OF THE HIPPOCAMPAL-CA1-REGION IN THE RAT.
003903 04-03

THE EFFECT OF ACETYLCHOLINE RELEASE ON CHOLINE FLUXES IN ISOLATED SYNAPTIC TERMINALS.
003924 04-03

L ASPARTATE BINDING-SITES IN RAT-CEREBELLUM: A COMPARISON OF THE BINDING OF L (3H)ASPARTATE AND L (3H)GLUTAMATE TO SYNAPTIC MEMBRANES.
004000 04-03

5' TRIPHOSPHATE RECYCLES INDEPENDENTLY OF ACETYLCHOLINE IN CHOLINERGIC SYNAPTIC VESICLES.
004063 04-03

SYNAPTOSOMAL
ANTIHISTAMINE EFFECT ON SYNAPTOSOMAL UPTAKE OF SEROTONIN, NOREPINEPHRINE AND DOPAMINE.
000035 01-03

INHIBITION OF BRAIN SYNAPTOSOMAL UPTAKE OF CHOLINE BY SOME 2 CARBOXAMIDOSTRYCHNINE DERIVATIVES WITH MUSCLE-RELAXANT PROPERTIES.
000084 01-03

CHARACTERIZATION OF 3H GABA-RECEPTOR BINDING TO RAT-BRAIN SYNAPTOSOMAL MEMBRANES: EFFECT OF NONGABAERGIC COMPOUNDS.
000139 01-03

THE MONOAMINE-OXIDASE-INHIBITORS CLORGYLINE AND L DEPRENYL ALSO AFFECT THE UPTAKE OF DOPAMINE, NORADRENALINE AND SEROTONIN BY RAT-BRAIN SYNAPTOSOMAL PREPARATIONS.
000171 01-03

ACTION OF BARBITURATES ON ACTIVITY OF ACETYLCHOLINESTERASE FROM SYNAPTOSOMAL MEMBRANES.
000224 01-03

LONG-TERM EFFECTS OF CONTINUOUS EXPOSURE TO AMPHETAMINE ON BRAIN DOPAMINE CONCENTRATION AND SYNAPTOSOMAL UPTAKE IN MICE.
000287 01-03

INHIBITION OF (3H)DIAZEPAM BINDING TO RAT-BRAIN CORTICAL SYNAPTOSOMAL MEMBRANES BY ADENOSINE UPTAKE BLOCKERS.
000330 01-03

DIVERGENT RESERPINE EFFECTS ON AMFONELIC-ACID AND AMPHETAMINE STIMULATION OF SYNAPTOSOMAL DOPAMINE FORMATION FROM PHENYLALANINE.
001113 02-03

PHENCYCLIDINE-INDUCED STIMULATION OF SYNAPTOSOMAL TYROSINE-HYDROXYLASE ACTIVITY.
001304 02-03

INTERACTIONS OF NARCOTICS WITH SYNAPTOSOMAL CALCIUM TRANSPORT.
002712 03-03

INHIBITION OF SYNAPTOSOMAL CALCIUM UPTAKE BY ETHANOL.
003827 04-03

EFFECT OF INHIBITORS OF GABA-AMINOTRANSFERASE ON THE METABOLISM OF GABA IN BRAIN TISSUE AND SYNAPTOSOMAL FRACTIONS.
003914 04-03

THE HIGH-AFFINITY CHOLINE UPTAKE SYSTEM WITH RESPECT TO THE MUSCARINIC-RECEPTORS USING A SYNAPTOSOMAL FRACTION ABUNDANT IN PRESYNAPTIC MEMBRANES.
004028 04-03

SYNAPTOSOMES
EFFECTS OF PSYCHOTROPIC-DRUGS ON THE DISTRIBUTION OF 3H DOPAMINE INTO COMPARTMENTS OF RAT STRIATAL SYNAPTOSOMES

AND ON SUBSEQUENT DEPOLARIZATION-INDUCED 3H DOPAMINE
RELEASE.
000067 01-03
EFFECT OF MORPHINE ON CALCIUM UPTAKE BY LYSED SYNAPTOSOMES.
000117 01-03.
EFFECTS OF CHLORDIAZEPOXIDE ON DEPOLARIZATION-INDUCED CALCIUM
INFLUX INTO SYNAPTOSOMES.
000183 01-03
TETRAHYDRO-BETA-CARBOLINES AND CORRESPONDING TRYPTAMINES:
IN VITRO INHIBITION OF SEROTONIN, DOPAMINE AND
NORADRENALINE UPTAKE IN RAT-BRAIN SYNAPTOSOMES.
001078 02-02
EFFECTS OF GABA AND DIAZEPAM ON 3H SEROTONIN RELEASE FROM
HIPPOCAMPAL SYNAPTOSOMES.
001116 02-03
BIPHASIC ACTIVITY OF MEMBRANE-BOUND ENZYMES IN BRAIN
MITOCHONDRIA AND SYNAPTOSOMES DURING THE DEVELOPMENT OF
TOLERANCE TO AND PHYSICAL-DEPENDENCE ON CHRONIC MORPHINE
ADMINISTRATION TO RATS.
001285 02-03
THE EFFECT OF PSYCHOTROPIC-SUBSTANCES AND NARCOTIC ANALGESIC-
DRUGS ON 14C NORADRENALINE UPTAKE BY SYNAPTOSOMES OF THE
CEREBRAL-CORTEX OF RATS.
001363 02-03
UPTAKE OF PIPERIDINE AND PIPECOLIC-ACID BY SYNAPTOSOMES FROM
MOUSE-BRAIN.
001396 02-03
IN VIVO CHANGES IN THE GABA CONTENT OF NERVE-ENDINGS
(SYNAPTOSOMES) INDUCED BY INHIBITORS OF GABA UPTAKE.
001540 02-03
EFFECTS OF NEOMYCIN ON CALCIUM AND POLYPHOSPHOINOSITIDE
METABOLISM OF GUINEA-PIG SYNAPTOSOMES.
002741 03-03
EFFECT OF TAURINE ON 45CA2 ACCUMULATION IN RAT BRAIN
SYNAPTOSOMES.
002855 03-03
KINETIC DATA ON THE INHIBITION OF HIGH-AFFINITY CHOLINE
TRANSPORT INTO RAT-FOREBRAIN SYNAPTOSOMES BY CHOLINE-LIKE
COMPOUNDS AND NITROGEN-MUSTARD ANALOGUES.
002879 03-03
RELEASE OF ACETYLCHOLINE FROM RAT-BRAIN SYNAPTOSOMES
STIMULATED WITH LEPTINOTARSIN, A NEW NEUROTOXIN.
003148 03-06
INHIBITION OF (3H)DIAZEPAM BINDING BY AN ENDOGENOUS FRACTION
FROM RAT-BRAIN SYNAPTOSOMES.
003768 04-03
CATECHOLAMINE SYNTHESIS REGULATION IN HYPOTHALAMIC
SYNAPTOSOMES. (UNPUBLISHED PAPER).
003829 04-03
EFFECT OF VERAPAMIL ON 45CA UPTAKE BY SYNAPTOSOMES.
003856 04-03
CORRELATIONS BETWEEN NA-K-ATPASE ACTIVITY AND ACETYLCHOLINE
RELEASE IN RAT CORTICAL SYNAPTOSOMES.
003937 04-03
EFFECTS OF IN VIVO AMPHETAMINE ADMINISTRATION ON DOPAMINE
SYNTHESIS REGULATION IN RAT-BRAIN STRIATAL SYNAPTOSOMES.
(UNPUBLISHED PAPER).
003960 04-03
EFFECTS OF CANNABINOIDS ON CATECHOLAMINE UPTAKE AND RELEASE
IN HYPOTHALAMIC AND STRIATAL SYNAPTOSOMES.
003970 04-03
STUDIES ON THE MECHANISM-OF-ACTION OF AVERMECTIN-B1A:
STIMULATION OF RELEASE OF GAMMA AMINOBUTYRIC-ACID FROM
BRAIN SYNAPTOSOMES.
003973 04-03

SYNCHRONIZATION
SYNCHRONIZATION OF EEG ACTIVITY OF MALE RHESUS-MONKEYS
MACACA-MULATTA TREATED WITH OVOCYCLIN.
001312 02-03

SYNDROME
ACUTE VERSUS CHRONIC EFFECTS OF SEROTONIN UPTAKE BLOCKERS ON
POTENTIATION OF THE SEROTONIN SYNDROME.
000050 01-03
RECLASSIFICATION OF THE TARDIVE-DYSKINESIA SYNDROME.
002374 02-15
ATTENUATION OF THE LITHIUM-INDUCED DIABETES-INSIPIDUS-LIKE
SYNDROME BY AMILORIDE IN RATS.
002717 03-03
NEUROLEPTIC-INDUCED SYNDROME MIMICKING MYASTHENIA-GRAVIS.
003474 03-15
A TARDIVE-DYSKINESIA-LIKE SYNDROME AFTER AMITRIPTYLINE
TREATMENT.
003552 03-15
A PRELIMINARY OPEN-STUDY OF THE USE OF AMINEPTINE OF THE
DEFICIENT SYNDROME OF HEBEPHRENICS AND OF ADDICTS DURING
WITHDRAWAL.
004445 04-11
HYPERVENTILATION-SYNDROME AND BETA-RECEPTOR FUNCTION –
CLINICAL-EFFECT OF BETA BLOCKER UPON THE SYNDROME.
004459 04-11

SYNERGISM
SYNERGISM OF COMBINED LITHIUM NEUROLEPTIC THERAPY: A DOUBLE-
BLIND, PLACEBO-CONTROLLED CASE-STUDY.
003165 03-08

SYNERGISTIC
SYNERGISTIC ACTIONS OF PROPANTHELINE-BROMIDE WITH CIMETIDINE
AND THIOPROPAZATE-HYDROCHLORIDE IN THE PREVENTION OF
STRESS-ULCER FORMATION IN RATS.
000064 01-03

SYNTHESES
PRODRUGS OF SOME DOPAMINERGIC 2 AMINOTETRALINS: A REVIEW OF
THEIR SYNTHESES AND NEUROCHEMICAL PROFILES.
000004 01-01

SYNTHESIS
THE ROLE OF INTRANEURONAL 5 HT AND OF TRYPTOPHAN-
HYDROXYLASE ACTIVATION IN THE CONTROL OF 5 HT SYNTHESIS IN
RAT-BRAIN SLICES INCUBATED IN K-ENRICHED MEDIUM.
000123 01-03
DIMETHYLAMINOETHANOL (DEANOL) METABOLISM IN RAT-BRAIN AND
ITS EFFECT ON ACETYLCHOLINE SYNTHESIS.
000150 01-03
STREET PCP SCENE: ISSUES ON SYNTHESIS AND CONTAMINATION.
000744 01-12
GABA SYNTHESIS BY CULTURED FIBROBLASTS OBTAINED FROM PERSONS
WITH HUNTINGTONS-DISEASE.
000765 01-13
SYNTHESIS OF SOME 5 PHENYLHEXAHYDROAZEPINOINDOLES AS
POTENTIAL NEUROLEPTIC-AGENTS.
001019 02-01
SYNTHESIS OF 180 ANALOGS OF BIOGENIC-AMINES. (UNPUBLISHED
PAPER).
001044 02-01
SYNTHESIS AND PHARMACOLOGY OF 2 AMINO-3-ETHOXYCARBONYL-4-
PHENYLTHIOPHENE DERIVATIVES.
001083 02-02
SYNTHESIS AND ANXIOLYTIC-ACTIVITY OF A SERIES OF
PYRAZINOBENZODIAZEPINE DERIVATIVES.
001089 02-02
CORTICOSTERONE INCREASES THE SYNTHESIS OF A SOLUBLE PROTEIN IN
PITUITARY-GLANDS FROM ADRENALECTOMIZED MALE RATS WHICH
PRECIPITATES WITH ANTI-RAT GROWTH-HORMONE ANTISERUM.
(UNPUBLISHED PAPER).
001122 02-03
FURTHER STUDIES ON THE INHIBITION OF MONOAMINE SYNTHESIS BY
MONOFLUOROMETHYLDOPA.
001128 02-03
DOPAMINE SYNTHESIS: TOLERANCE TO HALOPERIDOL AND
SUPERSENSITIVITY TO APOMORPHINE DEPEND ON PRESYNAPTIC-
RECEPTORS.
001129 02-03
BRAIN SEROTONIN AND 5 HYDROXYINDOLEACETIC-ACID
CONCENTRATIONS AND SEROTONIN SYNTHESIS FOLLOWING
TETRAHYDRO-BETA-CARBOLINE ADMINISTRATION IN MICE.
001152 02-03
DEVELOPMENTAL ASPECTS OF CATECHOLESTROGEN SYNTHESIS.
(UNPUBLISHED PAPER).
001282 02-03
THE ROLE OF PROTEIN SYNTHESIS IN THE HYPOTHALAMIC MECHANISM
MEDIATING PYROGEN FEVER.
001454 02-03
LONG-TERM APPLICATION OF HALOPERIDOL: EFFECT OF ANTICHOLINERGIC
TREATMENT ON THE RATE OF DOPAMINE SYNTHESIS.
001490 02-03
ROLE OF NEUROTRANSMITTERS AND PROTEIN SYNTHESIS IN SHORT-
TERM AND LONG-TERM MEMORY.
001573 02-04
THE SYNTHESIS AND ACTIVITY OF CIS AND TRANS 2
AMINOMETHYLCYCLOPROPANECARBOXYLIC-ACID AS
CONFORMATIONALLY RESTRICTED ANALOGUES OF GABA.
002633 03-01
PHENYLETHYLAMINE EFFECTS ON DOPAMINE SYNTHESIS. STRUCTURE-
ACTIVITY RELATIONSHIPS.
002649 03-02
EFFECTS OF AN EPINEPHRINE SYNTHESIS INHIBITOR, SKF-64139, ON THE
SECRETION OF LUTEINIZING-HORMONE IN OVARIECTOMIZED FEMALE
RATS.
002693 03-03
SELECTIVE EFFECTS OF LSD AND HYPERTHERMIA ON THE SYNTHESIS OF
SYNAPTIC PROTEINS AND GLYCOPROTEINS.
002721 03-03
A QUANTITATIVE REGIONAL ANALYSIS OF PROTEIN SYNTHESIS
INHIBITION IN THE RAT-BRAIN FOLLOWING LOCALIZED INJECTION OF
CYCLOHEXIMIDE.
002780 03-03
LEVONANTRADOL, A POTENT CANNABINOID RELATED ANALGESIC,
ANTAGONIZES HALOPERIDOL-INDUCED ACTIVATION OF STRIATAL
DOPAMINE SYNTHESIS.
002786 03-03

SYNTHESIS AND STRUCTURE-ACTIVITY RELATIONSHIP OF A
PYRIMIDOPYRIMIDINE DERIVATIVE WITH ANTIDEPRESSANT ACTIVITY.
003653 04-01

SYNTHESIS AND BIOLOGICAL-ACTIVITY OF HUMAN BETA ENDORPHIN
ANALOGS WITH DISULFIDE BRIDGES.
003655 04-01

SYNTHESIS OF CYTOSKELETAL PROTEINS IN BULK ISOLATED NEURONAL
PERIKARYA.
003672 04-01

SYNTHESIS AND PHARMACOLOGICAL-STUDY OF SOME ENKEPHALIN
ANALOGS IN RELATION TO THE PLURALITY OF OPIATE-RECEPTORS.
003682 04-02

SYNTHESIS AND BIOCHEMICAL AND PHARMACOLOGIC PROPERTIES OF
ANALOGUES AND DERIVATIVES OF P CHLOROPHENYLALANINE.
003691 04-02

SYNTHESIS AND GABA-RECEPTOR BINDING-ACTIVITY OF TWO
FLUOROAMINOMETHYLPHENOLS.
003693 04-02

SYNTHESIS OF PHENYLURETHANS OF 1,2 DIALKYL-4-PYRAZOLIDINOLS AS
ANTICONVULSANT-AGENTS.
003695 04-02

SYNTHESIS AND PHARMACOLOGICAL ACTIVITY OF SOME 2 IMINO-3-
ALKYLTHIAZOLINE DERIVATIVES.
003698 04-02

SYNTHESIS OF POTENTIAL ANTICONVULSANTS: CONDENSATION OF
ISATINS WITH ACETONE AND RELATED KETONES.
003699 04-02

SYNTHESIS AND PHARMACOLOGICAL PROPERTIES OF N-4 1
AZETIDINYLBUTYNYL 2 PYRROLIDONE, A HIGHLY POTENT
OXOTREMORINE-LIKE-AGENT.
003701 04-02

EFFECT OF ALPHA METHYLPHENYLALANINE AND PHENYLALANINE ON
BRAIN POLYRIBOSOMES AND PROTEIN SYNTHESIS.
003733 04-03

EFFECT OF INTRAVENOUS ADMINISTRATION OF D LYSERGIC-ACID-
DIETHYLAMIDE ON SUBSEQUENT PROTEIN SYNTHESIS IN A CELL-FREE
SYSTEM DERIVED FROM BRAIN.
003761 04-03

CATECHOLAMINE AND 5 HYDROXYTRYPTAMINE SYNTHESIS AND
METABOLISM FOLLOWING INTRACEREBROVENTRICULAR INJECTION OF
DIBUTYRYL-CYCLIC-AMP.
003769 04-03

OPPOSITE EFFECTS OF NALOXONE ON SUBSTANCE-P-INDUCED IN BRAIN
DOPA SYNTHESIS AND IN LOCOMOTOR-ACTIVITY IN RATS.
003799 04-03

CATECHOLAMINE SYNTHESIS REGULATION IN HYPOTHALAMIC
SYNAPTOSOMES. (UNPUBLISHED PAPER).
003829 04-03

STIMULATION OF FRUCTOSEBIPHOSPHATASE ACTIVITY AND SYNTHESIS
IN THE CEREBRAL-CORTEX OF RATS SUBMITTED TO THE CONVULSANT
METHIONINE-SULFOXIMINE.
003838 04-03

PHENYLALAMINE EFFECTS ON DOPAMINE SYNTHESIS: STRUCTURE-
ACTIVITY RELATIONSHIPS. (UNPUBLISHED PAPER).
003959 04-03

EFFECTS OF IN VIVO AMPHETAMINE ADMINISTRATION ON DOPAMINE
SYNTHESIS REGULATION IN RAT-BRAIN STRIATAL SYNAPTOSOMES.
(UNPUBLISHED PAPER).
003960 04-03

INHIBITION OF THE SYNTHESIS OF ACETYLCHOLINE IN RAT-BRAIN SLICES
BY (-) HYDROXYCITRATE AND CITRATE.
004044 04-03

ANTITREMOR ACTION OF C10DICHOL, A PERIPHERAL ACETYLCHOLINE
SYNTHESIS INHIBITOR.
004096 04-04

SYNTHESIZE
REGIONAL AND SUBCELLULAR LOCALIZATION IN RAT-BRAIN OF THE
ENZYMES THAT CAN SYNTHESIZE GAMMA HYDROXYBUTYRIC-ACID.
003675 04-01

SYNTHESIZED
EFFECT OF ACUTE ADMINISTRATION OF MORPHINE ON NEWLY
SYNTHESIZED 5 HYDROXYTRYPTAMINE IN SPINAL-CORD OF THE RAT.
000110 01-03

NEWLY SYNTHESIZED CHOLECYSTOKININ IN SUBCELLULAR FRACTIONS OF
THE RAT-BRAIN.
003805 04-03

SYNTHESIZING
IMMUNOCYTOCHEMICAL LOCALIZATION OF CATECHOLAMINE
SYNTHESIZING ENZYMES AND NEUROPEPTIDES IN AREA POSTREMA
AND MEDIAL NUCLEUS-TRACTUS-SOLITARIUS OF RAT-BRAIN.
002634 03-01

DIFFERENTIAL-EFFECTS OF ALPHA METHYLDOPAMINE, CLONIDINE AND
HYDRALAZINE ON NOREPINEPHRINE AND EPINEPHRINE SYNTHESIZING
ENZYMES IN THE BRAINSTEM NUCLEI OF SPONTANEOUSLY
HYPERTENSIVE-RATS.
003947 04-03

SYNTHETIC
APPLICATION OF A SYNTHETIC ENKEPHALIN ANALOGUE DURING HEROIN
WITHDRAWAL.
000685 01-11

PREPARATION AND CHARACTERIZATION OF SYNTHETIC MODELS FOR THE
DENSE-BODIES OF HUMAN PLATELETS. (UNPUBLISHED PAPER).
001013 02-01

SYNTHETIC IMMUNOSTIMULANTS DERIVED FROM THE BACTERIAL CELL
WALL.
001080 02-02

QUINACRINE AND SEROTONIN BINDING BY SYNTHETIC MODELS FOR
HUMAN PLATELET DENSE-BODIES: EVALUATION OF THE ROLE OF
BINDING IN AMINE STORAGE. (UNPUBLISHED PAPER).
002219 02-13

A SINGLE-DOSE STUDY OF NABILONE, A SYNTHETIC CANNABINOID.
002328 02-14

NEUROPHARMACOLOGY OF SYNTHETIC ERGOT DERIVATIVES IN MAN.
002429 02-15

OPERANT FEEDING AND DRINKING IN PIGS FOLLOWING
INTRACEREBROVENTRICULAR INJECTION OF SYNTHETIC
CHOLECYSTOKININ-OCTAPEPTIDE.
003064 03-04

PRENATAL EXPOSURE TO SYNTHETIC PROGESTINS INCREASES POTENTIAL
FOR AGGRESSION IN HUMANS.
003527 03-15

A SYNTHETIC ACTH4-9 ANALOGUE (ORGANON-2766) AND SLEEP IN
HEALTHY MAN.
004574 04-14

SYNTHETICALLY-MODIFIED
CLASSIFICATION OF ENDORPHINS/ENKEPHALINS IN BRAIN PHYSIOLOGY
AND PATHOLOGY (BASED ON EEG AND CLINICAL-STUDY OF
SYNTHETICALLY-MODIFIED METHIONINE-ENKEPHALIN).
002286 02-13

SYRINGE
AN IMPROVED PNEUMATIC SYRINGE FOR SELF-ADMINISTRATION OF
DRUGS BY RATS.
004304 04-06

SYRUP
RECTAL VALPROATE SYRUP AND STATUS-EPILEPTICUS.
000727 01-11

SYSTEMIC
DOES SYSTEMIC MORPHINE INCREASE DESCENDING INHIBITORY
CONTROLS OF DORSAL-HORN NEURONES INVOLVED IN NOCICEPTION?
000175 01-03

SYSTEMIC DIPIPERIDINOETHANE MIMICS THE CONVULSANT AND
NEUROTOXIC-ACTIONS OF KAINIC-ACID.
000222 01-03

EFFECTS OF SYSTEMIC AND INTRAVENTRICULAR ADMINISTRATION OF
CANNABINOIDS ON SCHEDULE-CONTROLLED RESPONDING IN THE
SQUIRREL-MONKEY.
000354 01-04

SYSTEMIC AND INTRAVENTRICULAR PROLACTIN INDUCES EXCESSIVE
GROOMING.
000378 01-04

SYSTEMIC INSULIN DECREASES LATERAL HYPOTHALAMIC UNIT ACTIVITY.
001275 02-03

DIFFERENTIAL-EFFECTS OF SYSTEMIC VERSUS INTRACRANIAL INJECTION
OF OPIATES ON CENTRAL, OROFACIAL AND LOWER BODY
NOCICEPTION: SOMATOTYPY IN BULBAR ANALGESIA SYSTEMS.
001446 02-03

ACTIVATION AND LATERALIZATION OF SENSORIMOTOR FIELD FOR
PERIORAL BITING-REFLEX BY INTRANIGRAL GABA AGONIST AND BY
SYSTEMIC APOMORPHINE IN THE RAT.
001657 02-04

DOSE-RESPONSE STUDY OF THE PRECIPITATED ABSTINENCE-SYNDROME
FOR MORPHINE: SYSTEMIC VS PERIAQUEDUCTAL GRAY NALOXONE.
(PH.D. DISSERTATION).
002979 03-04

THE DYNAMICS OF SYSTEMIC VENOUS, ARTERIAL, AND CEREBROSPINAL-
FLUID PRESSURE UNDER I.V. ADMINISTRATION OF POLYETHYLENE-
GLYCOL.
004045 04-03

SYSTEMICALLY
EFFECTS OF CENTRALLY-ADMINISTERED AND SYSTEMICALLY
ADMINISTERED L TYROSINE AND L LEUCINE ON OVARIAN FUNCTION IN
THE OLD RAT.
001180 02-03

METKEPHAMID, A SYSTEMICALLY ACTIVE ANALOG OF METHIONINE-
ENKEPHALIN WITH POTENT OPIOID DELTA-RECEPTOR ACTIVITY.
002720 03-03

T-MAZE
INTRAHYPOTHALAMIC MICROINJECTIONS OF NORADRENALINE WITH AND
WITHOUT INDUCTION OF THE ALIMENTARY DRIVE AS A REWARD IN A
T-MAZE LEARNING IN RATS.
001604 02-04

T-SCORES
EFFECTS OF SINGLE-ORAL-DOSAGES OF STEROIDS ON HUMAN EEG
BASELINE CROSSING T-SCORES SHOWN BY MULTIVARIATE STATISTICS
AND STANDARD PROFILES.
002239 02-13

TABERNANTHINE
EFFECT OF TABERNANTHINE ON THE TURNOVER TIME OF BRAIN
CATECHOLAMINES IN NORMAL AND HYPOBARIC HYPOXIC RATS.
001187 02-03

TACHYCARDIA
INTERMITTENT DECORTICATION AND PROGRESSIVE HYPERTHERMIA,
HYPERTENSION AND TACHYCARDIA FOLLOWING METHYLGLUCAMINE
IOTHALAMATE VENTRICULOGRAM.
003520 03-15
MODULATORY EFFECT OF BRAIN ACETYLCHOLINE ON REFLEX-INDUCED
BRADYCARDIA AND TACHYCARDIA IN CONSCIOUS RATS.
003744 04-03

TACRINE
DIAZEPAM IN COMBINATION WITH TACRINE DERIVATIVES ANTAGONIZES
BEHAVIOURAL-EFFECTS OF ANTICHOLINERGIC PSYCHOTOMIMETICS IN
RATS.
000420 01-04

TACTICS
CHOICE OF TACTICS IN TREATING ALCOHOLIC-DELIRIUM.
000688 01-11

TACTILE
A COMPARISON OF HUMAN TACTILE STIMULUS VELOCITY
DISCRIMINATION WITH THE ABILITY OF S-I CORTICAL NEURONS IN
AWAKE RHESUS-MONKEYS TO SIGNAL THE SAME VELOCITY
DIFFERENCES BEFORE AND AFTER NONANESTHETIC DOSES OF
PENTOBARBITAL.
000055 01-03

TAGLUTIMIDE
PHARMACOLOGICAL-PROPERTIES OF TAGLUTIMIDE, A NEW SEDATIVE
HYPNOTIC-DRUG.
001087 02-02

TAIL
EFFECTS OF ANALGESICS AND CNS-ACTING DRUGS ON STRUGGLING
FOLLOWING REPETITIVE STIMULATION OF THE TAIL, AND FLEXOR
REFLEX TO A SINGLE STIMULATION OF THE SCIATIC-NERVE IN RATS.
004148 04-04

TAIL-SHOCK
TITRATION PROCEDURE WITH RATS USING A NOSE-POKE RESPONSE AND
TAIL-SHOCK.
001862 02-06

TAILORED
A NOVEL PSYCHOMETRIC-TEST MODEL APPLYING TAILORED TESTING FOR
ECONOMIC AND EFFICIENT COLLECTION OF
PSYCHOPHARMACOLOGICAL-EFFECTS.
002479 02-16

TAIPOXIN
EFFECTS OF TAIPOXIN ON THE ULTRASTRUCTURE OF CHOLINERGIC AXON
TERMINALS IN THE MOUSE ADRENAL-MEDULLA.
003916 04-03

TALAPOIN-MONKEYS
BEHAVIOURAL-EFFECTS AND ENDOCRINE-EFFECTS OF NALTREXONE IN
MALE TALAPOIN-MONKEYS.
001718 02-04

TAP
A NOVEL THREE-WAY TAP.
001863 02-06

TARDIVE
THE OCCURRENCE OF TARDIVE EXTRAPYRAMIDAL SYMPTOMS IN
SCHIZOPHRENIC-PATIENTS UNDERGOING PROLONGED NEUROLEPTIC
TREATMENT.
000885 01-15
TARDIVE TOURETTE-SYNDROME IN AN AUTISTIC-PATIENT AFTER LONG-
TERM NEUROLEPTIC ADMINISTRATION.
000887 01-15

TARDIVE-DYSKINESIA
ORAL DYSKINESIA IN BRAIN-DAMAGED RATS WITHDRAWN FROM A
NEUROLEPTIC: IMPLICATION FOR MODELS OF TARDIVE-DYSKINESIA.
000393 01-04
OXIPEROMIDE IN TARDIVE-DYSKINESIA.
000540 01-07
CLOZAPINE IN THE TREATMENT OF TARDIVE-DYSKINESIA: AN INTERIM
REPORT.
000677 01-11
TREATMENT OF TARDIVE-DYSKINESIA WITH OXYPERTINE – PRELIMINARY
CLINICAL-EXPERIENCE AND A BRIEF REVIEW OF THE LITERATURE.
000692 01-11
IDENTIFICATION OF A SUBGROUP OF TARDIVE-DYSKINESIA PATIENTS BY
PHARMACOLOGIC-PROBES.
000708 01-11
THE EFFECTS OF CHOLINERGIC-DRUGS ON THE INVOLUNTARY-
MOVEMENTS OF TARDIVE-DYSKINESIA.
000726 01-11
SPONT.,NEOUS DYSKINESIA IN THE ELDERLY AND TARDIVE-DYSKINESIA
FROM NEUROLEPTICS. A SURVEY OF 270 ELDERLY-PATIENTS.
000834 01-15
NEUROLEPTIC-INDUCED TARDIVE-DYSKINESIA: RECENT
PATHOPHYSIOLOGICAL-DATA, THERAPEUTIC TRIALS.
000842 01-15
DRUG-VARIABLES IN THE ETIOLOGY OF TARDIVE-DYSKINESIA:
APPLICATION OF DISCRIMINANT FUNCTION ANALYSIS.
000844 01-15

TARDIVE-DYSKINESIA AND LITHIUM ASSOCIATED NEPHROPATHY: ARE
YOU LIABLE?
000846 01-15
TARDIVE-DYSKINESIA AND OTHER MOVEMENT-DISORDERS IN CHILDREN
TREATED WITH PSYCHOTROPIC-DRUGS.
000849 01-15
REVERSIBILITY OF TARDIVE-DYSKINESIA.
000854 01-15
STRATEGY FOR THE STUDY OF PATIENTS AT HIGH-RISK FOR TARDIVE-
DYSKINESIA.
000858 01-15
TARDIVE-DYSKINESIA: REVIEW AND UPDATE.
000862 01-15
TARDIVE-DYSKINESIA: SUMMARY OF A TASK-FORCE-REPORT OF THE
AMERICAN-PSYCHIATRIC-ASSOCIATION.
000875 01-15
A NEUROENDOCRINE-STUDY OF SUPERSENSITIVITY IN TARDIVE-
DYSKINESIA.
000908 01-16
TARDIVE-DYSKINESIA RESULTING FROM CHRONIC NARCOTIC
TREATMENT.
000922 01-17
CHOLINERGIC ASPECTS OF TARDIVE-DYSKINESIA: HUMAN AND ANIMAL
STUDIES.
000928 01-17
TARDIVE-DYSKINESIA: RESEARCH & TREATMENT.
000934 01-17
EFFECTS OF CHOLINE CONTAINING COMPOUNDS ON TARDIVE-DYSKINESIA
AND OTHER MOVEMENT-DISORDERS.
000942 01-17
DOPAMINERGIC-SUPERSENSITIVITY: INFLUENCE OF DOPAMINE AGONISTS
AND DRUGS USED FOR THE TREATMENT OF TARDIVE-DYSKINESIA.
001169 02-03
ANTICHOLINERGICS PROMOTE NEUROLEPTIC-INDUCED TARDIVE-
DYSKINESIA.
001834 02-05
TARDIVE-DYSKINESIA IN DEPRESSED-PATIENTS: SUCCESSFUL THERAPY
WITH ANTIDEPRESSANTS AND LITHIUM.
002037 02-09
TREATMENT OF TARDIVE-DYSKINESIA IN AN AGITATED, DEPRESSED-
PATIENT.
002038 02-09
GAMMA ACETYLENIC-GABA IN TARDIVE-DYSKINESIA.
002101 02-11
CHOLINERGIC ASPECTS OF TARDIVE-DYSKINESIA.
002102 02-11
PATHOPHYSIOLOGICAL-ASPECTS OF REVERSIBLE AND IRREVERSIBLE
TARDIVE-DYSKINESIA.
002124 02-11
PHARMACOLOGIC-PROBES INTO TARDIVE-DYSKINESIA.
002179 02-11
TARDIVE-DYSKINESIA: BIOCHEMICAL-STUDIES. (UNPUBLISHED PAPER).
002245 02-13
PATHOPHYSIOLOGIC-BASIS OF TARDIVE-DYSKINESIA.
002373 02-15
RECLASSIFICATION OF THE TARDIVE-DYSKINESIA SYNDROME.
002374 02-15
DOPAMINE ANTAGONIST AND AGONIST TREATMENT OF TARDIVE-
DYSKINESIA.
002377 02-15
LECITHIN IN THE TREATMENT OF TARDIVE-DYSKINESIA.
002380 02-15
PHARMACOLOGIC-STUDIES OF TARDIVE-DYSKINESIA.
002387 02-15
TARDIVE-DYSKINESIA: RECOGNITION, MANAGEMENT, AND PREVENTION.
002392 02-15
TARDIVE-DYSKINESIA FROM NEUROLEPTIC-DRUGS: REVIEW OF THE
LITERATURE.
002398 02-15
TARDIVE-DYSKINESIA FOLLOWING LOW-DOSES OF PIPERACETAZINE.
002399 02-15
ABSENCE OF SEVERE TARDIVE-DYSKINESIA IN HUNGARIAN
SCHIZOPHRENIC-OUTPATIENTS.
002404 02-15
THE PREVALENCE OF PRESUMED TARDIVE-DYSKINESIA IN PSYCHIATRIC-
INPATIENTS AND PSYCHIATRIC-OUTPATIENTS.
002417 02-15
SUBSYNDROMES OF TARDIVE-DYSKINESIA.
002421 02-15
BRADYCARDIA, PERSISTENT DIABETES-INSIPIDUS, AND TARDIVE-
DYSKINESIA WITH LITHIUM INTOXICATION.
002427 02-15
FAILURE OF LITHIUM TREATMENT IN ESTABLISHED TARDIVE-DYSKINESIA.
002432 02-15
HALOPERIDOL-INDUCED TARDIVE-DYSKINESIA IN A CHILD WITH GILLES-
DE-LA-TOURETTES-DISEASE.
002437 02-15
TARDIVE-DYSKINESIA.
002440 02-15

EFFECT OF SODIUM-VALPROATE AND BACLOFEN IN TARDIVE-DYSKINESIA: CLINICAL-STUDIES AND NEUROENDOCRINE-STUDIES.
002441 02-15

TARDIVE-DYSKINESIA ON HUNGARIAN PSYCHIATRIC-WARDS.
002447 02-15

CHANGES IN PREVALENCE, SEVERITY, AND RECOVERY IN TARDIVE-DYSKINESIA WITH AGE.
002455 02-15

NEUROLEPTIC-INDUCED REINNERVATION SPROUTING IN THE CENTRAL-NERVOUS-SYSTEM (A MODEL FOR THE DEVELOPMENT OF TARDIVE-DYSKINESIA AND SUPERSENSITIVITY PSYCHOSIS).
002459 02-15

PROPRANOLOL (INDERAL) FOR TARDIVE-DYSKINESIA AND EXTRAPYRAMIDAL SIDE-EFFECTS FROM NEUROLEPTICS: POSSIBLE INVOLVEMENT OF BETA-ADRENERGIC MECHANISMS.
002470 02-15

USE OF CHOLINE AND LECITHIN IN THE TREATMENT OF TARDIVE-DYSKINESIA.
002473 02-15

CLONAZEPAM AND PHENOBARBITAL IN TARDIVE-DYSKINESIA.
003294 03-11

DOPAMINERGIC AND GABAERGIC ASPECTS OF TARDIVE-DYSKINESIA.
003302 03-11

TARDIVE-DYSKINESIA.
003464 03-15

PHARMACOLOGICAL-STUDIES OF TARDIVE-DYSKINESIA: IMPLICATIONS FOR FUTURE RESEARCH.
003465 03-15

TARDIVE-DYSKINESIA: CLINICOEPIDEMIOLOGICAL REVISION AND CONTRIBUTION.
003466 03-15

EFFECTS OF GRADUAL DECREASE AND DISCONTINUATION OF NEUROLEPTICS ON CLINICAL CONDITION AND TARDIVE-DYSKINESIA.
003469 03-15

EFFECT OF DES-TYR-GAMMA-ENDORPHIN IN TARDIVE-DYSKINESIA.
003472 03-15

ANIMAL-MODELS OF TARDIVE-DYSKINESIA.
003476 03-15

TARDIVE-DYSKINESIA IN SCHIZOPHRENIC-OUTPATIENTS: PREVALENCE AND SIGNIFICANT VARIABLES.
003483 03-15

THE EFFECTS OF A DRUG-HOLIDAY ON RELAPSE AND TARDIVE-DYSKINESIA IN CHRONIC-SCHIZOPHRENICS.
003487 03-15

LECITHIN ADMINISTRATION IN TARDIVE-DYSKINESIA: CLINICAL AND BIOMEDICAL-CORRELATES.
003496 03-15

LYMPHOCYTE MONOAMINE-OXIDASE AND PLASMA PROLACTIN AND GROWTH-HORMONE IN TARDIVE-DYSKINESIA.
003499 03-15

PRELIMINARY-FINDINGS WITH REGARD TO RISK-FACTORS IN THE DEVELOPMENT OF TARDIVE-DYSKINESIA.
003501 03-15

TARDIVE-DYSKINESIA: TWO-YEAR RECOVERY.
003535 03-15

FAMILIAL OCCURRENCE OF TARDIVE-DYSKINESIA.
003548 03-15

ANTAGONISM OF DOPAMINE SUPERSENSITIVITY BY ESTROGEN: NEUROCHEMICAL-STUDIES IN AN ANIMAL-MODEL OF TARDIVE-DYSKINESIA.
004268 04-05

THE BIOCHEMICAL BACKGROUND TO TARDIVE-DYSKINESIA.
004588 04-15

TARDIVE-DYSKINESIA: RECENT DEVELOPMENTS.
004592 04-15

EFFECTS OF NEUROLEPTIC ADJUSTMENT ON CLINICAL CONDITION AND TARDIVE-DYSKINESIA IN SCHIZOPHRENIC-PATIENTS.
004595 04-15

PREVENTION OF TARDIVE-DYSKINESIA AND OTHER DRUG RELATED ADVERSE-EFFECTS.
004601 04-15

CLINICAL STRATEGIES FOR ANTIPSYCHOTIC-DRUG TREATMENT, TARDIVE-DYSKINESIA, AND THE TRAINING OF RESEARCH PSYCHIATRISTS.
004603 04-15

CLINICAL AND PRECLINICAL EXPERIENCE WITH CHOLINE-CHLORIDE IN HUNTINGTONS-DISEASE AND TARDIVE-DYSKINESIA: UNANSWERED QUESTIONS.
004604 04-15

A CONTROLLED-TRIAL OF OXYPERTINE IN TARDIVE-DYSKINESIA.
004611 04-15

LECITHIN FOR THE TREATMENT OF TARDIVE-DYSKINESIA.
004612 04-15

TARDIVE-DYSKINESIA AND OTHER DRUG-INDUCED MOVEMENT-DISORDERS AMONG HANDICAPPED CHILDREN AND YOUTH.
004614 04-15

TREATMENT OF TARDIVE-DYSKINESIA.
004616 04-15

BACLOFEN IN THE TREATMENT OF TARDIVE-DYSKINESIA: OPEN LABEL STUDY.
004619 04-15

TARDIVE-DYSKINESIA.
004624 04-15

ON THE THERAPY OF NEUROLEPTIC-INDUCED TARDIVE-DYSKINESIA WITH DIMETHYLAMINOETHANOL (DEANOL).
004627 04-15

PRESENT ATTEMPTS AT TREATING TARDIVE-DYSKINESIA.
004629 04-15

TARDIVE-DYSKINESIA: PROBLEMS OF PATHOGENESIS, THERAPY, AND PREVENTION.
004644 04-15

TARDIVE-DYSKINESIA-LIKE
A TARDIVE-DYSKINESIA-LIKE SYNDROME AFTER AMITRIPTYLINE TREATMENT.
003552 03-15

TARDIVE-DYSKINESIAS
TARDIVE-DYSKINESIAS (OBSERVATIONS CONCERNING THREE CASES).
000861 01-15

NEUROLEPTIC-INDUCED TARDIVE-DYSKINESIAS.
002382 02-15

TARDIVE-HYPERKINESIA
TARDIVE-HYPERKINESIA. EFFECTS OF SULPIRIDE AND GABA SYSTEM AGONISTS.
002405 02-15

TASK-FORCE-REPORT
TARDIVE-DYSKINESIA: SUMMARY OF A TASK-FORCE-REPORT OF THE AMERICAN-PSYCHIATRIC-ASSOCIATION.
000875 01-15

TASTE-AVERSION
HANDLING IN INFANCY, TASTE-AVERSION, AND BRAIN LATERALITY IN RATS.
000375 01-04

ABSENCE OF LITHIUM-INDUCED TASTE-AVERSION AFTER AREA-POSTREMA LESION.
000456 01-04

MODULATION OF CONDITIONED TASTE-AVERSION BY SODIUM-PENTOBARBITAL.
001596 02-04

PREEXPOSURE TO DELTA9 THC BLOCKS THC-INDUCED CONDITIONED TASTE-AVERSION IN RATS.
001618 02-04

ACTH POTENTIATES MORPHINE-INDUCED CONDITIONED TASTE-AVERSION.
001781 02-04

THE RELATIONSHIP BETWEEN POSITIVE REINFORCEMENT AND CONDITIONED TASTE-AVERSION PRODUCED BY SELF-ADMINISTERED DRUGS. (PH.D. DISSERTATION).
001798 02-04

EFFECTS OF DESGLYCINAMIDE-LYSINE-VASOPRESSIN ON A CONDITIONED TASTE-AVERSION IN RATS.
001811 02-04

BOMBESIN PRODUCES TASTE-AVERSION IN RATS.
002702 03-03

DOPAMINE DEPLETION BY 6 HYDROXYDOPAMINE PREVENTS CONDITIONED TASTE-AVERSION INDUCED BY METHYLAMPHETAMINE BUT NOT LITHIUM-CHLORIDE.
003110 03-04

NALOXONE FAILS TO BLOCK AMPHETAMINE-INDUCED ANOREXIA AND CONDITIONED TASTE-AVERSION.
004121 04-04

TASTE-AVERSIONS
EFFECTS OF DORSOLATERAL TEGMENTAL LESIONS ON AMPHETAMINE-INDUCED AND LITHIUM-INDUCED TASTE-AVERSIONS.
003114 03-04

TAURINE
LOCALIZATION OF SENSITIVE SITES TO TAURINE, GAMMA AMINOBUTYRIC-ACID, GLYCINE AND BETA ALANINE IN THE MOLECULAR LAYER OF GUINEA-PIG CEREBELLAR SLICES.
001402 02-03

CONTRALATERAL CIRCLING-BEHAVIOUR INDUCED BY INTRANIGRAL INJECTION OF TAURINE IN RATS.
001670 02-04

INHIBITORY ACTIONS OF TAUROCYAMINE, HYPOTAURINE, HOMOTAURINE, TAURINE AND GABA ON SPIKE DISCHARGES OF PURKINJE-CELLS, AND LOCALIZATION OF SENSITIVE SITES, IN GUINEA-PIG CEREBELLAR SLICES.
002846 03-03

EFFECT OF TAURINE ON 45CA2 ACCUMULATION IN RAT BRAIN SYNAPTOSOMES.
002855 03-03

THE EFFECT OF COLCHICINE AND CYTOCHALASIN B ON THE RELEASE OF TAURINE FROM THE CHICK RETINA.
002856 03-03

MODULATORY INTERACTIONS BETWEEN NOREPINEPHRINE AND TAURINE, BETA ALANINE, GAMMA AMINOBUTYRIC-ACID AND MUSCIMOL APPLIED IONTOPHORETICALLY TO CEREBELLAR PURKINJE-CELLS.
004058 04-03

TAUROCYAMINE
INHIBITORY ACTIONS OF TAUROCYAMINE, HYPOTAURINE, HOMOTAURINE, TAURINE AND GABA ON SPIKE DISCHARGES OF

PURKINJE-CELLS, AND LOCALIZATION OF SENSITIVE SITES, IN GUINEA-PIG CEREBELLAR SLICES.
002846 03-03

TEA
NEUROLEPTICS: INTERACTIONS WITH FOOD -- CHEMICAL AND PHARMACODYNAMIC STUDIES ON THE INTERACTIONS OF COFFEE AND TEA.
003612 03-17

TEACHER
PSYCHOACTIVE-DRUG-EFFECTS IN A HYPERACTIVE-CHILD: A CASE-STUDY ANALYSIS OF BEHAVIOR-CHANGE AND TEACHER ATTENTION.
002313 02-14

TEACHERS
UNDERSTANDING AND USE OF CHEMOTHERAPY BY LEARNING-DISABILITIES AND BEHAVIOR-DISORDERS TEACHERS.
000965 01-17

TEACHING
THE TEACHING OF PSYCHOPHARMACOLOGY.
002597 02-17

TEAMWORK
PARAPROFESSIONAL AND PROFESSIONAL TEAMWORK AND TRAINING IN MANAGING PCP AND OTHER DRUG-ABUSE PROBLEMS.
000924 01-17

TECHNICAL-ASPECT
BINDING OF PHENCYCLIDINE TO RAT-BRAIN MEMBRANES: TECHNICAL-ASPECT.
001882 02-06

TECHNIQUE
INTRATHECAL MORPHINE IN MICE: A NEW TECHNIQUE.
001868 02-06
MODIFIED CUP TECHNIQUE FOR MICROESTIMATION OF THE RELEASE AND UPTAKE OF NEUROTRANSMITTERS IN BRAIN SLICES.
003147 03-06
A SYMPTOM-PROFILE-ANALYSIS OF ANTIPSYCHOTIC-DRUG TREATMENT: NONPARAMETRIC MULTIDIMENSIONAL TECHNIQUE.
003196 03-08
USE OF THE INTRACEREBRAL INJECTION TECHNIQUE TO ELUCIDATE MECHANISMS OF APOMORPHINE CLIMBING AND ITS ANTAGONISM IN THE MOUSE.
004092 04-04

TECHNIQUES
INVESTIGATION OF NARCOTICS AND ANTITUSSIVES USING DRUG DISCRIMINATION TECHNIQUES.
000447 01-04
TECHNIQUES FOR PLASMA PROTEIN BINDING OF DEMETHYLCHLORIMIPRAMINE.
000897 01-16
NEW EXPERIMENTAL TECHNIQUES IN THE PHARMACOLOGICAL EVALUATION OF CNS ACTING DRUGS.
001479 02-03
GLC/TLC ANALYSIS OF CODEINE AND MORPHINE IN URINE VIA DERIVATIZATION TECHNIQUES.
004687 04-16
RECEPTOR TECHNIQUES IN THE STUDY OF PLASMA LEVELS OF NEUROLEPTICS AND ANTIDEPRESSANT-DRUGS.
004694 04-16

TEGMENTAL
INFLUENCE OF AMPHETAMINE AND PHENYLPROPANOLAMINE ON FOOD INTAKE, ACTIVITY, AND BODY-TEMPERATURE IN RATS WITH VENTROMEDIAL HYPOTHALAMIC OR DORSOLATERAL TEGMENTAL DAMAGE.
000322 01-03
EFFECT OF PICROTOXIN AND NIPECOTIC-ACID ON INHIBITORY RESPONSE OF DOPAMINERGIC NEURONS IN THE VENTRAL TEGMENTAL AREA TO STIMULATION OF THE NUCLEUS-ACCUMBENS.
000331 01-03
LOCOMOTOR-ACTIVITY ELICITED BY INJECTIONS OF PICROTOXIN INTO THE VENTRAL TEGMENTAL AREA IS ATTENUATED BY INJECTIONS OF GABA INTO THE GLOBUS-PALLIDUS.
000436 01-04
DORSAL TEGMENTAL BUNDLE DESTRUCTION: EFFECTS ON OPERANT-BEHAVIOR, BRAIN CATECHOLAMINE LEVELS, AND BEHAVIORAL-SUPPRESSION PRODUCED BY ADRENERGIC AGONISTS.
001726 02-04
EFFECTS OF AMPHETAMINE AND PHENYLPROPANOLAMINE ON FOOD INTAKE IN RATS WITH VENTROMEDIAL HYPOTHALAMIC OR DORSOLATERAL TEGMENTAL DAMAGE.
001818 02-04
A TOPOGRAPHIC LOCALIZATION OF ENKEPHALIN ON THE DOPAMINE NEURONS OF THE RAT SUBSTANTIA-NIGRA AND VENTRAL TEGMENTAL AREA DEMONSTRATED BY COMBINED HISTOFLUORESCENCE IMMUNOCYTOCHEMISTRY.
002639 03-01
INTRACRANIAL SELF-ADMINISTRATION OF MORPHINE INTO THE VENTRAL TEGMENTAL AREA IN RATS.
002960 03-04
EFFECTS OF DORSOLATERAL TEGMENTAL LESIONS ON AMPHETAMINE-INDUCED AND LITHIUM-INDUCED TASTE-AVERSIONS.
003114 03-04

MORPHINE DIFFERENTIALLY AFFECTS VENTRAL TEGMENTAL AND SUBSTANTIA-NIGRA BRAIN REWARD THRESHOLDS.
004187 04-04

TEGMENTUM
5 HT BLOCKADE AND THE STIMULANT-EFFECTS OF D-AMPHETAMINE AND L-AMPHETAMINE: NO INTERACTION IN SELF-STIMULATION OF PREFRONTAL-CORTEX, HYPOTHALAMUS, OR DORSAL TEGMENTUM. UNEXPECTED LETHALITY IN HIPPOCAMPAL SITES.
000387 01-04

TELE-METHYLHISTAMINE
TELE-METHYLHISTAMINE IS A SPECIFIC MAO-B SUBSTRATE IN MAN.
002230 02-13

TELENCEPHALON
THE INFLUENCE OF UNILATERAL 6 HYDROXYDOPAMINE LESIONS OF THE SUBSTANTIA-NIGRA IN THE ABSENCE OF THE TELENCEPHALON.
004197 04-04

TELEOST
DOPAMINERGIC MECHANISMS IN THE TELEOST RETINA. II. FACTORS AFFECTING THE ACCUMULATION OF CYCLIC-AMP IN PIECES OF INTACT CARP RETINA.
003776 04-03
DOPAMINERGIC MECHANISMS IN THE TELEOST RETINA. I. DOPAMINE-SENSITIVE ADENYLATE-CYCLASE IN HOMOGENATES OF CARP RETINA; EFFECTS OF AGONISTS, ANTAGONISTS AND ERGOTS.
004051 04-03

TEMAZEPAM
RESIDUAL-EFFECTS OF TEMAZEPAM AND OTHER HYPNOTIC-COMPOUNDS ON COGNITIVE FUNCTION.
000879 01-15
EFFICACY AND SIDE-EFFECTS OF LORAZEPAM, OXAZEPAM, AND TEMAZEPAM AS SLEEPING-AIDS IN PSYCHOGERIATRIC-INPATIENTS.
002076 02-10
EUHYPNOS-FORTE, HIGH-DOSE TEMAZEPAM FOR RESISTANT INSOMNIA: POSTMARKETING SURVEILLANCE IN 10,057 PATIENTS UNRESPONSIVE TO CONVENTIONAL HYPNOTIC DOSAGE.
002324 02-14

TEMPERATURE
INFLUENCE OF NARCOTIC-AGENTS ON TEMPERATURE REGULATION.
001108 02-03
ROLE OF BRAIN CATECHOLAMINES AND 5 HYDROXYTRYPTAMINE IN MORPHINE-INDUCED TEMPERATURE CHANGES IN NORMAL AND TOLERANT RATS AND MICE.
001476 02-03
CORE TEMPERATURE CHANGES FOLLOWING ADMINISTRATION OF NALOXONE AND NALTREXONE TO RATS EXPOSED TO HOT AND COLD AMBIENT TEMPERATURES. EVIDENCE FOR THE PHYSIOLOGICAL ROLE OF ENDORPHINS IN HOT AND COLD ACCLIMATIZATION.
004034 04-03

TEMPERATURES
EFFECTS OF BRAIN-MONOAMINE DEPLETION ON THERMOREGULATORY RESPONSES OF RABBITS TO DIFFERENT HYPOTHALAMIC TEMPERATURES.
000190 01-03
BIOCHEMICAL-EFFECTS AND BEHAVIORAL-EFFECTS OF ACUTE ETHANOL IN RATS AT DIFFERENT ENVIRONMENTAL TEMPERATURES.
002864 03-03
THE EFFECTS OF THEOPHYLLINE AND CAFFEINE ON THERMOREGULATORY FUNCTIONS OF RATS AT DIFFERENT AMBIENT TEMPERATURES.
003907 04-03
CORE TEMPERATURE CHANGES FOLLOWING ADMINISTRATION OF NALOXONE AND NALTREXONE TO RATS EXPOSED TO HOT AND COLD AMBIENT TEMPERATURES. EVIDENCE FOR THE PHYSIOLOGICAL ROLE OF ENDORPHINS IN HOT AND COLD ACCLIMATIZATION.
004034 04-03

TEMPORAL
REWARDING AND AVERSIVE-EFFECTS OF MORPHINE: TEMPORAL AND PHARMACOLOGICAL-PROPERTIES.
000470 01-04
TEMPORAL PROPERTIES OF THE REWARDING AND AVERSIVE-EFFECTS OF AMPHETAMINE IN RATS.
000471 01-04
EFFECTS OF TRIFLUOPERAZINE, CHLORPROMAZINE, AND HALOPERIDOL UPON TEMPORAL INFORMATION-PROCESSING BY SCHIZOPHRENIC-PATIENTS.
000554 01-08
TEMPORAL AND ENVIRONMENTAL CUES IN CONDITIONED HYPOTHERMIA AND HYPERTHERMIA ASSOCIATED WITH MORPHINE.
002709 03-03
TEMPORAL PATTERNING OF NEURONAL ACTIVITY DURING THERMAL AND NEUROCHEMICAL STIMULATION OF THE PREOPTIC/ANTERIOR HYPOTHALAMUS OF THE AWAKE RABBIT.
002737 03-03
CNS EFFECTS OF CHOLINE ADMINISTRATION: EVIDENCE FOR TEMPORAL DEPENDENCE.
003996 04-03
METHADONE-INDUCED ATTENUATION OF THE EFFECTS OF DELTA9 TETRAHYDROCANNABINOL ON TEMPORAL DISCRIMINATION IN PIGEONS.
004095 04-04

CORRECTION OF HORMONAL ACTIVITY OF THE THYROID-GLAND AS A METHOD OF PATHOGENIC THERAPY IN A COMPREHENSIVE TREATMENT OF PATIENTS WITH TEMPORAL EPILEPSY.
004579 04-14

TENDENCY
CHANGES IN THE AUGMENTER REDUCER TENDENCY AND IN PAIN MEASURES AS A RESULT OF TREATMENT WITH A SEROTONIN REUPTAKE INHIBITOR ZIMELIDINE.
002305 02-13

TENSION
THE EFFECT OF DIAZEPAM ON TENSION AND ELECTROLYTE DISTRIBUTION IN FROG MUSCLE.
000069 01-03

TENTANUS
EFFECT OF TENTANUS TOXIN ON TRANSMITTER RELEASE FROM THE SUBSTANTIA-NIGRA AND STRIATUM IN VITRO.
002691 03-03

TENURE
FACTORS DETERMINING PATIENT TENURE ON A 3-YEAR DOUBLE-BLIND INVESTIGATION OF PIMOZIDE VERSUS FLUPHENAZINE-HCL.
002513 02-17

TEPLICE
COMPARISON OF DRUG PRESCRIPTIONS FOR PSYCHIATRIC-PATIENTS AFTER HOSPITAL DISCHARGE IN THE DISTRICTS TEPLICE AND UHERSKE-HRADISTE.
002518 02-17

TERATOGENICITY
TERATOGENICITY OF IMIPRAMINE AND AMITRIPTYLINE IN FETAL HAMSTERS.
002410 02-15

MULTIINSTITUTIONAL-STUDY ON THE TERATOGENICITY AND FETAL TOXICITY OF ANTIEPILEPTIC-DRUGS: A REPORT OF A COLLABORATIVE-STUDY GROUP IN JAPAN.
002442 02-15

TERATOLOGICAL
TOXICOLOGICAL AND TERATOLOGICAL STUDIES OF CHLORODIMETHYLAMINOETHOXYDIBENZOTHIEPINE (ZOTEPINE), A NEW NEUROLEPTIC-DRUG.
000515 01-05

TERMINAL-FIELDS
MESOLIMBICOCORTICAL DOPAMINE TERMINAL-FIELDS ARE NECESSARY FOR NORMAL LOCOMOTOR AND INVESTIGATORY EXPLORATION IN RATS.
000383 01-04

RELATIONSHIPS BETWEEN SELECTIVE DENERVATION OF DOPAMINE TERMINAL-FIELDS IN THE ANTERIOR-FOREBRAIN AND BEHAVIORAL-RESPONSES TO AMPHETAMINE AND APOMORPHINE.
000384 01-04

TERMINAL-RICH
EFFECTS OF CHRONIC-TREATMENT WITH L SULPIRIDE AND HALOPERIDOL ON CENTRAL DOPAMINE TURNOVER EVALUATED IN DOPAMINE CELL BODY AND NERVE TERMINAL-RICH AREAS.
001096 02-03

TERMINALS
EFFECTS OF CHRONIC NEUROLEPTIC TREATMENT ON TYROSINE-HYDROXYLASE IN DOPAMINERGIC TERMINALS: COMPARISONS BETWEEN DRUGS AND BRAIN REGIONS REVEALS DIFFERENT MECHANISMS OF TOLERANCE.
001243 02-03

A NOVEL GABA-RECEPTOR MODULATES STIMULUS-INDUCED GLUTAMATE RELEASE FROM CORTICOSTRIATAL TERMINALS.
001376 02-03

DECREASE OF GAD IMMUNOREACTIVE NERVE TERMINALS IN THE SUBSTANTIA-NIGRA AFTER KAINIC-ACID LESION OF THE STRIATUM. (UNPUBLISHED PAPER).
001400 02-03

EFFECT OF REPEATED TREATMENT WITH NEUROLEPTICS ON DOPAMINE METABOLISM IN CELL BODIES AND TERMINALS OF DOPAMINERGIC-SYSTEMS IN THE RAT-BRAIN.
001464 02-03

MEASUREMENT OF THE MEMBRANE POTENTIAL OF ISOLATED NERVE TERMINALS BY THE LIPOPHILIC CATION (3H)TRIPHENYLMETHYLPHOSPHONIUM-BROMIDE.
002746 03-03

FLUORESCENCE HISTOCHEMISTRY INDICATES DAMAGE OF STRIATAL DOPAMINE NERVE TERMINALS IN RATS AFTER MULTIPLE DOSES OF METHAMPHETAMINE.
002812 03-03

SELECTIVE NEUROTOXIC-ACTION OF CAPSAICIN ON GLOMERULAR C-TYPE TERMINALS IN RAT SUBSTANTIA-GELATINOSA.
003143 03-06

EFFECTS OF TAIPOXIN ON THE ULTRASTRUCTURE OF CHOLINERGIC AXON TERMINALS IN THE MOUSE ADRENAL-MEDULLA.
003916 04-03

THE EFFECT OF ACETYLCHOLINE RELEASE ON CHOLINE FLUXES IN ISOLATED SYNAPTIC TERMINALS.
003924 04-03

THE RELATIONSHIP BETWEEN LOSS OF DOPAMINE NERVE TERMINALS, STRIATAL (3H)SPIROPERIDOL BINDING AND ROTATIONAL-BEHAVIOR IN UNILATERALLY 6 HYDROXYDOPAMINE LESIONED RATS.
004129 04-04

TERMINATING
THE PROGNOSIS OF EPILEPSY AND THE STRATEGY FOR TERMINATING ANTIEPILEPTIC THERAPY.
004724 04-17

TERMINATION
FIXED-RATIO SCHEDULES OF FOOD PRESENTATION AND STIMULUS-SHOCK TERMINATION: EFFECTS OF D-AMPHETAMINE, MORPHINE, AND CLOZAPINE.
000431 01-04

TERTIARY
TRICYCLIC-ANTIDEPRESSANT DRUGS AND INDIVIDUAL DIFFERENCES IN THE EXPLORATORY-ACTIVITY OF RATS: CONTRASTING-EFFECTS OF TERTIARY AND SECONDARY AMINE COMPOUNDS.
000401 01-04

IMPAIRMENT OF AVOIDANCE-BEHAVIOR FOLLOWING SHORT-TERM INGESTION OF ETHANOL, TERTIARY BUTANOL, OR PENTOBARBITAL IN MICE.
000479 01-04

A RAPID AND SENSITIVE RADIORECEPTOR ASSAY FOR TERTIARY AMINE TRICYCLIC-ANTIDEPRESSANTS.
004689 04-16

TEST
EFFECTS OF CHLORDIAZEPOXIDE AND DIAZEPAM ON FEEDING PERFORMANCE IN A FOOD PREFERENCE TEST.
000367 01-04

EFFECTS OF EXPERIMENTER AND TEST LOCATION NOVELTY ON NONSPECIFIC ACTIVITY IN RATS AND ITS MODIFICATION BY METHAMPHETAMINE.
000409 01-04

EFFECTS OF ANTIDEPRESSANTS ON PITUITARY HORMONAL SECRETIONS IN HEALTHY TEST SUBJECTS, NEUROTIC-PATIENTS, AND ENDOGENOUS DEPRESSIVE-PATIENTS.
002009 02-09

THE EFFECTS OF ALCOHOL AND CAFFEINE ON CONCENTRATION TEST PERFORMANCE.
002337 02-14

A SIMPLE SYSTEM FOR CONTROL OF THE CONTINUOUS PERFORMANCE TEST IN PSYCHOPHARMACOLOGICAL-RESEARCH.
002474 02-16

A TEST OF A NEUROTRANSMITTER MODEL OF THE AFFECTIVE-DISORDERS. (PH.D. DISSERTATION).
003063 03-04

PROGNOSIS IN SCHIZOPHRENIA: INDIVIDUAL DIFFERENCES IN PSYCHOLOGICAL RESPONSE TO A TEST DOSE OF ANTIPSYCHOTIC-DRUG AND THEIR RELATIONSHIP TO BLOOD AND SALIVA LEVELS AND TREATMENT OUTCOME.
003189 03-08

STATISTICAL ANALYSES OF PHYSIOLOGIC DATA FROM FEMALE PATIENTS WITH AN ENDORMORPHOUS DEPRESSIVE COURSE: A TRIAL, INTERACTIONS BETWEEN PHYSIOLOGIC PARAMETERS, TEST JUNCTURES IN THIS PHASE.
003251 03-09

TYRAMINE PRESSOR TEST AND CARDIOVASCULAR-EFFECTS OF CHLORIMIPRAMINE AND NORTRIPTYLINE IN HEALTHY VOLUNTEERS.
003428 03-13

EFFECTS OF PENTAZOCINE AND NALORPHINE ON MOTILITY IN CHRONICALLY MORPHINE TREATED RATS: A POTENTIAL SUBSTITUTION TEST TO DETECT THE NARCOTIC CHARACTER OF A DRUG.
003555 03-16

STUDIES ON THE TREATMENT AND DIAGNOSIS OF NEUROTIC VERTIGO FROM THE VIEWPOINT OF NEUROOTOLOGY: OBSERVATION OF THE BALANCE TEST FOR ANALYZING NEUROTIC VERTIGO.
004387 04-09

AN EVALUATION OF THE USEFULNESS OF THE ACYLASE TEST IN NEUROLEPTIC TREATMENT.
004426 04-10

TESTED
PLASMA DOPAMINE-BETA-HYDROXYLASE ACTIVITY IN CHRONIC SCHIZOPHRENIC-PATIENTS TESTED WITH SINGLE-DOSE OF 2 BROMO-ALPHA-ERGOCRIPTINE (PARLODEL).
004343 04-08

TESTES
ADENOSINE-RECEPTORS IN RAT TESTES: LABELING WITH 3H CYCLOHEXYLADENOSINE.
002835 03-03

TESTING
IN VITRO ACETYLCHOLINE RELEASE FROM RAT CAUDATE-NUCLEUS AS A NEW MODEL FOR TESTING DRUGS WITH DOPAMINE-RECEPTOR ACTIVITY.
000289 01-03

REINNERVATION OF THE DENERVATED STRIATUM BY SUBSTANTIA-NIGRA TRANSPLANTS: FUNCTIONAL CONSEQUENCES AS REVEALED BY PHARMACOLOGICAL AND SENSORIMOTOR TESTING.
000347 01-04

SERIAL COGNITIVE TESTING IN CANCER-PATIENTS RECEIVING CHEMOTHERAPY.
000876 01-15

ORIENTATIONAL TESTING OF CHLORPROMAZINE-HCL ON HOSPITALIZED MENTAL-PATIENTS.
002131 02-11

THE USE OF BROMOCRIPTINE FOR TESTING CENTRAL DOPAMINERGIC REACTIVITY.
002205 02-13

A NOVEL PSYCHOMETRIC-TEST MODEL APPLYING TAILORED TESTING FOR ECONOMIC AND EFFICIENT COLLECTION OF PSYCHOPHARMACOLOGICAL-EFFECTS.
002479 02-16

ANALGESIC TOLERANCE PRODUCED BY MORPHINE PELLETS IS FACILITATED BY ANALGESIC TESTING.
002943 03-04

TESTOSTERONE
THE ACUTE AND CHRONIC EFFECT OF LITHIUM ON SERUM TESTOSTERONE IN RATS.
000238 01-03

TESTOSTERONE AND PERSISTENCE OF SOCIAL INVESTIGATION IN LABORATORY RATS.
000488 01-04

PLASMA PROLACTIN AND TESTOSTERONE DURING PENFLURIDOL TREATMENT.
000874 01-15

LONG-TERM EFFECTS OF TESTOSTERONE INJECTIONS ON THE SOCIAL-BEHAVIOUR OF MALE DUCKS AND THEIR PHYSIOLOGICAL-CORRELATES.
001565 02-04

INCREASES IN TESTOSTERONE LEVELS AND IN COPULATORY-BEHAVIOR OF MALE RHESUS-MONKEYS FOLLOWING TREATMENT WITH HUMAN CHORIONIC GONADOTROPHIN.
003012 03-04

RAT PUP-KILLING AND MATERNAL-BEHAVIOR IN MALE LONG-EVANS-RATS: PRENATAL STIMULATION AND POSTNATAL TESTOSTERONE.
003054 03-04

TESTOSTERONE POTENTIATION OF THE EFFECTIVENESS OF ACTH1-24 ON THE INDUCTION OF THE STRETCH-YAWNING-SYNDROME (SYS) IN MALE GUINEA-PIGS.
003074 03-04

EFFECTS OF NEONATAL TESTOSTERONE AND ESTROGEN ON OPEN-FIELD BEHAVIOUR IN RATS.
003098 03-04

FAILURE TO FIND SEX-DIFFERENCES IN TESTOSTERONE ACTIVATED AGGRESSION IN TWO STRAINS OF RATS.
003107 03-04

TESTOSTERONE-LIKE
MORPHINE EXERTS TESTOSTERONE-LIKE EFFECTS IN THE HYPOTHALAMUS OF THE CASTRATED MALE RAT.
000051 01-03

TESTS
MORPHINE-DEPENDENCE AND DOPAMINERGIC-ACTIVITY: TESTS OF CIRCLING RESPONSES IN RATS WITH UNILATERAL NIGRAL LESIONS.
001641 02-04

MINI-SYMPOSIUM: III. SIMPLE IN VIVO TESTS THAT DIFFERENTIATE PROTOTYPE AGONISTS AT OPIATE-RECEPTORS.
004289 04-06

TETANUS-TOXIN
PAPAIN-DERIVED FRAGMENT IIC TETANUS-TOXIN: ITS BINDING TO-ISOLATED SYNAPTIC MEMBRANES AND RETROGRADE AXONAL TRANSPORT.
003734 04-03

TETRABAMATE
COMPARATIVE-STUDY OF THE INDUCTIVE EFFECT OF TWO PSYCHOMODERATORS -- TETRABAMATE AND COMPLEXE-1656 -- AND OF PHENOBARBITAL ON LIVER MICROSOMAL ENZYMES IN RATS.
001874 02-06

TETRABENAZINE
BIOCHEMICAL-STUDY OF THE ANIMAL-MODEL DEPRESSION INDUCED BY TETRABENAZINE.
001506 02-03

TETRABENAZINE-INDUCED
EFFECTS OF TRICYCLIC-ANTIDEPRESSANTS ON TETRABENAZINE-INDUCED DEPLETION OF BRAIN MONOAMINES IN RATS. 1. NOREPINEPHRINE.
004062 04-03

TETRACYCLIC
CLINICAL-TRIALS WITH NEW BICYCLIC AND TETRACYCLIC COMPOUNDS: ZIMELIDINE AND MAPROTILINE.
003213 03-09

TETRACYCLIC-ANTIDEPRESSANT
THE TETRACYCLIC-ANTIDEPRESSANT MIANSERIN: EVALUATION OF ITS BLOCKADE OF PRESYNAPTIC ALPHA-ADRENOCEPTORS IN A SELF-STIMULATION MODEL USING CLONIDINE.
003016 03-04

NEUROTROPIC-DRUGS AS COMEDICATION TO PSYCHOTROPICS: COMBINED ADMINISTRATION OF A NEUROTROPIC-DRUG AND A TETRACYCLIC-ANTIDEPRESSANT.
004396 04-09

TETRACYCLIC-ANTIDEPRESSANTS
DETERMINATION OF TRICYCLIC-ANTIDEPRESSANTS AND TETRACYCLIC-ANTIDEPRESSANTS AND OF THEIR METABOLIC PRODUCTS IN BIOLOGICAL FLUIDS.
002498 02-16

DIFFERENT EFFECTS OF TRICYCLIC-ANTIDEPRESSANTS AND TETRACYCLIC-ANTIDEPRESSANTS ON THE RELEASE OF TSH, PROLACTIN, AND GROWTH-HORMONE AFTER ADMINISTRATION OF THYROSTIMULATING-RELEASING-HORMONE IN MANIC-DEPRESSIVES.
004407 04-09

TETRAETHYL-LEAD
THE CLINICAL DYNAMICS OF TETRAETHYL-LEAD POISONING.
003500 03-15

TETRAHYDRO-BETA-CARBOLINE
BRAIN SEROTONIN AND 5 HYDROXYINDOLEACETIC-ACID CONCENTRATIONS AND SEROTONIN SYNTHESIS FOLLOWING TETRAHYDRO-BETA-CARBOLINE ADMINISTRATION IN MICE.
001152 02-03

IDENTIFICATION AND QUANTIFICATION OF 1,2,3,4 TETRAHYDRO-BETA-CARBOLINE, 2 METHYL-TETRAHYDRO-BETA-CARBOLINE, AND 6 METHOXY-TETRAHYDRO-BETA-CARBOLINE AS IN VIVO CONSTITUENTS OF RAT-BRAIN AND ADRENAL-GLAND.
002636 03-01

ACTIONS OF TETRAHYDRONORHARMANE (TETRAHYDRO-BETA-CARBOLINE) ON 5 HYDROXYTRYPTAMINE AND DOPAMINE-MEDIATED MECHANISMS.
002854 03-03

TETRAHYDRO-BETA-CARBOLINES
TETRAHYDRO-BETA-CARBOLINES AND CORRESPONDING TRYPTAMINES: IN VITRO INHIBITION OF SEROTONIN AND DOPAMINE UPTAKE BY HUMAN BLOOD-PLATELETS.
001067 02-02

TETRAHYDRO-BETA-CARBOLINES AND CORRESPONDING TRYPTAMINES: IN VITRO INHIBITION OF SEROTONIN, DOPAMINE AND NORADRENALINE UPTAKE IN RAT-BRAIN SYNAPTOSOMES.
001078 02-02

TETRAHYDROCANNABINOL
THE EFFECT OF DELTA9 TETRAHYDROCANNABINOL ON THE POSITIVE AND NEGATIVE FEEDBACK CONTROL OF LUTEINIZING-HORMONE RELEASE.
000286 01-03

EFFECTS OF CHRONIC ADMINISTRATION OF DELTA9 TETRAHYDROCANNABINOL ON THE CARDIOVASCULAR SYSTEM, AND PRESSOR AND BEHAVIORAL-RESPONSES TO BRAIN-STIMULATION IN FREELY-MOVING-RATS.
000417 01-04

THE MECHANISM-OF-ACTION OF DELTA9 TETRAHYDROCANNABINOL ON BODY-TEMPERATURE IN MICE.
001190 02-03

INFLUENCE OF THYROTROPIN-RELEASING-HORMONE AND HISTIDYL-PROLINE-DIKETOPIPERAZINE ON SPONTANEOUS LOCOMOTOR-ACTIVITY AND ANALGESIA INDUCED BY DELTA9 TETRAHYDROCANNABINOL IN THE MOUSE.
001575 02-04

THE EFFECTS OF DELTA9 TETRAHYDROCANNABINOL ALONE AND IN COMBINATION WITH CANNABIDIOL ON FIXED-INTERVAL PERFORMANCE IN RHESUS-MONKEYS.
001582 02-04

ACUTE AND CHRONIC EFFECTS OF DELTA9 TETRAHYDROCANNABINOL ON COMPLEX BEHAVIOR OF SQUIRREL-MONKEYS.
001583 02-04

AN ABSTINENCE-SYNDROME FOLLOWING CHRONIC ADMINISTRATION OF DELTA9 TETRAHYDROCANNABINOL IN RHESUS-MONKEYS.
001621 02-04

EFFECTS OF DELTA9 TETRAHYDROCANNABINOL ON THE CARDIOVASCULAR-SYSTEM, AND PRESSOR AND BEHAVIORAL-RESPONSES TO BRAIN-STIMULATION IN RATS.
001681 02-04

CHRONIC DELTA9 TETRAHYDROCANNABINOL IN RATS: EFFECT ON SOCIAL-INTERACTIONS, MOUSE-KILLING, MOTOR-ACTIVITY, CONSUMMATORY-BEHAVIOR, AND BODY-TEMPERATURE.
001722 02-04

THE EFFECT OF CONDITIONS INFLUENCING ENDOGENOUS PROSTAGLANDINS ON THE ACTIVITY OF DELTA9 TETRAHYDROCANNABINOL.
002196 02-12

PLASMA DELTA9 TETRAHYDROCANNABINOL CONCENTRATIONS AND CLINICAL-EFFECTS AFTER ORAL AND INTRAVENOUS ADMINISTRATION AND SMOKING.
002201 02-12

INFLUENCE OF CANNABIS AND DELTA9 TETRAHYDROCANNABINOL ON THE BIOCHEMISTRY OF THE MALE REPRODUCTIVE ORGANS.
002686 03-03

ANTAGONISM BY CHLORNALTREXAMINE OF SOME EFFECTS OF DELTA9 TETRAHYDROCANNABINOL IN RATS.
003104 03-04

NEUTRALIZATION OF THE EFFECT OF DELTA9 TETRAHYDROCANNABINOL ON BARBITURATE SLEEPING-TIME BY SPECIFIC ACTIVE IMMUNIZATION.
003803 04-03

EFFECTS OF DELTA9 TETRAHYDROCANNABINOL AND CANNABIDIOL ON SODIUM-DEPENDENT HIGH-AFFINITY CHOLINE UPTAKE IN THE RAT HIPPOCAMPUS.
003908 04-03

METHADONE-INDUCED ATTENUATION OF THE EFFECTS OF DELTA9
TETRAHYDROCANNABINOL ON TEMPORAL DISCRIMINATION IN
PIGEONS.
004095 04-04
ATTENUATION OF DELTA9 TETRAHYDROCANNABINOL-INDUCED
WITHDRAWAL-LIKE BEHAVIOUR BY DELTA9
TETRAHYDROCANNABINOL.
004243 04-04
CHARACTERISTICS OF THE STIMULUS PRODUCED BY THE MIXTURE OF
CANNABIDIOL WITH DELTA9 TETRAHYDROCANNABINOL.
004263 04-04
BEHAVIORAL-PHARMACOLOGY OF TETRAHYDROCANNABINOL
CONVULSIONS IN RABBITS.
004288 04-06

TETRAHYDROCANNABINOL-INDUCED
RELATIONSHIP BETWEEN DELTA9 TETRAHYDROCANNABINOL-INDUCED
MOUSE-KILLING-BEHAVIOR ON THE RAT AND THE METABOLISM OF
MONOAMINES IN THE BRAIN, PARTICULARLY THE OLFACTORY-BULB.
000472 01-04
ATTENUATION OF DELTA9 TETRAHYDROCANNABINOL-INDUCED
WITHDRAWAL-LIKE BEHAVIOUR BY DELTA9
TETRAHYDROCANNABINOL.
004243 04-04

TETRAHYDROCANNABINOLS
BIOLOGICAL-ACTIVITY OF THE TETRAHYDROCANNABINOLS.
002556 02-17

TETRAHYDROFURYLALKYL
N TETRAHYDROFURYLALKYL AND N ALKOXYALKYL DERIVATIVES OF (-)
NORMETAZOCINE, COMPOUNDS WITH DIFFERENTIATED OPIOID ACTION
PROFILES.
000013 01-02

TETRAHYDROISOQUINOLINE-7-SULFONANILIDES
INHIBITORS OF PHENYLETHANOLAMINE-N-METHYLTRANSFERASE AND
EPINEPHRINE BIOSYNTHESIS. 2. 1,2,3,4 TETRAHYDROISOQUINOLINE-7-
SULFONANILIDES.
001069 02-02

TETRAHYDRONORHARMANE
ACTIONS OF TETRAHYDRONORHARMANE (TETRAHYDRO-BETA-
CARBOLINE) ON 5 HYDROXYTRYPTAMINE AND DOPAMINE-MEDIATED
MECHANISMS.
002854 03-03

TETRAPEPTIDE
POTENT TETRAPEPTIDE ENKEPHALINS.
003684 04-02

TETRAPHENYLPHOSPHONIUM
DEMONSTRATION OF A MUSCARINIC-RECEPTOR-MEDIATED CYCLIC-GMP-
DEPENDENT HYPERPOLARIZATION OF THE MEMBRANE POTENTIAL OF
MOUSE NEUROBLASTOMA CELLS USING
(3H)TETRAPHENYLPHOSPHONIUM.
004049 04-03

TEXTBOOK
TEXTBOOK OF CLINICAL PSYCHOPHARMACOLOGY.
000929 01-17

TEXTURES
EFFECTS OF ACUTE OR CHRONIC ADMINISTRATION OF
CHLORDIAZEPOXIDE ON FEEDING PARAMETERS USING TWO FOOD
TEXTURES IN THE RAT.
000368 01-04

THA
USE OF THA IN TREATMENT OF ALZHEIMER-LIKE DEMENTIA: PILOT-STUDY
IN TWELVE PATIENTS.
003377 03-11
THA — A REVIEW OF THE LITERATURE AND ITS USE IN TREATMENT OF
FIVE OVERDOSE PATIENTS.
003539 03-15

THALAMOCORTICAL
INFLUENCE OF CARBAMAZEPINE ON THALAMOCORTICAL AND
HIPPOCAMPOCORTICAL SELF-SUSTAINED AFTERDISCHARGES IN RATS.
001356 02-03
INFLUENCE OF DIPROPYLACETIC-ACID ON THALAMOCORTICAL RESPONSES
IN RATS.
001419 02-03

THALAMUS
NORADRENALINE RELEASE FROM SLICES OF THE THALAMUS OF NORMAL
AND MORPHINE-DEPENDENT RATS.
001142 02-03
ACUTE AND CHRONIC OPIATE-EFFECTS ON SINGLE UNITS AND EEG OF
MEDIAL THALAMUS AND HIPPOCAMPUS: A LATENCY ANALYSIS.
001344 02-03
OPIATE-RECEPTORS AND SLEEP. II. EFFECTS OF MICROINJECTIONS OF
ETHYL-ALCOHOL AND PENTOBARBITAL IN THE MEDIAN THALAMUS,
PERIAQUEDUCTAL GRAY MATTER AND NUCLEUS-TRACTUS-SOLITARIUS
OF THE RABBIT.
002917 03-03
EXCITATORY EFFECTS OF DIHYDROCAPSAICIN ON NOCICEPTIVE NEURONS
IN THE MEDIAL THALAMUS.
003714 04-03
UNIT ACTIVITY IN MEDIAL THALAMUS: COMPARATIVE-EFFECTS OF
CAFFEINE AND AMPHETAMINE.
003752 04-03

THE EFFECT OF CHOLINERGIC SUBSTANCES ON NOCICEPTIVE EVOKED-
RESPONSES IN SPECIFIC NUCLEI OF THE THALAMUS.
003770 04-03
THE ROLE OF NIGRAL PROJECTIONS TO THE THALAMUS IN DRUG-
INDUCED CIRCLING-BEHAVIOUR IN THE RAT.
004205 04-04

THALLIUM
ELECTROPHYSIOLOGICAL-CHANGES AT A CENTRAL NORADRENERGIC
SYNAPSE DURING THALLIUM TOXICOSIS.
001848 02-05
THE NEUROLOGICAL FORENSIC ASPECTS OF THALLIUM POISONING.
002438 02-15
PRUSSIAN-BLUE: SPECIFIC TREATMENT OF THALLIUM, ARSENIC,
INDUSTRIAL-SOLVENT INTOXICATION, AND OTHER
POLYNEUROPATHOLOGIES. A POSSIBLE ANTIPSYCHOTIC-AGENT.
003348 03-11

THC
DELTA9 THC IN PIGEONS: A REPLICATION AND EXTENSION.
000394 01-04
PREEXPOSURE TO DELTA9 THC BLOCKS THC-INDUCED CONDITIONED
TASTE-AVERSION IN RATS.
001618 02-04
DELTA9 THC AS A DISCRIMINATIVE-STIMULUS IN RATS AND PIGEONS:
GENERALIZATION TO THC METABOLITES AND SP-111.
001666 02-04
PLASMA AND BRAIN LEVELS OF DELTA6 THC AND SEVEN
MONOOXYGENATED METABOLITES CORRELATED TO THE CATALEPTIC-
EFFECT IN THE MOUSE.
001737 02-04
LITHIUM-CHLORIDE AND DELTA9 THC LEAD TO CONDITIONED AVERSIONS
IN THE PIGEON.
003003 03-04

THC-INDUCED
PREEXPOSURE TO DELTA9 THC BLOCKS THC-INDUCED CONDITIONED
TASTE-AVERSION IN RATS.
001618 02-04

THEOPHYLLINE
EFFECTS OF THREE ANTIBIOTICS ON THEOPHYLLINE KINETICS.
000784 01-13
THE INFLUENCE OF PENTIFYLLINE AND THEOPHYLLINE ON REACTION
KINETICS OF CATECHOLAMINE STIMULATED ATPASE FROM RAT-BRAIN.
001052 02-01
AMINOPHYLLINE AND THEOPHYLLINE DERIVATIVES AS ANTAGONISTS OF
NEURONAL DEPRESSION BY ADENOSINE: A MICROIONTOPHORETIC-
STUDY.
001410 02-03
THEOPHYLLINE AND DEPRESSION.
002439 02-15
THE EFFECTS OF THEOPHYLLINE AND CAFFEINE ON THERMOREGULATORY
FUNCTIONS OF RATS AT DIFFERENT AMBIENT TEMPERATURES.
003907 04-03

THEORETICAL
PRACTICAL AND THEORETICAL ASPECTS OF PHENYTOIN
ADMINISTRATION. I. RELATIONSHIP BETWEEN DOSE AND PLASMA
CONCENTRATION.
000760 01-13
TWENTY YEARS HALOPERIDOL: CLINICAL-EFFECTIVENESS AND
THEORETICAL IMPLICATIONS.
000938 01-17

THEORIES
SYNAPTIC AND BEHAVIOURAL-ACTIONS OF ANTIDEPRESSANT-DRUGS:
FURTHER THOUGHTS ON THE IMPLICATIONS FOR THEORIES OF
DEPRESSION.
003229 03-09

THEORY
CASE-REPORT: USING ATTRIBUTION THEORY TO LIMIT NEED FOR
NEUROLEPTIC-MEDICINE.
000559 01-08
ROTTING WITH THEIR RIGHTS ON: CONSTITUTIONAL THEORY AND
CLINICAL REALITY IN DRUG-REFUSAL BY PSYCHIATRIC-PATIENTS.
000911 01-17
AN INTERFERENCE REDUCTION THEORY OF THE EFFECTS OF ETHANOL ON
CONFLICT-BEHAVIOR.
001586 02-04
THEORY, PROCEDURE, AND APPLICATIONS OF THE RADIOACTIVE
DEOXYGLUCOSE METHOD FOR THE MEASUREMENT OF LOCAL GLUCOSE
UTILIZATION IN THE CENTRAL-NERVOUS-SYSTEM. (UNPUBLISHED
PAPER).
001877 02-06
EFFECTS OF ANXIETY REDUCTION BY BEHAVIOURAL-TECHNIQUES AND
MEPROBAMATE ON CERTAIN PARAMETERS OF INFORMATION THEORY.
003108 03-04
A CONTROLLED-STUDY OF L-DOPA IN SCHIZOPHRENIA WITH REFERENCE
TO THE THEORY OF DOPAMINERGIC-RECEPTOR HYPERSENSITIVITY.
004312 04-08

THERAPEUTIC
FLASH-EVOKED AFTERDISCHARGE IN RAT AS A MODEL OF THE ABSENCE
SEIZURE: DOSE-RESPONSE STUDIES WITH THERAPEUTIC DRUGS.
000160 01-03

LITHIUM LEVEL IN SOME BIOLOGICAL FLUIDS AT ITS PROPHYLACTIC THERAPEUTIC APPLICATION.
000605 01-09

LITHIUM TREATMENT IN AFFECTIVE-DISORDERS: THERAPEUTIC PLASMA LEVEL.
000635 01-09

LITHIUM TREATMENT IN AFFECTIVE-DISORDERS FROM VIEWPOINT OF TRANSCULTURAL PSYCHOPHARMACOLOGY: THERAPEUTIC PLASMA LEVEL.
000636 01-09

TRICYCLIC-ANTIDEPRESSANTS: THERAPEUTIC PLASMA LEVEL.
000646 01-09

THERAPEUTIC APPLICATION OF PHYSOSTIGMINE IN NEUROSIS.
000651 01-10

CONTROLLED-COMPARISON OF THE THERAPEUTIC EFFECTS OF NATRIUM-OXYBUTYRATE AND OXAZEPAM.
000658 01-10

THERAPEUTIC ASPECTS OF MARIHUANA.
000667 01-11

CONVERSION SCALES FOR COMMONLY REQUESTED SERUM CONCENTRATIONS OF DRUGS AND OTHER SUBSTANCES OF THERAPEUTIC AND TOXICOLOGICAL IMPORTANCE, AND OF HORMONES.
000759 01-13

NEUROLEPTIC-INDUCED TARDIVE-DYSKINESIA: RECENT PATHOPHYSIOLOGICAL-DATA, THERAPEUTIC TRIALS.
000842 01-15

TWENTY YEARS CLINICAL THERAPEUTIC EXPERIENCE WITH CALCIUM GLUTAMATES EFFICACY.
000963 01-17

ON THE MECHANISM OF THERAPEUTIC ACTIONS OF PSYCHOTROPIC-DRUGS.
000964 01-17

THE INFLUENCE OF EXTERNAL SODIUM AND POTASSIUM ON LITHIUM UPTAKE BY PRIMARY BRAIN CELL CULTURES AT THERAPEUTIC LITHIUM CONCENTRATION.
001300 02-03

DISORDERS OF SMOOTH-PURSUIT EYE-MOVEMENTS IN SCHIZOPHRENICS AND THE EFFECT OF NEUROLEPTICS IN THERAPEUTIC DOSES.
001912 02-08

PLASMA LEVELS AND THERAPEUTIC EFFICACY OF FLUPHENAZINE-HCL AND FLUPHENAZINE-DECANOATE.
001913 02-08

NEUROLEPTICS AND DOPAMINE-RECEPTORS, THERAPEUTIC IMPLICATIONS.
001942 02-08

MIANSERIN: DETERMINATION OF THERAPEUTIC DOSE RANGE.
002026 02-09

BLOOD LEVEL OF AMITRIPTYLINE, NORTRIPTYLINE, NORADRENALINE, SEROTONIN AND THERAPEUTIC RESPONSE.
002057 02-09

THERAPEUTIC RESULTS IN A PSYCHOGERIATRIC-WARD AFTER CHANGE OF MEDICATION.
002136 02-11

CLOMIPRAMINE AND DOXEPIN IN DEPRESSIVE-NEUROSIS: PLASMA LEVELS AND THERAPEUTIC RESPONSE.
002258 02-13

BEHAVIORAL-DISTURBANCES IN PSYCHIATRY: A THERAPEUTIC APPROACH.
002321 02-14

CARDIOVASCULAR-EFFECTS OF THERAPEUTIC DOSES OF TRICYCLIC-ANTIDEPRESSANTS: IMPORTANCE OF BLOOD LEVEL MONITORING.
002456 02-15

NEUROLEPTIC BLOOD LEVELS AND THERAPEUTIC EFFECT.
002480 02-16

PLASMA LEVODOPA, DOPAMINE AND THERAPEUTIC RESPONSE FOLLOWING LEVODOPA THERAPY OF PARKINSONIAN-PATIENTS.
002504 02-16

BENZODIAZEPINES: CLINICAL-PHARMACOLOGY AND THERAPEUTIC USE.
002521 02-17

CLASSIFICATION OF DRUGS AND PATIENTS TO ACHIEVE MAXIMUM THERAPEUTIC RESPONSE.
002560 02-17

REGULATION OF NEUROTRANSMISSION THROUGH PRESYNAPTIC-RECEPTORS AND OTHER MECHANISMS: POSSIBLE CLINICAL RELEVANCE AND THERAPEUTIC POTENTIAL.
002569 02-16

THERAPEUTIC PROFILE OF HALOPERIDOL.
002603 02-17

STUDY OF METABOLISM AND BLOOD LEVELS OF ANTIDEPRESSANTS: TOWARDS A RATIONALIZATION OF THEIR THERAPEUTIC USE.
002625 02-17

THERAPEUTIC TRIAL OF A NEW ANTIDEPRESSANT: MIANSERIN.
003208 03-09

THERAPEUTIC EFFECT OF MIANSERINE AND IMIPRAMINE IN ENDOGENOUS DEPRESSIONS (CONTROLLED-COMPARISON).
003264 03-09

THE THERAPEUTIC ACTIVITY OF TRYPTOPHAN AND ITS EFFECT ON SEROTONIN METABOLISM IN EPILEPTIC-PATIENTS.
003289 03-11

THE THERAPEUTIC PROFILE OF MIANSERIN IN MILD ELDERLY DEPRESSIVES.
003297 03-11

CLINICAL PHARMACOKINETICS IN NEWBORNS AND INFANTS: AGE-RELATED DIFFERENCES AND THERAPEUTIC IMPLICATIONS.
003343 03-11

LITHIUM NEUROTOXICITY AT THERAPEUTIC LEVELS: A CASE-REPORT.
003533 03-15

NATURAL AND THERAPEUTIC ENVIRONMENTAL INDICATORS OF MAINTENANCE DOSAGE REQUIREMENTS.
003561 03-16

THERAPEUTIC INTEREST OF BLOOD LEVELS DETERMINATION FOR ANTIDEPRESSANTS: METHODOLOGICAL APPROACH.
003571 03-16

DEBATE: THERAPEUTIC TRIALS IN A NATURAL ENVIRONMENT.
003635 03-17

THERAPEUTIC (III): GENERAL CHARACTERISTICS OF ANTIPSYCHOTIC-DRUGS.
003644 03-17

THERAPEUTIC NEWS.
004308 04-07

CLINICAL DEPRESSIONS: DIAGNOSTIC AND THERAPEUTIC CHALLENGES.
004350 04-09

THERAPEUTIC PLASMA LEVELS OF SOME ANTICONVULSANTS IN FOCAL EPILEPSY IN RELATION TO COMPUTERIZED-AXIAL-TOMOGRAPHY.
004439 04-11

SOME THERAPEUTIC EFFECTS OF NOOTROPYL.
004458 04-11

A COMPARATIVE EVALUATION OF THE EFFICACY OF SOME THERAPEUTIC METHODS USED IN DELIRIUM-TREMENS.
004486 04-11

NEUROLEPTIC TRICYCLIC-ANTIDEPRESSANT COMBINATION: PHARMACOLOGICAL-ASPECTS AND THERAPEUTIC INTEREST.
004501 04-13

PHARMACOLOGICAL PECULIARITIES OF A BENZODIAZEPINE/ATARACTIC-DRUG AND ITS THERAPEUTIC RELEVANCE: THE SPECIAL STATUS OF CLORAZEPATE-DIPOTASSIUM (TRANXILIUM).
004527 04-13

PROBLEMS OF TREATING DEFORMING MYODYSTONIA WITH L-DOPA, AND PREDICTION OF ITS THERAPEUTIC EFFECT.
004536 04-13

COMPUTER-ANALYZED ELECTROENCEPHALOGRAM TO PREDICT THE THERAPEUTIC OUTCOME IN SCHIZOPHRENIA.
004680 04-16

THERAPEUTIC MONITORING OF PLASMA CONCENTRATIONS OF TRICYCLIC-ANTIDEPRESSANTS: PERSPECTIVE OF THE CLINICAL LABORATORY.
004681 04-16

THERAPEUTIC TREATMENT OF INSUFFICIENT PERFORMANCE IN CEREBROVASCULAR-DISEASES.
004718 04-17

THERAPEUTIC-EFFICACY
NOMIFENSINE IN THE TREATMENT OF OBSESSIVE-COMPULSIVE-NEUROSIS. THERAPEUTIC-EFFICACY AND TOLERABILITY IN COMPARISON TO IMIPRAMINE.
002078 02-10

ON A POSSIBLE ROLE OF GABA IN MANIA. THERAPEUTIC-EFFICACY OF SODIUM-VALPROATE.
003219 03-09

DEPRESSION SUBTYPES AFFECT THE STEADY-STATE PLASMA LEVELS AND THERAPEUTIC-EFFICACY OF AMITRIPTYLINE AND NORTRIPTYLINE.
003244 03-09

THERAPEUTIC-EFFICACY OF DOXEPIN IN DIVIDED AND SINGLE-DOSE REGIME.
003259 03-09

THERAPEUTIC-PERSPECTIVES
PHARMACOLOGIC AND THERAPEUTIC-PERSPECTIVES ON DEMENTIA: AN EXPERIMENTAL APPROACH.
003065 03-04

THERAPEUTICALLY-RESISTANT
TREATMENT OF THERAPEUTICALLY-RESISTANT PARANOID SCHIZOPHRENIC-PATIENTS WITH FLUPHENAZINE DEPOT COMBINED WITH OTHER PSYCHOTROPIC-DRUGS AND CLOZAPINE.
003172 03-08

THERAPEUTICS
THERAPEUTICS (II): LITHIUM.
000641 01-09

THERAPEUTICS V -- THE UNWANTED EFFECTS OF ANTIPSYCHOTICS.
000892 01-15

RESPECTIVE POSITION OF ANTIDEPRESSANTS IN THERAPEUTICS.
002581 02-17

THERAPEUTICS (I) -- PHARMACOLOGICAL-TREATMENT OF DEPRESSIONS.
003270 03-09

PHENYTOIN: PHARMACOKINETICS AND CLINICAL THERAPEUTICS.
003353 03-11

THERAPEUTICS VI -- ANXIOLYTICS (BENZODIAZEPINES).
003546 03-15

Subject Index

THERAPIES

COMPARATIVE ENZYME-INDUCING EFFECTS OF CHLORPROMAZINE AND FLUPHENAZINE THERAPIES IN PSYCHOTIC-PATIENTS.
000682 01-11

DRUG AND DIETETIC THERAPIES FOR HYPERKINETIC-CHILDREN. (PH.D. DISSERTATION).
003576 03-17

THERAPIST

THE EFFECT OF ASSERTIVENESS TRAINING, PROVERA AND SEX OF THERAPIST IN THE TREATMENT OF GENITAL EXHIBITIONISM.
000697 01-11

THERAPY

STUDY ON VISUALLY-EVOKED-POTENTIALS IN SCHIZOPHRENIC-PATIENTS IN SULPIRIDE THERAPY.
000550 01-08

AFFECTIVE-EPISODE FREQUENCY AND LITHIUM THERAPY.
000587 01-09

HANDBOOK OF LITHIUM THERAPY.
000597 01-09

AMITRIPTYLINE THERAPY OF OBSESSIVE-COMPULSIVE-NEUROSIS.
000656 01-10

CLINICAL-EXPERIENCE WITH PIRACETAM THERAPY IN GERONTOLOGY.
000686 01-11

VASOPRESSIN THERAPY IN PARKINSONS-DISEASE.
000689 01-11

THE LONG-TERM RESULTS OF STEREOTAXIC SURGERY AND L-DOPA THERAPY IN PATIENTS WITH PARKINSONS-DISEASE: A 10-YEAR FOLLOWUP STUDY.
000693 01-11

INTRAVENOUS PHENOBARBITAL THERAPY IN BARBITURATE AND OTHER HYPNOSEDATIVE WITHDRAWAL REACTIONS: A KINETIC APPROACH.
000703 01-11

CYPROTERONACETATE IN THE THERAPY OF SEXUAL-DEVIATIONS.
000735 01-11

A COMPUTER OCULOGRAPHIC AND EEG DOUBLE-BLIND STUDY INCLUDING WELL-BEING FOR DETERMINING CHANGED VIGILANCE UNDER THERAPY WITH TIAPRIDE.
000751 01-13

THE AUTOINDUCTION OF CARBAMAZEPINE DURING LONG-TERM THERAPY.
000785 01-13

ASSESSMENT OF MULTIVARIATE RELATIONSHIPS IN REACTIVITY OF PATIENTS RECEIVING LITHIUM THERAPY.
000819 01-14

RENAL FUNCTION AND BIOPSY IN PATIENTS ON LITHIUM THERAPY.
000830 01-15

A CASE OF CARDIOVASCULAR COLLAPSE DURING LITHIUM-CARBONATE THERAPY.
000860 01-15

SEIZURES DURING TRICYCLIC THERAPY.
000868 01-15

BILATERAL PAPILLOEDEMA IN LONG-TERM THERAPY WITH LITHIUM-CARBONATE.
000878 01-15

CLINICAL HANDBOOK OF ANTIPSYCHOTIC-DRUG THERAPY.
000961 01-17

INFUSION THERAPY IN THERAPY-RESISTANT DEPRESSION.
002007 02-09

TARDIVE-DYSKINESIA IN DEPRESSED-PATIENTS: SUCCESSFUL THERAPY WITH ANTIDEPRESSANTS AND LITHIUM.
002037 02-09

THE USE OF CLOROTEPIN AND DIAZEPAM IN A COMPLEX THERAPY OF NEUROSES (CONTROLLED-COMPARISON).
002064 02-10

CLINICAL-ASPECTS OF ANXIETY AND ITS THERAPY.
002089 02-10

AN ATTEMPT TO TREAT THE SIDE-EFFECTS OF PSYCHOTROPIC THERAPY WITH BROMOCRIPTINE.
002094 02-11

CONCENTRATION OF SEROTONIN METABOLITES IN THE CEREBROSPINAL-FLUID FROM ALCOHOLICS BEFORE AND DURING SULFIRAM THERAPY.
002095 02-11

NOMIFENSINE AS CONCOMITANT THERAPY IN THE TREATMENT OF PARKINSON-PATIENTS. A DOUBLE-BLIND PLACEBO-CONTROLLED-STUDY.
002130 02-11

MEDICAL PSYCHOLOGICAL AND COMBINED THERAPY IN THE CASES OF ENURESIS: A COMPARATIVE-STUDY.
002175 02-11

CARBAMAZEPINE THERAPY IN TRIGEMINAL-NEURALGIA: CLINICAL-EFFECTS IN RELATION TO PLASMA CONCENTRATION.
002181 02-11

LITHIUM THERAPY IN AGGRESSIVE MENTALLY-SUBNORMAL-PATIENTS.
002316 02-14

BIOCHEMICAL-EVIDENCE FOR OSTEOMALACIA WITH CARBAMAZEPINE THERAPY.
002445 02-15

INDIVIDUALIZATION OF PHENYTOIN THERAPY.
002495 02-16

PHENYTOIN THERAPY FOR EPILEPTIC-CHILDREN: EVALUATION OF
SALIVARY AND PLASMA CONCENTRATIONS AND OF METHODS OF
ASSESSING COMPLIANCE.
                                                    004495 04-11
THE EFFECTS OF ESTROGEN THERAPY ON THE SEX-LIFE OF
POSTMENOPAUSAL-WOMEN.
                                                    004573 04-14
CORRECTION OF HORMONAL ACTIVITY OF THE THYROID-GLAND AS A
METHOD OF PATHOGENIC THERAPY IN A COMPREHENSIVE TREATMENT
OF PATIENTS WITH TEMPORAL EPILEPSY.
                                                    004579 04-14
ANTIEPILEPTIC THERAPY WITH PHENYTOIN: WHICH IS THE OPTIMUM
SERUM LEVEL?
                                                    004586 04-14
ON THE QUESTION OF PARENCHYMAL DAMAGE CAUSED BY LONG-TERM
THERAPY WITH PSYCHOTROPICS IN ADOLESCENCE.
                                                    004626 04-15
ON THE THERAPY OF NEUROLEPTIC-INDUCED TARDIVE-DYSKINESIA WITH
DIMETHYLAMINOETHANOL (DEANOL).
                                                    004627 04-15
TARDIVE-DYSKINESIA: PROBLEMS OF PATHOGENESIS, THERAPY, AND
PREVENTION.
                                                    004644 04-15
KIDNEY FUNCTION IN PATIENTS WITH AFFECTIVE-DISORDERS WITH AND
WITHOUT LITHIUM THERAPY.
                                                    004664 04-15
THE PROGNOSIS OF EPILEPSY AND THE STRATEGY FOR TERMINATING
ANTIEPILEPTIC THERAPY.
                                                    004724 04-17
THERAPY-RESISTANT
INFUSION THERAPY IN THERAPY-RESISTANT DEPRESSION.
                                                    002007 02-09
TREATMENT OF THERAPY-RESISTANT DEPRESSED-PATIENTS WITH IV.
INFUSIONS OF NOMIFENSINE CONTROLLED BY GALVANIC-SKIN-
RESISTANCE.
                                                    002012 02-09
ON THE ANTICONVULSANT BLOOD LEVEL IN THERAPY-RESISTANT
EPILEPTIC-PATIENTS.
                                                    003300 03-11
POLYPHARMACY REGIMEN AS AN EXACERBATING RISK IN THERAPY-
RESISTANT EPILEPTIC-SEIZURES AND BEHAVIORAL-DISORDERS.
                                                    004720 04-17·
THERMAL
TEMPORAL PATTERNING OF NEURONAL ACTIVITY DURING THERMAL AND
NEUROCHEMICAL STIMULATION OF THE PREOPTIC/ANTERIOR
HYPOTHALAMUS OF THE AWAKE RABBIT.
                                                    002737 03-03
THERMOREGULATION
EFFECTS OF CENTRALLY-ADMINISTERED PENTAZOCINE AND
ETHYLKETOCYCLAZOCINE ON THERMOREGULATION IN THE CAT.
                                                    000361 01-04
THE EFFECTS OF INJECTIONS OF BOMBESIN INTO THE CEREBRAL
VENTRICLES ON BEHAVIORAL THERMOREGULATION.
                                                    002952 03-04
BOMBESIN ALTERS BEHAVIORAL THERMOREGULATION IN FISH.
                                                    003026 03-04
EFFECTS OF OLFACTORY-BULBECTOMY AND PERIPHERALLY-INDUCED
ANOSMIA ON THERMOREGULATION IN THE RAT: SUSCEPTIBILITY TO
ANTIDEPRESSANT-DRUGS.
                                                    004113 04-04
THERMOREGULATORY
EFFECTS OF BRAIN-MONOAMINE DEPLETION ON THERMOREGULATORY
RESPONSES OF RABBITS TO DIFFERENT HYPOTHALAMIC
TEMPERATURES.
                                                    000190 01-03
THERMOREGULATORY AND LOCOMOTOR-EFFECTS OF DSIP:
PARADOXICAL-INTERACTION WITH D-AMPHETAMINE.
                                                    001827 02-04
EVIDENCE FOR THERMOREGULATORY DOPAMINERGIC-RECEPTORS
LOCATED IN THE PREOPTICUS-MEDIALIS-NUCLEUS OF THE RAT
HYPOTHALAMUS.
                                                    003754 04-03
THE EFFECTS OF THEOPHYLLINE AND CAFFEINE ON THERMOREGULATORY
FUNCTIONS OF RATS AT DIFFERENT AMBIENT TEMPERATURES.
                                                    003907 04-03
THERMOREGULATORY-EFFECTS
NEUROPHYSIOLOGICAL-EFFECTS AND THERMOREGULATORY-EFFECTS OF
CAPSAICIN.
                                                    001421 02-03
REDUCED TOLERANCE TO MORPHINE THERMOREGULATORY-EFFECTS IN
SENESCENT RATS.
                                                    002822 03-03
THESHOLD
EFFECT OF AMITRIPTYLINE ANTIDOTES ON REPETITIVE EXTRASYSTOLE
THESHOLD.
                                                    001856 02-05
THETA
IDENTICAL RESPONSES OF THE TWO HIPPOCAMPAL THETA GENERATORS
TO PHYSIOLOGICAL AND PHARMACOLOGICAL ACTIVATION.
                                                    002792 03-03

THEURER
TREATMENT OF ORGANIC-BRAIN-DISTURBANCES IN ELDERLY-PATIENTS. A
CLINICAL DOUBLE-BLIND STUDY WITH MACROMOLECULAR ORGAN
LYSATES (CYTOPLASMATIC THERAPY ACCORDING TO THEURER).
                                                    003327 03-11
THIAZIDE-INDUCED
THIAZIDE-INDUCED HYPERCALCEMIA IN A MANIC-DEPRESSIVE-PATIENT.
                                                    000843 01-15
THIAZIDES
FENFLURAMINE POTENTIATION OF ANTIHYPERTENSIVE-EFFECTS OF
THIAZIDES.
                                                    002138 02-11
THIN-FIBER
NALOXONE EFFECTS ON THE BLOOD-PRESSURE RESPONSE INDUCED BY
THIN-FIBER MUSCULAR AFFERENTS.
                                                    002794 03-03
THIN-LAYER-CHROMATOGRAPHY
SEPARATION OF BARBITURATES USING REVERSE PHASE THIN-LAYER-
CHROMATOGRAPHY.
                                                    004670 04-16
MASS SCREENING AND CONFIRMATION OF DIAZEPAM IN URINE BY EMIT
THIN-LAYER-CHROMATOGRAPHY.
                                                    004672 04-16
THINKING
CHANGE IN OVERINCLUSIVE THINKING OF SCHIZOPHRENIC-PATIENTS IS
RELATED TO PLASMA PHENOTHIAZINE CONCENTRATION.
                                                    001941 02-08
THIOLS
THIOLS LIBERATE COVALENTLY-BONDED FLAVIN FROM MONOAMINE-
OXIDASE. (UNPUBLISHED PAPER).
                                                    001060 02-01
THIOPENTAL-SODIUM
BEHAVIORAL-DESENSITIZATION OF PHOBIC-ANXIETY USING THIOPENTAL-
SODIUM.
                                                    002352 02-14
THIOPENTONE
VALUE OF PROPANIDID IN ELECTROCONVULSIVE-THERAPY (COMPARISON
WITH THIOPENTONE).
                                                    004379 04-09
THIOPROPAZATE-HYDROCHLORIDE
SYNERGISTIC ACTIONS OF PROPANTHELINE-BROMIDE WITH CIMETIDINE
AND THIOPROPAZATE-HYDROCHLORIDE IN THE PREVENTION OF
STRESS-ULCER FORMATION IN RATS.
                                                    000064 01-03
THIOPROPERAZINE
THE USE OF THIOPROPERAZINE, A PHENOTHIAZINE DERIVATIVE, AS A
LIGAND FOR NEUROLEPTIC-RECEPTORS -- I. IN VITRO STUDIES.
                                                    001133 02-03
THE USE OF THIOPROPERAZINE, A PHENOTHIAZINE DERIVATIVE, AS A
LIGAND FOR NEUROLEPTIC-RECEPTORS -- II. IN VIVO STUDIES.
                                                    001137 02-03
THE EFFECT OF THIOPROPERAZINE ON DELAYED REACTIONS IN LOWER
MONKEYS.
                                                    004125 04-04
THIORIDAZINE
PROLONGATION OF THE EJACULATION LATENCY IN THE MALE RAT BY
THIORIDAZINE AND CHLORIMIPRAMINE.
                                                    000335 01-04
EFFECTS OF THIORIDAZINE ON APOMORPHINE-ELICITED STEREOTYPIC-
BEHAVIOR AND MOTOR-ACTIVITY.
                                                    000424 01-04
A COMPARISON OF THE CARDIOVASCULAR EFFECTS OF HALOPERIDOL,
THIORIDAZINE AND CHLORPROMAZINE-HCL.
                                                    000512 01-05
THE RELATIONSHIP BETWEEN THE THIORIDAZINE LEVEL IN THE PLASMA
AND SYMPTOMS OF PARANOID SCHIZOPHRENIA.
                                                    000546 01-08
EFFECTS OF THIORIDAZINE ON THE COGNITIVE FUNCTIONING OF A
HYPOTONIC SCHIZOPHRENIC-BOY.
                                                    000557 01-08
THE EFFECT OF THIORIDAZINE ON PROLACTIN LEVELS IN ACUTELY
SCHIZOPHRENIC-PATIENTS: CHALLENGE-DOSE AND STEADY-STATE
LEVELS.
                                                    000558 01-08
AN UNUSUAL OCULAR-COMPLICATION OF THIORIDAZINE.
                                                    000848 01-15
CHANGES IN CEREBRAL DOPAMINE FUNCTION INDUCED BY A YEARS
ADMINISTRATION OF TRIFLUOPERAZINE OR THIORIDAZINE AND THEIR
SUBSEQUENT WITHDRAWAL.
                                                    001175 02-03
STUDIES ON THIORIDAZINE AND MESORIDAZINE METABOLISM. II. IN
VIVO METABOLISM OF TRITIATED DRUGS IN RHESUS-MONKEYS.
                                                    001229 02-0.
STUDIES ON THIORIDAZINE AND MESORIDAZINE METABOLISM. I.
PROTEIN BINDING.
                                                    001867 02-06
COMPARISON OF SCH-12679 AND THIORIDAZINE IN AGGRESSIVE
MENTAL-RETARDATES.
                                                    002119 02-11

A CONTROLLED DOUBLE-BLIND STUDY OF HALOPERIDOL VERSUS THIORIDAZINE IN THE TREATMENT OF RESTLESS MENTALLY-SUBNORMAL-PATIENTS: SERUM LEVELS AND CLINICAL-EFFECTS.
002185 02-11

ON THE CLINICAL PHARMACOKINETICS OF THIORIDAZINE AND ITS METABOLITES.
002207 02-13

EFFECTS OF THIORIDAZINE (MELLARIL) ON TITRATING DELAYED MATCHING-TO-SAMPLE PERFORMANCE IN MENTALLY-RETARDED ADULTS.
002471 02-15

THE EFFECTS OF THIORIDAZINE ON ELECTRICAL AND ISCHEMIC VENTRICULAR FIBRILLATION IN THE DOG HEART IN SITU.
002697 03-03

EFFECTS OF THIORIDAZINE (MELLARIL) ON TITRATING DELAYED MATCHING-TO-SAMPLE PERFORMANCE IN MENTALLY-RETARDED ADULTS.
003392 03-11

SELF-STIMULATION AND LOCOMOTOR CHANGES INDICATING LATENT ANTICHOLINERGIC-ACTIVITY BY AN ATYPICAL NEUROLEPTIC (THIORIDAZINE).
003560 03-16

CEREBROSPINAL-FLUID CONCENTRATIONS OF THIORIDAZINE AND ITS MAIN METABOLITES IN PSYCHIATRIC-PATIENTS.
003569 03-16

AN UNUSUAL CASE OF THIORIDAZINE AND LEVOMEPROMAZINE DEPENDENCE.
004634 04-15

THIOTHIXENE
DOUBLE-BLIND COMPARISON OF HALOPERIDOL AND THIOTHIXENE WITH AFTERCARE TREATMENT EVALUATION IN PSYCHIATRIC-OUTPATIENTS WITH SCHIZOPHRENIA.
000574 01-08

THIP
GABAERGIC ACTIONS OF THIP IN VIVO AND IN VITRO: A COMPARISON WITH MUSCIMOL AND GABA.
000319 01-03

DIFFERENTIAL REVERSAL BY SCOPOLAMINE AND THIP OF THE ANTISTEREOTYPIC AND CATALEPTIC-EFFECTS OF NEUROLEPTICS.
002948 03-04

ANALGESIC PROPERTIES OF THE GABAMIMETIC THIP.
003013 03-04

HYPERACTIVITY FOLLOWING INJECTION OF A GLUTAMATE AGONIST AND 6,7 ADTN INTO RAT NUCLEUS-ACCUMBENS AND ITS INHIBITION BY THIP.
004066 04-04

THIRST
INCREASED HUNGER AND THIRST DURING GLUCOPRIVATION IN HUMANS.
000828 01-14

THORAZINE
CONDITIONING AND RETENTION OF DEFENSIVE BURYING AS A FUNCTION OF ELAVIL AND THORAZINE INJECTION.
002974 03-04

THOUGHTS
SYNAPTIC AND BEHAVIOURAL-ACTIONS OF ANTIDEPRESSANT-DRUGS: FURTHER THOUGHTS ON THE IMPLICATIONS FOR THEORIES OF DEPRESSION.
003229 03-09

THREE-WAY
A NOVEL THREE-WAY TAP.
001863 02-06

THREO-3-HYDROXYASPARTATE
POTENTIATION OF L GLUTAMATE AND L ASPARTATE EXCITATION OF CAT SPINAL NEURONES BY THE STEREOISOMERS OF THREO-3-HYDROXYASPARTATE.
002768 03-03

THRESHOLD
REVERSIBLE INACTIVATION OF RAPHE-MAGNUS NEURONS: EFFECTS ON NOCICEPTIVE THRESHOLD AND MORPHINE-INDUCED ANALGESIA.
000240 01-03

PENTYLENETETRAZOL SEIZURE THRESHOLD: A QUANTITATIVE MEASURE OF ETHANOL DEPENDENCE IN RATS.
001750 02-04

LOWERING OF THE CONVULSIVE THRESHOLD BY NONSTEROIDAL ANTIINFLAMMATORY-DRUGS.
002904 03-03

ETHYL-BETA-CARBOLINE-CARBOXYLATE LOWERS SEIZURE THRESHOLD AND ANTAGONIZES FLURAZEPAM-INDUCED SEDATION IN RATS.
002971 03-04

EFFECT OF FLURAZEPAM, PENTOBARBITAL, AND CAFFEINE ON AROUSAL THRESHOLD.
003439 03-14

THE EFFECT OF ELECTRICAL-STIMULATION OF THE LOCUS-COERULEUS AND INTRAPERITONEAL INJECTION OF CERTAIN PHARMACOLOGICAL SUBSTANCES ON THE THRESHOLD OF HIPPOCAMPAL AFTERDISCHARGES.
003885 04-03

NEW ANTIDEPRESSANT-DRUGS AND THE SEIZURE THRESHOLD.
004662 04-15

THRESHOLDS
RELATION OF MONOMETHYLHYDRAZINE (MMH) SEIZURE THRESHOLDS TO AFTERDISCHARGE THRESHOLDS WITH AMYGDALOID STIMULATION IN CATS.
000474 01-04

AUDITORY AROUSAL THRESHOLDS OF GOOD SLEEPERS AND POOR SLEEPERS WITH AND WITHOUT FLURAZEPAM.
003446 03-14

REWARD AND DETECTION THRESHOLDS FOR BRAIN-STIMULATION: DISSOCIATIVE-EFFECTS OF COCAINE.
004160 04-04

MORPHINE DIFFERENTIALLY AFFECTS VENTRAL TEGMENTAL AND SUBSTANTIA-NIGRA BRAIN REWARD THRESHOLDS.
004187 04-04

THROMBOCYTOSIS
THROMBOCYTOSIS IN THE OFFSPRING OF FEMALE MICE RECEIVING DL METHADONE.
001836 02-05

THYMIDINE
EFFECT OF AMPHETAMINE ON THE METABOLISM AND INCORPORATION OF (3H) THYMIDINE INTO DNA OF DEVELOPING RAT-BRAIN.
003729 04-03

THYMOANALEPTIC
THYMOANALEPTIC TREATMENT CONTROL THROUGH MEASUREMENT OF PLASMA CONCENTRATIONS OF AMITRIPTYLINE AND ITS METABOLITE NORTRIPTYLINE.
002304 02-13

THYMOLEPTIC
NEUROLEPTIC AND THYMOLEPTIC TREATMENT OF PSYCHOTIC-OUTPATIENTS.
000556 01-08

PHARMACOLOGICAL-STUDIES ON A NEW THYMOLEPTIC ANTIDEPRESSANT. DIMETHYLAMINOPROPYL-5-METHYL-3-PHENYL-1H-INDAZOLE (FS-32).
001659 02-04

THYMUS-GLAND
POSSIBLE ROLE OF THE THYMUS-GLAND IN MENTAL-ILLNESS.
002273 02-13

THYREOTROPIN
INFLUENCE OF NOMIFENSINE ON GROWTH-HORMONE, PROLACTIN, LUTEINISING-HORMONE AND THYREOTROPIN IN HEALTHY SUBJECTS AND HYPERPROLACTINAEMIC-PATIENTS.
002137 02-11

THYROID-ACTIVITY
ANXIETY AND THYROID-ACTIVITY IN PSYCHIATRIC-PATIENTS.
000786 01-13

THYROID-FUNCTION
SINEMET AND THYROID-FUNCTION IN PARKINSON-DISEASE.
000733 01-11

SEROTONERGIC AND CATECHOLAMINERGIC INFLUENCE ON THYROID-FUNCTION IN THE VERVET-MONKEY.
001385 02-03

LITHIUM THERAPY AND THYROID-FUNCTION: A LONG-TERM STUDY.
003504 03-15

NEUROTRANSMITTER CONTROL OF HYPOTHALAMIC PITUITARY THYROID-FUNCTION IN RATS.
003942 04-03

EFFECTS OF CAFFEINE ON ANTERIOR PITUITARY AND THYROID-FUNCTION IN THE RAT.
004014 04-03

THYROID-GLAND
CORRECTION OF HORMONAL ACTIVITY OF THE THYROID-GLAND AS A METHOD OF PATHOGENIC THERAPY IN A COMPREHENSIVE TREATMENT OF PATIENTS WITH TEMPORAL EPILEPSY.
004579 04-14

THYROID-HORMONES
ENDOCRINE CHANGES AND BEHAVIORAL-CHANGES IN DEPRESSION AFTER THYROTROPIN-RELEASING-HORMONE (TRH): ALTERATION BY PRETREATMENT WITH THYROID-HORMONES.
002259 02-13

REGULATION OF ALPHA1-ADRENOCEPTORS IN THE CEREBRAL-CORTEX OF THE RAT BY THYROID-HORMONES.
003816 04-03

THYROID-INDUCED
THYROID-INDUCED MANIA IN HYPOTHYROID-PATIENTS.
000857 01-15

THYROLIBERIN
EFFECT OF MELANOSTATIN AND THYROLIBERIN ON THE BIOSYNTHESIS AND RELEASE OF DOPAMINE BY RAT-BRAIN STRIATAL P2-FRACTIONS.
001472 02-03

THYROSTIMULATING-RELEASING-HORMONE
DIFFERENT EFFECTS OF TRICYCLIC-ANTIDEPRESSANTS AND TETRACYCLIC-ANTIDEPRESSANTS ON THE RELEASE OF TSH, PROLACTIN, AND GROWTH-HORMONE AFTER ADMINISTRATION OF THYROSTIMULATING-RELEASING-HORMONE IN MANIC-DEPRESSIVES.
004407 04-09

THYROTOXICOSIS
EXTRAPYRAMIDAL REACTION OF FLUPHENAZINE POTENTIATED BY
THYROTOXICOSIS.
003551 03-15

THYROTROPHIN
THYROTROPHIN RESPONSE TO THYROTROPHIN-RELEASING-HORMONE IN
UNIPOLAR AND BIPOLAR AFFECTIVE-ILLNESS.
003237 03-09

THYROTROPHIN-RELEASING-FACTOR
HORMONAL STIMULATION AFTER INJECTION OF THYROTROPHIN-
RELEASING-FACTOR (TRF) AND ACTH1-24 IN PATIENTS FOLLOWING
CHRONIC-TREATMENT WITH NEUROLEPTICS: PRELIMINARY-STUDY.
004505 04-13

THYROTROPHIN-RELEASING-HORMONE
THYROTROPHIN RESPONSE TO THYROTROPHIN-RELEASING-HORMONE IN
UNIPOLAR AND BIPOLAR AFFECTIVE-ILLNESS.
003237 03-09

THYROTROPIN
MODIFICATION OF GABAERGIC ACTIVITY AND THYROTROPIN SECRETION
IN MALE RATS.
001362 02-03

THYROTROPIN-RELEASING-HORMONE
AN ANALOGUE OF THYROTROPIN-RELEASING-HORMONE WITH IMPROVED
BIOLOGICAL-STABILITY BOTH IN VITRO AND IN VIVO.
000032 01-03

GROWTH-HORMONE (GH) RELEASE FOLLOWING THYROTROPIN-
RELEASING-HORMONE (TRH) INJECTION IN MANIC-PATIENTS
RECEIVING LITHIUM-CARBONATE.
000645 01-09

THE EEG EFFECTS OF THYROTROPIN-RELEASING-HORMONE IN HEALTHY
SUBJECTS AND CHRONIC SCHIZOPHRENICS.
000770 01-13

THYROTROPIN-RELEASING-HORMONE: NEUROCHEMICAL EVIDENCE FOR
THE POTENTIATION OF IMIPRAMINE EFFECTS ON THE METABOLISM
AND UPTAKE OF BRAIN CATECHOLAMINES.
001427 02-03

INFLUENCE OF THYROTROPIN-RELEASING-HORMONE AND HISTIDYL-
PROLINE-DIKETOPIPERAZINE ON SPONTANEOUS LOCOMOTOR-ACTIVITY
AND ANALGESIA INDUCED BY DELTA9 TETRAHYDROCANNABINOL IN
THE MOUSE.
001575 02-04

INVESTIGATIONS ON THE INTERACTION OF THYROTROPIN-RELEASING-
HORMONE (TRH) AND MK-771 WITH CENTRAL NORADRENERGIC
MECHANISMS.
001701 02-04

BIPHASIC-EFFECTS OF THYROTROPIN-RELEASING-HORMONE ON
EXPLORATORY-BEHAVIOR IN MICE.
001808 02-04

PSYCHOTROPIC-ACTION OF THYROTROPIN-RELEASING-HORMONE.
002023 02-09

ENDOCRINE CHANGES AND BEHAVIORAL-CHANGES IN DEPRESSION AFTER
THYROTROPIN-RELEASING-HORMONE (TRH): ALTERATION BY
PRETREATMENT WITH THYROID-HORMONES.
002259 02-13

INDIVIDUAL VARIATIONS IN THE EFFECTS OF FLURAZEPAM,
CLORAZEPATE, L-DOPA AND THYROTROPIN-RELEASING-HORMONE ON
REM SLEEP IN MAN.
002349 02-14

EFFECT OF LITHIUM ON PROLACTIN RESPONSES TO THYROTROPIN-
RELEASING-HORMONE IN PATIENTS WITH MANIC-STATE.
003266 03-09

THE EFFECTS OF THYROTROPIN-RELEASING-HORMONE ON CYCLIC-AMP
ACCUMULATION IN RABBIT CEREBROCORTICAL TISSUE IN THE
PRESENCE AND ABSENCE OF CNS DEPRESSANTS.
004010 04-03

PASSAGE THROUGH THE BLOOD-BRAIN-BARRIER OF THYROTROPIN-
RELEASING-HORMONE ENCAPSULATED IN LIPOSOMES.
004298 04-06

THYROXIN
THYROXIN SENSITIVITY OF SENSORIMOTOR CORTICAL NEURONS AND THE
HYPOTHALAMIC VENTROMEDIAL NUCLEUS.
003713 04-03

THYROXINE
EFFECTS OF PERINATAL THYROXINE AND/OR CORTICOSTERONE
TREATMENT ON THE ONTOGENESIS OF HYPOTHALAMIC AND
MESENCEPHALIC NOREPINEPHRINE AND DOPAMINE CONTENT.
000180 01-03

INFLUENCE OF CARBAMAZEPINE ON SERUM THYROXINE AND
TRIIODOTHYRONINE IN PATIENTS WITH EPILEPSY.
004488 04-11

TIADIPONE
A DOUBLE-BLIND CROSSED CLINICAL-STUDY WITH A NEW
PSYCHOPHARMACEUTICAL: TIADIPONE (QM-6008), DIAZEPAM, AND
A PLACEBO.
003153 03-07

TIAPRIDE
COMPUTERIZING THE MMPI IN THE STUDY OF A NEW PSYCHOTROPIC-
AGENT: TIAPRIDE.
000585 01-09

A COMPUTER OCULOGRAPHIC AND EEG DOUBLE-BLIND STUDY INCLUDING
WELL-BEING FOR DETERMINING CHANGED VIGILANCE UNDER THERAPY
WITH TIAPRIDE.
000751 01-13

EFFECTS OF TIAPRIDE ON HOMOVANILLIC-ACID LEVELS IN HUMAN
CEREBROSPINAL-FLUID DRAWN AT PNEUMOENCEPHALOGRAPHY.
001483 02-03

ALCOHOL WITHDRAWAL USING TIAPRIDE: QUANTITATIVE
PSYCHOPATHOLOGY.
003293 03-11

A TRIAL TREATMENT WITH TIAPRIDE FOR SOME EXTRAPYRAMIDAL-
SYNDROMES CAUSED BY NEUROLEPTIC-AGENTS.
003553 03-15

TICS
THE TREATMENT AND ETIOLOGY OF TICS AND TOURETTE-SYNDROME.
003372 03-11

DO STIMULANTS PROVOKE, CAUSE, OR EXACERBATE TICS AND
TOURETTE-SYNDROME?
004485 04-11

TIME
HOSPITAL AND OUTPATIENT CARE FOR PSYCHOTIC-PATIENTS DURING THE
LAST THREE DECADES: SUBSEQUENT HOSPITAL AND OUTPATIENT
TREATMENT OF PSYCHOTIC-PATIENTS HOSPITALIZED FOR THE FIRST
TIME IN 1949-50, 1959-60 OR 1969-70.
000571 01-08

EFFECT OF TABERNANTHINE ON THE TURNOVER TIME OF BRAIN
CATECHOLAMINES IN NORMAL AND HYPOBARIC HYPOXIC RATS.
001187 02-03

METHAMPHETAMINE AND TIME ESTIMATION.
003040 03-04

RAPID ACQUISITION OF A TWO-DRUG DISCRIMINATION: TIME OF DAY
EFFECT UPON SALINE STATE.
004214 04-04

TIME-BLIND
TIME-BLIND ANALYSIS AND OTHER VIDEO-STRATEGIES IN PHASE II
TRIALS OF PSYCHOTROPIC-DRUGS.
003568 03-16

TIME-COURSE
TIME-COURSE OF ETORPHINE LEVELS IN TISSUES OF OPIATE-TOLERANT
AND NONTOLERANT RATS.
000301 01-03

WATER INTAKE AND TIME-COURSE OF DRINKING AFTER SINGLE OR
REPEATED CHLORDIAZEPOXIDE INJECTIONS.
000369 01-04

THE TIME-COURSE OF NORADRENERGIC PRESYNAPTIC AND
POSTSYNAPTIC ACTIVITY DURING CHRONIC DESIPRAMINE
TREATMENT.
001289 02-03

MODULATION OF APOMORPHINE-INDUCED STEREOTYPY BY ESTROGEN:
TIME-COURSE AND DOSE-RESPONSE.
001636 02-04

TIME-COURSE OF THE ANTIPSYCHOTIC-EFFECT IN SCHIZOPHRENIA AND
SOME CHANGES IN POSTMORTEM BRAIN AND THEIR RELATION TO
NEUROLEPTIC-MEDICATION.
001911 02-08

TIME-COURSE OF CHRONIC HALOPERIDOL AND CLOZAPINE UPON
OPERANT RATE AND DURATION.
002989 03-04

TIME-COURSE OF CLINICAL CHEMICAL PARAMETERS UNDER LONG-TERM
LITHIUM TREATMENT.
003515 03-15

CORRECTION OF THE EXTRAPYRAMIDAL NEUROLEPTIC-SYNDROME BY
TRYPTOPHAN AND THE TIME-COURSE OF ITS CONTENT IN THE BLOOD
OF PATIENTS.
004434 04-11

TIME-DEPENDENT
EFFECT OF PHENTOLAMINE ADMINISTRATION INTO THE AMYGDALA
COMPLEX OF RATS ON TIME-DEPENDENT MEMORY PROCESSES.
002998 03-04

TIME-DEPENDENT CHANGES IN ANTEROGRADE SCOPOLAMINE-INDUCED
AMNESIA IN RATS.
004182 04-04

TIMID-BEHAVIOUR
BICUCULLINE ANTAGONIZES EFFECTS OF DIAZEPAM ON AGGRESSIVE AND
TIMID-BEHAVIOUR IN MICE.
000485 01-04

TIMING
APOMORPHINE: EFFECTS ON THE TIMING AND SEQUENCING OF PECKING-
BEHAVIOR IN CHICKS.
000428 01-04

TISSUE
DISTRIBUTION OF 14C PHENYTOIN IN RAT PURKINJE-CELLS, CEREBELLAR
AND CEREBRAL NEURONAL TISSUE AFTER A SINGLE INTRAPERITONEAL
INJECTION.
000261 01-03

EFFECT OF PYRITINOL AND PIRACETAM ON CHANGES IN FREE AMMONIA
LEVEL IN CNS TISSUE AFTER PARADOXICAL SLEEP-DEPRIVATION IN
RATS.
001199 02-03

EFFECTS OF RATE OF BLOOD FLOW ON FRACTIONAL EXTRACTION AND ON
UPTAKE OF INFUSED NORADRENALINE BY BROWN ADIPOSE TISSUE IN
VIVO.
001231 02-03
SEX-DIFFERENCES IN THE AMPHETAMINE STIMULATED RELEASE OF
CATECHOLAMINES FROM RAT STRIATAL TISSUE IN VITRO.
002668 03-03
THE EFFECTS OF D-AMPHETAMINE AND POTASSIUM ON SEROTONIN
RELEASE AND METABOLISM IN RAT-CEREBRAL-CORTEX TISSUE.
002754 03-03
A RAPID AND SIMPLE METHOD FOR THE DETERMINATION OF PICOGRAM
LEVELS OF 3 METHOXYTYRAMINE IN BRAIN TISSUE USING LIQUID-
CHROMATOGRAPHY WITH ELECTROCHEMICAL DETECTION.
003674 04-01
TISSUE CHOLINE STUDIED USING A SIMPLE CHEMICAL ASSAY.
003828 04-03
INHIBITION OF DOPAMINE D-1 AND D-2 BINDING-SITES IN NEURONAL
TISSUE BY ASCORBATE.
003876 04-03
EFFECT OF INHIBITORS OF GABA-AMINOTRANSFERASE ON THE
METABOLISM OF GABA IN BRAIN TISSUE AND SYNAPTOSOMAL
FRACTIONS.
003914 04-03
THE EFFECTS OF THYROTROPIN-RELEASING-HORMONE ON CYCLIC-AMP
ACCUMULATION IN RABBIT CEREBROCORTICAL TISSUE IN THE
PRESENCE AND ABSENCE OF CNS DEPRESSANTS.
004010 04-03
BENZODIAZEPINE-RECEPTORS: EFFECT OF TISSUE PREINCUBATION AT 37
DEGREES C.
004013 04-03
EFFECT OF DESMETHYLIMIPRAMINE ON TISSUE DISTRIBUTION AND
ANORECTIC-ACTIVITY OF CHLORPHENTERMINE IN RATS.
004179 04-04

TISSUES
COMPARISON OF BETA-ADRENERGIC-RECEPTOR SUBTYPES IN
MAMMALIAN TISSUES.
000207 01-03
TIME-COURSE OF ETORPHINE LEVELS IN TISSUES OF OPIATE-TOLERANT
AND NONTOLERANT RATS.
000301 01-03
RECEPTOR BINDING INTERACTIONS OF THE ANGIOTENSIN-II ANTAGONIST,
125I SARCOSINE1-LEUCINE8-ANGIOTENSIN-II, WITH MAMMALIAN
BRAIN AND PERIPHERAL TISSUES.
001125 02-03
DEVELOPMENTALLY REGULATED LECTINS IN SLIME MOULDS AND CHICK
TISSUES -- ARE THEY CELL ADHESION MOLECULES?
003724 04-03
ON THE IMPORTANCE OF AGONIST CONCENTRATION GRADIENTS WITHIN
ISOLATED TISSUES. INCREASED MAXIMAL RESPONSES OF RAT VASA-
DEFERENTIA TO (-) NORADRENALINE AFTER BLOCKADE OF NEURONAL
UPTAKE.
003879 04-03
OPIOID BINDING PROPERTIES OF BRAIN AND PERIPHERAL TISSUES:
EVIDENCE FOR HETEROGENEITY IN OPIOID LIGAND BINDING SITES.
003902 04-03

TITRATING
EFFECTS OF THIORIDAZINE (MELLARIL) ON TITRATING DELAYED
MATCHING-TO-SAMPLE PERFORMANCE IN MENTALLY-RETARDED
ADULTS.
002471 02-15
EFFECTS OF THIORIDAZINE (MELLARIL) ON TITRATING DELAYED
MATCHING-TO-SAMPLE PERFORMANCE OF MENTALLY-RETARDED
ADULTS.
003392 03-11

TITRATION
NALORPHINES EFFECT UNDER SEVERAL SCHEDULES OF ELECTRIC-SHOCK
TITRATION.
000379 01-04
EFFECTS OF MORPHINE, PENTAZOCINE AND CYCLAZOCINE ALONE AND IN
COMBINATION WITH NALOXONE ON ELECTRIC-SHOCK TITRATION IN
THE SQUIRREL-MONKEY.
001611 02-04
TITRATION PROCEDURE WITH RATS USING A NOSE-POKE RESPONSE AND
TAIL-SHOCK.
001862 02-06

TLC
GLC/TLC ANALYSIS OF CODEINE AND MORPHINE IN URINE VIA
DERIVATIZATION TECHNIQUES.
004687 04-16

TOAD
ACUTE AND CHRONIC EFFECTS OF MORPHINE ON TRANSMEMBRANE
POTENTIAL AND ON SHORT-CIRCUIT CURRENT IN ISOLATED TOAD
SKIN: APPARENT MORPHINE-DEPENDENCE.
001176 02-03

TOBACCO
SMOKING AND VIGILANCE: THE EFFECTS OF TOBACCO SMOKING ON CFF
AS RELATED TO PERSONALITY AND SMOKING HABITS.
002368 02-14
PSYCHOTOMIMETIC USE OF TOBACCO IN SURINAM AND FRENCH-
GUIANA.
002592 02-17

TOFISOPAM
OUR EXPERIENCE WITH TOFISOPAM (GRANDAXIN-EGYPT).
000647 01-10
ACTION OF TOFISOPAM ON THE ERGONOMIC VIGILANCE LEVEL. ITS
INTERACTION WITH THE EFFECTS OF ALCOHOL. CLINICAL
PHARMACOLOGICAL-STUDY.
001891 02-07
TOFISOPAM IN PSEUDONEURASTHENIA WITH HEADACHES.
002075 02-10
TO THE CLINICAL-EVALUATION OF ANXIOLYTICS (TOFISOPAM).
002494 02-16

TOFIZOPAM
THE TREATMENT OF ANXIOUS-DEPRESSIVE-SYNDROMES WITH
TOFIZOPAM.
000615 01-09
TOFIZOPAM IN THE TREATMENT OF CHRONIC ALCOHOLISM.
000706 01-11

TOLERABILITY
NOMIFENSINE IN THE TREATMENT OF OBSESSIVE-COMPULSIVE-NEUROSIS.
THERAPEUTIC-EFFICACY AND TOLERABILITY IN COMPARISON TO
IMIPRAMINE.
002078 02-10

TOLERANCE
REDUCTION OF OPIATE BINDING TO BRAINSTEM SLICES ASSOCIATED
WITH THE DEVELOPMENT OF TOLERANCE TO MORPHINE IN RATS.
000066 01-03
TOLERANCE TO SUPPRESSIVE EFFECTS OF CHLORDIAZEPOXIDE ON
OPERANT-BEHAVIOR: LACK OF CROSS-TOLERANCE TO PENTOBARBITAL.
000356 01-04
ASSESSMENT OF TOLERANCE TO AND PHYSICAL-DEPENDENCE ON
PENTOBARBITAL, INDUCED BY MULTIPLE PELLET IMPLANTATION.
000385 01-04
TOLERANCE OF MICE TO NITROUS-OXIDE.
000418 01-04
REPEATED ADMINISTRATION OF NALTREXONE PRODUCES TOLERANCE TO
NALOXONE-INDUCED HYPERALGESIA.
000453 01-04
TOLERANCE TO INCREASES IN STRIATAL ACETYLCHOLINE
CONCENTRATIONS AFTER REPEATED ADMINISTRATION OF
APOMORPHINE-DIPIVALOYL-ESTER.
000464 01-04
TRICYCLIC-ANTIDEPRESSANT DRUG TOLERANCE IN ORIENTAL AND
OCCIDENTAL POPULATIONS.
000590 01-09
IMPAIRED GLUCOSE TOLERANCE IN LONG-TERM LITHIUM TREATED
PATIENTS.
000611 01-09
DOPAMINE SYNTHESIS: TOLERANCE TO HALOPERIDOL AND
SUPERSENSITIVITY TO APOMORPHINE DEPEND ON PRESYNAPTIC-
RECEPTORS.
001129 02-03
TOLERANCE TO BARBITURATE-INDUCED CENTRAL-NERVOUS-SYSTEM
DEPRESSION: INVOLVEMENT OF STIMULUS SECRETION COUPLING IN
DISCRETE BRAIN AREAS. (PH.D. DISSERTATION).
001213 02-03
EFFECTS OF CHRONIC NEUROLEPTIC TREATMENT ON TYROSINE-
HYDROXYLASE IN DOPAMINERGIC TERMINALS: COMPARISONS
BETWEEN DRUGS AND BRAIN REGIONS REVEALS DIFFERENT
MECHANISMS OF TOLERANCE.
001243 02-03
BIPHASIC ACTIVITY OF MEMBRANE-BOUND ENZYMES IN BRAIN
MITOCHONDRIA AND SYNAPTOSOMES DURING THE DEVELOPMENT OF
TOLERANCE TO AND PHYSICAL-DEPENDENCE ON CHRONIC MORPHINE
ADMINISTRATION TO RATS.
001285 02-03
TOLERANCE TO ETHANOL-INDUCED IMPAIRMENT OF WATER-ESCAPE IN
RATS BRED FOR ETHANOL SENSITIVITY.
001567 02-04
TOLERANCE DEVELOPMENT TO PHENCYCLIDINE BY CHRONIC
ADMINISTRATION.
001619 02-04
APPARENT TOLERANCE TO SOME ASPECTS OF AMPHETAMINE
STEREOTYPY WITH LONG-TERM-TREATMENT.
001758 02-04
TOLERANCE TO FLUPHENAZINE AND SUPERSENSITIVITY TO APOMORPHINE
IN CENTRAL DOPAMINERGIC-SYSTEMS AFTER CHRONIC FLUPHENAZINE-
DECANOATE TREATMENT.
001820 02-04
TOLERANCE TO DEXTROAMPHETAMINE-SULFATE IN HYPERACTIVE-
CHILDREN: ASSESSMENT USING AN EMPIRICAL NEUROPSYCHOLOGICAL
PARADIGM -- A PILOT-STUDY.
002126 02-11
LITHIUM: PROBLEMS OF APPLICATION, TOLERANCE, AND EFFICACY.
002434 02-15
DEVELOPMENT OF TOLERANCE TO THE EXCITATORY EFFECT OF MORPHINE
AND CROSS-TOLERANCE TO THE INHIBITORY ACTION OF BETA
ENDORPHIN IN THE ISOLATED RAT VAS-DEFERENS.
002756 03-03

REDUCED TOLERANCE TO MORPHINE THERMOREGULATORY-EFFECTS IN
SENESCENT RATS.
                                                   002822 03-03
DEVELOPMENT OF ACUTE TOLERANCE TO THE EFFECTS OF NALOXONE ON
THE HYPOTHALAMIC PITUITARY LUTEINIZING-HORMONE AXIS IN THE
MALE RAT.
                                                   002853 03-03
ANALGESIC TOLERANCE PRODUCED BY MORPHINE PELLETS IS
FACILITATED BY ANALGESIC TESTING.
                                                   002943 03-04
ENVIRONMENTAL MODULATION OF ANALGESIC TOLERANCE INDUCED BY
MORPHINE PELLETS.
                                                   002944 03-04
TOLERANCE TO THE DISCRIMINATIVE-STIMULUS PROPERTIES OF D-
AMPHETAMINE.
                                                   002953 03-04
CATS DEVELOP TOLERANCE TO D-AMPHETAMINES EFFECTS UPON
LOCOMOTION AND STEREOTYPED-BEHAVIORS.
                                                   003018 03-04
DIFFERENTIATION OF OPIATE-RECEPTORS IN THE BRAIN BY THE SELECTIVE
DEVELOPMENT OF TOLERANCE.
                                                   003088 03-04
DIFFERENCE IN THE DEVELOPMENT OF TOLERANCE TO MORPHINE AND D
ALA2-METHIONINE-ENKEPHALIN IN C57 BL/6J AND DBA/2J MICE.
                                                   003126 03-05
TOLERANCE IN A COMPRESSED GASTRORESISTANT FORM IN
PSYCHIATRIC-PATIENTS.
                                                   003157 03-07
TOLERANCE STUDY IN PSYCHIATRIC-PATIENTS OF A NEW PREPARATION
OF SODIUM-DIPROPYLACETATE.
                                                   003158 03-07
DIFFERENTIAL TOLERANCE TO THE EFFECTS OF MORPHINE ON EVOKED
ACTIVITY IN THE HIPPOCAMPAL SLICE.
                                                   003760 04-03
EFFECT OF P CHLOROPHENYLALANINE ON THE ACQUISITION OF
TOLERANCE TO THE HYPNOTIC-EFFECTS OF PENTOBARBITAL, BARBITAL,
AND ETHANOL.
                                                   003883 04-03
THE EFFECTS OF PEPTIDES ON TOLERANCE TO THE CATALEPTIC-EFFECTS
AND HYPOTHERMIC-EFFECTS OF MORPHINE IN THE RAT.
                                                   004072 04-04
FOOD PREFERENCE FOLLOWING ACUTE OR CHRONIC CHLORDIAZEPOXIDE
ADMINISTRATION: TOLERANCE TO AN ANTINEOPHOBIC ACTION.
                                                   004090 04-04
NEUROLOGICAL TOLERANCE OF LITHIUM AND PSYCHOTROPIC-DRUGS IN
COMBINATION: 265 CASES.
                                                  ·004594 04-15

TOLERANT
ROLE OF BRAIN CATECHOLAMINES AND 5 HYDROXYTRYPTAMINE IN
MORPHINE-INDUCED TEMPERATURE CHANGES IN NORMAL AND
TOLERANT RATS AND MICE.
                                                   001476 02-03
POTENTIATION OF BARBITURATE HYPNOSIS BY PROBENECID:
DIFFERENTIAL-EFFECT IN TOLERANT ANIMALS.
                                                   003038 03-04

TOLOXATONE
MONOAMINE-OXIDASE-INHIBITION AND BRAIN-AMINE METABOLISM
AFTER ORAL TREATMENT WITH TOLOXATONE IN THE RAT.
                                                   000156 01-03

TOLUENE
BRIEF COMMUNICATION: BEHAVIORAL RECOVERY AFTER TOLUENE
EXPOSURE IN RATS.
                                                   002969 03-04

TONIC
MORPHINE AND SUPRASPINAL INHIBITION OF SPINAL NEURONES:
EVIDENCE THAT MORPHINE DECREASES TONIC DESCENDING INHIBITION
IN THE ANESTHETIZED CAT.
                                                   001203 02-03
EVIDENCE FOR A TONIC GABAERGIC CONTROL OF SEROTONIN NEURONS
IN THE MEDIAN RAPHE NUCLEUS.
                                                   002719 03-03
CATECHOLAMINERGIC INVOLVEMENT IN PHASIC VERSUS TONIC
ELECTROCORTICAL AROUSAL.
                                                   002723 03-03
PHARMACOLOGIC EVIDENCE FOR A TONIC MUSCARINIC INHIBITORY
INPUT TO THE EDINGER-WESTPHAL NUCLEUS IN THE DOG.
                                                   002889 03-03
THE EFFECTS OF TRYPTOPHAN AND MANIPULATIONS OF SEROTONERGIC-
RECEPTORS ON TONIC IMMOBILITY IN CHICKENS.
                                                   004245 04-04
TONIC IMMOBILITY IN DOMESTIC FOWL: POSSIBLE INTERACTION OF
SEROTONERGIC AND DOPAMINERGIC MECHANISMS.
                                                   004246 04-04
DOSE-EFFECT OF DEAE ON SUBJECTIVE PROBLEMS, VERTIGO,
DEPRESSION, ASTHENIA, CEPHALALGIA, AND TONIC POSTURAL
ACTIVITY PROBLEMS RECORDED WITH STATOKINESIMETER IN
POSTCONCUSSIONAL-SYNDROME.
                                                   004472 04-11

TOOTH-PULP
MORPHINE AND ELECTROACUPUNCTURE: COMPARISON OF THE EFFECTS
ON THE CORTICAL EVOKED-RESPONSES AFTER TOOTH-PULP
STIMULATION IN RATS.
                                                   001294 02-03
EFFECTS OF MORPHINE ON EVOKED-POTENTIALS RECORDED FROM THE
AMYGDALA BY TOOTH-PULP STIMULATION IN CATS.
                                                   001379 02-03
FURTHER STUDIES ON OPIATE-RECEPTORS THAT MEDIATE
ANTINOCICEPTION: TOOTH-PULP STIMULATION IN THE DOG.
                                                   001782 02-04

TOPICS
RECENT REVIEWS OF BIOCHEMICAL, NEUROCHEMICAL, AND
PHARMACOLOGICAL TOPICS.
                                                   003649 03-17

TOPOGRAPHIC
A TOPOGRAPHIC LOCALIZATION OF ENKEPHALIN ON THE DOPAMINE
NEURONS OF THE RAT SUBSTANTIA-NIGRA AND VENTRAL TEGMENTAL
AREA DEMONSTRATED BY COMBINED HISTOFLUORESCENCE
IMMUNOCYTOCHEMISTRY.
                                                   002639 03-01

TOURETTE-SYNDROME
CLONIDINE IN TOURETTE-SYNDROME.
                                                   000672 01-11
TARDIVE TOURETTE-SYNDROME IN AN AUTISTIC-PATIENT AFTER LONG-
TERM NEUROLEPTIC ADMINISTRATION.
                                                   000887 01-15
PHYSOSTIGMINE IN TOURETTE-SYNDROME: EVIDENCE FOR CHOLINERGIC
UNDERACTIVITY.
                                                   003286 03-10
THE TREATMENT AND ETIOLOGY OF TICS AND TOURETTE-SYNDROME.
                                                   003372 03-11
CLONIDINE IN TOURETTE-SYNDROME.
                                                   003420 03-13
FACT-SHEET: TOURETTE-SYNDROME.
                                                   004474 04-11
DO STIMULANTS PROVOKE, CAUSE, OR EXACERBATE TICS AND
TOURETTE-SYNDROME?
                                                   004485 04-11

TOXIC
THE ETIOLOGY OF TOXIC PERIPHERAL NEUROPATHIES: IN VITRO EFFECTS
OF ACRYLAMIDE AND 2,5 HEXANEDIONE ON BRAIN ENOLASE AND
OTHER GLYCOLYTIC ENZYMES.
                                                   000131 01-03
HEMODYNAMIC FAILURE INDUCED BY NARCOTIC AND TOXIC DOSES OF
12 CNS DEPRESSANTS IN INTACT AND PITHED RATS.
                                                   001855 02-05
TOXIC EFFECTS OF ALPHA AMINOADIPATE ON CULTURED CEREBELLAR
CELLS.
                                                   002729 03-03
TOXIC PSYCHOSIS FOLLOWING USE OF QUINACRINE.
                                                   003507 03-15
MEASUREMENTS OF NERVE CONDUCTION VELOCITY DURING DECREASING
TOXIC DIPHENYLHYDANTOIN LEVELS AND THE BEGINNING OF
CARBAMAZEPINE MEDICATION: A CLINICAL NEUROPHYSIOLOGICAL
REPORT.
                                                   004441 04-11

TOXICANTS
USING PROFILES OF SACCHARIN AND WATER DRINKING TO DETECT AND
DISCRIMINATE ACTIONS OF DRUGS AND TOXICANTS.
                                                   000503 01-04

TOXICITY
CIMETIDINE TOXICITY MANIFESTED AS PARANOIA AND
HALLUCINATIONS.
                                                   000829 01-15
RETINAL TOXICITY OF MAM-ACETATE IS DEVELOPMENTALLY SPECIFIC.
(UNPUBLISHED PAPER).
                                                   001212 02-03
ADRENERGIC NONSPECIFIC POTENTIATION OF YOHIMBINE TOXICITY IN
MICE BY ANTIDEPRESSANTS AND RELATED DRUGS AND
ANTIYOHIMBINE ACTION OF ANTIADRENERGIC AND SEROTONERGIC
DRUGS.
                                                   001330 02-03
TOXICITY OF OXYGEN IN IRON RICH AREAS OF RAT-BRAIN.
(UNPUBLISHED PAPER).
                                                   001498 02-03
PSYCHIATRIC MORBIDITY AND PHYSICAL TOXICITY ASSOCIATED WITH
ADJUVANT CHEMOTHERAPY AFTER MASTECTOMY.
                                                   002433 02-15
MULTIINSTITUTIONAL-STUDY ON THE TERATOGENICITY AND FETAL
TOXICITY OF ANTIEPILEPTIC-DRUGS: A REPORT OF A COLLABORATIVE-
STUDY GROUP IN JAPAN.
                                                   002442 02-15
A CASE OF REVERSIBLE PURE-WORD DEAFNESS DURING LITHIUM
TOXICITY.
                                                   003481 03-15
PHENYTOIN TOXICITY IN A BRAIN-DAMAGE ADOLESCENT: A CASE-
REPORT.
                                                   003512 03-15

HOW TO TREAT AND PREVENT DRUG TOXICITY.
003541 03-15
MICROPROPERTIES OF OPERANT-BEHAVIOR AS ASPECTS OF TOXICITY.
004666 04-15

TOXICOLOGIC
TOXICOLOGIC AND PHARMACOLOGIC-EFFECTS OF PHENCYCLIDINE-HCL IN THE DOG. (PH.D. DISSERTATION).
000519 01-05

TOXICOLOGICAL
TOXICOLOGICAL AND TERATOLOGICAL STUDIES OF CHLORODIMETHYLAMINOETHOXYDIBENZOTHIEPINE (ZOTEPINE), A NEW NEUROLEPTIC-DRUG.
000515 01-05
CONVERSION SCALES FOR COMMONLY REQUESTED SERUM CONCENTRATIONS OF DRUGS AND OTHER SUBSTANCES OF THERAPEUTIC AND TOXICOLOGICAL IMPORTANCE, AND OF HORMONES.
000759 01-13
A COMPARATIVE REVIEW OF THE PHARMACOLOGICAL AND TOXICOLOGICAL PROPERTIES OF DISULFIRAM AND CALCIUM-CARBIMIDE.
003522 03-15

TOXICOLOGY
TOXICOLOGY -- PHARMACOLOGY -- METABOLISM.
002252 02-13
THE BRAINSTEM AUDITORY EVOKED-RESPONSE AS A TOOL IN NEUROBEHAVIORAL TOXICOLOGY AND MEDICINE.
004277 04-05

TOXICOSIS
ELECTROPHYSIOLOGICAL-CHANGES AT A CENTRAL NORADRENERGIC SYNAPSE DURING THALLIUM TOXICOSIS.
001848 02-05

TOXIN
HYBRID PROTEINS USED TO STUDY THE MECHANISM OF TOXIN ENTRANCE INTO CELLS. (UNPUBLISHED PAPER).
001063 02-01
ANTI-THY-1-2 MONOCLONAL ANTIBODY LINKED TO RICIN IS A POTENT CELL TYPE SPECIFIC TOXIN. (UNPUBLISHED PAPER).
001064 02-01
EFFECT OF TENTANUS TOXIN ON TRANSMITTER RELEASE FROM THE SUBSTANTIA-NIGRA AND STRIATUM IN VITRO.
002691 03-03

TOXINS
ACTIONS OF TREMORGENIC FUNGAL TOXINS ON NEUROTRANSMITTER RELEASE.
002843 03-03
A CRITICAL EVALUATION OF THE USE OF TOXINS FROM DENDROASPIS VIRIDIS TO BLOCK NICOTINIC RESPONSES AT CENTRAL AND GANGLIONIC SYNAPSES.
002870 03-03

TRACE
PHARMACOLOGY OF PHENETHYLAMINE TRACE AMINES IN THE DOG -- DISCUSSION.
000469 01-04

TRACT
DRUG-INDUCED DISORDERS OF THE URINARY TRACT.
002393 02-15
COMPARISON OF THE POTENCIES OF CLEBOPRIDE AND OTHER SUBSTITUTED BENZAMIDE DRUGS ON ISOLATED GASTROINTESTINAL TRACT OF THE GUINEA-PIG AND RAT.
003928 04-03

TRAINING
EXTINCTION AND DOPAMINE-RECEPTOR BLOCKADE AFTER INTERMITTENT REINFORCEMENT TRAINING: FAILURE TO OBSERVE FUNCTIONAL EQUIVALENCE.
000490 01-04
THE EFFECT OF ASSERTIVENESS TRAINING, PROVERA AND SEX OF THERAPIST IN THE TREATMENT OF GENITAL EXHIBITIONISM.
000697 01-11
PARAPROFESSIONAL AND PROFESSIONAL TEAMWORK AND TRAINING IN MANAGING PCP AND OTHER DRUG-ABUSE PROBLEMS.
000924 01-17
DEPENDENCE OF THE AVFAIL EFFECT ON THE SEQUENCE OF TRAINING OPERATIONS.
001086 02-02
BETA ENDORPHIN CAUSES RETROGRADE AMNESIA AND IS RELEASED FROM THE RAT-BRAIN BY VARIOUS FORMS OF TRAINING AND STIMULATION.
001664 02-04
DISCUSSION OF WHO ACTIVITY IN BIOLOGICAL-PSYCHIATRY WITH SPECIAL REFERENCE TO TRAINING.
002520 02-17
LECITHIN AND MEMORY TRAINING IN ALZHEIMERS-DISEASE. (PH.D. DISSERTATION).
003299 03-11
FACTORS REGULATING DRUG CUE SENSITIVITY: LIMITS OF DISCRIMINABILITY AND THE ROLE OF A PROGRESSIVELY DECREASING TRAINING DOSE IN FENTANYL SALINE DISCRIMINATION.
004088 04-04

CLINICAL STRATEGIES FOR ANTIPSYCHOTIC-DRUG TREATMENT, TARDIVE-DYSKINESIA, AND THE TRAINING OF RESEARCH PSYCHIATRISTS.
004603 04-15

TRAIT
PERSONALITY TRAIT AND ANTIANXIETY-DRUG EFFECTS ON PSYCHOMOTOR PERFORMANCE.
002336 02-14

TRANQUILIZER
USE OF THE NEW TRANQUILIZER PHENAZEPAM IN PSYCHIATRIC-PRACTICE.
000578 01-09
THE TRANQUILIZER DEMETRIN (PRAZEPAM).
003331 03-11
A COMPARATIVE CLINICAL-TRIAL WITH THE TRANQUILIZER TRAZODONE AND THE TRICYCLIC-ANTIDEPRESSANT CLOMIPRAMINE.
004380 04-09

TRANQUILIZERS
STUDIES ON THE COMPREHENSIVE MEDICAL TREATMENT OF PEPTIC-ULCERS (3) -- UTILIZATION OF TRANQUILIZERS IN THE TREATMENT OF GASTRIC-ULCERS.
000653 01-10
INFLUENCE OF BENZODIAZEPINE TRANQUILIZERS ON AMPHETAMINE-INDUCED LOCOMOTOR-STIMULATION IN MICE.
001767 02-04
INFLUENCE OF BENZODIAZEPINE TRANQUILIZERS ON SCOPOLAMINE-INDUCED LOCOMOTOR-STIMULATION IN MICE.
001768 02-04
THE ACTION OF BENZODIAZEPINES ON THE LIMBIC-SYSTEM COMPARED TO OTHER TRANQUILIZERS.
002731 03-03
DEPENDENCE ON TRANQUILIZERS (AN OVERVIEW WITH (CASE-STUDIES).
003580 03-17

TRANQUILIZING
THE TRANQUILIZING OF AMERICA.
003602 03-17
THE PHARMACOLOGICAL CHARACTERISTICS OF THE TRANQUILIZING EFFECT OF HYDIPHEN.
004261 04-04

TRANQUILIZING-DRUGS
METHODS AND METHODOLOGICAL-CONSIDERATIONS IN MEASURING ANTIANXIETY-EFFECTS OF TRANQUILIZING-DRUGS.
002537 02-17

TRANS-ISOMERS
THE PHOTOCHEMICAL-STABILITY OF CIS-ISOMERS AND TRANS-ISOMERS OF TRICYCLIC NEUROLEPTIC-DRUGS.
001872 02-06
PLASMA LEVELS OF THE CIS-ISOMERS AND TRANS-ISOMERS OF DOXEPIN AND DESMETHYLDOXEPIN AFTER ADMINISTRATION OF DOXEPIN TO PATIENTS.
004355 04-09

TRANSCALLOSAL
THE EFFECT OF NOOTROPIL ON THE TRANSCALLOSAL AND PRIMARY EVOKED-RESPONSES OF THE CAT CEREBRAL-CORTEX.
003780 04-03

TRANSCULTURAL
LITHIUM TREATMENT IN AFFECTIVE-DISORDERS FROM VIEWPOINT OF TRANSCULTURAL PSYCHOPHARMACOLOGY: THERAPEUTIC PLASMA LEVEL.
000636 01-09
TRANSCULTURAL PHARMACOKINETIC STUDY ON LI CONCENTRATION IN PLASMA AND SALIVA.
000769 01-13

TRANSDUCER
ELECTROLYTIC MICROINFUSION TRANSDUCER SYSTEM: AN ALTERNATIVE METHOD OF INTRACRANIAL DRUG APPLICATION.
001861 02-06

TRANSDUCTION
BIOCHEMICAL-MECHANISM OF SIGNAL TRANSDUCTION ACROSS BIOMEMBRANES. (UNPUBLISHED PAPER).
001026 02-01
PHOSPHOLIPID METHYLATION: A BIOCHEMICAL-EVENT OF SIGNAL TRANSDUCTION. (UNPUBLISHED PAPER).
001279 02-03

TRANSECTION
DENERVATION SUPERSENSITIVITY TO 5 HYDROXYTRYPTOPHAN IN RATS FOLLOWING SPINAL TRANSECTION AND 5,7 DIHYDROXYTRYPTAMINE INJECTION.
003722 04-03
DOPAMINE-ACTIVATED ADENYLATE-CYCLASE OF SPINAL-CORD: SUPERSENSITIVITY FOLLOWING TRANSECTION OF THE CORD.
003800 04-03

TRANSFER
TRANSFER OF LORAZEPAM AND ITS CONJUGATE ACROSS THE HUMAN PLACENTA.
000774 01-13
ENHANCED TRANSFER OF EXPERIMENTAL ALLERGIC-ENCEPHALOMYELITIS WITH STRAIN-13 GUINEA-PIG LYMPH-NODE CELLS: REQUIREMENT FOR

CULTURE WITH SPECIFIC ANTIGEN AND ALLOGENIC PERITONEAL EXUDATE CELLS. (UNPUBLISHED PAPER).
001201 02-03
ENHANCED TRANSFER OF EXPERIMENTAL ALLERGIC-ENCEPHALOMYELITIS WITH LEWIS-RAT LYMPH-NODE CELLS. (UNPUBLISHED PAPER).
001434 02-03
THE EFFECTS OF PIMOZIDE DURING PAIRING ON THE TRANSFER OF CLASSICAL CONDITIONING TO AN OPERANT DISCRIMINATION.
002956 03-04
EXTENDED SCHEDULE TRANSFER OF ETHANOL DISCRIMINATION.
003087 03-04
TRANSFER FROM MULTIPLE TO SINGLE ANTIEPILEPTIC DRUG-THERAPY.
003316 03-11
NMR SPECTRAL STUDY OF PROTON TRANSFER IN AMITRIPTYLINE-HYDROCHLORIDE CHLORDIAZEPOXIDE-HYDROCHLORIDE COMBINATIONS IN DIPOLAR APROTIC SOLVENTS.
003654 04-01

TRANSFORMATION
THE EFFECT OF LITHIUM ON THE INCORPORATION OF 3H GLUCOSAMINE INTO GLYCOPEPTIDES AND THE TRANSFORMATION OF 3H GLUCOSAMINE INTO SIALIC-ACID IN RAT-BRAIN.
001209 02-03

TRANSIENT
TRANSIENT ABOLITION OF GENERALIZED PHOTOSENSITIVE EPILEPTIC-DISCHARGE IN HUMANS BY APOMORPHINE, A DOPAMINE-RECEPTOR AGONIST.
000714 01-11
TRANSIENT HYPERKINESIA AFTER A SINGLE INTRAVENOUS PERFUSION OF DIPHENYLHYDANTOIN: REPORT OF A CASE ASSOCIATED WITH NONTOXIC PLASMA LEVELS OF DIPHENYLHYDANTOIN.
004638 04-15

TRANSIENT-EFFECT
TRANSIENT-EFFECT OF L TRYPTOPHAN IN PROGRESSIVE MYOCLONUS EPILEPSY WITHOUT LAFORA-BODIES: CLINICAL-STUDY AND ELECTROPHYSIOLOGICAL-STUDY.
000694 01-11

TRANSIENT-SYNDROMES
PSYCHOPATHOMETRIC DOUBLE-BLIND COURSE STUDY WITH NICERGOLINE VERSUS PLACEBO IN GERIATRIC-PATIENTS WITH TRANSIENT-SYNDROMES.
000665 01-11

TRANSLATION
CELL-FREE TRANSLATION OF FREE AND MEMBRANE-BOUND POLYSOMES AND POLYADENYLATED MRNA FROM RABBIT BRAIN FOLLOWING ADMINISTRATION OF D LYSERGIC-ACID-DIETHYLAMIDE IN VIVO.
003832 04-03

TRANSMEMBRANE
PHOSPHOLIPID METHYLATION AND TRANSMEMBRANE SIGNALLING. (UNPUBLISHED PAPER).
001001 02-01
ACUTE AND CHRONIC EFFECTS OF MORPHINE ON TRANSMEMBRANE POTENTIAL AND ON SHORT-CIRCUIT CURRENT IN ISOLATED TOAD SKIN: APPARENT MORPHINE-DEPENDENCE.
001176 02-03

TRANSMETHYLATION
DUAL-EFFECTS OF MESCALINE: THE TRANSMETHYLATION HYPOTHESIS REVISITED.
001584 02-04
ABNORMAL TRANSMETHYLATION REACTION DURING THE METABOLISM OF DOPAMINE, TRYPTAMINE, AND SEROTONIN, AND SCHIZOPHRENIC-SYMPTOMS: A CRITICAL REVIEW.
003404 03-13

TRANSMISSION
REDUCTION OF GAMMA AMINOBUTYRIC-ACID-MEDIATED (GABA) TRANSMISSION BY A CONVULSANT BENZODIAZEPINE.
000015 01-02
EFFECT OF MIANSERIN ON NORADRENERGIC TRANSMISSION IN THE RAT ANOCOCCYGEUS-MUSCLE.
000075 01-03
ADENINE-NUCLEOTIDES AND SYNAPTIC TRANSMISSION IN THE IN VITRO RAT HIPPOCAMPUS.
000080 01-03
THE EFFECTS OF TWO ANALOGS OF DOPAMINE ON GANGLIONIC TRANSMISSION IN THE SYMPATHETIC-NERVOUS-SYSTEM.
000162 01-03
ENKEPHALINS PRESYNAPTICALLY INHIBIT CHOLINERGIC TRANSMISSION IN SYMPATHETIC GANGLIA.
000167 01-03
INTERACTION OF DIAZEPAM WITH SYNAPTIC TRANSMISSION IN THE IN VITRO RAT HIPPOCAMPUS.
000178 01-03
BEHAVIORAL-EFFECTS AND ELECTROCORTICAL-EFFECTS AFTER INTRASTRIATAL CEFAZOLIN IN RATS ARE ANTAGONIZED BY DRUGS ENHANCING GABAERGIC TRANSMISSION.
000443 01-04
REGULATION OF CHOLINERGIC TRANSMISSION IN ADRENAL-MEDULLA. (UNPUBLISHED PAPER).
001182 02-03
AN EXAMINATION OF FACTORS INFLUENCING ADRENERGIC TRANSMISSION IN THE PITHED RAT, WITH SPECIAL REFERENCE TO

NORADRENALINE UPTAKE MECHANISMS AND POSTJUNCTIONAL ALPHA-ADRENOCEPTORS.
001196 02-03
ROLE OF CALMODULIN IN DOPAMINERGIC TRANSMISSION. (UNPUBLISHED PAPER).
001270 02-03
INHIBITORY ACTION OF ADENOSINE ON SYNAPTIC TRANSMISSION IN THE HIPPOCAMPUS OF THE GUINEA-PIG IN VITRO.
001401 02-03
ENHANCED BEHAVIOURAL-EFFECTS, ELECTROCORTICAL-EFFECTS AND HYPERTHERMIC-EFFECTS OF SEROTONIN-LIKE AGENTS AFTER IMPAIRMENT OF SEROTONIN TRANSMISSION IN FOWL BRAIN.
001733 02-04
DOPAMINE DEPLETION SLOWS RETINAL TRANSMISSION.
002708 03-03
METHYSERGIDE AND SUPRASPINAL INHIBITION OF THE SPINAL TRANSMISSION OF NOCICEPTIVE INFORMATION IN THE ANESTHETIZED CAT.
002740 03-03
NONSEROTONERGIC DEPRESSION OF SPINAL MONOSYNAPTIC REFLEX TRANSMISSION BY 5 HYDROXYTRYPTOPHAN.
002745 03-03
EVIDENCE THAT THE OPIATE-RECEPTORS OF THE SUBSTANTIA-GELATINOSA CONTRIBUTE TO THE DEPRESSION, BY INTRAVENOUS MORPHINE, OF THE SPINAL TRANSMISSION OF IMPULSES IN UNMYELINATED PRIMARY AFFERENTS.
002767 03-03
ANTIANXIETY-AGENTS AND SYNAPTIC TRANSMISSION IN THE BRAIN: ELECTROPHYSIOLOGICAL-STUDIES. (PH.D. DISSERTATION).
002840 03-03
CHANGES IN NORADRENERGIC TRANSMISSION ALTER THE CONCENTRATION OF CYTOPLASMIC PROGESTIN-RECEPTORS IN HYPOTHALAMUS.
002842 03-03
CALMODULIN: ITS ROLE IN SYNAPTIC TRANSMISSION.
003162 03-07
THE EFFECTS OF ALPHA AND BETA NEUROTOXINS FROM THE VENOMS OF VARIOUS SNAKES ON TRANSMISSION IN AUTONOMIC GANGLIA.
003750 04-03
INFLUENCE OF THE DOPAMINERGIC AGONISTS BROMOCRIPTINE, PIRIBEDIL AND NOMIFENSINE ON THE SYMPATHETIC NEURAL TRANSMISSION IN THE NICTITATING MEMBRANE OF THE CAT.
003822 04-03
PRESYNAPTIC MODULATION OF SYNAPTIC TRANSMISSION IN HELIX-POMATIA: THE EFFECTS OF SEROTONIN AND DOPAMINE ANTAGONISTS.
003869 04-03
DIFFERENTIAL-EFFECTS OF PENTOBARBITAL AND ETHER ON THE SYNAPTIC TRANSMISSION OF THE HIPPOCAMPAL-CA1-REGION IN THE RAT.
003903 04-03
ELECTROPHYSIOLOGICAL EVIDENCE FOR PRESYNAPTIC ACTIONS OF PHENCYCLIDINE ON NORADRENERGIC TRANSMISSION IN RAT CEREBELLUM.
003926 04-03

TRANSMITTER
CATECHOLAMINE TRANSMITTER SYSTEMS.
000580 01-09
EVIDENCE SUGGESTING A TRANSMITTER OR NEUROMODULATORY ROLE FOR SUBSTANCE-P AT THE FIRST SYNAPSE OF THE BARORECEPTOR REFLEX.
001264 02-03
DIRECT EVIDENCE AGAINST ACETYLCHOLINE AS THE DILATOR TRANSMITTER IN THE CAT CEREBRAL-ARTERY.
001336 02-03
EFFECT OF TENTANUS TOXIN ON TRANSMITTER RELEASE FROM THE SUBSTANTIA-NIGRA AND STRIATUM IN VITRO.
002691 03-03
ACTIONS OF BETA BUNGAROTOXIN ON AMINO-ACID TRANSMITTER RELEASE.
002897 03-03
INFUSIONS INTO THE OCULOMOTOR NUCLEUS OR NERVE: A METHOD OF ESTIMATING THE DOSAGE AT WHICH TRANSMITTER ANTAGONISTS INFUSED INTRACRANIALLY PRODUCE NONSPECIFIC BLOCKING OF NEURAL ACTIVITY.
003134 03-06

TRANSMITTERS
. EXCITATORY AMINO-ACID TRANSMITTERS.
003648 03-17
DRUGS, TRANSMITTERS AND HORMONES, AND MATING-BEHAVIOR.
004721 04-17

TRANSPLANTED
SEIZURES AND RELATED EPILEPTIFORM ACTIVITY IN HIPPOCAMPUS TRANSPLANTED TO THE ANTERIOR-CHAMBER OF THE EYE: MODULATION BY CHOLINERGIC AND ADRENERGIC INPUT.
000095 01-03

Subject Index

TRANSPLANTS
REINNERVATION OF THE DENERVATED STRIATUM BY SUBSTANTIA-NIGRA TRANSPLANTS: FUNCTIONAL CONSEQUENCES AS REVEALED BY PHARMACOLOGICAL AND SENSORIMOTOR TESTING.
000347 01-04

TRANSPORT
BIOSYNTHESIS, AXONAL TRANSPORT AND RELEASE OF POSTERIOR PITUITARY-HORMONES. (UNPUBLISHED PAPER).
001148 02-03
CERTAIN MECHANISMS OF THE ACTION OF PSYCHOTROPIC-DRUGS ON TRANSPORT ATPASES.
001331 02-03
NEURONAL TRANSPORT OF 5 HYDROXYTRYPTAMINE.
001451 02-03
DISCUSSION OF CLINICAL-PAPERS ON LITHIUM TRANSPORT IN AFFECTIVE-DISORDERS.
001987 02-09
LITHIUM TRANSPORT STUDIES IN AFFECTIVE-DISORDERS.
002024 02-09
ABNORMALITIES OF LITHIUM TRANSPORT IN PATIENTS WITH AFFECTIVE-DISORDERS.
002269 02-13
INTERACTIONS OF NARCOTICS WITH SYNAPTOSOMAL CALCIUM TRANSPORT.
002712 03-03
TRANSPORT OF NEUTRAL AMINO-ACIDS AT THE BLOOD-BRAIN-BARRIER.
002764 03-03
KINETIC DATA ON THE INHIBITION OF HIGH-AFFINITY CHOLINE TRANSPORT INTO RAT-FOREBRAIN SYNAPTOSOMES BY CHOLINE-LIKE COMPOUNDS AND NITROGEN-MUSTARD ANALOGUES.
002879 03-03
PAPAIN-DERIVED FRAGMENT IIC TETANUS-TOXIN: ITS BINDING TO ISOLATED SYNAPTIC MEMBRANES AND RETROGRADE AXONAL TRANSPORT.
003734 04-03
STUDIES ON AXONAL TRANSPORT IN DOPAMINERGIC NEURONS: EFFECT OF NEUROPHARMACOLOGIC LESIONS.
003858 04-03
THE EFFECT OF CHRONIC NICOTINE AND WITHDRAWAL ON INTRAAXONAL TRANSPORT OF ACETYLCHOLINE AND RELATED ENZYMES IN SCIATIC-NERVE OF THE RAT.
003897 04-03
RESERPINE EFFECT ON THE AXONAL TRANSPORT OF DOPAMINE-BETA-HYDROXYLASE AND TYROSINE-HYDROXYLASE IN RAT-BRAIN.
003904 04-03
STUDIES ON GAMMA AMINOBUTYRIC-ACID TRANSPORT IN COBALT EXPERIMENTAL EPILEPSY IN THE RAT.
003990 04-03
PROPERTIES OF THE OPTICAL-ISOMERS AND METABOLITES OF KETAMINE ON THE HIGH-AFFINITY TRANSPORT AND CATABOLISM OF MONOAMINES.
004009 04-03
THE EFFECT OF NORADRENALINE ON NA-K TRANSPORT IN RAT-CEREBRAL-CORTICAL SLICES.
004056 04-03
EFFECTS OF A SINGLE-THERAPEUTIC-DOSE OF GLYCEROL ON CEREBRAL METABOLISM IN THE BRAINS OF YOUNG MICE: POSSIBLE INCREASE IN BRAIN GLUCOSE TRANSPORT AND GLUCOSE UTILIZATION.
004281 04-05
INTERACTION OF CHLORPROMAZINE WITH THE TRANSPORT SYSTEM OF GLUCOSE IN HUMAN ERYTHROCYTES.
004529 04-13

TRANSSYNAPTIC
INTERACTIONS OF NEUROPEPTIDES WITH CHOLINERGIC SEPTOHIPPOCAMPAL PATHWAY: INDICATION FOR A POSSIBLE TRANSSYNAPTIC REGULATION. (UNPUBLISHED PAPER).
001062 02-01

TRANXENE
EVALUATION OF CLORAZEPATE (TRANXENE) AS AN ANTICONVULSANT — A PILOT-STUDY.
000728 01-11

TRANXILIUM
PHARMACOLOGICAL PECULIARITIES OF A BENZODIAZEPINE/ATARACTIC-DRUG AND ITS THERAPEUTIC RELEVANCE: THE SPECIAL STATUS OF CLORAZEPATE-DIPOTASSIUM (TRANXILIUM).
004527 04-13

TRANYLCYPROMINE
TRANYLCYPROMINE STEREOISOMERS, MONOAMINERGIC NEUROTRANSMISSION AND BEHAVIOR. A MINIREVIEW.
000016 01-02
THE NEW ANTIDEPRESSANT PIRLINDOLE: A COMPARISON WITH IMIPRAMINE AND TRANYLCYPROMINE.
001360 02-03
THE BEHAVIOR OF RATS IN THE OPEN-FIELD WITHOUT STRESS, UNDER ACUTE AND PERSISTING INFLUENCE OF IMIPRAMINE AND TRANYLCYPROMINE AS WELL AS ON THE INDIVIDUAL REACTION TYPE (EMOTIVE AND NONEMOTIVE).
001624 02-04
EFFECT OF CITALOPRAM (LU-10-171) ON TRANYLCYPROMINE AND TRYPTOPHAN-INDUCED WET-DOG-SHAKES IN RATS.
001682 02-04

A CASE OF TRIGEMINAL-NEURALGIA TREATED WITH LITHIUM-CARBONATE.
000690 01-11

SOCIAL AND CLINICAL SIGNIFICANCE OF DETERMINING THE BARBITURATE LEVEL IN THE BLOOD SERUM OF PATIENTS TREATED WITH ANTIEPILEPTIC-DRUGS.
000695 01-11

RENAL FUNCTION IN LITHIUM AND NONLITHIUM TREATED PATIENTS WITH AFFECTIVE-DISORDERS.
000837 01-15

TARDIVE-DYSKINESIA AND OTHER MOVEMENT-DISORDERS IN CHILDREN TREATED WITH PSYCHOTROPIC-DRUGS.
000849 01-15

DYSKINETIC AND NEUROLOGICAL-COMPLICATIONS IN CHILDREN TREATED WITH PSYCHOTROPIC-MEDICATIONS.
000880 01-15

RESPONSIVENESS TO VASOACTIVE-AGENTS OF CEREBRAL-ARTERIES AND MESENTERIC-ARTERIES ISOLATED FROM CONTROL AND RESERPINE TREATED DOGS.
001273 02-03

SYNCHRONIZATION OF EEG ACTIVITY OF MALE RHESUS-MONKEYS MACACA-MULATTA TREATED WITH OVOCYCLIN.
001312 02-03

DOWN REGULATION OF DIHYDROALPRENOLOL AND IMIPRAMINE BINDING-SITES IN BRAIN OF RATS REPEATEDLY TREATED WITH IMIPRAMINE.
001317 02-03

HEROIN, BUT NOT LEVORPHANOL, PRODUCES EXPLOSIVE MOTOR-BEHAVIOR IN NALOXONE TREATED RATS.
001579 02-04

THE EFFECTS OF D LYSERGIC-ACID-DIETHYLAMIDE (LSD), 2,5 DIMETHOXY-4-METHYLAMPHETAMINE (DOM) AND D-AMPHETAMINE ON OPERANT-RESPONDING IN CONTROL AND 6 HYDROXYDOPAMINE TREATED RATS.
001595 02-04

ELECTROMYOGRAPHIC-ASSESSMENT OF SPINAL REFLEXES IN EXPERIMENTALLY DEPRESSED DOGS TREATED WITH ANTIDEPRESSANTS.
001620 02-04

CHANGES OF PHYSICAL MORPHINE-DEPENDENCE IN RATS CHRONICALLY TREATED WITH DRUGS ACTING ON BRAIN 5 HYDROXYTRYPTAMINE.
001764 02-04

BASAL AND STIMULATED LEVELS OF PROLACTIN, TSH AND LH IN SERUM OF CHRONIC SCHIZOPHRENIC-PATIENTS, LONG-TERM TREATED WITH NEUROLEPTICS.
001935 02-08

BASAL AND STIMULATED LEVELS OF PROLACTIN, TSH, AND LH IN SERUM OF CHRONIC SCHIZOPHRENIC-PATIENTS LONG-TERM TREATED WITH NEUROLEPTICS; RELATIONS TO PSYCHOPATHOLOGY.
001936 02-08

RELATIONSHIPS AMONG BIOCHEMICAL-VARIABLES, CLINICAL-VARIABLES, AND PHARMACOKINETIC-VARIABLES IN NEUROLEPTIC TREATED SCHIZOPHRENIC-PATIENTS.
001946 02-08

DRUG-INDUCED ARTERIAL HYPOTENSION IN PSYCHIATRIC-PATIENTS TREATED WITH DIHYDROERGOTAMINE.
001950 02-08

ACTH4-10 AND MEMORY IN ECT TREATED AND UNTREATED PATIENTS. I. EFFECT ON CONSOLIDATION.
001982 02-09

ACTH4-10 AND MEMORY IN ECT TREATED PATIENTS AND UNTREATED CONTROLS. II. EFFECT ON RETRIEVAL.
001983 02-09

MOTOR-LEARNING ABILITIES IN SUBJECTS TREATED WITH LITHIUM-SALTS AND TRICYCLIC-ANTIDEPRESSANTS.
002058 02-09

TRICHOTILLOMANIA TREATED WITH AMITRIPTYLINE.
002083 02-10

EEG CHANGES IN CHILDREN WITH TREATED PHENYLKETONURIA AFTER PHENYLALANINE LOAD.
002115 02-11

THE RELATIONSHIP OF ALPHA AND DELTA EEG FREQUENCIES TO PAIN AND MOOD IN FIBROSITIS-PATIENTS TREATED WITH CHLORPROMAZINE AND L TRYPTOPHAN.
002152 02-11

STUDY OF PROLACTIN VARIATIONS IN PSYCHIATRIC-PATIENTS TREATED WITH FLUPHENAZINE-DECANOATE.
002226 02-13

SALIVARY IMMUNOGLOBULIN CONCENTRATIONS IN PATIENTS WITH EPILEPSY TREATED WITH CARBAMAZEPINE.
002234 02-13

PLASMA HDL CHOLESTEROL AND GROWTH-HORMONE IN EPILEPTICS TREATED WITH ANTICONVULSANTS.
002260 02-13

BROMOCRIPTINE IN PARKINSONS-DISEASE: REPORT ON 106 PATIENTS TREATED FOR UP TO 5 YEARS.
002342 02-14

EDEMAS AND MYOCLONIES IN A PATIENT WITH PARKINSONS-DISEASE TREATED BY AMANTADINE: PROBLEM WITH ASSOCIATED MEDICATIONS.
002389 02-15

PLASMA FLUPHENAZINE LEVELS BY RADIOIMMUNOASSAY IN SCHIZOPHRENIC-PATIENTS TREATED WITH DEPOT INJECTIONS OF FLUPHENAZINE-DECANOATE.
002510 02-16

SUPPRESSION OF AMPHETAMINE-INDUCED EEG AROUSAL IN THE HIPPOCAMPUS OF HALOPERIDOL TREATED RABBITS.
002683 03-03

EFFECT OF MAZINDOL ON BRAIN DOPAMINE TURNOVER IN SPIPERONE TREATED RATS.
002726 03-03

MULTIDIMENSIONAL ANALYSES OF BEHAVIOR IN MICE TREATED WITH ALPHA ENDORPHIN.
003020 03-04

COPULATORY-BEHAVIOR AND SEXUAL-REFLEXES OF MALE RATS TREATED WITH NALOXONE.
003077 03-04

INTERACTIONS OF DIAZEPAM AND COCAINE IN THE MORPHINE TREATED RAT. (PH.D. DISSERTATION).
003115 03-04

DEPRESSED-OUTPATIENTS TREATED WITH COGNITIVE-THERAPY OR PHARMACOTHERAPY: A ONE-YEAR FOLLOWUP.
003235 03-09

THE TREATMENT OF DEPRESSION USING CLOMIPRAMINE IN GENERAL-MEDICAL-PRACTICE: 48 CASES TREATED ON AN OUTPATIENT BASIS.
003268 03-09

ADULT-ONSET STUTTERING TREATED WITH ANTICONVULSANTS.
003290 03-11

ON A CASE OF MEMORY-DISTURBANCES TREATED WITH VASOPRESSIN.
003301 03-11

COMPARISON OF STANDARD AND HOLTOR-MONITORED EKGS IN A PATIENT TREATED WITH SEVERAL ANTIDEPRESSANTS.
003304 03-11

THE EFFECT OF AMANTADINE ON PROLACTIN LEVELS AND GALACTORRHEA ON NEUROLEPTIC TREATED PATIENTS.
003373 03-11

RESPIRATORY-DISEASE AND NASAL IMMUNOGLOBULIN CONCENTRATIONS IN PHENYTOIN TREATED EPILEPTIC-PATIENTS.
003486 03-15

PREDICTORS OF ADOLESCENT HEIGHT AND WEIGHT IN HYPERKINETIC-BOYS TREATED WITH METHYLPHENIDATE.
003509 03-15

EFFECTS OF PENTAZOCINE AND NALORPHINE ON MOTILITY IN CHRONICALLY MORPHINE TREATED RATS: A POTENTIAL SUBSTITUTION TEST TO DETECT THE NARCOTIC CHARACTER OF A DRUG.
003555 03-16

ALTERATIONS OF ACETYLCHOLINE AND CHOLINE METABOLISM IN MAMMALIAN PREPARATIONS TREATED WITH BETA BUNGAROTOXIN.
003820 04-03

DEVELOPMENTAL-CHANGE IN REARING RESPONSE TO ATROPINE IN RATS TREATED WITH 6 HYDROXYDOPA.
004191 04-04

CATECHOLAMINE SEROTONIN INTERACTION EFFECTS ON ACTIVITY IN RATS NEONATALLY TREATED WITH 6 HYDROXYDOPAMINE.
004194 04-04

NEUROTRANSMITTER-RECEPTORS IN BRAIN REGIONS OF ACRYLAMIDE TREATED RATS. I: EFFECTS OF A SINGLE EXPOSURE TO ACRYLAMIDE.
004264 04-05

NEUROTRANSMITTER-RECEPTORS IN BRAIN REGIONS OF ACRYLAMIDE TREATED RATS. II: EFFECTS OF EXTENDED EXPOSURE TO ACRYLAMIDE.
004265 04-05

A FOLLOWUP STUDY OF SCHIZOPHRENIC-OUTPATIENTS TREATED WITH DEPOT NEUROLEPTICS.
004342 04-08

NORMAL PLASMA DOPAMINE-BETA-HYDROXYLASE IN NONTREATED AND TREATED PARKINSON-PATIENTS.
004471 04-11

PECULIARITIES OF THE CEREBRAL PATHOMORPHOLOGY OF PATIENTS WITH SCHIZOPHRENIA TREATED WITH PSYCHOTROPIC-DRUGS (PHARMACOLOGICAL PATHOMORPHOSIS).
004528 04-13

ELECTROENCEPHALOGRAPHIC CHANGE IN PARKINSONIAN-PATIENTS TREATED WITH LEVODOPA CARBIDOPA.
004557 04-13

CONCENTRATIONS OF CHLORPROMAZINE AND TWO OF ITS ACTIVE METABOLITES IN PLASMA AND CEREBROSPINAL-FLUID OF PSYCHOTIC-PATIENTS TREATED WITH FIXED DRUG DOSES.
004559 04-13

TREATING
CHOICE OF TACTICS IN TREATING ALCOHOLIC-DELIRIUM.
000688 01-11

CORONARY-HEART-DISEASE: TREATING THE ANXIETY COMPONENT.
002088 02-10

FAMILY-TREE GIVES CLUES TO TREATING PSYCHOSES.
002363 02-13

PSYCHOPHARMACEUTICALS FOR TREATING PAIN.
002548 02-17

THE USE OF LITHIUM-CARBONATE FOR TREATING KUGELBERG-WELANDER SPINAL AMYOTROPHY PATIENTS.
003326 03-11

EFFICACY OF LITHIUM IN TREATING MOOD-DISORDER OCCURRING AFTER BRAINSTEM INJURY.
003354 03-11
ACTION ON THE EMOTIONALLY-REINFORCED BRAIN SYSTEM AS A MEANS OF TREATING ALCOHOLISM AND DRUG ADDICTION PATHOGENETICALLY.
003641 03-17
PROBLEMS OF TREATING DEFORMING MYODYSTONIA WITH L-DOPA, AND PREDICTION OF ITS THERAPEUTIC EFFECT.
004536 04-13
PRESENT ATTEMPTS AT TREATING TARDIVE-DYSKINESIA.
004629 04-15

TREATMENT
THE SENSITIVITY OF THE RAT CORTICOSTERONE RESPONSE TO ENVIRONMENTAL MANIPULATIONS AND TO CHRONIC CHLORDIAZEPOXIDE TREATMENT.
000092 01-03
HYPOPHYSECTOMY PREVENTS THE STRIATAL DOPAMINE-RECEPTOR SUPERSENSITIVITY PRODUCED BY CHRONIC HALOPERIDOL TREATMENT.
000132 01-03
MONOAMINE-OXIDASE-INHIBITION AND BRAIN-AMINE METABOLISM AFTER ORAL TREATMENT WITH TOLOXATONE IN THE RAT.
000156 01-03
EFFECTS OF PERINATAL THYROXINE AND/OR CORTICOSTERONE TREATMENT ON THE ONTOGENESIS OF HYPOTHALAMIC AND MESENCEPHALIC NOREPINEPHRINE AND DOPAMINE CONTENT.
000180 01-03
STRIATAL DOPAMINERGIC ACTIVITY DURING WITHDRAWAL FROM CHRONIC NEUROLEPTIC TREATMENT IN RATS.
000203 01-03
LONG-TERM ANTIDEPRESSANT TREATMENT DECREASES SPIROPERIDOL-LABELED SEROTONIN-RECEPTOR BINDING.
000230 01-03
LONG-TERM ANTIDEPRESSANT TREATMENT: ALTERATIONS IN CEREBRAL CAPILLARY PERMEABILITY.
000239 01-03
REDUCTION OF VOLUNTARY MORPHINE CONSUMPTION FOLLOWING TREATMENT WITH ZIMELIDINE.
000253 01-03
FUNCTIONAL AND STRUCTURAL CONSEQUENCES OF LONG-TERM DIETARY L-DOPA TREATMENT IN MICE.
000257 01-03
FUNCTIONAL EVIDENCE FOR SUBSENSITIVITY OF NORADRENERGIC-ALPHA2-RECEPTORS AFTER CHRONIC DESIPRAMINE TREATMENT.
000283 01-03
ALTERATION OF PHARMACOKINETIC PARAMETERS FOR PENTOBARBITAL BY ISCHEMIC STROKE AND REVERSION TO NORMAL BY DEXAMETHASONE TREATMENT.
000321 01-03
THE INTERACTION OF ANTICHOLINESTERASES AND DIAZEPAM IN THE TREATMENT OF ANTICHOLINERGIC-SYNDROME IN DOGS.
000389 01-04
OPEN-FIELD PERFORMANCE OF RATS AFTER ENDOTOXIN TREATMENT.
000473 01-04
MORPHINE TREATMENT AT DIFFERENT INFANT AGES: INFLUENCE ON LATER MORPHINE EFFECTS IN RATS. (PH.D. DISSERTATION).
000511 01-05
OUR EXPERIENCE WITH PIRACETAM (NOOTROPIL-UCB) TREATMENT IN CHILDREN FROM HIGH-RISK PREGNANCIES WITH SUBSEQUENT MINIMAL-BRAIN-DYSFUNCTION.
000544 01-07
ANTIDEPRESSANT TREATMENT BY INTRAVENOUS ADMINISTRATION COMPARED TO PERORAL ADMINISTRATION: A DOUBLE-BLIND STUDY OF QUINUPRAMINE.
000552 01-08
NEUROLEPTIC AND THYMOLEPTIC TREATMENT OF PSYCHOTIC-OUTPATIENTS.
000556 01-08
THE PLACE OF LONG-ACTING NEUROLEPTICS IN THE TREATMENT OF SCHIZOPHRENIA.
000563 01-08
PREDICTING OUTCOME OF ANTIPSYCHOTIC-DRUG TREATMENT FROM EARLY-RESPONSE.
000565 01-08
HOSPITAL AND OUTPATIENT CARE FOR PSYCHOTIC-PATIENTS DURING THE LAST THREE DECADES: SUBSEQUENT HOSPITAL AND OUTPATIENT TREATMENT OF PSYCHOTIC-PATIENTS HOSPITALIZED FOR THE FIRST TIME IN 1949-50, 1959-60 OR 1969-70.
000571 01-08
DOUBLE-BLIND COMPARISON OF HALOPERIDOL AND THIOTHIXENE WITH AFTERCARE TREATMENT EVALUATION IN PSYCHIATRIC-OUTPATIENTS WITH SCHIZOPHRENIA.
000574 01-08
LITHIUM TREATMENT IN POSTPSYCHOTIC DEPRESSION.
000575 01-08
ADVANTAGE OF PHARMACOKINETIC DATA DURING TREATMENT OF PSYCHOSES WITH HALOPERIDOL.
000577 01-08
TREATMENT OF DEPRESSION IN THE MEDICALLY-ILL ELDERLY WITH METHYLPHENIDATE.
000602 01-09

THE TREATMENT OF SCHIZOAFFECTIVE-PSYCHOSES WITH LITHIUM-CARBONATE.
000607 01-09
THE TREATMENT OF DEPRESSIVE-CONDITIONS WITH NOMIFENSINE.
000609 01-09
NOMIFENSIN IN THE TREATMENT OF ENDOGENOUS DEPRESSIONS. CLINICAL-EXPERIENCE AND EEG FINDINGS.
000613 01-09
THE TREATMENT OF ANXIOUS-DEPRESSIVE-SYNDROMES WITH TOFIZOPAM.
000615 01-09
IMIPRAMINE TREATMENT OF PREPUBERTAL MAJOR DEPRESSIVE-DISORDERS: PLASMA LEVELS AND CLINICAL-RESPONSE – PRELIMINARY REPORT.
000620 01-09
OUR EXPERIENCE WITH MAPROTILIN TREATMENT OF DEPRESSIVE-STATES.
000623 01-09
VILOXAZINE IN THE TREATMENT OF DEPRESSIVE-STATES.
000626 01-09
SINTAMIL IN THE TREATMENT OF DEPRESSION; A COMPARISON OF SINGLE VS. DIVIDED DOSE ADMINISTRATION.
000629 01-09
ANTIDEPRESSIVE TREATMENT AND MOOD-SWING-PATTERNS IN ENDOGENOUS DEPRESSION.
000633 01-09
LITHIUM TREATMENT IN AFFECTIVE-DISORDERS: THERAPEUTIC PLASMA LEVEL.
000635 01-09
LITHIUM TREATMENT IN AFFECTIVE-DISORDERS FROM VIEWPOINT OF TRANSCULTURAL PSYCHOPHARMACOLOGY: THERAPEUTIC PLASMA LEVEL.
000636 01-09
COMBINED MONOAMINE-OXIDASE-INHIBITOR TRICYCLIC-ANTIDEPRESSANT TREATMENT: A PILOT-STUDY.
000644 01-09
STUDIES ON THE COMPREHENSIVE MEDICAL TREATMENT OF PEPTIC-ULCERS (3) – UTILIZATION OF TRANQUILIZERS IN THE TREATMENT OF GASTRIC-ULCERS.
000653 01-10
CLINICAL-EXPERIENCE WITH LOW-DOSES OF HALOPERIDOL IN THE TREATMENT OF NEUROSES.
000654 01-10
ANTIDEPRESSIVE TREATMENT IN PARKINSONS-DISEASE: A CONTROLLED-TRIAL OF THE EFFECT OF NORTRIPTYLINE IN PATIENTS WITH PARKINSONS-DISEASE TREATED WITH L-DOPA.
000659 01-11
ANTICONVULSANTS AND TREATMENT OF EPILEPSY.
000661 01-11
LITHIUM-CARBONATE IN THE TREATMENT OF CLUSTER-HEADACHES.
000670 01-11
PYRITINOL ADMINISTRATION AS PART OF EPILEPSY TREATMENT IN CHILDREN.
000671 01-11
BIOCHEMICAL-MEASUREMENTS DURING (-)DEPRENYL TREATMENT OF PARKINSONISM.
000673 01-11
CHOLINE-BITARTRATE TREATMENT OF ALZHEIMER-TYPE DEMENTIAS.
000675 01-11
CLOZAPINE IN THE TREATMENT OF TARDIVE-DYSKINESIA: AN INTERIM REPORT.
000677 01-11
TREATMENT OF TARDIVE-DYSKINESIA WITH OXYPERTINE – PRELIMINARY CLINICAL-EXPERIENCE AND A BRIEF REVIEW OF THE LITERATURE.
000692 01-11
THE EFFECT OF ASSERTIVENESS TRAINING, PROVERA AND SEX OF THERAPIST IN THE TREATMENT OF GENITAL EXHIBITIONISM.
000697 01-11
TOFIZOPAM IN THE TREATMENT OF CHRONIC ALCOHOLISM.
000706 01-11
THE TREATMENT OF PARKINSONS-DISEASE USING A COMBINATION OF L-DOPA AND DECARBOXYLASE INHIBITORS (CARBIDOPA, BENSERASIDE). A CLINICAL AND BIOCHEMICAL COMPARATIVE INVESTIGATION.
000712 01-11
FLUNITRAZEPAM IN THE TREATMENT OF DELIRIUM-TREMENS – PRELIMINARY REPORT.
000719 01-11
CONTROLLED-TRIAL OF BEHAVIOUR-THERAPY, PHARMACOTHERAPY, AND THEIR COMBINATION IN THE TREATMENT OF OBESITY.
000725 01-11
COMPARISON OF SUSTAINED-RELEASE AND STANDARD METHYLPHENIDATE IN THE TREATMENT OF MINIMAL-BRAIN-DYSFUNCTION.
000732 01-11
ISSUES FOR INPATIENT TREATMENT OF CHRONIC PCP ABUSE.
000736 01-12
LITHIUM-INDUCED COGWHEEL RIGIDITY: TREATMENT WITH AMANTADINE.
000748 01-13

METHODOLOGICAL REMARKS ON LONG-TERM LITHIUM TREATMENT.
000749 01-13

TREATMENT OF DRUG-INDUCED DRYNESS OF MOUTH IN PSYCHIATRIC-PATIENTS – A CONTROLLED-COMPARATIVE-STUDY.
000799 01-13

PROLACTIN RESPONSE AND EXTRAPYRAMIDAL SIDE-EFFECTS DURING PROPRANOLOL AND NEUROLEPTIC-DRUGS TREATMENT IN CHRONIC SCHIZOPHRENIC-PATIENTS.
000841 01-15

HYPNAGOGIC AND HYPNOPOMPIC HALLUCINATIONS DURING AMITRIPTYLINE TREATMENT.
000850 01-15

PLASMA PROLACTIN AND TESTOSTERONE DURING PENFLURIDOL TREATMENT.
000874 01-15

ELECTROCARDIOGRAPHIC-CHANGES DURING LITHIUM TREATMENT.
000881 01-15

THE OCCURRENCE OF TARDIVE EXTRAPYRAMIDAL SYMPTOMS IN SCHIZOPHRENIC-PATIENTS UNDERGOING PROLONGED NEUROLEPTIC TREATMENT.
000885 01-15

CLINICALLY SIGNIFICANT SIDE-EFFECTS OF LITHIUM TREATMENT.
000893 01-15

DEXAMETHASONE-SUPPRESSION-TESTS IN DEPRESSION AND RESPONSE TO TREATMENT.
000899 01-16

ENDOCRINOLOGICAL CHANGES IN PATIENTS WITH SEXUAL-DYSFUNCTION UNDER LONG-TERM NEUROLEPTIC TREATMENT.
000912 01-17

OUTPATIENT TREATMENT ISSUES AND STRATEGIES FOR ACUTE AND CHRONIC PCP ABUSERS.
000919 01-17

TARDIVE-DYSKINESIA RESULTING FROM CHRONIC NARCOTIC TREATMENT.
000922 01-17

TARDIVE-DYSKINESIA: RESEARCH & TREATMENT.
000934 01-17

FOLLOWUP TREATMENT AND AFTERCARE OF DISCHARGED SCHIZOPHRENIC-PATIENTS.
000944 01-17

PROTOCOLS FOR THE USE OF PSYCHOACTIVE-DRUGS – PART I: PROTOCOL FOR THE TREATMENT OF PSYCHOSIS WITH ANTIPSYCHOTICS.
000949 01-17

PSYCHOPHARMACOLOGICAL AND PSYCHOTHERAPEUTIC-APPROACHES TO THE TREATMENT OF FUNCTIONAL PSYCHOSES.
000977 01-17

A REVISED CHECKLIST TO OBTAIN CONSENT TO TREATMENT WITH MEDICATION.
000984 01-17

DEPRESSION IN THE ELDERLY: RESEARCH DIRECTIONS IN PSYCHOPATHOLOGY, EPIDEMIOLOGY, AND TREATMENT.
000998 01-17

CENTRAL LEVELS OF NORADRENALINE, 3 METHOXY-4-HYDROXYPHENYLETHYLENEGLYCOL AND CYCLIC-AMP IN THE RAT AFTER ACTIVATION OF LOCUS-COERULEUS NEURONS: INFLUENCE OF SINGLE AND REPEATED NEUROLEPTIC TREATMENT.
001095 02-03

EFFECT OF CHRONIC TRICYCLIC-ANTIDEPRESSANT TREATMENT ON THE SEROTONINERGIC-AUTORECEPTOR: A MICROIONTOPHORETIC-STUDY IN THE RAT.
001135 02-03

GLUCOSE OXIDATION IN THE VENTROMEDIAL HYPOTHALAMUS IS NOT AFFECTED BY INSULIN OR OUABAIN BUT DEPRESSED BY ALLOXAN TREATMENT.
001145 02-03

ACUTE AND CHRONIC HALOPERIDOL TREATMENT: EFFECTS ON NIGROSTRIATAL DOPAMINERGIC-SYSTEM ACTIVITY.
001153 02-03

DOPAMINERGIC-SUPERSENSITIVITY: INFLUENCE OF DOPAMINE AGONISTS AND DRUGS USED FOR THE TREATMENT OF TARDIVE-DYSKINESIA.
001169 02-03

DOPAMINE-SENSITIVE ADENYLATE-CYCLASE AND RECEPTOR BINDING-ACTIVITIES FOLLOWING ACUTE AND CHRONIC NEUROLEPTIC-DRUG TREATMENT. (UNPUBLISHED PAPER).
001172 02-03

LONG-TERM HALOPERIDOL TREATMENT OF MICE: A CHANGE IN BETA-ADRENERGIC-RECEPTOR RESPONSIVENESS.
001206 02-03

EFFECTS OF CHRONIC NEUROLEPTIC TREATMENT ON TYROSINE-HYDROXYLASE IN DOPAMINERGIC TERMINALS: COMPARISONS BETWEEN DRUGS AND BRAIN REGIONS REVEALS DIFFERENT MECHANISMS OF TOLERANCE.
001243 02-03

CALMODULIN RELEASE FROM STRIATAL MEMBRANES AFTER ACUTE AND CHRONIC TREATMENT WITH BUTACLAMOL.
001249 02-03

THE TIME-COURSE OF NORADRENERGIC PRESYNAPTIC AND POSTSYNAPTIC ACTIVITY DURING CHRONIC DESIPRAMINE TREATMENT.
001289 02-03

THE HYPERKINETIC-SYNDROME FOLLOWING LONG-TERM HALOPERIDOL TREATMENT: INVOLVEMENT OF DOPAMINE AND NORADRENALINE.
001299 02-03

INTERACTION OF TRIAZOLAM WITH DESIPRAMINE: EFFECTS OF SINGLE AND REPEATED TREATMENT ON CERTAIN PHARMACOLOGIC-RESPONSES AND BRAIN CATECHOLAMINE LEVELS.
001323 02-03

LONG-TERM HALOPERIDOL TREATMENT AND FACTORS EFFECTING THE ACTIVITY OF STRIATAL TYROSINE-HYDROXYLASE.
001348 02-03

ALTERED LEVELS OF BETA ENDORPHIN FRAGMENTS AFTER CHRONIC MORPHINE TREATMENT OF GUINEA-PIG ILEUM IN VITRO AND IN VIVO.
001404 02-03

EFFECT OF REPEATED TREATMENT WITH NEUROLEPTICS ON DOPAMINE METABOLISM IN CELL BODIES AND TERMINALS OF DOPAMINERGIC-SYSTEMS IN THE RAT-BRAIN.
001464 02-03

LONG-TERM APPLICATION OF HALOPERIDOL: EFFECT OF ANTICHOLINERGIC TREATMENT ON THE RATE OF DOPAMINE SYNTHESIS.
001490 02-03

ENHANCED SENSITIVITY OF AMYGDALOID NEURONS TO SEROTONIN AND NOREPINEPHRINE AFTER CHRONIC ANTIDEPRESSANT TREATMENT.
001523 02-03

BEHAVIORAL-EFFECTS, ANTIDOPAMINERGIC-EFFECTS, AND PROHYPNOTIC-EFFECTS OF NEUROLEPTICS DURING AND AFTER PROLONGED TREATMENT.
001577 02-04

INTERACTION OF PSYCHOPHARMALOGIC-FACTORS AND PSYCHOSOCIAL-FACTORS IN THE TREATMENT OF ANIMAL-MODELS OF HYPOINHIBITORY (HYPERKINETIC) BEHAVIOR.
001602 02-04

SWIMMING CAPACITY OF MICE AFTER PROLONGED TREATMENT WITH PSYCHOSTIMULANTS: II. EFFECT OF METHAMPHETAMINE ON SWIMMING PERFORMANCE AND AVAILABILITY OF METABOLIC SUBSTRATES.
001613 02-04

SUBACUTE CANNABINOID TREATMENT: ANTICONVULSANT ACTIVITY AND WITHDRAWAL EXCITABILITY IN MICE.
001671 02-04

NEUROCHEMICAL-EFFECTS AND BEHAVIORAL-EFFECTS OF CHRONIC D-AMPHETAMINE TREATMENT IN GENETICALLY OBESE (OBOB) MICE. (PH.D. DISSERTATION).
001739 02-04

EMERGENCE OF APOMORPHINE-INDUCED VACUOUS CHEWING DURING 6 MONTHS CONTINUOUS TREATMENT WITH FLUPHENAZINE-DECANOATE.
001817 02-04

TOLERANCE TO FLUPHENAZINE AND SUPERSENSITIVITY TO APOMORPHINE IN CENTRAL DOPAMINERGIC-SYSTEMS AFTER CHRONIC FLUPHENAZINE-DECANOATE TREATMENT.
001820 02-04

CHRONIC NEUROLEPTIC TREATMENT AND DOPAMINE-RECEPTOR REGULATION.
001837 02-05

3H APOMORPHINE-RECEPTORS IN VARIOUS RAT-BRAIN REGIONS: A STUDY OF SPECIFIC AND NONSPECIFIC BINDING AND THE INFLUENCE OF CHRONIC NEUROLEPTIC TREATMENT.
001846 02-05

NEUROLEPTIC TREATMENT FOR A SUBSTANTIAL PROPORTION OF ADULT LIFE: BEHAVIOURAL-SEQUELAE OF 9 MONTHS HALOPERIDOL ADMINISTRATION.
001858 02-05

ANTIPSYCHOTIC-EFFECT OF PROPRANOLOL ON CHRONIC SCHIZOPHRENICS: STUDY OF A GRADUAL TREATMENT REGIMEN.
001915 02-08

EFFECT OF PROPRANOLOL TREATMENT ON SERUM PROLACTIN LEVEL IN SCHIZOPHRENIC-PATIENTS.
001916 02-08

OXYPROTHEPINE-DECANOATE COMPARED WITH FLUPHENAZINE-DECANOATE IN THE TREATMENT OF SCHIZOPHRENIA: PRELIMINARY-COMMUNICATION.
001934 02-08

USE OF LARGE-SINGLE-DOSES OF BROMOCRIPTINE IN SCHIZOPHRENIC-PATIENTS WITH ELEVATED SERUM PROLACTIN LEVELS AND EXTRAPYRAMIDAL SIDE-EFFECTS ASSOCIATED WITH NEUROLEPTIC TREATMENT.
001944 02-08

PLASMA FLUPHENAZINE AND PROLACTIN LEVELS IN SCHIZOPHRENIC-PATIENTS DURING TREATMENT WITH LOW-DOSES AND HIGH-DOSES OF FLUPHENAZINE-ENANTHATE.
001956 02-08

PRELIMINARY-STUDIES ON CSF GAMMA AMINOBUTYRIC-ACID LEVELS IN PSYCHIATRIC-PATIENTS BEFORE AND DURING TREATMENT WITH DIFFERENT PSYCHOTROPIC-DRUGS.
001959 02-08

STUDY OF MAPROTILINE IN OUTPATIENT TREATMENT OF DEPRESSIVE-STATES BY THE GENERAL-PRACTITIONER: ADVANTAGE OF SINGLE-NIGHTLY-DOSE.
001961 02-09

Subject Index

RESULTS OF A SURVEY ON THE PRESENT TREATMENT OF DEPRESSION IN SPAIN.
001963 02-09

NOMIFENSINE IN THE TREATMENT OF VARIOUS TYPES OF DEPRESSION.
001968 02-09

THE PLACE OF SURVECTOR AMONG THE VARIOUS DRUGS USED IN TREATMENT OF MOOD-DISORDERS.
001969 02-09

ATTEMPT AT PSYCHOLOGICAL UNDERSTANDING AND TREATMENT OF PSYCHOLOGICAL ASTHENIA AND ASTHENO-DEPRESSIVE-SYNDROMES USING ERGADYL.
001974 02-09

NOMIFENSINE IN THE TREATMENT OF ENDOGENOUS DEPRESSION. A CONTROLLED-STUDY VS. NORTRIPTYLINE.
001978 02-09

TREATMENT OF ASTHENO-DEPRESSIVE-DISORDERS WITH MINAPRINE (CANTOR). MULTICENTER-STUDY OF 248 CASES EVALUATED WITH THE FATIGUE STUDY GROUPS NO. 4 CLINICAL-SCALE.
001980 02-09

A COMPARISON OF HALOPERIDOL, LITHIUM-CARBONATE AND THEIR COMBINATION IN THE TREATMENT OF MANIA.
001990 02-09

TRAZODONE IN THE TREATMENT OF NEUROTIC DEPRESSION.
001994 02-09

AN OVERVIEW OF SEVENTEEN YEARS OF EXPERIENCE WITH DOTHIEPIN IN THE TREATMENT OF DEPRESSION IN EUROPE.
001995 02-09

IS IT POSSIBLE TO SET UP ANY RULES FOR A COMPREHENSIVE TREATMENT OF DEPRESSIVE-STATES?
001997 02-09

THE IMPORTANCE OF AMINEPTINE IN THE TREATMENT OF NONPSYCHOTIC DEPRESSIVE-STATES IN THE ELDERLY.
001999 02-09

EVALUATION OF NOMIFENSINE IN THE TREATMENT OF GERIATRIC DEPRESSION USING PSYCHOMETRIC-TESTS AND PLASMA LEVEL CONTROLS.
002004 02-09

TREATMENT OF THERAPY-RESISTANT DEPRESSED-PATIENTS WITH IV INFUSIONS OF NOMIFENSINE CONTROLLED BY GALVANIC-SKIN-RESISTANCE.
002012 02-09

INNOVATIONS IN TREATMENT WITH ANTIDEPRESSANTS.
002019 02-09

LARGE-DOSES OF DIBENZEPINE NOVERIL IN THE TREATMENT OF DEPRESSIVE-STATES.
002020 02-09

TREATMENT OF ANXIOUS-DEPRESSED OUTPATIENTS WITH A FIXED COMBINATION (NOMIFENSINE/CLOBAZAM) IN COMPARISON TO A MONOSUBSTANCE (DOXEPINE).
002028 02-09

SENSITIZATION AND OSCILLATION FOLLOWING REPEATED STIMULATION: RELATIONSHIP TO AFFECTIVE-ILLNESS AND ITS TREATMENT WITH LITHIUM AND CARBAMAZEPINE.
002031 02-09

TREATMENT OF TARDIVE-DYSKINESIA IN AN AGITATED, DEPRESSED-PATIENT.
002038 02-09

THE PHARMACOTHERAPY OF MAJOR DEPRESSIVE-SYNDROME. PART 1: TREATMENT OF ACUTE DEPRESSION.
002044 02-09

TREATMENT OF CHRONIC PAIN WITH ANTIDEPRESSANT-DRUGS.
002048 02-09

A TEN YEAR FOLLOWUP OF LITHIUM-CARBONATE TREATMENT OF MANIC-DEPRESSIVE-ILLNESS: PRELIMINARY-RESULTS.
002053 02-09

PYRAZIDOL IN THE TREATMENT OF DEPRESSIONS.
002055 02-09

INFUSION OF MAPROTILIN AND CLOMIPRAMIN AND THEIR COMBINATION IN THE TREATMENT OF DEPRESSION.
002056 02-09

INHIBITION AND APATHY: TREATMENT WITH SURVECTOR.
002066 02-10

PIMOZIDE IN THE TREATMENT OF SOME SOCIAL-MALADJUSTMENTS IN PERSONALITY-DISORDERS.
002068 02-10

DOUBLE-BLIND CLINICAL ASSESSMENT OF ALPRAZOLAM, A NEW BENZODIAZEPINE DERIVATIVE, IN THE TREATMENT OF MODERATE TO SEVERE ANXIETY.
002070 02-10

FLUSPIRILENE (IMAP) IN THE TREATMENT OF PSYCHOSOMATIC-COMPLAINTS IN HYPOCHONDRIACAL-PATIENTS.
002072 02-10

KETAZOLAM COMPARED TO DIAZEPAM AND PLACEBO IN THE TREATMENT OF ANXIETY.
002074 02-10

NOMIFENSINE IN THE TREATMENT OF OBSESSIVE-COMPULSIVE-NEUROSIS. THERAPEUTIC-EFFICACY AND TOLERABILITY IN COMPARISON TO IMIPRAMINE.
002078 02-10

THYMOANALEPTIC TREATMENT CONTROL THROUGH MEASUREMENT OF PLASMA CONCENTRATIONS OF AMITRIPTYLINE AND ITS METABOLITE NORTRIPTYLINE.
002304 02-13

CHANGES IN THE AUGMENTER REDUCER TENDENCY AND IN PAIN MEASURES AS A RESULT OF TREATMENT WITH A SEROTONIN REUPTAKE INHIBITOR ZIMELIDINE.
002305 02-13

THE QUESTION OF MINIMUM-DOSES OF ANTICONVULSANTS IN THE TREATMENT OF EPILEPSY.
002306 02-13

SHORT-TERM AND LONG-TERM EFFECTS ON GABA AND DOPAMINE NEURONS DURING TREATMENT WITH SULPIRIDE.
002311 02-13

PAROXYSTIC-DYSKINESIAS DURING TREATMENT WITH DIPHENYLHYDANTOIN.
002319 02-14

L HTP AND THE SEROTONIN HYPOTHESIS: THEIR MEANING FOR TREATMENT OF DEPRESSION.
002326 02-14

ALCOHOL WITHDRAWAL-SYNDROME: TREATMENT WITH TRAZODONE.
002356 02-14

NEUROPEPTIDE TREATMENT OF SOCIOPATHY: RESEARCH IN PROGRESS.
002369 02-14

DOPAMINE ANTAGONIST AND AGONIST TREATMENT OF TARDIVE-DYSKINESIA.
002377 02-15

LECITHIN IN THE TREATMENT OF TARDIVE-DYSKINESIA.
002380 02-15

LEVODOPA COMPARED WITH BROMOCRIPTINE IN THE TREATMENT OF PARKINSONS-DISEASE.
002406 02-15

CASE 3: ASSESSMENT AND TREATMENT OF DRUG-INDUCED TREMOR.
002407 02-15

COMPARATIVE-STUDY OF VARIATIONS IN PROLACTIN LEVELS DURING TREATMENT WITH ANTIPSYCHOTIC-DRUGS.
002412 02-15

AN INVESTIGATION OF SOME SIDE-EFFECTS IN 47 PSYCHOTIC-PATIENTS DURING TREATMENT WITH CLOZAPINE AND DISCONTINUING OF THE TREATMENT.
002424 02-15

APPROACHES TO THE PROBLEM OF PREVENTING HAZARDS OF LONG-TERM NEUROLEPTIC TREATMENT AND OF AVOIDING UNNECESSARY DRUGS.
002426 02-15

TREATMENT OF PSYCHOTROPIC-CAUSED ORTHOSTATIC HYPOTENSION.
002428 02-15

MALIGNANT-HYPERTHERMIC-SYNDROMES IN THE COURSE OF TREATMENT WITH LONG-ACTING NEUROLEPTICS.
002430 02-15

FAILURE OF LITHIUM TREATMENT IN ESTABLISHED TARDIVE-DYSKINESIA.
002432 02-15

TREATMENT OF IATROGENIC DRUG DEPENDENCE IN THE GENERAL-HOSPITAL.
002460 02-15

RECENT DEVELOPMENTS IN LITHIUM TREATMENT: IS IT DANGEROUS FOR THE KIDNEY?
002465 02-15

USE OF CHOLINE AND LECITHIN IN THE TREATMENT OF TARDIVE-DYSKINESIA.
002473 02-15

ERGOTS IN THE TREATMENT OF MENTAL-DISORDERS OF OLD-AGE.
002545 02-17

PLACEBO, MEDICINE AND PAIN, OR THE RELATIVE FUNCTION OF MEDICATION IN THE TREATMENT OF PAIN.
002577 02-17

THE TREATMENT OF OPIATE ADDICTION USING METHADONE-CHLORHYDRATE.
002600 02-17

REPEATED ANTIDEPRESSANT TREATMENTS INDUCE A LONG-LASTING DOPAMINE-AUTORECEPTOR SUBSENSITIVITY: IS DAILY TREATMENT NECESSARY FOR CLINICAL EFFICACY?
002659 03-03

DURING ONE YEARS NEUROLEPTIC TREATMENT IN RATS STRIATAL DOPAMINE-RECEPTOR BLOCKADE DECREASES BUT SERUM PROLACTIN LEVELS REMAIN ELEVATED.
002707 03-03

EFFECTS OF FETAL TREATMENT WITH METHYLAZOXYMETHANOL-ACETATE AT VARIOUS GESTATIONAL DATES ON THE NEUROCHEMISTRY OF THE ADULT NEOCORTEX OF THE RAT.
002770 03-03

INFLUENCE OF A CHRONIC NEW POTENTIAL ANTIDEPRESSANT, DIMETHYLAMINOPROPYL-5-METHYL-3-PHENYL-1H-INDAZOLE (FS-32) AND ITS N DESMETHYLATED-COMPOUND (FS-97): TREATMENT ON MONOAMINERGIC-RECEPTOR SENSITIVITY IN THE RAT-BRAIN.
002787 03-03

AN ENHANCED SENSITIVITY OF MUSCARINIC CHOLINERGIC-RECEPTOR ASSOCIATED WITH DOPAMINERGIC-RECEPTOR SUBSENSITIVITY AFTER CHRONIC ANTIDEPRESSANT TREATMENT.
002788 03-03

PHARMACOLOGIC APPROACHES TO THE TREATMENT OF SENILE-DEMENTIA.
002809 03-03

EFFECTS OF PROLONGED TREATMENT WITH LITHIUM AND TRICYCLIC-ANTIDEPRESSANTS ON DISCHARGE FREQUENCY, NOREPINEPHRINE RESPONSES AND BETA-RECEPTOR BINDING IN RAT-CEREBELLUM: ELECTROPHYSIOLOGICAL AND BIOCHEMICAL COMPARISON.
002884 03-03

DIFFERENTIAL-EFFECT OF CHRONIC DESIPRAMINE AND AMITRIPTYLINE TREATMENT ON RAT-BRAIN ADRENERGIC AND SEROTONERGIC-RECEPTORS.
002914 03-03

MEPACRINE TREATMENT PREVENTS IMMOBILIZATION-INDUCED DESENSITIZATION OF BETA-ADRENERGIC-RECEPTORS IN RAT HYPOTHALAMUS AND BRAINSTEM.
002919 03-03

INDUCTION OF HYPERSENSITIVITY OF BRAIN BY HYDRALAZINE TREATMENT IN RATS.
003008 03-04

INCREASES IN TESTOSTERONE LEVELS AND IN COPULATORY-BEHAVIOR OF MALE RHESUS-MONKEYS FOLLOWING TREATMENT WITH HUMAN CHORIONIC GONADOTROPHIN.
003012 03-04

THE EFFECTS OF IMIPRAMINE TREATMENT ON THE UNCONDITIONED ALIMENTARY BEHAVIOR AND CLASSICAL CONDITIONED SALIVARY REACTIONS IN DOGS.
003030 03-04

EFFECTS OF CHRONIC NALOXONE TREATMENT ON BRAIN-STIMULATION REWARD.
003066 03-04

ACETYLCHOLINESTERASE AND CHOLINESTERASE ACTIVITIES IN THE MOUSE CEREBELLUM FOLLOWING MISONIDAZOLE TREATMENT.
003123 03-05

AN OPEN-STUDY OF MAPROTILINE 75MG IN THE TREATMENT OF DEPRESSIVE-STATES.
003152 03-07

TREATMENT OF THERAPEUTICALLY-RESISTANT PARANOID SCHIZOPHRENIC-PATIENTS WITH FLUPHENAZINE DEPOT COMBINED WITH OTHER PSYCHOTROPIC-DRUGS AND CLOZAPINE.
003172 03-08

LATE RESULTS OF LITHIUM TREATMENT OF ADOLESCENTS WITH ATTACK LIKE SCHIZOPHRENIA.
003177 03-08

CHLORPROMAZINE LEVELS AND THE OUTCOME OF TREATMENT IN SCHIZOPHRENIC-PATIENTS.
003188 03-08

PROGNOSIS IN SCHIZOPHRENIA: INDIVIDUAL DIFFERENCES IN PSYCHOLOGICAL RESPONSE TO A TEST DOSE OF ANTIPSYCHOTIC-DRUG AND THEIR RELATIONSHIP TO BLOOD AND SALIVA LEVELS AND TREATMENT OUTCOME.
003189 03-08

DIAGNOSIS AND TREATMENT OF ACUTE SCHIZOPHRENIC-PSYCHOSES.
003191 03-08

THE USE OF A MORPHINE ANTAGONIST (NALOXONE) IN THE TREATMENT OF DISSOCIATIVE-SYNDROMES.
003194 03-08

A SYMPTOM-PROFILE-ANALYSIS OF ANTIPSYCHOTIC-DRUG TREATMENT: NONPARAMETRIC MULTIDIMENSIONAL TECHNIQUE.
003196 03-08

CLINICAL-STUDY OF MAPROTILINE IN THE TREATMENT OF DEPRESSIVE-STATES: COMPILATION OF 1520 OBSERVATIONS.
003206 03-09

PROTOCOLS FOR THE USE OF PSYCHOACTIVE-DRUGS -- PART II: PROTOCOL FOR THE TREATMENT OF DEPRESSION WITH TRICYCLIC-ANTIDEPRESSANTS.
003214 03-09

AMOXAPINE AND AMITRIPTYLINE IN THE OUTPATIENT TREATMENT OF ENDOGENOUS DEPRESSION.
003217 03-09

THE REPRESSION OF THE LITHIUM-PUMP AS AN INDICATOR OF RESPONSE TO PROPHYLACTIC TREATMENT.
003221 03-09

HISTORICAL-PERSPECTIVES AND CURRENT HIGHLIGHTS ON LITHIUM TREATMENT IN MANIC-DEPRESSIVE-ILLNESS.
003224 03-09

DOSAGE OF INTRATUMORAL LITHIUM (CEREBRAL GLIOBLASTOMA): ON A FAILURE OF TREATMENT OF MANIC-DEPRESSIVE-PSYCHOSIS.
003226 03-09

SLEEP AND TREATMENT PREDICTION IN ENDOGENOUS DEPRESSION.
003236 03-09

AMOXAPINE AND IMIPRAMINE IN THE TREATMENT OF DEPRESSED-OUTPATIENTS: A CONTROLLED-STUDY.
003254 03-09

CEREBRAL EVOKED-POTENTIAL CHANGES PRODUCED BY TREATMENT WITH LITHIUM-CARBONATE.
003263 03-09

THE TREATMENT OF DEPRESSION USING CLOMIPRAMINE IN GENERAL-MEDICAL-PRACTICE: 48 CASES TREATED ON AN OUTPATIENT BASIS.
003268 03-09

DEPRESSED-OUTPATIENTS: RESULTS ONE YEAR AFTER TREATMENT WITH DRUGS AND/OR INTERPERSONAL PSYCHOTHERAPY.
003272 03-09

RECENT ADVANCES IN THE DIAGNOSIS AND TREATMENT OF ANXIETY-DISORDERS.
003275 03-10

CHANGES IN THE PSYCHOPATHOLOGY OF PSYCHOSIS DUE TO NEUROLEPTIC TREATMENT.
003281 03-10

BENZODIAZEPINE TREATMENT OF SPECIFIC ANXIETY STATES.
003284 03-10

PHENELZINE AND EXPOSURE IN THE TREATMENT OF PHOBIAS.
003285 03-10

SEXUAL-DIFFICULTIES AMONG CONVALESCING ALCOHOLICS: INTEREST IN PRAZEPAM TREATMENT IN 30 CASES.
003296 03-11

EVALUATION OF THE RELATIVE EFFECTIVENESS OF METHYLPHENIDATE AND COGNITIVE BEHAVIOR-MODIFICATION IN THE TREATMENT OF KINDERGARTEN-AGED HYPERACTIVE-CHILDREN.
003306 03-11

RECENT ADVANCES IN THE TREATMENT OF EPILEPSY.
003307 03-11

INCREASED SERUM PROLACTIN LEVELS DURING PHENOTHIAZINE AND BUTYROPHENONE TREATMENT OF SIX POSTPARTUM WOMEN.
003318 03-11

MOLINDONE-HYDROCHLORIDE IN THE TREATMENT OF AGGRESSIVE, HOSPITALIZED CHILDREN.
003321 03-11

TREATMENT OF TRAUMATIC WAR-NEUROSIS WITH PHENELZINE.
003325 03-11

TREATMENT OF ORGANIC-BRAIN-DISTURBANCES IN ELDERLY-PATIENTS. A CLINICAL DOUBLE-BLIND STUDY WITH MACROMOLECULAR ORGAN LYSATES (CYTOPLASMATIC THERAPY ACCORDING TO THEURER).
003327 03-11

A CLINICAL, CONTROLLED-STUDY OF L ALPHA ACETYLMETHADOL IN THE TREATMENT OF NARCOTIC ADDICTION.
003335 03-11

THE EFFECTIVENESS OF IMIPRAMINE IN THE TREATMENT OF ENURESIS: THE SIGNIFICANCE OF TYPE OF ENURESIS AND REPORTED LEVEL OF SLEEP. (PH.D. DISSERTATION).
003337 03-11

THE EFFECT OF WITHDRAWAL FROM PROLONGED PROPHYLACTIC TREATMENT WITH LITHIUM.
003339 03-11

NALOXONE IN THE TREATMENT OF ANOREXIA-NERVOSA: EFFECT ON WEIGHT-GAIN AND LIPOLYSIS.
003342 03-11

RAPID TREATMENT OF ACUTE PSYCHOTIC-SYMPTOMS WITH HIGH-DOSE AND LOW-DOSE HALOPERIDOL: BEHAVIORAL-CONSIDERATIONS.
003346 03-11

PHARMACOLOGIC CHARACTERIZATION AND LECITHIN TREATMENT OF A PATIENT WITH SPONTANEOUS ORAL FACIAL DYSKINESIA AND DEMENTIA.
003347 03-11

PRUSSIAN-BLUE: SPECIFIC TREATMENT OF THALLIUM, ARSENIC, INDUSTRIAL-SOLVENT INTOXICATION, AND OTHER POLYNEUROPATHOLOGIES. A POSSIBLE ANTIPSYCHOTIC-AGENT.
003348 03-11

TREATMENT OF ANXIETY IN CHILDREN AND ADOLESCENTS.
003349 03-11

HYPNOTIC-DRUGS AND TREATMENT OF INSOMNIA.
003350 03-11

THE USE OF PHENAZEPAM IN THE TREATMENT OF PSYCHOTIC-PATIENTS.
003351 03-11

PROGRESSIVE SUPRANUCLEAR PALSY: PNEUMOENCEPHALOGRAPHY, ELECTRONYSTAGMOGRAPHY AND TREATMENT WITH METHYSERGIDE.
003355 03-11

IMIPRAMINE TREATMENT OF BORDERLINE-CHILDREN: CASE-REPORTS WITH A CONTROLLED-STUDY.
003356 03-11

PHYSOSTIGMINE FOR TREATMENT OF DELIRIUM-TREMENS.
003364 03-11

THE ROLE OF PSYCHOPHARMACOTHERAPY IN THE TREATMENT OF ELDERLY-PATIENTS WITH ORGANIC-MENTAL-SYNDROMES.
003368 03-11

THE TREATMENT AND ETIOLOGY OF TICS AND TOURETTE-SYNDROME.
003372 03-11

USE OF THA IN TREATMENT OF ALZHEIMER-LIKE DEMENTIA: PILOT-STUDY IN TWELVE PATIENTS.
003377 03-11

ON THE INTENSIVE TREATMENT OF ENDOGENOUS PSYCHOSES.
003384 03-11

LITHIUM TREATMENT OF THE KLEINE-LEVIN-SYNDROME.
003390 03-11

PROPRANOLOL IN THE TREATMENT OF RAGE AND VIOLENT-BEHAVIOR IN PATIENTS WITH CHRONIC-BRAIN-SYNDROMES.
003394 03-11

FLUNITRAZEPAM IN THE TREATMENT OF INSOMNIA: A STUDY OF 50 PSYCHIATRIC-PATIENTS.
003444 03-14

EFFECTS OF SUBCHRONIC DESMETHYLIMIPRAMINE (DMI) TREATMENT OF THE CLASSICALLY CONDITIONED EYEBLINK RESPONSE IN RABBITS.
004180 04-04

TREATMENT OF UNSTABLE ANGINA BY DILTIAZEM.
004307 04-07

CORRELATIONS BETWEEN VISUAL-EVOKED-POTENTIALS AND PSYCHOPATHOLOGICAL-FINDINGS IN SCHIZOPHRENIC-PATIENTS UNDER TREATMENT WITH VARIOUS PSYCHOPHARMACOLOGICAL-DRUGS.
004315 04-08

PRELIMINARY TRIAL OF CLONIDINE TREATMENT IN TWO PATIENTS SUFFERING FROM CHRONIC SCHIZOPHRENIA.
004320 04-08

PLASMA LEVELS OF BETA ENDORPHIN UNDER CHRONIC NEUROLEPTIC TREATMENT IN SCHIZOPHRENIC-PATIENTS: FAILURE OF NALOXONE TO COUNTERACT CURATIVE EFFECTS OF NEUROLEPTIC-DRUGS.
004321 04-08

THE TREATMENT OF CHRONIC SCHIZOPHRENIC-PATIENTS: AN INTERVIEW WITH DR. J. HUSSER.
004328 04-08

NEUROENDOCRINE-TESTS DURING TREATMENT WITH NEUROLEPTIC-DRUGS: I. PLASMA PROLACTIN RESPONSE TO CHLORPROMAZINE CHALLENGE.
004329 04-08

HALOPERIDOL AND DROPERIDOL TREATMENT IN SCHIZOPHRENICS: CLINICAL APPLICATION OF THE PROLACTIN MODEL.
004332 04-08

A DOUBLE-BLIND COMPARISON OF THREE DOSAGES OF FLUTROLINE (CP-36584) IN THE TREATMENT OF SCHIZOPHRENIA.
004333 04-08

THE USE OF SODIUM-NUCLEINATE IN THE TREATMENT OF SCHIZOPHRENIC-PATIENTS.
004339 04-08

LONG-TERM NEUROLEPTIC TREATMENT OF CHRONIC SCHIZOPHRENIC-PATIENTS: CLINICAL AND BIOCHEMICAL-EFFECTS OF WITHDRAWAL.
004344 04-08

EVALUATIONS OF LOXAPINE-SUCCINATE IN THE AMBULATORY TREATMENT OF ACUTE SCHIZOPHRENIC-EPISODES.
004345 04-08

CLINICAL-RESPONSE AND BLOOD LEVELS IN THE TREATMENT OF DEPRESSION WITH A NEW ANTIDEPRESSANT-DRUG, AMOXAPINE.
004356 04-09

GUIDELINES ON THE DIAGNOSIS AND TREATMENT OF DEPRESSION.
004376 04-09

TREATMENT OF DEPRESSION WITH AN MAO-INHIBITOR FOLLOWED BY 5 HTP -- AN UNFINISHED RESEARCH PROJECT.
004377 04-09

CEREBROSPINAL-FLUID VALUES OF HVA AND 5 HIAA IN PATIENTS WITH ENDOGENOUS DEPRESSION DURING THE COURSE OF TREATMENT.
004382 04-09

AN EVALUATION OF TRAZODONE IN THE TREATMENT OF DEPRESSION.
004386 04-09

STUDIES ON THE TREATMENT AND DIAGNOSIS OF NEUROTIC VERTIGO FROM THE VIEWPOINT OF NEUROOTOLOGY: OBSERVATION OF THE BALANCE TEST FOR ANALYZING NEUROTIC VERTIGO.
004387 04-09

VILOXAZINE IN THE TREATMENT OF DEPRESSIVE-NEUROSIS: A PLACEBO AND STANDARD (IMIPRAMINE) CONTROLLED CLINICAL-STUDY.
004392 04-09

ALTERATIONS IN NORADRENERGIC FUNCTION DURING CLORGYLINE TREATMENT.
004393 04-09

LITHIUM TREATMENT OF MANIC-DEPRESSIVE-ILLNESS. A PRACTICAL GUIDE.
004408 04-09

ELECTROCARDIOGRAM-CHANGES AND PLASMA DESIPRAMINE LEVELS DURING TREATMENT OF DEPRESSION.
004411 04-09

CHANGES IN PSYCHOPATHOLOGIC SYMPTOMS DURING 20 DAYS OF TREATMENT WITH ANTIDEPRESSANTS AND NEUROLEPTIC-DRUGS.
004415 04-09

CONTROLLED CLINICAL-TRIAL OF NOMIFENSINE IN THE TREATMENT OF DEPRESSION.
004417 04-09

PRAZEPAM: A NEW BENZODIAZEPINE FOR THE TREATMENT OF ANXIOUS-DEPRESSIVE STATES.
004419 04-10

DIFFERENTIAL DIAGNOSIS AND TREATMENT OF PANIC ATTACKS AND PHOBIC-STATES.
004424 04-10

AN EVALUATION OF THE USEFULNESS OF THE ACYLASE TEST IN NEUROLEPTIC TREATMENT.
004426 04-10

DRUG-THERAPY FOR HYPERACTIVITY: TREATMENT PROCEDURES IN NATURAL SETTINGS.
004449 04-11

TREATMENT OF SEX-OFFENDERS WITH MEDROXYPROGESTERONE-ACETATE.
004450 04-11

TREATMENT OF ENCOPRESIS WITH IMIPRAMINE.
004451 04-11

METHADONE TREATMENT OF HEROIN ADDICTS IN SWITZERLAND.
004452 04-11

HYPERVENTILATION-SYNDROME, TREATMENT WITH L TRYPTOPHAN AND PYRIDOXINE; PREDICTIVE VALUES OF XANTHURENIC-ACID EXCRETION.
004456 04-11

THE CLASSIFICATION OF SLEEP-DISORDERS AND THE TREATMENT OF VARIOUS FORMS OF SOMNAMBULISM.
004461 04-11

EFFECT OF TREATMENT WITH SODIUM-VALPROATE AND DIAZEPAM ON PLASMA CORTICOTROPIN IN NELSONS-SYNDROME.
004463 04-11

SCOPOLAMINE IN CHOLINOLYTIC TREATMENT.
004468 04-11

TREATMENT OF EPILEPSIES WITH CLONAZEPAM (ANTELEPSIN).
004481 04-11

THE TREATMENT OF INSOMNIA THROUGH HOMEOPATHY IN A CLINIC.
004484 04-11

SINGLE-CASE STUDY OF CLINICAL-RESPONSE TO HIGH-DOSE ERGOT ALKALOID TREATMENT FOR DEMENTIA. PRELIMINARY REPORT.
004493 04-11

CEREBROSPINAL-FLUID HOMOVANILLIC-ACID PATTERNS DURING NEUROLEPTIC TREATMENT. (UNPUBLISHED PAPER).
004502 04-13

A MECHANISM FOR THE ACCUMULATION OF CHOLINE IN ERYTHROCYTES DURING TREATMENT WITH LITHIUM.
004520 04-13

TREATMENT OF UNDERNUTRITION AND ELECTROLYTE-DISTURBANCES IN ANOREXIA-NERVOSA.
004531 04-13

TREATMENT OF NARCOLEPSY AND SLEEP-APNEA WITH GAMMA HYDROXYBUTYRATE: A CLINICAL AND POLYSOMNOGRAPHIC CASE-STUDY.
004571 04-14

PROSPECTS FOR THE TREATMENT OF POSTENCEPHALITIC PARKINSONISM WITH ANTILYMPHOCYTIC IMMUNOGLOBULIN.
004572 04-14

CORRECTION OF HORMONAL ACTIVITY OF THE THYROID-GLAND AS A METHOD OF PATHOGENIC THERAPY IN A COMPREHENSIVE TREATMENT OF PATIENTS WITH TEMPORAL EPILEPSY.
004579 04-14

USE OF LYSINE-VASOPRESSIN IN THE TREATMENT OF POSTTRAUMATIC AMNESIA.
004583 04-14

OPIOID DEPENDENCE: MECHANISMS AND TREATMENT.
004587 04-14

CLINICAL STRATEGIES FOR ANTIPSYCHOTIC-DRUG TREATMENT, TARDIVE-DYSKINESIA, AND THE TRAINING OF RESEARCH PSYCHIATRISTS.
004603 04-15

LECITHIN FOR THE TREATMENT OF TARDIVE-DYSKINESIA.
004612 04-15

NEUROLEPTIC TREATMENT AS EXPERIENCED BY A PSYCHIATRIST.
004613 04-15

TREATMENT OF TARDIVE-DYSKINESIA.
004616 04-15

A STUDY ON MENTAL-SYMPTOMS DEVELOPED DURING THE TREATMENT OF PARKINSONS-DISEASE.
004618 04-15

BACLOFEN IN THE TREATMENT OF TARDIVE-DYSKINESIA: OPEN LABEL STUDY.
004619 04-15

A CASE OF ACUTE AGRANULOCYTOSIS DURING TREATMENT WITH CLOZAPINE.
004642 04-15

RESULTS OF TREATMENT BY MODITEN DEPOT IN OUTPATIENTS-WARDS IN THE SOUTH MORAVIAN REGION.
004648 04-15

APOMORPHINE-INDUCED STEREOTYPY IN MATURE AND SENESCENT RATS FOLLOWING CESSATION OF CHRONIC HALOPERIDOL TREATMENT.
004651 04-15

LITHIUM-CARBONATE IN THE TREATMENT OF MOVEMENT-DISORDERS. A CRITICAL REVIEW.
004668 04-15

THE USE OF CLINICAL KINETIC DATA IN TREATMENT WITH ANTIDEPRESSANT-DRUGS.
004686 04-16

STUDY ON THE STABILITY OF THE FACTORIAL STRUCTURE OF THE AMP SYSTEM DURING TREATMENT.
004696 04-16

ANOREXIA-NERVOSA. SYMPTOMS, COURSE AND POSSIBILITIES FOR TREATMENT.
004711 04-17

PSYCHOPHARMACOLOGY AND PSYCHOTHERAPY IN THE TREATMENT OF ANXIETY.
004712 04-17

THERAPEUTIC TREATMENT OF INSUFFICIENT PERFORMANCE IN CEREBROVASCULAR-DISEASES.
004718 04-17

Subject Index

EMOTIONAL-DISORDERS IN CHILDREN AND ADOLESCENTS: MEDICAL AND PSYCHOLOGICAL APPROACHES TO TREATMENT.
004743 04-17

CURRENT TRENDS IN TREATMENT IN PSYCHIATRY.
004747 04-17

TREATMENTS
LITHIUM LEVELS IN BLOOD-PLATELETS, SERUM, RED-BLOOD-CELLS AND BRAIN REGIONS IN RATS GIVEN ACUTE OR CHRONIC LITHIUM-SALT TREATMENTS.
000082 01-03

PRINCIPAL AND DIFFERENTIAL-EFFECTS OF HALOPERIDOL AND PLACEBO TREATMENTS UPON SPEECH DISFLUENCIES IN STUTTERERS.
000713 01-11

ATTEMPTS TO DEVELOP SUPERSENSITIVITY OR SUBSENSITIVITY RETINAL DOPAMINE-RECEPTORS AFTER VARIOUS TREATMENTS WITH ANTAGONISTS OR AGONISTS.
001350 02-03

TREATMENTS FOR SLEEP-WAKE-DISORDERS IN THE ELDERLY.
002157 02-11

REPEATED ANTIDEPRESSANT TREATMENTS INDUCE A LONG-LASTING DOPAMINE-AUTORECEPTOR SUBSENSITIVITY: IS DAILY TREATMENT NECESSARY FOR CLINICAL EFFICACY?
002659 03-03

BEHAVIOURAL-RESPONSES TO DRUGS RELEASING 5 HYDROXYTRYPTAMINE AND CATECHOLAMINES: EFFECTS OF TREATMENTS ALTERING PRECURSOR CONCENTRATIONS IN BRAIN.
002990 03-04

THE BEHAVIORAL-EFFECTS OF D-AMPHETAMINE ALONE AND IN COMBINATION WITH ACUTE AND CHRONIC MORPHINE TREATMENTS IN RATS.
003915 04-03   TR

ALTERATIONS IN GAMMA AMINOBUTYRIC-ACID-RECEPTOR SENSITIVITY FOLLOWING ACUTE AND CHRONIC ETHANOL TREATMENTS.
004037 04-03

CLASSICAL NEUROLEPTICS AND DECONDITIONING ACTIVITY AFTER SINGLE   TR
OR REPEATED TREATMENTS: ROLE OF DIFFERENT CEREBRAL NEUROTRANSMITTERS.
004115 04-04

PREVALENCE OF HYPERACTIVITY AND RELATED TREATMENTS AMONG ELEMENTARY SCHOOL CHILDREN.
004469 04-11

TREMOR
HARMALINE-INDUCED TREMOR: THE BENZODIAZEPINE-RECEPTOR AS A SITE-OF-ACTION.
001436 02-03

CASE 3: ASSESSMENT AND TREATMENT OF DRUG-INDUCED TREMOR.
002407 02-15

TREMORGENIC
ACTIONS OF TREMORGENIC FUNGAL TOXINS ON NEUROTRANSMITTER RELEASE.
002843 03-03

TREMORS
MODIFICATION OF DRUG-INDUCED CATATONIA AND TREMORS BY QUIPAZINE IN RATS AND MICE.
004164 04-04

TRENDS
TRENDS IN THE PRESCRIPTION OF PSYCHOTROPIC-DRUGS (1970-1977) IN A STATE-HOSPITAL.
000926 01-17

ANTIPSYCHOTICS AND ANTIDEPRESSANTS: NEW TRENDS AND EXPECTED FUTURE.
002539 02-17

COMPUTERIZED MONITORING OF PSYCHOTROPIC-DRUG ORDERS: SOME TRENDS AND REVELATIONS.
003566 03-16

NEW TRENDS CONCERNING THE BIOCHEMICAL-MECHANISM OF ACTION OF BENZODIAZEPINES.
003642 03-17

PSYCHOPHARMACOTHERAPY: THE PRESENT STATE AND THE DEVELOPMENT OF TRENDS.
004723 04-17

CURRENT TRENDS IN TREATMENT IN PSYCHIATRY.
004747 04-17

TRH
MODIFICATION OF THE PROLINE RESIDUE OF TRH ENHANCES BIOLOGICAL-ACTIVITY AND INHIBITS DEGRADATION.
000351 01-04

PROLACTIN AND SOMATOTROPIN RESPONSES TO TRH IN SCHIZOPHRENIC-PATIENTS.
000570 01-08

GROWTH-HORMONE AFTER TRH IN WOMEN WITH DEPRESSIVE-ILLNESS.   TR
000606 01-09

GROWTH-HORMONE (GH) RELEASE FOLLOWING THYROTROPIN-RELEASING-HORMONE (TRH) INJECTION IN MANIC-PATIENTS RECEIVING LITHIUM-CARBONATE.
000645 01-09

SOME PHARMACOLOGICAL-ASPECTS AND BIOCHEMICAL-ASPECTS OF TRH: EXPERIMENTAL AND CLINICAL DATA.
001189 02-03

TRIAZOLAM
CHRONIC USE OF TRIAZOLAM: THE EFFECTS ON THE SLEEP PATTERNS OF INSOMNIACS.
000710 01-11
INTERACTION OF TRIAZOLAM WITH DESIPRAMINE: EFFECTS OF SINGLE AND REPEATED TREATMENT ON CERTAIN PHARMACOLOGIC-RESPONSES AND BRAIN CATECHOLAMINE LEVELS.
001323 02-03
COMPARISON OF NITRAZEPAM 5 MG WITH TRIAZOLAM 0.5 MG IN YOUNG PSYCHIATRIC INSOMNIAC-INPATIENTS.
002096 02-11
THE EFFICACY OF TRIAZOLAM AND CHLORAL-HYDRATE IN GERIATRIC INSOMNIACS.
002160 02-11
THE EFFECTS OF TRIAZOLAM AND NITRAZEPAM ON SLEEP QUALITY, MORNING VIGILANCE, AND PSYCHOMOTOR PERFORMANCE.
002330 02-14
THE EFFECTS OF FLURAZEPAM, LORAZEPAM, AND TRIAZOLAM ON SLEEP AND MEMORY.
002357 02-14
DIFFICULTIES ENCOUNTERED DURING A CONTROLLED STUDY OF A NEW HYPNOTIC-DRUG (TRIAZOLAM) BY A GROUP OF GENERAL-PRACTITIONERS.
003155 03-07

TRIAZOLOTHIENODIACEPINE
EEG ASSESSMENTS OF DOSAGE AND SLEEP PROFILES FOR A HYPNOTIC-DRUG OF THE TRIAZOLOTHIENODIACEPINE SERIES.
002338 02-14

TRICHLOROPHENOXYACETIC-ACID
2,4,5 TRICHLOROPHENOXYACETIC-ACID CAUSES BEHAVIORAL-EFFECTS IN CHICKENS AT ENVIRONMENTALLY RELEVANT DOSES.
003079 03-04

TRICHOTILLOMANIA
TRICHOTILLOMANIA TREATED WITH AMITRIPTYLINE.
002083 02-10

TRICYCLIC
FLUORINATED ANALOGUES OF THE TRICYCLIC NEUROLEPTICS: 2,3 DIFLUORO DERIVATIVE OF CLOROTEPIN.
000001 01-01
THE EFFECT OF A NEW FLUORINATED TRICYCLIC NEUROLEPTIC-DRUG ISOFLOXYTHEPIN ON THE RAT STRIATAL DOPAMINE METABOLISM.
000306 01-03
SEIZURES DURING TRICYCLIC THERAPY.
000868 01-15
THE PHOTOCHEMICAL-STABILITY OF CIS-ISOMERS AND TRANS-ISOMERS OF TRICYCLIC NEUROLEPTIC-DRUGS.
001872 02-06
CHILDHOOD-ENURESIS: II. PSYCHOPATHOLOGY, TRICYCLIC CONCENTRATION IN PLASMA, AND ANTIENURETIC-EFFECT.
002354 02-14
PSYCHIATRIC-ASPECTS OF ACUTE POISONING WITH TRICYCLIC AND RELATED ANTIDEPRESSANTS – 1980.
002458 02-15
BLOOD LEVEL MEASUREMENTS OF TRICYCLIC DRUGS AS A DIAGNOSTIC TOOL.
004368 04-09

TRICYCLIC-ANTIDEPRESSANT
TRICYCLIC-ANTIDEPRESSANT DRUGS AND INDIVIDUAL DIFFERENCES IN THE EXPLORATORY-ACTIVITY OF RATS: CONTRASTING-EFFECTS OF TERTIARY AND SECONDARY AMINE COMPOUNDS.
000401 01-04
ATTENUATION OF AMPHETAMINE ANOREXIA IN RATS FOLLOWING SUBCHRONIC-TREATMENT WITH A TRICYCLIC-ANTIDEPRESSANT.
000501 01-04
HYPOMANIA AND TRICYCLIC-ANTIDEPRESSANT CHOICE.
000545 01-07
TRICYCLIC-ANTIDEPRESSANT DRUG TOLERANCE IN ORIENTAL AND OCCIDENTAL POPULATIONS.
000590 01-09
COMBINED MONOAMINE-OXIDASE-INHIBITOR TRICYCLIC-ANTIDEPRESSANT TREATMENT: A PILOT-STUDY.
000644 01-09
TRICYCLIC-ANTIDEPRESSANT DRUG-INTERACTIONS WITH HISTAMINE AND ALPHA-ADRENERGIC-RECEPTORS.
000791 01-13
EXPERIMENTAL EVALUATION OF ANTIDEPRESSANT ACTIVITY OF CLOMIPRAMINE, A NEW TRICYCLIC-ANTIDEPRESSANT DRUG.
001068 02-02
EFFECT OF CHRONIC TRICYCLIC-ANTIDEPRESSANT TREATMENT ON THE SEROTONINERGIC-AUTORECEPTOR: A MICROIONTOPHORETIC-STUDY IN THE RAT.
001135 02-03
PRESYNAPTIC ALPHA-ADRENOCEPTORS AND THE ACTION OF TRICYCLIC-ANTIDEPRESSANT DRUGS IN BEHAVIOURAL-DESPAIR IN RATS.
001829 02-04
LONG-TERM MONITORING OF TRICYCLIC-ANTIDEPRESSANT PLASMA CONCENTRATIONS.
002014 02-09
RELEVANCY OF TRICYCLIC-ANTIDEPRESSANT PLASMA LEVELS.
003246 03-09

THE BENEFITS AND RISKS OF COMBINING AN MAO-INHIBITOR AND A TRICYCLIC-ANTIDEPRESSANT.
003273 03-09
TRICYCLIC-ANTIDEPRESSANT DRUG-TREATMENT DECREASES ALPHA2-ADRENORECEPTORS ON HUMAN PLATELET MEMBRANES.
003408 03-13
EXCEPTIONAL CASES OF DEATH CAUSED BY TRICYCLIC-ANTIDEPRESSANT AGENTS.
003490 03-15
ARRHYTHMIA INDUCED BY A TRICYCLIC-ANTIDEPRESSANT IN A PATIENT WITH UNDIAGNOSED MITRAL-VALVE PROLAPSE.
003521 03-15
INTERACTION OF THE TRICYCLIC-ANTIDEPRESSANT AMITRIPTYLINE WITH PREJUNCTIONAL ALPHA AND MUSCARINIC-RECEPTORS IN THE DOG SAPHENOUS VEIN.
003756 04-03
DOXEPIN, A TRICYCLIC-ANTIDEPRESSANT, BINDS TO NORMAL, INTACT ASTROGLIAL CELLS IN CULTURES AND INHIBITS THE ISOPROTERENOL-INDUCED INCREASE IN CYCLIC-AMP PRODUCTION.
003836 04-03
ALPHA2-ADRENORECEPTORS IN RAT-BRAIN ARE DECREASED AFTER LONG-TERM TRICYCLIC-ANTIDEPRESSANT DRUG-TREATMENT.
004008 04-03
EFFECT OF CHRONIC-TREATMENT WITH TRICYCLIC-ANTIDEPRESSANT DRUGS ON IDENTIFIED BRAIN NORADRENERGIC AND SEROTONERGIC NEURONS.
004026 04-03
SUBCHRONIC-TREATMENT WITH THE TRICYCLIC-ANTIDEPRESSANT DMI INCREASES ISOLATION-INDUCED FIGHTING IN RATS.
004252 04-04
A COMPARATIVE CLINICAL-TRIAL WITH THE TRANQUILIZER TRAZODONE AND THE TRICYCLIC-ANTIDEPRESSANT CLOMIPRAMINE.
004380 04-09
NEUROLEPTIC TRICYCLIC-ANTIDEPRESSANT COMBINATION: PHARMACOLOGICAL-ASPECTS AND THERAPEUTIC INTEREST.
004501 04-13
SYMPATHOMIMETIC-AMINES AND TRICYCLIC-ANTIDEPRESSANT DRUGS.
004678 04-16

TRICYCLIC-ANTIDEPRESSANT-INDUCED
TRICYCLIC-ANTIDEPRESSANT-INDUCED MANIA.
004656 04-15

TRICYCLIC-ANTIDEPRESSANTS
REPEATED TRICYCLIC-ANTIDEPRESSANTS INDUCE A PROGRESSIVE SWITCH IN THE ELECTROPHYSIOLOGICAL RESPONSE OF DOPAMINE NEURONS TO AUTORECEPTOR STIMULATION.
000046 01-03
TRICYCLIC-ANTIDEPRESSANTS INDUCE SUBSENSITIVITY OF PRESYNAPTIC DOPAMINE-AUTORECEPTORS.
000048 01-03
ANTIDEPRESSANT PROPERTIES OF 2 4 ETHYL-2-PIPERAZINYL-4-PHENYLQUINOLINE-HCL (AD-1308) AND ITS MECHANISM-OF-ACTION AS COMPARED WITH TRICYCLIC-ANTIDEPRESSANTS.
000152 01-03
POSTAMPHETAMINE DEPRESSION OF SELF-STIMULATION RESPONDING FROM THE SUBSTANTIA-NIGRA: REVERSAL BY TRICYCLIC-ANTIDEPRESSANTS.
000419 01-04
TRICYCLIC-ANTIDEPRESSANTS: THERAPEUTIC PLASMA LEVEL.
000646 01-09
DOPAMINE-RECEPTOR BLOCKADE IN RAT-BRAIN AFTER ACUTE AND SUBCHRONIC-TREATMENT WITH TRICYCLIC-ANTIDEPRESSANTS.
001314 02-03
CONFORMATIONALLY RESTRICTED TRICYCLIC-ANTIDEPRESSANTS. 1. OCTAHYDRODIBENZAZEPINONAPHTHYRIDINES AS RIGID IMIPRAMINE ANALOGUES.
001710 02-04
HIGH-AFFINITY BINDING OF TRICYCLIC-ANTIDEPRESSANTS TO HISTAMINE H1-RECEPTORS: FACT AND ARTIFACT.
001880 02-06
EFFECT OF TRICYCLIC-ANTIDEPRESSANTS ON INDIVIDUAL SYMPTOMS.
002052 02-09
MOTOR-LEARNING ABILITIES IN SUBJECTS TREATED WITH LITHIUM-SALTS AND TRICYCLIC-ANTIDEPRESSANTS.
002058 02-09
THE PERIPHERAL ANTICHOLINERGIC-ACTIVITY OF TRICYCLIC-ANTIDEPRESSANTS: COMPARISON OF AMITRIPTYLINE AND DESIPRAMINE IN HUMAN VOLUNTEERS.
002298 02-13
CARDIOVASCULAR-EFFECTS OF THERAPEUTIC DOSES OF TRICYCLIC-ANTIDEPRESSANTS: IMPORTANCE OF BLOOD LEVEL MONITORING.
002456 02-15
DETERMINATION OF TRICYCLIC-ANTIDEPRESSANTS AND TETRACYCLIC-ANTIDEPRESSANTS AND OF THEIR METABOLIC PRODUCTS IN BIOLOGICAL FLUIDS.
002498 02-16
INTERACTIONS OF TRICYCLIC-ANTIDEPRESSANTS WITH A SYNAPTIC ION-CHANNEL.
002660 03-03

EFFECTS OF PROLONGED TREATMENT WITH LITHIUM AND TRICYCLIC-ANTIDEPRESSANTS ON DISCHARGE FREQUENCY, NOREPINEPHRINE RESPONSES AND BETA-RECEPTOR BINDING IN RAT-CEREBELLUM: ELECTROPHYSIOLOGICAL AND BIOCHEMICAL COMPARISON.
002884 03-03

PROTOCOLS FOR THE USE OF PSYCHOACTIVE-DRUGS -- PART II: PROTOCOL FOR THE TREATMENT OF DEPRESSION WITH TRICYCLIC-ANTIDEPRESSANTS.
003214 03-09

EFFECTS OF TRICYCLIC-ANTIDEPRESSANTS ON INTERPERSONAL LEARNING.
003225 03-09

HYPOMANIA AND MANIA AFTER WITHDRAWAL OF TRICYCLIC-ANTIDEPRESSANTS.
003243 03-09

EXCESSIVE PLASMA CONCENTRATIONS OF TRICYCLIC-ANTIDEPRESSANTS RESULTING FROM USUAL DOSES: A REPORT OF SIX CASES.
003479 03-15

THE EFFECT OF DIBENZAZEPINES (TRICYCLIC-ANTIDEPRESSANTS) ON CEREBRAL CAPILLARY PERMEABILITY IN THE RAT IN VIVO.
003974 04-03

TRICYCLIC-ANTIDEPRESSANTS AND HISTAMINE H1-RECEPTORS.
003986 04-03

EFFECTS OF TRICYCLIC-ANTIDEPRESSANTS ON TETRABENAZINE-INDUCED DEPLETION OF BRAIN MONOAMINES IN RATS. 1. NOREPINEPHRINE.
004062 04-03

THE EFFECTS OF TRICYCLIC-ANTIDEPRESSANTS ON PERFORMANCE UNDER A DIFFERENTIAL-REINFORCEMENT-OF-LOW-RATES SCHEDULE IN RATS.
004175 04-04

INDIVIDUAL DIFFERENCES IN EFFECTS OF TRICYCLIC-ANTIDEPRESSANTS AND ANTICHOLINERGIC-DRUGS ON OPERANT-BEHAVIOR IN THE SQUIRREL-MONKEY.
004176 04-04

MECHANISM OF MEMBRANE STABILIZING AND LYTIC-EFFECTS OF TRICYCLIC-ANTIDEPRESSANTS.
004283 04-05

PHARMACOKINETICS AND CLINICAL-RESPONSE TO TRICYCLIC-ANTIDEPRESSANTS.
004370 04-09

DIFFERENT EFFECTS OF TRICYCLIC-ANTIDEPRESSANTS AND TETRACYCLIC-ANTIDEPRESSANTS ON THE RELEASE OF TSH, PROLACTIN, AND GROWTH-HORMONE AFTER ADMINISTRATION OF THYROSTIMULATING-RELEASING-HORMONE IN MANIC-DEPRESSIVES.
004407 04-09

THE EFFECT OF FIVE TRICYCLIC-ANTIDEPRESSANTS ON SALIVARY FLOW AND MOOD IN HEALTHY VOLUNTEERS.
004560 04-14

TRICYCLIC-ANTIDEPRESSANTS AND ALCOHOLIC BLACKOUTS.
004617 04-15

RADIOIMMUNOASSAY OF TRICYCLIC-ANTIDEPRESSANTS.
004674 04-16

THERAPEUTIC MONITORING OF PLASMA CONCENTRATIONS OF TRICYCLIC-ANTIDEPRESSANTS: PERSPECTIVE OF THE CLINICAL LABORATORY.
004681 04-16

A RAPID AND SENSITIVE RADIORECEPTOR ASSAY FOR TERTIARY AMINE TRICYCLIC-ANTIDEPRESSANTS.
004689 04-16

TRICYCLICS
REPEATED TRICYCLICS INDUCE A PROGRESSIVE DOPAMINE-AUTORECEPTOR SUBSENSITIVITY INDEPENDENT OF DAILY DRUG-TREATMENT.
000047 01-03

TRIETHYLTIN-INDUCED
BRAINSTEM AUDITORY EVOKED-POTENTIALS AND MYELIN CHANGES IN TRIETHYLTIN-INDUCED EDEMA IN YOUNG ADULT RATS.
000509 01-05

TRIFLUOPERAZINE
EFFECTS OF TRIFLUOPERAZINE, CHLORPROMAZINE, AND HALOPERIDOL UPON TEMPORAL INFORMATION-PROCESSING BY SCHIZOPHRENIC-PATIENTS.
000554 01-08

A COMPARISON OF STRIATAL AND MESOLIMBIC DOPAMINE FUNCTION IN THE RAT DURING 6-MONTH TRIFLUOPERAZINE ADMINISTRATION.
001174 02-03

CHANGES IN CEREBRAL DOPAMINE FUNCTION INDUCED BY A YEARS ADMINISTRATION OF TRIFLUOPERAZINE OR THIORIDAZINE AND THEIR SUBSEQUENT WITHDRAWAL.
001175 02-03

FLUPHENAZINE, TRIFLUOPERAZINE AND PERPHENAZINE IN VACUTAINERS.
003565 03-16

TRIFLUOROETHYL-DIHYDROXYPHENYLETHYLAMINE
PREPARATION AND BIOLOGICAL ACTIONS OF N 2,2,2 TRIFLUOROETHYL-DIHYDROXYPHENYLETHYLAMINE.
003697 04-02

TRIFLUOROMETHYLTHIODIBENZOCYCLOHEPTENYLIDENEPIPERIDINE
STEREOSPECIFIC INHIBITION OF DOPAMINE-SENSITIVE ADENYLATE-CYCLASE IN CARP RETINA BY THE ENANTIOMERS OF (/-) 1 CYCLOPROPYLMETHYL TRIFLUOROMETHYLTHIODIBENZOCYCLOHEPTENYLIDENEPIPERIDINE.
003706 04-02

TRIGEMINAL-NEURALGIA
A CASE OF TRIGEMINAL-NEURALGIA TREATED WITH LITHIUM-CARBONATE.
000690 01-11

BACLOFEN IN TRIGEMINAL-NEURALGIA: ITS EFFECT ON THE SPINAL TRIGEMINAL-NUCLEUS: A PILOT-STUDY.
002122 02-11

CARBAMAZEPINE THERAPY IN TRIGEMINAL-NEURALGIA: CLINICAL-EFFECTS IN RELATION TO PLASMA CONCENTRATION.
002181 02-11

TRIGEMINAL-NUCLEUS
MICROIONTOPHORETIC STUDIES ON NORADRENERGIC INHIBITION FROM LOCUS-COERULEUS OF SPINAL TRIGEMINAL-NUCLEUS NEURONS.
000260 01-03

BACLOFEN IN TRIGEMINAL-NEURALGIA: ITS EFFECT ON THE SPINAL TRIGEMINAL-NUCLEUS: A PILOT-STUDY.
002122 02-11

TRIGGER
A BARBITURATE-EVOKED INTENSIFICATION OF POSTSYNAPTIC INHIBITION IN THE PREOPTIC OVULATORY TRIGGER REGION OF THE HYPOTHALAMUS.
002818 03-03

THE NA-K-ATPASE: A PLAUSIBLE TRIGGER FOR VOLTAGE-INDEPENDENT RELEASE OF CYTOPLASMIC NEUROTRANSMITTERS.
003953 04-03

TRIHYDROXY
DIHYDROXY AND TRIHYDROXY ANALOGS OF CHLORPROMAZINE INFLUENCE THE CENTRAL-ACTIVITY OF ADENYLATE-CYCLASE AND CYCLIC-AMP-PHOSPHODIESTERASE.
001405 02-03

TRIHYDROXYBENZYLHYDRAZINE
THE INTERACTION OF 2,3,4 TRIHYDROXYBENZYLHYDRAZINE WITH DOPA-DECARBOXYLASE FROM PIG KIDNEY.
002925 03-03

TRIIODOTHYRONINE
EFFECT OF ACUTE AND CHRONIC TRIIODOTHYRONINE (T3) ADMINISTRATION TO RATS ON CENTRAL 5 HT AND DOPAMINE-MEDIATED BEHAVIOURAL-RESPONSES AND RELATED BRAIN-BIOCHEMISTRY.
002951 03-04

INFLUENCE OF CARBAMAZEPINE ON SERUM THYROXINE AND TRIIODOTHYRONINE IN PATIENTS WITH EPILEPSY.
004488 04-11

TRIMETHADIONE
TRIMETHADIONE EFFECTS ON CHOLINERGIC RESPONSES IN APLYSIA NEURONS.
002782 03-03

TRIMIPRAMINE
TRIMIPRAMINE: TWENTY YEARS WORLDWIDE CLINICAL-EXPERIENCE.
000985 01-17

DOUBLE-BLIND CONTROLLED-STUDY: AMINEPTINE VERSUS TRIMIPRAMINE.
002051 02-09

TRIPELENNAMINE
POTENTIATION OF LETHALITY IN MICE BY COMBINATIONS OF PENTAZOCINE AND TRIPELENNAMINE.
000529 01-05

MEDICAL AND PSYCHIATRIC-COMPLICATIONS OF PENTAZOCINE AND TRIPELENNAMINE ABUSE.
000955 01-17

TRIPEPTIDE
A TRIPEPTIDE FOR CONTROL OF SCHIZOPHRENIC-SYMPTOMS.
001919 02-08

TRIPHENYLMETHYLPHOSPHONIUM-BROMIDE
MEASUREMENT OF THE MEMBRANE POTENTIAL OF ISOLATED NERVE TERMINALS BY THE LIPOPHILIC CATION (3H)TRIPHENYLMETHYLPHOSPHONIUM-BROMIDE.
002746 03-03

TRIPHOSPHATE
5' TRIPHOSPHATE RECYCLES INDEPENDENTLY OF ACETYLCHOLINE IN CHOLINERGIC SYNAPTIC VESICLES.
004063 04-03

TRITIATED
STUDIES ON THIORIDAZINE AND MESORIDAZINE METABOLISM. II. IN VIVO METABOLISM OF TRITIATED DRUGS IN RHESUS-MONKEYS.
001229 02-03

COMPARISON OF THE BINDING CHARACTERISTICS OF TRITIATED OPIATES AND OPIOID-PEPTIDES.
003802 04-03

TROTTING
DIAZEPAM-INDUCED ATAXIA IN TROTTING SQUIRREL-MONKEYS.
004138 04-04

TRYPTAMINE
ABNORMAL TRANSMETHYLATION REACTION DURING THE METABOLISM OF DOPAMINE, TRYPTAMINE, AND SEROTONIN, AND SCHIZOPHRENIC-SYMPTOMS: A CRITICAL REVIEW.
003404 03-13

N,N DIISOPROPYLTRYPTAMINE (DIPT) AND 5
METHOXYDIISOPROPYLTRYPTAMINE (5 MEO-DIPT). TWO ORALLY
ACTIVE TRYPTAMINE ANALOGS WITH CNS ACTIVITY.
004310 04-07

TRYPTAMINERGIC
PHARMACOLOGICAL EVIDENCE OF A POSSIBLE TRYPTAMINERGIC
REGULATION OF OPIATE-RECEPTORS BY USING INDALPINE, A SELECTIVE
5 HT UPTAKE INHIBITOR.
001517 02-03

TRYPTAMINES
TETRAHYDRO-BETA-CARBOLINES AND CORRESPONDING TRYPTAMINES:
IN VITRO INHIBITION OF SEROTONIN AND DOPAMINE UPTAKE BY
HUMAN BLOOD-PLATELETS.
001067 02-02
TETRAHYDRO-BETA-CARBOLINES AND CORRESPONDING TRYPTAMINES:
IN VITRO INHIBITION OF SEROTONIN, DOPAMINE AND
NORADRENALINE UPTAKE IN RAT-BRAIN SYNAPTOSOMES.
001078 02-02

TRYPTOPHAN
L TRYPTOPHAN INJECTION ENHANCES PULSATILE GROWTH-HORMONE
SECRETION IN THE RAT. (UNPUBLISHED PAPER).
000020 01-03
ENHANCEMENT OF RAT-BRAIN METABOLISM OF A TRYPTOPHAN LOAD
BY CHRONIC ETHANOL ADMINISTRATION.
000022 01-03
ACUTE CHANGES IN BRAIN TRYPTOPHAN AND SEROTONIN FOLLOWING
CARBOHYDRATE OR PROTEIN INGESTION BY DIABETIC RATS.
(UNPUBLISHED PAPER).
000060 01-03
THE CONVERSION OE (3H)TRYPTOPHAN TO 5 (3H)HYDROXYTRYPTAMINE
IN MOUSE-BRAIN FOLLOWING DEPLETION OF PHENYLALANINE AND
TYROSINE.
000148 01-03
PROSPECTIVE-TRIAL OF L TRYPTOPHAN IN MATERNITY-BLUES.
000683 01-11
TRANSIENT-EFFECT OF L TRYPTOPHAN IN PROGRESSIVE MYOCLONUS
EPILEPSY WITHOUT LAFORA-BODIES: CLINICAL-STUDY AND
ELECTROPHYSIOLOGICAL-STUDY.
000694 01-11
PAIN AND TRYPTOPHAN.
000775 01-13
LITHIUM EFFECTS ON HIGH-AFFINITY TRYPTOPHAN UPTAKE: EVIDENCE
AGAINST A STABILIZATION MECHANISM.
001496 02-03
CLINICAL-STUDIES AND BIOLOGICAL-STUDIES OF L TRYPTOPHAN IN
DEPRESSION.
001977 02-09
EFFICACY AND SIDE-EFFECTS OF CHLORAL-HYDRATE AND TRYPTOPHAN
AS SLEEPING-AIDS IN PSYCHOGERIATRIC-PATIENTS.
002077 02-10
THE RELATIONSHIP OF ALPHA AND DELTA EEG FREQUENCIES TO PAIN
AND MOOD IN FIBROSITIS-PATIENTS TREATED WITH CHLORPROMAZINE
AND L TRYPTOPHAN.
002152 02-11
METHOD FOR THE DETERMINATION OF TRYPTOPHAN IN SERUM AND
CEREBROSPINAL-FLUID.
002208 02-13
EFFECT OF L TRYPTOPHAN ON APOMORPHINE-INDUCED GROWTH-
HORMONE SECRETION IN NORMAL SUBJECTS.
002253 02-13
EFFECTS OF ALBUMIN, AMINO-ACIDS, AND CLOFIBRATE ON THE UPTAKE
OF TRYPTOPHAN BY THE RAT-BRAIN.
002673 03-03
THE FUNCTIONAL IMPORTANCE OF INCREASED BRAIN TRYPTOPHAN IN
THE SEROTONERGIC RESPONSE TO RESTRAINT STRESS.
002779 03-03
EFFECTS OF BENSERAZIDE AND CARBIDOPA ON THE METABOLISM OF L
TRYPTOPHAN BY ISOLATED RAT LIVER CELLS.
002899 03-03
DIFFERENTIAL-EFFECTS OF SHORT-TERM AND LONG-TERM LITHIUM ON
TRYPTOPHAN UPTAKE AND SEROTONERGIC FUNCTION IN CAT BRAIN.
002911 03-03
EFFECT OF P CHLOROPHENYLALANINE AND TRYPTOPHAN ON SLEEP, EEG
AND MOTOR-ACTIVITY IN THE RAT.
002958 03-04
THE THERAPEUTIC ACTIVITY OF TRYPTOPHAN AND ITS EFFECT ON
SEROTONIN METABOLISM IN EPILEPTIC-PATIENTS.
003289 03-11
PLASMA FREE AND TOTAL TRYPTOPHAN, BLOOD SEROTONIN, AND THE
HYPERACTIVITY-SYNDROME: NO EVIDENCE FOR THE SEROTONIN
DEFICIENCY HYPOTHESIS.
003312 03-11
LEVELS OF 5 HYDROXYINDOLEACETIC-ACID AND TRYPTOPHAN IN
LUMBAR CEREBROSPINAL-FLUID AND BLOOD OF PATIENTS WITH
DEMENTIA AND NORMAL PRESSURE HYDROCEPHALUS AFTER
TRYPTOPHAN ADMINISTRATION.
003419 03-13
DAYTIME EFFECTS OF L TRYPTOPHAN.
003455 03-14

STRESS-MODULATED ALTERATION OF BRAIN BIOGENIC-AMINES IN THE
RAT: EFFECTS OF L TRYPTOPHAN.
003978 04-03
EFFECT OF PRENATAL PHENYTOIN ADMINISTRATION ON BRAIN
TRYPTOPHAN METABOLISM OF RAT OFFSPRING DURING THE
PREWEANING PERIOD.
004108 04-04
THE EFFECTS OF TRYPTOPHAN AND MANIPULATIONS OF SEROTONERGIC-
RECEPTORS ON TONIC IMMOBILITY IN CHICKENS.
004245 04-04
POTENTIATION   THE EFFECT OF ANTIDEPRESSANT-DRUGS BY
TRYPTOPHANOF
004412 04-09
CORRECTION OF THE EXTRAPYRAMIDAL NEUROLEPTIC-SYNDROME BY
TRYPTOPHAN AND THE TIME-COURSE OF ITS CONTENT IN THE BLOOD
OF PATIENTS.
004434 04-11
HYPERVENTILATION-SYNDROME, TREATMENT WITH L TRYPTOPHAN AND
PYRIDOXINE; PREDICTIVE VALUES OF XANTHURENIC-ACID EXCRETION.
004456 04-11

TRYPTOPHAN-HYDROXYLASE
THE ROLE OF INTRANEURONAL 5 HT AND OF TRYPTOPHAN-
HYDROXYLASE ACTIVATION IN THE CONTROL OF 5 HT SYNTHESIS IN
RAT-BRAIN SLICES INCUBATED IN K-ENRICHED MEDIUM.
000123 01-03
GLUCOCORTICOIDS AS A REGULATORY FACTOR FOR BRAIN TRYPTOPHAN-
HYDROXYLASE DURING DEVELOPMENT.
001500 02-03
LONG-TERM EFFECTS OF MULTIPLE DOSES OF METHAMPHETAMINE ON
TRYPTOPHAN-HYDROXYLASE AND TYROSINE-HYDROXYLASE ACTIVITY
IN RAT-BRAIN.
003850 04-03
STUDIES ON THE KINETIC PROPERTIES OF TRYPTOPHAN-HYDROXYLASE OF
RABBIT MESENCEPHALON AND PONS-MEDULLA: EFFECT OF LONG-
TERM-TREATMENT WITH NEUROLEPTICS AND ANTIDEPRESSANTS.
003852 04-03 ·
() 6 FLUOROTRYPTOPHAN, AN INHIBITOR OF TRYPTOPHAN-
HYDROXYLASE: SLEEP AND WAKEFULNESS IN THE RAT.
004189 04-04

TRYPTOPHAN-INDUCED
EFFECT OF CITALOPRAM (LU-10-171) ON TRANYLCYPROMINE AND
TRYPTOPHAN-INDUCED WET-DOG-SHAKES IN RATS.
001682 02-04

TRYPTOPHOL-INDUCED
TRYPTOPHOL-INDUCED CHANGE IN BRAIN 5 HYDROXYTRYPTAMINE
METABOLISM.
001236 02-03

TSH
CHANGES OF ACTH, STH, TSH AND PROLACTIN LEVELS IN ENDOTOXIN
SHOCK IN RATS.
000119 01-03
BASAL AND STIMULATED LEVELS OF PROLACTIN, TSH AND LH IN SERUM
OF CHRONIC SCHIZOPHRENIC-PATIENTS, LONG-TERM TREATED WITH
NEUROLEPTICS.
001935 02-08
BASAL AND STIMULATED LEVELS OF PROLACTIN, TSH, AND LH IN SERUM
OF CHRONIC SCHIZOPHRENIC-PATIENTS LONG-TERM TREATED WITH
NEUROLEPTICS: RELATIONS TO PSYCHOPATHOLOGY.
001936 02-08
THE TSH RESPONSE TO TRH INJECTION IN PSYCHIATRIC-PATIENTS: A
REVIEW.
002145 02-11
TSH, HGH, HPR, AND CORTISOL RESPONSE TO TRH IN DEPRESSED-
PATIENTS.
004399 04-09
DIFFERENT EFFECTS OF TRICYCLIC-ANTIDEPRESSANTS AND TETRACYCLIC-
ANTIDEPRESSANTS ON THE RELEASE OF TSH, PROLACTIN, AND
GROWTH-HORMONE AFTER ADMINISTRATION OF THYROSTIMULATING-
RELEASING-HORMONE IN MANIC-DEPRESSIVES.
004407 04-09

TUBERCLE
CROSS-TOLERANCE OF DOPAMINE METABOLISM TO BACLOFEN, GAMMA
BUTYROLACTONE AND HA-966 IN THE STRIATUM AND OLFACTORY
TUBERCLE OF THE RAT.
002681 03-03
SLEEP ELICITED BY OLFACTORY TUBERCLE STIMULATION AND THE EFFECT
OF ATROPINE.
002955 03-04

TUBEROINFUNDIBULAR
DISRUPTION OF 5 HYDROXYTRYPTAMINERGIC NEURONAL FUNCTION
BLOCKS THE ACTION OF MORPHINE ON TUBEROINFUNDIBULAR
DOPAMINERGIC NEURONS.
002700 03-03

TUBOCURARINE
ANTAGONISM OF SOME CENTRAL-EFFECTS OF D TUBOCURARINE BY
GAMMA AMINOBUTYRIC-ACID.
004102 04-04

TUMOUR
DIAZEPAM AS TUMOUR PROMOTER.
003495 03-15
TUMOURS
ABSENCE OF EFFECT OF DIAZEPAM ON TUMOURS.
003497 03-15
TURNING
TURNING ON THE ENDORPHINS.
001489 02-03
TURNOVER
ACUTE AND CHRONIC EFFECTS OF NEUROLEPTICS AND ACUTE EFFECTS OF
APOMORPHINE AND AMPHETAMINE ON DOPAMINE TURNOVER IN
CORPUS-STRIATUM AND SUBSTANTIA-NIGRA OF THE RAT-BRAIN.
000215 01-03
EFFECTS OF CHRONIC-TREATMENT WITH L SULPIRIDE AND HALOPERIDOL
ON CENTRAL DOPAMINE TURNOVER EVALUATED IN DOPAMINE CELL
BODY AND NERVE TERMINAL-RICH AREAS.
001096 02-03
EFFECT OF TABERNANTHINE ON THE TURNOVER TIME OF BRAIN
CATECHOLAMINES IN NORMAL AND HYPOBARIC HYPOXIC RATS.
001187 02-03
EFFECT OF MOXESTROL ON HALOPERIDOL-INDUCED CHANGES IN
STRIATAL ACETYLCHOLINE LEVELS AND DOPAMINE TURNOVER.
001218 02-03
CHOLECYSTOKININ-PEPTIDES PRODUCE MARKED REDUCTION OF
DOPAMINE TURNOVER IN DISCRETE AREAS IN THE RAT-BRAIN
FOLLOWING INTERAVENTRICULAR INJECTION.
001239 02-03
INFLUENCE OF MORPHINE ON MEMBRANE TURNOVER AND FUNCTION.
001280 02-03
THE EFFECT OF CARBIDINE ON DOPAMINE TURNOVER IN THE CORPUS-
STRIATUM OF THE BRAINS OF RATS.
001352 02-03
SHORT-TERM AND LONG-TERM MODIFICATION OF SKELETAL-MUSCLE
SODIUM-PUMP ACTIVITY AND MUSCLE PROTEIN TURNOVER.
(UNPUBLISHED PAPER).
001519 02-03
ACTIONS OF ENKEPHALIN, MU AND PARTIAL AGONIST ANALGESICS ON
ACETYLCHOLINE TURNOVER IN RAT-BRAIN.
001541 02-03
EFFECT OF APOMORPHINE ON MORPHINE-INDUCED DECREASE IN
LOCOMOTOR-ACTIVITY AND INCREASE IN DOPAMINE TURNOVER IN
RATS.
001728 02-04
EFFECTS OF 4 AMINOPYRIDINE ON THE TURNOVER OF MONOAMINES IN
THE CENTRAL-NERVOUS-SYSTEM OF THE RAT.
002658 03-03
EFFECT OF MAZINDOL ON BRAIN DOPAMINE TURNOVER IN SPIPERONE
TREATED RATS.
002726 03-03
GABA ANTAGONISTS ENHANCE DOPAMINE TURNOVER IN THE RAT
RETINA IN VIVO.
002772 03-03
ACCELERATED METABOLISM OF PROBENECID DURING LONG-TERM-
TREATMENT OF RATS WITH ANTICONVULSANT-DRUGS: EFFECT ON
CENTRAL SEROTONIN TURNOVER STUDIES.
002890 03-03
MYOINOSITOL TURNOVER IN THE INTACT RAT-BRAIN: INCREASED
PRODUCTION AFTER D-AMPHETAMINE.
003723 04-03
CATECHOLAMINE TURNOVER IN RAT-CEREBRAL-CORTEX AND CAUDATE
FOLLOWING REPEATED TREATMENT WITH DIHYDROERGOTOXINE.
003765 04-03
SOME BARBITURATES ENHANCE THE EFFECT OF MUSCIMOL ON
DOPAMINE TURNOVER IN THE RAT RETINA.
003873 04-03
EFFECT OF IMIPRAMINE ON CENTRAL 5 HYDROXYTRYPTAMINE
TURNOVER AND METABOLISM IN RATS.
003999 04-03
ONTOGENY OF HISTAMINERGIC NEUROTRANSMISSION IN THE RAT-
BRAIN: CONCOMITANT DEVELOPMENT OF NEURONAL HISTAMINE, H1-
RECEPTORS, AND H1-RECEPTOR-MEDIATED STIMULATION OF
PHOSPHOLIPID TURNOVER.
004021 04-03
ACETYLCHOLINE TURNOVER AND AGGRESSION IN RELATED THREE
STRAINS OF MICE.
004151 04-04
TURNOVER-RATE
THE EFFECTS OF MUSCARINIC-RECEPTOR BLOCKERS ON THE TURNOVER-
RATE OF ACETYLCHOLINE IN VARIOUS REGIONS OF THE RAT-BRAIN.
000328 01-03
EFFECT OF ANTINOCICEPTIVE DOSES OF OXOTREMORINE ON MOUSE-
BRAIN ACETYLCHOLINE TURNOVER-RATE.
001513 02-03
ESTIMATING IN VIVO THE TURNOVER-RATE OF BRAIN ENKEPHALINS.
001884 02-06
TURNOVER-RATES
DOSE-DEPENDENT PHARMACOKINETICS OF ALPHA METHYL-P-TYROSINE
(ALPHA MT) AND COMPARISON OF CATECHOLAMINE TURNOVER-
RATES AFTER TWO DOSES OF ALPHA MT.
001532 02-03

TWO-COMPONENT
SIMULTANEOUS HIGH-PERFORMANCE LIQUID-CHROMATOGRAPHIC-
DETERMINATION OF AMITRIPTYLINE-HYDROCHLORIDE IN TWO-
COMPONENT TABLET FORMULATIONS.
004673 04-16
TWO-DRUG
RAPID ACQUISITION OF A TWO-DRUG DISCRIMINATION: TIME OF DAY
EFFECT UPON SALINE STATE.
004214 04-04
TWO-SHOCK
A SIGNAL-DETECTION-ANALYSIS OF MORPHINE EFFECTS ON THE
RESPONSE BIAS OF RATS IN A TWO-SHOCK DISCRIMINATION TASK.
004124 04-04
TWO-WAY
TWO-WAY AVOIDANCE LEARNING UNDER THE INFLUENCE OF NOOTROPIC-
DRUGS.
001647 02-04
TYPE-1
BIOCHEMICAL-EVIDENCE FOR TYPE-1 AND TYPE-2 OPIATE-RECEPTORS.
(UNPUBLISHED PAPER).
001050 02-01
SIMILARITIES AND DISSIMILARITIES BETWEEN DOPAMINE AND
NEUROLEPTIC-RECEPTORS: FURTHER EVIDENCE FOR TYPE-1 AND TYPE-2
DOPAMINE-RECEPTORS IN THE CNS.
001480 02-03
INTERCONVERTING MU AND DELTA-FORMS OF TYPE-1 OPIATE-RECEPTORS
IN THE RAT STRIATAL PATCHES.
003737 04-03
TYPE-2
BIOCHEMICAL-EVIDENCE FOR TYPE-1 AND TYPE-2 OPIATE-RECEPTORS.
(UNPUBLISHED PAPER).
001050 02-01
SIMILARITIES AND DISSIMILARITIES BETWEEN DOPAMINE AND
NEUROLEPTIC-RECEPTORS: FURTHER EVIDENCE FOR TYPE-1 AND TYPE-2
DOPAMINE-RECEPTORS IN THE CNS.
001480 02-03
TYPICAL
THE EFFECT OF TYPICAL AND ATYPICAL NEUROLEPTICS ON BINDING OF
(3H)SPIROPERIDOL IN CALF CAUDATE.
003906 04-03
TYRAMINE
THE EFFECT OF MONOAMINE-OXIDASE-INHIBITORS ON FIRST-PASS
METABOLISM OF TYRAMINE IN DOG INTESTINE.
000141 01-03
RESPONSES TO TYRAMINE AND NOREPINEPHRINE AFTER IMIPRAMINE
AND TRAZODONE.
000864 01-15
THE EFFECT OF PHENELZINE AND SOME OF ITS PARA HALOGENATED
DERIVATIVES ON THE LEVELS OF BRAIN TYRAMINE AND OCTOPAMINE
IN THE MOUSE.
001077 02-02
A COMPARISON OF THE EFFECTS OF METHYLPHENIDATE AND
AMPHETAMINE ON THE SIMULTANEOUS RELEASE OF RADIOLABELLED
DOPAMINE AND P OR M TYRAMINE FROM RAT STRIATAL SLICES.
001207 02-03
TYRAMINE CONTENT OF CANNED AND PACKET SOUPS.
002394 02-15
BETA PHENYLETHYLAMINE, PHENYLETHANOLAMINE, TYRAMINE AND
OCTOPAMINE. (UNPUBLISHED PAPER).
002601 02-17
TYRAMINE PRESSOR TEST AND CARDIOVASCULAR-EFFECTS OF
CHLORIMIPRAMINE AND NORTRIPTYLINE IN HEALTHY VOLUNTEERS.
003428 03-13
INFLUENCE OF CALCIUM ON NORADRENALINE RELEASE EVOKED BY 5
HYDROXYTRYPTAMINE, TYRAMINE AND POTASSIUM FROM GOAT
PIAL-ARTERIES.
003925 04-03
TYRAMINES
METHYLPHENIDATE-LIKE STIMULANTS IN VITRO RELEASE
(3H)TYRAMINES BUT NOT (14C)DOPAMINE.
002706 03-03
TYROSINE
THE CONVERSION OF (3H)TRYPTOPHAN TO 5 (3H)HYDROXYTRYPTAMINE
IN MOUSE-BRAIN FOLLOWING DEPLETION OF PHENYLALANINE AND
TYROSINE.
000148 01-03
TYROSINE ADMINISTRATION REDUCES BLOOD-PRESSURE AND ENHANCES
BRAIN NOREPINEPHRINE RELEASE IN SPONTANEOUSLY HYPERTENSIVE-
RATS.
000296 01-03
EFFECTS OF CENTRALLY-ADMINISTERED AND SYSTEMICALLY
ADMINISTERED L TYROSINE AND L LEUCINE ON OVARIAN FUNCTION IN
THE OLD RAT.
001180 02-03
THE HYPOTENSIVE-EFFECT OF CENTRALLY-ADMINISTERED TYROSINE.
001548 02-03

ULTRASTRUCTURE
ELECTRON MICROSCOPIC STUDIES OF BRAIN SLICES: THE EFFECTS OF
HIGH-FREQUENCY STIMULATION ON DENDRITIC ULTRASTRUCTURE.
(UNPUBLISHED PAPER).
001036 02-01

CANNABIS-SATIVA: EFFECTS ON BRAIN FUNCTION AND ULTRASTRUCTURE
IN RHESUS-MONKEYS.
002747 03-03

EFFECTS OF TAIPOXIN ON THE ULTRASTRUCTURE OF CHOLINERGIC AXON
TERMINALS IN THE MOUSE ADRENAL-MEDULLA.
003916 04-03

UMBILICAL-CORD-SERUM
CONCENTRATIONS OF CIS(Z) FLUPENTHIXOL IN MATERNAL SERUM,
AMNIOTIC-FLUID, UMBILICAL-CORD-SERUM, AND MILK.
002423 02-15

UNANESTHETIZED
CONVERGENT PROPERTIES AND CHEMICAL SENSITIVITY OF MIDBRAIN
RETICULAR FORMATION NEURONS OF UNANESTHETIZED RABBITS.
003972 04-03

UNCONDITIONED
THE EFFECTS OF IMIPRAMINE TREATMENT ON THE UNCONDITIONED
ALIMENTARY BEHAVIOR AND CLASSICAL CONDITIONED SALIVARY
REACTIONS IN DOGS.
003030 03-04

UNCONDITIONED-STIMULUS
INTERFERENCE WITH INGESTIONAL AVERSION LEARNING PRODUCED BY
PREEXPOSURE TO THE UNCONDITIONED-STIMULUS: ASSOCIATIVE-
ASPECTS AND NONASSOCIATIVE-ASPECTS.
001610 02-04

UNDERACTIVITY
PHYSOSTIGMINE IN TOURETTE-SYNDROME: EVIDENCE FOR CHOLINERGIC
UNDERACTIVITY.
003286 03-10

UNDERCUT
ASTHMA THERAPY MAY UNDERCUT KIDS AT SCHOOL.
004475 04-11

UNDERNUTRITION
TREATMENT OF UNDERNUTRITION AND ELECTROLYTE-DISTURBANCES IN
ANOREXIA-NERVOSA.
004531 04-13

UNDERSTANDING
UNDERSTANDING AND USE OF CHEMOTHERAPY BY LEARNING-
DISABILITIES AND BEHAVIOR-DISORDERS TEACHERS.
000965 01-17

ATTEMPT AT PSYCHOLOGICAL UNDERSTANDING AND TREATMENT OF
PSYCHOLOGICAL ASTHENIA AND ASTHENO-DEPRESSIVE-SYNDROMES
USING ERGADYL.
001974 02-09

UNDESIRABLE
UNDESIRABLE EFFECTS OF MEDICINES: A REVIEW OF SEVERAL
PUBLICATIONS ISSUED FROM 1977-1979.
004632 04-15

SIDE-EFFECTS AND UNDESIRABLE COMBINATIONS OF PSYCHOTROPIC-
MEDICATIONS.
004663 04-15

UNDIAGNOSED
ARRHYTHMIA INDUCED BY A TRICYCLIC-ANTIDEPRESSANT IN A PATIENT
WITH UNDIAGNOSED MITRAL-VALVE PROLAPSE.
003521 03-15

UNILATERAL
ROTATIONAL-BEHAVIOR INDUCED BY COCAINE ANALOGS IN RATS WITH
UNILATERAL 6 HYDROXYDOPAMINE LESIONS OF THE SUBSTANTIA-
NIGRA: DEPENDENCE UPON DOPAMINE UPTAKE INHIBITION.
000404 01-04

FACTORS INFLUENCING SEIZURE DURATION AND NUMBER OF SEIZURES
APPLIED IN UNILATERAL ELECTROCONVULSIVE-THERAPY: ANESTHETICS
AND BENZODIAZEPINES.
000792 01-13

UNILATERAL 5,7 DIHYDROXYTRYPTAMINE LESIONS OF THE DORSAL
RAPHE NUCLEUS (DRN) AND RAT ROTATIONAL-BEHAVIOUR.
001578 02-04

MORPHINE-DEPENDENCE AND DOPAMINERGIC-ACTIVITY: TESTS OF
CIRCLING RESPONSES IN RATS WITH UNILATERAL NIGRAL LESIONS.
001641 02-04

HANDEDNESS IN RATS: BLOCKADE OF REACHING-BEHAVIOR BY
UNILATERAL 6 OHDA INJECTIONS INTO SUBSTANTIA-NIGRA AND
CAUDATE-NUCLEUS.
001778 02-04

THE STRIATONIGRAL GABA PATHWAY: FUNCTIONAL AND
NEUROCHEMICAL CHARACTERISTICS IN RATS WITH UNILATERAL
STRIATAL KAINIC-ACID LESIONS.
001816 02-04

THE EFFECT OF DOPAMINE UPTAKE BLOCKING-AGENTS ON THE
AMPHETAMINE-INDUCED CIRCLING-BEHAVIOR IN MICE WITH
UNILATERAL NIGROSTRIATAL LESIONS.
004117 04-04

THE INFLUENCE OF UNILATERAL 6 HYDROXYDOPAMINE LESIONS OF THE
SUBSTANTIA-NIGRA IN THE ABSENCE OF THE TELENCEPHALON.
004197 04-04

UNILATERALLY
THE RELATIONSHIP BETWEEN LOSS OF DOPAMINE NERVE TERMINALS, STRIATAL (3H)SPIROPERIDOL BINDING AND ROTATIONAL-BEHAVIOR IN UNILATERALLY 6 HYDROXYDOPAMINE LESIONED RATS.
004129 04-04

UNIMPAIRED
UNIMPAIRED QUININE METABOLISM IN RATS WITH VENTROMEDIAL HYPOTHALAMIC LESIONS.
003821 04-03

UNIPOLAR
THREE CASES OF UNIPOLAR DELUSIONAL DEPRESSION RESPONSIVE TO L-DOPA.
000628 01-09
THYROTROPHIN RESPONSE TO THYROTROPHIN-RELEASING-HORMONE IN UNIPOLAR AND BIPOLAR AFFECTIVE-ILLNESS.
003237 03-09
LITHIUM AND IMIPRAMINE IN THE PROPHYLAXIS OF UNIPOLAR AND BIPOLAR-II DEPRESSION: A PROSPECTIVE, PLACEBO-CONTROLLED COMPARISON.
003252 03-09
LITHIUM UPTAKE IN RED CELLS OF CYCLOID AND UNIPOLAR DYSTHYMIC-PATIENTS.
003258 03-09

UNITARY
EVIDENCE FOR, AND LOCALIZATION OF, A UNITARY DOPAMINE-RECEPTOR COMPOSED OF COOPERATIVELY LINKED SUBUNIT BINDING-SITES IN RAT STRIATUM.
000186 01-03
UNITARY DOPAMINERGIC-RECEPTOR COMPOSED OF COOPERATIVELY LINKED AGONIST AND ANTAGONIST SUBUNIT BINDING-SITES.
001342 02-03
MUSCARINIC-RECEPTOR: MULTIPLE SITES OR UNITARY CONCEPT?
003896 04-03

UNITS
ACUTE AND CHRONIC OPIATE-EFFECTS ON SINGLE UNITS AND EEG OF MEDIAL THALAMUS AND HIPPOCAMPUS: A LATENCY ANALYSIS.
001344 02-03
GABA-RECEPTORS AS SUPRAMOLECULAR UNITS.
002819 03-03

UNIVERSITY-OF-LEEDS
PROCEEDINGS OF THE BRITISH-PHARMACOLOGICAL-SOCIETY, 12TH-14TH SEPTEMBER, 1979, UNIVERSITY-OF-LEEDS.
000966 01-17

UNMASKING
CONSISTENT UNMASKING OF DOPAMINE-INDUCED DILATION OF THE CANINE FEMORAL VASCULAR BED.
003911 04-03

UNMYELINATED
EVIDENCE THAT THE OPIATE-RECEPTORS OF THE SUBSTANTIA-GELATINOSA CONTRIBUTE TO THE DEPRESSION, BY INTRAVENOUS MORPHINE, OF THE SPINAL TRANSMISSION OF IMPULSES IN UNMYELINATED PRIMARY AFFERENTS.
002767 03-03
SUPRASPINAL INHIBITION OF THE EXCITATION OF DORSAL-HORN NEURONES BY IMPULSES IN UNMYELINATED PRIMARY AFFERENTS: LACK OF EFFECT BY STRYCHNINE AND BICUCULLINE.
003778 04-03

UNRESTRAINED
THE EFFECT OF CORTISOL MICROIONOPHORETIC-APPLICATIONS ON THE ACTIVITY OF HIPPOCAMPAL NEURONS IN UNRESTRAINED RABBITS.
001123 02-03

UNSTABLE
NEUROTRANSMITTERS AND DEPRESSION: TOO MUCH, TOO LITTLE, TOO UNSTABLE -- OR NOT UNSTABLE ENOUGH?
002931 03-03
TREATMENT OF UNSTABLE ANGINA BY DILTIAZEM.
004307 04-07

UNSTRESSED
SUPPRESSION OF SERUM PROLACTIN BY NALOXONE BUT NOT BY ANTI-BETA-ENDORPHIN ANTISERUM IN STRESSED AND UNSTRESSED RATS.
002871 03-03

UNTREATED
ACTH4-10 AND MEMORY IN ECT TREATED AND UNTREATED PATIENTS. I. EFFECT ON CONSOLIDATION.
001982 02-09
ACTH4-10 AND MEMORY IN ECT TREATED PATIENTS AND UNTREATED CONTROLS. II. EFFECT ON RETRIEVAL.
001983 02-09

UNWANTED
THERAPEUTICS V -- THE UNWANTED EFFECTS OF ANTIPSYCHOTICS.
000892 01-15
UNWANTED EFFECTS OF LITHIUM-CARBONATE USED IN THE PREVENTION OF RELAPSES OF AFFECTIVE-ILLNESS.
004625 04-15

UPDATE
TARDIVE-DYSKINESIA: REVIEW AND UPDATE.
000862 01-15
UPDATE ON LITHIUM: 1979-1980.
002450 02-15
HALOPERIDOL UPDATE: 1958-1980.
002517 02-17

THE BENZODIAZEPINE-RECEPTOR: AN UPDATE.
002833 03-03
PSYCHOPHARMACOLOGY UPDATE.
003583 03-17

UPHOLDS
FEDERAL-COURT UPHOLDS RIGHT-TO-REFUSE PSYCHOTROPIC-DRUGS, ORDERS IMPROVEMENTS AT LIMA-STATE-HOSPITAL.
002583 02-17

UPTAKE
ARYLDIALKENYLPIPERAZINES AS SELECTIVE AND VERY POTENT INHIBITORS OF DOPAMINE UPTAKE.
000005 01-01
MATURATION OF SYMPATHETIC NEUROTRANSMISSION IN THE RAT HEART. III. DEVELOPMENTAL-CHANGES IN RESERPINE INHIBITION OF NOREPINEPHRINE UPTAKE INTO ISOLATED SYNAPTIC VESICLES.
000025 01-03
INHIBITION OF HIGH-AFFINITY CHOLINE UPTAKE: STRUCTURE-ACTIVITY STUDIES.
000026 01-03
ANTIHISTAMINE EFFECT ON SYNAPTOSOMAL UPTAKE OF SEROTONIN, NOREPINEPHRINE AND DOPAMINE.
000035 01-03
ACUTE VERSUS CHRONIC EFFECTS OF SEROTONIN UPTAKE BLOCKERS ON POTENTIATION OF THE SEROTONIN SYNDROME.
000050 01-03
INHIBITION OF BRAIN SYNAPTOSOMAL UPTAKE OF CHOLINE BY SOME 2 CARBOXAMIDOSTRYCHNINE DERIVATIVES WITH MUSCLE-RELAXANT PROPERTIES.
000084 01-03
COMPARISON OF THE EFFECTS OF THE ISOMERS OF AMPHETAMINE, METHYLPHENIDATE AND DEOXYPIPRADROL ON THE UPTAKE OF L (3H)NOREPINEPHRINE AND (3H)DOPAMINE BY SYNAPTIC VESICLES FROM RAT-WHOLE-BRAIN, STRIATUM AND HYPOTHALAMUS.
000091 01-03
EFFECT OF MORPHINE ON CALCIUM UPTAKE BY LYSED SYNAPTOSOMES.
000117 01-03
THE MONOAMINE-OXIDASE-INHIBITORS CLORGYLINE AND L DEPRENYL ALSO AFFECT THE UPTAKE OF DOPAMINE, NORADRENALINE AND SEROTONIN BY RAT-BRAIN SYNAPTOSOMAL PREPARATIONS.
000171 01-03
INHIBITION OF NEURONAL UPTAKE REDUCES THE PRESYNAPTIC EFFECTS OF CLONIDINE BUT NOT OF ALPHA METHYLNORADRENALINE ON THE STIMULATION-EVOKED RELEASE OF 3H NORADRENALINE FROM RAT OCCIPITAL-CORTEX SLICES.
000227 01-03
RELATION BETWEEN THE EFFECTS OF ANTIDEPRESSANT-DRUGS ON THE UPTAKE OF MONOAMINES AND ON THE SPONTANEOUS ACTIVITY OF CENTRAL NEURONS.
000267 01-03
LONG-TERM EFFECTS OF CONTINUOUS EXPOSURE TO AMPHETAMINE ON BRAIN DOPAMINE CONCENTRATION AND SYNAPTOSOMAL UPTAKE IN MICE.
000287 01-03
ANALYSIS OF THE ACTIVATION OF DOPAMINE METABOLISM BY A SEROTONIN UPTAKE INHIBITOR.
000315 01-03
CGP-6085-A, A NEW, SPECIFIC, INHIBITOR OF SEROTONIN UPTAKE: NEUROCHEMICAL CHARACTERIZATION AND COMPARISON WITH OTHER SEROTONIN UPTAKE BLOCKERS.
000316 01-03
INHIBITION OF (3H)DIAZEPAM BINDING TO RAT-BRAIN CORTICAL SYNAPTOSOMAL MEMBRANES BY ADENOSINE UPTAKE BLOCKERS.
000330 01-03
ROTATIONAL-BEHAVIOR INDUCED BY COCAINE ANALOGS IN RATS WITH UNILATERAL 6 HYDROXYDOPAMINE LESIONS OF THE SUBSTANTIA-NIGRA: DEPENDENCE UPON DOPAMINE UPTAKE INHIBITION.
000404 01-04
NOREPINEPHRINE UPTAKE INHIBITORS AS BIOCHEMICALLY-SELECTIVE AND BEHAVIORALLY-SELECTIVE ANTAGONISTS OF THE LOCOMOTOR-STIMULATION INDUCED BY INDIRECTLY ACTING SYMPATHOMIMETIC-AMINES IN MICE.
000492 01-04
DECREASED UPTAKE OF 5 HYDROXYTRYPTAMINE IN BLOOD-PLATELETS FROM PATIENTS WITH ENDOGENOUS DEPRESSION.
000637 01-09
IN VITRO EFFECT OF PHENCYCLIDINE AND OTHER PSYCHOMOTOR STIMULANTS ON SEROTONIN UPTAKE IN HUMAN PLATELETS.
000750 01-13
EFFECT OF NEUROLEPTIC-DRUGS ON LITHIUM UPTAKE BY THE HUMAN ERYTHROCYTE.
000973 01-17
TETRAHYDRO-BETA-CARBOLINES AND CORRESPONDING TRYPTAMINES: IN VITRO INHIBITION OF SEROTONIN AND DOPAMINE UPTAKE BY HUMAN BLOOD-PLATELETS.
001067 02-02
TETRAHYDRO-BETA-CARBOLINES AND CORRESPONDING TRYPTAMINES: IN VITRO INHIBITION OF SEROTONIN, DOPAMINE AND NORADRENALINE UPTAKE IN RAT-BRAIN SYNAPTOSOMES.
001078 02-02

GABA AGONISTS AND UPTAKE INHIBITORS DESIGNED AS AGENTS WITH IRREVERSIBLE ACTIONS.
001079 02-02

LONG-TERM EFFECT OF NEUROLEPTICS ON CORTICOSTERONE SEPTOHIPPOCAMPAL UPTAKE IN RATS.
001107 02-03

AN EXAMINATION OF FACTORS INFLUENCING ADRENERGIC TRANSMISSION IN THE PITHED RAT, WITH SPECIAL REFERENCE TO NORADRENALINE UPTAKE MECHANISMS AND POSTJUNCTIONAL ALPHA-ADRENOCEPTORS.
001196 02-03

EFFECTS OF RATE OF BLOOD FLOW ON FRACTIONAL EXTRACTION AND ON UPTAKE OF INFUSED NORADRENALINE BY BROWN ADIPOSE TISSUE IN VIVO.
001231 02-03

THE INFLUENCE OF EXTERNAL SODIUM AND POTASSIUM ON LITHIUM UPTAKE BY PRIMARY BRAIN CELL CULTURES AT THERAPEUTIC LITHIUM CONCENTRATION.
001300 02-03

THE EFFECT OF PSYCHOTROPIC-SUBSTANCES AND NARCOTIC ANALGESIC-DRUGS ON 14C NORADRENALINE UPTAKE BY SYNAPTOSOMES OF THE CEREBRAL-CORTEX OF RATS.
001363 02-03

UPTAKE OF PIPERIDINE AND PIPECOLIC-ACID BY SYNAPTOSOMES FROM MOUSE-BRAIN.
001396 02-03

THYROTROPIN-RELEASING-HORMONE: NEUROCHEMICAL EVIDENCE FOR THE POTENTIATION OF IMIPRAMINE EFFECTS ON THE METABOLISM AND UPTAKE OF BRAIN CATECHOLAMINES.
001427 02-03

STRUCTURAL REQUIREMENTS FOR UPTAKE INTO SEROTONINERGIC NEURONES.
001452 02-03

MULTIVARIATE APPROACHES APPLIED TO STUDIES OF NOREPINEPHRINE AND SEROTONIN UPTAKE.
001460 02-03

LITHIUM EFFECTS ON HIGH-AFFINITY TRYPTOPHAN UPTAKE: EVIDENCE AGAINST A STABILIZATION MECHANISM.
001496 02-03

PHARMACOLOGICAL EVIDENCE OF A POSSIBLE TRYPTAMINERGIC REGULATION OF OPIATE-RECEPTORS BY USING INDALPINE, A SELECTIVE 5 HT UPTAKE INHIBITOR.
001517 02-03

IN VIVO CHANGES IN THE GABA CONTENT OF NERVE-ENDINGS (SYNAPTOSOMES) INDUCED BY INHIBITORS OF GABA UPTAKE.
001540 02-03

MOTOR-ACTIVITY AND ROTATIONAL-BEHAVIOR AFTER ANALOGS OF COCAINE: CORRELATION WITH DOPAMINE UPTAKE BLOCKADE.
001650 02-04

THE EFFECTS OF 5 HT UPTAKE AND MAO-INHIBITORS ON L 5 HTP-INDUCED EXCITATION IN RATS.
001740 02-04

PLATELET AGGREGATION, 5 HYDROXYTRYPTAMINE UPTAKE AND RELEASE IN HUNTINGTONS-CHOREA.
002112 02-11

EFFECT OF DOXEPIN ON SEROTONIN METABOLISM IN RAT-BRAIN AND SEROTONIN UPTAKE BY HUMAN BLOOD-PLATELETS.
002243 02-13

INFLUENCE OF CICLAZINDOL ON MONOAMINE UPTAKE AND CNS FUNCTION IN NORMAL SUBJECTS.
002268 02-13

BRAIN GLUCOCORTICOID-RECEPTOR: CORRELATION OF IN VIVO UPTAKE OF CORTICOSTERONE WITH BEHAVIORAL-EVENTS, ENDOCRINE-EVENTS, AND NEUROPHARMACOLOGICAL EVENTS.
002515 02-17

DU-24565, A QUIPAZINE DERIVATIVE, A POTENT SELECTIVE SEROTONIN UPTAKE INHIBITOR.
002651 03-02

EFFECTS OF ALBUMIN, AMINO-ACIDS, AND CLOFIBRATE ON THE UPTAKE OF TRYPTOPHAN BY THE RAT-BRAIN.
002673 03-03

DIFFERENTIAL-EFFECTS OF SHORT-TERM AND LONG-TERM LITHIUM ON TRYPTOPHAN UPTAKE AND SEROTONERGIC FUNCTION IN CAT BRAIN.
002911 03-03

DO BENZODIAZEPINES BIND AT ADENOSINE UPTAKE SITES IN CNS?
002933 03-03

MODIFIED CUP TECHNIQUE FOR MICROESTIMATION OF THE RELEASE AND UPTAKE OF NEUROTRANSMITTERS IN BRAIN SLICES.
003147 03-06

LITHIUM UPTAKE IN RED CELLS OF CYCLOID AND UNIPOLAR DYSTHYMIC-PATIENTS.
003258 03-09

INDICATIONS FOR A BRAIN UPTAKE OF LABELLED VASOPRESSIN AND OCYTOCIN AND THE PROBLEM OF THE BLOOD-BRAIN-BARRIER.
003669 04-01

NONCOMPETITIVE AMINE UPTAKE INHIBITION BY THE NEW ANTIDEPRESSANT PRIDEFINE.
003771 04-03

A STUDY OF GAMMA AMINOBUTYRIC-ACID UPTAKE IN NORMAL AND DOWNS-SYNDROME PLATELETS.
003787 04-03

EFFECTS OF CONFORMATIONALLY RESTRAINED ANALOGUES OF SEROTONIN ON ITS UPTAKE AND BINDING IN RAT-BRAIN.
003794 04-03

UPTAKE OF RADIOCALCIUM BY NERVE-ENDINGS ISOLATED FROM RAT-BRAIN: KINETIC STUDIES.
003814 04-03

UPTAKE OF RADIOCALCIUM BY NERVE-ENDINGS ISOLATED FROM RAT-BRAIN: PHARMACOLOGICAL-STUDIES.
003815 04-03

INHIBITION OF SYNAPTOSOMAL CALCIUM UPTAKE BY ETHANOL.
003827 04-03

THE UPTAKE OF CARNITINE BY SLICES OF RAT-CEREBRAL-CORTEX.
003853 04-03

EFFECT OF VERAPAMIL ON 45CA UPTAKE BY SYNAPTOSOMES.
003856 04-03

ON THE IMPORTANCE OF AGONIST CONCENTRATION GRADIENTS WITHIN ISOLATED TISSUES. INCREASED MAXIMAL RESPONSES OF RAT VASA-DEFERENTIA TO (-) NORADRENALINE AFTER BLOCKADE OF NEURONAL UPTAKE.
003879 04-03

THE IMPORTANCE OF CATECHOLAMINE UPTAKE INHIBITION IN THE REVERSAL OF GUANETHIDINE BLOCKADE OF ADRENERGIC NEURONS.
003900 04-03

EFFECTS OF DELTA9 TETRAHYDROCANNABINOL AND CANNABIDIOL ON SODIUM-DEPENDENT HIGH-AFFINITY CHOLINE UPTAKE IN THE RAT HIPPOCAMPUS.
003908 04-03

EFFECTS OF HALOPEMIDE ON GABA-RECEPTOR BINDING, UPTAKE AND RELEASE.
003913 04-03

AMINE UPTAKE INHIBITORS: CRITERIA OF SELECTIVITY.
003921 04-03

THE HUMAN PLATELET AS A MODEL FOR THE GLUTAMATERGIC NEURON: PLATELET UPTAKE OF L GLUTAMATE.
003923 04-03

ADENOSINE AND CYCLIC-AMP IN RAT-CEREBRAL-CORTICAL SLICES: EFFECTS OF ADENOSINE UPTAKE INHIBITORS AND ADENOSINE-DEAMINASE INHIBITORS.
003950 04-03

EFFECTS OF CANNABINOIDS ON CATECHOLAMINE UPTAKE AND RELEASE IN HYPOTHALAMIC AND STRIATAL SYNAPTOSOMES.
003970 04-03

THE HIGH-AFFINITY CHOLINE UPTAKE SYSTEM WITH RESPECT TO THE MUSCARINIC-RECEPTORS USING A SYNAPTOSOMAL FRACTION ABUNDANT IN PRESYNAPTIC MEMBRANES.
004028 04-03

INHIBITION BY CAFFEINE OF CALCIUM UPTAKE BY BRAIN MICROSOMAL VESICLES.
004042 04-03

ANORECTIC-PROPERTIES OF A NEW LONG ACTING SEROTONIN UPTAKE INHIBITOR.
004105 04-04

THE EFFECT OF DOPAMINE UPTAKE BLOCKING-AGENTS ON THE AMPHETAMINE-INDUCED CIRCLING-BEHAVIOR IN MICE WITH UNILATERAL NIGROSTRIATAL LESIONS.
004117 04-04

DIFFERENTIAL-EFFECTS OF SEVERAL DOPAMINE UPTAKE INHIBITORS AND RELEASING-AGENTS ON LOCOMOTOR-ACTIVITY IN NORMAL AND IN RESERPINIZED MICE.
004130 04-04

A SIMPLE HISTOCHEMICAL SCREENING METHOD FOR AMINE UPTAKE.
004295 04-06

EFFECT OF NOREPINEPHRINE UPTAKE BLOCKERS ON NOREPINEPHRINE KINETICS.
004506 04-13

EFFECTS OF RO-11-2465, A NEW PSYCHOTROPIC-AGENT ON THE UPTAKE OF SEROTONIN BY HUMAN PLATELETS -- IN VITRO DETERMINATION OF THE IC50.
004532 04-13

SPECIFIC GABA-RECEPTOR AGONISTS AND UPTAKE INHIBITORS: DESIGN, DEVELOPMENT AND STRUCTURE-ACTIVITY STUDIES.
004725 04-17

ANTIDEPRESSANTS AND THE SEROTONIN UPTAKE IN PLATELETS.
004727 04-17

URBAN
THE URBAN EPIDEMIC OF PHENCYCLIDINE USE: LABORATORY EVIDENCE FROM A PUBLIC PSYCHIATRIC-HOSPITAL INPATIENT-SERVICE.
003554 03-16

UREA
EFFECTS OF UREA ON HEXOBARBITAL AND ANTIPYRINE DISPOSITION IN RATS.
000307 01-03

URETHANE
PRESSURE REVERSAL OF THE EFFECT OF URETHANE ON THE EVOKED SOMATOSENSORY CORTICAL RESPONSE IN THE RAT.
001106 02-03

URINARY
INCREASED URINARY EXCRETION OF CATECHOLAMINES AND THEIR
METABOLITES IN STREPTOZOTOCIN DIABETIC RAT.
000154 01-03
URINARY MHPG AND CLINICAL-RESPONSE TO AMITRIPTYLINE IN
DEPRESSED-PATIENTS.
000631 01-09
VARIATIONS IN URINARY EXCRETION OF 3 METHOXY-4-
HYDROXYPHENYLGLYCOL-SULFATE IN DEPRESSIVE-CONDITIONS.
002013 02-09
EFFECTS OF CAFFEINE ON PLASMA FREE FATTY-ACIDS, URINARY
CATECHOLAMINES, AND DRUG BINDING.
002272 02-13
DRUG-INDUCED DISORDERS OF THE URINARY TRACT.
002393 02-15
INFLUENCE OF PSYCHOTROPIC-DRUGS ON THE URINARY ELIMINATION OF
LITHIUM.
002895 03-03
TOWARD A BIOCHEMICAL CLASSIFICATION OF DEPRESSIVE-DISORDERS
IV: PRETREATMENT URINARY MHPG LEVELS AS PREDICTORS OF
ANTIDEPRESSANT RESPONSE TO IMIPRAMINE.
004406 04-09
VARIATIONS IN URINARY LEVELS OF 3 METHOXY-4-
HYDROXYPHENYLGLYCOL-SULFATE IN PATIENTS WITH DEPRESSIVE-
SYNDROMES.
004533 04-13

URINE
1-M CHLOROPHENYLPIPERAZINE: A METABOLITE OF TRAZODONE
ISOLATED FROM RAT URINE.
000204 01-03
QUANTITATIVE ANALYSIS OF 6 HYDROXYMELATONIN IN HUMAN URINE
BY GAS-CHROMATOGRAPHY NEGATIVE CHEMICAL-IONIZATION MASS-
SPECTROMETRY. (UNPUBLISHED PAPER).
001058 02-01
EFFECT OF FLUPHENAZINE ON THE CIRCADIAN-EXCRETION OF CYCLIC-
NUCLEOTIDES AND ELECTROLYTES IN THE URINE OF CHRONIC
SCHIZOPHRENICS.
001927 02-08
EFFECT OF LITHIUM ON POTASSIUM AND CALCIUM IN SERUM,
ERYTHROCYTES AND IN URINE.
002054 02-09
KINETICS AND BIOTRANSFORMATION OF LORMETAZEPAM: II.
RADIOIMMUNOLOGIC DETERMINATIONS IN PLASMA AND URINE OF
YOUNG AND ELDERLY SUBJECTS: FIRST-PASS EFFECT.
004516 04-13
ACUTE PHENCYCLIDINE (PCP) INTOXICATION: QUANTITATIVE URINE
LEVELS AND CLINICAL MANAGEMENT.
004665 04-15
MASS SCREENING AND CONFIRMATION OF DIAZEPAM IN URINE BY EMIT
THIN-LAYER-CHROMATOGRAPHY.
004672 04-16
GLC/TLC ANALYSIS OF CODEINE AND MORPHINE IN URINE VIA
DERIVATIZATION TECHNIQUES.
004687 04-16

USAGE
PSYCHIATRIC-DISTURBANCE IN MENTALLY-HANDICAPPED-PATIENTS: A
PROSPECTIVE STUDY OF CURRENT CLINICAL USAGE OF DEPOT
FLUPHENAZINE IN HOSPITALS FOR THE MENTALLY-HANDICAPPED.
000668 01-11

USEFULNESS
THE USEFULNESS OF THE ERYTHROCYTE LITHIUM INDEX IN THE
EVALUATION OF DISORDERS OF ION-TRANSFER IN PATIENTS WITH
DEPRESSIVE-SYNDROMES.
000625 01-09
AN EVALUATION OF THE USEFULNESS OF THE ACYLASE TEST IN
NEUROLEPTIC TREATMENT.
004426 04-10
A COMPARATIVE EVALUATION OF THE USEFULNESS OF
PSYCHOPHYSIOLOGICAL-TESTS DURING VARIOUS LEVELS OF
ACTIVATION OF THE CENTRAL-NERVOUS-SYSTEM.
004543 04-13

UTERINE
SURGICAL MANIPULATION OF THE UTERINE ENVIRONMENT OF RAT
FETUSES.
002478 02-16

UTILIZATION
STUDIES ON THE COMPREHENSIVE MEDICAL TREATMENT OF PEPTIC-
ULCERS (3) -- UTILIZATION OF TRANQUILIZERS IN THE TREATMENT OF
GASTRIC-ULCERS.
000653 01-10
LOCAL CEREBRAL GLUCOSE UTILIZATION (LCGU) IN RAT-BRAIN DURING
HYPOXEMIA. (UNPUBLISHED PAPER).
001380 02-03
REGIONAL CHANGES IN BRAIN GLUCOSE UTILIZATION IN RATS GIVEN A
PYRETHROID INSECTICIDE.
001838 02-05
THEORY, PROCEDURE, AND APPLICATIONS OF THE RADIOACTIVE
DEOXYGLUCOSE METHOD FOR THE MEASUREMENT OF LOCAL GLUCOSE
UTILIZATION IN THE CENTRAL-NERVOUS-SYSTEM. (UNPUBLISHED
PAPER).
001877 02-06

UTILIZATION OF PSYCHOTROPIC-DRUGS. AN INTERNATIONAL
COMPARISON.
002616 02-16
HETEROGENEOUS DEPRESSION OF GLUCOSE UTILIZATION IN THE
CAUDATE-NUCLEUS BY GABA AGONISTS.
002640 03-01
IMPACT OF DRUG SCHEDULING ON UTILIZATION.
003601 03-17
EFFECTS OF A SINGLE-THERAPEUTIC-DOSE OF GLYCEROL ON CEREBRAL
METABOLISM IN THE BRAINS OF YOUNG MICE: POSSIBLE INCREASE IN
BRAIN GLUCOSE TRANSPORT AND GLUCOSE UTILIZATION.
004281 04-05

UTILIZING
A COMPARISON OF HUMAN MUSCARINIC CHOLINERGIC-RECEPTOR
RESPONSE TO A NUMBER OF PSYCHOTROPICS UTILIZING THE
RADIOLABELED ANTAGONIST, (3H) QUINUCLIDINYL-BENZILATE. (PH.D.
DISSERTATION).
002918 03-03

VACUTAINERS
FLUPHENAZINE, TRIFLUOPERAZINE AND PERPHENAZINE IN VACUTAINERS.
003565 03-16

VALENCE
EFFICACY AND PATTERN VALENCE OF PSYCHOACTIVE-DRUGS: A NEW
METHOD OF COMPARING DRUGS APPLIED TO IDENTICAL PATIENTS IN
RANDOMIZED-ORDER.
000699 01-11

VALIDITY
THE VALIDITY OF MODELS IN PSYCHOPHARMACOLOGY.
003633 03-17

VALIUM
CHRONIC-TREATMENT WITH VALIUM (DIAZEPAM) FAILS TO AFFECT THE
REPRODUCTIVE SYSTEM OF THE MALE RAT.
001535 02-03
PUBLIC JUDGMENTS ON THE IMPORTANCE OF VALIUM INFORMATION.
003590 03-17

VALPROATE
RECTAL VALPROATE SYRUP AND STATUS-EPILEPTICUS.
000727 01-11
INTRAVENOUS VALPROATE: EFFECTS ON PLASMA AND SALIVA
PHENYTOIN LEVELS.
003359 03-11
MECHANISM OF VALPROATE PHENOBARBITAL INTERACTION IN EPILEPTIC-
PATIENTS.
004522 04-13

VALPROIC-ACID
DISPOSITION OF VALPROIC-ACID IN THE RAT: DOSE-DEPENDENT
METABOLISM, DISTRIBUTION, ENTEROHEPATIC RECIRCULATION AND
CHOLERETIC-EFFECT.
000073 01-03
VALPROIC-ACID DOSAGE AND PLASMA PROTEIN BINDING AND
CLEARANCE.
000755 01-13
VALPROIC-ACID AND PLASMA LEVELS OF PHENYTOIN.
000756 01-13
DETERMINATION OF VALPROIC-ACID BY FLAME-IONIZATION GAS-LIQUID-
CHROMATOGRAPHY.
000906 01-16
INTERACTION BETWEEN PHENYTOIN AND VALPROIC-ACID: PLASMA
PROTEIN BINDING AND METABOLIC-EFFECTS.
002276 02-13
CLINICAL-TRIALS OF DEPAKENE (VALPROIC-ACID) COADMINISTERED WITH
OTHER ANTICONVULSANTS IN EPILEPTIC-PATIENTS.
002367 02-14
PHENYTOIN VALPROIC-ACID INTERACTION IN RHESUS-MONKEY.
002785 03-03
PHARMACOKINETIC PROFILE OF VALPROIC-ACID IN RHESUS-MONKEYS
FOLLOWING SINGLE BOLUS AND CONSTANT RATE INTRAVENOUS
ADMINISTRATIONS.
002797 03-03
VALPROIC-ACID SERUM LEVELS AND PROTECTION AGAINST KINDLED
AMYGDALOID SEIZURES IN THE RAT.
002946 03-04
ANTICONVULSANT ACTIVITY OF METABOLITES OF VALPROIC-ACID.
004168 04-04
VALPROIC-ACID IN CHILDHOOD-EPILEPSY: ANTICONVULSIVE EFFICACY IN
RELATION TO ITS PLASMA LEVELS.
004525 04-13

VALUE
VALUE OF SALIVA SAMPLES IN MONITORING CARBAMAZEPINE
CONCENTRATIONS IN EPILEPTIC-PATIENTS.
000903 01-16
DIFFERENTIAL-EFFECTS OF IMIPRAMINE IN RATS AS A FUNCTION OF DRL
SCHEDULE VALUE.
001714 02-04
LIMITS, VALUE AND PERSPECTIVES OF THE PSYCHIATRIC-DIAGNOSIS IN
CLINICAL PSYCHOPHARMACOLOGY.
002631 02-17

INTRACELLULAR LITHIUM: ITS VALUE IN THE PREDICTION OF A POSITIVE RESPONSE TO LITHIUM.
003382 03-11

VALUE OF PROPANIDID IN ELECTROCONVULSIVE-THERAPY (COMPARISON WITH THIOPENTONE).
004379 04-09

VALUES
ENHANCEMENT OF ETORPHINE BRAIN CONCENTRATIONS AND CHANGES IN ETORPHINE NALOXONE PA2 VALUES IN MORPHINE PRETREATED MICE.
002800 03-03

CEREBROSPINAL-FLUID VALUES OF HVA AND 5 HIAA IN PATIENTS WITH ENDOGENOUS DEPRESSION DURING THE COURSE OF TREATMENT.
004382 04-09

HYPERVENTILATION-SYNDROME, TREATMENT WITH L TRYPTOPHAN AND PYRIDOXINE; PREDICTIVE VALUES OF XANTHURENIC-ACID EXCRETION.
004456 04-11

VAL5-ENKEPHALIN
COMPARATIVE-STUDY OF ANALGESIA INDUCED BY N VAL5-ENKEPHALIN AND PRO5-ENKEPHALIN ANALOGS.
000021 01-03

VAPOUR
GLIAL CELL EFFECTS OF SUBACUTE FORMIC-ACID VAPOUR EXPOSURE.
000527 01-05

VARIABILITY
STRUCTURE OF VARIABILITY AND CORRELATION IN LEARNING AFTER DRUG ADMINISTRATION.
002562 02-17

VARIABLES
TWO OR MORE CONFORMATIONS OF BENZODIAZEPINE-RECEPTORS DEPENDING ON GABA-RECEPTORS AND OTHER VARIABLES.
001139 02-03

TARDIVE-DYSKINESIA IN SCHIZOPHRENIC-OUTPATIENTS; PREVALENCE AND SIGNIFICANT VARIABLES.
003483 03-15

VARIANCE
CONSISTENCY IN CATECHOLAMINE EXCRETION IN LABORATORY AND NATURAL SETTINGS: CORRELATIONAL AND VARIANCE COMPONENTS ANALYSES.
004508 04-13

VARIATION
INTERSUBJECT AND INTRASUBJECT VARIATION IN DIAZEPAM FREE FRACTION.
000747 01-13

INTERINDIVIDUAL VARIATION OF CLINICAL-RESPONSE TO HALOPERIDOL.
001230 02-03

CAPACITIES OF ATTENTION, STRESS-RESISTANCE, AND SLOW CEREBRAL POTENTIALS: EFFECTS OF CARPIPRAMINE ON CONTINGENT NEGATIVE VARIATION WAVES AND P-300.
003451 03-14

VARIATIONS
VARIATIONS IN PSYCHOPHYSIOLOGICAL ACTIVATION RESPONSES IN DEPRESSIVE-STATES.
001965 02-09

VARIATIONS IN URINARY EXCRETION OF 3 METHOXY-4-HYDROXYPHENYLGLYCOL-SULFATE IN DEPRESSIVE-CONDITIONS.
002013 02-09

STUDY OF PROLACTIN VARIATIONS IN PSYCHIATRIC-PATIENTS TREATED WITH FLUPHENAZINE-DECANOATE.
002226 02-13

INDIVIDUAL VARIATIONS IN THE EFFECTS OF FLURAZEPAM, CLORAZEPATE, L-DOPA AND THYROTROPIN-RELEASING-HORMONE ON REM SLEEP IN MAN.
002349 02-14

CNV VARIATIONS INDUCED BY THE ADMINISTRATION OF DIAZEPAM, HALOPERIDOL, PHENELZINE AND D-AMPHETAMINE.
002355 02-14

COMPARATIVE-STUDY OF VARIATIONS IN PROLACTIN LEVELS DURING TREATMENT WITH ANTIPSYCHOTIC-DRUGS.
002412 02-15

TWO DISTINCT SEROTONIN-RECEPTORS; REGIONAL VARIATIONS IN RECEPTOR BINDING IN MAMMALIAN BRAIN.
002861 03-03

GENETIC VARIATIONS IN MIDBRAIN DOPAMINE CELL NUMBER; PARALLEL WITH DIFFERENCES IN RESPONSES TO DOPAMINERGIC AGONISTS AND IN NATURALISTIC BEHAVIORS MEDIATED BY CENTRAL DOPAMINERGIC-SYSTEMS. (UNPUBLISHED PAPER).
004112 04-04

VARIATIONS IN URINARY LEVELS OF 3 METHOXY-4-HYDROXYPHENYLGLYCOL-SULFATE IN PATIENTS WITH DEPRESSIVE-SYNDROMES.
004533 04-13

EFFECT OF LITHIUM ON REACTION-TIME -- A STUDY OF DIURNAL VARIATIONS.
004607 04-15

VARIES
THE SPECIFIC ACTIVITY OF PLATELET MONOAMINE-OXIDASE VARIES WITH PLATELET COUNT DURING SEVERE EXERCISE AND NORADRENALINE INFUSION.
004509 04-13

VAS-DEFERENS
THE EFFECTS OF BROMOCRIPTINE ON PRESYNAPTIC AND POSTSYNAPTIC ALPHA-ADRENOCEPTORS IN THE MOUSE VAS-DEFERENS.
000108 01-03

EXCITATORY AND INHIBITORY-EFFECTS OF OPIATES IN THE RAT VAS-DEFERENS; A DUAL-MECHANISM OF OPIATE ACTION.
000143 01-03

INTERACTIONS BETWEEN MORPHINE AND THE OPIOID-LIKE PEPTIDES IN THE RAT VAS-DEFERENS.
001290 02-03

COMPARATIVE-EFFECTS OF SOMATOSTATIN AND ENKEPHALINS ON THE GUINEA-PIG ILEUM AND THE RAT VAS-DEFERENS.
001302 02-03

DEVELOPMENT OF TOLERANCE TO THE EXCITATORY EFFECT OF MORPHINE AND CROSS-TOLERANCE TO THE INHIBITORY ACTION OF BETA ENDORPHIN IN THE ISOLATED RAT VAS-DEFERENS.
002756 03-03

COMPARATIVE-STUDY ON THE EFFECT OF MORPHINE AND THE OPIOID-LIKE PEPTIDES IN THE VAS-DEFERENS OF RODENTS; STRAIN AND SPECIES-DIFFERENCES, EVIDENCE FOR MULTIPLE OPIATE-RECEPTORS.
002757 03-03

DIFFERENTIAL-EFFECTS OF POTASSIUM ON THE POTENCY OF DIFFERENT OPIOIDS IN THE MOUSE VAS-DEFERENS.
002935 03-03

VASA-DEFERENTIA
ON THE IMPORTANCE OF AGONIST CONCENTRATION GRADIENTS WITHIN ISOLATED TISSUES. INCREASED MAXIMAL RESPONSES OF RAT VASA-DEFERENTIA TO (-) NORADRENALINE AFTER BLOCKADE OF NEURONAL UPTAKE.
003879 04-03

VASCULAR
COMPARISON OF MIANSERIN WITH DESIPRAMINE, MAPROTILINE AND PHENTOLAMINE ON CARDIAC PRESYNAPTIC AND VASCULAR POSTSYNAPTIC ALPHA-ADRENOCEPTORS AND NORADRENALINE REUPTAKE IN PITHED NORMOTENSIVE-RATS.
000044 01-03

EFFECTS OF 3',4' DIHYDROXYNOMIFENSINE ON THE DOPAMINE VASCULAR RECEPTOR.
003890 04-03

CONSISTENT UNMASKING OF DOPAMINE-INDUCED DILATION OF THE CANINE FEMORAL VASCULAR BED.
003911 04-03

VASCULATURE
NONLINEAR REGRESSION ANALYSIS OF NOREPINEPHRINE RESPONSE KINETICS IN CEREBRAL VASCULATURE.
000256 01-03

VASOACTIVE-AGENTS
RESPONSIVENESS TO VASOACTIVE-AGENTS OF CEREBRAL-ARTERIES AND MESENTERIC-ARTERIES ISOLATED FROM CONTROL AND RESERPINE TREATED DOGS.
001273 02-03

VASOCONSTRICTION
PARASYMPATHOMIMETIC-INFLUENCE OF CARBACHOL ON LOCAL CEREBRAL BLOOD FLOW IN THE RABBIT BY A DIRECT VASODILATOR ACTION AND AN INHIBITION OF THE SYMPATHETIC MEDIATED VASOCONSTRICTION.
001109 02-03

VASODILATOR
PARASYMPATHOMIMETIC-INFLUENCE OF CARBACHOL ON LOCAL CEREBRAL BLOOD FLOW IN THE RABBIT BY A DIRECT VASODILATOR ACTION AND AN INHIBITION OF THE SYMPATHETIC MEDIATED VASOCONSTRICTION.
001109 02-03

ANTAGONISM OF THE RENAL VASODILATOR ACTIVITY OF DOPAMINE BY METOCLOPRAMIDE.
001265 02-03

VASOMOTOR
EFFECTS OF GAMMA HYDROXYBUTYRIC-ACID ON METABOLIC, RESPIRATORY AND VASOMOTOR ACTIVITIES AND BODY-TEMPERATURE IN RATS.
000189 01-03

VASOPRESSIN
NALOXONE PROMOTES STIMULUS-EVOKED VASOPRESSIN RELEASE IN VIVO.
000165 01-03

VASOPRESSIN THERAPY IN PARKINSONS-DISEASE.
000689 01-11

EVIDENCE THAT VASOPRESSIN IS INVOLVED IN THE ISOPRENALINE-INDUCED BETA ENDORPHIN RELEASE.
001319 02-03

THE EFFECT OF NEUROPEPTIDE FRAGMENTS OF ADRENOCORTICOTROPIN AND VASOPRESSIN ON BEHAVIORAL-ACTIVITY IN RATS.
001812 02-04

VASOPRESSIN AND SCHIZOPHRENIA.
001954 02-08

INHIBITION OF VASOPRESSIN RELEASE TO CAROTID OCCLUSION BY GAMMA AMINOBUTYRIC-ACID AND GLYCINE.
002715 03-03

ON A CASE OF MEMORY-DISTURBANCES TREATED WITH VASOPRESSIN.
003301 03-11

EFFECTS OF VASOPRESSIN ON HUMAN MEMORY FUNCTIONS.
003388 03-11

INDICATIONS FOR A BRAIN UPTAKE OF LABELLED VASOPRESSIN AND
OCYTOCIN AND THE PROBLEM OF THE BLOOD-BRAIN-BARRIER.
003669 04-01

VASOPRESSIN STIMULATES RELEASE OF BETA LIPOTROPIN AND BETA
ENDORPHIN IN CONSCIOUS RATS AS MEASURED BY
RADIOIMMUNOASSAY OF UNEXTRACTED PLASMA.
003715 04-03

VASOTOCIN
VASOTOCIN, PROSTAGLANDIN, AND FEMALE REPRODUCTIVE BEHAVIOR
IN THE FROG, RANA-PIPIENS.
002978 03-04

VEIN
INTERACTION OF THE TRICYCLIC-ANTIDEPRESSANT AMITRIPTYLINE WITH
PREJUNCTIONAL ALPHA AND MUSCARINIC-RECEPTORS IN THE DOG
SAPHENOUS VEIN.
003756 04-03

VELOCITY
A COMPARISON OF HUMAN TACTILE STIMULUS VELOCITY
DISCRIMINATION WITH THE ABILITY OF S-I CORTICAL NEURONS IN
AWAKE RHESUS-MONKEYS TO SIGNAL THE SAME VELOCITY
DIFFERENCES BEFORE AND AFTER NONANESTHETIC DOSES OF
PENTOBARBITAL.
000055 01-03

MEASUREMENTS OF NERVE CONDUCTION VELOCITY DURING DECREASING
TOXIC DIPHENYLHYDANTOIN LEVELS AND THE BEGINNING OF
CARBAMAZEPINE MEDICATION: A CLINICAL NEUROPHYSIOLOGICAL
REPORT.
004441 04-11

VENOMS
THE EFFECTS OF ALPHA AND BETA NEUROTOXINS FROM THE VENOMS OF
VARIOUS SNAKES ON TRANSMISSION IN AUTONOMIC GANGLIA.
003750 04-03

VENOUS
ABSORPTION OF 14C LABELED METHADONE BY PORTAL AND
EXTRAPORTAL VENOUS CIRCULATIONS FOLLOWING INTRAPERITONEAL
AND INTRODUODENAL ADMINISTRATION.
000094 01-03

ORAL BIOAVAILABILITY OF APOMORPHINE IN THE RAT WITH A
PORTACAVAL VENOUS ANASTOMOSIS.
001158 02-03

PHENYTOIN CONCENTRATIONS IN VENOUS VERSUS CAPILLARY BLOOD OF
GERIATRIC-PATIENTS.
003381 03-11

THE DYNAMICS OF SYSTEMIC VENOUS, ARTERIAL, AND CEREBROSPINAL-
FLUID PRESSURE UNDER I.V. ADMINISTRATION OF POLYETHYLENE-
GLYCOL.
004045 04-03

VENTRAL
EFFECT OF PICROTOXIN AND NIPECOTIC-ACID ON INHIBITORY RESPONSE
OF DOPAMINERGIC NEURONS IN THE VENTRAL TEGMENTAL AREA TO
STIMULATION OF THE NUCLEUS-ACCUMBENS.
000331 01-03

LOCOMOTOR-ACTIVITY ELICITED BY INJECTIONS OF PICROTOXIN INTO THE
VENTRAL TEGMENTAL AREA IS ATTENUATED BY INJECTIONS OF GABA
INTO THE GLOBUS-PALLIDUS.
000436 01-04

EFFECTS OF LILLY-110140 (FLUOXETINE) ON SELF-STIMULATION
BEHAVIOR IN THE DORSAL AND VENTRAL REGIONS OF THE LATERAL
HYPOTHALAMUS IN THE MOUSE.
001590 02-04

A TOPOGRAPHIC LOCALIZATION OF ENKEPHALIN ON THE DOPAMINE
NEURONS OF THE RAT SUBSTANTIA-NIGRA AND VENTRAL TEGMENTAL
AREA DEMONSTRATED BY COMBINED HISTOFLUORESCENCE
IMMUNOCYTOCHEMISTRY.
002639 03-01

DEPRESSION OF VENTRAL ROOT DORSAL ROOT POTENTIAL BY DL ALPHA
AMINOADIPATE IN FROG SPINAL-CORD.
002755 03-03

CHOLINERGIC, DOPAMINERGIC, NORADRENERGIC, OR GLUTAMINERGIC
STIMULATION VENTRAL TO THE ANTERIOR SEPTUM DOES NOT
SPECIFICALLY SUPPRESS DEFENSIVE-BEHAVIOR.
002945 03-04

INTRACRANIAL SELF-ADMINISTRATION OF MORPHINE INTO THE VENTRAL
TEGMENTAL AREA IN RATS.
002960 03-04

SENSITIVITY TO GABA OF NEURONS OF THE DORSAL AND VENTRAL
LATERAL GENICULATE NUCLEI IN THE RAT.
003877 04-03

MORPHINE DIFFERENTIALLY AFFECTS VENTRAL TEGMENTAL AND
SUBSTANTIA-NIGRA BRAIN REWARD THRESHOLDS.
004187 04-04

VENTRICLE
STUDIES ON GABA RELEASE IN VIVO USING A SIMPLE METHOD FOR
PERFUSION OF THE FOURTH VENTRICLE OF THE RAT.
001881 02-06

VENTRICLES
COMPARATIVE-STUDY OF AGGRESSIVE-BEHAVIOUR AFTER INJECTION OF
CHOLINOMIMETICS, ANTICHOLINESTERASES, NICOTINIC, AND
MUSCARINIC GANGLIONIC STIMULANTS INTO THE CEREBRAL
VENTRICLES OF CONSCIOUS CATS: FAILURE OF NICOTINIC-DRUGS TO
EVOKE AGGRESSION.
001568 02-04

THE PHARMACOLOGY OF AGGRESSIVE-BEHAVIOURAL-PHENOMENA
ELICITED BY MUSCARINE INJECTED INTO THE CEREBRAL VENTRICLES OF
CONSCIOUS CATS.
001569 02-04

CEREBRAL VENTRICLES AND DOPAMINE IN SCHIZOPHRENIA.
(UNPUBLISHED PAPER).
001928 02-08

THE EFFECTS OF INJECTIONS OF BOMBESIN INTO THE CEREBRAL
VENTRICLES ON BEHAVIORAL THERMOREGULATION.
002952 03-04

VENTRICULAR
PROTECTIVE EFFECT OF PRENYLAMINE AGAINST VULNERABILITY TO
VENTRICULAR FIBRILLATION IN THE NORMAL AND ISCHEMIC CANINE
MYOCARDIUM.
000265 01-03

5,7 DIHYDROXYTRYPTAMINE-INDUCED MOUSE-KILLING AND
BEHAVIORAL-REVERSAL WITH VENTRICULAR ADMINISTRATION OF
SEROTONIN IN RATS.
001562 02-04

EFFECTS OF IMIPRAMINE ON LEFT VENTRICULAR PERFORMANCE IN
CHILDREN.
002385 02-15

THE EFFECTS OF THIORIDAZINE ON ELECTRICAL AND ISCHEMIC
VENTRICULAR FIBRILLATION IN THE DOG HEART IN SITU.
002697 03-03

VENTRICULAR-MUSCLE
ELECTROPHYSIOLOGICAL-EFFECTS OF IMIPRAMINE ON BOVINE
VENTRICULAR-MUSCLE AND PURKINJE-FIBRES.
003988 04-03

VENTRICULOGRAM
INTERMITTENT DECORTICATION AND PROGRESSIVE HYPERTHERMIA,
HYPERTENSION AND TACHYCARDIA FOLLOWING METHYLGLUCAMINE
IOTHALAMATE VENTRICULOGRAM.
003520 03-15

VENTROMEDIAL
INFLUENCE OF AMPHETAMINE AND PHENYLPROPANOLAMINE ON FOOD
INTAKE, ACTIVITY, AND BODY-TEMPERATURE IN RATS WITH
VENTROMEDIAL HYPOTHALAMIC OR DORSOLATERAL TEGMENTAL
DAMAGE.
000322 01-03

GLUCOSE OXIDATION IN THE VENTROMEDIAL HYPOTHALAMUS IS NOT
AFFECTED BY INSULIN OR OUABAIN BUT DEPRESSED BY ALLOXAN
TREATMENT.
001145 02-03

EFFECTS OF AMPHETAMINE AND PHENYLPROPANOLAMINE ON FOOD
INTAKE IN RATS WITH VENTROMEDIAL HYPOTHALAMIC OR
DORSOLATERAL TEGMENTAL DAMAGE.
001818 02-04

THYROXIN SENSITIVITY OF SENSORIMOTOR CORTICAL NEURONS AND THE
HYPOTHALAMIC VENTROMEDIAL NUCLEUS.
003713 04-03

UNIMPAIRED QUININE METABOLISM IN RATS WITH VENTROMEDIAL
HYPOTHALAMIC LESIONS.
003821 04-03

VEP
THE EFFECT OF SODIUM-VALPROATE ON THE PHOTOSENSITIVE VEP.
004513 04-13

VERAPAMIL
EFFECT OF VERAPAMIL ON 45CA UPTAKE BY SYNAPTOSOMES.
003856 04-03

VERATRINE
RELEASE OF GONADOTROPIN-RELEASING-HORMONE BY VERATRINE IN A
HYPOTHALAMIC PITUITARY COINCUBATION.
000237 01-03

VERBAL-ASSOCIATIONS
ACUTE EFFECT OF BENZOCTAMINE (10 MG), SODIUM-
HYDROXYBUTYRATE (2 G) AND FENCAMFAMINE (10 MG) ON VERBAL-
ASSOCIATIONS.
000806 01-14

ACUTE EFFECT OF CLOROTEPIN (0.5MG AND 1.0MG) AND
METHAQUALONE (300MG) ON VERBAL-ASSOCIATIONS.
002333 02-14

VERBAL-MEMORY
DISSOCIATION OF THE STRYCHNINE EFFECT ON VISUAL-MEMORY AND
VERBAL-MEMORY IN ORGANIC-PSYCHOSYNDROMES.
000816 01-14

DISSOCIATION OF THE STRYCHNINE EFFECT ON VISUAL-MEMORY AND
VERBAL-MEMORY IN ORGANIC-PSYCHOSYNDROMES.
002155 02-11

VERONA
PSYCHOTROPIC-DRUGS AND PSYCHIATRIC-HOSPITAL ADMISSIONS IN VERONA, ITALY.
004717 04-17

VERTEBRAL-ARTERY
THE SIMULTANEOUS INFUSION OF DRUGS VIA THE LEFT AND RIGHT VERTEBRAL-ARTERY OF THE CAT; A MODIFIED ANIMAL-MODEL FOR THE STUDY OF POSSIBLE CENTRAL-ACTIONS OF DRUGS UPON THE LOWER BRAINSTEM.
004297 04-06

VERTEBRATE
RIA AND HPLC EVIDENCE FOR THE PRESENCE OF METHIONINE-ENKEPHALIN AND CHOLECYSTOKININ IN THE NEURAL RETINA OF SEVERAL VERTEBRATE SPECIES. (UNPUBLISHED PAPER).
001017 02-01

VERTIGO
STUDIES ON THE TREATMENT AND DIAGNOSIS OF NEUROTIC VERTIGO FROM THE VIEWPOINT OF NEUROOTOLOGY: OBSERVATION OF THE BALANCE TEST FOR ANALYZING NEUROTIC VERTIGO.
004387 04-09

DOSE-EFFECT OF DEAE ON SUBJECTIVE PROBLEMS, VERTIGO, DEPRESSION, ASTHENIA, CEPHALALGIA, AND TONIC POSTURAL ACTIVITY PROBLEMS RECORDED WITH STATOKINESIMETER IN POSTCONCUSSIONAL-SYNDROME.
004472 04-11

THE EFFICACY OF PIRACETAM IN VERTIGO: A DOUBLE-BLIND STUDY IN PATIENTS WITH VERTIGO OF CENTRAL ORIGIN.
004478 04-11

VERVET-MONKEY
SEROTONERGIC AND CATECHOLAMINERGIC INFLUENCE ON THYROID-FUNCTION IN THE VERVET-MONKEY.
001385 02-03

VERVET-MONKEYS
PERIPHERAL-CORRELATES OF SEROTONERGICALLY-INFLUENCED BEHAVIORS IN VERVET-MONKEYS (CERCOPITHECUS-AETHIOPS-SABAEUS).
004204 04-04

VESICLES
MATURATION OF SYMPATHETIC NEUROTRANSMISSION IN THE RAT HEART. III. DEVELOPMENTAL-CHANGES IN RESERPINE INHIBITION OF NOREPINEPHRINE UPTAKE INTO ISOLATED SYNAPTIC VESICLES.
000025 01-03

COMPARISON OF THE EFFECTS OF THE ISOMERS OF AMPHETAMINE, METHYLPHENIDATE AND DEOXYPIPRADROL ON THE UPTAKE OF L (3H)NOREPINEPHRINE AND (3H)DOPAMINE BY SYNAPTIC VESICLES FROM RAT-WHOLE-BRAIN, STRIATUM AND HYPOTHALAMUS.
000091 01-03

REGIONAL DISTRIBUTION AND BIOCHEMICAL-PROPERTIES OF 125I TYR8-SUBSTANCE-P BINDING-SITES IN SYNAPTIC VESICLES.
000259 01-03

ASCORBIC-ACID, AN ENDOGENOUS FACTOR REQUIRED FOR ACETYLCHOLINE RELEASE FROM THE SYNAPTIC VESICLES.
001322 02-03

DISTRIBUTION OF MEMBRANE GLYCOPROTEINS AMONG THE ORGANELLES OF A SINGLE IDENTIFIED NEURON OF APLYSIA. II. ISOLATION AND CHARACTERIZATION OF A GLYCOPROTEIN ASSOCIATED WITH VESICLES.
002657 03-03

INHIBITION BY CAFFEINE OF CALCIUM UPTAKE BY BRAIN MICROSOMAL VESICLES.
004042 04-03

5' TRIPHOSPHATE RECYCLES INDEPENDENTLY OF ACETYLCHOLINE IN CHOLINERGIC SYNAPTIC VESICLES.
004063 04-03

VESSEL
EFFECT OF PAPAVERINE ON REGIONAL CEREBRAL BLOOD FLOW AND SMALL VESSEL BLOOD CONTENT.
001177 02-03

VESTIBULAR
ETHANOL-INDUCED CHANGES IN CYCLIC-GUANOSINE-PHOSPHATE METABOLISM IN MOUSE VESTIBULAR REGION.
003784 04-03

SELECTIVE EFFECT OF ETHANOL ON THE VESTIBULAR NUCLEUS NEURONS IN THE CAT.
004139 04-04

VESTIBULO-OCULAR
VESTIBULO-OCULAR REFLEXES IN RABBITS: REDUCTION BY INTRAVENOUS INJECTION OF DIAZEPAM.
001566 02-04

CHANGES IN THE HORIZONTAL VESTIBULO-OCULAR REFLEX OF THE RHESUS-MONKEY WITH BEHAVIORAL AND PHARMACOLOGICAL ALERTING.
002997 03-04

VIDEO-ANALYSIS
ON THE RELATIONSHIP BETWEEN MEASURES OBTAINED BY VIDEO-ANALYSIS OF NONVERBAL-BEHAVIOR AND SELF-RATING OF MOOD.
004410 04-09

VIDEO-STRATEGIES
TIME-BLIND ANALYSIS AND OTHER VIDEO-STRATEGIES IN PHASE II TRIALS OF PSYCHOTROPIC-DRUGS.
003568 03-16

VIEWPOINT
LITHIUM TREATMENT IN AFFECTIVE-DISORDERS FROM VIEWPOINT OF TRANSCULTURAL PSYCHOPHARMACOLOGY: THERAPEUTIC PLASMA LEVEL.
000636 01-09

STUDIES ON THE TREATMENT AND DIAGNOSIS OF NEUROTIC VERTIGO FROM THE VIEWPOINT OF NEUROOTOLOGY: OBSERVATION OF THE BALANCE TEST FOR ANALYZING NEUROTIC VERTIGO.
004387 04-09

VIGILANCE
STUDY OF VIGILANCE AFTER INGESTION OF ZOPICLONE IN COMPARISON WITH NITRAZEPAM AND PLACEBO. METHODOLOGY OF THE STUDY: SELF-EVALUATION QUESTIONNAIRE AND PSYCHOMETRIC-TESTS.
000543 01-07

A COMPUTER OCULOGRAPHIC AND EEG DOUBLE-BLIND STUDY INCLUDING WELL-BEING FOR DETERMINING CHANGED VIGILANCE UNDER THERAPY WITH TIAPRIDE.
000751 01-13

ACTION OF TOFISOPAM ON THE ERGONOMIC VIGILANCE LEVEL. ITS INTERACTION WITH THE EFFECTS OF ALCOHOL. CLINICAL PHARMACOLOGICAL-STUDY.
001891 02-07

CORTICAL-CORRELATES OF VIGILANCE REGULATION AND THEIR USE IN EVALUATING THE EFFECTS OF TREATMENT.
002147 02-11

THE EFFECTS OF TRIAZOLAM AND NITRAZEPAM ON SLEEP QUALITY, MORNING VIGILANCE, AND PSYCHOMOTOR PERFORMANCE.
002330 02-14

VIGILANCE IMPAIRING DRUGS: ANALYSIS OF SUBJECTIVE RESPONSES.
002332 02-14

EFFECTS OF AMPHETAMINE ON VIGILANCE PERFORMANCE IN NORMAL AND HYPERACTIVE-CHILDREN.
002359 02-14

SMOKING AND VIGILANCE: THE EFFECTS OF TOBACCO SMOKING ON CFF AS RELATED TO PERSONALITY AND SMOKING HABITS.
002368 02-14

CORRELATED STUDY OF THE EFFECTS OF SE-5023 IN AN HYPOXIC ATMOSPHERE ON QUANTIFIED EEG, VIGILANCE, MEMORY, AND MOOD.
003440 03-14

VILOXAZINE
CLINICAL-TRIAL OF VILOXAZINE IN DEPRESSIVE-CONDITIONS.
000589 01-09

VILOXAZINE PLASMA CONCENTRATIONS AND CLINICAL-RESPONSE.
000614 01-09

VILOXAZINE IN THE TREATMENT OF DEPRESSIVE-STATES.
000626 01-09

LONG-TERM ADMINISTRATION OF ATROPINE, IMIPRAMINE, AND VILOXAZINE ALTERS RESPONSIVENESS OF RAT-CORTICAL-NEURONES TO ACETYLCHOLINE.
001306 02-03

VILOXAZINE: A REVIEW OF THE LITERATURE.
001964 02-09

CLINICAL-STUDY OF VILOXAZINE.
001972 02-09

THE USE OF VILOXAZINE IN HOSPITALIZED DEPRESSED-PATIENTS: RANDOM COMPARISON WITH IMIPRAMINE IN A DOUBLE-BLIND TRIAL.
001998 02-09

RESULTS OF CLINICAL-TESTS OF VILOXAZINE (VIVALAN ICI): PART OF A MULTICLINICAL-STUDY.
002006 02-09

VILOXAZINE IN THE TREATMENT OF DEPRESSIVE-NEUROSIS: A CONTROLLED CLINICAL-STUDY WITH DOXEPIN AND PLACEBO.
002080 02-10

VILOXAZINE AND THE DEPRESSED SCHIZOPHRENIC – METHODOLOGICAL-ISSUES.
003181 03-08

COMBINED ADMINISTRATION OF NIALAMIDE AND VILOXAZINE TO DEPRESSIVE-PATIENTS.
003232 03-09

MULTICENTRE-STUDY WITH VILOXAZINE (VIVALAN) IN DEPRESSED-PATIENTS.
004375 04-09

VILOXAZINE IN THE TREATMENT OF DEPRESSIVE-NEUROSIS: A PLACEBO AND STANDARD (IMIPRAMINE) CONTROLLED CLINICAL-STUDY.
004392 04-09

VINBLASTINE
THE EFFECTS OF COLCHICINE AND VINBLASTINE ON MEMORY IN CHICKS.
004069 04-04

VINYL-GABA
EFFECTS OF GAMMA ACETYLENIC-GABA AND GAMMA VINYL-GABA ON ELECTRICALLY-INDUCED SPINAL-CORD CONVULSIONS AND ON SPINAL-CORD GABA CONCENTRATION.
000145 01-03

INCREASED CSF GAMMA AMINOBUTYRIC-ACID AFTER TREATMENT WITH GAMMA VINYL-GABA.
002237 02-13

EFFECT OF GAMMA VINYL-GABA ON BICUCULLINE-INDUCED SEIZURES.
004157 04-04

VIOLENT
ACUTE MANAGEMENT OF THE VIOLENT AGGRESSIVE-PATIENT.
000586 01-09
PCP AND VIOLENT CRIME: THE PEOPLE VS. PEACE.
000986 01-17

VIOLENT-BEHAVIOR
PROPRANOLOL IN THE TREATMENT OF RAGE AND VIOLENT-BEHAVIOR IN
PATIENTS WITH CHRONIC-BRAIN-SYNDROMES.
003394 03-11

VIOLENT-BEHAVIOUR
BIOLOGY AND THERAPY OF VIOLENT-BEHAVIOUR IN CHILDREN.
002608 02-17

VIRIDIS
A CRITICAL EVALUATION OF THE USE OF TOXINS FROM DENDROASPIS
VIRIDIS TO BLOCK NICOTINIC RESPONSES AT CENTRAL AND
GANGLIONIC SYNAPSES.
002870 03-03

VISUAL
AN OLD SIDE-EFFECT REVISITED: VISUAL HALLUCINATIONS.
000886 01-15
EFFECTS OF HIPPOCAMPAL BRAIN-DAMAGE ON AUDITORY AND VISUAL
RECENT MEMORY: COMPARISON WITH MARIJUANA INTOXICATED
SUBJECTS.
002320 02-14
PSYCHOACTIVE-DRUG QUANTIFICATION BY VISUAL FLICKER SENSITIVITY
MEASUREMENT. (PH.D. DISSERTATION).
002485 02-16
SELECTIVE SYNAPTIC ANTAGONISM BY ATROPINE AND ALPHA
AMINOADIPATE OF PULVINAR AND CORTICAL AFFERENTS TO THE
SUPRASYLVIAN VISUAL AREA (CLARE-BISHOP AREA).
002752 03-03
THE STIMULATING EFFECT OF AMPHETAMINE ON THE VISUAL SYSTEM.
003398 03-13
HABITUATION OF ELECTRODERMAL AND RESPIRATORY RESPONSES TO
VISUAL STIMULI AS A FUNCTION OF PERSONALITY DIFFERENCES IN
AFFECT LEVEL.
003414 03-13
THE EFFECT OF PSYCHOSTIMULANTS ON CHANGES IN THE EXCITABILITY
OF THE VISUAL CEREBRAL-CORTEX.
003919 04-03
AN ANALYSIS OF VISUAL OBJECT REVERSAL LEARNING IN THE
MARMOSET AFTER AMPHETAMINE AND HALOPERIDOL.
004208 04-04
PERSONALITY AND DRUGS IN VISUAL FIGURAL AFTEREFFECTS.
004581 04-14

VISUAL-EVOKED-POTENTIALS
CORRELATIONS BETWEEN VISUAL-EVOKED-POTENTIALS AND
PSYCHOPATHOLOGICAL-FINDINGS IN SCHIZOPHRENIC-PATIENTS UNDER
TREATMENT WITH VARIOUS PSYCHOPHARMACOLOGICAL-DRUGS.
004315 04-08

VISUAL-MEMORY
DISSOCIATION OF THE STRYCHNINE EFFECT ON VISUAL-MEMORY AND
VERBAL-MEMORY IN ORGANIC-PSYCHOSYNDROMES.
000816 01-14
DISSOCIATION OF THE STRYCHNINE EFFECT ON VISUAL-MEMORY AND
VERBAL-MEMORY IN ORGANIC-PSYCHOSYNDROMES.
002155 02-11
INFLUENCE OF STRYCHNINE ON THE CONSOLIDATION PHASE OF VISUAL-
MEMORY IN GERONTOPSYCHIATRIC-PATIENTS.
002156 02-11

VISUALLY-EVOKED-POTENTIALS
STUDY ON VISUALLY-EVOKED-POTENTIALS IN SCHIZOPHRENIC-PATIENTS
IN SULPIRIDE THERAPY.
000550 01-08

VITAMIN
VITAMIN RESPONSIVE GENETIC ABNORMALITIES. (UNPUBLISHED PAPER).
001388 02-03

VITAMIN-B6
HOMOCYSTEINE-INDUCED CONVULSIONS: ENHANCEMENT BY VITAMIN-B6
AND INHIBITION BY HYDRAZINE.
002758 03-03
THE BIOLOGICAL-EFFECTS AND CLINICAL-EFFECTS OF ORAL MAGNESIUM
AND ASSOCIATED MAGNESIUM VITAMIN-B6 ADMINISTRATION ON
CERTAIN DISORDERS OBSERVED IN INFANTILE AUTISM.
003291 03-11

VITAMINS
LARGE-DOSES OF VITAMINS AND BEHAVIORAL-CONSEQUENCES. (PH.D.
DISSERTATION).
001633 02-04

VIVALAN
RESULTS OF CLINICAL-TESTS OF VILOXAZINE (VIVALAN ICI): PART OF A
MULTICLINICAL-STUDY.
002006 02-09
MULTICENTRE-STUDY WITH VILOXAZINE (VIVALAN) IN DEPRESSED-
PATIENTS.
004375 04-09

VOCABULARY
EFFECTS OF METHYLPHENIDATE ON LEARNING A BEGINNING READING
VOCABULARY BY NORMAL ADULTS.
000812 01-14

VOCALIZATION
ASCENDING ENDORPHIN INHIBITION OF DISTRESS VOCALIZATION.
003011 03-04

VOLTAGE
MONOAMINE REPLACEMENT AFTER RESERPINE: CATECHOLAMINERGIC
AGONISTS RESTORE MOTOR-ACTIVITY BUT PHENYLETHYLAMINE
RESTORES ATROPINE-RESISTANT NEOCORTICAL LOW VOLTAGE FAST-
ACTIVITY.
000309 01-03
RESERPINE ABOLISHES MOVEMENT CORRELATED ATROPINE-RESISTANT
NEOCORTICAL LOW VOLTAGE FAST-ACTIVITY.
000310 01-03
VOLTAGE CLAMP STUDY OF CAT SPINAL MOTONEURONS DURING
STRYCHNINE-INDUCED SEIZURES.
002886 03-03

VOLTAGE-INDEPENDENT
THE NA-K-ATPASE: A PLAUSIBLE TRIGGER FOR VOLTAGE-INDEPENDENT
RELEASE OF CYTOPLASMIC NEUROTRANSMITTERS.
003953 04-03

VOLTAMMETRIC
IN VIVO VOLTAMMETRIC INVESTIGATIONS INTO THE ACTION OF HA-966
ON CENTRAL DOPAMINERGIC NEURONS.
002832 03-03

VOLTAMMETRY
DOPAMINE HYPOACTIVITY MEASURED BY IN VIVO VOLTAMMETRY.
001149 02-03

VOLUNTARY
REDUCTION OF VOLUNTARY MORPHINE CONSUMPTION FOLLOWING
TREATMENT WITH ZIMELIDINE.
000253 01-03
VOLUNTARY INTOXICATION FROM PHENCYCLIDINE. WILL IT RAISE A
REASONABLE-DOUBT OF THE MENTAL-CAPACITY OF A PERSON
CHARGED WITH A CRIME REQUIRING SPECIFIC INTENT OR MENTAL-
STATE?.
000914 01-17

VOLUNTEERS
CHRONIC ADMINISTRATION OF CANNABIDIOL TO HEALTHY VOLUNTEERS
AND EPILEPTIC-PATIENTS.
000669 01-11
PHARMACOKINETICS OF CHLORPROMAZINE IN NORMAL VOLUNTEERS.
000778 01-13
PHARMACOKINETICS OF NORTRIPTYLINE IN ELDERLY VOLUNTEERS.
002184 02-11
LEVELS OF MINERAL-ELEMENTS IN THE SERUM AND SALIVA OF HEALTHY
MALE VOLUNTEERS AFTER A SINGLE-DOSE OF LI2CO3.
002297 02-13
THE PERIPHERAL ANTICHOLINERGIC-ACTIVITY OF TRICYCLIC-
ANTIDEPRESSANTS: COMPARISON OF AMITRIPTYLINE AND
DESIPRAMINE IN HUMAN VOLUNTEERS.
002298 02-13
SINGLE-DOSE PHARMACOKINETICS OF DOXEPIN IN HEALTHY
VOLUNTEERS.
002303 02-13
SUBJECTIVE DRUG-EFFECTS AND DRUG PREFERENCE IN HEALTHY
VOLUNTEERS AS A MODEL OF A DRUGS REINFORCING EFFECTS:
STUDIES ON NOMIFENSINE, AMPHETAMINE AND PLACEBO.
002362 02-14
CARDIOVASCULAR-EFFECTS OF MIANSERIN AND AMITRIPTYLINE IN
HEALTHY VOLUNTEERS.
002469 02-15
DESIPRAMINE AND 2 HYDROXYDESIPRAMINE PHARMACOKINETICS IN
NORMAL VOLUNTEERS.
003154 03-07
TYRAMINE PRESSOR TEST AND CARDIOVASCULAR-EFFECTS OF
CHLORIMIPRAMINE AND NORTRIPTYLINE IN HEALTHY VOLUNTEERS.
003428 03-13
APOMORPHINE, HALOPERIDOL AND THE AVERAGE EVOKED-POTENTIALS
IN NORMAL HUMAN VOLUNTEERS.
004549 04-13
THE EFFECT OF FIVE TRICYCLIC-ANTIDEPRESSANTS ON SALIVARY FLOW
AND MOOD IN HEALTHY VOLUNTEERS.
004560 04-14

VOMITING
INTRAVENOUS LORAZEPAM TO PREVENT NAUSEA AND VOMITING
ASSOCIATED WITH CANCER CHEMOTHERAPY.
003614 03-17

VULNERABILITY
PROTECTIVE EFFECT OF PRENYLAMINE AGAINST VULNERABILITY TO
VENTRICULAR FIBRILLATION IN THE NORMAL AND ISCHEMIC CANINE
MYOCARDIUM.
000265 01-03
INCREASED VULNERABILITY TO CHOLINERGIC STIMULATION IN
AFFECTIVE-DISORDER PATIENTS.
002003 02-09

WAKEFULNESS
CHARACTERIZATION OF ERGOT AND NONERGOT SEROTONIN
ANTAGONISTS BY PROLACTIN AND GROWTH-HORMONE PROFILES
DURING WAKEFULNESS AND SLEEP.
002217 02-13

() 6 FLUOROTRYPTOPHAN, AN INHIBITOR OF TRYPTOPHAN-
HYDROXYLASE: SLEEP AND WAKEFULNESS IN THE RAT.
004189 04-04

WAKING
THE CLOCK AND THE BLUE GUITAR: STUDIES OF HUMAN GROWTH-
HORMONE SECRETION IN SLEEP AND WAKING. (UNPUBLISHED PAPER).
002346 02-14
DOES P CHLOROPHENYLALANINE PRODUCE DISTURBED WAKING,
DISTURBED SLEEP OR ACTIVATION BY PONTO-GENICULO-OCCIPITAL
WAVES IN CATS?
003704 04-02

WALL
SYNTHETIC IMMUNOSTIMULANTS DERIVED FROM THE BACTERIAL CELL
WALL.
001080 02-02

WAR-NEUROSIS
TREATMENT OF TRAUMATIC WAR-NEUROSIS WITH PHENELZINE.
003325 03-11

WARFARIN
DRUG-INTERACTIONS OF AMITRIPTYLINE AND NORTRIPTYLINE WITH
WARFARIN IN THE RAT.
003912 04-03

WASTAGE
FAILURE OF CLORAZEPATE TO CAUSE MALFORMATIONS OR FETAL
WASTAGE IN THE RAT.
000514 01-05

WATER
WATER INTAKE AND TIME-COURSE OF DRINKING AFTER SINGLE OR
REPEATED CHLORDIAZEPOXIDE INJECTIONS.
000369 01-04
USING PROFILES OF SACCHARIN AND WATER DRINKING TO DETECT AND
DISCRIMINATE ACTIONS OF DRUGS AND TOXICANTS.
000503 01-04
REVERSAL BY PHENYTOIN OF CARBAMAZEPINE-INDUCED WATER
INTOXICATION: A PHARMACOKINETIC-INTERACTION.
000783 01-13
NALOXONE: EFFECTS ON FOOD AND WATER CONSUMPTION IN THE
NONDEPRIVED AND DEPRIVED RAT.
001599 02-04
DIFFERENTIAL-EFFECTS OF MORPHINE ON FOOD AND WATER INTAKE IN
FOOD DEPRIVED AND FREELY-FEEDING RATS.
001765 02-04
ANTECEDENTS OF SELF-INDUCED WATER INTOXICATION: A PRELIMINARY-
REPORT.
002414 02-15
SINGLE OR REPEATED ADMINISTRATION OF SMALL DOSES OF
APOMORPHINE ON WATER INTAKE AND ACTIVITY IN WATER-
DEPRIVED RATS.
002981 03-04
PIMOZIDE ATTENUATES LEVER-PRESSING FOR WATER REINFORCEMENT IN
RATS.
003000 03-04
EFFECTS OF CAFFEINE ADMINISTRATION ON FOOD AND WATER
CONSUMPTION UNDER VARIOUS EXPERIMENTAL CONDITIONS.
003049 03-04
CENTRAL-EFFECTS OF ANGIOTENSIN-II IN WATER AND SALINE LOADED
RATS.
003845 04-03
NALOXONE SUPPRESSES FOOD/WATER CONSUMPTION IN THE DEPRIVED
CAT.
004114 04-04
THE SITE OF ACTION OF NALOXONE IN SUPPRESSING FOOD AND WATER
INTAKE IN RATS.
004146 04-04
IN NORMAL YOUNG MEN ACUTE DOPAMINERGIC BLOCKADE DOES NOT
IMPAIR FREE WATER EXCRETION FOLLOWING A STANDARD WATER
LOAD.
004600 04-15

WATER-DEPRIVED
SINGLE OR REPEATED ADMINISTRATION OF SMALL DOSES OF
APOMORPHINE ON WATER INTAKE AND ACTIVITY IN WATER-
DEPRIVED RATS.
002981 03-04

WATER-ESCAPE
TOLERANCE TO ETHANOL-INDUCED IMPAIRMENT OF WATER-ESCAPE IN
RATS BRED FOR ETHANOL SENSITIVITY.
001567 02-04

WAVES
CAPACITIES OF ATTENTION, STRESS-RESISTANCE, AND SLOW CEREBRAL
POTENTIALS: EFFECTS OF CARPIPRAMINE ON CONTINGENT NEGATIVE
VARIATION WAVES AND P-300.
003451 03-14
DOES P CHLOROPHENYLALANINE PRODUCE DISTURBED WAKING,
DISTURBED SLEEP OR ACTIVATION BY PONTO-GENICULO-OCCIPITAL
WAVES IN CATS?
003704 04-02

WB-4101
(3H)QUINUCLIDINYL-BENZILATE BINDING TO MUSCARINIC-RECEPTORS
AND (3H)WB-4101 BINDING TO ALPHA-ADRENERGIC-RECEPTORS IN

RABBIT IRIS: COMPARISON OF RESULTS IN SLICES AND MICROSOMAL
FRACTIONS.
000299 01-03

WEANING
BIOELECTRICAL-ACTIVITY OF THE RAT BRAIN AFTER PREMATURE
WEANING AND AFTER RNA ADMINISTRATION.
002865 03-03

WEIGHT
PREDICTORS OF ADOLESCENT HEIGHT AND WEIGHT IN HYPERKINETIC-
BOYS TREATED WITH METHYLPHENIDATE.
003509 03-15
DEPOT FLUPHENAZINE MAINTENANCE-TREATMENT AND ASSOCIATED
WEIGHT CHANGES.
004635 04-15

WEIGHT-CONTROL
DOUBLE-BLIND EVALUATION OF REINFORCING AND ANORECTIC-ACTIONS
OF WEIGHT-CONTROL MEDICATIONS: INTERACTION OF
PHARMACOLOGICAL-TREATMENT AND BEHAVIORAL-TREATMENTS.
002314 02-14

WEIGHT-GAIN
PHENOBARBITAL EFFECTS ON WEIGHT-GAIN AND CIRCADIAN-CYCLING OF
FOOD INTAKE AND BODY-TEMPERATURE.
001409 02-03
LITHIUM-CARBONATE AND WEIGHT-GAIN.
002448 02-15
NALOXONE IN THE TREATMENT OF ANOREXIA-NERVOSA: EFFECT ON
WEIGHT-GAIN AND LIPOLYSIS.
003342 03-11

WEIGHTS
COCAINE AND SEIZURE PROTECTION IN MICE OF VARYING BRAIN
WEIGHTS.
004103 04-04

WELL-BEING
A COMPUTER OCULOGRAPHIC AND EEG DOUBLE-BLIND STUDY INCLUDING
WELL-BEING FOR DETERMINING CHANGED VIGILANCE UNDER THERAPY
WITH TIAPRIDE.
000751 01-13

WELLBUTRIN
CLINICAL-EFFICACY OF THE NEW ANTIDEPRESSANT BUPROPION
(WELLBUTRIN).
003227 03-09

WET-DOG-SHAKE
STUDIES OF CARBACHOL-INDUCED WET-DOG-SHAKE BEHAVIOR IN RATS.
004241 04-04

WET-DOG-SHAKES
EFFECT OF CITALOPRAM (LU-10-171) ON TRANYLCYPROMINE AND
TRYPTOPHAN-INDUCED WET-DOG-SHAKES IN RATS.
001682 02-04
KAINIC-ACID-INDUCED WET-DOG-SHAKES IN RATS: THE RELATION TO
CENTRAL NEUROTRANSMITTERS.
001685 02-04

WHEEL
NALOXONE SUPPRESSES FEEDING AND DRINKING BUT NOT WHEEL
RUNNING IN RATS.
004080 04-04

WIDOWERS
WIDOWS AND WIDOWERS AND THEIR MEDICATION USE: NURSING
IMPLICATIONS.
003626 03-17

WIDOWS
WIDOWS AND WIDOWERS AND THEIR MEDICATION USE: NURSING
IMPLICATIONS.
003626 03-17

WINGS
FDA CLIPS PSYCHODRUG PIONEERS IND WINGS.
003160 03-07

WITHDRAWAL
SEROTONIN PARTICIPATION IN GUT WITHDRAWAL FROM OPIATES.
000109 01-03
STRIATAL DOPAMINERGIC ACTIVITY DURING WITHDRAWAL FROM
CHRONIC NEUROLEPTIC TREATMENT IN RATS.
000203 01-03
APPLICATION OF A SYNTHETIC ENKEPHALIN ANALOGUE DURING HEROIN
WITHDRAWAL.
000685 01-11
INTRAVENOUS PHENOBARBITAL THERAPY IN BARBITURATE AND OTHER
HYPNOSEDATIVE WITHDRAWAL REACTIONS: A KINETIC APPROACH.
000703 01-11
MANIC-PSYCHOSIS FOLLOWING RAPID WITHDRAWAL FROM BACLOFEN.
000832 01-15
THE ROLE OF CHOLINERGIC-SUPERSENSITIVITY IN THE MEDICAL
SYMPTOMS ASSOCIATED WITH WITHDRAWAL OF ANTIPSYCHOTIC-
DRUGS.
000869 01-15
A CASE-REPORT OF LORAZEPAM WITHDRAWAL.
000889 01-15
INTROVERSION AND SEVERITY OF THE BENZODIAZEPINE WITHDRAWAL.
000923 01-17

INTERACTION-STUDIES BETWEEN NARCOTIC ANALGESICS, NARCOTIC ANTAGONISTS AND ETHANOL: STUDIES DURING ACUTE AND CHRONIC-TREATMENT AND WITHDRAWAL STATES IN RATS AND MICE. (PH.D. DISSERTATION).
001165 02-03
CHANGES IN CEREBRAL DOPAMINE FUNCTION INDUCED BY A YEARS ADMINISTRATION OF TRIFLUOPERAZINE OR THIORIDAZINE AND THEIR SUBSEQUENT WITHDRAWAL.
001175 02-03
A DEMONSTRATION OF NALOXONE PRECIPITATED OPIATE WITHDRAWAL ON SINGLE NEURONES IN THE MORPHINE-TOLERANT/DEPENDENT RAT-BRAIN.
001234 02-03
NARCOTIC ANTAGONIST PRECIPITATED ABSTINENCE: RELATIONSHIP TO WITHDRAWAL INDUCING BENZAZOCINES. (PH.D. DISSERTATION).
001518 02-03
EFFECTS OF MORPHINE WITHDRAWAL ON FOOD COMPETITION HIERARCHIES AND FIGHTING-BEHAVIOR IN RATS.
001632 02-04
SUBACUTE CANNABINOID TREATMENT: ANTICONVULSANT ACTIVITY AND WITHDRAWAL EXCITABILITY IN MICE.
001671 02-04
EFFECT OF P CHLOROPHENYLALANINE ON DIAZEPAM WITHDRAWAL SIGNS IN RATS.
001797 02-04
THE EFFECTS OF ETHANOL, PHENOBARBITAL, AND BACLOFEN ON ETHANOL WITHDRAWAL IN THE RHESUS-MONKEY.
001802 02-04
RAPID RECURRENCE OF MANIA FOLLOWING LITHIUM WITHDRAWAL.
002010 02-09
ADVANTAGE OF MONOTHERAPY WITH CLOBAZAM IN THE TREATMENT AND POSTTREATMENT OF ALCOHOLIC WITHDRAWAL.
002140 02-11
USE OF INJECTABLE LORAZEPAM IN ALCOHOL WITHDRAWAL.
002176 02-11
CHANGES IN CEREBRAL DOPAMINE METABOLISM AND RECEPTORS DURING ONE-YEAR NEUROLEPTIC ADMINISTRATION AND SUBSEQUENT WITHDRAWAL: RELEVANCE TO BRAIN-BIOCHEMISTRY IN SCHIZOPHRENIA.
002390 02-15
SPONTANEOUS ACTIVITY AND APOMORPHINE STEREOTYPY DURING AND AFTER WITHDRAWAL FROM 3 1/2 MONTHS CONTINUOUS ADMINISTRATION OF HALOPERIDOL: SOME METHODOLOGICAL-ISSUES.
002509 02-16
THE CHANGE OF BLOOD PROLACTIN LEVEL DUE TO THE WITHDRAWAL OF MAINTENANCE NEUROLEPTICS.
002559 02-17
MORPHINE WITHDRAWAL CAUSES SUBSENSITIVITY OF ADRENERGIC-RECEPTOR RESPONSE.
002838 03-03
LOW SERUM PROLACTIN AND EARLY RELAPSE FOLLOWING NEUROLEPTIC WITHDRAWAL.
003166 03-08
HYPOMANIA AND MANIA AFTER WITHDRAWAL OF TRICYCLIC-ANTIDEPRESSANTS.
003243 03-09
ALCOHOL WITHDRAWAL USING TIAPRIDE: QUANTITATIVE PSYCHOPATHOLOGY.
003293 03-11
EFFICACY OF CLONIDINE IN OPIATE WITHDRAWAL: A STUDY OF THIRTY PATIENTS.
003317 03-11
DOUBLE-BLIND COMPARISON OF ALPRAZOLAM AND DIAZEPAM FOR SUBCHRONIC WITHDRAWAL FROM ALCOHOL.
003332 03-11
THE EFFECT OF WITHDRAWAL FROM PROLONGED PROPHYLACTIC TREATMENT WITH LITHIUM.
003339 03-11
BENZODIAZEPINE WITHDRAWAL SYMPTOMS AND PROPRANOLOL.
003543 03-15
EFFECT OF LOW-DOSE LITHIUM ADMINISTRATION AND SUBSEQUENT WITHDRAWAL ON BIOGENIC-AMINES IN RAT-BRAIN.
003708 04-03
THE EFFECT OF CHRONIC NICOTINE AND WITHDRAWAL ON INTRAAXONAL TRANSPORT OF ACETYLCHOLINE AND RELATED ENZYMES IN SCIATIC-NERVE OF THE RAT.
003897 04-03
EFFECTS OF ETHANOL ADMINISTRATION AND WITHDRAWAL ON NEUROTRANSMITTER-RECEPTOR SYSTEMS IN C57 MICE.
003979 04-03
THE EFFECTS OF ACUTE AND CHRONIC ETHANC ADMINISTRATION AND ITS WITHDRAWAL ON GAMMA AMINOBUTYRIC-ACID-RECEPTOR BINDING IN RAT-BRAIN.
004035 04-03
CHARACTER AND MEANING OF QUASI-MORPHINE WITHDRAWAL PHENOMENA ELICITED BY METHYLXANTHINES.
004087 04-04
EFFECTS OF WITHDRAWAL FROM LONG-TERM DIPHENYLHYDANTOIN TREATMENT ON AUDIOGENIC-SEIZURES AND MAXIMAL ELECTROSHOCK-INDUCED SEIZURES IN RATS.
004101 04-04

OPIATE-DEPENDENCE FOLLOWING ACUTE INJECTIONS OF MORPHINE AND NALOXONE: THE ASSESSMENT OF VARIOUS WITHDRAWAL SIGNS.
004209 04-04
PHARMACOLOGICAL-ASPECTS OF SHAKING-BEHAVIOR PRODUCED BY TRH, AG-3-5, AND MORPHINE WITHDRAWAL,
004248 04-04
LONG-TERM NEUROLEPTIC TREATMENT OF CHRONIC SCHIZOPHRENIC-PATIENTS: CLINICAL AND BIOCHEMICAL-EFFECTS OF WITHDRAWAL.
004344 04-08
A PRELIMINARY OPEN-STUDY OF THE USE OF AMINEPTINE OF THE DEFICIENT SYNDROME OF HEBEPHRENICS AND OF ADDICTS DURING WITHDRAWAL.
004445 04-11
ADVERSE-EFFECTS OF ANTIPARKINSON-DRUG WITHDRAWAL. (UNPUBLISHED PAPER).
004623 04-15
WITHDRAWAL SYMPTOMS AFTER GRADUATED CESSATION OF IMIPRAMINE IN CHILDREN.
004630 04-15
WITHDRAWAL-LIKE
HIPPOCAMPAL INVOLVEMENT IN THE PHARMACOLOGIC INDUCTION OF WITHDRAWAL-LIKE BEHAVIORS.
004140 04-04
ATTENUATION OF DELTA9 TETRAHYDROCANNABINOL-INDUCED WITHDRAWAL-LIKE BEHAVIOUR BY DELTA9 TETRAHYDROCANNABINOL.
004243 04-04
WITHDRAWAL-SYNDROME
BARBITURATE-DEPENDENCE IN MICE: EFFECTS OF PROPRANOLOL ON THE WITHDRAWAL-SYNDROME (40798).
000313 01-03
SODIUM-VALPROATE IN THE TREATMENT OF ALCOHOL WITHDRAWAL-SYNDROME.
002139 02-11
ALCOHOL WITHDRAWAL-SYNDROME: TREATMENT WITH TRAZODONE.
002356 02-14
SEVERE WITHDRAWAL-SYNDROME AFTER CESSATION OF BENZODIAZEPINE TREATMENT: SIX CLINICAL CASES.
003505 03-15
RX-336-M, A NEW CHEMICAL TOOL IN THE ANALYSIS OF THE QUASI-MORPHINE WITHDRAWAL-SYNDROME.
004093 04-04
PHYSIOLOGICAL AND BEHAVIORAL APPROACHES TO THE STUDY OF THE QUASI-MORPHINE WITHDRAWAL-SYNDROME.
004242 04-04
WITHDRAWAL-SYNDROMES
CHOLINERGIC REBOUND IN NEUROLEPTIC WITHDRAWAL-SYNDROMES.
003506 03-15
WITHDRAWN '
ORAL DYSKINESIA IN BRAIN-DAMAGED RATS WITHDRAWN FROM A NEUROLEPTIC: IMPLICATION FOR MODELS OF TARDIVE-DYSKINESIA.
000393 01-03
WOMEN
GROWTH-HORMONE AFTER TRH IN WOMEN WITH DEPRESSIVE-ILLNESS.
000606 01-09
AMITRIPTYLINE, NORTRIPTYLINE PLASMA LEVELS AND CLINICAL-RESPONSE IN WOMEN WITH AFFECTIVE-DISORDERS.
000757 01-13
EFFECTS OF NALOXONE UPON PROLACTIN AND CORTISOL IN NORMAL WOMEN.
002213 02-13
INCREASED SERUM PROLACTIN LEVELS DURING PHENOTHIAZINE AND BUTYROPHENONE TREATMENT OF SIX POSTPARTUM WOMEN.
003318 03-11
ELECTROPHYSIOLOGICAL AND PSYCHOLOGICAL CHANGES INDUCED BY STEROID-HORMONES IN MEN AND WOMEN.
004500 04-13
WORLD
THE WORLD OF HALLUCINOGENIC PLANTS.
003396 03-12
WORLD-HEALTH-ORGANIZATION
AMITRIPTYLINE PLASMA CONCENTRATION AND CLINICAL-EFFECT: A WORLD-HEALTH-ORGANIZATION COLLABORATIVE-STUDY.
001976 02-09
WORLDWIDE
TRIMIPRAMINE: TWENTY YEARS WORLDWIDE CLINICAL-EXPERIENCE.
000985 01-17
XANTHURENIC-ACID
HYPERVENTILATION-SYNDROME, TREATMENT WITH L TRYPTOPHAN AND PYRIDOXINE; PREDICTIVE VALUES OF XANTHURENIC-ACID EXCRETION.
004646 04-11
XQ-FRAGILE-SITE
FRAGILE SITES IN HUMAN CHROMOSOMES I. THE EFFECT OF METHIONINE ON THE XQ-FRAGILE-SITE.
004515 04-13
Y-MAZE
Y-MAZE BEHAVIOR AFTER AN ANALOG OF ACTH4-9, EVIDENCE FOR AN ATTENTIONAL-ALTERATION.
001676 02-04

YAWNING-BEHAVIOR
SEX-HORMONE INFLUENCES ON YAWNING-BEHAVIOR.
000407 01-04
INTERACTION OF CHOLINERGIC AND DOPAMINERGIC INFLUENCES ON YAWNING-BEHAVIOR.
001656 02-04

YOHIMBINE
ADMINISTRATION OF ANTISOMATOSTATIN SERUM TO RATS REVERSES THE INHIBITION OF PULSATILE GROWTH-HORMONE SECRETION PRODUCED BY INJECTION OF METERGOLINE BUT NOT YOHIMBINE. (UNPUBLISHED PAPER).
000019 01-03
ACCELERATION OF DESIPRAMINE-INDUCED DECREASE OF RAT CORTICOCEREBRAL BETA-ADRENERGIC-RECEPTORS BY YOHIMBINE.
000326 01-03
EFFECTS OF DESIPRAMINE AND YOHIMBINE ON ALPHA2-ADRENOCEPTOR AND BETA-ADRENOCEPTOR SENSITIVITY.
001305 02-03
ADRENERGIC NONSPECIFIC POTENTIATION OF YOHIMBINE TOXICITY IN MICE BY ANTIDEPRESSANTS AND RELATED DRUGS AND ANTIYOHIMBINE ACTION OF ANTIADRENERGIC AND SEROTONERGIC DRUGS.
001330 02-03
FUNCTIONAL CHARACTERIZATION OF CENTRAL ALPHA-ADRENOCEPTORS BY YOHIMBINE DIASTEREOMERS.
002748 03-03
ANTIDOPAMINERGIC PROPERTIES OF YOHIMBINE.
003995 04-03
HUMAN PLATELET ALPHA2-ADRENERGIC-RECEPTORS: LABELING WITH 3H YOHIMBINE, A SELECTIVE ANTAGONIST LIGAND.
004676 04-16

YOUNG
INHIBITION OF GROWTH IN YOUNG MICE TREATED WITH PENTAZOCINE: REVERSAL BY NALTREXONE.
000318 01-03
BRAINSTEM AUDITORY EVOKED-POTENTIALS AND MYELIN CHANGES IN TRIETHYLTIN-INDUCED EDEMA IN YOUNG ADULT RATS.
000509 01-05
PIRACETAM AND RETRIEVAL OF MEMORY IN YOUNG RATS.
000803 01-14
DIFFERENTIAL DOPAMINERGIC FUNCTION IN YOUNG AND OLD FEMALE RATS AS MEASURED BY THREE BEHAVIORS.
001683 02-04
BRIEF SOCIAL-ISOLATION, PAIN RESPONSIVITY, AND MORPHINE ANALGESIA IN YOUNG RATS.
001744 02-04
COMPARISON OF NITRAZEPAM 5 MG WITH TRIAZOLAM 0.5 MG IN YOUNG PSYCHIATRIC INSOMNIAC-INPATIENTS.
002096 02-11
5 HYDROXYTRYPTOPHAN AND PYRIDOXINE: THEIR EFFECTS IN YOUNG CHILDREN WITH DOWNS-SYNDROME.
002161 02-11
DIURNAL GROWTH-HORMONE RESPONSES TO DEXTROAMPHETAMINE IN NORMAL YOUNG MEN AND POSTMENOPAUSAL-WOMEN.
003411 03-13
EFFECTS OF A SINGLE-THERAPEUTIC-DOSE OF GLYCEROL ON CEREBRAL METABOLISM IN THE BRAINS OF YOUNG MICE: POSSIBLE INCREASE IN BRAIN GLUCOSE TRANSPORT AND GLUCOSE UTILIZATION.
004281 04-05
HYPERACTIVES AS YOUNG ADULTS: PROSPECTIVE TEN-YEAR FOLLOWUP.
004454 04-11
KINETICS AND BIOTRANSFORMATION OF LORMETAZEPAM: II. RADIOIMMUNOLOGIC DETERMINATIONS IN PLASMA AND URINE OF YOUNG AND ELDERLY SUBJECTS: FIRST-PASS EFFECT.
004516 04-13
IN NORMAL YOUNG MEN ACUTE DOPAMINERGIC BLOCKADE DOES NOT IMPAIR FREE WATER EXCRETION FOLLOWING A STANDARD WATER LOAD.
004600 04-15

YOUTH
TARDIVE-DYSKINESIA AND OTHER DRUG-INDUCED MOVEMENT-DISORDERS AMONG HANDICAPPED CHILDREN AND YOUTH.
004614 04-15

ZIMELIDINE
REDUCTION OF VOLUNTARY MORPHINE CONSUMPTION FOLLOWING TREATMENT WITH ZIMELIDINE.
000253 01-03
BIOCHEMICAL-EFFECTS OF ZIMELIDINE IN MAN.
001967 02-09
A CLINICAL-TRIAL OF ZIMELIDINE IN DEPRESSION.
001992 02-09
CARDIOVASCULAR-EFFECTS OF AMITRIPTYLINE, MIANSERIN AND ZIMELIDINE IN DEPRESSED-PATIENTS.
002215 02-13
CHANGES IN THE AUGMENTER REDUCER TENDENCY AND IN PAIN MEASURES AS A RESULT OF TREATMENT WITH A SEROTONIN REUPTAKE INHIBITOR ZIMELIDINE.
002305 02-13
CLINICAL-TRIALS WITH NEW BICYCLIC AND TETRACYCLIC COMPOUNDS: ZIMELIDINE AND MAPROTILINE.
003213 03-09
CROSS-OVER STUDY OF ZIMELIDINE AND DESIPRAMINE IN DEPRESSION: EVIDENCE FOR AMINE SPECIFICITY.
003250 03-09
EFFECTS OF ZIMELIDINE ON SEROTONINERGIC AND NORADRENERGIC NEURONS AFTER REPEATED ADMINISTRATION IN THE RAT.
003991 04-03
ATTENUATION OF PETHIDINE-INDUCED ANTINOCICEPTION BY ZIMELIDINE, AN INHIBITOR OF 5 HYDROXYTRYPTAMINE REUPTAKE.
004118 04-04
SINGLE-DOSE PHARMACOKINETIC DATA ON ZIMELIDINE IN DEPRESSED-PATIENTS.
004385 04-09
MAPROTILINE, NOMIFENSINE, MIANSERIN, ZIMELIDINE: A REVIEW OF ANTIDEPRESSANT EFFICACY IN INPATIENTS.
004731 04-17

ZONA-COMPACTA
THE PARTICIPATION OF SUBSTANTIA-NIGRA ZONA-COMPACTA AND ZONA-RETICULATA NEURONS IN MORPHINE SUPPRESSION OF CAUDATE SPONTANEOUS NEURONAL ACTIVITIES IN THE RAT.
002718 03-03

ZONA-RETICULATA
THE PARTICIPATION OF SUBSTANTIA-NIGRA ZONA-COMPACTA AND ZONA-RETICULATA NEURONS IN MORPHINE SUPPRESSION OF CAUDATE SPONTANEOUS NEURONAL ACTIVITIES IN THE RAT
002718 03-03

ZONE-SPECIFIC
ROTATION INDUCED BY INTRANIGRAL INJECTIONS OF GABA AGONISTS AND ANTAGONISTS: ZONE-SPECIFIC EFFECTS.
000422 01-04

ZONES
LSD-INDUCED ULTRASTRUCTURAL MODIFICATIONS OF LIMBIC-SYSTEM NUCLEI AND OTHER CEREBRAL ZONES.
002198 02-12

ZOPICLONE
STUDY OF VIGILANCE AFTER INGESTION OF ZOPICLONE IN COMPARISON WITH NITRAZEPAM AND PLACEBO. METHODOLOGY OF THE STUDY: SELF-EVALUATION QUESTIONNAIRE AND PSYCHOMETRIC-TESTS.
000543 01-07

ZOTEPINE
PHARMACOKINETICS AND METABOLISM OF CHLORODIMETHYLAMINOETHOXYDIBENZOTHIEPINE (ZOTEPINE) IN RAT, MOUSE, DOG AND MAN.
000219 01-03
PHARMACOLOGICAL-STUDY OF CHLORODIMETHYLAMINOETHOXYDIBENZOTHIEPINE (ZOTEPINE), A NEW NEUROLEPTIC-DRUG.
000493 01-04
TOXICOLOGICAL AND TERATOLOGICAL STUDIES OF CHLORODIMETHYLAMINOETHOXYDIBENZOTHIEPINE (ZOTEPINE), A NEW NEUROLEPTIC-DRUG.
000515 01-05

ZUCKER
METABOLIC AND SYMPATHOADRENAL ABNORMALITIES IN THE OBESE ZUCKER RAT: EFFECT OF CHRONIC PHENOXYBENZAMINE TREATMENT.
003905 04-03

ZWITTERION
THE IONIZATION OF 5 HYDROXYTRYPTAMINE AND RELATED COMPOUNDS AND AN APPRAISAL OF METHODS FOR THE ESTIMATION OF ZWITTERION CONSTANTS.
001859 02-06

125I
REGIONAL DISTRIBUTION AND BIOCHEMICAL-PROPERTIES OF 125I TYR8-SUBSTANCE-P BINDING-SITES IN SYNAPTIC VESICLES.
000259 01-03
REGULATION OF RECEPTOR BINDING INTERACTIONS OF 125I ANGIOTENSIN-II AND 125I SARCOSINE1-LEUCINE8-ANGIOTENSIN-II, AN ANGIOTENSIN ANTAGONIST, BY SODIUM-ION.
001124 02-03
RECEPTOR BINDING INTERACTIONS OF THE ANGIOTENSIN-II ANTAGONIST, 125I SARCOSINE1-LEUCINE8-ANGIOTENSIN-II, WITH MAMMALIAN BRAIN AND PERIPHERAL TISSUES.
001125 02-03
ABUNDANCE AND LOCATION OF 125I SALMON CALCITONIN BINDING-SITE IN RAT-BRAIN.
001320 02-03

1694
ANTIDEPRESSANT ACTION OF INJECTABLE 1694.
001960 02-09

45-0088-S
PHARMACOLOGY OF 2 O CHLOROBENZOYL-CHLORO-METHYL-NA-GLYCYLGLYCINANILIDE HYDRATE (45-0088-S), A COMPOUND WITH BENZODIAZEPINE-LIKE PROPERTIES.
003692 04-02

45CA
EFFECT OF VERAPAMIL ON 45CA UPTAKE BY SYNAPTOSOMES.
003856 04-03

45CA2

EFFECT OF TAURINE ON 45CA2 ACCUMULATION IN RAT BRAIN SYNAPTOSOMES.

002855 03-03

INCREASE OF C-GMP AND ACCUMULATION OF 45CA2 EVOKED BY DRUGS ACTING ON SODIUM OR POTASSIUM CHANNELS.

003709 04-03

77BR

SPECIFIC IN VIVO BINDING OF 77BR P BROMOSPIROPERIDOL IN RAT-BRAIN: A POTENTIAL TOOL FOR GAMMA-RAY IMAGING.

004293 04-06

82BR

DISTRIBUTION AND EXCRETION IN THE RAT AND MONKEY OF (82BR) BROMOCRIPTINE.

000196 01-03

AUTHOR INDEX

A

AABRO E 000659 01-11
AALTONEN L 000774 01-13
AAMODT RL 000196 01-03
AANDERUD S 004488 04-11
AARLI JA 002234 02-13 , 003486 03-15
ABBRUZZESE G 004382 04-09
ABDALA NE 002018 02-09
ABDEL-LATIF AA 000299 01-03
ABDUL-GHANI A 000058 01-03
ABEL EL 001830 02-05
ABEL JG 000747 01-13
ABELSON JS 001557 02-04
ABHYANKAR RR 002158 02-11
ABIKOFF H 000678 01-11
ABRAHAM LD 004226 04-04
ABRAHAM RR 004463 04-11
ABRAHAM SF 002062 02-10
ABRAMETS II 002790 03-03
ABRAMOVA LI 003176 03-08
ABRAMS AA 000748 01-13
ABRIOL C 004530 04-13
ABUZZAHAB FS 002513 02-17
ACHILLI G 003674 04-01
ACHTE K 000910 01-17 , 003573 03-17
ACKENHEIL M 001935 02-08 , 001936 02-08 ,
  001959 02-08 , 002311 02-13 , 002370
  02-15 , 004344 04-08
ACKERMAN L 000945 01-17
ACKERMAN PT 002118 02-11
ACOSTA E 001930 02-08
ACOSTA J 001558 02-04
ADAM K 002446 02-15
ADAMEC RE 002202 02-12 , 003133 03-06
ADAMS C 004376 04-09
ADAMS L 002803 03-03
ADAMS PM 002942 03-04 , 003121 03-05 ,
  004083 04-04
ADER JP 001095 02-03
ADEY M 002512 02-16
ADINOLFI M 003071 03-04
ADLER DS 004498 04-13
ADLER LE 000829 01-15
ADLER MW 004697 04-17
ADNEY K 003509 03-15
ADOLPHE AB 004560 04-14
ADRIEN J 000214 01-03 , 000423 01-04
ADVOKAT C 002943 03-04 , 002944 03-04
AELLIG A 000759 01-13
AESCHLIMANN JM 000759 01-13
AFELTOWICZ Z 000546 01-08
AGARKOVA VP 003994 04-03
AGARWAL PK 000583 01-09
AGHAJANIAN GK 000024 01-03 , 000068 01-
  03 , 001364 02-03 , 001523 02-03
AGID Y 003458 03-14
AGNATI LF 001096 02-03 , 001238 02-03 ,
  001239 02-03 , 001240 02-03 , 002727
  03-03
AGNOLI A 002090 02-11 , 002312 02-14 ,
  002371 02-15 , 003085 03-04 , 004431
  04-11
AGRANOFF BW 003987 04-03
AGRAWAL AK 004264 04-05 , 004265 04-05
AGUIAR M 000407 01-04
AGUILAR JS 001097 02-03
AGUILERA LI 000102 01-03
AGUILLAUME-TORRES R 002078 02-10
AGURELL S 002201 02-12
AHERN G 000896 01-15
AHLENIUS S 000334 01-04 , 000335 01-04
AHLFORS UG 000637 01-09
AHLUWALIA P 003708 04-03
AHMED M 000007 01-02
AHN HS 001447 02-03
AHNERT-HILGER G 003709 04-03
AHRENDSEN K 004235 04-04
AHTEE L 001098 02-03
AIGNER TG 004073 04-04
AIRAKSINEN MM 001067 02-02 , 001078 02-
  02
AKAIKE A 001691 02-04 , 003083 03-04
AKASU T 003710 04-03
AKBARALY R 000777 01-13
AKERA T 000066 01-03

AKERT K 003734 04-03
AKHALKATSI RG 004107 04-04
AKHTAR RA 000299 01-03
AKIL H 003112 03-04
AKIMOV GA 003438 03-14
AKIYAMA A 000636 01-09 , 004636 04-15
AKPINAR S 002203 02-13 , 004460 04-11
AKSAMIT RR 001099 02-03 , 001100 02-03
AL-YASSIRI MM 004346 04-09 , 004707 04-
  17
ALAM AS 000017 01-03 , 001101 02-03
ALAMO C 001189 02-03
ALANDER T 001102 02-03 , 004065 04-04
ALBALA A 004359 04-09
ALBANO C 000700 01-11 , 002356 02-14 ,
  004382 04-09
ALBARELLO B 004347 04-09
ALBERT DJ 002945 03-04 , 003134 03-06
ALBERT E 004698 04-17
ALBERT J 002119 02-11
ALBERT V 004194 04-04
ALBERT W 000633 01-09
ALBERTSON TE 001559 02-04 , 002653 03-03
  , 002862 03-03 , 002946 03-04
ALBIN H 002395 02-15
ALBINIAK BA 001560 02-04
ALBIZZATI MG 002121 02-11
ALBOU P 003574 03-17
ALBRECHT J 000830 01-15
ALBY JM 001960 02-09 , 001961 02-09 ,
  001965 02-09 , 003206 03-09
ALEKSANDROVSKIY YA 000578 01-09
ALEKSEYEVA LP 003994 04-03
ALEVIZOS B 004059 04-03
ALEXANDER BK 000530 01-06
ALEXANDER JR 001914 02-08
ALEXANDER MS 001914 02-08
ALEXANDER PE 000575 01-08
ALFREDSSON G 001905 02-08 , 004311 04-08
  , 004559 04-13
ALGERI S 001103 02-03 , 001325 02-03 ,
  003674 04-01 , 004019 04-03
ALI BH 003711 04-03
ALI SF 001831 02-05
ALIYEV MN 004161 04-04 , 004162 04-04 ,
  004163 04-04
ALKALAY D 002204 02-13
ALLAIN N 002255 02-13
ALLAN JA 002424 02-17
ALLAN RD 001104 02-03 , 002633 03-01
ALLARIA E 002731 03-03
ALLEGRE G 003419 03-13
ALLEGRI G 000418 01-04 , 003826 04-03
ALLEN MD 000766 01-13 , 000831 01-15 ,
  002206 02-13 , 002442 04-11
ALLEN RE 003554 03-16
ALLEN WC 003012 03-04
ALLERS G 000640 01-09 , 002304 02-13
ALLEVA E 000336 01-04
ALLEVA FR 001849 02-05
ALLISON JH 003712 04-03
ALLMAN TFM 002516 02-16
ALLUMAY KD 003131 03-05 , 003981 04-03
ALMAZAN G 002246 01-03
ALMGREN O 004126 04-04
ALPERT JE 000452 01-04 , 001752 02-04
ALPERT M 003277 03-03 , 004312 J4-08
ALPHS L 001348 02-03 , 002654 03-03 ,
  002867 03-03 , 003826 04-03
ALPS BJ 001091 02-02
ALSTON C 002942 03-04
ALSTON J 004745 04-17
ALTAMURA AC 004439 04-11
ALTAMURA C 002912 04-03 , 003324 03-11
ALTESMAN RI 002480 02-16
ALTMAN FJ 003539 03-15
ALTMAN JL 001561 02-04
ALTSHULER HL 002947 03-04
ALTSHULER RA 001520 02-03 , 003681 04-02
ALTSTEIN M 002655 03-03 , 002656 03-03
ALTURA BM 001105 02-03
ALVAN G 002282 02-13
ALVORD EC 001201 02-03 , 001434 02-03
AMABILE G 002355 02-14
AMADYAN MG 000607 01-09
AMAN MG 002474 02-16

AMBRON RT 002657 03-03
AMDISEN A 000893 01-15 , 002465 02-15
AMOUR MA 003582 03-17
AMIR S 000337 01-04
AMIRAGOVA MG 003713 04-03
AMIT Z 000253 01-03 , 000337 01-04 ,
  001579 02-04 , 001781 02-04
AMMENDOLA D 003075 03-04
AMOCHAEV A 000509 01-05
AMORY MC 000018 01-03
AMSTERDAM J 000582 01-09
ANANDAM N 000510 01-05
ANANTH J 001000 01-17 , 001886 02-07 ,
  003461 03-15 , 004348 04-09 , 004668
  04-15
ANATOL J 003689 04-02
ANDEN N 001102 02-03 , 002372 02-15 ,
  002658 03-03 , 004065 04-04
ANDERMANN F 000714 01-11
ANDERSEN HB 002400 02-15
ANDERSEN J 000659 01-11
ANDERSON C 000697 01-11
ANDERSON EG 000174 01-03
ANDERSON M 003321 03-11
ANDERSON PJ 003663 04-01
ANDERSON RE 000295 01-03
ANDERSSON K 001096 02-03 , 001238 02-03
  , 001239 02-03 , 001240 02-03 , 002727
  03-03
ANDO K 004459 04-11
ANDO R 001379 02-03
ANDO T 000444 01-04
ANDOH R 003714 04-03
ANDRASIK F 000657 01-10
ANDRE A 001227 02-03
ANDREJEVA NI 004174 04-04
ANDREWS PR 001029 02-01
ANDREYEVA NI 000008 01-02
ANDREYEVA OG 003398 03-13
ANDRULONIS PA 000539 01-07
ANGEL A 001106 02-03
ANGELERGUES R 003575 03-17
ANGELO H 004326 03-11
ANGELUCCI L 001107 02-03 , 002515 02-17
ANGERSON WJ 003817 04-03
ANGGARD E 004534 04-13 ,
ANGRIST B 000251 01-08 , 001906 02-08 ,
  002453 02-15 , 003552 03-15
ANGST J 000749 01-13 , 001962 02-09 ,
  003608 03-17
ANHALT HS 000660 01-11
ANHUT H 000165 01-03 , 001319 02-03 ,
  003715 04-03
ANIELLO R 004384 04-09
ANILINE O 003554 03-16
ANISMAN H 000490 01-04
ANISSIMOV JZ 003716 04-03
ANKIER SI 004386 04-09
ANLEZARK G 004137 04-04
ANNABLE L 003305 03-11
ANNITTO W 002516 02-16
ANSELL GB 004588 04-15
ANSELMI B 004533 04-13
ANSSEAU M 004308 04-07 , 004589 04-15
ANTELMAN SM 000046 01-03 , 000047 01-03
  , 000048 01-03 , 002659 03-03 , 002891
  03-03 , 003122 03-05
ANTHONY SG 000487 01-04
ANTIPOVA RI 003326 03-11
ANTKIEWICZ-MICHALUK L 004210 04-04
ANTONOVA LV 002949 03-04
ANTONYAN MN 002663 03-03
ANWAR J 001831 02-05
APPEL IB 000499 01-04 , 001561 02-04 ,
  001652 02-04 , 001753 02-04 , 001754
  02-04 , 004250 04-04
APPEL NM 002924 03-03
APPELBAUM PS 000991 01-17
APPELBAUM E 002947 03-04
APPLEGATE CD 001562 02-04
APRISON MH 001730 02-04
APUD J 001422 02-03 , 002690 03-03
ARAI M 002844 03-03
ARAI S 000661 01-11
ARAI Y 000159 01-03

A-1

ARANA GW 001114 02-03
ARANOVICH AG 003172 03-08
ARASZKIEWICZ A 000719 01-11
ARATO M 000912 01-17 , 002447 02-15 , 004499 04-13
ARBILLA S 000235 01-03
ARDAILLOU R 004505 04-13
ARDITO P 004417 04-09
AREFOLOV VA 001352 02-03
ARENA R 002091 02-11
ARENDT R 003352 03-11
ARGENTIERI TM 000131 01-03
ARKFELD DF 004647 04-15
ARMOCIDA G 003382 03-11
ARMSTRONG DM 002634 03-01
ARMSTRONG MJ 001695 02-04
ARMSTRONG-JAMES M 002475 02-16
ARNDT R 004481 04-11
ARNOLD ES 000832 01-15
ARNOLD MA 000019 01-03 , 000020 01-03 , 004014 04-03
ARNT J 002948 03-04 , 004066 04-04
AROCHA L 001930 02-08
ARONOW WS 001856 02-05
ARONSON JK 003399 03-13
ARORA RC 001468 02-03
ARRIGO-REINA R 001468 02-03
ARRIGONI E 001126 02-03 , 003730 04-03
ARTAUD F 000123 01-03 , 004011 04-03
ARUSHANYAN EB 004067 04-04
ARY M 001108 02-03 , 003024 03-04
ARZI A 004164 04-04
ARZU D 004694 04-16
ASAM U 003288 03-11
ASANO T 003717 04-03
ASANO Y 004646 01-09
ASARCH KB 004349 04-09
ASBERG M 002086 02-10 , 002300 02-13
ASCH RH 000286 01-03
ASCHOFF JC 000751 01-13
ASHCROFT GW 001708 02-04
ASHMARIN IP 002949 03-04
ASHTON D 000496 01-04
ASHTON H 004669 04-16
ASIN KE 004098 04-04
ASK A 001452 02-03
ASNIS G 000752 01-13 , 000874 01-15 , 002238 02-13 , 003411 03-13 , 004405 04-09
ASPES F 000105 01-03
ASSICOT M 001887 02-07
ASSIMACOPOULOS T 004615 04-15
ASTRACHAN DI 001605 02-04 , 002950 03-04
ATAMER-SIMSEK S 001216 02-03 , 001217 02-03
ATRENS D 002476 02-16 , 003016 03-04
ATSMON A 001915 02-08
ATTERWILL CK 002951 03-04
ATTILA LMJ 001098 02-03
AUBINEAU P 001109 02-03
AUBREE JC 000662 01-11
AUDIBERT A 001954 02-08
AUDIGIER Y 000021 01-03 , 001110 02-03 , 003682 04-02
AUDINOT M 003825 04-03
AUGER RG 002037 02-09 , 002038 02-09
AUGUSTYN DH 002932 03-03
AULAKH CS 001601 02-04
AUVINEN J 002076 02-10 , 002077 02-10
AVANESOVA TS 003289 03-11
AVERY DD 001544 02-03 , 002952 03-04
AVIRAM U 002171 02-11
AVRUTSKIY GY 000578 01-09 , 004433 04-11 , 004699 04-17
AWOUTERS F 002648 03-02
AXELROD J 001001 02-01 , 001002 02-01 , 001026 02-01 , 001027 02-01 , 001118 02-03 , 001188 02-03 , 001279 02-03 , 001282 02-03 , 001318 02-03 , 001502 02-03 , 002919 03-03
AXELSON J 001111 02-03
AXELSSON R 002207 02-13 , 002590 02-17 , 003569 03-16 , 004700 04-17
AYA K 002837 03-03
AYALA GF 002750 03-03
AYALA-GUERRERO F 002661 03-03
AYCOCK E 001637 02-04
AYD FJ 000985 01-17 , 002517 02-17 , 004350 04-09 , 004590 04-15

AYGEN M 002443 02-15
AYHAN IH 003104 03-04
AYVAZASHVILI IM 004068 04-04 , 004107 04-04
AZMITIA EC 002929 03-03
AZUMA H 003718 04-03
AZZARO AJ 003697 04-02 , 004009 04-03

B

BABBINI M 000338 01-04 , 003555 03-16
BABOROVA E 000548 01-08 , 001925 02-08
BACH NJ 001538 02-03
BACHMAN J 002209 02-13
BACHMANN E 004284 04-05
BACHMANN K 000307 01-03
BACIKOVA B 002518 02-17
BACK OJ 001832 02-05
BACKWELL B 004560 04-14
BACOPOULOS NG 001112 02-03 , 002285 02-13 , 002662 03-03
BACOTTI AV 000339 01-04
BADAWY AA 000022 01-03
BADGER TM 002821 03-03
BAERT F 003653 04-01
BAETTIG K 001202 02-03 , 002984 03-04
BAEZ LA 001702 02-04
BAGCHI SP 001113 02-03
BAGGHI SP 001113 02-03
BAGGIO G 000340 01-04
BAHARY C 002443 02-15
BAILEY DN 004591 04-15
BAILEY J 000837 01-15 , 001976 02-09 , 004338 04-08
BAIN GT 001563 02-04
BAJAJ N 002158 02-11
BAJGAR J 000127 01-03 , 000389 01-04
BAJUSZ S 002650 03-02
BAK IJ 001374 02-03
BAKER GB 003137 03-06 , 003719 04-03
BAKER HF 001759 02-04 , 003072 03-04 , 004208 04-04
BAKER J 001941 02-08
BAKHAREV VD 001812 02-04 , 003438 03-14
BAKHUIS WL 001564 02-04
BAKKER EAD 001370 02-03
BALIK J 000674 01-11
BALITSKIY KP 001520 02-03
BALK KP 002343 02-14
BALLANTINE HT 002551 02-17
BALLARD BL 003212 03-09
BALLDIN J 002664 03-03
BALLENGER J 003237 03-01 , 003388 03-11
BALLUS C 001963 02-09 , 002588 02-17 , 002589 02-17 , 004351 04-09
BALON R 000542 01-07 , 001888 02-07 , 001924 02-08 , 002025 02-09
BALSARA JJ 001068 02-02 , 004147 04-04
BALSTER RL 000341 01-04 , 000354 01-04 , 001582 02-04 , 002520 02-17 , 002961 03-04
BALTHAZART J 001565 02-04
BAN TA 000622 01-09 , 001964 02-09 , 002026 02-09 , 002080 02-10 , 002431 02-15 , 003274 03-10 , 004333 04-08 , 004392 04-09 , 004700 04-17
BANAY-SCHWARTZ M 004606 04-15
BANCAUD J 003334 03-11
BANDUHN N 000753 01-13
BANGERTER FW 003980 04-03
BANNET J 003720 04-03

BANNON MJ 000023 01-03 , 001117 02-03
BAQUER NZ 002868 03-03 , 003891 04-03
BAR PR 003721 04-03
BAR-ON E 004564 04-14
BARABAN JM 000024 01-03 , 000372 01-04
BARACZKA K 003193 03-08
BARAILLER J 003691 04-02
BARALDI M 000397 01-04
BARASH HM 003576 03-17
BARATTI CM 001658 02-04
BARATZ R 003290 03-11
BARBEAU A 000950 01-17
BARBEAU H 003722 04-03
BARBER HE 003400 03-13
BARBIN G 001054 02-01
BARBOUR B 000756 01-13
BARCHAS JD 001423 02-03 , 001707 02-04 , 003006 03-04 , 003477 03-15 , 003663 04-01 , 003935 04-03 , 004314 04-08 , 004514 04-13
BARCHAS PR 003006 03-04
BARDEN N 002635 03-01
BARDO MT 000511 01-05
BAREIS DL 000025 01-03 , 001002 02-01 , 001118 02-03
BARFIELD RJ 000430 01-04
BARGTEYL BA 000506 01-04
BARK NM 002380 02-15
BARKA AI 002683 03-03
BARKAI A 003723 04-03 , 004005 04-03
BARKER JL 000116 01-03 , 000194 01-03 , 000198 01-03 , 000275 01-03 , 002665 03-03 , 002666 03-03 , 002896 03-03
BARKER S 002636 03-01 , 004221 04-04
BARKIN RM 003401 03-13
BARKLEY P 001702 02-04
BARKLEY RA 002092 02-11
BARKOV NK 003919 04-03
BARLOW OH 004425 04-10
BARLOW RB 001859 02-06
BARMACK JE 003321 03-11
BARMACK NH 001566 02-04
BARNARD G 003439 03-14
BARNES RJ 002059 02-10
BARNES TRE 002374 02-15 , 002375 02-15 , 002421 02-15
BARNETT A 003857 04-03
BARNETTE MS 004052 04-03
BARON C 003895 04-03
BARON J 003564 03-16 , 004387 04-09 , 004472 04-11
BARONDES SH 003724 04-03
BARR GA 001584 02-04
BARRECA T 003425 03-13
BARRES M 004395 04-09
BARRETT JE 000508 01-04 , 000649 01-10 , 003105 03-04
BARRETT RE 002401 02-15
BARRETT RJ 000342 01-04 , 001699 02-04 , 002953 03-04
BARRIO A 000223 01-03
BARROS-PINTO MCD 003464 03-15
BARRY RJ 003414 03-13
BARSUHN C 000170 01-03 , 003034 03-04
BARTAKOVA L 000595 01-09
BARTELS K 001606 02-04
BARTFAI T 002667 03-03 , 003860 04-03
BARTHELEMY C 003291 03-11
BARTHOLINI G 001119 02-03 , 001907 02-08
BARTKE A 002695 03-03
BARTLET AL 003711 04-03
BARTLETT MF 002214 02-13
BARTOLETTI M 000338 01-04 , 003555 03-16
BARTOLINI A 000104 01-03
BARTOLINI L 003065 03-04
BARTOLINI R 000104 01-03
BARTOLOMEO JG 001375 02-03
BARTOVA D 000663 01-11
BARUCHE F 002170 02-11
BASBAUM AI 002638 03-01
BASELT RC 001559 02-04 , 002946 03-04
BASHORE TR 003131 03-05
BASOMBRIO J 002018 02-09
BASOVA J 000595 01-09
BASS MB 001567 02-04 , 001625 02-04
BASS NH 003025 03-04
BASSECHES PJ 003725 04-03
BASSET P 000543 01-07

BASSETT EG 000916 01-17
BASSI S 002121 02-11
BASTECKY J 000548 01-08 , 000976 01-17 ,
   001908 02-08 , 001925 02-08
BATEMAN WBJ 000913 01-17
BATHIEN N 001965 02-09 , 004652 04-15
BATT JR 002320 02-14
BATTA SK 000447 01-04
BATTAINI F 001512 02-03
BATTERSBY MK 001381 02-09
BATTIG K 003042 03-04 , 003577 03-17
BATZOLD F 000026 01-03
BAUDRY M 001120 02-03 , 001147 02-03 ,
   003726 04-03
BAUER AC 001860 02-06
BAUERLE U 000029 01-03
BAUM MJ 002821 03-03
BAUMAN J 000798 01-13
BAUMANN PA 000316 01-03 , 003921 04-03
BAUTISTA S 002969 03-04
BAVAZZANO A 002093 02-11
BAXLEY GB 002313 02-14
BAXLEY RC 000914 01-17
BAXTER CF 004352 04-09
BAXTER DE 003148 03-06
BEACH RC 004455 04-11
BEAINI AY 000579 01-09
BEAN NJ 001745 02-04
BEAR G 000698 01-11
BEARD OW 000866 01-15
BEARDEN LJ 000477 01-04 , 000478 01-04
BEATTY WW 003084 03-04
BEAU Y 002094 02-11
BEAUCHAMP R 002942 03-04
BEAUDOIN D 000033 01-03 , 000093 01-03
BEAULIEU M 001324 02-03
BECA ET 000915 01-17
BECH P 002033 02-09
BECHTEL P 000640 01-09 , 002304 02-13
BECK AT 003235 03-09
BECK O 002095 02-11 , 002208 02-13
BECK SG 000343 01-04
BECKER BF 002227 02-13
BECKER D 004500 04-13
BECKER FT 002476 02-16
BECKER J 000459 01-04 , 001059 02-01 ,
   001121 02-03 , 002668 03-03
BECKER KL 002637 03-01
BECKER W 000751 01-13
BECKFORD U 004463 04-11
BECKMANN H 001909 02-08
BECLE J 002108 02-11
BECU R 003268 03-09
BEDARD P 003722 04-03
BEDFORD JA 000344 01-04 , 002954 03-04 ,
   003127 03-05
BEDNAR BR 004352 04-09
BEECHING M 004552 04-13
BEERS RFJ 000916 01-17
BEHAR R 000926 01-17
BEHBEHANI MM 003127 04-03
BEINFELD MC 001003 02-01 , 001004 02-01 ,
   001005 02-01 , 001017 02-01 , 001122
   02-03
BELESLIN DB 001568 02-04 , 001569 02-04
BELKNAP JK 000313 01-03
BELL GA 004069 04-04
BELL RD 000051 01-03
BELLACK AS 000657 01-10
BELLANTUONO C 002521 02-17
BELMAKER RH 000083 01-03 , 001966 02-09
   , 003720 04-03 , 004167 04-04 , 004353
   04-09
BELYAYEV BS 004335 04-08 , 004381 04-09 ,
   004390 04-09
BELYI VP 001123 02-03
BEMIS KG 002720 03-03
BEN-BARAK Y 001833 02-05
BEN-DAVID M 000841 01-15 , 001916 02-08
BENAKIS A 001874 02-06
BENARDO LS 003728 04-03
BENDEK G 003729 04-03
BENDER AS 000330 01-03 , 002933 03-03
BENDER W 001570 02-04
BENDERLY A 003719 04-03
BENEDEK G 002955 03-04
BENEDETTI MS 003874 04-03
BENESOVA O 000144 01-03 , 000595 01-09 ,
   000800 01-14 , 000917 01-17 , 001571
   02-04

BENFENATI F 001096 02-03
BENGHEZAL A 001954 02-08
BENINGER RJ 000345 01-04 , 001572 02-04 ,
   002956 03-04 , 004070 04-04
BENKERT O 002137 02-11 , 004435 04-11
BENMAMAN JD 004558 04-13
BENNETT B 000537 01-06
BENNETT C 001053 02-01
BENNETT EL 001573 02-04 , 004097 04-04 ,
   004578 04-14
BENNETT JP 001124 02-03 , 001125 02-03
BENNETT WF 001147 02-03
BENNIE EH 003504 03-15
BENOWITZ NL 000796 01-13 , 001621 02-04 ,
   002209 02-13
BENSON DI 001484 02-03
BENSON RM 004743 04-17
BENTAL E 004564 04-14
BENTLEY GA 000263 01-03
BENTUE-FERRER D 002205 02-13
BENVENUTI P 004365 04-09
BENYACOUB A 002014 02-09 , 002600 02-17
   004445 04-11
BENZI G 001126 02-03 , 003730 04-03
BERAMENDI V 004312 04-08
BERARDI N 002894 03-03
BERCHOU RC 003367 03-11
BERDE B 002522 02-17
BRECOECHEA J 003689 04-02
BERECZ JM 000672 01-11
BEREGI L 002541 02-17
BERENDSEN HHG 000441 01-04
BERETTA G 003295 03-11
BEREZOVA NY 000578 01-09
BERGER FM 000801 01-14
BERGER G 003564 03-16
BERGER L 003702 04-02
BERGER PA 000928 01-17 , 002488 02-16 ,
   003286 03-10 , 003465 03-15 , 003477
   03-15 , 003663 04-01 , 004313 04-08 ,
   004314 04-08 , 004327 04-08 , 004442
   04-11 , 004314 04-13 , 004592 04-15 ,
   004604 04-15 , 004703 04-17
BERGER TW 002916 03-03
BERGEY GK 002669 03-03
BERGGREN U 004110 04-04
BERGHMANS W 000758 01-13
BERGLUND M 002210 02-13
BERGMAN J 004077 04-04
BERGMANN F 001574 02-04
BERGMANN M · 004321 04-08
BERGSTROM L 000027 01-03
BERKMAN K 000169 01-03
BERKOWITZ AL 003960 04-03
BERLISS H 001929 02-08
BERMAN R 002780 03-03
BERNADT MW 002060 02-10
BERNARD PS 000188 01-03
BERNARDINA BD 002319 02-14
BERNASCONI R 003135 03-06
BERNASCONI S 003705 04-02
BERNEY S 004333 04-08
BERNHARDT W 004586 04-14
BERNIER JL 003653 04-01
BERNSTEIN JG 003292 03-11
BERNTSON GG 003111 03-04 , 003112 03-04
BERRY SD 002916 03-03
BERSANI G 002226 02-13 , 003466 03-15 ,
   004318 04-08
BERTACCINI G 004535 04-13
BERTHON G 002061 02-10
BERTILSSON L 000754 01-13 , 000897 01-16 ,
   001967 02-09 , 002181 02-11 , 002282
   02-13 , 002300 02-13
BERTLER A 002211 02-13
BERTOLETTI P 004354 04-09 , 004419 04-10
BERTOLINI R 002650 03-02
BERZETEI IP 002650 03-02
BESIO G 000700 01-11 , 002013 02-09 ,
   004533 04-13
BESSER GM 001016 02-01 , 001127 02-03 ,
   003731 04-03 , 003732 04-03 , 004363
   04-09
BESSON J 000028 01-03 , 000110 01-03 ,
   000513 01-03 , 002791 03-03
BEST MR 001610 02-04
BETT JHN 002232 02-13   ,
BEUDIN P 004479 04-11
BEUMONT PJV 002062 02-10
BEVAN JA 002670 03-03

BEVERIDGE IJ 000409 01-04
BEY P 001128 02-03
BEYER C 002957 03-04
BEYER S 002523 02-17
BEZZI G 002058 02-09
BHARGAVA HN 001435 02-03 , 001575 02-04
   , 001576 02-04 , 004072 04-04
BHARGAVA KP 002247 01-03 , 002186 02-11
BHATTACHARYA SK 001769 02-04
BHATTACHARYYA AK 000346 01-04 , 001601
   02-04
BHATTACHARYYA PK 003654 04-01
BHAVSAR VH 003772 04-03 , 004102 04-04
BHAWAN J 000257 01-03
BHUTA SI 002291 02-13
BIANCHETTI G 000549 01-08 , 002267 02-13
BIANCHI CP 000069 01-03
BIANCHI G 002063 02-10 , 004477 04-11
BIANCHI M 000105 01-03
BIANCHI RG 000064 01-03
BIAZZI A 001577 02-04
BIDZINSKI A 004546 04-13
BIEGER D 001821 02-04
BIELSKI R 004411 04-09
BIERTUEMPHEL H 003217 03-09
BIGELOW GE 002314 02-14 , 004566 04-14 ,
   004582 04-14
BIGELOW L 001928 02-08 , 001945 02-08 ,
   003165 03-08 , 003168 03-08 , 003184
   03-08
BIGGER JT 002697 03-03
BIGGIO G 001129 02-03 , 002477 02-16 ,
   002743 03-03 , 003739 04-03
BIGGS C 003095 03-04
BIGGS JSG 002424 02-17
BIGNAMI G 002671 03-03
BIGON E 002682 03-03
BILLE J 003578 03-17
BINEK PA 003733 04-03
BING LA 001622 02-04 , 002992 03-04
BINYILDIZ P 001217 02-03
BJORN-HENRIKSEN T 004734 04-17
BIOULAC B 000272 01-03
BIRCH NJ 002212 02-13
BIRCHER J 002525 02-17 , 004495 04-11
BIRD ED 000564 01-08 , 002575 02-17
BIRD KD 002193 02-12
BIRDSALL N 000026 01-03
BIRKEMO LS 004111 04-04
BIRKMAYER W 000712 01-11
BIRKNER R 004319 04-08
BIRNKRANDT D 002928 03-03
BIRSEL S 001130 02-03
BISCHOFF S 001131 02-03
BISHOP M 000837 01-15 , 001943 02-08 ,
   004338 04-08
BISHOP P 001745 02-04
BISMUTH C 003505 03-15
BISWAS B 002672 03-03
BITETTI R 000378 01-04
BITTENCOURT PRM 002376 02-15 , 003467
   03-15
BITTER I 003193 03-08
BITTIGER H 002131 02-03 , 003135 03-06
BITTNER SE 004073 04-04
BITTNER-MANICKA M 000664 01-11
BIXLER EO 000945 01-17
BIZZINI B 003734 04-03
BJORKLUND A 000347 01-04
BJORNDAL N 001968 02-09 , 002377 02-15
BLACK IB 000149 01-03 , 003881 04-03
BLACK KL 000321 01-03
BLACKBURN TP 001578 02-04
BLADIN PF 003433 03-13
BLAHA L 000665 01-11
BLAIR IA 001132 02-03
BLAIR R 000337 01-04 , 001579 02-04
BLAKE J 003655 04-01
BLAKELY RD 003012 03-04
BLAKEMORE CB 002360 02-14
BLAMPIED NM 000353 01-04
BLANC M 003559 03-16
BLANCHARD J 001133 02-03 , 001137 02-03
BLANCO J 003553 03-15
BLANK AC 000089 01-03
BLANK B 001069 02-02
BLANKSTEIN J 002213 02-13
BLASER SM 004352 04-09

BLASIG J 000029 01-03 , 003740 04-03 , 004104 04-04
BLASS EM 002478 02-16
BLATNICK RA 001539 02-03
BLAUSTEIN JD 002842 03-03
BLAUWBLOMME J 003208 03-09
BLAZEK J 004648 04-15
BLEEKER JAC 002526 02-17
BLENNOW G 001134 02-03
BLIER P 001135 02-03
BLINDER BJ 004743 04-17
BLINDERMANN J 002878 03-03
BLODGETT ALN 004403 04-09
BLOOM F 000580 01-09 , 001136 02-03 , 002599 02-17 , 002884 03-03 , 003136 03-06 , 003735 04-03
BLOOM V 004411 04-09
BLOXAM DL 002673 03-03
BLUET-PAJOT MT 000262 01-03
BLUM A 001229 02-03 , 001867 02-06 , 004395 04-09
BLUM I 004320 04-08
BLUME HW 002674 03-03
BLUMENTHAL M 002096 02-11
BLUNDELL C 001476 02-03 , 001784 02-04
BLUNDELL JE 002527 02-17
BOARATO E 002682 03-03
BOBIK A 004506 04-13
BOBON DP 002528 02-17 , 003293 03-11
BOBRITSKAYA ZM 004633 04-15
BOBRUFF A 003294 03-11
BOCCI U 003295 03-11
BOCKAERT J 000213 01-03 , 000214 01-03
BODEM G 003161 03-07
BODENSTEINER JB 003468 03-15
BODNAR RJ 003348 01-04 , 004074 04-04
BODNER AJ 001006 02-01
BODNER L 003338 03-11
BOER GJ 004091 04-04
BOERNGEN R 001712 02-04
BOGAERT MG 004355 04-09
BOGDAL J 001844 02-05
BOGETTO F 002872 03-03 , 002873 03-03
BOHL I 004481 04-11
BOHLEN P 003458 03-14 , 004285 04-06 , 004296 04-06
BOHLIN L 000084 01-03
BOHN MC 000030 01-03
BOHRER RE 003363 03-11
BOIREAU A 001133 02-03 , 001137 02-03
BOISSIER JR 001070 02-02 , 001218 02-03 , 002635 03-01 , 003789 04-03 , 004105 04-04
BOKOR JT 004063 04-03
BOKSA J 000204 01-03
BOLANDER K 001594 02-04
BOLDYREV AI 003209 03-09 , 004593 04-15
BOLE GG 000779 01-13
BOLELOUCKY Z 000976 01-17 , 002064 02-10
BOLEYN T 002193 02-12
BOLLE P 002664 03-03
BOLLEA E 000833 01-15
BOLLES RC 001615 02-04
BOLTER A 000736 01-12
BOND NW 001580 02-04
BONDY B 003556 03-16
BONDY SC 004264 04-05 , 004265 04-05
BONETTI EP 002646 03-02
BONICALZI M 001985 02-09
BONILLA E 002112 02-11
BONING J 003579 02-15
BONNAFOUX D 002140 02-11 , 003296 03-11
BONNET AM 003458 03-14
BONNET JJ 004173 04-04
BONNET KA 004300 04-06
BONNET MH 003439 03-14
BOOJ S 003897 04-03
BORBE HO 001440 02-03 , 004211 04-04
BORBELY AA 002958 03-04
BORDASH GD 004245 04-04 , 004246 04-04
BORDES MM 002395 02-15
BORENSTEIN P 001170 02-03 , 002731 03-03
BOREYSHA LB 003100 03-04
BORG S 002095 02-11
BORGA O 000897 01-16
BORIOVA M 002064 02-10
BORISON RL 001834 02-05
BORN-LEVEQUE M 003293 03-11
BORNE RF 002954 03-04
BORNHEIM LM 002675 03-03

BORNSTEIN JC 000063 01-03 , 002768 03-03
BORNSTEIN S 002065 02-10
BORODKIN YS 004075 04-04
BORRI P 002925 03-03
BORYS HK 002675 03-03
BOSCHE J 002438 02-15
BOSCREDON J 000616 01-09 , 000782 01-13 , 001980 02-09
BOSHANS RL 003712 04-03
BOSHART G 000705 01-11
BOSI E 002277 02-13
BOSOV AM 004340 04-08
BOSSI L 003334 03-11 , 003343 03-11
BOSSI M 000105 01-03
BOSZORMENYI Z 004436 04-11
BOTTARI R 004622 04-15
BOTTICELLI LJ 004076 04-04
BOUBLI S 003559 03-16
BOUCHARLAT J 002379 02-15 , 003149 03-07
BOUDOURESQUE F 003759 04-03
BOUEILH P 000834 01-15
BOULENGER J 001090 02-02 , 004501 04-13
BOULTON AA 001077 02-02 , 001207 02-03
BOUMAN HJ 001370 02-03
BOUR HL 001564 02-04 , 003056 03-04
BOUR HLMG 004091 04-04
BOURGEOIS M 000834 01-15
BOURGOIN S 000123 01-03 , 004011 04-03
BOURN WM 001138 02-03
BOURNE RC 004282 04-05 , 004423 04-10
BOURQUE C 000253 01-03
BOUSQUET B 000018 01-03
BOUTELLE WE 004356 04-09
BOUTILLIER H 001090 02-02
BOUVIER G 003341 03-11
BOUYARD P 013371 02-03
BOUYER J 001581 02-04
BOWDLE TA 000755 01-13
BOWDLER JM 003736 04-03
BOWEN WD 003737 04-03
BOWERS MB 000708 01-11 , 000764 01-13 , 002097 02-11 , 002098 02-11 , 003738 04-03 , 004502 04-13
BOWERY NG 003839 04-03
BOWES GM 001472 02-03
BOWYER JF 000106 01-03 , 002959 03-04
BOXENBAUM HG 002248 02-13
BOYAN-SALYERS BD 001007 02-01
BOYD EJS 004306 04-07
BOYD JL 000644 01-09
BOYER P 002498 02-16 , 002529 02-17
BOYESON MG 004135 04-04
BOZAK M 004519 04-13 , 004567 04-14
BOZARTH MA 001861 02-06 , 002960 03-04 , 002999 03-04
BRACCINI T 002023 02-09 , 003210 03-09 , 004357 04-09 , 004594 04-15
BRACHET-LIERMAIN A 000777 01-13
BRACKEN J 002391 02-15
BRACONNIER A 002344 02-14
BRADFORD HF 000058 01-03 , 002843 03-03 , 002897 03-03
BRADFORD LD 000395 01-04
BRADLEY EL 001793 02-04
BRADSHAW CM 002298 02-13
BRADY JV 000395 01-04 , 004123 04-04
BRADY KT 001582 02-04 , 002961 03-04
BRADY LS 000349 01-04 , 004077 04-04
BRAESTRUP C 000216 01-03 , 000918 01-17 , 001139 02-03 , 001395 02-03 , 002676 03-03 , 003579 03-17 , 003739 04-03
BRAFF DL 000748 01-13 , 002194 02-12
BRAGG L 000919 01-17
BRAGIN AG 002941 03-03
BRAGIN E 002641 03-01
BRAHMAPURIKAR MT 001361 02-03
BRAITHWAITE R 000897 01-16 , 002266 02-13 , 002284 02-13
BRAMMER GL 001385 02-03 , 003942 04-03 , 004204 04-04
BRANCH BJ 000180 01-03
BRANCH MN 000350 01-04 , 001583 02-04
BRANCHEY LB 002380 02-15 , 003469 03-15 , 004595 04-15
BRANCHEY MH 002380 02-15 , 003469 03-15 , 004595 04-15
BRANCONNIER RJ 003297 03-11 , 003557 03-16
BRANDENBERGER H 003490 03-15
BRANDT J 000767 01-13 , A-1

BRANDT M 002677 03-03
BRANNAN MD 000512 01-05
BRANTE G 003542 03-15
BRANTL V 003740 04-03
BRASE DA 001140 02-03 , 003741 04-03
BRASIL MAA 003470 03-15
BRASSEUR R 000581 01-09
BRAUER H 004626 04-15
BRAUMAN H 000606 01-09 , 002099 02-11 , 003237 03-09
BRAUN G 003683 04-02
BRAUN H 001729 02-04 , 003061 03-04
BRAUN U 003683 04-02
BRAUTIGAM M 002962 03-04
BRAVKOV MF 001514 02-03
BRECKENRIDGE AM 001832 02-05 , 003621 03-17
BREESE G 001141 02-03 , 001389 02-03 , 001813 02-04 , 003037 03-04 , 003748 04-03 , 003917 04-03 , 004195 04-04
BREHM L 001079 02-02
BREIMER DD 000920 01-17
BRENDLE A 000867 01-15
BRENENGEN EE 002037 02-09
BRENNAN MJW 002678 03-03
BRENOT P 002170 02-11 , 003451 03-14
BRESOLIN N 002902 03-03
BRESS W 004670 04-16
BRESSLER B 002381 02-15
BREUNING SE 003298 03-11 , 003392 03-11 , 004437 04-11 , 004438 04-11
BREWARD J 000031 01-03
BREWIN R 003602 03-17
BREWSTER D 000032 01-03 , 000351 01-04
BREYER-PFAFF U 002214 02-13
BREZENOFF HE 003744 04-03
BRICK J 000481 01-04
BRICOLO R 004717 04-17
BRIDENBAUGH RH 003347 03-11
BRIDGE TP 001928 02-08 , 003169 03-08 , 003499 03-15 , 004671 04-16
BRIDGER WH 001584 02-04
BRIDGES PK 002375 02-15 , 004346 04-09
BRIEF D 004098 04-04
BRIEN JF 003522 03-15
BRIGGS RS 002679 03-03
BRILEY M 000033 01-03 , 000235 01-03 , 002254 02-13 , 002569 02-16 , 003427 03-13 , 003610 03-17 , 003955 04-03 , 004358 04-09 , 004707 04-17
BRINDEAU F 002731 03-03
BRINKMAN S 003095 03-04 , 003299 03-11 , 003385 03-11
BRINKSCHULTE M 002214 02-13
BRION S 001969 02-09 , 002389 02-15
BROCHE JP 002100 02-11
BROCHET D 003424 03-13
BROCKMAN R 000896 01-15
BRODDE O 003816 04-03
BRODEMANN R 002792 03-03
BRODIE M 001142 02-03 , 004203 04-04
BRODIE RR 004504 04-13
BRODY TM 000066 01-03
BROEKER H 003300 03-11
BROEKKAMP CL 001585 02-04 , 002986 03-04
BROENG-NIELSEN B 003484 03-15
BRON B 004596 04-15
BROOKE M 002433 02-15
BROOKS AD 004496 04-12
BROONER RK 003308 03-11
BROPHY TO 004555 04-13
BROSEMER RW 003953 04-03
BROSSET P 002395 02-15
BROSTEANU ER 000550 01-08 , 004315 04-08
BROSTOFF SW 003665 04-01
BROWDER S 002700 03-03
BROWN DA 000034 01-03 , 001143 02-03 , 001144 02-03
BROWN DF 001145 02-03 , 003821 04-03
BROWN DL 002683 03-03
BROWN DR 002963 03-04
BROWN GB 002636 03-01
BROWN GL 003340 03-11
BROWN GM 003402 03-13
BROWN HK 003143 03-06
BROWN IR 002721 03-03 , 003761 04-03 , 003831 04-03 , 003832 04-03

BROWN J 001146 02-03 , 001586 02-04 ,
  004078 04-04
BROWN K 004090 04-04
BROWN MJ 002504 02-16
BROWN PA 000035 01-03
BROWN RD 003865 04-03
BROWN RM 002641 03-01
BROWN WA 001970 02-09 , 001971 02-09 ,
  002511 02-16 , 003166 03-08 , 003211
  03-09
BROWN WJ 001587 02-04
BROWN ZW 000253 01-03 , 000337 01-04
BROWNELL J 002217 02-13
BROWNING M 001147 02-03
BROWNSTEIN M 001003 02-01 , 001005 02-
  01 , 001008 02-01 , 001053 02-01 ,
  001148 02-03 , 001211 02-03 , 001400
  02-03 , 002645 03-01
BROXTERMAN HJ 001149 02-03 , 001150 02-
  03 , 002681 03-03 , 002832 03-03
BROZEK G 004064 04-03
BRUCKNER GW 002004 02-09 , 003327 03-11
BRUCKNER H 004481 04-11
BRUCKWICK E 001348 02-03 , 001423 02-03
BRUGUEROLLE B 001371 02-03
BRUINVELS J 001606 02-04 , 001809 02-04
BRUMBACK RA 002459 02-15
BRUN A 003451 03-14
BRUNE GG 002501 02-16
BRUNEAUX J 001980 02-09
BRUNI A 002682 03-03
BRUNI J 000756 01-13 , 000762 01-13
BRUNNER H 001972 02-09 , 002382 02-15
BRUNO F 001422 02-03 , 003126 03-05
BRUNS RF 003766 04-03
BRUNSWICK D 000582 01-09 , 003246 03-09
BRUST JCM 000835 01-15
BRUST-CARMONA H 003101 03-04
BRUTUS M 000348 01-04
BUCH HP 001151 02-03
BUCHANAN D 000622 01-09
BUCHEN C 002677 03-03
BUCHSBAUM M 000612 01-09 , 000716 01-
  1 , 001910 02-08 , 002222 02-13 ,
  002359 02-14 , 002366 02-14 , 003167
  03-08 , 003242 03-09 , 003310 03-11 ,
  004316 04-08 , 004549 04-13
BUCHT G 004664 04-15
BUCHWALD NA 001340 02-03
BUCK SH 001421 02-03
BUCKALEW LW 004704 04-17
BUCKETT WR 002964 03-04 , 003620 03-17
BUCKHOLTZ NS 001152 02-03
BUCKLE PJ 003742 04-03
BUCKLEY JP 003707 04-02
BUDD RD 003656 04-01 , 003657 04-01 ,
  003658 04-01 , 003659 04-01 , 004672
  04-16 , 004687 04-16
BUDEK M 002683 03-03
BUENO OFA 004263 04-04
BUESCHER H 003013 03-04
BUGARD P 001980 02-09
BUGAT R 003441 03-14
BUGATTI A 001422 02-03
BUGGY J 002891 03-03
BULLARD WP 003922 04-03
BULON VV 004075 04-04
BUMBIER EE 003151 03-07
BUNAG RD 003099 03-04
BUNNEY BS 000023 01-03 , 001153 02-03
BUNNEY EB 001117 02-03
BUNNEY WE 000575 01-08 , 001443 02-03 ,
  001951 02-08 , 001973 02-09 , 001984
  02-09 , 022221 02-13 , 003275 03-10 ,
  003276 03-10 , 004316 04-08 , 004317
  04-08 , 004398 04-09 , 004705 04-17
BUNTING PR 002533 02-17
BURBACH RV 004671 04-16
BURBAYEVA GS 003176 03-08
BURCH T 001154 02-03 , 004037 04-03
BURCHFIEL JL 002684 03-03
BURDICK BM 000921 01-17
BURES J 000352 01-04 , 001778 02-04
BURESOVA A 000613 01-09
BURESOVA O 000352 01-04
BURGESS CD 002215 02-13 , 004597 04-15
BURGESS CE 004707 04-17
BURGESS SK 001155 02-03
BURGEVIN MC 003898 04-03
BURIAN W 003580 03-17

BURKARD G 000665 01-11
BURKARD WP 001314 02-03
BURKE D 004673 04-16
BURKE MP 003537 03-15
BURKI HR 001156 02-03
BURKITT M 004509 04-13
BURKS TF 002366 02-03 , 001421 02-03 ,
  002822 03-03 , 003773 04-03
BURNAZYAN GA 000607 01-09
BURNE TA 001862 02-06
BURNER M 001974 02-09
BURNETT G 004090 04-04
BURNHAM WM 000160 01-03 , 000416 01-04
  002493 02-16
BURNS RH 003688 04-02
BURNS RJ 001835 02-05
BURRIGHT RG 004103 04-04
BURROWS GD 000614 01-09 , 002184 02-11 ,
  002383 02-15 , 002497 02-16 , 004477
  04-11 , 004639 04-15
BURROWS GH 002685 03-03
BURSTEIN Y 001836 02-05
BURSTON KN 001859 02-06
BURTEN W 003212 03-09
BURTON JS 000007 01-02
BURWELL B 000278 01-03
BUSCH D 003190 03-08 , 004538 04-13 ,
  004540 04-13
BUSCH M 002479 02-16
BUSH D 001992 02-09
BUSH H 002433 02-15
BUSH LG 002780 03-03
BUSH PJ 004706 04-17
BUSTAMI F 001183 02-03
BUSTOS G 002285 02-13
BUTLER LJ 002713 03-03
BUTLER JA 003878 04-03
BUU NT 004286 04-06
BUVAT J 004503 04-13
BUVAT-HERBAUT M 004503 04-13
BUXTON M 000745 01-12 , 000924 01-17
BYMASTER FP 001538 02-03
BYRING RG 002096 02-11
BYRSKA B 001417 02-03 , 001788 02-04

C

CABBAT FS 000404 01-04 , 001650 02-04
CABRAS PL 004365 04-09
CACCIA S 000036 01-03 , 001157 02-03
CAGGIULA AR 001167 02-03 , 002968 03-04
CAILLE E 003403 03-13
CAILLE J 003440 03-14
CAIN DP 000037 01-03
CAIN M 004221 04-04
CALANCA A 004615 04-15
CALANDRA C 003150 03-07 , 003301 03-11
CALDWELL HC 003151 03-07
CALHOUN DW 000064 01-03
CALIARI S 001386 02-03
CALIL HM 002654 02-03
CALLAGHAN DA 001588 02-04
CALLAGHAN JT 002257 02-13
CALLAGHAN N 002445 02-15
CALLAWAY JT 000649 01-17 , 003214 03-09
CALNE DB 000673 01-11 , 002384 02-15 ,
  003309 03-11 , 003319 03-11 , 003406
  03-13
CALO M 000443 01-04
CALOGERO M 000161 02-03
CALOINESCU C 002295 02-13
CALVAINI M 003157 03-07 , 003158 03-07
CALVERLEY DG 003137 03-06 , 003719 04-03
CAMAGNA A 002226 02-13
CAMERON DB 000353 01-04
CAMMANN G 004481 04-11
CAMP JA 000443 01-04
CAMPBELL A 001158 02-03
CAMPBELL BA 002965 03-04
CAMPBELL IC 000038 01-09 , 000612 01-09 ,
  001536 02-03 , 002081 02-10
CAMPBELL JL 003304 03-11
CAMPBELL K 003304 03-11
CAMPBELL M 003360 03-11 , 003361 03-11
CAMPBELL RG 000828 01-14
CAMPOS CJR 000039 01-03
CAMPOS F 003163 03-07
CANCHOLA E 002957 03-04
CANCRO R 003471 03-15
CANDELORA K 003377 03-11

CANGER R 004439 04-11
CANNON JG 002236 02-13
CANO J 002625 02-17 , 003571 03-16
CANONICO PL 000378 01-04
CANTONI GL 001006 02-01 , 001021 02-01 ,
  001100 02-03 , 001415 02-03
CANTOR S 000557 01-08
CANTRILL RC 002678 03-03
CAPDEVILLE C 002108 02-11
CAPLAN LR 000947 01-17
CAPLOVA T 000609 01-09 , 000707 01-11 ,
  001934 02-08 , 002020 02-09 , 004375
  04-09
CAPONERI MA 001985 02-09
CAPPARELLI HV 000657 01-10
CAPPELIEZ P 004079 04-04
CAPPELLAZZO G 002682 03-03
CAPUTI AP 003744 04-03
CARBONE JJ 002248 02-13
CARCHMAN RA 002712 03-03
CARDENAS HL 001450 02-03
CARDINALI DP 001159 02-03
CARDOT A 000205 01-03
CARENINI G 001051 02-01
CARENZI A 001422 02-03 , 003126 03-05
CAREY MP 004080 04-04
CARIDROIT M 003404 03-13 , 003404 03-13
CARILLI L 004318 04-08
CARINO MA 000424 01-04
CARISSIMI M 001051 02-01
CARLEO R 003124 03-05
CARLI G 004081 04-04
CARLI M 000036 01-03
CARLINI EA 000669 01-11 , 003163 03-07
CARLSEN S 002204 02-13
CARLSON KR 000257 01-03 , 000922 01-17
CARLSSON A 000399 01-04 , 001392 02-03 ,
  003799 04-03 , 004412 04-09
CARLSSON S 001737 02-04
CARMAN AB 002770 03-03
CARMAN JS 002216 02-13 , 002637 03-01 ,
  003168 03-08
CARMEN RD 001442 02-03
CARMONA E 000040 01-03
CARNEY JM 000354 01-04
CARNEY K 003744 04-03
CARON MG 001009 02-01
CARONNA P 002058 02-09
CARPENTER L 004611 04-15
CARPENTER WT 000836 01-15
CARPENTIER P 002379 02-15
CARPORALI M 002355 02-14
CARRANZA J 004598 04-15
CARRASCO MA 000071 01-03 , 001664 02-04
CARRAZ G 001160 02-03
CARROLL B 000588 01-09 , 001792 02-04 ,
  004359 04-09 , 004403 04-09 , 004674
  04-16
CARROLL JA 000206 01-03
CARROLL ME 004287 04-06
CARRON R 004615 04-15
CARRUBA MO 000041 01-03 , 000042 01-03
  000355 01-04 , 001161 02-03 , 001733
  02-04 , 002863 03-03
CARTER CJ 001589 02-04 , 002869 03-03 ,
  002966 03-04
CARTER MF 004310 04-07
CARTY SE 003866 04-03
CARUSO TP 001162 02-03 , 004082 04-04
CARVER CS 003405 03-13
CARVEY P 001845 02-05 , 004249 04-04
CARWILE S 002149 02-11
CARY MD 000923 01-17
CASACCHIA M 004384 04-09
CASAIS L 001189 02-03
CASANUEVA F 002690 03-03
CASAZZA G 001424 02-03
CASCIO CS 003878 04-03
CASE WG 003254 03-09 , 004400 04-09
CASEY D 000043 01-03 , 000540 01-07 ,
  002101 02-11 , 002102 02-11 , 002377
  02-15 , 002405 02-15 , 003302 03-11 ,
  003472 03-15
CASH C 003675 04-01
CASO C 003553 03-15
CASPER R 000555 01-08 , 001913 02-08 ,
  002386 02-15 , 004215 04-04 ,
CASSAGNES J 004307 04-07

CASSANO G 000563 01-08
CASSON I 000698 01-11 , 002342 02-14
CASTAIGNE P 003303 03-11
CASTANAS E 003759 04-03
CASTANEDA E 002500 02-16
CASTELLANI S 004083 04-04
CASTELLANO C 000336 01-04 , 000382 01-04
CASTELLO E 002591 02-17
CASTON TV 000056 01-03
CASTRO A 003645 03-17
CASTROGIOVANNI P 004507 04-13
CASU M 001129 02-03
CATALANI A 002515 02-17
CATLIN DH 004360 04-09
CATTABENI F 001422 02-03
CATTELL WR 000837 01-15
CATTO E 004019 04-03
CAVALHEIRO EA 000039 01-03
CAVERO I 000044 01-03
CAVIEZEL F 002277 02-13
CAYREYRE M 002530 02-17
CAZALA P 001590 02-04
CAZZULLO CL 002293 02-13 , 004361 04-09 ,
  004439 04-11
CELANI T 003444 03-14
CENAJEK D 004599 04-15
CENRAUD B 000777 01-13 , 000873 01-15
CEPEDA C 003564 03-16
CERCIELLO A 003124 03-05
CERF FA 000713 01-11
CERNA V 000623 01-09
CERRITO F 001163 02-03 , 001424 02-03 ,
  003745 04-03
CERVANTES P 000560 01-08 , 002253 02-13
CERVENA I 000001 01-01
CERVO L 000258 01-03 , 001764 02-04
CESARE DA 000356 01-04
CESKOVA E 000567 01-08 , 000568 01-08 ,
  000613 01-09 , 000634 01-09 , 001937
  02-08 , 001949 02-08 , 001975 02-09
  002021 02-09 , 002519 02-17 , 003245
  03-09 , 003264 03-09
CESURA AM 002863 03-03
CHABRAND P 003152 03-07
CHADWICK D 001164 02-03
CHAI H 003538 03-15
CHAKRABARTI JK 001591 02-04 , 001592 02-
  04
CHAKRAVARTI SN 002186 02-11
CHAKRAVARTY I 002686 03-03
CHALLENOR Y 000835 01-15
CHALMERS RJ 003504 03-15
CHAMBERS WJ 000619 01-09 , 000620 01-09
CHAMPNEY TC 003111 03-04
CHAN SHH 001225 02-03 , 002718 03-03
CHANDLER S 002171 02-11
CHANDORKAR AG 001068 02-02 , 004147 04-
  04
CHANDRA A 000189 01-03 , 002806 03-03 ,
  003907 04-03
CHANDRA P 000449 01-04
CHANG J 001698 02-04 , 003746 04-03
CHANG K 003581 03-17 , 003746 04-03
CHANG N 002937 03-03
CHANG P 003747 04-03
CHANG S 000555 01-08 , 001913 02-08 ,
  002179 02-11 , 002386 02-15 , 002481
  02-16
CHANG W 003655 04-01
CHANG Y 002967 03-04
CHANKOTADZE IS 001640 02-04
CHANNABASAVANNA SM 000621 01-09 ,
  000627 01-09
CHAPIN JK 002642 03-01
CHAPIN RE 003748 04-03
CHAPMAN CR 002195 02-12
CHAPMAN DB 000357 01-04
CHAPMAN RJ 003592 03-17
CHAPPEL JN 000924 01-17
CHAPRON C 002231 02-13
CHARAZAC P 001980 02-09
CHARBAUT J 004395 04-09
CHARBIT J 003524 03-15
CHARETTE C 002499 02-16
CHARIGNON Y 002379 02-15
CHARLEBOIS AT 000513 01-05
CHARMES JP 002395 02-15
CHARNEY D 000666 01-11 , 000945 01-17
CHASE TN 002387 02-15 , 003198 03-08
CHASSEAUD LF 004504 04-13

CHATTHA AS 002122 02-11 , 002724 03-03
CHATURVEDI MK 000583 01-09
CHAU LSK 000292 01-03
CHAU TT 004084 04-04
CHAUDHARI A 000081 01-03
CHAUVOT B 002103 02-11
CHAVEZ E 000045 01-03
CHAVKIN C 003902 04-03
CHAZOT G 003458 03-14
CHEAL M 003358 01-04
CHECKLEY SA 004362 04-09
CHELACK BJ 000234 01-03 , 000451 01-04 ,
  003864 04-03 , 003969 04-03
CHEN ACN 002195 02-12
CHEN FF 004085 04-04
CHEN HT 000298 01-03
CHEN P 001822 02-04
CHEN RC 001165 02-03
CHEN TC 001313 02-03
CHEN YM 002806 03-03
CHENEY DL 000328 01-03 , 001062 02-01 ,
  001166 02-03
CHENG CS 004489 04-11
CHERAMAT R 001070 02-02 , 001072 02-02
CHERN YF 000189 01-03
CHESHER GB 000359 01-04 , 002193 02-12
CHESS Q 000220 01-03
CHEUNG MN 003363 03-11
CHEUNG SW 004048 04-03 , 004303 04-06
CHEVALIER JF 002388 02-15 , 002389 02-15
CHEVAUX G 001902 02-07
CHEVILLARD C 003749 04-03
CHIANG P 001006 02-01 , 001010 02-01 ,
  001021 02-01 , 001415 02-03
CHIAPPINELLI VA 003750 04-03
CHIARAVIGLIO E 001749 02-04
CHIAROTTI M 003751 04-03 , 003803 04-03
CHIBA S 000444 01-04
CHIDLEY LJ 003753 04-03
CHIELI T 001391 02-03 , 004115 04-04
CHIHARA K 003187 03-08 , 003266 03-09
CHILDERS SR 002613 02-17 , 002688 03-03 ,
  002985 03-04 , 004198 04-04
CHINAGLIA L 004440 04-11
CHIODO LA 000413 01-03 , 000047 01-03 ,
  000048 01-03 , 001167 02-03 , 002659
  03-03 , 002880 03-03 , 002968 03-04 ,
  003122 03-05
CHIPKIN RE 003684 04-02
CHITOUR D 000175 01-03
CHIU S 000360 01-04
CHLOPOCKA-WOZNIAK M 002040 02-09 ,
  004404 04-09
CHMELA Z 000274 01-03 , 001474 02-03
CHO A 000826 01-14 , 002235 02-13 ,
  003338 03-11
CHO D 000798 01-13 , 003383 03-11
CHO TM 001168 02-03
CHODERA A 004599 04-15
CHOJNACKI J 004660 04-15
CHOJNACKI M 002456 02-15 , 003304 03-11
CHOM P 000660 02-11 , 004658 04-15
CHOU DT 003752 04-03
CHOUINARD G 003305 03-11
CHRAEMMER JB 002400 02-15
CHRISTENSEN AV 001169 02-03 , 001465 02-
  03 , 002948 03-04
CHRISTENSEN JM 000767 01-13
CHRISTENSEN NJ 003805 04-03
CHRISTENSEN TR 002101 02-11 , 003302 03-
  11
CHRISTENSSON E 000043 01-03
CHRISTIAN ST 002636 03-01
CHRISTIANSEN J 001976 02-09 , 002033 02-
  09
CHRISTODOULOU GN 000786 01-13
CHU N 002689 03-03
CHUANG D 001317 02-03
CHUDLER R 001676 02-04
CHUMCHAL O 000690 01-11
CHUNG EH 000050 01-03
CHURCH MW 003446 03-14
CHURCH RM 003040 03-04
CHWEH A 001208 02-03
CIARLONE AE 003795 04-03
CICCONE JR 002419 02-15
CICERO TJ 000051 01-03 , 002853 03-03
CICHOCKI T 001844 02-05
CIMINO M 004052 04-03 , 004750 04-17
CINCIRIPINI PM 002104 02-11

CIOFFI LA 003124 03-05
CIOTTI T 000185 01-03
CIRAULO DA 003284 03-10 , 003526 03-15
CITRON D 003523 03-15
CIUREZU T 001979 02-09
CIVATI C 002690 03-03
CIVRAN E 000105 01-03
CLAGHORN JL 001995 02-09 , 002531 02-17 ,
  003213 03-09 , 004739 04-17
CLANACHAN AS 004266 04-05
CLANCY J 002073 02-10
CLAPP JF 004027 04-03
CLARENBACH P 002217 02-13
CLARET-TOURNIER T 002105 02-11
CLARK BD 002721 03-03 , 003761 04-03
CLARK DB 000718 01-11
CLARK HB 000239 01-03 , 003974 04-03
CLARK MSG 004086 04-04
CLARK TK 001593 02-04
CLARK WG 000361 01-04 , 000433 01-04 ,
  002532 02-17
CLARK YL 002532 02-17
CLARKE A 002991 03-04
CLARKE C 003123 03-05
CLAUS G 001594 02-04
CLAVERE JL 003226 03-09
CLAVERIE B 003451 03-14
CLAYCOMB JB 002454 02-15
CLEAU M 001170 02-03
CLEDES A 002135 02-11
CLEMENS JA 001171 02-03
CLEMENT JG 004272 04-05
CLEMENT-CORMIER Y 000052 01-03 , 001007
  02-01 , 001011 02-01 , 001172 02-03 ,
  003660 04-01 , 003661 04-01
CLEMENTO AJ 003103 03-04
CLEMENTS-JEWERY S 003753 04-03 , 003851
  04-03 , 004707 04-17
CLERC G 001594 02-04
CLICK M 003238 03-09 , 004345 04-08
CLINESCHMIDT BV 000053 01-03 , 001701 02-
  04 , 002533 02-17
CLOUET DH 000220 01-03 , 001173 02-03
CLOW A 001174 02-03 , 001175 02-03 ,
  001301 02-03 , 002390 02-15 , 002707
  03-03 , 002789 03-03 , 004033 04-03
CLYDE CA 002330 02-14
COALE EH 004132 04-04
COAMBS RB 000530 01-06
COAT C 004594 04-15
COBBETT P 001863 02-06
COBLE P 002339 02-14 , 003236 03-09
COCCHI D 001391 02-03 , 002690 03-03
COCCHI R 000584 01-09
COCHE B 002066 02-10
COELLE C 000054 01-03
COENEGRACHT J 004298 04-06
COFFINET P 002140 02-11
COHEN BM 002480 02-16
COHEN DJ 000452 01-04 , 001752 02-04 ,
  004058 04-15
COHEN IL 003360 03-11 , 003361 03-11
COHEN JB 003750 04-03
COHEN M 002107 02-11 , 003582 03-17 ,
  004600 04-15
COHEN NJ 003306 03-11
COHEN NL 003277 03-10
COHEN RA 003496 03-15 , 003768 04-03
COHEN RM 002280 02-13 , 003255 03-09 ,
  004393 04-09 , 004659 04-15
COHEN S 000667 01-11
COHN JB 002067 02-10
COKER ST 000518 01-05
COLASANTI BK 003078 03-04 , 003908 04-03
COLBOC O 003754 04-03
COLBURN RW 000196 01-03 , 001058 02-01
COLBURN WA 002248 02-13
COLE JO 000787 01-13 , 000844 01-15 ,
  002404 02-15 , 003294 03-11 , 003297
  03-11 , 003557 03-16 , 003583 03-17
  004323 04-08 , 004406 04-09 , 004601
  04-15 , 004623 04-15
COLE S 001197 02-03
COLEMAN JH 000949 01-17 , 003214 03-09
COLEMAN MD 002138 02-11
COLEMAN RR 000183 01-03
COLHOUN EH 002879 03-03
COLINET A 001920 02-08
COLLA P 004456 04-11

COLLARD J 000585 01-09 , 002068 02-10 ,
  004589 04-15
COLLIER B 002870 03-03
COLLIER HOJ 004087 04-04
COLLINGRIDGE GL 002691 03-03
COLLINS AC 001648 02-04
COLLINS GGS 000034 01-03 , 002691 03-03
COLLINS JG 000055 01-03 , 003755 04-03
COLLINS JP 001339 02-03
COLLINS RC 000056 01-03 , 000222 01-03
COLLINS RJ 000497 01-04
COLLIS MG 003756 04-03
COLLORA M 000677 01-11
COLLU R 000285 01-03
COLONI F 001947 02-08
COLONNA L 000362 01-04
COLOTLA VA 002969 03-04
COLPAERT FC 000363 01-04 , 004088 04-04
COLT EWD 003473 03-15
COMAI K 003905 04-03
COMAR D 003564 03-16
COMINSKY NC 001810 02-04
COMIS SD 003757 04-03
COMMISSARIS RL 000364 01-04 , 000365 01-
  04 , 000386 01-04 , 001595 02-04 ,
  004089 04-04
COMMISSIONG JW 003800 04-03 , 004188
  04-04
CONCANNON JT 001596 02-04 , 001597 02-
  04 , 002970 03-04
CONCAS A 002743 03-03
CONCHA GL 000102 01-03
CONCHA J 001176 02-03
CONDE-LOPEZ V 003153 03-07
CONE EJ 000469 01-04
CONGIA S 001483 02-03
CONNERS CK 002339 02-14
CONNOLLY J 003174 03-08
CONNOR JD 001787 02-04 , 003094 03-04 ,
  004007 04-03
CONNOR TM 001623 02-04 , 004237 04-04
CONNORS BW 002692 03-03
CONRADSON S 003663 04-01
CONSO F 003513 03-15
CONSOLAZIONE A 001103 02-03
CONSOLO S 001325 02-03 , 003758 04-03
CONSROE P 004288 04-06
CONSTABLE I 002592 02-17
CONSTANTI A 001143 02-03
CONSTANTINIDIS J 002218 02-13
CONTE G 001460 02-03
CONTE-DEVOLX B 003759 04-03
CONTEL NR 002866 03-03
CONTI L 002090 02-11
CONTRERAS E 001176 02-03
CONTRERAS G 001176 02-03
CONWAY RS 001177 02-03
COOK J 004221 04-04
COOK L 000057 01-03 , 000468 01-04
COOK MR 004585 04-14
COOKSON JC 004363 04-09
COOLS AR 000366 01-04 , 001178 02-03
COOMBES S 001086 02-02
COOPER AJ 002315 02-14
COOPER BR 001141 02-03
COOPER BY 001179 02-03
COOPER JK 000905 01-16 , 003565 03-16
COOPER JR 003937 04-03
COOPER KE 004034 04-03
COOPER PH 000396 01-04
COOPER RL 001180 02-03 , 001683 02-04
COOPER SF 002119 02-11
COOPER SJ 000367 01-04 , 000368 01-04 ,
  000369 01-04 , 001598 02-04 , 001599
  02-04 , 001600 02-04 , 002981 03-04 ,
  002982 03-04 , 004090 04-04
COPELAND RL 001601 02-04
COPPEN A 000837 01-15 , 001943 02-08 ,
  001976 02-09 , 001977 02-09 , 004338
  04-08 , 004364 04-09 , 004707 04-17
COQUILLAT G 003458 03-14
CORBETTA G 001998 02-09
CORDA MG 002477 02-16 , 002743 03-03
CORDASCO F 004651 04-15
CORDON JJ 001595 02-04
CORNAGGIA CM 004439 04-11
CORNER MA 003056 03-04 , 004091 04-04
CORNFIELD RB 003325 03-11
CORONA GL 000757 01-13 , 002057 02-09 ,
  004675 04-16

CORREA F 001459 02-03 , 003685 04-02
CORRIGAL WA 003760 04-03
CORSO P 004245 04-04 , 004246 04-04
CORSON EO 001602 02-04
CORSON SA 001602 02-04
CORTELLI P 001096 02-03
CORTESE I 002973 03-04
CORTEZ A 000425 01-04
CORTHAY J 001874 02-06
CORTI H 004357 04-09
CORWIN H 000514 01-05
COSCINA D 000268 01-03 , 004131 04-04
COSGROVE JW 003761 04-03 , 003832 04-03
COSSUM PA 003558 03-16
COSTA C 003419 03-13
COSTA D 001979 02-09
COSTA E 000397 01-04 , 000925 01-17 ,
  001012 02-01 , 001045 02-01 , 001062
  02-01 , 001166 02-03 , 001181 02-03 ,
  001182 02-03 , 001263 02-03 , 001284
  02-03 , 001317 02-03 , 001403 02-03 ,
  001884 02-06 , 002642 03-01 , 002819
  03-03 , 003808 04-03
COSTA G 000105 01-03
COSTA JL 001013 02-01 , 001014 02-01 ,
  002219 02-13
COSTA MF 004029 04-03
COSTA-E-CASTRO M 003185 03-08
COSTA-MOLINARI JM 001978 02-09
COSTAKIS E 003698 04-02
COSTALL B 000370 01-04 , 001603 02-04 ,
  002220 02-13 , 004092 04-04
COSTELLO DJ 000256 01-03
COSTENTIN J 003754 04-03 , 004173 04-04
COTE IL 003762 04-03
COTE LJ 002401 02-15
COTE TE 001313 02-03
COTES PM 001923 02-08
COTONAT J 003559 03-16
COTTEREAU MJ 000551 01-08 , 000577 01-08
  , 002267 02-13 , 002398 02-15
COTTRAUX J 003584 03-17
COUDERT D 000110 01-03
COUPAL A 001771 02-04
COUPAR IM 001334 02-03
COUPET J 004122 04-04
COUPLAND RE 001183 02-03
COURJON J 004638 04-15
COURTNEY KR 000195 01-03
COUTINHO-NETTO J 000058 01-03
COUTTS RT 003137 03-06 , 003719 04-03
COWAN A 002701 03-03 , 004093 04-04 ,
  004289 04-06
COWDRY RW 004708 04-17
COWEN PJ 001184 02-03 , 002444 02-15 ,
  002971 03-04
COX B 002804 03-03 , 003785 04-03 ,
  003786 04-03 , 003902 04-03 , 004113
  04-04
COX JR 002232 02-13
COY DH 000402 01-04 , 001673 02-04 ,
  001674 02-04 , 001827 02-04
COYLE JT 000059 01-03 , 000566 01-08 ,
  001885 02-06 , 002770 03-03 , 002939
  03-04
CRABBE JC 004094 04-04
CRABTREE R 002257 02-13 , 002429 02-15
CRAFT MJ 000668 01-11
CRAIG CR 003078 03-04 , 003990 04-03
CRAIG TJ 000088 01-15 , 000926 01-17 ,
  002391 02-15
CRAIGHEAD LW 000725 01-11
CRAIGMILL AL 000437 01-04
CRAIN SM 004300 04-06
CRAMER H 002217 02-13 , 002311 02-13
CRANDALL EA 000060 01-03
CRAVES FB 001335 02-03
CRAWFORD FE 001832 02-05
CRAWLEY J 002910 03-03 , 002972 03-04 ,
  004221 04-04
CRAYTON J 002179 02-11
CREASEY DE 003243 03-09
CREESE I 000041 01-08 , 001185 02-03 ,
  001186 02-03 , 001837 02-05 , 002575
  02-17 , 002613 02-17 , 002803 03-03 ,
  002922 03-03 , 003199 03-08 , 003585
  03-17 , 004003 04-03
CREMA A 002276 02-13
CREMER JE 001838 02-04

CRETET E 001187 02-03
CREUTZFELDT OD 002752 03-03 , 004500 04-
  13
CREWS EL 002216 02-13 , 002392 02-15 ,
  003474 03-15
CREWS FT 001188 02-03 , 003763 04-03
CREWS T 000898 01-16
CRIADO M 001097 02-03
CRILL WE 002886 03-03
CROCKETT G 003504 03-15
CROCQ L 001980 02-09
CRONENBERGER L 001227 02-03
CRONHOLM B 001981 02-09 , 002086 02-10
CRONK CE 002161 02-11
CROOK T 002125 02-11
CROOKS J 002534 02-17
CROS J 000021 01-03 , 000797 01-13 ,
  001110 02-03 , 003682 04-02
CROSS AJ 000062 01-03 , 000325 01-03 ,
  001816 02-04 , 001911 02-08
CROW TJ 001911 02-08 , 001923 02-08 ,
  004423 04-10
CROWDER MK 000839 01-15
CROWE RR 002073 02-10
CROWLEY WR 001528 02-03 , 002693 03-03
CRUZ TF 002721 03-03
CRUZ-MORALES SE 000371 01-04
CSANALOSI I 000655 01-10 , 003254 03-09
CUATRECASAS P 002580 02-17 , 003581 03-
  17 , 003746 04-03
CUCCHI ML 000757 01-13 , 004675 04-16
CUCHE H 000577 01-08 , 001907 02-08 ,
  002015 02-09 , 002267 02-13 , 002694
  03-03 , 003175 03-08 , 004709 04-17
CUELLAR A 000045 01-03
CUENCA E 001189 02-03
CUENDET J 004615 04-15
CULLARI S 003298 03-11 , 004437 04-11
CULLEN EI 000779 01-13
CULLERRE P 001889 02-07
CULVENOR AJ 003764 04-03
CUMIN R 001381 02-03 , 002646 03-02
CUMMINGS AJ 003549 03-15
CUNHA AM 000669 01-11
CUNNINGHAM CE 002092 02-11
CUNNINGHAM VJ 001838 02-05
CUOMO V 002973 03-04
CUPANO J 002486 02-16
CURRO F 001259 02-03
CURTI D 003730 04-03
CURTIS DR 000063 01-03 , 002633 03-01 ,
  002647 03-02 , 002768 03-03
CURTIS JR 002393 02-15
CURTIS SD 003981 04-03
CURZON G 002673 03-03 , 002990 03-04
CUSACK B 004014 04-03
CUTHBERT NJ 004087 04-04
CUTLER NR 002221 02-13
CVEJIC V 003765 04-03
CYTAWA J 001604 02-04
CYTRYN L 003242 03-09
CYTRYNIAK H 001579 02-04
CZUCZWAR SJ 000163 01-03 , 002921 03-03
  , 004241 04-04

D

DA PRADA M 001314 02-03 , 002863 03-03
DACHARY JM 001090 02-02
DAFNY N 001421 02-03
DAFTER RE 000380 01-04
DAGANI F 003730 04-03
DAHL JL 003909 04-03
DAHLBOM R 003701 04-02
DAHLSTROM A 003897 04-03
DAIGUJI M 004676 04-16
DAILEY G 004600 04-15
DAILEY JW 003865 04-03
DAINOSON K 003450 03-14
DAISLEY RW 002394 02-15
DAJANI EZ 000064 01-03
DAL BELLO A 001200 02-03
DALE PG 002316 02-14
DALERY J 004638 04-15
DALESSANDRO R 001096 02-03
DALILA-Y-CASTILLO E 002173 02-11
DALLOCCHIO M 002395 02-15
DALLY S 003505 03-15
DALTERIO SL 002695 03-03

DALTON K 000927 01-17
DALY JW 003766 04-03 , 003950 04-03
DAM H 004537 04-13
DAM M 000767 01-13 , 003307 03-11 ,
   004602 04-15
DAMASIO H 000670 01-11
DAMBROSIA JM 003319 03-11
DAMIANO BP 003094 03-04 , 004007 04-03
DANA SL 000765 01-13
DANCKWARDT JF 002535 02-17
DANDIYA PC 001682 02-04
DANGOUMAU J 002395 02-15
DANIEL SA 004095 04-04
DANIELCZYK W 003475 03-15
DANIELS MP 000065 01-03
DANIELS S 001686 02-04
DANION J 001904 02-07 , 002895 03-03 ,
   004270 04-05
DANNER R 004441 04-11
DANTONIO J 001991 02-09
DANY F 002395 02-15
DARBINYAN AG 002663 03-03
DARCOURT G 002023 02-09 , 002108 02-11 ,
   002536 02-17 , 003210 03-09 , 004357
   04-09
DARCY-GOMEZ G 001409 02-03
DARDA S 001259 02-03
DARONDEL A 001980 02-09
DARRAGH A 004532 04-13
DAS M 004096 04-04
DASBERG H 003196 03-08
DASCOURT G 004594 04-15
DASHWOOD MR 002976 03-04
DATTA N 000002 01-01 , 000003 01-01 ,
   001015 02-01
DAUSSE J 000205 01-03 , 003944 04-03
DAVID I 001912 02-08
DAVIDOW B 000859 01-15
DAVIDSON AB 003476 03-15
DAVIDSON J 004745 04-17
DAVIDSON PP 000518 01-05
DAVIDSON S 001915 02-08 , 002396 02-15
DAVIES B 000114 01-09 , 002184 02-11 ,
   004707 04-17
DAVIES DS 000141 01-03
DAVIES J 001190 02-03 , 001191 02-03 ,
   002691 03-03 , 002696 03-03
DAVIES S 001707 02-04 , 003769 04-03 ,
   003241 03-09
DAVILA K 003918 04-03
DAVIS A 003767 04-03
DAVIS BA 001077 02-02
DAVIS BM 002317 02-14 , 003215 03-09
DAVIS CM 000530 01-06
DAVIS G 003357 03-11
DAVIS GA 003017 03-04
DAVIS GC 001910 02-08 , 001984 02-09 ,
   002222 02-13 , 003167 03-08 , 004316
   04-08 , 004317 04-08
DAVIS HP 003636 03-17 , 004097 04-04
DAVIS JC 002697 03-03
DAVIS JD 004098 04-04
DAVIS JM 000135 01-03 , 000547 01-08 ,
   000572 01-08 , 000672 01-11 , 000675
   01-11 , 000726 01-11 , 000908 01-16 ,
   000934 01-17 , 000973 01-17 , 001073
   02-02 , 001913 02-08 , 002024 02-09 ,
   002179 02-11 , 002269 02-13 , 002386
   02-15 , 002481 02-16 , 002491 02-16 ,
   003142 03-06 , 003471 03-15 , 004215
   04-04 , 004374 04-09 , 004577 04-14 ,
   004603 04-15 , 004682 04-16
DAVIS JS 003119 03-04
DAVIS KL 000928 01-17 , 002317 02-14 ,
   002488 02-16 , 003215 03-09 , 003465
   03-15 , 003477 03-15 , 004099 04-04 ,
   004327 04-08 , 004442 04-11 , 004514
   04-13 , 004604 04-15 , 004703 04-17
DAVIS LG 003496 03-15 , 003768 04-03
DAVIS M 000066 01-03 , 003480 03-15 ,
   001605 02-04 , 002397 02-15 , 002950
   03-04
DAVIS SF 002974 03-04
DAVIS VJ 003392 03-11
DAVIS WC 001192 02-03
DAVISON AN 000171 01-03
DAVISON K 000201 02-09
DAVISON M 001193 02-03
DAW J 003474 03-15
DAWBARN D 004100 04-04

DAWLING S 002266 02-13 , 002284 02-13
DAWSON SD 000432 01-04
DAY IP 001093 02-02
DAY N 001830 02-05
DAYICAN G 004460 04-11 , 004519 04-13
DE ANTONI A 003419 03-13
DE BASTIANI P 002283 02-13
DE BELLEROCHE J 002843 03-03
DE BOER T 001606 02-04
DE BRUIJN JPC 003107 03-04
DE BUCK RP 001890 02-07
DE CATANZARO D 002975 03-04
OE CUYPER HJA 003216 03-09
DE GIOVANNI L 003122 03-05
DE GORI N 003075 03-04
DE GROAT WC 000162 01-03
DE GROOT MHL 000586 01-09
DE GUBAREFF T 000222 01-03
DE JONG AP 002698 03-03
DE JONGHE F 002526 02-17 , 003107 03-04
DE LA FUENTE-RAMIREZ JR 002109 02-11
DE LA FUENTE-RAMIREZ R 003478 03-15
DE LA MORA P 003101 03-04
DE LANGEN CDJ 000067 01-03 , 000323 01-
   03
DE LIMA TCM 004101 04-04
DE LUCA B 003124 03-05
DE MAIO D 001985 02-09
DE MONTIGNY C 000068 01-03 , 001135 02-
   03
DE MONTIS G 002477 02-16
DE ROBERTIS E 001097 02-03
DE ROSA A 001460 02-03
DE ROSSETT SE 002320 02-14
DE SARRO GB 000442 01-04 , 000443 01-04
DE VAUS JE 001607 02-04
DE VILLARD R 002110 02-11 , 004638 04-15
DE WIED D 001953 02-08
DE ZEEUW RA 003216 03-09
DEACON RMJ 003073 03-04
DEAKIN JFW 000373 01-04 , 002976 03-04
DEAN P 001755 02-04
DEAN S 004114 04-04
DEANOVIC Z 002243 02-13
DEARING ME 001583 02-04
DEBELJUK L 001194 02-03
DEBERDT R 000758 01-13 , 004355 04-09
DEBUS G 002537 02-17 , 003769 04-03
DECOSKEY D 003364 03-11
DEDEK J 001202 02-03 , 003995 04-03
DEFEUDIS FV 002538 02-17 , 002699 03-03
DEFRAITES EG 003198 03-08
DEGIROLAMI U 000257 01-03
DEGROOF RC 000069 01-03
DEGTYAREV VP 003797 04-03
DEHAVEN R 000026 01-03
DEIMAN-VAN AALST WMA 002651 03-02
DEISENHAMMER E 004443 04-11
DEISER R 004605 04-15
DEJOHN C 004694 04-16
DEKIRMENJIAN H 002386 02-15 , 002491 02-
   16
DEL BIANCO PL 004553 04-13
DEL POZO E 002217 02-13
DEL RIO J 000398 01-04
DEL ROSCIO S 004431 04-11
DELANOY RL 001250 02-03
DELARUE M 003268 03-09
DELASHAW JBJ 000374 01-04
DELEVA JI 003716 04-03
DELIA G 001982 02-09 , 001983 02-09
DELIAC P 003451 03-14
DELINI-STULA A 001740 02-04
DELISI L 001945 02-08 , 002245 02-13 ,
   003169 03-08 , 003184 03-08
DELITALA G 001016 02-01 , 001127 02-03 ,
   003731 04-03 , 003732 04-03
DELLEN RG 000650 01-10
DELOT D 003313 03-11
DELONG M 002223 02-13 , 004561 04-14
DEMANGE J 001891 02-07
DEMAREST KT 002700 03-03
DEMELLWEEK C 004121 04-04
DEMENGE P 000070 01-03
DEMENT WC 000374 01-04
DEMENTYEVA NF 004444 04-11
DEMET EM 000312 01-03 , 003771 04-03
DEMICHEL P 002876 03-03
DEMIRIAN L 002928 03-03
DEMYER W 000514 01-05 , 000521 01-05

DENBER HCB 000929 01-17
DENCKER SJ 000890 01-15 , 001956 02-08
DENDEL PS 000182 01-03
DENENBERG VH 000375 01-04
DENES Z 000930 01-17
DENFORD J 002164 02-11
DENGLER HJ 000968 01-17
DENIJS EL 004562 04-14
DENIKER P 000549 01-08 , 000551 01-08 ,
   000577 01-08 , 001195 02-03 , 001892
   02-07 , 002016 02-09 , 002267 02-13 ,
   002398 02-15 , 002539 02-17 , 004445
   04-11 , 004709 04-17
DENIS B 002379 02-15
DENVER D 002596 02-17
DEOM A 000759 01-13
DEPAULO JR 003199 03-08
DEPOCAS F 001231 02-03
DEPRY D 003346 03-11
DEROSSETT SE 002983 03-04
DERYCK M 000376 01-04
DESAGER JP 000181 01-03
DESHMUKH PP 001373 02-03 , 002902 03-03
DESMOND PV 002224 02-13 , 002272 02-13
DESOUSA G 003367 03-11
DESSAIGNE S 003089 03-04
DESTRADE C 003051 03-04
DETAILLE J 003293 03-11
DETLOR J 002106 02-11
DETTMAR PW 000351 01-04 , 002701 03-03 ,
   003662 04-01
DEUTSCH JA 002702 03-03 , 002977 03-04 ,
   004182 04-04
DEUTSCH SI 004606 04-15
DEVANE CL 002225 02-13 , 003154 03-07 ,
   003479 03-15
DEVICHE P 001565 02-04
DEVITT D 003557 03-16
DEVLIN MC 002322 02-14
DEVOITILLE JM 004561 04-14
DEVOIZE JL 004479 04-11
DEVOTO P 000285 01-03
DEWEY WL 001513 02-03 , 002712 03-03 ,
   003970 04-03 , 004610 04-15
DEWHURST WG 003137 03-06 , 003719 04-03
DEWIED D 003074 03-04
DEWITT JR 001608 02-04
DEWITT L 000435 01-04
DEWS PB 002364 02-14 , 004228 04-04 ,
   004280 04-05
DEY PK 001429 02-03
DEZE J 002111 02-11
DHUMAL VR 003772 04-03 , 004102 04-04
DI GIORGIO RM 000218 01-03 , 002762 03-03
   , 003952 04-03
DI MARCO E 003222 03-09
DI PAOLO T 001324 02-03
DI PERRI RG 003359 03-11
DIAKOW C 002978 03-04
DIAMOND BI 001834 02-05 , 004268 04-05
DIAMOND EL 003405 03-13
DIAMOND I 001257 02-03
DIAMOND JM 004521 04-13
DIAMOND L 004400 04-09
DIAMOND RJ 003308 03-11
DIAMOND RL 002005 02-09
DIAMOND SG 003336 03-11
DIAS RD 000071 01-03 , 001664 02-04
DIAZ MC 001194 02-03
DIBNER MD 000072 01-03 , 002932 03-03 ,
   003979 04-03
DICKINSON RG 000073 01-03
DICKINSON WA 002979 03-04
DICKISON SE 003686 04-02
DICKSON VAT 002974 03-04
DIEPART E 002398 02-15
DIETL H 002703 03-03 , 003968 04-03
DIETRICHSON P 000701 01-11
DIETZ AJ 003480 03-15
DIETZ DD 002887 03-03
DIEZ-EWALD M 002112 02-11
DIFFLEY D 000074 01-03
DIFNY N 003773 04-03
DIGGORY GL 003686 04-02
DIGREGORIO GJ 003725 04-03
DIJKSTRA D 000004 01-01 , 000324 01-03
DILLMAN CE 004643 04-15
DILLON A 002439 02-15
DILLON D 004427 04-10

DINERSTEIN RJ 004293 04-06
DINGLEDINE R 001864 02-06 , 002704 03-03
DINGWALL JM 001932 02-08
DINTCHEFF BA 001830 02-05
DIRGO JA 004281 04-05
DIRICO S 004308 04-07 , 004589 04-15
OIRLICH G 004322 04-08
DITTRICH A 004696 04-16
DIVAKARAN P 003774 04-03
DIXON R 000898 01-16
DIXON WJ 003188 03-08 , 003189 03-08
DLABAC A 000242 01-03 , 000306 01-03 ,
  001720 02-04 , 002279 02-13 , 002540
  02-17
DOAMARAL JR 003663 04-01 , 004514 04-13
DOBIAS J 004748 04-17
DOBRY PJK 002980 03-04 , 004200 04-04
DOBRZYNSKA L 000931 01-17
DOCHERTY JP 000843 01-15 , 001951 02-08
DOCHERTY JR 001196 02-03
DOCKRAY GJ 001291 02-03
DODA M 003822 04-03
DODD J 001864 02-06 , 002704 03-03
DODSON WE 002113 02-11
DOGGRELL SA 000075 01-03
DOHN HH 002216 02-13
DOI T 001609 02-04
DOLANSKY J 000671 01-11
DOLE VP 002114 02-11
DOLEZAL V 004044 04-03
DOLLERY CT 002504 02-16
DOLPHIN AC 000931 01-17
DOMENECH J 003291 03-11
DOMENGIE B 003268 03-09
DOMER FR 000076 01-03 , 001197 02-03
DOMINGUEZ RA 002399 02-15
DOMINO EF 000462 01-04 , 000737 01-12 ,
  000934 01-17 , 001198 02-03
DOMINY BW 001687 02-04
DOMJAN M 001610 02-04 , 003055 03-04
DONALD RA 004545 04-13
DONALDSON JO 003481 03-15
DONG DE 000418 01-04
DONIGAN BE 003699 04-02
DONINI G 000833 01-15
DONLON PT 003217 03-09
DONNAN GA 003433 03-13
DONNELLY J 000539 01-07
DONOVICK PJ 004103 04-04
DOOGAN DP 003775 04-03
DOONGAJI DR 002158 02-11
DOOT DL 003690 04-02
DORDAIN G 003155 03-07
DORE CJ 002365 02-13
DORMANDY J 002598 02-17
DORMHORST A 004463 04-11
DORSEY R 003586 03-17
DORUS E 001987 02-09
DOSSENA M 001126 02-03 , 003730 04-03
DOSTAL T 000600 01-09 , 001888 02-07 ,
  002006 02-09 , 002131 02-11 , 004375
  04-09
DOSTALOVA J 000658 01-10
DOSTALOVA K 000077 01-03 , 000805 01-14
  , 001199 02-03 , 002333 02-14
DOTTI A 002226 02-13 , 003466 03-15 ,
  004318 04-08
DOUGLAS R 002154 02-11
DOURISH CT 002981 03-04 , 002982 03-04
DOW RC 001708 02-04
DOWLING JE 001296 02-03 , 003776 04-03 ,
  004051 04-03
DOWNING RW 000840 01-15 , 002482 02-16
  , 004420 04-10
DOXEY JC 001146 02-03
DOYLE RL 000377 01-04 , 001677 02-04
DRACHMAN DA 000802 01-14
DRACHMAN DB 000232 01-03
DRAGO F 000378 01-04 , 001200 02-03 ,
  003301 03-11
DRAHOKOUPIL L 000686 01-11 , 002188 02-
DRAPER RJ 002318 02-14
DRASGOW F 003363 03-11
DRAVET C 000873 01-15 , 002319 02-14
DRAY A 000738 01-12 , 001191 02-03
DREIFUSS FE 003378 03-11
DREOSTI IE 001986 02-09
DRESCHER K 003515 03-15
DRESSE A 000267 01-03

DREVET M 001980 02-09
DREW WG 002320 02-14 , 002983 03-04
DREWETT RF 000483 01-04
DREXLER G 002775 03-03
DRIESENS F 000758 01-13
DRIESSEN O 000760 01-13
DRISCOLL BF 001201 02-03
DRISCOLL P 001202 02-03 , 002852 03-03 ,
  002984 03-04 , 003042 03-04
DROGUETT PA 000102 01-03
DROSS K 000078 01-03 , 002240 02-13
DRTILKOVA I 000729 01-11 , 002115 02-11 ,
  002190 02-11
DRUFF JH 000949 01-17 , 003214 03-09
DRUST EG 001787 02-04 , 004007 04-03
DRY J 004505 04-13
DSOUZAS BJ 004447 04-11
DU CHESNE H 004481 04-11
DUANE DD 002037 02-09 , 002038 02-09
DUBNITSKAYA EB 004340 04-08
DUBOCOVICH ML 000227 01-03 , 002801 03-
  03 , 003777 04-03
DUBOIS JP 002232 02-13
DUCHE D 002116 02-11 , 002321 02-14 ,
  002344 02-14
DUCHEMIN AM 000241 01-03 , 001054 02-01
DUCKLES SP 000079 01-03
DUDAI Y 001833 02-05 , 002655 03-03
DUFFY FH 002684 03-03
DUFOUR H 002619 02-17 , 003524 03-15
DUFRASNE M 000585 01-09
DUGGAN AW 001203 02-03 , 002740 03-03 ,
  002767 03-03 , 003778 04-03
DUGGAN B 002445 02-15
DUHAIME J 004286 04-06
DUHAULT J 002030 02-03 , 002541 02-17
DUHM J 001987 02-09 , 002227 02-13
DUIZABO P 003156 03-07
DUK T 003837 04-03
DUM J 004104 04-04
DUMAS M 000865 01-15
DUMBRILLE A 001303 02-03
DUMBRILLE-ROSS A 001204 02-03
DUMOND J 000865 01-15
DUMONT C 004105 04-04
DUMVIC P 004639 04-15
DUN NJ 001205 02-03 , 003779 04-03
DUNCAN W 002341 02-14
DUNLAP CE 002804 03-03
DUNLAP WP 000402 01-04
DUNLEAVY RA 003482 03-15
DUNN AJ 003044 03-03 , 003109 03-04
DUNN GD 002272 02-13
DUNNER DL 000587 01-09 , 001893 02-07 ,
  001987 02-09 , 001989 02-09 , 002228
  02-13 , 002448 02-15 , 003221 03-09 ,
  004369 04-09 , 004391 04-09
DUNNER FJ 000868 01-15
DUNNETT SB 000347 01-04
DUNSTAN R 001206 02-03 , 001299 02-03 ,
  002986 03-04
DUNWIDDIE TV 000800 01-03 , 000178 01-03
DUPELJ M 002705 03-03
DUPONT A 002635 03-01
DURAN E 004319 04-08
DURAND A 002625 02-17 , 003571 03-16
DURIASZ H 003050 03-04
DURSO R 000698 01-11 , 002342 02-14 ,
  002371 02-15 , 004431 04-11
DURST N 004573 04-14
DUSEK K 000548 01-08 , 001925 02-08
DUSLAK B 004682 04-16
DUSTICIER N 000217 01-03
DUVOISIN RC 000404 01-04 , 001650 02-04 ,
  002117 02-11 , 004129 04-04
DVORKIN B 002814 03-03
DWINGER H 001917 02-08
DWIVEDI C 000261 01-03
DYCK LE 001207 02-03 , 002706 03-03
DYER RG 002708 03-03
DYER RS 002708 03-03
DYKMAN RA 002118 02-11
DYKSTRA LA 000379 01-04 , 000403 01-04 ,
  001611 02-04 , 004106 04-04
DYRENFURTH I 000874 01-15
DYSKEN M 001913 02-08 , 002407 02-15 ,
  002481 02-16 , 002491 02-16
DYSKEN MW 000672 01-11 , 000675 01-11
DZHAFARLI MT 004125 04-04

DZHALIASHVILI TA 004107 04-04
DZHOKHADZE LD 003780 04-03

E

EADIE MJ 004555 04-13
EANES ED 001013 02-01 , 002219 02-13
EATWELL JC 000517 01-05
EBADI M 001208 02-03
EBARA T 000082 01-03
EBERT MH 000182 01-03 , 000673 01-11,
  003309 03-11 , 003340 03-11 , 003362
  03-11
EBSTEIN RP 000083 01-03 , 003720 04-03 ,
  004167 04-04
ECKERNAS S 000084 01-03
EDELFORS S 001209 02-03
EDELMAN AM 001423 02-03
EDEN S 002664 03-03
EDVINSSON L 000200 01-03 , 003781 04-03
EDWARDS D 000631 01-09 , 002891 03-03
EDWARDS JG 000638 01-09 , 001914 02-08
EFTHYMIOU ML 003513 03-15
EGER EII 000418 01-04
EGUCHI T 000199 01-03
EHLERS CL 001210 02-03
EHLERT FJ 000279 01-03
EHRENSING RH 001311 02-03
EHRET CF 001409 02-03
EHRLICH BE 004521 04-13
EHSANULLAH RSB 002268 02-13
EICHELBAUM M 000754 01-13 , 003314 03-11
EICHELMAN B 002987 03-04 , 003021 03-04
EIDEN LE 001017 02-01 , 001018 02-01 ,
  001211 02-03 , 001212 02-03
EIGEMAN L 002651 03-02
EIGYO M 003692 04-02
EIKELBOOM R 002709 03-03 , 002710 03-03,
  002906 03-03
EINSPAHR FJ 003782 04-03 , 004200 04-04
EISDORFER C 004710 04-17
EISENBERG RM 000085 01-03 , 003888 04-03
EISERT A 003968 04-03
EISINGER S 001664 02-04
EISLER T 000673 01-11 , 002384 02-15 ,
  003309 03-11 , 003406 03-13
EKBOM K 002181 02-11
EL HAIT MAS 000900 01-16
EL-FAKHANY E 003783 04-03
EL-SOHLY MA 001022 02-01 , 001023 02-01
ELAM R 001574 02-04
ELDER JK 004215 04-04
ELENS P 000758 01-13
ELGHOZI J 003944 04-03
ELIANDER H 000086 01-03
ELIASSON SG 003784 04-03
ELIE R 001929 02-08 , 002119 02-11
ELIS J 002542 02-17
ELISABETSKY E 001664 02-04
ELISEO C 003466 03-15
ELIZUR A 000841 01-15 , 001915 02-08 ,
  001916 02-08 , 004320 04-08
ELKINS R 003310 03-11 , 004657 04-15
ELLEY J 002633 02-09
ELLINWOOD EH 001683 02-04 , 002711 03-03
  , 003005 03-04
ELLIOTT AJ 001019 02-01
ELLIOTT EJ 000638 01-09
ELLIOTT J 001302 02-03 , 003862 04-03
ELLIOTT M 003760 04-03
ELLIS DB 002059 02-11
ELLIS KO 003687 04-02 , 003688 04-02
ELLISON G 000216 01-03 , 001395 02-03 ,
  001875 02-06 , 002988 03-04
ELMASSIAN BJ 003651 03-17
ELMAZAR MMA 004108 04-04
ELONEN E 003428 03-13
ELOVAARA E 000261 01-03
ELROD SV 001213 02-03
ELSASS P 002229 02-13 , 002329 02-14 ,
  004607 04-15
ELSOHLY MA 000344 01-04
ELSWORTH JD 000983 01-17 , 002230 02-13
  , 002365 02-14
ELTON RA 004677 04-16
EMERSON R 004447 04-11
EMERY C 004690 04-16
EMI Y 000515 01-05
EMLEY GS 002759 03-03

EMMETT-OGLESBY MW 000380 01-04
EMORY LE 004324 04-08
EMRICH HM 001917 02-08, 001918 02-08,
003218 03-09, 003219 03-09, 004321
04-08, 004322 04-08
EMSON PC 001296 02-03, 004184 04-04
END DW 002712 03-03
ENDO M 004608 04-15
ENDO S 002350 02-14
ENDO Y 004301 04-06
ENDROCZI E 004109 04-04
ENEROTH P 002727 03-03
ENG N 003406 03-13
ENGBERG G 001214 02-03
ENGEL J 000087 01-03, 001839 02-05,
004110 04-04, 004120 04-04, 004126
04-04
ENGELHARDT DM 000880 01-15
ENGELMANN W 000772 01-13
ENGELSMANN F 004348 04-09
ENGLISH MG 003684 04-02
ENGQUIST A 002400 02-15
ENJALBERT A 000213 01-03
ENJALBERT M 000864 01-15
ENNA SJ 001215 02-03, 002713 03-03,
002716 03-03, 002778 03-03, 004157
04-04
ENNIS C 003785 04-03, 003786 04-03
ENNS L 003787 04-03
ENNS MP 000480 04-04
ENULESCU O 002295 02-13
EPSTEIN LH 002104 02-11
ERARD R 000739 01-12
ERBAN L 000600 01-09, 003170 03-08
ERCILLA R 004319 04-08
ERDMANN JF 002072 02-10
ERDOS A 000912 01-17
ERICKSON CK 001865 02-06
ERIKSSON E 002664 03-03
ERINOFF L 001340 02-03
ERMISCH A 003669 04-01
EROGLU L 001216 02-03, 001217 02-03,
003788 04-03
ERVIN FR 001049 02-01, 001612 02-04
ERVIN GN 004111 04-04
ERWIN CW 000867 01-15, 000895 01-15
ERWIN VG 003146 03-06
ESCANDE M 003559 03-16
ESCOBAR J 001931 02-08
ESCURET E 002231 02-13
ESKAY R 000277 01-03, 001017 02-01,
001018 02-01
ESLER M 004506 04-13
ESPAGNO J 003226 03-09
ESPINOSA L 001558 02-04
ESPOSITO RU 003066 03-04, 004160 04-04
ESSMAN WB 000932 01-17
ESTEBAN A 003311 03-11
ESTLER C 001613 02-04
ETEMAD B 002079 02-10
ETTLIN R 004284 04-05
EUVRARD C 001218 02-03, 003789 04-03
EVANS HL 003128 03-05, 004271 04-05
EVANS L 001988 02-09, 002232 02-13
EVANS M 000022 01-03, 001840 02-05
EVANS RH 001104 02-03, 003587 03-17,
004348 03-17
EVARTS JV 003319 03-11
EVEN P 001920 02-08
EVENSON GN 001076 02-02
EVENSON RC 002414 02-15
EVERED MD 001614 02-04
EVERSMANN T 002137 02-11
EVES F 003174 03-08
EWING FE 001092 02-02
EXTEIN I 000899 01-16, 000933 01-17,
001984 02-09, 003203 03-09, 003250
03-09, 003357 03-11
EYSTER ME 000945 01-17
EZRIN-WATERS C 003483 03-15

F

FABRICANT JD 003121 03-05
FADDA F 001483 02-03
FADEN AI 002714 03-03
FAGES C 004029 04-03
FAHN S 002401 02-15
FAIMAN C 002213 02-13
FAIN JN 002728 03-03

FAINGOLD CL 001219 02-03
FAIRBAIRN JW 002196 02-12
FAIRCHILD AD 001220 02-03
FAIRHURST JI 001591 02-04
FAISON E 000053 01-03
FAIT V 000686 01-11, 002188 02-11
FALASCHI P 002371 02-15, 004431 04-11
FALCH E 001139 02-03, 002647 03-02
FALETTI MV 001242 02-03
FALK JL 004235 04-04
FALK W 001099 02-03, 001100 02-03
FALKO JM 003521 03-15
FALKUM E 002550 02-17
FALTUS F 004375 04-09
FAN KJ 003436 03-13
FANELLI CJ 000187 01-03
FANELLI RJ 004103 04-04
FANG V 003190 03-08, 003318 03-11,
003790 04-03, 004538 04-13
FANGET M 004307 04-07
FANN E 002179 02-11
FANN WE 000934 01-17, 002486 02-16,
004710 04-17
FANSELOW MS 001615 02-04
FAORE E 003194 03-08
FARABOLLINI F 004081 04-04
FARARUNI M 000562 01-08
FARAVELLI C 004365 04-09
FARB DH 003980 04-03
FARELLI S 002356 02-14
FARIELLO RG 003853 04-03, 004609 04-15
FARRIS RD 003525 03-15
FARRIS TS 000088 01-03
FARSANG C 003791 04-03
FARSKA I 003739 03-03, 003696 04-02
FATHERAZI S 001144 02-03
FAULL KF 003477 03-15, 003663 04-01
FAUMAN BJ 000935 01-17
FAUMAN MA 000935 01-17
FAUSTMAN W 002989 03-04
FAVARO M 003441 03-14
FAY DD 001013 02-01, 001014 02-01,
002219 02-13
FEDER HH 002842 03-03
FEDERSPIEL CF 000979 01-17
FEENSTRA MGP 000004 01-01, 000324 01-03
FEHSKE KJ 001440 02-03, 004211 04-04
FEIGHNER JP 000936 01-17
FEIGL P 000728 01-11
FEINBERG M 000588 01-09, 004359 04-09,
004674 04-16
FEKETE MIK 003792 04-03
FELDBERG W 002715 03-03
FELDMAN B 002318 02-14
FELDON J 001757 02-04
FELEGI W 000510 01-05
FELINE A 000543 01-07
FELIX A 001740 02-04
FELNER A 001740 02-04
FENELLI A 003157 03-07, 003158 03-07
FENNESSY MR 001841 02-05, 004243 04-04
FENOGLIO L 000757 01-13, 002057 02-04,
002058 02-09, 004675 04-16
FERGUSON DG 003298 03-11, 004437 04-11
004438 04-11
FERGUSON HB 002120 02-11, 003312 03-11
FERKANY JW 001215 02-03, 001221 02-03,
002713 03-03, 002716 03-03
FERLAND L 001324 02-03
FERNANDEZ R 002849 03-03, 002850 03-03,
002851 03-03
FERNANDEZ-ALONSO JI 003673 04-01
FERNANDEZ-TOME P 000398 01-04
FERNANDO JCR 002990 03-04
FERNSTROM JD 000019 01-03, 000020 01-03
000060 01-03, 000296 01-03, 004025
04-03
FERRARA M 004417 04-04
FERRARA P 002081 02-04
FERRARI F 000340 01-04
FERRARO DP 000381 01-04
FERRENDELLI JA 000089 01-03, 000090 01-
03, 000115 01-03
FERRER-VIDAL L 001978 02-09
FERRERI M 001960 02-09, 001961 02-09,
001965 02-09, 003206 03-09, 003588
03-17
FERRETY G 000552 01-08
FERRI P 000282 01-03
FERRI S 000282 01-03, 001468 02-03

FERRIER BM 002322 02-14
FERRIS O 003898 04-03, 003899 04-03
FERRIS RM 000091 01-03
FERRIS S 002125 02-11, 004482 04-11
FESSLER RG 001616 02-04, 001719 02-04
FEUERSTEIN C 000070 01-03
FEUERSTEIN G 001222 02-03, 001223 02-03,
001224 02-03, 002250 02-13, 002717
03-03
FIBIGER HC 000283 01-03, 000345 01-04,
000463 01-04, 004070 04-04
FICHTE K 000768 01-13
FICHTER MM 004711 04-17
FIDELL LS 003589 03-17
FIELDING LT 000937 01-17
FIELDS HL 000425 01-04
FIEVE RR 000587 01-09, 001893 02-07,
001989 02-09, 002228 02-13, 002448
02-15, 002543 02-17, 002683 03-03,
003221 03-09, 003473 03-15, 004369
04-09, 004391 04-09, 004606 04-15
FIGUEROA AM 002402 02-15
FILE SE 000092 01-03, 001617 02-04,
001866 02-06, 002991 03-04
FILETTI S 003301 03-11
FILIBECK U 000382 01-04
FILINGER E 001658 02-04
FILIP V 000570 01-08, 000674 01-11,
000761 01-13, 000770 01-13
FILIPOVA M 000674 01-11
FILLION G 000033 01-03, 000093 01-03
FILLION M 000033 01-03
FINCH CE 004217 04-04
FINCHAM J 004580 04-14
FINK JS 000383 01-04, 000384 01-04,
004112 04-04
FINK M 001071 02-02, 001894 02-07,
004366 04-09
FINKEL S 000675 01-11
FINKELFARB E 004263 04-04
FINN AL 003353 03-11, 003421 03-13
FINNERTY EP 001225 02-03, 002718 03-03
FINNERTY RJ 001994 02-09
FIREMARK HM 003338 03-11
FISCHER B 004344 04-08
FISCHER C 003458 03-14
FISCHER GJ 001618 02-04
FISCHER H 001935 02-08, 002311 02-13
FISCHER J 001419 02-03, 002764 03-03
FISCHER JM 003539 03-15
FISCHER W 004481 04-11
FISCHER-CORNELSSEN KA 002483 02-16
FISCHMAN MW 002323 02-14, 002328 02-14
FISH BS 004288 04-06
FISHER RW 000206 01-03
FISHER S 003590 03-17, 003987 04-03
FISHKIN SM 000879 01-15
FISHMAN J 000400 01-04
FITZGERALD M 001226 02-03, 002439 02-15
FITZGERALD SC 002669 03-03
FITZJARRELL AT 002747 03-03
FJELDBORG N 000792 01-13
FLAGG HC 003077 03-04
FLANNERY J 001385 02-03, 004204 04-04
FLATAKER LM 000053 01-03
FLATMAN JA 002799 03-03
FLECHTER S 004343 04-08
FLEISS JL 001989 02-09, 003221 03-09
FLEITMAN JS 000762 01-13
FLETCHER A 000158 01-03
FLEYS EP 004593 04-15
FLIEGEROVA O 000761 01-13
FLINT BA 000385 01-04, 001619 02-04,
002753 03-03
FLOOD JF 001573 02-04, 004578 04-14
FLOREA-CIOCOIU V 002281 02-13
FLORENCE JE 000094 01-03
FLORU L 000550 01-08, 004315 04-08
FLOSBACH CW 002962 03-04
FLUCH N 003503 03-15
FLYNN D 001318 02-03
FLYNN JR 002236 02-13, 004244 04-04
FOBES JL 004194 04-04
FOG R 000890 01-15
FOGARI R 002070 02-10
FOGH-ANDERSEN P 003484 03-15
FOLBERGROVA J 001134 02-03
FOLEY K 000898 01-16
FOLEY TL 004196 04-04

FOLGERING H 004456 04-11
FOLLATH F 000909 01-16
FOLTIN RW 003110 03-04
FONBERG E 001620 02-04 , 003030 03-04
FONDARAI J 001980 02-09
FONG JC 003664 04-01
FONLUPT P 001227 02-03 , 002816 03-03
FONNUM F 002774 03-03
FONTAGNE J 004632 04-15
FONTAINE F 003305 03-11
FONTAINE J 001228 02-03
FONTAN M 000589 01-09 , 003313 03-11 ,
  003404 03-13
FONTANA CJ 002747 03-03
FONTANI G 004081 04-04
FOO SH 006698 01-11 , 002342 02-14
FORCHETTI C 002090 02-11 , 002312 02-14 ,
  002371 02-15 , 002719 03-03 , 003085
  03-04
FORD DH 001367 02-03
FORD KE 003125 03-05
FORD RD 000386 01-04
FORDE JH 003752 04-03
FORETTE F 000596 01-09 , 003324 03-11
FORINO V 003591 03-17
FORLONI GL 003758 04-03
FORN J 000291 01-03
FORNARO P 004507 04-13
FORREST IS 001229 02-03 , 001867 02-06
FORSMAN A 000888 01-15 , 001230 02-03 ,
  002590 02-17
FORSMAN L 004508 04-13
FORSTER A 003342 03-11
FORSTER B 002505 02-16 , 004403 04-09
FORSTER C 004113 04-04
FORTUNE D 000370 01-04 , 003662 04-01
FOSSOM L 001790 02-04
FOSTER DO 001231 02-03
FOSTER GA 001578 02-04
FOSTER JA 004114 04-04
FOURCADE J 003441 03-14
FOURNIER E 003513 03-15
FOUSSARD-BLANPIN O 003689 04-02
FOUTZ AS 003374 01-04
FOVALL P 000675 01-11
FOWLER LK 002324 02-14
FOWLER S 002989 03-04
FOX DA 004157 04-04
FOX PC 000738 01-12
FRAJESE G 004431 04-11
FRANCES H 001072 02-02 , 001232 02-03 ,
  003633 03-17
FRANCIS DL 004087 04-04
FRANCIS IB 004620 04-15
FRANCIS RL 000368 01-04 , 000369 01-04 ,
  001600 02-04
FRANCO A 002379 02-15
FRANCO S 000015 01-02
FRANCO-MORSELLI R 003343 03-11
FRANCOIS M 002030 02-09
FRANK LA 003278 03-10
FRANK M 003054 03-04
FRANKE L 002049 02-09
FRANKLIN KBJ 000387 01-04
FRANKLIN M 001956 02-08 , 004329 04-08
FRANKS GJ 003363 03-11
FRANTIK E 002332 02-14
FRANTZ AG 002871 03-03
FRANZ DN 004040 04-03
FRANZEN G 003542 03-15
FRASER HF 004610 04-15
FRASER S 004329 04-08 , 004520 04-13
FRATTINI P 000757 01-13 , 004675 04-16
FRATTOLA L 002121 02-11
FRAUD J 001902 02-07
FRAY PJ 002484 02-16
FRAYSSINET R 003524 03-15
FRAZER A 000940 01-17 , 001463 02-03 ,
  001991 02-09
FRAZINGARO S 004717 04-17
FRECKER RC 004552 04-14
FREDA J 001596 02-04
FREDERICKS AB 001621 02-04
FREDERICKSON RCA 002720 03-03
FREDERIKSEN S 001982 02-09 , 001983 02-09
FREDHOLM B 001238 02-03
FREDRICKSON JW 003413 03-13 , 004619 04-
  15 , 004620 04-15
FREED W 000255 01-03 , 000869 01-15 ,
  001233 02-03 , 001622 02-04 , 001672

  02-04 , 001928 02-08 , 002992 03-04 ,
  002993 03-04
FREEDMAN AM 004712 04-17
FREEDMAN DX 004448 04-11
FREEDMAN MS 002721 03-03
FREEDMAN R 000095 01-03 , 000197 01-03 ,
  000209 01-03 , 001848 02-05 , 003793
  04-03 , 003926 04-03
FREEDMAN SB 002722 03-03 , 004055 04-03
FREEMAN CG 003867 04-03
FREEMAN H 002544 02-17 , 003171 03-08 ,
  004611 04-15
FREEMAN JM 004447 04-11
FREGLY MJ 001623 02-04 , 004237 04-04
FREGNAN GB 001391 02-03 , 001577 02-04 ,
  004115 04-04 , 004116 04-04
FREIRE GL 004042 04-03
FRENK H 000494 01-04 , 004114 04-04
FRESIA P 001481 02-03
FREUND D 001624 02-04
FREUND JL 001624 02-04
FREWIN DB 000682 01-11
FREY H 000096 01-03 , 000097 01-03 ,
  000785 01-13
FREY WH 002825 03-03
FREYHAN FA 000938 01-17 , 000939 01-17 ·
FREZZA G 003222 03-09
FRIDMAN AL 000506 01-04
FRIED PA 000513 01-05
FRIEDEL RO 004411 04-09
FRIEDHOFF A 003277 03-10 , 003407 03-13 ,
  003927 04-03 , 003939 04-03 , 003989
  04-03 , 004312 04-08
FRIEDMAN AM 004293 04-06
FRIEDMAN DP 002723 03-03
FRIEDMAN E 000203 01-03 , 003794 04-03 ,
  004383 04-09
FRIEDMAN HJ 001625 02-04 , 002994 03-04
FRIEDMAN J 000013 01-13
FRIEDMAN MB 000183 01-03
FRIEDMAN P 002784 01-13
FRIEL P 000177 01-03 , 000728 01-11
FRIGENI V 003126 03-05
FRIGERIO C 001391 02-03
FRIGO GM 002276 02-13
FRIIS ML 002127 02-11 , 003484 03-15
FRISCHKNECHT HR 001626 02-04 , 001776
  02-04 , 001777 02-04
FRITH CD 004423 04-10
FRITZ LC 003973 04-03
FRITZ RR 000148 01-03
FROHMAN CE 001919 02-08
FROHMAN LA 000908 01-16 , 003920 04-03
FROLICH JC 000622 01-09
FROMM GH 002122 02-11 , 002724 03-03
FROSCHER W 003314 03-11
FROWEIN HW 004563 04-14
FRY BW 003795 04-03
FRY JP 001234 02-03 , 001235 02-03
FRYDMAN ML 001231 02-03
FRYE GD 001813 02-04 , 003037 03-04 ,
  004195 04-04
FUCHS CZ 000594 01-09
FUENTES AM 001159 02-03
FUJII I 004636 04-15
FUJII T 000515 01-05
FUJIMOTO JM 002800 03-03
FUJIMOTO M 002725 03-03
FUJIMOTO S 000098 01-03 , 000199 01-03 ,
  000260 01-03
FUJIMURA Y 001659 02-04
FUJISAKI T 003692 04-02
FUJITA A 003692 04-02
FUJITA N 000099 01-03
FUJITA T 003187 03-08 , 003266 03-09
FUJIWARA M 000210 01-03 , 001548 02-03
FUJIWARA T 001472 02-03
FUKUDA H 003807 04-03
FUKUDA N 003052 03-04
FUKUDA T 002174 02-11 , 003093 03-04
FUKUDA Y 003877 04-03
FUKUHARA K 000515 01-05
FUKUHARA T 003179 03-08 , 003315 03-11 ,
  003415 03-13 , 003416 03-13
FUKUMORI R 001236 02-03 , 001797 02-04
FUKUSHIMA H 004448 04-11
FUKUSHIMA Y 002442 02-15
FULLE D 001126 02-03
FULLER RW 000100 01-03 , 000101 01-03 ,
  001237 02-03 , 002726 03-03 , 002995
  03-04 , 003796 04-03

FULLER TA 000222 01-03
FULTON T 000191 01-03 , 000388 01-04
FUMAGALLI P 003801 04-03
FUNG D 000734 01-11
FUNG YK 002996 03-04 , 004117 04-04
FUQUA W 003392 03-11
FURMAN JM 002997 03-04
FURUKAWA K 000152 01-03
FURUKAWA S 001320 02-03
FURUKAWA T 000515 01-05 , 001808 02-04 ,
  004256 04-04
FUSEK J 000127 01-03 , 000389 01-04 ,
  000420 01-04 , 001274 02-03 , 001689
  02-04
FUXE K 001096 02-03 , 001238 02-03 ,
  001239 02-03 , 001240 02-03 , 002727
  03-03
FYER A 000632 01-09 , 003240 03-09 ,
  003241 03-09
FYER AF 003409 03-13

G

GABAY S 001271 02-03
GABRIEL E 003251 03-09
GABRIEL SM 000051 01-03
GABRYS MC 001613 02-04
GACHY B 004307 04-07
GADOW KD 000676 01-11 , 000812 01-14 ,
  004449 04-11 , 004713 04-17 , 004714
  04-17
GAGE FH 000390 01-04
GAGLIARDI R 000669 01-11
GAGNE P 004450 04-11
GAGNIERE B 002108 02-11
GAGNON A 002010 02-09
GAHWILER BH 001241 02-03
GAIARDI M 000338 01-04 , 003555 03-16
GAIDE MS 001242 02-03
GAILLARD J 002325 02-14
GAILLARD P 000842 01-15
GAILLARD-SIZARET C 000842 01-15
GAINER H 001053 02-01 , 001148 02-03
GAITZ CM 002545 02-17
GAJEWSKA S 003050 03-04
GAL EM 004715 04-17
GAL J 002235 02-13
GALDABINI JJ 004655 04-15
GALDAMES DG 000102 01-03
GALE K 001140 01-03 , 001243 02-03 ,
  001627 02-04 , 002163 02-11 , 003797
  04-03 , 004018 04-03
GALEAZZI G 003466 03-15
GALIANA J 001189 02-03
GALINA ZH 000337 01-04
GALLAGER DW 000038 01-03 , 000103 01-03 ,
  001502 02-03 , 001503 02-03 , 001504
  02-03 , 001842 02-05 , 002912 03-03
GALLAGHER AM 001628 02-04 , 002998 03-04 ,
  003798 04-03
GALLAGHER RM 003592 03-17
GALLAND MC 002319 02-14
GALLET G 002123 02-11
GALLI A 000104 01-03
GALLIVAN JV 000448 01-04
GALLO V 000185 01-03
GALTEAU MM 001507 02-03
GALVA MD 002863 03-03
GALVAN M 000034 01-03 , 001244 02-03
GALZIGNA L 000105 01-03
GAMBLE S 001817 02-04 , 001858 02-05 ,
  002509 02-16 , 004204 04-05 , 004423
  04-10
GAMBOA A 002855 03-03
GAMBURG AL 003172 03-08
GAMMEL G 002004 02-09
GAMMON GD 000843 01-15
GANDER RE 002485 02-16
GANGULY DK 004096 04-04
GANNAWAY AJ 003316 03-11
GANZ AJ 000705 01-11
GARATTINI S 000036 01-03 , 001157 02-03 ,
  002521 02-17 , 002546 02-17 , 002602
  02-17 , 003758 04-03
GARBANATI JA 000375 01-04
GARBARG M 001054 02-01
GARBER HI 001337 02-03
GARCEAU D 001547 02-03
GARCIA AG 001357 02-03

GOMES C 000040 01-03
GOMES UCR 002735 03-03
GOMEZ B 001355 02-03
GOMEZ F 001930 02-08
GOMEZ M 003338 03-11
GOMEZ-JARABO G 001558 02-04
GOMITA Y 003004 03-04
GOMMEREN W 000186 01-03 , 004033 04-03
GONCALVES N 001996 02-09
GONNARD P 004029 04-03
GONZALEZ C 001176 02-03
GONZALEZ JP 002736 03-03
GONZALEZ JV 002112 02-11
GONZALEZ LP 001683 02-04 , 003005 03-04
GONZALEZ MONCLUS E 002588 02-17 ,
  002589 02-17
GONZALEZ-VILCHES J 002849 03-03 , 002850
  03-03 , 002851 03-03
GOODALE DB 002236 02-13 , 004244 04-04
GOODE DJ 003318 03-11
GOODE PG 000516 01-05
GOODMAN RR 000990 01-17
GOODNICK PJ 004367 04-09 , 004369 04-09
GOODWIN F 003357 03-11 , 003388 03-11
GOODWIN FK 000225 01-03 , 001536 02-03 ,
  001984 02-09 , 002628 02-17 , 002972
  03-04 , 003250 03-09 , 004689 04-16 ,
  004708 04-17
GOODWIN PJ 000517 01-05
GOOTJES J 000005 01-01
GOPINATHAN G 002342 02-14 , 002384 02-
  15 , 003319 03-11
GORBATKO LG 004633 04-15
GORDIYENKO ZP 004633 04-15
GORDON A 001257 02-03 , 001914 02-08
GORDON C 002737 03-03 , 003488 03-15
GORDON J 001636 02-04 , 003385 03-11 ,
  004268 04-05
GORDON LS 002862 03-03
GORDON W 000913 01-17
GORELICK DA 004360 04-09
GORGONE G 001200 02-03
GORI E 003801 04-03
GORI G 003065 03-04
GORISSEN H 002489 02-16 , 003896 04-03
GORKIN RA 001433 02-03
GORMAN J 003394 03-11 , 003409 03-13
GORMEZANO I 001637 02-04
GORODETZKY ÇW 003594 03-17 , 004610 04-
  15
GORSKI H 004660 04-15
GORZALKA BB 002975 03-04
GOSENFELD LF 004352 04-09 , 004521 04-13
GOSLING JA 001955 02-08
GOSPE SM 003806 04-03
GOSSAITI P 004503 04-13
GOTESTAM KG 000804 01-14
GOTHERT M 000111 01-03 , 001258 02-03
GOTO M 003807 04-03
GOTSICK JE 002983 03-04
GOTTBERG E 001275 02-03
GOTTESMAN II 002825 03-03
GOTTLIEB P 000591 01-09
GOTTSCHALK LA 002067 02-10
GOUDEMAND M 000589 01-09
GOUDIE AJ 004121 04-04
GOUREVITCH M 004613 04-15
GOUT R 000021 01-03 , 003682 04-02
GOUVIER WD 000394 01-04
GOUZOU A 000680 01-11
GOVONI S 001480 02-03 , 003808 04-03
GOWDEY CW 001746 02-04
GOY RW 003017 03-04
GOYA N 000696 01-11
GOZDALSKA J 000719 01-11
GRAB EL 000787 01-13
GRABOWSKA-ANDEN M 001102 02-03 ,
  002372 02-15 , 004065 04-04
GRACE AA 000023 01-03 , 001153 02-03
GRADY RW 001836 02-05
GRAF L 003193 03-08
GRAFE P 001244 02-03
GRAHAM J 003552 03-15
GRAHAM JDP 001190 02-03
GRAHAM LTJ 000145 01-03
GRAHAME-SMITH DG 001412 02-03 , 001486
  02-03 , 001487 02-03 , 003399 03-13
GRAM LF 002033 02-09 , 004370 04-09
GRAMSCH C 003837 04-03
GRANACHER RP 000961 01-17

GRANATA AR 000223 01-03
GRANDADAM A 004105 04-04
GRANDISON L 002738 03-03 , 003809 04-03
GRANT SJ 002910 03-03 , 003810 04-03
GRASSI A 003801 04-03
GRATTON OA 001106 02-03
GRATTON I 002928 03-03
GRAU JW 001707 02-04
GRAVEL G 002119 02-11
GRAVEM AO 000890 01-15
GRAY DS 002975 03-04
GRAY JA 001757 02-04 , 002069 02-10
GRAY PN 000765 01-13
GRAZE KK 003489 03-15
GREDAL O 002676 03-03
GREDEN J 004359 04-09
GREELEY GH 003811 04-03
GREEN AL 000900 01-16
GREEN AR 001184 02-03 , 001686 02-04 ,
  002444 02-15 , 002971 03-04 , 003736
  04-03
GREEN DE 001229 02-03 , 001867 02-06
GREEN DJ 001438 02-03
GREEN J 000112 01-03 , 001369 02-03 , ·
  002413 02-15 , 004557 04-13
GREEN KF 001811 02-04 , 003812 04-03
GREEN L 003320 03-11
GREEN V 002739 03-03
GREEN WH 003361 03-11
GREENBERG LH 000113 01-03 , 001529 02-03
GREENBERG S 001259 02-03
GREENBLATT DJ 000114 01-03 , 000681 01-
  11 , 000766 01-13 , 000784 01-13 ,
  000789 01-13 , 000790 01-13 , 000831
  01-15 , 000968 01-17 , 002206 02-13 ,
  003161 03-07 , 003284 03-10 , 003352
  03-11 , 003410 03-13 , 004432 04-11
GREENBLÄTT EN 001093 02-02 , 004122 04-
  04
GREENFIELD AA 002212 02-13
GREENFIELD S 003665 04-01
GREENGARD P 000291 01-03
GREENHILL L 003321 03-11
GREGOIRE F 002099 02-11
GREGSON AN 003071 03-04
GREIL W 001570 02-04 , 002227 02-13
GREISMAN P 000655 01-11
GREISS KC 002070 02-10
GREIST JH 002005 02-09 , 002244 02-13 ,
  003498 03-15
GRESTY MA 002376 02-15
GREWAL RS 000154 01-03
GRIAUZDE ML 001260 02-03
GRIEB P 003971 04-03   ····
GRIERSMITH BT 001203 02-03 , 002740 03-
  03 , 003778 04-03
GRIESBACH PH 000717 01-11
GRIFFI PG 001460 02-03
GRIFFIN HD 002741 03-03
GRIFFITH DNW 002071 02-10
GRIFFITHS RR 000395 01-04 , 002314 02-14 ,
  004123 04-04 , 004566 04-14 , 004582
  04-14
GRIGNOLO A 003813 04-03
GRIJALVA CV 000096 01-04 , 001638 02-04
GRILLY DM 001639 02-04 , 004124 04-04
GRIMALDI LF 003571 03-16
GRIPENBERG J 003814 04-03 , 003815 04-03
GRISAR T 004694 04-16
GRISOLIA S 002744 03-03
GRISSETTE DP 000518 01-05
GRISSOM T 002160 02-11
GRITTI P 003042 03-14
GROB P 003734 04-03
GROF E 003402 03-13
GROF P 003402 03-13
GROFOVA I 002774 03-03
GROH J 002054 02-09
GROH KR 001409 02-03
GROH U 002127 02-11
GROOM GP 003529 03-15 , 003530 03-15
GROPPETTI A 001422 02-03
GROSS C 003451 03-14
GROSS G 002744 03-03 , 003816 04-03 ,
  004325 04-08
GROSS K 001793 02-04
GROSS PM 003817 04-03
GROSS RA 000089 01-03 , 000115 01-03

GROSSMAN A 001127 02-03 , 003731 04-03 ,
  003732 04-03
GROTH J 004300 04-06
GROUILLER A 003691 04-02
GROVE J 002237 02-13
GROVES PM 004229 04-04
GROVESTINE D 001535 02-03
GROWDON JH 000942 01-17 , 002473 02-15 ,
  004612 04-15
GRUBE E 003352 03-11
GRUENAU C 002354 02-14
GRUNBAUM A 003595 03-17
GRUNBERGER J 000720 01-11 , 000788 01-13
  001895 02-07 , 002166 02-11
GRÜOL DL 000116 01-03
GRUPP LA 001344 02-03
GRUSZCZYNSKI W 000626 01-09 , 000719
  01-11
GRUZELIER J 003174 03-08 , 003443 03-14
GUALTIERI CT 000849 01-15 , 002409 02-15 ,
  004614 04-15
GUANDALINI A 004717 04-17
GUARDUCCI R 002093 02-11
GUARINO RA 002059 02-10
GUARNERI P 002743 03-03
GUBERMAN AS 004732 04-17
GUCHHAIT RB 003818 04-03
GUDKA HV 002394 02-15
GUEDES RCA 002752 03-03
GUELEN PJM 000541 01-07
GUELFI JD 003596 03-17
GUENSBERGER E 001997 02-09
GUEREMY C 003898 04-03
GUERIN B 000070 01-03
GUERRERO MD 000117 01-03
GUERRERO-MUNOZ F 000117 01-03
GUERRET M 004530 04-13
GUERRI C 002744 03-03
GUERRINI A 001998 02-09
GUEST JF 000171 01-03
GUGLER R 003314 03-11
GUGUSHVILI LN 001640 02-04 , 004125 04-04
GUIDI E 003114 03-04
GUIDOTTI A 000397 01-04 , 001012 02-01 ,
  001045 02-01 , 001182 02-03 , 001261
  02-03 , 001262 02-03 , 001263 02-03 ,
  001849 02-05 , 002642 03-01 , 002819
  03-03 , 003809 04-03
GUILBAUD G 000175 01-03
GUILLARD P 002094 02-11
GUILLEMINAULT C 000374 01-04
GUILLERY T 002137 02-11
GUILLOUX F 000176 01-03 , 003899 04-03
GUILMOT PH 001920 02-08
GUIMON J 004312 04-08
GUINN MM 003127 03-05
GUISADO E 000398 01-04
GUISO G 001157 02-03
GUIVERNAU M 000439 01-04
GULATI OD 003772 04-03
GULMANN NC 000659 01-11
GULUMOGLU A 001059 02-01
GUNDERSEN CB 003819 04-03 , 003820 04-03
GUNDERSON CH 002415 02-15
GUNGOR M 000169 01-03
GUNION MW 003821 04-03
GUNNE LM 000685 01-11
GUPTA BS 004581 04-14
GUPTA G 003180 03-08
GURAM MS 002410 02-15
GURANOWSKI A 001010 02-01 , 001021 02-
  01
GURBANI NK 001682 02-04
GURD JW 002721 03-03
GUREVICH M 000236 01-03
GUREVICH ZP 003384 03-11
GURWICH E 000872 01-15
GUSTAFSSON J 000273 01-03
GUTHEIL TG 000911 01-17
GUTIERREZ M 004312 04-08
GUTJAHR CL 004467 04-11
GUTTERIDGE NJA 001591 02-04
GUY W 002026 02-09 , 002080 02-10 ,
  004333 04-08 , 004392 04-09
GUYDA H 002253 02-13
GUYOT M 000777 01-13
GUZ A 002164 02-11
GUZIK H 001019 02-01
GUZMAN-FLORES C 001612 02-04

GYMOESE E 002229 02-13
GYORGY L 003822 04-03
GYORY AN 000943 01-17

H

HAARMANN I 001283 02-03 , 003846 04-03
HAAS AE 002830 03-03 , 002831 03-03
HAAS S 001909 02-08
HAASE H 000944 01-17 , 002548 02-17 ,
  003234 03-09
HABARA T 004551 04-13
HABER S 003006 03-04 , 003007 03-04
HABERMAN SJ 002481 02-16
HABERMANN E 003709 04-03
HABLE CP 001531 02-03
HACKENBERG P 000118 01-03
HACKETT RB 000519 01-05
HACKSELL U 000399 01-04
HADAWAY PF 000530 01-06
HADGRAFT J 000007 01-02
HADJICHRISTOS C 003466 03-15
HADJIKONSTANTINOU M 004471 04-11
HADZHIKOSTOVA H 000119 01-03
HAEFELY W 002646 03-02
HAEUSLER G 001264 02-03
HAFLER D 004653 04-15
HAGA K 003823 04-03
HAGA T 003823 04-03
HAGEMAN WE 000512 01-05
HAGERMAN LM 000017 01-03 , 001101 02-
  03
HAHN EF 000400 01-04
HAHN J 004075 04-04
HAHN RA 001265 02-03
HAHN Z 003729 04-03
HAIDUKEWYCH D 003367 03-11
HAIER RJ 001971 02-09 , 003211 03-09
HAIGH E 001266 02-03
HAIGLER HJ 001267 02-03 , 003849 04-03
HAILER AW 001013 02-01 , 002219 02-13
HAILSTONE MH 003867 04-03
HAINER V 000570 01-08
HAJNOVA R 000663 01-11
HAKANSSON CG 004012 04-03
HAKER O 004343 04-08
HALARIS AE 000125 01-03 , 000312 01-03 ,
  003227 03-09 , 003771 04-03
HALASZ B 002817 03-03
HALBREICH U 000752 01-13 , 000874 01-15 ,
  002238 02-13 , 003228 03-09 , 003411
  03-13 , 004685 04-19
HALDEMAN S 003322 03-11
HALDERS SG 004298 04-06
HALE MS 003481 03-15
HALKOVA E 000548 01-08 , 001908 02-08 ,
  001925 02-08
HALL ED 002745 03-03
HALL H 000120 01-03 , 001238 02-03 ,
  001240 02-03 , 003824 04-03 , 003991
  04-03
HALL KR 002216 02-13
HALL MD 004032 04-03
HALL PV 003853 04-03
HALLBERG H 004126 04-04
HALLCHER LM 003712 04-03
HALLER C 001999 02-09
HALLETT M 001164 02-03
HALLIWELL JV 001641 02-04
HALLOCK M 003794 04-03
HALPERIN DA 004326 04-08
HALPERN F 000752 01-13 , 000776 01-13 ,
  000874 01-15 , 002238 02-13 , 003321
  03-11 , 003411 03-13 , 004405 04-09
HALPERN LM 003327 03-03
HALSEY MJ 001106 02-03
HAMALA K 001268 02-03
HAMER R 003487 03-15
HAMET P 000864 01-15
HAMILTON HE 000538 01-06
HAMILTON M 002487 02-16
HAMILTON W 001984 02-05
HAMMER GV 000907 01-16
HAMMER JS 000835 01-15
HAMMETT S 001822 02-04
HAMMOND DL 000121 01-03 , 000122 01-03
HAMMOND EJ 002758 03-03
HAMMOND NV 003443 03-14
HAMON M 000123 01-03 , 000213 01-03 ,
  000214 01-03 , 001269 02-03 , 003825
  04-03

HAMOUZ W 000592 01-09
HAMOVIT J 003242 03-09
HAMPRECHT B 000308 01-03 , 002677 03-03 ,
  003975 04-03
HANBAUER I 001182 02-03 , 001270 02-03 ,
  001403 02-03
HANDELMANN GE 001398 02-03
HANDFORD HA 000945 01-17
HANDLEY S 001146 02-03 , 004078 04-04
HANER H 003490 03-15
HANIN I 000631 01-09 , 004290 04-06 ,
  004511 04-13 , 004679 04-16
HANING RV 003017 03-04
HANKE H 004516 04-13
HANLON TE 000904 01-16 , 003182 03-08
HANSEN BS 000767 01-13
HANSEN EL 001716 02-04
HANSEN HE 002465 02-15
HANSEN T 002229 02-13 , 002329 02-14
HANSLICEK L 000600 01-09
HANSON DR 001572 02-04
HANSON G 003826 04-03
HANSSON E 002746 03-03
HANTZBERG P 002600 02-17
HANUS H 000593 01-09 , 002000 02-09
HANUS L 001022 02-01 , 001023 02-01
HANZLICEK L 000542 01-07
HARA S 003008 03-04
HARA T 002559 02-17
HARACZ JL 001642 02-04 , 001643 02-04
HARADA Y 001691 02-04
HARBERT CA 001092 02-02
HARDEBO JE 003781 04-03
HARDEN TK 002820 03-03
HARDING GFA 004513 04-13
HARDING JW 003953 04-03
HARDT W 000780 01-13
HARDY C 001644 02-04
HARDY RA 001093 02-02
HARIHARASUBRAMANIAN N 000881 01-15
HARIK SI 002798 03-03
HARLAND RC 000073 01-02
HARMAN AW 000682 01-11
HARMANT J 004487 04-17
HARMAR AJ 004100 04-04
HARMATZ JS 000766 01-13 , 004432 04-11
HARMS D 003491 03-15
HARPER AM 003817 04-03
HARPF H 003503 03-15
HARRER G 003597 03-17 , 004718 04-17
HARRIS B 000683 01-11
HARRIS DW 000124 01-03
HARRIS GJ 001853 02-05
HARRIS J 001271 02-03
HARRIS LS 000354 01-04 , 004084 04-04
HARRIS PA 003497 03-15
HARRIS PQ 002480 02-16
HARRIS RA 000479 01-04 , 001645 02-04 ,
  003600 03-17 , 003827 04-03 , 004127
  04-04
HARRIS SC 000906 01-16
HARRISON REW 002636 03-01
HARRISON-READ PE 000401 01-04 , 001646
  02-04 , 003229 03-09
HARSTON CT 002328 02-14
HART SL 001245 02-03 , 002783 03-03
HARTFORD JT 002545 02-17
HARTMAN BK 000239 01-03 , 003974 04-03
HARTMAN E 000946 01-17
HARTMAN J 000125 01-03 , 002549 02-17
HARTMANN G 000803 01-14
HARTMANN H 003490 03-15
HARTO-TRUAX N 003227 03-09
HARTSE KM 000822 01-14 , 002357 02-14
HARTUNG M 000711 01-11
HARVAN PA 001795 02-04
HARVENGT C 000181 01-03
HARVEY JA 000646 01-04 , 001637 02-04
HARZER K 003671 04-01
HASAN AM 001831 02-05
HASAN MZ 001831 02-05
HASEGAWA AT 001853 02-05
HASKETT R 003459 04-09
HASSANYEH F 002001 02-09
HASSMANNOVA J 000803 01-14 , 000815 01-
  14 , 001647 02-04
HASUE I 003544 03-15
HASUZAWA H 002349 02-14 , 003450 03-14
HATA F 001272 02-03

HATCHELL PC 001648 02-04
HATCHER J 004324 04-08
HAUBRICH DR 003828 04-03
HAUG T 000804 01-14
HAUGE M 003484 03-15
HAUGHTON H 002318 02-14
HAUHART RE 004281 04-05
HAUPTMANN M 004547 04-13
HAUSEN AC 002411 02-15
HAVEMANN U 001649 02-04
HAWK B 004614 04-15
HAWKING F 002546 02-17
HAWKINS MF 001544 02-03 , 002952 03-04 ,
  003026 03-04
HAWKSWORTH GM 004740 04-17
HAWTHORNE JN 002741 03-03
HAYASHI S 001273 02-03
HAYASHI T 001293 02-03 , 004128 04-04
HAYCOCK DA 003829 04-03
HAYCOOK W 004557 04-13
HAYS SE 003830 04-03
HAYSTEAD TAJ 001759 02-04 , 003072 03-04 ,
  004208 04-04
HAYWARD TL 003757 04-03
HAZAMA H 000860 01-15 , 003179 03-08 ,
  003315 03-11 , 003415 03-13 , 003416
  03-13 , 004388 04-09
HAZUM E 003581 03-17 , 003746 04-03
HEADLEY PM 002633 03-01
HEALEY ML 000403 01-04
HEALTON EB 000835 01-15
HEAPY CG 001578 02-04
HEATH E 003857 04-03
HEATH JE 002737 03-03
HEATH RG 002747 03-03
HEAULME M 003898 04-03
HEBDIGE S 002276 02-13
HECHT M 004467 04-11
HECHTMAN L 004454 04-11
HECK DG 002974 03-04
HECKL K 000561 01-08
HECQUET S 003155 03-07
HEDBERG A 000207 01-03
HEDLER L 002748 03-03 , 003983 04-03
HEDLEY-WHYTE J 003894 04-03
HEDLUND B 003022 03-03 , 003860 04-03
HEDRYCH A 000290 01-03
HEFFNER TG 002632 02-17
HEFTI F 000202 01-03 , 003323 03-11
HEGDE R 003259 03-09
HEGLI D 002749 03-03
HEGSTRAND LR 003021 03-04
HEID J 003135 03-06
HEIDRICH H 004309 04-07
HEIKKILA JJ 003831 04-03 , 003832 04-03
HEIKKILA RE 000404 01-04 , 001650 02-04 ,
  004129 04-04 , 004130 04-04
HEIKKINEN ER 004542 04-13
HEIMAN EM 003598 03-17
HEIMANN M 000335 01-04
HEIN DW 004132 04-04
HEINONEN E 003814 04-03 , 003815 04-03
HEINRICH K 000562 01-08
HEINZ G 000414 01-04
HEINZE WJ 000135 01-03 , 001073 02-02
HEIWALL PO 003897 04-03
HELKE CJ 001024 02-01 , 001222 02-03
HELLER A 001340 02-03 , 002654 03-03
HELMCHEN H 004371 04-09
HELMESTE DM 000300 01-03 , 004131 04-04
HELWIG C 003306 03-11
HEMMENDINGER R 002717 03-03
HEMMINGSEN R 000126 01-03 , 000850 01-
  15
HEMMINKI E 002550 02-17 , 003599 03-17
HEMRICK-LUECKE SK 000100 01-03
HENDEL J 002229 02-13 , 002329 02-14
HENDERSON G 001408 02-03
HENDERSON JD 001534 02-03
HENDERSON VW 003492 03-15
HENDLEY ED 002685 03-03
HENDRICK JC 001565 02-04
HENDRICKS C 004233 04-04
HENICHART JP 003653 04-01
HENINGER GR 001496 02-03 , 002098 02-11 ,
  002911 03-03 , 003418 03-13 , 004502
  04-13
HENNEBERRY RC 001279 02-03
HENNING JM 003009 03-04

HENNING M 000231 01-03 , 003965 04-03
HENRIET I 003895 04-03
HENRIKSEN SJ 000580 01-09 , 003136 03-06
HENRY J 002254 02-13 , 003175 03-08 ,
003324 03-11
HENRY JF 000596 01-09
HENSBY CN 001132 02-03
HENSCHEN A 003740 04-03
HENSELING M 000535 01-06
HENSLEY MJ 002128 02-11
HERBERG LJ 003560 03-16
HERBERT J 001718 02-04
HERBERT M 002365 02-14
HERBET A 000213 01-03 , 000214 01-03 ,
001269 02-03 , 003825 04-03
HEREDIA E 002217 02-13
HERETIK A 000707 01-11
HERINK J 000127 01-03 , 000389 01-04 ,
001274 02-03 , 001689 02-04
HERKEN H 002962 03-04
HERKENHAM M 001025 02-01 , 001050 02-
01 , 003737 04-03 , 003833 04-03
HERKERT E 004619 04-15
HERLING S 001651 02-04 , 003010 03-04 ,
003106 03-04 , 004132 04-04 , 004133
04-04 , 004134 04-04 , 004719 04-17
HERMAN BH 003011 03-04
HERMAN JP 003792 04-03
HERMANN A 003834 04-03
HERNANDEZ L 001275 02-03 , 001652 02-04 ,
003015 03-04
HERNANDEZ MF 002967 03-04
HERNANDEZ RJ 001276 02-03
HERNDON JG 003012 03-04
HERNING RI 002209 02-13 , 004512 04-13
HERRICK CE 004513 04-13
HERRMANN PW 004650 04-15
HERRMANN WM 000768 01-13 , 002239 02-
13 , 003412 03-13 , 004455 04-11
HERTZ L 003836 04-03
HERVY C 003279 03-10
HERVY M 000596 01-09 , 003324 03-11
HERZ A 000029 01-03 , 001234 02-03 ,
001235 02-03 , 001283 02-03 , 001918
02-08 , 003088 03-04 , 003837 04-03 ,
004104 04-04 , 004321 04-08 , 004322
04-08
HESPE W 000005 01-01
HESS J 003669 04-01
HESSELGREN T 002208 02-13
HESTER JB 001074 02-02 , 001075 02-02 ,
001076 02-02
HESTNESS J 000740 01-12
HEUCKE U 001082 02-02
HEURTEAUX C 002299 02-13
HEVOR T 003838 04-03
HEWITT J 004027 04-03
HEXUM T 001182 02-03
HEY L 002003 02-09
HEYKANTS J 000758 01-13 , 001932 02-08
HEYM J 003018 03-04
HICKS TP 002752 03-03
HIEBLE JP 001255 02-03
HIEP A 004635 04-15
HIER DB 000947 01-17
HIKIJI A 004618 04-15
HIKITA T 003416 03-13
HILAKIVI I 000405 01-04
HILDENBRAND G 003314 03-11
HILL DR 003839 04-03
HILL HF 001277 02-03
HILL JM 001278 02-03
HILL M 004114 04-04
HILL RC 003013 03-04
HILL SY 000406 01-04
HILLER JM 000128 01-03 , 003840 04-03 ,
004300 04-06
HILLIER K 003841 04-03
HILMY M 000738 01-12
HIMMELHOCH JM 000594 01-09 , 004511 04-
13

HINDMARCH I 000579 01-09 , 002330 02-14
, 002331 02-14 , 002351 02-14
HINGTGEN J 000521 01-05 , 001730 02-04
HINKOVA L 000473 01-04
HINOKI M 003842 04-03 , 004387 04-09
HIRAI K 003710 04-03 , 003843 04-03
HIRANO M 000212 01-03 , 002781 03-03 ,
004608 04-15
HIRATA A 000099 01-03
HIRATA F 001001 02-01 , 001002 02-01 ,
001026 02-01 , 001118 02-03 , 001188
02-03 , 001279 02-03 , 001502 02-03 ,
001546 02-03 , 002919 03-03
HIRAYAMA K 002309 02-13
HIROSE K 003692 04-02
HIROTA R 003893 04-03
HIROZ C 004615 04-15
HIRSCH JD 002836 03-03 , 002915 03-03 ,
003844 04-03
HIRSCH S 001921 02-08 , 002182 02-11 ,
003174 03-08
HIRSCHOWITZ J 000555 01-08
HIRSH KR 003752 04-03
HIRST M 001746 02-04
HITCHCOCK ER 002551 02-17
HITOMI M 000493 01-04
HITRI A 001845 02-05
HITZEMANN R 001280 02-03 , 001653 02-04
HIZAL A 003788 04-03
HJEDS H 003693 04-02
HJELMELAND LM 001056 02-01
HJELMSTED A 000659 01-11
HJERPE C 004142 04-04
HJORTH S 000399 01-04
HO AKS 004269 04-05
HO BT 001779 02-04 , 001789 02-04
HO C 001281 02-03 , 004269 04-05
HO IK 003085 01-04 , 001619 02-04 ,
002753 03-03 , 003600 03-17
HO L 004150 04-04
HOBBIGER F 003123 03-05
HOBI V 004623 04-15
HOBUSCH D 004481 04-11
HODDES ES 003014 03-04
HODGE GK 004135 04-04
HODGES KK 002418 02-15
HOEBEL BG 003015 03-04
HOEFKE W 001259 02-03
HOES MJAJM 000541 01-07 , 004456 04-11
HOFER MA 001654 02-04
HOFFER B 000080 01-03 , 000095 01-03 ,
000107 01-03 , 000178 01-03 , 000197
01-03 , 000209 01-03 , 001382 02-03 ,
001848 02-05 , 002502 02-16 , 003926
04-03 , 003957 04-03
HOFFET H 004457 04-11
HOFFMAN AR 001282 02-03 , 001318 02-03
HOFFMAN BB 000901 01-16
HOFFMAN BF 003493 03-15
HOFFMAN SJ 001055 02-01 , 001088 02-02
HOFFMAN WE 003845 04-03
HOFFMANN A 003396 03-12
HOFFMANN I 002751 03-03
HOFFMANN R 001624 02-04
HOFFMANN WE 003844 03-15
HOFFMEISTER F 000684 01-11 , 001655 02-04
HOFMANN A 004497 04-12
HOFMANN M 000375 01-04
HOFMANN W 003412 03-13
HOFMANN WE 001869 02-06
HOGAN EL 003665 04-01
HOGARTY GE 003561 03-16
HOGBEN GL 003325 03-11
HOKFELT T 001239 02-03
HOKIN-NEAVERSON M 000129 01-03
HOKKANEN E 004542 04-13
HOKKANEN TEJ 002260 02-13
HOLADAY JW 002552 02-17 , 002714 03-03
HOLCK MI 000302 01-03
HOLCOMB H 003190 03-08
HOLDEN KR 004447 04-11
HOLINGER PC 002053 02-09
HOLKESVICK R 004661 04-15
HOLLAND RPC 004375 04-09
HOLLINGER MA 000106 01-03
HOLLINGSWORTH PJ 004008 04-03
HOLLISTER LE 000928 01-17 , 002201 02-12 ,
002488 02-16 , 003477 03-15 , 004327
04-08 , 004442 04-11 , 004514 04-13 ,

HOLLON SD 003235 03-09
HOLLOWAY DA 002593 02-17
HOLLT V 001283 02-03 , 003837 04-03 ,
003846 04-03 , 004321 04-08
HOLM-JENSEN J 000126 01-03
HOLMAN EW 000470 01-04 , 000471 01-04
HOLMBERG G 004372 04-09
HOLMES CB 000921 01-17
HOLMES R 000053 01-03
HOLMGREN B 000407 01-04 , 001656 02-04
HOLMSTEDT B 002095 02-11 , 003847 04-03
HOLMSTRAND J 000685 01-11
HOLOHEAN AM 000499 01-04 , 004250 04-04
HOLT JM 003601 03-17
HOLTZMAN D 002437 02-15
HOLTZMAN SG 000349 01-04 , 000391 01-04
, 001803 02-04 , 002963 03-04 , 003086
03-04 , 004077 04-04 , 004136 04-04 ,
004236 04-04
HOLZMAN PS 003448 03-14
HOM D 001653 02-04
HOMAN HD 002754 03-03
HOMICK JL 004138 04-04
HOMMA S 002755 03-03
HOMMEL M 002379 02-15
HONDA F 000493 01-04 , 004295 04-06
HONDA Y 000769 01-13
HONG JS 001284 02-03 , 003808 04-03
HONMA T 000408 01-04
HONORE T 003693 04-02 , 003848 04-03
HONZA R 001819 02-04
HOOD WF 003827 04-03
HOPE V 002149 02-11
HOPE A 000078 01-03 , 002240 02-13
HOPKINS J 004454 04-11
HOPPENER RJ 000760 01-13 , 000851 01-15
HORAK J 000595 01-09
HORI M 000012 01-02 , 000142 01-03
HORI N 003141 03-06
HORIE R 001548 02-03
HORIKAWA J 001323 02-03
HORIKAWA S 002349 02-14
HORISAKA K 000009 01-02
HORITA A 000624 01-04
HORKA E 000623 01-09 , 000883 01-15 ,
002452 02-15
HORN AS 000004 01-01 , 000324 01-03 ,
001359 02-03 , 001390 02-03 , 001710
02-04
HORN CA 001793 02-04
HORN KM 000392 01-04
HORNE JA 002241 02-13
HORNUNG R 001246 02-03
HORNYKIEWICZ O 001471 02-03
HOROWITZ SG 002814 03-03
HORROBIN DF 003495 03-15
HORSBURGH RJ 003138 03-06
HORSMAN LI 001591 02-04 , 001592 02-04
HORTON R 003976 04-03 , 004137 04-04
HORVATH FE 002723 03-03
HORVATH M 002332 02-14
HORVATH TB 002317 02-14
HORWITZ C 004169 04-04
HORWITZ M 003268 03-04
HOSEIN EA 001285 02-03
HOSEK K 000556 01-08 , 002518 02-17
HOSFORD DA 003849 04-03
HOSHINO AY 002367 02-14
HOSTETLER RM 004560 04-14
HOTCHKISS A 000130 01-03 , 001027 02-01 ,
003850 04-03
HOTTEN TM 001592 02-04
HOUGH LB 000112 01-03
HOUGHTEN RA 001028 02-01
HOUILLON P 004458 04-11
HOUSE CR 000031 01-03
HOUSLAY MD 001286 02-03
HOWARD A 003233 03-09 , 003252 03-09
HOWARD-PEEBLES PN 004515 04-15
HOWAT JMT 002433 02-15
HOWELL WE 002708 03-03
HOWELLS RB 001661 02-04
HOWELLS RD 001287 02-03
HOWLAND RD 000131 01-03
HOXTER AL 003054 03-04
HOYUMPA AM 002224 02-13 , 002272 02-13

JAVAID JI 001913 02-08 , 002481 02-16 ,
 002491 02-16 , 004682 04-16
JAVID MJ 000288 01-03 , 004232 04-04
JAWAHARLAL K 001773 02-04
JAWORSKI MT 000517 01-05
JEANNEAU A 003604 03-17
JEANPARIS F 003296 03-11
JEDLICKA S 003580 03-17
JEFFERSON JW 002005 02-09 , 002244 02-13
 003498 03-15
JELINEK R 000144 01-03 , 000595 01-09
JELLINEK T 004623 04-15
JEN M 002994 03-04
JENA K 004486 04-11
JENDEN DJ 000150 01-03 , 000826 01-14 ,
 001220 02-03 , 002235 02-13 , 003188
 03-08 , 003189 03-08 , 003201 03-08 ,
 003819 04-03 , 003820 04-03 , 004514
 04-13 , 004520 04-13 , 004521 04-13 ,
 004683 04-16
JENKINS LM 003647 03-17
JENNER P 000413 01-04 , 001164 02-03 ,
 001174 02-03 , 001175 02-03 , 001301
 02-03 , 002358 02-14 , 002390 02-15 ,
 002707 03-03 , 002789 03-03 , 004032
 04-03 , 004033 04-03 , 004205 04-04
JENSEN A 002424 02-15
JENSEN JPA 000689 01-11
JENSEN RA 000195 01-03 , 001711 02-04 ,
 002823 03-03 , 003861 04-03 , 003918
 04-03 , 003936 04-03 , 004143 04-04 ,
 004177 04-04
JENSEN RT 001005 02-01
JEPPSSON B 001158 02-03
JERLICZ M 003846 04-03
JESSEL HJ 003231 03-09
JESSEL I 003231 03-09
JESTE DV 001958 02-08 , 002245 02-13 ,
 003499 03-15
JEZIERSKA A 003500 03-15
JHAMANDAS K 001302 02-03 , 001303 02-03
 , 003862 04-03 , 003863 04-03
JIANG ZG 000234 01-03 , 000451 01-04 ,
 003864 04-03 , 003969 04-03
JIMERSON DC 000618 01-09 , 001223 02-03 ,
 004393 04-09 , 004565 04-14
JINDAL MN 001748 02-04
JINDAL SP 004291 04-06
JINDROVA O 002793 03-03
JO M 000856 01-15
JOBE PC 000145 01-03 , 000146 01-03 ,
 003865 04-03 , 004144 04-04 , 004145
 04-04
JOBERT A 000480 01-04
JOCHEMSEN R 000920 01-17
JOH TH 002634 03-01
JOHANNESSEN J 001043 02-01
JOHANNESSEN S 004462 04-11 , 004488 04-
 11
JOHANSON CE 001542 02-03 , 002334 02-14
 , 002335 02-14 , 003445 03-14 , 004071
 04-04
JOHANSSON BB 000147 01-03
JOHANSSON F 002305 02-13
JOHANSSON R 001956 02-08
JOHN R 003504 03-15
JOHN TM 003893 04-03
JOHNSON AL 002432 02-15
JOHNSON AM 004086 04-04
JOHNSON C 003310 03-11
JOHNSON D 000237 01-03 , 001280 02-03
JOHNSON EE 003894 04-03
JOHNSON FN 000597 01-09
JOHNSON GFS 000558 01-08 , 003016 03-04
 004624 04-15
JOHNSON HG 004576 04-14
JOHNSON KM 000148 01-03 , 001304 02-03 ,
 002766 03-03
JOHNSON LC 003446 03-14 , 004568 04-14
JOHNSON MK 003510 03-15
JOHNSON RC 000509 01-05
JOHNSON RF 002272 02-13
JOHNSON RG 003866 04-03
JOHNSON RH 002139 02-11 , 002402 02-15 ,
 003333 03-11 , 003371 03-11
JOHNSON RL 002500 02-16
JOHNSON RP 002639 03-01
JOHNSON RW 001305 02-03
JOHNSON SM 002767 03-03 , 003778 04-03
JOHNSON TC 003733 04-03

JOHNSSON A 000772 01-13
JOHNSTON GAR 001104 02-03 , 002633 03-
 01 , 002768 03-03 , 002769 03-03 ,
 003867 04-03
JOHNSTON JA 000949 01-17 , 003214 03-09
JOHNSTON MV 000059 01-03 , 002770 03-03
JOHNSTON R 000569 01-08
JOHNSTONE EC 001911 02-08 , 001923 02-08
JOLICOEUR FB 003049 03-04
JONAKAIT GMBMC 000149 01-03
JONASON J 004126 04-04
JONES A 001016 02-01
JONES BA 003521 03-15
JONES BE 001760 02-04
JONES BJ 001399 02-03
JONES DL 000436 01-04 , 003019 03-04
JONES GP 001029 02-01
JONES JG 004146 04-04
JONES KL 004576 04-14
JONES MT 004463 04-11
JONES R 001207 02-03 , 001306 02-03 ,
 001475 02-03 , 001667 02-04 , 002209
 02-13 , 004512 04-13
JONES SM 004201 04-04
JONES SW 003868 04-03
JONSSON G 002672 03-03
JOO F 002765 03-03
JOPE R 000150 01-03 , 000675 01-11 ,
 004520 04-13 , 004521 04-13
JORGENSEN A 002423 02-15 , 003472 03-15
JORNESTEDT L 002086 02-10
JOSE CJ 002414 02-15
JOSEPH J 001668 02-04
JOSEPH MH 002779 03-03
JOSEPHSON AM 000857 01-15
JOSHI VV 004147 04-04
JOSIFKO M 001702 02-04 , 002332 02-14
JOUANNIGOT R 004458 04-11
JOUVENT R 000598 01-09
JOVANOVIC UJ 001869 02-06 , 004309 04-07
JOY RM 002862 03-03
JOYCE RP 002415 02-15
JUDD L 000824 01-14 , 002003 02-09 ,
 003178 03-08
JUEL C 003869 04-03
JUHASZ A 001300 02-03 , 002765 03-03
JUILLET P 002553 02-17
JULIEN D 000817 01-14
JULOU L 001133 02-03 , 001137 02-03
JUNG D 000773 01-13
JUNG F 000799 01-13
JUNG L 002246 02-13 , 002492 02-16
JUNG MJ 000248 01-03 , 001128 02-03
JUNGKUNZ G 000599 01-09
JUORIO AV 001077 02-02 , 003870 04-03
JURGENS R 000751 01-13
JURKOWLANIEC E 001604 02-04
JURNA I 000414 01-04
JUSKO WJ 002225 02-13 , 003154 03-07 ,
 003479 03-15
JUSTICE JB 001873 02-06
JYOYAMA H 003692 04-02

K

KAAKKOLA S 000415 01-04 , 001669 02-04 ,
 001670 02-04
KAARIAINEN I 001670 02-04
KABES J 000542 01-07 , 000600 01-09 ,
 001888 02-07 , 001924 02-08 , 002006
 02-09 , 002025 02-09 , 002131 02-11 ,
 002132 02-11 , 003232 03-09 , 004375
 04-09
KABOUCHE M 001517 02-03 , 003899 04-03
KACIAN J 003335 03-11
KACZ D 004227 04-04
KADAR D 000747 01-13
KAFFEMAN ME 000822 01-14
KAFKA MS 001536 02-03
KAGAWA K 004022 04-03
KAGEYAMA H 000151 01-03 , 003893 04-03
KAHLAU F 001624 02-04
KAHN RL 000675 01-11
KAHRILAS PJ 003364 03-11
KAISER C 001237 02-03
KAKEGAWA N 004720 04-17
KAKITA K 000522 01-05
KALAB Z 002115 02-11
KALANT H 001387 02-03 , 001425 02-03 ,
 003883 04-03

KALICHMAN MW 000416 01-04
KALIN NH 002280 02-13 , 003255 03-09
KALIR A 001030 02-01
KALIS D 002072 02-10
KALISZAK JE 002314 02-14 , 004566 04-14
KALIX P 001307 02-03 , 003694 04-02
KALLOS M 002404 02-15
KALVACH Z 000548 01-08 , 000690 01-11 ,
 001908 02-08 , 001925 02-08
KAMATA K 003871 04-03 , 004148 04-04
KAMATA M 003871 04-03
KAMBURO RA 004262 04-04
KAMEI C 004149 04-04
KAMENKA JM 001031 02-01
KAMENSKIY AA 002949 03-04
KAMER RS 003872 04-03
KAMEYAMA T 002771 03-03 , 003020 03-04
 , 003871 04-03 , 004148 04-04
KAMIJO K 000159 01-03
KAMIYA H 004028 04-03
KAMMERER F 002416 02-15
KAMMERER T 004395 04-09
KAMOUN A 001896 02-07 , 001969 02-09 ,
 002247 02-13 , 004445 04-11
KAMP CW 002772 03-03 , 003873 04-03
KAMP D 000830 01-15
KAMRAJ-MAZURKIEWICZ K 000931 01-17
KAN JP 000156 01-03 , 003874 04-03
KANAREK RB 004150 04-04
KANARKOWSKI R 000601 01-09
KANE J 000808 01-14 , 000858 01-15 ,
 002339 02-14 , 002417 02-15 , 003233
 03-09 , 003252 03-09 , 003501 03-15 ,
 003548 03-15
KANENO S 002773 03-03
KANG JC 002994 03-04
KANGAS L 000702 01-11 , 003330 03-11 ,
 004524 04-13
KANOWSKI S 000691 01-11
KANTAK KM 003021 03-04
KANTO J 000702 01-11 , 000774 01-13 ,
 003330 03-11 , 004524 04-13
KANYICSKA B 003792 04-03
KANZLER M 002413 02-15
KAPELSKI Z 000625 01-09 , 002040 02-09 ,
 004404 04-09 , 004416 04-09
KAPETANOVIC IM 004522 04-13
KAPFER MT 004407 04-09
KAPINAS K 000665 01-11
KAPLAN H 000790 01-13
KAPLAN LJ 003874 04-03
KAPLIN GP 004732 04-17
KAPP BS 001628 02-04 , 002998 03-04 ,
 003798 04-03
KAPUR BM 000703 01-11
KARACAN I 004556 04-13
KARAMAT ALI F 001508 02-03
KARASAWA T 000012 01-02 , 000152 01-03
KARASKOVA M 002008 02-09
KARCZAG I 003193 03-08
KARCZMAR AG 003779 04-03 , 004151 04-
 04 , 004721 04-17
KARI I 001078 02-02
KARLBERG BE 000604 01-09
KARLER R 001671 02-04 , 002675 03-03 ,
 004040 04-03
KARLOV VA 003605 03-17
KARLSEN RL 002774 03-03
KARNIOL IG 004263 04-04
KAROBATH M 000561 01-08 , 001308 02-03
 , 001309 02-03 , 002307 03-03 , 002775
 03-03 , 002893 03-03 , 002909 03-03 ,
 004023 04-03
KAROUM F 000153 01-03 , 001310 02-03 ,
 001957 02-08 , 001958 02-08
KARPIAK SE 003025 03-04
KARRAS A 000808 01-14
KARRASZ W 003288 03-11
KARSON C 001672 02-04 , 001928 02-08 ,
 001945 02-08 , 002022 03-04 , 003023
 03-04 , 003193 03-08
KARTALOVSKI B 001521 02-03 , 001882 02-
 06
KARTZINEL R 003606 03-17
KASAMATSU T 003024 03-04
KASARSKIS EJ 003025 03-04
KASHANI JH 002418 02-15
KASICKI S 001620 02-04
KASKEY GB 002419 02-15

KASPARKOVA E 002055 02-09
KASTIN AJ 001311 02-03 , 001327 02-03 ,
 001673 02-04 , 001674 02-04 , 001827
 02-04 , 003112 03-04
KATHOL RG 002073 02-10
KATO E 000098 01-03
KATO R 000211 01-03 , 001393 02-03 ,
 002834 03-03 , 003946 04-03
KATON W 000602 01-09
KATORI M 004518 04-13
KATSUDA N 003141 03-06
KATSUMATA Y 004024 04-03
KATZ JL 004152 04-04 , 004224 04-04
KATZ NL 000529 01-05
KATZ RJ 001675 02-04 , 001676 02-04
 001677 02-04 , 001678 02-04 , 001679
 02-04 , 001680 02-04 , 001792 02-04 ,
 004153 04-04 , 004154 04-04 , 004155
 04-04 , 004156 04-04
KATZ S 000678 01-11
KATZNAN R 001447 02-03 , 002180 02-11
KAU D 001538 02-03
KAUFMAN IA 004576 04-14
KAUFMAN KR 003539 03-15
KAUFMAN S 003883 04-03 , 001519 02-03 ,
 002087 02-10
KAUFMANN K 003875 04-03
KAUL B 000859 01-15
KAUL CL 000154 01-03
KAUL PN 004164 04-04
KAUMEIER HS 003234 03-09
KAUR C 000155 01-03 , 001312 02-03
KAUROV OA 003438 03-14
KAVALIERS M 003026 03-04
KAWAHARA R 000860 01-15 , 003179 03-08
 003315 03-11 , 003415 03-13 , 003416
 03-13
KAWAI I 000628 01-09
KAWAI T 004257 04-04 , 004258 04-04
KAWAI Y 004608 04-15
KAWASAKI H 000417 01-04 , 001681 02-04
KAWASAKI K 003027 03-04
KAWASHIMA K 000902 01-16 , 004684 04-
 16
KAWAZU Y 002336 02-14
KAY OC 004610 04-15
KAY DSG 003365 03-11
KAY EJ 003003 03-04
KAYAALP SO 003876 04-03
KAYAMA Y 003877 04-03
KAYANO M 003416 03-13
KAYMAKCALAN S 002554 02-17
KAZAMATSURI H 000692 01-11
KAZARYAN KA 003882 04-03
KAZDIN AE 004630 04-15
KEANE PE 000156 01-03
KEBABIAN JW 001313 02-03
KEETON TK 002776 03-03
KEHR W 003769 04-03
KELLAMS JJ 003430 03-15
KELLAR KJ 000304 01-03 , 003878 04-03
KELLAWAY IW 000007 01-02
KELLEHER RT 003096 02-04 , 004012 04-03 ,
 004225 04-04
KELLER A 003668 04-03
KELLER HH 001314 02-03
KELLER W 004696 04-16 , 004722 04-17
KELLEY KW 000456 01-04 , 002777 03-03 ,
 003048 03-04
KELLY CJ 003733 04-03
KELLY D 000348 01-04 , 004376 04-09 ,
 004464 04-11
KELLY JS 001864 02-06 , 002704 03-03
KELLY P 000693 01-11 , 002640 03-01
KEMALI D 001315 02-03 , 002198 02-12 ,
 022274 02-13
KEMALI M 001315 02-03 , 002198 02-12
KEMEL ML 002733 03-03
KEMENY V 000010 01-02
KEMP JA 002894 03-03
KEMP JD 001578 02-04
KENAKIN TP 003879 04-03
KENDALL DA 002778 03-03 , 004157 04-04
KENNEDY C 001380 02-03
KENNEDY P 002555 02-17
KENNETT DJ 002322 02-14
KENNETT GA 002779 03-03
KENNIS L 002648 03-02
KENT JL 001050 02-01
KENT S 003447 03-14 , 004465 04-11

KEOGH NJ 002606 02-17
KERBER RE 002073 02-03
KEREN G 003363 03-11
KERESZTES-NAGY P 003028 03-04
KERGUERIS M 003563 03-16
KERR FWL 003432 03-13
KERRY RJ 002420 02-15
KERWIN R 000157 01-03 , 002869 03-03 ,
 003880 04-03
KESHAVAN HJH 001682 02-04
KESNER RP 002780 03-03
KESSLER JA 003881 04-03
KESSLER KA 003280 03-10 , 003607 03-17
KETTENES-VAN DEN BOSCH JJ 002556 02-17
KETTLER D 002263 02-13
KETTLER R 001381 02-03
KEUCHEL I 002337 02-14
KEVERNE EB 001718 02-04
KEYER-UYSAL M 000169 01-03
KHACHATURYAN AAM 000607 01-09
KHACHATURYAN GS 003882 04-03
KHAJAWALL A 002273 02-13
KHAN I 002556 02-17
KHAN MM 004620 04-15
KHANNA JM 003883 04-03
KHAYALI M 000698 01-11 , 002342 02-14
KAZAN N 000505 01-04 , 004038 04-03 ,
 004170 04-04 , 004259 04-04
KHEMANI L 002204 02-13
KHODOROV BI 003884 04-03
KHOKHLOV AP 003326 03-11
KHOO K 002248 02-13
KIDGER T 002374 02-15 , 002421 02-15
KIECHEL JR 004530 04-13
KIELCZAWA J 000861 01-15
KIELHOLZ P 000603 01-09 , 002007 02-09 ,
 004376 04-09
KIES MW 001201 02-03 , 001434 02-03
KIESSLING LA 003784 04-03
KIKTA DC 001623 02-04 , 004237 04-04
KIKVADZE IN 003885 04-03
KILBEY MM 001683 02-04 , 002711 03-03
KILGORE M 004557 04-13
KILIAN A 004625 04-15
KILLAM EK 000106 01-03 , 001210 02-03
KILLIAN A 003746 04-03
KILLIAN GA 002481 02-16 , 004523 04-13 ,
 004603 04-15
KILPATRICK IC 000158 01-03 , 004158 04-04
KILTS CD 004195 04-04
KIM J 000212 01-03 , 002781 03-03
KIM K 002794 03-03
KIM SH 001359 02-03
KIM YI 001316 02-03
KIM YJ 001316 02-03
KIMBALL CP 002557 02-17
KIMBALL JG 002133 02-11
KIMBRELL D 003473 03-15
KINDEL GH 004151 04-04
KINDERNAYOVA H 000576 01-08 , 002000
 02-09 , 002054 02-09
KINEMUCHI H 000159 01-03
KING AG 001870 02-06
KING C 003044 03-04
KING D 001926 02-08 , 002558 02-17 ,
 003409 03-13
KING GA 000160 01-03 , 002493 02-16 ,
 003133 03-06
KING RB 000775 01-13
KING WB 003029 03-04
KING WM 002782 03-03
KINGSLEY E 002422 02-15
KINKADE PT 004097 04-04
KINNEY CD 001926 02-08
KINNEY MJ 003180 03-08
KINNIER WJ 001317 02-03
KINSBOURNE M 002134 02-11
KINSCHERF DA 000090 01-03
KINSTON W 004626 04-15
KINZE W 004626 04-15
KIRALY E 003859 04-03
KIRBY MJ 002268 02-13
KIRBY ML 001161 01-03
KIRCHMAYER S 001844 02-05
KIRIAKOS R 004348 04-09
KIRK L 002423 02-15
KIRKEGAARD A 002424 02-15
KIRSHIN SV 002462 04-04
KIRSHNER H 000832 01-15
KISARA K 001379 02-03 , 002837 03-03 ,
 003714 04-03 , 004301 04-06

KISHORE MK 002186 02-11
KISSLING W 001917 02-08 , 001918 02-08 ,
 003218 03-09 , 003219 03-09 , 004321
 04-08 , 004322 04-08
KITAGAWA H 001236 02-03 , 001797 02-04 ,
 003008 03-04
KITAGAWA K 001394 02-03
KITAMURA T 002559 02-17
KITAZATO K 001857 02-05
KITCHEN I 002783 03-03
KITENGE A 004458 04-11
KITZEN JM 000162 01-03
KITZROW W 002049 02-09
KIZER JS 003811 04-03
KIZZORT BL 001873 02-06
KJELLMAN BF 000604 01-09
KLAGGE E 003344 03-11
KLAPETEK J 003331 03-11
KLAPPROTH HE 002479 02-16
KLAU M 003481 03-15
KLAWANS HL 000498 01-04 , 000862 01-15 ,
 000950 01-17 , 001845 02-05 , 002159
 02-11 , 002407 02-15 , 002468 02-15 ,
 003471 03-15 , 003502 03-15 , 003516
 03-15 , 004249 04-04
KLEBER HD 000666 01-11 , 000820 01-14 ,
 003317 03-11
KLEBER RJ 002074 02-10
KLEE WA 001032 02-01 , 001033 02-01 ,
 001035 02-01 , 001056 02-01
KLEIN DF 000632 01-09 , 000678 01-11 ,
 000951 01-17 , 003228 03-09 , 003233
 03-09 , 003240 03-09 , 003252 03-09 ,
 003262 03-09 , 003409 03-13 , 004424
 04-10 , 004427 04-10 , 004752 04-17
KLEIN ST 003184 03-08
KLEIN W 002425 02-15 , 003503 03-15
KLEINBERG D 001948 02-08
KLEINE TO 001927 02-08
KLEINMAN J 001672 02-04 , 001928 02-08 ,
 001957 02-08 , 001958 02-08 , 003022
 03-04 , 003023 03-04
KLEINROK Z 000163 01-03 , 001515 02-03 ,
 001684 02-04 , 001685 02-04 , 002921
 03-03 , 004166 04-04 , 004241 04-04
KLEMKE W 000711 01-11 , 000772 01-13
KLEMM WR 003886 04-03
KLEPNER CA 001484 02-03
KLERMAN GL 003256 03-09 , 003272 03-09 ,
 004401 04-09
KLESHCHINOV VN 002784 03-03
KLEVAN T 000187 01-03
KLICPERA C 000633 01-09
KLIMEK V 001647 02-04
KLIMOVA H 001647 02-04
KLINE N 002560 02-17 , 003608 03-17 ,
 004377 04-09
KLING A 001594 02-04 , 004651 04-15
KLING PJ 000502 01-04
KLIR T 004486 04-11
KLOOG Y 001318 02-03
KLORMAN R 002419 02-15
KLOSE KJ 001242 02-03
KLOTZ U 000164 01-03 , 002249 02-13 ,
 004524 04-13 , 004525 04-13
KLUGMAN KP 003887 04-03
KNAAPE H 004481 04-11
KNEPEL W 000165 01-03 , 001319 02-03 ,
 003715 04-03
KNOX J 004329 04-08
KNYCH ET 003888 04-03
KO WC 002806 03-03
KOBLIN DD 000418 01-04 , 001686 02-04
KOCAN D 003122 03-05
KOCH B 000193 01-03
KOCH K 001865 02-06 , 002785 03-03
KOCH SW 001687 02-04
KOCH-WESER J 001128 02-03 , 002237 02-13 ,
 003458 03-14 , 003620 03-17
KOCHER R 004627 04-15
KOCSIS JD 000166 01-03
KOCUR J 004660 04-15
KOE BK 001092 02-02 , 001687 02-04 ,
 002786 03-03
KOE KW 004159 04-04
KOELZ A 000909 01-16
KOEPKE KM 001813 02-04
KOEPPEN D 002028 02-09
KOGER HS 000005 01-01

KOHJIMOTO Y 004028 04-03
KOHLER C 001238 02-03 , 001240 02-03 ,
 002727 03-03 , 003889 04-03
KOHLI JD 001252 02-03 , 003890 04-03 ,
 003911 04-03
KOHNEN R 002337 02-14 , 002561 02-17
KOIDA M 001320 02-03
KOIDE T 001659 02-04 , 002787 03-03 ,
 002788 03-03
KOIVULA K 002096 02-11
KOJA T 003093 03-04
KOJIMA M 000212 01-03
KOKETSU K 003710 04-03 , 003843 04-03
KOKKINIDIS L 000419 01-04 , 001688 02-04 ,
 002010 02-09
KOLAKOWSKA T 004329 04-08
KOLASSA N 001087 02-02
KOLATA GB 004378 04-09
KOLBE H 002789 03-03
KOLIBAS E 000707 01-11
KOLIN IS 003332 03-11
KOLLER WC 002159 02-11 , 002468 02-15 ,
 003502 03-15 , 003516 03-15
KOLOBOV NA 000506 01-04
KOLOMAZNIK K 002297 02-13
KOLOMAZNIK M 000605 01-09 , 000852 01-
15 , 002008 02-09 , 002129 02-11
KOLYÁSKINA GI 004324 04-08 , 004541 04-
13
KOMENDA S 000651 01-10 , 000805 01-14 ,
 000806 01-14 , 001731 02-04 , 002333
 02-14 , 002562 02-17
KOMISSAROV IV 002790 03-03
KOMULAINEN H 001067 02-02 , 001078 02-
02
KONDO T 002309 02-13
KONIG L 004380 04-09 , 004723 04-17
KONIKOVA M 000615 01-09 , 000706 01-11 ,
 002020 02-09
KONISHI S 000167 01-03
KOOB GF 002484 02-16
KOPERA H 000863 01-15 , 002425 02-15 ,
 003503 03-15
KOPIN IJ 000196 01-03 , 000673 01-11 ,
 001304 02-01 , 001047 02-01 , 001048
 02-01 , 001058 02-01 , 001222 02-03 ,
 001223 02-03 , 001224 02-03 , 001279
 02-03 , 001400 02-03 , 001528 02-03 ,
 001546 02-03 , 002138 02-11 , 002250
 02-13 , 002546 02-17 , 002919 03-03 ,
 003310 03-11 , 003362 03-11 , 004057
 04-03
KOPP U 004511 04-13
KORCZYN AD 004001 04-03
KORCZYNSKI R 001620 02-04 , 003030 03-04
KORF J 001095 02-03 , 002923 03-03
KORINKOVA V 002020 02-09
KORIVI P 004694 04-16
KORNER P 004506 04-13
KORNET MJ 003695 04-02
KORNETSKY C 003066 03-04 , 004160 04-04
KORNFELD EC 001538 02-03
KORSGAARD S 003472 03-15
KOSH JW 003700 04-02
KOSKI G 001035 02-01 , 001056 02-01
KOSKINIEMI M 000694 01-11
KOSLOW SH 004679 04-16 , 004685 04-16
KOSS M 001193 02-03 , 001321 02-03
KOSSEN SP 001508 02-03
KOSTERLITZ HW 000168 01-03 , 003802 04-
03
KOSTRZEWA RM 001673 02-04 , 001717 02-
04
KOTANCHIK NL 002104 02-11
KOTANI Y 001293 02-03
KOTELKEVICH YN 003172 03-08
KOTELNIKOVA NV 001331 02-03
KOTORII M 002349 02-14
KOTORII T 002349 02-14 , 003450 03-14
KOUKKOU M 001962 02-09
KOUP JR 003562 03-16
KOUPERNIK C 002563 02-17
KOUPILOVA M 000389 01-04 , 000420 01-04
 , 001689 02-04
KOURETAS N 002454 02-15
KOUTRAS DA 000786 01-13
KOVACS GL 003031 03-04
KOVACS M 003235 03-09
KOVERECH A 003157 03-07 , 003158 03-07
KOVES K 002817 03-03

KOW L 000421 01-04
KOWALCZYK K 000695 01-11
KOYA D 000872 01-15
KOYAMA T 003938 04-03
KOYUNCUOGLU H 000169 01-03 , 003788 04-
03
KOZAKOVA H 000542 01-07
KOZICKA M 000163 01-03
KOZLOVSKAYA MM 004261 04-04
KOZLOWSKI MR 000422 01-04
KRAEMER GW 001850 02-05
KRAEMER H 003007 03-04
KRAGH-SORENSEN P 002251 02-13 , 004686
 04-16
KRAKIEWICZ A 000573 01-08
KRAL VA 004466 04-11
KRAMARCY NR 002985 03-03
KRAMER JC 000952 01-15
KRAMER M 002160 02-11 , 002357 02-14
KRAUPP O 001087 02-02
KRAUS E 002791 03-03
KRAUSS J 001131 02-03
KRAUTWALD O 002033 02-09
KRAVTSOV AN 002940 03-03
KREBS BP 002023 02-09
KREBS E 002286 02-13
KREBS H 003309 03-11
KREEK MJ 000796 01-13 , 001836 02-05 ,
 004467 04-11
KREISBERG R 004600 04-15
KREISMAN NR 002782 03-03
KREJCI I 000809 01-14 , 002540 02-17
KREJCOVA H 000674 01-11
KRESS J 002135 02-11
KRIEBEL GWJ 000559 01-08
KRIEGER-FINANCE F 001904 02-07
KRIKORIAN A 002252 02-13
KRIPKE D 000455 01-04
KRIPPNER S 002199 02-12
KRISHNAN H 003891 04-03
KRISIAK M 001796 02-04
KRISTENSEN O 000722 01-11 , 000903 01-16
KRISTJANSEN P 000890 01-15 , 001968 02-09
 002426 02-15
KRISTOF M 004724 04-17
KRIVOBOK GK 003100 03-04
KROG AJ 001069 02-02
KROGSGAARD-LARSEN P 001079 02-02 ,
 001139 02-03 , 001309 02-03 , 001540
 02-03 , 002647 03-02 , 002678 03-03 ,
 002727 03-03 , 003848 04-03 , 004725
 04-17
KROH U 001927 02-08
KRONFOL Z 004359 04-09
KROPF D 000768 01-13 , 000810 01-14
KRSIAK M 000485 01-04 , 000658 01-10',
 001690 02-04 , 001805 02-04
KRUG M 002792 03-03
KRUGER ER 004460 04-09
KRUK ZL 002475 02-16
KRULIK R 000630 01-09 , 000761 01-13 ,
 002793 03-03 , 003696 04-02
KRUPENINA LB 004308 04-08 , 004526 04-13
KRUPKA LR 000953 01-17
KRUTZIK S 003215 03-09
KRUTZSCH H 001048 02-01 , 002776 03-03
KRYL L 002008 02-09
KRYNICKI V 004387 04-09
KRYZHANOVSKY GN 003070 03-04 , 003984
 04-03 , 004161 04-04 , 004162 04-04 ,
 004163 04-04
KRZYMINSKI S 004468 04-11
KRZYSKO K 002564 02-17
KUBA K 000098 01-03
KUBA S 000639 01-09
KUBACKI A 002565 02-17
KUBICKI S 002338 02-14 , 003412 03-13
KUBO S 003271 03-09
KUBOS KL 000532 01-06
KUBOTA K 000211 01-03
KUCEROVA H 002000 02-09
KUCHEL O 004286 04-06
KUCHERENKO RP 001354 02-03
KUDRNOVA K 000654 01-10 , 002056 02-09
KUEHNLE JC 003449 03-14
KUHAR MJ 000026 01-03 , 002566 02-17 ,
 002644 03-01 , 002938 03-03 , 004292
 04-06
KUHN C 000461 01-04 , 001813 02-04
KUHN DM 003117 03-04 , 003892 04-03

KUKSGAUS NE 003713 04-03
KUKWA L 004527 04-13
KULA NS 001114 02-03 , 001158 02-03
KULCSAR A 004349 04-09
KULIK FA 002470 02-15
KULKARNI MR 004379 04-09
KULKARNI SK 004164 04-04
KULMALA HK 004293 04-06
KUMAR R 000438 01-04 , 001641 02-04 ,
 001871 02-06
KUMAR YV 003533 03-15
KUMASHIRO H 002442 02-15
KUMAZAWA T 002794 03-03
KUMMER P 001490 02-03
KUMPEL Q 000811 01-14 , 000917 01-17 ,
 002136 02-11
KUNOS G 003791 04-03
KUO C 001322 02-03
KUO M 004690 04-16
KUPERSMITH M 000698 01-11 , 002342 02-
14 , 002795 03-03
KUPFER A 004495 04-11
KUPFER DJ 000406 01-04 , 000631 01-09 ,
 002339 02-14 , 003236 03-09
KUPFERBERG HJ 004061 04-03 , 004522 04-
13
KUPIETZ SS 000812 01-14
KUPKOVA B 000809 01-14
KURAISHI Y 001691 02-04
KURAN W 004628 04-15 , 004629 04-15
KURGYIS J 002650 03-02
KURIBARA H 001692 02-04 , 001693 02-04 ,
 003032 03-04 , 004165 04-04
KURIHARA M 003544 03-15
KURIYAMA K 000522 01-05
KURLAND AA 000904 01-16 , 003181 03-08 ,
 003182 03-08
KUROKAWA T 000696 01-11
KUROMARU S 000645 01-09
KUROSAWA A 000151 01-03 , 003893 04-03
KURSAWE H 004380 04-09
KURTZKE RN 003878 04-03
KURUMA I 002309 02-13
KURUVILLA A 002796 03-03 , 003033 03-04
KUSAKA M 001323 02-03
KUSAKA Y 001394 02-03
KUSCHINSKY K 001649 02-04 , 003417 03-13
KUSS H 000599 01-09
KUTSCHER CL 000503 01-04
KUTT H 002567 02-17 , 004653 04-15
KUTZ I 004001 04-03
KUYAMA C 003271 03-09
KUYAMA H 000199 01-03
KUYER A 002851 01-15
KUZMA RJ 004560 04-14
KUZNETSOV ON 000578 01-09
KUZNETSOVA VI 004528 04-13
KVAENDE H 002095 02-11
KVETINA J 000332 01-03
KWAN S 002914 03-03
KYRIAKIDES M 000807 01-14 , 004580 04-14
KYUNNAPU IV 003384 03-11

L

LA BRIE RA 000844 01-15
LA PAGLIA NA 002231 02-13
LAAKMANN G 001935 02-08 , 001936 02-08
 , 002009 02-09 , 002137 02-11
LAASBERG LH 003894 04-03
LABELLA FS 002882 03-03
LABORIT G 003895 04-03
LABRIE F 001218 02-03 , 001324 02-03 ,
 002635 03-03
LABRIE RA 004323 04-08
LACASSE Y 000831 01-15
LACELLE S 001231 02-03
LACIGA Z 000686 01-11 , 002188 02-11
LACKO I 004529 04-13
LACKO L 004529 04-13
LACKOVIC Z 003139 03-06
LADER M 000622 01-11 , 000954 01-17
LADINSKY H 001325 02-03 , 003758 04-03
LADISICH W 004331 04-08
LADOGANA L 003494 03-15
LADURON P 000186 01-03 , 001326 02-03 ,
 002489 02-16 , 002648 03-02 , 003896
 04-03
LAFUENTE L 001189 02-03

LAGIER G 003505 03-15 , 004632 04-15
LAGNADO JR 003652 03-17
LAGRANGE J 001947 02-08
LAGUNAS MA 002288 02-13
LAGUZZI RF 000423 01-04
LAHAV M 004320 04-08
LAHMEYER HW 000955 01-17 , 002427 02-15
LAHOSTE GJ 001327 02-03
LAHTI RA 000170 01-03 , 003034 03-04
LAI AA 002797 03-03
LAI H 000424 01-04
LAI JCK 000171 01-03
LAI M 001407 02-03
LAIANI L 001182 02-03
LAJTHA A 001772 02-04 , 004039 04-03
LAKE CR 001952 02-08 , 002034 02-09 ,
002138 02-11 , 003309 03-11 , 003340
03-11 , 004393 04-09
LAXIN ML 002653 03-03
LAKOSKI JM 001328 02-03
LAL H 002611 02-17 , 003053 03-04 ,
004219 04-04
LAL S 000560 01-08 , 000714 01-11 ,
002253 02-13 , 002441 02-15
LALLEMAND A 004530 04-13
LAMAISON D 004307 04-07
LAMANNA JC 002798 03-03
LAMBERT JDC 002799 03-03
LAMBERT NM 004469 04-11
LAMBERT PA 003609 03-17
LAMBIE DG 002139 02-11 , 002402 02-15 ,
003333 03-11 , 003371 03-11
LAMM MCL 002859 03-03
LAMMINSIVU U 002076 02-10
LAMOUR M 003242 03-09
LANDAUER AA 002340 02-14
LANDER CM 002177 02-11
LANDER N 000669 01-11
LANDGRAF W 003669 04-01
LANE PT 001538 02-03
LANG WJ 004054 04-03
LANGE DG 002800 03-03
LANGE E 004380 04-09 , 004723 04-17
LANGE SC 000172 01-03
LANGER D 003310 03-11
LANGER G 000575 01-13 , 002568 02-17 ,
004332 04-08
LANGER SZ 000033 01-03 , 000227 01-03 ,
000235 01-03 , 002254 02-13 , 002569
02-16 , 002801 03-03 , 003427 03-13 ,
003610 03-11 , 003777 04-03 , 003955
04-03 , 004358 04-09
LANGEVIN R 000697 01-11
LANGLOIS Y 002119 02-11
LANGWINSKI R 000429 01-04 , 001694 02-04
001709 02-04
LANOTTE M 003952 04-03
LANSDOWN MJR 001329 02-03
LANTHORN TH 004140 04-04
LAPALME M 001285 02-03
LAPALUS P 004357 04-09
LAPIERRE YD 001427 02-03 , 001428 02-03 ,
001929 02-08 , 002007 02-09 , 002010
02-09 , 003285 03-10 , 003354 03-11 ,
003565 03-16 , 004539 04-13
LAPIN IP 000173 01-03 , 001330 02-03
LAPINA IA 004075 04-04
LAPORTE P 002140 02-11
LAPP JE 000956 01-17
LAROCHELLE P 000864 01-15
LAROUSSE C 003563 03-16
LARROW RW 004027 04-03
LARSEN HF 000903 01-16
LARSEN J 001079 02-02 , 002011 02-09
LARSEN N 002251 02-13
LARSON AA 000174 01-03 , 001695 02-04
LARSON DL 001162 02-03 , 004082 04-04
LARSSON K 000335 01-04 , 002957 03-04
LARSSON PA 003897 04-03
LARUE-ACHAGIOTIS C 003035 03-04
LASCELLES PT 003961 04-03
LASKA FJ 001841 02-05
LASKOVA NB 000578 01-09 , 004433 04-11
LASPE H 001917 02-08
LASSERRE M 003563 03-16
LASSOFF S 003128 03-05 , 004271 04-05
LATHAM CJ 002527 02-17
LATIES VG 003128 03-05 , 004271 04-05
LATKER C 001212 02-03
LAU A 001285 02-03

LAU C 000278 01-03 , 002802 03-03
LAU YS 001249 02-03
LAUDER JM 000030 01-03
LAUGHREN T 001970 02-09 , 003166 03-08
LAURENT J 004105 04-04
LAURIDSEN J 003848 04-03
LAURO R 002226 02-13
LAURSEN AM 002763 03-03
LAUTIN A 000561 01-08 , 001948 02-08 ,
002448 02-15 , 002877 03-03 , 004391
04-09
LAUX G 002012 02-09
LAVAGNA J 00*BAD MAG TAPE**ERR01*2108
02-11 , 004357 04-09 , 004594 04-15
LAVARENNE J 002570 02-17
LAVENE D 004530 04-13
LAVERDIERE M 003341 03-11
LAVERTY R 001142 02-03
LAVIE P 004569 04-14
LAVRETSKAYA EF 001331 02-03
LAW PY 001168 02-03
LAW S 001114 02-03
LAW W 004630 04-15
LAWALL JS 002428 02-15
LAWRENCE RC 004631 04-15
LAWSON AAH 002458 02-15
LAWTON NF 002255 02-13
LAYTON B 001443 02-03
LAZAROVA M 004166 04-04 ,[18004227 04-
04[I02LAZARUS JH[18003504 03-
15[I02LAZARUS LW[18000675 01-
11[I02LAZDUINSKI M 001521 02-03 ,
001882 02-06[I02LAZER ES 004012 04-
03[I02LAZZARI R 002312 02-14
LE AD 003883 04-03
LE BARS D 000028 01-03 , 000175 01-03 ,
002791 03-03
LE BELLEC M 003505 03-15
LE FUR G 000176 01-03 , 001517 02-03 ,
002256 02-13 , 003898 04-03 , 003899
04-03
LE MAGNEN J 001721 02-04 , 003035 03-04
LE MOAL M 001696 02-04
LE NORMAND Y 003316 03-16
LE PERA G 003157 03-07 , 003158 03-07
LEAL KW 000177 01-03
LEANDER JD 003046 03-04 , 003915 04-03
LEANDER S 002658 03-03
LEBLANC AE 003883 04-03
LEBOUTILLIER JC 000525 01-05
LEBRECHT U 001332 02-03 , 001697 02-04
LECCHINI S 002276 02-13
LECHAT P 004632 04-15
LECHIN F 001930 02-08
LECKMAN JF 002341 02-14 , 003418 03-13
LECRUBIER Y 000598 01-09 , 001232 02-03 ,
001942 02-08 , 002278 02-13 , 003424
03-13
LEDDET I 003291 03-11
LEDERER E 001080 02-02
LEE CH 003900 04-03
LEE DM 001583 02-04
LEE EHY 001333 02-03
LEE HK 000178 01-03
LEE HS 004009 04-03
LEE I 000638 01-09
LEE JH 001316 02-03
LEE K 001036 02-01
LEE MJ 002472 02-05
LEE MK 001334 02-03
LEE NM 001335 02-03 , 001698 02-04 ,
002994 03-04
LEE T 001336 02-03 , 002236 02-13
LEEB-LUNDBERG F 000848 01-03
LEELAVATHI DE 000134 01-03 , 000882 01-15
001789 02-04 , 003901 04-03 , 004694
04-15
LEENEN FH 000484 01-04
LEES AJ 002177 02-11
LEFEBVRE J 004531 04-13
LEFEVRE-BORG F 000044 01-03
LEFF S 002803 03-03
LEFKOWITZ RJ 000901 01-16 , 001009 02-01
LEGATOR MS 003121 03-05
LEGENDRE JL 001405 02-03 , 003956 04-03
LEGER J 000865 01-15
LEGNANI G 001998 02-09
LEGROS JJ 004583 04-14
LEGUAY D 002571 02-17 , 003208 03-09
LEHMANN E 000562 01-08 , 004342 04-08

LEHMANN HE 000847 01-15 , 002572 02-17
LEHRL S 000665 01-11
LEIBOWITZ M 003240 03-09
LEIBOWITZ S 003071 03-04
LEIGH N 004205 04-04
LEIGHTON M 002268 02-13
LEIGHTY EG 000179 01-03
LEITH NJ 001699 02-04 , 002953 03-04
LELORD G 003291 03-11
LEMAIRE A 004503 04-13
LEMBECK F 000259 01-03 , 003887 04-03
LEMBERGER L 002257 02-13 , 002429 02-15
LEME-LOPES J 002141 02-11 , 003281 03-10
LEMKIN PF 001037 02-01
LEMPERIERE T 000543 01-07 , 002430 02-15
LENEHAN T 004532 04-13
LENELLE J 001920 02-08
LENGVARI I 000180 01-03
LENZ G 000819 01-14
LEON A 000397 01-04 , 001045 02-01 ,
002682 03-03
LEONARD BE 004707 04-17 , 004726 04-17
LEONARD EJ 001099 02-03
LEONARD JP 000181 01-03
LEONARD P 004506 04-13
LEPAGE D 004470 04-11
LEPINE JP 002449 02-15
LEPPAVUORI A 000405 01-04
LERER B 004167 04-04
LERMAN SH 001337 02-03
LERNER P 000182 01-03 , 001952 02-08
LERNER Y 003196 03-08
LESHER A 002204 02-13
LESIEUR P 002449 02-15
LESLIE FM 002804 03-03 , 003902 04-03
LESLIE SW 000183 01-03
LESSE H 001338 02-03 , 001339 02-03
LESSER RP 000835 01-15
LESTER D 001567 02-04 , 001625 02-04
LEUNEN A 003293 03-11
LEUNG LS 000184 01-03 , 003903 04-03
LEUNG TKC 000171 01-03
LEUNG WJ 003659 04-01
LEVANDER S 002368 02-14
LEVEN M 002289 02-13
LEVENSON AJ 000866 01-15 , 002573 02-17
LEVI G 000185 01-03 , 001424 02-03
LEVIN BE 003904 04-03 , 003905 04-03
LEVINE AS 001725 02-04 , 003059 03-04 ,
003943 04-03 , 004181 04-04
LEVINE J 000425 01-04 , 000563 01-08 ,
001931 02-08 , 002574 02-17
LEVINE MS 001340 02-03
LEVINE R 000673 01-11 , 001348 02-03
LEVINE S 004273 04-05
LEVITT M 004427 04-10
LEVITT R 001793 02-04
LEVRON M 002169 02-11 , 002271 02-13
LEVY A 004320 04-08
LEVY DL 003448 03-14
LEVY JK 004138 04-04
LEVY MI 002317 02-14
LEVY RA 000121 01-03 , 000122 01-03
LEVY RH 000728 01-11 , 000755 01-13 ,
000777 01-13 , 002785 03-03 , 002797
03-03 , 004558 04-13
LEVY RM 001341 02-03
LEW JY 001254 02-03 , 001255 02-03 ,
004120 04-04
LEWANDER T 003701 04-02
LEWINSOHN R 000983 01-17
LEWIS DV 002805 03-03
LEWIS JW 003611 03-17
LEWIS ME 000347 01-04 , 002641 03-01
LEWIS PD 001407 02-03
LEWIS RF 004453 04-11
LEWIS SV 001059 02-01
LEWIS VA 001631 02-04 , 001700 02-04
LEWY AJ 000432 01-04 , 001043 02-01 ,
002628 02-17
LEYBIN L 001698 02-04
LEYSEN J 000186 01-03 , 001342 02-03 ,
001846 02-05 , 002648 03-02 , 003896
04-03 , 004033 04-03
LEZANSKA M 000885 01-15
LHAMON WT 000554 01-08
LHUILLIER J 002571 02-17 , 003208 03-09
LI CH 001028 02-01 , 001038 02-01 ,
001081 02-02 , 003193 03-08 , 003655

04-01 , 004238 04-04 , 004360 04-09 ,
  004489 04-11
LI PP 004048 04-03 , 004303 04-06
LI S 002728 03-03
LI-WAN-PO A 001872 02-06
LIANG NY 001343 02-03
LIBIGER J 002055 02-09 , 002431 02-15 ,
LIBUS J 000647 01-10 , 002075 02-10 ,
  002494 02-16
LIBUSOVA E 000647 01-10 , 002075 02-10 ,
  002494 02-16
LICATA SM 000594 01-09
LICHTENBERG D 002717 03-03
LICHTIGFELD FJ 003442 03-14
LIDDLE J 001926 02-08
LIDEMAN RR 004381 04-09
LIEB J 001993 02-09
LIEBERMAN A 000698 01-11 , 001254 02-03 ,
  002342 02-14 , 002453 02-15 , 002795
  03-03
LIEBERMAN J 003506 03-15
LIEBERMAN KW 000187 01-03
LIEBESKIND JC 000470 01-04
LIEBMAN JM 000188 01-03
LIEBOWITZ J 001398 02-03
LIEBOWITZ M 000632 01-09 , 003241 03-09 ,
  003262 03-09 , 004424 04-10
LIEBSON I 002314 02-14 , 004566 04-14 ,
  004582 04-14
LIEFKE T 004380 04-09
LIENERT GA 000699 01-11 , 002337 02-14 ,
  002561 02-17
LIGHT AI 002798 03-03
LIGHT KC 003813 04-03
LILAVIVATHANA U 000828 01-14
LILES IC 001700 02-04
LILJEQUIST S 001839 02-05
LIM L 000171 01-03
LIN C 003906 04-03
LIN CS 004489 04-11
LIN H 000779 01-13 , 003666 04-01
LIN M 000189 01-03 , 000190 01-03 ,
  002806 03-03 , 004085 04-04
LIN MT 003907 04-03
LIND MD 003118 03-04
LINDAMOOD C 003908 04-03
LINDBERG D 003183 03-08
LINDBERG I 003909 04-03
LINDBERG P 000399 01-04
LINDE OK 003612 03-17
LINDENBERG EDJ 002526 02-17
LINDENMAYER J 003507 03-15
LINDER M 004627 04-15
LINDERGARD B 003542 03-15
LINDGREN J 002201 02-12
LINDGREN S 002211 02-13
LINDHOLM T 003542 03-15
LINDROS KO 004220 04-04
LINDSAY WS 001873 02-06
LINDVALL M 002807 03-03
LINDVALL O 003910 04-03
LINET OI 003332 03-11
LING MHM 003508 03-15
LING NC 000226 01-03
LINGJAERDE O 004727 04-17
LINKOWSKI P 000606 01-09 , 003237 03-09
LINN RT 004135 04-04
LINNOILA M 000867 01-15 , 001180 02-03 ,
  002076 02-10 , 002077 02-10 , 002258
  02-13 , 003428 03-13
LINSEMAN MA 001344 02-03 , 003760 04-03
LINTON P 000710 01-11 , 002142 02-11
LINZMAYER L 000720 01-11 , 000788 01-13
LIPINSKI JF 002480 02-16
LIPKIN L 001037 02-01
LIPPER S 000612 01-09
LIPPITSCH M 001309 02-03
LIPPMAN L 000882 01-15
LIPPMANN SB 000997 01-17
LIPSITT DR 000957 01-17
LIPSKA B 000794 01-13
LIPTON JM 001247 02-03 , 001248 02-03
LIPTON MA 002144 02-11
LIPTON ME 002143 02-11
LIPTON RB 003448 03-14
LIPTON S 000426 01-04 , 003613 03-17
LIS B 000885 01-15
LISSAK K 004075 04-04
LISSITZKY J 003759 04-03
LIST S 001509 02-03 , 001847 02-05

LISTINSKY JJ 003911 04-03
LITTLE HJ 001686 02-04
LITVINOVA NM 004633 04-15
LIU GG 003907 04-03
LIU L 002175 02-11
LIUKKO P 000774 01-13
LIVINGSTON KE 000160 01-03
LLOYD BL 000114 01-03
LLOYD C 003238 03-09
LLOYD H 002907 03-03
LLOYD KG 001345 02-03 , 001585 02-04 ,
  001826 02-04 , 002986 03-04 , 003334
  03-11
LLUCH S 001355 02-03
LO S 000734 01-11
LOCATELLI V 001239 02-03 , 001391 02-03 ,
  002690 03-03
LOCK K 001475 02-03
LOCKFELD A 002866 03-03
LOCNISKAR A 000766 01-13
LODGE D 000063 01-03 , 002633 03-01 ,
  002647 03-02 , 002768 03-03 , 002808
  03-03
LODHI R 003367 03-11
LOEB C 000700 01-11 , 002013 02-09 ,
  004382 04-09 , 004533 04-13
LOEBER JG 001404 02-03
LOEFFLER KO 001229 02-03 , 001867 02-06
LOEW DM 001346 02-03 , 002809 03-03
LOFTHOUSE R 004423 04-10
LOFTUS EF 004570 04-14
LOGIN IS 002810 03-03
LOGOTHETIS J 003186 03-08
LOGUE JN 003239 03-09
LOH H 000433 01-04 , 001168 02-03 ,
  001280 02-03 , 001653 02-04 , 001698
  02-04 , 002552 02-17 , 002994 03-04 ,
  004238 04-04 , 004489 04-11
LOH HL 000958 01-17
LOH YP 001398 02-03
LOHR N 004359 04-09
LOISEAU P 000777 01-13
LOMAX P 001108 02-03
LOMBERTIE E 000865 01-15
LONEY J 003509 03-15 , 004714 04-17
LONG JP 000162 01-03 , 002236 02-13 ,
  004244 04-04
LONG W 004670 04-16
LONGMAN DA 001785 02-04
LONGSHORE MA 002811 03-03
LOO H 000551 01-08 , 000577 01-08 ,
  001090 02-02 , 001195 02-03 , 001969
  02-09 , 002014 02-09 , 002015 02-09 ,
  002016 02-09 , 003175 03-08 , 004445
  04-11
LOO JCK 000778 01-13
LOO YH 000191 01-03 , 000388 01-04
LOOMIS CW 003522 03-15 , 003912 04-03
LOONEN AJM 001347 02-03 , 003913 04-03
LOOSEN PT 002145 02-11 , 002259 02-13
LOPATA A 001039 02-01
LOPEZ JR 000449 01-04
LOPEZ-COLOME AM 002856 03-03
LOPEZ-ZANON A 002078 02-10
LORD JAH 000168 01-03
LORENS SA 004118 04-04
LORENZINI R 003194 03-08
LOREZ H 002812 03-03
LOSCHER W 000096 01-03 , 000097 01-03 ,
  000192 01-03 , 003036 03-04 , 003914
  04-03 , 004168 04-04
LOSSIUS R 000701 01-11
LOSSNER B 001819 02-04
LOTTI M 003510 03-15
LOTTI VJ 001701 02-04
LOTTSPEICH F 003740 04-03
LOUIS WJ 000536 01-06
LOUPPE A 002123 02-11
LOUS P 000767 01-13
LOVALLO WR 000879 01-15
LOVELL DK 000344 01-04
LOVENBERG W 001348 02-03 , 001415 02-03
  , 001423 02-03 , 001548 02-03 , 002654
  03-03 , 002776 03-03 , 002867 03-03 ,
  003117 03-04 , 003652 03-17 , 003826
  04-03 , 003892 04-03
LOVERING EG 004631 04-15
LOVETT EJ 001473 02-03
LOWE D 003308 03-11

LOWERY HW 003355 03-11
LOWERY SP 001702 02-04
LOWN B 000265 01-03
LOWNDES HE 000131 01-03
LOWRY MR 000868 01-15
LOWRY MT 001703 02-04
LU KS 003666 04-01
LUCA N 002281 02-13
LUCAS LA 001704 02-04
LUCAS RA 001089 02-02
LUCAS TS 003068 03-04
LUCATO R 003760 04-03
LUCEK R 002248 02-13
LUCHINS DJ 000869 01-15 , 001233 02-03 ,
  003184 03-08
LUCKER PW 002479 02-16
LUCOT JB 000427 01-04 , 003915 04-03 ,
  004169 04-04
LUDDEN TM 002495 02-16
LUDIN HP 000813 01-14
LUDLOW JM 002420 02-15
LUDMER LM 000132 01-03
LUDWICK BT 002785 03-03
LUE FA 002152 02-11
LUHAR J 004619 04-15
LUINI A 000301 01-03
LUISADA PV 000739 01-12
LUKANINA SK 004335 04-08
LUKAS SE 004170 04-04
LUKASH L 004670 04-16
LUKOVITS I 000010 01-02 , 001039 02-01
LUKS A 002562 02-17
LULLIEN L 004458 04-11
LULLMANN-RAUCH R 003916 04-03
LUND A 002496 02-16
LUND HI 000722 01-11
LUND M 003484 03-15
LUNDBERG D 001389 02-03 , 003917 04-03
LUNDBORG P 000087 01-03
LUNDE PKM 000701 01-11
LUNDH H 003781 04-03
LUNDIN L 001956 02-08
LUNDT PV 000650 01-10
LUOMA PV 002260 02-13
LUPATKIN W 000619 01-09
LUPCZYNSKI G 003268 03-09
LUSSON JR 004307 04-07
LUSTIG A 001944 02-08
LUTHER J 002149 02-11
LUTTGE WG 002927 03-03
LUTTINGER D 003037 03-04
LUTZ T 002160 02-11 , 004291 04-06
LUTZ-BUCHER B 000193 01-03
LUU DUC C 001083 02-02
LYKETSOS G 004337 04-08
LYKOURAS E 002294 02-13
LYNCH G 001036 02-01 , 001120 02-03 ,
  001147 02-03 , 003726 04-03 , 003918
  04-03
LYNCH KL 001853 02-05
LYNESS WH 000364 01-04 , 001595 02-04 ,
  002813 03-03 , 003038 03-04 , 004171
  04-04
LYNN AG 000351 01-04 , 003662 04-01
LYNN K 002284 02-13
LYNN RK 000073 01-03
LYON L 000670 01-11
LYON M 002988 03-04
LYUBIMOV BI 001705 02-04

M

MAAS JW 000297 01-03 , 001289 02-03 ,
  001496 02-03 , 002910 03-03 , 002911
  03-03 , 003418 03-13
MAAYANI S 000112 01-03 , 001368 02-03 ,
  001369 02-03 , 001706 02-04 , 003906
  04-03
MACAROVA J 000805 01-14 , 000806 01-14
  , 001731 02-04 , 002333 02-14 , 002562
  02-17
MACDERMOT J 001132 02-03 , 002255 02-13
  , 002897 03-03
MACDONALD JF 001349 02-03
MACDONALD RL 000194 01-03 , 002885 03-
  03
MACH T 001844 02-05
MACHLIS LE 000428 01-04
MACHULA AI 003919 04-03

MACKAY AVP 000564 01-08 , 002432 02-15 , 002575 02-17
MACKENZIE TB 000857 01-15
MACKLIN D 002164 02-11
MACLEOD NK 000158 01-03
MACLEOD RM 002810 03-03
MACLEOD SM 000790 01-13
MACMILLAN BT 002695 03-03
MACPHAIL RC 002708 03-03
MADDEN J 001707 02-04
MADDOX VH 001040 02-01
MADERDRUT JL 004206 04-04
MADRAS B 003767 04-03
MADRUGA WS 003185 03-08
MADSEN BW 000524 01-05 , 004179 04-04
MADSEN J 000870 01-15
MAEDA K 003266 03-09 , 003920 04-03
MAEJIMA S 000856 01-15
MAEKAWA K 000661 01-11
MAENO H 002936 03-03
MAENPAA K 000774 01-13
MAERZ JC 000959 01-17
MAFFINI M 002356 02-14
MAGELUND G 002101 02-11 , 003302 03-11
MAGIL SG 002934 03-03
MAGISTRETTI PJ 001350 02-03 , 003735 04-03
MAGNANI G 003425 03-13
MAGNUS RV 002146 02-11
MAGNUSSEN I 000138 01-03 , 002261 02-13
MAGNUSSON T 003799 04-03
MAGUIRE GP 002433 02-15
MAGUIRE KP 000614 01-09 , 002184 02-11 , 002497 02-16 , 004477 04-11
MAGUN H 000909 01-16
MAHAR PJ 000848 01-15
MAHEO M 002135 02-11
MAHER J 003614 03-17
MAHLER HR 003948 04-03
MAHUZIER G 002498 02-16
MAHUZIER P 002529 02-17
MAIKXEL RP 003978 04-03
MAIER SF 001707 02-04
MAILLARD M 002576 02-17
MAILMAN RB 001813 02-04 , 004195 04-04
MAINARD F 000018 01-03
MAININI E 004535 04-13
MAIRE F 003401 03-13
MAITAI CK 001084 02-02
MAITRE L 000316 01-03 , 003921 04-03
MAITRE M 002878 03-03 , 003675 04-01
MAJ J 000204 01-03
MAJEWSKA Z 000931 01-17
MAJOCHA R 001351 02-03 , 002932 03-03
MAJOR LF 000612 01-09
MAKANJUOLA ROA 001708 02-04
MAKINO Y 004720 04-17
MAKK G 001423 02-03
MAKMAN MH 001447 02-03 , 001448 02-03 , 001629 02-04 , 002811 03-03 , 002814 03-03
MAKSAY G 000010 01-02 , 000011 01-02
MAKSIMOVA LA 002949 03-04
MAKSIMOWSKA M 004634 04-15
MALCOLM RE 002343 02-14
MALEC D 000429 01-04 , 001709 02-04
MALEN CE 002262 02-13
MALETZKY BM 000648 01-10
MALGA A 001978 02-09
MALIK R 000195 01-03
MALIKOVA LA 001352 02-03
MALINOVSKAYA NB 004572 04-14
MALLAT M 003825 04-03
MALLINGER AG 004511 04-13
MALLORGA P 000103 01-03 , 001502 02-03 , 001503 02-03 , 001504 02-03 , 001842 02-05 , 002912 03-03
MALLYA A 002273 02-13
MALM U 001956 02-08
MALMBERG-AIELLO P 000104 01-03
MALMGREN H 002211 02-13
MALONE MH 004186 04-04
MALONEY R 001597 02-04
MALTBIE AA 003511 03-15
MALTHE-SORENSSEN D 002774 03-03
MALTZMAN I 002369 02-14
MAMELAK M 004571 04-14
MAMELOK RD 003650 03-17
MANANI G 000105 01-03
MANARA L 000301 01-03

MANCHANDA R 001921 02-08
MANDEL M 000870 01-15 , 001931 02-08
MANDEL P 001371 02-03 , 001499 02-03 , 001756 02-04 , 002699 03-03 , 002878 03-03 , 003675 04-01
MANDELKORN T 000713 01-11
MANDELL AJ 003922 04-03
MANGANIELLO V 001002 02-01
MANGANO RM 003923 04-03
MANGAT HK 000155 01-03 , 001312 02-03
MANGONI A 001483 02-03
MANIAN AA 001405 02-03
MANIER DH 002353 02-03
MANINA AA 001354 02-03
MANKOVSKIY NB 004572 04-14
MANN E 000882 01-15 , 002456 02-15 , 003304 03-11
MANN J 001992 02-09 , 002017 02-09 , 004383 04-09
MANN LI 004027 04-03
MANN M 003159 03-07
MANNING DE 002167 02-11
MANNING T 004670 04-16
MANNISTO PT 001362 02-03
MANOS N 003186 03-08
MANSBRIDGE B 003590 03-17
MANSFIELD JG 001586 02-04
MANSHIEM P 003512 03-15
MANSIKKA M 000702 01-11
MANSOUR A 000348 01-04
MANTANUS H 004583 04-14
MANTEGAZZA P 000041 01-03 , 000042 01-03 , 000355 01-04 , 001161 02-03
MANTLE PG 002843 02-03
MANZINO L 000404 01-04
MAOZ B 004573 04-14
MARAINI G 000878 01-15
MARANGOS PJ 000225 01-03 , 000276 01-03 , 001041 02-01 , 001475 02-03 , 001536 02-03 , 002645 03-01 , 002857 03-03 , 002972 03-04 , 004172 04-04
MARCAIS H 004173 04-04
MARCELLI D 002344 02-14
MARCETICH JR 002005 02-09
MARCHBANKS RM 003924 04-03
MARCHETTI G 004365 04-09
MARCHISIO AM 000285 01-03
MARCHMONT RJ 001286 02-03
MARCO EJ 001355 02-03
MARCO-GRANEL F 002434 02-15
MARCOVICI M 003335 03-11
MARDER SR 001951 02-08 , 003202 03-08
MARDH G 003454 04-13
MAREGHA MG 003194 03-08
MAREK J 000570 01-08 , 000761 01-13
MARES P 000460 01-04 , 001356 02-03 , 001419 02-03 , 001439 02-03 , 003039 03-04 , 004064 04-03
MARESCAUX C 002237 02-13
MARESOVA D 001356 02-03
MARFAING-JALLAT P 001721 02-04
MARGOLIS FL 002836 03-03
MARGOLIS R 000871 01-15
MARICQ AV 003040 03-04
MARIE-CARDINE M 002577 02-17
MARIN J 001355 02-03 , 001357 02-03 , 003925 04-03
MARINI JL 000297 01-03 , 001496 02-03 , 004409 04-09
MARK VH 003520 03-15
MARKESBERY WR 000718 01-11
MARKEY SP 000196 01-03 , 001042 02-01 , 001043 02-01 , 001044 02-01 , 001058 02-01
MARKHAM CH 003336 03-11
MARKIANOS M 004471 04-11
MARKOFF RA 003223 03-09
MARKOWITZ S 003887 04-03
MARKS BH 000302 01-03
MARKS J 000960 01-17
MARKS RC 000894 01-15
MARMO E 000442 01-04
MAROLI AN 001795 02-04 , 003041 03-04
MARQUES PR 001366 02-03 , 002822 03-03
MARRIOTT P 004635 04-15
MARSDEN CD 000413 01-04 , 001164 02-03 , 001174 02-03 , 001175 02-03 , 001301 02-03 , 002168 02-11 , 002358 02-14 , 002390 02-15 , 002432 02-15 , 002707 03-03 , 002789 03-03 , 003422 03-13 ,

004032 04-03 , 004033 04-03 , 004205 04-04
MARSH GM 003377 03-11
MARSH VR 004669 04-16
MARSHALL AM 001358 02-03
MARSHALL EF 000038 01-03 , 002081 02-10
MARSHALL JF 000422 01-04 , 002815 03-03
MARSHALL RJ 004266 04-05
MARTENSSON E 002207 02-13 , 003569 03-16
MARTIN AR 001359 02-03 , 001710 02-04
MARTIN BR 000354 01-04
MARTIN D 002037 02-09 , 003220 03-09
MARTIN E 000909 01-16
MARTIN I 001378 02-03 , 002971 03-04 , 003615 03-17
MARTIN J 001202 02-03 , 002018 02-09 , 002852 03-03 , 003042 03-04 , 003441 03-14
MARTIN P 000703 01-11 , 003135 03-06
MARTIN WR 004728 04-17
MARTIN-DEL-CAMPO E 003638 03-17
MARTINELLI I 004535 04-13
MARTINET M 002816 03-03
MARTINEZ AJ 002724 03-03
MARTINEZ JL 001711 02-04 , 002823 03-03 , 003861 04-03 , 003936 04-03 , 004143 04-04 , 004177 04-04
MARTINEZ-CAMPOS A 002690 03-03
MARTINEZ-ROLDAN C 003043 03-04
MARTINI L 001418 02-03
MARTINO AM 004172 04-04
MARTINSSON L 000147 01-03
MARTIS L 002797 03-03
MARTON J 002817 03-03
MARTORANA PA 001082 02-02 , 001360 02-03
MARTRES MP 002900 03-03
MARTUCCI N 002090 02-11 , 002312 02-14
MARUMO H 004192 04-04
MARUTA T 000787 01-13 , 002037 02-09 , 004406 04-09
MARUYAMA Y 001323 02-03
MARWAHA J 000197 01-03 , 001848 02-05 , 003793 04-03 , 003926 04-03
MARZATICO F 003730 04-03
MARZILLI RA 003337 03-11
MARZULLO G 003927 04-03
MASEK K 000485 01-04
MASHKOVSKY MD 000008 01-02 , 001520 02-03 , 003681 04-02 , 003934 04-03 , 004174 04-04
MASIREVIC G 003703 04-02
MASON AS 000961 01-17
MASON GA 003037 03-04
MASON GR 001337 02-03
MASON NR 002995 03-04
MASON ST 000345 01-04 , 004070 04-04
MASSAROTTI M 003419 03-13
MASSERANO JM 003044 03-04
MASSO JL 003928 04-03
MASSOTTI M 001012 02-01 , 001045 02-01 , 001263 02-03 , 001849 02-05 , 002642 03-01 , 002819 03-03
MASTAGLIA FL 002435 02-15
MASTEN LW 000280 01-03
MASUDA Y 000012 01-02 , 000142 01-03 , 004149 04-04
MASUR H 002567 02-17
MASUR J 001712 02-04
MATEENUDDIN M 001361 02-03
MATEJCEK M 002147 02-11
MATEO D 003311 03-11
MATHERS DA 000198 01-03 , 002665 03-03 , 002666 03-03
MATHEW RJ 002531 02-17 , 003213 03-09
MATHIEU MN 003749 04-03
MATHIS DF 004687 04-16
MATIN MA 004274 04-05
MATSUBARA K 003692 04-02
MATSUKURA S 003187 03-08
MATSUMOTO A 000199 01-03
MATSUMOTO K 001293 02-03
MATSUMOTO T 000212 01-03 , 002781 03-03
MATSUMOTO Y 003129 03-05
MATSUNAGA F 004636 04-15
MATSUO H 004283 04-05
MATSUSHITA A 003027 03-04 , 003692 04-02

MATSUSHITA H 001659 02-04 , 002787 03-03
  002788 03-03
MATTES J 000678 01-11
MATTHEWS KL 002436 02-15
MATTHEWS WD 003045 03-04 , 003929 04-03
MATTHIES H 001819 02-04
MATTILA J 001362 02-03
MATTILA MJ 002258 02-13 , 003428 03-13
MATTSON M 004251 04-04
MATTSON RH 000687 01-11
MATTSSON A 004637 04-15
MATWYSHYN GA 001575 02-04
MAUGUIERE F 004638 04-15
MAUK MD 001674 02-04
MAURER R 003013 03-04
MAUTNER HG 003930 04-03
MAVISSAKALIAN M 004425 04-10
MAWER GE 003316 03-11
MAY CN 000949 01-17 , 003214 03-09
MAY JG 001717 02-04
MAY PRA 000565 01-08 , 000826 01-14 ,
  000891 01-15 , 003188 03-08 , 003189
  03-08 , 003201 03-08 , 003202 03-08
MAY SJ 000594 01-09
MAYA A 002288 02-13
MAYER A 002151 02-11
MAYER J 003883 04-03
MAYER ML 002818 03-03 , 003931 04-03
MAYER N 000259 01-03
MAYER WJW 001044 02-01
MAYERON MA 003382 03-11
MAYO JA 003247 03-09
MAYOL RF 004691 04-16
MAYSOV NI 001363 02-03
MAZARGUIL H 000021 01-03 , 001110 02-03
  003682 04-02
MAZIERE M 003564 03-16
MAZUREK K 004599 04-15
MAZURKIEWICZ-KWILECKI IM 003932 04-03
MAZURSKIY MB 004732 04-17
MAZZARI S 001012 02-01 , 001045 02-01 ,
  002819 03-03
MAZZI C 004535 04-13
MCAULEY R 002266 02-13
MCCAFFERTY GP 003045 03-04 , 003929 04-03
MCCAFFERTY MR 004267 04-05
MCCALL RB 001364 02-03
MCCALLUM P 000763 01-13
MCCARRON JA 002148 02-11
MCCARTHY BW 002735 03-03 , 002839 03-03
MCCARTHY KD 002820 03-03
MCCARTHY PS 001765 02-04 , 003080 03-04
MCCARTY R 001251 02-03
MCCAUGHRAN JA 004294 04-06
MCCAUL ME 001713 02-04
MCCLEARY PE 003046 03-04
MCCLELLAND GR 004086 04-04
MCCLURE WO 003148 03-06 , 003676 04-01
MCCONNELL SK 002821 03-03
MCCOY EE 003787 04-03
MCCRAY DS 002118 02-11
MCCREADIE RG 001932 02-08
MCCREERY RL 000014 01-02
MCCULLOCH J 000200 01-03 , 001365 02-03 ,
  002640 03-01
MCCURDY L 000962 01-17
MCDONALD AC 004199 04-04
MCDONALD R 000484 01-04 , 000704 01-11
MCDOUGAL JN 001366 02-03 , 002822 03-03
MCDOWELL F 002567 02-17
MCEVILLY JP 002079 02-10
MCEVOY JP 001964 02-09 , 002080 02-10 ,
  004333 04-08 , 004392 04-09 , 004702
  04-17
MCFADYEN IR 003549 03-15
MCGAUGH JL 001711 02-04 , 002345 02-14 ,
  002823 03-03 , 003861 04-03 , 003918
  04-03 , 003936 04-03 , 004143 04-04 ,
  004177 04-04
MCGEER EG 002824 03-03 , 004294 04-06
MCGEER PL 002824 03-03
MCGILL M 001014 02-01
MCGILVERAY IJ 000778 01-13
MCGIMSEY J 000849 01-15
MCGINITY JW 001865 02-06
MCGINTY JF 001367 02-03
MCGIVNEY A 001188 02-03

MCGIVNEY WT 003047 03-04
MCGLONE JJ 000456 01-04 , 003048 03-04
MCGOUGH JP 000426 01-04
MCGOWAN EB 000290 01-03
MCGOWAN WT 001561 02-04
MCGRATH JC 001196 02-03
MCGRATH P 000632 01-09 , 003240 03-09 ,
  003241 03-09 , 003262 03-09
MCGUFFIN P 001933 02-08
MCGUIRE MT 004204 04-04
MCGUIRE PS 001714 02-04 , 004175 04-04
MCILWAIN H 002578 02-17
MCINTOSH P 003114 03-04
MCINTOSH TK 004030 01-04
MCINTYRE HB 003338 03-11
MCINTYRE IM 004639 04-15
MCKEARNEY JW 000339 01-04 , 000356 01-04 , 000431 01-04 , 001715 02-04 ,
  004376 04-04
MCKEITH IG 003420 03-13
MCKELVEY J 001597 02-04
MCKENZIE GM 001716 02-04
MCKERNAN T 003381 03-11
MCKIM HR 003719 04-03
MCKIMMEY C 000220 01-03
MCKINNEY WT 001850 02-05 , 003140 03-06
MCKNEW DH 003242 03-09
MCLEAN JH 001717 02-04
MCLELLAN AT 003335 03-11
MCLENNAN PL 003933 04-03
MCMASTER SB 002500 02-16
MCMILLAN DE 001666 02-04 , 003915 04-03
MCMILLEN BA 000201 01-03
MCNAIR DM 000649 01-10 , 003282 03-10
MCNALL CL 003798 04-03
MCNAMARA JO 002149 02-11
MCNEELY BU 004655 04-15
MCQUEEN EG 001142 02-03
MCSWIGAN JD 002825 03-03
MEADE RG 004057 04-04
MEARELLI S 004431 04-11
MEARES R 000763 01-13
MECHLER L 004487 04-11
MECHOULAM R 000669 01-11
MECO G 004384 04-09
MEDEK A 001731 02-04
MEDIAVILLA JL 002200 02-12
MEDILANSKI P 001874 02-06
MEDINA JH 003130 03-05
MEDVEDEV BA 003934 04-03
MEDVEDEV VI 001812 02-04 , 003438 03-14
MEDZIHRADSKY F 000779 01-13
MEEK JL 002719 03-03
MEERT C 001920 02-08
MEFFORD IN 003935 04-03
MEGRABYAN AA 000607 01-09
MEHENDALE HM 002845 03-03
MEHROTRA AN 003536 03-15
MEHROTRA SN 002175 02-11
MEIBACH RC 001368 02-03 , 001369 02-03 ,
  001706 02-04 , 003280 03-04
MEIER KD 001959 02-08
MEIER JWA 000851 01-15
MEINCK H 002263 02-13
MEINERT JC 001409 02-03
MEINHOLD JM 000872 01-15
MEISEL-KOSIK I 001917 02-08
MEITES J 000298 01-03
MELAMED BR 004267 04-05
MELAMED E 000202 01-03 , 003323 03-11
MELCHIOR C 003979 04-03
MELDRUM B 000182 02-11 , 002826 03-03 ,
  004137 04-04
MELDRUM MJ 002827 03-03
MELIS W 001985 02-09
MELLADO C 001985 02-09
MELLER E 000203 01-03 , 003794 04-03
MELLER RE 001718 02-04
MELLERUP ET 004537 04-13 , 004607 04-15
MELLITS ED 004447 04-11
MELLO NK 003449 03-14
MELLSTROM B 000754 01-15 , 002282 02-13 ,
  002300 02-13
MELNICHUK PV 004536 04-13
MELNIKOVA LI 001354 02-03
MELTZER HL 001893 02-07 , 001989 02-09 ,
  002228 02-13 , 003221 03-09 , 004369 04-09
MELTZER HY 000750 01-13 , 001616 02-04 ,
  001719 02-04 , 002098 02-11 , 002264
  04-04

02-13 , 002265 02-13 , 003190 03-08
  003318 03-11 , 004538 04-13 , 004540 04-13 , 004676 04-16
MELVILLE A 002579 02-17
MELVILLE ID 003371 03-11
MELZACKA M 000204 01-03
MEMO M 001480 02-03 , 001481 02-03 ,
  001482 02-03 , 001512 02-03 , 002828 03-03
MENCER DL 003521 03-15
MENCHETTI G 002091 02-11
MENDELS J 000582 01-09 , 000940 01-17 ,
  001463 02-03 , 001991 02-09 , 002248
  02-13 , 003263 03-09 , 003570 03-16
MENDELSON JH 003449 03-14
MENDELSON W 000432 01-04 , 002150 02-11
  002346 02-14 , 002354 02-14
MENDELSON WB 004729 04-17
MENDENHALL CL 004473 04-11
MENDIS N 004640 04-15
MENDIS T 001000 01-17
MENDLEWICZ J 000606 01-09 , 000608 01-09
  002347 02-14 , 003237 03-09
MENDOZA MM 002117 02-11
MENIA A 004472 04-11
MENINI C 003564 03-16
MENNINI T 000258 01-03 , 002602 02-17
MENON GN 004519 04-13
MENON MK 000433 01-04
MENS WBJ 001370 02-03
MENTASTI M 000712 01-11
MERALI Z 004539 04-13
MERANO Y 002635 03-01
MERCIER J 003089 03-04
MERKEL AD 003049 03-04
MERLE L 002395 02-15
MERLIE JP 003670 04-01
MERMET A 003668 04-01
MERRIGAN KP 004074 04-04
MERRIL C 001037 02-01
MERZ H 000013 01-02
MESDJIAN E 001015 01-15 , 001371 02-03 ,
  002319 02-14
MESHAD M 004600 04-15
MESHI T 001323 02-03
MESSIHA FS 000523 01-05
MESSING RB 002823 03-03 , 003861 04-03 ,
  003936 04-03 , 004143 04-04 , 004177 04-04
MESULAM M 003290 03-11
MESZAROS J 003050 03-04
METCALF G 000351 01-04 , 003080 03-04 ,
  003662 04-01
METSELAAR HJ 001606 02-04
METYS J 001720 02-04
METYSOVA J 000001 01-01 , 000306 01-03 ,
  001720 02-04 , 002279 02-13
METZ J 000473 01-04 , 004540 04-13
MEUNIER GF 000284 01-03
MEYER DK 001003 02-01 , 001372 02-03
MEYER EM 003937 04-03
MEYER ER 000051 01-03
MEYER LY 000386 01-04
MEYER P 000205 01-04 , 003944 04-03
MEYERS B 000616 04-08
MEYERSON BA 002551 02-17
MEYERSON BJ 004178 04-04
MEYERSON LR 002898 03-03
MEYERSON YA 003398 03-13
MIACH PJ 000205 01-03
MICELI D 001721 02-04
MICHAEL SD 003295 03-03 , 003159 03-07
MICHEAU J 003051 03-04
MICHENFELDER JD 000295 01-03
MICHOS GA 002367 02-14
MICKEY MR 001220 02-03
MICZEK KA 000434 01-04 , 001722 02-04 ,
  003052 03-04
MIDDELHOFF HD 000799 01-13
MIDDLEMISS DN 000206 01-03 , 001940 02-08
MIDHA KK 000778 01-13 , 000905 01-16 ,
  002499 02-16 , 003565 03-16
MIELKE DH 002348 02-14
MIGLECZ E 001799 02-04 , 002650 03-02
MIGNEE C 003513 03-15
MIKES F 000705 01-11
MIKHAYLOVA NM 003339 03-11 , 004390 04-09

MIKKELSEN E 002354 02-14
MIKKELSON E 003340 03-11
MIKKLESON PL 001976 02-09
MIKSIC S 003053 03-04
MIKUNI M 003938 04-03
MIKUNI N 001297 02-03
MILANOV S 000119 01-03
MILECH T 003524 03-15
MILES NJ 003687 04-02
MILESI GM 003425 03-13
MILEWSKA G 000885 01-15
MILEY WM 003054 03-04
MILFAY D 001257 02-03
MILIUS W 004516 04-13
MILLAR J 002475 02-16
MILLER AL 000870 01-15
MILLER DA 000228 01-03
MILLER JC 003407 03-13 , 003939 04-03
MILLER JQ 003378 03-11
MILLER K 000191 01-03
MILLER P 002149 02-11
MILLER R 002580 02-17 , 002634 03-01 ,
    003145 03-06 , 003253 03-09 , 003667
    04-01
MILLER V 003055 03-04
MILLER WC 003015 03-04
MILLET Y 003759 04-03
MILLMAN JE 004669 04-16
MILLS IH 003342 03-11
MILLS MJ 004730 04-17
MILSON JA 002894 03-03
MILSTEIN V 003430 03-13
MIMAKI T 001373 02-03 , 002902 03-03
MIMS ME 000145 01-03
MIMYUKOVA TA 004434 04-11
MIN BH 002248 02-13 , 002486 02-16
MINAMIURA N 001060 02-01
MINCHIN RF 000524 01-05 , 004179 04-04
MINDE K 003306 03-11
MINEGISHI A 001236 02-03
MINELLI A 002925 03-03
MINICH LN 003636 04-13
MINNE P 001954 02-08
MINNEMA DJ 000435 01-04
MINNEMAN KP 000207 01-03 , 002829 03-03
MINSKER EI 004335 04-08
MINTY K 002164 02-11
MINTZ M 002154 02-11 , 003060 03-04
MINTZ R 003049 03-04
MINZI AL 001985 02-09
MIRANDA H 001290 02-03 , 002756 03-03
MIRIN SM 003243 03-09
MIRMAN MJ 000655 01-10
MIRMIRAN M 003056 03-04 , 004091 04-04
MISGELD U 001374 02-03
MISHKIN M 002641 03-01
MISHRA R 000208 01-03 , 000360 01-04 ,
    001358 02-03 , 001447 02-03 , 001493
    02-03
MISKA RM 003132 03-05
MISRA AL 001375 02-03
MISRA CH 001789 02-04 , 003901 04-03 ,
    003940 04-03 , 004694 04-16
MISRA RS 000081 01-03
MISSIK T 000706 01-11
MISUREC J 000567 01-08 , 000613 01-09 ,
    000623 01-09 , 000634 01-09 , 002115
    02-11 , 002190 02-11
MITCHELL E 002436 02-15
MITCHELL G 003887 04-03
MITCHELL JE 003514 03-15
MITCHELL R 001376 02-03 , 001377 02-03 ,
    001378 02-03
MITKEVICH SP 004541 04-13
MITRANI N 000176 01-03 , 003899 04-03
MITROFANOV VS 001705 02-04
MITSUDOME A 000696 01-11
MITTEL NS 003566 03-16
MITTERMEIER RA 002592 02-17
MITTMAN S 002656 03-03
MIURA A 000210 01-03
MIURA S 002844 03-03 , 004422 04-10 ,
    004518 04-13
MIYAGAWA T 001379 02-03 , 003714 04-03
MIYAKAWA T 000814 01-14
MIYAKODA J 000860 01-15
MIYAKOSHI N 003941 04-03
MIYAMOTO M 003057 03-04
MIYAMOTO T 003129 03-05
MIYAOKA M 001380 02-03

MIYAZAKI M 001273 02-03
MIZOULE J 000176 01-03 , 003898 04-03
MIZRAHI EM 002437 02-15
MIZUGUCHI R 002559 02-17
MIZUTA T 003999 04-03
MIZUTANI A 003717 04-03
MLCAKOVA K 002136 02-11
MO K 000963 01-17
MOBLEY PL 001493 02-03 , 004746 04-17
MOCCETTI T 003490 03-15
MODE A 000273 01-03
MODIGH K 002664 03-03
MODRZEWSKA R 004426 04-10
MOEGLEN JM 001954 02-08
MOERSCHBAECHER JM 001723 02-04
MOGENSON GJ 000331 01-03 , 000436 01-04
    000457 01-04 , 003019 03-04
MÖGER WH 001535 02-03
MOGILNICKA E 003058 03-04
MOHASCI E 000898 01-16 , 003702 04-02
MOHLENHOF O 002263 02-13
MOHLER H 001381 02-03 , 002643 03-01 ,
    002646 03-02
MOHRLAND JS 000437 01-04 , 001328 02-03
    001724 02-04
MÖHS RC 002317 02-14
MOISES HC 000209 01-03 , 001382 02-03 ,
    004058 04-03
MOLCAN J 000609 01-09 , 000615 01-09 ,
    000706 01-11 , 000707 01-11 , 001934
    02-08 , 001997 02-09 , 002019 02-09 ,
    002020 02-09 , 002151 02-11 , 003567
    03-16 , 004375 04-09
MOLCZADZKI M 004395 04-09
MOLDOFSKY H 002152 02-11
MOLINOFF PB 000272 01-03 , 000207 01-03 ,
    002829 03-03 , 002932 03-03 , 003979
    04-03 , 004229 04-04
MOLLER H 000610 01-09 , 001917 02-08 ,
    003218 03-13 , 003219 03-09
MOLLER IW 002329 02-14
MOLLHOFF G 002438 02-15
MOLLORGA P 001279 02-03
MOLNAR J 002817 03-03
MON MJ 002830 03-03 , 002831 03-03
MONACO AP 003015 03-04
MONACO F 000533 01-06
MONCADA V 000450 01-04 , 002896 03-03
MONDAL P 000002 01-01 , 000003 01-01 ,
    001015 02-01
MONETI G 001386 02-03
MONPREMIER P 001929 02-08
MONTASTRUC J 000411 04-03
MONTGOMERY A 004252 04-04
MONTGOMERY D 002215 02-13 , 002266 02-
    13
MONTGOMERY JA 001021 02-01
MONTGOMERY S 001976 02-09 , 002215 02-
    13 , 002266 02-13 , 004385 04-09 ,
    004707 04-17 , 004731 04-17
MONTGOMERY T 000501 01-04 , 002931 03-
    03 , 004180 04-04
MONTI JA 002636 03-01
MONTPLAISIR J 003341 03-11
MOODY AH 001437 02-03
MOODY TW 001064 02-01 , 001383 02-03
MOON CD 003537 03-15
MOORE CF 002637 03-01
MOORE DC 000708 01-11
MOORE DP 004641 04-15
MOORE KE 000614 01-04 , 000365 01-04 ,
    001595 02-04 , 002700 03-03 , 004089
    04-04 , 004171 04-04
MOORE P 002164 02-11
MOORE R 003342 03-11
MOORE SL 000709 01-11
MORALES ER 000102 01-03
MORAN EC 001850 02-05
MORAN TJ 003593 03-17
MORENO G 004535 04-13
MORENO L 001421 02-03
MORETON JE 004038 04-03 , 004170 04-04
MORETTI P 002091 02-11
MORETTI-OJEMANN L 000728 01-11
MORGAN BA 000351 01-04 , 003662 04-01
MORGAN DD 004473 04-11
MORGAN IG 004069 04-04
MORGAN JP 001851 02-05
MORGAN ME 001384 02-03

MORGAN V 004519 04-13 , 004567 04-14
MORGAN WW 002772 03-03 , 003873 04-03
MORI A 004388 04-09
MORI J 000493 01-04 , 003141 03-06 ,
    004278 04-05 , 004295 04-06
MORIHISA J 001945 02-08 , 003169 03-08 ,
    003184 03-08
MORIOKA T 004551 04-13
MORITA H 004618 04-15
MORITA K 00009B 01-03
MORITA Y 001188 02-03
MORKOVKIN VM 004732 04-17
MORLEY JE 001385 02-03 , 001725 02-04 ,
    003059 03-04 , 003942 04-03 , 003943
    04-03 , 004181 04-04
MORO F 001200 02-03
MOROCUTTI C 002355 02-14
MOROJI T 000964 01-17
MORONI F 001386 02-03
MORRIS DH 003684 04-02
MORRIS HH 003468 03-15
MORRIS M 000537 01-06 , 001726 02-04
MORRIS MJ 003944 04-03
MORRIS RJ 000655 01-10
MORRIS RW 000529 01-05
MORRISON DH 001707 02-04
MORRISON M 004114 04-04
MORSE WH 003096 03-04 , 004012 04-03
MORSELLI PL 000549 01-08 , 000596 01-09 ,
    000777 01-13 , 001907 02-08 , 002014
    02-09 , 002254 02-13 , 002267 02-13 ,
    003175 03-08 , 003324 03-11 , 003334
    03-11 , 003343 03-11 , 003616 03-17
MORTIER L 002600 02-17
MORTON AK 004279 04-05
MORTON L 002084 02-10 , 003285 03-10
MOS J 001149 02-03 , 002832 03-03
MOSCOVICI M 001944 02-08
MOSER C 000745 01-12
MOSER L 000650 01-10
MOSER P 003686 04-02 , 003921 04-03
MOSHKAVOVSKIY YS 001331 02-03
MOSKOWITZ MA 002503 02-16
MOSS DE 002500 02-16 , 004182 04-04
MOSS WW 004688 04-16
MOTLEY B 002432 02-15
MOTOYOSHI S 004185 04-04
MOTTA M 001418 02-03
MOUCHET P 000070 01-03
MOUNIER F 000262 01-03
MOUNSEY IJ 000206 01-03
MOUNTJOY CQ 002081 02-10
MOUSSAOUI D 002581 02-17
MOUZAKIS D 004337 04-08
MOYE T 001707 02-04
MOZHAYEVA YG 004444 04-11
MRSKOS A 002115 02-11
MRSULJA BB 003765 04-03
MUCCI L 003791 04-03
MUCCINO RR 002486 02-16
MUCHA RF 001387 02-03
MUCK-SELER D 002243 02-13
MUDD SH 001388 02-03
MUELLER C 001970 02-09
MUELLER K 001727 02-04
MUELLER RA 001389 02-03 , 001813 02-04 ,
    003748 04-03 , 003917 04-03 , 004195
    04-04
MUENTER MD 003432 03-13
MUESER KT 004577 04-14
MUH JP 003291 03-11
MUHI-ELDEEN Z 003701 04-02
MUHLBAUER H 000780 01-13
MUIR B 002164 02-11
MUKERJI S 003836 04-03
MUKHOPADHYAY S 004674 04-16
MULAY VP 004379 04-09
MULBRY LW 001210 02-03
MULDER AH 000067 01-03 , 000289 01-03 ,
    000323 01-03 , 001390 02-03
MULDER TBA 004305 04-06
MULDER-HAJONIDES WREM 003216 03-09
MULLER C 000684 01-11
MULLER D 003300 03-11
MULLER E 000042 01-03 , 001391 02-03 ,
    002690 03-03 , 003191 03-08 , 003344
    03-11
MULLER H 003671 04-01
MULLER J 003300 03-11

MULLER M 000308 01-03
MULLER P 001392 02-03
MULLER WE 001440 02-03 , 002833 03-03 ,
  004211 04-04
MULLER-OERLINGHAUSEN B 000611 01-09 ,
  000749 01-13 , 000753 01-13 , 000768
  01-13 , 000830 01-15 , 002290 02-13 ,
  003515 03-15   003568 03-16
MULOPULOS GP 003463 03-15
MULVANEY DE 000284 01-03
MUMFORD L 000438 01-04
MUNARI C 003334 03-11
MUNEKIYO K 000260 01-03
MUNOZ C 000439 01-04
MUNSON E 003346 03-11
MURAKAMI H 001728 02-04
MURAKI T 000211 01-03 , 001393 02-03 ,
  002834 03-03 , 003946 04-03
MURAMATSU I 000210 01-03
MURATORIO A 001295 02-03
MURIE N 002153 02-11
MURONOVA J 000643 01-09
MURPHY D 000038 01-03 , 000587 01-09 ,
  000612 01-09 000673 01-11 , 002233
  02-13 , 002280 02-13 , 003255 03-09 ,
  004393 04-09 , 004659 04-15
MURPHY DT 000425 01-04
MURPHY JE 004386 04-09
MURPHY K 002164 02-11 , 002835 03-03
MURPHY MB 002439 02-15
MURPHY ML 000866 01-15
MURPHY MR 004183 04-04
MURPHY RJ 000937 01-17
MURRAY HW 002567 02-17
MURRAY JB 002440 02-15
MURRAY JN 000965 01-17
MURUGAIAH K 002707 03-03
MUSA MN 003244 03-09
MUSACCHIO JM 000061 01-03
MUSCETTOLA G 003250 03-09
MUSIL F 000605 01-09
MUSTY RE 004263 04-04
MUTH EA 001528 02-03
MUTT V 001239 02-03
MYCEK MJ 002813 03-03 , 003038 03-04
MYERS JK 000998 01-17
MYERS MM 002685 03-03
MYERS RD 001454 02-03
MYGUEL M 004594 04-15
MYKING OL 004488 04-11
MYLLYLA VV 002260 02-13 , 004542 04-13
MYQUEL M 004357 04-04
MYQUEL-SIDER M 002108 02-11
MYSLINSKI NR 002967 03-04
MYSLIVECEK J 000803 01-14 , 000815 01-14
  001647 02-04
MYSLOBODSKY MS 001729 02-04 , 002154
  02-11 , 003060 03-04 , 003061 03-04

N

NABELEK L 001934 02-08
NABER D 001536 02-03 , 001935 02-08 ,
  001936 02-08 , 002222 02-13 , 003357
  03-11
NABESHIMA T 002771 03-03
NACCARI F 000443 01-04 , 001733 02-04 ,
  003075 03-04
NACHTMAN V 004642 04-15
NADI NS 002836 03-03
NAG D 002186 02-11
NAGAI Y 003057 03-04
NAGARAJU A 000904 01-16 , 003181 03-08 ,
  003182 03-08
NAGASHIMA R 001659 02-04
NAGAWA Y 003057 03-04
NAGAYAMA H 001730 02-04
NAGY A 003945 04-03
NAGY BR 004643 04-15
NAGY JI 004184 04-04
NAHORSKI SR 001878 02-06 , 002679 03-03
NAHUNEK K 000567 01-08 , 000568 01-08 ,
  000613 01-09 , 000634 01-09 , 000663
  01-11 , 000729 01-11 , 001937 02-08 ,
  001949 02-08 , 001975 02-09 , 002021
  02-09 , 002064 02-10 , 002115 02-11 ,
  002190 02-11 , 003245 03-09 , 003264
  03-09 , 004375 04-09
NAIDER F 001059 02-01
NAIL GL 002954 03-04

NAIR NPV 000560 01-08 , 001428 02-03 ,
  002441 02-15
NAKADATE T 000211 01-03 , 001393 02-03 ,
  002834 03-03 , 003946 04-03
NAKAHAMA H 002837 03-03
NAKAHARA H 000472 01-04
NAKAHARA T 000212 01-03 , 002781 03-03
NAKAJIMA E 004551 04-13
NAKAMURA H 004185 04-04
NAKAMURA I 004608 04-15
NAKAMURA K 003947 04-03 , 003947 04-03
NAKAMURA S 003129 03-05
NAKAMUTA H 001320 02-03
NAKANE Y 000636 01-09 002442 02-15
NAKANISHI K 003842 04-03 , 004387 04-09
NAKANO M 004517 04-13
NAKANO S 002336 02-14 004247 04-04
NAKASONE C 003345 03-11
NAKATA Y 001394 02-03
NAKAYAMA T 003672 04-01
NAKAZAWA H 003083 03-04
NAKAZAWA Y 002349 02-14 , 003450 03-14
NAMBA MMQ 004186 04-04
NAMBA S 003345 03-11
NANDA RN 003371 03-11
NANDY K 002582 02-17
NANZ C 001440 02-03 , 004211 04-04
NAQUET R 003564 03-16
NARABAYASHI H 002309 02-13
NARANJO CA 000747 01-13 , 000789 01-13 ,
  000790 01-13 , 004552 04-13
NARAYAN S 000069 01-03
NARAYANAN HS 003533 03-15
NARCISSE G 001083 02-02
NARUMI S 003057 03-04
NASH H 004047 04-03
NASH HL 001329 02-03
NASR S 004538 04-13
NASRALLAH HA 001938 02-08
NATHAN RS 000752 01-13 , 000776 01-13 ,
  000874 01-15 , 002238 02-13 , 004405
  04-09
NATHANSON JA 002838 03-03
NATION RL 002508 02-16
NATSUKA K 004185 04-04
NATSUKI R 001280 02-03
NAUSIEDA P 000498 01-04 , 001845 02-05 ,
  002159 02-11 002468 02-15 , 003502
  03-15 , 003516 03-15 , 004249 04-04
NAUTSCH J 002501 02-16
NAVA D 003157 03-07 003158 03-07
NAVRATIL J 000651 01-10 , 001731 02-04 ,
  002333 02-14
NAYLOR GJ 003365 03-11
NAYLOR RJ 000370 01-04 , 001603 02-04 ,
  002220 02-13 , 004092 04-04
NAZZARO JM 000467 01-04 , 004187 04-04
NEAFSEY EJ 000172 01-03
NEAL MJ 002691 03-03
NEALE JH 004002 04-03
NEALE SE 001461 02-03
NEAR JA 003948 04-03
NEBORSKY R 003346 03-11
NECKERS LM 000255 01-03 , 003499 03-15 ,
  004285 04-06 , 004296 04-06
NEE L 002354 02-14
NEELY P 000742 01-12
NEETHLING AC 002839 03-03
NEF B 001657 02-04 , 004197 04-04
NEFF NH 003139 03-06 , 003800 04-03 ,
  003876 04-03 , 003949 04-03 , 003958
  04-03 , 004188 04-04
NEGREANU J 001161 02-03
NEIL A 003062 03-04
NEIL JH 000594 01-09 000631 01-09 ,
  003236 03-09 , 004511 04-13
NEILL DB 001873 02-06
NELSON DL 000213 01-03 , 000214 01-03 ,
  001269 02-03 , 003825 04-03
NELSON DR 004086 04-04
NELSON ED 000740 01-12
NELSON JC 000781 01-13
NELSON JL 004196 04-04
NELSON M 002939 03-03
NELSON PG 002669 03-03
NELSON R 003309 03-11
NEMCOVA J 000332 01-03
NEMEROFF CB 003037 03-04 , 004111 04-04
NEMIROFF A 002978 03-04
NEOPHYTIDES A 000698 01-11 , 002342 02-
  14

NERAD J 000816 01-14 , 002155 02-11
NERI A 002443 02-15
NESTOROS JN 002840 03-03 , 004733 04-17
NEUHAUS HU 002958 03-04
NEUHOFF V 000054 01-03
NEUMAN J 002156 02-11
NEUMEYER JL 001114 02-03
NEVILLE DM 001063 02-01 , 001064 02-01
NEWHOUSE P 003347 03-11
NEWMAN S 000697 01-11
NEWMEYER JA 000741 01-12
NEZIROGLU F 002082 02-10
NG K 001607 02-04 , 003182 03-08
NGUYEN T 002209 02-13
NICHOLSON AN 000440 01-04 , 004189 04-04
  004574 04-14
NICKOLSON VJ 000264 01-03 , 000441 01-04
NICOL AR 003420 03-13
NICOL SE 002825 03-03
NICOLAOU NM 000215 01-03
NICOLLE MH 000817 01-14
NICOLOV N 000473 01-04 , 003716 04-03
NIEDZIELSKI J 001694 02-04
NIEFORTH KA 004012 04-03
NIELSEN EB 000216 01-03 , 001395 02-03 ,
  001875 02-06 , 002988 03-04
NIELSEN F 001950 02-08
NIELSEN IM 001169 02-03
NIELSEN J 001732 02-04 , 004734 04-17 ,
  004734 04-17
NIELSEN M 000216 01-03 , 000918 01-17 ,
  001139 02-03 , 001395 02-03 , 002676
  03-03 , 003579 03-17 , 003739 04-03
NIELSEN-KUDSK F 001852 02-05 , 002261 02-
  13
NIELSON HC 000392 01-04 , 001608 02-04
NIEMEGEERS CJE 000363 01-04 , 004088 04-
  04
NIEOULLON A 000217 01-03
NIETO D 003348 03-11
NIEUWEBOER B 004516 04-13
NIGAM A 002175 02-11
NIGHTINGALE JH 000638 01-09
NIKANDROVA LR 004543 04-13
NIKOLAISHVILI MI 004068 04-04
NIKOLETSEAS MM 004190 04-04
NIKOLOV N 000119 01-03
NILSEN S 003180 03-08
NILSSON B 001134 02-03
NILSSON JLG 000399 01-04
NIMIT Y 003950 04-03
NIOCHE J 003691 04-02
NISHI H 003951 04-03
NISHIURA M 000219 01-03
NISHIURA N 000219 01-03
NISSEN C 001311 02-03
NISSEN G 003349 03-11
NISTICO GO 000041 01-03 , 000218 01-03 ,
  000442 01-04 , 000443 01-04 , 001733
  02-04 , 001734 02-04 , 002762 03-03 ,
  003952 04-03
NISTICO GO 003075 03-04
NISTRI A 002841 03-03
NITANAI T 004551 04-13
NITZ R 001082 02-02 , 001360 02-03
NIWA G 000661 01-11
NOACH EL 001150 02-03 , 002681 03-03
NOBLE EP 001499 02-03
NOBLE RG 001735 02-04
NOCERA F 003466 03-15
NOCK B 002842 03-03
NODA K 000219 01-03
NODA Y 001808 02-04
NOGUCHI H 000219 01-03
NOGUCHI Y 000099 01-03 , 000444 01-04
NOGUIERA AB 003185 03-08
NOHRIA V 000370 01-04 , 004092 04-04
NOLL KLM 003063 03-04
NOMURA Y 000445 01-04 , 001396 02-03 ,
  004191 04-04
NONAKA K 003450 03-14
NOORDHUIZEN GJM 002022 02-09
NORDGREN I 003847 04-03
NORDSTROM O 002667 03-03
NORELL SE 003618 03-17
NORMAN TR 000614 01-09 , 002184 02-11 ,
  002383 02-15 , 002497 02-16 , 004477
  04-11 , 004639 04-15
NORRIS PJ 002843 03-03

NORTH RA 001203 02-03 , 002740 03-03
NOSEK I 004642 04-15
NOVAK C 003306 03-11
NOVAKOVA V 002865 03-03
NOVIN D 000396 01-04 , 003821 04-03
NOVOTNA J 002507 02-16
NOVOTNY V 000615 01-09 , 000706 01-11 ,
  000707 01-11 , 002020 02-09 , 002151
  02-11
NOWAK JZ 001332 02-03 , 001397 02-03 ,
  001697 02-04
NOWAK MJ 001639 02-04
NOYES R 002073 02-10 , 003619 03-17
NULLER YL 003351 03-11
NUMMINEN A 002077 02-10
NUNN PB 002858 03-03
NURMAND LB 001736 02-04
NURNBERGER JI 004565 04-14
NUSSER W 003456 03-14
NUTT DJ 001184 02-03 , 002444 02-15 ,
  002971 03-04
NUTTALL EA 003496 03-15
NUTTER D 003246 03-09
NUTTO D 000165 01-03 , 001319 02-03 ,
  003715 04-03
NUZZI G 000878 01-15
NYBACK H 001905 02-08
NYBERG G 003569 03-16
NYHAN WL 004576 04-14

O

O-UCHI T 004138 04-04
OAKLEY NR 001399 02-03
OANA Y 002844 03-03
OATES JA 002734 03-03
OBAL F 002955 03-04 , 002955 03-04
OBE G 000753 01-13
OBERLANDER C 003789 04-03
OBERMAN Z 004343 04-08
OBIOLS J 002588 02-17 , 002589 02-17
OBRIEN CP 003335 03-11
OBRIEN JH 000343 01-04
OBRIEN R 000725 01-11
OBRIST PA 003813 04-03
OCALLAGHAN JP 000220 01-03 , 001173 02-
  03
OCHI Y 000152 01-03
OCHS HR 000114 01-03 , 000968 01-17 ,
  003161 03-07 , 003352 03-11
OCONNELL RA 003247 03-09
OCONNOR MK 002038 02-09
ODA D 000639 01-09
ODEJIDE AO 004334 04-08
ODIO M 003978 04-03
ODIO-YGLESIAS M 003794 04-03
ODONNELL JM 000434 01-04
ODONNELL JP 003697 04-02
ODONOHUE TL 001046 02-01 , 001398 02-03
  001528 02-03
ODORIZZI F 004717 04-17
ODRISCOLL D 002445 02-15
OECHSNER R 001917 02-08
OEFFINGER KC 002766 03-03
OEI TPS 000446 01-04
OERTEL WH 001047 02-01 , 001048 02-01 ,
  001400 02-03
OFALLON JV 003953 04-03
OGAWA N 002336 02-14 , 004247 04-04
OGREN S 001096 02-03 , 001238 02-03 ,
  001240 02-03 , 002727 03-03 , 003824
  04-03
OGREN SO 002523 01-03
OGURA C 000639 01-09
OH VMS 002268 02-13
OHARE JA 002445 02-15
OHASHI K 004128 04-04
OHIZUMI Y 001280 02-03
OHKAWA T 003450 03-14
OHLSSON A 001737 02-04 , 002201 02-12
OHMAN R 001230 02-03 , 002590 02-17 ,
  004700 04-17
OHMIYA Y 002845 03-03
OHMORI K 004192 04-04
OHMOTO T 003129 03-05
OHSAWA K 003714 04-03
OHSHIMA M 002349 02-14
OISHI R 001681 02-04
OITZL M 004015 04-03
OKA M 001293 02-03 , 004149 04-04 ,
  004193 04-04

OKA T 000221 01-03
OKABAYASHI T 002725 03-03
OKADA K 003856 04-03
OKADA T 003947 04-03
OKADA Y 001401 02-03
OKAMOTO K 001402 02-03 , 002846 03-03
OKASHA A 003192 03-08
OKRUHLICA L 001934 02-08 , 002151 02-11
OKTABA-POLKOWSKA A 001684 02-04
OKTAY S 004275 04-05
OKUDAIRA N 002350 02-14
OKUI M 000219 01-03
OKUMA T 002442 02-15 , 004388 04-09
OKUSE S 000653 01-10
OKUYAMA S 004148 04-04
OLAJOSSY M 004426 04-10 , 004644 04-15
OLANOW CW 003353 03-11 , 003421 03-13
OLDHAM AJ 000818 01-14
OLDS ME 001738 02-04 , 004194 04-04
OLEARY DP 002997 03-04
OLEYNIK LI 003643 03-17
OLIANAS MC 003949 04-03 , 003958 04-03
OLIVER C 003759 04-03
OLIVER M 001036 02-01 , 003918 04-03
OLIVERIO A 000336 01-04 , 001766 02-04
OLIVIER M 003305 03-11
OLLER FV 002288 02-13
OLLER-DAURELLA L 002288 02-13
OLNEY JW 000222 01-03
OLPE H 002847 03-03 , 003880 04-03
OLSAUSKAS RS 001739 02-04
OLSEN RW 002848 03-03
OLSHAN A 004695 04-16
OLSHAN GA 001327 02-03
OLSON L 000095 01-03
OLSON RD 001327 02-03
OLTON DS 001398 02-03
OMER LMO 004532 04-13
OMOROKOV BM 003172 03-08
ONALI P 001403 02-03
ONBE H 000199 01-03
ONDRUSEK MG 004195 04-04
ONEILL JJ 004267 04-05
ONEILL KJ 004267 04-05
ONEILL MJ 004438 04-11
ONO H 003807 04-03
ONO T 000493 01-04 , 002442 02-15
ONODA K 002753 03-03
ONUR R 004275 04-05
OOSTERVELD WJ 004478 04-11
OPGENOORTH E 000819 01-14 , 003251 03-09
OPMEER FA 001404 02-03
ORBACHEVSKAYA IY 002892 03-03
ORLOV IV 002940 03-03
ORLOWSKI RC 001320 02-03
ORME ML 001832 02-05
ORMSBEE HS 001327 02-03
ORNE EC 004585 04-14
ORNE MT 004585 04-14
ORNSTEIN K 004015 04-03
ORR ML 004645 04-15
ORSULAK PJ 000787 01-13 , 004406 04-09
ORTEGA J 001558 02-04
ORTEGA-BEVIA F 002849 03-03 , 002850 03-
  03 , 002851 03-03
ORTEGA-MONASTERIO L 001963 02-09
ORTH JP 002023 02-09
ORTIZ A 003673 04-01
ORTIZ MA 001740 02-04
ORTMANN J 002033 02-09
ORTMANN R 001740 02-04
OSAWA K 000661 01-11
OSBORNE M 003837 04-03
OSBORNE RH 000054 01-03 , 003954 04-03
OSBORNE VL 003045 03-04
OSHINO N 003718 04-03
OSSOLA L 002699 03-03
OSTERWALDER R 001264 02-03
OSTOW M 000969 01-17 , 000970 01-17 ,
  000971 01-17 , 000972 01-17
OSTROUMOVA LI 004389 04-09
OSTROVSKAYA RU 000485 01-04 , 001705
  02-04
OSTROW DG 001987 02-09 , 002024 02-09 ,
  002269 02-13 , 003142 03-06
OSTROW LC 004874 01-15
OSTROWSKI NL 004196 04-04
OSUIDE G 001741 02-04
OSWALD I 002446 02-15
OTSUKA M 000167 01-03 , 000493 01-04

OTSUKI S 004388 04-09
OTT H 004309 04-07
OTT J 000742 01-12
OTT T 002792 03-03
OTTER MY 001736 02-04
OTVOS L 000010 01-02 , 000011 01-02
OULES MJ 000616 01-09 , 000782 01-13
OVERALL JE 004324 04-08
OVERO KF 000591 01-09
OVERSTREET DH 000226 01-03 , 002163 02-
  11 , 002852 03-03 , 003042 03-04
OVERTON DA 000447 01-04
OWEN F 000062 01-03 , 001911 02-08 ,
  004423 04-10
OWEN G 002420 02-15
OWEN JE 002995 03-04
OWENS DGC 004423 04-10
OWENS DP 002853 03-03
OWENS K 003993 04-03
OWMAN C 002807 03-03
OXMAN TE 000876 01-15
OYA M 004024 04-03
OYEWUMI LK 003354 03-11
OZAKI Y 002503 02-16
OZAWA S 001401 02-03

P

PABST J 000968 01-17
PABST M 000259 01-03
PACHECO H 001227 02-03 , 002816 03-03 ,
  003691 04-02
PACHECO P 001612 02-04
PACKMAN PM 001122 02-03 , 003712 04-03
PADEL U 000483 01-04
PADIAN N 003272 03-09 , 004418 04-09
PADJEN AL 002870 03-03
PAITICH D 000697 01-11
PAKARINEN A 002258 02-13
PAKKENBERG H 002127 02-11
PAKOVITS M 003792 04-03
PAKSZYS W 004494 04-11
PALACIOS JM 001054 02-01 , 002644 03-01
PALCOUX MC 004307 04-07
PALERMO NN 003143 03-06
PALERMO-NETO J 004101 04-04
PALET JL 000517 01-05
PALFAI T 001742 02-04
PALFREYMAN MG 000248 01-03 , 000458 01-
  04 , 001128 02-03 , 003620 03-17
PALKOVITS M 003955 04-03
PALMER FB 000732 01-11
PALMER GC 001259 02-03 , 001405 02-03 ,
  003956 04-03
PALMER MR 001406 02-03 , 002502 02-16 ,
  003926 04-03 , 003957 04-03
PALMER S 001259 02-03 , 003956 04-03 ,
  004009 04-03
PALMERY M 001107 02-03 , 002515 02-17
PALMOUR RM 001049 02-01 , 001612 02-04 ,
  001743 02-04
PALOSI E 000010 01-02
PANAHON NC 003479 03-15
PANDELON R 003152 03-07
PANDEY G 000135 01-03 , 000908 01-16 ,
  000973 01-17 , 002269 02-13 , 004682
  04-16
PANISSIDI G 001200 02-03
PANKSEPP J 001644 02-04 , 001744 02-04 ,
  001745 02-04 , 003011 03-04
PANNIER L 002854 03-03
PANSA M 004635 04-15
PANTELEYEVA GP 004335 04-08 , 004381 04-
  09 , 004390 04-09
PAOLINO E 002283 02-13
PAPADAKIS N 003520 03-15
PAPADOPOULOS G 001657 02-04 , 004197
  04-04
PAPADOPOULOU-DAIFOTIS Z 003698 04-02
PAPE D 002205 02-13
PAPEZOVA H 001888 02-07 , 001924 02-08 ,
  002025 02-09
PAPPAS BA 000309 01-03 , 000310 01-03 ,
  000448 01-04 , 003142 03-06
PARADKAR VM 001710 02-04
PARDAL JF 000223 01-03
PARDO A 003673 04-01
PARE CMB 004640 04-15
PAREEK NK 000583 01-09

PARENTI M 001422 02-03 , 003139 03-06 ,
   003800 04-03 , 003949 04-03 , 003958
   04-03 , 004188 04-04
PARIKH MD 002158 02-11
PARISER SF 003521 03-15
PARK BK 003621 03-17
PARK RN 001746 02-04
PARKER D 002003 02-09 , 003178 03-08
PARKER LA 001747 02-04
PARKER RE 000740 01-12
PARKER RR 003249 03-09 , 044402 04-09
PARKES J 002168 02-11 , 002358 02-14 ,
   003422 03-13 , 004113 04-04
PARMAR SS 000081 01-03 , 003119 03-04
PARROTT AC 002331 02-14 , 002351 02-14
PARROTT EL 004554 04-13
PARROTT RF 003064 03-04
PARSON R 003699 04-02
PARSONS DS 001793 02-04
PARSONS SL 002702 03-03
PARTLOW LM 002780 03-03
PARY R 001945 02-08
PASANTES-MORALES H 002855 03-03 ,
   002856 03-03
PASCOE JP 003798 04-03
PASI A 003490 03-15
PASSOTH P 000611 01-09
PASTERNAK GW 001554 02-03 , 003685 04-
   02 , 004198 04-04
PASTOR G 000188 01-03
PASTORIS O 001126 02-03
PASTUSZKO A 000224 01-03
PATACCHIOLI F 001107 02-03 , 002515 02-17
PATAY M 001902 02-07 , 002270 02-13 ,
   002271 02-13
PATE JK 000839 01-15
PATEL AJ 001407 02-03 , 002673 03-03
PATEL IH 000755 01-13
PATEL NB 001748 02-04
PATEL VK 001748 02-04
PATERSON SJ 000168 01-03 , 003802 04-03
PATOCKA J 000389 01-04
PATON DM 000974 01-17
PATON WDM 001686 02-04
PATRICK RL 002649 03-02 , 003829 04-03 ,
   003959 04-03 , 003960 04-03
PATSALOS PN 003961 04-03
PATTERSON T 004544 04-13
PATURAUD JP 003155 03-07
PATWARDHAN RV 002224 02-13 , 002272
   02-13
PATY J 003451 03-14
PAUGH BA 000450 01-04
PAUL A 000449 01-04
PAUL S 000225 01-03 , 000275 01-03 ,
   000276 01-03 , 000277 01-03 , 000450
   01-04 , 001475 02-03 , 002645 03-01 ,
   002857 03-03 , 002896 03-03 , 002972
   03-04 , 003962 04-03 , 004172 04-04
   004221 04-04 , 004251 04-04 , 004689
   04-16
PAULING P 000002 01-01 , 000003 01-01 ,
   001015 02-01
PAULSON GW 000950 01-17 , 003355 03-11
PAULUCCI TS 003111 03-04
PAUR R 000691 01-11
PAVLOVICOVA E 001804 02-04
PAWLICKI R 001844 02-05
PAXTON JW 004545 04-13
PAYKEL ES 003248 03-09 , 003249 03-09 ,
   004336 04-08 , 004402 04-09
PAZO JH 003130 03-05
PEACHEY JE 003522 03-15
PEARCE C 001743 02-04
PEARCE D 004690 04-16
PEARLMAN T 002352 02-14
PEARSON S 002858 03-03
PECHADRE JC 004479 04-11
PECKNOLD J 003285 03-10
PEDERSEN HE 000659 01-11
PEDERSEN PE 002478 02-16
PEDIGO NW 000226 01-03
PEELE R 000739 01-12
PEET LA 000092 01-03
PEET M 001940 02-08
PEGRAM V 000710 01-11
PEKKARINEN A 000086 01-03
PELAYO F 000227 01-03
PELICIER Y 000877 01-15
PELLERIN-MILLECAMPS E 000589 01-09

PENDLETON RG 000228 01-03 , 001069 02-02
   001255 02-03
PENG C 004489 04-11
PENG GW 001710 02-04
PENIN H 003314 03-11
PENKE B 003031 03-04
PENNY RHC 002843 03-03
PENRY JK 003375 03-11 , 004522 04-13
PEPEU G 001386 02-03 , 003065 03-04
PEPPER CM 001408 02-03
PERAINO C 001409 02-03
PERCIVAL JE 002241 02-13
PERCY VA 002859 03-03
PEREIRA AE 000669 01-11
PEREL JM 000619 01-09 , 000620 01-09 ,
   000776 01-13
PERÉNYI A 002447 02-15
PERERA-ORTIZ Y 002661 03-03
PEREZ VJ 000517 01-05
PEREZ-CRUET J 002273 02-13
PEREZ-DE-LA-MORA M 002727 03-03
PEREZ-GUAITA MD 001749 02-04
PERHACH JL 003103 03-04
PERKINS MN 000229 01-03 , 001410 02-03 ,
   003963 04-03
PERLIK S 000862 01-15 , 002159 02-11 ,
   002468 02-15 , 003502 03-15
PERLMAN T 004454 04-11
PERLMUTTER R 000717 01-11
PERLOW MJ 000255 01-03
PERON P 004445 04-11
PEROSSINI M 004507 04-13
PEROUTKA SJ 002230 01-03 , 002860 03-03 ,
   002861 03-03 , 003964 04-03
PERRIER D 000773 01-13
PERRIN JH 000762 01-13
PERRIN MH 003985 04-03
PERRINGTON A 001299 02-03
PERRIS C 002274 02-13
PERRISSIN M 001083 02-02
PERRON J 002600 02-17
PERRY KW 003796 04-03
PERRY ML 001960 02-08
PERRY PJ 003508 03-15
PERRY R 003361 03-11
PERRY W 003066 03-04
PERSAD E 001990 02-09
PERSSON B 000231 01-03 , 003965 04-03
PERSSON R 004412 04-09
PERT A 001050 02-01 , 001411 02-03
   001443 02-03 , 002275 02-13 , 002641
   03-01 , 003067 03-04
PERT CB 001025 02-01 , 001050 02-01 ,
   001383 02-03 , 001444 02-03 , 002641
   03-01 , 003737 04-03
PERUCCA E 000783 01-13 , 002276 02-13 ,
   003622 03-17
PESANDO P 000878 01-15
PESELOW ED 002017 02-09 , 002448 02-15 ,
   004391 04-09 , 004606 04-15
PESTRONK A 000232 01-03
PETERKA M 000144 01-03
PETERS DAV 003312 03-11
PETERS JE 001750 02-04
PETERS JR 001412 02-03
PETERS MA 000094 01-03
PETERS RH 001818 02-04 , 003821 04-03
PETERSEN C 003966 04-03
PETERSEN KP 001413 02-03
PETERSEN LR 001634 02-04
PETERSEN RC 000743 01-12
PETERSON CM 001836 02-05
PETERSON DW 001084 02-02
PETERSON GR 004560 04-14
PETERSON RC 004688 04-16
PETERSON SL 001559 02-04 , 002653 03-03 ,
   002862 03-03 , 002946 03-04
PETERSON TL 000937 01-17
PETHO B 003193 03-08
PETIT E 004742 04-17
PETIT M 003362 01-04 , 002449 02-15
PETIT TL 000525 01-05
PETOVA J 000544 01-07
PETR R 001635 02-04
PETRANOVA T 002008 02-09
PETRESCOU L 000817 01-14
PETRIE JC 003400 03-13
PETRIE WM 002026 02-09 , 004392 04-09 ,
   004646 04-15
PETTI T 002339 02-14 , 003356 03-11 ,
   004630 04-15

PETTIGREW JD 003024 03-04
PETTOROSSI VE 001566 02-04
PETTY F 001751 02-04 , 001775 02-04 ,
   003743 04-03
PEURA P 001078 02-02
PEVNICK J 000798 01-13
PEYER M 003967 04-03
PEYTON GA 000906 01-16
PFAFF DW 000421 01-04
PFEFFERBAUM A 003215 03-09
PFEIFER HJ 000784 01-13
PFLUEGER AB 003828 04-03
PFLUG B 000711 01-11 , 000772 01-13
PHILIPP M 000617 01-09 , 004480 04-11
PHILIPPU A 000520 01-05 , 002703 03-03 ,
   003968 04-03
PHILLIPS AG 000345 01-04 , 001572 02-04 ,
   002956 03-04 , 004070 04-04 , 004199
   04-04
PHILLIPS J 003433 03-13
PHILLIPS MI 003845 04-03
PHILLIPSON OT 001941 02-08
PHILLIS JW 000233 01-03 , 000234 01-03 ,
   000329 01-03 , 000330 01-03 , 000451
   01-04 , 001414 02-03 , 002933 03-03 ,
   003864 04-03 , 003969 04-03 , 004056
   04-03
PHYALL W 001415 02-03
PIAFSKY KM 000975 01-17
PICCARDI MP 001483 02-03
PICCIOLA G 001051 02-01
PICCIONE P 002160 02-11 , 002357 02-14
PICCIRILLO M 000452 01-04 , 001752 02-04
PICHAT L 003825 04-03
PICKAR D 003220 03-09 , 003357 03-11 ,
   004393 04-09
PICKARD JD 001416 02-03
PICKEL VM 002634 03-01
PICKENS JT 002196 02-12
PICKHOLZ D 000083 01-03
PICKMAN C 000470 01-04
PICKWORTH WB 002889 03-03
PICOTTI GB 002863 03-03
PIEGLER T 000799 01-13
PIERCE D 004394 04-09
PIERCEY MF 002980 03-04 , 003782 04-03 ,
   004200 04-04
PIERELLI F 002355 02-14 , 003157 03-07 ,
   003158 03-07
PIERI L 001381 02-03 , 002646 03-02
PIERSON RN 002928 03-03
PIETRUSZEWSKA I 004625 04-15
PIETTE LH 001065 02-01 , 001066 02-01
PIHL RO 002202 02-12
PILATE C 000543 01-07
PILC A 001256 02-03 , 001417 02-03
PILCHER CWT 000453 01-04 , 004201 04-04
PIMENTEL C 000669 01-11
PIMOULE C 000235 01-03
PINA AM 002591 02-17
PINDER RM 000592 01-09 , 004395 04-09
PINEGIN LY 004045 04-03
PINELLI P 000757 01-13 , 004675 04-16
PIPERNO R 000833 01-15
PIQUET J 003313 03-11
PIQUET V 004505 04-13
PIREDDA S 003533 01-06
PIRES-DE-OLIVEIRA RS 003358 03-11
PISANI FD 003359 03-11
PISANI G 001386 02-03
PISANTI N 000443 01-04
PISHKIN V 000879 01-15
PISTOLE T 000644 01-09
PISVEJC J 002132 02-11
PITTMAN KA 004691 04-16
PITTMAN QJ 002674 03-03
PITTMAN R 000197 01-03 , 002829 03-03
PITTONI G 000105 01-03
PITTS AF 003554 03-16
PITTS FN 003554 03-16
PIVA F 001418 02-03
PLACHETA P 001309 02-03 , 002893 03-03
PLANANSKY K 000569 01-08
PLANCHE R 002027 02-09
PLANTARD-NÉAU C 003563 03-16
PLATT JE 003360 03-11 , 003361 03-11
PLAZNIK A 001103 02-03
PLENAT M 003523 03-15
PLENGE P 004537 04-13

PLESHKOVA NM 004579 04-14
PLETSCHER A 003967 04-03
PLEUVRY BJ 004279 04-05
PLEVOVA J 000976 01-17
PLOTKIN C 003406 03-13
PLOTKIN MJ 002592 02-17
POAT JA 002722 03-03 , 004055 04-03
POCOCK DA 002340 02-14
PODDAR MK 003970 04-03
PODHRADSKA O 002115 02-11
PODIWINSKY F 000712 01-11
POE WD 002593 02-17
POELDINGER W 002286 02-13
POGGESI E 000036 01-03 , 000258 01-03
POGSON CI 002899 03-03
POHL M 001419 02-03
POHORECKY LA 002864 03-03
POIGNANT JC 001085 02-02 , 001898 02-07 ,
  001969 02-09
POINTIS D 001170 02-03
POIRIER J 001891 02-07 , 001969 02-09
POIRIER MA 004631 04-15
POIRIER MF 000551 01-08
POIRIER-LITTRE MF 000549 01-08
POKORNY J 002865 03-03
POKORSKI M 003971 04-03
POKRYSHKIN VI 003919 04-03
POLACEK J 004642 04-15
POLAND RE 003830 04-03 , 004403 04-09
POLC P 001381 02-03 , 002646 03-02
POLDINGER W 000603 01-09 , 002028 02-09
  004396 04-09
POLESSKAYA MM 003972 04-03
POLGAR M 000912 01-17
POLGATT M 003730 04-03
POLI M 002277 02-13
POLIMANTI S 004397 04-09
POLING A 001753 02-04 , 001754 02-04
POLINSKY RJ 003362 03-11
POLIZOS P 000880 01-15
POLLACK E 000678 01-11
POLLACK J 002928 03-03
POLLARD HB 001027 02-01
POLLARI L 001078 02-02
POLLERI A 002371 02-15
POLVAN N 004567 04-14
POMERANZ B 000236 01-03
PONDER SW 000361 01-04
PONG S 003688 04-02 , 003973 04-03
PONOMAREVA-STEPNAYA MA 001812 02-04
PONTANI RB 001375 02-03
PONTO LB 003509 03-15
PONTONNIER G 000797 01-13
PONZIO F 001325 02-03 , 003674 04-01
POPE HG 002480 02-16
POPE S 000697 01-11 , 001755 02-04
POPKIN N 000871 01-15
POPOV N 001819 02-04
POPOVIC M 002594 02-17
POPP FD 003699 04-02
POPPAY M 002663 03-03
PORGES SW 003363 03-11
POROT M 001969 02-09 , 002029 02-09 ,
  002030 02-09 , 003523 03-15
PORSCHE E 001052 02-03
PORSIUS AJ 004297 04-06
PORTA R 004116 04-04
PORTER RJ 004522 04-13
PORTOGHESE PS 001162 02-03 , 003104 03-
  04 , 004082 04-04
PORTUGAL H 003524 03-15
POSER W 000611 01-09
POSEY FT 004688 04-16
POSHIVALOV VP 004202 04-04
POSMUROVA M 000570 01-08 , 000761 01-
  13
POST R 000618 01-09 , 001984 02-09 ,
  002031 02-09 , 002034 02-09 , 002221
  02-13 , 002353 02-14 , 002366 02-14 ,
  002637 03-01 , 002866 03-03 , 003067
  03-04 , 003388 03-11 , 004398 04-09 ,
  004549 04-13
POSTMES TJ 004298 04-06
POTH MA 001282 02-03
POTKIN S 001928 02-08 , 001957 02-08 ,
  001958 02-08 , 003169 03-08 , 003499
  03-15
POTTASH ALC 000899 01-16 , 003220 03-09 ,
  003317 03-11
POTTER WZ 003250 03-09

POTVIN AR 002182 02-11
POTVIN JH 002182 02-11
POUEYTO P 002170 02-11
POWELL DA 001560 02-04 , 001668 02-04
POWELL JR 000773 01-13
POWERS CA 000237 01-03
POWERS DL 003700 04-02
POWERS JS 003364 03-11
POZDNYAKOV VS 003209 03-09
POZZA G 002277 02-13
PRADALIER A 004505 04-13
PRADHAN S 000346 01-04 , 001270 02-03 ,
  001348 02-03 , 001601 02-04 , 002867
  03-03 , 003826 04-03
PRAIGROTH A 002170 02-11
PRAKASH MR 002868 03-03
PRAKASH R 004656 04-15
PRANGE AJ 001850 02-05 , 002145 02-11 ,
  002259 02-13 , 003037 03-04 , 004111
  04-04
PRASAD C 004181 04-04
PRASAD V 000238 01-03
PRATT SR 003757 04-03
PREDESCU V 001979 02-09
PREDY PA 000419 01-04
PREINIGEROVA O 000654 01-10
PRELEVIC S 000714 01-11
PREODOR D 002053 02-09
PRESKORN SH 000239 01-03 , 003974 04-03
PRESSLICH O 003251 03-09
PRESTON PR 001329 02-03
PRIBRAM HFW 003322 03-11
PRICE RG 000837 01-15
PRIEN R 002450 02-15 , 002516 02-16
PRIESTLY BG 000682 01-11
PRIKRYL P 003423 03-13
PRIKRYL T 002507 02-16
PRIMROSE DA 003452 03-14
PRINCE DA 003728 04-03
PRINGUEY D 003524 03-15 , 003642 03-17
PRINS D 000713 01-11
PRINZ P 004695 04-16
PRIOUX-GUYONNEAU M 001187 02-03
PROHL L 004626 04-15
PROKES J 003170 03-08 , 003696 04-02
PROKHOROVA IS 004330 04-08
PROPST F 003975 04-03
PROSTAKOVA TI 004579 04-14
PROTIVA M 000001 01-01
PROTT FW 002540 01-13
PROUDFIT HK 000121 01-03 , 000122 01-03 ,
  000240 01-03 , 001420 02-03
PROZIALECK W 004052 04-03 , 004750 04-17
PRUDHOMME B 001899 02-07
PRUNERI C 004439 04-11
PRUSOFF BA 000624 01-09 , 003272 03-09 ,
  004418 04-09
PRUSS TP 000512 01-05
PRUSSAK C 003421 03-13
PRYOR JC 004515 04-13
PRZEWLOCKA B 003058 03-04
PRZEWLOCKI R 003837 04-03 , 003846 04-03
PRZYSLO FR 001253 02-03
PSARAS M 003744 04-03
PUDEL V 000611 01-09
PUECH AJ 000598 01-09 , 001942 02-08 ,
  002278 02-13 , 002992 02-13 , 003155
  03-07 , 003424 03-13 , 003633 03-17
PUERTO AX 001539 02-03
PUERTO R 001539 02-03
PUESCHEL SM 002161 02-11
PUGLISI-ALLEGRA S 001756 02-04
PUHRINGER W 004332 04-08
PUIG-ANTICH J 000619 01-09 , 000620 01-09
PUJOL J 002162 02-11 , 002588 02-17 ,
  002589 02-17 , 003668 04-01
PULLAR IA 001591 02-04 , 001592 02-04
PULLEN G 002595 02-17
PUNJANI NF 000022 01-03
PURI JN 000247 01-03
PURI SK 000049 01-03
PURVES R 003144 03-06
PURVES RD 000344 01-04
PUTKONEN PTS 000405 01-04
PUZYNSKI S 004546 04-13 , 004547 04-13 ,
  004548 04-13
PYCOCK CJ 000157 01-03 , 001589 02-04 ,
  002869 03-03 , 002966 03-04 , 003976
  04-03 , 004 00 04-04
PYNNONEN S 000785 01-13

QUACH TT 000241 01-03 , 001054 02-01
QUADBECK H 000562 01-08
QUADRI AA 000621 01-09
QUALLS CB 001971 02-09 , 003211 03-09
QUEISNEROVA M 000242 01-03 , 002279 02-
  13
QUERE J 002135 02-11
QUESNEY LF 000714 01-11
QUIK M 001296 02-03 , 002870 03-03
QUINAUX N 000267 01-03
QUINONES NQ 001093 02-02
QUINQUIS M 002600 02-17
QUIRCE CM 003977 04-03 , 003978 04-03
QUIRION R 000243 01-03
QUIST S 001852 02-05
QUITKIN F 000632 01-09 , 003228 03-09 ,
  003233 03-09 , 003240 03-09 , 003241
  03-09 , 003252 03-09 , 003262 03-09
QUOCK RM 003068 03-04

RAABE WA 004276 04-05
RABE A 000388 01-04
RABE LS 001421 02-03
RABENDING G 004481 04-11
RABIN RA 003979 04-03
RABINS P 003374 03-11
RACADOT A 004503 04-13
RACAGNI G 001422 02-03 , 002690 03-03 ,
  002973 03-04 , 003126 03-05
RACKHAM A 004053 04-03 , 004218 04-04
RACZ WJ 003912 04-03
RADEKE E 001740 02-04
RADOUCO-THOMAS C 002596 02-17
RADOUCO-THOMAS S 002596 02-17
RADOVANCEVIC L 000977 01-17
RADULOVACKI M 000244 01-03 , 004203 04-
  04
RADWAN S 001843 02-05
RAESE JD 001423 02-03
RAFAELSEN OJ 000850 01-15 , 000978 01-17
  002011 02-09 , 002597 02-17 , 004537
  04-13 , 004607 04-15
RAFF G 000825 01-14 , 003456 03-14
RAFTER J 000273 01-03
RAGAN P 000226 01-03
RAGAVAN VV 002871 03-03
RAGHEB M 000622 01-09
RAICHLE ME 003974 04-03
RAIMONDO S 001126 02-03 , 003730 04-03
RAINES A 000140 01-03
RAISANEN P 002185 02-11
RAISMAN R 002254 02-13 , 002569 02-16 ,
  003427 03-13 , 003955 04-03 , 004358
  04-09
RAITERI M 000185 01-03 , 001163 02-03 ,
  001424 02-03 , 003745 04-03
RAJKOWSKI J 000245 01-03
RAJTAR G 004166 04-04
RAKUS A 000609 01-09 , 003567 03-16
RALEIGH MJ 001385 02-03 , 004204 04-04
RAMA RAO VA 001943 02-08 , 001976 02-09
RAMADANOGLU E 004519 04-13
RAMIREZ VD 000459 01-04 , 001121 02-03 ,
  002668 03-03
RAMIREZ-GONZALEZ MD 000246 01-03 ,
  003791 04-03
RAMOS OL 000669 01-11
RAMOS-LORENZI JR 003233 03-09 , 003252
  03-09
RAMOT O 002875 03-03
RAMSAY G 000697 01-11
RAMSEIER F 004399 04-09
RAMSEY P 002417 02-15
RAMSEY TA 000940 01-17 , 001991 02-09 ,
  003263 03-09 , 003570 03-16
RANCE MJ 000032 01-03 , 000351 01-04 ,
  003611 03-17
RANDALL PK 004217 04-04
RANDO RR 003980 04-03
RANE A 002181 02-11
RANELLI CJ 003253 03-09
RANGARAJ N 001425 02-03
RANI SJ 002266 02-13
RANSOM DH 001048 02-01 , 001400 02-03
RAO AV 000881 01-15

RAO BSSR 000627 01-09 , 003533 03-15
RAO VAR 004338 04-08
RAPISARDA V 003150 03-07
RAPKIN RM 003294 03-11
RAPOPORT JL 000715 01-11 , 000716 01-11 ,
002354 02-14 , 002359 02-14 , 003242
03-09 , 033310 03-11 , 003437 03-13
RAPOPORT R 000079 01-03
RAPPAPORT MS 001426 02-03
RAPPOLT RT 003525 03-15
RAPPORT MM 003025 03-04
RAPPORT RL 000177 01-03
RASKIN LA 002965 03-04
RASKIN NH 003623 03-17
RASKIND M 000602 01-09
RASNYUK VA 003172 03-08
RASTOGI JK 002172 02-11
RASTOGI RB 001427 02-03 , 001428 02-03
RASTOGI SK 000247 01-03
RATAUD J 001517 02-03
RATEY JJ 003526 03-15
RATHJE J 002229 02-13
RATTAN P 000675 01-11
RAUH E 004122 04-04
RAUSEN AR 001836 02-05
RAVAZZANI C 002863 03-03
RAVENNA F 001051 02-01
RAVIZZA L 002032 02-09 , 002872 03-03 ,
002873 03-03
RAWLE FC 003736 04-03
RAWLINS JNP 001757 02-04
RAWLINS MD 004669 04-16
RAWSON RA 000827 01-14
RAY AK 001429 02-03
RAY DE 001838 02-05
RAY TB 000145 01-03 , 000146 01-03 ,
004144 04-04 , 004144 04-04
RAY WA 000079 01-17
RAYKHMAN LM 001331 02-03
RAYMOND V 001324 02-03
RAYNAUD G 001090 02-02
READER TA 000068 01-03
REAGAN MW 000937 01-17
REAVES BJ 001057 02-01
REAVILL C 001301 02-03 , 004205 04-04
REBARD R 003220 03-09
REBAUDENGO P 002872 03-03 , 002873 03-03
REBEC GV 000454 01-04 , 001758 02-04 ,
003131 03-05 , 003981 04-03
REBERT CS 004277 04-05
RECASENS M 002878 03-03
RECH R 000036 01-03 , 000364 01-04 ,
000365 01-04 , 000386 01-04 , 001595
02-04 , 004089 04-04
RECHTMAN MP 004054 04-03
RECOMMIS D 003749 04-03
REDDY RAMANA SV 004206 04-04
REDGRAVE P 001755 02-04 , 002679 03-03
REDMOND DE 000372 01-04 , 002285 02-13 ,
002838 03-03 , 003810 04-03 , 003982
04-03
REDMOND FC 003551 03-15
REECE S 000734 01-11
REED D 004692 04-16
REED JP 003624 03-17
REED K 000882 01-15
REED RB 002161 02-11
REES L 003283 03-10
REES M 002598 02-17
REGAN CM 002729 03-03
REGAN JW 001430 02-03 , 002874 03-03
REGENSTEIN AC 003960 04-03
REGGI V 002521 02-17
REGGIANI A 001512 02-03
REGNAULT H 002123 02-11
REGOLI D 000243 01-03
REHAVI M 002875 03-03 , 003962 04-03 ,
004689 04-16
REHFELD JF 003805 04-03
REICHENBERG K 001788 02-04
REICHL R 001431 02-03
REID AH 003365 03-11
REID JL 002504 02-16
REID LD 000371 01-04 , 003118 03-04 ,
004196 04-04
REID WH 004647 04-15
REIDENBERG MM 002451 02-15
REIGEL CE 001138 02-03
REIGLE TG 000136 01-03
REIMANN I 000164 01-03 , 002249 02-13

REIMANN W 003983 04-03
REIMHERR FW 003389 03-11
REINHARD JF 002503 02-16
REINHARDT B 004396 04-09
REINISCH JM 003527 03-15
REINSTEIN DK 002934 03-03 , 003069 03-04
REIS DJ 002634 03-01 , 004112 04-04
REISBERG B 002125 02-11 , 004482 04-11
REISBY N 002033 02-09
REISINE T 000226 01-03 , 001305 02-03 ,
002163 02-11 , 004011 04-03 , 004013
04-03
REITH MEA 001772 02-04
REKER D 000798 01-13 , 003383 03-11
REKHTMAN MB 003070 03-04 , 003984 04-
03
REKTOR L 000623 01-09 , 000883 01-15 ,
002452 02-15 , 004648 04-15
REME JM 000797 01-13
REMIEN J 003556 03-16
RENAUD LP 002674 03-03
RENFORDT E 003568 03-16
RENICK J 004600 04-15
RENIER E 002389 02-15
RENNICK PM 002126 02-11 , 004453 04-11
RENSHAW DC 004483 04-11
RENYI AL 003991 04-03
RENZI G 000104 01-03
RESELE L 001460 02-03
RESNICK RB 000731 01-11 , 000827 01-14
RESUL B 003701 04-02
RETTORI VB 001194 02-03
REUBI J 003985 04-03
REUS VI 001984 02-09 , 002034 02-09
REUSE J 001228 02-03
REVELEY MA 000983 01-17
REVENKO SV 003884 04-03
REVUELTA AV 001166 02-03
REVUSKY S 001086 02-02
REVVA LI 003531 03-15
REY AC 000836 01-15 , 004549 04-13
REYES FI 002213 02-13
REYES RB 000406 01-04
REYMANN JM 002205 02-13
REYNOLDS EH 003366 03-11 , 004649 04-15
REYNOLDS JC 003521 03-15
REYNOLDS NC 003132 03-05
REYNOLDS PC 004650 04-15
REYNTJENS A 000758 01-13
REZNICEK V 000658 01-10
RHODES KF 000516 01-05
RIBELLES M 002744 03-03
RIBEREAU-GAYON G 000248 01-03
RICCARDI F 002828 03-03
RICCIARDI S 000600 01-03 , 000355 01-04 ,
001161 02-03
RICCIO DC 001597 02-04
RICE A 000470 01-04
RICE K 003962 04-03 , 004221 04-04 ,
004251 04-04
RICHARD JW 004053 04-03
RICHARDS GE 000088 01-03
RICHARDS JG 001381 02-03 , 002643 03-01
RICHARDS RK 000249 01-03
RICHARDSON E 000612 01-14
RICHARDSON JS 003836 04-03
RICHARDSON MA 001614 02-04 , 002380 02-
15 , 003469 03-15 , 004595 04-15
RICHELLE M 000250 01-03
RICHELSON E 000250 01-03 , 000980 01-17 ,
001432 02-03 , 001433 02-03 , 001880
02-06 , 003783 04-03 , 003986 04-03 ,
004030 04-03 , 004049 04-04 , 004737
04-17
RICHENS A 000783 01-13 , 002376 02-15 ,
003467 03-15 , 004738 04-17
RICHERT JR 001434 02-03
RICHTER JA 000251 01-03 , 004146 04-04
RICHTROVA E 003170 03-08
RICK JT 003071 03-04
RICKELS K 000655 01-10 , 000840 01-15 ,
002482 02-16 , 003254 03-09 , 004400
04-09 , 004420 04-10
RIDLEY PT 000228 01-03
RIDLEY RM 001759 02-04 , 001911 02-08 ,
003072 03-04 , 004208 04-04
RIEDEL C 004380 04-09
RIEDERER P 000712 01-11
RIFFEE WH 001822 02-04
RIFKIN A 000632 01-09 , 003233 03-09 ,
003252 03-09 , 003625 03-17 , 004427
04-10

RIGAUD A 004395 04-09
RIGGS JJ 000512 01-05
RIGOR BM 003774 04-03
RIGTER H 004094 04-04
RIMANOCZY A 001300 02-03 , 002765 03-03
RIMON R 002185 02-11
RINGDAHL B 003701 04-02
RINGWALD E 001944 02-08
RINIERIS PM 000786 01-13
RINNE UK 003528 03-15
RIORDAN CE 000820 01-14
RIOUX F 000243 01-03
RISBERG J 002210 02-13
RISCH C 000455 01-04 , 002003 02-09 ,
003603 03-17
RISCH SC 002280 02-13 , 003255 03-09 ,
003529 03-15 , 003530 03-15
RISNER ME 000469 01-04 , 001760 02-04
RITCH MA 001806 02-04
RITSCHEL WA 000907 01-16
RITTA MN 001159 02-03
RITTENHOUSE HG 003987 04-03
RITTER S 000456 01-04
RITZ A 004103 04-04
RITZMANN RF 001435 02-03 , 001576 02-04
, 001780 02-04 , 004209 04-04
RIVA LP 004535 04-13
RIVERA-CALIMLIM L 000717 01-11 , 001938
02-08
RIVIER JE 003985 04-03
RIZEK AE 002864 03-03
RIZZO PA 002355 02-14
ROACH AG 000044 01-03
ROACH CA 003522 03-15
ROBBINS TW 002484 02-16
ROBERT G 001900 02-07 , 001901 02-07
ROBERT O 003441 03-14
ROBERTS DJ 003928 04-03
ROBERTS MB 001824 02-04
ROBERTS MS 003558 03-16
ROBERTS PJ 002888 03-03 , 004000 04-03
ROBERTS S 003040 03-04
ROBERTS T 000471 01-04
ROBERTSON A 000387 01-04 , 000457 01-04
ROBERTSON D 002272 02-13 , 002734 03-03
ROBERTSON HA 000252 01-03 , 001436 02-03
ROBERTSON TW 001242 02-03
ROBERTSON WCJ 000718 01-11
ROBIN MM 000458 01-04
ROBINS E 002052 02-09
ROBINSON DS 002035 02-09
ROBINSON GMH 000574 01-08
ROBINSON J 001437 02-03 , 004423 04-10 ,
004473 04-11
ROBINSON K 004693 04-16
ROBINSON MM 001614 02-04
ROBINSON TE 000309 01-03 , 000459 01-04 ,
001438 02-03
ROBISON GA 001445 02-03
ROBSON PA 003753 04-03
ROCCATAGLIATA G 000700 01-11 , 002013
02-09 , 002356 02-14 , 004382 04-09 ,
004533 04-13
ROCCELLA P 003419 03-13
ROCHA E SILVA M 002175 03-03
ROCHAT C 000258 01-03 , 001764 02-04
ROCHE M 001227 02-03 , 003691 04-02
ROCKMAN GE 000253 01-03
RODE A 004548 04-13
RODGERS RJ 003073 03-04
RODGERS RM 000073 01-03
RODIN EA 000367 03-11
RODNY J 000674 01-11
RODRIGUEZ F 002272 01-03
RODRIGUEZ R 000407 01-04
RODRIGUEZ S 003988 04-03
RODRIGUEZ-SANABRA F 001558 02-04
RODRIGUEZ-SIERRA JF 003074 03-04
ROED A 002749 03-03
ROEHRS TA 004695 04-16
ROEMER D 003013 03-04
ROEMER RA 003263 03-09
ROERIG DL 001853 02-05
ROERIG SC 002800 03-03
ROESKE WR 000279 01-03 , 001430 02-03 ,
001441 02-03 , 001545 02-03 , 002874
03-03
ROFFMAN M 004619 04-15 , 004651 04-15
ROGER J 000873 01-15 , 002319 02-14

ROGERS J 001136 02-03 , 004182 04-04
ROGERS LJ 003079 03-04
ROGERS PJ 002527 02-17
ROGINSKY M 000660 01-11
ROGOL A 001928 02-08 , 003499 03-15
ROGOWSKI Z 004564 04-14
ROGOZ Z 001417 02-03
ROGOZEA R 002281 02-13
ROJAHN J 002409 02-15
ROKOSZ-PELC A 004210 04-04
ROKYTA R 000460 01-04 , 001439 02-03
ROLANDI E 003425 03-13
ROLF L 002501 02-16
ROLLAND B 004029 04-03
ROLLEMA H 000004 01-01 , 000324 01-03
ROLLINS OE 002282 02-13
ROLSTEN C 000134 01-03
ROMACH MK 000747 01-13
ROMAIN M 001902 02-07
ROMAN F 002541 02-17
ROMANIUK A 001761 02-04
ROMANO C 000254 01-03
ROMEL TE 004732 04-17
ROMMELSPACHER H 001440 02-03 , 002854 03-03 , 004211 04-04
ROMO R 004046 04-03
ROMOLINIOVA A 000803 01-14
RONAI AZ 001799 02-04 , 002650 03-02
RONDOT P 004652 04-15
ROOSE S 000590 01-09
ROPERT R 002036 02-09
ROPPOLO JR 000055 01-03 , 003755 04-03
ROQUEBERT J 002876 03-03
ROQUEFEUIL B 002231 02-13
RORSMAN B 003542 03-15
ROSAMOND JD 003684 04-02
ROSATI G 002283 02-13
ROSE BW 003566 03-16
ROSE C 000241 01-03 , 001054 02-01
ROSE FC 004509 04-13
ROSE GJ 001634 02-04
ROSE JE 001416 02-03
ROSE SE 004060 04-03
ROSECRANS JA 000435 01-04 , 001020 02-01 , 004260 04-04
ROSEN AJ 004577 04-14
ROSEN GD 000375 01-04
ROSENBAUM AH 000787 01-13 , 002037 02-09 , 002038 02-09 , 004406 04-09
ROSENBAUM J 003626 03-17
ROSENBAUM R 004512 04-13
ROSENBERG GS 002317 02-14 , 004099 04-04
ROSENBERG HC 000526 01-05
ROSENBERG RD 001057 02-01
ROSENBERGER LB 001441 02-03
ROSENBERGER PB 000821 01-14
ROSENBLATT JE 000255 01-03 , 001442 02-03 , 001443 02-03 , 001444 02-03 , 001945 02-08 , 003169 03-08 , 004671 04-16
ROSENDORFF C 003887 04-03
ROSENFELD GC 001445 02-03
ROSENFELD JP 001446 02-03 , 003028 03-04
ROSENFELD MR 001447 02-03 , 001448 02-03
ROSENGARTEN H 003989 04-03
ROSENTHAL M 003789 03-03
ROSENZWEIG MR 001573 02-04 , 004097 04-04 , 004578 04-14
ROSHCHINA LF 001449 02-03 , 004212 04-04
ROSKAM SE 000471 01-04
ROSNICK L 000632 01-09
ROSS B 003487 03-15
ROSS DH 000958 01-17 , 001450 02-03
ROSS JA 004080 04-04
ROSS RJ 003220 03-09
ROSS S 000120 01-03 , 001451 02-03 , 001452 02-03 , 003990 04-03 , 003991 04-03 , 004704 04-17
ROSS-CHOUINARD A 003305 03-11
ROSSEEL MT 004355 04-09
ROSSER RM 002164 02-11 , 002284 02-13
ROSSI F 003744 04-03
ROSSI J 001644 02-04
ROSSIE GV 003627 03-17
ROSSIER J 001110 02-03 , 002599 02-17
ROSSIO J 004324 04-08
ROSSITER VS 003446 03-15
ROSSOR M 000564 01-08 , 002163 02-11 , 002504 02-16
ROSZKOWSKI AP 001091 02-02
ROTH KA 003935 04-03

ROTH M 002081 02-10
ROTH RH 000023 01-03 , 000764 01-13 , 001117 02-03 , 001453 02-03 , 001820 02-04 , 002097 02-11 , 002285 02-13 , 002662 03-03 , 002911 03-03
ROTH T 000822 01-14 , 002160 02-11 , 002357 02-14
ROTHBART M 000582 01-09 , 002248 02-13
ROTIROTI D 002218 01-03 , 000442 01-04 , 000443 01-04 , 001733 02-04 , 001734 02-04 , 002762 03-03 , 003075 03-04 , 003952 04-03
ROTROSEN J 000461 01-04 , 001906 02-08 , 001948 02-08 , 002877 03-03 , 004606 04-15
ROUBAL Z 000242 01-03 , 002279 02-13
ROUBICEK J 002601 02-17
ROUFOGALIS BD 003162 03-07
ROUGEUL A 001581 02-04
ROUILLON F 003628 03-17
ROULEAU D 002635 03-01
ROUNSAVILLE BJ 000624 01-09 , 003256 03-09 , 004401 04-09
ROUOT B 003685 04-02 , 003992 04-03
ROUSSELLE JC 000093 01-03
ROUSSINOV K 004166 04-04
ROUTLEDGE PA 000867 01-15
ROUVEIX B 004632 04-15
ROUX J 002600 02-17 , 004445 04-11
ROVEI V 000596 01-09 , 002014 02-09 , 002324 03-11
ROVERE RA 003479 03-15
ROVINSKAYA SA 003531 03-15
ROWAN P 003249 03-09 , 004402 04-09
ROWE PH 001832 02-05
ROWLAND N 002891 03-03 , 003122 03-05 , 004196 04-04
ROWLEY VN 001630 02-04
ROXAS M 003150 03-07
ROY D 002654 03-01
ROYER RJ 003629 03-17
ROYZIN L 003532 03-15
ROZITIS A 003738 04-03
RUBENSTEIN JS 003876 04-03
RUBICSEK K 002945 03-04
RUBIN JJ 002930 03-03
RUBIN RT 002287 02-13 , 002505 02-16 , 003830 04-03 , 004403 04-09
RUBINO IA 004318 04-08
RUBINOW D 003388 03-11
RUBIU MA 003924 04-03
RUCINE MO 000543 01-07
RUDD SM 000832 01-15
RUDEBERG A 004495 04-11
RUDEBERG C 001762 02-04
RUDEEN PK 003076 03-04
RUDELL RL 004287 04-06
RUDORFER MV 000884 01-15 , 002039 02-09 , 004550 04-13
RUDZIK AD 001074 02-02 , 001075 02-02
RUFF RL 004653 04-15
RUFFING DM 000462 01-04
RUGGERI S 003085 03-04 , 004431 04-11
RULLIERE R 004530 04-13
RUMBACH L 002237 02-13
RUMIGNY J 002878 03-03 , 003675 04-01
RUNDELL O 003460 03-14
RUSH AJ 003235 03-09 , 003257 03-09
RUSH L 003393 03-11
RUSSELL B 004213 04-04
RUSSELL JA 001053 02-01 , 001148 02-03
RUSSO PV 003922 04-03
RUSTERHOLZ DB 002236 02-13
RUTH RC 003993 04-03
RUTHER E 001570 02-04
RUTHERFORD D 003543 03-15
RUTTERFORD MG 004693 04-16
RUWE WD 001454 02-03
RYABUKHA VN 001520 02-03
RYAN R 003676 04-01
RYBAKOWSKI J 000625 01-09 , 000885 01-15 , 002040 02-09 , 004404 04-09 , 004416 04-09
RYDZYNSKI Z 000626 01-09 , 000719 01-11
RYLETT BJ 002879 03-03
RYMAN T 001737 02-04
RYMASZEWSKA G 000861 01-15
RYPKA M 000274 01-11

RYSANEK K 003423 03-13
RYSANEK R 000568 01-08 , 000613 01-09 , 000634 01-09 , 001949 02-08 , 002021 02-09 , 003264 03-09
RZHEVSKAYA GF 004261 04-04

S

SAAB PG 002357 02-14
SAARI M 000448 01-04
SAARMA MM 003368 03-11
SAARMA YM 003368 03-11
SAAVEDRA IN 000102 01-03
SAAVEDRA JM 001455 02-03 , 001456 02-03 , 001457 02-03 , 001458 02-03 , 001459 02-03 , 002762 03-03
SABATER J 002288 02-13
SABBATINI F 003194 03-08
SABOURAUD O 002205 02-13
SACCHETTI E 001460 02-03 , 004361 04-09
SACHAIS BA 003239 03-09
SACHAR EJ 000752 01-13 , 000776 01-13 , 000874 01-15 , 002238 02-13 , 003411 03-13 , 003426 03-13 , 004405 04-09
SACHS BD 003077 03-04
SACKELLARES JC 003378 03-11
SACKETT PH 000014 01-02
SACKS W 004377 04-09
SADJA L 000829 01-15
SADLER A 003487 03-15
SADRE NL 001361 02-03
SAELENS JK 000188 01-03 , 001461 02-03
SAFFITZ MS 000256 01-03
SAHA BK 002432 02-15
SAHAI J 004656 04-15
SAHAKIAN BJ 000257 01-03 , 000802 01-14 , 002484 02-16
SAHGAL A 001763 02-04
SAHLEY TL 001745 02-04
SAHLIN L 000273 01-03
SAHLSTROM L 000084 01-03
SAIANI L 001482 02-03
SAINGRA S 003524 03-15
SAINIO K 000694 01-11
SAINT-HILAIRE JM 003341 03-11
SAITO K 000099 01-03 , 003807 04-03
SAITO M 001255 02-03 , 002165 02-11 , 002781 03-03
SAITO Y 003938 04-03
SAITOH R 004295 04-06
SAJI Y 003057 03-04
SAKAI KK 000302 01-03
SAKAI T 000856 01-15
SAKAI Y 001402 02-03 , 002846 03-03
SAKAMOTO K 004283 04-05
SAKURADA H 003450 03-14
SAKURADA S 001379 02-03 , 002837 03-03 , 003714 04-03
SALA A 003705 04-02
SALA P 002093 02-11
SALAICES M 001357 02-03
SALAMONE JD 001873 02-06
SALAMY A 000509 01-05
SALCEDA R 002856 03-03
SALEM RB 000889 01-15
SALEMINK CA 002556 02-17
SALETU B 000720 01-11 , 000786 01-13 , 001895 02-07 , 002166 02-11
SALIS PJ 004556 04-13
SALLEMARK M 000120 01-03
SALLER CF 002880 03-03 , 002968 03-04
SALLES KSS 003078 03-04
SALMI T 000694 01-11
SALMON P 001757 02-04
SALOKANGAS RKR 000571 01-08
SALOME RR 004182 04-04
SALZMAN C 000981 01-17 , 003369 03-11
SALZMAN LF 002419 02-15
SAMADASHVILI ZV 003780 04-03
SAMANIEGO B 003936 04-03
SAMANIN R 000036 01-03 , 000258 01-03 , 001157 02-03 , 001325 02-03 , 001764 02-04 , 002042 02-09 , 002017 02-09
SAMARDZIC R 001568 02-04 , 001569 02-04
SAMARZA A 000672 01-11
SAMINI M 000108 01-03
SAMPATH G 000627 01-09 , 003533 03-15
SAMSONOVA NA 003070 03-04 , 003984 04-03

SAMU I 002404 02-15
SANBERG PR 000463 01-04
SANCHEZ CF 003925 04-03
SANCHEZ D 000399 01-04
SANCHEZ-TURET M 003453 03-14
SAND DJ 000792 01-13
SANDERS-BUSH E 002287 01-03
SANDERSON CA 003079 03-04
SANDFORD DA 000982 01-17
SANDLER K 000582 01-09
SANDLER M 000721 01-11 , 000983 01-17 ,
  002230 02-13 , 004509 04-13 , 004640
  04-15
SANDMAN CA 003112 03-04
SANDOVAL J 004469 04-11
SANES JN 003319 03-11
SANGDEE C 004040 04-03
SANGER DJ 001765 02-04 , 003080 03-04
SANKAR R 001197 02-03
SANSONE M 001766 02-04 , 001767 02-04 ,
  001768 02-04
SANTAGOSTINO A 003801 04-03
SANTAGOSTINO G 000757 01-13 , 004675 04-
  16
SANTI PA 004287 04-06
SANTINI V 001422 02-03
SANTOS AB 002167 02-11
SANVITO WL 000669 01-11
SANYAL AK 001769 02-04
SAR M 002639 03-01
SARAF K 003233 03-09 , 003252 03-09
SARAI K 004388 04-09
SARANAK J 003081 03-04
SARATIKOV AS 003994 04-03
SARIA A 000259 01-03
SARNA GS 001838 02-05
SARNA S 000694 01-11
SARRAZIN A 000543 01-07
SASA M 000260 01-03 , 004139 04-04
SASAHARA K 004551 04-13
SASAKI T 004618 04-15
SASS SW 003067 03-04
SASSONE DM 004469 04-11
SATINDER KP 003082 03-04
SATO E 000902 01-16 , 004684 04-16
SATO H 001462 02-03
SATO S 000444 01-04
SATO T 002442 02-15
SATO Y 002442 02-15
SATOH M 001691 02-04 , 003083 03-04
SATOH T 001236 02-03 , 001797 02-04 ,
  003008 03-04
SATOH Y 000493 01-04 , 004278 04-05
SAUNDERS NA 002128 02-11
SAUTER A 001254 02-03
SAUVAGE D 003291 03-11
SAVAGE C 003308 03-11
SAVAGE OD 001463 02-03 , 002881 03-03
SAVAGEAU MM 003084 03-04
SAVAKI HE 001365 02-03
SAVARD C 004286 04-06
SAVETT M 003154 03-07
SAVOLAINEN H 000261 01-03 , 000527 01-05
SAWA N 001609 02-04
SAWE J 000754 01-13
SAWYNOK J 002882 03-03
SCAPAGNINI U 000378 01-04 , 001200 02-03
SCARNA H 003668 04-01
SCARNATI E 003085 03-04
SCARPA A 003866 04-03
SCARPELLINI JD 003784 04-03
SCATTON B 000464 01-04 , 001119 02-03 ,
  001464 02-03 , 003995 04-03
SCHACHT U 002289 02-13
SCHACHTER M 002168 02-11 , 002358 02-14
  003422 03-13
SCHAEFER GJ 003086 03-04
SCHAFFER C 001913.02-08
SCHAFFER JD 002026 02-09 , 002080 02-10
SCHAFFER MH 000572 01-08 , 003198 03-08
SCHAFFNER R 002646 03-02
SCHAFFNER W 000979 01-17
SCHALLERT T 000226 01-03 , 000376 01-04
SCHALLY AV 001311 02-03 , 001673 02-04 ,
  001674 02-04
SCHALOCK RL 001587 02-04
SCHARBACH H 001090 02-02 , 002169 02-11
  002271 02-13 , 044428 04-10
SCHATZ RA 002883 03-03
SCHATZBERG AF 000787 01-13 , 003243 03-
  09 , 004406 04-09

SCHAUB C 000262 01-03
SCHAUMBURG K 001079 02-02
SCHECHTER MD 000465 01-04 , 001770 02-04
  002970 03-04 , 003087 03-04 , 004214
  04-04
SCHECHTER PJ 000458 01-04 , 002237 02-13
  003458 03-14 , 003620 03-17
SCHECTER AJ 004467 04-11
SCHEEL-KRUGER J 001465 02-03
SCHEININ M 002303 02-13
SCHELL D 000849 01-15
SCHENK H 002425 02-15
SCHENK S 001771 02-04
SCHENKER S 002224 02-13 , 002272 02-13
SCHICKEROVA R 003039 03-04
SCHIELE B 002603 02-17
SCHIER E 002604 02-17
SCHIFF AA 000668 01-11
SCHIFFMANN E 001118 02-03
SCHILDKRAUT JJ 000787 01-13 , 004406 04-
  09
SCHILKRUT R 004319 04-08
SCHILLER M 002324 02-14
SCHIMMEL GT 001584 02-04
SCHIMMEL KC 004484 04-11
SCHINDLER R 004605 04-15
SCHLEMMER RF 001073 02-02 , 004215 04-
  04
SCHLEN H 000263 01-03
SCHLESINGER K 001791 02-04
SCHLESS A 000582 01-09 , 003254 03-09
SCHLEY J 002290 02-13
SCHLIENGER JL 004407 04-09
SCHLOSBERG AJ 000646 01-04
SCHLOSSER W 000015 01-02
SCHMALTZ K 001678 02-04 , 004154 04-04 ,
  004155 04-04 , 004156 04-04
SCHMECHEL DE 001047 02-01 , 001048 02-01
  001400 02-03
SCHMID E 002041 02-09
SCHMID PG 003845 04-03
SCHMID W 004321 04-08
SCHMIDT DE 003996 04-03
SCHMIDT G 002438 02-15
SCHMIDT M 002895 03-03 , 003853 04-03 ,
  004270 04-05
SCHMIDT R 003677 04-01
SCHMIDT-GLENEWINKEL T 001396 02-03
SCHMITT G 002699 03-03
SCHMITZ H 002479 02-16
SCHMITZ I 002130 02-11
SCHMUCKER DL 003997 04-03
SCHMUTZ M 003880 04-03
SCHNEIDER SJ 003413 03-13 , 004619 04-15 ,
  004620 04-15
SCHNEIDERMAN N 001242 02-03
SCHNELLE K 001570 02-04
SCHNOLL SH 000744 01-12
SCHOCKER FW 002884 03-03
SCHOEMAKER H 002170 02-11
SCHOENEBERGER AS 000265 01-03
SCHOLFIELD CN 001466 02-03
SCHONBECK G 001308 02-03
SCHONFELD AR 001876 02-06 , 004216 04-04
SCHOOLAR J 003082 03-04 , 003385 03-11 ,
  004694 04-16 , 004739 04-17
SCHOOLER NR 000563 01-08 , 001931 02-08 ,
  003195 03-08
SCHORDERET M 001350 02-03
SCHOTTLER F 001036 02-01
SCHOU M 000893 01-15 , 002465 02-15 ,
  003534 03-15 , 003630 03-17 , 004408
  04-09
SCHOUSBOE A 001540 02-03 , 002647 03-02
SCHRAN HF 002291 02-13
SCHRATZER M 004309 04-07
SCHREIBER RA 001467 02-03
SCHRIER BK 002669 03-03
SCHRIVER RC 003151 03-07
SCHROEDER LA 002980 03-04 , 004200 04-04
SCHUBERT DSP 004654 04-15
SCHUBERT E 001020 02-01
SCHUHMACHER P 000266 01-03
SCHULMAN E 004522 04-13
SCHUUMAN JA 001136 02-03
SCHULTZ J 000580 01-09 , 001136 02-03 ,
  002884 03-03
SCHULTZES RE 003396 03-12
SCHULZ C 003357 03-11

SCHULZ DW 002885 03-03
SCHULZ H 000754 01-13
SCHULZ R 002935 03-03 , 003088 03-04 ,
  003837 04-03
SCHULZECK S 001819 02-04
SCHUMANN H 002742 03-03 , 003816 04-03
SCHUSTER CR 000427 01-04 , 002323 02-14 ,
  022328 02-14 , 002926 03-03 , 003110
  03-04
SCHUSTER P 003251 03-09
SCHUTTLER R 004325 04-08
SCHUTZENBERGER WG 001087 02-02
SCHWABE U 001860 02-06
SCHWAN TJ 003687 04-02
SCHWARCZ R 001240 02-03 , 003889 04-03 ,
  003923 04-03
SCHWARK WS 001588 02-04
SCHWARTZ G 002441 02-15
SCHWARTZ JC 000241 01-03 , 001054 02-01
  002900 03-03
SCHWARTZ JH 002657 03-03
SCHWARTZ JP 001403 02-03 , 003998 04-03
SCHWARZ ED 000984 01-17
SCHWARZ HJ 002291 02-13
SCHWEIZER C 004525 04-13
SCHWERTNER HA 000006 01-01 , 000538 01-
  06
SCHWIBBE M 004500 04-13
SCHWINDT PC 002886 03-03
SCOGGINS BA 002497 02-16
SCOLLO-LAVIZZARI G 000909 01-16
SCORZA-SMERALDI R 002293 02-13
SCOTO GM 000282 01-03 , 001468 02-03
SCOTT AK 004740 04-17
SCOTT CS 003631 03-17
SCOTT J 001027 02-01 , 001704 02-04
SCOTT RH 001793 02-04
SCOTTO DI TELLA AM 003089 03-04
SCOTTO JC 002296 02-13
SCULLY RE 004655 04-15
SCUVEE-MOREAU J 000267 01-03
SEALES DM 003446 03-14
SEAMAN SF 003090 03-04
SEBASTIANI G 003258 03-09
SEBBAN M 002895 03-03
SEBENS JB 001095 02-03
SECHTER D 003427 03-13 , 004358 04-09
SEDMAK T 002594 02-17
SEDVALL G 001905 02-08 , 001946 02-08 ,
  004311 04-08
SEED M 004463 04-11
SEEGER TF 000467 01-04 , 001469 02-03 ,
  004187 04-04
SEELER W 003231 03-09
SEEMAN MV 003483 03-15 , 003535 03-15
SEEMAN P 000268 01-03 , 001204 02-03 ,
  001509 02-03 , 001510 02-03 , 001511
  02-03 , 001847 02-05 , 002914 03-03 ,
  003483 03-15 , 003767 04-03 , 004131
  04-04 , 004741 04-17
SEGAL DS 001758 02-04 , 003178 03-08
SEGAL R 004343 04-08
SEGAL S 000841 01-15 , 002171 02-11
SEGAL Z 001915 02-08 , 001916 02-08
SEGALEN A 002642 01-03
SEGALL JE 001010 02-01
SEGAWA M 000472 01-04
SEGAWA T 001394 02-03 , 001728 02-04 ,
  003999 04-03 , 004191 04-04
SEGUIN EB 003987 04-03
SEHESTED P 000722 01-11
SEIDEL K 002049 02-09
SEIDEN LS 000427 01-04 , 001714 02-04 ,
  002926 03-03 , 003110 03-04 , 004073
  04-04 , 004169 04-04 , 004175 04-04
SEIDENWURM D 000425 01-04
SEIDLER FJ 004021 04-03
SEIGER A 000095 01-03
SEILICOVICH A 001194 02-03
SEINE P 001999 02-09
SEIZINGER B 001283 02-03
SELLECK SB 000534 01-06
SELLERS EM 000703 01-11 , 000747 01-13 ,
  000789 01-13 , 000790 01-13 , 004552
  04-13
SELLERS MS 003449 03-14
SELLINGER OZ 000377 01-04 , 002883 03-03 ,
  002887 03-03
SELLSTROM A 002746 03-03

SELLWOOD RA 002433 02-15
SELTZER RL 004637 04-15
SELWYN M 001461 02-03
SEMEYN DR 004089 04-04
SEMKE VY 004429 04-10
SENGOKU A 004720 04-17
SENON J 001999 02-09
SENTENAC H 001187 02-03
SEPINWALL J 000057 01-03 , 000468 01-04
SEPPALA T 002258 02-13 , 003428 03-13
SERBY M 002453 02-15
SERCOMBE R 001109 02-03
SERRA MT 001229 02-03 , 001867 02-06
SERRANO AC 003370 03-11
SERRANO MI 001189 02-03
SERSHEN H 001772 02-04
SESSO M 001985 02-09
SETH PK 004264 04-05
SETHI BB 004656 04-15
SETHI PK 002172 02-11
SETHY VH 000124 01-03 , 000269 01-03
SETLER PE 003929 04-03
SETTLE ECJ 000985 01-17
SEVERE J 001931 02-08
SEVERINOVA NP 003172 03-08
SEVERNYY AA 003339 03-11
SEVERSON JA 004217 04-04
SEVESTRE P 001947 02-08
SEWELL RDE 001773 02-04 , 002736 03-03
SEWELL WR 000394 01-04
SEYLAZ J 001109 02-03
SFAGOS C 004471 04-11
SFARTI M 000552 01-08
SHABIB A 001245 02-03
SHADER RI 000681 01-11 , 000766 01-13 ,
  000831 01-15 , 003284 03-10 , 003526
  03-15 , 004432 04-11 , 004657 04-15
SHAFIQ SA 000290 01-03
SHAGASS C 003263 03-09
SHAH SN 000509 01-05
SHAH U 000732 01-11
SHAKIR RA 002402 02-15 , 003371 03-11 ,
  003374 03-11
SHALIF I 003196 03-08
SHALINI K 000621 01-09
SHANLEY BC 002735 03-03
SHANNAK KS 001471 02-03
SHANNON HE 000469 01-04
SHAPIRO AK 003372 03-11 , 004485 04-11
SHAPIRO AP 002891 03-03
SHAPIRO BH 000281 01-03
SHAPIRO BS 004129 04-04
SHAPIRO DM 004567 04-14
SHAPIRO E 003372 03-11 , 004485 04-11
SHAPIRO LM 001472 02-03
SHAPIRO-ACKERMAN E 002173 02-11
SHARE NN 004218 04-04
SHARER DR 004742 04-17
SHARIF NA 002888 03-03 , 004000 04-03
SHARKAWI M 000270 01-03
SHARMA M 004656 04-15
SHARMA S 003259 03-09
SHARMA UC 003536 03-15
SHARMAN DF 003652 03-17
SHARP B 003942 04-03
SHARPE LG 001491 02-03 , 002889 03-03
SHARPLESS NS 002180 02-11 , 002890 03-03 ,
  003432 03-13
SHASHOUA VE 003677 04-01
SHASKAN EG 001473 02-03
SHAVIT S 004001 04-03
SHAW DH 003236 03-09
SHAW J 000747 01-13
SHAW KM 002177 02-11
SHAW MDM 001416 02-03
SHAYWITZ BA 000426 01-04 , 000452 01-04
  001752 02-04 , 002106 02-11 , 004658
  04-15
SHAYWITZ SE 004658 04-15
SHCHELKUNOV YL 003398 03-13
SHEA C 000619 01-09
SHEARD MH 000238 01-03 , 000297 01-03 ,
  001496 02-03 , 003091 03-04 , 004219 04-04
  04-09
SHEARMAN GT 003092 03-04 , 004219 04-04
SHEEHAN DV 002454 02-15
SHEEHY MP 002168 02-11
SHEKIM WO 002418 02-15
SHELAT H 003901 04-03

SHELDON PW 003123 03-05
SHENKMAN L 003664 04-01
SHENOY RS 003487 03-15
SHEPHERD DT 001806 02-04
SHEPHERD JT 003756 04-03
SHEPHERD M 002605 02-17
SHEPPARD GP 002432 02-15
SHERBANY AA 002657 03-03
SHERIDAN WF 002080 02-10
SHERMAN AD 001631 02-04 , 001751 02-04 ,
  001775 02-04 , 003743 04-03
SHERMAN G 000375 01-04 , 003053 03-04
SHERMAN JE 000470 01-04 , 000471 01-04
SHERMAN WR 003712 04-03
SHERSTNEV VV 003716 04-03
SHESTAKOV SV 004339 04-08
SHIBATA R 000696 01-11
SHIBATA S 000210 01-03
SHIBATA T 001691 02-04
SHIBLA DB 004002 04-03
SHIFRIN S 001037 02-01
SHIH JC 004349 04-09
SHIH T 004290 04-06
SHIKAI I 000814 01-14
SHIMA K 001379 02-03 , 002837 03-03 ,
  003714 04-03
SHIMEK ELJ 000006 01-01 , 000538 01-06
SHIMIZU M 000012 01-02 , 000142 01-03 ,
  000152 01-03 , 004149 04-04 , 004185
  04-04 , 004193 04-04
SHIMIZU T 000271 01-03 , 002174 02-11 ,
  003093 03-04
SHIMOMURA K 004278 04-05 , 004295 04-06
SHIMOYAMA N 000639 01-09
SHIMOYAMA S 000639 01-09
SHINDO H 003941 04-03
SHINDO M 001659 02-04
SHINGU K 000628 01-09
SHINODA M 000856 01-15
SHINOHARA M 001380 02-03
SHIOMI H 000472 01-04
SHIOMI T 003702 04-02
SHIPLEY JE 002891 03-03
SHIPPENBERG TS 002947 03-04
SHIRAISHI Y 000012 01-02
SHIRAKI Y 001659 02-04
SHISHLYANNIKOVA LV 004067 04-04
SHIZGAL P 001579 02-04 , 001771 02-04
SHKODROVA D 000473 01-04
SHOEMAKER WJ 003735 04-03
SHOGAN G 004343 04-08
SHOLEVAR GP 004743 04-17
SHOLOMSKAS AJ 000886 01-15
SHOLOMSKAS D 000624 01-09 , 003272 03-
  09
SHOPSIN B 000677 01-11 , 002042 02-09 ,
  002043 02-09 , 002044 02-09 , 003632
  03-17
SHORE D 000255 01-03 , 001444 02-03
SHORE PA 000201 01-03 , 002680 03-03
SHORVON SD 003366 03-11
SHOUSE MN 000474 01-04
SHPANSKAYA LS 004016 04-03
SHRABERG D 002629 02-17
SHUG AL 003853 04-03
SHUKLA GD 003536 03-15
SHULGIN AT 003683 04-02 , 004310 04-07
SHUMAN R 002720 03-03
SHUMILINA AI 002892 03-03
SHURLEY JT 000879 01-15
SHUTO K 004192 04-04
SHUTOV AA 003304 03-11
SHVARTSBURD A 003304 03-11
SHYBUT G 001542 02-03
SIBLEY DR 001186 02-03 , 003585 03-17 ,
  004003 04-03
SICUTERI F 004553 04-13
SIDDALL JW 002606 02-17
SIDDIQUI RA 004274 04-05
SIDOROWICZ S 000573 01-08
SIEBER B 001626 02-04 , 001776 02-04 ,
  001777 02-04
SIEGEL RK 000986 01-17
SIEGERS C 002469 02-15
SIEGERT M 002290 02-13
SIEGFRIED B 001778 02-04
SIEGHART W 002893 03-03
SIEMENS MK 001414 02-03
SIEMKOWICZ E 000475 01-04
SIESJO BK 001134 02-03

SIEST G 001507 02-03
SIEVER LJ 002366 02-14 , 003373 03-11 ,
  004659 04-15
SIGELL LT 000740 01-12
SIGGINS GR 000580 01-09 , 001136 02-03 ,
  002884 03-03 , 003136 03-06 , 003735
  04-03
SIGMUNDI RA 001615 02-04
SIHM F 002033 02-09
SIKORA J 002132 02-11
SILBERFARB PM 000876 01-15
SILBERGELD EK 000132 01-03 , 000133 01-03
  001288 02-03
SILBERMAN EK 000618 01-09
SILBRET M 001242 02-03
SILER-KHODR TM 000286 01-03
SILLANPAA M 000785 01-13
SILLETT RW 002343 02-14
SILLITO AM 002894 03-03
SILVA CC 003163 03-07
SILVA OL 002637 03-01
SILVERMAN AY 000286 01-03
SILVERMAN PB 001779 02-04
SILVERMAN RB 001055 02-01 , 001088 02-02
SILVERSTONE T 000807 01-14 , 002060 02-10
  002607 02-17 , 004363 04-09 , 004580
  04-14
SILVESTRI R 000442 01-04 , 000443 01-04
SIMANTOV R 004234 04-04
SIMEON J 001903 02-07 , 002608 02-17 ,
  003383 03-11
SIMEON S 003383 03-11
SIMKE JP 001461 02-03
SIMKO A 000987 01-17
SIMMELSGAARD H 003472 03-15
SIMMONS MA 000499 01-04
SIMMONS WH 001780 02-04
SIMON EJ 000128 01-03 , 001287 02-03 ,
  002609 02-17 , 003702 04-02 , 003840
  04-03 , 004300 04-06
SIMON FR 003702 04-02
SIMON H 001696 02-04
SIMON J 000543 01-07
SIMON LD 003702 04-02
SIMON P 000598 01-09 , 001070 02-02 ,
  001072 02-02 , 001232 02-03 , 001942
  02-08 , 002278 02-13 , 002292 02-13 ,
  003155 03-07 , 003424 03-13 , 003633
  03-17
SIMONDS WF 001035 02-01 , 001056 02-01
SIMONNET G 000272 01-03
SIMONOVIC M 001719 02-04
SIMONTON S 001885 02-06
SIMPSON JA 003429 03-13
SIMPSON JB 000534 01-06
SIMPSON LL 004004 04-03 , 004005 04-03
SIMPSON M 004554 04-13
SINCLAIR JD 004220 04-04
SINCZUK-WALCZAK H 003500 03-15
SINDRUP EH 003484 03-15
SING J 003000 03-04
SINGER G 001801 02-04
SINGER HS 003374 03-11
SINGER L 001904 02-07 , 002895 03-03 ,
  004270 04-05 , 004407 04-09
SINGH G 000629 01-09
SINGH MM 002611 02-17
SINGH R 003891 04-03
SINGH SB 002175 02-11
SINGH VK 004581 04-14
SINGHAL RL 001427 02-03 , 001428 02-03 ,
  003708 04-03
SINGLETON W 002060 02-10
SINHA JN 000247 01-03 , 002703 03-03
SINYOR D 001781 02-04
SIOMOUPOULOS V 003260 03-09
SIPKOVSKA E 000615 01-09
SIRACUSANO A 002187 02-11
SIRAGANIAN RP 001188 02-03
SIROKA A 000806 01-14 , 002333 02-14
SITARAM N 002341 02-14 , 002506 02-16 ,
  003255 03-09
SIWERS B 001967 02-09
SJOERDSMA A 001128 02-03
SJOGREN C 004006 04-03
SJOQUIST B 004534 04-13
SJOQVIST F 000754 01-13 , 002282 02-13 ,
  002300 02-13
SJOSTEDT L 003542 03-15

SKARICIC V 000977 01-17
SKETT P 000273 01-03
SKEWS H 004506 04-13
SKINGLE M 001782 02-04
SKINNER JT 002258 02-13
SKINNER T 000867 01-15
SKIRBOLL L 001117 02-03 , 001153 02-03 ,
  001239 02-03
SKLENOVSKY A 000077 01-03 , 000274 01-03
  001474 02-03
SKLODWOSKI H 004660 04-15
SKODA C 002612 02-17
SKOGLUND RR 000723 01-11
SKOLNICK P 000225 01-03 , 000275 01-03 ,
  000276 01-03 , 000277 01-03 , 000450
  01-04 , 001475 02-03 , 002645 03-01 ,
  002857 03-03 , 002896 03-03 , 002972
  03-04 , 003950 04-03 , 003962 04-03
  004172 04-04 , 004221 04-04 , 004251
  04-04 , 004689 04-16
SKONDIA V 000600 01-09 , 000988 01-17 ,
  002132 02-11
SKORIK AJ 003384 03-11
SKOVAJSOVA M 000542 01-07 , 002131 02-
  1
SKOVBJERG H 002676 03-03
SKRODER R 002095 02-11
SKRYMA RN 004041 04-03
SKULA E 002507 02-16
SKURDAL AJ 001586 02-04
SLANGEN JL 004159 04-04
SLATER P 001476 02-03 , 001783 02-04 ,
  001784 02-04 , 001785 02-04
SLATER SL 000612 01-09
SLAUGHTER MM 003145 03-06
SLAVNEY PR 003199 03-08
SLIFER BE 001786 02-04
SLOTKIN TA 000025 01-03 , 000278 01-03 ,
  002802 03-03 , 004021 04-03
SLOVITER RS 001787 02-04 , 003094 03-04 ,
  004007 04-03
SLYMEN DJ 002073 02-10
SMALL IF 003430 03-13
SMALL JG 003430 03-13
SMALLBERG S 003388 03-11
SMERALDI E 001460 02-03 , 002293 02-13 ,
  004361 04-09
SMIALOWSKA M 001477 02-03 , 001788 02-
  04
SMIALOWSKI A 001788 02-04
SMIGAN L 004664 04-15
SMIT MH 000279 01-03
SMITH AA 000318 01-03
SMITH B 003422 03-13
SMITH CB 003408 03-13 , 003763 04-03 ,
  004008 04-03 , 004242 04-04
SMITH CCT 002843 03-03 , 002897 03-03
SMITH CE 000052 01-03
SMITH CM 003454 03-14
SMITH CP 002898 03-03
SMITH CW 001591 02-04
SMITH OE 000745 01-12 , 000746 01-12 ,
  000924 01-17
SMITH DF 000016 01-02 , 000082 01-03 ,
  004222 04-04 , 004223 04-04
SMITH DJ 004009 04-03
SMITH DL 003143 03-06
SMITH DW 003462 03-15
SMITH EB 001686 02-04
SMITH ES 000476 01-04
SMITH GC 001478 02-03
SMITH GP 000383 01-04 , 000384 01-04
SMITH JM 000989 01-17 , 002455 02-15 ,
  003537 03-15
SMITH JR 000280 01-03 , 004010 04-03 ,
  004300 04-06
SMITH LT 003460 03-14
SMITH MT 004555 04-13
SMITH N 000745 01-12
SMITH PA 002870 03-03
SMITH PR 000528 01-05
SMITH R 002179 02-11
SMITH RC 000134 01-03 , 000572 01-08 ,
  000726 01-11 , 000882 01-15 , 000908
  01-16 , 000934 01-17 , 001789 02-04 ,
  002456 02-15 , 003095 03-04 , 003304
  03-11 , 003385 03-11 , 003901 04-03 ,
  003940 04-03 , 004694 04-16
SMITH RG 001089 02-02
SMITH RK 000031 01-03
SMITH RN 004693 04-16
SMITH RV 001822 02-04
SMITH SA 002899 03-03
SMITH TG 000116 01-03
SMITH TM 001113 02-03
SMITHWICK EL 002720 03-03
SMOLNIKOVA NM 001854 02-05
SMULEVICH AB 004340 04-08
SMYTH RD 004691 04-16
SNAITH RP 000579 01-09
SNEAD OCI 000477 01-04 , 000478 01-04
SNELL D 000479 01-04 , 001645 02-04
SNIDER RH 002637 03-01
SNIDER SR 002401 02-15
SNODDY HD 000101 01-03 , 002726 03-03 ,
  002995 03-04 , 003796 04-03
SNYDER S 000074 01-03 , 000230 01-03 ,
  000564 01-08 , 000656 01-10 , 000791
  01-13 , 000990 01-17 , 001124 02-03 ,
  001125 02-03 , 001837 02-05 , 002083
  02-10 , 002613 02-17 , 002688 03-03 ,
  002730 03-03 , 002835 03-03 , 002860
  03-03 , 002861 03-03 , 002922 03-03 ,
  003197 03-08 , 003199 03-08 , 003685
  04-02 , 003766 04-03 , 003964 04-03 ,
  003992 04-03 , 004198 04-04 , 004430
  04-10 , 004554 04-13 , 004744 04-17
SNYDERMAN S 002017 02-09
SO EL 003375 03-11
SO R 003190 03-08
SOBCZYK P 004486 04-11
SOBOTKA P 000460 01-04 , 001439 02-03
SOE-AGNIE CJ 003913 04-03
SOKOLOFF H 004673 04-16
SOKOLOFF L 001365 02-03 , 001380 02-03 ,
  002083 02-10
SOKOLOFF P 002900 03-03
SOKOLOVSKY M 002875 03-03
SOLDATOS C 002614 02-17 , 004373 04-09 ,
  004519 04-13 , 004567 04-14
SOLOMON PR 003872 04-03
SOLYOM C 002084 02-10 , 003285 03-10
SOLYOM L 002084 02-10 , 003285 03-10
SOM CW 000450 01-04
SOMJEN GG 000738 01-12
SOMMER R 004443 04-11
SONAWANE BR 000281 01-03
SONDERGAARD I 003428 03-13
SONI SD 004611 04-15
SONTAG K 000054 01-03
SONTAG N 000516 01-03
SOOKMAN D 002084 02-10
SOREL L 004487 04-11
SORENSEN KH 002329 02-14
SOSTEK AJ 002359 02-14
SOTANIEMI EA 002260 02-13
SOUBRIE P 000048 01-03 , 004011 04-03
SOUCEK K 000595 01-09 , 000630 01-09 ,
  002457 02-15 , 003261 03-09
SOUDIJN W 001347 02-03 , 002698 03-03 ,
  003913 04-03
SOUKUP K 002084 02-10
SOULAIRAC A 001479 02-03
SOULAIRAC M 001479 02-03
SOUMIREU-MOURAT B 003051 03-04
SOURANDER L 002260 02-14
SOURKES TL 000246 01-03 , 000500 01-04
SOUTHAM AS 003142 03-06
SOUVATZOGLOU AM 000786 01-13
SOUZA DO 000071 01-03 , 001664 02-04
SOVNER R 001931 02-08 , 003376 03-11
SOWELL JW 003700 04-02
SOWINSKI R 004273 04-05
SPADARO C 000282 01-03 , 001468 02-03
SPADARO M 002355 02-14
SPALLONE L 002226 02-13
SPALTEN D 003321 03-11
SPAMPINATO S 000285 01-03
SPANO PF 000285 01-03 , 001480 02-03 ,
  000481 02-03 , 001482 02-03 , 001512
  02-03 , 002121 02-11 , 002828 03-03
SPARBER SB 000085 01-03 , 001084 02-02 ,
  001632 02-04 , 001794 02-04
SPATZ H 002018 02-09
SPEALMAN RD 003096 03-04 , 004012 04-03
  004224 04-04 , 004225 04-04
SPEAR LP 000481 01-04 , 000482 01-04 ,
  001470 02-03 , 001774 02-04 , 002901
  03-03
SPECIALE SG 000153 01-03 , 001310 02-03
SPECTOR S 000317 01-03
SPENCE I 003742 04-03
SPENCER J 002176 02-11
SPENCER PS 002736 03-03 , 002905 03-03
SPERK G 001308 02-03
SPERLICH S 000819 01-14
SPERRY R 000424 01-04
SPETH RC 001710 02-04 , 002902 03-03 ,
  004013 04-03
SPIEGEL D 000823 01-14
SPIEGEL R 001944 02-08 , 002217 02-13
SPIEHLER VR 004143 04-04 , 004177 04-04
SPIKER DG 000631 01-09 , 003236 03-09 ,
  003634 03-17
SPINA F 001200 02-03
SPINDEL E 004014 04-03
SPINWEBER CL 003455 03-14 , 004568 04-14
SPIRDUSO WW 004226 04-04
SPIRTES MA 000402 01-04
SPISSU A 001483 02-03
SPITERI NJ 000483 01-04
SPOKES EG 000564 01-08 , 002575 02-17
SPOTNITZ S 001305 02-03
SPRICK U 004015 04-03
SPRIET A 002045 02-09 , 002615 02-17 ,
  003635 03-17
SPRING DD 001267 02-03
SPRINGER PK 000889 01-15
SPUNT A 000872 01-15
SPYRAKI C 000283 01-03
SQUIBB RE 004264 04-05
SQUILLACE KM 002866 03-03 , 003067 03-04
SQUIRE LR 000824 01-14 , 003636 03-17
SQUIRES RF 001484 02-03 , 002903 03-03 ,
  003739 04-03
SRAMKOVA J 000570 01-08 , 000761 01-13
SRINIVASAN V 001009 02-01
SRIVASTAVA DN 001769 02-04
SRIVASTAVA JR 002175 02-11
SRIWATANAKUL K 001878 02-06
ST-PIERRE S 000243 01-03
STAAK M 000825 01-14 , 003456 03-14
STABROVSKIY YM 004016 04-03
STACH R 004227 04-04
STACHURA J 001844 02-05
STADLER R 000720 01-11
STAHL SM 000887 01-15 , 003286 03-10 ,
  004442 04-11
STAINTHORP SF 004279 04-05
STALLONE F 000587 01-09
STAMM ER 001791 02-04
STAMM G 002748 03-03
STAMMER CH 003684 04-02
STANCEL GM 002778 03-03
STANCER HC 000300 01-03 , 001990 02-09
STANISHEVSKAYA AV 004017 04-03
STANLEY M 000461 01-04 , 000561 01-08 ,
  001533 02-03 , 001948 02-08 , 002877
  03-03
STAPLETON JM 003118 03-04
STARK LG 001559 02-04 , 002653 03-03 ,
  002862 03-03 , 002946 03-04
STARK P 004228 04-04 , 004280 04-05
STARK-ADAMEC C 002202 02-12
STARKE K 000535 01-06 , 001298 02-03 ,
  002748 03-03 , 002751 03-03 , 003637
  03-17 , 003983 04-03
STARKEY IR 002458 02-15
STARMARK J 000888 01-15
STARMER GA 002193 02-12
STAROBINETS MK 003457 03-14
STARR BJ 004704 04-17
STARR MS 000158 01-03 , 004141 04-04 ,
  004158 04-04
STARRATT C 000284 01-03
STASSEN HH 001962 02-09
STASTNA D 000815 01-14
STATON RD 002459 02-15
STAUB RA 001672 02-04 , 003022 03-04 ,
  003023 03-04 , 003499 03-15
STAUDERMAN K 001794 02-04
STAUNTON DA 001485 02-03 , 003735 04-03
  004229 04-04
STAVERIS S 002492 02-16
STAYE J 002409 02-15
STEELE TE 000545 01-07
STEELE WJ 001750 02-04
STEFANINI E 000285 01-03 , 001481 02-03

STEFANIS C 000786 01-13 , 002294 02-13 , 004059 04-03
STEFANOVICH V 001052 02-01 , 001499 02-03
STEFANYSYN H 001285 02-03
STEGER RW 000286 01-03
STEGGLES DJ 001591 02-04
STEIN F 001920 02-08
STEIN GS 002830 03-03 , 002831 03-03
STEIN JL 002830 03-03 , 002831 03-03
STEIN L 000991 01-17
STEINBERG B 000638 01-09
STEINBERG D 000992 01-17
STEINBERG H 000401 01-04 , 001646 02-04
STEINBOCK R 001931 02-08
STEINBRENNER J 001490 02-03
STEINER JA 001486 02-03 , 001487 02-03
STEINER M 001792 02-04
STEINER S 004341 04-08
STEINFELD AS 001059 02-01
STEINFELS GF 000505 01-04 , 003097 03-04 , 004230 04-04 , 004259 04-04
STEINGOLD RG 000955 01-17
STEINHAUER HB 002904 03-03 , 003983 04-03
STENBERG D 001879 02-06
STENEVI U 000347 01-04 , 003910 04-03
STENGAARD-PEDERSEN K 003805 04-03
STENZLER S 002417 02-15
STEPHAN F 004407 04-09
STEPHAN K 004309 04-07
STEPHENS JH 000836 01-15
STEPHENS R 003686 04-02 , 004557 04-13
STEPHENSON JD 001734 02-04
STEPOVIK NV 003438 03-14
STEPPELER A 000535 01-04
STERANKA LR 000287 01-03
STERC J 002865 03-03
STERMAN AB 002905 03-03
STERMAN MB 000474 01-04
STERN GM 002177 02-11 , 002365 02-14 , 004640 04-11
STERN JM 000510 01-05
STERN S 003164 03-07 , 003570 03-16
STERN W 003227 03-09
STERNBERG D 001251 02-03 , 001488 02-03 , 001952 02-08 , 002098 02-11 , 004231 04-04
STERNBERG S 000083 01-03
STERNER U 004142 04-04
STEVENS R 003098 03-04
STEVENSON IH 002534 02-17
STEWART A 000553 01-08 , 001489 02-03
STEWART J 000632 01-09 , 002709 03-03 , 002710 03-03 , 002906 03-03 , 003228 03-09 , 003240 03-09 , 003241 03-09 , 003262 03-09 , 003684 04-02
STEWART RB 000889 01-15
STEWART SE 000518 01-05
STEWART WRC 002080 02-10
STIKA L 000993 01-17 , 002542 02-17 , 002616 02-16
STILLER RL 000619 01-09
STILWELL DJ 001793 02-04
STINUS L 001696 02-04
STITZER ML 004582 04-14
STOCCO S 001446 02-03
STOCK G 001490 02-03
STOCKHAUS K 000013 01-02
STOFF DM 001794 02-04 , 001957 02-08 , 001958 02-08 , 004018 04-04
STOICA E 002295 02-13
STOKES KB 001335 02-03
STOKES PE 000187 01-03
STOLBERG-ACOSTA R 003638 03-17
STONE AL 001057 02-01
STONE BM 004574 04-14
STONE TW 000229 01-03 , 001410 02-03 , 002907 03-03 , 003963 04-03
STONE WE 000288 01-03 , 004232 04-04
STOOF JC 000289 01-03 , 001390 02-03
STOSCH R 003344 03-11
STOTLAND LM 001541 02-03
STOTLAND M 004053 04-03
STRACHER A 000290 01-03
STRADA SJ 001445 02-03
STRAIT MR 000162 01-03
STRAJELEVICH D 000083 01-03
STRAMENTINOLI G 002883 03-03 , 004019 04-03

STRAND S 003570 03-16
STRANDJORD RE 002234 02-13 , 004488 04-11
STRANGE PG 001253 02-03
STRANSKY P 000593 01-09
STRATHDEE A 001416 02-03
STRAUGHAN DW 003931 04-03
STRAUMANIS JJ 003263 03-09
STREATY RA 001033 02-01 , 001056 02-01
STRECKO A 000609 01-09 , 001934 02-08
STREICHENWEIN SM 002012 02-09
STREKALOVA SN 001854 02-05
STRELKOV RB 001354 02-03
STRELTZER J 002460 02-15
STRIAN F 000633 01-09
STRICKER EM 000484 01-04 , 002632 02-17 , 003120 03-04
STRICKLAND R 004745 04-17
STRID C 001737 02-04
STRIPLING JS 004233 04-04
STRITTMATTER W 001279 02-03 , 001502 02-03
STRNAD P 000724 01-11
STROEBEL CF 000539 01-07
STROHL KP 002128 02-11
STROHM H 000825 01-14
STROLIN BENEDETTI M 000156 01-03
STROMBOM U 000291 01-03
STROMGREN L 000792 01-13
STRONGE R 001215 02-03 , 002716 03-03
STROSBERG AM 003900 04-03
STROTHER A 000292 01-03
STRUBELT O 001855 02-05
STRUVE F 000858 01-15 , 003501 03-15
STRZYZEWSKI W 000625 01-09 , 002040 02-09
STUART WK 003319 03-11
STUBBS WA 001016 02-01 , 003731 04-03
STUDER K 004627 04-15
STUDY RE 004020 04-03
STULEMEIJER SM 000592 01-09 , 003503 03-15 , 004395 04-09
STULNIKOV M 003713 04-03
STUMPF C 003804 04-03
STUMPF WE 002639 03-01
STUNKARD AJ 000725 01-11
STURGEON RD 001616 02-04 , 001719 02-04
STUTZ RM 001795 02-04
SU CY 004489 04-11
SU T 001491 02-03
SUBA P 001635 02-04
SUBASH M 000627 01-09
SUBRAMANIAN N 004021 04-03
SUDAKOV KV 003716 04-03
SUDKOVA M 000544 01-07
SUEOKA S 003187 03-08
SUESS WM 003538 03-15
SUGERMAN AA 003180 03-08
SUGIHARA K 000639 01-09
SUGIKAWA M 004022 04-03
SUGRUE MF 000293 01-03 , 001492 02-03 , 002908 03-03
SULCOVA A 000485 01-04 , 001796 02-04
SULLIVAN AC 003377 03-11 , 004044 04-03
SULLIVAN FM 004108 04-04
SULLIVAN J 003306 03-11
SULSER F 000208 01-03 , 000793 01-13 , 001353 02-03 , 001493 02-03 , 002617 02-17 , 004746 04-17
SUMIKAWA K 003868 04-03
SUMMERLIN J 002618 02-17
SUMMERS R 000536 01-06 , 003388 03-11
SUMMERS W 003377 03-11 , 003539 03-15
SUNDARAM Y 004490 04-11
SUNDBERG DK 000537 01-06
SUNDERMANN RH 000294 01-03
SUNDT TMJ 000295 01-03
SUPAVILAI P 002775 03-03 , 002893 03-03 , 002909 03-03 , 004023 04-03
SUPPRIAN U 003540 03-15
SURIVILLO WW 003431 03-13
SUSIC V 003703 04-02
SUSSMAN S 004577 04-14
SUTAK M 003863 04-03
SUTFIN TA 003378 03-15
SUTTER J 002296 02-13 , 002619 02-17
SUTULA TP 003378 03-15
SUVA J 000605 01-09 , 001494 02-03 , 002297 02-13
SUZUKI A 000219 01-03

SUZUKI J 004491 04-11
SUZUKI O 004024 04-03
SUZUKI S 001659 02-04
SUZUKI T 000769 01-13 , 001797 02-04 , 004257 04-04 , 004258 04-04
SUZUKI Y 004518 04-13
SVARE B 003159 03-07
SVATEK E 002279 02-13
SVED AF 000296 01-03 , 004025 04-03
SVEJKOVSKA J 000576 01-08 , 000654 01-10
SVEJNOHOVA D 001494 02-03
SVENDSEN O 000890 01-15
SVENSK H 001067 02-02
SVENSSON TH 001214 02-03 , 001392 02-03 , 004026 04-03
SVENSSON U 000399 01-04
SVESTKA J 000567 01-08 , 000568 01-08 , 000613 01-09 , 000634 01-09 , 000663 01-11 , 001937 02-08 , 001975 02-09 , 002021 02-09 , 003245 03-09 , 003264 03-09 , 004375 04-09
SVIRIDOVA YI 003289 03-11
SVORAD D 001268 02-03 , 001495 02-03 , 001551 02-03
SWAN H 001544 02-03
SWANN AC 000297 01-03 , 001496 02-03 , 002910 03-03 , 002911 03-03
SWANSON JM 002134 02-11
SWARTZ CM 001879 02-06 , 004661 04-15
SWASH M 003454 03-14
SWEENEY DR 000899 01-16 , 003220 03-09 , 003317 03-11
SWEENEY DW 000764 01-13
SWEENEY KF 001598 02-04
SWEET WH 001497 02-03
SWIGAR M 003667 04-01
SWITZER RC 001498 02-03
SWITZMAN L 001781 02-04 , 001798 02-04
SYAPIN PJ 000450 01-04 , 001499 02-03
SYKES M 002741 03-03
SYLVESTER PW 000298 01-03
SYMCHOWICZ B 004103 04-04
SYMMES SK 003076 03-04
SYMONDS RL 003265 03-09
SYNDER SH 002575 02-17
SYNDULKO K 002182 02-11
SYNKOVA J 002064 02-10
SZABADI E 002298 02-13
SZABO G 003031 03-04
SZAJNERMAN Z 004416 04-09
SZAREK BL 000539 01-07
SZCZUDRAWA J 001844 02-05
SZE PY 001500 02-03
SZECHTMAN H 004234 04-04
SZEKELY JI 000486 01-04 , 001799 02-04 , 002650 03-02
SZENTISTVANYI I 001300 02-03 , 002765 03-03
SZERB JC 001130 02-03
SZEREDA-PRZESTASZEWSKA M 001501 02-03
SZETO HH 004027 04-03
SZORADY I 002461 02-15
SZRENIAWSKI Z 003050 03-04
SZUCS-MYERS VA 004122 04-04
SZUKALSKI B 000794 01-13

T

TABERNER PV 002361 02-14
TABRIZI MA 000619 01-09 , 000776 01-13 , 003411 03-13
TACHI N 000856 01-15
TACHIKAWA S 002936 03-03
TACHIKI KH 004352 04-09
TADAKI E 002794 03-03
TADANO T 004301 04-06
TADOKORO S 001693 02-04 , 003032 03-04 , 004128 04-04 , 004165 04-04
TAEUBER K 002362 02-14
TAFT WCJ 000299 01-03
TAGASHIRA E 001800 02-04
TAIT A 002433 02-15
TAKAGI H 000472 01-04 , 001691 02-04 , 003083 03-04
TAKAHASHI DM 004302 04-06
TAKAHASHI H 003099 03-04
TAKAHASHI M 003714 04-03
TAKAHASHI N 001379 02-03

TAKAHASHI R 000635 01-09 , 000636 01-09 ,
    001801 02-04 , 002442 02-15 , 004388
    04-09 , 004422 04-10
TAKAHASHI Y 003679 04-01
TAKANO N 001659 02-04
TAKANO Y 004028 04-03
TAKAORI S 000260 01-03 , 004139 04-04
TAKASHIMA S 000696 01-11
TAKAYANAGUI OM 003328 03-11
TAKEMORI AE 000311 01-03 , 001162 02-03
    003104 03-04 , 004082 04-04
TAKESHITA H 003179 03-08 , 003415 03-13 ,
    003416 03-13
TAKEUCHI Y 000795 01-13
TAKEYASU K 001272 02-03
TALAIRACH J 003334 03-11
TALALAYENKO AN 003100 03-04
TALJAARD JJF 002839 03-03 , 002859 03-03
TALLMAN JF 000038 01-03 , 000103 01-03 ,
    001279 02-03 , 001502 02-03 , 001503
    02-03 , 001504 02-03 , 002912 03-03 ,
    004705 04-17
TAMARGO J 003988 04-03
TAMMINGA C 000572 01-08 , 000726 01-11
    000908 01-16 , 002178 02-11 , 002179
    02-11 , 002387 02-15 , 003198 03-08
TAMMISTO P 000261 01-03
TAMURA T 003415 03-13
TANABE H 003544 03-15
TANABE K 000502 01-04
TANAKA K 004518 04-13
TANAKA M 003941 04-03
TANAKA S 002913 03-03 , 002920 03-03
TANCREDI L 003471 03-15
TANDBERG D 003541 03-15
TANG FLM 000091 01-03
TANG M 004235 04-04
TANG SW 000300 01-03 , 001204 02-03 ,
    002914 03-03
TANIGUCHI T 000317 01-03
TANIMOTO K 000645 01-09 , 003187 03-08 ,
    003266 03-09
TANSELLA CZ 002085 02-10
TAPPAZ ML 001047 02-01 , 001048 02-01
TARCHALSKA B 003050 03-04
TARDI M 004384 04-09
TARDY M 004029 04-03
TARGONSKA A 000601 01-09
TARGUM SD 002363 02-14
TARIKA J 001802 02-04 , 004359 04-09
TARNAWA I 000486 01-04
TARNAWSKI A 001844 02-05
TARNOPOLSKY A 003647 03-17
TARONI PL 001460 02-03
TARSY D 002373 02-15 , 003294 03-11
TARTARO T 002342 02-14
TARTER R 003180 03-08
TASAKI I 001505 02-03
TATARELLI R 002187 02-11
TATEISHI N 001506 02-03
TATURYAN IK 002663 03-03
TATYANENKO LV 001331 02-03
TAUB H 003312 03-11
TAUKULIS HK 001086 02-02
TAUSSIGOVA D 002131 02-11
TAUZIEDE-CASTEL C 003404 03-13
TAVANI A 000301 01-03
TAYLOR AN 000180 01-03
TAYLOR CI 000545 01-07
TAYLOR DA 000095 01-03 , 000107 01-03 ,
    004243 04-04
TAYLOR DP 001050 02-01 , 001383 02-03 ,
    003103 03-04 , 003855 04-03
TAYLOR GC 003355 03-11
TAYLOR JE 001880 02-06 , 004030 04-03
TAYLOR KE 000380 01-04
TAYLOR MA 003463 03-15
TAYLOR P 001043 02-01 , 002374 02-15 ,
    002421 02-15
TAYLOR SP 001233 02-03
TAYLOR T 004504 04-13
TAYLOR WJ 004031 04-03
TAZI A 001507 02-03
TEAL JJ 001803 02-04 , 004236 04-04
TEASDALE GM 003817 04-03
TEELKEN AW 001959 02-08 , 002311 02-13
TEGELER J 000562 01-08 , 004342 04-08
TEGYEY Z 000010 01-02 , 000011 01-02
TEITELBAUM P 000376 01-04
TELEGDY G 003031 03-04

TELFORD R 004669 04-16
TELL G 002237 02-13 , 003458 03-14 ,
    003620 03-17
TELLEZ-VILLAGRA C 003101 03-04
TEMPLETON WW 003841 04-03
TEN BRUGGENCATE G 001244 02-03
TEN OEVER GHM 002072 02-10
TENEN SS 002915 03-03
TENNENT TG 004747 04-17
TEO RKC 002193 02-12
TEPPER S 002102 02-11
TERAO M 003856 04-03
TERASAWA E 003074 03-04
TERAVAINEN H 003309 03-11 , 003319 03-11
TERENIUS L 000027 01-03 , 002620 02-17 ,
    003062 03-04
TERRENCE CF 002122 02-11
TERRY LC 002693 03-03
TERRY WS 000487 01-04
TERZANI S 000603 01-09 , 002007 02-09
TESCHEMACHER H 003740 04-03
TESSEL RE 000492 01-04 , 001155 02-03
TESTA B 002358 02-14
TETSUO M 001043 02-01 , 001058 02-01
TEYSSONEYRE B 004307 04-07
THAL LJ 001447 02-03 , 002180 02-11 ,
    002814 03-03
THANKI CM 000413 01-04
THARP B 002437 02-15
THARP VK 002369 02-14
THAVUNDAYIL JX 002441 02-15
THEILGAARD A 004607 04-15
THELLIER M 002299 02-13
THEODORE W 004522 04-13
THEODOROU A 001174 02-03 , 001175 02-03
    001301 02-03 , 002390 02-15 , 002707
    03-03 , 004032 04-03 , 004033 04-03 ,
    004252 04-04
THESLEFF S 003916 04-03
THIEBOT MH 000480 01-04 , 003633 03-17
THIELS C 002462 02-15
THIEME RE 000289 01-03
THILL R 002046 02-09
THIVEL-CHAMCHAM H 003441 03-14
THOLOSE A 002576 02-17 , 002621 02-17
THOMAS AJ 002843 03-03
THOMAS C 002433 02-15
THOMAS J 000103 01-03 , 000302 01-03 ,
    001502 02-03 , 001503 02-03 , 001504
    02-03 , 002508 02-16 , 002912 03-03
THOMAS LW 000348 01-04
THOMAS NU 003511 03-15
THOMASOVA E 002136 02-11
THOMPSON CL 003437 03-13
THOMPSON DA 000828 01-14
THOMPSON DM 001723 02-04
THOMPSON EJ 002897 03-03
THOMPSON JW 004669 04-16
THOMPSON RF 002916 03-03
THOMPSON RG 000390 01-04
THOMPSON T 002364 02-14 , 004095 04-04
THOMSEN A 000792 01-13
THOMSEN K 003547 03-15
THOR DH 000488 01-04
THORELL L 000604 01-09
THOREN P 002086 02-10 , 002300 02-13
THORN BE 003102 03-04
THORNER MO 002291 02-13
THORNHILL JA 004034 04-03
THORNTON C 002725 02-14
THORPY MJ 000727 01-11
THREATTE RM 001623 02-04 , 004237 04-04
THULESIUS O 001950 02-08
THURMAN GB 004324 04-08
THURSTON JH 004281 04-05
THYSELL H 003542 03-15
TI J 001059 02-01
TICKU MK 000303 01-03 , 001154 02-03
    001192 02-03 , 002301 02-13 , 004035
    04-03 , 004036 04-03 , 004037 04-03
TIGHE PJ 003198 03-08
TIGNOL J 000834 01-15
TIKAL K 001804 02-04
TILSON HA 001862 02-06 , 004264 04-05 ,
    004265 04-05
TIMKO J 001991 02-09
TIMMERMANS PBMWM 001508 02-03
TIMOTIJEVIC-MARKOVIC I 002047 02-09
TIMSIT-BERTHIER M 004583 04-14
TINKLENBERG JR 002317 02-14 , 004493 04-
    11 , 004665 04-15

TIPLADY B 004385 04-09 , 004677 04-16
TIPTON KF 003639 03-17
TIRELLI AS 003758 04-03
TISSOT R 002218 02-13 , 002917 03-03
TITELER M 001509 02-03 , 001510 02-03 ,
    001511 02-03
TITOV SA 002949 03-04
TIWARI S 003462 03-15
TOBIN JM 000574 01-08
TOBIS JM 001856 02-05
TOBLER I 002958 03-04
TOCCO DJ 000502 01-04
TOCHILOV VA 003351 03-11
TODA K 001294 02-03
TODA N 001273 02-03
TODOROKI M 001808 02-04
TOFFANO G 002682 03-03 , 003419 03-13
TOGNONI G 002521 02-17
TOIDE K 001857 02-05
TOKUNAGA Y 001393 02-03 , 002834 03-03
TOLBERT LC 002302 02-13
TOLLEFSON G 002463 02-15 , 002918 03-03
TOLLENAERE JP 002197 02-12
TOLNACHEVA NS 001363 02-03 , 001705 02-
    04
TOLMAN KG 002422 02-15
TOLNA J 003193 03-08
TOLPYSHEV BA 000489 01-04
TOMASETTI F 003466 03-15
TOMASIKOVA Z 001690 02-04 , 001805 02-
    04
TOMBAUGH J 000490 01-04
TOMBAUGH TN 000490 01-04 , 001806 02-04
TOMBROS E 002527 02-17
TOMIZAWA S 004022 04-03
TOMPKINS EC 003103 03-04
TOMSON T 002181 02-11
TONDA K 004062 04-03
TONG TG 000796 01-13
TONGROACH P 002691 03-03
TOPAL G 003895 04-03
TOPIAR A 000643 01-09
TORDA T 001279 02-03 , 001546 02-03 ,
    002919 03-03
TORII S 002350 02-14
TORRE E 002872 03-03 , 002873 03-03
TORRES-CHAZARO 9 002969 03-04
TORTELLA FC 004038 04-03
TOSCA P 002057 02-09 , 002058 02-09
TOSTESON DC 003640 03-17
TOTH J 004039 04-03
TOURNILHAC M 002048 02-09
TOURTELLOTTE WW 002182 02-11
TOVAREK J 003423 03-13
TOWELL JF 003146 03-06
TOY LY 001810 02-04
TRABUCCHI M 001480 02-03 , 001481 02-03
    001482 02-03 , 001512 02-03 , 002121
    02-11 , 002828 03-03
TRAMPOSCH A 004040 04-03
TRAN VT 000074 01-03
TRASKMAN L 002086 02-10 , 002282 02-13 ,
    002300 02-13
TRAUER T 002374 02-15 , 002421 02-15
TRAYNOR JR 002241 02-13
TREISER S 000304 01-03
TREISSER C 001902 02-07
TRENDELENBURG U 000535 01-06
TRESSEL WR 000530 01-04
TRIANO T 000388 01-04
TRICKLEBANK MD 002673 03-03
TRICOU BJ 004538 04-13
TRIMBLE MR 002183 02-11 , 004662 04-15
TRINER L 000305 01-03
TRINUS KF 004041 04-03
TRIPATHI HL 001513 02-03
TRITES RL 002120 02-11 , 003312 03-11
TROJABORG W 000126 01-03
TROLIN G 000828 01-11
TROTTA EE 004042 04-03
TROUPIN AS 000728 01-11
TRUBNIKOV VI 003176 03-08
TRULSON ME 000491 01-04 , 003018 03-04
TRUONG L 004286 04-06
TSAMIS M 002529 02-17
TSANG WK 001795 02-04
TSATSAS G 003698 04-02

TSENG L   000433 01-04 ,   001081 02-02 ,
  001642 02-04 ,   001643 02-04 ,   004238
  04-04
TSIRKIN SY   004335 04-08
TSITINI-TSAMIS M   002498 02-16
TSKHADADZE LV   004043 04-03
TSUANG MT   003508 03-15
TSUCHIE H   000639 01-09
TSUCHIMOTO S   000199 01-03
TSUEI SE   002508 02-16
TSUJIMOTO A   002913 03-03 ,   002920 03-03
TSUKINOKI Y   003692 04-02
TSUNOO A   000167 01-03
TSUTSULKOVSKAYA MY   003176 03-08 ,
  004381 04-09
TSYGANKOV BD   004584 04-14
TSYRLIN VA   001514 02-03
TU J   003380 03-11
TUASON VB   002825 03-03
TUCEK S   004044 04-03
TUCK JR   001967 02-09
TUFIK S   004239 04-04
TUISL E   001087 02-02
TUKIAINEN E   000637 01-09
TULUNAY FC   003104 03-04
TUMA I   002055 02-09
TUMILASCI OR   003130 03-05
TUMMINELLO MC   001126 02-03
TUNE LE   000566 01-08 ,   003199 03-08 ,
  003374 03-11
TUOMISTO J   000637 01-09 ,   001067 02-02 ,
  001078 02-02
TUPPER DE   001591 02-04 ,   001592 02-04
TURBOTT J   002184 02-11
TURCK M   002884 03-03
TUR AR   003872 04-03
TURKANIS SA   001671 02-04 ,   004040 04-03
TURKER RK   004275 04-05
TURKSON SNA   001926 02-08
TURNBULL MJ   004240 04-04
TURNER CE   000344 01-04 ,   001022 02-01 ,
  001023 02-01
TURNER JAM   002343 02-14
TURNER P   000807 01-14 ,   004597 04-15
TURNER SM   000657 01-10
TURSKA-KOEPPE G   003500 03-15
TURSKI L   001515 02-03 ,   001685 02-04 ,
  002921 03-03 ,   004241 04-04
TURSKI W   002921 03-03 ,   004241 04-04
TURTLE JR   002062 02-10
TWEEDALE R   002422 02-15
TWITCHIN B   002633 03-01
TYBRING G   000897 01-16 ,   002181 02-11
TYCE GM   003432 03-13
TYERS MB   001782 02-04 ,   001807 02-04
TYKVA R   003696 04-02
TYLER TD   000492 01-04
TYRER P   000638 01-09 ,   002464 02-15 ,
  003543 03-15

U

UCHIDA S   000493 01-04 ,   001272 02-03
UCHIDA-ERNOUF G   003689 04-02
UCHIGATA M   003544 03-15
UCHIMURA H   000212 01-03 ,   002781 03-03
UCHTENHAGEN A   004452 04-11
UDINSKY J   000017 01-03
UEBELHACK R   002049 02-09
UEDA I   004283 04-05
UEKI S   000417 01-04 ,   001681 02-04 ,
  003004 03-04 ,   003397 03-12 ,   003951
  04-03
UENO K   002937 03-03
UESUGI J   004258 04-04
UETRECHT JP   003545 03-15
UHDE TW   002366 02-14
UHL GR   002566 02-17
UHLENHUTH EH   002328 02-14 ,   002334 02-14 ,
  002335 02-14 ,   003445 03-14
UKAI M   003020 03-04
ULLMANN RK   002313 02-14
ULRICH G   004410 04-09
ULRICH R   003236 03-09
UMEZAWA Y   000639 01-09
UMSTEAD GS   003381 03-11
UNEMI N   001857 02-05
UNIS A   003356 03-11
UNNERSTALL JR   002644 03-01
UOTILA L   000694 01-11

UPHOUSE LL   004264 04-05
UPRICHARD DC   001516 02-03 ,   003992 04-03
  004676 04-16
URBA-HOLMAGREN R   000407 01-04 ,   001656
  02-04
URCA G   000494 01-04
URETSKY N   002796 03-03 ,   003033 03-04 ,
  004117 04-04
URQUILLA PR   003697 04-02
URSILLO R   000326 01-03 ,   001305 02-03
URSIN R   003704 04-02
USDIN TB   002922 03-03
USHIJIMA I   001808 02-04
USO T   003230 03-09
UYLINGS HBM   004091 04-04
UZAN A   000176 01-03 ,   001517 02-03 ,
  003898 04-03 ,   003899 04-03

V

VAATSTRA WJ   002651 03-02
VACEK J   003267 03-09
VADROT M   001090 02-02 ,   002014 02-09
VAGNUCCI AH   000484 01-04
VAGOGNE L   002430 02-15
VAIL BJ   001618 02-04
VAISANEN K   002185 02-11
VAISH SC   002186 02-11
VAJDA FJE   003433 03-13
VALCHAR M   000306 01-03 ,   001720 02-04
VALCOURT RJ   003077 03-04
VALDES JJ   000390 01-04
VALDMAN AV   003641 03-17 ,   004261 04-04
VALE W   003985 04-03
VALENTINE JO   003105 03-04
VALENTINO RJ   001518 02-03 ,   001651 02-04
  003106 03-04 ,   004132 04-04 ,   004242
  04-04
VALENTOVIC M   000307 01-03
VALENZUELA AL   000102 01-03
VALERI P   001107 02-03 ,   002515 02-17
VALETTE A   000797 01-13
VALLA JP   000994 01-17
VALLANO ML   000430 01-04
VALLI M   001371 02-03 ,   003642 03-17
VALLICK D   003173 03-08
VALLS JM   001930 02-08
VALLVE C   001978 02-09
VALMIKINATHAN K   004490 04-11
VALOVIRTA E   003330 03-11
VALZELLI L   000932 01-17 ,   000995 01-17 ,
  002622 02-17 ,   003705 04-02
VAMOS E   001944 02-08
VAN AMERONGEN P   002050 02-09
VAN BENNEKOM WP   002832 03-03
VAN CALKER D   000308 01-03
VAN DE POEL F   001976 02-09
VAN DE POLL NE   003056 03-04 ,   003107 03-
  04 ,   004091 04-04
VAN DEN BOGAARD AEJM   004298 04-06
VAN DEN BROECK WAE   000495 01-04
VAN DEN DRIESSCHE J   002205 02-13
VAN DEN STEEN N   001886 02-07
VAN DER DIJS B   001930 02-08
VAN DER HEYDEN JAM   002923 03-03
VAN DER KOLK BA   000981 01-17
VAN DER LAAN JW   001809 02-04
VAN DER LINDEN L   000181 01-03
VAN DER LUGT JC   000323 01-03
VAN DER VELDE CD   003287 03-10
VAN DER VELDE EA   000760 01-13
VAN DER ZEE P   000005 01-01
VAN HEES T   002232 02-13
VAN HOUTTE JP   003268 03-09
VAN KAMMEN DP   000575 01-08 ,   001910
  02-08 ,   001952 02-08 ,   001952 02-08
  002222 02-13 ,   003167 03-08 ,   003357
  03-11
VAN LOON GR   002924 03-03
VAN MAANEN EF   001851 02-05
VAN NOORDWIJK J   002556 02-17
VAN OENE JC   001530 02-03
VAN OYEN HG   003056 03-04 ,   003107 03-04
  004091 04-04
VAN PELT J   003107 03-04
VAN PRAAG HM   000996 01-17 ,   001953 02-
  08 ,   001966 02-09 ,   001976 02-09 ,
  002347 02-14 ,   003203 03-08 ,   003203
  03-08 ,   003216 03-09 ,   003269 03-09
VAN PUTTEN T   000565 01-08 ,   000826 01-14
  ,   000891 01-15 ,   003188 03-08 ,   003189
  03-08 ,   003201 03-08 ,   003202 03-08

VAN REE JM   001404 02-03 ,   001953 02-08
VAN VALKENBURG CFM   001150 02-03 ,
  002681 03-03
VAN WIJNGAARDEN I   000758 01-13
VAN WIMERSMA GREIDANUS TB   001370 02-03
  ,   003854 04-03
VAN WOERT MH   000050 01-03 ,   000138 01-
  03 ,   003854 04-03
VAN ZERSSEN D   004322 04-08
VAN ZWIETEN PA   001508 02-03
VANDEGRIFF KD   001810 02-04
VANDEL B   000640 01-09 ,   002304 02-13
VANDEL S   000640 01-09 ,   002304 02-13
VANDENBERK J   002648 03-02
VANDENBURGH H   001519 02-03 ,   002087 02-
  10
VANDERWOLF CH   000184 01-03 ,   000309 01-
  03 ,   000310 01-03
VANKOVA H   000686 01-11 ,   002188 02-11
VAPAATALO H   004542 04-13
VARDI J   004343 04-08
VARGA E   003180 03-08
VARGA V   003180 03-08
VARGAS L   002661 03-03
VARGAS P   003507 03-15
VARIA IG   003511 03-15
VARMA R   002367 02-14 ,   002367 02-14
VARONOS D   003698 04-02
VARSOU E   002294 02-13
VARTANIAN FE   002623 02-17
VARTANYAN FY   004381 04-09 ,   004663 04-
  15
VASER EE   001736 02-04
VASHENIN MM   004434 04-11
VASQUEZ B   001711 02-04 ,   002823 03-03 ,
  003861 04-03 ,   003936 04-03 ,   004143
  04-04 ,   004177 04-04
VASSELLA F   004495 04-11
VAUDRY H   002635 03-01
VAUGHAN PFT   001472 02-03
VAUGHT JL   000311 01-03
VAUPEL DB   000469 01-04
VAUTERIN C   002051 02-09
VAWTER MP   001811 02-04
VAYNSHTEYN GB   004045 04-03
VAYNSHTOK AB   003643 03-17
VAYNTRUB MY   004593 04-15
VAZQUEZ F   003101 03-04
VEALE WL   004034 04-03
VEDASIROMONI JR   004096 04-04
VEITH RC   004411 04-09
VEKSHINA NL   004017 04-03
VEKSLER IG   001520 02-03
VELASCO F   004046 04-03
VELASCO M   004046 04-03
VELLA G   002187 02-11
VELLUCCI SV   001881 02-06
VENABLES PH   003203 03-08
VENCOVSKY E   000686 01-11 ,   002188 02-11
  ,   004748 04-17
VENDITE DA   001664 02-04
VENEMA K   002923 03-03
VENEMA R   002746 03-03
VENER AM   000953 01-17
VENKATAKRISHNA-BHATT H   001748 02-04
VENKATARAMAIAH SR   003108 03-04
VENN RD   002624 02-17
VENTO AL   000928 01-17
VERBERNE AJM   004243 04-04
VERGHESE JP   000894 01-15
VERHOEVEN WMA   001953 02-08 ,   003200
  03-08 ,   003203 03-08
VERIMER T   004244 04-04
VERNALEONE F   000285 01-03
VERNIKOS J   000035 01-03
VEROSKY M   000305 01-03
VERRIER RL   000265 01-03
VERSIANI M   000641 01-09 ,   000892 01-15 ,
  003270 03-09 ,   003546 03-15 ,   003644
  03-17
VERTES Z   001407 02-03
VESTERGAARD P   000893 01-15 ,   002465 02-
  15 ,   003534 03-15 ,   003547 03-15 ,
  004291 04-06
VETULANI J   001256 02-03 ,   001788 02-04 ,
  004210 04-04
VIAIA A   003571 03-16
VIALA A   002625 02-17
VIAUD B   002061 02-10
VIAUD P   004472 04-11

VICKROY TW 000148 01-03 , 001304 02-03
VIDALES JE 003434 03-13
VIESSELMAN JO 003377 03-11
VIGEVANI F 003751 04-03 , 003803 04-03
VIGNON J 001521 02-03 , 001882 02-06
VIGOURET J 001346 02-03
VIHKO R 002258 02-13
VIJAYASENAN ME 002139 02-11
VILAR AN 001459 02-03
VILBERG T 001745 02-04
VILES JM 001145 02-03 , 003678 04-01
VILLA D 003382 03-11
VILLA RF 001126 02-03 , 003730 04-03
VILLARREAL JE 003645 03-17
VILLENEUVE A 002416 02-15
VILLIGER JW 002985 03-04 , 003109 03-04
VINAR O 000642 01-09 , 000643 01-09 ,
   000658 01-10 , 000993 01-17 , 002616
   02-16 , 002626 02-17 , 003646 03-17 ,
   004749 04-17
VINCENS M 004632 04-15
VINCENT J 001521 02-03 , 001882 02-06
VINCENT JD 000272 01-03
VINING EP 004447 04-11
VINOGRADOV MV 000578 01-09 , 004526 04-
   13
VINOGRADOV VM 001812 02-04
VINOGRADOVA OS 002941 03-03
VINSOVA M 000544 01-07
VIRGILI P 001295 02-03 , 002091 02-11
VIRGILD J 004606 04-15
VIRTANEN R 002303 02-13 , 003435 03-13
VIRUS RM 001726 02-04
VISAN-IONESCU I 001979 02-09
VISHEVA N 000119 01-03
VISHNYAKOVA YS 000578 01-09
VITALIANO PP 004695 04-16
VITIELLO MV 004695 04-16
VIUKARI M 002076 02-10 , 002077 02-10 ,
   002185 02-11
VOCCI FJ 001513 02-03
VOGEL RA 001813 02-04
VOGEL Z 000065 01-03 , 002655 03-03 ,
   002656 03-03
VOHRA J 004639 04-15
VOICULESCU V 004451 04-11
VOITH K 001814 02-04
VOJTECHOVSKY M 000816 01-14 , 002155
   02-11 , 002156 02-11
VOLAVKA J 000798 01-13 , 003383 03-11
VOLKER L 000049 01-03
VOLK J 002204 02-13
VOLKOVA LD 003457 03-14
VOLLER GW 002111 02-11
VOLMAT R 000640 01-09 , 002304 02-13
VOLSAN O 002131 02-11
VOLTATTORNI CB 002925 03-03
VOLTERRA V 002189 02-11
VON ALBERT HH 000920 01-17
VON KNORRING L 002274 02-13 , 002305 02-
   13 , 004664 04-15
VON LITTROV K 001815 02-04
VON LUCKNER N 004696 04-16
VON VOIGTLANDER P 001074 02-02 , 001075
   02-02 , 001076 02-02
VON WERDER K 000735 02-08
VON ZERSSEN D 001917 02-08 , 001918 02-
   08 , 003218 03-09 , 003219 03-09
VORONINA TA 001815 02-04
VOSMER G 000312 01-03 , 003771 04-03
VOSTALOVA V 001647 02-04
VOVIN RY 003384 03-11
VOZEH S 000909 01-16
VRANCKX C 001954 02-08 , 004355 04-09
VREE TB 000541 01-07
VRIJMOED-DE VRIES MC 000289 01-03
VROULIS G 003095 03-04 , 003385 03-11 ,
   004694 04-16
VULLIEMOZ Y 000305 01-03
VYAS BK 000583 01-09
VYAS IL 000131 01-03
VYBOROVA L 000729 01-11 , 002115 02-11 ,
   002190 02-11

W

WADA JA 002466 02-15
WADA T 002442 02-15
WADDINGHAM S 000313 01-03
WADDINGTON JL 002452 02-03 , 001816 02-
   04 , 001817 02-04 , 001858 02-05 ,
   002509 02-16 , 004282 04-05

WADSWORTH J 002215 02-13
WAEHRENS J 001968 02-09
WAGEMAKER H 000997 01-17
WAGGONER RJ 000730 01-11
WAGNER GC 000427 01-04 , 002926 03-03 ,
   003110 03-04 , 004073 04-04
WAGNER J 000248 01-03 , 000321 01-03 ,
   001128 02-03
WAGNER R 001945 02-08 , 002245 02-13 ,
   003169 03-08 , 003184 03-08 , 003357
   03-11 , 003499 03-15
WAGNER WE 002204 02-13
WAHLEN A 002201 02-12
WAHLIN A 004664 04-15
WAHLSTROM J 000888 01-15
WAI M 001824 02-04
WAID WM 004585 04-14
WAITE JG 002273 02-13
WAJDICKOVA K 002020 02-09
WAJSBORT J 004569 04-14
WAKADE AR 000314 01-03
WAKEMAN P 002474 02-16
WAKO M 000661 01-11
WAKUI Y 000159 01-03
WALDMEIER PC 000315 01-03 , 000316 01-03
   001740 02-04 , 003921 04-03
WALDROP WM 002167 02-11
WALETZKY JP 003607 03-17
WALINDER J 004412 04-09
WALKER C 002989 03-04
WALKER JM 003111 03-04 , 003112 03-04
WALKER MK 003386 03-11 , 003459 03-14
WALKER S 004665 04-15
WALKIN E 004672 04-16
WALL KD 000909 01-11
WALLACE JE 000006 01-01 , 000538 01-06 ,
   000906 01-16
WALLACE MM 004074 04-04
WALLACE TL 004052 04-03 , 004751 04-17
WALLACH MB 001091 02-02
WALLAND A 000266 01-03 , 001431 02-03
WALLER D 000529 01-05 , 002368 02-14
WALLIN L 004412 04-09
WALLIS CJ 002927 03-03
WALLIS D 001329 02-03 , 004047 04-03
WALLNAU LB 004245 04-04 , 004246 04-04
WALOVITCH R 002244 01-03 , 004203 04-04
WALSH B 002236 02-13
WALSH JT 003341 03-11
WALSH TJ 001742 02-04
WALSON P 000773 01-13
WALTER DS 002701 03-03
WALTER L 003387 03-11
WALTERS JR 000319 01-03 , 000320 01-03
WALTHER H 003300 03-11
WALTON KG 002932 03-03
WALZ MA 003113 03-04
WAMBEBE C 001741 02-04
WAN O 001285 02-03
WANDALL T 000591 01-09
WANG CC 003574 03-03
WANG HS 000189 01-03
WANG J 000317 01-03 , 002928 03-03
WANG RIH 001853 02-05 , 002800 03-03
WANG RK 003997 04-03
WANG RY 000068 01-03 , 001523 02-03
WANIEWSKI RA 001524 02-03
WANNAMAKER BB 004558 04-13
WANNARKA GL 001525 02-03
WARD CD 003319 03-11
WARDELL JR 001265 02-03
WARDLEY-SMITH B 001106 02-03
WARE PL 001112 02-03
WARIN V 003653 04-01
WARREN JW 004558 04-13
WARREN LA 003900 04-03
WARSH JJ 002268 01-03 , 004048 04-03 ,
   004303 04-06
WARSHAUER D 003320 03-11
WARTEL R 003208 03-09
WARTER JM 002237 02-13
WASER PG 000705 01-11 , 001626 02-04 ,
   001776 02-04 , 001777 02-04
WASHTON AM 000731 01-11 , 000827 01-14
WASILEWSKI R 000664 01-11
WASLEY JWF 001089 02-02
WASSEF NM 000318 01-03
WASSERMAN S 002472 02-15
WASTEK GJ 004013 04-03 , 004049 04-03
WASZCZAK BL 000319 01-03 , 000320 01-03

WATANABE H 004247 04-04
WATANABE K 000009 01-02 , 001060 02-01 ,
   001065 02-01 , 001066 02-01
WATANABE N 000515 01-05
WATANABE S 000417 01-04 , 001681 02-04 ,
   003271 03-09 , 003951 04-03 , 004388
   04-09
WATANABE Y 004050 04-03
WATERBURY LD 001091 02-02
WATERFALL JF 000516 01-05
WATERFIELD AA 000168 01-03
WATERHOUSE BD 002687 03-03 , 004058 04-
   03
WATERS B 002043 02-09 , 002044 02-09
WATERS IW 000280 01-03
WATKINS G 003647 03-17
WATKINS J 002504 02-16 , 002696 03-03 ,
   003587 03-17 , 003648 03-17
WATKINS JT 003257 03-09
WATLING KJ 001296 02-03 , 003706 04-02 ,
   003776 04-03 , 004051 04-03
WATSON JR 004631 04-15
WATZMAN N 003707 04-02
WAUQUIER A 000495 01-04 , 000496 01-04 ,
   001526 02-03
WAWCZK S 003463 03-15
WAXMAN SG 000166 01-03
WAY EL 000117 01-03 , 000137 01-03 ,
   000357 01-03 , 001662 02-04 , 002627
   02-17 , 002757 03-03 , 003649 03-17 ,
   004489 04-11
WAYNER MJ 003049 03-04
WAZER D 000461 01-04 , 002877 03-03
WEAVER LM 003002 03-04
WEBB WB 003439 03-14
WEBER HP 001527 02-03
WEBER KA 002191 02-11
WEBER R 004221 04-04
WEBSTER P 000571 01-09
WEBSTER RA 001881 02-06
WECKER L 001061 02-01 , 003996 04-03
WEDDINGTON WW 000894 01-15 , 002408
   02-15
WEEKS BJ 001461 02-03
WEEKS JR 000497 01-04 , 004304 04-06
WEET CR 002320 02-14
WEET JF 003845 04-03
WEGENER G 001996 02-09
WEGLICKI WB 003993 04-03
WEGNER J 002417 02-15 , 003548 03-15
WEHR TA 001536 02-03 , 002628 02-17
WEI ET 003572 03-15 , 004238 04-04 ,
   004248 04-04
WEIDLER DJ 000321 01-03
WEIGHT ML 001759 02-04
WEIL-FUGAZZA J 000110 01-03
WEILER MH 001374 02-03
WEINBERG U 003228 03-09
WEINBERGER DR 001622 02-04 , 001928 02-
   08 , 003165 03-08 , 003184 03-08
WEINER G 001069 02-02
WEINER RD 000895 01-15
WEINER WJ 000498 01-04 , 001845 02-05 ,
   002159 02-11 , 002468 02-15 , 003502
   03-15 , 003516 03-15 , 004249 04-04
WEINGARTNER H 000716 01-11 , 003310 03-
   11 , 003388 03-11
WEINHOLD P 000858 01-15 , 003501 03-15 ,
   003548 03-15
WEINSTEIN H 000112 01-03 , 001706 02-04
WEINSTOCK AB 004572 04-14
WEINSTOCK M 001528 02-03
WEIR RL 003436 03-13
WEISE CC 000655 01-10 , 003254 03-09
WEISE V 000309 03-11 , 003362 03-11
WEISE VK 001042 02-03
WEISNER B 004586 04-14
WEISS B 000113 01-03 , 001529 02-03 ,
   004052 04-03 , 004666 04-15 , 004750
   04-17 , 004751 04-17
WEISS G 000655 01-10 , 004454 04-11
WEISS HR 001177 02-03
WEISSMAN A 001092 02-02
WEISSMAN MM 000998 01-17 , 003256 03-
   09 , 003272 03-09 , 004401 04-09 ,
   004413 04-09 , 004418 04-09
WEITZEL WD 002629 02-17
WEITZELL R 002748 03-03
WEITZMAN ED 003228 03-09

WELBEL L   003204 03-08
WELCH WM   001092 02-02
WELLE SL   000828 01-14
WELLER M   001543 02-03 ,   001921 02-08 ,
003174 03-08
WELLMAN PJ   000322 01-03 ,   001818 02-04 ,
003114 03-04
WELLMEYER D   001197 02-03
WELLS B   004580 04-14
WELNER A   002052 02-09
WELNER Z   002052 02-09
WELZL H   001657 02-04
WEMER J   000323 01-03
WENDEL OT   000537 01-06
WENDER PH   003389 03-11 ,   004752 04-17
WENDT H   004516 04-13
WENDT U   002306 02-13
WENER A   004454 04-11
WENGER GR   001883 02-06
WENZEL U   003390 03-11
WEPIERRE J   001187 02-03
WERBLOWSKY J   003254 03-09
WERNER C   000617 01-09
WERQUIN G   001902 02-07
WESSELS FL   003687 04-02 ,   003688 04-02
WESSELS WH   001955 02-08
WESSON DR   000746 01-12
WEST DP   000872 01-15
WEST E   004402 04-09
WEST KB   000499 01-04
WESTENBERG HGM   003216 03-09
WESTER H   002469 02-15
WESTERINK BHC   000004 01-01 ,   000324 01-
03 ,   001530 02-03 ,   004305 04-06
WESTERLUND D   003991 04-03
WESTLAKE WJ   003151 03-07
WESTMAN K   000268 01-03
WESTON WL   000401 03-13
WESTPHAL J   003393 03-11
WETZEL W   001819 02-04
WHALEY-KLAHN MA   003509 03-15
WHANGER AD   000895 01-15
WHEATLEY D   002088 02-10 ,   002307 02-13 ,
004414 04-09
WHEELER H   004240 04-04
WHEELER SC   001820 02-04
WHETZEL N   003309 03-11
WHITAKER PM   000325 01-03
WHITE DK   003342 01-04
WHITE FJ   000499 01-04 ,   004250 04-04
WHITE JH   002192 02-11
WHITE K   000644 01-09 ,   003273 03-09
WHITE N   004079 04-04
WHITE RD   001144 02-03
WHITE SR   001821 02-04
WHITEHOUSE D   000732 01-11
WHITELAW AGL   003509 03-15
WHITESIDE DA   002974 03-04
WHITESIDE EA   000703 01-11 ,   002139 02-11
WHITMORE WL   004021 04-03
WHITMORE SR   002685 03-03
WICHLINSKI L   000601 01-09 ,   002564 02-17
WIDELITZ MM   001531 02-03
WIDEMAN J   003971 04-03
WIDERLOV E   001532 02-03
WIDLOCHER D   000246 01-03 ,   000500
01-04
WIECH N   000326 01-03 ,   001305 02-03
WIECHMAN BE   003115 03-04
WIECK HH   003550 03-15
WIENER H   001087 02-02
WIENIAWSKA-SZEWCZYK E   000794 01-13
WIERASZKO A   003147 03-06
WIERSEMA S   004690 04-16
WIERUSZ-WYSOCKA B   004416 04-09
WIGGINS RC   003774 04-03
WIJLING A   002681 03-03
WIKLER A   004587 04-14
WIKSTROM H   000399 01-04
WILBUR R   002470 02-15
WILCOX CE   000051 01-03
WILCOX GL   001868 02-06
WILCOX RE   001822 02-04
WILDER BJ   000756 01-13 ,   000762 01-13 ,
002758 03-03
WILENSKY AJ   000177 01-03 ,   000728 01-11 ,
000755 01-13
WILES DH   001932 02-08 ,   001956 02-08 ,
002510 02-16

WILETS G   000829 01-15
WILK S   001533 02-03 ,   003906 04-03
WILKERSON RD   001534 02-03
WILKIE DM   004199 04-04
WILKIE FL   004492 04-11
WILKINS JN   000891 01-15
WILKINSON EH   003182 03-08
WILKINSON M   001535 02-03
WILKISON DM   003327 01-03
WILLENBRING M   003217 03-09
WILLIAMS A   002384 02-15 ,   003420 03-13
WILLIAMS BB   000518 01-05
WILLIAMS BW   002511 02-16
WILLIAMS D   003394 03-11
WILLIAMS EA   001073 02-02
WILLIAMS EF   004251 04-04
WILLIAMS HL   003460 03-14
WILLIAMS JH   002929 03-03
WILLIAMS KN   001738 02-04
WILLIAMS M   001941 02-08
WILLIAMS P   003265 03-09
WILLIAMS RG   001329 02-03
WILLIAMS RL   003650 03-17
WILLIAMS S   004363 04-09
WILLIAMS T   001771 02-04
WILLIAMSON J   000999 01-17
WILLMORE LJ   000756 01-13 ,   002930 03-03
WILLNER P   000501 01-04 ,   002931 03-03 ,
004180 04-04 ,   004252 04-04
WILLOW M   002769 03-03
WILSKA M   000573 01-08
WILSON A   003422 03-13
WILSON IC   002145 02-11 ,   002259 02-13
WILSON JH   001813 02-04
WILSON MC   000344 01-04 ,   002954 03-04 ,
003127 03-05
WILSON RW   003651 03-17
WILSON WA   003762 04-03 ,   003806 04-03
WILSON WH   001964 02-09 ,   002026 02-09 ,
002080 02-10 ,   004333 04-08 ,   004392
04-09 ,   004702 04-17
WILSON WP   000895 01-15
WINDORFER A   003218 03-09
WINGER G   001651 02-04 ,   001802 02-04
WINGERT TD   000733 01-11
WINGFIELD CW   003304 03-11
WINKLER M   001649 02-04
WINSBERG BG   000812 01-14 ,   002385 02-15
WINSTON RA   004403 04-09
WINTER CA   000502 01-04
WINTER JC   003116 03-04
WINTER JSD   002213 02-13
WINTERS WD   002653 03-03 ,   002959 03-03
WIRTH JF   002016 02-09
WIRTSHAFTER D   004098 04-04
WIRZ-JUSTICE A   001536 02-03 ,   002628 02-
17
WISE CD   001928 02-08 ,   003169 03-08 ,
003499 03-15
WISE RA   001861 02-06 ,   002960 03-04 ,
002999 03-04 ,   003000 03-04
WISHART TB   001823 02-04 ,   003560 03-16
WISNIEWSKI HM   000191 01-03
WISSOCQ J   002299 02-13
WITKIN JM   001537 02-03
WITSCHY JK   003551 03-15
WITTENBORN JR   003391 03-11
WITTENBRINK A   004529 04-13
WITTMANN LA   003202 03-08
WODE-HELGODT B   001905 02-08 ,   004559 04-
13
WOERNER M   000858 01-15 ,   003501 03-15
WOESTENBORGHS R   000758 01-13
WOGGON B   004415 04-09 ,   004667 04-15 ,
004696 04-16
WOJCIK JD   004612 04-15
WOJCIK WJ   004203 04-04
WOJTOWICZ JM   001349 02-03
WOLF A   004031 04-03
WOLF CL   000076 01-03
WOLF DL   002259 02-13
WOLF MO   004226 04-04
WOLF WA   003117 03-04 ,   003892 04-03
WOLFE BB   002932 03-03 ,   003979 04-03 ,
004229 04-04
WOLFE JW   002997 03-04
WOLFF I   001151 02-03
WOLFF P   002699 03-03
WOLFSON L   002180 02-11
WOLIN RE   002225 02-13 ,   003479 03-15

WOLLERT U   001440 02-03 ,   004211 04-04
WOLPERT E   000799 01-13 ,   002053 02-09
WOLPERT GY   002053 02-09
WONG C   001824 02-04
WONG DT   001538 02-03
WONG KC   001539 02-03
WONNACOTT S   003924 04-03
WOO JH   001316 02-03
WOO S   000305 01-03
WOOD DR   003389 03-11
WOOD G   003598 03-17
WOOD JD   001540 02-03
WOOD K   001977 02-09 ,   004364 04-09
WOOD MD   003686 04-02
WOOD PL   000328 01-03 ,   001062 02-01 ,
001541 02-03 ,   004053 04-03
WOODBURY DM   004061 04-03
WOODMAN OL   004054 04-03
WOODRUFF GN   002722 03-03 ,   004055 04-03
WOODS JH   001557 02-04 ,   001828 02-04 ,
003106 03-04 ,   004132 04-04 ,   004133
04-04 ,   004134 04-04 ,   004242 04-04 ,
004253 04-04 ,   004719 04-17
WOODS TW   004145 04-04
WOODWARD DJ   000209 01-03 ,   001382 02-
03 ,   002687 03-03 ,   003926 04-03 ,
004058 04-03
WOOGEN S   003552 03-15
WOOLF CJ   001226 02-03 ,   004254 04-04
WOOLVERTON WL   000341 01-04 ,   001542 02-
03 ,   001825 02-04
WOOSLEY RL   003545 03-15
WOOTEN GF   000294 01-03 ,   003492 03-15
WORK J   002629 02-17
WORMS P   000464 01-04 ,   001345 02-03 ,
001826 02-04 ,   003334 03-11
WORMSLEY KG   004306 04-07
WRIGHT CM   000440 01-04 ,   004189 04-04
WRIGHT DJM   001543 02-03
WRIGHT FC   001591 02-04 ,   001592 02-04
WRIGHT WB   001093 02-02
WU J   001653 02-04 ,   002643 03-01
WU M   000436 01-04 ,   003019 03-04 ,
003118 03-04
WU PH   000234 01-03 ,   000329 01-03 ,
000330 01-03 ,   000451 01-04 ,   001414
02-03 ,   002933 03-03 ,   004056 04-03
WUERTHELE SM   002502 02-16
WUNDER BA   001544 02-03 ,   002952 03-04
WURM JME   000614 01-09 ,   004477 04-11
WURSTER RM   004123 04-04
WURTMAN RJ   000202 01-03 ,   000296 01-03
000942 01-17 ,   002473 02-15 ,   002934
03-03 ,   004014 04-04 ,   004076 04-04
WUSCHNER-STOCKHEIM M   004711 04-17
WUSTER M   002935 03-03 ,   003088 03-04 ,
003837 04-04
WUTTKE W   004500 04-13
WYATT ES   002216 02-13
WYATT RJ   000153 01-03 ,   000255 01-03 ,
000432 01-04 ,   000869 01-15 ,   001233
02-03 ,   001310 02-03 ,   001442 02-03 ,
001444 02-03 ,   001622 02-04 ,   001672
02-04 ,   001794 02-04 ,   001938 02-08 ,
001945 02-08 ,   001957 02-08 ,   001958
02-08 ,   002245 02-13 ,   002341 02-14 ,
002992 03-04 ,   002993 03-04 ,   003022
03-04 ,   003023 03-04 ,   003165 03-08 ,
003168 03-08 ,   003169 03-08 ,   003184
03-08 ,   003499 03-15 ,   004671 04-16
WYLER AR   000172 01-03
WYNN V   004463 04-11
WYSOCKI H   004416 04-09
WYSOCKI T   002471 02-15 ,   003392 03-11
WYTEK R   000819 01-14 ,   003251 03-09

Y

YAFFE SJ   000281 01-03
YAGI G   000854 01-15
YAGI K   004720 04-17
YAGO LS   003554 03-16
YAHR MD   002117 02-11 ,   002467 02-15
YAJIMA H   001394 02-03
YAKIMOVSKIY AF   004255 04-04
YAKSH TL   004206 04-04 ,   004213 04-04
YALE C   000565 01-08 ,   000826 01-14 ,
001220 02-03 ,   003188 03-08 ,   003189
03-08

YAMADA K 000628 01-09 , 001808 02-04 ,
   004193 04-04 , 004256 04-04
YAMADA S 001430 02-03 , 001545 02-03 ,
   002874 03-03
YAMADA T 003942 04-03
YAMAGUCHI I 001224 02-03 , 001279 02-03
   , 001546 02-03 , 002919 03-03 , 004057
   04-03
YAMAGUCHI K 002771 03-03
YAMAGUCHI N 000645 01-09 , 001547 02-03
   , 003266 03-09
YAMAMOTO BK 000503 01-04
YAMAMOTO H 003679 04-01
YAMAMOTO J 000734 01-11
YAMAMOTO K 000098 01-03
YAMAMOTO M 002936 03-03
YAMAMOTO T 003397 03-12
YAMAMURA HI 000226 01-03 , 000279 01-
   03 , 001305 02-03 , 001359 02-03 ,
   001373 02-03 , 001430 02-03 , 001441
   02-03 , 001545 02-03 , 001710 02-04 ,
   002163 02-11 , 002852 03-03 , 002874
   03-03 , 002902 03-03 , 004013 04-03
YAMAMURA S 000279 01-03
YAMANAMI S 004192 04-04
YAMASHIRO D 001028 02-01 , 001081 02-02
YAMASHITA I 000646 01-09 , 003938 04-03
YAMORI Y 001548 02-03
YANAGIHARA T 004060 04-03
YANAURA S 001236 02-03 , 001797 02-04 ,
   001800 02-04 , 004257 04-04 , 004258
   04-04
YANG FC 003659 04-01
YANG HT 001182 02-03 , 001270 02-03 ,
   001284 02-03 , 001884 02-06
YANG HYT 003808 04-03
YANIK G 000244 01-03
YARBROUGH GG 001701 02-04
YARDIM M 004460 04-11
YAROWSKY P 002308 02-13
YARYURA-TOBIAS JA 002630 02-17
YASSA K 001000 01-17 , 004668 04-15
YASUHARA H 004283 04-05
YASUNOBU KT 001060 02-01 , 001065 02-01
   , 001066 02-01 , 003680 04-01
YATES RA 001940 02-08
YAVETZ B 002875 03-03
YAVORSKII AN 001549 02-03
YEH HH 004058 04-03
YEH SY 004610 04-15
YEHLE AL 000394 01-04
YEHUDA S 001827 02-04
YELLIN JB 003922 04-03
YEO T 001016 02-01 , 001127 02-03 ,
   003731 04-03 , 003732 04-03
YERET A 000841 01-15 , 001915 02-0B ,
   001916 02-08
YERMOLINA LA 004444 04-11
YEROUKALIS D 004059 04-03
YESAVAGE JA 002512 02-16 , 003393 03-11
   004493 04-11 , 004665 04-15
YEZHKOVA VA 004444 04-11
YIM CY 000331 01-03
YIM GKW 001703 02-04
YLIEFF M 004561 04-14
YOHE HC 002937 03-03
YOKOCHI M 002309 02-13
YOKOI I 004060 04-03
YOKOTA K 000696 01-11
YOKOYAMA S 003271 03-09
YOKOYAMA Y 004185 04-04
YONEKAWA WD 004061 04-03
YORK EJ 003684 04-02
YORKSTON N 003174 03-08
YOSHIDA H 000099 01-03 , 001272 02-03 ,
   001322 02-03 , 004050 04-03

YOSHIDA K 000012 01-02 , 000142 01-03 ,
   000152 01-03 , 004149 04-04 , 004193
   04-04
YOSHIDA N 002771 03-03
YOSHII T 001797 02-04
YOSHIMI H 003187 03-08
YOSHIMIZU N 000902 01-16 , 004684 04-16
YOSHIMURA H 000504 01-04
YOSHINAGA J 004618 04-15
YOSHINO JE 003148 03-06
YOSHIZAKI T 004062 04-03
YOTIS A 001550 02-03
YOUDIM MBH 000608 01-09 , 003652 03-17 ,
   004569 04-14
YOULE RJ 001063 02-01 , 001064 02-01
YOUNG AM 001828 02-04
YOUNG ER 004094 04-04
YOUNG GA 000505 01-04 , 004230 04-04 ,
   004259 04-04
YOUNG JG 002106 02-11
YOUNG JM 001266 02-03 , 004031 04-03
YOUNG M 004538 04-13
YOUNG R 000660 01-11 , 000884 01-15 ,
   002039 02-09 , 003690 04-02 , 004260
   04-04 , 004550 04-13
YOUNG SN 002253 02-13
YOUNG WS 002644 03-01 , 002938 03-03
YU RK 002937 03-03 , 003025 03-04
YUDOFSKY S 000896 01-15 , 003394 03-11
YUMATOV YA 003972 04-03
YUTRZENKA GJ 003119 03-04
YUTZEY DA 000375 01-04
YUWILER A 001385 02-03 , 003942 04-03 ,
   004204 04-04
YVONNEAU M 002472 02-15
YZOMBARD G 003524 03-15

Z

ZACCARA G 004417 04-09
ZACHARKO RM 000419 01-04 , 001688 02-04
   , 001823 02-04
ZACKOVA P 000332 01-03
ZACZEK R 001885 02-06 , 002939 03-03
ZADINA JE 001311 02-03
ZAGRYADSKIY PV 003438 03-14
ZAHN T 003205 03-08 , 003310 03-11 ,
   003437 03-13
ZAHNISER NR 003979 04-03
ZAIKONNIKOVA IV 004261 04-04
ZAKHAROV ND 002940 03-03
ZAKI S 003174 03-08
ZAKUSOV VV 001094 02-02
ZALCIK J 001551 02-03
ZALCMAN S 001945 02-08 , 002245 02-13
ZALDIVAR SB 004009 04-03
ZALEJSKI S 004494 04-11
ZALESOV VS 000506 01-04
ZALESOV VV 000506 01-04
ZALUSKA M 004546 04-13 , 004547 04-13 ,
   004548 04-13
ZAMOSHCHINA TA 003994 04-03
ZANASI M 002355 02-14
ZANDER KJ 001959 02-08 , 002311 02-13 ,
   004344 04-08
ZAPLETALEK M 000576 01-08 , 000593 01-09
   , 000654 01-10 , 000735 01-11 , 002000
   02-09 , 002054 02-09 , 002055 02-09 ,
   002056 02-09 , 002089 02-10
ZARAFIAN E 001969 02-09
ZARIFIAN E 000549 01-08 , 000577 01-08 ,
   001195 02-03 , 001907 02-08 , 002016
   02-09 , 002267 02-13 , 002310 02-13 ,
   002539 02-17 , 002631 02-17 , 003175
   03-08 , 003427 03-13 , 004358 04-09 ,
   004445 04-11 , 004501 04-13

ZAROR-BEHRENS G 001231 02-03
ZARRANZ JJ 003553 03-15
ZATECKA I 000595 01-09 , 000630 01-09
ZATONSKAYA MS 003384 03-11
ZATZ M 000277 01-03 , 001212 02-03 ,
   001552 02-03
ZAUDIG M 001918 02-08 , 004322 04-08
ZAVADIL A 001528 02-03 , 002354 02-14
ZAWILSLAK R 004270 04-05
ZAWOISKI EJ 001553 02-03
ZBINDEN G 004284 04-05
ZBYTOVSKY J 000576 01-08 , 000735 01-11
   , 002056 02-09
ZEBROWSKA-LUPINA I 001829 02-04
ZEIDAN H 001065 02-01 , 001066 02-01
ZEISEL SH 002473 02-15
ZELNIK TC 003408 03-13
ZEMLAN FP 000421 01-04
ZENTALL TR 003009 03-04
ZERBI F 000757 01-13 , 002057 02-09 ,
   002058 02-09 , 004675 04-16
ZERSSEN DV 004321 04-08
ZETLER G 000507 01-04 , 002652 03-02
ZETTERSTROM T 003701 04-02
ZHADINA SD 002941 03-03
ZHANG A 001554 02-03
ZHURAVLEV BV 002892 03-03
ZIANCE RJ 002754 03-03
ZIEGLER M 000182 01-03 , 000673 01-11 ,
   002138 02-11 , 003340 03-11
ZIEGLGANSBERGER W 001234 02-03 , 001235
   02-03
ZIGMOND MJ 002632 02-17 , 003120 03-04
ZIGMOND RE 000333 01-03 , 003750 04-03
ZIGUN JR 001117 02-03
ZILBERMAN Y 002717 03-03
ZIMAKOVA IY 004262 04-04
ZIMINSKI K 004670 04-16
ZIMMER R 001959 02-08 , 002311 02-13 ,
   004344 04-08
ZIMMERMAN KS 000454 01-04
ZIMMERMANN H 004063 04-03
ZIMMERMANN RL 002513 02-17
ZIPPARRI L 000833 01-15
ZIS AP 003408 03-13
ZISKIND E 002369 02-14
ZISOOK S 003238 03-09 , 004345 04-08
ZISSIS NP 004337 04-08
ZITTING A 000527 01-05
ZIVKOVIC B 001119 02-03 , 003995 04-03
ZIZOLFI S 003444 03-14
ZOLOVICK AJ 001644 02-04
ZORICK F 000822 01-14 , 002160 02-11
ZORRETTA D 004318 04-08
ZOUHAR A 004064 04-03
ZRAIKA M 000248 01-03 , 000458 01-04 ,
   001128 02-03
ZUARDI AW 004263 0' 04
ZUCCARELLI RR 0005ob 01-04
ZUCHA I 003567 03-16
ZUCKER J 001285 02-03
ZUCKERMAN DM 004418 04-09
ZUKERMAN Z 002443 02-15
ZUKIN RS 001555 02-03 , 001629 02-04
ZUKIN SR 001555 02-03
ZUMSTEIN A 000535 01-06 , 001298 02-03 ,
   002751 03-03
ZUTCHI T 001914 02-08
ZVARTAU EE 001556 02-03 , 003641 03-17
ZVOLSKY P 002457 02-15 , 003261 03-09
ZWEIG M 003828 04-03
ZYSSET T 004495 04-11

☆ U.S. GOVERNMENT PRINTING OFFICE : 1983 O - 412-525

PSYCHOPHARMACOLOGY ABSTRACTS

Questions about Clearinghouse service should be addressed o:t

    Psychopharmacology Abstracts
    National Clearinghouse for Mental Health Information
    Alcohol, Drug Abuse, and Mental Health Administration
    5600 Fishers Lane
    Rockville, Maryland 20857

For information on subscriptions and the purchase of single copies of the *Abstracts* (Vol. 7 onward), please refer to page ii of this issue.

DEPARTMENT OF
HEALTH AND HUMAN SERVICES
PUBLIC HEALTH SERVICE

ALCOHOL, DRUG ABUSE, AND
MENTAL HEALTH ADMINISTRATION
5600 FISHERS LANE
ROCKVILLE, MARYLAND 20857

OFFICIAL BUSINESS
PENALTY FOR PRIVATE USE, $300

POSTAGE AND FEES PAID
U.S. DEPARTMENT OF H.H.S.
HHS 396

Fourth-Class/Book

NOTICE OF MAILING CHANGE

☐ Check here if you wish to discontinue receiving this type of publication.

☐ Check here if your address has changed and you wish to continue receiving the type of publication. (Be sure to furnish your complete address including zip code.)

Tear off cover with address label still affixed and send to:

Alcohol, Drug Abuse, and Mental Health Administration
Printing and Publications Management Section
5600 Fishers Lane (Rm. 6-105)
Rockville, Maryland 20857

DHHS Publication No. (ADM) 83-150
Printed 1983

Lightning Source UK Ltd.
Milton Keynes UK
UKHW012221070119
334855UK00010BA/1671/P